BAIRD'S MANUAL

OF AMERICAN COLLEGE FRATERNITIES

William Raimond Baird

The 20th Edition of
Baird's Manual
of
American College Fraternities
is dedicated to
Jack L. Anson
Phi Kappa Tau
1924–1990

Fraternity Leader
Author
Sportsman
Interfraternity Friend
"Mr. Fraternity"

*"Fraternity is understanding,
it is recognition,
it is a joining with men,
in common enterprises,
it is a willingness
to share and to participate,
it is discipline.
It is selflessness.
It is these things
and many more.
It is above all an attitude."*

JACK ANSON, 1965

Baird's Manual OF

AMERICAN COLLEGE

FRATERNITIES

Twentieth Edition

EDITED BY

Jack L. Anson
and
Robert F. Marchesani Jr.

BAIRD'S MANUAL FOUNDATION, INC.

INDIANAPOLIS, INDIANA • NINETEEN NINETY-ONE

Preface

As you review the Baird's Manual of American College Fraternities, it would be easy to dismiss it as being simply a reference book to be used solely in research and then relegated to the dusty shelves of a library.

The fact is, the Baird's Manual is a living and vibrant record of the more than 215-year-old American college fraternity system. Its many pages celebrate the oldest form of student self-governance in the centuries-old American system of higher education.

Throughout the years, fraternities have thrived because of their ability to unite in common purpose students from different backgrounds. The Baird's Manual is record of that diversity, and the growth of the American college fraternity system.

This 20th edition was prepared during a period of unprecedented growth in the fraternity system. Between 1977, when the 19th edition of Baird's was published, and 1991, hundreds of thousands of young men and women joined the ranks of NIC, NPC, NPHC, PFA and ACHS fraternities and sororities. During the same period, hundreds of new chapters of these organizations were started and established, demonstrating the widespread interest in additional opportunities for membership among students.

How can we explain the growth? A number of reasons come to mind. First and foremost, the interest in belonging to an organization that simulates the family structure or at least reduces the overwhelming nature of many of today's large college campuses. Being a part of an organization of "brothers" or "sisters" who care about your well-being certainly helps to create what former Penn State President John Oswald called "an island of smallness on the large ocean that is today's college campus."

In addition, fraternities and sororities offer today's students opportunities for personal development unmatched in most campus organizations. The leadership opportunities alone have caused some to call the American college fraternity a "laboratory" where students can test and develop their skills as organizational leaders, public speakers, community servants and good citizens.

Underlying the whole experience is the ritual that is exclusive to each fraternity. While often incorrectly associated with illegal and immoral hazing activities, a fraternity ritual is the solemn and historical rationale for an organization's existence. The ritual is often presented to new members during a serious church-like ceremony where new members learn the underlying meaning of their respective organizations.

While these ceremonies are usually attended by members only because of the esoteric nature of most fraternities, a visitor at such a service would learn that college fraternities stand for some lofty ideals. . . scholastic achievement, public service, respect for one's fellow man and so on.

The conflict between these stated ideals and the behavior of undergraduate members on the campus often is caused confusion and a lack of support for the fraternity system. Only through cooperative effort among undergraduate and alumni members, general fraternity leaders, campus administrators and other concerned parties will college fraternities meet their stated purposes. During the period between editions of Baird's Manuals both constructive and destructive relationships have resulted in mixed results for fraternities on a number of campuses.

It's clear, however, that in the cases where the true mission of fraternity is understood and supported by all concerned, positive constructive relationships can be built between fraternities and host institutions. The counter is also true, and the small number of campuses which chose to "wash their hands" of the fraternity system through "derecognition" exemplify the result of uncooperative relationships between supporters and detractors of the fraternity movement.

One final reason can be cited for the unprecedented growth experienced by all fraternities. . . namely that men's and women's fraternities are fun. Survey after survey highlights that a primary motivation of students in seeking affiliation with any campus organization is fun. Fraternities in all forms offer an organized and varied schedule of activities including intramural sports, community service projects, dances, formals and theme functions. When properly planned and supervised, these activities are fun, constructive and developmental in many ways. However, these same activities when not properly planned, supervised and executed can result in criticism.

The fact remains that during the period of 1977–1991, students joined fraternities at a greater rate than at any previous time in the system's history. And as long as fraternities continue to offer students a niche on the campus, a chance to develop personal skills, an organized agenda of activities and friendship with students of similar interests, these organizations will continue to be as popular with the students of tomorrow as they are with those of today.

It's to the spirit of self-governance and fraternalism that is exemplified by the young men and women on the college campus today that this 20th edition of Baird's Manual is dedicated.

As with any project of this magnitude, there are a number of people to acknowledge and thank.

Sadly, the one person who is most responsible for this edition of Baird's Manual will never see the fruits of his labor. Jack Anson served as editor of this edition of the manual until his untimely death in 1990. Jack, the epitome of the loyal lifelong fraternity member, did the majority of the groundwork for this edition and it's to his memory that this 20th Baird's Manual is dedicated.

After taking over for Jack Anson, my single greatest source of assistance and inspiration has been Jonathan Brant. Despite the demands of his role as the NIC's executive vice president, Jonathan has always been there to share in the work, offer an encouraging word or help solve a problem.

I want to also extend my deepest appreciation to Frank Ruck, the chairman of the Baird's Manual Foundation, as well as the members of the board of the foundation. Frank's confidence in this project and me was always motivating.

Several additional people deserve special recognition as well: Mike Moxley of Maury Boyd and Associates for his patience and undying interest in seeing the 20th edition completed; Jody Toth of Shepard Poorman Communications for boundless enthusiasm and persistence; Kent Owen for writing the section on "The Nature of the College Fraternity;" Betty Mullins Jones for editing the "Origins and Evolution" section; Harriet Rodenberg for her assistance with the professional fraternity section; and Jayne Wade Anderson for her help with the honor society section.

I especially thank the fraternity and sorority staff members and volunteers, and college and university administrators who offered the updated information which constitutes most of what Baird's Manual is.

On a personal note, I must thank my wife, Marlene, and daughter, Allison, for allowing me to devote time to this project and to all the fraternity activities that play such an important role in my life.

It's interesting to note that when William Raimond Baird first published his Manual in 1879 he declared that such a book would be one of the means to attain the goal of common friendship among fraternities and to bring about a better understanding of the system by fraternity men and women, college faculties and the general public.

Baird, initiated as a member of Alpha Sigma Chi at Stevens Institute of Technology, led his fraternity's merger into Beta Theta Pi in 1879, the same year he published the small volume titled "American College Fraternities." He preferred the title author rather than editor of that first manual, and subsequent editions in 1880, 1883, 1890, 1898, 1905, 1912 and 1915. He was also a member of Tau Beta Pi and Phi Delta Phi, and between 1882 and 1893 served as secretary of the council of the latter. Professionally, he was a patent lawyer and a mineralogist.

The ninth and 10th editions of 1920 and 1923 were edited by James Taylor Brown, Beta Theta Pi, and the 11th, 12th and 13th editions of 1927, 1930 and 1935 by Francis W. Shephardson, Beta Theta Pi. Alvan E. Duerr, Delta Delta Delta, edited the 14th edition of 1940, Harold J. Bailey, Beta Theta Pi, the 15th edition of 1949, and George Starr Lasher, Theta Chi, the 16th edition of 1957. The editor of the 17th, 18th and 19th editions of 1963, 1968 and 1977 was John Robson, Sigma Phi Epsilon, the longtime chief editor of Banta publishing company. The editor of this 20th edition is Robert F. Marchesani Jr., Phi Kappa Psi, who assumed the role after the death of Jack L. Anson, Phi Kappa Tau. Anson served as editor of the project from the time the decision was made to publish the 20th edition until his untimely death in September 1990.

In closing, let me share one sentiment that hopefully will continue to be the foundation upon which the fraternity movement stands. It is a quotation from Ralph D. "Dud" Daniel of Phi Kappa Psi and one of the greatest fraternity men in the history of the movement. When speaking before a group of young fraternity men, Dud will often say, "Let's be what we say we are . . . a fraternity, not a club . . . made-up of men, not boys . . . based on ideals, not expediency."

Here's hoping we can all be what we say we are.

                                              Bob Marchesani

Table of Contents

PART V   PROFESSIONAL FRATERNITIES

PART VI   HONOR SOCIETIES

PART VII   RECOGNITION SOCIETIES

PART VIII   FRATERNITIES THAT ARE NO MORE

APPENDIX

INDEX

Part I

The American College Fraternity

Reflections on the College Fraternity and its Changing Nature

Kent Christopher Owen
© 1991

Free association is a curious notion. In America it is a constitutionally protected right, exercised vigorously by a free people to create all sorts of organizations for all sorts of purposes. What makes it curious is that the experience is at once an act of individualism and a preference for community. An individual can freely choose to belong to a group.

In the language of psychoanalysis, free association means spontaneously bringing to consciousness whatever perceptions, memories, and impressions a single word can summon. In common parlance, it is saying the first thing that comes to mind whenever a given word is spoken. Whether as a term of art or a parlor game, it tries to reveal the dominant meaning one keeps of something, deeply or superficially, true or false.

For the American college fraternity, both meanings are to the point. In the 1990s—if media reports are a valid measure—popular impressions of the fraternity dwell on alcohol-drenched, drug-infested tenements full of reckless louts, wild parties, gang rapes, brutal hazing, and like outrages.

Indeed, whenever the word "fraternity" comes up, the immediate images are almost certain to be offensive: the callous impudence of smug whites mocking poor blacks, the crass oafishness of Greek-lettered rowdies at sports events, the feral insolence of vain lordlings. Usually, the least objectionable is of a peppy fund-raising event: bouncing a basketball from Tuscaloosa to Memphis or choosing the shapeliest legs in Champaign-Urbana. Of course, the proceeds always go to charity.

If it were possible to write a history of what Americans think about "the college fraternity," it would disclose the vagaries of our collective beliefs in the idealism of youth, the formation of character, the soundness of academic institutions as moral agencies, the perfectibility of man and the idea of progress, and the struggle between good and evil. Admittedly, this raises the matter to a higher level of abstraction. However, it gets at what is ultimately at stake.

In any case there is no denying that in the 1990s the very mention of fraternity sets off a barrage of reactions: scornful condemnation through wary misgivings and partial approvals to defensive sentimentality or stubborn loyalty. Only one thing is certain: almost no one is indifferent. Sad to say, not many take the trouble to think through the matter for the sake of a fair and accurate understanding. Hence a mass of instant perceptions, usually based on lurid and appalling instances, obscure the full nature of the college fraternity.

For much of the early and mid-nineteenth century, largely because of its secrecy, the fraternity had gained the reputation of being a subversive, even ungodly organization. Chiefly to professors and trustees, the fraternity appeared to threaten the academic monopoly on the thinking and conduct of students, which colleges took as their moral duty. Owing mainly to the anti-Masonic political movement, it was seen as a disruptive conspiracy against the academic order.

And in a sense it was. Then as now, college students were often dissatisfied with stodgy teaching, arbitrary requirements, and courses that took little notice of current issues and events. In reaction students organized their own literary and debating societies so that they could express themselves freely on the foremost topics of the day as well as the more enduring questions prompted by their studies. Within such societies controversy energized young minds that had been made to learn orthodox opinions by rote. Within some classrooms it was often hard to tell where the lecture began and the sermon left off.

All the same it should be noted that several colleges where fraternities were founded—e.g., Union, Jefferson, Hamilton, and Miami—were rather advanced, even experimental in teaching methods and curricula, encouraging students to think for themselves beyond the bounds of academic conventionality. What these colleges had in common to a varying extent was the reforming influence of evangelical Presbyterians and the common sense empiricism of the Scottish Enlightenment. It is probable that Scottish Freemasonry was also a motive force, helping to shape the collegiate ethos through the boot-legged doctrines of liberal humanism, then not yet wholly secularized.

Inevitably, what had begun as shared yearning for a livelier life of the mind grew into a broader fellowship. Intellectual pastimes persisted at the center of fraternity life until nearly the end of the nineteenth century: orations, debates, the reading of original poems as well as scientific and scholarly papers. But for all the earnestness that the young scholars applied to the high-minded business of fraternity, they found plenty of time for parties, games, dancing, sports, outings, and the kindred pleasures of one another's company.

From the outset, fraternity chapters grew differing histories and personalities. Some were zealously religious, some keenly political, some boisterously athletic, some giddily social. There were serious scholars and indifferent ones; young men of principled purpose and those of aimless disposition; sons of the rich and high-born, proud of their privilege; sons of middling families and less, ambitious to advance. Were such students truly the brightest and the best of their generation? If so, when? In the 1850s? or the 1890s? the 1930s? the 1980s?

Throughout nearly the whole of the nineteenth century fraternity chapters remained small in numbers and selective in quality: their size seldom exceeded thirty members and was often half that. Some of the members usually lived together in boarding houses and college lodgings, but few chapters occupied their own houses until the 1890s. Once fraternity alumni had grown prosperous enough to rent or build chapter houses and, more important, influential enough in college affairs to get permission for such arrangements, chapter sizes slowly started to increase.

It is tempting to see the arrival of the fraternity chapter house as the closing of the fraternity's intellectual, moral, and cultural "golden age." When a fraternity got together only once a week or so for a chapter meeting, the occasion was extraordinary. Gathering in a rented hall or classroom, fraternity brothers could invest their time together with a sense of special purpose. Whether they met to discuss a passage from Aristotle's *Nicomachean Ethics* or Erasmus's *Adagia* or the Missouri Compromise, they could engage each topic, serious or not, with undistracted freedom.

But as soon as a chapter settled under one roof and took on the duties of housekeeping, the main emphasis in fraternity affairs became starkly practical. Alumni raised money to build the house and, as corporation trustees, handled mortgage payments, large-scale maintenance, and legal matters. It was up to the undergraduates to manage internal affairs and routine business, which they did largely by trial and error.

In a period of about fifty years the chapter's foremost concerns had changed from an express emphasis on intellectual development and moral education to social, recreational, and extracurricular activities. Romantic idealists and intellectuals gave way to good fellows. When the chapter's daily life became centered in a common residence and shaped by it, economic considerations began to take priority, for good or ill. Yet the establishment of the chapter in its own house brought about at the same time the establishment of more systematic self-governance through both leadership and stewardship.

In effect the moral principles and ethical theories propounded by the founders had at last taken concrete form in the actual community of a self-governing chapter. Fraternity was no longer an abstract proposition of building utopias; it was now a tangible problem of managing relationships among frequently conflicting personalities and interests.

In the best tradition of American pragmatism the ideals on which the fraternity was based—justice, honor, truth, loyalty, love of wisdom, brotherly love, unselfish service, and the like—were daily put to the test. Granted, the test was merely the workaday routines of ordinary undergraduates—hardly a valid sample of urgent complexities in "the real world." Still, the advent of the chapter house marked a decisive shift from fraternity as speculation and personal friendships to fraternity as practical experience and communal relationships.

The move to the chapter house produced other structural changes. It had been customary to offer formal invitations, one by one, to students proposed for membership; upon their acceptance they were then initiated shortly thereafter, usually one at a time and often on separate occasions. But because a chapter house had to be kept full, incoming freshmen were recruited as pledges in classes or delegations—often "rushed" on arrival at the train station, then "spiked" with buttons or ribbons—and carted off to the house. Once there and settled in, the pledges were soon put to work, doing menial chores and running errands for upperclassmen; the latter duties were in the "fagging" tradition of the English public schools, which American boarding schools had discovered handy to imitate and passed along to fraternities.

While the mere existence of the chapter house can scarcely be blamed for hazing, it certainly made the fraternity's most troubling and reviled custom all the easier. Unless chapter officers were vigilant and chapter discipline diligently enforced, there were simply too many opportunities for a few bullies and rowdies to harass pledges in their power. Old-fashioned hazing was generally of the rough-and-tumble sort: swats with paddles, harmless scraps, coltish free-for-alls. It was left to later generations to introduce road trips, snipe and scavenger hunts, asinine public stunts and practical jokes, humiliating games, punishing physical exercises, and ingenious forms of psychological discomfort.

What all this has to do with fostering brotherhood through shared moral ideals and principles is a subject that belongs more appropriately to the history of military training and perhaps certain cultic orders. Nonetheless, in the history of academic institutions hazing dates back at least to the medieval universities of Europe and Britain. Hazing in American schools and colleges, not alone in fraternities, emerged on a broad scale after the Civil War, when it had been a common feature of military camp life. Afterwards, "rough play" became an occasional diversion in chapter and college life, which general fraternities first began to oppose by edict in the late 1860s.

By the start of the twentieth century the fraternities that chapter houses were built to sustain had already changed almost beyond recognition from the early, simple bands of brothers. Just as public and private universities had begun to overshadow smaller, church-related colleges, so had the new vocational curricula of commerce, engineering, and the applied sciences overtaken the traditional studies of the liberal arts and the learned professions. College education in America had outgrown the rarefied day of the gentleman and the scholar.

It could no longer be assumed that college students in general, let alone fraternity men in particular, were well schooled in the classics. With little Latin and less Greek, few chapters contained students who were prepared to understand the deeper meanings and broader implications of their ceremonies. Or, more's the pity, who were intellectually curious enough to make the effort. Many of the fraternities founded in the middle decades of the nineteenth century derived the essential elements of their rituals from the philosophy and literature of ancient Greece and Rome as well as the Jewish and Christian Scriptures. Some drew on the chivalric traditions of the Middle Ages, military codes of honor, precepts and forms of Freemasonry, and, after the Civil War, the conciliatory endeavors of universal brotherhood. There was also evidence of the teachings of Enlightenment science and philosophy, especially in the Scottish tradition, and the projects of European and British Romanticism.

Seldom having little more than a slight acquaintance with such sources, chapters were inclined to stress the awe-inspiring and theatrical aspects of initiatory rites at the expense of profounder significance. Spectacle and mystery, rather than humane learning and ancient wisdom, came to prevail. Primeval myths, powerful in austerity, were distorted into gorgeous but ludicrous pageants. What the Greeks of old may have inspired, latterday vulgarians did their damnedest to obscure and confuse.

Coffins and hooded robes, burning crosses and stakes, swords and armor, cauldrons and grails, lions and dragons, terrifying oaths and incantations, the regalia of crusaders, cavaliers, feudal knights, holy pilgrims and sainted martyrs, stage machinery and special effects—all these were elevated into the mystical means that transformed lowly pledges into bonded brothers. What light and truth may have failed to accomplish, sensation dared to attempt.

At the outbreak of World War I the college fraternity movement—for a movement it had indeed become—was an immense success. Plainly, the fraternity had long since grown far beyond its modest origins as a secret society brought into being by little groups of student idealists. At last a presence across the whole continent extending into Canada, the movement comprised women's fraternities (or sororities as some wished to be known), Jewish as well as Christian fraternities (Catholic and Protestant), fraternities for blacks as well as whites, secret and non-secret, aggressively expansive and determinedly limited, democratic and elitist. In brief a sprawling assortment of free associations almost as variegated as American democracy itself.

Chapter houses were by now standard points of reference on the campus, welcomed by administrators and trustees as useful adjuncts. An inescapable presence, fraternities set the social tone, dominated campus politics and extracurricular activities, and defined whatever the collegiate experience was supposed to be all about. Fraternity dances and serenades, fraternity pranks and stunts, fraternity songs and cheers, fraternity parties and reunions—the confounded ubiquity of Greek letters.

For many colleges and universities, the customs and traditions carried on by fraternities were virtually the only customs and traditions that the institutions possessed, the only vital history there was. Without the Greeks they were just so many lackluster, nondescript academies. Fortunately, fraternity alumni felt intense loyalty to both alma mater and fraternity, believing that generous support for one clearly benefited the other. Over the years fraternities and academic institutions—after their initial resistance to one another—had grown ever more intertwined, practically to a condition of mutual dependency. In the late nineteenth century and again in the early twentieth, populist legislatures in South Carolina and Mississippi forced fraternities to disband temporarily at the state universities, and private colleges such as Carleton and Wooster dismissed them as inimical to academic purposes.

But elsewhere in the nation, especially because of a judicial decision involving Purdue, fraternities were securely in place.

As fraternity alumni achieved affluence and prominence in disproportionate numbers—Greek journals and public prints were ever ready to point that out—it became common opinion that a college education was not in itself sufficient for success. One had to belong to a good fraternity if one really wanted to succeed in American society. There was apparently something magical about secret handshakes and passwords that admitted an able young man to the inner sanctum of business, industry, and the professions—or, at the very least, afforded him a privileged opportunity to prove his merit. Hence, apart from the glamour that fraternities seemed to radiate on campus, there was the widely held notion that fraternities were able to guarantee successful careers and, for all one knew, the total fulfillment of the American dream—riches, fame, power, prestige, and the love of beautiful women.

Broadway comedies and operettas, novels and short stories (ah, dear old Siwash), and fraternity ballads (SAE's "Violets," "White Star of Sigma Nu," and, inexorably, "Sweetheart of Sigma Chi") presented young Greeks as irresistibly charming. By the mid-twenties, Hollywood was showing the American public pretty pictures of fraternity life. The rose-tinted images were wholesome and appealing: manly good fellows and winsome young ladies, one and all well-mannered, high-spirited, slightly naughty but discreet, and always ready to give it the old college try. If the American public had to give any thought to fraternities, it was bound to be one of carefree gaiety and ceaseless happiness. From the Greeks there was always good news.

Even so, observers of higher education knew that the golden Greeks had fallen far short of recreating Athenian civilization on the campuses of America. Most academics were willing to treat them with benign forbearance, content with their docility and the stable order they gave to collegiate life. All the same, full of their success and acclaim, fraternities had provoked severe critics and forthright opponents: impassioned college teachers, student journalists and politicians, social activists, who rallied the independents or "barbarians" to challenge the supremacy of the Greeks.

What these antagonists thought they saw when they looked hard was bumptious pride, lordly arrogance, self-indulgence, plutocratic ostentation, snobbery, social apathy, crass materialism, anti-intellectualism, and an ugly array of prejudices. Ironically, these charges resembled nothing so much as the syllabus of vices that a good many fraternity founders had originally set out to counteract. Obviously, the way to the Good, the True, and the Beautiful did not necessarily lead to fraternity row.

And there to this day, for unyielding opponents of the fraternity, the matter yet remains. On their view the fraternity is inherently and irredeemably corrupt. Their bill of particulars, admittedly overstated, goes something like this. Left to govern themselves, young men inevitably fall prey to evil, unable to withstand the temptations to misuse authority and to harm their fellow creatures. Granted the moral sanctions of ritual and tradition, they act arbitrarily to suit their own pleasure and convenience, ignoring the demands of justice, honor, and decency. Separated from the larger academic community, they mislead themselves into believing the illusion of their own superiority, acknowledging only themselves and others like themselves as worthy of dignity and respect. Secure in the sanctuary of a chapter house, they are impervious to the enlightened influences that circulate freely and constantly throughout the rest of academic society. All in all, there is in the nature of young men a capacity for evil, which is activated by the very nature of the fraternity; therefore, because the fraternity causes young men to do evil, the fraternity must be abolished. Q.E.D.

Put that boldly, this radical critique forces even the most complacent loyalist to sit up and take notice. Faulty logic and false premises aside, the perennial criticism of the fraternity as a social organization is that it overestimates the ability of young men to govern themselves, whatever the circumstances. The argument strikes at the heart of the American assumption, grounded in the work of Jefferson, Hamilton, and Madison, that a free man is fully capable of choosing his associates and then of proceeding to conduct his own life in cooperation with theirs without endangering the health and safety of the larger community as a whole.

Must the state or its agencies—academy, public assembly, police, or other civil authorities—supervise the conduct of those persons who are law-abiding citizens? Is the adult citizen entitled to enjoy his privacy without interference? What conditions present such a clear and present danger that the freedom of association must be abridged?

Seen in these terms, the college fraternity as a continuing experiment in free association and self-governance raises greater issues about the fate of representative democracy and moral education? Are young men becoming increasingly ungovernable and ineducable? Is it reasonable to entrust the authority and responsibility of the self-governing fraternity to the rising generations whose behavior seems to indicate otherwise.?

These were the questions that were raised about the nature of the fraternity and the moral capacity of its members—insistently raised in the mid-prohibition twenties and the post-prohibition thirties when excessive drinking and reckless partying were thought to have dragged down the Greeks to the lowest depths of iniquity and degradation. When the fraternity system—the community of chapters had somehow evolved into a system, supposedly indicative of intensive organization and centralized control—survived first the great Depression and then World War II and returned in full force to campus, its durability perplexed the opposition. How in the world could such an antiquated and enervated relic of the bad old social order muster the strength to keep going?

Of course, the perennial criticisms persisted, particularly about lax academic performance, dangerous hazing, and overactive social life. As American higher education became more relentlessly democratic—thanks in great measure to the returning veterans who took full advantage of the G.I. Bill or Rights—the fraternity movement had to confront the fact that its membership policies were by and large offensively discriminatory. After initial resistance and consequent embarrassment, fraternities gradually dismantled the barriers and began to admit men from a broader spectrum of racial, social, religious, and ethnic backgrounds.

From the many-layered mixture of changes in post-war America came a variety of renovated, more broadly representative fraternities—more broadly representative fraternities, that is, of the nation's college-attending population. In fact, the nature of the fraternity had changed once again, this time in scope. If fraternities had chosen to narrow themselves in membership, they might have failed to adapt to the new realities, withdrawing to themselves and dwindling to eventual inconsequence. In the main, however, the fraternity movement had the good sense, or good luck, to choose breadth—if by breadth one means a richer selection of qualities and abilities—and accordingly to choose growth—if by growth one means vitality, not merely expansion in quantity.

No matter how wisely fraternities might have planned and acted, neither they nor any other segment of American society, especially one identified with "the establishment," could have come through the social turbulence and political turmoil of the sixties and seventies in firm command of its own destiny. The war in Vietnam and its aftermath, campus revolts and radical initiatives, and the civil rights, feminist, and gay liberation movements—to note only a few of the major elements—unsettled virtually everything and strongly affected its subsequent course, whether in reform or reaction.

As convenient symbols of social oppression, fraternities suddenly found themselves the direct objects of fierce hostility and nearly violent contempt. While chapters collapsed and members disappeared, Greeks in many parts of the country were understandably discouraged, but seldom actually panic-stricken.

In retrospect the worst damage done to fraternities and, by extension, to colleges and universities was less the loss of chapters and members than the loss of an assured identity, of a secure position in collegiate life. What the Greeks had actually achieved, what they had come to represent over long years of association—historical continuity, venerable traditions, rooted values, stability, institutional loyalties, vitality of collegiate culture,

leadership and stewardship, richly textured community, an ethic of civic responsibility and public service, and much else besides—all that was in one way or another displaced and disrupted, although not totally destroyed.

During the late seventies and well into the eighties a considerable amount of what fraternities had either lost or been forced to surrender was reclaimed—at least there was the appearance of reestablished continuities and traditions—but in a deeper sense the real nature of the relationship, the wholeness itself that had once organically connected fraternity life with the greater life of the academic institution, was irretrievably different and strange.

What had gone wrong did not become fully evident until the eighties were well under way. Most fraternities grew extravagantly, some prodigiously in record numbers of new chapters, pledges, initiates, alumni contributions—all the statistical and financial measures of corporate success. Indeed, the fraternity business had never been better.

But the signs were not uniformly auspicious. Seemingly, one chapter after another, first in this part of the country and then in that, was involved in a bad hazing incident or a case of gang rape or a drunken brawl or a drug raid or a racial confrontation or mindless vandalism. Here a pledge died of alcohol poisoning and there a young woman was sexually assaulted. And nearly everywhere that there was trouble on campus, there were plenty of Greek letters on display. Or so it appeared, if one watched television, went to movies, read newspapers and magazines, and ventured into public, thus putting oneself at the disposal of media-driven mass culture and designer-opinion.

Were fraternities in fact instigating most of the evils that infected American campuses? Were fraternity members going berserk on booze and drugs to wreak havoc in every direction? Did the academy's student-appeasing decision in the late sixties to do away with in loco parentis and parietal regulations set loose a rampaging monster into its midst? Did the fraternities' partial downfall in the time of the Dire Paroxysm cause them to abandon whatever remained of self-governance and moral education? Have their own alumni and other adherents finally given up on them altogether? Most important, is there any longer a safe place for fraternities in the reconstructed, deconstructed, post-structural academic community, where multicultural, politically correct behavior is the enforced order of the day?

In the eighties a few colleges such as Amherst and Colby felt sure they knew the truth about fraternities and banished the chapters one and all. Oddly enough, a few returned not many years later to reestablish extramural, almost sub rosa chapters, much to the chagrin of the college authorities. Before long a passel of college and universities, mainly in the Northeast but notably in Pennsylvania, scrutinized fraternities, found them deficient in many respects, and moved to withdraw official recognition and support or to curtail them in various ways.

Gathering momentum into the nineties, the "Greek Life Movement" spread rapidly to both public and private institutions throughout the nation, suprisingly even to several in the Midwest and the South, which had long maintained hospitable, mutually beneficial relations with the fraternities in residence. Fortunately for the chapters involved, such old-line institutions elected to apply sensible, construction reforms instead of the punitive sanctions imposed in the Northeast.

Still, there is no mistaking the intentions of the academy: fraternities must change their ways or die. In most circumstances, if academic administrations can be believed and trusted, gradual reforms should be sufficient if they are reasonably effective. But in those institutions, for the time being, under the sway of the eclectic New Left and allied radicals no amount of the most effective reforms on the part of the Greeks, achieved by them in good faith, will ever satisfy what are becoming "nonnegotiable demands."

For such willful intransigents the only acceptable ideological solution to the fraternity problem is total, permanent extinction. Thus alone will the class struggle on campus be advanced toward power to the people; thus alone will social justice be perfected.

Where, then, does all this leave America's college fraternities? More to the point, why should ordinary citizens concern themselves with what are, after all, private, voluntary organizations? Is there actually any important question of public policy? Or are these rhetorical questions meant only to forward inquiry and discussion? Isn't the entire problem in the final analysis, well, rather academic?

The modern dictum that all politics is local applies just as well to fraternities, also in their way political entities. Despite the hierarchies of general fraternities—national governing councils and assemblies, professional executive staffs, and extensive networks of alumni volunteers—the life of the fraternity is centered in each local chapter, occupied, managed, and governed by undergraduates. No matter how many and disparate are the ties that bind the local chapter to the general fraternity, the fact remains that decentralized operation is the reality of the situation. By the way, this condition seldom affects the overwhelming majority of women's fraternity chapters, and usually not at all; their systems of centralized control and supervised operation involve alumnae members to an extent unmatched by any known men's fraternity.

Given what is the rough equivalent of local autonomy within a federation, each chapter is, in effect, free to do and be pretty much whatever it damned well pleases. Of course, this is at once the joy and the sorrow of free association. So long as what a chapter chooses is lawful and responsible, there need be no cause for complaint. Once a chapter ignores its legitimate obligations, resists its own history and traditions, defies the authority of alumni, general fraternity, and institution, violates the civil order and outrages common decency, that chapter—more especially, the present undergrauate generation—must forfeit the freedom of association and suffer the penalty of banishment, fittingly the punishment of ostracism imposed by the ancient Greeks on their own outlaws.

All the zany, reckless nihilism that made the 1979 movie "Animal House" the prevalent image of fraternities for millions of Americans, including rising generations of would-be and initiated Greeks, has brought strange consequences. In one coarsely hilarious movie after another, film-makers and television producers gorge the public's insatiable appetite for hot stuff about the partying and mating habits of rich, wild, and crazy Greek-letter frat kids. The art falls somewhat short of Aristophanes and Plautus, although Petronius and Rabelais might have been enormously amused. At the very least, it all goes to show that satire is a tricky genre for even clever hacks.

But to the literal-minded young and others of similar impairment, the rollicking, roguish images have been accepted as a quasi-documentary representation of fraternity life. As a result or as a metaphor, the kind of fraternity experience that students desire and expect—and tend to create for themselves—appears to be based largely on the constant pursuit of pleasure, good times, and fun. Which, one must concede, is not quite unnatural, but after awhile rather tedious.

One may be led to believe that the social customs of latterday Greeks resemble frenzied Dionysian revels more than the drinking parties of Socrates, where the conversation was bright and lively, but women were almost never present. Admittedly, excessive drinking has become the contemporary campus's most serious problem, and the Greeks, no strangers to fashion, have made it their central and common ritual. Nearly all their own woes are related in some way to the promiscuous consumption of alcohol, despite the fact that every general fraternity has made efforts to place limits on its use. Here again, the de facto existence of local autonomy for chapters brings with it a sort of local option about drinking, how a chapter chooses to use the option and accept the consequences.

If nothing else is entirely clear about the present-day state of the American college fraternity, it can be said that the experience it makes available is neither monolithic, assuredly beneficial, nor risk-free. When most fraternities came into being, founders and pioneering members seemed convinced that the essential principles, precepts, and ideals would somehow enable their brotherhoods to transcend the wicked circumstances of the surrounding society.

Once, according to Socrates, one had achieved true knowledge of the Good, virtue was certain to ensue. Nevertheless, there was the Socratic Paradox: having come to know the Good, one could not then turn away from it because the will would never let one act against the best interests of one's own soul. It would be left to later minds to figure out why one would deliberately choose to ignore the Good and, worse yet, choose to forsake virtue.

Social scientists may explain it all away as cognitive dissonance, Freudians as the brutish clutch of the id, Marxians as the cultural contradiction of capitalism, theologians as original sin, and academic radicals as the fallacy of America. Whatever the cause, the human propensity for misdoing is a fact of nature from which not even the most enlightened and humane fraternity can redeem the natural yahoo. Only rush chairmen and social workers believe otherwise.

Perhaps the right question to ask about the fraternity is not: what can one learn through it about the Good, the True, and the Beautiful or about Justice, Honor, and Magnanimity or about Compassion, Generosity, and Brotherly Love or about Loyalty, Constancy, and Dedication or about Courage, Discipline, and Perseverance or about Moral Responsibility, Personal Integrity, and Noble Service?

Rather, it may well be: what can one learn about Evil, Falsehood, and Vulgarity or about Injustice, Dishonor, and Meanness of Spirit or about Callousness, Avarice, and Inhumanity or about Treachery, Faithlessness, and Aimlessness or about Cowardice, Disorderliness, and Vacillation or about Irresponsibility, Weakness of Character, and Base Selfishness?

Suprisingly, neither of these catalogues is culled from *The Pilgrim's Progress*. Nor is either an exercise in cynicism or a counsel of despair. Instead, this gets at the difficulty and complexity of the human condition and of human nature itself as that is discovered sooner or later in any endeavor, the fraternity providing no exception.

What such an awareness may foster is a certain measure of understanding and acceptance, not the arrogant illusion of complete knowledge or comprehension, but a deeper humility before the mysteries of the human spirit. What it may also foster is a well-tempered sense of regret and resignation about human frailty. That, too, is worth having. One should not lose much time in coming to terms with the tragic. The human comedy makes precious little sense without it.

Although it seems a peculiar way of dealing with such questions, perhaps the soundest approach may be, after all, by indirection. There is a good deal to be said in favor of going roundabout to look aslant at things. Anything as manifold and multifaceted as fraternities have grown to become during two centuries requires a fair amount of modesty when it comes to considering their lasting values and significance.

Let it be said that fraternities are about what matters most: enduring friendships founded on shared principles and personal affinities; living out good lives, not just having good times; cordial laughter, delightful gaiety, robust merriment; the lively pleasures of good companions; the sustaining loyalty of old comrades through whatever fortune or adversity may appear; the settled conviction that lives are lived to the best effect when firmly secured by mutual bonds of deep affection, administration, and respect. In freedom, if wisely chosen, there is fraternity, and in fraternity, if rightly used, there is joy.

Interfraternalism

"Cooperative efforts among chapters are a priority. Activities unifying the fraternity system and fostering an understanding of common purpose must be developed and maintained. Unhealthy competition should be minimized."

William Raimond Baird, Beta Theta Pi, the author of the first edition of this MANUAL in 1879, is the father of the interfraternity movement. It is evident in the current literature of the time that Mr. Baird's correspondence with other fraternity leaders, like the appearance of the MANUAL itself, resulted in a setting of the stage.

After the appearance of the first edition, Willis O. Robb, newly appointed editor of *The Beta Theta Pi* magazine, began to stimulate interest through correspondence with fellow editors, for an interfraternity meeting at which topics of mutual interest might be discussed, particularly public relations. Robb wrote an editorial in November, 1881, proposing an inter-Greek meeting. He said: "We look forward with confidence to a not distant time when an ecumenical conference of fraternity men will be held and arrangements made which will greatly strengthen the good feeling now developing so rapidly." The December, 1881, issue followed up this suggestion by an editorial, "Pan-Hellenic Council," in which Robb swept away objections that had been voiced to such a council and named topics which it might be useful to discuss at such a conference.

On February 22, 1883, thirteen editors of fraternity journals convened at the old Colonnade Hotel, Philadelphia. This was the first meeting of what is known today as the College Fraternity Editors Association. A resolution was adopted recommending that "a Panhellenic Conference be held in New York City to begin July 4, 1884, provided that ten fraternities shall signify their intention to participate on or before January 1, 1884." Though fewer than ten fraternities pledged to attend and thus this conference died a-borning, the movement was discussed in the fraternity journals. The discussion itself served to bring about many of the results which it was hoped might be accomplished by the meeting. From that time in several colleges the chapters of the different fraternities therein established held an annual panhellenic banquet. Tacit agreements and in many cases written contracts were made regarding the pledging and initiation of certain classes of students and a number of customs grew relative to matters of common interest. Panhellenic clubs, composed of members of different fraternities, were formed in many cities.

In 1891 at the call of Kappa Kappa Gamma a panhellenic convention of seven women's fraternities met at Boston. It lasted three days and concluded with a banquet.

Against the background of the Philadelphia meeting of 1883, some of the leaders arranged a modest get-together in July, 1893, at the Chicago World's Fair, which they called College Fraternities Congress. Joseph C. Nate, historian of Sigma Chi, wrote: "A Congress was held for discussion of fraternity problems; an exhibit maintained in the educational section of the fair under the direction of the associated fraternities and there was a group meeting of the editors of fraternity journals." A paper read at this Congress was "Legal Status of the Fraternities," given by Mr. Baird himself. Elsewhere it is reported that a number of representatives from women's national fraternities were present. A similar and somewhat informal meeting took place at the Cotton States and International Exposition, Atlanta, Georgia, on November 18, 1895. On that day, about three hundred fraternity members, presided over by W. W. Davies, Phi Delta Theta, formed The American Panhellenic Society, though its purposes were not definitely expressed. No representatives from the women's groups participated. The National Panhellenic Conference of women's fraternities was formed in 1902.

In February, 1909, at a meeting of the Religious Education Association held at Chicago, a series of resolutions was presented by George D. Kimball, Sigma Alpha Epsilon, suggesting that steps should be taken to bring about a panhellenic union of the different men's fraternities. In consequence to this resolution, a call was sent out by W. H. P. Faunce, Delta Upsilon, president of Brown University, representing the Association, to all fraternities for men whose addresses he could ascertain. In response representatives of twenty-six fraternities met at the University Club in New York City on November 17, 1909. An organization was effected with Hamilton W. Mabie, Alpha Delta Phi, as chairman, and Francis W. Shepardson, Beta Theta Pi, as secretary. That was the beginning of the National Interfraternity Conference.

Business of the campus interfraternity council was transacted decades before there was such a thing as a national conference. For example, at Monmouth College at the opening of the college year in 1870, a meeting was called of the chapters of Beta Theta Pi, Delta Tau Delta, Kappa Phi Lambda, Phi Gamma Delta, and Phi Sigma. The following resolution was adopted: "We promise neither to vote

upon, bid, or initiate, nor in any wise electioneer for, or with, any outsider for membership in our fraternities until after January 1, 1871."

The hand of Mr. Baird is also seen, and not faintly, in the evolution of the campus interfraternity council. Baird was chairman of a Conference committee appointed in 1911 to study campus rushing agreements and the following year presented a printed report of 47 pages, which gives information about rushing methods at 78 institutions. "We believe that if each fraternity in this Conference," said Baird in his report, "should through its officials urge its several chapters to actively promote and enthusiastically assist in the organization of local conferences they would be speedily formed everywhere." He went on to warn: "It is plainly evident that unless they remedy the admitted evils of rushing that the college authorities will assume control of such matters and put such limitations upon the activities of the different fraternities as to cripple their membership and interfere with their progress."

Evidence of the increased strength and unity of fraternities and sororities on the undergraduate level is reflected in the international organizations, the National Panhellenic Conference, the National Interfraternity Conference, the Professional Fraternity Association, the National Interfraternity Foundation, the Center for the Study of the College Fraternity, the Association of Fraternity Advisors, and the National Pan Hellenic Council.

Interfraternity and Panhellenic cohesiveness has received additional impetus in recent years through outstanding Regional Interfraternity Conferences. They are: Mid-American Interfraternity Council Association (MIFCA), Mid-American Panhellenic Council Association (MAPCA), Northeast Interfraternity Conference (NEIFC), Northeast Panhellenic Conference (NEPC), Southeastern Interfraternity Conference (SEIFC), Southeastern Panhellenic Conference (SEPC), and Western Regional Greek Conference (WRGC). Each is an association of campus councils, offering an annual educational and legislative conference as well as a variety of support services throughout the year.

Greek Week has steadily become a symbol of cooperation between the campus and the Greeks. Its place of origin was appropriately Athens, Ohio. Impressed by the friendly spirit and helpful attitude being generated among fraternities at the National Interfraternity Conference, George Starr Lasher, Theta Chi, in 1929 returned to Ohio University where he was in charge of the journalism program, with the conviction that the need for such cooperation was on the campus as well as among national leaders. As a result, the next year, 1930, Ohio University held an undergraduate interfraternity conference with two of the most outstanding fraternity men in the nation as speakers, Francis W. Shepardson, national president of Beta Theta Pi, and Alvan E. Duerr, past national president of Delta Tau Delta. Panel discussions were guided by representatives of six other national fraternities. The success of the experiment warranted its continuance. Other campuses adopted the idea. The title Greek Week was used first by Ohio State in 1933. John O. Moseley, Sigma Alpha Epsilon, outlined a constructive program to cover a week's activities that provided a pattern which influenced the events that now are held in many schools throughout the country. In most of them both fraternity and sorority chapters combine for the program.

Greek Weeks through friendly relations, service, and exercise in understanding should increase the prestige of the IFC and the Panhellenic on many campuses.

The Kinds of Fraternities and Sororities

From the origin of the college fraternity in the 18th century, the evolution of the system has created a number of different kinds of fraternities. The characteristics that differentiate the types of fraternities relate to their purposes, membership requirements or field of interest.

The various kinds of fraternities are best identified by the coordinating conferences or associations to which they belong. These organizations include the National Interfraternity Conference, National Panhellenic Conference, National Pan Hellenic Council, Professional Fraternity Association and the Association of College Honor Societies.

One type of fraternal organization without an umbrella group is the recognition society, which differs from a fraternity in that it exists mainly to recognize achievement or interest in a specific field.

The fraternity, whether for men or women — the latter typically known as a sorority — is considered a general fraternity if it offers membership to students without regard to field of study, class year or grade attainment above the typical minimum requirement.

General fraternities are commonly called "social" fraternities, but while the initial use of the term social referred to social development, the term has been mistakenly thought to refer to social functions by members and non-members alike. Actually, the intent was to suggest that a student needed to be "socialized," that is, directed with a proper consideration of one's future responsibilities in society.

Fraternity leaders, therefore, prefer the term general fraternity when referring to organizations that offer membership to students from all academic backgrounds. One additional difference between general fraternities and other types of groups is the single-sex nature of the memberships. As a result of the same legislation that protected the single-sex nature of the Boy Scouts and Girl Scouts, fraternities are able to remain as single-sex organizations.

The professional fraternity differs from the general fraternity in a few respects as far as membership is concerned. First, it selects all its members from students pursuing a similar course of study. The professional groups also organize social activities that are in harmony with their specific and common educational goals. Lastly, professional fraternities are all co-educational.

Nith relatively few exceptions, both the general and professional fraternities have been mutually exclusive in their memberships; and no fraternities initiate any member of another fraternity in the same category.

While general fraternities elect membership by mutual choice, the societies confer membership upon the individual, regardless of membership in any other organization and without solicitation of any kind to insure acceptance of election. Moreover, since the fraternity offers an organized social life for its members, congeniality is essential, and therefore personal qualifications of the candidate assume importance. The societies, on the other hand, ordinarily do not attempt to organize activities for their members; they exist more to give recognition to interest and merit.

The following definitions will help differentiate the kinds of fraternities in existence:

Men's general college fraternities are mutually exclusive, self-perpetuating groups which provide an organized social life for their members in college and universities as a contributing aspect of their educational experience. They draw their members primarily from the undergraduate student body.

Women's general college fraternities are primarily groups of women at colleges and universities which, in addition to their individual purposes, are committed to cooperation with college administrators to maintain high social and scholastic standards and which do not limit membership to any one academic field.

Professional fraternities are specialized organizations which limit membership to a students in a specific field of study; which maintain mutually exclusive membership in that field, but may initiate members of the general fraternities; and which organizes its group life specifically to promote professional competency and achievement within its field. Professional fraternities are typically open to male and female students, have minimum scholastic requirements for membership, and sponsor professional development programs that are of interest to student and/or alumni members of the fraternities.

An honor society is an association of primarily collegiate members and chapters whose purposes are to encourage and recognize superior scholarship and/or leadership achievement either in broad fields of education or in departmental fields at either the undergraduate or graduate levels.

A recognition society is an organization which confers members in recognition of a student's interest and participation in some field of collegiate study or activity with more liberal membership requirements than are prescribed for general and departmental honor societies.

Origins and Evolution of the College Fraternity

Men's Groups The year 1776 saw the birth both of the United States of America and Phi Beta Kappa, the first American society bearing a Greek-letter name. Phi Beta Kappa was founded December 5, 1776, at the College of William and Mary in Williamsburg, Virginia, the second oldest college in America, where it had been preceded by a society of somewhat uncertain nature called The Flat Hat which saw birth in 1750 and is believed to have continued in existence for at least twenty years. Phi Beta Kappa had all the characteristics of the present-day fraternity: the charm and mystery of secrecy, a ritual, oaths of fidelity, a grip, a motto, a badge for external display, a background of high idealism, a strong tie of friendship and comradeship, an urge for sharing its values through nation-wide expansion. It was formed for social and literary purposes and held regular and frequent meetings. In December, 1779, the parent chapter authorized the establishment of branches at Yale and Harvard, and in January, 1781, as the contending armies in the Revolutionary War became increasingly active in the Virginia peninsula it ceased its own operations.

The chapter at Yale was to have been called Zeta, but when it was actually established, November 13, 1780, it took the name of Alpha of Connecticut. It was quite formal in its nature, its membership being confined to the two upper classes, and it soon lost whatever of vitality and fraternal spirit had existed in the original organization. The Harvard chapter, called Alpha of Massachusetts, was established September 5, 1781, and these two chapters together organized Alpha of New Hampshire at Dartmouth in 1787. There was no further expansion for thirty years, and, when half a century of the fraternity's life had passed, there were only five active chapters. It soon became and since has remained a scholarly honor society.

The first of several orders of Kappa Alpha originated at the University of North Carolina in 1812, and it established a number of chapters throughout the Carolinas and other southern states.[1] Pi Beta Phi, a local, was established at Union in 1813 with a "hope to equal the learned societies of this country, both in fame and utility," Chi Delta Theta, a local, at Yale in 1821, and Chi Phi, a local, at Princeton in 1924. The first of these had no continuing influence, but Chi Phi was the basis for the Chi Phi Society at Princeton in 1854, which has had a continuous existence since that date.

In many colleges a different type of society developed early. These were mostly of a literary character and bore names of distinctly classical origin such as Adelphian, Calliopean, Ciceronian, Erosophian, Philolethean, or of a special sort such as Franklin and Linonian. Some of them were secret and some were not. Some had Greek mottoes expressing their ideals. Their object was training and drill in composition and oratory. Their exercises consisted of debates, orations, essays, and the reading and discussion of papers on literary subjects. They were encouraged by the faculties. They were given prominent places in college catalogues, their worth being suggested by a quotation from one of these publications: "Each of these societies has thus far been fully equal to a professorship; and the manner in which mind comes into contact with mind in these voluntary democratic associations is admirably well adapted for the development of every natural talent with which any young man may be endowed." The student joined them as a matter of course; their work was mainly educational. As a usual thing there were two such societies in a college, and the entire body of students was divided about equally between them. Their rivalries were fierce at times, competition being keen on the occasion of joint debate, as it was within the individual societies in anticipation of "publics." The meetings afforded opportunity for promoting acquaintance among the students, but usually the societies were too large to foster close friendships.

Such were the societies existing in the colleges when, in the autumn of 1825, the Kappa Alpha Society was formed at Union by John Hunter and other members of the class of 1826. In external features at least this society bore a close resemblance to Phi Beta Kappa, which had established its fifth chapter at Union in 1817. It was secret, it had a Greek name, it displayed a badge of similar shape, and it named its chapters on the same system. The new society, though exceedingly small, met with much opposition, but was secretly popular with the students, who paid it the

[1] This fraternity is described in Fraternities That Are No More. A somewhat unauthentic fragment of history which would help bridge the gap between the establishment of Phi Beta Kappa and Kappa Alpha and that of other Greek-letter societies may be of passing interest. *Banta's Greek Exchange* in April, 1940, pictured the obverse and reverse of a silver fraternity charm bearing the date 1786, the Greek letters AΣ, two hearts in outline, and other marks. The picture was received from Hubert W. Swender, Sigma Nu, who said the charm had belonged to his grandfather, a physician educated in New York.

sincere compliment of imitation by the foundation in the same college of Sigma Phi, March 4, 1827, and of Delta Phi, November 17, 1827. These three fraternities, called sometimes the "Union Triad," were the pattern for the American fraternity system.

In 1829 the I. K. A. Society, similar in aims and purposes to these societies, was established at Washington (now Trinity) College, Hartford, Connecticut, and continued its independent existence until 1917, when it became a chapter of Delta Phi. Sigma Phi was the first of the fraternities to establish a branch organization, and in 1831, calling itself the Alpha Chapter of New York, it placed its Beta Chapter at Hamilton College. This act probably resulted one year later in the foundation of Alpha Delta Phi at the college. In November, 1833, Psi Upsilon was founded at Union, and in the same year Kappa Alpha established a chapter at Williams, being followed one year later at the same place by Sigma Phi. Here they found a new rival in the shape of an anti-secret society called the Social Fraternity, which afterwards united with similar organizations to form Delta Upsilon. In 1837 the Mystical Seven Fraternity, not Greek in name, but similar otherwise, originated at Wesleyan. Alpha Delta Phi's second chapter was established at Miami in 1833, and in 1839 Beta Theta Pi, the first fraternity organized west of the Alleghenies, was founded there. A fifth society at Union, Chi Psi, was formed in 1841. This same year the first fraternity chapter in the South was placed at Emory College in Georgia by the Mystical Seven, and the second one by the same fraternity in 1844 at Franklin College, now the University of Georgia; but this extension in the South does not seem to have been the immediate cause of the foundation of any new societies, unless the origin of the first distinctively southern fraternity, the W.W.W., or Rainbow, which was founded at the University of Mississippi in 1848, may be so explained. Its name being English, and its nomenclature, symbols, and customs being very similar to those of the Mystical Seven, it is difficult to believe that its establishment was not due in some manner to the older society.

Alpha Delta Phi placed a chapter at Yale in 1836, and in 1839 Psi Upsilon planted a rival chapter which soon became firmly established. Delta Kappa Epsilon was founded at Yale in 1844, and immediately placed branch chapters in other colleges. Alpha Sigma Phi was founded in 1845 at Yale as a sophomore society; however, its early chapters at Harvard, Amherst, Marietta, and Ohio Wesleyan were open to all classes. In 1847 the first New York City fraternity, Zeta Psi, was founded at the University of the City of New York (now New York University), and the same year Delta Psi originated simultaneously at the same university and at Columbia College, while Union College witnessed the birth of Theta Delta Chi, its sixth society. In 1848

Phi Gamma Delta originated at Jefferson, where Beta Theta Pi had established a chapter in 1842, and in December of 1848 Phi Delta Theta was founded at Miami, while Alpha Delta Phi and Beta Theta Pi were temporarily inactive in that institution.

In 1849 Delta Phi placed a chapter at the University of Pennsylvania, and Phi Kappa Sigma was founded there in 1850; in 1852 Phi Kappa Psi originated at Jefferson; in 1854 the first of the three orders of Chi Phi made its appearance at Princeton; in 1855 Sigma Chi arose at Miami as the result of a split in a recently established chapter of Delta Kappa Epsilon. Sigma Chi was the third fraternity originating at Miami, and Beta Theta Pi, Phi Delta Theta and Sigma Chi, from their home and birthplace called the Miami Triad, spread over the West and South as the members of the Union Triad had spread over the eastern states.

The second southern fraternity, Sigma Alpha Epsilon, was founded at the University of Alabama in 1856, after several fraternities had established chapters there. The same year Theta Chi was founded at Norwich University in Vermont, but did not start to expand until 1902. In 1857 Phi Sigma was founded at Lombard University, and in 1858 Sigma Delta Pi was established at Dartmouth. In 1858 a second order of Chi Phi was founded at the University of North Carolina; the Sigma Alpha, or the Black Badge Fraternity, was founded at Roanoke College and Delta Tau Delta at Bethany College. In 1860 a third Chi Phi order was founded at Hobart, where other fraternities had existed for many years.

During the Civil War collegiate activity everywhere was weakened and in the South practically was suspended. In the North Theta Xi, founded at Rensselaer Polytechnic Institute in 1864, was the only fraternity originating in that period. It also was the first fraternity aiming to restrict its membership to persons intending to engage in a particular profession.

After the war the state of affairs in the South was so uncertain that the re-establishment of chapters by the northern fraternities was not at once generally undertaken. It was natural, therefore, that new southern fraternities should be created, especially at institutions made prominent by their military character. At the Virginia Military Institute, Lexington, Virginia, Alpha Tau Omega was founded in 1865, Kappa Sigma Kappa in 1867, and Sigma Nu in 1869; Kappa Alpha Order was founded at Washington and Lee University, located in the same town, in 1865. In 1867 Alpha Gamma originated at Cumberland University, and in 1869 Kappa Sigma at the University of Virginia, where in 1868 Pi Kappa Alpha was founded.

In 1868 D. G. K., an agricultural society, was established at the Massachusetts Agricultural College, where Q. T. V., a similar society, was founded the next year, and Phi Sigma Kappa, a third, in 1873.

In 1890 Delta Chi, originally legal in tendency, but reformed as a social fraternity, was founded at Cornell. In 1895 Pi Lambda Phi was founded at Yale, and Alpha Chi Rho at Trinity. In 1897 Sigma Pi was established at Vincennes, and in December, 1899, Delta Sigma Phi at the College of the City of New York. Other fraternities for men were founded in the nineteenth century but were not incorporated or chartered under their present names until the twentieth century.

Women's Groups The "firsts" among women's fraternities are three. Alpha Delta Pi is counted as the first sisterhood, having been founded as the Adelphean Society in 1851. Pi Beta Phi came into being in 1867 as the first organization of college women established as a national college fraternity. Kappa Alpha Theta was organized in January, 1870, as the first Greek-letter society for women.

While there were scattered cases of women elected to the men's fraternities, it early became evident that there was a distinct field for similar organizations for women. For many years in schools for young women societies bearing Greek or classical names were common, such as Adelphean, already named, Euterpean, and Philomathean. These became founding-chapters of national bodies and claimed precedence by virtue of the initial dates of their parent local organizations.

The I. C. Sorosis, similar in purpose to the Greek-letter societies, was founded at Monmouth College in 1867. In 1870 at Indiana Asbury University, now DePauw, Kappa Alpha Theta was born. In the same year Kappa Kappa Gamma was established at Monmouth, Illinois. Alpha Phi originated at Syracuse University in New York in 1872, and in 1873 Delta Gamma began at Lewis Institute for Young Women in Oxford, Mississippi. On November 9, 1874, Sigma Kappa was founded at Colby College in Waterville, Maine, and on November 11 Gamma Phi Beta followed Alpha Phi at Syracuse. Alpha Chi Omega was founded at DePauw University in 1885 and Delta Delta Delta was organized at Boston University in 1888. That same year, I.C. Sorosis officially adopted the Greek name Pi Beta Phi which it had used from the beginning as a secret motto.

Other women's sororities founded in the nineteenth century are Alpha Xi Delta in 1893 at Lombard College (now Knox) in Galesburg, Illinois; Chi Omega in 1895 at the University of Arkansas, Fayetteville; Alpha Omicron Pi in 1897 at Barnard College, New York City; Kappa Delta in 1897 at Longwood College, Farmville, Virginia; and Zeta Tau Alpha in 1898, also at Longwood. Two other women's fraternities were founded at Longwood College—Sigma Sigma Sigma in 1898 and Alpha Sigma Alpha in 1901—but until 1947 they limited their chapters to teacher colleges. National Panhellenic Conference was organized in 1902 and now includes twenty-six women's fraternities.

All of the women's groups were called fraternities in the beginning because no other word existed. Then in 1882, Gamma Phi Beta was named a "soror-ity," a coined word suggested by their advisor who was a professor of Latin, and who thought the word "fraternity" was ill-advised for a group of young ladies. However, the other Greek-letter societies for women had already been incorporated as fraternities, and in 1909 the National Panhellenic Conference revised its Constitution to use the word "fraternity" throughout. This usage still prevails.

Greek-letter Names The name of a fraternity usually is composed of two or three Greek letters, as Sigma Chi, Alpha Delta Phi, Beta Theta Pi, Phi Delta Theta, Lambda Chi Alpha, and Sigma Phi Epsilon. These letters commonly represent a motto, which is supposed to be unknown to all but the fraternity's members and which indicates briefly the purposes or aims of the organization. The branches situated in the various colleges are affiliated and with a few exceptions are termed chapters.

The chapters receive various names sometimes from the Greek letters in the order of their establishment, as Alpha, Beta, Gamma, Delta and so on. Sometimes they are named from the colleges, as *Union* chapter, *Hamilton* chapter, or from the college towns, as *Waterville* chapter, *Middletown* chapter, or after some individual prominent in relation to the field into which the organization is extending its ranks.

Several of the fraternities have adopted the state system, naming the first chapter established in a state the Alpha of that state, the second the Beta, and so on. When chapters have become so numerous that the letters of the alphabet are exhausted, combinations are used, either arbitrarily, as Theta Zeta, Beta Chi, or by design in the addition of supplementary letters, as, Alpha Alpha, Alpha Beta, Alpha Gamma, or Beta Alpha, Beta Beta, Beta Gamma, and so on. In other cases a regular system is employed, and some word or combination of words is used to denote the repetition, as Alpha Deuteron, Beta Deuteron, or in case the alphabet is being used the third time, Alpha Triteron, Beta Triteron, the supplemental words being generally denoted by their initial letters, "Delta" and "Tau," respectively. Some chapters having their origin in pre-existing organizations have perpetuated the memory of this fact in a chapter name embodying that of the original fraternity.

Membership Members of social fraternities are normally drawn from the four undergraduate classes. In the early days upperclassmen only were admitted to membership. At Yale the chapters of the social fraternities for many years were merely junior societies; and at Dartmouth for a time, though members were pledged, they were not admitted until the sophomore year.

The constant rivalry among chapters and the multiplication of fraternities have led in many cases to an indiscriminate scramble for members at the beginning of each year. Both fraternities and colleges have perceived the shortcomings of this sort of "rushing" as the contest for members is called, and are constantly striving to set up systems which will permit the sensible recruitment of new members. The deferred pledging of students until a fixed data and the deferred initiation of pledged members until they have completed a prescribed portion of their college course or secured a predetermined grade have been adopted in a number of places. Such procedure is in striking contrast with earlier custom in some of the larger western and southern colleges where the preparatory schools being intimately connected with the colleges, "preps" were not only pledged, but initiated before they entered the college.

Many chapters are old enough to admit great-grandchildren of early members, and frequently a student before entering college has already decided if opportunity comes to join the fraternity to which a parent or other relative belongs. "Legacies" of this type have made some chapters extremely powerful, giving them representation in families and in communities in successive generations.

Some men's fraternities elect prominent public figures to honorary membership, and some elect and initiate members who are not undergraduates. Some of the women's fraternities elect and initiate alumnae members, especially in instances when a local becomes a chapter in the organization, or when one group merges with another. These practices are not consistent among fraternities and each organization follows its own customs and traditions.

Professional fraternities draw their members from the particular discipline followed, and members of social fraternities are free to belong to professional and honorary groups. But National Interfraternity Conference now forbids membership in more than one social fraternity.

At Harvard, for example, the chapter of Delta Kappa Epsilon declined into a sophomore society, informally dubbed the "Dickey" Club. While it was still connected with Delta Kappa Epsilon and recognized as a chapter, its members joined Alpha Delta Phi, Delta Upsilon, or other fraternities later in their college life. Acacia, too, founded in 1904 on the teachings of Masonry, took initiates of other fraternities as members until 1919. In 1905 the National Panhellenic Conference adopted an agreement forbidding membership in more than one NPC group.

The Ritual and Other Characteristics of Fraternity When Phi Beta Kappa began in 1776, it was secret. It had a secret ritual, a secret motto, grip, and password. Almost every fraternity founded since that time has followed its example, and almost every fraternity has a ritual which is frankly imitative of that used in Freemasonry.

Various types of ritual are used in the conduct of fraternity business. A ritual is used in initiating new members; many groups use a ritual in conducting formal chapter meetings, in the ceremonies for installing officers, and for memorial services.

Although each fraternity has its own ceremonies, the initiation ritual usually includes an explanation of the secret signs and symbols, the meaning of the secret motto, and a charge or challenge to the new member to be of good character and to be loyal to the other members of the society. High ideals and high moral and ethical teachings are central to the theme of most rituals, and each new member is given an oath to swear by and repeats a vow in the initiation proceedings. The new member is instructed as to the high purposes of the group and of the responsibility which membership requires.

In the early years of fraternity organization, the constitution and bylaws were usually secret, but in recent years these papers have been printed in handbooks and other publications. And civil rights legislation has determined that fraternities may no longer exclude from their membership persons of a particular race, creed, or ethnic persuasion. The constitutions are open to perusal.

Among the equipment or trappings of fraternity are the badges and jewelry worn by members. Only authorized persons—that is, initiated members—may wear the badge. A notable exception to this rule is seen in the old tradition wherein a young woman wears the fraternity badge of her sweetheart. It is a symbol of fidelity and an intention of engagement. On the other hand, young women never give their badges to the men. It is strictly a male custom.

Some badges are symbols such as shields, stars, maltese crosses, keys, or crescents—either plain or jeweled. Some are monograms or letters. Whatever the form of the badge, it carries great symbolism for the wearer. Early badges were large and many were ornate. Women's fraternities wore their early badges as ornaments at the throat of their blouses, or as tie pins. Later on, in the early part of the twentieth century, strict rules for the placement of the badge were observed. But modern usage again permits the badge to be worn as jewelry. Modern badges are small and many are plain. Most fraternities have rulings on the size and ornamentation allowed.

Almost all fraternities have pledge pins or pledge buttons which are worn by the provisional members who are not yet initiated. Many of these carry symbols of the fraternity. And almost all fraternities have crests or coats-of-arms which are used as wall plaques or are reproduced on jewelry.

Fraternity jewelry has created an intensely competitive industry and some companies base their entire business enterprise on the production and sale of badges and necklaces, bracelets, lavalieres, rings, and other jewelry. Most fraternities have an official jeweler who cooperates with the national or international organization in offering items to be sold to members.

Other businesses have developed in providing clothing such as jackets, hats, sweaters, and shirts bearing the fraternity monogram or logo or other symbols; and in providing stationery, cards, cups, or decals imprinted with the fraternity symbols. In recent years it has become a custom on most campuses to have a large composite photograph, made up of individual pictures of the members, and prominently displayed in the meeting rooms or chapter houses. Many photographers specialize in providing these composites.

The Chapter House In the early years of fraternity, chapters were small enough to hold their meetings in a student's dormitory room or in a home. As the groups grew larger, some rented halls and in some cases these "temples" were elaborately decorated.

At the University of Michigan in 1846, the members of Chi Psi built a 20 by 14 foot log cabin in the woods near the campus in order to have a place for chapter meetings. This is generally conceded to be the "first fraternity house." At Kenyon College in 1854, Delta Kappa Epsilon built a hut on land provided by the college. In 1864, the Kappa Alpha Society at Williams College occupied the first chapter house.

A combination of circumstances provided the thrust for fraternities to occupy their own chapter houses. First, many colleges and universities were turning away from the English custom of providing rooming and boarding facilities for their students, and were adopting the German philosophy which was deliberately detached from concern for the student and his out-of-class existence. The chancellors at both the University of Michigan and the University of Wisconsin in the mid-nineteenth century demanded that the dormitory system be ended "at once, thoroughly, and forever."

Added to this was the clash of town-and-gown and the unfriendly relations between the students, who were many times unruly and destructive, and the landlords and merchants, who sometimes cheated and unfairly charged the students.

Then at the same time the Civil War pushed many schools toward bankruptcy. Schools could barely manage to pay the faculties and certainly had no funds to construct housing for the students.

The fraternities, already organized and functioning, thus became an instrument of assistance to their members. They decided to house and feed their members.

First they rented houses. Zeta Psi at the University of California rented what they called the Berkeley Farm House in 1873. In 1876 they moved into a building constructed for them.

By 1883 thirty chapters of ten separate fraternities for men owned their own houses. In 1886, Alpha Phi built the first women's fraternity house at Syracuse University.

Fraternities were not created to be in the business of housing and feeding students, but this feature of fraternity life has had a tremendous impact on the fraternity movement. The interest of the alumni had never been so fully roused and maintained by any other feature of fraternity life as by the efforts which have been made to build chapter lodges and houses. The creation of building funds, the frequent consultation as to plans, and the con-

sideration of ways and means have intensified the interest of alumni both in chapter and in college in a way that nothing else has done. All of this has resulted in direct benefit to the colleges, and the wiser college officials are encouraging the development of this feature of fraternity life in every way possible. For the advantages of the chapter-house system are not altogether on the side of the student. They relieve the colleges from the necessity of increasing the dormitory accommodations and also from many of the details of supervision of the actions of the students. The chapter house has localized the fraternity and has made the honor and reputation of the chapter a powerful factor in discipline. The head of the house, usually the chapter president, has become an important official, frequently being made the medium for communication of college administrative information or advice regarding individual members.

The fraternity houses have added much to the equipment and attractiveness of many colleges and have stimulated the building of dormitories to house nonfraternity students. In most of them room and board may be obtained at the average cost of the college community, and club dues are kept within reasonable limits.

Chapter-house life is having a great influence upon fraternity character. It has its advantages and its disadvantages. It varies greatly in different institutions. It fosters pride of organization; it promotes fraternal sentiment; it develops social discipline; it inculcates business habits; it stimulates the individual's ambition; it affords many opportunities for mutual helpfulness; it encourages close and abiding friendships; it brings the individual student under observant eyes; it generally promotes college loyalties. On the other hand, it may engender and foster social exclusiveness; it makes some students narrow and conceited because they assume for themselves, often unjustifiably, the reputation which the chapter may have established by the worthy performances of its members. In some places it increases the expense of college life; it increases the average size of chapters and makes in many cases a large chapter a necessity where a smaller one would be more effective and more advantageous.

The fraternities make increasing efforts to have chapter life wholesome and helpful. Under normal leadership they discountenance any form of dissipation in the chapter houses. Most of them cause a thorough supervision to be made of the scholarship of the members. They encourage study hours, correct deportment, show regard for the interests of others, and in general seek to make the house a comfortable college home to be cherished in pleasing memory with the passing years.

Organization and Administration Before the Civil War the fraternities were comprised largely of chapters united only by a common name and common principles. Each chapter was independent to the verge of anarchy and did pretty much as it pleased, even at times in opposition to the expressed wish of the fraternity of which it was a member. It was not uncommon for one chapter to establish another at a neighboring college without going through the formality of asking the consent of other chapters or of any common authority. Means of intercommunication were inadequate and not used, and chapters were often established and became inactive before the fact of their existence became generally known throughout the organization of which they were supposed to constitute an integral part. Again, many chapters were organized in such an imperfect manner that they learned little of the organization to which they belonged, and, being swept out of existence by some cause, they were lost sight of by their fraternity, which remained ignorant of their existence.

In a few instances chapters were established at places which did not meet the approval of the fraternity when the fact of such existence became known, and the chapters were repudiated, leaving perplexing questions of membership to be settled by future historians. Few of the fraternities had any centralized form of government and fewer still thought of pursuing a settled policy in any of their actions. The idea prevalent was that each chapter was to work out its own salvation.

The first step toward an organized government in most of the fraternities was the selection of one chapter, either the parent chapter if functioning, or each of the chapters in turn, to be what was called the "grand" or "presiding" chapter. This chapter was supposed to be the repository of facts, from which other chapters might derive information and to be the governing body of the fraternity, subject only to the directions of the assembly of delegates from the chapters, termed the convention, and was to preserve and maintain some sort of settled policy in the administration of fraternity affairs. In general, however, when the fraternities held conventions, authority of all kinds was vested in that body during its sessions, and this system has remained practically unchanged. These conventions or reunions were made up of delegates from the various chapters and within the fraternities were frequently known by some high sounding name as "grand conclave." As presiding officer some old and well-known member was usually chosen, and in addition to the transaction of business public exercises were held during which the assembly was addressed, poems were read, and so on. The sessions usually concluded with a banquet. Few changes were made in this plan until after the Civil War, but about 1870 or 1872 the fraternities, recovering their activity and beginning to extend and multiply saw plainly that the old system was no longer adequate to supply a growing organization.

A new system of government began to appear. The convention still retained the supreme legislative power and in many cases reserved to itself the right to grant new charters, but the administrative and executive and in some cases the judicial functions of the government were gradually vested in a body of alumni, sometimes elected from one locality and sometimes connected with one chapter, who acted in precisely the same way as the board of trustees of a college would in directing the affairs of its institution. And some of these "boards" resembled in dignity and complexion the board of trustees of a college. Under the designation of "executive council," or some similar name, such bodies quite generally became incorporated either under general laws or by special legislation. Such corporations now hold the legal title to whatever property the general fraternity possesses. The executive head of the fraternity or some member of the governing council came to be the secretary.

With a rapid increase in the number of chapters and the spread of accurate information concerning the fraternities, other features were introduced. Some of the fraternities deliberately mapped out the territory in which they were situated or which they proposed to occupy and established chapters in the colleges within such territorial lines with a sound judgment which was often a sure index of the future prosperity of the institution. The territory which a fraternity occupied was also divided up into districts, divisions, provinces, or regions, and executives known as chiefs, governors, or presidents were appointed for each of these. In some of the fraternities the organization, nearly perfect for administrative purposes, is completed on the local undergraduate level by the chapter counselor, faculty adviser, and alumni board officers.

The Central Office The great increase of campuses on which fraternities and sororities are functioning with the resultant increase in membership and activities made central offices and supervisory staffs essential. As a result, practically every organization nowadays has central headquarters with field workers ranging from one to five in number. Several of the men's fraternities employ men for the purpose of forming new groups and encouraging locals to petition. A period of aggressive expansion begun in the 1950s continues, leaders recognizing the need of meeting the challenge created by the development of new institutions of learning and the enlargement of existing ones.

The central office, which had its beginning in a modest fashion, now handles numerous business activities, such as maintenance of membership records and mailing lists, issuing of various publications, preservation of historical material, checking the financial operations of undergraduate chapters, arranging for conventions and conferences, issuing reports of national officers, directing the field staff, participating in interfraternity activities, and taking care of voluminous correspondence.

Raising standards of efficiency in chapter management constitutes an everyday challenge to fraternity and sorority national leaders. The chief contact between the national administration of a fraternity and the undergraduate chapters was once through national conventions, publications, and executive offices, some of which had visitation officers, but no longer. While conventions have become somewhat less important, most being held either biennially or triennially instead of annually because of the heavy expense involved, training schools for officers have become highly important. Since Sigma Alpha Epsilon and Chi Omega pioneered in this field in 1935, scores of the Greek organizations have followed example. The training schools are held in connection with conventions by some fraternities; others are conducted for a week in one or more sections of the country. Persons chosen because of their ability to instruct deal with the most important problems of chapter life: social, business, public relations, house management, kitchen management, pledge training, rushing, bidding, ritualistic work, publications, accounting, and chapter morale.

Training programs and panel discussions are also featured at annual regional conferences, which have proved an effective agency for officer training.

The Role of Alumni and Alumnae Members Fraternities assume that the members they initiate will maintain a bond within the fraternity throughout their lives. Even rushees are told this. It is emphasized in pledge training that membership is for life. Many fraternities have a ceremony to conduct graduating seniors into alumni and alumnae status. And most fraternities have a special ceremony to recognize members of fifty years' standing or longer.

Fraternities usually insist that their undergraduate chapters maintain contact with former members of the chapter and urge them to keep an accurate file of addresses. Many chapters publish newsletters in which they report not only the activities of the current chapter but news of the alumni and alumnae.

All fraternities have volunteers and many have professional staff members who work with the alumni and alumnae. These staff people work with the undergraduate chapters to help them develop better relationships with their alumni and alumnae for every chapter needs strong support from its graduated members.

Alumni interfraternity councils and alumnae panhellenic councils have been organized in many college and university cities to supplement the work of the undergraduate councils.

The structure and organization of alumni and alumnae chapters depends on the individual fraternity and will vary from group to group and even from chapter to chapter. Some are "clubs" which hold meetings—usually luncheon or dinner—at times. Some have carefully planned programs and others are more casual.

A single chapter may have its alumni or alumnae organized into an "association" which meets at the chapter house at stated times like homecoming or commencement. And another type of "association" is the house corporation or chapter house associa-

tion—a legal entity which owns and manages the property of the chapter. These "House Boards" make the mortgage payments, pay the insurance, oversee the physical plant, and pay the employees. Trustees or directors are usually elected by the alumni or alumnae at a meeting or by mail once each year.

The Housemother and Mothers' Clubs Women's fraternities sought housemothers at an early date to participate in house management. The men's houses followed the sororities frequently at the behest of the college, and sometimes reluctantly. Alpha Chi Omega published its first *Housemothers' Manual* in 1926. Today the fraternity or sorority that does not have a housemothers' manual is rare.

Mothers' clubs and mothers' and wives' clubs existed on an informal basis for many years before organizations were formed and definite programs conducted.

Housemothers provide social training as well as general house management. Summer schools for housemothers are conducted by many universities.

In the upheaval of the 1960's and 1970's, many fraternity chapters decided to dispense with housemothers, as well as house staff. But in recent years, the chapters are discovering that housemothers are a necessary adjunct to chapter life and many universities, faced with complaints from parents, are requiring the chapters to engage housemothers—who are now known as "house directors." The sorority national officers have always required their chapters to have house directors. In some schools, house "parents" are engaged to plan the meals and supervise the staff.

The Greek Press One of the delightful forerunners of national fraternity journalism is a modest newsletter first published at Wesleyan Female College by the Adelphean Society in the early 1850s. Known as the "Adelphean Chronicle," it took the form of both serious and lighthearted essays, college and local news, poetry, geometric and algebraic problems, and miscellaneous enigmas (whose answers were sometimes tantalizingly omitted the following week). But the tiny publication bestowed a rich heritage in reflecting an atmosphere of sisterly fellowship and the devoted spirit and dedication of highminded purpose on the part of a group of unusual young women.

The idea of founding a periodical national in scope was introduced at an early date in the conventions of Sigma Phi, Alpha Delta Phi, Beta Theta Pi, and Delta Kappa Epsilon, and probably the early records of other fraternity conventions show similar resolutions. These early schemes were almost always based upon the notion that such a periodical would afford a vehicle for the publication of literary articles written by the members and that it would add to the cultural equipment of a people who lacked magazines and still craved intellectual improvement. None of these materialized. The convention of Delta Upsilon, held in 1867, authorized the publication of a semi-annual called *Our Record*.

The two numbers were issued under one cover in the spring of 1868, and bore the double date of October, 1867, and April, 1868. It met with no success. In 1860 Theta Delta Chi directed the publication of a fraternity journal to be known as the *Shield* and to be edited by the Grand Lodge. The first number appeared in July, 1869, and bore the legend "Published in the interest of the Theta Delta Chi." Only one number was printed; it was not adequately supported, and it was merged into the *College Review*.

The first fraternity journal, however, which had a continuous existence and possessed the features and aims of the current fraternity periodicals, is the *Beta Theta Pi*. This was founded in December, 1872, by the Rev. Charles Duy Walker, professor at the Virginia Military Institute. He had been made general secretary of Beta Theta Pi at the convention held the preceding September. He chafed at the amount of time which the duties of his position demanded and determined to found a journal that should do part of his work for him and relieve him of much of his writing. The journal was named after the fraternity. It was a four-page monthly of the size known as "small quarto" and was filled with chapter news, reports, constitutional discussions, and personals. In 1874 it was made the official organ of the fraternity, its size was reduced, and the number of pages was increased.

During the years 1868, 1869, and 1873 the Pennsylvania chapters of Chi Phi issued an annual known as the *Chi Phi Chakett* containing lists of the members of those chapters. This was succeeded by the *Chi Phi Quarterly* in 1874, upon the union of the northern and southern orders, which was first issued at Carlisle, Pennsylvania, and subsequently removed to Trinity College, North Carolina (now Duke University).

In 1875 Phi Delta Theta established the *Scroll* as a monthly. Although frequency of issue has varied, it has always been published at least five times a year. At first its circulation was limited to members of the fraternity, but this restriction was removed in 1881.

The *Phi Kappa Psi Monthly* followed in 1875. In 1876 it was changed to a quarterly and the next year on the death of its editor it ceased publication. In 1879 the *Shield* was commenced as a private enterprise. It met with varying fortunes and suspended in April, 1882. In 1883 it was made the official organ of the fraternity and has since been published as such.

In 1877 Delta Tau Delta entered the field with a monthly called the *Crescent*. It was a success, and the next year it was officially adopted as the organ of the fraternity, being placed under the control of the Alpha Chapter. In February, 1886, its name was changed to the *Rainbow*, out of compliment to a southern fraternity which at that time united with Delta Tau Delta.

Down to 1878 this feature of fraternity administration was monopolized by the fraternities of western origin. At this date the Cornell chapter of

Psi Upsilon began the issue of a periodical called the *Diamond*. It met with little support and soon suspended. In 1882 it was revived by members of the chapter at Union College. Its place of publication soon afterwards was changed to New York, and in 1886 it was placed under the control of the Executive Council of the fraternity. Soon after this it suspended, but was revived in recent years.

Phi Gamma Delta in 1879 published at Delaware, Ohio, an official journal called the *Phi Gamma Delta* issued under authority of the convention held the preceding year.

Kappa Alpha Order began publication of the *Kappa Alpha Journal* in 1879 at Richmond, Virginia. Three numbers were published when it suspended. In November, 1883, a quarterly periodical was begun under the name of the *Kappa Alpha Magazine*. In 1885 it resumed its original name, which it has carried since.

These were the pioneers. Now almost every fraternity, except those in a group of smaller societies of eastern origin, issues a journal.

The women's fraternities began publishing journals in 1882, when Kappa Kappa Gamma issued the first *Golden Key* (later called simply *The Key*). In 1884 Delta Gamma started *Anchora*, closely followed by *The Arrow* of Pi Beta Phi and the *Kappa Alpha Theta* quarterly in 1885. Today every women's fraternity in National Panhellenic Conference publishes a magazine or journal and in 1913 the editors formed the NPC Editors Conference.

Editors of men's fraternity journals began the College Fraternity Editors Association in 1924, and the editors of women's journals are welcome as members.

The national quarterly interfraternity journal known as *Banta's Greek Exchange* was launched by George Banta in December, 1912. It was born out of the man's devotion to the fraternity and a love for printing which began when he was a boy of eight and had no decline until his death in 1935 at the age of seventy-eight. Although Mr. Banta laid the foundation of what was to become one of the nation's greatest educational printing institutions, business was secondary with him. He was first president of the General Council of his fraternity Phi Delta Theta and counted scores upon scores of fraternity and sorority leaders as his close friends. Throughout his lifetime, editors of the men's and women's magazines brought their problems to him; he introduced quality to Greek-letter journalism. Publication of the *Exchange* was suspended in July, 1973, after other than Greek-letter areas had become the center of Company interest.

In 1933, Leland F. Leland, editor of the quarterly journal of Tau Kappa Epsilon, established the Fraternity Press in St. Paul, Minnesota, and began publication of a five-times-a-year periodical which he called *The Fraternity Month*. The magazine was discontinued in 1971.

A most useful paper for Greeks is the *Interfraternity Bulletin*, published by the National Interfraternity Foundation and appearing monthly September through May. It was begun as the *IRAC Bulletin* as a service of the Interfraternity Research and Advisory Council and publication was assumed by the Foundation in 1986 when IRAC ceased to exist.

The undergraduates in most colleges publish annually one or more books which frequently are elaborately illustrated and devoted mainly to the exposition of the features of college life not included in the curriculum. These yearbooks may properly be mentioned here because much information about fraternities in general may be obtained from them and when studied in series they are valuable aids to knowledge of local fraternity history.

Because of the high cost of production, the catalogue of membership, once considered an imperative factor in a national fraternity's service to its members, began to experience a decline in the 1950s.

In 1878 Psi Upsilon appointed Charles W. Smiley of its Wesleyan chapter to prepare its catalogue. He had had previous experience in the compilation of the admirable alumni record of Wesleyan University, and, adopting the standard set by that publication, he produced a fraternity catalogue which was published in 1879 and gave a full biography of every member, living or dead, the facts about whom could be ascertained by personal research.

This publication set an unusual standard of completeness. Other fraternities at once took up the work in this same direction. Two years later Beta Theta Pi produced a catalogue not so complete in detail, but involving more labor on account of the imperfect records of southern and western colleges in which a majority of its chapters were situated. Phi Delta Theta soon completed a similar task under the same or greater difficulties. Alpha Delta Phi in 1882 published a semi-centennial catalogue, added to the elaborate detail of the catalogues just mentioned the record of its members who served in the Civil War, a bibliography of its literature and much historical matter. Delta Tau Delta, Delta Upsilon, Zeta Psi, Chi Psi, Sigma Chi, and other fraternities also produced catalogues which are monuments of painstaking research and intellectual labor. In 1889 Psi Upsilon issued another catalogue superior even to its predecessor in the elaborateness of its detail, and in 1890 Delta Kappa Epsilon after long preparation published a bulky volume of some 1,700 pages, leaving nothing to be desired in the way of completeness and probably marking the point of extreme advance in this direction. The Vernon catalogue of Phi Gamma Delta published in 1898, a volume of more than 1,450 pages profusely illustrated, was a monumental work.

In 1905 Beta Theta Pi published a catalogue with the information much condensed and in two forms, one on thin paper and with edges closely trimmed. In 1912 and 1917 it published revisions with the names arranged in double columns on thin paper making a compact and handy book, notwithstanding the large number of names printed. The same general plan has been followed by Alpha Delta Phi, Chi Psi, and Kappa Alpha Order, which, in several editions each, have issued convenient catalogues easily carried in the coat pocket. In 1921 Kappa Sigma published an "Address Book" of 500 pages. In 1926 Phi Delta Theta issued a notable volume giving a complete directory of members arranged by chapters, alphabetically, and by geographical distribution. In 1928 Phi Kappa Psi, following the same general plan, published a catalogue of marked distinction. A high standard for such publications was set by the Sigma Chi catalogue of 1929. In recent years a number of fraternities have published their membership lists as special numbers of their fraternity magazines, Phi Gamma Delta leading in this. When the names only of members are given, sometimes under alphabetic, geographic, and professional heads, the compilation is commonly called a directory.

Songbooks with and without music have been issued by practically all of the fraternities. The songs are of all degrees of excellence from unmeaning ditties, designed simply as a vent for enthusiasm and animal spirits, to lyrics of genuine poetic and musical worth.

The widely popular "fraternity sings" in many institutions have extended the knowledge of the songs of the fraternities and have served to stimulate the production of many pleasing lyrics.

Miscellaneous publications by fraternities have rapidly increased in number, in scope, and in physical attractiveness in recent years. They include fraternity manuals, manuals for pledges, guides to study methods, chapter histories, convention addresses and poems, biographies of members, chapter lists, chapter house rules, chapter library catalogues, section and city alumni lists, and the like.

Among the earlier volumes of miscellaneous type several are worth noting. *The History of the Omega Chapter of Sigma Chi*, published in 1885, was an interesting account of fraternity life at Northwestern University. The *Epitome of Psi Upsilon*, published in 1884, was a complete and painstaking record by an enthusiastic member of the more salient features of Psi Upsilon down to that time. In 1942 *Annals of Psi Upsilon 1833-1941* was published, a history and directory of living members. *The Manual of Phi Delta Theta*, smaller in size, contained much valuable and timely information. *Fraternity Studies*, published in 1894 by William Raimond Baird, was an account of the history and public activities of Beta Theta Pi. A second edition, much enlarged and entitled *The Hand-book of Beta Theta Pi*, was published by the same author in 1907. A history of Phi Kappa Psi by C. L. Van Cleve was published in 1902, a history of Phi Delta Theta by Walter B. Palmer in 1906, and a history of Sigma Alpha Epsilon by William C. Levere in 1911.

A *Detailed Record of Delta Delta Delta, 1888-1907*, by Bessie Leach Priddy, was a well-illustrated cloth-bound volume of 268 pages. When it was published in 1907, it was the first such publication by any women's organization—being preceded only by a 64-page pamphlet entitled *Kappa's Record*, published in 1903. A *Detailed Record of Delta Delta Delta, 1888–1931*, also by Mrs. Priddy and totaling 690 pages, was published in 1931.

Funds and Philanthropies The fraternity system has helped itself immeasurably through the establishment of funds and welfare projects. There is scarcely a national fraternity or sorority today which does not energetically promote a program of scholarships and awards, student loans, and preceptorships, as well as such social welfare projects as orthopedics, muscular dystrophy, the deaf, the paralyzed, the retarded, the underprivileged, and so on.

Phi Kappa Sigma founded a scholarship in 1888, setting an example that has been followed by practically all Greek organizations with varying degrees of success.

Pi Beta Phi was the pioneer in adopting a social welfare project when in 1912 as a memorial to its founders it established a settlement school in the Appalachian highlands at Gatlinburg, Tennessee. That prompted other sororities to turn their attention to the needs of underprivileged groups, to the physically afflicted, particularly children, and to missions of various character.

Sigma Chi organized the first of the foundations in 1939, and most fraternities and sororities have done likewise. Not only are hundreds of undergraduates receiving prizes and scholarships because of their scholastic achievements, but chapters and schools are getting grants; also students are being given scholarships for graduate study.

Because of worthwhile programs carried on by these foundations they are receiving generous gifts and bequests. Individual chapters are also being remembered in the wills of alumni and alumnae to a much greater extent than in earlier years. In increasing numbers members of Greek organizations are giving evidence of their loyalty and appreciation for what fraternity life meant to them by contributing money and property to be used in support of the college organization to which they belonged as undergraduates.

Professional and Honor Groups Phi Delta Phi, a legal fraternity established in 1869 at the University of Michigan, is the first of the professional groups having a formal history.[2]

By 1870 professional schools were being established by many universities, and with them fraternities were founded which restricted their

membership to students pursuing only professional courses. These societies became known as professional fraternities to distinguish them from the general fraternities, which admitted students from all departments. After Phi Delta Phi in law there came, in 1897, another law fraternity, Lambda Epsilon, in Chicago. It existed until November 8, 1902, at which time it was reorganized as Phi Alpha Delta. About the same time Delta Theta Phi and several others were founded.

The University of Michigan might be well called the "mother" of the professional fraternity, for several in each of several fields were founded there. Nu Sigma Nu, the first organization admitting medical students only, was established at Michigan in 1882. Within the next nine years four other medical fraternities were established. Alpha Kappa Kappa in 1888, Phi Chi in 1889, Phi Rho Sigma in 1890, and Phi Beta Pi in 1891. Kappa Psi was established in 1879 at New Haven, Connecticut, but for many years it admitted students in both fields of pharmacy and medicine. It separated in 1925 into two distinct organizations, the pharmacy group retaining the name of Kappa Psi and the medical group taking the name of Theta Kappa Psi.

The first professional dental fraternity was also founded at Michigan, Delta Sigma Delta in 1882. It was closely followed by Xi Psi Phi in 1889 and Psi Omega in 1892. Alpha Chi Sigma was founded at the University of Wisconsin in chemistry in 1902; Alpha Kappa Psi in commerce and business administration in 1904, closely followed by Delta Sigma Pi in 1907, both at New York University. Theta Tau started at the University of Minnesota in 1904 in the field of engineering. Then followed Phi Delta Kappa at Indiana University in 1906 in education and Scarab Fraternity in 1909 in architecture at the University of Illinois.

The professional fraternity is unusual in that it provides all of the advantages of fraternal affiliation, yet offers the real benefits which accrue to a membership comprised exclusively of those who have chosen the same profession for their life work. Professional fraternity chapters have strong faculty support because the professional fraternity offers association with members in their chosen profession.

Satisfactory scholarship is perhaps the primary requisite of collegiate training. An examination of the records of professional fraternity members will reveal that they usually maintain scholastic averages higher than the general student body. This is the result not only of their efforts to secure better than average students as members, but also because they are encouraged to achieve scholastic excellence in order to qualify as capable and respected representatives of the profession for which they are educating themselves.

Professional fraternities emphasize the value and necessity of their chapters' conducting professional and educational programs in addition to their regular undergraduate scholastic work. The types of

---

[2]The first professional fraternity of which any account at all may be found was Kappa Lambda, a secret society of medical students founded at Transylvania University in 1803 and extending to the College of Physicians and Surgeons of New York, the Rutgers University Medical School, Jefferson Medical College, and elsewhere. It continued to be active in New York until 1858 or later, but having no useful purpose faded into oblivion. Consolidated with Phi Beta Pi with the fraternities retaining the name Phi Beta Pi.

these projects vary as to the fraternity, the chapter, and the profession, but their aim is the same: namely, to educate and broaden their members. Addresses by people prominent in various fields of endeavor, research projects, open forums, discussion meetings, inspection trips, debates, educational motion pictures, joint meetings with professional societies, awards for unusual professional or scholastic achievement, and the publication of departmental or professional literature are among the forms these programs take. Another phase of the professional fraternity's activities is the sponsoring of social occasions to develop in their members that social grace, poise, and confidence so necessary to success.

One of the most important benefits of professional fraternity membership comes after graduation. Most professional fraternities have active alumni associations which offer valuable social and professional contacts, and many provide placement services for employment. Members moving from one city to another find these contacts of exceptional value. Many law fraternities have excellent facilities for the interchange of business between members in different cities. Education fraternities help their members make academic connections. Medical fraternities provide contacts of great importance to a physician, especially for consultation. The scope and character of these services will vary with the profession and with the fraternity, but many persons trained in a profession will testify that the professional fraternity was one of the most important factors in their careers.

Through the years, many of the professional fraternities have changed their purposes, and some have changed their names. They have even changed their conferences. On October 21, 1977, the Professional Panhellenic Association which was made up of women's fraternities in nine professional fields, and the Professional Interfraternity Conference of men's fraternities in eleven fields met in joint session and merged into the Professional Fraternity Association. This merger represented 35 national and international fraternities which at that time had more than one and a half million members.

The Honor Society Not counting Phi Beta Kappa, which did not originate as an honor society but became one, the first of the honor groups is Tau Beta Pi, engineering society for men, established at Lehigh University in 1885.

The honor society has followed the expansion and specialization of higher education in America. When Phi Beta Kappa was organized in 1776 there was no thought given to its proper "field," since all colleges then in existence were for the training of men for "the service of the church and the state." With the expansion of education into new fields, a choice had to be made, and Phi Beta Kappa elected at the end of the first half century of its existence to operate in the field of the liberal arts and sciences. Although this was not finally voted until 1898, the trend was evident some years earlier, and the 1880s saw the establishment of Tau Beta Pi in the field of engineering and Sigma Xi in scientific research.

In the early years of the twentieth century other honor societies came into being. One of these, Phi Kappa Phi, was started by the presidents of three state universities with the thought that these institutions should have their honor society; later, its field was wisely extended to include any institution of university scope, accepting into membership superior students of all schools or colleges of which they are a part. With this exception, and with the exception of Alpha Kappa Mu, which had its origins in Negro colleges and universities, scholarship honor societies have followed the earlier tradition of selecting a specific field of coverage. Thus Alpha Omega Alpha elects in the field of medicine, Beta Gamma Sigma in commerce, Tau Beta Pi and Sigma Tau in engineering, and Omicron Nu in home economics.

Honor societies exist to recognize the attainment of scholarship of a superior quality; and to recognize leadership, character, and good campus citizenship.

An honor society must define and maintain a high standard of eligibility for membership and achieve sufficient status so that membership becomes something to be valued highly.

Three interesting variations have developed since 1900. One of these recognizes the values of extracurricular activities and the development of general campus citizenship, and its prime requisite for election is meritorious attainments in all-round leadership in college life. In this field, Omicron Delta Kappa for men and Mortar Board for women achieved excellent reputations. Both have a strong secondary requirement of scholarship.

A second variation is represented by the numerous societies which draw their membership from the various departments of study, recognizing chiefly good work in the field of the student's major interest or special field of study. These societies are generally known as departmental honor societies and are represented by such societies as Sigma Pi Sigma, in physics; Alpha Epsilon Delta, in premedicine; Delta Sigma Rho in speech and forensics; Pi Kappa Lambda in music; Phi Alpha Theta in history; Eta Kappa Nu in electrical engineering; Pi Tau Sigma in mechanical engineering; Rho Chi in pharmacy; Tau Sigma Delta in architecture and allied arts; Pi Sigma Alpha in political science; Phi Sigma in biology; Phi Sigma Iota in romance languages; Alpha Pi Mu in industrial engineering; Pi Gamma Mu in social science; Chi Epsilon in civil engineering; and Kappa Tau Alpha in journalism.

The third variation recognizes scholastic achievement during the freshman year and encourages its members toward higher goals. This field of freshman scholarship honor societies is represented by

Phi Eta Sigma, Alpha Lambda Delta, and Sigma Epsilon Sigma.

Omicron Delta Kappa was originally a men's honorary, and Mortar Board was a women's honorary. The freshman scholarship honorary Phi Eta Sigma was founded for men, and Alpha Lambda Delta and Sigma Epsilon Sigma was for women. But when the provisions of Title IX of the Education Amendments of 1972 were interpreted to mean that fraternities and sororities could no longer be single sex organizations, several senators introduced legislation to exempt fraternities and sororities because they are private organizations that are not federally funded. Specifically excluded were organizations such as the Boy Scouts and Girl Scouts, YMCA, YWCA, and "social" fraternities and "social" sororities. Unfortunately, these provisions did not cover professional fraternities and sororities or the honorary groups. Consequently, some professional groups amended their constitutions to make membership available to any student, and Mortar Board admitted men, Blue Key and other erstwhile men's honoraries admitted women, and Phi Eta Sigma and Alpha Lambda Delta became "person" groups.

In the wake of the honor society came the so-called **Recognition Society,** which recognizes the diligence of its members in such areas as service to others in neighborly deeds, journalism, dramatics, leadership, wholesome extracurricular effort, literature, language, science, the arts, and thus on. Many of these societies are not at all clearcut in their emphases, some vary in manner of operation from campus to campus, and hence to classify them properly under the established characters is, to understate the problem, difficult. The first of such societies, Gamma Alpha, a graduate science "recognition society" for men, was launched at Cornell University in 1899. A number of its chapters maintain houses, and the members live together in fellowship. Hence the springs of its true nature are like those of the professional fraternity.

Mergers[3] A merger is the answer for a fraternity desiring to become larger as it is for one which decides it is too depressed to continue its own existence. In 1879 when the five eastern chapters of Alpha Sigma Chi were united with Beta Theta Pi, Mr. Baird considered that a "defect was remedied" in that Beta Theta Pi previously had no eastern

---

[3]*Merger* is used as a term of convenience. Its use is admittedly erroneous in the case of such consolidations as that of Phi Kappa and Theta Kappa Phi on April 29, 1959, when these two sizable men's fraternities—the former with thirty chapters and four colonies and the latter thirty-four chapters and three colonies—effected a "unification" under a new name—Phi Kappa Theta; or as that of Lambda Chi Alpha and Theta Kappa Nu in 1939 when a large group "absorbed" a small; or as that of Delta Zeta and Theta Upsilon in 1962, when the small group was "accepted into membership" by the large. Accounts of approximately a hundred fraternities and societies are given in another section of this manual. Few of them met outright death, since in the majority of the instances of the fraternities that are no more a part of them—in some cases a sizable part—continues life under another name.

chapters and would now have "a strong wing." Within a twenty-year period following the depression of 1929, no fewer than twenty-four fraternities were principals in mergers; as a result, the number of national fraternities was reduced by fourteen; in the same period ten sororities were involved in mergers, a loss of national sororities resulting. Only two national fraternities developed in this period, and no sororities. Kappa Sigma Kappa, a fraternity which existed from 1867 to 1886, was revived in 1935. Beta Sigma Tau was founded as an interracial fraternity in 1948 but was in turn absorbed by Pi Lambda Phi in 1960, while the following year saw Kappa Nu absorbed by Phi Epsilon Pi. Many of the mergers of NPC fraternities were "leap-frogging" combinations. Pi Sigma Tau was absorbed by Beta Sigma Omicron which in turn was absorbed by Zeta Tau Alpha (1964). Lambda Omega was absorbed by Theta Upsilon which was absorbed by Delta Zeta (1962). Delta Zeta absorbed Beta Phi Alpha (1941), Delta Sigma Epsilon (1956), and Phi Omega Pi (1946) which also had chapters absorbed by Alpha Omicron Pi, Alpha Gamma Delta. Sigma Kappa, and Kappa Alpha Theta. Alpha Delta Theta was absorbed by Phi Mu (1939) and Pi Kappa Sigma was absorbed by Sigma Kappa (1959). Iota Alpha Pi disbanded in 1971 and its chapters were not reaffiliated with any other group.

On August 20, Kappa Sigma Kappa brought twenty-one of its active college chapters located at accredited schools into merger with Theta Xi, a 62–chapter fraternity; meanwhile it was agreed that eight chapters at unaccredited institutions might continue to operate as Kappa Sigma Kappa. In 1964, Delta Kappa was taken into Sigma Pi.

The last merger of the '60s was that of Phi Sigma Delta with Zeta Beta Tau in March, 1969. The following year Zeta Beta Tau absorbed Phi Epsilon Pi. In 1972 Beta Sigma Rho was taken into union with Pi Lambda Phi.

An Era of Great Change Since 1900 the development of fraternities has been so rapid that the twentieth-century organizations outnumber those established in the century and a quarter preceding. At the same time the great growth of education institutions and the tremendous increase in the number of students led to notable expansion of some of the older organizations.

World War I, the depression of the 1930s, and World War II were periods of crisis which the fraternities weathered gallantly but which nevertheless helped mold them into a changed institution. During World War II, to counteract the effect of depleted manpower, the national boards of a number of fraternities voted to increase rather than decrease their staffs in order to be of greater service to undermanned chapters. The V-12 program and other such programs of the military gave encouragement to Fraternity Row. Fraternity magazines were filled with service news, and in some cases published special overseas editions. Only a few reduced the size and number of issues to keep within limited budgets, for officers recognized the value of the publications in keeping in touch with their members in service.

While many sorority members entered war service, the chapters carried on in normal fashion, the members taking over many campus activities which had been largely in charge of men. Members and alumnae sold more than two billion dollars' worth of war bonds and stamps and raised huge sums of money for Red Cross and other welfare agencies. It is estimated that 325,000 fraternity men and women were in uniform. Many of them gave their lives.

With the close of World War II, the fraternity situation changed almost overnight from a famine to a feast. Men flocked back to the campuses not only to resume their studies, but to enjoy college life and particularly fraternity life. Contrary to all the predictions of columnists and editorial writers, these men, matured by the serious business of war, nevertheless wanted the joys and satisfaction that come with collegiate brotherhood, and they flocked into the chapter houses. Not only were these men eager to resume fraternity life, but they wanted some of their service "buddies" to share it with them. Many who ordinarily could not have afforded college, let alone fraternity experiences, were able to do so because the GI bill largely took care of their expenses.

As a result, chapters became large, often unwieldy. They found annexes to take care of the overflow. In some cases chapter meetings had to be held in shifts, as no room available was large enough to take care of the number of members. Men back to the campus, however, were eager to complete the work for their degrees as rapidly as possible, and so the chapters were gradually reduced to something like normal size.

Service men brought a serious attitude toward their courses, an impatience with juvenile hazing tactics, and an appreciation of the real values of fraternity life.

Universities, coming to realize the potential of the Greek chapters, began to employ advisors in student personnel who concentrated their attention to this field. Today a number of persons work with Greeks in making their chapters of greater service to their members, their campus, and their national structure.

In 1976, the Association of Fraternity Advisors (AFA) was organized for professional advisors to college social fraternities and sororities. It offers mutual support and promotes the advancement of the college fraternity. The association meets annually and has among its members approximately 600 campus fraternity professionals.

In the twenty years prior to the campus unrest which began in 1964, Fraternity Row experienced the greatest development in size in its history: more campuses opened to national fraternities: more chapters were installed than in any previous period; more members initiated; more chapter houses

were built and remodeled; more foundations and endowment funds were established. In addition, better relationships were developed between the Greeks and educational administrations and the Greeks and the communities of which they are a part partially because of Help Week programs.

Immeasurable good will has been produced by fraternities that have instituted a Community Service Day. In some places the chapters bring their alumni into the effort.

The amelioration of Hell Week has done much to create and maintain worthwhile public relations. Newspapers and the radio will give the Greeks publicity for constructive efforts.

Obstacles on the Path   Since their earliest days the fraternities have faced many obstacles.

In their early and middle years, the fraternities suffered from a rivalry among themselves that was at times incredibly intense and bitter and they suffered much ill will from the public because they concealed their activities in a manner which evoked mistrust in the average American citizen.

The progress of Greekdom suffered from the wave of anti-Freemasonry following the alleged murder in 1827 of a man named William Morgan who claimed to be a royal arch Mason who threatened to betray the secrets of his order and publish them to the world. In 1831 Phi Beta Kappa was compelled by public opinion to expose its secrets.

At the close of the 1890s, the Populist movement, which originated among farmers, swept the country and in South Carolina obtained full control of the state and local governments. The radical measures enacted included, in 1897, "An act to prohibit Greek-letter fraternities, or any organization of like nature in State institutions"—which meant the University of South Carolina and Clemson College, the agricultural college established by the legislature in 1893. This enactment was the severest blow fraternities had thus far received. Arkansas followed South Carolina's example in 1901, Mississippi in 1912.[4]

Fraternities were banished from Virginia Military Institute and Virginia Polytechnic Institute in 1878. They were driven from Monmouth in 1884 and from Wooster in 1913. The trustees of Wooster were seduced by an offer of a large endowment, on condition that fraternities be banished. But Wooster did not get the money it expected, which was humiliating for the trustees; and the sympathetic interest of loyal alumni was estranged, which was unfortunate for the college.

Fraternities have been ostracized practically continually at Princeton and they have never been permitted at Oberlin.

There were already more than a score of national fraternities on April 12, 1861, when the first shot was fired in the War Between the States. The war put an end to college enterprise everywhere. Many

[4]A Review of Legislation Affecting Fraternities is a part of the Appendix.

of the Southern colleges were destroyed, and their faculties disbanded, and in the North some closed their doors because they lacked professors and students.

Prior to 1880 and in a few cases afterwards, the fraternities evaded antifraternity rules and conducted sub rosa chapters. Few institutions prohibit fraternities today. Norwich University disbanded its fraternity chapters during 1960, while in the same year Randolph-Macon Woman's College denationalized its sororities. When the University of Buffalo became a part of the University of the State of New York system in 1962, the fraternities on that campus were automatically denationalized by an existing anti-national law.[5]

It was almost Armistice time of World War I when the War Department, "considering that fraternity activities are incompatible with military discipline," issued a memorandum that fraternities be suspended in institutions where units of the Student's Army Training Corps had been established. Two fraternity leaders interceded with Newton D. Baker of Phi Gamma Delta, who then headed the War Department, and the ruling was altered to permit the business operation of fraternities as before, including pledgings, initiations, and meetings.

Following World War I fraternities encountered no great adversities until the economic depression of 1929. The financial situation, became so serious that college enrollments suffered, and the majority of those who did attend college felt that they could not afford to belong to a fraternity. Some chapter houses were closed because of resulting financial difficulties. Chapters were necessarily withdrawn in a number of cases. Membership slumped. Expansion came to a standstill. Fraternities were extremely cautious in adding new chapters to their rolls, not infrequently keeping petitioning groups on the waiting list for years.

With the advent of World War II came further adversity. The effect of war was to decimate chapter manpower so drastically that many chapters closed for the duration. While one fraternity ordered all its chapters to close down for the duration, most governing bodies urged their chapters to continue on a limited basis if at all possible. One fraternity official promoted the slogan, "The time to rebuild is NOW!" Only 68 fraternity undergraduates out of the normal 500 were left on one campus, but they pooled their interests, carried on a Greek Week program, and kept the identity of their chapters. Chapters on the same campus occasionally carried out cooperative housing and boarding programs. On some campuses resident alumni took over chapter Offices. Sympathetic college administrators were helpful, offering to store records, rituals, and initia-

[5]In late 1976, SUNY trustees repealed this ruling, thus reversing a 23-year-old policy and permitting national social groups on SUNY campuses once more, provided the group did not discriminate on the basis of race, creed, national origin, sex, or disability. However, following HEW guidelines, men's social groups would not be forced to accept women as members, nor the women's groups men.

tion paraphernalia. The V-12 and similar programs also encouraged continuation of effort. In some cases the colleges even assisted chapters to meet financial obligations. Banks and individuals that held chapter house mortgages postponed contract and even interest payments in some cases.

The period following World War II was one of great popularity for the fraternity system. The GI bill enabled many to seek college educations and the colleges and universities enjoyed an unprecedented era of prosperity which was also accompanied by a rise in the membership of fraternities. But this period was followed in the 1960's and early 1970's by a change in attitude of the students. Campuses became centers of unrest and rebellion against "the establishment." One of the catch phrases was "Don't trust anyone over 30," and another was, "The Greeks are dying." Fraternities and sororities were favorite targets of the student dissidents, despite the fact that some of the members of fraternities and sororities were also active in protest groups. Students demanded an end to the tradition of "in loco parentis," and held marches to force administrators to grant unlimited parietal hours—which came to be known as "open visitation." It was a time of upheaval in the colleges and universities and was reflected in low numbers going through rush and low numbers pledging Greek organizations. Many chapters failed and in 1973 statistics showed the lowest percentage of growth, or increase in membership, since the conferences began keeping records, and for the first time the conferences had fewer chapters at the end of the year than they did at the beginning.

But once again the pendulum swung back, and fraternities were popular. Membership in the men's fraternities increased from 230,000 in 1980 to more than 400,000 in 1986. Sororities showed similar gains and added 131 new chapters in three years.

And right along with this popularity and rise in membership came more problems. Some colleges and universities brought charges against fraternities and sororities and a few schools abolished the Greek system from their campuses, the most prominent of which were probably Colby, Amherst, the University of Lowell, and Franklin and Marshall. These charges, pin-pointed at Dartmouth by the faculty in an attempt to close out the chapters' were racism, sexism, destructive behavior, anti-intellectualism, and abuse of alcohol.

All Greek organizations can refute the charge of racism. All fraternities and sororities have eliminated any ethnic or religious requirements or qualifications. The charge of sexism may logically be leveled because most fraternities restrict their membership to men and all sororities restrict their membership to women—and they are determined to keep that ruling in force, despite the objections of some schools which are attempting to make the chapters accept members of both sexes or face expulsion.

But the charges of destructive behavior, anti-intellectualism, and abuse of alcohol are being met head-on by every national or international sorority or fraternity.

Hazing is one of the biggest problems, even for sororities which in past years had never considered mistreating their pledges. Now every fraternity and every sorority has stringent prohibitions against the practice. Members have been expelled and chapters have been closed when such charges have been proved. Most states have passed anti-hazing legislation and some have made it a felony to practice dangerous or degrading activities against pledges or members. And most states have raised the age when it is legal to consume alcoholic beverages to 21-or-over.

Fraternity administrators are agreed that the abuse of alcohol is a contributing factor to hazing and is usually the cause of property destruction and vandalism. To help fraternities and sororities combat the problem, chapter programming usually includes sessions with groups such as BACCHUS or GADD (Greeks Against Drunk Driving).

Greek organizations are determined not only to get the abuse of alcohol under control but have required chapters to instruct the members in risk management. In recent years it has become very difficult for chapters to get liability insurance unless it can be proved that rules against the abuse of alcohol are in place and are rigorously enforced. Ruinous law suits brought against fraternities following accidents have the potential for bankrupting a fraternity.

The charges of anti-intellectualism are hard to prove. Every Greek organization has requirements for a specific grade-point-average before a member can be initiated, and some chapters have grade requirements before a member is considered in good standing or can hold a chapter office or participate in extra-curricular activities. Many groups have required study tables, a tutoring service, and scholarship recognition awards.

All of these problems have presented colleges and universities with a dilemma. Some institutions wish to control the students' behavior and enforce rules and regulations. On the other hand, no school wishes to be included in ruinous law suits which have been levied in the case of property damage or wrongful injury or death arising from a fraternity prank or negligence. And schools which attempt to put restrictions on the students—in the spirit of the old "in loco parentis" mode—are putting themselves in the risk of being named "responsible."

Nobody denies the attraction of fraternity life. The picture of young men and young women united in the bonds of brotherhood and sisterhood is appealing. And the emotional experiences are something no classroom or laboratory can offer.

Hell Week on most campuses has been renamed Help Week or Inspiration Week. Greeks as individual chapters or united in cooperative efforts have raised millions of dollars and given millions of hours in volunteer time to countless charities, both locally and nationally.

Statistics have proved that 65 to 70 per cent of the students who belong to Greek organizations stay in school to graduate, while only 30 to 35 per cent of the unaffiliated students remain to graduation. Statistics show that most of the donations made to alma mater are given by members of Greek organizations. It is not difficult to marshall arguments favoring the Greek system.

But so long as the chapters are made up of human beings, there will be problems to solve and crises to be met. For 200 years this has been true.

Center for the Study of the College Fraternity

On April 28, 1979, nine interfraternity leaders met in Covington, Kentucky, to discuss the formation of an organization that could encourage and support research on the fraternity and sorority experience. That group included representatives of higher education associations, fraternity executives, and representatives of fraternity and sorority alumni organizations. The founders of the organization anticipated that the Center for the Study of the College Fraternity would become a clearing house for related research, a library of research projects completed, a consulting service for member associations, and a publisher of research monographs.

Funds to begin the center came from gifts from national fraternity foundations and a grant from the Commission on the American College Fraternity for the Year 2000. It was agreed that on-going operational funds would come from membership fees from interested individuals, national fraternity and sorority organizations, college and university institutional memberships, and IFC and Panhellenic Association memberships.

The Center was officially incorporated in 1981 as a not-for-profit, tax exempt corporation in the state of Indiana. An external agency agreement was negotiated with Indiana University to locate the offices of the Center in Bloomington, Indiana.

Update, the research newsletter of the Center was first published in 1979. *Update* is now published two to four times a year and includes summaries of recent research articles on fraternities or sororities, and periodically provides a research agenda identifying priority concerns for coming years.

Currently, the Board of Directors for the Center for the Study of the College Fraternity includes two University Presidents, two university faculty members, several at-large members, and representatives of the American College Personnel Association, the Association of Fraternity Advisors, the College Fraternity Editor's Association, the Fraternity Executives Association, the National Association of Student Personnel Administrators, the National Association of Women in Education, The National Interfraternity conference, the National Interfraternity Foundation, the National panhellenic conference, the National Pan Hellenic Council, and the professional Fraternities Association.

In 1982, the center began a longitudinal study on the status of college fraternities and sororities, surveying institutional Greek systems on over 100 items of interest, including size of membership, university support services, scholastic achievement, rush systems, and campus policies. The most recent status report provides information from 398 colleges and universities.

Center monographs also include annotated bibliographies of research articles on fraternities and sororities published between 1950 and 1985. The annotated bibliography on research published between 1985 and 1990 will be published in the coming year. Four other monographs issued by the center have covered topics such as enhancing the guality of Greek life, the influence of student involvement by sorority membership, student development applications to Greek letter organizations, and an analysis of alumni giving to higher education and its relationship to participation in undergraduate activities.

At the end of its first decade of service, the center Board affirmed that the mission of the center for the Study of the College Fraternity is to encourage and support study and dissemination of research of high quality in educational significance on the role of the fraternity and sorority in higher education. current topics of research interest include: What is the impact of membership in a Greek organization upon the personal development of individual members? What are the factors which are associated with or produce satisfaction with the Greek experience? What are the characteristicS of individuals that selectively propel them toward Greek life in a particular setting? What is known on & given campus about the ways and the degree in which the Greek experience contributes to open mindedness, willingness to change and lifelong growth? How does the process of re-enforcement of values and ideals modeling desirable life styles and providing satisfying, rewarding individual behavior opportunities operate in various groups on a given campus? What is the image of the fraternity and sorority system in general? With what goals, values, attitudes and behaviors are new members of Greek organizations being socialized? How does membership in Greek organizations affect the freshman year experience?

Address: Center for the Study of the College Fraternity
           Franklin Hall 002
           Bloomington, Indiana 47405
Phone: 812 855–1228

Center Leadership:
  Board Chairpersons
    1979–1983   E. Garth Jenkins
    1983–1984   Dr. Robert H. Shaffer
    1984–1990   Mrs. Adele Williamson
    1991–Present Dr. Caryl Smith

  Executive Directors
    1979–1983   Dr. Robert H. Shaffer
    1983–Present Dr. Richard N. McKaig

National Interfraternity Conference

National Interfraternity Conference

The National Interfraternity Conference (NIC) is a confederation of 62 men's college fraternities with over 5,200 chapters on more than 800 campuses throughout Canada and the United States. The NIC represents 400,000 collegiate members and four and one half million alumni. Its volunteer leadership and professional staff based in Indianapolis serve fraternities in university, government and media relations. The promotion of scholarship, leadership, service, and friendship among fraternity members is the NIC's purpose.

History of NIC

The Greek-letter fraternity is a uniquely American institution. It is found almost exclusively in educational institutions of the United States and Canada and traces its origin to a year already well-remembered in the annals of the free world–1776.

On December 5 in that year, five students of The College of William and Mary at Williamsburg, the colonial capital of Virginia, established Phi Beta Kappa. Their motive was to arrange, within the bonds of strict secrecy and of tested friendship, for opportunities to discuss freely the exciting issues of their times, including the recently proclaimed Declaration of Independence. Directly or indirectly, all present-day fraternities trace their origin to Phi Beta Kappa's example, including Kappa Alpha Society, Sigma Phi and Delta Phi. These have continued, since the 1820s, as general fraternities for men, while Phi Beta Kappa evolved into an honor society, recognizing high scholastic attainment.

Jealousy, suspicion and intense rivalry characterized fraternity relations in their early years. Abuse developed, including the affiliating of preparatory school students, the initiation of men already obligated to rival societies, and even the "lifting" of whole chapters.

The publication, in 1879, of the first of many editions of BAIRD'S MANUAL OF AMERICAN COLLEGE FRATERNITIES stimulated interest in more harmonious and ethical relationships. On February 22, 1883 at Philadelphia a Panhellenic Conference was organized, with the Reverend Otis A. Glazebrook, a founder of Alpha Tau Omega, as its first chairman; but a majority of the 14 fraternities represented did not support the call for a second meeting.

Fraternity journals continued to discuss the advisability of cooperation. In Chicago, during the World's Fair of 1893, a Congress of Fraternities brought together prominent leaders of both the men's and women's fraternities. In that city on May 24, 1902, the women's groups effected an Interfraternity Conference, which has continued to the present time, although now renamed as the National Panhellenic Conference.

For their present Conference, the men's fraternities are indebted to the Department of Universities and Colleges of the Religious Education Association. This organization, on February 11, 1909, sponsored a meeting at Chicago to which 17 fraternities sent representatives. The discussions proved to be so worthwhile that these gentlemen requested R.E.A. to call another meeting to discuss mutual problems and to consider a "Panhellenic Union."

This was convened on November 27, 1909 in New York by W. H. P. Faunce, Delta Upsilon, then president of Brown University and the chairman of the R.E.A.'s Department of Colleges and Universities. Twenty-six fraternities, represented by about sixty delegates, responded to Dr. Faunce's call.

As the discussions proceeded, sentiments of narrow rivalry gave way and the fact of common aims and interests emerged. Unanimously, those in attendance voted to make the proposed Conference permanent; Hamilton W. Mable, Alpha Delta Phi, and Francis W. Shepardson, Beta Theta Pi, were chosen, as chairman and secretary respectively, to insure this result. Formal organization was completed in 1910 with the adoption of a simple constitution. The basic principle of representation—one fraternity, one vote—has remained unchanged. Amendments and bylaws were adopted however to provide for a junior class of member and to define criteria for admission to and retention of membership privilege, a principal requirement being the chartering of collegiate chapters only at accredited, four-year, degree-granting institutions.

In 1931 the organization's name was changed from Interfraternity Conference to National Interfraternity Conference. A substantive reorganiza-tion plan was authorized in 1955, including the creation of a House of Delegates in which all legislative and policy making powers are now vested. Between its meetings, however, its elected Executive committee may fulfill the executive and administrative functions of the Conference and carry forward necessary business. All officers (except the executive vice president) serve without compensation.

Because of the mounting burden of correspondence and communication and the need to allocate many committee functions to a minimum office staff, the establishment of such a central office has been urged from 1921 forward. The first step was successfully accomplished in 1956. The second stage was consummated in 1965 with the employment of the first full-time administrative secretary; the move of the office to large, better equipped quarters at 271 Madison Avenue, New York; the application of most of the recommendations of the Study of the Reorganization Committee reports of 1963 and 1964 and the approval of budgetary provisions for this enlarged service.

In 1968 with the support of the College Fraternity Secretaries Association the House of Delegates amended the constitution and bylaws to change the purpose and simplify the organizational structure. "The purpose of the National Interfraternity Conference shall be to promote the well-being of its member fraternities by providing such services to them as the House of Delegates may determine, these services to include, but not to be limited to, promotion of cooperative action in dealing with fraternity matters of mutual concern, research in areas of fraternity operations and procedures, fact-finding and data gathering, and the dissemination of such data to the member fraternities. Conference action shall not in any way abrogate the right of its member fraternities to self-determination."

In January 1971, the Headquarters of the Conference was relocated in Indianapolis, Indiana and Jack L. Anson, Phi Kappa Tau, became the executive director.

The '70s saw established a category of associate membership for those persons and companies that provide products and services to national fraternities. Approval has been given for the establishment of chapters at accredited two-year institutions.

In 1982, Jonathan J. Brant, Beta Theta Pi, accepted leadership of the Conference as its executive director. In 1989, this title was changed to executive vice president.

The '80s presented the best of times and worst of times for fraternities. Tremendous growth in membership and the number of chapters illustrate an increasing interest in fraternity. At the same time, a litigious society and public opinion focused on student abuse of alcohol, substances, property and fellow human beings in the form of hazing and sexual misconduct. Fortunately, the vast majority of fraternity activity is meritorious and within the mission of higher education.

During this decade, the Conference has made

great strides largely through long-range planning. It has a new look of a modern graphic identification program. The Conference established INTER-CHANGE: STRATEGIES FOR IMPROVEMENT, a program of services for Interfraternity Councils and Alumni Interfraternity Councils. Further, a Commission on Values and Ethics was established to promulgate basic and ultimate expectations of fraternity members through Challenges&Choices programming.

The outlook for the National Interfraternity Conference and its member fraternities is bright, confirming the desirability of college fraternities on campuses throughout the United States and Canada.

- There are more men in American college fraternities now than at any other time in their existence, since Phi Beta Kappa was formed at Williamsburg in 1776!
- Nearly four and one-half million are members including more than 400,000 collegians on campuses throughout Canada and the United States.
- 62 NIC member fraternities have 5,238 chapters and 418 colonies at over 800 colleges and universities.
- Growth: Since fraternities were reorganized following World War II, there have been more chapters each year than existed the year before.

Year	Total Chapters	Average Number of Men per Chapter	Totals of Collegiate Initiates & Associates
1990	5,238	54	282,852 & 118,608
1989	5,194	52	270,088 & 113,748
1988	5,120	52	266,240 & 107,247
1987	4,850	50	242,500
1986	4,695	49	230,055
1985	4,599	47	216,153
1984	4,500	45	202,500
1981	4,448	44	195,712
1971	4,247	34	144,398
1951	3,055	—	—
1941	2,455	—	—

- Three chapters have been chartered for every one closed in the last several years—158 were opened in 1989–90; 160 in 1988–89; 178 in 1987–88; and 163 in 1986–87. This means that there has been a net increase (chapters opened minus chapters closed in the same year) of 64 last year, 105 in 1988–89; 121 in 1987–88; and 115 in 1986–87. There has been a 65% increase to 91 chapters closed; 55 in 1988–89; 57 in 1987–88; and 48 in 1986–87.
- Each chapter has an average of 54 student brothers; over a 50% increase since 1972 (in 1972 there were 34 men per chapter; the previous high was 49 per chapter in 1965).
- The total number of fraternity members on campus has increased by 178% since 1972. In that year there were 144,398 students in fraternities and today there are 401,460 collegiate members and associates.
- NIC fraternities have experienced 3% increase in the number of initiates this year (98,290 total in 1989–90; 95,395 in 1988–89 and 7.2% increase over 1987–88).
- "The American college fraternity is an American institution and the chapter in the form it ideally exists on the college campus is a miniature of the larger American democracy . . . The fraternity group is formed by mutual selection, based on congeniality and common purpose. Here the young member learns, perhaps for the first time, to submit to the will of the majority and to shape his own conduct by the interests and standards of the others with whom he lives. In assuming his share of work in the group, he develops a sense of responsibility for the well-being of something outside himself. He is merged with the group; must work with and for it; must fight to emerge as a leader who will direct it. He learns the great lesson of subordinating self and selfish desires for the good of others. He thus learns to lend his strength to those who have less, thus fulfilling an educational goal than which there is not higher . . ." *Baird's Manual of American College Fraternities, Bicentennial Edition.*

INTERCHANGE: Strategies for Improvement

Mission Statement:

INTERCHANGE, the National Interfraternity Conference's program of services to campus Interfraternity Councils and Greek Advisors, is designed to enhance the quality of undergraduate, interfraternal cooperation with an emphasis on self-regulation.

INTERCHANGE Philosophy:

Step One:
INTERCHANGE Self-Appraisal

The Self-Appraisal begins the INTERCHANGE process by providing a tool for annual assessment, evaluation, and goal setting. Emphasis is placed on participation of all chapter presidents and IFC officers.

The 1990–91 Self-Appraisal is a self-scoring instrument to provide campuses with *immediate* feedback.

Step Two:
INTERCHANGE Resource Manual

The Resource Manual is to provide a comprehensive guidebook on IFC operations. The Resource Manual restates the appraisal guidelines and offers a "nuts and bolts" explanation of each guideline and specific, pragmatic suggestions for implementation.

The Resource Manual provides clarification of guidelines when completing the Self-Appraisal and offers immediate suggestions once priority areas are identified.

Step Three:
INTERCHANGE Directory of Resource Files

The Directory of Resource Files brings a variety of quality Greek resources under one listing. The 1990–91 directory contains 600+ listings.

Once priority areas are identified after using the Self-Appraisal, the Directory provides instant access to similar programs from campuses throughout the country.

Step Four:
Campus Commentary

Campus Commentary is the official INTERCHANGE newsletter. *Campus Commentary* provides updated, current information ten times annually (August–May) to build upon the annual reprintings of the Resource Manual and Directory of Resource Files.

The goal of *Campus Commentary* has become the compilation of "good" news about Greek systems and IFCs. Each issue contains approximately 30–40 ready-to-implement ideas from campuses throughout the country.

Step Five:
Undergraduate Interfraternity Institute (UIFI)

As a method to reinforce use of INTERCHANGE services, influence undergraduate attitudes on the IFC role, empower leaders to accept the challenges of change, and offer a quality, intimate leadership experience the Undergraduate Interfraternity Institute (UIFI) was created.

Using a model of live-in group facilitators (1 facilitator for each 5–6 participants), delegates (men and women with a target audience of current and emerging IFC, Panhellenic, and Black Greek Council leaders) complete a comprehensive case study. A "faculty-like" panel of fraternity/sorority executives and chief student affairs officers hear case study presentations and offer critical feedback which is a critical learning opportunity of UIFI.

NIC Commission on Values and Ethics

The National Interfraternity Conference is committed to enhancing the benefits of fraternity membership. We exist to promote the importance of fraternal relationships, character-building, leadership development and the nurturing of responsible and accountable men and women.

As an outcome of that commitment, the NIC's Commission on Values and Ethics has developed a statement on basic expectations of fraternity membership. This nine-point statement summarizes the guidelines by which fraternity men and women should govern their individual fraternal experiences. The National Panhellenic Conference has resolved to encourage all panhellenic women to foster behavior that fulfills these Basic Expectations.

To communicate these expectations to college students, alumni and fraternal organization leaders, the Commission designed *Challenges&Choices*. *Challenges&Choices* develops awareness and appreciation of the Basic Expectations and encourages their implementation in the daily lives of fraternity members.

Basic Expectations

In an effort to lessen the disparity between fraternity ideals and individual behavior and to personalize these ideals in the daily undergraduate experience, the following Basic Expectations of fraternity membership have been established:

  I. I will know and understand the ideals expressed in my fraternity Ritual and will strive to incorporate them in my daily life.

 II. I will strive for academic achievement and practice academic integrity.

III. I will respect the dignity of all persons; therefore I will not physically, mentally, psychologically or sexually abuse or haze any human being.

 IV. I will protect the health and safety of all human beings.

  V. I will respect my property and the property of others; therefore, I will neither abuse nor tolerate the abuse of property.

 VI. I will meet my financial obligations in a timely manner.

VII. I will neither use nor support the use of illegal drugs; I will neither misuse nor support the misuse of alcohol.

VIII. I acknowledge that a clean and attractive environment is essential to both physical and mental health; therefore I will do all in my power to see that the chapter property is properly cleaned and maintained.

IX. I will challenge all my fraternity members to abide by these fraternal expectations and will confront those who violate them.

How *Challenges & Choices* Helps

Chapters will benefit in many ways from hosting a *Challenges&Choices* Workshop. *Challenges&Choices*

- fine tunes your individual and collective value systems.
- allows participants to explore choices in given life situations.
- helps participants think through responses *before* decisions *have* to be made.
- creates an environment for open and frank discussion.
- encourages fraternal bonding and learning from one another through group interaction.
- reinforces commitment and accountability to the fraternity.
- provides interesting and adaptable teaching materials for use in your organization.

- provides leadership training in ethical decision making.

How *Challenges&Choices* Works

Since there is no better time to establish value-based patterns for lifetime decision-making, *Challenges&Choices* was created with collegiate men and women in mind.

Challenges&Choices is a structured dialog-focused program. Most often, participants belong to a local fraternal chapter. The program is equally effective, however, with groups of students and alumni, campus-wide Greek organization leaders and student development groups.

In a *Challenges&Choices* Workshop, participants practice the Basic Expectations by becoming involved in simulated life experiences called *case studies*. The Workshop leader—who may be a Greek advisor, a chapter officer, an alumnus or an IFC/Panhellenic officer—guides small-group discussion about the case studies to demonstrate the practicality of the Basic Expectations for daily living.

National Interfraternity Conference Member Fraternities

Acacia	Delta Kappa Epsilon	Phi Delta Theta	Sigma Chi
Alpha Chi Rho	Delta Phi	Phi Gamma Delta	Sigma Nu
Alpha Delta Gamma	Delta Psi	Phi Kappa Psi	Sigma Phi Epsilon
Alpha Delta Phi	Delta Sigma Phi	Phi Kappa Sigma	Sigma Phi Society
Alpha Epsilon Pi	Delta Tau Delta	Phi Kappa Tau	Sigma Pi
Alpha Gamma Rho	Delta Upsilon	Phi Kappa Theta	Sigma Tau Gamma
Alpha Gamma Sigma	FarmHouse	Phi Lambda Chi	Tau Delta Phi
Alpha Kappa Lambda	Iota Phi Theta	Phi Mu Delta	Tau Epsilon Phi
Alpha Phi Delta	Kappa Alpha Order	Phi Sigma Kappa	Tau Kappa Epsilon
Alpha Sigma Phi	Kappa Alpha Psi	Pi Kappa Alpha	Theta Chi
Alpha Tau Omega	Kappa Alpha Society	Pi Kappa Phi	Theta Delta Chi
Beta Sigma Psi	Kappa Delta Phi	Pi Lambda Phi	Theta Xi
Beta Theta Pi	Kappa Delta Rho	Psi Upsilon	Triangle
Chi Phi	Kappa Sigma	Sigma Alpha Epsilon	Zeta Beta Tau
Chi Psi	Lambda Chi Alpha	Sigma Alpha Mu	Zeta Psi
Delta Chi	Lambda Phi Epsilon		

The Constitution of the National Interfraternity Conference

ARTICLE I
NAME

The name of this Conference shall be the National Interfraternity Conference.

ARTICLE II
PURPOSE

The purpose of the National Interfraternity Conference shall be to promote the well-being of its member fraternities by providing such services to

them as the House of Delegates may determine, these services to include, but not be limited to, promotion of cooperative action in dealing with fraternity matters of mutual concern, research in areas of fraternity operations and procedures, fact-finding and data gathering, and the dissemination of such data to the member fraternities. Conference action shall not in any way abrogate the right of its member fraternities to self-determination.

ARTICLE III
MEMBERSHIP

The Conference shall be composed of those men's general college fraternities which (a) were members on December 1, 1921, of (b) are thereafter admitted in conformity with this Constitution. Provisions may be made in the By-Laws for Associate Membership and Foundation Membership.

ARTICLE IV
HOUSE OF DELEGATES

The Powers of the Conference shall be vested in a House of Delegates.

Section 1. **Composition.** The House of Delegates shall be composed of one delegate from each member fraternity, chosen by that fraternity for such term and upon such qualifications as it may determine. Each member fraternity may also choose an alternate delegate who shall represent it in the absence of the delegate.

Section 2. **Voting.** Each delegate present, or in his absence the alternate delegate, is vested with one vote. Each Past Chairman and Past President of the Conference shall have the privilege of a seat in the House of Delegates with voice and shall have the right to participate in all discussions, but in such capacity may not vote.

Section 3. **Responsibilities.** The House of Delegates shall be responsible for the broad general policies of the Conference, for electing a Board of Directors and certain officers as herein provided, and for instructing the Board as to activities in behalf of the Conference. All such activities shall preserve the autonomous right of each member fraternity over its own affairs.

ARTICLE V
BOARD OF DIRECTORS

The executive and administrative powers of the House of Delegates shall be vested in a Board of fifteen Directors, fourteen of whom shall be elected as herein provided and the other of whom shall be the most recent living Past President in good standing.

Section 1. **Qualification; term.** Directors shall have served as members of the governing board or administrative staff of their respective fraternities. Seven Directors shall be elected at each Annual Meeting, and their term of office shall be two years. No Director shall serve more than four full terms, except as hereinafter provided. Eight Directors shall constitute a quorum. The most recent living Past President in good standing shall serve as a voting Director, without regard to any other provision of the Constitution limiting the duration of his service as a Director.

Section 2. **Eligibility.** No person shall be elected or chosen as a Director unless he is a member of a fraternity which is a member of the Conference with its dues, paid and in good standing. For this purpose, a fraternity which has been granted an extension by the Board of Directors as provided in the By-Laws for the payment of dues, shall not be deemed a member in good standing. An elected member of the Board of Directors whose fraternity is not in good standing because of failure to pay its dues shall have his office vacated forthwith.

Section 3. **Vacancies.** In the event of the death or resignation of a Director between the Annual Meetings, such vacancy shall be filled by a majority vote of the remaining Directors, and the person thus chosen shall serve only until the next regularly assembled Annual Meeting at which time a successor to the deceased or resigned Director shall be elected to fill the remainder, if any, of his expired term. The resignation of a Director shall be submitted to the House of Delegates, if assembled; otherwise, the resignation shall be submitted to the Board of Directors through the Executive Vice President and CEO (Chief Executive Officer). A Director chosen to fill an unexpired term may be elected for four full terms following the completion of the incomplete term.

Section 4. **Duties.** The Board of Directors shall be responsible for carrying out the purposes and policies of the Conference, for the election of such officers as it may determine in addition to those elected by the House of Delegates, for the employment of an Executive Vice President and CEO, and for defining and fixing the responsibilities of its officers and employees.

ARTICLE VI
OFFICERS

From the membership of the Board of Directors, the House of Delegates shall elect a President-elect who shall serve a term of one year and who shall succeed to the office of President at the next Annual Meeting of the House of Delegates. In the event of the death or resignation of the President, the President-elect shall become the President, and the Board of Directors shall elect a Vice President from among its members to serve until the next Annual Meeting. At the next Annual Meeting following the death or resignation of the President, the House of Delegates shall elect a President, who may be the man who succeeded to that office by reason of the death or resignation of his predecessor, and a President-elect. In the event of the death or resignation of the President-elect, the Board of Directors shall elect a Vice President who shall serve until the next Annual Meeting of the House of Delegates, and at such meeting the House of Delegates shall elect a President and a President-elect. The Board of Directors shall elect from among its members a Secretary and a Treasurer for terms of one year.

ARTICLE VII
COMMITTEES

Regular committees shall consist of an Executive Committee and a Nominating Committee.

Section 1. **Executive Committee.** Between meetings of the Board of Directors, the executive and administrative duties of the Board may be carried out by an Executive Committee of five of its members: The President, President-elect or Vice President, Secretary, Treasurer, and one member at large elected by the Board. Three members shall constitute a quorum. The Executive Committee shall report to and be responsible to the Board, and through the Board to the House of Delegates.

Section 2. **Nominating Committee.** A Nominating Committee shall consist of the immediate living Past President, who shall serve as Chairman, and not less than six men, each of whom has been a delegate or an alternate who has served in the absence of a delegate at any one of the five immediately preceding Annual Meetings, appointed by the President with the concurrence of the Board of Directors. Each member fraternity shall be represented on the Nominating Committee at least once in ten years, if a member is qualified. The Nominating Committee shall prepare and present for election to the Board at each Annual Meeting a slate of seven nominees for two year terms, plus such additional number of nominees, if any, as may be required to fill unexpired terms of Board positions vacated by resignation, death, or by reason of the immediate Past President becoming an ex officio member of the Board.

Section 3. **Other Committees.** The Board of Directors may form such other committees as it deems necessary to perform the work of the Conference. The President shall appoint the chairman and members of such other committees with the concurrence of the Board of Directors.

Section 4. **Fraternity Executives Advisory Committee.** The President, with the concurrence of the Board, shall appoint a Fraternity Executives Advisory Committee, with members nominated by the Fraternity Executives Association, which committee shall meet as required with the Board of Directors and the Executive Committee.

ARTICLE VIII
ANNUAL MEETINGS

The Annual Meeting of the National Interfraternity Conference shall be held at such time and place as is designated by the Board of Directors. The Annual Meeting of the House of Delegates shall be held at the same time and place as the Annual Meeting of the Conference, but special meetings may be held at such time and place as it may decide in annual session or by the Board of Directors or by petition signed by at least one-third of its regular delegates.

Section 1. **Notices.** Notices of the Annual Meeting of the conference and of the House of Delegates shall be issued by the Conference not less than sixty days preceding the Annual Meetings, and thirty days preceding special meetings.

Section 2. **Registration.** Registration for the Annual Meeting shall be limited to representatives of member fraternities, representatives of associate members and foundation members, and guests specifically invited by the Conference. A person who is not registered shall not be admitted to an official function of the Annual Meeting.

ARTICLE IX
ADMISSION TO MEMBERSHIP

Every general college fraternity eligible for membership in the Conference under Article III of this Constitution and under Section 1 of the By-Laws may be admitted to membership upon two-thirds vote of the Board of Directors in attendance at the meeting when the vote is taken. In the event of the failure by the applicant fraternity to obtain the approval of the Board of Directors for admission to membership in the Conference, such fraternity may thereafter appeal to the House of Delegates, which by a two-thirds vote of the member fraternities represented at such meeting, may approve the application for admission and admit the fraternity to membership in the Conference. Failure to obtain a two-thirds vote in the House of Delegates shall affirm the action of the Board in rejecting the application for admission.

ARTICLE X
CONDUCT; DISCIPLINARY ACTION

No member fraternity, associate member or foundation member shall engage in any conduct or activity which is detrimental or prejudicial to the general college fraternity system or the Conference. A violation of this Constitution or of the By-Laws shall be deemed evidence per se that the conduct or activity is detrimental or prejudicial.

Section 1. **Investigation and Hearing.** The Board of Directors shall investigate all complaints which come to it in writing and shall forthwith communicate any such complaint to the alleged offender. Such written complaint shall specify the section of the Constitution or By-Laws alleged to have been violated and shall, in general, set forth the conduct or activity complained of. Both the complainant and the alleged offender shall be afforded a reasonable opportunity to appear and be heard before the Board of Directors or such special committee as the Board shall appoint to investigate, hear evidence and report to the Board. The Board of Directors, by a two-thirds vote of all of its members, may expel or impose lesser disciplinary action against the offender for conduct or activity found by the Board to be detrimental or prejudicial to the general college fraternity system or the Conference.

Section 2. **Appeal.** The member fraternity, associate member or foundation member shall have the right to appeal the disciplinary action of the Board of Directors to the House of Delegates at its Annual Meeting next following the notice of appeal. Appeal may be taken by the filing of a written notice of appeal with the office of the National Interfraternity Conference within sixty days from the date of the notice of the disciplinary action. The disciplinary action of the Board of Directors shall stand until the appeal shall be heard by the House of Delegates. The House of Delegates, by a majority vote of the members in attendance, may affirm or reverse the action of the Board of Directors and may lessen or increase the disciplinary action imposed by the Board.

ARTICLE XI
DUES

The annual dues of members shall be as fixed from time to time by action of the House of Delegates.

Section 1. **Payment; delinquency.** All dues shall be payable in January of each year. On any amount unpaid on the first day of June next following, a charge of ten percent (10%) will be imposed. An additional charge of one percent (1%) will be added on the first day of each calendar month thereafter in which default continues, to and including the first day of December of that year. Thereafter, an additional charge of one and one-half percent (1 1/2%) will be added on the first day of each calendar month in which default continues. If the charges for unpaid dues exceed those permitted by the applicable law, the said charges shall be the maximum so permitted.

Section 2. **Suspension of Representation.** No member that is in arrears for dues or other indebtedness to the Conference shall have representation at the Annual Meeting of the House of Delegates. If dues have not been fully paid for the current year prior to the Board of Directors meeting immediately preceding the Annual Meeting of the House of Delegates, the delinquent member shall be denied representation in the House of Delegates and shall be dropped from membership in the Conference unless granted an extension by the Board of Directors.

ARTICLE XII
AMENDMENTS

This Constitution may be amended at any meeting by a two-thirds vote of all the member fraternities entitled to vote in the House of Delegates, whether or not present at the meeting. If written notice of any proposed amendment has been mailed to all member fraternities at least 30 days before such meeting, then such amendment may be adopted by a two-thirds vote of all member fraternities present and voting on such amendment, provided that such two-thirds vote is not less than one-half of all members entitled to vote in the House of Delegates, whether or not present at the meeting. Amendments may be proposed by means of such advance written notice upon proper authorization of the governing body of any member fraternity or of the Board of Directors. Amendments may be adopted without a meeting by the written approval of two-thirds of all member fraternities entitled to vote in the House of Delegates. The Board of Directors may make recommendations to the House of Delegates regarding action to be taken on any proposed amendment.

ARTICLE XII
INCORPORATION

The Conference shall be incorporated under the membership corporation laws of the state of New York under the title "National Interfraternity Conference, Inc."

The By-Laws of The National Interfraternity Conference

SECTION 1
MEMBERSHIP REQUIREMENTS

(a) **Fraternity Membership:** To be eligible for membership in the Conference, a fraternity must:
1. Be devoted to general fraternity ideals;
2. Be national, as distinct from local, in character, meaning that it shall (i) consist of no fewer than five undergraduate chapters, each of which has a current undergraduate membership of at least ten members, (ii) include not less than three undergraduate chapters, which have been part of the fraternity for at least five years, and (iii) have constitutional provisions for national conventions or equivalent with interim authority in trustees, directors or other officers who supervise the affairs of the fraternity.
3. Be mutually exclusive of and in competition with other general college fraternities, meaning that no member fraternity shall initiate a member of any other member fraternity until such time as the second fraternity shall have been formally notified in writing by the national office of the first fraternity that a candidate for membership in the second fraternity is no longer regarded as a member of the fraternity.
4. Have no undergraduate chapters related to institutions other than accredited (i) four-year colleges or universities which grant Bachelor Decrees, or (ii) two-year degree granting junior colleges.

For the purpose of these By-Laws, "accredited" shall mean, in the United States, institutions which are accredited by one of the following regional associations: Middle States, New England, North Central, Northwest, Southern or Western, and the accrediting agencies recognized by the American Council on Education; and, other than in the United States, institutions which are accredited or approved in some similar manner.

For the purpose of these By-Laws, a chapter is "related to" an institution if its membership is drawn from students enrolled at such institution, and no formal agreement with or recognition by such institution shall be required or implied.

This subsection shall not be deemed to prohibit undergraduate chapters related to extension, branches or regional campuses of accredited institutions.

(b) **Associate Membership:** To be eligible for Associate Membership, the member must be either an individual, a firm, an association, a partnership, a corporation, or an officer or an employee of a corporation, or a member or employee of a partnership actively engaged in the business of manufacturing, selling, distributing, or providing supplies, products, or services to member fraternities. Election to Associate Membership shall be by majority vote of the Board of Directors. The Board of Directors shall fix dues, and establish and publish rules and procedures pertaining to Associate Membership in the Conference.

(c) **Foundation Membership:** To be eligible for Foundation Membership, the member must be organized and operate exclusively for educational purposes as an adjunct of a member fraternity or as an adjunct of a member in good standing of the National Panhellenic Conference, and exempt from Federal income taxes under Section 501(c)(3) of Internal Revenue Code of 1954 or corresponding provisions of Canadian Law. Election to Foundation Membership shall be by majority vote of the Board of Directors. The Board of Directors shall fix dues, and establish and publish rules and procedures pertaining to Foundation Membership in the Conference.

Section 2
Colonies

A colony, meaning a newly-formed group or association of students sponsored, organized or assisted by a fraternity with the intent of it becoming a chapter or otherwise affiliated in any manner with that fraternity, may be established by a member fraternity only in relation to an accredited college or university. No member fraternity shall sponsor, organize, assist or participate in any manner in the formation, organization or establishment of a colony related to an accredited college or university, unless such college or university shall hold an approved candidacy status with the appropriate regional association, and such colony may become chartered only upon full accreditation of the institution.

Section 3
Comity

No member fraternity shall accept a petition for membership, grant colony or other affiliated status, or grant a charter to any group substantially representing an existing or previously resigned or disassociated colony or active chapter of another member fraternity, until the fraternity with which such group was previously connected has officially given written notice to the Conference that all rights have been waived by them, or until five years have elapsed from the date of resignation or disassociation.

Section 4
Affiliation of Local Chapter

Member fraternities may accept petitions for a charter from and grant charters to eligible local chapters in accredited colleges or universities. Upon receipt and acceptance of such petition, a member fraternity may give written notice to the Conference of such acceptance, identifying the local chapter and the institution with which it is related. Upon receipt by the Conference of such notice, the local chapter shall be subject to the rules of comity set forth in Section 3, except that the elapsed time from the date of resignation or disassociation shall be three years instead of five years.

The Conference, upon receipt of notice from a member fraternity that it has accepted the application of a local fraternity, shall forthwith give notice thereof to all member fraternities.

A "local chapter" shall mean any local fraternity, club or group previously formed and existing as a fraternal or common-interest organization, other than a colony.

Section 5
Fiscal Year

The fiscal year of the Conference shall begin September 1.

Section 6
Governing Rules

The business of the Conference shall be governed by Robert's Rules of Order, except as hereinafter noted.

Section 7
Educational Advisory Council

The Board of Directors may appoint an educational advisory council of such number as it may determine.

Section 8
Amendments

Amendments to By-Laws relating to membership in the Conference, the qualifications, or privileges of membership of members may be made in the same manner as amendments to the Constitution are made. Other amendments to the By-Laws may be made by the House of Delegates by a majority of the members voting thereon, with or without notice of the proposed amendment.

National Interfraternity Conference—Risk Management Policy

The Risk Management Policy of the National Interfraternity Conference includes the provisions which follow and shall apply to all fraternity entities and all levels of fraternity membership.

Alcohol and Drugs

1. The possession, use and/or consumption of ALCOHOLIC BEVERAGES, while on chapter premises, during an official fraternity event, or in any situation sponsored or endorsed by the chapter, must be in compliance with any and all applicable laws of the state, province, county, city and university.
2. No alcoholic beverages may be purchased through the chapter treasury nor may the purchase of same for members or guests be undertaken or coordinated by any member in the name of or on behalf of the chapter. The purchase and/or use of a bulk quantity of such alcoholic beverages, i.e., kegs, is prohibited.
3. No chapter members, collectively or individually, shall purchase for, serve to, or sell alcoholic beverages to any minor (i.e., those under legal "drinking age").
4. The possession, sale and/or use of an ILLEGAL DRUG OR CONTROLLED SUBSTANCE at any chapter house, sponsored event or at any event that an observer would associate with the fraternity, is strictly prohibited.
5. No chapter may co-sponsor an event with an alcohol distributor, charitable organization or tavern (tavern is defined as an establishment generating more than half of annual gross sales from alcohol) where alcohol is given away, sold or otherwise provided to those present.
6. No chapter may co-sponsor or co-finance a function where alcohol is purchased by any of the host chapters, groups or organizations.
7. All rush activities associated with any chapter will be a DRY function.
8. OPEN PARTIES where alcohol is present, meaning those with unrestricted access by non-members of the fraternity, without specific invitation, shall be prohibited.
9. No member shall permit, tolerate, encourage or participate in "drinking games."
10. No alcohol shall be present at any pledge/associate member/novice program or activity of the chapter.

Hazing

No chapter shall conduct hazing activities. Hazing activities are defined as:
   "Any action taken or situation created, intentionally, whether on or off fraternity premises, to produce mental or physical discomfort, embarrassment, harassment, or ridicule. Such activities may include, but are not limited to the following: use of alcohol; paddling in any form; creation of excessive fatigue; physical and psychological shocks; quests, treasure hunts, scavenger hunts, road trips or any other such activities carried on outside or inside of the confines of the chapter house; wearing of public apparel which is conspicuous and not normally in good taste; engaging in public stunts and buffoonery; morally degrading or humiliating games and activities; and any other activities which are not consistent with fraternal law, ritual or policy or the regulations and policies of the educational institution."

Sexual Abuse

The fraternity will not tolerate or condone any form of sexually abusive behavior on the part of its members, whether physical, mental or emotional. This is to include any actions which are demeaning to women including but not limited to date rape, gang rape, or verbal harassment.

Fire, Health, and Safety

1. All chapter houses shall, prior to, during, and following occupancy, meet all local fore and health codes and standards.
2. All chapters must have posted by common phones emergency numbers for fire, police and ambulance and must have posted evacuation routes on the back of the door of each sleeping room.
3. All chapters shall comply with engineering recommendations as reported by the insurance company.
4. The possession and/or use of firearms or explosive devices of any kind within the confines and premises of the chapter house is expressly forbidden.

Education

Each student member, associate member and pledge shall be instructed annually on the Risk Management Policy of the National Interfraternity Conference.

Chairmen and Presidents of the National Interfraternity Conference

1909–10	Hamilton W. Mabie, Alpha Delta Phi		1955	Herbert L. Brown, Phi Sigma Kappa
1911	William H. P. Faunce, Delta Upsilon		1956	Horace G. Nichol, Delta Upsilon
1912	Oscar H. Rogers, Sigmi Phi		1957	Francis S. Van Derbur, Kappa Sigma
1913	William A. Trimpe, Sigma Chi		1958	Houston T. Karnes, Lambda Chi Alpha
1914	Francis W. Shepardson, Beta Theta Pi		1959	J. Edward Murphy, Sigma Nu
1915	James B. Curtis, Delta Tau Delta		1960	Roland Maxwell, Phi Kappa Tau
1916	Henry H. McCorkle, Phi Kappa Psi		1961	Joel W. Reynolds, Delta Tau Delta
1917	Orion H. Cheney, Phi Gamma Delta		1962	Earl D. Rhodes, Theta Chi
1918–19	James D. Livingston, Delta Phi		1963	Robert W. Kelly, Sigma Phi Epsilon
1920	Albert S. Bard, Chi Psi		1964	Bertram W. Bennett, Beta Theta Pi
1921	Don R. Almy, Sigma Alpha Epsilon		1965	J. Dwight Peterson, Sigma Chi
1922	F. H. Nymeyer, Zeta Psi		1966	Robert W. Krovitz, Alpha Epsilon Pi
1923	John J. Kuhn, Delta Chi		1967	Fred H. Turner, Sigma Alpha Epsilon
1924	A. Bruce Bielaski, Delta Tau Delta		1968	Louis L. Roth, Sigma Nu
1925	Walter H. Conley, Phi Sigma Kappa		1969	Zeke L. Loflin, Theta Xi
1926	Henry R. Johnston, Delta Kappa Epsilon		1970	Tozier Brown, Lambda Chi Alpha
1927	William R. Bayes, Phi Delta Theta		1971	Robert D. Lynn, Pi Kappa Alpha
1928	Harold Riegelman, Zeta Beta Tau		1972	Lewis S. Armstrong, Delta Chi
1929	Clifford M. Swan, Delta Upsilon		1973	Robert K. Ausman, Alpha Epsilon Pi
1930	Charles W. Gerstenberg, Delta Chi		1974	William J. Cutbirth, Jr., Sigma Pi
1931–32	Alvan E. Duerr, Delta Tau Delta		1975	George F. Patterson, Jr., Acacia
1933	Edward T. T. Williams, Delta Phi		1976	George F. Jelen, Jr., Alpha Delta Gamma
1934	Cecil J. Wilkinson, Phi Gamma Delta		1977	Peter F. Greiner, Beta Theta Pi
1935	LeRoy E. Kimball, Sigma Nu		1978	Richard H. Sudheimer, Triangle
1936	Harold J. Baily, Beta Theta Pi		1979	Norman C. Brewer, Jr., Sigma Chi
1937	H. Maurice Darling, Delta Kappa Epsilon		1979–80	George M. Mills, Alpha Chi Rho
1938	Russell C. MacFall, Delta Chi		1981	James H. McLaughlin, Zeta Psi
1939	Harry S. Rogers, Alpha Tau Omega		1982	David C. Bland, Jr., Phi Gamma Delta
1940–41	Lloyd G. Balfour, Sigma Chi		1983	Sidney H. Guller, Sigma Alpha Mu
1942	John M. MacGregor, Alpha Tau Omega		1984	J. Glenn Hahn, Alpha Kappa Lambda
1943	Scott Turner, Psi Upsilon		1985	Rodney Williams Jr., Tau Kappa Epsilon
1944	Leroy A. Wilson, Lambda Chi Alpha		1986	Edwin L. Heminger, Delta Tau Delta
1945	Verling C. Enteman, Delta Phi		1987	Clay Myers, Lambda Chi Alpha
1946	Maurice Jacobs, Phi Epsilon Pi		1988	Chuck V. Loring, Phi Sigma Kappa
1947	David Embury, Acacia		1989	Patrick I. Brown, Alpha Tau Omega
1948	Gilbert W. Mead, Phi Gamma Delta		1990	Henry L. Bauer, Kappa Sigma
1949	Frank H. Myers, Kappa Alpha Order		1991	Dr. William R. Nester, Pi Kappa Alpha
1950	William J. Barnes, Theta Xi		1992	Robert L. Marchman III, Sigma Nu
1951	A. Ray Warnock, Beta Theta Pi			
1952	Charles E. Pledger, Jr., Theta Delta Chi			
1953	C. Robert Yeager, Pi Kappa Alpha			
1954	Lloyd S. Cochran, Alpha Sigma Phi			

An amendment providing for the change in the title of the chief officer of the NIC from Chairman to President was adopted at the 1961 Conference.

Recipients of the National Interfraternity Conference Gold Medal

1940	Albert S. Bard, Chi Psi		1949	Leroy A. Wilson, Lambda Chi Alpha
	Alvan E. Duerr, Delta Tau Delta		1950	Joseph A. Bursley (nonfraternity)
1941	H. Maurice Darling, Delta Kappa Epsilon		1951	Arthur Ray Warnock, Beta Theta Pi
1946	Lloyd G. Balfour, Sigma Chi			Joseph A. Park, Alpha Tau Omega
1947	John Mosely, Sigma Alpha Epsilon			William R. Bayes, Phi Delta Theta
1948	G. Herbert Smith, Beta Theta Pi		1952	Henry M. Wriston, Delta Tau Delta

1953 Verling C. Enteman, Delta Phi
1954 Frank H. Myers, Kappa Alpha Order
      Maurice Jacobs, Phi Epsilon Pi
1955 Cecil J. Wilkinson, Phi Gamma Delta
1956 Fred H. Turner, Sigma Alpha Epsilon
1957 Herbert L. Brown, Phi Sigma Kappa
      John M. MacGregor, Alpha Tau Omega
1959 Horace G. Nichol, Delta Upsilon
1960 Francis S. Van Derbur, Kappa Sigma
1961 George S. Ward, Phi Delta Theta
1962 Herman B Wells, Sigma Nu
      J. Edward Murphy, Sigma Nu
1964 Henry R. Johnston, Delta Kappa Epsilon
1965 Tom C. Clark, Delta Tau Delta
1966 Dr. Seth R. Brooks, Beta Theta Pi
      Joel W. Reynolds, Delta Tau Delta
1967 Roland Maxwell, Phi Kappa Tau
      Scott Turner, Psi Upsilon
1968 George W. Chapman, Theta Chi
1969 Houston T. Karnes, Lambda Chi Alpha
1970 J. Dwight Peterson, Sigma Chi
      Stewart D. Daniels, Alpha Tau Omega
1971 Joe D. Waggonner, Jr., Kappa Sigma
      Earl D. Rhodes, Theta Chi

1972 Robert W. Krovitz, Alpha Epsilon Pi
      Zeke L. Loflin, Theta Xi
1975 Tozier Brown, Lambda Chi Alpha
1976 John D. Millett, Phi Delta Theta
      Ralph F. Burns, Alpha Sigma Phi
1977 Richard R. Fletcher, Sigma Nu
1978 George S. Toll, Alpha Epsilon Pi
1979 Ralph D. Daniel, Phi Kappa Psi
      George F. Patterson, Jr., Acacia
1981 Robert K. Ausman, M.D., Alpha Epsilon Pi
1982 Dr. Norman Vincent Peale, Phi Gamma
         Delta
1983 Ronald W. Reagan, Tau Kappa Epsilon
1984 Harold Jacobsen, Sigma Pi
      Robert B. Stewart, Alpha Chi Rho
1985 Ewing T. Bowles, Phi Kappa Tau
      Barry Goldwater, Sigma Chi
1986 Jack L. Anson, Phi Kappa Tau
1987 Dr. Ronald W. Roskens, Sigma Tau Gamma
      Richard H. Sudhelmer, Triangle
1988 Paul K. Addams, Alpha Chi Rho
      Sidney H. Guller, Sigma Alpha Mu
1989 Stanley I. Fishel, Zeta Beta Tau
      William S. Zerman, Phi Gamma Delta
1990 Dr. John L. Blackburn, Alpha Sigma Phi

Recipients of the National Interfraternity Conference Silver Medal

1980 Hugh D. Scott, Jr., Alpha Chi Rho
      Carroll K. Simons, Phi Kappa Sigma
      Marsh White, Delta Chi
1981 John J. Rhodes, Beta Theta Pi
1982 James H. McLaughlin, Zeta Psi
      Robert H. Shaffer, Sigma Chi
1984 Fred L. Dixon, Phi Gamma Delta
1985 James S. Brady, Sigma Chi
      George Bush, Delta Kappa Epsilon
      John W. Galbreath, Delta Tau Delta

1986 Dr. John W. Ryan, Kappa Sigma
1987 Ellison S. Onizuka, Triangle
      Samuel H. Shapiro, Alpha Epsilon Pi
1989 Edward M. King, Sigma Chi
      Eileen C. Stevens, Alpha Phi
1990 Edward A. Pease, Pi Kappa Alpha

Recipients of the National Interfraternity Conference Interfraternal Awards

1989 Albert D. Shonk, Phi Sigma Kappa
      Dr. Charles E. Wicks, Phi Delta Theta
      George W. Spasyk, Lambda Chi Alpha
      Sigma Phi Epsilon Educational Foundation
      Balfour Company

1990 Joseph F. Lacchia, Delta Chi
      Colonel Paul J. B. Murphy, Jr., Sigma Nu
      Dr. John D. Wilson, Sigma Nu
      Will S. Kelm, Ph.D., Delta Upsilon

National Panhellenic Conference

What is NPC?

As the name implies, National Panhellenic is a Conference body. Its members are women's fraternities, each of which is autonomous as a social, Greek-letter society of college women, undergraduates and alumnae.

Purpose

National Panhellenic Conference is an organization established to foster interfraternity relationships, to assist collegiate chapters of the NPC member groups, and to cooperate with colleges and universities in maintaining the highest scholastic and social standards.

Members

Twenty-six women's fraternities, national or international in scope, comprise National Panhellenic Conference. They are:

Alpha Chi Omega	Delta Zeta
Alpha Delta Pi	Gamma Phi Beta
Alpha Epsilon Phi	Kappa Alpha Theta
Alpha Gamma Delta	Kappa Delta
Alpha Omicron Pi	Kappa Kappa Gamma
Alpha Phi	Phi Mu
Alpha Sigma Alpha	Phi Sigma Sigma
Alpha Sigma Tau	Pi Beta Phi
Alpha Xi Delta	Sigma Delta Tau
Chi Omega	Sigma Kappa
Delta Delta Delta	Sigma Sigma Sigma
Delta Gamma	Theta Phi Alpha
Delta Phi Epsilon	Zeta Tau Alpha

How NPC Functions

National Panhellenic Conference functions as a conference, not as a convention. In 1988, twenty-six groups affirmed the concept that National Panhellenic Conference continue to operate as a Conference.

Each fraternity selects one delegate to represent it at NPC meetings. The delegate casts the fraternity vote, serves on a standing committee and acts as liaison between her fraternity and the other NPC groups. Each fraternity may name three alternate delegates, one of whom is often the National (International) President.

Business is conducted at biennial conferences and interim sessions (held only if delegates vote to convene). A three-member Executive Committee administers NPC (Chairman, Secretary, and Treasurer). The NPC officers are delegates of member groups, holding office for six years, beginning with Treasurer, progressing to Secretary and then to Chairman. Delegates serve on the Executive Committee in an established rotation order. Between biennial conferences, the Executive Committee administers those concerns having the approval of the Conference and directs the work of standing and special committees.

Powers of NPC

National Panhellenic Conference legislative powers are limited to enactment of laws for its own government.

It is empowered to make recommendations to member fraternities, such recommendations becoming law only after ratification by the member groups. Through such recommendations have come the UNANIMOUS AGREEMENTS of the Conference: The Panhellenic Creed, Panhellenic Compact, Standards of Ethical Conduct, Agreement on Questionnaires and Constitutions, College Panhellenics Agreement, Jurisdiction of a College Panhellenic Council and NPC Declaration for Freedom.

Because they have been ratified, the UNANIMOUS AGREEMENTS must be followed by all fraternities in NPC until such time as they are amended or rescinded. College Panhellenics and Alumnae Panhellenics also are required to abide by them.

National Panhellenic Conference formulates policies on matters of interfraternity interest and concern; studies changing educational outlooks; and through discussions, panels special programs at biennial meetings, contributes to interfraternity understanding and friendship.

NPC is a conference body. NPC cannot transgress or supersede in any way the rights and powers of the individual fraternities which comprise it except as provided above.

History of National Panhellenic Conference

National Panhellenic Conference evolved gradually through a cooperative spirit among women's fraternities. As early as 1891, Kappa Kappa Gamma invited all of the Greek-letter women's college fraternities (there were seven at the time) to a meeting in Boston on April 16 and 17. The groups discussed interfraternity courtesy, fraternity jewelry and stationery and Greek journalism. A second meeting was planned for 1893 at the Chicago

World's Fair, and although some representatives were there, no records exist of the session.

Early histories of women's fraternities contain accounts of "rushing and pledging agreements" or "compacts" among fraternities on various campuses, and also many stories of cooperation and mutual assistance. However, no actual Panhellenic organization existed and no uniform practices were observed. By 1902, it was obvious that some standards were needed, so Alpha Phi invited Pi Beta Phi, Kappa Alpha Theta, Kappa Kappa Gamma, Delta Gamma, Gamma Phi Beta, Delta Delta Delta, Alpha Chi Omega and Chi Omega to a conference in Chicago on May 24. Although Alpha Chi Omega and Chi Omega were not able to send delegates to this meeting, the session resulted in the organization of the first interfraternity association and the first inter-group organization on college campuses. (National Interfraternity Conference for men's fraternities was organized in 1909.)

This meeting and the next few resulted in several mutual agreements, especially regarding pledging. Up to this time no guidelines had been set, and women could be pledged to groups before enrolling in college and, indeed, even belong to more than one group.

First called the Interfraternity Conference, the organization has been variously named and renamed the Inter-Sorority Conference (until 1908); the National Panhellenic Conference (until 1911); the National Panhellenic Congress (until 1917); the National Panhellenic Conference (until 1921); the National Panhellenic Congress (until 1945); and finally the National Panhellenic Conference.

The name change is significant to the NPC philosophy because the organization is a conference, not a congress. It enacts no legislation except for the conduct of its own meetings. Other than the basic UNANIMOUS AGREEMENTS which all groups have voted to observe, NPC confines itself to recommendations and advice, and acts as a court of final appeal in any College Panhellenic difficulty. One of its greatest services is providing Area Advisers for College Panhellenics and Alumnae Panhellenics.

The conference met annually until 1914, when it was voted to have biennial sessions beginning in 1915. While some interim sessions had been held prior to 1971, provision in the Constitution was made at that time for the necessary sessions. The chairmanship is held in rotation according to each member group's entrance into NPC.

Constitution of the National Panhellenic Conference

As amended 1978, 1979, 1983, Revised 1985, and amended 1987, 1988, and 1989

ARTICLE I
NAME

The name of this organization shall be the National Panhellenic Conference.

ARTICLE II
OBJECT

The object of this organization shall be to maintain on a high plane fraternity and interfraternity relationships, to cooperate with college and university authorities in their effort to maintain high social and scholarship standards throughout the whole college or university, and to be a forum for the discussion of questions of interest to the college or university and the fraternity world.

ARTICLE III
MEMBERSHIP

Section I. Membership in the National Panhellenic Conference shall be open to Women's National College Fraternities which meet the qualifications specified in the Bylaws.

The following fraternities are members of the National Panhellenic Conference:

1. Pi Beta Phi
2. Kappa Alpha Theta
3. Kappa Kappa Gamma
4. Alpha Phi
5. Delta Gamma
6. Gamma Phi Beta
7. Alpha Chi Omega
8. Delta Delta Delta
9. Alpha Xi Delta
10. Chi Omega
11. Sigma Kappa
12. Alpha Omicron Pi
13. Zeta Tau Alpha
14. Alpha Gamma Delta
15. Alpha Delta Pi
16. Delta Zeta
17. Phi Mu
18. Kappa Delta
19. Sigma Sigma Sigma
20. Alpha Sigma Tau
21. Alpha Sigma Alpha
22. Alpha Epsilon Phi
23. Theta Phi Alpha
24. Phi Sigma Sigma
25. Delta Phi Epsilon
26. Sigma Delta Tau

Additional fraternities admitted to the National Panhellenic Conference shall be listed in order of their admission. If two or more are admitted at the same Conference, they shall be listed in the order of their founding date.

Section II. Classification of members.

a. Active members shall be those fraternities which have fully qualified for membership as specified in the Bylaws and which have been duly admitted to membership in the National Panhellenic Conference.

b. Associate members shall be those fraternities which have not fully qualified for active membership but which the National Panhellenic Conference has admitted to associate membership.

ARTICLE IV
REPRESENTATION

Section 1. The voting body of the National Panhellenic Conference shall be composed of one delegate from each fraternity holding membership.

Section 2. One representative from each fraternity holding associate membership may have a voice but not a vote in the National Panhellenic Conference.

ARTICLE V
SESSIONS

Section 1. Regular sessions of the National Panhellenic Conference shall be held biennially.

Section 2. Special sessions of the National Panhellenic Conference may be called by the Executive Committee upon unanimous vote of the Committee or upon a three-fourths vote of the member fraternities.

Section 3. An interim session shall be held between regular sessions upon a two-thirds vote of the delegates.

Section 4. An Executive Session may be called by the Executive Committee upon unanimous vote of the Committee.

ARTICLE VI
OFFICERS

The officers of the National Panhellenic Conference shall be a Chairman, a Secretary, and a Treasurer who shall accede to office by rotation according to the official membership list and who shall serve from the end of one biennial session until the end of the next succeeding biennial session. These three officers shall constitute the Executive Committee of the National Panhellenic Conference.

ARTICLE VII
POWERS

Section 1. The powers of the National Panhellenic Conference shall be:
a. To make laws that pertain to its own government;

b. To admit, at its own discretion, petitioning fraternities to membership in the National Panhellenic Conference;
c. To levy and collect annual dues;
d. To make recommendations to the National Presidents of the member fraternities for legislation, and to refer to fraternities for discussion matters which are of interest to the college and fraternity world.
e. To serve as a court of final appeal in any College Panhellenic difficulty;
f. To empower the Executive Committee to administer the business of the Conference to include publications, Central Office, and the activities necessary to carry out the mission and purposes of the Conference.
g. To empower the Executive Committee to invoke the Discipline process as provided for in the Bylaws, Article VIII.

Section 2. Except as otherwise provided in this Constitution and Bylaws, a two-thirds vote of all the delegates shall be necessary to carry out these powers.

ARTICLE VIII
AMENDMENTS

Section 1. This Constitution may be amended by a five-sixths vote of delegates with the subsequent ratification of the National Presidents of the member fraternities, a five-sixths vote being necessary for ratification.

Section 2. A proposed amendment shall be presented to the member fraternities at least sixty (60) days prior to the session of the National Panhellenic Conference which is to act upon the amendment. A proposed amendment shall be in the hands of the Chairman of National Panhellenic Conference at least ninety (90) days prior to the session which is to act upon the amendment.

ARTICLE IX
PARLIAMENTARY AUTHORITY

In all matters not provided for in the Constitution and Bylaws, the National Panhellenic Conference shall be governed by current *Robert's Rules of Order, Newly Revised.*

Chairmen of the National Panhellenic Conference

1902	Margaret M. Whitney, Alpha Phi
1903	Laura B. Norton, Kappa Alpha Theta
1904	Grace Telling, Delta Gamma
1905	Amy H. Olgen, Delta Delta Delta
1906	Ella Boston Leib, Alpha Xi Delta
1907	Jobelle Holcombe, Chi Omega
1908	Anna Webster Lytle, Pi Beta Phi
1909	L. Pearle Green, Kappa Alpha Theta
1910	Florence Burton Roth, Kappa Kappa Gamma
1911	Marguerite Lake, Delta Gamma
1912	Cora A. McElroy, Alpha Phi
1913	Lillian W. Thompson, Gamma Phi Beta
1914	Lois Smith Crann, Alpha Chi Omega
1915	Amy Olgen Parmelee, Delta Delta Delta
1917	Lena Grandin Baldwin, Alpha Xi Delta
1919	Mary Love Collins, Chi Omega
1921	Ethel Hayward Weston, Sigma Kappa
1923	Lillian MacQuillan McCausland, Alpha Omicron Pi[1]
1925	May Agness Hopkins, Zeta Tau Alpha[2]
1927	Louise Leonard, Alpha Gamma Delta[3]
1929	Irma Tapp, Alpha Delta Pi[4]
1931	Rennie Sebring-Smith, Delta Zeta

1933	Clara Raynor Radar, Phi Mu
1933	Nellie Hart Prince, Phi Mu[5]
1935	Gladys Pugh Redd, Kappa Delta
1937	Harriet Williamson Tuft, Beta Phi Alpha
1939	Violet Young Gentry, Alpha Delta Theta
1941	Beatrice M. Moore, Theta Upsilon
1943	Juelda Burnaugh, Beta Sigma Omicron
1945	Helen Hambley Cunningham, Phi Omega Pi
1947	Amy B. Onken, Pi Beta Phi
1949	L. Pearle Green, Kappa Alpha Theta
1951	Edith Reese Crabtree, Kappa Kappa Gamma
1953	Margaret C. Hutchinson, Alpha Phi
1955	Helen R. Byars, Delta Gamma
1957	Beatrice Locke Hogan, Gamma Phi Beta
1959	Rosita Hopps Nordwall, Alpha Chi Omega
1961	Ernestine B. Grigsby, Delta Delta Delta
1963	Mary Burt Brooks Nash, Alpha Xi Delta
1965	Miss Elizabeth Dyer, Chi Omega
1967	Ruth Rysdon Miller, Sigma Kappa
1969	Mary Louise Roller, Alpha Omicron Pi
1971	Harriet Ross Frische, Zeta Tau Alpha
1973	Myra Vedder Foxworthy, Alpha Gamma Delta
1975	Virginia Friese Jacobsen, Alpha Delta Pi
1977	Gwen McKeeman, Delta Zeta
1979	Adele R. Williamson, Phi Mu
1981	Minnie Mae Prescott, Kappa Delta
1983	Mary K. Barbee, Sigma Sigma Sigma
1985	Cynthia K. McCrory, Alpha Sigma Tau
1987	Sidney G. Allen, Alpha Sigma Alpha
1989	Beth Saul, Alpha Epsilon Phi
1991	Louise E. Kier, Phi Sigma Sigma

[1] Mrs. McCausland died shortly before the meeting.
[2] The meeting was held January, 1926.
[3] The meeting was held February, 1928.
[4] The meeting was held February, 1930.
[5] Mrs. Radar substituted for Mrs. Prince who was absent due to illness.

The National Panhellenic Editors Conference

The National Panhellenic Editors Conference was organized in October, 1913, during the twelfth National Panhellenic Congress, now National Panhellenic Conference, which was held in Chicago that year.

The NPC Chairman had summoned the "Greek Journalism" ladies to meet concurrently with NPC. Thirteen editors were present at the first meeting and, according to the report, "Those fraternities whose editors were unable to attend were represented by other council officers. The whole field of fraternity journalism—purpose and methods—was open for discussion, and much profitable interchange of ideas resulted."

Louise Fitch, Delta Delta Delta, was the Conference's first chairman. Pearle Green, Kappa Alpha Theta, was elected secretary. First mention was made of a committee on publicity and the organizing group thought that the Editors Conference would "become a permanent feature."

The next meeting produced the editors' first assignment from NPC. The Congress "moved to send the 'Code of Ethics' to the editors to reword." This resulted in the Panhellenic Creed which exists to this day.

From 1913 on the Editors Conference has met regularly in conjunction with NPC. It has knit the editors into a congenial group bound by the ties of similar interests. The personal associations and friendships resulting are valued highly. There is much interchange of ideas, techniques and craft information.

As would be expected, the Conference's program has expanded through the years and extends over the several days the NPC meeting is in session. There are workshop type meetings, a "brasstacks" dinner and occasional presentations of programs for the National Panhellenic Conference. The editors have provided the expertise for many NPC brochures and booklets and produced a program for one session at the Bicentennial Celebration in Williamsburg, Virginia, in 1976.

"Campus Sights and Sounds" is a current release available quarterly for all fraternity editors.

There are four officers of the Conference, with the vice president automatically succeeding to the chairmanship.

Chairmen of the NPC Editors' Conference

1913–15	R. Louis Fitch, Delta Delta Delta
1915–17	L. Pearle Green, Kappa Alpha Theta
1917–19	Florence A. Armstrong, Alpha Chi Omega
1919–21	Arema O'Brien, Delta Zeta
1921–23	Ruth Sanders Thomson, Alpha Phi
1923–26	Lindsey Barbee, Gamma Phi Beta
1926–28	Emily Butterfield, Alpha Gamma Delta
1928–30	Hazel Eckhart, Alpha Chi Omega
1930–31	Florence Merdian, Phi Mu
1931–33	Wilma Smith Leland, Alpha Omicron Pi
1933–35	Shirley Kreasan (Kreig) Strout, Zeta Tau Alpha
1935–37	Frances Warren Baker, Sigma Kappa
1937–39	Alta Gwinn Saunders, Delta Gamma
1939–41	Helen C. Bower, Kappa Kappa Gamma
1941–43	Christelle Ferguson, Chi Omega
1943–45	Adele Taylor Alford, Pi Beta Phi

1945–47	Airdrie Kincaid Pinkerton, Gamma Phi Beta		1967–69	Betty Hellex Foellinger, Zeta Tau Alpha
1947–49	Charlotte Wheeler Verplank, Delta Zeta		1969–71	Frances Lewis Stevenson, Delta Gamma
1949–51	Marian Wiley Keys, Alpha Phi		1971–73	Virginia Glover Zoerb, Phi Mu
1951–53	Ann L. Hall, Alpha Chi Omega		1973–75	Betty Luker Haverfield, Gamma Phi Beta
1953–55	Josephine Ganson Burr, Sigma Sigma Sigma		1975–77	Phyllis Seidler McIntyre, Sigma Sigma Sigma
1955–57	Tonie Whitcomb Eberhardt, Alpha Gamma Delta		1977–79	Ellen Hartman Gast, Alpha Xi Delta
1957–59	Sarah Cabot Pierce, Phi Mu		1979–81	Eleanor Bailey Hyatt, Chi Omega
1959–61	Ardis McBroom Marek, Gamma Phi Beta		1981–83	Marilyn Simpson Ford, Pi Beta Phi
1961–63	Margaret Knights Hultch, Alpha Phi		1983–85	Diane Miller Selby, Kappa Kappa Gamma
1963–65	Isabel Hatton Simmons, Kappa Kappa Gamma		1985–87	Kris Brandt Riske, Gamma Phi Beta
1965–67	Frances Priddy McDonald, Delta Delta Delta		1987–89	Miriam Rosenbloum Grant, Sigma Delta Tau
			1989–91	Gwen Moss McKeeman, Delta Zeta

National Panhellenic Association of Central Office Executives

The national Panhellenic Association of Central Office Executives was formed in 1943 for purposes of providing a channel of exchange of ideas and information pertinent to all fraternity officers; to foster interfraternity cooperation; to provide means of handling business matters of mutual concern; and to unify policies of procedure.

Presidents of the Association of Central Office Executives

1943–45	Clara O. Pierce, Kappa Kappa Gamma		1967–69	Louise Rider Horn, Phi Mu
1945–47	Margaret Hazlett Taggart, Sigma Kappa		1969–71	Dorothy Schulze Vaaler, Kappa Alpha Theta
1947–49	Helen E. Sackett, Kappa Alpha Theta		1971–73	Betty Wert, Alpha Xi Delta
1949–51	Irene Boughton, Delta Zeta		1973–77	Carmalieta Brown, Delta Gamma
1951–53	Gertrude M. Anderson, Alpha Xi Delta		1977–79	Mrs. James Gillespie, Alpha Delta Pi
1953–55	Helen Glenn, Alpha Delta Pi		1979–81	Mrs. Earl Rauen, Alpha Gamma Delta
1955–57	Roberta Abernethy, Delta Gamma		1981–83	Mrs. James Shumway, Alpha Phi
1957–59	Helen Winton Jenkins, Zeta Tau Alpha		1983–85	Nancy Leonard, Alpha Chi Omega
1959–61	Haanah Keenan, Alpha Chi Omega		1985–87	Virginia Fry, Pi Beta Phi
1961–63	J. Ann Hughes, Alpha Omicron Pi		1987–89	Diane Gregory, Alpha Xi Delta
1963–65	Minnie Mae Prescott, Kappa Delta		1989–91	Cindy Menges, Delta Zeta
1965–67	Mary Jane Flemmer, Alpha Gamma Delta			

National Pan-Hellenic Council

What is the National Pan-Hellenic Council?

The National Pan-Hellenic Council (**NPHC**) is composed of eight (8) National Greek letter community service Fraternities and Sororities. They are Alpha Kappa Alpha, Delta Sigma Theta, Sigma Gamma Rho and Zeta Phi Beta Sororities and Alpha Phi Alpha, Kappa Alpha Psi, Phi Beta Sigma and Omega Psi Phi Fraternities.

The NPHC currently is composed of over 900,000 affiliated members in undergraduate and alumni councils in all regions of the United States and abroad. The NPHC stresses and provides action strategies on matters of mutual concern and serves as the conduit through which these action plans are put into effect.

History of NPHC

The Black Greek letter movement commenced in 1906 on a predominantly white college campus as a means by which cultural interaction and community service could be maintained. Over the next 16 years the opportunity to form NPHC organizations would occur on seven other occasions. Each of these eight organizations evolved during a period when Blacks were being denied essential rights and services afforded others. These Black Greek organizations were designed to foster brotherhood and/or sisterhood and to serve as a conduit by which collective action plans could be coordinated.

In 1930 a number of these organizations recognized a need to form an umbrella organization that would provide coordination of philosophies and activities. This umbrella group became known as the National Pan-Hellenic Council. The eight organizations which would eventually comprise the NPHC made a pledge to devote their resources and services in an effort to enhance their communities. Despite the diversity inherent in the individual groups, the NPHC provided the forum and impetus for addressing items of mutual concern. The organizations soon discovered that the effect of their educational, social, and economic programs on their respective constituencies was greatly enhanced by the collective coordination through NPHC.

Philosophy of NPHC

The eight organizations which compose NPHC have mandated that, where there are two or more NPHC member chapters, an attempt should be made to form a NPHC council.

NPHC organizations are unique with respect to other Greek letter organizations in that they have a profound commitment to providing community service and to uplifting/promoting the general public welfare. Projects sponsored by NPHC organizations include: voter registration and education, aid to the needy and elderly, programs to eliminate illiteracy, legislative briefings, career training, fellowships and scholarships for educational study and research, economic development seminars, health care awareness programs, tutorial programs, and support of civil rights, educational, and community service organizations.

NPHC councils are designed to assure that member organizations maintain their distinct identity of promoting and providing community services. NPHC organizations embrace a service for life philosophy and aim to assure the continuance of social action, political empowerment and economic development. NPHC is a crucial means by which these services can be assured within the local, national, and the international communities.

Objectives of NPHC coordination are:
- to provide an opportunity for discussion regarding the common cultural heritage of the NPHC organizations
- to provide leadership coordination for NPHC organizations in addressing items of mutual con-

cern and to serve as the conduit for joint acton programs when requested
- to interact with other national Greek federations and associations and discuss items of common interest to the general college community
- to collect and disseminate general information, services, and materials for the purpose of assisting the NPHC affiliate organizations in the fulfillment of individual and joint objectives
- to coordinate the common activities of NPHC organizations in a manner that will allow the most effective utilization of resources and permit the maximization of benefits to the fraternity/sorority world
- to foster an understanding of the structure and method of operation among the affiliate organizations

Organization of the NPHC

The NPHC organizational structure consists of: 1. The General Convention. 2. The Executive Board. 3. The Regional Office and 4. Member Undergraduate and Alumni councils.

The policies, programs, and practices of the NPHC are established by voting delegates during the biennial General Convention. The delegates include the elected officers of the NPHC, the National Presidents and Executive Directors/Secretaries of the affiliate organizations, and at least two representatives of each of the undergraduate and alumni councils.

Between General Conventions, the NPHC Executive Board assures that the mandates of the Convention are carried out and deliberates upon policies coming before NPHC.

The NPHC Executive Board is composed of the following:

Nine (9) elected officers—President, First Vice President, Second Vice President (undergraduate), Treasurer, Financial Secretary, Recording Secretary, Correspondence Secretary, Graduate Member-At-Large, and Undergraduate Member-At-Large.

Sixteen (16) Executive Officers of the Affiliate Organizations—The National President/Basilei/Polemarch and the Executive Director/Executive Secretary of each of the eight affiliate organizations.

Four (4) Appointed National Officers—Parliamentarian, Legal Counsel, National Program Chairperson, and Historian.

Regional NPHC

The NPHC has six regional offices which provide resources and governance for undergraduate and alumni councils. In addition to providing information and service, these regions conduct biennial conferences with undergraduate and alumni councils and also recommend appropriate legislation for action at the General Convention.

Each region has a Regional Office which has the

responsibility of assuring that the councils are in accordance with the mandate of the General convention. The regional director also provides coordination of regional programs and establishes a working relationship with the regional directors/representatives of the eight affiliate organizations.

The six NPHC regions are: Northern, Southwestern, Southern, Western, Central, and Eastern.

NORTHERN
Iowa
Kansas
Minnesota
Missouri
Nebraska
North Dakota
South Dakota

SOUTHERN
Alabama
Florida
Georgia
Kentucky
Mississippi
North Carolina
South Carolina
Tennessee

SOUTHWESTERN
Arkansas
Louisiana
Oklahoma
Texas

CENTRAL
Illinois
Indiana
Michigan
Ohio
West Virginia
Wisconsin

WESTERN
Alaska
Arizona
California
Colorado
Hawaii
Idaho
Montana
Nevada
New Mexico
Oregon
Utah
Washington
Wyoming

EASTERN
Connecticut
Delaware
Maine
Maryland
Massachusetts
New Hampshire
New Jersey
New York
Pennsylvania
Rhode Island
Vermont
Virginia
Washington, D.C.

Campus NPHC

The NPHC campus council is composed of undergraduate chapters of the eight NPHC organizations. The campus NPHC, as well as the individual chapters, is a valuable asset to the university. Studies show that fraternity and sorority members are among the most loyal alumni following graduation and tend to provide the bulk of the alumni contributions. Also, most of the campus student leadership is provided by fraternity and sorority members. The campus council of NPHC provides:

- Encouragement of scholarship, and enhancement of loyalty to the alma mater
- A harmonious working relationship among NPHC groups and a learning environment which will help eradicate intergreek rivalry
- Preservation of the cultural heritage of the historically established community service greek organizations

- Promotion of the programs of the university
- Educational programs on operations, academic excellence, leadership, health care, drug awareness, and code of conduct
- A forum for addressing items of mutual concern to the NPHC organizations
- Uniform guidelines for pledge, rush, and standards of conduct for NPHC organizations
- Administrative arm for NPHC organizations
- Joint programming with campus IFC and NPC groups
- Promotion of the service philosophy of the NPHC organizations
- Programs designed to enhance the social and educational life of the minority community and the general college community at large

Alumni NPHC

The Alumni Council of NPHC is composed of alumni chapters of the eight NPHC affiliate organizations. The alumni councils serve as the means by which the organized activities of the professional and intellectual leaders in the Black community become a reality. At a time when Blacks are afflicted with high poverty levels, large school dropout rates, and overall economic deprivation, the NPHC alumni councils carry the leadership banner in the minority communities. By combining resources, NPHC organizations make a much more significant impact. Among many other projects, the alumni councils provide:

- Financial support for civil rights, educational and social service organizations and/or projects
- Coordination of programs for minority youth and the aged
- A significant voice regarding many issues confronting local, national, and international communities
- College scholarships that are based on academic excellence and demonstrated financial need
- A forum for addressing items of mutual concern to the NPHC organizations
- Preservation of the philosophy and cultural heritage of the historically established community service organizations

Services Provided by NPHC

- Monitors federal and state legislative and regulatory activities and other matters of mutual concern to NPHC organizations.
- Spearheads joint action by NPHC member organizations, where appropriate, and maintains active and open communication with the executive offices of each of the eight member organizations.
- Publishes national and regional newsletters which allow NPHC undergraduate and alumni councils to exchange ideas and resources.
- Conducts national and campus workshops on issues specific to NPHC member chapters and councils.

- Serves as a resource sharing body and engages in constructive discussions on areas of mutual interest with other greek federations, associations, and university greek administrators.
- Provides sample bylaws and rules of operations for alumni and undergraduate councils. The regional directors work directly with alumni councils and campus councils and advise on NPHC organization, rushing, standards of conduct, and constitutional revisions.
- Provides consultation to councils and universities on NPHC matters.
- Assists the eight member organizations in meeting their individual objectives, where requested.
- Conducts awards programs which recognizes councils and member organizations for outstanding service.
- Conducts regional and national conventions which provide the opportunity for NPHC members to exchange ideas and solutions to common problems.

Affiliate Organizations Facts

Year established
Alpha Phi Alpha	1906
Alpha Kappa Alpha	1908
Kappa Alpha Psi	1911
Omega Psi Phi	1911
Delta Sigma Theta	1913
Phi Beta Sigma	1914
Zeta Phi Beta	1920
Sigma Gamma Rho	1922

Total membership
Delta Sigma Theta	175,000
Omega Psi Phi	120,500
Alpha Kappa Alpha	120,000
Alpha Phi Alpha	105,000
Phi Beta Sigma	85,000
Kappa Alpha Psi	80,000
Zeta Phi Beta	75,000
Sigma Gamma Rho	70,900

Undergraduate Chapters
Delta Sigma Theta	379
Kappa Alpha Psi	325
Omega Psi Phi	315
Alpha Phi Alpha	315
Alpha Kappa Alpha	314
Phi Beta Sigma	300
Zeta Phi Beta	240
Sigma Gamma Rho	160

Alumni Chapters
Delta Sigma Theta	422
Alpha Kappa Alpha	415
Omega Psi Phi	351
Alpha Phi Alpha	350
Phi Beta Sigma	350
Kappa Alpha Psi	318
Zeta Phi Beta	290
Sigma Gamma Rho	190

*based on 1987–88 figures

STATEMENTS

Statement on formation of NPHC campus and alumni councils

In order to form a NPHC council, the participants must abide by the following criteria:

1. The objectives and activities of the council must be in direct accord with the established objectives of the National office.
2. Undergraduate councils must abide by all applicable provisions set forth by their respective universities.
3. Councils agree that they will not arbitrarily exclude any area chapters which are recognized by the eight NPHC organizations.
4. Campus councils agree to attempt to plan joint educational activities with other campus greek governing bodies.
5. Councils agree that at no time will derogatory statements be made about other NPHC organizations. This includes greek shows, interest programs, etc.
6. Councils agree that no rule or penalty will be imposed which will violate any established policy or procedure of one or more of the eight NPHC organizations.
7. Campus councils agree to work with college administrators in an effort to build a constructive working relationship which will lead to the furtherance of their joint objectives.
8. Councils will actively recruit any chapters in their immediate area which are inactive with respect to NPHC.
9. Campus and Alumni councils will ensure that each NPHC chapter is granted equal voting privileges within the established council.
10. Councils agree to abide by all the provisions of NPHC handbooks and constitution.

Statement on Hazing

Hazing in any form is a violation of National Pan-Hellenic Council rules. Additionally, each of the eight Pan-Hellenic organizations have established rules which strictly prohibit hazing.

The NPHC expects each of its member organizations to impose immediate and severe penalties for any proven violations of hazing. In the event a campus or alumni council becomes aware of any potential hazing incident, it has a responsibility to immediately notify university administrators as well as the appropriate fraternity or sorority in which the incident is suspected. A NPHC council, whether college or alumni, shall not consider or address any alleged incident of hazing.

Statement on Alcohol usage

The NPHC is concerned about the growing consumption of alcohol on college campuses and the incidents in which alcohol plays a part.

NPHC has taken the position that the sale or consumption of alcohol at any NPHC sponsored event on the college campus is strictly prohibited.

NPHC further suggests that college councils offer educational programs that address the problems of alcohol and drug abuse.

Statement on the role of College/University Greek Advisors

The role of advisors with respect to NPHC member chapters is unique from that of advising other national Greek organizations.

In order to provide local assistance and advisories to undergraduate chapters, the eight NPHC organizations all provide area chapter advisors. The advisors are often members of local alumni chapters. The role of these alumni advisors is to provide guidance and any needed assistance to area undergraduate chapters in helping them accomplish chapter objectives and programs, as well as the objectives set by the university. NPHC organizations also have elected and/or appointed State and Regional Directors/ Representatives. These line authorities should be consulted before contacting a National Office. The role of these officers is to ensure that their respective organizations are operating and performing according to national mandates and those prescribed by the university.

University administrators and appointed Greek advisors are encouraged to develop and maintain a working relationship with the locally provided alumni chapter advisors. Campus Greek advisors should meet periodically with the chapter advisors and discuss university goals and policies. University personnel should also develop a working relationship with the Regional and State Directors/Representatives of each of the NPHC organizations. This relationship will assure that university objectives are properly communicated to the organizations' officers.

NPHC sees the university advisor as being responsible for providing long-term continuity within the groups. Therefore, the advisors must be familiar with each of the organizations' history and policies, including major changes in the group's programs. NPHC and its members organizations offer area workshops and other informational exchanges that are useful to university personnel who serve as Greek advisors. Greek advisors are encouraged to actively participate in these programs.

Presidents of the National Pan-Hellenic Council

1930–33	Atty. Matthew W. Bullock, Omega Psi Phi	1954–56	Dr. Ernest Wilkins, Jr., Kappa Alpha Psi
1933–36	Atty. J. Ernest Williams, Kappa Alpha Psi	1956–58	Mrs. Geraldine Elliot, Zeta Phi Beta
1936–38	Ms. Maude E. Porter, Alpha Kappa Alpha	1958–60	Mr. Julius Simmons, Phi Beta Sigma
1938–40	Mr. William C. Pyant, Alpha Phi Alpha	1960–62	Ms. Edna Douglas, Sigma Gamma Rho
1940–41	Mrs. Joanna H. Ranson, Zeta Phi Beta	1962–64	Dr. Alvin J. McNeil, Phi Beta Sigma
1941–43	Atty. George W. Lawrence, Phi Beta Sigma	1964–67	Dr. Walter J. Washington, Alpha Phi Alpha
1944–46	Mrs. Bertha Black Rhoda, Sigma Gamma Rho	1967–69	Mrs. Carey B. Preston, Alpha Kappa Alpha
1946–48	Mr. Ellsworth J. Evans, Kappa Alpha Psi	1969–71	Mrs. Mildred C. Bradham, Zeta Phi Beta
1948–50	Mrs. Mae Wright Downs, Delta Sigma Theta	1971–72	Mr. Earl A. Morris, Kappa Alpha Psi
1950–52	Atty. Victor J. Ashe, Kappa Alpha Psi	1972–74	Mr. James T. Bailey, Omega Psi Phi
1952–54	Mrs. Arnetta G. Wallace, Alpha Kappa Alpha	1974–78	Mrs. Alice M. Swain, Sigma Gamma Rho
		1976–78	Mr. Charles B. Wright, Phi Beta Sigma
		1978–83	Mrs. Beatrice Jett, Alpha Kappa Alpha
		1983–88	Dr. Gilbert Francis, Phi Beta Sigma
		1985–89	Dr. Ada J. Jackson, Alpha Kappa Alpha
		1989——	Ms. Daisy M. Wood, Delta Sigma Theta

Professional Fraternity Association

The Professional Fraternity Association was formed in 1977 with the merger of the Professional Panhellenic Association and the Professional Interfraternity Conference.

The purposes of this organization shall be to advocate and encourage excellence in scholarship; advancement of professional and interfraternity ethics; cooperation among member fraternities for the advancement of fraternal ideals, and loyalty to alma mater.

To encourage formation of area/campus professional fraternity councils on campus of recognized colleges, universities, and professional schools;

To identify and advise member fraternities of social, political and economic legislation which could affect their operations.

Membership is open to a professional fraternity, national or international in character, which charters its chapters only at appropriately accredited colleges, universities, or professional schools. The fraternity shall be identified by, or related to, a specific discipline, but may initiate members of general fraternities and of other professional disciplines.

The officers of the Professional Fraternity Association are elected at the annual convention which is held in the fall. At this time the career achievement award winner is named. This is presented to a fraternity member who has achieved distinction not only in his/her fraternity but in the profession as well.

Publications include the PFA Today newsletter which is published five times a year and a pamphlet entitled The Professional Fraternity . . . Real Answers for a Real Life.

The Professional Fraternity Association has a membership of 34 professional freaternities. The Central Office for PFA is located in Indianapolis, IN where an executive secretary handles the administrative work of the association.

Professional Fraternity Association Constitution

ARTICLE I
NAME

The name of this organization shall be the Professional Fraternity Association.

ARTICLE II
PURPOSES

The purposes of this organization shall be to advocate and encourage excellence in scholarship; advancement of professional and interfraternity ethics; cooperation among member fraternities for the advancement of fraternal ideals; and loyalty to the alma mater.

To encourage formation of area/campus professional fraternity councils on campuses of recognized colleges, universities, and professional schools.

To identify and advise member fraternities of social, political, and economic legislation which could affect their operations.

ARTICLE III
MEMBERSHIP

To be eligible for membership, a fraternity shall be national or international in character and shall charter its institutional chapters only at appropriately accredited colleges, universities, or professional schools. The fraternity shall be identified by, or related to, a specific discipline, but may initiate members of general fraternities and of other professional disciplines.

ARTICLE IV
OFFICERS

The officers of the Professional Fraternity Association shall be a President, a President-Elect, a Secretary and a Treasurer.

ARTICLE V
CONVENTIONS

The Professional Fraternity Association shall meet annually in convention. The convention shall be composed of the delegates of the member fraternities and shall be the governing body of the Association.

ARTICLE VI
AMENDMENTS

The Constitution may be amended at any convention by a two-thirds vote of the member fraternities present and entitled to vote, provided, that notice and content of proposed amendment(s) be submitted to the Executive Secretary and distributed to members at least thirty (30) days prior to the opening date of convention, at which such amendment(s) is (are) to be considered.

In the interim between conventions, proposed amendments may be mailed by the Executive Secretary to the president of each member fraternity, specifying the vote to be returned to sender within sixty (60) days. A favorable vote on three-fourths of the ballots returned by member fraternities shall be necessary for any amendments submitted by mail; results will be reported.

ARTICLE VII
DISSOLUTION

This Association shall use its funds only to accomplish the objectives and purposes as specified in the Constitution and Bylaws and no part of said funds shall inure or be distributed to the members of the Association. On dissolution of the Association, and funds remaining shall be distributed to one or more regularly organized and qualified educational organization(s) to be selected by the Board of Directors.

Professional Fraternity Association Bylaws

ARTICLE I
MEMBERSHIP

Sec. 1 - There shall be two classes of membership: organizational and associate.

Sec. 2 - The charter organizational membership in this Association shall be those national or international professional or professionally oriented college fraternities which are in the Professional Interfraternity Conference or the Professional Panhellenic Association at the time of organization.

Sec. 3 - A fraternity which meets the definition contained in Article III of the Constitution shall file an application for membership with the Board of Directors together with a copy of its Constitution and Bylaws.

The Board of Directors shall thereafter conduct an investigation of the eligibility of the applicant and shall submit the name of the applicant fraternity together with its investigation to the member fraternities of PFA.

Any member fraternity may file an objection to the granting of membership to the applicant. Such objections together with reasons therefor shall be filed with the Executive Secretary of the PFA within a period of 60 days from the date of mailing by the Board of Directors. If any objections shall be so received, all other member fraternities shall forthwith be notified of such objection.

If an objection shall be received, then balloting on the applicant shall be deferred until the next succeeding convention, at which time a secret ballot shall be taken.

If no objection shall be received, then member fraternities shall, within the next 30 days, indicate by mail ballot either approval, disapproval, or a desire to defer vote thereon until the next succeeding convention.

Membership shall be conferred upon receipt of ballots of approval by two thirds of those voting.

Sec. 4 - Associate membership shall be granted to any person, partnership, or corporation that furnishes equipment, supplies, or services to member fraternities, subject to approval by the Board of Directors. Associate members shall have no voting privileges, nor may they hold elective office.

Sec. 5 - Resignation, Suspension, or Expulsion
a. Any member of the Association may voluntarily withdraw from the Association upon due notice by certified mail to the Executive Secretary of the Association.
b. The Association may, by two-thirds vote at any convention, after a hearing, suspend any member until the next convention for violations of any provisions of the Constitution and Bylaws of this Association.
c. The Association may, by three-fourths vote at any convention, expel any member for willful or negligent violations of any provisions of the Constitution and Bylaws of this Association. Before a member may be expelled from membership in this Association, the Executive Secretary shall send to the president and secretary of the said member due notice thereof, in writing. This said notice shall contain a statement of the alleged violations and the advice that it is on suspension pending official action after a hearing thereon at the next scheduled convention of the Association.

Sec. 6 - Reinstatement of Members - Reinstatement of any constituent member fraternity of the Professional Fraternity Association which has voluntarily withdrawn its membership or which has been expelled by the Association shall be in accordance with the procedure set forth in Section 3 of the Article for the admission of new members. Reinstatement of any former associate member of the Professional Fraternity Association shall be in accordance with the procedures set forth in Section 4 of Article I.

ARTICLE II
OFFICERS AND DIRECTORS

The officers of the Professional Fraternity Association shall be as set forth in Article IV of the Constitution.

Sec. 1. - Description of Officers and Directors
a. The officers of the Association shall be as described in Article IV of the Constitution.
b. The Board of Directors shall consist of the officers, the immediate Past President and two Directors at Large.
c. The Associate Members shall select from among their number a representative who shall serve as Associate Member Liaison to the Board of Directors. The Associate Member Liaison shall

participate in meetings of the Board of Directors but shall have no vote in Association matters.

Sec. 2. - Election and Term of Office

a. Officers, except the president, shall be elected at each annual convention from among the membership of the constituent member fraternities in good standing of the Association. A member fraternity may have no more than one of its members serving as an officer of the Association at any given time.

b. Wherever practical, the Directors at Large shall not be members of the same fraternity nor from the same discipline. They shall be elected at each annual convention from among the membership of the constituent member fraternities in good standing of the Association.

c. All officers and directors shall be elected for a term of one year effective with the close of the annual convention at which the elections occur.

d. Officers and directors with the exception of the President and the President-Elect shall be eligible for election to the same office for a maximum of two consecutive terms. The President and the President-Elect may not be re-elected to consecutive terms.

Sec. 3. - Duties of the Officers, Directors and the Associate Member Liaison

a. Duties of the President - The President shall be the chief executive officer of the Association and shall preside at all meetings of the Association and of its Board of Directors. The President shall oversee the work of all committees.

b. Duties of President-Elect - The President-Elect shall perform the duties of the President in the absence or disability of the latter and shall serve as the program chairman for the annual convention of the Association. The President-Elect shall assume the office of President at the conclusion of the next annual convention and shall, prior to that meeting, appoint the committees for the following year and shall arrange for committee meetings to occur during the convention.

c. Duties of the Secretary - The Secretary shall keep a complete and accurate record of all meetings of the Association and of its Board of Directors.

d. Duties of the Treasurer - The Treasurer shall oversee the financial records of the Association and shall report on its financial condition on a periodic basis and in such form as prescribed by the Board of Directors.

e. Duties of the Directors at Large - The Directors at Large shall be assigned committee and special task responsibilities by the President or the President-Elect.

f. Duties of the Past President - The Past President shall be assigned committee and special task responsibilities by the President or the President-Elect.

g. Duties of the Associate Member Liaison - The Associate Member Liaison shall serve in an advisory capacity to the Board of Directors especially on matters related to the Associate Members; shall coordinate and be responsible for all Associate Member sponsored events at the annual convention and shall co-chair with the President a meeting of the Associate Members at the annual convention.

Sec. 4 - Vacancies

a. A vacancy of any of the above offices may be declared by a two-thirds vote of the voting delegates at convention or by a five-sixths vote of the Board of Directors.

b. Vacancies occurring in any of the above offices may be filled by a majority vote of the Board of Directors.

ARTICLE III
EXECUTIVE SECRETARY

An Executive Secretary may be appointed by the Board of Directors to perform necessary functions of the Association. This appointee will be a non-voting member of the Board, and will be reimbursed for all actual expenses incurred in this office, and in addition may receive an honorarium, the amount to be determined by the Board of Directors. The Executive Secretary need not be a member of a constituent member of the Association.

ARTICLE IV
CONVENTION

Sec. 1 - The Professional Fraternity Association shall meet annually, except when the Board of Directors deems it unwise because of unusual circumstances. The time, length of meeting, and place shall be determined by the Board of Directors.

Sec. 2 - Special meetings may be called by a majority of the Board of Directors with notice specifying date, place, and purpose sent to all member fraternities no less than thirty (30) days in advance of the proposed meeting.

ARTICLE V
GOVERNMENT

Sec. 1 - The Professional Fraternity Association, in convention, composed of the voting delegates of the members as herein provided, shall be the governing body of the Association.

Sec. 2 - Convention delegates: Each member fraternity, in good standing, through its representation, shall be entitled to one vote. Said fraternity shall designate its voting member.

Sec. 3 - Quorum: A quorum shall consist of a majority of the members in good standing.

ARTICLE VI
COMMITTEES

The following standing committees shall be appointed by the President-Elect with the approval of the Board of Directors: (1) Membership, (2) Local Professional Fraternity Council, (3) Legal and Legislative, (4) Nominating, (5) Public Relations, (6) Convention Planning, (7) Audit. Each of these committees shall be appointed at least forty-five days prior to the annual convention. Special Committees may be appointed by the President as they are required.

ARTICLE VII
FINANCES

Sec. 1 - Annual dues, payable to the Professional Fraternity Association, for each constituent member fraternity shall be $200.

Sec. 2 - Membership dues for associate members shall be payable annually in the amount of $300 for the first year, and $200 for each consecutive year thereafter.

Sec. 3 - The fiscal year shall be from July 1 through June 30, inclusive.

Sec. 4 - Dues shall be payable July 1, and member fraternities and associate members shall become delinquent if dues have not been paid as of the opening session of the annual meeting.

ARTICLE VIII
DISBURSEMENTS

Sec. 1 - The Board of Directors is authorized to designate a depository bank or banks for the funds of the Professional Fraternity Association, shall determine the manner of withdrawals therefrom, and the officer or officers required to sign checks and to write drafts thereon.

Sec. 2 - The expenses as authorized by the convention, by the President, or by the Board of Directors, shall be paid out of funds of the Professional Fraternity Association. Expenses of the Board of Directors including transportation, housing, scheduled meals, and registration for attendance at interim meetings, and half of these same expenses for attendance at conventions shall be reimbursed.

Sec. 3 - The Treasurer shall make a full report to the Association at the convention, and to the Board of Directors as requested, of the revenues, disbursements, assets, liabilities, and equity of the Professional Fraternity Association.

ARTICLE IX
PARLIAMENTARY PROCEDURE

Robert's Rules of Order, latest revision, shall be the parliamentary authority with respect to all procedures not specifically provided for in the Constitution and Bylaws of the Professional Fraternity Association.

ARTICLE X
AMENDMENTS

The Bylaws may be amended at any convention by a two-thirds vote of the member fraternities present and entitled to vote, provided, that notice and content of proposed amendment(s) be submitted to the Executive Secretary and distributed to members at least thirty (30) days prior to the opening date of the convention, at which such amendments (s) is (are) to be considered.

In the interim between conventions, proposed amendments may be mailed by the Executive Secretary to the president of each member fraternity, specifying the vote to be returned to sender within sixty (60) days. A favorable vote on three-fourths of the ballots returned by member fraternities shall be necessary for any amendments submitted by mail; results will be reported.

Presidents of the Professional Fraternity Association

1977–78	Mary Ellin Frohmader, Phi Beta
1978–79	Frederick J. Weltkamp, Phi Alpha Delta
1979–80	Marilyn Haberle, Lambda Kappa Sigma
1980–81	Dan Beeman, Ph.D, Phi Mu Alpha Sinfonia
1981–82	Angela Sattell, Phi Chi Theta
1982–83	G.W. Roach, Alpha Zeta
1983–84	Fannie E. Hicklin, Ph.D, Zeta Phi Eta
1984–85	Dewey D. Garner, Ph.D, Kappa Psi
1985–86	Mary R. Greer, Lambda Kappa Sigma
1986–87	Michael, J. Mazur, Jr., Delta Sigma Pi
1987–88	Jill Campbell, Phi Chi Theta
1988–89	Alan C. Williams, Ph.D, Gamma Iota Sigma
1989–90	Daryl Hendrix, Kappa Epsilon

The Founding of the Association of College Honor Societies

The growth of the honor society movement since 1900 has been rapid and varied. Many groups were of local campus significance only, while a number expanded to other colleges and universities and sought to be recognized as national in scope. Their multiplicity, and in many cases their duplication, low standards, and competition presented a burdensome problem to students, faculty members, and administrators, as well as to college life generally.

For a number of years before 1925, leaders of college fraternities were concerned about the growing proliferation of "honor societies" and so-called "honorary fraternities." A comprehensive report of a special committee to the 15th annual meeting of the National Interfraternity Conference recommended that representatives of all professional, honorary, and honorary fraternities be invited to a conference in November 1924 and that the National Interfraternity Conference define what should constitute (a) an honorary fraternity, (b) a professional fraternity, and (c) an honorary-professional fraternity. Evidently this report elicited no definite action. However, officers of some of the older honor societies were still concerned about the problem.

At a meeting of the executive committee of Sigma Xi, the scientific honor society, held in New York, May 2, 1925, William W. Root, M.D., secretary-treasurer of Alpha Omega Alpha, the medical honor society, who was present on invitation, suggested that a conference of delegates from honorary fraternities might result in advantage to all. The executive committee voted to cooperate in arranging and attending such a conference. Rev. Oscar M. Voorhees, D.D., secretary of Phi Beta Kappa, who with Dr. Root, was a guest at lunch, was asked by Dr. Edward Ellery, secretary of Sigma Xi, what he thought of Dr. Root's suggestion; he replied that he believed that the need for such a conference was pressing but declined to take any positive steps until authorization was sought from his National Council.

The subject was brought to the attention of the 15th triennial session of the Phi Beta Kappa National Council in New York, September 8, 1925, and the officers were authorized to represent Phi Beta Kappa in any conferences that should be planned. This action was reported to the officers of other leading honor societies, and a conference was held at the Pennsylvania Hotel, New York, on October 2, 1925, with four societies represented: Alpha Omega Alpha, Order of the Coif, Phi Beta Kappa, and Sigma Xi. Officers of Phi Kappa Phi indicated their interest but could not be represented. After some discussion it was decided to hold a general conference to which other honor societies would be invited the last week in 1925 in Kansas City, in conjunction with the annual meeting of the American Association for the Advancement of Science.

The meeting was held on December 30, 1925, in the Athletic Club Building of the Chamber of Commerce of Kansas City, with seventeen persons present, representing eighteen organizations and including Alpha Omega Alpha, Phi Beta Kappa, Phi Kappa Phi, Sigma Xi, and Tau Beta Phi, among others. The Order of the Coif could not be represented. After a thorough discussion, a permanent organization was effected with Dr. Francis W. Shepardson, vice-president of Phi Beta Kappa, as president, and Dr. Root as secretary-treasurer, with an executive committee of six members, three of whom should be Drs. Shepardson, Voorhees, and Root, they to choose the other three. This they did after conference and correspondence, completing the committee for the first year by adding Prof. Floyd K. Richtmyer, a past president of Sigma Xi, Prof. Arthur D. Moore, president of Tau Beta Pi, and Dr. Henry B. Ward, for many years the notable secretary of Sigma Xi. A committee on constitution was appointed, consisting of Walter L. Bierring, M.D., president of Alpha Omega Alpha, Prof. Richtmyer, and Dr. Root.

The next session was held in Williamsburg, Virginia, November 26 and 27, 1926, in connection with the sesquicentennial celebration of the founding of Phi Beta Kappa and in the memorial building presented to the College of William and Mary by that organization. Attendance was limited and it was agreed that the initial charter members should be the following six societies: Alpha Omega Alpha (medicine), represented by Dr. Root, secretary-treasurer; Order of the Coif (law), represented by Prof. Walter W. Cook, president; Phi Beta Kappa (liberal arts), represented by Dr. Voorhees, secretary; Phi Kappa Phi (all academic fields), represented by Dr. Charles H. Gordon, secretary; Sigma Xi (science), represented by Dr. Ellery, secretary; and Tau Beta Pi (engineering), represented by Prof. A.D. Moore, president, with a Council comprising the above six representatives and three members-at-large elected by the societies' representatives. The new organization was named the Association of College Honor Societies, with responsibility lodged in the Council. The representatives elected Dr. Shepherdson of Phi Beta Kappa, Prof. Richtmyer and Dr. Ward of Sigma Xi as members-at-large of the Council. The committee on constitution appointed at the Kansas City meeting was continued and the following officers elected: president, Dr. Shepardson; vice president, Dr. Ellery; and secretary-treasurer, Dr. Root. The new organization was recognized in *Baird's Manual of American College Fraternities*, Eleventh Edition, 1927, p. 302.

Meetings in November 1927 and January 1929 were devoted to discussion of the eligibility of other societies and the drafting of the constitution, which was adopted in 1929.

The purposes as stated in the first constitution were, as they are now, to consider problems of mutual interest, such as those arising from the confusion prevailing on college campuses concerning the character, function, standards for membership, multiplicity, and undesirable duplication of honor societies; to recommend action leading to appropriate classification, higher standards, reasonable costs of membership, and consolidation or elimination of duplicating honor societies; and to promote the highest interest of honor societies. Provisions were made for meetings, attendance of representatives of other societies as observers, admission of other societies found to have proper qualifications for membership, admission fees, annual dues, and needed studies, reports, and recommendations.

Initially, membership was limited to organizations requiring superior work in broad fields of study. However, at the Council meeting in 1930, provision was made for the admission of leadership honor societies with strong scholarship requirements, and Omicron Delta Kappa (leadership—men) was elected to membership, along with Sigma Tau (engineering). Prof. A. D. Moore, Tau Beta Pi, succeeded Dr. Ellery, Sigma Xi, as vice-president in 1930. Dr. Root, Alpha Omega Alpha, served as secretary-treasurer from 1925 until his death in 1932. Dr. Shepardson, Phi Beta Kappa, served as president until 1933, when he was succeeded by Prof. A. D. Moore, and then served as secretary-treasurer until the Council meeting on February 27, 1937, with Dr. William Moseley Brown, secretary-treasurer of Omicron Delta Kappa, as vice-president. On August 9, 1937, Dr. Shepardson died, and ACHS lost another of its founding members and long time leaders.

At the Council meeting in June 1933, Sigma Xi submitted its resignation stating that it had decided to devote itself primarily to research and no longer considered itself strictly a college honor society. However, Dr. Ward continued as a member-at-large of the Council until 1945. Four new member societies were elected in 1937, including the first freshman honor society, Phi Eta Sigma (freshman scholarship—men); Beta Gamma Sigma (commerce); Mortar Board (student leadership—women); and Tau Kappa Alpha (forensics). New officers elected were president, Dr. Henry B. Ward, member-at-large, vice president, Josiah J. Moore, M.D., secretary-treasurer of Alpha Omega Alpha; and secretary-treasurer, Dr. Brown, Omega Delta Kappa. Following this meeting Phi Beta Kappa

withdrew in December 1937, although Dr. Voorhees continued as a member-at-large until 1944.

Definitions and standards continued to occupy the attention of the ACHS Council and in 1939, it finally spelled out the definition of an honor society and set the standards for membership in Scholarship Honor Societies to students ranking in the highest 20 per cent of scholarship and for Leadership Honor Societies to students ranking in the highest 35 per cent of scholarship. This was a significant step forward as these requirements affected several of the member societies. At this meeting, Dr. Josiah J. Moore, Alpha Omega Alpha, was elected president; Prof. P. W. Ott, Tau Beta Pi, vice-president; and Dr. Lawrence R. Guild, Phi Kappa Phi, secretary-treasurer.

In 1937, the Association of Deans of Men and Deans of Women established a committee to try to classify and control the large number of honorary organizations. A conference of representatives of several honor societies and the committee was held in the Office of Education, Department of the Interior, April 21–22, 1939, to seek ways of enhancing the value of college honor societies. Evidently, little action resulted from these efforts. However, under the leadership of President L. G. Balfour, the National Interfraternity Conference set up a National Committee of College Fraternities and Societies (NCCFS) in 1941 composed of representatives of the Associations of Deans and Advisors of Men, the Association of College Honor Societies, the Professional Interfraternity Conference, the professional Panhellenic Association, and the National Interfraternity Conference. The ACHS officers, consisting of president, Dr. Josiah J. Moore; vice president, Dr. Robert W. Bishop, Omicron Delta Kappa; and secretary-treasurer, Dr. Lawrence W. Guild, with Mrs. F. D. (Katherine W.) Coleman, Mortar Board, of the Executive Committee, spearheaded the work with the NCCFS and by 1944 had expanded the definitions, classifications, standards, and functions of honor societies to include General Scholarship, Leadership, and Departmental or Specialized Honor Societies.

With the election of three departmental honor societies in 1945, Alpha Epsilon Delta (premedicine), Phi Alpha Theta (history), and Sigma Pi Sigma (physics), ACHS began a new era of expanded membership and activities under the leadership of Dr. Guild, president, and Dr. Bishop, secretary-treasurer.

Further information about ACHS is available in the ACHS archives which has been established as a historical repository at Muhlenberg College, Allentown, Pennsylvania, and is maintained by Phi Alpha Theta, the history honor society.

The Organization and Purpose of the Association of College Honor Societies

The problem faced by higher education and by the ACHS of developing and maintaining high standards in college honor societies covers the whole college field and all categories of Greek letter organizations. Individual associations and conferences in the general social and professional fields are also studying ways and means of improving conditions. Educational associations and councils are cooperating. While progress was slow and difficult at times during the early history of the ACHS, great progress has been made since 1945 by joint action of college administrators and faculty members and representatives of the major societies and fraternities and their respective associations. The real solution of the problem requires such a cooperative combination of forces.

The objective of the ACHS now is to encourage all general and specialized honor societies to join forces for the establishment and maintenance of desirable standards and useful functions in higher education, and for the achievement of appropriate recognition of member societies of the Council of ACHS. To this end, the ACHS invites qualified societies to affiliate with it. Societies which do not meet the standards will be helped in every way possible to come up to them. Special attention is called to the Constitution and Bylaws of the ACHS and to their statements of definitions, standards, and requirements for membership and functions of honor societies.

Progress toward achieving the present objective of the ACHS is found in two specific developments. The first of these is that the editor of Baird's Manual has sought and gained editorial assistance in the problem of classifying the numerous societies which are in existence, and has accepted the distinctions as the basis for classification. This extension of common categories is an instance of cooperation toward the goal of maintaining standards for honor societies.

The second development is closely related to the question of honor society standards. In a letter dated April 13, 1973, the U.S. Civil Service Commission stated, "Membership in a national honorary society meets one of the requirements for entrance at the GS-7 level in numerous professional and technical occupations in the Federal service. However, applicants must meet all of the requirements as described in the particular Federal Job Announcement covering the positions for which they apply." This affords a very tangible acknowledgment that organizations maintaining honor societies standards merit distinction.

The Constitution of the Association of College Honor Societies

(Adopted and as amended through February 27, 1971)

ARTICLE I
NAME

Section 1. The name of the Association shall be The Association of College Honor Societies.

ARTICLE II
PURPOSES

Section 1. The purposes of the Association shall be
a. To act as the coordinating agency for college and university honor societies, as hereinafter provided;
b. To provide facilities for the consideration of matters of mutual interest, such as administrative problems, establishment and maintenance of scholastic and other standards, membership costs, functions of honor societies, and prevention of undesirable duplication and competition among honor societies;
c. To define honor societies of the several types and to classify existing societies into their proper categories under these definitions;
d. To cooperate with college and university faculties and administrative officers in developing and maintaining high standards and useful functions within honor societies which are organized or seek to be organized;
e. To collect, publish, and distribute information and data of value to honor societies, colleges and universities, and publishers of directories and journals.

ARTICLE III
MEMBERSHIP

Section 1. The Association of College Honor Societies shall consist of such national (or international) honor societies as meet the standards as hereinafter defined. In general these societies shall require for membership superior scholarship and/or leadership achievement either in broad fields of education or in departmental fields at either undergraduate or graduate levels.

Section 2. There shall be two classes of member societies: first, active voting member societies which meet all requirements for membership in the Association; and second, associate non-voting member societies which do not meet the requirements of age or size but meet all other membership requirements.

ARTICLE IV
COUNCIL

Section 1. There shall be a Council, to consist of one representative, preferably an executive, from each active voting member society. This person shall be chosen by his society to serve one year, or until his successor is chosen. In addition, there shall be elected by the Council three members-at-large to serve one year.

Section 2. It shall be the duty of the Council to investigate and determine all matters in regard to qualifications for representation in the Association. Any charges or complaints regarding a constituent society may be submitted by any member of the Council, and when so submitted, shall be investigated by the Council. For the election of a society to representation in the Association, or for suspension, or for expulsion, an affirmative vote of four-fifths of the official Council members present shall be required. Election, suspension, or expulsion, may take place at any regularly called meeting of the Council.

Section 3. The Council shall meet annually at a time and place to be selected by the Executive Committee.

Section 4. A quorum for the transaction of business at Council meetings shall be official representatives from two-thirds of the societies which have membership in the Association.

Section 5. The Council may, at its discretion, invite to its sessions representatives of other organizations, such representatives to have the liberty of the floor, but without vote. All meetings are at the call of the President, or on written request of any three members.

Section 6. The order of business and program at the annual Council meeting shall be arranged by the Executive Committee.

ARTICLE V—OFFICERS

Section 1. The officers of this association shall be (a) President, (b) Vice President, and (c) Secretary-Treasurer, to be chosen by the Council from its own membership to serve for one year, or until their successors are elected. At the discretion of the Council, the post of Secretary-Treasurer may be separated into those of Secretary and Treasurer, each of whom shall perform the duties incident to those offices and have membership on the Executive Committee in the event of such separation.

Section 2. There shall be an Executive Committee which shall consist of the President, the Vice President, the Secretary-Treasurer, the immediate Past President, and two members elected from the Council, one member from the general honor society group, and one member from the specialized honor society group. In the initial election, after the adoption of this section, these members shall be elected to the Executive Committee for a term of one year and thereafter for a term of two years. Each elected member shall serve until a successor shall be elected. The Executive Committee shall meet regularly at the time and the place of each annual meeting of the Council, and at such special meetings as a majority of its members shall deem necessary and proper. The expense of attendance of these persons at special meetings of the Executive Committee shall be met from the Association's Treasury.

ARTICLE VI—AMENDMENTS

Section 1. This Constitution may be amended by a four-fifths vote of the societies represented at any regularly called meeting of the Council provided notice of the proposed amendment is sent out with the call for the meeting at least 30 days prior to the meeting.

The Bylaws of the Association of College Honor Societies

(Adopted and as amended through February 25, 1984)

ARTICLE I
DEFINITIONS AND CLASSIFICATIONS

Section 1. **Honor Society.** An honor society is an association of primarily collegiate chapters whose purposes are to recognize and encourage high scholarship and/or leadership achievement in some broad or specialized field of study.

Section 2. Societies which are members of the Association shall be classified as

a. General Honor Societies

b. Specialized Honor Societies

Section 3. **General Honor Societies.** A general honor society is one which receives into membership individuals from one or all schools and colleges of an institution who have achieved high scholarship and who fulfill such additional requirements of distinction in some broad field of study, research, and culture or in general leadership as the society has established. A broad field of study is one in which a systematic development of the mind and cultural values are acquired through instruction, training, example, and experience.

Section 4. A specialized honor society is one which receives into membership persons who have demonstrated achievement within a given department of a school, college, or larger unit of a university or within a department of a two-year college.

Section 5. **Recognition Societies.** A recognition society is one which confers membership in recognition of a student's interest and participation in some field of collegiate study or activity, with more liberal membership requirements than are prescribed for general and specialized honor societies. Accordingly, recognition societies are not eligible for membership in the Association of College Honor Societies.

ARTICLE II
STANDARDS AND REQUIREMENTS FOR MEMBERSHIP

For membership in the Association, a society shall conform to the following minimal standards:

Section 1. Election to membership shall be irrespective of membership in or affiliation with other organizations and associations.

Section 2. Membership shall be conferred solely on the basis of character and specified eligibility.

Section 3. No solicitation or propaganda, such as rushing and social pressure, shall be used to ensure acceptance or invitation to membership.

Section 4. General Honor Societies which base eligibility primarily upon scholarship shall elect undergraduates who rank not lower than the highest twenty percent of their class in scholarship.

Section 5. General Honor Societies which base eligibility primarily upon all-around leadership in student affairs shall elect from the entire institution undergraduates who rank not lower than the highest thirty-five percent of their class in scholarship.

Section 6. Specialized Honor Societies which elect persons actively interested in a specific field shall elect only those who have demonstrated superior scholarship in this field; undergraduates who are elected shall rank not lower than the highest thirty five percent of their class in general scholarship, and shall have completed at least three semesters or five quarters of the college course.

Section 7. The cumulative scholastic record of the student as interpreted by the institution where membership is to be conferred shall be the basis for computing scholastic eligibility for the purpose of classification in ranks as specified in the preceding sections 4, 5, and 6 of this Article.

Section 8. Election to membership in general honor societies other than freshman honor societies and two-year college honor societies shall be held not earlier than the fifth semester or the seventh quarter of the college course.

Section 9. An active voting member society and an associate nonvoting member society shall have ten or more active collegiate chapters located in two or more regions in the country.

Section 10. An active chapter shall be one which holds elections to membership at least annually, except in national emergencies, and includes active student members. An inactive chapter shall be one in which no elections have been held during a two-year period. Any chapter which has held no election for a period of five years may be dropped from the listing of active and inactive chapters of that society.

Section 11. A society shall have existed as a national organization for at least ten years before becoming an active voting member of the Association and for at least five years before becoming an associate nonvoting member of the Association.

Section 12. The constitution and bylaws of a society shall provide for national conventions or other equivalents at least every three years. At these conventions national officers shall be elected and authority established for an interim control of the affairs of the society. The convention shall include a report of national finances covering the period from the immediately preceding convention.

Section 13. Each member society of the Association shall furnish the Secretary-Treasurer with a copy of its constitution and bylaws and shall inform him periodically of any amendments therein. Each member society of the Association shall submit an annual report of its society.

Section 14. Admission fees and dues charged by each member society shall not be more than is deemed reasonable by the Council of the Association.

Section 15. Collegiate chapters of member societies shall be established, maintained, or reactivated only in colleges and universities that grant the associate, baccalaureate, or higher degrees and that are accredited by the appropriate national or regional accrediting agency. Such agencies include the New England Association of Colleges, the Middle States Association, the North Central Association, the Southern Association, the Northwest Association, the Western College Association, certain appropriate professional accrediting agencies, and by those specialized accrediting bodies also recognized by the Council on Postsecondary Accreditation. Two-year vocational, technical, and career institutions offering general or specialized programs which lead to career opportunities shall not be eligible.

Section 16. No member society shall hereafter grant a charter to a chapter in any institution which fails to meet fully the standards and requirements of the Association.

ARTICLE III
ADMISSION FEE AND DUES

Section 1. The dues from each active voting member society and each associate nonvoting member society shall be set by the Council, the fiscal year to begin February 1.

Section 2. Admission fee shall be $50.00.

ARTICLE IV
FUNCTIONS OF HONOR SOCIETIES

Section 1. The functions of honor societies are not social as in the case of general college fraternities. Social activities of honor societies are incidental and may obtain occasionally in connection with their major functions.

Section 2. The following functions are properly served by an Honor Society:

a. It confers distinction for high achievement in undergraduate, graduate, and professional studies; in student leadership; and in the various fields of research.
b. It fosters the spirit of liberal culture.
c. It stimulates and encourages mental development.
d. It stands for freedom of mind and spirit and for democracy of learning.
e. It provides spiritual and intellectual leadership.
f. It preserves valuable traditions and customs.
g. It associates outstanding leaders in mutual understanding for the advancement of society in the art of democratic living.
h. It stimulates worthy attitudes for the improvement of the general welfare of the institution.
i. It imposes upon members high citizenship responsibilities and emphasizes deeper study and discussion of the American tradition—its characteristics, ideals, and possibilities.

ARTICLE V
PARLIAMENTARY AUTHORITY

Section 1. In all parliamentary situations not herein specified, *Roberts' Rules of Order* will obtain.

ARTICLE VI
DISSOLUTION

Section 1. In the event of dissolution, the residual assets of the Association will be turned over to one or more organizations which themselves are exempt as organizations described in sections 501(c)(3) and 170(c)(2) of the Internal Revenue Code of 1954 or corresponding sections of any prior or future law or to the Federal, State, or local government for exclusive public purpose.

ARTICLE VII
AMENDMENTS

Section 1. These bylaws may be amended at any annual or special meeting of the Council by an affirmative vote of three-fourths of the Council members present, provided that written notice of the proposed changes shall have been mailed by the Secretary-Treasurer to Council members at least 30 days prior to the meeting, or by the affirmative vote of four-fifths of the Council members present if no such notice has been given.

The Presidents of the Association of College Honor Societies

1925–26	Francis W. Shepardson	1957–59	Robert H. Nagel
1926–30	Francis W. Shepardson	1959–61	David S. Clark
1930–32	Francis W. Shepardson	1961–63	George W. Gore
1932–33	Francis W. Shepardson	1963–65	Ruth H. Weimer
1933–37	Arthur D. Moore	1965–67	James E. Foy
1937–39	Henry B. Ward	1967–69	Theodore W. Zillman
1939–40	Josiah J. Moore	1969–71	Franklin Burdette
1940–41	Josiah J. Moore	1971–73	Edward J. Rowe
1941–45	Josiah J. Moore	1973–75	James W. Bayne
1945–47	Lawrence R. Guild	1975–77	Eileen C. Maddex
1947–49	Lawrence R. Guild	1977–79	Donald B. Hoffman
1949–50	Robert W. Bishop	1979–81	Karlem Riess
1950–51	Marsh W. White	1981–83	William W. Scott
1951–52	George L. Webster	1983–85	Dexter C. Jameson, Jr.
1952–53	Maurice L. Moore	1985–87	Jayne Wade Anderson
1953–55	Harvey L. Johnson	1987–89	Angelo J. Perna
1955–57	Rosemary Ginn	1989–90	George L. Robertson

The Fraternity Executives Association

The Fraternity Executives Association, at first named the College Fraternity Secretaries Association, met unofficially "for mutual benefit and assistance" some years before a formal organization was effected. Philip E. Lyon, traveling secretary of Phi Gamma Delta, served as chairman for a dinner and program held on November 26, 1920, in conjunction with the Conference of that year, but no organization was formed. For some years the traveling secretaries had been meeting informally for dinner and a discussion of common problems. In 1930, Harrold P. Flint, executive secretary of Tau Kappa Epsilon and a member of the Conference executive committee, called a group together with the assistance of Robert H. Hogue, then executive secretary of Theta Chi, and the meeting was held in conjunction with the Conference on November 28, 1930. Dean of the fraternity executive secretaries, Arthur R. Priest, Phi Delta Theta, was elected the first president.

Meetings at which mutual problems were discussed were held at the time of the Conference for many years. When it was discovered that a summer workshop program was of greater value, the College Fraternity Secretaries Association met in the summer jointly with the College Fraternity Editors Association. A number of secretaries also serve their fraternities as editors.

Feeling the desirability of an opportunity for the secretaries to consider fraternity problems was the deans of men a joint dinner was established in 1955, which became a regular feature of the NIC annual meeting. One of the results of these get-togethers was the inauguration of the first Training School for Field Secretaries, held in Indianapolis, January 4–5, 1957, to improve the visitation program of national fraternities.

In recent years, FEA has expanded its programs and operations by sponsoring research, educational, and promotional projects and has enhanced the professionalism of its members through sound programming, publications, and workshops.

Articles of Incorporation Fraternity Executives Association, Inc.

The undersigned incorporator, desiring to form a corporation pursuant to the provisions of the Indiana Not-For-Profit Corporation Act of 1971 ("Act"), hereby executes the following Articles of Incorporation:

ARTICLE I
NAME

The name of the corporation is Fraternity Executives Association, Inc.

ARTICLE II
PURPOSE

Fraternity Executives Association, Inc. ("Corporation"), is organized and shall at all times be operated exclusively to further the common business interest of the members of the Corporation by promoting, supporting, and encouraging the free discussion and exchange of ideas relating to college fraternal organizations.

ARTICLE III
POWERS

In furtherance of the purpose for which it is organized, the Corporation shall possess, in addition to the powers conferred by the Act, all of the following powers:

Section 1. To continue as a corporation under its corporate name perpetually;

Section 2. To sue and be sued in its corporate name;

Section 3. To acquire, own, hold, lease, mortgage, pledge, sell, convey, or otherwise dispose of property, real or personal, tangible or intangible;

Section 4. To borrow money and to issue, sell, or pledge its obligations and evidences of in-debtedness, and to mortgage its property and franchises to secure the payment thereof;

Section 5. To carry out its purposes in this state and elsewhere; to have one or more offices inside or outside of this state; and to acquire, own, hold and use, and to lease, mortgage, pledge, sell, convey, or otherwise dispose of property, real or personal, tangible or intangible, inside or outside of this state.

Section 6. To acquire, hold, own, and vote and to sell, assign, transfer, mortgage, pledge, or otherwise dispose of the capital stock, bonds, securities, or evidences of indebtedness of any other corporation, domestic or foreign, insofar as the same shall be consistent with the purposes of the Corporation;

Section 7. To appoint such officers and agents as the affairs of the Corporation may require and to define their duties and fix their compensation;

Section 8. To indemnify any director or officer or former director or officer of the Corporation, or any person who may have served at its request as a director or officer of another corporation, against liability and expense in accordance with Article XII, Section 9 of the Articles of Incorporation;

Section 9. To purchase and maintain insurance on behalf of any person who is or was a director, officer, employee, or agent of the Corporation, or is or was serving at the request of the Corporation as a director, officer, employee, or agent of another corporation, partnership, joint venture, trust, or other enterprise against any liability asserted against him and incurred by him in any such capacity, or arising out of his status as such, whether or not the Corporation would have the power to indemnify him against liability under the provisions of these Articles;

Section 10. To make by-laws for the government and regulation of its affairs;

Section 11. To cease its activities and to dissolve and surrender its corporate franchise;

Section 12. To do all acts and things necessary, convenient, or expedient to carry out the charitable purposes for which it is formed, including, without limitation, the making of gifts, donations, contributions, loans, and grants by the Corporation of all or any part of its income, assets, and property.

ARTICLE IV
PERIOD OF EXISTENCE

The period during which the Corporation shall continue is perpetual.

ARTICLE V
RESIDENT AGENT AND PRINCIPAL OFFICE

Section 1. Resident Agent. The name and address of the resident agent in charge of the Corporation's principal office are C.T. Corporation System, One North Capitol Avenue, Indianapolis, IN 46204.

Section 2. Principal Office. The address of the principal office of the Corporation is One North Capitol Avenue, Indianapolis, IN 46204.

ARTICLE VI
INCORPORATOR

Name and Post Office Address. The name and address of the incorporator of the Corporation is James E. Greer, Jr., 114 Fifth Avenue, New York, New York 10011.

ARTICLE VII
STATEMENT OF PROPERTY

The following is a statement of the property to be taken over by this Corporation at or upon its incorporation and an estimate of the value of that property: $25,000.

ARTICLE VIII
MEMBERS

Section 1. The members of the Corporation shall be those employees of administrative offices of college fraternal organizations who from time to time are admitted by the Corporation to membership and meet the duly adopted requirements of membership. The members of the Corporation shall determine membership requirements.

Section 2. Each member of the Corporation who serves as the chief administrative officers of an organization eligible for membership in the National Interfraternity Conference or National Panhellenic Conference and the Executive Director of the National Interfraternity Conference shall be entitled to one vote on each issue to come before a meeting of members.

Section 3. There shall be no classes of membership, except that there shall be honorary members as provided in the By-Laws.

ARTICLE IX
DIRECTORS

Section 1. The exact number of directors of the Corporation shall be prescribed from time to time by the By-Laws of the Corporation at a number no greater than thirteen (13) and no smaller than three (3). Whenever the By-Laws do not prescribe the exact number of directors, the number of directors shall be nine (9).

Section 2. Only those voting members of this Corporation shall be eligible to serve as an officer or director of the Corporation.

ARTICLE X
INITIAL BOARD OF DIRECTORS

The names and addresses of the initial Board of Directors of the Corporation are as follows:
1. William P. Bernier, P.O. Box 54, Warrensburg, Missouri 64093.
2. Wilford A. Butler, P.O. Box 40108, Indianapolis, Indiana 46240.
3. James E. Greer, Jr., 114 Fifth Avenue, New York, New York 10011.
4. Philip Josephson, P.O. Box 20246, Kansas City, Missouri 64195.
5. Maurice E. Littlefield, P.O. Box 1869, Lexington, Virginia 24450.
6. Gregory E. McElroy, 35 Orchard Street, White Plains, New York 10603.
7. Robert L. Off, 2400 Frederick, Suite 110, St. Joseph, Missouri 64506.
8. Stephen R. Siders, 4001 West Kirby Avenue, Champaign, Illinois 61821.
9. Charles N. White, Jr., P.O. Box 1901, Richmond, Virginia 23215.

ARTICLE XI
ELECTION OF DIRECTORS AND OFFICERS

Section 1. The members of the initial Board of Directors shall serve until the first annual meeting of the members of the Corporation. Thereafter, a director shall serve for a term of one year and until his successor is elected and qualified. A director may serve any number of consecutive terms.

Section 2. At each annual meeting, the voting members of the Corporation shall elect the members of the Corporation's Board of Directors and the officers of the Corporation. Each director and officer shall be elected by majority vote of the voting members of the Corporation.

Section 3. The Board of Directors shall at times be comprised of the Corporation's President, president-Elect, Secretary, Treasurer, Immediate Past President, and three other persons, all of whom shall be elected as directors by the voting members of the Corporation as provided in this Article XI.

Section 4. When a vacancy occurs on the Board of Directors or in an office of the Corporation by reason of death, resignation, removal or incapacity of a director or officer or an increase in the number of directors or officers prescribed in the Corporation's Articles of Incorporation or By-Laws, the directors serving immediately after such vacancy occurs shall by majority vote elect a director or officer to fill such vacancy.

ARTICLE XII
REGULATION OF CORPORATE AFFAIRS

The affairs of the Corporation shall be subject to the following provisions:

Section 1. Neither the members of the Corporation nor the Board of Directors shall have power or authorization to do any act that will prevent the Corporation from being an organization described in section 501(c)(6) of the Internal Revenue Code or corresponding provisions of any subsequent federal tax laws.

Section 2. No part of the net earnings of the Corporation shall inure to the benefit of, or be distributable to, its members or any other private person, except that the Corporation shall be authorized and empowered to pay reasonable compensation for services rendered and to make payments and distributions in furtherance of the purpose set forth in Article II of these Articles.

Section 3. Subject to the provisions of these Articles of Incorporation and applicable law, the Board of Directors shall have complete and plenary power to manage, control, and conduct all the affairs of the Corporation.

Section 4. The power to make, alter, amend, and repeal the Corporation's By-Laws shall be vested in the voting members of the Corporation.

Section 5. No member or director of the Corporation shall be liable for any of its obligations.

Section 6. Meetings of the members and meetings of the Board of Directors may be held at any location.

Section 7. A director may be removed, with or without cause, by a vote of a majority of the voting members of the Corporation, at a meeting of the voting members called expressly for that purpose.

Section 8. If the Corporation is dissolved, all of its property remaining after payment and discharge of its obligations shall be transferred and conveyed to one or more not-for-profit corporations which are organized for purposes substantially similar to those of the Corporation and which are exempt from federal income tax under Section 501(a) of the Code or corresponding provisions of any subsequent federal tax laws.

Section 9. To the extent permitted by the Act, the Corporation indemnified each director, advisor, officer, former director, former advisor, and former officer of the Corporation, and each person who may have served at its request as a director or officer of another corporation against expenses actually and reasonably incurred by him in connection with the defense of any civil action, suit, or proceeding in which he is made or threatened to be made a party by reason of bing or having been a director, advisor, or officer, except in relation to matters as to which he is adjudged in the action, suit or proceeding to b liable for negligence or misconduct in the performance of duty to the Corporation.

Section 10. Any action required or permitted to be taken at any meeting of the members or of the Board of Directors may be taken without a meeting, if prior to such action a written consent to such action is signed by all members or all directors, as the case may be, and such written consent is filed with the minutes of proceedings of the members or of the board.

The undersigned incorporator hereby adopts these Articles of Incorporation, representing beforehand to the Secretary of State of the State of Indiana and all persons whom it may concern that a membership list of the above-named corporation has been opened in accordance with the law and that at least three persons have signed that membership list.

The undersigned Incorporator, this 3rd day of May, 1985, hereby verifies subject to penalties of perjury that the facts contained herein are true.

S/James E. Greer, Jr.

Fraternity Executives Association, Inc. Bylaws

ARTICLE I
GENERAL

Section 1. The name of the corporation is Fraternity Executives Association, Inc. (hereinafter referred to as the "Corporation").

Section 2. The post office address of the Corporation is one North Capitol Avenue, Indianapolis, Indiana 46204. The Resident Agent is C.T. Corporation System.

Section 3. The fiscal year of the Corporation shall begin on the first day of May and end on the last day of the following April.

ARTICLE II
MEMBERS

Section 1. Membership in the Corporation is governed by the Articles of Incorporation.

Section 2. The meeting of the subscribing members shall be the first annual meeting of the members. Thereafter, unless otherwise determined by the Board of Directors, the annual meeting of the members shall be held each year on the first Wednesday in June or at such other date within six months after the end of the Corporation's fiscal year at such place and time as may be specified by the Board of Directors of the Corporation.

Section 3. Special meetings of the members may be called at any time by the President of the Corporation or by a majority of the Board of Directors. A special meeting shall be held at a time and place specified by the caller or callers of the special meeting.

Section 4. A written notice, stating the place, day, and hour of any meeting of the members and, in the case of a special meeting, the purpose or purposes for which the meeting is called, shall be delivered or mailed by the Secretary of the Corporation or by the caller or callers of the meeting to the members entitled to vote at such meeting at least ten (10) days before the date of the meeting. Notice of any meeting may be waived by a written waiver filed with the Secretary or by attendance at the meeting in person or by proxy.

Section 5. Each voting member of the Corporation shall be entitled to one vote upon each question which properly comes before a meeting of the members. Each question shall be determined by a majority vote of the members present at a meeting at which a quorum is present.

Section 6. At all meetings of the members, the members present shall constitute a quorum. Any meeting of members including annual and special meetings or any adjournments thereof, may be adjourned to a later date although less than a quorum is present.

Section 7. Any voting member of the Corporation who has been a voting member of the Corporation or its predecessor for a period of at least ten years or has served as President of the Corporation may become an honorary member of the Corporation upon retirement from or upon leaving the active employment of his fraternity subject to the approval of the Corporation's Board of Directors.

ARTICLE III
DIRECTORS

Section 1. The affairs of the Corporation shall be managed by the Board of Directors. The Board of Directors shall have nine members, who shall be elected in the manner prescribed in the Articles of Incorporation.

Section 2. A majority of the Board of Directors shall be necessary to constitute a quorum for the transaction of any business except the filling of vacancies on the Board of Directors and in the office of the Corporation which shall be filled in accordance with the provisions of Article XI, Section 3, of the Corporation's Articles of Incorporation. Except as otherwise provided by law, the Corporation's Articles of Incorporation, or these By-Laws, the act of a majority of directors present at a meeting at which a quorum is present shall be the act of the Board of Directors.

Section 3. The Board of Directors shall meet immediately following the annual meeting of the members for the purpose of transacting such business as properly may come before the meeting.

Section 4. Special meetings of the Board of Directors may be called by the President of the Corporation or by a majority of the Board of Directors upon not less than fourteen (14) days' written notice. A special meeting may be held at such place as is specified in the call of the special meeting. The purpose of any such meeting need not be specified. Notice of the time, place, and call of any meeting of the Board may be waived in writing if the waiver sets out in reasonable detail the purpose or purposes for which the meeting is called and the time and place thereof. Attendance at any meeting of the Board shall constitute a waiver of notice of such meeting and of the time, place, and call thereof.

ARTICLE IV
OFFICERS

Section 1. The Corporation shall have a President, a President-elect, a Secretary, a Treasurer, and such other officers as the voting members of the Corporation may from time to time elect. Each officer shall be elected by the voting members of the Corporation at the annual meeting of the members and shall serve until the next annual meeting and until the officer's successor is elected and qualified. No person may hold more than one office at any given time. Any vacancy occurring in any office prior to an annual election shall be filled by the Board of Directors at a special meeting, and the person elected to fill such vacancy shall serve until the next annual meeting and until that person's successor is elected and qualified.

Section 2. The President shall be the principal executive officer of the Corporation and shall be responsible for the day-to-day operation and performance of the Corporation's routine activities pursuant to the policies established by the members of the Corporation and the Board of Directors. He shall perform such other duties as the members of the Corporation and the Board of Directors may prescribe.

Section 3. The President-Elect of the Corporation shall perform such duties as the members, the Board of Directors, and the President shall from time to time prescribe.

Section 4. The Secretary shall attend all meetings of the members and the Board of Directors and shall keep a true and complete record of the proceedings of such meetings. The Secretary shall give and serve all notices, keep a roll of the members, file and preserve all important documents, records, reports, and communications, and shall perform such other duties as the members, the Board of Directors, or the president may prescribe.

Section 5. The Treasurer shall keep correct and complete records of account, showing accurately the financial condition of the Corporation. The Treasurer shall be the legal custodian of all moneys, notes, securities and other valuables which may from time to time come into the possession of the Corporation. The Treasurer shall promptly deposit all funds of the Corporation in the Corporation's accounts in reliable banks or other depositories designated by the Board of Directors. The Treasurer shall furnish at meetings of the Board of Directors, or whenever requested by the President, a statement of the financial condition of the Corporation and shall perform such other duties as the members, the Board of Directors, or the President may prescribe.

Section 6. The Editor of *News & Notes* shall be an ex-officio member, without vote.

Section 7. Each other officer of the Corporation shall perform such duties as the members, the Board of Directors, and the President may from time to time prescribe.

ARTICLE V
OBLIGATIONS AND FISCAL MATTERS

Section 1. The Board of Directors may authorize any officer or agent or agents of the Corporation to enter into any contract or execute any instrument on its behalf. Such authorization may be general or confined to specific instances. Except as provided in these By-Laws, no officer, agent, or employee shall have any power to bind the Corporation or to render it liable for any purpose or amount unless so authorized by the Board of Directors.

Section 2. All checks, drafts, or other orders for payment of money by the Corporation shall be signed by such person or persons as the Board of Directors may from time to time designate by resolution.

Section 3. The fiscal year of the Corporation shall be from May 1 to April 30 of the succeeding year.

Section 4. The *News & Notes* shall be the official publication of the Fraternity Executives Association with the Editor appointed annually by the President with the approval of the Board of Directors.

ARTICLE VI
AMENDMENTS

The power to make, alter, amend, or repeal the By-Laws is vested in the members of the Corporation.

STANDING ORDERS
FRATERNITY EXECUTIVES ASSOCIATION, INC.

Standing Order Number One. The rules and procedures of the Fraternity Executives Association not stated in the Articles of Incorporation or the By-Laws shall be set forth as Standing Orders; Standing Orders are created and amended only by the membership of the Association by a majority vote of the voting members present at a regular or special meeting of the Association.

Standing Order Number Two. Membership in the Fraternity Executives Association shall consist of employees of administrative offices of those college fraternal organizations eligible for membership in the National Interfraternity Conference, National Panhellenic Conference and the employees (Executive Director) of the National Interfraternity Conference, who have paid current Association dues.

Standing Order Number Three. The dues of the Fraternity Executives Association shall be set by the Board of Directors.

Standing Order Number Four. Attendance at meetings of the Fraternity Executives Association shall be open to all members (the Chief Administrative Officer, but may be represented by any staff member designated by the Chief Administrative Officer upon written notice to the President). Executive sessions may be held with attendance restricted to voting members of the corporation (the Chief Administrative Officers). Honorary members may attend meetings of the association as non-voting members and special guests may be invited by the FEA president.

Standing Order Number Five. Amendments to the By-Laws can be made only by the two-thirds majority vote of the voting members present and voting at the annual or a special meeting of the members.

Standing Order Number Six. Each voting member of his designated representative shall be entitled to one vote. Designated representatives shall be approved by the President only after a written notice is provided the president authorizing the designation to an employee of the voting member's fraternity. No voting members shall have more than one vote regardless of the number of fraternities served. Proxy, phone, mail, and wire voting is not permitted at membership meetings.

Standing Order Number Seven. A quorum for all meetings of the Association shall be defined as being at least twenty voting members or their designated representatives in attendance and in good standing.

Standing Order Number Eight. To assure an orderly transition in the business of the Association, the secretary and the treasurer elected at the annual meeting, in accordance with Article IV of the By-Laws, shall assume their operating responsibili-ties on October 1 of the year elected. In the interim, they shall serve on the Board of Directors with all responsibilities of a director. The outgoing secretary and treasurer of the Association shall continue with their operating responsibilities through September 30 of the year their term of office ends.

Standing Order Number Nine. The membership of the Association shall be grouped into "sections" for the purpose of conducting educational programming. The number and governance of "sections" shall be determined by the Board of Directors.

Presidents of the Fraternity Executives Association

*	Deceased
1930–31 *	Arthur R. Priest, Phi Delta Theta
1931–33 *	Bruce H. McIntosh, Lambda Chi Alpha
1933–34 *	Malcolm C. Sewell, Sigma Nu
1934–35 *	Norman Hackett, Theta Delta Chi
1935–36 *	Stewart D. Daniels, Alpha Tau Omega
1936–37	Harold H. Jacobsen, Sigma Pi
1937–38 *	Wilbur M. Walden, Alpha Chi Rho
1938–39 *	A. H. Aldridge, Theta Chi
1939–40 *	William H. Phillips, Sigma Phi Epsilon
1940–41 *	Richard J. Young, Phi Kappa Tau
1941–42 *	G. Herbert Smith, Beta Theta Pi
1942–43 *	C. F. Williams, Phi Kappa Psi
1943–44 *	H. Seger Slifer, Chi Psi
1944–45 *	Cecil J. Wilkinson, Phi Gamma Delta
1945–46 *	Lauren Foreman, Sigma Alpha Epsilon
1946–47 *	Earl F. Schoening, Phi Sigma Kappa
1947–48 *	William W. Elder, Delta Kappa Epsilon
1948–49 *	Harold P. Davison, Theta Xi
1949–50 *	Luther Z. Rosser, Chi Phi
1950–51 *	J. Russell Easton, Sigma Chi
1951–52	William W. Hindman, Jr., Sigma Phi Epsilon
1952–53	Ralph F. Burns, Alpha Sigma Phi
1953–54 *	Ransom M. Bassett, Kappa Alpha Order
1954–55 *	Paul C. Beam, Phi Delta Theta
1955–56 *	Cyril F. Flad, Lambda Chi Alpha
1956–57 *	Francis Wacker, Delta Sigma Phi
1957–58 *	George W. Chapman, Theta Chi
1958–59 *	George V. Uihlein, Phi Kappa Theta
1959–60 *	Robert D. Lynn, Pi Kappa Alpha
1960–61 *	Roy C. Clark, Acacia
1961–62	Ralph D. Daniel, Phi Kappa Psi
1962–63	Robert J. Miller, Phi Delta Theta
1963–64	George S. Toll, Alpha Epsilon Pi
1964–65	William T. Bringham, CAE, Sigma Chi
1965–66	William E. Forester, Kappa Alpha Order
1966–67	Lewis J. Bacon, Alpha Kappa Lambda
1967–68 *	Rex A. Smith, CAE, Sigma Alpha Epsilon
1968–69 *	Jack L. Anson, Phi Kappa Tau
1969–70 *	Richard R. Fletcher, Sigma Nu
1970–71	Donald M. Johnson, Sigma Phi Epsilon
1971–72	William S. Zerman, Phi Gamma Delta
1972	Bruce B. Melchert, Tau Kappa Epsilon (Partial Term)
1972–73	Durward W. Owen, CAE, Pi Kappa Phi
1973–74	William M. Henderson, Delta Kappa Epsilon
1974–75	William P. Schwartz, Sigma Alpha Mu
1975–76 *	Alfred P. Sheriff, III, Delta Tau Delta
1976–77	Wilford A. Butler, CAE, Delta Upsilon
1977–78	Sidney S. Suntag, Tau Epsilon Phi
1978–79	Howard R. Alter, Jr., Theta Chi
1979–80	George W. Spasyk, Lambda Chi Alpha
1980–81	George A. Beck, Pi Lambda Phi
1981–82	T. J. Schmitz, CAE, Tau Kappa Epsilon
1982–83	Henry B. Poor, Psi Upsilon
1983–84	William P. Bernier, Sigma Tau Gamma
1984–85	James E. Greer, Jr., Zeta Beta Tau
1985–86	Gregory E. McElroy, Zeta Psi
1986–87	Philip Josephson, Alpha Gamma Rho
1987–88	Robert L. Off, FarmHouse
1988–89	Charles N. White, Jr., Sigma Phi Epsilon
1989–90	Maurice E. Littlefield, Sigma Nu
1990–91	Sidney N. Dunn, Alpha Epsilon Pi
1991–92	Kenneth D. Tracey, Sigma Alpha Epsilon

Association of Fraternity Advisors

The Association of Fraternity Advisors (AFA) is a professional association for campus advisors to men's and women's fraternities. AFA was founded December 1, 1976 during the bicentennial gathering of the National Interfraternity Conference in Williamsburg, Virginia. In June of 1977, an organizational meeting was held in Indianapolis at which bylaws were adopted and officers elected. John Mohr was elected as the first president.

The purposes as stated in the AFA bylaws are:

1. to provide for the cooperative association and professional stimulation of those persons engaged in the advisement of fraternities and sororities,
2. to formulate and maintain high professional standards in the advisement of fraternities and sororities,
3. to provide a forum through publications, conferences, and informal interactions for the sharing of ideas and concerns related to the advisement of fraternities and sororities,
4. to stimulate educational programming and student development concepts within local chapters of fraternities and sororities and local interfraternity organizations,
5. to promote research and experimentation related to fraternities and sororities,
6. to encourage interested and qualified persons to seek student personnel positions in post-secondary educational institutions which include advisement of fraternities and sororities, and
7. to maintain positive and supportive working relationships with related Student Affairs associations, with national fraternity and sorority organizations, and with national interfraternity organizations.

From the original 35 members, the organization has grown to over 900 members in 1991, including over 700 regular members and 200 affiliate members. Regular members include student personnel professionals and graduate students at institutions of higher education. Affiliate members include staff members of (inter)national fraternities and sororities; (inter)national, regional and local fraternity and sorority alumni volunteers; and others interested in the enhancement of the advisement of fraternities and sororities.

Since its inception, the Annual Conference of the Association is held at a concurrent date and location with the Annual Meeting of the National Interfraternity Conference. The attendance at the Annual Conference has grown from about 70 in 1977 to over 450 in 1990. In addition, area conferences are organized on a state or regional basis.

When it was founded, AFA assumed responsibility for publishing *The Fraternity Newsletter*, which had been edited by Jerry Lilly since July 1974. In 1991, the name of the publication was changed to *AFA Perspectives*. The Association also published the *Greek Advisor's Manual* and other publications.

Association of Fraternity Advisors, Inc.
Bylaws

(As of December, 1990)

ARTICLE I
NAME

The name of the Corporation shall be the Association of Fraternity Advisors, Inc. The Corporation may also utilize the following assumed names: Association of Fraternity Advisors; AFA.

ARTICLE II
PURPOSES

A. To provide for the cooperative association and professional stimulation of those persons engaged in the advisement of fraternities and sororities;
B. to formulate and maintain high professional standards in the advisement of fraternities and sororities;
C. to provide a forum through publications, conferences, and informal interactions for the sharing of ideas and concerns related to the advisement of fraternities and sororities;
D. to stimulate educational programming and student development concepts within local chapters of fraternities and sororities and local interfraternity organizations;
E. to promote research and experimentation related to fraternities and sororities;
F. to encourage interested and qualified persons to seek student personnel positions in post-secondary educational institutions which include advisement of fraternities and sororities; and
G. to maintain positive and supportive working relationships with related professional Student Affairs associations, with national fraternity and sorority organizations, and with national interfraternity organizations.

ARTICLE III
MEMBERSHIP

The classes of membership in the Association among persons in the United States and Canada shall be Regular, Associate, and Affiliate.

A. **Regular.** Regular members shall be those persons who maintain the primary advising role to the men's and/or women's fraternity system associated with a post-secondary educational institution. Chief student personnel officers and other student personnel workers not directly involved with but actively interested in men's or women's fraternities shall be considered Regular members. Regular members shall pay the annual dues, shall be entitled to one vote in all business of the Association, and shall be eligible to hold elected or appointed office.

B. **Affiliate.** Affiliate members shall be all other persons who are actively concerned with enhancement of the advisement of men's or women's fraternities, including but not limited to, professional executives of national organizations as well as volunteer advisors and officers on the campus, regional or national level. Affiliate members shall pay the annual dues and shall receive all benefits of the Association, except they shall neither possess the vote nor hold office. Affiliate members are eligible to serve on committees.

C. **Associate Member.** Associate members shall be those individuals, organizations, companies, manufacturers, or suppliers of goods and services that support the policies, purposes, and activities of the Association. Associate members shall be subject to the approval of the Executive Board. They shall pay an annual affiliate member fee, which will entitle them to receive the newsletter and have the opportunity to have a display table at the annual conference. Associate members shall neither possess the right to vote nor hold office. They are not eligible to serve on committees.

D. **Transfer of Membership.** All memberships are individual in nature and are to remain with the individual throughout the term of the membership. No transfer of membership shall be granted regardless of the given situation.

ARTICLE IV
FINANCE

A. **Dues.** The annual dues for Regular and Affiliate members of the Association shall be recommended by the Executive Committee and ratified by a plurality vote of the Regular members in attendance at the business session at the annual conference.

B. **Membership year.** The membership year of the Association for the purposes of the annual dues shall be July 1 through June 30. Failure to pay the annual dues by **September 15** shall cause the Secretary to drop the member's name from the roll of the Association.

C. **Fiscal year.** The fiscal year of the Association for the purposes of accounting shall be January 1 through December 31.

D. **Funds.** To implement their programs, the officers and committee chairs may request funds from the President of the Association. Such programs shall not include reimbursement for travel to the annual conference of the Association. The officers and chairs shall not exceed the amounts approved in the budget without prior special approval of the Executive Committee. A written account of the expenditure shall be made at the annual business session by the Treasurer.

ARTICLE V
OFFICERS

A. **Officers.** The Officers of the Association shall be the President, the President-Elect, the Executive Vice President, the Regional Vice Presidents, the Secretary, and the Treasurer.

B. **Qualifications.**
   1. Each officer shall be a regular member during his or her term of office.
   2. The President, President-Elect, Executive Vice President, Secretary, and Treasurer shall have been members of the Association for a minimum of two (2) years prior to nomination (except as provided in V.B.5. below).
   3. The Regional Vice Presidents shall have been members of the Association for a minimum of one (1) year immediately prior to nomination.
   4. The Regional Vice Presidents shall be located at a college or university within the region they represent.
   5. The President, President-Elect, Executive Vice President, the Secretary, and the Treasurer shall have served as an elected or appointed officer, committee chair, or state coordinator of the Association for at least one (1) year prior to nomination. In lieu of service in one of the aforementioned positions, a nominee may substitute a minimum of three years Regular membership in the Association.

C. **Term of Office.** The term of office of the President, President-Elect, Executive Vice President, and Regional Vice Presidents shall be one (1) year. The Secretary and the Treasurer shall serve for a term of two (2) years. The Secretary shall be elected in even numbered years. The Treasurer shall be elected in odd numbered years. The President-Elect shall not be eligible to elected to consecutive regular terms in the same office. The Secretary, Treasurer, Executive Vice President, and Regional Vice Presidents shall serve no more than two (2) consecutive terms in office.

D. **Assumption of Office.** Newly elected officers shall take office at the close of the annual conference and shall serve through the next annual conference or until their successors are elected. Retiring officers shall be responsible for the completion of the details of the annual conference for which they are responsible and for the presentation to the new officers all necessary reports and information required for the smooth transition of responsibility.

E. **Vacancies.**

1. If the Office of President becomes vacant the President-Elect shall succeed to that office.

2. If the Office of President-Elect becomes vacant because of the incumbent's inability to complete his/her term or because the incumbent succeeds to the Office of President within thirty (30) days after the beginning of a term of office, the Executive Committee shall call for the election of a new President-Elect by the eligible voting membership. If the President-Elect succeeds to the Office of President more than thirty (30) but less than one-hundred-twenty (120) days after the beginning of a term, the Executive Committee may, but is not required to call for an election of a new President-Elect by the eligible voting membership.

   In any of the above situations the President-Elect shall succeed to the Office of President at the next annual conference.

   In the event the Executive Committee elects not to call for the election of a new President-Elect under the guidelines or if the President-Elect succeeds to the Office of President more than one-hundred-twenty (120) days after the beginning of a term, the new President, with approval of the Executive Committee, shall appoint an Interim President-Elect who shall serve until the next annual conference. An Interim-President-Elect shall assume all regular duties of the President-Elect, but shall not succeed to the Office of President, unless that office becomes vacant and then only until the next annual conference, when both a President and a President-Elect shall be elected. Interim Presidents-Elect shall be eligible to succeed themselves for a regular term.

3. If the Office of Executive Vice President becomes vacant, the President, with the approval of the Executive Committee, shall appoint an Interim Executive Vice President. Interim Vice Presidents for Projects shall be eligible to succeed themselves for a regular term.

4. If the Office of Secretary becomes vacant during the first year of a regular term of office, the Executive Committee shall call for the election of a new Secretary by the eligible voting membership. If the Office of Secretary becomes vacant during the second year of a regular term of office, the Presi-

dent, with the approval of the Executive Committee shall appoint an Interim Secretary. Interim Secretaries shall be eligible to succeed themselves for a regular term.

5. If the Office of Treasurer becomes vacant during the first year of a regular term of office, the Executive Committee shall call for the election of a new Treasurer by the eligible voting membership. If the Office of Treasurer becomes vacant during the second year of a regular term of office, the President, with the approval of the Executive Committee shall appoint an Interim Treasurer. Interim Treasurers shall be eligible to succeed themselves for a regular term.

6. If the Office of Regional Vice President becomes vacant, the President, with the approval of the Executive Committee shall appoint an Interim Regional Vice President. The Interim Regional Vice President shall serve until the next annual conference and shall be eligible for election to a regular term of office.

7. **Resignation of an Officer-Elect Prior to Assumption of Office.** In the event that an officer-elect resigns his/her position after the completion of the official mail ballot and prior to the business session of the annual conference, the Executive Committee shall call for the election of a new officer-elect by the eligible voting membership in attendance at the business session of the annual conference. This election shall be conducted in accordance with the applicable provisions of Article VIII, Nominations and Elections.

8. **Emergency Order of Succession.** In the event the Offices of the President and President-Elect become vacant, the next person available shall assume office as Acting President according to the following Order of Succession: Executive Vice President, Secretary, Treasurer, Northern Regional Vice President, Southern Regional Vice President, Mid American Regional Vice President, and Western Regional Vice President. The Acting President shall hold office until the Executive Committee can act as specified above.

F. **Duties.**

1. The **President** shall serve as the chief executive officer of the Association, Chair of the Executive Committee, and presiding officer at all business sessions of the Association. The President shall appoint all members of committees, subject the approval of the Executive Committee, and shall hold ex-officio membership on all committees. The President, with the Treasurer, shall present an annual operating budget for the Association to the Executive Committee for its approval prior to the beginning of the fiscal year. The

President shall be bonded, at the expense of the Association, in such amount as shall be determined by the Executive Committee.

2. The **President-Elect,** in the absence of the President or his/her inability to serve, shall perform the duties of the President. The President-Elect shall serve as the liaison from the Executive Committee to all Association liaisons/liaison committees, as well as such other duties as delegated by the President. The President-Elect shall succeed to the Office of President.

3. The **Executive Vice President** shall coordinate the activities and programs of all committees which provide direct services to the Association membership; the activities and programs of all special projects undertaken by the Association; and shall recommend to the Executive Committee the undertaking of appropriate projects.

4. The **Secretary** shall take and publish the minutes of all Executive Committee meetings and the annual meeting. The Secretary shall organize all official documents of the Association, maintain a file of all committee and officer reports and update the operations manual as needed. The Secretary shall maintain all membership records and produce an annual membership report complete with demographic information regarding members. The Secretary shall develop and implement programs and procedures to secure and increase membership in the Association. The Secretary shall serve as the liaison from the Executive Committee to the Bylaws Committee.

5. The **Treasurer** shall collect and disburse all funds of the Association as authorized by the Executive Committee and approved by the President. The Treasurer shall maintain all necessary records and shall prepare written quarterly and annual financial reports on the financial condition of the Association. The annual report and annual budget shall be distributed at the annual conference. The Treasurer shall handle conference registration. The Treasurer shall supervise preparation of all tax forms and oversee Association investments. The Treasurer shall serve as the Chair of the Finance Committee. The Treasurer shall, at Association expense, be bonded in such amount as shall be determined by the Executive Committee.

6. The **Regional Vice Presidents** shall have the primary responsibility for promoting the purposes and programs of the Association within their respective regions. They shall attend their regional IFC and Panhellenic meetings as the official representatives of the Association. If they are unable to attend one of these meetings they are responsible for ensuring that another member

of the Association attends that meeting as the official representative of the Association.

ARTICLE VI
EXECUTIVE COMMITTEE

A. **Membership.** The Executive Committee shall consist of the nine (9) elected officers, the immediate Past President, the Editor and the Director of Conferences and Meetings. The Executive Committee shall serve as a board of Directors in accordance with the laws of the State of Indiana.

B. **Editor and Director of Conferences and Meetings.**
   1. **Editor.** The Editor shall have been a Regular member of the Association for a minimum of one (1) year immediately prior to appointment by the President and approval by the Executive Committee. The Editor shall be responsible for publication of *The Fraternity Newsletter* and such other materials as may be approved by the Executive Committee at a cost and frequency determined by the Executive Committee.
   2. **Director of Conferences and Meetings.** The Director of Conferences and Meetings shall have been a regular member of the Association for a minimum of two (2) years immediately prior to appointment by the President and approval by the Executive Committee. The Director of Conferences and Meetings shall be responsible for site inspections and negotiations; all physical arrangements for conferences and Association meetings; and will be responsible for overseeing the work of the Conference Program Chair and Program Chair-Elect.

C. **Assumption and Terms of Office.**
   1. The Editor shall take office on June 1 and serve until the following May 31. The Editor, not an elected officer of this body, shall be eligible for reappointment with majority approval by the Executive Committee.
   2. The Director of Conferences and Meetings shall take office at the annual conference and shall serve through the next annual conference or until a successor is appointed. A retiring Director of Conferences shall be responsible for the completion of the details of the annual conference(s) for which the appointment is made, and for the presentation to the new Director of Conferences all necessary reports and information required for the smooth transition of responsibility. The Director of Conferences and Meetings, not an elected officer of this body, shall be eligible for reappointment with majority approval by the Executive Committee.

D. **Duties.** The Executive Committee shall serve as a Board for the formulation and recommendation of policies to the Association between business sessions of the annual conference, shall have the power to propose amendments to these Bylaws, and shall carry on business for the Association.

ARTICLE VII
MEETINGS

A. **Annual Conference.** Unless prevented by a national emergency, there shall be an annual conference of the Association at which the annual business session shall be conducted. The annual conference may be held at a time and place that coincides with, yet not delimited by, the annual conference of the National Interfraternity Conference. Notice of the annual conference of the Association shall be sent to all Regular and Associate members of record at least forty-five (45) days in advance of the conference.

B. **Executive Committee.** The Executive Committee shall meet at such times and places as it shall determine, to include at least one (1) meeting in the interim of the annual conference. A majority of the Executive Committee shall constitute a quorum for the transaction of business. The Executive Committee may, at its discretion, authorize Association funds to support such committee meetings.

C. **Quorum.** The Regular members present at the business session of the annual conference shall constitute a quorum for the transaction of business, provided proper notice of the business session has been given.

D. **Required Attendance.** All officers and chairs of the Association shall be present at the annual conference at which they are elected or appointed and at the annual conference for which they are responsible. Failure to attend these meetings, unless excused by a unanimous vote of the Executive Committee shall constitute cause for Removal Without Notice as provided under Article IX of these Bylaws.

ARTICLE VIII
NOMINATIONS AND ELECTIONS

A. **Nominating Committee.** The Nominating Committee normally shall be chaired by the Past President. In the event that the Past President is unable to assume or continue his/her responsibilities, a Regular member shall be appointed by the President at the approval of the Executive Committee. During the Regional Meetings conducted at the Annual Conference, a plurality of regular members in attendance the respective Regional Meetings, shall elect the Region's representatives to a Nominating Committee of eight (8) Regular members; two (2) from each of the Regions of the Association; with all elected to have been Regular members of the Association for a minimum of three (3) years prior to election. The membership of the Nominating Committee shall be announced in the next issue of *The Fraternity Newsletter* following the Annual Conference.

B. **Procedure.** The mechanics and details of the nominating and election procedure shall be established by the Nominating Committee and approved by the Executive Committee, unless otherwise specified by these Bylaws.

C. **Nominations.** In *The Fraternity Newsletter,* the Nominating Committee shall call for nominations for all Regular members for elected positions to be filled on the Executive Committee and shall submit to the Secretary of the Association its nominations at least forty-five (45) days prior to the annual conference. In selecting the nominees, the Committee shall consider the qualifications for office (including professional training and experience, geographic location, and type of institution at which employed) rather than the number of nominations received. The Committee need not limit its nominations to those received from the membership. The Committee shall nominate two (2) candidates for each position if reasonably possible. To be eligible for nominatin, a candidate must be a paid member of the Association by September 15.

D. **Balloting.** No later than thirty (30) days prior to the annual conference the Chair of the Nominating Committee shall mail a printed ballot to all Regular members who were listed on the roll of the Association as of September 15, specifying that the ballot be returned postmarked not later than twenty-one (21) days after the mailing date. Regional Vice Presidents will be elected by those Regular members of the Association who work in their respective regions.

The Regional composition of the Association shall be as follows:

1. **Eastern**—Maine, New Hampshire, Vermont, New York, Pennsylvania, Massachusetts, Connecticut, Rhode Island, New Jersey, Delaware, Maryland, West Virginia, Washington, D.C., Quebec, Newfoundland, New Brunswick, and Nova Scotia.
2. **Southern**—Virginia, Kentucky, North Carolina, Tennessee, South Carolina, Georgia, Florida, Alabama, Mississippi, and Louisiana.
3. **Mid American**—Ontario, Manitoba, North Dakota, South Dakota, Minnesota, Wisconsin, Michigan, Ohio, Indiana, Illinois, Iowa, Nebraska, Kansas, Missouri, Arkansas, Oklahoma, and Texas.
4. **West**—New Mexico, Arizona, Colorado, Wyoming, Montana, Utah, Idaho, Nevada, California, Oregon, Washington, Alaska, Hawaii, British Columbia, Alberta, and Saskatchewan.

E. **Teller.** All ballots shall be mailed directly to the Teller for the Association. Ballots shall be opened and tabulated only by the Teller. The Teller shall be appointed at least thirty (30) days prior to the annual conference by the President, subject to the approval of the Executive Committee.

F. **Election.** A plurality vote shall constitute election to office. In the event that two (2) candidates receive an identical number of votes, the Teller Committee shall conduct further balloting among Regular members in attendance at the business session of the annual conference. Further balloting shall require a new election among the same candidates. The results of all elections shall be announced by the Chair of the Teller Committee at the business session of the annual conference, and subsequently shall be printed in the issue of *The Fraternity Newsletter* following the annual conference.

ARTICLE IX
REMOVAL AND IMPEACHMENT

A. **Removal Without Notice.** Officers, Chairs, and committee members who cease to be members in good financial standing, who cease to be Regular members as defined in Article III, Paragraph A or as provided in Article VII Paragraph D in these Bylaws, in reference to removal, shall be removed from their positions by a majority vote of the Executive Committee.

B. **Removal With Notice.** Appointed Officers, Chairs, and committee members who do not carry out their duties as assigned in these Bylaws may be removed by a four-fifths (4/5) majority of the Executive Committee, provided sufficient notice has been given, and the individual has been given a reasonable opportunity to defend him/herself before the Executive Committee.

C. **Impeachment and Removal.** Elected Officers of the Association may be impeached and removed for failure to carry out their duties as assigned by these Bylaws under the following procedures:
   1. Charges are brought before the Executive Committee.
   2. The Executive Committee conducts a hearing and provides the Officer an opportunity to defend against the charge.
   3. The Executive Committee, in closed session, in the absence of the accused officer who has no vote, votes unanimously to impeach.
   4. The Bill of Impeachment, along with an explanatory statement from the Executive Committee and a statement from the accused officer, is submitted to all Regular members. A majority agreement of those voting within four (4) weeks of the date of the mailing shall be sufficient to effect removal from office.

ARTICLE X
STANDING AND SPECIAL COMMITTEES, REPRESENTATIVES, AND AREA COORDINATORS

A. **Appointment of Committee Members.** The President, with the prior approval of the Executive Committee, shall appoint the Chairs and Members of the standing and special committees determined appropriate to carry out the purposes of the Association. All persons serving on committees shall be Regular or Affiliate Members of the Association during their terms of office. The Chairs of all committees shall have been Regular members of the Association a minimum of one (1) year immediately prior to the appointment. The term of office for all committees and Chairs (with the exception of the Conference Program Chair) shall be one (1) year. Committee Chairs and members may be reappointed to their positions.

The **Conference Program Chair** shall be appointed a minimum of eighteen (18) months prior to the conference for which this Chair is responsible, and will serve as Conference Program Chair-Elect until the completion of the annual conference immediately prior to the conference for which this Chair is responsible.

B. **Reporting.** Committees shall not obligate the Association to any undertaking not specifically approved in advance by the Executive Committee or the membership at the business session of the annual conference. Committees shall submit to the President and membership an interim and an annual report of their work.

C. **Standing Committees.** The standing committees of the Association shall be: Bylaws, Information Services, Current Affairs, Nominating, Professional Development, Conference Program Committee, Resolutions, Teller, Awards, Newsletter Advisory Board, Finance, and Commuter Greeks.
   1. **Bylaws.** The Bylaws Committee shall recommend to the Executive Committee any amendments determined appropriate for consideration by the membership in accordance with the provisions of Article XI and Article XII.
   2. **Information Services.** The Information Services Committee is to research and report to the Executive Committee and/or the annual conference issues or other pertinent matters concerning Fraternity/Sorority organizations.
   3. **Current Affairs.** The Current Affairs Committee will provide information and resources to the membership, as requested.
   4. **Nominating.** The Nominating Committee shall perform the duties provided for in Article VIII.
   5. **Professional Development.** The Professional Development Committee shall develop and implement such programs as will enhance the skills and competencies of the members of the Association as well as to carry out the purposes of the Association.
   6. **Conference Program.** The Conference Program Committee shall solicit, promote, and select programs for the annual conference, shall develop a schedule of these programs

and shall conduct appropriate evaluation of the programs at the annual conference.

7. **Resolutions.** The Resolutions Committee will research and prepare appropriate resolutions to be considered at the annual business session for adoption.

8. **Teller.** The Teller will count the ballots of the annual election of officers and any other balloting or voting of the Association.

9. **Awards.** The Awards Committee shall determine all awards as well as tabulate and report winners of these awards at the annual conference.

10. **Newsletter Advisory Board.** The Newsletter Advisory Board shall: assist in the determination of topical issues for publication; write articles for publication; collect copy from outside sources; serve as a resource group/sounding board for the Editor.

11. **Finance Committee.** The Finance Committee shall review the annual audit; review quarterly and annual financial reports; make recommendations regarding financial matters to the Executive Committee and the general membership; and prepare the proposed budget to be presented at the annual business meeting.

12. **Commuter Greeks.** The committee on Commuter Greeks shall research and report to the Executive Committee and/or the annual conference issues or other pertinent matters concerning Fraternity/Sorority organizations on commuter campuses. Where appropriate, the committee shall develop programs which may be of assistance to those Association members working on commuter campuses, and shall serve as a forum for the concerns expressed by those who work at commuter campuses.

D. **Special Committees.** Special Committees shall be appointed by the President, with the approval of the Executive Committee.

E. **Representatives.**

1. **Appointment.** The President, with the prior approval of the Executive Committee, shall appoint the individuals who shall represent the Association to other organizations and committees. The Representatives shall have been a Regular members of the Association for a minimum of one (1) year immediately prior to the appointment and maintain Regular member status during the term of appointment. The term for all Representatives normally shall be one (1) year; however, terms may vary in cases where the term is set by a host organization or committee. Representatives may be reappointed to their positions.

2. **Reporting.** Representatives shall not obligate the Association to any undertaking not specifically approved in advance by the Executive Committee or the membership at the business session of the annual conference. Representatives shall submit to the President and membership an interim report and an annual report of their work.

3. The **Standing Representatives** are: Representative to the Center for the Study of the College Fraternity (CSCF); Liaison to the National Panhellenic Conference (NPC); Liaison to the National Interfraternity Conference (NIC); Liaison to the Fraternity Executives Association (FEA); Liaison to the National Pan-Hellenic Council (NPHC); Liaison to the National Association of Student Personnel Administrators (NASPA); Liaison to the National Association for Women Deans, Administrators; and Counselors (NAWDAC); Liaison to Project GAMMA; Liaison to the College Fraternity Editors Association (CFEA); Liaison to the Association of College Personnel Administrators (ACPA); Liaison to the National Association for Campus Activities (NACA); Representative to the Council for the Advancement of Standards (CAS); and Representative to the Inter-Association Task Force on Alcohol and other Drug Issues.

4. **Special Representatives.** Special Representatives shall be appointed by the President with the approval of the Executive Committee.

F. **Area Coordinators.**

1. **Appointment.** The Regional Vice Presidents, in consultation with the Membership Committee Chair, shall appoint the individuals who will represent the Association as Area Coordinators. Area Coordinators may be reappointed to their positions.

2. **Reporting.** Area Coordinators shall not obligate the Association to any undertaking not specifically approved in advance by the Executive Committee or the membership at the business session of the annual conference. Area Coordinators shall submit to their respective Regional Vice Presidents and Executive Committee an interim report and an annual report of their work.

ARTICLE XI
PARLIAMENTARY AUTHORITY

In all situations not provided for in the Articles or the Bylaws the rules contained in the current edition of *Robert's Rules of Order, Newly Revised* shall govern the Association in operations.

ARTICLE XII
AMENDMENTS

A. **Proposing.** Amendments to or a repeal of these Bylaws may be proposed by the Executive Committee on its own initiative or upon petition by 2 1/2% of the regular members. The Executive Committee shall present all such proposals to the regular members with or without endorsement.

B. **Approval.** Amendments to or a repeal of these Bylaws shall be approved by: a 2/3 affirmative vote of the regular members present at the annual business meeting of the Association duly called, provided written notice of proposed changes have been sent to the regular members thirty (30) days before such meeting; or by majority vote of the regular members voting by a thirty (30) day mail ballot.

ARTICLE XIII
BUDGET

A. The Executive Committee shall present a projected Annual Budget for the succeeding fiscal year at the business session of the annual conference.

B. The Executive Committee shall approve expenditures in accordance with the projected Annual Budget, except that the Executive Committee may deviate from the Annual Budget in unforeseen circumstances, provided such deviation does not exceed overall projected income.

C. The Association shall not be in a deficit budget condition at any time. No expenditures shall be authorized which shall produce such deficit condition.

ARTICLE XIV
PROFESSIONAL DEVELOPMENT PROGRAM

A. **Research.** The Executive Committee may approve the expenditure of funds to support research projects related to Fraternity/Sorority Affairs.

B. **Scholarships.** The Executive Committee may approve scholarships for Association members to attend Fraternity/Sorority oriented seminars and institutes.

C. **Professional Affiliations.** At Association expense, the Executive Committee may joint and/or send delegates or observers to other professional organizations.

ARTICLE XV
COMMITTEE MEETINGS

The Executive Committee may authorize committee meetings at times and places deemed most appropriate and may, at its discretion, authorize Association funds to support such committee meetings.

ARTICLE XVI
IMPEACHMENT CHARGES

A. Charges may be brought by any Regular member of the Association in good standing.

B. Charges will be filed with the Secretary of the Association, except that if the Secretary is the affected Officer, charges will be filed with the President-Elect.

C. Impeachment proceedings shall be in accordance with Article IX(C).

ARTICLE XVII
WRITE-IN CANDIDATES

A. Write-in candidates shall be permitted in all elections.

B. Ballots shall be arranged so as to provide for write-in candidates.

ARTICLE XVIII
CONSTRUCTION

These Bylaws shall be construed and enforced in accordance with the laws of the State of Indiana.

Presidents of the Association of Fraternity Advisors

1977	John Mohr	1985	Barb Robel
1978	Barbara Tootle	1986	Gayle Beyers
1979	Larry Lunsford	1987	Gary Bonas
1980	Larry Lunsford	1988	Terry Appolonia
1981	Bill Brennan	1989	Bridget Guernsey
	Doug Lange	1990	Paul DeWine
1982	Doug Lange	1991	Douglas Case
1983	Shelley Sutherland	1992	Richard Walker
1984	Vic Boschini		

CFEA History

As early as 1883, editors of 14 men's fraternity magazines met in Philadelphia to promote the concept of interfraternal cooperation. Editors of National Interfraternity Conference member organizations met at an annual dinner for many years before officially organizing in 1923.

In the late 1960s, discussions with editors of National Panhellenic Conference and Professional Fraternity Association publications brought about the realization that all editors would benefit from belonging to a single association. Since 1969, the CFEA has actively sought the participation of all Greek-letter society editors and their staffs.

Constitution of the CFEA

(As revised June 1990)

PURPOSE

To stimulate and encourage those engaged in college fraternity journalism and communications; to form a center for the communication and exchange of views of all those interested in fraternity communications; to establish a community of interest through personal contacts; to raise the standard of fraternity journalism and communications; to publish information helpful to its members; and generally to do those things that will aid in elevating our profession and tend toward an intelligent understanding of the general college and professional fraternities and sororities and honor societies by administrators, students, and the general public this College Fraternity Editors Association is formed.

ARTICLE I
NAME

Section 1. The name of this Association shall be the College Fraternity Editors Association.

Section 2. This Association shall be governed by this Constitution and by the procedures set forth in *Robert's Rules of Order.*

ARTICLE II
MEMBERSHIP

Section 1. Regular membership in this Association shall be open to all general college and professional fraternities and sororities and honor societies operating chapters on college and university campuses in the United States and Canada. Only those fraternities and sororities which have paid the annual dues of the Association shall be considered members. Each organization holding regular membership in good standing shall have one vote. Membership includes two (2) representatives, but additional representatives, regardless of their positions within the member organization, may also be included at an additional annual cost per person as determined by the Board of Directors.

Section 2. Affiliate membership may be extended to interfraternity organizations. Affiliate members shall not be entitled to vote or to hold office.

Section 3. Associate membership may be extended upon payment of annual dues as established by the Board of Directors, to any person, commercial suppliers, vendors, and others whose resources enhance fraternalism. Associate members will not be entitled to a vote or to hold office. Individual associate members or representatives of organizations holding associate membership who attend the annual meeting shall pay the same registration fee as members.

Section 4. Honorary membership may be extended to any individual by the Board of Directors based upon past outstanding service to the Association, including but not limited to, service as an elected member of the Board of Directors. Such members shall be entitled to attend annual or special meetings by paying the regular registration fee, but they may not vote except as provided in Section 1 of this article. Additionally, they shall receive *The Fraternity Editor* and other information mailed to the membership for an annual fee, if any, as determined by the Board of Directors.

ARTICLE III
GOVERNMENT

Section 1. This Association shall be governed by the meetings thereof by those members in attendance, and ad interim by the Board of Directors.

Section 2. The fiscal year for this Association shall be from September 1 to August 31, or such other time as the Board of Directors shall designate.

ARTICLE IV
OFFICERS

Section 1. The officers of this Association shall consist of a President, President-Elect, Secretary, and Treasurer, all constituting the Executive Committee. Actions of the Executive Committee shall be reviewed by the Board of Directors.

Section 2. The President, President-Elect, Secretary, Treasurer and four members of the Board of Directors shall be elected by the Association at its annual meeting, for a period of one year. In addition to the officers and the four elected Directors, the immediate past president of the Association shall be a member of the Board of Directors. Should the immediate past president discontinue membership in the Association at the completion of the term or should the immediate past president not wish to continue to serve on the Board of Directors, the membership will elect an additional member to the Board of Directors.

Section 3. Vacancies in the elective office shall be filled by the Executive Committee for the remainder of the term. Any officer or director may be removed for cause by a vote of at least seven members of the Board of Directors or by at least two-thirds mail vote of the regular membership.

Section 4. The President shall preside at all meetings of the Association, of the Executive Committee, and of the Board of Directors.

Section 5. The President-Elect shall perform the duties of the President at all meetings at which the latter is absent.

Section 6. The Secretary shall keep accurate minutes of the meetings of the Association, of the Executive Committee, and of the Board of Directors.

Section 7. The Treasurer shall be in charge of the Association's funds, subject to the supervision of the Board of Directors.

Section 8. The President shall have the authority to appoint, with the approval of the Board, other such offices and committees as deemed necessary for a period of one year.

ARTICLE V
ELECTIONS

Section 1. Three months prior to an annual meeting, the President, with the approval of the Board of Directors, shall appoint a nominations committee of three individual members and shall designate one from among them as chairperson. The nominations committee shall be responsible for reviewing and soliciting from among the Association's membership those willing to serve in elective office and for presenting its recommendations to the membership at the annual meeting. The nominations committee shall endeavor to ensure that its recommendations for elective office include at minimum one individual from each of the categories of fraternal organizations represented in the membership of the Association.

Section 2. The nominations committee shall present its recommended slate to the membership. Nominations may be made from the floor provided that the nominator submit to the Secretary a signed acknowledgement from the person to be nominated that said person is willing to fulfill the responsibilities of the office. Should nominations from the floor be made, election shall be by secret ballot. Election of non-contested offices may be made by acclamation.

ARTICLE VI
MEETINGS

Section 1. The Association shall hold an annual meeting for the conduct of business and for an editors' conference.

Section 2. Special meetings may be held from time to time as the Board of Directors shall determine, but, only such business shall therein be transacted as shall be specified in the call.

Section 3. The Executive Committee and Board of Directors shall meet at such times and places as the President may determine, or by agreement of a majority of the Committee.

Section 4. Special meetings may also be called from time to time on the petition of five or more members, to be received by the Secretary not less than thirty (30) days before the date set for such meeting in the petition. Such petitions shall also state the business to be transacted at the called meeting.

ARTICLE VII
DUES AND ASSESSMENTS

Section 1. Annual dues may be fixed by the membership at a general meeting, to be assessed against members. Such dues shall be devoted only to payment of actual expenses of the Association.

Section 2. The Board of Directors shall determine the registration fee to be levied for individuals attending the annual or special meetings of the Association.

ARTICLE VIII
AMENDMENTS

Section 1. This Constitution may be amended by at least a two-thirds vote of the member fraternities and sororities attending the annual meeting, or at least a two-thirds vote of the member organizations in a mail vote. Proposed amendments shall be received in writing by the President and Secretary at least 60 days prior to the time of voting. The President and Secretary shall be responsible for distributing proposed amendments to the membership at least 30 days prior to the time of voting. Other amendments may be introduced at the annual meeting if at least two-thirds of the members present vote to consider them. No amendment shall be considered unless it meets either of the previous criteria.

Presidents of the College Fraternity Editors Association

1924–26	William C. Levere, Sigma Alpha Epsilon
1926–28	Chester W. Cleveland, Sigma Chi
1928–29	Cecil J. Wilkinson, Phi Gamma Delta
1929–30	George Banta, Jr., Phi Delta Theta
1930–32	Leland F. Leland, Tau Kappa Epsilon
1932–33	Francis W. Shepardson, Beta Theta Pi
1933–34	C. F. Williams, Phi Kappa Psi
1934–35	Charles Edward Thomas, Sigma Nu
1935–36	K. D. Pulcipher, Pi Kappa Alpha
1936–37	Linn C. Lightner, Lambda Chi Alpha
1937–38	George Starr Lasher, Theta Chi
1938–39	Lauren Forman, Sigma Alpha Epsilon
1939–40	F. James Barnes, II, Sigma Phi Epsilon
1940–41	C. W. May, Kappa Alpha Order
1941	Oswald W. Hering, Delta Kappa Epsilon (Died in Office)
1941–42	Leland F. Leland, Tau Kappa Epsilon
1942–43	Robert J. Pilgrim, Phi Kappa Sigma
1943–44	Dr. Hugh J. Ryan, Delta Sigma Phi
1944–45	Lee B. Dover, Zeta Beta Tau
1945–46	Earl F. Schoening, Phi Sigma Kappa
1946–47	John Robson, Sigma Phi Epsilon
1947–48	Frank C. Ferguson, Kappa Sigma
1948–49	Don Gable, Sigma Alpha Epsilon
1949–50	Judge Luther Z. Rosser, Chi Phi
1950–51	Harold P. Davison, Theta Xi
1951–52	Don C. Wolfe, Kappa Delta Rho
1952–53	Francis Wacker, Delta Sigma Phi
1953–54	Robert D. Lynn, Pi Kappa Alpha
1954–55	James Hammerstein, Sigma Alpha Mu
1955–56	Richard J. Young, Phi Kappa Tau
1956–57	Robert J. Simonds, Alpha Tau Omega
1957–58	Hayward S. Biggers, Phi Delta Theta
1958–59	George S. Toll, Alpha Epsilon Pi
1959–60	James F. Hudson, Phi Gamma Delta
1960–61	Jack L. Anson, Phi Kappa Tau
1961–62	Robert E. Jepson, Acacia
1962–63	Ralph F. Burns, Alpha Sigma Phi
1963–64	Harold Jacobsen, Sigma Pi
1964–65	Frank L. Chinery, Phi Kappa Theta
1965–66	Carl J. Gladfelter, Chi Phi
1966–67	Durward W. Owen, Pi Kappa Phi
1967–68	Harry L. Bird, Alpha Tau Omega
1968–69	Tom Cunning, Alpha Chi Rho
1969–70	Haldon C. Dick, Phi Kappa Psi
1970–71	Fred F. Yoder, Sigma Chi
1971–72	Jack W. Jareo, Phi Kappa Tau
1972–73	James M. Brasher, III, Lambda Chi Alpha
1973–74	Stephen Christensen, Kappa Sigma
1974–75	Ernest J. White, Delta Theta Phi
1975–76	R. John Kaegi, Pi Kappa Alpha
1976–77	Dale A. Slivinske, Theta Chi
1977–78	L. David Dickensheets, Tau Kappa Epsilon
1978–79	Dr. James F. Miller, Alpha Chi Sigma
1979–80	Robert L. Off, FarmHouse
1980–81	Robert E. Bernier, Sigma Tau Gamma
1981–82	Evin C. Varner, Alpha Sigma Phi
1982–83	Michael A. Moxley, Tau Kappa Epsilon
1983–84	Robert E. Lyon, Kappa Alpha Order
1984–85	V. Randall McLeary, Lambda Chi Alpha
1985–86	Dr. Charles H. Lippy, Alpha Chi Rho
1986–87	Eleanor B. Hyatt, Chi Omega
1987–88	William D. Krahling, Alpha Tau Omega
1988–89	Dr. Anthony Palmieri III, Kappa Psi
1989–90	William C. Schilling, Alpha Gamma Rho
1990–91	Kris Brandt Riske, Gamma Phi Beta

Part II

CAMPUSES AND THEIR FRATERNITIES

ABILENE CHRISTIAN COLLEGE Abilene, TX. College of liberal arts; coeducational; private; related to Church of Christ; chartered 1906.

PROFESSIONAL
1962 Mu Phi Epsilon

ACHS HONORS
1927 Alpha Chi
1950 Sigma Tau Delta
1954 Kappa Delta Pi
1956 Phi Alpha Theta
1973 Sigma Pi Sigma
1986 Kappa Tau Alpha
1986 Phi Eta Sigma
1990 Kappa Omicron Nu

SERVICE
1960 Alpha Phi Omega

RECOGNITION
1935 Alpha Psi Omega
1958 Blue Key
1959 Kappa Pi
1966 National Block and Bridle
     Club

INACTIVE
1970–85 Phi Mu Alpha—
        Sinfonia

ADAMS STATE COLLEGE OF COLORADO Alamosa, CO. College of liberal arts; teachers college; pre-professional school; coeducational; state control; established 1921.

PROFESSIONAL
1964 Kappa Kappa Psi

ACHS HONORS
1978 Phi Sigma Iota

SERVICE
     The National Spurs

1962 Alpha Phi Omega

RECOGNITION
1950 Alpha Psi Omega
1960 Blue Key

INACTIVE
1985–88 Lambda Chi Alpha

ADELPHI UNIVERSITY Garden City, L.I., NY. Founded 1896; first degree-granting liberal arts college on Long Island; undergraduate, graduate, and evening programs; private, nonsectarian, coeducational.

A Panhellenic Site (individual offices, a lounge, a meeting room) is provided for sororities in one of the residence halls and a meeting room is provided for men's fraternities in one of the men's residence halls. Interfraternity Office is located in the University Center. Individual houses are neither permitted nor planned for.

NIC MEN'S
1963 Pi Lambda Phi
1963 Tau Epsilon Phi

NPHC MEN'S
     Phi Beta Sigma
1972 Alpha Phi Alpha

NPC WOMEN'S
1908 Delta Gamma
1911 Delta Delta Delta
1916 Alpha Epsilon Phi

NPHC WOMEN'S
1975 Alpha Kappa Alpha

PROFESSIONAL
1952 Delta Omicron
1958 Pi Sigma Epsilon
1982 Delta Sigma Pi

ACHS HONORS
     Omicron Delta Epsilon
1931 Sigma Delta Pi
1950 Psi Chi
1952 Alpha Epsilon Delta
1956 Phi Alpha Theta
1959 Pi Delta Phi
1962 Alpha Kappa Delta
1962 Sigma Pi Sigma
1970 Sigma Theta Tau
1974 Delta Mu Delta

1975 Kappa Delta Pi
1982 Pi Sigma Alpha

OTHER HONORS
1964 Pi Mu Epsilon

RECOGNITION
1951 Alpha Psi Omega
1952 Delta Phi Alpha
1957 Beta Beta Beta
1960 Kappa Pi

INACTIVE
1905–54 Kappa Kappa Gamma
1907–51 Kappa Alpha Theta
1913–73 Phi Mu
1920   Phi Sigma Sigma
1922–78 Delta Zeta
1923–77 Sigma Kappa
1926–71 Delta Phi Epsilon
1929–58 Pi Gamma Mu
1951   Eta Sigma Phi
1953–60 Gamma Sigma Epsilon
1965–90 Tau Kappa Epsilon
1967–72 Zeta Beta Tau
1969–74 Sigma Alpha Epsilon

COLONIES
     Alpha Epsilon Pi
1982 Theta Chi

ADRIAN COLLEGE Adrian, MI. College of Liberal Arts; coeducational; private control; related to the Methodist Church. Founded in 1845 as Michigan Union College; incorporated as Adrian College in 1859.

Three (Alpha Tau Omega, Sigma Alpha Epsilon, and Theta Chi) fraternities occupy college-owned houses for which they pay rent, and two (Pi Kappa Alpha and Tau Kappa Epsilon) occupy houses they own. Sororities are housed in college-owned sorority complexes.

NIC MEN'S
1887 Sigma Alpha Epsilon
1961 Tau Kappa Epsilon
1964 Theta Chi
1969 Phi Kappa Sigma

NPC WOMEN'S
1961 Alpha Phi
1961 Chi Omega
1965 Alpha Sigma Alpha

PROFESSIONAL
1966 Alpha Kappa Psi
1971 Sigma Alpha Iota

ACHS HONORS
1950 Pi Delta Phi
1956 Lambda Iota Tau
1964 Alpha Chi
1969 Kappa Delta Pi
1969 Phi Alpha Theta
1973 Psi Chi

1974 Kappa Omicron Nu
1988 Phi Eta Sigma

OTHER HONORS
      National Order of Omega

RECOGNITION
1967 Beta Beta Beta
1971 Pi Kappa Delta

INACTIVE
1878–84 Delta Tau Delta
1881–79 Alpha Tau Omega
1882–44 Kappa Kappa Gamma
1890–46 Delta Delta Delta
1921–34 Theta Alpha Phi
1961–89 Sigma Sigma Sigma
1966–77 Pi Kappa Alpha
1967–73 Phi Gamma Nu
1967–83 Phi Mu Alpha—
            Sinfonia
1969–84 Sigma Kappa

AGNES SCOTT COLLEGE Decatur, GA. College of liberal arts for women; private control; nondenominational. Established 1889.

ACHS HONORS
1931 Mortar Board
1979 Phi Sigma Tau
1985 Phi Sigma Iota
1990 Psi Chi

OTHER HONORS
1926 Phi Beta Kappa

RECOGNITION
1928 Eta Sigma Phi
1933 Chi Beta Phi

INACTIVE
1958–68 Sigma Alpha Iota

AIR FORCE INSTITUTE OF TECHNOLOGY Wright-Patterson Air Force Base, OH. Founded 1926.

ACHS HONORS
      Omicron Delta Epsilon

1959 Tau Beta Pi
1962 Eta Kappa Nu

UNIVERSITY OF AKRON Akron, OH. Fully state supported effective July, 1967, institution of higher learning; organized in 1870; nonsectarian, coeducational; colleges of liberal arts, engineering, education, business administration, nursing, fine and applied arts, and law as well as a general college, evening and adult education division and graduate division; one of two institutions in the U.S. offering the Ph.D. in polymer chemistry. Fraternities and sororities occupy houses and property which they own.

NIC MEN'S
1873 Delta Tau Delta
1875 Phi Delta Theta
1919 Lambda Chi Alpha
1938 Phi Kappa Tau
1942 Phi Sigma Kappa
1942 Theta Chi
1948 Tau Kappa Epsilon
1966 Sigma Pi
1970 Phi Kappa Psi
1985 Sigma Tau Gamma
1986 Phi Gamma Delta

NPHC MEN'S
      Phi Beta Sigma
1925 Alpha Phi Alpha

NPC WOMEN'S
1877 Kappa Kappa Gamma
1879 Delta Gamma
1922 Alpha Gamma Delta
1938 Alpha Delta Pi
1967 Chi Omega
1986 Alpha Phi

NPHC WOMEN'S
1961 Alpha Kappa Alpha
1978 Sigma Gamma Rho

PROFESSIONAL
1962 Phi Alpha Delta
1970 Delta Sigma Pi
1973 Delta Theta Phi
1973 Kappa Kappa Psi
1973 Tau Beta Sigma

1985 Phi Alpha Delta

OTHER PROFESSIONAL
1967 Beta Alpha Psi
1968 Pi Lambda Theta

ACHS HONORS
      Omicron Delta Epsilon
1921 Phi Sigma
1922 Omicron Delta Kappa
1925 Kappa Delta Pi
1932 Pi Sigma Alpha
1940 Phi Eta Sigma
1941 Alpha Lambda Delta
1950 Psi Chi
1953 Phi Alpha Theta
1962 Phi Sigma Tau
1964 Mortar Board
1967 Beta Gamma Sigma
1967 Gamma Theta Upsilon
1968 Sigma Delta Pi
1969 Pi Delta Phi
1969 Sigma Pi Sigma
1971 Eta Kappa Nu
1974 Tau Beta Pi
1977 Kappa Omicron Nu

OTHER HONORS
      National Order of Omega
1962 National Collegiate
      Players

UNIVERSITY OF ALABAMA Tuscaloosa, AL. First instruction at college level, 1831. State institution, coeducational; chartered 1820. Divisions: arts and sciences, chemistry, commerce, dentistry, education, engineering, graduate, home economics, law, medicine, nursing. Extension divisions in six major cities.

The fraternities and sororities own houses built on college-owned land.

NIC MEN'S
1847 Delta Kappa Epsilon
1850 Alpha Delta Phi
1855 Phi Gamma Delta
1856 Sigma Alpha Epsilon
1874 Sigma Nu
1876 Sigma Chi
1877 Phi Delta Theta
1885 Alpha Tau Omega
1885 Kappa Alpha Order
1899 Kappa Sigma
1903 Phi Kappa Sigma
1916 Zeta Beta Tau
1917 Lambda Chi Alpha
1917 Pi Kappa Phi
1920 Chi Phi
1924 Pi Kappa Alpha
1925 Delta Tau Delta
1925 Phi Sigma Kappa
1926 Theta Chi
1927 Delta Chi
1927 Sigma Phi Epsilon
1929 Alpha Phi Delta
1932 Delta Sigma Phi
1964 Beta Theta Pi
1964 Phi Kappa Psi
1975 Kappa Alpha Psi (A)
1975 Tau Kappa Epsilon

NPHC MEN'S
      Phi Beta Sigma
      Phi Beta Sigma

1969 Pi Mu Epsilon
1969 Sigma Xi

RECOGNITION
      Angel Flight
      Arnold Air Society (E-2)
1922 Pi Kappa Delta
1923 Society for Collegiate
      Journalists—Pi Delta
      Epsilon-Alpha Phi Gamma
      (A)
1925 Scabbard and Blade (6)

INACTIVE
1912–78 Phi Mu
1924–31 Alpha Epsilon Phi
1924–37 Phi Epsilon Kappa
1924–39 Pi Gamma Mu
1929   Delta Psi Kappa
1929–72 Zeta Tau Alpha
1931–87 Theta Phi Alpha
1932–62 Alpha Kappa Alpha
1941–73 Alpha Epsilon Pi
1942–68 Pi Omega Pi
1954–84 Alpha Chi Sigma
1962–80 Delta Zeta
1963–70 Sigma Delta Tau
1975–81 Phi Chi Theta

1974 Alpha Phi Alpha
1974 Alpha Phi Alpha

NPC WOMEN'S
1904 Kappa Delta
1907 Alpha Delta Pi
1910 Zeta Tau Alpha
1914 Delta Delta Delta
1921 Alpha Gamma Delta
1922 Chi Omega
1922 Delta Zeta
1924 Alpha Chi Omega
1927 Kappa Kappa Gamma
1931 Phi Mu
1932 Sigma Kappa
1935 Sigma Delta Tau
1949 Pi Beta Phi
1967 Alpha Omicron Pi
1967 Kappa Alpha Theta
1989 Gamma Phi Beta

NPHC WOMEN'S
1972 Delta Sigma Theta (B)
1974 Alpha Kappa Alpha
1974 Delta Sigma Theta (B)
1975 Sigma Gamma Rho

PROFESSIONAL
1922 Phi Alpha Delta
1922 Phi Delta Phi
1922 Theta Tau
1924 Alpha Kappa Psi
1926 Delta Sigma Pi

1951 Psi Omega
1961 Kappa Delta Epsilon
1965 Mu Phi Epsilon
1966 Phi Mu Alpha—Sinfonia
1972 Gamma Iota Sigma
1978 Delta Theta Phi
1983 Phi Alpha Delta

OTHER PROFESSIONAL
1936 Phi Upsilon Omicron
1945 Alpha Epsilon Rho
1948 Beta Alpha Psi
1948 Sigma Delta Chi
1952 Delta Sigma Delta
1953 Alpha Beta Alpha

ACHS HONORS
Omicron Delta Epsilon
1915 Delta Sigma Rho-Tau Kappa Alpha
1922 Kappa Delta Pi
1924 Omicron Delta Kappa
1926 Tau Beta Pi
1929 Mortar Board
1929 Psi Chi
1930 Alpha Lambda Delta
1930 Phi Eta Sigma
1931 Beta Gamma Sigma
1938 Alpha Kappa Delta
1945 Sigma Delta Pi
1948 Chi Epsilon
1948 Phi Alpha Theta
1948 Pi Tau Sigma
1949 Alpha Pi Mu
1949 Sigma Pi Sigma
1956 Pi Sigma Alpha
1957 Pi Kappa Lambda
1958 Sigma Theta Tau
1961 Alpha Sigma Mu
1962 Eta Kappa Nu
1968 Gamma Theta Upsilon
1971 Omega Chi Epsilon
1972 Lambda Iota Tau
1973 Pi Delta Phi
1974 Kappa Tau Alpha
1975 Beta Phi Mu
1979 Phi Sigma Iota
1981 Pi Omega Pi
1982 Pi Sigma Alpha
1988 Lambda Sigma Society

OTHER HONORS
National Order of Omega

UNIVERSITY OF ALABAMA IN BIRMINGHAM
Birmingham, AL. Opened as an extension center of University of Alabama, 1936; designated as an independent campus in University of Alabama System, 1966; consists of University College, Medical Center, and Graduate School.

NIC MEN'S
1975 Lambda Chi Alpha
1979 Tau Kappa Epsilon
1980 Alpha Tau Omega
1980 Kappa Alpha Psi (A)
1982 Theta Chi
1985 Pi Kappa Phi
1986 Delta Sigma Phi
1990 Kappa Sigma

NPC WOMEN'S
1970 Alpha Sigma Tau
1978 Alpha Gamma Delta
1987 Alpha Omicron Pi

1851 Phi Beta Kappa
1922 Pi Mu Epsilon
1939 Sigma Xi
1949 Sigma Gamma Epsilon
1954 Omicron Kappa Upsilon
1970 Order of the Coif

SERVICE
1948 Alpha Phi Omega

RECOGNITION
Arnold Air Society (C-2)
1921 Chi Delta Phi
1924 Gamma Sigma Epsilon
1924 Scabbard and Blade (5)
1930 Alpha Psi Omega
1930 Iota Lambda Sigma
1936 Sigma Delta Psi
1951 Delta Phi Alpha
1951 Kappa Pi
1966 Beta Beta Beta

INACTIVE
1904 Phi Chi
1905 Phi Beta Pi and Theta Kappa Psi (B)
1906 Phi Beta Pi and Theta Kappa Psi (a)
1919-61 Sigma Alpha Mu
1925-40 Chi Beta Phi
1926 Sigma Delta Kappa
1927-40 Pi Lambda Phi
1927-73 Delta Phi Epsilon
1927-88 Alpha Xi Delta
1928-39 Pi Gamma Mu
1930-71 Alpha Sigma Phi
1931 Kappa Beta Pi
1931-51 Zeta Phi Eta
1932-63 Alpha Phi
1932-82 Theta Xi
1937-51 National Collegiate Players
1938-83 Phi Chi Theta
1942-82 Alpha Epsilon Pi
1945-67 Alpha Epsilon Phi
1947-78 Delta Gamma
1952-65 Alpha Chi Sigma
1953 Sigma Gamma Tau
1953-61 Xi Psi Phi
1966-70 Acacia

COLONIES
1986 Phi Kappa Phi

NPHC WOMEN'S
1975 Alpha Kappa Alpha

PROFESSIONAL
1975 Kappa Delta Epsilon
1986 Kappa Delta Epsilon

ACHS HONORS
Omicron Delta Epsilon
1971 Alpha Lambda Delta
1971 Kappa Delta Pi
1973 Beta Gamma Sigma
1975 Omicron Delta Kappa
1975 Phi Kappa Phi
1976 Phi Alpha Theta

1977 Tau Beta Pi
1983 Eta Kappa Nu

OTHER HONORS
National Order of Omega

SERVICE
1969 Alpha Phi Omega

INACTIVE
1972-84 Pi Kappa Alpha
1975-89 Sigma Phi Epsilon
1980-85 Sigma Kappa

UNIVERSITY OF ALABAMA IN HUNTSVILLE
Huntsville, AL. Established 1950; designated an autonomous institution within the University of Alabama System, 1960; Schools: humanities and behavioral sciences, science and engineering, nursing, graduate, and primary medical care.

NIC MEN'S
1977 Delta Chi
1979 Alpha Tau Omega
1979 Pi Kappa Alpha
1988 Kappa Alpha Psi (A)

NPC WOMEN'S
1977 Chi Omega
1977 Delta Zeta
1977 Kappa Delta

NPHC WOMEN'S
1987 Alpha Kappa Alpha

ACHS HONORS
Omicron Delta Epsilon
1969 Sigma Pi Sigma

1973 Phi Alpha Theta
1973 Phi Kappa Phi
1974 Alpha Lambda Delta
1974 Sigma Tau Delta
1976 Sigma Theta Tau
1977 Psi Chi
1978 Eta Kappa Nu
1980 Tau Beta Pi
1982 Omicron Delta Kappa

OTHER HONORS
National Order of Omega

SERVICE
1970 Gamma Sigma Sigma

ALABAMA AGRICULTURAL AND MECHANICAL UNIVERSITY Normal, AL. Land-grant College organized in 1873 and controlled by the State Board of Education; coeducational; offers bachelor of science and master degrees.

NIC MEN'S
1950 Kappa Alpha Psi (A)

NPHC MEN'S
Phi Beta Sigma
1936 Omega Psi Phi
1948 Alpha Phi Alpha
1948 Omega Psi Phi

NPHC WOMEN'S
Zeta Phi Beta
1949 Alpha Kappa Alpha
1949 Delta Sigma Theta (B)
1987 Sigma Gamma Rho

ACHS HONORS
Omicron Delta Epsilon
1948 Alpha Kappa Mu
1971 Delta Mu Delta
1972 Kappa Delta Pi
1974 Sigma Tau Delta
1975 Kappa Omicron Nu

SERVICE
1965 Alpha Phi Omega
1970 Gamma Sigma Sigma

INACTIVE
1972-84 Phi Chi Theta
1980-81 Beta Phi Mu

ALABAMA STATE UNIVERSITY Montgomery, AL. State College; coeducational; founded 1874. Administration does not permit special quarters for fraternities and sororities.

NIC MEN'S
1938 Kappa Alpha Psi (A)

NPHC MEN'S
Phi Beta Sigma
1936 Alpha Phi Alpha

NPHC WOMEN'S
Zeta Phi Beta
1937 Delta Sigma Theta (B)
1938 Alpha Kappa Alpha
1958 Sigma Gamma Rho

PROFESSIONAL
1967 Kappa Kappa Psi
1969 Phi Mu Alpha—Sinfonia
1970 Tau Beta Sigma
1976 Delta Omicron

ACHS HONORS
1947 Alpha Kappa Mu
1963 Sigma Delta Pi
1973 Kappa Delta Pi
1975 Pi Gamma Mu
1977 Delta Mu Delta
1978 Pi Omega Pi

1982 Pi Kappa Lambda
1987 Phi Eta Sigma

OTHER HONORS
1976 Pi Mu Epsilon

SERVICE
1973 Alpha Phi Omega
1975 Gamma Sigma Sigma

RECOGNITION
1939 Alpha Psi Omega
1948 Sigma Delta Psi

INACTIVE
1934–72 Zeta Phi Eta
1947–60 Beta Kappa Chi

UNIVERSITY OF ALASKA Anchorage, AK. University and land-grant college; coeducational; state control; founded 1917.

OTHER PROFESSIONAL
1974 Sigma Delta Chi

ACHS HONORS
Omicron Delta Epsilon

1980 Psi Chi
1983 Phi Alpha Theta

UNIVERSITY OF ALASKA, FAIRBANKS Fairbanks, AK.

ACHS HONORS
Omicron Delta Epsilon
1976 Phi Kappa Phi

1979 Psi Chi
1987 Gamma Theta Upsilon

ALBANY COLLEGE OF PHARMACY Albany, NY. Founded 1881 as the Department of Pharmacy of Union University; coeducational.

PROFESSIONAL
1918 Lambda Kappa Sigma
1921 Rho Pi Phi
1931 Phi Delta Chi

ACHS HONORS
1976 Rho Chi

COLONIES
Kappa Epsilon

ALBANY MEDICAL COLLEGE Albany, NY. Founded 1839; united with Union College in 1873.

OTHER HONORS
1949 Alpha Omega Alpha

INACTIVE
1924   Phi Lambda Kappa

ALBANY STATE COLLEGE Albany, GA. College of liberal arts and teachers college; coeducational; state control. Established 1903 as normal school.

NIC MEN'S
1956 Kappa Alpha Psi (A)

NPHC MEN'S
Phi Beta Sigma
1948 Alpha Phi Alpha
1949 Omega Psi Phi

NPHC WOMEN'S
Zeta Phi Beta
1949 Alpha Kappa Alpha
1952 Delta Sigma Theta (B)
1975 Sigma Gamma Rho

ACHS HONORS
1952 Alpha Kappa Mu
1969 Phi Alpha Theta
1975 Kappa Delta Pi

SERVICE
1974 Alpha Phi Omega

RECOGNITION
1962 Beta Beta Beta

COLONIES
1989 Delta Chi

UNIVERSITY OF ALBERTA Edmonton, AB. Provincially controlled and supported; founded 1908; the largest of the three degree-granting institutions in the province; coeducational; all major disciplines represented through to Ph.D. degree.

Fraternities and sororities may occupy houses owned by them.

NIC MEN'S
1930 Phi Delta Theta
1930 Zeta Psi
1932 Delta Kappa Epsilon
1935 Delta Upsilon
1939 Kappa Sigma
1945 Lambda Chi Alpha
1965 Theta Chi
1970 Phi Gamma Delta
1974 FarmHouse
1989 Kappa Alpha Society

NPC WOMEN'S
1931 Delta Gamma
1931 Kappa Alpha Theta
1931 Pi Beta Phi

OTHER WOMEN'S
1986 CERES

ACHS HONORS
1966 Phi Alpha Theta
1980 Xi Sigma Pi

OTHER HONORS
National Order of Omega
1958 Alpha Omega Alpha

RECOGNITION
1963 Eta Sigma Phi

INACTIVE
1932–59 Delta Delta Delta
1941–72 Sigma Alpha Mu
1964–79 Alpha Gamma Delta
1965–71 Delta Sigma Phi

ALBERTUS MAGNUS COLLEGE New Haven, CT.

ACHS HONORS
1974 Sigma Delta Pi

1979 Phi Sigma Iota

ALBION COLLEGE Albion, MI. Founded in 1835. Liberal arts, four-year institution affiliated with the Methodist Church. Coeducational with an enrollment of 1,650. Offers the B.A. degree as well as pre-professional courses in law, medicine, dentistry and engineering.

Fraternity houses and property are owned by college. The sororities have lodges only and members are required to live in the dormitories.

NIC MEN'S
1876 Delta Tau Delta
1886 Sigma Chi
1889 Alpha Tau Omega
1895 Sigma Nu
1917 Delta Sigma Phi
1926 Tau Kappa Epsilon

NPC WOMEN'S
1887 Alpha Chi Omega
1887 Kappa Alpha Theta
1915 Alpha Xi Delta
1923 Kappa Delta
1990 Phi Mu

PROFESSIONAL
1930 Phi Mu Alpha—Sinfonia
1943 Sigma Alpha Iota

ACHS HONORS
Omicron Delta Epsilon
1911 Delta Sigma Rho-Tau
    Kappa Alpha
1937 Kappa Mu Epsilon
1940 Alpha Lambda Delta
1941 Mortar Board
1942 Omicron Delta Kappa
1958 Phi Alpha Theta

1964 Psi Chi
1979 Phi Sigma Tau
1982 Pi Sigma Alpha
1983 Pi Kappa Lambda

OTHER HONORS
National Order of Omega
1940 Phi Beta Kappa
1971 Sigma Gamma Epsilon

RECOGNITION
1928 Society for Collegiate
    Journalists—Pi Delta
    Epsilon-Alpha Phi Gamma
    (A)
1929 Theta Alpha Phi
1945 Kappa Pi
1949 Sigma Delta Psi
1950 Beta Beta Beta

INACTIVE
1883–87 Delta Gamma
1929–68 Zeta Tau Alpha
1940–70 Delta Zeta
1949–88 Phi Eta Sigma
1952   Eta Sigma Phi
1959–85 Pi Beta Phi
1964–74 Sigma Pi Sigma

ALBRIGHT COLLEGE Reading, PA. College of liberal arts; coeducational; private control; Evangelical United Brethren Church; founded 1856.

NIC MEN'S
1970 Tau Kappa Epsilon
1987 Alpha Chi Rho
1987 Sigma Phi Epsilon
1988 Pi Lambda Phi
1990 Pi Kappa Phi

NPC WOMEN'S
1986 Phi Mu
1987 Alpha Delta Pi
1987 Sigma Kappa

ACHS HONORS
Omicron Delta Epsilon
1965 Phi Alpha Theta

1973 Kappa Omicron Nu
1990 Psi Chi

SERVICE
1957 Alpha Phi Omega
1967 Gamma Sigma Sigma

RECOGNITION
1942 Delta Phi Alpha
1951 Alpha Psi Omega

INACTIVE
1928–59 Pi Gamma Mu
1929–59 Sigma Tau Delta

UNIVERSITY OF ALBUQUERQUE
Albuquerque, NM. College of liberal arts; coeducational; private: Roman Catholic; established 1920; named College of St. Joseph on the Rio Grande until 1966.

ACHS HONORS
1962 Delta Epsilon Sigma

ALCORN STATE UNIVERSITY
Lorman, MS. Land-grant college; coeducational; state control; chartered 1871 as Alcorn University.

NIC MEN'S
1949 Kappa Alpha Psi (A)

NPHC MEN'S
Phi Beta Sigma
1950 Alpha Phi Alpha

NPHC WOMEN'S
1946 Sigma Gamma Rho
1950 Alpha Kappa Alpha
1972 Sigma Gamma Rho

ACHS HONORS
1949 Alpha Kappa Mu
1972 Kappa Omicron Nu

SERVICE
1980 Alpha Phi Omega

RECOGNITION
1975 Beta Beta Beta

ALDERSON-BROADDUS COLLEGE
Philippi, WV. Founded in 1871. Undergraduate college for men and women; private control; affiliated with the American Baptist Churches, USA; located on site of first land battle of the Civil War.

The administration does not permit the fraternities to occupy special quarters.

RECOGNITION
1932 Alpha Psi Omega

ALFRED UNIVERSITY
Alfred, NY. Founded 1836/Chartered 1857. The nonsectarian coeducational university comprises the privately endowed College of Liberal Arts and Sciences, College of Nursing, College of Business and Administration, School of Engineering and the Graduate School; and the publicly funded New York State College of Ceramics.

Ownership of houses and property is by the fraternities and sororities.

NIC MEN'S
1920 Delta Sigma Phi
1925 Lambda Chi Alpha
1933 Zeta Beta Tau
1952 Tau Delta Phi
1971 Alpha Chi Rho

1989 Sigma Alpha Mu

OTHER PROFESSIONAL
1926 Keramos

ACHS HONORS
1927 Pi Gamma Mu

1954 Alpha Lambda Delta
1964 Psi Chi
1969 Phi Sigma Iota
1970 Phi Kappa Phi
1973 Delta Mu Delta

SERVICE
1947 Alpha Phi Omega

RECOGNITION
1936 Blue Key

INACTIVE
1933–54 Theta Alpha Phi
1959–77 Lambda Sigma Society

ALICE LLOYD COLLEGE
Pippa Passes, KY.

PROFESSIONAL
1988 Kappa Delta Epsilon

ALLEGHENY COLLEGE
Meadville, PA. Founded 1815 by citizens of Meadville 27 years after settlement; women admitted 1870; independent coeducational liberal arts college; historical affiliation with United Methodist Church. Graduate and undergraduate summer session.

Five fraternities own the houses and property which they occupy. Two fraternities rent from the college. Members of sororities reside in residence halls. The Greek system operates on a deferred rush system; formal rush occurs during second term. College rents suites on top floor of residence hall to sororities for their meetings and social activities.

NIC MEN'S
1855 Phi Kappa Psi
1860 Phi Gamma Delta
1864 Delta Tau Delta
1879 Phi Delta Theta
1942 Theta Chi

NPHC MEN'S
Phi Beta Sigma

NPC WOMEN'S
1881 Kappa Alpha Theta
1888 Kappa Kappa Gamma
1891 Alpha Chi Omega
1912 Alpha Gamma Delta
1983 Alpha Delta Pi

OTHER PROFESSIONAL
1923 Kappa Phi Kappa

ACHS HONORS
1913 Delta Sigma Rho-Tau
Kappa Alpha
1922 Phi Sigma Iota

1927 Lambda Sigma Society
1990 Psi Chi

OTHER HONORS
National Order of Omega
1902 Phi Beta Kappa

SERVICE
1971 Alpha Phi Omega

RECOGNITION
Angel Flight
Arnold Air Society (E-1)
1933 Sigma Delta Psi

INACTIVE
1887–90 Sigma Alpha Epsilon
1908–09 Sigma Phi Epsilon
1913–34 Alpha Chi Sigma
1914–87 Alpha Chi Rho
1926–70 Alpha Xi Delta
1928–39 Omicron Delta Kappa
1933–79 Kappa Delta Epsilon
1950–84 Pi Gamma Mu

ALLEN UNIVERSITY
Columbia, SC. University; coeducational; private control; African Methodist Episcopal Church. Established 1870 as Paine Institute.

NIC MEN'S
1947 Kappa Alpha Psi (A)

NPHC MEN'S
Phi Beta Sigma
1938 Omega Psi Phi
1946 Alpha Phi Alpha

NPHC WOMEN'S
Zeta Phi Beta
1947 Alpha Kappa Alpha
1948 Delta Sigma Theta (B)
1950 Sigma Gamma Rho

INACTIVE
1949–74 Alpha Kappa Mu

ALLENTOWN COLLEGE OF ST. FRANCIS DE SALES
Center Valley, PA.

ACHS HONORS
1971 Delta Epsilon Sigma
1985 Phi Sigma Iota
1987 Psi Chi

1990 Theta Alpha Kappa

INACTIVE
1979-79 Theta Alpha Kappa

ALLIANCE COLLEGE Cambridge Springs, PA. College of liberal arts; coeducational; private control; nonsectarian; established 1912.

ACHS HONORS
    Sigma Tau Delta

RECOGNITION
1970 Beta Beta Beta

INACTIVE
1959-87 Sigma Tau Gamma

1959-87 Tau Kappa Epsilon
1966-79 Delta Zeta
1968-73 Alpha Kappa Lambda
1968-88 Pi Lambda Phi
1969-79 Pi Gamma Mu

ALMA COLLEGE Alma, MI. College of liberal arts; coeducational; private control; Presbyterian Church. Established 1886.

The fraternities and three of the sororities occupy houses which are leased from the college. Each house has nine to fifteen residents, the other chapter members live in college residence halls. One sorority occupies a section of a residence hall and has a chapter room in the basement of that hall.

NIC MEN'S
1957 Tau Kappa Epsilon
1973 Theta Chi
1984 Sigma Alpha Epsilon
1984 Sigma Chi

NPC WOMEN'S
1984 Gamma Phi Beta
1985 Alpha Gamma Delta
1986 Alpha Xi Delta

PROFESSIONAL
1972 Phi Mu Alpha—Sinfonia

ACHS HONORS
    Omicron Delta Epsilon
1941 Delta Sigma Rho-Tau
    Kappa Alpha
1954 Lambda Iota Tau

1960 Psi Chi
1966 Phi Alpha Theta
1967 Omicron Delta Kappa
1977 Pi Sigma Alpha
1981 Sigma Pi Sigma

SERVICE
1965 Alpha Phi Omega
1971 Gamma Sigma Sigma

RECOGNITION
1932 Alpha Psi Omega
1957 Beta Beta Beta

INACTIVE
1954-73 Delta Sigma Phi
1959-66 Sigma Tau Gamma
1959-71 Alpha Sigma Tau

ALVERNO COLLEGE Milwaukee, WI. College of liberal arts for women and teachers college; privately controlled by the Roman Catholic Church. Established 1887.

PROFESSIONAL
1973 Delta Omicron

ACHS HONORS
1949 Delta Epsilon Sigma

1973 Psi Chi
1973 Sigma Tau Delta
1974 Lambda Iota Tau

AMARILLO COLLEGE Amarillo, TX.

NPHC MEN'S
    Phi Beta Sigma

SERVICE
1970 Alpha Phi Omega

AMERICAN CONSERVATORY OF MUSIC Chicago, IL. Coeducational; founded 1886.

PROFESSIONAL
1906 Sigma Alpha Iota

1923 Mu Phi Epsilon
1929 Delta Omicron

INACTIVE
1900-01 Phi Mu Alpha—
    Sinfonia

1919-63 Phi Beta
1920-83 Phi Mu Alpha—
    Sinfonia

AMERICAN INTERNATIONAL COLLEGE Springfield, MA. College of liberal arts, business administration, and teacher-training; coeducational; private control; nonsectarian. Chartered as French-Protestant College 1885; changed to French-American College 1894; to present name 1905.

Ownership of fraternity property is by the fraternity.

PROFESSIONAL
1974 Phi Gamma Nu

ACHS HONORS
    Omicron Delta Epsilon
1947 Alpha Chi
1965 Phi Alpha Theta
1967 Psi Chi
1978 Psi Chi

SERVICE
1950 Alpha Phi Omega

INACTIVE
-77   Alpha Sigma Tau
1959-84 Tau Kappa Epsilon
1964-69 Phi Sigma Kappa
1966-72 Theta Chi

AMERICAN UNIVERSITY Washington, DC. University, college of liveral arts; professional schools; coeducational; private control; Methodist Church; chartered 1893; Washington College of Law became part of the university in 1949.

The fraternities may own houses which stand on college-owned land. Sororities are given social rooms in residence halls.

NIC MEN'S
1936 Phi Sigma Kappa
1940 Alpha Sigma Phi
1943 Alpha Tau Omega
1960 Tau Epsilon Phi
1963 Zeta Beta Tau
1969 Alpha Epsilon Pi
1981 Kappa Alpha Psi (A)
1989 Sigma Alpha Mu

NPC WOMEN'S
1933 Phi Mu
1936 Delta Gamma
1937 Alpha Chi Omega
1959 Alpha Epsilon Phi
1962 Phi Sigma Sigma
1987 Sigma Delta Tau

NPHC WOMEN'S
1976 Delta Sigma Theta (B)
1977 Alpha Kappa Alpha

PROFESSIONAL
1941 Delta Theta Phi
1959 Mu Phi Epsilon
1960 Phi Alpha Delta
1962 Pi Sigma Epsilon
1965 Phi Delta Phi
1969 Alpha Chi Sigma

OTHER PROFESSIONAL
1916 Kappa Beta Pi
1952 Sigma Delta Chi
1954 Kappa Phi Kappa
1957 Women in Communications

ACHS HONORS
    Omicron Delta Epsilon
    Pi Alpha Alpha
1932 Delta Sigma Rho-Tau
    Kappa Alpha

1938 Omicron Delta Kappa
1954 Pi Sigma Alpha
1956 Phi Alpha Theta
1958 Psi Chi
1964 Phi Kappa Phi
1966 Kappa Tau Alpha
1968 Mortar Board
1971 Sigma Pi Sigma
1974 Alpha Epsilon Delta
1981 Alpha Lambda Delta

OTHER HONORS
    National Order of Omega

SERVICE
1949 Alpha Phi Omega
1965 Gamma Sigma Sigma

RECOGNITION
1923 Phi Delta Gamma
1945 Alpha Psi Omega
1949 Delta Phi Alpha
1960 Rho Epsilon

INACTIVE
1904-44 Sigma Nu Phi
1931-78 Pi Gamma Mu
1932-76 Beta Beta Beta
1937-44 Alpha Phi
1943-74 Kappa Delta
1954   Alpha Eta Rho
1955-67 Kappa Delta Epsilon
1959   Zeta Phi Eta
1969-71 Zeta Psi
1969-77 Phi Mu Alpha—
    Sinfonia

COLONIES
1990 Delta Tau Delta

AMERICAN UNIVERSITY OF BEIRUT Beirut, LE.

OTHER PROFESSIONAL	OTHER HONORS
1927 Delta Sigma Theta (C)	1958 Alpha Omega Alpha

AMERICAN UNIVERSITY IN CAIRO Cairo, EG.

RECOGNITION	INACTIVE
1950 Alpha Psi Omega	–86 Omicron Delta Epsilon

UNIVERSITY OF THE AMERICAS Toluca, MX. Established 1956. Formerly Mexico City College.

OTHER WOMEN'S	1971 Alpha Chi
1961 Kappa Beta Gamma	
ACHS HONORS	INACTIVE
Omicron Delta Epsilon	1958–75 Delta Sigma Pi

AMHERST COLLEGE Amherst, MA. College of liberal arts and sciences; private control; nonsectarian. Founded 1821; chartered 1825; board of trustees also manage the Folger Shakespeare Memorial Library in Washington, D.C.

Ownership of fraternity house and lot has been transferred to the college by 12 fraternities, and then leased back to the fraternity corporations. By terms of the lease, the fraternities operate the houses, and remain responsible for maintenance and upkeep. The lease calls for a nominal fee as rent. The college pays the taxes and insurance, assumes costs of certain safety expenses, and remits an in lieu or room-rent to each chapter. Room rent for all students is collected as part of the college fee. Until a few years ago, all of the Amherst fraternities owned their own buildings on their own land.

NIC MEN'S	INACTIVE
1841 Psi Upsilon	1836–89 Alpha Delta Phi
1846 Delta Kappa Epsilon	1847–71 Delta Upsilon
1864 Chi Psi	1858–59 Zeta Psi
1885 Theta Delta Chi	1873–80 Chi Phi
	1883–68 Beta Theta Pi
ACHS HONORS	1888–56 Phi Delta Theta
1913 Delta Sigma Rho-Tau	1893–62 Phi Gamma Delta
Kappa Alpha	1895–48 Phi Kappa Psi
	1918–46 Delta Tau Delta
OTHER HONORS	1922–49 Alpha Phi Alpha
National Order of Omega	1927–31 Pi Lambda Phi
1853 Phi Beta Kappa	1932–57 Theta Xi
1950 Sigma Xi	

ANDERSON COLLEGE Anderson, IN. College of liberal arts; theological seminary; coeducational; private control; Church of God. Established 1917.

ACHS HONORS	RECOGNITION
1947 Sigma Tau Delta	1948 Alpha Psi Omega
1957 Kappa Mu Epsilon	1948 Sigma Zeta
1959 Alpha Chi	1963 Society for Collegiate
1966 Phi Eta Sigma	Journalists—Pi Delta
1970 Alpha Lambda Delta	Epsilon-Alpha Phi Gamma
1971 Kappa Delta Pi	(A)
1975 Pi Kappa Lambda	
1977 Delta Mu Delta	INACTIVE
	1965–77 Pi Gamma Mu

ANDREWS UNIVERSITY Berrien Springs, MI.

ACHS HONORS	1987 Theta Alpha Kappa
Omicron Delta Epsilon	1989 Phi Kappa Phi
1969 Phi Alpha Theta	1990 Kappa Omicron Nu
1970 Delta Mu Delta	
1974 Sigma Pi Sigma	
1978 Psi Chi	OTHER HONORS
1982 Pi Kappa Lambda	1970 Pi Mu Epsilon

ANGELO STATE COLLEGE San Angelo, TX. Founded 1936 as a two-year institution; became four-year state-supported undergraduate college in 1965; coeducational.

NIC MEN'S	1969 Sigma Delta Pi
1970 Lambda Chi Alpha	1971 Alpha Lambda Delta
1971 Pi Kappa Alpha	1976 Sigma Tau Delta
1974 Sigma Phi Epsilon	1977 Sigma Pi Sigma
	1982 Pi Gamma Mu
NPC WOMEN'S	
1975 Delta Zeta	OTHER HONORS
1977 Sigma Kappa	1971 Pi Mu Epsilon
PROFESSIONAL	SERVICE
1967 Delta Sigma Pi	1976 Alpha Phi Omega
1968 Kappa Kappa Psi	
1975 Sigma Alpha Iota	RECOGNITION
1978 Phi Mu Alpha—Sinfonia	1970 Gamma Sigma Epsilon
	1971 Pi Kappa Delta
ACHS HONORS	
1968 Alpha Chi	INACTIVE
1968 Phi Alpha Theta	1968–76 Phi Eta Sigma
1969 Kappa Delta Pi	1972–77 Alpha Kappa Lambda

ANNA MARIA COLLEGE FOR WOMEN Paxton, MA. College of liberal arts for women; private control; Roman Catholic Church; founded 1946.

ACHS HONORS	1956 Delta Epsilon Sigma
1955 Lambda Iota Tau	

ANNHURST COLLEGE South Woodstock, CT. College of liberal arts for men and women; private control; fully accredited. Established 1941.

ACHS HONORS	RECOGNITION
1949 Delta Epsilon Sigma	1973 Sigma Zeta
1968 Lambda Iota Tau	1976 Kappa Pi

APPALACHIAN STATE UNIVERSITY Boone, NC. Chartered in 1903, became part of the sixteen campus UNC System in 1967. ASU is a comprehensive university composed of five colleges offering over 200 undergraduate and graduate majors.

Some fraternities own their own houses, some rent facilities and some fraternities and all sororities live in residence halls.

NIC MEN'S	NPC WOMEN'S
1973 Pi Kappa Phi	1973 Delta Zeta
1973 Tau Kappa Epsilon	1973 Kappa Delta
1974 Kappa Sigma	1974 Chi Omega
1975 Lambda Chi Alpha	1975 Alpha Delta Pi
1975 Sigma Phi Epsilon	1983 Phi Mu
1976 Kappa Alpha Order	1985 Sigma Kappa
1986 Delta Chi	
1986 Kappa Alpha Psi (A)	NPHC WOMEN'S
	1987 Alpha Kappa Alpha

PROFESSIONAL
1967 Phi Mu Alpha—Sinfonia
1968 Sigma Alpha Iota
1979 Gamma Iota Sigma

OTHER PROFESSIONAL
1977 Alpha Epsilon Rho

ACHS HONORS
     Omicron Delta Epsilon
1957 Pi Gamma Mu
1962 Alpha Chi
1963 Pi Delta Phi
1964 Sigma Delta Pi
1967 Kappa Delta Pi
1969 Phi Alpha Theta
1969 Sigma Pi Sigma
1971 Pi Kappa Lambda
1974 Gamma Theta Upsilon
1974 Phi Kappa Phi
1976 Kappa Omicron Nu

1976 Pi Sigma Alpha
1982 Psi Chi
1986 Phi Eta Sigma

OTHER HONORS
     National Order of Omega
1976 Pi Mu Epsilon

SERVICE
1967 Alpha Phi Omega
1971 Gamma Sigma Sigma

RECOGNITION
1948 Alpha Psi Omega
1950 Pi Kappa Delta
1954 Beta Beta Beta

INACTIVE
1955–73 Pi Omega Pi

COLONIES
     Pi Lambda Phi

AQUINAS COLLEGE Grand Rapids, MI. College of liberal arts; coeducational; private control; Roman Catholic Church. Established 1886.

ACHS HONORS
     Omicron Delta Epsilon
1950 Delta Epsilon Sigma
1954 Lambda Iota Tau
1962 Phi Alpha Theta

1972 Gamma Theta Upsilon
1981 Psi Chi

RECOGNITION
1966 Beta Beta Beta

ARAPAHOE COMMUNITY COLLEGE Littleton, CO.

SERVICE
1969 Alpha Phi Omega

UNIVERSITY OF ARIZONA Tucson, AZ. Founded by the territorial legislature in 1885; first instruction 1891; land-grant institution; coeducational university; fourteen colleges and divisions including a graduate college, state control; nonsectarian.

A number of fraternities own their houses on their own land; others lease their houses. Some which lease rent from the university houses which are built on land owned by the university. They have an option to purchase the houses at the end of forty years. One sorority has such an arrangement. All other sororities own their houses and the land on which they are built.

NIC MEN'S
1915 Kappa Sigma
1917 Sigma Alpha Epsilon
1918 Sigma Nu
1921 Sigma Chi
1922 Phi Delta Theta
1925 Delta Chi
1925 Pi Kappa Alpha
1926 Zeta Beta Tau
1930 Alpha Tau Omega
1931 Phi Gamma Delta
1947 Lambda Chi Alpha
1947 Phi Kappa Psi
1947 Tau Delta Phi
1951 Phi Kappa Theta
1954 Sigma Phi Epsilon
1956 Kappa Alpha Psi (A)
1959 Alpha Gamma Rho

1959 Delta Tau Delta
1961 Alpha Kappa Lambda
1962 Sigma Alpha Mu
1964 Alpha Epsilon Pi
1968 Phi Sigma Kappa
1989 Beta Theta Pi

NPHC MEN'S
1968 Alpha Phi Alpha

NPC WOMEN'S
1917 Kappa Alpha Theta
1917 Pi Beta Phi
1920 Kappa Kappa Gamma
1922 Chi Omega
1922 Gamma Phi Beta
1923 Delta Gamma
1926 Alpha Phi
1930 Alpha Chi Omega

1940 Alpha Epsilon Phi
1957 Alpha Delta Pi
1959 Alpha Omicron Pi
1959 Sigma Delta Tau
1978 Sigma Kappa

NPHC WOMEN'S
1975 Alpha Kappa Alpha
1975 Delta Sigma Theta (B)

OTHER WOMEN'S
     Lambda Delta Sigma

PROFESSIONAL
1923 Alpha Kappa Psi
1923 Phi Alpha Delta
1927 Sigma Alpha Iota
1929 Kappa Kappa Psi
1929 Phi Delta Phi
1930 Theta Tau
1950 Kappa Psi
1950 Phi Delta Chi
1950 Tau Beta Sigma
1951 Delta Sigma Pi
1952 Kappa Epsilon
1958 Phi Chi Theta
1959 Delta Psi Kappa
1967 Alpha Chi Sigma
1986 Phi Alpha Delta

OTHER PROFESSIONAL
1927 Alpha Zeta
1928 Pi Lambda Theta
1932 Kappa Beta Pi
1951 Alpha Tau Alpha
1962 Beta Alpha Psi
1963 Sigma Delta Chi

ACHS HONORS
     Omicron Delta Epsilon
     Pi Alpha Alpha
1916 Phi Kappa Phi
1926 Mortar Board
1926 Tau Beta Pi
1930 Sigma Delta Pi
1941 Pi Delta Phi
1947 Pi Omega Pi
1948 Beta Gamma Sigma
1950 Sigma Pi Sigma
1953 Alpha Kappa Delta
1954 Rho Chi
1957 Psi Chi
1958 Phi Alpha Theta
1959 Phi Eta Sigma
1961 Kappa Omicron Nu
1962 Pi Sigma Alpha
1966 Kappa Delta Pi
1967 Alpha Epsilon Delta

1970 Kappa Tau Alpha
1974 Sigma Theta Tau
1977 Beta Phi Mu
1979 Sigma Lambda Alpha
1983 Gamma Theta Upsilon
1987 Sigma Lambda Alpha

OTHER HONORS
     National Order of Omega
1926 National Collegiate
          Players
1928 Sigma Xi
1932 Phi Beta Kappa
1941 Pi Mu Epsilon
1958 Gamma Sigma Delta
1959 Sigma Gamma Epsilon
1970 Order of the Coif
1971 Alpha Omega Alpha

SERVICE
     The National Spurs
1949 Alpha Phi Omega

RECOGNITION
     Angel Flight
     Arnold Air Society (I)
1923 Scabbard and Blade (4)
1926 Phi Lambda Upsilon
1933 Blue Key
1936 Sigma Delta Psi
1956 Beta Beta Beta
1961 Delta Phi Alpha
1961 Pi Kappa Delta

INACTIVE
1920–34 Theta Alpha Phi
1927–42 Kappa Omicron Nu
1927–87 Phi Mu Alpha—
          Sinfonia
1930–78 Delta Zeta
1939   Zeta Phi Eta
1941–72 Theta Chi
1946–84 Delta Delta Delta
1948–63 Delta Sigma Phi
1949–61 Kappa Alpha Order
1950–71 Acacia
1951–58 Rho Chi
1951–61 Alpha Xi Delta
1951–63 Pi Kappa Phi
1955–69 Alpha Sigma Phi
1958–81 Alpha Lambda Delta
1959–69 Beta Theta Pi
1959–70 Delta Upsilon
1962–77 Phi Mu
1966–70 Chi Phi
1967–86 Tau Kappa Epsilon

ARIZONA STATE UNIVERSITY Tempe, AZ. Founded as a territorial school in old Arizona Territory in 1885. Oldest institution of higher learning in the state. Coeducational; full graduate and undergraduate programs; state control.

Fifteen fraternities lease their houses from the University, through Federal government financing; four fraternities rent their houses or have none. Sorority members are housed in a university residence hall; each group has its own floor.

NIC MEN'S
1948 Delta Sigma Phi
1948 Kappa Alpha Psi (A)
1948 Tau Kappa Epsilon

1949 Delta Chi
1949 Phi Sigma Kappa
1951 Alpha Epsilon Pi
1951 Alpha Tau Omega

1951 Lambda Chi Alpha
1951 Pi Kappa Alpha
1951 Sigma Pi
1952 Sigma Phi Epsilon
1953 Theta Chi
1955 Sigma Nu
1958 Phi Delta Theta
1960 Sigma Chi
1961 Sigma Alpha Epsilon
1961 Theta Delta Chi
1962 Phi Kappa Psi
1963 Kappa Sigma
1965 Phi Gamma Delta
1977 Beta Theta Pi
1985 Delta Kappa Epsilon
1987 Sigma Alpha Mu
1988 Delta Tau Delta

OTHER MEN'S
    Sigma Gamma Chi

NPHC MEN'S
    Phi Beta Sigma
1976 Alpha Phi Alpha

NPC WOMEN'S
1949 Gamma Phi Beta
1950 Alpha Delta Pi
1950 Sigma Sigma Sigma
1951 Chi Omega
1952 Kappa Delta
1958 Alpha Phi
1958 Delta Gamma
1959 Kappa Alpha Theta
1959 Kappa Kappa Gamma
1965 Delta Delta Delta
1965 Pi Beta Phi
1982 Alpha Chi Omega
1987 Alpha Gamma Delta
1989 Sigma Kappa

NPHC WOMEN'S
1952 Sigma Gamma Rho
1970 Alpha Kappa Alpha
1972 Delta Sigma Theta (B)

OTHER WOMEN'S
    Lambda Delta Sigma

PROFESSIONAL
1949 Kappa Kappa Psi
1949 Tau Beta Sigma
1951 Delta Sigma Pi
1958 Pi Sigma Epsilon
1959 Sigma Alpha Iota
1961 Phi Mu Alpha—Sinfonia
1963 Pi Sigma Epsilon
1971 Delta Theta Phi
1971 Phi Delta Phi
1972 Alpha Kappa Psi
1972 Phi Alpha Delta
1975 Alpha Chi Sigma
1984 Phi Alpha Delta

OTHER PROFESSIONAL
1956 Phi Epsilon Kappa
1960 Phi Upsilon Omicron
1960 Sigma Delta Chi
1963 Beta Alpha Psi
1964 Alpha Zeta
1966 Delta Pi Epsilon

1967 Pi Lambda Theta
1971 Alpha Epsilon Rho

ACHS HONORS
    Omicron Delta Epsilon
    Pi Alpha Alpha
1930 Kappa Delta Pi
1932 Gamma Theta Upsilon
1932 Sigma Tau Delta
1938 Pi Omega Pi
1951 Psi Chi
1954 Phi Kappa Phi
1958 Alpha Lambda Delta
1960 Alpha Epsilon Delta
1961 Alpha Kappa Delta
1961 Pi Sigma Alpha
1962 Alpha Pi Mu
1963 Beta Gamma Sigma
1963 Eta Kappa Nu
1963 Mortar Board
1963 Phi Alpha Theta
1963 Tau Beta Pi
1964 Pi Tau Sigma
1969 Sigma Delta Pi
1976 Sigma Theta Tau
1980 Omicron Delta Kappa
1983 Sigma Pi Sigma
1985 Chi Epsilon
1990 Pi Kappa Lambda

OTHER HONORS
    National Order of Omega
1963 National Collegiate
    Players
1965 Sigma Xi
1973 Phi Beta Kappa

SERVICE
1949 Alpha Phi Omega

RECOGNITION
    Angel Flight
    Arnold Air Society (I)
1932 Lambda Delta Lambda
1936 Pi Kappa Delta
1938 Sigma Delta Psi
1941 Blue Key
1954 Beta Beta Beta
1963 Sigma Iota Epsilon
1971 Phi Lambda Upsilon

INACTIVE
1939–46 Pi Gamma Mu
1950   Kappa Phi Kappa
1950   Sigma Epsilon Sigma
1950–54 Kappa Delta Epsilon
1951–55 Delta Phi Kappa
1952–64 Alpha Sigma Alpha
1952–80 Phi Eta Sigma
1953–70 Alpha Beta Alpha
1958–72 Alpha Epsilon Phi
1958–80 Alpha Gamma Rho
1962–70 Alpha Rho Chi
1968–79 Phi Chi Theta
1969–72 Zeta Beta Tau
1975–84 Gamma Iota Sigma

COLONIES
    Alpha Tau Omega
1990 Delta Upsilon

UNIVERSITY OF ARKANSAS Fayetteville, AR. State land-grant university; established in 1871 at Fayetteville. Coeducational; instruction in five undergraduate colleges, four professional schools, and many graduate programs. Medical center located at Little Rock.

A number of fraternities and sororities occupy houses on their own land; however, the majority are owned by the university and are leased to them.

NIC MEN'S
1890 Kappa Sigma
1894 Sigma Alpha Epsilon
1904 Pi Kappa Alpha
1904 Sigma Nu
1905 Sigma Chi
1907 Sigma Phi Epsilon
1925 Lambda Chi Alpha
1934 Alpha Gamma Rho
1948 Phi Delta Theta
1949 Kappa Alpha Psi (A)
1954 FarmHouse
1961 Tau Kappa Epsilon
1969 Phi Gamma Delta
1973 Tau Kappa Epsilon
1975 Delta Upsilon
1979 Kappa Alpha Psi (A)
1984 Sigma Tau Gamma
1985 Phi Kappa Tau

NPHC MEN'S
    Phi Beta Sigma
1975 Alpha Phi Alpha

NPC WOMEN'S
1895 Chi Omega
1903 Zeta Tau Alpha
1909 Pi Beta Phi
1913 Delta Delta Delta
1923 Phi Mu
1925 Kappa Kappa Gamma
1930 Delta Gamma
1957 Alpha Delta Pi
1973 Alpha Xi Delta
1989 Kappa Delta

NPHC WOMEN'S
1943 Sigma Gamma Rho
1951 Alpha Kappa Alpha
1970 Alpha Kappa Alpha
1973 Alpha Kappa Alpha
1974 Alpha Kappa Alpha
1974 Delta Sigma Theta (B)
1975 Delta Sigma Theta (B)
1976 Alpha Kappa Alpha

PROFESSIONAL
1906 Phi Alpha Delta
1908 Delta Theta Phi
1924 Kappa Kappa Psi
1925 Phi Mu Alpha—Sinfonia
1925 Sigma Alpha Iota
1928 Alpha Chi Sigma
1928 Alpha Kappa Psi
1928 Theta Tau
1941 Delta Theta Phi
1950 Tau Beta Sigma
1955 Kappa Psi
1967 Phi Delta Chi
1981 Alpha Rho Chi
1985 Phi Alpha Delta
1990 Sigma Alpha

OTHER PROFESSIONAL
1917 Alpha Zeta

1943 Phi Upsilon Omicron
1951 Beta Alpha Psi
1954 Alpha Tau Alpha
1967 Kappa Beta Pi

ACHS HONORS
    Omicron Delta Epsilon
1914 Delta Sigma Rho-Tau
    Kappa Alpha
1914 Tau Beta Pi
1921 Phi Alpha Theta
1924 Kappa Delta Pi
1931 Phi Eta Sigma
1932 Beta Gamma Sigma
1936 Kappa Tau Alpha
1938 Alpha Epsilon Delta
1939 Omicron Delta Kappa
1940 Mortar Board
1948 Sigma Pi Sigma
1950 Alpha Kappa Delta
1950 Sigma Delta Pi
1955 Rho Chi
1956 Alpha Pi Mu
1959 Eta Kappa Nu
1959 Pi Tau Sigma
1961 Alpha Epsilon
1962 Chi Epsilon
1963 Gamma Theta Upsilon
1968 Pi Sigma Alpha
1970 Omega Chi Epsilon
1975 Pi Delta Phi
1977 Tau Sigma Delta
1982 Phi Kappa Phi
1984 Pi Kappa Lambda
1988 Sigma Lambda Alpha

OTHER HONORS
    National Order of Omega
1931 Pi Mu Epsilon
1932 Phi Beta Kappa
1947 National Collegiate
    Players
1949 Sigma Gamma Epsilon
1953 Sigma Xi
1954 Gamma Sigma Delta
1955 Alpha Omega Alpha

SERVICE
1939 Alpha Phi Omega
1972 Gamma Sigma Sigma

RECOGNITION
    Angel Flight
    Arnold Air Society (G-1)
1916 Scabbard and Blade (2)
1927 Sigma Delta Psi
1928 Blue Key
1941 Kappa Pi
1970 Sigma Iota Epsilon
1971 Sigma Phi Alpha
1973 Pi Kappa Delta
1976 Pi Kappa Delta

INACTIVE
1882–64 Alpha Tau Omega

1895–60 Kappa Alpha Order
1906–39 Phi Rho Sigma
1915   Phi Chi
1922   Phi Alpha Tau
1923–49 Phi Beta Pi and Theta
         Kappa Psi (B)
1929–77 Psi Chi
1932–55 Zeta Beta Tau
1938   Phi Beta Pi and Theta
         Kappa Psi (a)
1942–82 Alpha Lambda Delta

1945–60 Phi Sigma
1948–54 Delta Sigma Phi
1948–77 Sigma Pi
1950   Eta Sigma Phi
1950   Phi Gamma Nu
1951–74 Acacia
1961–77 Alpha Chi Omega
1964–85 Alpha Kappa Lambda
1966–89 Kappa Alpha Theta
1970–75 Delta Sigma Pi
1979–91 Phi Kappa Psi

UNIVERSITY OF ARKANSAS AT LITTLE ROCK

Little Rock, AR. Founded 1927; coeducational; private control.

The fraternities and sororities own lodges on their property which are used for meetings and entertainment.

NIC MEN'S
1963 Kappa Sigma
1965 Pi Kappa Alpha
1974 Sigma Phi Epsilon
1975 Kappa Alpha Psi (A)

NPHC MEN'S
1976 Alpha Phi Alpha

NPC WOMEN'S
1963 Delta Delta Delta
1963 Pi Beta Phi
1964 Chi Omega

PROFESSIONAL
1964 Kappa Epsilon
1967 Phi Alpha Delta
1971 Delta Theta Phi
1971 Sigma Alpha Iota

OTHER PROFESSIONAL
1967 Kappa Beta Pi

1975 Sigma Delta Chi
1977 Alpha Epsilon Rho

ACHS HONORS
1963 Phi Alpha Theta
1972 Phi Kappa Phi
1976 Kappa Delta Pi
1977 Beta Gamma Sigma
1977 Kappa Tau Alpha
1979 Pi Sigma Alpha
1981 Sigma Pi Sigma

OTHER HONORS
      National Order of Omega
1963 Sigma Xi

INACTIVE
1963–81 Kappa Kappa Gamma
1965–80 Sigma Alpha Epsilon
1968–78 Phi Mu Alpha—
         Sinfonia

UNIVERSITY OF ARKANSAS AT MONTICELLO

Monticello, AR. College of liberal arts and technological institution; coeducational; state control; established 1909. The college furnishes suites for the fraternities in college dormitories.

NIC MEN'S
1938 Sigma Tau Gamma
1940 Phi Lambda Chi
1980 Kappa Alpha Psi (A)

NPHC MEN'S
      Phi Beta Sigma

NPC WOMEN'S
1962 Alpha Sigma Tau
1984 Sigma Sigma Sigma

PROFESSIONAL
1971 Kappa Kappa Psi

1985 Phi Alpha Delta

SERVICE
1984 Alpha Phi Omega

INACTIVE
1942–88 Theta Xi
1974–79 Sigma Kappa
1982–84 Phi Mu Alpha—
         Sinfonia

UNIVERSITY OF ARKANSAS AT PINE BLUFF

Pine Bluff, AR. Four-year land-grant college; coeducational; state control; created by legislative act 1873; established as normal school 1875; became four-year college in 1929.

NPHC MEN'S
      Phi Beta Sigma

NPHC WOMEN'S
      Zeta Phi Beta

PROFESSIONAL
1970 Kappa Kappa Psi

OTHER PROFESSIONAL
1966 Alpha Tau Alpha

ACHS HONORS
1938 Alpha Kappa Mu

1973 Phi Alpha Theta
1975 Sigma Tau Delta
1990 Kappa Omicron Nu

SERVICE
1975 Alpha Phi Omega

ARKANSAS COLLEGE

Batesville, AR. College of liberal arts; coeducational; private control; Presbyterian Synod. Chartered 1872.

NIC MEN'S
1973 Kappa Sigma

ACHS HONORS
1960 Alpha Chi

1971 Sigma Tau Delta

RECOGNITION
1927 Alpha Psi Omega

ARKANSAS BAPTIST COLLEGE   Little Rock, AR.

NPHC MEN'S
      Phi Beta Sigma

ARKANSAS STATE UNIVERSITY

Jonesboro, AR. Multipurpose institution; coeducational; state control; established 1909.

The university furnishes space for fraternity and sorority suites.

NIC MEN'S
1948 Pi Kappa Alpha
1948 Sigma Pi
1949 Tau Kappa Epsilon
1955 Sigma Phi Epsilon
1959 Lambda Chi Alpha
1967 Kappa Alpha Order
1968 Alpha Tau Omega
1973 Alpha Gamma Rho
1975 Kappa Alpha Psi (A)
1987 Sigma Chi

NPHC MEN'S
1973 Alpha Phi Alpha

NPC WOMEN'S
1948 Alpha Gamma Delta
1949 Alpha Omicron Pi
1951 Phi Mu
1961 Chi Omega
1968 Kappa Delta
1968 Zeta Tau Alpha

NPHC WOMEN'S
1973 Delta Sigma Theta (B)

PROFESSIONAL
1960 Alpha Kappa Psi
1964 Kappa Kappa Psi
1965 Tau Beta Sigma
1967 Phi Mu Alpha—Sinfonia
1967 Sigma Alpha Iota
1978 Gamma Iota Sigma

OTHER PROFESSIONAL
1964 Alpha Tau Alpha

1971 Sigma Delta Chi
1976 Alpha Epsilon Rho

ACHS HONORS
      Omicron Delta Epsilon
1934 Pi Gamma Mu
1939 Pi Omega Pi
1951 Kappa Delta Pi
1960 Phi Alpha Theta
1960 Phi Eta Sigma
1965 Alpha Lambda Delta
1965 Kappa Mu Epsilon
1966 Lambda Iota Tau
1971 Sigma Pi Sigma
1972 Phi Kappa Phi
1978 Pi Sigma Alpha
1979 Psi Chi
1981 Kappa Tau Alpha
1988 Pi Kappa Lambda

SERVICE
1978 Alpha Phi Omega

RECOGNITION
1935 Alpha Psi Omega
1938 Scabbard and Blade (7)
1946 Sigma Delta Psi
1948 Alpha Psi Omega
1959 National Block and Bridle
      Club

INACTIVE
1931–37 Lambda Delta Lambda
1932   Phi Beta

ARKANSAS TECH UNIVERSITY

Russellville, AR. Colleges of Business Education, Liberal and Fine Arts, Physical and Life Sciences, Systems Science; coeducational; state control; established 1909 as agricultural and engineering school.

NIC MEN'S
1977 Lambda Chi Alpha
1977 Phi Lambda Chi
1977 Sigma Phi Epsilon
1977 Theta Chi

NPC WOMEN'S
1977 Delta Zeta
1977 Phi Mu
1977 Zeta Tau Alpha

PROFESSIONAL
1958 Kappa Kappa Psi
1958 Tau Beta Sigma
1975 Phi Mu Alpha—Sinfonia
1975 Sigma Alpha Iota

ACHS HONORS
1968 Kappa Delta Pi

1969 Alpha Chi
1989 Phi Eta Sigma

OTHER HONORS
National Order of Omega
1961 National Collegiate
Players

SERVICE
1969 Alpha Phi Omega

RECOGNITION
1954 Blue Key
1958 Cardinal Key
1962 Scabbard and Blade (15)
1966 Kappa Pi

INACTIVE
1983–86 Alpha Sigma Tau

ARMSTRONG COLLEGE Berkeley, CA. Founded by J. Evan Armstrong in 1918; undergraduate colleges of accounting, business administration, and secretarial administration. Graduate school of business administration. Coeducational, private control, nonsectarian.

Fraternities and sororities do not have houses. Meetings are held at the college or in members' homes. No restriction about ownership or use of houses if groups do with to own house.

NIC MEN'S
1973 Sigma Nu

NPC WOMEN'S
1969 Phi Mu
1970 Alpha Gamma Delta

ACHS HONORS
1971 Phi Alpha Theta
1971 Pi Delta Phi

OTHER HONORS
1974 Pi Mu Epsilon

SERVICE
1966 Alpha Phi Omega

INACTIVE
1970–84 Pi Kappa Phi

ARMSTRONG STATE COLLEGE Savannah, GA. Established in 1935 as a municipal junior college; became a two-year unit of the University System of Georgia in 1959 and a four-year college in 1964 offering more than twenty majors leading to B.A. or B.S. degrees.

NIC MEN'S
1972 Phi Kappa Theta

ACHS HONORS
1974 Kappa Delta Pi

1978 Phi Eta Sigma

INACTIVE
1970–85 Sigma Kappa
1971–80 Pi Kappa Alpha

ASBURY COLLEGE Wilmore, KY.

ACHS HONORS
1975 Phi Alpha Theta
1983 Phi Sigma Tau

RECOGNITION
1970 Sigma Zeta

ASHLAND COLLEGE Ashland, OH. Founded 1878, related to Brethren Church; private control; coeducational; offering baccalaureate degrees in arts, humanities, business, economics, radio/TV, sciences, education, nursing; graduate degrees in business, education, theology.

NIC MEN'S
1966 Kappa Sigma

1966 Phi Delta Theta
1966 Phi Kappa Psi

1967 Sigma Nu
1978 Tau Kappa Epsilon

NPC WOMEN'S
1965 Delta Zeta
1967 Alpha Delta Pi
1967 Alpha Phi
1968 Phi Mu

NPHC WOMEN'S
1974 Delta Sigma Theta (B)

ACHS HONORS
Omicron Delta Epsilon

1966 Kappa Delta Pi
1969 Phi Alpha Theta
1984 Kappa Omicron Nu
1986 Delta Mu Delta

OTHER HONORS
National Order of Omega

RECOGNITION
1936 Alpha Psi Omega

INACTIVE
–69   Sigma Tau Delta

ASSUMPTION COLLEGE Worcester, MA.

ACHS HONORS
1956 Delta Epsilon Sigma

1968 Kappa Mu Epsilon

ATHENS STATE COLLEGE Athens, AL. College of liberal arts; coeducational; private control; Methodist Church. Established as Athens Female Academy 1822; chartered 1843; named Athens College 1948; named Athens State College in 1975.

NIC MEN'S
1969 Tau Kappa Epsilon

NPC WOMEN'S
1966 Phi Mu

ACHS HONORS
1956 Sigma Tau Delta
1970 Delta Mu Delta
1984 Phi Alpha Theta
1985 Psi Chi

INACTIVE
1935–53 Kappa Mu Epsilon
1966–72 Sigma Kappa
1966–82 Zeta Tau Alpha
1967–67 Pi Kappa Phi
1968–77 Alpha Tau Omega
1968–79 Delta Tau Delta
1969–75 Alpha Epsilon Pi

ATLANTA UNIVERSITY Atlanta, GA.

NIC MEN'S
1980 Kappa Alpha Psi (A)

NPHC MEN'S
Phi Beta Sigma
1922 Omega Psi Phi

NPHC WOMEN'S
1970 Delta Sigma Theta (B)

PROFESSIONAL
1914 Delta Theta Phi

ACHS HONORS
1946 Alpha Kappa Delta
1956 Pi Sigma Alpha
1960 Beta Phi Mu
1975 Beta Gamma Sigma

INACTIVE
1964–73 Delta Mu Delta

ATLANTIC CHRISTIAN COLLEGE Wilson, NC. College of liberal arts; coeducational; private control; related to Christian (Disciples of Christ) Church. Established 1902.

Fraternity houses are privately owned; sorority members live in residence halls.

NIC MEN'S
1958 Alpha Sigma Phi
1958 Delta Sigma Phi
1958 Sigma Phi Epsilon
1990 Pi Kappa Phi

NPC WOMEN'S
1965 Delta Zeta
1965 Sigma Sigma Sigma
1967 Phi Mu

NPHC WOMEN'S
1981 Alpha Kappa Alpha

ACHS HONORS
1968 Alpha Chi
1968 Pi Gamma Mu
1979 Theta Alpha Kappa

INACTIVE
1959–82 Sigma Pi
1980–84 Phi Mu Alpha—
Sinfonia

ATLANTIC UNION COLLEGE South Lancaster, MA.

ACHS HONORS
1990 Phi Alpha Theta

AUBURN UNIVERSITY Auburn, AL. Alabama's land-grant university. Founded 1856 as Alabama A & M College, became Alabama Polytechnic Institute in 1899 until 1960 to Auburn. Coeducational; undergraduate, masters, and doctoral programs.

In some cases ownership of fraternity house and land is by the fraternity; in others it is by the fraternity on university-owned land. Women's social fraternities occupy space in university residence halls.

NIC MEN'S
1878 Sigma Alpha Epsilon
1879 Alpha Tau Omega
1879 Phi Delta Theta
1883 Kappa Alpha Order
1890 Sigma Nu
1895 Pi Kappa Alpha
1900 Kappa Sigma
1908 Delta Sigma Phi
1908 Sigma Phi Epsilon
1915 Lambda Chi Alpha
1918 Theta Chi
1919 Alpha Gamma Rho
1926 Pi Kappa Phi
1926 Sigma Pi
1927 Phi Kappa Tau
1934 Sigma Chi
1947 Tau Kappa Epsilon
1951 Delta Chi
1952 Delta Tau Delta
1954 Theta Xi
1962 Phi Gamma Delta
1964 Beta Theta Pi
1967 Chi Phi
1971 FarmHouse
1975 Kappa Alpha Psi (A)

NPHC MEN'S
Phi Beta Sigma

NPC WOMEN'S
1922 Kappa Delta
1923 Chi Omega
1939 Alpha Gamma Delta
1940 Delta Zeta
1942 Alpha Delta Pi
1946 Alpha Omicron Pi
1946 Phi Mu
1951 Zeta Tau Alpha
1954 Delta Delta Delta
1957 Kappa Alpha Theta
1957 Pi Beta Phi
1963 Kappa Kappa Gamma
1967 Alpha Chi Omega
1980 Alpha Xi Delta
1989 Sigma Kappa

NPHC WOMEN'S
1974 Delta Sigma Theta (B)
1976 Alpha Kappa Alpha
1980 Alpha Kappa Alpha

PROFESSIONAL
1921 Phi Delta Chi
1931 Delta Sigma Pi
1940 Omega Tau Sigma
1949 Phi Mu Alpha—Sinfonia
1954 Delta Omicron
1956 Kappa Epsilon
1956 Pi Sigma Epsilon
1963 Kappa Psi

OTHER PROFESSIONAL
1912 Alpha Psi
1932 Scarab
1936 Phi Psi
1941 Alpha Zeta
1966 Alpha Eta Rho
1976 Alpha Epsilon Rho

ACHS HONORS
Omicron Delta Epsilon
1914 Phi Kappa Phi
1920 Eta Kappa Nu
1921 Tau Beta Pi
1925 Rho Chi
1928 Kappa Delta Pi
1928 Omicron Delta Kappa
1932 Alpha Epsilon Delta
1935 Delta Sigma Rho-Tau Kappa Alpha
1938 Chi Epsilon
1940 Pi Tau Sigma
1950 Phi Eta Sigma
1950 Sigma Pi Sigma
1951 Kappa Omicron Nu
1952 Alpha Lambda Delta
1952 Xi Sigma Pi
1955 Mortar Board
1957 Lambda Sigma Society
1960 Sigma Tau Delta
1961 Psi Chi
1965 Phi Alpha Theta
1965 Pi Delta Phi
1965 Sigma Gamma Tau
1968 Alpha Pi Mu
1969 Sigma Delta Pi
1970 Pi Sigma Alpha
1975 Omega Chi Epsilon
1977 Beta Gamma Sigma
1985 Sigma Lambda Alpha
1987 Gamma Theta Upsilon
1990 Pi Kappa Lambda

OTHER HONORS
National Order of Omega
1916 Gamma Sigma Delta
1950 Sigma Xi
1953 Pi Mu Epsilon
1975 Sigma Gamma Epsilon

SERVICE
1927 Alpha Phi Omega
1972 Gamma Sigma Sigma

RECOGNITION
Angel Flight
Arnold Air Society (C-2)
1924 Scabbard and Blade (5)
1933 Phi Lambda Upsilon
1948 Phi Zeta
1949 National Block and Bridle Club
1962 Lambda Tau

INACTIVE
1916–20 Zeta Beta Tau
1921–34 Theta Alpha Phi

1921–84 Alpha Epsilon Pi
1923–33 Gamma Sigma Epsilon
1932 Cardinal Key
1956 Alpha Alpha Gamma
1961–70 Delta Upsilon
1968–83 Gamma Phi Beta
1972–88 Delta Gamma
1974–85 Phi Chi Theta
1974–88 Phi Kappa Psi
1981–88 Tau Kappa Epsilon

COLONIES
Alpha Kappa Lambda
Pi Lambda Phi
Sigma Kappa

AUBURN UNIVERSITY AT MONTGOMERY Montgomery, AL. Founded in 1967. Public institution. Schools of Science, Business, Education, Liberal Arts, and Nursing. Cross-registration with Auburn (at Auburn) and Huntington College.

Limited housing available in university-owned apartments.

NIC MEN'S
1977 Sigma Phi Epsilon
1980 Pi Kappa Phi
1984 Lambda Chi Alpha

NPC WOMEN'S
1977 Delta Zeta
1978 Zeta Tau Alpha
1979 Alpha Gamma Delta

ACHS HONORS
Omicron Delta Epsilon
1977 Phi Alpha Theta
1979 Pi Sigma Alpha
1980 Omicron Delta Kappa
1981 Phi Eta Sigma
1986 Psi Chi
1990 Phi Kappa Phi

AUGSBURG COLLEGE Minneapolis, MN. College of liberal arts; coeducational; private control; American Lutheran Church. Established 1869.

PROFESSIONAL
1956 Alpha Delta Theta
1975 Phi Beta

ACHS HONORS
1955 Lambda Iota Tau
1959 Pi Gamma Mu
1976 Sigma Pi Sigma
1987 Omicron Delta Kappa

1989 Delta Mu Delta

OTHER HONORS
1958 National Collegiate Players

SERVICE
1976 Alpha Phi Omega

AUGUSTA COLLEGE Augusta, GA. College of liberal arts and general studies; teacher preparatory and professional; coeducational. Established 1925; state control.

NIC MEN'S
1971 Pi Kappa Phi
1983 Delta Chi

NPC WOMEN'S
1972 Zeta Tau Alpha

NPHC WOMEN'S
1975 Delta Sigma Theta (B)
1978 Alpha Kappa Alpha

ACHS HONORS
1974 Phi Kappa Phi

1983 Psi Chi

SERVICE
1966 Alpha Phi Omega

RECOGNITION
1973 Beta Beta Beta

INACTIVE
1972–83 Alpha Delta Pi
1980–83 Phi Mu Alpha— Sinfonia

AUGUSTANA COLLEGE Rock Island, IL. Founded in 1860 by Swedish immigrants whose educational origins may be traced to the Old World universities of Uppsala and Lund in Sweden. Supported by the Lutheran Church of America.

PROFESSIONAL
1965 Sigma Alpha Iota
1970 Phi Mu Alpha—Sinfonia

ACHS HONORS
1946 Phi Alpha Theta
1962 Omicron Delta Kappa
1965 Mortar Board
1965 Sigma Delta Pi

1969 Psi Chi

OTHER HONORS
1938 Sigma Gamma Epsilon

SERVICE
1955 Alpha Phi Omega

RECOGNITION
1948 Beta Beta Beta

AUGUSTANA COLLEGE Sioux Falls, SD. Founded 1860; Four-year liberal arts coeducational program; institution of the American Lutheran Church; master's degree education program began summer 1963; master's degree selected studies program began summer 1983.

ACHS HONORS
1958 Phi Alpha Theta
1976 Pi Sigma Alpha

RECOGNITION
1948 Blue Key

1959 Beta Beta Beta

INACTIVE
1971–80 Phi Mu Alpha—
Sinfonia

AURARIA HIGHER EDUCATION CENTER Denver, CO.

INACTIVE
1984–87 Delta Sigma Phi

AURORA UNIVERSITY Aurora, IL.

NIC MEN'S
1987 Delta Sigma Phi

NPHC MEN'S
Phi Beta Sigma

NPHC WOMEN'S
1985 Alpha Kappa Alpha

AUSTIN COLLEGE Sherman, TX. College of liberal arts; coeducational; private control; Presbyterian Church. Chartered 1849.

ACHS HONORS
1922 Alpha Chi
1961 Sigma Delta Pi
1966 Pi Delta Phi
1967 Pi Gamma Mu
1972 Sigma Pi Sigma
1976 Psi Chi
1979 Phi Sigma Iota

SERVICE
1970 Alpha Phi Omega

RECOGNITION
1952 Alpha Psi Omega
1960 Eta Sigma Phi
1964 Beta Beta Beta
1976 Kappa Pi

INACTIVE
1853–54 Phi Delta Theta
1865–65 Phi Kappa Sigma
1895–00 Alpha Tau Omega
1935–36 Chi Beta Phi

AUSTIN PEAY STATE UNIVERSITY Clarksville, TN. Regional state university; coeducational; state control; established 1927. Became state college in 1943, and a university in 1967.

NIC MEN'S
1972 Pi Kappa Alpha
1973 Sigma Chi
1975 Kappa Alpha Psi (A)

1983 Alpha Gamma Rho
1985 Kappa Sigma

NPHC MEN'S
Phi Beta Sigma

1973 Alpha Phi Alpha

NPC WOMEN'S
1972 Chi Omega
1973 Kappa Delta
1983 Alpha Delta Pi
1986 Alpha Omicron Pi

NPHC WOMEN'S
1973 Delta Sigma Theta (B)
1976 Alpha Kappa Alpha

PROFESSIONAL
1959 Phi Mu Alpha—Sinfonia
1965 Alpha Kappa Psi
1965 Sigma Alpha Iota

OTHER PROFESSIONAL
1970 Alpha Beta Alpha

ACHS HONORS
        Omicron Delta Epsilon
1953 Kappa Delta Pi
1960 Gamma Theta Upsilon

1961 Phi Alpha Theta
1969 Sigma Pi Sigma
1976 Phi Kappa Phi
1979 Omicron Delta Kappa
1980 Alpha Lambda Delta
1980 Pi Sigma Alpha
1990 Psi Chi

OTHER HONORS
        National Order of Omega

SERVICE
1968 Alpha Phi Omega

RECOGNITION
1973 Pi Kappa Delta

INACTIVE
1969–72 Kappa Omicron Nu
1971–89 Alpha Tau Omega
1973–76 Sigma Phi Epsilon
1973–83 Alpha Phi
1974–81 Phi Chi Theta

AVERETT COLLEGE Danville, VA. Private institution. Founded in 1859. Four-year; coeducational; liberal arts college. Affiliated with Southern Baptist Church.

Housing is available on campus in single-sex dormitories.

NIC MEN'S
1989 Pi Kappa Phi

ACHS HONORS
1972 Alpha Chi
1987 Phi Eta Sigma

RECOGNITION
1976 Beta Beta Beta

INACTIVE
1979–81 Sigma Sigma Sigma

COLONIES
        Phi Sigma Sigma
        Sigma Pi

AVILA COLLEGE Kansas City, MO.

ACHS HONORS
1974 Sigma Theta Tau

1975 Psi Chi

BABSON COLLEGE OF MANAGEMENT Babson Park, MA. Professional school for men and women; private control; nonsectarian. Established 1919.

NIC MEN'S
1971 Theta Chi
1976 Zeta Beta Tau
1984 Tau Kappa Epsilon

NPC WOMEN'S
1976 Sigma Kappa
1980 Kappa Kappa Gamma

ACHS HONORS
        Omicron Delta Epsilon

RECOGNITION
1951 Blue Key

INACTIVE
1951–81 Delta Sigma Pi

BAKER UNIVERSITY Baldwin City, KS. Chartered February 12, 1858. Oldest four-year college in Kansas. Undergraduate; coeducational; controlled and maintained by the Kansas conference of the Methodist Church.

The fraternities and the sororities own their own houses on their own land.

NIC MEN'S
1865 Phi Gamma Delta
1903 Delta Tau Delta
1903 Kappa Sigma
1910 Sigma Phi Epsilon

NPC WOMEN'S
1895 Delta Delta Delta
1907 Alpha Chi Omega
1912 Zeta Tau Alpha
1916 Phi Mu

NPHC WOMEN'S
1982 Sigma Gamma Rho

ACHS HONORS
1966 Pi Gamma Mu
1979 Phi Eta Sigma
1980 Phi Sigma Tau

RECOGNITION
1926 Alpha Psi Omega
1950 Kappa Pi

INACTIVE
1910–34 Delta Zeta
1924–34 Lambda Chi Alpha
1972–76 Tau Kappa Epsilon

BAKERSFIELD COLLEGE Bakersfield, CA. Public institution. Founded in 1913. Coeducational; liberal arts college.

NPC WOMEN'S
1988 Phi Sigma Sigma

BALDWIN-WALLACE COLLEGE Berea, OH. Coeducational; founded 1845; affiliated with United Methodist Church; Baldwin University and German-Wallace College merged in 1913.

Fraternities and sororities occupy individual sections of college residence halls built specifically for this purpose.

NIC MEN'S
1926 Lambda Chi Alpha
1939 Alpha Sigma Phi
1941 Alpha Tau Omega
1942 Phi Kappa Tau
1948 Pi Lambda Phi
1948 Sigma Phi Epsilon
1979 Kappa Alpha Psi (A)

NPC WOMEN'S
1940 Alpha Gamma Delta
1941 Alpha Xi Delta
1941 Delta Zeta
1942 Phi Mu
1957 Zeta Tau Alpha
1964 Alpha Phi

NPHC WOMEN'S
1973 Delta Sigma Theta (B)
1980 Sigma Gamma Rho

PROFESSIONAL
1926 Mu Phi Epsilon

ACHS HONORS
Omicron Delta Epsilon
1937 Sigma Delta Pi

1947 Kappa Mu Epsilon
1948 Delta Mu Delta
1952 Omicron Delta Kappa
1953 Phi Alpha Theta
1954 Lambda Iota Tau
1956 Psi Chi
1966 Kappa Delta Pi
1981 Pi Sigma Alpha

OTHER HONORS
National Order of Omega

SERVICE
1965 Alpha Phi Omega

RECOGNITION
1920 Theta Alpha Phi
1921 Pi Kappa Delta
1937 Delta Phi Alpha
1956 Sigma Delta Psi
1967 Kappa Pi

INACTIVE
1929–38 Pi Gamma Mu
1937–85 Phi Mu Alpha—
Sinfonia
1949–54 Phi Sigma Kappa

BALL STATE UNIVERSITY Muncie, IN. Coeducational; state control; established 1918 as normal school; land given by Ball brothers; name changed to present 1965.

Fraternities occupy their own houses on their own land. Sororities are provided meeting rooms in residence halls.

NIC MEN'S
1930 Sigma Tau Gamma
1947 Theta Xi
1948 Phi Sigma Kappa
1951 Lambda Chi Alpha

1951 Theta Chi
1953 Kappa Alpha Psi (A)
1953 Sigma Phi Epsilon
1958 Delta Chi
1962 Sigma Chi

1965 Beta Theta Pi
1966 Delta Tau Delta
1967 Sigma Alpha Epsilon
1969 Phi Delta Theta
1970 Sigma Pi
1971 Sigma Nu
1972 Alpha Tau Omega
1989 Kappa Delta Rho

NPHC MEN'S
Phi Beta Sigma
1973 Alpha Phi Alpha

NPC WOMEN'S
1945 Sigma Sigma Sigma
1950 Alpha Chi Omega
1952 Alpha Omicron Pi
1952 Chi Omega
1952 Pi Beta Phi
1953 Delta Zeta
1954 Sigma Kappa
1964 Alpha Phi
1970 Kappa Alpha Theta
1980 Delta Delta Delta
1988 Alpha Gamma Delta
1990 Phi Mu

NPHC WOMEN'S
1940 Sigma Gamma Rho
1953 Delta Sigma Theta (B)
1968 Alpha Kappa Alpha

PROFESSIONAL
1946 Sigma Alpha Iota
1948 Phi Mu Alpha—Sinfonia
1962 Delta Sigma Pi
1969 Mu Phi Epsilon
1974 Phi Gamma Nu
1982 Gamma Iota Sigma

OTHER PROFESSIONAL
1948 Delta Pi Epsilon
1954 Pi Lambda Theta
1956 Phi Upsilon Omicron
1966 Sigma Delta Chi

ACHS HONORS
Omicron Delta Epsilon
1929 Pi Omega Pi
1931 Kappa Delta Pi
1931 Pi Gamma Mu
1950 Delta Sigma Rho-Tau
Kappa Alpha
1955 Pi Kappa Lambda
1967 Phi Alpha Theta
1968 Gamma Theta Upsilon
1968 Kappa Tau Alpha
1968 Sigma Pi Sigma
1971 Mortar Board
1972 Lambda Iota Tau
1972 Pi Sigma Alpha
1974 Sigma Theta Tau
1977 Psi Chi
1978 Alpha Lambda Delta
1981 Sigma Lambda Alpha

OTHER HONORS
National Order of Omega
1944 Delta Phi Delta

SERVICE
1947 Alpha Phi Omega
1970 Gamma Sigma Sigma

RECOGNITION
Angel Flight
Arnold Air Society (D-2)
1931 Society for Collegiate
Journalists—Pi Delta
Epsilon-Alpha Phi Gamma
(A)
1932 Blue Key
1937 Alpha Psi Omega
1938 Sigma Zeta
1948 Sigma Delta Psi

INACTIVE
1938–69 Sigma Tau Delta
1945–72 Alpha Sigma Tau
1952 Eta Sigma Phi
1970–85 Delta Gamma

UNIVERSITY OF BALTIMORE Baltimore, MD.

PROFESSIONAL
1973 Phi Alpha Delta
1983 Delta Theta Phi

ACHS HONORS
Pi Alpha Alpha

1972 Phi Alpha Theta
1975 Psi Chi
1978 Delta Mu Delta
1981 Pi Sigma Alpha
1984 Pi Gamma Mu

BAPTIST COLLEGE AT CHARLESTON Charleston, SC.

NPHC MEN'S
Phi Beta Sigma

ACHS HONORS
1972 Pi Gamma Mu

SERVICE
1969 Alpha Phi Omega

INACTIVE
1975–86 Alpha Kappa Alpha

BARBER-SCOTIA COLLEGE Concord, NC. College of liberal arts; coeducational; private control; United Presbyterian Church. Established as seminary in 1867.

NIC MEN'S
1972 Kappa Alpha Psi (A)

NPHC MEN'S
Phi Beta Sigma
1967 Alpha Phi Alpha

NPHC WOMEN'S
Zeta Phi Beta
1966 Alpha Kappa Alpha
1966 Delta Sigma Theta (B)
1971 Sigma Gamma Rho

ACHS HONORS
1954 Alpha Kappa Mu

SERVICE
1980 Alpha Phi Omega

BARD COLLEGE   Annadale-On-Hudson, NY.

INACTIVE
1895–42 Sigma Alpha Epsilon

BARNARD COLLEGE   New York, NY. Named for Frederick A. P. Barnard, tenth president of Columbia University; established 1889; women's undergraduate college of Columbia University; independent; own faculty, campus, board of trustees; faculty in 1916 resolved against Greek-letter fellowship societies.

INACTIVE
1891–17 Kappa Kappa Gamma
1897–15 Alpha Omicron Pi
1898–15 Kappa Alpha Theta
1901–15 Gamma Phi Beta
1903–13 Delta Delta Delta
1903–16 Alpha Phi
1904–15 Pi Beta Phi
1907–13 Chi Omega
1909–14 Alpha Epsilon Phi
1920–22 Delta Phi Epsilon

BARRY UNIVERSITY   Miami Shores, FL. A world class Catholic international university; Coeducational; 52 undergraduate and 20 graduate majors.

NPC WOMEN'S
1989 Delta Phi Epsilon

ACHS HONORS
1945 Delta Epsilon Sigma
1965 Lambda Iota Tau
1968 Phi Alpha Theta
1974 Psi Chi
1976 Kappa Delta Pi

1977 Theta Alpha Kappa
1990 Pi Gamma Mu

RECOGNITION
1969 Beta Beta Beta

INACTIVE
1972–77 Kappa Omicron Nu

BARUCH COLLEGE   New York, NY. Formerly a part of City College as the Bernard M. Baruch School of Business and Public Administration, the school became a separate college in 1976. College of liberal arts and general studies.

NIC MEN'S
1935 Tau Delta Phi

NPHC MEN'S
      Phi Beta Sigma

ACHS HONORS
      Omicron Delta Epsilon

1974 Sigma Delta Pi

SERVICE
1939 Alpha Phi Omega

INACTIVE
1966–68 Zeta Beta Tau
1967–70 Delta Phi Epsilon

BATES COLLEGE   Lewiston, ME. College of liberal arts; coeducational; private control; nonsectarian; established 1855 as Maine State Seminary.

ACHS HONORS
1915 Delta Sigma Rho-Tau
      Kappa Alpha
1926 Phi Sigma Iota
1973 Sigma Delta Pi

OTHER HONORS
1917 Phi Beta Kappa

INACTIVE
1929   Delta Phi Alpha

BAYLOR UNIVERSITY   Waco, TX. University; coeducational; private control; property of Baptist General Convention of Texas.

NIC MEN'S
1856 Phi Gamma Delta

1858 Sigma Alpha Epsilon
1976 Kappa Alpha Order

1976 Kappa Sigma
1976 Lambda Chi Alpha
1976 Sigma Phi Epsilon
1976 Tau Kappa Epsilon
1977 Alpha Tau Omega
1977 Phi Delta Theta
1977 Pi Kappa Alpha
1977 Sigma Tau Gamma
1978 Delta Upsilon
1978 Sigma Chi

NPHC MEN'S
      Phi Beta Sigma

NPC WOMEN'S
1976 Kappa Alpha Theta
1977 Chi Omega
1977 Delta Delta Delta
1977 Kappa Kappa Gamma
1977 Pi Beta Phi
1977 Zeta Tau Alpha
1980 Alpha Delta Pi
1983 Kappa Delta
1985 Alpha Chi Omega
1989 Sigma Kappa

PROFESSIONAL
1920 Psi Omega
1921 Xi Psi Phi
1930 Delta Sigma Pi
1939 Mu Phi Epsilon
1940 Phi Mu Alpha—Sinfonia
1943 Phi Chi
1945 Alpha Omega
1948 Delta Psi Kappa
1948 Kappa Kappa Psi
1948 Tau Beta Sigma
1949 Delta Theta Phi
1949 Phi Alpha Delta
1949 Phi Delta Phi
1958 Alpha Kappa Psi
1970 Zeta Phi Eta

OTHER PROFESSIONAL
1922 Delta Sigma Delta
1929 Phi Delta Epsilon
1929 Sigma Delta Chi
1955 Beta Alpha Psi

ACHS HONORS
      Omicron Delta Epsilon
1922 Alpha Chi
1925 Sigma Tau Delta
1928 Alpha Kappa Delta

1928 Sigma Delta Pi
1929 Alpha Epsilon Delta
1929 Kappa Delta Pi
1942 Psi Chi
1955 Phi Sigma Tau
1955 Pi Sigma Alpha
1958 Alpha Lambda Delta
1959 Sigma Pi Sigma
1960 Beta Gamma Sigma
1962 Omicron Delta Kappa
1965 Pi Delta Phi
1971 Mortar Board
1972 Phi Alpha Theta
1973 Kappa Omicron Nu
1974 Pi Kappa Lambda
1986 Theta Alpha Kappa

OTHER HONORS
      National Order of Omega
1925 Omicron Kappa Upsilon
1949 Alpha Omega Alpha
1968 Sigma Xi
1977 Phi Beta Kappa

SERVICE
1948 Alpha Phi Omega

RECOGNITION
      Angel Flight
      Arnold Air Society (G-1)
1930 Alpha Psi Omega
1931 Beta Beta Beta
1945 Kappa Pi
1958 Sigma Phi Alpha
1972 Sigma Iota Epsilon

INACTIVE
1920   Phi Beta Pi and Theta
            Kappa Psi (a)
1924–69   Pi Gamma Mu
1933   Phi Lambda Kappa
1942–50   Phi Beta Pi and Theta
            Kappa Psi (B)
1944   Phi Gamma Nu
1948–70   Alpha Kappa Kappa
1960   Eta Sigma Phi
1961–67   Pi Omega Pi
1962–84   Phi Eta Sigma
1977–86   Delta Gamma
1980–88   Beta Theta Pi

COLONIES
      Sigma Kappa

BEAVER COLLEGE   Glenside, PA. College of liberal arts for men and women; private control; Presbyterian Church (U.S.A.); established 1853.

ACHS HONORS
1939 Psi Chi
1948 Kappa Delta Pi
1958 Pi Delta Phi

1964 Phi Alpha Theta

RECOGNITION
1950 Alpha Psi Omega

BEHREND COLLEGE   Erie, PA.

NIC MEN'S
1986 Kappa Delta Rho

1990 Delta Chi

BELHAVEN COLLEGE   Jackson, MS. College of liberal arts; coeducational; private control; Synod of Mississippi, Presbyterian Church. Established 1883.

PROFESSIONAL
1947 Mu Phi Epsilon
1950 Kappa Delta Epsilon

ACHS HONORS
1964 Phi Alpha Theta

RECOGNITION
1945 Alpha Psi Omega

1963 Eta Sigma Phi
1965 Kappa Pi

INACTIVE
1965–83 Phi Mu Alpha—
           Sinfonia

BELLARMINE COLLEGE   Louisville, KY. Founded by the Catholic Archdiocese of Louisville, 1950, chartered and first instruction 1950; liberal arts and sciences; coeducational; private control; Catholic.

NIC MEN'S
1961 Alpha Delta Gamma

PROFESSIONAL
1983 Delta Sigma Pi

ACHS HONORS
     Omicron Delta Epsilon

1958 Delta Sigma Rho-Tau
       Kappa Alpha
1959 Delta Epsilon Sigma
1964 Phi Sigma Tau
1968 Psi Chi

BELMONT COLLEGE   Nashville, TN. Established 1951; coeducational.

PROFESSIONAL
1966 Phi Mu Alpha—Sinfonia
1969 Sigma Alpha Iota

ACHS HONORS
1968 Phi Alpha Theta
1971 Alpha Chi
1976 Kappa Delta Pi

1982 Pi Kappa Lambda

RECOGNITION
1947 Alpha Psi Omega
1965 Blue Key

INACTIVE
1907–11 Phi Mu

BELMONT ABBEY COLLEGE   Belmont, NC. College of liberal arts; private control; Roman Catholic; affiliated with the Catholic University of America; established 1876.

Students are assigned to the dormitories of their choice. Administration requires that fraternity members occupy residence halls. The college rents lodges to the fraternities.

NIC MEN'S
     Tau Kappa Epsilon
1959 Phi Kappa Theta
1965 Sigma Phi Epsilon
1969 Pi Kappa Phi

ACHS HONORS
1959 Delta Epsilon Sigma
1972 Pi Gamma Mu

1979 Phi Sigma Tau

SERVICE
1967 Alpha Phi Omega

INACTIVE
1960–88 Tau Kappa Epsilon
1978–80 Zeta Tau Alpha

BELOIT COLLEGE   Beloit, WI. College of liberal arts; coeducational; private control; nonsectarian; chartered 1846.

The fraternities and sororities occupy college-owned buildings on college-owned land on a lease basis.

NIC MEN'S
1860 Beta Theta Pi
1881 Phi Kappa Psi
1882 Sigma Chi
1915 Sigma Alpha Epsilon
1917 Tau Kappa Epsilon
1931 Sigma Pi

ACHS HONORS
1909 Delta Sigma Rho-Tau
       Kappa Alpha
1926 Phi Sigma Iota
1948 Omicron Delta Kappa
1951 Mortar Board
1982 Psi Chi

OTHER HONORS
1911 Phi Beta Kappa

1947 National Collegiate
       Players

SERVICE
1978 Alpha Phi Omega

INACTIVE
1915–26 Sigma Delta Chi
1917–64 Pi Kappa Alpha
1919–71 Pi Beta Phi
1920–70 Kappa Delta
1922–63 Delta Gamma
1925–63 Delta Delta Delta
1927–35 Sigma Alpha Iota
1947–70 Kappa Alpha Theta
1948–70 Phi Eta Sigma
1951–69 Alpha Lambda Delta

BEMIDJI STATE UNIVERSITY   Bemidji, MN. Co-educational; liberal arts with seven divisions; behavioral sciences; business and industry; education; fine arts; humanities; health, physical education and recreation; math and science. Established 1913; state controlled.

Fraternities and sororities do not have houses.

NIC MEN'S
1973 Tau Kappa Epsilon

ACHS HONORS
1971 Sigma Pi Sigma
1985 Gamma Theta Upsilon

SERVICE
1971 Alpha Phi Omega

RECOGNITION
1939 Alpha Phi Sigma (E)
1966 Delta Phi Alpha

INACTIVE
1970–76 Phi Sigma Kappa
1971–75 Alpha Tau Omega
1971–84 Alpha Omicron Pi

BENEDICT COLLEGE   Columbia, SC. Founded 1870. Coeducational.

NIC MEN'S
1949 Kappa Alpha Psi (A)

NPHC MEN'S
     Phi Beta Sigma
1947 Alpha Phi Alpha
1947 Omega Psi Phi

NPHC WOMEN'S
     Zeta Phi Beta
1947 Alpha Kappa Alpha
1947 Sigma Gamma Rho
1948 Delta Sigma Theta (B)

PROFESSIONAL
1987 Phi Mu Alpha—Sinfonia

ACHS HONORS
1947 Alpha Kappa Mu
1973 Delta Mu Delta
1976 Sigma Tau Delta
1983 Sigma Pi Sigma

SERVICE
1973 Alpha Phi Omega

INACTIVE
1948–60 Beta Kappa Chi

BENEDICTINE COLLEGE   Atchison, KS. College of liberal arts for men and women; private control (Roman Catholic); established 1863. Merged from St. Benedict's College and Mount St. Scholastica College 1971.

PROFESSIONAL
1946 Sigma Alpha Iota
1971 Alpha Kappa Psi

ACHS HONORS
     Omicron Delta Epsilon

1940 Kappa Mu Epsilon
1964 Psi Chi
1971 Sigma Pi Sigma

BENNETT COLLEGE Greensboro, NC. College of liberal arts for women; private control; related to Methodist Church; founded 1873.

NPHC WOMEN'S
1971 Alpha Kappa Alpha

1963 Pi Gamma Mu

ACHS HONORS
1948 Beta Kappa Chi

INACTIVE
1937–73 Alpha Kappa Mu

BENTLEY COLLEGE Waltham, MA. College of business and finance, coeducational; private, non-profit. Established 1917.

NIC MEN'S
1971 Tau Kappa Epsilon
1976 Zeta Beta Tau
1978 Sigma Phi Epsilon
1990 Phi Delta Theta

PROFESSIONAL
1987 Delta Sigma Pi

ACHS HONORS
Omicron Delta Epsilon

NPC WOMEN'S
1982 Alpha Phi
1988 Delta Phi Epsilon

OTHER HONORS
National Order of Omega

BEREA COLLEGE Berea, KY. College of liberal arts; coeducational; private control; nonsectarian. Founded 1855.

ACHS HONORS
Omicron Delta Epsilon
1924 Delta Sigma Rho-Tau Kappa Alpha
1924 Pi Gamma Mu
1937 Sigma Pi Sigma
1953 Phi Kappa Phi
1957 Psi Chi

1962 Kappa Delta Pi
1973 Mortar Board
1985 Phi Alpha Theta

RECOGNITION
1927 Alpha Psi Omega
1930 Delta Phi Alpha
1954 Beta Beta Beta

BERRY COLLEGE Mt. Berry, GA. College of liberal arts and teacher education; coeducational; established 1902.

PROFESSIONAL
1974 Phi Mu Alpha—Sinfonia
1974 Sigma Alpha Iota

ACHS HONORS
Omicron Delta Epsilon
1965 Sigma Tau Delta
1969 Alpha Chi
1969 Phi Alpha Theta

1981 Lambda Sigma Society
1986 Omicron Delta Kappa
1986 Psi Chi

SERVICE
1972 Alpha Phi Omega

RECOGNITION
1946 Alpha Psi Omega

BETHANY COLLEGE Lindsborg, KS. Four-year college of liberal arts; coeducational; private control; Lutheran Church in America; chartered as academy 1881.

PROFESSIONAL
1927 Sigma Alpha Iota
1940 Phi Mu Alpha—Sinfonia

ACHS HONORS
1970 Lambda Iota Tau
1973 Phi Alpha Theta
1973 Pi Delta Phi

OTHER HONORS
1920 Delta Phi Delta

RECOGNITION
1935 Alpha Psi Omega

INACTIVE
1930–42 Pi Gamma Mu

BETHANY COLLEGE Bethany, WV. College of liberal arts; coeducational; private control; nonsectarian; affiliated with Disciples of Christ Church. Chartered 1840.

Three (Alpha Sigma Phi, Beta Theta Pi, and Sigma Nu) fraternities own their own houses and land; all other social fraternities are provided individual residences.

NIC MEN'S
1859 Delta Tau Delta
1860 Beta Theta Pi
1923 Phi Kappa Tau
1929 Alpha Sigma Phi

NPC WOMEN'S
1903 Alpha Xi Delta
1905 Zeta Tau Alpha
1923 Kappa Delta
1939 Phi Mu

ACHS HONORS
Omicron Delta Epsilon
1938 Pi Gamma Mu

1967 Phi Alpha Theta
1972 Lambda Iota Tau
1973 Sigma Delta Pi
1975 Kappa Mu Epsilon
1980 Psi Chi

RECOGNITION
1928 Alpha Psi Omega
1974 Kappa Pi

INACTIVE
1859–82 Phi Kappa Psi
1903–05 Sigma Phi Epsilon
1968–81 Pi Beta Phi
1969–83 Sigma Alpha Epsilon

BETHANY NAZARENE COLLEGE Bethany, OK. College of liberal arts; coeducational; private; Church of the Nazarene; established 1908; was Bethany-Peniel College until 1955.

ACHS HONORS
1979 Delta Mu Delta

1980 Mortar Board

BETHEL COLLEGE St. Paul, MN. Private control: Baptist General Conference. Founded in 1871. Divisions of Humanities, Social & Behavioral Sciences, Mathematics & Natural Sciences, Nursing, Fine & Performing Arts, and Education & Physical Education.

Freshmen must live in college housing. Dormitories are single-sex.

RECOGNITION
1971 Pi Kappa Delta

INACTIVE
1963–81 Pi Gamma Mu

BETHEL COLLEGE McKenzie, TN. College of liberal arts; coeducational; private: Cumberland Presbyterian Church; established 1842.

RECOGNITION
1946 Alpha Psi Omega
1961 Society for Collegiate Journalists—Pi Delta Epsilon-Alpha Phi Gamma (A)

INACTIVE
1966–82 Phi Mu Alpha— Sinfonia
1969–77 Pi Kappa Phi

BETHUNE-COOKMAN COLLEGE Daytona Beach, FL. College of liberal arts; coeducational; private control; related to the Methodist Church. Established 1923 by merger of Cookman Institute and Daytona Normal.

NIC MEN'S
1948 Kappa Alpha Psi (A)

NPHC MEN'S
Phi Beta Sigma
1948 Alpha Phi Alpha
1948 Omega Psi Phi

NPHC WOMEN'S
Zeta Phi Beta

1949 Alpha Kappa Alpha
1949 Delta Sigma Theta (B)
1950 Sigma Gamma Rho

ACHS HONORS
1950 Alpha Kappa Mu
1951 Beta Kappa Chi
1971 Sigma Delta Pi
1972 Phi Alpha Theta
1975 Psi Chi

1981 Psi Chi

SERVICE
1961 Alpha Phi Omega
1976 Gamma Sigma Sigma

RECOGNITION
1975 Beta Beta Beta

INACTIVE
1953–76 Pi Omega Pi

COLONIES
1991 Phi Kappa Psi

BIOLA UNIVERSITY   La Mirada, CA.

ACHS HONORS
1981 Phi Alpha Theta

1981 Psi Chi

BIRMINGHAM-SOUTHERN COLLEGE   Birmingham, AL. Four-year collegiate liberal arts institution founded in 1856 and operating under the auspices of the Alabama-West Florida and North Alabama Conferences of the United Methodist Church.

Five men's national social fraternities, with four having houses on college land. There are six national sororities, each having its own chapter room in Stockham's Woman's Building.

NIC MEN'S
1878 Sigma Alpha Epsilon
1885 Alpha Tau Omega
1942 Theta Chi

NPC WOMEN'S
1922 Zeta Tau Alpha
1925 Alpha Omicron Pi
1926 Alpha Chi Omega
1930 Kappa Delta
1989 Chi Omega
1989 Chi Omega

NPHC WOMEN'S
1979 Alpha Kappa Alpha

PROFESSIONAL
1933 Kappa Delta Epsilon
1950 Kappa Delta Epsilon

OTHER PROFESSIONAL
1924 Kappa Phi Kappa

ACHS HONORS
1924 Omicron Delta Kappa
1927 Delta Sigma Rho-Tau
      Kappa Alpha
1931 Phi Sigma Iota
1934 Alpha Lambda Delta
1935 Mortar Board
1956 Phi Eta Sigma
1974 Psi Chi

1976 Phi Alpha Theta
1981 Kappa Mu Epsilon
1981 Pi Kappa Lambda
1984 Pi Sigma Alpha

OTHER HONORS
      National Order of Omega
1937 Phi Beta Kappa

SERVICE
1961 Alpha Phi Omega

RECOGNITION
1926 Kappa Pi
1927 Eta Sigma Phi
1930 Delta Phi Alpha
1975 Beta Beta Beta

INACTIVE
1871–69 Pi Kappa Alpha
1882–74 Kappa Alpha Order
1924–40 Pi Gamma Mu
1924–84 Lambda Chi Alpha
1927–89 Pi Beta Phi
1928–39 Beta Beta Beta
1928–61 Delta Sigma Phi
1930–57 Gamma Phi Beta
1958–63 Phi Chi Theta
1959–69 Alpha Kappa Psi
1962–74 Delta Zeta
1969–77 Sigma Pi Sigma

BISHOP COLLEGE   Dallas, TX. Founded 1880; coeducational; college of liberal arts.

NIC MEN'S
1956 Kappa Alpha Psi (A)
1989 Beta Theta Pi

NPHC MEN'S
      Phi Beta Sigma
1957 Alpha Phi Alpha
1957 Omega Psi Phi

NPC WOMEN'S
1989 Alpha Phi

NPHC WOMEN'S
      Zeta Phi Beta

1955 Alpha Kappa Alpha
1955 Delta Sigma Theta (B)
1962 Sigma Gamma Rho

ACHS HONORS
1951 Alpha Kappa Mu
1973 Pi Omega Pi

SERVICE
1972 Alpha Phi Omega
1975 Gamma Sigma Sigma

INACTIVE
1952–60 Beta Kappa Chi

BLACK HILLS COLLEGE   Spearfish, SD. Chartered as Dakota Normal School 1883; name changed to Spearfish Normal School 1889; name changed to Black Hills Teachers College 1940; to present 1964. B.S., B.A., and master's in education; about half the students enrolled in liberal arts; coeducational; state control.

Sigma Tau Gamma and Phi Sigma Epsilon own houses on their own land.

NIC MEN'S
1928 Sigma Tau Gamma
1955 Phi Sigma Kappa

ACHS HONORS
1929 Kappa Delta Pi

RECOGNITION
1958 Alpha Psi Omega

INACTIVE
1959–69 Sigma Kappa
1966–74 Tau Kappa Epsilon

BLACKBURN COLLEGE   Carlinville, IL. Private control: Presbyterian Church. Founded in 1837. Four-year; coeducational; liberal arts college.

On-campus housing is available for all unmarried students.

ACHS HONORS
1971 Alpha Chi

BLINN COLLEGE   Brenham, TX.

SERVICE
1972 Alpha Phi Omega

BLOOMFIELD COLLEGE   Bloomfield, NJ. Founded 1868. Four-year coeducational college of liberal arts. Private control; affiliated with the Presbyterian Church.

Fraternities occupy college-owned houses. Sorority members are required to live in dormitories.

PROFESSIONAL
1964 Alpha Kappa Psi

ACHS HONORS
1965 Phi Alpha Theta

1984 Psi Chi

BLOOMSBURG STATE COLLEGE   Bloomsberg, PA. State college; coeducational; state control. Founded 1839 as private academy; became normal school in 1869, state teachers college in 1927, state college in 1960.

NIC MEN'S
1969 Zeta Psi
1970 Phi Sigma Kappa
1972 Lambda Chi Alpha
1978 Tau Kappa Epsilon
1981 Kappa Alpha Psi (A)
1990 Pi Kappa Phi
1990 Theta Chi

NPC WOMEN'S
1971 Sigma Sigma Sigma
1979 Alpha Sigma Tau
1988 Phi Sigma Sigma

PROFESSIONAL
1971 Kappa Kappa Psi

OTHER PROFESSIONAL
1930 Phi Sigma Pi

ACHS HONORS
      Omicron Delta Epsilon
1931 Gamma Theta Upsilon
1931 Kappa Delta Pi
1935 Pi Omega Pi
1966 Sigma Tau Delta
1967 Phi Alpha Theta
1970 Psi Chi
1970 Sigma Pi Sigma
1973 Delta Mu Delta
1973 Kappa Mu Epsilon
1976 Phi Sigma Iota

1977 Phi Kappa Phi

SERVICE
1963 Alpha Phi Omega

RECOGNITION
1927 Alpha Psi Omega

1962 Pi Kappa Delta

INACTIVE
1970–73 Sigma Pi

BLUEFIELD STATE COLLEGE Bluefield, WV.
College of liberal arts; teachers college and technological institute; coeducational; state control; chartered 1896.

Fraternities and sororities do not have houses.

NIC MEN'S
1935 Kappa Alpha Psi (A)

NPHC MEN'S
  Phi Beta Sigma
1932 Alpha Phi Alpha
1936 Omega Psi Phi

NPHC WOMEN'S
  Zeta Phi Beta
1938 Alpha Kappa Alpha

1938 Delta Sigma Theta (B)

ACHS HONORS
1947 Beta Kappa Chi
1951 Pi Omega Pi
1971 Alpha Chi
1990 Phi Eta Sigma

INACTIVE
1940–66 Alpha Kappa Mu
1971–77 Tau Kappa Epsilon

BOISE STATE UNIVERSITY Boise, ID. College of liberal arts and general; professional; coeducational. Established 1932. State control.

NIC MEN'S
1969 Kappa Sigma

NPC WOMEN'S
1970 Alpha Chi Omega
1970 Gamma Phi Beta

OTHER WOMEN'S
  Lambda Delta Sigma

ACHS HONORS
  Omicron Delta Epsilon
1974 Phi Kappa Phi
1980 Phi Alpha Theta
1984 Pi Sigma Alpha

SERVICE
1940 Intercollegiate Knights

RECOGNITION
1968 Kappa Pi
1971 Pi Kappa Delta

INACTIVE
1969–73 Alpha Xi Delta
1969–84 Delta Delta Delta
1969–87 Alpha Omicron Pi
1970–90 Tau Kappa Epsilon
1976–78 Phi Mu Alpha—
    Sinfonia
1978–90 Sigma Phi Epsilon

BOSTON COLLEGE Chestnut Hill, MA. University; coeducational; private control; Roman Catholic. Established 1863.

NIC MEN'S
1892 Sigma Alpha Epsilon

PROFESSIONAL
1955 Alpha Kappa Psi

OTHER PROFESSIONAL
1967 Kappa Phi Kappa
1977 Alpha Epsilon Rho

ACHS HONORS
  Omicron Delta Epsilon
1939 Alpha Sigma Nu
1953 Sigma Pi Sigma

1957 Beta Gamma Sigma
1960 Phi Alpha Theta
1977 Alpha Epsilon Delta

OTHER HONORS
1963 Order of the Coif
1966 Sigma Xi

SERVICE
1969 Alpha Phi Omega

INACTIVE
1957–75 Delta Sigma Pi
1968–70 Kappa Delta Epsilon

BOSTON COLLEGE OF LAW Brighton, MA.

PROFESSIONAL
1974 Phi Alpha Delta

INACTIVE
1958   Kappa Beta Pi

BOSTON CONSERVATORY OF MUSIC Boston, MA. Established 1867; coeducational.

PROFESSIONAL
1963 Phi Mu Alpha—Sinfonia
1968 Sigma Alpha Iota

ACHS HONORS
1975 Pi Kappa Lambda

BOSTON UNIVERSITY Boston, MA. A Methodist Theological Seminary from 1839–69, the University received its charter in 1869. Fifteen undergraduate schools and colleges; coeducational; private control; nonsectarian.

Fraternities may own their own houses on their own property. Transition under way from fraternity-owned houses to ownership by university.

NIC MEN'S
1889 Delta Tau Delta
1909 Lambda Chi Alpha
1917 Tau Delta Phi
1927 Alpha Phi Delta
1940 Alpha Epsilon Pi
1959 Tau Kappa Epsilon
1968 Sigma Alpha Mu
1986 Pi Lambda Phi
1987 Kappa Sigma
1990 Sigma Chi

NPHC MEN'S
  Phi Beta Sigma

NPC WOMEN'S
1887 Gamma Phi Beta
1888 Delta Delta Delta
1911 Alpha Delta Pi
1951 Alpha Epsilon Phi
1959 Sigma Delta Tau
1984 Alpha Phi
1988 Delta Gamma

PROFESSIONAL
1915 Delta Theta Phi
1916 Delta Sigma Pi
1965 Phi Alpha Delta
1977 Alpha Omega

OTHER PROFESSIONAL
1942 Delta Pi Epsilon
1947 Sigma Delta Chi

ACHS HONORS
  Omicron Delta Epsilon
1952 Phi Alpha Theta
1953 Psi Chi
1955 Pi Kappa Lambda
1956 Phi Sigma Iota
1956 Pi Sigma Alpha
1970 Gamma Theta Upsilon
1974 Mortar Board

1975 Tau Beta Pi
1981 Sigma Pi Sigma
1982 Phi Sigma Tau

OTHER HONORS
  National Order of Omega

SERVICE
1948 Alpha Phi Omega
1953 Gamma Sigma Sigma

RECOGNITION
1928 Scabbard and Blade (6)

INACTIVE
1876–15 Beta Theta Pi
1877–12 Theta Delta Chi
1882–71 Kappa Kappa Gamma
1883–70 Alpha Phi
1896–85 Pi Beta Phi
1908–89 Zeta Beta Tau
1912–68 Zeta Tau Alpha
1913–61 Alpha Gamma Delta
1920–41 Delta Sigma Phi
1921–70 Theta Phi Alpha
1923–27 Beta Alpha Psi
1924–51 Kappa Alpha Psi (A)
1924–64 Phi Chi Theta
1927–29 Phi Mu Delta
1927–60 Kappa Delta Phi (C)
1932–55 Pi Gamma Mu
1941–66 Phi Sigma Sigma
1946–68 Pi Omega Pi
1948–53 Phi Sigma Kappa
1948–75 Phi Mu Alpha—
    Sinfonia
1950–70 Sigma Phi Epsilon
1954–55 Kappa Alpha Mu
1962–71 Acacia

COLONIES
1904 Sigma Kappa
1990 Chi Phi

BOWDOIN COLLEGE Brunswick, ME. Founded 1794, first instruction 1802. Undergraduate liberal arts college for men and women; private; nonsectarian. All Bowdoin fraternities are coeducational.

NIC MEN'S
1841 Alpha Delta Phi
1843 Psi Upsilon
1844 Chi Psi
1844 Delta Kappa Epsilon
1854 Theta Delta Chi
1867 Zeta Psi
1900 Beta Theta Pi

OTHER HONORS
1825 Phi Beta Kappa

INACTIVE
1857–52 Delta Upsilon
1895–65 Kappa Sigma
1918–70 Sigma Nu
1929–62 Alpha Tau Omega

BOWIE STATE COLLEGE Bowie, MD. Teachers college; coeducational; state control; established 1867.

NIC MEN'S
1969 Kappa Alpha Psi (A)

NPHC MEN'S
     Phi Beta Sigma
1971 Alpha Phi Alpha

NPHC WOMEN'S
1968 Delta Sigma Theta (B)
1969 Alpha Kappa Alpha
1973 Sigma Gamma Rho

ACHS HONORS
1965 Alpha Kappa Mu
1971 Phi Alpha Theta
1974 Psi Chi
1975 Alpha Chi
1976 Sigma Tau Delta
1977 Delta Mu Delta
1977 Kappa Delta Pi

BOWLING GREEN STATE UNIVERSITY Bowling Green, OH. Established as a state normal school, 1910, classes began in 1914. Became Bowling Green State College in 1929 and Bowling Green State University in 1935. There are five undergraduate colleges: liberal arts, education, business administration, musical arts, health, and community services; graduate school; all colleges coeducational; state supported.

The university owns most houses occupied by the fraternities and sororities. Each member living in the house pays room rent to the university at the same rate as students living in residence halls. The houses are furnished by the university with the exception of the lounges which each group must furnish. The fraternities and sororities operate their own dining rooms.

NIC MEN'S
1942 Pi Kappa Alpha
1943 Alpha Tau Omega
1945 Sigma Alpha Epsilon
1946 Sigma Nu
1947 Kappa Sigma
1947 Sigma Chi
1948 Delta Tau Delta
1948 Theta Chi
1948 Zeta Beta Tau
1949 Delta Upsilon
1950 Alpha Sigma Phi
1950 Phi Delta Theta
1950 Phi Kappa Psi
1950 Phi Kappa Tau
1950 Sigma Phi Epsilon
1962 Beta Theta Pi
1971 Kappa Alpha Psi (A)
1976 Pi Kappa Phi
1982 Lambda Chi Alpha
1984 Phi Gamma Delta
1990 Phi Sigma Kappa

NPHC MEN'S
     Phi Beta Sigma

NPC WOMEN'S
1943 Alpha Phi
1943 Alpha Xi Delta
1943 Delta Gamma
1943 Gamma Phi Beta
1944 Alpha Chi Omega
1945 Alpha Gamma Delta
1946 Kappa Delta
1946 Phi Mu
1947 Chi Omega
1950 Delta Zeta

1983 Kappa Kappa Gamma
1986 Pi Beta Phi
1989 Alpha Omicron Pi

NPHC WOMEN'S
1965 Delta Sigma Theta (B)
1973 Sigma Gamma Rho
1975 Alpha Kappa Alpha

PROFESSIONAL
1949 Kappa Kappa Psi
1952 Delta Psi Kappa
1959 Sigma Alpha Iota
1960 Phi Mu Alpha—Sinfonia
1967 Gamma Iota Sigma
1970 Delta Sigma Pi
1984 Phi Alpha Delta

OTHER PROFESSIONAL
1952 Phi Upsilon Omicron
1953 Phi Epsilon Kappa
1955 Beta Alpha Psi
1965 Sigma Delta Chi
1971 Delta Pi Epsilon

ACHS HONORS
     Omicron Delta Epsilon
1936 Sigma Tau Delta
1937 Kappa Mu Epsilon
1939 Kappa Delta Pi
1941 Pi Omega Pi
1947 Pi Sigma Alpha
1947 Psi Chi
1948 Gamma Theta Upsilon
1948 Sigma Delta Pi
1949 Alpha Epsilon Delta
1949 Omicron Delta Kappa
1950 Phi Alpha Theta

1953 Alpha Kappa Delta
1954 Phi Eta Sigma
1955 Beta Gamma Sigma
1962 Pi Delta Phi
1963 Phi Sigma Tau
1964 Phi Kappa Phi
1966 Alpha Lambda Delta
1969 Mortar Board
1969 Sigma Pi Sigma
1971 Kappa Tau Alpha
1977 Pi Kappa Lambda

OTHER HONORS
     National Order of Omega
1948 Delta Phi Delta
1959 Sigma Gamma Epsilon

SERVICE
1948 Alpha Phi Omega

RECOGNITION
     Angel Flight
     Arnold Air Society (E-2)
1930 Pi Kappa Delta
1934 Sigma Delta Psi
1952 Beta Beta Beta
1952 Eta Sigma Phi
1963 Delta Phi Alpha

INACTIVE
1947–55 Kappa Alpha Mu
1951–53 Theta Xi
1951–90 Alpha Delta Pi
1958–85 Tau Kappa Epsilon
1969–81 Alpha Epsilon Pi
1978–80 Zeta Tau Alpha

COLONIES
1990 Phi Sigma Kappa

BRADLEY UNIVERSITY Peoria, IL. University; coeducational; private control; nonsectarian; chartered 1897; graduate school. Most fraternities own their own houses on college-owned land. Four sororities own their own houses and two are on college land.

NIC MEN'S
1946 Tau Kappa Epsilon
1948 Theta Xi
1949 Alpha Epsilon Pi
1949 Sigma Chi
1949 Sigma Phi Epsilon
1949 Theta Chi
1950 Pi Kappa Alpha
1951 Delta Upsilon
1955 Sigma Nu
1962 Tau Epsilon Phi
1965 Phi Kappa Tau
1967 Sigma Alpha Epsilon
1978 Kappa Alpha Psi (A)
1982 Phi Gamma Delta
1982 Pi Kappa Phi
1988 Delta Tau Delta

NPHC MEN'S
     Phi Beta Sigma
1962 Alpha Phi Alpha

NPC WOMEN'S
1947 Chi Omega
1947 Pi Beta Phi
1947 Sigma Kappa
1948 Gamma Phi Beta
1962 Sigma Delta Tau
1978 Alpha Chi Omega

NPHC WOMEN'S
1968 Alpha Kappa Alpha
1971 Delta Sigma Theta (B)
1975 Sigma Gamma Rho

PROFESSIONAL
1948 Phi Mu Alpha—Sinfonia
1948 Sigma Alpha Iota
1951 Alpha Kappa Psi
1959 Phi Chi Theta
1965 Sigma Phi Delta

OTHER PROFESSIONAL
1921 Phi Sigma Pi
1958 Pi Lambda Theta
1958 Sigma Delta Chi

ACHS HONORS
     Omicron Delta Epsilon

1927 Pi Gamma Mu
1949 Phi Alpha Theta
1949 Pi Sigma Alpha
1950 Omicron Delta Kappa
1951 Alpha Lambda Delta
1951 Phi Eta Sigma
1961 Kappa Omicron Nu
1961 Pi Tau Sigma
1962 Eta Kappa Nu
1963 Phi Kappa Phi
1964 Alpha Pi Mu
1964 Kappa Tau Alpha
1964 Tau Beta Pi
1967 Mortar Board
1969 Chi Epsilon
1970 Sigma Tau Delta
1971 Sigma Pi Sigma
1978 Gamma Theta Upsilon
1987 Phi Sigma Iota

OTHER HONORS
     National Order of Omega
1951 Delta Phi Delta

SERVICE
1948 Alpha Phi Omega

RECOGNITION
     Angel Flight
     Arnold Air Society (D-2)
1921 Pi Kappa Delta
1924 Theta Alpha Phi
1946 Sigma Delta Psi

INACTIVE
1927–89 Lambda Chi Alpha
1954   Kappa Alpha Mu
1957–87 Delta Zeta
1962–66 Sigma Sigma Sigma
1966–73 Zeta Beta Tau
1967–80 Kappa Delta Rho
1968–70 Psi Chi
1968–83 Alpha Epsilon Phi
1985–87 Delta Gamma

COLONIES
1975 Sigma Gamma Rho

BRANDEIS UNIVERSITY Waltham, MA. University; coeducational; private control; nonsectarian; chartered 1948.

NIC MEN'S	OTHER HONORS
Tau Kappa Epsilon	1962 Phi Beta Kappa
1987 Alpha Epsilon Pi	
1987 Sigma Alpha Mu	RECOGNITION
1991 Phi Kappa Psi	1962 Delta Phi Alpha
ACHS HONORS	
Omicron Delta Epsilon	INACTIVE
1990 Psi Chi	1988–89 Zeta Beta Tau

BRENAU COLLEGE Gainesville, GA. College of liberal arts for women; private control; nonsectarian. Established 1878 as Georgia Female Institute.

Sorority houses are owned by the college. There are no dining halls in the houses but small kitchens are furnished for the use of the occupants. The college charges no rental, as such, but each girl pays the regular charge for board and room charged to all resident students. The sorority, usually through the national office, contributes to capital outlay for maintenance and additions to the house. The college shares in this expense.

NPC WOMEN'S	1980 Alpha Lambda Delta
1910 Alpha Delta Pi	
1910 Phi Mu	RECOGNITION
1911 Alpha Chi Omega	1946 Kappa Pi
1913 Alpha Gamma Delta	
1914 Delta Delta Delta	INACTIVE
1962 Chi Omega	1909–14 Alpha Sigma Alpha
	1924–78 Delta Zeta
PROFESSIONAL	1926 Delta Psi Kappa
1911 Mu Phi Epsilon	1926–30 Delta Phi Epsilon
1917 Zeta Phi Eta	1927–41 Alpha Xi Delta
	1928–37 Pi Gamma Mu
ACHS HONORS	1933–41 Beta Beta Beta
1972 Phi Alpha Theta	1938–60 Gamma Sigma Epsilon

BRESCIA COLLEGE Owensboro, KY. Private control: Roman Catholic. Four-year.

On campus housing is available in single-sex dormitories.

ACHS HONORS
1974 Alpha Chi

BREVARD COMMUNITY COLLEGE Cocoa, FL.

PROFESSIONAL
1968 Phi Mu Alpha—Sinfonia

BRIAR CLIFF COLLEGE Sioux City, IA.

ACHS HONORS	INACTIVE
1967 Gamma Theta Upsilon	1947–69 Sigma Tau Delta
1985 Phi Alpha Theta	
1987 Psi Chi	

RECOGNITION
1946 Alpha Psi Omega

UNIVERSITY OF BRIDGEPORT Bridgeport, CT. Founded in 1927 as the first chartered junior college in New England; chartered as a university in 1947; coeducational; nonsectarian; nonprofit; fully accredited; private institution. Colleges: Arts and Humanities, Business and Public Management, Health Sciences, Metropolitan, Science and Engineering, and the School of Law. Baccalaureate and Master's degree programs in liberal arts, business administration, education, engineering, sciences, and law. Sixth Year Diploma in Education and doctoral degrees in Educational Management and Law.

Fraternities and sororities do not have houses. On-campus fraternal housing permitted.

NIC MEN'S	1980 Phi Sigma Iota
1971 Tau Kappa Epsilon	1981 Eta Kappa Nu
NPC WOMEN'S	SERVICE
1989 Alpha Epsilon Phi	1950 Alpha Phi Omega
PROFESSIONAL	RECOGNITION
1973 Mu Phi Epsilon	1958 Sigma Phi Alpha
1977 Delta Theta Phi	1961 Delta Tau Kappa
1980 Phi Alpha Delta	1962 Kappa Pi
OTHER PROFESSIONAL	
1972 Sigma Delta Chi	INACTIVE
	1954–68 Pi Gamma Mu
ACHS HONORS	1968–71 Pi Lambda Phi
1963 Psi Chi	1970–73 Alpha Sigma Phi
1965 Phi Alpha Theta	1973–80 Phi Mu Alpha—
1967 Kappa Delta Pi	Sinfonia
1970 Beta Gamma Sigma	
1971 Sigma Pi Sigma	COLONIES
1979 Phi Kappa Phi	Sigma Pi

BRIDGEWATER COLLEGE Bridgewater, VA. Founded by D. C. Flory in 1880; coeducational; private control; related to Church of the Brethren; college of liberal arts.

NIC MEN'S	1985 Omicron Delta Kappa
1983 Sigma Chi	1986 Psi Chi
1989 Sigma Pi	1988 Gamma Theta Upsilon
NPC WOMEN'S	RECOGNITION
1987 Gamma Phi Beta	1939 Alpha Psi Omega
1989 Phi Sigma Sigma	
ACHS HONORS	INACTIVE
1925 Delta Sigma Rho-Tau	1900–76 Kappa Delta Phi (C)
Kappa Alpha	
1968 Phi Alpha Theta	COLONIES
1972 Alpha Chi	Sigma Tau Gamma
	1988 Theta Chi

BRIGHAM YOUNG UNIVERSITY Provo, UT. University; coeducational; private control; Church of Jesus Christ of Latter-day Saints. Founded in 1875 as Brigham Young Academy.

PROFESSIONAL	ACHS HONORS
1974 Phi Alpha Delta	Omicron Delta Epsilon
1976 Delta Theta Phi	1922 Delta Sigma Rho-Tau
	Kappa Alpha
OTHER PROFESSIONAL	1936 Sigma Pi Sigma
1959 Sigma Delta Chi	1947 Phi Eta Sigma
1965 Beta Alpha Psi	1948 Phi Alpha Theta
1969 Delta Pi Epsilon	1951 Phi Kappa Phi
1970 Alpha Zeta	1952 Kappa Tau Alpha
	1952 Pi Sigma Alpha

1954 Psi Chi
1959 Sigma Delta Pi
1961 Kappa Omicron Nu
1962 Alpha Kappa Delta
1963 Pi Delta Phi
1964 Beta Gamma Sigma
1964 Tau Beta Pi
1967 Gamma Theta Upsilon
1969 Alpha Epsilon Delta
1969 Pi Kappa Lambda
1971 Eta Kappa Nu
1975 Beta Phi Mu

OTHER HONORS
1948 Sigma Gamma Epsilon
1950 Sigma Xi
1968 Pi Mu Epsilon

SERVICE
    The National Spurs

1941 Intercollegiate Knights
1949 Alpha Phi Omega

RECOGNITION
    Angel Flight
    Arnold Air Society (H-1)
1924 Theta Alpha Phi
1932 Blue Key
1962 Delta Phi Alpha
1968 Sigma Delta Psi

INACTIVE
1928–52 Alpha Kappa Psi
1929–76 Delta Phi Kappa
1931–74 Beta Beta Beta
1938–65 Phi Chi Theta
1950–77 Alpha Lambda Delta
1953–73 Phi Mu Alpha—
        Sinfonia
1955–60 Mu Phi Epsilon

Hawaii Campus Laie, Oahu, HI. Private control: Church of Jesus Christ of Latter-Day Saints (Mormons). Founded in 1955. Affiliated with Brigham Young University in 1974.

Freshmen and foreign sponsored students must live on campus. Pledge of conduct is required. Dress and hair code.

ACHS HONORS
1968 Phi Alpha Theta

1970 Alpha Chi

UNIVERSITY OF BRITISH COLUMBIA Vancouver, BC. Established 1908; coeducational.

The fraternities may own the houses and property which they occupy.

NIC MEN'S
    Alpha Epsilon Pi
1926 Alpha Delta Phi
1926 Zeta Psi
1929 Phi Gamma Delta
1930 Phi Delta Theta
1935 Psi Upsilon
1936 Beta Theta Pi
1936 Phi Kappa Sigma
1941 Kappa Sigma
1942 Zeta Beta Tau
1949 Delta Kappa Epsilon
1949 Sigma Chi

NPC WOMEN'S
1928 Delta Gamma
1928 Gamma Phi Beta
1929 Alpha Phi
1929 Kappa Kappa Gamma

1930 Alpha Gamma Delta
1931 Alpha Delta Pi
1946 Delta Phi Epsilon

PROFESSIONAL
1926 Phi Alpha Delta
1932 Sigma Phi Delta
1956 Lambda Kappa Sigma

OTHER HONORS
1954 Alpha Omega Alpha

INACTIVE
1930–80 Kappa Alpha Theta
1932–84 Alpha Omicron Pi
1935–72 Delta Upsilon
1947–71 Alpha Tau Omega
1948–53 Sigma Delta Pi
1949–59 Sigma Alpha Mu
1950–62 Lambda Chi Alpha

BROOKLYN COLLEGE OF THE CITY UNIVERSITY OF NEW YORK Brooklyn, NY. College of liberal arts; coeducational; public control; municipal; governed by the board of higher education of the College of the City of New York; established 1930.

NIC MEN'S
1914 Tau Delta Phi
1921 Alpha Phi Delta
1934 Alpha Phi Delta
1956 Alpha Epsilon Pi
1957 Sigma Alpha Mu

1958 Tau Epsilon Phi
1959 Tau Delta Phi
1960 Zeta Beta Tau

NPHC MEN'S
    Phi Beta Sigma

Phi Beta Sigma
1924 Omega Psi Phi
1953 Alpha Phi Alpha

NPC WOMEN'S
1959 Sigma Delta Tau

OTHER PROFESSIONAL
1971 Alpha Epsilon Rho

ACHS HONORS
    Omicron Delta Epsilon
1936 Eta Kappa Nu
1940 Tau Beta Pi
1946 Eta Kappa Nu
1946 Phi Alpha Theta
1949 Chi Epsilon
1951 Psi Chi
1961 Psi Chi
1964 Omega Chi Epsilon
1967 Pi Sigma Alpha
1990 Phi Alpha Theta

SERVICE
1939 Alpha Phi Omega
1940 Alpha Phi Omega

INACTIVE
1855–13 Alpha Delta Phi
1856–73 Delta Kappa Epsilon
1857–73 Chi Psi
1865–06 Phi Gamma Delta
1874–78 Delta Upsilon
1881–31 Theta Delta Chi
1884–91 Phi Delta Theta
1896–73 Phi Sigma Kappa
1899–14 Delta Sigma Phi
1910–20 Zeta Beta Tau
1919–34 Pi Lambda Phi
1931–72 Alpha Delta Pi
1931–84 Delta Phi Epsilon
1933–69 Kappa Delta
1954–69 Phi Sigma Sigma
1954–76 Alpha Epsilon Phi
1958–73 Alpha Epsilon Pi
1958–73 Pi Lambda Phi
1960–72 Alpha Sigma Tau
1966–71 Alpha Epsilon Phi
1966–74 Tau Kappa Epsilon
1974–83 Kappa Omicron Nu

BROOKLYN LAW SCHOOL Brooklyn, NY.

PROFESSIONAL
1907 Phi Delta Phi

1922 Delta Theta Phi
1922 Phi Alpha Delta

BROWARD COMMUNITY COLLEGE Fort Lauderdale, FL.

SERVICE
1987 Alpha Phi Omega

INACTIVE
1974–88 Tau Kappa Epsilon

BROWN UNIVERSITY Providence, RI. Founded and chartered in 1764. University; undergraduate college for men; graduate school coeducational; private control; nonsectarian.

All fraternities are housed in a residential quadrangle owned by the university. Each student is responsible to the university for his room rent.

NIC MEN'S
1836 Alpha Delta Phi
1838 Delta Phi
1840 Psi Upsilon
1852 Delta Psi
1853 Theta Delta Chi
1868 Delta Upsilon
1896 Delta Tau Delta
1898 Kappa Sigma
1902 Phi Kappa Psi
1914 Sigma Chi
1983 Kappa Alpha Psi (A)

NPHC MEN'S
    Phi Beta Sigma
1947 Omega Psi Phi

NPC WOMEN'S
1897 Kappa Alpha Theta
1908 Alpha Omicron Pi
1979 Alpha Chi Omega

NPHC WOMEN'S
1974 Alpha Kappa Alpha

ACHS HONORS
    Omicron Delta Epsilon

1909 Delta Sigma Rho-Tau
    Kappa Alpha
1954 Tau Beta Pi

OTHER HONORS
1830 Phi Beta Kappa
1900 Sigma Xi

SERVICE
1963 Alpha Phi Omega

RECOGNITION
    Arnold Air Society (A-1)

INACTIVE
1849–73 Beta Theta Pi
1850–63 Delta Kappa Epsilon
1852–87 Zeta Psi
1860–71 Chi Psi
1872–95 Chi Phi
1889–30 Phi Kappa Theta
1889–68 Phi Delta Theta
1894–40 Alpha Tau Omega
1902–68 Phi Gamma Delta
1906–39 Phi Sigma Kappa
1908–11 Sigma Kappa
1912–19 Sigma Phi Epsilon
1912–64 Sigma Nu

1912–68 Lambda Chi Alpha
1916–18 Zeta Beta Tau

1921–48 Alpha Phi Alpha
1929–63 Pi Lambda Phi

BRYANT COLLEGE   Smithfield, RI.

NIC MEN'S
1967 Tau Epsilon Phi
1968 Tau Kappa Epsilon
1969 Phi Kappa Tau
1985 Kappa Delta Rho
1989 Sigma Phi Epsilon
1990 Phi Kappa Sigma

NPC WOMEN'S
1990 Alpha Phi
1990 Theta Phi Alpha

ACHS HONORS
Omicron Delta Epsilon

1970 Delta Mu Delta

INACTIVE
1969–71 Alpha Sigma Tau
1970–72 Theta Chi
1970–74 Delta Sigma Phi

COLONIES
Pi Kappa Phi
1989 Delta Chi
1990 Delta Zeta

BUCKNELL UNIVERSITY   Lewisburg, PA.
Founded 1846, charter granted the same year. Management committed to a board of trustees; undergraduate college, coeducational; private control; nonsectarian.

Seven fraternities occupy houses and property which they own, three own and occupy houses on college-owned land and, three reside in university-owned and operated residence halls. Sororities have suites in a residence hall in which their members live.

NIC MEN'S
1855 Phi Kappa Psi
1864 Sigma Chi
1882 Phi Gamma Delta
1893 Sigma Alpha Epsilon
1896 Kappa Sigma
1913 Lambda Chi Alpha
1921 Kappa Delta Rho
1930 Alpha Phi Delta
1932 Sigma Alpha Mu
1938 Sigma Phi Epsilon
1947 Tau Kappa Epsilon
1947 Theta Chi
1950 Delta Upsilon
1984 Chi Phi

NPHC MEN'S
Phi Beta Sigma

NPC WOMEN'S
1895 Pi Beta Phi
1898 Alpha Chi Omega
1904 Delta Delta Delta
1922 Phi Mu
1948 Kappa Kappa Gamma
1978 Delta Gamma
1978 Gamma Phi Beta
1984 Kappa Alpha Theta

PROFESSIONAL
1916 Mu Phi Epsilon

OTHER PROFESSIONAL
1930 Kappa Phi Kappa

ACHS HONORS
Omicron Delta Epsilon
1921 Delta Sigma Rho-Tau
Kappa Alpha
1930 Pi Sigma Alpha
1931 Phi Sigma
1932 Delta Mu Delta

1938 Alpha Lambda Delta
1939 Phi Eta Sigma
1941 Mortar Board
1941 Phi Alpha Theta
1943 Sigma Delta Pi
1946 Alpha Kappa Delta
1946 Omicron Delta Kappa
1947 Tau Beta Pi
1950 Psi Chi
1951 Pi Delta Phi
1955 Phi Sigma Tau
1961 Kappa Delta Pi

OTHER HONORS
National Order of Omega
1925 Pi Mu Epsilon
1940 Phi Beta Kappa

SERVICE
1950 Alpha Phi Omega

RECOGNITION
1919 Theta Alpha Phi
1932 Delta Phi Alpha

INACTIVE
1865–77 Theta Delta Chi
1915–70 Kappa Delta
1925–50 Phi Mu Alpha—
Sinfonia
1927–69 Sigma Tau Delta
1928–33 Phi Kappa Theta
1930–78 Delta Zeta
1932–69 Alpha Chi Sigma
1938–60 Kappa Delta Epsilon
1948–74 Sigma Pi Sigma
1948–78 Alpha Phi
1953–64 Alpha Sigma Alpha
1980–82 Delta Phi Epsilon

COLONIES
1991 Psi Upsilon

BUENA VISTA COLLEGE   Storm Lake, IA.
Founded 1891. Coeducational; private control; Presbyterian related; grants B.A. and B.S. degrees.

ACHS HONORS
1937 Sigma Tau Delta
1966 Phi Alpha Theta
1970 Alpha Chi
1970 Pi Delta Phi

RECOGNITION
1924 Pi Kappa Delta

1926 Alpha Psi Omega

INACTIVE
1965–89 Phi Mu Alpha—
Sinfonia

BUTLER UNIVERSITY   Indianapolis, IN. University; coeducational; private control; chartered as Northwestern Christian University 1850; name changed in 1877 in honor of Ovid Butler. Includes colleges of liberal arts, education, business administration, fine arts and pharmacy. Butler also has a University College.

The fraternities and sororities occupy houses and property they own.

NIC MEN'S
1859 Phi Delta Theta
1865 Sigma Chi
1875 Delta Tau Delta
1915 Lambda Chi Alpha
1926 Sigma Nu
1951 Tau Kappa Epsilon
1971 Phi Kappa Psi

NPC WOMEN'S
1874 Kappa Alpha Theta
1878 Kappa Kappa Gamma
1897 Pi Beta Phi
1914 Delta Delta Delta
1925 Alpha Chi Omega
1925 Delta Gamma
1928 Alpha Sigma Alpha
1967 Alpha Phi

NPHC WOMEN'S
1922 Sigma Gamma Rho

PROFESSIONAL
1906 Mu Phi Epsilon
1911 Sigma Alpha Iota
1930 Kappa Psi
1938 Lambda Kappa Sigma
1945 Delta Psi Kappa
1955 Phi Delta Chi

OTHER PROFESSIONAL
1926 Sigma Delta Chi
1927 Women in Communications

ACHS HONORS
Omicron Delta Epsilon
1908 Delta Sigma Rho-Tau
Kappa Alpha
1922 Phi Kappa Phi
1931 Kappa Delta Pi
1931 Phi Eta Sigma

1935 Sigma Tau Delta
1949 Alpha Lambda Delta
1952 Kappa Mu Epsilon
1953 Rho Chi
1956 Mortar Board
1960 Sigma Delta Pi
1970 Phi Alpha Theta
1976 Pi Kappa Lambda
1977 Kappa Omicron Nu
1982 Lambda Sigma Society
1986 Phi Sigma Iota

SERVICE
The National Spurs
1936 Alpha Phi Omega

RECOGNITION
Angel Flight
Arnold Air Society (D-2)
1926 Blue Key
1950 Eta Sigma Phi

INACTIVE
1878–81 Beta Theta Pi
1891–80 Kappa Sigma
1920–56 Zeta Tau Alpha
1924–35 Delta Zeta
1925–33 Alpha Delta Pi
1926–35 National Collegiate
Players
1926–86 Phi Mu Alpha—
Sinfonia
1927–40 Alpha Omicron Pi
1928–33 Sigma Sigma Sigma
1928–37 Kappa Delta Rho
1931 Phi Beta
1931–35 Kappa Delta
1948–57 Sigma Alpha Mu
1949–80 Kappa Sigma
1953–76 Phi Kappa Theta

CABRINI COLLEGE Radnor, PA. Private control: Roman Catholic. Founded in 1957. Four-year; coeducational; liberal arts college.

On campus housing is available.

ACHS HONORS
1966 Lambda Iota Tau
1974 Phi Alpha Theta
1980 Theta Alpha Kappa

1983 Psi Chi

RECOGNITION
1974 Beta Beta Beta

CALDWELL COLLEGE FOR WOMEN Caldwell, NJ. College of liberal arts for women; private control; Roman Catholic Church; incorporated 1939.

PROFESSIONAL
1989 Kappa Delta Epsilon

ACHS HONORS
1944 Delta Epsilon Sigma
1957 Sigma Tau Delta
1971 Alpha Chi

1977 Theta Alpha Kappa
1987 Phi Sigma Iota
1989 Phi Alpha Theta

INACTIVE
1907-08 Kappa Delta

UNIVERSITY OF CALGARY Calgary, AB. A provincial university; coeducational; nondenominational; government supported. Established 1945.

There is no formal recognition of fraternities by the University Administration, and there are no provisions for fraternity housing on campus.

NIC MEN'S
1967 Zeta Psi
1984 Kappa Sigma
1984 Phi Gamma Delta
1988 Lambda Chi Alpha
1990 Delta Upsilon

NPC WOMEN'S
1983 Alpha Gamma Delta
1985 Alpha Omicron Pi

INACTIVE
1968-70 Theta Delta Chi
1970-76 Phi Delta Theta

UNIVERSITY OF CALIFORNIA Oakland, CA.

NIC MEN'S
1921 Zeta Beta Tau
1947 Kappa Alpha Psi (A)

NPHC WOMEN'S
1984 Alpha Kappa Alpha

INACTIVE
1922-41 Delta Theta Phi
1925-34 Phi Mu Delta

UNIVERSITY OF CALIFORNIA, BERKELEY Berkeley, CA. State university; coeducational; founded 1868; selected as site for College of California 1857.

Fraternities and sororities own their own houses on their own land.

NIC MEN'S
1870 Zeta Psi
1873 Phi Delta Theta
1875 Chi Phi
1876 Delta Kappa Epsilon
1879 Beta Theta Pi
1881 Phi Gamma Delta
1886 Sigma Chi
1894 Sigma Alpha Epsilon
1895 Chi Psi
1896 Delta Upsilon
1898 Delta Tau Delta

1899 Phi Kappa Psi
1900 Alpha Tau Omega
1900 Theta Delta Chi
1901 Kappa Sigma
1902 Psi Upsilon
1903 Phi Kappa Sigma
1905 Acacia
1908 Alpha Delta Phi
1909 Phi Sigma Kappa
1909 Pi Kappa Phi
1910 Delta Chi
1910 Sigma Phi Epsilon

1910 Theta Xi
1912 Pi Kappa Alpha
1912 Sigma Phi Society
1913 Alpha Sigma Phi
1913 Lambda Chi Alpha
1913 Sigma Pi
1913 Theta Chi
1914 Alpha Kappa Lambda
1915 Delta Sigma Phi
1919 Tau Kappa Epsilon
1921 Phi Kappa Tau
1922 Pi Lambda Phi
1924 Kappa Delta Rho
1929 Sigma Alpha Mu
1949 Alpha Epsilon Pi

NPHC MEN'S
    Phi Beta Sigma

NPC WOMEN'S
1880 Kappa Kappa Gamma
1890 Kappa Alpha Theta
1894 Gamma Phi Beta
1900 Delta Delta Delta
1900 Pi Beta Phi
1901 Alpha Phi
1902 Chi Omega
1907 Alpha Omicron Pi
1907 Delta Gamma
1909 Alpha Chi Omega
1910 Sigma Kappa
1913 Alpha Delta Pi
1915 Alpha Gamma Delta
1916 Phi Mu
1923 Alpha Epsilon Phi

NPHC WOMEN'S
1922 Alpha Kappa Alpha

PROFESSIONAL
1911 Phi Alpha Delta
1913 Alpha Chi Sigma
1913 Phi Delta Phi
1920 Alpha Omega
1922 Delta Sigma Pi

ACHS HONORS
    Omicron Delta Epsilon
1907 Tau Beta Pi
1915 Eta Kappa Nu
1924 Xi Sigma Pi
1925 Chi Epsilon
1925 Mortar Board
1926 Pi Sigma Alpha
1938 Phi Alpha Theta
1941 Psi Chi
1979 Phi Sigma Iota
1984 Sigma Pi Sigma

OTHER HONORS
    National Order of Omega

SERVICE
1939 Alpha Phi Omega

INACTIVE
1909-69 Alpha Xi Delta
1911-75 Theta Tau
1915-69 Delta Zeta
1915-69 Zeta Tau Alpha
1917-69 Kappa Delta
1923-69 Alpha Chi Rho
1925-84 Phi Chi Theta
1926-66 Phi Sigma Sigma
1947-62 Phi Eta Sigma
1948-68 Delta Phi Epsilon

UNIVERSITY OF CALIFORNIA, DAVIS Davis, CA. Founded 1908 as branch of College of Agriculture; in 1951 became a general campus of the University of California. Undergraduate and graduate education in Colleges of Letters and Science, Agriculture, Engineering; School of Veterinary Medicine, School of Law, and School of Medicine. Coeducational, state university, administered by Board of Regents.

Fraternities are permitted to own their own houses on their own land.

NIC MEN'S
1923 Alpha Gamma Rho
1951 Kappa Sigma
1952 Sigma Nu
1952 Theta Xi
1954 Delta Sigma Phi
1954 Phi Delta Theta
1963 Sigma Phi Epsilon
1967 Theta Chi
1969 Chi Phi
1979 Kappa Alpha Psi (A)
1979 Phi Kappa Psi
1979 Sigma Alpha Mu
1981 Zeta Psi
1982 Sigma Pi
1985 Pi Kappa Alpha
1985 Sigma Chi
1987 FarmHouse
1987 Lambda Chi Alpha
1988 Alpha Epsilon Pi
1989 Zeta Beta Tau
1990 Pi Kappa Phi

NPHC MEN'S
    Phi Beta Sigma
1972 Alpha Phi Alpha

NPC WOMEN'S
1974 Alpha Phi
1974 Delta Delta Delta
1974 Phi Mu
1975 Alpha Omicron Pi
1975 Chi Omega
1975 Delta Gamma
1975 Kappa Kappa Gamma
1980 Alpha Epsilon Phi
1986 Alpha Chi Omega

NPHC WOMEN'S
1974 Delta Sigma Theta (B)
1978 Alpha Kappa Alpha

PROFESSIONAL
1970 Phi Delta Phi
1972 Phi Alpha Delta
1990 Sigma Alpha

OTHER PROFESSIONAL
1940 Alpha Zeta

ACHS HONORS
    Omicron Delta Epsilon
1944 Kappa Omicron Nu
1954 Phi Kappa Phi
1966 Pi Sigma Alpha
1969 Tau Beta Pi
1974 Pi Delta Phi
1981 Phi Alpha Theta
1981 Sigma Pi Sigma
1982 Psi Chi
1982 Sigma Lambda Alpha

OTHER HONORS
1972 Alpha Omega Alpha

1972 Order of the Coif

SERVICE
1951 Alpha Phi Omega

RECOGNITION
1951 Scabbard and Blade (9)

INACTIVE
1948–73 Phi Sigma Kappa
1952–89 Sigma Alpha Epsilon
1966–71 Delta Upsilon
1967–71 Phi Kappa Tau

COLONIES
    Kappa Alpha Order
1989 Delta Chi
1989 Tau Kappa Epsilon

UNIVERSITY OF CALIFORNIA, IRVINE Irvine, CA. Established 1961; general campus of the University of California.

NIC MEN'S
1949 Chi Psi
1975 Beta Theta Pi
1975 Phi Delta Theta
1975 Sigma Chi
1982 Kappa Alpha Psi (A)
1982 Kappa Sigma
1982 Phi Gamma Delta
1987 Sigma Alpha Epsilon
1988 Alpha Epsilon Pi

NPC WOMEN'S
1974 Delta Gamma
1974 Gamma Phi Beta
1974 Pi Beta Phi
1977 Alpha Chi Omega
1979 Delta Delta Delta
1982 Kappa Kappa Gamma
1985 Kappa Alpha Theta
1988 Alpha Phi

NPHC WOMEN'S
1977 Alpha Kappa Alpha

PROFESSIONAL
1985 Phi Alpha Delta

ACHS HONORS
1970 Sigma Pi Sigma
1976 Eta Kappa Nu
1982 Tau Beta Pi
1986 Phi Alpha Theta
1988 Chi Epsilon
1988 Psi Chi

OTHER HONORS
    National Order of Omega

SERVICE
1967 Alpha Phi Omega

COLONIES
    Pi Kappa Phi
1991 Phi Kappa Psi

UNIVERSITY OF CALIFORNIA, LOS ANGELES Los Angeles, CA. State university; coeducational; established as normal school, 1881; transferred to university by legislature, 1919, as the University of California-Southern Branch; became UCLA, 1927.

Most of the NPC and NIC groups own or lease chapter houses.

NIC MEN'S
1923 Kappa Alpha Psi (A)
1923 Sigma Pi
1924 Phi Delta Theta
1924 Zeta Psi
1926 Alpha Sigma Phi
1926 Alpha Tau Omega
1926 Beta Theta Pi
1926 Delta Tau Delta
1926 Kappa Sigma
1926 Phi Kappa Sigma
1926 Sigma Alpha Mu
1927 Delta Sigma Phi
1927 Zeta Beta Tau
1928 Tau Delta Phi
1928 Theta Xi
1929 Sigma Alpha Epsilon
1929 Theta Delta Chi
1930 Lambda Chi Alpha
1930 Sigma Nu

1931 Chi Phi
1931 Phi Gamma Delta
1931 Phi Kappa Psi
1931 Theta Chi
1947 Sigma Chi
1947 Tau Epsilon Phi
1947 Tau Kappa Epsilon
1957 Triangle
1984 Sigma Phi Epsilon

NPHC MEN'S
    Phi Beta Sigma
    Phi Beta Sigma
    Phi Beta Sigma

NPC WOMEN'S
1923 Chi Omega
1924 Alpha Epsilon Phi
1924 Alpha Phi
1924 Gamma Phi Beta
1925 Alpha Delta Pi

1925 Delta Delta Delta
1925 Delta Gamma
1925 Delta Zeta
1925 Kappa Alpha Theta
1925 Kappa Kappa Gamma
1925 Sigma Kappa
1926 Alpha Chi Omega
1926 Kappa Delta
1927 Pi Beta Phi

NPHC WOMEN'S
1925 Alpha Kappa Alpha

PROFESSIONAL
1925 Sigma Alpha Iota
1926 Alpha Kappa Psi
1928 Alpha Tau Delta
1929 Kappa Kappa Psi
1935 Alpha Chi Sigma
1938 Mu Phi Epsilon
1951 Phi Alpha Delta
1951 Phi Delta Phi
1970 Alpha Omega
1971 Delta Theta Phi
1973 Tau Beta Sigma

OTHER PROFESSIONAL
1926 Phi Epsilon Kappa
1931 Pi Lambda Theta
1950 Nu Beta Epsilon
1953 Phi Delta Epsilon
1954 Sigma Delta Chi
1957 Alpha Lambda Gamma
1964 Delta Pi Epsilon
1969 Delta Sigma Delta

ACHS HONORS
    Omicron Delta Epsilon
1923 Pi Sigma Alpha
1925 Kappa Omicron Nu
1926 Pi Delta Phi
1926 Sigma Delta Pi
1929 Psi Chi
1932 Pi Gamma Mu
1936 Phi Eta Sigma
1939 Mortar Board
1940 Alpha Lambda Delta
1940 Beta Gamma Sigma
1952 Tau Beta Pi
1953 Sigma Pi Sigma
1962 Phi Alpha Theta
1984 Eta Kappa Nu
1985 Beta Phi Mu

OTHER HONORS
    National Order of Omega
1925 Pi Mu Epsilon

1933 Sigma Xi
1938 Phi Beta Kappa
1954 Order of the Coif
1956 Alpha Omega Alpha

SERVICE
1931 Alpha Phi Omega

RECOGNITION
    Angel Flight
    Arnold Air Society (I)
1923 Pi Kappa Delta
1925 Scabbard and Blade (6)
1930 Blue Key
1932 Delta Phi Alpha
1935 Phi Lambda Upsilon
1958 Iota Tau Tau

INACTIVE
1921   Phi Sigma Sigma
1922–69 Pi Lambda Phi
1924–80 Alpha Xi Delta
1925–69 Phi Beta
1925–73 Alpha Omicron Pi
1925–82 Alpha Gamma Delta
1926–51 Alpha Sigma Alpha
1926–54 Theta Phi Alpha
1926–86 Zeta Tau Alpha
1927–87 Phi Mu
1927–87 Sigma Delta Tau
1929–52 Delta Upsilon
1930   Zeta Phi Eta
1931–60 Kappa Alpha Order
1932–47 Sigma Gamma Epsilon
1932–52 Delta Kappa Epsilon
1934–58 Delta Chi
1936   Alpha Eta Rho
1937–61 Alpha Zeta
1937–73 Phi Mu Alpha—
    Sinfonia
1938–70 Phi Chi Theta
1947–54 Phi Sigma
1947–59 Alpha Phi Alpha
1948–83 Acacia
1950–87 Phi Kappa Tau
1951–65 Sigma Phi Delta
1952   Phi Chi
1953–57 Rho Epsilon
1953–61 Pi Omega Pi
1956–71 Delta Phi Epsilon
1967–71 Beta Alpha Psi

COLONIES
    Pi Kappa Alpha
1948 Alpha Epsilon Pi

UNIVERSITY OF CALIFORNIA, RIVERSIDE Riverside, CA. Academic divisions of the University of California, Riverside, include college of letters and science, school of agricultural sciences, graduate division, and summer session; school of administration and engineering will begin 1969; established 1907 as Citrus Experiment Station; college of letters and sciences added 1948; became general campus of the University of California 1959.

NIC MEN'S
1974 Kappa Alpha Psi (A)
1977 Phi Gamma Delta
1978 Phi Kappa Sigma
1987 Phi Delta Theta
1989 Alpha Tau Omega

1990 Sigma Alpha Epsilon

NPC WOMEN'S
1976 Gamma Phi Beta
1976 Kappa Alpha Theta
1976 Kappa Kappa Gamma
1986 Sigma Kappa

1988 Pi Beta Phi
1990 Delta Gamma

NPHC WOMEN'S
1976 Alpha Kappa Alpha

PROFESSIONAL
1974 Mu Phi Epsilon
1989 Delta Sigma Pi

ACHS HONORS
    Omicron Delta Epsilon

1968 Sigma Delta Pi
1987 Psi Chi

OTHER HONORS
    National Order of Omega
1965 Phi Beta Kappa
1965 Pi Mu Epsilon

COLONIES
    Beta Theta Pi
    Kappa Alpha Order

UNIVERSITY OF CALIFORNIA, SAN DIEGO La Jolla, CA. Public institution. Founded in 1964. Four-year; coeducational.

NIC MEN'S
    Alpha Epsilon Pi
1947 Sigma Phi Epsilon
1982 Phi Delta Theta
1984 Delta Sigma Phi
1985 Zeta Beta Tau
1986 Pi Kappa Phi
1986 Sigma Alpha Mu
1987 Sigma Alpha Epsilon
1987 Sigma Pi
1988 Delta Tau Delta
1988 Sigma Phi Epsilon
1991 Sigma Chi

NPC WOMEN'S
1949 Alpha Phi

1977 Alpha Omicron Pi
1978 Sigma Kappa
1981 Delta Gamma
1987 Pi Beta Phi
1989 Delta Delta Delta

OTHER HONORS
    National Order of Omega

SERVICE
1967 Alpha Phi Omega

COLONIES
    Beta Theta Pi
1992 Alpha Chi Omega

UNIVERSITY OF CALIFORNIA, SANTA BARBARA Santa Barbara, CA. Established 1891 as a private school, later taken over by the city; 1909 as Santa Barbara State Normal School of Manual Arts and Home Economics came under state control; in 1921 became Santa Barbara State Teachers College; changed to Santa Barbara State College 1935; to Santa Barbara College of the University of California 1944; moved to present site 1954; became a general campus of the University of California 1958. Coeducational; both undergraduate and graduate; nonsectarian.

Fraternities and sororities occupy their own houses on their own land.

NIC MEN'S
1947 Sigma Phi Epsilon
1949 Lambda Chi Alpha
1949 Sigma Alpha Epsilon
1964 Phi Kappa Psi
1965 Sigma Chi
1966 Phi Sigma Kappa
1967 Phi Delta Theta
1968 Zeta Beta Tau
1988 Alpha Epsilon Pi
1988 Delta Upsilon
1989 Pi Kappa Alpha

NPHC MEN'S
1976 Alpha Phi Alpha

NPC WOMEN'S
1950 Alpha Delta Pi
1950 Alpha Phi
1950 Chi Omega
1950 Delta Gamma
1950 Kappa Alpha Theta
1950 Pi Beta Phi

1950 Sigma Kappa
1965 Alpha Chi Omega
1978 Kappa Kappa Gamma
1982 Kappa Delta
1983 Gamma Phi Beta
1987 Delta Delta Delta

PROFESSIONAL
1965 Mu Phi Epsilon

ACHS HONORS
    Omicron Delta Epsilon
1927 Kappa Delta Pi
1941 Delta Sigma Rho-Tau
    Kappa Alpha
1949 Phi Alpha Theta
1950 Pi Sigma Alpha
1965 Mortar Board
1967 Alpha Lambda Delta
1969 Eta Kappa Nu
1979 Psi Chi
1981 Tau Beta Pi

OTHER HONORS
    National Order of Omega

SERVICE
1931 Alpha Phi Omega

RECOGNITION
1951 Scabbard and Blade (9)

INACTIVE
1925–67 Delta Zeta
1928–61 Kappa Omicron Nu
1943–56 Sigma Tau Gamma
1947–70 Kappa Sigma

1948–63 Delta Sigma Phi
1948–76 Sigma Pi
1949–88 Delta Tau Delta
1964–86 Pi Kappa Lambda
1966–71 Alpha Delta Phi
1966–76 Sigma Pi Sigma
1968–71 Alpha Epsilon Phi
1968–80 Theta Delta Chi
1981–84 Alpha Gamma Delta

COLONIES
    Beta Theta Pi

UNIVERSITY OF CALIFORNIA, SANTA CRUZ Santa Cruz, CA.

NIC MEN'S
1989 Sigma Alpha Epsilon
1989 Theta Chi

NPC WOMEN'S
1990 Gamma Phi Beta

ACHS HONORS
1989 Psi Chi

INACTIVE
1981–86 Sigma Pi Sigma

UNIVERSITY OF CALIFORNIA, SAN FRANCISCO MEDICAL CENTER San Francisco, CA. Founded 1864 as Toland Medical College; became part of University 1902; colleges of pharmacy, dentistry, medicine, and nursing.

PROFESSIONAL
1902 Phi Delta Chi

1919 Lambda Kappa Sigma

UNIVERSITY OF CALIFORNIA, SAN FRANCISCO San Francisco, CA.

ACHS HONORS
1949 Rho Chi

1964 Sigma Theta Tau

CALIFORNIA BAPTIST COLLEGE Riverside, CA. Private control: Southern Baptist Church. Founded in 1950. Four-year; coeducational; liberal arts college.

On campus housing is available in single-sex dormitories.

ACHS HONORS
1969 Alpha Chi

CALIFORNIA COLLEGE OF MEDICINE Irvine, CA.

SERVICE
1961 Alpha Phi Omega

INACTIVE
1963   Phi Chi

1964–74 Phi Rho Sigma

CALIFORNIA UNIVERSITY OF PENNSYLVANIA California, PA. Public institution. Founded in 1852. Four-year; coeducational.

Fraternities and sororities own their own houses.

NIC MEN'S
    Tau Kappa Epsilon
1959 Sigma Tau Gamma

1960 Alpha Kappa Lambda
1962 Delta Sigma Phi
1965 Theta Xi

1971 Kappa Alpha Psi (A)
1974 Delta Chi
1985 Phi Mu Delta
1987 Phi Kappa Sigma
1990 Acacia

NPHC MEN'S
    Phi Beta Sigma

NPC WOMEN'S
1958 Delta Zeta
1959 Sigma Kappa
1960 Sigma Sigma Sigma
1983 Alpha Sigma Tau
1985 Theta Phi Alpha
1990 Phi Sigma Sigma

NPHC WOMEN'S
1975 Alpha Kappa Alpha

OTHER PROFESSIONAL
1930 Phi Sigma Pi

ACHS HONORS
    Omicron Delta Epsilon
1933 Pi Gamma Mu
1941 Kappa Delta Pi
1958 Sigma Tau Delta
1961 Gamma Theta Upsilon
1970 Phi Alpha Theta
1989 Psi Chi

SERVICE
1956 Alpha Phi Omega

RECOGNITION
1964 Pi Kappa Delta

INACTIVE
1959–82 Tau Kappa Epsilon
1961–78 Zeta Tau Alpha
1963–81 Alpha Xi Delta
1970–83 Kappa Delta Epsilon
1972–79 Theta Delta Chi

CALIFORNIA INSTITUTE OF TECHNOLOGY

Pasadena, CA. A college, graduate school, and institute of research, in science, engineering, and the humanities; private control; coeducational; nonsectarian. Established 1891.

ACHS HONORS
    Omicron Delta Epsilon
1921 Tau Beta Pi

RECOGNITION
1952 Blue Key

1963 Society for Collegiate Journalists—Pi Delta Epsilon-Alpha Phi Gamma (A)

CALIFORNIA LUTHERAN COLLEGE

Thousand Oaks, CA. College of liberal arts; coeducational; private control; affiliated with American Lutheran Church and Lutheran Church in America; incorporated 1959.

ACHS HONORS
1971 Pi Delta Phi

SERVICE
    The National Spurs

RECOGNITION
1967 Alpha Psi Omega

INACTIVE
1968–81 Pi Gamma Mu

CALIFORNIA POLYTECHNIC STATE UNIVERSITY

Pomona, CA. Kellogg Campus; established 1901 as California Polytechnic School.

NIC MEN'S
1980 Sigma Phi Epsilon
1981 Acacia
1982 FarmHouse
1984 Phi Kappa Tau
1985 Sigma Chi
1986 Beta Theta Pi
1987 Phi Delta Theta
1989 Alpha Tau Omega
1990 Delta Sigma Phi

NPHC MEN'S
1974 Alpha Phi Alpha

NPC WOMEN'S
1980 Zeta Tau Alpha
1981 Kappa Delta
1981 Sigma Kappa
1983 Chi Omega

OTHER WOMEN'S
1986 CERES

PROFESSIONAL
1980 Alpha Rho Chi
1990 Sigma Alpha

OTHER PROFESSIONAL
1971 Sigma Delta Chi

ACHS HONORS
    Omicron Delta Epsilon
1964 Kappa Mu Epsilon
1966 Pi Gamma Mu
1969 Sigma Pi Sigma
1971 Eta Kappa Nu
1971 Pi Tau Sigma
1972 Eta Kappa Nu
1972 Tau Beta Pi
1973 Phi Alpha Theta
1973 Phi Kappa Phi
1979 Pi Sigma Alpha
1979 Sigma Lambda Alpha
1980 Xi Sigma Pi
1981 Delta Mu Delta
1982 Chi Epsilon

1982 Psi Chi
1984 Omega Chi Epsilon
1984 Pi Sigma Alpha

OTHER HONORS
    National Order of Omega

SERVICE
1948 Alpha Phi Omega
1969 Alpha Phi Omega

RECOGNITION
1963 Beta Beta Beta

INACTIVE
1969–89 Delta Sigma Pi
1973–86 Phi Chi Theta

COLONIES
    Alpha Epsilon Pi

CALIFORNIA POLYTECHNIC STATE UNIVERSITY

San Luis Obispo, CA. State college of agriculture, engineering, arts and sciences; coeducational; state control; established 1901; became four-year college in 1940.

Administration does not recognize social fraternities and sororities. No special quarters permitted.

NIC MEN'S
1923 Alpha Gamma Rho
1966 Phi Kappa Psi
1969 Alpha Epsilon Pi
1969 Delta Sigma Phi
1969 Theta Chi
1970 Delta Chi
1979 Lambda Chi Alpha
1984 Sigma Alpha Epsilon
1986 Sigma Chi
1987 Tau Kappa Epsilon
1988 Sigma Pi
1989 Kappa Sigma
1989 Pi Kappa Alpha
1990 Sigma Phi Epsilon

NPHC MEN'S
    Phi Beta Sigma

NPC WOMEN'S
1973 Sigma Kappa
1975 Alpha Phi
1975 Gamma Phi Beta
1975 Zeta Tau Alpha
1976 Kappa Delta
1978 Alpha Chi Omega
1986 Alpha Omicron Pi

1989 Kappa Alpha Theta

NPHC WOMEN'S
1977 Alpha Kappa Alpha

PROFESSIONAL
1981 Delta Sigma Pi
1982 Alpha Chi Sigma

ACHS HONORS
    Omicron Delta Epsilon
1958 Kappa Mu Epsilon
1965 Phi Kappa Phi
1968 Pi Gamma Mu
1969 Sigma Pi Sigma
1972 Tau Beta Pi
1979 Sigma Lambda Alpha
1986 Chi Epsilon

OTHER HONORS
    National Order of Omega

RECOGNITION
1960 Cardinal Key

COLONIES
    Phi Sigma Kappa
    Theta Xi
1970 Delta Upsilon

CALIFORNIA STATE COLLEGE, STANISLAUS

Turlock, CA. Public institution. Founded in 1959. Four-year; coeducational.

97% of students live off-campus or commute.

NIC MEN'S
1979 Theta Chi

ACHS HONORS
1984 Psi Chi
1990 Phi Alpha Theta

INACTIVE
1977–81 Sigma Kappa
1982–86 Phi Mu Alpha— Sinfonia

CALIFORNIA STATE COLLEGE OF PENNSYLVANIA

California, PA. Founded as an Academy in 1852; in 1914 became Southwestern Normal School, a state-owned institution; in 1928 name changed to California State Teachers College which was granted the right to offer a four-year curriculum and a degree of bachelor of science in education; in 1961 name was changed to California State College which now offers both bachelor's and master's degrees in education. The college has recently been granted the right to establish a liberal arts program. California State College is coeducational, state controlled.

NPHC WOMEN'S
1972 Delta Sigma Theta (B)

OTHER PROFESSIONAL
1969 Kappa Phi Kappa

SERVICE
1978 Alpha Phi Omega

RECOGNITION
1929 Alpha Psi Omega
1966 Society for Collegiate Journalists—Pi Delta Epsilon-Alpha Phi Gamma (P)

CALIFORNIA STATE UNIVERSITY, BAKERSFIELD Bakersfield, CA.

NIC MEN'S
1985 Sigma Pi
1987 Delta Upsilon

NPC WOMEN'S
1983 Gamma Phi Beta

NPHC WOMEN'S
1977 Sigma Gamma Rho

ACHS HONORS
  Omicron Delta Epsilon
  Pi Alpha Alpha
1976 Beta Gamma Sigma
1977 Phi Alpha Theta

CALIFORNIA STATE UNIVERSITY, CHICO
Chico, CA. State-supported liberal arts and teacher training college; founded as normal school in 1887; status changed in 1921 to state teachers college; became four-year college in 1924, granting baccalaureate degree and, in 1949, the master of arts degree.

Fraternities own their own houses on their own land. Sorority members rent or own their houses on private land.

NIC MEN'S
1958 Phi Kappa Tau
1961 Tau Kappa Epsilon
1975 Sigma Nu
1978 Alpha Gamma Rho
1981 Kappa Alpha Psi (A)
1982 Theta Chi
1984 Lambda Chi Alpha
1987 Beta Theta Pi
1987 Delta Chi
1988 Phi Delta Theta
1988 Pi Kappa Phi

NPHC MEN'S
  Phi Beta Sigma

NPC WOMEN'S
1924 Delta Zeta
1959 Alpha Gamma Delta
1959 Sigma Kappa
1975 Zeta Tau Alpha
1986 Pi Beta Phi
1988 Gamma Phi Beta
1990 Alpha Delta Pi

PROFESSIONAL
1960 Delta Sigma Pi
1976 Phi Chi Theta

OTHER PROFESSIONAL
1973 Beta Alpha Psi

ACHS HONORS
  Omicron Delta Epsilon
1926 Kappa Delta Pi
1959 Gamma Theta Upsilon
1962 Phi Kappa Phi
1963 Phi Sigma Tau
1964 Psi Chi
1967 Phi Eta Sigma
1973 Beta Gamma Sigma
1983 Sigma Pi Sigma
1985 Eta Kappa Nu
1988 Phi Alpha Theta

OTHER HONORS
  National Order of Omega

SERVICE
  The National Spurs
1949 Alpha Phi Omega
1971 Gamma Sigma Sigma

RECOGNITION
1936 Blue Key
1937 Cardinal Key

INACTIVE
1950–78 Pi Omega Pi
1968–87 Sigma Phi Epsilon

COLONIES
1956 Delta Sigma Phi

CALIFORNIA STATE UNIVERSITY, DOMINGUEZ HILLS Carson, CA.

NIC MEN'S
  Tau Kappa Epsilon

PROFESSIONAL
1976 Mu Phi Epsilon

1984 Phi Alpha Delta

ACHS HONORS
  Pi Alpha Alpha
1972 Phi Alpha Theta
1972 Psi Chi

1974 Pi Delta Phi
1984 Phi Kappa Phi
1989 Delta Mu Delta

COLONIES
  Sigma Pi

CALIFORNIA STATE UNIVERSITY, FRESNO
Fresno, CA. Founded in 1911, under the Board of Trustees of the California State Colleges. Enrollment 14,900 with Bachelor Degrees in 80 fields and Master Degrees in 27; 1400-acre campus. College of liberal arts; coeducational.

Fraternities and sororities own their own houses on their own land.

NIC MEN'S
1942 Theta Chi
1949 Sigma Alpha Epsilon
1951 Kappa Sigma
1951 Sigma Nu
1952 Lambda Chi Alpha
1952 Sigma Chi
1963 Alpha Gamma Rho
1968 Delta Upsilon
1986 Pi Kappa Alpha
1987 Phi Gamma Delta

NPHC MEN'S
  Phi Beta Sigma
1952 Omega Psi Phi
1957 Alpha Phi Alpha

NPC WOMEN'S
1928 Delta Zeta
1951 Delta Gamma
1951 Phi Mu
1952 Alpha Xi Delta
1953 Kappa Alpha Theta
1954 Kappa Kappa Gamma

NPHC WOMEN'S
1959 Alpha Kappa Alpha

OTHER WOMEN'S
1987 CERES

PROFESSIONAL
1964 Phi Chi Theta
1965 Pi Sigma Epsilon
1980 Delta Sigma Pi

OTHER PROFESSIONAL
1962 Alpha Zeta
1969 Beta Alpha Psi
1971 Alpha Tau Alpha

1975 Phi Upsilon Omicron

ACHS HONORS
  Omicron Delta Epsilon
1929 Pi Gamma Mu
1935 Kappa Delta Pi
1935 Sigma Delta Pi
1951 Psi Chi
1953 Phi Kappa Phi
1968 Gamma Theta Upsilon
1974 Tau Beta Pi
1979 Eta Kappa Nu
1982 Sigma Pi Sigma
1984 Phi Sigma Iota
1987 Kappa Tau Alpha

OTHER HONORS
  National Order of Omega

RECOGNITION
  Arnold Air Society (I)
1936 Blue Key
1950 Sigma Delta Psi
1951 Beta Beta Beta
1957 National Block and Bridle Club
1976 Sigma Iota Epsilon

INACTIVE
1939–56 Kappa Delta Rho
1941–83 Phi Mu Alpha— Sinfonia
1947–59 Phi Sigma Kappa
1948–59 Sigma Pi
1951–56 Sigma Sigma Sigma
1953–71 Pi Omega Pi

COLONIES
1947 Delta Sigma Phi

CALIFORNIA STATE UNIVERSITY, FULLERTON
Fullerton, CA. Established in 1957 as Orange County State College; became part of the California System in 1964; coeducational state college; grants bachelor degrees in 24 major fields, and master's in 11 fields.

NIC MEN'S
1966 Phi Kappa Tau
1966 Phi Sigma Kappa
1967 Delta Chi
1969 Sigma Alpha Epsilon
1976 Delta Sigma Phi
1977 Lambda Chi Alpha
1978 Sigma Pi
1984 Kappa Sigma
1990 Pi Kappa Phi

NPHC MEN'S
  Phi Beta Sigma

NPC WOMEN'S
1968 Alpha Chi Omega
1968 Delta Zeta
1970 Alpha Delta Pi
1971 Gamma Phi Beta
1971 Sigma Kappa
1979 Zeta Tau Alpha

PROFESSIONAL
1965 Mu Phi Epsilon
1966 Phi Mu Alpha—Sinfonia
1986 Delta Sigma Pi

OTHER PROFESSIONAL
1968 Sigma Delta Chi
1972 Beta Alpha Psi

ACHS HONORS
Omicron Delta Epsilon
1962 Phi Alpha Theta
1965 Beta Gamma Sigma
1967 Psi Chi
1968 Phi Kappa Phi
1968 Pi Sigma Alpha

1969 Pi Kappa Lambda
1985 Kappa Tau Alpha
1988 Omicron Delta Kappa

OTHER HONORS
National Order of Omega

RECOGNITION
1967 Blue Key
1967 Kappa Pi

INACTIVE
1965–70 Phi Beta
1969–89 Tau Kappa Epsilon
1984–90 Sigma Alpha Mu

CALIFORNIA STATE UNIVERSITY, HAYWARD

Hayward, CA. College of liberal arts and teachers college; coeducational; state control; established as Alameda County State College in 1957; name changed to present 1963.

NIC MEN'S
1984 Delta Sigma Phi
1989 Kappa Alpha Psi (A)
1990 Delta Chi

NPHC MEN'S
Phi Beta Sigma

NPC WOMEN'S
1984 Sigma Sigma Sigma
1987 Alpha Phi

PROFESSIONAL
1966 Mu Phi Epsilon

OTHER PROFESSIONAL
1976 Sigma Delta Chi

ACHS HONORS
Omicron Delta Epsilon

1978 Sigma Pi Sigma

SERVICE
1964 Alpha Phi Omega

RECOGNITION
1966 Pi Kappa Delta

INACTIVE
1966–76 Delta Sigma Pi
1967–69 Pi Gamma Mu
1967–74 Phi Mu Alpha—
          Sinfonia
1971–84 Delta Mu Delta

COLONIES
1988 Theta Chi

CALIFORNIA STATE UNIVERSITY, LONG BEACH

Long Beach, CA. Established in 1949; largest of the nineteen campus California State University system; focus is on instruction through the Master's Degree in liberal arts and sciences, applied fields and the professions, as well as teacher preparation. Housing for fraternities and sororities is off-campus where the majority of the organizations own or lease houses.

NIC MEN'S
Tau Kappa Epsilon
1954 Tau Kappa Epsilon
1955 Acacia
1955 Sigma Alpha Epsilon
1955 Sigma Pi
1956 Phi Kappa Tau
1959 Kappa Sigma
1965 Theta Chi
1968 Delta Chi
1970 Sigma Chi
1987 Delta Upsilon
1988 Alpha Epsilon Pi
1988 Pi Kappa Alpha

NPHC MEN'S
Phi Beta Sigma

NPC WOMEN'S
1954 Delta Zeta
1954 Sigma Kappa
1955 Delta Delta Delta

1956 Alpha Phi
1959 Delta Gamma
1962 Gamma Phi Beta
1965 Alpha Omicron Pi

NPHC WOMEN'S
1969 Sigma Gamma Rho
1976 Alpha Kappa Alpha

OTHER WOMEN'S
Lambda Delta Sigma

PROFESSIONAL
1960 Pi Sigma Epsilon
1961 Phi Mu Alpha—Sinfonia
1966 Alpha Tau Delta
1988 Delta Sigma Pi

OTHER PROFESSIONAL
1967 Alpha Epsilon Rho
1970 Sigma Delta Chi
1972 Beta Alpha Psi

ACHS HONORS
Omicron Delta Epsilon
Pi Alpha Alpha
1951 Gamma Theta Upsilon
1953 Delta Sigma Rho-Tau
      Kappa Alpha
1954 Psi Chi
1963 Phi Kappa Phi
1964 Phi Sigma Tau
1965 Eta Kappa Nu
1965 Pi Sigma Alpha
1965 Tau Beta Pi
1966 Alpha Lambda Delta
1966 Phi Eta Sigma
1969 Kappa Delta Pi
1969 Kappa Omicron Nu
1969 Phi Alpha Theta
1969 Pi Delta Phi
1969 Sigma Pi Sigma
1972 Beta Gamma Sigma
1972 Mortar Board
1973 Chi Epsilon
1975 Kappa Tau Alpha
1983 Pi Kappa Lambda

OTHER HONORS
1963 National Collegiate
      Players

SERVICE
1966 Alpha Phi Omega

RECOGNITION
1960 Blue Key

INACTIVE
1955–70 Phi Beta
1956–70 Pi Omega Pi
1956–74 Zeta Tau Alpha
1957–63 Pi Gamma Mu
1960–75 Zeta Beta Tau
1963–73 Sigma Phi Epsilon
1966–71 Alpha Epsilon Phi
1968–73 Alpha Delta Phi
1969–74 Sigma Phi Delta
1969–76 Phi Chi Theta

COLONIES
1965 Sigma Gamma Rho
1990 Phi Gamma Delta

CALIFORNIA STATE UNIVERSITY, LOS ANGELES

Los Angeles, CA. Chartered by State of California 1947 as Los Angeles State College; coeducational undergraduate and graduate programs in arts and sciences. Became California State in 1964.

Administration does not recognize fraternity or sorority housing; however, the organizations do occupy rented or leased houses.

NIC MEN'S
1962 Phi Sigma Kappa
1965 Sigma Alpha Epsilon
1966 Sigma Nu
1968 Zeta Beta Tau

NPC WOMEN'S
1966 Delta Zeta

PROFESSIONAL
1954 Phi Mu Alpha—Sinfonia
1965 Alpha Tau Delta

OTHER PROFESSIONAL
1966 Sigma Delta Chi
1968 Phi Upsilon Omicron

ACHS HONORS
Omicron Delta Epsilon
1954 Sigma Delta Pi
1956 Psi Chi
1960 Phi Alpha Theta
1960 Pi Sigma Alpha

1962 Kappa Delta Pi
1965 Phi Kappa Phi
1966 Eta Kappa Nu
1967 Pi Delta Phi
1967 Tau Beta Pi
1970 Chi Epsilon

SERVICE
1954 Alpha Phi Omega

RECOGNITION
1950 Blue Key
1965 Rho Epsilon

INACTIVE
Lambda Delta Sigma
1960–75 Theta Chi
1960–77 Tau Kappa Epsilon
1963–74 Sigma Pi Sigma
1964–79 Phi Chi Theta
1966–69 Kappa Sigma
1970–85 Lambda Chi Alpha

CALIFORNIA STATE UNIVERSITY, NORTHRIDGE

Northridge, CA. Founded 1958; baccalaureate and master's degrees; coeducational; state control. Fraternities and sororities occupy houses in the vicinity.

NIC MEN'S
1963 Sigma Phi Epsilon
1964 Zeta Beta Tau
1966 Phi Delta Theta
1966 Sigma Alpha Mu
1966 Sigma Chi
1967 Phi Kappa Psi
1967 Pi Kappa Alpha

1967 Sigma Alpha Epsilon
1972 Lambda Chi Alpha
1977 Sigma Pi
1984 Theta Chi
1985 Alpha Epsilon Pi
1989 Pi Kappa Phi

NPHC MEN'S
Phi Beta Sigma

NPC WOMEN'S
1964 Alpha Xi Delta
1967 Alpha Omicron Pi
1967 Delta Delta Delta
1974 Alpha Phi
1974 Kappa Kappa Gamma
1976 Sigma Kappa
1978 Zeta Tau Alpha
1986 Alpha Chi Omega

NPHC WOMEN'S
1973 Sigma Gamma Rho

PROFESSIONAL
1980 Delta Sigma Pi

OTHER PROFESSIONAL
1973 Alpha Epsilon Rho

ACHS HONORS
　　　Omicron Delta Epsilon
1962 Phi Alpha Theta
1965 Pi Sigma Alpha
1966 Sigma Pi Sigma
1967 Psi Chi
1968 Tau Beta Pi

CALIFORNIA STATE UNIVERSITY, SACRAMENTO
Sacramento, CA. Founded 1947; member of the California State University system; coeducational; undergraduate and graduate programs.

NIC MEN'S
1961 Tau Kappa Epsilon
1963 Sigma Phi Epsilon
1964 Theta Chi
1967 Sigma Alpha Epsilon
1971 Delta Chi
1977 Kappa Alpha Psi (A)
1980 Lambda Chi Alpha
1981 Pi Kappa Alpha
1982 Pi Kappa Phi
1985 Sigma Chi
1987 Chi Phi
1987 Delta Sigma Phi
1988 Phi Delta Theta
1988 Sigma Pi

NPHC MEN'S
　　　Phi Beta Sigma

NPC WOMEN'S
1966 Delta Gamma
1967 Alpha Chi Omega
1968 Alpha Phi
1983 Gamma Phi Beta
1988 Alpha Delta Pi

NPHC WOMEN'S
1950 Delta Sigma Theta (B)
1972 Alpha Kappa Alpha

PROFESSIONAL
1963 Delta Sigma Pi
1970 Kappa Kappa Psi
1984 Phi Alpha Delta

OTHER PROFESSIONAL
1964 Beta Alpha Psi

CALIFORNIA STATE UNIVERSITY, SAN BERNADINO
San Bernadino, CA.

NIC MEN'S
1987 Delta Sigma Phi
1987 Sigma Chi

1970 Kappa Tau Alpha
1971 Pi Kappa Lambda
1974 Phi Kappa Phi
1976 Pi Gamma Mu
1977 Gamma Theta Upsilon
1979 Kappa Omicron Nu
1980 Omicron Delta Kappa

OTHER HONORS
　　　National Order of Omega

SERVICE
1962 Alpha Phi Omega

RECOGNITION
1958 Blue Key

INACTIVE
1961–76 Phi Mu Alpha—
　　　　　Sinfonia
1964–71 Delta Upsilon
1965　　 Phi Sigma Sigma
1966–74 Phi Eta Sigma
1966–79 Phi Chi Theta
1967–70 Phi Sigma Kappa
1968–71 Alpha Epsilon Phi

ACHS HONORS
　　　Omicron Delta Epsilon
1956 Kappa Delta Pi
1958 Psi Chi
1960 Pi Omega Pi
1963 Phi Kappa Phi
1969 Pi Delta Phi
1970 Sigma Pi Sigma
1971 Phi Alpha Theta
1971 Sigma Delta Pi
1972 Pi Sigma Alpha
1977 Pi Kappa Lambda
1984 Tau Beta Pi

OTHER HONORS
　　　National Order of Omega
1967 National Collegiate
　　　Players

SERVICE
1952 Alpha Phi Omega

RECOGNITION
1950 Alpha Psi Omega
1956 Blue Key

INACTIVE
1957–87 Phi Mu Alpha—
　　　　　Sinfonia
1961–71 Alpha Sigma Phi
1963–87 Phi Kappa Tau
1965–70 Alpha Xi Delta
1967–75 Sigma Kappa
1975　　 Phi Gamma Nu

1989 Tau Kappa Epsilon

NPHC MEN'S
　　　Phi Beta Sigma

NPC WOMEN'S
1986 Alpha Phi
1988 Alpha Delta Pi
1990 Kappa Delta

ACHS HONORS
　　　Omicron Delta Epsilon

1976 Psi Chi
1977 Pi Sigma Alpha
1979 Phi Kappa Phi
1988 Phi Alpha Theta

OTHER HONORS
　　　National Order of Omega

CALIFORNIA WESTERN SCHOOL OF LAW
San Diego, CA.

PROFESSIONAL
1962 Phi Alpha Delta
1964 Phi Delta Phi

OTHER PROFESSIONAL
1982 Sigma Nu Phi

ACHS HONORS
1963 Alpha Kappa Delta

RECOGNITION
1963 Blue Key
1965 Alpha Psi Omega

CALUMET COLLEGE
Whiting, IN. College of liberal arts and general; teacher preparatory; coeducational; Roman Catholic affiliation; coeducational. Established 1951.

SERVICE
1965 Alpha Phi Omega

INACTIVE
1971–86 Zeta Beta Tau

CAMERON UNIVERSITY
Lawton, OK. Public institution. Founded in 1908. Four-year; coeducational.

90% of students live off campus or commute.

NIC MEN'S
1974 Kappa Alpha Psi (A)

NPHC MEN'S
1975 Alpha Phi Alpha

NPHC WOMEN'S
1975 Delta Sigma Theta (B)
1982 Alpha Kappa Alpha

PROFESSIONAL
1974 Kappa Kappa Psi
1974 Tau Beta Sigma

ACHS HONORS
1974 Sigma Pi Sigma
1975 Phi Kappa Phi
1982 Phi Alpha Theta

1985 Phi Eta Sigma
1988 Phi Sigma Iota

SERVICE
1969 Alpha Phi Omega
1971 Gamma Sigma Sigma

RECOGNITION
1975 Pi Kappa Delta

INACTIVE
1972–78 Sigma Tau Gamma
1977–87 Alpha Gamma Delta
1984–88 Tau Kappa Epsilon

COLONIES
1990 Phi Delta Theta

CAMPBELL UNIVERSITY
Buies Creek, NC.

PROFESSIONAL
1979 Delta Theta Phi
1979 Phi Alpha Delta
1987 Kappa Epsilon
1988 Phi Delta Chi

ACHS HONORS
1974 Phi Eta Sigma

1975 Phi Kappa Phi
1977 Omicron Delta Kappa
1983 Pi Gamma Mu
1983 Pi Gamma Mu

SERVICE
1961 Alpha Phi Omega
1967 Gamma Sigma Sigma

CANISIUS COLLEGE
Buffalo, NY. College of liberal arts and school of business administration; coeducational; private control; conducted by the Society of Jesus; established 1870.

NIC MEN'S
1982 Sigma Phi Epsilon

NPC WOMEN'S
1987 Alpha Omicron Pi

PROFESSIONAL
1957 Alpha Kappa Psi
1962 Phi Gamma Nu
1983 Phi Alpha Delta

ACHS HONORS
1955 Alpha Sigma Nu
1964 Phi Alpha Theta
1974 Psi Chi
1978 Pi Sigma Alpha
1982 Theta Alpha Kappa

RECOGNITION
1941 Beta Beta Beta

COLONIES
    Phi Sigma Sigma

CAPITAL UNIVERSITY Columbus, OH. University; coeducational; private control; American Lutheran Church controlled and owned. Founded at Canton in 1830, moved to Columbus 1831.

NPHC MEN'S
    Phi Beta Sigma

NPHC WOMEN'S
1981 Alpha Kappa Alpha

PROFESSIONAL
1932 Phi Beta
1951 Phi Mu Alpha—Sinfonia
1969 Phi Alpha Delta
1972 Delta Theta Phi
1983 Phi Alpha Delta

ACHS HONORS
1929 Delta Sigma Rho-Tau
    Kappa Alpha

1988 Pi Kappa Lambda

OTHER HONORS
1951 National Collegiate
    Players

SERVICE
1966 Alpha Phi Omega

RECOGNITION
    Arnold Air Society (D-1)

INACTIVE
1977–82 Psi Chi

CARDINAL STRITCH COLLEGE Milwaukee, WI.

ACHS HONORS
1948 Delta Epsilon Sigma

1970 Sigma Tau Delta
1979 Psi Chi

CARLETON COLLEGE Northfield, MN.

NIC MEN'S
1989 Acacia

ACHS HONORS
1911 Delta Sigma Rho-Tau
    Kappa Alpha
1951 Mortar Board

OTHER HONORS
1914 Phi Beta Kappa
1936 Sigma Xi

1961 Pi Mu Epsilon

RECOGNITION
1930 Sigma Delta Psi

INACTIVE
1883–88 Phi Kappa Psi

COLONIES
    Beta Theta Pi

CARLOW COLLEGE Pittsburgh, PA. College of liberal arts and professional preparation for women; Roman Catholic; established 1929. Name changed to Carlow College in 1969.

PROFESSIONAL
1975 Kappa Delta Epsilon
1977 Phi Chi Theta

ACHS HONORS
1969 Lambda Iota Tau

CARNEGIE-MELLON UNIVERSITY Pittsburgh, PA. Founded by Andrew Carnegie in 1900 as Carnegie Technical Schools; state approved to give degrees in 1912; merged with Mellon Institute to form Carnegie University in 1967; prifately supported, coeducational university.

Twelve fraternities occupy school-owned dormitories.

NIC MEN'S
1912 Theta Xi
1917 Delta Upsilon
1919 Sigma Alpha Epsilon

1920 Beta Theta Pi
1921 Kappa Sigma
1921 Pi Kappa Alpha
1922 Pi Lambda Phi

1923 Alpha Tau Omega
1923 Delta Tau Delta
1926 Alpha Phi Delta
1929 Tau Delta Phi
1930 Kappa Delta Rho
1987 Alpha Epsilon Pi
1987 Sigma Tau Gamma

NPC WOMEN'S
1944 Chi Omega
1944 Delta Delta Delta
1944 Delta Gamma
1944 Kappa Alpha Theta
1944 Kappa Kappa Gamma

PROFESSIONAL
1928 Phi Mu Alpha—Sinfonia

ACHS HONORS
    Omicron Delta Epsilon
    Pi Alpha Alpha
1916 Tau Beta Pi
1923 Eta Kappa Nu
1923 Mortar Board
1929 Lambda Sigma Society
1952 Kappa Omicron Nu

1973 Phi Alpha Theta
1975 Psi Chi
1982 Chi Epsilon
1988 Phi Eta Sigma

OTHER HONORS
    National Order of Omega
1947 Pi Mu Epsilon

SERVICE
1929 Alpha Phi Omega

INACTIVE
1922–48 Theta Tau
1923–33 Acacia
1924–36 Alpha Rho Chi
1925–36 Alpha Sigma Phi
1925–37 Sigma Phi Epsilon
1926–40 Phi Sigma Kappa
1927–34 Phi Kappa Psi
1929–35 Lambda Chi Alpha
1933–84 Phi Kappa Phi
1942–70 Omicron Delta Kappa
1944–71 Alpha Epsilon Phi
1945–68 Sigma Kappa
1974–85 Zeta Beta Tau

CARROLL COLLEGE Waukesha, WI. Founded 1846 in honor of Charles Carroll. College of liberal arts; coeducational; affiliated with United Presbyterian Church.

Three fraternities occupy their own houses on their own land; the two others rent or lease their dwellings from the college. Sorority members occupy dormitory rooms; they rent a chapter room and workroom from the college.

NIC MEN'S
1919 Tau Kappa Epsilon

NPC WOMEN'S
1947 Delta Zeta
1948 Alpha Xi Delta
1948 Chi Omega
1952 Alpha Gamma Delta

ACHS HONORS
1948 Phi Alpha Theta
1956 Gamma Theta Upsilon
1959 Kappa Delta Pi
1964 Alpha Kappa Delta
1969 Lambda Iota Tau
1972 Pi Sigma Alpha
1979 Phi Alpha Theta
1979 Theta Alpha Kappa
1980 Psi Chi
1989 Psi Chi

OTHER HONORS
1941 Sigma Epsilon Sigma

SERVICE
    The National Spurs

RECOGNITION
1924 Pi Kappa Delta
1927 Beta Beta Beta
1939 Alpha Psi Omega
1960 Pi Kappa Delta
1964 Eta Sigma Phi

INACTIVE
1923–54 Theta Alpha Phi
1929–42 Pi Gamma Mu
1931–50 Sigma Tau Delta
1932   Phi Beta
1940–83 Sigma Phi Epsilon
1955–71 Alpha Kappa Psi
1959–68 Sigma Kappa
1969–86 Phi Eta Sigma

COLONIES
1988 Sigma Pi Sigma

CARSON-NEWMAN COLLEGE Jefferson City, TN. In 1851 chartered as The Mossy Creek Missionary Baptist Seminary; name later changed to Carson College. Newman College for girls opened 1882. The two schools consolidated in 1889. Liberal arts college; coeducational; church-related (Baptist).

PROFESSIONAL
1962 Alpha Kappa Psi
1963 Phi Mu Alpha—Sinfonia
1966 Delta Omicron

ACHS HONORS
1954 Sigma Delta Pi
1955 Pi Delta Phi
1961 Phi Alpha Theta

1964 Sigma Tau Delta	**SERVICE**
1965 Psi Chi	1963 Alpha Phi Omega
1968 Alpha Chi	1970 Gamma Sigma Sigma
1968 Alpha Lambda Delta	
1968 Kappa Delta Pi	**RECOGNITION**
1968 Kappa Omicron Nu	1937 Alpha Psi Omega
1968 Phi Sigma Tau	1940 Pi Kappa Delta
1968 Sigma Pi Sigma	1956 Blue Key
1970 Pi Kappa Lambda	1960 Beta Beta Beta
1971 Kappa Mu Epsilon	1969 Kappa Pi
1971 Phi Eta Sigma	
1974 Mortar Board	**INACTIVE**
	1963–88 Phi Chi Theta

CARTHAGE COLLEGE   Kenosha, WI. College of liberal arts; coeducational; private control; related to Lutheran Church; founded 1847 as Hillsboro College. Campus moved from Carthage, IL to Kenosha, WI in 1964.

NIC MEN'S	**SERVICE**
1984 Phi Kappa Sigma	1965 Alpha Phi Omega
	1965 Gamma Sigma Sigma
NPHC MEN'S	
1976 Alpha Phi Alpha	**RECOGNITION**
	1920 Pi Kappa Delta
PROFESSIONAL	1930 Beta Beta Beta
1935 Sigma Alpha Iota	1938 Alpha Psi Omega
1978 Phi Mu Alpha—Sinfonia	1948 Kappa Pi
	1968 Blue Key
ACHS HONORS	
1956 Sigma Tau Delta	**INACTIVE**
1968 Alpha Lambda Delta	1882–88 Pi Beta Phi
1968 Phi Alpha Theta	1942–43 Alpha Sigma Phi
1972 Psi Chi	1948–64 Alpha Epsilon Delta
1977 Gamma Theta Upsilon	1949–62 Kappa Omicron Nu

CASE WESTERN RESERVE UNIVERSITY   Cleveland, OH. Founded 1826 at Hudson, OH, as a college; moved to Cleveland 1882 and became Western Reserve University. Western Reserve federated with Case Institute of Technology in 1967 to form Case Western Reserve University. Today the university comprises two undergraduate colleges and eight graduate and professional schools, all located in the University Circle area of Cleveland.

The fraternities own their own land and homes, except in some instances where ownership is by the college on rental basis.

NIC MEN'S	1906 Alpha Chi Sigma
1851 Delta Upsilon	1906 Delta Theta Phi
1868 Delta Kappa Epsilon	1906 Phi Alpha Delta
1876 Phi Gamma Delta	
1884 Zeta Psi	**OTHER PROFESSIONAL**
1905 Sigma Alpha Epsilon	1919 Phi Delta Epsilon
1906 Phi Kappa Psi	1919 Tau Epsilon Rho
1909 Sigma Chi	1926 Phi Lambda Kappa
1909 Zeta Beta Tau	1930 Beta Alpha Psi
1925 Phi Kappa Tau	
1942 Theta Chi	**ACHS HONORS**
1945 Sigma Alpha Mu	Omicron Delta Epsilon
1960 Pi Kappa Alpha	1900 Tau Beta Pi
1979 Beta Theta Pi	1910 Eta Kappa Nu
	1949 Psi Chi
NPC WOMEN'S	1950 Pi Sigma Alpha
1982 Alpha Phi	1952 Mortar Board
1983 Alpha Chi Omega	1956 Phi Sigma Iota
1985 Phi Mu	
	OTHER HONORS
PROFESSIONAL	National Order of Omega
1901 Phi Delta Phi	

SERVICE	1917–33 Sigma Delta Chi
1950 Alpha Phi Omega	1918–63 Lambda Chi Alpha
1969 Alpha Phi Omega	1931–50 Rho Chi
	1939–40 Alpha Sigma Phi
INACTIVE	1946–66 Phi Upsilon Omicron
1901–29 Alpha Tau Omega	1947–70 Delta Sigma Pi
1909–57 Alpha Kappa Kappa	1947–70 Omicron Delta Kappa
1911–90 Theta Tau	

Western Reserve College   Cleveland, OH.

NIC MEN'S	**RECOGNITION**
1882 Delta Tau Delta	1925 Sigma Delta Psi
1922 Alpha Phi Delta	1932 Phi Delta Gamma
1936 Kappa Alpha Psi (A)	
	INACTIVE
NPHC MEN'S	1841–64 Alpha Delta Phi
1914 Alpha Phi Alpha	1841–79 Beta Theta Pi
	1906–11 Phi Beta Pi and Theta
PROFESSIONAL	Kappa Psi (a)
1896 Psi Omega	1906–41 Phi Chi
1901 Phi Rho Sigma	1909–53 Sigma Nu
1936 Alpha Omega	1915–59 Pi Kappa Alpha
	1922 Xi Psi Phi
OTHER PROFESSIONAL	1923–37 Phi Delta Chi
1897 Delta Sigma Delta	1926–45 National Collegiate
1926 Alpha Zeta Omega	Players
	1927–45 National Collegiate
ACHS HONORS	Players
1911 Delta Sigma Rho-Tau	1927–69 Sigma Tau Delta
Kappa Alpha	1928–49 Kappa Epsilon
1958 Beta Gamma Sigma	1930–32 Gamma Eta Gamma
1959 Phi Alpha Theta	1940–47 Phi Mu Alpha—
1966 Sigma Theta Tau	Sinfonia
	1947–74 Alpha Epsilon Pi
OTHER HONORS	1955 Beta Beta Beta
1903 Alpha Omega Alpha	1963–70 Sigma Chi
1913 Order of the Coif	
1925 Iota Sigma Pi	
1929 Omicron Kappa Upsilon	
1932 Sigma Xi	

College Of Case Institute Of Technology   Cleveland, OH.

NIC MEN'S	**RECOGNITION**
1896 Phi Delta Theta	Angel Flight
1907 Sigma Nu	Arnold Air Society (E-2)
1941 Phi Kappa Theta	1932 Blue Key
ACHS HONORS	**INACTIVE**
1942 Delta Sigma Rho-Tau	1903–34 Kappa Sigma
Kappa Alpha	1905–79 Beta Theta Pi
1961 Alpha Sigma Mu	
OTHER HONORS	
1904 Sigma Xi	

CASTLETON STATE COLLEGE   Castleton, VT.

OTHER PROFESSIONAL	**ACHS HONORS**
1968 Kappa Delta Phi (C)	1983 Phi Eta Sigma

CATAWBA COLLEGE   Salisbury, NC.

ACHS HONORS	1974 Psi Chi
1958 Kappa Delta Pi	

CATONSVILLE COMMUNITY COLLEGE   Catonsville, MD.

NPHC MEN'S
    Phi Beta Sigma

THE CATHOLIC UNIVERSITY OF AMERICA

Washington, DC. Approved in 1887 by Pope Leo XIII, incorporated in that same year and classes began in November, 1889. Coeducational. Five undergraduate schools and ten graduate schools; schools of arts and sciences comprise 23 departments; two-thirds of the degrees conferred each year are advanced degrees.

NIC MEN'S
1930 Phi Kappa Theta
1950 Alpha Delta Gamma
1979 Alpha Phi Delta

NPHC WOMEN'S
1972 Delta Sigma Theta (B)

PROFESSIONAL
1954 Sigma Alpha Iota
1962 Phi Alpha Delta
1965 Delta Theta Phi
1984 Phi Alpha Delta

OTHER PROFESSIONAL
1931 Gamma Eta Gamma

ACHS HONORS
1929 Phi Eta Sigma
1929 Pi Gamma Mu
1953 Sigma Theta Tau
1955 Delta Epsilon Sigma
1955 Pi Gamma Mu
1958 Psi Chi

1962 Phi Alpha Theta
1962 Tau Beta Pi
1964 Beta Phi Mu
1968 Pi Kappa Lambda
1981 Pi Sigma Alpha
1985 Phi Sigma Tau

OTHER HONORS
1942 Phi Beta Kappa

SERVICE
1948 Alpha Phi Omega

RECOGNITION
Angel Flight
Arnold Air Society (B-1)
1932 Blue Key

INACTIVE
1945–64 Sigma Beta Kappa
1955–82 Phi Mu Alpha—
          Sinfonia
1956–70 Theta Phi Alpha
1965–77 Tau Kappa Epsilon

CATHOLIC UNIVERSITY OF PUERTO RICO

Ponce, PR. University; coeducational; private control; Roman Catholic Church. Established 1948.

PROFESSIONAL
1969 Phi Alpha Delta
1970 Delta Theta Phi
1983 Phi Alpha Delta

ACHS HONORS
1955 Phi Alpha Theta
1968 Delta Epsilon Sigma

SERVICE
1970 Alpha Phi Omega

RECOGNITION
1960 Beta Beta Beta

INACTIVE
1957–69 Sigma Tau Delta

CEDAR CREST COLLEGE

Allentown, PA. Liberal arts college for women founded in 1867; private control; affiliated with United Church of Christ.

ACHS HONORS
1947 Phi Alpha Theta
1966 Sigma Tau Delta
1990 Kappa Mu Epsilon
1990 Psi Chi

RECOGNITION
1943 Alpha Psi Omega
1965 Beta Beta Beta

CENTENARY COLLEGE OF LOUISIANA

Shreveport, LA. College of liberal arts; coeducational; private control; established as College of Louisiana 1825; name changed to present 1845; college moved from Jackson, LA to Shreveport in 1907.

The fraternities occupy houses off campus.

NIC MEN'S
1885 Kappa Sigma
1891 Kappa Alpha Order
1963 Tau Kappa Epsilon
1977 Theta Chi

NPC WOMEN'S
1927 Zeta Tau Alpha
1928 Chi Omega

PROFESSIONAL
1954 Phi Beta
1957 Phi Mu Alpha—Sinfonia

ACHS HONORS
1926 Alpha Chi
1928 Pi Gamma Mu
1949 Omicron Delta Kappa
1950 Phi Sigma Iota
1955 Alpha Epsilon Delta
1969 Lambda Iota Tau
1983 Phi Alpha Theta
1990 Phi Eta Sigma

OTHER HONORS
1950 Sigma Gamma Epsilon

SERVICE
1948 Alpha Phi Omega

RECOGNITION
1933 Alpha Psi Omega
1960 Kappa Pi

INACTIVE
1840–61 Beta Theta Pi
1855–61 Phi Kappa Sigma
1858–61 Chi Phi
1860–61 Sigma Alpha Epsilon
1902–51 Pi Kappa Alpha
1925–58 Lambda Chi Alpha
1927–77 Sigma Pi Sigma
1931–77 Alpha Xi Delta
1947–51 Alpha Omicron Pi
1947–69 Sigma Tau Delta

UNIVERSITY OF CENTRAL ARKANSAS

Conway, AR. Teachers college; coeducational; state control; chartered 1907 as normal school; became four-year college in 1920; named Arkansas State Teachers College in 1925; name changed to present 1967.

The college furnishes rent-free rooms in the dormitories in which fraternities and sororities carry on their activities.

NIC MEN'S
1934 Sigma Tau Gamma
1935 Phi Sigma Kappa
1963 Pi Kappa Alpha
1977 Kappa Alpha Psi (A)
1988 Sigma Phi Epsilon

NPHC MEN'S
Phi Beta Sigma

NPC WOMEN'S
1935 Alpha Sigma Tau
1935 Sigma Sigma Sigma
1944 Delta Zeta
1959 Sigma Kappa

PROFESSIONAL
1967 Kappa Kappa Psi
1967 Tau Beta Sigma
1976 Phi Mu Alpha—Sinfonia
1986 Phi Alpha Delta

ACHS HONORS
1932 Alpha Chi

1932 Phi Alpha Theta
1952 Pi Omega Pi
1967 Gamma Theta Upsilon
1970 Psi Chi
1981 Phi Sigma Iota
1983 Sigma Pi Sigma

OTHER HONORS
National Order of Omega

SERVICE
1971 Alpha Phi Omega

RECOGNITION
1968 Kappa Pi

INACTIVE
1962–82 Theta Xi
1980–90 Pi Kappa Phi

COLONIES
1990 Kappa Sigma

CENTRAL COLLEGE

Pella, IA. Founded in 1853. Coeducational, liberal arts college; fully accredited, related to the Reformed Church in America. Study abroad and individual research programs.

NPC WOMEN'S
1941 Alpha Sigma Alpha

RECOGNITION
1914 Pi Kappa Delta
1921 Pi Kappa Delta
1927 Alpha Psi Omega

INACTIVE
1876–78 Phi Delta Theta
1883–01 Sigma Nu
1884–90 Alpha Tau Omega
1885–01 Phi Delta Theta
1947–69 Sigma Tau Delta

CENTRAL CONNECTICUT STATE COLLEGE

New Britain, CT. Oldest of the state's public institutions; established as a normal school in 1850; relocated to present campus in 1923; became teachers college in 1933; four-year liberal arts; to present name in 1961; coeducational; controlled by Board of Trustees for State Colleges since 1965.

NPHC MEN'S
Phi Beta Sigma

PROFESSIONAL
1975 Sigma Alpha Iota

OTHER PROFESSIONAL
1972 Delta Pi Epsilon

ACHS HONORS
Omicron Delta Epsilon
1943 Kappa Delta Pi
1968 Gamma Theta Upsilon
1968 Psi Chi
1976 Phi Alpha Theta

1982 Pi Sigma Alpha
1983 Delta Mu Delta

SERVICE
1947 Alpha Phi Omega
1964 Gamma Sigma Sigma

RECOGNITION
1971 Pi Kappa Delta

INACTIVE
1972–84 Phi Mu Alpha—
Sinfonia
1973–82 Tau Kappa Epsilon

UNIVERSITY OF CENTRAL FLORIDA Orlando, FL. Four-year state university; coeducational. Established 1963. Degree programs in humanities and fine arts, social sciences, natural sciences, general studies, business administration, education, and engineering.

Fraternities and sororities have their own houses.

NIC MEN'S
1971 Alpha Tau Omega
1971 Kappa Sigma
1971 Lambda Chi Alpha
1971 Tau Kappa Epsilon
1973 Pi Kappa Alpha
1973 Sigma Alpha Epsilon
1974 Sigma Chi
1975 Delta Tau Delta
1981 Phi Delta Theta
1984 Kappa Alpha Psi (A)
1985 Sigma Phi Epsilon

NPHC MEN'S
Phi Beta Sigma

NPC WOMEN'S
1971 Zeta Tau Alpha
1972 Delta Delta Delta
1978 Kappa Delta
1981 Pi Beta Phi
1982 Alpha Delta Pi
1985 Delta Gamma

NPHC WOMEN'S
1990 Sigma Gamma Rho

PROFESSIONAL
1970 Delta Sigma Pi

1979 Phi Mu Alpha—Sinfonia

ACHS HONORS
Omicron Delta Epsilon
Pi Alpha Alpha
1974 Omicron Delta Kappa
1975 Eta Kappa Nu
1977 Tau Beta Pi
1981 Pi Sigma Alpha
1981 Psi Chi
1982 Phi Kappa Phi
1989 Phi Eta Sigma

OTHER HONORS
National Order of Omega

SERVICE
1975 Alpha Phi Omega

INACTIVE
1973–81 Phi Chi Theta
1973–84 Alpha Chi Omega
1974–84 Chi Phi

CENTRAL METHODIST COLLEGE Fayette, MO. College of liberal arts; coeducational; private control; Methodist Church; established 1854.

Administration requires fraternity and sorority members to occupy residence halls.

PROFESSIONAL
1931 Phi Beta

ACHS HONORS
1934 Alpha Epsilon Delta
1935 Pi Gamma Mu
1949 Kappa Mu Epsilon
1958 Alpha Lambda Delta
1960 Omicron Delta Kappa
1971 Sigma Tau Delta

1976 Delta Mu Delta

SERVICE
1948 Alpha Phi Omega

RECOGNITION
1956 Beta Beta Beta

INACTIVE
1949–77 Pi Omega Pi

CENTRAL MICHIGAN UNIVERSITY Mt. Pleasant, MI. Founded as Central Michigan Normal

School and Business Institute in 1892, brought under control of State Board of Education in 1896. University; undergraduate schools and graduate school; coeducational; state control.

Fraternities and sororities own their own houses on their own land.

NIC MEN'S
1941 Phi Sigma Kappa
1941 Sigma Tau Gamma
1948 Delta Sigma Phi
1954 Tau Kappa Epsilon
1956 Sigma Phi Epsilon
1962 Theta Chi
1967 Sigma Chi
1969 Sigma Pi
1970 Lambda Chi Alpha
1974 Kappa Alpha Psi (A)
1980 Alpha Chi Rho
1985 Beta Theta Pi
1988 Delta Chi

NPHC MEN'S
Phi Beta Sigma

NPC WOMEN'S
1905 Alpha Sigma Tau
1942 Sigma Sigma Sigma
1951 Zeta Tau Alpha
1953 Delta Zeta
1958 Alpha Chi Omega
1959 Alpha Gamma Delta
1959 Sigma Kappa
1984 Phi Sigma Sigma
1985 Phi Mu

NPHC WOMEN'S
1971 Alpha Kappa Alpha
1971 Delta Sigma Theta (B)

PROFESSIONAL
1944 Delta Omicron
1953 Delta Psi Kappa
1964 Alpha Kappa Psi
1965 Phi Mu Alpha—Sinfonia
1975 Phi Chi Theta
1977 Gamma Iota Sigma
1987 Phi Alpha Delta

OTHER PROFESSIONAL
1961 Phi Epsilon Kappa
1971 Sigma Delta Chi

1972 Alpha Epsilon Rho

ACHS HONORS
Omicron Delta Epsilon
1941 Kappa Delta Pi
1942 Kappa Mu Epsilon
1964 Phi Kappa Phi
1966 Gamma Theta Upsilon
1966 Phi Eta Sigma
1969 Phi Alpha Theta
1970 Psi Chi
1970 Sigma Delta Pi
1971 Pi Delta Phi
1973 Kappa Omicron Nu
1973 Mortar Board
1976 Sigma Pi Sigma
1979 Pi Omega Pi

OTHER HONORS
National Order of Omega

SERVICE
1947 Alpha Phi Omega
1972 Gamma Sigma Sigma

RECOGNITION
1940 Pi Kappa Delta
1946 Alpha Psi Omega
1961 Sigma Delta Psi
1962 Beta Beta Beta
1971 Sigma Iota Epsilon

INACTIVE
1940–69 Sigma Tau Delta
1956–75 Pi Kappa Phi
1959–76 Alpha Xi Delta
1960–70 Alpha Beta Alpha
1961–87 Alpha Lambda Delta
1965–89 Phi Kappa Tau
1968–73 Beta Sigma Psi
1969–70 Alpha Phi

COLONIES
Theta Xi

CENTRAL MISSOURI STATE UNIVERSITY Warrensburg, MO. Founded 1871. University; undergraduate coeducational; graduate school coeducational; state control.

Eight fraternities live in a college owned complex of eight units with separate living, dining, and sleeping areas. Seven sororities live in college owned Panhellenic Hall with separate living and sleeping areas for each unit and a common dining area for all units. The members of the fraternities and sororities have individual housing contracts with the university.

NIC MEN'S
1920 Sigma Tau Gamma
1931 Phi Sigma Kappa
1954 Tau Kappa Epsilon
1957 Alpha Kappa Lambda

1962 Sigma Pi
1962 Theta Chi
1967 Lambda Chi Alpha
1968 Sigma Phi Epsilon
1969 Beta Sigma Psi

1971 Delta Chi
1972 Kappa Alpha Psi (A)

NPHC MEN'S
Phi Beta Sigma
1966 Alpha Phi Alpha

NPC WOMEN'S
1915 Sigma Sigma Sigma
1919 Alpha Sigma Alpha
1927 Delta Zeta
1959 Alpha Gamma Delta
1959 Sigma Kappa
1962 Alpha Omicron Pi
1985 Zeta Tau Alpha

NPHC WOMEN'S
1969 Delta Sigma Theta (B)
1970 Sigma Gamma Rho

PROFESSIONAL
1930 Phi Mu Alpha—Sinfonia
1963 Delta Psi Kappa
1970 Phi Mu Alpha—Sinfonia
1971 Sigma Alpha Iota
1979 Delta Sigma Pi

OTHER PROFESSIONAL
1916 Phi Sigma Pi
1974 Sigma Delta Chi

ACHS HONORS
Omicron Delta Epsilon
1922 Kappa Delta Pi
1923 Kappa Omicron Nu
1938 Kappa Mu Epsilon
1948 Pi Omega Pi

1956 Pi Kappa Lambda
1958 Sigma Tau Delta
1965 Lambda Sigma Society
1965 Phi Alpha Theta
1966 Gamma Theta Upsilon
1967 Psi Chi
1970 Sigma Pi Sigma
1972 Phi Eta Sigma
1972 Phi Kappa Phi
1973 Pi Sigma Alpha
1984 Mortar Board
1990 Kappa Tau Alpha

OTHER HONORS
National Order of Omega

SERVICE
1938 Alpha Phi Omega
1977 Gamma Sigma Sigma

RECOGNITION
1924 Pi Kappa Delta
1935 Alpha Psi Omega
1956 Beta Beta Beta
1956 Sigma Zeta

INACTIVE
1925–34 Theta Alpha Phi
1929 Delta Phi Alpha
1957–71 Acacia
1961–78 Alpha Lambda Delta
1962–83 Alpha Sigma Tau
1969–90 Alpha Xi Delta
1970–89 Delta Upsilon
1973–78 Alpha Epsilon Pi

CENTRAL STATE UNIVERSITY Edmond, OK.

Oldest state educational institution in Oklahoma, established as the Territorial Normal School by the Territorial Legislature December 24, 1890; raised to the rank of four-year college in 1919; coeducational. Designated as a university in 1971.

General fraternities and sororities own or lease houses.

NIC MEN'S
1957 Tau Kappa Epsilon
1959 Sigma Tau Gamma
1962 Alpha Tau Omega
1963 Kappa Alpha Psi (A)
1969 Kappa Sigma

NPHC MEN'S
Phi Beta Sigma

NPC WOMEN'S
1950 Delta Zeta
1959 Sigma Kappa
1961 Alpha Gamma Delta

NPHC WOMEN'S
1972 Delta Sigma Theta (B)

PROFESSIONAL
1967 Delta Psi Kappa

OTHER PROFESSIONAL
1968 Alpha Beta Alpha
1972 Sigma Delta Chi

ACHS HONORS
Omicron Delta Epsilon

1935 Kappa Delta Pi
1939 Pi Omega Pi
1950 Alpha Chi
1970 Sigma Pi Sigma
1971 Phi Alpha Theta
1973 Alpha Lambda Delta
1974 Phi Eta Sigma
1976 Psi Chi
1978 Mortar Board
1979 Phi Sigma Iota
1981 Kappa Tau Alpha

RECOGNITION
1939 Kappa Pi
1949 Alpha Psi Omega

INACTIVE
1933–69 Sigma Tau Delta
1950–79 Sigma Sigma Sigma
1954–59 Phi Lambda Chi
1960–66 Alpha Omicron Pi
1961–84 Phi Mu Alpha—
Sinfonia
1964–83 Acacia

CENTRAL STATE UNIVERSITY Wilberforce, OH.

College of liberal arts and education; coeducational; state control; established as normal and industrial school in 1887.

Fraternities and sororities do not occupy special quarters.

NIC MEN'S
1952 Kappa Alpha Psi (A)

NPHC MEN'S
Phi Beta Sigma
1951 Alpha Phi Alpha
1951 Omega Psi Phi

NPHC WOMEN'S
Zeta Phi Beta
1952 Alpha Kappa Alpha
1971 Sigma Gamma Rho
1981 Sigma Gamma Rho

PROFESSIONAL
1972 Mu Phi Epsilon

1973 Phi Mu Alpha—Sinfonia

ACHS HONORS
1948 Alpha Kappa Mu
1948 Beta Kappa Chi
1954 Phi Alpha Theta
1978 Phi Sigma Tau
1982 Psi Chi

SERVICE
1950 Alpha Phi Omega

RECOGNITION
1964 Delta Tau Kappa

CENTRAL TEXAS Killeen, TX.

SERVICE
1971 Alpha Phi Omega

CENTRAL WASHINGTON UNIVERSITY Ellensburg, WA.

Established in 1890. Offers undergraduate degrees in arts and sciences, business, and professional education at all levels. Offers graduate degrees at the master's level in arts and sciences and professional education. In a national survey of college and university presidents published in *U.S. News and World Report*, Central was recognized as one of the top ten comprehensive liberal arts colleges west of the Mississippi.

ACHS HONORS
1938 Kappa Delta Pi
1962 Psi Chi
1965 Gamma Theta Upsilon
1971 Phi Sigma
1972 Phi Alpha Theta
1976 Phi Kappa Phi
1981 Pi Sigma Alpha

SERVICE
1935 Intercollegiate Knights

1949 Alpha Phi Omega

RECOGNITION
Angel Flight
Arnold Air Society (H-2)
1941 Kappa Pi
1951 Alpha Psi Omega

COLONIES
1987 Sigma Pi Sigma

CENTRE COLLEGE OF KENTUCKY Danville, KY.

Founded and chartered 1819; first instruction 1820; Central University merged with Centre 1901; college of liberal arts; coeducational; private control.

The college owns the fraternity houses; rental is on same basis as student living in dormitories; they are required to fill the house with their own members or students whom they elect to have live with them.

NIC MEN'S
1848 Beta Theta Pi
1854 Delta Kappa Epsilon
1876 Sigma Chi
1882 Sigma Alpha Epsilon

1901 Phi Delta Theta
1914 Phi Kappa Tau

NPC WOMEN'S
1980 Delta Delta Delta
1980 Kappa Alpha Theta

1980 Kappa Kappa Gamma
1988 Chi Omega

ACHS HONORS
    Omicron Delta Epsilon
1921 Omicron Delta Kappa
1965 Phi Alpha Theta
1967 Phi Sigma Tau
1967 Sigma Delta Pi
1976 Phi Sigma Iota
1983 Pi Sigma Alpha

OTHER HONORS
    National Order of Omega

SERVICE
1949 Alpha Phi Omega

INACTIVE
1850–01 Phi Delta Theta
1856–56 Phi Gamma Delta
1860–62 Phi Kappa Sigma
1883–33 Kappa Alpha Order
1932–36 Alpha Sigma Phi

CHABOT COLLEGE   Hayward, CA.

SERVICE
1967 Alpha Phi Omega

CHADRON STATE COLLEGE   Chadron, NB. College of liberal arts; teachers college; coeducational; state control; established 1911 as normal school. Formerly Nebraska State Teachers College.

NIC MEN'S
1963 Phi Sigma Kappa

ACHS HONORS
1938 Pi Omega Pi
1949 Gamma Theta Upsilon
1962 Kappa Mu Epsilon
1969 Phi Alpha Theta

SERVICE
1962 Alpha Phi Omega

INACTIVE
1950–82 Sigma Tau Gamma
1963–80 Alpha Xi Delta
1964–81 Chi Omega
1969–77 Alpha Omicron Pi
1972–85 Theta Chi

CHAMINADE UNIVERSITY OF HONOLULU   Honolulu, HI.

ACHS HONORS
1966 Phi Alpha Theta

1968 Delta Mu Delta
1983 Pi Sigma Alpha

CHAPMAN COLLEGE   Orange, CA.

NIC MEN'S
1981 Sigma Phi Epsilon
1985 Pi Kappa Alpha
1987 Alpha Delta Phi
1989 Delta Sigma Phi

NPC WOMEN'S
1988 Phi Sigma Sigma
1989 Alpha Phi

1989 Delta Gamma
1989 Gamma Phi Beta

ACHS HONORS
1971 Sigma Delta Pi
1988 Psi Chi

SERVICE
1967 Alpha Phi Omega

COLLEGE OF CHARLESTON   Charleston, SC. Founded 1770; charter granted 1785; twelfth oldest college in America. State-supported, liberal arts college; coeducational; first municipal college in America.

One fraternity and one sorority own houses on their own land. The other fraternities and sororities rent houses from the college.

NIC MEN'S
1881 Sigma Alpha Epsilon
1889 Alpha Tau Omega
1904 Pi Kappa Phi
1962 Tau Kappa Epsilon
1970 Kappa Sigma
1974 Kappa Alpha Psi (A)
1988 Sigma Chi

NPHC MEN'S
    Phi Beta Sigma
    Phi Beta Sigma

NPC WOMEN'S
1928 Chi Omega
1931 Delta Delta Delta
1939 Phi Mu
1972 Zeta Tau Alpha

1979 Alpha Delta Pi
1990 Kappa Alpha Theta

NPHC WOMEN'S
1974 Delta Sigma Theta (B)
1975 Alpha Kappa Alpha

PROFESSIONAL
1981 Alpha Chi Sigma

ACHS HONORS
    Omicron Delta Epsilon
1975 Omicron Delta Kappa
1976 Phi Kappa Phi
1979 Pi Sigma Alpha

1979 Psi Chi
1981 Phi Alpha Theta

SERVICE
1980 Alpha Phi Omega

INACTIVE
1901–05 Phi Kappa Sigma
1904–39 Kappa Alpha Order
1934–53 Delta Zeta
1970–89 Zeta Beta Tau

COLONIES
1987 Sigma Pi Sigma

UNIVERSITY OF CHARLESTON   Charleston, WV.

ACHS HONORS
1963 Pi Gamma Mu
1966 Alpha Lambda Delta
1968 Phi Alpha Theta
1971 Gamma Theta Upsilon
1988 Psi Chi

INACTIVE
1960–87 Alpha Sigma Phi
1962–85 Delta Zeta
1970–87 Sigma Phi Epsilon

CHATHAM COLLEGE   Pittsburgh, PA. College of liberal arts for women; private control; nonsectarian. Chartered 1869.

ACHS HONORS
    Omicron Delta Epsilon
1957 Mortar Board

OTHER HONORS
1962 Phi Beta Kappa

INACTIVE
1902–04 Kappa Delta

CHATTANOOGA STATE TECHNICAL COMMUNITY COLLEGE   Chattanooga, TN.

SERVICE
1973 Alpha Phi Omega

1975 Gamma Sigma Sigma

CHESTNUT HILL COLLEGE   Philadelphia, PA.

ACHS HONORS
1942 Delta Epsilon Sigma

1981 Psi Chi

CHEYNEY STATE COLLEGE   Cheyney, PA. Teachers college; coeducational; state control; established 1837.

NIC MEN'S
1950 Kappa Alpha Psi (A)

NPHC MEN'S
    Phi Beta Sigma
1950 Omega Psi Phi
1951 Alpha Phi Alpha

NPHC WOMEN'S
    Zeta Phi Beta
1953 Delta Sigma Theta (B)

1954 Alpha Kappa Alpha
1957 Sigma Gamma Rho

ACHS HONORS
1973 Alpha Kappa Mu
1977 Psi Chi
1979 Kappa Omicron Nu
1980 Gamma Theta Upsilon

RECOGNITION
1956 Alpha Phi Sigma (E)

CHICAGO-KENT COLLEGE OF LAW   Chicago, IL. Founded by Joseph M. Bailey, chief justice, Illinois Supreme Court, 1887, as the Chicago Evening Law Class. Chartered as an educational corporation 1888. Professional law college, coeducational; private control; nonsectarian.

PROFESSIONAL
1896 Phi Delta Phi
1902 Phi Alpha Delta
1909 Delta Theta Phi
1915 Delta Theta Phi

OTHER PROFESSIONAL
1908 Kappa Beta Pi

INACTIVE
1896–34 Delta Chi

CHICAGO COLLEGE OF OSTEOPATHY Chicago, IL.

OSTEOPATHIC
1911 Iota Tau Sigma
1914 Atlas Club
1921 Delta Omega
1939 Lambda Omicron Gamma

1939 Sigma Sigma Phi

INACTIVE
1915 Phi Sigma Gamma
1919–43 Theta Psi

CHICAGO CONSERVATORY COLLEGE Chicago, IL. Founded 1857. Undergraduate and graduate courses in music and music education. Private control; nonprofit; nonsectarian.

PROFESSIONAL
1924 Sigma Alpha Iota

1906–09 Mu Phi Epsilon

INACTIVE
1902–04 Phi Mu Alpha—
        Sinfonia

CHICAGO STATE UNIVERSITY Chicago, IL. Teachers college; coeducational; municipal control; state-supported. Established as Cook County Normal School in 1869; reorganized as teachers college 1938. Formerly Illinois Teachers College Chicago-South.

NIC MEN'S
1975 Kappa Alpha Psi (A)

NPHC MEN'S
     Phi Beta Sigma

PROFESSIONAL
1974 Mu Phi Epsilon

ACHS HONORS
1968 Lambda Iota Tau
1969 Phi Alpha Theta
1970 Gamma Theta Upsilon

INACTIVE
1942–75 Kappa Mu Epsilon

UNIVERSITY OF CHICAGO Chicago, IL. Controlled by private corporation; nonsectarian; incorporated 1890; William Rainey Harper appointed first president; instruction started 1892; undergraduate, professional schools, and graduate divisions coeducational; quarter system.

Fraternities own their own houses on their own land.

NIC MEN'S
1865 Phi Delta Theta
1865 Phi Kappa Psi
1869 Psi Upsilon
1879 Delta Kappa Epsilon
1896 Alpha Delta Phi
1901 Delta Upsilon
1902 Phi Gamma Delta
1904 Alpha Tau Omega
1918 Kappa Alpha Psi (A)
1921 Tau Delta Phi
1990 Pi Kappa Alpha

NPHC MEN'S
1910 Alpha Phi Alpha
1923 Omega Psi Phi

NPC WOMEN'S
1985 Alpha Omicron Pi
1986 Kappa Alpha Theta

NPHC WOMEN'S
     Zeta Phi Beta
1947 Delta Sigma Theta (B)
1982 Alpha Kappa Alpha

PROFESSIONAL
1902 Phi Alpha Delta
1903 Phi Delta Phi

OTHER PROFESSIONAL
1920 Gamma Eta Gamma
1921 Pi Lambda Theta
1949 Phi Delta Epsilon

ACHS HONORS
     Omicron Delta Epsilon
1906 Delta Sigma Rho-Tau
     Kappa Alpha
1940 Beta Gamma Sigma

OTHER HONORS
1899 Phi Beta Kappa
1902 Alpha Omega Alpha
1903 Sigma Xi
1911 Order of the Coif

SERVICE
1940 Alpha Phi Omega

RECOGNITION
1908 Gamma Alpha
1962 Alpha Psi Omega
1969 Sigma Delta Epsilon

INACTIVE
1864–87 Zeta Psi
1868–65 Beta Theta Pi
1895 Phi Rho Sigma
1895–98 Sigma Nu
1897–52 Sigma Chi
1898–35 Delta Tau Delta
1901 Phi Beta Pi and Theta
      Kappa Psi (a)

1903–29 Delta Chi
1903–41 Sigma Alpha Epsilon
1904 Sigma Nu
1904–47 Kappa Sigma
1906–43 Phi Kappa Sigma
1909–33 Acacia
1909–34 Delta Theta Phi
1910–32 Delta Sigma Phi
1915–17 Sigma Delta Chi
1916 Kappa Beta Pi
1916–75 Zeta Beta Tau
1917–35 Tau Kappa Epsilon
1918–49 Phi Delta Epsilon
1919–49 Pi Lambda Phi
1920–35 Alpha Sigma Phi
1920–37 Lambda Chi Alpha
1924 Eta Sigma Phi
1925 Sigma Delta Epsilon
1928–34 Alpha Kappa Psi
1928–46 Delta Sigma Pi
1929 Nu Beta Epsilon
1929–48 Psi Chi
1932–34 Sigma Pi Sigma
1945–48 Phi Delta Gamma
1947–48 Sigma Gamma Epsilon

CHRISTIAN BROTHERS COLLEGE Memphis, TN. Colleges of engineering, business administration, and science for men; private; Roman Catholic Church; established 1854 as Memphis Female College, and became Christian Brothers College 1871.

NIC MEN'S
1981 Tau Kappa Epsilon
1983 Pi Kappa Phi
1989 Sigma Alpha Epsilon

NPHC WOMEN'S
1978 Alpha Kappa Alpha

PROFESSIONAL
1964 Delta Sigma Pi

ACHS HONORS
1974 Tau Beta Pi
1975 Alpha Chi
1987 Psi Chi
1989 Phi Alpha Theta

COLONIES
     Zeta Tau Alpha

CHRISTOPHER NEWPORT COLLEGE Newport News, VA. Public institution. Founded in 1961. Four-year; coeducational; liberal arts college.

No housing available on campus.

NIC MEN'S
1981 Sigma Pi
1987 Sigma Tau Gamma

NPC WOMEN'S
1988 Gamma Phi Beta

NPHC WOMEN'S
1980 Alpha Kappa Alpha

PROFESSIONAL
1972 Alpha Kappa Psi

ACHS HONORS
     Omicron Delta Epsilon
1976 Alpha Chi
1976 Phi Sigma Tau
1989 Psi Chi

OTHER HONORS
     National Order of Omega

UNIVERSITY OF CINCINNATI Cincinnati, OH. Coeducational; first municipal university in the United States; Cincinnati College and the Medical College of Ohio founded in 1819. University of Cincinnati incorporated as municipal institution in 1870. Known as the home of the co-operative system of education, established in 1906 by the late Dr.

Herman Schneider. Three of UC's colleges, business administration; design, architecture, and art; and engineering, on co-operative basis. The plan provides for three-month periods of structured internship assignments alternating with three-month study periods after an initial period of fulltime study.

Most fraternities and sororities occupy their own houses on their own land.

NIC MEN'S
1840 Beta Theta Pi
1882 Sigma Chi
1889 Sigma Alpha Epsilon
1898 Phi Delta Theta
1909 Delta Tau Delta
1910 Pi Kappa Alpha
1917 Sigma Alpha Mu
1919 Lambda Chi Alpha
1920 Alpha Epsilon Pi
1920 Tau Delta Phi
1921 Triangle
1922 Alpha Tau Omega
1925 Phi Kappa Theta
1939 Kappa Alpha Psi (A)
1942 Theta Chi
1949 Sigma Phi Epsilon
1967 Tau Kappa Epsilon
1971 Phi Gamma Delta

NPHC MEN'S
     Phi Beta Sigma
1920 Alpha Phi Alpha
1947 Omega Psi Phi

NPC WOMEN'S
1885 Kappa Kappa Gamma
1892 Delta Delta Delta
1913 Chi Omega
1913 Kappa Alpha Theta
1913 Kappa Delta
1919 Alpha Chi Omega
1919 Theta Phi Alpha
1921 Zeta Tau Alpha
1923 Sigma Delta Tau
1935 Alpha Delta Pi

NPHC WOMEN'S
     Zeta Phi Beta
1920 Delta Sigma Theta (B)
1921 Alpha Kappa Alpha
1978 Sigma Gamma Rho

PROFESSIONAL
1886 Phi Delta Phi
1908 Phi Alpha Delta
1914 Alpha Kappa Psi
1918 Phi Beta
1924 Delta Sigma Pi
1927 Delta Theta Phi
1927 Kappa Psi
1928 Kappa Kappa Psi
1947 Tau Beta Sigma
1949 Kappa Epsilon
1955 Mu Phi Epsilon
1955 Phi Mu Alpha—Sinfonia
1969 Gamma Iota Sigma
1982 Phi Chi Theta
1984 Phi Alpha Delta

OTHER PROFESSIONAL
1924 Alpha Zeta Omega
1928 Phi Delta Epsilon
1929 Scarab
1930 Phi Epsilon Kappa

1942 Delta Pi Epsilon
1955 Beta Alpha Psi
1977 Alpha Epsilon Rho

ACHS HONORS
     Omicron Delta Epsilon
1908 Delta Sigma Rho-Tau
     Kappa Alpha
1915 Tau Beta Pi
1917 Kappa Delta Pi
1922 Beta Gamma Sigma
1923 Eta Kappa Nu
1925 Delta Mu Delta
1926 Pi Tau Sigma
1931 Alpha Lambda Delta
1931 Omicron Delta Kappa
1932 Mortar Board
1934 Alpha Kappa Delta
1936 Pi Kappa Lambda
1939 Kappa Omicron Nu
1950 Chi Epsilon
1950 Phi Alpha Theta
1953 Sigma Delta Pi
1956 Rho Chi
1958 Pi Delta Phi
1959 Psi Chi
1965 Gamma Theta Upsilon
1968 Sigma Gamma Tau
1969 Alpha Sigma Mu
1969 Sigma Pi Sigma
1972 Sigma Theta Tau

OTHER HONORS
     National Order of Omega
1899 Phi Beta Kappa
1916 Alpha Omega Alpha
1923 Iota Sigma Pi
1926 Sigma Xi
1928 Order of the Coif
1941 Delta Phi Delta

SERVICE
1942 Alpha Phi Omega

RECOGNITION
     Angel Flight
     Arnold Air Society (D-1)
1923 Scabbard and Blade (4)
1930 Sigma Delta Psi
1931 Delta Phi Alpha
1939 Phi Lambda Upsilon
1941 Theta Alpha Phi
1947 Iota Lambda Sigma
1973 Sigma Phi Alpha

INACTIVE
1901–69 Alpha Kappa Kappa
1913–13 Pi Kappa Phi
1916–77 Delta Zeta
1917–74 Alpha Chi Sigma
1918   Phi Chi
1919–28 Phi Beta Pi and Theta
        Kappa Psi (B)
1920–35 Zeta Beta Tau
1923–71 Alpha Gamma Delta

1926   Eta Sigma Phi
1926–51 Delta Phi Epsilon
1926–71 Phi Sigma Sigma
1927–35 Phi Rho Sigma
1929–58 Alpha Omicron Pi
1929–71 Acacia
1931–51 Phi Mu
1932   Sigma Gamma Epsilon

1933–76 Phi Eta Sigma
1937–80 Alpha Sigma Phi
1961   Sigma Iota Epsilon
1963–73 Sigma Nu

COLONIES
1920 Pi Lambda Phi
1959 Phi Kappa Tau

College-Conservatory Of Music Cincinnati, OH.

PROFESSIONAL
1909 Delta Omicron
1955 Sigma Alpha Iota

INACTIVE
1903–55 Phi Mu Alpha—
        Sinfonia

1914–55 Phi Mu Alpha—
        Sinfonia
1915–55 Sigma Alpha Iota
1918–50 Delta Omicron

THE CITADEL Charleston, SC. Liberal arts military college for men; state control; established 1842. Formerly South Carolina Military Academy.

ACHS HONORS
1941 Sigma Pi Sigma
1951 Pi Sigma Alpha
1955 Phi Alpha Theta
1979 Phi Kappa Phi
1981 Tau Beta Pi

SERVICE
1953 Alpha Phi Omega

RECOGNITION
     Arnold Air Society (C-1)
1960 Sigma Delta Psi

INACTIVE
1883–91 Alpha Tau Omega
1889–90 Pi Kappa Alpha

CITY UNIVERSITY OF NEW YORK CITY COLLEGE New York, NY. Largest unit of the City University of New York System. Coeducational, municipal control. Undergraduate and graduate programs, including doctorate.

NIC MEN'S
1925 Phi Kappa Theta

NPHC MEN'S
     Phi Beta Sigma

NPHC WOMEN'S
1924 Delta Sigma Theta (B)

PROFESSIONAL
1960 Pi Sigma Epsilon
1964 Pi Sigma Epsilon

OTHER PROFESSIONAL
1949 Beta Alpha Psi

ACHS HONORS
1929 Sigma Delta Pi
1931 Kappa Delta Pi
1935 Beta Gamma Sigma
1942 Pi Tau Sigma

1952 Pi Delta Phi

OTHER HONORS
1867 Phi Beta Kappa

SERVICE
1957 Gamma Sigma Sigma

RECOGNITION
1947 Eta Mu Pi
1953 Scabbard and Blade (10)
1965 Blue Key

INACTIVE
1856–57 Theta Delta Chi
1896–71 Pi Lambda Phi
1903–71 Zeta Beta Tau
1909–83 Sigma Alpha Mu
1959–60 Rho Epsilon
1967–72 Delta Phi Epsilon

CITY UNIVERSITY OF NEW YORK, BERNARD M. BARUCH COLLEGE New York, NY. Public college established as an independent school in 1968.

No housing available on campus.

ACHS HONORS
     Pi Alpha Alpha
1947 Psi Chi

INACTIVE
1960–73 Alpha Epsilon Pi

CITY UNIVERSITY OF NEW YORK, HERBERT H. LEHMAN COLLEGE New York, NY. Public institution. Founded in 1931. Four-year; coeducational; liberal arts college.

No housing available on campus.

ACHS HONORS	INACTIVE
1969 Psi Chi	1959–73 Alpha Epsilon Pi
1970 Phi Alpha Theta	1966–70 Sigma Alpha Mu
1971 Pi Sigma Alpha	

CLAFLIN COLLEGE Orangeburg, SC. College of liberal arts; coeducational; private control; related to Methodist Church. Chartered 1869.

NIC MEN'S	1948 Delta Sigma Theta (B)
1949 Kappa Alpha Psi (A)	1949 Alpha Kappa Alpha
	1950 Sigma Gamma Rho
NPHC MEN'S	
1938 Omega Psi Phi	
1948 Alpha Phi Alpha	ACHS HONORS
	1951 Alpha Kappa Mu
NPHC WOMEN'S	1974 Pi Gamma Mu
Zeta Phi Beta	

CLAREMONT COLLEGE Claremont, CA. College of liberal arts and teachers college; coeducational; private control; nonsectarian; founded 1925.

NIC MEN'S	Omicron Delta Epsilon
1991 Zeta Psi	1961 Pi Sigma Alpha
	1979 Psi Chi
OTHER PROFESSIONAL	
1935 Pi Lambda Theta	
ACHS HONORS	
Omicron Delta Epsilon	

CLARION UNIVERSITY OF PENNSYLVANIA Clarion, PA. Founded as Carrier Seminary in 1866; name changed to Clarion Normal School in 1887; to State Teachers College in 1929; to Clarion State in 1960; to Clarion University in 1983. Clarion University is a multi-purpose public institution offering associate degrees in three areas, more than sixty baccalaureate programs leading to a B.A., B.F.A., and B.S.; and twelve graduate programs leading to Master of Arts, Master of Education, Master of Science, and Master of Science in Library Science.

Several fraternities own their houses off campus or lease them from a private owner. Several sororities have houses off campus; leased from private owners, or occupy particular floors in a residence hall.

NIC MEN'S	1987 Kappa Delta Rho
1946 Sigma Tau Gamma	
1959 Phi Sigma Kappa	NPHC MEN'S
1960 Theta Chi	Phi Beta Sigma
1963 Theta Xi	
1964 Alpha Chi Rho	NPC WOMEN'S
1967 Phi Sigma Kappa	1932 Delta Zeta
1967 Tau Kappa Epsilon	1935 Sigma Sigma Sigma
1978 Sigma Chi	1960 Zeta Tau Alpha
1982 Sigma Phi Epsilon	1966 Alpha Sigma Tau
1986 Delta Chi	1967 Alpha Sigma Alpha
1986 Kappa Alpha Psi (A)	1971 Phi Sigma Sigma
	1987 Delta Phi Epsilon

NPHC WOMEN'S	1983 Phi Eta Sigma
1974 Delta Sigma Theta (B)	
1976 Alpha Kappa Alpha	OTHER HONORS
	1971 Pi Mu Epsilon
PROFESSIONAL	
1970 Kappa Kappa Psi	SERVICE
	1977 Alpha Phi Omega
OTHER PROFESSIONAL	
1930 Phi Sigma Pi	RECOGNITION
	1928 Alpha Psi Omega
ACHS HONORS	1964 Pi Kappa Delta
Omicron Delta Epsilon	
Sigma Tau Delta	INACTIVE
1967 Kappa Delta Pi	1930–71 Pi Gamma Mu
1969 Gamma Theta Upsilon	1970–85 Alpha Xi Delta
1975 Psi Chi	
1976 Phi Alpha Theta	COLONIES
1980 Beta Phi Mu	Theta Phi Alpha

CLARK COLLEGE Atlanta, GA. Founded as Clark University in 1869 by the Freedmen's Aid Society of the Methodist Episcopal Church. Named in honor of Bishop Davis W. Clark, first president of the Society, and moving aegis in the Methodist Church's interest in the ex-slaves. Name changed to Clark College in 1940. Coeducational; church related (Methodist); nonsectarian. A unit of the Atlanta University Center.

NIC MEN'S	ACHS HONORS
1948 Kappa Alpha Psi (A)	1944 Alpha Kappa Mu
	1982 Pi Gamma Mu
NPHC MEN'S	
Phi Beta Sigma	SERVICE
1923 Omega Psi Phi	1969 Alpha Phi Omega
1927 Alpha Phi Alpha	
NPHC WOMEN'S	
Zeta Phi Beta	

CLARK UNIVERSITY Worcester, MA. University; co-ordinate college for men and women; private control; nonsectarian. Established 1887.

NIC MEN'S	1960 Psi Chi
Alpha Epsilon Pi	1962 Sigma Pi Sigma
Alpha Epsilon Pi	1963 Phi Sigma Tau
1961 Tau Epsilon Phi	1977 Psi Chi
NPHC WOMEN'S	OTHER HONORS
1924 Delta Sigma Theta (B)	1953 Phi Beta Kappa
1930 Alpha Kappa Alpha	
1952 Sigma Gamma Rho	SERVICE
	1989 Alpha Phi Omega
PROFESSIONAL	
1982 Kappa Delta Epsilon	INACTIVE
	1924–69 Zeta Beta Tau
ACHS HONORS	1925–70 Lambda Chi Alpha
Omicron Delta Epsilon	1933 Delta Phi Alpha
1916 Delta Sigma Rho-Tau	
Kappa Alpha	COLONIES
1951 Gamma Theta Upsilon	Sigma Pi

CLARKE COLLEGE Dubuque, IA. Founded 1843; liberal arts college with selected professional majors; coeducational (1979); Roman Catholic; confers Associate (A.A.), Bachelor (B.A., B.S., B.F.A.), and Master's degrees (M.A.).

ACHS HONORS
1940 Delta Epsilon Sigma

CLARKSON UNIVERSITY Potsdam, NY. Founded by the sisters of Thomas S. Clarkson as a memorial to him in 1896. Coeducational institution offering undergraduate degrees in chemical, civil and environmental, electrical and computer, and mechanical and industrial engineering; biology, chemistry, computer science, industrial hygiene-environmental toxicology, mathematics, and physics; accounting and law, applied psychology, computer-based management systems, economics and finance, industrial management, management and marketing; industrial distribution; economics, history, humanities, social sciences, political science, sociology, and technical communications; private control; nonsectarian; graduate school.

NIC MEN'S
1952 Theta Chi
1956 Alpha Chi Rho
1961 Delta Upsilon
1963 Tau Kappa Epsilon
1967 Delta Sigma Phi
1968 Alpha Epsilon Pi
1968 Tau Epsilon Phi
1981 Phi Kappa Sigma
1988 Sigma Chi

NPC WOMEN'S
1977 Phi Sigma Sigma
1984 Phi Mu
1986 Delta Zeta

ACHS HONORS
1941 Omega Chi Epsilon
1941 Tau Beta Pi
1950 Eta Kappa Nu

1950 Pi Tau Sigma
1951 Chi Epsilon
1969 Phi Alpha Theta
1969 Sigma Pi Sigma
1972 Phi Kappa Phi

OTHER HONORS
     National Order of Omega
1965 Pi Mu Epsilon

SERVICE
1958 Alpha Phi Omega

RECOGNITION
1965 Gamma Sigma Epsilon

INACTIVE
1957–63 Pi Kappa Phi
1957–70 Triangle
1958–73 Alpha Kappa Psi
1958–88 Theta Xi

CLEMSON UNIVERSITY Clemson, SC. A land-grant, state-supported university; chartered in 1889 as Clemson Agricultural and Mechanical College; formally opened 1893; name changed to Clemson University in 1964. The campus is the old farm site of John C. Calhoun, willed to the state by Thomas G. Clemson, the first secretary of agriculture and the son-in-law of Mr. Calhoun. Originally an all-male military academy, the university became coeducational in 1955.

Two fraternities have houses in the city. Fourteen fraternities and ten sororities are furnished resident hall floors and lounges. The fraternity and sorority chapters were local groups from 1956 through 1970.

NIC MEN'S
1970 Beta Theta Pi
1970 Kappa Alpha Order
1970 Kappa Sigma
1970 Phi Delta Theta
1970 Pi Kappa Alpha
1970 Sigma Alpha Epsilon
1970 Sigma Nu
1970 Sigma Phi Epsilon
1970 Theta Chi
1971 Alpha Tau Omega
1971 Chi Psi
1974 Alpha Gamma Rho
1977 Sigma Chi
1980 Kappa Alpha Psi (A)

1988 Pi Kappa Phi
1990 Delta Chi

NPHC MEN'S
     Phi Beta Sigma

NPC WOMEN'S
1970 Chi Omega
1970 Delta Delta Delta
1970 Kappa Kappa Gamma
1972 Kappa Alpha Theta
1976 Alpha Delta Pi
1976 Pi Beta Phi
1980 Kappa Delta
1981 Delta Gamma
1985 Alpha Chi Omega

1988 Gamma Phi Beta

NPHC WOMEN'S
1977 Alpha Kappa Alpha

PROFESSIONAL
1982 Delta Sigma Pi

OTHER PROFESSIONAL
1927 Phi Psi
1930 Alpha Zeta
1951 Kappa Phi Kappa
1958 Keramos

ACHS HONORS
     Omicron Delta Epsilon
1928 Tau Beta Pi
1938 Phi Kappa Phi
1940 Phi Eta Sigma
1949 Sigma Pi Sigma
1963 Tau Sigma Delta
1965 Delta Sigma Rho-Tau
     Kappa Alpha
1965 Xi Sigma Pi
1971 Alpha Epsilon Delta
1971 Alpha Lambda Delta
1972 Eta Kappa Nu
1972 Kappa Delta Pi
1972 Sigma Delta Pi
1974 Chi Epsilon
1975 Pi Delta Phi

1975 Psi Chi
1976 Pi Sigma Alpha
1977 Mortar Board
1985 Phi Alpha Theta
1987 Omicron Delta Kappa

OTHER HONORS
     National Order of Omega
1966 Sigma Xi
1973 Pi Mu Epsilon

SERVICE
1940 Alpha Phi Omega
1974 Gamma Sigma Sigma

RECOGNITION
     Arnold Air Society (C-1)
1930 Iota Lambda Sigma
1932 Blue Key
1933 Scabbard and Blade (7)
1937 Mu Beta Psi
1937 National Block and Bridle
     Club
1947 Alpha Psi Omega

INACTIVE
1939–56 Alpha Chi Sigma
1974–88 Phi Gamma Delta

COLONIES
     Lambda Chi Alpha

CLEVELAND INSTITUTE OF MUSIC Cleveland, OH. Established 1920; coeducational.

PROFESSIONAL
1939 Mu Phi Epsilon

ACHS HONORS
1965 Pi Kappa Lambda

CLEVELAND STATE UNIVERSITY Cleveland, OH. Formerly Fenn College, founded in 1923; state control under board of trustees; coeducational; four undergraduate colleges; graduate curricula.

Fraternities own their own houses on their own land; no sorority owns or rents quarters, for the college makes available a room which all sororities use.

NIC MEN'S
1953 Tau Kappa Epsilon
1961 Sigma Tau Gamma
1963 Delta Sigma Phi

NPHC MEN'S
     Phi Beta Sigma
1960 Alpha Phi Alpha

NPC WOMEN'S
1979 Theta Phi Alpha
1983 Sigma Kappa
1988 Alpha Epsilon Phi

NPHC WOMEN'S
1925 Alpha Kappa Alpha
1925 Delta Sigma Theta (B)
1929 Sigma Gamma Rho
1981 Sigma Gamma Rho

PROFESSIONAL
1962 Phi Alpha Delta

ACHS HONORS
     Omicron Delta Epsilon
1953 Tau Beta Pi
1963 Eta Kappa Nu
1972 Phi Alpha Theta
1972 Sigma Delta Pi
1978 Pi Kappa Lambda
1984 Psi Chi

SERVICE
1949 Alpha Phi Omega

RECOGNITION
1969 Blue Key

INACTIVE
1964–90 Sigma Phi Epsilon
1967–74 Alpha Epsilon Pi
1969–86 Sigma Pi Sigma
1975–90 Phi Kappa Tau

CLINCH VALLEY COLLEGE Wise, VA. Liberal arts and general college of the University of Virginia. Coeducational. State control. Established 1954.

NIC MEN'S
1976 Phi Sigma Kappa
1980 Pi Kappa Phi

ACHS HONORS
1972 Sigma Tau Delta

RECOGNITION
1971 Sigma Zeta

INACTIVE
1970–74 Beta Beta Beta

COE COLLEGE Cedar Rapids, IA. Founded as the Cedar Rapids Collegiate Institute in 1851 and first instruction in 1851. Liberal arts college, coeducational, private control, Presbyterian. Fraternity and sorority members are required by the administration to occupy dormitories.

NIC MEN'S
1916 Tau Kappa Epsilon
1920 Phi Kappa Tau
1928 Alpha Sigma Phi
1946 Lambda Chi Alpha

NPC WOMEN'S
1912 Delta Delta Delta
1914 Chi Omega
1969 Alpha Omicron Pi

PROFESSIONAL
1926 Mu Phi Epsilon
1930 Phi Mu Alpha—Sinfonia

ACHS HONORS
   Omicron Delta Epsilon
1925 Phi Kappa Phi
1926 Phi Sigma Iota
1938 Alpha Lambda Delta
1982 Phi Eta Sigma
1985 Mortar Board

OTHER HONORS
1949 Phi Beta Kappa

SERVICE
1946 Alpha Phi Omega

RECOGNITION
1923 Pi Kappa Delta
1945 Alpha Psi Omega

INACTIVE
1911–66 Kappa Delta
1917–64 Alpha Gamma Delta
1918–74 Alpha Xi Delta
1921   Scabbard and Blade
        (3)
1924–37 Zeta Phi Eta
1927   Eta Sigma Phi
1937–39 Kappa Phi Kappa
1938–58 Pi Gamma Mu

COKER COLLEGE Hartsville, SC. College of liberal arts for women; private control; nonsectarian; chartered 1894.

NPHC MEN'S
   Phi Beta Sigma

RECOGNITION
1927 Alpha Psi Omega

INACTIVE
1931–70 Sigma Tau Delta
1940–62 Kappa Mu Epsilon

COLBY COLLEGE Waterville, ME. College of liberal arts; coeducational; private control; nonsectarian. Established 1813 as Maine Literary and Theological Institution; became Colby College 1899; women admitted 1871.

Social or general fraternities and sororities were abolished by the college in 1984.

NIC MEN'S
1933 Tau Delta Phi

ACHS HONORS
1929 Phi Sigma Iota
1948 Sigma Pi Sigma
1971 Sigma Delta Pi
1972 Pi Sigma Alpha
1981 Psi Chi

OTHER HONORS
1896 Phi Beta Kappa

RECOGNITION
   Arnold Air Society (A-1)
1949 Delta Phi Alpha

INACTIVE
1846–84 Delta Kappa Epsilon
1850–88 Zeta Psi
1852–84 Delta Upsilon

1874–84 Sigma Kappa
1884–86 Phi Delta Theta
1892–84 Alpha Tau Omega
1906–84 Chi Omega
1908–64 Delta Delta Delta
1915–74 Alpha Delta Pi
1918–44 Phi Mu

1918–84 Lambda Chi Alpha
1923–37 Kappa Phi Kappa
1926–54 Pi Gamma Mu
1926–83 Kappa Delta Rho
1959–84 Pi Lambda Phi
1961–69 Alpha Delta Phi

COLGATE UNIVERSITY Hamilton, NY. Liberal arts undergraduate institution for men and women founded in 1819 as Baptist Education Society; named Madison University in 1846; renamed Colgate University in 1890; enrollment about 2,600 students; private control; nonsectarian.

Most fraternities occupy their own houses on their own land. The college requires all first-year students to live in university residence halls; upperclass students may reside in chapter houses or in private accommodations in the community.

NIC MEN'S
1856 Delta Kappa Epsilon
1865 Delta Upsilon
1880 Beta Theta Pi
1912 Theta Chi
1917 Alpha Tau Omega
1917 Kappa Delta Rho
1918 Phi Delta Theta
1930 Sigma Chi

NPC WOMEN'S
1981 Gamma Phi Beta
1986 Pi Beta Phi
1988 Alpha Chi Omega
1988 Kappa Alpha Theta
1988 Kappa Kappa Gamma

ACHS HONORS
   Omicron Delta Epsilon
1910 Delta Sigma Rho-Tau
     Kappa Alpha
1950 Psi Chi
1955 Pi Sigma Alpha
1965 Phi Alpha Theta
1976 Sigma Delta Pi
1977 Gamma Theta Upsilon
1982 Phi Eta Sigma

OTHER HONORS
1878 Phi Beta Kappa

SERVICE
1956 Alpha Phi Omega

RECOGNITION
   Arnold Air Society (E-1)
1925 Sigma Delta Psi
1927 Alpha Psi Omega
1935 Delta Phi Alpha
1963 Eta Sigma Phi
1971 Beta Beta Beta

INACTIVE
1850–72 Alpha Delta Phi
1874–76 Delta Phi
1887–82 Phi Kappa Psi
1887–88 Phi Gamma Delta
1916–68 Lambda Chi Alpha
1917–68 Sigma Nu
1924–55 Alpha Chi Sigma
1928–40 Sigma Gamma Epsilon
1928–46 Kappa Phi Kappa
1937–71 Phi Kappa Tau
1956–72 Tau Kappa Epsilon
1966–75 Kappa Mu Epsilon

COLLEGE OF THE OZARKS Clarksville, AR. Private control: Presbyterian Church. Founded in 1834. Four-year; coeducational; liberal arts college.

ACHS HONORS
1932 Alpha Chi
1951 Phi Alpha Theta
1969 Sigma Delta Pi
1973 Phi Alpha Theta
1973 Sigma Tau Delta

SERVICE
1966 Alpha Phi Omega

RECOGNITION
1935 Alpha Psi Omega

UNIVERSITY OF COLORADO Boulder, CO. Established in 1876, main campus at Boulder, CO, medical center in Denver, undergraduate campuses in Denver and Colorado Springs. More than 120 fields of study are offered at the undergraduate and graduate levels through the university's ten schools and colleges.

Fraternities occupy their own houses on their own land.

NIC MEN'S
Tau Kappa Epsilon
1891 Sigma Alpha Epsilon
1900 Beta Theta Pi
1901 Alpha Tau Omega
1902 Phi Delta Theta
1902 Sigma Nu
1904 Sigma Phi Epsilon
1911 Acacia
1912 Phi Gamma Delta
1914 Phi Kappa Psi
1914 Sigma Chi
1916 Kappa Sigma
1919 Zeta Beta Tau
1920 Chi Psi
1923 Lambda Chi Alpha
1924 Delta Sigma Phi
1924 Phi Kappa Tau
1929 Theta Xi
1931 Kappa Alpha Psi (A)
1950 Tau Kappa Epsilon
1953 Delta Upsilon
1977 Alpha Epsilon Pi
1983 Delta Chi
1984 Sigma Pi
1990 Zeta Psi

NPHC MEN'S
Phi Beta Sigma

NPC WOMEN'S
Alpha Phi
1884 Pi Beta Phi
1886 Delta Gamma
1901 Kappa Kappa Gamma
1906 Chi Omega
1907 Alpha Chi Omega
1910 Delta Delta Delta
1921 Kappa Alpha Theta
1927 Alpha Omicron Pi
1947 Kappa Delta
1952 Alpha Epsilon Phi
1954 Gamma Phi Beta

NPHC WOMEN'S
1982 Alpha Kappa Alpha

PROFESSIONAL
1907 Phi Delta Phi
1910 Phi Alpha Delta
1914 Phi Delta Chi
1926 Delta Sigma Pi
1932 Kappa Kappa Psi
1936 Sigma Alpha Iota
1946 Tau Beta Sigma
1950 Alpha Kappa Psi
1980 Alpha Omega

OTHER PROFESSIONAL
1919 Sigma Delta Chi
1926 Phi Delta Epsilon
1927 Beta Alpha Psi
1927 Women in Communications
1959 Delta Pi Epsilon
1976 Delta Sigma Delta

ACHS HONORS
Omicron Delta Epsilon
Pi Alpha Alpha
1905 Tau Beta Pi
1910 Delta Sigma Rho-Tau
Kappa Alpha
1912 Kappa Delta Pi
1922 Eta Kappa Nu
1924 Mortar Board
1929 Chi Epsilon
1930 Sigma Pi Sigma
1932 Pi Tau Sigma
1934 Alpha Epsilon Delta

1934 Kappa Tau Alpha
1939 Beta Gamma Sigma
1941 Phi Sigma
1947 Rho Chi
1948 Phi Alpha Theta
1949 Psi Chi
1953 Gamma Theta Upsilon
1958 Pi Kappa Lambda
1959 Pi Sigma Alpha
1961 Alpha Kappa Delta
1969 Alpha Epsilon
1970 Sigma Delta Pi
1974 Sigma Gamma Tau
1980 Omega Chi Epsilon

OTHER HONORS
National Order of Omega
1904 Phi Beta Kappa
1905 Sigma Xi
1918 Iota Sigma Pi
1926 Alpha Omega Alpha
1930 Delta Phi Delta
1942 Order of the Coif
1963 Gamma Sigma Delta

SERVICE
1941 Alpha Phi Omega

RECOGNITION
Arnold Air Society (H-1)
1928 Sigma Delta Psi
1934 Delta Phi Alpha
1950 Phi Lambda Upsilon
1958 Scabbard and Blade (14)
1958 Sigma Iota Epsilon
1961 Blue Key
1967 Rho Epsilon

INACTIVE
1883–89 Delta Tau Delta
1903–12 Alpha Kappa Kappa
1908–72 Alpha Chi Sigma
1909–72 Phi Rho Sigma
1914–85 Alpha Delta Pi
1915–57 Alpha Sigma Phi
1920   Phi Beta Pi and Theta
Kappa Psi (a)
1921–37 Phi Chi
1922–69 Pi Kappa Alpha
1924–34 Delta Zeta
1924–82 Alpha Phi
1926–32 Delta Theta Phi
1929   Sigma Epsilon Sigma
1929–63 Pi Lambda Phi
1930–86 Kappa Epsilon
1932–57 Pi Gamma Mu
1934   Sigma Gamma Epsilon
1936   Pi Mu Epsilon
1936–38 Phi Chi Theta
1937–85 Phi Mu Alpha—
Sinfonia
1940–66 Delta Phi Epsilon
1947–71 Sigma Delta Tau
1947–72 Zeta Tau Alpha
1950   Alpha Delta Theta
1953–60 Sigma Alpha Mu
1958–88 Alpha Gamma Delta
1964–74 Alpha Lambda Delta
1966–72 Kappa Beta Pi
1967–70 Alpha Kappa Lambda
1969–70 Omicron Delta Kappa
1969–70 Triangle

COLONIES
Chi Phi
Pi Kappa Phi
1990 Chi Phi

UNIVERSITY OF COLORADO, COLORADO SPRINGS Colorado Springs, CO.

ACHS HONORS
Pi Alpha Alpha
1973 Phi Alpha Theta
1975 Psi Chi

1982 Eta Kappa Nu

COLONIES
1986 Sigma Pi Sigma

UNIVERSITY OF COLORADO, DENVER Denver, CO.

PROFESSIONAL
1971 Phi Chi Theta

ACHS HONORS
Omicron Delta Epsilon
1966 Sigma Theta Tau
1969 Phi Sigma
1978 Eta Kappa Nu

1982 Chi Epsilon
1984 Psi Chi
1985 Phi Alpha Theta
1985 Pi Sigma Alpha
1985 Tau Beta Pi
1988 Sigma Lambda Alpha

COLORADO COLLEGE Colorado Springs, CO.
Founded in 1874 in Colorado Territory, first instruction, 1874. Privately endowed; nonsectarian; coeducational college of liberal arts granting the A.B. degree.

The college owns four of the five fraternity houses and provides maintenance and upkeep of them. In addition, it provides for the meal service in each of the houses although the meals are prepared and served in the houses. At registration the college collects room and board charges directly from each resident of the fraternity houses. The fraternities have exclusive use of the houses, provided they are maintained at 90 per cent. No charge is made against the fraternities for the use of the houses.

Sorority lodges are owned by the sorority on college-owned land and do not provide living quarters except for the housemother. Members are assigned to college residence halls, except for seniors who may live off campus.

NIC MEN'S
1904 Kappa Sigma
1905 Sigma Chi
1908 Phi Gamma Delta
1913 Phi Delta Theta
1914 Beta Theta Pi

1957 Alpha Lambda Delta
1967 Phi Sigma Iota

NPC WOMEN'S
1932 Delta Gamma
1932 Gamma Phi Beta
1932 Kappa Alpha Theta
1932 Kappa Kappa Gamma

OTHER HONORS
1904 Phi Beta Kappa

RECOGNITION
1935 Sigma Delta Psi

ACHS HONORS
1916 Delta Sigma Rho-Tau
Kappa Alpha
1956 Pi Gamma Mu

INACTIVE
1919–66 Alpha Kappa Psi
1920–34 Theta Alpha Phi
1921–33 Pi Kappa Alpha
1926   Eta Sigma Phi
1934–42 Lambda Chi Alpha
1954–61 Alpha Phi

COLORADO SCHOOL OF MINES Golden, CO.
Founded in 1869 as a wing of Episcopal university, it came under territorial control in 1874. Ranks as oldest and largest college devoted exclusively to the education of mineral engineers. Coeducational undergraduate and graduate college.

Fraternities own their own houses and land.

NIC MEN'S
1901 Sigma Nu
1903 Sigma Alpha Epsilon
1904 Kappa Sigma
1908 Beta Theta Pi
1923 Sigma Phi Epsilon
1929 Alpha Tau Omega
1985 Phi Gamma Delta

NPC WOMEN'S
1980 Sigma Kappa
1986 Pi Beta Phi

PROFESSIONAL
1925 Kappa Kappa Psi

ACHS HONORS
1905 Tau Beta Pi
1965 Alpha Sigma Mu
1971 Kappa Mu Epsilon

1978 Sigma Pi Sigma

OTHER HONORS
1922 Sigma Gamma Epsilon
1965 Sigma Xi

SERVICE
1958 Alpha Phi Omega

RECOGNITION
1926 Blue Key
1932 Scabbard and Blade (7)
1935 Sigma Delta Psi

INACTIVE
1907–85 Theta Tau
1951–61 Theta Chi
1951–63 Pi Kappa Alpha
1977–82 Alpha Gamma Delta

COLORADO STATE UNIVERSITY Fort Collins, CO. Founded by territorial legislature in 1870; nine colleges in university plus graduate school; coeducational; land-grant college. Fraternities and sororities occupy their own houses on their own land. Occasionally they occupy rental property as a temporary situation.

NIC MEN'S
1915 Sigma Nu
1915 Sigma Phi Epsilon
1917 Sigma Alpha Epsilon
1919 Sigma Chi
1920 Alpha Tau Omega
1920 Phi Delta Theta
1921 Alpha Gamma Rho
1922 Lambda Chi Alpha
1929 Phi Kappa Tau
1949 FarmHouse
1956 Pi Kappa Alpha
1967 Delta Tau Delta
1967 Triangle
1968 Phi Gamma Delta
1988 Beta Theta Pi
1990 Pi Kappa Phi

NPHC MEN'S
Phi Beta Sigma

NPC WOMEN'S
1915 Gamma Phi Beta
1916 Kappa Delta
1917 Delta Delta Delta
1917 Kappa Alpha Theta
1947 Sigma Kappa
1954 Pi Beta Phi
1956 Kappa Kappa Gamma
1957 Chi Omega
1965 Alpha Chi Omega
1979 Alpha Phi

OTHER WOMEN'S
1985 CERES

PROFESSIONAL
1928 Delta Omicron
1967 Phi Mu Alpha—Sinfonia
1991 Sigma Alpha

OTHER PROFESSIONAL
1906 Alpha Zeta
1930 Alpha Tau Alpha
1970 Sigma Delta Chi
1971 Beta Alpha Psi

ACHS HONORS
Omicron Delta Epsilon
1920 Kappa Omicron Nu
1927 Phi Kappa Phi
1943 Xi Sigma Pi
1948 Kappa Mu Epsilon
1950 Chi Epsilon
1956 Alpha Lambda Delta
1961 Mortar Board
1961 Pi Tau Sigma
1962 Eta Kappa Nu
1962 Phi Alpha Theta
1962 Sigma Pi Sigma
1964 Alpha Kappa Delta
1964 Psi Chi
1965 Phi Eta Sigma
1965 Phi Sigma Iota
1966 Pi Sigma Alpha
1970 Beta Gamma Sigma
1974 Tau Beta Pi
1984 Omega Chi Epsilon
1988 Pi Kappa Lambda
1989 Sigma Lambda Alpha

OTHER HONORS
National Order of Omega
1953 Sigma Xi
1973 Phi Beta Kappa

SERVICE
The National Spurs
1947 Alpha Phi Omega
1953 Intercollegiate Knights

RECOGNITION
Arnold Air Society (H-1)
1915 Pi Kappa Delta
1923 Scabbard and Blade (4)
1931 Beta Beta Beta
1931 Iota Lambda Sigma
1950 Phi Zeta

INACTIVE
1910   Alpha Psi
1928–69 Alpha Sigma Tau
1932–65 Pi Gamma Mu
1945–78 Delta Zeta
1949–75 Tau Kappa Epsilon
1950–71 Acacia
1950–72 Theta Chi
1952–70 Omicron Delta Kappa
1952–75 Zeta Beta Tau
1956–60 Lambda Iota Tau
1961–69 Sigma Tau Delta
1961–72 Pi Omega Pi
1964–74 Alpha Kappa Lambda
1966–68 Sigma Delta Tau
1971–87 Delta Upsilon

COLUMBIA COLLEGE Columbia, MO. Private control: Disciples of Christ Church. Founded in 1851. Four-year; coeducational; liberal arts college.

On campus housing is available in single-sex dormitories.

ACHS HONORS
1976 Alpha Chi

COLUMBIA COLLEGE Columbia, SC. College of liberal arts for women; private control; Methodist Church; chartered 1854.

PROFESSIONAL
1957 Delta Omicron

ACHS HONORS
1928 Sigma Tau Delta
1948 Phi Alpha Theta
1975 Pi Delta Phi
1976 Sigma Delta Pi

1985 Omicron Delta Kappa

RECOGNITION
1945 Alpha Psi Omega

INACTIVE
1904–09 Alpha Sigma Alpha

COLUMBIA COLLEGE, COLUMBIA UNIVERSITY
New York, NY. Founded as Kings Collge, 1754; undergraduate college for men.

Nine fraternities own their own houses; five are owned by the college; and one is jointly owned by the college and fraternity.

NIC MEN'S
1836 Alpha Delta Phi
1842 Delta Phi
1842 Psi Upsilon
1847 Delta Psi
1866 Phi Gamma Delta
1872 Phi Kappa Psi
1879 Zeta Psi
1881 Beta Theta Pi
1894 Sigma Chi
1900 Alpha Chi Rho
1904 Zeta Beta Tau
1911 Sigma Alpha Mu
1916 Alpha Phi Delta
1916 Tau Delta Phi
1921 Kappa Alpha Psi (A)
1982 Kappa Delta Rho
1990 Pi Kappa Alpha

NPC WOMEN'S
1984 Alpha Phi
1986 Kappa Alpha Theta
1988 Delta Gamma

1989 Alpha Chi Omega

PROFESSIONAL
1914 Alpha Omega
1916 Phi Alpha Delta
1921 Rho Pi Phi
1955 Kappa Delta Epsilon

OTHER PROFESSIONAL
1923 Alpha Zeta Omega

ACHS HONORS
Omicron Delta Epsilon
1902 Tau Beta Pi
1929 Pi Sigma Alpha
1949 Gamma Theta Upsilon
1954 Eta Kappa Nu
1963 Psi Chi
1967 Beta Phi Mu
1982 Chi Epsilon
1983 Sigma Pi Sigma
1985 Alpha Lambda Delta

SERVICE
1954 Alpha Phi Omega

1982 Alpha Phi Omega

INACTIVE
1846–85 Chi Psi
1855–34 Phi Kappa Sigma
1874–35 Delta Kappa Epsilon
1881–10 Alpha Tau Omega
1882–28 Delta Tau Delta
1883–29 Theta Delta Chi
1884–35 Phi Delta Theta
1885–64 Delta Upsilon
1895–60 Sigma Alpha Epsilon
1896–64 Pi Lambda Phi
1897–33 Phi Sigma Kappa
1898–40 Phi Delta Chi
1899–33 Theta Xi

1901–13 Delta Sigma Phi
1909–33 Acacia
1910–57 Alpha Sigma Phi
1914–32 Delta Theta Phi
1914–70 Theta Tau
1915–17 Alpha Epsilon Phi
1923–43 Delta Chi
1924–51 Phi Chi Theta
1928–76 Phi Mu Alpha—
        Sinfonia
1931–69 Lambda Kappa Sigma
1954–76 Rho Chi

COLONIES
1923 Alpha Epsilon Pi

COLUMBIA UNION COLLEGE   Takoma Park, MD. College of liberal arts; coeducational; private control; Seventh-day Adventist Church; established 1904.

ACHS HONORS
1965 Phi Alpha Theta

1985 Phi Eta Sigma
1989 Psi Chi

COLUMBUS COLLEGE   Columbus, GA. College of liberal arts and general; teacher preparatory; professional; educational. State control. Established 1958.

NIC MEN'S
1974 Kappa Alpha Psi (A)
1977 Tau Kappa Epsilon

NPHC MEN'S
    Phi Beta Sigma
1972 Alpha Phi Alpha

NPHC WOMEN'S
1971 Delta Sigma Theta (B)
1972 Alpha Kappa Alpha

PROFESSIONAL
1948 Delta Theta Phi
1988 Phi Mu Alpha—Sinfonia

ACHS HONORS
1970 Lambda Iota Tau
1973 Psi Chi
1975 Phi Alpha Theta
1976 Phi Kappa Phi
1989 Phi Eta Sigma

SERVICE
1971 Alpha Phi Omega

INACTIVE
1970–84 Delta Sigma Pi
1975–85 Delta Zeta
1975–86 Sigma Pi
1980–86 Delta Chi

COLUMBUS STATE COMMUNITY COLLEGE   Columbus, OH.

SERVICE
1990 Alpha Phi Omega

CONCORD COLLEGE   Athens, WV. Founded 1875; state-supported liberal arts college with a strong concentration in teacher education. Third largest institution of higher education in West Virginia.

Some fraternities and sororities occupy their own lodges on their own land; others have long-range plans for owning them. Freshmen and sophomores in fraternities and sororities are required to live in the dormitories.

NIC MEN'S
    Tau Kappa Epsilon
1949 Sigma Tau Gamma
1960 Phi Sigma Kappa

NPC WOMEN'S
1925 Sigma Sigma Sigma
1928 Delta Zeta
1930 Alpha Sigma Tau
1947 Alpha Sigma Alpha

OTHER PROFESSIONAL
1953 Alpha Beta Alpha

ACHS HONORS
1935 Kappa Delta Pi
1937 Gamma Theta Upsilon
1969 Alpha Chi

RECOGNITION
1929 Alpha Psi Omega
1930 Chi Beta Phi
1938 Cardinal Key
1954 Kappa Pi

INACTIVE
1932–57 Pi Gamma Mu
1942–79 Kappa Omicron Nu
1946–78 Theta Xi
1948–60 Pi Omega Pi
1963–87 Tau Kappa Epsilon
1966–84 Alpha Sigma Phi
1969–86 Pi Kappa Alpha

COLONIES
    Pi Kappa Phi

CONCORDIA COLLEGE   River Forest, IL.

ACHS HONORS
1968 Phi Alpha Theta

CONCORDIA COLLEGE   Moorhead, MN. College of liberal arts; coeducational; private control; affiliated with American Lutheran Church. Chartered 1891.

ACHS HONORS
1957 Pi Gamma Mu
1961 Psi Chi

1970 Sigma Delta Pi
1973 Sigma Pi Sigma
1987 Omicron Delta Kappa

CONCORDIA LUTHERAN COLLEGE   Austin, TX.

SERVICE
1987 Alpha Phi Omega

CONCORDIA UNIVERSITY   Loyola Campus, Montreal, QB. Established 1974 by merger of Loyola College (1896) and Sir George Williams University (1929). Coeducational.

NIC MEN'S
1967 Tau Kappa Epsilon

UNIVERSITY OF CONNECTICUT   Storrs, CT. University and land-grant college; coeducational; state control; established by act of General Assembly in 1881.

A university ruling in 1970 to eliminate selective housing in university facilities displaced most of the twenty men's general fraternities and seven women's general sororities. Some were able to procure off-campus housing; others, who were not, disbanded. In 1979, the Board of Trustees passed a resolution stating that the university should provide housing for fraternities and sororities. The university then began to lease university owned houses to fraternities and sororities. Inactive organizations began to return, and new national organizations began to colonize in response to the growing interest in Greek life, and the support given to the fraternal organizations by the administration.

NIC MEN'S
1922 Alpha Gamma Rho
1932 Tau Epsilon Phi
1942 Kappa Sigma
1943 Sigma Alpha Epsilon
1943 Sigma Chi

1947 Lambda Chi Alpha
1952 Tau Kappa Epsilon
1955 Delta Chi
1956 Alpha Epsilon Pi
1956 Chi Phi
1956 Sigma Phi Epsilon

1958 Alpha Gamma Rho
1960 Zeta Psi
1982 Triangle
1990 Kappa Alpha Psi (A)
1990 Tau Kappa Epsilon

NPHC MEN'S
      Phi Beta Sigma
1975 Alpha Phi Alpha

NPC WOMEN'S
1883 Kappa Alpha Theta
1942 Kappa Alpha Theta
1942 Kappa Kappa Gamma
1943 Delta Zeta
1943 Pi Beta Phi
1983 Delta Gamma
1990 Kappa Delta

NPHC WOMEN'S
1977 Alpha Kappa Alpha

PROFESSIONAL
1926 Rho Pi Phi
1928 Kappa Psi
1949 Lambda Kappa Sigma
1949 Phi Delta Chi
1962 Kappa Kappa Psi
1964 Tau Beta Sigma
1970 Delta Sigma Pi
1973 Phi Alpha Delta
1978 Gamma Iota Sigma
1984 Alpha Omega
1990 Sigma Alpha

OTHER PROFESSIONAL
1929 Alpha Zeta Omega
1948 Phi Upsilon Omicron
1952 Alpha Zeta

ACHS HONORS
      Omicron Delta Epsilon
      Pi Alpha Alpha
1942 Rho Chi
1948 Pi Tau Sigma
1949 Chi Epsilon
1949 Eta Kappa Nu
1949 Mortar Board
1949 Tau Beta Pi
1950 Sigma Pi Sigma

1951 Phi Kappa Phi
1952 Delta Sigma Rho-Tau
      Kappa Alpha
1952 Phi Alpha Theta
1954 Sigma Delta Pi
1955 Pi Sigma Alpha
1955 Sigma Theta Tau
1959 Beta Gamma Sigma
1959 Kappa Delta Pi
1964 Alpha Lambda Delta
1965 Pi Delta Phi
1980 Gamma Theta Upsilon
1983 Omega Chi Epsilon
1983 Psi Chi
1989 Pi Kappa Lambda

OTHER HONORS
      National Order of Omega
1945 Sigma Xi
1956 Phi Beta Kappa
1963 Pi Mu Epsilon

SERVICE
1947 Alpha Phi Omega
1956 Gamma Sigma Sigma

RECOGNITION
      Arnold Air Society (A-1)
1938 National Block and Bridle
      Club
1951 Phi Lambda Upsilon
1952 Scabbard and Blade (10)

INACTIVE
1916–70 Zeta Beta Tau
1918–47 Phi Mu Delta
1943   Phi Sigma Sigma
1943–51 Sigma Nu
1943–63 Phi Mu
1943–70 Alpha Delta Pi
1943–71 Alpha Sigma Phi
1943–72 Theta Xi
1944–70 Alpha Epsilon Phi
1947–69 Zeta Beta Tau
1947–72 Phi Sigma Kappa
1948–51 Alpha Xi Delta
1948–66 Theta Chi
1961–71 Phi Kappa Tau
1979–83 Phi Chi Theta

CONNECTICUT COLLEGE   New London, CT.

ACHS HONORS
1984 Pi Sigma Alpha

1988 Psi Chi

CONNECTICUT WESLEYAN   Middletown, CT.

INACTIVE
1895–13 Delta Delta Delta

CONNERS STATE COLLEGE   Warner, OK.

SERVICE
1971 Alpha Phi Omega

CONVERSE COLLEGE   Spartanburg, SC. College of liberal arts for women; men admitted at graduate level; private control; nonsectarian; established 1889.

PROFESSIONAL
1966 Delta Omicron

ACHS HONORS
1938 Pi Kappa Lambda
1967 Mortar Board

1970 Pi Gamma Mu
1981 Phi Sigma Iota
1982 Alpha Lambda Delta

RECOGNITION
1957 Alpha Psi Omega

THE COOPER UNION FOR THE ADVANCEMENT OF SCIENCE AND ART   New York, NY. Founded by Peter Cooper, board of trustees organized, chartered and first instruction 1859. School of engineering; school of art and architecture; coeducational; private control; nonsectarian.

Fraternities occupy houses on a rental basis.

NIC MEN'S
1975 Tau Delta Phi
1984 Zeta Psi

ACHS HONORS
1947 Tau Beta Pi
1949 Chi Epsilon
1949 Pi Tau Sigma

1962 Eta Kappa Nu

SERVICE
1953 Alpha Phi Omega

INACTIVE
-90   Delta Phi Epsilon
1968–86 Sigma Pi Sigma

COPPIN STATE COLLEGE   Baltimore, MD. Established 1900 as a city normal school; became a city teachers college in 1938; a state teachers college in 1950, and a liberal arts program added in 1963.

NIC MEN'S
1970 Kappa Alpha Psi (A)

NPHC MEN'S
      Phi Beta Sigma

NPHC WOMEN'S
1968 Delta Sigma Theta (B)
1968 Sigma Gamma Rho

1969 Alpha Kappa Alpha

ACHS HONORS
1963 Alpha Kappa Mu
1972 Sigma Tau Delta
1982 Phi Alpha Theta
1987 Pi Gamma Mu

CORNELL COLLEGE   Mount Vernon, IA. College of liberal arts; private control; affiliated with the Methodist Church; nonsectarian; founded in 1853.

ACHS HONORS
1943 Mortar Board
1948 Pi Kappa Lambda

SERVICE
1977 Alpha Phi Omega

INACTIVE
1868–71 Phi Kappa Psi
1888–13 Sigma Nu
1930–41 National Collegiate
        Players

CORNELL UNIVERSITY   Ithaca, NY. University and land-grant college; coeducational; private control; nonsectarian; main campus at Ithaca; Cornell Aeronautical Laboratory at Buffalo; Agricultural experimental station at Geneva. Incorporated in 1865.

Many fraternities and sororities occupy their own houses on their own land. However, the university has instituted a group housing plan by which a fraternity or sorority deeds its property to the university and the university then leases the property back to the fraternity or sorority. With this arrangement, alumni can make contributions directly to the university for building projects of fraternities and sororities on a tax-deductible basis.

NIC MEN'S
1868 Chi Phi
1868 Kappa Alpha Society

1868 Zeta Psi
1869 Alpha Delta Phi
1869 Chi Psi

1869 Delta Upsilon
1869 Phi Kappa Psi
1870 Delta Kappa Epsilon
1870 Theta Delta Chi
1872 Phi Delta Theta
1876 Psi Upsilon
1879 Beta Theta Pi
1887 Alpha Tau Omega
1888 Phi Gamma Delta
1889 Phi Sigma Kappa
1890 Delta Chi
1890 Delta Tau Delta
1890 Sigma Chi
1890 Sigma Phi Society
1891 Delta Phi
1891 Sigma Alpha Epsilon
1892 Kappa Sigma
1901 Sigma Nu
1907 Acacia
1907 Zeta Beta Tau
1909 Alpha Sigma Phi
1911 Phi Kappa Sigma
1911 Sigma Alpha Mu
1912 Sigma Phi Epsilon
1912 Theta Chi
1913 Kappa Delta Rho
1913 Lambda Chi Alpha
1913 Tau Epsilon Phi
1914 Alpha Gamma Rho
1917 Alpha Epsilon Pi
1917 Pi Kappa Alpha
1917 Sigma Pi
1921 Pi Kappa Phi
1922 Alpha Phi Delta
1923 Tau Kappa Epsilon
1930 Phi Kappa Tau
1934 Tau Delta Phi
1972 Alpha Gamma Sigma
1979 Kappa Alpha Psi (A)

NPHC MEN'S
     Phi Beta Sigma
1906 Alpha Phi Alpha

NPC WOMEN'S
1881 Kappa Alpha Theta
1883 Kappa Kappa Gamma
1885 Delta Gamma
1889 Alpha Phi
1908 Alpha Omicron Pi
1913 Delta Delta Delta
1917 Chi Omega
1917 Kappa Delta
1917 Sigma Delta Tau
1919 Pi Beta Phi
1920 Alpha Epsilon Phi
1984 Alpha Chi Omega
1985 Alpha Gamma Delta

NPHC WOMEN'S
1979 Alpha Kappa Alpha
1990 Sigma Gamma Rho

PROFESSIONAL
1911 Omega Tau Sigma
1913 Alpha Chi Sigma
1925 Phi Alpha Delta

OTHER PROFESSIONAL
1901 Alpha Zeta
1907 Alpha Psi

ACHS HONORS
     Omicron Delta Epsilon

1910 Tau Beta Pi
1911 Delta Sigma Rho-Tau
     Kappa Alpha
1912 Eta Kappa Nu
1918 Mortar Board
1919 Kappa Omicron Nu
1920 Phi Kappa Phi
1925 Alpha Kappa Delta
1925 Chi Epsilon
1936 Pi Delta Phi
1948 Pi Tau Sigma
1948 Psi Chi
1968 Sigma Theta Tau
1975 Sigma Delta Pi

OTHER HONORS
     National Order of Omega
1882 Phi Beta Kappa
1886 Sigma Xi
1910 Alpha Omega Alpha
1914 Order of the Coif
1921 Sigma Gamma Epsilon
1923 Phi Beta Kappa
1953 Pi Mu Epsilon
1960 National Collegiate
     Players

SERVICE
1927 Alpha Phi Omega

RECOGNITION
     Arnold Air Society (E-1)
1899 Gamma Alpha
1906 Scabbard and Blade (1)
1921 Sigma Delta Epsilon
1923 Pi Alpha Xi
1925 Phi Zeta
1937 National Block and Bridle
     Club

INACTIVE
1896–76 Pi Lambda Phi
1901–41 Alpha Kappa Kappa
1903–53 Delta Theta Phi
1903–70 Theta Xi
1904–55 Phi Delta Epsilon
1907–43 Delta Sigma Phi
1908–32 Delta Zeta
1908–71 Alpha Chi Rho
1909–18 Gamma Eta Gamma
1912–15 Sigma Alpha Mu
1918–64 Alpha Xi Delta
1920–59 Sigma Delta Chi
1921   Phi Chi
1921–39 Kappa Beta Pi
1921–56 Sigma Kappa
1927–31 Phi Kappa Theta
1928   Phi Lambda Kappa
1933   Delta Phi Alpha
1933–60 Kappa Delta Epsilon
1934–56 Kappa Phi Kappa
1937–52 Alpha Kappa Alpha
1940–53 Phi Delta Gamma
1942–85 Triangle
1946–72 Alpha Epsilon Delta
1954–69 Phi Sigma Sigma
1960–88 Delta Phi Epsilon
1961–73 Phi Eta Sigma
1961–86 Alpha Lambda Delta
1963–85 Phi Sigma Kappa
1968–72 Alpha Pi Mu

CORPUS CHRISTI STATE UNIVERSITY Corpus
Christi, TX. Formerly Texas A&I University at Corpus Christi.

NIC MEN'S
1968 Tau Delta Phi

NPHC WOMEN'S
1938 Delta Sigma Theta (B)

PROFESSIONAL
1981 Delta Sigma Pi

THE CREIGHTON UNIVERSITY Omaha, NB.
Founded 1878 through a bequest from the Edward
and John Creighton families. Administered by the
Jesuits; coeducational; private control: Roman
Catholic. Seven schools and colleges.

Professional school fraternities occupy their own
houses on their own land. Undergraduate fraternities are not permitted to occupy houses.

NIC MEN'S
1965 Phi Kappa Psi
1968 Sigma Alpha Epsilon
1969 Delta Upsilon
1970 Delta Chi
1977 Pi Kappa Alpha
1986 Sigma Phi Epsilon

NPC WOMEN'S
1952 Theta Phi Alpha
1962 Delta Zeta
1986 Alpha Gamma Delta
1986 Gamma Phi Beta
1990 Alpha Phi

PROFESSIONAL
1912 Delta Theta Phi
1915 Xi Psi Phi
1916 Phi Chi
1920 Lambda Kappa Sigma
1950 Phi Alpha Delta
1966 Phi Gamma Nu

OTHER PROFESSIONAL
1910 Delta Sigma Delta
1912 Gamma Eta Gamma
1953 Beta Alpha Psi

ACHS HONORS
     Omicron Delta Epsilon
1921 Alpha Sigma Nu
1934 Delta Sigma Rho-Tau
     Kappa Alpha
1941 Rho Chi
1961 Phi Alpha Theta

ACHS HONORS
1989 Psi Chi

INACTIVE
1969–74 Tau Kappa Epsilon
1970–73 Sigma Pi

1963 Beta Gamma Sigma
1971 Phi Sigma Tau
1977 Pi Sigma Alpha
1979 Psi Chi
1982 Sigma Pi Sigma
1988 Omicron Delta Kappa

OTHER HONORS
1916 Omicron Kappa Upsilon
1957 Alpha Omega Alpha
1973 Pi Mu Epsilon

SERVICE
1953 Alpha Phi Omega

RECOGNITION
1951 Alpha Psi Omega
1951 Phi Delta Gamma

INACTIVE
1900–73 Phi Rho Sigma
1907   Phi Beta Pi and Theta
         Kappa Psi (a)
1920–71 Phi Delta Chi
1921–35 Psi Omega
1925   Kappa Beta Pi
1925–59 Phi Delta Epsilon
1926–35 Kappa Psi
1928–52 Pi Lambda Phi
1930–75 Delta Sigma Pi
1948–53 Kappa Beta Gamma
1955–71 Alpha Sigma Alpha
1957–72 Alpha Kappa Psi
1961–84 Sigma Sigma Sigma

CULVER-STOCKTON COLLEGE Canton, MO.
Founded 1853, first chartered coeducational liberal
arts college west of the Mississippi. Church related,
Christian Church (Disciples of Christ); privately
supported; nonsectarian.

The fraternities may, and some do, occupy their
own houses on their own land. Three sororities own
houses situated on college-owned land.

NIC MEN'S
     Tau Kappa Epsilon
1926 Lambda Chi Alpha
1952 Sigma Phi Epsilon
1959 Tau Kappa Epsilon
1971 Alpha Tau Omega
1974 Kappa Alpha Psi (A)
1988 Delta Upsilon

NPHC MEN'S
     Phi Beta Sigma

NPC WOMEN'S
1927 Chi Omega
1943 Alpha Xi Delta
1947 Sigma Kappa

NPHC WOMEN'S
1971 Delta Sigma Theta (B)

ACHS HONORS
1963 Sigma Tau Delta
1972 Alpha Chi
1984 Phi Eta Sigma

OTHER HONORS
National Order of Omega

RECOGNITION
1922 Pi Kappa Delta

CUMBERLAND COLLEGE Williamsburg, KY.
Four-year college; coeducational; private control;
Baptist Church; formerly junior college. Founded
1889.

ACHS HONORS
1974 Phi Alpha Theta
1988 Alpha Lambda Delta

SERVICE
1967 Alpha Phi Omega

RECOGNITION
1967 Alpha Psi Omega

INACTIVE
1857–61 Alpha Delta Phi

1857–74 Delta Kappa Epsilon
1858–61 Delta Psi
1859–61 Phi Kappa Sigma
1860–49 Sigma Alpha Epsilon
1892–08 Pi Kappa Alpha
1969–87 Phi Mu Alpha—
          Sinfonia

CUMBERLAND UNIVERSITY Lebanon, TN.

INACTIVE
1854–89 Beta Theta Pi
1860–79 Phi Kappa Psi
1868–02 Alpha Tau Omega
1869–78 Phi Gamma Delta
1872–80 Sigma Chi

1880–84 Kappa Sigma
1887–17 Kappa Sigma
1912–60 Delta Sigma Phi
1916–40 Sigma Nu Phi
1917–48 Lambda Chi Alpha
1941   Cardinal Key

C. W. POST COLLEGE OF LONG ISLAND
UNIVERSITY Greenvale, Long Island, NY. College
of liberal arts; coeducational; private control; nonsectarian; established 1954.

NIC MEN'S
1961 Tau Kappa Epsilon
1962 Alpha Epsilon Pi
1968 Tau Delta Phi

NPHC MEN'S
     Phi Beta Sigma
1975 Alpha Phi Alpha

NPHC WOMEN'S
1975 Alpha Kappa Alpha

PROFESSIONAL
1965 Delta Sigma Pi

ACHS HONORS
     Pi Alpha Alpha
1957 Sigma Tau Delta
1959 Psi Chi
1964 Delta Mu Delta
1964 Delta Sigma Rho-Tau
     Kappa Alpha
1969 Sigma Delta Pi

1978 Phi Alpha Theta
1981 Pi Sigma Alpha
1983 Kappa Mu Epsilon
1984 Phi Eta Sigma
1984 Phi Sigma Tau

RECOGNITION
1944 Alpha Psi Omega
1966 Kappa Pi
1974 Beta Beta Beta

INACTIVE
1960–71 Phi Sigma Kappa
1960–88 Kappa Delta Rho
1962–72 Alpha Epsilon Phi
1962–77 Alpha Xi Delta
1964–74 Phi Kappa Tau
1964–90 Zeta Beta Tau
1967–72 Sigma Delta Tau
1968–74 Alpha Sigma Alpha
1969–77 Sigma Alpha Epsilon
1978–84 Sigma Kappa

DAEMEN COLLEGE Amherst, NY. Founded as
Rosary Hill College, Buffalo, 1947. Name changed in
1976 in honor of the founder of the Order of St.
Francis, Catherine Daemen. Private coeducational
liberal arts college.

NIC MEN'S
1981 Sigma Phi Epsilon

ACHS HONORS
1961 Pi Gamma Mu

1973 Delta Mu Delta

DAKOTA STATE COLLEGE Madison, SD.

ACHS HONORS
1979 Delta Mu Delta

DAKOTA WESLEYAN UNIVERSITY Mitchell, SD.
Founded by Dakota Mission Conference, Methodist
Episcopal Church, 1882. Chartered and first instruction 1883; university; undergraduate coeducational; related to Methodist Church.

ACHS HONORS
1922 Sigma Tau Delta
1924 Phi Kappa Phi
1967 Pi Gamma Mu

RECOGNITION
1920 Theta Alpha Phi

1972 Sigma Zeta

INACTIVE
1925–37 Pi Gamma Mu

DALHOUSIE UNIVERSITY Halifax, NS. Founded
1818; coeducational university.

NIC MEN'S
1930 Phi Delta Theta
1933 Sigma Chi

NPC WOMEN'S
1932 Alpha Gamma Delta

PROFESSIONAL
1925 Phi Rho Sigma
1928 Phi Chi

INACTIVE
1925–40 Phi Delta Phi
1929–32 Psi Omega
1930–47 Phi Delta Epsilon
1931–37 Delta Sigma Pi
1934–76 Pi Beta Phi
1938–88 Zeta Psi

UNIVERSITY OF DALLAS Dallas, TX. Univer-
sity; coeducational; private control; Roman Catholic; established 1955.

NPHC WOMEN'S
1935 Delta Sigma Theta (B)

ACHS HONORS
     Omicron Delta Epsilon
1965 Phi Alpha Theta

1975 Kappa Delta Pi
1984 Sigma Pi Sigma

RECOGNITION
1971 Sigma Iota Epsilon

DALLAS BAPTIST UNIVERSITY Dallas, TX. Uni-
versity of liberal arts and general; teacher preparatory; masters degree; coeducational. Southern
Baptist affiliation. Established as College in Dallas
1965—became a University in 1985.

NPC WOMEN'S
1975 Alpha Sigma Alpha

PROFESSIONAL
1973 Mu Phi Epsilon

ACHS HONORS
1972 Alpha Chi

SERVICE
1969 Alpha Phi Omega

INACTIVE
1972–80 Kappa Sigma
1974–78 Alpha Phi
1974–80 Lambda Chi Alpha

DANA COLLEGE Blair, NB. College of liberal
arts; coeducational; private control; related to The
American Lutheran Church; established 1884.

ACHS HONORS
1960 Alpha Chi
1967 Phi Alpha Theta

RECOGNITION
1965 Alpha Psi Omega

DARTMOUTH COLLEGE Hanover, NH. College of
liberal arts for men; with three associated professional graduate schools; private control; nonsectar-

ian; chartered 1769, by authority of George III, by the Province of New Hampshire.

Of the 22 fraternities, 20 own their own houses on their own land; one rents a college-owned house.

NIC MEN'S
1842 Psi Upsilon
1853 Zeta Psi
1869 Theta Delta Chi
1889 Beta Theta Pi
1908 Sigma Alpha Epsilon
1909 Sigma Phi Epsilon
1987 Kappa Alpha Psi (A)

NPHC MEN'S
1972 Alpha Phi Alpha

NPC WOMEN'S
1978 Kappa Kappa Gamma
1980 Alpha Chi Omega
1982 Kappa Alpha Theta
1984 Delta Delta Delta
1987 Delta Gamma

NPHC WOMEN'S
1983 Alpha Kappa Alpha

OTHER PROFESSIONAL
1922 Kappa Phi Kappa

ACHS HONORS
    Omicron Delta Epsilon
1910 Delta Sigma Rho-Tau
    Kappa Alpha

OTHER HONORS
    National Order of Omega
1787 Phi Beta Kappa

1968 Sigma Xi

INACTIVE
1846–69 Alpha Delta Phi
1853–70 Delta Kappa Epsilon
1884–60 Phi Delta Theta
1893–60 Sigma Chi
1896–67 Phi Kappa Psi
1901–60 Delta Tau Delta
1901–65 Phi Gamma Delta
1902–87 Chi Phi
1905–55 Phi Sigma Kappa
1905–80 Kappa Sigma
1906–08 Acacia
1906–37 Gamma Alpha
1907–61 Sigma Nu
1914–31 Lambda Chi Alpha
1919–63 Alpha Chi Rho
1920–22 Zeta Beta Tau
1921–52 Theta Chi
1923–33 Alpha Chi Sigma
1924–36 Alpha Tau Omega
1924–71 Pi Lambda Phi
1926–66 Delta Upsilon
1928–36 Alpha Sigma Phi
1929–38 Phi Kappa Sigma
1930–35 Sigma Alpha Mu
1977–88 Sigma Kappa
1984–90 Delta Phi Epsilon

DARTMOUTH MEDICAL COLLEGE Hanover, NH. Established in 1797.

OTHER HONORS
1973 Alpha Omega Alpha

INACTIVE
1888–62 Alpha Kappa Kappa

DAVID LIPSCOMB COLLEGE Nashville, TN. College of liberal arts; coeducational; private control; affiliated with churches of Christ; established 1891.

PROFESSIONAL
1956 Alpha Kappa Psi
1973 Phi Mu Alpha—Sinfonia
1974 Sigma Alpha Iota
1985 Phi Alpha Delta

ACHS HONORS
1956 Phi Alpha Theta

1956 Sigma Tau Delta
1971 Psi Chi

RECOGNITION
1956 Pi Kappa Delta

DAVIDSON COLLEGE Davidson, NC. Liberal arts college founded 1837; coeducational; an institution of the Presbyterian Church in the United States.

Lodge system; college owns houses. Each fraternity member pays a fraternity housing fee to the college each semester. Fraternities eat, meet, and socialize in houses. Members live in dormitories. There are no fraternity "sections" or halls in the dormitories. Only person living in fraternity house is housemother-dietician. Phi Gamma Delta and Sigma Phi Epsilon are housed off campus.

NIC MEN'S
1869 Pi Kappa Alpha
1880 Kappa Alpha Order
1883 Sigma Alpha Epsilon
1890 Kappa Sigma
1923 Phi Gamma Delta
1928 Phi Delta Theta
1930 Sigma Phi Epsilon

ACHS HONORS
    Omicron Delta Epsilon
1917 Omicron Delta Kappa
1921 Sigma Pi Sigma
1931 Sigma Delta Pi
1936 Alpha Epsilon Delta
1953 Delta Sigma Rho-Tau
    Kappa Alpha

OTHER HONORS
1923 Phi Beta Kappa

SERVICE
1962 Alpha Phi Omega

RECOGNITION
1923 Scabbard and Blade (5)
1930 Delta Phi Alpha
1934 Sigma Delta Psi
1944 Alpha Psi Omega

INACTIVE
1858–71 Beta Theta Pi
1859–69 Chi Phi
1912–70 Pi Kappa Phi
1919–72 Gamma Sigma Epsilon
1929   Eta Sigma Phi
1929–31 Mu Beta Psi
1938–43 Pi Gamma Mu
1940–69 Phi Mu Alpha—
    Sinfonia
1948–69 Sigma Chi
1951–71 Alpha Tau Omega
1958–71 Sigma Nu
1962–86 Phi Eta Sigma

DAVIS AND ELKINS COLLEGE Elkins, WV. College of liberal arts; coeducational; private control; related to the Presbyterian Church. Chartered 1903. Founded by U.S. Senators Henry G. Davis and Stephen B. Elkins in 1904.

All fraternities and sororities reside on campus with members living in residence halls.

NIC MEN'S
1946 Tau Kappa Epsilon
1949 Alpha Sigma Phi
1949 Sigma Phi Epsilon

NPC WOMEN'S
1949 Phi Mu
1963 Zeta Tau Alpha
1980 Pi Beta Phi

ACHS HONORS
1947 Sigma Tau Delta
1948 Phi Alpha Theta
1968 Alpha Chi

1969 Psi Chi
1971 Sigma Delta Pi

SERVICE
1967 Alpha Phi Omega

RECOGNITION
1925 Chi Beta Phi
1945 Alpha Psi Omega

INACTIVE
1948–84 Chi Omega
1950–55 Pi Beta Phi
1983–90 Kappa Sigma

UNIVERSITY OF DAYTON Dayton, OH. University; coeducational; private control; Roman Catholic. Established 1850.

NIC MEN'S
1972 Phi Sigma Kappa
1972 Tau Kappa Epsilon
1975 Lambda Chi Alpha
1978 Kappa Alpha Psi (A)
1988 Sigma Chi
1990 Delta Sigma Phi

NPHC MEN'S
    Phi Beta Sigma
1947 Alpha Phi Alpha

NPC WOMEN'S
1985 Alpha Phi
1987 Theta Phi Alpha
1987 Zeta Tau Alpha
1989 Pi Beta Phi
1990 Chi Omega

NPHC WOMEN'S
1946 Delta Sigma Theta (B)

PROFESSIONAL
1963 Delta Sigma Pi

1965 Sigma Alpha Iota
1969 Alpha Delta Theta
1969 Phi Gamma Nu
1969 Phi Mu Alpha—Sinfonia
1975 Phi Alpha Delta
1985 Phi Alpha Delta

ACHS HONORS
    Omicron Delta Epsilon
    Pi Alpha Alpha
1940 Delta Epsilon Sigma
1951 Phi Alpha Theta
1959 Psi Chi
1961 Tau Beta Pi
1962 Alpha Epsilon Delta
1968 Phi Sigma Tau
1968 Sigma Pi Sigma
1969 Sigma Delta Pi
1972 Pi Sigma Alpha
1974 Kappa Omicron Nu
1977 Theta Alpha Kappa

OTHER HONORS
National Order of Omega
1960 Pi Mu Epsilon
1975 Sigma Xi

RECOGNITION
1949 Scabbard and Blade (9)
1960 Pi Kappa Delta

1962 Beta Beta Beta

INACTIVE
1931–39 Alpha Kappa Alpha
1950–68 Alpha Kappa Alpha
1971–73 Kappa Delta Rho
1971–82 Delta Upsilon
1986   Phi Sigma Sigma

DEFIANCE COLLEGE Defiance, OH. Founded 1850; coeducational

Fraternities have houses of their own.

NIC MEN'S
1949 Theta Xi
1964 Tau Kappa Epsilon
1970 Sigma Phi Epsilon

NPC WOMEN'S
1964 Alpha Xi Delta

ACHS HONORS
1970 Phi Alpha Theta
1971 Alpha Chi

RECOGNITION
1929 Alpha Psi Omega

UNIVERSITY OF DELAWARE Newark, DE. University and land-grant college. Established as an academy, 1743; right to confer degrees granted 1833 as Newark College; changed to Delaware College, 1843. Women's College established, 1913. Colleges united under name University of Delaware, 1921; became coeducational 1945; eight undergraduate colleges and two graduate colleges; private; state-assisted university.

Of the fifteen fraternities, five live in their own houses on their own land; five own houses on college-owned land.

NIC MEN'S
1904 Kappa Alpha Order
1907 Sigma Phi Epsilon
1910 Sigma Nu
1924 Phi Kappa Tau
1925 Alpha Epsilon Pi
1948 Delta Tau Delta
1948 Pi Kappa Alpha
1965 Lambda Chi Alpha
1971 Tau Kappa Epsilon
1982 Zeta Beta Tau
1985 Phi Kappa Psi
1986 Kappa Delta Rho
1989 Kappa Alpha Psi (A)

NPHC MEN'S
Phi Beta Sigma

NPC WOMEN'S
1972 Alpha Chi Omega
1972 Alpha Omicron Pi
1972 Alpha Phi
1972 Alpha Sigma Alpha
1982 Phi Sigma Sigma
1986 Sigma Kappa
1988 Chi Omega
1989 Alpha Epsilon Phi
1990 Alpha Xi Delta

NPHC WOMEN'S
1975 Delta Sigma Theta (B)
1977 Alpha Kappa Alpha
1981 Sigma Gamma Rho

PROFESSIONAL
1975 Delta Theta Phi
1975 Phi Alpha Delta

OTHER PROFESSIONAL
1949 Alpha Zeta

ACHS HONORS
Omicron Delta Epsilon
1905 Phi Kappa Phi
1933 Tau Beta Pi
1949 Kappa Delta Pi
1949 Omicron Delta Kappa
1949 Sigma Pi Sigma
1950 Psi Chi
1954 Alpha Kappa Delta
1960 Mortar Board
1963 Kappa Omicron Nu
1966 Eta Kappa Nu
1967 Beta Gamma Sigma
1973 Pi Delta Phi
1973 Pi Sigma Alpha
1974 Sigma Delta Pi
1974 Sigma Theta Tau
1979 Phi Alpha Theta
1985 Chi Epsilon

OTHER HONORS
National Order of Omega
1941 Pi Mu Epsilon
1956 Phi Beta Kappa
1959 Sigma Xi

SERVICE
1948 Alpha Phi Omega
1967 Gamma Sigma Sigma

RECOGNITION
1928 Alpha Psi Omega
1932 Scabbard and Blade (7)
1955 Beta Beta Beta
1962 Delta Phi Alpha

INACTIVE
1923–89 Theta Chi
1949–85 Alpha Tau Omega
1954–65 Alpha Chi Sigma
1970–83 Delta Upsilon

COLONIES
Pi Lambda Phi
1990 Delta Chi

DELAWARE STATE COLLEGE Dover, DE. College of liberal arts; teachers college; land-grant college; coeducational; state control; chartered 1891.

Fraternity and sorority members reside in residence halls.

NIC MEN'S
1947 Kappa Alpha Psi (A)

NPHC MEN'S
Phi Beta Sigma
1948 Alpha Phi Alpha
1949 Omega Psi Phi

NPHC WOMEN'S
1955 Alpha Kappa Alpha
1958 Delta Sigma Theta (B)
1974 Sigma Gamma Rho

PROFESSIONAL
1975 Phi Gamma Nu

ACHS HONORS
1963 Alpha Kappa Mu
1971 Delta Mu Delta
1971 Phi Alpha Theta
1981 Psi Chi

SERVICE
1968 Alpha Phi Omega

DELTA STATE COLLEGE Cleveland, MS. College of liberal arts; teachers college; coeducational; state control; chartered 1924.

Sororities and fraternities have chapter rooms in the dormitories in which their members live.

NIC MEN'S
1963 Pi Kappa Alpha
1965 Kappa Alpha Order
1968 Phi Kappa Tau
1975 Kappa Sigma
1988 Kappa Alpha Psi (A)

NPHC MEN'S
Phi Beta Sigma

NPC WOMEN'S
1962 Delta Delta Delta
1962 Kappa Delta
1966 Phi Mu
1985 Zeta Tau Alpha

NPHC WOMEN'S
1973 Delta Sigma Theta (B)
1978 Alpha Kappa Alpha

PROFESSIONAL
1960 Phi Mu Alpha—Sinfonia
1972 Mu Phi Epsilon

OTHER PROFESSIONAL
1974 Alpha Epsilon Rho

ACHS HONORS
1954 Kappa Delta Pi
1958 Pi Gamma Mu
1960 Pi Omega Pi
1971 Omicron Delta Kappa
1972 Phi Alpha Theta
1972 Phi Kappa Phi
1973 Kappa Omicron Nu
1974 Lambda Iota Tau
1975 Delta Mu Delta
1977 Phi Eta Sigma
1989 Pi Kappa Lambda

OTHER HONORS
National Order of Omega

RECOGNITION
1935 Alpha Psi Omega
1950 Beta Beta Beta
1961 Pi Kappa Delta
1964 Kappa Pi

DENISON UNIVERSITY Granville, OH. Founded by the Ohio Baptist Education Society, chartered and first instruction as Granville Literary and Theological Institution 1831. Name changed to Denison University 1856; undergraduate college for men becoming coeducational 1900; private control; nonsectarian.

The fraternities own houses on college-owned land in all but two cases where the college owns and rents. Most of the fraternities and sororities have 99-year renewable leases. Houses built since 1950 are technically owned by the university although built and paid for by the groups holding the leases. The sorority houses have no dormitory facilities.

NIC MEN'S
1868 Beta Theta Pi
1868 Sigma Chi
1885 Phi Gamma Delta
1911 Kappa Sigma
1914 Phi Delta Theta
1919 Lambda Chi Alpha
1919 Sigma Alpha Epsilon
1958 Alpha Tau Omega
1969 Delta Chi

NPC WOMEN'S
1929 Delta Delta Delta
1929 Kappa Alpha Theta
1929 Kappa Kappa Gamma
1938 Delta Gamma
1954 Pi Beta Phi
1961 Alpha Chi Omega

ACHS HONORS
     Omicron Delta Epsilon
1924 Delta Sigma Rho-Tau
     Kappa Alpha
1928 Phi Alpha Theta
1931 Sigma Delta Pi
1933 Omicron Delta Kappa
1936 Mortar Board
1946 Psi Chi

UNIVERSITY OF DENVER   Denver, CO. Founded by John Evans; chartered and first instruction as Colorado Seminary in 1864; board of trustees elected by Rocky Mountain Conference of the Methodist Church on recommendation of the board; coeducational; private control. The fraternities own houses on college-owned land, as do the sororities in the majority of cases.

NIC MEN'S
1889 Beta Theta Pi
1891 Sigma Alpha Epsilon
1902 Kappa Sigma
1913 Sigma Phi Epsilon
1917 Lambda Chi Alpha
1920 Zeta Beta Tau
1947 Sigma Chi
1949 Phi Kappa Sigma
1951 Alpha Tau Omega
1989 Chi Phi

NPHC MEN'S
     Phi Beta Sigma
1922 Alpha Phi Alpha

NPC WOMEN'S
1897 Gamma Phi Beta
1908 Sigma Kappa
1917 Delta Zeta
1928 Alpha Gamma Delta
1946 Delta Gamma

NPHC WOMEN'S
1939 Delta Sigma Theta (B)
1969 Delta Sigma Theta (B)

PROFESSIONAL
1902 Phi Delta Phi
1910 Alpha Kappa Psi
1913 Phi Alpha Delta
1923 Mu Phi Epsilon
1952 Alpha Delta Theta

1947 Pi Sigma Alpha
1949 Pi Delta Phi
1950 Alpha Epsilon Delta
1953 Kappa Delta Pi
1964 Alpha Kappa Delta
1968 Sigma Pi Sigma

OTHER HONORS
1963 Pi Mu Epsilon

SERVICE
1965 Alpha Phi Omega

RECOGNITION
     Arnold Air Society (D-1)
1926 Eta Sigma Phi
1952 Delta Phi Alpha

INACTIVE
1912–69 Phi Mu Alpha—
         Sinfonia
1915–53 Delta Omicron
1928–30 Alpha Sigma Alpha
1928–69 Chi Omega
1930–70 Alpha Omicron Pi
1930–79 Alpha Phi
1931–49 Alpha Xi Delta
1949–84 Delta Upsilon

1982 Delta Theta Phi

OTHER PROFESSIONAL
1931 Kappa Beta Pi
1942 Delta Pi Epsilon
1950 Beta Alpha Psi

ACHS HONORS
     Omicron Delta Epsilon
1909 Delta Sigma Rho-Tau
     Kappa Alpha
1917 Phi Sigma
1917 Phi Sigma Iota
1926 Beta Gamma Sigma
1926 Kappa Delta Pi
1929 Psi Chi
1934 Omicron Delta Kappa
1934 Sigma Pi Sigma
1935 Alpha Lambda Delta
1937 Mortar Board
1947 Alpha Kappa Delta
1960 Phi Alpha Theta
1965 Gamma Theta Upsilon
1966 Alpha Epsilon Delta
1968 Alpha Sigma Mu

OTHER HONORS
     National Order of Omega
1924 Iota Sigma Pi
1940 Phi Beta Kappa
1950 Pi Mu Epsilon
1950 Sigma Xi

SERVICE
     The National Spurs
1951 Intercollegiate Knights

RECOGNITION
1967 Sigma Iota Epsilon

INACTIVE
1885–80 Pi Beta Phi
1897–32 Psi Omega
1910–24 Sigma Delta Chi
1912   Phi Lambda Upsilon
1914–74 Kappa Delta
1920–24 Alpha Epsilon Phi
1921–34 Zeta Tau Alpha
1924–62 Phi Chi Theta
1925–58 Acacia
1925–72 Pi Kappa Alpha
1925–90 Delta Sigma Pi
1926–37 Tau Epsilon Rho
1926–50 National Collegiate
         Players
1926–51 Theta Phi Alpha
1926–53 Sigma Alpha Iota

1926–57 Delta Phi Epsilon
1926–67 Pi Lambda Phi
1927   Eta Sigma Phi
1927–57 Phi Kappa Theta
1927–83 Pi Gamma Mu
1928   Phi Gamma Nu
1929–52 Alpha Xi Delta
1945   Zeta Phi Eta
1946–87 Alpha Chi Omega
1948–80 Theta Chi
1949   Scabbard and Blade
        (8)
1949–65 Alpha Eta Rho
1949–85 Phi Mu Alpha—
        Sinfonia
1951–78 Tau Kappa Epsilon
1954–75 Tau Beta Pi
1960–75 Eta Kappa Nu
1965–84 Sigma Delta Tau
1970–85 Beta Phi Mu
1981–90 Phi Gamma Delta
1985–87 Pi Kappa Phi

DE PAUL UNIVERSITY   Chicago, IL. University; coeducational; private control; Roman Catholic Church; chartered as St. Vincent's College 1898; new charter in 1907 authorized De Paul University; first Catholic university in Illinois. American College of Physical Education consolidated with De Paul in 1946, now the College of Physical Education.

NIC MEN'S
1950 Alpha Phi Delta
1968 Phi Kappa Theta

NPC WOMEN'S
1960 Theta Phi Alpha
1962 Delta Zeta
1971 Alpha Sigma Alpha

PROFESSIONAL
1902 Phi Alpha Delta
1904 Delta Theta Phi
1928 Delta Sigma Pi
1944 Mu Phi Epsilon
1984 Phi Alpha Delta

OTHER PROFESSIONAL
1916 Kappa Beta Pi
1934 Gamma Eta Gamma

ACHS HONORS
     Omicron Delta Epsilon
1941 Delta Epsilon Sigma
1954 Delta Mu Delta
1958 Beta Gamma Sigma
1958 Pi Delta Phi
1962 Kappa Delta Pi
1965 Alpha Lambda Delta
1966 Psi Chi

1972 Sigma Pi Sigma
1974 Phi Alpha Theta
1977 Theta Alpha Kappa
1983 Pi Sigma Alpha
1987 Pi Kappa Lambda

OTHER HONORS
1956 Pi Mu Epsilon

SERVICE
1969 Alpha Phi Omega

RECOGNITION
1927 Blue Key
1954 Sigma Delta Psi

INACTIVE
1926   Sigma Delta Kappa
1928–73 Alpha Delta Gamma
1929–86 Pi Gamma Mu
1931   Phi Gamma Nu
1956   Scabbard and Blade
        (13)
1956–69 Sigma Delta Pi
1962–83 Phi Mu Alpha—
        Sinfonia
1962–86 Phi Eta Sigma
1967–27 Zeta Beta Tau
1968–79 Tau Kappa Epsilon

DEPAUW UNIVERSITY   Greencastle, IN. College of liberal arts, school of music, and school of nursing; coeducational; founded by Methodist Church; private control. Established 1832; chartered 1837; first named Indiana Asbury University, but changed to DePauw in recognition of gift from Washington C. DePauw.

NIC MEN'S
1845 Beta Theta Pi

1856 Phi Gamma Delta
1859 Sigma Chi

1865 Phi Kappa Psi
1866 Delta Kappa Epsilon
1868 Phi Delta Theta
1871 Delta Tau Delta
1887 Delta Upsilon
1890 Sigma Nu
1892 Delta Chi
1915 Lambda Chi Alpha
1924 Alpha Tau Omega
1949 Sigma Alpha Epsilon

NPC WOMEN'S
1870 Kappa Alpha Theta
1875 Kappa Kappa Gamma
1885 Alpha Chi Omega
1887 Alpha Phi
1907 Alpha Omicron Pi
1908 Alpha Gamma Delta
1908 Delta Delta Delta
1909 Delta Zeta
1942 Pi Beta Phi
1949 Delta Gamma

PROFESSIONAL
1905 Mu Phi Epsilon

OTHER PROFESSIONAL
1909 Sigma Delta Chi
1919 Women in Communications

ACHS HONORS
Omicron Delta Epsilon
1914 Delta Sigma Rho-Tau
Kappa Alpha

1919 Mortar Board
1927 Alpha Lambda Delta
1929 Phi Eta Sigma
1930 Phi Sigma Iota
1932 Pi Sigma Alpha
1936 Pi Kappa Lambda
1948 Alpha Kappa Delta
1962 Sigma Theta Tau
1966 Sigma Pi Sigma

OTHER HONORS
National Order of Omega
1889 Phi Beta Kappa
1923 National Collegiate
Players

SERVICE
1936 Alpha Phi Omega

RECOGNITION
Arnold Air Society (D-2)
1944 Kappa Pi

INACTIVE
1870–79 Pi Beta Phi
1911–82 Phi Mu Alpha—
Sinfonia
1923   Scabbard and Blade
(5)
1926–33 Kappa Delta
1949–73 Beta Beta Beta
1954–82 Psi Chi

DETROIT INSTITUTE OF TECHNOLOGY Detroit, MI. Established in 1891, the Detroit Institute of Technology is an accredited independent, private coeducational institution of higher learning comprising three colleges: The College of Arts & Sciences, the College of Business Administration, and the College of Engineering.

No fraternity has a house of its own.

NPHC MEN'S
1959 Omega Psi Phi

PROFESSIONAL
1962 Pi Sigma Epsilon

OTHER PROFESSIONAL
1930 Alpha Zeta Omega

INACTIVE
1930–66 Alpha Sigma Phi
1947–56 Lambda Kappa Sigma
1967–72 Alpha Epsilon Pi

DETROIT SCHOOL OF LAW Detroit, MI.

PROFESSIONAL
1903 Delta Theta Phi
1916 Delta Theta Phi

OTHER PROFESSIONAL
1916 Sigma Nu Phi

1920 Kappa Beta Pi
1947 Tau Epsilon Rho

UNIVERSITY OF DETROIT Detroit, MI. Founded 1877 by the Jesuit fathers; undergraduate college for men and women; graduate school coeducational; privately supported and controlled; Roman Catholic.

Fraternities and sororities do not maintain their own houses, due in part to city zoning regulations in University area.

NIC MEN'S
1950 Delta Sigma Phi
1956 Sigma Phi Epsilon
1957 Phi Kappa Theta
1962 Sigma Pi

NPHC MEN'S
1971 Alpha Phi Alpha

NPC WOMEN'S
1953 Sigma Sigma Sigma

NPHC WOMEN'S
Zeta Phi Beta
1954 Delta Sigma Theta (B)
1974 Alpha Kappa Alpha

OTHER WOMEN'S
1948 Kappa Beta Gamma

PROFESSIONAL
1930 Alpha Kappa Psi
1931 Phi Gamma Nu
1933 Alpha Omega
1939 Psi Omega
1960 Pi Sigma Epsilon
1964 Theta Tau
1968 Phi Alpha Delta
1978 Phi Alpha Delta
1985 Phi Alpha Delta

OTHER PROFESSIONAL
1919 Gamma Eta Gamma
1920 Kappa Beta Pi
1921 Sigma Delta Kappa
1939 Delta Sigma Delta
1954 Beta Alpha Psi
1963 Sigma Delta Chi
1965 Alpha Epsilon Rho

ACHS HONORS
1924 Alpha Sigma Nu
1941 Alpha Epsilon Delta
1941 Tau Beta Pi

DICKINSON COLLEGE Carlisle, PA. Founded 1773 as grammar school; chartered 1783 as Dickinson College; women admitted 1884; college of liberal arts; private control. Dickinson College is a residential liberal arts college with approximately 90–95% of its students living in college-owned housing.

Fraternities rent college-owned housing units; sororities rent suites of rooms in town for their meeting and social purposes.

NIC MEN'S
1854 Phi Kappa Sigma
1859 Phi Kappa Psi
1859 Sigma Chi
1874 Beta Theta Pi
1880 Phi Delta Theta
1890 Sigma Alpha Epsilon
1902 Kappa Sigma
1916 Theta Chi

NPC WOMEN'S
1903 Pi Beta Phi
1979 Kappa Kappa Gamma
1982 Kappa Alpha Theta
1986 Delta Delta Delta

ACHS HONORS
Omicron Delta Epsilon
1915 Delta Sigma Rho-Tau
Kappa Alpha

1943 Pi Tau Sigma
1947 Eta Kappa Nu
1950 Chi Epsilon
1952 Beta Gamma Sigma
1953 Pi Delta Phi
1955 Psi Chi
1958 Phi Alpha Theta
1960 Phi Sigma Tau
1963 Sigma Pi Sigma
1965 Alpha Kappa Delta
1965 Omega Chi Epsilon
1977 Pi Sigma Alpha

OTHER HONORS
1941 Omicron Kappa Upsilon
1965 Pi Mu Epsilon

SERVICE
1949 Alpha Phi Omega

RECOGNITION
Angel Flight
Arnold Air Society (E-2)
1942 Blue Key
1962 Sigma Phi Alpha

INACTIVE
1921–68 Delta Sigma Pi
1923–47 Alpha Kappa Alpha
1930–42 Zeta Beta Tau
1949–76 Theta Xi
1950–87 Delta Sigma Pi
1951–72 Theta Phi Alpha
1952–73 Delta Zeta
1953   Gamma Sigma Sigma
1953–62 Alpha Kappa Alpha
1957–67 Xi Psi Phi
1957–70 Pi Omega Pi
1957–73 Phi Sigma Kappa
1957–75 Tau Kappa Epsilon
1959–74 Alpha Sigma Tau
1964–80 Phi Eta Sigma

1927 Omicron Delta Kappa
1962 Pi Delta Phi
1962 Sigma Delta Pi
1968 Sigma Pi Sigma
1975 Psi Chi
1983 Pi Sigma Alpha
1984 Phi Alpha Theta

OTHER HONORS
1887 Phi Beta Kappa

SERVICE
1989 Alpha Phi Omega

RECOGNITION
1948 Delta Phi Alpha
1948 Society for Collegiate
Journalists—Pi Delta
Epsilon-Alpha Phi Gamma
(P)
1949 Alpha Psi Omega

1964 Eta Sigma Phi

INACTIVE
1852–71 Zeta Psi
1861–95 Theta Delta Chi
1869–93 Chi Phi
1893–33 Delta Chi
1905–89 Alpha Chi Rho
1907–71 Chi Omega

1914–85 Zeta Beta Tau
1919–20 Sigma Alpha Mu
1919–67 Phi Mu
1924–67 Zeta Tau Alpha
1959–88 Pi Gamma Mu
1960–71 Phi Mu Alpha—
        Sinfonia
1980–87 Gamma Phi Beta

DICKINSON SCHOOL OF LAW   Carlisle, PA. Founded 1834; coeducational.

PROFESSIONAL
1903 Delta Theta Phi
1923 Phi Alpha Delta

INACTIVE
1924–35 Tau Epsilon Rho

DICKINSON STATE COLLEGE   Dickinson, ND. College of liberal arts and teachers college; coeducational; state control; established as State Normal School 1917; name changed to present 1963.

PROFESSIONAL
1967 Mu Phi Epsilon

OTHER PROFESSIONAL
1932 Phi Sigma Pi

ACHS HONORS
1971 Lambda Iota Tau

RECOGNITION
1968 Kappa Pi

INACTIVE
1947–52 Sigma Tau Delta
1964–88 Tau Kappa Epsilon
1966–81 Delta Zeta
1966–82 Theta Chi
1976–87 Phi Mu Alpha—
        Sinfonia

DILLARD UNIVERSITY   New Orleans, LA. College of liberal arts; coeducational; private control; Congregational and Methodist; established 1930 by merger of New Orleans University and Straight College.

NIC MEN'S
1937 Kappa Alpha Psi (A)

NPHC MEN'S
     Phi Beta Sigma
1936 Omega Psi Phi
1938 Alpha Phi Alpha

NPHC WOMEN'S
     Zeta Phi Beta
1937 Delta Sigma Theta (B)
1938 Alpha Kappa Alpha
1940 Sigma Gamma Rho

PROFESSIONAL
1972 Phi Gamma Nu

ACHS HONORS
1942 Alpha Kappa Mu
1957 Beta Kappa Chi
1970 Alpha Chi
1973 Phi Alpha Theta
1973 Psi Chi
1973 Sigma Delta Pi
1974 Lambda Iota Tau

SERVICE
1971 Alpha Phi Omega
1974 Gamma Sigma Sigma

RECOGNITION
1973 Beta Beta Beta

DISTRICT OF COLUMBIA TEACHERS COLLEGE Washington, DC. Teachers college; coeducational; municipal control; established 1955 by merger of Wilson and Miner Teachers Colleges, founded 1873 and 1851, respectively.

NIC MEN'S
1940 Kappa Alpha Psi (A)

NPHC MEN'S
1962 Omega Psi Phi

NPHC WOMEN'S
     Zeta Phi Beta
1936 Alpha Kappa Alpha

1937 Delta Sigma Theta (B)
1948 Sigma Gamma Rho

ACHS HONORS
1956 Kappa Delta Pi

INACTIVE
1935–47 Sigma Tau Delta

DISTRICT OF COLUMBIA UNIVERSITY   Washington, DC.

NPHC MEN'S
     Phi Beta Sigma

ACHS HONORS
1956 Gamma Theta Upsilon

OTHER HONORS
1915 Sigma Xi

INACTIVE
1938–54 Sigma Sigma Sigma

DOANE COLLEGE   Crete, NB. Liberal arts college; coeducational; private control; affiliated with United Church of Christ; chartered 1872.

PROFESSIONAL
1954 Kappa Kappa Psi
1954 Tau Beta Sigma

ACHS HONORS
1930 Sigma Tau Delta
1931 Alpha Lambda Delta
1949 Phi Eta Sigma

1951 Phi Alpha Theta
1987 Psi Chi

RECOGNITION
1920 Pi Kappa Delta
1934 Alpha Psi Omega
1935 Cardinal Key
1972 Beta Beta Beta

DOMINICAN COLLEGE OF SAN RAFAEL   San Rafael, CA. The oldest Catholic college for women in California; liberal arts; undergraduate and graduate studies. Founded 1889.

ACHS HONORS
1936 Pi Delta Phi
1980 Psi Chi
1989 Pi Gamma Mu

SERVICE
1967 Alpha Phi Omega

INACTIVE
1931–69 Sigma Delta Pi

DORDT COLLEGE   Sioux Center, IA.

ACHS HONORS
1972 Sigma Pi Sigma

DOWLING COLLEGE   Oakdale, NY.

ACHS HONORS
     Omicron Delta Epsilon

1977 Psi Chi
1984 Delta Mu Delta

DRAKE UNIVERSITY   Des Moines, IA. Founded 1881; private control; nonsectarian; coeducational; ten colleges and divisions; undergraduate and graduate programs. Ownership of fraternity and sorority houses and lots is by the fraternities and sororities.

NIC MEN'S
1921 Sigma Alpha Epsilon
1925 Kappa Alpha Psi (A)
1932 Tau Kappa Epsilon
1948 Sigma Phi Epsilon
1949 Pi Kappa Phi
1949 Theta Chi
1950 Pi Kappa Alpha
1961 Phi Delta Theta
1980 Sigma Chi

NPC WOMEN'S
1921 Chi Omega
1921 Delta Gamma
1921 Kappa Alpha Theta
1921 Kappa Kappa Gamma
1958 Alpha Phi
1983 Pi Beta Phi

NPHC WOMEN'S
1925 Delta Sigma Theta (B)
1973 Alpha Kappa Alpha
1981 Sigma Gamma Rho

PROFESSIONAL
1917 Mu Phi Epsilon
1920 Sigma Alpha Iota
1921 Delta Theta Phi
1921 Phi Alpha Delta
1921 Phi Delta Chi
1921 Zeta Phi Eta
1922 Phi Mu Alpha—Sinfonia
1924 Delta Sigma Pi
1925 Lambda Kappa Sigma
1930 Kappa Psi
1949 Alpha Kappa Psi
1954 Phi Gamma Nu

1966 Alpha Delta Theta
1982 Gamma Iota Sigma

OTHER PROFESSIONAL
1924 Sigma Delta Chi
1932 Women in Communications
1940 Kappa Beta Pi
1967 Beta Alpha Psi

ACHS HONORS
   Omicron Delta Epsilon
   Pi Alpha Alpha
1917 Kappa Delta Pi
1926 Phi Sigma Iota
1928 Pi Kappa Lambda
1929 Omicron Delta Kappa
1929 Psi Chi
1938 Alpha Lambda Delta
1940 Kappa Mu Epsilon
1950 Alpha Kappa Delta
1951 Rho Chi
1953 Beta Gamma Sigma
1954 Mortar Board
1957 Phi Eta Sigma
1970 Phi Kappa Phi
1971 Kappa Tau Alpha
1980 Pi Sigma Alpha

OTHER HONORS
   National Order of Omega
1922 Delta Phi Delta
1923 Phi Beta Kappa

1952 Order of the Coif

SERVICE
1931 Alpha Phi Omega

RECOGNITION
   Angel Flight
   Arnold Air Society (F-2)
1926 Pi Kappa Delta
1929 Theta Alpha Phi
1937 Delta Phi Alpha
1947 Beta Beta Beta
1953 Sigma Delta Psi

INACTIVE
1891–95 Sigma Nu
1921–33 Alpha Chi Omega
1921–76 Alpha Xi Delta
1922–36 Alpha Sigma Alpha
1922–52 Phi Mu
1923–87 Alpha Tau Omega
1925–30 Pi Lambda Phi
1925–36 Kappa Phi Kappa
1925–46 Sigma Tau Delta
1927 Eta Sigma Phi
1946–79 Delta Zeta
1952–73 Alpha Epsilon Phi
1968–83 Gamma Phi Beta
1969–76 Zeta Beta Tau

COLONIES
1937 Alpha Epsilon Pi

DREW UNIVERSITY Madison, NJ. The College of Liberal Arts was formerly called Brothers College; founded 1928; coeducational; church-related but nonsectarian. The university also imcludes the theological school and the graduate school.

ACHS HONORS
   Omicron Delta Epsilon
1974 Pi Sigma Alpha
1980 Psi Chi
1983 Phi Alpha Theta

SERVICE
1966 Alpha Phi Omega

RECOGNITION
1937 Beta Beta Beta

1948 Alpha Psi Omega
1954 Kappa Pi

INACTIVE
1940–60 Pi Gamma Mu

COLONIES
1988 Sigma Pi Sigma

DREXEL UNIVERSITY Philadelphia, PA. Founded in 1891 by Anthony J. Drexel. Originally named the Drexel Institute of Art, Science, and Industry.

Fraternity houses are owned by the alumni corporations in every case but the title is retained by the university. In many cases the university holds a first mortgage on the property, and in all cases financial assistance from the school has been a major factor in fraternity growth. The Panhellenic House is a joint project of all sororities and each has a chapter suite in the building.

NIC MEN'S
1933 Pi Kappa Phi
1939 Tau Kappa Epsilon
1940 Theta Chi
1941 Lambda Chi Alpha
1947 Sigma Alpha Mu
1950 Sigma Pi
1955 Tau Epsilon Phi

1956 Delta Sigma Phi
1965 Phi Sigma Kappa
1965 Pi Lambda Phi
1971 Sigma Alpha Epsilon
1983 Phi Kappa Sigma

NPC WOMEN'S
1925 Alpha Sigma Alpha

1928 Delta Zeta
1954 Phi Mu
1961 Phi Sigma Sigma

OTHER PROFESSIONAL
1976 Beta Alpha Psi

ACHS HONORS
1930 Tau Beta Pi
1935 Eta Kappa Nu
1936 Phi Kappa Phi
1938 Kappa Omicron Nu
1953 Chi Epsilon
1965 Sigma Pi Sigma
1968 Beta Gamma Sigma
1969 Beta Phi Mu
1969 Phi Eta Sigma
1973 Psi Chi
1980 Phi Alpha Theta

OTHER HONORS
   National Order of Omega
1966 Pi Mu Epsilon
1972 Sigma Xi

SERVICE
1948 Alpha Phi Omega
1953 Gamma Sigma Sigma

INACTIVE
1926–74 Sigma Sigma Sigma
1941–70 Pi Omega Pi
1947–51 Delta Phi Epsilon
1968–73 Alpha Kappa Psi
1968–74 Phi Gamma Nu

COLONIES
1990 Alpha Chi Rho

DRURY COLLEGE Springfield, MO. Organized in 1873 and opened on September 25 of that year. A private, coeducational, four-year liberal arts institution founded by Congregationalists, but not controlled by any religious body. The control is vested in a self-perpetuating board of trustees.

Ownership of two fraternity houses is by the fraternities; three houses are owned by the college and rented to the fraternities. Ownership is by college on rental basis to sorority. Administration requires fraternities to fill residence halls before the fraternity houses may be occupied.

NIC MEN'S
1906 Kappa Alpha Order
1919 Sigma Nu
1924 Lambda Chi Alpha
1982 Sigma Pi

NPC WOMEN'S
1909 Zeta Tau Alpha
1913 Delta Delta Delta
1914 Pi Beta Phi
1931 Kappa Delta

PROFESSIONAL
1942 Sigma Alpha Iota
1982 Phi Alpha Delta

ACHS HONORS
1948 Phi Alpha Theta
1949 Alpha Lambda Delta
1950 Omicron Delta Kappa
1951 Phi Eta Sigma
1951 Sigma Delta Pi

1965 Pi Delta Phi
1966 Mortar Board
1975 Kappa Delta Pi
1978 Psi Chi
1984 Kappa Mu Epsilon

OTHER HONORS
1946 National Collegiate
   Players

RECOGNITION
1929 Beta Beta Beta
1945 Pi Kappa Delta

INACTIVE
1925–34 Sigma Tau Delta
1925–64 Pi Gamma Mu
1949–88 Sigma Phi Epsilon
1950–83 Alpha Phi
1959–87 Phi Mu Alpha—
   Sinfonia
1964–83 Phi Kappa Sigma

UNIVERSITY OF DUBUQUE Dubuque, IA. University; college of liberal arts; theological seminary; coeducational; affiliated with the United Presbyterian Church. Chartered 1871.

ACHS HONORS
1953 Phi Alpha Theta
1962 Kappa Delta Pi

SERVICE
1965 Alpha Phi Omega
1977 Gamma Sigma Sigma

RECOGNITION
1932 Alpha Psi Omega
1936 Sigma Delta Psi

INACTIVE
-90 Phi Sigma Kappa

DUKE UNIVERSITY

DUKE UNIVERSITY Durham, NC. University; co-educational; private control; affiliated with the Methodist Church; first instruction 1838; chartered as Union Institute 1841; became Trinity College 1859; Duke University created in 1924; Trinity College continued as undergraduate college for men, and is currently undergraduate College of Arts and Sciences, along with School of Engineering.

NIC MEN'S
1872 Alpha Tau Omega
1873 Kappa Sigma
1878 Phi Delta Theta
1901 Pi Kappa Alpha
1909 Sigma Phi Epsilon
1912 Sigma Chi
1915 Pi Kappa Phi
1920 Delta Sigma Phi
1928 Delta Tau Delta
1931 Sigma Alpha Epsilon
1934 Phi Kappa Psi
1936 Phi Kappa Sigma
1939 Beta Theta Pi
1949 Theta Chi
1973 Psi Upsilon
1979 Kappa Alpha Psi (A)
1983 Delta Kappa Epsilon
1985 Alpha Epsilon Pi
1988 Chi Psi

NPHC MEN'S
1975 Alpha Phi Alpha

NPC WOMEN'S
1911 Alpha Delta Pi
1912 Kappa Delta
1915 Zeta Tau Alpha
1928 Kappa Alpha Theta
1930 Kappa Kappa Gamma
1931 Delta Delta Delta
1933 Pi Beta Phi
1934 Alpha Epsilon Phi
1939 Delta Gamma
1976 Chi Omega
1979 Alpha Omicron Pi

NPHC WOMEN'S
1975 Alpha Kappa Alpha
1975 Delta Sigma Theta (B)

PROFESSIONAL
1931 Phi Delta Phi
1946 Phi Alpha Delta
1947 Delta Theta Phi

OTHER PROFESSIONAL
1929 Gamma Eta Gamma

ACHS HONORS
Omicron Delta Epsilon
1914 Delta Sigma Rho-Tau
Kappa Alpha

1925 Sigma Pi Sigma
1926 Omicron Delta Kappa
1927 Kappa Delta Pi
1932 Phi Eta Sigma
1936 Sigma Delta Pi
1944 Pi Tau Sigma
1948 Tau Beta Pi
1955 Pi Sigma Alpha
1959 Psi Chi
1961 Eta Kappa Nu
1964 Chi Epsilon
1972 Sigma Theta Tau

OTHER HONORS
National Order of Omega
1920 Phi Beta Kappa
1931 Alpha Omega Alpha
1932 Pi Mu Epsilon
1933 Order of the Coif
1933 Sigma Xi

SERVICE
1955 Alpha Phi Omega

RECOGNITION
Arnold Air Society (B-2)
1931 Delta Phi Alpha
1944 Phi Lambda Upsilon
1950 Eta Sigma Phi
1968 Sigma Delta Psi

INACTIVE
1871–52 Chi Phi
1901–70 Kappa Alpha Order
1923–35 Sigma Nu Phi
1924–69 Lambda Chi Alpha
1925–54 Theta Alpha Phi
1926–42 Phi Sigma
1928–30 Sigma Tau Delta
1929–66 Alpha Kappa Psi
1930 Phi Chi
1931–38 Phi Beta Pi and Theta
Kappa Psi (a)
1931–55 Alpha Kappa Kappa
1931–67 Sigma Kappa
1933–43 Pi Gamma Mu
1934–87 Phi Mu
1935–70 Alpha Phi
1935–71 Zeta Beta Tau
1939–42 Alpha Eta Rho
1942–76 Alpha Chi Omega

DUQUESNE UNIVERSITY

DUQUESNE UNIVERSITY Pittsburgh, PA. University; coeducational; private control; Roman Catholic Church. Established as Pittsburgh Catholic College of the Holy Ghost in 1878; became Duquesne University in 1911.

University does not permit occupancy of special quarters by fraternities or sororities.

NIC MEN'S
1927 Zeta Beta Tau

1929 Alpha Phi Delta
1957 Phi Kappa Theta

1973 Alpha Tau Omega
1978 Sigma Tau Gamma

NPC WOMEN'S
1969 Delta Zeta
1970 Alpha Phi
1970 Zeta Tau Alpha
1971 Alpha Gamma Delta
1971 Alpha Sigma Tau

NPHC WOMEN'S
1946 Delta Sigma Theta (B)

PROFESSIONAL
1932 Lambda Kappa Sigma
1938 Alpha Tau Delta
1953 Mu Phi Epsilon
1957 Kappa Delta Epsilon
1960 Phi Delta Chi
1960 Phi Mu Alpha—Sinfonia
1963 Phi Alpha Delta
1967 Kappa Psi
1970 Delta Sigma Pi
1971 Delta Theta Phi
1973 Phi Chi Theta

OTHER PROFESSIONAL
1954 Kappa Phi Kappa
1958 Sigma Delta Chi
1962 Women in Communications

ACHS HONORS
Omicron Delta Epsilon
1940 Pi Omega Pi
1941 Rho Chi
1950 Psi Chi

1956 Phi Alpha Theta
1958 Alpha Kappa Delta
1962 Beta Gamma Sigma
1962 Kappa Tau Alpha
1964 Phi Sigma
1969 Lambda Sigma Society
1971 Phi Sigma Iota
1973 Alpha Epsilon Delta
1976 Mortar Board
1976 Phi Kappa Phi
1978 Omicron Delta Kappa
1981 Pi Sigma Alpha
1983 Phi Eta Sigma
1983 Theta Alpha Kappa
1988 Pi Kappa Lambda

SERVICE
1966 Alpha Phi Omega
1969 Gamma Sigma Sigma

RECOGNITION
Angel Flight
Arnold Air Society (E-1)
1941 Scabbard and Blade (8)
1951 Alpha Psi Omega
1966 Delta Phi Alpha

INACTIVE
1953–59 Pi Gamma Mu
1965–73 Sigma Pi Sigma
1971–74 Alpha Sigma Phi
1971–82 Tau Kappa Epsilon
1972–73 Kappa Beta Pi
1972–76 Sigma Phi Epsilon

EARLHAM COLLEGE

EARLHAM COLLEGE Richmond, IN. College of liberal arts; coeducational; private control; affiliated with Society of Friends; opened 1847, reorganized as Earlham College 1859.

ACHS HONORS
1929 Delta Sigma Rho-Tau
Kappa Alpha

OTHER HONORS
1929 National Collegiate
Players

1965 Phi Beta Kappa

EAST CAROLINA UNIVERSITY

EAST CAROLINA UNIVERSITY Greenville, NC. Established by the General Assembly, ratified March 8, 1907, under the name of East Carolina Teachers Training School; name changed to East Carolina Teachers College in 1921; became East Carolina College in 1951. State-supported; undergraduate and graduate courses for men and women.

Fraternities and sororities are permitted to own their own houses on their own land and in most cases do so.

NIC MEN'S
1958 Kappa Alpha Order
1958 Theta Chi
1959 Lambda Chi Alpha
1959 Sigma Nu
1961 Sigma Phi Epsilon
1962 Phi Kappa Tau
1963 Pi Kappa Phi
1966 Kappa Sigma
1968 Tau Kappa Epsilon
1971 Delta Sigma Phi
1975 Kappa Alpha Psi (A)

1978 Sigma Tau Gamma
1979 Alpha Sigma Phi
1983 Beta Theta Pi
1990 Sigma Pi

NPHC MEN'S
Phi Beta Sigma
1971 Alpha Phi Alpha

NPC WOMEN'S
1960 Alpha Delta Pi
1960 Alpha Omicron Pi
1960 Alpha Phi

1960 Alpha Xi Delta
1960 Chi Omega
1960 Delta Zeta
1960 Sigma Sigma Sigma
1987 Zeta Tau Alpha

NPHC WOMEN'S
1973 Alpha Kappa Alpha
1973 Delta Sigma Theta (B)
1977 Sigma Gamma Rho

PROFESSIONAL
1955 Phi Mu Alpha—Sinfonia
1955 Sigma Alpha Iota

OTHER PROFESSIONAL
1936 Phi Sigma Pi
1967 Alpha Beta Alpha
1968 Phi Upsilon Omicron

ACHS HONORS
    Omicron Delta Epsilon
1944 Pi Omega Pi
1953 Kappa Delta Pi
1955 Gamma Theta Upsilon
1961 Sigma Tau Delta
1964 Pi Kappa Lambda
1965 Phi Sigma Tau
1966 Alpha Kappa Delta
1966 Phi Alpha Theta
1966 Psi Chi
1967 Alpha Chi
1968 Beta Gamma Sigma
1969 Phi Sigma Iota
1969 Pi Sigma Alpha
1970 Phi Kappa Phi
1972 Sigma Pi Sigma
1974 Sigma Theta Tau

EAST CENTRAL STATE UNIVERSITY Ada, OK.
Liberal arts college; coeducational; state control;
chartered 1909.

College rents to fraternities and sororities. Fraternities and sororities may own property.

NIC MEN'S
1938 Sigma Tau Gamma
1963 Pi Kappa Alpha
1966 Phi Kappa Tau

NPHC MEN'S
1971 Alpha Phi Alpha

NPC WOMEN'S
1964 Chi Omega
1966 Zeta Tau Alpha
1968 Alpha Gamma Delta

ACHS HONORS
1950 Gamma Theta Upsilon
1963 Alpha Chi
1978 Pi Gamma Mu
1978 Psi Chi

RECOGNITION
1928 Alpha Psi Omega

INACTIVE
1922–56 Sigma Sigma Sigma
1973–84 Alpha Kappa Alpha

EAST STROUDSBURG STATE COLLEGE East
Stroudsburg, PA. Teachers college; coeducational;
state control; established 1893; became state teachers college 1927.

NIC MEN'S
1961 Sigma Pi
1963 Phi Sigma Kappa
1964 Tau Kappa Epsilon
1974 Theta Chi
1976 Alpha Chi Rho
1982 Pi Lambda Phi
1984 Kappa Alpha Psi (A)
1987 Delta Sigma Phi

NPHC MEN'S
    Phi Beta Sigma

NPC WOMEN'S
1968 Alpha Sigma Alpha
1969 Alpha Omicron Pi
1981 Phi Sigma Sigma
1984 Delta Phi Epsilon
1986 Sigma Sigma Sigma

ACHS HONORS
1931 Kappa Delta Pi
1948 Gamma Theta Upsilon
1955 Sigma Tau Delta
1960 Phi Alpha Theta

1975 Phi Eta Sigma
1976 Alpha Epsilon Delta

OTHER HONORS
    National Order of Omega
1960 Delta Phi Delta
1966 National Collegiate
    Players
1968 Pi Mu Epsilon
1974 Sigma Xi

SERVICE
1953 Alpha Phi Omega
1974 Gamma Sigma Sigma

RECOGNITION
    Angel Flight
    Arnold Air Society (B-2)
1964 Alpha Psi Omega
1965 Sigma Delta Psi
1969 Society for Collegiate
    Journalists—Pi Delta
    Epsilon-Alpha Phi Gamma
    (A)

INACTIVE
1955–72 Delta Sigma Pi
1958–86 Pi Kappa Alpha
1960–84 Kappa Delta
1965–72 Alpha Epsilon Pi
1966–69 Alpha Kappa Psi
1970–74 Lambda Tau
1971–78 Pi Lambda Phi
1983–88 Zeta Beta Tau

COLONIES
1988 Phi Kappa Psi

1970 Sigma Pi Sigma
1979 Pi Sigma Alpha
1980 Psi Chi

SERVICE
1947 Alpha Phi Omega

RECOGNITION
1945 Alpha Psi Omega
1967 Pi Kappa Delta

EAST TENNESSEE STATE UNIVERSITY
Johnson City, TN. Founded in 1911 by the State
Board of Education; undergraduate college, coeducational; graduate school, coeducational.

Fraternities are permitted to own their own houses
on their own land. Sororities are housed in a Panhellenic Building which is on college-owned land
and belongs jointly to the sororities and the college.

NIC MEN'S
1954 Phi Sigma Kappa
1954 Sigma Phi Epsilon
1955 Pi Kappa Alpha
1956 Lambda Chi Alpha
1966 Kappa Alpha Order
1969 Sigma Chi
1973 Sigma Nu
1978 Kappa Alpha Psi (A)
1979 Tau Kappa Epsilon

NPC WOMEN'S
1954 Alpha Delta Pi
1954 Kappa Delta
1955 Phi Mu
1956 Sigma Kappa

NPHC WOMEN'S
    Alpha Kappa Alpha

PROFESSIONAL
1957 Delta Omicron
1958 Delta Sigma Pi
1963 Phi Mu Alpha—Sinfonia

OTHER PROFESSIONAL
1972 Sigma Delta Chi

ACHS HONORS
1947 Kappa Delta Pi
1950 Gamma Theta Upsilon
1959 Kappa Mu Epsilon

1961 Pi Gamma Mu
1965 Alpha Lambda Delta
1969 Kappa Omicron Nu
1970 Phi Kappa Phi
1970 Sigma Delta Pi
1976 Pi Delta Phi
1976 Pi Sigma Alpha
1977 Psi Chi
1980 Omicron Delta Kappa
1990 Phi Alpha Theta

OTHER HONORS
    National Order of Omega

SERVICE
1953 Alpha Phi Omega
1973 Gamma Sigma Sigma

RECOGNITION
1932 Pi Kappa Delta
1948 Alpha Psi Omega

INACTIVE
1955–78 Alpha Omicron Pi
1956–78 Alpha Xi Delta
1956–89 Delta Zeta
1963–83 Sigma Alpha Epsilon
1964–87 Pi Kappa Phi
1970–78 Alpha Kappa Lambda
1971–84 Kappa Sigma

EAST TEXAS BAPTIST UNIVERSITY Marshall, TX. College of liberal arts; coeducational; private control; Baptist Church; established 1917.

ACHS HONORS
1958 Alpha Chi
1970 Phi Alpha Theta
1972 Sigma Tau Delta

1973 Sigma Delta Pi

SERVICE
1965 Alpha Phi Omega

EAST TEXAS STATE UNIVERSITY Commerce, TX. Multipurpose liberal arts and teachers
training institution; coeducational; state control.
Established 1889. Graduate school.

Fraternities make arrangements for their own
quarters; houses are rented from institutions or approved housing. Administration requires sorority
members to occupy dormitories.

NIC MEN'S
1960 Kappa Alpha Order
1961 Delta Tau Delta

1962 Lambda Chi Alpha
1963 Pi Kappa Phi
1963 Sigma Chi

1970 Phi Kappa Theta
1975 Kappa Alpha Psi (A)
1978 Pi Kappa Alpha

NPHC MEN'S
     Phi Beta Sigma

NPC WOMEN'S
1959 Chi Omega
1960 Alpha Phi
1960 Kappa Delta
1962 Gamma Phi Beta

NPHC WOMEN'S
1970 Alpha Kappa Alpha
1971 Delta Sigma Theta (B)

PROFESSIONAL
1963 Delta Psi Kappa
1967 Mu Phi Epsilon
1967 Phi Mu Alpha—Sinfonia
1972 Kappa Kappa Psi

OTHER PROFESSIONAL
1961 Sigma Delta Chi

ACHS HONORS
     Omicron Delta Epsilon
1922 Alpha Chi
1929 Sigma Tau Delta
1948 Kappa Delta Pi
1949 Pi Omega Pi
1956 Alpha Lambda Delta
1959 Phi Alpha Theta
1960 Phi Eta Sigma
1963 Alpha Kappa Delta

1969 Sigma Delta Pi
1970 Psi Chi
1971 Pi Delta Phi
1972 Pi Sigma Alpha
1972 Sigma Pi Sigma
1976 Beta Gamma Sigma
1983 Psi Chi
1989 Phi Alpha Theta

OTHER HONORS
     National Order of Omega

SERVICE
1937 Alpha Phi Omega
1972 Gamma Sigma Sigma

RECOGNITION
     Angel Flight
     Arnold Air Society (G-1)
1924 Pi Kappa Delta
1950 Alpha Psi Omega
1961 Beta Beta Beta
1962 Iota Lambda Sigma
1970 Sigma Delta Psi

INACTIVE
1959–65 Delta Sigma Phi
1960–87 Delta Sigma Pi
1961–82 Alpha Delta Pi
1961–88 Sigma Phi Epsilon
1964–80 Phi Chi Theta
1970–76 Acacia
1973–81 Delta Chi
1980–85 Alpha Gamma Rho

EASTERN COLLEGE   St. Davids, PA.

NIC MEN'S
1985 Alpha Phi Delta

ACHS HONORS
1966 Phi Alpha Theta
1976 Pi Gamma Mu
1978 Phi Sigma Iota
1979 Delta Mu Delta

1984 Psi Chi

SERVICE
1967 Alpha Phi Omega

RECOGNITION
1976 Sigma Zeta

EASTERN CONNECTICUT STATE COLLEGE
Willimantic, CT. College of Liberal arts and teachers college; coeducational; state control; established 1889; formerly Willimantic State College.

ACHS HONORS
     Omicron Delta Epsilon
1981 Kappa Mu Epsilon

1982 Psi Chi
1985 Delta Mu Delta

EASTERN ILLINOIS UNIVERSITY   Charleston, IL. Established by act of General Assembly of Illinois 1895. First instruction 1899. Grants A.B., B.S., and B.S. in Ed. undergraduate degrees; graduate school, M.S., in ed.; coeducational; state control.

Fraternities and sororities rent or own the chapter houses. Four fraternities do not have housing, four rent, and the remainder own their houses. Except for four sororities which do not have housing, all own their houses.

NIC MEN'S
1930 Phi Sigma Kappa
1941 Sigma Tau Gamma
1949 Sigma Pi
1952 Tau Kappa Epsilon

1962 Delta Sigma Phi
1964 Pi Kappa Alpha
1967 Delta Chi
1971 Sigma Chi
1975 Kappa Alpha Psi (A)

1977 Lambda Chi Alpha
1981 Delta Tau Delta

NPHC MEN'S
     Phi Beta Sigma
1968 Alpha Phi Alpha

NPC WOMEN'S
1942 Sigma Sigma Sigma
1949 Delta Zeta
1956 Sigma Kappa
1961 Alpha Gamma Delta
1969 Alpha Sigma Alpha
1976 Alpha Phi
1982 Alpha Sigma Tau
1985 Phi Sigma Sigma

NPHC WOMEN'S
1971 Delta Sigma Theta (B)
1971 Sigma Gamma Rho
1972 Alpha Kappa Alpha

PROFESSIONAL
1964 Delta Sigma Pi
1966 Phi Mu Alpha—Sinfonia
1968 Sigma Alpha Iota
1969 Delta Psi Kappa
1976 Kappa Kappa Psi
1976 Phi Gamma Nu

OTHER PROFESSIONAL
1969 Alpha Beta Alpha
1975 Delta Pi Epsilon

ACHS HONORS
     Omicron Delta Epsilon
1931 Kappa Delta Pi

1932 Sigma Tau Delta
1935 Kappa Mu Epsilon
1940 Gamma Theta Upsilon
1940 Pi Omega Pi
1950 Kappa Omicron Nu
1955 Phi Alpha Theta
1966 Pi Sigma Alpha
1967 Delta Mu Delta
1967 Sigma Delta Pi
1969 Psi Chi
1970 Phi Sigma
1970 Sigma Pi Sigma
1976 Pi Delta Phi
1983 Kappa Tau Alpha

OTHER HONORS
     National Order of Omega
1974 Sigma Gamma Epsilon

SERVICE
1947 Alpha Phi Omega

RECOGNITION
1949 Society for Collegiate
     Journalists—Pi Delta
     Epsilon-Alpha Phi Gamma
     (P)
1961 Beta Beta Beta
1983 Gamma Sigma Epsilon

INACTIVE
1957–79 Alpha Kappa Lambda
1964–84 Kappa Delta
1966–84 Beta Sigma Psi
1972–74 Alpha Omicron Pi
1972–77 Acacia

EASTERN KENTUCKY UNIVERSITY   Richmond, KY. A coeducational university offering general and liberal arts programs and professional training in education and other fields at undergraduate and graduate levels; established as normal school in 1906; remained a teachers college until 1948; became university 1966.

All sorority members live in dormitories; some fraternities are housed in dormitories, while others rent lodges within the community.

NIC MEN'S
1969 Kappa Alpha Order
1969 Phi Delta Theta
1969 Pi Kappa Alpha
1969 Tau Kappa Epsilon
1970 Sigma Chi
1970 Sigma Nu
1971 Beta Theta Pi
1971 Theta Chi
1973 Kappa Alpha Psi (A)
1973 Sigma Alpha Epsilon
1978 Lambda Chi Alpha
1978 Sigma Pi
1982 Phi Kappa Tau

NPHC MEN'S
     Phi Beta Sigma

NPC WOMEN'S
1968 Alpha Gamma Delta
1968 Kappa Delta
1969 Alpha Delta Pi
1969 Chi Omega
1972 Kappa Alpha Theta
1973 Phi Mu
1976 Pi Beta Phi
1982 Delta Zeta

1987 Alpha Omicron Pi
1990 Alpha Chi Omega

NPHC WOMEN'S
1970 Delta Sigma Theta (B)
1971 Alpha Kappa Alpha

PROFESSIONAL
1967 Delta Omicron
1967 Phi Mu Alpha—Sinfonia
1973 Delta Psi Kappa
1983 Gamma Iota Sigma

OTHER PROFESSIONAL
1973 Phi Upsilon Omicron

ACHS HONORS
     Omicron Delta Epsilon
1935 Pi Omega Pi
1948 Lambda Sigma Society
1950 Sigma Tau Delta
1968 Phi Alpha Theta
1968 Psi Chi
1969 Sigma Delta Pi
1971 Kappa Mu Epsilon
1971 Phi Kappa Phi
1975 Gamma Theta Upsilon
1976 Phi Sigma

1978 Pi Sigma Alpha
1983 Kappa Tau Alpha
1983 Mortar Board
1984 Sigma Pi Sigma

OTHER HONORS
    National Order of Omega

RECOGNITION
1968 Society for Collegiate
    Journalists—Pi Delta
    Epsilon-Alpha Phi Gamma
    (A)

INACTIVE
1970–83 Delta Upsilon

EASTERN MICHIGAN UNIVERSITY Ypsilanti, MI. Created by state legislature 1849 as Michigan State Normal School; first building completed and instruction begun 1852; name changed to Eastern Michigan College in 1955, and became university in 1959. Undergraduate colleges and graduate school coeducational; under authority of the State Board of Education.

NIC MEN'S
    Alpha Epsilon Pi
1934 Phi Sigma Kappa
1952 Delta Sigma Phi
1955 Kappa Alpha Psi (A)
1955 Tau Kappa Epsilon
1960 Theta Chi
1969 Alpha Epsilon Pi
1976 Lambda Chi Alpha
1989 Sigma Phi Epsilon

NPHC MEN'S
    Phi Beta Sigma
1959 Alpha Phi Alpha

NPC WOMEN'S
1899 Alpha Sigma Tau
1917 Sigma Sigma Sigma
1954 Alpha Xi Delta
1955 Delta Zeta
1959 Sigma Kappa
1974 Alpha Gamma Delta

NPHC WOMEN'S
1947 Alpha Kappa Alpha
1970 Sigma Gamma Rho

PROFESSIONAL
1950 Mu Phi Epsilon
1963 Delta Psi Kappa
1964 Alpha Kappa Psi
1965 Kappa Kappa Psi
1967 Phi Gamma Nu
1967 Tau Beta Sigma

OTHER PROFESSIONAL
1975 Delta Pi Epsilon

ACHS HONORS
    Omicron Delta Epsilon
1922 Kappa Delta Pi
1949 Pi Omega Pi
1962 Gamma Theta Upsilon

1972 Mortar Board
1973 Phi Kappa Phi
1974 Pi Sigma Alpha
1975 Beta Gamma Sigma
1978 Psi Chi
1984 Phi Alpha Theta

OTHER HONORS
    National Order of Omega

SERVICE
1956 Alpha Phi Omega

RECOGNITION
1918 Sigma Delta Psi
1954 Alpha Psi Omega
1965 Scabbard and Blade (16)
1965 Society for Collegiate
    Journalists—Pi Delta
    Epsilon-Alpha Phi Gamma
    (A)

INACTIVE
1932–62 Pi Gamma Mu
1948–75 Sigma Tau Gamma
1948–82 Alpha Sigma Phi
1948–88 Phi Mu Alpha—
    Sinfonia
1957–62 Pi Kappa Phi
1962–72 Sigma Pi
1962–79 Alpha Omicron Pi
1963–76 Zeta Tau Alpha
1968–70 Delta Phi Epsilon
1968–71 Sigma Alpha Mu
1968–77 Phi Sigma Kappa
1969–72 Alpha Epsilon Phi
1969–84 Delta Sigma Pi
1980–86 Alpha Chi Sigma
1981–83 Phi Sigma Sigma

COLONIES
1985 Sigma Pi Sigma

EASTERN MONTANA COLLEGE Billings, MT. A four-year state college with programs in the sciences, liberal arts, education, and a graduate education and vocational program. Established 1927.

NIC MEN'S
1973 Kappa Sigma

NPC WOMEN'S
1985 Alpha Chi Omega

PROFESSIONAL
1959 Kappa Delta Epsilon

OTHER PROFESSIONAL
1958 Kappa Phi Kappa

ACHS HONORS
1970 Phi Alpha Theta
1972 Psi Chi

SERVICE
1959 Intercollegiate Knights

RECOGNITION
1938 Alpha Psi Omega

INACTIVE
1977–79 Alpha Gamma Delta

EASTERN NAZARENE COLLEGE Quincy, MS.

ACHS HONORS
1989 Psi Chi

EASTERN NEW MEXICO UNIVERSITY Portales, NM. Founded 1934 as junior college; university; coeducational; state control; accredited by North Central Association.

Fraternities use lodges with limited residence capacity. Sororities have chapter rooms on campus and live in residence halls. Eastern Village (a development tract) has been created with one house completed and two more currently under consideration. Organizations lease land, own the houses.

NIC MEN'S
1962 Kappa Sigma
1963 Sigma Alpha Epsilon
1966 Sigma Nu
1967 Sigma Chi
1969 Phi Kappa Psi

NPC WOMEN'S
1962 Chi Omega
1962 Zeta Tau Alpha

PROFESSIONAL
1949 Kappa Kappa Psi
1950 Tau Beta Sigma
1959 Sigma Alpha Iota
1961 Phi Gamma Nu

ACHS HONORS
1955 Gamma Theta Upsilon
1958 Phi Alpha Theta
1967 Alpha Lambda Delta
1967 Psi Chi
1971 Phi Kappa Phi
1971 Sigma Pi Sigma
1977 Pi Kappa Lambda
1981 Delta Mu Delta

OTHER HONORS
    National Order of Omega

SERVICE
    The National Spurs
1961 Alpha Phi Omega

RECOGNITION
1947 Alpha Psi Omega
1949 Kappa Pi
1958 Sigma Delta Psi
1966 Pi Kappa Delta
1969 Blue Key
1972 Beta Beta Beta

INACTIVE
1960–86 Phi Mu Alpha—
    Sinfonia
1960–87 Delta Sigma Pi
1962–90 Pi Kappa Alpha
1964–87 Alpha Delta Pi
1968–74 Kappa Delta
1969–72 Zeta Beta Tau
1973–90 Phi Eta Sigma

EASTERN OREGON COLLEGE La Grande, OR. College of liberal arts and teachers college; coeducational; state control; established 1929.

ACHS HONORS
1976 Sigma Pi Sigma
1982 Psi Chi
1986 Phi Alpha Theta

SERVICE
1951 Intercollegiate Knights

RECOGNITION
1942 Alpha Psi Omega
1958 Kappa Pi
1964 Blue Key

EASTERN WASHINGTON UNIVERSITY Cheney, WA. Established 1882. College of Letters & Sciences; Schools of Business, Fine Arts, Health Sciences, Human Learning & Development, Mathematical Sciences & Technology, Public Affairs, Social Work & Human Services; Intercollegiate Center for Nursing Education. Located seventeen miles from Spokane.

Five residence halls and three unfurnished apartment complexes for married students.

NIC MEN'S
1984 Delta Chi

NPHC MEN'S
1974 Alpha Phi Alpha

NPC WOMEN'S
1989 Alpha Omicron Pi
1990 Alpha Phi

PROFESSIONAL
1949 Mu Phi Epsilon

ACHS HONORS
1936 Kappa Delta Pi
1962 Psi Chi
1965 Alpha Kappa Delta
1976 Beta Gamma Sigma
1981 Phi Alpha Theta
1981 Phi Eta Sigma
1982 Phi Kappa Phi
1982 Pi Sigma Alpha

SERVICE
1937 Intercollegiate Knights

1948 Alpha Phi Omega

RECOGNITION
1949 Kappa Pi
1961 Alpha Psi Omega
1969 Pi Kappa Delta

INACTIVE
1948–53 Phi Sigma Kappa
1950–74 Phi Mu Alpha—
        Sinfonia
1965–72 Pi Gamma Mu
1966–71 Alpha Xi Delta
1966–77 Chi Omega
1966–78 Pi Kappa Alpha
1967–83 Phi Chi Theta
1968–76 Lambda Chi Alpha
1970–73 Sigma Nu
1970–77 Sigma Kappa
1976–78 Zeta Tau Alpha

COLONIES
1990 Phi Delta Theta

EASTFIELD COLLEGE Mesquite, TX.

SERVICE
1982 Alpha Phi Omega

ECKERD COLLEGE ST. Petersburg, FL.

ACHS HONORS
    Omicron Delta Epsilon
1983 Omicron Delta Kappa

OTHER HONORS
1965 Pi Mu Epsilon

EDGEWOOD COLLEGE Madison, WI.

PROFESSIONAL
1963 Alpha Delta Theta

ACHS HONORS
1961 Delta Epsilon Sigma

INACTIVE
1964–76 Pi Omega Pi

EDINBORO UNIVERSITY OF PENNSYLVANIA
Edinboro, PA. Founded as an academy in 1856, chartered as a normal school 1861, recognized as a four-year degree-granting college in 1926. Undergraduate programs, bachelor of science in education and bachelor of arts degrees; graduate programs; coeducational; state public institution.

Plans for fraternity and sorority housing are being studied at the college.

NIC MEN'S
1959 Delta Sigma Phi
1964 Sigma Tau Gamma
1966 Tau Kappa Epsilon
1967 Phi Sigma Kappa
1971 Lambda Chi Alpha
1971 Theta Chi
1977 Alpha Chi Rho
1984 Phi Kappa Psi
1986 Sigma Pi
1987 Kappa Alpha Psi (A)
1989 Pi Lambda Phi

NPC WOMEN'S
1959 Alpha Gamma Delta
1965 Delta Zeta
1969 Alpha Sigma Alpha
1969 Alpha Sigma Tau

1970 Zeta Tau Alpha

NPHC WOMEN'S
1970 Alpha Kappa Alpha

PROFESSIONAL
1976 Phi Mu Alpha—Sinfonia
1976 Sigma Alpha Iota

OTHER PROFESSIONAL
1938 Phi Sigma Pi
1969 Alpha Beta Alpha

ACHS HONORS
1951 Kappa Delta Pi
1959 Gamma Theta Upsilon
1970 Sigma Delta Pi
1971 Pi Delta Phi
1971 Psi Chi

1971 Sigma Pi Sigma
1972 Phi Alpha Theta
1980 Phi Eta Sigma

OTHER HONORS
1932 Delta Phi Delta
1974 Pi Mu Epsilon

SERVICE
1951 Alpha Phi Omega
1967 Gamma Sigma Sigma

RECOGNITION
1930 Alpha Psi Omega
1950 Beta Beta Beta

1975 Pi Kappa Delta

INACTIVE
1867–70 Chi Phi
1938–60 Kappa Delta Phi (C)
1967–76 Sigma Sigma Sigma
1970–82 Alpha Xi Delta
1971–82 Delta Phi Epsilon

COLONIES
    Kappa Delta Rho
    Theta Xi
1990 Delta Chi

EDWARD WATERS COLLEGE Jacksonville, FL.

NIC MEN'S
1960 Kappa Alpha Psi (A)

NPHC MEN'S
    Phi Beta Sigma
1961 Omega Psi Phi

1975 Alpha Phi Alpha

NPHC WOMEN'S
    Zeta Phi Beta
1971 Sigma Gamma Rho
1980 Alpha Kappa Alpha

EL CENTRO COLLEGE Dallas, TX.

SERVICE
1967 Alpha Phi Omega

ELIZABETH CITY STATE UNIVERSITY
Elizabeth City, NC. Founded 1891; coeducational; state control.

NIC MEN'S
1961 Kappa Alpha Psi (A)

NPHC MEN'S
    Phi Beta Sigma
1954 Omega Psi Phi

NPHC WOMEN'S
    Zeta Phi Beta
1953 Delta Sigma Theta (B)
1970 Sigma Gamma Rho

ACHS HONORS
1942 Alpha Kappa Mu

1964 Kappa Delta Pi
1975 Alpha Chi
1975 Sigma Tau Delta

SERVICE
1971 Alpha Phi Omega

RECOGNITION
1963 Beta Beta Beta

INACTIVE
1902–04 Kappa Delta

ELIZABETHTOWN COLLEGE Elizabethtown, PA.

ACHS HONORS
1969 Phi Alpha Theta
1970 Sigma Pi Sigma
1971 Alpha Lambda Delta
1977 Psi Chi
1978 Pi Sigma Alpha

RECOGNITION
1967 Alpha Psi Omega

INACTIVE
1932–42 Sigma Zeta

ELMHURST COLLEGE Elmhurst, IL. College of liberal arts; coeducational; private; United Church of Christ; chartered 1865.

NIC MEN'S
1970 Tau Kappa Epsilon
1977 Alpha Tau Omega

NPC WOMEN'S
1977 Sigma Kappa
1980 Alpha Phi

ACHS HONORS
1962 Pi Gamma Mu
1963 Delta Mu Delta

1964 Gamma Theta Upsilon
1965 Psi Chi
1972 Sigma Tau Delta
1976 Alpha Epsilon Delta
1976 Omicron Delta Kappa
1977 Phi Kappa Phi
1979 Sigma Pi Sigma

OTHER HONORS
    National Order of Omega

SERVICE
1986 Alpha Phi Omega

RECOGNITION
1963 Pi Kappa Delta

1965 Beta Beta Beta

COLONIES
1989 Delta Chi

ELMIRA COLLEGE Elmira, NY. College of liberal arts coeducational; private control; nonsectarian; chartered 1855.

ACHS HONORS
1931 Delta Sigma Rho-Tau
     Kappa Alpha
1971 Psi Chi
1978 Phi Alpha Theta
1990 Phi Eta Sigma

OTHER HONORS
1940 Phi Beta Kappa

1956 National Collegiate
     Players

INACTIVE
1927–43 Pi Gamma Mu

ELON COLLEGE Elon College, NC. College of liberal arts; coeducational; private control; United Church of Christ. Chartered 1889.

NIC MEN'S
1973 Kappa Sigma
1973 Sigma Phi Epsilon
1977 Sigma Pi
1987 Sigma Chi
1988 Kappa Alpha Psi (A)
1989 Alpha Kappa Lambda

NPC WOMEN'S
1970 Sigma Sigma Sigma
1971 Phi Mu
1971 Zeta Tau Alpha
1977 Alpha Sigma Alpha
1987 Alpha Omicron Pi

NPHC WOMEN'S
1987 Alpha Kappa Alpha

ACHS HONORS
1929 Pi Gamma Mu
1968 Alpha Chi

1977 Omicron Delta Kappa
1978 Phi Alpha Theta
1981 Theta Alpha Kappa
1990 Kappa Mu Epsilon

SERVICE
1967 Alpha Phi Omega

RECOGNITION
1949 Alpha Psi Omega

INACTIVE
1950–69 Sigma Mu Sigma
1968–89 Tau Kappa Epsilon
1972–73 Delta Zeta
1979–89 Pi Kappa Phi

COLONIES
     Lambda Chi Alpha
     Pi Kappa Phi

ELLSWORTH COMMUNITY COLLEGE Iowa City, IA.

INACTIVE
1927–27 Alpha Sigma Phi

EMBRY RIDDLE AERONAUTICAL UNIVERSITY Prescott, AZ. Private institution. Founded in 1926. Four-year; coeducational. Majors offered are: aeronautical science, aeronautical engineering, electrical engineering, aviation business administration, computer science with aviation applications.

NIC MEN'S
1982 Sigma Pi

COLONIES
     Theta Xi

EMBRY RIDDLE AERONAUTICAL UNIVERSITY Bunnell, FL. Private institution. Founded in 1926. Four-year; coeducational. Majors offered are: aeronautical science, aeronautical engineering, engineering physics, aviation business administration, computer science with aviation applications, aviation maintenance, avionics.

NIC MEN'S
1971 Sigma Chi
1972 Delta Chi
1974 Lambda Chi Alpha
1984 Sigma Pi

NPC WOMEN'S
1986 Theta Phi Alpha

PROFESSIONAL
1960 Sigma Phi Delta

OTHER PROFESSIONAL
1961 Alpha Eta Rho

ACHS HONORS
1975 Omicron Delta Kappa

EMERSON COLLEGE Boston, MA. Specialized college with emphasis on the communication and performing arts; coeducational; private control; nonsectarian. Established 1880.

PROFESSIONAL
1908 Zeta Phi Eta

ACHS HONORS
1967 Delta Sigma Rho-Tau
     Kappa Alpha

RECOGNITION
1966 Alpha Psi Omega

COLONIES
1989 Alpha Epsilon Phi
1990 Alpha Epsilon Pi

EMMANUEL COLLEGE Boston, MA. College of liberal arts for women; private control; Roman Catholic; established 1919.

ACHS HONORS
1940 Delta Epsilon Sigma
1959 Phi Alpha Theta

RECOGNITION
1949 Alpha Psi Omega

1959 Beta Beta Beta

INACTIVE
1953   Delta Phi Alpha
1965–79 Psi Chi

EMORY UNIVERSITY Atlanta, GA. University; coeducational; private control; affiliated with Methodist Church; chartered as Emory College, 1836; incorporated as Emory University, 1915; moved to Atlanta campus 1919.

Fraternities occupy college-owned houses on rental basis; administration requires sorority members to occupy dormitories.

NIC MEN'S
1869 Chi Phi
1869 Kappa Alpha Order
1871 Phi Delta Theta
1881 Alpha Tau Omega
1881 Sigma Alpha Epsilon
1882 Delta Tau Delta
1884 Sigma Nu
1919 Pi Kappa Alpha
1919 Tau Epsilon Phi
1920 Alpha Epsilon Pi
1921 Sigma Chi
1924 Sigma Pi
1948 Beta Theta Pi
1965 Phi Gamma Delta
1987 Kappa Alpha Psi (A)

NPHC MEN'S
1976 Alpha Phi Alpha

NPC WOMEN'S
1959 Alpha Delta Pi
1959 Alpha Epsilon Phi
1959 Chi Omega
1959 Delta Delta Delta
1959 Delta Gamma
1959 Kappa Alpha Theta
1959 Kappa Kappa Gamma
1977 Delta Phi Epsilon

NPHC WOMEN'S
1979 Alpha Kappa Alpha

PROFESSIONAL
1905 Phi Chi
1912 Xi Psi Phi
1918 Psi Omega
1923 Phi Delta Phi
1927 Phi Alpha Delta
1973 Delta Theta Phi

OTHER PROFESSIONAL
1921 Delta Sigma Delta
1930 Phi Delta Epsilon
1949 Kappa Beta Pi

ACHS HONORS
     Omicron Delta Epsilon
1922 Delta Sigma Rho-Tau
     Kappa Alpha
1925 Omicron Delta Kappa
1925 Phi Sigma
1930 Phi Sigma Iota
1938 Pi Sigma Alpha
1948 Sigma Pi Sigma
1950 Beta Gamma Sigma
1956 Alpha Kappa Delta
1964 Sigma Theta Tau
1969 Mortar Board
1975 Phi Alpha Theta
1976 Psi Chi

1979 Phi Sigma Tau
1987 Theta Alpha Kappa

OTHER HONORS
      National Order of Omega
1921 Omicron Kappa Upsilon
1929 Phi Beta Kappa
1939 Alpha Omega Alpha
1944 Sigma Xi
1971 Order of the Coif

SERVICE
1946 Alpha Phi Omega

RECOGNITION
      Arnold Air Society (C-1)
1933 Eta Sigma Phi
1949 Alpha Psi Omega
1951 Sigma Delta Psi

INACTIVE
1887–35 Kappa Sigma
1904–59 Phi Rho Sigma
1909–53 Phi Beta Pi and Theta
        Kappa Psi (B)

1912–57 Pi Kappa Phi
1914–63 Alpha Kappa Kappa
1921–25 Chi Beta Phi
1923   Scabbard and Blade
        (4)
1923–34 Phi Beta Pi and Theta
        Kappa Psi (a)
1925–35 Kappa Sigma
1926–63 Alpha Kappa Psi
1927–54 Kappa Phi Kappa
1928–88 Alpha Omega
1929–37 Lambda Chi Alpha
1938   Delta Phi Alpha
1941–53 Sigma Delta Chi
1948   Sigma Gamma Epsilon
1949   Kappa Kappa Psi
1959–73 Phi Mu
1959–85 Kappa Delta
1959–86 Kappa Delta Epsilon
1959–88 Alpha Chi Omega
1962–69 Alpha Epsilon Delta

EMORY AND HENRY COLLEGE   Emory, VA. Founded by the Holston Conference of the Methodist Church in 1836; first instruction in 1838. A coeducational liberal arts college.

OTHER PROFESSIONAL
1924 Kappa Phi Kappa

ACHS HONORS
      Omicron Delta Epsilon
1917 Delta Sigma Rho-Tau
     Kappa Alpha
1928 Pi Gamma Mu
1937 Gamma Theta Upsilon
1988 Phi Sigma Iota

SERVICE
1966 Alpha Phi Omega

RECOGNITION
1925 Blue Key
1927 Alpha Psi Omega
1942 Cardinal Key
1958 Beta Beta Beta

INACTIVE
1856–61 Phi Kappa Sigma
1874–95 Kappa Sigma
1884–96 Sigma Alpha Epsilon
1893–95 Kappa Alpha Order
1936–69 Alpha Epsilon Delta
1950–71 Kappa Delta Epsilon

EMPORIA STATE UNIVERSITY   Emporia, KS. Teachers college; coeducational; state control; chartered as normal school in 1863.

Fraternities and sororities own their own houses and property.

NIC MEN'S
1922 Sigma Tau Gamma
1951 Sigma Phi Epsilon
1951 Tau Kappa Epsilon
1968 Phi Delta Theta
1976 Sigma Pi
1977 Kappa Sigma
1984 Kappa Alpha Psi (A)

NPC WOMEN'S
1917 Sigma Sigma Sigma
1923 Alpha Sigma Tau
1961 Chi Omega

NPHC WOMEN'S
1969 Sigma Gamma Rho
1979 Alpha Kappa Alpha

PROFESSIONAL
1962 Kappa Kappa Psi

ACHS HONORS
1920 Kappa Delta Pi
1929 Pi Omega Pi
1934 Kappa Mu Epsilon

1956 Sigma Delta Pi
1963 Pi Delta Phi
1964 Psi Chi
1966 Sigma Pi Sigma
1973 Beta Phi Mu
1978 Kappa Omicron Nu
1980 Phi Kappa Phi
1985 Phi Alpha Theta

OTHER HONORS
1951 National Collegiate
     Players

SERVICE
1947 Alpha Phi Omega

RECOGNITION
1961 Blue Key

INACTIVE
1910–89 Phi Sigma Kappa
1917–82 Delta Zeta
1927–46 Pi Gamma Mu
1928–67 Kappa Omicron Nu

1929–73 Phi Mu Alpha—
        Sinfonia
1937–84 Phi Mu Alpha—
        Sinfonia
1959–74 Sigma Kappa
1963–70 Theta Xi

1970–77 Phi Kappa Tau
1971–76 Acacia

COLONIES
1949 Alpha Kappa Lambda

ERSKINE COLLEGE   Due West, SC. College of liberal arts and theological seminary; college coeducational; seminary for men; private control; Associate Reformed Presbyterian; established 1839.

ACHS HONORS
1964 Omicron Delta Kappa
1978 Phi Alpha Theta

RECOGNITION
1963 Alpha Psi Omega

1969 Beta Beta Beta

INACTIVE
1860–61 Sigma Chi
1883–93 Kappa Alpha Order
1884–94 Sigma Alpha Epsilon

EUREKA COLLEGE   Eureka, IL. Founded 1855.

NIC MEN'S
1917 Tau Kappa Epsilon
1925 Lambda Chi Alpha
1985 Delta Sigma Phi

NPHC WOMEN'S
1972 Delta Sigma Theta (B)
1974 Alpha Kappa Alpha

ACHS HONORS
1969 Alpha Chi

1971 Sigma Tau Delta

RECOGNITION
1915 Pi Kappa Delta
1948 Sigma Zeta

COLONIES
1917 Delta Zeta

EVANGEL COLLEGE   Springfield, MO. College of arts and sciences owned and operated by the Genral Council of the Assemblies of God; coeducational; estblished in 1955.

PROFESSIONAL
1971 Mu Phi Epsilon

ACHS HONORS
1971 Kappa Mu Epsilon
1972 Pi Gamma Mu
1972 Sigma Tau Delta
1979 Theta Alpha Kappa

1985 Pi Kappa Lambda

RECOGNITION
1966 Pi Kappa Delta

INACTIVE
1961–86 Phi Mu Alpha—
        Sinfonia

UNIVERSITY OF EVANSVILLE   Evansville, IN. College of liberal arts with schools of engineering, nursing; coeducational; private control; affiliated with Methodist Church; incorporated 1854 as Moores Hill Male and Female Collegiate Institute at Moores Hill, Ind.; charter granted and name changed to Evansville College 1919. Became University of Evansville in 1967.

Ownership of fraternity house and land is by the fraternity; for sorority, ownership is by college on rental basis.

NIC MEN'S
1955 Sigma Phi Epsilon
1956 Lambda Chi Alpha
1957 Sigma Alpha Epsilon
1957 Tau Kappa Epsilon
1965 Kappa Alpha Psi (A)
1968 Phi Kappa Tau

NPHC MEN'S
     Phi Beta Sigma

NPC WOMEN'S
1951 Alpha Omicron Pi
1951 Chi Omega
1952 Phi Mu
1964 Zeta Tau Alpha

PROFESSIONAL
1948 Sigma Alpha Iota
1951 Phi Mu Alpha—Sinfonia
1963 Pi Sigma Epsilon
1966 Alpha Tau Delta

1980 Delta Sigma Pi
1984 Phi Alpha Delta

OTHER PROFESSIONAL
1973 Pi Lambda Theta

ACHS HONORS
1928 Delta Sigma Rho-Tau
     Kappa Alpha
1949 Sigma Pi Sigma
1960 Kappa Mu Epsilon
1963 Phi Kappa Phi
1964 Psi Chi
1971 Lambda Iota Tau
1975 Mortar Board
1976 Phi Eta Sigma
1979 Pi Kappa Lambda
1979 Pi Sigma Alpha
1988 Phi Alpha Theta

OTHER HONORS
     National Order of Omega

SERVICE
1940 Alpha Phi Omega

RECOGNITION
     Angel Flight
     Arnold Air Society (D-2)
1952 Alpha Psi Omega
1954 Kappa Pi
1964 Blue Key

INACTIVE
1929–73 Pi Gamma Mu
1950–58 Acacia
1951–69 Alpha Kappa Alpha
1962–87 Alpha Lambda Delta
1974–83 Alpha Phi

FAIRFIELD UNIVERSITY Fairfield, CT. University offering three schools of study: Arts & Sciences, Business & Nursing; coeducational; private control: Roman Catholic, established 1942.

NIC MEN'S
1967 Phi Kappa Theta

ACHS HONORS
     Omicron Delta Epsilon
1961 Alpha Sigma Nu
1962 Alpha Epsilon Delta
1968 Sigma Delta Pi
1969 Pi Delta Phi

1973 Phi Sigma Tau
1977 Phi Alpha Theta
1977 Psi Chi
1977 Theta Alpha Kappa
1981 Pi Sigma Alpha

SERVICE
1976 Alpha Phi Omega

FAIRLEIGH DICKINSON UNIVERSITY Rutherford, NJ. University; coeducational; private control; nonsectarian. Established 1941.

Additional campuses at Teaneck, Madison, and Edward Williams College at Research Park.

NIC MEN'S
1971 Tau Kappa Epsilon
1979 Sigma Pi
1983 Tau Kappa Epsilon
1984 Zeta Beta Tau
1985 Alpha Chi Rho

NPHC MEN'S
     Phi Beta Sigma

NPC WOMEN'S
1980 Phi Sigma Sigma
1986 Delta Phi Epsilon
1988 Alpha Epsilon Phi

PROFESSIONAL
1987 Alpha Omega

ACHS HONORS
     Omicron Delta Epsilon
     Pi Alpha Alpha
1963 Psi Chi
1969 Phi Alpha Theta
1977 Eta Kappa Nu
1977 Phi Alpha Theta
1978 Delta Mu Delta
1980 Pi Sigma Alpha
1985 Omicron Delta Kappa

INACTIVE
1970–73 Alpha Epsilon Pi

COLONIES
     Pi Lambda Phi

FAIRLEIGH DICKINSON UNIVERSITY, FLORHAM PARK-MADISON CAMPUS Madison, NJ.

NIC MEN'S
     Tau Kappa Epsilon
1984 Phi Sigma Kappa
1984 Zeta Beta Tau
1988 Sigma Chi

NPC WOMEN'S
1984 Zeta Tau Alpha
1988 Theta Phi Alpha
1990 Delta Phi Epsilon

ACHS HONORS
     Omicron Delta Epsilon
1968 Psi Chi
1983 Pi Sigma Alpha

SERVICE
1963 Alpha Phi Omega

RECOGNITION
1967 Beta Beta Beta

INACTIVE
1974–76 Sigma Phi Epsilon

1974–88 Phi Chi Theta

FAIRLEIGH DICKINSON UNIVERSITY, TEANECK-HACKENSACK CAMPUS Teaneck, NJ. Private institution. Four-year; coeducational.

NIC MEN'S
1972 Zeta Beta Tau
1973 Phi Sigma Kappa
1979 Alpha Chi Rho

NPC WOMEN'S
1990 Delta Phi Epsilon
1990 Theta Phi Alpha

NPHC WOMEN'S
1980 Alpha Kappa Alpha

ACHS HONORS
     Omicron Delta Epsilon
1967 Psi Chi

SERVICE
1965 Alpha Phi Omega

COLONIES
     Phi Mu

FAIRMONT STATE COLLEGE Fairmont, WV. Founded in 1865 as private teacher training institution; became a state normal school 1867; coeducational; degrees in education and liberal arts.

Fraternities and sororities rent properties from private citizens or companies.

NIC MEN'S
1945 Theta Xi
1960 Tau Kappa Epsilon
1963 Sigma Pi
1973 Alpha Phi Delta

NPC WOMEN'S
1930 Sigma Sigma Sigma
1934 Delta Zeta
1966 Phi Mu

ACHS HONORS
1928 Pi Gamma Mu
1931 Kappa Delta Pi
1964 Sigma Tau Delta
1978 Phi Alpha Theta

SERVICE
1982 Alpha Phi Omega

RECOGNITION
1925 Alpha Psi Omega
1925 Lambda Delta Lambda
1957 Beta Beta Beta
1959 Kappa Pi

INACTIVE
1877–80 Delta Gamma
1903–12 Kappa Delta
1929–80 Sigma Tau Gamma
1959–74 Sigma Kappa
1963–82 Alpha Xi Delta

FAYETTEVILLE STATE UNIVERSITY Fayetteville, NC. Teachers college; coeducational; state control; established 1867, chartered 1877.

NIC MEN'S
1962 Kappa Alpha Psi (A)

NPHC MEN'S
     Phi Beta Sigma
1951 Omega Psi Phi
1959 Alpha Phi Alpha

NPHC WOMEN'S
     Zeta Phi Beta
1952 Alpha Kappa Alpha
1952 Delta Sigma Theta (B)
1970 Sigma Gamma Rho

ACHS HONORS
     Omicron Delta Epsilon
1940 Alpha Kappa Mu
1972 Sigma Tau Delta
1973 Pi Omega Pi
1976 Delta Mu Delta

SERVICE
1970 Alpha Phi Omega
1973 Gamma Sigma Sigma

INACTIVE
1974–85 Pi Gamma Mu

FERRIS STATE COLLEGE Big Rapids, MI. Founded by Woodbridge N. Ferris 1884, became a state college 1950. College; coeducational; three-degree granting programs—commerce, education, pharmacy—general education through sophomore year, and a diverse assortment of trade-technical programs.

Fraternities are encouraged to own their own property. There is no residential plan for sororities.

NIC MEN'S
1962 Delta Sigma Phi
1962 Sigma Phi Epsilon
1963 Lambda Chi Alpha
1966 Pi Kappa Alpha
1968 Phi Kappa Theta
1968 Phi Sigma Kappa
1969 Kappa Alpha Psi (A)
1973 Sigma Alpha Epsilon
1989 Pi Lambda Phi

NPHC MEN'S
    Phi Beta Sigma
1966 Alpha Phi Alpha

NPC WOMEN'S
1961 Delta Zeta
1964 Alpha Xi Delta
1970 Zeta Tau Alpha
1985 Alpha Sigma Tau
1988 Phi Sigma Sigma

NPHC WOMEN'S
1969 Delta Sigma Theta (B)
1970 Sigma Gamma Rho
1971 Alpha Kappa Alpha

PROFESSIONAL
1951 Phi Delta Chi
1952 Kappa Psi
1953 Lambda Kappa Sigma

1959 Delta Sigma Pi
1966 Kappa Kappa Psi
1966 Tau Beta Sigma
1981 Gamma Iota Sigma

OTHER PROFESSIONAL
1974 Alpha Zeta Omega

ACHS HONORS
1955 Rho Chi
1961 Pi Omega Pi
1971 Omicron Delta Kappa

OTHER HONORS
    National Order of Omega

SERVICE
1963 Alpha Phi Omega

RECOGNITION
1946 Alpha Psi Omega
1960 Pi Kappa Delta
1967 Sigma Delta Psi

INACTIVE
1951–77 Theta Xi
1962–79 Sigma Alpha Mu
1962–87 Tau Kappa Epsilon
1963–79 Alpha Gamma Delta
1964–85 Phi Eta Sigma
1966–78 Phi Sigma Kappa

FINDLAY COLLEGE Findlay, OH. Founded 1882; coeducational.

All fraternity houses are privately owned. All sororities rent college-owned houses.

NIC MEN'S
1963 Tau Kappa Epsilon
1967 Sigma Pi
1972 Theta Chi

NPC WOMEN'S
1965 Delta Zeta
1965 Sigma Kappa

NPHC WOMEN'S
1975 Delta Sigma Theta (B)

PROFESSIONAL
1968 Delta Omicron

ACHS HONORS
    Sigma Tau Delta
1969 Phi Alpha Theta

RECOGNITION
1953 Alpha Psi Omega
1961 Sigma Delta Psi

INACTIVE
1964–83 Alpha Sigma Phi
1965–77 Alpha Xi Delta
1968–79 Phi Mu Alpha—
        Sinfonia
1983–85 Alpha Gamma Delta

FISK UNIVERSITY Nashville, TN. Founded by John Ogden, Erastus Milo Cravath, and E. P. Smith, in collaboraton with the Freedmen's Aid Commission of Cincinnati, and assisted by General Clinton B. Fisk; board of trustees organized 1866; chartered and first instruction 1866. University; undergraduate coeducational; graduate school coeducational; private control; nonsectarian.

No special housing is maintained for fraternities and sororities.

NIC MEN'S
1927 Kappa Alpha Psi (A)

NPHC MEN'S
    Phi Beta Sigma
1925 Omega Psi Phi

1927 Alpha Phi Alpha

NPHC WOMEN'S
    Zeta Phi Beta
1925 Delta Sigma Theta (B)
1927 Alpha Kappa Alpha

1945 Sigma Gamma Rho

ACHS HONORS
    Omicron Delta Epsilon
1945 Alpha Kappa Delta
1945 Beta Kappa Chi
1973 Lambda Iota Tau
1975 Mortar Board
1981 Psi Chi
1990 Delta Mu Delta

OTHER HONORS
1953 Phi Beta Kappa

SERVICE
1977 Alpha Phi Omega

INACTIVE
1953–87 Phi Mu Alpha—
        Sinfonia

FITCHBURG STATE COLLEGE Fitchburg, MA. College of liberal arts and teachers college; coeducational; state control; chartered as normal school 1894.

NPHC MEN'S
    Phi Beta Sigma

ACHS HONORS
1969 Phi Alpha Theta
1983 Psi Chi

SERVICE
1965 Alpha Phi Omega

INACTIVE
–86   Omicron Delta Epsilon

COLONIES
    Phi Sigma Sigma
    Sigma Tau Gamma

UNIVERSITY OF FLORIDA Gainesville, FL. University and land-grant college; coeducational; state control; authorized by legislature 1853; first instruction as East Florida Seminary; named University of Florida 1905.

Eight fraternities own their houses on their own land; sixteen occupy their houses on college land; twelve sororities own houses on college land; two sororities own their houses and property; three fraternities and one sorority rent.

NIC MEN'S
1884 Alpha Tau Omega
1884 Sigma Alpha Epsilon
1904 Kappa Alpha Order
1904 Pi Kappa Alpha
1916 Theta Chi
1920 Sigma Nu
1922 Kappa Sigma
1924 Phi Delta Theta
1924 Pi Kappa Phi
1924 Sigma Chi
1925 Alpha Gamma Rho
1925 Delta Tau Delta
1925 Pi Lambda Phi
1925 Sigma Phi Epsilon
1925 Tau Epsilon Phi
1926 Delta Chi
1926 Phi Kappa Tau
1930 Beta Theta Pi
1930 Delta Sigma Phi
1933 Lambda Chi Alpha
1935 Chi Phi
1940 Phi Gamma Delta
1950 Tau Kappa Epsilon
1951 Alpha Epsilon Pi
1957 Delta Upsilon
1967 Phi Kappa Psi
1972 Kappa Alpha Psi (A)
1973 Phi Kappa Theta
1984 Sigma Pi
1986 Sigma Alpha Mu

NPHC MEN'S
    Phi Beta Sigma
1973 Alpha Phi Alpha

NPC WOMEN'S
1948 Alpha Delta Pi
1948 Alpha Epsilon Phi
1948 Alpha Omicron Pi
1948 Chi Omega
1948 Delta Delta Delta
1948 Kappa Delta
1949 Alpha Chi Omega
1949 Delta Gamma
1949 Sigma Kappa
1949 Zeta Tau Alpha
1955 Delta Phi Epsilon
1962 Kappa Alpha Theta
1967 Phi Sigma Sigma
1969 Pi Beta Phi
1978 Kappa Kappa Gamma
1981 Alpha Xi Delta

NPHC WOMEN'S
1975 Alpha Kappa Alpha
1975 Delta Sigma Theta (B)
1990 Sigma Gamma Rho

PROFESSIONAL
1919 Phi Delta Phi
1924 Phi Alpha Delta
1926 Alpha Kappa Psi
1929 Delta Sigma Pi
1931 Kappa Kappa Psi
1939 Kappa Epsilon
1947 Delta Theta Phi
1949 Kappa Psi
1956 Rho Pi Phi
1958 Phi Mu Alpha—Sinfonia
1958 Pi Sigma Epsilon
1958 Tau Beta Sigma

1962 Sigma Alpha Iota
1974 Alpha Omega
1986 Alpha Rho Chi
1986 Phi Alpha Delta

OTHER PROFESSIONAL
1922 Alpha Zeta
1929 Sigma Delta Chi
1938 Beta Alpha Psi
1947 Delta Pi Epsilon
1955 Pi Lambda Theta
1975 Delta Sigma Delta
1976 Keramos

ACHS HONORS
    Omicron Delta Epsilon
1912 Phi Kappa Phi
1923 Kappa Delta Pi
1925 Phi Sigma
1926 Delta Sigma Rho-Tau
    Kappa Alpha
1928 Rho Chi
1930 Alpha Epsilon Delta
1930 Beta Gamma Sigma
1930 Phi Eta Sigma
1948 Xi Sigma Pi
1949 Phi Alpha Theta
1950 Alpha Kappa Delta
1950 Alpha Lambda Delta
1950 Pi Sigma Alpha
1951 Kappa Tau Alpha
1957 Sigma Pi Sigma
1960 Mortar Board
1961 Psi Chi
1961 Tau Beta Pi
1964 Sigma Theta Tau
1966 Alpha Sigma Mu
1966 Gamma Theta Upsilon
1966 Tau Sigma Delta
1967 Alpha Pi Mu
1967 Eta Kappa Nu
1968 Omicron Delta Kappa
1968 Pi Tau Sigma
1970 Pi Kappa Lambda
1971 Lambda Iota Tau

1979 Sigma Lambda Alpha
1980 Rho Chi

OTHER HONORS
    National Order of Omega
1938 Phi Beta Kappa
1938 Sigma Xi
1948 National Collegiate
    Players
1955 Gamma Sigma Delta
1956 Order of the Coif
1960 Alpha Omega Alpha
1962 Sigma Gamma Epsilon
1965 Pi Mu Epsilon

SERVICE
1931 Alpha Phi Omega

RECOGNITION
    Angel Flight
1920 Scabbard and Blade (2)
1936 Sigma Delta Psi
1937 National Block and Bridle
    Club
1962 Lambda Tau

INACTIVE
–52   Kappa Delta Rho
1921–65 Gamma Sigma Epsilon
1929–31 Omicron Delta Kappa
1929–35 Kappa Phi Kappa
1929–39 Pi Gamma Mu
1929–63 Alpha Tau Alpha
1940–43 Eta Mu Pi
1948–52 Sigma Tau Delta
1948–87 Zeta Beta Tau
1949   Delta Phi Alpha
1949–50 Sigma Delta Pi
1949–87 Phi Mu
1951–59 Phi Sigma Kappa
1953–74 Alpha Chi Sigma
1956–86 Phi Chi Theta
1958   Zeta Phi Eta
1959–59 Rho Epsilon
1975–83 Sigma Delta Tau

FLORIDA A & M UNIVERSITY Tallahassee, FL. University and land-grant college; coeducational; state control. Chartered as Florida State Normal and Industrial School for Negro Youth 1887; name changed to present 1953; accredited by SA.

One fraternity owns its house; others lease their houses all are located near campus.

NIC MEN'S
1933 Kappa Alpha Psi (A)

NPHC MEN'S
    Phi Beta Sigma
1932 Alpha Phi Alpha

NPHC WOMEN'S
    Zeta Phi Beta
1932 Alpha Kappa Alpha
1937 Delta Sigma Theta (B)
1946 Sigma Gamma Rho

PROFESSIONAL
1960 Kappa Kappa Psi
1960 Tau Beta Sigma
1971 Kappa Epsilon

OTHER PROFESSIONAL
1957 Alpha Beta Alpha
1969 Alpha Tau Alpha

ACHS HONORS
1944 Alpha Kappa Mu
1953 Beta Kappa Chi
1955 Kappa Delta Pi
1958 Lambda Iota Tau
1969 Psi Chi
1977 Pi Omega Pi
1987 Phi Eta Sigma

SERVICE
1952 Alpha Phi Omega
1969 Gamma Sigma Sigma

RECOGNITION
1952 Scabbard and Blade (10)
1959 Sigma Delta Psi

INACTIVE
1962–85 Pi Gamma Mu

FLORIDA ATLANTIC UNIVERSITY Boca Raton, FL. State university; established 1961; coeducational.

NIC MEN'S
    Alpha Epsilon Pi
1969 Alpha Tau Omega
1987 Pi Lambda Phi

PROFESSIONAL
1968 Phi Gamma Nu

ACHS HONORS
    Omicron Delta Epsilon
    Pi Alpha Alpha
1968 Phi Sigma Tau
1969 Phi Alpha Theta
1971 Phi Kappa Phi
1975 Pi Sigma Alpha
1985 Tau Beta Pi

OTHER HONORS
1972 Pi Mu Epsilon

RECOGNITION
1967 Sigma Delta Psi
1970 Blue Key

INACTIVE
1966–90 Delta Sigma Pi
1969–71 Alpha Omicron Pi
1969–76 Delta Gamma
1970–75 Phi Mu
1971–76 Lambda Chi Alpha
1983–83 Phi Chi Theta

COLONIES
    Phi Sigma Sigma
1989 Tau Kappa Epsilon

FLORIDA INSTITUTE OF TECHNOLOGY Melbourne, FL. Founded 1958.

NIC MEN'S
1968 Chi Phi
1970 Alpha Epsilon Pi
1972 Lambda Chi Alpha
1973 Theta Xi
1975 Tau Kappa Epsilon
1984 Kappa Alpha Psi (A)
1987 Delta Sigma Phi

NPHC MEN'S
    Phi Beta Sigma

NPC WOMEN'S
1981 Gamma Phi Beta
1982 Sigma Kappa

ACHS HONORS
1971 Eta Kappa Nu

1981 Psi Chi
1986 Tau Beta Pi
1987 Delta Mu Delta

OTHER HONORS
    National Order of Omega

RECOGNITION
1973 Beta Beta Beta

INACTIVE
1954–54 Alpha Kappa Alpha
1972–72 Theta Delta Chi

COLONIES
    Pi Lambda Phi

FLORIDA INTERNATIONAL UNIVERSITY Miami, FL. Founded in 1965. State liberal arts college; upper division only; Bachelor's and Master's Degrees.

There presently are no fraternity or sorority houses. 92% of students live off campus or commute.

NIC MEN'S
1987 Sigma Phi Epsilon
1987 Tau Epsilon Phi
1988 Phi Delta Theta
1988 Tau Kappa Epsilon

NPHC MEN'S
    Phi Beta Sigma

NPC WOMEN'S
1984 Phi Sigma Sigma
1988 Phi Mu
1989 Delta Phi Epsilon

ACHS HONORS
    Omicron Delta Epsilon

    Pi Alpha Alpha
1975 Psi Chi
1976 Sigma Pi Sigma
1978 Phi Kappa Phi
1982 Phi Eta Sigma
1985 Omicron Delta Kappa
1985 Phi Alpha Theta

OTHER HONORS
    National Order of Omega

SERVICE
1978 Alpha Phi Omega

COLONIES
1989 Delta Chi

FLORIDA MEMORIAL COLLEGE   Miami, FL.

NIC MEN'S
1966 Kappa Alpha Psi (A)

NPHC WOMEN'S
1954 Alpha Kappa Alpha
1964 Sigma Gamma Rho
1969 Delta Sigma Theta (B)

ACHS HONORS
1954 Alpha Kappa Mu
1964 Lambda Iota Tau

SERVICE
1970 Alpha Phi Omega
1975 Gamma Sigma Sigma

FLORIDA SOUTHERN COLLEGE   Lakeland, FL.
Founded 1885 as The Florida Conference College by the Methodist Church. Coeducational; undergraduate liberal arts college; private control; became Florida Southern 1935.

Fraternities occupy college-owned houses on rental basis; sorority members are required to live in dormitories.

NIC MEN'S
1938 Lambda Chi Alpha
1946 Theta Chi
1947 Pi Kappa Alpha
1948 Pi Kappa Phi
1949 Sigma Alpha Epsilon
1950 Phi Sigma Kappa
1958 Kappa Alpha Order
1959 Sigma Chi

NPC WOMEN'S
1936 Alpha Chi Omega
1946 Alpha Delta Pi
1946 Alpha Omicron Pi
1954 Phi Mu
1955 Kappa Delta
1957 Zeta Tau Alpha

PROFESSIONAL
1957 Delta Sigma Pi
1959 Phi Mu Alpha—Sinfonia
1966 Phi Chi Theta
1972 Delta Omicron

OTHER PROFESSIONAL
1977 Sigma Delta Chi

ACHS HONORS
　　　Omicron Delta Epsilon
1928 Pi Gamma Mu
1940 Kappa Delta Pi
1951 Omicron Delta Kappa

1962 Psi Chi
1969 Sigma Pi Sigma
1973 Sigma Delta Pi
1976 Kappa Mu Epsilon
1984 Phi Eta Sigma

OTHER HONORS
　　　National Order of Omega

RECOGNITION
1933 Alpha Psi Omega
1944 Kappa Pi
1953 Society for Collegiate Journalists—Pi Delta Epsilon-Alpha Phi Gamma (P)
1955 Beta Beta Beta

INACTIVE
1937–79 Delta Zeta
1938–49 Kappa Omicron Nu
1947–53 Phi Sigma Sigma
1948–85 Tau Kappa Epsilon
1949–53 National Collegiate Players
1949–90 Sigma Phi Epsilon
1951–69 Sigma Tau Delta
1955–75 Sigma Sigma Sigma
1958–76 Alpha Gamma Delta
1959–69 Kappa Sigma

FLORIDA STATE UNIVERSITY   Tallahassee, FL.
Established 1859 by the Florida Legislature; coeducational; state supported; graduate school and four undergraduate divisions.

Ten fraternities own their own houses and property, and eight fraternities occupy college-owned houses on rental basis; sororities own their own houses and property.

NIC MEN'S
1949 Alpha Tau Omega
1949 Delta Tau Delta
1949 Kappa Alpha Order
1949 Phi Kappa Tau
1949 Sigma Alpha Epsilon
1949 Theta Chi
1950 Lambda Chi Alpha
1950 Phi Delta Theta
1950 Pi Kappa Phi

1950 Sigma Nu
1950 Sigma Phi Epsilon
1951 Kappa Sigma
1961 Delta Chi
1962 Phi Kappa Psi
1967 Phi Gamma Delta
1968 Alpha Epsilon Pi
1968 Chi Phi
1968 Tau Kappa Epsilon
1969 Beta Theta Pi

1975 Kappa Alpha Psi (A)
1988 Sigma Pi
1990 Phi Sigma Kappa
1990 Zeta Beta Tau

NPHC MEN'S
　　　Phi Beta Sigma
1974 Alpha Phi Alpha

NPC WOMEN'S
1904 Kappa Delta
1908 Chi Omega
1909 Alpha Delta Pi
1916 Delta Delta Delta
1920 Sigma Kappa
1921 Pi Beta Phi
1924 Delta Zeta
1924 Kappa Alpha Theta
1924 Zeta Tau Alpha
1925 Alpha Gamma Delta
1929 Alpha Chi Omega
1929 Phi Mu
1950 Gamma Phi Beta
1951 Delta Gamma
1961 Kappa Kappa Gamma
1989 Sigma Delta Tau

NPHC WOMEN'S
1971 Alpha Kappa Alpha
1972 Sigma Gamma Rho

PROFESSIONAL
1947 Sigma Alpha Iota
1949 Alpha Kappa Psi
1949 Delta Sigma Pi
1949 Phi Mu Alpha—Sinfonia
1955 Kappa Kappa Psi
1955 Tau Beta Sigma
1968 Delta Theta Phi
1968 Phi Alpha Delta
1968 Phi Delta Phi
1969 Mu Phi Epsilon
1970 Delta Psi Kappa
1975 Gamma Iota Sigma
1978 Alpha Chi Sigma

OTHER PROFESSIONAL
1958 Phi Epsilon Kappa
1962 Beta Alpha Psi

ACHS HONORS
　　　Omicron Delta Epsilon
　　　Pi Alpha Alpha
1922 Kappa Omicron Nu
1925 Kappa Delta Pi
1925 Phi Kappa Phi
1926 Phi Alpha Theta
1931 Mortar Board
1935 Sigma Delta Pi
1938 Pi Delta Phi

1943 Pi Kappa Lambda
1949 Alpha Kappa Delta
1950 Omicron Delta Kappa
1951 Delta Sigma Rho-Tau Kappa Alpha
1954 Pi Sigma Alpha
1954 Sigma Pi Sigma
1955 Phi Eta Sigma
1956 Gamma Theta Upsilon
1956 Phi Sigma
1957 Beta Phi Mu
1959 Psi Chi
1963 Beta Gamma Sigma
1963 Phi Sigma Tau
1972 Lambda Iota Tau
1974 Sigma Theta Tau
1976 Pi Gamma Mu

OTHER HONORS
　　　National Order of Omega
1935 Phi Beta Kappa
1955 Sigma Xi
1956 Pi Mu Epsilon

SERVICE
1951 Alpha Phi Omega
1963 Gamma Sigma Sigma

RECOGNITION
　　　Angel Flight
1926 Eta Sigma Phi
1939 Iota Lambda Sigma
1955 Scabbard and Blade (12)
1964 Delta Tau Kappa
1967 Phi Delta Gamma
1968 Sigma Iota Epsilon

INACTIVE
1903–05 Kappa Alpha Order
1920–90 Sigma Sigma Sigma
1925–71 Delta Phi Epsilon
1928–80 Alpha Omicron Pi
1929–80 Alpha Xi Delta
1937　　Zeta Phi Eta
1939–52 Gamma Sigma Epsilon
1941–86 Alpha Lambda Delta
1946–69 Alpha Epsilon Delta
1949–88 Pi Kappa Alpha
1950–69 Sigma Tau Delta
1950–76 Pi Omega Pi
1951–88 Sigma Chi
1956–58 Kappa Alpha Mu
1957–83 Phi Chi Theta
1959–72 Alpha Phi
1976–79 Alpha Epsilon Phi

COLONIES
　　　Theta Xi
1990 Delta Upsilon

FLORIDA TECHNOLOGICAL UNIVERSITY   Orlando, FL. Four-year state university; coeducational. Established 1963. Degree programs in humanities and fine arts, social sciences, natural sciences, general studies, business administration, education, and engineering.

NIC MEN'S
1968 Pi Kappa Alpha

NPHC WOMEN'S
1975 Delta Sigma Theta (B)

PROFESSIONAL
1976 Sigma Alpha Iota

OTHER PROFESSIONAL
1972 Sigma Delta Chi

ACHS HONORS
1969 Sigma Pi Sigma
1973 Alpha Pi Mu

RECOGNITION
1966 Blue Key
1976 Sigma Iota Epsilon

FONTBONNE COLLEGE   St. Louis, MO. College of liberal arts for men and women; private control: Roman Catholic; chartered 1917.

ACHS HONORS
1940 Delta Epsilon Sigma
1968 Pi Delta Phi
1988 Delta Mu Delta

INACTIVE
1962–74 Pi Gamma Mu
1968–70 Sigma Delta Pi

FORDHAM UNIVERSITY   Bronx, NY. Founded as St. John's College, Fordham, June 24, 1841, under the direction of the Fathers of the Society of Jesus (Jesuits). Undergraduate liberal arts college, business, education, graduate arts and sciences, law, social service, general studies, coeducational; private control; Roman Catholic open to all qualified students regardless of race or religion, with no compulsory religious courses.

Administration does not permit national social fraternities or sororities on campus.

NIC MEN'S
1979 Kappa Alpha Psi (A)
1987 Alpha Phi Delta
1990 Delta Kappa Epsilon

PROFESSIONAL
1912 Delta Theta Phi
1940 Rho Pi Phi
1963 Alpha Kappa Psi
1964 Phi Alpha Delta

OTHER PROFESSIONAL
1920 Gamma Eta Gamma
1929 Alpha Zeta Omega
1957 Beta Alpha Psi
1970 Sigma Delta Chi

ACHS HONORS
     Omicron Delta Epsilon
1939 Beta Gamma Sigma
1961 Pi Sigma Alpha
1965 Alpha Kappa Delta
1968 Kappa Delta Pi
1970 Sigma Pi Sigma
1977 Phi Alpha Theta

1980 Psi Chi
1983 Phi Kappa Phi
1983 Psi Chi

OTHER HONORS
1958 Sigma Xi
1962 Phi Beta Kappa
1965 Iota Sigma Pi

SERVICE
1963 Alpha Phi Omega

RECOGNITION
     Angel Flight
     Arnold Air Society (A-2)
1959 Phi Lambda Upsilon

INACTIVE
1907–21 Phi Delta Epsilon
1918–34 Pi Lambda Phi
1956   Rho Chi
1963–70 Kappa Beta Pi
1966–74 Alpha Epsilon Delta

COLONIES
     Kappa Delta Rho

FORT HAYS STATE UNIVERSITY   Hays, KS. Founded in 1902 as a normal school to serve the people of Western Kansas. State, tax-supported liberal and applied arts college; coeducational; state control under Board of Regents; nonsectarian. Confers B.A., B.S., M.A., M.S., and Ed.S. degrees.

Fraternities and sororities own their own houses on their own land.

NIC MEN'S
     Tau Kappa Epsilon
1930 Phi Sigma Kappa
1942 Tau Kappa Epsilon
1953 Delta Sigma Phi
1958 Sigma Phi Epsilon
1967 Sigma Chi

NPC WOMEN'S
1925 Delta Zeta
1925 Sigma Sigma Sigma
1959 Alpha Gamma Delta

PROFESSIONAL
1927 Phi Mu Alpha—Sinfonia
1931 Sigma Alpha Iota

ACHS HONORS
     Omicron Delta Epsilon
1924 Kappa Omicron Nu
1929 Pi Omega Pi
1939 Sigma Pi Sigma
1952 Kappa Mu Epsilon
1954 Phi Kappa Phi
1956 Lambda Iota Tau
1958 Phi Eta Sigma

1959 Alpha Lambda Delta
1960 Phi Alpha Theta
1970 Psi Chi
1971 Mortar Board
1988 Phi Sigma Iota

OTHER HONORS
     National Order of Omega

SERVICE
     The National Spurs
1959 Alpha Phi Omega

RECOGNITION
1924 Pi Kappa Delta

1949 Alpha Psi Omega

INACTIVE
1926–83 Sigma Tau Gamma
1928–61 Alpha Sigma Alpha
1931–54 Pi Gamma Mu
1959–76 Sigma Kappa
1962–72 Beta Beta Beta
1962–89 Alpha Kappa Lambda
1979–83 Phi Sigma Sigma

COLONIES
1989 Kappa Sigma

FORT LEWIS COLLEGE   Durango, CO. College of liberal arts; coeducational; state control; established 1910; junior college of Colorado State University until 1948.

ACHS HONORS
1964 Phi Alpha Theta
1974 Sigma Delta Pi

1975 Beta Gamma Sigma
1978 Phi Sigma Iota
1985 Kappa Mu Epsilon

FORT VALLEY STATE COLLEGE   Fort Valley, GA. College of liberal arts; land-grant college; teachers college; coeducational; state control; established 1895.

NIC MEN'S
1948 Kappa Alpha Psi (A)

NPHC MEN'S
     Phi Beta Sigma
1946 Alpha Phi Alpha
1946 Omega Psi Phi

NPHC WOMEN'S
     Zeta Phi Beta
1941 Alpha Kappa Alpha
1944 Delta Sigma Theta (B)
1975 Sigma Gamma Rho

PROFESSIONAL
1971 Phi Mu Alpha—Sinfonia

ACHS HONORS
1951 Beta Kappa Chi
1952 Alpha Kappa Mu
1975 Phi Alpha Theta

SERVICE
1969 Alpha Phi Omega
1972 Gamma Sigma Sigma

INACTIVE
1925–33 Alpha Kappa Alpha

FORT WRIGHT COLLEGE OF THE HOLY NAMES   Spokane, WA. College of liberal arts and teachers college for women; private; Roman Catholic; established 1907.

ACHS HONORS
1969 Alpha Chi

INACTIVE
1966–82 Phi Alpha Theta

FRAMINGHAM STATE COLLEGE   Framingham, MA. Teachers and liberal arts college; coeducational; state control; established 1839.

OTHER PROFESSIONAL
1971 Phi Upsilon Omicron

ACHS HONORS
     Omicron Delta Epsilon
1966 Kappa Delta Pi
1973 Phi Alpha Theta

1976 Gamma Theta Upsilon

RECOGNITION
1961 Alpha Psi Omega

INACTIVE
1969–82 Kappa Delta Phi (C)

FRANCIS MARION COLLEGE   Florence, SC. College of liberal arts and general with limited professional programs; teacher preparatory; limited graduate program for teachers and a continuing education program, also cooperative programs with other institutions; coeducational; state supported. Established 1970.

NIC MEN'S
1974 Kappa Alpha Order
1974 Pi Kappa Alpha
1978 Alpha Tau Omega
1979 Sigma Phi Epsilon
1985 Kappa Alpha Psi (A)

NPHC MEN'S
Phi Beta Sigma
1975 Alpha Phi Alpha

NPC WOMEN'S
1974 Zeta Tau Alpha
1980 Alpha Delta Pi
1985 Kappa Delta

NPHC WOMEN'S
1975 Alpha Kappa Alpha

ACHS HONORS
Omicron Delta Epsilon
1977 Pi Gamma Mu
1978 Phi Kappa Phi
1978 Psi Chi
1979 Omicron Delta Kappa

INACTIVE
1974-82 Phi Mu
1982-85 Alpha Sigma Phi

COLONIES
Pi Kappa Phi
1986 Sigma Pi Sigma

FRANCISCAN UNIVERSITY OF STEUBENVILLE Steubenville, OH.

ACHS HONORS
1989 Psi Chi

INACTIVE
1964-89 Tau Kappa Epsilon

FRANKLIN COLLEGE OF INDIANA Franklin, IN. Founded in 1834 by pioneer Baptists. Coeducational, residential, liberal arts college, voluntarily associated with the American Baptist Convention; private control.

Fraternities own their own houses on their own land; sororities are housed in residence halls.

NIC MEN'S
1860 Phi Delta Theta
1892 Sigma Alpha Epsilon
1919 Kappa Delta Rho
1925 Lambda Chi Alpha
1988 Tau Kappa Epsilon

NPC WOMEN'S
1888 Pi Beta Phi
1912 Delta Delta Delta
1927 Zeta Tau Alpha

OTHER PROFESSIONAL
1946 Women in Communications

ACHS HONORS
1948 Phi Alpha Theta
1975 Delta Mu Delta

RECOGNITION
1921 Pi Kappa Delta
1923 Theta Alpha Phi
1927 Blue Key
1953 Chi Beta Phi
1957 Society for Collegiate Journalists—Pi Delta Epsilon-Alpha Phi Gamma (A)

INACTIVE
1871-77 Delta Tau Delta
1878-85 Delta Gamma
1879-84 Kappa Kappa Gamma
1920-90 Delta Zeta
1925   Eta Sigma Phi
1927-40 Kappa Delta Pi

FRANKLIN AND MARSHALL COLLEGE Lancaster, PA. Founded in 1787 by Benjamin Franklin and a group of Lancaster and Philadelphia citizens. Undergraduate liberal arts college for men and women; graduate programs in geology and physics in evening division only; private; nonsectarian.

Fraternities own their own houses on their own land.

NIC MEN'S
1854 Chi Phi
1854 Phi Kappa Sigma
1860 Phi Kappa Psi
1903 Phi Sigma Kappa

1915 Delta Sigma Phi
1918 Sigma Pi
1921 Phi Kappa Tau
1928 Kappa Sigma
1947 Pi Lambda Phi

NPC WOMEN'S
1978 Sigma Sigma Sigma
1982 Alpha Phi
1987 Chi Omega

ACHS HONORS
Omicron Delta Epsilon
1937 Pi Gamma Mu
1938 Sigma Pi Sigma
1948 Phi Alpha Theta

1977 Psi Chi

OTHER HONORS
1908 Phi Beta Kappa

INACTIVE
1874-95 Delta Tau Delta
1917-80 Lambda Chi Alpha
1931-88 Zeta Beta Tau
1936-48 Alpha Sigma Phi

FRANKLIN PIERCE COLLEGE Rindge, NH.

PROFESSIONAL
1974 Phi Alpha Delta

ACHS HONORS
1976 Phi Alpha Theta

FREED-HARDEMAN COLLEGE Henderson, TN. Private control: Church of Christ. Founded in 1869.

Students must live on campus or at home. No co-ed dormitories.

ACHS HONORS
1976 Alpha Chi

1985 Delta Mu Delta

FRIENDS UNIVERSITY Wichita, KS. College of liberal arts; coeducational; private control; Quakers, Established 1898.

PROFESSIONAL
1953 Mu Phi Epsilon

ACHS HONORS
1974 Sigma Delta Pi

RECOGNITION
1957 Alpha Psi Omega

1970 Kappa Pi

INACTIVE
1954-83 Phi Mu Alpha—Sinfonia

FROSTBURG STATE COLLEGE Frostburg, MD. Opened as the State Normal School at Frostburg, September 15, 1902. Became teachers college 1932, two years liberal arts added 1932, four years liberal arts added 1960. Graduate school in education; coeducational state-controlled.

Administration does not permit occupancy of special quarters by fraternities or sororities.

NIC MEN'S
1960 Sigma Tau Gamma
1983 Kappa Alpha Psi (A)

NPHC MEN'S
Phi Beta Sigma

NPC WOMEN'S
1961 Alpha Xi Delta
1989 Phi Sigma Sigma

NPHC WOMEN'S
1974 Delta Sigma Theta (B)
1977 Alpha Kappa Alpha

PROFESSIONAL
1966 Phi Mu Alpha—Sinfonia
1967 Delta Omicron

ACHS HONORS
1964 Gamma Theta Upsilon
1964 Phi Alpha Theta
1967 Pi Delta Phi
1971 Sigma Tau Delta

1972 Sigma Delta Pi
1973 Sigma Pi Sigma
1976 Psi Chi
1978 Kappa Mu Epsilon
1979 Pi Sigma Alpha
1981 Phi Eta Sigma

OTHER HONORS
National Order of Omega

RECOGNITION
1967 Beta Beta Beta
1971 Pi Kappa Delta

INACTIVE
-80   Omicron Delta Epsilon
1962-88 Tau Kappa Epsilon

COLONIES
Kappa Delta Rho
Phi Sigma Kappa
Sigma Alpha Epsilon
1989 Delta Chi

FURMAN UNIVERSITY Greenville, SC. College of liberal arts; coeducational; private control; chartered 1826; merged with Greenville Woman's College 1937.

Beginning September, 1962, the social fraternities pledged no more men, following a resolution adopted by the board of trustees of the university in June that aimed to terminate the system.

NIC MEN'S
1868 Sigma Alpha Epsilon
1909 Pi Kappa Phi
1950 Tau Kappa Epsilon
1989 Sigma Chi

NPHC MEN'S
Phi Beta Sigma

PROFESSIONAL
1938 Phi Mu Alpha—Sinfonia
1963 Mu Phi Epsilon

OTHER PROFESSIONAL
1951 Kappa Phi Kappa

ACHS HONORS
1926 Pi Gamma Mu
1927 Sigma Pi Sigma
1938 Alpha Epsilon Delta
1958 Phi Sigma Iota
1970 Pi Kappa Lambda
1971 Psi Chi
1977 Kappa Delta Pi
1981 Omicron Delta Kappa

1982 Phi Eta Sigma
1990 Phi Alpha Theta

OTHER HONORS
1973 Phi Beta Kappa

RECOGNITION
1928 Chi Beta Phi
1932 Sigma Delta Psi
1939 Alpha Psi Omega
1939 Eta Sigma Phi
1948 Blue Key
1954 Scabbard and Blade (11)
1958 Society for Collegiate Journalists—Pi Delta Epsilon-Alpha Phi Gamma (A)

INACTIVE
1858–98 Chi Psi
1872–63 Kappa Alpha Order
1915–53 Delta Sigma Phi
1942–64 Theta Chi
1951–85 Kappa Delta Epsilon

GALLAUDET UNIVERSITY Washington, DC.

NIC MEN'S
1983 Kappa Sigma

NPC WOMEN'S
1988 Delta Phi Epsilon

ACHS HONORS
1980 Phi Sigma Iota

SERVICE
1979 Alpha Phi Omega

GANNON UNIVERSITY Erie, PA. Founded in 1933, incorporated by the Commonwealth of Pennsylvania. Middle States accredited in liberal arts, business administration, science, with mechanical and electrical engineering. Undergraduate and graduate studies, coeducational; private control: Roman Catholic Diocese of Erie.

Fraternities own their own houses on their own land.

NIC MEN'S
1954 Delta Sigma Phi
1955 Tau Kappa Epsilon
1959 Alpha Phi Delta
1962 Pi Kappa Alpha
1971 Delta Chi
1982 Kappa Delta Rho

NPC WOMEN'S
1976 Alpha Gamma Delta
1985 Sigma Sigma Sigma

PROFESSIONAL
1967 Pi Sigma Epsilon
1968 Alpha Kappa Psi

OTHER PROFESSIONAL
1977 Alpha Epsilon Rho

ACHS HONORS
Omicron Delta Epsilon
1972 Sigma Pi Sigma
1982 Psi Chi
1987 Lambda Sigma Society
1987 Phi Eta Sigma
1988 Phi Sigma Iota

SERVICE
1967 Alpha Phi Omega

RECOGNITION
1958 Blue Key
1958 Scabbard and Blade (14)
1966 Beta Beta Beta

INACTIVE
1970–72 Theta Phi Alpha
1971–90 Pi Gamma Mu

GARDNER-WEBB COLLEGE Boiling Springs, NC. Private control: Baptist Church, Baptist State Convention of North Carolina. Founded in 1905. Four-year; coeducational; liberal arts college.

On campus housing available in single-sex dormitories.

ACHS HONORS
1971 Alpha Chi

1971 Sigma Tau Delta
1987 Psi Chi

GENEVA COLLEGE Beaver Falls, PA.

ACHS HONORS
1964 Lambda Iota Tau

RECOGNITION
1975 Beta Beta Beta

GEORGE MASON UNIVERSITY Fairfax, VA. A state university; College of Arts and Sciences; Professional Studies; Business Administration; Nursing; Information Technology and Engineering; School of Law; Graduate School; Continuing Education. Coeducational. Established 1957.

NIC MEN'S
1970 Kappa Sigma
1970 Tau Kappa Epsilon
1980 Sigma Phi Epsilon
1982 Theta Chi
1985 Kappa Alpha Psi (A)
1986 Pi Kappa Phi
1988 Beta Theta Pi
1989 Alpha Chi Rho
1989 Chi Phi
1989 Phi Kappa Sigma
1989 Sigma Chi

NPHC MEN'S
Phi Beta Sigma

NPC WOMEN'S
1970 Chi Omega
1972 Phi Mu
1978 Alpha Omicron Pi
1980 Zeta Tau Alpha
1988 Alpha Phi

1990 Gamma Phi Beta

NPHC WOMEN'S
1987 Alpha Kappa Alpha

PROFESSIONAL
1974 Phi Beta
1976 Delta Theta Phi

ACHS HONORS
Omicron Delta Epsilon
1970 Sigma Pi Sigma
1971 Alpha Chi
1972 Kappa Delta Pi
1974 Psi Chi
1983 Phi Sigma Tau
1983 Pi Sigma Alpha
1987 Phi Alpha Theta
1989 Gamma Theta Upsilon

COLONIES
Alpha Kappa Lambda

GEORGE PEABODY COLLEGE FOR TEACHERS Nashville, TN. Teachers college and graduate school; coeducational; private control; nonsectarian; founded as academy 1785; established as normal institute 1875; survey, and field services.

PROFESSIONAL
1946 Sigma Alpha Iota

OTHER PROFESSIONAL
1926 Phi Sigma Pi
1953 Delta Pi Epsilon

ACHS HONORS
1927 Kappa Delta Pi
1942 Pi Omega Pi

RECOGNITION
1941 Alpha Psi Omega
1959 Sigma Delta Psi

INACTIVE
1904–11 Sigma Sigma Sigma
1928 Delta Psi Kappa
1928–37 Alpha Tau Alpha
1947–81 Phi Mu Alpha—Sinfonia

THE GEORGE WASHINGTON UNIVERSITY Washington, DC. University; coeducational; private control; nonsectarian; founded 1821 as Columbian College; became George Washington University 1904.

Fraternities are permitted to own their own houses on their own land.

NIC MEN'S
1858 Sigma Alpha Epsilon
1864 Sigma Chi
1892 Kappa Sigma
1896 Theta Delta Chi
1899 Phi Sigma Kappa
1903 Delta Tau Delta
1909 Sigma Phi Epsilon
1914 Zeta Beta Tau
1915 Sigma Nu
1932 Tau Epsilon Phi
1935 Tau Kappa Epsilon
1947 Alpha Epsilon Pi
1967 Sigma Alpha Mu
1977 Alpha Phi Delta

NPC WOMEN'S
1906 Sigma Kappa
1924 Phi Sigma Sigma
1929 Kappa Kappa Gamma
1930 Alpha Epsilon Phi
1945 Delta Gamma
1961 Sigma Delta Tau
1966 Delta Phi Epsilon

NPHC WOMEN'S
1975 Delta Sigma Theta (B)
1978 Alpha Kappa Alpha

PROFESSIONAL
1884 Phi Delta Phi
1904 Phi Chi
1916 Delta Theta Phi
1920 Phi Alpha Delta
1933 Alpha Kappa Psi
1935 Theta Tau
1984 Phi Alpha Delta

OTHER PROFESSIONAL
1920 Kappa Beta Pi
1920 Phi Delta Epsilon
1930 Alpha Zeta Omega
1931 Gamma Eta Gamma
1931 Nu Beta Epsilon
1935 Pi Lambda Theta
1968 Sigma Delta Chi

ACHS HONORS
    Omicron Delta Epsilon
    Pi Alpha Alpha
1908 Delta Sigma Rho-Tau
    Kappa Alpha
1929 Omicron Delta Kappa
1929 Phi Eta Sigma
1949 Psi Chi
1952 Alpha Kappa Delta

1956 Sigma Delta Pi
1963 Tau Beta Pi
1972 Alpha Epsilon Delta
1972 Pi Delta Phi
1974 Pi Sigma Alpha
1975 Phi Alpha Theta
1979 Eta Kappa Nu

OTHER HONORS
    National Order of Omega
1926 Order of the Coif
1937 Iota Sigma Pi
1937 Sigma Xi
1945 National Collegiate
    Players
1966 Pi Mu Epsilon

SERVICE
1950 Alpha Phi Omega

RECOGNITION
    Angel Flight
1927 Phi Delta Gamma

INACTIVE
1874–88 Alpha Tau Omega
1889–68 Pi Beta Phi
1894–54 Kappa Alpha Order
1903–19 Psi Omega
1903–68 Chi Omega
1905–41 Alpha Kappa Kappa
1915–50 Phi Mu
1917 Xi Psi Phi
1920–60 Acacia
1922–30 Delta Zeta
1922–68 Alpha Delta Pi
1922–68 Kappa Delta
1923 Phi Lambda Kappa
1924–69 Zeta Tau Alpha
1925 Phi Beta Gamma
1925–34 Sigma Mu Sigma
1926 Scarab
1926–73 Alpha Chi Sigma
1927–47 Sigma Gamma Epsilon
1930–59 Pi Gamma Mu
1930–76 Alpha Lambda Delta
1936–74 Sigma Pi Sigma
1938–79 Mortar Board
1946–75 Kappa Alpha Theta
1950–63 Kappa Psi
1955–64 Rho Chi
1961–64 Kappa Epsilon

COLONIES
1868 Phi Kappa Psi
1941 Pi Kappa Alpha

GEORGETOWN COLLEGE Georgetown, KY. Founded in 1829; coeducational; Southern Baptist related; liberal arts A.B. and B.S.; M.A. in educational.

College owns fraternity and sorority houses; students are charged rent in same manner as independents living in dormitories.

NIC MEN'S
1904 Kappa Alpha Order
1906 Pi Kappa Alpha
1928 Lambda Chi Alpha
1970 Phi Kappa Tau

NPC WOMEN'S
1929 Sigma Kappa
1946 Kappa Delta
1969 Phi Mu

PROFESSIONAL
1960 Phi Mu Alpha—Sinfonia

1970 Delta Psi Kappa

ACHS HONORS
1925 Sigma Tau Delta
1950 Phi Alpha Theta
1953 Sigma Delta Pi
1956 Pi Delta Phi
1968 Alpha Lambda Delta
1989 Psi Chi

RECOGNITION
1946 Kappa Pi

GEORGETOWN UNIVERSITY Washington, DC. Founded by John Carroll in 1789; formally chartered by Congress in 1844. University; undergraduate colleges for men and women; graduate school coeducational; private control; Catholic.

Delta Phi Epsilon, the only fraternity which occupies a house, rents it from a private owner.

PROFESSIONAL
1909 Phi Alpha Delta
1910 Delta Theta Phi
1917 Alpha Omega
1921 Delta Sigma Pi

ACHS HONORS
    Omicron Delta Epsilon
1948 Phi Alpha Theta
1961 Pi Sigma Alpha
1973 Psi Chi

THE UNIVERSITY OF GEORGIA Athens, GA. Incorporated by an act of the General Assembly on January 27, 1785. Georgia was the first state to provide for establishment of a state-supported university. Doors opened to students in 1801. University; coeducational; under control of board of regents of university system of Georgia.

Fraternities and sororities have chapter houses. A majority of the houses are owned by the chapters. In some cases, the houses are owned by the university and rented to the fraternity.

1947 Alpha Psi Omega
1950 Beta Beta Beta
1953 Eta Sigma Phi
1962 Delta Phi Alpha

INACTIVE
1857–76 Phi Delta Theta
1929–68 Gamma Sigma Epsilon
1971–86 Kappa Omicron Nu

SERVICE
1956 Alpha Phi Omega

INACTIVE
1903–43 Delta Chi
1903–44 Sigma Nu Phi
1916–47 Zeta Beta Tau
1932–51 Pi Gamma Mu
1967–73 Phi Eta Sigma

NIC MEN'S
1865 Sigma Alpha Epsilon
1867 Chi Phi
1868 Kappa Alpha Order
1871 Phi Delta Theta
1871 Phi Gamma Delta
1872 Sigma Chi
1873 Sigma Nu
1878 Alpha Tau Omega
1882 Delta Tau Delta
1890 Chi Psi
1901 Kappa Sigma
1908 Pi Kappa Alpha
1915 Lambda Chi Alpha
1915 Pi Kappa Phi
1919 Tau Epsilon Phi
1926 Alpha Epsilon Pi
1927 Alpha Gamma Rho
1949 Theta Chi
1950 Phi Kappa Tau
1963 Sigma Phi Epsilon
1966 Acacia
1967 Phi Kappa Theta
1971 Kappa Alpha Psi (A)
1972 Tau Kappa Epsilon

1976 Phi Kappa Psi
1987 Beta Theta Pi

NPHC MEN'S
    Phi Beta Sigma
1969 Alpha Phi Alpha

NPC WOMEN'S
1921 Phi Mu
1922 Chi Omega
1923 Alpha Gamma Delta
1924 Kappa Delta
1924 Sigma Delta Tau
1933 Alpha Delta Pi
1934 Delta Delta Delta
1935 Alpha Omicron Pi
1935 Delta Phi Epsilon
1937 Kappa Alpha Theta
1938 Alpha Chi Omega
1939 Pi Beta Phi
1948 Kappa Kappa Gamma
1949 Zeta Tau Alpha
1961 Delta Zeta
1964 Sigma Kappa
1967 Delta Gamma
1983 Gamma Phi Beta

NPHC WOMEN'S
1969 Delta Sigma Theta (B)
1972 Alpha Kappa Alpha
1973 Alpha Kappa Alpha
1976 Alpha Kappa Alpha
1988 Sigma Gamma Rho

PROFESSIONAL
1903 Phi Rho Sigma
1904 Delta Theta Phi
1922 Alpha Kappa Psi
1922 Delta Sigma Pi
1922 Phi Delta Phi
1930 Phi Chi
1937 Phi Delta Chi
1940 Sigma Alpha Iota
1943 Zeta Phi Eta
1947 Phi Alpha Delta
1947 Phi Chi Theta
1948 Omega Tau Sigma
1950 Phi Mu Alpha—Sinfonia
1951 Kappa Psi
1954 Lambda Kappa Sigma
1954 Pi Sigma Epsilon
1956 Kappa Delta Epsilon
1975 Gamma Iota Sigma
1984 Phi Alpha Delta

OTHER PROFESSIONAL
1904 Alpha Kappa Kappa
1914 Alpha Zeta
1920 Phi Beta Pi and Theta
        Kappa Psi (B)
1928 Sigma Delta Chi
1929 Phi Delta Epsilon
1930 Women in Communications
1936 Phi Upsilon Omicron
1949 Alpha Psi
1956 Kappa Phi Kappa
1963 Beta Alpha Psi
1969 Delta Pi Epsilon

ACHS HONORS
      Omicron Delta Epsilon
      Pi Alpha Alpha
1918 Beta Gamma Sigma
1923 Phi Kappa Phi
1929 Kappa Delta Pi
1930 Kappa Tau Alpha
1930 Psi Chi
1932 Alpha Epsilon Delta
1934 Alpha Lambda Delta
1935 Omicron Delta Kappa
1938 Phi Eta Sigma
1939 Mortar Board
1941 Xi Sigma Pi

MEDICAL COLLEGE OF GEORGIA Augusta, GA. Established 1828 as Medical Academy of Georgia. Coeducational since 1920.

NPHC WOMEN'S
1976 Delta Sigma Theta (B)

ACHS HONORS
1974 Sigma Theta Tau

OTHER HONORS
1975 Sigma Xi

GEORGIA COLLEGE Milledgeville, GA. A residential comprehensive senior college founded in 1889 of the University System of Georgia, comprised of four schools: Arts and Sciences, Education, Business, and Graduate Studies; majors in over fifty areas, including undergraduate, graduate and specialist degrees.

1948 Pi Sigma Alpha
1949 Rho Chi
1951 Phi Sigma
1952 Pi Omega Pi
1955 Sigma Delta Pi
1956 Phi Alpha Theta
1964 Delta Sigma Rho-Tau
        Kappa Alpha
1965 Alpha Kappa Delta
1966 Gamma Theta Upsilon
1968 Pi Kappa Lambda
1969 Pi Delta Phi
1973 Phi Sigma Tau
1976 Phi Alpha Theta
1980 Sigma Lambda Alpha

OTHER HONORS
      National Order of Omega
1914 Phi Beta Kappa
1926 Alpha Omega Alpha
1934 Pi Mu Epsilon
1946 Sigma Xi
1961 Gamma Sigma Delta

SERVICE
1938 Alpha Phi Omega
1958 Gamma Sigma Sigma

RECOGNITION
      Angel Flight
      Arnold Air Society (C-1)
1920 Scabbard and Blade (2)
1926 Blue Key
1937 Kappa Pi
1940 Gamma Sigma Epsilon
1950 Delta Phi Alpha
1951 Iota Lambda Sigma
1959 Phi Zeta
1960 National Block and Bridle
        Club
1961 Rho Epsilon
1966 Beta Beta Beta
1973 Sigma Iota Epsilon

INACTIVE
1846–56 Beta Theta Pi
1915–85 Zeta Beta Tau
1922   Sigma Delta Kappa
1928   Alpha Psi Omega
1941–74 Sigma Pi Sigma
1948–88 Sigma Pi
1960–74 Alpha Xi Delta
1965–74 FarmHouse
1965–83 Delta Chi

COLONIES
      Sigma Tau Gamma

NIC MEN'S
1974 Kappa Sigma
1974 Pi Kappa Alpha
1975 Phi Delta Theta
1984 Pi Kappa Phi
1987 Kappa Alpha Psi (A)

NPHC MEN'S
      Phi Beta Sigma
      Phi Beta Sigma
1976 Alpha Phi Alpha

NPC WOMEN'S
1973 Phi Mu
1974 Alpha Delta Pi

1974 Delta Zeta

PROFESSIONAL
1953 Sigma Alpha Iota
1971 Phi Mu Alpha—Sinfonia

OTHER PROFESSIONAL
1946 Phi Upsilon Omicron

ACHS HONORS
1973 Phi Kappa Phi
1974 Sigma Delta Pi

INACTIVE
1929–71 Pi Gamma Mu
1977–88 Delta Sigma Pi

GEORGIA INSTITUTE OF TECHNOLOGY Atlanta, GA. Founded by Legislature, 1885; first instruction, 1888. Member of University System of Georgia, state control; undergraduate, coeducational. Fraternities own their own houses on their own land.

NIC MEN'S
1888 Alpha Tau Omega
1890 Sigma Alpha Epsilon
1895 Kappa Sigma
1896 Sigma Nu
1899 Kappa Alpha Order
1902 Phi Delta Theta
1904 Chi Phi
1904 Phi Kappa Sigma
1904 Pi Kappa Alpha
1907 Sigma Phi Epsilon
1913 Pi Kappa Phi
1916 Zeta Beta Tau
1917 Beta Theta Pi
1920 Alpha Epsilon Pi
1920 Delta Sigma Phi
1921 Delta Tau Delta
1922 Sigma Chi
1923 Chi Psi
1923 Phi Sigma Kappa
1923 Theta Chi
1926 Phi Gamma Delta
1929 Phi Kappa Tau
1942 Lambda Chi Alpha
1948 Tau Kappa Epsilon
1951 Theta Xi
1957 Delta Upsilon
1969 Phi Kappa Theta
1970 Psi Upsilon
1982 Kappa Alpha Psi (A)

NPHC MEN'S
      Phi Beta Sigma

NPC WOMEN'S
1954 Alpha Xi Delta
1972 Alpha Gamma Delta
1975 Alpha Chi Omega
1977 Alpha Delta Pi
1984 Zeta Tau Alpha
1989 Phi Mu

NPHC WOMEN'S
1979 Alpha Kappa Alpha

PROFESSIONAL
1924 Kappa Kappa Psi

1932 Alpha Chi Sigma
1962 Alpha Kappa Psi
1962 Pi Sigma Epsilon
1973 Tau Beta Sigma

OTHER PROFESSIONAL
1925 Phi Psi
1949 Delta Kappa Phi
1950 Keramos

ACHS HONORS
      Omicron Delta Epsilon
1914 Phi Kappa Phi
1925 Tau Beta Pi
1930 Phi Eta Sigma
1932 Omicron Delta Kappa
1932 Pi Tau Sigma
1941 Chi Epsilon
1941 Eta Kappa Nu
1949 Alpha Pi Mu
1949 Sigma Pi Sigma
1953 Sigma Gamma Tau
1956 Tau Sigma Delta
1978 Lambda Sigma Society
1983 Omega Chi Epsilon

OTHER HONORS
      National Order of Omega
1953 Sigma Xi
1959 Pi Mu Epsilon

SERVICE
1939 Alpha Phi Omega

RECOGNITION
      Arnold Air Society (C-1)
1921 Scabbard and Blade (2)
1947 Sigma Delta Psi
1968 Beta Beta Beta
1975 Sigma Iota Epsilon

INACTIVE
1927–33 Beta Gamma Sigma
1928   Kappa Eta Kappa
1951–60 Phi Lambda Upsilon
1965–73 Delta Sigma Pi

COLONIES
1990 Delta Chi

GEORGIA MILITARY COLLEGE Milledgeville, GA.

INACTIVE
1857–65 Sigma Alpha Epsilon

1861–65 Zeta Psi

GEORGIA SOUTHERN COLLEGE Statesboro, GA. Teachers College founded in 1908; became Georgia Southern College in 1959; member of University System of Georgia; state control; undergraduate and graduate; coeducational.

Fraternities and sororities established 1968.

NIC MEN'S
1968 Alpha Tau Omega
1968 Kappa Alpha Order
1968 Kappa Sigma
1968 Pi Kappa Phi
1968 Tau Kappa Epsilon
1969 Delta Tau Delta
1970 Sigma Chi
1970 Sigma Nu
1971 Phi Delta Theta
1979 Kappa Alpha Psi (A)

NPHC MEN'S
Phi Beta Sigma

NPC WOMEN'S
1968 Alpha Delta Pi
1968 Delta Zeta
1968 Kappa Delta
1968 Phi Mu
1968 Zeta Tau Alpha
1976 Chi Omega
1988 Alpha Omicron Pi
1990 Kappa Kappa Gamma

NPHC WOMEN'S
1977 Alpha Kappa Alpha

PROFESSIONAL
1953 Phi Mu Alpha—Sinfonia
1958 Sigma Alpha Iota
1963 Delta Sigma Pi
1973 Delta Psi Kappa

OTHER PROFESSIONAL
1957 Kappa Phi Kappa

1969 Phi Upsilon Omicron

ACHS HONORS
Omicron Delta Epsilon
Pi Alpha Alpha
1968 Sigma Delta Pi
1969 Phi Alpha Theta
1970 Pi Delta Phi
1971 Phi Kappa Phi
1981 Psi Chi
1981 Sigma Pi Sigma

OTHER HONORS
National Order of Omega

SERVICE
1960 Alpha Phi Omega

RECOGNITION
1941 Alpha Psi Omega
1971 Pi Kappa Delta
1971 Sigma Delta Psi

INACTIVE
1958–79 Kappa Delta Epsilon
1958–81 Pi Omega Pi
1968–79 Alpha Xi Delta
1968–89 Sigma Pi
1969–89 Sigma Phi Epsilon
1980–84 Alpha Gamma Delta

COLONIES
Sigma Alpha Epsilon
1972 Delta Chi

GEORGIA SOUTHWESTERN COLLEGE Americus, GA. College of liberal arts and general studies; coeducational. Established 1908.

NIC MEN'S
1969 Kappa Sigma
1969 Pi Kappa Phi
1970 Sigma Chi
1984 Kappa Alpha Psi (A)

NPHC MEN'S
1976 Alpha Phi Alpha

NPC WOMEN'S
1969 Kappa Delta
1970 Zeta Tau Alpha

NPHC WOMEN'S
1971 Delta Sigma Theta (B)
1980 Alpha Kappa Alpha

ACHS HONORS
1971 Pi Delta Phi
1973 Sigma Delta Pi
1975 Sigma Tau Delta
1976 Alpha Lambda Delta
1983 Pi Sigma Alpha
1989 Psi Chi

SERVICE
1950 Alpha Phi Omega

RECOGNITION
1970 Blue Key

INACTIVE
1972–87 Alpha Chi Omega
1974–90 Lambda Chi Alpha

GEORGIA STATE UNIVERSITY Atlanta, GA. Founded in 1914 as the Georgia Tech Evening School of Commerce; University System of Georgia, Atlanta Center, 1932; 1947–55, Atlanta division of University of Georgia. In 1955, it became Georgia State College, undergraduate college for men and women; Graduate School; state control. Became Georgia State University in 1969.

Fraternity and sorority chapter rooms are located in the Student Activities Building, and each organization rents the space from the college. Several of the fraternities own rural property with party lodges.

NIC MEN'S
1952 Alpha Epsilon Pi
1954 Pi Kappa Phi
1955 Sigma Phi Epsilon
1958 Kappa Sigma
1959 Sigma Nu
1960 Pi Kappa Alpha
1968 Tau Kappa Epsilon
1980 Kappa Alpha Psi (A)
1987 Lambda Chi Alpha

NPHC MEN'S
Phi Beta Sigma
1968 Alpha Phi Alpha

NPC WOMEN'S
1955 Delta Zeta
1956 Alpha Omicron Pi
1961 Zeta Tau Alpha
1963 Alpha Xi Delta
1987 Phi Mu

NPHC WOMEN'S
1969 Delta Sigma Theta (B)

PROFESSIONAL
1917 Alpha Kappa Psi
1921 Delta Sigma Pi
1929 Phi Chi Theta
1969 Mu Phi Epsilon
1973 Gamma Iota Sigma
1983 Delta Theta Phi
1984 Phi Alpha Delta

OTHER PROFESSIONAL
1961 Beta Alpha Psi
1969 Sigma Delta Chi
1973 Delta Pi Epsilon

ACHS HONORS
Omicron Delta Epsilon

Pi Alpha Alpha
1955 Alpha Lambda Delta
1956 Phi Eta Sigma
1960 Beta Gamma Sigma
1960 Psi Chi
1964 Sigma Tau Delta
1966 Alpha Kappa Delta
1967 Phi Alpha Theta
1968 Omicron Delta Kappa
1969 Sigma Delta Pi
1969 Sigma Pi Sigma
1970 Lambda Iota Tau
1971 Phi Kappa Phi
1972 Mortar Board
1983 Pi Sigma Alpha

OTHER HONORS
National Order of Omega

RECOGNITION
1931 Alpha Psi Omega
1940 Alpha Psi Omega
1951 Blue Key
1954 Scabbard and Blade (11)

INACTIVE
1956–78 Alpha Phi
1958–60 Delta Phi Epsilon
1959–60 Delta Mu Delta
1964 Beta Beta Beta
1965 Phi Sigma Sigma
1967–87 Delta Gamma
1968–87 Alpha Tau Omega
1968–89 Kappa Delta Epsilon
1969–76 Phi Mu Alpha—Sinfonia
1970–87 Chi Phi

GEORGIAN COURT COLLEGE Lakewood, NJ. College of liberal arts for women; private control; Roman Catholic; established 1908.

ACHS HONORS
1964 Pi Delta Phi
1964 Sigma Delta Pi
1974 Sigma Tau Delta

1977 Theta Alpha Kappa
1978 Psi Chi
1987 Delta Mu Delta
1988 Phi Alpha Theta

GETTYSBURG COLLEGE Gettysburg, PA. Founded by Rev. Samuel Simon Schmucker in 1832. First Lutheran college in America, originally named Pennsylvania College. Gettysburg College legally adopted as name in 1921. Coeducational.

Ownership of fraternity house and lot is by respective chapter alumni corporations with three exceptions; these chapters own houses on college lot. Each sorority has room in a resident hall which is rented.

NIC MEN'S
1855 Phi Kappa Psi
1858 Phi Gamma Delta
1863 Sigma Chi
1875 Phi Delta Theta
1882 Alpha Tau Omega
1883 Sigma Alpha Epsilon
1924 Lambda Chi Alpha
1925 Phi Sigma Kappa
1926 Tau Kappa Epsilon
1952 Theta Chi
1954 Sigma Nu

NPC WOMEN'S
1937 Chi Omega
1939 Delta Gamma
1949 Alpha Xi Delta
1956 Sigma Kappa
1959 Gamma Phi Beta
1961 Alpha Delta Pi

PROFESSIONAL
1967 Sigma Alpha Iota

OTHER PROFESSIONAL
1923 Kappa Phi Kappa

ACHS HONORS
     Omicron Delta Epsilon
1931 Phi Sigma Iota
1939 Phi Alpha Theta
1949 Psi Chi
1983 Pi Sigma Alpha

OTHER HONORS
     National Order of Omega
1923 Phi Beta Kappa

SERVICE
1951 Alpha Phi Omega

RECOGNITION
     Arnold Air Society (B-1)
1928 Beta Beta Beta
1931 Eta Sigma Phi
1939 Society for Collegiate
     Journalists—Pi Delta
     Epsilon-Alpha Phi Gamma
     (P)
1942 Delta Phi Alpha
1955 Alpha Psi Omega

INACTIVE
1867–72 Chi Phi
1922   Scabbard and Blade
        (3)
1926–39 Pi Gamma Mu
1939–60 Kappa Delta Epsilon
1945–70 Phi Mu
1949–61 Sigma Pi Sigma
1958–89 Alpha Chi Rho
1967–89 Phi Mu Alpha—
        Sinfonia
1979–90 Sigma Sigma Sigma

COLONIES
1928 Kappa Delta Rho

GLASSBORO STATE COLLEGE Glassboro, NJ. Coeducational; state control; established 1923; graduate division.

NIC MEN'S
1974 Tau Kappa Epsilon
1978 Alpha Phi Delta
1980 Sigma Phi Epsilon
1982 Delta Kappa Epsilon
1988 Sigma Pi

NPHC MEN'S
     Phi Beta Sigma

NPC WOMEN'S
1978 Delta Zeta
1985 Alpha Epsilon Phi
1988 Sigma Sigma Sigma

NPHC WOMEN'S
1977 Alpha Kappa Alpha
1980 Sigma Gamma Rho

OTHER PROFESSIONAL
1968 Alpha Beta Alpha
1976 Alpha Epsilon Rho

ACHS HONORS
1953 Kappa Delta Pi
1965 Pi Delta Phi
1972 Sigma Delta Pi
1977 Phi Alpha Theta
1978 Kappa Omicron Nu
1978 Pi Kappa Lambda

SERVICE
1961 Alpha Phi Omega

RECOGNITION
1962 Alpha Psi Omega

INACTIVE
1959–73 Pi Gamma Mu
1970–80 Phi Mu Alpha—
        Sinfonia
1983–89 Zeta Beta Tau

COLONIES
1989 Alpha Chi Rho
1989 Theta Chi

GLENVILLE STATE COLLEGE Glenville, WV. College of liberal arts; teachers college; coeducational; state control; established 1872.

NIC MEN'S
1964 Tau Kappa Epsilon
1971 Lambda Chi Alpha

NPC WOMEN'S
1963 Delta Zeta
1970 Sigma Sigma Sigma

ACHS HONORS
1966 Kappa Delta Pi

1974 Sigma Tau Delta
1979 Pi Gamma Mu

INACTIVE
1947–86 Theta Xi
1950–56 Sigma Tau Gamma

GMI ENGINEERING & MANAGEMENT INSTITUTE Flint, MI. Founded 1919; co-operative programs grant degrees in mechanical, industrial, and electrical engineering and management systems; all students enrolled in the programs are sponsored by plants of General Motors Corporation and over 200 companies internationally; the co-operative plan involves alternating periods of twelve weeks of class instruction at the Institute and related work experience in sponsoring units.

Fraternities and sororities own their own houses on their own land.

NIC MEN'S
1954 Theta Xi
1963 Alpha Tau Omega
1963 Delta Tau Delta
1963 Pi Kappa Alpha
1963 Sigma Chi
1963 Sigma Nu
1964 Beta Theta Pi
1964 Lambda Chi Alpha
1964 Phi Delta Theta
1964 Phi Gamma Delta
1965 Sigma Alpha Epsilon
1974 Kappa Alpha Psi (A)

NPHC MEN'S
1973 Alpha Phi Alpha

NPC WOMEN'S
1974 Theta Phi Alpha
1975 Alpha Sigma Alpha
1986 Alpha Gamma Delta

ACHS HONORS
1971 Tau Beta Pi
1978 Eta Kappa Nu
1979 Phi Eta Sigma

OTHER HONORS
     National Order of Omega

INACTIVE
1969–83 Theta Tau
1974–84 Alpha Kappa Alpha

GOLDEN GATE UNIVERSITY San Francisco, CA.

PROFESSIONAL
1972 Phi Alpha Delta

1986 Phi Alpha Delta

GONZAGA UNIVERSITY Spokane, WA. University; coeducational; private control; Roman Catholic. Established 1887.

PROFESSIONAL
1968 Phi Alpha Delta

ACHS HONORS
     Omicron Delta Epsilon
1939 Alpha Sigma Nu
1966 Kappa Delta Pi
1968 Phi Alpha Theta

1983 Theta Alpha Kappa

OTHER HONORS
1968 Pi Mu Epsilon

COLONIES
1988 Sigma Pi Sigma

GOUCHER COLLEGE Towson, Baltimore, MD. Founded 1885, liberal arts college for women; graduate school in education; private control; nonsectarian.

OTHER HONORS
1905 Phi Beta Kappa

INACTIVE
1891–50 Alpha Phi
1891–50 Delta Gamma
1893–50 Gamma Phi Beta

1896–50 Kappa Alpha Theta
1897–50 Pi Beta Phi
1898–41 Delta Delta Delta
1908–50 Alpha Gamma Delta
1933–42 Kappa Kappa Gamma

GRACELAND COLLEGE Lamoni, IA. College of liberal arts; coeducational; private control; affiliated with Reorganized Church of Jesus Christ of Latter Day Saints; established 1895.

ACHS HONORS
1967 Phi Alpha Theta

SERVICE
1948 Alpha Phi Omega

GRAMBLING STATE UNIVERSITY

Grambling, LA. College of liberal arts and teachers college; coeducational; state control; established 1901 as industrial school.

NIC MEN'S
1970 Kappa Alpha Psi (A)

NPHC MEN'S
   Phi Beta Sigma
1951 Omega Psi Phi
1952 Alpha Phi Alpha

NPHC WOMEN'S
   Zeta Phi Beta
1950 Delta Sigma Theta (B)
1951 Alpha Kappa Alpha
1960 Sigma Gamma Rho

PROFESSIONAL
1968 Delta Psi Kappa
1970 Kappa Kappa Psi
1971 Phi Mu Alpha—Sinfonia

ACHS HONORS
1950 Alpha Kappa Mu

1956 Beta Kappa Chi
1962 Kappa Delta Pi
1965 Gamma Theta Upsilon
1966 Lambda Iota Tau
1967 Kappa Omicron Nu
1971 Pi Gamma Mu
1971 Sigma Pi Sigma
1974 Pi Omega Pi
1980 Pi Sigma Alpha

OTHER HONORS
1970 Pi Mu Epsilon

SERVICE
1971 Alpha Phi Omega

RECOGNITION
1960 Sigma Delta Psi
1974 Beta Beta Beta

GRAND CANYON COLLEGE

Phoenix, AZ. Private control: Arizona Southern Baptist Convention. Founded in 1949.

Single students under 20 must live at home or on campus. Single-sex dormitories.

ACHS HONORS
1971 Alpha Chi

RECOGNITION
1963 Alpha Psi Omega

GRAND VALLEY STATE COLLEGE

Allendale, MI. Public institution. Founded in 1960.

NIC MEN'S
1970 Delta Sigma Phi
1979 Pi Kappa Phi
1983 Sigma Phi Epsilon
1987 Tau Kappa Epsilon

NPHC MEN'S
   Phi Beta Sigma
1974 Alpha Phi Alpha

NPC WOMEN'S
1984 Sigma Sigma Sigma
1987 Delta Zeta
1989 Alpha Omicron Pi

NPHC WOMEN'S
1974 Delta Sigma Theta (B)
1980 Alpha Kappa Alpha

PROFESSIONAL
1986 Delta Sigma Pi

ACHS HONORS
1974 Delta Mu Delta
1979 Phi Alpha Theta
1980 Phi Kappa Phi
1980 Pi Sigma Alpha
1990 Psi Chi

GREAT FALLS COLLEGE   Great Falls, MT.

ACHS HONORS
1965 Delta Epsilon Sigma

SERVICE
1956 Alpha Phi Omega

1959 Gamma Sigma Sigma

RECOGNITION
1969 Pi Kappa Delta

GREATER NEW HAVEN STATE TECHNICAL COLLEGE   New Haven, CT.

NPHC WOMEN'S
1984 Alpha Kappa Alpha

GREENSBORO COLLEGE   Greensboro, NC. Liberal arts college founded 1838; private: Methodist affiliated; became coeducational 1956.

NPHC WOMEN'S
1969 Delta Sigma Theta (B)

SERVICE
1964 Alpha Phi Omega

RECOGNITION
1947 Alpha Psi Omega

INACTIVE
1965–67 Pi Gamma Mu

GREENVILLE COLLEGE   Greenville, IL. College of liberal arts; coeducational; private control; affiliated with Free Methodist Church. Chartered 1892.

ACHS HONORS
1959 Phi Alpha Theta

RECOGNITION
1951 Pi Kappa Delta

1957 Beta Beta Beta

INACTIVE
1957–69 Sigma Tau Delta

GRINNELL COLLEGE   Grinnell, IA. Founded in 1846; liberal arts; coeducational; residential; private control.

OTHER PROFESSIONAL
1919 Sigma Delta Chi

ACHS HONORS
1937 Mortar Board
1951 Delta Sigma Rho-Tau
     Kappa Alpha
1962 Alpha Kappa Delta

OTHER HONORS
1908 Phi Beta Kappa

1928 National Collegiate
     Players

SERVICE
1952 Alpha Phi Omega

INACTIVE
1929–70 Pi Kappa Lambda

GROVE CITY COLLEGE   Grove City, PA. College of liberal arts and sciences; coeducational; private control; United Presbyterian Church. Chartered 1879.

ACHS HONORS
1926 Pi Gamma Mu
1947 Omicron Delta Kappa
1965 Lambda Iota Tau
1967 Kappa Mu Epsilon
1970 Sigma Pi Sigma
1972 Mortar Board
1973 Delta Mu Delta
1982 Phi Alpha Theta

SERVICE
1986 Alpha Phi Omega

RECOGNITION
   Angel Flight
   Arnold Air Society (E-1)
1957 Beta Beta Beta

INACTIVE
1953–78 Lambda Sigma Society

GUILFORD COLLEGE   Guilford College, NC.

ACHS HONORS
1963 Phi Alpha Theta
1977 Sigma Pi Sigma

SERVICE
1966 Alpha Phi Omega

INACTIVE
1977–79 Pi Gamma Mu

GUSTAVUS ADOLPHUS COLLEGE   St. Peter, MN. College of liberal arts; coeducational; church control; Minnesota Synod of Lutheran Church in America; founded 1862.

PROFESSIONAL
1959 Alpha Kappa Psi

ACHS HONORS
   Omicron Delta Epsilon
1988 Psi Chi
1989 Pi Kappa Lambda

OTHER HONORS
1949 National Collegiate
     Players

SERVICE
1948 Alpha Phi Omega

RECOGNITION
1923 Pi Kappa Delta

INACTIVE
1929–46 Pi Gamma Mu

HAHNEMANN MEDICAL COLLEGE AND HOSPITAL   Philadelphia, PA. Founded 1848.

INACTIVE
1947	Phi Beta Pi and Theta Kappa Psi (a)	1948 Phi Chi

HAMILTON COLLEGE   Clinton, NY. Founded by Samuel Kirkland in 1793 as Hamilton-Oneida Academy. Chartered as a college in 1812. Undergraduate college for men and women; private control; nonsectarian; enrollment 1,600. A.B. degree.

Ownership of fraternity house and land is by the fraternity in some instances; in others the house is owned by the fraternity but is on college-owned land.

NIC MEN'S
1831 Sigma Phi Society
1832 Alpha Delta Phi
1843 Psi Upsilon
1845 Chi Psi
1847 Delta Upsilon
1856 Delta Kappa Epsilon
1868 Theta Delta Chi
1950 Delta Phi

NPC WOMEN'S
1989 Phi Sigma Sigma

ACHS HONORS
Omicron Delta Epsilon

1922 Delta Sigma Rho-Tau Kappa Alpha
1977 Phi Sigma Iota
1977 Psi Chi

OTHER HONORS
1870 Phi Beta Kappa
1965 Sigma Xi

RECOGNITION
1952 Alpha Psi Omega

INACTIVE
1924–58 Lambda Chi Alpha
1930–71 Tau Kappa Epsilon

HAMLINE UNIVERSITY   St. Paul, MN. College of liberal arts; coeducational; private control; related to Methodist Church; chartered 1854.

One fraternity owns its house on its own land; two houses are owned by college and rented to the fraternities.

NIC MEN'S
1942 Theta Chi
1965 Alpha Tau Omega

PROFESSIONAL
1975 Phi Alpha Delta
1983 Delta Theta Phi

OTHER PROFESSIONAL
1975 Sigma Nu Phi

ACHS HONORS
1924 Pi Gamma Mu
1925 Alpha Kappa Delta
1968 Psi Chi
1976 Sigma Delta Pi

OTHER HONORS
1938 National Collegiate Players

SERVICE
1950 Alpha Phi Omega

RECOGNITION
1923 Pi Kappa Delta
1939 Beta Beta Beta

INACTIVE
1926–54 Kappa Phi Kappa
1936–52 Kappa Delta Epsilon
1956–63 Alpha Kappa Psi
1959–82 Tau Kappa Epsilon

HAMPDEN-SYDNEY COLLEGE   Hampden-Sydney, VA. College of liberal arts for men; private control; related to Southern Presbyterian Church. Chartered 1775.

Ownership of houses is by fraternities on college-owned land.

NIC MEN'S
1860 Sigma Alpha Epsilon
1867 Chi Phi
1870 Phi Gamma Delta

1872 Sigma Chi
1883 Kappa Sigma
1885 Pi Kappa Alpha
1899 Kappa Alpha Order

1914 Theta Chi
1926 Lambda Chi Alpha
1965 Sigma Nu

PROFESSIONAL
1971 Alpha Chi Sigma

ACHS HONORS
Omicron Delta Epsilon
1923 Delta Sigma Rho-Tau Kappa Alpha
1924 Omicron Delta Kappa
1962 Psi Chi
1978 Phi Alpha Theta
1978 Pi Sigma Alpha
1979 Phi Sigma Iota

OTHER HONORS
1949 Phi Beta Kappa

RECOGNITION
1921 Chi Beta Phi
1932 Alpha Psi Omega
1939 Society for Collegiate Journalists—Pi Delta Epsilon-Alpha Phi Gamma (P)
1942 Eta Sigma Phi

INACTIVE
1850–12 Beta Theta Pi
1855–00 Phi Kappa Psi
1890–94 Alpha Tau Omega

HAMPTON INSTITUTE   Hampton, VA. College of liberal arts; teachers college; technological institute; coeducational; private control; nonsectarian. Founded as Hampton Normal and Agricultural Institute 1868; name changed to present 1930.

Administration does not permit occupancy of speical quarters by fraternities or sororities.

NIC MEN'S
1947 Kappa Alpha Psi (A)

NPHC MEN'S
Phi Beta Sigma
1947 Alpha Phi Alpha
1947 Omega Psi Phi

NPHC WOMEN'S
Zeta Phi Beta
1947 Alpha Kappa Alpha
1947 Delta Sigma Theta (B)
1975 Sigma Gamma Rho

OTHER PROFESSIONAL
1950 Alpha Zeta Omega

ACHS HONORS
1940 Alpha Kappa Mu
1943 Beta Kappa Chi
1966 Delta Sigma Rho-Tau Kappa Alpha
1974 Phi Alpha Theta
1975 Psi Chi
1980 Kappa Omicron Nu
1981 Kappa Tau Alpha

COLONIES
1985 Sigma Pi Sigma

HANOVER COLLEGE   Hanover, IN. College of liberal arts; coeducational; private control; affiliated with Presbyterian Church. Chartered 1827.

There is a combination of ownership of house and land by the fraternity and of ownership by college on rental basis to fraternity and sorority.

NIC MEN'S
1853 Beta Theta Pi
1861 Phi Delta Theta
1864 Phi Gamma Delta
1871 Sigma Chi
1924 Lambda Chi Alpha

NPC WOMEN'S
1882 Kappa Alpha Theta
1913 Alpha Delta Pi
1913 Phi Mu
1987 Chi Omega

ACHS HONORS
1936 Delta Sigma Rho-Tau Kappa Alpha
1953 Alpha Lambda Delta
1957 Phi Eta Sigma
1969 Sigma Pi Sigma

1976 Mortar Board
1977 Psi Chi
1981 Pi Sigma Alpha

SERVICE
1952 Alpha Phi Omega

RECOGNITION
1928 Society for Collegiate Journalists—Pi Delta Epsilon-Alpha Phi Gamma (A)
1950 Theta Alpha Phi

INACTIVE
1872–95 Delta Tau Delta
1881–87 Delta Gamma
1930–63 Pi Gamma Mu
1950–85 Alpha Omicron Pi

HARDIN-SIMMONS UNIVERSITY   Abilene, TX. University; coeducational; private control; Baptist General Convention of Texas. Established 1891.

PROFESSIONAL
1959 Phi Mu Alpha—Sinfonia
1961 Sigma Alpha Iota
1966 Alpha Kappa Psi

ACHS HONORS
1925 Alpha Chi
1929 Pi Gamma Mu
1949 Sigma Delta Pi
1949 Sigma Tau Delta
1975 Kappa Mu Epsilon
1984 Pi Kappa Lambda

1987 Phi Alpha Theta

SERVICE
1949 Alpha Phi Omega

RECOGNITION
1928 Pi Kappa Delta
1935 Alpha Psi Omega
1954 Kappa Pi
1967 Beta Beta Beta

INACTIVE
1907–11 Phi Mu

HARDING UNIVERSITY Searcy, AR. Founded 1924 as an independent, nonsectarian school; coeducational; bachelor degrees and three degrees in the master's areas.

ACHS HONORS
1957 Alpha Chi
1960 Phi Alpha Theta
1971 Delta Mu Delta
1974 Sigma Tau Delta
1975 Kappa Delta Pi
1976 Psi Chi
1982 Pi Sigma Alpha

RECOGNITION
1940 Alpha Psi Omega

1957 Pi Kappa Delta
1957 Sigma Delta Psi
1967 Society for Collegiate
    Journalists—Pi Delta
    Epsilon-Alpha Phi Gamma
    (A)
1968 Kappa Pi

HARRIS-STOWE STATE COLLEGE St. Louis, MO. Teachers college; coeducational; municipal control; established 1857.

NIC MEN'S
1942 Kappa Alpha Psi (A)

NPHC MEN'S
    Phi Beta Sigma

NPHC WOMEN'S
1937 Sigma Gamma Rho

ACHS HONORS
1965 Gamma Theta Upsilon

RECOGNITION
1954 Kappa Pi

INACTIVE
1928–75 Delta Zeta
1930–75 Alpha Sigma Tau
1930–75 Sigma Sigma Sigma
1942–75 Sigma Tau Gamma

UNIVERSITY OF HARTFORD West Hartford, CT. Private, coeducational university founded in 1957; College of Arts and Sciences, Barney School of Business and Public Administration, College of Basic Studies, College of Education and Allied Services, College of Engineering, Hartford Art School, Hartt School of Music, Ward Technical College, Graduate Programs.

NIC MEN'S
1966 Tau Kappa Epsilon
1967 Tau Epsilon Phi
1967 Zeta Beta Tau
1969 Theta Chi
1986 Alpha Epsilon Pi
1989 Sigma Phi Epsilon

NPC WOMEN'S
1968 Alpha Xi Delta
1984 Alpha Epsilon Phi
1984 Zeta Tau Alpha
1989 Sigma Delta Tau
1990 Sigma Kappa

ACHS HONORS
    Omicron Delta Epsilon
1966 Delta Sigma Rho-Tau
    Kappa Alpha

1969 Phi Sigma Iota
1969 Psi Chi
1973 Pi Tau Sigma
1974 Alpha Chi
1981 Pi Kappa Lambda
1984 Eta Kappa Nu

OTHER HONORS
    National Order of Omega

INACTIVE
1966–69 Pi Lambda Phi
1968–72 Phi Sigma Kappa
1968–77 Delta Phi Epsilon
1969–74 Sigma Alpha Epsilon

COLONIES
1967 Sigma Alpha Mu

HARTWICK COLLEGE Oneonta, NY. Four-year liberal arts college; coeducational; thirty-one major programs of college study offered; private control; established 1928; outgrowth of Hartwick Seminary, oldest Lutheran school in U.S.; founded 1797.

The fraternities and sororities own their own houses on their own lots.

NIC MEN'S
1935 Alpha Sigma Phi
1966 Alpha Chi Rho

NPC WOMEN'S
1952 Alpha Omicron Pi

PROFESSIONAL
1950 Phi Mu Alpha—Sinfonia
1952 Sigma Alpha Iota

ACHS HONORS
    Omicron Delta Epsilon
1951 Psi Chi
1968 Phi Alpha Theta

1981 Pi Sigma Alpha

OTHER HONORS
    National Order of Omega

RECOGNITION
1950 Beta Beta Beta
1952 Alpha Psi Omega

INACTIVE
1948–55 Phi Sigma Kappa
1948–90 Delta Sigma Phi
1949–63 Zeta Tau Alpha
1949–82 Tau Kappa Epsilon

HARVARD UNIVERSITY Cambridge, MA. University for men; women admitted to graduate school of business administration, dental medicine, design, education, law, medicine, and public health. Private control; nonsectarian. Founded 1636 by general court of Massachusetts Bay Colony; named for John Harvard.

NIC MEN'S
1852 Zeta Psi
1916 Sigma Alpha Mu
1918 Tau Delta Phi
1928 Alpha Phi Delta

PROFESSIONAL
1912 Alpha Omega
1981 Phi Alpha Delta

OTHER PROFESSIONAL
1933 Pi Lambda Theta

ACHS HONORS
    Omicron Delta Epsilon
1909 Delta Sigma Rho-Tau
    Kappa Alpha

OTHER HONORS
1781 Phi Beta Kappa
1906 Alpha Omega Alpha
1930 Omicron Kappa Upsilon
1931 Sigma Xi

INACTIVE
1837–07 Alpha Delta Phi
1843–01 Beta Theta Pi
1845–01 Delta Phi
1850–73 Psi Upsilon
1850–32 Alpha Sigma Phi

1851–91 Delta Kappa Epsilon
1856–16 Theta Delta Chi
1865–67 Phi Kappa Sigma
1881–42 Delta Upsilon
1885–87 Chi Phi
1887–09 Phi Delta Phi
1891–44 Delta Sigma Delta
1893–79 Sigma Alpha Epsilon
1896–00 Pi Lambda Phi
1897–65 Psi Omega
1899   Xi Psi Phi
1902–23 Phi Rho Sigma
1905–33 Kappa Sigma
1906–34 Acacia
1912–45 Alpha Chi Sigma
1913   Phi Beta Pi and Theta
        Kappa Psi (a)
1914–33 Zeta Beta Tau
1916–18 Alpha Kappa Psi
1916–32 Lambda Chi Alpha
1916–33 Phi Delta Epsilon
1921   Phi Beta Pi and Theta
        Kappa Psi (B)
1921–35 Phi Chi
1923   Gamma Alpha
1923–36 Tau Beta Pi
1927   Phi Lambda Kappa

HASTINGS COLLEGE Hastings, NB. Chartered 1882, college of liberal arts; coeducational; private control; affiliated with Presbyterian Church.

The administration does not permit occupancy of special housing.

PROFESSIONAL
1911 Phi Alpha Delta
1986 Phi Mu Alpha—Sinfonia

ACHS HONORS
1947 Alpha Chi
1982 Psi Chi

1987 Phi Alpha Theta
1989 Phi Sigma Iota

1959 Kappa Pi

RECOGNITION
1920 Pi Kappa Delta
1942 Alpha Psi Omega

INACTIVE
1887–87 Pi Beta Phi
1928–46 Pi Gamma Mu

HASTINGS COLLEGE OF LAW San Francisco, CA.

PROFESSIONAL
1949 Delta Theta Phi
1983 Phi Delta Phi

INACTIVE
1924–57 Kappa Beta Pi
1926 Sigma Delta Kappa

OTHER HONORS
1954 Order of the Coif

HAVERFORD COLLEGE Haverford, PA. College of liberal arts for men; private control; Quaker Society of Friends; chartered 1832.

OTHER HONORS
1899 Phi Beta Kappa

1891–92 Alpha Tau Omega

INACTIVE
1884–90 Phi Kappa Sigma

UNIVERSITY OF HAWAII Honolulu, HI. University and land-grant college; coeducational; state control; established 1907.

PROFESSIONAL
1961 Pi Sigma Epsilon
1969 Sigma Alpha Iota
1982 Delta Theta Phi

OTHER PROFESSIONAL
1964 Phi Upsilon Omicron
1964 Pi Lambda Theta
1970 Sigma Delta Chi
1974 Beta Alpha Psi

ACHS HONORS
Omicron Delta Epsilon
1930 Phi Kappa Phi
1947 Delta Sigma Rho-Tau
Kappa Alpha
1957 Chi Epsilon
1959 Psi Chi
1963 Eta Kappa Nu
1964 Phi Eta Sigma
1965 Pi Delta Phi
1966 Alpha Lambda Delta
1968 Beta Gamma Sigma
1968 Beta Phi Mu
1969 Pi Tau Sigma
1971 Sigma Delta Pi

1979 Pi Sigma Alpha
1984 Pi Kappa Lambda

OTHER HONORS
1947 Sigma Xi
1952 Phi Beta Kappa
1968 Gamma Sigma Delta

SERVICE
1957 Alpha Phi Omega

RECOGNITION
Angel Flight
Arnold Air Society (I)
1938 Sigma Delta Psi
1962 Delta Phi Alpha
1967 Sigma Phi Alpha

INACTIVE
1921–35 Theta Alpha Phi
1929–60 Pi Gamma Mu
1954–63 Sigma Pi Sigma
1955–70 Omicron Delta Kappa
1958–60 Pi Omega Pi

COLONIES
Beta Theta Pi

UNIVERSITY OF HAWAII AT HILO Hilo, HI.

PROFESSIONAL
1989 Delta Sigma Pi

1985 Phi Alpha Theta

ACHS HONORS
1976 Gamma Theta Upsilon

UNIVERSITY OF HAWAII AT MANOA Manoa, HI.

ACHS HONORS
1965 Mortar Board

1978 Kappa Tau Alpha
1984 Phi Alpha Theta

HAWAII PACIFIC COLLEGE Honolulu, HI.

ACHS HONORS
1983 Delta Mu Delta

HEIDELBERG COLLEGE Tiffin, OH. Founded by the Ohio Synod of the Reformed Church in the United States; now affiliated with the United Church of Christ. Formally opened on November 11, 1850. Undergraduate; coeducational.

ACHS HONORS
1928 Kappa Delta Pi
1951 Phi Alpha Theta
1965 Phi Sigma Iota
1972 Sigma Tau Delta
1975 Sigma Pi Sigma
1984 Psi Chi
1986 Alpha Lambda Delta
1988 Omicron Delta Kappa

RECOGNITION
1921 Pi Kappa Delta
1936 Alpha Psi Omega
1951 Kappa Pi
1954 Eta Sigma Phi
1965 Delta Phi Alpha

INACTIVE
1922–34 Theta Alpha Phi

OTHER HONORS
National Order of Omega

HENDERSON STATE UNIVERSITY Arkadelphia, AR. Founded in 1929; supported largely by legislative appropriations; coeducational; offers degrees of B.S.E.; B.A.; B.S.; B.M.; and B.M.E.; B.S., B.A. at undergraduate level and M.S.Ed. at the graduate level.

The fraternities share an IFC facility. One group owns its house. Sorority members live in residence halls.

NIC MEN'S
1946 Phi Lambda Chi
1946 Phi Sigma Kappa
1946 Sigma Tau Gamma
1954 Sigma Phi Epsilon
1975 Kappa Alpha Psi (A)

NPHC MEN'S
Phi Beta Sigma
1973 Alpha Phi Alpha

NPC WOMEN'S
1946 Alpha Sigma Alpha
1946 Alpha Sigma Tau
1946 Delta Zeta
1961 Alpha Xi Delta

NPHC WOMEN'S
1972 Delta Sigma Theta (B)
1973 Alpha Kappa Alpha

PROFESSIONAL
1967 Delta Omicron
1968 Phi Mu Alpha—Sinfonia

ACHS HONORS
1938 Kappa Delta Pi
1946 Phi Alpha Theta
1953 Alpha Chi
1973 Sigma Pi Sigma
1974 Sigma Tau Delta

OTHER HONORS
National Order of Omega

RECOGNITION
1963 Scabbard and Blade (15)
1976 Beta Beta Beta

INACTIVE
1934–39 Pi Gamma Mu
1946–74 Sigma Sigma Sigma

COLONIES
Kappa Alpha Order
Theta Xi
1947 Theta Xi

HENDRIX COLLEGE Conway, AR. Founded as Central Collegiate at Altus, AR, in 1884; moved to Conway in 1890; liberal arts; coeducational; Methodist; 600 enrollment.

PROFESSIONAL
1948 Mu Phi Epsilon

ACHS HONORS
1926 Alpha Chi
1957 Alpha Epsilon Delta

OTHER HONORS
1976 Pi Mu Epsilon

SERVICE
1949 Alpha Phi Omega

RECOGNITION
1936 Alpha Psi Omega
1941 Blue Key
1949 Cardinal Key

INACTIVE
1940–55 Phi Mu Alpha—
     Sinfonia

HERBERT H. LEHMAN COLLEGE Bronx, NY.
Dedicated as a separate college of the City University of New York in 1968. Beginning in 1931 as a division of Hunter College. Lehman College has become a coeducational senior liberal arts institution offering baccalaureate and advanced degree programs. A nonresidential college in a residence area of the northern Bronx, the student body is drawn largely from the five boroughs of New York City and the New York counties north of the city. Situated upon a 37-acre campus, Herbert H. Lehman College has the atmosphere and facilities of a non-urban campus.

NPHC WOMEN'S
1983 Alpha Kappa Alpha

1971 Phi Beta Kappa

ACHS HONORS
     Omicron Delta Epsilon
1969 Sigma Delta Pi
1970 Pi Delta Phi
1971 Kappa Delta Pi

SERVICE
1954 Alpha Phi Omega

OTHER HONORS
1968 Pi Mu Epsilon

INACTIVE
1968   Phi Sigma Sigma
1968–72 Delta Phi Epsilon
1968–73 Sigma Delta Tau

HIGH POINT COLLEGE High Point, NC.
College of liberal arts and teachers college; coeducational; private control; nonsectarian; affiliated with Methodist Church. Chartered 1920.

NIC MEN'S
1953 Pi Kappa Alpha
1954 Lambda Chi Alpha
1954 Theta Chi
1956 Delta Sigma Phi

NPC WOMEN'S
1953 Phi Mu
1955 Alpha Gamma Delta
1955 Kappa Delta
1957 Zeta Tau Alpha

ACHS HONORS
1965 Kappa Delta Pi
1970 Delta Mu Delta
1976 Alpha Chi

1984 Phi Sigma Iota
1988 Psi Chi

SERVICE
1958 Alpha Phi Omega

RECOGNITION
1966 Society for Collegiate Journalists—Pi Delta Epsilon-Alpha Phi Gamma (A)

INACTIVE
1953–65 Sigma Phi Epsilon
1954–66 Tau Kappa Epsilon

HILLSDALE COLLEGE Hillsdale, MI. Founded
1844 at Spring Arbor, the first college in Michigan to admit women on a par with men; in 1853 moved to Hillsdale; Dickerson, the first gymnasium in the state; college of liberal arts; coeducational; privately endowed.

The fraternities occupy their own houses on land which they own; the sororities occupy college-owned quarters on rental basis.

NIC MEN'S
1867 Delta Tau Delta
1883 Sigma Chi
1888 Alpha Tau Omega
1915 Delta Sigma Phi
1963 Tau Kappa Epsilon

NPC WOMEN'S
1881 Kappa Kappa Gamma
1887 Pi Beta Phi
1924 Chi Omega
1983 Alpha Xi Delta

PROFESSIONAL
1925 Sigma Alpha Iota
1965 Phi Mu Alpha—Sinfonia

ACHS HONORS
1949 Omicron Delta Kappa
1967 Lambda Iota Tau
1976 Phi Alpha Theta
1977 Psi Chi

RECOGNITION
1949 Alpha Psi Omega
1976 Beta Beta Beta
1976 Sigma Zeta

INACTIVE
1882–98 Phi Delta Theta
1922–34 Theta Alpha Phi
1927–38 Sigma Tau Delta
1965–89 Phi Sigma Kappa

HIRAM COLLEGE Hiram, OH. College of liberal
arts; coeducational; private control; founded by members of the Disciples of Christ, but not under church control; nonsectarian; chartered 1850.

ACHS HONORS
     Omicron Delta Epsilon
1954 Phi Sigma Iota
1962 Delta Sigma Rho-Tau Kappa Alpha
1962 Omicron Delta Kappa
1963 Kappa Delta Pi
1963 Pi Gamma Mu
1984 Alpha Lambda Delta

OTHER HONORS
1971 Phi Beta Kappa

SERVICE
1950 Alpha Phi Omega

RECOGNITION
1930 Theta Alpha Phi
1935 Sigma Delta Psi
1952 Beta Beta Beta

HOBART COLLEGE Geneva, NY. The oldest liberal
arts college in western New York. Founded in 1822 by John Henry Hobart, Bishop of the Episcopal Diocese of New York. Undergraduate college for men, private control.

The fraternities own their own houses on their own land.

NIC MEN'S
1840 Alpha Delta Phi
1840 Sigma Phi Society
1844 Kappa Alpha Society
1857 Theta Delta Chi
1860 Chi Phi
1892 Sigma Chi
1935 Kappa Sigma
1948 Delta Chi
1950 Phi Sigma Kappa

ACHS HONORS
     Omicron Delta Epsilon

1940 Phi Sigma Iota

OTHER HONORS
1871 Phi Beta Kappa

RECOGNITION
     Arnold Air Society (E-1)

INACTIVE
1881–92 Phi Kappa Psi
1952–85 Phi Kappa Tau
1954–79 Pi Gamma Mu
1965–79 Tau Kappa Epsilon
1968–75 Pi Lambda Phi

HOFSTRA UNIVERSITY Hempstead, NY. Coeducational
at undergraduate and graduate levels; private control; nonsectarian; residence facilities. Founded in 1935 as a memorial to William S. Hofstra, first known as Nassau College Hofstra Memorial, and under the academic jurisdiction of New York University during its first four years. In 1939, Hofstra became independent and in 1940 was granted an absolute charter by the New York State Board of Regents. With another charter change in 1963, Hofstra attained university status. Within the university there now are: the Hofstra College of Liberal Arts and Sciences; a school of business; a school of education; New College, an experimental branch; and University College for the more mature students, most of whom study during evening hours. Hofstra received approval of the Regents to open a law school in 1970.

NIC MEN'S
1969 Phi Sigma Kappa
1969 Tau Epsilon Phi
1969 Tau Kappa Epsilon
1969 Zeta Beta Tau
1979 Kappa Alpha Psi (A)
1985 Kappa Delta Rho
1987 Alpha Epsilon Pi
1988 Sigma Alpha Mu
1988 Sigma Pi

NPC WOMEN'S
1986 Sigma Delta Tau
1987 Sigma Sigma Sigma
1988 Delta Phi Epsilon
1989 Alpha Epsilon Phi
1989 Phi Sigma Sigma

NPHC WOMEN'S
1976 Alpha Kappa Alpha

PROFESSIONAL
1958 Pi Sigma Epsilon
1976 Phi Alpha Delta

OTHER PROFESSIONAL
1976 Beta Alpha Psi

ACHS HONORS
      Omicron Delta Epsilon
1941 Sigma Delta Pi
1942 Kappa Mu Epsilon
1944 Phi Alpha Theta

1949 Pi Gamma Mu
1950 Psi Chi
1951 Sigma Pi Sigma
1954 Kappa Delta Pi
1959 Alpha Epsilon Delta
1963 Pi Delta Phi
1969 Beta Gamma Sigma
1974 Pi Kappa Lambda
1976 Pi Sigma Alpha

OTHER HONORS
      National Order of Omega
1973 Phi Beta Kappa

RECOGNITION
1943 Beta Beta Beta
1951 Alpha Psi Omega
1953 Society for Collegiate
      Journalists—Pi Delta
      Epsilon-Alpha Phi Gamma
      (P)
1954 Kappa Pi
1954 Scabbard and Blade (11)

INACTIVE
1962–65 Phi Beta

COLONIES
      Pi Lambda Phi
1989 Kappa Sigma
1990 Chi Phi

HOLLINS COLLEGE   Hollins College, VA. College of liberal arts for women; private control; nonsectarian; established 1842.

ACHS HONORS
      Omicron Delta Epsilon
1959 Psi Chi
1977 Phi Alpha Theta
1980 Omicron Delta Kappa

OTHER HONORS
1962 Phi Beta Kappa

INACTIVE
1902–12 Kappa Delta

1904–29 Phi Mu
1905–14 Sigma Sigma Sigma
1914–29 Delta Delta Delta
1916–29 Gamma Phi Beta
1917–30 Pi Beta Phi
1919–29 Chi Omega
1921–29 Zeta Tau Alpha

COLLEGE OF THE HOLY CROSS   Worcester, MA. College of liberal arts; coeducational; private control; Roman Catholic Church; established by Bishop of Boston and first instruction 1843.

ACHS HONORS
      Omicron Delta Epsilon
1940 Alpha Sigma Nu
1941 Delta Epsilon Sigma
1965 Psi Chi
1966 Phi Alpha Theta
1970 Sigma Pi Sigma
1971 Phi Sigma Iota
1975 Pi Sigma Alpha

OTHER HONORS
1967 Pi Mu Epsilon
1974 Phi Beta Kappa

RECOGNITION
1964 Eta Sigma Phi

INACTIVE
1970–72 Kappa Delta Epsilon

HOLY FAMILY COLLEGE   Philadelphia, PA. College of liberal arts for women; private control; related to Roman Catholic Church; chartered in 1954.

ACHS HONORS
1959 Lambda Iota Tau
1968 Psi Chi
1971 Kappa Mu Epsilon

1983 Phi Sigma Iota

RECOGNITION
1970 Beta Beta Beta

HOLY NAMES COLLEGE   Oakland, CA. College of liberal arts; graduate school; coeducational; Roman Catholic; established 1868.

PROFESSIONAL
1959 Mu Phi Epsilon

ACHS HONORS
1954 Pi Gamma Mu

1959 Pi Delta Phi
1989 Psi Chi

HOOD COLLEGE   Frederick, MD. College of liberal arts for women; private control; affiliated with United Church of Christ; organized 1893.

ACHS HONORS
      Omicron Delta Epsilon
1948 Mortar Board
1974 Psi Chi
1975 Phi Kappa Phi
1975 Sigma Delta Pi
1976 Kappa Omicron Nu

1976 Pi Delta Phi

RECOGNITION
1940 Alpha Psi Omega
1947 Beta Beta Beta

INACTIVE
1906–07 Sigma Sigma Sigma

HOPE COLLEGE   Holland, MI. College of liberal arts; coeducational; private control; Reformed Church of America. Established 1851.

PROFESSIONAL
1972 Delta Omicron

ACHS HONORS
      Omicron Delta Epsilon
1950 Phi Alpha Theta
1960 Alpha Epsilon Delta
1961 Mortar Board
1962 Pi Delta Phi
1965 Psi Chi
1965 Sigma Delta Pi
1971 Lambda Iota Tau
1975 Pi Sigma Alpha
1982 Sigma Pi Sigma
1987 Pi Kappa Lambda

OTHER HONORS
1951 National Collegiate
      Players
1971 Phi Beta Kappa
1972 Pi Mu Epsilon

SERVICE
1960 Alpha Phi Omega

RECOGNITION
1932 Blue Key
1950 Beta Beta Beta
1951 Delta Phi Alpha
1958 Eta Sigma Phi

INACTIVE
1961–82 Phi Mu Alpha—
        Sinfonia

HOUGHTON COLLEGE   Houghton, NY.

ACHS HONORS
1979 Phi Alpha Theta
1988 Pi Kappa Lambda

SERVICE
1953 Alpha Phi Omega

UNIVERSITY OF HOUSTON   Houston, TX. University; coeducational; legally public, administered and financed by State; established as a junior college 1927; became four-year college in 1934.

Fraternities and sororities are permitted to own their own houses on their own land.

NIC MEN'S
      Alpha Epsilon Pi
1956 Phi Kappa Theta
1956 Phi Sigma Kappa
1956 Pi Kappa Alpha
1956 Sigma Alpha Epsilon
1956 Sigma Chi
1956 Sigma Nu
1956 Sigma Phi Epsilon
1956 Tau Kappa Epsilon
1967 Sigma Alpha Mu
1968 Alpha Epsilon Pi

1973 Delta Upsilon
1974 Kappa Alpha Psi (A)
1977 Beta Theta Pi

NPHC MEN'S
      Phi Beta Sigma
      Phi Beta Sigma

NPC WOMEN'S
1956 Alpha Chi Omega
1956 Chi Omega
1956 Delta Gamma
1956 Delta Zeta

1956 Phi Mu
1956 Zeta Tau Alpha

NPHC WOMEN'S
1969 Alpha Kappa Alpha
1969 Delta Sigma Theta (B)
1973 Sigma Gamma Rho
1986 Alpha Kappa Alpha

PROFESSIONAL
1948 Phi Beta
1950 Kappa Kappa Psi
1950 Tau Beta Sigma
1953 Kappa Epsilon
1953 Phi Delta Chi
1953 Phi Delta Phi
1953 Sigma Alpha Iota
1955 Delta Theta Phi
1958 Alpha Chi Sigma
1963 Kappa Psi
1963 Phi Alpha Delta
1966 Phi Mu Alpha—Sinfonia
1969 Delta Sigma Pi
1973 Delta Psi Kappa
1973 Phi Gamma Nu

OTHER PROFESSIONAL
1947 Kappa Alpha Mu
1949 Sigma Delta Chi
1950 Women in Communications
1955 Kappa Beta Pi
1956 Delta Pi Epsilon
1960 Phi Upsilon Omicron
1966 Beta Alpha Psi

ACHS HONORS
     Omicron Delta Epsilon
1949 Phi Kappa Phi
1951 Kappa Delta Pi
1952 Pi Delta Phi
1952 Sigma Delta Pi
1956 Alpha Epsilon Delta
1956 Alpha Kappa Delta
1956 Sigma Pi Sigma
1957 Phi Alpha Theta
1958 Psi Chi
1958 Rho Chi
1960 Alpha Pi Mu
1960 Omicron Delta Kappa

UNIVERSITY OF HOUSTON AT CLEAR LAKE
Clear Lake, TX.

ACHS HONORS
     Pi Alpha Alpha
1980 Phi Kappa Phi
1984 Omicron Delta Kappa
1985 Psi Chi
1989 Phi Alpha Theta

UNIVERSITY OF HOUSTON AT VICTORIA Victoria, TX.

PROFESSIONAL
1990 Delta Sigma Pi

ACHS HONORS
1982 Phi Kappa Phi

1989 Psi Chi

HOUSTON BAPTIST UNIVERSITY Houston, TX.
College of liberal arts and general; teacher preparatory; professional; coeducational. Southern Baptist affiliation. Established 1960.

NIC MEN'S
1972 Kappa Alpha Order
1973 Alpha Tau Omega

NPC WOMEN'S
1977 Kappa Delta
1978 Phi Mu

1962 Pi Omega Pi
1962 Tau Beta Pi
1964 Beta Gamma Sigma
1964 Eta Kappa Nu
1965 Alpha Lambda Delta
1965 Phi Eta Sigma
1966 Pi Tau Sigma
1970 Mortar Board
1972 Chi Epsilon
1974 Gamma Theta Upsilon
1975 Omega Chi Epsilon
1989 Pi Kappa Lambda
1990 Pi Gamma Mu

OTHER HONORS
     National Order of Omega
1951 Sigma Gamma Epsilon
1966 Iota Sigma Pi
1966 Sigma Xi
1974 Pi Mu Epsilon

SERVICE
1947 Alpha Phi Omega
1953 Gamma Sigma Sigma

RECOGNITION
1926 Alpha Psi Omega
1955 Kappa Pi
1956 Scabbard and Blade (13)
1957 Sigma Iota Epsilon
1961 Delta Phi Alpha
1967 Beta Beta Beta

INACTIVE
1956–59 Pi Kappa Phi
1956–60 Alpha Delta Pi
1956–60 Alpha Phi
1956–60 Kappa Alpha Order
1956–66 Zeta Beta Tau
1957–86 Lambda Chi Alpha
1961–88 Theta Tau
1965–71 Sigma Delta Tau
1969–71 Acacia
1972–82 Alpha Rho Chi

COLONIES
     Theta Tau
1956 Delta Chi
1956 Delta Sigma Phi

PROFESSIONAL
1972 Sigma Alpha Iota

ACHS HONORS
1971 Alpha Chi
1971 Sigma Tau Delta
1972 Omicron Delta Kappa
1975 Psi Chi
1976 Alpha Epsilon Delta
1987 Theta Alpha Kappa

SERVICE
1990 Alpha Phi Omega

RECOGNITION
1969 Pi Kappa Delta

INACTIVE
1969–88 Phi Mu Alpha—Sinfonia

HOWARD UNIVERSITY Washington, DC.
Founded by General Oliver Otis Howard, chartered in 1867. Private control, coeducational nonsectarian; consisting of 17 schools and colleges; undergraduate, graduate, and professional.

NIC MEN'S
1879 Sigma Nu
1976 Kappa Alpha Psi (A)

NPHC MEN'S
     Phi Beta Sigma
1907 Alpha Phi Alpha
1911 Omega Psi Phi
1926 Omega Psi Phi

NPHC WOMEN'S
     Zeta Phi Beta
1908 Alpha Kappa Alpha
1913 Delta Sigma Theta (B)
1938 Sigma Gamma Rho

PROFESSIONAL
1935 Kappa Psi
1952 Phi Mu Alpha—Sinfonia
1959 Alpha Omega
1965 Sigma Alpha Iota
1966 Phi Alpha Delta
1970 Delta Theta Phi
1980 Delta Sigma Pi
1981 Gamma Iota Sigma
1984 Kappa Epsilon

OTHER PROFESSIONAL
1929 Kappa Phi Kappa

ACHS HONORS
     Omicron Delta Epsilon
     Pi Alpha Alpha
1929 Beta Kappa Chi
1947 Psi Chi
1948 Pi Kappa Lambda
1949 Sigma Pi Sigma
1952 Alpha Kappa Delta
1952 Pi Delta Phi

1954 Kappa Delta Pi
1956 Phi Alpha Theta
1956 Pi Sigma Alpha
1956 Tau Beta Pi
1958 Delta Sigma Rho-Tau Kappa Alpha
1959 Sigma Delta Pi
1960 Rho Chi
1963 Kappa Omicron Nu
1970 Sigma Delta Pi
1971 Tau Sigma Delta
1976 Sigma Theta Tau
1977 Beta Gamma Sigma
1982 Omega Chi Epsilon

OTHER HONORS
1948 Omicron Kappa Upsilon
1951 Pi Mu Epsilon
1953 Phi Beta Kappa
1955 Alpha Omega Alpha
1957 Sigma Xi

SERVICE
1948 Alpha Phi Omega
1963 Gamma Sigma Sigma

RECOGNITION
     Angel Flight
     Arnold Air Society (B-1)
1949 Delta Phi Alpha
1950 Scabbard and Blade (9)
1956 Eta Sigma Phi
1959 Sigma Phi Alpha

INACTIVE
1961–69 Kappa Mu Epsilon
1963–74 Kappa Beta Pi
1975–88 Alpha Omega

HOWARD PAYNE UNIVERSITY Brownwood, TX.
College of liberal arts; coeducational; private control; established 1889; graduate division instituted 1959.

NIC MEN'S
1920 Kappa Alpha Psi (A)

PROFESSIONAL
1965 Phi Mu Alpha—Sinfonia
1966 Delta Omicron
1971 Kappa Kappa Psi

ACHS HONORS
     Sigma Tau Delta
1925 Alpha Chi

1958 Kappa Delta Pi
1962 Alpha Lambda Delta
1976 Pi Gamma Mu

SERVICE
1967 Alpha Phi Omega

RECOGNITION
1924 Pi Kappa Delta
1963 Blue Key

HUMBOLDT STATE UNIVERSITY Arcata, CA. Public institution. Founded in 1913. Four-year; coeducational.

84% of students live off-campus or commute.

NIC MEN'S
1958 Delta Sigma Phi
1987 Chi Phi

NPC WOMEN'S
1988 Delta Phi Epsilon

OTHER PROFESSIONAL
1976 Sigma Delta Chi

ACHS HONORS
1973 Xi Sigma Pi
1981 Pi Gamma Mu
1984 Psi Chi
1986 Kappa Tau Alpha

1986 Omicron Delta Kappa
1987 Phi Kappa Phi

SERVICE
1949 Intercollegiate Knights
1968 Alpha Phi Omega

RECOGNITION
1928 Alpha Psi Omega
1956 Pi Kappa Delta

INACTIVE
1959–71 Delta Zeta
1960–77 Tau Kappa Epsilon
1967–76 Phi Mu

HUNTER COLLEGE New York, NY. Opened as Female Normal and High School, 1870; by legislative action became Normal College of the City of New York with Thomas Hunter as first president. In 1914, name changed to Hunter College of the City of New York; in 1961, to Hunter College of the City University of New York (CUNY). Evening classes began in 1917; graduate studies were introduced in 1921, open to women and men; in 1964 the entire college, with its professional schools of nursing, social work, and health sciences, became coeducational; in 1968, its Bronx campus became independent under the name of Lehman College/CUNY. Second oldest college in CUNY, Hunter is today the largest of the CUNY units and the only one with a residence hall.

NIC MEN'S
1952 Tau Delta Phi
1987 Zeta Beta Tau

PROFESSIONAL
1951 Delta Omicron

OTHER PROFESSIONAL
1964 Delta Pi Epsilon

ACHS HONORS
Omicron Delta Epsilon
1928 Sigma Delta Pi
1928 Sigma Tau Delta
1931 Phi Sigma
1946 Pi Delta Phi
1950 Psi Chi
1954 Phi Alpha Theta
1958 Kappa Delta Pi
1960 Pi Sigma Alpha
1970 Sigma Pi Sigma
1970 Sigma Theta Tau

OTHER HONORS
1920 Phi Beta Kappa
1925 Pi Mu Epsilon
1951 Iota Sigma Pi
1969 Sigma Xi

SERVICE
1989 Alpha Phi Omega

RECOGNITION
1936 Delta Phi Alpha
1954 Kappa Pi
1974 Pi Kappa Delta

INACTIVE
1909–70 Alpha Epsilon Phi
1913–64 Kappa Delta
1913–76 Phi Sigma Sigma
1922–40 Chi Omega
1922–83 Delta Phi Epsilon
1925–71 Alpha Xi Delta
1927–64 Alpha Delta Pi
1928 Eta Sigma Phi
1937–63 Alpha Gamma Delta
1946–71 Delta Zeta
1952–65 Phi Upsilon Omicron
1960–73 Sigma Delta Tau
1966–71 Sigma Alpha Mu
1967–70 Pi Lambda Phi
1968–70 Alpha Epsilon Pi

COLONIES
1990 Tau Kappa Epsilon

HUNTINGDON COLLEGE Montgomery, AL. College of liberal arts; coeducational; private control; related to the Methodist Episcopal Church. Estab-

lished as Tuskegee Female College 1854; to present name 1935.

NIC MEN'S
1978 Sigma Phi Epsilon
1982 Kappa Sigma

NPC WOMEN'S
1976 Alpha Omicron Pi
1976 Chi Omega

ACHS HONORS
1965 Kappa Mu Epsilon

1965 Psi Chi
1986 Phi Eta Sigma

RECOGNITION
1930 Chi Delta Phi
1946 Beta Beta Beta
1966 Lambda Tau

HUNTINGTON COLLEGE Huntington, IN. Liberal arts college sponsored by the Church of the United Brethren in Christ; fully accredited. Founded 1897 as Central College.

ACHS HONORS
1966 Alpha Chi

RECOGNITION
1928 Alpha Psi Omega

HURON COLLEGE Huron, SD. College of liberal arts; coeducational; private control; United Presbyterian Church. Established as Pierre University in 1883.

ACHS HONORS
1932 Pi Gamma Mu

RECOGNITION
1918 Pi Kappa Delta

INACTIVE
1920–37 Theta Alpha Phi
1971–75 Tau Kappa Epsilon

HUSSON COLLEGE Bangor, ME. Private college of business; coeducational; established 1898; two-year A.B.A.; four-year B.S. and M.S. programs in accounting, business administration, recreation management, secretarial science, and business teacher education.

Fraternities and sororities have special accommodations in residence halls.

NIC MEN'S
1975 Tau Kappa Epsilon
1976 Tau Epsilon Phi

OTHER PROFESSIONAL
1952 Kappa Delta Phi (C)

HUSTON-TILLOTSON COLLEGE Austin, TX. College of liberal arts; coeducational; private control by the Methodist Church and Congregational and Christian Churches; established 1877.

NIC MEN'S
1949 Kappa Alpha Psi (A)

NPHC MEN'S
1939 Alpha Phi Alpha
1950 Omega Psi Phi

NPHC WOMEN'S
Zeta Phi Beta
1930 Delta Sigma Theta (B)
1945 Sigma Gamma Rho
1953 Alpha Kappa Alpha
1953 Alpha Kappa Alpha

THE COLLEGE OF IDAHO Caldwell, ID. Founded in 1891 as Idaho's first institution of higher education. Four-year, privately endowed, coeducational, church-related (Presbyterian), liberal arts, nonsectarian in instruction.

NIC MEN'S
1979 Kappa Sigma

ACHS HONORS
1984 Phi Eta Sigma

SERVICE
1935 Intercollegiate Knights

RECOGNITION
1927 Pi Kappa Delta

INACTIVE
1925–40 Sigma Tau Delta
1930–35 Lambda Chi Alpha

UNIVERSITY OF IDAHO   Moscow, ID. Created by act of territorial legislature in 1889. Letters and science (the liberal arts college), agriculture, engineering, law, mines, forestry, education, business administration, and the graduate school. Master's degrees offered in all divisions, and doctorate degrees in agriculture, forestry, education and letters and science.

Fraternities and sororities are permitted to occupy houses on property of their ownership and most of them do so. Four fraternities and two sororities own houses on university land leased for 99 years.

NIC MEN'S
1905 Kappa Sigma
1908 Phi Delta Theta
1914 Beta Theta Pi
1915 Sigma Nu
1919 Sigma Alpha Epsilon
1920 Phi Gamma Delta
1924 Delta Chi
1924 Sigma Chi
1925 Alpha Tau Omega
1927 Lambda Chi Alpha
1927 Tau Kappa Epsilon
1931 Delta Tau Delta
1947 Phi Kappa Tau
1950 Delta Sigma Phi
1957 FarmHouse
1959 Theta Chi
1966 Pi Kappa Alpha
1968 Alpha Kappa Lambda

NPC WOMEN'S
1910 Gamma Phi Beta
1911 Delta Gamma
1916 Kappa Kappa Gamma
1920 Kappa Alpha Theta
1923 Pi Beta Phi
1928 Alpha Phi
1929 Delta Delta Delta
1958 Alpha Gamma Delta
1987 Kappa Kappa Gamma

OTHER WOMEN'S
     Lambda Delta Sigma

PROFESSIONAL
1914 Phi Alpha Delta
1923 Alpha Kappa Psi
1924 Sigma Alpha Iota
1983 Delta Theta Phi

OTHER PROFESSIONAL
1918 Phi Upsilon Omicron
1920 Alpha Zeta
1948 Sigma Delta Chi
1955 Women in Communications
1957 Phi Epsilon Kappa

ACHS HONORS
1920 Xi Sigma Pi
1923 Mortar Board
1928 Kappa Delta Pi
1933 Alpha Lambda Delta
1934 Phi Eta Sigma
1950 Pi Gamma Mu
1960 Phi Kappa Phi
1960 Sigma Pi Sigma
1962 Phi Sigma
1964 Pi Kappa Lambda
1970 Phi Alpha Theta
1974 Tau Beta Pi
1975 Gamma Theta Upsilon
1978 Psi Chi
1978 Sigma Lambda Alpha

OTHER HONORS
     National Order of Omega
1922 Sigma Xi
1926 Phi Beta Kappa

SERVICE
     The National Spurs
1922 Intercollegiate Knights
1941 Alpha Phi Omega

RECOGNITION
     Angel Flight
1926 Blue Key
1934 Sigma Delta Psi
1957 National Block and Bridle
     Club

INACTIVE
1924–88 Alpha Chi Omega
1925   Scabbard and Blade
         (6)
1925–40 Sigma Delta Pi
1926–57 Phi Chi Theta
1928–36 Alpha Tau Delta
1929   Sigma Gamma Epsilon
1934   Cardinal Key
1936–75 Phi Mu Alpha—
         Sinfonia
1939–62 Alpha Epsilon Delta

IDAHO STATE UNIVERSITY   Pocatello, ID. Formerly Academy of Idaho, 1901; Idaho Technical Institute, 1915; University of Idaho Southern Branch, 1927; Idaho State, 1947; coeducational; college of liberal arts, including a two-year division of agri-culture, engineering, and forestry; graduate division, 1955. Became university 1963.

Fraternities own their own houses on their own land. The sororities occupy an on-campus college-owned residence hall as a Panhellenic house.

NIC MEN'S
1949 Phi Sigma Kappa
1961 Sigma Nu
1964 Kappa Alpha Psi (A)

OTHER MEN'S
     Sigma Gamma Chi

NPHC WOMEN'S
1974 Delta Sigma Theta (B)

OTHER WOMEN'S
     Lambda Delta Sigma

PROFESSIONAL
1928 Phi Delta Chi
1936 Lambda Kappa Sigma
1957 Alpha Kappa Psi

OTHER PROFESSIONAL
1954 Kappa Phi Kappa
1972 Phi Upsilon Omicron

ACHS HONORS
     Omicron Delta Epsilon
1949 Pi Sigma Alpha
1951 Rho Chi
1969 Sigma Pi Sigma
1970 Phi Kappa Phi
1972 Mortar Board
1976 Phi Alpha Theta
1989 Psi Chi

OTHER HONORS
1966 Sigma Xi

SERVICE
     The National Spurs
1932 Intercollegiate Knights
1949 Alpha Phi Omega

RECOGNITION
1947 Alpha Psi Omega
1948 Sigma Delta Psi
1949 Pi Kappa Delta
1957 Scabbard and Blade (13)
1959 Blue Key

INACTIVE
1949–85 Gamma Phi Beta
1949–87 Tau Kappa Epsilon
1950–58 Phi Mu Alpha—
         Sinfonia
1950–61 Phi Kappa Tau
1950–65 Sigma Kappa
1950–81 Alpha Omicron Pi
1950–84 Alpha Chi Omega
1954–60 Kappa Delta Epsilon
1958–72 Sigma Phi Epsilon
1961–70 Pi Kappa Alpha
1966   Delta Phi Kappa
1970–81 Delta Chi
1970–82 Phi Chi Theta
1975–83 Phi Gamma Delta
1977–85 Kappa Delta

UNIVERSITY OF ILLINOIS   Urbana, IL. University; land-grant institution; coeducational; state control; supported by state, federal and private funds. Main campuses situated in Urbana-Champaign and Chicago. Satellite medical campuses at Peoria and Rockford. Incorporated as Illinois Industrial University 1867; first instruction 1868. Name changed to present 1885.

NIC MEN'S
1872 Delta Tau Delta
1881 Sigma Chi
1891 Kappa Sigma
1892 Phi Kappa Sigma
1893 Phi Delta Theta
1895 Alpha Tau Omega
1897 Phi Gamma Delta
1899 Sigma Alpha Epsilon
1902 Beta Theta Pi
1902 Sigma Nu
1903 Sigma Phi Epsilon
1904 Phi Kappa Psi
1905 Delta Upsilon
1906 Acacia
1906 Alpha Gamma Rho
1907 Triangle
1908 Alpha Sigma Phi
1908 Sigma Pi
1908 Theta Delta Chi
1909 Zeta Psi
1910 Phi Sigma Kappa
1910 Psi Upsilon

1911 Alpha Delta Phi
1912 Chi Phi
1912 Chi Psi
1912 Phi Kappa Theta
1912 Tau Kappa Epsilon
1912 Zeta Beta Tau
1913 Kappa Alpha Psi (A)
1914 FarmHouse
1915 Lambda Chi Alpha
1916 Alpha Chi Rho
1916 Phi Kappa Tau
1916 Theta Chi
1917 Pi Kappa Alpha
1918 Sigma Alpha Mu
1919 Delta Sigma Phi
1920 Alpha Epsilon Pi
1920 Delta Phi
1921 Alpha Kappa Lambda
1921 Kappa Delta Rho
1921 Pi Kappa Phi
1922 Theta Xi
1923 Delta Chi
1924 Tau Delta Phi

1924 Tau Epsilon Phi
1925 Beta Sigma Psi
1934 Pi Lambda Phi
1953 Sigma Tau Gamma
1958 Phi Sigma Kappa
1981 Alpha Gamma Sigma

NPHC MEN'S
    Phi Beta Sigma
1917 Alpha Phi Alpha
1928 Omega Psi Phi

NPC WOMEN'S
1895 Kappa Alpha Theta
1895 Pi Beta Phi
1899 Alpha Chi Omega
1899 Kappa Kappa Gamma
1900 Chi Omega
1905 Alpha Xi Delta
1906 Delta Gamma
1906 Sigma Kappa
1911 Alpha Omicron Pi
1912 Alpha Delta Pi
1913 Gamma Phi Beta
1918 Alpha Gamma Delta
1920 Alpha Epsilon Phi
1920 Delta Delta Delta
1921 Delta Zeta
1921 Phi Mu
1921 Zeta Tau Alpha
1922 Alpha Phi
1923 Kappa Delta
1923 Phi Sigma Sigma
1926 Sigma Delta Tau
1927 Delta Phi Epsilon

NPHC WOMEN'S
1914 Alpha Kappa Alpha
1932 Delta Sigma Theta (B)
1969 Sigma Gamma Rho

PROFESSIONAL
1901 Phi Delta Phi
1908 Alpha Chi Sigma
1910 Kappa Psi
1913 Alpha Kappa Psi
1914 Alpha Rho Chi
1918 Lambda Kappa Sigma
1922 Delta Sigma Pi
1924 Sigma Alpha Iota
1925 Delta Theta Phi
1925 Phi Mu Alpha—Sinfonia
1928 Alpha Omega
1928 Sigma Phi Delta
1937 Zeta Phi Eta
1951 Mu Phi Epsilon
1956 Omega Tau Sigma
1959 Rho Pi Phi
1974 Phi Gamma Nu
1984 Phi Alpha Delta

OTHER PROFESSIONAL
1900 Alpha Zeta
1901 Delta Sigma Delta
1902 Phi Beta Pi and Theta
    Kappa Psi (a)
1908 Phi Lambda Kappa
1909 Scarab
1912 Sigma Delta Chi
1915 Keramos
1918 Phi Delta Epsilon
1918 Women in Communications
1919 Beta Alpha Psi
1921 Alpha Tau Alpha
1926 Phi Upsilon Omicron
1929 Nu Beta Epsilon
1929 Phi Epsilon Kappa
1954 Alpha Eta Rho

1955 Delta Pi Epsilon

ACHS HONORS
    Omicron Delta Epsilon
1897 Tau Beta Pi
1904 Eta Kappa Nu
1906 Delta Sigma Rho-Tau
    Kappa Alpha
1911 Kappa Delta Pi
1914 Kappa Omicron Nu
1916 Pi Tau Sigma
1918 Mortar Board
1922 Chi Epsilon
1923 Phi Eta Sigma
1923 Pi Kappa Lambda
1924 Alpha Lambda Delta
1925 Kappa Tau Alpha
1925 Phi Sigma
1926 Sigma Delta Pi
1927 Phi Alpha Theta
1927 Pi Delta Phi
1928 Alpha Kappa Delta
1933 Phi Kappa Phi
1939 Psi Chi
1940 Alpha Sigma Mu
1949 Beta Phi Mu
1953 Sigma Gamma Tau
1956 Pi Sigma Alpha
1960 Alpha Epsilon
1962 Omicron Delta Kappa
1965 Xi Sigma Pi
1966 Lambda Iota Tau
1969 Alpha Epsilon Delta
1974 Gamma Theta Upsilon
1974 Phi Alpha Theta
1976 Alpha Pi Mu
1980 Phi Sigma Tau
1982 Sigma Lambda Alpha

OTHER HONORS
    National Order of Omega
1902 Alpha Omega Alpha
1902 Order of the Coif
1907 Phi Beta Kappa
1918 Iota Sigma Pi
1922 National Collegiate
    Players
1923 Gamma Sigma Delta
1924 Pi Mu Epsilon
1928 Omicron Kappa Upsilon

RECOGNITION
    Angel Flight
    Arnold Air Society (D-2)
1899 Phi Lambda Upsilon
1908 Gamma Alpha
1909 Scabbard and Blade (1)
1920 Sigma Delta Psi
1924 Pi Alpha Xi
1924 Sigma Delta Epsilon
1927 Sigma Iota Epsilon
1931 Delta Phi Alpha
1953 Phi Zeta
1955 National Block and Bridle
    Club

INACTIVE
1894–69 Phi Rho Sigma
1899–69 Alpha Kappa Kappa
1901–16 Phi Beta Pi and Theta
    Kappa Psi (B)
1902–55 Xi Psi Phi
1904–86 Delta Kappa Epsilon
1913 Beta Gamma Sigma
1916–39 Theta Tau
1917–18 Tau Sigma Delta
1918 Phi Chi
1919–53 Theta Phi Alpha

1921 Kappa Beta Pi
1921–31 Gamma Eta Gamma
1923–39 Phi Mu Delta
1925 Alpha Alpha Gamma
1925–34 Sigma Mu Sigma
1927 Sigma Delta Kappa

1927–58 Phi Chi Theta
1928 Eta Sigma Phi
1929–35 Kappa Phi Kappa
1929–52 Phi Beta
1931–36 Omega Chi Epsilon
1957–87 Sigma Sigma Sigma

UNIVERSITY OF ILLINOIS AT CHICAGO
Chicago, IL. Formed by the merger of the former Medical Center (1890s) and Chicago Circle (1965) campuses of the University of Illinois; 15 colleges, 25,000 students; doctorates in 46 fields; masters in 79; bachelors in 98; coeducational; state supported.

NIC MEN'S
1968 Tau Delta Phi
1970 Sigma Alpha Mu
1970 Zeta Psi
1979 Alpha Phi Delta
1981 Kappa Alpha Psi (A)

PROFESSIONAL
1952 Phi Delta Chi
1958 Alpha Tau Delta

ACHS HONORS
    Omicron Delta Epsilon
1934 Rho Chi
1965 Alpha Lambda Delta
1966 Sigma Theta Tau
1967 Phi Eta Sigma
1970 Gamma Theta Upsilon

1972 Beta Gamma Sigma
1973 Phi Kappa Phi
1981 Pi Sigma Alpha
1984 Tau Beta Pi
1986 Psi Chi

OTHER HONORS
    National Order of Omega

SERVICE
1967 Alpha Phi Omega

INACTIVE
1969–72 Alpha Epsilon Pi
1970–87 Tau Kappa Epsilon

COLONIES
    Theta Xi

ILLINOIS BENEDICTINE COLLEGE Lisle, IL.

ACHS HONORS
1963 Sigma Pi Sigma
1979 Kappa Mu Epsilon
1979 Psi Chi
1980 Pi Gamma Mu

1989 Phi Sigma Iota

RECOGNITION
1970 Blue Key
1975 Beta Beta Beta

ILLINOIS CENTRAL COLLEGE East Peoria, IL.

SERVICE
1972 Alpha Phi Omega

RECOGNITION
1970 Sigma Zeta

ILLINOIS COLLEGE
Jacksonville, IL. College of liberal arts; coeducational; private control; affiliated with Presbyterian and Congregational Churches; founded 1829.

ACHS HONORS
    Omicron Delta Epsilon
1980 Phi Sigma Iota
1981 Delta Mu Delta

SERVICE
1949 Alpha Phi Omega

INACTIVE
1856–66 Beta Theta Pi
1927–38 Pi Gamma Mu

ILLINOIS COLLEGE OF OPTOMETRY
Chicago, IL. Formed in 1955 by the consolidation of the Northern Illinois College of Ophthalmology and Otology founded in 1872, and the Chicago College of Optometry founded in 1937.

INACTIVE
1954 Omega Epsilon Phi

ILLINOIS INSTITUTE OF TECHNOLOGY

ILLINOIS INSTITUTE OF TECHNOLOGY Chicago, IL. Formed in 1940 through merger of Armour Institute of Technology, 1892, and Lewis Institute, 1896. Curricula include engineering, physical sciences, liberal studies, architecture, and design. Graduate and undergraduate divisions coeducational. Privately supported; nonsectarian affiliated organizations include IIT Research Institute, Association of American Railroads Technology Center, and Institute of Gas Technology.

Housing plan includes ownership of the house by the fraternity on college-owned land, and ownership by college on rental basis to the fraternity.

NIC MEN'S
1898 Phi Kappa Sigma
1901 Delta Tau Delta
1922 Theta Xi
1923 Triangle
1925 Alpha Epsilon Pi
1935 Pi Kappa Phi
1939 Alpha Sigma Phi
1947 Tau Epsilon Phi
1948 Sigma Phi Epsilon

NPC WOMEN'S
1978 Delta Phi Epsilon

ACHS HONORS
1906 Tau Beta Pi
1909 Eta Kappa Nu
1923 Chi Epsilon
1924 Pi Tau Sigma
1948 Phi Eta Sigma
1965 Alpha Pi Mu

OTHER HONORS
1942 Sigma Xi

SERVICE
1945 Alpha Phi Omega

RECOGNITION
     Arnold Air Society (D-2)
     Arnold Air Society (F-2)
1920 Phi Lambda Upsilon

INACTIVE
1915   Scarab
1922–52 Sigma Alpha Mu
1930–85 Alpha Chi Sigma
1946   Sigma Iota Epsilon
1947–60 Sigma Kappa
1948–69 Delta Zeta
1949–66 Sigma Pi Sigma
1955–68 Psi Chi

ILLINOIS STATE UNIVERSITY

ILLINOIS STATE UNIVERSITY Normal, IL. Founded by the State of Illinois in 1857 as the first state-supported institution of higher education; coeducational. Undergraduate and graduate programs leading to bachelor's, master's, and doctor's degrees.

NIC MEN'S
1969 Tau Kappa Epsilon
1970 Alpha Kappa Lambda
1971 Delta Sigma Phi
1971 Lambda Chi Alpha
1971 Sigma Phi Epsilon
1972 Sigma Nu
1973 Alpha Gamma Rho
1973 Delta Chi
1975 Alpha Tau Omega
1975 Sigma Tau Gamma
1977 Sigma Pi
1980 Beta Sigma Psi
1980 Kappa Alpha Psi (A)
1982 Alpha Epsilon Pi
1982 Kappa Delta Rho
1982 Phi Sigma Kappa
1983 FarmHouse
1985 Phi Kappa Psi
1985 Sigma Chi
1988 Alpha Sigma Phi
1990 Sigma Alpha Epsilon

NPHC MEN'S
     Phi Beta Sigma
1972 Alpha Phi Alpha

NPC WOMEN'S
1973 Alpha Delta Pi
1973 Alpha Gamma Delta
1973 Delta Zeta
1973 Kappa Delta
1974 Chi Omega
1974 Delta Delta Delta
1974 Pi Beta Phi
1974 Zeta Tau Alpha
1980 Gamma Phi Beta
1983 Alpha Phi
1988 Phi Sigma Sigma
1989 Sigma Sigma Sigma

NPHC WOMEN'S
1971 Delta Sigma Theta (B)
1972 Alpha Kappa Alpha
1973 Sigma Gamma Rho

PROFESSIONAL
1933 Kappa Delta Epsilon
1965 Delta Omicron
1976 Tau Beta Sigma
1980 Delta Sigma Pi

OTHER PROFESSIONAL
1935 Alpha Tau Alpha
1956 Alpha Beta Alpha
1971 Delta Pi Epsilon

1974 Alpha Zeta

ACHS HONORS
     Omicron Delta Epsilon
1928 Gamma Theta Upsilon
1928 Pi Omega Pi
1930 Pi Gamma Mu
1936 Sigma Tau Delta
1951 Kappa Omicron Nu
1965 Phi Eta Sigma
1966 Alpha Lambda Delta
1966 Omicron Delta Kappa
1966 Phi Sigma
1967 Phi Alpha Theta
1969 Sigma Delta Pi

1976 Mortar Board
1980 Pi Sigma Alpha
1984 Psi Chi
1985 Pi Kappa Lambda

OTHER HONORS
     National Order of Omega

SERVICE
1949 Alpha Phi Omega

INACTIVE
1933–81 Kappa Mu Epsilon
1965–84 Phi Mu Alpha—
         Sinfonia
1972–78 Acacia

ILLINOIS WESLEYAN UNIVERSITY

ILLINOIS WESLEYAN UNIVERSITY Bloomington, IL. Founded 1850; chartered 1853. Methodist related; private control; coeducaitonal; college of liberal arts and college of fine arts; collegiate school of nursing; graduate division in music.

Fraternities and sororities are permitted to occupy their own houses on fraternity property and all but one fraternity do so.

NIC MEN'S
1866 Phi Gamma Delta
1883 Sigma Chi
1899 Tau Kappa Epsilon
1942 Theta Chi
1975 Sigma Pi

NPHC MEN'S
     Phi Beta Sigma

NPC WOMEN'S
1873 Kappa Kappa Gamma
1906 Sigma Kappa
1908 Kappa Delta
1914 Alpha Gamma Delta
1956 Alpha Omicron Pi

NPHC WOMEN'S
1972 Delta Sigma Theta (B)
1982 Alpha Kappa Alpha

PROFESSIONAL
1924 Phi Mu Alpha—Sinfonia
1924 Sigma Alpha Iota
1926 Delta Omicron
1958 Alpha Kappa Psi
1965 Alpha Tau Delta
1975 Phi Gamma Nu

ACHS HONORS
     Omicron Delta Epsilon
1922 Phi Kappa Phi
1926 Phi Sigma Iota

1949 Alpha Lambda Delta
1965 Kappa Delta Pi
1966 Alpha Kappa Delta
1967 Phi Alpha Theta
1967 Phi Eta Sigma
1974 Pi Kappa Lambda
1975 Psi Chi
1985 Pi Sigma Alpha

OTHER HONORS
1948 Delta Phi Delta

SERVICE
1976 Alpha Phi Omega

RECOGNITION
1914 Pi Kappa Delta
1923 Theta Alpha Phi
1943 Blue Key
1964 Beta Beta Beta
1971 Blue Key

INACTIVE
1875–95 Kappa Alpha Theta
1877–80 Delta Tau Delta
1878–97 Phi Delta Theta
1878–28 Phi Delta Phi
1931–52 Pi Gamma Mu
1937–60 Alpha Epsilon Delta

COLONIES
1957 Acacia

IMMACULATA COLLEGE

IMMACULATA COLLEGE Immaculata, PA.

ACHS HONORS
1940 Delta Epsilon Sigma
1944 Kappa Omicron Nu
1957 Lambda Iota Tau
1977 Psi Chi

1980 Pi Kappa Lambda
1983 Phi Alpha Theta

RECOGNITION
1944 Alpha Psi Omega

IMMACULATE HEART COLLEGE

IMMACULATE HEART COLLEGE Los Angeles, CA. College of liberal arts for men and women; coeducational graduate school; private control; non-denominational. Chartered 1916.

ACHS HONORS
1940 Delta Epsilon Sigma
1985 Phi Sigma Iota

INACTIVE
1951–69 Sigma Alpha Iota
1956–81 Phi Alpha Theta

INCARNATE WORD COLLEGE San Antonio, TX. Private control: Roman Catholic. Founded in 1891. Four-yer; coeducational; liberal arts college.

80% of students live off campus or commute.

PROFESSIONAL
1971 Delta Omicron

ACHS HONORS
1926 Alpha Chi
1937 Alpha Lambda Delta

SERVICE
1980 Alpha Phi Omega

RECOGNITION
1944 Alpha Psi Omega

INDIANA UNIVERSITY Bloomington, IN. Founded in 1820; university, undergraduate colleges; graduate school; coeducational; state-supported. Most of the fraternities and sororities occupy their houses on property which they own; however, the university owns and rents several houses to fraternities and sororities on a short-term basis until the chapters are able to acquire their own properties.

NIC MEN'S
1845 Beta Theta Pi
1849 Phi Delta Theta
1858 Sigma Chi
1869 Phi Kappa Psi
1870 Delta Tau Delta
1871 Phi Gamma Delta
1887 Kappa Sigma
1892 Sigma Nu
1907 Sigma Alpha Epsilon
1911 Kappa Alpha Psi (A)
1915 Alpha Tau Omega
1915 Delta Upsilon
1917 Lambda Chi Alpha
1920 Acacia
1921 Theta Chi
1922 Sigma Alpha Mu
1924 Sigma Pi
1925 Delta Chi
1926 Kappa Delta Rho
1931 Sigma Phi Epsilon
1939 Phi Kappa Theta
1947 Pi Kappa Phi
1947 Zeta Beta Tau
1949 Phi Kappa Tau
1950 Pi Kappa Alpha
1950 Tau Kappa Epsilon
1958 Alpha Epsilon Pi
1958 Chi Phi
1968 Alpha Sigma Phi
1970 Kappa Alpha Psi (A)

NPHC MEN'S
Phi Beta Sigma
1947 Alpha Phi Alpha
1947 Omega Psi Phi

NPC WOMEN'S
1870 Kappa Alpha Theta
1872 Kappa Kappa Gamma
1893 Pi Beta Phi
1898 Delta Gamma
1909 Delta Zeta
1916 Alpha Omicron Pi
1917 Delta Delta Delta
1918 Sigma Kappa
1920 Phi Mu
1922 Alpha Chi Omega
1922 Chi Omega
1922 Zeta Tau Alpha
1923 Kappa Delta
1926 Alpha Delta Pi
1940 Sigma Delta Tau
1946 Alpha Xi Delta
1947 Alpha Gamma Delta
1947 Alpha Phi
1957 Gamma Phi Beta
1958 Alpha Epsilon Phi
1989 Sigma Sigma Sigma

NPHC WOMEN'S
1922 Alpha Kappa Alpha
1947 Delta Sigma Theta (B)
1971 Alpha Kappa Alpha
1971 Sigma Gamma Rho

PROFESSIONAL
1893 Xi Psi Phi
1900 Phi Delta Phi
1903 Phi Chi
1903 Phi Rho Sigma
1908 Alpha Chi Sigma
1925 Delta Sigma Pi
1927 Alpha Kappa Psi
1928 Alpha Omega
1928 Delta Theta Phi
1931 Kappa Kappa Psi
1939 Sigma Alpha Iota
1947 Phi Delta Phi
1947 Phi Mu Alpha—Sinfonia
1948 Phi Alpha Delta
1949 Tau Beta Sigma
1951 Mu Phi Epsilon
1966 Delta Omicron
1966 Phi Alpha Delta
1972 Delta Psi Kappa
1984 Phi Alpha Delta

OTHER PROFESSIONAL
1900 Delta Sigma Delta
1911 Gamma Eta Gamma
1913 Women in Communications

1914 Sigma Delta Chi
1920 Pi Lambda Theta
1932 Sigma Delta Kappa
1934 Phi Epsilon Kappa
1945 Delta Pi Epsilon
1957 Beta Alpha Psi
1973 Alpha Epsilon Rho

ACHS HONORS
Omicron Delta Epsilon
Pi Alpha Alpha
1908 Delta Sigma Rho-Tau Kappa Alpha
1921 Mortar Board
1922 Sigma Theta Tau
1923 Beta Gamma Sigma
1923 Kappa Omicron Nu
1930 Phi Eta Sigma
1931 Alpha Lambda Delta
1936 Alpha Kappa Delta
1937 Pi Sigma Alpha
1948 Gamma Theta Upsilon
1948 Pi Kappa Lambda
1948 Psi Chi
1949 Alpha Epsilon Delta
1951 Phi Alpha Theta
1952 Phi Sigma Iota
1962 Alpha Epsilon
1962 Sigma Pi Sigma
1970 Beta Phi Mu

OTHER HONORS
National Order of Omega
1904 Sigma Xi
1911 Phi Beta Kappa
1916 Alpha Omega Alpha
1925 Order of the Coif

1926 Sigma Gamma Epsilon
1934 Omicron Kappa Upsilon
1964 Pi Mu Epsilon

SERVICE
1929 Alpha Phi Omega

RECOGNITION
Angel Flight
Arnold Air Society (D-2)
1912 Sigma Delta Psi
1920 Scabbard and Blade (2)
1922 Theta Alpha Phi
1926 Eta Sigma Phi
1926 Phi Lambda Upsilon
1929 Blue Key
1933 Delta Phi Alpha
1955 Sigma Iota Epsilon
1958 Sigma Phi Alpha
1959 Sigma Delta Epsilon

INACTIVE
1905 Phi Beta Pi and Theta Kappa Psi (a)
1908 Phi Beta Pi and Theta Kappa Psi (a)
1920–59 Theta Phi Alpha
1924–44 Phi Beta Pi and Theta Kappa Psi (B)
1924–56 Phi Delta Epsilon
1928–59 Pi Lambda Phi
1930 Iota Sigma Pi
1946–52 Delta Phi Epsilon
1949–72 Phi Sigma Kappa
1949–79 Theta Xi
1954–57 Kappa Alpha Mu
1955 Omega Epsilon Phi

INDIANA UNIVERSITY AT EVANSVILLE Evansville, IN.

RECOGNITION
1970 Sigma Zeta

INACTIVE
1982–84 Sigma Alpha Epsilon

INDIANA UNIVERSITY NORTHWEST Gary, IN.

NPHC WOMEN'S
1966 Sigma Gamma Rho
1976 Delta Sigma Theta (B)

PROFESSIONAL
1971 Delta Sigma Pi

ACHS HONORS
Omicron Delta Epsilon

1978 Psi Chi
1984 Phi Eta Sigma

INACTIVE
1974–78 Phi Chi Theta

INDIANA UNIVERSITY, PURDUE UNIVERSITY AT FORT WAYNE Fort Wayne, IN.

NIC MEN'S
1977 Sigma Phi Epsilon

NPC WOMEN'S
1973 Delta Gamma
1974 Pi Beta Phi

PROFESSIONAL
1977 Delta Sigma Pi

SERVICE
1969 Alpha Phi Omega

RECOGNITION
1966 Sigma Phi Alpha

INDIANA UNIVERSITY, PURDUE UNIVERSITY AT INDIANAPOLIS Indianapolis, IN.

NIC MEN'S
1982 Kappa Alpha Psi (A)

1991 Pi Kappa Phi

NPC WOMEN'S
1989 Phi Mu

NPHC WOMEN'S
1920 Alpha Kappa Alpha

PROFESSIONAL
1923 Delta Theta Phi
1982 Delta Sigma Pi

ACHS HONORS
1971 Sigma Tau Delta

1972 Phi Sigma Tau
1980 Pi Sigma Alpha
1981 Psi Chi
1985 Alpha Lambda Delta
1985 Phi Eta Sigma

SERVICE
1968 Alpha Phi Omega

INDIANA UNIVERSITY AT SOUTH BEND South Bend, IN. Public institution. Founded in 1962. Four-year; coeducational.

Fraternity has its own house. No campus housing available.

ACHS HONORS
     Omicron Delta Epsilon
1969 Phi Alpha Theta
1975 Psi Chi
1977 Pi Sigma Alpha
1981 Phi Eta Sigma

RECOGNITION
1975 Sigma Phi Alpha

INACTIVE
1970–77 Alpha Xi Delta
1971–88 Sigma Pi

INDIANA UNIVERSITY SOUTHEAST New Albany, IN. Public institution. Founded in 1941. Four-year; coeducational.

Fraternities and sororities have offices. No housing available.

NIC MEN'S
1976 Tau Kappa Epsilon
1977 Pi Kappa Alpha

NPC WOMEN'S
1973 Sigma Kappa
1978 Alpha Phi
1990 Phi Sigma Sigma

ACHS HONORS
1971 Phi Alpha Theta

1972 Kappa Delta Pi
1977 Phi Eta Sigma
1987 Gamma Theta Upsilon
1989 Psi Chi

SERVICE
1983 Alpha Phi Omega

COLONIES
     Theta Xi

INDIANA UNIVERSITY OF PENNSYLVANIA Indiana, PA. Founded in 1875; coeducational; state owned and controlled; nonsectarian; undergraduate and graduate degree programs.

IFC fraternities occupy houses off-campus; eight fraternities own their own houses; eight rent houses. Panhellenic sororities have chapter rooms in residence halls provided rent-free by the university. The eight national fraternities and sororities and one local fraternity forming the Black Greek Council utilize two university-owned houses for meetings and programs.

NIC MEN'S
1953 Delta Sigma Phi
1955 Kappa Delta Rho
1955 Tau Kappa Epsilon
1957 Theta Chi
1961 Theta Xi
1965 Phi Sigma Kappa
1968 Kappa Sigma
1970 Lambda Chi Alpha
1970 Phi Kappa Psi
1973 Sigma Chi

1974 Phi Kappa Theta
1974 Sigma Nu
1976 Delta Tau Delta
1982 Alpha Tau Omega
1983 Kappa Alpha Psi (A)
1984 Phi Delta Theta
1986 Alpha Chi Rho
1988 Pi Kappa Phi

NPHC MEN'S
     Phi Beta Sigma

NPC WOMEN'S
1914 Alpha Sigma Alpha
1915 Sigma Sigma Sigma
1916 Alpha Sigma Tau
1950 Phi Mu
1951 Zeta Tau Alpha
1952 Delta Zeta
1952 Sigma Kappa
1959 Alpha Gamma Delta
1963 Alpha Xi Delta
1966 Alpha Omicron Pi
1968 Delta Phi Epsilon
1968 Kappa Delta
1981 Delta Gamma
1986 Theta Phi Alpha

NPHC WOMEN'S
1983 Sigma Gamma Rho

PROFESSIONAL
1953 Delta Omicron
1953 Phi Mu Alpha—Sinfonia

OTHER PROFESSIONAL
1929 Phi Sigma Pi
1969 Delta Pi Epsilon

ACHS HONORS
     Omicron Delta Epsilon
1928 Kappa Delta Pi
1929 Pi Omega Pi

1940 Kappa Omicron Nu
1962 Pi Gamma Mu
1964 Gamma Theta Upsilon
1965 Kappa Mu Epsilon
1968 Phi Alpha Theta
1968 Pi Delta Phi
1970 Psi Chi
1972 Sigma Delta Pi
1972 Sigma Pi Sigma

OTHER HONORS
     National Order of Omega
1946 Delta Phi Delta
1976 Sigma Gamma Epsilon

SERVICE
1959 Alpha Phi Omega
1969 Gamma Sigma Sigma

RECOGNITION
1953 Alpha Psi Omega

INACTIVE
1930–86 Sigma Tau Gamma
1952–74 Sigma Phi Epsilon
1965–83 Alpha Phi
1966–78 Alpha Delta Pi

COLONIES
1969 Phi Sigma Sigma

INDIANA INSTITUTE OF TECHNOLOGY Fort Wayne, IN. Established in 1930; reorganized as nonprofit college in 1948. College of engineering, computer science, and business for men and women; private control; nonsectarian.

Fraternities with exceptions own their own land and homes.

NIC MEN'S
1958 Kappa Alpha Psi (A)
1963 Phi Kappa Theta
1963 Sigma Phi Epsilon
1966 Sigma Pi

NPHC MEN'S
     Phi Beta Sigma
     Phi Beta Sigma

PROFESSIONAL
1951 Sigma Phi Delta

INACTIVE
1932–77 Alpha Sigma Phi
1946–75 Theta Xi
1963–82 Tau Kappa Epsilon
1970–76 Alpha Epsilon Pi

INDIANA STATE UNIVERSITY Terre Haute, IN. Founded 1870; state institution; coeducational; undergraduate and graduate programs.

The fraternities are located in off-campus houses, owned by the fraternities, and in residence hall floors. Sororities rent suite space in residence halls; these suites provide sorority meeting room facilities.

NIC MEN'S
1869 Phi Delta Theta
1951 Tau Kappa Epsilon
1952 Lambda Chi Alpha
1952 Theta Chi
1954 Sigma Phi Epsilon
1958 Pi Lambda Phi
1963 Alpha Tau Omega
1967 Sigma Pi
1969 Sigma Alpha Epsilon
1971 Phi Gamma Delta
1979 Pi Kappa Alpha

1985 Sigma Chi
1987 Phi Kappa Psi
1990 Sigma Tau Gamma

NPHC MEN'S
     Phi Beta Sigma
1969 Alpha Phi Alpha

NPC WOMEN'S
1949 Chi Omega
1951 Alpha Sigma Alpha
1951 Sigma Kappa
1952 Gamma Phi Beta

1953 Alpha Omicron Pi
1953 Zeta Tau Alpha
1954 Delta Gamma
1964 Alpha Phi
1971 Alpha Chi Omega

NPHC WOMEN'S
1923 Sigma Gamma Rho
1969 Alpha Kappa Alpha
1969 Delta Sigma Theta (B)
1971 Sigma Gamma Rho
1973 Delta Sigma Theta (B)

PROFESSIONAL
1943 Sigma Alpha Iota
1947 Phi Mu Alpha—Sinfonia
1959 Delta Sigma Pi
1968 Delta Psi Kappa
1970 Alpha Kappa Psi
1990 Gamma Iota Sigma

OTHER PROFESSIONAL
1952 Alpha Beta Alpha
1960 Phi Upsilon Omicron
1965 Sigma Delta Chi
1971 Delta Pi Epsilon
1971 Pi Lambda Theta

ACHS HONORS
    Omicron Delta Epsilon
1926 Kappa Delta Pi
1934 Pi Omega Pi
1941 Delta Sigma Rho-Tau
    Kappa Alpha
1955 Phi Sigma Iota
1963 Alpha Kappa Delta
1964 Sigma Tau Delta
1967 Alpha Lambda Delta

INDIANA WESLEYAN UNIVERSITY   Marion, IN.

ACHS HONORS
1976 Pi Gamma Mu

UNIVERSITY OF INDIANAPOLIS   Indianapolis, IN.

NPHC WOMEN'S
1925 Delta Sigma Theta (B)

PROFESSIONAL
1916 Delta Psi Kappa

ACHS HONORS
1983 Phi Alpha Theta

1985 Delta Mu Delta

SERVICE
1950 Alpha Phi Omega

INACTIVE
1972–84 Phi Mu Alpha—
    Sinfonia

INTER-AMERICAN UNIVERSITY OF PUERTO RICO   San German, PR. College of liberal arts; teacher-training institution; coeducational; private control; nonsectarian; related to Presbyterian Church. Founded 1912 as Polytechnic Institute of Puerto Rico.

PROFESSIONAL
1970 Delta Theta Phi
1976 Phi Alpha Delta
1986 Phi Alpha Delta

ACHS HONORS
1950 Phi Alpha Theta

SERVICE
1972 Alpha Phi Omega
1974 Alpha Phi Omega

RECOGNITION
1945 Beta Beta Beta
1962 Delta Tau Kappa

IONA UNIVERSITY   Iona, NY.

1969 Gamma Theta Upsilon
1970 Sigma Pi Sigma
1972 Sigma Delta Pi
1973 Phi Alpha Theta
1977 Pi Kappa Lambda
1980 Phi Kappa Phi
1980 Pi Sigma Alpha
1980 Psi Chi
1982 Mortar Board

OTHER HONORS
    National Order of Omega
1966 Pi Mu Epsilon
1972 Sigma Gamma Epsilon

SERVICE
1938 Alpha Phi Omega

RECOGNITION
1938 Society for Collegiate
    Journalists—Pi Delta
    Epsilon-Alpha Phi Gamma
    (A)
1939 Blue Key
1940 Kappa Pi
1952 Eta Sigma Phi
1969 Sigma Zeta

INACTIVE
1928–38 Kappa Alpha Psi (A)
1932–71 Pi Gamma Mu
1966–85 Alpha Xi Delta
1968–84 Kappa Sigma
1968–85 Delta Delta Delta
1971–76 Alpha Epsilon Pi

COLONIES
    Pi Kappa Phi

NIC MEN'S
1985 Tau Kappa Epsilon

NPHC MEN'S
    Phi Beta Sigma

NPC WOMEN'S
1985 Phi Sigma Sigma

ACHS HONORS
    Omicron Delta Epsilon
1968 Psi Chi
1970 Sigma Pi Sigma
1971 Delta Epsilon Sigma
1971 Sigma Delta Pi

1977 Theta Alpha Kappa
1982 Phi Sigma Tau
1983 Phi Alpha Theta

OTHER HONORS
1971 Pi Mu Epsilon

RECOGNITION
1963 Beta Beta Beta

INACTIVE
1966–88 Delta Mu Delta

COLONIES
    Delta Upsilon

THE UNIVERSITY OF IOWA   Iowa City, IA. Created on February 25, 1847, 59 days after Iowa became a state, by an Act of the First General Assembly, passed in the Old Capitol Building, which is the central administrative building of the University today. Coeducational, state university, organized into 10 colleges, 6 schools, and more than 100 departments.

Fraternities and sororities are permitted to occupy their own houses on their own property and nearly all do so.

NIC MEN'S
1866 Beta Theta Pi
1867 Phi Kappa Psi
1873 Phi Gamma Delta
1880 Delta Tau Delta
1882 Phi Delta Theta
1882 Sigma Chi
1902 Kappa Sigma
1905 Sigma Alpha Epsilon
1909 Acacia
1912 Delta Chi
1912 Theta Xi
1914 Kappa Alpha Psi (A)
1915 Alpha Tau Omega
1917 Sigma Phi Epsilon
1918 Sigma Pi
1925 Delta Upsilon
1929 Pi Kappa Alpha
1951 Alpha Epsilon Pi
1962 Lambda Chi Alpha
1968 Tau Kappa Epsilon
1985 Sigma Alpha Mu
1985 Sigma Tau Gamma
1990 Alpha Kappa Lambda

NPHC MEN'S
    Phi Beta Sigma

NPC WOMEN'S
1882 Kappa Kappa Gamma
1882 Pi Beta Phi
1886 Delta Gamma
1904 Delta Delta Delta
1911 Alpha Chi Omega
1912 Alpha Xi Delta
1913 Delta Zeta
1915 Alpha Delta Pi
1915 Gamma Phi Beta
1919 Chi Omega
1922 Zeta Tau Alpha
1924 Sigma Kappa
1926 Kappa Alpha Theta
1961 Alpha Phi
1964 Alpha Gamma Delta

NPHC WOMEN'S
1919 Delta Sigma Theta (B)
1974 Delta Sigma Theta (B)
1983 Sigma Gamma Rho

PROFESSIONAL
1893 Phi Delta Phi
1902 Phi Rho Sigma
1906 Psi Omega
1907 Phi Delta Chi
1908 Phi Alpha Delta
1920 Delta Sigma Pi
1921 Alpha Chi Sigma
1921 Delta Theta Phi
1921 Kappa Epsilon
1923 Alpha Kappa Psi
1923 Theta Tau
1928 Phi Gamma Nu
1972 Phi Mu Alpha—Sinfonia
1972 Sigma Alpha Iota

OTHER PROFESSIONAL
1912 Sigma Delta Chi
1914 Delta Sigma Delta
1918 Women in Communications
1920 Pi Lambda Theta
1921 Alpha Kappa Kappa
1923 Gamma Eta Gamma
1925 Phi Epsilon Kappa
1947 Delta Pi Epsilon
1954 Beta Alpha Psi
1962 Phi Upsilon Omicron
1971 Alpha Zeta Omega
1982 Sigma Nu Phi

ACHS HONORS
    Omicron Delta Epsilon
1909 Tau Beta Pi
1920 Beta Gamma Sigma
1923 Rho Chi
1926 Mortar Board
1926 Phi Sigma Iota
1929 Sigma Theta Tau
1930 Kappa Omicron Nu
1935 Pi Tau Sigma
1936 Kappa Tau Alpha

1939 Eta Kappa Nu
1940 Chi Epsilon
1945 Phi Eta Sigma
1947 Omicron Delta Kappa
1950 Alpha Kappa Delta
1950 Pi Delta Phi
1953 Phi Alpha Theta
1954 Pi Sigma Alpha
1955 Gamma Theta Upsilon
1960 Pi Kappa Lambda
1971 Alpha Epsilon
1983 Sigma Pi Sigma
1984 Omega Chi Epsilon
1985 Psi Chi
1988 Beta Phi Mu

OTHER HONORS
    National Order of Omega
1895 Phi Beta Kappa
1900 Sigma Xi
1908 Order of the Coif
1920 Alpha Omega Alpha
1923 Omicron Kappa Upsilon
1926 Iota Sigma Pi
1969 Sigma Gamma Epsilon

SERVICE
1930 Alpha Phi Omega

RECOGNITION
    Angel Flight
    Arnold Air Society (F-2)
1919 National Block and Bridle
    Club

1925 Eta Sigma Phi
1936 Delta Phi Alpha
1950 Sigma Delta Psi
1958 Sigma Phi Alpha

INACTIVE
1893–51 Xi Psi Phi
1906   Scabbard and Blade
       (1)
1914–63 Phi Kappa Theta
1920   Gamma Alpha
1920–90 Phi Kappa Sigma
1921   Kappa Beta Pi
1921–71 Zeta Beta Tau
1922–48 Alpha Phi Alpha
1922–48 Triangle
1923   Kappa Eta Kappa
1923   Phi Chi
1923–33 Kappa Delta
1925–41 Phi Mu
1926–34 Theta Phi Alpha
1927–37 Pi Lambda Phi
1927–80 Pi Omega Pi
1929–42 Phi Delta Epsilon
1932–50 National Collegiate
       Players
1933–88 Sigma Delta Tau
1934–41 Pi Gamma Mu
1936   Zeta Phi Eta
1945–77 Alpha Lambda Delta
1950–51 Sigma Delta Pi
1966   Sigma Iota Epsilon
1968–74 Alpha Epsilon Phi

1905 Phi Beta Pi and Theta
    Kappa Psi (a)
1914 Sigma Delta Chi
1917 Women in Communications
1926 Phi Upsilon Omicron
1941 Keramos

ACHS HONORS
    Omicron Delta Epsilon
1907 Tau Beta Pi
1909 Delta Sigma Rho-Tau
    Kappa Alpha
1911 Phi Kappa Phi
1913 Kappa Omicron Nu
1916 Eta Kappa Nu
1925 Mortar Board
1929 Psi Chi
1930 Tau Sigma Delta
1932 Omega Chi Epsilon
1942 Pi Tau Sigma
1947 Phi Eta Sigma
1950 Alpha Kappa Delta
1953 Sigma Gamma Tau
1957 Alpha Lambda Delta
1963 Phi Sigma Iota
1965 Chi Epsilon
1965 Phi Alpha Theta
1965 Xi Sigma Pi
1970 Pi Sigma Alpha
1971 Kappa Delta Pi
1973 Pi Kappa Lambda
1976 Alpha Pi Mu
1976 Sigma Pi Sigma
1986 Kappa Tau Alpha

OTHER HONORS
    National Order of Omega
1907 Gamma Sigma Delta
1920 Iota Sigma Pi
1921 Sigma Xi
1923 Pi Mu Epsilon
1928 Delta Phi Delta
1973 Phi Beta Kappa

SERVICE
1930 Alpha Phi Omega

RECOGNITION
    Angel Flight
    Arnold Air Society (F-2)
1912 Phi Lambda Upsilon
1915 Scabbard and Blade (2)
1925 Phi Lambda Upsilon
1931 Lambda Delta Lambda
1931 Phi Zeta

INACTIVE
1911–39 Phi Sigma Kappa
1922–49 Alpha Phi Alpha
1922–74 Chi Phi
1923–34 National Collegiate
       Players
1924–39 Pi Gamma Mu
1925   Sigma Delta Epsilon
1929–68 Alpha Chi Sigma
1932–72 Alpha Chi Rho
1949–70 Alpha Kappa Alpha
1958–72 Alpha Kappa Psi

IOWA STATE UNIVERSITY OF SCIENCE AND TECHNOLOGY
Ames, IA. Land-grant college established in 1858. Coeducational; graduate school; public control; nonsectarian. Formerly Iowa State College of Agriculture and Mechanic Arts; changed to present name in 1959.

Fraternities and sororities occupy their own houses on property which they own.

NIC MEN'S
1875 Delta Tau Delta
1904 Sigma Nu
1905 Beta Theta Pi
1905 Sigma Alpha Epsilon
1907 Phi Gamma Delta
1908 Alpha Tau Omega
1909 Acacia
1909 Kappa Sigma
1909 Theta Xi
1913 Delta Upsilon
1913 Phi Delta Theta
1913 Phi Kappa Psi
1913 Pi Kappa Alpha
1914 Alpha Gamma Rho
1915 Tau Kappa Epsilon
1916 Sigma Chi
1916 Sigma Phi Epsilon
1917 Lambda Chi Alpha
1919 Theta Delta Chi
1920 Alpha Sigma Phi
1922 Sigma Pi
1922 Theta Chi
1923 Delta Chi
1924 Phi Kappa Theta
1927 Delta Sigma Phi
1927 FarmHouse
1928 Phi Kappa Tau
1929 Pi Kappa Phi
1949 Beta Sigma Psi

1961 Alpha Kappa Lambda
1964 Triangle

NPC WOMEN'S
1877 Pi Beta Phi
1890 Delta Delta Delta
1908 Kappa Delta
1911 Alpha Delta Pi
1917 Alpha Gamma Delta
1918 Gamma Phi Beta
1921 Sigma Kappa
1922 Chi Omega
1926 Zeta Tau Alpha
1931 Delta Zeta
1946 Kappa Kappa Gamma
1948 Kappa Alpha Theta
1961 Alpha Chi Omega
1968 Alpha Omicron Pi
1969 Alpha Xi Delta
1977 Alpha Phi

NPHC WOMEN'S
1982 Sigma Gamma Rho

PROFESSIONAL
1922 Phi Mu Alpha—Sinfonia
1925 Sigma Alpha Iota
1965 Omega Tau Sigma
1986 Sigma Alpha

OTHER PROFESSIONAL
1905 Alpha Zeta

IOWA WESLEYAN COLLEGE
Mt. Pleasant, IA. College of liberal arts; coeducational; private control; affiliated with Methodist Church. Chartered as literary institute in 1842.

Fraternity and sorority members live in residence halls. Sororities own lodges off campus.

NIC MEN'S
1871 Phi Delta Theta

NPC WOMEN'S
1868 Pi Beta Phi
1902 Alpha Xi Delta

NPHC WOMEN'S
1969 Alpha Kappa Alpha

PROFESSIONAL
1960 Delta Omicron

ACHS HONORS
1925 Sigma Tau Delta

RECOGNITION
1926 Beta Beta Beta

1927 Alpha Psi Omega
1927 Blue Key
1928 Kappa Pi

INACTIVE
1868–15 Beta Theta Pi
1875–80 Delta Tau Delta
1913–76 Sigma Phi Epsilon
1914–43 Phi Mu
1918–87 Zeta Tau Alpha
1924–74 Lambda Chi Alpha
1947–54 Tau Kappa Epsilon
1966–74 Phi Mu Alpha—
    Sinfonia
1968–84 Phi Kappa Tau

ITHACA COLLEGE
Ithaca, NY. Founded 1892; coeducational and nonsectarian. Schools of Humanities and Sciences; Music; Health, Physical Education, and Recreation; Communications; Business; and Allied Health Professions.

NPHC WOMEN'S
1975 Delta Sigma Theta (B)

PROFESSIONAL
1901 Phi Mu Alpha—Sinfonia
1909 Sigma Alpha Iota

OTHER PROFESSIONAL
1926 Phi Epsilon Kappa
1960 Alpha Epsilon Rho

ACHS HONORS
    Omicron Delta Epsilon
1956 Pi Kappa Lambda

1966 Delta Mu Delta
1969 Phi Alpha Theta
1972 Sigma Delta Pi
1977 Phi Kappa Phi

OTHER HONORS
1969 Pi Mu Epsilon

RECOGNITION
1934 Theta Alpha Phi

1936 Sigma Delta Psi
1965 Pi Kappa Delta

INACTIVE
1957–71 Delta Sigma Pi

COLONIES
1990 Alpha Epsilon Pi

JACKSON STATE UNIVERSITY Jackson, MS. College of liberal arts and teachers college; coeducational; state control; established 1877.

NIC MEN'S
1951 Kappa Alpha Psi (A)

NPHC MEN'S
　　　Phi Beta Sigma
1949 Omega Psi Phi
1953 Alpha Phi Alpha

NPHC WOMEN'S
　　　Zeta Phi Beta
1940 Sigma Gamma Rho
1949 Alpha Kappa Alpha
1952 Delta Sigma Theta (B)

OTHER PROFESSIONAL
1971 Alpha Beta Alpha

ACHS HONORS
1949 Alpha Kappa Mu
1965 Gamma Theta Upsilon

1971 Delta Mu Delta
1973 Pi Omega Pi
1975 Alpha Chi
1976 Phi Kappa Phi
1977 Alpha Lambda Delta
1978 Sigma Pi Sigma
1979 Phi Alpha Theta
1980 Psi Chi
1982 Pi Gamma Mu
1982 Pi Sigma Alpha

SERVICE
1979 Alpha Phi Omega

RECOGNITION
1968 Beta Beta Beta

INACTIVE
1907–57 Alpha Xi Delta

JACKSONVILLE STATE UNIVERSITY Jacksonville, AL. University of liberal arts and general studies; teacher preparatory; professional; state control; coeducational. Established 1883.

NIC MEN'S
1968 Delta Chi
1969 Alpha Tau Omega
1971 Kappa Sigma
1971 Pi Kappa Phi
1972 Pi Kappa Phi
1974 Kappa Alpha Psi (A)
1976 Kappa Alpha Order

NPHC MEN'S
　　　Phi Beta Sigma

NPC WOMEN'S
1968 Alpha Xi Delta
1969 Zeta Tau Alpha
1970 Phi Mu
1977 Delta Zeta
1987 Gamma Phi Beta

NPHC WOMEN'S
1973 Delta Sigma Theta (B)

PROFESSIONAL
1950 Phi Mu Alpha—Sinfonia

ACHS HONORS
1972 Phi Alpha Theta
1978 Gamma Theta Upsilon
1978 Omicron Delta Kappa
1980 Phi Eta Sigma

SERVICE
1979 Alpha Phi Omega

INACTIVE
1959–75 Pi Gamma Mu
1973–80 Delta Tau Delta

JACKSONVILLE UNIVERSITY Jacksonville, FL. Founded 1934; coeducational. Became four-year college in 1956.

NIC MEN'S
1968 Phi Delta Theta
1968 Sigma Phi Epsilon
1971 Pi Lambda Phi
1983 Phi Gamma Delta
1988 Sigma Chi
1989 Sigma Phi Epsilon

NPC WOMEN'S
1968 Delta Delta Delta
1968 Zeta Tau Alpha
1969 Alpha Delta Pi

1982 Alpha Epsilon Phi
1990 Alpha Omicron Pi

NPHC WOMEN'S
1977 Alpha Kappa Alpha
1987 Alpha Kappa Alpha

PROFESSIONAL
1954 Kappa Delta Epsilon
1962 Alpha Kappa Psi
1965 Mu Phi Epsilon
1966 Phi Mu Alpha—Sinfonia

1988 Kappa Delta Epsilon

ACHS HONORS
1965 Psi Chi
1967 Phi Alpha Theta
1968 Gamma Theta Upsilon
1970 Sigma Pi Sigma
1975 Phi Kappa Phi
1981 Omicron Delta Kappa
1984 Pi Kappa Lambda
1986 Phi Sigma Iota

OTHER HONORS
　　　National Order of Omega

RECOGNITION
1968 Beta Beta Beta

INACTIVE
1968–86 Delta Zeta
1970–77 Alpha Xi Delta
1979–86 Delta Chi

JAMES MADISON UNIVERSITY Harrisonburg, VA. State-supported comprehensive coeducational institution. Established in 1908.

Fraternity and sorority chapters are housed in university-owned or -operated housing.

NIC MEN'S
1972 Alpha Chi Rho
1977 Pi Kappa Phi
1987 Alpha Kappa Lambda
1987 Sigma Chi

NPHC WOMEN'S
1989 Sigma Gamma Rho

OTHER PROFESSIONAL
1976 Alpha Epsilon Rho

ACHS HONORS
1969 Pi Gamma Mu
1977 Mortar Board
1977 Theta Alpha Kappa

OTHER HONORS
　　　National Order of Omega

SERVICE
1970 Alpha Phi Omega

JAMESTOWN COLLEGE Jamestown, ND. College of liberal arts; coeducational; private control: related to Presbyterian Church; chartered 1884.

ACHS HONORS
1975 Alpha Chi

SERVICE
　　　The National Spurs

INACTIVE
1923–34 Theta Alpha Phi

1925–36 Sigma Tau Delta
1970–82 Psi Chi
1971–79 Sigma Pi Sigma

JARVIS CHRISTIAN COLLEGE Hawkins, TX. College of liberal arts; coeducational; private control; related to Christian Church; established 1912.

NIC MEN'S
1971 Kappa Alpha Psi (A)

NPHC MEN'S
　　　Phi Beta Sigma
1972 Alpha Phi Alpha

NPHC WOMEN'S
1971 Delta Sigma Theta (B)

1972 Sigma Gamma Rho

ACHS HONORS
1953 Alpha Kappa Mu
1974 Pi Omega Pi

INACTIVE
–71　　　Alpha Kappa Alpha

JEFFERSON COLLEGE Hillsboro, MO.

INACTIVE
1858–62 Delta Kappa Epsilon

1858–69 Sigma Chi

JEFFERSON MEDICAL COLLEGE AND MEDICAL CENTER Philadelphia, PA. Founded in 1825 by Dr. George McClellan. Also offers graduate courses in the basic medical sciences, leading to M.S. and Ph.D. degrees.

OTHER PROFESSIONAL
1900 Alpha Kappa Kappa

OTHER HONORS
1903 Alpha Omega Alpha
1967 Sigma Xi

INACTIVE
1903–12 Sigma Phi Epsilon

1907–09 Zeta Beta Tau

JERSEY CITY STATE COLLEGE Jersey City, NJ. Established by act of New Jersey State Legislature, 1925; first instruction, 1929. Teachers college; undergraduate and graduate coeducational; state control; public.

NPHC MEN'S
Phi Beta Sigma
ACHS HONORS
Omicron Delta Epsilon
1938 Kappa Delta Pi

1971 Phi Alpha Theta
1974 Pi Sigma Alpha
1979 Psi Chi

COLONIES
1990 Tau Kappa Epsilon

JOHN BROWN UNIVERSITY Siloam Springs, AR. Private control: Independent/Christian. Founded in 1911. Four-year; coeducational; liberal arts college.

ACHS HONORS
1975 Alpha Chi

JOHN CARROLL UNIVERSITY Cleveland, OH. University; college of liberal arts, and business school for men; private control; Roman Catholic. Founded 1886.

PROFESSIONAL
1956 Alpha Kappa Psi

ACHS HONORS
Omicron Delta Epsilon
1939 Alpha Sigma Nu
1956 Lambda Iota Tau
1958 Delta Sigma Rho-Tau
Kappa Alpha
1959 Phi Alpha Theta
1963 Alpha Epsilon Delta
1965 Psi Chi
1972 Beta Gamma Sigma
1975 Sigma Pi Sigma

1979 Theta Alpha Kappa
1981 Pi Sigma Alpha

OTHER HONORS
1965 Pi Mu Epsilon

RECOGNITION
1948 Society for Collegiate
Journalists—Pi Delta
Epsilon-Alpha Phi Gamma
(P)
1950 Alpha Psi Omega
1953 Scabbard and Blade (10)

JOHN JAY COLLEGE OF CRIMINAL JUSTICE New York, NY.

ACHS HONORS
Pi Alpha Alpha

1974 Psi Chi

JOHN MARSHALL LAW SCHOOL Atlanta, GA.

OTHER PROFESSIONAL
1938 Sigma Delta Kappa

RECOGNITION
1956 Iota Tau Tau

JOHN MARSHALL LAW SCHOOL Chicago, IL.

PROFESSIONAL
1908 Delta Theta Phi
1953 Phi Alpha Delta

OTHER PROFESSIONAL
1916 Kappa Beta Pi

THE JOHNS HOPKINS UNIVERSITY Baltimore, MD. Founded by Johns Hopkins in 1876. Undergraduate college for men. Graduate school, coeducational; private control; nonsectarian.

Fraternities occupy their own houses on their own property.

NIC MEN'S
1877 Alpha Tau Omega
1879 Phi Kappa Psi
1885 Delta Phi
1889 Alpha Delta Phi
1891 Phi Gamma Delta
1920 Kappa Sigma
1925 Pi Lambda Phi
1928 Delta Upsilon
1929 Sigma Phi Epsilon
1959 Tau Epsilon Phi
1969 Sigma Nu

NPHC MEN'S
Phi Beta Sigma

NPC WOMEN'S
1981 Alpha Phi
1982 Phi Mu
1990 Delta Gamma

NPHC WOMEN'S
1976 Delta Sigma Theta (B)
1984 Alpha Kappa Alpha

PROFESSIONAL
1922 Delta Sigma Pi

OTHER PROFESSIONAL
1926 Pi Lambda Theta

ACHS HONORS
Omicron Delta Epsilon
1916 Omicron Delta Kappa
1921 Tau Beta Pi
1949 Pi Tau Sigma
1956 Alpha Epsilon Delta
1957 Pi Sigma Alpha
1958 Eta Kappa Nu
1968 Sigma Pi Sigma

OTHER HONORS
National Order of Omega
1895 Phi Beta Kappa
1906 Alpha Omega Alpha
1924 Sigma Xi

SERVICE
1952 Alpha Phi Omega

RECOGNITION
1920 Scabbard and Blade (2)
1926 Alpha Psi Omega
1928 Phi Delta Gamma
1932 Phi Lambda Upsilon
1954 Delta Phi Alpha

INACTIVE
1891–75 Kappa Alpha Order
1903–04 Phi Rho Sigma
1905	Gamma Alpha
1909	Phi Chi
1909–33 Phi Delta Epsilon
1913	Phi Beta Pi and Theta
Kappa Psi (a)
1917–48 Alpha Kappa Kappa
1920–26 Phi Beta Pi and Theta
Kappa Psi (B)
1923–24 Gamma Sigma Epsilon
1936–71 Alpha Epsilon Pi
1937–42 Alpha Chi Rho
1939–47 Sigma Gamma Epsilon
1957–80 Psi Chi
1958–90 Zeta Beta Tau
1976–81 Alpha Chi Sigma

COLONIES
Acacia
1877 Beta Theta Pi

JOHNSON C. SMITH UNIVERSITY Charlotte, NC. University; coeducational; private control; affiliated with United Presbyterian Church. Established 1867.

NIC MEN'S
1927 Kappa Alpha Psi (A)

NPHC MEN'S
Phi Beta Sigma
1921 Omega Psi Phi
1923 Alpha Phi Alpha

NPHC WOMEN'S
1943 Delta Sigma Theta (B)
1944 Alpha Kappa Alpha
1955 Sigma Gamma Rho

ACHS HONORS
1931 Beta Kappa Chi

1939 Alpha Kappa Mu
1972 Sigma Tau Delta
1976 Alpha Chi
1980 Pi Gamma Mu
1987 Psi Chi

SERVICE
1947 Alpha Phi Omega

INACTIVE
Zeta Phi Beta

JOHNSON SCHOOL OF TECHNOLOGY Scranton, PA.

INACTIVE
1976–89 Alpha Chi Rho

JUDSON COLLEGE Marion, AL. College of liberal arts for women; private control; Baptist Church. Established 1838.

PROFESSIONAL
1955 Delta Omicron
1982 Kappa Delta Epsilon

ACHS HONORS
1946 Sigma Delta Pi
1954 Phi Alpha Theta
1956 Pi Delta Phi

RECOGNITION
1934 Alpha Psi Omega
1967 Lambda Tau
1976 Beta Beta Beta

INACTIVE
1904–19 Kappa Delta
1905–19 Zeta Tau Alpha
1913–19 Delta Delta Delta

JUNIATA COLLEGE   Huntington, PA.

PROFESSIONAL
1987 Phi Chi Theta

ACHS HONORS
1975 Sigma Pi Sigma

RECOGNITION
1928 Sigma Delta Psi

1967 Society for Collegiate
Journalists—Pi Delta
Epsilon-Alpha Phi Gamma
(A)
1970 Beta Beta Beta

KALAMAZOO COLLEGE   Kalamazoo, MI. College of liberal arts; coeducational; private control; related to Baptist Church. Chartered as Michigan and Huron Institute 1833; name changed to present 1855.

ACHS HONORS
1942 Alpha Lambda Delta

OTHER HONORS
1958 Phi Beta Kappa

RECOGNITION
1918 Pi Kappa Delta

INACTIVE
1965–78 Phi Eta Sigma

KANSAS CITY COLLEGE OF OSTEOPATHIC MEDICINE   Kansas City, MO. Founded 1916. Coeducational.

NPHC MEN'S
Phi Beta Sigma

OSTEOPATHIC
1915 Phi Sigma Gamma
1916 Iota Tau Sigma

1923 Atlas Club
1930 Psi Sigma Alpha
1932 Sigma Sigma Phi
1953 Delta Omega
1964 Lambda Omicron Gamma

THE UNIVERSITY OF KANSAS   Lawrence, KS. University; coeducational; state control; main campus at Lawrence; medical center at Kansas City, KS. Established 1864; first instruction 1866.

The administration permits fraternities and sororities the right of ownership of property and nearly all avail themselves of the advantage of this right.

NIC MEN'S
1873 Beta Theta Pi
1876 Phi Kappa Psi
1881 Phi Gamma Delta
1882 Phi Delta Theta
1884 Sigma Chi
1884 Sigma Nu
1901 Alpha Tau Omega
1903 Sigma Alpha Epsilon
1904 Acacia
1912 Kappa Sigma
1914 Delta Tau Delta
1914 Pi Kappa Alpha
1915 Phi Kappa Theta
1920 Delta Upsilon
1920 Kappa Alpha Psi (A)
1922 Alpha Kappa Lambda
1923 Delta Chi
1923 Sigma Phi Epsilon
1927 Triangle
1942 Tau Kappa Epsilon
1947 Lambda Chi Alpha
1949 Alpha Epsilon Pi

1954 Theta Chi
1984 Zeta Beta Tau

NPHC MEN'S
Phi Beta Sigma
1917 Alpha Phi Alpha

NPC WOMEN'S
1873 Pi Beta Phi
1881 Kappa Alpha Theta
1883 Kappa Kappa Gamma
1902 Chi Omega
1912 Alpha Delta Pi
1913 Sigma Kappa
1914 Alpha Chi Omega
1915 Gamma Phi Beta
1916 Alpha Xi Delta
1918 Alpha Omicron Pi
1922 Alpha Gamma Delta
1941 Delta Gamma
1946 Delta Delta Delta
1985 Sigma Delta Tau
1990 Kappa Delta

NPHC WOMEN'S
1916 Alpha Kappa Alpha
1925 Delta Sigma Theta (B)
1976 Alpha Kappa Alpha

PROFESSIONAL
1897 Phi Delta Phi
1909 Alpha Chi Sigma
1909 Phi Alpha Delta
1911 Mu Phi Epsilon
1912 Theta Tau
1914 Phi Mu Alpha—Sinfonia
1916 Delta Theta Phi
1920 Alpha Kappa Psi
1920 Psi Omega
1921 Delta Sigma Pi
1932 Kappa Psi
1942 Kappa Epsilon
1948 Sigma Alpha Iota
1984 Alpha Rho Chi

OTHER PROFESSIONAL
1910 Sigma Delta Chi
1913 Women in Communications
1918 Pi Lambda Theta
1921 Scarab
1954 Kappa Alpha Mu
1957 Phi Epsilon Kappa
1959 Alpha Epsilon Rho
1965 Alpha Tau Alpha
1966 Alpha Alpha Gamma

ACHS HONORS
Pi Alpha Alpha
1910 Delta Sigma Rho-Tau
Kappa Alpha
1914 Tau Beta Pi
1915 Kappa-Omicron Nu
1921 Phi Sigma
1922 Pi Sigma Alpha
1924 Mortar Board
1926 Beta Gamma Sigma
1927 Pi Kappa Lambda
1929 Psi Chi
1930 Pi Delta Phi
1931 Sigma Theta Tau
1941 Pi Tau Sigma
1946 Phi Alpha Theta
1947 Omicron Delta Kappa
1949 Sigma Delta Pi
1950 Sigma Pi Sigma
1950 Tau Sigma Delta
1951 Rho Chi
1952 Eta Kappa Nu
1953 Sigma Gamma Tau
1961 Alpha Kappa Delta
1961 Lambda Sigma Society
1967 Chi Epsilon
1967 Gamma Theta Upsilon

1967 Kappa Tau Alpha
1975 Phi Kappa Phi

OTHER HONORS
National Order of Omega
1890 Phi Beta Kappa
1890 Sigma Xi
1909 Delta Phi Delta
1915 Sigma Gamma Epsilon
1924 Order of the Coif
1927 National Collegiate
Players
1928 Pi Mu Epsilon
1930 Alpha Omega Alpha

SERVICE
1929 Alpha Phi Omega

RECOGNITION
Angel Flight
Arnold Air Society (G-2)
1923 Kappa Eta Kappa
1923 Scabbard and Blade (4)
1948 Phi Lambda Upsilon
1949 Delta Phi Alpha
1968 Sigma Delta Epsilon

INACTIVE
1904–13 Phi Beta Pi and Theta
Kappa Psi (a)
1910   Phi Beta Pi and Theta
Kappa Psi (a)
1915   Phi Chi
1915–76 Delta Zeta
1916   Phi Alpha Tau
1917–30 Phi Delta Chi
1920   Phi Beta Pi and Theta
Kappa Psi (a)
1921–55 Theta Phi Alpha
1923–36 Sigma Alpha Mu
1924   Iota Sigma Pi
1925–80 Phi Chi Theta
1926   Eta Sigma Phi
1926–32 Phi Delta Epsilon
1926–36 Delta Zeta
1927   Phi Lambda Kappa
1929   Phi Chi
1949–84 Phi Kappa Sigma
1950–61 Sigma Pi
1950–89 Alpha Phi
1956–69 Delta Sigma Phi
1960–66 Pi Omega Pi
1967–72 Beta Sigma Psi
1970–71 Alpha Epsilon Phi

COLONIES
1920 Lambda Kappa Sigma
1948 Phi Kappa Tau
1977 Sigma Gamma Rho

Medical Center   Kansas City, KS.

PROFESSIONAL
1931 Alpha Omega

INACTIVE
1927–87 Phi Mu Alpha—
Sinfonia

1948–52 Kappa Mu Epsilon
1950–59 Phi Mu Alpha—
Sinfonia

KANSAS STATE COLLEGE OF PITTSBURG   Pittsburg, KS. Founded in 1903 for the purpose of instruction in liberal arts and teacher education. Coeducational; undergraduate and graduate program; state control.

Those who own houses own them outright; some are leasing.

NPC WOMEN'S
1920 Alpha Sigma Alpha

PROFESSIONAL
1930 Sigma Alpha Iota
1946 Delta Psi Kappa
1959 Alpha Kappa Psi

OTHER PROFESSIONAL
1920 Phi Upsilon Omicron
1974 Delta Pi Epsilon

ACHS HONORS
1925 Kappa Delta Pi
1926 Sigma Tau Delta

RECOGNITION
1921 Pi Kappa Delta
1955 Scabbard and Blade (12)
1960 Beta Beta Beta

INACTIVE
1948–53 Alpha Phi Alpha
1950–60 Phi Lambda Chi

KANSAS STATE UNIVERSITY OF AGRICULTURE AND APPLIED SCIENCE   Manhattan, KS. University and land-grant college; coeducational; state control. Established as Kansas State Agricultural College 1863; name changed 1959.

Administration requires fraternities and sororities to occupy their own houses on their own land and all of them do so. Freshman students must live in either a residence hall or Greek chapter house.

NIC MEN'S
1913 Acacia
1913 Pi Kappa Alpha
1913 Sigma Alpha Epsilon
1914 Beta Theta Pi
1918 Sigma Phi Epsilon
1919 Delta Tau Delta
1919 Kappa Sigma
1920 Alpha Tau Omega
1920 Phi Delta Theta
1921 FarmHouse
1921 Phi Kappa Theta
1924 Lambda Chi Alpha
1925 Delta Sigma Phi
1925 Phi Kappa Tau
1927 Alpha Gamma Rho
1930 Alpha Kappa Lambda
1931 Tau Kappa Epsilon
1931 Theta Xi
1947 Kappa Alpha Psi (A)
1949 Sigma Chi
1951 Beta Sigma Psi
1956 Delta Upsilon
1964 Triangle
1968 Phi Gamma Delta
1978 Pi Kappa Phi

NPHC MEN'S
        Phi Beta Sigma
1975 Alpha Phi Alpha

NPC WOMEN'S
1915 Alpha Delta Pi
1915 Chi Omega
1915 Delta Delta Delta
1915 Pi Beta Phi
1916 Kappa Kappa Gamma
1920 Kappa Delta
1922 Alpha Xi Delta
1947 Alpha Chi Omega
1957 Gamma Phi Beta
1961 Kappa Alpha Theta
1982 Sigma Sigma Sigma

NPHC WOMEN'S
1969 Delta Sigma Theta (B)

PROFESSIONAL
1922 Mu Phi Epsilon
1926 Alpha Kappa Psi
1946 Alpha Delta Theta
1965 Alpha Chi Sigma
1970 Kappa Kappa Psi
1970 Tau Beta Sigma
1972 Delta Psi Kappa

OTHER PROFESSIONAL
1909 Alpha Zeta
1915 Sigma Delta Chi
1916 Women in Communications
1925 Phi Sigma Pi
1930 Phi Epsilon Kappa
1950 Alpha Alpha Gamma
1952 Alpha Epsilon Rho
1960 Kappa Alpha Mu
1960 Phi Upsilon Omicron

ACHS HONORS
        Omicron Delta Epsilon
1915 Kappa Omicron Nu
1915 Phi Kappa Phi
1928 Mortar Board
1939 Eta Kappa Nu
1939 Pi Tau Sigma
1946 Pi Gamma Mu
1950 Tau Sigma Delta
1951 Delta Sigma Rho-Tau Kappa Alpha
1953 Phi Alpha Theta
1957 Phi Eta Sigma
1958 Alpha Lambda Delta
1959 Gamma Theta Upsilon
1960 Chi Epsilon
1961 Kappa Delta Pi
1964 Sigma Delta Pi
1969 Alpha Pi Mu
1970 Psi Chi
1973 Beta Gamma Sigma
1974 Tau Beta Pi
1976 Alpha Epsilon Delta
1976 Omega Chi Epsilon
1976 Sigma Pi Sigma
1977 Pi Kappa Lambda
1979 Pi Sigma Alpha

1981 Sigma Lambda Alpha
1983 Pi Omega Pi

OTHER HONORS
        National Order of Omega
1914 Gamma Sigma Delta
1928 Sigma Xi
1935 Pi Mu Epsilon
1945 National Collegiate Players
1947 Sigma Gamma Epsilon
1952 Delta Phi Delta
1974 Phi Beta Kappa

SERVICE
        The National Spurs
1930 Alpha Phi Omega

RECOGNITION
        Angel Flight
        Arnold Air Society (G-2)
1914 Scabbard and Blade (1)
1919 National Block and Bridle Club

INACTIVE
1931 Phi Lambda Upsilon
1934 Blue Key
1937 Lambda Delta Lambda
1953 Phi Delta Gamma
1969 Phi Zeta

INACTIVE
1912   Alpha Psi
1916   Phi Alpha Tau
1921–85 Phi Mu Alpha—Sinfonia
1923–35 Alpha Rho Chi
1923–41 Phi Sigma Kappa
1931–40 Zeta Tau Alpha
1934–41 Alpha Kappa Alpha
1935   Kappa Eta Kappa
1937–86 Alpha Kappa Alpha
1949–63 Alpha Epsilon Pi
1957–84 Phi Chi Theta
1964–81 Delta Chi
1966–74 Delta Mu Delta
1985–89 Alpha Gamma Delta

KANSAS WESLEYAN UNIVERSITY   Salina, KS. College of liberal arts; coeducational; private control; related to Methodist Church; established 1885; first instruction 1886.

ACHS HONORS
1964 Lambda Iota Tau

RECOGNITION
1926 Alpha Psi Omega
1946 Kappa Pi
1970 Beta Beta Beta

INACTIVE
1925–31 Sigma Tau Delta
1928–46 Pi Gamma Mu
1970–82 Delta Mu Delta
1972–86 Sigma Pi Sigma

KEAN COLLEGE OF NEW JERSEY   Union, NJ.

NPHC MEN'S
        Phi Beta Sigma

PROFESSIONAL
1972 Sigma Alpha Iota

ACHS HONORS
        Omicron Delta Epsilon
        Pi Alpha Alpha
1974 Psi Chi
1976 Pi Sigma Alpha

1977 Phi Kappa Phi
1979 Phi Alpha Theta

SERVICE
1969 Alpha Phi Omega
1971 Alpha Phi Omega

INACTIVE
1971–86 Phi Mu Alpha—Sinfonia

KEARNEY STATE COLLEGE   Kearney, NB. Founded in 1905 as Western State Normal School. Became four-year degree-granting institution 1922; coeducational; baccalaureate and master's degrees; state-supported.

NIC MEN'S
1962 Sigma Tau Gamma
1962 Theta Xi
1965 Sigma Phi Epsilon
1966 Alpha Tau Omega
1966 Phi Delta Theta
1967 Beta Sigma Psi
1967 Phi Kappa Tau
1987 Pi Kappa Alpha

NPC WOMEN'S
1962 Chi Omega
1963 Alpha Phi
1963 Gamma Phi Beta
1969 Alpha Omicron Pi

ACHS HONORS
        Omicron Delta Epsilon
1955 Kappa Omicron Nu
1959 Kappa Mu Epsilon
1970 Phi Alpha Theta
1973 Psi Chi
1975 Sigma Pi Sigma
1982 Gamma Theta Upsilon
1984 Phi Eta Sigma

SERVICE
        The National Spurs
1962 Alpha Phi Omega

RECOGNITION
1944 Beta Beta Beta
1972 Lambda Tau

INACTIVE
1929-79 Pi Omega Pi
1956-72 Pi Gamma Mu
1960-86 Phi Mu Alpha—
    Sinfonia

1962-69 Alpha Xi Delta
1963-67 Delta Zeta
1970-72 Alpha Kappa Lambda
1972-74 Acacia

KEENE STATE COLLEGE Keene, NH. State control; coeducational; established as Keene Normal School 1909; first baccalaureate 1928; master's degree in education.

NIC MEN'S
1968 Tau Kappa Epsilon
1970 Phi Mu Delta

NPC WOMEN'S
1983 Delta Phi Epsilon

OTHER PROFESSIONAL
1921 Kappa Delta Phi (C)

ACHS HONORS
    Sigma Pi Sigma
1943 Kappa Delta Pi
1985 Phi Alpha Theta
1989 Psi Chi

SERVICE
1948 Alpha Phi Omega

RECOGNITION
1948 Alpha Psi Omega
1966 Beta Beta Beta

INACTIVE
1948-54 Sigma Tau Gamma
1972-74 Delta Zeta
1980-85 Zeta Beta Tau

COLONIES
1989 Sigma Pi Sigma

KENT STATE UNIVERSITY Kent, OH. Founded by an act of the Ohio General Assembly, 1910. Board of trustees organized 1911, first instruction 1913. University; coeducational; semester; accredited; state control; graduate and undergraduate programs.

Fraternities and sororities are permitted to own their own houses on their own land.

NIC MEN'S
1948 Delta Upsilon
1949 Alpha Epsilon Pi
1949 Kappa Alpha Psi (A)
1949 Phi Kappa Theta
1950 Delta Tau Delta
1950 Phi Sigma Kappa
1953 Alpha Tau Omega
1953 Sigma Alpha Epsilon
1953 Theta Chi
1954 Phi Delta Theta
1963 Tau Kappa Epsilon
1965 Sigma Chi
1982 Alpha Chi Rho
1990 Delta Chi

NPHC MEN'S
    Phi Beta Sigma
1957 Alpha Phi Alpha

NPC WOMEN'S
1947 Alpha Xi Delta
1947 Chi Omega
1947 Delta Gamma
1948 Alpha Phi
1948 Delta Zeta

NPHC WOMEN'S
1962 Sigma Gamma Rho
1964 Delta Sigma Theta (B)
1968 Alpha Kappa Alpha
1973 Sigma Gamma Rho

PROFESSIONAL
1942 Delta Sigma Pi
1951 Kappa Kappa Psi
1982 Phi Alpha Delta

OTHER PROFESSIONAL
1934 Phi Epsilon Kappa
1951 Women in Communications
1952 Sigma Delta Chi
1964 Beta Alpha Psi

ACHS HONORS
    Omicron Delta Epsilon
    Pi Alpha Alpha
1935 Kappa Delta Pi
1938 Phi Alpha Theta
1939 Pi Gamma Mu
1941 Psi Chi
1948 Pi Delta Phi
1948 Sigma Delta Pi
1950 Gamma Theta Upsilon
1950 Pi Sigma Alpha
1954 Alpha Kappa Delta
1955 Kappa Omicron Nu
1960 Alpha Lambda Delta
1964 Beta Gamma Sigma
1965 Omicron Delta Kappa
1968 Beta Phi Mu
1972 Mortar Board
1972 Sigma Pi Sigma
1973 Sigma Tau Delta
1980 Pi Kappa Lambda
1990 Kappa Tau Alpha

OTHER HONORS
    National Order of Omega
1956 Pi Mu Epsilon
1967 Sigma Xi
1968 Sigma Gamma Epsilon
1977 Phi Beta Kappa

SERVICE
1948 Alpha Phi Omega

RECOGNITION
    Angel Flight
    Arnold Air Society (E-2)
1930 Iota Lambda Sigma
1932 Blue Key
1933 Cardinal Key
1949 Scabbard and Blade (8)
1950 Delta Phi Alpha
1966 Beta Beta Beta

INACTIVE
1925-81 Sigma Sigma Sigma
1926-39 Alpha Sigma Alpha
1927-39 Alpha Sigma Tau
1927-87 Sigma Tau Gamma
1947-54 Kappa Alpha Mu
1947-72 Gamma Phi Beta

1947-78 Alpha Gamma Delta
1949-70 Sigma Nu
1950-73 Alpha Chi Omega
1950-83 Kappa Sigma
1953-80 Pi Omega Pi
1953-83 Sigma Phi Epsilon
1957-74 Phi Eta Sigma
1960-80 Phi Gamma Delta
1965-84 Alpha Epsilon Phi
1967-82 Phi Mu Alpha—
    Sinfonia
1970-71 Zeta Beta Tau
1971-78 Phi Kappa Psi

COLONIES
1949 Phi Kappa Tau

UNIVERSITY OF KENTUCKY Lexington, KY. University and land-grant college; coeducational; state control; chartered as agricultural and mechanical college 1865; became University of Kentucky 1916.

The majority of the fraternities and sororities occupy houses leased from the University on a long-term basis. These houses are constructed according to specifications agreed upon by the group to occupy the house and the University.

NIC MEN'S
    Tau Kappa Epsilon
1893 Kappa Alpha Order
1893 Sigma Chi
1900 Sigma Alpha Epsilon
1901 Kappa Sigma
1901 Phi Delta Theta
1901 Pi Kappa Alpha
1902 Sigma Nu
1909 Alpha Tau Omega
1920 Alpha Gamma Rho
1920 Phi Kappa Tau
1924 Delta Tau Delta
1926 Phi Sigma Kappa
1930 Lambda Chi Alpha
1933 Sigma Phi Epsilon
1951 FarmHouse
1951 Tau Kappa Epsilon
1968 Theta Chi
1973 Sigma Pi
1981 Kappa Alpha Psi (A)
1988 Phi Kappa Psi
1989 Beta Theta Pi

NPHC MEN'S
    Phi Beta Sigma
1965 Alpha Phi Alpha

NPC WOMEN'S
1908 Alpha Gamma Delta
1908 Alpha Xi Delta
1909 Kappa Delta
1910 Kappa Kappa Gamma
1914 Chi Omega
1923 Delta Delta Delta
1923 Delta Zeta
1924 Zeta Tau Alpha
1941 Alpha Delta Pi
1945 Kappa Alpha Theta
1962 Delta Gamma
1962 Pi Beta Phi
1982 Alpha Omicron Pi
1990 Sigma Kappa

NPHC WOMEN'S
1975 Alpha Kappa Alpha
1975 Delta Sigma Theta (B)

PROFESSIONAL
1909 Kappa Psi
1914 Phi Alpha Delta
1923 Phi Delta Chi
1925 Phi Delta Phi
1958 Lambda Kappa Sigma
1961 Delta Psi Kappa
1966 Delta Theta Phi
1967 Sigma Alpha Iota

OTHER PROFESSIONAL
1912 Alpha Zeta
1920 Women in Communications
1922 Phi Upsilon Omicron
1923 Alpha Zeta Omega
1952 Beta Alpha Psi
1956 Alpha Epsilon Rho
1956 Sigma Delta Chi

ACHS HONORS
    Omicron Delta Epsilon
    Pi Alpha Alpha
1902 Tau Beta Pi
1913 Delta Sigma Rho-Tau
    Kappa Alpha
1920 Mortar Board
1923 Pi Sigma Alpha
1924 Kappa Delta Pi
1925 Omicron Delta Kappa
1928 Beta Gamma Sigma
1930 Sigma Pi Sigma
1931 Kappa Tau Alpha
1931 Lambda Sigma Society
1937 Phi Alpha Theta
1940 Alpha Lambda Delta
1946 Phi Eta Sigma
1947 Pi Tau Sigma
1948 Eta Kappa Nu
1948 Gamma Theta Upsilon
1949 Rho Chi
1950 Phi Sigma Iota

1959 Alpha Epsilon Delta
1959 Alpha Kappa Delta
1961 Psi Chi
1962 Chi Epsilon
1965 Pi Delta Phi
1965 Sigma Delta Pi
1969 Alpha Sigma Mu
1970 Beta Phi Mu
1970 Pi Kappa Lambda
1971 Omega Chi Epsilon
1975 Tau Sigma Delta
1976 Xi Sigma Pi
1977 Alpha Epsilon
1989 Sigma Lambda Alpha

OTHER HONORS
     National Order of Omega
1922 Sigma Xi
1926 Phi Beta Kappa
1927 Pi Mu Epsilon
1928 Sigma Gamma Epsilon
1931 Order of the Coif
1955 Gamma Sigma Delta
1964 Alpha Omega Alpha
1966 Omicron Kappa Upsilon

SERVICE
1933 Alpha Phi Omega

RECOGNITION
     Angel Flight

     Arnold Air Society (D-2)
1923 National Block and Bridle
     Club
1923 Scabbard and Blade (4)
1925 Chi Delta Phi
1927 Eta Sigma Phi
1960 Delta Phi Alpha

INACTIVE
1913–81 Delta Chi
1915–24 Sigma Alpha Mu
1917–60 Alpha Sigma Phi
1917–70 Alpha Chi Sigma
1920–68 Delta Sigma Pi
1920–83 Triangle
1922–89 Phi Mu Alpha—
         Sinfonia
1925–73 Phi Beta
1927–36 Sigma Delta Chi
1942–73 Zeta Beta Tau
1949–53 Pi Lambda Phi
1952–57 Phi Sigma Sigma
1958–83 Phi Gamma Delta
1960   Kappa Beta Pi
1963–71 Kappa Beta Pi
1966–76 Alpha Chi Omega
1966–82 Gamma Phi Beta
1969   Sigma Phi Alpha
1972–87 Alpha Epsilon Pi

KENTUCKY STATE UNIVERSITY   Frankfort, KY.
Founded as a result of an act passed by the General
Assembly of Kentucky in 1886. It is an undergradu-
ate coeducational teacher training college.

Fraternities and sororities do not own housing, but
the administration does not prohibit individual
ownership.

NIC MEN'S
1935 Kappa Alpha Psi (A)

NPHC MEN'S
     Phi Beta Sigma
1932 Alpha Phi Alpha
1934 Omega Psi Phi

NPHC WOMEN'S
1932 Alpha Kappa Alpha
1934 Delta Sigma Theta (B)
1947 Sigma Gamma Rho

ACHS HONORS
1945 Alpha Kappa Mu
1945 Beta Kappa Chi
1972 Sigma Tau Delta

SERVICE
1966 Alpha Phi Omega
1975 Gamma Sigma Sigma

INACTIVE
     Zeta Phi Beta

KENTUCKY WESLEYAN COLLEGE   Owens-
boro, KY. College of liberal arts; coeducational; private control; affiliated with the Methodist Church;
established 1858; first instruction 1866.

NIC MEN'S
1959 Sigma Phi Epsilon
1960 Sigma Nu
1969 Sigma Alpha Mu

NPC WOMEN'S
1958 Kappa Delta
1958 Sigma Kappa

PROFESSIONAL
1967 Delta Omicron

ACHS HONORS
1968 Alpha Chi

1968 Lambda Iota Tau
1968 Phi Alpha Theta

RECOGNITION
1955 Alpha Psi Omega

INACTIVE
1902–07 Kappa Alpha Order
1959–81 Alpha Omicron Pi
1963–86 Phi Mu Alpha—
        Sinfonia
1964–74 Phi Delta Theta

KENNESAW STATE COLLEGE   Marietta, GA.

NIC MEN'S
1987 Theta Chi

NPC WOMEN'S
1989 Delta Phi Epsilon
1989 Phi Mu

ACHS HONORS
     Phi Kappa Phi
1982 Phi Alpha Theta

1982 Pi Sigma Alpha
1982 Psi Chi
1984 Phi Eta Sigma

INACTIVE
1983–87 Phi Mu Alpha—
        Sinfonia

COLONIES
     Pi Kappa Phi

KENYON COLLEGE   Gambier, OH. Founded by
Philander Chase. Chartered 1827; first instruction
1824; first baccalaureate degree awarded 1829. College of liberal arts; coeducational; related to the
Protestant Episcopal Church.

The administration requires fraternity members to
live in dormitories.

NIC MEN'S
1852 Delta Kappa Epsilon
1858 Alpha Delta Phi
1860 Psi Upsilon
1879 Beta Theta Pi
1881 Delta Tau Delta
1937 Phi Kappa Sigma
1940 Delta Phi

ACHS HONORS
     Omicron Delta Epsilon

OTHER HONORS
1858 Phi Beta Kappa

RECOGNITION
     Arnold Air Society (D-1)

INACTIVE
1854–98 Theta Delta Chi
1861–65 Chi Phi
1916–70 Sigma Pi

KEUKA COLLEGE   Keuka Park, NY. College of
liberal arts and professional studies for women; private control. Established 1890.

ACHS HONORS
1932 Pi Gamma Mu
1963 Sigma Tau Delta

RECOGNITION
1930 Alpha Psi Omega

1950 Society for Collegiate
     Journalists—Pi Delta
     Epsilon-Alpha Phi Gamma
     (P)
1954 Chi Beta Phi
1967 Kappa Pi

KING'S COLLEGE   Wilkes-Barre, PA. Four-year,
coeducational, independent undergraduate college
of 1,700 full-time and 600 part-time students.

ACHS HONORS
1963 Delta Epsilon Sigma
1967 Phi Alpha Theta
1973 Psi Chi
1977 Theta Alpha Kappa
1979 Phi Sigma Tau
1984 Pi Sigma Alpha
1990 Delta Mu Delta

RECOGNITION
1962 Society for Collegiate
     Journalists—Pi Delta
     Epsilon-Alpha Phi Gamma
     (P)

INACTIVE
1984–88 Pi Lambda Phi

KIRKSVILLE COLLEGE OF OSTEOPATHIC
MEDICINE   Kirksville, MO. The American School
of Osteopathy was founded in Kirksville by Andrew Taylor Still and chartered by the State of Missouri on May 10, 1892. In 1922 Andrew T. Still
College of Osteopathy was founded and in 1926 the
two schools were merged to form the present institution. Professional coeducational; nonsectarian.

OSTEOPATHIC
1898 Atlas Club

1902 Iota Tau Sigma
1903 Theta Psi

1904 Delta Omega
1921 Sigma Sigma Phi
1924 Psi Sigma Alpha

SERVICE
1936 Alpha Phi Omega

INACTIVE
1915   Phi Sigma Gamma

KNOX COLLEGE Galesburg, IL. College of liberal arts; coeducational; private control; nonsectarian; chartered 1837.

Five fraternities have houses owned by the college and rented on a long-term lease basis.

NIC MEN'S
1855 Beta Theta Pi
1867 Phi Gamma Delta
1912 Tau Kappa Epsilon
1930 Phi Delta Theta

NPC WOMEN'S
1884 Pi Beta Phi
1889 Delta Delta Delta
1930 Pi Beta Phi

PROFESSIONAL
1923 Sigma Alpha Iota

ACHS HONORS
1920 Mortar Board
1921 Pi Kappa Lambda
1953 Pi Sigma Alpha
1975 Sigma Delta Pi

OTHER HONORS
1917 Phi Beta Kappa

SERVICE
1984 Alpha Phi Omega

RECOGNITION
1923 Scabbard and Blade (5)
1928 Sigma Delta Psi

INACTIVE
1871–30 Phi Delta Theta
1893–73 Alpha Xi Delta
1912–89 Phi Mu
1915–34 Lambda Chi Alpha
1915–64 Delta Zeta
1917–27 Sigma Delta Chi
1922–34 Theta Alpha Phi
1926–67 Phi Beta
1927–37 Pi Gamma Mu
1928–53 Phi Sigma Kappa
1929–42 Beta Beta Beta

KNOXVILLE COLLEGE Knoxville, TN. College of liberal arts; coeducational; private control; affiliated with United Presbyterian Church; established 1863.

Sorority and fraternity members occupy residence halls.

NIC MEN'S
1947 Kappa Alpha Psi (A)

NPHC MEN'S
   Phi Beta Sigma
1946 Omega Psi Phi
1947 Alpha Phi Alpha

NPHC WOMEN'S
1946 Alpha Kappa Alpha
1947 Delta Sigma Theta (B)
1962 Sigma Gamma Rho
1975 Delta Sigma Theta (B)

ACHS HONORS
1938 Alpha Kappa Mu
1958 Beta Kappa Chi
1966 Lambda Iota Tau

RECOGNITION
1963 Sigma Delta Psi

INACTIVE
   Zeta Phi Beta
1969–83 Phi Mu Alpha—
   Sinfonia

KUTZTOWN STATE COLLEGE Kutztown, PA. Established as normal school in 1866; in 1926 designated as state teachers college; became state college in 1960; coeducational; state control.

NIC MEN'S
1972 Lambda Chi Alpha
1989 Alpha Chi Rho

NPC WOMEN'S
1972 Delta Zeta

PROFESSIONAL
1973 Kappa Kappa Psi

OTHER PROFESSIONAL
1957 Alpha Beta Alpha

ACHS HONORS
1941 Kappa Delta Pi
1965 Gamma Theta Upsilon
1965 Kappa Mu Epsilon
1967 Phi Alpha Theta
1972 Psi Chi
1975 Sigma Tau Delta

1987 Phi Sigma Iota

SERVICE
1964 Alpha Phi Omega

RECOGNITION
1963 Alpha Psi Omega

INACTIVE
1973–77 Tau Kappa Epsilon

LAFAYETTE COLLEGE Easton, PA. College of liberal arts, sciences, and engineering; chartered 1826; private control; affiliated with the Presbyterian Church. Coeducational.

Ownership of houses is on college-owned land for the most part.

NIC MEN'S
1855 Delta Kappa Epsilon
1857 Zeta Psi
1867 Sigma Chi
1867 Theta Delta Chi
1869 Phi Kappa Psi
1873 Phi Delta Theta
1874 Chi Phi
1883 Phi Gamma Delta
1900 Sigma Nu
1919 Sigma Alpha Epsilon
1928 Kappa Delta Rho
1930 Theta Chi

NPC WOMEN'S
1980 Kappa Kappa Gamma
1980 Pi Beta Phi
1981 Alpha Gamma Delta
1982 Delta Gamma
1989 Alpha Phi

OTHER PROFESSIONAL
1922 Kappa Phi Kappa

ACHS HONORS
   Omicron Delta Epsilon
1921 Tau Beta Pi

1948 Phi Alpha Theta
1959 Eta Kappa Nu
1960 Psi Chi
1971 Pi Tau Sigma
1984 Pi Sigma Alpha

OTHER HONORS
1890 Phi Beta Kappa

SERVICE
1925 Alpha Phi Omega

RECOGNITION
1928 Alpha Psi Omega
1932 Scabbard and Blade (7)

INACTIVE
1853–85 Phi Kappa Sigma
1874–88 Delta Tau Delta
1885–88 Delta Upsilon
1903–86 Alpha Chi Rho
1921–86 Kappa Sigma
1923–35 Alpha Chi Sigma
1928–75 Phi Kappa Tau
1931–72 Theta Xi
1940–83 Pi Lambda Phi
1980–90 Sigma Kappa

LAGRANGE COLLEGE LaGrange, GA. College of liberal arts; coeducational; private control (Methodist); chartered 1831.

NIC MEN'S
1969 Kappa Sigma
1969 Pi Kappa Phi
1970 Delta Tau Delta

NPC WOMEN'S
1971 Alpha Omicron Pi
1971 Kappa Delta
1971 Phi Mu

ACHS HONORS
   Omicron Delta Epsilon

1959 Pi Gamma Mu
1979 Omicron Delta Kappa
1988 Phi Alpha Theta

RECOGNITION
1940 Alpha Psi Omega

INACTIVE
1859–60 Phi Kappa Psi

LAKE FOREST COLLEGE Lake Forest, IL. Liberal arts college; coeducational; private control; affiliated with United Presbyterian Church. Chartered as Lind University 1857; first instruction at college level 1861; name changed to Lake Forest University, 1865; first baccalaureate awarded 1879; became Lake Forest College 1902.

ACHS HONORS
   Omicron Delta Epsilon
1929 Phi Sigma Iota
1930 Sigma Pi Sigma

1960 Psi Chi
1971 Pi Sigma Alpha
1981 Phi Sigma Tau

OTHER HONORS
1962 Phi Beta Kappa

RECOGNITION
1935 Beta Beta Beta
1954 Alpha Psi Omega

INACTIVE
1880–67 Kappa Sigma
1893–95 Phi Kappa Sigma
1926–68 Phi Eta Sigma
1930–40 Sigma Tau Delta

1932–61 Alpha Xi Delta
1934–61 Gamma Phi Beta
1934–62 Alpha Lambda Delta
1936–61 Alpha Delta Pi
1938–61 Chi Omega
1950–61 Phi Delta Theta
1950–66 Delta Chi
1952–61 Alpha Phi
1952–72 Tau Kappa Epsilon
1978–81 Theta Delta Chi

LAKE SUPERIOR STATE COLLEGE Sault Ste. Marie, MI. Public institution. Founded in 1946. Four-year; coeducational.

Fraternities and sororities have their own houses.

NIC MEN'S
1984 Delta Sigma Phi
1987 Tau Kappa Epsilon
1988 Theta Xi

NPC WOMEN'S
1987 Alpha Sigma Tau
1989 Delta Phi Epsilon

LAKELAND COLLEGE Sheboygan, WI. College of liberal arts and general studies; teachers preparatory; coeducational. United Church of Christ affiliation. Established 1862.

ACHS HONORS
1972 Phi Alpha Theta

RECOGNITION
1974 Sigma Phi Alpha

INACTIVE
1977–88 Tau Kappa Epsilon

LAMAR UNIVERSITY Beaumont, TX. Founded in 1923 by the South Park Independent School District as South Park Junior College. In 1932, a Union Junior College District was created in a county election; the name was changed to Lamar College. In September, 1951, Lamar College became Lamar State College of Technology, a four-year, coeducational college. In August, 1971, the institution gained university status and the name was changed to Lamar University.

NIC MEN'S
1957 Alpha Tau Omega
1957 Sigma Nu
1957 Sigma Phi Epsilon
1958 Pi Kappa Alpha
1965 Phi Delta Theta
1968 Phi Kappa Theta
1970 Delta Tau Delta
1972 Kappa Sigma
1973 Kappa Alpha Psi (A)

NPHC MEN'S
   Phi Beta Sigma
1963 Alpha Phi Alpha

NPC WOMEN'S
1956 Alpha Chi Omega
1956 Alpha Delta Pi
1963 Zeta Tau Alpha
1965 Gamma Phi Beta

NPHC WOMEN'S
1970 Alpha Kappa Alpha
1970 Delta Sigma Theta (B)

PROFESSIONAL
1954 Kappa Kappa Psi

1954 Tau Beta Sigma
1956 Delta Sigma Pi
1956 Phi Mu Alpha—Sinfonia
1958 Delta Psi Kappa

ACHS HONORS
   Omicron Delta Epsilon
1959 Alpha Pi Mu
1960 Eta Kappa Nu
1965 Kappa Omicron Nu
1965 Phi Kappa Phi
1965 Sigma Pi Sigma
1967 Alpha Lambda Delta
1967 Omega Chi Epsilon
1967 Phi Alpha Theta
1967 Pi Delta Phi
1968 Chi Epsilon
1968 Phi Eta Sigma
1968 Pi Tau Sigma
1968 Sigma Delta Pi
1968 Tau Beta Pi
1973 Pi Sigma Alpha
1974 Sigma Tau Delta
1986 Psi Chi

OTHER HONORS
   National Order of Omega
1965 Pi Mu Epsilon

SERVICE
1951 Alpha Phi Omega

RECOGNITION
1956 Alpha Psi Omega
1961 Blue Key

INACTIVE
1956–83 Kappa Delta
1957–70 Kappa Alpha Order
1957–85 Delta Zeta
1961–83 Sigma Chi
1969–79 Zeta Beta Tau
1971–77 Lambda Chi Alpha

LAMBUTH COLLEGE Jackson, TN. Chartered as Memphis Conference Female Institute 1843; became coeducational 1924. Undergraduate college of liberal arts; church related (Methodist); nonsectarian.

Fraternity and sorority members are required to reside in dormitories.

NIC MEN'S
1957 Kappa Alpha Order
1958 Kappa Sigma
1971 Sigma Phi Epsilon

NPC WOMEN'S
1957 Alpha Omicron Pi
1957 Sigma Kappa
1969 Phi Mu

NPHC WOMEN'S
1988 Alpha Kappa Alpha

ACHS HONORS
1955 Lambda Iota Tau
1970 Phi Alpha Theta

INACTIVE
1957–84 Alpha Xi Delta
1962–74 Delta Sigma Phi

LANDER COLLEGE Greenwood, SC. College of liberal arts; coeducational; established 1872 as a private institution; came under State College Board of Trustees of the State of South Carolina 1973; over 2300 students.

NIC MEN'S
1970 Pi Kappa Phi
1973 Sigma Nu
1980 Kappa Sigma
1986 Alpha Tau Omega

NPC WOMEN'S
1971 Phi Mu
1972 Alpha Phi

NPHC WOMEN'S
1973 Delta Sigma Theta (B)
1977 Alpha Kappa Alpha

ACHS HONORS
1957 Alpha Chi

1968 Phi Alpha Theta
1986 Psi Chi

RECOGNITION
1962 Lambda Tau
1971 Blue Key

INACTIVE
1972–78 Tau Kappa Epsilon

COLONIES
   Alpha Tau Omega
   Zeta Tau Alpha

LANE COLLEGE Jackson, TN. Coeducational; founded 1882.

NIC MEN'S
1940 Kappa Alpha Psi (A)

NPHC MEN'S
   Phi Beta Sigma
1936 Alpha Phi Alpha
1940 Omega Psi Phi

NPHC WOMEN'S
1939 Alpha Kappa Alpha
1939 Delta Sigma Theta (B)

1939 Sigma Gamma Rho

PROFESSIONAL
1972 Tau Beta Sigma

ACHS HONORS
1962 Alpha Kappa Mu
1972 Sigma Tau Delta

INACTIVE
1943–60 Beta Kappa Chi

LANGSTON UNIVERSITY Langston, OK. Established 1897; land-grant institution; undergraduate, coeducational.

NIC MEN'S
1933 Kappa Alpha Psi (A)

NPHC MEN'S
   Phi Beta Sigma

1932 Alpha Phi Alpha
1932 Omega Psi Phi

NPHC WOMEN'S
1939 Alpha Kappa Alpha
1939 Delta Sigma Theta (B)
1941 Sigma Gamma Rho

PROFESSIONAL
1957 Kappa Kappa Psi
1969 Tau Beta Sigma

ACHS HONORS
1953 Kappa Delta Pi

1957 Alpha Kappa Mu
1966 Alpha Chi

SERVICE
1970 Alpha Phi Omega

RECOGNITION
1963 Beta Beta Beta

INACTIVE
        Zeta Phi Beta

LASALLE COLLEGE   Philadelphia, PA. College of liberal arts; coeducational; private control (Roman Catholic); founded 1863.

Off-campus fraternity houses permitted.

NIC MEN'S
1963 Tau Kappa Epsilon
1968 Phi Kappa Theta
1969 Phi Sigma Kappa
1975 Alpha Chi Rho
1982 Pi Kappa Phi
1985 Phi Gamma Delta

OTHER MEN'S
1947 Sigma Beta Kappa

NPHC MEN'S
        Phi Beta Sigma

NPC WOMEN'S
1983 Gamma Phi Beta
1985 Delta Phi Epsilon

PROFESSIONAL
1960 Pi Sigma Epsilon
1963 Delta Sigma Pi
1975 Phi Gamma Nu
1989 Gamma Iota Sigma

ACHS HONORS
        Omicron Delta Epsilon
1950 Alpha Epsilon Delta
1953 Kappa Mu Epsilon
1958 Lambda Iota Tau
1964 Psi Chi
1968 Phi Alpha Theta
1978 Phi Sigma Tau
1986 Phi Sigma Iota
1990 Pi Gamma Mu

SERVICE
1955 Alpha Phi Omega
1974 Gamma Sigma Sigma

INACTIVE
1881–82 Kappa Kappa Gamma
1968–71 Phi Kappa Tau
1972–78 Phi Sigma Kappa
1976–82 Zeta Beta Tau
1977–85 Theta Alpha Kappa

UNIVERSITY OF LA VERNE   La Verne, CA.

NIC MEN'S
1985 Sigma Alpha Epsilon
1987 Delta Sigma Phi

NPC WOMEN'S
1986 Sigma Kappa
1988 Alpha Delta Pi

PROFESSIONAL
1977 Delta Theta Phi

1979 Delta Theta Phi

ACHS HONORS
1969 Pi Gamma Mu
1990 Psi Chi

RECOGNITION
1936 Alpha Psi Omega

LAWRENCE INSTITUTE OF TECHNOLOGY   Southfield, MI. Professional institute; coeducational; independent. Established 1932.

NIC MEN'S
1971 Sigma Phi Epsilon
1986 Sigma Pi

NPHC MEN'S
        Phi Beta Sigma

PROFESSIONAL
1947 Theta Tau

ACHS HONORS
1972 Sigma Pi Sigma

1978 Tau Beta Pi
1982 Eta Kappa Nu

INACTIVE
1968–77 Theta Xi
1968–77 Theta Xi
1968–91 Alpha Sigma Phi

LAWRENCE UNIVERSITY   Appleton, WI. College of liberal arts; coeducational; private control; non-

sectarian. Established as Lawrence Institute 1847; became Lawrence College of Wisconsin 1913; Institute of Paper Chemistry affiliated with college 1929. Milwaukee Downer College was merged to form Lawrence University in 1964.

Fraternities occupy college-owned houses on a quadrangle on rental basis; sorority members live in residence halls.

NIC MEN'S
1859 Phi Delta Theta
1915 Sigma Phi Epsilon
1920 Phi Kappa Tau
1935 Delta Tau Delta
1936 Beta Theta Pi

NPC WOMEN'S
1915 Delta Gamma
1915 Kappa Alpha Theta
1981 Kappa Kappa Gamma

PROFESSIONAL
1917 Sigma Alpha Iota
1938 Phi Mu Alpha—Sinfonia

ACHS HONORS
        Omicron Delta Epsilon
1922 Mortar Board
1927 Phi Sigma Iota
1929 Phi Sigma
1951 Pi Kappa Lambda

1984 Lambda Sigma Society

OTHER HONORS
1927 National Collegiate
        Players
1964 Phi Beta Kappa

RECOGNITION
        Arnold Air Society (F-2)
1929 Eta Sigma Phi

INACTIVE
1908–69· Alpha Delta Pi
1912–42 Mu Phi Epsilon
1914–35 Phi Mu
1918–68 Kappa Delta
1921–39 Zeta Tau Alpha
1924–37 Pi Gamma Mu
1928–34 Delta Omicron
1930–80 Alpha Chi Omega
1940–83 Pi Beta Phi
1958–88 Phi Gamma Delta

LEBANON VALLEY COLLEGE   Annville, PA. College of liberal arts; coeducational; private control; related to Evangelical United Brethren Church. Established 1866.

NIC MEN'S
1988 Tau Kappa Epsilon

PROFESSIONAL
1960 Phi Mu Alpha—Sinfonia
1961 Sigma Alpha Iota

ACHS HONORS
1938 Pi Gamma Mu
1964 Psi Chi

1980 Phi Sigma Iota

SERVICE
1960 Alpha Phi Omega
1969 Gamma Sigma Sigma

RECOGNITION
1953 Beta Beta Beta
1960 Alpha Psi Omega

LEE COLLEGE   Cleveland, TN. Private control: Church of God. Founded in 1918.

Freshmen must live on campus or at home.

ACHS HONORS
1971 Alpha Chi

SERVICE
1971 Alpha Phi Omega

LEHIGH UNIVERSITY   Bethlehem, PA. Founded by Asa Packer, board of trustees organized 1865, chartered the first instruction 1866. University; undergraduate colleges for men; Graduate School coeducational; private control; nonsectarian.

Fraternities are permitted to own their own property, which some do, others own houses on college lots, and most occupy college-owned houses on a rental basis.

NIC MEN'S
1872 Chi Phi

1876 Phi Delta Theta
1882 Alpha Tau Omega

1884 Delta Phi
1884 Psi Upsilon
1884 Theta Delta Chi
1885 Delta Upsilon
1885 Sigma Nu
1887 Phi Gamma Delta
1887 Sigma Chi
1887 Sigma Phi Society
1891 Beta Theta Pi
1894 Chi Psi
1894 Kappa Alpha Society
1900 Kappa Sigma
1901 Phi Sigma Kappa
1904 Theta Xi
1907 Sigma Phi Epsilon
1915 Pi Lambda Phi
1919 Phi Kappa Theta
1923 Sigma Alpha Mu
1926 Lambda Chi Alpha
1927 Tau Delta Phi
1929 Alpha Sigma Phi
1929 Pi Kappa Alpha
1931 Delta Sigma Phi
1942 Theta Chi
1952 Delta Chi
1967 Tau Epsilon Phi
1973 Zeta Psi
1979 Alpha Epsilon Pi
1985 Phi Kappa Psi

NPC WOMEN'S
1975 Alpha Phi
1976 Alpha Gamma Delta
1976 Gamma Phi Beta
1982 Delta Gamma
1984 Alpha Omicron Pi
1984 Kappa Alpha Theta
1989 Alpha Chi Omega
1989 Delta Zeta

OTHER PROFESSIONAL
1959 Beta Alpha Psi

ACHS HONORS
     Omicron Delta Epsilon
1885 Tau Beta Pi
1925 Omicron Delta Kappa
1926 Eta Kappa Nu
1927 Pi Tau Sigma
1930 Phi Eta Sigma
1940 Phi Alpha Theta
1950 Beta Gamma Sigma
1952 Alpha Pi Mu
1952 Chi Epsilon
1955 Psi Chi
1960 Delta Sigma Rho-Tau
     Kappa Alpha
1964 Pi Sigma Alpha
1976 Sigma Tau Delta
1984 Phi Sigma Iota

OTHER HONORS
     National Order of Omega
1887 Phi Beta Kappa
1928 Sigma Xi
1929 Pi Mu Epsilon

SERVICE
1936 Alpha Phi Omega

RECOGNITION
     Arnold Air Society (B-1)
1922 Scabbard and Blade (3)
1928 Eta Sigma Phi
1966 Delta Phi Alpha

INACTIVE
1870–89 Phi Kappa Sigma
1918–89 Alpha Chi Rho
1924–71 Alpha Kappa Psi
1925–33 Zeta Beta Tau
1935–70 Alpha Epsilon Delta
1948–60 Pi Gamma Mu

COLONIES
1874 Delta Tau Delta

LEMOYNE-OWEN COLLEGE   Memphis, TN. Established 1870; accredited, private, liberal arts, coeducational. Affiliated with Congregational Christian Church; supported by American Missionary Association, under whose auspices it was founded, and by the United Negro College Fund.

Sigma Gamma Rho owns its sorority house which is adjacent to the property owned by the college.

NIC MEN'S
1940 Kappa Alpha Psi (A)

NPHC MEN'S
     Phi Beta Sigma
1933 Omega Psi Phi
1934 Alpha Phi Alpha

NPHC WOMEN'S
     Zeta Phi Beta
1934 Delta Sigma Theta (B)
1938 Alpha Kappa Alpha
1938 Sigma Gamma Rho

ACHS HONORS
     Omicron Delta Epsilon

1944 Alpha Kappa Mu
1945 Beta Kappa Chi
1951 Alpha Sigma Nu
1954 Pi Gamma Mu
1982 Phi Sigma Tau
1983 Delta Mu Delta
1985 Phi Alpha Theta

SERVICE
1950 Alpha Phi Omega

RECOGNITION
1960 Eta Sigma Phi

LENOIR-RHYNE COLLEGE   Hickory, NC. College of liberal arts; coeducational; private control; related to United Evangelical Lutheran Synod of North Carolina. Chartered 1891 as Lenoir College.

NIC MEN'S
1950 Theta Xi
1954 Tau Kappa Epsilon
1954 Theta Chi
1983 Pi Kappa Phi

NPC WOMEN'S
1961 Delta Zeta
1962 Kappa Delta
1962 Sigma Kappa
1962 Zeta Tau Alpha

ACHS HONORS
     Omicron Delta Epsilon
1981 Pi Sigma Alpha

SERVICE
1987 Alpha Phi Omega

RECOGNITION
1952 Chi Beta Phi

INACTIVE
1953–84 Sigma Phi Epsilon

LEWIS UNIVERSITY   Lockport, IL. Colleges of liberal arts for men; private control; Roman Catholic Church; established as Holy Name Technical School 1932; became Lewis College of Science and Technology 1946; Lewis College 1961; Lewis University 1973.

NIC MEN'S
1934 Kappa Alpha Psi (A)
1967 Phi Kappa Theta
1978 Kappa Alpha Psi (A)

NPHC MEN'S
     Phi Beta Sigma

NPHC WOMEN'S
1936 Sigma Gamma Rho
1974 Sigma Gamma Rho
1975 Delta Sigma Theta (B)
1978 Alpha Kappa Alpha

PROFESSIONAL
1965 Delta Sigma Pi
1974 Phi Gamma Nu

ACHS HONORS
1965 Delta Epsilon Sigma
1967 Phi Alpha Theta
1968 Phi Sigma Tau
1972 Sigma Tau Delta
1975 Sigma Pi Sigma
1981 Psi Chi
1982 Theta Alpha Kappa

INACTIVE
1873–89 Delta Gamma
1964–84 Phi Mu Alpha—
     Sinfonia
1967–83 Tau Kappa Epsilon
1971–79 Kappa Delta Rho
1976–84 Sigma Phi Epsilon

LEWIS AND CLARK COLLEGE   Portland, OR. Established as Albany College under the auspices of the Presbyterian Church 1867. Name changed to Lewis and Clark College 1942. Four-year liberal arts college; coeducational. Offers degrees B.S., B.A.

Fraternity members live in residence halls.

NIC MEN'S
1957 Sigma Phi Epsilon
1965 Sigma Alpha Epsilon

PROFESSIONAL
1921 Delta Theta Phi
1947 Mu Phi Epsilon
1972 Phi Alpha Delta

ACHS HONORS
1960 Phi Alpha Theta
1974 Delta Mu Delta
1977 Phi Kappa Phi
1986 Psi Chi

RECOGNITION
1947 Alpha Psi Omega
1948 Pi Kappa Delta
1949 Blue Key
1954 Kappa Pi

INACTIVE
1949–73 Phi Mu Alpha—
     Sinfonia
1953–72 Alpha Kappa Psi
1959–71 Theta Chi

COLONIES
1986 Sigma Pi Sigma

LIBERTY UNIVERSITY   Lynchburg, VA.

ACHS HONORS
1982 Phi Alpha Theta
1986 Alpha Lambda Delta

1987 Kappa Mu Epsilon
1988 Psi Chi

LIMESTONE COLLEGE   Gaffney, SC.

RECOGNITION
1932 Chi Delta Phi
1941 Chi Beta Phi

INACTIVE
1946   Phi Gamma Nu

1956–88 Kappa Delta Epsilon
1972–80 Delta Zeta
1976–87 Phi Mu Alpha—
     Sinfonia

LINCOLN MEMORIAL UNIVERSITY Harrogate, TN. College of liberal arts; coeducational; private control; nonsectarian; established 1897.

ACHS HONORS
1936 Delta Sigma Rho-Tau
    Kappa Alpha
1949 Pi Delta Phi
1951 Pi Omega Pi
1967 Phi Alpha Theta
1968 Alpha Chi

SERVICE
1966 Alpha Phi Omega

1968 Gamma Sigma Sigma

INACTIVE
1950–70 Sigma Delta Pi
1980–84 Sigma Phi Epsilon
1981–87 Sigma Sigma Sigma
1983–85 Alpha Xi Delta

THE LINCOLN UNIVERSITY Lincoln University, PA. Founded by John Miller Dickey as Ashman Institute 1854; named The Lincoln University 1866; undergraduate college; coeducational; private control; state aided; nonsectarian.

Fraternity houses are not prohibited, but none has ever been built.

NIC MEN'S
1915 Kappa Alpha Psi (A)

NPHC MEN'S
    Phi Beta Sigma
1912 Alpha Phi Alpha

NPHC WOMEN'S
1969 Alpha Kappa Alpha
1969 Delta Sigma Theta (B)

OTHER PROFESSIONAL
1972 Sigma Delta Chi

ACHS HONORS
    Omicron Delta Epsilon

1923 Beta Kappa Chi
1971 Alpha Chi
1975 Phi Alpha Theta
1978 Phi Sigma Iota
1982 Psi Chi

SERVICE
1967 Alpha Phi Omega

COLONIES
1987 Sigma Pi Sigma

LINCOLN UNIVERSITY Jefferson City, MO. Established 1866; became state institution 1879; land-grant college 1890. In 1954 opened doors to any qualified person who wished to enroll.

NIC MEN'S
1932 Kappa Alpha Psi (A)

NPHC MEN'S
    Phi Beta Sigma
1930 Alpha Phi Alpha
1936 Omega Psi Phi

NPHC WOMEN'S
    Zeta Phi Beta
1928 Alpha Kappa Alpha
1937 Sigma Gamma Rho

ACHS HONORS
    Omicron Delta Epsilon

1932 Beta Kappa Chi
1963 Delta Mu Delta
1974 Phi Alpha Theta

INACTIVE
1953–77 Phi Mu Alpha—
    Sinfonia
1966–74 Sigma Alpha Iota
1972–84 Kappa Omicron Nu

COLONIES
    FarmHouse

LINDENWOOD COLLEGE St. Charles, MO. Colleges of liberal arts for men and women; private control; established 1827.

PROFESSIONAL
1932 Mu Phi Epsilon

ACHS HONORS
1949 Alpha Lambda Delta
1967 Phi Sigma Tau
1970 Pi Delta Phi
1972 Sigma Delta Pi

RECOGNITION
1927 Alpha Psi Omega
1928 Kappa Pi

INACTIVE
1928–44 Sigma Tau Delta
1929–49 Pi Gamma Mu
1961–64 Kappa Omicron Nu

LINFIELD COLLEGE McMinnville, OR. College of liberal arts; coeducational; private control; related to American Baptist Church; established 1849; chartered 1858.

NIC MEN'S
1949 Theta Chi
1950 Pi Kappa Alpha
1983 Kappa Sigma

NPC WOMEN'S
1981 Phi Sigma Sigma
1990 Alpha Phi

PROFESSIONAL
1949 Mu Phi Epsilon

ACHS HONORS
    Omicron Delta Epsilon
1929 Pi Gamma Mu

1959 Sigma Pi Sigma
1983 Psi Chi
1989 Phi Alpha Theta

SERVICE
1939 Intercollegiate Knights

RECOGNITION
1924 Pi Kappa Delta
1926 Alpha Psi Omega

INACTIVE
1950–54 Phi Sigma Kappa
1952–73 Alpha Tau Omega

LIVINGSTON UNIVERSITY Livingston, AL. State college; chartered 1840; coeducational.

NIC MEN'S
1964 Pi Kappa Phi
1964 Tau Kappa Epsilon
1967 Delta Chi
1978 Kappa Alpha Psi (A)

NPHC MEN'S
    Phi Beta Sigma

NPC WOMEN'S
1969 Phi Mu
1987 Alpha Sigma Tau

NPHC WOMEN'S
1978 Alpha Kappa Alpha

PROFESSIONAL
1986 Delta Sigma Pi

ACHS HONORS
1985 Phi Eta Sigma
1987 Omicron Delta Kappa

RECOGNITION
1967 Blue Key

INACTIVE
1963–82 Phi Mu Alpha—
    Sinfonia
1971–78 Zeta Tau Alpha
1971–83 Delta Zeta

LIVINGSTONE COLLEGE Salisbury, NC. College of liberal arts; theological seminary; coeducational; incorporated 1879.

NPHC MEN'S
    Phi Beta Sigma
1927 Omega Psi Phi
1947 Alpha Phi Alpha

NPHC WOMEN'S
    Zeta Phi Beta
1930 Alpha Kappa Alpha

1947 Delta Sigma Theta (B)

ACHS HONORS
1962 Alpha Kappa Mu

INACTIVE
1945–60 Beta Kappa Chi
1948–53 Kappa Alpha Psi (A)

LOCK HAVEN STATE COLLEGE Lock Haven, PA. Founded 1877; public control; coeducational; undergraduate college teacher education and liberal arts.

Fraternities occupy houses on property which they own; the sorority members are required to live in dormitories.

NIC MEN'S
1958 Kappa Delta Rho
1960 Tau Kappa Epsilon
1964 Lambda Chi Alpha
1969 Phi Mu Delta
1983 Alpha Chi Rho
1987 Alpha Sigma Phi
1989 Kappa Alpha Psi (A)

NPHC MEN'S
    Phi Beta Sigma

NPC WOMEN'S
1921 Alpha Sigma Tau
1935 Sigma Sigma Sigma
1959 Sigma Kappa
1968 Zeta Tau Alpha

PROFESSIONAL
1975 Kappa Kappa Psi

ACHS HONORS
1938 Kappa Delta Pi
1971 Gamma Theta Upsilon
1975 Phi Kappa Phi

1983 Psi Chi

OTHER HONORS
National Order of Omega

SERVICE
1963 Alpha Phi Omega

INACTIVE
1961–88 Sigma Pi
1963–77 Delta Zeta

LOMA LINDA UNIVERSITY Loma Linda, CA.
Founded 1905, incorporated 1909. University; professional schools of dentistry, medicine, nursing, dietetics, medical technology, physical therapy, x-ray technology; divisions of religion, public health and tropical medicine, general studies; professional programs in occupational therapy, dental hygiene; graduate school. Private, Seventh-day Adventist.

ACHS HONORS
1976 Sigma Theta Tau

OTHER HONORS
1957 Alpha Omega Alpha
1976 Sigma Xi

RECOGNITION
1962 Sigma Phi Alpha

INACTIVE
1967–74 Sigma Pi Sigma

LON MORRIS COLLEGE Jacksonville, TX.

SERVICE
1976 Alpha Phi Omega

LONG ISLAND UNIVERSITY Brooklyn, NY.
Founded by Brooklyn civic leaders in 1926. Zeckendorf Campus named for president of the board of trustees. William Zeckendorf. Additional units at Brooklyn College of Pharmacy (1929), CW Post College (1955), and Southampton College (1963). University, graduate school, coeducational—college of liberal arts and sciences, college of business administration, school of education. Independent and nonsectarian.

Fraternities and sororities on the Brooklyn Center campus of Long Island University rent their meeting and social rooms from private landlords; there are no resident fraternities or sororities on campus.

NIC MEN'S
1949 Alpha Phi Delta
1955 Kappa Alpha Psi (A)
1956 Tau Delta Phi

NPHC MEN'S
Phi Beta Sigma

NPHC WOMEN'S
1983 Sigma Gamma Rho

PROFESSIONAL
1925 Rho Pi Phi
1951 Lambda Kappa Sigma

OTHER PROFESSIONAL
1919 Phi Lambda Kappa
1962 Sigma Delta Chi

ACHS HONORS
Omicron Delta Epsilon
Omicron Delta Epsilon
1955 Rho Chi
1956 Phi Alpha Theta
1956 Sigma Tau Delta
1957 Alpha Epsilon Delta
1957 Phi Sigma
1958 Pi Gamma Mu

1961 Psi Chi
1967 Kappa Tau Alpha
1974 Phi Sigma Tau
1976 Beta Phi Mu
1982 Pi Sigma Alpha
1988 Psi Chi

SERVICE
1948 Alpha Phi Omega
1979 Alpha Phi Omega

RECOGNITION
1943 Eta Mu Pi

INACTIVE
1876–80 Phi Kappa Sigma
1901–50 Phi Beta Pi and Theta
        Kappa Psi (B)
1903–14 Zeta Beta Tau
1911–34 Sigma Alpha Mu
1929   Phi Sigma Sigma
1930–70 Delta Phi Epsilon
1958–87 Sigma Alpha Mu
1962–73 Alpha Epsilon Pi
1963–68 Zeta Beta Tau
1963–81 Phi Delta Chi
1967–70 Pi Lambda Phi

BROOKLYN COLLEGE OF PHARMACY CUNY,
Brooklyn, NY. Division of Long Island University; established 1886.

OTHER PROFESSIONAL
1917 Delta Sigma Theta (C)

LONGWOOD COLLEGE Farmville, VA. Incorporated by the General Assembly March 5, 1839, as Farmville Female Seminary Association, outgrowth of the Farmville Female Seminary established 1833; became a state teachers college 1884; present name chosen 1949, derived from Longwood Estate, a property now owned by the college, the birthplace of General Joseph E. Johnston, Confederate military figure. A coeducational comprehensive institution. Longwood offers eight baccalaureate degrees and two master's degrees.

Sorority members live in a Panhellic residence hall. Each fraternity and sorority chapter has a chapter room in the residence halls.

NIC MEN'S
1978 Sigma Phi Epsilon
1979 Pi Kappa Phi
1980 Alpha Chi Rho
1980 Alpha Sigma Phi
1987 Tau Kappa Epsilon

NPHC MEN'S
Phi Beta Sigma

NPC WOMEN'S
1897 Kappa Delta
1898 Sigma Sigma Sigma
1898 Zeta Tau Alpha
1901 Alpha Sigma Alpha
1935 Alpha Sigma Tau
1949 Delta Zeta
1959 Alpha Gamma Delta
1959 Sigma Kappa
1969 Alpha Delta Pi

NPHC WOMEN'S
1977 Alpha Kappa Alpha

PROFESSIONAL
1959 Sigma Alpha Iota
1968 Delta Psi Kappa
1979 Phi Mu Alpha—Sinfonia
1981 Delta Sigma Pi

ACHS HONORS
1927 Pi Gamma Mu
1928 Kappa Delta Pi
1961 Pi Omega Pi
1966 Alpha Lambda Delta
1966 Lambda Iota Tau
1972 Phi Kappa Phi
1988 Psi Chi

OTHER HONORS
National Order of Omega
1976 Pi Mu Epsilon

SERVICE
1981 Alpha Phi Omega

RECOGNITION
1945 Alpha Psi Omega
1950 Society for Collegiate
     Journalists—Pi Delta
     Epsilon-Alpha Phi Gamma
     (P)
1974 Beta Beta Beta

INACTIVE
1961–83 Phi Mu
1962–88 Kappa Omicron Nu
1969–78 Alpha Phi
1982–89 Delta Sigma Phi

LORAS COLLEGE Dubuque, IA. College of liberal arts for men; private control; Roman Catholic; established 1839; Iowa's oldest college.

NIC MEN'S
1974 Sigma Phi Epsilon

NPHC MEN'S
Phi Beta Sigma

ACHS HONORS
Omicron Delta Epsilon

1940 Delta Epsilon Sigma
1957 Phi Alpha Theta
1969 Phi Sigma Tau
1970 Lambda Iota Tau

SERVICE
1954 Alpha Phi Omega

LOS ANGELES CITY COLLEGE Los Angeles, CA.

RECOGNITION
1960 Kappa Pi   1953   Gamma Sigma Sigma

INACTIVE
1951   Alpha Eta Rho

LOS ANGELES HARBOR COLLEGE Wilmington, CA.

SERVICE
1965 Alpha Phi Omega

LOUISIANA COLLEGE Pineville, LA. College of liberal arts; coeducational; private control; affiliated with Baptist Convention (La.); Established 1906.

PROFESSIONAL
1959 Delta Omicron

OTHER PROFESSIONAL
1965 Kappa Phi Kappa

ACHS HONORS
1929 Alpha Chi
1949 Psi Chi
1959 Kappa Delta Pi
1971 Omicron Delta Kappa

SERVICE
1968 Alpha Phi Omega

RECOGNITION
1925 Pi Kappa Delta
1928 Alpha Psi Omega
1953 Eta Sigma Phi

INACTIVE
1938–45 Sigma Delta Pi
1939–52 Kappa Omicron Nu
1965–71 Kappa Delta Epsilon

LOUISIANA STATE UNIVERSITY Baton Rouge, LA. Founded January 2, 1860 at Pineville, LA, chartered under its present name in 1870 and merged with the Agricultural and Mechanical College January 2, 1877. Undergraduate colleges, graduate and professional schools.

Ownership of house is by fraternity on college-owned land, leased to the fraternity.

NIC MEN'S
1858 Delta Kappa Epsilon
1867 Sigma Alpha Epsilon
1885 Kappa Alpha Order
1887 Kappa Sigma
1887 Sigma Nu
1902 Pi Kappa Alpha
1914 Lambda Chi Alpha
1921 Theta Xi
1925 Sigma Chi
1926 Alpha Gamma Rho
1936 Sigma Pi
1938 Phi Delta Theta
1938 Phi Kappa Theta
1940 Alpha Tau Omega
1941 Delta Chi
1948 Phi Gamma Delta
1949 Tau Kappa Epsilon
1956 Acacia
1966 Delta Tau Delta
1966 Phi Kappa Psi
1988 Kappa Alpha Psi (A)

NPHC MEN'S
Phi Beta Sigma
1973 Alpha Phi Alpha

NPC WOMEN'S
1909 Kappa Delta

1917 Delta Zeta
1924 Chi Omega
1934 Delta Delta Delta
1934 Phi Mu
1935 Kappa Kappa Gamma
1936 Pi Beta Phi
1948 Delta Gamma
1959 Zeta Tau Alpha
1963 Kappa Alpha Theta
1984 Sigma Kappa

NPHC WOMEN'S
1956 Sigma Gamma Rho
1972 Alpha Kappa Alpha
1972 Alpha Kappa Alpha
1972 Delta Sigma Theta (B)

PROFESSIONAL
1926 Sigma Alpha Iota
1927 Phi Delta Phi
1929 Delta Sigma Pi
1932 Phi Chi
1938 Phi Mu Alpha—Sinfonia
1939 Delta Psi Kappa
1948 Kappa Kappa Psi
1963 Phi Alpha Delta
1969 Kappa Delta Epsilon
1973 Delta Theta Phi
1989 Sigma Alpha

OTHER PROFESSIONAL
1915 Sigma Delta Chi
1916 Alpha Zeta
1927 Women in Communications
1930 Gamma Eta Gamma
1931 Phi Upsilon Omicron
1932 Alpha Tau Alpha
1934 Kappa Phi Kappa
1938 Phi Delta Epsilon
1939 Beta Alpha Psi
1954 Alpha Beta Alpha

ACHS HONORS
Omicron Delta Epsilon
1912 Delta Sigma Rho-Tau
    Kappa Alpha
1926 Pi Sigma Alpha
1930 Phi Kappa Phi
1932 Phi Eta Sigma
1933 Alpha Lambda Delta
1933 Beta Gamma Sigma
1933 Omicron Delta Kappa
1934 Kappa Delta Pi
1934 Mortar Board
1936 Phi Sigma Iota
1936 Tau Beta Pi
1937 Sigma Delta Pi
1940 Xi Sigma Pi
1945 Psi Chi
1950 Sigma Pi Sigma
1951 Pi Tau Sigma
1952 Alpha Kappa Delta
1954 Alpha Epsilon Delta
1956 Phi Alpha Theta
1961 Eta Kappa Nu
1965 Pi Kappa Lambda
1968 Chi Epsilon
1974 Beta Phi Mu
1977 Kappa Omicron Nu
1978 Kappa Tau Alpha
1978 Sigma Lambda Alpha
1987 Phi Alpha Theta
1988 Omega Chi Epsilon

OTHER HONORS
National Order of Omega
1939 Pi Mu Epsilon
1942 Order of the Coif
1942 Sigma Xi
1949 Alpha Omega Alpha

1949 Iota Sigma Pi
1961 Gamma Sigma Delta
1977 Phi Beta Kappa

SERVICE
1932 Alpha Phi Omega

RECOGNITION
Angel Flight
Arnold Air Society (C-2)
1923 Scabbard and Blade (5)
1931 National Block and Bridle
    Club
1934 Sigma Delta Psi
1937 Phi Lambda Upsilon
1948 Delta Phi Alpha
1961 Lambda Tau
1976 Pi Kappa Delta
1977 Phi Zeta

INACTIVE
1909–89 Zeta Beta Tau
1914–85 Alpha Delta Pi
1914–86 Alpha Chi Sigma
1924–69 Sigma Delta Tau
1926–70 Alpha Chi Omega
1927–33 Phi Sigma Sigma
1931–62 Delta Omicron
1933   Phi Beta Pi and Theta
    Kappa Psi (a)
1934–54 Alpha Kappa Kappa
1935–41 Phi Rho Sigma
1935–58 Pi Gamma Mu
1936   Eta Sigma Phi
1936   Phi Lambda Kappa
1936–47 Kappa Mu Epsilon
1938–72 Alpha Epsilon Pi
1938–80 Alpha Omicron Pi
1938–84 Alpha Epsilon Phi
1938–88 Alpha Xi Delta
1939   Phi Beta
1957–69 Sigma Tau Delta
1961–79 Sigma Phi Epsilon
1964–77 Gamma Phi Beta
1965–80 Alpha Phi
1968–72 Pi Kappa Phi
1975–84 Gamma Iota Sigma
1976–85 Phi Chi Theta
1979–83 Delta Upsilon
1979–85 Alpha Gamma Delta

Louisiana State University Medical School New Orleans, LA.

RECOGNITION
1966 Alpha Psi Omega

LOUISIANA STATE UNIVERSITY AT SHREVEPORT Shreveport, LA. University of liberal arts, business administration, education, sciences, and general studies; coeducational; state control. Established 1965.

NIC MEN'S
1976 Delta Sigma Phi
1976 Kappa Alpha Order
1979 Phi Delta Theta
1984 Kappa Sigma

NPC WOMEN'S
1961 Zeta Tau Alpha
1975 Delta Delta Delta
1975 Zeta Tau Alpha
1984 Phi Mu

ACHS HONORS
1983 Omicron Delta Kappa
1983 Pi Sigma Alpha
1984 Phi Sigma Iota
1985 Phi Kappa Phi

OTHER HONORS
1973 Alpha Omega Alpha

INACTIVE
1974–81 Alpha Phi

LOUISIANA TECH UNIVERSITY Ruston, LA.
Founded by the General Assembly of Louisiana in 1895. Coeducational; university divided into six colleges and a division of admissions, basic and career studies. All six colleges offer the master's degree, one college offers the specialist's degree, and two colleges offer the doctorate.

Ownership of fraternity house and land is by the fraternity and sorority.

NIC MEN'S
1925 Lambda Chi Alpha
1940 Pi Kappa Alpha
1943 Kappa Sigma
1947 Kappa Alpha Order
1947 Tau Kappa Epsilon
1961 Sigma Nu
1966 Alpha Tau Omega
1970 Sigma Pi
1976 Kappa Alpha Psi (A)
1983 Sigma Alpha Epsilon
1984 Delta Kappa Epsilon
1987 Delta Chi

NPHC MEN'S
     Phi Beta Sigma
1971 Alpha Phi Alpha

NPC WOMEN'S
1931 Kappa Delta
1940 Sigma Kappa
1943 Phi Mu
1944 Alpha Chi Omega
1962 Delta Zeta
1986 Delta Gamma

NPHC WOMEN'S
1973 Alpha Kappa Alpha
1974 Delta Sigma Theta (B)
1974 Sigma Gamma Rho

PROFESSIONAL
1948 Delta Sigma Pi
1962 Phi Beta
1964 Phi Mu Alpha—Sinfonia
1967 Alpha Kappa Psi
1969 Sigma Alpha Iota

OTHER PROFESSIONAL
1956 Beta Alpha Psi
1966 Alpha Beta Alpha
1974 Alpha Zeta
1975 Delta Pi Epsilon

ACHS HONORS
     Omicron Delta Epsilon
1931 Sigma Tau Delta
1949 Omicron Delta Kappa

1951 Phi Kappa Phi
1951 Tau Beta Pi
1957 Pi Tau Sigma
1960 Eta Kappa Nu
1963 Beta Gamma Sigma
1964 Lambda Sigma Society
1966 Phi Alpha Theta
1967 Sigma Pi Sigma
1971 Omega Chi Epsilon
1973 Alpha Pi Mu
1974 Alpha Epsilon Delta
1974 Mortar Board
1976 Chi Epsilon
1976 Kappa Omicron Nu
1976 Psi Chi

OTHER HONORS
1945 National Collegiate
     Players
1973 Pi Mu Epsilon

SERVICE
1941 Alpha Phi Omega

RECOGNITION
     Angel Flight
     Arnold Air Society (G-1)
1944 Pi Kappa Delta
1955 National Block and Bridle
     Club
1958 Beta Beta Beta
1967 Kappa Pi

INACTIVE
1928–39 Pi Gamma Mu
1944–70 Sigma Delta Pi
1948–54 Delta Sigma Phi
1949–60 Sigma Iota Epsilon
1949–84 Theta Xi
1955   Sigma Gamma Epsilon
1967–81 Zeta Tau Alpha
1974–85 Phi Chi Theta
1975–90 Phi Kappa Sigma

COLONIES
1990 Alpha Gamma Rho

UNIVERSITY OF LOUISVILLE Louisville, KY.
Established in 1798 by grant of public lands, chartered by state legislature in 1846; university; coeducational colleges; nonsectarian. Became state university in 1970.

Fraternities and sororities occupy houses of their own on their own property as well as lease homes on university property.

NIC MEN'S
     Alpha Epsilon Pi
     Alpha Epsilon Pi
1933 Kappa Alpha Psi (A)

1941 Triangle
1942 Tau Kappa Epsilon
1947 Phi Kappa Tau
1947 Sigma Phi Epsilon

1948 Lambda Chi Alpha
1949 Delta Upsilon
1949 Pi Kappa Phi
1971 Beta Theta Pi
1982 Delta Chi
1983 Kappa Sigma
1989 Sigma Chi

NPHC MEN'S
     Phi Beta Sigma

NPC WOMEN'S
1922 Sigma Kappa
1925 Pi Beta Phi
1928 Delta Zeta
1928 Kappa Delta
1929 Chi Omega
1983 Alpha Omicron Pi

NPHC WOMEN'S
1922 Delta Sigma Theta (B)
1932 Alpha Kappa Alpha
1979 Sigma Gamma Rho

PROFESSIONAL
1894 Phi Chi
1918 Delta Omicron
1935 Phi Alpha Delta
1948 Delta Theta Phi
1982 Phi Alpha Delta

OTHER PROFESSIONAL
1914 Delta Sigma Delta
1921 Phi Delta Epsilon

ACHS HONORS
1942 Phi Kappa Phi
1943 Omicron Delta Kappa
1945 Alpha Epsilon Delta
1948 Psi Chi
1949 Mortar Board
1952 Sigma Pi Sigma
1953 Kappa Delta Pi
1959 Phi Eta Sigma
1960 Pi Sigma Alpha
1968 Phi Alpha Theta
1971 Eta Kappa Nu
1974 Tau Beta Pi

1975 Pi Delta Phi
1978 Chi Epsilon

OTHER HONORS
     National Order of Omega
1924 Omicron Kappa Upsilon
1926 Alpha Omega Alpha
1955 Sigma Xi

SERVICE
1946 Alpha Phi Omega
1973 Gamma Sigma Sigma

RECOGNITION
     Angel Flight
     Arnold Air Society (D-2)
1939 Delta Phi Alpha
1956 Sigma Delta Psi
1962 Phi Lambda Upsilon

INACTIVE
1909–76 Alpha Kappa Kappa
1913   Phi Beta Pi and Theta
         Kappa Psi (a)
1914–59 Xi Psi Phi
1921–60 Kappa Alpha Order
1923–60 Alpha Phi Alpha
1925–61 Sigma Alpha Iota
1925–87 Alpha Omega
1927–33 Pi Kappa Lambda
1927–38 Pi Gamma Mu
1927–51 Delta Phi Epsilon
1927–77 Zeta Tau Alpha
1928   Sigma Delta Kappa
1930   Phi Lambda Kappa
1939–78 Theta Tau
1952–84 Lambda Sigma Society
1952–85 Phi Mu Alpha—
         Sinfonia
1953   Sigma Mu Sigma
1965   Sigma Phi Alpha
1965–72 Zeta Beta Tau
1974–80 Phi Chi Theta

COLONIES
1945 Sigma Alpha Mu

UNIVERSITY OF LOWELL Lowell, MA.
Formed June 9, 1975, through merger of Lowell Technological Institute (1895) and Lowell State College (1894). Undergraduate and graduate and doctoral programs; coeducational; state-supported.

NIC MEN'S
1969 Tau Kappa Epsilon

NPC WOMEN'S
1975 Alpha Sigma Tau

ACHS HONORS
1964 Eta Kappa Nu
1968 Sigma Pi Sigma
1973 Sigma Delta Pi
1975 Omega Chi Epsilon
1983 Chi Epsilon

1985 Tau Beta Pi
1990 Psi Chi

RECOGNITION
     Arnold Air Society (A-1)

INACTIVE
1949–86 Pi Lambda Phi
1968–83 Kappa Delta Phi (C)
1969–78 Kappa Sigma
1983–87 Delta Phi Epsilon

LOYOLA COLLEGE Baltimore, MD.
College of liberal arts; coeducational; private control; established 1852.

ACHS HONORS
     Omicron Delta Epsilon
1942 Alpha Sigma Nu

1948 Delta Sigma Rho-Tau
     Kappa Alpha
1971 Sigma Pi Sigma
1973 Phi Alpha Theta

1973 Psi Chi
1982 Theta Alpha Kappa
1985 Pi Sigma Alpha

RECOGNITION
1951 Eta Sigma Phi
1965 Beta Beta Beta

LOYOLA UNIVERSITY Chicago, IL. Founded 1870 as St. Ignatius College and operated by the Society of Jesus; a Roman Catholic institution; coeducational; ten undergraduate and graduate colleges.

The fraternities and sororities are permitted to occupy quarters on land of their ownership and they do so.

NIC MEN'S
1924 Alpha Delta Gamma
1950 Tau Delta Phi
1956 Tau Kappa Epsilon
1960 Sigma Pi
1965 Phi Kappa Theta
1968 Alpha Sigma Phi
1968 Delta Sigma Phi
1976 Theta Xi
1983 Sigma Alpha Epsilon

NPHC MEN'S
Phi Beta Sigma

NPC WOMEN'S
1964 Alpha Sigma Alpha

OTHER WOMEN'S
1954 Kappa Beta Gamma

PROFESSIONAL
1902 Phi Alpha Delta
1925 Delta Theta Phi
1932 Alpha Omega
1950 Delta Sigma Pi
1957 Alpha Tau Delta

OTHER PROFESSIONAL
1885 Delta Sigma Delta
1924 Kappa Beta Pi
1932 Nu Beta Epsilon

ACHS HONORS
Omicron Delta Epsilon
1928 Alpha Kappa Delta
1938 Alpha Sigma Nu
1940 Delta Epsilon Sigma
1952 Psi Chi

1956 Phi Sigma Tau
1960 Delta Sigma Rho-Tau
      Kappa Alpha
1962 Beta Gamma Sigma
1963 Pi Delta Phi
1963 Sigma Theta Tau
1972 Sigma Delta Pi
1973 Pi Sigma Alpha
1976 Phi Alpha Theta
1977 Alpha Epsilon Delta
1977 Theta Alpha Kappa
1980 Sigma Pi Sigma

OTHER HONORS
1955 Sigma Xi

SERVICE
1966 Alpha Phi Omega
1976 Alpha Phi Omega

RECOGNITION
1926 Blue Key
1966 Scabbard and Blade (16)
1970 Beta Beta Beta

INACTIVE
1907   Phi Chi
1921   Phi Beta Pi and Theta
          Kappa Psi (a)
1925–43 Sigma Nu Phi
1929–66 Pi Gamma Mu
1943–90 Theta Phi Alpha
1965–71 Phi Mu
1967–73 Phi Chi Theta
1968–75 Kappa Delta Epsilon
1969–84 Alpha Kappa Lambda

LOYOLA MARYMOUNT UNIVERSITY Los Angeles, CA. Roman Catholic; founded in 1911 under the direction of the Society of Jesus. Undergraduate men's colleges of arts and sciences, business administration and engineering; graduate division includes school of law.

All fraternities occupy houses on a rent-lease arrangement with private owners.

NIC MEN'S
1952 Alpha Delta Gamma
1956 Phi Kappa Theta
1976 Pi Kappa Alpha
1982 Sigma Pi

NPHC MEN'S
Phi Beta Sigma

NPC WOMEN'S
1976 Alpha Phi
1981 Delta Gamma

1986 Delta Zeta

PROFESSIONAL
1937 Phi Alpha Delta
1949 Delta Theta Phi
1959 Delta Sigma Pi
1970 Sigma Phi Delta

ACHS HONORS
Omicron Delta Epsilon
1939 Alpha Sigma Nu
1963 Pi Gamma Mu

1969 Phi Alpha Theta
1970 Phi Alpha Theta
1974 Tau Beta Pi
1979 Psi Chi
1979 Sigma Pi Sigma
1981 Theta Alpha Kappa

OTHER HONORS
National Order of Omega

RECOGNITION
Arnold Air Society (I)

INACTIVE
1959–89 Phi Sigma Kappa
1960–67 Tau Kappa Epsilon
1978–84 Sigma Sigma Sigma

COLONIES
1958 Delta Sigma Phi

LOYOLA UNIVERSITY IN NEW ORLEANS New Orleans, LA. University; coeducational; private control; Roman Catholic College; founded 1849; chartered 1912 as Loyola University.

NIC MEN'S
1932 Alpha Delta Gamma
1969 Phi Kappa Theta
1983 Sigma Phi Epsilon

NPC WOMEN'S
1959 Theta Phi Alpha
1984 Alpha Chi Omega
1984 Delta Gamma
1989 Gamma Phi Beta

NPHC WOMEN'S
1972 Alpha Kappa Alpha

PROFESSIONAL
1921 Psi Omega
1926 Delta Theta Phi
1932 Alpha Omega
1958 Delta Sigma Pi
1963 Alpha Delta Theta
1965 Phi Alpha Delta

OTHER PROFESSIONAL
1917 Delta Sigma Delta

ACHS HONORS
1949 Kappa Delta Pi
1954 Sigma Pi Sigma
1967 Psi Chi

1975 Pi Sigma Alpha
1985 Theta Alpha Kappa
1990 Kappa Tau Alpha
1990 Phi Eta Sigma

OTHER HONORS
National Order of Omega
1929 Omicron Kappa Upsilon
1970 Pi Mu Epsilon

RECOGNITION
1931 Blue Key
1956 Beta Beta Beta

INACTIVE
1925–40 Sigma Nu Phi
1926   Phi Beta Gamma
1942–65 Kappa Epsilon
1953   Cardinal Key
1953–67 Phi Mu Alpha—
          Sinfonia
1961   Kappa Beta Gamma
1962–75 Phi Chi Theta
1962–81 Sigma Sigma Sigma

COLONIES
1990 Phi Kappa Psi

LUBBOCK CHRISTIAN COLLEGE Lubbock, TX. Private control: Church of Christ. Founded in 1957. Four-year; coeducational.

Must be over 21 to live off-campus. Single-sex dormitories.

ACHS HONORS
1972 Alpha Chi

LUTHER COLLEGE Decora, IA.

ACHS HONORS
Omicron Delta Epsilon
1966 Phi Alpha Theta
1984 Sigma Pi Sigma
1985 Pi Kappa Lambda
1990 Psi Chi

SERVICE
1957 Alpha Phi Omega

RECOGNITION
1962 Alpha Psi Omega

INACTIVE
1962   Beta Beta Beta

LYCOMING COLLEGE Williamsport, PA. Founded in 1812 as Williamsport Academy, then Williamsport Dickinson Seminary, then Williamsport Dickinson Junior College, then Lycoming College in 1948; undergraduate liberal arts coeducational college; private; Methodist-related; 1,250 students.

Fraternities reside in two campus residence halls, in which each chapter maintains its own chapter rooms and rooms for residence.

NIC MEN'S	
1951 Alpha Sigma Phi	1976 Psi Chi
1953 Kappa Delta Rho	1978 Pi Gamma Mu
1953 Lambda Chi Alpha	1979 Phi Kappa Phi
1953 Sigma Pi	1979 Pi Sigma Alpha
1955 Theta Chi	1980 Phi Sigma Tau
1969 Tau Kappa Epsilon	1989 Phi Sigma Iota

ACHS HONORS	SERVICE
Omicron Delta Epsilon	1963 Alpha Phi Omega
1956 Phi Alpha Theta	RECOGNITION
1973 Sigma Pi Sigma	1951 Alpha Psi Omega

LYNDON STATE COLLEGE Lyndonville, VT. Public institution. Four-year; coeducational; liberal arts college.

Students must live on campus unless 23 or with Dean of Students permission.

OTHER PROFESSIONAL
1960 Kappa Delta Phi (C)

LYNCHBURG COLLEGE Lynchburg, VA. College of liberal arts; coeducational; private control; affiliated with Christian Church; chartered 1903.

NPHC WOMEN'S
Alpha Kappa Alpha

1969 Gamma Sigma Sigma

ACHS HONORS	RECOGNITION
1953 Kappa Delta Pi	1926 Alpha Psi Omega
1972 Sigma Pi Sigma	1948 Chi Beta Phi
1980 Phi Eta Sigma	1960 Blue Key
1985 Phi Alpha Theta	1961 Cardinal Key
1986 Pi Sigma Alpha	1962 Sigma Mu Sigma
1987 Phi Sigma Iota	
1989 Psi Chi	

SERVICE	INACTIVE
1957 Alpha Phi Omega	1928–46 Sigma Tau Delta

MACALESTER COLLEGE Saint Paul, MN. Founded by Dr. Edward Duffield Neill in 1853 as the Baldwin Academy. Macalester College as a collegiate institution opened its doors to students on September 15, 1885; private undergraduate liberal arts coeducational college; Presbyterian-related.

PROFESSIONAL	OTHER HONORS
1945 Alpha Delta Theta	1951 National Collegiate Players
ACHS HONORS	1968 Phi Beta Kappa
Omicron Delta Epsilon	1968 Pi Mu Epsilon
1951 Kappa Delta Pi	
1965 Alpha Kappa Delta	RECOGNITION
1966 Phi Alpha Theta	1921 Pi Kappa Delta
1966 Pi Sigma Alpha	1938 Sigma Delta Psi
1975 Gamma Theta Upsilon	

INACTIVE
1923–41 Sigma Alpha Iota
1946–65 Pi Gamma Mu

MCGILL UNIVERSITY Montreal, QB. Founded 1821; coeducational.

In matters of housing, the university permits the fraternities to depend on their own resources.

NIC MEN'S	OTHER HONORS
1883 Zeta Psi	1911 Alpha Omega Alpha
1897 Alpha Delta Phi	1922 Sigma Xi
1898 Delta Upsilon	
1899 Kappa Alpha Society	INACTIVE
1902 Phi Delta Theta	1900–89 Delta Kappa Epsilon
1921 Pi Lambda Phi	1901–08 Phi Beta Pi and Theta Kappa Psi (a)
1927 Sigma Chi	1901–72 Theta Delta Chi
1928 Psi Upsilon	1904–65 Alpha Kappa Kappa
1953 Lambda Chi Alpha	1913–38 Phi Rho Sigma
1988 Beta Theta Pi	1913–69 Zeta Beta Tau
1990 Alpha Epsilon Pi	1919–86 Sigma Alpha Mu
NPC WOMEN'S	1921–30 Psi Omega
1922 Delta Phi Epsilon	1922–27 Delta Sigma Pi
1930 Kappa Kappa Gamma	1922–44 Phi Chi
1931 Gamma Phi Beta	1922–72 Delta Sigma Phi
1932 Kappa Alpha Theta	1926–33 Phi Delta Epsilon
1939 Alpha Omicron Pi	1926–71 Sigma Delta Tau
PROFESSIONAL	1930–85 Alpha Gamma Delta
1956 Alpha Omega	1931–73 Delta Gamma
	1948–68 Phi Gamma Delta
OTHER PROFESSIONAL	1958–72 Alpha Epsilon Delta
1923 Alpha Zeta Omega	
ACHS HONORS	COLONIES
Omicron Delta Epsilon	1989 Phi Sigma Kappa

MACMURRAY COLLEGE Jacksonville, IL. College of liberal arts; co-ordinated colleges for men and women; private control (Methodist); chartered 1846; 1955 established for men and women.

ACHS HONORS	SERVICE
Omicron Delta Epsilon	1964 Alpha Phi Omega
1956 Alpha Lambda Delta	1980 Alpha Phi Omega
1960 Psi Chi	
1968 Mortar Board	INACTIVE
1987 Kappa Mu Epsilon	1926–35 Sigma Alpha Iota
	1959–61 Pi Gamma Mu
OTHER HONORS	
1943 National Collegiate Players	

MCMURRY COLLEGE Abilene, TX. College of liberal arts; coeducational; private control (Methodist). Established 1923 as junior college, became four-year college 1925.

PROFESSIONAL	RECOGNITION
1967 Delta Omicron	1943 Alpha Psi Omega
	1965 Gamma Sigma Epsilon
ACHS HONORS	1966 Pi Kappa Delta
1926 Alpha Chi	1968 Kappa Pi
1951 Kappa Delta Pi	
1951 Sigma Tau Delta	
1962 Sigma Pi Sigma	INACTIVE
1971 Phi Alpha Theta	1985–88 Phi Mu Alpha— Sinfonia
1975 Sigma Delta Pi	

MCNEESE STATE COLLEGE Lake Charles, LA. College of liberal arts; professional schools; coeducational; state control; established 1939 as junior college of Louisiana State University; became four-year college 1950.

Fraternities and sororities own their own houses on their own land.

NIC MEN'S
1955 Pi Kappa Phi
1966 Kappa Sigma
1969 Kappa Alpha Order
1970 Kappa Alpha Psi (A)
1972 Phi Kappa Theta

NPHC MEN'S
      Phi Beta Sigma
1973 Alpha Phi Alpha

NPC WOMEN'S
1958 Alpha Delta Pi
1958 Chi Omega
1958 Phi Mu

NPHC WOMEN'S
      Zeta Phi Beta
1971 Alpha Kappa Alpha

PROFESSIONAL
1955 Phi Mu Alpha—Sinfonia
1955 Sigma Alpha Iota
1969 Delta Sigma Pi

ACHS HONORS
1956 Sigma Tau Delta

1971 Phi Kappa Phi
1972 Kappa Omicron Nu
1975 Phi Alpha Theta
1985 Alpha Lambda Delta

OTHER HONORS
      National Order of Omega
1964 Pi Mu Epsilon

RECOGNITION
1955 Alpha Psi Omega
1956 Blue Key
1956 National Block and Bridle
      Club
1958 Pi Kappa Delta
1959 Scabbard and Blade (14)

INACTIVE
1957–77 Tau Kappa Epsilon
1958–65 Delta Zeta
1962–87 Phi Chi Theta
1963–72 Alpha Kappa Lambda
1971–82 Zeta Tau Alpha

MCPHERSON COLLEGE McPherson, KS. College of liberal arts; coeducational; private control: affiliated with Church of the Brethren; established 1887.

ACHS HONORS
1954 Phi Alpha Theta

RECOGNITION
1940 Alpha Psi Omega

1942 Pi Kappa Delta

UNIVERSITY OF MAINE AT AUGUSTA Augusta, ME.

OTHER PROFESSIONAL
1968 Kappa Delta Phi (C)

UNIVERSITY OF MAINE AT FARMINGTON Farmington, ME.

ACHS HONORS
1966 Gamma Theta Upsilon
1968 Alpha Chi
1968 Kappa Delta Pi
1984 Psi Chi

RECOGNITION
1968 Beta Beta Beta

INACTIVE
1931–71 Kappa Delta Phi (C)

UNIVERSITY OF MAINE AT FORT KENT Fort Kent, ME.

OTHER PROFESSIONAL
1966 Kappa Delta Phi (C)

UNIVERSITY OF MAINE AT MACHIAS Machias, ME.

OTHER PROFESSIONAL
1931 Kappa Delta Phi (C)

SERVICE
1972 Alpha Phi Omega

UNIVERSITY OF MAINE AT ORONO Orono, ME. Multi-purpose college; coeducational; state control; established as normal school 1908; became Madison College 1938.

Fraternity and sorority members live in college-owned housing and pay rent as individuals.

NIC MEN'S
1879 Beta Theta Pi
1886 Kappa Sigma
1891 Alpha Tau Omega
1898 Phi Kappa Sigma
1899 Phi Gamma Delta
1901 Sigma Alpha Epsilon
1902 Sigma Chi
1907 Theta Chi
1908 Delta Tau Delta
1913 Sigma Nu
1924 Alpha Gamma Rho
1929 Tau Epsilon Phi
1948 Sigma Phi Epsilon
1948 Tau Kappa Epsilon
1970 Delta Upsilon
1985 Tau Kappa Epsilon

NPC WOMEN'S
1908 Alpha Omicron Pi
1912 Phi Mu
1917 Delta Delta Delta
1920 Pi Beta Phi
1921 Chi Omega
1924 Delta Zeta
1963 Alpha Phi

PROFESSIONAL
1970 Kappa Kappa Psi

OTHER PROFESSIONAL
1906 Alpha Zeta
1923 Kappa Phi Kappa

ACHS HONORS
      Omicron Delta Epsilon
      Pi Alpha Alpha
1897 Phi Kappa Phi
1911 Tau Beta Pi
1917 Xi Sigma Pi
1931 Kappa Omicron Nu
1932 Kappa Delta Pi
1949 Sigma Pi Sigma

1961 Eta Kappa Nu
1967 Pi Sigma Alpha
1967 Sigma Delta Pi
1970 Alpha Lambda Delta
1974 Beta Gamma Sigma
1974 Phi Alpha Theta
1975 Phi Sigma Iota
1980 Chi Epsilon
1986 Psi Chi
1989 Pi Kappa Lambda

OTHER HONORS
      National Order of Omega
1923 Phi Beta Kappa
1948 Sigma Xi
1965 Pi Mu Epsilon

SERVICE
1967 Alpha Phi Omega

RECOGNITION
1949 Pi Kappa Delta

INACTIVE
1894–02 Kappa Sigma
1901   Gamma Eta Gamma
1908–19 Phi Delta Phi
1911–41 Alpha Chi Sigma
1915–24 Sigma Delta Chi
1916   Scabbard and Blade
          (2)
1916–25 Zeta Beta Tau
1917–35 Phi Sigma
1923–74 Phi Mu Delta
1926–35 Phi Kappa Theta
1959–88 Alpha Chi Omega
1968–84 Alpha Delta Pi
1968–85 Sigma Kappa
1972–74 Kappa Delta Phi (C)

COLONIES
1913 Lambda Chi Alpha

COLLEGE OF THE MAINLAND Texas City, TX.

NPHC MEN'S
      Phi Beta Sigma

UNIVERSITY OF MAINE AT PRESQUE ISLE Presque Isle, ME.

OTHER PROFESSIONAL
1952 Kappa Delta Phi (C)

ACHS HONORS
1982 Phi Eta Sigma

MADISON COLLEGE Harrisonburg, VA. Land-grant institution; board of trustees organized 1865, first instruction 1868. University; coeducational undergraduate colleges and graduate study; state control; school of law, school of business administration. Branches at Augusta, Bangor, Farmington, Fort Kent, Machias, Portland-Gorham, and Presque Isle.

Fraternities are permitted to possess their own houses and property; most do; however, in some cases ownership is by the fraternity on college-owned land. Administration requires sorority members to occupy dormitories.

NIC MEN'S
1969 Tau Kappa Epsilon
1970 Sigma Phi Epsilon
1976 Kappa Sigma
1978 Sigma Pi
1982 Lambda Chi Alpha
1988 Chi Phi
1988 Kappa Alpha Psi (A)

NPHC MEN'S
Phi Beta Sigma

NPC WOMEN'S
1939 Alpha Sigma Alpha
1939 Sigma Sigma Sigma
1944 Alpha Sigma Tau
1949 Zeta Tau Alpha
1959 Alpha Gamma Delta
1959 Sigma Kappa
1982 Delta Gamma
1987 Alpha Chi Omega

NPHC WOMEN'S
1971 Delta Sigma Theta (B)
1978 Alpha Kappa Alpha

PROFESSIONAL
1958 Sigma Alpha Iota
1969 Phi Mu Alpha—Sinfonia
1974 Delta Sigma Pi

1976 Phi Chi Theta

OTHER PROFESSIONAL
1961 Alpha Beta Alpha

ACHS HONORS
Omicron Delta Epsilon
Pi Alpha Alpha
1928 Kappa Delta Pi
1945 Pi Omega Pi
1964 Phi Sigma Iota
1971 Psi Chi
1972 Phi Alpha Theta
1974 Phi Kappa Phi
1976 Omicron Delta Kappa
1980 Pi Sigma Alpha
1981 Phi Sigma Tau
1983 Sigma Pi Sigma
1985 Kappa Tau Alpha

RECOGNITION
1959 Kappa Pi

INACTIVE
1960–87 Phi Mu
1969–81 Kappa Delta
1972–89 Theta Chi

COLONIES
Kappa Delta Rho

UNIVERSITY OF MAINE OF PORTLAND-GORHAM
Portland, ME. College of liberal arts and general studies; teacher preparatory; professional; state control; coeducational. Established 1970.

NIC MEN'S
1975 Sigma Nu

NPC WOMEN'S
1968 Alpha Xi Delta

INACTIVE
1966–84 Kappa Delta Epsilon

MANCHESTER COLLEGE
North Manchester, IN. College of liberal arts; coeducational; private control (Church of the Brethren). Established 1889.

ACHS HONORS
1936 Delta Sigma Rho-Tau Kappa Alpha
1948 Sigma Pi Sigma
1950 Kappa Mu Epsilon

RECOGNITION
1945 Alpha Psi Omega
1964 Beta Beta Beta

MANHATTAN COLLEGE
Riverdale, NY. College of liberal arts; professional school; men; private control (Roman Catholic); founded 1853.

The college does not recognize fraternity houses.

NIC MEN'S
1929 Alpha Phi Delta
1950 Phi Kappa Theta
1969 Phi Sigma Kappa

OTHER PROFESSIONAL
1943 Phi Epsilon Kappa

ACHS HONORS
Omicron Delta Epsilon
1949 Chi Epsilon
1950 Eta Kappa Nu
1951 Phi Alpha Theta
1951 Sigma Pi Sigma
1967 Tau Beta Pi

1969 Pi Tau Sigma
1970 Delta Mu Delta
1971 Kappa Delta Pi
1975 Psi Chi
1977 Theta Alpha Kappa
1984 Pi Sigma Alpha
1985 Omega Chi Epsilon

OTHER HONORS
1961 Pi Mu Epsilon
1968 Sigma Xi
1971 Phi Beta Kappa

SERVICE
1953 Alpha Phi Omega

RECOGNITION
Arnold Air Society (A-2)
1955 Delta Phi Alpha
1972 Sigma Delta Psi
1975 Beta Beta Beta

INACTIVE
1948 Sigma Beta Kappa
1961–82 Phi Mu Alpha—Sinfonia
1966–71 Delta Sigma Pi

MANHATTANVILLE COLLEGE
Manhattan, NY.

ACHS HONORS
1979 Psi Chi

RECOGNITION
1972 Beta Beta Beta

THE UNIVERSITY OF MANITOBA
Winnipeg, MB. Founded 1877. Coeducational.

The college permits the fraternities to depend on their own resources in matters of housing.

NIC MEN'S
1921 Zeta Psi
1925 Delta Kappa Epsilon
1926 Sigma Alpha Mu
1929 Delta Upsilon
1930 Phi Delta Theta
1932 Tau Delta Phi

NPC WOMEN'S
1928 Alpha Phi
1929 Zeta Tau Alpha
1930 Alpha Delta Pi
1930 Alpha Gamma Delta

PROFESSIONAL
1953 Sigma Phi Delta
1959 Alpha Omega

OTHER HONORS
1961 Omicron Kappa Upsilon

INACTIVE
1923   Phi Beta Pi and Theta Kappa Psi (B)
1925–75 Gamma Phi Beta
1928–76 Kappa Kappa Gamma
1929–44 Phi Rho Sigma
1929–76 Pi Beta Phi
1930–55 Phi Sigma Sigma
1931–52 Delta Delta Delta
1933–56 Sigma Kappa
1948–72 Zeta Beta Tau
1958–81 Tau Kappa Epsilon

COLONIES
1948 Alpha Epsilon Pi

MANKATO STATE UNIVERSITY
Mankato, MN. Schools of arts and science, business, education, graduate school, health and physical education, and nursing; coeducational; state control; established 1867 as normal school.

Fraternities and sororities have chapter houses.

NIC MEN'S
1964 Phi Delta Theta
1969 Phi Kappa Psi
1971 Delta Tau Delta

NPC WOMEN'S
1965 Alpha Chi Omega
1966 Gamma Phi Beta
1990 Sigma Sigma Sigma

PROFESSIONAL
1960 Delta Sigma Pi

OTHER PROFESSIONAL
1965 Phi Upsilon Omicron
1969 Delta Pi Epsilon

ACHS HONORS
Omicron Delta Epsilon
1955 Delta Sigma Rho-Tau Kappa Alpha
1964 Sigma Tau Delta
1966 Phi Alpha Theta
1968 Kappa Delta Pi
1970 Pi Omega Pi
1974 Phi Kappa Phi
1984 Gamma Theta Upsilon

OTHER HONORS
National Order of Omega
1950 National Collegiate Players

SERVICE
1961 Alpha Phi Omega
1963 Gamma Sigma Sigma

RECOGNITION
1961 Sigma Delta Psi
1962 Kappa Pi

INACTIVE
1961–80 Tau Kappa Epsilon
1963–79 Phi Mu Alpha—Sinfonia
1964–72 Sigma Alpha Iota
1965–75 Delta Delta Delta
1967–73 Alpha Gamma Delta
1967–75 Sigma Alpha Epsilon
1968–86 Alpha Tau Omega

COLONIES
1966 Lambda Chi Alpha
1990 Delta Chi

MANSFIELD UNIVERSITY Mansfield, PA. Multi-purpose university; coeducational; state control. Established 1854 as Mansfield Classical Seminary.

NIC MEN'S
1962 Phi Sigma Kappa
1965 Sigma Tau Gamma
1971 Tau Kappa Epsilon
1972 Lambda Chi Alpha
1987 Alpha Chi Rho

NPHC MEN'S
Phi Beta Sigma

NPC WOMEN'S
1965 Alpha Sigma Tau
1966 Delta Zeta
1970 Alpha Sigma Alpha
1971 Zeta Tau Alpha

PROFESSIONAL
1931 Phi Mu Alpha—Sinfonia
1968 Kappa Kappa Psi

OTHER PROFESSIONAL
1930 Phi Sigma Pi
1970 Alpha Beta Alpha

ACHS HONORS
1930 Kappa Delta Pi
1931 Pi Gamma Mu
1948 Kappa Omicron Nu
1955 Gamma Theta Upsilon
1967 Pi Delta Phi
1973 Psi Chi
1974 Lambda Sigma Society

RECOGNITION
1949 Alpha Psi Omega
1962 Delta Phi Alpha
1971 Pi Kappa Delta

INACTIVE
1968–85 Phi Sigma Kappa

MARIAN COLLEGE Indianapolis, IN. Founded 1937 by the Sisters of St. Francis of Oldenburg, IN, as a liberal arts college for women; coeducational 1954; private control.

ACHS HONORS
1945 Delta Epsilon Sigma
1957 Lambda Iota Tau
1983 Psi Chi

MARIAN COLLEGE OF FOND DU LAC Fond du Lac, WI. College of liberal arts for women; private; Roman Catholic; chartered 1936.

PROFESSIONAL
1961 Alpha Delta Theta

ACHS HONORS
1966 Sigma Tau Delta

MARIETTA COLLEGE Marietta, OH. Chartered in 1835; fully accredited; liberal arts and science, co-educational, private control, nonsectarian; offers six degrees, A.A., A.B., B.F.A., B.S., B.S. in petroleum engineering and M.A. in liberal learning.

Seven fraternities occupy college-owned houses. One sorority occupies a college-owned house; and three own their own houses on their own land.

NIC MEN'S
1860 Alpha Sigma Phi
1870 Delta Upsilon
1890 Alpha Tau Omega
1925 Lambda Chi Alpha
1959 Tau Kappa Epsilon
1960 Tau Epsilon Phi
1968 Delta Tau Delta

NPC WOMEN'S
1923 Chi Omega
1944 Sigma Kappa
1945 Alpha Xi Delta
1963 Sigma Sigma Sigma

ACHS HONORS
Omicron Delta Epsilon
1950 Omicron Delta Kappa
1950 Phi Alpha Theta
1953 Sigma Delta Pi
1960 Kappa Mu Epsilon
1981 Psi Chi

OTHER HONORS
1860 Phi Beta Kappa

SERVICE
1964 Alpha Phi Omega
1966 Gamma Sigma Sigma

RECOGNITION
1926 Beta Beta Beta
1926 Pi Kappa Delta
1937 Alpha Psi Omega
1949 Society for Collegiate Journalists—Pi Delta Epsilon-Alpha Phi Gamma (P)
1956 Chi Delta Phi

INACTIVE
1855–97 Phi Gamma Delta
1952–56 Sigma Tau Gamma
1959–65 Pi Gamma Mu
1961–75 Alpha Gamma Delta
1961–83 Alpha Sigma Tau

MARIST COLLEGE Poughkeepsie, NY. Liberal arts college for men and women; private control. Established 1946.

NIC MEN'S
Tau Kappa Epsilon
1979 Sigma Phi Epsilon

ACHS HONORS
1967 Phi Alpha Theta

1979 Psi Chi
1985 Pi Sigma Alpha

COLONIES
1989 Tau Epsilon Phi

MARQUETTE UNIVERSITY Milwaukee, WI. Founded 1881. Catholic, Jesuit, coeducational. Offers graduate studies, medicine, dentistry, law, liberal arts, speech, journalism, nursing, business administration, engineering, dental hygiene.

Fraternities own their own houses on their own land.

NIC MEN'S
1937 Triangle
1954 Kappa Alpha Psi (A)
1969 Phi Kappa Theta
1977 Delta Chi
1988 Phi Delta Theta
1989 Sigma Chi
1990 Tau Kappa Epsilon

NPC WOMEN'S
1989 Alpha Chi Omega
1989 Alpha Phi

NPHC WOMEN'S
1975 Delta Sigma Theta (B)
1978 Alpha Kappa Alpha
1980 Sigma Gamma Rho

PROFESSIONAL
1897 Psi Omega
1920 Delta Sigma Pi
1921 Delta Theta Phi
1931 Sigma Phi Delta
1938 Alpha Tau Delta
1952 Zeta Phi Eta
1957 Phi Delta Phi
1962 Pi Sigma Epsilon
1966 Phi Alpha Delta
1985 Phi Alpha Delta

OTHER PROFESSIONAL
1918 Delta Sigma Delta
1920 Sigma Delta Chi
1922 Phi Delta Epsilon
1923 Women in Communications
1942 Beta Alpha Psi
1973 Pi Lambda Theta

ACHS HONORS
Omicron Delta Epsilon
1915 Alpha Sigma Nu
1929 Beta Gamma Sigma
1930 Delta Sigma Rho-Tau Kappa Alpha
1930 Kappa Tau Alpha
1932 Tau Beta Pi
1938 Phi Sigma
1939 Alpha Kappa Delta
1941 Phi Alpha Theta
1942 Pi Tau Sigma
1945 Eta Kappa Nu
1947 Sigma Pi Sigma
1950 Chi Epsilon
1950 Sigma Delta Pi
1951 Pi Delta Phi

1959 Pi Gamma Mu
1960 Psi Chi
1961 Phi Sigma Tau
1968 Alpha Epsilon Delta
1970 Pi Sigma Alpha
1977 Theta Alpha Kappa

OTHER HONORS
1924 Omicron Kappa Upsilon
1933 Pi Mu Epsilon
1949 Alpha Omega Alpha
1960 Sigma Xi
1971 Phi Beta Kappa

SERVICE
1949 Alpha Phi Omega

RECOGNITION
1948 Phi Delta Gamma
1949 Delta Phi Alpha
1950 Eta Sigma Phi
1956 Scabbard and Blade (12)
1960 Sigma Phi Alpha

INACTIVE
1900–68 Alpha Kappa Kappa
1903–21 Phi Rho Sigma
1907–42 Phi Beta Pi and Theta Kappa Psi (a)
1917 Kappa Beta Gamma
1921 Phi Chi
1922–46 Sigma Nu Phi
1924 Kappa Beta Pi
1924–87 Alpha Omega
1925–31 Delta Omicron
1925–74 Alpha Epsilon Pi
1926–72 Alpha Kappa Psi
1934–69 Sigma Tau Delta
1936 Tau Epsilon Rho
1939–76 Phi Chi Theta
1941–69 Theta Phi Alpha
1944 Alpha Delta Theta
1964–73 Phi Mu
1965–73 Alpha Delta Gamma
1965–84 Alpha Delta Pi
1969–85 Sigma Sigma Sigma
1970–75 Delta Upsilon
1970–79 Delta Tau Delta
1970–85 Sigma Phi Epsilon
1971–73 Theta Chi
1973–83 Zeta Beta Tau

COLONIES
1988 Phi Delta Theta

MARS HILL COLLEGE
Mars Hills, NC. Founded 1856; coeducational; junior college until 1965; four-year liberal arts college; affiliated with Southern Baptist College.

NIC MEN'S
1986 Kappa Alpha Psi (A)

PROFESSIONAL
1967 Phi Mu Alpha—Sinfonia
1970 Delta Omicron

ACHS HONORS
1971 Alpha Chi
1976 Phi Alpha Theta

1981 Pi Sigma Alpha

SERVICE
1967 Alpha Phi Omega

INACTIVE
1973–79 Pi Kappa Phi

COLONIES
1989 Theta Chi

MARSHALL UNIVERSITY
Huntington, WV. Chartered as Marshall Academy 1837; became Marshall College 1858 under the West Virginia Conference of the Methodist Episcopal Church, South. Coeducational; state control; university.

Fraternities and sororities own houses on their own land.

NIC MEN'S
1927 Kappa Alpha Order
1929 Alpha Sigma Phi
1946 Lambda Chi Alpha
1947 Sigma Phi Epsilon
1947 Tau Kappa Epsilon
1948 Pi Kappa Alpha
1962 Kappa Alpha Psi (A)
1978 Alpha Tau Omega
1987 Phi Delta Theta
1989 Pi Kappa Phi

NPHC MEN'S
Phi Beta Sigma

NPC WOMEN'S
1922 Delta Zeta
1922 Sigma Sigma Sigma
1927 Alpha Sigma Alpha
1950 Alpha Xi Delta
1952 Alpha Chi Omega
1966 Phi Mu

NPHC WOMEN'S
1971 Delta Sigma Theta (B)
1972 Alpha Kappa Alpha
1983 Sigma Gamma Rho

PROFESSIONAL
1945 Delta Omicron
1965 Alpha Kappa Psi
1972 Kappa Kappa Psi
1972 Tau Beta Sigma
1982 Phi Alpha Delta
1985 Alpha Chi Sigma

OTHER PROFESSIONAL
1972 Sigma Delta Chi

ACHS HONORS
Omicron Delta Epsilon
1923 Kappa Delta Pi

1926 Kappa Omicron Nu
1937 Pi Sigma Alpha
1947 Omicron Delta Kappa
1948 Phi Eta Sigma
1948 Psi Chi
1950 Alpha Epsilon Delta
1950 Alpha Kappa Delta
1950 Phi Alpha Theta
1951 Pi Delta Phi
1952 Pi Omega Pi
1955 Gamma Theta Upsilon
1963 Sigma Tau Delta

OTHER HONORS
National Order of Omega
1970 Pi Mu Epsilon

SERVICE
1949 Alpha Phi Omega

RECOGNITION
1925 Alpha Psi Omega
1925 Chi Beta Phi
1949 Eta Mu Pi
1950 Pi Kappa Delta
1951 Eta Sigma Phi
1951 Kappa Pi
1956 Scabbard and Blade (12)

INACTIVE
1926–37 Pi Gamma Mu
1946–59 Alpha Sigma Tau
1948–70 Sigma Delta Pi
1952–78 Phi Mu Alpha—Sinfonia
1953–76 Alpha Lambda Delta
1953–82 Sigma Alpha Epsilon
1956–75 Alpha Beta Alpha
1959–83 Sigma Kappa
1965–78 Zeta Beta Tau
1970–71 Phi Kappa Tau

MARY BALDWIN COLLEGE
Staunton, VA. College of liberal arts for women; private control (Presbyterian); established 1842.

ACHS HONORS
Omicron Delta Epsilon
1965 Phi Alpha Theta

1975 Psi Chi
1976 Omicron Delta Kappa

OTHER HONORS
1971 Phi Beta Kappa

RECOGNITION
1948 Beta Beta Beta

INACTIVE
1904–06 Zeta Tau Alpha
1905–07 Alpha Sigma Alpha
1906–10 Alpha Delta Pi

MARY HARDIN-BAYLOR COLLEGE
Belton, TX. College of liberal arts for women; private control (Baptist General Convention of Texas). Chartered 1845 as Female Department of Baylor University.

ACHS HONORS
1922 Alpha Chi
1927 Sigma Tau Delta
1928 Pi Gamma Mu
1931 Sigma Delta Pi
1960 Phi Alpha Theta

SERVICE
1973 Alpha Phi Omega

RECOGNITION
1925 Pi Kappa Delta
1933 Alpha Psi Omega
1942 Kappa Pi

INACTIVE
1964–66 Pi Omega Pi

MARY WASHINGTON COLLEGE
Fredericksburg, VA. College of liberal arts for men and women; state control; chartered as normal school 1908; became part of university 1944; separated from university 1972.

PROFESSIONAL
1946 Mu Phi Epsilon

ACHS HONORS
Omicron Delta Epsilon
1936 Pi Omega Pi
1948 Pi Gamma Mu
1950 Phi Sigma Iota
1954 Psi Chi
1959 Mortar Board
1968 Lambda Iota Tau
1971 Gamma Theta Upsilon
1973 Phi Alpha Theta
1975 Kappa Delta Pi
1980 Pi Sigma Alpha

OTHER HONORS
1971 Phi Beta Kappa

RECOGNITION
1930 Alpha Phi Sigma (E)
1937 Alpha Psi Omega
1945 Chi Beta Phi
1950 Eta Sigma Phi

INACTIVE
1945–69 Sigma Tau Delta
1951 Zeta Phi Eta
1962–68 Kappa Omicron Nu

COLONIES
1986 Sigma Pi Sigma

MARYGROVE COLLEGE
Detroit, MI.

ACHS HONORS
1959 Alpha Lambda Delta
1961 Sigma Delta Pi
1964 Pi Delta Phi

RECOGNITION
1956 Alpha Psi Omega

UNIVERSITY OF MARYLAND
College Park, MD. Founded at Baltimore 1807, and the Maryland Agriculture College, founded at College Park, 1856, were consolidated by 1920 Act of the Maryland State Legislature as a state-supported, coeducational, land-grant institution of higher learning. Located on the College Park campus are eight undergraduate colleges, the graduate school, the experiment station and various institutes and bureaus. Situated on its Baltimore campus are six professional schools and the University Hospital.

Eleven fraternities own their own houses on their own land; six sororities do so. Nine fraternities and twelve sororities rent houses on college-owned land. Two fraternities privately rent chapter houses. Eleven groups do not have chapter houses.

NIC MEN'S
1874 Kappa Sigma
1878 Phi Gamma Delta
1897 Phi Sigma Kappa
1899 Phi Kappa Sigma
1914 Kappa Alpha Order
1917 Sigma Nu
1919 Zeta Beta Tau
1924 Delta Sigma Phi
1925 Tau Epsilon Phi
1928 Alpha Gamma Rho
1929 Theta Chi
1930 Alpha Tau Omega
1930 Phi Delta Theta
1933 Sigma Alpha Mu
1940 Alpha Epsilon Pi
1942 Sigma Chi
1943 Sigma Alpha Epsilon
1947 Tau Kappa Epsilon
1948 Delta Tau Delta
1949 Sigma Phi Epsilon
1949 Sigma Pi
1950 Phi Kappa Tau
1952 Pi Kappa Alpha
1972 Delta Upsilon
1975 Kappa Alpha Psi (A)
1976 Zeta Psi
1982 Beta Theta Pi

NPHC MEN'S
 Phi Beta Sigma
1974 Alpha Phi Alpha

NPC WOMEN'S
1924 Alpha Omicron Pi
1929 Kappa Delta
1929 Kappa Kappa Gamma
1934 Alpha Xi Delta
1934 Delta Delta Delta
1936 Phi Sigma Sigma
1940 Alpha Delta Pi
1940 Gamma Phi Beta
1940 Sigma Kappa
1943 Alpha Epsilon Phi
1944 Pi Beta Phi
1945 Delta Gamma
1947 Alpha Gamma Delta
1947 Kappa Alpha Theta
1948 Alpha Chi Omega
1952 Sigma Delta Tau
1960 Delta Phi Epsilon
1961 Alpha Phi

NPHC WOMEN'S
1974 Alpha Kappa Alpha
1974 Delta Sigma Theta (B)
1976 Sigma Gamma Rho

PROFESSIONAL
1893 Xi Psi Phi
1905 Phi Delta Chi
1919 Lambda Kappa Sigma
1922 Delta Theta Phi
1923 Alpha Omega
1926 Kappa Psi
1927 Alpha Chi Sigma
1950 Delta Sigma Pi
1955 Kappa Kappa Psi
1957 Sigma Alpha Iota
1957 Tau Beta Sigma
1958 Phi Alpha Delta
1962 Rho Pi Phi

OTHER PROFESSIONAL
1912 Phi Delta Epsilon
1918 Nu Beta Epsilon
1920 Alpha Zeta
1920 Gamma Eta Gamma

1923 Alpha Zeta Omega
1936 Beta Alpha Psi
1956 Sigma Delta Chi

ACHS HONORS
 Omicron Delta Epsilon
1920 Phi Kappa Phi
1922 Sigma Delta Pi
1927 Omicron Delta Kappa
1929 Tau Beta Pi
1930 Rho Chi
1932 Alpha Lambda Delta
1934 Mortar Board
1937 Kappa Omicron Nu
1938 Pi Sigma Alpha
1940 Beta Gamma Sigma
1940 Phi Eta Sigma
1946 Alpha Kappa Delta
1948 Phi Alpha Theta
1948 Sigma Pi Sigma
1955 Psi Chi
1956 Pi Tau Sigma
1957 Eta Kappa Nu
1957 Gamma Theta Upsilon
1958 Delta Sigma Rho-Tau
 Kappa Alpha
1959 Sigma Theta Tau
1960 Alpha Sigma Mu
1961 Chi Epsilon
1961 Phi Sigma
1962 Kappa Delta Pi
1962 Kappa Tau Alpha
1964 Beta Phi Mu
1966 Sigma Gamma Tau
1973 Omega Chi Epsilon
1977 Alpha Epsilon
1978 Pi Kappa Lambda
1980 Phi Sigma Iota
1987 Gamma Theta Upsilon

OTHER HONORS
1928 Sigma Xi
1938 Order of the Coif
1947 National Collegiate
 Players
1949 Alpha Omega Alpha
1964 Phi Beta Kappa

SERVICE
1947 Alpha Phi Omega
1957 Gamma Sigma Sigma

RECOGNITION
 Angel Flight
 Arnold Air Society (B-1)
1930 Society for Collegiate
 Journalists—Pi Delta
 Epsilon-Alpha Phi Gamma
 (P)
1938 National Block and Bridle
 Club
1940 Iota Lambda Sigma
1949 Pi Alpha Xi
1956 Phi Delta Gamma
1973 Sigma Phi Alpha

INACTIVE
1895–95 Phi Chi
1898–31 Phi Beta Pi and Theta
 Kappa Psi (B)
1900–24 Psi Omega
1901 Phi Beta Pi and Theta
 Kappa Psi (a)
1904–36 Phi Rho Sigma
1922 Phi Lambda Kappa
1922 Scabbard and Blade
 (3)
1923–23 Chi Omega

1923–28 Alpha Kappa Kappa
1924–39 Psi Omega
1929–36 Kappa Phi Kappa
1931–38 Delta Sigma Delta
1932–74 Lambda Chi Alpha
1952–60 Delta Kappa Epsilon
1955–86 Phi Chi Theta
1958–76 Phi Mu Alpha—
 Sinfonia

School Of Pharmacy College Park, MD.

NIC MEN'S
1969 Tau Delta Phi

OTHER HONORS
 National Order of Omega

UNIVERSITY OF MARYLAND, BALTIMORE COUNTY Cantonsville, MD. Public institution. Founded in 1966. Four-year; coeducational.

79% of students live off campus or commute.

NIC MEN'S
1976 Kappa Alpha Psi (A)
1980 Lambda Chi Alpha
1987 Sigma Alpha Epsilon
1988 Alpha Tau Omega
1988 Phi Kappa Psi

NPHC MEN'S
 Phi Beta Sigma

NPC WOMEN'S
1979 Phi Sigma Sigma
1983 Delta Phi Epsilon
1989 Phi Mu

NPHC WOMEN'S
1974 Delta Sigma Theta (B)
1977 Alpha Kappa Alpha

1990 Sigma Gamma Rho

ACHS HONORS
 Omicron Delta Epsilon
1973 Psi Chi
1977 Phi Alpha Theta
1980 Sigma Pi Sigma
1981 Omicron Delta Kappa
1984 Pi Sigma Alpha

RECOGNITION
1960 Phi Delta Gamma

INACTIVE
1874–18 Kappa Sigma

COLONIES
1990 Tau Epsilon Phi

1959 Kappa Alpha Mu

COLONIES
 Pi Kappa Phi
1978 Triangle
1987 Delta Chi
1988 Delta Chi

UNIVERSITY OF MARYLAND, EASTERN SHORE Princess Anne, MD. Land-grant college; coeducational; state control; part of University of Maryland; chartered 1886.

NIC MEN'S
1949 Kappa Alpha Psi (A)

NPHC MEN'S
 Phi Beta Sigma
1950 Alpha Phi Alpha

NPHC WOMEN'S
1951 Alpha Kappa Alpha

OTHER PROFESSIONAL
1971 Alpha Tau Alpha

ACHS HONORS
1955 Alpha Kappa Mu

1974 Sigma Tau Delta
1985 Kappa Omicron Nu

SERVICE
1967 Alpha Phi Omega

RECOGNITION
 Arnold Air Society (B-1)

INACTIVE
 Zeta Phi Beta

MARYMONT COLLEGE Salina, KS. Private institution. Four-year; coeducational; liberal arts college.

Must live at home or on campus if under 21.

ACHS HONORS
1974 Alpha Chi

MARYMOUNT COLLEGE Terrytown, NY.

ACHS HONORS
1959 Delta Epsilon Sigma
1969 Pi Delta Phi

1970 Psi Chi
1981 Psi Chi

MARYMOUNT MANHATTAN COLLEGE New York, NY.

NPHC WOMEN'S
1987 Alpha Kappa Alpha

ACHS HONORS
1979 Psi Chi

MARYVILLE COLLEGE Maryville, TN. College of liberal arts; coeducational; private: United Presbyterian Church; founded 1819.

ACHS HONORS
1964 Pi Delta Phi
1973 Lambda Iota Tau
1976 Alpha Lambda Delta
1986 Omicron Delta Kappa

SERVICE
1979 Alpha Phi Omega

INACTIVE.
1957–85 Pi Gamma Mu
1966–85 Phi Mu Alpha—
        Sinfonia
1967–67 Sigma Delta Pi

MARYVILLE COLLEGE OF ST LOUIS St. Louis, MO. Private control. Founded in 1872. Four-year; graduate; coeducational; liberal arts college.

66% of students live off campus or commute.

ACHS HONORS
1969 Pi Delta Phi

1982 Pi Gamma Mu

MARYWOOD COLLEGE Scranton, PA. College of liberal arts for women; private control; Roman Catholic; established 1915.

ACHS HONORS
     Pi Alpha Alpha
1944 Delta Epsilon Sigma
1947 Kappa Omicron Nu
1964 Kappa Mu Epsilon
1964 Lambda Iota Tau
1965 Phi Alpha Theta
1966 Psi Chi

1972 Pi Gamma Mu
1982 Theta Alpha Kappa
1987 Pi Kappa Lambda

RECOGNITION
1962 Eta Sigma Phi

INACTIVE
1944–69 Sigma Tau Delta

UNIVERSITY OF MASSACHUSETTS Amherst, MA. State university of the Commonwealth; founded in 1863 under provisions of the Morrill Land Grant Act passed by the United States Congress one year earlier. Coeducational.

The fraternities and sororities own their own houses on their own land.

NIC MEN'S
1873 Phi Sigma Kappa
1912 Lambda Chi Alpha
1912 Sigma Phi Epsilon
1933 Alpha Epsilon Pi
1953 Phi Mu Delta
1969 Delta Chi
1975 Zeta Psi
1977 Pi Kappa Alpha
1978 Alpha Delta Phi
1980 Delta Upsilon
1987 Alpha Chi Rho

1989 Kappa Alpha Psi (A)

NPHC MEN'S
     Phi Beta Sigma

NPC WOMEN'S
1941 Chi Omega
1942 Kappa Kappa Gamma
1944 Sigma Kappa
1945 Sigma Delta Tau
1961 Alpha Chi Omega
1963 Sigma Sigma Sigma
1981 Delta Zeta

PROFESSIONAL
1968 Alpha Delta Theta
1969 Kappa Kappa Psi
1969 Tau Beta Sigma

OTHER PROFESSIONAL
1956 Alpha Zeta
1975 Beta Alpha Psi

ACHS HONORS
     Omicron Delta Epsilon
     Omicron Delta Epsilon
1904 Phi Kappa Phi
1952 Kappa Omicron Nu
1955 Mortar Board
1956 Tau Beta Pi
1959 Beta Gamma Sigma
1960 Alpha Lambda Delta
1960 Eta Kappa Nu
1962 Xi Sigma Pi
1963 Pi Sigma Alpha
1964 Delta Sigma Rho-Tau
        Kappa Alpha
1965 Kappa Delta Pi
1966 Alpha Pi Mu
1972 Sigma Theta Tau
1979 Psi Chi
1984 Phi Alpha Theta
1988 Chi Epsilon
1990 Kappa Tau Alpha
1990 Sigma Lambda Alpha

OTHER HONORS
1938 Sigma Xi
1965 Phi Beta Kappa

SERVICE
1952 Alpha Phi Omega
1963 Gamma Sigma Sigma

RECOGNITION
     Angel Flight
     Arnold Air Society (A-1)
1955 Sigma Delta Psi
1964 Scabbard and Blade (15)

INACTIVE
1854–60 Alpha Sigma Phi
1904–84 Kappa Sigma
1911–88 Theta Chi
1917–62 Alpha Gamma Rho
1937–82 Sigma Alpha Epsilon
1943–79 Kappa Alpha Theta
1944–73 Pi Beta Phi
1951   Sigma Gamma Epsilon
1955–81 Phi Eta Sigma
1956–72 Tau Kappa Epsilon
1957–72 Zeta Beta Tau
1967–81 Pi Lambda Phi
1984–90 Phi Mu

COLONIES
1965 Sigma Alpha Mu

MASSACHUSETTS COLLEGE OF PHARMACY Boston, MA. Founded 1823, the second college of pharmacy in the United States; coeducational, nonsectarian, private control.

PROFESSIONAL
1902 Phi Delta Chi
1907 Kappa Psi
1913 Lambda Kappa Sigma
1919 Rho Pi Phi
1988 Kappa Epsilon

ACHS HONORS
1939 Rho Chi

1967 Psi Chi
1976 Sigma Pi Sigma

INACTIVE
1924   Delta Sigma Theta (C)
1967–83 Phi Alpha Theta

MASSACHUSETTS INSTITUTE OF TECHNOLOGY Cambridge, MA. Founded by William Barton Rogers, chartered 1861. Instruction began 1865. Originally located in Boston; moved to Cambridge in 1916. Schools of architecture and planning, science, engineering, humanities and social science, and management. Coeducational; private control; nonsectarian.

Fraternities own their own houses on their own land.

NIC MEN'S
1873 Chi Phi
1882 Sigma Chi
1885 Alpha Tau Omega
1885 Theta Xi
1889 Delta Psi
1889 Delta Tau Delta
1889 Phi Gamma Delta
1890 Delta Kappa Epsilon
1890 Theta Delta Chi
1891 Delta Upsilon
1892 Sigma Alpha Epsilon
1897 Pi Lambda Phi
1902 Phi Sigma Kappa

1902 Theta Chi
1903 Phi Kappa Sigma
1911 Zeta Beta Tau
1912 Lambda Chi Alpha
1913 Beta Theta Pi
1914 Kappa Sigma
1918 Phi Kappa Theta
1919 Tau Delta Phi
1919 Tau Epsilon Phi
1928 Alpha Phi Delta
1932 Phi Delta Theta
1951 Alpha Epsilon Pi
1952 Sigma Phi Epsilon
1975 Kappa Alpha Psi (A)

1977 Alpha Delta Phi
1979 Zeta Psi

NPC WOMEN'S
1984 Alpha Phi
1986 Alpha Chi Omega
1989 Sigma Kappa

NPHC WOMEN'S
1977 Alpha Kappa Alpha

PROFESSIONAL
1919 Alpha Chi Sigma

ACHS HONORS
1922 Tau Beta Pi
1928 Chi Epsilon
1939 Eta Kappa Nu
1947 Pi Tau Sigma
1956 Delta Sigma Rho-Tau
    Kappa Alpha
1982 Sigma Pi Sigma

OTHER HONORS
1934 Sigma Xi
1971 Phi Beta Kappa

SERVICE
1936 Alpha Phi Omega

RECOGNITION
    Angel Flight
    Arnold Air Society (A-1)
1924 Scabbard and Blade (5)
1956 Phi Lambda Upsilon
1966 Sigma Delta Psi

INACTIVE
1904–08 Delta Sigma Phi
1912–30 Theta Tau
1917–73 Sigma Alpha Mu
1921   Scarab
1922–74 Sigma Nu
1922–77 Phi Mu Delta
1924   Kappa Eta Kappa
1929–39 Alpha Sigma Phi
1970–82 Pi Kappa Alpha

COLONIES
    Sigma Kappa

MEHARRY MEDICAL COLLEGE Nashville, TN. Established 1876.

NIC MEN'S
1919 Kappa Alpha Psi (A)

NPHC MEN'S
    Phi Beta Sigma
1919 Alpha Phi Alpha
1919 Omega Psi Phi

NPHC WOMEN'S
1949 Delta Sigma Theta (B)

PROFESSIONAL
1971 Alpha Omega

OTHER HONORS
1957 Alpha Omega Alpha

RECOGNITION
1960 Sigma Phi Alpha

INACTIVE
1921–27 Alpha Kappa Alpha

MEMPHIS STATE UNIVERSITY Memphis, TN. University; coeducational; state control; established 1909 as West Tennessee State Normal School.

Fraternities occupy houses on land which they own and houses owned by the university. Sororities are housed in a Panhellenic Building owned by the university.

NIC MEN'S
1947 Pi Kappa Alpha
1948 Kappa Alpha Order
1949 Lambda Chi Alpha
1949 Sigma Phi Epsilon
1950 Kappa Sigma
1953 Sigma Alpha Epsilon
1954 Sigma Chi
1965 Alpha Tau Omega
1966 Pi Kappa Phi
1969 Phi Kappa Theta
1969 Phi Sigma Kappa
1972 Phi Gamma Delta
1980 Kappa Alpha Psi (A)

NPHC MEN'S
    Phi Beta Sigma
1975 Alpha Phi Alpha

NPC WOMEN'S
1947 Alpha Delta Pi
1947 Alpha Gamma Delta
1947 Phi Mu
1947 Sigma Kappa

1948 Delta Zeta
1962 Pi Beta Phi
1965 Delta Gamma
1985 Alpha Chi Omega

NPHC WOMEN'S
1963 Delta Sigma Theta (B)
1968 Alpha Kappa Alpha
1968 Sigma Gamma Rho

PROFESSIONAL
1921 Delta Theta Phi
1949 Delta Sigma Pi
1951 Phi Gamma Nu
1958 Pi Sigma Epsilon
1959 Phi Mu Alpha—Sinfonia
1962 Sigma Alpha Iota
1965 Phi Delta Phi
1966 Phi Alpha Delta
1970 Alpha Kappa Psi

OTHER PROFESSIONAL
1966 Sigma Delta Chi
1966 Sigma Delta Kappa
1969 Alpha Epsilon Rho

1971 Beta Alpha Psi
1972 Delta Pi Epsilon

ACHS HONORS
    Omicron Delta Epsilon
1950 Sigma Delta Pi
1955 Phi Alpha Theta
1958 Alpha Lambda Delta
1963 Omicron Delta Kappa
1965 Pi Delta Phi
1967 Kappa Delta Pi
1967 Sigma Pi Sigma
1970 Beta Gamma Sigma
1971 Phi Kappa Phi
1971 Pi Kappa Lambda
1972 Pi Sigma Alpha
1973 Kappa Tau Alpha
1973 Mortar Board
1974 Gamma Theta Upsilon
1974 Kappa Omicron Nu
1974 Phi Eta Sigma
1977 Tau Beta Pi

OTHER HONORS
    National Order of Omega

SERVICE
1956 Alpha Phi Omega

RECOGNITION
    Angel Flight
    Arnold Air Society (C-2)
1947 Chi Beta Phi
1950 Alpha Psi Omega
1952 Society for Collegiate
    Journalists—Pi Delta
    Epsilon-Alpha Phi Gamma
    (P)
1970 Beta Beta Beta

INACTIVE
1949–77 Alpha Xi Delta
1954–78 Psi Chi
1958–84 Gamma Phi Beta
1961–70 Delta Mu Delta
1962–71 Acacia
1962–76 Sigma Delta Tau
1963–76 Alpha Phi
1967–72 Zeta Beta Tau
1970–85 Phi Kappa Psi

COLONIES
1959 Alpha Epsilon Pi

MENLO COLLEGE Menlo Park, CA. Founded in 1914; two separate divisions; a two-year college; and a School of Business Administration (a four-year college); coeducational.

ACHS HONORS
1975 Alpha Chi

INACTIVE
1966–83 Delta Sigma Pi

1975–77 Phi Chi Theta

MERCER UNIVERSITY Macon, GA. University; coeducational; private control (Baptist). Founded as Mercer Institute 1833; became university 1837. College of Pharmacy located in Atlanta (formerly Southern College of Pharmacy).

Administration requires fraternity and sorority members to reside in dormitories. Eight fraternities have lodges on college-owned land but they are not housed there nor permitted to have their regular meals there. Sororities meet and have social functions in a Panhellenic House.

NIC MEN'S
1872 Phi Delta Theta
1873 Kappa Alpha Order
1874 Kappa Sigma
1880 Alpha Tau Omega
1884 Sigma Nu
1923 Pi Kappa Phi
1927 Sigma Pi
1950 Lambda Chi Alpha
1976 Kappa Alpha Psi (A)

NPHC MEN'S
1974 Alpha Phi Alpha

NPC WOMEN'S
1937 Alpha Delta Pi
1938 Phi Mu
1943 Chi Omega
1960 Alpha Gamma Delta

NPHC WOMEN'S
1973 Delta Sigma Theta (B)
1974 Alpha Kappa Alpha

PROFESSIONAL
1927 Delta Sigma Pi
1928 Delta Theta Phi
1928 Phi Alpha Delta
1940 Kappa Delta Epsilon
1951 Phi Delta Chi
1953 Kappa Psi
1958 Delta Omicron
1960 Kappa Epsilon
1963 Phi Mu Alpha—Sinfonia
1964 Phi Delta Phi
1985 Phi Alpha Delta

OTHER PROFESSIONAL
1929 Kappa Phi Kappa

ACHS HONORS
1932 Phi Eta Sigma
1940 Delta Sigma Rho-Tau
     Kappa Alpha
1967 Rho Chi
1979 Phi Sigma Iota
1981 Phi Sigma Tau
1982 Phi Kappa Phi

OTHER HONORS
     National Order of Omega

SERVICE
1946 Alpha Phi Omega

RECOGNITION
1928 Blue Key
1934 Cardinal Key
1936 Alpha Psi Omega
1942 Gamma Sigma Epsilon
1951 Scabbard and Blade (9)
1954 Beta Beta Beta

INACTIVE
1869–80 Chi Phi
1870–89 Sigma Alpha Epsilon
1923–41 Pi Kappa Alpha
1982–89 Kappa Delta Epsilon

MERCY COLLEGE Dobbs Ferry, NY. Private control. Founded in 1950. Four-year; coeducational; liberal arts college.

95% of students live off campus or commute.

ACHS HONORS
1974 Phi Alpha Theta
1974 Phi Sigma Iota

1975 Delta Mu Delta
1976 Pi Gamma Mu
1978 Psi Chi

MERCY COLLEGE OF DETROIT Detroit, MI. College of liberal arts; coeducational; private; Roman Catholic; chartered as Mercy College 1941; became coeducational and name changed to present 1963.

PROFESSIONAL
1961 Alpha Delta Theta

ACHS HONORS
1951 Delta Epsilon Sigma
1965 Kappa Delta Pi
1980 Phi Sigma Tau

1981 Psi Chi

RECOGNITION
1957 Alpha Psi Omega

INACTIVE
1964–86 Kappa Omicron Nu

MARCYHURST COLLEGE Erie, PA.

ACHS HONORS
1942 Delta Epsilon Sigma
1963 Pi Delta Phi
1985 Delta Mu Delta

1986 Phi Eta Sigma

INACTIVE
1949–58 Kappa Omicron Nu

MEREDITH COLLEGE Raleigh, NC. College of liberal arts for women; private control (Baptist). Established 1891.

PROFESSIONAL
1949 Sigma Alpha Iota

ACHS HONORS
1973 Pi Kappa Lambda
1975 Phi Alpha Theta

1975 Psi Chi
1980 Delta Mu Delta
1981 Kappa Omicron Nu

RECOGNITION
1938 Alpha Psi Omega

MERRIMACK COLLEGE North Andover, MA. College of liberal arts; coeducational; private control (Roman Catholic); established 1947.

Fraternity members occupy residence halls.

NIC MEN'S
1962 Phi Kappa Theta
1985 Alpha Delta Gamma
1990 Tau Kappa Epsilon

OTHER MEN'S
1953 Sigma Beta Kappa

ACHS HONORS
     Omicron Delta Epsilon

1966 Phi Alpha Theta
1985 Psi Chi

RECOGNITION
1964 Alpha Psi Omega

INACTIVE
1969–72 Theta Xi

MESA STATE COLLEGE Grand Junction, CO.

ACHS HONORS
1985 Phi Alpha Theta
1988 Psi Chi
1990 Kappa Mu Epsilon

INACTIVE
1978–83 Sigma Sigma Sigma

1982–83 Tau Kappa Epsilon

COLONIES
1989 Sigma Pi Sigma

METHODIST COLLEGE Fayetteville, NC. College of liberal arts and general studies; teacher preparatory; United Methodist affiliation; coeducational. Established 1956.

NIC MEN'S
1975 Lambda Chi Alpha

ACHS HONORS
1976 Alpha Chi
1976 Pi Gamma Mu
1981 Omicron Delta Kappa
1983 Psi Chi

1985 Phi Sigma Iota
1986 Phi Eta Sigma

INACTIVE
1974–81 Pi Kappa Phi
1974–87 Alpha Xi Delta
1977–82 Kappa Delta

MIAMI UNIVERSITY Oxford, OH. Founded by act of Ohio general assembly 1809. University; undergraduate and graduate coeducational; state university; nonsectarian.

Ownership of fraternity house and land is by the fraternity; sororities rent suite space in residence halls.

NIC MEN'S
1835 Alpha Delta Phi
1839 Beta Theta Pi
1848 Phi Delta Theta
1852 Delta Kappa Epsilon
1855 Sigma Chi
1868 Delta Upsilon
1906 Phi Kappa Tau
1916 Delta Tau Delta
1919 Sigma Alpha Epsilon
1927 Sigma Nu
1932 Delta Chi
1936 Zeta Beta Tau
1946 Sigma Alpha Epsilon
1947 Pi Kappa Alpha
1948 Sigma Phi Epsilon
1948 Theta Chi
1949 Acacia
1950 Lambda Chi Alpha
1954 Tau Kappa Epsilon
1957 Phi Gamma Delta
1959 Sigma Alpha Mu
1964 Alpha Epsilon Pi
1967 Kappa Sigma
1972 Phi Kappa Psi
1977 Alpha Tau Omega
1980 Kappa Alpha Psi (A)
1990 Psi Upsilon

NPC WOMEN'S
1902 Delta Zeta
1911 Delta Delta Delta
1911 Sigma Sigma Sigma
1913 Chi Omega
1914 Alpha Sigma Alpha
1919 Alpha Omicron Pi
1922 Sigma Kappa
1923 Delta Gamma
1926 Zeta Tau Alpha
1940 Alpha Epsilon Phi

1940 Kappa Kappa Gamma
1941 Alpha Chi Omega
1945 Pi Beta Phi
1947 Gamma Phi Beta
1951 Kappa Alpha Theta
1957 Alpha Phi
1958 Kappa Delta
1976 Phi Mu
1980 Alpha Xi Delta
1982 Alpha Gamma Delta
1984 Alpha Delta Pi

NPHC WOMEN'S
1969 Delta Sigma Theta (B)
1977 Alpha Kappa Alpha

PROFESSIONAL
1923 Delta Omicron
1924 Phi Mu Alpha—Sinfonia
1927 Delta Sigma Pi
1965 Delta Psi Kappa
1969 Tau Beta Sigma

OTHER PROFESSIONAL
1925 Kappa Phi Kappa
1942 Beta Alpha Psi
1949 Phi Epsilon Kappa
1963 Phi Upsilon Omicron

ACHS HONORS
     Omicron Delta Epsilon
1908 Delta Sigma Rho-Tau
     Kappa Alpha
1922 Kappa Delta Pi
1922 Mortar Board
1925 Alpha Kappa Delta
1925 Lambda Sigma Society
1926 Phi Sigma
1928 Phi Eta Sigma
1932 Sigma Delta Pi
1932 Sigma Pi Sigma

1934 Omicron Delta Kappa
1940 Psi Chi
1949 Pi Delta Phi
1960 Alpha Lambda Delta
1963 Phi Alpha Theta
1964 Pi Sigma Alpha
1966 Gamma Theta Upsilon
1972 Phi Kappa Phi
1974 Pi Kappa Lambda
1976 Sigma Tau Delta
1984 Chi Epsilon

OTHER HONORS
    National Order of Omega
1930 Delta Phi Delta
1934 Sigma Gamma Epsilon
1949 Pi Mu Epsilon

SERVICE
1935 Alpha Phi Omega

1948 Alpha Phi Omega

RECOGNITION
    Angel Flight
    Arnold Air Society (D-1)
1935 Delta Phi Alpha
1949 Sigma Delta Psi

INACTIVE
1916–24 Sigma Delta Chi
1924–29 Alpha Sigma Tau
1927   Eta Sigma Phi
1940–72 Pi Omega Pi
1955–69 Alpha Kappa Psi
1963–87 Sigma Delta Tau
1968–78 Kappa Delta Epsilon
1969–88 Chi Phi

COLONIES
    Sigma Tau Gamma

1969 Sigma Xi

SERVICE
1958 Gamma Sigma Sigma

RECOGNITION
    Angel Flight
    Arnold Air Society (C-1)
1947 Beta Beta Beta
1948 Kappa Pi
1949 Delta Phi Alpha
1952 Scabbard and Blade (10)
1969 Sigma Delta Psi

INACTIVE
1927–32 Mu Phi Epsilon
1936–54 Theta Alpha Phi
1936–84 Chi Omega
1938–69 Zeta Tau Alpha
1939–69 Sigma Kappa
1939–78 Delta Zeta

1946–63 Pi Lambda Phi
1947   Phi Sigma Sigma
1947–69 Pi Kappa Phi
1947–76 Alpha Delta Pi
1948–63 Phi Kappa Tau
1948–67 Sigma Nu
1948–80 Delta Delta Delta
1949–58 Delta Sigma Phi
1950–51 Delta Chi
1950–63 Kappa Alpha Order
1950–63 Theta Chi
1950–64 Sigma Pi
1954–82 Phi Delta Theta
1955   Phi Beta Pi and Theta
        Kappa Psi (a)
1956–71 Pi Omega Pi
1958   Zeta Phi Eta
1958–70 Alpha Chi Omega

UNIVERSITY OF MIAMI Coral Gables, FL.
Founded in 1925; first instruction 1926. Undergraduate colleges; university college, college of arts and sciences, school of business administration, school of education, school of engineering, school of music; graduate school, school of law, school of medicine. Coeducational; private control; nonsectarian.

Fraternities purchase house and land (or it is donated) with reverter clause to the university. Sorority members live in dormitories and have private meeting rooms in Panhellenic House.

NIC MEN'S
    Kappa Alpha Psi (A)
1939 Kappa Sigma
1940 Lambda Chi Alpha
1940 Pi Kappa Alpha
1942 Sigma Chi
1946 Sigma Alpha Mu
1946 Zeta Beta Tau
1947 Alpha Epsilon Pi
1949 Sigma Phi Epsilon
1949 Tau Kappa Epsilon
1950 Alpha Phi Delta
1952 Alpha Sigma Phi
1952 Alpha Tau Omega
1952 Tau Delta Phi

NPHC MEN'S
    Phi Beta Sigma
1970 Alpha Phi Alpha

NPC WOMEN'S
1938 Alpha Epsilon Phi
1938 Kappa Kappa Gamma
1939 Delta Phi Epsilon
1946 Delta Gamma
1957 Sigma Delta Tau

NPHC WOMEN'S
1972 Delta Sigma Theta (B)
1975 Alpha Kappa Alpha

PROFESSIONAL
1926 Sigma Alpha Iota
1937 Phi Mu Alpha—Sinfonia
1941 Alpha Kappa Psi
1946 Phi Alpha Delta
1947 Phi Delta Phi
1948 Delta Sigma Pi
1949 Delta Theta Phi
1953 Phi Chi
1970 Delta Psi Kappa

OTHER PROFESSIONAL
1932 Phi Beta Gamma
1946 Nu Beta Epsilon
1947 Kappa Alpha Mu
1947 Sigma Delta Chi
1949 Kappa Beta Pi
1950 Alpha Epsilon Rho
1951 Tau Epsilon Rho
1953 Alpha Kappa Kappa
1953 Phi Delta Epsilon
1961 Beta Alpha Psi

ACHS HONORS
    Omicron Delta Epsilon
1944 Sigma Delta Pi
1948 Alpha Epsilon Delta
1949 Gamma Theta Upsilon
1949 Omicron Delta Kappa
1950 Alpha Kappa Delta
1950 Alpha Lambda Delta
1950 Phi Eta Sigma
1950 Psi Chi
1951 Phi Alpha Theta
1954 Phi Kappa Phi
1958 Delta Sigma Rho-Tau
    Kappa Alpha
1958 Kappa Tau Alpha
1963 Pi Kappa Lambda
1964 Tau Beta Pi
1965 Eta Kappa Nu
1965 Mortar Board
1965 Pi Sigma Alpha
1969 Sigma Pi Sigma
1970 Pi Tau Sigma
1974 Sigma Tau Delta

OTHER HONORS
    National Order of Omega
1951 Pi Mu Epsilon
1959 Alpha Omega Alpha

MIAMI-DADE COMMUNITY COLLEGE Miami, FL. Two-year college; coeducational; local control. Established 1959.

NIC MEN'S
1972 Sigma Phi Epsilon
1972 Tau Kappa Epsilon

SERVICE
1967 Alpha Phi Omega

THE UNIVERSITY OF MICHIGAN Ann Arbor, MI. University; coeducational; state control; founded in Detroit in 1817 as University of Michigania: state constitution provided that legislature support university; University of Michigan was established at Ann Arbor in 1837, soon after Michigan was admitted to the Union.

The fraternities and sororities own their own houses on their own land.

NIC MEN'S
1845 Beta Theta Pi
1845 Chi Psi
1846 Alpha Delta Phi
1855 Delta Kappa Epsilon
1858 Sigma Phi Society
1858 Zeta Psi
1864 Phi Delta Theta
1865 Psi Upsilon
1872 Delta Tau Delta
1876 Delta Upsilon
1876 Phi Kappa Psi
1877 Sigma Chi
1882 Chi Phi
1885 Phi Gamma Delta
1888 Alpha Tau Omega
1889 Sigma Alpha Epsilon
1889 Theta Delta Chi
1892 Delta Chi
1892 Kappa Sigma
1902 Sigma Nu
1904 Acacia
1908 Alpha Sigma Phi
1912 Sigma Phi Epsilon
1913 Lambda Chi Alpha
1915 Phi Sigma Kappa
1916 Zeta Beta Tau
1919 Theta Chi
1920 Delta Sigma Phi
1922 Kappa Alpha Psi (A)
1923 Alpha Phi Delta
1923 Phi Kappa Tau

1923 Sigma Alpha Mu
1925 Tau Kappa Epsilon
1925 Triangle
1927 Pi Kappa Phi
1949 Alpha Epsilon Pi

NPHC MEN'S
    Phi Beta Sigma
1909 Alpha Phi Alpha
1922 Omega Psi Phi

NPC WOMEN'S
1882 Gamma Phi Beta
1885 Delta Gamma
1888 Pi Beta Phi
1890 Kappa Kappa Gamma
1892 Alpha Phi
1894 Delta Delta Delta
1898 Alpha Chi Omega
1905 Chi Omega
1920 Alpha Xi Delta
1920 Zeta Tau Alpha
1921 Alpha Epsilon Phi
1921 Alpha Omicron Pi
1922 Alpha Gamma Delta
1923 Delta Zeta
1924 Sigma Kappa
1929 Alpha Delta Pi
1944 Sigma Delta Tau
1954 Delta Phi Epsilon

NPHC WOMEN'S
1921 Delta Sigma Theta (B)
1932 Alpha Kappa Alpha

1980 Sigma Gamma Rho
1984 Alpha Kappa Alpha

PROFESSIONAL
1869 Phi Delta Phi
1883 Phi Delta Chi
1897 Phi Rho Sigma
1903 Sigma Alpha Iota
1904 Mu Phi Epsilon
1905 Phi Alpha Delta
1905 Phi Chi
1912 Delta Theta Phi
1914 Alpha Rho Chi
1916 Alpha Chi Sigma
1920 Alpha Kappa Psi
1921 Delta Sigma Pi
1925 Kappa Kappa Psi
1926 Alpha Omega
1948 Tau Beta Sigma
1978 Rho Pi Phi

OTHER PROFESSIONAL
1882 Delta Sigma Delta
1910 Sigma Delta Chi
1921 Kappa Beta Pi
1921 Phi Delta Epsilon
1922 Pi Lambda Theta
1925 Phi Epsilon Kappa
1926 Tau Epsilon Rho
1926 Women in Communications
1946 Delta Pi Epsilon
1951 Beta Alpha Psi

ACHS HONORS
    Omicron Delta Epsilon
1906 Delta Sigma Rho-Tau
    Kappa Alpha
1906 Tau Beta Pi
1916 Phi Sigma
1918 Mortar Board
1922 Rho Chi
1927 Alpha Kappa Delta
1930 Beta Gamma Sigma
1931 Kappa Tau Alpha
1937 Eta Kappa Nu
1945 Pi Kappa Lambda
1948 Chi Epsilon
1948 Pi Tau Sigma
1949 Pi Sigma Alpha
1957 Alpha Pi Mu
1958 Xi Sigma Pi
1959 Sigma Theta Tau
1964 Phi Sigma Iota
1966 Gamma Theta Upsilon
1967 Beta Phi Mu
1970 Sigma Theta Tau
1971 Alpha Sigma Mu
1973 Alpha Epsilon
1982 Phi Alpha Theta
1982 Psi Chi
1990 Sigma Lambda Alpha

OTHER HONORS
    National Order of Omega
1903 Sigma Xi
1907 Alpha Omega Alpha

UNIVERSITY OF MICHIGAN, DEARBORN Dearborn, MI. Established in 1959 on the 210-acre site which was donated by the Ford Motor Company to the University of Michigan; programs in liberal arts, teaching, business administration, and engineering incorporating the work-study program; coeducational.

1907 Phi Beta Kappa
1925 Order of the Coif
1930 Omicron Kappa Upsilon

SERVICE
1940 Alpha Phi Omega

RECOGNITION
    Arnold Air Society (E-2)
1909 Phi Lambda Upsilon
1914 Gamma Alpha
1923 Scabbard and Blade (4)
1928 Sigma Delta Psi
1941 Iota Lambda Sigma
1957 Delta Phi Alpha
1959 Sigma Phi Alpha

INACTIVE
1855–36 Delta Phi
1874–75 Sigma Chi
1879–86 Kappa Alpha Theta
1888–40 Phi Beta Pi and Theta
    Kappa Psi (B)
1889–50 Xi Psi Phi
1898–45 Phi Beta Pi and Theta
    Kappa Psi (a)
1902–67 Phi Mu Alpha—
    Sinfonia
1905–36 Psi Omega
1905–63 Phi Kappa Sigma
1906–61 Alpha Kappa Kappa
1911–29 Gamma Eta Gamma
1912–44 Theta Phi Alpha
1913 Tau Sigma Delta
1914 Sigma Delta Kappa
1914–86 Theta Xi
1916 Phi Alpha Tau
1917 Iota Sigma Pi
1921 Sigma Gamma Epsilon
1921–33 Alpha Chi Rho
1921–69 Kappa Delta
1922 Phi Lambda Kappa
1922 Phi Sigma Sigma
1922–33 Phi Mu Delta
1922–74 Pi Kappa Alpha
1924–35 Phi Kappa Theta
1924–70 Alpha Kappa Lambda
1925–36 Delta Omicron
1925–40 Kappa Delta Rho
1925–70 Sigma Pi
1926–78 Phi Eta Sigma
1926–80 Phi Kappa Phi
1928 Alpha Alpha Gamma
1928 Eta Sigma Phi
1928–33 Beta Sigma Psi
1928–74 Alpha Lambda Delta
1930–68 Zeta Phi Eta
1948–70 Sigma Delta Pi
1950–68 Lambda Kappa Sigma
1955–69 Phi Chi Theta
1957–64 Phi Mu

COLONIES
1913 Pi Lambda Phi
1986 Sigma Pi Sigma

NIC MEN'S
1987 Delta Sigma Phi
1988 Tau Kappa Epsilon
1989 Kappa Alpha Psi (A)

NPC WOMEN'S
1989 Phi Mu
1990 Delta Phi Epsilon

PROFESSIONAL
1966 Alpha Kappa Psi

UNIVERSITY OF MICHIGAN, FLINT Flint, MI. Public institution. Founded in 1956. Four-year; coeducational.

No housing available.

NIC MEN'S
1922 Tau Delta Phi
1969 Theta Chi

NPHC MEN'S
    Phi Beta Sigma

ACHS HONORS
    Omicron Delta Epsilon

1975 Psi Chi
1977 Phi Alpha Theta
1979 Phi Sigma Iota

COLONIES
    Theta Phi Alpha
1990 Tau Kappa Epsilon

MICHIGAN STATE UNIVERSITY East Lansing, MI. University and land-grant college; coeducational; state control; chartered 1855.

Fraternities and sororities own their own houses and land.

NIC MEN'S
1872 Delta Tau Delta
1873 Phi Delta Theta
1922 Alpha Gamma Rho
1922 Lambda Chi Alpha
1924 Delta Sigma Phi
1924 Phi Kappa Tau
1925 Pi Kappa Phi
1927 Sigma Alpha Epsilon
1934 Alpha Epsilon Pi
1934 Sigma Nu
1935 Delta Chi
1936 FarmHouse
1937 Kappa Sigma
1939 Theta Chi
1940 Alpha Tau Omega
1942 Sigma Chi
1943 Psi Upsilon
1949 Delta Upsilon
1950 Beta Theta Pi
1954 Phi Kappa Psi
1955 Triangle
1956 Kappa Alpha Psi (A)
1959 Phi Gamma Delta
1959 Sigma Alpha Mu
1960 Sigma Phi Epsilon
1964 Theta Delta Chi
1966 Tau Delta Phi
1984 Pi Lambda Phi
1985 Alpha Delta Phi
1986 Tau Kappa Epsilon
1989 Pi Kappa Alpha

NPHC MEN'S
    Phi Beta Sigma
1948 Alpha Phi Alpha
1961 Omega Psi Phi

NPC WOMEN'S
1921 Alpha Gamma Delta

1973 Phi Gamma Nu
1988 Theta Tau

ACHS HONORS
    Omicron Delta Epsilon
1980 Psi Chi
1981 Eta Kappa Nu
1982 Tau Beta Pi
1989 Phi Alpha Theta

1922 Alpha Phi
1924 Kappa Delta
1926 Chi Omega
1926 Kappa Alpha Theta
1927 Sigma Kappa
1928 Alpha Chi Omega
1930 Kappa Kappa Gamma
1931 Zeta Tau Alpha
1934 Alpha Omicron Pi
1934 Alpha Xi Delta
1944 Gamma Phi Beta
1945 Pi Beta Phi
1946 Delta Gamma
1948 Delta Delta Delta
1955 Phi Mu
1964 Sigma Delta Tau

NPHC WOMEN'S
1954 Alpha Kappa Alpha
1960 Delta Sigma Theta (B)
1968 Sigma Gamma Rho

PROFESSIONAL
1930 Sigma Alpha Iota
1938 Phi Mu Alpha—Sinfonia
1945 Alpha Delta Theta
1946 Delta Psi Kappa
1949 Delta Omicron
1950 Phi Gamma Nu
1952 Alpha Kappa Psi
1971 Kappa Kappa Psi
1985 Sigma Alpha

OTHER PROFESSIONAL
1902 Alpha Zeta
1940 Sigma Delta Chi
1944 Women in Communications
1950 Phi Epsilon Kappa
1954 Beta Alpha Psi
1961 Delta Pi Epsilon

ACHS HONORS

Omicron Delta Epsilon
Pi Alpha Alpha
1892 Tau Beta Pi
1912 Kappa Omicron Nu
1916 Xi Sigma Pi
1927 Phi Kappa Phi
1934 Mortar Board
1935 Sigma Pi Sigma
1942 Kappa Delta Pi
1945 Sigma Delta Pi
1947 Phi Alpha Theta
1948 Pi Sigma Alpha
1950 Pi Tau Sigma
1951 Chi Epsilon
1951 Eta Kappa Nu
1953 Alpha Kappa Delta
1954 Beta Gamma Sigma
1956 Kappa Tau Alpha
1957 Gamma Theta Upsilon
1958 Delta Sigma Rho-Tau
Kappa Alpha
1963 Pi Kappa Lambda
1964 Phi Sigma Iota
1965 Psi Chi
1977 Omega Chi Epsilon
1978 Sigma Lambda Alpha

OTHER HONORS

National Order of Omega
1927 Sigma Xi
1940 Pi Mu Epsilon
1948 Delta Phi Delta
1968 Phi Beta Kappa

SERVICE

1937 Alpha Phi Omega

RECOGNITION

Angel Flight

Arnold Air Society (E-2)
1914 Scabbard and Blade (1)
1924 Theta Alpha Phi
1927 Blue Key
1929 Pi Alpha Xi
1930 National Block and Bridle
Club
1936 Sigma Delta Psi
1950 Phi Zeta
1955 Beta Beta Beta
1956 Delta Phi Alpha
1970 Sigma Iota Epsilon

INACTIVE

1915   Alpha Psi
1921–37 Phi Sigma
1928–85 Alpha Chi Sigma
1929–34 Sigma Mu Sigma
1930–59 Alpha Kappa Alpha
1931–42 Mu Phi Epsilon
1941–79 Delta Zeta
1947   Sigma Gamma Epsilon
1947–61 Kappa Alpha Mu
1947–71 Zeta Beta Tau
1947–73 Pi Gamma Mu
1949–71 Phi Kappa Sigma
1949–74 Delta Sigma Pi
1950–59 Theta Xi
1950–80 Psi Chi
1952–73 Alpha Epsilon Phi
1954   Sigma Delta Epsilon
1954–76 Phi Eta Sigma
1956–64 Alpha Sigma Phi
1956–78 Alpha Delta Pi
1957–74 Pi Omega Pi
1957–80 Alpha Lambda Delta
1958–69 Sigma Phi Delta
1959–73 Phi Sigma Kappa
1963–70 Omicron Delta Kappa

MICHIGAN TECHNOLOGICAL UNIVERSITY

Houghton, MI. The university was founded in 1885 and has developed an international reputation as one of the finest schools of engineering and science in the United States. The campus is located near Lake Superior in the historic "Copper Country" of Michigan's Upper Peninsula. Michigan Tech offers undergraduate and graduate programs in engineering, science, business, forestry, liberal arts, and secondary science teaching. Associate degrees are offered in four field of technology. Recreational facilities include: downhill and cross country ski areas, eighteen-hole golf course, indoor and outdoor tennis courts, ice arena, and new athletic complex.

NIC MEN'S

1948 Delta Sigma Phi
1959 Phi Kappa Tau
1965 Sigma Phi Epsilon
1968 Phi Kappa Theta
1969 Tau Kappa Epsilon
1974 Sigma Tau Gamma
1980 Lambda Chi Alpha
1984 Sigma Pi
1986 Delta Upsilon
1988 Triangle

NPC WOMEN'S

1975 Delta Zeta
1979 Alpha Gamma Delta
1980 Alpha Sigma Tau
1987 Delta Phi Epsilon

PROFESSIONAL

1906 Theta Tau
1968 Alpha Kappa Psi

ACHS HONORS

1904 Tau Beta Pi
1932 Alpha Sigma Mu
1936 Eta Kappa Nu
1948 Chi Epsilon
1954 Phi Eta Sigma
1955 Phi Kappa Phi
1967 Pi Tau Sigma
1971 Xi Sigma Pi
1975 Phi Sigma
1976 Sigma Pi Sigma
1980 Omicron Delta Kappa

OTHER HONORS

1971 Sigma Xi

SERVICE

1947 Alpha Phi Omega

RECOGNITION

Angel Flight
Arnold Air Society (F-1)

1932 Blue Key
1942 Phi Lambda Upsilon
1967 Mu Beta Psi

INACTIVE

1957   Sigma Gamma Epsilon
1962–73 Beta Sigma Psi

MIDDLE GEORGIA COLLEGE   Cochran, GA.

INACTIVE

1888–90 Alpha Tau Omega

MIDDLE TENNESSEE STATE UNIVERSITY   Murfreesboro, TN. State control; coeducational; enrollment 11,500; founded 1911.

NIC MEN'S

1969 Kappa Alpha Order
1969 Kappa Sigma
1969 Sigma Alpha Epsilon
1970 Sigma Chi
1970 Sigma Nu
1971 Pi Kappa Alpha
1972 Delta Tau Delta
1973 Kappa Alpha Psi (A)
1976 Alpha Gamma Rho
1977 Sigma Phi Epsilon
1988 Beta Theta Pi
1990 Tau Kappa Epsilon

NPHC MEN'S

Phi Beta Sigma
1975 Alpha Phi Alpha

NPC WOMEN'S

1967 Delta Zeta
1969 Alpha Delta Pi
1969 Chi Omega
1969 Kappa Delta
1985 Alpha Omicron Pi

NPHC WOMEN'S

1973 Alpha Kappa Alpha
1973 Delta Sigma Theta (B)

PROFESSIONAL

1965 Alpha Kappa Psi
1965 Delta Omicron
1965 Pi Sigma Epsilon
1966 Phi Mu Alpha—Sinfonia
1984 Gamma Iota Sigma

OTHER PROFESSIONAL

1974 Sigma Delta Chi

ACHS HONORS

Omicron Delta Epsilon

1956 Kappa Delta Pi
1956 Kappa Omicron Nu
1958 Pi Gamma Mu
1970 Phi Alpha Theta
1972 Psi Chi
1973 Pi Sigma Alpha
1975 Sigma Tau Delta
1986 Phi Sigma Iota
1987 Phi Kappa Phi

OTHER HONORS

1971 Pi Mu Epsilon

SERVICE

1983 Alpha Phi Omega

RECOGNITION

1948 Alpha Psi Omega
1952 Pi Kappa Delta
1959 National Block and Bridle
Club
1967 Beta Beta Beta
1967 Kappa Pi
1967 Sigma Delta Psi
1968 Society for Collegiate
Journalists—Pi Delta
Epsilon-Alpha Phi Gamma
(A)

INACTIVE

1954–80 Pi Omega Pi
1967–84 Delta Mu Delta
1969–85 Alpha Gamma Delta
1970–86 Alpha Tau Omega
1973–80 Pi Kappa Phi

COLONIES

1987 Sigma Pi Sigma

MIDDLEBURY COLLEGE   Middlebury, VT. College of liberal arts; coeducational; private control; nonsectarian; chartered 1800. Main campus at Middlebury. Bread Loaf Mountain campus at Bread Loaf Mountain, Vt.

NIC MEN'S

1843 Chi Psi
1854 Delta Kappa Epsilon
1856 Delta Upsiion
1905 Kappa Delta Rho
1956 Zeta Psi

ACHS HONORS

Omicron Delta Epsilon

1920 Delta Sigma Rho-Tau
Kappa Alpha

OTHER HONORS

1868 Phi Beta Kappa

INACTIVE

1893–69 Pi Beta Phi
1911–69 Sigma Kappa
1917–69 Delta Delta Delta

1923–69 Kappa Kappa Gamma
1925–39 Kappa Phi Kappa
1925–47 Alpha Sigma Phi
1925–52 Phi Mu
1925–65 Alpha Xi Delta
1925–90 Sigma Phi Epsilon

1927–45 Sigma Delta Pi
1928–85 Mortar Board
1940–56 Kappa Delta
1942–70 Theta Chi
1947–65 Alpha Tau Omega
1950–72 Phi Kappa Tau

MIDWESTERN STATE UNIVERSITY Wichita Falls, TX. Coeducational, state-supported; chartered in 1922 as Wichita Falls Junior College; renamed Hardin Junior College in 1937; senior college division established in 1946, changing name to Hardin College; became Midwestern University in 1950; in January 1952 the Graduate School was authorized; by action of 56th Legislature of the State of Texas, Midwestern University became a state-supported institution on September 1, 1961.

No sorority houses; fraternities allowed to lease houses off-campus.

NIC MEN'S
1959 Kappa Sigma
1960 Phi Sigma Kappa
1964 Kappa Alpha Order
1966 Sigma Nu
1969 Tau Kappa Epsilon

NPC WOMEN'S
1959 Alpha Phi
1959 Sigma Kappa
1963 Gamma Phi Beta
1966 Chi Omega

PROFESSIONAL
1951 Kappa Kappa Psi
1959 Mu Phi Epsilon
1964 Phi Chi Theta

ACHS HONORS
1951 Alpha Chi
1969 Kappa Delta Pi
1972 Phi Alpha Theta
1974 Alpha Lambda Delta
1974 Psi Chi
1975 Phi Eta Sigma

1975 Sigma Pi Sigma
1977 Pi Kappa Lambda
1977 Pi Sigma Alpha
1981 Mortar Board

OTHER HONORS
    National Order of Omega

SERVICE
1951 Alpha Phi Omega

RECOGNITION
1954 Beta Beta Beta
1955 Alpha Psi Omega
1961 Pi Kappa Delta
1961 Scabbard and Blade (15)
1972 Gamma Sigma Epsilon

INACTIVE
1953–67 Pi Gamma Mu
1954–55 Sigma Delta Pi
1959–81 Phi Mu Alpha—
    Sinfonia
1960–74 Delta Sigma Pi

MILES COLLEGE Birmingham, AL.

NIC MEN'S
1957 Kappa Alpha Psi (A)

NPHC MEN'S
    Phi Beta Sigma
1947 Alpha Phi Alpha
1947 Omega Psi Phi

NPHC WOMEN'S
1970 Alpha Kappa Alpha

1970 Delta Sigma Theta (B)
1970 Sigma Gamma Rho

PROFESSIONAL
1978 Delta Theta Phi

ACHS HONORS
1956 Alpha Kappa Mu

MILLERSVILLE STATE COLLEGE Millersville, PA. Teachers college; coeducational; state control; chartered as Millersville Academy 1854; first Pennsylvania normal school 1859.

NIC MEN'S
1972 Sigma Tau Gamma
1983 Kappa Alpha Psi (A)
1984 Sigma Pi
1988 Acacia
1988 Phi Kappa Sigma
1988 Tau Kappa Epsilon

1989 Alpha Chi Rho

NPHC MEN'S
    Phi Beta Sigma
1974 Alpha Phi Alpha

NPC WOMEN'S
1976 Alpha Sigma Tau

1988 Delta Zeta
1988 Phi Sigma Sigma
1989 Delta Phi Epsilon
1990 Alpha Xi Delta

NPHC WOMEN'S
1974 Delta Sigma Theta (B)
1988 Sigma Gamma Rho

OTHER PROFESSIONAL
1934 Phi Sigma Pi
1970 Pi Lambda Theta

ACHS HONORS
1979 Phi Kappa Phi

1981 Phi Sigma Iota
1981 Sigma Pi Sigma
1982 Pi Gamma Mu
1989 Psi Chi

SERVICE
1949 Alpha Phi Omega

RECOGNITION
1962 Alpha Psi Omega

INACTIVE
1935   Iota Lambda Sigma
1954–72 Alpha Beta Alpha
1975–84 Alpha Kappa Alpha

MILLIGAN COLLEGE Milligan College, TN.

ACHS HONORS
1968 Phi Sigma Tau

SERVICE
1966 Alpha Phi Omega

RECOGNITION
1955 Alpha Psi Omega
1967 Sigma Delta Psi

MILLIKIN UNIVERSITY Decatur, IL. Founded by James Millikin of Decatur in 1901, opened for first classes on September 15, 1903. Coeducational university with college of arts and sciences, Tabor School of Business and Engineering, college of fine arts; private, nonsectarian, related to Presbyterian Church (U.S.A.).

The social fraternities and sororities occupy their own houses on their own land.

NIC MEN'S
1909 Tau Kappa Epsilon
1911 Sigma Alpha Epsilon
1966 Kappa Sigma
1975 Alpha Tau Omega

NPHC MEN'S
1973 Alpha Phi Alpha

NPC WOMEN'S
1912 Delta Delta Delta
1912 Pi Beta Phi
1912 Zeta Tau Alpha
1913 Alpha Chi Omega

NPHC WOMEN'S
1973 Delta Sigma Theta (B)

PROFESSIONAL
1917 Sigma Alpha Iota
1929 Phi Mu Alpha—Sinfonia
1965 Alpha Kappa Psi

ACHS HONORS
1949 Phi Kappa Phi

1957 Pi Kappa Lambda
1968 Alpha Epsilon Delta
1971 Phi Alpha Theta
1980 Alpha Lambda Delta
1980 Phi Sigma Iota
1982 Omicron Delta Kappa

OTHER HONORS
    National Order of Omega

SERVICE
1949 Alpha Phi Omega

RECOGNITION
1925 Sigma Delta Psi

INACTIVE
1924–36 Kappa Phi Kappa
1927–33 Delta Omicron
1955–65 Alpha Kappa Lambda

COLONIES
1921 Delta Sigma Phi

MILLS COLLEGE Oakland, CA. Founded 1852. Undergraduate residence college for women; Graduate School coeducational; private control; nonsectarian.

ACHS HONORS
    Omicron Delta Epsilon

OTHER HONORS
1929 Phi Beta Kappa

MILLSAPS COLLEGE Jackson, MS. College of liberal arts; coeducational; private control; Methodist Church; established 1890.

NIC MEN'S
1893 Kappa Alpha Order
1895 Kappa Sigma
1905 Pi Kappa Alpha
1924 Lambda Chi Alpha
1990 Sigma Alpha Epsilon

NPC WOMEN'S
1914 Kappa Delta
1914 Phi Mu
1934 Chi Omega
1986 Delta Delta Delta

NPHC WOMEN'S
1977 Alpha Kappa Alpha

ACHS HONORS
　Omicron Delta Epsilon
1926 Omicron Delta Kappa
1935 Alpha Epsilon Delta
1957 Pi Delta Phi

1968 Sigma Delta Pi
1969 Phi Alpha Theta
1981 Phi Eta Sigma

OTHER HONORS
　National Order of Omega

SERVICE
1950 Alpha Phi Omega

RECOGNITION
1928 Alpha Psi Omega
1935 Eta Sigma Phi
1975 Beta Beta Beta

INACTIVE
1926–36 Delta Zeta
1941–78 Kappa Delta Epsilon
1964–74 Zeta Tau Alpha

COLONIES
1988 Sigma Pi Sigma

MILTON COLLEGE Milton, WI.

INACTIVE
1940–76 Alpha Sigma Phi

1968–77 Sigma Pi
1973–77 Tau Kappa Epsilon

MILWAUKEE SCHOOL OF ENGINEERING Milwaukee, WI. Established 1903; for men.

NIC MEN'S
1965 Triangle
1987 Delta Sigma Phi

NPHC MEN'S
　Phi Beta Sigma

ACHS HONORS
1983 Eta Kappa Nu
1990 Tau Beta Pi

INACTIVE
1925　Sigma Mu Sigma

UNIVERSITY OF MINNESOTA Minneapolis, MN. Land-grant university chartered in 1851 by Legislative Assembly, 7 years before Minnesota Territory became a state. Fourth largest university in U.S. Students in graduate and undergraduate schools; four coeducational campuses.

Fraternities and sororities own the houses and property which they occupy.

NIC MEN'S
1874 Chi Psi
1881 Phi Delta Theta
1883 Delta Tau Delta
1888 Phi Kappa Psi
1888 Sigma Chi
1889 Beta Theta Pi
1889 Delta Kappa Epsilon
1890 Phi Gamma Delta
1891 Psi Upsilon
1892 Alpha Delta Phi
1892 Delta Chi
1899 Zeta Psi
1901 Kappa Sigma
1902 Alpha Tau Omega
1902 Sigma Alpha Epsilon
1904 Sigma Nu
1906 Acacia
1910 Phi Sigma Kappa
1915 Sigma Alpha Mu
1916 Sigma Phi Epsilon

1917 Alpha Gamma Rho
1922 Pi Kappa Alpha
1922 Triangle
1924 Kappa Alpha Psi (A)
1924 Theta Chi
1928 Chi Phi
1928 Tau Delta Phi
1931 FarmHouse

NPHC MEN'S
　Phi Beta Sigma
1912 Alpha Phi Alpha

NPC WOMEN'S
1880 Kappa Kappa Gamma
1882 Delta Gamma
1889 Kappa Alpha Theta
1890 Alpha Phi
1890 Pi Beta Phi
1894 Delta Delta Delta
1902 Gamma Phi Beta
1908 Alpha Gamma Delta

1912 Alpha Omicron Pi
1921 Alpha Chi Omega
1929 Sigma Delta Tau

NPHC WOMEN'S
1970 Sigma Gamma Rho

PROFESSIONAL
1891 Phi Delta Phi
1900 Phi Rho Sigma
1904 Alpha Chi Sigma
1904 Phi Delta Chi
1904 Theta Tau
1905 Delta Theta Phi
1905 Xi Psi Phi
1916 Alpha Rho Chi
1918 Psi Omega
1920 Phi Chi
1921 Kappa Epsilon
1922 Alpha Kappa Psi
1922 Alpha Omega
1922 Phi Alpha Delta
1924 Delta Sigma Pi
1926 Sigma Alpha Iota
1927 Alpha Tau Delta
1928 Kappa Psi
1929 Phi Beta
1944 Alpha Delta Theta
1962 Pi Sigma Epsilon

OTHER PROFESSIONAL
1894 Delta Sigma Delta
1898 Alpha Kappa Kappa
1909 Phi Upsilon Omicron
1916 Sigma Delta Chi
1918 Pi Lambda Theta
1922 Alpha Alpha Gamma
1923 Phi Delta Epsilon
1924 Gamma Eta Gamma
1925 Phi Beta Gamma
1930 Phi Epsilon Kappa
1931 Beta Alpha Psi
1951 Delta Pi Epsilon
1956 Alpha Psi
1957 Kappa Alpha Mu
1963 Alpha Tau Alpha

ACHS HONORS
　Omicron Delta Epsilon
1906 Delta Sigma Rho-Tau
　Kappa Alpha
1909 Tau Beta Pi
1917 Tau Sigma Delta
1919 Mortar Board
1920 Eta Kappa Nu
1920 Xi Sigma Pi
1921 Beta Gamma Sigma
1922 Pi Tau Sigma
1923 Chi Epsilon
1923 Kappa Omicron Nu
1930 Rho Chi
1934 Sigma Theta Tau
1936 Psi Chi
1937 Phi Alpha Theta
1948 Kappa Tau Alpha
1950 Pi Delta Phi
1953 Sigma Gamma Tau
1956 Alpha Kappa Delta
1958 Pi Kappa Lambda
1960 Alpha Epsilon
1974 Phi Kappa Phi
1976 Omicron Delta Kappa
1979 Sigma Lambda Alpha

1979 Sigma Pi Sigma

OTHER HONORS
　National Order of Omega
1892 Phi Beta Kappa
1896 Sigma Xi
1908 Alpha Omega Alpha
1915 Order of the Coif
1917 Gamma Sigma Delta
1919 Delta Phi Delta
1922 National Collegiate
　Players
1923 Iota Sigma Pi
1930 Sigma Epsilon Sigma

SERVICE
1902 Alpha Phi Omega
1942 Alpha Phi Omega
1957 Gamma Sigma Sigma
1963 Gamma Sigma Sigma

RECOGNITION
　Angel Flight
　Arnold Air Society (F-1)
1905 Scabbard and Blade (1)
1910 Phi Lambda Upsilon
1912 Sigma Delta Psi
1923 Kappa Eta Kappa
1945 Sigma Delta Epsilon
1952 Phi Zeta
1958 Sigma Phi Alpha

INACTIVE
1892–84 Theta Delta Chi
1896–03 Psi Omega
1904　Phi Beta Pi and Theta
　Kappa Psi (a)
1905–73 Alpha Zeta
1907–87 Alpha Xi Delta
1908　Phi Beta Pi and Theta
　Kappa Psi (B)
1915–43 Phi Kappa Sigma
1916　Gamma Alpha
1916–35 Alpha Sigma Phi
1917–87 Tau Kappa Epsilon
1918–72 Kappa Delta
1920–66 Theta Xi
1921–61 Sigma Kappa
1921–89 Chi Omega
1922　Sigma Gamma Epsilon
1923　Kappa Beta Pi
1923–59 Zeta Tau Alpha
1923–65 Delta Zeta
1923–87 Alpha Delta Pi
1924–74 Phi Mu Alpha—
　Sinfonia
1925–59 Lambda Chi Alpha
1925–70 Phi Mu
1926　Scarab
1927–45 Mu Phi Epsilon
1929–32 Delta Phi Epsilon
1934–38 Omega Chi Epsilon
1934–69 Zeta Phi Eta
1938–78 Alpha Epsilon Phi
1947–61 Phi Kappa Theta
1949–70 Zeta Beta Tau
1949–73 Alpha Epsilon Pi
1958–75 Phi Mu Alpha—
　Sinfonia
1963–83 Beta Sigma Psi

COLONIES
1890 Delta Upsilon

UNIVERSITY OF MINNESOTA, DULUTH Duluth, MN. Founded as normal school 1902; became Duluth State Teachers College 1926; campus of the

Unviersity of Minnesota 1947. Liberal arts, education, two-year associate in arts, pre-professional programs. Master's degree in eight fields.

PROFESSIONAL	SERVICE
1947 Sigma Alpha Iota	1961 Alpha Phi Omega

ACHS HONORS	
Omicron Delta Epsilon	
1936 Gamma Theta Upsilon	RECOGNITION
1946 Kappa Delta Pi	Angel Flight
1949 Phi Alpha Theta	Arnold Air Society (F-1)
1956 Pi Gamma Mu	1941 Alpha Psi Omega
1958 Psi Chi	1945 Kappa Pi
1976 Kappa Omicron Nu	1975 Sigma Phi Alpha

UNIVERSITY OF MINNESOTA, MORRIS   Morris, MN. College of liberal arts; coeducational; state control; established 1960.

NIC MEN'S	INACTIVE
1969 Phi Sigma Kappa	1964–88 Phi Mu Delta
1989 Chi Phi	1966–87 Tau Kappa Epsilon
	1969–84 Beta Sigma Psi
ACHS HONORS	1970–80 Sigma Sigma Sigma
1984 Psi Chi	

MINOT STATE COLLEGE   Minot, ND. Coeducational; state control; established as a normal school 1913.

The fraternities are permitted to occupy their own houses on their own land.

PROFESSIONAL	INACTIVE
1963 Phi Mu Alpha—Sinfonia	1945–54 Alpha Sigma Tau
1964 Sigma Alpha Iota	1947–88 Sigma Sigma Sigma
	1957–83 Tau Kappa Epsilon
ACHS HONORS	1964–69 Sigma Tau Delta
1964 Pi Omega Pi	1966–88 Sigma Tau Gamma
	1967–85 Delta Zeta
RECOGNITION	
1967 Kappa Pi	

THE UNIVERSITY OF MISSISSIPPI   University, MS. Located at Oxford, MS. Chartered 1844, first instruction 1848; coeducational; nine colleges and schools; state control.

The university maintains ownership of property with each fraternity responsible for construction of its house.

NIC MEN'S	NPHC MEN'S
1855 Delta Psi	Phi Beta Sigma
1857 Phi Kappa Psi	
1857 Sigma Chi	NPC WOMEN'S
1866 Sigma Alpha Epsilon	1899 Chi Omega
1877 Phi Delta Theta	1904 Delta Delta Delta
1879 Beta Theta Pi	1926 Phi Mu
1900 Kappa Alpha Order	1927 Delta Gamma
1926 Kappa Sigma	1927 Kappa Delta
1927 Alpha Tau Omega	1947 Kappa Kappa Gamma
1927 Pi Kappa Alpha	1958 Alpha Omicron Pi
1927 Sigma Nu	1961 Alpha Delta Pi
1928 Sigma Phi Epsilon	1962 Pi Beta Phi
1951 Phi Kappa Theta	1979 Kappa Alpha Theta
1953 Sigma Pi	
1969 Phi Kappa Tau	NPHC WOMEN'S
1983 Kappa Alpha Psi (A)	1974 Alpha Kappa Alpha
	1977 Alpha Kappa Alpha

PROFESSIONAL	
1926 Kappa Psi	1966 Pi Delta Phi
1926 Phi Chi	1969 Tau Beta Pi
1927 Delta Sigma Pi	1971 Eta Kappa Nu
1927 Phi Delta Chi	1973 Kappa Omicron Nu
1927 Phi Delta Phi	1975 Sigma Tau Delta
1929 Phi Alpha Delta	1978 Kappa Tau Alpha
1937 Sigma Alpha Iota	1979 Sigma Pi Sigma
1950 Phi Gamma Nu	1984 Psi Chi
1959 Tau Beta Sigma	
1960 Kappa Epsilon	OTHER HONORS
1962 Phi Mu Alpha—Sinfonia	National Order of Omega
1963 Pi Sigma Epsilon	1957 Alpha Omega Alpha
1967 Delta Theta Phi	1964 Gamma Sigma Delta
1976 Gamma Iota Sigma	1968 Pi Mu Epsilon
1980 Phi Alpha Delta	1972 Sigma Gamma Epsilon

OTHER PROFESSIONAL	SERVICE
1947 Alpha Kappa Kappa	1948 Alpha Phi Omega
1951 Beta Alpha Psi	
1951 Delta Pi Epsilon	RECOGNITION
1952 Women in Communications	Angel Flight
1963 Sigma Delta Chi	Arnold Air Society (C-2)
1970 Kappa Beta Pi	1926 Eta Sigma Phi
	1927 Alpha Psi Omega
ACHS HONORS	1940 Scabbard and Blade (8)
Omicron Delta Epsilon	1941 Beta Beta Beta
Pi Alpha Alpha	1946 Sigma Delta Psi
1917 Delta Sigma Rho-Tau	1976 Kappa Pi
Kappa Alpha	
1930 Alpha Lambda Delta	INACTIVE
1930 Phi Eta Sigma	1850–85 Delta Kappa Epsilon
1936 Omicron Delta Kappa	1859–61 Phi Kappa Sigma
1937 Chi Epsilon	1868–79 Phi Gamma Delta
1937 Rho Chi	1886–42 Delta Tau Delta
1938 Alpha Epsilon Delta	1926 Phi Beta Pi and Theta
1941 Lambda Sigma Society	Kappa Psi (B)
1942 Mortar Board	1927 Sigma Delta Kappa
1944 Beta Gamma Sigma	1927–49 Pi Kappa Phi
1947 Kappa Delta Pi	1928–53 Delta Zeta
1948 Pi Sigma Alpha	1935–85 Zeta Beta Tau
1955 Phi Sigma Tau	1937–57 Gamma Sigma Epsilon
1957 Sigma Delta Pi	1939–86 Zeta Tau Alpha
1959 Phi Kappa Phi	1948 Kappa Kappa Psi
1965 Phi Alpha Theta	1962–76 Pi Omega Pi
	1971–76 Alpha Xi Delta
	1978–79 Pi Omega Pi

MISSISSIPPI COLLEGE   Clinton, MS. College of liberal arts; coeducational; private control (Baptist). Established 1826. Oldest institution of higher learning in Mississippi.

PROFESSIONAL	1978 Mortar Board
1958 Delta Omicron	1990 Psi Chi
1964 Delta Sigma Pi	
1975 Delta Theta Phi	OTHER HONORS
1984 Phi Alpha Delta	1974 Pi Mu Epsilon

ACHS HONORS	RECOGNITION
1957 Sigma Tau Delta	1957 Alpha Psi Omega
1958 Pi Gamma Mu	1958 Eta Sigma Phi
1959 Alpha Chi	1971 Beta Beta Beta
1959 Kappa Delta Pi	
1960 Alpha Lambda Delta	INACTIVE
1960 Omicron Delta Kappa	1860–61 Phi Kappa Psi
1961 Phi Alpha Theta	1869–72 Sigma Alpha Epsilon
1965 Alpha Epsilon Delta	1873–74 Sigma Chi
1970 Sigma Pi Sigma	1959–85 Phi Mu Alpha—
	Sinfonia

MISSISSIPPI STATE UNIVERSITY   State College, MS. University; land-grant college; coeducational; state control; chartered 1878 as Mississippi Agricultural and Mechanical College; schools of agriculture, engineering, arts and sciences, business, education, forestry and graduate.

Of the nineteen fraternities, nine own houses on college land; and the others own houses on their own land. The sororities have chapter rooms in residence halls.

NIC MEN'S
1887 Sigma Alpha Epsilon
1927 Kappa Alpha Order
1927 Pi Kappa Alpha
1936 Kappa Sigma
1937 Alpha Tau Omega
1937 Sigma Pi
1938 Phi Kappa Tau
1938 Sigma Chi
1938 Sigma Phi Epsilon
1939 Lambda Chi Alpha
1964 Delta Chi
1964 FarmHouse
1970 Phi Gamma Delta
1972 Triangle
1974 Sigma Nu
1975 Kappa Alpha Psi (A)

NPHC MEN'S
Phi Beta Sigma
1974 Alpha Phi Alpha

NPC WOMEN'S
1936 Chi Omega
1940 Zeta Tau Alpha
1962 Phi Mu
1969 Delta Gamma
1971 Kappa Delta
1972 Delta Delta Delta
1989 Alpha Gamma Delta

NPHC WOMEN'S
1976 Delta Sigma Theta (B)
1982 Sigma Gamma Rho

PROFESSIONAL
1949 Delta Sigma Pi
1956 Alpha Kappa Psi
1963 Phi Mu Alpha—Sinfonia
1964 Theta Tau
1971 Sigma Alpha Iota
1978 Gamma Iota Sigma

OTHER PROFESSIONAL
1928 Alpha Zeta
1960 Beta Alpha Psi
1974 Pi Lambda Theta

ACHS HONORS
Omicron Delta Epsilon
Pi Alpha Alpha
Sigma Tau Delta
1928 Tau Beta Pi
1932 Kappa Mu Epsilon
1935 Phi Eta Sigma
1937 Omicron Delta Kappa
1938 Alpha Epsilon Delta
1939 Pi Omega Pi
1950 Phi Alpha Theta
1951 Phi Kappa Phi
1954 Alpha Kappa Delta

1957 Pi Tau Sigma
1958 Kappa Delta Pi
1959 Eta Kappa Nu
1961 Beta Gamma Sigma
1965 Alpha Lambda Delta
1965 Pi Delta Phi
1970 Sigma Pi Sigma
1971 Alpha Pi Mu
1971 Chi Epsilon
1971 Sigma Gamma Tau
1971 Xi Sigma Pi
1972 Kappa Omicron Nu
1977 Pi Sigma Alpha
1978 Lambda Sigma·Society
1978 Omega Chi Epsilon
1988 Sigma Lambda Alpha

OTHER HONORS
National Order of Omega
1948 Sigma Gamma Epsilon
1966 Sigma Xi

SERVICE
1947 Alpha Phi Omega

RECOGNITION
Angel Flight
Arnold Air Society (C-2)
1928 Blue Key
1928 Scabbard and Blade (7)
1934 Alpha Psi Omega
1934 Pi Kappa Delta
1938 National Block and Bridle Club
1939 Alpha Psi Omega
1939 Iota Lambda Sigma
1947 Society for Collegiate Journalists—Pi Delta Epsilon-Alpha Phi Gamma (P)
1954 Cardinal Key
1966 Delta Phi Alpha
1975 Kappa Pi

INACTIVE
1926–42 Pi Gamma Mu
1936   Beta Beta Beta
1937–50 Sigma Alpha Mu
1938–56 Alpha Tau Alpha
1940–60 Theta Xi
1948–60 Phi Kappa Theta
1961–80 Acacia
1962–67 Sigma Delta Pi
1966–84 Phi Chi Theta
1966–88 Alpha Delta Pi
1974–84 Alpha Chi Omega
1977–84 Kappa Kappa Gamma

COLONIES
1990 Phi Delta Theta

MISSISSIPPI UNIVERSITY FOR WOMEN Columbus, MS. College of liberal arts; state control; established 1884; oldest state college for women in the U.S.

PROFESSIONAL
1941 Sigma Alpha Iota
1946 Kappa Delta Epsilon

OTHER PROFESSIONAL
1940 Phi Upsilon Omicron
1950 Alpha Beta Alpha

ACHS HONORS
1927 Pi Delta Phi
1932 Kappa Mu Epsilon
1935 Pi Omega Pi
1942 Mortar Board
1949 Phi Alpha Theta
1949 Sigma Tau Delta
1951 Alpha Epsilon Delta
1957 Phi Kappa Phi
1959 Sigma Delta Pi

RECOGNITION
1927 Eta Sigma Phi
1928 Beta Beta Beta
1935 Gamma Sigma Epsilon
1948 Pi Kappa Delta
1971 Lambda Tau

INACTIVE
1928–82 Pi Gamma Mu

MISSISSIPPI VALLEY STATE UNIVERSITY Itta Bena, MS.

NIC MEN'S
1970 Kappa Alpha Psi (A)

NPHC MEN'S
Phi Beta Sigma
1970 Alpha Phi Alpha

NPHC WOMEN'S
1969 Alpha Kappa Alpha
1969 Delta Sigma Theta (B)
1985 Sigma Gamma Rho

PROFESSIONAL
1962 Kappa Kappa Psi
1962 Tau Beta Sigma

ACHS HONORS
1969 Alpha Kappa Mu
1972 Sigma Tau Delta

INACTIVE
1975–76 Pi Omega Pi

UNIVERSITY OF MISSOURI Columbia, MO. Oldest state university west of the Mississippi River, founded 1839. World's first school of journalism established 1908. Four colleges and ten schools at the Columbia division.

Fraternities and sororities occupy their own houses on their land.

NIC MEN'S
1869 Phi Kappa Psi
1870 Phi Delta Theta
1884 Sigma Alpha Epsilon
1886 Sigma Nu
1890 Beta Theta Pi
1891 Kappa Alpha Order
1896 Sigma Chi
1898 Kappa Sigma
1899 Phi Gamma Delta
1905 Delta Tau Delta
1905 FarmHouse
1906 Alpha Tau Omega
1909 Pi Kappa Alpha
1914 Sigma Phi Epsilon
1916 Alpha Gamma Rho
1917 Zeta Beta Tau
1923 Alpha Gamma Sigma
1923 Phi Kappa Theta
1924 Delta Upsilon
1926 Lambda Chi Alpha
1927 Delta Sigma Phi
1928 Sigma Alpha Mu
1929 Alpha Sigma Phi
1947 Alpha Epsilon Pi
1947 Tau Kappa Epsilon
1949 Pi Kappa Phi
1951 Delta Chi
1958 Sigma Tau Gamma
1961 Kappa Alpha Psi (A)
1962 Beta Sigma Psi

NPHC MEN'S
Phi Beta Sigma
1966 Alpha Phi Alpha

NPC WOMEN'S
1875 Kappa Kappa Gamma
1899 Pi Beta Phi

1909 Delta Gamma
1909 Kappa Alpha Theta
1910 Alpha Phi
1913 Chi Omega
1915 Alpha Delta Pi
1915 Delta Delta Delta
1921 Gamma Phi Beta
1922 Alpha Chi Omega
1922 Alpha Gamma Delta
1924 Zeta Tau Alpha
1929 Alpha Epsilon Phi
1968 Sigma Kappa
1976 Kappa Delta
1986 Alpha Omicron Pi

NPHC WOMEN'S
1964 Alpha Kappa Alpha
1966 Delta Sigma Theta (B)
1973 Sigma Gamma Rho
1974 Delta Sigma Theta (B)
1980 Sigma Gamma Rho
1981 Alpha Kappa Alpha

PROFESSIONAL
1890 Phi Delta Phi
1907 Alpha Chi Sigma
1907 Phi Mu Alpha—Sinfonia
1909 Phi Alpha Delta
1920 Alpha Kappa Psi
1921 Delta Theta Phi
1923 Delta Sigma Pi
1926 Phi Chi Theta
1941 Sigma Alpha Iota
1984 Phi Alpha Delta

OTHER PROFESSIONAL
1907 Alpha Zeta
1911 Women in Communications
1913 Sigma Delta Chi
1918 Pi Lambda Theta

1929 Phi Upsilon Omicron
1934 Alpha Tau Alpha
1944 Kappa Alpha Mu
1946 Kappa Beta Pi
1967 Beta Alpha Psi
1969 Alpha Zeta Omega

ACHS HONORS
    Omicron Delta Epsilon
    Pi Alpha Alpha
1902 Tau Beta Pi
1908 Delta Sigma Rho-Tau
    Kappa Alpha
1910 Kappa Tau Alpha
1911 Eta Kappa Nu
1918 Mortar Board
1921 Sigma Delta Pi
1922 Phi Sigma Iota
1925 Pi Tau Sigma
1926 Phi Eta Sigma
1927 Alpha Kappa Delta
1931 Beta Gamma Sigma
1933 Omicron Delta Kappa
1934 Chi Epsilon
1934 Psi Chi
1952 Xi Sigma Pi
1955 Gamma Theta Upsilon
1955 Pi Sigma Alpha
1959 Alpha Epsilon
1963 Alpha Pi Mu
1964 Sigma Theta Tau
1970 Kappa Delta Pi
1970 Pi Kappa Lambda
1970 Pi Kappa Lambda
1971 Beta Phi Mu
1972 Kappa Omicron Nu
1972 Phi Kappa Phi
1973 Mortar Board
1975 Pi Sigma Alpha
1984 Phi Alpha Theta

OTHER HONORS
    National Order of Omega

1901 Phi Beta Kappa
1905 Order of the Coif
1905 Sigma Xi
1909 Gamma Sigma Delta
1922 Pi Mu Epsilon
1924 Delta Phi Delta
1928 Sigma Epsilon Sigma
1957 Alpha Omega Alpha

SERVICE
1938 Alpha Phi Omega

RECOGNITION
    Angel Flight
    Arnold Air Society (G-1)
1911 Scabbard and Blade (1)
1919 National Block and Bridle
    Club
1928 Eta Sigma Phi
1933 Blue Key
1965 Phi Zeta
1972 Phi Lambda Upsilon

INACTIVE
1906   Phi Beta Pi and Theta
        Kappa Psi (a)
1907–84 Acacia
1913–44 Phi Mu
1914   Gamma Alpha
1917–35 Alpha Kappa Kappa
1919–39 Sigma Gamma Epsilon
1920–34 Theta Alpha Phi
1921–27 Theta Phi Alpha
1924   Sigma Delta Epsilon
1924–33 Triangle
1925–36 Lambda Sigma Society
1928–38 Mu Phi Epsilon
1935–55 Phi Sigma Sigma
1955   Phi Chi
1957–64 Theta Xi
1957–68 Sigma Delta Tau
1967–90 Sigma Pi
1978–84 Delta Phi Epsilon

UNIVERSITY OF MISSOURI-KANSAS CITY

Kansas City, MO. Coeducational, public, state university. Chartered 1929. Became state university 1963. Law School established 1938 by merger of Kansas City School of Law (founded 1895). School of Dentistry established 1941 by merger of Kansas City-Western Dental College (founded 1881) with the university. Conservatory of Music established 1959 by merger of the Conservatory of Music of Kansas City (founded 1914). The UMKC School of Pharmacy established in 1943 by merger with the Kansas City College of Pharmacy (founded 1889). Also during this period, the School of Business and Public Administration (1953), the School of Education (1954), the Division of Continuing Education (1958), the School of Graduate Studies (1964), the School of Medicine (1970), the School of Nursing (1980), and the School of Basic Life Sciences (1985) were organized.

NIC MEN'S
1956 Delta Chi
1969 Sigma Tau Gamma
1976 Lambda Chi Alpha
1977 Sigma Phi Epsilon
1987 Kappa Alpha Psi (A)
1988 Beta Theta Pi

NPC WOMEN'S
1961 Chi Omega
1962 Alpha Delta Pi
1987 Delta Zeta

NPHC WOMEN'S
1982 Sigma Gamma Rho

PROFESSIONAL
1907 Phi Alpha Delta
1915 Delta Theta Phi
1958 Kappa Epsilon
1960 Phi Delta Chi

OTHER PROFESSIONAL
1973 Pi Lambda Theta

ACHS HONORS
    Omicron Delta Epsilon
1954 Rho Chi
1955 Psi Chi
1956 Omicron Delta Kappa
1962 Pi Kappa Lambda
1969 Beta Gamma Sigma
1969 Phi Kappa Phi

1970 Phi Alpha Theta
1971 Sigma Pi Sigma
1976 Gamma Theta Upsilon
1980 Eta Kappa Nu

OTHER HONORS
1963 National Collegiate
    Players

SERVICE
1934 Alpha Phi Omega

INACTIVE
1956–72 Alpha Epsilon Pi
1956–80 Tau Kappa Epsilon
1967–71 Sigma Delta Tau
1972–74 Zeta Phi Eta

UNIVERSITY OF MISSOURI-ROLLA   Rolla, MO. Division of the University of Missouri. Founded 1870.

Nineteen fraternities own their properties, in some instances subject to mortgage; six of these facilities are situated on land leased from the university. Three sororities own facilities.

NIC MEN'S
1903 Kappa Alpha Order
1903 Kappa Sigma
1905 Pi Kappa Alpha
1917 Lambda Chi Alpha
1927 Triangle
1933 Sigma Pi
1947 Alpha Epsilon Pi
1947 Sigma Phi Epsilon
1947 Tau Kappa Epsilon
1949 Theta Xi
1952 Beta Sigma Psi
1956 Delta Sigma Phi
1956 Sigma Tau Gamma
1958 Acacia
1966 Delta Tau Delta
1968 Pi Kappa Phi
1980 Kappa Alpha Psi (A)
1983 Sigma Chi

NPHC MEN'S
1965 Alpha Phi Alpha

NPC WOMEN'S
1972 Kappa Delta
1973 Zeta Tau Alpha
1979 Chi Omega

PROFESSIONAL
1936 Alpha Chi Sigma

1958 Kappa Kappa Psi

OTHER PROFESSIONAL
1947 Keramos

ACHS HONORS
    Omicron Delta Epsilon
1906 Tau Beta Pi
1920 Phi Kappa Phi
1950 Chi Epsilon
1950 Sigma Pi Sigma
1952 Eta Kappa Nu
1958 Alpha Sigma Mu
1961 Kappa Mu Epsilon
1963 Phi Eta Sigma
1974 Omega Chi Epsilon
1979 Psi Chi

SERVICE
1939 Alpha Phi Omega
1964 Intercollegiate Knights

RECOGNITION
1965 Scabbard and Blade (16)

INACTIVE
1916–75 Theta Tau
1963–74 Theta Chi

UNIVERSITY OF MISSOURI-ST. LOUIS   St. Louis, MO. Established 1963; state-supported public institution.

Totally a commuter institution therefore the fraternities and sororities who occupy fraternity houses either own or rent facilities in the surrounding community.

NIC MEN'S
1968 Sigma Tau Gamma
1969 Pi Kappa Alpha
1969 Sigma Pi
1976 Tau Kappa Epsilon

NPC WOMEN'S
1968 Alpha Xi Delta
1968 Delta Zeta
1977 Zeta Tau Alpha

NPHC WOMEN'S
1970 Delta Sigma Theta (B)

PROFESSIONAL
1968 Delta Sigma Pi

OTHER PROFESSIONAL
1972 Beta Alpha Psi

ACHS HONORS
     Omicron Delta Epsilon
1967 Psi Chi

1970 Kappa Delta Pi
1971 Beta Gamma Sigma
1977 Pi Sigma Alpha
1980 Phi Kappa Phi

SERVICE
1967 Alpha Phi Omega

MISSOURI SOUTHERN STATE COLLEGE   Joplin, MO. College of liberal arts and general studies; teacher preparatory; professional; coeducational. State control. Established 1965.

NIC MEN'S
1971 Kappa Alpha Order
1974 Sigma Nu
1990 Sigma Pi

NPC WOMEN'S
1974 Zeta Tau Alpha

ACHS HONORS
     Omicron Delta Epsilon
1975 Kappa Mu Epsilon
1976 Pi Omega Pi

1977 Pi Gamma Mu
1980 Psi Chi
1987 Omicron Delta Kappa
1988 Phi Eta Sigma
1990 Phi Alpha Theta

RECOGNITION
1973 Beta Beta Beta

INACTIVE
1972–84 Delta Gamma

MISSOURI VALLEY COLLEGE   Marshall, MO. College of liberal arts; coeducational; private control (United Presbyterian Church). Chartered 1888.

NIC MEN'S
1891 Sigma Nu
1945 Alpha Sigma Phi
1955 Tau Kappa Epsilon

NPHC MEN'S
     Phi Beta Sigma

NPC WOMEN'S
1945 Alpha Xi Delta
1967 Alpha Sigma Alpha

ACHS HONORS
1948 Sigma Tau Delta

SERVICE
1947 Alpha Phi Omega

1968 Gamma Sigma Sigma

RECOGNITION
1937 Beta Beta Beta
1942 Alpha Psi Omega
1951 Sigma Zeta
1954 Society for Collegiate
     Journalists—Pi Delta
     Epsilon-Alpha Phi Gamma
     (P)

INACTIVE
1931–79 Pi Gamma Mu
1945–80 Delta Zeta

MISSOURI WESTERN STATE COLLEGE   St. Joseph, MO. College of liberal arts and sciences, education, technology, and business administration; state control; established 1915; became four-year college in 1969.

NIC MEN'S
1971 Phi Sigma Kappa
1985 Sigma Tau Gamma

NPC WOMEN'S
1976 Sigma Kappa

PROFESSIONAL
1981 Phi Mu Alpha—Sinfonia

ACHS HONORS
1974 Sigma Tau Delta
1989 Psi Chi

SERVICE
1970 Alpha Phi Omega

RECOGNITION
1977 Pi Kappa Delta

INACTIVE
1970–87 Phi Mu
1971–80 Delta Zeta
1971–83 Tau Kappa Epsilon
1972–85 Lambda Chi Alpha
1973–82 Sigma Phi Epsilon
1976–79 Delta Chi

MOBILE COLLEGE   Mobile, AL.

NPHC MEN'S
     Phi Beta Sigma

NPHC WOMEN'S
1972 Delta Sigma Theta (B)

PROFESSIONAL
1983 Kappa Delta Epsilon

ACHS HONORS
1982 Phi Alpha Theta

1983 Psi Chi
1989 Theta Alpha Kappa

SERVICE
1966 Alpha Phi Omega

MOLLOY COLLEGE   Rockville Centre, NY.

ACHS HONORS
1968 Delta Epsilon Sigma
1973 Psi Chi

1979 Phi Sigma Tau
1979 Theta Alpha Kappa
1983 Phi Alpha Theta

MONMOUTH COLLEGE   Monmouth, IL. Established 1853, first instruction 1856, chartered 1857. Undergraduate college of liberal arts; coeducational; private control (United Presbyterian).

Ownership of house and land is by the fraternity, though college retains posession of deed. Administration requires sorority members to occupy dormitories.

NIC MEN'S
1928 Tau Kappa Epsilon
1942 Theta Chi
1947 Alpha Tau Omega
1948 Sigma Phi Epsilon
1971 Zeta Beta Tau

NPHC MEN'S
     Phi Beta Sigma

NPC WOMEN'S
1867 Pi Beta Phi
1870 Kappa Kappa Gamma
1936 Kappa Delta
1986 Alpha Sigma Tau

ACHS HONORS
1948 Phi Alpha Theta
1956 Alpha Lambda Delta
1971 Eta Kappa Nu

1972 Mortar Board
1972 Psi Chi
1979 Pi Sigma Alpha
1982 Delta Mu Delta

OTHER HONORS
     National Order of Omega

INACTIVE
1865–71 Delta Tau Delta
1865–78 Beta Theta Pi
1869–71 Phi Gamma Delta
1871–84 Phi Delta Theta
1871–84 Phi Kappa Psi
1874–78 Sigma Chi
1932–80 Alpha Xi Delta
1959–81 Pi Gamma Mu
1963–81 Sigma Alpha Epsilon

MONMOUTH COLLEGE   West Long Branch, NJ. College of liberal arts and professional education; coeducational; private control; nonsectarian; established 1933 as junior college; became four-year college 1956.

NIC MEN'S
     Alpha Epsilon Pi
1966 Tau Kappa Epsilon
1967 Phi Kappa Psi
1969 Sigma Pi
1983 Phi Sigma Kappa

NPC WOMEN'S
1967 Delta Phi Epsilon
1971 Zeta Tau Alpha
1986 Theta Phi Alpha
1987 Phi Sigma Sigma

ACHS HONORS
1964 Phi Alpha Theta
1964 Psi Chi
1967 Sigma Pi Sigma
1976 Kappa Delta Pi
1976 Phi Sigma Tau

1985 Omicron Delta Kappa
1987 Phi Eta Sigma

SERVICE
1964 Alpha Phi Omega
1973 Gamma Sigma Sigma

RECOGNITION
1962 Alpha Psi Omega
1976 Beta Beta Beta

INACTIVE
1962–71 Delta Sigma Pi
1967–71 Delta Zeta
1968–89 Delta Sigma Phi
1969–77 Sigma Alpha Mu
1973–75 Zeta Beta Tau
1973–75 Zeta Tau Alpha

UNIVERSITY OF MONTANA
UNIVERSITY OF MONTANA Missoula, MT. Authorized by legislature in 1892, first classes held in 1895; liberal arts, coeducational undergraduate and graduate.

Ownership of fraternity house and land and sorority house and land is by the organization.

NIC MEN'S
1905 Sigma Nu
1906 Sigma Chi
1918 Sigma Phi Epsilon
1920 Phi Delta Theta
1923 Alpha Tau Omega
1927 Sigma Alpha Epsilon
1937 Theta Chi
1987 Phi Gamma Delta

NPC WOMEN'S
1909 Kappa Alpha Theta
1909 Kappa Kappa Gamma
1911 Delta Gamma
1918 Alpha Phi

PROFESSIONAL
1917 Alpha Kappa Psi
1922 Phi Delta Phi
1950 Phi Alpha Delta
1952 Mu Phi Epsilon

OTHER PROFESSIONAL
1915 Sigma Delta Chi
1916 Women in Communications
1928 Phi Epsilon Kappa
1974 Beta Alpha Psi

ACHS HONORS
Omicron Delta Epsilon
1921 Phi Sigma
1927 Mortar Board
1930 Psi Chi
1936 Alpha Lambda Delta
1948 Phi Alpha Theta
1952 Beta Gamma Sigma
1953 Kappa Tau Alpha
1958 Alpha Kappa Delta
1960 Rho Chi
1962 Kappa Omicron Nu
1963 Pi Kappa Lambda
1964 Phi Eta Sigma
1966 Pi Delta Phi
1967 Sigma Delta Pi
1969 Pi Sigma Alpha

OTHER HONORS
1925 Pi Mu Epsilon
1952 National Collegiate Players
1964 Sigma Xi

SERVICE
The National Spurs
1949 Alpha Phi Omega

RECOGNITION
Angel Flight
Arnold Air Society (H-2)
1964 Delta Tau Kappa
1967 Sigma Delta Psi
1973 Pi Kappa Delta

INACTIVE
1918   Delta Phi Delta
1920   Delta Psi Kappa
1922   Scabbard and Blade (4)
1923–52 Alpha Chi Omega
1923–72 Phi Sigma Kappa
1924–38 Alpha Xi Delta
1924–42 Kappa Delta
1924–54 Pi Gamma Mu
1924–82 Sigma Kappa
1926–33 Sigma Alpha Iota
1926–71 Delta Delta Delta
1927–37 Kappa Sigma
1927–67 Phi Sigma
1933–43 Alpha Delta Pi
1947–74 Phi Chi Theta
1948–81 Phi Mu Alpha—Sinfonia
1950   Sigma Gamma Epsilon
1954–84 Phi Kappa Phi
1956–73 Delta Sigma Phi
1965–71 Alpha Kappa Lambda
1965–87 Alpha Omicron Pi
1975–83 Phi Kappa Psi

COLONIES
Pi Kappa Alpha

MONTANA COLLEGE OF MINERAL SCIENCE & TECHNOLOGY
MONTANA COLLEGE OF MINERAL SCIENCE & TECHNOLOGY Butte, MT. Mineral industry engineering college with engineering degrees (B.S.) in engineering science, geology, geophysics, metallurgy, mineral dressing, mining, and petroleum. Formerly Montana School of Mines.

ACHS HONORS
1984 Tau Beta Pi

SERVICE
The National Spurs

RECOGNITION
1973 Pi Kappa Delta

INACTIVE
1932–88 Theta Tau

MONTANA STATE UNIVERSITY
MONTANA STATE UNIVERSITY Bozeman, MT. University, seven coeducational undergraduate colleges; coeducational college of graduate studies; state control through Board of Regents; established 1893; became university 1965.

Most fraternities and sororities own their own houses and land; two fraternities and one sorority occupy houses rented from the university.

NIC MEN'S
1917 Sigma Chi
1919 Sigma Alpha Epsilon
1925 Alpha Gamma Rho
1926 Kappa Sigma
1928 Pi Kappa Alpha
1931 Lambda Chi Alpha
1939 Phi Sigma Kappa
1952 Sigma Nu
1956 Delta Sigma Phi
1979 FarmHouse

NPC WOMEN'S
1917 Alpha Omicron Pi
1920 Chi Omega
1921 Pi Beta Phi
1924 Alpha Gamma Delta
1924 Kappa Delta
1948 Delta Gamma

OTHER WOMEN'S
1989 CERES

PROFESSIONAL
1920 Kappa Kappa Psi
1920 Kappa Psi
1922 Kappa Epsilon
1940 Alpha Tau Delta
1960 Tau Beta Sigma

OTHER PROFESSIONAL
1917 Phi Upsilon Omicron
1922 Alpha Zeta

ACHS HONORS
1910 Delta Sigma Rho-Tau Kappa Alpha
1922 Phi Kappa Phi
1926 Tau Beta Pi
1927 Mortar Board

1931 Alpha Lambda Delta
1942 Pi Omega Pi
1958 Pi Tau Sigma
1960 Xi Sigma Pi
1965 Psi Chi
1971 Chi Epsilon
1973 Alpha Pi Mu
1973 Phi Alpha Theta
1974 Sigma Pi Sigma
1975 Lambda Iota Tau
1976 Sigma Delta Pi
1978 Pi Sigma Alpha

OTHER HONORS
National Order of Omega
1950 Sigma Xi
1959 Pi Mu Epsilon

SERVICE
The National Spurs
1949 Alpha Phi Omega

RECOGNITION
Arnold Air Society (H-2)
1921 Pi Kappa Delta
1930 Sigma Delta Psi
1931 Alpha Psi Omega

INACTIVE
1923–34 Theta Alpha Phi
1925   Scabbard and Blade (6)
1926–59 Alpha Chi Sigma
1930–81 Phi Eta Sigma
1932–35 Alpha Delta Pi
1961–87 Sigma Phi Epsilon
1968–76 Phi Delta Theta
1971–83 Kappa Alpha Theta

MONTCLAIR STATE COLLEGE
MONTCLAIR STATE COLLEGE Upper Montclair, NJ. Teachers college, coeducational; state control; established as normal school in 1908; merged with Panzer College in 1958.

No fraternities or sororities are allowed to own properties for housing or chapter house uses. This is a New Jersey State educational policy in operation on all six New Jersey State College campuses. State College campuses do not rent facilities to any social or professional groups.

NIC MEN'S
1978 Kappa Alpha Psi (A)
1986 Tau Kappa Epsilon
1989 Zeta Beta Tau

NPHC MEN'S
Phi Beta Sigma

NPC WOMEN'S
1988 Phi Sigma Sigma
1989 Delta Phi Epsilon

1989 Zeta Tau Alpha
1990 Sigma Delta Tau

PROFESSIONAL
1962 Phi Mu Alpha—Sinfonia
1963 Sigma Alpha Iota
1972 Alpha Kappa Psi
1974 Phi Chi Theta
1987 Phi Alpha Delta

OTHER PROFESSIONAL
1974 Delta Pi Epsilon

ACHS HONORS
 Omicron Delta Epsilon
1931 Kappa Delta Pi
1933 Gamma Theta Upsilon
1944 Kappa Mu Epsilon
1948 Pi Omega Pi
1961 Sigma Delta Pi
1962 Pi Delta Phi
1965 Pi Gamma Mu
1971 Psi Chi
1973 Phi Alpha Theta
1974 Pi Sigma Alpha
1976 Phi Kappa Phi

1989 Kappa Omicron Nu

SERVICE
1962 Alpha Phi Omega

RECOGNITION
1958 Kappa Pi

INACTIVE
1955   Eta Sigma Phi

COLONIES
 Alpha Phi Delta
 Theta Xi
1989 Delta Chi
1990 Alpha Chi Rho

UNIVERSITY OF MONTEVALLO Montevallo, AL.
Coeducational since 1956; state control; established 1893. There are four colleges: Arts and Sciences, Business, Education, and Fine Arts.

NIC MEN'S
1971 Pi Kappa Phi
1972 Alpha Tau Omega
1972 Delta Chi
1972 Lambda Chi Alpha
1974 Pi Kappa Alpha

NPC WOMEN'S
1971 Alpha Delta Pi
1971 Chi Omega
1972 Alpha Gamma Delta
1972 Phi Mu

NPHC WOMEN'S
1978 Alpha Kappa Alpha

PROFESSIONAL
1967 Alpha Kappa Psi
1973 Phi Chi Theta

ACHS HONORS
1931 Kappa Omicron Nu
1937 Kappa Mu Epsilon
1939 Alpha Lambda Delta
1948 Pi Kappa Lambda
1961 Phi Alpha Theta
1967 Sigma Tau Delta
1978 Omicron Delta Kappa
1978 Phi Kappa Phi
1981 Psi Chi

RECOGNITION
1944 Society for Collegiate Journalists—Pi Delta Epsilon-Alpha Phi Gamma (P)

MOORHEAD STATE UNIVERSITY Moorhead, MN. College of liberal arts; coeducational; state control; established as normal school 1887, master's in English, history, music, biology, chemistry, and education.

Fraternities and sororities are permitted to own their own houses and property. All sororities own houses within one block of the campus. Three fraternities own houses.

NIC MEN'S
1970 Phi Sigma Kappa

NPC WOMEN'S
1963 Delta Zeta
1964 Gamma Phi Beta

PROFESSIONAL
1959 Sigma Alpha Iota

ACHS HONORS
1931 Kappa Delta Pi
1933 Gamma Theta Upsilon
1966 Alpha Lambda Delta
1971 Delta Mu Delta
1972 Pi Omega Pi
1982 Phi Kappa Phi
1982 Pi Kappa Lambda
1984 Psi Chi

SERVICE
 The National Spurs

1972 Alpha Phi Omega

RECOGNITION
1927 Alpha Psi Omega
1964 Kappa Pi

INACTIVE
1931–41 Sigma Tau Delta
1938 Delta Psi Kappa
1956–86 Phi Mu Alpha—Sinfonia
1960–87 Sigma Tau Gamma
1963–88 Tau Kappa Epsilon
1964–84 Alpha Delta Pi
1966–88 Alpha Phi
1967–76 Phi Eta Sigma
1973–86 Sigma Pi Sigma

MORAVIAN COLLEGE Bethlehem, PA. Established by the Moravian Church. Men's college 1807; women's program 1742; coeducational; undergraduate.

The college rents quarters to the fraternities and sororities.

OTHER PROFESSIONAL
1937 Kappa Phi Kappa

ACHS HONORS
1963 Phi Alpha Theta
1967 Lambda Iota Tau
1968 Sigma Pi Sigma
1976 Psi Chi
1983 Omicron Delta Kappa
1983 Phi Sigma Iota

SERVICE
1961 Alpha Phi Omega
1976 Gamma Sigma Sigma

RECOGNITION
1944 Alpha Psi Omega

INACTIVE
1956–65 Tau Kappa Epsilon
1957–74 Kappa Delta Epsilon

MOREHEAD STATE UNIVERSITY Morehead, KY. Colleges of Applied Sciences and Technology, Arts and Sciences, and Professional Studies; coeducational; state-supported since it was established in 1922.

NIC MEN'S
1969 Tau Kappa Epsilon
1970 Delta Tau Delta
1970 Sigma Phi Epsilon
1971 Kappa Alpha Psi (A)
1971 Lambda Chi Alpha
1971 Sigma Alpha Epsilon
1971 Sigma Pi
1971 Theta Chi
1973 Pi Kappa Phi
1973 Sigma Nu
1988 FarmHouse

NPC WOMEN'S
1969 Chi Omega
1969 Kappa Delta
1969 Sigma Sigma Sigma
1970 Delta Gamma
1970 Delta Zeta

NPHC WOMEN'S
1970 Delta Sigma Theta (B)
1973 Alpha Kappa Alpha

PROFESSIONAL
1959 Phi Mu Alpha—Sinfonia
1960 Sigma Alpha Iota
1982 Phi Alpha Delta

OTHER PROFESSIONAL
1962 Alpha Beta Alpha
1975 Alpha Epsilon Rho

ACHS HONORS
1961 Gamma Theta Upsilon
1965 Lambda Iota Tau
1968 Kappa Omicron Nu
1970 Phi Alpha Theta
1971 Pi Gamma Mu
1973 Phi Kappa Phi
1976 Pi Kappa Lambda
1979 Psi Chi

OTHER HONORS
 National Order of Omega

RECOGNITION
1966 Blue Key

INACTIVE
1961–85 Lambda Sigma Society
1967–77 Sigma Pi Sigma
1970–82 Zeta Tau Alpha
1970–84 Alpha Omicron Pi
1971–76 Chi Phi
1971–84 Pi Kappa Alpha

COLONIES
1989 Kappa Sigma

MOREHOUSE COLLEGE Atlanta, GA. College of liberal arts for men; private control (Baptist); established 1867.

NIC MEN'S
1921 Kappa Alpha Psi (A)

NPHC MEN'S
 Phi Beta Sigma
1922 Omega Psi Phi
1924 Alpha Phi Alpha

ACHS HONORS
 Omicron Delta Epsilon
1956 Pi Delta Phi
1959 Delta Sigma Rho-Tau Kappa Alpha

1970 Phi Alpha Theta
1976 Sigma Pi Sigma
1976 Sigma Tau Delta
1984 Psi Chi

OTHER HONORS
1968 Phi Beta Kappa

SERVICE
1974 Alpha Phi Omega

RECOGNITION
1958 Sigma Delta Psi

MORGAN STATE UNIVERSITY Baltimore, MD. In 1975, Morgan State College became Morgan State University. It evolved from being a predominantly Negro college to a multi-racial university. However, Morgan retains its historical commitment to train Black stutdents in the liberal arts, selected professions, and graduate study. Morgan is one of three doctoral degree-granting institutions in the state of Maryland and has become the state's first urban-oriented university.

NIC MEN'S
1931 Kappa Alpha Psi (A)

NPHC MEN'S
     Phi Beta Sigma
1923 Omega Psi Phi
1926 Alpha Phi Alpha

NPHC WOMEN'S
     Zeta Phi Beta
1925 Alpha Kappa Alpha
1925 Delta Sigma Theta (B)
1954 Sigma Gamma Rho

PROFESSIONAL
1976 Kappa Kappa Psi
1976 Tau Beta Sigma

ACHS HONORS
1934 Beta Kappa Chi
1940 Alpha Kappa Mu
1955 Delta Sigma Rho-Tau
     Kappa Alpha
1955 Gamma Theta Upsilon

1955 Phi Sigma Tau
1956 Kappa Delta Pi
1956 Lambda Iota Tau
1956 Pi Gamma Mu
1958 Psi Chi
1960 Phi Alpha Theta
1969 Sigma Pi Sigma
1974 Pi Sigma Alpha
1978 Delta Mu Delta
1980 Kappa Omicron Nu
1982 Alpha Lambda Delta
1982 Phi Eta Sigma
1983 Sigma Lambda Alpha

OTHER HONORS
1970 Pi Mu Epsilon

SERVICE
1956 Alpha Phi Omega
1964 Gamma Sigma Sigma

RECOGNITION
1954 Alpha Psi Omega

MORNINGSIDE COLLEGE Sioux City, IA. College of liberal arts; coeducational; private control; Methodist Church; chartered as University of the Northwest 1889.

The fraternities and sororities rent quarters from the college.

NIC MEN'S
1956 Delta Sigma Phi

NPC WOMEN'S
1957 Alpha Delta Pi
1966 Alpha Omicron Pi

PROFESSIONAL
1929 Mu Phi Epsilon
1941 Phi Mu Alpha—Sinfonia

ACHS HONORS
1926 Alpha Kappa Delta
1927 Sigma Tau Delta
1929 Phi Sigma Iota
1930 Sigma Pi Sigma
1939 Psi Chi
1959 Alpha Lambda Delta
1965 Kappa Mu Epsilon
1967 Phi Eta Sigma

1983 Omicron Delta Kappa

RECOGNITION
1927 Alpha Psi Omega
1960 Sigma Delta Psi
1962 Blue Key
1964 Society for Collegiate
     Journalists—Pi Delta
     Epsilon-Alpha Phi Gamma
     (A)

INACTIVE
1926   Eta Sigma Phi
1928   Beta Beta Beta
1929–60 Pi Gamma Mu
1954–85 Sigma Phi Epsilon
1955–87 Tau Kappa Epsilon
1957–79 Delta Zeta
1960–67 Phi Chi Theta

MORRIS COLLEGE Sumter, SC.

NIC MEN'S
1982 Kappa Alpha Psi (A)

NPHC MEN'S
     Phi Beta Sigma

NPHC WOMEN'S
1979 Alpha Kappa Alpha

1983 Sigma Gamma Rho

SERVICE
1985 Alpha Phi Omega

MORRIS BROWN COLLEGE Atlanta, GA. (African Methodist Episcopal); chartered 1885; part of Atlanta University Center.

NIC MEN'S
1937 Kappa Alpha Psi (A)

NPHC MEN'S
     Phi Beta Sigma
1910 Alpha Phi Alpha
1935 Omega Psi Phi

NPHC WOMEN'S
     Zeta Phi Beta
1942 Alpha Kappa Alpha
1942 Delta Sigma Theta (B)

1952 Sigma Gamma Rho

PROFESSIONAL
1973 Delta Omicron
1973 Phi Mu Alpha—Sinfonia

ACHS HONORS
1945 Alpha Kappa Mu
1976 Omicron Delta Kappa
1980 Phi Sigma Iota
1983 Phi Eta Sigma

MORRIS HARVEY COLLEGE Charleston, WV. Founded 1888 by Methodist Episcopal Church, South. Moved to Charleston in 1935 and in 1942 became an independent college. Four-year liberal arts college; coeducational.

College has a "live in" policy and does not permit fraternity and sorority houses at the present time.

ACHS HONORS
1964 Kappa Delta Pi
1965 Sigma Tau Delta
1970 Pi Delta Phi
1973 Sigma Delta Pi

RECOGNITION
1923 Chi Beta Phi

1948 Alpha Psi Omega
1956 Pi Kappa Delta

INACTIVE
1947–77 Theta Xi
1961–78 Alpha Omicron Pi
1965–83 Alpha Xi Delta

MOUNT HOLYOKE COLLEGE South Hadley, MA. Private control. Founded in 1837. Four-year; women's; liberal arts college.

99% of students live on campus. Single-sex dorms.

ACHS HONORS
     Omicron Delta Epsilon
1980 Psi Chi
1990 Phi Alpha Theta

OTHER HONORS
1967 Sigma Xi

MOUNT MARY COLLEGE Milwaukee, WI. College of liberal arts for women; private control (Roman Catholic) established 1872.

PROFESSIONAL
1948 Alpha Delta Theta

ACHS HONORS
1942 Delta Epsilon Sigma
1947 Kappa Mu Epsilon
1951 Sigma Tau Delta
1953 Phi Alpha Theta
1956 Lambda Iota Tau
1965 Alpha Kappa Delta
1986 Phi Alpha Theta

1989 Theta Alpha Kappa

OTHER HONORS
1956 Delta Phi Delta

RECOGNITION
1950 Eta Sigma Phi
1955 Alpha Psi Omega
1961 Beta Beta Beta

INACTIVE
1949–65 Kappa Omicron Nu

MOUNT ST. MARY'S COLLEGE Emmitsburg, MD. Four-year liberal arts college for men; founded 1808, second oldest Catholic college in the United States; private.

ACHS HONORS
1957 Lambda Iota Tau
1963 Phi Alpha Theta
1976 Psi Chi

1981 Phi Sigma Tau
1982 Theta Alpha Kappa
1990 Delta Mu Delta

MOUNT ST. MARY'S COLLEGE Los Angeles, CA. College of liberal arts for women; men admitted to music school, nursing school, and graduate school; private control (Roman Catholic); established 1925.

ACHS HONORS
1949 Pi Delta Phi
1955 Lambda Iota Tau
1959 Sigma Delta Pi
1964 Phi Alpha Theta
1975 Delta Mu Delta
1981 Pi Sigma Alpha

1984 Psi Chi

SERVICE
1981 Alpha Phi Omega

INACTIVE
1955–68 Sigma Alpha Iota
1972–80 Pi Gamma Mu

MOUNT UNION COLLEGE Alliance, OH. Founded by Orville Nelson Hartshorn in 1846; chartered by State of Ohio in 1858; pioneered summer school program in 1870. Coeducational; liberal arts college. Methodist-affiliated, nonsectarian in admissions.

Fraternities occupy houses on property which they own. Sorority houses serve as meeting places and headquarters for social affairs; the women are housed in the residence halls.

NIC MEN'S
1882 Alpha Tau Omega
1885 Sigma Alpha Epsilon
1915 Phi Kappa Tau

NPHC MEN'S
1974 Alpha Phi Alpha

NPC WOMEN'S
1903 Alpha Xi Delta
1914 Delta Delta Delta
1920 Alpha Chi Omega
1947 Alpha Delta Pi

PROFESSIONAL
1915 Mu Phi Epsilon

ACHS HONORS
     Omicron Delta Epsilon
1928 Phi Sigma
1934 Pi Gamma Mu
1947 Alpha Lambda Delta

1966 Lambda Sigma Society

SERVICE
1964 Alpha Phi Omega

RECOGNITION
1928 Alpha Psi Omega
1947 Sigma Delta Psi
1960 Blue Key
1963 Pi Kappa Delta

INACTIVE
1875–86 Delta Tau Delta
1882–08 Delta Gamma
1924–43 Kappa Delta
1929–60 Alpha Sigma Phi
1965–85 Phi Mu Alpha—
     Sinfonia

COLONIES
1986 Sigma Pi Sigma

MUHLENBERG COLLEGE Allentown, PA. College of liberal arts, coeducational; private control; Lutheran Church in America. Established as Allentown Seminary 1848; name changed to Muhlenberg College 1867.

Ownership of fraternity house and ground is by the fraternity or ownership is by college on rental basis to fraternity.

NIC MEN'S
1881 Alpha Tau Omega
1916 Phi Kappa Tau
1932 Zeta Beta Tau
1938 Sigma Phi Epsilon
1958 Tau Kappa Epsilon
1988 Alpha Epsilon Pi

NPC WOMEN'S
1932 Zeta Tau Alpha
1984 Alpha Chi Omega
1984 Delta Zeta
1984 Phi Sigma Sigma

ACHS HONORS
     Omicron Delta Epsilon
1928 Phi Sigma Iota
1929 Phi Alpha Theta
1930 Omicron Delta Kappa
1959 Psi Chi
1963 Sigma Tau Delta
1976 Pi Sigma Alpha

OTHER HONORS
     National Order of Omega
1968 Phi Beta Kappa

SERVICE
1962 Alpha Phi Omega

RECOGNITION
1930 Alpha Psi Omega
1932 Eta Sigma Phi
1953 Society for Collegiate Journalists—Pi Delta Epsilon-Alpha Phi Gamma (P)
1961 Delta Phi Alpha

INACTIVE
1867–94 Phi Gamma Delta
1868–85 Chi Phi
1927–53 Kappa Phi Kappa
1931–78 Lambda Chi Alpha
1949–55 Phi Sigma Kappa
1972–77 Sigma Pi Sigma

MUNDELEIN COLLEGE Chicago, IL. College of liberal arts for women; private control (Roman Catholic). Chartered 1930.

ACHS HONORS
1949 Delta Sigma Rho-Tau Kappa Alpha
1960 Pi Delta Phi
1971 Phi Alpha Theta

1974 Psi Chi
1982 Phi Sigma Tau

RECOGNITION
1963 Beta Beta Beta

MURRAY STATE UNIVERSITY Murray, KY. College of liberal arts and teachers college; coeducational; state control; established 1922 as normal school.

The administration permits fraternities and sororities to own and operate their own houses.

NIC MEN'S
1958 Pi Kappa Alpha
1959 Alpha Tau Omega
1959 Sigma Chi
1959 Tau Kappa Epsilon
1968 Alpha Gamma Rho
1968 Lambda Chi Alpha
1968 Sigma Pi
1969 Kappa Alpha Order
1969 Sigma Nu
1969 Sigma Phi Epsilon
1973 Delta Sigma Phi
1973 Kappa Alpha Psi (A)

NPHC MEN'S
     Phi Beta Sigma
1969 Alpha Phi Alpha

NPC WOMEN'S
1942 Sigma Sigma Sigma
1946 Alpha Sigma Alpha
1961 Alpha Omicron Pi
1966 Alpha Gamma Delta
1968 Alpha Delta Pi

NPHC WOMEN'S
1970 Delta Sigma Theta (B)
1971 Alpha Kappa Alpha

PROFESSIONAL
1938 Phi Mu Alpha—Sinfonia
1939 Sigma Alpha Iota
1966 Alpha Kappa Psi

OTHER PROFESSIONAL
1953 Alpha Beta Alpha
1960 Alpha Epsilon Rho
1973 Sigma Delta Chi

ACHS HONORS
1939 Kappa Delta Pi
1941 Delta Sigma Rho-Tau Kappa Alpha
1953 Pi Omega Pi
1961 Kappa Omicron Nu
1963 Sigma Pi Sigma
1965 Alpha Chi
1965 Psi Chi
1966 Gamma Theta Upsilon
1967 Alpha Lambda Delta
1968 Phi Alpha Theta
1968 Sigma Delta Pi
1970 Omicron Delta Kappa
1970 Pi Delta Phi
1974 Pi Sigma Alpha

OTHER HONORS
     National Order of Omega
1975 Pi Mu Epsilon

SERVICE
1964 Alpha Phi Omega

RECOGNITION
1930 Alpha Psi Omega
1947 Beta Beta Beta
1950 Kappa Pi
1956 Scabbard and Blade (13)

INACTIVE
1967–84 Kappa Delta
1978–90 Alpha Phi
1982–87 Phi Kappa Tau

COLONIES
Sigma Tau Gamma

MUSKINGUM COLLEGE New Concord, OH. College of liberal arts; coeducational; private control (United Presbyterian); chartered 1837.

NIC MEN'S
1966 Kappa Sigma
1971 Phi Kappa Tau

NPC WOMEN'S
1988 Theta Phi Alpha

ACHS HONORS
     Omicron Delta Epsilon
1912 Delta Sigma Rho-Tau
     Kappa Alpha
1926 Sigma Tau Delta
1928 Lambda Sigma Society
1947 Phi Alpha Theta
1948 Phi Sigma Iota
1966 Phi Sigma Tau
1968 Psi Chi
1969 Kappa Mu Epsilon

OTHER HONORS
1927 National Collegiate
     Players

RECOGNITION
1948 Sigma Delta Psi

INACTIVE
1928–50 Pi Gamma Mu
1928–61 Sigma Alpha Iota
1930–69 Phi Mu Alpha—
        Sinfonia
1940–82 Sigma Pi Sigma
1951–68 Alpha Epsilon Delta

COLONIES
1990 Tau Kappa Epsilon

NASHVILLE STATE TECHNICAL INSTITUTE Nashville, TN.

NPHC MEN'S
     Phi Beta Sigma

INACTIVE
1850–50 Phi Gamma Delta

1870–75 Phi Kappa Psi
1871–72 Alpha Tau Omega

NATIONAL COLLEGE OF EDUCATION Evanston, IL. Liberal arts college and teacher education; coeducational; private control; nonsectarian; established 1886.

ACHS HONORS
1955 Kappa Delta Pi

INACTIVE
1974–82 Alpha Kappa Alpha

NAZARETH COLLEGE OF ROCHESTER Rochester, NY. An independent, coeducational, liberal arts college that offers up-to-date career programs solidly based in the liberal arts. Its suburban campus is located in Pittsford in western upstate New York, approximately seven miles from Rochester. Founded in 1924, the college has conferred over 11,000 baccalaureate and master's degrees.

PROFESSIONAL
1966 Mu Phi Epsilon

ACHS HONORS
1954 Lambda Iota Tau
1959 Pi Gamma Mu

1965 Pi Delta Phi
1979 Psi Chi

RECOGNITION
1959 Beta Beta Beta

UNIVERSITY OF NEBRASKA Lincoln, NB. A land-grant college established in February, 1869, by an act of state legislature. State university; undergraduate and graduate colleges. Coeducational.

The fraternities and sororities occupy houses and land of their ownership. Four fraternities and sororities rent houses.

NIC MEN'S
1875 Phi Delta Theta
1883 Sigma Chi
1888 Beta Theta Pi
1893 Delta Tau Delta
1893 Sigma Alpha Epsilon
1895 Phi Kappa Psi
1897 Alpha Tau Omega
1897 Kappa Sigma
1898 Delta Upsilon
1898 Phi Gamma Delta
1905 Acacia
1909 Sigma Nu
1911 FarmHouse
1911 Sigma Phi Epsilon
1915 Pi Kappa Phi
1916 Kappa Alpha Psi (A)
1917 Alpha Gamma Rho
1921 Lambda Chi Alpha
1925 Tau Kappa Epsilon
1925 Theta Chi
1926 Sigma Alpha Mu
1927 Theta Xi
1929 Beta Sigma Psi
1932 Chi Phi
1953 Alpha Gamma Sigma
1963 Triangle

NPC WOMEN'S
1884 Kappa Kappa Gamma
1887 Kappa Alpha Theta
1888 Delta Gamma
1894 Delta Delta Delta
1895 Pi Beta Phi
1903 Alpha Omicron Pi
1903 Chi Omega
1906 Alpha Phi
1907 Alpha Chi Omega
1912 Alpha Xi Delta
1914 Gamma Phi Beta
1915 Alpha Delta Pi
1920 Kappa Delta
1921 Phi Mu

NPHC WOMEN'S
1922 Delta Sigma Theta (B)

PROFESSIONAL
1895 Phi Delta Phi
1901 Phi Rho Sigma
1914 Alpha Kappa Psi
1915 Phi Alpha Delta
1915 Sigma Alpha Iota
1916 Phi Chi
1919 Mu Phi Epsilon
1920 Kappa Psi
1921 Delta Omicron
1921 Kappa Epsilon
1921 Phi Mu Alpha—Sinfonia
1922 Delta Theta Phi
1924 Delta Sigma Pi
1927 Phi Chi Theta

OTHER PROFESSIONAL
1904 Alpha Zeta
1914 Sigma Delta Chi
1916 Women in Communications
1923 Pi Lambda Theta
1925 Alpha Tau Alpha
1925 Phi Upsilon Omicron
1930 Phi Epsilon Kappa
1945 Kappa Beta Pi
1946 Alpha Epsilon Rho
1966 Delta Pi Epsilon
1980 Sigma Nu Phi

ACHS HONORS
     Omicron Delta Epsilon

1906 Delta Sigma Rho-Tau
     Kappa Alpha
1914 Kappa Omicron Nu
1920 Pi Kappa Lambda
1921 Mortar Board
1924 Beta Gamma Sigma
1929 Psi Chi
1931 Alpha Lambda Delta
1931 Pi Sigma Alpha
1936 Alpha Kappa Delta
1938 Phi Sigma Iota
1938 Pi Tau Sigma
1943 Rho Chi
1947 Kappa Tau Alpha
1948 Alpha Lambda Delta
1949 Eta Kappa Nu
1951 Pi Gamma Mu
1952 Gamma Theta Upsilon
1957 Phi Alpha Theta
1960 Phi Eta Sigma
1961 Chi Epsilon
1962 Phi Sigma Tau
1965 Psi Chi
1965 Tau Sigma Delta
1966 Alpha Epsilon
1974 Alpha Pi Mu
1974 Tau Beta Pi

OTHER HONORS
1895 Phi Beta Kappa
1897 Sigma Xi
1904 Order of the Coif
1914 Alpha Omega Alpha
1918 Gamma Sigma Delta
1924 National Collegiate
     Players
1928 Pi Mu Epsilon
1930 Omicron Kappa Upsilon
1936 Delta Phi Delta

SERVICE
1935 Alpha Phi Omega

RECOGNITION
     Angel Flight
     Arnold Air Society (F-2)
1919 National Block and Bridle
     Club
1922 Phi Lambda Upsilon
1925 Sigma Delta Psi
1927 Sigma Delta Epsilon
1933 Lambda Delta Lambda
1936 Lambda Delta Lambda
1957 Delta Phi Alpha
1958 Kappa Pi
1960 Phi Delta Gamma
1962 Lambda Tau
1967 Sigma Phi Alpha

INACTIVE
1905–71 Xi Psi Phi
1907   Phi Alpha Tau
1909–34 Alpha Chi Sigma
1909–53 Delta Chi
1910–71 Delta Zeta
1912   Iota Sigma Pi
1912–24 Phi Delta Chi
1913   Delta Sigma Delta
1913–50 Alpha Sigma Phi
1917   Sigma Gamma Epsilon
1920–39 Phi Beta Pi and Theta
        Kappa Psi (a)
1921   Scabbard and Blade
        (3)
1921–55 Alpha Kappa Kappa
1922–62 Zeta Beta Tau
1922–62 Zeta Tau Alpha
1923–73 Sigma Kappa

1924-37 Theta Phi Alpha
1924-77 Pi Kappa Alpha
1925-34 Phi Kappa Theta
1925-40 Phi Sigma Kappa
1925-70 Sigma Delta Tau
1925-84 Delta Sigma Phi

1927-51 Alpha Kappa Alpha
1927-58 Alpha Phi Alpha
1927-80 Zeta Tau Alpha
1944-54 Phi Delta Epsilon
1947-60 Kappa Alpha Mu
1964-65 Sigma Pi Sigma

UNIVERSITY OF NEBRASKA SCHOOL OF TECHNICAL AGRICULTURE Curtis, NE.

NIC MEN'S
1985 FarmHouse

UNIVERSITY OF NEBRASKA AT OMAHA
Omaha, NB. University; coeducational; state control. Incorporated 1908 as University of Omaha; became municipal 1928 by act of Nebraska legislature; became affiliated with the University of Nebraska in 1968.

NIC MEN'S
Tau Kappa Epsilon
1950 Theta Chi
1951 Sigma Phi Epsilon
1952 Pi Kappa Alpha
1954 Lambda Chi Alpha
1956 Tau Kappa Epsilon
1974 Sigma Nu

NPC WOMEN'S
1949 Chi Omega
1950 Alpha Xi Delta
1950 Sigma Kappa
1950 Zeta Tau Alpha

PROFESSIONAL
1951 Phi Mu Alpha—Sinfonia
1959 Phi Chi Theta

OTHER PROFESSIONAL
1973 Sigma Delta Chi

ACHS HONORS
Omicron Delta Epsilon

1934 Phi Alpha Theta
1948 Phi Eta Sigma
1950 Omicron Delta Kappa
1964 Gamma Theta Upsilon
1966 Phi Kappa Phi
1988 Chi Epsilon

SERVICE
1934 Alpha Phi Omega

RECOGNITION
1974 Beta Beta Beta

INACTIVE
1949-78 Delta Sigma Pi
1950-55 Zeta Beta Tau
1950-55 Zeta Tau Alpha
1967-72 Alpha Epsilon Pi
1970-76 Gamma Phi Beta
1972-77 Sigma Pi Sigma
1972-87 Sigma Tau Gamma
1972-90 Pi Kappa Phi
1977-79 Acacia

NEBRASKA WESLEYAN UNIVERSITY Lincoln, NB. College of liberal arts; coeducational; private control (Methodist); chartered 1887.

NIC MEN'S
1923 Phi Kappa Tau
1949 Theta Chi
1957 Tau Kappa Epsilon
1958 Zeta Psi

NPC WOMEN'S
1927 Alpha Gamma Delta
1942 Delta Zeta

NPHC WOMEN'S
1976 Sigma Gamma Rho

PROFESSIONAL
1968 Mu Phi Epsilon

ACHS HONORS
Omicron Delta Epsilon
1913 Phi Kappa Phi
1926 Pi Gamma Mu
1930 Psi Chi
1947 Sigma Pi Sigma

1956 Kappa Delta Pi
1972 Phi Alpha Theta
1986 Kappa Mu Epsilon

OTHER HONORS
National Order of Omega

RECOGNITION
1913 Pi Kappa Delta
1923 Theta Alpha Phi
1927 Blue Key
1948 Cardinal Key
1964 Beta Beta Beta

INACTIVE
1923-33 Sigma Alpha Iota
1939-84 Phi Mu
1968-80 Alpha Kappa Lambda
1969-84 Phi Mu Alpha—Sinfonia

UNIVERSITY OF NEVADA Reno, NV. Established in Elko, NV, in 1864. Land-grant institution. Moved to Reno 1874. First classes enrolled for sessions 1887 in Morrill Hall. Has a division in Las Vegas. Coeducational, undergraduate and graduate school. Master's and doctoral programs offered in certain colleges.

Fraternities and sororities are housed in dwellings and on land which they themselves own.

NIC MEN'S
1914 Sigma Nu
1917 Phi Sigma Kappa
1917 Sigma Alpha Epsilon
1921 Alpha Tau Omega
1929 Lambda Chi Alpha
1972 Phi Delta Theta
1982 Tau Kappa Epsilon
1988 Pi Kappa Alpha
1988 Sigma Pi

NPC WOMEN'S
1913 Delta Delta Delta
1915 Pi Beta Phi
1921 Gamma Phi Beta
1922 Kappa Alpha Theta
1971 Alpha Chi Omega

NPHC WOMEN'S
1970 Delta Sigma Theta (B)

OTHER WOMEN'S
Lambda Delta Sigma

PROFESSIONAL
1959 Delta Sigma Pi
1985 Phi Alpha Delta
1989 Phi Mu Alpha—Sinfonia

OTHER PROFESSIONAL
1947 Sigma Delta Chi
1963 Alpha Zeta

ACHS HONORS
Omicron Delta Epsilon
1912 Phi Kappa Phi
1936 Kappa Tau Alpha
1938 Alpha Epsilon Delta
1945 Phi Alpha Theta
1948 Delta Sigma Rho-Tau Kappa Alpha

1950 Psi Chi
1958 Sigma Pi Sigma
1962 Beta Gamma Sigma
1964 Pi Sigma Alpha
1967 Sigma Delta Pi
1970 Pi Delta Phi
1973 Gamma Theta Upsilon
1974 Tau Beta Pi
1979 Phi Sigma Iota
1982 Eta Kappa Nu
1987 Kappa Omicron Nu

OTHER HONORS
1955 Pi Mu Epsilon
1966 Gamma Sigma Delta
1969 Sigma Xi

SERVICE
The National Spurs
1969 Alpha Phi Omega

RECOGNITION
1926 Blue Key
1948 Sigma Delta Psi

INACTIVE
1924-36 Sigma Gamma Epsilon
1929 Scabbard and Blade (7)
1931-55 Chi Delta Phi
1942-71 Theta Chi
1949-58 Beta Beta Beta
1950-51 Delta Sigma Phi
1962-63 Sigma Phi Epsilon

COLONIES
1989 Delta Chi

UNIVERSITY OF NEVADA AT LAS VEGAS Las Vegas, NV. Established 1855 as the Southern Regional Division of the University of Nevada; became university 1965; coeducational; undergraduate and graduate programs.

No fraternity housing is available; fraternities are encouraged to live in the residence hall.

NIC MEN'S
1967 Kappa Sigma
1968 Alpha Epsilon Pi
1968 Alpha Tau Omega
1969 Delta Sigma Phi
1969 Sigma Chi
1975 Sigma Nu
1976 Kappa Alpha Psi (A)
1982 Tau Kappa Epsilon
1985 Sigma Alpha Epsilon
1987 Sigma Phi Epsilon

NPHC MEN'S
Phi Beta Sigma

NPC WOMEN'S
1968 Alpha Delta Pi
1968 Delta Zeta
1984 Zeta Tau Alpha
1987 Sigma Kappa
1989 Alpha Gamma Delta

NPHC WOMEN'S
1976 Alpha Kappa Alpha

PROFESSIONAL
1967 Phi Gamma Nu
1989 Delta Sigma Pi
1989 Kappa Delta Epsilon

ACHS HONORS
      Omicron Delta Epsilon
1967 Phi Kappa Phi
1969 Gamma Theta Upsilon
1970 Psi Chi
1971 Kappa Delta Pi
1976 Alpha Epsilon Delta

NEW ENGLAND COLLEGE   Henniker, NH.

NIC MEN'S
1983 Sigma Phi Epsilon

INACTIVE
1979–83 Phi Sigma Sigma

NEW ENGLAND CONSERVATORY OF MUSIC
Boston, MA. Established in 1867. The oldest private conservatory in the United States; grants Bachelor of Music and Master of Music degrees.

There are no fraternity or sorority houses; however, there is no administrative policy prohibiting such housing.

PROFESSIONAL
1903 Mu Phi Epsilon
1915 Sigma Alpha Iota
1950 Delta Omicron

ACHS HONORS
1927 Pi Kappa Lambda

INACTIVE
1895–50 Alpha Chi Omega
1898–70 Phi Mu Alpha—
         Sinfonia

NEW ENGLAND SCHOOL OF LAW   Boston, MA.

PROFESSIONAL
1920 Phi Alpha Delta

1970 Delta Theta Phi
1972 Delta Theta Phi

UNIVERSITY OF NEW HAMPSHIRE   Durham, NH. Founded first in 1866 at Dartmouth College in Hanover. Moved to Durham 1892 as the New Hampshire College of Agriculture and Mechanic Arts. Became the state university 1923. A land-grant and sea-grant institution. Composed of the colleges and Life Sciences and Agriculture, Engineering and Physical Sciences, Liberal Arts, School of Health Studies, Whittemore School of Business and Economics, Thompson School of Applied Science (two-year Associate degree program), and a graduate school. Coeducational; state-supported; nonsectarian.

Sorority and fraternity membership is at 10% and 21% respectively. Greek societies own housing and land or rent off-campus facilities. All sororities but one have dining programs; fraternities have dining programs or use one of several university dining plans.

NIC MEN'S
1901 Kappa Sigma
1910 Theta Chi
1917 Alpha Tau Omega
1917 Sigma Alpha Epsilon
1918 Lambda Chi Alpha
1924 Alpha Gamma Rho

1924 Phi Kappa Theta
1929 Pi Kappa Alpha
1949 Acacia
1983 Phi Delta Theta
1984 Sigma Phi Epsilon
1986 Delta Chi

1978 Phi Alpha Theta
1978 Pi Sigma Alpha

OTHER HONORS
      National Order of Omega
1972 Sigma Gamma Epsilon

INACTIVE
1967–73 Phi Mu

COLONIES
      Lambda Chi Alpha
1989 Phi Delta Theta

NPC WOMEN'S
1914 Alpha Xi Delta
1915 Chi Omega
1919 Phi Mu
1924 Alpha Chi Omega
1962 Delta Zeta
1986 Alpha Phi

OTHER PROFESSIONAL
1903 Alpha Zeta
1945 Phi Upsilon Omicron

ACHS HONORS
      Omicron Delta Epsilon
1922 Phi Kappa Phi
1926 Delta Sigma Rho-Tau
      Kappa Alpha
1926 Phi Sigma
1938 Mortar Board
1939 Alpha Kappa Delta
1941 Pi Gamma Mu
1949 Alpha Epsilon Delta
1949 Psi Chi
1950 Tau Beta Pi
1954 Pi Sigma Alpha
1966 Xi Sigma Pi
1969 Sigma Delta Pi
1974 Pi Omega Pi
1978 Phi Alpha Theta
1981 Phi Sigma Iota

OTHER HONORS
      National Order of Omega
1948 Pi Mu Epsilon
1952 Phi Beta Kappa
1954 Sigma Xi

SERVICE
1949 Alpha Phi Omega

RECOGNITION
      Angel Flight
      Arnold Air Society (A-1)
1966 Delta Phi Alpha

INACTIVE
1911–71 Alpha Chi Sigma
1918–81 Phi Mu Delta
1924–62 Zeta Beta Tau
1924–62 Zeta Tau Alpha
1926   Scabbard and Blade
         (6)
1928–65 Kappa Delta Pi
1929–62 Kappa Delta
1931–34 Alpha Sigma Phi
1932–89 Tau Kappa Epsilon
1950–57 Sigma Pi Sigma
1970–75 Alpha Epsilon Pi
1979–83 Phi Chi Theta

COLONIES
      Phi Kappa Sigma

NEW HAMPSHIRE COLLEGE   Manchester, NH.
College of liberal arts and general studies; teacher preparatory; professional; independent control; coeducational. Established 1932.

NIC MEN'S
1973 Kappa Sigma

OTHER PROFESSIONAL
1968 Kappa Delta Phi (C)

ACHS HONORS
1978 Delta Mu Delta

SERVICE
1977 Alpha Phi Omega

INACTIVE
1979–86 Alpha Phi

UNIVERSITY OF NEW HAVEN   New Haven, CT.
Private, independent, coeducational university with schools of arts and sciences; business; engineering; hotel, restaurant and tourism administration; and professional studies. Established 1920.

NIC MEN'S
1969 Zeta Beta Tau
1981 Delta Chi

NPC WOMEN'S
1969 Zeta Tau Alpha

ACHS HONORS
1969 Alpha Chi
1973 Pi Tau Sigma
1974 Eta Kappa Nu
1975 Phi Alpha Theta

1976 Psi Chi
1984 Alpha Lambda Delta

SERVICE
1964 Alpha Phi Omega

RECOGNITION
1975 Beta Beta Beta

INACTIVE
1969–83 Tau Kappa Epsilon

NEW JERSEY INSTITUTE OF TECHNOLOGY
Newark, NJ. Founded in 1881 by board of trade of Newark and civic-minded citizens. Undergraduate and graduate coeducational engineering and architecture education; public support; nonsectarian.

The fraternities either own houses on their own land or rent them from private owners.

NIC MEN'S
1921 Alpha Sigma Phi
1938 Sigma Pi
1947 Tau Delta Phi
1947 Tau Epsilon Phi
1948 Pi Kappa Phi
1952 Alpha Phi Delta
1963 Theta Chi
1965 Tau Kappa Epsilon

NPHC MEN'S
Phi Beta Sigma
1974 Alpha Phi Alpha

NPC WOMEN'S
1983 Alpha Sigma Tau

ACHS HONORS
1941 Tau Beta Pi
1950 Omicron Delta Kappa
1952 Phi Eta Sigma
1953 Eta Kappa Nu
1957 Omega Chi Epsilon
1958 Chi Epsilon

OTHER HONORS
1976 Sigma Xi

SERVICE
1953 Alpha Phi Omega

RECOGNITION
1971 Pi Kappa Delta

COLLEGE OF MEDICINE AND DENTISTRY OF NEW JERSEY Newark, NJ. Incorporated in 1954 as the Seton Hall College of Medicine and Dentistry; in 1965 became College of Medicine and Dentistry of New Jersey, a state supported institution. Class of 1965 was first to receive Doctor of Dental Medicine degree which replaced Doctor of Dental Surgery degree.

PROFESSIONAL
1958 Psi Omega
1959 Alpha Omega

OTHER HONORS
1977 Alpha Omega Alpha

INACTIVE
1824–25 Chi Phi

UNIVERSITY OF NEW MEXICO Albuquerque, NM. University; coeducational; state control; chartered 1889; first instruction 1892.

The fraternities and sororities own their houses on premises which they own with the exception of one fraternity and three sororities which have houses on university-owned land.

NIC MEN'S
1915 Pi Kappa Alpha
1916 Sigma Chi
1925 Kappa Sigma
1929 Kappa Alpha Order
1929 Sigma Phi Epsilon
1946 Sigma Alpha Epsilon
1949 Lambda Chi Alpha
1966 Phi Gamma Delta
1969 Alpha Tau Omega
1989 Phi Delta Theta

NPHC MEN'S
1965 Omega Psi Phi

NPC WOMEN'S
1918 Alpha Chi Omega
1918 Kappa Kappa Gamma
1925 Chi Omega
1946 Pi Beta Phi
1949 Delta Delta Delta
1983 Zeta Tau Alpha

NPHC WOMEN'S
1970 Delta Sigma Theta (B)

PROFESSIONAL
1935 Sigma Alpha Iota
1948 Kappa Psi
1949 Delta Sigma Pi
1968 Kappa Epsilon
1972 Delta Theta Phi

OTHER PROFESSIONAL
1939 Pi Lambda Theta
1949 Sigma Delta Chi

ACHS HONORS
Omicron Delta Epsilon
Pi Alpha Alpha
1916 Phi Kappa Phi
1929 Pi Sigma Alpha
1935 Kappa Mu Epsilon
1935 Phi Sigma
1936 Kappa Omicron Nu
1936 Mortar Board
1936 Phi Alpha Theta
1938 Delta Sigma Rho-Tau Kappa Alpha
1940 Alpha Kappa Delta
1948 Phi Sigma Iota
1948 Pi Tau Sigma
1951 Chi Epsilon
1955 Phi Sigma Tau
1962 Eta Kappa Nu
1968 Rho Chi
1969 Gamma Theta Upsilon
1973 Phi Eta Sigma
1974 Alpha Sigma Mu
1974 Tau Beta Pi
1975 Pi Sigma Alpha
1981 Psi Chi
1987 Kappa Tau Alpha

OTHER HONORS
National Order of Omega
1953 Sigma Gamma Epsilon
1954 Sigma Xi
1965 Phi Beta Kappa
1968 Alpha Omega Alpha
1971 Order of the Coif

SERVICE
The National Spurs
1947 Alpha Phi Omega
1969 Gamma Sigma Sigma

RECOGNITION
Angel Flight
Arnold Air Society (I)
1957 Blue Key

INACTIVE
1911–78 Phi Mu
1920–82 Alpha Delta Pi

1928–40 Pi Gamma Mu
1928–45 Theta Alpha Phi
1936 Delta Phi Delta
1946–82 Phi Delta Theta
1947–55 Kappa Alpha Mu
1947–65 Alpha Epsilon Pi
1948–54 Phi Kappa Tau
1948–70 Alpha Kappa Psi
1948–78 Kappa Alpha Theta
1949 Phi Gamma Nu
1950–64 Tau Kappa Epsilon
1961–73 Delta Gamma
1961–73 Pi Kappa Lambda
1961–74 Phi Mu Alpha—Sinfonia
1963–77 Phi Sigma Kappa
1968–72 Alpha Kappa Lambda

COLONIES
1947 Delta Sigma Phi

NEW MEXICO HIGHLANDS UNIVERSITY Las Vegas, NM. University; teachers college; coeducational; state control; chartered as a normal school 1898.

ACHS HONORS
1933 Phi Sigma Iota
1948 Psi Chi
1960 Delta Sigma Rho-Tau Kappa Alpha
1965 Phi Eta Sigma
1969 Phi Kappa Phi
1973 Phi Alpha Theta
1974 Sigma Pi Sigma

SERVICE
The National Spurs

RECOGNITION
1930 Alpha Psi Omega

1950 Kappa Pi

INACTIVE
1919–78 Delta Zeta
1921–64 Sigma Sigma Sigma
1942–78 Pi Omega Pi
1951–83 Pi Gamma Mu
1964–75 Tau Kappa Epsilon
1968–72 Pi Lambda Phi
1968–74 Alpha Sigma Alpha
1970–75 Phi Kappa Tau
1971–75 Sigma Alpha Epsilon
1974 Sigma Gamma Epsilon

NEW MEXICO STATE UNIVERSITY Las Cruces, NM. University; land-grant college. Established as Las Cruces College in 1888; chartered as New Mexico College of Agriculture and Mechanic Arts in 1889; name changed to the current one in 1958. Colleges of arts and sciences, agriculture and home economics, business administration and economics, engineering, education, and human and community services; and the graduate school.

Two fraternities and five sororities now lease university-owned houses on campus.

NIC MEN'S
1934 Tau Kappa Epsilon
1941 Sigma Alpha Epsilon
1946 Lambda Chi Alpha
1948 Phi Kappa Tau
1948 Theta Chi
1951 Alpha Gamma Rho
1973 Sigma Nu
1976 Alpha Tau Omega
1977 Kappa Alpha Psi (A)
1987 FarmHouse
1990 Kappa Sigma

NPC WOMEN'S
1928 Zeta Tau Alpha
1939 Chi Omega
1949 Delta Zeta
1972 Pi Beta Phi

1979 Alpha Chi Omega

NPHC WOMEN'S
1975 Delta Sigma Theta (B)

PROFESSIONAL
1954 Kappa Kappa Psi
1956 Tau Beta Sigma
1963 Delta Sigma Pi
1971 Phi Gamma Nu

OTHER PROFESSIONAL
1927 Alpha Zeta
1969 Sigma Delta Chi
1974 Beta Alpha Psi

ACHS HONORS
Omicron Delta Epsilon
1947 Sigma Delta Pi

1955 Sigma Delta Pi
1959 Eta Kappa Nu
1960 Sigma Pi Sigma
1962 Phi Kappa Phi
1967 Mortar Board
1968 Chi Epsilon
1968 Gamma Theta Upsilon
1970 Phi Alpha Theta
1972 Alpha Pi Mu
1974 Tau Beta Pi
1979 Omega Chi Epsilon

OTHER HONORS
    National Order of Omega
1957 Sigma Xi
1960 Pi Mu Epsilon
1975 Sigma Gamma Epsilon

SERVICE
    The National Spurs
1954 Alpha Phi Omega

RECOGNITION
    Angel Flight
    Arnold Air Society (I)
1932 Blue Key
1936 Sigma Delta Psi
1956 Blue Key
1957 Beta Beta Beta
1964 Pi Kappa Delta

INACTIVE
    Lambda Delta Sigma
1955–86 Sigma Pi
1957–72 Pi Gamma Mu
1961–73 Alpha Kappa Lambda
1962–77 Psi Chi
1964–72 Phi Mu Alpha—
    Sinfonia
1968–85 Sigma Chi

COLONIES
1990 Phi Kappa Tau

UNIVERSITY OF NEW ORLEANS Lakefront,
New Orleans, LA. Established by legislative act as a
metropolitan campus of the Louisiana State University system, starting operations in 1958. Two campus sites on Lakeshore Drive totaling 300 acres.
Undergraduate studies offered by colleges of liberal
arts, sciences, business administration, education
and engineering.

NIC MEN'S
1961 Tau Kappa Epsilon
1963 Theta Xi
1964 Lambda Chi Alpha
1971 Phi Kappa Sigma
1983 Kappa Alpha Psi (A)

NPHC MEN'S
    Phi Beta Sigma

NPC WOMEN'S
1962 Alpha Xi Delta
1962 Sigma Kappa
1963 Delta Zeta

NPHC WOMEN'S
1976 Delta Sigma Theta (B)

PROFESSIONAL
1962 Delta Sigma Pi
1963 Phi Chi Theta
1974 Mu Phi Epsilon

OTHER PROFESSIONAL
1971 Beta Alpha Psi

ACHS HONORS
    Omicron Delta Epsilon

1962 Psi Chi
1967 Phi Eta Sigma
1969 Beta Gamma Sigma
1969 Sigma Pi Sigma
1970 Phi Kappa Phi
1971 Omicron Delta Kappa
1971 Pi Sigma Alpha
1980 Gamma Theta Upsilon

OTHER HONORS
    National Order of Omega
1972 Sigma Gamma Epsilon

SERVICE
1986 Alpha Phi Omega

RECOGNITION
1969 Beta Beta Beta

INACTIVE
–69   Sigma Tau Delta
1966–72 Sigma Alpha Mu
1971–85 Alpha Lambda Delta

COLLEGE OF NEW ROCHELLE New Rochelle, NY.

ACHS HONORS
1971 Sigma Delta Pi
1975 Psi Chi
1978 Theta Alpha Kappa

1980 Phi Sigma Iota

RECOGNITION
1962 Beta Beta Beta

NEW YORK INSTITUTE OF TECHNOLOGY Old
Westbury, NY. Teacher Preparatory; professional;
coeducational. Independent control. Established
1955.

NIC MEN'S
1925 Lambda Chi Alpha
1971 Tau Kappa Epsilon
1972 Delta Sigma Phi
1989 Delta Sigma Phi
1990 Alpha Chi Rho
1990 Kappa Delta Rho

NPC WOMEN'S
1990 Theta Phi Alpha

ACHS HONORS
    Omicron Delta Epsilon
1960 Omega Chi Epsilon
1971 Delta Mu Delta
1971 Sigma Pi Sigma
1974 Psi Chi
1984 Psi Chi

INACTIVE
1970–83 Alpha Epsilon Pi

NEW YORK LAW SCHOOL New York, NY.

PROFESSIONAL
1899 Phi Delta Phi
1968 Phi Alpha Delta

INACTIVE
1902–07 Delta Chi
1907–55 Delta Theta Phi

NEW YORK MEDICAL COLLEGE Valhalla, NY.

NIC MEN'S
1914 Tau Delta Phi

OTHER PROFESSIONAL
1913 Phi Delta Epsilon
1929 Phi Lambda Kappa

OTHER HONORS
1957 Alpha Omega Alpha

INACTIVE
1937–69 Alpha Kappa Kappa
1948   Phi Chi

NEW YORK UNIVERSITY New York, NY.
Founded by Albert Gallatin and others and chartered in 1831. University; undergraduate and graduate schools coeducational; private control;
nonsectarian. Metropolitan university of 13 colleges, schools, and divisions at five major centers in
Manhattan. The University Heights Center, one of
the six main original divisions, situated at 181st
Street and University Avenue, The Bronx, was
closed in 1972.

NIC MEN'S
1841 Delta Phi
1847 Zeta Psi
1892 Phi Gamma Delta
1913 Alpha Epsilon Pi
1914 Tau Delta Phi
1917 Theta Chi
1921 Alpha Phi Delta
1930 Alpha Phi Delta
1930 Sigma Phi Epsilon
1943 Tau Delta Phi
1949 Sigma Alpha Mu

NPC WOMEN'S
1917 Alpha Epsilon Phi
1917 Delta Phi Epsilon

PROFESSIONAL
1904 Alpha Kappa Psi
1907 Delta Sigma Pi
1909 Phi Alpha Delta
1911 Alpha Omega
1924 Phi Chi Theta
1954 Sigma Alpha Iota

OTHER PROFESSIONAL
1924 Pi Lambda Theta
1926 Beta Alpha Psi
1930 Kappa Phi Kappa
1936 Delta Pi Epsilon
1975 Alpha Epsilon Rho

ACHS HONORS
    Omicron Delta Epsilon
1930 Kappa Delta Pi
1932 Alpha Kappa Delta
1933 Psi Chi

1937 Sigma Pi Sigma
1938 Eta Kappa Nu
1943 Pi Tau Sigma
1946 Kappa Tau Alpha
1950 Pi Sigma Alpha
1960 Alpha Sigma Mu
1968 Phi Alpha Theta
1971 Beta Gamma Sigma
1975 Pi Tau Sigma
1984 Pi Kappa Lambda

OTHER HONORS
1923 Alpha Omega Alpha
1926 Sigma Xi
1930 Omicron Kappa Upsilon
1958 Order of the Coif
1964 Pi Mu Epsilon

SERVICE
1938 Alpha Phi Omega
1953 Gamma Sigma Sigma

RECOGNITION
    Angel Flight
1922 Eta Mu Pi
1926 Scabbard and Blade (6)
1935 Phi Lambda Upsilon
1939 Eta Mu Pi
1956 Iota Tau Tau
1959 Rho Epsilon
1962 Blue Key

INACTIVE
1835–39 Alpha Delta Phi
1835–48 Sigma Phi Society
1837–89 Psi Upsilon
1847–53 Delta-Psi

1865–45 Delta Upsilon
1891–43 Delta Chi
1893–72 Xi Psi Phi
1896–73 Pi Lambda Phi
1900–61 Alpha Omicron Pi
1902–34 Delta Sigma Phi
1912–32 Pi Kappa Alpha
1916–16 Delta Theta Phi
1918–63 Phi Sigma Sigma
1923   Phi Beta Pi and Theta
            Kappa Psi (B)
1924–43 Phi Kappa Tau
1928–80 Phi Mu Alpha—
            Sinfonia
1931–37 Pi Gamma Mu
1931–74 Tau Beta Pi
1935–37 Phi Mu Delta

1935–69 Delta Zeta
1941–64 Pi Omega Pi
1949–71 Alpha Pi Mu
1951–66 Pi Lambda Phi
1952–69 Kappa Delta Epsilon
1954–73 Chi Epsilon
1955   Sigma Mu Sigma
1955–65 Phi Delta Epsilon
1960–70 Sigma Delta Tau
1960–73 Sigma Pi Sigma
1961–72 Zeta Tau Alpha
1962–65 Alpha Epsilon Phi

COLONIES
1905 Kappa Sigma
1989 Tau Kappa Epsilon
1990 Kappa Sigma

Washington Square Center New York, NY.

ACHS HONORS
1912 Delta Sigma Rho-Tau
      Kappa Alpha

STATE UNIVERSITY OF NEW YORK New York, NY. First normal school in the state. Oldest unit and one of four University centers for graduate and undergraduate studies. Coeducational; state control; chartered 1844.

NPHC WOMEN'S
1990 Sigma Gamma Rho

ACHS HONORS
1971 Sigma Delta Pi

RECOGNITION
1928 Sigma Delta Epsilon

STATE UNIVERSITY OF NEW YORK AT ALBANY Albany, NY.

NIC MEN'S
1981 Kappa Alpha Psi (A)
1985 Pi Lambda Phi
1986 Alpha Epsilon Pi
1986 Sigma Alpha Mu
1986 Tau Epsilon Phi
1986 Tau Kappa Epsilon
1986 Zeta Beta Tau
1987 Sigma Phi Epsilon
1988 Sigma Chi
1989 Phi Kappa Sigma
1990 Sigma Alpha Epsilon
1990 Sigma Pi

NPHC MEN'S
      Phi Beta Sigma

NPC WOMEN'S
1917 Alpha Epsilon Phi
1985 Sigma Delta Tau
1986 Delta Phi Epsilon
1987 Phi Sigma Sigma
1989 Alpha Omicron Pi
1989 Alpha Phi

NPHC WOMEN'S
1981 Alpha Kappa Alpha

PROFESSIONAL
1967 Delta Sigma Pi
1974 Phi Gamma Nu

OTHER PROFESSIONAL
1963 Delta Pi Epsilon

ACHS HONORS
      Omicron Delta Epsilon
      Pi Alpha Alpha
1942 Pi Omega Pi
1951 Delta Sigma Rho-Tau
      Kappa Alpha
1960 Sigma Pi Sigma
1966 Psi Chi
1967 Alpha Kappa Delta
1967 Pi Sigma Alpha
1969 Gamma Theta Upsilon
1969 Pi Delta Phi
1969 Sigma Delta Pi
1976 Phi Alpha Theta

OTHER HONORS
1969 Pi Mu Epsilon
1974 Phi Beta Kappa

INACTIVE
1927–71 Pi Gamma Mu
1957–69 Kappa Mu Epsilon
1960–66 Kappa Delta Epsilon

COLONIES
1915 Kappa Delta Rho
1988 Theta Chi
1990 Chi Phi

STATE UNIVERSITY OF NEW YORK AT BINGHAMTON Binghamton, NY.

NIC MEN'S
1970 Tau Epsilon Phi
1985 Alpha Epsilon Pi
1985 Kappa Alpha Psi (A)
1986 Sigma Alpha Epsilon
1986 Sigma Alpha Mu
1986 Sigma Phi Epsilon
1987 Tau Kappa Epsilon
1987 Zeta Beta Tau
1990 Pi Lambda Phi

NPHC MEN'S
      Phi Beta Sigma

NPC WOMEN'S
1985 Alpha Epsilon Phi
1985 Delta Phi Epsilon
1985 Phi Sigma Sigma
1985 Sigma Delta Tau
1987 Alpha Phi
1987 Alpha Xi Delta

NPHC WOMEN'S
1984 Alpha Kappa Alpha
1989 Sigma Gamma Rho

PROFESSIONAL
1981 Delta Sigma Pi

ACHS HONORS
      Omicron Delta Epsilon
      Pi Alpha Alpha
1972 Pi Sigma Alpha
1974 Sigma Pi Sigma
1982 Gamma Theta Upsilon
1982 Psi Chi

OTHER HONORS
1971 Phi Beta Kappa

SERVICE
1949 Alpha Phi Omega

COLONIES
1990 Chi Phi

STATE UNIVERSITY OF NEW YORK AT BUFFALO Buffalo, NY. Name changed from The University of Buffalo in 1962 when the institution was taken into the State system. Originally chartered in 1846; coeducational; private control; nonsectarian. Main campus on outskirts of Buffalo; law school in city.

SUNY trustees in November, 1976, lifted the 1953 ban on national Greek societies. Procedures were established to reconstitute national chapters on campus.

NIC MEN'S
1897 Delta Chi
1916 Sigma Alpha Mu
1917 Zeta Beta Tau
1921 Alpha Phi Delta
1943 Pi Lambda Phi
1949 Theta Chi
1950 Phi Kappa Psi
1958 Alpha Epsilon Pi
1979 Sigma Pi
1984 Kappa Sigma
1985 Alpha Delta Phi
1987 Alpha Chi Rho

NPC WOMEN'S
1920 Phi Sigma Sigma
1921 Sigma Delta Tau
1940 Chi Omega
1985 Alpha Epsilon Phi

PROFESSIONAL
1916 Alpha Omega
1922 Rho Pi Phi
1925 Delta Sigma Pi
1952 Lambda Kappa Sigma
1968 Phi Alpha Delta

ACHS HONORS
      Omicron Delta Epsilon
1931 Kappa Delta Pi

1953 Gamma Theta Upsilon
1959 Phi Eta Sigma
1967 Tau Beta Pi
1969 Chi Epsilon
1971 Sigma Pi Sigma
1973 Beta Phi Mu
1974 Eta Kappa Nu
1976 Phi Alpha Theta
1983 Psi Chi
1988 Phi Alpha Theta

OTHER HONORS
1951 Pi Mu Epsilon

SERVICE
1948 Alpha Phi Omega

RECOGNITION
1943 Chi Delta Phi

INACTIVE
1920–64 Sigma Kappa
1922–72 Alpha Gamma Delta
1924–25 Kappa Alpha Psi (A)
1926–54 Alpha Sigma Alpha
1954–89 Sigma Phi Epsilon
1958–85 Alpha Lambda Delta

COLONIES
1950 Alpha Sigma Phi

STATE UNIVERSITY OF NEW YORK AT STONY BROOK Stony Brook, NY. Established 1957; state university.

NIC MEN'S
1977 Zeta Beta Tau
1986 Alpha Epsilon Pi

1987 Alpha Phi Delta
1987 Tau Kappa Epsilon
1989 Alpha Chi Rho

NPHC MEN'S
    Phi Beta Sigma

NPC WOMEN'S
1984 Sigma Delta Tau
1987 Theta Phi Alpha
1988 Phi Sigma Sigma
1989 Alpha Phi

NPHC WOMEN'S
    Alpha Kappa Alpha
1990 Sigma Gamma Rho

PROFESSIONAL
1986 Alpha Omega

ACHS HONORS
    Omicron Delta Epsilon

1967 Phi Alpha Theta
1967 Phi Sigma Iota
1967 Phi Sigma Iota
1969 Sigma Pi Sigma
1970 Tau Beta Pi
1975 Pi Sigma Alpha
1979 Eta Kappa Nu
1979 Phi Sigma Tau
1988 Psi Chi

OTHER HONORS
1974 Phi Beta Kappa

COLONIES
1990 Tau Delta Phi

STATE UNIVERSITY OF NEW YORK COLLEGE AT BUFFALO
Buffalo, NY. The State University College at Buffalo, founded 1871 as Buffalo State Normal School.

NIC MEN'S
1933 Sigma Tau Gamma
1957 Tau Kappa Epsilon
1982 Tau Kappa Epsilon
1983 Phi Kappa Sigma
1989 Phi Kappa Tau
1990 Alpha Epsilon Pi

NPC WOMEN'S
1925 Alpha Sigma Tau
1988 Sigma Delta Tau
1990 Alpha Phi
1990 Phi Sigma Sigma

NPHC WOMEN'S
1984 Alpha Kappa Alpha
1987 Sigma Gamma Rho

OTHER PROFESSIONAL
1923 Phi Upsilon Omicron
1976 Alpha Epsilon Rho

ACHS HONORS
    Omicron Delta Epsilon
1940 Rho Chi
1979 Psi Chi
1980 Phi Sigma Iota
1983 Pi Sigma Alpha
1989 Pi Kappa Lambda

INACTIVE
1911–53 Sigma Sigma Sigma
1939–71 Pi Lambda Theta

COLONIES
1990 Phi Delta Theta

STATE UNIVERSITY OF NEW YORK COLLEGE AT BROCKPORT
Brockport, NY.

NIC MEN'S
1984 Kappa Alpha Psi (A)
1986 Delta Sigma Phi
1987 Alpha Chi Rho
1989 Tau Kappa Epsilon

NPHC MEN'S
    Phi Beta Sigma

NPC WOMEN'S
1987 Delta Phi Epsilon
1987 Phi Sigma Sigma

NPHC WOMEN'S
1982 Alpha Kappa Alpha

ACHS HONORS
    Omicron Delta Epsilon
1949 Kappa Delta Pi
1982 Pi Sigma Alpha
1986 Phi Alpha Theta

SERVICE
1951 Alpha Phi Omega
1972 Gamma Sigma Sigma

INACTIVE
1975–78 Psi Chi

STATE UNIVERSITY OF NEW YORK COLLEGE AT CORTLAND
Cortland, NY. Teachers college; coeducational; state control; established 1863.

NIC MEN'S
    Alpha Epsilon Pi
1986 Pi Lambda Phi
1988 Tau Kappa Epsilon
1989 Pi Kappa Phi

NPC WOMEN'S
1987 Delta Phi Epsilon
1988 Sigma Delta Tau
1989 Alpha Phi

ACHS HONORS
    Omicron Delta Epsilon
1945 Kappa Delta Pi
1967 Psi Chi
1968 Phi Alpha Theta
1972 Pi Sigma Alpha
1978 Phi Eta Sigma
1978 Sigma Pi Sigma
1983 Phi Kappa Phi

INACTIVE
1946–53 Alpha Sigma Alpha
1946–82 Sigma Sigma Sigma

1952–54 Sigma Tau Gamma
1982–90 Sigma Phi Epsilon
1983–85 Zeta Beta Tau

STATE UNIVERSITY OF NEW YORK COLLEGE OF AGRICULTURE AT COBLESKILL
Cobleskill, NY.

SERVICE
1968 Alpha Phi Omega

COLONIES
    Alpha Phi Delta

STATE UNIVERSITY OF NEW YORK COLLEGE OF TECHNOLOGY AT FARMINGDALE
Farmingdale, NY.

NIC MEN'S
1976 Tau Delta Phi

NPHC MEN'S
    Phi Beta Sigma

OTHER PROFESSIONAL
1957 Alpha Eta Rho

ACHS HONORS
1976 Phi Sigma Tau
1979 Eta Kappa Nu

STATE UNIVERSITY OF NEW YORK COLLEGE OF TECHNOLOGY UTICA
Utica, NY.

NIC MEN'S
1978 Alpha Phi Delta

STATE UNIVERSITY OF NEW YORK COLLEGE AT FREDONIA
Fredonia, NY. Founded in 1967. Liberal arts college with programs in fine and performing arts, teaching and professional studies.

NIC MEN'S
1980 Sigma Phi Epsilon
1987 Phi Kappa Sigma

NPC WOMEN'S
1986 Delta Phi Epsilon
1987 Sigma Kappa

PROFESSIONAL
1964 Sigma Alpha Iota
1967 Phi Mu Alpha—Sinfonia

ACHS HONORS
    Omicron Delta Epsilon
1950 Kappa Delta Pi
1960 Delta Sigma Rho-Tau
    Kappa Alpha
1968 Pi Delta Phi
1968 Sigma Delta Pi
1969 Phi Alpha Theta

1970 Sigma Pi Sigma
1972 Alpha Lambda Delta
1974 Phi Eta Sigma
1974 Psi Chi
1980 Pi Kappa Lambda
1985 Delta Mu Delta

OTHER HONORS
    National Order of Omega
1965 Pi Mu Epsilon

SERVICE
1971 Alpha Phi Omega

RECOGNITION
1943 Alpha Psi Omega
1968 Beta Beta Beta

COLONIES
1988 Delta Chi

STATE UNIVERSITY OF NEW YORK OF ARTS AND SCIENCE
Geneseo, NY. Coeducational; state control; established 1867.

NIC MEN'S
1980 Alpha Chi Rho
1980 Sigma Phi Epsilon
1981 Phi Kappa Sigma

NPHC MEN'S
    Phi Beta Sigma

NPC WOMEN'S
1986 Delta Phi Epsilon
1989 Sigma Kappa

ACHS HONORS
    Omicron Delta Epsilon
1944 Kappa Delta Pi
1969 Phi Alpha Theta
1970 Psi Chi
1971 Sigma Tau Delta
1972 Sigma Pi Sigma
1981 Phi Sigma Iota
1983 Delta Mu Delta
1984 Pi Sigma Alpha
1986 Gamma Theta Upsilon

SERVICE
1986 Alpha Phi Omega

RECOGNITION
1936 Alpha Psi Omega

1966 Pi Kappa Delta

INACTIVE
1952–54 Phi Sigma Kappa
1969–83 Beta Phi Mu

STATE UNIVERSITY OF NEW YORK AT NEW PALTZ
New Paltz, NY. Teachers college; coeducational; state control; established 1887 as normal school.

NIC MEN'S
1970 Tau Epsilon Phi
1980 Kappa Alpha Psi (A)
1990 Tau Kappa Epsilon

NPHC MEN'S
Phi Beta Sigma

NPC WOMEN'S
1989 Alpha Epsilon Phi
1989 Delta Phi Epsilon
1989 Sigma Delta Tau

NPHC WOMEN'S
1983 Alpha Kappa Alpha

1987 Sigma Gamma Rho

ACHS HONORS
1946 Kappa Delta Pi
1979 Pi Sigma Alpha
1987 Phi Sigma Iota

SERVICE
1990 Alpha Phi Omega

RECOGNITION
1962 Kappa Pi

INACTIVE
1951–54 Sigma Tau Gamma

STATE UNIVERSITY OF NEW YORK AT ONEONTA
Oneonta, NY. Teachers college and liberal arts college; coeducational; state control; established as normal school 1899.

Fraternities and sororities presently are renting houses from private owners.

NIC MEN'S
1950 Sigma Tau Gamma
1987 Alpha Epsilon Pi
1987 Phi Kappa Sigma
1989 Sigma Alpha Mu
1989 Tau Kappa Epsilon

NPC WOMEN'S
1987 Alpha Epsilon Phi
1987 Delta Phi Epsilon
1988 Sigma Delta Tau
1989 Phi Sigma Sigma

OTHER PROFESSIONAL
1971 Phi Upsilon Omicron

ACHS HONORS
Omicron Delta Epsilon
1944 Kappa Delta Pi
1975 Sigma Pi Sigma

1979 Psi Chi
1982 Phi Sigma Iota

SERVICE
1963 Alpha Phi Omega
1968 Gamma Sigma Sigma

RECOGNITION
1949 Alpha Psi Omega

INACTIVE
1946–54 Alpha Sigma Alpha
1968–79 Pi Gamma Mu
1988–89 Zeta Beta Tau
1988–89 Zeta Tau Alpha

COLONIES
Theta Xi
1989 Phi Delta Theta
1990 Tau Epsilon Phi

STATE UNIVERSITY OF NEW YORK AT OSWEGO
Oswego, NY. Teachers college and liberal arts college; coeducational; state control; first instruction 1861.

All of the social fraternities and sororities own (or are buying) their own house or rent from private individuals off campus. Because of a State University of New York ruling in 1954, all social fraternities must only exist on campus with local status.

NIC MEN'S
1950 Phi Sigma Kappa
1987 Alpha Epsilon Pi
1987 Tau Kappa Epsilon
1988 Sigma Phi Epsilon
1989 Phi Kappa Tau

NPHC MEN'S
Phi Beta Sigma

NPC WOMEN'S
1985 Alpha Epsilon Phi
1987 Delta Phi Epsilon

1989 Phi Sigma Sigma
1989 Sigma Delta Tau

OTHER PROFESSIONAL
1972 Alpha Epsilon Rho

ACHS HONORS
Omicron Delta Epsilon
1945 Kappa Delta Pi
1968 Psi Chi
1973 Sigma Pi Sigma
1975 Pi Delta Phi
1979 Delta Mu Delta
1979 Phi Alpha Theta
1982 Pi Sigma Alpha

1983 Phi Eta Sigma
1986 Phi Sigma Iota

SERVICE
1947 Alpha Phi Omega

RECOGNITION
1950 Alpha Psi Omega

INACTIVE
1951–54 Alpha Sigma Alpha
1951–54 Sigma Tau Gamma
1959–79 Kappa Mu Epsilon
1965–70 Pi Gamma Mu

STATE UNIVERSITY OF NEW YORK OF EDUCATION AT PLATTSBURGH
Plattsburgh, NY. Teachers college; coeducational; state control; established 1890. State affiliated 1948.

NIC MEN'S
1981 Alpha Chi Rho
1985 Sigma Pi
1988 Alpha Sigma Phi
1989 Tau Kappa Epsilon

NPC WOMEN'S
1988 Alpha Epsilon Phi
1988 Delta Phi Epsilon

OTHER PROFESSIONAL
1967 Phi Upsilon Omicron

ACHS HONORS
Omicron Delta Epsilon
1955 Kappa Delta Pi
1968 Psi Chi

1977 Gamma Theta Upsilon
1980 Sigma Pi Sigma
1981 Omicron Delta Kappa
1983 Phi Eta Sigma
1985 Phi Alpha Theta

OTHER HONORS
National Order of Omega
National Order of Omega
National Order of Omega

SERVICE
1987 Alpha Phi Omega

INACTIVE
1968–71 Kappa Delta Epsilon

STATE UNIVERSITY OF NEW YORK OF ENVIRONMENTAL SCIENCE AND FORESTRY
Syracuse, NY.

ACHS HONORS
1979 Sigma Lambda Alpha

STATE UNIVERSITY OF NEW YORK AT POTSDAM
Potsdam, NY. Established as St. Lawrence Academy in 1816; coeducational; state control; undergraduate preparation in music, elementary and secondary teaching; liberal arts 1964; graduate programs. Crane Institute of Music was incorporated in 1926.

Fraternities and sororities own their own houses and property.

NIC MEN'S
1979 Phi Kappa Sigma
1983 Sigma Pi

PROFESSIONAL
1958 Phi Mu Alpha—Sinfonia

ACHS HONORS
Omicron Delta Epsilon
1944 Kappa Delta Pi
1980 Pi Sigma Alpha

1980 Sigma Pi Sigma
1984 Phi Alpha Theta
1988 Pi Kappa Lambda
1989 Phi Eta Sigma

SERVICE
1973 Gamma Sigma Sigma

RECOGNITION
1967 Beta Beta Beta
1979 Gamma Sigma Epsilon

STATE UNIVERSITY OF NEW YORK AT PURCHASE Purchase, NY.

NPHC MEN'S
    Phi Beta Sigma

STATE UNIVERSITY OF NEW YORK AT OLD WESTBURY Old Westbury, NY.

NIC MEN'S
1986 Kappa Alpha Psi (A)

NPHC MEN'S
    Phi Beta Sigma

NPHC WOMEN'S
1987 Sigma Gamma Rho

COLLEGE OF STATEN ISLAND OF THE CITY UNIVERSITY OF NEW YORK Staten Island, NY.

NIC MEN'S
1987 Alpha Phi Delta

ACHS HONORS
1978 Psi Chi

NEW YORK DOWNSTATE MEDICAL CENTER IN NEW YORK CITY Brooklyn, NY. Division of state university in 1950; established 1860; coeducational.

OTHER HONORS
1969 Sigma Xi

INACTIVE
1938   Phi Chi

NEWBERRY COLLEGE Newberry, SC. College of liberal arts; coeducational; private control; affiliated with Lutheran Church; established 1956.

NIC MEN'S
1966 Kappa Alpha Order
1967 Alpha Tau Omega
1972 Theta Chi
1974 Tau Kappa Epsilon

NPC WOMEN'S
1967 Alpha Xi Delta
1968 Kappa Delta

PROFESSIONAL
1971 Phi Mu Alpha—Sinfonia

1972 Delta Omicron

ACHS HONORS
1976 Phi Alpha Theta

RECOGNITION
1929 Alpha Psi Omega
1951 Blue Key

INACTIVE
1873-74 Kappa Alpha Order
1978-81 Alpha Phi

NIAGARA UNIVERSITY Niagara, NY. Coeducational; liberal arts university in the Vincentian tradition; established in 1856.

NPHC MEN'S
    Phi Beta Sigma

PROFESSIONAL
1955 Alpha Kappa Psi
1975 Phi Gamma Nu
1984 Phi Alpha Delta

ACHS HONORS
    Omicron Delta Epsilon
1940 Delta Epsilon Sigma
1968 Kappa Mu Epsilon
1981 Phi Sigma Iota
1981 Theta Alpha Kappa

1983 Psi Chi
1988 Phi Alpha Theta

SERVICE
1960 Alpha Phi Omega

RECOGNITION
1952 Alpha Psi Omega
1954 Scabbard and Blade (11)

INACTIVE
1969-70 Delta Zeta
1970-77 Tau Kappa Epsilon

NICHOLLS STATE UNIVERSITY Thibodaux, LA. Established in 1948 as Francis T. Nicholls Junior College, became four-year college in 1956, university in 1970; coeducational; major colleges are arts and sciences, life sciences and technology, education, and business administration; there is a freshman division. Three colleges offer the master's degree and one the specialist's degree. Some fraternities rent off-campus houses.

NIC MEN'S
1966 Phi Kappa Theta
1969 Tau Kappa Epsilon
1971 Delta Sigma Phi
1973 Phi Sigma Kappa
1977 Kappa Alpha Order
1983 Kappa Alpha Psi (A)
1989 Theta Xi

NPHC MEN'S
    Phi Beta Sigma
1975 Alpha Phi Alpha

NPC WOMEN'S
1967 Phi Mu
1967 Sigma Sigma Sigma
1968 Delta Zeta

PROFESSIONAL
1967 Delta Sigma Pi
1967 Pi Sigma Epsilon
1972 Delta Psi Kappa

OTHER PROFESSIONAL
1961 Alpha Beta Alpha

ACHS HONORS
    Omicron Delta Epsilon
1968 Alpha Lambda Delta
1969 Phi Alpha Theta
1971 Delta Mu Delta
1971 Kappa Delta Pi
1971 Phi Eta Sigma
1974 Delta Mu Delta
1974 Phi Kappa Phi
1979 Psi Chi
1982 Kappa Omicron Nu

OTHER HONORS
1968 Pi Mu Epsilon

INACTIVE
1957-69 Sigma Tau Delta
1968-74 Alpha Sigma Alpha
1969-71 Sigma Tau Gamma
1969-87 Pi Kappa Alpha
1974-83 Alpha Gamma Delta
1975-83 Pi Kappa Phi

NORFOLK STATE COLLEGE Norfolk, VA. The Norfolk Unit of Virginia Union University was established in 1935 to provide training on the junior college level for high school graduates of the Norfolk-Portsmouth area. The Norfolk Division of Virginia State College was created in 1944 and in February, 1969, Norfolk State College was named an independent institution.

NIC MEN'S
1963 Kappa Alpha Psi (A)

NPHC MEN'S
    Phi Beta Sigma

NPHC WOMEN'S
1962 Alpha Kappa Alpha
1964 Sigma Gamma Rho

OTHER PROFESSIONAL
1976 Alpha Epsilon Rho

ACHS HONORS
    Omicron Delta Epsilon
1966 Pi Omega Pi
1970 Alpha Kappa Mu
1975 Psi Chi
1976 Sigma Tau Delta

SERVICE
1970 Alpha Phi Omega

UNIVERSITY OF NORTH ALABAMA Florence, AL. College of liberal arts and professional programs; coeducational; state control; founded 1872.

NIC MEN'S
1974 Alpha Tau Omega
1974 Phi Gamma Delta
1974 Pi Kappa Alpha
1974 Sigma Chi
1975 Kappa Sigma
1976 Kappa Alpha Psi (A)
1989 Sigma Alpha Epsilon

NPHC MEN'S
1975 Alpha Phi Alpha

NPC WOMEN'S
1973 Alpha Delta Pi
1973 Phi Mu
1973 Zeta Tau Alpha
1977 Alpha Gamma Delta

NPHC WOMEN'S
1980 Alpha Kappa Alpha

ACHS HONORS
Omicron Delta Epsilon
1935 Kappa Mu Epsilon
1963 Kappa Omicron Nu
1970 Phi Alpha Theta
1971 Phi Kappa Phi
1973 Phi Eta Sigma
1974 Alpha Lambda Delta
1976 Omicron Delta Kappa

1976 Sigma Pi Sigma
1980 Gamma Theta Upsilon
1987 Phi Sigma Iota
1988 Psi Chi

INACTIVE
1973–83 Alpha Omicron Pi
1974–81 Lambda Chi Alpha
1974–84 Pi Kappa Phi

NORTH ADAMS STATE COLLEGE North Adams, MA. Public institution. Founded in 1894. Four-year; coeducational; liberal arts college.

All dormitories are co-ed.

NIC MEN'S
1988 Alpha Chi Rho

OTHER PROFESSIONAL
1961 Kappa Delta Phi (C)

ACHS HONORS
1966 Lambda Iota Tau

1970 Alpha Chi
1978 Gamma Theta Upsilon
1985 Phi Alpha Theta

INACTIVE
1971–75 Tau Kappa Epsilon

UNIVERSITY OF NORTH CAROLINA Chapel Hill, NC. University; coeducational; co-ordinate colleges for men and women; women admitted as freshmen and sophomores to nursing, dental hygiene, medical technology, physical therapy, or pharmacy; state control; chartered 1789.

Fraternities and sororities occupy their own houses on their own premises with the exception of several which occupy privately rented houses.

NIC MEN'S
Alpha Epsilon Pi
1851 Delta Kappa Epsilon
1851 Phi Gamma Delta
1852 Beta Theta Pi
1854 Delta Psi
1855 Chi Psi
1856 Phi Kappa Sigma
1858 Chi Phi
1858 Zeta Psi
1879 Alpha Tau Omega
1881 Kappa Alpha Order
1885 Phi Delta Theta
1888 Sigma Nu
1889 Sigma Chi
1893 Kappa Sigma
1895 Pi Kappa Alpha
1914 Pi Kappa Phi
1920 Delta Sigma Phi
1920 Theta Chi
1921 Delta Tau Delta
1921 Sigma Phi Epsilon
1924 Tau Epsilon Phi
1926 Lambda Chi Alpha
1937 Alpha Epsilon Pi
1953 Delta Upsilon
1976 Kappa Alpha Psi (A)

NPHC MEN'S
Phi Beta Sigma
1976 Alpha Phi Alpha

NPC WOMEN'S
1923 Chi Omega
1923 Pi Beta Phi
1939 Alpha Delta Pi
1943 Delta Delta Delta

1951 Kappa Delta
1958 Kappa Kappa Gamma
1964 Phi Mu
1966 Kappa Alpha Theta
1974 Delta Phi Epsilon
1977 Alpha Chi Omega
1979 Zeta Tau Alpha
1988 Delta Zeta
1989 Sigma Sigma Sigma

NPHC WOMEN'S
1931 Alpha Kappa Alpha
1971 Delta Sigma Theta (B)
1973 Delta Sigma Theta (B)
1974 Alpha Kappa Alpha
1976 Alpha Kappa Alpha
1980 Alpha Kappa Alpha
1987 Sigma Gamma Rho

PROFESSIONAL
1912 Alpha Chi Sigma
1915 Kappa Psi
1919 Phi Delta Phi
1921 Phi Alpha Delta
1923 Phi Delta Chi
1924 Delta Theta Phi
1925 Alpha Kappa Psi
1925 Delta Sigma Pi
1926 Phi Mu Alpha—Sinfonia
1940 Kappa Epsilon
1951 Psi Omega
1952 Xi Psi Phi
1973 Phi Mu Alpha—Sinfonia
1985 Phi Alpha Delta

OTHER PROFESSIONAL
1951 Delta Sigma Delta
1958 Sigma Delta Chi

1973 Alpha Tau Alpha

ACHS HONORS
Omicron Delta Epsilon
1909 Delta Sigma Rho-Tau
Kappa Alpha
1929 Rho Chi
1931 Alpha Kappa Delta
1933 Beta Gamma Sigma
1936 Alpha Epsilon Delta
1940 Pi Kappa Lambda
1942 Pi Tau Sigma
1947 Phi Eta Sigma
1949 Pi Sigma Alpha
1952 Alpha Kappa Delta
1952 Phi Alpha Theta
1952 Pi Delta Phi
1952 Psi Chi
1953 Phi Alpha Theta
1955 Kappa Tau Alpha
1957 Beta Phi Mu
1962 Sigma Theta Tau
1966 Alpha Epsilon
1968 Sigma Delta Pi
1972 Pi Tau Sigma
1975 Sigma Delta Pi
1983 Gamma Theta Upsilon
1983 Sigma Pi Sigma

OTHER HONORS
1904 Phi Beta Kappa
1920 Sigma Xi
1928 Order of the Coif
1948 Pi Mu Epsilon
1953 Omicron Kappa Upsilon
1954 Alpha Omega Alpha

SERVICE
1930 Alpha Phi Omega

1972 Gamma Sigma Sigma

RECOGNITION
Angel Flight
Arnold Air Society (B-2)
1938 Delta Phi Alpha
1949 Scabbard and Blade (8)
1950 Kappa Pi
1959 Sigma Phi Alpha
1976 Sigma Delta Psi

INACTIVE
1855–61 Delta Phi
1856–60 Theta Delta Chi
1857–90 Sigma Alpha Epsilon
1905 Phi Chi
1915–39 Phi Beta Pi and Theta
Kappa Psi (B)
1920–22 Sigma Delta Chi
1923–32 Acacia
1923–64 Alpha Kappa Kappa
1926–35 Phi Sigma Kappa
1927–85 Zeta Beta Tau
1927–85 Zeta Tau Alpha
1928–38 Tau Beta Pi
1931–33 Phi Delta Gamma
1932 Sigma Gamma Epsilon
1939–84 Pi Lambda Phi
1940–42 Chi Beta Phi
1945–65 Alpha Gamma Delta
1946–55 Sigma Alpha Iota
1970–89 Sigma Sigma Sigma

COLONIES
1987 Phi Delta Theta
1990 Phi Kappa Tau

NORTH CAROLINA AGRICULTURAL AND TECHNICAL STATE UNIVERSITY Greensboro, NC. Land-grant university; coeducational; state control; established 1891.

The college provides rooms for eight fraternities and sororities to conduct meetings and other activities.

NIC MEN'S
1933 Kappa Alpha Psi (A)

NPHC MEN'S
Phi Beta Sigma
1927 Omega Psi Phi
1929 Alpha Phi Alpha

NPHC WOMEN'S
Zeta Phi Beta
1931 Alpha Kappa Alpha
1932 Delta Sigma Theta (B)
1951 Sigma Gamma Rho

PROFESSIONAL
1972 Phi Mu Alpha—Sinfonia
1976 Mu Phi Epsilon

ACHS HONORS
Omicron Delta Epsilon
1937 Alpha Kappa Mu
1946 Beta Kappa Chi

1954 Pi Omega Pi
1955 Pi Delta Phi
1957 Kappa Delta Pi
1972 Alpha Chi
1973 Phi Alpha Theta
1978 Alpha Lambda Delta
1978 Kappa Omicron Nu
1979 Psi Chi
1980 Eta Kappa Nu
1986 Tau Beta Pi

OTHER HONORS
1974 Gamma Sigma Delta

SERVICE
1953 Alpha Phi Omega
1968 Gamma Sigma Sigma

RECOGNITION
Arnold Air Society (B-2)
1951 Scabbard and Blade (10)

UNIVERSITY OF NORTH CAROLINA AT ASHEVILLE
North Carolina, Asheville, NC. Public institution. Founded in 1927. Graduate; coeducational.

Fraternities and sororities have houses, suites or designated dormitory areas.

NIC MEN'S
1983 Pi Lambda Phi
1988 Theta Chi

NPC WOMEN'S
1983 Alpha Xi Delta
1987 Alpha Delta Pi

ACHS HONORS
    Omicron Delta Epsilon
1973 Psi Chi

1974 Phi Alpha Theta
1974 Pi Delta Phi
1987 Omicron Delta Kappa
1988 Phi Eta Sigma

SERVICE
1971 Alpha Phi Omega

COLONIES
    Sigma Pi
1985 Sigma Pi Sigma

UNIVERSITY OF NORTH CAROLINA AT CHARLOTTE
Charlotte, NC. University of liberal arts and general studies; specialized professional colleges; coeducational; state control. Established 1965.

NIC MEN'S
1970 Chi Phi
1970 Kappa Alpha Psi (A)
1970 Kappa Sigma
1972 Lambda Chi Alpha
1973 Pi Kappa Phi
1973 Sigma Phi Epsilon
1979 Alpha Sigma Phi
1987 Phi Kappa Sigma
1990 Delta Sigma Phi

NPHC MEN'S
    Phi Beta Sigma

NPC WOMEN'S
1971 Alpha Delta Pi
1971 Delta Zeta
1974 Zeta Tau Alpha
1982 Chi Omega
1989 Sigma Kappa

NPHC WOMEN'S
1972 Delta Sigma Theta (B)
1976 Alpha Kappa Alpha

PROFESSIONAL
1968 Alpha Kappa Psi

ACHS HONORS
    Omicron Delta Epsilon
    Pi Alpha Alpha
1974 Sigma Pi Sigma
1976 Phi Alpha Theta
1977 Pi Sigma Alpha
1979 Tau Beta Pi
1980 Phi Kappa Phi
1982 Omicron Delta Kappa
1983 Phi Eta Sigma
1984 Gamma Theta Upsilon
1990 Psi Chi

OTHER HONORS
    National Order of Omega

SERVICE
1967 Alpha Phi Omega

INACTIVE
1972–77 Delta Delta Delta

COLONIES
    Sigma Kappa
1990 Tau Kappa Epsilon

UNIVERSITY OF NORTH CAROLINA AT GREENSBORO
Greensboro, NC. College of liberal arts for men and women; state control; chartered 1891 as State Normal and Industrial College; incorporated in the University of North Carolina.

NIC MEN'S
1981 Pi Kappa Phi
1982 Sigma Phi Epsilon
1983 Lambda Chi Alpha
1985 Kappa Alpha Psi (A)
1986 Tau Kappa Epsilon

NPHC MEN'S
    Phi Beta Sigma

NPC WOMEN'S
1981 Alpha Delta Pi
1981 Chi Omega
1981 Phi Mu

1982 Alpha Chi Omega

PROFESSIONAL
1960 Mu Phi Epsilon
1981 Delta Sigma Pi

OTHER PROFESSIONAL
1942 Delta Pi Epsilon

ACHS HONORS
    Omicron Delta Epsilon
1942 Kappa Omicron Nu
1949 Phi Alpha Theta
1958 Psi-Chi
1969 Gamma Theta Upsilon

1976 Sigma Theta Tau
1977 Sigma Pi Sigma
1984 Beta Phi Mu
1988 Alpha Lambda Delta

OTHER HONORS
1969 Pi Mu Epsilon

SERVICE
1969 Alpha Phi Omega
1975 Gamma Sigma Sigma

INACTIVE
1979–87 Sigma Tau Gamma

UNIVERSITY OF NORTH CAROLINA AT WILMINGTON
Wilmington, NC. University of liberal arts and general studies; teacher preparatory; coeducational; state control. Established 1947.

NIC MEN'S
1968 Pi Kappa Phi
1979 Chi Phi
1981 Sigma Alpha Epsilon
1983 Kappa Sigma
1984 Delta Tau Delta
1985 Kappa Alpha Psi (A)
1986 Delta Sigma Phi

NPHC MEN'S
    Phi Beta Sigma

NPC WOMEN'S
1979 Delta Zeta
1983 Alpha Delta Pi
1987 Alpha Xi Delta
1989 Alpha Phi
1990 Chi Omega

NPHC WOMEN'S
    Alpha Kappa Alpha

ACHS HONORS
1969 Sigma Pi Sigma

1979 Phi Eta Sigma
1980 Phi Kappa Phi
1980 Pi Sigma Alpha
1981 Psi Chi

OTHER HONORS
    National Order of Omega
1974 Pi Mu Epsilon

SERVICE
1969 Alpha Phi Omega

INACTIVE
1968–74 Phi Mu
1969–75 Zeta Tau Alpha
1970–85 Tau Kappa Epsilon
1974–77 Delta Upsilon

COLONIES
    Alpha Gamma Delta
    Lambda Chi Alpha

NORTH CAROLINA CENTRAL UNIVERSITY
Durham, NC. College of liberal arts; coeducational; state control; chartered 1909.

Fraternity and sorority members live in residence halls.

NIC MEN'S
1931 Kappa Alpha Psi (A)

NPHC MEN'S
    Phi Beta Sigma
1941 Alpha Phi Alpha

NPHC WOMEN'S
1952 Sigma Gamma Rho

PROFESSIONAL
1971 Phi Alpha Delta
1972 Delta Theta Phi
1974 Kappa Kappa Psi

1974 Tau Beta Sigma

ACHS HONORS
1940 Alpha Kappa Mu
1955 Pi Gamma Mu
1961 Psi Chi
1965 Gamma Theta Upsilon
1973 Kappa Omicron Nu
1976 Beta Phi Mu

SERVICE
1967 Alpha Phi Omega
1971 Gamma Sigma Sigma

NORTH CAROLINA STATE UNIVERSITY
Raleigh, NC. Founded by legislative act of March 7, 1887; a comprehensive university featuring science, technology, and liberal studies. Schools of agriculture and life sciences, design, education, engineering, forest resources, humanities and social sciences, physical and mathematical sciences, textiles, veterinary medicine and graduate. Coeducational.

A university owned Fraternity Court houses fourteen chapters. Nine others rent or own off campus.

NIC MEN'S
1895 Sigma Nu
1903 Kappa Alpha Order
1903 Kappa Sigma
1904 Pi Kappa Alpha
1905 Sigma Phi Epsilon
1915 Delta Sigma Phi
1919 Alpha Gamma Rho
1920 Pi Kappa Phi
1921 Sigma Pi
1923 Phi Kappa Tau
1924 Lambda Chi Alpha
1938 Sigma Alpha Mu
1943 Sigma Chi
1947 Sigma Alpha Epsilon
1947 Tau Kappa Epsilon
1952 Theta Chi
1954 FarmHouse
1977 Delta Upsilon
1980 Kappa Alpha Psi (A)
1988 Phi Delta Theta
1990 Delta Chi

NPHC MEN'S
Phi Beta Sigma
1971 Alpha Phi Alpha

NPC WOMEN'S
1960 Sigma Kappa
1971 Alpha Delta Pi
1984 Chi Omega

NPHC WOMEN'S
1975 Delta Sigma Theta (B)

PROFESSIONAL
1924 Theta Tau

OTHER PROFESSIONAL
1904 Alpha Zeta
1924 Keramos
1924 Phi Psi
1931 Kappa Phi Kappa
1948 Delta Kappa Phi

ACHS HONORS
Omicron Delta Epsilon
Pi Alpha Alpha

1923 Phi Kappa Phi
1925 Tau Beta Pi
1930 Phi Eta Sigma
1938 Eta Kappa Nu
1940 Xi Sigma Pi
1948 Chi Epsilon
1950 Alpha Kappa Delta
1953 Sigma Pi Sigma
1955 Alpha Pi Mu
1962 Alpha Sigma Mu
1963 Phi Sigma
1968 Psi Chi
1970 Alpha Lambda Delta
1970 Sigma Gamma Tau
1972 Pi Sigma Alpha
1975 Alpha Epsilon Delta
1980 Phi Sigma Iota
1983 Phi Alpha Theta

OTHER HONORS
National Order of Omega
1944 Sigma Xi
1955 Gamma Sigma Delta
1960 Pi Mu Epsilon

SERVICE
1950 Alpha Phi Omega

RECOGNITION
Angel Flight
Arnold Air Society (B-2)
1922 Scabbard and Blade (3)
1925 Mu Beta Psi
1928 Blue Key
1956 National Block and Bridle Club
1976 Phi Lambda Upsilon

INACTIVE
1921–51 Gamma Sigma Epsilon
1929–38 Delta Sigma Pi
1930–86 Alpha Sigma Phi
1975–82 Alpha Phi
1983–85 Zeta Beta Tau
1983–85 Zeta Tau Alpha
1983–90 Alpha Xi Delta

NORTH CAROLINA WESLEYAN COLLEGE
Rocky Mount, NC.

NIC MEN'S
1986 Sigma Pi

ACHS HONORS
1972 Omicron Delta Kappa
1979 Theta Alpha Kappa
1983 Psi Chi

1985 Phi Eta Sigma

SERVICE
1965 Alpha Phi Omega

COLONIES
Pi Kappa Phi

NORTH CENTRAL COLLEGE Naperville, IL. College of liberal arts; coeducational; affiliated with Evangelical United Brethren Church; chartered as Plainfield College, 1861.

PROFESSIONAL
1965 Sigma Alpha Iota

ACHS HONORS
1955 Phi Sigma Iota
1974 Psi Chi
1975 Lambda Iota Tau
1980 Phi Alpha Theta

RECOGNITION
1924 Pi Kappa Delta

1932 Alpha Psi Omega
1937 Beta Beta Beta

INACTIVE
1924–69 Pi Gamma Mu
1970–83 Phi Mu Alpha— Sinfonia

THE UNIVERSITY OF NORTH DAKOTA Grand Forks, ND. Coeducational; state-supported university. Founded six years before North Dakota became state. Governor Ordway signed bill 1883. Eleven separate colleges which include the graduate school.

The sororities and fraternities with one exception, occupy their own houses on their own land.

NIC MEN'S
1909 Sigma Chi
1913 Phi Delta Theta
1922 Alpha Tau Omega
1922 Beta Theta Pi
1923 Sigma Alpha Epsilon
1923 Sigma Nu
1926 Kappa Sigma
1928 Lambda Chi Alpha
1929 Tau Delta Phi
1935 Delta Tau Delta
1938 Tau Kappa Epsilon
1961 Delta Upsilon
1968 Pi Kappa Alpha
1986 Pi Kappa Phi

NPC WOMEN'S
1911 Alpha Phi
1911 Kappa Alpha Theta
1916 Delta Gamma
1920 Gamma Phi Beta
1921 Pi Beta Phi
1923 Alpha Chi Omega
1929 Delta Delta Delta

PROFESSIONAL
1911 Phi Alpha Delta
1911 Phi Delta Phi
1916 Sigma Alpha Iota
1949 Delta Psi Kappa
1954 Alpha Delta Theta
1979 Delta Theta Phi

OTHER PROFESSIONAL
1922 Sigma Delta Chi
1923 Beta Alpha Psi
1925 Pi Lambda Theta
1944 Phi Upsilon Omicron
1949 Phi Epsilon Kappa
1963 Delta Pi Epsilon
1966 Alpha Eta Rho

ACHS HONORS
Omicron Delta Epsilon
1911 Delta Sigma Rho-Tau Kappa Alpha
1930 Phi Eta Sigma
1932 Mortar Board
1948 Gamma Theta Upsilon
1948 Phi Alpha Theta
1950 Alpha Lambda Delta

1951 Pi Omega Pi
1961 Psi Chi
1962 Eta Kappa Nu
1964 Alpha Epsilon
1964 Alpha Kappa Delta
1974 Tau Beta Pi
1974 Tau Sigma Delta
1982 Pi Sigma Alpha
1986 Kappa Tau Alpha

OTHER HONORS
National Order of Omega
1914 Phi Beta Kappa
1920 Sigma Xi
1922 Delta Phi Delta
1925 Order of the Coif
1926 National Collegiate Players
1930 Sigma Epsilon Sigma
1950 Sigma Gamma Epsilon

SERVICE
1947 Alpha Phi Omega

RECOGNITION
1926 Blue Key
1940 Lambda Delta Lambda
1959 Sigma Delta Psi

INACTIVE
1919–83 Delta Zeta
1921 Scabbard and Blade (3)
1924–29 Phi Sigma
1925–59 Phi Chi Theta
1925–74 Delta Sigma Pi
1926 Beta Gamma Sigma
1926–42 Zeta Phi Eta
1928–37 Sigma Kappa
1931 Kappa Beta Pi
1931–33 Sigma Tau Delta
1932–89 Theta Chi
1948 Phi Beta Pi and Theta Kappa Psi (a)
1968–75 Phi Mu Alpha— Sinfonia

COLONIES
Acacia
1988 Delta Chi

NORTH DAKOTA STATE UNIVERSITY
Fargo, ND. University and land grant college; coeducational; state control; chartered 1889 as North Dakota Agricultural College.

The fraternities and sororities occupy their own houses on their own land.

NIC MEN'S
1913 Alpha Gamma Rho
1917 Theta Chi

1931 Alpha Tau Omega
1934 Sigma Chi
1935 Sigma Alpha Epsilon

1955 FarmHouse
1955 Tau Kappa Epsilon
1962 Sigma Nu
1970 Delta Upsilon

NPC WOMEN'S
1924 Kappa Delta
1930 Alpha Gamma Delta
1930 Gamma Phi Beta
1932 Phi Mu
1947 Kappa Alpha Theta

PROFESSIONAL
1920 Sigma Alpha Iota
1923 Kappa Psi
1928 Sigma Phi Delta
1930 Kappa Epsilon
1935 Kappa Kappa Psi
1951 Tau Beta Sigma

OTHER PROFESSIONAL
1909 Alpha Zeta
1914 Phi Upsilon Omicron

ACHS HONORS
1913 Phi Kappa Phi
1928 Rho Chi

1931 Kappa Delta Pi
1950 Tau Beta Pi
1958 Eta Kappa Nu
1964 Alpha Lambda Delta
1964 Mortar Board
1964 Phi Eta Sigma
1973 Sigma Pi Sigma
1974 Psi Chi

OTHER HONORS
        National Order of Omega
1963 Sigma Xi

SERVICE
1934 Alpha Phi Omega

RECOGNITION
        Angel Flight
        Arnold Air Society (F-1)
1922 Scabbard and Blade (3)
1927 Blue Key

INACTIVE
1927–42 Pi Gamma Mu
1929–85 Kappa Kappa Gamma
1935–40 Lambda Delta Lambda

UNIVERSITY OF NORTH FLORIDA   Jacksonville, FL.

NIC MEN'S
1987 Lambda Chi Alpha
1987 Pi Kappa Phi

NPC WOMEN'S
1977 Zeta Tau Alpha
1987 Alpha Chi Omega

NPHC WOMEN'S
1978 Alpha Kappa Alpha

PROFESSIONAL
1981 Delta Sigma Pi

ACHS HONORS
        Omicron Delta Epsilon
1977 Beta Gamma Sigma
1977 Phi Alpha Theta
1980 Phi Kappa Phi
1985 Psi Chi

OTHER HONORS
1974 Pi Mu Epsilon

SERVICE
1974 Alpha Phi Omega

NORTH GEORGIA COLLEGE   Dahlonega, GA.
College of liberal arts; coeducational; state control; military; established 1873 as agricultural college.

NIC MEN'S
1881 Sigma Nu
1971 Pi Kappa Phi
1972 Sigma Phi Epsilon
1982 Sigma Chi

NPC WOMEN'S
1973 Kappa Delta
1973 Phi Mu
1983 Alpha Gamma Delta
1989 Delta Zeta

ACHS HONORS
1958 Phi Alpha Theta

1975 Phi Kappa Phi
1976 Sigma Pi Sigma
1982 Psi Chi
1983 Pi Sigma Alpha
1989 Phi Eta Sigma

RECOGNITION
1954 Alpha Psi Omega
1956 Scabbard and Blade (12)

INACTIVE
1879–88 Sigma Alpha Epsilon
1885–91 Kappa Sigma
1900–33 Pi Kappa Alpha

NORTH PARK COLLEGE   Chicago, IL.

ACHS HONORS
1963 Kappa Mu Epsilon
1967 Phi Sigma Tau
1971 Delta Mu Delta

1985 Psi Chi

RECOGNITION
1963 Beta Beta Beta

NORTH TEXAS STATE UNIVERSITY   Denton, TX. Founded 1890 as Texas Normal College, a private normal school. By acts of Texas state legislature became North Texas State Normal College in 1899, North Texas State Teachers College in 1923, North Texas State College in 1949, North Texas State University in 1961. University; undergraduate colleges; graduate school; coeducational; state control.

Ownership of fraternity house and land is by the fraternity; administration requires sorority members to occupy dormitories.

NIC MEN'S
1952 Delta Sigma Phi
1952 Kappa Sigma
1952 Lambda Chi Alpha
1952 Sigma Phi Epsilon
1953 Kappa Alpha Order
1953 Sigma Nu
1954 Theta Chi
1955 Phi Kappa Sigma
1955 Pi Kappa Alpha
1967 Phi Kappa Theta
1972 Kappa Alpha Psi (A)
1985 Sigma Tau Gamma
1988 Sigma Alpha Epsilon
1990 Sigma Chi

NPHC MEN'S
        Phi Beta Sigma
1970 Alpha Phi Alpha

NPC WOMEN'S
1953 Alpha Delta Pi
1953 Chi Omega
1953 Zeta Tau Alpha
1954 Alpha Phi
1968 Delta Zeta
1976 Pi Beta Phi
1989 Kappa Kappa Gamma

NPHC WOMEN'S
1968 Delta Sigma Theta (B)
1969 Alpha Kappa Alpha
1976 Sigma Gamma Rho

PROFESSIONAL
1928 Delta Psi Kappa
1940 Phi Mu Alpha—Sinfonia
1941 Sigma Alpha Iota
1945 Mu Phi Epsilon
1952 Alpha Chi Sigma
1954 Delta Sigma Pi
1957 Phi Chi Theta

OTHER PROFESSIONAL
1947 Phi Upsilon Omicron
1953 Women in Communications
1954 Sigma Delta Chi
1957 Delta Pi Epsilon
1962 Beta Alpha Psi

ACHS HONORS
        Omicron Delta Epsilon

Pi Alpha Alpha
1922 Alpha Chi
1926 Kappa Delta Pi
1928 Pi Omega Pi
1940 Sigma Tau Delta
1945 Phi Alpha Theta
1948 Pi Kappa Lambda
1948 Psi Chi
1949 Gamma Theta Upsilon
1950 Pi Delta Phi
1952 Alpha Lambda Delta
1953 Phi Eta Sigma
1954 Pi Sigma Alpha
1959 Alpha Kappa Delta
1962 Beta Gamma Sigma
1965 Sigma Pi Sigma
1968 Mortar Board
1972 Kappa Tau Alpha
1976 Beta Phi Mu
1979 Phi Sigma Iota
1982 Phi Kappa Phi

OTHER HONORS
        National Order of Omega

SERVICE
1942 Alpha Phi Omega

RECOGNITION
        Angel Flight
        Arnold Air Society (G-1)
1927 Pi Kappa Delta
1947 Beta Beta Beta
1950 Blue Key
1951 Kappa Pi
1964 Alpha Psi Omega

INACTIVE
1927–37 Pi Gamma Mu
1951–82 Kappa Mu Epsilon
1953–76 Delta Gamma
1954–75 Kappa Delta
1960–73 Alpha Beta Alpha
1967–87 Sigma Alpha Mu
1968–83 Tau Kappa Epsilon
1969–73 Delta Phi Epsilon
1969–89 Alpha Xi Delta
1970–75 Pi Kappa Phi

NORTHEAST LOUISIANA UNIVERSITY   Monroe, LA. Founded 1931 as part of Ouachita Parish school system. Original name Ouachita Parish Junior College; became part of Louisiana State University and designated as Northeast Center of Louisiana State University 1934; name changed to Northeast Junior College 1939. In 1950 legislature

established the Junior College as four-year institution transferring supervision to the state board of education and changing the name to Northeast Louisiana State College; graduate program in education established 1961.

Ownership of fraternity house and land is by the fraternity.

NIC MEN'S
1957 Kappa Alpha Order
1967 Kappa Sigma
1972 Pi Kappa Alpha
1974 Kappa Alpha Psi (A)
1984 Delta Sigma Phi

NPHC MEN'S
Phi Beta Sigma
1972 Alpha Phi Alpha

NPC WOMEN'S
1956 Phi Mu
1967 Kappa Delta
1986 Sigma Kappa

NPHC WOMEN'S
1973 Alpha Kappa Alpha
1974 Delta Sigma Theta (B)
1986 Sigma Gamma Rho

PROFESSIONAL
1955 Phi Mu Alpha—Sinfonia
1956 Delta Omicron
1957 Pi Sigma Epsilon
1959 Phi Delta Chi
1960 Kappa Epsilon
1968 Kappa Kappa Psi
1969 Delta Sigma Pi
1970 Tau Beta Sigma

OTHER PROFESSIONAL
1974 Alpha Epsilon Rho

ACHS HONORS
Omicron Delta Epsilon
1955 Sigma Tau Delta

1956 Phi Alpha Theta
1960 Omicron Delta Kappa
1961 Rho Chi
1965 Alpha Lambda Delta
1968 Sigma Pi Sigma
1969 Psi Chi
1970 Phi Kappa Phi
1972 Phi Eta Sigma
1973 Beta Gamma Sigma
1974 Alpha Epsilon Delta
1974 Kappa Omicron Nu
1975 Gamma Theta Upsilon
1976 Pi Omega Pi
1976 Sigma Delta Pi
1977 Mortar Board
1988 Kappa Tau Alpha

OTHER HONORS
1970 Sigma Gamma Epsilon

SERVICE
1981 Alpha Phi Omega

RECOGNITION
1956 Scabbard and Blade (13)
1961 Kappa Pi

INACTIVE
1956–88 Tau Kappa Epsilon
1959–73 Phi Beta
1960–83 Sigma Tau Gamma
1965–86 Zeta Tau Alpha
1969–73 Zeta Beta Tau
1969–73 Zeta Tau Alpha
1969–81 Acacia

NORTHEAST MISSOURI STATE UNIVERSITY

Kirksville, MO. Public liberal arts and sciences; co-educational; state control; chartered as normal school 1867. Graduate school.

The general fraternities occupy houses which they own on their own ground. The general sorority members live in a Panhellenic residence hall.

NIC MEN'S
1921 Sigma Tau Gamma
1928 Phi Sigma Kappa
1953 Alpha Kappa Lambda
1962 Tau Kappa Epsilon
1963 Kappa Alpha Psi (A)
1972 Pi Kappa Phi
1978 Alpha Gamma Rho
1978 Delta Chi
1979 Alpha Tau Omega
1981 Sigma Phi Epsilon
1986 Lambda Chi Alpha
1987 Phi Kappa Tau

NPHC MEN'S
Phi Beta Sigma
1974 Alpha Phi Alpha

NPC WOMEN'S
1914 Alpha Sigma Alpha
1915 Sigma Sigma Sigma
1921 Delta Zeta
1959 Sigma Kappa
1968 Alpha Sigma Tau
1990 Alpha Phi

NPHC WOMEN'S
1968 Delta Sigma Theta (B)
1970 Sigma Gamma Rho
1979 Alpha Kappa Alpha

PROFESSIONAL
1968 Phi Mu Alpha—Sinfonia
1969 Sigma Alpha Iota
1978 Delta Sigma Pi
1985 Alpha Chi Sigma

ACHS HONORS
1923 Kappa Delta Pi
1923 Pi Omega Pi
1968 Kappa Mu Epsilon
1968 Kappa Omicron Nu
1968 Phi Alpha Theta
1970 Sigma Tau Delta
1976 Psi Chi
1978 Pi Sigma Alpha
1990 Phi Eta Sigma

OTHER HONORS
National Order of Omega

SERVICE
1927 Alpha Phi Omega

RECOGNITION
1926 Blue Key
1927 Sigma Zeta
1930 Alpha Phi Sigma (E)
1934 Cardinal Key

COLONIES
1987 Sigma Pi Sigma

NORTHEASTERN ILLINOIS UNIVERSITY Chicago, IL.

NIC MEN'S
1968 Tau Kappa Epsilon

PROFESSIONAL
1970 Sigma Alpha Iota

ACHS HONORS
Omicron Delta Epsilon
1967 Gamma Theta Upsilon

1968 Psi Chi
1970 Phi Alpha Theta
1977 Pi Sigma Alpha

INACTIVE
1969–84 Phi Mu Alpha—
Sinfonia

NORTHEASTERN OKLAHOMA STATE UNIVERSITY

Tahlequah, OK. Established 1846 as Cherokee National Female Seminary; chartered by state 1909 as Northeastern State Normal; became Northeastern State College 1939; and Northeastern Oklahoma State University in 1974. University of liberal arts, business, and service areas.

Fraternity housing must conform to approved housing regulations.

NIC MEN'S
1930 Phi Sigma Kappa
1939 Phi Lambda Chi
1972 Kappa Alpha Psi (A)
1975 Pi Kappa Alpha
1990 Tau Kappa Epsilon

NPHC MEN'S
1970 Alpha Phi Alpha

NPC WOMEN'S
1923 Delta Zeta
1929 Sigma Sigma Sigma
1937 Alpha Sigma Alpha

PROFESSIONAL
1938 Kappa Kappa Psi

ACHS HONORS
1931 Kappa Mu Epsilon
1937 Alpha Chi
1964 Sigma Tau Delta

1965 Pi Gamma Mu
1966 Kappa Delta Pi
1970 Phi Alpha Theta
1978 Pi Sigma Alpha
1978 Sigma Pi Sigma
1982 Psi Chi

SERVICE
1938 Alpha Phi Omega
1965 Gamma Sigma Sigma

RECOGNITION
1975 Lambda Tau

INACTIVE
–83 Alpha Sigma Tau
1924–90 Sigma Tau Gamma
1930–67 Pi Omega Pi
1973–89 Acacia

COLONIES
Lambda Chi Alpha

NORTHEASTERN UNIVERSITY

Boston, MA. Co-educational, privately endowed, operating on Co-operative Plan of Education. Established 1898. Ph.D. programs in chemistry, biology mathematics, psychology, chemical engineering, mechanical engineering, electrical engineering, and physics; master's degrees and bachelor's degrees in business administration, computer science, education, arts and sciences, professional accounting, actuarial science, pharmacy, engineering; bachelor's degree in nursing and criminal justice.

Ownership of fraternity house and lot is by the fraternity.

NIC MEN'S
1961 Tau Epsilon Phi
1962 Alpha Epsilon Pi
1963 Phi Sigma Kappa
1968 Phi Kappa Tau
1968 Sigma Alpha Mu
1969 Tau Kappa Epsilon
1990 Theta Delta Chi

NPC WOMEN'S
1968 Delta Phi Epsilon
1989 Delta Zeta
1990 Alpha Epsilon Phi
1990 Sigma Delta Tau

NPHC WOMEN'S
1974 Alpha Kappa Alpha
1984 Sigma Gamma Rho

PROFESSIONAL
1957 Rho Pi Phi
1958 Kappa Psi

OTHER PROFESSIONAL
1951 Alpha Zeta Omega
1968 Beta Alpha Psi
1971 Sigma Delta Chi

ACHS HONORS
    Omicron Delta Epsilon
1941 Tau Beta Pi
1950 Eta Kappa Nu
1952 Pi Tau Sigma
1958 Phi Alpha Theta

1960 Alpha Pi Mu
1960 Pi Sigma Alpha
1961 Rho Chi
1963 Beta Gamma Sigma
1963 Phi Kappa Phi
1964 Alpha Kappa Delta
1964 Kappa Delta Pi
1965 Chi Epsilon
1965 Omega Chi Epsilon
1968 Phi Sigma
1976 Phi Sigma Iota
1976 Sigma Theta Tau
1986 Kappa Tau Alpha

OTHER HONORS
    National Order of Omega
1965 Sigma Xi

RECOGNITION
1954 Alpha Psi Omega
1954 Scabbard and Blade (11)
1971 Pi Kappa Delta

INACTIVE
1963–69 Lambda Kappa Sigma
1969–73 Alpha Omicron Pi
1969–77 Alpha Sigma Tau
1969–84 Zeta Beta Tau
1969–84 Zeta Tau Alpha
1971–83 Delta Chi

COLONIES
1986 Sigma Pi Sigma

NORTHERN ARIZONA UNIVERSITY Flagstaff, AZ. Coeducational; state control; chartered 1899 as Northern Arizona Normal School; became Arizona State College; chartered 1966 to present name. College of Arts and Sciences, Business Administration, Creative and Communication Arts, Design and Technology, Center for Excellence in Education, Engineering and Technology, School of Forestry, School of Health Professions, Social and Behavioral Sciences; Graduate.

Sorority members are not required to live in dormitories. Fraternity members may rent, own private houses, or live in resident halls.

NIC MEN'S
    Tau Kappa Epsilon
1951 Sigma Pi
1956 Tau Kappa Epsilon
1959 Delta Chi
1962 Sigma Nu
1967 Sigma Chi
1968 Kappa Sigma
1969 Kappa Alpha Psi (A)
1974 Sigma Phi Epsilon
1975 Sigma Alpha Epsilon
1980 Pi Kappa Alpha
1981 Phi Sigma Kappa
1990 Alpha Tau Omega

OTHER MEN'S
    Sigma Gamma Chi

NPC WOMEN'S
1958 Delta Delta Delta
1958 Gamma Phi Beta
1963 Alpha Omicron Pi

1968 Alpha Delta Pi
1990 Pi Beta Phi

OTHER WOMEN'S
    Lambda Delta Sigma

PROFESSIONAL
1930 Delta Psi Kappa
1954 Kappa Kappa Psi
1954 Tau Beta Sigma
1961 Phi Mu Alpha—Sinfonia
1963 Sigma Alpha Iota
1967 Delta Sigma Pi
1983 Phi Alpha Delta

OTHER PROFESSIONAL
1968 Sigma Delta Chi

ACHS HONORS
    Omicron Delta Epsilon
1930 Kappa Delta Pi
1950 Phi Eta Sigma
1959 Phi Kappa Phi

1965 Phi Alpha Theta
1968 Sigma Pi Sigma
1969 Gamma Theta Upsilon
1971 Mortar Board
1972 Sigma Delta Pi
1975 Xi Sigma Pi
1976 Psi Chi
1978 Pi Sigma Alpha
1981 Tau Beta Pi
1983 Kappa Tau Alpha
1986 Alpha Lambda Delta
1987 Phi Sigma Iota

OTHER HONORS
    National Order of Omega

SERVICE
    The National Spurs

RECOGNITION
1949 Blue Key
1959 Beta Beta Beta

INACTIVE
1931–77 Pi Omega Pi
1933–40 Pi Gamma Mu
1952–84 Delta Sigma Phi
1958–75 Phi Kappa Theta
1968–75 Alpha Epsilon Pi
1968–79 Sigma Tau Gamma

UNIVERSITY OF NORTHERN COLORADO Greeley, CO. Founded in 1890. Degrees offered are bachelor of arts, bachelor of science, specialist in education, master of arts, and doctor of education. Coeducational; state supported.

The fraternities and sororities may occupy college-owned houses on a rental basis or purchase their own houses.

NIC MEN'S
1953 Tau Kappa Epsilon
1958 Sigma Chi
1970 Sigma Alpha Epsilon
1981 Delta Sigma Phi
1984 Delta Chi
1987 Sigma Pi
1989 Delta Upsilon

NPHC MEN'S
    Phi Beta Sigma

NPC WOMEN'S
1916 Delta Zeta
1950 Sigma Kappa
1960 Alpha Phi
1962 Alpha Delta Pi
1967 Alpha Xi Delta

NPHC WOMEN'S
1976 Sigma Gamma Rho

PROFESSIONAL
1931 Kappa Kappa Psi
1950 Tau Beta Sigma

OTHER PROFESSIONAL
1954 Delta Pi Epsilon
1976 Sigma Delta Chi

ACHS HONORS
    Omicron Delta Epsilon
1923 Phi Sigma Iota

1928 Pi Omega Pi
1929 Phi Alpha Theta
1968 Gamma Theta Upsilon
1972 Mortar Board
1973 Pi Kappa Lambda
1982 Psi Chi

OTHER HONORS
    National Order of Omega
1971 Pi Mu Epsilon

SERVICE
    The National Spurs
1956 Alpha Phi Omega

RECOGNITION
1933 Blue Key

INACTIVE
1915–84 Sigma Sigma Sigma
1934–84 Phi Mu Alpha—
        Sinfonia
1952–80 Sigma Phi Epsilon
1956–74 Acacia
1957–72 Alpha Kappa Lambda
1959–80 Alpha Gamma Delta
1963–64 Pi Gamma Mu
1976–88 Lambda Chi Alpha

COLONIES
    Theta Xi
1954 Theta Xi

NORTHERN ILLINOIS UNIVERSITY DeKalb, IL. University; coeducational; state control; established 1895 as normal school. Graduate school.

NIC MEN'S
1947 Phi Sigma Kappa
1954 Phi Kappa Theta
1959 Sigma Pi
1961 Theta Chi
1966 Delta Upsilon
1967 Phi Sigma Kappa
1968 Kappa Alpha Psi (A)
1968 Phi Kappa Sigma
1970 Sigma Nu
1971 Pi Kappa Alpha

1971 Sigma Phi Epsilon
1972 Sigma Chi
1981 Lambda Chi Alpha
1982 Sigma Alpha Mu
1987 Delta Sigma Phi
1989 Delta Chi
1989 Kappa Sigma

NPHC MEN'S
    Phi Beta Sigma
1964 Alpha Phi Alpha

NPC WOMEN'S
1944 Sigma Sigma Sigma
1948 Alpha Sigma Alpha
1950 Delta Zeta
1952 Kappa Delta
1954 Sigma Kappa
1964 Alpha Delta Pi
1969 Alpha Phi
1969 Delta Gamma
1981 Delta Phi Epsilon

NPHC WOMEN'S
1960 Alpha Kappa Alpha
1968 Delta Sigma Theta (B)
1975 Sigma Gamma Rho

PROFESSIONAL
1951 Sigma Alpha Iota
1968 Delta Sigma Pi
1977 Delta Theta Phi
1978 Phi Alpha Delta
1984 Phi Alpha Delta

OTHER PROFESSIONAL
1963 Pi Lambda Theta
1967 Delta Pi Epsilon
1967 Sigma Delta Chi
1971 Beta Alpha Psi
1975 Alpha Epsilon Rho

ACHS HONORS
Omicron Delta Epsilon
Pi Alpha Alpha
1935 Kappa Delta Pi
1938 Sigma Tau Delta
1949 Sigma Delta Pi
1954 Lambda Sigma Society
1957 Pi Omega Pi
1959 Phi Alpha Theta
1960 Alpha Kappa Delta
1960 Phi Sigma
1963 Psi Chi
1965 Gamma Theta Upsilon
1968 Pi Sigma Alpha
1970 Beta Gamma Sigma
1971 Kappa Tau Alpha

1971 Mortar Board
1972 Omicron Delta Kappa
1973 Phi Sigma Tau
1973 Sigma Pi Sigma
1974 Phi Kappa Phi
1976 Kappa Omicron Nu
1976 Sigma Theta Tau
1978 Phi Sigma Iota
1986 Pi Kappa Lambda

OTHER HONORS
National Order of Omega
1969 National Collegiate
Players
1972 Pi Mu Epsilon

SERVICE
1928 Alpha Phi Omega

RECOGNITION
1931 Alpha Psi Omega
1934 Pi Kappa Delta
1963 Sigma Iota Epsilon
1968 Sigma Delta Psi

INACTIVE
1927   Omega Epsilon Phi
1937–72 Sigma Zeta
1950–83 Phi Mu Alpha—
Sinfonia
1953–82 Tau Kappa Epsilon
1958–60 Pi Kappa Phi
1958–64 Alpha Beta Alpha
1959–85 Alpha Xi Delta
1966–77 Phi Eta Sigma
1966–88 Sigma Alpha Epsilon
1967–75 Sigma Delta Tau
1967–85 Chi Omega
1969–71 Zeta Beta Tau
1969–71 Zeta Tau Alpha
1970–74 Alpha Chi Omega
1976–81 Alpha Epsilon Pi

COLONIES
1954 Alpha Omicron Pi
1964 Alpha Kappa Lambda

UNIVERSITY OF NORTHERN IOWA Cedar
Falls, IA. Chartered as Iowa State Normal School,
1876; Iowa State Teachers College, 1909; State College of Iowa, 1961; University of Northern Iowa,
1967. Bachelor of arts, master of arts, master of
arts in education, and specialist in education degrees; graduate college and college of humanities
and fine arts, business and behavioral sciences, natural sciences, education; master of arts in Industrial
Arts and in Technology; doctorate in Industrial
Technology; doctorate in education. State control;
coeducational.

NIC MEN'S
1938 Phi Sigma Kappa
1955 Tau Kappa Epsilon
1965 Sigma Alpha Epsilon
1968 Delta Upsilon
1970 Delta Chi
1975 Pi Kappa Alpha
1985 Kappa Sigma
1988 Kappa Alpha Psi (A)

NPC WOMEN'S
1965 Alpha Xi Delta
1967 Alpha Delta Pi
1968 Gamma Phi Beta
1970 Alpha Phi

PROFESSIONAL
1931 Phi Mu Alpha—Sinfonia

OTHER PROFESSIONAL
1966 Delta Pi Epsilon
1970 Phi Upsilon Omicron

ACHS HONORS
Omicron Delta Epsilon
1925 Pi Omega Pi
1928 Gamma Theta Upsilon
1931 Kappa Mu Epsilon
1969 Sigma Delta Pi
1970 Phi Alpha Theta
1974 Pi Kappa Lambda

1982 Omicron Delta Kappa
1982 Phi Eta Sigma
1983 Psi Chi
1983 Sigma Pi Sigma

OTHER HONORS
National Order of Omega
1974 Sigma Gamma Epsilon

SERVICE
1938 Alpha Phi Omega

RECOGNITION
1934 Beta Beta Beta

NORTHERN KENTUCKY UNIVERSITY Highland
Heights, KY. College of liberal arts and general
studies; teacher preparatory; professional; educational. State control. Established 1968.

NIC MEN'S
1972 Pi Kappa Alpha
1973 Alpha Delta Gamma
1982 Sigma Phi Epsilon
1983 Alpha Tau Omega
1983 Tau Kappa Epsilon

NPC WOMEN'S
1972 Delta Zeta
1974 Theta Phi Alpha
1979 Phi Sigma Sigma

PROFESSIONAL
1955 Phi Alpha Delta
1973 Delta Theta Phi

ACHS HONORS
1981 Psi Chi
1984 Pi Sigma Alpha
1985 Phi Alpha Theta

OTHER HONORS
National Order of Omega

NORTHERN MICHIGAN UNIVERSITY Mar-
quette, MI. Founded in 1899. State supported, comprehensive, residential, coeducational; bachelor's,
master's and specialist's degrees.

Some fraternities own their own houses off-
campus; housing on campus is amply available.

NIC MEN'S
Tau Kappa Epsilon
1961 Phi Kappa Tau
1962 Delta Sigma Phi
1968 Kappa Alpha Psi (A)
1968 Lambda Chi Alpha

NPHC MEN'S
1966 Alpha Phi Alpha

NPC WOMEN'S
1962 Alpha Xi Delta
1989 Alpha Gamma Delta

NPHC WOMEN'S
1969 Delta Sigma Theta (B)

PROFESSIONAL
1967 Alpha Kappa Psi
1969 Sigma Alpha Iota

ACHS HONORS
Omicron Delta Epsilon
1935 Kappa Delta Pi
1967 Pi Omega Pi
1969 Phi Alpha Theta
1971 Delta Mu Delta
1972 Phi Kappa Phi
1979 Mortar Board

1979 Phi Sigma Iota

SERVICE
1951 Alpha Phi Omega
1964 Gamma Sigma Sigma

RECOGNITION
1961 Blue Key
1972 Sigma Delta Psi

INACTIVE
1963–82 Delta Zeta
1965–86 Theta Chi
1968–82 Chi Omega
1968–90 Phi Mu Alpha—
Sinfonia
1969–72 Delta Tau Delta
1969–73 Sigma Kappa
1969–75 Sigma Alpha Mu
1969–82 Alpha Kappa Alpha
1969–82 Alpha Sigma Phi
1970–76 Kappa Sigma
1970–79 Sigma Sigma Sigma
1975–80 Kappa Omicron Nu

COLONIES
1988 Delta Chi

1948 Society for Collegiate
Journalists—Pi Delta
Epsilon-Alpha Phi Gamma
(A)
1954 Kappa Pi

INACTIVE
–71   Alpha Sigma Tau
1928–84 Pi Gamma Mu
1947–78 Sigma Tau Gamma
1956–71 Alpha Beta Alpha
1966–72 Sigma Sigma Sigma
1968–79 Alpha Gamma Delta
1968–87 Alpha Chi Omega

NORTHERN STATE COLLEGE Aberdeen, SD.
Liberal arts and general studies; coeducational; state control; established as normal school 1901.

PROFESSIONAL
1959 Phi Mu Alpha—Sinfonia
1960 Sigma Alpha Iota

ACHS HONORS
    Omicron Delta Epsilon
1922 Kappa Delta Pi
1972 Pi Kappa Lambda
1980 Pi Gamma Mu
1989 Psi Chi

OTHER HONORS
1964 Delta Phi Delta

RECOGNITION
1960 Blue Key

INACTIVE
1929–68 Pi Omega Pi
1970–78 Alpha Xi Delta

NORTHLAND COLLEGE Ashland, WI. College of
liberal arts; coeducational; private control (United Church of Christ); chartered as North Wisconsin Academy 1892.

One of the fraternities has a house.

NIC MEN'S
1959 Phi Sigma Kappa

1965–83 Tau Kappa Epsilon
1968–69 Delta Zeta

INACTIVE
1960–83 Sigma Tau Gamma

NORTHROP UNIVERSITY Inglewood, CA: A private engineering college 1942; nonsectarian, undergraduate, coeducational; present enrollment 1800.

NIC MEN'S
1968 Tau Kappa Epsilon

PROFESSIONAL
1980 Delta Theta Phi

ACHS HONORS
1973 Eta Kappa Nu

1974 Sigma Gamma Tau
1974 Tau Beta Pi
1975 Pi Tau Sigma

INACTIVE
1972–76 Sigma Phi Epsilon

NORTHWEST MISSOURI STATE UNIVERSITY
Maryville, MO. University of liberal arts and general studies; coeducational; state control; established 1905; master's degree in education, guidance, and counseling.

Fraternities occupy houses on premises which they themselves own; sorority members live in dormitories as none of the groups own houses and the college does not provide them.

NIC MEN'S
1927 Sigma Tau Gamma
1938 Phi Sigma Kappa
1954 Tau Kappa Epsilon
1963 Alpha Kappa Lambda
1968 Delta Sigma Phi
1971 Delta Chi
1980 Sigma Phi Epsilon
1985 Kappa Alpha Psi (A)

NPC WOMEN'S
1927 Sigma Sigma Sigma
1928 Alpha Sigma Alpha
1947 Delta Zeta
1961 Phi Mu

NPHC WOMEN'S
1976 Delta Sigma Theta (B)
1976 Sigma Gamma Rho

PROFESSIONAL
1962 Delta Psi Kappa
1968 Phi Mu Alpha—Sinfonia
1971 Sigma Alpha Iota

OTHER PROFESSIONAL
1969 Alpha Beta Alpha

ACHS HONORS
    Omicron Delta Epsilon
1922 Kappa Omicron Nu
1924 Pi Omega Pi
1930 Sigma Tau Delta
1948 Kappa Delta Pi
1980 Gamma Theta Upsilon
1981 Phi Alpha Theta
1982 Phi Eta Sigma
1982 Psi Chi
1984 Pi Sigma Alpha

OTHER HONORS
    National Order of Omega

SERVICE
1939 Alpha Phi Omega
1961 Gamma Sigma Sigma

RECOGNITION
1932 Pi Kappa Delta
1947 Alpha Psi Omega
1954 Kappa Pi
1958 Pi Kappa Delta
1960 Blue Key

1966 Beta Beta Beta
1968 Society for Collegiate
    Journalists—Pi Delta
    Epsilon-Alpha Phi Gamma
    (P)

INACTIVE
1927–87 Pi Gamma Mu
1959–65 Phi Lambda Chi
1971–82 Alpha Omicron Pi

COLONIES
1990 Alpha Gamma Rho

NORTHWESTERN UNIVERSITY Evanston and
Chicago, IL. Chartered 1851; first instruction 1855. University; coeducational; private control; nonsectarian; related to the Methodist Episcopal Church. Evanston Campus: graduate school of management, school of education, school of journalism, college of liberal arts, school of music, school of speech, technological institute, graduate school. Chicago Campus: school of medicine, school of dentistry, school of law, graduate division school of business, evening division.

The university owns the houses and the fraternities and sororities occupy them on a rental basis.

NIC MEN'S
1859 Phi Delta Theta
1864 Phi Kappa Psi
1867 Phi Gamma Delta
1869 Sigma Chi
1872 Phi Kappa Sigma
1873 Beta Theta Pi
1880 Delta Upsilon
1893 Delta Tau Delta
1894 Sigma Alpha Epsilon
1898 Chi Psi
1898 Sigma Nu
1917 Kappa Alpha Psi (A)
1917 Lambda Chi Alpha
1920 Zeta Beta Tau
1923 Tau Delta Phi
1932 Pi Kappa Alpha
1939 Alpha Delta Phi
1941 Kappa Sigma
1947 Alpha Tau Omega
1947 Zeta Psi
1949 Psi Upsilon
1950 Theta Chi
1952 Chi Phi
1989 Sigma Phi Epsilon

NPHC MEN'S
    Phi Beta Sigma
1922 Alpha Phi Alpha

NPC WOMEN'S
1881 Alpha Phi
1882 Delta Gamma
1882 Kappa Kappa Gamma
1887 Kappa Alpha Theta
1888 Gamma Phi Beta
1890 Alpha Chi Omega
1894 Pi Beta Phi
1895 Delta Delta Delta
1901 Chi Omega
1907 Kappa Delta
1913 Alpha Gamma Delta
1920 Delta Zeta
1920 Zeta Tau Alpha

NPHC WOMEN'S
1939 Sigma Gamma Rho
1968 Alpha Kappa Alpha
1971 Delta Sigma Theta (B)

PROFESSIONAL
1880 Phi Delta Phi
1890 Phi Rho Sigma
1893 Zeta Phi Eta
1896 Phi Delta Chi
1896 Psi Omega
1900 Xi Psi Phi
1902 Phi Alpha Delta
1904 Sigma Alpha Iota
1910 Phi Mu Alpha—Sinfonia
1912 Phi Beta
1924 Phi Gamma Nu
1932 Alpha Omega

OTHER PROFESSIONAL
1892 Delta Sigma Delta
1918 Phi Delta Epsilon
1919 Gamma Eta Gamma
1921 Beta Alpha Psi
1922 Sigma Delta Chi
1923 Women in Communications
1933 Pi Lambda Theta
1946 Delta Pi Epsilon

ACHS HONORS
    Omicron Delta Epsilon
1906 Delta Sigma Rho-Tau
    Kappa Alpha
1918 Pi Kappa Lambda
1920 Beta Gamma Sigma
1922 Mortar Board
1923 Alpha Kappa Delta
1932 Phi Eta Sigma
1933 Alpha Lambda Delta
1936 Phi Sigma Iota
1941 Tau Beta Pi
1948 Eta Kappa Nu
1949 Kappa Tau Alpha
1950 Gamma Theta Upsilon
1970 Sigma Pi Sigma

1974 Alpha Sigma Mu
1975 Omega Chi Epsilon
1976 Sigma Theta Tau
1982 Pi Sigma Alpha

OTHER HONORS
National Order of Omega
1890 Phi Beta Kappa
1903 Alpha Omega Alpha
1906 Sigma Xi
1907 Order of the Coif
1914 Omicron Kappa Upsilon
1944 Pi Mu Epsilon

SERVICE
1931 Alpha Phi Omega

RECOGNITION
1916 Sigma Delta Psi
1927 Phi Lambda Upsilon
1951 Beta Beta Beta
1958 Sigma Phi Alpha

INACTIVE
-87   Alpha Epsilon Pi
1893-09 Delta Chi
1901-68 Alpha Kappa Kappa
1902   Phi Beta Pi and Theta
            Kappa Psi (a)
1902-51 Delta Theta Phi
1909-73 Alpha Omicron Pi
1911-68 Alpha Kappa Psi
1911-90 Acacia
1913-68 Alpha Chi Sigma
1914   Phi Lambda Kappa
1914-68 Mu Phi Epsilon

1914-77 Delta Sigma Pi
1915   Kappa Beta Pi
1919   Nu Beta Epsilon
1920   Phi Chi
1920-67 Delta Sigma Pi
1921   Sigma Delta Kappa
1921-48 Phi Mu Delta
1921-72 Alpha Xi Delta
1921-88 Alpha Epsilon Phi
1922   Scabbard and Blade
            (3)
1922-32 National Collegiate
            Players
1922-70 Delta Mu Delta
1923-56 Delta Omicron
1923-69 Zeta Tau Alpha
1924   Eta Sigma Phi
1924-72 Phi Chi Theta
1929   Sigma Delta Epsilon
1931   Phi Beta Pi and Theta
            Kappa Psi (B)
1932-88 Theta Xi
1935-87 Triangle
1936   Tau Epsilon Rho
1936-42 Alpha Eta Rho
1938-83 Sigma Delta Tau
1945-71 Alpha Delta Pi
1948   Delta Phi Alpha
1948-59 Delta Kappa Epsilon
1951-89 Theta Delta Chi
1958-74 Alpha Pi Mu
1967-76 Phi Sigma Kappa
1967-90 Sigma Alpha Mu
1975-76 Alpha Epsilon Delta

NORTHWESTERN OKLAHOMA STATE UNIVERSITY

Alva, OK. University of liberal arts and teachers college; coeducational; state control; chartered as normal school in 1897; became four-year college in 1919.

NIC MEN'S
1960 Phi Lambda Chi

1965 Blue Key

OTHER PROFESSIONAL
1931 Phi Sigma Pi

ACHS HONORS
1936 Kappa Delta Pi
1967 Phi Alpha Theta

RECOGNITION
1931 Alpha Psi Omega
1960 Kappa Pi

INACTIVE
1915-63 Sigma Sigma Sigma
1916-52 Alpha Sigma Alpha
1916-88 Delta Zeta
1927-62 Sigma Tau Gamma
1959-75 Sigma Kappa
1970-74 Pi Kappa Phi
1982-84 Phi Mu Alpha—
            Sinfonia

NORTHWESTERN STATE UNIVERSITY OF LOUISIANA

Natchitoches, LA. Six colleges and a graduate school; coeducational; state control. Established 1884.

Two fraternities have off-campus houses, six fraternities/sororities have on-campus lodges and shrine rooms are available to fraternities/sororities in a residence hall.

NIC MEN'S
1929 Sigma Tau Gamma
1957 Tau Kappa Epsilon
1963 Kappa Alpha Order
1966 Kappa Sigma
1973 Theta Chi
1975 Kappa Alpha Psi (A)

NPHC MEN'S
Phi Beta Sigma
1973 Alpha Phi Alpha

NPC WOMEN'S
1928 Sigma Sigma Sigma
1958 Alpha Omicron Pi
1959 Sigma Kappa

1968 Phi Mu

NPHC WOMEN'S
1972 Delta Sigma Theta (B)
1973 Alpha Kappa Alpha
1989 Sigma Gamma Rho

PROFESSIONAL
1942 Phi Mu Alpha—Sinfonia
1950 Sigma Alpha Iota
1971 Delta Psi Kappa

OTHER PROFESSIONAL
1950 Alpha Beta Alpha

ACHS HONORS
1934 Phi Alpha Theta
1939 Pi Omega Pi
1953 Phi Kappa Phi
1963 Phi Eta Sigma

1964 Sigma Tau Delta
1965 Alpha Lambda Delta
1969 Psi Chi
1971 Sigma Pi Sigma
1976 Kappa Omicron Nu
1976 Sigma Delta Pi

RECOGNITION
1931 Lambda Delta Lambda
1932 Alpha Psi Omega
1951 Pi Kappa Delta
1959 Blue Key
1959 Kappa Pi

INACTIVE
1927-85 Delta Zeta
1930-71 Alpha Sigma Alpha
1956-81 Pi Kappa Phi
1959-63 Alpha Gamma Delta

NORWICH UNIVERSITY

Northfield, VT. Founded 1819 by Capt. Alden Partridge, father of the ROTC program; oldest military college in the United States. First collegiate institution in U.S. to offer civil engineering and agriculture.

The fraternities owned their own houses on their own land until the board of trustees effected liquidation of the fraternity system in 1959.

NIC MEN'S
1950 Tau Delta Phi

PROFESSIONAL
1953 Alpha Kappa Psi

ACHS HONORS
Omicron Delta Epsilon
1951 Chi Epsilon
1965 Tau Beta Pi
1967 Phi Alpha Theta
1980 Eta Kappa Nu
1981 Pi Gamma Mu

RECOGNITION
1935 Alpha Psi Omega
1957 Alpha Psi Omega
1964 Pi Kappa Delta

INACTIVE
1856-60 Theta Chi
1908-60 Sigma Phi Epsilon
1927-60 Sigma Alpha Epsilon
1949-60 Sigma Nu
1950-60 Lambda Chi Alpha
1957-65 Alpha Eta Rho

NORTHWOOD INSTITUTE

Midland, MI.

NIC MEN'S
1978 Sigma Phi Epsilon
1983 Phi Delta Theta
1986 Tau Kappa Epsilon
1988 Theta Chi
1990 Alpha Chi Rho

NPHC MEN'S
Phi Beta Sigma

NPC WOMEN'S
1983 Alpha Chi Omega

1984 Delta Zeta
1988 Alpha Gamma Delta

ACHS HONORS
1984 Delta Mu Delta

INACTIVE
1982-87 Phi Chi Theta
1985-87 Alpha Phi

UNIVERSITY OF NOTRE DAME

Notre Dame, IN. Founded by Father Edward Sorin in 1842; chartered by state of Indiana in 1844. University for men and women; undergraduate college, graduate school, law school. Private control: Roman Catholic.

PROFESSIONAL
1977 Phi Alpha Delta

OTHER PROFESSIONAL
1962 Beta Alpha Psi

ACHS HONORS
Omicron Delta Epsilon

1908 Delta Sigma Rho-Tau
      Kappa Alpha
1955 Pi Sigma Alpha
1960 Tau Beta Pi
1961 Tau Sigma Delta
1962 Alpha Sigma Mu
1962 Eta Kappa Nu
1962 Pi Tau Sigma

1963 Alpha Epsilon Delta
1963 Beta Gamma Sigma
1966 Chi Epsilon
1968 Psi Chi
1971 Phi Alpha Theta
1984 Theta Alpha Kappa

OTHER HONORS
1952 Sigma Xi

1968 Phi Beta Kappa

SERVICE
1967 Alpha Phi Omega

RECOGNITION
Arnold Air Society (E-2)

NOTRE DAME COLLEGE   Cleveland, OH.

PROFESSIONAL
1987 Phi Chi Theta

ACHS HONORS
1964 Pi Delta Phi

1969 Phi Alpha Theta

RECOGNITION
1963 Alpha Psi Omega

COLLEGE OF NOTRE DAME OF MARYLAND
Baltimore, MD.

ACHS HONORS
1940 Delta Epsilon Sigma
1948 Pi Delta Phi
1963 Kappa Mu Epsilon
1968 Phi Alpha Theta
1974 Psi Chi

1974 Sigma Delta Pi

RECOGNITION
1947 Beta Beta Beta
1949 Eta Sigma Phi

NOVA UNIVERSITY   Fort Lauderdale, FL.

PROFESSIONAL
1975 Phi Alpha Delta

1982 Delta Theta Phi
1986 Phi Alpha Delta

OAKLAND UNIVERSITY   Rochester, MI. Public institution. Founded in 1957. Four-year; coeducational.

Fraternities have houses. All dormitories are co-ed. 83% of students live off campus or commute.

NIC MEN'S
1981 Kappa Alpha Psi (A)
1981 Theta Chi
1986 Sigma Pi

NPHC MEN'S
     Phi Beta Sigma
     Phi Beta Sigma

NPC WOMEN'S
1980 Alpha Delta Pi
1983 Phi Sigma Sigma
1984 Gamma Phi Beta

NPHC WOMEN'S
1981 Alpha Kappa Alpha

PROFESSIONAL
1976 Delta Omicron

ACHS HONORS
     Omicron Delta Epsilon

1971 Sigma Delta Pi
1979 Tau Beta Pi
1983 Pi Sigma Alpha
1984 Psi Chi

OTHER HONORS
1975 Sigma Xi

SERVICE
1967 Alpha Phi Omega
1971 Alpha Phi Omega

INACTIVE
1852–61 Delta Kappa Epsilon
1915–18 Phi Beta Pi and Theta
         Kappa Psi (a)

COLONIES
     Theta Tau
1987 Sigma Gamma Rho

OBERLIN COLLEGE   Oberlin, OH. College of liberal arts, and conservatory of music. Coeducational; private control; nonsectarian; established 1833. School of theology merged with Vanderbilt Divinity School 1965.

ACHS HONORS
1926 Pi Kappa Lambda
1936 Delta Sigma Rho-Tau
     Kappa Alpha

OTHER HONORS
1907 Phi Beta Kappa
1941 Sigma Xi

RECOGNITION
1921 Sigma Delta Psi

OCCIDENTAL COLLEGE   Los Angeles, CA. College of liberal arts; coeducational; private control (United Presbyterian). Chartered 1887; graduate instruction 1922.

The fraternities and sororities own their houses and the land which they occupy.

NIC MEN'S
1926 Alpha Tau Omega
1931 Sigma Alpha Epsilon
1933 Kappa Sigma
1979 Phi Sigma Kappa
1983 Kappa Alpha Psi (A)

PROFESSIONAL
1931 Sigma Alpha Iota
1954 Alpha Chi Sigma

OTHER PROFESSIONAL
1931 Phi Epsilon Kappa

ACHS HONORS
     Omicron Delta Epsilon
1917 Delta Sigma Rho-Tau
     Kappa Alpha
1947 Mortar Board
1947 Psi Chi
1948 Sigma Pi Sigma

1951 Phi Alpha Theta
1955 Alpha Kappa Delta

OTHER HONORS
1926 Phi Beta Kappa
1969 Pi Mu Epsilon

RECOGNITION
     Angel Flight
     Arnold Air Society (I)
1926 Sigma Delta Psi
1975 Beta Beta Beta

INACTIVE
1920–30 Theta Alpha Phi
1926–69 Phi Gamma Delta
1947   Zeta Phi Eta
1952   Delta Psi Kappa
1954–69 Kappa Mu Epsilon
1955–85 Phi Mu Alpha—
         Sinfonia

OGLETHORPE UNIVERSITY   Atlanta, GA. College of liberal arts; coeducational; private control; nonsectarian; established 1835.

NIC MEN'S
1859 Sigma Alpha Epsilon
1922 Delta Sigma Phi
1969 Chi Phi

NPC WOMEN'S
1969 Chi Omega
1987 Sigma Sigma Sigma

ACHS HONORS
1964 Sigma Tau Delta
1971 Alpha Chi
1971 Phi Alpha Theta
1976 Omicron Delta Kappa
1985 Psi Chi
1988 Phi Eta Sigma

SERVICE
1958 Alpha Phi Omega

RECOGNITION
1926 Blue Key
1971 Sigma Zeta

INACTIVE
1859–61 Beta Theta Pi
1871–72 Chi Phi
1871–72 Phi Delta Theta
1871–73 Kappa Alpha Order
1917–43 Pi Kappa Phi
1918–38 Kappa Alpha Order
1924–45 Chi Omega
1925–34 Lambda Chi Alpha
1930–74 Kappa Delta
1930–86 Delta Zeta
1968–73 Delta Phi Epsilon
1969–74 Sigma Alpha Mu
1969–76 Alpha Epsilon Pi

OHIO UNIVERSITY   Athens, OH. Founded 1804, oldest institution of higher learning in the Northwest Territory; first instruction 1808; five undergraduate degree colleges; a graduate school; state control under board of trustees. Coeducational.

The fraternities and sororities occupy their own houses on land which they own.

NIC MEN'S
1841 Beta Theta Pi
1862 Delta Tau Delta
1868 Phi Delta Theta
1911 Phi Kappa Tau
1918 Lambda Chi Alpha
1925 Theta Chi
1928 Phi Kappa Theta
1930 Pi Kappa Alpha
1933 Alpha Phi Delta

1949 Acacia
1949 Sigma Chi
1951 Sigma Nu
1953 Sigma Alpha Epsilon
1955 Delta Upsilon
1966 Kappa Alpha Psi (A)
1966 Phi Gamma Delta
1967 Sigma Phi Epsilon
1978 Alpha Epsilon Pi

NPHC MEN'S
Phi Beta Sigma
1919 Alpha Phi Alpha

NPC WOMEN'S
1889 Pi Beta Phi
1908 Alpha Gamma Delta
1911 Alpha Xi Delta
1913 Chi Omega
1914 Alpha Delta Pi
1927 Phi Mu
1941 Phi Sigma Sigma
1949 Sigma Kappa
1988 Alpha Omicron Pi
1990 Delta Zeta

NPHC WOMEN'S
1963 Delta Sigma Theta (B)
1964 Alpha Kappa Alpha
1980 Sigma Gamma Rho

PROFESSIONAL
1924 Phi Mu Alpha—Sinfonia
1924 Sigma Alpha Iota
1925 Delta Sigma Pi
1931 Kappa Kappa Psi
1951 Tau Beta Sigma
1969 Phi Gamma Nu
1982 Phi Alpha Delta
1989 Theta Tau

OTHER PROFESSIONAL
1921 Phi Upsilon Omicron
1932 Sigma Delta Chi
1941 Women in Communications
1947 Kappa Alpha Mu
1952 Beta Alpha Psi

ACHS HONORS
Omicron Delta Epsilon
1916 Delta Sigma Rho-Tau
Kappa Alpha
1923 Kappa Delta Pi
1926 Alpha Kappa Delta
1929 Psi Chi
1930 Kappa Tau Alpha
1936 Phi Eta Sigma
1938 Mortar Board
1940 Alpha Epsilon Delta
1941 Alpha Lambda Delta

OHIO NORTHERN UNIVERSITY Ada, OH. Founded in 1871 by Henry Solomon Lehr and has been affiliated with the United Methodist Church since 1898; fully accredited undergraduate colleges of arts and sciences, engineering, pharmacy, and business administration, as well as a graduate college of law.

Five of the eight fraternities are on land leased from the university in houses that are fraternity-owned. The remaining three are located off-campus at fraternity owned locations; the four sororities have off-campus houses and women reside in the houses as well as in residence halls.

NIC MEN'S
1905 Sigma Phi Epsilon
1912 Sigma Pi
1920 Delta Sigma Phi
1925 Phi Kappa Theta
1926 Phi Mu Delta
1942 Alpha Sigma Phi
1966 Theta Chi

1951 Beta Gamma Sigma
1951 Omicron Delta Kappa
1953 Tau Beta Pi
1954 Phi Alpha Theta
1956 Phi Kappa Phi
1956 Pi Gamma Mu
1958 Sigma Pi Sigma
1960 Eta Kappa Nu
1965 Alpha Epsilon
1966 Phi Sigma Iota
1969 Pi Kappa Lambda
1978 Pi Sigma Alpha

OTHER HONORS
National Order of Omega
1922 Delta Phi Delta
1922 National Collegiate
Players
1929 Phi Beta Kappa
1961 Sigma Xi
1969 Pi Mu Epsilon

SERVICE
1942 Alpha Phi Omega

RECOGNITION
Angel Flight
Arnold Air Society (D-1)
1925 Eta Sigma Phi
1927 Blue Key
1939 Scabbard and Blade (8)
1957 Delta Phi Alpha

INACTIVE
1876–86 Kappa Alpha Theta
1910–82 Sigma Pi
1912–31 Sigma Sigma Sigma
1917–32 Alpha Sigma Alpha
1919–71 Theta Phi Alpha
1922–85 Zeta Tau Alpha
1927–77 Tau Kappa Epsilon
1943–69 Zeta Beta Tau
1943–69 Zeta Tau Alpha
1951–56 Alpha Kappa Lambda
1951–84 Alpha Epsilon Phi
1953–73 Phi Kappa Sigma
1955–75 Kappa Delta
1970–72 Sigma Alpha Mu

NPC WOMEN'S
1959 Alpha Xi Delta
1959 Delta Zeta
1959 Zeta Tau Alpha
1966 Alpha Omicron Pi

PROFESSIONAL
1910 Delta Theta Phi
1920 Kappa Psi

1923 Rho Pi Phi
1927 Kappa Kappa Psi
1955 Phi Delta Chi
1957 Kappa Epsilon
1960 Phi Alpha Delta
1964 Tau Beta Sigma

OTHER PROFESSIONAL
1922 Sigma Delta Kappa
1952 Alpha Zeta Omega
1966 Kappa Beta Pi

ACHS HONORS
Omicron Delta Epsilon
1960 Kappa Delta Pi
1962 Rho Chi
1963 Sigma Tau Delta
1966 Alpha Lambda Delta
1966 Phi Eta Sigma
1967 Phi Kappa Phi
1968 Phi Alpha Theta
1968 Sigma Delta Pi
1969 Pi Delta Phi

THE OHIO STATE UNIVERSITY Columbus, OH. Founded in 1873 under the Land Grant Act of 1862, governed by a board of trustees. Coeducational; five undergraduate colleges, a graduate school, five professional colleges, nine special schools and research centers.

The fraternities and sororities occupy houses and premises of their ownership.

NIC MEN'S
1878 Phi Gamma Delta
1880 Phi Kappa Psi
1882 Sigma Chi
1883 Chi Phi
1883 Phi Delta Theta
1885 Beta Theta Pi
1891 Sigma Nu
1892 Alpha Tau Omega
1892 Sigma Alpha Epsilon
1894 Delta Tau Delta
1895 Kappa Sigma
1902 Delta Chi
1904 Alpha Gamma Rho
1904 Delta Upsilon
1906 Acacia
1908 Alpha Sigma Phi
1908 Sigma Phi Epsilon
1908 Sigma Pi
1911 Triangle
1912 Phi Kappa Tau
1912 Pi Kappa Alpha
1915 Kappa Alpha Psi (A)
1920 Delta Sigma Phi
1920 Phi Kappa Theta
1920 Sigma Alpha Mu
1921 Alpha Epsilon Pi
1921 Tau Kappa Epsilon
1921 Theta Chi
1922 Alpha Gamma Sigma
1923 Alpha Phi Delta
1923 Lambda Chi Alpha
1924 Tau Delta Phi
1925 Phi Kappa Sigma
1925 Phi Sigma Kappa
1927 Tau Epsilon Phi
1950 Alpha Kappa Lambda

NPHC MEN'S
Phi Beta Sigma
1910 Alpha Phi Alpha

1970 Omicron Delta Kappa
1973 Delta Mu Delta
1973 Tau Beta Pi
1975 Mortar Board
1987 Kappa Mu Epsilon

OTHER HONORS
National Order of Omega

RECOGNITION
1919 Society for Collegiate
Journalists—Pi Delta
Epsilon-Alpha Phi Gamma
(A)
1924 Theta Alpha Phi
1959 Sigma Delta Psi
1966 Beta Beta Beta
1967 Pi Kappa Delta
1970 Kappa Pi

INACTIVE
1886–88 Kappa Sigma
1924–81 Alpha Epsilon Pi

1926 Omega Psi Phi

NPC WOMEN'S
1888 Kappa Kappa Gamma
1892 Kappa Alpha Theta
1894 Pi Beta Phi
1896 Delta Delta Delta
1911 Delta Gamma
1911 Delta Zeta
1912 Alpha Phi
1913 Phi Mu
1916 Alpha Xi Delta
1919 Chi Omega
1921 Alpha Delta Pi
1921 Alpha Epsilon Phi
1921 Sigma Delta Tau
1921 Zeta Tau Alpha
1922 Kappa Delta
1923 Alpha Chi Omega
1928 Delta Phi Epsilon
1946 Alpha Gamma Delta

NPHC WOMEN'S
1919 Delta Sigma Theta (B)
1921 Alpha Kappa Alpha
1971 Sigma Gamma Rho

PROFESSIONAL
1893 Phi Delta Phi
1896 Xi Psi Phi
1901 Psi Omega
1908 Phi Delta Chi
1911 Omega Tau Sigma
1913 Delta Theta Phi
1915 Alpha Kappa Psi
1915 Alpha Rho Chi
1921 Delta Sigma Pi
1921 Phi Alpha Delta
1923 Kappa Kappa Psi
1923 Rho Pi Phi
1924 Theta Tau
1925 Kappa Psi

1926 Alpha Omega
1926 Kappa Epsilon
1928 Delta Omicron
1931 Phi Mu Alpha—Sinfonia
1950 Tau Beta Sigma
1953 Alpha Tau Delta
1959 Alpha Delta Theta
1966 Gamma Iota Sigma
1978 Sigma Alpha
1983 Phi Alpha Delta

OTHER PROFESSIONAL
1897 Alpha Zeta
1902 Keramos
1903 Phi Beta Pi and Theta
     Kappa Psi (B)
1907 Alpha Psi
1911 Sigma Delta Chi
1913 Women in Communications
1915 Phi Upsilon Omicron
1921 Phi Delta Epsilon
1922 Gamma Eta Gamma
1922 Pi Lambda Theta
1926 Delta Sigma Delta
1926 Kappa Beta Pi
1928 Kappa Phi Kappa
1929 Beta Alpha Psi
1948 Delta Pi Epsilon
1985 Alpha Zeta Omega

ACHS HONORS
     Omicron Delta Epsilon
     Pi Alpha Alpha
1907 Eta Kappa Nu
1910 Delta Sigma Rho-Tau
     Kappa Alpha
1918 Mortar Board
1921 Tau Beta Pi
1922 Beta Gamma Sigma
1927 Phi Alpha Theta
1928 Kappa Omicron Nu
1928 Phi Eta Sigma
1929 Alpha Kappa Delta
1929 Pi Sigma Alpha
1932 Sigma Theta Tau
1934 Rho Chi
1936 Kappa Tau Alpha
1936 Sigma Pi Sigma
1945 Alpha Lambda Delta
1948 Pi Tau Sigma
1949 Alpha Pi Mu
1949 Chi Epsilon
1951 Psi Chi
1953 Sigma Gamma Tau
1954 Gamma Theta Upsilon
1957 Pi Kappa Lambda
1962 Alpha Sigma Mu
1973 Phi Kappa Phi
1980 Sigma Lambda Alpha

OTHER HONORS
     National Order of Omega
1898 Sigma Xi

OHIO WESLEYAN UNIVERSITY Delaware, OH. University; college of liberal arts; coeducational; private control (Methodist); established 1841; chartered 1842; Ohio Wesleyan Female College merged with Ohio Wesleyan Univesity 1877.

One fraternity and five sororities occupy their own houses on land of their ownership; ten fraternities occupy college-owned houses.

1904 Phi Beta Kappa
1905 Gamma Sigma Delta
1914 Order of the Coif
1916 Omicron Kappa Upsilon
1919 Pi Mu Epsilon
1933 Alpha Omega Alpha
1939 Delta Phi Delta
1952 National Collegiate
     Players
1963 Iota Sigma Pi

SERVICE
1934 Alpha Phi Omega

RECOGNITION
     Angel Flight
     Arnold Air Society (D-1)
1911 Phi Lambda Upsilon
1915 Scabbard and Blade (1)
1917 Sigma Delta Psi
1922 Gamma Alpha
1926 Chi Delta Phi
1927 Sigma Delta Epsilon
1929 Pi Alpha Xi
1930 Phi Delta Gamma
1934 Eta Sigma Phi
1934 Phi Zeta
1958 Sigma Phi Alpha
1965 National Block and Bridle
     Club
1967 Iota Lambda Sigma

INACTIVE
          Lambda Delta Sigma
1902–72 Alpha Kappa Kappa
1910–36 Alpha Chi Sigma
1911–89 Zeta Beta Tau
1911–89 Zeta Tau Alpha
1913   Phi Chi
1913–43 Phi Rho Sigma
1915–24 Phi Sigma
1919–40 Sigma Kappa
1919–44 Theta Phi Alpha
1920   Tau Epsilon Rho
1920–57 Theta Xi
1922–34 Alpha Sigma Alpha
1922–35 Tau Sigma Delta
1922–76 Kappa Delta Rho
1923–82 Alpha Chi Rho
1926   Sigma Gamma Epsilon
1926–60 Phi Mu Delta
1927–36 Pi Kappa Phi
1927–77 Pi Lambda Phi
1928   Phi Lambda Kappa
1928–58 Phi Sigma Sigma
1928–85 Phi Chi Theta
1932–36 Phi Epsilon Kappa
1939–63 Pi Omega Pi
1941   Omega Epsilon Phi
1941   Zeta Phi Eta
1948   Delta Phi Alpha
1951–67 Gamma Phi Beta
1979–83 Zeta Psi

NIC MEN'S
1853 Beta Theta Pi
1855 Sigma Chi
1860 Phi Delta Theta
1861 Phi Kappa Psi
1866 Delta Tau Delta
1869 Phi Gamma Delta
1873 Chi Phi
1887 Alpha Tau Omega
1888 Sigma Alpha Epsilon
1915 Sigma Phi Epsilon
1931 Tau Kappa Epsilon

NPC WOMEN'S
1880 Kappa Kappa Gamma
1881 Kappa Alpha Theta
1924 Delta Gamma
1925 Delta Delta Delta
1925 Pi Beta Phi

PROFESSIONAL
1923 Mu Phi Epsilon

ACHS HONORS
     Omicron Delta Epsilon
1907 Delta Sigma Rho-Tau
     Kappa Alpha
1923 Kappa Delta Pi
1923 Pi Kappa Lambda
1927 Omicron Delta Kappa
1929 Mortar Board
1929 Sigma Pi Sigma
1932 Alpha Kappa Delta
1932 Pi Sigma Alpha
1951 Psi Chi
1954 Phi Alpha Theta
1978 Phi Sigma Iota

THE UNIVERSITY OF OKLAHOMA Norman, OK. Chartered 1890, first classes 1892. Undergraduate and graduate state-supported coeducational university. Governing body, board of regents appointed by governor. Eight degree-granting colleges and schools of medicine and nursing.

The fraternities and sororities own their houses and the land which they occupy.

NIC MEN'S
1905 Kappa Alpha Order
1906 Kappa Sigma
1907 Beta Theta Pi
1909 Sigma Nu
1912 Sigma Chi
1916 Phi Gamma Delta
1918 Phi Delta Theta
1920 Phi Kappa Psi
1920 Pi Kappa Alpha
1921 Alpha Tau Omega
1922 Delta Tau Delta
1923 Pi Kappa Phi
1926 Lambda Chi Alpha
1927 Delta Chi
1927 Delta Upsilon
1929 Phi Kappa Sigma
1934 Phi Kappa Theta
1946 Sigma Phi Epsilon
1953 Delta Kappa Epsilon
1959 Alpha Epsilon Pi
1973 Kappa Alpha Psi (A)
1979 Triangle

NPHC MEN'S
     Phi Beta Sigma
1967 Alpha Phi Alpha

1985 Phi Eta Sigma

OTHER HONORS
     National Order of Omega
1907 Phi Beta Kappa
1922 Delta Phi Delta
1927 Pi Mu Epsilon

RECOGNITION
     Angel Flight
     Arnold Air Society (D-1)
1919 Theta Alpha Phi

INACTIVE
1863–70 Alpha Sigma Phi
1922–82 Phi Mu Alpha—
        Sinfonia
1923–67 Alpha Delta Pi
1923–84 Gamma Phi Beta
1924–37 Phi Mu
1924–68 Zeta Tau Alpha
1924–77 Alpha Chi Omega
1924–79 Alpha Xi Delta
1924–84 Alpha Gamma Delta
1925–41 Sigma Kappa
1925–44 Kappa Delta
1925–75 Chi Omega
1926–82 Kappa Sigma
1928–58 Phi Kappa Tau
1930–31 Kappa Omicron Nu
1931   Phi Epsilon Kappa
1948–68 Pi Lambda Phi
1949–71 Phi Upsilon Omicron

COLONIES
1924 Delta Zeta

NPC WOMEN'S
1909 Kappa Alpha Theta
1910 Delta Delta Delta
1910 Pi Beta Phi
1914 Kappa Kappa Gamma
1916 Alpha Chi Omega
1917 Alpha Phi
1918 Delta Gamma
1918 Gamma Phi Beta
1919 Alpha Gamma Delta
1919 Chi Omega
1953 Zeta Tau Alpha
1955 Kappa Delta

NPHC WOMEN'S
1962 Alpha Kappa Alpha
1973 Alpha Kappa Alpha
1973 Delta Sigma Theta (B)
1976 Alpha Kappa Alpha

PROFESSIONAL
1911 Phi Delta Phi
1912 Phi Mu Alpha—Sinfonia
1913 Phi Delta Chi
1916 Phi Alpha Delta
1921 Kappa Kappa Psi
1922 Mu Phi Epsilon
1929 Delta Sigma Pi

1929 Sigma Alpha Iota
1946 Tau Beta Sigma
1947 Delta Theta Phi
1960 Phi Alpha Delta
1965 Kappa Epsilon
1981 Alpha Rho Chi
1984 Phi Alpha Delta

OTHER PROFESSIONAL
1911 Sigma Delta Chi
1915 Women in Communications
1926 Kappa Beta Pi
1949 Delta Pi Epsilon
1963 Alpha Tau Alpha

ACHS HONORS
     Omicron Delta Epsilon
     Pi Alpha Alpha
1913 Delta Sigma Rho-Tau
     Kappa Alpha
1915 Kappa Delta Pi
1922 Pi Sigma Alpha
1922 Rho Chi
1925 Mortar Board
1926 Kappa Omicron Nu
1926 Tau Beta Pi
1927 Phi Eta Sigma
1928 Phi Sigma
1929 Alpha Lambda Delta
1930 Sigma Pi Sigma
1933 Beta Gamma Sigma
1936 Alpha Epsilon Delta
1936 Psi Chi
1940 Pi Tau Sigma
1942 Eta Kappa Nu
1950 Gamma Theta Upsilon
1951 Kappa Tau Alpha
1953 Sigma Gamma Tau
1955 Omicron Delta Kappa
1955 Pi Kappa Lambda
1957 Phi Alpha Theta
1958 Alpha Kappa Delta
1967 Beta Phi Mu
1968 Alpha Pi Mu
1968 Tau Sigma Delta
1969 Lambda Sigma Society
1970 Sigma Theta Tau
1983 Chi Epsilon
1990 Phi Kappa Phi

OTHER HONORS
     National Order of Omega
1916 Sigma Gamma Epsilon
1920 Phi Beta Kappa
1921 Iota Sigma Pi
1925 Order of the Coif
1929 Pi Mu Epsilon

1930 Sigma Xi
1936 Delta Phi Delta
1953 Alpha Omega Alpha

SERVICE
1942 Alpha Phi Omega
1968 Gamma Sigma Sigma

RECOGNITION
     Angel Flight
     Arnold Air Society (G-1)
1921 Scabbard and Blade (3)
1928 Sigma Delta Psi
1942 Lambda Tau
1948 Delta Phi Alpha
1952 Phi Lambda Upsilon

INACTIVE
1909–89 Sigma Alpha Epsilon
1912   Phi Beta Pi and Theta
        Kappa Psi (a)
1915–33 Alpha Kappa Psi
1918   Delta Psi Kappa
1919–69 Alpha Chi Sigma
1920–42 Alpha Kappa Kappa
1920–82 Sigma Alpha Mu
1920–89 Acacia
1921–58 Kappa Psi
1921–85 Alpha Xi Delta
1922   Phi Chi
1922–63 Pi Lambda Phi
1923–65 Phi Mu
1923–86 Alpha Sigma Phi
1924–33 Alpha Omicron Pi
1924–34 Sigma Mu Sigma
1928   Eta Sigma Phi
1929–75 Sigma Delta Tau
1939–72 Pi Omega Pi
1945–57 Kappa Alpha Mu
1947–70 Alpha Delta Pi
1949–60 Theta Xi
1950–54 Kappa Delta Rho
1951–58 Pi Gamma Mu
1951–70 Sigma Delta Pi
1956–79 Alpha Epsilon Phi
1959   Zeta Phi Eta
1966–69 Delta Phi Epsilon
1970–72 Zeta Beta Tau
1970–72 Zeta Tau Alpha
1975–75 Phi Gamma Nu
1977–87 Tau Kappa Epsilon
1980–82 Sigma Sigma Sigma

COLONIES
1920 Lambda Kappa Sigma
1956 Delta Sigma Phi

OKLAHOMA BAPTIST UNIVERSITY Shaw-
nee, OK. Founded by Baptist General Convention of
Oklahoma, board of trustees organized 1907, chartered 1910, first instruction 1911. University; coeducational; church-related.

PROFESSIONAL
1928 Sigma Alpha Iota
1967 Kappa Kappa Psi
1967 Phi Mu Alpha—Sinfonia
1973 Tau Beta Sigma

ACHS HONORS
1928 Kappa Delta Pi
1941 Sigma Tau Delta
1958 Phi Eta Sigma
1961 Alpha Lambda Delta
1963 Omicron Delta Kappa

1968 Mortar Board
1968 Psi Chi
1989 Pi Kappa Lambda

SERVICE
1939 Alpha Phi Omega

RECOGNITION
1922 Pi Kappa Delta
1922 Theta Alpha Phi
1947 Kappa Pi
1954 Beta Beta Beta

INACTIVE
1929–37 Pi Gamma Mu

OKLAHOMA CHRISTIAN COLLEGE Oklahoma
City, OK. Private control: Church of Christ.
Founded in 1950. Four-year; coeducational; liberal
arts college.

ACHS HONORS
1966 Alpha Chi
1972 Phi Alpha Theta
1974 Sigma Tau Delta

RECOGNITION
1964 Alpha Psi Omega

OKLAHOMA CITY UNIVERSITY Oklahoma
City, OK. University; coeducational; private control
(Methodist Church); established 1904 as Epworth
University.

Kappa Alpha Order and Lambda Chi Alpha own
their houses and the land which they occupy.
Kappa Sigma and Sigma Alpha Epsilon are housed
in facilities rented from the college. Each national
sorority has an apartment in a building provided by
the university for which it pays rent by contract.

NIC MEN'S
1924 Lambda Chi Alpha
1952 Kappa Alpha Order
1967 Kappa Sigma

NPC WOMEN'S
1951 Gamma Phi Beta
1955 Alpha Chi Omega
1961 Alpha Phi

NPHC WOMEN'S
     Zeta Phi Beta

PROFESSIONAL
1928 Sigma Alpha Iota
1961 Phi Delta Phi
1964 Delta Theta Phi
1985 Phi Alpha Delta

ACHS HONORS
1960 Pi Kappa Lambda
1963 Sigma Pi Sigma
1967 Psi Chi
1971 Phi Alpha Theta

1981 Phi Eta Sigma

SERVICE
1939 Alpha Phi Omega

RECOGNITION
1922 Beta Beta Beta
1928 Kappa Pi
1933 Blue Key
1934 Cardinal Key
1943 Iota Tau Tau
1959 Alpha Psi Omega
1960 Alpha Psi Omega

INACTIVE
1928–65 Pi Gamma Mu
1948–79 Phi Mu Alpha—
        Sinfonia
1951–87 Delta Zeta
1952–61 Sigma Phi Epsilon
1956–83 Delta Sigma Pi
1975–86 Sigma Alpha Epsilon

OKLAHOMA PANHANDLE STATE UNIVERSITY
Goodwell, OK. College of liberal arts; teachers college, and technological institute; coeducational;
state control; established 1909.

ACHS HONORS
1985 Phi Alpha Theta

OKLAHOMA STATE UNIVERSITY Stillwa-
ter, OK. Founded 1890 as Oklahoma Agricultural
and Mechanical College by act of first territorial
legislature as land-grant school. Name changed to
Oklahoma State University 1957. Coeducational; divisions and colleges as follows: agriculture, arts and
sciences, business, education, engineering home
economics, veterinary medicine, graduate school.
Other branches of the university include the School
of Technical training at Okmulgee, and the Technical Institute at Oklahoma City.

Most fraternities and sororities own their houses and the land which they occupy.

NIC MEN'S
1917 Lambda Chi Alpha
1920 Kappa Sigma
1920 Sigma Nu
1920 Sigma Phi Epsilon
1921 Alpha Gamma Rho
1922 Sigma Chi
1923 Beta Theta Pi
1928 FarmHouse
1931 Sigma Alpha Epsilon
1937 Phi Kappa Theta
1939 Pi Kappa Alpha
1946 Phi Delta Theta
1947 Alpha Tau Omega
1948 Delta Chi
1949 Delta Tau Delta
1949 Phi Kappa Tau
1960 Delta Upsilon
1962 Phi Gamma Delta
1964 Triangle
1970 Pi Kappa Phi
1971 Kappa Alpha Psi (A)

NPHC MEN'S
1958 Alpha Phi Alpha

NPC WOMEN'S
1919 Kappa Alpha Theta
1919 Kappa Delta
1919 Pi Beta Phi
1920 Chi Omega
1921 Alpha Delta Pi
1922 Delta Zeta
1923 Zeta Tau Alpha
1947 Alpha Chi Omega
1947 Kappa Kappa Gamma
1958 Gamma Phi Beta
1962 Delta Delta Delta
1979 Phi Mu

NPHC WOMEN'S
1971 Delta Sigma Theta (B)

PROFESSIONAL
1919 Kappa Kappa Psi
1920 Alpha Kappa Psi
1926 Alpha Rho Chi
1938 Sigma Alpha Iota
1946 Tau Beta Sigma
1949 Delta Sigma Pi
1949 Phi Mu Alpha—Sinfonia
1958 Omega Tau Sigma
1985 Phi Alpha Delta

OTHER PROFESSIONAL
1916 Alpha Zeta
1938 Delta Pi Epsilon
1939 Beta Alpha Psi
1942 Women in Communications
1946 Sigma Delta Chi
1950 Phi Upsilon Omicron
1954 Alpha Psi
1963 Alpha Beta Alpha
1973 Alpha Epsilon Rho

ACHS HONORS
Omicron Delta Epsilon
1920 Phi Kappa Phi
1921 Kappa Delta Pi
1921 Kappa Omicron Nu
1930 Eta Kappa Nu
1930 Phi Sigma
1931 Phi Eta Sigma
1931 Pi Tau Sigma
1932 Phi Alpha Theta
1940 Mortar Board
1941 Chi Epsilon
1946 Sigma Tau Delta
1948 Gamma Theta Upsilon
1948 Psi Chi
1948 Sigma Pi Sigma
1951 Alpha Pi Mu
1954 Kappa Tau Alpha
1954 Omicron Delta Kappa
1959 Beta Gamma Sigma
1963 Pi Sigma Alpha
1964 Omega Chi Epsilon
1966 Alpha Epsilon Delta
1967 Alpha Lambda Delta
1971 Tau Sigma Delta
1973 Xi Sigma Pi
1974 Tau Beta Pi
1985 Sigma Lambda Alpha

OTHER HONORS
National Order of Omega
1938 Pi Mu Epsilon
1949 Sigma Gamma Epsilon
1949 Sigma Xi

SERVICE
1950 Alpha Phi Omega
1961 Intercollegiate Knights

RECOGNITION
Angel Flight
Arnold Air Society (G-1)
1916 Pi Kappa Delta
1920 National Block and Bridle Club
1920 Scabbard and Blade (2)
1929 Phi Lambda Upsilon
1930 Iota Lambda Sigma
1932 Blue Key
1950 Lambda Delta Lambda
1958 Phi Zeta

INACTIVE
1919–34 Theta Alpha Phi
1920–72 Kappa Alpha Order
1923–88 Acacia
1929–58 Pi Gamma Mu
1938–70 Pi Omega Pi
1947–68 Theta Chi
1947–71 Tau Kappa Epsilon
1967–91 Phi Kappa Psi
1968–81 Alpha Xi Delta
1970–79 Beta Sigma Psi

OLD DOMINION UNIVERSITY   Norfolk, VA. Schools of arts and letters, science and health professions, business administration, education, and engineering; coeducational; state control; formerly Norfolk division of College of William and Mary.

NIC MEN'S
1964 Pi Kappa Phi
1965 Alpha Tau Omega
1965 Kappa Alpha Order
1965 Tau Kappa Epsilon
1967 Sigma Nu
1968 Theta Chi
1973 Lambda Chi Alpha
1975 Kappa Alpha Psi (A)
1978 Phi Gamma Delta
1985 Sigma Phi Epsilon
1989 Kappa Delta Rho

NPHC MEN'S
Phi Beta Sigma

NPC WOMEN'S
1964 Alpha Xi Delta
1964 Chi Omega
1965 Pi Beta Phi
1966 Delta Zeta
1970 Alpha Phi
1987 Zeta Tau Alpha

NPHC WOMEN'S
1974 Delta Sigma Theta (B)
1975 Alpha Kappa Alpha
1982 Sigma Gamma Rho

PROFESSIONAL
1957 Sigma Alpha Iota
1959 Alpha Kappa Psi
1960 Phi Mu Alpha—Sinfonia
1975 Delta Psi Kappa
1990 Theta Tau

ACHS HONORS
Omicron Delta Epsilon

Pi Alpha Alpha
1962 Phi Alpha Theta
1971 Sigma Pi Sigma
1972 Psi Chi
1974 Alpha Chi
1974 Kappa Delta Pi
1974 Pi Sigma Alpha
1975 Beta Gamma Sigma
1975 Eta Kappa Nu
1976 Omicron Delta Kappa
1976 Sigma Delta Pi
1977 Phi Kappa Phi
1979 Chi Epsilon
1979 Tau Beta Pi
1985 Gamma Theta Upsilon

OTHER HONORS
National Order of Omega

SERVICE
1988 Alpha Phi Omega

RECOGNITION
1962 Pi Kappa Delta
1969 Beta Beta Beta
1969 Sigma Phi Alpha

INACTIVE
1949–72 Theta Xi
1963–72 Alpha Epsilon Pi
1966–85 Pi Kappa Alpha
1967–73 Phi Kappa Tau
1967–82 Delta Sigma Phi
1969–77 Alpha Epsilon Phi
1972–85 Phi Mu

OLIVET COLLEGE   Olivet, MI.

PROFESSIONAL
1974 Phi Mu Alpha—Sinfonia
1975 Mu Phi Epsilon
1986 Gamma Iota Sigma

ACHS HONORS
1967 Phi Alpha Theta

1968 Alpha Chi
1973 Phi Sigma Tau
1974 Omicron Delta Kappa
1979 Psi Chi

RECOGNITION
1969 Sigma Zeta

OLIVET NAZARENE COLLEGE   Kankakee, IL. College of liberal arts; coeducational; private control; Church of the Nazarene. Established 1907.

ACHS HONORS
1962 Sigma Tau Delta
1967 Phi Alpha Theta

1973 Kappa Delta Pi
1980 Sigma Pi Sigma
1982 Kappa Omicron Nu

ORAL ROBERTS COLLEGE   Tulsa, OK.

PROFESSIONAL
1970 Kappa Kappa Psi
1972 Mu Phi Epsilon

ACHS HONORS
1973 Alpha Lambda Delta

1974 Sigma Delta Pi
1976 Phi Alpha Theta
1990 Kappa Mu Epsilon

RECOGNITION
1976 Beta Beta Beta

UNIVERSITY OF OREGON   Eugene, OR. University; coeducational; state control; main campus at

Eugene, and medical, dental, and norsing school at Portland; established 1872, and first instruction 1876.

Fraternities and sororities occupy houses on property which is theirs with a few exceptions where ownership is by the college on rental basis to fraternity.

NIC MEN'S
Tau Kappa Epsilon
1900 Sigma Nu
1904 Kappa Sigma
1909 Beta Theta Pi
1910 Alpha Tau Omega
1910 Sigma Chi
1911 Phi Gamma Delta
1912 Phi Delta Theta
1913 Delta Tau Delta
1919 Sigma Alpha Epsilon
1921 Chi Psi
1923 Phi Kappa Psi
1925 Theta Chi
1926 Sigma Phi Epsilon
1931 Pi Kappa Alpha
1934 Delta Upsilon
1947 Tau Kappa Epsilon
1948 Lambda Chi Alpha
1950 Kappa Alpha Psi (A)

NPHC MEN'S
Phi Beta Sigma

NPC WOMEN'S
1908 Gamma Phi Beta
1909 Chi Omega
1909 Kappa Alpha Theta
1910 Delta Delta Delta
1913 Delta Gamma
1913 Kappa Kappa Gamma
1915 Alpha Phi
1915 Pi Beta Phi
1920 Delta Zeta
1921 Alpha Chi Omega

NPHC WOMEN'S
1973 Sigma Gamma Rho

PROFESSIONAL
1891 Phi Delta Phi
1900 Psi Omega
1908 Phi Alpha Delta
1908 Xi Psi Phi
1911 Mu Phi Epsilon
1913 Delta Theta Phi
1915 Alpha Kappa Psi
1929 Phi Beta

OTHER PROFESSIONAL
1907 Delta Sigma Delta
1913 Sigma Delta Chi
1915 Women in Communications
1921 Beta Alpha Psi
1921 Pi Lambda Theta
1928 Phi Epsilon Kappa

ACHS HONORS
Pi Alpha Alpha
1914 Delta Sigma Rho-Tau Kappa Alpha
1921 Beta Gamma Sigma
1923 Mortar Board
1926 Alpha Kappa Delta
1928 Pi Delta Phi
1949 Phi Eta Sigma
1951 Pi Sigma Alpha

1953 Alpha Lambda Delta
1960 Kappa Tau Alpha
1964 Pi Kappa Lambda
1973 Beta Phi Mu
1976 Alpha Epsilon
1976 Sigma Theta Tau
1983 Pi Gamma Mu
1988 Phi Alpha Theta

OTHER HONORS
National Order of Omega
1923 Alpha Omega Alpha
1923 Phi Beta Kappa
1923 Sigma Xi
1931 Pi Mu Epsilon
1934 Order of the Coif

SERVICE
1948 Alpha Phi Omega

RECOGNITION
Angel Flight
Arnold Air Society (H-2)
1925 Sigma Delta Psi
1928 Scabbard and Blade (6)
1949 Eta Mu Pi
1952 Chi Delta Phi

INACTIVE
1903–64 Alpha Kappa Kappa
1909–13 Acacia
1913–31 Phi Chi
1915–17 Gamma Eta Gamma
1920–86 Alpha Delta Pi
1921 Kappa Beta Pi
1921–49 Phi Beta Pi and Theta Kappa Psi (B)
1921–74 Phi Mu Alpha—Sinfonia
1922–60 National Collegiate Players
1922–66 Sigma Delta Pi
1922–68 Alpha Xi Delta
1923–89 Alpha Omicron Pi
1924–69 Alpha Gamma Delta
1924–81 Phi Chi Theta
1926–33 Kappa Delta
1926–36 Phi Delta Epsilon
1926–66 Phi Sigma Kappa
1927–37 Phi Mu
1929–71 Zeta Tau Alpha
1930–62 Sigma Alpha Mu
1936 Delta Phi Alpha
1938–52 Alpha Phi Alpha
1947–72 Pi Kappa Phi
1948–52 Sigma Pi Sigma
1948–64 Phi Kappa Sigma
1953–71 Psi Chi
1955 Phi Beta Pi and Theta Kappa Psi (a)
1962–70 Chi Phi
1963–71 Delta Chi

COLONIES
1928 Sigma Kappa

University Of Oregon Medical School And University Of Oregon Dental School Portland, OR. Established 1887; coeducational; schools of medicine, dentistry, and nursing.

PROFESSIONAL
1932 Alpha Tau Delta

OREGON INSTITUTE OF TECHNOLOGY Klamath Falls, OR. Public institution. Founded in 1947. Four-year; coeducational; technical institution.

All dorms are co-ed. 82% of students live off campus or commute.

NIC MEN'S
1982 Phi Delta Theta

1978–83 Zeta Beta Tau
1978–83 Zeta Tau Alpha

INACTIVE
1977–81 Phi Sigma Kappa

OREGON STATE UNIVERSITY Corvallis, OR. Founded as Corvallis College in 1858 and designated as the agricultural college of the State of Oregon in 1868, Oregon State University is a comprehensive research university with over 15,000 students enrolled in its 12 colleges and schools. It is also one of the nation's few land- and sea-grant universities. The 400-acre main campus is noted for its natural beauty of rolling green lawns, tall shade trees, and flowering shrubs. The university also maintains the OSU Hatfield Marine Science Center on the Oregon coast. Within the state and throughout the northwest, OSU is recognized for a long-standing commitment to academic excellence and has a dynamic tradition of student involvement in campus governance, campus and community service organizations, and in Greek honor societies and living groups.

NIC MEN'S
1882 Alpha Tau Omega
1915 Kappa Sigma
1915 Sigma Alpha Epsilon
1916 Sigma Chi
1916 Theta Chi
1917 Lambda Chi Alpha
1917 Sigma Nu
1918 Phi Delta Theta
1918 Sigma Phi Epsilon
1920 Alpha Sigma Phi
1920 Pi Kappa Alpha
1921 Phi Gamma Delta
1921 Phi Sigma Kappa
1922 Delta Upsilon
1923 Beta Theta Pi
1924 Acacia
1924 Alpha Gamma Rho
1924 Pi Kappa Phi
1924 Tau Kappa Epsilon
1928 Kappa Delta Rho
1930 Delta Tau Delta
1931 Chi Phi
1931 Delta Chi
1948 Phi Kappa Psi
1951 Phi Kappa Theta
1958 Alpha Kappa Lambda

1964 FarmHouse
1978 Kappa Alpha Psi (A)

NPC WOMEN'S
1915 Alpha Chi Omega
1917 Chi Omega
1917 Kappa Alpha Theta
1917 Pi Beta Phi
1918 Delta Delta Delta
1918 Gamma Phi Beta
1918 Sigma Kappa
1919 Alpha Xi Delta
1921 Alpha Gamma Delta
1924 Kappa Kappa Gamma
1926 Alpha Delta Pi
1926 Alpha Omicron Pi
1926 Kappa Delta
1946 Delta Gamma
1947 Alpha Phi

PROFESSIONAL
1911 Kappa Psi
1924 Phi Chi Theta
1930 Lambda Kappa Sigma
1967 Zeta Phi Eta
1982 Phi Delta Chi

OTHER PROFESSIONAL
1918 Alpha Zeta

1920 Sigma Delta Chi
1923 Beta Alpha Psi
1925 Women in Communications

ACHS HONORS
    Omicron Delta Epsilon
1919 Kappa Omicron Nu
1921 Eta Kappa Nu
1921 Xi Sigma Pi
1922 Delta Sigma Rho-Tau
    Kappa Alpha
1922 Rho Chi
1924 Phi Kappa Phi
1924 Tau Beta Pi
1928 Kappa Delta Pi
1933 Alpha Lambda Delta
1933 Mortar Board
1933 Phi Sigma
1934 Sigma Pi Sigma
1941 Pi Tau Sigma
1949 Phi Eta Sigma
1951 Beta Gamma Sigma
1954 Phi Alpha Theta
1957 Gamma Theta Upsilon
1959 Sigma Delta Pi
1962 Pi Delta Phi
1969 Alpha Pi Mu
1976 Kappa Tau Alpha
1980 Pi Sigma Alpha

OTHER HONORS
    National Order of Omega
1923 National Collegiate
    Players

1937 Sigma Xi
1938 Pi Mu Epsilon
1960 Iota Sigma Pi

SERVICE
1946 Alpha Phi Omega

RECOGNITION
    Angel Flight
    Arnold Air Society (H-2)
1920 Scabbard and Blade (2)
1927 Phi Lambda Upsilon
1928 Sigma Delta Psi
1934 Blue Key
1949 Kappa Pi
1962 National Block and Bridle
    Club

INACTIVE
1909–43 Gamma Sigma Delta
1914–33 Alpha Kappa Psi
1919–77 Delta Zeta
1920   Delta Psi Kappa
1923–70 Zeta Tau Alpha
1924–85 Sigma Pi
1925–87 Phi Kappa Tau
1927–43 Alpha Chi Rho
1927–72 Theta Xi
1928–85 Delta Sigma Phi
1931–35 Phi Mu Delta
1934–53 Sigma Gamma Epsilon
1949–75 Phi Kappa Sigma
1962–70 Zeta Psi

OSGOODE HALL LAW SCHOOL Toronto, ON. Founded 1873; coeducational.

PROFESSIONAL
1896 Phi Delta Phi

OTHER PROFESSIONAL
1925 Kappa Beta Pi

COLLEGE OF OSTEOPATHIC MEDICINE AND SURGERY Des Moines, IA. Incorporated 1898; coeducational, nonsectarian. Four-year course in osteopathic medicine, leading to the degree Doctor of Osteopathy.

OSTEOPATHIC
1912 Delta Omega
1915 Phi Sigma Gamma
1918 Atlas Club
1925 Sigma Sigma Phi

INACTIVE
1903   Iota Tau Sigma
1932   Psi Sigma Alpha
1938   Lambda Omicron
      Gamma

OTTAWA UNIVERSITY Ottawa, KS. College of liberal arts; coeducational; private control (American Baptist Convention). Chartered 1865.

OTHER PROFESSIONAL
1974 Kappa Beta Pi

ACHS HONORS
1967 Phi Alpha Theta

OTHER HONORS
1971 Alpha Omega Alpha

RECOGNITION
1913 Pi Kappa Delta

1926 Alpha Psi Omega
1966 Kappa Pi

INACTIVE
1930–43 Pi Gamma Mu
1971–88 Sigma Pi Sigma

OTTERBEIN COLLEGE Westerville, OH. Established 1847; first college in U.S. to begin as a coeducational institution, and the first to employ women on faculty. Classes open to students of all races, nationalities, and creeds.

A comprehensive study of the Greek system has been launched to better serve the needs of the members.

PROFESSIONAL
1955 Delta Omicron

ACHS HONORS
    Omicron Delta Epsilon
1933 Phi Sigma Iota
1948 Alpha Epsilon Delta
1948 Phi Alpha Theta
1960 Alpha Lambda Delta
1965 Phi Eta Sigma

OTHER HONORS
    National Order of Omega

RECOGNITION
    Angel Flight
    Arnold Air Society (D-1)
1923 Pi Kappa Delta
1927 Theta Alpha Phi
1929 Sigma Zeta

OUACHITA BAPTIST UNIVERSITY Arkadelphia, AR. Founded by Arkansas Baptist Convention in 1885; classes began in 1886. Coeducational; liberal arts; undergraduate and graduate degrees.

PROFESSIONAL
1964 Phi Mu Alpha—Sinfonia
1967 Sigma Alpha Iota

ACHS HONORS
1930 Sigma Tau Delta
1958 Kappa Delta Pi
1976 Phi Alpha Theta
1981 Pi Kappa Lambda

OTHER HONORS
1961 National Collegiate
    Players

RECOGNITION
1957 Gamma Sigma Epsilon
1958 Scabbard and Blade (14)
1961 Blue Key
1962 Beta Beta Beta

INACTIVE
1930–37 Pi Gamma Mu

OUR LADY OF HOLY CROSS COLLEGE New Orleans, LA. Private control. Roman Catholic. Founded in 1916. Four-year; coeducational; liberal arts college.

No housing available.

ACHS HONORS
1975 Alpha Chi

RECOGNITION
1972 Blue Key

OUR LADY OF THE LAKE UNIVERSITY San Antonio, TX. Liberal arts college undergraduate; coeducational; three professional schools: social work, communication disorders, education. Founded 1896.

PROFESSIONAL
1934 Sigma Alpha Iota

ACHS HONORS
1922 Alpha Chi
1984 Delta Mu Delta

RECOGNITION
1943 Sigma Zeta

1945 Alpha Psi Omega
1946 Kappa Pi

INACTIVE
1937–69 Sigma Tau Delta
1937–83 Pi Gamma Mu
1943–76 Kappa Omicron Nu
1957–67 Alpha Beta Alpha

PACE UNIVERSITY New York, NY. Six schools: arts and sciences; business administration; nursing; education; continuing education; and law. Coeducational; nonsectarian; established 1906.

NIC MEN'S
1979 Alpha Phi Delta
1983 Delta Kappa Epsilon
1990 Tau Kappa Epsilon

NPHC MEN'S
Phi Beta Sigma

NPC WOMEN'S
1987 Phi Sigma Sigma
1990 Delta Phi Epsilon

PROFESSIONAL
1961 Pi Sigma Epsilon
1973 Phi Chi Theta
1977 Delta Theta Phi
1979 Phi Alpha Delta

ACHS HONORS
Omicron Delta Epsilon
Pi Alpha Alpha
1968 Phi Alpha Theta
1968 Pi Gamma Mu
1969 Psi Chi
1970 Phi Sigma Iota
1972 Pi Delta Phi
1974 Kappa Mu Epsilon
1976 Delta Mu Delta
1985 Phi Eta Sigma

SERVICE
1966 Alpha Phi Omega

RECOGNITION
1968 Beta Beta Beta

Pleasantville/Briarcliff Campus Pleasantville, NY.

NIC MEN'S
1987 Alpha Phi Delta

1984 Phi Sigma Iota

ACHS HONORS
1978 Phi Eta Sigma

UNIVERSITY OF THE PACIFIC Stockton, CA. Formerly College of the Pacific; University; coeducational; private control. Chartered 1851. Schools of liberal arts and sciences, music, education, engineering, pharmacy, business and public administration.

One fraternity occupies a house which stands on college-owned land; three occupy college-owned houses on college property; one rents off-campus from private owner; one occupies privately-owned house off-campus. Two sororities own houses which stand on college-owned land; two occupy college-owned houses on college property.

NIC MEN'S
1970 Sigma Alpha Epsilon
1986 Phi Delta Theta

NPC WOMEN'S
1889 Kappa Alpha Theta
1959 Delta Delta Delta
1959 Delta Gamma
1962 Alpha Chi Omega

NPHC WOMEN'S
1974 Delta Sigma Theta (B)
1978 Alpha Kappa Alpha

PROFESSIONAL
1931 Phi Mu Alpha—Sinfonia
1959 Lambda Kappa Sigma
1960 Alpha Chi Sigma
1969 Phi Alpha Delta
1969 Phi Delta Phi
1983 Delta Theta Phi
1984 Delta Sigma Pi

ACHS HONORS
Omicron Delta Epsilon
Pi Alpha Alpha
1921 Pi Kappa Lambda
1951 Phi Kappa Phi
1955 Phi Sigma Tau
1960 Alpha Lambda Delta
1964 Rho Chi

1966 Sigma Delta Pi
1967 Mortar Board
1982 Eta Kappa Nu
1988 Tau Beta Pi

OTHER HONORS
National Order of Omega

SERVICE
1981 Alpha Phi Omega

RECOGNITION
1922 Pi Kappa Delta
1931 Beta Beta Beta
1931 Society for Collegiate
Journalists—Pi Delta
Epsilon-Alpha Phi Gamma
(A)
1937 Sigma Delta Psi
1950 Blue Key

INACTIVE
1881–92 Phi Kappa Psi
1924–58 Pi Gamma Mu
1959–73 Delta Upsilon
1960–66 Phi Sigma Kappa
1960–74 Alpha Epsilon Delta
1961–78 Phi Kappa Tau
1963–72 Gamma Phi Beta
1963–74 Phi Eta Sigma

College Of Physicians And Surgeons Of San Francisco And School Of Dentistry San Francisco, CA. Established 1896; coeducational. Became part of the University of the Pacific 1962.

PROFESSIONAL
1918 Alpha Omega

OTHER HONORS
1933 Omicron Kappa Upsilon

PACIFIC UNIVERSITY Forest Grove, OR. University; coeducational; private control (United Church of Christ, Congregational); chartered as Tualatin Academy 1849; became Pacific University 1957; college of optometry.

NIC MEN'S
1955 Alpha Kappa Lambda

PROFESSIONAL
1956 Phi Delta Chi

RECOGNITION
1926 Blue Key

INACTIVE
1948 Omega Epsilon Phi
1965–70 Sigma Alpha Iota
1965–82 Phi Mu Alpha—
Sinfonia

PACIFIC LUTHERAN UNIVERSITY Tacoma, WA. University; coeducational; private control; related to Lutheran Church. Founded 1890.

PROFESSIONAL
1953 Mu Phi Epsilon
1963 Alpha Kappa Psi

OTHER PROFESSIONAL
1976 Beta Alpha Psi

ACHS HONORS
Omicron Delta Epsilon
1971 Beta Gamma Sigma
1987 Psi Chi

SERVICE
The National Spurs

1950 Alpha Phi Omega
1964 Intercollegiate Knights

RECOGNITION
1942 Alpha Psi Omega
1949 Pi Kappa Delta
1951 Blue Key

INACTIVE
1961–70 Pi Gamma Mu
1966–79 Phi Chi Theta
1967–75 Phi Beta

PACIFIC UNION COLLEGE Angwin, CA.

ACHS HONORS
1981 Psi Chi

INACTIVE
1968–86 Sigma Pi Sigma

PAINE COLLEGE Augusta, GA. College of liberal arts; coeducational; private control (Methodist); established 1882.

NIC MEN'S
1970 Kappa Alpha Psi (A)

NPHC MEN'S
Phi Beta Sigma
1970 Alpha Phi Alpha

NPHC WOMEN'S
1970 Delta Sigma Theta (B)
1970 Sigma Gamma Rho
1971 Alpha Kappa Alpha

ACHS HONORS
1947 Alpha Kappa Mu

PAN AMERICAN UNIVERSITY Edinburg, TX. Began as Edinburg Junior College 1927; first instruction 1927; chartered as senior college 1952. Coeducational; became a part of the Texas College and University System under full state support September, 1965.

NIC MEN'S
1964 Phi Sigma Kappa
1970 Phi Kappa Theta

NPC WOMEN'S
1966 Delta Zeta
1966 Kappa Delta

PROFESSIONAL
1969 Alpha Kappa Psi
1972 Mu Phi Epsilon

ACHS HONORS
1958 Alpha Chi
1969 Kappa Delta Pi
1972 Phi Alpha Theta
1975 Pi Omega Pi
1982 Phi Alpha Theta
1983 Phi Kappa Phi
1983 Psi Chi

SERVICE
1955 Alpha Phi Omega

1959 Intercollegiate Knights

RECOGNITION
1966 Alpha Psi Omega

INACTIVE
1964–83 Tau Kappa Epsilon
1966–71 Alpha Omicron Pi
1967–86 Sigma Pi Sigma
1968–88 Kappa Sigma
1974–77 Phi Chi Theta
1975–78 Phi Mu Alpha—
         Sinfonia
1975–86 Phi Kappa Tau

PARK COLLEGE   Parksville, MO.

ACHS HONORS
     Omicron Delta Epsilon
1958 Phi Alpha Theta
1959 Pi Gamma Mu
1971 Sigma Delta Pi

SERVICE
1929 Alpha Phi Omega

RECOGNITION
1923 Theta Alpha Phi

INACTIVE
1930–79 Sigma Pi Sigma
1957–74 Phi Mu Alpha—
         Sinfonia

PARKS COLLEGE OF ST. LOUIS UNIVERSITY
Cahokia, IL. Private control: Reorganized Church of Jesus Christ of the Latter Day Saints Campus. Founded in 1875. Divisions of liberal studies, life science, social sciences, math sciences, communications and performing arts.

Single-sex dormitories.

NIC MEN'S
1985 Kappa Delta Rho

NPC WOMEN'S
1988 Alpha Omicron Pi

OTHER PROFESSIONAL
1950 Alpha Eta Rho

ACHS HONORS
1971 Alpha Chi

SERVICE
1950 Alpha Phi Omega

RECOGNITION
     Arnold Air Society (G-2)

PARSONS SCHOOL OF DESIGN   New York, NY.

NIC MEN'S
1966 Delta Sigma Phi

RECOGNITION
1951 Alpha Psi Omega

INACTIVE
1920–54 Theta Alpha Phi
1925–30 Sigma Tau Delta
1928–76 Phi Kappa Phi
1951–72 Chi Beta Phi
1951–73 Tau Kappa Epsilon
1956–72 Phi Sigma Kappa
1956–73 Sigma Phi Epsilon
1957–71 Delta Zeta
1957–73 Alpha Gamma Delta

1959–72 Alpha Xi Delta
1959–73 Alpha Chi Rho
1962–73 Beta Beta Beta
1963–73 Lambda Chi Alpha
1964–66 Alpha Omicron Pi
1964–73 Pi Kappa Alpha
1964–73 Sigma Pi
1965–72 Alpha Epsilon Pi
1965–72 Delta Chi
1966–72 Zeta Beta Tau
1966–72 Zeta Tau Alpha
1967–69 Sigma Delta Tau
1967–72 Psi Chi
1967–73 Theta Chi

PAUL QUINN COLLEGE   Waco, TX. Four-year coeducational college; church related: African Methodist Episcopal Church; established 1872.

NIC MEN'S
1982 Kappa Alpha Psi (A)

NPHC MEN'S
     Phi Beta Sigma
1974 Alpha Phi Alpha

NPHC WOMEN'S
     Zeta Phi Beta
1964 Sigma Gamma Rho
1973 Alpha Kappa Alpha
1974 Delta Sigma Theta (B)

ACHS HONORS
1975 Alpha Kappa Mu

PEABODY CONSERVATORY OF MUSIC   Baltimore, MD. Founded 1857; coeducational.

PROFESSIONAL
1927 Mu Phi Epsilon

ACHS HONORS
1983 Pi Kappa Lambda

INACTIVE
1911–85 Phi Mu Alpha—
         Sinfonia
1929–38 Delta Omicron

PEMBROKE STATE UNIVERSITY   Pembroke, NC. College of liberal arts and general studies; teacher preparatory; coeducational. State control. Established 1887.

NIC MEN'S
1973 Tau Kappa Epsilon
1989 Kappa Alpha Psi (A)

NPHC MEN'S
     Phi Beta Sigma

NPC WOMEN'S
1973 Kappa Delta
1973 Zeta Tau Alpha
1974 Sigma Sigma Sigma

NPHC WOMEN'S
1988 Alpha Kappa Alpha

PROFESSIONAL
1971 Phi Mu Alpha—Sinfonia

ACHS HONORS
1971 Sigma Delta Pi
1975 Alpha Chi
1978 Pi Sigma Alpha
1978 Psi Chi
1988 Phi Alpha Theta

INACTIVE
1973–91 Pi Kappa Phi
1974–86 Pi Kappa Alpha

UNIVERSITY OF PENNSYLVANIA   Philadelphia, PA. Founded 1740. Benjamin Franklin first president of the board of trustees. University; composite of 19 undergraduate, graduate, and professional schools; coeducational except separate undergraduate liberal arts and sciences colleges for men and women; provate control; nonsectarian.

Fraternities and sororities own their own houses and the land which they occupy except for several instances where ownership of the house is by the organization of college-owned land or where ownership is by college on rental basis to fraternity and sorority.

NIC MEN'S
1849 Delta Phi
1850 Phi Kappa Sigma
1850 Zeta Psi
1854 Delta Psi
1875 Sigma Chi
1877 Phi Kappa Psi
1880 Beta Theta Pi
1881 Alpha Tau Omega
1881 Phi Gamma Delta
1883 Phi Delta Theta
1888 Delta Upsilon
1892 Kappa Sigma
1894 Sigma Nu
1896 Alpha Chi Rho
1896 Pi Lambda Phi
1899 Delta Kappa Epsilon
1900 Phi Sigma Kappa
1901 Sigma Alpha Epsilon
1904 Sigma Phi Epsilon
1906 Acacia
1907 Zeta Beta Tau
1912 Theta Xi
1913 Kappa Alpha Society
1914 Sigma Alpha Mu
1919 Alpha Epsilon Pi
1920 Pi Kappa Alpha

1920 Tau Delta Phi
1921 Tau Epsilon Phi
1922 Alpha Phi Delta
1928 Triangle
1952 Kappa Alpha Psi (A)

NPHC MEN'S
1920 Alpha Phi Alpha

NPC WOMEN'S
1904 Delta Delta Delta
1907 Zeta Tau Alpha
1919 Alpha Chi Omega
1919 Chi Omega
1919 Kappa Alpha Theta
1920 Sigma Delta Tau
1921 Kappa Delta
1926 Phi Sigma Sigma
1988 Alpha Phi

NPHC WOMEN'S
1918 Delta Sigma Theta (B)

PROFESSIONAL
1896 Psi Omega
1910 Alpha Omega
1932 Delta Sigma Pi
1947 Delta Omicron
1989 Gamma Iota Sigma

OTHER PROFESSIONAL
1891 Delta Sigma Delta
1907 Phi Delta Epsilon
1907 Phi Lambda Kappa
1908 Alpha Psi
1918 Pi Lambda Theta
1924 Kappa Phi Kappa
1949 Beta Alpha Psi

ACHS HONORS
　Omicron Delta Epsilon
1909 Delta Sigma Rho-Tau
　Kappa Alpha
1913 Eta Kappa Nu
1916 Beta Gamma Sigma
1921 Mortar Board
1921 Tau Beta Pi
1923 Phi Alpha Theta
1927 Pi Gamma Mu
1930 Psi Chi
1938 Pi Delta Phi
1951 Alpha Epsilon Delta
1953 Pi Sigma Alpha
1958 Sigma Theta Tau
1962 Alpha Kappa Delta
1968 Pi Tau Sigma
1970 Alpha Epsilon
1974 Sigma Theta Tau

OTHER HONORS
　National Order of Omega
1892 Phi Beta Kappa
1903 Alpha Omega Alpha
1914 Order of the Coif
1916 Omicron Kappa Upsilon
1921 Pi Mu Epsilon
1930 Iota Sigma Pi

SERVICE
1945 Alpha Phi Omega

RECOGNITION
1922 Scabbard and Blade (3)
1929 Phi Zeta
1931 Delta Phi Alpha
1951 Phi Lambda Upsilon

INACTIVE
1861–72 Zeta Psi
1883–85 Chi Phi
1886–34 Phi Delta Phi
1890–77 Kappa Kappa Gamma
1891–90 Psi Upsilon
1897–71 Delta Tau Delta
1899–59 Xi Psi Phi
1901–56 Alpha Kappa Kappa
1901–73 Phi Rho Sigma
1904–49 Delta Chi
1906　Omega Tau Sigma
1908　Phi Chi
1908–42 Delta Sigma Phi
1909–13 Phi Beta Pi and Theta
　Kappa Psi (a)
1909–38 Sigma Pi
1910–28 Delta Theta Phi
1912–29 Sigma Delta Chi
1912–56 Lambda Chi Alpha
1912–60 Theta Chi
1914–78 Alpha Sigma Phi
1915–34 Theta Delta Chi
1917–70 Alpha Epsilon Phi
1918　Tau Sigma Delta
1918–54 Zeta Tau Alpha
1918–58 Alpha Omicron Pi
1919　Phi Beta Pi and Theta
　Kappa Psi (a)
1921–29 Phi Beta Pi and Theta
　Kappa Psi (B)
1921–72 Alpha Chi Sigma
1925–47 Alpha Kappa Alpha
1926–42 Phi Kappa Tau
1926–70 Delta Phi Epsilon
1927　Eta Sigma Phi
1927–43 Tau Epsilon Rho
1927–66 Alpha Xi Delta
1928–34 Delta Zeta
1930–43 Tau Kappa Epsilon
1946–58 Delta Gamma
1952–69 Kappa Delta Epsilon
1952–70 Sigma Delta Pi
1961–73 Alpha Kappa Psi

PENNSYLVANIA STATE UNIVERSITY
University Park, PA. University and land-grant college; coeducational; state control. Chartered 1855; master's and doctor's degrees.

Ownership of fraternity house and land is by the fraternity; sorority members are required to occupy dormitories.

NIC MEN'S
1872 Delta Tau Delta
1888 Beta Theta Pi
1888 Phi Gamma Delta
1890 Phi Kappa Sigma
1891 Sigma Chi
1892 Kappa Sigma
1892 Sigma Alpha Epsilon
1899 Phi Sigma Kappa
1904 Phi Delta Theta
1905 Delta Sigma Phi
1907 Theta Xi
1909 Acacia
1909 Sigma Nu
1911 Alpha Gamma Rho
1911 Delta Upsilon
1912 Lambda Chi Alpha
1912 Phi Kappa Psi
1912 Sigma Pi
1913 Phi Kappa Theta
1913 Pi Kappa Alpha
1914 Alpha Tau Omega
1915 Sigma Phi Epsilon
1917 Alpha Chi Rho
1918 Alpha Sigma Phi
1919 Theta Chi
1920 Kappa Delta Rho
1921 Alpha Epsilon Pi
1922 Phi Kappa Tau
1922 Tau Kappa Epsilon
1924 Chi Phi
1927 Pi Kappa Phi
1929 Alpha Phi Delta
1929 Delta Chi
1930 Phi Mu Delta
1942 Pi Lambda Phi
1946 Zeta Beta Tau
1949 Sigma Alpha Mu

1952 Kappa Alpha Psi (A)
1954 Theta Delta Chi
1956 Sigma Tau Gamma
1957 Alpha Kappa Lambda
1960 Delta Phi
1960 Zeta Psi
1963 Tau Epsilon Phi
1965 Tau Delta Phi
1989 Psi Upsilon
1989 Tau Kappa Epsilon

NPHC MEN'S
　Phi Beta Sigma
1921 Omega Psi Phi
1947 Alpha Phi Alpha

NPC WOMEN'S
1926 Chi Omega
1929 Alpha Omicron Pi
1929 Phi Mu
1930 Delta Gamma
1930 Kappa Kappa Gamma
1931 Kappa Alpha Theta
1932 Alpha Chi Omega
1932 Gamma Phi Beta
1939 Zeta Tau Alpha
1941 Kappa Delta
1942 Alpha Xi Delta
1943 Sigma Delta Tau
1946 Delta Zeta
1947 Alpha Gamma Delta
1947 Delta Delta Delta
1953 Pi Beta Phi
1954 Sigma Sigma Sigma
1958 Alpha Phi
1962 Alpha Sigma Alpha

NPHC WOMEN'S
1953 Alpha Kappa Alpha
1960 Delta Sigma Theta (B)
1987 Sigma Gamma Rho

PROFESSIONAL
1911 Alpha Chi Sigma
1923 Delta Sigma Pi
1923 Phi Mu Alpha—Sinfonia
1950 Alpha Kappa Psi
1955 Alpha Rho Chi
1955 Phi Chi Theta
1959 Mu Phi Epsilon
1989 Gamma Iota Sigma
1989 Gamma Iota Sigma
1989 Sigma Alpha

OTHER PROFESSIONAL
1898 Alpha Zeta
1916 Scarab
1927 Kappa Phi Kappa
1931 Alpha Tau Alpha
1932 Sigma Delta Chi
1934 Phi Epsilon Kappa
1934 Women in Communications
1936 Pi Lambda Theta
1948 Keramos
1948 Phi Upsilon Omicron
1951 Delta Pi Epsilon
1960 Beta Alpha Psi

ACHS HONORS
　Omicron Delta Epsilon
1900 Phi Kappa Phi

PENNSYLVANIA STATE UNIVERSITY, ALTOONA
Altoona, PA.

NIC MEN'S
1971 Pi Lambda Phi

1909 Eta Kappa Nu
1912 Tau Beta Pi
1917 Delta Sigma Rho-Tau
　Kappa Alpha
1924 Kappa Omicron Nu
1924 Xi Sigma Pi
1925 Phi Sigma Iota
1925 Pi Tau Sigma
1926 Sigma Pi Sigma
1927 Chi Epsilon
1929 Phi Eta Sigma
1930 Alpha Lambda Delta
1930 Psi Chi
1935 Mortar Board
1938 Alpha Epsilon Delta
1949 Alpha Kappa Delta
1950 Alpha Pi Mu
1951 Gamma Theta Upsilon
1953 Pi Sigma Alpha
1955 Kappa Tau Alpha
1955 Omicron Delta Kappa
1955 Phi Sigma
1956 Phi Alpha Theta
1957 Beta Gamma Sigma
1957 Sigma Gamma Tau
1974 Alpha Sigma Mu
1979 Sigma Lambda Alpha
1988 Omega Chi Epsilon
1988 Pi Kappa Lambda

OTHER HONORS
　National Order of Omega
1908 Gamma Sigma Delta
1930 Pi Mu Epsilon
1930 Sigma Xi
1937 Phi Beta Kappa

SERVICE
1932 Alpha Phi Omega
1957 Gamma Sigma Sigma

RECOGNITION
　Angel Flight
　Arnold Air Society (E-1)
1912 Scabbard and Blade (1)
1914 Phi Lambda Upsilon
1923 Theta Alpha Phi
1924 National Block and Bridle
　Club
1925 Iota Lambda Sigma
1926 Pi Alpha`Xi
1936 Sigma Delta Epsilon
1956 Delta Phi Alpha

INACTIVE
1913–84 Pi Lambda Phi
1922　Sigma Gamma Epsilon
1923–36 Kappa Delta Pi
1927–29 Xi Sigma Pi
1927–77 Lambda Sigma Society
1928–71 Pi Gamma Mu
1929–69 Theta Phi Alpha
1937–78 Alpha Epsilon Phi
1946–70 Phi Sigma Sigma
1950　Omega Epsilon Phi
1951–62 Pi Omega Pi
1956–72 Sigma Tau Delta
1958–75 Alpha Delta Pi
1960–66 Delta Phi Epsilon
1961　Rho Epsilon

ACHS HONORS
1980 Alpha Lambda Delta

PENNSYLVANIA STATE UNIVERSITY, BEAVER CAMPUS Monaca, PA.

ACHS HONORS
1983 Lambda Sigma Society

PENNSYLVANIA STATE UNIVERSITY, BEHREND Erie, PA.

NIC MEN'S
1980 Alpha Phi Delta
1990 Sigma Tau Gamma

SERVICE
1986 Alpha Phi Omega

ACHS HONORS
1970 Lambda Sigma Society
1985 Omicron Delta Kappa

COLONIES
Sigma Pi Sigma

PENNSYLVANIA STATE UNIVERSITY, HARRISBURG CAPITOL COLLEGE Middletown, PA.

ACHS HONORS
Pi Alpha Alpha

PENNSYLVANIA STATE UNIVERSITY, HAZLETON CAMPUS Hazleton, PA.

SERVICE
1974 Alpha Phi Omega

PEPPERDINE UNIVERSITY Malibu, CA. Liberal arts college; coeducational; private control; affiliated with the Churches of Christ. Established 1937. Main liberal arts facility within the University is Seaver College.

PROFESSIONAL
1972 Phi Alpha Delta
1973 Delta Theta Phi
1986 Phi Alpha Delta

1976 Pi Gamma Mu
1977 Psi Chi
1982 Phi Eta Sigma

OTHER PROFESSIONAL
1973 Sigma Delta Chi

SERVICE
1970 Alpha Phi Omega

ACHS HONORS
Omicron Delta Epsilon
1952 Psi Chi
1968 Alpha Chi
1968 Kappa Delta Pi
1973 Pi Delta Phi
1975 Phi Alpha Theta

INACTIVE
1950–70 Phi Beta
1951–70 Phi Mu Alpha—
·Sinfonia
1955–66 Pi Gamma Mu
1955–67 Phi Chi Theta
1955–81 Kappa Omicron Nu
1959–83 Phi Alpha Theta

PERU STATE COLLEGE Peru, NB. Established in 1867, state's oldest institution of higher education; teacher education; liberal arts.

ACHS HONORS
1927 Pi Omega Pi
1929 Kappa Delta Pi
1959 Phi Alpha Theta
1969 Gamma Theta Upsilon

INACTIVE
1929–41 Pi Gamma Mu
1930–45 Kappa Omicron Nu

PFEIFFER COLLEGE Misenheimer, NC. College of liberal arts; coeducational; private control (Methodist). Established 1885.

PROFESSIONAL
1970 Alpha Kappa Psi

SERVICE
1965 Alpha Phi Omega

ACHS HONORS
1975 Phi Alpha Theta
1982 Psi Chi

RECOGNITION
1958 Alpha Psi Omega

PHILADELPHIA COLLEGE OF OSTEOPATHIC MEDICINE Philadelphia, PA. Founded 1898; coeducational. Was Philadelphia College of Osteopathy from 1921-1967.

OSTEOPATHIC
1909 Iota Tau Sigma
1917 Phi Sigma Gamma
1924 Atlas Club
1929 Lambda Omicron Gamma

1966 Delta Omega

INACTIVE
1922–43 Theta Psi

PHILADELPHIA COLLEGE OF PHARMACY AND SCIENCE Philadelphia, PA. Founded 1821.

NIC MEN'S
1969 Pi Lambda Phi

1952 Rho Pi Phi
1967 Alpha Delta Theta

PROFESSIONAL
1901 Phi Delta Chi
1902 Kappa Psi
ł920 Lambda Kappa Sigma
1945 Kappa Epsilon

OTHER PROFESSIONAL
1921 Alpha Zeta Omega

ACHS HONORS
1951 Rho Chi

PHILADELPHIA COLLEGE OF TEXTILES AND SCIENCE Philadelphia, PA. Founded 1884. Undergraduate programs leading to B.S. degrees in business administration, chemistry, textile engineering, textile management and marketing, textile chemistry and fabric design. Coeducational, private control, nonsectarian.

Zeta Beta Tau owns its own home and property.

NIC MEN'S
1964 Sigma Phi Epsilon

NPC WOMEN'S
1989 Delta Phi Epsilon

PROFESSIONAL
1968 Delta Sigma Pi

OTHER PROFESSIONAL
1899 Delta Kappa Phi

1903 Phi Psi

ACHS HONORS
1985 Delta Mu Delta

RECOGNITION
1973 Blue Key

INACTIVE
1966–77 Tau Kappa Epsilon
1967–71 Delta Zeta

PHILADELPHIA MUSICAL ACADEMY Philadelphia, PA. Coeducational; founded 1870.

PROFESSIONAL
1963 Delta Omicron

INACTIVE
1965–77 Phi Mu Alpha—
Sinfonia

PHILANDER SMITH COLLEGE Little Rock, AR. College of liberal arts; coeducational; private control (Methodist); founded 1877, chartered 1883.

Fraternities and sororities have no houses; the college supplies meeting rooms.

NIC MEN'S
1947 Kappa Alpha Psi (A)

NPHC MEN'S
Phi Beta Sigma
1938 Alpha Phi Alpha
1942 Omega Psi Phi

NPHC WOMEN'S
Zeta Phi Beta

1940 Alpha Kappa Alpha
1941 Delta Sigma Theta (B)
1943 Sigma Gamma Rho

ACHS HONORS
1940 Alpha Kappa Mu
1944 Beta Kappa Chi

SERVICE
1965 Alpha Phi Omega

UNIVERSITY OF THE PHILIPPINES Quezon City, LU. Founded 1908; coeducational university.

ACHS HONORS
1932 Pi Gamma Mu
1933 Phi Kappa Phi
1958 Phi Alpha Theta

INACTIVE
1932–62 Sigma Pi Sigma

PHILIPPINE WOMEN'S UNIVERSITY Manila, PI.

PROFESSIONAL
1962 Mu Phi Epsilon

PHILLIPS UNIVERSITY Enid, OK. University; coeducational; private control (Disciples of Christ); chartered 1906.

PROFESSIONAL
1962 Mu Phi Epsilon

ACHS HONORS
1954 Kappa Delta Pi

RECOGNITION
1943 Cardinal Key

1949 Kappa Pi

INACTIVE
1947–83 Phi Mu Alpha—
Sinfonia

PIEDMONT COLLEGE Demorest, GA. Private control: Congregational Christian Church. Founded in 1897. Four-year; coeducational; liberal arts college.

Students must live at home or on campus. Single-sex dormitories.

ACHS HONORS
1975 Alpha Chi

PIKEVILLE COLLEGE Pikeville, KY. Liberal arts college; founded 1889; affiliated with United Presbyterian College.

ACHS HONORS
1965 Phi Alpha Theta

1977 Lambda Iota Tau
1983 Phi Eta Sigma

UNIVERSITY OF PITTSBURGH Pittsburgh, PA. Founded by Hugh Brackenridge, chartered as the Pittsburgh Academy 1787, became Western University of Pennsylvania 1819, changed to University of Pittsburgh 1908. University; coeducational; nonsectarian.

Several fraternities lease fraternity houses built by the Universtiy in 1984. Some fraternities and sororities own their houses and the land which they oc-cupy. Several sororities occupy floors with living quarters and suites in Amos Hall, a campus residence hall.

NIC MEN'S
1864 Delta Tau Delta
1909 Sigma Chi
1913 Sigma Alpha Epsilon
1914 Pi Lambda Phi
1916 Delta Sigma Phi
1916 Phi Gamma Delta
1918 Phi Delta Theta
1919 Lambda Chi Alpha
1919 Sigma Alpha Mu
1919 Theta Chi
1920 Kappa Sigma
1923 Alpha Phi Delta
1923 Phi Kappa Theta
1934 Pi Kappa Alpha
1937 Kappa Alpha Psi (A)
1962 Zeta Beta Tau
1968 Delta Phi
1970 Alpha Epsilon Pi
1970 Triangle
1978 Pi Kappa Phi
1990 Phi Sigma Kappa

NPHC MEN'S
Phi Beta Sigma
1913 Alpha Phi Alpha
1928 Omega Psi Phi

NPC WOMEN'S
1915 Kappa Alpha Theta
1916 Delta Delta Delta
1916 Delta Zeta
1919 Chi Omega
1919 Kappa Kappa Gamma
1920 Alpha Delta Pi
1920 Alpha Epsilon Phi
1920 Kappa Delta
1922 Theta Phi Alpha
1925 Delta Phi Epsilon
1949 Sigma Sigma Sigma
1950 Sigma Delta Tau

NPHC WOMEN'S
1918 Alpha Kappa Alpha
1921 Delta Sigma Theta (B)
1927 Delta Sigma Theta (B)
1971 Delta Sigma Theta (B)
1983 Sigma Gamma Rho

PROFESSIONAL
1897 Psi Omega
1907 Phi Delta Chi
1913 Kappa Psi
1916 Delta Theta Phi
1918 Lambda Kappa Sigma
1921 Delta Sigma Pi
1924 Phi Chi Theta
1925 Phi Alpha Delta
1945 Alpha Tau Delta
1948 Kappa Kappa Psi
1969 Tau Beta Sigma

OTHER PROFESSIONAL
1891 Phi Beta Pi and Theta
Kappa Psi (a)
1903 Delta Sigma Delta
1911 Phi Delta Epsilon
1918 Pi Lambda Theta
1926 Kappa Phi Kappa
1926 Tau Epsilon Rho
1928 Alpha Zeta Omega
1940 Delta Pi Epsilon

ACHS HONORS
Omicron Delta Epsilon
1916 Omicron Delta Kappa
1920 Beta Gamma Sigma
1920 Delta Sigma Rho-Tau
Kappa Alpha
1922 Lambda Sigma Society
1922 Phi Alpha Theta
1923 Mortar Board
1928 Pi Sigma Alpha
1936 Alpha Kappa Delta
1937 Eta Kappa Nu
1937 Phi Eta Sigma
1938 Sigma Pi Sigma
1940 Pi Tau Sigma
1946 Sigma Theta Tau
1948 Alpha Epsilon Delta
1949 Psi Chi
1950 Rho Chi
1958 Alpha Pi Mu
1959 Omega Chi Epsilon
1967 Beta Phi Mu
1970 Chi Epsilon
1971 Gamma Theta Upsilon
1974 Tau Beta Pi
1979 Phi Sigma Iota

OTHER HONORS
National Order of Omega
1916 Omicron Kappa Upsilon
1927 Order of the Coif
1953 Phi Beta Kappa

SERVICE
1927 Alpha Phi Omega
1970 Gamma Sigma Sigma

RECOGNITION
Angel Flight
Arnold Air Society (E-1)
1917 Phi Lambda Upsilon
1929 Scabbard and Blade (7)
1936 Phi Delta Gamma
1947 Eta Mu Pi
1950 Sigma Delta Psi
1952 Beta Beta Beta

INACTIVE
1903–63 Sigma Phi Epsilon
1908–70 Phi Rho Sigma
1909–59 Phi Delta Phi
1911–12 Alpha Kappa Kappa
1915–34 Alpha Chi Sigma
1915–65 Zeta Tau Alpha
1918–31 Pi Beta Phi
1918–35 Alpha Xi Delta
1919–35 Sigma Delta Chi
1920 Delta Psi Kappa
1920–61 Phi Mu
1920–88 Alpha Omega
1921–60 Delta Mu Delta
1922 Phi Lambda Kappa
1923–60 Sigma Pi
1924 Phi Sigma Sigma
1924 Xi Psi Phi
1929–66 Phi Sigma
1931–52 Alpha Kappa Alpha
1955–67 Beta Alpha Psi
1972–73 Kappa Beta Pi

COLONIES
Kappa Delta Rho

UNIVERSITY OF PITTSBURGH AT BRADFORD
Bradford, PA.

ACHS HONORS	SERVICE
1988 Alpha Lambda Delta	1987 Alpha Phi Omega

UNIVERSITY OF PITTSBURGH AT GREENSBURG Greensburg, PA.

NIC MEN'S
1987 Kappa Delta Rho

UNIVERSITY OF PITTSBURGH AT JOHNSTOWN
Johnstown, PA. Founded in 1927, UPJ is a four-year degree-granting college of the University of Pittsburgh. UPJ offers academic programs in the humanities, natural sciences, social sciences, education, and engineering technology. Coeducational: private control: state-related.

NIC MEN'S	1979 Pi Sigma Alpha
1972 Delta Chi	1980 Phi Eta Sigma
1973 Acacia	
1982 Kappa Delta Rho	
1988 Sigma Tau Gamma	INACTIVE
NPC WOMEN'S	1973–79 Alpha Xi Delta
1972 Delta Zeta	
1982 Alpha Gamma Delta	
ACHS HONORS	COLONIES
1972 Psi Chi	Phi Sigma Sigma

PITTSBURG STATE UNIVERSITY Pittsburg, KS.
Founded in 1903 for the purpose of instruction in liberal arts and teacher education. Coeducational; undergraduate and graduate program; state control.

Fraternities and sororities who own houses own them outright; some are leasing.

NIC MEN'S	1965 Lambda Sigma Society
1924 Sigma Tau Gamma	1968 Delta Mu Delta
1927 Phi Sigma Kappa	1969 Sigma Pi Sigma
1936 Kappa Alpha Psi (A)	1978 Pi Sigma Alpha
1963 Pi Kappa Alpha	1979 Phi Kappa Phi
1969 Lambda Chi Alpha	
1973 Sigma Phi Epsilon	SERVICE
	1946 Alpha Phi Omega
NPC WOMEN'S	
1922 Sigma Sigma Sigma	INACTIVE
1959 Alpha Gamma Delta	1927–37 Pi Gamma Mu
	1928–84 Phi Mu Alpha—
ACHS HONORS	Sinfonia
Omicron Delta Epsilon	1930–78 Pi Omega Pi
1930 Phi Alpha Theta	1954–88 Tau Kappa Epsilon
1932 Kappa Mu Epsilon	1959–73 Alpha Delta Pi
1941 Psi Chi	1968–74 Alpha Kappa Lambda
1963 Omicron Delta Kappa	

PLYMOUTH STATE COLLEGE OF THE UNIVERSITY OF NEW HAMPSHIRE Plymouth, NH. Founded 1870; coeducational; liberal arts, teacher education; business administration. Became division of the University of New Hampshire 1963.

Members live in dorms or approved off-campus housing.

NPC WOMEN'S	1980 Phi Kappa Phi
1972 Delta Zeta	1981 Phi Sigma Iota
OTHER PROFESSIONAL	1981 Pi Gamma Mu
1966 Kappa Delta Phi (C)	1984 Psi Chi
ACHS HONORS	INACTIVE
1966 Kappa Delta Pi	1968–78 Tau Kappa Epsilon

POINT LOMA COLLEGE Pasadena, CA. College of liberal arts; coeducational; private control (Church of the Nazarene); chartered 1902; became Point Loma College in 1973.

PROFESSIONAL	ACHS HONORS
1954 Kappa Delta Epsilon	1978 Phi Alpha Theta

POINT PARK COLLEGE Pittsburgh, PA. Private control. Founded in 1960. Four-year; coeducational; liberal arts college.

NIC MEN'S	ACHS HONORS
1973 Sigma Tau Gamma	1990 Psi Chi
PROFESSIONAL	SERVICE
1970 Alpha Kappa Psi	1967 Alpha Phi Omega
OTHER PROFESSIONAL	INACTIVE
1973 Sigma Delta Chi	1971–72 Lambda Chi Alpha

POLYTECHNIC INSTITUTE OF NEW YORK
Brooklyn, NY. Incorporated in 1854, first instruction 1855. College of engineering and science for men and women; private control; nonsectarian.

Ownership of fraternity house and ground is by the fraternity.

NIC MEN'S	1974 Eta Kappa Nu
1920 Alpha Phi Delta	1974 Tau Beta Pi
1928 Pi Kappa Phi	
1969 Tau Delta Phi	INACTIVE
ACHS HONORS	1896–50 Alpha Chi Rho
1949 Chi Epsilon	1926–51 Alpha Sigma Phi
1955 Sigma Gamma Tau	1931–74 Tau Beta Pi
1959 Sigma Pi Sigma	1953–73 Alpha Epsilon Pi

POMONA COLLEGE Claremont, CA. College of liberal arts; coeducational; private control; nonsectarian; chartered 1887.

The seven local fraternities have meeting rooms in the residence halls.

ACHS HONORS	OTHER HONORS
1928 Delta Sigma Rho-Tau	1914 Phi Beta Kappa
Kappa Alpha	RECOGNITION
1930 Alpha Kappa Delta	1957 Delta Phi Alpha
1930 Mortar Board	1959 Sigma Delta Psi
1962 Sigma Delta Pi	
1988 Psi Chi	INACTIVE
	1948–63 Kappa Mu Epsilon

UNIVERSITY OF PORTLAND Portland, OR. University; coeducational; private control (Roman Catholic). Established 1901.

NPC WOMEN'S	1988 Zeta Tau Alpha
1961 Alpha Chi Omega	

NPHC WOMEN'S
1940 Delta Sigma Theta (B)

PROFESSIONAL
1952 Alpha Kappa Psi
1953 Phi Beta
1961 Alpha Tau Delta

ACHS HONORS
1940 Delta Epsilon Sigma
1959 Sigma Delta Pi
1969 Pi Delta Phi
1971 Phi Alpha Theta

1977 Eta Kappa Nu
1977 Theta Alpha Kappa

RECOGNITION
    Angel Flight
    Arnold Air Society (H-2)
1947 Alpha Psi Omega
1951 Blue Key

INACTIVE
1943–72 Beta Beta Beta
1961–86 Phi Chi Theta
1962   Zeta Phi Eta

PORTLAND STATE UNIVERSITY   Portland, OR. Established 1955 from an extension center of the Oregon State System of Higher Education; formerly Vanport College, Portland Extension Centr, and Portland State Extension Center. Became Portland State College in 1955 and Portland State University in 1969, as a four-year institution granting both undergraduate and graduate degrees.

The University does not have student housing; fraternities and sororities may rent or buy houses.

NIC MEN'S
1958 Tau Kappa Epsilon
1961 Kappa Sigma

NPC WOMEN'S
1969 Phi Sigma Sigma

PROFESSIONAL
1959 Mu Phi Epsilon
1963 Alpha Kappa Psi

OTHER PROFESSIONAL
1971 Delta Pi Epsilon
1972 Pi Lambda Theta

ACHS HONORS
1974 Phi Alpha Theta
1979 Phi Sigma Iota
1980 Phi Kappa Phi
1982 Pi Sigma Alpha

OTHER HONORS
1963 Pi Mu Epsilon

1974 Sigma Xi

SERVICE
1950 Alpha Phi Omega
1960 Intercollegiate Knights

RECOGNITION
1970 Sigma Delta Psi

INACTIVE
1959–73 Alpha Phi
1960–80 Pi Beta Phi
1961–64 Delta Delta Delta
1961–65 Delta Zeta
1961–72 Alpha Omicron Pi
1962–70 Phi Beta
1966–82 Phi Mu Alpha—
        Sinfonia
1967–71 Sigma Alpha Mu

PRAIRIE VIEW A & M UNIVERSITY   Prairie View, TX. Land-grant college; coeducational; state control; established 1876.

NIC MEN'S
1970 Kappa Alpha Psi (A)

NPHC MEN'S
    Phi Beta Sigma
1970 Alpha Phi Alpha

NPHC WOMEN'S
1969 Sigma Gamma Rho
1970 Alpha Kappa Alpha

OTHER PROFESSIONAL
1969 Alpha Tau Alpha

ACHS HONORS
    Omicron Delta Epsilon
1940 Alpha Kappa Mu
1947 Beta Kappa Chi
1963 Kappa Omicron Nu

1966 Gamma Theta Upsilon
1972 Sigma Tau Delta
1973 Delta Mu Delta
1973 Eta Kappa Nu
1973 Pi Omega Pi
1974 Phi Alpha Theta
1974 Sigma Pi Sigma
1974 Tau Beta Pi
1979 Phi Eta Sigma

OTHER HONORS
1969 Pi Mu Epsilon

SERVICE
1967 Alpha Phi Omega

INACTIVE
1970–70 Sigma Delta Pi

PRATT INSTITUTE   Brooklyn, NY. Professional institution; coeducational; private control; nonsectarian; established 1887.

NIC MEN'S
1962 Tau Delta Phi
1990 Kappa Sigma

ACHS HONORS
1952 Tau Beta Pi
1958 Pi Tau Sigma
1961 Eta Kappa Nu
1962 Beta Phi Mu

OTHER HONORS
1967 Pi Mu Epsilon

SERVICE
1957 Alpha Phi Omega

RECOGNITION
1956 Scabbard and Blade (12)

INACTIVE
1956–71 Zeta Beta Tau
1970–72 Sigma Pi Sigma

PRESBYTERIAN COLLEGE   Clinton, SC. College of liberal arts; coeducational; private control; affiliated with the Presbyterian Church. Established 1880 as Clinton College; 1890 became Presbyterian College.

Fraternities occupy houses on rental basis from college.

NIC MEN'S
1890 Pi Kappa Alpha
1907 Pi Kappa Phi
1924 Kappa Alpha Order
1928 Alpha Sigma Phi
1942 Theta Chi
1951 Sigma Nu

NPHC MEN'S
    Phi Beta Sigma

NPC WOMEN'S
1990 Alpha Delta Pi
1990 Sigma Sigma Sigma

ACHS HONORS
1972 Psi Chi
1982 Sigma Pi Sigma
1985 Omicron Delta Kappa
1985 Phi Alpha Theta
1985 Pi Gamma Mu

RECOGNITION
1932 Blue Key
1953 Scabbard and Blade (10)
1957 Sigma Delta Psi

INACTIVE
1905–10 Kappa Delta
1925–40 Chi Beta Phi

PRINCETON UNIVERSITY   Princeton, NJ. University for men; nonsectarian; private control; established 1746; became university in 1896.

NIC MEN'S
1845 Delta Kappa Epsilon
1850 Zeta Psi
1851 Delta Psi
1854 Chi Phi
1863 Theta Delta Chi
1983 Sigma Alpha Epsilon

NPC WOMEN'S
1983 Kappa Alpha Theta
1990 Pi Beta Phi

NPHC WOMEN'S
1988 Alpha Kappa Alpha

ACHS HONORS
    Omicron Delta Epsilon
1972 Tau Beta Pi

OTHER HONORS
1899 Phi Beta Kappa
1932 Sigma Xi

SERVICE
1962 Alpha Phi Omega

INACTIVE
1843–45 Beta Theta Pi
1851–57 Chi Psi
1852–84 Kappa Alpha Society
1853–58 Sigma Phi Society
1853–81 Phi Kappa Sigma
1854–77 Delta Phi
1869–82 Sigma Chi
1870–71 Delta Upsilon
1967–78 Eta Kappa Nu

PROVIDENCE COLLEGE   Providence, RI. College of liberal arts for men; private control (Roman Catholic); chartered 1917.

NPHC WOMEN'S
1974 Delta Sigma Theta (B)

ACHS HONORS
    Omicron Delta Epsilon

1940 Delta Epsilon Sigma
1954 Alpha Epsilon Delta
1963 Phi Sigma Tau
1972 Pi Sigma Alpha

1983 Phi Sigma Iota

INACTIVE
1962–86 Sigma Pi Sigma

UNIVERSITY OF PUERTO RICO   Mayaguez, PR.
Schools of agriculture, engineering, and arts and sciences. Founded in 1912 as the College of Agriculture and Mechanic Arts.

Fraternal groups rent off-campus residences from private owners.

SERVICE
1969 Alpha Phi Omega

UNIVERSITY OF PUERTO RICO   Rio Piedras, PR.
University and land-grant institution; coeducational; government control; established 1900, became university 1903. Colleges of general studies, humanities, natural science, social science, business, education, pharmacy, and law.

PROFESSIONAL
1984 Phi Alpha Delta

ACHS HONORS
1948 Phi Alpha Theta

SERVICE
1970 Gamma Sigma Sigma

RECOGNITION
1952 Beta Beta Beta

INACTIVE
1962–68 Kappa Epsilon

UNIVERSITY OF PUERTO RICO   San Juan, PR.
School of medicine, tropical medicine, and dentistry.

ACHS HONORS
    Omicron Delta Epsilon
1969 Phi Kappa Phi
1969 Tau Beta Pi
1987 Kappa Omicron Nu

SERVICE
1965 Alpha Phi Omega

INACTIVE
1962   Phi Chi

UNIVERSITY OF PUGET SOUND   Tacoma, WA.
Established in 1888; a nonsectarian program committed to comprehensive liberal learning and academic excellence in the arts and sciences and in five professional schools.

Fraternities and some sororities occupy university-owned group housing units on a regular residence hall fee basis. Houses are furnished, maintained, and supervised by the occupants; a centrally located subterranean kitchen serves all units, though the type of service is determined by joint-fraternity action. Other sorority women live in sections of the college-owned residence halls, with chapter rooms in those same facilities.

NIC MEN'S
1948 Kappa Sigma
1948 Sigma Nu
1950 Sigma Chi
1951 Sigma Alpha Epsilon
1952 Phi Delta Theta
1962 Beta Theta Pi

NPC WOMEN'S
1948 Pi Beta Phi
1952 Delta Delta Delta
1953 Alpha Phi
1961 Gamma Phi Beta
1963 Kappa Alpha Theta
1966 Kappa Kappa Gamma

PROFESSIONAL
1948 Sigma Alpha Iota
1949 Phi Mu Alpha—Sinfonia
1959 Alpha Kappa Psi

1973 Delta Theta Phi
1974 Phi Alpha Delta

ACHS HONORS
    Omicron Delta Epsilon
1948 Phi Sigma
1959 Mortar Board
1972 Sigma Pi Sigma
1975 Phi Kappa Phi
1975 Sigma Tau Delta
1985 Pi Sigma Alpha
1985 Psi Chi

OTHER HONORS
    National Order of Omega
1949 Delta Phi Delta

SERVICE
    The National Spurs
1946 Intercollegiate Knights

RECOGNITION
    Angel Flight
    Arnold Air Society (H-2)
1922 Pi Kappa Delta

INACTIVE
1922–35 Theta Alpha Phi
1928–68 Pi Gamma Mu
1949–80 Theta Chi
1953–82 Chi Omega
1963–63 Kappa Omicron Nu
1965–84 Phi Chi Theta
1966–71 Phi Gamma Delta

PURDUE UNIVERSITY   West Lafayette, IN. University; land-grant college; coeducational; state control; university centers at Fort Wayne, Hammond, Indianapolis, and Westville. Chartered 1865 by general assembly under name of the trustees of Indiana Agricultural College; in 1869 John Purdue donated money and 100 acres of land for present site of university in Tippecanoe County.

The fraternities and sororities own their houses with few exceptions; annexes are also permitted.

NIC MEN'S
1875 Sigma Chi
1885 Kappa Sigma
1891 Sigma Nu
1893 Phi Delta Theta
1893 Sigma Alpha Epsilon
1901 Phi Kappa Psi
1902 Phi Gamma Delta
1903 Beta Theta Pi
1904 Alpha Tau Omega
1905 Phi Kappa Sigma
1905 Sigma Phi Epsilon
1905 Theta Xi
1907 Acacia
1907 Delta Tau Delta
1909 Triangle
1911 Alpha Gamma Rho
1912 Sigma Pi
1914 Delta Upsilon
1915 Lambda Chi Alpha
1918 Phi Kappa Theta
1920 Kappa Alpha Psi (A)
1920 Phi Kappa Tau
1920 Theta Chi
1921 Kappa Delta Rho
1922 Pi Kappa Alpha
1922 Pi Kappa Phi
1925 Beta Sigma Psi
1927 Delta Chi
1928 Tau Kappa Epsilon
1930 Phi Sigma Kappa
1934 Alpha Kappa Lambda
1936 Alpha Chi Rho
1939 Alpha Sigma Phi
1952 FarmHouse
1954 Alpha Epsilon Pi
1956 Delta Sigma Phi
1959 Sigma Tau Gamma
1968 Zeta Psi
1988 Chi Phi

NPHC MEN'S
    Phi Beta Sigma
1942 Omega Psi Phi

1948 Alpha Phi Alpha

NPC WOMEN'S
1915 Kappa Alpha Theta
1918 Alpha Chi Omega
1919 Chi Omega
1919 Kappa Kappa Gamma
1921 Alpha Xi Delta
1921 Pi Beta Phi
1921 Zeta Tau Alpha
1929 Phi Mu
1940 Delta Gamma
1947 Alpha Delta Pi
1948 Sigma Kappa
1963 Alpha Omicron Pi
1963 Alpha Phi
1968 Alpha Gamma Delta
1975 Gamma Phi Beta
1988 Delta Delta Delta
1988 Delta Zeta

NPHC WOMEN'S
1968 Delta Sigma Theta (B)
1969 Alpha Kappa Alpha
1972 Sigma Gamma Rho

PROFESSIONAL
1916 Phi Delta Chi
1928 Kappa Psi
1928 Theta Tau
1948 Kappa Epsilon
1955 Alpha Chi Sigma
1956 Kappa Kappa Psi
1959 Tau Beta Sigma
1984 Delta Sigma Pi
1984 Sigma Alpha

OTHER PROFESSIONAL
1908 Alpha Zeta
1911 Sigma Delta Chi
1954 Women in Communications
1962 Alpha Eta Rho
1962 Alpha Tau Alpha

ACHS HONORS
    Omicron Delta Epsilon

Omicron Delta Epsilon
1893 Tau Beta Pi
1906 Eta Kappa Nu
1913 Kappa Omicron Nu
1916 Delta Sigma Rho-Tau
    Kappa Alpha
1919 Kappa Delta Pi
1922 Pi Tau Sigma
1926 Alpha Lambda Delta
1926 Mortar Board
1929 Chi Epsilon
1932 Sigma Pi Sigma
1934 Xi Sigma Pi
1943 Omega Chi Epsilon
1945 Rho Chi
1948 Phi Eta Sigma
1950 Alpha Epsilon Delta
1953 Sigma Gamma Tau
1954 Lambda Iota Tau
1959 Alpha Pi Mu
1960 Sigma Delta Pi
1961 Omicron Delta Kappa
1963 Alpha Sigma Mu
1963 Pi Delta Phi
1964 Psi Chi
1967 Pi Sigma Alpha
1968 Phi Alpha Theta
1970 Beta Gamma Sigma
1971 Phi Kappa Phi
1979 Sigma Lambda Alpha

OTHER HONORS
    National Order of Omega
1909 Sigma Xi
1949 Sigma Gamma Epsilon
1960 Delta Phi Delta
1963 Iota Sigma Pi
1971 Phi Beta Kappa
1972 Gamma Sigma Delta

SERVICE
1932 Alpha Phi Omega

RECOGNITION
    Angel Flight
    Arnold Air Society (D-2)
1908 Scabbard and Blade (1)
1917 Phi Lambda Upsilon
1929 Sigma Delta Psi
1929 Theta Alpha Phi
1940 Iota Lambda Sigma
1949 Sigma Delta Epsilon
1956 National Block and Bridle
    Club
1962 Phi Zeta

INACTIVE
1922–89 Sigma Alpha Mu
1925–34 Sigma Mu Sigma
1948–53 Sigma Delta Tau
1948–76 Alpha Epsilon Phi

PURDUE UNIVERSITY CALUMET CAMPUS

Hammond, IN. College of liberal arts and general studies; teacher preparatory; professional; coeducational. State control. Established 1943.

NIC MEN'S
1969 Phi Kappa Theta
1971 Phi Sigma Kappa

NPC WOMEN'S
1970 Theta Phi Alpha

NPHC WOMEN'S
1976 Sigma Gamma Rho

ACHS HONORS
1990 Phi Alpha Theta

RECOGNITION
1972 Sigma Delta Psi

INACTIVE
1972–82 Sigma Kappa

QUEENS COLLEGE

Charlotte, NC. Four-year liberal arts college for women; affiliated with Presbyterian Church through synods of North Carolina, South Carolina, and Georgia. Founded 1957.

The sororities occupy self-owned lodges on college property.

NIC MEN'S
1952 Tau Delta Phi

NPC WOMEN'S
1928 Chi Omega
1928 Kappa Delta
1929 Phi Mu
1931 Alpha Delta Pi

PROFESSIONAL
1959 Delta Omicron

ACHS HONORS
1985 Phi Alpha Theta

OTHER HONORS
    National Order of Omega
1968 Sigma Xi

INACTIVE
1930–77 Alpha Gamma Delta
1946–52 Mu Phi Epsilon
1959–65 Alpha Chi Omega

COLONIES
    Pi Kappa Phi

QUEENS COLLEGE

Flushing, NY. College of liberal arts; coeducational; municipal control. Chartered 1937; graduate division 1948.

NIC MEN'S
1949 Alpha Epsilon Pi
1956 Tau Epsilon Phi

NPHC MEN'S
    Phi Beta Sigma

NPC WOMEN'S
1955 Delta Phi Epsilon
1967 Sigma Delta Tau

PROFESSIONAL
1963 Delta Omicron

ACHS HONORS
    Omicron Delta Epsilon
1948 Phi Alpha Theta
1950 Pi Sigma Alpha
1951 Psi Chi
1954 Sigma Delta Pi
1963 Kappa Delta Pi
1964 Delta Sigma Rho-Tau
    Kappa Alpha
1967 Pi Delta Phi
1971 Beta Phi Mu

1975 Pi Kappa Lambda

OTHER HONORS
1961 National Collegiate
    Players

SERVICE
1940 Alpha Phi Omega
1953 Gamma Sigma Sigma

RECOGNITION
1952 Kappa Pi
1956 Delta Phi Alpha

INACTIVE
1940–71 Alpha Delta Pi
1955–73 Sigma Alpha Mu
1955–80 Delta Zeta
1956–67 Phi Sigma Sigma
1956–71 Alpha Epsilon Phi
1957–71 Alpha Sigma Alpha
1957–71 Sigma Sigma Sigma
1958–70 Alpha Sigma Tau
1966–73 Zeta Beta Tau
1967–71 Pi Lambda Phi

QUEENS COLLEGE

Ontario, CN.

INACTIVE
1903–14 Phi Sigma Kappa

QUINCY COLLEGE

Quincy, IL. Private control: Roman Catholic. Founded in 1860. Four-year; coeducational; liberal arts college.

PROFESSIONAL
1989 Delta Sigma Pi

ACHS HONORS
1956 Delta Epsilon Sigma

1968 Phi Alpha Theta

INACTIVE
1947–60 Alpha Delta Gamma
1954–60 Theta Phi Alpha

QUINNIPIAC COLLEGE

Hamden, CT. College of accounting, business administration, and medical technology; junior college with above curricula plus liberal arts and secretarial studies; coeducational; private control; nonsectarian. Incorporated 1929 as Junior College of Commerce 1935; 4-year program added and name changed to present 1951; first baccalaureate awarded 1952. Merged with Larson College, founded 1911, in 1952.

Housing plans for fraternities are being studied.

NIC MEN'S
1964 Alpha Chi Rho
1967 Tau Kappa Epsilon

NPC WOMEN'S
1988 Alpha Gamma Delta

ACHS HONORS
1960 Delta Mu Delta
1986 Psi Chi

SERVICE
1960 Alpha Phi Omega

RECOGNITION
1964 Lambda Tau

INACTIVE
1968–72 Sigma Pi
1968–75 Alpha Epsilon Pi
1968–75 Pi Lambda Phi
1968–76 Phi Sigma Kappa
1972–79 Delta Zeta

RADCLIFFE COLLEGE Cambridge, MA. Liberal arts college; since 1879, its founding, women have been offered a Harvard education; separately incorporated and financed, both undergraduates and graduates study under the Harvard University faculty; has undergraduate library, residence facilities, deans, and student services of its own.

OTHER HONORS　　　　　1943 Sigma Xi
1914 Phi Beta Kappa

RADFORD COLLEGE Radford, VA. College of liberal arts; coeducational; state control; chartered 1910.

The college provides chapter rooms for the sororities.

NIC MEN'S
1976 Phi Sigma Kappa
1977 Alpha Chi Rho
1977 Tau Kappa Epsilon
1978 Pi Kappa Phi
1980 Alpha Sigma Phi
1981 Sigma Phi Epsilon
1982 Phi Kappa Sigma
1985 Kappa Delta Rho

NPHC MEN'S
　　Phi Beta Sigma

NPC WOMEN'S
1929 Sigma Sigma Sigma
1942 Alpha Sigma Alpha
1953 Alpha Sigma Tau
1959 Sigma Kappa
1972 Zeta Tau Alpha
1983 Delta Zeta
1990 Phi Sigma Sigma

NPHC WOMEN'S
1974 Alpha Kappa Alpha

PROFESSIONAL
1959 Mu Phi Epsilon
1984 Phi Alpha Delta

OTHER PROFESSIONAL
1969 Alpha Beta Alpha

ACHS HONORS
　　Omicron Delta Epsilon
1928 Pi Gamma Mu
1931 Kappa Delta Pi
1959 Kappa Mu Epsilon
1966 Pi Delta Phi
1966 Sigma Tau Delta
1968 Gamma Theta Upsilon
1968 Pi Omega Pi
1969 Kappa Omicron Nu
1969 Phi Kappa Phi
1972 Phi Alpha Theta
1973 Alpha Lambda Delta
1976 Delta Mu Delta
1978 Omicron Delta Kappa
1979 Psi Chi
1980 Phi Sigma Iota
1981 Pi Sigma Alpha

OTHER HONORS
　　National Order of Omega

SERVICE
1984 Alpha Phi Omega

RECOGNITION
1941 Chi Beta Phi

INACTIVE
1974–77 Alpha Delta Pi

RAMAPO COLLEGE OF NEW JERSEY Mahwah, NJ.

NIC MEN'S
1990 Zeta Beta Tau

ACHS HONORS
　　Omicron Delta Epsilon

1983 Pi Sigma Alpha
1986 Delta Mu Delta
1988 Phi Alpha Theta

RANDOLPH-MACON COLLEGE Ashland, VA. College of liberal arts for men and women; private control (Methodist). Chartered 1830.

The majority of the fraternities own houses and land; several have constructed houses on land leased from the college.

NIC MEN'S
1872 Phi Kappa Sigma
1874 Phi Delta Theta
1888 Kappa Sigma
1906 Sigma Phi Epsilon

1926 Lambda Chi Alpha
1949 Theta Chi
1967 Sigma Alpha Epsilon
1969 Kappa Alpha Order
1988 Pi Kappa Alpha

NPC WOMEN'S
1982 Phi Mu
1984 Kappa Alpha Theta
1987 Alpha Gamma Delta

ACHS HONORS
1913 Delta Sigma Rho-Tau
　　Kappa Alpha
1933 Omicron Delta Kappa
1970 Pi Delta Phi
1983 Phi Alpha Theta
1985 Sigma Pi Sigma
1990 Psi Chi

OTHER HONORS
1923 Phi Beta Kappa

SERVICE
1950 Alpha Phi Omega

RECOGNITION
1916 Chi Beta Phi

1945 Beta Beta Beta
1964 Alpha Psi Omega

INACTIVE
1853–61 Delta Psi
1871–79 Phi Kappa Psi
1873–93 Beta Theta Pi
1874–76 Alpha Tau Omega
1874–01 Sigma Chi
1903–60 Alpha Omicron Pi
1905–60 Delta Delta Delta
1908–13 Alpha Sigma Alpha
1910–60 Alpha Delta Pi
1910–60 Phi Mu
1924–38 Delta Zeta
1928–46 Alpha Xi Delta
1949–84 Pi Gamma Mu
1966–85 Alpha Epsilon Pi

RANDOLPH-MACON WOMAN'S COLLEGE Lynchburg, VA. College of liberal arts for women; private control (Methodist); established 1891.

OTHER HONORS
1917 Phi Beta Kappa

RECOGNITION
1961 Eta Sigma Phi

INACTIVE
1899–60 Chi Omega
1902–60 Zeta Tau Alpha

1903–60 Kappa Delta
1904–11 Sigma Sigma Sigma
1913–60 Pi Beta Phi
1916–60 Kappa Alpha Theta
1917–41 Sigma Kappa
1926–40 Pi Gamma Mu
1930–51 Gamma Phi Beta

UNIVERSITY OF REDLANDS Redlands, CA. University; coeducational; private control (American Baptist Founded). Chartered 1907.

Fraternities own meeting houses on university-owned land; sororities meet in alumni houses.

NPHC MEN'S
　　Phi Beta Sigma
1974 Alpha Phi Alpha

PROFESSIONAL
1924 Sigma Alpha Iota
1949 Phi Mu Alpha—Sinfonia

OTHER PROFESSIONAL
1969 Pi Lambda Theta

ACHS HONORS
　　Omicron Delta Epsilon
1938 Pi Kappa Lambda
1954 Omicron Delta Kappa
1955 Mortar Board
1958 Pi Gamma Mu
1959 Psi Chi
1978 Phi Alpha Theta

OTHER HONORS
1955 Sigma Gamma Epsilon

SERVICE
　　The National Spurs
1967 Alpha Phi Omega

RECOGNITION
1914 Pi Kappa Delta
1920 Theta Alpha Phi
1928 Society for Collegiate
　　Journalists—Pi Delta
　　Epsilon-Alpha Phi Gamma
　　(A)

INACTIVE
1926–69 Sigma Tau Delta
1939–75 Alpha Epsilon Delta
1947–51 Sigma Pi Sigma
1960　Beta Beta Beta
1969–76 Phi Eta Sigma

REED COLLEGE Portland, OR. Founded by trustees of Reed Institute, created by the will of Amanda W. Reed; first classes in 1911. Private, nonsectarian, coeducational, undergraduate college of liberal arts and sciences.

OTHER HONORS
1938 Phi Beta Kappa

REGIS COLLEGE Denver, CO. College of liberal arts for men; women admitted to evening and summer session; private control (Roman Catholic); established 1877.

ACHS HONORS	INACTIVE
1963 Pi Delta Phi	1950–70 Alpha Delta Gamma
1966 Alpha Sigma Nu	
1989 Psi Chi	

REGIS COLLEGE Weston, MA. College of liberal arts for women; privte control (Roman Catholic); chartered 1927.

ACHS HONORS	1971 Psi Chi
Omicron Delta Epsilon	
1940 Delta Epsilon Sigma	INACTIVE
1952 Pi Gamma Mu	1951–56 Kappa Omicron Nu
1958 Alpha Lambda Delta	1952–68 Phi Upsilon Omicron

RENSSELAER POLYTECHNIC INSTITUTE Troy, NY. Founded by Stephen Van Rensselaer 1824. Engineering, science, architecture, humanities, and social sciences, graduate school. Private control; coeducational; nonsectarian.

Twenty fraternities own their houses and land, three lease their homes and land from the Institute, one owns its house but leases land from the Institute, and one rents facilities from a private landlord. The sorority was permitted to rent facilities in 1977.

NIC MEN'S	1989 Kappa Alpha Psi (A)
1864 Delta Phi	
1864 Theta Xi	NPC WOMEN'S
1865 Zeta Psi	1976 Phi Sigma Sigma
1879 Delta Tau Delta	1980 Alpha Gamma Delta
1908 Theta Chi	1984 Pi Beta Phi
1918 Zeta Beta Tau	
1921 Alpha Phi Delta	ACHS HONORS
1922 Phi Kappa Tau	Omicron Delta Epsilon
1929 Phi Mu Delta	1908 Tau Beta Pi
1931 Pi Kappa Phi	1940 Chi Epsilon
1935 Pi Kappa Alpha	1940 Pi Tau Sigma
1937 Lambda Chi Alpha	1942 Eta Kappa Nu
1938 Sigma Phi Epsilon	1961 Alpha Sigma Mu
1940 Alpha Sigma Phi	1963 Sigma Pi Sigma
1948 Alpha Chi Rho	1976 Alpha Epsilon Delta
1949 Acacia	
1949 Tau Kappa Epsilon	OTHER HONORS
1950 Phi Sigma Kappa	National Order of Omega
1950 Sigma Chi	
1951 Alpha Epsilon Pi	SERVICE
1951 Sigma Alpha Epsilon	1947 Alpha Phi Omega
1954 Pi Lambda Phi	
1957 Tau Epsilon Phi	INACTIVE
1982 Psi Upsilon	1853–96 Theta Delta Chi
1984 Phi Gamma Delta	1867–65 Delta Kappa Epsilon
	1878–87 Chi Phi
	1922–64 Alpha Tau Omega

UNIVERSITY OF RHODE ISLAND Kingston, RI. Land-grant college 1892. Rhode Island State College 1909, became university 1951. Governed by board of regents, state control; undergraduate colleges coeducational; graduate school coeducational; nonsectarian.

Fraternity and sorority houses self-owned on college-owned land.

NIC MEN'S	1951 Kappa Omicron Nu
1911 Theta Chi	1954 Tau Beta Pi
1914 Lambda Chi Alpha	1955 Pi Sigma Alpha
1928 Alpha Epsilon Pi	1959 Alpha Kappa Delta
1929 Sigma Alpha Epsilon	1959 Rho Chi
1937 Tau Kappa Epsilon	1962 Kappa Delta Pi
1948 Phi Sigma Kappa	1966 Phi Alpha Theta
1948 Sigma Pi	1967 Mortar Board
1949 Sigma Chi	1969 Beta Gamma Sigma
1950 Phi Gamma Delta	1969 Sigma Delta Pi
1954 Sigma Nu	1969 Sigma Pi Sigma
1961 Zeta Beta Tau	1970 Pi Tau Sigma
1962 Chi Phi	1971 Eta Kappa Nu
1963 Theta Delta Chi	1971 Pi Delta Phi
1965 Sigma Phi Epsilon	1976 Beta Phi Mu
1966 Phi Kappa Psi	1979 Phi Eta Sigma
1969 Tau Epsilon Phi	1979 Phi Sigma Iota
	1984 Psi Chi
NPC WOMEN'S	1988 Chi Epsilon
1919 Sigma Kappa	1989 Pi Kappa Lambda
1922 Chi Omega	
1928 Delta Zeta	OTHER HONORS
1946 Sigma Delta Tau	National Order of Omega
1948 Alpha Delta Pi	1953 Sigma Xi
1948 Alpha Xi Delta	1962 Pi Mu Epsilon
1955 Alpha Chi Omega	1977 Phi Beta Kappa
PROFESSIONAL	
1911 Kappa Psi	SERVICE
1922 Rho Pi Phi	1966 Alpha Phi Omega
1927 Lambda Kappa Sigma	
	RECOGNITION
OTHER PROFESSIONAL	1963 Lambda Tau
1936 Alpha Zeta	
1971 Beta Alpha Psi	INACTIVE
	1929–77 Phi Mu Delta
ACHS HONORS	1961–82 Delta Delta Delta
Omicron Delta Epsilon	1962–86 Alpha Epsilon Phi
1913 Phi Kappa Phi	1965–73 Kappa Alpha Theta
1919 Delta Sigma Rho-Tau	1969–73 Kappa Delta Rho
Kappa Alpha	1970–74 Pi Lambda Phi
1935 Phi Sigma	1973 Phi Sigma Sigma
1947 Phi Alpha Theta	
1947 Phi Alpha Theta	COLONIES
	Beta Theta Pi

RHODE ISLAND COLLEGE Providence, RI. General college; coeducational; state control; chartered as normal school 1854.

OTHER PROFESSIONAL	OTHER HONORS
1928 Kappa Delta Phi (C)	1967 Pi Mu Epsilon
ACHS HONORS	
1982 Phi Sigma Iota	

RHODES COLLEGE Memphis, TN. Private control: Presbyterian Church. Founded in 1848. Four-year; coeducational; liberal arts college.

62% of men and 65% of women join fraternities. Single-sex dormitories.

NIC MEN'S	1931 Delta Delta Delta
1878 Pi Kappa Alpha	1989 Gamma Phi Beta
1882 Alpha Tau Omega	
1882 Kappa Sigma	NPHC WOMEN'S
1882 Sigma Alpha Epsilon	Alpha Kappa Alpha
NPC WOMEN'S	ACHS HONORS
1922 Chi Omega	Omicron Delta Epsilon
1925 Alpha Omicron Pi	Omicron Delta Epsilon
1925 Kappa Delta	1927 Omicron Delta Kappa

1949 Pi Kappa Lambda
1952 Psi Chi
1963 Sigma Pi Sigma
1964 Mortar Board
1990 Phi Alpha Theta

OTHER HONORS
    National Order of Omega

INACTIVE
1929–77 Zeta Tau Alpha

RICE UNIVERSITY
Houston, TX. Founded by William Marsh Rice, chartered 1891 as the Rice Institute; name changed to William Marsh Rice University 1960. First instruction 1912. Undergraduate and graduate school coeducational; private control, nonsectarian.

ACHS HONORS
    Omicron Delta Epsilon
1930 Pi Delta Phi
1940 Tau Beta Pi
1970 Sigma Pi Sigma
1981 Eta Kappa Nu
1990 Psi Chi

OTHER HONORS
1929 Phi Beta Kappa
1938 Sigma Xi

1958 Sigma Gamma Epsilon

SERVICE
1949 Alpha Phi Omega

RECOGNITION
1926 Phi Lambda Upsilon
1949 Delta Phi Alpha

INACTIVE
1953–69 Sigma Delta Pi

UNIVERSITY OF RICHMOND
Richmond, VA. Founded and first instruction 1830; chartered as Richmond College 1840; chartered as University of Richmond 1920. University; Richmond College for men and Westhampton College for women are coordinate colleges of liberal arts and sciences; graduate and professional divisions coeducational; private control (Baptist).

Fraternities own lodges on college land.

NIC MEN'S
1870 Kappa Alpha Order
1873 Phi Kappa Sigma
1875 Phi Delta Theta
1884 Sigma Alpha Epsilon
1890 Phi Gamma Delta
1891 Pi Kappa Alpha
1898 Kappa Sigma
1901 Sigma Phi Epsilon
1915 Theta Chi
1918 Lambda Chi Alpha
1958 Sigma Chi

NPHC MEN'S
    Phi Beta Sigma
    Phi Beta Sigma

NPC WOMEN'S
1987 Delta Delta Delta
1987 Delta Gamma
1987 Kappa Alpha Theta
1987 Kappa Kappa Gamma
1987 Pi Beta Phi
1989 Alpha Phi

PROFESSIONAL
1911 Delta Theta Phi
1948 Phi Alpha Delta
1955 Alpha Kappa Psi
1962 Phi Delta Phi
1983 Phi Alpha Delta

ACHS HONORS
    Omicron Delta Epsilon
1912 Delta Sigma Rho-Tau
    Kappa Alpha
1921 Omicron Delta Kappa
1932 Sigma Pi Sigma
1948 Phi Alpha Theta

1950 Psi Chi
1953 Pi Sigma Alpha
1955 Kappa Delta Pi
1965 Beta Gamma Sigma
1975 Phi Eta Sigma
1975 Phi Sigma Iota
1982 Phi Sigma Tau
1985 Theta Alpha Kappa

OTHER HONORS
    National Order of Omega
1929 Phi Beta Kappa
1948 Pi Mu Epsilon

SERVICE
1965 Alpha Phi Omega

RECOGNITION
1926 Society for Collegiate
    Journalists—Pi Delta
    Epsilon-Alpha Phi Gamma
    (P)
1939 Beta Beta Beta
1940 Eta Sigma Phi
1948 Gamma Sigma Epsilon
1953 Scabbard and Blade (11)
1976 Sigma Delta Psi

INACTIVE
1871–96 Beta Theta Pi
1878–84 Alpha Tau Omega
1880–82 Sigma Chi
1921–40 Sigma Nu Phi
1925–72 Zeta Beta Tau
1954–72 Alpha Epsilon Pi
1971–76 Phi Mu Alpha—
    Sinfonia
1987–88 Chi Omega

RICHMOND PROFESSIONAL INSTITUTE
Richmond, VA. Affiliate of College of William and Mary.

PROFESSIONAL
1964 Pi Sigma Epsilon

1967 Delta Omicron

RICKER COLLEGE
Houlton, ME. College of liberal arts and general studies; teacher preparatory; coeducational; independent control. Established 1848.

ACHS HONORS
1968 Alpha Chi

INACTIVE
1970–76 Pi Lambda Phi

RICKS COLLEGE
Rexburg, ID. Coeducational; founded 1888.

OTHER MEN'S
1949 Delta Phi Kappa

OTHER WOMEN'S
    Lambda Delta Sigma

RECOGNITION
1973 Sigma Delta Psi

RIDER COLLEGE
Trenton, NJ. Founded 1865. Coeducational; private control; nonsectarian. Undergraduate college in liberal arts, commerce and education; graduate programs in education and business. Relocated on suburban campus in Lawrenceville, since September, 1964.

The fraternity and sorority houses are owned by the college and rented to the individual organizations.

NIC MEN'S
1956 Phi Sigma Kappa
1957 Zeta Beta Tau
1961 Theta Chi
1965 Phi Kappa Psi
1986 Phi Kappa Tau

NPC WOMEN'S
1962 Delta Phi Epsilon
1967 Alpha Xi Delta
1967 Zeta Tau Alpha

NPHC WOMEN'S
1980 Alpha Kappa Alpha

PROFESSIONAL
1934 Delta Sigma Pi
1965 Phi Chi Theta

OTHER PROFESSIONAL
1968 Delta Pi Epsilon
1977 Sigma Delta Chi

ACHS HONORS
    Omicron Delta Epsilon
1963 Phi Alpha Theta
1965 Psi Chi
1966 Pi Delta Phi
1966 Pi Gamma Mu

1967 Sigma Delta Pi
1968 Pi Omega Pi
1976 Alpha Lambda Delta
1976 Omicron Delta Kappa
1979 Phi Sigma Tau
1979 Pi Sigma Alpha

OTHER HONORS
    National Order of Omega

SERVICE
1966 Alpha Phi Omega
1968 Gamma Sigma Sigma

RECOGNITION
1962 Society for Collegiate
    Journalists—Pi Delta
    Epsilon-Alpha Phi Gamma
    (P)
1966 Beta Beta Beta
1975 Sigma Iota Epsilon

INACTIVE
1956–87 Tau Kappa Epsilon
1967–88 Delta Zeta

COLONIES
1990 Alpha Epsilon Pi

RIO GRANDE COLLEGE
Rio Grande, OH. Founded in 1876 as a denominational college; became completely private and independent in 1952; coeducational, liberal arts institution which emphasizes teacher education.

NIC MEN'S
1972 Alpha Sigma Phi
1987 Tau Kappa Epsilon

NPC WOMEN'S
1985 Alpha Sigma Tau

ACHS HONORS
1982 Phi Alpha Theta

1985 Alpha Lambda Delta

RECOGNITION
1973 Pi Kappa Delta

INACTIVE
1986   Phi Sigma Sigma

RIPON COLLEGE   Ripon, WI. Founded as the Lyceum of Ripon 1850, chartered 1851 as Brockway College. Renamed Ripon College 1864. Independent, coeducational, residential liberal arts college; nonsectarian.

NIC MEN'S
1954 Theta Chi
1955 Sigma Chi
1960 Phi Delta Theta

NPC WOMEN'S
1959 Alpha Chi Omega
1960 Alpha Delta Pi

ACHS HONORS
     Omicron Delta Epsilon
1957 Phi Sigma Iota
1965 Phi Alpha Theta
1969 Sigma Pi Sigma
1970 Psi Chi

OTHER HONORS
1952 Phi Beta Kappa

SERVICE
1954 Alpha Phi Omega

RECOGNITION
1913 Pi Kappa Delta
1965 Delta Phi Alpha
1966 Scabbard and Blade (16)
1967 Beta Beta Beta

INACTIVE
1919–47 Theta Alpha Phi
1954–76 Sigma Nu
1958–80 Sigma Alpha Epsilon
1958–87 Alpha Xi Delta
1959–70 Alpha Phi
1959–84 Delta Upsilon
1960–67 Kappa Delta

RIVIER COLLEGE   Nashua, NH. College of liberal arts for women; undergraduate and graduate; private control (Roman Catholic). Establsihed 1933.

ACHS HONORS
1948 Delta Epsilon Sigma

ROANOKE COLLEGE   Salem, VA. Founded by Dr. David Bittle and Dr. Christopher C. Baughman, near Staunton, VA, 1842. Moved to Salem, VA, 1847. Chartered as a degree-granting institution 1853. Liberal arts college; coeducational; independent college affiliated with the Lutheran Church in America.

Designated fraternity and sorority housing provided by the college.

NIC MEN'S
1872 Sigma Chi
1916 Pi Kappa Phi
1924 Kappa Alpha Order
1959 Pi Lambda Phi

NPC WOMEN'S
1955 Chi Omega
1955 Delta Gamma
1955 Phi Mu

ACHS HONORS
     Omicron Delta Epsilon
1922 Delta Sigma Rho-Tau
     Kappa Alpha
1966 Sigma Pi Sigma
1967 Delta Mu Delta
1972 Pi Delta Phi
1973 Sigma Delta Pi
1974 Alpha Chi

1974 Phi Alpha Theta
1976 Alpha Lambda Delta
1976 Pi Sigma Alpha
1980 Psi Chi
1981 Pi Gamma Mu

OTHER HONORS
1972 Pi Mu Epsilon

SERVICE
1988 Alpha Phi Omega

RECOGNITION
1930 Blue Key
1931 Alpha Psi Omega
1949 Cardinal Key
1957 Beta Beta Beta

INACTIVE
1866–05 Phi Gamma Delta
1869–92 Alpha Tau Omega

1869–96 Phi Delta Theta
1896–09 Pi Kappa Alpha

1903–05 Sigma Phi Epsilon
1962–78 Alpha Phi

ROBERT MORRIS COLLEGE   Coraopolis, PA. Private control. Founded in 1921. Four-year; coeducational; specialized institution.

70% of students live off campus or commute. Single-sex dormitories.

NIC MEN'S
1970 Alpha Chi Rho
1971 Phi Sigma Kappa
1973 Delta Tau Delta
1977 Tau Kappa Epsilon
1981 Kappa Delta Rho

NPC WOMEN'S
1980 Zeta Tau Alpha
1981 Delta Zeta
1982 Delta Phi Epsilon
1985 Theta Phi Alpha

PROFESSIONAL
1980 Delta Sigma Pi

ACHS HONORS
1987 Lambda Sigma Society

OTHER HONORS
     National Order of Omega

SERVICE
1987 Alpha Phi Omega

INACTIVE
1971–73 Pi Kappa Alpha
1972–74 Phi Mu

COLONIES
     Sigma Tau Gamma

ROCHESTER INSTITUTE OF TECHNOLOGY Rochester, NY. Founded 1829 a Rochester Athenaeum; merged with the Mechanics Institute 1891; name changed to present 1944; coeducational; private control; nonsectarian.

Administration requires fraternities and sororities to occupy residence halls.

NIC MEN'S
1949 Theta Xi
1959 Tau Epsilon Phi
1960 Phi Sigma Kappa
1960 Sigma Pi
1966 Alpha Epsilon Pi
1966 Phi Kappa Tau
1967 Triangle
1973 Tau Kappa Epsilon
1986 Phi Delta Theta
1987 Delta Sigma Phi
1990 Kappa Delta Rho

NPHC MEN'S
     Phi Beta Sigma

NPC WOMEN'S
1963 Alpha Xi Delta
1964 Alpha Sigma Alpha

PROFESSIONAL
1966 Alpha Chi Sigma
1967 Phi Gamma Nu

ACHS HONORS
     Omicron Delta Epsilon
1959 Delta Sigma Rho-Tau
     Kappa Alpha
1969 Sigma Pi Sigma
1970 Phi Kappa Phi
1971 Tau Beta Pi

OTHER HONORS
     National Order of Omega

SERVICE
1963 Alpha Phi Omega

RECOGNITION
1960 Eta Mu Pi

INACTIVE
1961–83 Delta Sigma Pi
1979   Phi Sigma Sigma

COLONIES
1990 Phi Kappa Psi

UNIVERSITY OF ROCHESTER   Rochester, NY. Founded by Ira Harris 1850. University; colleges of arts and science; engineering, business administration, education. Eastman School of Music, medicine and dentistry; undergraduate and graduate education; private control; nonsectarian.

Eight fraternities occupy self-owned houses on college land; several others occupy dormitory wings. The four sororities are in the women's residence hall.

NIC MEN'S
1850 Alpha Delta Phi
1856 Delta Kappa Epsilon
1858 Psi Upsilon
1867 Theta Delta Chi
1884 Chi Psi
1911 Zeta Beta Tau
1920 Theta Chi
1929 Alpha Phi Delta
1932 Sigma Chi
1957 Sigma Alpha Mu
1957 Tau Kappa Epsilon
1966 Chi Phi
1981 Delta Sigma Phi
1985 Phi Kappa Tau
1986 Sigma Phi Epsilon

NPC WOMEN'S
1977 Delta Zeta
1978 Sigma Delta Tau
1979 Kappa Delta
1981 Phi Sigma Sigma
1987 Delta Gamma

OTHER PROFESSIONAL
1925 Omega Epsilon Phi

ACHS HONORS
   Omicron Delta Epsilon
1947 Tau Beta Pi
1964 Beta Gamma Sigma
1967 Phi Sigma Iota

OTHER HONORS
   National Order of Omega
1887 Phi Beta Kappa
1929 Alpha Omega Alpha
1930 Sigma Xi

SERVICE
1958 Alpha Phi Omega

RECOGNITION
   Arnold Air Society (E-1)
1930 Delta Phi Alpha
1976 Sigma Delta Epsilon

INACTIVE
1851–95 Delta Psi
1926–36 Kappa Phi Kappa
1932–38 Phi Rho Sigma
1964–73 Alpha Epsilon Pi

COLONIES
1852 Delta Upsilon

ROCKFORD COLLEGE Rockford, IL. College of liberal arts; coeducational; private control; nonsectarian. Chartered 1847.

ACHS HONORS
   Omicron Delta Epsilon
1933 Delta Sigma Rho-Tau
   Kappa Alpha

1987 Phi Alpha Theta

OTHER HONORS
1953 Phi Beta Kappa

ROCKHURST COLLEGE Kansas City, MO. College of liberal arts for men and women; private control; Roman Catholic; established 1910.

NIC MEN'S
1932 Alpha Delta Gamma
1966 Tau Kappa Epsilon
1972 Sigma Alpha Epsilon

NPHC MEN'S
1952 Alpha Phi Alpha

ACHS HONORS
1942 Delta Epsilon Sigma
1953 Alpha Sigma Nu

1968 Phi Sigma Tau
1983 Phi Alpha Theta

SERVICE
1940 Alpha Phi Omega

RECOGNITION
1948 Pi Kappa Delta

INACTIVE
1954–55 Alpha Kappa Psi

ROLLINS COLLEGE Winter Park, FL. Founded 1885 under the auspices of the Congregational Church; now nonsectarian, private, liberal arts, coeducational; graduate programs in business administration, and education.

Fraternities and sororities reside in residence halls.

NIC MEN'S
   Tau Kappa Epsilon
1927 Kappa Alpha Order
1934 Phi Delta Theta
1959 Tau Kappa Epsilon
1967 Sigma Phi Epsilon
1977 Chi Psi
1989 Alpha Tau Omega

NPC WOMEN'S
1929 Phi Mu
1931 Chi Omega

1932 Kappa Kappa Gamma
1933 Kappa Alpha Theta

ACHS HONORS
   Omicron Delta Epsilon
   Omicron Delta Epsilon
1932 Omicron Delta Kappa
1935 Pi Kappa Lambda
1961 Phi Sigma Iota
1967 Kappa Delta Pi
1975 Sigma Pi Sigma
1987 Phi Eta Sigma

RECOGNITION
1938 Theta Alpha Phi

INACTIVE
1923–67 Phi Beta
1924–70 Lambda Chi Alpha
1928–71 Gamma Phi Beta

1929–70 Pi Beta Phi
1931–88 Alpha Phi
1932–73 Pi Gamma Mu
1937–72 Sigma Nu
1941–70 Delta Chi

ROOSEVELT UNIVERSITY Chicago, IL. University; coeducational; private control; nonsectarian; established 1945.

NIC MEN'S
1957 Tau Delta Phi

PROFESSIONAL
1960 Mu Phi Epsilon
1968 Phi Gamma Nu

ACHS HONORS
1947 Psi Chi

1964 Beta Gamma Sigma
1965 Phi Alpha Theta
1989 Delta Mu Delta

INACTIVE
1949–73 Phi Mu Alpha—
   Sinfonia

ROSARY COLLEGE River Forest, IL. College of liberal arts; coeducational; private control (Roman Catholic); as Sinsinawa Academy, granted charter by State of Wisconsin in 1848, and incorporated 1901. Moved to River Forest and incorporated by State of Illinois 1918.

ACHS HONORS
1948 Sigma Delta Pi
1951 Pi Delta Phi
1953 Pi Gamma Mu
1965 Phi Alpha Theta

1967 Kappa Mu Epsilon
1978 Kappa Omicron Nu
1980 Psi Chi
1983 Beta Phi Mu
1983 Theta Alpha Kappa

ROSARY HILL COLLEGE Buffalo, NY. College of liberal arts for women; private control (Roman Catholic); chartered 1947.

PROFESSIONAL
1973 Delta Omicron

ACHS HONORS
1956 Delta Epsilon Sigma
1965 Lambda Iota Tau

1968 Lambda Iota Tau

RECOGNITION
1964 Beta Beta Beta
1966 Lambda Tau

ROSE-HULMAN INSTITUTE OF TECHNOLOGY Terre Haute, IN. Founded by Chauncey Rose 1874. First instruction 1875. College of engineering and science for men; undergraduate curriculum leading to a B.S., and graduate curriculum leading to a M.S. degree. Private control, nonsectarian.

The fraternities own their houses.

NIC MEN'S
1893 Alpha Tau Omega
1907 Theta Xi
1925 Lambda Chi Alpha
1968 Triangle
1969 Phi Gamma Delta
1982 Delta Sigma Phi
1988 Pi Kappa Alpha

PROFESSIONAL
1909 Alpha Chi Sigma

ACHS HONORS
1928 Tau Beta Pi

1965 Eta Kappa Nu
1966 Sigma Pi Sigma
1968 Pi Tau Sigma
1969 Omega Chi Epsilon
1988 Alpha Lambda Delta

OTHER HONORS
1966 Pi Mu Epsilon

SERVICE
1968 Alpha Phi Omega

RECOGNITION
1932 Blue Key

RUSSELL SAGE COLLEGE Troy, NY.

ACHS HONORS
Omicron Delta Epsilon
Pi Alpha Alpha
1970 Phi Alpha Theta
1972 Psi Chi

1975 Phi Kappa Phi

RECOGNITION
1934 Alpha Psi Omega
1975 Beta Beta Beta

RUST COLLEGE Holly Springs, MS. Established 1866; coeducational; four-year accredited college.

NIC MEN'S
1972 Kappa Alpha Psi (A)

NPHC MEN'S
Phi Beta Sigma
1973 Alpha Phi Alpha

NPHC WOMEN'S
Zeta Phi Beta

1971 Delta Sigma Theta (B)
1974 Alpha Kappa Alpha

ACHS HONORS
1973 Phi Alpha Theta
1975 Alpha Kappa Mu

SERVICE
1973 Alpha Phi Omega

RUTGERS—THE STATE UNIVERSITY New Brunswick, NJ. Founded 1766 as Queen's College. Undergraduate residential colleges: Rutgers College, Douglass College, Livingston College, Cook College. Professional nonresidential undergraduate colleges: engineering; pharmacy. Graduate schools of education, library science, social work, psychology, and fine arts.

Twenty-six chapter houses are owned by chapter corporations; sixteen chapters operate without houses.

NIC MEN'S
1845 Delta Phi
1848 Zeta Psi
1858 Delta Upsilon
1867 Chi Phi
1879 Beta Theta Pi
1879 Chi Psi
1917 Phi Gamma Delta
1918 Kappa Sigma
1921 Sigma Alpha Mu
1930 Tau Kappa Epsilon
1931 Alpha Sigma Phi
1932 Theta Chi
1934 Tau Delta Phi
1937 Alpha Chi Rho
1944 Sigma Phi Epsilon
1947 Zeta Beta Tau
1949 Delta Sigma Phi
1951 Tau Delta Phi
1956 Alpha Epsilon Pi
1959 Phi Sigma Kappa
1964 Sigma Pi
1965 Tau Epsilon Phi
1974 Kappa Alpha Psi (A)
1984 Kappa Delta Rho
1987 Phi Kappa Psi
1988 Phi Delta Theta
1990 Phi Kappa Sigma
1991 Sigma Chi

NPHC MEN'S
Phi Beta Sigma
Phi Beta Sigma

NPC WOMEN'S
1977 Gamma Phi Beta
1978 Phi Sigma Sigma
1978 Zeta Tau Alpha
1981 Sigma Delta Tau

1982 Sigma Kappa
1985 Delta Gamma
1988 Alpha Chi Omega

NPHC WOMEN'S
1975 Alpha Kappa Alpha
1978 Sigma Gamma Rho

PROFESSIONAL
1924 Kappa Psi
1925 Rho Pi Phi
1930 Lambda Kappa Sigma
1942 Delta Sigma Pi
1950 Phi Delta Phi

OTHER PROFESSIONAL
1922 Alpha Zeta
1923 Alpha Zeta Omega
1947 Keramos
1968 Alpha Tau Alpha

ACHS HONORS
Omicron Delta Epsilon
1929 Delta Sigma Rho-Tau Kappa Alpha
1929 Psi Chi
1934 Sigma Delta Pi
1934 Tau Beta Pi
1938 Kappa Delta Pi
1947 Rho Chi
1948 Phi Alpha Theta
1950 Eta Kappa Nu
1952 Pi Tau Sigma
1953 Pi Sigma Alpha
1964 Alpha Kappa Delta
1965 Alpha Pi Mu
1968 Sigma Theta Tau
1969 Phi Sigma Iota
1970 Beta Phi Mu
1970 Chi Epsilon

1973 Kappa Omicron Nu
1976 Phi Alpha Theta
1980 Gamma Theta Upsilon
1981 Sigma Lambda Alpha
1986 Phi Eta Sigma
1990 Pi Kappa Lambda

OTHER HONORS
National Order of Omega
1869 Phi Beta Kappa
1922 Sigma Xi
1954 Pi Mu Epsilon

SERVICE
1947 Alpha Phi Omega

RECOGNITION
Arnold Air Society (B-1)
1922 Phi Lambda Upsilon
1923 Scabbard and Blade (S)
1928 Alpha Psi Omega
1931 Delta Phi Alpha

1933 Pi Alpha Xi
1948 National Block and Bridle Club

INACTIVE
1848–50 Delta Psi
1861–85 Delta Kappa Epsilon
1913–59 Pi Kappa Alpha
1913–88 Lambda Chi Alpha
1934–55 Kappa Phi Kappa
1937–72 Delta Sigma Pi
1950–60 Alpha Phi Alpha
1952 Beta Beta Beta
1952–67 Alpha Gamma Rho
1960–86 Phi Chi Theta
1961–69 Pi Lambda Phi
1962–70 Kappa Beta Pi
1978–83 Sigma Sigma Sigma

COLONIES
1988 Sigma Pi Sigma

RUTGERS THE STATE UNIVERSITY Newark, NJ. Founded 1946 comprised of the New Jersey College of Pharmacy and the former University of Newark. Colleges of arts and sciences, law, nursing, business administration, and pharmacy.

Fraternities and sororities may occupy facilities with university approval.

NIC MEN'S
1960 Tau Kappa Epsilon

PROFESSIONAL
1955 Phi Alpha Delta

ACHS HONORS
Omicron Delta Epsilon
Pi Alpha Alpha
1938 Kappa Delta Pi
1942 Beta Gamma Sigma
1964 Phi Alpha Theta
1969 Psi Chi

SERVICE
1950 Alpha Phi Omega

RECOGNITION
1954 Alpha Psi Omega
1966 Beta Beta Beta

INACTIVE
1935–83 Pi Lambda Phi
1962–73 Alpha Epsilon Pi
1964–65 Sigma Pi Sigma
1970–72 Zeta Beta Tau

COLONIES
1981 Phi Sigma Sigma

RUTGERS THE STATE UNIVERSITY Camden, NJ. The State University; founded 1927, and became part of Rutgers in 1950.

NIC MEN'S
1966 Tau Epsilon Phi
1985 Tau Kappa Epsilon
1990 Phi Kappa Sigma

NPC WOMEN'S
1971 Phi Sigma Sigma
1981 Delta Phi Epsilon

PROFESSIONAL
1966 Phi Alpha Delta

ACHS HONORS
Omicron Delta Epsilon
1968 Psi Chi
1969 Sigma Pi Sigma
1976 Kappa Delta Pi
1981 Pi Sigma Alpha

OTHER HONORS
1967 Pi Mu Epsilon

ST. AMBROSE COLLEGE Davenport, IA. Private control: Roman Catholic. Founded in 1882. Four-year; coeducational.

73% of students live off campus or commute. Single-sex dormitories.

PROFESSIONAL
1970 Delta Sigma Pi

ACHS HONORS
1940 Delta Epsilon Sigma

1963 Kappa Delta Pi
1967 Phi Eta Sigma
1969 Alpha Chi
1980 Psi Chi

SERVICE
1980 Alpha Phi Omega

RECOGNITION
1963 Beta Beta Beta

INACTIVE
1973–76 Phi Chi Theta

ST. ANSELM'S COLLEGE   Manchester, NH. College of liberal arts for men; women admitted to nursing school; private control (Roman Catholic); chartered 1889.

ACHS HONORS
    Omicron Delta Epsilon
1940 Delta Epsilon Sigma
1960 Delta Sigma Rho-Tau
    Kappa Alpha

1962 Pi Gamma Mu
1972 Phi Alpha Theta
1976 Gamma Theta Upsilon
1990 Psi Chi

ST. AUGUSTINE'S COLLEGE   Raleigh, NC. College of liberal arts; coeducational private control (Protestant Episcopal); incorporated 1867.

Administration requires sorority and fraternity members to occupy residence halls.

NIC MEN'S
1949 Kappa Alpha Psi (A)
NPHC MEN'S
    Phi Beta Sigma
1947 Omega Psi Phi
1948 Alpha Phi Alpha
NPHC WOMEN'S
    Zeta Phi Beta
1948 Delta Sigma Theta (B)
1949 Alpha Kappa Alpha
1950 Sigma Gamma Rho
ACHS HONORS
1950 Alpha Kappa Mu

1971 Sigma Tau Delta
1972 Delta Mu Delta
1973 Pi Delta Phi
1977 Phi Alpha Theta

SERVICE
1969 Alpha Phi Omega

RECOGNITION
1973 Mu Beta Psi

INACTIVE
1952–60 Beta Kappa Chi

ST. BONAVENTURE UNIVERSITY   St. Bonaventure, NY. University; coeducational; incorporated 1855.

OTHER PROFESSIONAL
1966 Sigma Delta Chi

ACHS HONORS
    Omicron Delta Epsilon
1959 Delta Epsilon Sigma
1960 Sigma Pi Sigma
1967 Psi Chi
1971 Phi Alpha Theta
1972 Pi Delta Phi
1974 Kappa Tau Alpha
1983 Pi Gamma Mu

1985 Delta Mu Delta

SERVICE
1983 Alpha Phi Omega

RECOGNITION
1967 Society for Collegiate
    Journalists—Pi Delta
    Epsilon-Alpha Phi Gamma
    (P)

INACTIVE
1951–53 Delta Sigma Pi

THE COLLEGE OF ST. CATHERINE   St. Paul, MN. College of liberal arts for women; private control (Roman Catholic); founded as a junior college 1905, became four-year college 1911.

ACHS HONORS
    Omicron Delta Epsilon
1941 Pi Gamma Mu
1949 Pi Delta Phi
1978 Kappa Omicron Nu
1979 Psi Chi
1979 Theta Alpha Kappa
1985 Delta Mu Delta

OTHER HONORS
1938 Phi Beta Kappa
1942 National Collegiate
    Players
1964 Delta Phi Delta

INACTIVE
1946–58 Mu Phi Epsilon

ST. CLOUD STATE UNIVERSITY   St. Cloud, MN. State college; coeducational; state control; established 1869 as normal school; centennial celebration, 1968-69; masters degrees, M.S., M.A., M.B.A.

Fraternities and sororities have housing of their own; Tau Kappa Epsilon and Alpha Phi own their houses.

NIC MEN'S
1961 Phi Sigma Kappa
1961 Tau Kappa Epsilon
1965 Theta Chi
1977 Acacia
1983 Delta Sigma Phi
1988 Alpha Delta Gamma

NPC WOMEN'S
1966 Delta Zeta

PROFESSIONAL
1969 Sigma Alpha Iota
1970 Delta Sigma Pi
1974 Phi Chi Theta

OTHER PROFESSIONAL
1976 Sigma Delta Chi

ACHS HONORS
    Omicron Delta Epsilon
1932 Kappa Delta Pi
1939 Pi Omega Pi

1968 Gamma Theta Upsilon
1969 Psi Chi
1974 Lambda Iota Tau
1974 Phi Kappa Phi
1977 Beta Gamma Sigma

OTHER HONORS
1959 National Collegiate
    Players

SERVICE
1953 Alpha Phi Omega
1961 Gamma Sigma Sigma

INACTIVE
1960–74 Sigma Tau Gamma
1963–77 Alpha Xi Delta
1964–78 Alpha Phi
1965–82 Sigma Sigma Sigma
1968–76 Phi Mu Alpha—
    Sinfonia
1969–79 Phi Kappa Tau

ST. EDWARD'S UNIVERSITY   Austin, TX. Private control: Holy Cross brothers. Founded in 1885. Became coeducational in 1966.

75% of students live off campus or commute.

PROFESSIONAL
1972 Delta Sigma Pi

ACHS HONORS
1926 Alpha Chi

1973 Delta Mu Delta
1977 Theta Alpha Kappa

SERVICE
1966 Alpha Phi Omega

ST. FRANCIS COLLEGE   Brooklyn, NY. College of liberal arts for men; private control (Roman Catholic); established 1858 as St. Francis Academy.

NIC MEN'S
1962 Alpha Phi Delta

NPC WOMEN'S
1990 Delta Phi Epsilon

PROFESSIONAL
1964 Alpha Kappa Psi

ACHS HONORS
    Omicron Delta Epsilon

1962 Phi Alpha Theta
1967 Sigma Delta Pi
1977 Theta Alpha Kappa

RECOGNITION
1976 Pi Kappa Delta

INACTIVE
1969–87 Kappa Mu Epsilon

ST. FRANCIS COLLEGE   Fort Wayne, IN. Founded 1890 as normal training school for members of Franciscan sisterhood; open to lay students 1940; liberal arts college; teacher education; coeducational; private; Roman Catholic.

ACHS HONORS
1942 Delta Epsilon Sigma

RECOGNITION
1967 Lambda Tau

ST. FRANCIS COLLEGE   Joliet, IL.

ACHS HONORS
1940 Delta Epsilon Sigma

1945 Kappa Mu Epsilon
1969 Phi Alpha Theta

ST. FRANCIS COLLEGE   Loretto, PA. College of arts and science, with teacher education; coeducational; private control (Roman Catholic); established 1847.

NIC MEN'S
1948 Delta Sigma Phi
1949 Alpha Phi Delta
1955 Tau Kappa Epsilon

NPC WOMEN'S
1990 Theta Phi Alpha

PROFESSIONAL
1964 Alpha Kappa Psi

ACHS HONORS
1940 Delta Epsilon Sigma
1976 Psi Chi
1977 Phi Sigma Iota
1979 Kappa Mu Epsilon

1979 Theta Alpha Kappa
1981 Phi Alpha Theta
1984 Delta Mu Delta

SERVICE
1969 Alpha Phi Omega

RECOGNITION
1956 Society for Collegiate
Journalists—Pi Delta
Epsilon-Alpha Phi Gamma
(P)

INACTIVE
1948–57 Sigma Beta Kappa
1974–87 Phi Chi Theta

UNIVERSITY OF ST. THOMAS   Houston, TX.

PROFESSIONAL
1976 Mu Phi Epsilon

ACHS HONORS
Omicron Delta Epsilon
1955 Delta Epsilon Sigma

1962 Pi Delta Phi
1971 Sigma Delta Pi
1975 Pi Gamma Mu
1977 Psi Chi

ST. JOHN'S COLLEGE   Annapolis, MD. Private control. Founded in 1784. Four-year; coeducational; liberal arts college.

Freshmen must live on campus. Co-ed dormitories.

INACTIVE
1903–40 Phi Sigma Kappa

1916–42 Kappa Alpha Order
1937–47 Zeta Beta Tau

ST. JOHN'S UNIVERSITY   Collegeville, MN.

ACHS HONORS
Omicron Delta Epsilon
1940 Delta Epsilon Sigma

INACTIVE
1973–76 Psi Chi

ST. JOHN'S UNIVERSITY   Jamaica, NY. University; coeducational; private control (Roman Catholic); established 1870 as St. John's College; chartered 1871. There are two campuses.

NIC MEN'S
1959 Alpha Phi Delta
1960 Phi Kappa Tau
1961 Tau Kappa Epsilon
1965 Phi Kappa Theta
1968 Pi Lambda Phi
1986 Kappa Alpha Psi (A)
1990 Sigma Phi Epsilon

NPHC MEN'S
Phi Beta Sigma

NPC WOMEN'S
1960 Theta Phi Alpha
1990 Phi Sigma Sigma

PROFESSIONAL
1924 Rho Pi Phi
1928 Delta Theta Phi
1957 Phi Alpha Delta
1958 Phi Delta Chi
1959 Pi Sigma Epsilon
1961 Lambda Kappa Sigma
1962 Alpha Delta Theta
1962 Phi Chi Theta
1986 Phi Chi Theta

OTHER PROFESSIONAL
1975 Alpha Zeta Omega

ACHS HONORS
Omicron Delta Epsilon

1963 Sigma Delta Pi
1964 Alpha Kappa Delta
1964 Kappa Delta Pi
1964 Psi Chi
1965 Pi Delta Phi
1973 Sigma Pi Sigma
1977 Beta Phi Mu
1977 Phi Alpha Theta
1979 Theta Alpha Kappa

SERVICE
1949 Alpha Phi Omega

RECOGNITION
1930 Iota Tau Tau

1965 Society for Collegiate
Journalists—Pi Delta
Epsilon-Alpha Phi Gamma
(P)

INACTIVE
1932–39 Alpha Sigma Phi
1932–68 Delta Mu Delta
1935–43 Sigma Alpha Epsilon
1938–59 Zeta Beta Tau
1966–78 Delta Zeta
1967–85 Delta Sigma Phi
1969–72 Alpha Sigma Alpha

Jamaica Campus Jamaica, NY. The fraternities and sororities may not occupy their own special quarters.

INACTIVE
1965–73 Alpha Kappa Psi

ST. JOHN FISHER COLLEGE   Rochester, NY. College of liberal arts, science, and commerce for men and women; private control (Roman Catholic); established 1949.

ACHS HONORS
Omicron Delta Epsilon
1959 Pi Gamma Mu

1965 Delta Epsilon Sigma
1971 Phi Alpha Theta
1973 Pi Delta Phi

ST. JOSEPH'S COLLEGE   Rensselaer, IN.

ACHS HONORS
1956 Delta Epsilon Sigma
1979 Psi Chi

SERVICE
1985 Alpha Phi Omega

INACTIVE
1960–61 Phi Eta Sigma

ST. JOSEPH'S COLLEGE   Philadelphia, PA. College of liberal arts for men; Roman Catholic; established 1851.

NIC MEN'S
1976 Phi Sigma Kappa
1978 Lambda Chi Alpha
1983 Pi Kappa Phi
1988 Sigma Phi Epsilon

NPC WOMEN'S
1983 Sigma Sigma Sigma
1987 Alpha Gamma Delta

PROFESSIONAL
1978 Phi Chi Theta

ACHS HONORS
Omicron Delta Epsilon
1939 Alpha Sigma Nu
1951 Sigma Pi Sigma
1967 Phi Alpha Theta
1968 Alpha Epsilon Delta

1974 Psi Chi
1976 Phi Sigma Tau
1976 Pi Sigma Alpha
1980 Theta Alpha Kappa
1985 Alpha Lambda Delta
1987 Phi Alpha Theta
1987 Phi Sigma Iota

RECOGNITION
Arnold Air Society (B-1)
1963 Alpha Psi Omega

INACTIVE
1965–83 Delta Sigma Pi
1970–73 Kappa Mu Epsilon
1982–84 Alpha Delta Gamma

COLONIES
Pi Kappa Alpha

ST. LAWRENCE UNIVERSITY   Canton, NY. University; college of liberal arts, nonsectarian; graduate; coeducational; private control; chartered 1856.

The fraternities and sororities are permitted to own their houses and land and most do; however, in several instances ownership is by the college on rental basis to the fraternity and sorority. Men and women may not live in the houses during the freshman year.

NIC MEN'S
1879 Beta Theta Pi
1882 Alpha Tau Omega
1902 Phi Sigma Kappa
1919 Sigma Alpha Epsilon
1930 Sigma Pi
1953 Sigma Chi
1959 Phi Kappa Sigma

NPC WOMEN'S
1881 Kappa Kappa Gamma
1891 Delta Delta Delta
1914 Pi Beta Phi
1981 Chi Omega

ACHS HONORS
    Omicron Delta Epsilon
1916 Delta Sigma Rho-Tau
    Kappa Alpha
1947 Alpha Kappa Delta
1949 Pi Sigma Alpha
1954 Omicron Delta Kappa
1955 Phi Sigma Tau
1955 Psi Chi

1970 Phi Alpha Theta
1970 Sigma Delta Pi
1971 Pi Delta Phi

OTHER HONORS
1899 Phi Beta Kappa
1935 Pi Mu Epsilon

SERVICE
1953 Alpha Phi Omega

RECOGNITION
1942 Beta Beta Beta
1953 Scabbard and Blade (11)

INACTIVE
1884–87 Delta Gamma
1921–69 Kappa Delta
1924–30 Delta Zeta
1929–73 Sigma Pi Sigma
1933–65 Gamma Sigma Epsilon
1935–83 Alpha Delta Pi
1955–76 Mortar Board
1960–70 Delta Gamma

ST. LOUIS UNIVERSITY St. Louis, MO. Founded in 1818, private control, Society of Jesus, Roman Catholic. Coeducational, colleges of arts and sciences, technology, commerce and finance, aeronautical technology; schools of law, medicine, dentistry, nursing, philosophy and letters, graduate school.

There are no undergraduate fraternity or sorority houses.

NIC MEN'S
1916 Delta Sigma Phi
1927 Alpha Delta Gamma
1948 Phi Kappa Theta
1955 Tau Kappa Epsilon
1983 Phi Delta Theta
1984 Sigma Chi
1990 Pi Kappa Alpha

NPHC MEN'S
1955 Omega Psi Phi

NPC WOMEN'S
1967 Gamma Phi Beta
1984 Alpha Sigma Tau
1988 Alpha Delta Pi

NPHC WOMEN'S
    Zeta Phi Beta

PROFESSIONAL
1906 Phi Rho Sigma
1910 Phi Chi
1922 Delta Theta Phi
1949 Phi Alpha Delta
1949 Phi Delta Phi
1951 Alpha Delta Theta
1957 Alpha Kappa Psi
1985 Phi Alpha Delta

OTHER PROFESSIONAL
1903 Phi Beta Pi and Theta
    Kappa Psi (a)
1924 Phi Delta Epsilon
1952 Delta Sigma Theta (C)

1955 Kappa Phi Kappa
1970 Pi Lambda Theta
1980 Sigma Nu Phi

ACHS HONORS
    Omicron Delta Epsilon
1923 Alpha Sigma Nu
1950 Phi Sigma Iota
1951 Gamma Theta Upsilon
1955 Psi Chi
1963 Beta Gamma Sigma
1966 Phi Alpha Theta
1967 Pi Delta Phi
1969 Pi Sigma Alpha
1974 Sigma Delta Pi
1979 Theta Alpha Kappa
1988 Phi Eta Sigma

OTHER HONORS
    National Order of Omega
1924 Alpha Omega Alpha
1934 Omicron Kappa Upsilon
1944 Sigma Xi
1945 Pi Mu Epsilon
1968 Phi Beta Kappa

SERVICE
1944 Alpha Phi Omega

RECOGNITION
    Angel Flight
1941 Eta Sigma Phi
1949 Sigma Delta Psi
1969 Beta Beta Beta

INACTIVE
1901   Delta Sigma Delta
1909–69 Alpha Kappa Kappa
1922–29 Phi Beta Pi and Theta
    Kappa Psi (B)
1922–43 Sigma Nu Phi
1924   Phi Lambda Kappa
1925   Kappa Beta Pi
1943–74 Xi Psi Phi

1946–68 Delta Sigma Pi
1947   Kappa Beta Gamma
1947–49 Pi Gamma Mu
1948–80 Phi Chi Theta
1955–73 Theta Phi Alpha
1956–71 Delta Zeta
1963–74 Eta Kappa Nu
1969–82 Sigma Pi

ST. LOUIS COLLEGE OF PHARMACY AND APPLIED SCIENCES St. Louis, MO. Founded 1864; coeducational.

Fraternities own their own or rent houses and property.

PROFESSIONAL
1932 Rho Pi Phi
1946 Kappa Psi
1951 Lambda Kappa Sigma
1960 Phi Delta Chi
1980 Kappa Epsilon

OTHER PROFESSIONAL
1942 Alpha Zeta Omega

ACHS HONORS
1955 Rho Chi

ST. MARTIN'S COLLEGE Olympia, WA. College of liberal arts coeducational; private: Roman Catholic Church; established 1895.

ACHS HONORS
    Omicron Delta Epsilon

INACTIVE
1967–69 Sigma Tau Delta

ST. MARY, COLLEGE OF Omaha, NE. College of liberal arts for women; private control (Roman Catholic); established 1923.

ACHS HONORS
1962 Sigma Tau Delta
1968 Phi Alpha Theta
1978 Phi Alpha Theta

SERVICE
1980 Alpha Phi Omega

ST. MARY OF THE PLAINS Dodge City, KS. Private control: Roman Catholic. Controlled by the Sisters of St. Joseph of Wichita. Founded in 1952.

Underclassmen must live at home or on campus.

ACHS HONORS
1968 Alpha Chi
1973 Phi Alpha Theta

RECOGNITION
1976 Pi Kappa Delta

ST. MARY-OF-THE-WOODS COLLEGE St. Mary-Of-The-Woods, IN. College of liberal arts for women; private, Catholic; founded 1840, chartered 1846.

PROFESSIONAL
1963 Phi Gamma Nu

ACHS HONORS
1927 Sigma Tau Delta
1940 Delta Epsilon Sigma

1968 Phi Alpha Theta
1977 Psi Chi
1979 Phi Sigma Tau

INACTIVE
1949–76 Kappa Omicron Nu

ST. MARY'S COLLEGE Winona, MN. Liberal arts college; coed since 1969; private (Roman Catholic); founded 1913.

NIC MEN'S
1970 Alpha Delta Gamma

NPC WOMEN'S
1986 Theta Phi Alpha

PROFESSIONAL
1956 Phi Mu Alpha—Sinfonia

ACHS HONORS
1940 Delta Epsilon Sigma
1966 Phi Alpha Theta
1969 Psi Chi

1970 Pi Gamma Mu

SERVICE
1967 Alpha Phi Omega

RECOGNITION
1959 Beta Beta Beta

INACTIVE
1973–80 Tau Kappa Epsilon

COLONIES
Lambda Iota Tau

ST. MARY'S COLLEGE OF CALIFORNIA
Moraga, CA. Private control: Roman Catholic. Founded in 1863. Four-year, coeducational; liberal arts college.

PROFESSIONAL
1970 Phi Alpha Delta

ACHS HONORS
Omicron Delta Epsilon

INACTIVE
1931–33 Alpha Delta Gamma

ST. MARY'S UNIVERSITY Halifax, NS. Established 1841.

NIC MEN'S
1969 Phi Kappa Theta

NPC WOMEN'S
1989 Delta Zeta

ACHS HONORS
1982 Pi Sigma Alpha

ST. MARY'S DOMINICAN COLLEGE New Orleans, LA. College of liberal arts for women; private control (Roman Catholic); established 1860.

ACHS HONORS
1958 Kappa Delta Pi

RECOGNITION
1953 Alpha Psi Omega
1954 Cardinal Key

INACTIVE
1962–73 Phi Beta
1976–85 Phi Alpha Theta
1978–84 Kappa Omicron Nu

ST. MARY'S UNIVERSITY OF SAN ANTONIO
San Antonio, TX. University for men and women; school of law coeducational; private control (Roman Catholic); established 1852.

Delta Sigma Phi has its own house and lot.

NIC MEN'S
1962 Delta Sigma Phi
1970 Sigma Phi Epsilon
1973 Lambda Chi Alpha
1980 Kappa Sigma
1988 Chi Phi

NPHC MEN'S
1964 Alpha Phi Alpha

NPC WOMEN'S
1976 Alpha Sigma Tau

PROFESSIONAL
1950 Delta Theta Phi

OTHER PROFESSIONAL
1952 Kappa Beta Pi

ACHS HONORS
Omicron Delta Epsilon
1940 Delta Epsilon Sigma
1965 Phi Alpha Theta
1972 Psi Chi
1983 Delta Mu Delta
1987 Phi Sigma Iota

INACTIVE
1958–81 Pi Gamma Mu
1965–67 Sigma Alpha Mu

ST. MICHAEL'S COLLEGE Winooski, VT. College of liberal arts for men; private control (Roman Catholic); chartered 1904.

OTHER PROFESSIONAL
1960 Kappa Phi Kappa

ACHS HONORS
Omicron Delta Epsilon
1942 Delta Epsilon Sigma
1975 Phi Sigma Tau

RECOGNITION
Arnold Air Society (A-1)

INACTIVE
1960–71 Alpha Epsilon Delta
1961–70 Phi Eta Sigma

ST. NORBERT COLLEGE West DePere, WI. Founded by Abbot Bernard H. Pennings, O. Praem., 1898. Liberal arts college; coeducational; private control; nonsectarian.

Administration does not permit special quarters for fraternities and sororities.

NIC MEN'S
1948 Alpha Delta Gamma
1966 Sigma Tau Gamma
1968 Phi Sigma Kappa
1990 Tau Kappa Epsilon

PROFESSIONAL
1965 Alpha Delta Theta

ACHS HONORS
Omicron Delta Epsilon
1940 Delta Epsilon Sigma

1979 Phi Sigma Iota
1980 Psi Chi

SERVICE
1935 Alpha Phi Omega

INACTIVE
1960–71 Theta Phi Alpha
1960–76 Sigma Beta Kappa
1963 Kappa Beta Gamma
1963–70 Delta Zeta
1966–68 Alpha Omicron Pi

ST. OLAF COLLEGE Northfield, MN. College of liberal arts; coeducational; private control (American Lutheran); founded 1874.

ACHS HONORS
Omicron Delta Epsilon
1950 Sigma Pi Sigma
1964 Pi Kappa Lambda
1972 Psi Chi
1976 Phi Alpha Theta
1984 Pi Sigma Alpha

OTHER HONORS
1941 National Collegiate Players
1949 Phi Beta Kappa

SERVICE
1951 Alpha Phi Omega

RECOGNITION
Angel Flight
Arnold Air Society (F-1)
1922 Pi Kappa Delta
1928 Sigma Delta Psi
1932 Blue Key

INACTIVE
1949–65 Pi Gamma Mu

ST. PAUL'S COLLEGE Lawrenceville, VA. College of liberal arts and teachers college; coeducational; private control (Episcopal); established 1888; formerly St. Paul's Polytechnic Institute.

NIC MEN'S
1954 Kappa Alpha Psi (A)

NPHC MEN'S
Phi Beta Sigma
1951 Omega Psi Phi
1952 Alpha Phi Alpha

NPHC WOMEN'S
1952 Alpha Kappa Alpha
1952 Delta Sigma Theta (B)
1952 Sigma Gamma Rho

ACHS HONORS
1954 Alpha Kappa Mu

ST. PETER'S COLLEGE Jersey City, NJ. College of liberal arts for men; coeducational evening session; private control (Roman Catholic); chartered 1872.

PROFESSIONAL
1964 Delta Sigma Pi

ACHS HONORS
Omicron Delta Epsilon
1967 Alpha Sigma Nu
1969 Sigma Pi Sigma
1970 Phi Alpha Theta

1978 Pi Sigma Alpha
1979 Theta Alpha Kappa
1980 Phi Sigma Tau
1985 Psi Chi

OTHER HONORS
1968 Pi Mu Epsilon

SERVICE
1965 Alpha Phi Omega
1969 Gamma Sigma Sigma

INACTIVE
1957   Eta Sigma Phi
1970–71 Theta Phi Alpha

COLLEGE OF ST. SCHOLASTICA Duluth, MN.
College of liberal arts for women; private control
(Roman Catholic); established 1902.

PROFESSIONAL
1939 Alpha Tau Delta

1969 Alpha Chi

ACHS HONORS
1940 Delta Epsilon Sigma
1955 Lambda Iota Tau

INACTIVE
1948   Alpha Delta Theta
1961–76 Pi Gamma Mu

ST. TERESA COLLEGE Winona, MN. College of
liberal arts for women; private control; Roman
Catholic. Established 1907.

PROFESSIONAL
1954 Alpha Delta Theta

RECOGNITION
1954 Alpha Psi Omega
1964 Eta Sigma Phi

ACHS HONORS
1950 Sigma Delta Pi
1951 Pi Delta Phi
1966 Lambda Iota Tau
1971 Phi Alpha Theta

INACTIVE
1953–89 Pi Gamma Mu
1978–89 Theta Alpha Kappa

COLLEGE OF SAINT THOMAS St. Paul, MN.
Catholic coeducational liberal arts college founded
in 1885 by Archbishop John Ireland; located by the
Mississippi in the heart of St. Paul.

NIC MEN'S
1970 Phi Sigma Kappa
1990 Sigma Chi

1942 Delta Epsilon Sigma
1950 Pi Gamma Mu
1973 Phi Alpha Theta
1987 Theta Alpha Kappa

NPC WOMEN'S
1989 Delta Phi Epsilon

NPHC WOMEN'S
      Alpha Kappa Alpha
1975 Sigma Gamma Rho

SERVICE
1969 Alpha Phi Omega

PROFESSIONAL
1957 Alpha Kappa Psi
1985 Delta Theta Phi

RECOGNITION
Angel Flight
Arnold Air Society (F-1)

OTHER PROFESSIONAL
1966 Sigma Delta Chi

ACHS HONORS
      Omicron Delta Epsilon

INACTIVE
1970–84 Tau Kappa Epsilon
1979–85 Alpha Gamma Delta

ST. THOMAS AQUINAS COLLEGE Sparkill, NY.
Private control. Founded in 1952. Four-year; graduate; coeducational; liberal arts college.

94% of students live off campus or commute. The
only on-campus housing available is non-married
student apartments.

ACHS HONORS
1972 Alpha Chi
1986 Delta Mu Delta

1987 Kappa Mu Epsilon
1987 Pi Gamma Mu
1988 Phi Sigma Iota

ST. VINCENT COLLEGE Latrobe, PA. College of
liberal arts for men; private control (Roman Catholic); established 1846.

ACHS HONORS
1940 Delta Epsilon Sigma

1968 Phi Alpha Theta

SAGINAW VALLEY STATE UNIVERSITY
University Center, MI.

NPHC MEN'S
      Phi Beta Sigma

ACHS HONORS
1973 Sigma Pi Sigma
1984 Psi Chi

NPHC WOMEN'S
1977 Sigma Gamma Rho

SALEM COLLEGE Winston-Salem, NC. College of
liberal arts for women; private control (Moravian).
Founded 1772.

ACHS HONORS
1952 Phi Alpha Theta
1974 Sigma Tau Delta
1980 Pi Gamma Mu
1984 Mortar Board

1986 Omicron Delta Kappa

INACTIVE
1905–09 Alpha Delta Pi

SALEM COLLEGE Salem, WV. Private control.
Founded in 1888. Four-year; coeducational; liberal
arts college.

Fraternities and sororities have suites. Underclassmen must live on campus.

NIC MEN'S
1970 Sigma Pi
1970 Sigma Tau Gamma

INACTIVE
1956–81 Pi Omega Pi
1968–72 Sigma Pi Sigma
1971–74 Phi Sigma Kappa
1971–83 Alpha Tau Omega
1971–83 Tau Kappa Epsilon
1973–82 Phi Mu Alpha—
          Sinfonia

ACHS HONORS
1970 Phi Alpha Theta
1979 Alpha Lambda Delta
1989 Phi Sigma Iota

SALEM STATE COLLEGE Salem, MA. Teachers
college; coeducational; state control; established as
normal school 1854.

ACHS HONORS
1973 Phi Alpha Theta
1975 Delta Mu Delta
1976 Phi Kappa Phi
1980 Psi Chi
1986 Alpha Lambda Delta

1988 Gamma Theta Upsilon

RECOGNITION
1966 Delta Tau Kappa

INACTIVE
1914–80 Kappa Delta Phi (C)

SALISBURY STATE COLLEGE Salisbury, MD.
Teachers college; coeducational; state control;
founded 1925 as normal school.

NIC MEN'S
      Kappa Alpha Psi (A)
      Tau Kappa Epsilon
1977 Sigma Alpha Epsilon
1986 Pi Lambda Phi

1974 Phi Kappa Phi
1974 Psi Chi
1975 Omicron Delta Kappa
1980 Gamma Theta Upsilon
1982 Delta Mu Delta
1983 Phi Eta Sigma
1983 Phi Sigma Tau
1983 Pi Gamma Mu

NPHC MEN'S
      Phi Beta Sigma

NPC WOMEN'S
1975 Zeta Tau Alpha
1978 Alpha Sigma Tau
1989 Phi Mu

SERVICE
1980 Alpha Phi Omega

NPHC WOMEN'S
1979 Alpha Kappa Alpha

RECOGNITION
1972 Beta Beta Beta

ACHS HONORS
1959 Phi Alpha Theta

INACTIVE
1978–80 Phi Kappa Sigma

SALVE REGINA COLLEGE Newport, RI. College of liberal arts and sciences; coeducational; private control; Roman Catholic; chartered 1934; established 1947.

ACHS HONORS
1965 Sigma Delta Pi
1968 Delta Epsilon Sigma

1975 Pi Delta Phi
1983 Theta Alpha Kappa

SAMFORD UNIVERSITY Birmingham, AL. Formerly Howard College, renamed in honor of Frank Park Samford in 1965; university: liberal arts, pharmacy, law, teacher education, physical education and graduate school; coeducational; private control; Alabama Baptist Convention. Chartered 1841, named in honor of John Howard, English philanthropist and reformer.

Ownership of lodge is by fraternity on college-owned land; administration requires sorority members to occupy residence hall suites.

NIC MEN'S
1872 Sigma Chi
1911 Pi Kappa Alpha
1924 Lambda Chi Alpha
1925 Pi Kappa Phi

NPC WOMEN'S
1910 Alpha Delta Pi
1924 Delta Zeta
1924 Phi Mu
1963 Chi Omega
1964 Zeta Tau Alpha

NPHC WOMEN'S
1988 Alpha Kappa Alpha

PROFESSIONAL
1948 Delta Theta Phi
1949 Alpha Kappa Psi
1949 Phi Alpha Delta
1950 Lambda Kappa Sigma
1954 Kappa Delta Epsilon
1956 Delta Omicron
1965 Phi Delta Phi
1967 Phi Mu Alpha—Sinfonia

OTHER PROFESSIONAL
1963 Sigma Delta Kappa

ACHS HONORS
1928 Alpha Epsilon Delta
1928 Pi Gamma Mu

1951 Omicron Delta Kappa
1954 Rho Chi
1956 Phi Alpha Theta
1958 Alpha Lambda Delta
1959 Sigma Tau Delta
1962 Kappa Omicron Nu
1966 Delta Sigma Rho-Tau
        Kappa Alpha
1972 Phi Eta Sigma
1972 Phi Kappa Phi
1974 Pi Kappa Lambda

OTHER HONORS
1967 Pi Mu Epsilon

SERVICE
1941 Alpha Phi Omega
1973 Gamma Sigma Sigma

RECOGNITION
1940 Kappa Pi
1958 Beta Beta Beta

INACTIVE
1930–35 Sigma Phi Epsilon
1947–66 Kappa Delta Pi
1948–66 Delta Sigma Phi
1956–87 Phi Delta Chi
1960–87 Phi Chi Theta
1968–85 Kappa Delta

Cumberland Law School Birmingham, AL. Formerly Cumberland University, now a part of Samford University, Birmingham, AL.

OTHER PROFESSIONAL
1982 Sigma Nu Phi

SAM HOUSTON STATE UNIVERSITY Huntsville, TX. Created by legislature act 1879 as Sam Houston Normal Institute; first instruction 1879. Became four-year college and name changed to Sam Houston State College in 1965. In 1969 Sam Houston became a university. Undergraduate programs are offered in 76 disciplines, graduate program in 58. A doctor's degree in criminal justice was authorized in 1972. Coeducational; state control.

All fraternities rent off-campus houses in the City of Huntsville or Walker County. The sororities live in university-owned houses. Each house and kitchen is managed by the chapter under university housing policy.

NIC MEN'S
1960 Alpha Tau Omega
1960 Delta Tau Delta
1960 Kappa Alpha Order
1961 Pi Kappa Alpha
1961 Sigma Chi
1962 Sigma Phi Epsilon
1977 Delta Sigma Phi
1978 Kappa Sigma
1980 Kappa Alpha Psi (A)
1985 Sigma Tau Gamma
1987 Tau Kappa Epsilon
1989 Theta Chi

NPHC MEN'S
        Phi Beta Sigma
1973 Alpha Phi Alpha

NPC WOMEN'S
1959 Alpha Chi Omega
1959 Alpha Delta Pi
1959 Kappa Delta
1959 Zeta Tau Alpha
1965 Chi Omega

NPHC WOMEN'S
1973 Alpha Kappa Alpha
1973 Delta Sigma Theta (B)
1984 Sigma Gamma Rho

PROFESSIONAL
1948 Kappa Kappa Psi
1950 Sigma Alpha Iota
1963 Phi Chi Theta
1976 Alpha Kappa Psi

OTHER PROFESSIONAL
1958 Sigma Delta Chi
1970 Alpha Beta Alpha

ACHS HONORS
        Omicron Delta Epsilon

1923 Alpha Chi
1930 Gamma Theta Upsilon
1931 Pi Gamma Mu
1934 Pi Omega Pi
1935 Sigma Tau Delta
1936 Kappa Delta Pi
1958 Alpha Kappa Delta
1962 Kappa Omicron Nu
1965 Sigma Pi Sigma
1968 Pi Kappa Lambda
1970 Alpha Lambda Delta
1972 Phi Alpha Theta
1972 Pi Delta Phi
1973 Psi Chi
1973 Sigma Delta Pi
1976 Pi Sigma Alpha

OTHER HONORS
        National Order of Omega
1970 Pi Mu Epsilon

SERVICE
1950 Alpha Phi Omega

RECOGNITION
1944 Alpha Psi Omega
1945 Kappa Pi
1956 Scabbard and Blade (13)
1965 Beta Beta Beta

INACTIVE
1930–55 Alpha Kappa Alpha
1954–90 Phi Mu Alpha—
        Sinfonia
1959–89 Delta Zeta
1962–75 Delta Sigma Pi
1975–85 Lambda Chi Alpha

COLONIES
1990 Phi Delta Theta

UNIVERSITY OF SAN DIEGO San Diego, CA. College of arts and sciences, school of nursing, business, law, and education; coeducational, private; incorporated 1949.

NIC MEN'S
1947 Kappa Sigma
1947 Theta Chi
1948 Lambda Chi Alpha
1949 Sigma Pi
1950 Alpha Tau Omega
1969 Delta Chi
1970 Alpha Epsilon Pi
1983 Sigma Alpha Mu
1983 Sigma Pi
1984 Beta Theta Pi
1986 Phi Gamma Delta
1988 Alpha Epsilon Pi
1989 Phi Delta Theta

NPHC MEN'S
        Phi Beta Sigma

NPC WOMEN'S
1949 Alpha Gamma Delta
1949 Kappa Delta
1949 Pi Beta Phi
1950 Chi Omega

1950 Delta Zeta
1950 Sigma Kappa
1951 Kappa Alpha Theta
1977 Alpha Delta Pi
1979 Zeta Tau Alpha
1984 Gamma Phi Beta
1985 Delta Gamma
1985 Kappa Kappa Gamma
1989 Alpha Phi

PROFESSIONAL
1950 Phi Mu Alpha—Sinfonia
1961 Phi Alpha Delta
1962 Phi Delta Phi
1966 Delta Theta Phi
1979 Delta Sigma Pi
1982 Phi Alpha Delta
1986 Delta Sigma Pi

ACHS HONORS
        Omicron Delta Epsilon
        Omicron Delta Epsilon
        Pi Alpha Alpha

1940 Sigma Pi Sigma
1948 Phi Alpha Theta
1950 Psi Chi
1955 Phi Eta Sigma
1959 Pi Sigma Alpha
1963 Gamma Theta Upsilon
1965 Mortar Board
1965 Phi Kappa Phi
1967 Chi Epsilon
1970 Phi Alpha Theta
1972 Kappa Tau Alpha
1973 Phi Sigma Tau
1973 Tau Beta Pi
1974 Eta Kappa Nu
1975 Psi Chi
1977 Pi Sigma Alpha

1982 Theta Alpha Kappa

INACTIVE
1932–39 Pi Gamma Mu
1935–53 Alpha Kappa Alpha
1948–87 Pi Kappa Alpha
1949–59 Phi Sigma Kappa
1949–71 Pi Omega Pi
1950–53 Phi Kappa Tau
1956–77 Alpha Lambda Delta
1963–70 Alpha Delta Gamma
1964–71 Alpha Epsilon Phi
1966–80 Tau Kappa Epsilon

COLONIES
1990 Delta Tau Delta

SAN DIEGO STATE UNIVERSITY San Diego, CA.
Chartered and first instruction 1897. College of liberal arts; schools of business, education, social work, engineering, and graduae school; coeducational; state control.

NIC MEN'S
1948 Delta Sigma Phi
1949 Sigma Alpha Epsilon
1949 Sigma Chi
1950 Tau Kappa Epsilon
1951 Kappa Alpha Psi (A)
1951 Zeta Beta Tau
1963 Sigma Nu
1968 Delta Upsilon
1983 Tau Kappa Epsilon

NPC WOMEN'S
1949 Alpha Xi Delta
1949 Gamma Phi Beta
1950 Alpha Chi Omega

NPHC WOMEN'S
1938 Delta Sigma Theta (B)

PROFESSIONAL
1939 Sigma Alpha Iota

OTHER PROFESSIONAL
1957 Sigma Delta Chi
1958 Alpha Epsilon Rho
1960 Beta Alpha Psi
1962 Pi Lambda Theta
1973 Phi Upsilon Omicron

ACHS HONORS
1927 Kappa Delta Pi

1953 Alpha Kappa Delta
1960 Beta Gamma Sigma
1967 Pi Delta Phi
1967 Pi Tau Sigma
1968 Sigma Delta Pi
1976 Sigma Theta Tau

OTHER HONORS
    National Order of Omega
1974 Phi Beta Kappa

SERVICE
1932 Alpha Phi Omega

RECOGNITION
    Angel Flight
    Arnold Air Society (I)
1932 Blue Key
1949 Pi Kappa Delta
1950 Sigma Delta Psi
1961 Kappa Pi
1966 Delta Phi Alpha
1966 Sigma Iota Epsilon

INACTIVE
1931–50 Lambda Delta Lambda
1932–39 Alpha Sigma Alpha
1939–42 Alpha Eta Rho
1950–61 Kappa Alpha Order

UNIVERSITY OF SAN FRANCISCO San Francisco, CA. University; college of lieberal arts, science, business administration, and law; private control (Roman Catholic).

NIC MEN'S
1969 Sigma Alpha Epsilon
1980 Zeta Beta Tau

NPHC MEN'S
1925 Omega Psi Phi

NPC WOMEN'S
1983 Delta Zeta
1989 Delta Phi Epsilon

NPHC WOMEN'S
    Zeta Phi Beta

PROFESSIONAL
1938 Phi Alpha Delta
1950 Delta Sigma Pi

1959 Phi Delta Phi
1983 Delta Theta Phi

OTHER PROFESSIONAL
1925 Sigma Delta Kappa

ACHS HONORS
1935 Pi Sigma Alpha
1941 Alpha Sigma Nu
1963 Beta Gamma Sigma
1970 Sigma Theta Tau
1972 Phi Alpha Theta
1973 Psi Chi
1977 Theta Alpha Kappa
1981 Sigma Pi Sigma

RECOGNITION
1941 Scabbard and Blade (8)
1969 Beta Beta Beta

INACTIVE
1946   Kappa Beta Pi

1955–70 Alpha Delta Gamma
1972–86 Phi Chi Theta

COLONIES
    Pi Kappa Phi

CITY COLLEGE OF SAN FRANCISCO San Francisco, CA.

SERVICE
1951 Alpha Phi Omega

INACTIVE
1958   Gamma Sigma Sigma

SAN FRANCISCO STATE UNIVERSITY San Francisco, CA. College of liberal arts; coeducational; state control; established 1899.

NIC MEN'S
1981 Sigma Phi Epsilon
1987 Tau Kappa Epsilon
1990 Phi Kappa Tau

NPHC MEN'S
    Phi Beta Sigma

NPC WOMEN'S
1981 Phi Sigma Sigma
1988 Alpha Phi

PROFESSIONAL
1955 Mu Phi Epsilon
1959 Delta Sigma Pi
1976 Phi Chi Theta

OTHER PROFESSIONAL
1960 Delta Pi Epsilon
1962 Pi Lambda Theta
1964 Beta Alpha Psi
1969 Sigma Delta Chi

ACHS HONORS
1960 Pi Sigma Alpha
1961 Delta Sigma Rho-Tau
    Kappa Alpha

1964 Alpha Kappa Delta
1964 Psi Chi
1965 Phi Alpha Theta
1966 Gamma Theta Upsilon
1969 Beta Gamma Sigma
1984 Phi Sigma Iota

SERVICE
1956 Alpha Phi Omega

RECOGNITION
    Angel Flight
    Arnold Air Society (I)
1941 Alpha Psi Omega

INACTIVE
–90   Pi Lambda Phi
1931–51 Alpha Kappa Alpha
1934–65 Kappa Delta Pi
1957–81 Phi Mu Alpha—
    Sinfonia
1964–67 Phi Eta Sigma

COLONIES
    Alpha Gamma Delta

SAN JOSE STATE UNIVERSITY San Jose, CA. Founded 1857 as Minns' Evening Normal School. Oldest and one of largest of California's state colleges and universities. Coeducational, under trustees of the State University System of California; confers B.A., B.S., and M.S. degree and teaching credentials.

The fraternities and sororities own their own land and homes.

NIC MEN'S
1947 Sigma Alpha Epsilon
1948 Delta Upsilon
1948 Theta Chi
1949 Delta Sigma Phi
1950 Alpha Tau Omega
1950 Pi Kappa Alpha
1950 Sigma Pi
1951 Sigma Nu
1952 Sigma Chi
1956 Kappa Alpha Psi (A)
1963 Sigma Alpha Mu
1965 Kappa Sigma
1978 Phi Delta Theta
1987 Tau Kappa Epsilon
1989 Phi Gamma Delta

NPHC MEN'S
    Phi Beta Sigma
1962 Alpha Phi Alpha
1962 Omega Psi Phi

NPC WOMEN'S
1948 Alpha Omicron Pi
1948 Chi Omega
1948 Delta Gamma
1948 Delta Zeta
1956 Kappa Delta

NPHC WOMEN'S
1972 Alpha Kappa Alpha
1973 Sigma Gamma Rho

PROFESSIONAL
1938 Mu Phi Epsilon
1971 Delta Sigma Pi

1981 Phi Chi Theta

OTHER PROFESSIONAL
1939 Phi Epsilon Kappa
1940 Alpha Eta Rho
1954 Sigma Delta Chi
1955 Phi Upsilon Omicron
1957 Kappa Alpha Mu
1961 Pi Lambda Theta
1969 Delta Pi Epsilon

ACHS HONORS
1928 Kappa Delta Pi
1948 Phi Alpha Theta
1948 Psi Chi
1954 Phi Kappa Phi
1955 Kappa Tau Alpha
1960 Alpha Kappa Delta
1961 Gamma Theta Upsilon
1962 Phi Sigma Tau
1963 Alpha Lambda Delta
1963 Sigma Theta Tau
1964 Tau Beta Pi
1965 Eta Kappa Nu
1968 Beta Gamma Sigma
1968 Pi Sigma Alpha
1971 Chi Epsilon
1972 Beta Phi Mu
1986 Phi Sigma Iota

OTHER HONORS
1946 Delta Phi Delta

SERVICE
1939 Alpha Phi Omega

SANTA CLARA UNIVERSITY   Santa Clara, CA.
Founded in 1851 by the Society of Jesus and has the distinction of being the first institution of higher learning in California. This Jesuit and Catholic University became the first coeducational Catholic University in the state in Fall 1961 when women were accepted as undergraduates. Santa Clara is distinguished by its Jesuit and Catholic heritage and by its promise to provide value-oriented education.

NIC MEN'S
1975 Sigma Phi Epsilon
1985 Sigma Pi
1986 Sigma Alpha Epsilon
1987 Theta Chi

NPC WOMEN'S
1976 Alpha Phi
1986 Alpha Chi Omega
1987 Delta Gamma

PROFESSIONAL
1966 Phi Alpha Delta
1984 Delta Theta Phi

OTHER PROFESSIONAL
1931 Gamma Eta Gamma

ACHS HONORS
      Phi Sigma Iota
1942 Alpha Sigma Nu
1955 Beta Gamma Sigma

RECOGNITION
      Angel Flight
      Arnold Air Society (I)
1948 Blue Key
1964 Rho Epsilon

INACTIVE
1929–81 Phi Mu Alpha—
         Sinfonia
1934–78 Pi Omega Pi
1941–55 Eta Mu Pi
1942–74 Beta Beta Beta
1948–59 Kappa Alpha Order
1948–66 Phi Sigma Kappa
1948–71 Sigma Kappa
1948–72 Kappa Kappa Gamma
1948–74 Alpha Chi Omega
1948–74 Phi Eta Sigma
1948–75 Kappa Alpha Theta
1948–84 Gamma Phi Beta
1950–70 Lambda Chi Alpha
1951–70 Theta Xi
1956   Scabbard and Blade
        (13)
1956–66 Phi Mu
1958–73 Sigma Phi Epsilon
1966–68 Alpha Epsilon Phi
1966–71 Acacia

COLONIES
1987 Sigma Pi Sigma

1956 Tau Beta Pi
1966 Phi Alpha Theta
1969 Sigma Pi Sigma
1971 Eta Kappa Nu
1982 Theta Alpha Kappa

OTHER HONORS
      National Order of Omega
1967 Pi Mu Epsilon

SERVICE
1948 Alpha Phi Omega

RECOGNITION
1955 Scabbard and Blade (12)

INACTIVE
1950–71 Delta Sigma Pi
1979–83 Zeta Tau Alpha

COLONIES
      Pi Kappa Alpha

COLLEGE OF SANTA FE   Santa Fe, NM. College of liberal arts and general studies: coeducational; private control (Roman Catholic). Established 1947.

NIC MEN'S
1973 Phi Kappa Theta
INACTIVE
1968–77 Tau Kappa Epsilon

1969–75 Pi Gamma Mu
1972–83 Phi Kappa Tau

SAVANNAH STATE COLLEGE   Savannah, GA. College of applied arts and sciences, teachers college, and technological institution. Coeducational; state control; established 1892.

NIC MEN'S
1970 Kappa Alpha Psi (A)
NPHC MEN'S
      Phi Beta Sigma
1949 Alpha Phi Alpha
1949 Omega Psi Phi
NPHC WOMEN'S
      Zeta Phi Beta
1949 Alpha Kappa Alpha
1949 Sigma Gamma Rho
1952 Delta Sigma Theta (B)

PROFESSIONAL
1983 Delta Sigma Pi

ACHS HONORS
1952 Alpha Kappa Mu
1971 Sigma Tau Delta
1974 Pi Gamma Mu

SERVICE
1966 Alpha Phi Omega
1970 Gamma Sigma Sigma

UNIVERSITY OF SCRANTON   Scranton, PA. University for men; private control; Roman Catholic; established as College of St. Thomas 1888; coeducational evening and summer sessions.

ACHS HONORS
      Omicron Delta Epsilon
1943 Alpha Sigma Nu
1967 Phi Alpha Theta
1968 Delta Mu Delta
1969 Psi Chi
1969 Sigma Pi Sigma
1971 Pi Gamma Mu
1976 Alpha Epsilon Delta
1980 Pi Sigma Alpha

1980 Theta Alpha Kappa
1982 Phi Sigma Tau

OTHER HONORS
1973 Pi Mu Epsilon

SERVICE
1981 Alpha Phi Omega

RECOGNITION
1975 Phi Lambda Upsilon

SCRIPPS COLLEGE   Claremont, CA. College of liberal arts for women; private control; nonsectarian; chartered 1926.

OTHER HONORS
1962 Phi Beta Kappa

SEATTLE UNIVERSITY   Seattle, WA. University; coeducational; private control (Roman Catholic); established 1891.

NPHC MEN'S
      Phi Beta Sigma
NPHC WOMEN'S
1932 Delta Sigma Theta (B)
PROFESSIONAL
1955 Alpha Kappa Psi
1968 Phi Beta
OTHER PROFESSIONAL
1973 Beta Alpha Psi
ACHS HONORS
      Omicron Delta Epsilon
1941 Alpha Epsilon Delta
1951 Kappa Delta Pi
1966 Beta Gamma Sigma

1966 Sigma Theta Tau
1966 Tau Beta Pi
1971 Sigma Pi Sigma
1985 Psi Chi

OTHER HONORS
1960 Pi Mu Epsilon
SERVICE
1940 Intercollegiate Knights
1952 Alpha Phi Omega
RECOGNITION
1956 Scabbard and Blade (13)
INACTIVE
1948–65 Alpha Tau Delta
1966–75 Phi Chi Theta

SEATTLE PACIFIC UNIVERSITY   Seattle, WA.

PROFESSIONAL
1969 Mu Phi Epsilon

ACHS HONORS
1969 Lambda Iota Tau
1981 Phi Alpha Theta

RECOGNITION
1940 Pi Kappa Delta
1954 Kappa Pi

INACTIVE
1950–59 Sigma Tau Delta

SETON HALL UNIVERSITY   South Orange, NJ. University; coeducational; private control (Roman Catholic); established 1856.

NIC MEN'S
1962 Phi Kappa Theta
1963 Tau Kappa Epsilon
1967 Tau Delta Phi
1968 Sigma Tau Gamma
1969 Sigma Pi
1970 Pi Kappa Alpha
1970 Sigma Phi Epsilon
1980 Pi Kappa Phi
1986 Phi Kappa Sigma

NPC WOMEN'S
1988 Alpha Phi
1989 Alpha Gamma Delta
1989 Delta Phi Epsilon

NPHC WOMEN'S
1948 Alpha Kappa Alpha

PROFESSIONAL
1954 Alpha Kappa Psi
1964 Phi Alpha Delta
1966 Pi Sigma Epsilon
1986 Phi Alpha Delta

OTHER PROFESSIONAL
1962 Kappa Beta Pi

ACHS HONORS
Omicron Delta Epsilon
1942 Delta Epsilon Sigma
1964 Alpha Epsilon Delta
1966 Phi Alpha Theta
1969 Psi Chi
1969 Sigma Pi Sigma
1970 Sigma Delta Pi
1977 Kappa Delta Pi
1978 Pi Sigma Alpha
1980 Theta Alpha Kappa

OTHER HONORS
1957 Omicron Kappa Upsilon
1968 Pi Mu Epsilon

RECOGNITION
1967 Scabbard and Blade (16)

INACTIVE
1958–69 Phi Rho Sigma
1959–73 Xi Psi Phi
1968–70 Delta Sigma Phi
1968–89 Zeta Beta Tau
1977–87 Phi Chi Theta

SETON HILL COLLEGE   Greensburg, PA. College of liberal arts for women; Roman Catholic; founded 1883.

ACHS HONORS
1936 Alpha Lambda Delta
1947 Pi Gamma Mu
1948 Kappa Omicron Nu
1981 Theta Alpha Kappa
1983 Psi Chi

RECOGNITION
1964 Eta Sigma Phi

INACTIVE
1942–75 Sigma Alpha Iota
1945–56 Lambda Sigma Society

SHAW UNIVERSITY   Raleigh, NC. University; coeducational; private control (Baptist); established 1865.

The fraternities and sororities are not permitted their own special housing.

NIC MEN'S
1951 Kappa Alpha Psi (A)

NPHC MEN'S
Phi Beta Sigma
1923 Omega Psi Phi
1936 Alpha Phi Alpha

NPHC WOMEN'S
Zeta Phi Beta
1934 Delta Sigma Theta (B)
1938 Alpha Kappa Alpha

1950 Sigma Gamma Rho

OTHER PROFESSIONAL
1976 Alpha Epsilon Rho

ACHS HONORS
1940 Alpha Kappa Mu
1972 Alpha Chi

INACTIVE
1952–60 Beta Kappa Chi

SHENANDOAH CONSERVATORY OF MUSIC   Winchester, VA. Founded 1875; coeducational.

PROFESSIONAL
1957 Sigma Alpha Iota
1965 Phi Mu Alpha—Sinfonia

SERVICE
1969 Alpha Phi Omega

INACTIVE
1978–86 Theta Alpha Kappa

SHEPHERD COLLEGE   Shepherdstown, WV. College of liberal arts; teacher education; coeducational; state control; established 1872 as normal school.

The fratenities and sororities are not permitted their own special housing.

NIC MEN'S
1956 Tau Kappa Epsilon
1960 Phi Sigma Kappa
1972 Theta Xi
1977 Lambda Chi Alpha

NPC WOMEN'S
1945 Sigma Sigma Sigma
1973 Delta Zeta

PROFESSIONAL
1961 Delta Sigma Pi
1972 Phi Gamma Nu

OTHER PROFESSIONAL
1958 Alpha Beta Alpha

ACHS HONORS
1939 Kappa Delta Pi
1963 Kappa Omicron Nu
1970 Phi Alpha Theta
1974 Lambda Iota Tau

INACTIVE
1940–86 Alpha Sigma Tau

SHIPPENSBURG UNIVERSITY   Shippensburg, PA. Founded in 1871. Undergraduate school coeducational; graduate school coeducational; nonsectarian; public institution.

NIC MEN'S
1959 Phi Sigma Kappa
1959 Sigma Tau Gamma
1959 Tau Kappa Epsilon
1960 Sigma Pi
1966 Acacia
1969 Kappa Sigma
1981 Kappa Alpha Psi (A)
1982 Lambda Chi Alpha
1984 Pi Lambda Phi
1986 Pi Kappa Phi

NPC WOMEN'S
1971 Alpha Sigma Tau
1972 Delta Zeta
1984 Alpha Omicron Pi
1987 Phi Sigma Sigma

OTHER PROFESSIONAL
1931 Phi Sigma Pi
1965 Alpha Beta Alpha
1972 Delta Pi Epsilon

ACHS HONORS
Omicron Delta Epsilon

1937 Gamma Theta Upsilon
1941 Kappa Delta Pi
1944 Pi Omega Pi
1969 Kappa Mu Epsilon
1973 Sigma Pi Sigma
1976 Phi Alpha Theta
1976 Psi Chi
1977 Pi Sigma Alpha

OTHER HONORS
National Order of Omega

SERVICE
1954 Alpha Phi Omega

RECOGNITION
1957 Alpha Psi Omega
1975 Pi Kappa Delta

INACTIVE
1968–88 Theta Chi

COLONIES
1990 Alpha Chi Rho

SHORTER COLLEGE   Rome, GA. College of liberal arts; coeducational; private control: Baptists; chartered 1873.

PROFESSIONAL
1970 Phi Mu Alpha—Sinfonia
1975 Mu Phi Epsilon

ACHS HONORS
1963 Pi Gamma Mu
1981 Pi Kappa Lambda

RECOGNITION
1965 Beta Beta Beta

INACTIVE
1910–12 Alpha Sigma Alpha
1911–12 Phi Mu

SIENA COLLEGE Loudonville, NY.

PROFESSIONAL
1971 Delta Sigma Pi

ACHS HONORS
1954 Delta Epsilon Sigma

1974 Sigma Pi Sigma
1975 Pi Gamma Mu
1979 Psi Chi
1969 Phi Alpha Theta

SIENA HEIGHTS COLLEGE Adrian, MI. Coeducational liberal arts college; undergraduate and graduate programs; private control (Roman Catholic). Incorporated 1919.

NIC MEN'S
1986 Pi Lambda Phi

NPC WOMEN'S
1987 Phi Sigma Sigma

ACHS HONORS
1940 Delta Epsilon Sigma
1954 Lambda Iota Tau
1979 Phi Sigma Tau

SIMPSON COLLEGE Indianola, IA. Founded 1860, chartered and first instruction 1860. Undergraduate college for men and women; private control (Methodist Church).

Lambda Chi Alpha owns its own land and home. Two new houses were constructed by college in 1962 for occupation by Alpha Tau Omega and Sigma Alpha Epsilon on rental basis. The sororities own their own land and homes.

NIC MEN'S
1885 Alpha Tau Omega
1889 Sigma Alpha Epsilon
1924 Lambda Chi Alpha

NPHC MEN'S
Phi Beta Sigma

NPC WOMEN'S
1874 Pi Beta Phi
1880 Kappa Kappa Gamma
1889 Delta Delta Delta
1907 Alpha Chi Omega

PROFESSIONAL
1915 Phi Mu Alpha—Sinfonia
1917 Mu Phi Epsilon

ACHS HONORS
1925 Sigma Tau Delta

1983 Alpha Lambda Delta
1985 Phi Alpha Theta

SERVICE
1948 Alpha Phi Omega

RECOGNITION
1918 Pi Kappa Delta
1925 Beta Beta Beta
1935 Alpha Psi Omega

INACTIVE
1873-94 Delta Tau Delta
1880-91 Kappa Alpha Theta
1882-89 Phi Kappa Psi
1928-53 Pi Gamma Mu
1950-52 Pi Kappa Phi
1962-77 Delta Zeta
1964-76 Delta Upsilon

SIOUX FALLS COLLEGE Sioux Falls, SD. Established 1883; four-year, fully accredited, liberal arts college, providing undergraduate work for men and women. Private control; church-related.

ACHS HONORS
1954 Lambda Iota Tau
1966 Alpha Chi

RECOGNITION
1920 Pi Kappa Delta
1962 Alpha Psi Omega

SKIDMORE COLLEGE Saratoga Springs, NY.

ACHS HONORS
Omicron Delta Epsilon
1969 Psi Chi

1979 Phi Sigma Iota
1989 Phi Alpha Theta

SLIPPERY ROCK STATE COLLEGE Slippery Rock, PA. Founded in 1889. Undergraduate, graduate programs.

The fraternities are permitted to own their own land and homes. Sorority members live in wings of dormitories.

NIC MEN'S
1962 Sigma Pi
1966 Theta Xi
1968 Lambda Chi Alpha
1970 Alpha Sigma Phi
1970 Phi Sigma Kappa
1981 Kappa Delta Rho
1985 Pi Kappa Phi
1986 Delta Sigma Phi

NPC WOMEN'S
1961 Sigma Sigma Sigma
1963 Alpha Xi Delta
1963 Delta Zeta
1963 Kappa Delta
1966 Alpha Omicron Pi
1966 Alpha Sigma Alpha
1966 Alpha Sigma Tau

NPHC WOMEN'S
1978 Alpha Kappa Alpha

PROFESSIONAL
1956 Delta Psi Kappa
1977 Phi Chi Theta

OTHER PROFESSIONAL
1930 Phi Sigma Pi
1970 Alpha Beta Alpha

ACHS HONORS
1932 Gamma Theta Upsilon

1935 Sigma Tau Delta
1938 Kappa Delta Pi
1963 Pi Delta Phi
1964 Sigma Delta Pi
1970 Phi Alpha Theta
1970 Psi Chi
1972 Delta Mu Delta
1974 Lambda Sigma Society
1975 Sigma Pi Sigma
1982 Phi Eta Sigma
1984 Phi Sigma Tau

OTHER HONORS
National Order of Omega

SERVICE
1951 Alpha Phi Omega

RECOGNITION
1970 Beta Beta Beta

INACTIVE
1929-71 Pi Gamma Mu
1961-71 Sigma Tau Gamma
1961-72 Alpha Chi Rho
1963-87 Tau Kappa Epsilon
1964-88 Theta Chi
1966-82 Zeta Tau Alpha
1972-80 Phi Mu Delta

COLONIES
Phi Sigma Sigma

SMITH COLLEGE Northampton, MA. College of liberal arts for women; private control; chartered 1871.

ACHS HONORS
1975 Psi Chi

OTHER HONORS
1935 Sigma Xi

SONOMA STATE UNIVERSITY Rohnert Park, CA. Established in 1960 as one of the 19 campuses of the California State University system; coeducational; emphasis on liberal arts and sciences.

93% of students live off campus or commute.

NIC MEN'S
1987 Kappa Alpha Psi (A)
1989 Delta Sigma Phi
1990 Sigma Alpha Epsilon

NPC WOMEN'S
1989 Alpha Xi Delta

ACHS HONORS
1970 Phi Alpha Theta
1980 Pi Sigma Alpha

COLONIES
1990 Tau Kappa Epsilon

UNIVERSITY OF THE SOUTH Sewanee, TN. Coeducational; private control (Protestant Episcopal). Established 1857; chartered 1858; college of arts and sciences founded 1868; school of theology 1878.

The fraternities own houses on college property, but these are recreation centers only; members live in the dormitories and eat in the dining hall where special tables may be reserved.

NIC MEN'S
1881 Sigma Alpha Epsilon
1883 Delta Tau Delta
1883 Kappa Alpha Order
1949 Beta Theta Pi
1963 Lambda Chi Alpha
1964 Chi Psi

ACHS HONORS
Omicron Delta Epsilon

1929 Omicron Delta Kappa
1958 Pi Sigma Alpha
1958 Sigma Pi Sigma
1987 Phi Alpha Theta

INACTIVE
1882–70 Kappa Sigma
1898–10 Pi Kappa Alpha
1929–35 Pi Kappa Phi
1930–62 Pi Gamma Mu

UNIVERSITY OF SOUTH ALABAMA Mobile, AL.
Public university with the colleges of arts & sciences, business & management, education, engineering, allied health, nursing, medicine, continuing education. Established 1963. Coed; 9,500 students.

NIC MEN'S
1968 Phi Kappa Sigma
1969 Kappa Sigma
1970 Sigma Chi
1970 Sigma Nu
1970 Tau Kappa Epsilon
1971 Pi Kappa Alpha
1971 Pi Kappa Phi
1971 Sigma Alpha Epsilon
1974 Kappa Alpha Psi (A)
1977 Kappa Alpha Order
1987 Sigma Phi Epsilon

NPHC MEN'S
1972 Alpha Phi Alpha

NPC WOMEN'S
1969 Alpha Omicron Pi
1969 Chi Omega
1969 Kappa Delta
1969 Phi Mu
1969 Zeta Tau Alpha
1984 Alpha Gamma Delta

NPHC WOMEN'S
1970 Alpha Kappa Alpha

PROFESSIONAL
1969 Alpha Kappa Psi
1969 Phi Chi Theta
1972 Sigma Alpha Iota
1984 Phi Alpha Delta

ACHS HONORS
1969 Phi Eta Sigma

1970 Phi Alpha Theta
1971 Alpha Lambda Delta
1972 Psi Chi
1973 Gamma Theta Upsilon
1975 Alpha Chi
1976 Sigma Delta Pi
1977 Beta Gamma Sigma
1977 Omicron Delta Kappa
1977 Phi Kappa Phi
1978 Pi Omega Pi
1979 Eta Kappa Nu
1979 Mortar Board
1979 Sigma Pi Sigma
1980 Pi Sigma Alpha
1990 Tau Beta Pi

OTHER HONORS
National Order of Omega
1972 Pi Mu Epsilon
1977 Alpha Omega Alpha
1977 Sigma Gamma Epsilon

SERVICE
1975 Alpha Phi Omega

RECOGNITION
1970 Beta Beta Beta

INACTIVE
1879–82 Sigma Chi
1970–83 Phi Mu Alpha—
    Sinfonia
1974–84 Theta Xi
1977–82 Lambda Chi Alpha

UNIVERSITY OF SOUTH CAROLINA Columbia, SC. University; coeducational; state control. Chartered as South Carolina College 1801; became university 1906.

Ownership of fraternity and sorority houses is by college on rental basis.

NIC MEN'S
1857 Phi Kappa Psi
1880 Kappa Alpha Order
1882 Phi Delta Theta
1882 Sigma Alpha Epsilon
1883 Alpha Tau Omega
1886 Sigma Nu
1890 Kappa Sigma
1891 Pi Kappa Alpha
1904 Sigma Phi Epsilon
1910 Pi Kappa Phi
1928 Zeta Beta Tau
1929 Sigma Chi
1945 Lambda Chi Alpha

1970 Kappa Alpha Psi (A)
1983 Delta Upsilon

NPHC MEN'S
Phi Beta Sigma
1973 Alpha Phi Alpha

NPC WOMEN'S
1928 Alpha Delta Pi
1928 Chi Omega
1928 Delta Delta Delta
1928 Delta Zeta
1929 Zeta Tau Alpha
1940 Kappa Delta
1967 Kappa Kappa Gamma

1985 Delta Gamma
1988 Alpha Chi Omega
1990 Kappa Alpha Theta

NPHC WOMEN'S
1973 Alpha Kappa Alpha
1973 Delta Sigma Theta (B)
1974 Sigma Gamma Rho

PROFESSIONAL
1906 Phi Rho Sigma
1927 Phi Chi
1927 Phi Delta Phi
1929 Delta Sigma Pi
1948 Delta Omicron
1949 Phi Alpha Delta
1949 Phi Mu Alpha—Sinfonia
1950 Kappa Delta Epsilon
1961 Kappa Psi
1966 Kappa Epsilon
1966 Pi Sigma Epsilon
1971 Tau Beta Sigma
1972 Xi Psi Phi
1974 Kappa Kappa Psi
1976 Gamma Iota Sigma
1981 Phi Delta Chi
1982 Delta Theta Phi
1986 Phi Alpha Delta

OTHER PROFESSIONAL
1960 Sigma Delta Chi
1965 Beta Alpha Psi
1970 Alpha Epsilon Rho
1972 Delta Sigma Delta

ACHS HONORS
Omicron Delta Epsilon
1927 Omicron Delta Kappa
1928 Alpha Epsilon Delta
1931 Sigma Delta Pi
1952 Psi Chi
1954 Rho Chi
1956 Delta Sigma Rho-Tau
    Kappa Alpha
1956 Sigma Pi Sigma
1958 Tau Beta Pi
1962 Alpha Lambda Delta
1962 Eta Kappa Nu
1963 Beta Gamma Sigma
1966 Phi Eta Sigma
1966 Sigma Theta Tau
1967 Mortar Board
1968 Kappa Tau Alpha
1969 Gamma Theta Upsilon

1969 Phi Alpha Theta
1971 Pi Kappa Lambda
1971 Pi Kappa Lambda
1974 Phi Sigma Iota
1975 Pi Delta Phi
1979 Omega Chi Epsilon
1980 Chi Epsilon
1982 Beta Phi Mu

OTHER HONORS
National Order of Omega
1926 Phi Beta Kappa
1957 Gamma Sigma Delta
1958 Sigma Xi
1959 Pi Mu Epsilon

SERVICE
1951 Alpha Phi Omega

RECOGNITION
Angel Flight
Arnold Air Society (C-1)
1927 Blue Key
1931 Alpha Psi Omega
1947 Kappa Pi
1951 Eta Mu Pi

INACTIVE
1850–61 Delta Psi
1852–61 Delta Kappa Epsilon
1858–61 Beta Theta Pi
1859–59 Theta Delta Chi
1889–97 Chi Phi
1928   Eta Sigma Phi
1928–35 Sigma Delta Chi
1928–50 Pi Lambda Phi
1929–62 Phi Sigma Kappa
1929–89 Phi Kappa Sigma
1930–47 Kappa Phi Kappa
1931–85 Pi Beta Phi
1932–38 Delta Phi Alpha
1932–43 Sigma Kappa
1933–82 Alpha Omicron Pi
1935–49 Pi Gamma Mu
1945–78 Alpha Epsilon Phi
1947   Delta Psi Kappa
1948–55 Alpha Kappa Psi
1949–59 Phi Delta Epsilon
1957–62 Sigma Delta Tau
1967–69 Sigma Tau Delta
1977–83 Sigma Sigma Sigma

COLONIES
1990 Delta Tau Delta

UNIVERSITY OF SOUTH CAROLINA AT AIKEN
Aiken, SC. Established in 1961 under authority granted by the South Carolina General Assembly and the Aiken County Commission for Higher Education; four-year campus of the University of South Carolina System; coeducational; public control.

Only on campus housing available is non-married student apartments. 85% of students live off campus or commute.

NIC MEN'S
1988 Kappa Alpha Psi (A)
1989 Tau Kappa Epsilon

NPC WOMEN'S
1990 Phi Mu

NPHC WOMEN'S
1978 Alpha Kappa Alpha

UNIVERSITY OF SOUTH CAROLINA, COASTAL CAROLINA Conway, SC.

NIC MEN'S
1979 Sigma Phi Epsilon

ACHS HONORS
1978 Phi Alpha Theta
1979 Phi Sigma Tau

1980 Omicron Delta Kappa
1990 Phi Eta Sigma
1990 Psi Chi

SERVICE
1977 Alpha Phi Omega

UNIVERSITY OF SOUTH CAROLINA AT SPARTANBURG Spartanburg, SC. Public institution. Founded in 1967. Four-year; coeducational.

Only on-campus housing available is non-married student apartments. 85% of students live off campus or commute.

NIC MEN'S
1988 Lambda Chi Alpha

ACHS HONORS
1979 Omicron Delta Kappa
1982 Pi Sigma Alpha

INACTIVE
1981–88 Pi Kappa Phi

COLONIES
Pi Kappa Phi

MEDICAL UNIVERSITY OF SOUTH CAROLINA Charleston, SC.

PROFESSIONAL
1927 Kappa Psi
1947 Phi Delta Chi
1948 Lambda Kappa Sigma

ACHS HONORS
1947 Rho Chi

SOUTH CAROLINA STATE COLLEGE Orangeburg, SC. College of liberal arts; land-grant college; coeducational; state control; established as normal school 1895.

NIC MEN'S
1931 Kappa Alpha Psi (A)

NPHC MEN'S
      Phi Beta Sigma
1927 Omega Psi Phi
1929 Alpha Phi Alpha

NPHC WOMEN'S
      Zeta Phi Beta
1934 Delta Sigma Theta (B)
1938 Alpha Kappa Alpha
1974 Sigma Gamma Rho

PROFESSIONAL
1971 Kappa Kappa Psi
1975 Tau Beta Sigma
1984 Phi Mu Alpha—Sinfonia

OTHER PROFESSIONAL
1973 Alpha Beta Alpha

ACHS HONORS
1948 Beta Kappa Chi
1951 Alpha Kappa Mu
1967 Kappa Mu Epsilon
1970 Delta Mu Delta
1975 Kappa Omicron Nu
1975 Pi Gamma Mu
1979 Psi Chi

RECOGNITION
1955 Scabbard and Blade (12)
1970 Society for Collegiate
      Journalists—Pi Delta
      Epsilon-Alpha Phi Gamma
      (A)

INACTIVE
1982–86 Phi Chi Theta

UNIVERSITY OF SOUTH DAKOTA Vermillion, SD. Organized 1882; undergraduate colleges coeducational; graduate schools coeducational; state control; nonsectarian.

The fraternities own their own land and homes.

NIC MEN'S
1906 Phi Delta Theta
1911 Sigma Alpha Epsilon
1912 Beta Theta Pi

1916 Lambda Chi Alpha
1924 Delta Tau Delta
1926 Alpha Tau Omega
1960 Tau Kappa Epsilon

1968 Sigma Nu
1971 Delta Upsilon

NPC WOMEN'S
1903 Alpha Xi Delta
1912 Kappa Alpha Theta
1920 Alpha Phi
1924 Chi Omega
1927 Pi Beta Phi

PROFESSIONAL
1904 Delta Theta Phi
1911 Phi Delta Phi
1924 Delta Sigma Pi
1924 Mu Phi Epsilon
1927 Phi Alpha Delta
1947 Zeta Phi Eta
1985 Phi Alpha Delta

OTHER PROFESSIONAL
1948 Kappa Beta Pi

ACHS HONORS
      Omicron Delta Epsilon
1916 Delta Sigma Rho-Tau
      Kappa Alpha
1928 Mortar Board
1928 Phi Sigma
1929 Phi Sigma Iota
1930 Alpha Lambda Delta
1930 Phi Eta Sigma
1951 Beta Gamma Sigma
1956 Pi Sigma Alpha
1956 Pi Sigma Alpha
1957 Omicron Delta Kappa
1957 Phi Alpha Theta
1961 Pi Tau Sigma
1964 Lambda Iota Tau

1966 Alpha Epsilon
1967 Psi Chi

OTHER HONORS
      National Order of Omega
1926 Phi Beta Kappa
1948 National Collegiate
      Players
1957 Gamma Sigma Delta
1960 Pi Mu Epsilon

RECOGNITION
1924 Scabbard and Blade (5)
1929 Sigma Delta Psi
1938 Eta Sigma Phi
1944 Society for Collegiate
      Journalists—Pi Delta
      Epsilon-Alpha Phi Gamma
      (P)
1970 Lambda Tau
1970 Sigma Phi Alpha

INACTIVE
1921–34 Theta Alpha Phi
1921–42 Phi Chi
1926   Sigma Phi Delta
1926–31 Pi Gamma Mu
1926–32 Sigma Delta Chi
1926–41 Kappa Sigma
1933–38 Delta Delta Delta
1947–59 Sigma Pi Sigma
1948–86 Phi Mu Alpha—
              Sinfonia
1949–62 Theta Xi
1951–82 Pi Omega Pi
1966–70 Alpha Gamma Delta

SOUTH DAKOTA SCHOOL OF MINES AND TECHNOLOGY Rapid City, SD. Established 1885; state-supported; B.S. and M.S. degrees in chemical, civil, electrical, geological, mechanical, metallurgical, and mining engineering; and in chemistry, geology, mathematics, and physics. M.S. degrees in paleontology and meteorology; Ph.D. in electrical engineering, geological engineering, and geology.

Delta Sigma Phi, Theta Tau, and Triangle own their own land and homes. Alpha Chi Sigma rents a chapter house.

NIC MEN'S
1930 Triangle
1954 Delta Sigma Phi

NPC WOMEN'S
1986 Alpha Delta Pi

PROFESSIONAL
1932 Theta Tau
1970 Alpha Chi Sigma

ACHS HONORS
1949 Eta Kappa Nu
1951 Sigma Pi Sigma
1974 Tau Beta Pi

OTHER HONORS
1965 Sigma Xi
1970 Pi Mu Epsilon

RECOGNITION
1955 Scabbard and Blade (12)

SOUTH DAKOTA STATE UNIVERSITY Brookings, SD. State-supported, land-grant; established 1881. Coeducational; divisions of instruction in agriculture and biological sciences, engineering, home economics, nursing, pharmacy, arts and sciences, general registration, education, and graduate school. B.A., M.A., B.S., M.S., and Ph.D. degrees.

Fraternities own their own houses with two located on a state-owned Greek Row.

NIC MEN'S
1964 Alpha Gamma Rho
1966 FarmHouse
1968 Lambda Chi Alpha
1971 Sigma Alpha Epsilon

NPC WOMEN'S
1967 Chi Omega
1968 Alpha Xi Delta

PROFESSIONAL
1956 Kappa Epsilon
1968 Kappa Psi

OTHER PROFESSIONAL
1924 Alpha Zeta
1934 Phi Upsilon Omicron
1937 Sigma Delta Chi
1949 Women in Communications
1975 Alpha Tau Alpha

ACHS HONORS
Omicron Delta Epsilon
1929 Pi Gamma Mu
1931 Rho Chi
1947 Sigma Pi Sigma
1949 Phi Kappa Phi
1955 Kappa Delta Pi
1957 Eta Kappa Nu
1961 Chi Epsilon
1961 Sigma Theta Tau
1962 Kappa Tau Alpha

1966 Alpha Lambda Delta
1970 Gamma Theta Upsilon
1972 Mortar Board
1974 Tau Beta Pi
1979 Psi Chi
1982 Phi Alpha Theta

OTHER HONORS
National Order of Omega
1957 Sigma Xi

SERVICE
1959 Alpha Phi Omega

RECOGNITION
Angel Flight
Arnold Air Society (F-1)
1920 Pi Kappa Delta
1927 Scabbard and Blade (6)
1928 Blue Key
1929 Sigma Delta Psi
1946 National Block and Bridle Club
1949 Alpha Psi Omega
1955 Pi Kappa Delta
1970 Phi Lambda Upsilon
1970 Sigma Delta Psi

INACTIVE
1973–90 Tau Kappa Epsilon
1975–78 Kappa Delta

UNIVERSITY OF SOUTH FLORIDA Tampa, FL.
Founded December 18, 1956. When it was opened to a charter class of 2,000 freshmen on September 26, 1960, it became the first state university in the United States to be totally planned and initiated in this century. Coeducational undergraduate colleges: arts and letters, business administration, education, engineering, fine arts, medicine, natural sciences, nursing, social and behavioral sciences, and school of continuing education; 78 master's programs, 19 doctoral programs and a professional M.D. degree.

NIC MEN'S
1967 Alpha Tau Omega
1967 Phi Delta Theta
1967 Sigma Nu
1967 Tau Epsilon Phi
1968 Delta Tau Delta
1968 Kappa Sigma
1968 Lambda Chi Alpha
1968 Pi Kappa Alpha
1968 Sigma Alpha Epsilon
1968 Sigma Phi Epsilon
1969 Zeta Beta Tau
1973 Kappa Alpha Psi (A)
1979 Sigma Chi
1983 Chi Phi
1987 Alpha Epsilon Pi
1988 Pi Kappa Phi
1988 Sigma Alpha Mu

NPHC MEN'S
Phi Beta Sigma
1972 Alpha Phi Alpha

NPC WOMEN'S
1966 Delta Delta Delta
1967 Alpha Delta Pi
1967 Kappa Delta

1968 Chi Omega
1968 Delta Gamma
1985 Alpha Omicron Pi
1988 Sigma Delta Tau

NPHC WOMEN'S
1971 Alpha Kappa Alpha
1973 Delta Sigma Theta (B)
1981 Sigma Gamma Rho

PROFESSIONAL
1966 Sigma Alpha Iota
1968 Phi Mu Alpha—Sinfonia
1971 Delta Sigma Pi

OTHER PROFESSIONAL
1972 Beta Alpha Psi
1973 Sigma Delta Chi

ACHS HONORS
Omicron Delta Epsilon
Pi Alpha Alpha
1966 Sigma Pi Sigma
1967 Psi Chi
1968 Gamma Theta Upsilon
1968 Kappa Delta Pi
1970 Beta Gamma Sigma
1970 Omicron Delta Kappa

1971 Phi Alpha Theta
1971 Phi Kappa Phi
1972 Mortar Board
1972 Psi Chi
1973 Phi Sigma
1973 Pi Sigma Alpha
1974 Sigma Tau Delta
1974 Tau Beta Pi
1975 Alpha Epsilon Delta
1977 Kappa Tau Alpha
1979 Pi Gamma Mu
1980 Beta Phi Mu
1984 Chi Epsilon

OTHER HONORS
National Order of Omega

1966 Pi Mu Epsilon
1976 Alpha Omega Alpha

SERVICE
1968 Alpha Phi Omega

INACTIVE
1967–78 Delta Zeta
1967–84 Tau Kappa Epsilon
1969–79 Alpha Epsilon Phi
1969–80 Kappa Alpha Theta
1971–81 Phi Gamma Delta
1972–80 Phi Chi Theta
1984–88 Phi Eta Sigma

COLONIES
Sigma Tau Gamma

SOUTH TEXAS COLLEGE OF LAW Houston, TX.
Established 1923; coeducational.

PROFESSIONAL
1956 Delta Theta Phi
1959 Phi Alpha Delta

RECOGNITION
1966 Iota Tau Tau

SOUTHAMPTON COLLEGE OF LONG ISLAND UNIVERSITY Southampton, NY. Liberal arts college; part of the multiuniversity system of Long Island Univesity; founded in 1963.

ACHS HONORS
1972 Sigma Tau Delta
1980 Delta Mu Delta

INACTIVE
1969–72 Tau Kappa Epsilon

1969–76 Sigma Alpha Mu
1971–78 Zeta Beta Tau

SOUTHEAST MISSOURI STATE UNIVERSITY
Cape Girardeau, MO. College of liberal arts and teachers college; coeducational; state control; chartered 1873 as normal school.

The administration requires the fraternities and sororities to occupy dormitories designed for Greek groups.

NIC MEN'S
1952 Sigma Tau Gamma
1958 Pi Kappa Alpha
1960 Sigma Chi
1969 Phi Sigma Kappa
1977 Delta Chi
1984 Theta Xi
1985 Kappa Alpha Psi (A)

NPHC MEN'S
Phi Beta Sigma

NPC WOMEN'S
1951 Sigma Sigma Sigma
1957 Delta Delta Delta
1958 Alpha Chi Omega
1958 Alpha Xi Delta
1959 Alpha Delta Pi
1985 Zeta Tau Alpha

NPHC WOMEN'S
1981 Alpha Kappa Alpha
1989 Sigma Gamma Rho

PROFESSIONAL
1961 Phi Mu Alpha—Sinfonia
1963 Sigma Alpha Iota
1965 Alpha Kappa Psi
1967 Phi Gamma Nu

OTHER PROFESSIONAL
1960 Alpha Beta Alpha

ACHS HONORS
Omicron Delta Epsilon
1925 Kappa Delta Pi
1925 Kappa Omicron Nu
1934 Sigma Tau Delta
1942 Phi Alpha Theta
1957 Pi Omega Pi
1969 Sigma Pi Sigma
1978 Psi Chi
1979 Pi Sigma Alpha
1984 Phi Eta Sigma
1988 Kappa Tau Alpha

OTHER HONORS
National Order of Omega
1948 National Collegiate Players

SERVICE
1939 Alpha Phi Omega
1966 Gamma Sigma Sigma

RECOGNITION
1932 Pi Kappa Delta
1951 Kappa Pi
1965 Iota Lambda Sigma

INACTIVE
1932–39 Sigma Zeta
1953–89 Sigma Phi Epsilon
1953–90 Tau Kappa Epsilon

COLONIES
Lambda Chi Alpha

SOUTHEASTERN LOUISIANA UNIVERSITY
Hammond, LA. Colleges of business, education, humanities, science and technology; graduate school; coeducational, state control. Chartered 1925.

NIC MEN'S
1939 Sigma Tau Gamma
1961 Tau Kappa Epsilon
1963 Theta Xi
1969 Delta Tau Delta
1972 Alpha Tau Omega
1989 Kappa Sigma

NPHC MEN'S
Phi Beta Sigma
1975 Alpha Phi Alpha

NPC WOMEN'S
1940 Alpha Sigma Tau
1962 Phi Mu
1963 Alpha Omicron Pi
1964 Sigma Sigma Sigma
1990 Theta Phi Alpha

NPHC WOMEN'S
1976 Delta Sigma Theta (B)
1977 Alpha Kappa Alpha

PROFESSIONAL
1949 Phi Mu Alpha—Sinfonia
1956 Delta Omicron

OTHER PROFESSIONAL
1956 Phi Epsilon Kappa

ACHS HONORS
Omicron Delta Epsilon
1948 Kappa Delta Pi
1956 Phi Kappa Phi
1967 Pi Gamma Mu
1971 Phi Alpha Theta
1973 Psi Chi
1989 Phi Eta Sigma

OTHER HONORS
National Order of Omega
1957 National Collegiate
Players
1964 Pi Mu Epsilon

RECOGNITION
1955 Pi Kappa Delta
1969 Lambda Tau

INACTIVE
–69   Sigma Tau Delta
1941–48 Phi Lambda Chi
1966–84 Delta Sigma Pi
1969   Phi Kappa Theta

SOUTHEASTERN MASSACHUSETTS UNIVERSITY
North Dartmouth, MA. Founded 1895; undergraduate programs leading to the degrees of Bachelor of Science, Bachelor of Arts, Bachelor of Fine Arts, Bachelor of Business Administration, Master of Science, Master of Arts, Master of Fine Arts. Coeducational, nonsectarian, state supported.

NIC MEN'S
1970 Tau Kappa Epsilon

NPHC WOMEN'S
1976 Delta Sigma Theta (B)

OTHER PROFESSIONAL
1904 Phi Psi

ACHS HONORS
1974 Eta Kappa Nu

1981 Pi Sigma Alpha
1983 Sigma Pi Sigma
1989 Delta Mu Delta

INACTIVE
–88   Alpha Sigma Tau

SOUTHEASTERN OKLAHOMA STATE UNIVERSITY
Durant, OK. Established by act of legislature and opened for admission in 1909. State college; coeducational; state control; nonsectarian.

Fraternities and sororities may own their own land and homes.

NIC MEN'S
1929 Sigma Tau Gamma
1956 Tau Kappa Epsilon

NPC WOMEN'S
1932 Alpha Sigma Tau

NPHC WOMEN'S
1973 Delta Sigma Theta (B)

ACHS HONORS
1928 Kappa Delta Pi
1931 Pi Omega Pi
1973 Kappa Mu Epsilon

OTHER HONORS
National Order of Omega

SERVICE
1952 Alpha Phi Omega

RECOGNITION
1932 Blue Key
1932 Pi Kappa Delta
1937 Cardinal Key

INACTIVE
1931–85 Phi Sigma Kappa
1958–74 Delta Zeta
1959–87 Sigma Kappa
1985–88 Sigma Pi

UNIVERSITY OF SOUTHERN CALIFORNIA
Los Angeles, CA. Founded 1880; first students admitted 1880. Undergraduate and graduate schools coeducational; private control; nonsectarian.

The fraternities and sororities are permitted to own their own land and homes and do so except in a few instances where ownership is by the college on rental basis. Freshman women pledges must occupy residence halls.

NIC MEN'S
1889 Sigma Chi
1910 Delta Chi
1921 Sigma Alpha Epsilon
1925 Delta Sigma Phi
1925 Kappa Sigma
1926 Kappa Alpha Order
1926 Tau Epsilon Phi
1927 Phi Kappa Psi
1927 Tau Delta Phi
1928 Phi Sigma Kappa
1928 Sigma Phi Epsilon
1930 Sigma Nu
1931 Alpha Epsilon Pi
1934 Chi Phi
1940 Theta Xi
1941 Delta Tau Delta
1942 Theta Chi
1947 Beta Theta Pi
1947 Kappa Alpha Psi (A)
1948 Lambda Chi Alpha
1948 Phi Delta Theta
1948 Phi Gamma Delta
1948 Sigma Alpha Mu
1948 Tau Kappa Epsilon
1951 Alpha Tau Omega
1985 Sigma Pi

NPHC MEN'S
1921 Alpha Phi Alpha

NPC WOMEN'S
1887 Kappa Alpha Theta
1895 Alpha Chi Omega
1917 Pi Beta Phi
1921 Alpha Epsilon Phi
1921 Delta Delta Delta
1922 Delta Gamma
1925 Alpha Delta Pi
1938 Gamma Phi Beta
1940 Chi Omega
1945 Alpha Phi
1947 Kappa Kappa Gamma
1989 Sigma Kappa

NPHC WOMEN'S
1924 Delta Sigma Theta (B)
1924 Delta Sigma Theta (B)
1974 Alpha Kappa Alpha
1980 Sigma Gamma Rho

PROFESSIONAL
1900 Psi Omega

1907 Phi Delta Phi
1909 Phi Delta Chi
1911 Phi Alpha Delta
1912 Delta Theta Phi
1918 Delta Psi Kappa
1921 Lambda Kappa Sigma
1921 Zeta Phi Eta
1922 Alpha Rho Chi
1922 Delta Sigma Pi
1923 Mu Phi Epsilon
1923 Rho Pi Phi
1924 Alpha Omega
1924 Sigma Phi Delta
1925 Phi Beta
1926 Sigma Alpha Iota
1941 Kappa Kappa Psi
1983 Phi Alpha Delta

OTHER PROFESSIONAL
1906 Delta Sigma Delta
1918 Phi Delta Epsilon
1922 Gamma Eta Gamma
1925 Beta Alpha Psi
1929 Alpha Eta Rho
1930 Women in Communications
1934 Sigma Delta Chi
1941 Nu Beta Epsilon
1953 Delta Pi Epsilon
1954 Alpha Epsilon Rho

ACHS HONORS
Omicron Delta Epsilon
Pi Alpha Alpha
1914 Delta Sigma Rho-Tau
Kappa Alpha
1920 Alpha Kappa Delta
1923 Beta Gamma Sigma
1923 Pi Kappa Lambda
1924 Chi Epsilon
1924 Phi Kappa Phi
1925 Eta Kappa Nu
1925 Pi Delta Phi
1925 Rho Chi
1925 Sigma Delta Pi
1927 Pi Sigma Alpha
1928 Phi Sigma
1929 Mortar Board
1929 Psi Chi
1932 Phi Alpha Theta
1939 Alpha Epsilon Delta
1939 Alpha Lambda Delta
1947 Tau Beta Pi

1949 Pi Tau Sigma
1956 Beta Phi Mu
1958 Alpha Pi Mu
1964 Phi Sigma Tau
1972 Sigma Pi Sigma
1974 Omega Chi Epsilon

OTHER HONORS
    National Order of Omega
1914 Iota Sigma Pi
1916 Omicron Kappa Upsilon
1926 National Collegiate
    Players
1929 Order of the Coif
1929 Phi Beta Kappa
1949 Alpha Omega Alpha
1972 Pi Mu Epsilon

SERVICE
1934 Alpha Phi Omega

RECOGNITION
    Arnold Air Society (I)
1916 Sigma Delta Psi
1926 Phi Lambda Upsilon
1930 Blue Key
1947 Rho Epsilon
1950 Phi Delta Gamma
1952 Iota Tau Tau
1959 Sigma Delta Epsilon

INACTIVE
1887–97 Delta Gamma
1896–69 Phi Rho Sigma
1909–40 Kappa Psi
1909–42 Phi Beta Pi and Theta
    Kappa Psi (B)
1910–61 Zeta Tau Alpha
1913–55 Alpha Kappa Kappa

1913–67 Xi Psi Phi
1915–50 Phi Mu
1917–41 Sigma Nu Phi
1917–64 Kappa Delta
1918–72 Zeta Beta Tau
1920–52 Pi Lambda Phi
1922–88 Phi Kappa Tau
1923–49 Kappa Beta Pi
1923–53 Delta Zeta
1923–85 Phi Mu Alpha—
    Sinfonia
1923–86 Alpha Gamma Delta
1925 Sigma Delta Kappa
1925–85 Phi Chi Theta
1926–72 Pi Kappa Alpha
1927 Scarab
1927–35 Sigma Delta Tau
1929 Phi Chi
1930–38 Phi Beta Pi and Theta
    Kappa Psi (a)
1931 Delta Phi Delta
1931 Tau Sigma Delta
1931–56 Alpha Tau Delta
1934 Delta Phi Alpha
1935–52 Phi Epsilon Kappa
1936–76 Phi Eta Sigma
1940–47 Delta Omicron
1940–61 Pi Omega Pi
1945–53 Phi Sigma Sigma
1945–90 Alpha Omicron Pi
1947–61 Acacia
1952–62 Psi Upsilon
1976–83 Pi Kappa Phi

COLONIES
    Sigma Kappa

UNIVERSITY OF SOUTHERN COLORADO

Pueblo, CO. Evolving from Pueblo Junio College, Southern Colorado State College was established by the Colorado General Assembly in an act which was signed into law by the Governor on March 25, 1961. Southern Colorado State College is a multipurpose institution offering the following degrees: Bachelor of Arts, Bachelor of Science, Associate in Arts, and Associate in Applied Science.

There are no fraternity or sorority houses.

NIC MEN'S
1981 Kappa Sigma

PROFESSIONAL
1967 Delta Omicron

OTHER PROFESSIONAL
1971 Sigma Delta Chi

ACHS HONORS
    Omicron Delta Epsilon
1967 Alpha Chi

1968 Pi Delta Phi
1968 Psi Chi
1974 Sigma Pi Sigma
1988 Alpha Lambda Delta

INACTIVE
1965–82 Phi Mu Alpha—
    Sinfonia
1970–79 Tau Kappa Epsilon
1979–85 Delta Sigma Phi
1980–84 Sigma Kappa

SOUTHERN UNIVERSITY

Baton Rouge, LA. University and land grant college; coeducational; state control; established 1880 as Southern University; moved from New Orleans to Baton Rouge 1914.

There are no fraternity or sorority houses.

NIC MEN'S
1935 Kappa Alpha Psi (A)
1968 Kappa Alpha Psi (A)

NPHC MEN'S
    Phi Beta Sigma
    Phi Beta Sigma
    Phi Beta Sigma
1936 Alpha Phi Alpha
1936 Omega Psi Phi
1964 Alpha Phi Alpha

NPHC WOMEN'S
    Zeta Phi Beta
1934 Delta Sigma Theta (B)
1940 Alpha Kappa Alpha
1950 Sigma Gamma Rho
1968 Sigma Gamma Rho
1971 Alpha Kappa Alpha

PROFESSIONAL
1965 Phi Mu Alpha—Sinfonia
1966 Mu Phi Epsilon
1972 Delta Theta Phi
1973 Kappa Kappa Psi
1975 Kappa Delta Epsilon
1980 Phi Alpha Delta

OTHER PROFESSIONAL
1969 Phi Upsilon Omicron

ACHS HONORS
1941 Alpha Kappa Mu
1944 Beta Kappa Chi
1954 Gamma Theta Upsilon
1957 Pi Gamma Mu
1959 Pi Omega Pi
1961 Psi Chi
1964 Alpha Kappa Delta
1971 Phi Alpha Theta
1972 Sigma Pi Sigma
1975 Alpha Chi
1975 Pi Tau Sigma
1976 Eta Kappa Nu
1976 Phi Sigma
1978 Phi Sigma Iota
1983 Pi Sigma Alpha

OTHER HONORS
1960 Pi Mu Epsilon

SERVICE
1952 Alpha Phi Omega
1963 Gamma Sigma Sigma
1967 Alpha Phi Omega

RECOGNITION
1958 Beta Beta Beta

INACTIVE
1887–96 Phi Delta Theta

SOUTHERN ARKANSAS UNIVERSITY

Magnolia, AR. Schools of liberal and performing arts, science and technology, business, and education. Coeducational; state control; established 1909.

NIC MEN'S
1977 Sigma Pi
1982 Kappa Alpha Psi (A)
1985 Sigma Tau Gamma

NPHC MEN'S
    Phi Beta Sigma
1975 Alpha Phi Alpha

NPC WOMEN'S
1986 Sigma Sigma Sigma

NPHC WOMEN'S
1974 Alpha Kappa Alpha

ACHS HONORS
1953 Pi Delta Phi

1958 Alpha Chi
1959 Sigma Tau Delta
1962 Phi Alpha Theta
1972 Sigma Pi Sigma

RECOGNITION
1951 Alpha Psi Omega

INACTIVE
1971–83 Phi Mu Alpha—
    Sinfonia

COLONIES
    Phi Lambda Chi

SOUTHWEST BAPTIST UNIVERSITY

Southwest Baptist, MO. Private control: Baptist Church. Founded in 1878. Four-year; coeducational; liberal arts college.

Freshmen must live on campus. Single-sex dormitories.

PROFESSIONAL
1971 Kappa Kappa Psi
1971 Tau Beta Sigma
1983 Phi Alpha Delta

ACHS HONORS
1972 Alpha Chi

1987 Pi Kappa Lambda

RECOGNITION
1969 Pi Kappa Delta

INACTIVE
1878–81 Delta Gamma

SOUTHERN CONNECTICUT STATE COLLEGE
New Haven, CT. College of liberal arts; teachers college, and professional library school; coeducational; state control; chartered 1893.

NIC MEN'S
1987 Alpha Phi Delta
1988 Sigma Pi

NPHC MEN'S
Phi Beta Sigma

NPC WOMEN'S
1989 Phi Sigma Sigma
1990 Delta Phi Epsilon

PROFESSIONAL
1969 Delta Psi Kappa

ACHS HONORS
Omicron Delta Epsilon

1972 Psi Chi
1975 Gamma Theta Upsilon

OTHER HONORS
1959 National Collegiate
Players

RECOGNITION
1968 Sigma Delta Psi

INACTIVE
1950–67 Kappa Delta Phi (C)
1953–81 Kappa Delta Epsilon
1967–86 Kappa Mu Epsilon
1970–78 Alpha Chi Rho

SOUTHERN ILLINOIS UNIVERSITY Carbondale, IL. University; coeducational; state control; established 1869. Formerly Southern Illinois Normal University.

Five fraternities and three sororities occupy university-owned houses on rental basis. Five fraternities rent houses from private owners. Meeting rooms are available at no cost to those organizations without houses.

NIC MEN'S
1949 Tau Kappa Epsilon
1950 Kappa Alpha Psi (A)
1951 Sigma Tau Gamma
1951 Theta Xi
1955 Delta Chi
1955 Sigma Pi
1957 Phi Sigma Kappa
1970 Alpha Gamma Rho
1971 Tau Kappa Epsilon
1972 Kappa Alpha Psi (A)
1973 Alpha Tau Omega
1979 Sigma Phi Epsilon
1983 Alpha Epsilon Pi
1990 Alpha Chi Rho
1990 Pi Kappa Alpha

NPHC MEN'S
Phi Beta Sigma
1934 Alpha Phi Alpha

NPC WOMEN'S
1931 Sigma Sigma Sigma
1953 Delta Zeta
1955 Sigma Kappa
1957 Alpha Gamma Delta
1972 Alpha Sigma Alpha

NPHC WOMEN'S
1938 Sigma Gamma Rho
1952 Alpha Kappa Alpha
1968 Sigma Gamma Rho
1969 Alpha Kappa Alpha
1969 Delta Sigma Theta (B)

PROFESSIONAL
1949 Phi Mu Alpha—Sinfonia
1950 Mu Phi Epsilon
1959 Alpha Kappa Psi
1962 Pi Sigma Epsilon
1966 Mu Phi Epsilon
1974 Phi Alpha Delta
1982 Delta Theta Phi

OTHER PROFESSIONAL
1955 Pi Lambda Theta
1956 Sigma Delta Chi
1960 Alpha Zeta
1963 Alpha Eta Rho
1966 Beta Alpha Psi
1968 Alpha Epsilon Rho
1969 Delta Pi Epsilon

ACHS HONORS
Omicron Delta Epsilon
1936 Gamma Theta Upsilon
1939 Kappa Delta Pi
1941 Pi Omega Pi
1947 Alpha Kappa Delta
1949 Sigma Pi Sigma
1954 Phi Eta Sigma
1955 Pi Sigma Alpha
1956 Alpha Lambda Delta
1956 Phi Kappa Phi
1958 Kappa Tau Alpha
1961 Lambda Iota Tau
1963 Beta Gamma Sigma
1964 Xi Sigma Pi
1965 Pi Kappa Lambda
1967 Kappa Delta Pi
1971 Phi Alpha Theta
1976 Tau Beta Pi

OTHER HONORS
National Order of Omega
1948 National Collegiate
Players
1966 Sigma Xi

SERVICE
1948 Alpha Phi Omega
1963 Gamma Sigma Sigma

RECOGNITIQN
Angel Flight
Arnold Air Society (G-2)

1939 Society for Collegiate
Journalists—Pi Delta
Epsilon-Alpha Phi Gamma
(P)
1942 Pi Kappa Delta
1956 Iota Lambda Sigma
1959 National Block and Bridle
Club
1963 Sigma Delta Psi
1964 National Block and Bridle
Club
1969 Sigma Phi Alpha

INACTIVE
1651–85 Kappa Omicron Nu

1939–42 Sigma Tau Delta
1953–79 Phi Kappa Tau
1954 Kappa Alpha Mu
1956 Zeta Phi Eta
1968–72 Phi Gamma Nu
1969–86 Delta Sigma Pi
1970–73 Alpha Omicron Pi
1971–73 Sigma Alpha Mu
1971–80 Delta Upsilon
1973–82 Alpha Kappa Lambda
1975–84 Alpha Chi Sigma
1982–89 Alpha Epsilon Phi

COLONIES
1976 Triangle

SOUTHERN ILLINOIS UNIVERSITY Edwardsville, IL. Opened the fall quarter of 1965; also campuses in Alton and East St. Louis; coeducational; state-supported; degrees offered are bachelor of arts, bachelor of science, master of arts, master of science, and the certificate of specialist.

Does not offer on-campus housing for fraternities and sororities.

NIC MEN'S
1972 Sigma Pi
1973 Sigma Phj Epsilon
1989 Alpha Kappa Lambda

NPHC MEN'S
Phi Beta Sigma
1974 Alpha Phi Alpha

NPC WOMEN'S
1972 Alpha Sigma Tau
1974 Alpha Phi

PROFESSIONAL
1966 Phi Mu Alpha—Sinfonia

OTHER PROFESSIONAL
1973 Sigma Delta Chi

ACHS HONORS
1963 Gamma Theta Upsilon
1966 Pi Omega Pi

1968 Psi Chi
1969 Pi Delta Phi
1976 Beta Gamma Sigma
1976 Pi Kappa Lambda
1978 Phi Kappa Phi
1980 Eta Kappa Nu
1982 Phi Eta Sigma

OTHER HONORS
1973 Pi Mu Epsilon

SERVICE
1948 Alpha Phi Omega

RECOGNITION
1967 Pi Kappa Delta

INACTIVE
1966–75 Zeta Phi Eta
1973–79 Phi Chi Theta
1974–79 Delta Chi

SOUTHERN INDIANA UNIVERSITY Evansville, IN. Public institution. Founded in 1965. Four-year; coeducational.

Fraternities and sororities have their own houses.

NIC MEN'S
1970 Tau Kappa Epsilon
1973 Sigma Tau Gamma
1984 Lambda Chi Alpha
1986 Phi Delta Theta
1988 Alpha Kappa Lambda

NPC WOMEN'S
1976 Delta Zeta
1985 Alpha Gamma Delta

ACHS HONORS
Omicron Delta Epsllon
1984 Psi Chi
1988 Phi Alpha Theta

OTHER HONORS
National Order of Omega

INACTIVE
1971–83 Sigma Kappa
1972–86 Sigma Sigma Sigma

UNIVERSITY OF SOUTHERN MAINE Gorham, ME. University; coeducational; private control (Methodist); chartered 1911.

The fraternities and sororities own their houses but the university owns the land.

NIC MEN'S
1967 Tau Kappa Epsilon
1969 Delta Chi
1975 Phi Mu Delta

NPC WOMEN'S
1972 Phi Mu

OTHER PROFESSIONAL
1938 Kappa Delta Phi (C)

ACHS HONORS
1975 Phi Kappa Phi
1982 Psi Chi
1986 Phi Alpha Theta
1987 Phi Sigma Iota

INACTIVE
1972-85 Delta Zeta

SOUTHERN METHODIST UNIVERSITY Dallas, TX.

NIC MEN'S
1915 Kappa Alpha Order
1916 Pi Kappa Alpha
1918 Alpha Tau Omega
1921 Lambda Chi Alpha
1922 Phi Delta Theta
1923 Sigma Alpha Epsilon
1927 Kappa Sigma
1948 Phi Gamma Delta
1948 Sigma Chi
1951 Beta Theta Pi
1974 Sigma Nu
1985 Sigma Phi Epsilon
1987 Kappa Alpha Psi (A)
1988 Phi Kappa Psi

NPHC MEN'S
Phi Beta Sigma
1974 Alpha Phi Alpha

NPC WOMEN'S
1915 Alpha Delta Pi
1915 Phi Mu
1916 Chi Omega
1916 Delta Delta Delta
1916 Pi Beta Phi
1916 Zeta Tau Alpha
1926 Delta Gamma
1929 Gamma Phi Beta
1929 Kappa Alpha Theta
1929 Kappa Kappa Gamma

NPHC WOMEN'S
1976 Alpha Kappa Alpha
1976 Delta Sigma Theta (B)

PROFESSIONAL
1919 Zeta Phi Eta
1926 Mu Phi Epsilon
1927 Delta Theta Phi
1932 Phi Alpha Delta
1948 Delta Sigma Pi
1959 Phi Delta Tau
1990 Theta Tau

OTHER PROFESSIONAL
1930 Women in Communications
1931 Sigma Delta Chi
1940 Kappa Beta Pi
1950 Beta Alpha Psi

ACHS HONORS
Omicron Delta Epsilon
1917 Delta Sigma Rho-Tau Kappa Alpha
1926 Pi Sigma Alpha
1927 Phi Alpha Theta
1930 Psi Chi

1931 Alpha Lambda Delta
1931 Kappa Tau Alpha
1932 Alpha Kappa Delta
1932 Mortar Board
1933 Beta Gamma Sigma
1936 Sigma Delta Pi
1940 Kappa Mu Epsilon
1948 Pi Delta Phi
1950 Pi Kappa Lambda
1955 Chi Epsilon
1957 Eta Kappa Nu
1958 Pi Tau Sigma
1974 Tau Beta Pi
1975 Kappa Delta Pi
1978 Sigma Pi Sigma

OTHER HONORS
National Order of Omega
1949 Phi Beta Kappa
1967 Order of the Coif
1976 Sigma Xi

SERVICE
1935 Alpha Phi Omega

RECOGNITION
Angel Flight
Arnold Air Society (G-1)
1932 Beta Beta Beta
1932 Blue Key
1951 Sigma Iota Epsilon

INACTIVE
1910   Phi Beta Pi and Theta Kappa Psi (B)
1915-42 Alpha Omicron Pi
1916-75 Kappa Delta
1917-63 Sigma Kappa
1923-62 Alpha Kappa Psi
1926   Delta Psi Kappa
1926-70 Delta Zeta
1927   Eta Sigma Phi
1927-85 Delta Chi
1931-90 Phi Eta Sigma
1934   Delta Phi Alpha
1939-76 Sigma Alpha Mu
1944-86 Phi Chi Theta
1947-53 Phi Sigma Sigma
1948-61 Delta Kappa Epsilon
1949-52 Kappa Phi Kappa
1949-86 Phi Mu Alpha— Sinfonia
1950   Scabbard and Blade (9)
1961-69 Sigma Tau Delta
1969-71 Alpha Epsilon Phi

UNIVERSITY OF SOUTHERN MISSISSIPPI Hattiesburg, MS. Founded 1910; first instruction 1912. Graduate and undergraduate schools and doctoral program in education and psychology. Coeducational; state-supported.

Ownership of house is by fraternity on college land; sorority members are required to occupy an 8-story Panhellenic dormitory.

NIC MEN'S
1948 Kappa Sigma
1948 Phi Kappa Tau
1949 Alpha Tau Omega
1949 Kappa Alpha Order
1949 Pi Kappa Alpha
1953 Sigma Phi Epsilon
1965 Sigma Alpha Epsilon
1968 Sigma Nu
1980 Kappa Alpha Psi (A)
1981 Sigma Chi
1986 Tau Kappa Epsilon
1988 Delta Tau Delta

NPHC MEN'S
Phi Beta Sigma

NPC WOMEN'S
1938 Alpha Sigma Alpha
1940 Delta Zeta
1949 Chi Omega
1949 Kappa Delta
1950 Phi Mu
1951 Delta Delta Delta
1961 Pi Beta Phi
1971 Delta Gamma
1985 Alpha Delta Pi

NPHC WOMEN'S
1975 Alpha Kappa Alpha
1975 Delta Sigma Theta (B)
1978 Sigma Gamma Rho

PROFESSIONAL
1950 Delta Sigma Pi
1956 Pi Sigma Epsilon
1957 Kappa Kappa Psi
1957 Mu Phi Epsilon
1957 Phi Mu Alpha—Sinfonia
1957 Tau Beta Sigma

OTHER PROFESSIONAL
1975 Sigma Delta Chi

ACHS HONORS
Omicron Delta Epsilon

1940 Pi Omega Pi
1949 Alpha Epsilon Delta
1949 Kappa Mu Epsilon
1949 Pi Kappa Lambda
1949 Sigma Delta Pi
1950 Phi Eta Sigma
1950 Pi Delta Phi
1951 Kappa Omicron Nu
1954 Kappa Delta Pi
1954 Omicron Delta Kappa
1956 Lambda Iota Tau
1957 Alpha Lambda Delta
1962 Phi Alpha Theta
1963 Psi Chi
1965 Gamma Theta Upsilon
1967 Phi Kappa Phi
1970 Lambda Sigma Society
1971 Sigma Pi Sigma
1977 Beta Gamma Sigma
1981 Beta Phi Mu
1990 Kappa Tau Alpha

OTHER HONORS
National Order of Omega

SERVICE
1952 Alpha Phi Omega

RECOGNITION
1948 Alpha Psi Omega
1949 Kappa Pi
1949 Pi Kappa Delta
1950 Beta Beta Beta
1959 Scabbard and Blade (14)
1960 Sigma Delta Psi
1962 Rho Epsilon

INACTIVE
1937-85 Sigma Sigma Sigma
1955-82 Pi Gamma Mu
1958   Iota Lambda Sigma
1961-68 Acacia
1961-87 Phi Chi Theta

SOUTHERN OREGON STATE COLLEGE Ashland, OR. General college for teacher education, and preprofessional and semiprofessional studies; coeducational; state control; established 1926 as normal school.

PROFESSIONAL
1973 Sigma Alpha Iota

ACHS HONORS
Omicron Delta Epsilon
1955 Gamma Theta Upsilon
1961 Kappa Delta Pi
1980 Phi Kappa Phi
1981 Sigma Pi Sigma
1982 Psi Chi
1983 Phi Sigma Iota

1984 Alpha Lambda Delta

SERVICE
1948 Alpha Phi Omega

RECOGNITION
1955 Alpha Psi Omega

INACTIVE
1962-76 Tau Kappa Epsilon
1971-84 Phi Mu Alpha— Sinfonia

SOUTHERN TECHNICAL INSTITUTE Marietta, GA. Public institution. Founded in 1948. Four-year, coeducational, technical institution.

87% of students live off campus or commute.

NIC MEN'S
1972 Sigma Pi
1973 Tau Kappa Epsilon
1975 Lambda Chi Alpha
1976 Sigma Nu
1981 Pi Kappa Phi

1981 Sigma Phi Epsilon

NPC WOMEN'S
1980 Gamma Phi Beta
1983 Alpha Delta Pi

SOUTHERN STATE COLLEGE Magnolia, AK. College of liberal arts, teachers college, and technological institute; coeducational; state control; established 1909.

NPHC WOMEN'S
1974 Delta Sigma Theta (B)
PROFESSIONAL
1966 Kappa Kappa Psi

1966 Tau Beta Sigma
1973 Sigma Alpha Iota

SOUTHWEST MISSOURI STATE UNIVERSITY Springfield, MO. Colleges of arts and letters, business administration, education and psychology, health and applied sciences, humanities and social sciences, science and mathematics; state assisted; established as normal school in 1905; graduate program through master's and specialist level.

The fraternities and sororities own their own homes or rent.

NIC MEN'S
1947 Kappa Alpha Order
1948 Sigma Pi
1949 Tau Kappa Epsilon
1957 Sigma Phi Epsilon
1967 Phi Sigma Kappa
1969 Pi Kappa Alpha
1970 Alpha Gamma Sigma
1971 Sigma Chi
1972 Lambda Chi Alpha
1972 Sigma Nu
1981 Delta Upsilon
1984 Kappa Sigma
1985 Kappa Alpha Psi (A)
1985 Phi Delta Theta
1986 Delta Chi
NPHC MEN'S
  Phi Beta Sigma
NPC WOMEN'S
1941 Delta Zeta
1945 Sigma Sigma Sigma
1947 Alpha Sigma Alpha
1949 Alpha Delta Pi
1959 Sigma Kappa
1977 Gamma Phi Beta
1983 Alpha Chi Omega
PROFESSIONAL
1953 Delta Psi Kappa
1960 Mu Phi Epsilon
1960 Phi Mu Alpha—Sinfonia
1970 Kappa Kappa Psi
1981 Delta Sigma Pi
1981 Phi Alpha Delta
ACHS HONORS
  Omicron Delta Epsilon

1931 Gamma Theta Upsilon
1932 Kappa Mu Epsilon
1937 Pi Omega Pi
1945 Kappa Omicron Nu
1961 Delta Sigma Rho-Tau
  Kappa Alpha
1962 Phi Alpha Theta
1964 Alpha Kappa Delta
1966 Kappa Delta Pi
1970 Psi Chi
1972 Sigma Pi Sigma
1973 Pi Delta Phi
1974 Phi Kappa Phi
1974 Sigma Tau Delta
1976 Omicron Delta Kappa
1976 Pi Sigma Alpha
1982 Phi Eta Sigma
1986 Pi Kappa Lambda

OTHER HONORS
  National Order of Omega
1945 Delta Phi Delta

SERVICE
1938 Alpha Phi Omega
1972 Gamma Sigma Sigma

RECOGNITION
1946 Alpha Psi Omega
1967 Sigma Delta Psi

INACTIVE
1929–54 Pi Gamma Mu
1941–87 Sigma Tau Gamma
1948–70 Alpha Sigma Tau
1971–74 Phi Mu
1982–90 Delta Sigma Phi

SOUTHWEST STATE UNIVERSITY Marshall, MN.

ACHS HONORS
1984 Pi Gamma Mu

1987 Psi Chi

SOUTHWEST TEXAS STATE UNIVERSITY San Marcos, TX. College of liberal arts with teacher education emphasized; coeducational; state control; established 1898.

Administration permission exists for special quarters; currently all dormitory residency.

NIC MEN'S
1965 Pi Kappa Alpha
1965 Theta Xi
1966 Kappa Sigma
1966 Lambda Chi Alpha
1966 Sigma Nu
1969 Phi Kappa Psi
1970 Delta Tau Delta
1972 Tau Kappa Epsilon
1980 Phi Delta Theta
1981 Sigma Phi Epsilon
1982 Kappa Alpha Psi (A)
1983 Sigma Tau Gamma
1986 Alpha Tau Omega
1986 Sigma Chi
1988 Phi Kappa Sigma
NPHC MEN'S
  Phi Beta Sigma
NPC WOMEN'S
1964 Chi Omega
1964 Delta Zeta
1965 Alpha Xi Delta
1966 Alpha Delta Pi
1968 Gamma Phi Beta
1980 Zeta Tau Alpha
1988 Delta Gamma
NPHC WOMEN'S
1973 Alpha Kappa Alpha
1973 Delta Sigma Theta (B)
PROFESSIONAL
1947 Phi Mu Alpha—Sinfonia
1948 Delta Psi Kappa
1961 Mu Phi Epsilon
1970 Alpha Kappa Psi
1975 Phi Chi Theta
OTHER PROFESSIONAL
1976 Alpha Epsilon Rho
ACHS HONORS
  Pi Alpha Alpha
1922 Alpha Chi
1928 Pi Gamma Mu

1951 Kappa Delta Pi
1951 Pi Omega Pi
1952 Sigma Tau Delta
1962 Sigma Delta Pi
1968 Pi Delta Phi
1969 Gamma Theta Upsilon
1971 Phi Alpha Theta
1973 Phi Eta Sigma
1974 Alpha Lambda Delta
1976 Sigma Pi Sigma
1978 Phi Sigma Iota
1981 Kappa Tau Alpha
1982 Phi Sigma Tau
1982 Psi Chi
1984 Pi Kappa Lambda

OTHER HONORS
  National Order of Omega
1927 National Collegiate
  Players

SERVICE
1960 Alpha Phi Omega
1971 Gamma Sigma Sigma

RECOGNITION
  Angel Flight
  Arnold Air Society (G-1)
1934 Pi Kappa Delta
1944 Alpha Psi Omega
1946 Kappa Pi
1962 Delta Phi Alpha
1967 Beta Beta Beta

INACTIVE
1968–88 Phi Kappa Tau
1969–84 Sigma Kappa
1972–77 Delta Upsilon
1979–89 Alpha Phi
1980–86 Kappa Mu Epsilon

COLONIES
  Alpha Tau Omega
1988 Theta Chi
1990 Phi Gamma Delta

SOUTHWESTERN COLLEGE Winfield, KS. College of liberal arts; coeducational; private control (Methodist) founded 1885.

PROFESSIONAL
1964 Mu Phi Epsilon

1948 Kappa Pi

ACHS HONORS
1924 Pi Gamma Mu

RECOGNITION
1925 Beta Beta Beta

INACTIVE
1929–77 Kappa Omicron Nu
1965–78 Phi Mu Alpha—
  Sinfonia

SOUTHWESTERN UNIVERSITY Georgetown, TX. College of liberal arts and fine arts; coeducational; private control (Methodist); chartered 1840 as Ruterville College.

Fraternities own their own houses on college-owned land; administration provides chapter rooms for sororities at small rental fee.

NIC MEN'S
1883 Kappa Alpha Order
1886 Kappa Sigma
1886 Phi Delta Theta
1910 Pi Kappa Alpha

NPC WOMEN'S
1906 Zeta Tau Alpha
1907 Alpha Delta Pi
1911 Delta Delta Delta
1946 Delta Zeta

PROFESSIONAL
1907 Phi Chi

OTHER PROFESSIONAL
1943 Phi Delta Epsilon

ACHS HONORS
1922 Alpha Chi

1970 Pi Delta Phi
1971 Sigma Delta Pi
1975 Psi Chi

RECOGNITION
1948 Cardinal Key
1975 Blue Key

INACTIVE
1887–88 Sigma Alpha Epsilon
1905–11 Sigma Sigma Sigma
1908–82 Phi Mu
1924–78 Pi Gamma Mu
1927–40 Sigma Tau Delta

COLONIES
1990 Delta Chi

UNIVERSITY OF SOUTHWESTERN LOUISIANA Lafayette, LA. Established 1898 as Southwestern Louisiana Industrial Institute; name changed to Southwestern Louisiana Institute 1921; to present name 1961. University; coeducational; state control.

The fraternities rent houses off campus.

NIC MEN'S
1941 Phi Kappa Theta
1946 Theta Xi
1948 Sigma Pi
1956 Kappa Sigma
1960 Kappa Alpha Order
1962 Lambda Chi Alpha
1963 Sigma Nu
1968 Phi Delta Theta
1968 Sigma Alpha Epsilon
1969 Delta Tau Delta
1975 Kappa Alpha Psi (A)
1987 Sigma Pi

NPHC MEN'S
1968 Alpha Phi Alpha

NPC WOMEN'S
1931 Sigma Sigma Sigma
1940 Alpha Sigma Alpha
1956 Kappa Delta
1956 Phi Mu
1957 Delta Delta Delta
1967 Chi Omega

NPHC WOMEN'S
1967 Alpha Kappa Alpha
1971 Delta Sigma Theta (B)

PROFESSIONAL
1943 Sigma Alpha Iota
1947 Phi Mu Alpha—Sinfonia
1968 Delta Psi Kappa
1981 Delta Sigma Pi

OTHER PROFESSIONAL
1964 Alpha Zeta

ACHS HONORS
    Omicron Delta Epsilon
1928 Pi Gamma Mu
1936 Kappa Delta Pi
1940 Sigma Delta Pi
1951 Phi Kappa Phi
1955 Phi Alpha Theta
1956 Sigma Tau Delta
1959 Psi Chi
1960 Sigma Pi Sigma
1960 Tau Beta Pi
1961 Phi Eta Sigma
1961 Pi Tau Sigma
1962 Eta Kappa Nu
1965 Alpha Lambda Delta
1967 Phi Sigma
1975 Kappa Omicron Nu
1976 Pi Kappa Lambda
1979 Omega Chi Epsilon
1985 Chi Epsilon

OTHER HONORS
    National Order of Omega
1954 Sigma Gamma Epsilon
1966 Pi Mu Epsilon

SERVICE
1939 Alpha Phi Omega

RECOGNITION
    Arnold Air Society (C-2)
1932 Blue Key
1942 Alpha Psi Omega
1948 Blue Key
1976 Blue Key

INACTIVE
1948–74 Delta Sigma Phi
1951–68 Kappa Mu Epsilon
1956–77 Delta Zeta
1966–72 Sigma Kappa
1969–90 Pi Kappa Alpha

1969–91 Phi Kappa Psi
1974–88 Tau Kappa Epsilon

COLONIES
1956 Alpha Omicron Pi

SOUTHWESTERN AT MEMPHIS Memphis, TN. Founded 1848 at Clarksville, TN; moved to Memphis in 1925; coeducational college of lieberal arts and sciences; church related (Synods of Alabama, Louisiana, Mississippi, and Tennessee in the Pesbyterian Church in the United States).

Fraternity and sorority houses are lodges only; all students required to live in college residence halls.

NIC MEN'S
1887 Kappa Alpha Order
1934 Sigma Nu

RECOGNITION
1935 Chi Beta Phi
1946 Alpha Psi Omega

SOUTHWESTERN STATE UNIVERSITY Weatherford, OK. College of liberal arts; teachers college; professional schools; coeducational; state control; chartered as normal school in 1901.

One fraternity owns its own land and home; others hope to follow example.

NIC MEN'S
1956 Tau Kappa Epsilon
1962 Sigma Tau Gamma
1971 Phi Delta Theta

PROFESSIONAL
1956 Phi Delta Chi
1960 Kappa Epsilon
1963 Kappa Psi
1967 Kappa Kappa Psi
1968 Phi Mu Alpha—Sinfonia
1972 Mu Phi Epsilon

ACHS HONORS
1934 Phi Alpha Theta
1961 Rho Chi
1968 Phi Alpha Theta
1969 Sigma Pi Sigma
1970 Kappa Delta Pi

SERVICE
1974 Alpha Phi Omega

RECOGNITION
1931 Alpha Psi Omega
1934 Alpha Phi Sigma (E)
1948 Kappa Pi
1950 Pi Kappa Delta
1952 Beta Beta Beta
1974 Lambda Tau

INACTIVE
1928–41 Pi Gamma Mu
1939–68 Delta Zeta
1962–70 Alpha Xi Delta
1962–90 Sigma Kappa
1965–90 Pi Kappa Alpha
1973–89 Gamma Phi Beta
1974–90 Alpha Gamma Delta

SPELMAN COLLEGE   Atlanta, GA.

NPHC WOMEN'S
1973 Sigma Gamma Rho
1978 Alpha Kappa Alpha

PROFESSIONAL
1986 Kappa Delta Epsilon

ACHS HONORS
    Omicron Delta Epsilon
1974 Pi Kappa Lambda
1974 Psi Chi
1976 Sigma Delta Pi
1986 Alpha Lambda Delta

SPRING GARDEN COLLEGE Philadelphia, PA. Private control. Founded in 1851. Four-year, coeducational; technical institution.

No special housing for fraternities and sororities.

ACHS HONORS
1976 Alpha Chi

COLONIES
1989 Tau Kappa Epsilon

SPRING HILL COLLEGE Spring Hill, AL. College of liberal arts; coeducational; private control (Jesuit); established 1830, chartered 1836.

No fraternity or sorority housing is available.

NIC MEN'S
1955 Phi Kappa Theta
1966 Alpha Delta Gamma
1967 Phi Kappa Tau
1984 Sigma Chi

NPC WOMEN'S
1985 Delta Delta Delta
1987 Phi Mu

ACHS HONORS
    Omicron Delta Epsilon
1937 Alpha Sigma Nu
1965 Phi Eta Sigma
1966 Delta Sigma Rho-Tau
    Kappa Alpha
1966 Phi Alpha Theta
1973 Sigma Delta Pi

1976 Phi Sigma Tau
1979 Pi Sigma Alpha
1990 Psi Chi

RECOGNITION
1937 Alpha Psi Omega
1956 Lambda Tau
1957 Scabbard and Blade (14)

INACTIVE
1932–36 Alpha Delta Gamma
1937–72 Beta Beta Beta
1967–69 Kappa Sigma
1967–70 Kappa Alpha Order

COLONIES
    Lambda Chi Alpha

SPRINGFIELD COLLEGE Springfield, MA. Teachers college and professional school; coeducational; private control; nonsectarian. Established 1885.

ACHS HONORS
1965 Psi Chi

RECOGNITION
1913 Sigma Delta Psi

1957 Alpha Psi Omega

INACTIVE
1936–46 Pi Gamma Mu

STANFORD UNIVERSITY Stanford, CA. University; coeducational; private control; nonsectarian; chartered as Leland Stanford Junior University 1885; branch campuses at various European centers.

Some fraternities own their houses (on university land); others rent Stanford-owned houses.

NIC MEN'S
    Alpha Epsilon Pi
1891 Phi Delta Theta
1891 Phi Kappa Psi
1891 Sigma Chi
1892 Sigma Alpha Epsilon
1893 Delta Tau Delta
1894 Beta Theta Pi
1895 Kappa Alpha Order
1899 Kappa Sigma
1901 Delta Kappa Epsilon
1903 Theta Delta Chi
1914 Theta Xi
1916 Alpha Delta Phi
1983 Kappa Alpha Psi (A)
1985 Sigma Phi Epsilon
1986 Sigma Alpha Mu

NPHC MEN'S
1951 Alpha Phi Alpha

NPC WOMEN'S
1886 Delta Gamma
1892 Kappa Alpha Theta
1892 Kappa Kappa Gamma
1893 Pi Beta Phi
1908 Delta Delta Delta
1978 Alpha Phi

1983 Sigma Delta Tau

NPHC WOMEN'S
1981 Alpha Kappa Alpha

PROFESSIONAL
1897 Phi Delta Phi
1911 Phi Alpha Delta
1922 Delta Theta Phi
1955 Sigma Alpha Iota

ACHS HONORS
    Omicron Delta Epsilon
1911 Delta Sigma Rho-Tau
    Kappa Alpha
1926 Pi Sigma Alpha
1934 Pi Delta Phi
1935 Tau Beta Pi
1947 Phi Alpha Theta
1948 Gamma Theta Upsilon

OTHER HONORS
    National Order of Omega
1901 Sigma Xi
1904 Phi Beta Kappa
1911 Order of the Coif
1913 Iota Sigma Pi

SERVICE
1928 Alpha Phi Omega

RECOGNITION
    Angel Flight
    Arnold Air Society (I)
1913 Phi Lambda Upsilon
1964 Sigma Delta Psi

INACTIVE
1891–61 Alpha Tau Omega
1891–63 Sigma Nu
1891–71 Phi Gamma Delta
1892–87 Zeta Psi
1895–71 Chi Psi
1896–87 Delta Upsilon
1899–44 Alpha Phi
1904–16 Acacia
1905–70 Delta Chi
1907   Phi Alpha Tau
1910–44 Alpha Omicron Pi
1911–37 Phi Chi
1915–31 Sigma Kappa

1915–44 Chi Omega
1915–62 Sigma Delta Chi
1915–72 Phi Kappa Sigma
1916–55 Alpha Chi Sigma
1917–81 Alpha Sigma Phi
1920–66 Alpha Kappa Lambda
1920–88 Theta Chi
1923   Scabbard and Blade
    (5)
1923–59 Phi Rho Sigma
1923–73 Phi Sigma Kappa
1926–63 Sigma Delta Pi
1932–62 Alpha Kappa Kappa
1939–54 Gamma Alpha
1955–57 Psi Chi
1956–69 Phi Beta
1979–82 Alpha Chi Omega

COLONIES
1905 Gamma Phi Beta

STEPHEN F. AUSTIN STATE COLLEGE Nacogdoches, TX. Established 1921 by the thirty-sixth Texas legislature, began opration 1928. State college, graduate, undergraduate, and coeducational.

Fraternity and sorority members are required to live in the dormitories and no houses are maintained.

NIC MEN'S
1960 Delta Sigma Phi
1960 Pi Kappa Alpha
1961 Theta Chi
1962 Phi Delta Theta
1968 Kappa Alpha Order
1969 Alpha Tau Omega
1970 Sigma Tau Gamma
1974 Lambda Chi Alpha
1975 Sigma Chi
1976 Sigma Phi Epsilon
1986 Kappa Alpha Psi (A)
1988 Delta Tau Delta

NPHC MEN'S
    Phi Beta Sigma
1974 Alpha Phi Alpha

NPC WOMEN'S
1963 Chi Omega
1963 Delta Zeta
1967 Alpha Chi Omega
1972 Delta Delta Delta
1977 Zeta Tau Alpha
1990 Gamma Phi Beta

NPHC WOMEN'S
1971 Delta Sigma Theta (B)
1972 Alpha Kappa Alpha

PROFESSIONAL
1950 Delta Psi Kappa
1957 Kappa Kappa Psi
1957 Tau Beta Sigma
1964 Phi Mu Alpha—Sinfonia
1965 Mu Phi Epsilon
1966 Alpha Kappa Psi
1968 Phi Chi Theta

OTHER PROFESSIONAL
1973 Phi Upsilon Omicron

1976 Sigma Delta Chi

ACHS HONORS
    Omicron Delta Epsilon
1926 Alpha Chi
1959 Kappa Delta Pi
1960 Phi Alpha Theta
1965 Psi Chi
1965 Sigma Tau Delta
1966 Sigma Pi Sigma
1968 Gamma Theta Upsilon
1968 Xi Sigma Pi
1976 Beta Gamma Sigma
1977 Pi Kappa Lambda
1978 Pi Sigma Alpha
1980 Phi Eta Sigma

OTHER HONORS
    National Order of Omega
1970 Pi Mu Epsilon
1974 Sigma Gamma Epsilon

SERVICE
1961 Alpha Phi Omega
1970 Gamma Sigma Sigma

RECOGNITION
1929 Alpha Psi Omega
1934 Pi Kappa Delta
1952 Kappa Pi
1961 Beta Beta Beta
1981 Gamma Sigma Epsilon

INACTIVE
1960–89 Sigma Kappa
1971–88 Tau Kappa Epsilon
1975–75 Acacia

STERLING COLLEGE Sterling, KS. Founded in 1887 by the co-operation of citizens of Sterling and the United Presbyterian Church. Liberal arts college; coeducational; affiliated with the Presbyterian Church (U.S.A.).

ACHS HONORS
1961 Pi Gamma Mu
1961 Sigma Tau Delta
1965 Alpha Chi

SERVICE
1969 Alpha Phi Omega

RECOGNITION
1923 Pi Kappa Delta
1957 Alpha Psi Omega

STETSON UNIVERSITY   DeLand, FL. Founded by Henry DeLand in 1883. University; undergraduate and graduate schools coeducational; private control; affiliated with the Florida Baptist Convention. College of Law at St. Petersburg.

Two fraternities own their houses while five others live in University-owned fraternity houses. The Fraternity Row complex completed in 1962 houses five nationals in five separate houses. The sororities are housed in university-owned houses.

NIC MEN'S
1913 Sigma Nu
1921 Pi Kappa Phi
1925 Delta Sigma Phi
1949 Lambda Chi Alpha
1949 Sigma Phi Epsilon
1974 Phi Sigma Kappa
1983 Alpha Tau Omega

NPC WOMEN'S
1913 Delta Delta Delta
1913 Pi Beta Phi
1917 Alpha Xi Delta
1934 Zeta Tau Alpha
1949 Phi Mu
1957 Alpha Chi Omega
1981 Kappa Alpha Theta

PROFESSIONAL
1915 Phi Alpha Delta
1921 Phi Beta
1947 Phi Delta Phi
1948 Delta Theta Phi
1968 Alpha Kappa Psi
1970 Phi Chi Theta
1972 Delta Theta Phi
1985 Phi Alpha Delta

OTHER PROFESSIONAL
1921 Sigma Nu Phi

ACHS HONORS
1937 Sigma Pi Sigma

1942 Phi Alpha Theta
1950 Kappa Delta Pi
1953 Omicron Delta Kappa
1955 Sigma Tau Delta
1956 Gamma Theta Upsilon
1957 Psi Chi
1958 Mortar Board
1963 Pi Kappa Lambda
1973 Sigma Delta Pi
1978 Phi Eta Sigma

OTHER HONORS
      National Order of Omega

RECOGNITION
1919 Theta Alpha Phi
1932 Gamma Sigma Epsilon
1938 Pi Kappa Delta
1946 Kappa Pi
1947 Beta Beta Beta
1952 Scabbard and Blade (10)
1958 Pi Kappa Delta

INACTIVE
1917   Delta Psi Kappa
1929–42 Pi Gamma Mu
1937–70 Sigma Delta Pi
1951–89 Pi Kappa Alpha
1960–74 Kappa Mu Epsilon
1969–82 Alpha Kappa Alpha

COLLEGE OF STEUBENVILLE   Steubenville, OH. Founded 1946; coeducational. Private control; Roman Catholic, Franciscan.

Administration requires fraternity and sorority members to occupy dormitories.

NIC MEN'S
1948 Alpha Phi Delta

NPC WOMEN'S
1963 Theta Phi Alpha

ACHS HONORS
1964 Alpha Chi

RECOGNITION
1966 Alpha Psi Omega

INACTIVE
1964–69 Sigma Tau Delta
1964–70 Phi Mu
1965–83 Delta Zeta
1965–87 Alpha Chi Rho
1966–73 Lambda Chi Alpha
1978–83 Kappa Delta Epsilon

STEVENS INSTITUTE OF TECHNOLOGY   Hoboken, NJ. Founded in 1870; undergraduate school of science and engineering, management, and computer science; coeducational. Graduate school coeducational; private control; nonsectarian.

The fraternities own their own land and homes.

NIC MEN'S
1874 Delta Tau Delta
1874 Theta Xi
1879 Beta Theta Pi
1883 Chi Phi
1883 Chi Psi
1899 Phi Sigma Kappa
1916 Pi Lambda Phi
1926 Alpha Sigma Phi
1938 Sigma Phi Epsilon

NPC WOMEN'S
1982 Phi Sigma Sigma
1985 Delta Phi Epsilon

ACHS HONORS
1896 Tau Beta Pi

1972 Psi Chi
1983 Eta Kappa Nu

OTHER HONORS
1954 Sigma Xi

SERVICE
1949 Alpha Phi Omega

RECOGNITION
      Arnold Air Society (B-1)

INACTIVE
1881–96 Alpha Tau Omega
1883–91 Sigma Chi

STILLMAN COLLEGE   Tuscaloosa, AL. College of liberal arts; coeducational; private control; chartered 1876. Presbyterian.

NIC MEN'S
1963 Kappa Alpha Psi (A)

NPHC MEN'S
      Phi Beta Sigma
1962 Alpha Phi Alpha
1963 Omega Psi Phi

NPHC WOMEN'S
      Zeta Phi Beta
1962 Delta Sigma Theta (B)
1963 Alpha Kappa Alpha
1977 Sigma Gamma Rho

ACHS HONORS
1956 Alpha Kappa Mu

STOCKTON STATE COLLEGE   Pomona, NJ. Public institution. Founded in 1971. Four-year; coeducational; liberal arts college.

NIC MEN'S
1980 Alpha Chi Rho
1984 Alpha Sigma Phi
1984 Tau Kappa Epsilon
1987 Alpha Phi Delta
1988 Pi Kappa Phi

NPC WOMEN'S
1985 Alpha Gamma Delta
1985 Sigma Sigma Sigma
1990 Delta Zeta

NPHC WOMEN'S
1982 Sigma Gamma Rho

ACHS HONORS
      Omicron Delta Epsilon
1979 Psi Chi
1982 Sigma Pi Sigma

INACTIVE
–90   Delta Phi Epsilon

STONEHILL COLLEGE   North Easton, MA. College of liberal arts for men and women; private control; Roman Catholic; chartered 1948.

ACHS HONORS
      Omicron Delta Epsilon
1960 Delta Epsilon Sigma
1968 Phi Alpha Theta
1976 Sigma Delta Pi
1977 Delta Mu Delta

1983 Psi Chi

RECOGNITION
1936 Alpha Psi Omega
1972 Sigma Zeta

SUFFOLK UNIVERSITY   Boston, MA. University; coeducational; private control; nonsectarian. Established 1906 as law school.

NIC MEN'S
1970 Tau Kappa Epsilon

NPC WOMEN'S
1970 Phi Sigma Sigma

PROFESSIONAL
1965 Phi Alpha Delta
1969 Delta Theta Phi
1976 Phi Delta Phi

OTHER PROFESSIONAL
1967 Phi Alpha Tau
1976 Sigma Delta Chi

ACHS HONORS
Omicron Delta Epsilon
Pi Alpha Alpha

1962 Phi Alpha Theta
1965 Phi Sigma Tau
1970 Pi Gamma Mu
1978 Delta Mu Delta
1978 Psi Chi

SERVICE
1964 Alpha Phi Omega
1967 Gamma Sigma Sigma

RECOGNITION
1970 Sigma Zeta

INACTIVE
1960–88 Delta Sigma Pi
1975–84 Phi Chi Theta

SUL ROSS STATE COLLEGE Alpine, TX. College of liberal arts; teachers college; coeducational; state control; founded 1917.

Sororities occupy college housing.

PROFESSIONAL
1949 Kappa Kappa Psi

ACHS HONORS
1926 Alpha Chi
1946 Kappa Delta Pi
1954 Sigma Tau Delta
1966 Phi Alpha Theta
1986 Pi Sigma Alpha

RECOGNITION
1930 Alpha Psi Omega
1972 Beta Beta Beta

INACTIVE
1961–61 Gamma Sigma Epsilon
1968–83 Tau Kappa Epsilon
1969–76 Phi Mu
1970–81 Alpha Kappa Lambda

SUSQUEHANNA UNIVERSITY Selinsgrove, PA. Founded by leaders of the Lutheran Church 1858; supported in its purposes and objectives by the Central Pennsylvania Synod of the Lutheran Church in America. Liberal arts college; additional curricula in music education, business administration.

Ownership of house is by fraternity on college-owned land. Two fraternities housed in college-owned buildings. Sorority members are required to live in dormitories.

NIC MEN'S
1924 Phi Mu Delta
1942 Theta Chi
1957 Lambda Chi Alpha
1971 Phi Sigma Kappa
1984 Sigma Phi Epsilon

NPC WOMEN'S
1950 Alpha Delta Pi
1950 Kappa Delta
1964 Sigma Kappa

PROFESSIONAL
1927 Sigma Alpha Iota
1976 Phi Mu Alpha—Sinfonia

ACHS HONORS
1927 Pi Gamma Mu
1966 Phi Alpha Theta
1968 Psi Chi
1969 Kappa Mu Epsilon

1969 Pi Delta Phi
1977 Alpha Lambda Delta
1977 Pi Sigma Alpha
1980 Delta Mu Delta
1987 Phi Sigma Iota

OTHER HONORS
National Order of Omega

SERVICE
1963 Alpha Phi Omega

RECOGNITION
1942 Alpha Psi Omega

INACTIVE
1957–83 Alpha Xi Delta
1962–82 Tau Kappa Epsilon

COLONIES
Zeta Tau Alpha
1988 Sigma Pi Sigma

SWARTHMORE COLLEGE Swarthmore, PA. College of liberal arts and engineering; coeducational; private control. Chartered and incorporated 1864; first instruction 1869.

Phi Sigma Kappa and Phi Omega Psi own houses on college-owned land. Delta Upsilon occupies a college-owned house.

NIC MEN'S
1894 Delta Upsilon
1906 Phi Sigma Kappa

ACHS HONORS
1974 Tau Beta Pi

OTHER HONORS
1896 Phi Beta Kappa
1923 Sigma Xi

INACTIVE
1888–62 Kappa Sigma

1889–63 Phi Kappa Psi
1891–34 Kappa Alpha Theta
1892–34 Pi Beta Phi
1893–34 Kappa Kappa Gamma
1912–34 Delta Gamma
1918–58 Phi Delta Theta
1918–65 Mortar Board
1919–32 Chi Omega
1919–34 Phi Mu
1930–34 Delta Zeta

SYRACUSE UNIVERSITY Syracuse, NY. University; coeducational; private; chartered as Syracuse University 1870.

Two types of ownership prevail; in most cases ownership of land and home is by the fraternity and sorority, but in a few cases ownership is in university hands and the group occupies the house on a rental basis.

NIC MEN'S
1871 Delta Kappa Epsilon
1873 Delta Upsilon
1875 Psi Upsilon
1875 Zeta Psi
1884 Phi Kappa Psi
1887 Phi Delta Theta
1889 Beta Theta Pi
1901 Phi Gamma Delta
1904 Sigma Chi
1905 Alpha Chi Rho
1905 Sigma Phi Epsilon
1906 Kappa Sigma
1907 Sigma Alpha Epsilon
1910 Delta Tau Delta
1911 Zeta Beta Tau
1913 Pi Kappa Alpha
1913 Sigma Alpha Mu
1914 Alpha Phi Delta
1918 Lambda Chi Alpha
1922 Tau Epsilon Phi
1928 Theta Chi
1947 Alpha Epsilon Pi
1949 Pi Lambda Phi
1949 Tau Delta Phi
1950 Alpha Tau Omega
1951 Kappa Alpha Psi (A)
1963 Tau Kappa Epsilon

NPHC MEN'S
Phi Beta Sigma

NPC WOMEN'S
1872 Alpha Phi
1874 Gamma Phi Beta
1883 Kappa Kappa Gamma
1889 Kappa Alpha Theta
1896 Delta Delta Delta
1896 Pi Beta Phi
1901 Delta Gamma
1904 Alpha Gamma Delta
1904 Alpha Xi Delta
1905 Sigma Kappa
1906 Alpha Chi Omega
1911 Chi Omega
1914 Alpha Omicron Pi
1919 Alpha Epsilon Phi

1921 Delta Phi Epsilon
1927 Phi Sigma Sigma
1946 Sigma Delta Tau

NPHC WOMEN'S
1973 Delta Sigma Theta (B)
1975 Alpha Kappa Alpha
1981 Sigma Gamma Rho

PROFESSIONAL
1899 Phi Delta Phi
1912 Alpha Chi Sigma
1914 Zeta Phi Eta
1925 Sigma Alpha Iota
1954 Phi Alpha Delta

OTHER PROFESSIONAL
1918 Pi Lambda Theta
1925 Kappa Phi Kappa
1926 Sigma Delta Chi
1929 Beta Alpha Psi
1943 Alpha Epsilon Rho
1945 Delta Pi Epsilon
1950 Phi Epsilon Kappa
1980 Sigma Nu Phi

ACHS HONORS
Omicron Delta Epsilon
1906 Tau Beta Pi
1910 Delta Sigma Rho-Tau
Kappa Alpha
1916 Phi Kappa Phi
1922 Beta Gamma Sigma
1928 Alpha Kappa Delta
1932 Psi Chi
1941 Kappa Omicron Nu
1946 Phi Sigma Iota
1947 Alpha Epsilon Delta
1948 Pi Tau Sigma
1950 Pi Sigma Alpha
1951 Alpha Pi Mu
1951 Eta Kappa Nu
1959 Beta Phi Mu
1959 Sigma Theta Tau
1964 Pi Kappa Lambda
1966 Phi Alpha Theta
1967 Phi Eta Sigma
1977 Kappa Tau Alpha

1978 Chi Epsilon

OTHER HONORS
    National Order of Omega
1896 Phi Beta Kappa
1906 Sigma Xi
1914 Pi Mu Epsilon
1952 Order of the Coif

SERVICE
1931 Alpha Phi Omega

RECOGNITION
    Angel Flight
    Arnold Air Society (E-1)
1922 Scabbard and Blade (4)
1948 Delta Phi Alpha
1951 Phi Lambda Upsilon

INACTIVE
1899–65 Alpha Kappa Kappa
1899–70 Delta Chi
1904–77 Phi Mu Alpha—
    Sinfonia
1905–16 Mu Phi Epsilon
1906–70 Sigma Nu
1907–18 Phi Beta Pi and Theta
    Kappa Psi (a)
1908–32 Gamma Eta Gamma
1911–85 Acacia
1915   Phi Alpha Tau

1918   Tau Sigma Delta
1919–58 Phi Delta Epsilon
1920–69 Phi Mu
1921   Kappa Beta Pi
1922–57 Phi Kappa Tau
1923–68 Theta Phi Alpha
1923–69 Alpha Kappa Psi
1923–71 Kappa Delta
1923–76 Zeta Tau Alpha
1924–57 Delta Zeta
1924–71 Alpha Delta Pi
1925–35 Phi Kappa Theta
1925–59 Alpha Sigma Phi
1925–89 Theta Tau
1927   Sigma Iota Epsilon
1929–44 Phi Chi
1929–55 Pi Gamma Mu
1933   Sigma Delta Epsilon
1933–60 Sigma Pi Sigma
1946–47 Kappa Alpha Mu
1949–52 Alpha Phi Alpha
1950–53 Sigma Pi
1960–71 Alpha Sigma Tau
1964–70 Alpha Sigma Alpha
1970–78 Alpha Lambda Delta

COLONIES
    Alpha Tau Omega
    Kappa Delta Rho

TALLADEGA COLLEGE   Talladega, AL. College of liberal arts; coeducational; private control (Congregational Christian); established 1867.

Administration requires fraternities and sororities to occupy residence halls.

NIC MEN'S
1948 Kappa Alpha Psi (A)

NPHC MEN'S
    Phi Beta Sigma
1921 Omega Psi Phi

NPHC WOMEN'S
1924 Alpha Kappa Alpha

1927 Delta Sigma Theta (B)
1972 Sigma Gamma Rho

ACHS HONORS
1956 Beta Kappa Chi
1968 Alpha Chi
1981 Phi Alpha Theta

UNIVERSITY OF TAMPA   Tampa, FL. College of liberal arts; coeducational; private control; nonsectarian; chartered 1930.

The fraternities own their own land and homes; sororities are not permitted to house themselves.

NIC MEN'S
1953 Sigma Phi Epsilon
1955 Pi Kappa Phi
1957 Theta Chi
1970 Alpha Epsilon Pi
1979 Phi Delta Theta
1982 Sigma Alpha Epsilon

NPC WOMEN'S
1954 Alpha Chi Omega
1954 Delta Zeta
1981 Delta Gamma

PROFESSIONAL
1941 Kappa Kappa Psi
1953 Sigma Alpha Iota
1963 Delta Sigma Pi
1971 Tau Beta Sigma
1972 Phi Gamma Nu

ACHS HONORS
    Omicron Delta Epsilon
1956 Sigma Tau Delta
1961 Phi Alpha Theta
1964 Psi Chi
1966 Kappa Delta Pi
1968 Alpha Chi
1972 Omicron Delta Kappa
1975 Phi Eta Sigma
1983 Pi Sigma Alpha

OTHER HONORS
    National Order of Omega

SERVICE
1960 Alpha Phi Omega

RECOGNITION
1927 Alpha Psi Omega
1948 Kappa Pi

INACTIVE
1952–77 Zeta Tau Alpha
1953–63 Sigma Sigma Sigma
1955–79 Tau Kappa Epsilon
1965–76 Delta Phi Epsilon

TARKIO COLLEGE   Tarkio, MO. Founded 1883. Liberal arts, coeducational; affiliated with United Presbyterian Church.

NIC MEN'S
1973 Theta Chi
1987 Tau Kappa Epsilon

ACHS HONORS
1966 Phi Alpha Theta
1972 Sigma Tau Delta

SERVICE
1975 Alpha Phi Omega

RECOGNITION
1927 Alpha Psi Omega

INACTIVE
1970–75 Alpha Sigma Phi
1971–78 Psi Chi
1975–76 Phi Mu Delta

TARLETON STATE UNIVERSITY   Stephenville, TX.

NIC MEN'S
    Tau Kappa Epsilon
1986 Lambda Chi Alpha
1988 Delta Chi
1989 Kappa Delta Rho

NPC WOMEN'S
1985 Alpha Gamma Delta
1985 Delta Zeta

PROFESSIONAL
1979 Phi Mu Alpha—Sinfonia

ACHS HONORS
1969 Alpha Chi
1981 Phi Eta Sigma

1985 Phi Alpha Theta

OTHER HONORS
    National Order of Omega

SERVICE
1963 Alpha Phi Omega
1967 Gamma Sigma Sigma

RECOGNITION
1968 Beta Beta Beta

INACTIVE
1967–79 Kappa Mu Epsilon

COLONIES
1990 Alpha Gamma Rho

1969–71 Alpha Sigma Alpha
1972–84 Zeta Beta Tau

COLONIES
    Sigma Delta Tau

TEMPLE UNIVERSITY   Philadelphia, PA. Founded 1884 by Russell H. Conwell. Chartered 1888. Undergraduate and graduate schools and colleges coeducational; private, state-related institution; nonsectarian.

The fraternities own their own land and homes; the sororities do not maintain individual houses but use the Panhellenic House for meetings.

NIC MEN'S
1909 Sigma Pi
1927 Pi Lambda Phi
1929 Zeta Beta Tau
1930 Alpha Phi Delta
1932 Phi Kappa Theta
1955 Alpha Chi Rho
1956 Alpha Epsilon Pi
1956 Tau Delta Phi
1984 Delta Tau Delta
1985 Kappa Delta Rho
1987 Phi Kappa Psi
1987 Sigma Alpha Mu
1990 Delta Kappa Epsilon

NPHC MEN'S
    Phi Beta Sigma
1914 Alpha Phi Alpha

NPC WOMEN'S
1921 Delta Zeta
1922 Alpha Sigma Alpha
1926 Phi Sigma Sigma

1959 Delta Phi Epsilon
1984 Alpha Epsilon Phi

NPHC WOMEN'S
1955 Alpha Kappa Alpha
1960 Delta Sigma Theta (B)

PROFESSIONAL
1893 Xi Psi Phi
1896 Psi Omega
1914 Alpha Omega
1923 Delta Sigma Pi
1928 Delta Psi Kappa
1930 Kappa Psi
1933 Phi Rho Sigma
1937 Phi Delta Phi
1939 Phi Alpha Delta
1948 Lambda Kappa Sigma
1951 Phi Delta Chi
1952 Rho Pi Phi
1960 Alpha Delta Theta
1964 Sigma Alpha Iota
1980 Gamma Iota Sigma

OTHER PROFESSIONAL
1916 Phi Delta Epsilon
1921 Phi Epsilon Kappa
1922 Alpha Zeta Omega
1927 Kappa Phi Kappa
1930 Sigma Delta Chi
1932 Alpha Kappa Kappa
1933 Women in Communications
1934 Tau Epsilon Rho
1945 Delta Sigma Delta
1956 Beta Alpha Psi
1958 Delta Pi Epsilon

ACHS HONORS
Omicron Delta Epsilon
1935 Beta Gamma Sigma
1947 Phi Alpha Theta
1948 Psi Chi
1950 Delta Sigma Rho-Tau
Kappa Alpha
1954 Pi Delta Phi
1954 Sigma Pi Sigma
1955 Rho Chi
1958 Sigma Delta Pi
1960 Alpha Lambda Delta
1963 Alpha Kappa Delta
1963 Pi Omega Pi
1965 Pi Sigma Alpha
1974 Kappa Tau Alpha

OTHER HONORS
National Order of Omega
1937 Omicron Kappa Upsilon
1949 Sigma Xi

1950 Alpha Omega Alpha
1960 Pi Mu Epsilon
1974 Phi Beta Kappa

SERVICE
1948 Alpha Phi Omega

RECOGNITION
1933 Phi Delta Gamma
1933 Theta Alpha Phi
1949 Delta Phi Alpha
1950 Scabbard and Blade (9)
1958 Sigma Phi Alpha

INACTIVE
1909   Phi Chi
1919   Nu Beta Epsilon
1919–60 Alpha Sigma Tau
1920–60 Kappa Alpha Psi (A)
1922–45 Alpha Kappa Alpha
1928   Phi Lambda Kappa
1929   Phi Gamma Nu
1929–54 Pi Gamma Mu
1933–73 Kappa Delta Epsilon
1934   Phi Beta Pi and Theta
Kappa Psi (a)
1938–72 Sigma Phi Epsilon
1959–79 Alpha Gamma Delta
1962–74 Phi Eta Sigma
1967–80 Phi Mu Alpha—
Sinfonia

COLONIES
Sigma Tau Gamma
1990 Delta Upsilon

TEMPLE UNIVERSITY, AMBLER BRANCH Ambler, PA. Public institution. Extension campus of Temple University (Philadelphia). Founded in 1910.

95% of students live off campus or commute.

NIC MEN'S
1981 Alpha Chi Rho

UNIVERSITY OF TENNESSEE Knoxville, TN. Founded in 1794 as Blount College by the legislature of this federal territory; public; coeducational. University and land-grant college.

Thirteen fraternities are situated in a Fraternity Park financed by the institution with the chapters subsequently leasing and paying the debt service; eight chapters lease the land and the house; two own both the land and the house; one owns the house but leases the land. Sororities occupy a university-owned panhellenic building; all but two sororities have suites in the building, each with a meeting room, a kitchen, and a smaller room for files and equipment.

NIC MEN'S
1872 Alpha Tau Omega
1873 Pi Kappa Alpha
1879 Sigma Alpha Epsilon
1880 Kappa Sigma
1883 Kappa Alpha Order
1890 Phi Gamma Delta
1913 Sigma Phi Epsilon
1917 Sigma Chi
1921 Sigma Nu
1924 Delta Tau Delta

1925 Phi Sigma Kappa
1931 Pi Kappa Phi
1932 Lambda Chi Alpha
1949 Alpha Epsilon Pi
1951 Alpha Gamma Rho
1959 FarmHouse
1963 Phi Delta Theta
1966 Acacia
1967 Beta Theta Pi
1967 Phi Kappa Psi
1969 Chi Phi

1969 Delta Upsilon
1971 Phi Kappa Tau
1986 Kappa Alpha Psi (A)

NPHC MEN'S
Phi Beta Sigma
1976 Alpha Phi Alpha

NPC WOMEN'S
1900 Chi Omega
1902 Alpha Omicron Pi
1904 Zeta Tau Alpha
1908 Phi Mu
1920 Alpha Delta Pi
1921 Sigma Kappa
1923 Delta Delta Delta
1925 Kappa Delta
1933 Delta Zeta
1947 Delta Gamma
1948 Pi Beta Phi
1958 Alpha Xi Delta
1961 Alpha Chi Omega
1961 Alpha Gamma Delta
1967 Kappa Kappa Gamma

NPHC WOMEN'S
1970 Alpha Kappa Alpha
1971 Delta Sigma Theta (B)

PROFESSIONAL
1906 Phi Rho Sigma
1913 Kappa Psi
1914 Phi Chi
1916 Phi Alpha Delta
1919 Phi Delta Phi
1921 Xi Psi Phi
1922 Phi Delta Chi
1924 Delta Sigma Pi
1926 Psi Omega
1929 Alpha Chi Sigma
1951 Lambda Kappa Sigma
1959 Phi Mu—Sinfonia
1960 Sigma Alpha Iota
1964 Alpha Kappa Psi
1966 Delta Theta Phi
1967 Phi Chi Theta
1984 Phi Alpha Delta
1990 Sigma Alpha

OTHER PROFESSIONAL
1903 Alpha Kappa Kappa
1912 Alpha Zeta
1921 Delta Sigma Delta
1940 Pi Lambda Theta
1946 Delta Pi Epsilon
1951 Beta Alpha Psi
1956 Sigma Delta Chi

ACHS HONORS
Omicron Delta Epsilon
1899 Phi Kappa Phi
1916 Delta Sigma Rho-Tau
Kappa Alpha
1929 Tau Beta Pi
1930 Phi Eta Sigma
1932 Alpha Lambda Delta
1935 Kappa Omicron Nu
1937 Mortar Board
1944 Sigma Delta Pi
1947 Beta Gamma Sigma
1947 Omicron Delta Kappa

1948 Alpha Epsilon Delta
1948 Eta Kappa Nu
1948 Rho Chi
1949 Chi Epsilon
1949 Gamma Theta Upsilon
1949 Pi Delta Phi
1950 Pi Sigma Alpha
1950 Pi Tau Sigma
1952 Kappa Tau Alpha
1954 Alpha Pi Mu
1954 Sigma Pi Sigma
1966 Alpha Kappa Delta
1966 Gamma Theta Upsilon
1968 Pi Tau Sigma
1969 Phi Sigma
1969 Pi Kappa Lambda
1972 Sigma Theta Tau
1972 Xi Sigma Pi
1973 Kappa Delta Pi
1973 Lambda Iota Tau
1977 Beta Phi Mu
1978 Psi Chi

OTHER HONORS
National Order of Omega
1930 Omicron Kappa Upsilon
1941 Alpha Omega Alpha
1950 Sigma Xi
1952 Order of the Coif
1964 Gamma Sigma Delta
1965 Phi Beta Kappa
1967 Sigma Gamma Epsilon

SERVICE
1948 Alpha Phi Omega
1950 Alpha Phi Omega
1970 Gamma Sigma Sigma

RECOGNITION
Angel Flight
Arnold Air Society (D-2)
1923 Scabbard and Blade (4)
1928 Sigma Delta Psi
1929 Iota Lambda Sigma
1940 Alpha Psi Omega
1946 National Block and Bridle
Club
1963 Rho Epsilon

INACTIVE
1904–13 Delta Theta Phi
1920–34 Theta Alpha Phi
1925   Phi·Lambda Kappa
1928   Phi Beta Pi and Theta
Kappa Psi (a)
1928   Sigma Delta Kappa
1928–69 Zeta Beta Tau
1929–56 Phi Delta Epsilon
1935–84 Alpha Omega
1936   Delta Phi Alpha
1940   Eta Sigma Phi
1941–63 Pi Omega Pi
1942–60 Theta Chi
1948–77 Alpha Epsilon Phi
1950   Alpha Eta Rho
1960–68 Alpha Beta Alpha
1965–77 Gamma Phi Beta
1969–79 Alpha Kappa Lambda
1969–85 Kappa Alpha Theta

UNIVERSITY OF TENNESSEE AT CHATTANOOGA Chattanooga, TN. Chartered as Chattanooga University in 1886. Coeducational college of Arts and Sciences and college of Applied Arts; graduate instruction in mathematics, physics, education and business administration; private control; nonsectarian. Known as U. S. Grant University from 1889-07.

NIC MEN'S
1947 Sigma Chi
1948 Lambda Chi Alpha
1949 Kappa Sigma
1982 Kappa Alpha Psi (A)

NPHC MEN'S
     Phi Beta Sigma
1972 Alpha Phi Alpha

NPC WOMEN'S
1919 Chi Omega
1926 Alpha Delta Pi

NPHC WOMEN'S
1971 Alpha Kappa Alpha

PROFESSIONAL
1969 Phi Mu Alpha—Sinfonia
1975 Delta Omicron

ACHS HONORS
     Omicron Delta Epsilon
1929 Sigma Pi Sigma
1947 Alpha Lambda Delta
1947 Phi Eta Sigma

1953 Mortar Board
1966 Phi Alpha Theta
1969 Kappa Delta Pi
1976 Kappa Omicron Nu
1976 Psi Chi
1986 Pi Sigma Alpha
1990 Tau Beta Pi

OTHER HONORS
1971 Pi Mu Epsilon

RECOGNITION
1932 Gamma Sigma Epsilon

INACTIVE
1907–42 Delta Theta Phi
1923–89 Pi Beta Phi
1928–81 Pi Gamma Mu
1937–70 Phi Mu
1945–63 Kappa Delta
1947–90 Pi Kappa Alpha
1962–72 Alpha Epsilon Pi
1976   Phi Sigma Sigma
1980–87 Alpha Tau Omega

UNIVERSITY OF TENNESSEE AT MARTIN
Martin, TN. University and land-grant college; coeducational; state control; Martin Branch founded 1927.

NIC MEN'S
1960 Phi Sigma Kappa
1961 Pi Kappa Alpha
1963 Alpha Gamma Rho
1964 Alpha Tau Omega
1971 Kappa Alpha Psi (A)
1972 Sigma Alpha Epsilon
1975 Kappa Alpha Order
1982 Sigma Pi

NPHC MEN'S
     Phi Beta Sigma
1976 Alpha Phi Alpha

NPC WOMEN'S
1961 Alpha Delta Pi
1961 Chi Omega
1961 Zeta Tau Alpha
1966 Alpha Omicron Pi
1989 Alpha Gamma Delta

NPHC WOMEN'S
1970 Delta Sigma Theta (B)
1971 Alpha Kappa Alpha
1986 Sigma Gamma Rho

PROFESSIONAL
1965 Alpha Kappa Psi

1966 Phi Chi Theta
1968 Phi Mu Alpha—Sinfonia
1969 Sigma Alpha Iota

OTHER PROFESSIONAL
1972 Phi Upsilon Omicron
1976 Alpha Zeta

ACHS HONORS
1962 Sigma Tau Delta
1971 Phi Kappa Phi
1974 Phi Eta Sigma
1974 Psi Chi
1981 Pi Sigma Alpha
1987 Phi Alpha Theta

SERVICE
1970 Alpha Phi Omega
1975 Gamma Sigma Sigma

RECOGNITION
1958 Alpha Psi Omega
1967 Scabbard and Blade (16)

INACTIVE
1974–88 Sigma Kappa
1984–89 Phi Kappa Tau

TENNESSEE STATE UNIVERSITY
Nashville, TN. Land-grant university; professional schools; coeducational; state control, established 1912.

NPHC MEN'S
     Phi Beta Sigma
1930 Omega Psi Phi

NPHC WOMEN'S
     Zeta Phi Beta
1931 Alpha Kappa Alpha
1942 Sigma Gamma Rho

PROFESSIONAL
1956 Phi Mu Alpha—Sinfonia
1973 Kappa Kappa Psi

ACHS HONORS
     Pi Alpha Alpha
1937 Alpha Kappa Mu
1950 Pi Omega Pi
1970 Kappa Omicron Nu

1970 Phi Alpha Theta
1973 Eta Kappa Nu
1973 Psi Chi
1975 Alpha Lambda Delta
1976 Delta Mu Delta

SERVICE
1975 Alpha Phi Omega

RECOGNITION
1971 Pi Kappa Delta

TENNESSEE TECHNOLOGICAL UNIVERSITY
Cookeville, TN. Founded as Tennessee Polytechnic Institute 1915; name changed and university status granted 1965; public, state controlled; coeducational; graduate and undergraduate degrees.

NIC MEN'S
1961 Alpha Gamma Sigma
1969 Alpha Tau Omega
1969 Kappa Sigma
1969 Phi Delta Theta
1969 Sigma Alpha Epsilon
1969 Tau Kappa Epsilon
1970 Sigma Chi
1971 Lambda Chi Alpha
1981 Phi Gamma Delta
1981 Pi Kappa Alpha
1983 FarmHouse

NPC WOMEN'S
1969 Alpha Delta Pi
1969 Kappa Delta
1969 Phi Mu
1969 Zeta Tau Alpha
1980 Delta Gamma

NPHC WOMEN'S
1981 Alpha Kappa Alpha

PROFESSIONAL
1965 Alpha Kappa Psi
1966 Mu Phi Epsilon
1966 Phi Mu Alpha—Sinfonia
1968 Phi Gamma Nu
1968 Theta Tau

OTHER PROFESSIONAL
1974 Pi Lambda Theta

ACHS HONORS
     Omicron Delta Epsilon
1941 Kappa Mu Epsilon
1952 Kappa Delta Pi
1957 Sigma Tau Delta
1965 Phi Alpha Theta
1967 Eta Kappa Nu

1968 Kappa Omicron Nu
1968 Tau Beta Pi
1970 Phi Kappa Phi
1973 Alpha Lambda Delta
1975 Chi Epsilon
1975 Mortar Board
1975 Omicron Delta Kappa
1976 Sigma Pi Sigma
1979 Psi Chi
1988 Pi Kappa Lambda

SERVICE
1967 Alpha Phi Omega

RECOGNITION
1940 Pi Kappa Delta
1952 Sigma Iota Epsilon
1954 National Block and Bridle
     Club
1957 Alpha Psi Omega
1961 Scabbard and Blade (15)
1969 Sigma Delta Psi
1975 Society for Collegiate
     Journalists—Pi Delta
     Epsilon-Alpha Phi Gamma
     (A)
1976 Beta Beta Beta

INACTIVE
1945–81 Pi Omega Pi
1950–57 Alpha Tau Alpha
1969–71 Alpha Sigma Alpha
1969–77 Sigma Sigma Sigma
1969–88 Sigma Phi Epsilon
1970–76 Delta Tau Delta

COLONIES
     Beta Theta Pi

TENNESSEE WESLEYAN COLLEGE
Athens, TN. Sponsored as Athens Female College by Holston Conference of the Methodist Episcopal Church, S. Chartered as East Tennessee Wesleyan College 1866; chartered 1925 as Tennessee Wesleyan College, a coeducational junior college; changed to a senior college 1954; controlled by the United Methodist Church. Interdenominational.

The fraternities are permitted to rent houses which they use for meeting purposes and study rooms but which have sleeping quarters for no more than six. Each of the sororities occupies a permanent room in the women's dormitory at a small rental fee.

NPC WOMEN'S
1961 Sigma Kappa

ACHS HONORS
1968 Alpha Chi

RECOGNITION
1960 Alpha Psi Omega
1964 Pi Kappa Delta

INACTIVE
1959–79 Phi Sigma Kappa
1960–82 Sigma Phi Epsilon
1961–78 Kappa Delta

1961–79 Alpha Xi Delta
1962–70 Pi Gamma Mu
1964–82 Pi Kappa Phi
1968–78 Phi Mu

UNIVERSITY OF TEXAS Austin, TX. University; coeducational; state control. Organized by legislative act 1881. *Austin*, main campus; *Galveston*, school of medicine and nursing; *Dallas*, Southwestern Medical School; *Houston*, school of dentistry; *Port Arkansas*, institute of marine science; *Fort Davis*, McDonald Observatory.

Fraternities and sororities with rare exceptions own their own land and homes.

NIC MEN'S
1882 Sigma Alpha Epsilon
1883 Kappa Alpha Order
1883 Phi Delta Theta
1883 Phi Gamma Delta
1884 Kappa Sigma
1884 Sigma Chi
1886 Beta Theta Pi
1886 Sigma Nu
1892 Chi Phi
1897 Alpha Tau Omega
1904 Delta Tau Delta
1904 Phi Kappa Psi
1907 Delta Chi
1907 Delta Sigma Phi
1912 Delta Kappa Epsilon
1916 Acacia
1917 Lambda Chi Alpha
1920 Pi Kappa Alpha
1920 Zeta Beta Tau
1922 Sigma Alpha Mu
1926 Tau Delta Phi
1930 Sigma Phi Epsilon
1939 Alpha Epsilon Pi
1940 Phi Kappa Sigma
1949 Delta Upsilon
1951 Tau Kappa Epsilon
1951 Theta Chi
1959 Phi Kappa Theta
1977 Kappa Alpha Psi (A)
1978 Sigma Tau Gamma
1979 Zeta Psi
1988 Pi Kappa Phi
1990 Psi Upsilon

NPHC MEN'S
Phi Beta Sigma
Phi Beta Sigma
1961 Alpha Phi Alpha

NPC WOMEN'S
1902 Kappa Kappa Gamma
1902 Pi Beta Phi
1904 Chi Omega
1904 Kappa Alpha Theta
1906 Alpha Delta Pi
1906 Zeta Tau Alpha
1912 Delta Delta Delta
1920 Alpha Phi
1921 Kappa Delta
1924 Alpha Chi Omega
1925 Alpha Epsilon Phi
1929 Alpha Xi Delta
1939 Delta Gamma
1939 Sigma Delta Tau
1940 Alpha Gamma Delta

NPHC WOMEN'S
1959 Alpha Kappa Alpha
1960 Delta Sigma Theta (B)
1972 Delta Sigma Theta (B)
1975 Delta Sigma Theta (B)

PROFESSIONAL
1903 Phi Chi
1905 Phi Delta Chi
1909 Phi Delta Phi
1915 Alpha Kappa Psi
1916 Delta Theta Phi
1920 Mu Phi Epsilon
1924 Phi Mu Alpha—Sinfonia
1930 Delta Sigma Pi
1930 Xi Psi Phi
1934 Kappa Psi
1939 Phi Rho Sigma
1941 Kappa Kappa Psi
1943 Kappa Epsilon
1947 Phi Alpha Delta
1951 Sigma Alpha Iota
1973 Xi Psi Phi
1975 Phi Chi Theta
1987 Phi Alpha Delta

OTHER PROFESSIONAL
1906 Alpha Kappa Kappa
1910 Phi Beta Pi and Theta
        Kappa Psi (a)
1913 Sigma Delta Chi
1919 Women in Communications
1922 Alpha Alpha Gamma
1923 Phi Delta Epsilon
1924 Beta Alpha Psi
1927 Pi Lambda Theta
1947 Delta Sigma Delta
1959 Delta Pi Epsilon
1973 Delta Sigma Delta

ACHS HONORS
        Omicron Delta Epsilon
1909 Delta Sigma Rho-Tau
        Kappa Alpha
1916 Kappa Delta Pi
1916 Tau Beta Pi
1920 Pi Sigma Alpha
1922 Beta Gamma Sigma
1923 Mortar Board
1924 Kappa Omicron Nu
1925 Sigma Delta Pi
1928 Eta Kappa Nu
1929 Alpha Epsilon Delta
1930 Rho Chi
1931 Phi Eta Sigma
1931 Pi Tau Sigma
1934 Alpha Kappa Delta
1934 Chi Epsilon

1935 Alpha Lambda Delta
1938 Sigma Delta Pi
1941 Omega Chi Epsilon
1944 Pi Delta Phi
1946 Sigma Pi Sigma
1947 Phi Alpha Theta
1948 Pi Kappa Lambda
1950 Psi Chi
1955 Pi Omega Pi
1957 Sigma Gamma Tau
1959 Beta Gamma Sigma
1961 Kappa Tau Alpha
1962 Phi Kappa Phi
1963 Gamma Theta Upsilon
1966 Omicron Delta Kappa
1969 Alpha Epsilon
1969 Pi Tau Sigma
1971 Pi Tau Sigma
1974 Beta Phi Mu
1976 Alpha Epsilon

OTHER HONORS
        National Order of Omega
1905 Phi Beta Kappa
1915 Sigma Xi
1920 Alpha Omega Alpha
1920 Sigma Gamma Epsilon
1927 Order of the Coif
1930 Iota Sigma Pi
1940 Omicron Kappa Upsilon
1975 Pi Mu Epsilon

SERVICE
1935 Alpha Phi Omega

RECOGNITION
        Angel Flight
        Arnold Air Society (G-1)
1920 Phi Lambda Upsilon
1927 Sigma Iota Epsilon
1947 Sigma Delta Psi
1949 Scabbard and Blade (8)
1950 Iota Lambda Sigma
1955 Delta Phi Alpha
1958 Eta Sigma Phi
1964 Sigma Phi Alpha

INACTIVE
1913–65 Phi Mu
1916   Kappa Beta Pi
1922–88 Gamma Phi Beta
1924–71 Alpha Rho Chi
1924–77 Delta Zeta
1926–39 Alpha Psi Omega
1927   Sigma Phi Delta
1929–33 Phi Sigma Sigma
1931   Tau Sigma Delta
1934–90 Delta Phi Epsilon
1941–73 Alpha Omicron Pi
1943–88 Phi Kappa Tau
1946   Phi Sigma
1947–76 Phi Sigma Kappa
1952–85 Alpha Chi Sigma
1965–72 Sigma Pi
1967–70 Alpha Kappa Lambda
1968–73 Pi Lambda Phi

COLONIES
        Theta Tau
1913 Theta Xi

The University Of Texas Medical Branch Galveston, TX. Ownership of house and lot is by the fraternity.

OTHER HONORS
1954 Sigma Xi

University Of Texas Southwestern Medical School Dallas, TX.

ACHS HONORS
1985 Psi Chi

School Of Dentistry; Dental Hygiene Houston, TX.

INACTIVE
1979–88 Alpha Omega

UNIVERSITY OF TEXAS AT ARLINGTON Arlington, TX. State university; coeducational; part of University of Texas system; established 1895; became state institution 1917; was junior college until 1959; formerly Arlington State College.

NIC MEN'S
1967 Kappa Sigma
1968 Delta Tau Delta
1968 Kappa Alpha Order
1968 Phi Delta Theta
1968 Phi Gamma Delta
1969 Delta Upsilon
1971 Beta Theta Pi
1972 Sigma Phi Epsilon
1973 Pi Kappa Alpha
1976 Sigma Nu
1977 Kappa Alpha Psi (A)

1978 Pi Kappa Phi
1984 Sigma Chi
1986 Triangle

NPHC MEN'S
        Phi Beta Sigma
1970 Alpha Phi Alpha

NPC WOMEN'S
1967 Delta Zeta
1967 Phi Mu
1969 Alpha Chi Omega
1969 Delta Delta Delta

1969 Zeta Tau Alpha

NPHC WOMEN'S
1971 Alpha Kappa Alpha

PROFESSIONAL
1964 Kappa Kappa Psi
1965 Delta Sigma Pi
1968 Phi Mu Alpha—Sinfonia
1974 Phi Gamma Nu
1974 Sigma Alpha Iota
1975 Zeta Phi Eta

OTHER PROFESSIONAL
1971 Beta Alpha Psi
1973 Sigma Delta Chi

ACHS HONORS
     Omicron Delta Epsilon
1966 Eta Kappa Nu
1966 Sigma Pi Sigma
1968 Alpha Chi
1969 Beta Gamma Sigma
1969 Chi Epsilon
1969 Phi Alpha Theta

1969 Tau Beta Pi
1970 Alpha Pi Mu
1970 Sigma Gamma Tau
1975 Phi Sigma
1977 Kappa Delta Pi
1977 Phi Eta Sigma
1977 Phi Sigma Iota
1980 Pi Sigma Alpha
1981 Psi Chi
1984 Kappa Tau Alpha
1988 Sigma Lambda Alpha

OTHER HONORS
     National Order of Omega
1972 Sigma Xi
1975 Pi Mu Epsilon

SERVICE
1950 Alpha Phi Omega
1974 Gamma Sigma Sigma

INACTIVE
1970–89 Alpha Rho Chi
1971–83 Alpha Phi

THE UNIVERSITY OF TEXAS AT EL PASO El
Paso, TX. College of liberal arts; coeducational;
state control; established 1913 as Texas School of
Mines; branch of University of Texas.

Sororities and fraternities own lodges, some of
which are within campus limits; others rent houses
off-campus which are used as lodges.

NIC MEN'S
1941 Phi Kappa Tau
1946 Lambda Chi Alpha
1947 Sigma Alpha Epsilon
1949 Kappa Sigma
1949 Tau Kappa Epsilon
1976 Kappa Alpha Psi (A)

NPHC MEN'S
     Phi Beta Sigma
1968 Alpha Phi Alpha

NPC WOMEN'S
1938 Zeta Tau Alpha
1939 Chi Omega

NPHC WOMEN'S
1972 Alpha Kappa Alpha

OTHER WOMEN'S
     Lambda Delta Sigma

PROFESSIONAL
1947 Kappa Kappa Psi
1951 Delta Sigma Pi
1967 Sigma Alpha Iota
1985 Phi Mu Alpha—Sinfonia

OTHER PROFESSIONAL
1975 Sigma Delta Chi

ACHS HONORS
     Omicron Delta Epsilon

1949 Phi Alpha Theta
1957 Psi Chi
1960 Alpha Lambda Delta
1965 Alpha Sigma Mu
1967 Pi Sigma Alpha
1969 Tau Beta Pi
1971 Eta Kappa Nu
1972 Mortar Board
1974 Phi Kappa Phi
1976 Chi Epsilon
1986 Pi Kappa Lambda

OTHER HONORS
1975 Sigma Xi

SERVICE
     The National Spurs
1969 Alpha Phi Omega
1972 Gamma Sigma Sigma

RECOGNITION
1956 Scabbard and Blade (12)
1966 Beta Beta Beta

INACTIVE
1938–77 Delta Delta Delta
1961–66 Delta Chi
1962–69 Alpha Epsilon Phi
1962–72 Sigma Alpha Mu
1964–76 Kappa Delta
1967–72 Alpha Kappa Lambda

UNIVERSITY OF TEXAS AT SAN ANTONIO San
Antonio, TX. University; coeducational; state control. Organized by legislative act in 1969. Undergraduate and graduate degree programs.

No fraternity homes. Some on-campus housing for
general student body.

NIC MEN'S
1979 Sigma Phi Epsilon
1981 Tau Kappa Epsilon
1983 Lambda Chi Alpha
1988 Alpha Tau Omega
1990 Phi Delta Theta

NPC WOMEN'S
1978 Alpha Omicron Pi
1978 Sigma Kappa

NPHC WOMEN'S
     Alpha Kappa Alpha

PROFESSIONAL
1980 Alpha Omega

ACHS HONORS
     Omicron Delta Epsilon

1974 Phi Sigma
1981 Alpha Lambda Delta
1985 Gamma Theta Upsilon
1985 Psi Chi

OTHER HONORS
1975 Alpha Omega Alpha

INACTIVE
1970   Phi Chi
1979–82 Alpha Sigma Tau
1982–87 Phi Mu Alpha—
     Sinfonia

COLONIES
     Sigma Tau Gamma

TEXAS A & M UNIVERSITY College Station, TX.
University and land-grant college; state control; coeducational; established 1876.

Fraternities and sororities are active in the com-
muity but are not recognized by the university.

NIC MEN'S
1973 Sigma Phi Epsilon
1976 Pi Kappa Alpha
1976 Sigma Chi
1979 Alpha Tau Omega
1979 Phi Gamma Delta
1979 Pi Kappa Phi
1980 Theta Chi
1981 Sigma Alpha Epsilon
1981 Tau Kappa Epsilon
1982 Kappa Sigma
1982 Sigma Alpha Mu
1984 Phi Kappa Sigma
1985 Phi Delta Theta
1986 Alpha Gamma Rho
1987 Beta Theta Pi
1987 Chi Phi
1987 Kappa Alpha Psi (A)
1987 Phi Kappa Tau
1988 Beta Sigma Psi
1988 Delta Chi
1988 Triangle
1990 Zeta Beta Tau

NPC WOMEN'S
1975 Alpha Delta Pi
1975 Alpha Gamma Delta
1975 Chi Omega
1975 Delta Zeta
1975 Zeta Tau Alpha
1976 Kappa Alpha Theta
1976 Kappa Kappa Gamma
1981 Alpha Chi Omega
1981 Delta Delta Delta
1985 Pi Beta Phi
1988 Alpha Phi

NPHC WOMEN'S
1985 Alpha Kappa Alpha
1990 Sigma Gamma Rho

PROFESSIONAL
1985 Delta Sigma Pi

OTHER PROFESSIONAL
1951 Alpha Zeta
1954 Sigma Delta Chi
1974 Beta Alpha Psi

ACHS HONORS
     Omicron Delta Epsilon

     Pi Alpha Alpha
1948 Tau Beta Pi
1949 Phi Eta Sigma
1949 Phi Kappa Phi
1955 Eta Kappa Nu
1957 Sigma Gamma Tau
1958 Alpha Pi Mu
1959 Sigma Pi Sigma
1961 Alpha Kappa Delta
1962 Chi Epsilon
1964 Pi Tau Sigma
1970 Omega Chi Epsilon
1970 Phi Sigma
1970 Psi Chi
1970 Tau Sigma Delta
1971 Phi Alpha Theta
1972 Kappa Delta Pi
1972 Lambda Sigma Society
1975 Alpha Lambda Delta
1976 Pi Delta Phi
1976 Sigma Delta Pi
1978 Pi Sigma Alpha
1978 Xi Sigma Pi
1979 Gamma Theta Upsilon
1979 Mortar Board
1979 Sigma Lambda Alpha
1982 Delta Mu Delta
1983 Kappa Tau Alpha

OTHER HONORS
     National Order of Omega
1951 Sigma Xi
1965 Gamma Sigma Delta
1972 Pi Mu Epsilon

SERVICE
1962 Alpha Phi Omega

RECOGNITION
1950 Phi Zeta
1951 National Block and Bridle
     Club
1955 Iota Lambda Sigma
1957 Phi Lambda Upsilon
1965 Pi Kappa Delta
1968 Sigma Delta Psi
1971 Sigma Iota Epsilon

INACTIVE
1963–69 Sigma Tau Delta
1973   Sigma Gamma Epsilon

1975–81 Phi Mu
1975–87 Alpha Phi
1982–85 Delta Tau Delta

COLONIES
Delta Upsilon

FarmHouse
Kappa Alpha Order
Lambda Chi Alpha
Sigma Pi ·

TEXAS A & I UNIVERSITY Kingsville, TX. Chartered 1917, first instruction 1925; state supported; coeducational; academic colleges: agriculture and home economics, arts and sciences, business administration, engineering, teacher education and graduate studies.

Most of the fraternities own lodges and the sororities have suites in the residence hall.

NIC MEN'S
1965 Kappa Sigma
1966 Alpha Tau Omega
1966 Delta Tau Delta
1967 Sigma Chi
1970 Lambda Chi Alpha
1973 Phi Kappa Theta
1974 Kappa Alpha Psi (A)

NPHC WOMEN'S
1973 Alpha Kappa Alpha
1973 Delta Sigma Theta (B)

PROFESSIONAL
1965 Delta Sigma Pi
1967 Delta Omicron
1967 Kappa Kappa Psi
1969 Phi Gamma Nu
1970 Tau Beta Sigma

OTHER PROFESSIONAL
1934 Alpha Tau Alpha

ACHS HONORS
1927 Alpha Chi
1927 Kappa Omicron Nu

1950 Phi Alpha Theta
1952 Sigma Delta Pi
1969 Alpha Lambda Delta
1971 Eta Kappa Nu
1973 Sigma Pi Sigma
1974 Tau Beta Pi
1975 Kappa Delta Pi

SERVICE
1947 Alpha Phi Omega

RECOGNITION
1947 Alpha Psi Omega
1947 Pi Kappa Delta

INACTIVE
1964–85 Chi Omega
1965–78 Alpha Chi Omega
1965–86 Alpha Delta Pi
1965–88 Zeta Tau Alpha
1967–88 Phi Mu Alpha—Sinfonia
1971–82 Tau Kappa Epsilon
1972–80 Alpha Gamma Rho

TEXAS CHRISTIAN UNIVERSITY Fort Worth, TX. University; coeducational; private control (Disciples of Christ); founded 1873. A medium sized teaching and research institution with the atmosphere of smaller college.

The fraternities and sororities lease chapter rooms and exclusively occupy one-half of a residence hall for living from the University in the Worth Hills area.

NIC MEN'S
1955 Delta Tau Delta
1955 Kappa Sigma
1955 Phi Delta Theta
1955 Phi Kappa Sigma
1955 Sigma Alpha Epsilon
1955 Sigma Chi
1956 Lambda Chi Alpha
1980 Kappa Alpha Psi (A)
1980 Phi Gamma Delta

NPHC MEN'S
1972 Alpha Phi Alpha

NPC WOMEN'S
1955 Alpha Delta Pi
1955 Chi Omega
1955 Delta Delta Delta
1955 Kappa Alpha Theta

1955 Kappa Delta
1955 Kappa Kappa Gamma
1955 Zeta Tau Alpha
1956 Delta Gamma
1956 Pi Beta Phi

NPHC WOMEN'S
1972 Delta Sigma Theta (B)
1976 Alpha Kappa Alpha

PROFESSIONAL
1948 Mu Phi Epsilon
1948 Phi Mu Alpha—Sinfonia
1957 Kappa Kappa Psi
1957 Tau Beta Sigma
1959 Delta Sigma Pi
1963 Phi Chi Theta
1971 Delta Psi Kappa

OTHER PROFESSIONAL
1960 Sigma Delta Chi
1965 Beta Alpha Psi
1967 Women in Communications
1968 Phi Upsilon Omicron

ACHS HONORS
Omicron Delta Epsilon
1926 Sigma Tau Delta
1927 Phi Sigma Iota
1952 Pi Sigma Alpha
1956 Psi Chi
1959 Phi Alpha Theta
1962 Alpha Lambda Delta
1963 Phi Sigma Tau
1963 Sigma Pi Sigma
1964 Beta Gamma Sigma
1965 Alpha Kappa Delta
1965 Phi Sigma
1966 Kappa Delta Pi
1968 Gamma Theta Upsilon
1970 Mortar Board
1970 Pi Kappa Lambda
1970 Sigma Theta Tau
1979 Kappa Tau Alpha

OTHER HONORS
National Order of Omega
1959 Pi Mu Epsilon
1967 Sigma Xi
1971 Phi Beta Kappa

SERVICE
1950 Alpha Phi Omega

RECOGNITION
Angel Flight
Arnold Air Society (G-1)
1926 Pi Kappa Delta
1931 Sigma Delta Psi
1934 Alpha Psi Omega

INACTIVE
1923 Alpha Chi
1926–39 Pi Gamma Mu
1947–59 Kappa Mu Epsilon
1955–76 Sigma Phi Epsilon
1955–77 Alpha Gamma Delta
1962–76 Phi Eta Sigma
1979–89 Alpha Phi

COLONIES
1990 Alpha Chi Omega

TEXAS COLLEGE Tyler, TX. Organized as liberal arts college by a group of ministers of the Christian Methodist Church 1894. Instruction began 1895, with O. T. Womack as first president.

Administration permits occupancy of special quarters by fraternities and sororities.

NIC MEN'S
1937 Kappa Alpha Psi (A)

NPHC MEN'S
1941 Alpha Phi Alpha
1942 Omega Psi Phi

NPHC WOMEN'S
Zeta Phi Beta
1942 Delta Sigma Theta (B)

1951 Sigma Gamma Rho

ACHS HONORS
1951 Alpha Kappa Mu
1977 Phi Alpha Theta
1988 Psi Chi

INACTIVE
1953–60 Beta Kappa Chi

TEXAS LUTHERAN COLLEGE Sequin, TX. College of liberal arts; coeducational; private control; American Lutheran Church; founded 1891.

PROFESSIONAL
1971 Kappa Kappa Psi
1971 Tau Beta Sigma

ACHS HONORS
1956 Alpha Chi
1960 Phi Alpha Theta
1962 Sigma Tau Delta
1974 Alpha Lambda Delta

1975 Psi Chi

SERVICE
1969 Alpha Phi Omega

RECOGNITION
1966 Pi Kappa Delta
1973 Beta Beta Beta

TEXAS SOUTHERN UNIVERSITY Houston, TX. University; coeducational; state control; established 1947.

NIC MEN'S
1947 Kappa Alpha Psi (A)

NPHC MEN'S
Phi Beta Sigma
1948 Omega Psi Phi
1950 Alpha Phi Alpha

NPHC WOMEN'S
Zeta Phi Beta

1938 Sigma Gamma Rho
1949 Delta Sigma Theta (B)
1950 Alpha Kappa Alpha

PROFESSIONAL
1957 Kappa Kappa Psi
1958 Tau Beta Sigma
1969 Phi Alpha Delta
1970 Lambda Kappa Sigma
1974 Phi Mu Alpha—Sinfonia

1976 Zeta Phi Eta

OTHER PROFESSIONAL
1972 Sigma Delta Chi
1975 Beta Alpha Psi

ACHS HONORS
1950 Alpha Kappa Mu
1952 Beta Kappa Chi
1960 Pi Delta Phi
1965 Phi Alpha Theta
1965 Sigma Delta Pi
1966 Kappa Delta Pi
1968 Beta Gamma Sigma
1971 Pi Omega Pi

1973 Lambda Iota Tau
1977 Rho Chi
1984 Sigma Pi Sigma
1985 Phi Sigma Iota
1988 Gamma Theta Upsilon

SERVICE
1968 Alpha Phi Omega

RECOGNITION
1965 Beta Beta Beta

INACTIVE
1964–82 Delta Mu Delta

1975 Chi Epsilon
1976 Kappa Delta Pi
1979 Sigma Lambda Alpha
1981 Omega Chi Epsilon
1984 Lambda Sigma Society

OTHER HONORS
       National Order of Omega
1932 Sigma Gamma Epsilon
1960 Sigma Xi
1972 Gamma Sigma Delta
1974 Order of the Coif

SERVICE
1939 Alpha Phi Omega

RECOGNITION
       Angel Flight
       Arnold Air Society (G-1)
1926 Alpha Psi Omega

1933 National Block and Bridle
       Club
1951 Sigma Iota Epsilon
1954 Scabbard and Blade (11)
1962 Delta Phi Alpha

INACTIVE
1927–37 Pi Gamma Mu
1928   Alpha Chi
1947   Kappa Alpha Mu
1952–54 Kappa Phi Kappa
1955–85 Sigma Kappa
1959–81 Phi Mu
1966–76 Beta Beta Beta
1972–78 Pi Lambda Phi
1985–86 Delta Upsilon

COLONIES
       Sigma Tau Gamma

TEXAS TECH UNIVERSITY   Lubbock, TX. Established 1923: first instruction 1925: coeducational: undergraduate schools: agriculture, arts and sciences, business administration, engineering, education, home economics; graduate school: law school, and medical school: state supported.

Fraternities and sororities have been permitted to purchase land adjacent to college on which to build lodges for use as meeting rooms.

NIC MEN'S
1953 Alpha Tau Omega
1953 Kappa Sigma
1953 Phi Delta Theta
1953 Phi Kappa Psi
1953 Pi Kappa Alpha
1953 Sigma Alpha Epsilon
1953 Sigma Nu
1954 Phi Gamma Delta
1955 Sigma Chi
1957 Delta Tau Delta
1961 Kappa Alpha Order
1970 Beta Theta Pi
1970 Sigma Phi Epsilon
1976 Lambda Chi Alpha
1976 Tau Kappa Epsilon
1977 Delta Sigma Phi
1978 FarmHouse
1979 Kappa Alpha Psi (A)
1982 Chi Psi
1983 Delta Chi
1986 Pi Kappa Phi
1987 Alpha Gamma Rho
1990 Theta Chi

NPHC MEN'S
1972 Alpha Phi Alpha

NPC WOMEN'S
1953 Delta Delta Delta
1953 Kappa Alpha Theta
1953 Kappa Kappa Gamma
1953 Pi Beta Phi
1953 Zeta Tau Alpha
1954 Alpha Chi Omega
1954 Delta Gamma
1955 Alpha Phi
1956 Gamma Phi Beta
1962 Chi Omega
1966 Alpha Delta Pi
1987 Kappa Delta

NPHC WOMEN'S
1970 Delta Sigma Theta (B)
1971 Alpha Kappa Alpha
1983 Sigma Gamma Rho

PROFESSIONAL
1937 Kappa Kappa Psi

1946 Tau Beta Sigma
1947 Delta Sigma Pi
1949 Phi Gamma Nu
1952 Mu Phi Epsilon
1953 Phi Mu Alpha—Sinfonia
1966 Alpha Kappa Psi
1967 Delta Psi Kappa
1969 Delta Theta Phi
1969 Phi Alpha Delta
1972 Phi Delta Phi

OTHER PROFESSIONAL
1931 Phi Psi
1937 Phi Upsilon Omicron
1941 Women in Communications
1951 Alpha Zeta
1958 Sigma Delta Chi
1959 Beta Alpha Psi
1960 Phi Epsilon Kappa
1970 Alpha Epsilon Rho
1971 Kappa Beta Pi

ACHS HONORS
       Omicron Delta Epsilon
       Pi Alpha Alpha
1937 Tau Beta Pi
1938 Alpha Epsilon Delta
1939 Pi Sigma Alpha
1940 Kappa Mu Epsilon
1943 Sigma Tau Delta
1944 Sigma Delta Pi
1946 Phi Eta Sigma
1949 Alpha Lambda Delta
1952 Pi Omega Pi
1953 Alpha Pi Mu
1953 Delta Sigma Rho-Tau
       Kappa Alpha
1954 Sigma Pi Sigma
1956 Eta Kappa Nu
1956 Phi Kappa Phi
1956 Pi Delta Phi
1957 Mortar Board
1957 Phi Alpha Theta
1960 Psi Chi
1962 Tau Sigma Delta
1967 Gamma Theta Upsilon
1967 Kappa Tau Alpha
1972 Omicron Delta Kappa

TEXAS WESLEYAN COLLEGE   Fort Worth, TX. College of liberal arts; coeducational; private control (Methodist); established 1890.

The fraternities occupy houses on their own land. The College provides space for sorority meetings and activities.

NIC MEN'S
1973 Lambda Chi Alpha
1973 Sigma Phi Epsilon

NPC WOMEN'S
1972 Phi Mu
1973 Gamma Phi Beta
1975 Alpha Xi Delta

NPHC WOMEN'S
1979 Alpha Kappa Alpha

PROFESSIONAL
1950 Sigma Alpha Iota

ACHS HONORS
1922 Alpha Chi
1956 Sigma Tau Delta
1979 Phi Alpha Theta
1979 Psi Chi
1980 Alpha Lambda Delta
1989 Pi Gamma Mu

OTHER HONORS
       National Order of Omega

SERVICE
1963 Alpha Phi Omega
1967 Gamma Sigma Sigma

RECOGNITION
1941 Alpha Psi Omega
1954 Kappa Pi
1969 Society for Collegiate
       Journalists—Pi Delta
       Epsilon-Alpha Phi Gamma
       (P)

INACTIVE
1947–87 Phi Mu Alpha—
       Sinfonia
1968–70 Sigma Delta Pi
1973–82 Pi Kappa Alpha

TEXAS WOMAN'S UNIVERSITY   Denton, TX. University for women; state control; established 1901.

NPC WOMEN'S
1984 Alpha Omicron Pi
1985 Alpha Gamma Delta

NPHC WOMEN'S
1976 Alpha Kappa Alpha
1979 Sigma Gamma Rho

PROFESSIONAL
1945 Zeta Phi Eta
1947 Sigma Alpha Iota

OTHER PROFESSIONAL
1932 Women in Communications
1938 Phi Upsilon Omicron
1947 Kappa Alpha Mu
1950 Pi Lambda Theta
1953 Alpha Beta Alpha

ACHS HONORS
       Omicron Delta Epsilon
1922 Alpha Chi
1933 Alpha Lambda Delta

1936 Alpha Kappa Delta
1945 Sigma Tau Delta
1947 Kappa Mu Epsilon
1955 Phi Sigma Iota
1960 Phi Alpha Theta
1970 Psi Chi
1970 Sigma Theta Tau
1972 Mortar Board
1976 Beta Phi Mu
1981 Phi Kappa Phi
1982 Pi Sigma Alpha

OTHER HONORS
1940 Delta Phi Delta

RECOGNITION
1946 Beta Beta Beta
1975 Sigma Phi Alpha

INACTIVE
1936–50 National Collegiate
       Players

THIEL COLLEGE Greenville, PA. Founded 1870. Christian institution of higher education open to qualified students, men and women, regardless of race or creed; liberal education in accordance with the Christian faith.

Men's groups occupy fraternity houses on a yearly lease basis. Sorority members are required to live in residence halls.

NIC MEN'S
1915 Delta Sigma Phi
1925 Lambda Chi Alpha
1948 Sigma Phi Epsilon
1959 Alpha Chi Rho

NPC WOMEN'S
1950 Chi Omega
1952 Sigma Kappa
1959 Alpha Xi Delta
1961 Alpha Gamma Delta
1964 Zeta Tau Alpha

ACHS HONORS
1956 Phi Alpha Theta
1959 Lambda Sigma Society
1962 Sigma Delta Pi

1971 Sigma Pi Sigma
1972 Pi Delta Phi
1973 Psi Chi
1979 Pi Sigma Alpha

RECOGNITION
1927 Beta Beta Beta
1938 Alpha Psi Omega
1953 Society for Collegiate Journalists—Pi Delta Epsilon-Alpha Phi Gamma (P)
1959 Delta Phi Alpha

INACTIVE
1872–73 Phi Gamma Delta

THOMAS COLLEGE Waterville, ME. Private control. Founded in 1894. Four-year; coeducational; professional institution.

Freshmen must live on campus. Co-ed dormitories.

OTHER PROFESSIONAL
1960 Kappa Delta Phi (C)

ACHS HONORS
1976 Alpha Chi

THOMAS MORE COLLEGE Crestview Hills, KY. Liberal arts college; private control, Catholic Diocese of Northern Kentucky. Established 1921 as Villa Madonna College.

NIC MEN'S
1966 Alpha Delta Gamma

NPC WOMEN'S
1986 Alpha Omicron Pi

ACHS HONORS
1966 Phi Alpha Theta

1970 Sigma Pi Sigma
1988 Psi Chi

INACTIVE
1968–74 Theta Phi Alpha

TIFT COLLEGE Forsyth, GA.

ACHS HONORS
1975 Alpha Chi

INACTIVE
1969–87 Alpha Lambda Delta

UNIVERSITY OF TOLEDO Toledo, OH. Established 1872; became a state university July 1, 1967; coeducational; six undergraduate colleges; graduate division and junior college.

The fraternities own their own land and homes. The sororities occupy off-campus housing.

NIC MEN'S
1937 Alpha Sigma Phi
1942 Kappa Alpha Psi (A)
1950 Phi Kappa Psi
1950 Sigma Phi Epsilon
1950 Tau Kappa Epsilon
1950 Theta Chi
1951 Pi Kappa Phi
1953 Sigma Alpha Epsilon
1955 Pi Kappa Alpha
1961 Sigma Alpha Mu
1971 Triangle
1984 Kappa Delta Rho

NPHC MEN'S
Phi Beta Sigma
1954 Alpha Phi Alpha

NPC WOMEN'S
1944 Alpha Omicron Pi
1944 Chi Omega
1944 Delta Delta Delta
1945 Alpha Chi Omega
1945 Pi Beta Phi
1946 Kappa Delta

NPHC WOMEN'S
1928 Alpha Kappa Alpha
1938 Delta Sigma Theta (B)

PROFESSIONAL
1905 Mu Phi Epsilon
1925 Kappa Psi
1941 Delta Theta Phi
1951 Alpha Kappa Psi
1956 Lambda Kappa Sigma
1960 Phi Alpha Delta
1984 Rho Pi Phi

OTHER PROFESSIONAL
1950 Alpha Zeta Omega
1956 Kappa Beta Pi
1965 Pi Lambda Theta
1966 Beta Alpha Psi
1970 Sigma Delta Chi

ACHS HONORS
Omicron Delta Epsilon
1924 Pi Gamma Mu
1945 Phi Alpha Theta
1946 Kappa Delta Pi
1946 Sigma Delta Pi
1947 Alpha Epsilon Delta

1952 Phi Kappa Phi
1954 Tau Beta Pi
1955 Beta Gamma Sigma
1955 Rho Chi
1956 Pi Delta Phi
1961 Phi Eta Sigma
1963 Eta Kappa Nu
1964 Alpha Kappa Delta
1966 Psi Chi
1969 Sigma Pi Sigma
1971 Alpha Pi Mu
1974 Pi Tau Sigma
1975 Alpha Lambda Delta
1981 Gamma Theta Upsilon
1982 Pi Sigma Alpha
1983 Mortar Board

OTHER HONORS
National Order of Omega
1936 Pi Mu Epsilon
1951 National Collegiate Players
1976 Sigma Xi

SERVICE
1948 Alpha Phi Omega

RECOGNITION
1923 Society for Collegiate Journalists—Pi Delta Epsilon-Alpha Phi Gamma (A)
1927 Society for Collegiate Journalists—Pi Delta Epsilon-Alpha Phi Gamma (A)
1950 Scabbard and Blade (9)
1952 Blue Key

INACTIVE
1946–81 Zeta Tau Alpha
1949–73 Beta Beta Beta
1950–73 Alpha Epsilon Pi
1964–76 Sigma Delta Tau
1970–73 Phi Mu Alpha—Sinfonia
1974–77 Phi Mu Delta

COLONIES
Beta Theta Pi
Theta Tau

UNIVERSITY OF TORONTO Toronto, ON. Founded 1843.

The administration permits the fraternities to look after their own housing requirments.

NIC MEN'S
1879 Zeta Psi
1892 Kappa Alpha Society
1893 Alpha Delta Phi
1895 Phi Kappa Sigma
1898 Delta Kappa Epsilon
1899 Delta Upsilon
1906 Beta Theta Pi
1906 Phi Delta Theta
1912 Theta Delta Chi
1920 Psi Upsilon
1923 Phi Gamma Delta
1926 Delta Tau Delta
1927 Lambda Chi Alpha
1949 Sigma Nu
1988 Alpha Epsilon Pi

NPC WOMEN'S
1906 Alpha Phi
1908 Pi Beta Phi
1911 Kappa Kappa Gamma
1919 Alpha Gamma Delta
1919 Gamma Phi Beta
1930 Alpha Omicron Pi
1930 Delta Delta Delta

PROFESSIONAL
1921 Alpha Omega
1926 Rho Pi Phi
1987 Lambda Kappa Sigma

OTHER PROFESSIONAL
1924 Phi Delta Epsilon

OTHER HONORS
1906 Alpha Omega Alpha
1950 Omicron Kappa Upsilon

INACTIVE
1887–41 Kappa Alpha Theta
1897–75 Delta Chi
1905–61 Alpha Kappa Kappa
1913–29 Sigma Delta Chi
1913–76 Delta Gamma
1920–40 Phi Beta Pi and Theta
          Kappa Psi (B)
1920–72 Sigma Alpha Mu
1922   Phi Chi

1922–42 Phi Rho Sigma
1922–89 Pi Lambda Phi
1924–58 Delta Phi Epsilon
1924–87 Kappa Sigma
1927–55 Alpha Epsilon Phi
1929–43 Alpha Delta Pi
1930–40 Tau Epsilon Rho
1930–53 Alpha Chi Omega
1932–41 Pi Gamma Mu
1951–63 Delta Sigma Phi

COLONIES
       Sigma Pi

TOUGALOO COLLEGE Tougaloo, MS. College of liberal arts; coeducational; private control; established 1869.

NIC MEN'S
1949 Kappa Alpha Psi (A)

NPHC MEN'S
      Phi Beta Sigma
1948 Omega Psi Phi

NPHC WOMEN'S
      Zeta Phi Beta

1949 Alpha Kappa Alpha
1980 Sigma Gamma Rho

ACHS HONORS
1954 Alpha Kappa Mu
1982 Alpha Lambda Delta

SERVICE
1978 Alpha Phi Omega

TOWSON STATE UNIVERSITY Baltimore, MD. Teachers and liberal arts college; graduate; coeducational; state control; established 1865.

NIC MEN'S
1979 Phi Kappa Sigma
1980 Sigma Alpha Mu
1981 Sigma Alpha Epsilon
1982 Kappa Alpha Psi (A)
1984 Lambda Chi Alpha
1985 Alpha Chi Rho
1985 Kappa Sigma
1985 Phi Sigma Kappa
1985 Pi Lambda Phi
1989 Delta Sigma Phi
1991 Pi Kappa Phi

NPHC MEN'S
      Phi Beta Sigma

NPC WOMEN'S
1977 Phi Sigma Sigma
1979 Alpha Gamma Delta
1981 Zeta Tau Alpha
1982 Delta Phi Epsilon
1986 Alpha Omicron Pi
1990 Alpha Phi
1990 Alpha Xi Delta

NPHC WOMEN'S
1975 Delta Sigma Theta (B)
1977 Alpha Kappa Alpha

1977 Sigma Gamma Rho

OTHER PROFESSIONAL
1977 Alpha Epsilon Rho

ACHS HONORS
1954 Gamma Theta Upsilon
1961 Phi Alpha Theta
1966 Psi Chi
1968 Sigma Delta Pi
1973 Lambda Iota Tau
1975 Sigma Pi Sigma
1987 Omicron Delta Kappa

SERVICE
1950 Alpha Phi Omega

RECOGNITION
1966 Pi Kappa Delta
1968 Beta Beta Beta

INACTIVE
1967–76 Phi Mu Alpha—
          Sinfonia
1979–85 Sigma Phi Epsilon
1985–89 Tau Kappa Epsilon

COLONIES
       Sigma Pi

TRANSYLVANIA UNIVERSITY Lexington, KY. Four-year private liberal arts, coeducational. Founded 1780, oldest college west of the Allegheny Mountains, and one of the oldest to be founded in the United States.

Each of the fraternities and sororities has a leased chapter room for meetings and social use in the residence halls.

NIC MEN'S
1888 Pi Kappa Alpha
1891 Kappa Alpha Order
1919 Phi Kappa Tau
1941 Delta Sigma Phi

NPC WOMEN'S
1899 Chi Omega
1908 Delta Delta Delta
1939 Phi Mu
1987 Alpha Omicron Pi

ACHS HONORS
      Omicron Delta Epsilon
1967 Phi Alpha Theta
1968 Sigma Delta Pi
1977 Omicron Delta Kappa
1979 Psi Chi

OTHER HONORS
      National Order of Omega

INACTIVE
1842–47 Beta Theta Pi
1860–62 Phi Gamma Delta
1865–66 Phi Kappa Psi
1894–01 Kappa Sigma
1948–72 Phi Beta
1954–54 Delta Zeta
1966–85 Sigma Kappa
1980–83 Phi Mu Alpha—
          Sinfonia

COLONIES
1989 Sigma Pi Sigma

TRENTON STATE COLLEGE Trenton, NJ. Multipurpose institution; coeducational; state control; established as New Jersey Normal and Model Schools 1855; master's degree.

NIC MEN'S
1974 Kappa Alpha Psi (A)
1978 Alpha Chi Rho
1984 Alpha Phi Delta
1986 Theta Chi
1988 Phi Kappa Tau
1990 Phi Kappa Psi

NPHC MEN'S
      Phi Beta Sigma
1974 Alpha Phi Alpha

NPC WOMEN'S
1977 Delta Zeta
1981 Zeta Tau Alpha
1988 Theta Phi Alpha

NPHC WOMEN'S
      Zeta Phi Beta
1971 Alpha Kappa Alpha
1972 Delta Sigma Theta (B)
1990 Sigma Gamma Rho

PROFESSIONAL
1964 Delta Omicron
1964 Delta Psi Kappa
1976 Phi Chi Theta

OTHER PROFESSIONAL
1924 Phi Epsilon Kappa
1976 Delta Pi Epsilon

ACHS HONORS
      Omicron Delta Epsilon
1931 Kappa Delta Pi
1934 Pi Omega Pi
1970 Psi Chi
1973 Phi Alpha Theta
1974 Sigma Pi Sigma
1977 Delta Mu Delta
1977 Gamma Theta Upsilon
1978 Phi Kappa Phi
1982 Pi Sigma Alpha

RECOGNITION
1975 Pi Kappa Delta
1976 Blue Key

INACTIVE
1962–80 Phi Mu Alpha—
          Sinfonia
1974–89 Zeta Beta Tau

COLONIES
       Phi Sigma Sigma

TRINITY COLLEGE Hartford, CT. Connecticut's second oldest college; founded as Washington College 1823 by the Episcopal Church; name changed to Trinity in 1845. College of liberal arts; coeducational; nonsectarian; private control.

Some of the fraternities own their own land and homes; others occupy space in the dormitories.

NIC MEN'S
1850 Delta Psi
1877 Alpha Delta Phi
1880 Psi Upsilon
1895 Alpha Chi Rho
1917 Delta Phi
1953 Pi Kappa Alpha
1966 Phi Mu Delta

NPC WOMEN'S
1982 Kappa Kappa Gamma

ACHS HONORS
1936 Pi Gamma Mu
1959 Psi Chi

RECOGNITION
1958 Delta Phi Alpha

INACTIVE
1870–76 Delta Upsilon
1879–90 Delta Kappa Epsilon
1892–99 Sigma Alpha Epsilon
1893–22 Phi Gamma Delta
1949–70 Theta Xi
1949–77 Sigma Pi Sigma
1956–70 Phi Kappa Psi
1976–88 Phi Mu Alpha—
          Sinfonia

TRINITY COLLEGE Washington, DC.

ACHS HONORS
1962 Pi Delta Phi

OTHER HONORS
1971 Phi Beta Kappa

RECOGNITION
1952 Alpha Psi Omega

INACTIVE
1951–68 Pi Gamma Mu
1966–77 Sigma Pi Sigma

TRINITY UNIVERSITY San Antonio, TX. College of liberal arts; coeducational; private control; sponsored by United Presbyterian Church. Established in 1869 at Tehuacana, and moved to San Antonio in 1942.

ACHS HONORS
        Omicron Delta Epsilon
1922 Alpha Chi
1935 Sigma Tau Delta
1955 Alpha Lambda Delta
1965 Pi Delta Phi
1966 Psi Chi
1966 Sigma Delta Pi
1966 Sigma Pi Sigma
1969 Kappa Delta Pi
1973 Mortar Board
1984 Pi Sigma Alpha

OTHER HONORS
1974 Phi Beta Kappa

SERVICE
1947 Alpha Phi Omega

RECOGNITION
1926 Blue Key
1930 Alpha Psi Omega
1968 Sigma Iota Epsilon

INACTIVE
1873–81 Beta Theta Pi
1878–83 Phi Delta Theta
1880–81 Delta Gamma
1909–83 Delta Sigma Phi
1930–38 Pi Gamma Mu
1945–57 Kappa Pi Sigma

TRI-STATE UNIVERSITY Angola, IN. Founded 1884. B.S. degrees in five fields of engineering, three fields of business, and in education; coeducational. Private control.

The fraternities own their own land and homes or lease from the University.

NIC MEN'S
1935 Alpha Sigma Phi
1947 Tau Kappa Epsilon
1966 Kappa Sigma
1967 Phi Kappa Theta
1968 Sigma Phi Epsilon
1969 Delta Chi

PROFESSIONAL
1947 Sigma Phi Delta
1969 Alpha Kappa Psi

ACHS HONORS
1972 Pi Tau Sigma
1973 Chi Epsilon
1975 Eta Kappa Nu
1975 Tau Beta Pi
1977 Delta Mu Delta

1980 Omega Chi Epsilon
1981 Pi Sigma Alpha
1983 Phi Eta Sigma

RECOGNITION
1965 Society for Collegiate
        Journalists—Pi Delta
        Epsilon-Alpha Phi Gamma
        (A)

INACTIVE
1921–66 Sigma Mu Sigma
1967–79 Acacia
1977–83 Sigma Kappa

COLONIES
1987 Triangle
1990 Delta Upsilon

TROY STATE UNIVERSITY Troy, AL. Four-year liberal arts university; founded 1887; coeducational; state-supported. One of three state university systems in Alabama.

Some fraternities own homes and land; others lease from the university. Some fraternity houses directly on campus. Sororities are housed in a Panhellenic residence hall with chapter rooms leased from the university.

NIC MEN'S
1966 Delta Chi
1966 Pi Kappa Phi
1967 Tau Kappa Epsilon
1971 Sigma Pi
1975 Lambda Chi Alpha
1976 Kappa Alpha Psi (A)
1977 Sigma Chi
1980 Sigma Alpha Epsilon

NPC WOMEN'S
1966 Kappa Delta
1966 Phi Mu
1967 Alpha Delta Pi
1971 Alpha Gamma Delta
1977 Chi Omega

NPHC WOMEN'S
1976 Delta Sigma Theta (B)
1978 Alpha Kappa Alpha

PROFESSIONAL
1960 Phi Mu Alpha—Sinfonia
1963 Sigma Alpha Iota
1968 Delta Sigma Pi
1974 Phi Gamma Nu
1974 Tau Beta Sigma

OTHER PROFESSIONAL
1976 Sigma Delta Chi

ACHS HONORS
        Omicron Delta Epsilon
1964 Phi Alpha Theta
1971 Phi Kappa Phi
1972 Sigma Tau Delta
1973 Omicron Delta Kappa
1974 Alpha Lambda Delta
1974 Phi Eta Sigma
1976 Psi Chi
1979 Mortar Board

SERVICE
1961 Alpha Phi Omega

RECOGNITION
1961 Lambda Tau
1967 Kappa Pi
1974 Beta Beta Beta
1976 Pi Kappa Delta

INACTIVE
1861–65 Delta Kappa Epsilon
1966–85 Theta Chi
1976–86 Delta Kappa Epsilon

TUFTS UNIVERSITY Medford, MA. University; college of liberal arts for men; Jackson College for women; other schools coeducational; private control; chartered 1852 by members of the Universalist denomination. The School of Dental Medicine (established 1868 as Boston Dental College) and School of Medicine (established 1893 as part of Tufts College) shares the Tufts-New England Medical Center in Boston.

Sigma Nu, Phi Sigma Kappa, and Theta Chi lease college-owned houses. The other fraternities own their own houses and property. Administration requires sorority members to occupy residence halls.

NIC MEN'S
1855 Zeta Psi
1856 Theta Delta Chi
1886 Delta Upsilon
1889 Delta Tau Delta
1916 Zeta Beta Tau
1940 Alpha Epsilon Pi
1950 Sigma Nu
1957 Theta Chi
1981 Psi Upsilon
1985 Sigma Phi Epsilon

NPC WOMEN'S
1908 Alpha Omicron Pi
1910 Chi Omega
1978 Alpha Phi

NPHC WOMEN'S
1916 Alpha Kappa Alpha

PROFESSIONAL
1911 Alpha Omega

OTHER PROFESSIONAL
1918 Phi Delta Epsilon
1920 Phi Lambda Kappa

ACHS HONORS
        Omicron Delta Epsilon
1927 Tau Beta Pi
1950 Psi Chi
1952 Alpha Kappa Delta

1955 Delta Sigma Rho-Tau
        Kappa Alpha
1964 Eta Kappa Nu

OTHER HONORS
        National Order of Omega
1892 Phi Beta Kappa
1940 Alpha Omega Alpha
1943 Sigma Xi
1944 Omicron Kappa Upsilon

RECOGNITION
        Arnold Air Society (A-1)

INACTIVE
1893–74 Alpha Tau Omega
1895–65 Psi Omega
1897   Delta Sigma Delta
1913   Phi Chi
1913–80 Sigma Kappa
1920–28 Phi Beta Pi and Theta
        Kappa Psi (B)
1924–31 Pi Lambda Phi
1934–41 Phi Mu Delta
1947–57 Sigma Pi Sigma
1954–52 Xi Psi Phi
1956–70 Delta Zeta
1957–76 Phi Sigma Kappa

COLONIES
1918 Phi Sigma Sigma

TULANE UNIVERSITY
New Orleans, LA. Founded as the Medical College of Louisiana 1834; later the University of Louisiana; name changed to the Tulane University of Louisiana 1884. Undergraduate college for men and women; professional schools; graduate school privately endowed; nonsectarian. Newcome College for women; professional schools graduate school; privately endowed; nonsectarian. Newcome College for women is a coordinate college.

The fraternities and sororities own their own land and homes.

NIC MEN'S
1858 Phi Kappa Sigma
1878 Pi Kappa Alpha
1882 Kappa Alpha Order
1886 Sigma Chi
1887 Alpha Tau Omega
1888 Sigma Nu
1889 Kappa Sigma
1897 Sigma Alpha Epsilon
1898 Delta Kappa Epsilon
1908 Beta Theta Pi
1909 Zeta Beta Tau
1920 Sigma Alpha Mu
1929 Sigma Phi Epsilon
1951 Alpha Epsilon Pi
1959 Tau Epsilon Phi
1964 Alpha Sigma Phi
1977 Zeta Psi
1982 Phi Gamma Delta

NPHC MEN'S
Phi Beta Sigma

NPC WOMEN'S
1891 Pi Beta Phi
1898 Alpha Omicron Pi
1899 Chi Omega
1904 Kappa Kappa Gamma
1906 Phi Mu
1914 Kappa Alpha Theta
1916 Alpha Epsilon Phi

PROFESSIONAL
1903 Phi Chi
1911 Phi Delta Phi
1924 Phi Alpha Delta
1969 Delta Theta Phi

OTHER PROFESSIONAL
1918 Phi Delta Epsilon
1924 Phi Lambda Kappa
1961 Beta Alpha Psi

ACHS HONORS
Omicron Delta Epsilon
1926 Beta Gamma Sigma
1932 Omicron Delta Kappa
1934 Psi Chi
1936 Tau Beta Pi
1940 Kappa Delta Pi
1947 Phi Sigma Iota
1949 Phi Alpha Theta
1949 Pi Sigma Alpha
1949 Tau Sigma Delta
1950 Sigma Pi Sigma
1953 Alpha Kappa Delta
1954 Phi Eta Sigma

1958 Alpha Epsilon Delta
1958 Mortar Board
1960 Delta Sigma Rho-Tau Kappa Alpha
1970 Pi Tau Sigma
1972 Alpha Lambda Delta
1973 Phi Sigma Tau
1976 Eta Kappa Nu
1978 Omega Chi Epsilon

OTHER HONORS
National Order of Omega
1909 Phi Beta Kappa
1914 Alpha Omega Alpha
1931 Order of the Coif
1934 Sigma Xi
1941 National Collegiate Players
1950 Sigma Gamma Epsilon
1961 Pi Mu Epsilon

SERVICE
1941 Alpha Phi Omega

RECOGNITION
Angel Flight
Arnold Air Society (C-2)
1933 Sigma Delta Psi
1936 Eta Sigma Phi
1942 Beta Beta Beta
1942 Scabbard and Blade (8)
1961 Delta Phi Alpha

INACTIVE
1889–70 Phi Delta Theta
1889–90 Delta Tau Delta
1903–72 Alpha Kappa Kappa
1906–77 Alpha Delta Pi
1907–29 Phi Beta Pi and Theta Kappa Psi (a)
1908   Phi Beta Pi and Theta Kappa Psi (B)
1916–63 Delta Sigma Phi
1918   Xi Psi Phi
1918–50 Phi Rho Sigma
1920–73 Sigma Pi
1923–35 Pi Kappa Phi
1925–33 Theta Alpha Phi
1927–52 Zeta Tau Alpha
1928–61 Delta Zeta
1928–71 Alpha Chi Sigma
1929   Sigma Phi Delta
1930   Kappa Beta Pi
1934–46 Phi Sigma Sigma
1949–63 Delta Sigma Pi
1956–65 Phi Chi Theta

UNIVERSITY OF TULSA
Tulsa, OK. University; coeducational; private control (Presbyterian). Established as Henry Kendall College 1894 at Muskogee, moved to Tulsa 1907; name changed to present 1920.

The fraternities own houses which are on college property. The sororities own lodges on college property which are used for meetings and entertainment and where there is a housemother in residence.

NIC MEN'S
1936 Pi Kappa Alpha
1937 Kappa Alpha Order
1937 Lambda Chi Alpha
1948 Kappa Sigma
1951 Sigma Chi
1951 Sigma Nu

NPC WOMEN'S
1929 Chi Omega
1931 Delta Delta Delta
1937 Kappa Delta
1946 Kappa Kappa Gamma
1947 Delta Gamma
1951 Kappa Alpha Theta

NPHC WOMEN'S
Zeta Phi Beta
1970 Delta Sigma Theta (B)

PROFESSIONAL
1924 Sigma Alpha Iota
1940 Delta Theta Phi
1948 Delta Sigma Pi
1954 Phi Alpha Delta
1959 Phi Delta Phi
1987 Phi Alpha Delta

OTHER PROFESSIONAL
1959 Alpha Epsilon Rho
1960 Sigma Delta Chi

ACHS HONORS
1929 Pi Gamma Mu
1931 Kappa Delta Pi
1946 Psi Chi
1948 Phi Eta Sigma
1949 Alpha Kappa Delta

1950 Mortar Board
1952 Phi Alpha Theta
1961 Omicron Delta Kappa
1963 Sigma Pi Sigma
1964 Beta Gamma Sigma
1964 Kappa Mu Epsilon
1965 Pi Kappa Lambda
1971 Tau Beta Pi
1973 Eta Kappa Nu
1974 Pi Sigma Alpha
1990 Phi Kappa Phi

OTHER HONORS
National Order of Omega

SERVICE
1939 Alpha Phi Omega

RECOGNITION
Angel Flight
Arnold Air Society (G-1)
1920 Theta Alpha Phi
1944 Lambda Tau
1951 Scabbard and Blade (10)
1962 Sigma Iota Epsilon

INACTIVE
1921–26 Pi Kappa Phi
1927–74 Phi Mu Alpha— Sinfonia
1939–89 Phi Mu
1944–71 Alpha Tau Omega
1946–59 Sigma Phi Epsilon
1953   Sigma Gamma Epsilon
1954–72 Alpha Kappa Psi
1974–86 Alpha Kappa Alpha

TUSCULUM COLLEGE
Greeneville, TN. College of liberal arts; coeducational; private control (United Presbyterian); chartered 1794.

ACHS HONORS
1960 Alpha Chi

SERVICE
1967 Alpha Phi Omega

RECOGNITION
1949 Alpha Psi Omega

INACTIVE
1946–69 Alpha Epsilon Delta
1962–71 Pi Gamma Mu

TUSKEGEE INSTITUTE
Tuskegee Institute, AL. Founded by Booker T. Washington in 1881; coeducational; technical, professional, and liberal arts college; graduate training on the master's level; private control; nonsectarian.

The fraternities and sororities do not have houses, but do have a special building in which they hold their meetings.

NIC MEN'S
1948 Kappa Alpha Psi (A)

NPHC MEN'S
    Phi Beta Sigma
1947 Omega Psi Phi
1948 Alpha Phi Alpha

NPHC WOMEN'S
1948 Alpha Kappa Alpha
1948 Delta Sigma Theta (B)
1973 Sigma Gamma Rho

PROFESSIONAL
1974 Kappa Kappa Psi
1976 Tau Beta Sigma

ACHS HONORS
1937 Alpha Kappa Mu
1944 Beta Kappa Chi

1967 Kappa Delta Pi
1967 Lambda Iota Tau
1969 Eta Kappa Nu
1970 Pi Tau Sigma
1972 Delta Mu Delta
1977 Kappa Omicron Nu

OTHER HONORS
1972 Pi Mu Epsilon
1974 Sigma Xi

SERVICE
1965 Alpha Phi Omega

RECOGNITION
    Angel Flight
    Arnold Air Society (C-1)
1964 Scabbard and Blade (15)
1967 Phi Zeta

TYLER JUNIOR COLLEGE Tyler, TX. Two-year college, terminal occupational below bachelor's; co-educational; state-local control. Established 1926.

NPHC WOMEN'S
1939 Alpha Kappa Alpha

PROFESSIONAL
1973 Kappa Kappa Psi
1973 Tau Beta Sigma

RECOGNITION
1976 Sigma Phi Alpha

INACTIVE
1971–89 Delta Upsilon
1972–88 Sigma Phi Epsilon
1973–81 Alpha Tau Omega
1976–86 Pi Kappa Alpha

UNION COLLEGE Barbourville, KY. College of liberal arts; coeducational; private control (Methodist); established 1879.

NIC MEN'S
1909 Zeta Beta Tau

ACHS HONORS
1926 Eta Kappa Nu
1979 Psi Chi

OTHER HONORS
    National Order of Omega

SERVICE
1948 Alpha Phi Omega

RECOGNITION
1936 Alpha Psi Omega
1960 Kappa Pi

INACTIVE
1955–66 Pi Gamma Mu
1961–80 Lambda Sigma Society
1965–83 Phi Mu Alpha—
    Sinfonia
1966–71 Sigma Alpha Iota

UNION COLLEGE Schenectady, NY. University; chartered as college 1795; coeducational; private control; nonsectarian.

Four fraternities own houses situated on college land; fourteen fraternities and sororities occupy college-owned houses on rental basis.

NIC MEN'S
1825 Kappa Alpha Society
1827 Delta Phi
1827 Sigma Phi Society
1833 Psi Upsilon
1838 Delta Upsilon
1841 Chi Psi
1847 Theta Delta Chi
1859 Alpha Delta Phi
1881 Beta Theta Pi
1883 Phi Delta Theta
1888 Phi Sigma Kappa
1893 Phi Gamma Delta
1901 Delta Chi
1921 Alpha Phi Delta

1923 Sigma Chi
1929 Kappa Sigma
1986 Alpha Epsilon Pi

NPC WOMEN'S
1977 Sigma Delta Tau
1978 Delta Gamma
1981 Delta Delta Delta
1986 Gamma Phi Beta

ACHS HONORS
    Omicron Delta Epsilon
1964 Tau Beta Pi
1974 Pi Sigma Alpha
1978 Phi Sigma Iota

SERVICE
1964 Alpha Phi Omega

INACTIVE
1856–69 Delta Kappa Epsilon
1856–71 Zeta Psi

1897–00 Pi Lambda Phi
1915–25 Zeta Beta Tau
1915–40 Lambda Chi Alpha
1926–37 Pi Gamma Mu

Albany Law School Albany, NY.

PROFESSIONAL
1979 Phi Alpha Delta

INACTIVE
1892–94 Delta Chi

UNION UNIVERSITY Jackson, TN. College of liberal arts; coeducational; private control (Tennessee Baptist Convention). Established as Jackson Academy, 1825; named Southwestern Baptist University in 1875; became Union University 1907.

NIC MEN'S
1857 Sigma Alpha Epsilon
1894 Alpha Tau Omega
1964 Lambda Chi Alpha

NPC WOMEN'S
1924 Chi Omega
1990 Kappa Delta

PROFESSIONAL
1960 Phi Mu Alpha—Sinfonia
1960 Sigma Alpha Iota

ACHS HONORS
1953 Phi Alpha Theta

1962 Alpha Chi
1965 Kappa Mu Epsilon
1976 Pi Gamma Mu

RECOGNITION
1928 Alpha Psi Omega
1976 Kappa Pi

INACTIVE
1851–73 Phi Gamma Delta
1861–62 Delta Kappa Epsilon
1867–78 Alpha Tau Omega
1892–08 Kappa Sigma
1909–24 Sigma Sigma Sigma

UNITED STATES NAVAL ACADEMY Annapolis, MD. Founded 1845 by the Honorable George Bancroft, then Secretary of the Navy. Fully accredited undergraduate college of the U.S. Navy.

The Brigade of Midshipmen is housed in the dormitory, Bancroft Hall, which along with the land and other buildings is owned by the U.S. Government.

ACHS HONORS
    Omicron Delta Epsilon
1966 Sigma Pi Sigma
1972 Sigma Tau Delta
1977 Phi Kappa Phi
1980 Phi Alpha Theta
1980 Pi Sigma Alpha

1984 Tau Beta Pi
1988 Phi Sigma Iota

INACTIVE
1863–63 Beta Theta Pi
1874–74 Zeta Psi

UPPER IOWA UNIVERSITY Fayette, IA. College of liberal arts; coeducational; private control; nonsectarian. Chartered 1850; established 1857.

NIC MEN'S
1891 Sigma Nu

ACHS HONORS
1926 Sigma Tau Delta
1968 Phi Alpha Theta

SERVICE
1959 Alpha Phi Omega

RECOGNITION
1922 Pi Kappa Delta
1928 Alpha Psi Omega

INACTIVE
1970–82 Pi Gamma Mu
1971–85 Tau Kappa Epsilon
1974–84 Acacia

UPSALA COLLEGE East Orange, NJ. College of liberal arts; coeducational; private control (Lutheran Church in America); established 1893.

NPHC MEN'S
    Phi Beta Sigma

PROFESSIONAL
1963 Alpha Kappa Psi

ACHS HONORS
1943 Phi Alpha Theta
1952 Psi Chi

SERVICE
1929 Alpha Phi Omega
1956 Gamma Sigma Sigma

RECOGNITION
1937 Alpha Psi Omega

1941 Delta Phi Alpha
1951 Society for Collegiate
    Journalists—Pi Delta
    Epsilon-Alpha Phi Gamma
    (P)
1963 Beta Beta Beta

INACTIVE
1940–69 Kappa Mu Epsilon
1954–77 Sigma Pi Sigma
1966   Phi Gamma Nu
1974–86 Phi Chi Theta

URSINUS COLLEGE Collegeville, PA. College of liberal arts; coeducational; private control (United Church of Christ); chartered 1869.

ACHS HONORS
    Omicron Delta Epsilon
1925 Delta Sigma Rho-Tau
    Kappa Alpha
1950 Pi Gamma Mu
1967 Psi Chi
1981 Sigma Pi Sigma
1983 Phi Sigma Iota

1987 Kappa Mu Epsilon
1987 Phi Alpha Theta

SERVICE
1956 Alpha Phi Omega

RECOGNITION
1934 Alpha Psi Omega

UNIVERSITY OF UTAH Salt Lake City, UT. University; coeducational; state control. Chartered as University of Deseret 1850, became University of Utah 1892.

Fraternities and sororities own their own land and houses in an off-campus area interspersed with single family residents. Older homes are available at a price.

NIC MEN'S
1908 Sigma Chi
1912 Pi Kappa Alpha
1913 Beta Theta Pi
1914 Phi Delta Theta
1924 Sigma Nu
1928 Kappa Sigma
1949 Sigma Alpha Epsilon
1950 Sigma Phi Epsilon
1963 Phi Sigma Kappa
1988 Phi Gamma Delta

OTHER MEN'S
    Sigma Gamma Chi

NPC WOMEN'S
1914 Chi Omega
1929 Pi Beta Phi
1932 Delta Delta Delta
1932 Delta Gamma
1932 Kappa Kappa Gamma
1934 Alpha Chi Omega

OTHER WOMEN'S
    Lambda Delta Sigma

PROFESSIONAL
1915 Delta Theta Phi
1922 Alpha Kappa Psi
1926 Phi Alpha Delta
1947 Phi Delta Phi
1950 Mu Phi Epsilon
1951 Phi Delta Chi

OTHER PROFESSIONAL
1946 Alpha Epsilon Rho

1954 Sigma Delta Chi

ACHS HONORS
    Omicron Delta Epsilon
    Pi Alpha Alpha
1910 Delta Sigma Rho-Tau
    Kappa Alpha
1922 Phi Kappa Phi
1932 Phi Sigma
1933 Kappa Omicron Nu
1933 Mortar Board
1933 Tau Beta Pi
1936 Phi Eta Sigma
1939 Psi Chi
1946 Beta Gamma Sigma
1946 Phi Alpha Theta
1946 Pi Sigma Alpha
1948 Chi Epsilon
1948 Pi Tau Sigma
1948 Sigma Pi Sigma
1949 Gamma Theta Upsilon
1950 Alpha Epsilon Delta
1951 Kappa Tau Alpha
1955 Rho Chi
1958 Eta Kappa Nu
1966 Sigma Delta Pi
1967 Phi Sigma Iota
1967 Pi Delta Phi
1975 Lambda Iota Tau

OTHER HONORS
    National Order of Omega
1935 Phi Beta Kappa
1937 Sigma Xi
1949 Alpha Omega Alpha

1953 Order of the Coif
1960 Pi Mu Epsilon

SERVICE
1937 Intercollegiate Knights
1951 Alpha Phi Omega

RECOGNITION
    Angel Flight
    Arnold Air Society (H-1)

INACTIVE
1913   Phi Beta Pi and Theta
    Kappa Psi (a)
1919–51 Sigma Alpha Mu
1920–45 Phi Chi
1920–54 Theta Alpha Phi
1920–74 Theta Tau
1920–75 Delta Phi Kappa
1920–76 Sigma Pi
1922   Sigma Gamma Epsilon
1922–79 Delta Sigma Pi
1925–57 Alpha Chi Sigma

UTAH STATE UNIVERSITY Logan, UT. Founded 1888; land-grant institution; eight resident colleges; graduate school; one-branch college. Coeducational; nonsectarian.

The fraternities and sororities own their own land and homes.

NIC MEN'S
1925 Pi Kappa Alpha
1926 Sigma Chi
1936 Sigma Phi Epsilon
1938 Sigma Nu
1959 Alpha Gamma Rho
1968 Phi Gamma Delta

OTHER MEN'S
    Sigma Gamma Chi
1927 Delta Phi Kappa

NPHC MEN'S
1974 Alpha Phi Alpha

NPC WOMEN'S
1930 Chi Omega
1934 Alpha Chi Omega
1937 Kappa Delta

OTHER WOMEN'S
    Lambda Delta Sigma

PROFESSIONAL
1922 Alpha Kappa Psi

OTHER PROFESSIONAL
1923 Phi Upsilon Omicron
1930 Alpha Zeta
1949 Alpha Tau Alpha
1972 Delta Pi Epsilon
1975 Sigma Delta Chi

ACHS HONORS
    Omicron Delta Epsilon
1920 Phi Kappa Phi
1921 Delta Sigma Rho-Tau
    Kappa Alpha
1939 Alpha Epsilon Delta
1939 Xi Sigma Pi
1946 Pi Sigma Alpha
1948 Psi Chi
1952 Phi Alpha Theta
1953 Alpha Lambda Delta

1925–68 Phi Chi Theta
1927–74 Alpha Delta Pi
1928–40 Delta Zeta
1930–87 Phi Mu
1932–43 Phi Sigma Sigma
1933–82 Alpha Lambda Delta
1945   Zeta Phi Eta
1946–65 Alpha Phi
1947–77 Alpha Xi Delta
1948–65 Phi Rho Sigma
1949–53 Alpha Tau Omega
1950–89 Lambda Chi Alpha
1953–55 Pi Sigma Epsilon
1955–61 Zeta Beta Tau
1957   Scabbard and Blade
    (5)
1957–65 Alpha Tau Delta
1959–81 Kappa Epsilon
1965–88 Kappa Alpha Theta
1970–73 Kappa Kappa Lambda
1970–78 Tau Kappa Epsilon

1959 Sigma Pi Sigma
1966 Lambda Iota Tau
1970 Mortar Board
1974 Tau Beta Pi
1979 Sigma Lambda Alpha
1982 Gamma Theta Upsilon

OTHER HONORS
    National Order of Omega
1942 Sigma Xi
1950 Sigma Gamma Epsilon
1962 Pi Mu Epsilon

SERVICE
    The National Spurs
1924 Intercollegiate Knights

RECOGNITION
    Angel Flight
    Arnold Air Society (H-1)
1927 Theta Alpha Phi
1932 Blue Key
1936 Sigma Delta Psi

INACTIVE
1909–22 Gamma Sigma Delta
1922   Scabbard and Blade
    (4)
1934–52 Pi Gamma Mu
1939–89 Sigma Alpha Epsilon
1947–64 Kappa Sigma
1947–71 Sigma Kappa
1948–53 Phi Epsilon Kappa
1949–62 Sigma Pi
1950–53 National Block and
    Bridle Club
1959–70 Delta Sigma Phi
1959–74 Delta Delta Delta
1960–66 Theta Tau
1960–70 Alpha Omicron Pi
1961–76 Phi Eta Sigma

UTICA COLLEGE OF SYRACUSE UNIVERSITY
Utica, NY. Founded 1946.

The college is primarily composed of commuting students and/or local residents; hence there is not the need or demand for fraternity houses. There is adequate room on campus for fraternity houses but no specific plans are contemplated for their erection either by fraternities or by the college.

NIC MEN'S
1949 Alpha Phi Delta
1966 Alpha Chi Rho
1968 Tau Kappa Epsilon

1950 Phi Alpha Theta
1971 Psi Chi

NPHC MEN'S
Phi Beta Sigma
1975 Alpha Phi Alpha

SERVICE
1949 Alpha Phi Omega
1969 Gamma Sigma Sigma

NPC WOMEN'S
1990 Phi Sigma Sigma

NPHC WOMEN'S
1975 Alpha Kappa Alpha

INACTIVE
1956–78 Theta Xi
1957–72 Beta Beta Beta
1958–65 Sigma Pi Sigma
1961–79 Kappa Mu Epsilon
1967–72 Alpha Epsilon Pi

ACHS HONORS
Omicron Delta Epsilon

VALDOSTA STATE COLLEGE
Valdosta, GA. Began operation in 1913 as a woman's college, coeducational since 1950. Senior liberal arts, unit of the state university system.

Fraternity and sorority housing is being planned.

NIC MEN'S
1959 Pi Kappa Phi
1959 Tau Kappa Epsilon
1968 Delta Chi
1972 Kappa Alpha Order
1973 Sigma Alpha Epsilon
1983 Kappa Alpha Psi (A)
1987 Theta Xi

1972 Sigma Alpha Iota

ACHS HONORS
1958 Alpha Chi
1971 Omicron Delta Kappa
1973 Alpha Lambda Delta
1974 Phi Kappa Phi
1976 Pi Delta Phi
1978 Phi Alpha Theta
1978 Sigma Pi Sigma
1980 Pi Gamma Mu

NPHC MEN'S
Phi Beta Sigma

NPC WOMEN'S
1958 Alpha Delta Pi
1958 Kappa Delta
1965 Phi Mu
1971 Zeta Tau Alpha
1984 Chi Omega

OTHER HONORS
National Order of Omega

SERVICE
1967 Alpha Phi Omega

NPHC WOMEN'S
1971 Delta Sigma Theta (B)
1976 Alpha Kappa Alpha
1988 Sigma Gamma Rho

RECOGNITION
1958 Alpha Psi Omega

INACTIVE
1958–82 Alpha Xi Delta
1960–74 Sigma Phi Epsilon
1971–74 Delta Sigma Phi

PROFESSIONAL
1970 Phi Mu Alpha—Sinfonia

VALENCIA COMMUNITY COLLEGE
Orlando, FL. Two-year college of liberal arts and occupational studies; coeducational. Local control. Established 1967.

INACTIVE
1973–77 Pi Kappa Alpha

VALLEY CITY STATE COLLEGE
Valley City, ND. Teachers college; coeducational; state control. Chartered as State Normal School 1889; first instruction 1890.

NIC MEN'S
1974 Sigma Nu

1977 Phi Alpha Theta

ACHS HONORS
1930 Pi Omega Pi
1934 Gamma Theta Upsilon

INACTIVE
1972–87 Tau Kappa Epsilon
1975–84 Sigma Sigma Sigma

VALPARAISO UNIVERSITY
Valparaiso, IN. University; coeducational; private control (Lutheran Church-Missouri Synod); chartered 1859.

The fraternities own their own land and homes. Sororities occupy college-owned housing on a rental basis.

NIC MEN'S
1952 Theta Chi
1953 Phi Kappa Psi
1953 Pi Kappa Alpha
1954 Lambda Chi Alpha
1954 Phi Delta Theta
1956 Sigma Phi Epsilon
1960 Sigma Pi
1960 Sigma Tau Gamma
1964 Phi Sigma Kappa
1973 Delta Sigma Phi
1990 Sigma Chi

1963 Tau Beta Pi
1968 Kappa Delta Pi
1969 Mortar Board
1974 Alpha Epsilon Delta
1975 Sigma Delta Pi
1976 Kappa Omicron Nu
1976 Phi Alpha Theta
1977 Sigma Pi Sigma
1990 Pi Kappa Lambda

PROFESSIONAL
1947 Phi Alpha Delta
1949 Delta Theta Phi
1951 Sigma Alpha Iota
1961 Phi Mu Alpha—Sinfonia
1983 Delta Sigma Pi

OTHER HONORS
National Order of Omega

SERVICE
1948 Alpha Phi Omega

OTHER PROFESSIONAL
1916 Sigma Delta Kappa

RECOGNITION
1928 Alpha Psi Omega
1961 Society for Collegiate Journalists—Pi Delta Epsilon-Alpha Phi Gamma (P)

ACHS HONORS
Omicron Delta Epsilon
1950 Gamma Theta Upsilon
1953 Pi Sigma Alpha
1955 Alpha Lambda Delta

INACTIVE
1932–58 Pi Gamma Mu
1951–88 Tau Kappa Epsilon
1957 Gamma Sigma Sigma

VANDERBILT UNIVERSITY
Nashville, TN. University; coeducational; private control; nonsectarian; chartered 1872 as Central University of Methodist Episcopal Church, south; founded as Vanderbilt in 1873.

All but two fraternities lease their homes from the university.

NIC MEN'S
1847 Delta Kappa Epsilon
1857 Sigma Alpha Epsilon
1876 Phi Delta Theta
1877 Phi Kappa Sigma
1883 Kappa Alpha Order
1884 Beta Theta Pi
1886 Sigma Nu
1889 Alpha Tau Omega
1891 Sigma Chi
1893 Pi Kappa Alpha
1901 Phi Kappa Psi
1902 Phi Kappa Sigma
1918 Zeta Beta Tau

1921 Tau Delta Phi
1929 Alpha Epsilon Pi
1989 Kappa Alpha Psi (A)

NPHC MEN'S
1975 Alpha Phi Alpha

NPC WOMEN'S
1904 Kappa Alpha Theta
1911 Delta Delta Delta
1917 Alpha Omicron Pi
1924 Gamma Phi Beta
1940 Pi Beta Phi
1949 Kappa Delta
1954 Chi Omega

1973 Kappa Kappa Gamma
1978 Alpha Delta Pi
1982 Alpha Chi Omega

NPHC WOMEN'S
1972 Alpha Kappa Alpha

PROFESSIONAL
1907 Phi Delta Phi
1921 Phi Alpha Delta
1922 Delta Theta Phi
1958 Kappa Delta Epsilon
1981 Alpha Chi Sigma

OTHER PROFESSIONAL
1981 Sigma Nu Phi

ACHS HONORS
     Omicron Delta Epsilon
1909 Delta Sigma Rho-Tau
     Kappa Alpha
1934 Omicron Delta Kappa
1938 Phi Sigma Iota
1938 Sigma Delta Pi
1940 Mortar Board
1946 Tau Beta Pi
1950 Phi Eta Sigma
1950 Pi Sigma Alpha
1953 Sigma Theta Tau
1966 Eta Kappa Nu
1967 Chi Epsilon
1969 Alpha Lambda Delta
1971 Pi Tau Sigma
1976 Alpha Sigma Mu
1980 Sigma Pi Sigma
1981 Psi Chi
1984 Phi Alpha Theta

OTHER HONORS
1901 Phi Beta Kappa
1923 Alpha Omega Alpha
1944 Sigma Xi
1948 Order of the Coif

SERVICE
1950 Alpha Phi Omega

RECOGNITION
1923 Sigma Delta Psi
1928 Eta Sigma Phi
1930 Delta Phi Alpha
1953 Scabbard and Blade (10)

INACTIVE
1883–42 Chi Phi
1886–30 Delta Tau Delta
1896–26 Delta Sigma Delta
1903–54 Alpha Kappa Kappa
1905   Phi Chi
1905   Xi Psi Phi
1906–26 Psi Omega
1906–44 Phi Beta Pi and Theta
        Kappa Psi (a)
1907–19 Phi Beta Pi and Theta
        Kappa Psi (B)
1916–65 Omicron Kappa
        Upsilon
1922–27 Delta Sigma Pi
1922–28 Gamma Eta Gamma
1922–38 Lambda Chi Alpha
1925–65 Alpha Epsilon Phi
1926–41 Sigma Kappa
1949–60 Theta Chi
1952   Beta Beta Beta

VASSAR COLLEGE Poughkeepsie, NY. Founded by Matthew Vassar 1861, opened 1865; independent liberal arts college; coeducational; residential; nonsectarian.

ACHS HONORS
     Omicron Delta Epsilon

OTHER HONORS
1899 Phi Beta Kappa

RECOGNITION
1972 Beta Beta Beta

UNIVERSITY OF VERMONT Burlington, VT. Chartered 1791; university and land-grant college; coeducational; state control; joined with State Agricultural College 1865; legislature established new charter 1955 as state university for the purposes of higher education.

Fraternity and sorority chapters maintain ownership of house and property.

NIC MEN'S
1845 Sigma Phi Society
1879 Phi Delta Theta
1887 Alpha Tau Omega
1893 Kappa Sigma
1898 Sigma Nu
1918 Phi Mu Delta
1929 Sigma Alpha Epsilon
1950 Acacia
1950 Sigma Phi Epsilon
1954 Alpha Epsilon Pi
1961 Alpha Gamma Rho
1969 Phi Gamma Delta

NPC WOMEN'S
1881 Kappa Alpha Theta

1893 Delta Delta Delta
1898 Pi Beta Phi
1921 Alpha Chi Omega
1951 Alpha Delta Pi
1980 Kappa Kappa Gamma

PROFESSIONAL
1975 Phi Alpha Delta
1983 Delta Theta Phi
1991 Sigma Alpha

OTHER PROFESSIONAL
1905 Alpha Zeta
1927 Kappa Phi Kappa

ACHS HONORS
     Omicron Delta Epsilon

1912 Delta Sigma Rho-Tau
     Kappa Alpha
1924 Mortar Board
1925 Kappa Omicron Nu
1953 Kappa Delta Pi
1958 Tau Beta Pi
1970 Chi Epsilon
1975 Xi Sigma Pi
1983 Phi Alpha Theta
1983 Phi Eta Sigma
1985 Gamma Theta Upsilon

OTHER HONORS
     National Order of Omega
1848 Phi Beta Kappa
1946 Sigma Xi
1951 National Collegiate
     Players
1952 Alpha Omega Alpha

SERVICE
1990 Alpha Phi Omega

RECOGNITION
1928 Sigma Delta Psi

1961 Sigma Phi Alpha

INACTIVE
1850–54 Delta Upsilon
1889   Phi Chi
1894–32 Alpha Kappa Kappa
1915–47 Alpha Xi Delta
1922   Scabbard and Blade
         (3)
1926   Eta Sigma Phi
1926–37 Kappa Delta
1930–61 Phi Delta Epsilon
1932–42 Pi Gamma Mu
1938–69 Zeta Beta Tau
1939–54 Delta Phi Epsilon
1945–70 Alpha Epsilon Phi
1950–74 Gamma Phi Beta
1951–78 Alpha Lambda Delta
1951–85 Theta Chi

COLONIES
1852 Theta Delta Chi

VILLANOVA UNIVERSITY Villanova, PA. Coeducational university; private control (Roman Catholic); established 1842.

NIC MEN'S
1971 Delta Tau Delta
1971 Lambda Chi Alpha
1973 Delta Kappa Epsilon
1977 Sigma Phi Epsilon
1982 Alpha Phi Delta
1982 Pi Kappa Phi
1984 Pi Kappa Alpha
1984 Zeta Psi
1985 Sigma Pi
1990 Phi Gamma Delta

NPC WOMEN'S
1982 Delta Delta Delta
1982 Kappa Kappa Gamma
1983 Alpha Chi Omega
1983 Kappa Alpha Theta
1985 Alpha Omicron Pi
1986 Delta Gamma
1987 Alpha Phi
1990 Pi Beta Phi

PROFESSIONAL
1963 Pi Sigma Epsilon

ACHS HONORS
     Omicron Delta Epsilon
1953 Delta Epsilon Sigma
1958 Pi Tau Sigma
1961 Eta Kappa Nu
1961 Tau Beta Pi

1966 Sigma Theta Tau
1968 Alpha Epsilon Delta
1972 Pi Sigma Alpha
1973 Phi Alpha Theta
1973 Phi Sigma Tau
1974 Phi Kappa Phi
1976 Beta Gamma Sigma
1977 Sigma Pi Sigma
1978 Psi Chi
1978 Theta Alpha Kappa
1982 Chi Epsilon
1988 Gamma Theta Upsilon
1988 Omicron Delta Kappa

OTHER HONORS
     National Order of Omega
1961 Order of the Coif
1967 Pi Mu Epsilon

SERVICE
1967 Alpha Phi Omega

RECOGNITION
1949 Alpha Psi Omega

INACTIVE
1950   Kappa Phi Kappa
1967–80 Tau Kappa Epsilon
1969–77 Alpha Xi Delta
1970–74 Kappa Sigma

VINCENNES UNIVERSITY Vincennes, IN. Junior college; coeducational; incorporated 1806; state-supported.

NIC MEN'S
1897 Sigma Pi
1972 Lambda Chi Alpha
1972 Sigma Phi Epsilon

1974 Sigma Nu

NPHC MEN'S
     Phi Beta Sigma

UNIVERSITY OF VIRGINIA Charlottesville, VA. Chartered 1819 by the General Assembly under sponsorship of Thomas Jefferson; first instruction 1825. College of arts and sciences 1819, law 1819, medicine 1819, graduate studies 1859, engineering 1868, education 1919, commerce 1952, medicine 1819, graduate school of business administration 1954, architecture 1954, nursing 1956. University, coeducational; state control.

Thirty-three of thirty-eight fraternities and fouteen of the twenty sororities own their own houses.

NIC MEN'S
1852 Delta Kappa Epsilon
1853 Phi Kappa Psi
1854 Phi Kappa Sigma
1855 Beta Theta Pi
1857 Sigma Alpha Epsilon
1857 Theta Delta Chi
1859 Chi Phi
1859 Phi Gamma Delta
1860 Chi Psi
1860 Delta Psi
1860 Sigma Chi
1868 Pi Kappa Alpha
1868 Zeta Psi
1869 Kappa Sigma
1870 Sigma Nu
1873 Kappa Alpha Order
1873 Phi Delta Theta
1889 Delta Tau Delta
1907 Phi Sigma Kappa
1907 Sigma Phi Epsilon
1908 Delta Phi
1914 Theta Chi
1921 Delta Sigma Phi
1922 Delta Upsilon
1925 Alpha Epsilon Pi
1932 Pi Lambda Phi
1936 Tau Epsilon Phi
1950 Tau Kappa Epsilon
1953 Sigma Phi Society
1959 Sigma Pi
1961 Pi Kappa Phi
1968 Sigma Alpha Mu
1974 Kappa Alpha Psi (A)
1987 Alpha Delta Phi

NPHC MEN'S
     Phi Beta Sigma
1973 Alpha Phi Alpha

NPC WOMEN'S
1927 Chi Omega
1932 Kappa Delta
1952 Zeta Tau Alpha
1975 Delta Delta Delta
1975 Pi Beta Phi
1976 Kappa Alpha Theta
1976 Kappa Kappa Gamma
1977 Alpha Delta Pi
1977 Delta Zeta
1978 Alpha Phi
1978 Delta Gamma
1980 Alpha Chi Omega
1981 Phi Mu
1982 Alpha Omicron Pi
1982 Sigma Sigma Sigma
1987 Alpha Xi Delta
1987 Sigma Kappa
1990 Alpha Gamma Delta

NPHC WOMEN'S
1973 Alpha Kappa Alpha
1973 Delta Sigma Theta (B)

PROFESSIONAL
1890 Phi Delta Phi
1910 Phi Alpha Delta

1919 Delta Theta Phi
1921 Alpha Kappa Psi
1922 Alpha Chi Sigma
1923 Theta Tau

OTHER PROFESSIONAL
1924 Phi Lambda Kappa
1950 Gamma Eta Gamma
1975 Beta Alpha Psi

ACHS HONORS
     Omicron Delta Epsilon
1908 Delta Sigma Rho-Tau
     Kappa Alpha
1921 Tau Beta Pi
1925 Omicron Delta Kappa
1929 Beta Gamma Sigma
1948 Phi Eta Sigma
1950 Gamma Theta Upsilon
1951 Kappa Delta Pi
1957 Eta Kappa Nu
1958 Phi Sigma
1963 Alpha Epsilon
1964 Alpha Epsilon Delta
1966 Sigma Pi Sigma
1967 Sigma Delta Pi
1972 Sigma Theta Tau
1973 Phi Alpha Theta
1977 Chi Epsilon
1979 Psi Chi
1980 Phi Sigma Iota
1983 Pi Sigma Alpha

OTHER HONORS
     National Order of Omega
1906 Order of the Coif
1908 Phi Beta Kappa
1919 Alpha Omega Alpha
1924 Sigma Xi
1970 Gamma Sigma Delta

SERVICE
1929 Alpha Phi Omega

RECOGNITION
     Arnold Air Society (B-1)
1935 Sigma Delta Psi

INACTIVE
1857–61 Kappa Alpha Society
1868–85 Alpha Tau Omega
1904–29 Phi Rho Sigma
1905–36 Delta Chi
1906   Phi Beta Pi and Theta
         Kappa Psi (a)
1907–31 Alpha Chi Rho
1909   Phi Beta Pi and Theta
         Kappa Psi (a)
1910–22 Sigma Delta Chi
1915–85 Zeta Beta Tau
1922   Phi Chi
1922–39 Alpha Kappa Kappa
1922–61 Alpha Rho Chi
1924–46 Phi Delta Epsilon
1925–70 Delta Sigma Pi
1928   Scarab
1950   Kappa Beta Pi
1952   Sigma Gamma Epsilon

1955 Beta Beta Beta
1955 Delta Phi Alpha

1981–88 Sigma Delta Tau

VIRGINIA COMMONWEALTH UNIVERSITY
Richmond, VA. Established 1838. The East Campus (Medical College of Virginia) offers health-related programs in the schools of allied health professions, basic sciences, dentistry, medicine, nursing, and pharmacy. The West Campus (Academic Campus) includes the schools of the arts, arts and sciences, business, community services, education, and social work.

NIC MEN'S
1902 Sigma Phi Epsilon
1970 Theta Delta Chi
1971 Kappa Sigma
1974 Kappa Alpha Psi (A)
1983 Pi Kappa Phi
1984 Pi Lambda Phi
1984 Sigma Tau Gamma
1985 Alpha Kappa Lambda
1987 Kappa Delta Rho
1988 Phi Sigma Kappa

NPHC MEN'S
1973 Alpha Phi Alpha

NPC WOMEN'S
1979 Phi Sigma Sigma
1986 Alpha Omicron Pi
1989 Phi Mu

NPHC WOMEN'S
1970 Delta Sigma Theta (B)
1972 Sigma Gamma Rho
1974 Alpha Kappa Alpha

PROFESSIONAL
1925 Phi Delta Chi
1967 Phi Mu Alpha—Sinfonia
1970 Delta Sigma Pi

OTHER PROFESSIONAL
1972 Sigma Delta Chi
1976 Delta Pi Epsilon

ACHS HONORS
     Omicron Delta Epsilon
1929 Rho Chi
1961 Psi Chi
1971 Kappa Delta Pi
1976 Phi Kappa Phi
1976 Pi Kappa Lambda
1978 Kappa Tau Alpha
1978 Sigma Pi Sigma
1983 Phi Eta Sigma
1984 Pi Sigma Alpha
1986 Omicron Delta Kappa

OTHER HONORS
     National Order of Omega

RECOGNITION
1971 Sigma Phi Alpha

INACTIVE
1970–73 Alpha Epsilon Pi

COLONIES
1990 Delta Chi
1990 Theta Chi

VIRGINIA MILITARY INSTITUTE
Lexington, VA. College of arts, sciences, and engineering for men, state control; chartered 1839.

ACHS HONORS
     Omicron Delta Epsilon
1966 Sigma Pi Sigma
1978 Phi Kappa Phi
1982 Eta Kappa Nu
1986 Phi Alpha Theta

INACTIVE
1865–81 Alpha Tau Omega

1868–13 Kappa Alpha Order
1869–80 Beta Theta Pi
1869–11 Sigma Nu
1874–84 Kappa Sigma
1874–11 Sigma Alpha Epsilon
1878–89 Phi Delta Theta
1884–85 Sigma Chi
1908–12 Sigma Phi Epsilon

VIRGINIA POLYTECHNIC INSTITUTE
Blacksburg, VA. Established 1872 as the Virginia Agricultural and Mechanical College. University; undergraduate colleges for men and women; graduate school; coeducational; state control; nonsectarian.

NIC MEN'S
1873 Pi Kappa Alpha
1874 Kappa Sigma
1877 Beta Theta Pi
1970 Sigma Phi Epsilon
1970 Theta Delta Chi
1971 Delta Kappa Epsilon
1971 Pi Kappa Phi

1971 Sigma Chi
1971 Sigma Nu
1971 Sigma Pi
1972 Phi Delta Theta
1972 Phi Gamma Delta
1972 Phi Sigma Kappa
1972 Theta Chi
1972 Theta Xi

1973 Alpha Tau Omega
1973 Lambda Chi Alpha
1973 Phi Kappa Sigma
1973 Tau Kappa Epsilon
1975 Alpha Gamma Rho
1975 Sigma Alpha Epsilon
1975 Zeta Psi
1976 Phi Kappa Psi
1977 Kappa Alpha Psi (A)
1980 Triangle
1983 Delta Upsilon
1984 Pi Lambda Phi
1989 Kappa Delta Rho

NPHC MEN'S
      Phi Beta Sigma
1973 Alpha Phi Alpha

NPC WOMEN'S
1971 Delta Gamma
1971 Delta Zeta
1972 Zeta Tau Alpha
1973 Delta Delta Delta
1973 Phi Mu
1974 Alpha Sigma Alpha
1979 Kappa Delta
1981 Pi Beta Phi
1983 Kappa Alpha Theta
1985 Kappa Kappa Gamma
1987 Chi Omega
1989 Alpha Phi
1990 Alpha Delta Pi

NPHC WOMEN'S
1974 Alpha Kappa Alpha
1975 Delta Sigma Theta (B)
1985 Sigma Gamma Rho

PROFESSIONAL
1939 Alpha Kappa Psi
1966 Delta Sigma Pi
1975 Delta Psi Kappa
1976 Kappa Kappa Psi
1986 Phi Alpha Delta
1987 Alpha Chi Sigma

OTHER PROFESSIONAL
1932 Alpha Zeta
1941 Keramos
1967 Beta Alpha Psi
1969 Delta Pi Epsilon
1969 Phi Upsilon Omicron
1976 Alpha Epsilon Rho

ACHS HONORS
      Omicron Delta Epsilon
1921 Phi Kappa Phi
1933 Tau Beta Pi
1934 Omicron Delta Kappa
1940 Eta Kappa Nu
1940 Pi Tau Sigma
1941 Alpha Sigma Mu
1941 Chi Epsilon

1947 Tau Sigma Delta
1949 Phi Sigma
1949 Sigma Pi Sigma
1950 Delta Sigma Rho-Tau
      Kappa Alpha
1953 Sigma Gamma Tau
1962 Xi Sigma Pi
1966 Phi Eta Sigma
1970 Phi Alpha Theta
1971 Pi Sigma Alpha
1972 Phi Sigma Iota
1976 Sigma Delta Pi
1977 Alpha Epsilon Delta
1977 Kappa Delta Pi
1977 Mortar Board
1977 Psi Chi
1979 Phi Sigma Tau
1982 Sigma Lambda Alpha
1984 Omega Chi Epsilon
1985 Kappa Omicron Nu
1986 Kappa Tau Alpha
1987 Gamma Theta Upsilon

OTHER HONORS
      National Order of Omega
1940 Sigma Xi
1961 Pi Mu Epsilon

SERVICE
1948 Alpha Phi Omega

RECOGNITION
      Arnold Air Society (B-2)
1930 Society for Collegiate
      Journalists—Pi Delta
      Epsilon-Alpha Phi Gamma
      (P)
1933 Phi Lambda Upsilon
1935 National Block and Bridle
      Club
1935 Sigma Delta Psi
1937 Alpha Psi Omega
1938 Scabbard and Blade (7)
1955 Sigma Mu Sigma
1967 Pi Alpha Xi

INACTIVE
1877–77 Kappa Alpha Order
1942   Sigma Gamma Epsilon
1951–64 Pi Omega Pi
1969–89 Alpha Rho Chi
1970–78 Alpha Lambda Delta
1971–85 Alpha Epsilon Pi
1972–83 Zeta Beta Tau
1972–88 Sigma Kappa
1973–74 Alpha Chi Omega
1978–80 Phi Mu Alpha—
          Sinfonia

COLONIES
      Kappa Alpha Order

VIRGINIA STATE COLLEGE Norfolk, VA. Established 1944; college of arts and sciences, education, commerce, agriculture, home economics, and graduate studies.

NIC MEN'S
1935 Kappa Alpha Psi (A)

NPHC MEN'S
      Phi Beta Sigma
1962 Omega Psi Phi
1963 Alpha Phi Alpha

NPHC WOMEN'S
      Zeta Phi Beta
1926 Alpha Kappa Alpha
1938 Sigma Gamma Rho

ACHS HONORS
      Omicron Delta Epsilon
1955 Kappa Mu Epsilon

1965 Psi Chi
1981 Pi Sigma Alpha
1982 Phi Alpha Theta

SERVICE
1974 Alpha Phi Omega

VIRGINIA STATE COLLEGE Petersburg, VA. College of liberal arts, teachers college, and land-grant college; coeducational; state control; founded 1882.

NPHC MEN'S
1926 Alpha Phi Alpha

NPHC WOMEN'S
      Zeta Phi Beta

ACHS HONORS
1951 Sigma Pi Sigma
1960 Pi Omega Pi
1964 Kappa Omicron Nu

VIRGINIA UNION UNIVERSITY Richmond, VA. Liberal arts college and theological seminary; coeducational; private control (Baptist); established 1865.

NIC MEN'S
1927 Kappa Alpha Psi (A)

NPHC MEN'S
      Phi Beta Sigma
1907 Alpha Phi Alpha
1919 Omega Psi Phi

NPHC WOMEN'S
1927 Alpha Kappa Alpha

1937 Delta Sigma Theta (B)
1951 Sigma Gamma Rho

ACHS HONORS
1933 Beta Kappa Chi
1941 Alpha Kappa Mu
1976 Sigma Tau Delta

SERVICE
1967 Alpha Phi Omega

VIRGINIA WESLEYAN COLLEGE Norfolk, VA. College of liberal arts, career and professional preparations; coeducational. United Methodist affiliation. Established 1961.

NIC MEN'S
1974 Sigma Nu
1988 Phi Kappa Tau

NPC WOMEN'S
1990 Phi Sigma Sigma

ACHS HONORS
1979 Psi Chi
1980 Phi Alpha Theta
1981 Omicron Delta Kappa
1983 Phi Eta Sigma

VOORHEES COLLEGE Denmark, SC. Liberal arts college; Private (Episcopal). Founded in 1897.

No special housing for fraternities and sororities.

NIC MEN'S
1970 Kappa Alpha Psi (A)

NPHC MEN'S
      Phi Beta Sigma
1971 Alpha Phi Alpha

NPHC WOMEN'S
1970 Delta Sigma Theta (B)
1973 Alpha Kappa Alpha
1977 Sigma Gamma Rho

ACHS HONORS
1970 Alpha Chi

WABASH COLLEGE Crawfordsville, IN. College of liberal arts for men; private control; nonsectarian; founded 1832 as the Wabash Teachers Seminary and Manual Labor College.

The fraternities maintain houses.

NIC MEN'S
1846 Beta Theta Pi
1850 Phi Delta Theta
1866 Phi Gamma Delta
1870 Phi Kappa Psi
1872 Delta Tau Delta
1880 Sigma Chi
1895 Kappa Sigma

1918 Lambda Chi Alpha
1927 Tau Kappa Epsilon

ACHS HONORS
      Omicron Delta Epsilon
1913 Delta Sigma Rho-Tau
      Kappa Alpha
1967 Psi Chi
1978 Phi Sigma Iota

OTHER HONORS
1898 Phi Beta Kappa

SERVICE
1947 Alpha Phi Omega

RECOGNITION
1923 Society for Collegiate
Journalists—Pi Delta
Epsilon-Alpha Phi Gamma
(P)

1925 Blue Key
1928 Sigma Delta Psi
1947 Delta Phi Alpha
1954 Alpha Psi Omega

INACTIVE
1879–82 Theta Delta Chi
1955–64 Sigma Pi Sigma

WAGNER COLLEGE   Staten Island, NY. College of liberal arts; coeducational; private, Lutheran affiliated. Wagner College is located on an 86-acre hilltop campus. Situated in a residential area, 30 minutes from Manhattan, the college offers small campus, suburban living near Manhattan's cultural and social advantages. Wagner also maintains a campus in Bregenz, Austria. At the start of its second century in the fall of 1984, Wagner College enrolled 2,250 Students in undergraduate and graduate programs, representing 18 states, 140 foreign countries and 22 religious denominations.

NIC MEN'S
    Tau Kappa Epsilon
1957 Tau Kappa Epsilon
1961 Theta Chi

NPHC MEN'S
    Phi Beta Sigma

NPC WOMEN'S
1950 Alpha Delta Pi
1951 Alpha Omicron Pi

ACHS HONORS
1954 Phi Alpha Theta
1960 Omicron Delta Kappa
1966 Psi Chi
1970 Delta Mu Delta
1971 Kappa Mu Epsilon
1972 Sigma Tau Delta

1973 Sigma Delta Pi

SERVICE
1952 Alpha Phi Omega

RECOGNITION
1948 Alpha Psi Omega
1955 Delta Phi Alpha
1961 Beta Beta Beta

INACTIVE
1926–82 Alpha Sigma Phi
1952–89 Phi Mu Alpha—
    Sinfonia
1958–67 Delta Zeta
1958–82 Phi Sigma Kappa
1958–85 Zeta Tau Alpha
1973–77 Sigma Pi Sigma

WAKE FOREST UNIVERSITY   Winston-Salem, NC. Founded 1834 in town of Wake Forest by Baptist State Convention. Began as college of liberal arts for men. Coeducation 1942. Moved to Winston-Salem 1956. Schools of law, medicine, and business management. Division of graduate studies. Baptist. Became university June, 1967.

Nine of the fraternities occupy space in college residence halls.

NIC MEN'S
    Tau Kappa Epsilon
1881 Kappa Alpha Order
1932 Alpha Sigma Phi
1937 Kappa Sigma
1938 Delta Sigma Phi
1939 Pi Kappa Alpha
1940 Sigma Phi Epsilon
1940 Sigma Pi
1948 Sigma Chi
1948 Theta Chi
1970 Delta Kappa Epsilon
1986 Chi Psi

NPC WOMEN'S
1989 Delta Delta Delta

PROFESSIONAL
1947 Phi Alpha Delta
1947 Phi Delta Phi
1985 Delta Theta Phi

OTHER PROFESSIONAL
1927 Gamma Eta Gamma
1949 Phi Epsilon Kappa

ACHS HONORS
    Omicron Delta Epsilon
1939 Omicron Delta Kappa
1948 Alpha Epsilon Delta
1956 Phi Alpha Theta
1958 Phi Sigma Iota
1963 Delta Sigma Rho-Tau
    Kappa Alpha

1969 Mortar Board
1971 Sigma Pi Sigma
1982 Pi Sigma Alpha
1987 Psi Chi

OTHER HONORS
1941 Phi Beta Kappa
1963 National Collegiate
    Players
1965 Sigma Xi

SERVICE
1952 Alpha Phi Omega

RECOGNITION
1926 Pi Kappa Delta
1942 Eta Sigma Phi
1948 Beta Beta Beta
1954 Scabbard and Blade (11)

1957 Sigma Delta Psi
1958 Delta Phi Alpha

INACTIVE
1923   Phi Beta Pi and Theta
    Kappa Psi (B)
1924–65 Phi Rho Sigma
1924–84 Lambda Chi Alpha
1926–36 Kappa Phi Kappa
1926–71 Gamma Sigma Epsilon
1929   Sigma Delta Kappa
1935   Phi Chi
1950–70 Alpha Kappa Psi
1950–72 Delta Sigma Pi
1951–82 Kappa Mu Epsilon
1961   Beta Gamma Sigma
1967–77 Phi Mu Alpha—
    Sinfonia

WARNER PACIFIC COLLEGE   Portland, OR. A private liberal arts Christian college.

Single-sex dormitories.

ACHS HONORS
1971 Alpha Chi

WARTBURG COLLEGE   Waverly, IA. College of liberal arts; coeducation; private control (American Lutheran Church); established 1852.

PROFESSIONAL
1968 Mu Phi Epsilon

ACHS HONORS
1960 Alpha Chi
1965 Kappa Delta Pi
1973 Kappa Mu Epsilon
1975 Delta Mu Delta
1987 Pi Gamma Mu

OTHER HONORS
1974 National Collegiate
    Players

RECOGNITION
1948 Alpha Psi Omega
1951 Beta Beta Beta

INACTIVE
1976–76 Phi Mu Alpha—
    Sinfonia

WASHBURN UNIVERSITY   Topeka, KS. University; college of liberal arts; law school; coeducational; municipal control; chartered 1865 as Lincoln College; became Washburn University in 1952.

Two fraternities own their own land and homes; the others are on campus.

NIC MEN'S
1909 Kappa Sigma
1910 Phi Delta Theta
1921 Kappa Alpha Psi (A)
1951 Sigma Phi Epsilon

NPHC MEN'S
1963 Alpha Phi Alpha

NPC WOMEN'S
1914 Kappa Alpha Theta
1916 Alpha Phi
1920 Delta Gamma
1922 Zeta Tau Alpha

NPHC WOMEN'S
1942 Delta Sigma Theta (B)

PROFESSIONAL
1912 Delta Theta Phi
1914 Sigma Alpha Iota
1921 Phi Alpha Delta
1961 Phi Mu Alpha—Sinfonia

1974 Phi Delta Phi

ACHS HONORS
    Omicron Delta Epsilon
1947 Kappa Mu Epsilon
1960 Sigma Pi Sigma
1968 Psi Chi
1971 Pi Kappa Phi
1983 Phi Alpha Theta
1984 Pi Sigma Alpha
1987 Phi Sigma Iota

OTHER HONORS
1920 Delta Phi Delta

SERVICE
1940 Alpha Phi Omega

RECOGNITION
    Angel Flight
    Arnold Air Society (G-2)
1913 Pi Kappa Delta
1938 Alpha Psi Omega

INACTIVE
1923–78 Alpha Kappa Alpha
1924–58 Pi Gamma Mu
1960–90 Delta Sigma Pi

1965–85 Alpha Kappa Lambda
1967–79 Tau Kappa Epsilon
1973–78 Phi Chi Theta

UNIVERSITY OF WASHINGTON   Seattle, WA.
Territorial University of Washington founded 1861, by bill sponsored by Senator A. A. Denny; became state university in 1889. University; coeducational undergraduate colleges; coeducational graduate school; state-supported; nonsectarian.

The fraternities and sororities own their own land and homes.

NIC MEN'S
1892 Sigma Alpha Epsilon
1896 Sigma Nu
1900 Phi Delta Theta
1900 Phi Gamma Delta
1901 Beta Theta Pi
1903 Kappa Sigma
1903 Sigma Chi
1906 Alpha Tau Omega
1906 Sigma Alpha Epsilon
1908 Delta Chi
1908 Delta Tau Delta
1910 Acacia
1910 Delta Upsilon
1912 Alpha Sigma Phi
1913 Theta Delta Chi
1914 Phi Kappa Psi
1914 Pi Kappa Alpha
1916 Psi Upsilon
1918 Lambda Chi Alpha
1919 Phi Kappa Sigma
1920 Zeta Psi
1921 Alpha Delta Phi
1921 Chi Psi
1922 Sigma Phi Epsilon
1922 Zeta Beta Tau
1923 Phi Sigma Kappa
1924 Pi Kappa Phi
1925 Theta Chi
1926 Sigma Alpha Mu
1926 Sigma Pi
1926 Tau Kappa Epsilon
1929 Phi Kappa Tau
1948 Kappa Alpha Psi (A)

NPHC MEN'S
    Phi Beta Sigma

NPC WOMEN'S
1903 Delta Gamma
1903 Gamma Phi Beta
1905 Kappa Kappa Gamma
1907 Alpha Xi Delta
1907 Pi Beta Phi
1908 Kappa Alpha Theta
1909 Alpha Gamma Delta
1909 Chi Omega
1909 Delta Delta Delta
1910 Alpha Chi Omega
1910 Sigma Kappa
1914 Alpha Phi
1914 Delta Zeta
1915 Alpha Omicron Pi
1917 Alpha Delta Pi
1917 Phi Mu

1917 Zeta Tau Alpha
1922 Kappa Delta

NPHC WOMEN'S
1976 Alpha Kappa Alpha

PROFESSIONAL
1905 Phi Delta Chi
1914 Phi Alpha Delta
1923 Delta Theta Phi
1941 Lambda Kappa Sigma
1985 Phi Alpha Delta

ACHS HONORS
    Omicron Delta Epsilon
1908 Xi Sigma Pi
1912 Tau Beta Pi
1922 Kappa Omicron Nu
1923 Alpha Kappa Delta
1925 Mortar Board
1928 Pi Sigma Alpha
1930 Psi Chi
1931 Rho Chi
1939 Phi Sigma Iota
1945 Kappa Tau Alpha
1948 Alpha Epsilon Delta
1951 Phi Alpha Theta
1953 Gamma Theta Upsilon
1983 Chi Epsilon
1990 Sigma Lambda Alpha

OTHER HONORS
    National Order of Omega

SERVICE
1936 Alpha Phi Omega
1939 Alpha Phi Omega

RECOGNITION
    Angel Flight

INACTIVE
1910–65 Delta Kappa Epsilon
1915–90 Theta Xi
1921–74 Phi Mu Alpha—
      Sinfonia
1924–59 Chi Phi
1926–59 Delta Sigma Phi
1930–34 Sigma Pi Sigma
1932–87 Alpha Epsilon Phi
1940   Phi Sigma Sigma
1947–61 Alpha Epsilon Pi
1959–80 Phi Eta Sigma
1963–71 Theta Tau
1963–74 Alpha Lambda Delta

COLONIES
1929 Alpha Kappa Lambda

WASHINGTON COLLEGE   Chestertown, MD.
Founded 1782, undergraduate, coeducational, liberal arts college, private control, nonsectarian.

Fraternity and sorority members are given preference of dormitory lodging in accordance to location of chapter rooms, which are provided free of charge to the organizations.

NIC MEN'S
1936 Kappa Alpha Order
1940 Theta Chi

NPC WOMEN'S
1937 Alpha Chi Omega
1938 Alpha Omicron Pi
1938 Zeta Tau Alpha

ACHS HONORS
1937 Omicron Delta Kappa
1968 Phi Alpha Theta
1979 Phi Sigma Tau

1982 Psi Chi

OTHER HONORS
    National Order of Omega

INACTIVE
1855–64 Phi Kappa Psi
1937–73 Lambda Chi Alpha
1941–42 Zeta Beta Tau

COLONIES
1952 Phi Sigma Kappa
1990 Phi Delta Theta

WASHINGTON UNIVERSITY   St. Louis, MO. University; coeducational; private control; nonsectarian; established 1853 as Eliot Seminary; became Washington University 1857.

On-campus fraternities are on renewable leases at a charge of one dollar; facilities are charged on a pro-rata basis. Sororities are all housed in one building with each sorority renting a room from the university.

NIC MEN'S
1869 Beta Theta Pi
1891 Phi Delta Theta
1902 Kappa Sigma
1903 Sigma Chi
1903 Sigma Nu
1905 Theta Xi
1919 Sigma Alpha Mu
1920 Tau Kappa Epsilon
1923 Zeta Beta Tau
1928 Alpha Epsilon Pi
1929 Sigma Phi Epsilon

NPHC MEN'S
    Phi Beta Sigma

NPC WOMEN'S
1907 Pi Beta Phi
1914 Delta Gamma
1917 Gamma Phi Beta
1920 Alpha Chi Omega
1921 Kappa Kappa Gamma
1925 Alpha Epsilon Phi
1983 Alpha Phi

PROFESSIONAL
1912 Delta Theta Phi
1922 Phi Alpha Delta
1923 Alpha Kappa Psi
1946 Alpha Omega
1953 Mu Phi Epsilon
1986 Phi Alpha Delta

OTHER PROFESSIONAL
1903 Phi Beta Pi and Theta
      Kappa Psi (a)
1904 Delta Sigma Delta
1922 Alpha Alpha Gamma
1928 Nu Beta Epsilon

ACHS HONORS
    Omicron Delta Epsilon
1922 Delta Sigma Rho-Tau
      Kappa Alpha
1922 Mortar Board
1922 Tau Beta Pi
1926 Pi Sigma Alpha
1930 Kappa Delta Pi
1933 Omicron Delta Kappa
1949 Pi Tau Sigma
1960 Eta Kappa Nu
1984 Phi Alpha Theta
1984 Psi Chi

OTHER HONORS
1905 Alpha Omega Alpha
1910 Sigma Xi
1914 Phi Beta Kappa
1916 Omicron Kappa Upsilon
1937 Order of the Coif
1975 Sigma Gamma Epsilon

RECOGNITION
    Angel Flight
    Arnold Air Society (G-2)
1932 Delta Phi Alpha
1946 Eta Mu Pi
1955 Alpha Psi Omega

INACTIVE
1905–12 Phi Beta Pi and Theta
      Kappa Psi (B)
1905–65 Kappa Alpha Order
1906–09 Delta Chi
1906–73 Kappa Alpha Theta
1909–12 Psi Omega
1914   Scarab
1917–72 Alpha Chi Sigma
1918–40 Alpha Tau Omega

1919	Delta Psi Kappa
1920–61	Pi Kappa Alpha
1921	Kappa Beta Pi
1921–67	Pi Lambda Phi
1922–39	Phi Chi
1922–58	National Collegiate Players
1922–59	Phi Delta Epsilon
1923–35	Alpha Kappa Kappa
1923–66	Phi Mu
1925–29	Gamma Eta Gamma
1926–54	Delta Delta Delta
1927	Phi Lambda Kappa
1927–53	Delta Sigma Pi
1928–36	Zeta Phi Eta
1929	Eta Sigma Phi
1929–63	Alpha Xi Delta
1931–57	Zeta Tau Alpha
1931–74	Phi Eta Sigma
1931–82	Alpha Lambda Delta
1950–61	Delta Sigma Phi
1950–65	Alpha Pi Mu
1950–69	Sigma Delta Pi
1951–62	Alpha Sigma Phi
1951–73	Sigma Delta Tau
1953–67	Phi Mu Alpha—Sinfonia
1963–71	Delta Phi Epsilon

WASHINGTON AND JEFFERSON COLLEGE

Washington, PA. College of liberal arts; private control; nonsectarian. Chartered 1787 as Washington Academy; Washington and Jefferson Academies united 1865 to form college.

Fraternities occupy a residential center of ten individual houses with private dining rooms in a Commons Building, occupied in 1968. W & J became coed in 1970; sororities, assigned "block housing," were introduced in 1979.

NIC MEN'S
1842 Beta Theta Pi
1848 Phi Gamma Delta
1852 Phi Kappa Psi
1854 Phi Kappa Sigma
1861 Delta Tau Delta
1875 Phi Delta Theta
1882 Alpha Tau Omega
1898 Kappa Sigma
1919 Lambda Chi Alpha
1963 Zeta Beta Tau
1941 Phi Sigma Tau
1947 Phi Alpha Theta
1952 Sigma Delta Pi
1981 Psi Chi

NPC WOMEN'S
1979 Delta Gamma
1979 Pi Beta Phi
1984 Kappa Kappa Gamma
1988 Kappa Alpha Theta

ACHS HONORS
Omicron Delta Epsilon
1917 Delta Sigma Rho-Tau Kappa Alpha
1922 Phi Sigma
1935 Pi Sigma Alpha

OTHER HONORS
1937 Phi Beta Kappa

SERVICE
1959 Alpha Phi Omega

RECOGNITION
1924 Society for Collegiate Journalists—Pi Delta Epsilon-Alpha Phi Gamma (P)
1926 Alpha Psi Omega
1936 Eta Sigma Phi
1956 Delta Phi Alpha

INACTIVE
1858–65 Theta Delta Chi
1860–71 Delta Upsilon
1902–06 Sigma Phi Epsilon
1948–81 Pi Lambda Phi

WASHINGTON AND LEE UNIVERSITY

Lexington, VA. University, coeducational; private control; nonsectarian; founded as Augusta Academy 1749; changed to Washington College 1813; to present name 1871 in honor of George Washington and Robert E. Lee.

Ownership of house is by fraternity on college-owned land or by college and leased to a fraternity.

NIC MEN'S
1855 Phi Kappa Psi
1856 Beta Theta Pi
1865 Kappa Alpha Order
1866 Sigma Chi
1867 Sigma Alpha Epsilon
1868 Phi Gamma Delta
1873 Kappa Sigma
1882 Sigma Nu
1887 Phi Delta Theta
1892 Pi Kappa Alpha
1895 Phi Kappa Sigma
1896 Delta Tau Delta
1906 Sigma Phi Epsilon
1920 Pi Kappa Phi
1922 Lambda Chi Alpha
1977 Chi Psi

NPHC MEN'S
1973 Alpha Phi Alpha

NPC WOMEN'S
1989 Chi Omega
1989 Kappa Alpha Theta

PROFESSIONAL
1908 Phi Delta Phi
1909 Delta Theta Phi
1912 Phi Alpha Delta

OTHER PROFESSIONAL
1929 Sigma Delta Chi

ACHS HONORS
Omicron Delta Epsilon
1913 Delta Sigma Rho-Tau Kappa Alpha
1914 Omicron Delta Kappa
1933 Beta Gamma Sigma
1937 Phi Eta Sigma
1948 Alpha Epsilon Delta
1954 Pi Sigma Alpha

OTHER HONORS
1911 Phi Beta Kappa
1950 Order of the Coif

SERVICE
1987 Alpha Phi Omega

RECOGNITION
1925 Alpha Psi Omega
1950 Sigma Delta Psi
1953 Scabbard and Blade (10)
1965 Mu Beta Psi

INACTIVE
1865–52 Alpha Tau Omega
1867–71 Delta Kappa Epsilon
1869–72 Theta Delta Chi
1869–88 Delta Psi
1872–75 Chi Phi
1906–14 Delta Sigma Phi
1907–34 Alpha Chi Rho
1920 Sigma Delta Kappa
1920–88 Zeta Beta Tau
1922–29 Alpha Kappa Psi
1925–36 Kappa Phi Kappa
1927–31 Gamma Sigma Epsilon
1930–71 Delta Upsilon
1930–76 Psi Chi
1970–74 Psi Upsilon

WASHINGTON STATE UNIVERSITY

Pullman, WA. Founded as a land-grant college on March 28, 1890. First instruction on January 13, 1892. University; undergraduate college; coeducational; graduate school; state control.

The fraternities and sororities own their own land and homes.

NIC MEN'S
1909 Kappa Sigma
1910 Sigma Nu
1911 Alpha Tau Omega
1912 Sigma Phi Epsilon
1914 Lambda Chi Alpha
1915 Sigma Alpha Epsilon
1918 Phi Delta Theta
1919 Sigma Chi
1920 Beta Theta Pi
1921 Alpha Gamma Rho
1924 Theta Chi
1926 Phi Sigma Kappa
1927 Alpha Kappa Lambda
1927 Phi Kappa Tau
1927 Tau Kappa Epsilon
1929 Pi Kappa Alpha
1933 Delta Upsilon
1935 Acacia
1943 Delta Chi
1946 Phi Kappa Theta
1949 Delta Sigma Phi
1950 Phi Gamma Delta
1955 FarmHouse
1956 Delta Tau Delta
1980 Kappa Alpha Psi (A)
1982 Phi Kappa Sigma
1990 Psi Upsilon

NPC WOMEN'S
Alpha Phi
1912 Alpha Delta Pi
1912 Pi Beta Phi
1913 Kappa Alpha Theta
1916 Alpha Chi Omega
1918 Delta Delta Delta
1920 Kappa Kappa Gamma
1921 Sigma Kappa
1923 Alpha Gamma Delta
1923 Chi Omega
1923 Kappa Delta
1926 Alpha Xi Delta
1932 Alpha Omicron Pi
1946 Delta Gamma
1955 Gamma Phi Beta

PROFESSIONAL
1916 Kappa Psi
1919 Mu Phi Epsilon
1921 Phi Mu Alpha—Sinfonia
1922 Lambda Kappa Sigma
1932 Alpha Kappa Psi
1933 Alpha Chi Sigma

OTHER PROFESSIONAL
1907 Alpha Zeta
1915 Alpha Psi
1923 Pi Lambda Theta
1924 Sigma Delta Chi
1925 Women in Communications
1932 Scarab
1934 Phi Epsilon Kappa
1951 Alpha Tau Alpha
1973 Beta Alpha Psi

ACHS HONORS
Omicron Delta Epsilon
1917 Delta Sigma Rho-Tau Kappa Alpha
1919 Kappa Omicron Nu
1919 Phi Kappa Phi
1923 Mortar Board
1923 Tau Beta Pi
1925 Rho Chi
1929 Psi Chi
1939 Alpha Kappa Delta
1939 Pi Sigma Alpha

1949 Gamma Theta Upsilon
1950 Phi Alpha Theta
1951 Beta Gamma Sigma
1959 Omicron Delta Kappa
1966 Xi Sigma Pi
1969 Pi Tau Sigma
1979 Pi Kappa Lambda
1980 Sigma Lambda Alpha

OTHER HONORS
    National Order of Omega
1923 National Collegiate
    Players
1930 Delta Phi Delta
1930 Sigma Xi
1931 Pi Mu Epsilon

SERVICE
    The National Spurs
1922 Intercollegiate Knights
1935 Alpha Phi Omega

RECOGNITION
    Angel Flight

    Arnold Air Society (H-2)
1916 Scabbard and Blade (2)
1926 Phi Lambda Upsilon
1936 Sigma Delta Psi
1949 Pi Alpha Xi
1952 Phi Zeta

INACTIVE
1919–58 Delta Zeta
1921–89 Theta Xi
1924   Sigma Gamma Epsilon
1928–38 Pi Gamma Mu
1928–39 Zeta Tau Alpha
1928–56 National Block and
    Bridle Club
1930–43 Phi Sigma
1945–85 Alpha Phi
1947–50 Sigma Alpha Mu
1947–76 Phi Chi Theta
1948–85 Phi Eta Sigma
1968–85 Alpha Lambda Delta

WAYLAND BAPTIST COLLEGE Plainview, TX. Founded by the Staked Plains Baptist Association under the leadership of Dr. J. H. Wayland, pioneer doctor; chartered 1908, board of trustees organized 1909, and first instruction 1909. College; coeducational undergraduate; Baptist General Convention of Texas control.

PROFESSIONAL
1961 Phi Mu Alpha—Sinfonia
1973 Sigma Alpha Iota

ACHS HONORS
1958 Alpha Chi
1958 Phi Alpha Theta

1959 Sigma Tau Delta

SERVICE
1968 Alpha Phi Omega

RECOGNITION
1948 Alpha Psi Omega

WAYNE STATE COLLEGE Wayne, NE. Coeducational; state control; established as summer normal school 1891, reorganized as state normal school 1910.

NIC MEN'S
1968 Tau Kappa Epsilon
1969 Phi Sigma Kappa
1969 Sigma Tau Gamma

NPC WOMEN'S
1985 Theta Phi Alpha

PROFESSIONAL
1953 Tau Beta Sigma
1969 Delta Sigma Pi

ACHS HONORS
1933 Kappa Mu Epsilon

1933 Pi Gamma Mu
1940 Pi Omega Pi
1963 Kappa Delta Pi
1967 Alpha Lambda Delta

INACTIVE
1969–74 Beta Sigma Psi
1969–83 Chi Omega
1969–83 Phi Mu

WAYNE STATE UNIVERSITY Detroit, MI. Institutional history that of originally unrelated schools—antecedents: Detroit Medical College, 1868; Detroit Normal Training School, 1881; Colleges of the City of Detroit, 1933; Wayne University, 1934; Wayne State University, 1956 (11 schools and colleges), coeducational.

The fraternities own their own land and houses but the sororities are not involved in their own housing.

NIC MEN'S
1927 Kappa Alpha Psi (A)
1930 Alpha Epsilon Pi
1950 Pi Kappa Alpha
1969 Sigma Pi

NPHC MEN'S
    Phi Beta Sigma

NPC WOMEN'S
1947 Delta Zeta
1958 Kappa Delta
1959 Alpha Gamma Delta
1988 Alpha Epsilon Phi

NPHC WOMEN'S
1936 Alpha Kappa Alpha
1938 Sigma Gamma Rho

PROFESSIONAL
1928 Delta Theta Phi
1928 Phi Delta Chi
1928 Rho Pi Phi
1930 Lambda Kappa Sigma
1941 Phi Mu Alpha—Sinfonia
1949 Delta Sigma Pi
1951 Theta Tau
1959 Phi Alpha Delta

OTHER PROFESSIONAL
1951 Alpha Zeta Omega

ACHS HONORS
    Omicron Delta Epsilon
    Pi Alpha Alpha
1931 Pi Sigma Alpha
1939 Alpha Kappa Delta

1946 Omicron Delta Kappa
1951 Psi Chi
1951 Tau Beta Pi
1952 Mortar Board
1956 Chi Epsilon
1960 Alpha Sigma Mu
1960 Eta Kappa Nu
1980 Phi Alpha Theta
1983 Pi Kappa Lambda
1986 Phi Eta Sigma

SERVICE
1948 Alpha Phi Omega

INACTIVE
1923–85 Alpha Sigma Tau
1930–70 Zeta Beta Tau
1938–73 Alpha Sigma Phi
1939–55 Sigma Pi Sigma
1942–63 Pi Omega Pi
1946–58 Kappa Mu Epsilon
1948–71 Sigma Alpha Mu
1948–79 Tau Kappa Epsilon
1950–70 Phi Sigma Sigma
1951–55 Sigma Tau Gamma
1951–72 Theta Xi
1953–59 Sigma Sigma Sigma
1955–71 Delta Phi Epsilon
1955–72 Alpha Chi Sigma
1956–74 Delta Chi
1958–72 Alpha Delta Pi
1959–74 Sigma Kappa
1969–71 Sigma Delta Tau
1979–85 Beta Phi Mu

WAYNESBURG COLLEGE Waynesburg, PA. College of liberal arts; coeducational; private control; related to United Presbyterian Church; established 1849.

The fraternities own their own land and homes. Sorority members are required to live in the dormitories.

NIC MEN'S
1910 Delta Sigma Phi
1958 Tau Kappa Epsilon
1960 Theta Chi
1980 Alpha Phi Delta

NPC WOMEN'S
1958 Alpha Delta Pi
1959 Sigma Kappa

PROFESSIONAL
1956 Alpha Kappa Psi
1973 Phi Chi Theta

ACHS HONORS
    Omicron Delta Epsilon
1928 Delta Sigma Rho-Tau
    Kappa Alpha
1937 Phi Alpha Theta

1941 Sigma Tau Delta
1959 Kappa Mu Epsilon
1975 Pi Gamma Mu
1976 Psi Chi

SERVICE
1949 Alpha Phi Omega

RECOGNITION
1940 Alpha Psi Omega
1967 Kappa Pi

INACTIVE
1865–66 Delta Tau Delta
1972   Phi Sigma Sigma

COLONIES
1961 Phi Sigma Kappa

WEBER STATE COLLEGE Ogden, UT. College of liberal arts; coeducational; state control; established as Weber State Academy 1908; became four-year college in 1963.

NIC MEN'S
1971 Beta Theta Pi
1971 Pi Kappa Alpha
1972 Sigma Alpha Epsilon

1972 Sigma Nu
1973 Tau Kappa Epsilon
1985 Kappa Alpha Psi (A)

OTHER MEN'S
     Sigma Gamma Chi

OTHER WOMEN'S
     Lambda Delta Sigma

PROFESSIONAL
1975 Kappa Kappa Psi
1985 Phi Alpha Delta

ACHS HONORS
     Omicron Delta Epsilon
1964 Lambda Iota Tau
1965 Delta Sigma Rho-Tau
     Kappa Alpha
1970 Alpha Epsilon Delta
1971 Phi Kappa Phi

1972 Gamma Theta Upsilon
1974 Psi Chi
1981 Pi Gamma Mu
1981 Pi Sigma Alpha
1986 Phi Alpha Theta
1986 Phi Sigma Iota

SERVICE
1980 Alpha Phi Omega

RECOGNITION
1964 Blue Key

INACTIVE
1927–65 Delta Phi Kappa
1968–82 Delta Sigma Pi
1974–75 Phi Gamma Nu

WEBBER COLLEGE Babson Park, FL. Private control. Four-year; coeducational; specialized institution.

Freshmen must live on campus. Single-sex dormitories.

NIC MEN'S
1982 Phi Kappa Tau

WEBSTER COLLEGE Webster Groves, MO. College of liberal arts for women; private control (Roman Catholic); established 1915 as Loretto College.

ACHS HONORS
1954 Pi Delta Phi
1985 Psi Chi

INACTIVE
1961–70 Sigma Alpha Iota

WELLESLEY COLLEGE Wellesley, MA. Founded 1870, opened 1875; residential liberal arts college for women; private control; nonsectarian.

OTHER HONORS
1904 Phi Beta Kappa
1938 Sigma Xi

COLONIES
1988 Sigma Pi Sigma

WELLS COLLEGE Aurora, NY. Founded by Henry Wells in 1868. Liberal arts college for women; private control; nonsectarian.

OTHER HONORS
1932 Phi Beta Kappa

WESLEYAN COLLEGE Macon, GA. College of liberal arts for women; fine arts; private control (Methodist); established 1836, oldest college chartered for women in the world.

PROFESSIONAL
1959 Sigma Alpha Iota

ACHS HONORS
1959 Pi Gamma Mu
1969 Phi Kappa Phi
1972 Mortar Board

1980 Psi Chi
1987 Alpha Lambda Delta

INACTIVE
1851–16 Alpha Delta Pi
1852–14 Phi Mu
1911–14 Zeta Tau Alpha

WESLEYAN UNIVERSITY Middletown, CT. Founded 1831; coeducational liberal arts college; private control; nonsectarian.

Ten fraternities own their land and homes; two fraternities occupy college-owned housing on rental basis.

NIC MEN'S
1843 Psi Upsilon
1844 Chi Psi
1856 Alpha Delta Phi
1867 Delta Kappa Epsilon
1890 Beta Theta Pi

PROFESSIONAL
1959 Kappa Delta Epsilon

ACHS HONORS
1966 Phi Sigma Iota

INACTIVE
1850–53 Delta Upsilon
1857–63 Theta Delta Chi
1885–86 Pi Beta Phi
1902–89 Delta Tau Delta
1906–12 Alpha Gamma Delta
1911–60 Alpha Chi Rho
1928–52 Phi Sigma Kappa
1928–59 Sigma Chi
1967–80 Kappa Alpha Society

WEST CHESTER UNIVERSITY OF PENNSYLVANIA West Chester, PA. College of liberal arts, music, and education (and graduate schools); coeducational; state control; established 1812; became normal school 1871; became university in 1983.

NIC MEN'S
1970 Theta Chi
1979 Sigma Phi Epsilon
1980 Kappa Alpha Psi (A)
1983 Alpha Chi Rho
1984 Sigma Pi
1986 Phi Kappa Sigma
1988 Phi Delta Theta
1989 Pi Kappa Phi
1990 Kappa Delta Rho

NPHC MEN'S
     Phi Beta Sigma
1970 Alpha Phi Alpha

NPC WOMEN'S
1969 Alpha Sigma Tau
1969 Delta Zeta
1970 Zeta Tau Alpha
1971 Alpha Phi
1971 Alpha Xi Delta
1989 Delta Phi Epsilon

NPHC WOMEN'S
1973 Alpha Kappa Alpha

PROFESSIONAL
1967 Phi Mu Alpha—Sinfonia
1968 Sigma Alpha Iota

ACHS HONORS
     Omicron Delta Epsilon
1963 Gamma Theta Upsilon

1966 Kappa Delta Pi
1967 Pi Gamma Mu
1968 Phi Alpha Theta
1968 Psi Chi
1978 Pi Kappa Lambda
1979 Phi Sigma Tau
1983 Phi Eta Sigma
1983 Pi Sigma Alpha

OTHER HONORS
     National Order of Omega
1970 Pi Mu Epsilon

SERVICE
1965 Alpha Phi Omega

RECOGNITION
1961 Alpha Psi Omega
1969 Pi Kappa Delta

INACTIVE
1968–73 Zeta Beta Tau
1968–76 Sigma Tau Gamma
1968–77 Pi Lambda Phi
1969–70 Sigma Delta Tau
1969–73 Alpha Sigma Alpha
1969–90 Tau Kappa Epsilon
1970–74 Alpha Omicron Pi
1970–80 Lambda Chi Alpha
1972–88 Alpha Lambda Delta

COLONIES
1986 Sigma Pi Sigma

UNIVERSITY OF WEST FLORIDA Pensacola, FL. State controlled; coed institution of liberal arts; teacher education, professional and science. Chartered in 1965. Centers in Eglin-Fort Walton Beach.

NIC MEN'S
1972 Alpha Tau Omega
1972 Delta Tau Delta
1973 Sigma Alpha Epsilon

NPHC MEN'S
1976 Alpha Phi Alpha

NPC WOMEN'S
1972 Alpha Delta Pi
1987 Phi Sigma Sigma
1990 Alpha Gamma Delta

NPHC WOMEN'S
1974 Alpha Kappa Alpha

1976 Delta Sigma Theta (B)

PROFESSIONAL
1969 Delta Sigma Pi

ACHS HONORS
    Pi Alpha Alpha
1970 Psi Chi
1971 Phi Alpha Theta
1973 Phi Kappa Phi

1973 Sigma Pi Sigma
1984 Omicron Delta Kappa
1985 Phi Eta Sigma

INACTIVE
1972–82 Pi Kappa Alpha
1973–74 Phi Delta Theta
1973–87 Phi Mu

WEST GEORGIA COLLEGE   Carrollton, GA. College of liberal arts; coeducational; state owned; established 1933.

NIC MEN'S
1971 Alpha Tau Omega
1971 Kappa Sigma
1971 Tau Kappa Epsilon
1972 Pi Kappa Alpha
1972 Sigma Nu
1973 Chi Phi
1975 Kappa Alpha Psi (A)

NPHC MEN'S
    Phi Beta Sigma

NPC WOMEN'S
1970 Delta Delta Delta
1971 Alpha Gamma Delta
1971 Chi Omega
1971 Kappa Delta
1971 Phi Mu
1989 Alpha Xi Delta

NPHC WOMEN'S
1973 Delta Sigma Theta (B)
1976 Alpha Kappa Alpha
1988 Sigma Gamma Rho

PROFESSIONAL
1970 Alpha Kappa Psi

1980 Phi Mu Alpha—Sinfonia

ACHS HONORS
    Omicron Delta Epsilon
1969 Alpha Lambda Delta
1969 Phi Alpha Theta
1969 Pi Gamma Mu
1973 Gamma Theta Upsilon
1973 Phi Eta Sigma
1973 Phi Kappa Phi
1975 Kappa Mu Epsilon
1979 Omicron Delta Kappa
1982 Phi Sigma Iota
1982 Pi Sigma Alpha
1985 Sigma Pi Sigma

OTHER HONORS
    National Order of Omega

SERVICE
1947 Alpha Phi Omega

RECOGNITION
1976 Blue Key

INACTIVE
1974–80 Delta Tau Delta

WEST LIBERTY STATE COLLEGE   West Liberty, WV. College of liberal arts; coeducational; state control. Chartered as West Liberty Academy 1837; name changed to West Liberty State Normal School 1870; named changed to present 1943.

Fraternity and sorority members live in residence halls.

NIC MEN'S
1966 Theta Xi
1972 Delta Chi
1989 Kappa Delta Rho

NPHC MEN'S
    Phi Beta Sigma

NPC WOMEN'S
1966 Alpha Xi Delta
1966 Chi Omega
1966 Delta Zeta

PROFESSIONAL
1960 Delta Sigma Pi
1961 Phi Gamma Nu
1970 Delta Psi Kappa

ACHS HONORS
    Omicron Delta Epsilon

1950 Pi Omega Pi
1968 Delta Mu Delta
1972 Phi Alpha Theta
1974 Gamma Theta Upsilon
1976 Sigma Tau Delta
1985 Pi Sigma Alpha

RECOGNITION
1935 Chi Beta Phi
1939 Alpha Psi Omega
1950 Kappa Pi
1958 Sigma Phi Alpha

INACTIVE
1859–62 Delta Tau Delta
1966–83 Alpha Delta Pi
1970–85 Lambda Chi Alpha
1971–77 Tau Kappa Epsilon
1976–77 Phi Sigma Kappa

WEST POINT ARMY ACADEMY   West Point, NY.

ACHS HONORS
1978 Phi Kappa Phi
1990 Phi Alpha Theta

COLONIES
1986 Sigma Pi Sigma

WEST TEXAS STATE UNIVERSITY   Canyon, TX. University composed of school of agricultiure, college of arts and sciences, school of business, college of education, school of fine arts, school of nursing and graduate school; coeducation; state control; established as a normal school in 1910.

Fraternity and sorority members are required to live in residence halls if under 21 years old. Most fraternities and sororities maintain off-campus lodges. All sororities maintain units (16-20 women) within the residence hall system.

NIC MEN'S
1959 Alpha Tau Omega
1959 Kappa Alpha Order
1959 Sigma Nu
1960 Lambda Chi Alpha
1964 Phi Delta Theta
1968 Kappa Alpha Psi (A)

NPHC MEN'S
1975 Alpha Phi Alpha

NPC WOMEN'S
1958 Chi Omega
1958 Delta Zeta
1958 Zeta Tau Alpha

NPHC WOMEN'S
1970 Delta Sigma Theta (B)

PROFESSIONAL
1947 Kappa Kappa Psi
1949 Tau Beta Sigma
1953 Phi Gamma Nu
1959 Alpha Kappa Psi
1960 Mu Phi Epsilon
1960 Phi Mu Alpha—Sinfonia
1964 Delta Psi Kappa
1985 Phi Alpha Delta

ACHS HONORS
    Omicron Delta Epsilon
1922 Alpha Chi
1952 Sigma Delta Pi
1953 Gamma Theta Upsilon
1958 Phi Alpha Theta

1959 Pi Omega Pi
1960 Kappa Delta Pi
1962 Sigma Tau Delta
1971 Pi Delta Phi
1971 Psi Chi
1972 Pi Gamma Mu
1973 Phi Eta Sigma
1981 Phi Sigma Iota
1985 Mortar Board
1990 Pi Kappa Lambda

OTHER HONORS
    National Order of Omega
1975 Pi Mu Epsilon

SERVICE
1949 Alpha Phi Omega
1971 Gamma Sigma Sigma

RECOGNITION
1933 Sigma Delta Psi
1938 Alpha Psi Omega
1954 Kappa Pi
1962 Pi Kappa Delta
1962 Scabbard and Blade (15)
1963 Beta Beta Beta
1964 National Block and Bridle Club

INACTIVE
1927–61 Kappa Omicron Nu
1958–84 Alpha Delta Pi
1973–80 Kappa Delta
1973–84 Sigma Phi Epsilon

WEST VIRGINIA UNIVERSITY   Morgantown, WV. Founded 1867 as land-grant institution. Coeducational; state university; state-approved board of governors.

Fraternities and sororities own their own land and homes.

NIC MEN'S
1860 Delta Tau Delta
1883 Kappa Sigma
1890 Phi Kappa Psi
1891 Phi Sigma Kappa
1895 Sigma Chi
1896 Phi Kappa Sigma
1897 Kappa Alpha Order
1900 Beta Theta Pi

1903 Sigma Phi Epsilon
1904 Pi Kappa Alpha
1904 Sigma Nu
1921 Theta Chi
1923 Alpha Phi Delta
1923 Tau Kappa Epsilon
1924 Alpha Gamma Rho
1926 Phi Delta Theta
1930 Pi Kappa Phi

1970 Kappa Alpha Psi (A)
1974 Phi Gamma Delta
1988 Sigma Pi

NPHC MEN'S
     Phi Beta Sigma

NPC WOMEN'S
1905 Alpha Xi Delta
1905 Chi Omega
1906 Kappa Kappa Gamma
1918 Pi Beta Phi
1922 Delta Gamma
1930 Alpha Phi
1951 Kappa Delta
1955 Delta Delta Delta
1986 Alpha Omicron Pi

NPHC WOMEN'S
1922 Alpha Kappa Alpha
1973 Alpha Kappa Alpha
1989 Sigma Gamma Rho

PROFESSIONAL
1922 Phi Delta Phi
1925 Kappa Kappa Psi
1925 Kappa Psi
1925 Phi Alpha Delta
1950 Mu Phi Epsilon
1957 Alpha Delta Theta
1960 Lambda Kappa Sigma
1962 Psi Omega
1962 Xi Psi Phi
1968 Zeta Phi Eta
1969 Tau Beta Sigma

OTHER PROFESSIONAL
1922 Alpha Zeta
1923 Phi Upsilon Omicron
1950 Alpha Tau Alpha
1957 Beta Alpha Psi
1959 Sigma Delta Chi
1961 Delta Sigma Delta

ACHS HONORS
     Omicron Delta Epsilon
     Pi Alpha Alpha
1922 Tau Beta Pi
1924 Delta Sigma Rho-Tau
     Kappa Alpha
1924 Mortar Board
1927 Kappa Delta Pi
1929 Sigma Pi Sigma
1930 Kappa Tau Alpha
1931 Alpha Epsilon Delta
1942 Pi Tau Sigma
1947 Eta Kappa Nu
1948 Psi Chi
1949 Chi Epsilon
1949 Rho Chi
1950 Pi Delta Phi
1952 Kappa Omicron Nu
1952 Phi Alpha Theta
1952 Xi Sigma Pi
1954 Sigma Gamma Tau
1955 Alpha Pi Mu

WEST VIRGINIA INSTITUTE OF TECHNOLOGY
Montgomery, WV. College of liberal arts and technological school; coeducational; state control; chartered 1895.

NIC MEN'S
1960 Sigma Phi Epsilon
1967 Pi Kappa Phi
1967 Sigma Pi
1978 Kappa Alpha Psi (A)

1983 Delta Chi
1987 Phi Kappa Tau

NPC WOMEN'S
1967 Delta Zeta

1957 Pi Sigma Alpha
1958 Omega Chi Epsilon
1960 Sigma Delta Pi
1966 Sigma Theta Tau
1971 Alpha Epsilon
1973 Pi Tau Sigma
1975 Phi Kappa Phi
1982 Pi Kappa Lambda
1984 Sigma Lambda Alpha

OTHER HONORS
     National Order of Omega
1910 Phi Beta Kappa
1925 Order of the Coif
1927 Sigma Gamma Epsilon
1939 Sigma Xi
1959 Gamma Sigma Delta
1961 Omicron Kappa Upsilon
1962 Alpha Omega Alpha
1966 National Collegiate
     Players
1967 Pi Mu Epsilon

SERVICE
1955 Alpha Phi Omega

RECOGNITION
     Angel Flight
     Arnold Air Society (E-1)
1916 Scabbard and Blade (2)
1920 National Block and Bridle
     Club
1924 Phi Lambda Upsilon
1926 Alpha Psi Omega
1959 Sigma Delta Psi
1967 Sigma Phi Alpha
1974 Beta Beta Beta

INACTIVE
1902–09 Delta Chi
1908   Phi Beta Pi and Theta
          Kappa Psi (B)
1922   Phi Beta Pi and Theta
          Kappa Psi (a)
1922–59 Pi Lambda Phi
1924–87 Alpha Delta Pi
1927   Eta Sigma Phi
1927–42 Phi Mu
1927–78 Zeta Beta Tau
1928–43 Phi Kappa Tau
1930–84 Gamma Phi Beta
1931   Delta Phi Alpha
1931–64 Alpha Sigma Phi
1932   Kappa Beta Pi
1933   Phi Chi
1934–69 Sigma Delta Tau
1943–69 Alpha Kappa Psi
1950–85 Phi Mu Alpha—
          Sinfonia
1953–76 Lambda Chi Alpha
1969–85 Chi Phi
1981–87 FarmHouse

COLONIES
1982 Kappa Delta Rho

NPHC WOMEN'S
1980 Alpha Kappa Alpha

PROFESSIONAL
1972 Kappa Kappa Psi

ACHS HONORS
1964 Phi Alpha Theta
1971 Alpha Chi
1971 Sigma Pi Sigma
1972 Tau Beta Pi
1974 Eta Kappa Nu

WEST VIRGINIA STATE COLLEGE Institute, WV. Multipurpose college; coeducational; state control; established 1891.

Kappa Alpha Psi, Alpha Phi Alpha, and Omega Psi Phi rent fraternity rooms on campus; Alpha Kappa Alpha and Delta Sigma Theta have a meeting room in the women's dormitory.

NIC MEN'S
1923 Kappa Alpha Psi (A)

NPHC MEN'S
     Phi Beta Sigma
1921 Alpha Phi Alpha
1922 Omega Psi Phi

NPC WOMEN'S
1977 Alpha Sigma Alpha

NPHC WOMEN'S
1932 Delta Sigma Theta (B)
1976 Sigma Gamma Rho

ACHS HONORS
     Omicron Delta Epsilon
1926 Beta Kappa Chi
1937 Alpha Kappa Mu
1949 Sigma Delta Pi

SERVICE
1959 Alpha Phi Omega

RECOGNITION
1947 Alpha Psi Omega

INACTIVE
1925–31 Chi Beta Phi
1966–69 Sigma Tau Delta
1968–89 Sigma Sigma Sigma
1974–78 Tau Kappa Epsilon

1954 Lambda Iota Tau
1956 Pi Delta Phi
1959 Phi Alpha Theta
1967 Kappa Delta Pi
1984 Psi Chi
1985 Pi Sigma Alpha
1986 Phi Eta Sigma

SERVICE
1964 Alpha Phi Omega

RECOGNITION
1937 Alpha Psi Omega
1949 Scabbard and Blade (8)

INACTIVE
     Zeta Phi Beta
1952 Delta Phi Alpha

WEST VIRGINIA WESLEYAN COLLEGE Buckhannon, WV. Founded by dedicated West Virginia Methodists in 1980; coeducational; owned and operated by the West Virginia Conference of the United Methodist Church.

The normal pattern for the college is to permit fraternities to purchase lot and house with college approval. All fraternities own their houses except Sigma Theta Epsilon. Holloway Hall primarily houses sorority women.

NIC MEN'S
1930 Kappa Alpha Order
1950 Theta Chi
1955 Theta Xi
1965 Chi Phi

NPC WOMEN'S
1947 Alpha Xi Delta
1948 Alpha Delta Pi
1948 Alpha Gamma Delta
1963 Zeta Tau Alpha

PROFESSIONAL
1947 Delta Psi Kappa
1972 Sigma Alpha Iota

OTHER PROFESSIONAL
1969 Alpha Beta Alpha

ACHS HONORS
     Omicron Delta Epsilon
     Sigma Tau Delta
1962 Psi Chi
1963 Omicron Delta Kappa
1970 Delta Mu Delta
1970 Kappa Delta Pi
1971 Kappa Omicron Nu
1971 Phi Alpha Theta
1972 Pi Gamma Mu
1974 Alpha Lambda Delta
1976 Mortar Board
1977 Phi Kappa Phi

RECOGNITION
1928 Alpha Psi Omega
1944 Beta Beta Beta
1961 Kappa Pi

1970 Society for Collegiate
    Journalists—Pi Delta
    Epsilon-Alpha Phi Gamma
    (A)

INACTIVE
1933–64 Alpha Sigma Phi

1959–85 Phi Sigma Kappa
1974–82 Phi Mu Alpha—
    Sinfonia

WESTERN CAROLINA UNIVERSITY Cullowhee, NC. Founded by Robert Lee Madison, board of directors organized 1888, chartered and first instruction 1889. Coeducational college; state-supported; nonsectarian.

NIC MEN'S
1958 Theta Xi
1959 Delta Sigma Phi
1959 Tau Kappa Epsilon
1964 Kappa Alpha Order
1966 Pi Kappa Phi
1967 Pi Kappa Alpha
1970 Lambda Chi Alpha
1978 Pi Lambda Phi
1981 Kappa Alpha Psi (A)
1983 Sigma Phi Epsilon

NPHC MEN'S
    Phi Beta Sigma

NPC WOMEN'S
1958 Sigma Kappa
1962 Delta Zeta
1966 Alpha Xi Delta
1966 Zeta Tau Alpha
1968 Phi Mu
1985 Alpha Chi Omega

NPHC WOMEN'S
1975 Alpha Kappa Alpha

PROFESSIONAL
1969 Kappa Kappa Psi

1975 Tau Beta Sigma
1984 Phi Alpha Delta

ACHS HONORS
    Omicron Delta Epsilon
1970 Phi Alpha Theta
1970 Psi Chi
1972 Alpha Lambda Delta
1972 Phi Kappa Phi
1973 Lambda Iota Tau
1983 Mortar Board
1983 Pi Gamma Mu
1983 Pi Gamma Mu

OTHER HONORS
    National Order of Omega
1975 Sigma Gamma Epsilon

SERVICE
1965 Alpha Phi Omega

RECOGNITION
1930 Alpha Phi Sigma (E)
1941 Alpha Psi Omega

INACTIVE
1975–82 Kappa Mu Epsilon

WESTERN CONNECTICUT STATE UNIVERSITY Danbury, CT.

NIC MEN'S
1988 Sigma Chi
1989 Sigma Pi

NPC WOMEN'S
1990 Alpha Delta Pi

PROFESSIONAL
1973 Sigma Alpha Iota

OTHER PROFESSIONAL
1974 Pi Lambda Theta

ACHS HONORS
    Omicron Delta Epsilon

1971 Phi Alpha Theta
1971 Psi Chi
1973 Delta Mu Delta
1978 Pi Gamma Mu

INACTIVE
1979–86 Phi Mu Alpha—
    Sinfonia

COLONIES
    Phi Sigma Sigma

WESTERN ILLINOIS UNIVERSITY Macomb, IL. A state-supported coeducational institution founded in 1899 as one of six state institutions of higher learning. Graduate school, school of education, and school of arts and sciences. Formerly Western Illinois State College.

The fraternities and sororities own their own land and homes.

NIC MEN'S
1943 Phi Sigma Kappa
1947 Theta Xi

1950 Delta Sigma Phi
1958 Tau Kappa Epsilon
1963 Alpha Gamma Rho

1970 Theta Chi
1971 Alpha Gamma Sigma
1971 Alpha Tau Omega
1971 Kappa Alpha Psi (A)
1971 Lambda Chi Alpha
1972 Delta Tau Delta
1974 Delta Upsilon
1976 Sigma Phi Epsilon
1976 Sigma Pi
1989 Sigma Chi

NPHC MEN'S
    Phi Beta Sigma
1971 Alpha Phi Alpha

NPC WOMEN'S
1943 Alpha Sigma Alpha
1946 Delta Zeta
1946 Sigma Sigma Sigma
1948 Alpha Sigma Tau
1959 Sigma Kappa
1970 Alpha Omicron Pi
1983 Chi Omega
1990 Phi Sigma Sigma

NPHC WOMEN'S
1970 Delta Sigma Theta (B)
1971 Alpha Kappa Alpha
1972 Sigma Gamma Rho

PROFESSIONAL
1962 Phi Mu Alpha—Sinfonia
1968 Mu Phi Epsilon
1969 Phi Gamma Nu
1986 Delta Sigma Pi

OTHER PROFESSIONAL
1966 Alpha Zeta
1972 Alpha Beta Alpha
1974 Delta Pi Epsilon

ACHS HONORS
    Omicron Delta Epsilon

    Sigma Tau Delta
1925 Kappa Delta Pi
1934 Pi Omega Pi
1953 Gamma Theta Upsilon
1959 Sigma Pi Sigma
1965 Kappa Omicron Nu
1969 Kappa Mu Epsilon
1969 Phi Alpha Theta
1969 Psi Chi
1972 Phi Kappa Phi
1972 Pi Sigma Alpha
1973 Phi Eta Sigma
1976 Mortar Board

OTHER HONORS
    National Order of Omega
1964 National Collegiate
    Players

SERVICE
1958 Alpha Phi Omega

RECOGNITION
1932 Pi Kappa Delta
1935 Sigma Zeta
1955 Beta Beta Beta
1962 Kappa Pi
1964 Blue Key
1965 National Block and Bridle
    Club
1971 Sigma Iota Epsilon

INACTIVE
1943–67 Sigma Tau Gamma
1955–69 Pi Gamma Mu
1973–79 Zeta Tau Alpha
1973–82 Alpha Lambda Delta

COLONIES
1989 Delta Chi

WESTERN KENTUCKY UNIVERSITY Bowling Green, KY. College of liberal arts; graduate and undergraduate schools; coeducational; state control; established 1906 as normal school. Became Western Kentucky State College in 1948, Western Kentucky University in 1966.

Fraternities own their own houses and property. The sororities will occupy houses of their own when financial arrangements are completed.

NIC MEN'S
1965 Kappa Sigma
1965 Lambda Chi Alpha
1965 Pi Kappa Alpha
1965 Sigma Alpha Epsilon
1965 Sigma Chi
1965 Sigma Nu
1966 Alpha Gamma Rho
1966 Phi Delta Theta
1967 Delta Tau Delta
1967 Sigma Phi Epsilon
1969 Kappa Alpha Psi (A)

NPHC MEN'S
    Phi Beta Sigma
1972 Alpha Phi Alpha

NPC WOMEN'S
1965 Alpha Delta Pi
1965 Alpha Omicron Pi
1965 Chi Omega
1965 Kappa Delta

1965 Phi Mu
1965 Sigma Kappa
1967 Alpha Xi Delta
1990 Alpha Gamma Delta

NPHC WOMEN'S
1968 Alpha Kappa Alpha
1970 Delta Sigma Theta (B)
1978 Sigma Gamma Rho

PROFESSIONAL
1960 Phi Mu Alpha—Sinfonia
1961 Delta Omicron
1964 Delta Sigma Pi
1965 Pi Sigma Epsilon
1969 Zeta Phi Eta

OTHER PROFESSIONAL
1966 Phi Upsilon Omicron
1974 Sigma Delta Chi

ACHS HONORS
    Omicron Delta Epsilon

1944 Sigma Pi Sigma
1960 Phi Alpha Theta
1963 Sigma Tau Delta
1964 Pi Delta Phi
1964 Sigma Delta Pi
1968 Alpha Epsilon Delta
1968 Gamma Theta Upsilon
1970 Phi Eta Sigma
1970 Pi Omega Pi
1971 Omicron Delta Kappa
1972 Pi Sigma Alpha
1973 Psi Chi
1981 Kappa Tau Alpha
1983 Phi Kappa Phi

OTHER HONORS
    National Order of Omega

1972 Pi Mu Epsilon

SERVICE
1964 Alpha Phi Omega
1968 Gamma Sigma Sigma

RECOGNITION
1954 Scabbard and Blade (11)
1960 Kappa Pi
1964 Delta Phi Alpha
1972 Beta Beta Beta

INACTIVE
1967–76 Alpha Tau Omega
1968–75 Phi Chi Theta
1974–84 Pi Kappa Phi

1968 Pi Kappa Lambda
1971 Beta Gamma Sigma
1984 Phi Alpha Theta
1989 Phi Kappa Phi
1989 Tau Beta Pi

OTHER HONORS
    National Order of Omega

SERVICE
1941 Alpha Phi Omega

RECOGNITION
1958 Beta Beta Beta
1965 Scabbard and Blade (16)
1969 Sigma Iota Epsilon

INACTIVE
1938–67 Pi Gamma Mu

1940–70 Sigma Tau Gamma
1953–76 Alpha Sigma Alpha
1957–74 Theta Xi
1958–70 Omicron Delta Kappa
1958–71 Alpha Beta Alpha
1962–70 Delta Sigma Pi
1962–74 Phi Kappa Tau
1964–73 Beta Sigma Psi
1966–83 Beta Phi Mu
1967–71 Zeta Beta Tau
1968–75 Gamma Phi Beta
1978–84 Beta Theta Pi
1980–82 Alpha Epsilon Pi

COLONIES
1956 Delta Upsilon

WESTERN MARYLAND COLLEGE Westminster, MD. College of liberal arts; coeducational; independent control; established 1869.

NIC MEN'S
1971 Phi Delta Theta
1983 Sigma Phi Epsilon

NPC WOMEN'S
1981 Phi Sigma Sigma
1989 Phi Mu

PROFESSIONAL
1957 Delta Omicron

ACHS HONORS
    Omicron Delta Epsilon
1960 Pi Gamma Mu

1963 Omicron Delta Kappa
1965 Kappa Mu Epsilon
1974 Psi Chi
1981 Phi Alpha Theta
1985 Pi Sigma Alpha

RECOGNITION
1932 Beta Beta Beta
1967 Phi Delta Gamma

COLONIES
1990 Delta Upsilon

WESTERN MICHIGAN UNIVERSITY Kalamazoo, MI. Founded 1903 as Western State Normal School. There are eight colleges, two schools, and fifty-three departments. In 1966, eight doctoral programs were initiated.

The fraternities and sororities own or rent their own land and houses. On-campus housing is optional to all students.

NIC MEN'S
1947 Delta Sigma Phi
1948 Kappa Alpha Psi (A)
1952 Tau Kappa Epsilon
1955 Delta Chi
1955 Sigma Phi Epsilon
1956 Phi Sigma Kappa
1961 Phi Sigma Kappa
1961 Sigma Alpha Epsilon
1963 Pi Kappa Alpha
1966 Sigma Chi
1967 Sigma Pi
1968 Lambda Chi Alpha
1972 Phi Gamma Delta
1989 Alpha Chi Rho

NPHC MEN'S
    Phi Beta Sigma
1962 Alpha Phi Alpha

NPC WOMEN'S
1950 Delta Zeta
1950 Sigma Kappa
1951 Alpha Chi Omega
1951 Alpha Omicron Pi
1952 Sigma Sigma Sigma
1960 Chi Omega
1962 Alpha Phi

1962 Phi Mu
1984 Delta Gamma

NPHC WOMEN'S
1953 Delta Sigma Theta (B)
1965 Alpha Kappa Alpha
1976 Sigma Gamma Rho

PROFESSIONAL
1948 Phi Mu Alpha—Sinfonia
1949 Sigma Alpha Iota
1954 Alpha Kappa Psi
1978 Phi Chi Theta

OTHER PROFESSIONAL
1971 Beta Alpha Psi
1973 Delta Pi Epsilon

ACHS HONORS
1928 Delta Sigma Rho-Tau
     Kappa Alpha
1929 Kappa Delta Pi
1948 Psi Chi
1949 Gamma Theta Upsilon
1950 Pi Omega Pi
1962 Alpha Lambda Delta
1962 Phi Eta Sigma
1963 Mortar Board
1965 Alpha Kappa Delta

WESTERN NEW ENGLAND COLLEGE Springfield, MA. Originally established 1919 as Springfield Division of Northeastern University; incorporated as Western New England 1951; coeducational; private; undergraduate and graduate programs.

NIC MEN'S
1969 Tau Epsilon Phi

PROFESSIONAL
1968 Alpha Kappa Psi
1974 Phi Alpha Delta

ACHS HONORS
1970 Delta Mu Delta
1974 Psi Chi

INACTIVE
1969–80 Zeta Beta Tau
1969–83 Tau Kappa Epsilon

WESTERN NEW MEXICO UNIVERSITY Silver City, NM. Established by act of New Mexico territorial legislature council as New Mexico Normal School 1893. Became New Mexico Western College 1949; coeducational college with graduate division. Became Western New Mexico University 1963.

ACHS HONORS
1962 Pi Gamma Mu
1982 Phi Eta Sigma

SERVICE
1952 Alpha Phi Omega

RECOGNITION
1929 Alpha Psi Omega

THE UNIVERSITY OF WESTERN ONTARIO London, ON. Founded by Legislature of the Province of Ontario 1878. Provincial charter 1908; university; undergraduate and graduate schools; coeducational; private control; undenominational.

The fraternities and sororities are permitted to provide their own land and houses.

NIC MEN'S
1931 Delta Upsilon
1945 Pi Lambda Phi
1947 Zeta Psi
1948 Kappa Alpha Society
1952 Beta Theta Pi
1957 Sigma Chi
1962 Phi Delta Theta
1968 Phi Gamma Delta
1972 Delta Kappa Epsilon
1985 Acacia
1985 Sigma Pi
1987 Alpha Epsilon Pi
1987 Delta Tau Delta

NPC WOMEN'S
1934 Pi Beta Phi
1936 Gamma Phi Beta
1937 Kappa Alpha Theta
1986 Alpha Omicron Pi

PROFESSIONAL
1976 Alpha Omega

OTHER HONORS
1942 Alpha Omega Alpha

INACTIVE
1924–74 Alpha Kappa Kappa
1931–47 Alpha Kappa Psi

COLONIES
    Sigma Alpha Epsilon
1989 Delta Chi

WESTERN OREGON STATE COLLEGE Monmouth, OR.

PROFESSIONAL
1977 Phi Mu Alpha—Sinfonia

ACHS HONORS
1970 Gamma Theta Upsilon

1980 Phi Kappa Phi
1980 Psi Chi
1985 Phi Sigma Iota

WESTERN STATE COLLEGE OF COLORADO
Gunnison, CO. Liberal arts college with a professional school of education; coeducational; state control; established as Colorado State Normal School 1901; name changed to present 1923.

Western State fraternities and sororites do not own or occupy any special housing. The women are required to live in college-operated dormitories, but the men may reside in provate homes, motels, and hotels. Freshman men students must occupy college-operated dormitories.

NIC MEN'S
1946 Theta Chi

PROFESSIONAL
1925 Delta Omicron
1965 Delta Sigma Pi

ACHS HONORS
1923 Kappa Delta Pi
1935 Sigma Delta Pi
1964 Phi Alpha Theta

SERVICE
1969 Alpha Phi Omega

RECOGNITION
1925 Beta Beta Beta

1925 Pi Kappa Delta
1926 Alpha Psi Omega
1931 Lambda Delta Lambda
1948 Kappa Pi

INACTIVE
1925–70 Delta Zeta
1925–82 Sigma Sigma Sigma
1927–71 Alpha Sigma Alpha
1928–37 Pi Gamma Mu
1929–33 Alpha Sigma Tau
1955–89 Tau Kappa Epsilon
1959–70 Sigma Kappa
1965–72 Sigma Pi
1976–84 Phi Chi Theta

WESTERN WASHINGTON STATE COLLEGE Bellingham, WA. College of liberal arts and teachers college; coeducational; state control; established 1893 as normal school.

ACHS HONORS
     Omicron Delta Epsilon
1951 Kappa Delta Pi
1964 Gamma Theta Upsilon
1966 Pi Sigma Alpha
1967 Phi Alpha Theta
1976 Sigma Pi Sigma
1983 Psi Chi

1989 Phi Kappa Phi

OTHER HONORS
1963 Pi Mu Epsilon

RECOGNITION
1951 Pi Kappa Delta
1963 Delta Phi Alpha

WESTFIELD STATE COLLEGE Westfield, MA. College of liberal arts and teachers college; coeducational; state control; chartered as normal school 1839.

ACHS HONORS
1965 Phi Alpha Theta
1971 Lambda Iota Tau
1977 Psi Chi

1981 Pi Sigma Alpha

SERVICE
1966 Gamma Sigma Sigma

WESTHAMPTON COLLEGE Richmond, VA. Coordinate college of University of Richmond; liberal arts for women; founded 1914.

ACHS HONORS
1930 Mortar Board

INACTIVE
1966–69 Sigma Tau Delta

WESTMAR COLLEGE LeMars, IA. Merger with York College, York, NE in 1954 dates the founding as 1890. Coeducational; private control (United Methodist Church).

ACHS HONORS
1924 Sigma Tau Delta
1966 Alpha Chi
1966 Psi Chi
1973 Phi Alpha Theta

RECOGNITION
1924 Pi Kappa Delta
1944 Alpha Psi Omega

INACTIVE
1971–75 Alpha Kappa Lambda

WESTMINSTER COLLEGE Fulton, MO. Founded in 1851; four-year, coeducational, church affiliated, preprofessional liberal arts college.

NIC MEN'S
1868 Beta Theta Pi
1880 Phi Delta Theta
1890 Kappa Alpha Order
1939 Delta Tau Delta
1949 Sigma Alpha Epsilon

NPC WOMEN'S
1982 Kappa Alpha Theta
1982 Kappa Kappa Gamma

ACHS HONORS
1935 Omicron Delta Kappa
1950 Phi Alpha Theta
1980 Phi Sigma Tau
1981 Psi Chi

SERVICE
1938 Alpha Phi Omega

RECOGNITION
1970 Beta Beta Beta

INACTIVE
1924–33 Lambda Chi Alpha
1935–42 Pi Gamma Mu
1942   Eta Sigma Phi
1948–88 Phi Gamma Delta
1960–76 Phi Kappa Psi

COLONIES
     Lambda Iota Tau

WESTMINSTER COLLEGE New Wilmington, PA. College of liberal arts; coeducational; private control (United Presbyterian Church); chartered 1852 as Westminster Collegiate Institute.

Fraternities own their own land and homes. College provides space for sorority chapter rooms.

NIC MEN'S
1938 Sigma Phi Epsilon
1939 Alpha Sigma Phi
1947 Sigma Nu
1952 Phi Kappa Tau
1966 Theta Chi

NPC WOMEN'S
1925 Alpha Gamma Delta
1926 Sigma Kappa
1931 Kappa Delta
1961 Phi Mu
1964 Zeta Tau Alpha

PROFESSIONAL
1946 Mu Phi Epsilon
1966 Phi Mu Alpha—Sinfonia

ACHS HONORS
     Omicron Delta Epsilon
1945 Lambda Sigma Society
1946 Phi Alpha Theta
1950 Kappa Mu Epsilon
1955 Mortar Board

1959 Sigma Pi Sigma
1960 Omicron Delta Kappa
1962 Psi Chi
1965 Pi Delta Phi
1965 Sigma Delta Pi
1969 Phi Sigma Tau
1976 Pi Sigma Alpha

SERVICE
1968 Alpha Phi Omega
1981 Alpha Phi Omega

RECOGNITION
1934 Society for Collegiate
     Journalists—Pi Delta
     Epsilon-Alpha Phi Gamma
     (P)
1950 Delta Phi Alpha
1952 Alpha Psi Omega
1954 Eta Sigma Phi

INACTIVE
1925–87 Chi Omega
1962–80 Delta Zeta

WESTMINSTER COLLEGE Salt Lake City, UT. College of liberal arts; coeducational; private control (United Methodist, United Church of Christ); founded 1875.

ACHS HONORS
1974 Phi Alpha Theta

1983 Phi Eta Sigma

WHEATON COLLEGE Norton, MA. A privately controlled endowed liberal arts college for women; nonsectarian. Founded by the Wheaton family in 1834; college charter granted 1912.

ACHS HONORS	1987 Psi Chi
Omicron Delta Epsilon	1990 Phi Alpha Theta
Omicron Delta Epsilon	
1930 Pi Gamma Mu	OTHER HONORS
1931 Sigma Pi Sigma	1932 Phi Beta Kappa
1955 Lambda Iota Tau	
1962 Phi Sigma Tau	RECOGNITION
1976 Sigma Delta Pi	1930 Pi Kappa Delta
1985 Psi Chi	1951 Sigma Delta Psi

WHITMAN COLLEGE Walla Walla, WA. Founded in 1859 in memory of the medical missionary, Marcus Whitman. Coeducational, liberal arts and sciences, privately endowed, nonsectarian, independent of church and public control.

The fraternities occupy homes on their own land. Sorority members have separate sections in the residence hall.

NIC MEN'S	1988 Phi Alpha Theta
1914 Phi Delta Theta	
1916 Beta Theta Pi	OTHER HONORS
1923 Sigma Chi	1920 Phi Beta Kappa
1930 Tau Kappa Epsilon	
1948 Delta Tau Delta	SERVICE
	The National Spurs
NPC WOMEN'S	
1916 Delta Gamma	RECOGNITION
1918 Kappa Kappa Gamma	1955 Pi Kappa Delta
1923 Delta Delta Delta	
1957 Kappa Alpha Theta	INACTIVE
	1913–55 Phi Mu
PROFESSIONAL	1928–83 Alpha Chi Omega
1920 Mu Phi Epsilon	1948–79 Alpha Phi
ACHS HONORS	
1926 Mortar Board	

WHITTIER COLLEGE Whittier, CA. College of liberal arts; coeducational; private control (Quakers); chartered 1901.

PROFESSIONAL	1965 Phi Alpha Theta
1963 Phi Beta	1967 Phi Sigma Tau
1977 Delta Theta Phi	1970 Pi Delta Phi
1979 Phi Alpha Delta	1976 Psi Chi
ACHS HONORS	
Omicron Delta Epsilon	RECOGNITION
1957 Alpha Kappa Delta	1976 Beta Beta Beta
1959 Pi Sigma Alpha	
1960 Omicron Delta Kappa	INACTIVE
1965 Delta Sigma Rho-Tau	1973–87 Kappa Omicron Nu
Kappa Alpha	

WHITWORTH COLLEGE Spokane, WA. College of liberal arts and sciences; coeducational; private control (Presbyterian); established 1890.

PROFESSIONAL	RECOGNITION
1965 Mu Phi Epsilon	1942 Alpha Psi Omega
	1949 Beta Beta Beta
OTHER PROFESSIONAL	
1969 Pi Lambda Theta	
ACHS HONORS	INACTIVE
1983 Phi Alpha Theta	1962–66 Psi Chi

WICHITA STATE UNIVERSITY Wichita, KS. Founded as Fairmount College 1895. University of Wichita created as municipal university 1926. Became a state school 1964. Coeducational; graduate school; undergraduate colleges: Liberal arts, education, fine arts, engineering, business administration, health related professions, and division of continuing education.

The fraternities and sororities own their land and houses. Students not housed in these facilities live in residence halls or in off-campus housing.

NIC MEN'S	1938 Pi Sigma Alpha
1958 Kappa Alpha Psi (A)	1948 Psi Chi
1959 Beta Theta Pi	1950 Phi Alpha Theta
1959 Delta Upsilon	1952 Alpha Kappa Delta
1959 Phi Delta Theta	1952 Sigma Delta Pi
1959 Sigma Phi Epsilon	1954 Mortar Board
1967 Kappa Sigma	1955 Phi Sigma Tau
1967 Sigma Alpha Epsilon	1958 Sigma Pi Sigma
1980 Alpha Tau Omega	1965 Tau Beta Pi
1982 Pi Kappa Alpha	1966 Eta Kappa Nu
	1968 Pi Delta Phi
NPHC MEN'S	1969 Phi Eta Sigma
Phi Beta Sigma	1970 Phi Kappa Phi
Phi Beta Sigma	1971 Omicron Delta Kappa
	1973 Pi Omega Pi
NPC WOMEN'S	1974 Alpha Lambda Delta
1958 Alpha Phi	
1958 Delta Delta Delta	OTHER HONORS
1958 Delta Gamma	National Order of Omega
1958 Gamma Phi Beta	1935 National Collegiate
	Players
NPHC WOMEN'S	1950 Pi Mu Epsilon
1934 Delta Sigma Theta (B)	
1967 Alpha Kappa Alpha	SERVICE
1970 Sigma Gamma Rho	1937 Alpha Phi Omega
PROFESSIONAL	RECOGNITION
1941 Mu Phi Epsilon	Arnold Air Society (G-2)
1950 Kappa Kappa Psi	1930 Scabbard and Blade (7)
1954 Alpha Kappa Psi	
1971 Sigma Alpha Iota	INACTIVE
	1930–51 Alpha Kappa Alpha
OTHER PROFESSIONAL	1947–85 Phi Mu Alpha—
1970 Sigma Delta Chi	Sinfonia
	1950–61 Alpha Phi Alpha
ACHS HONORS	1958–84 Alpha Chi Omega
Omicron Delta Epsilon	1972–74 Alpha Kappa Lambda
1932 Kappa Delta Pi	

WIDENER COLLEGE Chester, PA. Founded in Wilmington, DE, 1821, by John Bullock; given collegiate powers 1847. Moved 1862 to West Chester, PA, and to Chester 1865. Name changed to Pennsylvania Military College 1892; changed to PMC Colleges 1966; became nonprofit, nonproprietary institution operated and controlled by board of trustees 1934. Consists of coordinate colleges of Pennsylvania Military College for Men, and Penn Morton College (coeducational). Four centers of learning: liberal arts and science, engineering, management and applied economics, and nursing. Graduate programs in engineering and business management leading to master's. Merged with Delaware Law School 1975 and Brandywine Junior College 1976. Named Widener College 1972.

Fraternities and sororities may own and live in own houses but must take meals on campus.

NIC MEN'S
1956 Theta Chi
1962 Alpha Sigma Phi
1968 Kappa Sigma
1969 Tau Delta Phi
1972 Lambda Chi Alpha
1983 Sigma Pi
1985 Phi Delta Theta
1987 Pi Lambda Phi
1988 Alpha Tau Omega

NPC WOMEN'S
1977 Delta Phi Epsilon
1978 Phi Sigma Sigma
1982 Sigma Sigma Sigma
1989 Phi Mu

ACHS HONORS
Omicron Delta Epsilon

1968 Sigma Pi Sigma
1968 Tau Beta Pi
1969 Alpha Chi
1972 Pi Gamma Mu
1975 Phi Eta Sigma
1979 Phi Kappa Phi

OTHER HONORS
National Order of Omega

SERVICE
1984 Alpha Phi Omega

INACTIVE
1961–87 Tau Kappa Epsilon
1968–88 Zeta Beta Tau
1970–80 Alpha Sigma Tau

WILEY COLLEGE   Marshall, TX. Founded 1873; coeducational; college of liberal arts.

NIC MEN'S
1935 Kappa Alpha Psi (A)

NPHC MEN'S
Phi Beta Sigma
1922 Omega Psi Phi
1925 Alpha Phi Alpha

NPHC WOMEN'S
Zeta Phi Beta
1924 Alpha Kappa Alpha
1930 Delta Sigma Theta (B)

1946 Sigma Gamma Rho
1972 Sigma Gamma Rho

ACHS HONORS
1945 Alpha Kappa Mu
1945 Beta Kappa Chi
1977 Pi Omega Pi

SERVICE
1952 Alpha Phi Omega
1969 Gamma Sigma Sigma

WILLAMETTE UNIVERSITY   Salem, OR. University; coeducational; private control (Methodist Church); established as Oregon Institute 1824; became Willamette University 1853.

Administration requires fraternities to occupy houses which are a part of residence hall system.

NIC MEN'S
1946 Beta Theta Pi
1946 Phi Delta Theta
1947 Sigma Chi
1949 Sigma Alpha Epsilon
1961 Kappa Sigma
1963 Delta Tau Delta

NPC WOMEN'S
1944 Alpha Chi Omega
1944 Pi Beta Phi
1945 Delta Gamma

PROFESSIONAL
1924 Phi Alpha Delta
1928 Delta Theta Phi
1938 Mu Phi Epsilon
1947 Phi Delta Phi
1986 Phi Alpha Delta

ACHS HONORS
1926 Delta Sigma Rho-Tau
     Kappa Alpha
1947 Phi Eta Sigma
1948 Alpha Lambda Delta

1952 Psi Chi
1955 Kappa Delta Pi
1955 Omicron Delta Kappa
1955 Phi Sigma Iota
1957 Pi Kappa Lambda
1958 Mortar Board

OTHER HONORS
National Order of Omega

SERVICE
1947 Alpha Phi Omega

RECOGNITION
Angel Flight
Arnold Air Society (H-2)
1920 Theta Alpha Phi

INACTIVE
1924–78 Pi Gamma Mu
1945–72 Chi Omega
1947–70 Sigma Delta Pi
1956–76 Phi Mu Alpha—
       Sinfonia
1958–78 Alpha Phi

WILLIAM CAREY COLLEGE   Hattiesburg, MS. College of liberal arts; coeducational; private control; affiliated with Mississippi Baptist Convention; chartered as South Mississippi College, became Mississippi Woman's College, and name changed to present in 1954.

PROFESSIONAL
1964 Delta Omicron

ACHS HONORS
1967 Lambda Iota Tau
1969 Pi Gamma Mu
1970 Kappa Mu Epsilon
1971 Alpha Chi
1975 Omicron Delta Kappa

RECOGNITION
1967 Alpha Psi Omega
1973 Pi Kappa Delta

INACTIVE
1965–86 Phi Mu Alpha—
       Sinfonia

WILLIAM MITCHELL COLLEGE OF LAW   St. Paul, MN. Founded in 1900; merger of St. Paul College of Law and Minneapolis-Minnesota College of Law 1959.

PROFESSIONAL
1910 Delta Theta Phi
1962 Phi Alpha Delta

INACTIVE
1923–40 Sigma Nu Phi

COLLEGE OF WILLIAM AND MARY   Williamsburg, VA. College of liberal arts; coeducational; chartered 1693 by King William and Queen Mary; master's degree programs; state control.

Fraternity houses are owned by the college and leased to fraternities; each house accommodates 37 brothers. College-owned sorority houses are leased to the sororities; approximately twenty girls are housed in each.

NIC MEN'S
1853 Theta Delta Chi
1857 Sigma Alpha Epsilon
1871 Pi Kappa Alpha
1890 Kappa Alpha Order
1890 Kappa Sigma
1904 Sigma Phi Epsilon
1922 Sigma Nu
1927 Lambda Chi Alpha
1929 Pi Lambda Phi
1930 Alpha Phi Delta
1931 Sigma Pi
1968 Sigma Chi
1984 Psi Upsilon
1987 Delta Phi

NPHC MEN'S
1975 Alpha Phi Alpha

NPC WOMEN'S
1921 Chi Omega
1922 Kappa Alpha Theta
1923 Kappa Kappa Gamma
1925 Pi Beta Phi
1926 Phi Mu
1927 Alpha Chi Omega
1928 Delta Delta Delta
1928 Kappa Delta
1933 Gamma Phi Beta
1982 Delta Gamma

NPHC WOMEN'S
1976 Delta Sigma Theta (B)
1981 Alpha Kappa Alpha

PROFESSIONAL
1953 Phi Alpha Delta
1954 Delta Omicron
1965 Phi Delta Phi
1965 Phi Mu Alpha—Sinfonia
1973 Delta Theta Phi

ACHS HONORS
Omicron Delta Epsilon
1921 Delta Sigma Rho-Tau
     Kappa Alpha
1921 Omicron Delta Kappa
1927 Kappa Delta Pi
1927 Sigma Pi Sigma
1928 Mortar Board
1930 Phi Sigma
1952 Pi Delta Phi
1952 Sigma Delta Pi
1961 Alpha Lambda Delta
1961 Alpha Phi Theta
1961 Psi Chi
1965 Phi Eta Sigma
1973 Beta Gamma Sigma
1976 Pi Sigma Alpha

OTHER HONORS
1776 Phi Beta Kappa
1975 Sigma Gamma Epsilon

SERVICE
1961 Alpha Phi Omega

RECOGNITION
1922 Chi Delta Phi
1925 Theta Alpha Phi

1927 Eta Sigma Phi
1935 Society for Collegiate
    Journalists—Pi Delta
    Epsilon-Alpha Phi Gamma
    (P)
1949 Scabbard and Blade (8)
1981 Gamma Sigma Epsilon

INACTIVE
1876–77 Beta Theta Pi
1921–36 Alpha Kappa Psi

1921–39 Chi Beta Phi
1924–38 Pi Gamma Mu
1925–36 Kappa Phi Kappa
1927–39 Beta Alpha Psi
1927–54 Zeta Beta Tau
1933   Delta Psi Kappa
1934–46 Kappa Omicron Nu

COLONIES
1926 Phi Kappa Tau

WILLIAM JEWELL COLLEGE Liberty, MO. Founded in 1849 by the Baptists of Missouri; first building completed 1851; undergraduate; coeducational; granting A.B. degree; private control; chartered 1849.

Fraternities own their own land and homes. The sororities occupy a dormitory.

NIC MEN'S
1886 Phi Gamma Delta
1887 Kappa Alpha Order
1894 Sigma Nu
1942 Lambda Chi Alpha

NPC WOMEN'S
1946 Alpha Gamma Delta
1949 Alpha Delta Pi
1961 Delta Zeta
1964 Zeta Tau Alpha

PROFESSIONAL
1961 Phi Mu Alpha—Sinfonia
1961 Sigma Alpha Iota

ACHS HONORS
1930 Pi Gamma Mu
1930 Sigma Pi Sigma
1945 Phi Sigma Iota
1947 Kappa Mu Epsilon

1947 Phi Alpha Theta
1957 Alpha Lambda Delta
1970 Delta Mu Delta
1974 Phi Sigma Tau
1978 Mortar Board
1989 Psi Chi

OTHER HONORS
    National Order of Omega

SERVICE
1934 Alpha Phi Omega

RECOGNITION
1922 Pi Kappa Delta
1927 Beta Beta Beta
1929 Alpha Psi Omega

INACTIVE
1897–36 Kappa Sigma
1928–60 Sigma Tau Delta

WILLIAM PATERSON COLLEGE Wayne, NJ. Liberal arts college; coeducational; state control; established 1855.

NIC MEN'S
1971 Tau Kappa Epsilon
1986 Alpha Sigma Phi
1987 Alpha Phi Delta
1989 Phi Kappa Tau

NPHC MEN'S
    Phi Beta Sigma

NPC WOMEN'S
1985 Phi Sigma Sigma
1989 Delta Phi Epsilon

NPHC WOMEN'S
1971 Delta Sigma Theta (B)

OTHER PROFESSIONAL
1973 Pi Lambda Theta

ACHS HONORS
    Omicron Delta Epsilon
1970 Phi Alpha Theta
1975 Gamma Theta Upsilon
1976 Psi Chi
1979 Pi Sigma Alpha

INACTIVE
1973–80 Delta Zeta
1983–88 Zeta Beta Tau

COLONIES
    Kappa Delta Rho
1990 Tau Epsilon Phi

WILLIAM PENN COLLEGE Oskaloosa, IA. Private control: (Friends) Quaker. Founded in 1872. Four-year; coeducational; liberal arts college.

Students must live on campus, unless a senior or living at home.

NIC MEN'S
1972 Tau Kappa Epsilon

ACHS HONORS
1965 Alpha Chi
1971 Phi Alpha Theta

WILLIAM WOODS COLLEGE Fulton, MO. Four-year liberal arts college for women; private; founded in 1870; non-denominational; affiliated with the Christian Church.

Each sorority is assigned a college-owned residence hall for its sole occupancy.

NPC WOMEN'S
1965 Alpha Chi Omega
1965 Alpha Phi
1965 Chi Omega
1977 Delta Gamma

PROFESSIONAL
1928 Phi Beta

ACHS HONORS
1967 Alpha Chi

1971 Phi Alpha Theta
1972 Sigma Tau Delta
1976 Kappa Delta Pi

OTHER HONORS
    National Order of Omega

RECOGNITION
1972 Beta Beta Beta

WILLIAMS COLLEGE Williamstown, MA. Founded 1793; liberal arts college; coeducational; private control; nonsectarian.

In 1968, with the unanimous endorsement of the faculty, Williams College Trustees barred participation by undergraduates in fraternities at Williams College as a matter of educational policy. Those few fraternities which remained at Williams after the 1962 decision that the College would provide housing, dining, and social accommodations for the entire student body ended their activities by 1970. Fifteen residential houses, many of them occupying former fraternity properties transferred to the College, and averaging about 80 membes in size, provide living, study, dining, and social facilities for men and women students and their guests.

NIC MEN'S
1833 Kappa Alpha Society
1848 Zeta Psi

ACHS HONORS
1910 Delta Sigma Rho-Tau
    Kappa Alpha
1987 Psi Chi

OTHER HONORS
1864 Phi Beta Kappa

INACTIVE
1834–64 Delta Upsilon
1834–68 Sigma Phi Society

1842–63 Chi Psi
1847–66 Beta Theta Pi
1851–69 Alpha Delta Phi
1853–70 Delta Psi
1855–61 Delta Kappa Epsilon
1880–65 Phi Gamma Delta
1886–66 Phi Delta Theta
1891–96 Delta Tau Delta
1891–90 Theta Delta Chi
1906–66 Phi Sigma Kappa
1913–68 Psi Upsilon
1926–62 Delta Phi

WILMINGTON COLLEGE Wilmington, OH. College of liberal arts; coeducational; private control (Quakers). Founded as Franklin College at New Albany, Ohio; moved to Wilmington 1865; reorganized as Wilmington College 1870, first instruction 1871; chartered 1875; first class graduated 1875. National Normal University of Lebanon, Ohio, merged with college 1917.

ACHS HONORS
1954 Phi Alpha Theta

SERVICE
1968 Alpha Phi Omega

RECOGNITION
1923 Society for Collegiate
     Journalists—Pi Delta
     Epsilon-Alpha Phi Gamma
     (A)

1926 Alpha Psi Omega
1926 Chi Beta Phi

INACTIVE
1928–37 Pi Gamma Mu

UNIVERSITY OF WINDSOR Windsor, ON. Coeducational. Established 1857.

NIC MEN'S
     Tau Kappa Epsilon
1971 Delta Chi
1971 Tau Kappa Epsilon
1987 Pi Lambda Phi

NPC WOMEN'S
1981 Phi Sigma Sigma

PROFESSIONAL
1969 Phi Alpha Delta

OTHER PROFESSIONAL
1973 Kappa Beta Pi

ACHS HONORS
     Omicron Delta Epsilon

INACTIVE
1969–70 Sigma Tau Gamma
1970–70 Lambda Chi Alpha
1970–72 Pi Kappa Alpha

COLONIES
     Theta Tau

WINONA STATE UNIVERSITY Winona, MN. Normal school founded 1858, shortly after Minnesota's admission to the Union, by Governor Henry H. Sibley. Bachelor's degree and name changed to Winona State College 1957; changed to present name 1976.

No fraternity housing is maintained.

NIC MEN'S
1962 Phi Sigma Kappa
1970 Tau Kappa Epsilon

PROFESSIONAL
1983 Delta Sigma Pi

ACHS HONORS
1934 Kappa Delta Pi
1969 Phi Alpha Theta

OTHER HONORS
1962 National Collegiate
     Players

SERVICE
1966 Alpha Phi Omega

RECOGNITION
1971 Pi Kappa Delta

INACTIVE
1960–87 Sigma Tau Gamma
1962–83 Delta Zeta
1965–84 Alpha Xi Delta
1969–84 Alpha Delta Pi
1983–85 Alpha Kappa Lambda

COLONIES
     Pi Lambda Phi
1989 Tau Kappa Epsilon

WINSTON-SALEM STATE UNIVERSITY Winston-Salem, NC. Teachers college and school of nursing; coeducational; state control; established 1892.

NIC MEN'S
1960 Kappa Alpha Psi (A)

NPHC MEN'S
     Phi Beta Sigma

NPHC WOMEN'S
     Zeta Phi Beta
1949 Alpha Kappa Alpha
1951 Sigma Gamma Rho

ACHS HONORS
1950 Alpha Kappa Mu
1971 Phi Alpha Theta

1973 Pi Gamma Mu
1973 Sigma Tau Delta

SERVICE
1969 Alpha Phi Omega
1971 Gamma Sigma Sigma

INACTIVE
1906–09 Phi Mu
1979–87 Delta Sigma Pi
1979–87 Phi Mu Alpha—
        Sinfonia

WINTHROP COLLEGE Rock Hill, SC. College of arts and sciences; schools of education, consumer science and allied professions, business and music; coeducational; state assisted. Established 1886.

NIC MEN'S
1979 Sigma Phi Epsilon
1980 Pi Kappa Alpha
1980 Pi Kappa Phi
1982 Kappa Alpha Psi (A)
1986 Tau Kappa Epsilon
1987 Sigma Alpha Epsilon

NPHC MEN'S
     Phi Beta Sigma
     Phi Beta Sigma

NPC WOMEN'S
1977 Delta Zeta
1978 Zeta Tau Alpha
1979 Alpha Delta Pi
1979 Sigma Sigma Sigma
1985 Chi Omega

NPHC WOMEN'S
1978 Alpha Kappa Alpha
1989 Sigma Gamma Rho

PROFESSIONAL
1985 Phi Mu Alpha—Sinfonia

OTHER PROFESSIONAL
1934 Phi Upsilon Omicron

1976 Alpha Epsilon Rho

ACHS HONORS
     Omicron Delta Epsilon
1935 Kappa Delta Pi
1946 Alpha Kappa Delta
1947 Phi Alpha Theta
1950 Pi Delta Phi
1962 Sigma Delta Pi
1963 Psi Chi
1964 Phi Kappa Phi
1966 Alpha Lambda Delta
1972 Kappa Mu Epsilon
1972 Phi Sigma Tau
1973 Sigma Tau Delta
1981 Omicron Delta Kappa
1981 Pi Sigma Alpha
1990 Kappa Tau Alpha

RECOGNITION
1929 Beta Beta Beta
1933 Alpha Psi Omega
1944 Kappa Pi

INACTIVE
1927   Eta Sigma Phi
1938–52 Pi Gamma Mu

UNIVERSITY OF WISCONSIN Madison, WI. Organized by state legislature 1848; first instruction 1849; coeducational; state-controlled through board of regents.

The fraternities and sororities own their own land and homes.

NIC MEN'S
     Tau Kappa Epsilon
1857 Phi Delta Theta
1873 Beta Theta Pi
1884 Sigma Chi
1885 Delta Upsilon
1888 Delta Tau Delta
1893 Phi Gamma Delta
1895 Theta Delta Chi
1898 Kappa Sigma
1901 Phi Kappa Sigma
1902 Alpha Delta Phi
1903 Sigma Alpha Epsilon
1906 Acacia
1909 Sigma Phi Society
1913 Triangle
1916 Alpha Gamma Rho
1916 Chi Phi
1918 Theta Chi
1920 Pi Kappa Alpha
1920 Sigma Phi Epsilon
1922 Alpha Chi Rho
1922 Zeta Beta Tau
1923 Alpha Kappa Lambda
1923 Phi Kappa Theta
1924 Phi Kappa Tau
1926 Pi Lambda Phi
1927 Alpha Epsilon Pi
1966 Sigma Alpha Mu

NPHC MEN'S
     Phi Beta Sigma
     Phi Beta Sigma
1946 Alpha Phi Alpha

NPC WOMEN'S
1875 Kappa Kappa Gamma
1881 Delta Gamma
1885 Gamma Phi Beta
1890 Kappa Alpha Theta

1894 Pi Beta Phi
1896 Alpha Phi
1898 Delta Delta Delta
1902 Chi Omega
1903 Alpha Chi Omega
1905 Alpha Xi Delta
1921 Alpha Epsilon Phi
1958 Sigma Delta Tau

NPHC WOMEN'S
1968 Alpha Kappa Alpha
1973 Sigma Gamma Rho
1977 Alpha Kappa Alpha

PROFESSIONAL
1900 Phi Delta Chi
1902 Alpha Chi Sigma
1904 Phi Alpha Delta
1923 Delta Sigma Pi
1923 Theta Tau
1925 Phi Chi Theta
1949 Delta Theta Phi
1984 Phi Alpha Delta

ACHS HONORS
     Omicron Delta Epsilon
1899 Tau Beta Pi
1906 Delta Sigma Rho-Tau
     Kappa Alpha
1910 Eta Kappa Nu
1913 Beta Gamma Sigma
1915 Kappa Omicron Nu
1920 Mortar Board
1920 Phi Kappa Phi
1922 Alpha Kappa Delta
1925 Chi Epsilon
1925 Rho Chi
1927 Phi Eta Sigma
1929 Pi Sigma Alpha
1931 Sigma Delta Pi
1942 Psi Chi

1966 Phi Alpha Theta
1969 Alpha Sigma Mu
1974 Alpha Epsilon
1974 Xi Sigma Pi
1983 Pi Kappa Lambda
1984 Beta Phi Mu
1985 Sigma Lambda Alpha

OTHER HONORS
National Order of Omega
1899 Phi Beta Kappa
1927 Sigma Epsilon Sigma
1939 Pi Mu Epsilon

SERVICE
1938 Alpha Phi Omega
1966 Gamma Sigma Sigma

RECOGNITION
Angel Flight
1904 Scabbard and Blade (1)
1922 Sigma Delta Epsilon
1950 Pi Kappa Delta
1952 Eta Sigma Phi
1967 National Block and Bridle Club

INACTIVE
1875–39 Phi Kappa Psi
1896–87 Psi Upsilon
1902–62 Sigma Nu
1905–87 Alpha Gamma Delta

1906–54 Delta Kappa Epsilon
1907–70 Alpha Tau Omega
1909–39 Alpha Sigma Phi
1910–32 Zeta Psi
1917–41 Theta Xi
1917–42 Alpha Omicron Pi
1917–62 Phi Sigma
1917–68 Lambda Chi Alpha
1917–73 Phi Sigma Kappa
1918–71 Delta Zeta
1919–41 Phi Mu
1919–59 Sigma Kappa
1920–34 Alpha Delta Pi
1920–52 Delta Sigma Phi
1920–73 Kappa Delta
1921 Delta Phi Delta
1921–27 FarmHouse
1921–75 Phi Mu Alpha—Sinfonia
1922–88 Sigma Pi
1926–55 Theta Phi Alpha
1926–85 Kappa Epsilon
1930–69 Phi Sigma Sigma
1946–52 Kappa Alpha Psi (A)
1969–69 Sigma Delta Pi

COLONIES
1921 Delta Chi
1991 Phi Kappa Psi

UNIVERSITY OF WISCONSIN—EAU CLAIRE
Eau Claire, WI. Schools include: arts and sciences, education, business, nursing, graduate; coeducational; state control; established 1916.

NIC MEN'S
1952 Phi Sigma Kappa
1963 Alpha Kappa Lambda
1963 Tau Kappa Epsilon
1975 Phi Gamma Delta
1989 Delta Sigma Phi

NPC WOMEN'S
1956 Delta Zeta
1963 Sigma Sigma Sigma
1965 Alpha Xi Delta

PROFESSIONAL
1969 Phi Mu Alpha—Sinfonia
1969 Sigma Alpha Iota

OTHER PROFESSIONAL
1973 Delta Pi Epsilon
1974 Sigma Delta Chi

ACHS HONORS
Omicron Delta Epsilon
1943 Kappa Delta Pi
1955 Pi Delta Phi
1956 Sigma Tau Delta
1961 Sigma Delta Pi
1964 Psi Chi
1966 Phi Alpha Theta

1966 Phi Eta Sigma
1969 Phi Kappa Phi
1971 Alpha Lambda Delta
1971 Gamma Theta Upsilon
1974 Omicron Delta Kappa
1974 Pi Omega Pi
1976 Mortar Board
1977 Pi Kappa Lambda
1978 Kappa Mu Epsilon
1979 Kappa Tau Alpha
1979 Sigma Pi Sigma
1986 Pi Sigma Alpha

OTHER HONORS
1947 National Collegiate Players

SERVICE
1949 Alpha Phi Omega
1959 Gamma Sigma Sigma

RECOGNITION
1956 Sigma Delta Psi
1959 Kappa Pi

INACTIVE
1959–77 Sigma Tau Gamma

UNIVERSITY OF WISCONSIN—GREEN BAY
Green Bay, WI.

ACHS HONORS
1985 Alpha Lambda Delta
1987 Phi Alpha Theta
1989 Gamma Theta Upsilon

SERVICE
1966 Alpha Phi Omega

1968 Gamma Sigma Sigma

INACTIVE
–81 Alpha Sigma Tau

COLONIES
Phi Sigma Kappa

UNIVERSITY OF WISCONSIN—LA CROSSE La Crosse, WI. Baccalaureate degree and master's degree: premedical work, physical therapy, medical technology and nuclear medical technology; Graduate Programs: Adult Fitness-Cardiac Rehabilitation, biology, business administraation, college student personnel. Master of Education: professional development, educational media/technology, community health education, school health education, physical education (general, human performance and special physical education), reading, recreation & parks administration and therapeutic recreation, school psychology, special education-emotional disturbance/learning disabilities.

NIC MEN'S
1962 Alpha Kappa Lambda
1967 Delta Sigma Phi

NPHC MEN'S
Phi Beta Sigma

NPC WOMEN'S
1961 Alpha Xi Delta
1963 Alpha Phi

PROFESSIONAL
1930 Delta Psi Kappa
1969 Delta Sigma Pi
1973 Phi Gamma Nu

OTHER PROFESSIONAL
1926 Phi Epsilon Kappa

ACHS HONORS
1930 Kappa Delta Pi

1963 Sigma Delta Pi
1974 Gamma Theta Upsilon
1978 Pi Sigma Alpha
1979 Phi Sigma Tau
1984 Psi Chi

OTHER HONORS
National Order of Omega

SERVICE
1952 Alpha Phi Omega

INACTIVE
1960–86 Sigma Tau Gamma
1960–89 Phi Sigma Kappa
1961–81 Alpha Omicron Pi
1961–86 Delta Zeta
1962–83 Tau Kappa Epsilon
1971–86 Sigma Pi
1975–90 Phi Mu

UNIVERSITY OF WISCONSIN—MILWAUKEE
Milwaukee, WI. Established by the action of the state legislature 1955; merger of the Wisconsin State College and the University of Wisconsin Milwaukee Extension Division. Wisconsin State College was formerly known as Milwaukee State Teachers College; prior to that it was Milwaukee Normal School established 1880.

Three fraternities have houses; the sororities do not have houses.

NIC MEN'S
1958 Tau Kappa Epsilon
1970 Triangle

NPHC MEN'S
1964 Alpha Phi Alpha

NPC WOMEN'S
1958 Alpha Omicron Pi
1960 Gamma Phi Beta

NPHC WOMEN'S
1973 Delta Sigma Theta (B)
1974 Alpha Kappa Alpha

PROFESSIONAL
1941 Delta Omicron
1957 Alpha Kappa Psi
1965 Alpha Delta Theta
1965 Pi Sigma Epsilon
1976 Alpha Tau Delta
1989 Theta Tau

OTHER PROFESSIONAL
1963 Pi Lambda Theta

1965 Sigma Delta Chi

ACHS HONORS
Omicron Delta Epsilon
1930 Kappa Delta Pi
1950 Gamma Theta Upsilon
1953 Phi Alpha Theta
1958 Psi Chi
1960 Phi Kappa Phi
1960 Sigma Tau Delta
1962 Delta Sigma Rho-Tau Kappa Alpha
1963 Phi Eta Sigma
1963 Sigma Delta Pi
1970 Beta Gamma Sigma
1970 Pi Sigma Alpha
1973 Tau Beta Pi
1975 Mortar Board
1978 Beta Phi Mu

OTHER HONORS
1954 National Collegiate Players
1974 Phi Beta Kappa

SERVICE
1931 Alpha Phi Omega
1951 Alpha Phi Omega
1969 Gamma Sigma Sigma

RECOGNITION
1952 Eta Sigma Phi
1958 Scabbard and Blade (14)

INACTIVE
1941   Sigma Epsilon Sigma
1948–84 Phi Mu Alpha—
           Sinfonia
1949–70 Phi Sigma Kappa

1950–87 Sigma Sigma Sigma
1957–74 Alpha Epsilon Pi
1958–72 Alpha Phi
1958–73 Alpha Sigma Alpha
1958–73 Phi Mu
1958–78 Delta Zeta
1964–72 Sigma Pi
1966   Phi Sigma Sigma
1966–71 Phi Sigma Kappa
1966–74 Phi Chi Theta
1968–72 Zeta Beta Tau
1968–82 Delta Tau Delta
1970–73 Delta Chi

UNIVERSITY OF WISCONSIN—OSHKOSH Oshkosh, WI. Founded 1871; State Board of Regents; coeducational; colleges of letters and science, business administration, education, nursing, and graduate school, baccalaureate and master's degrees.

NIC MEN'S
1965 Delta Sigma Phi
1966 Sigma Pi
1969 Delta Chi

NPHC MEN'S
1971 Alpha Phi Alpha

NPC WOMEN'S
1965 Alpha Xi Delta
1966 Gamma Phi Beta
1987 Sigma Sigma Sigma

NPHC WOMEN'S
1973 Delta Sigma Theta (B)
1979 Sigma Gamma Rho

PROFESSIONAL
1961 Alpha Delta Theta
1965 Delta Omicron

OTHER PROFESSIONAL
1970 Alpha Epsilon Rho
1972 Sigma Delta Chi

ACHS HONORS
     Omicron Delta Epsilon
1929 Kappa Delta Pi
1963 Alpha Kappa Delta
1963 Psi Chi
1965 Phi Alpha Theta
1966 Alpha Lambda Delta
1969 Sigma Pi Sigma
1970 Beta Gamma Sigma

1973 Sigma Tau Delta
1979 Kappa Tau Alpha

OTHER HONORS
1961 National Collegiate
        Players

SERVICE
1948 Alpha Phi Omega
1960 Gamma Sigma Sigma

RECOGNITION
1965 Delta Tau Kappa
1975 Beta Beta Beta

INACTIVE
1960–80 Sigma Tau Gamma
1963–72 Alpha Kappa Lambda
1965–76 Phi Sigma Kappa
1966–72 Delta Zeta
1966–74 Phi Eta Sigma
1966–79 Alpha Phi
1966–79 Chi Omega
1966–84 Phi Mu Alpha—
           Sinfonia
1967–76 Sigma Phi Epsilon
1967–78 Tau Kappa Epsilon
1968–78 Phi Mu
1970–77 Delta Upsilon
1972–75 Zeta Beta Tau

COLONIES
1990 Kappa Sigma

UNIVERSITY OF WISCONSIN—PARKSIDE Kenosha, WI. Public liberal arts and teachers education. Bachelor's and Master's degrees.

94% of students live off campus or commute. Co-ed dormitories.

ACHS HONORS
1976 Phi Sigma Tau
1980 Phi Alpha Theta
1986 Psi Chi

RECOGNITION
1970 Sigma Delta Psi

INACTIVE
1973–75 Alpha Kappa Lambda

UNIVERSITY OF WISCONSIN—PLATTEVILLE Platteville, WI. Colleges of arts and science, agriculture, business and economics, engineering, industry, and education; coeducational; state control. Established 1866.

NIC MEN'S
1966 Delta Sigma Phi
1969 Phi Sigma Kappa
1969 Sigma Tau Gamma
1969 Tau Kappa Epsilon
1970 Sigma Pi
1972 Alpha Gamma Rho
1989 FarmHouse

NPHC MEN'S
1970 Alpha Phi Alpha

NPC WOMEN'S
1969 Gamma Phi Beta
1987 Theta Phi Alpha

OTHER WOMEN'S
1989 CERES

PROFESSIONAL
1975 Theta Tau

OTHER PROFESSIONAL
1971 Alpha Zeta

ACHS HONORS
     Omicron Delta Epsilon
1960 Phi Eta Sigma
1962 Kappa Delta Pi
1969 Sigma Pi Sigma
1970 Alpha Lambda Delta
1971 Chi Epsilon
1973 Phi Kappa Phi
1976 Gamma Theta Upsilon
1987 Psi Chi

SERVICE
1968 Alpha Phi Omega

RECOGNITION
1954 Alpha Psi Omega
1961 Beta Beta Beta
1963 Pi Kappa Delta

INACTIVE
1969–75 Delta Upsilon

UNIVERSITY OF WISCONSIN—RIVER FALLS River Falls, WI. Colleges of arts and sciences, agriculture, education; graduate school in education; coeducational; state control; established as normal school 1874; teacher college 1925; state college 1951; state university 1965.

NIC MEN'S
     Tau Kappa Epsilon
1968 Alpha Gamma Rho
1968 Phi Sigma Kappa
1968 Theta Chi

NPC WOMEN'S
1969 Sigma Sigma Sigma
1989 Phi Mu

PROFESSIONAL
1969 Delta Psi Kappa

OTHER PROFESSIONAL
1972 Alpha Zeta
1973 Alpha Tau Alpha
1975 Sigma Delta Chi

ACHS HONORS
     Omicron Delta Epsilon
1952 Kappa Delta Pi

1965 Kappa Mu Epsilon
1966 Phi Alpha Theta
1975 Sigma Pi Sigma
1976 Pi Sigma Alpha
1987 Psi Chi
1988 Phi Kappa Phi
1989 Gamma Theta Upsilon

OTHER HONORS
     National Order of Omega

RECOGNITION
1936 Pi Kappa Delta
1943 Alpha Psi Omega

INACTIVE
1961–75 Beta Beta Beta
1969–78 Sigma Tau Gamma
1969–84 Gamma Phi Beta

UNIVERSITY OF WISCONSIN—STEVENS POINT Stevens Point, WI. Organized 1894. Colleges of letters and science, fine aarts, professional studies and natural resources. Graduate programs, state supported; coeducational; formerly State Teachers College, Wisconsin State College, and Wisconsin State University.

NIC MEN'S
1931 Phi Sigma Kappa
1956 Tau Kappa Epsilon
1965 Sigma Tau Gamma

NPC WOMEN'S
1956 Alpha Sigma Alpha

PROFESSIONAL
1965 Delta Omicron
1965 Phi Mu Alpha—Sinfonia

ACHS HONORS
1963 Phi Alpha Theta
1969 Gamma Theta Upsilon

1974 Pi Kappa Lambda
1975 Xi Sigma Pi
1977 Psi Chi
1981 Phi Eta Sigma
1987 Phi Kappa Phi

SERVICE
1956 Alpha Phi Omega

RECOGNITION
1929 Sigma Zeta
1937 Alpha Psi Omega

1969 Pi Kappa Delta
1973 Beta Beta Beta

INACTIVE
1930–69 Sigma Tau Delta
1952–83 Sigma Phi Epsilon
1963–83 Delta Zeta
1964–83 Alpha Phi
1966–76 Sigma Pi
1968–72 Theta Phi Alpha
1968–74 Delta Sigma Phi

UNIVERSITY OF WISCONSIN—STOUT Meno-
monie, WI. Founded by James H. Stout in 1889; established as Stout Institute in 1903; teacher education; industrial technology; home economics; coeducational; state control; graduate study.

One fraternity owns its own land and home.

NIC MEN'S
1948 Sigma Tau Gamma

NPC WOMEN'S
1952 Sigma Sigma Sigma
1957 Delta Zeta
1958 Alpha Phi

SERVICE
1949 Alpha Phi Omega
1965 Gamma Sigma Sigma

RECOGNITION
1965 Pi Kappa Delta

INACTIVE
1952–85 Phi Sigma Kappa
1964–72 Sigma Pi
1966–84 Alpha Omicron Pi
1968–78 Tau Kappa Epsilon
1971–79 Sigma Phi Epsilon

UNIVERSITY OF WISCONSIN—SUPERIOR Superior, WI. College of liberal arts and teacher training; coeducational; state control; established 1893.

PROFESSIONAL
1967 Alpha Delta Theta

ACHS HONORS
1968 Sigma Pi Sigma
1970 Gamma Theta Upsilon

RECOGNITION
   Arnold Air Society (F-1)
1927 Alpha Psi Omega
1965 Pi Kappa Delta

INACTIVE
1960–76 Phi Sigma Kappa
1962–82 Tau Kappa Epsilon
1964–86 Sigma Tau Gamma
1965–81 Alpha Xi Delta
1968–74 Sigma Sigma Sigma
1971–73 Zeta Beta Tau
1977   Phi Sigma Sigma

UNIVERSITY OF WISCONSIN—WHITEWATER
Whitewater, WI. Coeducational; state-supported; teacher education, liberal arts, business administration, adult education, graduate program. Established as Whitewater State Normal School 1868; changed to Wisconsin State University—Whitewater 1964; changed to present name 1971.

Fraternities and sororities occupy privately owned houses which they lease or own.

NIC MEN'S
1950 Phi Sigma Kappa
1963 Tau Kappa Epsilon
1965 Lambda Chi Alpha
1970 Delta Chi

NPHC MEN'S
   Phi Beta Sigma
1968 Alpha Phi Alpha

NPC WOMEN'S
1932 Sigma Sigma Sigma
1936 Delta Zeta

NPHC WOMEN'S
1974 Delta Sigma Theta (B)
1974 Sigma Gamma Rho

PROFESSIONAL
1965 Delta Omicron
1965 Phi Mu Alpha—Sinfonia
1970 Delta Sigma Pi
1974 Zeta Phi Eta

OTHER PROFESSIONAL
1972 Alpha Beta Alpha
1972 Sigma Delta Chi

ACHS HONORS
   Omicron Delta Epsilon
1934 Pi Omega Pi
1938 Kappa Delta Pi
1965 Gamma Theta Upsilon
1967 Phi Alpha Theta
1967 Pi Delta Phi
1967 Sigma Delta Pi
1969 Phi Kappa Phi
1969 Sigma Pi Sigma
1973 Phi Sigma Tau
1975 Beta Gamma Sigma
1978 Phi Eta Sigma
1980 Psi Chi

OTHER HONORS
   National Order of Omega

RECOGNITION
1943 Pi Kappa Delta
1960 Beta Beta Beta
1976 Sigma Iota Epsilon

INACTIVE
1928–70 Sigma Tau Gamma
1931–44 Sigma Tau Delta
1959–80 Alpha Gamma Delta
1967–73 Alpha Omicron Pi
1967–73 Delta Sigma Phi
1968–77 Sigma Pi
1971–76 Alpha Sigma Alpha

WITTENBERG UNIVERSITY Springfield, OH. Founded by Ezra Keller in 1845; coeducational university with a college of arts and sciences, school of music, school of community education, and divinity school. Supported and controlled by the Luthern Church in America.

The fraternities and sororities own their own land and homes.

NIC MEN'S
1866 Phi Kappa Psi
1867 Beta Theta Pi
1883 Alpha Tau Omega
1884 Phi Gamma Delta
1932 Delta Sigma Phi
1932 Lambda Chi Alpha
1986 Kappa Alpha Psi (A)

NPC WOMEN'S
1904 Alpha Xi Delta
1913 Alpha Delta Pi
1924 Chi Omega
1927 Kappa Delta
1929 Gamma Phi Beta
1931 Delta Zeta
1956 Delta Gamma
1962 Sigma Kappa

PROFESSIONAL
1927 Phi Mu Alpha—Sinfonia
1928 Sigma Alpha Iota

OTHER PROFESSIONAL
1923 Kappa Phi Kappa

ACHS HONORS
   Omicron Delta Epsilon
1929 Psi Chi
1936 Phi Sigma Iota

1937 Alpha Lambda Delta
1938 Phi Eta Sigma
1947 Pi Sigma Alpha
1949 Phi Alpha Theta
1967 Mortar Board
1970 Gamma Theta Upsilon
1971 Phi Sigma Tau
1975 Sigma Delta Pi
1976 Omicron Delta Kappa

OTHER HONORS
   National Order of Omega

SERVICE
1948 Alpha Phi Omega

RECOGNITION
1922 Theta Alpha Phi
1928 Beta Beta Beta
1928 Blue Key
1931 Delta Phi Alpha

INACTIVE
1852–54 Phi Delta Theta
1905–06 Sigma Phi Epsilon
1926–83 Pi Kappa Alpha
1930–77 Phi Mu Delta
1956–79 Kappa Delta Epsilon
1960–63 Kappa Mu Epsilon

WOFFORD COLLEGE Spartanburg, SC. College of liberal arts; private control (Methodist); coeducational; chartered 1851.

The college owns fraternity lodges but the students are required to live in the dormitories.

NIC MEN'S
1869 Kappa Alpha Order
1885 Sigma Alpha Epsilon
1891 Pi Kappa Alpha
1894 Kappa Sigma
1911 Pi Kappa Phi
1964 Sigma Nu
1990 Kappa Alpha Psi (A)

NPC WOMEN'S
1978 Zeta Tau Alpha
1979 Kappa Delta
1989 Kappa Alpha Theta

ACHS HONORS
1939 Pi Gamma Mu
1952 Sigma Delta Pi
1976 Sigma Tau Delta

OTHER HONORS
1941 Phi Beta Kappa

SERVICE
1966 Alpha Phi Omega

RECOGNITION
1928 Blue Key
1928 Scabbard and Blade (6)
1929 Delta Phi Alpha
1950 Sigma Delta Psi

INACTIVE
1869–09 Chi Psi
1871–07 Chi Phi
1879–85 Phi Delta Theta
1891–96 Alpha Tau Omega
1916–81 Delta Sigma Phi
1925–39 Chi Beta Phi
1926–50 Lambda Chi Alpha
1940–63 Alpha Sigma Phi

WOODBURY COLLEGE Los Angeles, CA. Private control: Independent, non-profit. Founded in 1884. Four-year; coeducational; specialized institution.

93% of students live off campus or commute.

NPC WOMEN'S
1990 Phi Sigma Sigma

INACTIVE
1968–77 Zeta Tau Alpha

1969–75 Alpha Xi Delta
1971–75 Pi Kappa Alpha

COLONIES
1969 Delta Sigma Phi

COLLEGE OF WOOSTER Wooster, OH. College of liberal arts; coeducational; private control (United Presbyterian); chartered as University of Wooster 1866; name changed to College of Wooster 1914.

NIC MEN'S
1871 Phi Kappa Psi

ACHS HONORS
     Omicron Delta Epsilon
1922 Delta Sigma Rho-Tau
     Kappa Alpha
1924 Sigma Delta Pi
1926 Phi Sigma Iota
1941 Phi Alpha Theta
1941 Pi Kappa Lambda
1947 Pi Sigma Alpha
1983 Phi Sigma Tau

OTHER HONORS
1926 Phi Beta Kappa
1948 National Collegiate
     Players

RECOGNITION
1934 Eta Sigma Phi

1939 Delta Phi Alpha

INACTIVE
1872–97 Phi Delta Theta
1872–13 Beta Theta Pi
1873–13 Sigma Chi
1875–13 Kappa Alpha Theta
1876–14 Kappa Kappa Gamma
1880–14 Delta Tau Delta
1882–13 Phi Gamma Delta
1888–14 Alpha Tau Omega
1910–13 Pi Beta Phi
1912–13 Delta Delta Delta
1912–14 Sigma Phi Epsilon
1930–39 Kappa Phi Kappa
1930–43 Sigma Pi Sigma
1941–54 Kappa Mu Epsilon

WORCESTER POLYTECHNIC INSTITUTE Worcester, MA. Engineering and science degrees plus nontechnical programs. Private; nonsectarian; chartered 1865; graduate work.

Fraternities own their own land and homes except in two instances where the property is owned by the institute.

NIC MEN'S
1891 Phi Gamma Delta
1894 Sigma Alpha Epsilon
1906 Alpha Tau Omega
1909 Theta Chi
1915 Phi Sigma Kappa
1935 Phi Kappa Theta
1938 Sigma Phi Epsilon
1959 Tau Kappa Epsilon
1965 Sigma Pi
1976 Zeta Psi
1978 Alpha Chi Rho

NPC WOMEN'S
1977 Phi Sigma Sigma
1979 Delta Phi Epsilon
1980 Alpha Gamma Delta

ACHS HONORS
     Omicron Delta Epsilon
1910 Tau Beta Pi
1950 Eta Kappa Nu
1959 Pi Tau Sigma
1961 Chi Epsilon
1970 Sigma Pi Sigma
1973 Phi Alpha Theta
1973 Sigma Delta Pi

1974 Lambda Iota Tau
1981 Psi Chi
1982 Gamma Theta Upsilon

OTHER HONORS
     National Order of Omega
1908 Sigma Xi
1966 Pi Mu Epsilon

SERVICE
1964 Alpha Phi Omega

RECOGNITION
1948 Society for Collegiate
     Journalists—Pi Delta
     Epsilon-Alpha Phi Gamma
     (P)
1962 Alpha Psi Omega
1966 Scabbard and Blade (16)

INACTIVE
1913–88 Lambda Chi Alpha
1922–32 Pi Lambda Phi
1940–73 Alpha Epsilon Pi

WRIGHT STATE UNIVERSITY Dayton, OH. College of liberal arts and general studies; teacher preparatory; professional; coeducational; state control. Established 1964.

NIC MEN'S
1974 Sigma Phi Epsilon
1975 Phi Kappa Tau
1977 Beta Theta Pi

NPC WOMEN'S
1972 Alpha Xi Delta
1972 Delta Zeta
1973 Phi Mu
1973 Zeta Tau Alpha

PROFESSIONAL
1972 Phi Mu Alpha—Sinfonia
1973 Sigma Alpha Iota

ACHS HONORS
     Omicron Delta Epsilon
1969 Kappa Delta Pi
1969 Sigma Pi Sigma
1971 Phi Alpha Theta
1972 Sigma Delta Pi

1975 Pi Delta Phi
1976 Beta Gamma Sigma
1977 Pi Sigma Alpha
1987 Alpha Lambda Delta
1990 Phi Kappa Phi
1990 Tau Beta Pi

OTHER HONORS
1976 Sigma Gamma Epsilon

SERVICE
1985 Alpha Phi Omega

RECOGNITION
1973 Pi Kappa Delta

INACTIVE
1976–83 Pi Kappa Phi
1981–85 Alpha Omicron Pi

COLONIES
     Pi Kappa Phi

UNIVERSITY OF WYOMING Laramie, WY. University and land-grant college; coeducational; state control. Established 1886; incorporated 1891; governed by board of trustees.

Fraternities and sororites are housed on land purchased from the university.

NIC MEN'S
1913 Alpha Tau Omega
1917 Sigma Alpha Epsilon
1920 Sigma Nu
1921 Kappa Sigma
1930 Sigma Chi
1934 Phi Delta Theta
1945 Acacia
1950 FarmHouse
1984 Delta Tau Delta
1986 Pi Kappa Alpha
1988 Alpha Gamma Rho

OTHER MEN'S
     Sigma Gamma Chi

NPC WOMEN'S
1910 Pi Beta Phi
1913 Delta Delta Delta
1914 Kappa Delta
1927 Kappa Kappa Gamma
1933 Chi Omega

OTHER WOMEN'S
     Lambda Delta Sigma

PROFESSIONAL
1931 Phi Gamma Nu

1936 Alpha Kappa Psi
1949 Phi Delta Chi
1967 Delta Omicron
1983 Delta Theta Phi
1984 Phi Alpha Delta

OTHER PROFESSIONAL
1915 Phi Upsilon Omicron
1931 Alpha Tau Alpha
1933 Alpha Zeta
1961 Sigma Delta Chi
1972 Beta Alpha Psi

ACHS HONORS
     Omicron Delta Epsilon
1917 Delta Sigma Rho-Tau
     Kappa Alpha
1922 Phi Kappa Phi
1926 Kappa Delta Pi
1928 Phi Sigma Iota
1930 Psi Chi
1933 Mortar Board
1939 Alpha Epsilon Delta
1954 Omicron Delta Kappa
1957 Beta Gamma Sigma
1961 Rho Chi
1966 Pi Kappa Lambda

1966 Sigma Theta Tau
1967 Phi Alpha Theta
1967 Pi Sigma Alpha
1974 Tau Beta Pi
1987 Gamma Theta Upsilon

OTHER HONORS
     National Order of Omega
1930 Sigma Xi
1940 Phi Beta Kappa
1961 Gamma Sigma Delta

SERVICE
     The National Spurs
1962 Alpha Phi Omega

RECOGNITION
     Angel Flight
     Arnold Air Society (H-1)
1921 Theta Alpha Phi
1929 Scabbard and Blade (7)
1948 Society for Collegiate
     Journalists—Pi Delta
     Epsilon-Alpha Phi Gamma
     (P)
1965 Delta Phi Alpha

1968 Kappa Pi

INACTIVE
1924–39 Pi Gamma Mu
1925–42 Sigma Alpha Iota
1927   Phi Epsilon Kappa
1930–79 Alpha Chi Omega
1932–65 Gamma Sigma Epsilon
1943–63 Sigma Phi Epsilon
1949   Alpha Delta Theta
1949–74 Sigma Pi Sigma
1949–77 Tau Kappa Epsilon
1950–63 Phi Kappa Theta
1951–82 Phi Mu Alpha—
            Sinfonia
1961–73 Gamma Phi Beta
1964–74 Alpha Kappa Lambda
1965–87 Kappa Epsilon
1967–75 Phi Gamma Delta
1968–72 Delta Sigma Phi
1983–85 Delta Gamma

COLONIES
1989 Sigma Pi Sigma

XAVIER UNIVERSITY   Cincinnati, OH. University; coeducational; private control (Roman Catholic); established 1831.

NPHC MEN'S
     Phi Beta Sigma

NPC WOMEN'S
1983 Theta Phi Alpha

NPHC WOMEN'S
1941 Sigma Gamma Rho
1970 Alpha Kappa Alpha

PROFESSIONAL
1967 Pi Sigma Epsilon
1970 Delta Sigma Pi
1986 Phi Alpha Delta

ACHS HONORS
     Omicron Delta Epsilon
1939 Alpha Sigma Nu
1962 Psi Chi
1963 Sigma Pi Sigma
1965 Phi Alpha Theta

INACTIVE
1938–68 Alpha Kappa Alpha
1939–53 Kappa Alpha Psi (A)

COLONIES
1985 Alpha Delta Gamma

XAVIER UNIVERSITY OF LOUISIANA   New Orleans, LA.

PROFESSIONAL
1969 Alpha Delta Theta
1970 Kappa Epsilon

ACHS HONORS
     Omicron Delta Epsilon
1976 Alpha Epsilon Delta
1985 Psi Chi

SERVICE
1952 Alpha Phi Omega
1965 Gamma Sigma Sigma

INACTIVE
1936–55 Alpha Phi Alpha
1978–80 Phi Mu Alpha—
            Sinfonia

YALE UNIVERSITY   New Haven, CT. Coeducational university; private control; nonsectarian; chartered as Collegiate School 1701; became Yale College 1718, and a university 1887.

NIC MEN'S
1836 Alpha Delta Phi
1844 Delta Kappa Epsilon
1889 Zeta Psi
1919 Alpha Phi Delta
1986 Sigma Chi
1987 Kappa Alpha Psi (A)
1988 Sigma Alpha Epsilon

NPC WOMEN'S
1987 Kappa Kappa Gamma
1989 Pi Beta Phi

PROFESSIONAL
1887 Phi Delta Phi
1909 Phi Alpha Delta

OTHER PROFESSIONAL
1906 Alpha Kappa Kappa

ACHS HONORS
     Omicron Delta Epsilon
1909 Delta Sigma Rho-Tau
     Kappa Alpha
1923 Tau Beta Pi
1953 Pi Sigma Alpha

1990 Phi Alpha Theta

OTHER HONORS
1780 Phi Beta Kappa
1895 Sigma Xi
1915 Order of the Coif
1920 Alpha Omega Alpha

SERVICE
1946 Alpha Phi Omega

RECOGNITION
1914 Sigma Delta Psi

INACTIVE
1839–34 Psi Upsilon
1845–42 Alpha Sigma Phi
1865–36 Theta Xi
1875–65 Phi Gamma Delta
1877–59 Chi Phi
1887–00 Theta Delta Chi
1889–92 Sigma Nu
1893–29 Phi Sigma Kappa
1895–32 Pi Lambda Phi

YORK COLLEGE OF PENNSYLVANIA   York, PA. Private, non-demoninational college of liberal arts. Coeducational; 2,500 full-time students; degrees offered at Associate, Bachelor, and Master level. Established 1941.

NIC MEN'S
1977 Tau Kappa Epsilon
1979 Sigma Phi Epsilon
1989 Zeta Beta Tau

NPHC MEN'S
     Phi Beta Sigma

NPC WOMEN'S
1989 Delta Phi Epsilon
1989 Phi Sigma Sigma

ACHS HONORS
1976 Alpha Chi
1986 Delta Mu Delta

RECOGNITION
1974 Society for Collegiate
     Journalists—Pi Delta
     Epsilon-Alpha Phi Gamma
     (P)
1977 Pi Kappa Delta

INACTIVE
1884–88 Pi Beta Phi

COLONIES
     Sigma Delta Tau
     Sigma Pi
1990 Phi Delta Theta

YOUNGSTOWN STATE UNIVERSITY   Youngstown, OH. University; coeducational; public; established 1908 as Youngstown Association School of the YMCA.

NIC MEN'S
1946 Kappa Alpha Psi (A)
1953 Alpha Phi Delta
1954 Sigma Phi Epsilon
1956 Tau Kappa Epsilon
1956 Theta Chi
1959 Sigma Alpha Epsilon
1967 Phi Kappa Tau
1977 Sigma Chi

NPC WOMEN'S
1952 Phi Mu
1964 Zeta Tau Alpha
1968 Alpha Sigma Tau
1970 Delta Zeta

1905–37 Alpha Chi Rho
1907–19 Phi Rho Sigma
1909–28 Acacia
1909–57 Alpha Phi Alpha
1914–68 Alpha Chi Sigma
1915   Gamma Alpha
1917–34 Sigma Alpha Mu
1920   Iota Sigma Pi
1920–29 Kappa Beta Pi
1920–33 Zeta Beta Tau
1922–43 Phi Chi
1923–29 Delta Theta Phi
1924–60 Phi Delta Epsilon
1924–63 Chi Psi
1925   Phi Lambda Kappa
1956–64 Chi Epsilon
1985–87 Kappa Sigma

COLONIES
1892 Beta Theta Pi
1986 Kappa Alpha Theta
1990 Alpha Epsilon Pi

NPHC WOMEN'S
1953 Alpha Kappa Alpha
1968 Delta Sigma Theta (B)

ACHS HONORS
     Omicron Delta Epsilon
1972 Phi Kappa Phi
1972 Sigma Pi Sigma
1974 Tau Beta Pi
1978 Omega Chi Epsilon
1980 Psi Chi
1985 Phi Alpha Theta
1989 Phi Eta Sigma

SERVICE
1948 Alpha Phi Omega

Part III

The Mens Fraternities

Acacia

ACTIVE PIN

PLEDGE PIN

ACACIA was founded on May 12, 1904, at the University of Michigan by James M. Cooper, Benjamin E. DeRoy, Edward E. Gallup, J. Waldo Hawkins, Clarence G. Hill, Harvey J. Howard, George A. Malcolm, Ernest R. Ringo, William J. Marshall, Harlan P. Rowe, Ralph B. Scatterway, Charles A. Sink, Harvey B. Washburn, and William S. Wheeler. It is the only general fraternity to be founded at Ann Arbor. Most of these men had been associated in the the Masonic Club, organized in 1894, which had a flourishing existence on the university campus. They were all interested in fraternities; but, because of their Masonic bond and close friendship, they preferred to be together in the same fraternity. Consequently, they decided to found a new fraternity that would be distinctive and based on the teaching of Masonry. They chose for the name of their new fraternity, "Acacia," taken from the Greek word "Akakia," which means "everlasting." This word holds great significance in Masonry. The founders also made membership in a Masonic lodge a prerequisite to membership in Acacia, a membership requirement which was maintained until 1931. From the time of founding until 1919, members of other fraternities were eligible for membership in Acacia.

Growth The fraternity became national in the first year of its existence, and experienced a rapid growth by the establishment of chapters at many universities in the country. In the 1920s, a decline in the number of student Masons in undergraduate schools brought about a necessary relaxation of the Masonic membership requirement. The requirement was relaxed in 1931 and completely removed in 1933.

For a few years a Hebrew alphabet was used in chapter nomenclature because of the close connection between Semitic history and the traditions and ritual of Masonry. This plan was abandoned in 1913, and now the chapters are named for the institution at which they are located.

Government The government of the fraternity is vested in a National Conclave, which is composed of the National Council and two delegates from each chapter. The delegates are the chapter adviser, an alumnus chosen biennially by the undergraduate chapter and alumni at a joint meeting, and the venerable dean (president) of the undergraduate chapter. Conclaves convene biennially; expenses of all delegates are borne by the national organization. In alternate years, regional Leadership Academies are held in various parts of the country. These embody a training school for the undergraduate officers and advisers and are under the supervision of the National Council and the national headquarters staff. The National Council, elected by the Conclave, is the supreme executive and judicial body of the fraternity and is composed of six members who are elected for four-year terms and two undergraduate councelors elected for two-year terms. The national headquarters is under the direction of the executive director, who, along with the editor and leadership consultants, comprise the headquarters staff.

Alumni chapters, which hold regular meetings, but as such have no voice in the fraternity government, are located in the principal cities of the country.

Publications The official publication is *The Triad.* It is issued quarterly, and all initiates automatically become life subscribers to the magazine. Other publications include *Laws of Acacia, Pythagoras* (pledge manual), *The Acacia Song Book, Acacia Gold Books* (officers' manuals), *The Spirit of Excellence* (the chapter standards program), *Acacia Fraternity: The First Half Century,* and *Acacia Fraternity: The Third Quarter Century.*

Traditions and Insignia The fraternity awards a scholarship trophy to the chapter with the highest scholarship and one to the chapter with the most improved scholarship. There are ten other awards for outstanding achievement in particular fields. The highest recognition is the Founders Achievement Award, also known as the George A. Malcolm Award, given to the chapter best exemplifying the teaching of the fraternity. The Roy C. Clark Award is the highest recognition given an undergraduate. It honors the outstanding Acacian undergraduate of the year and pays tribute to the late Roy C. Clark, past national executive secretary.

The George F. Patterson Alumnus Award is given at most once annually to the Acacia alumnus of the year. This is the fraternity's highest individual award and is named after George F. Patterson, Jr., a past president of Acacia and of the National Interfraternity Conference. The Acacia Award of Merit, the second highest award of the fraternity, is presented to alumni for outstanding service to Acacia and for outstanding achievement in their chosen field. A similar award, The Order of Pythagoras, is made to undergraduates, as well as to alumni, for service above and beyond the ordinary call of duty.

The badge is a right-angled triangle of the first quadrant, proportioned 3, 4, and 5. The triangle is gold, the sides of which are set with pearls and the corners with garnets. Within the larger triangle are three right-angled triangles outlined in gold upon the black background. The pledge button is round with a black enameled background upon which is imposed a gold right-angled triangle and a gold outer circumference. The colors are black and gold, and the flower is the bloom of the Acacia evergreen.

Headquarters 3901 West 86th Street, #345, Indianapolis, Indiana 46268. Phone: (317) 872-8210. The headquarters was moved to Indianapolis from Boulder, Colorado, in December, 1981.

Membership Active chapters 40. Inactive chapters 44. Colonies 4. Total number of initiates 41,650. Chapter roll:

1904   Kansas, Kansas
1904   Michigan, Michigan (1970-1980)
1904   *Stanford, Stanford* (1916)
1905   California, Cal, Berkeley (1970-1980)
1905   Nebraska, Nebraska
1906   *Dartmouth, Dartmouth* (1908)
1906   Franklin, Penn (1966-1989)
1906   *Harvard, Harvard* (1934)
1906   Illinois, Illinois
1906   Minnesota, Minnesota (1971-1984)
1906   Ohio State, Ohio State (1979-1984)

1906   Wisconsin, Madison, Wisconsin, Madison (1971-1988)
1907   Cornell, Cornell
1907   *Missouri, Missouri* (1984)
1907   Purdue, Purdue
1909   *Chicago, Chicago* (1933)
1909   *Columbia, Columbia (NY)* (1933)
1909   Iowa, Iowa
1909   Iowa State, Iowa State
1909   *Oregon, Oregon* (1913)
1909   Penn State, Penn State
1909   *Yale, Yale* (1928)
1910   Washington (WA), Washington (WA) (1967-1985)
1911   Colorado, Colorado (1971-1990)
1911   *Northwestern, Northwestern* (1990)
1911   *Syracuse, Syracuse* (1985)
1913   Kansas State, Kansas State
1916   Texas, Texas
1920   *George Washington, George Washington* (1960)
1920   Indiana, Indiana
1920   *Oklahoma, Oklahoma* (1971) (1989)
1923   *Carnegie Tech, Carnegie-Mellon* (1933)
1923   *North Carolina, North Carolina* (1932)
1923   *Oklahoma State, Oklahoma State* (1988)
1924   Oregon State, Oregon State
1925   *Denver, Denver* (1958)
1929   *Cincinnati, Cincinnati* (1971)
1935   Washington State, Washington State
1945   Wyoming, Wyoming
1947   *USC, USC* (1961)
1948   *U.C.L.A., UCLA* (1971-1979) (1983)
1949   Miami (OH), Miami (OH) (1976-1986)
1949   New Hampshire, New Hampshire (1979-1982)
1949   Ohio, Ohio (1970-1989)
1949   Rensselaer, R.P.I.
1950   *Arizona, Arizona* (1971)
1950   *Colorado State, Colorado State* (1971)
1950   *Evansville, Evansville* (1958)
1950   Vermont, Vermont
1951   *Arkansas, Arkansas* (1974)
1955   Long Beach, Cal State, Long Beach
1956   L.S.U., L.S.U.
1956   *Northern Colorado, Northern Colorado* (1974)
1957   *Central Missouri State, Central Missouri State* (1971)
1958   Missouri/Rolla, Missouri, Rolla
1961   *Luther A. Smith, Southern Mississippi* (1968)
1961   *Mississippi State, Mississippi State* (1980)
1962   *Boston, Boston U.* (1971)
1962   *Memphis State, Memphis State* (1971)
1964   *Central State Oklahoma, Central State (OK)* (1983)
1966   *Alabama, Alabama* (1970)
1966   Georgia, Georgia (1971-1988)
1966   *San Jose State, San Jose* (1971)
1966   Shippensburg, Shippensburg
1966   Tennessee, Tennessee

1967 *Tri-State, Tri-State* (1979)
1969 *Houston, Houston* (1971)
1969 *Northeast Louisiana, Northeast Louisiana*
    (1981)
1970 *East Texas, East Texas* (1976)
1971 *Kansas St. Teacher's, Emporia* (1976)
1972 *Eastern Illinois, Eastern Illinois* (1977)
1972 *Illinois State, Illinois State* (1978)
1972 *Kearney State, Kearney* (1974)
1973 *Northeastern, Northeastern (OK)* (1989)
1973 Pittsburgh/Johnstown, Pitt, Johnstown
1974 *Upper Iowa, Upper Iowa* (1984)
1975 *Stephen F. Austin, Stephen F. Austin* (1975)
1977 *Nebraska at Omaha, Nebraska, Omaha*
    (1979)
1977 St. Cloud, St. Cloud
1981 Cal Poly/Pomona, Cal Poly, Pomona
1985 Western Ontario, Western Ontario
1988 Millersville, Millersville
1989 Carleton, Carleton
1990 C.U.P., California (PA)

Colonies: Central Florida, Johns Hopkins, North
Dakota, Illinois Wesleyan

Alpha Chi Rho

ACTIVE PIN

PLEDGE PIN

ALPHA CHI RHO was founded at Trinity College, Hartford, Connecticut, June 4, 1895, by the Rev. Paul Ziegler, 1872, Herbert T. Sherriff, 1897, William A. D. Eardeley, 1896, Carl G. Ziegler, 1897, and William H. Rouse, 1896. The father of Carl, the Rev. Paul Ziegler, was a member of the local Beta Beta Society at Trinity, which had become a chapter of Psi Upsilon in 1879. The new fraternity based itself on four Landmarks: "Membership from among those who are prepared to realize in word and deed the Brotherhood of all men; The insistence on a high and clean moral standard; The paramount duty of Brotherly love among members; Judgement not by externals, but by intrinsic worth. No one is denied membership in Alpha Chi Rho because of race, creed or nationality."

Growth The ideal of expanding the Fraternity based on the Landmarks came rapidly with chapters added at Brooklyn Polytechnical Institute and the University of Pennsylvania within one year of the original founding. New chapters were first to be added only at schools in states from the original 13 colonies, but by 1917 the fraternity had a chapter at the University of Illinois and with a total of 23 chapters had chapters as far west as Berkeley and Oregon State University by its 40th Anniversary. The expansion policy of the fraternity has been "Slow, But Sure." Expansion after World War II was geared towards rebuilding chapters seriously hurt during the war years. The present expansion "ideals" include locating new colonies within 300 miles of existing chapters. International expansion was started in 1985 with the founding of a chapter at the University of Windsor, Ontario, Canada. Expansion proceeds under the direction of the National Council and strives to achieve a steady and conservative pace.

Government Government is vested in the national convention, which meets annually in August. It is comprised of two delegates from each resident and each graduate chapter, all past presidents, and the National Council. Administration in the interim of sessions is carried on by the National Council, comprised of the president and vice-president, who are elected annually by the convention, the national secretary/executive director, and the national treasurer, who are appointed by the Council; three graduate councillors, who are elected by the convention in staggered terms of three years each, and two undergraduate councillors, who are elected to one year terms.

Other national offices include the national editor, the national scholarship officer, and the national chaplain, all of whom are appointed by the National Council. The national secretary, director of chapter services and the chapter consultants constitute the full time paid staff.

The vice-president serves as graduate editor for *The Garnet & White* and also oversees the graduate affairs committee.

The Annual Leadership/Scholarship Institute is held prior to the national convention each year. A fund to which each resident chapter contributes equally partially subsidizes transportation, meal, and room costs for two delegates per chapter or colony to attend the leadership school and national convention. The Alpha Chi Rho Educational Foundation provides additional funding for the Leadership School.

Regional scholarship conclaves are conducted three times per year by the national scholarship officer and national staff. Also funded by the educational foundation, these conclaves offer discussions on scholastic matters of both the chapter and individual members as well as other areas that affect chapter operations.

Traditions and Insignia The most distinctive characteristics of Alpha Chi Rho are the platform of principles and ideals on which the Fraternity was founded, called "Landmarks." They are the foundation of all aspects of the fraternity which promote brotherly love, service to others, high standards and non-discrimination in choosing members. They are set forth in the *EXOTERIC MANUAL*, the pledge manual and statement of all beliefs of the fraternity. The Landmarks are epitomized in the exoteric motto of the fraternity which is: *ANΔPIZEΣΘE*, "Be Men."

Each chapter is designated a Phi, and is composed of a resident chapter and its allied graduate chapter. Undergraduate members are called residents; all others are called graduates. The meeting of a resident chapter is called a council. Pledged candidates for membership are referred to as postulants.

The badge of Alpha Chi Rho is a modification of the ancient labarum and displays the letters A X P in the form of a monogram, on one side of which is an outstretched hand and on the other a torch. The colors are garnet and white; the flower, white carnations tipped in garnet. The pledge pin is a square lapel button of white enamel bearing the ancient form of the labarum in garnet.

The fraternity is also known as "the Crows," a derivative of the last two letters of the fraternity. Resident chapter houses are often referred to as Crow houses. The fraternity sponsors two interchapter sports events each year in both football and basketball, known as Crow Bowls.

Publications   The fraternity publishes a non-secret educational magazine quarterly, *The Garnet and White*, issued continuously since September, 1900.

Funds and Philanthropies   The Alpha Chi Rho Educational Foundation, Inc., established in 1950, is a public non-profit tax exempt organization which provides loans, scholarships, and promotes scholastic achievement for worthy students.

Headquarters   The national fraternity and the educational foundation maintain their offices in the Robert B. Stewart National Headquarters, 109 Oxford Way, Neptune, NJ 07753. Phone: (201) 776-5500.

Membership   Graduate/Alumni chapters 35. Total living membership 12,500. Undergraduate membership 1,500. Houses owned 15. Active chapters 50. Inactive chapters 19. Colonies 4. Total number of initiates 18,581.   Chapter roll:

1895   Phi Psi, Trinity (CT)
1896   *Phi Chi, New York Poly* (1950)
1896   Phi Phi, Penn
1900   Phi Omega, Columbia (NY) (1926-1940) (1971)
1903   *Phi Alpha, Lafayette* (1986)
1905   *Phi Beta, Dickinson* (1989)
1905   *Phi Delta, Yale* (1937)
1905   Phi Epsilon, Syracuse
1907   *Phi Eta, Washington and Lee* (1934)
1907   *Phi Zeta, Virginia* (1931)
1908   *Phi Theta, Cornell* (1971)
1911   *Phi Gamma, Wesleyan (CT)* (1960)
1914   *Phi Iota, Allegheny* (1987)
1916   Phi Kappa, Illinois
1917   Phi Lambda, Penn State
1918   *Phi Mu, Lehigh* (1989)
1919   *Phi Nu, Dartmouth* (1935-1957) (1963)

1921   *Phi Xi, Michigan* (1933)
1922   Phi Omicron, Wisconsin, Madison (1971-1977)
1923   *Phi Pi, Ohio State* (1936-1973) (1982)
1923   *Phi Rho, Cal, Berkeley* (1931-1951) (1969)
1927   *Phi Sigma, Oregon State* (1943)
1932   *Phi Tau, Iowa State* (1972)
1936   Alpha Phi, Purdue
1937   Beta Phi, Rutgers
1937   *Gamma Phi, Johns Hopkins* (1942)
1948   Delta Phi, R.P.I.
1955   Epsilon Phi, Temple
1956   Zeta Phi, Clarkson
1958   *Eta Phi, Gettysburg* (1989)
1959   *Iota Phi, Parsons* (1973)
1959   Theta Phi, Thiel (1980-1990)
1961   *Kappa Phi, Slippery Rock* (1972)
1964   Lambda Phi, Quinnipiac (1973-1990)
1964   Mu Phi, Clarion
1965   *Nu Phi, Steubenville* (1987)
1966   Omicron Phi, Utica
1966   Xi Phi, Hartwick
1970   Pi Phi, Robert Morris
1970   *Sigma Phi, Southern Connecticut* (1978)
1971   Tau Phi, Alfred
1972   Phi Kappa Beta, James Madison
1975   Omega Phi, LaSalle
1976   Phi Alpha Chi, East Stroudsburg
1976   *Rho Phi, Johnson Tech* (1989)
1977   Alphá Chi Phi, Edinboro
1977   Phi Beta Chi, Radford
1978   Delta Sigma Phi, Worcester Tech
1978   Phi Gamma Chi, Trenton
1979   Phi Epsilon Chi, Fairleigh Dickinson, Teaneck
1980   Phi Eta Chi, Stockton
1980   Phi Iota Chi, Central Michigan
1980   Phi Theta Chi, Longwood
1980   Phi Zeta Chi, SUNY Col., Geneseo
1981   Phi Kappa Chi, Temple, Ambler
1981   Sigma Tau Phi, SUNY Col., Plattsburgh
1982   Phi Lambda Chi, Kent
1983   Phi Mu Chi, Lock Haven
1983   Phi Nu Chi, West Chester
1985   Phi Omicron Chi, Fairleigh Dickinson, Rutherford
1985   Phi Xi Chi, Towson
1986   Phi Pi Chi, Indiana (PA)
1987   Alpha Beta Phi, Mansfield
1987   Delta Phi Chi, Albright
1987   Phi Rho Chi, Massachusetts
1987   Phi Sigma Chi, SUNY Col., Brockport
1987   Phi Tau Chi, SUNY, Buffalo
1988   Phi Omega Chi, North Adams
1989   Beta Chi Phi, Millersville
1989   Delta Chi Phi, Western Michigan
1989   Epsilon Chi Phi, SUNY, Stony Brook
1989   Gamma Chi Phi, George Mason
1989   Phi Sigma Tau, Kutztown
1990   Eta Chi Phi, New York Tech
1990   Phi Kappa Lambda, Northwood (MI)
1990   Zeta Chi Phi, Southern Illinois

Colonies: Glassboro, Drexel, Montclair, Shippensburg

COAT OF ARMS

Alpha Delta Gamma

ACTIVE PIN

PLEDGE PIN

ALPHA DELTA GAMMA was founded on the Lakeshore Campus of Loyola University in Chicago, Illinois, on the evening of October 10, 1924.

Francis Patrick Canary, John Joseph Dwyer, William S. Hallisey, and James Collins O'Brien, Jr., conceived the idea of founding a new fraternity based upon the traditions, ideals of true brotherhood, and missionary zeal of Ignatius Loyola and others. They saw five specific areas of development for students at Catholic colleges—the spiritual, the scholastic, service to college and the community, the encouragement of school spirit, and the social. These ideals were decreed in the purpose of Alpha Delta Gamma. The First Principle of the fraternity came from the *Spiritual Exercises* of Ignatius Loyola.

Daniel John Donohue, Hugh Gregory, George Anthony Hatton, and Rev. Charles A. Meehan, S.J. joined the original four in the Loyola Gymnasium to officially institute the fraternity on October 10, 1924.

Growth At St. Louis University an interested local fraternity, Delta Theta, on October 26, 1927, sent a delegation to Chicago and became affiliated. Gamma chapter was formed the following spring at De Paul University in Chicago by several transfer students from Loyola.

Delta chapter was added at St. Mary's College in Moraga, California, on February 17, 1931; however, the chapter became inactive two years later. In 1932 three local fraternities were invited to the national convention and agreed to affiliate. Delta Phi Sigma at Loyola University in New Orleans became Epsilon; Beta Sigma Kappa at Rockhurst College became Zeta; and Omicron Sigma at Spring Hill College became Omicron Sigma.

Following the Depression and deactivation during World War II, a period of expansion saw the addition of five chapters. Another five were added in the early 1960s.

Government The National Chapter, the supreme legislative body of the fraternity, meets annually in national convention hosted by an active chapter. It is composed of the national board of directors, three delegates from each active and alumni chapter, and all the past national presidents in attendance.

The national board of directors is composed of the elected officers and includes: president, vice-president, executive secretary, treasurer, moderator, and representative, an undergraduate member of an active chapter. Four regional advisers appointed by the national president administer the geographical areas of the fraternity. They are accountable to and report to the national board of directors.

Traditions and Insignia The badge is hexagonal and of pure gold which may be plain, beveled, or jeweled with pearls and ruby points. The base supports a black enameled field bearing the carved golden letters A Δ Γ. The badge is always worn at an angle of 45 degrees and with the appropriate chapter guard. The pledge button is a diamond shaped slab of gold with a bright red enamel center. The fraternity colors are scarlet red and gold. The fraternity flower is the red carnation.

Universal ADG Night is celebrated on the first Friday of December each year and commemorates the founding of the fraternity. National Laetare Sunday observances each year mark the annual Mass and Communion services for deceased brothers.

Active chapters annually support at least one function for the benefit of orphans such as a Christmas toy drive or a spring picnic. Each chapter will also donate its services to a community fund-raising campaign.

Annual awards presented at the national convention include: Alphadelt-of-the-year, Mac Boland Award (most outstanding undergraduate); alumnus-of-the-year (distinguished service by an alumnus to the fraternity); outstanding chapter; most improved chapter; the Rev. A. J. Kelly, S.J. scholastic averages award to the chapter with highest grade point average; national charitable activities award to the chapter with the most outstanding record of religious and community service projects; and the national convention attendance award.

Other awards include the Alpha Delta Gamma Man of the Year Award and the Alpha Delta Gamma Interfraternity Award. The Alpha Delta Gamma Award of Merit has been presented only four times.

Publications *Alphadelity*, the national magazine, was established in 1929; since 1938 it appeared quarterly, and now is published annually. A new pledge manual, *A Mark of Honor*, which in part is a history, was published in 1966. Other publications include a songbook, a record ("AGD in Song"), the *Alpha Delta Gamma Book of Rituals*, and directories of members (1935, 1937, 1938, 1962, and 1967).

Funds and Philanthropies Muscular dystrophy is the national philanthropy. The Housing and Education Fund is maintained as a sinking fund to provide the capitalization for housing loans.

The Alpha Delta Gamma Educational Fund, Inc. was chartered by the state of Illinois on July 20, 1965, as a nonprofit foundation. The goal of the corporation is to provide scholarship and loan assistance to undergraduates.

Headquarters P.O. Box 17605, Ft. Mitchell, KY 41017. Phone: (606) 441-7897.

Membership Graduate/Alumni chapters 6. Total undergraduate membership 275. Houses owned 2. Active chapters 12. Inactive chapters 9. Colonies 2. Total number of initiates 7,859. Chapter roll:

1924	Alpha, Loyola, Chicago	
1927	Beta, St. Louis	
1928	*Gamma, DePaul*	(1973)
1931	*Delta, St. Mary's (CA)*	(1933)
1932	Epsilon, Loyola, New Orleans	
1932	*Omicron Sigma, Spring Hill*	(1936)
1932	Zeta, Rockhurst	
1947	*Eta, Quincy*	(1960)
1948	Theta, St. Norbert	
1950	*Iota, Regis (CO)*	(1970)
1950	Kappa, Catholic	
1952	Lambda, Loyola Marymount, Los Angeles	
1955	*Nu, San Francisco*	(1970)
1961	Xi, Bellarmine	
1963	*Omicron, San Diego U*	(1970)
1965	*Pi, Marquette*	(1973)
1966	Mu, Spring Hill	
1966	Rho, Thomas More	
1970	Sigma, St. Mary's (MN)	
1973	Tau, Northern Kentucky	
1982	*Upsilon, St. Joseph's (PA)*	(1984)
1985	Phi, Merrimack	
1988	Chi, St. Cloud	

Colonies: Xavier (OH)

Alpha Delta Phi

ACTIVE PIN

PLEDGE PIN

ALPHA DELTA PHI was founded at Hamilton College in 1832 by Samuel Eells of the class of 1832. When he entered college in 1827 there were two literary societies at Hamilton, the Phoenix and the Philopeuthian, between which a bitter and active rivalry existed. He joined the Philopeuthian to escape importunity and persecution, but the struggle for supremacy became so desperate and the means of persuasion so unscrupulous that he determined to form a new society. In a history of the foundation of the fraternity, Mr. Eells writes:

"It was a contemplation of these and similar evils that first suggested to me the idea of establishing a society of a higher nature and more comprehensive and better principles, one that should combine all the advantages of a union for intellectual and literary purposes and at the same time maintain the integrity of youthful character and cultivate those finer feelings which the college society extinguished or enfeebled. The new association, first, must exclude that jealousy and angry competition, and, secondly, must be built on a more comprehensive scale providing for every variety of taste and talent, and, thirdly, it must be national and universal in its adaptations so as not merely to cultivate a taste for literature or furnish the mind with knowledge, but with a true philosophical spirit looking to the entire man so as to develop his whole being—moral, social, and intellectual.''

The attempt to establish a chapter of Kappa Alpha at Hamilton in 1830 and the establishment of a chapter of Sigma Phi there in 1831 probably suggested to Mr. Eells some of the details in the development of his plan.

Growth The fraternity was rapidly extended, the first chapters being established either by the founders of the parent chapter or those closely associated with them. It was the pioneer fraternity in eleven colleges and the second or third in ten others. As it sought students of decided literary tastes it soon acquired a distinctive literary character.

It may not be inappropriate to notice the extent of the fraternity system at the time of Miami, the first western chapter, was established in 1833. Kappa Alpha, the pioneer of the system, had chapters at Union and Williams; Delta Phi and Psi Upsilon were still local societies at Union, while Sigma Phi had chapters at Union and Hamilton. In other words, the system was then confined to two states, New York and Massachusetts, and to three colleges, Union, Hamilton, and Williams, when the founder of Alpha Delta Phi boldly planted its second chapter at Miami University, Oxford, Ohio, beyond the Alleghenies, in what was then emphatically the "West." Ohio was therefore the third state and Miami the fourth institution to serve as a home to the fraternities. The act of Alpha Delta Phi in establishing its second chapter at Miami was important in its results, as it led to the foundation of the three national fraternities, Beta Theta Pi, Phi Delta Theta, and Sigma Chi, forming the Miami Triad as Kappa Alpha, Delta Phi, and Sigma Phi formed a Union Triad.

Hamilton Chapter in 1882 erected the "Samuel Eells Memorial Hall," a stone building in honor of the founder, which served as the hall of the chapter until 1928 when a new house was built on the original site. Miami Chapter was established by the personal efforts of Mr. Eells; this chapter died at the suspension of the university in 1873. It was revived in 1951. In 1838 it admitted some six members from Cincinnati, and for some years it was supposed that a chapter had been established there, but none was chartered. After four years of existence the Urban Chapter was withdrawn in 1839 at the request of its own members to avoid the initiation of lower classmen in opposition to a rival society. Columbia Chapter was the first at that college and grew so strong immediately after its establishment that its prosperity incited the envy of the non-fraternity men, and its members surrendered its charter in 1840 to allay the resulting dissensions in the college. In 1881 the chapter was revived, nine other fraternities meanwhile having established chapters there.

Yale Chapter enjoyed a prosperous career down to 1869. It then began to decline, and this, in connection with the opposition to the system in Yale at that time, by which only juniors were eligible to membership in the general fraternities, led to the surrender of its charter in 1873. It was revived in 1888, but again became inactive in 1935, following the inauguration of the "college" plan at New Haven with its far-reaching changes in student life. Amherst Chapter was formed from a local society called Iota Pi Kappa in 1836. In its earliest years its membership was confined to the upper classmen. In 1845, in response to a demand that the faculty be permitted to inspect its constitution and records, the chapter offered to and did admit to membership the president of the college, thus averting the opposition of the college authorities.

Brunonian Chapter at Brown University was suspended in 1838 on account of the prejudice against initiating lower classmen. It was revived in 1851. Harvard Chapter was established on a literary basis, its earliest members being editors of the college monthly. It ceased to exist in 1865 on account of the existing opposition to the secret societies and was succeeded by the A.D. Club. The chapter was revived in 1879 and again withdrawn in 1907 at the instance of its own members, who found it difficult to fulfill their obligations to the fraternity and at the same time conform to the customs of the club system at Harvard. The members formed the Fly Club.

The charter of Geneva Chapter at Hobart College was withdrawn in 1876 at its own request on account of the decline in the number of eligible students in attendance at that time. Hudson Chapter, founded by Samuel Eells and named after the town in which the university was formerly located, was the first one established at Western Reserve. Its charter was withdrawn in 1964, due to the changing character of the university. Dartmouth Chapter sprang from a local society called Tau Delta Theta, which originated in 1842. Peninsular Chapter was the third chapter organized at the University of Michigan and passed through all vicissitudes of the conflict between the faculty and the students, known as the "fraternity war." The chapter at Rochester was originally at Colgate (then Madison) University where it existed less than a year. Soon after its establishment a large number of the professors and students left Madison and went to Rochester, where they established the University of Rochester. A majority of the new chapter located at the new seat of learning under the name of Empire Chapter, which was changed to Rochester Chapter in 1870.

Alabama Chapter at the University of Alabama

was killed by anti-fraternity laws in 1857. Under the advice of its graduate members a chapter was founded at Cumberland University in 1857, where it was killed by the Civil War. Williams Chapter has a fine memorial library, the gift on one of its members. It became inactive when fraternities were banned by the College in the late '60s. Manhattan Chapter was established at what was then called the New York Free Academy. For many years it maintained a summer camp at Lake George called Camp Manhattan. It became inactive in 1913. Middletown Chapter was formed from two societies at Wesleyan, one called Betrian, organized in 1849, and another called Lebanian, organized in 1854.

Union Chapter was derived from a local society called the Fraternal Society, founded in 1833, and the Phi Kappa Chapter from a similar society at Trinity, whose name it bears. The younger chapters were formed mainly from local societies organized for the express purpose of obtaining charters; Northwestern, however, succeeded the Wranglers Society, founded in 1903. During the '60s, chapters were established for short periods at Colby College, Colgate University, and the University of California. They were closed during the dissension of the late '60s. In 1976 the Lamda Phi Chapter was chartered at M.I.T.

Government Government for many years was in an unsettled condition, various expedients having been adopted and thrown aside. After trying in vain to unite the feature of entire independence in the chapters with strength and aggressiveness in the policy of the order as a whole, the problem was solved to the satisfaction of the fraternity in 1879 by the formation under a special act of the New York legislature of a corporation called the Executive Council of the Alpha Delta Phi Fraternity. This consisted of three general officers *ex officio*, of three members at large, all elected by the annual convention, the term of one of whom expired each year, and of one representative elected by each active chapter. This council transacted business through an executive committee of seven members. The actions of the council were subject to review by the annual conventions.

In 1911 the council established the position of traveling secretary supported by the alumni. An executive secretaryship was constituted in 1959. In 1968 the constitution was rewritten and the annual convention was confirmed as the seat of authority. It elects a twelve-man board of governors to administer the fraternity, one of whom is an undergraduate, who serves a one-year term. The other governors are alumni, who are elected for three-year terms. The officers of the fraternity are chosen from among the governors.

Traditions and Insignia The original badge is an oblong slab with rounded corners, displaying on a shield of black enamel a white crescent bearing the letters ΑΔΦ; above the crescent is a green star with a gold center, and below is the date 1832 in gold. On the back are engraved a monument with crossed sword and spear. This badge was partly superseded for some years by a jeweled crescent displaying the letters AΔΦ holding a star between its horns, which was at first used as a graduate symbol only. In 1912 the fraternity adopted a standard slab badge and restricted the wearing of its insignia to the standard badge in the case of undergraduates and to a badge or pendant by graduates.

Colors are emerald green and white with gold and black as subsidiary. The flower is the lily-of-the-valley. The pledge button is green and white.

Publications The first catalogue was issued in 1837 at New York. Succeeding editions were published in 1840, 1845, 1848, 1851, 1854, 1857, 1860, 1870, and 1876.

The semi-centennial edition, published at Boston in 1882, was a fine piece of work, complete in its information and ample in its details. In 1899 another edition was published. In 1909, 1915, 1922, 1928, 1936, 1941, 1949, 1956, 1966, and 1982, condensed catalogues without biographical detail were published by the Executive Council. Song books were published in 1885, 1859, 1860, 1864, 1875, 1896, 1904, 1912, and 1925. An official organ, the *Star and Crescent*, was published in New York from May, 1880, to July, 1885. Its five volumes contain many articles of general interest. In 1939 the official organ was named *The Executive Council Newsletter*. In 1975 its name was changed to *Xaipe*. In 1947, fourteen of the widely used songs were recorded and made available in albums of three records. An LP album was issued in 1974.

Funds and Philanthropies In 1897 when he was president of the fraternity Clarence A. Seward, Hobart, '48, founded the Seward Scholarships. One is always held by a member of Hamilton Chapter; the others are held for four years by members of the other chapters in rotation. In the fall of 1931 an international literary competition among the undergraduates of the fraternity was inaugurated.

After many years of preparation the Alpha Delta Phi Foundation, Inc. was chartered August 16, 1961, under the laws of the state of New York. It is a nonprofit membership corporation and was formed to strengthen the importance of the fraternity to its chapters and to its colleges and universities throughout the United States and Canada.

Headquarters 9211 Waukegan Road, Morton Grove, IL 60053. Phone: (708) 965-1832.

Membership Total living membership 22,000. Undergraduate membership 2,000. Houses owned 27. Active chapters 31. Inactive chapters 14. Total number of initiates 46,000. Chapter roll:

1832 Hamilton, Hamilton
1835 Miami, Miami (OH) (1873-1951)
1835 *Urban, N.Y.U.* (1839)
1836 *Amherst, Amherst* (1989)
1836 Brunonian, Brown (1841-1851)
1836 Columbia, Columbia (NY) (1840-1881)
1836 Yale, Yale (1873-1888) (1935-1990)
1837 *Harvard, Harvard* (1865-1879) (1907)

1840 Geneva, Hobart (1876)
1841 Bowdoin, Bowdoin (1972-1976)
1841 *Hudson, Western Reserve* (1964)
1846 *Dartmouth, Dartmouth* (1969)
1846 Peninsular, Michigan
1850 Alabama, Alabama (1857)
1850 *Madison Col, Colgate* (1852-1964) (1972)
1850 Rochester, Rochester
1851 *Williams, Williams* (1969)
1855 *Manhatten, CUNY, Brooklyn* (1913)
1856 Middletown, Wesleyan (CT)
1857 *Cumberland, Cumberland (KY)* (1861)
1858 Kenyon, Kenyon
1859 Union, Union (NY)
1869 Cornell, Cornell
1877 Phi Kappa, Trinity (CT)
1889 Johns Hopkins, Johns Hopkins (1969-1982)
1892 Minnesota, Minnesota
1893 Toronto, Toronto
1896 Chicago, Chicago
1897 McGill, McGill
1902 Wisconsin, Madison, Wisconsin, Madison
1908 California, Cal, Berkeley
1911 Illinois, Illinois
1916 Stanford, Stanford
1921 Washington (WA), Washington (WA)
1926 British Columbia, British Columbia
1939 Northwestern, Northwestern
1961 *Colby, Colby* (1969)
1966 *Santa Barbara, Cal, Santa Barbara* (1971)
1968 *Long Beach, Cal State, Long Beach* (1973)
1977 Lambda Phi, M.I.T.
1978 Massachusetts, Massachusetts
1985 Buffalo, SUNY, Buffalo
1985 Great Lakes, Michigan State
1987 Chapman, Chapman
1987 Virginia, Virginia

Alpha Epsilon Pi

COAT OF ARMS   ACTIVE PIN   PLEDGE PIN

ALPHA EPSILON PI was chartered at the Washington Square campus of New York University on November 7, 1913. Preliminary work leading to its formation had begun two years before, in 1911. It was incorporated as a membership corporation under the laws of New York on October 8, 1914. The founder and first national president was Charles C. Moskowitz '14. The other founders were Isador M. Glazer '15, Herman L. Kraus '15, Arthur E. Leopold '14, Arthur M. Lipkint '15, Emil J. Lustgarten '16, Benjamin N. Meyer '16, Charles J. Pintel '14, Maurice Plager '14, David K. Schafer '15, and Hyman Schulman '14.

Alpha Epsilon Pi's constitution and by-laws from

its inception have provided that any male student in good standing with his college or university is eligible for membership in the fraternity. However, the founders of the fraternity were all of the Jewish faith, and were concerned about the survival of the Jewish community and the development of leaders for it. The majority of Alpha Epsilon Pi's members have always been of the Jewish faith, but the fraternity's principles have found favor with men of all faiths, creeds and races, all of whom are represented in its membership.

Development and Growth From the beginning, the fraternity was planned by the founders as a national college fraternity. No other chapter was added, however, until 1917 when Beta Chapter was installed at Cornell University. Thereafter a consistent program of expansion added carefully selected chapters.

In 1940 Sigma Omega Psi and Alpha Epsilon Pi entered into an agreement to merge the two fraternities under the latter name. Seven years later Sigma Tau Phi, a junior member of the NIC, entered into a union with Alpha Epsilon Pi under the latter name.

Many of the chapters came from existing local organizations. When there was a decline of available material, the Xi Chapter was moved from the University of Detroit to Wayne State University, located in the same city. Zeta Chapter, inactive from 1923 to 1946, was revived by chartering the Sigma Gamma Club of Georgia Tech, which had been founded in 1936. Phi Chapter was formed from Delta Phi Alpha, founded in Massachusetts State College in 1915. It had been a local for eighteen years when chartered. Theta Deuteron at Akron was originally Phi Kappa Rho, founded in 1921, and was twenty years old when it became a chapter of Alpha Epsilon Pi. Sigma Phi at the University of Manitoba was installed in 1948 and was originally founded as a local fraternity in 1937. Also of interest is Upsilon Tau Chapter, which was chartered in 1950 at the University of Toledo. This sprang from the local Kappa Iota Chi, that had been organized at Toledo in 1923. Subsequently, Lambda Chi Fraternity, the principal competitor of Kappa Iota Chi, founded in 1925 at Toledo, was also merged into Alpha Epsilon Pi and Upsilon Tau Chapter.

The installation of Sigma Kappa Psi Chapter at Northeastern University is noteworthy. This institution had prohibited national fraternities in 1930, causing the Kappa chapter of Sigma Omega Psi to become a local fraternity under the name of Sigma Kappa Psi. In 1961, Northeastern University again permitted nationalization and Sigma Kappa Psi petitioned and was accepted under its local name of Alpha Epsilon Pi, which had in 1940 absorbed the former parent organization. Alumni of Sigma Omega Psi chapter at Northeastern University, who had been initiated prior to 1930, had joined Alpha Epsilon Pi when the merger took place, but had also remained as alumni of Sigma Kappa Psi. With the new affiliation, they were once again alumni of an active chapter at their alma mater.

Government and Administration The highest legal authority in the fraternity is the Supreme Council, the name given to the annual convention of Alpha Epsilon Pi. Each undergraduate chapter and alumni club is entitled to one vote at the Supreme Council sessions. The Supreme Council elects the Supreme Board of Governors of eleven men, nine alumni, and two undergraduates, annually. This board governs the fraternity between the meetings of the Supreme Council. The Supreme Board of Governors is chosen from alumni active in the work of the fraternity and from undergraduate delegates at the annual convention.

Under the direction of the Supreme Board of Governors are the regional governors, whose duties are to assist the Supreme Board of Governors in the supervision of chapters and alumni clubs in their areas. It is also the responsibility of the regional governor to plan a regional conclave at which all chapters in the area meet to discuss common problems and make recommendations for legislation to be presented to the Supreme Council.

The convention of the fraternity is usually held close to Labor Day and includes, as the first part of its program, a two-day Leadership Training Institute. The last two days are devoted to consideration of legislation necessary for the government of the fraternity. Convention sites are usually rotated among those cities where the fraternity is strongest in membership.

A board of seven trustees, known as the Fiscal Control Board, has jurisdiction over the endowment fund of the fraternity and its trust funds.

Alpha Epsilon Pi is especially proud of its record of interfraternity participation. Although it is one of the youngest members of the National Interfraternity Conference, AEΠs have twice served as NIC President, and three AEΠs have served on the NIC Executive Committee. In addition, the presidency of both the Fraternity Executives Association and the College Fraternity Editors Association have been held by a member of AEΠ. Three AEΠs have been awarded the NIC's highest honor, the Gold Medal.

Traditions and Insignia The fraternity's highest award in the Order of the Lion, symbolized by a gold key in the form of a lion, holding the staff and fleur-de-lis. This award is made only by the Supreme Council to an alumnus whose work, on behalf of the fraternity, has been of outstanding merit. Thus far, only 31 men have been so honored. The Gitelson Medallion is awarded annually by the Foundation, in silver to the alumnus and in bronze to the undergraduate whose work has been outstanding in the field of communal and interfaith activities. The I. E. Goldberg Ring is presented annually to that undergraduate whose work for his chapter and for the national fraternity has been outstanding. The Sidney Goldberg Ring is awarded to the undergraduate convention delegate who is selected as having contributed most to the success of the Supreme Council session.

The fraternity badge consists of the letters ΑΕΠ set in pearls on a gold base and the Ε and Π joined at the top. Optional equipment, joined by a chain of gold, is the chapter guard, consisting of the chapter letter set in sapphires on a gold base. The pledge button is diamond-shaped with the sides curved inward. It is of gold outline and blue enamel center. Colors are gold and blue. The sweetheart pin consists of a pearl bordered fleur-de-lis mounted with a miniature gold heart. The recognition button is available in two official styles, the staggered letter ΑΕΠ or a gold lion holding a staff and fleur-de-lis. An insignia is also provided for members of the fathers' clubs in the form of a gold watch charm mounted with the coat of arms. A special insignia for the members of the mothers' clubs is available in the shape of a gold fleur-de-lis inscribed with the letters ΑΕΠ. The official flag consists of the blue background with the figure of a rampant lion in gold holding a staff surmounted by a fleur-de-lis. In the upper left hand corner, also in gold, appear the letters ΑΕΠ. The coat of arms is a shield surmounted by a seven-branched candelabrum, which incorporates a six-pointed star. Within the shield there appear the following symbols: a rampant lion, a fleur-de-lis, the lamp of knowledge, and the fraternity pledge pin. Below the shield is a scroll on which appear the following Greek letters: ΕΠΟΝΑ.

Publications The first publication of the fraternity was designated *The Scroll*, a newspaper-type publication issued at irregular intervals in the early life of the fraternity. In 1924 its name was changed to *Alpha Epsilon Pi Quarterly*, and in 1948 to *The Lion of Alpha Epsilon Pi*. It has been published since 1919. The *Newsletter*, an esoteric pamphlet, is issued several times during the school year. It carries intra-fraternal news and messages to fraternity members. Membership directories were published in 1923, 1926, 1929, 1933, 1948, and 1952. A 50th anniversary edition was issued in 1964. In 1927 *Songs of Alpha Epsilon Pi* was first published, containing the words and music of all the fraternity songs and a number of college songs. This volume was enlarged and revised in 1939, and republished in 1948. The *Chapter Manual*, containing a complete outline of fraternity management, first published in 1929 for all workers and officers in the fraternity has undergone several revisions. The Constitution of the fraternity, formerly a separate volume, is now incorporated in *The Chapter Manual*.

The *Ritual Manuals* are separately printed and bound. The *Pledge Manual*, for the instruction of pledges, recites the history and structure of the fraternity, the fraternity system, and the pledge's duties and obligation to the fraternity. It was first published in 1933, successively revised and republished in 1935, 1939, 1945, 1948, 1952, 1958, and 1961. It was completely revised and reissued as *A Guide to Alpha Epsilon Pi"* in 1964, and is re-

printed annually. *About Alpha Epsilon Pi*, containing brief information pertinent to the fraternity and the fraternity system, was first published in 1937, the pamphlet, renamed *Alpha Epsilon Pi and You* in 1965, has been updated a number of times. Most of the chapters publish chapter papers for distribution to their alumni and to other chapters. The *Chapter Supervisor's Guide* was issued in 1959 and reissued in enlarged loose leaf form in 1966. In 1980, the Alpha Epsilon Pi Foundation issued a complete history of the fraternity's 65 years, 1913-1978. Authored by George S. Toll, who retired as executive vice-president in 1977, the 976-page volume contains the national history, individual chapter histories, and much statistical information about the fraternity.

Funds and Philanthropies The Alpha Epsilon Pi Foundation was established in 1946 to carry out the philanthropic program of the fraternity. Among its activities are the establishment of the chapter house libraries, grants for interfaith activity, publication of books ad pamphlets relating to interfaith activity, and grants-in-aid in the form of loan scholarships or outright grants to members and nonmembers of the fraternity who require financial assistance to complete their education. In this connection, the foundation now administers the Louis Moskowitz Scholarship Fund, which was created in 1940 by Charles C. Moskowitz, founder and first president of the fraternity. Other funds administered by the foundation include the Sol and Ella Savitt Fund, made possible by a gift of $50,000 by Mr. Savitt, an alumnus of the fraternity's Delta Chapter at Illinois. Over $15,000 a year is available for scholarship assistance through these funds. In the past the foundation has sponsored grants to assist in the housing and education of refugee students, and has also sponsored an exchange student program with graduate students from Israel.

The Alpha Epsilon Pi Foundation also cooperates with the International B'nai B'rith Foundation and the Union of American Hebrew Congregations. The foundation also administers a number of scholarship funds earmarked for various chapters through gifts of chapter alumni.

In 1984, the fraternity adopted as its national philanthropy, the Union of Councils for Soviet Jewry, the organization which seeks to ameliorate the condition of Soviet Jews and to facilitate their emigration from a land where they are not permitted to practice their religious beliefs or study their cultural heritage.

Headquarters 8815 Wesleyan Road, Indianapolis, IN 46268. Phone: (317) 876-1913.

Membership City/Area alumni associations 30. Total living membership 45,910. Total undergraduate membership 3,107. Houses owned 43. Active chapters 92. Inactive chapters 61. Colonies 11. Total number of initiates 57,679. Chapter roll:

British Columbia
Cal, San Diego
Clark
Eastern Michigan
Florida Atlantic
Houston
Louisville
Monmouth (NJ)
North Carolina
SUNY Col., Cortland
Stanford
Chi Mu, Clark
Tau Delta, Northwestern (1987)
Upsilon Lambda, Louisville

1913 Alpha, N.Y.U.
1917 Beta, Cornell
1919 Gamma, Penn
1920 Delta, Illinois
1920 Epsilon, Emory
1920 Omicron Deuteron, Cincinnati
1920 Zeta, Georgia Tech (1923-1946)
1921 Eta, Ohio State
1921 Pi Deuteron, Penn State (1974-1982)
1921 *Theta, Auburn* (1923-1965) (1984)
1924 *Kappa, Ohio Northern* (1981)
1925 Lambda, Illinois Tech (1932-1948) (Charter transferred to Illinois Tech)
1925 Mu, Virginia
1925 *Nu, Marquette* (1974)
1925 Rho Deuteron, Delaware
1926 Omicron, Georgia
1927 Pi, Wisconsin, Madison (1973-1982)
1928 Rho, Rhode Island
1928 Sigma, Washington (MO) (1972-1977)
1929 Tau, Vanderbilt
1930 Xi, Wayne State (MI) (1934-1947) (1973-1977)
1931 Upsilon, USC (1939-1946)
1933 Phi, Massachusetts (1973-1981)
1934 Chi, Michigan State (1972-1979)
1936 *Psi, Johns Hopkins* (1971)
1937 Omega, North Carolina (1951-1987)
1938 *Beta Deuteron, L.S.U.* (1952-1965) (1972)
1939 Gamma Deuteron, Texas
1940 Delta Deuteron, Maryland
1940 *Epsilon Deuteron, Worcester Tech* (1973)
1940 Eta Deuteron, Tufts
1940 Zeta Deuteron, Boston U. (1972-1984)
1941 *Theta Deuteron, Akron* (1973)
1942 *Iota Deuteron, Alabama* (1982)
1947 *Chi Deuteron, Washington (WA)* (1961)
1947 Kappa Deuteron, George Washington
1947 Lambda Deuteron, Miami (FL)
1947 Mu Deuteron, Missouri
1947 Nu Deuteron, Missouri, Rolla
1947 Sigma Deuteron, Syracuse (1973-1977)
1947 *Tau Deuteron, Western Reserve* (1974)
1947 *Upsilon Deuteron, New Mexico* (1965)
1948 *Alpha Upsilon, New York (Heights)* (1972)
1949 Beta Upsilon, Bradley
1949 Chi Alpha, Cal, Berkeley (1964-1985)
1949 Kappa Chi, Queens (NY) (1972-1987)

1949 *Kappa Sigma, Kansas State* (1963)
1949 Kappa Upsilon, Kansas (1977-1982)
1949 *Mu Upsilon, Minnesota* (1973)
1949 Omega Deuteron, Michigan
1949 Phi Deuteron, Kent (1972-1977)
1949 Psi Deuteron, Tennessee (1953-1962)
1950 *Upsilon Tau, Toledo* (1973)
1951 Alpha Sigma, Arizona State
1951 Iota Upsilon, Iowa
1951 Mu Tau, M.I.T.
1951 Phi Gamma, Florida
1951 Rho Pi, R.P.I.
1951 Tau Upsilon, Tulane (1974-1977)
1952 Gamma Alpha, Georgia State
1953 *Beta Pi, New York Poly* (1973)
1954 Pi Upsilon, Purdue (1970-1975)
1954 *Upsilon Rho, Richmond* (1972)
1954 Zeta Pi, Vermont (1972-1987)
1956 Alpha Pi, Temple (1972-1977)
1956 *Kappa Mu, Missouri, Kansas City* (1972)
1956 Phi Theta, CUNY, Brooklyn (1973-1988)
1956 Rho Upsilon, Rutgers
1956 Upsilon Kappa, Connecticut
1957 *Mu Epsilon, Wisconsin, Milwaukee* (1974)
1958 Beta Iota, Indiana
1958 *Sigma Chi, CUNY, Brooklyn* (1973)
1958 Upsilon Beta, SUNY, Buffalo (1972-1984)
1959 *Eta Chi, CUNY, Lehman* (1973)
1959 Omega Upsilon, Oklahoma (1973-1983)
1960 *Beta Sigma, CUNY, Baruch* (1973)
1962 Alpha Epsilon, C. W. Post (1973-1984)
1962 *Lambda Upsilon, Long Island* (1973)
1962 *Rho Beta, Rutgers, Newark* (1973)
1962 Sigma Kappa Psi, Northeastern
1962 *Upsilon Chi, Tennessee, Chattanooga* (1972)
1963 *Pi Zeta, Old Dominion* (1972)
1964 Alpha Tau, Miami (OH)
1964 *Rho Nu, Rochester* (1973)
1964 Upsilon Alpha, Arizona
1965 *Epsilon Kappa, East Carolina* (1972)
1965 *Pi Chi, Parsons* (1972)
1966 Rho Iota, Rochester Tech
1966 *Rho Mu, Randolph, Macon* (1985)
1967 *Delta Pi, Utica* (1972)
1967 *Delta Tau, Detroit Tech* (1972)
1967 *Phi Chi, Cleveland* (1974)
1967 *Upsilon Omicron, Nebraska, Omaha* (1972)
1968 Kappa Gamma, Clarkson
1968 *Nu Alpha, Northern Arizona* (1975)
1968 *Nu Eta, Quinnipiac* (1975)
1968 Nu Sigma, Nevada, Las Vegas (1971-1977)
1968 Phi Tau, Florida State
1968 *Rho Eta, Hunter* (1970)
1968 Upsilon Eta, Houston (1974-1988)
1969 *Alpha Chi, Athens* (1975)
1969 Epsilon Mu, Eastern Michigan (1973-1988)
1969 *Iota Chi, Illinois, Chicago* (1972)
1969 *Lambda Gamma, Bowling Green* (1981)
1969 *Omicron Chi, Oglethorpe* (1976)
1969 Sigma Omega, Cal Poly, San Luis Obispo
1969 Sigma Pi, American
1970 *Delta Beta, New Hampshire* (1975)

1970 *Epsilon Pi, Virginia Commonwealth* (1973)
1970 *Iota Tau, Indiana Tech* (1976)
1970 *Lambda Epsilon, Fairleigh Dickinson, Rutherford* (1973)
1970 Mu Phi, Florida Institute
1970 *Nu Tau, New York Tech* (1983)
1970 Phi Delta, Pitt
1970 Sigma Delta, San Diego U (1973-1983)
1970 Tau Phi, Tampa
1971 *Sigma Alpha, V.P.I.* (1985)
1971 *Tau Eta, Indiana State* (1976)
1972 *Lambda Kappa, Kentucky* (1987)
1973 *Sigma Mu, Central Missouri State* (1978)
1976 *Nu Iota, Northern Illinois* (1981)
1977 Chi Upsilon, Colorado (1985-1988)
1978 Omicron Upsilon, Ohio
1979 Sigma Eta, Lehigh
1980 *Kappa Xi, Western Michigan* (1982)
1982 Iota Beta, Illinois State
1983 Sigma Iota, Southern Illinois
1985 Beta Nu, SUNY, Binghamton
1985 Chi Nu, Cal State, Northridge
1985 Delta Kappa, Duke
1986 Alpha Nu, SUNY, Albany
1986 Eta Upsilon, Hartford
1986 Iota Delta, SUNY, Stony Brook
1986 Upsilon Sigma, Union (NY)
1987 Alpha Kappa, Carnegie-Mellon
1987 Lambda Beta, Brandeis
1987 Lambda Omega, Western Ontario
1987 Omega Nu, SUNY Col., Oneonta
1987 Omega Sigma, SUNY Col., Oswego
1987 Pi Beta, Hofstra
1987 Psi Phi, South Florida
1988 San Diego U
1988 Alpha Beta, Muhlenberg
1988 Chi Beta, Cal State, Long Beach
1988 Chi Delta, Cal, Davis
1988 Eta Pi, York (ON)
1988 Sigma Beta, Cal, Santa Barbara
1988 Tau Omega, Toronto
1988 Zeta Tau, Cal, Irvine
1990 McGill
1990 SUNY Col., Buffalo

Colonies: Adelphi, Cal Poly, Pomona, Columbia (NY), Drake, Manitoba, UCLA, Memphis State, Emerson, Ithaca, Rider, Yale

COAT OF ARMS

Alpha Gamma Rho

ACTIVE PIN

PLEDGE PIN

ALPHA GAMMA RHO was organized April 4, 1908, by the union of two prior societies: Alpha Gamma Rho founded in 1904 at Ohio State University by F. L. Allen, R. L. Fromme, W. A. Martin, E. S. Poston, G. T. Snyder, B. L. West, and R. C. E. Wallace; and Delta Rho Sigma founded in 1906 at the University of Illinois by R. E. Chambers, R. E. Taylor, E. E. Stultz, J. J. McKay, J. H. Craig, F. H. McKelvey, J. L. Martin, M. E. Greenleaf, and E. E. Chester. The Illinois chapter was named Alpha Chapter, and the Ohio State, Beta Chapter.

Prior to 1917 several chapters were conducted on the basis of a professional agricultural fraternity, electing members of social fraternities and permitting their own members to join such organizations. The other chapters, while limiting their membership to agricultural students, did not permit membership in other social fraternities. In February of 1917 legislation was passed barring dual membership. Since that time, although membership is still limited to agricultural students, the fraternity has usually been classed with other general fraternities. It is properly referred to as a professional-social agricultural fraternity.

The purposes of Alpha Gamma Rho are to make better men, and through them a broader and better agriculture by surrounding members with influences tending to encourage individual endeavor, resourcefulness, and aggressive effort along lines making for the development of better mental, social, moral and physical qualities and to promote a wider acquaintance and a broader outlook on the part of agricultural men through followship.

Government The government is vested in the convention which is held biennially and ad interim in the national board of directors consisting of six directors, who elect the grand president, executive vice president and financial vice president.

Until the late sixties, the fraternity did not employ a full-time staff. A professional staff, under the leadership of an executive director, is now responsible for administration, publications, fund raising, leadership seminars, conventions, expansion and visits to chapters.

Traditions and Insignia The badge is a gold crescent with a sickle and a sheaf of wheat placed inside of the points of the crescent, the handle of the sickle just touching the lower point of the crescent and the blade of the sickle being superimposed upon the sheaf. The letters A Γ P appear in black enamel on the middle of the crescent. The badge is worn so that the sheaf stands upright. The recognition pin consists of the letters A Γ P. The pledge pin is a small green circle, rimmed in gold, containing the letters AΓ P and two golden stems of wheat. The colors are dark green and gold; the flower a pink rose.

Publications A quarterly magazine, the *SICKLE & SHEAF*, has been continuously published since 1910. The sixth edition of the directory, the *GOLDEN CRESCENT* pledge manual, a songbook, a history and numerous membership and officer guides have been published.

Funds and Philanthropies The fraternity and its programs are administered by four separate leadership boards. A *SICKLE & SHEAF* Endowment Fund was established in 1929 to provide a free lifetime subscription to the quarterly *SICKLE & SHEAF* to all members. A Chapter House Loan Fund was established in 1958 to make and guarantee housing loans for chapters and colonies. The Educational Foundation of Alpha Gamma Rho was incorporated in 1965 to provide an endowment for scholarship and leadership development activities. The General Fraternity's National Board of Directors comprises the fourth fund.

Headquarters 10101 N. Executive Hills Blvd., Kansas City, MO 64153. Phone: (816) 891-9200.

Membership Graduate chapters 28. City/Area Alumni associations 54. Living membership 34,000. Houses owned 52. Active chapters 57. Inactive chapters 6. Colonies 3. Total number of initiates 44,661. Chapter roll:

1904	Beta, Ohio State
1906	Alpha, Illinois
1911	Delta, Purdue
1911	Gamma, Penn State
1913	Epsilon, North Dakota State
1914	Eta, Iowa State
1914	Zeta, Cornell
1916	Iota, Wisconsin, Madison
1916	Theta, Missouri
1917	Kappa, Nebraska
1917	Lambda, Minnesota
1917	*Mu, Massachusetts* (1962)
1919	Nu, North Carolina State
1919	Xi, Auburn
1920	Omicron, Kentucky
1921	Pi, Oklahoma State

1921	Rho, Colorado State
1921	Sigma, Washington State
1922	Tau, Michigan State
1922	Upsilon, Connecticut (1952-1958) (Reactivated as Alpha Nu)
1923	Chi, Cal Poly, San Luis Obispo (1940-1975) (Originally chartered as Cal, Berkeley, reopened at Cal Poly, San Luis Obispo in 1975)
1923	Phi, Cal, Davis
1924	Alpha Alpha, West Virginia
1924	Alpha Beta, Oregon State
1924	Omega, New Hampshire
1924	Psi, Maine
1925	Alpha Delta, Montana State
1925	Alpha Gamma, Florida
1926	Alpha Epsilon, L.S.U. (1951-1971)
1927	Alpha Eta, Georgia
1927	Alpha Zeta, Kansas State
1928	Alpha Theta, Maryland
1934	Alpha Iota, Arkansas
1951	Alpha Kappa, Tennessee
1951	Alpha Lambda, New Mexico State
1952	*Alpha Mu, Rutgers* (1967)
1958	Alpha Nu, Connecticut
1958	*Alpha Xi, Arizona State* (1980)
1959	Alpha Omicron, Utah State
1959	Alpha Pi, Arizona
1961	Alpha Rho, Vermont
1963	Alpha Sigma, Cal State, Fresno
1963	Alpha Tau, Western Illinois
1963	Alpha Upsilon, Tennessee, Martin
1964	Alpha Phi, South Dakota State
1966	Alpha Chi, Western Kentucky
1968	Alpha Omega, Murray State
1968	Alpha Psi, Wisconsin, River Falls
1970	Beta Alpha, Southern Illinois
1972	*Beta Beta, Texas A & I* (1980)
1972	Beta Gamma, Wisconsin, Platteville
1973	Beta Delta, Illinois State
1973	Beta Epsilon, Arkansas State
1974	Beta Zeta, Clemson
1975	Beta Eta, V.P.I.
1976	Beta Theta, Middle Tennessee
1978	Beta Iota, Northeast Missouri
1978	Beta Kappa, Cal State, Chico
1980	*Beta Lambda, East Texas* (1985)
1983	Beta Mu, Austin Peay
1986	Beta Nu, Texas A & M
1987	Beta Xi, Texas Tech.
1988	Wyoming

Colonies: Louisiana Tech, Northwest Missouri, Tarleton

Alpha Gamma Sigma

The professional agricultural fraternity, Alpha Gamma Sigma, was first organized as a local fraternity at Columbia, Missouri, on January 28, 1923. It was the outgrowth of a feeling among certain men that the other agricultural fraternities were disregarding the type of men essential to the proper forwarding of agriculture.

During the organization and growing period of Alpha Gamma Sigma, a similar organization was going through a period of development at Ohio State University. This organization was known as the National Agriculture Club. It was established October 23, 1922. During its first year its name was changed to Tau Gamma Phi Fraternity.

Tau Gamma Phi rapidly grew into prominence in Ohio State campus affairs, and ranked high in scholarship. It maintained as its ideals, the advancement of agriculture, scholarship, athletics and the social development of its members.

Unknown to each other, Alpha Gamma Sigma at Columbia, Missouri and Tau Gamma Phi at Columbus, Ohio, grew to be among the strongest fraternities on their respective campi. Each had opportunities to affiliate with national fraternities but the members of these two chapters believed that their ideals were high enough to form the foundation of a new and unique organization. In March, 1931, members and alumni of Tau Gamma Phi met with the members of Alpha Gamma Sigma at Columbia, and worked out a plan for joining the two groups in what now constitutes the National Chapter. A constitution was drawn up and officers consisted of the following: Clair E. Jones, president; Wayne Johnson, vice president; Don Rush, treasurer; O. E. Allen, secretary; and Delmer Glenn, historian, the Ohio chapter was designated as the Alpha chapter and the Missouri chapter as the Beta chapter.

The second General Convention was held in Columbus, Ohio, November 28 and 29, 1931. The constitution and by-laws were revised and adopted. The fraternity pin and pledge pin were also adopted. A new fraternity crest was designated and put into use. The ritual, secret grip, password, raps, and motto were adopted. Royal blue and silver were selected as the fraternity colors and the red rose as the fraternity flower. A committee was appointed to have a composer write a fraternity a sweetheart, and a pledge song.

At the Tenth National Convention in November 1951 procedures were approved for expansion of the fraternity. Possibilities for new chapters at recognized Land-Grant Colleges were reviewed.

November 7, 1953 marked another memorable occasion in the history of A.G.S. with the initiation of the charter members of the Gamma chapter. The first step in the organization of the Gamma chapter was taken when Assistant Dan Hixon of the University of Nebraska, College of Agriculture was contacted by members of the Beta chapter. Dean Hixon in turn approached the members of the Ag. Men's Club, and independent group of agricultural students at the University of Nebraska. The members of the Ag. Men's Club then asked Professor Donald R. Warner, an alumnus of the Beta chapter for additional information and advice. Professor Warner served as an advisor during the entire period of colonization. On March 14, 1953 a delegation from the Beta chapter met with the interested men at Nebraska to discuss plans for colonization. The Gamma Club of A.G.S. was established on April 20, 1953. On November 7, 1953 the Gamma Club became an active chapter, The Gamma Chapter of A.G.S.

The year 1961 was marked as another growth year for A.G.S. On Saturday, May 20th, a delegation of eight men from Alpha chapter and six men from Beta chapter plus Grand President Emil Malinovsky and Grand Vice President Alfred Lehmkuhi, initiated 19 charter members into Delta Chapter of Alpha Gamma Sigma, located on the campus of Tennessee Technological University at Cookeville, Tennessee. Dr. E. B. Knight served as advisor during the period of colonization and is now an active member of A.G.S. The founding of Delta chapter was the first chapter below the Mason-Dixon Line.

Sixteen men were initiated into the Epsilon Chapter of Alpha Gamma Sigma February 16, 1970. Through the work of two Beta alumni, Colin Collins and Van Ricketts, men at Southwest Missouri State University, Springfield, Missouri, were contacted and colonized by September 15, 1969. Ricketts remained in the capacity of advisor.

The Zeta Chapter of A.G.S. was colonized officially October 1, 1970, at Western Illinois University, Macomb, Illinois. On April 3, 1971, during an off-year conclave, members of the other chapters met at Macomb to formally initiate 21 men into active membership in the Zeta Chapter. Also initiated was Gary Posler, faculty member who served with Jack Riley, Beta alumnus, as advisor to the new chapter.

Shortly after the initiation of Zeta Chapter, Alpha Gamma Sigma was unanimously accepted as a member of the National Interfraternity Conference on June 19, 1971.

The history of IlliDell Cooperative Fraternity dates back to the spring of 1949. Twenty students and two faculty members purchased a house located at 706 South Goodwin. The twenty founding students each contributed $100, Mr. Warren Goodell, an interested Ag faculty member, contributed $3000 to total $5000 needed for the down payment on their first house. Because of his generous help, part of IlliDell's name is derived from mr. Goodell's name. The rest of the name (Illi) comes from the word, Illinois.

Since its founding in 1949, IlliDell has been home to over three hundred fifty University of Illinois students, IlliDell members have a golden heritage—

a heritage to be proud of. IlliDell probably has one of the most active alumni associations of any campus organization, and thanks to the wise planning of many students, faculty members, and to the faith and foresight of Mr. Warren Goodell, IlliDell has truly become a success.

In January, 1981 all present members of the IlliDell Fraternity became members of the IlliDell Chapter of Alpha Gamma Sigma. The decision to join a national organization came after the membership was assured that its place in A.G.S. would not hide the previous hard work and cooperation that preceded it. ID is proud to be associated with a group of men that places professionalism high on its list of priorities.

Headquarters 307 North Grimmell, Jefferson, IA 50129. Phone: (618) 675-3699.

Membership Active chapters 8. Total number of initiates 4,350. Chapter roll:

1922	Alpha,	Ohio State
1923	Beta,	Missouri
1953	Gamma,	Nebraska
1961	Delta,	Tennessee Tech.
1970	Epsilon,	Southwest Missouri
1971	Zeta,	Western Illinois
1972	Eta,	Cornell
1981	IlliDell,	Illinois

Alpha Kappa Lambda

ACTIVE PIN

PLEDGE PIN

ALPHA KAPPA LAMBDA, the first national college fraternity to be founded on the Pacific Coast, was established at the University of California in Berkeley on April 22, 1914. It was an outgrowth of a local club, Los Amigos Club, organized in January, 1907, by Herman Ritchie Bergh, Harold Alonzo Savage, Allen Holmes Kimball, Charles Oscar Perrine, Ludwig Rehfuess, Gail Cleland, Charles Junius Booth, William Floyd Barnum, Leonard Herrington Day, Harry Levi Osborne, and Joseph Leon Taylor. These eleven founders of the predecessor organization are honored in the traditions of the fraternity as its real founders.

Growth The early expansion program was disrupted by World War I. However, in 1920 Beta Chapter was founded by colonization at Stanford University. Charters were later granted to Bushnell Guild at Illinois, to Ochino at Kansas, to Cygnus at

Michigan, and to the Diversity Club at the State College of Washington. The depression and World War II disrupted rapid growth until 1949 when the fraternity's first full-time employee was hired and the fraternity embarked on an expansion program in 1950. The staff spends a considerable amount of time providing service to chapters by means of extensive chapter visitation programs and by up-to-date publications. Each year leadership training conferences are held for the undergraduate members.

Government Conferences known as national conclaves are held once a year, generally in the summer vacation season. Chapters are represented by official delegates. Collegiate chapters have two votes each, chapter corporate boards have one vote each, alumni chapters have one vote each, and each member of the National Executive Council has one vote. Government between conclaves is vested in the National Executive Council, consisting of six elected members and other appointive officers. One of the Council is an undergraduate member. The Executive Director is a full-time salaried officer selected by the National Executive Council. There is provision for the chapters to vote by referendum on certain questions.

Publications *The Logos* is the official publication. Monthly bulletins, *Inside AKL*, are sent to the chapters and corporate boards. Subscription to *The Logos* is free for life.

Traditions and Insignia No discriminatory bars exist in the national by-laws of the fraternity and a chapter is eligible to pledge any man meeting the qualifications of the fraternity, regardless of race, creed, or color. Self-support is another appeal of the fraternity, as a high percentage of the active members are working part-time. Scholastic achievement is a policy and a tradition in the fraternity. Alpha Kappa Lambda is a nonsecret order, there being no pledges of secrecy in the ritual, nor any grips, pass words, or other secret signs. Reliance upon the members' finer feelings is depended upon to safeguard the intimate things of the fraternity. The fraternity has been a leader in the elimination of "Hell Week," personal duties by pledges, and hazing. Such practices are viewed as a deterrent for the development of the whole man, intellectually, socially, physically, and spiritually. The fraternity has adopted an alcohol awareness policy, obligation members to responsible party practices and obeying state laws.

The motto of the fraternity is "Alethia Kai Logos." The badge consists of the three letters A K Λ with K superimposed upon the others and set with pearls. The pledge button is a small hollow diamond, with blue center, the diamond being the symbol of Los Amigos, the founder organization.

The flag consists of a purple and gold field, in two wide bands with the gold on top and purple on the bottom. The coat of arms is displayed in purple, centered in the top gold half. The letters A K Λ are displayed horizontally in gold, on the purple bottom half.

The official flower is the golden yellow Pernet rose. The coat of arms includes a scroll and a lamp in the upper cantons. In the base is a representation of the sun setting in San Francisco Bay, suggesting the origin of the fraternity at Berkeley.

Funds and Philanthropy The Alpha Kappa Lambda Educational Foundation was established in 1984. The new foundation will publish the fraternity's educational journal, provide scholarship, and support educational endeavors.

Headquarters 2902 N. Meridian Street, Indianapolis, IN 46208. Phone: (317) 924-4265.

Membership Graduate/Alumni chapters 7. City/Area alumni associations 17. Total living membership 16,062. Total undergraduate membership 1,200. Houses owned 21. Active chapters 34. Inactive chapters 28. Colonies 5. Total number of initiates 18,633. Chapter roll:

1914   Alpha, Cal, Berkeley (1969-1985)
1920   *Beta, Stanford* (1966)
1921   Gamma, Illinois
1922   Delta, Kansas (-1947)
1923   Epsilon, Wisconsin, Madison
1924   *Zeta, Michigan* (-1962) (1970)
1927   Eta, Washington State
1930   Iota, Kansas State
1934   Kappa, Purdue
1950   Mu, Ohio State (1976-1990)
1951   *Nu, Ohio* (1956)
1953   Xi, Northeast Missouri
1955   Omicron, Pacific (OR)
1955   *Pi, Millikin* (1965)
1957   *Rho, Eastern Illinois* (1979)
1957   Sigma, Central Missouri State
1957   Tau, Penn State
1957   *Upsilon, Northern Colorado* (1972)
1958   Phi, Oregon State
1960   Chi, California (PA)
1961   *Alpha Alpha, New Mexico State* (1973)
1961   Alpha Beta, Arizona (1985-1985)
1961   Psi, Iowa State
1962   *Alpha Delta, Fort Hays* (1989)
1962   Alpha Gamma, Wisconsin, La Crosse (1985-1987)
1963   *Alpha Epsilon, Wisconsin, Oshkosh* (1972)
1963   *Alpha Eta, McNeese* (1972)
1963   Alpha Theta, Wisconsin, Eau Claire (-1986)
1963   Alpha Zeta, Northwest Missouri
1964   *Alpha Iota, Wyoming* (1974)
1964   *Alpha Kappa, Colorado State* (1974)
1964   *Alpha Mu, Arkansas* (1985)
1965   *Alpha Nu, Washburn* (1985)
1965   *Alpha Xi, Montana* (1971)

1967   *Alpha Omicron, Colorado* (1970)
1967   *Alpha Pi, Texas* (1970)
1967   *Alpha Rho, Texas, El Paso* (1972)
1968   *Alpha Chi, Pittsburg State, Kansas* (1974)
1968   Alpha Phi, Idaho
1968   *Alpha Sigma, New Mexico* (1972)
1968   *Alpha Tau, Alliance* (1973)
1968   *Alpha Upsilon, Nebraska Wesleyan* (1980)
1969   *Alpha Psi, Tennessee* (1979)
1969   *Beta Alpha, Loyola, Chicago* (1984)
1970   *Beta Beta, Utah* (1973)
1970   Beta Delta, Illinois State
1970   *Beta Epsilon, Kearney* (1972)
1970   *Beta Gamma, Sul Ross* (1981)
1970   *Beta Zeta, East Tennessee* (1978)
1971   *Beta Eta, Westmar* (1975)
1972   *Beta Iota, Wichita* (1974)
1972   *Beta Theta, Angelo* (1977)
1973   *Beta Kappa, Southern Illinois* (1982)
1973   *Beta Lambda, Wisconsin, Parkside* (1975)
1983   *Beta Mu, Winona* (1985)
1985   Beta Nu, Virginia Commonwealth
1987   Beta Omicron, James Madison
1988   Beta Pi, Southern Indiana
1989   Beta Rho, Elon
1989   Beta Sigma, Northwood, Cedar Hill
1989   Beta Tau, Southern Illinois, Edwardsville
1990   Beta Upsilon, Iowa

Colonies: Auburn, George Mason, Washington (WA), Emporia, Northern Illinois

COAT OF ARMS

Alpha Phi Delta

ACTIVE PIN

PLEDGE PIN

ALPHA PHI DELTA was founded at Syracuse University on November 5, 1914. It did not start on a national program until its union on June 20, 1916, with Sigma Gamma Phi, a local fraternity of similar ideals at Columbia University.

The fraternity is governed through the National Council which meets annually at the national convention. The National Council is composed of delegates from each undergraduate chapter and alumni club. The Executive Council consists of the president, executive vice-president and executive secretary in addition to several national vice-presidents and district governors. The Executive Council which possesses administrative and supervisory functions between conventions meets once annually between conventions and at conventions. Meetings may also be called at the discretion of the President.

There are thirteen districts under the supervision of district governors. District conventions are also called annually for discussions of regional problems, to adopt resolutions for national consideration, and to elect district governors.

The offices of the president and executive vice-president are elective for one year with a tradition of re-election for a second year. All other national officers are appointed subject to the approval of the National Council at the national convention.

Traditions and Insignia The badge is a shield displaying upon its face a white scroll with the letters AΦΔ across the center. Vertically bisecting the scroll is a gold key upon a background of black; all this is mounted on a gold shield bordered with crown-set pearls, with a diamond star at the top and a flaming torch cutting the entire badge diagonally.

The seal of the fraternity, a vertically convex shield, beveled chiefs coming to a point at the base, purple field. Charges: A spread eagle, white key in dexter talon, torch in sinister talon, bendwise; fasces palewise in back of eagle; cresting, five pointed estoile rayonnant; scroll and mantling, or motto "Alpha Phi Delta." Motto on Grand Council Seal "Faciamus."

The pledge button is a shield divided diagonally into purple and white. The sister pin is a miniature of the regular pin. The flag is divided horizontally into purple and white; grand council seal in center. The colors are purple and white. The flower is the white carnation.

Publications The *Kleos* is the official publication of the fraternity and it is published quarterly. A monthly bulletin, *The Chapter Letter* is distributed during the academic year by Central Office. The first *Directory* was published in 1925, the most recent was produced in 1983. A comprehensive volume, *The History of Alpha Phi Delta Fraternity, 1914—1973* was published after many years of work and was up-dated in the introduction to the 1983 edition of the *Directory*. The pledge manual, the *Dokime* is revised regularly.

Funds and Philanthropies High scholastic achievement has always been a foremost ideal of Alpha Phi Delta. Throughout its history several scholarship funds have been established by individual alumni clubs. In 1973 the National Scholarship Foundation was instituted and since that time virtually all individual funds have merged into the one national fund. About a dozen awards are presented annually to brothers and non-brothers alike based upon academic excellence and need. In 1982 the Alpha Phi Delta Foundation was established which incorporated the fraternity's scholarship, housing, and cultural efforts.

Headquarters 404 Provincetown Drive, Cape May, NJ 08204. Phone: (609) 884-3226.

Membership Active chapters 34. Colonies 2. Total number of initiates 10,000. Chapter roll:

1914	Alpha, Syracuse
1916	Beta, Columbia (NY)
1919	Gamma, Yale
1920	Delta, New York Poly
1921	Epsilon, SUNY, Buffalo
1921	Eta, CUNY, Brooklyn
1921	Iota, Union (NY)
1921	Theta, N.Y.U.
1921	Zeta, R.P.I.
1922	Kappa, Western Reserve
1922	Lambda, Penn
1922	Mu, Cornell
1923	Nu, Pitt
1923	Omicron, Michigan
1923	Pi, West Virginia
1923	Xi, Ohio State
1926	Rho, Carnegie-Mellon
1927	Sigma, Boston U.
1928	Tau, M.I.T.
1928	Upsilon, Harvard
1929	Beta Beta, Manhattan
1929	Chi, Penn State
1929	Omega, Rochester
1929	Phi, Alabama
1929	Psi, Duquesne
1930	Beta Delta, Temple
1930	Beta Epsilon, Bucknell
1930	Beta Gamma, William and Mary
1930	Theta Beta, N.Y.U.
1933	Beta Zeta, Ohio
1934	Beta Eta, CUNY, Brooklyn
1948	Beta Theta, Steubenville
1949	Beta Iota, Utica
1949	Beta Kappa, Long Island
1949	Beta Lambda, St. Francis (PA)
1950	Beta Mu, DePaul
1950	Beta Nu, Miami (FL)
1952	Beta Xi, New Jersey Tech
1953	Beta Omicron, Youngstown State
1959	Beta Pi, St. John's (NY)
1959	Beta Rho, Gannon
1962	Beta Sigma, St. Francis (NY)
1973	Beta Tau, Fairmont
1977	Beta Upsilon, George Washington
1978	Beta Chi, SUNY Col. Tech, Utica
1978	Beta Phi, Glassboro
1979	Beta Omega, Pace
1979	Beta Psi, Catholic
1979	Gamma Beta, Illinois, Chicago
1980	Gamma Delta, Waynesburg
1980	Gamma Gamma, Penn State, Behrend
1982	Gamma Zeta, Villanova
1984	Gamma Eta, Trenton
1985	Gamma Theta, Eastern
1987	Gamma Iota, Pace, Pleasantville
1987	Gamma Kappa, CUNY, Staten Island
1987	Gamma Lambda, Fordham
1987	Gamma Mu, Stockton
1987	Gamma Nu, William Paterson
1987	Gamma Omicron, SUNY, Stony Brook
1987	Gamma Xi, Southern Connecticut

Colonies: Montclair, SUNY Col. Ag & Tech, Cobleskill

COAT OF ARMS

Alpha Sigma Phi

ACTIVE PIN

PLEDGE PIN

ALPHA SIGMA PHI from its founding at Yale in 1845 to its status as one of America's premier fraternities has a rich and exciting history. Three freshmen, Louis Manigault, Stephen Ormsby Rhea and Horace Spangler Weiser, founded Alpha Sigma Phi as the tenth oldest fraternity in the nation on December 6, 1845. The ideals of fostering scholarship, charity, and brotherhood brought the men together and still guide the fraternity today. Yale, in the 1840s, provided no extracurricular activities and Alpha Sigma Phi met a strong need on the part of the undergraduate men.

Alpha Sigma Phi at Yale quickly attracted the top students and became an integral force on campus. Two early members who later served as national president of Alpha Sigma Phi were Andrew Dickson White, who was the first president of Cornell University and Cyrus W. Northrup, former president of the University of Minnesota. In 1847 a chapter newsletter, *The Yale Tomahawk*, was started to promote the fraternity's purpose. *The Tomahawk* is the national magazine of Alpha Sigma Phi today and is the fraternity world's oldest publication still in existence.

Growth   In 1850, Alpha Sigma Phi spread its ideals to a second chapter, Beta at Harvard, where the members were sure their standards of excellence would be upheld. Charters were granted to Gamma at Amherst, Delta at Marietta, and Epsilon at Ohio Wesleyan during the next ten years. The membership was eager to expand when the Civil War broke out.

The war all but wiped out every chapter and faculty movements at Yale and Harvard to ban secret societies kept the chapters from revitalizing themselves. Nevertheless, Delta of Marietta managed to hang on. Two of the Delta brothers killed in the war bequeathed their swords to the chapter which still proudly displays them 125 years later. The surviving members and alumni built Alpha Sigma Phi back to its great strength on the Marietta campus. Still, Delta remained as the only existing chapter of the fraternity for 40 years.

In 1907 a young Yale law student, Wayne M. Musgrave, and his classmate, Edwin M. Waterbury, discovered documents outlining the proud history and traditions of Alpha Sigma Phi in the Yale library. Full of enthusiasm, they contacted Delta at Marietta to see if the same high standards and rich traditions still existed. Pleased at their discovery, the two "second founders" recruited a pledge class and refounded Alpha Chapter by March of that year.

The spark of the renewed Alpha Chapter spread quickly across the country to leading universities with the same high standards of excellence as in 1845. Harvard and Ohio Wesleyan were quickly revived. Chapters were added at Ohio State, Illinois, Michigan, Cornell, Wisconsin, Columbia, Washington, California, Nebraska, Penn, Stanford and on and on.

The continued growth of the fraternity was aided with a merger in 1939 with Phi Pi Phi Fraternity, consolidation in 1946 with Alpha Kappa Pi Fraternity, and another merger in 1965 with Alpha Gamma Upsilon. The additions of these fraternities' chapters maintained the standards and spread the influence of Alpha Sigma Phi.

The fraternity today continues the policy of selective growth and quality programs in every chapter. The motto "To Better The Man" serves as the guide and purpose of every chapter's existence as its members grow morally, intellectually, and spiritually in an atmosphere of true brotherhood. Aggressive programs in scholarship, leadership development, social responsibility, philanthropy, and campus involvement set a national standard.

Government   The parent-chapter type of administration was maintained during the period in which the early chapters received their charters but was supplanted in 1907 by the centralized form. Fraternity conventions are held biennially. The Grand Council of seven members is elected at the convention and has executive authority *ad interim* and operates through its central office on all internal matters, subject to referendum of the chapters. The national headquarters staff includes program professionals and traveling chapter leadership consultants who visit and help every chapter maintain the high standards and ideals of Alpha Sigma Phi.

Traditions and Insignia   The rituals written in 1845 by Founder Louis Manigault are still in use, and the history and traditions of the Fraternity in its earlier years have survived and are perpetuated in its present life. The fraternity elects no honorary members, but its constitution and by-laws provide for the initiation of faculty members and members of the collegiate administrative staff of universities where charters have been granted.

The original badge of the fraternity was a rectangular slab of gold, about an inch long, bearing on its face a black shield with an open book in white surmounted by a pen of gold, beneath which are the gold letters ΑΣΦ. The present badge is of the same design, but smaller, and it is never jeweled. Colors are cardinal and stone, and the flower is the talisman rose. The pledge pin is a seven-pointed gold star with black background and crossed sabers of gold appearing thereon.

Publications Every pledge to the fraternity receives a Scholarship Guide expressly written for new members as a signal to help assure that they maintain high academic standards. Pledges also receive a copy of the 114-page loose-leafed member's manual *To Better The Man.* This manual, with a title that expresses Alpha Sigma Phi's ultimate purpose, records the history of the fraternity, but more importantly serves as an educational tool for chapter operations and program beliefs. Topics ranging from career development to parliamentary procedure and from service to substance abuse prevention are covered and taught from this manual.

The Tomahawk is the Fraternity's quarterly national magazine and is the oldest fraternity publication still in existence today since its founding in 1847.

Manuals are available to help each officer with his duties and responsibilities. Of particular importance are those on membership recruitment and finance, the two areas most chapters need help with. Of highest importance is the Ritual Manual, copies of which are provided to every chapter.

Funds and Philanthropies The Alpha Sigma Phi Educational Foundation exists to promote the educational programs of the fraternity. Thousands of alumni give hundreds of thousands of dollars to support the foundation's annual programs and conferences. Scholarships and loans are also given through this fund.

The A-S-P Corporation is a separate mortgage loan organization associated with the fraternity. Loans for chapter housing and improvements are made to chapters.

Every year individual chapters provide their communities and colleges with thousands of man hours of free service and hundreds of thousands of dollars through fundraising efforts. While no nationally coordinated philanthropy exists, each chapter has numerous local efforts it champions.

Headquarters The executive offices are situated at 24 West William Street, Delaware, Ohio 43015. Phone: (614) 363-1911. Owned by the fraternity, these offices are housed in a one-story brick structure.

Membership Graduate/Alumni chapters 37. City/Area alumni associations 3. Total living membership 39,628. Undergraduate membership 1,747. Houses owned 30. Active chapters 53. Inactive chapters 53. Colonies 3. Total number of initiates 49,719. Chapter roll:

Year	Chapter
1845	*Alpha, Yale* (1942)
1850	*Beta, Harvard* (1932)
1854	*Gamma, Amherst* (1860)
1860	Delta, Marietta
1863	*Epsilon, Ohio Wesleyan* (1970)
1908	Eta, Illinois
1908	Theta, Michigan
1908	Zeta, Ohio State
1909	Iota, Cornell
1909	*Kappa, Wisconsin, Madison* (1939)

Year	Chapter
1910	*Lambda, Columbia (NY)* (1957)
1912	Mu, Washington (WA)
1913	*Gamma, Massachusetts* (1971)
1913	Nu, California
1913	*Xi, Nebraska* (1950)
1914	*Omicron, Penn* (1978)
1915	*Pi, Colorado* (1957)
1916	*Rho, Minnesota* (1935)
1917	*Sigma, Kentucky* (1960)
1917	*Tau, Stanford* (1981)
1918	Upsilon, Penn State
1920	*Chi, Chicago* (1935)
1920	Phi, Iowa State
1920	Psi, Oregon State
1921	Alpha Rho, New Jersey Tech (1954-1982)
1923	*Alpha Alpha, Oklahoma* (1986)
1924	*Alpha Beta, Iowa* (1940)
1925	*Alpha Delta, Middlebury* (1947)
1925	*Alpha Epsilon, Syracuse* (1959)
1925	*Alpha Gamma, Carnegie-Mellon* (1936)
1926	*Alpha Sigma, Wagner* (1982)
1926	Alpha Tau, Stevens Tech
1926	*Alpha Upsilon, New York Poly* (1951)
1926	Alpha Zeta, UCLA (1973-1984)
1927	*Alpha Phi, Ellsworth* (1927)
1928	Alpha Chi, Coe (1935-1937) (1957-1979)
1928	*Alpha Eta, Dartmouth* (1936)
1928	Alpha Psi, Presbyterian
1929	Alpha Theta, Missouri (1966-1980)
1929	*Beta Alpha, Mount Union* (1960)
1929	*Beta Beta, M.I.T.* (1939)
1929	Beta Delta, Marshall (1979-1980)
1929	Beta Epsilon, Lehigh
1929	Beta Gamma, Bethany (WV)
1930	*Alpha Iota, Alabama* (1971)
1930	*Beta Zeta, North Carolina State* (1986)
1930	*Gamma Sigma, Detroit Tech* (1966)
1931	*Alpha Kappa, West Virginia* (1964)
1931	*Beta Eta, New Hampshire* (1934)
1931	Beta Iota, Tufts
1931	Beta Theta, Rutgers
1932	*Beta Kappa, Centre College* (1936)
1932	*Beta Lambda, St. John's (NY)* (1939)
1932	Beta Mu, Wake Forest
1932	*Gamma Tau, Indiana Tech* (1977)
1933	*Beta Nu, West Virginia Wesleyan* (1964)
1935	Beta Omicron, Tri-State
1935	Beta Xi, Hartwick
1936	*Beta Pi (I), Franklin and Marshall* (1948)
1937	Beta Rho, Toledo
1937	*Beta Sigma, Cincinnati* (1980)
1938	*Beta Tau, Wayne State (MI)* (1973)
1939	*Alpha Lambda, Case Western Reserve* (1940)
1939	Alpha Mu, Baldwin-Wallace
1939	Alpha Nu, Westminster (PA)
1939	Alpha Pi, Purdue
1939	Alpha Xi, Illinois Tech
1940	Beta Chi, American
1940	*Beta Phi, Wofford* (1963)
1940	Beta Psi, R.P.I.
1940	*Beta Upsilon, Milton* (1976)

1942   Gamma Alpha, Ohio Northern
1942   *Gamma Beta, Carthage* (1943)
1943   *Gamma Gamma, Connecticut* (1971)
1945   Alpha Omicron, Missouri Valley
1948   *Gamma Upsilon, Eastern Michigan* (1982)
1949   Gamma Delta, Davis and Elkins
1950   *Gamma Epsilon, Buffalo* (1971)
1950   Gamma Zeta, Bowling Green (1954-1965)
1951   *Gamma Eta, Washington (MO)* (1962)
1951   Gamma Rho, Lycoming
1952   Gamma Theta, Miami (FL) (1959-1982)
1955   *Gamma Iota, Arizona* (1969)
1956   *Gamma Kappa, Michigan State* (1964)
1958   Gamma Lambda, Barton
1960   *Gamma Mu, Charleston (WV)* (1987)
1961   *Gamma Nu, Cal State, Sacramento* (1971)
1962   Gamma Xi, Widener
1964   Gamma Omicron, Tulane (1975-1978)
1964   *Gamma Pi, Findlay* (1983)
1966   *Gamma Phi, Concord* (1984)
1968   Delta Alpha, Loyola, Chicago
1968   Gamma Chi, Indiana
1968   *Gamma Psi, Lawrence Tech* (1991)
1969   *Delta Beta, Northern Michigan* (1982)
1970   Delta Delta, Slippery Rock
1970   *Delta Gamma, Tarkio* (1975)
1970   *Theta Sigma, Bridgeport* (1973)
1971   *Beta Pi (II), Duquesne* (1974)
1972   Delta Epsilon, Rio Grande
1979   Delta Eta, East Carolina
1979   Delta Zeta, North Carolina, Charlotte
1980   Delta Iota, Longwood
1980   Delta Theta, Radford
1982   *Delta Kappa, Francis Marion* (1985)
1984   Delta Lambda, Stockton
1986   Delta Mu, William Paterson
1987   Delta Nu, Lock Haven
1988   Delta Omicron, Illinois State
1988   Delta Xi, SUNY Col., Plattsburgh

Colonies: SUNY, Buffalo, SUNY, Binghamton, Central Michigan, Delaware, Findlay, Coastal Carolina College Interest Group

Alpha Tau Omega

ACTIVE PIN

PLEDGE PIN

ALPHA TAU OMEGA was founded at Richmond, Virginia, on September 11, 1865, by Otis Allan Glazebrook, Alfred Marshall, and Erskine Mayo Ross, three young Confederate soldiers, who had been cadets at Virginia Military Institute during the war. Their prime object was to restore the Union by uniting fraternally the young men of the South with those of the North and by fostering a Chris-tian brotherhood dedicated to the task of achieving and cherishing permanent peace.

It was the first fraternity to be established after the Civil War and projected as a national organiza-tion. Alpha or "Mother Society" was placed at the Virginia Military Institute at Lexington, Virginia, and Beta at Washington and Lee University in the same town. The first 22 chapters were in the South. In 1881 the first northern chapter was chartered.

Growth As this was the first fraternity of southern origin which was successful in maintain-ing chapters in the North, it is interesting to note that this was accomplished through members of other fraternities. Dr. Edgar F. Smith, Phi Kappa Psi, later provost of the University of Pennsylva-nia, who deplored the sectional prejudice which had balked Alpha Tau Omega in its purpose to be-come national, generously offered to pledge a suit-able northern nucleus. N. Wiley Thomas, a student at Pennsylvania, was initiated and within two years had established six northern chapters. A sud-den expansion of the fraternity resulted, 15 chap-ters being chartered in 1881-82.

The fraternity was originally intended as an or-ganization of college men as well as a college frater-nity, and that was the reason for the establishment of community chapters. These were not attached to any educational institution and were not long con-tinued. The first chapter at Union University was originally of this class, established at Murfrees-boro, Tennessee. This fraternity has not confined its membership strictly to undergraduates and has admitted faculty members when they are otherwise qualified. Membership has never been conferred ex-cept by initiation.

The chapters at Washington and Jefferson Col-lege and Southwestern Presbyterian University (later Southwestern at Memphis and now Rhodes College) were the last surviving chapters of Alpha Gamma, and the chapter at the University of Ala-bama was organized by former members of the same society. The membership of Alpha Gamma at other places was also largely absorbed by Alpha Tau Omega. The chapter at Lehigh, when revived in 1903, absorbed a chapter of Psi Alpha Kappa.

Expansion of ATO has been spasmodic rather than consistent, with periods of rapid growth fol-lowed by conservative policies. Under E.J. Shives, national president from 1886 to 1894, the frater-nity chartered 24 new chapters and reactivated 10 dormant ones. At the half-century mark in 1915 the fraternity had chartered 98 chapters of which 60 were then active. After 75 years, ATO had 94 active chapters and on its centennial date, September 11, 1965, a total of 122 active chapters of 165 char-tered. ATO's most aggressive decade of expansion was 1965-75 when 41 chapters were chartered.

The chapter at the University of the South in 1880 acquired the first house owned by Alpha Tau Omega and the first house owned by any fraternity at a southern college.

Associations of alumni are chartered by the fraternity and have a voice in its government. They are chapter, regional, or city associations, the latter predominating. The fraternity organized its ATO "Active for Life" program in the mid-1980s to focus on fraternity membership as a lifetime experience and to provide the opportunities to make it so.

Government The Alpha Chapter, or "Mother Society," ruled the fraternity for the first five years. The constitution, adopted in 1865, providing for the calling of a "Congress" in 1870, which convened in that year and to which was then transferred the reins of government. This was among the first attempts on the part of any fraternity to supersede the "presiding chapter" form of government. The central government was not immediately successful, and for several years the fraternity's life depended largely upon the vitality of individual chapters. The Congress of 1876 upon the insistence of Walter Hines Page elected, in his absence, Joseph Reid Anderson, as alumnus of Alpha, to be chief executive. He accepted the office in ignorance of the chaotic conditions, but, on learning the facts, earnestly set about the work of rehabilitation. He was the moving spirit of the Baltimore Congress of 1878, which established the present form of government and incorporated the fraternity under the name Alpha Tau Omega Fraternity of Baltimore City, the first fraternity to become incorporated. On November 1, 1948, the name was changed to the Alpha Tau Omega Fraternity, Incorporated.

The government of the fraternity is vested in executive, legislative, and judicial departments. Legislative power is primarily in a General Assembly of delegates from chapters and alumni associations which meets biennially at Congress. In the interim, the High Council—composed of five alumni elected to four-year terms and two undergraduates elected to two-year terms—acts in a general legislative and advisory capacity. Judicial authority is exercised by the Worthy High Chancellor who interprets the fraternity laws and decides cases. All national officers are elected by the General Assembly. There has been no basic change in government since 1878, but throughout attention has been given toward greater efficiency of administration. Examples of such steps include the creation in 1898 of administration districts, or Provinces, and the establishment in 1918 of a central office, conducted by an executive secretary appointed by the Worthy Grand Chief (national president), with the advice and consent of the High Council. The Province Chiefs are the personal representatives of the Worthy Grand Chief and make regular visits to each chapter. The coordination of local and national organization is a primary function for the National Headquarters' Member Services Dept. staff-members, in cooperation with Province Chiefs and other national officers. Province Conclaves are held annually. Since 1972, the Congress has met annually, having previously been held biennially. Congress in odd-numbered years is the Leadership Conference, ATO's undergraduate leadership training program, first held in 1946. Congress in even-numbered years includes both the Leadership Conference and the General Assembly.

New charters are issued at an institution of learning only after approval by chapters in the Province, the Province Chief, the Worthy Grand Chief, and the High Council.

Insignia The badge of the fraternity is a *cross pattee* of black enamel with a circular central panel upon which is shown in gold a crescent near the top, three stars immediately below the crescent, the letter T in the center, and at the bottom two hands clasped. The arms of the cross display the letters A and Ω vertically and the letters Ω and A horizontally. The original design has never been changed, but the size and type of mounting has been standardized. The fraternity presents a standard badge to each initiate.

The colors are sky blue and gold, and the flower is the white tea rose.

The flag has three equal horizontal stripes of gold, blue and gold respectively, and a blue field extending the width of the hoist and bearing three gold stars, the field and middle stripes taken together forming the letter T in blue.

The pledge pin consists of a circular field of white enamel (three-eights of an inch in diameter) upon which is inscribed a gold crescent and three stars of the same size and in the same relative position as in the central panel of the badge.

The colony badge for members of a colony, in progress toward becoming a chapter, is identical to the member's badge in size and shape. However, it is of sky blue enamel and does not carry the ATΩ letters, but does have a central panel similar to the pledge pin.

Publications The official organ is *The Palm*, published continuously since 1880. It appears four times a year.

The first songbook was published in 1886. A second edition was published in 1906; a third edition, in loose-leaf form was published in 1921; a fourth edition in 1947; a fifth edition in 1954 and a sixth edition, released in 1961. Several separately published pieces of vocal and instrumental music have been dedicated to the fraternity. A long-play record, including 11 favorite songs in Alpha Tau Omega, was released by the fraternity in 1957 and a cassette was released in 1985.

The first published list of members was issued at Richmond in 1878 by a committee of which Walter Hines Page was chairman. A similar list was put out by a self-appointed committee at Gettysburg in 1886. General directories of the fraternity have been published in 1897, 1903, 1907, 1911, 1921, 1928, 1937, and 1982.

A history of the fraternity, entitled *The ATO Story*, was begun in 1957 by Judge Claude T. Reno, long-time editor of *The Palm* and former national president. His death in 1961 interrupted the completion of the work. It was decided to issue *The ATO Story* in three parts instead of in one volume. Harry

L. Bird was appointed fraternity historian and produced the first volume, *The First 50 Years: 1865-1915* in 1962. He wrote the second volume, *From Gold to Diamond: 1915-1939*, and published it in 1965. *On to the Centennial*, the concluding volume, was published in 1967.

The Manual of the Alpha Tau Omega Fraternity was published by Claude T. Reno in 1911 containing an outline of the history of the fraternity, much statistical matter, and other material of interest and value for members and pledges. Revisions of this manual were published in 1929, 1939, and 1946. *The Manual* was succeeded in 1956 by the *Propylon* (meaning "a gateway before entrance to a temple"), edited by Warren Danford. Periodic revisions were made through 1973 when a third version of a handbook, also known as the *Propylon*, was edited by Robert E. Norris. That version, with revisions, served until 1985 when it was succeeded by *The Positive Experience: Leadership, Friendship, and Service*. The *Command Manual* is the basic instructional manual for chapter operations, supplemented by publications dealing with rush, member education, finance, public relations, and other topics.

In 1928 the minutes of the Congress from 1870 to 1896 inclusive were published in one volume by Claude T. Reno. The proceedings of the congresses since 1898 have been published or bound in individual volumes.

The fraternity's placement service functioned from 1935 to the 1960s, with the exception of the war years, publishing annually the *Placement Booklet*, which listed graduating seniors available for employment.

Funds and Philanthropies The tax-exempt Alpha Tau Omega Foundation was established in 1935 by a bequest from Erskine Mayo Ross, one of the fraternity's founders. It has been supported since by contributions from alumni for the purpose of providing educational assistance to Alpha Tau Omega, its members, and the youth of America through programs, scholarships, fellowships, and special grants.

The fraternity presents the Thomas Arkle Clark Award, named in memory of the pioneer dean of men and longtime Alpha Tau Omega leader, annually to a graduating senior from each of its chapters. The award is given in recognition of outstanding scholarship, leadership, and character. From the chapter recipients, Province honorees are selected, and from these a national winner is chosen.

Help Week, which substituted constructive campus and community service projects for the humiliating pre-initiation "hell week" practices, was originated by Alpha Tau Omega through Robert Lollar, chapter president at Indiana University, in February, 1950. In June of the same year the fraternity at its Congress adopted the program nationally and Help Week has since become the accepted standard for member education programs of fraternities and sororities. A bronze plaque presented by the fraternity, commemorating the birth of Help Week, hangs in the hall of the Indiana University Student Union.

ATO's Help Week concept has been expanded to year-long attention to social service. The Community Awareness Award annually recognizes the outstanding chapters in social service and grants are made to charities designated by the top chapters.

In the 1980s, the fraternity organized Leader-Shape—the trademarked contraction of "Leaders shape the future; ATO shapes leaders"—as its response to the nation's need for leadership skills in responsible service. The LeaderShape Campaign has a $6-million goal for the creation of The LeaderShape Institute, to be held at the National Headquarters where the developing complex of facilities will include The LeaderShape Center with more than 9,000 square feet of meeting space and housing accommodations for 66.

In weekly LeaderShape Institute seminars during the summer, young men and women from all backgrounds will meet with leaders from business and the professions to discuss leadership and social issues. The purpose is to significantly increase the young person's knowledge of, and ability to apply, basic leadership skills in a responsible manner in daily life.

Headquarters 4001 West Kirby Avenue, Champaign, Illinois 61821. Phone: (217) 351-1865. The fraternity dedicated the first headquarters building of its own at the fraternity's 100th anniversary in 1965. Then in 1982, the fraternity was able to acquire a new facility, originally developed for a fraternal order, which included a headquarters building with much more office space and an attractive layout that makes it a national "home", a swimming pool and bathhouse, two tennis courts, and 10 acres of landscaped grounds. It was this move that made the ambitious LeaderShape project possible.

Membership City/Area alumni associations 70. Total living membership 106,000. Total undergraduate membership 8,000. Houses owned 120. Active chapters 164. Inactive chapters 67. Colonies 4. Total number of initiates 156,035. Chapter roll:

1865	*Virginia Alpha, V.M.I.* (1881)
1865	*Virginia Beta, Washington and Lee* (1899-1906) (1952)
1867	*Tennessee Iota, Union (TN)* (1878)
1868	*Tennessee Lambda, Cumberland (TN)* (1872-1889) (1902)
1868	*Virginia Delta, Virginia* (1985)
1869	*Virginia Epsilon, Roanoke* (1876-1881) (1892)
1870	*Kentucky Mu, Kentucky Military Institute* (1872-1881) (1887)
1871	*Tennessee Nu, Nashville State* (1872)
1872	*Kentucky Omicron, Bethel (KY)* (1872)
1872	North Carolina Xi, Duke (1879-1890)
1872	Tennessee Pi, Tennessee (1873-1901)
1873	*Virginia Rho, Bethel (VA)* (1875)

1874 *District of Columbia Upsilon, George Washington* (1875-1887) (1888)
1874 *Virginia Tau, Randolph, Macon* (1876)
1877 Maryland Psi, Johns Hopkins (1882-1924)
1877 Tennessee Omega, Sewanee
1878 Georgia Alpha Beta, Georgia
1878 *Virginia Alpha Alpha, Richmond* (1884)
1879 Alabama Alpha Epsilon, Auburn
1879 North Carolina Alpha Delta, North Carolina
1880 Georgia Alpha Zeta, Mercer
1881 Georgia Alpha Theta, Emory
1881 *Michigan Alpha Mu, Adrian* (1971-1974) (1979)
1881 *New Jersey Alpha Kappa, Stevens Tech* (1884-1890) (1896)
1881 *New York Alpha Lambda, Columbia (NY)* (1884-1891) (1892-1900) (1910)
1881 *North Carolina Alpha Eta, Bingham's School* (1896)
1881 Pennsylvania Alpha Iota, Muhlenberg
1881 Pennsylvania Tau, Penn (1886-1891) (1896-1901)
1882 *Arkansas Alpha Xi, Arkansas* (1882-1951) (1964)
1882 New York Alpha Omicron, St. Lawrence
1882 Ohio Alpha Nu, Mount Union
1882 Oregon Alpha Sigma, Oregon State (1882-1916)
1882 Pennsylvania Alpha Pi, Washington and Jefferson (1883-1901)
1882 Pennsylvania Alpha Rho, Lehigh (1886-1890) (1897-1903)
1882 Pennsylvania Alpha Upsilon, Gettysburg
1882 Tennessee Alpha Tau, Rhodes
1883 Ohio Alpha Psi, Wittenberg
1883 *South Carolina Alpha Chi, Citadel* (1886-1888) (1891)
1883 South Carolina Alpha Phi, South Carolina (1897-1927)
1884 Florida Alpha Omega, Florida (1890-1904)
1884 *Kentucky Zeta, Central* (1890)
1885 Alabama Beta Beta, Birmingham-Southern
1885 Alabama Beta Delta, Alabama
1885 Iowa Beta Alpha, Simpson (1890-1905)
1885 Massachusetts Beta Gamma, M.I.T. (1886-1906)
1887 Louisiana Beta Epsilon, Tulane
1887 New York Beta Theta, Cornell
1887 Ohio Beta Eta, Ohio Wesleyan
1887 Vermont Beta Zeta, Vermont
1888 Georgia Beta Iota, Georgia Tech
1888 *Georgia Beta Nu, Middle Georgia* (1890)
1888 Michigan Beta Kappa, Hillsdale
1888 Michigan Beta Lambda, Michigan (1894-1904)
1888 *Ohio Beta Mu, Wooster* (1914)
1889 Michigan Beta Omicron, Albion
1889 South Carolina Beta Xi, Charleston (SC) (1895-1898)
1889 Tennessee Beta Pi, Vanderbilt
1890 Ohio Beta Rho, Marietta (1899-1920)

1890 *Virginia Beta Sigma, Hampden-Sydney* (1894)
1891 *California Beta Psi, Stanford* (1898-1911) (1961)
1891 Maine Beta Upsilon, Maine
1891 *Pennsylvania Beta Chi, Haverford* (1892)
1891 *South Carolina Beta Phi, Wofford* (1896)
1892 *Maine Gamma Alpha, Colby* (1984)
1892 Ohio Beta Omega, Ohio State
1893 Indiana Gamma Gamma, Rose-Hulman
1893 *Massachusetts Gamma Beta, Tufts* (1974)
1894 *Rhode Island Gamma Delta, Brown* (1940)
1894 Tennessee Beta Tau, Union (TN)
1895 Illinois Gamma Zeta, Illinois
1895 *Texas Gamma Epsilon, Austin* (1900)
1897 Nebraska Gamma Theta, Nebraska
1897 Texas Gamma Eta, Texas
1900 California Gamma Iota, Cal, Berkeley
1901 Colorado Gamma Lambda, Colorado (1969-1985)
1901 Kansas Gamma Mu, Kansas
1901 *Ohio Gamma Kappa, Case Western Reserve* (1929)
1902 Minnesota Gamma Nu, Minnesota
1904 Illinois Gamma Xi, Chicago (1940-1988)
1904 Indiana Gamma Omicron, Purdue
1906 Massachusetts Gamma Sigma, Worcester Tech
1906 Missouri Gamma Rho, Missouri
1906 Washington Gamma Pi, Washington (WA) (1975-1988)
1907 *Wisconsin Gamma Tau, Wisconsin, Madison* (1970)
1908 Iowa Gamma Upsilon, Iowa State
1909 Kentucky Mu Iota, Kentucky
1910 Oregon Gamma Phi, Oregon
1911 Washington Gamma Chi, Washington State
1913 Wyoming Gamma Psi, Wyoming
1914 Pennsylvania Gamma Omega, Penn State (1983-1987)
1915 Indiana Delta Alpha, Indiana
1915 Iowa Delta Beta, Iowa (1972-1987)
1917 New Hampshire Delta Delta, New Hampshire (1980-1987)
1917 New York Delta Gamma, Colgate
1918 *Missouri Delta Zeta, Washington (MO)* (1940)
1918 Texas Delta Epsilon, Southern Methodist (1985-1987)
1920 Colorado Delta Eta, Colorado State (1941-1948)
1920 Kansas Delta Theta, Kansas State
1921 Nevada Delta Iota, Nevada
1921 Oklahoma Delta Kappa, Oklahoma
1922 *New York Delta Mu, R.P.I.* (1964)
1922 North Dakota Delta Nu, North Dakota
1922 Ohio Delta Lambda, Cincinnati
1923 *Iowa Delta Omicron, Drake* (1987)
1923 Montana Delta Xi, Montana (1940-1947)
1923 Pennsylvania Delta Pi, Carnegie-Mellon
1924 Indiana Delta Rho, DePauw

1924 *New Hampshire Delta Sigma, Dartmouth* (1936)
1925 Idaho Delta Tau, Idaho
1926 California Delta Chi, UCLA
1926 California Delta Phi, Occidental (1969-1973)
1926 South Dakota Delta Upsilon, South Dakota
1927 Mississippi Delta Psi, Mississippi
1929 Colorado Epsilon Alpha, Colorado Mines
1929 *Maine Delta Omega, Bowdoin* (1962)
1930 Arizona Epsilon Beta, Arizona (1973-1979)
1930 Maryland Epsilon Gamma, Maryland
1931 North Dakota Epsilon Delta, North Dakota State
1937 Mississippi Epsilon Epsilon, Mississippi State
1940 Louisiana Epsilon Zeta, L.S.U.
1940 Michigan Epsilon Eta, Michigan State (1976-1977)
1941 Ohio Epsilon Theta, Baldwin-Wallace
1943 District of Col. Epsilon Iota, American
1943 Ohio Epsilon Kappa, Bowling Green
1944 *Oklahoma Epsilon Lambda, Tulsa* (1971)
1947 *British Columia Epsilon Pi, British Columbia* (1971)
1947 Illinois Epsilon Nu, Monmouth (IL)
1947 Illinois Epsilon Xi, Northwestern
1947 Oklahoma Epsilon Omicron, Oklahoma State (1972-1978)
1947 *Vermont Epsilon Mu, Middlebury* (1965)
1949 *Delaware Epsilon Rho, Delaware* (1985)
1949 Florida Epsilon Sigma, Florida State
1949 Mississippi Epsilon Upsilon, Southern Mississippi
1949 *Utah Epsilon Tau, Utah* (1953)
1950 California Epsilon Chi, San Jose (1970-1977)
1950 California Epsilon Psi, San Diego U
1950 New York Epsilon Phi, Syracuse (1974-1985)
1951 Arizona Zeta Alpha, Arizona State (1972-1986)
1951 California Zeta Beta, USC
1951 Colorado Zeta Gamma, Denver (1959-1966)
1951 *North Carolina Epsilon Omega, Davidson* (1971)
1952 Florida Zeta Epsilon, Miami (FL)
1952 *Oregon Zeta Delta, Linfield* (1973)
1953 Ohio Zeta Zeta, Kent (1970-1988)
1953 Texas Zeta Eta, Texas Tech.
1957 Texas Zeta Theta, Lamar
1958 Ohio Zeta Iota, Denison
1959 Kentucky Zeta Lambda, Murray State
1959 Texas Zeta Kappa, West Texas
1960 Texas Zeta Mu, Sam Houston
1962 Oklahoma Zeta Nu, Central State (OK)
1963 Indiana Zeta Omicron, Indiana State
1963 Michigan Zeta Xi, GMI
1964 Tennessee Zeta Pi, Tennessee, Martin
1965 Minnesota Zeta Sigma, Hamline
1965 Tennessee Zeta Rho, Memphis State (1980-1987)

1965 Virginia Zeta Tau, Old Dominion
1966 Louisiana Zeta Chi, Louisiana Tech
1966 Nebraska Zeta Upsilon, Kearney
1966 Texas Zeta Phi, Texas A & I
1967 Florida Eta Alpha, South Florida
1967 *Kentucky Zeta Omega, Western Kentucky* (1976)
1967 South Carolina Zeta Psi, Newberry
1968 *Alabama Eta Eta, Athens* (1977)
1968 Arkansas Eta Gamma, Arkansas State
1968 *Georgia Eta Beta, Georgia State* (1987)
1968 Goergia Eta Zeta, Georgia Southern
1968 *Minnesota Eta Delta, Mankato* (1986)
1968 Nevada Eta Epsilon, Nevada, Las Vegas
1969 Alabama Eta Theta, Jacksonville (AL)
1969 Florida Eta Mu, Florida Atlantic
1969 New Mexico Eta Kappa, New Mexico
1969 Tennessee Eta Lambda, Tennessee Tech
1969 Texas Eta Iota, Stephen F. Austin
1970 *Tennessee Eta Nu, Middle Tennessee* (1986)
1971 Florida Eta Rho, Central Florida
1971 Georgia Eta Phi, West Georgia
1971 Illinois Eta Upsilon, Western Illinois
1971 *Minnesota Eta Sigma, Bemidji* (1975)
1971 Missouri Eta Omicron, Culver-Stockton
1971 South Carolina Eta Pi, Clemson
1971 *Tennessee Eta Tau, Austin Peay* (1989)
1971 *West Virginia Eta Xi, Salem (WV)* (1983)
1972 Alabama Eta Omega, Montevallo
1972 Florida Eta Psi, West Florida (1976-1990)
1972 Indiana Theta Alpha, Ball State
1972 Louisiana Eta Chi, Southeastern Louisiana
1973 Illinois Theta Zeta, Southern Illinois
1973 Pennsylvania Theta Gamma, Duquesne
1973 *Texas Theta Beta, Tyler Junior* (1981)
1973 Texas Theta Epsilon, Houston Baptist
1973 Virginia Theta Delta, V.P.I.
1974 Alabama Theta Eta, North Alabama
1975 Illinois Theta Iota, Millikin
1975 Illinois Theta Theta, Illinois State
1976 New Mexico Theta Kappa, New Mexico State
1977 Illinois Theta Mu, Elmhurst
1977 Ohio Theta Lambda, Miami (OH)
1977 Texas Theta Nu, Baylor
1978 South Carolina Theta Xi, Francis Marion
1978 West Virginia Theta Omicron, Marshall
1979 Alabama Theta Pi, Alabama, Huntsville
1979 Missouri Theta Rho, Northeast Missouri
1979 Texas Theta Sigma, Texas A & M
1980 Alabama Theta Phi, Alabama, Birmingham
1980 Kansas Theta Tau, Wichita
1980 *Tennessee Theta Upsilon, Tennessee, Chattanooga* (1987)
1982 Pennsylvania Theta Chi, Indiana (PA)
1983 Florida Theta Psi, Stetson
1983 Kentucky Theta Omega, Northern Kentucky
1986 South Carolina Iota Beta, Lander
1986 Texas Iota Alpha, Southwest Texas
1988 Maryland Iota Gamma, Maryland, Baltimore County
1988 Pennsylvania Iota Delta, Widener

1988 Texas Iota Epsilon, Texas, San Antonio
1989 California Iota Eta, Cal Poly, Pomona
1989 California Iota Theta, Cal, Riverside
1989 Florida Iota Zeta, Rollins
1990 Arizona Iota Iota, Northern Arizona

Colonies: Arizona State, Lander, Southwest Texas, Syracuse

COAT OF ARMS

Beta Sigma Psi

ACTIVE PIN

BETA SIGMA PSI was organized as a national fraternity on April 17, 1925. The fraternity had its origins in the concern of a Lutheran pastor for the students who had been entrusted to his spiritual care at the University of Illinois. The Rev. V. Gustav Stiegemeyer in Champaign, Illinois was convinced that young men away from home for the first time were easily influenced by the opinions and actions of those around them. Since his chief concern was to help Lutheran students remain in contact with the church and to grow in the understanding and appreciation of it, he cast about for ways of increasing the knowledge of their heritage and arranging activities which would get them involved as a group. With a nucleus of ten students, he organized the Lutheran Illini League in the fall of 1919. At that time the intention was to do no more than to meet once or twice a week for discussion on contemporary issues. As the league grew in numbers during the first year, and as the members became better acquainted with each other, someone brought up the question of organizing as a living group and occupying a house of their own. By the fall of 1920 this suggestion had become a reality and the league was able to open its doors to twenty members. Early in 1921 the Lutheran Illini League was reorganized as the Concordia Club.

By 1923 the group regularly participated in campus activities; so much so that they were referred to as the "Concordia Fraternity." This was one of the circumstances which encouraged some of the members to give serious thought to once again reorganizing and becoming a part of the university fraternity system. There were those among the membership who argued that such a move would deprive the organization of its character and forfeit some of their most cherished objectives. To join the fraternity system would run the risk of becoming progressively secularized and ending up as just another fraternity. Those who were in favor of becoming a fraternity continued to agitate for it. They pointed out that by becoming full-fledged members of the university fraternity system the group would not only share in all privileges and advantages pertaining to fraternities, but would also have a voice in shaping future fraternity policy. Those who shared this conviction were Harold Ahlbrand, Wilbur E. Augustine, Norbert W. Behrens, Herman H. Gilster, Arden F. Henry, Russell Henry, Julius J. Seidel, and William H. Welge. In the end their point of view prevailed with the result of the filing of the incorporation papers in 1925. There were many individuals who shared in the formation of the Illini League, the Concordia Club and the fraternity, but the eight men listed above and The Rev. Stiegemeyer are considered the founders of Beta Sigma Psi.

Growth The Concordia Club at Champaign had been in correspondence with The Rev. Paul Schmidt who sponsored a similar organization at Purdue University. One month after the filing of incorporation papers in Illinois, the members of Alpha Chapter drove to Purdue to lend their presence to the formation of Beta Chapter. A National Council was elected with the first National Officers sometime in 1925. The two fledgling chapters promptly established the National Council as an indication of their optimism for the future.

They were soon joined by Gamma Chapter at the University of Michigan in 1928 and Delta Chapter at the University of Nebraska in 1929. Both of the new chapters had existed for four years as Concordia Clubs.

Economic depression caused Gamma and Alpha to become inactive in 1933 and 1940, respectively. The curtain came down on the first period of the fraternity's history. The loss of Alpha's house was a disaster of the first magnitude because it involved the loss of all of Alpha's and Concordia's trophies and memorabilia which were in the house when it was sold at public auction and the new owner refused to surrender them. Also lost were records pertaining to the early history of Beta Sigma Psi, including those which had been in possession of Rev. Stiegemeier until they were turned over to Alpha Chapter after his death in 1938.

Shortly, World War II necessarily disrupted campus life and Beta Sigma Psi was grievously wounded. Only two chapters, Beta and Delta, with a combined membership of fourteen remained. An undergraduate named Delmar Lienemann from the University of Nebraska stepped forward and was elected secretary treasurer, the forerunner of today's executive director. He started his job with no more than the National Constitution and a great determination to keep the fraternity alive. Del served loyally as a volunteer for twenty-two years and the fraternity's highest award is named in his honor.

In 1949 Epsilon Chapter was established at Iowa State University. The expansion was continued by the founding of Zeta Chapter at Kansas State in

1951 and Eta Chapter at the University of Missouri-Rolla in 1952. As a result of this growth, Beta Sigma Psi qualified as a junior member of the National Interfraternity Conference in 1952. Reactivation of Alpha Chapter was accomplished in 1956.

Government The National Council is the supreme legislative body of Beta Sigma Psi. It is composed of one representative, elected by secret ballot, from each active and alumni chapter and the national officers. Each active chapter delegate has two votes (the votes may be split) and alumni chapter votes are prorated so the total alumni votes do not exceed the active chapter votes. National Officers each have one-half vote. The National Council regularly meets once each year. Special sessions may be called by the National President. Administration of fraternity business between council meetings is vested in the Executive Committee which is comprised of the national officers and committees appointed by the national president.

The National Council establishes policies for the handling of problems at the chapter level; raises the funds necessary to conduct national business; grants charters to new chapters and is empowered by the constitution to discipline chapters and withdraw charters. National Officers are the president, vice presidents (minimum of four), executive director, publications director, scholarship director, and recruitment director. A national pastoral advisor advises the National Council on spiritual matters. Vice presidents assist the executive director in the areas of chapter services, protocol, and fraternity expansion.

Traditions and Insignia Since one objective of Beta Sigma Psi is to promote a fraternity for Lutheran college students, its traditions and activities foster this end. Members aim to recognize that a life rooted with Christ in God is the only true goal of human existence. Encouraged are those things which shall assist in the development of highly respected, well-adjusted, informed, socially acceptable gentlemen, such as: a well ordered home environment, insuring wholesome surroundings; attainment of high scholastic standing through good habits of study and industry; emphasis on a sterling code of moral and ethical values; stress on the teaching and need for good manners; fostering of cooperation through athletic competition and instilling the ideas of selflessness through group living.

Most chapters host a Gold Rose Formal each spring and sponsor Reformation Day activities in the fall. National Awards are presented each year at the National Council meeting. These awards are named after fraternity members who have made outstanding contributions to the operations of the national fraternity. They are as follows: Erck Award for the outstanding active, Welge Award for outstanding recruitment and membership education, Hingst Award for scholastic achievement, Edwards Award for outstanding chapter management, Baehr Award for best scrapbook, and the Lienemann Award for outstanding service to the fraternity, community, church, nation, and world.

A national basketball tournament is sponsored each year by a host chapter at its request. More than 100 fraternity members participate with some chapters sending as many as four teams.

The badge of the fraternity has a heart containing a black cross superimposed upon a gold rose (from Luther's family crest) which is nearly centered in the pin. The Greek Letters ΒΣΨ arch above the rose. Eighteen pearls border the badge. The national colors are cardinal red and white. Sisters pins are five-eighths the size of the regular badge. Such pins may be given in appropriate situations to mothers of active members, wives of alumni, sweethearts or chapter housemothers. The pledge button is red and white enamel with an edge of beveled gold. The red is to be worn to the outside at all times.

The real distinguishing characteristics of Beta Sigma Psi lie within the hearts of its members. Certain insignia and emblems have been adopted, however, to give external evidence of its brotherhood. These insignia are symbolic of the origin and objectives of the fraternity. Full meaning of these symbols is conveyed to the new member upon his activation. While initiation ceremonies are considered to be secret, they are open to any member of the Lutheran clergy.

The crest proper of the fraternity has in the upper left quadrant a shining star; the upper right quadrant a torch of learning; the lower right quadrant an anchor; and in the lower left quadrant a rising sun. A chain is directly centered above the crest proper and Luther's emblem is centered above the chain. Below the crest proper is the motto of Beta Sigma Psi, "Per Aspera Ad Astra." The crest of the fraternity appears on a recognition pin which is worn by actives and alumni. The official flower of the fraternity is the gold rose. While there are many fraternity songs, "Cross, Heart, & Rose" is the inspirational tune used in official ceremonies and major events.

Publications The Gold Rose, a fraternity newsmagazine to which all initiated members are life subscribers, is the official publication.

Funds and Philanthropies The fraternity maintains the Beta Sigma Psi Educational Foundation which was organized in 1982. Scholarships are presented in memory of William Welge, fraternity founder and life-time supporter. Educational grants are presented in memory of The Rev. H. Erck, first national pastoral advisor and student pastor at the University of Nebraska for 27 years.

Headquarters The national office of Beta Sigma Psi Fraternity is located at 12405 Old Halls Ferry Road, P.O. Box 38, Florissant (St. Louis County), Missouri 63032. Phone: (314) 355-2685.

Membership City/Area alumni associations 15. 5,665. Estimated living alumni 5,200. Houses owned 11. Active chapters 11. Inactive chapters 10. Total number of initiates 6,236. Chapter roll:

1925 Alpha, Illinois (1940-1955)
1925 Beta, Purdue
1928 *Gamma, Michigan* (1933)
1929 Delta, Nebraska
1949 Epsilon, Iowa State
1951 Zeta, Kansas State
1952 Eta, Missouri, Rolla
1962 Iota, Missouri
1962 *Theta, Michigan Tech* (1973)
1963 *Kappa, Minnesota* (1983)
1964 *Lambda, Western Michigan* (1973)
1966 *Mu, Eastern Illinois* (1984)
1967 *Nu, Kansas* (1972)
1967 Xi, Kearney
1968 *Omicron, Central Michigan* (1973)
1969 Pi, Central Missouri State
1969 *Rho, Minnesota, Morris* (1984)
1969 *Sigma, Wayne State (NE)* (1974)
1970 *Tau, Oklahoma State* (1979)
1980 Upsilon, Illinois State
1988 Phi, Texas A & M

COAT OF ARMS

Beta Theta Pi

ACTIVE PIN

PLEDGE PIN

BETA THETA PI was founded at Miami University, Oxford, Ohio, its first formal meeting being held August 8, 1839. Its constituent members were John Reily Knox, 1839; Samuel Taylor Marshall, 1840; David Linton, 1839; James George Smith, 1840; Charles Henry Hardin, 1841; John Holt Duncan, 1840; Michael Clarkson Ryan, 1839; and Thomas Boston Gordon, 1840. The first named, designated within the fraternity as "Pater" Knox, was the moving spirit.

Beta Theta Pi was the sixth college secret fraternity and the first to originate west of the Alleghenies. At the time of its organization, Alpha Delta Phi, which established a branch at Miami in 1833, was the only fraternity with a western chapter. Kappa Alpha was at Union and Williams, where anti-secret local societies also existed. Sigma Phi was at Union, Hamilton, Williams, and New York University. Psi Upsilon was at Union and New York University, and Brown, where rival chapters existed, but was without rivals as yet at Miami, Columbia, Yale, Amherst, and Harvard. The Mystical Seven had originated at Wesleyan. The fraternity system in 1839, therefore, existed in New York, New England, and Ohio only. The presence at Mi-

ami of Alpha Delta Phi and opposition to it led to the formation of Beta Theta Pi.

Growth The first branch or chapter was located in Cincinnati, nominally in the local law school, but actually it was not connected with any college, although it initiated only college men.

When the parent chapter was without undergraduates from 1873 until 1886, Miami University was closed. The chapter at Cincinnati as now constituted is considered the successor of that original Cincinnati chapter. The chapter at Transylvania died at an early date. The Washington and Jefferson chapter, Gamma 1842 and Nu 1855, was formed by the union of the two colleges named and was called Gamma Nu from 1865 until 1874 when the designation of the older chapter was adopted. The chapters at Princeton, Monmouth, Howard (Alabama), and Wooster colleges were killed by anti-fraternity laws. The period of the Civil War caused the suspension of the activities of all of the chapters south of the Ohio River. The Illinois College chapter closed in 1866. The chapter at the Naval Academy was formed when that institution was located at Newport, Rhode Island. It never had a real existence, facing a navy regulation against secret societies. The charters of the chapters at Harvard, Cumberland, Virginia Military Institute, Richmond, Trinity, Randolph-Macon, Virginia Polytechnic Institute, Butler, Iowa Wesleyan, and Boston were withdrawn by the fraternity. The William and Mary chapter surrendered its charter at a time when hopes for the institution were not realized. The Hampden-Sydney charter was surrendered in 1912 when attendance at the college was much reduced.

A number of the chapters were formed from existing organizations. The Brown chapter when revived in 1880 was the sole surviving chapter of Phi Kappa Alpha. The Denison chapter was a chapter of Kappa Phi Lambda; Mississippi the last one of Alpha Kappa Phi; Dartmouth the last of Sigma Delta Pi; and Missouri the last of Zeta Phi. Twice a union was effected with another fraternity, with Alpha Sigma Chi in 1879, and with the Mystical Seven in 1889. In the latter case, members of the chapters which had existed at the University of Georgia from 1844-59 and at Centenary College, Louisiana, 1850-61, were entitled to membership in Beta Theta Pi, 40 and 39, respectively. In each other instance the alumni of the uniting fraternity were received into full fellowship. From Alpha Sigma Chi came the chapters at Rutgers, Cornell, Stevens, St. Lawrence, and Maine. From the Mystical Seven came the chapter at Wesleyan and the present chapters at Davidson and North Carolina, previously existing Beta chapters at these places being then dormant. The active chapters of both fraternities at Virginia united their membership.

Alumni associations exist in many of the principal cities of the country. They have the right to a representation in the conventions, but have no power to initiate members. A number of them hold regular weekly luncheons and have proved valuable agencies for promoting fraternity friendships. For several years, 1884-93, a club of alumni maintained a summer resort at Wooglin, on Lake Chautauqua, New York, where it owned a plot of ground surrounding a clubhouse. Eight conventions of the fraternity were held there. The building was struck by lightning and burned to the ground in 1901, and the enterprise was abandoned, as were attempts at house-maintaining alumni fraternity clubs in New York and Chicago.

At the 145th General Convention in 1984, the delegates maintained Betas commitment to scholastic achievement by voting for a minimum 2.5 GPA on a 4 point scale for its chapters to remain in good standing. The chapters failure to meet this minimum for two consecutive years will result in the chapter being placed under suspension.

Government For eight years after the foundation of the fraternity, the parent chapter held the reins of government. In 1847 the convention of chapters established a "presiding chapter" system. Under this plan the convention remained the legislative body; but during its recess the affairs of the fraternity were administered by a chapter called the presiding chapter, selected usually in rotation with little consideration of its actual condition or the administrative capacity of its undergraduate members. In 1872 a general secretary was appointed, who shared the work of administration. The fraternity in 1874 was divided into districts, each with a district chief, but subordinate to the general secretary, the presiding chapter still retaining its position. The presiding plan was abandoned in 1879, and the affairs of the fraternity were confided to the Board of Directors, composed of nine members, three of whom retired from office each year. The offices of general secretary and of the subordinate chiefs of districts were retained, and the incorporation of the fraternity was secured. In 1879 the number of directors or trustees was reduced to six, three being administrative officers, president, general secretary, and general treasurer. The term of office is three years, two members retiring each year. Since 1925 the three non-officials have each been made a vice-president with special duties assigned by the board. The general convention is held annually. The fraternity pays travel allowances to all officers and chapter delegates and no registration fee is collected.

Traditions and Insignia The badge is an eight-sided shield, the sides of which curve inward. On a field of black enamel are displayed three stars of gold, a wreath of greenish gold encircling a diamond, the Greek letters, ΒΘΠ, and below, in smaller letters, αωλθ. The pledge button is a shield of white enamel the same shape as the badge and displays three gold stars.

The colors are light shades of pink and blue. The flower is the rose, the individual chapters choosing separate varieties. The flag displays three horizontal stripes of equal width of blue, white, and blue, a single white five-pointed star on the upper blue stripe, and two white five pointed stars in the lower blue stripe, the three stars forming an equilateral triangle, in the center a dragon seated in red.

The fraternity has a complete heraldic system perfected by Major George M. Chandler, Michigan '98, who designed also the standard badge, pledge button, and flag. The coat of arms of the general fraternity consists of the shield quartered white and red; and a blue chevron bearing three gold stars; crest, a gold dragon seated; motto: —kai—. For each chapter the coat of arms is the same shield with the same gold dragon crest, the white first quarter of the shield charged with a device of significance to the individual chapter, and the chapter motto, the Greek words of which begin with the Greek-letter designation of the chapter.

Publications A catalogue was first published in 1855, and subsequent editions in 1859, 1866, 1870, 1881, 1899, 1905, 1911, 1917, 1933, 1979 and 1984.

The fraternity first printed a collection of songs in 1847. Twenty-five editions of the songbook have been published, the later ones with full musical scores. The fraternity has an unusual number of original melodies.

The magazine of the fraternity, called the Βηθα Θητα Πι, was first issued December 15, 1872, and has been published continuously since. It began as a monthly and continued so for many years. Now identified as *The Beta Theta Pi*, it is a quarterly, with winter, spring, and fall issues plus the complete detailed minutes of the General Convention. The magazine publication expenses are met from the Baird Fund income. This endowment fund was established by the 1918 convention, and it has grown steadily through gifts and the life subscription fees of all members initiated since that time. The November 1928 issue of the magazine was the first finding list, or roll of members, of the Baird Fund.

In 1894, with the title *Fraternity Studies*, a manual of information concerning the fraternity was published giving its history to that date and other facts of interest. A second edition much more elaborate in form was issued in 1907 as the *Handbook of Beta Theta Pi. Betas of Achievement* was published in 1912. It contained 1,459 biographies of members of the fraternity who had become prominent in post-collegiate life, 494 of these being of deceased members. Nearly 600 names of living Betas are found in the current issue of Who's Who in America. The convention minutes from the beginning down to 1879 were published in 1916 as *Forty Years of Fraternity Legislation*. In 1918 *A Decade of Fraternity Reconstruction* brought the minutes down to 1889. In the very same year *Beta Letters* was printed, containing the correspondence passing between chapters or members from 1839 to 1884. All of these books were edited by William Raimond Baird.

In 1927 the handbook above mentioned was made the basis of *The Beta Book*, with a wider plan and with information brought down to date. A revised edition appeared in 1930, and a second revision in 1935. In 1928 Francis W. Shepardson, who edited *The Beta Book*, prepared *Beta Lore*, a miscellany of Beta sentiment, song, and story, richly illustrated and on a novel plan. *Beta Life*, a second illustrated miscellany describing fraternity individuals, incidents, and inspirations, appeared in 1929, and in 1936 *Beta Bards*, a collection of poetry and songs written by Betas. Ten addresses presented at consecutive general conventions by A. J. G. Priest, the ninth president of Beta Theta Pi, were compiled and published in 1956 as *The Great Ones*.

The Denison chapter published a history in 1885 and again in 1937, both volumes prepared by Francis W. Shepardson, 1882. In 1915 the Ohio Wesleyan Chapter published *The History of Theta Chapter*, prepared by Raymond Thornburg, 1915; and the Michigan Chapter in 1928 published *Beta Theta Pi at Michigan*, 1845-1928, an illustrated history in 270 pages prepared by Shelby B. Schurtz, 1908. More recent chapter publications include *One Hundred Years at Wabash* by Robert B. McCain, '23, published in '46; *The First Hundred Years of Beta Theta Pi at Indiana University* by Karl W. Fischer, '25; *The Westminster Beta* by Charles F. Lamkin; *Delta's First Century* by Robert T. Howard, '37, the last three being published in 1947. A history of the Oregon State chapter by David T. Doherty was published in 1963 under the title *True and Constant*.

The Mystics and Beta Theta Pi, an account of the Mystic Seven Fraternity, written by Karl W. Fischer, Indiana, '25, was published in 1940. *Son of the Stars*, a 214-page manual for pledges, was prepared in 1939 by G. Herbert Smith, DePauw, '27, and has been revised seven times since the original publication. The recent revisions of *Son of the Stars* were done by K. Warren Fawcett, Minnesota, '26, and H. Hiram Stephenson, Miami, '39, assisted by Jonathan J. Brant, Miami, '75. Fawcett's history of Beta Theta Pi, *Marching Along*, 1935-1960, was published in 1961.

In 1967 *Beta's Broad Domain*, a collection of the memoirs and written and spoken words of Dr. Seth R. Brooks, St. Lawrence, '22, former general secretary and president, was published with the assistance of editor-historian-archivist Fawcett. Also, in 1985 Dr. Brook's collection of *Inter Fratres* articles which have appeared in *The Beta Theta Pi* were published as a bound volume.

Funds In 1919 two endowment funds were established. The Baird Fund, designed primarily as a magazine endowment fund, now receives thirty dollars as a membership fee from each initiate, alumni being eligible upon the same terms, the magazine being furnished for life. The Founders Fund is invested primarily in chapter house loans. Its income is used largely for scholarship awards and Tutor-in-Residence stipends. A third fund provides scholarships for sons or daughters of Betas, honoring Seth R. Brooks and his wife, Corinne H. Brooks.

Headquarters The administrative office was es-

tablished in 1949 at 208 East High Street, P.O. Box 6277, Oxford, Ohio 45056. Phone: (513) 523-7591. In a century-old home, modern business and roll keeping facilities are maintained within sight of the fraternity's founding place on the Miami University campus. The operation of the administrative office is directed by the administrative secretary, an appointed officer of the fraternity.

Membership City/Area alumni associations 95. Total living membership 96,611. Undergraduate membership 7,198. Houses owned 97. Active chapters 126. Inactive chapters 34. Colonies 10. Total number of initiates 144,123. Chapter roll:

1839	Alpha, Miami (OH) (1848-1852) (1873-1886)
1840	Beta Nu, Cincinnati (1843-1890)
1840	*Mystic Seven, Centenary (1861)*
1841	*Beta, Western Reserve (1868-1881) (1979)*
1841	Beta Kappa, Ohio (1847-1854)
1842	*Epsilon, Transylvania (1847)*
1842	Gamma, Washington and Jefferson
1843	*Eta, Harvard (1901)*
1843	*Theta, Princeton (1845)*
1845	Delta, DePauw
1845	Lambda, Michigan (1856-1876)
1845	Pi, Indiana (1849-1855)
1846	*Mystic Seven, Georgia (1856)*
1846	Tau, Wabash (1849-1859)
1847	*Zeta, Williams (1851-1914) (1966)*
1848	Epsilon, Centre College (1861-1871)
1849	*Kappa, Brown (1851-1880) (1973)*
1850	*Zeta, Hampden-Sydney (1912)*
1852	Eta, North Carolina (1860-1889)
1853	Iota, Hanover
1853	Theta, Ohio Wesleyan
1854	*Mu, Cumberland (TN) (1860-1865) (1889)*
1855	Omicron, Virginia (1973-1980)
1855	Xi, Knox (1874-1888)
1856	Alpha Rho, Washington and Lee (1880-1917)
1856	*Sigma, Illinois College (1866)*
1858	*Phi Alpha, Davidson (1862-1890) (1971)*
1858	*Upsilon, South Carolina (1861)*
1859	*Chi, Oglethorpe (1861)*
1860	Chi, Beloit (1864-1872)
1860	Psi, Bethany (WV) (1864-1872)
1863	*Omega, Navy (1863)*
1865	*Alpha Alpha, Monmouth (IL) (1878)*
1866	Alpha Beta, Iowa (1873-1880)
1867	Alpha Gamma, Wittenberg
1868	Alpha Delta, Westminster (MO)
1868	*Alpha Epsilon, Iowa Wesleyan (1915)*
1868	Alpha Eta, Denison
1868	*Lambda Rho, Chicago (1875-1894) (1965)*
1869	Alpha Iota, Washington (MO) (1879-1900)
1869	*Alpha Theta, V.M.I. (1880)*
1871	*Alpha Kappa, Richmond (1896)*
1872	*Alpha Lambda, Wooster (1913)*
1872	*Alpha Mu, Howard (AL) (1879)*
1873	Alpha Nu, Kansas
1873	*Alpha Omicron, Trinity (TX) (1881)*
1873	Alpha Pi, Wisconsin, Madison

1873	*Alpha Xi, Randolph, Macon* (1893)	1923	Gamma Mu, Oregon State
1873	Rho, Northwestern	1926	Gamma Nu, UCLA
1874	Alpha Sigma, Dickinson	1930	Gamma Xi, Florida
1876	*Alpha Tau, William and Mary* (1877)	1936	Gamma Omicron, British Columbia
1876	*Upsilon, Boston U.* (1915)	1936	Gamma Pi, Lawrence
1877	Alpha Phi, V.P.I. (1880-1972)	1939	Gamma Rho, Duke
1878	*Alpha Psi, Butler* (1881)	1946	Gamma Sigma, Willamette
1879	Beta Alpha, Kenyon	1947	Gamma Tau, USC
1879	Beta Beta, Mississippi (1901-1928)	1948	Gamma Upsilon, Emory
1879	Beta Delta, Cornell	1949	Gamma Chi, U of the South
1879	Beta Eta, Maine	1950	Gamma Psi, Michigan State
1879	Beta Gamma, Rutgers	1951	Gamma Omega, Southern Methodist
1879	Beta Zeta, St. Lawrence	1952	Delta Alpha, Western Ontario
1879	Omega, Cal, Berkeley	1959	*Delta Beta, Arizona* (1969)
1879	Sigma, Stevens Tech	1959	Delta Gamma, Wichita
1880	Beta Theta, Colgate	1962	Delta Delta, Bowling Green
1880	Phi, Penn (1968-1976)	1962	Delta Epsilon, Puget Sound
1881	Alpha Alpha, Columbia (NY)	1964	Delta Eta, GMI
1881	Nu, Union (NY)	1964	Delta Theta, Alabama
1883	*Beta Iota, Amherst* (1968)	1964	Delta Zeta, Auburn
1884	Beta Lambda, Vanderbilt	1965	Delta Iota, Ball State
1885	Theta Delta, Ohio State	1967	Delta Kappa, Tennessee
1886	Beta Omicron, Texas	1969	Delta Lambda, Florida State
1888	Alpha Tau, Nebraska	1970	Delta Mu, Texas Tech.
1888	Alpha Upsilon, Penn State	1970	Delta Nu, Clemson
1889	Alpha Omega, Dartmouth	1971	Delta Omicron, Weber
1889	Alpha Zeta, Denver	1971	Delta Pi, Louisville
1889	Beta Epsilon, Syracuse (1956-1960)	1971	Delta Rho, Texas, Arlington
1889	Beta Pi, Minnesota	1971	Delta Xi, Eastern Kentucky
1890	Mu Epsilon, Wesleyan (CT)	1975	Delta Sigma, Cal, Irvine
1890	Zeta Phi, Missouri	1977	Delta Phi, Wright State
1891	Beta Chi, Lehigh	1977	Delta Tau, Arizona State
1894	Lambda Sigma Society, Stanford	1977	Delta Upsilon, Houston
1900	Beta Psi, West Virginia	1978	*Delta Chi, Western Michigan* (1984)
1900	Beta Sigma, Bowdoin	1979	Lambda Kappa Beta, Case Western Reserve
1900	Beta Tau, Colorado (1970-1978)	1980	*Delta Psi, Baylor* (1988)
1901	Beta Omega, Washington (WA)	1982	Delta Omega, Maryland
1902	Sigma Rho, Illinois	1983	Epsilon Alpha, East Carolina
1903	Beta Mu, Purdue	1984	Epsilon Beta, San Diego U.
1905	*Lambda Kappa, Case Tech* (1979)	1985	Epsilon Gamma, Central Michigan
1905	Tau Sigma, Iowa State	1986	Epsilon Delta, Cal Poly, Pomona
1906	Theta Zeta, Toronto	1986	Epsilon Zeta, Guelph
1907	Gamma Phi, Oklahoma	1987	Epsilon Epsilon, Georgia
1908	Beta Phi, Colorado Mines	1987	Epsilon Eta, Texas A & M
1908	Beta Xi, Tulane	1987	Epsilon Iota, Cal State, Chico
1909	Beta Rho, Oregon	1988	Epsilon Kappa, Colorado State
1912	Gamma Alpha, South Dakota	1988	Epsilon Lambda, Missouri, Kansas City
1913	Beta Upsilon, M.I.T.	1988	Epsilon Mu, George Mason
1913	Gamma Beta, Utah	1988	Epsilon Nu, McGill
1914	Gamma Delta, Colorado Col	1988	Epsilon Theta, Middle Tennessee
1914	Gamma Epsilon, Kansas State	1989	Bishop
1914	Gamma Gamma, Idaho	1989	Kentucky
1916	Gamma Zeta, Whitman	1989	Alpha Beta, Arizona
1917	Gamma Eta, Georgia Tech		
1920	Gamma Iota, Carnegie-Mellon		
1920	Gamma Theta, Washington State		
1922	Gamma Kappa, North Dakota		
1923	Gamma Lambda, Oklahoma State		

Colonies: Cal, Riverside, Cal, San Diego, Cal, Santa Barbara, Carleton, Hawaii, Rhode Island, Tennessee Tech., Toledo, Johns Hopkins, Yale

Chi Phi

ACTIVE PIN

PLEDGE PIN

CHI PHI as it exists today is the outgrowth of three older organizations, each of which bore the name of Chi Phi: Chi Phi Society, founded at the College of New Jersey; Chi Phi Fraternity, established at the University of North Carolina; and Secret Order of Chi Phi, founded at Hobart College.

The first of these older organizations, Chi Phi Society, which is known in the history of the fraternity as the Princeton Order of Chi Phi, was established at the College of New Jersey, later Princeton University, on December 24, 1824, by Robert Baird, then tutor in the college and later a prominent Presbyterian clergyman. He associated with himself in the formation of this secret Chi Phi Society a number of the faculties of both college and seminary as well as undergraduates of both institutions. This society ceased to be active in 1825.

Thirty years later, in the winter of 1853-54, John MacLean, Jr., found among the papers of his uncle, John MacLean, president of Princeton University, the old constitution, minute book, and ritual of the Chi Phi Society of 1824, and, with these as his guide, he united with Charles Smith DeGraw and Gustavus W. Mayer in reorganizing the old society at Princeton on what might have been called modern lines. The old motto and a great part of the ritual were retained. In the fall of 1854 Mayer organized a second chapter of this Chi Phi Society at Franklin and Marshall College, Joseph Henry Dubbs, later a distinguished professor of history at his *alma mater,* being the first initiate. The opposition of the Princeton faculty and the prohibitory pledge caused the death of the reorganized Princeton chapter in 1859 when its records were destroyed by the last active members, leaving the Lancaster chapter alone to represent the society.

The second of these older organizations, called Chi Phi Fraternity and now known as the Southern Order of Chi Phi, was founded at the University of North Carolina on August 21, 1858, by Thomas Capehart, Augustus Flythe, John C. Tucker, William H. Green, Fletcher T. Seymour, and James J. Cherry, who were students at the university. They organized this club to perpetuate their preparatory school friendships and named it Chi Phi Fraternity. The idea of expansion was early manifested, and chapters were rapidly organized. However, the war killed all but the parent chapter, which continued its existence throughout the struggle and from it, on the cessation of hostilities, sprang new chapters at Hampden-Sydney, Georgia, Edinburgh University in Scotland, Mercer, Emory, Oglethorpe, Trin-

ity, Kentucky Military Institute, and St. John's, while the extinct chapters at Virginia and Davidson were reorganized. This fraternity had a constitution providing for conventions and chapter referendum, but the primary authority rested in the parent chapter.

The Secret Order of Chi Phi, which is now known in the history of the fraternity as the Hobart Order of Chi Phi, was formed at Hobart College on November 14, 1860, by Amos Brunson and Alex J. Beach, who were students at the college. Being dissatisfied with the fraternities existing at Hobart, they associated themselves with John W. Jones, George G. Hopkins, Edward S. Lawson, Samuel W. Tuttle, David S. Hall, David P. Jackson, William H. Shepard, Harvey N. Loomis, William Sutphen, and Frank B. Wilson and founded Upsilon chapter of the Secret Order of Chi Phi. From Hobart, charters were issued to new chapters at Kenyon, Princeton, and Rutgers.

Five years later the Secret Order of Chi Phi at Hobart learned of the existence of Chi Phi Society in Pennsylvania, and on May 29, 1867, the two societies formally united. The Northern Order of Chi Phi Fraternity was thus formed, and later placed chapters at Muhlenberg, Cornell, Dickinson, Wofford, Washington and Lee, Lehigh, Brown, Massachusetts Institute of Technology, Amherst, Ohio Wesleyan, and Lafayette.

In the early winter of 1865-66 the Hobart alumni in New York learned of the existence of the Chi Phi Fraternity in the South through John R. D. Shepard, a member of the Alpha Chapter of the Chi Phi Fraternity at North Carolina. Negotiations for union were initiated, but languished until the northern Chi Phis in 1871 and 1872 placed chapters at Wofford and Washington and Lee. Particularly through the energy of the members of the latter chapter these negotiations were renewed, and after many mutual concessions the union was finally consummated at a meeting of a joint committee held in Washington, March 27, 1874, the new organization taking the name of Chi Phi Fraternity from the Southern Order, but the fabric of organization and the ritual from the Northern Order.

Chi Phi, like other fraternities, had lost heavily in both chapters and membership during the War Between the States, and immediately thereafter. Especially was this true in the Southern Order of Chi Phi, where entire chapters had volunteered for service, and where the effects of the war had largely destroyed southern institutions of higher learning. The period was one of strong sectional feeling, and the union of the Northern and the Southern Orders of Chi Phi in 1874 so shortly after conclusion of the conflict bears strong testimony to the strength of the common ideals which drew the two orders into union. Chi Phi was among the first to forget sectionalism and to extend the hand of brotherhood after the war; this wise step was largely attributable to the leadership of men like

Henry W. Grady of Georgia, Eta and Alpha, 1868, and northern Chi Phis of similar mind.

A unique result of the destruction of these times was the establishment of Theta Chapter of Chi Phi at Edinburgh University, Edinburgh, Scotland, in 1867. After the war, southern colleges and universities being largely destroyed, numbers of prominent students went abroad to complete their studies. A group of these men at Edinburgh University was granted a charter by Chi Phi Fraternity in 1867. The chapter was active for several years, but held no initiations. The re-opening of southern colleges soon after the war resulted in the withdrawal of the charter in 1870. However, this is thought to be the first chapter of an American college fraternity ever to have been established in Europe.

Government The supreme governing body of the Fraternity is the annual Congress composed of two delegates from each active chapter and one delegate from each chartered chapter and area alumni association.

The president and chief executive officer, known as the Grand Alpha, is elected to a two-year term by Congress. The Grand Alpha exercises supervision over all of the business of the fraternity and calls stated and special meetings of the Council. The Council is composed of the Grand Alpha and seven alumni, including the National Director, and two undergraduates who are appointed to serve a two-year term by the Grand Alpha. The National Director is the executive assistant to the Grand Alpha, and represents him at any time and in any capacity as the chief administrative officer of the fraternity. During the interval between Congresses, the administration of fraternity affairs is carried on by Council.

Traditions and Insignia In 1924, the fraternity celebrated at its annual congress in Chicago the centennial of the founding of the Chi Phi Society at Princeton in 1824, the 70th anniversary of the founding of its oldest undergraduate existing chapter at Franklin and Marshall College, and the semicentennial of the union of the Northern and Southern Orders. At these exercises the 16 general fraternities organized before 1854 were represented by official delegates as were the Interfraternity Conference and the Chicago Interfraternity Association.

The fraternity celebrated its 150th Anniversary with special alumni events around the country, culminating in a final celebration at the 1975 annual congress in Asheville, North Carolina.

The official badge issued through the Council is a monogrammed badge of gold, without jewels, consisting of the two Greek letters X and Φ. The colors upon it are scarlet and blue, the scarlet being upon the narrow and blue upon the broad bar of the letter X. The pledge button, called the chakett, consists of two superimposed six-pointed stars, the scarlet above the blue.

Publications The official publication of the fraternity is the *Chi Phi Chakett*, a quarterly magazine which is distributed without charge to all living members of Chi Phi Fraternity. The first publication of the fraternity, known as the *Chi Phi Chakett*, was an annual issued by the chapter at Franklin and Marshall College in 1868. It appeared in 1869 and again in 1872, edited by the Pennsylvania chapters. In 1874 appeared the *Chi Phi Quarterly*, which was issued regularly until 1891 when it was superseded by an official journal, again known as the *Chi Phi Chakett*. Until 1924 the *Chakett* was issued purely as an official bulletin, its place being filled as far as general interest was concerned by annual yearbooks, but, since then, it has appeared as an open quarterly.

In 1924 a memorial volume edited by Dr. Theodore B. Appel was issued, dedicated to Chi Phis who had lost their lives in the service of their country. In addition to a complete history of the fraternity, it contained full biographical details of the members.

In 1939 the fraternity published the *Chronicles of Chi Phi*, a monumental history of the fraternity prepared by Dr. Theodore B. Appel.

The fraternity supplies each pledge with a comprehensive fraternity/scholastic education guide. A series of chapter operations manuals are also published. Fraternity membership directories were published in 1967 and 1982.

Funds and Philanthropies At the request of Former Grand Alpha Joe Rice Dockery, Xi 1928, the 1971 Congress adopted the Muscular Dystrophy Association as the official charity of Chi Phi. The top fund raising chapters receive an incentive bonus from the Chi Phi Educational Trust.

The fraternity annually awards a medal known as the Sparks Memorial Medal to the member from each chapter who attains the chapter's best scholastic record for the year. The Congress of 1924 authorized the awarding of the Sparks Medal as a tribute to the memory and constructive work of Edwin E. Sparks, Alpha-Chi and Iota 1884, a former grand officer.

The Chi Phi Educational Trust was organized September 8, 1930, for the purpose of promoting scholarship and assistance of deserving students requiring such help. The Trust sponsors the annual Herman C. Krannert, Sigma 1912, Leadership Conference, and several regional workshops. In addition, the Trust provides study grants, student loans, annual student scholarships and grants to colleges and universities.

Headquarters The national office of the Chi Phi Fraternity is situated at 3400 Peachtree Road, N. E., Suite 1011, Atlanta, Ga. 30326. Phone: (404) 231-1824.

Membership Graduate/Alumni chapters 47. City/Area alumni associations 21. Total living membership 28,881. Total undergraduate membership 1,641. Houses owned 36. Active chapters 55. Inactive chapters 35. Colonies 6. Total number of initiates 45,912. Chapter roll:

1824 *Princeton Society, New Jersey Medicine and Dentistry (1825)*
1854 Alpha Sigma, Princeton (1859-1864) (1868-1987)
1854 Zeta, Franklin and Marshall
1858 Alpha-Alpha, North Carolina (1868-1924)
1858 *Beta, Centenary (1861)*
1859 Alpha, Virginia
1859 *Gamma, Davidson (1869)*
1860 *Epsilon, Nashville Military Col (1861)*
1860 Upsilon, Hobart (1880-1987)
1861 *Psi, Kenyon (1865)*
1867 Delta, Rutgers (1979-1981)
1867 Epsilon, Hampden-Sydney
1867 Eta, Georgia
1867 *Theta, Edinboro (1870)*
1867 *Theta, Gettysburg (1872)*
1868 *Beta, Muhlenberg (1885)*
1868 Xi, Cornell
1869 Gamma, Emory
1869 *Iota, Mercer (1880)*
1869 *Omega, Dickinson (1893)*
1871 *Alpha Mu, Duke (1952)*
1871 *Lambda, Oglethorpe (1872)*
1871 *Sigma, Wofford (1907)*
1872 *Kappa, Brown (1895)*
1872 *Nu, Washington and Lee (1875)*
1872 *Pi, Kentucky Military (1883)*
1872 Psi, Lehigh
1873 Alpha-Chi, Ohio Wesleyan (1890-1911)
1873 Beta, M.I.T.
1873 *Phi, Amherst (1980)*
1874 Rho, Lafayette
1875 Lambda, Cal, Berkeley
1877 *Omicron, Yale (1959)*
1878 *Theta, R.P.I. (1987)*
1882 Alpha-Tau, Michigan (1885-1921)
1883 *Alpha-Pi, Vanderbilt (1899-1924) (1942)*
1883 Iota, Ohio State
1883 Mu, Stevens Tech
1883 *Nu, Penn (1885)*
1885 *Beta, Harvard (1887)*
1889 *Tau, South Carolina (1897)*
1892 Nu, Texas (1972-1985)
1902 *Chi, Dartmouth (1968-1980) (1987)*
1904 Omega, Georgia Tech
1912 Sigma, Illinois (1978-1984)
1916 Kappa, Wisconsin, Madison
1920 Tau, Alabama
1922 *Alpha-Pi, Iowa State (1936-1970) (1974)*
1924 Alpha Delta, Penn State
1924 *Beta Delta, Washington (WA) (1959)*
1928 Gamma Delta, Minnesota
1931 Delta Delta, UCLA (1958-1989)
1931 Epsilon Delta, Oregon State
1932 Alpha Theta Chi, Nebraska (1942-1963)
1934 Eta Delta, USC
1935 Theta Delta, Florida
1952 Pi, Northwestern
1956 Zeta Delta, Connecticut (1969-1985)
1958 Iota Delta, Indiana
1962 Rho Iota Kappa, Rhode Island

1962 *Tau Delta, Oregon (1970)*
1965 Delta Xi, West Virginia Wesleyan
1966 Kappa Delta, Rochester (1971-1990)
1966 *Lambda Delta, Arizona (1970)*
1967 Mu Delta, Auburn (1979-1983)
1968 Nu Delta, Florida State
1968 Xi Delta, Florida Institute
1969 *Omicron Delta, Miami (OH) (1988)*
1969 Phi Delta, Tennessee
1969 *Pi Delta, West Virginia (1985)*
1969 Rho Delta, Oglethorpe
1969 Sigma Delta, Cal, Davis
1970 *Chi Delta, Georgia State (1987)*
1970 Psi Delta, North Carolina, Charlotte
1971 *Omega Delta, Morehead (1976)*
1973 Alpha Zeta, West Georgia
1974 *Beta Zeta, Central Florida (1984)*
1979 Gamma Zeta, North Carolina, Wilmington
1983 Delta Zeta, South Florida
1984 Phi Lambda Theta, Bucknell
1987 Epsilon Zeta, Humboldt
1987 Theta Zeta, Texas A & M
1987 Zeta Zeta, Cal State, Sacramento
1988 Kappa Zeta, Purdue
1988 Lambda Zeta, St. Mary's, San Antonio
1988 Nu Zeta, Madison Col
1989 Beta Sigma Rho, Minnesota, Morris
1989 Iota Zeta, George Mason
1989 Mu Zeta, Denver

Colonies: Colorado, SUNY, Binghamton, Hofstra, SUNY, Albany, Boston U., Colorado

Chi Psi

ACTIVE PIN

PLEDGE PIN

CHI PSI was founded at Union College, Schenectady, New York, on May 20th, 1841. While it was the eighth Greek-letter society in the country and the fifth to originate at Union, it was considered the first to be founded upon the fraternal and social principles of a brotherhood, rather than upon the literary characteristics on which existing societies had been started. The ten founders were Philip Spencer, Robert Heyward McFaddin, Jacob Henry Farrell, John Bush, Jr., Samuel Titus Taber, James Lafayette Witherspoon, William Force Terhune, Alexander Peter Berthoud, James Chatham Duane, and Patrick Upshaw Major.

Within the fraternity, each chapter is termed as "Alpha," and that letter is prefixed in each case to the chapter designation. All Alpha/chapter houses are called lodges, and all but one Alpha has its own lodge.

Chi Psi became a "national" fraternity on July 16, 1842, with the establishment of the Alpha at Williams College, and within five years had spread also to Middlebury, Wesleyan, Bowdoin, Hamilton, Michigan, and Columbia. Although the pattern of growth has been gradual, the fraternity was a pioneer at Middlebury (1843), Michigan (1845), Minnesota (1874), and California at Irvine (1964).

Almost at the outset of the Fraternity's career, it was dealt a severe blow. One of the founding members was Philip Spencer, son of a Cabinet officer in the Tyler Administration and a member of a family of high social position. On December 1, 1842, while serving as midshipman on the U.S. brig of war *Somers*, he was executed at sea for alleged mutiny. The circumstances surrounding his death and the character of the charges against him have always been shrouded in mystery. Senator Benton in his *Thirty Years View* shows the charge and arrest to have been unwarranted and is unsparing in his condemnation of the seizure and execution. James Fennimore Cooper, Gail Hamilton, and numerous others have been even more emphatic in denunciation of the steps which lead to Spencer's death. In his possession were found messages in Greek which the ship's officers took to be evidence of a plot to overthrow the ship, although some said the papers had to do with his fraternity, and when he refused to explain them he accordingly suffered the fate of a martyr. For many years after this, the Chi Psis were dubbed "Pirates" by their rivals.

Of the tragedy, an early Chi Psi wrote, "The death of Spencer was the crucial test of the coherence of the Chi Psi Fraternity. Here was a young man put to death for piracy. The press of the day was outspoken in upholding the justice of the sentence and popular prejudice sided with the press. But two ways were open for his brethren of the Fraternity: Either to repudiate their lost associate or defend his memory. What a trial they were subjected to! To express sympathy for him was to bring upon them public censure and derision. But Philip Spencer was their Brother. Boldly and manly they stood by his side to defend his memory. They showed to the world that the cohesion of Chi Psi embraced both the quick and the dead."

Growth After the founding of the original Alphas of the first five years, the fraternity extended to Princeton in 1851. Then, by reason of the fact that many of the members of the Alphas were southerners, Chi Psi extended into the South with Alphas at North Carolina, Furman, South Carolina, Mississippi, Virginia, and Wofford. As a result of the unsettled conditions of the Civil War or anti-fraternity legislation, a number of these new Alphas were inactive for a period of time. The Alphas at Furman, Wofford, and Princeton remain dormant.

On April 24, 1895, another milestone was passed with the establishment of Chi Psi at Stanford, placing the fraternity on the West Coast for the first time. The Yale Alpha was founded upon request by the college authorities and the other fraternities there represented, which made significant rush and other concessions for three years to help the new chapter. It was a notable illustration of the modern spirit of interfraternity cooperation.

About the middle of April, 1846, undergraduates from the Michigan Alpha built a log cabin in the woods near Ann Arbor, for the specific purpose of providing a meeting place for Chi Psi at a time when the faculty was hostile to fraternities. The cabin was 20 by 24 feet and was located on the present site of Forest Hill Cemetery. In a sense this building may be called the prototype of the modern fraternity house, as it was the first building to have been constructed specifically for fraternity purposes. The cabin resembled a hunting lodge, and hence the tradition of referring to all Chi Psi dwellings as lodges was begun.

The lodge of Alpha Pi at Union was erected by the Alpha fraternity as a memorial to Philip Spencer, one of the founders. The lodge at Stanford was destroyed in the earthquake of April 18, 1906, but was rebuilt. Prior to 1907, the Cornell lodge was the well-known Fiske-McGraw mansion in Ithaca. In a fire which completely destroyed it in the early morning hours of December 7, 1906, four members of the fraternity and three members of the Ithaca volunteer fire department lost their lives. Two of the four members who lost their lives had escaped from the burning building, but upon finding their roommates missing they, with rare devotion, returned to find them and perished with them. A new lodge was built upon the same site.

With the election of Edward C. Swift (Michigan '76) to the presidency of the fraternity in 1914, active efforts were made for the foundation of a permanent endowment fund for the fraternity. An initial fund was collected through the personal efforts of Swift by 1916. This fund was not formally incorporated until ten years later when the Executive Council formed the Chi Psi Educational Trust. For the two succeeding years, a campaign was carried on among alumni to increase the fund to $500,000, subscriptions to which were completed in September, 1928, with the fund oversubscribed. the fund from alumni contributions has grown to several million dollars for the benefit of fraternity undergraduates. Most of the Alphas also have their own educational endowment funds, some with assets approaching one-half million dollars.

Government Outside the annual conventions, the governing body of the fraternity is the Executive Council, which meets four times each year. This board is composed of at least nineteen members: twelve elected alumni, the national president, past presidents, and executive director, and five undergraduate members, one from each regional area. (In the 1960's, Chi Psi was one of the first fraternities to include undergraduates as full voting members of its national board.) Beyond its function as a governing board, the Executive Council also serves as the board of directors for the Philip Spencer Memorial Trust, which acts as trustee for the Alpha Building Fund.

In spite of the recognized local autonomy of its Alphas, Chi Psi was the pioneer in the policy of employing a paid traveling secretary to devote his entire time to fraternity work. This was in keeping with the desire to keep the fraternity closely knit and uniform. Chi Psi provides for "universal transfer" of members, so that any brother who has been initiated at one Alpha is automatically accepted as a full brother when he transfers to another school. The fraternity has no honorary members.

Chi Psi was also the first fraternity to establish a national financial control system for all its Alphas, called the Uniform Accounting System. And Chi Psi was the first fraternity to develop a student-exchange program, working with a privately endowed cultural exchange center in South America.

In the field of scholarship and pledge education, Chi Psi in 1952 initiated a special program of orientation conducted in each of its Alphas managed by a scholarship director and usually conducted by a faculty member. This program, called "The Man and His College," is proof of the fraternity's interest in creating within the undergraduates an appreciation of their fundamental reason for attendance in college.

In 1965, Chi Psi launched one of the most significant ventures in fraternity history, with a program concerned with meeting the needs of the human spirit. Developed by achievement motivation experts at a well-known university institute for human behavior, the *Program for Self Development* is a two-day course in which participants learn about themselves and the important tenets of goal setting, personal development and mutual assistance. By going beyond the scholarship training inherent in any undergraduate experience, the program assists in the development of leadership training designed to guarantee that the men of Chi Psi get into the habit of achieving useful goals in the classroom and beyond.

In the mid-1970's, National President Oliver Rowe introduced a new *"Program for Excellence"* in all the Alphas, stressing the importance of scholastic and extra-curricular achievement, fostered by self-discipline, as an adjunct of education that colleges did not provide. In 1982, Chi Psi instituted its Alpha Management Retreat Program, designed to train present and future officers in effective leadership and management techniques.

In May of 1941, over 700 members from all parts of the United States gathered at Union College to celebrate Chi Psi's Centennial. Many hundreds more in cities from coast to coast listed by network radio broadcast to the festivities. Prominent in the discussion were the new Central Office in Ann Arbor and the Philip Spencer Memorial Trust (a $100,000 endowment for the Headquarters building). Also on this occasion, as a memorial to the founders, Chi Psi presented Union College with a $5,000 endowment for a Chi Psi Alcove section in its library to be devoted to books on human relations.

The first central administrative headquarters for Chi Psi was established in New York City in 1912. It was moved to Madison for two years in 1919, and then finally to Ann Arbor in 1921. After years of rented quarters, the fraternity found a permanent home for its headquarters when a beautiful mansion property next to the university campus was donated in 1940.

In most large cities there are Regional Associations of alumni who get together frequently for social purposes and who annually celebrate Founders' Day on May 20th. Each Alpha also has its own alumni corporation, generally charged with supervising the lodge and its property, as well as its own local educational foundation, established to provide local scholarships.

Publications The first catalogue of the fraternity was published at Troy, New York, in 1849. Thirteen additional editions of the catalogue and ten editions of a membership directory have been published since then. The most complete catalogue was the 1941 version, which was a combined catalogue and history, depicting in print and picture the life of the fraternity and its members. This was released at the time of the Centennial Celebration in May of 1941, and a similar updated volume is planned for the Sesquicentennial in 1991.

The official journal of Chi Psi, *The Purple and Gold,* was first proposed on October 28, 1846, but regular publication was not begun until November, 1883. It is generally published for members only, and is sent without charge to each undergraduate and alumnus, and to the parents of each undergraduate so long as the man is in college. The Chi Psi Songbook has been published in six editions between 1878 and 1980.

Insignia The badge is a jeweled monogram, composed of a C laid upon a Ψ. The latter displays at its top a cross within a circle and at its bottom a skull and crossbones with three daggers above, while the former contains seventeen gems. The pledge button is a square in the form of an hourglass with the fraternity colors of purple and gold. The banner (flag) is similarly arranged with the Greek letters C and Ψ in a vertical placement. The national policy of Chi Psi has been very conservative in the use of the Chi Psi symbols and insignia.

Headquarters P.O. Box 1344, Ann Arbor, Michigan 48106. Phone: (313) 663-4204. The property is owned by Chi Psi and has provision for both the Central Office and some living quarters.

Membership Total living membership 19,000. Active chapters 33. Inactive chapters 10. Total number of initiates 50,000. Chapter roll:

1841 Pi, Union (NY)
1842 *Theta, Williams* (1963)
1843 Mu, Middlebury

1844   Alpha, Wesleyan (CT)
1844   Eta, Bowdoin
1845   Epsilon, Michigan
1845   Phi, Hamilton
1846   *Zeta, Columbia (NY)* (1885)
1851   *Delta, Princeton* (1857)
1855   Sigma, North Carolina
1857   *Kappa, CUNY, Brooklyn* (1873)
1858   *Upsilon, Furman* (1898)
1860   *Lambda, Brown* (1871)
1860   Omicron, Virginia
1864   Chi, Amherst
1869   Psi, Cornell
1869   *Tau, Wofford* (1909)
1874   Nu, Minnesota
1879   Rho, Rutgers
1883   Xi, Stevens Tech
1884   Omega, Rochester
1890   Alpha Delta, Georgia
1894   Beta Delta, Lehigh
1895   Delta Delta, Cal, Berkeley
1895   *Gamma Delta, Stanford* (1971)
1898   Epsilon Delta, Northwestern (At Chicago
       1898–1942)
1912   Zeta Delta, Illinois
1920   Psi Delta, Colorado
1921   Eta Delta, Oregon
1921   Theta Delta, Washington (WA)
1923   Iota Delta, Georgia Tech
1924   *Kappa Delta, Yale* (1963)
1949   Lambda Delta, Cal, Irvine (At UCLA 1949–
       1952)
1964   Tau Delta, U of the South
1971   Chi Delta, Clemson
1977   Mu Delta, Rollins
1977   Omicron Delta, Washington and Lee
1982   Xi Delta, Texas Tech.
1986   Upsilon Delta, Wake Forest
1988   Sigma Delta, Duke

Delta Chi

ACTIVE PIN

PLEDGE PIN

DELTA CHI was founded at Cornell University Law School in the spring of 1890 by Albert Sullard Barnes, Myron McKee Crandall, John Milton Gorham, Peter Schermerhorn Johnson, Edward Richard O'Malley, Owen Lincoln Potter, Alphonse Derwin Stillman, Thomas A. J. Sullivan, Monroe Marsh Sweetland, Thomas David Watkins, and Frederick Moore Whitney. It was recognized by the university on October 13, 1890, and this date is celebrated as Founders' Day. The Ritual was written by Alphonse D. Stillman and was adopted at a meeting held on October 20, 1890. With very few changes it is still in use. The purposes expressed by the Founders for creating Delta Chi were to promote friendship, develop character, advance justice, and assist in the acquisition of a sound education. These goals remain paramount to the fraternity today.

In the early years of the fraternity all members were engaged in the study of the law, in preparation for such study, or in the pursuit of related subjects. As a means of tightening the bonds among the members more securely, membership in other college fraternities, local as well as national, including professional fraternities, was prohibited by Delta Chi in 1909.

Growth In keeping with major changes in the educational world, many law schools became, in effect, graduate schools of recognized institutions. This development encouraged extension of membership into other collegiate departments of these universities. Consequently, in 1921, by action of the convention, membership was officially opened to students of all areas of study, and no longer restricted to students of law.

Conventions were held annually from 1894 to 1911 when the biennial plan was adopted. Delta Chi joined the NIC in 1911 and has maintained a continuous membership.

Government Government is vested in the convention, the Board of Regents, the Executive committee, and the chapters in that order. Each chapter is represented at the Convention by a fixed number of delegates. The Board of Regents is a body constituted of twelve members: three general officers, the retiring international president, and one member elected from each of the eight regions into which the United States and Canada are divided. The Board of Regents is the supreme legislative body of the fraternity in the interim between conventions. The Executive Committee, composed of the three general officers, has executive and administrative authority between conventions. The function of government reserved to the chapters consist of powers of acceptance or rejection.

Each undergraduate chapter has an alumnus adviser, who provides the liaison between the chapter he represents and the general fraternity. He is called the "BB" and is selected by the chapter he represents. Each chapter is also advised by an Alumni Board of Trustees which assist in overseeing the financial and administrative affairs of the chapter.

The general officers of the fraternity are designated by double letters as: "AA" (president), "CC" (secretary), and "DD" (treasurer). The administrative affairs of the fraternity are handled by the headquarters office staff under the direction of the executive director.

With the establishment of a headquarters in 1923, in Iowa City, Iowa, the fraternity developed and promoted a scholarship program in which each chapter is urged to plan for bettering chapter scholastic achievement. Recognition is given each year to the chapter with the highest scholastic achievement.

The fraternity also recognizes the most outstanding overall chapter each year, both nationally and in each region.

The headquarters also conducts a chapter visitation program, carried out by outstanding young graduates who, through periodic visits, provide each chapter with personal assistance in the development of programs and the solution of problems.

In 1938, the fraternity inaugurated a series of annual regional conferences in the eight administrative regions of the country. These are designed to provide a medium for the exchange of ideas, instill a national fraternity consciousness, provide leadership training and reinforce the goals of the fraternity.

The Jackson Leadership College, named after distinguished alumnus the late Senator Henry "Scoop" Jackson, is also conducted on an annual basis. The location of the college rotates throughout the regions of the fraternity based on need and concentrates on basic functional areas of leadership.

Funds and Philanthropies The Delta Chi Educational Foundation was organized in 1954 by action of the Executive Board. Incorporated as a nonprofit educational foundation, it has as its purposes: to aid, encourage, promote, and contribute to the education of students in colleges and universities throughout the United States and Canada; to provide educational advantages and opportunities for such students; to aid and assist such students, financially or otherwise, in the improvement of their education; to establish or finance endowments, fellowships, scholarship incentives, and awards for the furtherance of sound learning. The articles of incorporation are drafted to permit the foundation to make donations or loans to any college or university for the promotion of the overall aims of the foundation.

The Delta Chi Housing Fund loans money to both chapters and colonies to support their housing needs. The fund has been a significant influence in establishing and remodeling chapter housing.

The Boy Scouts of America was recognized by the convention in 1979 as the official national philanthropy of Delta Chi. Each chapter is encouraged to support BSA in its own way.

Publications The fraternity magazine, the *Delta Chi Quarterly*, was authorized and established at the Chicago convention in 1902, and was first published the following April. In addition to the *Quarterly*, the fraternity published a provisional catalogue in 1895, a biographical catalogue in 1899, and issues of the directory in 1904 and at regular intervals since then. *The Song Book*, first published in 1913, has been revised many times. *The Pledge Manual*, which first appeared in 1913, became *The Delta Chi Manual in 1966*. In 1976 it was substantially revised, redesigned, and renamed *The Cornerstone*.

Traditions and Insignia The badge is a mono-

gram of the two Greek letters, with the Δ superimposed upon the X. On the plain official badge the face of the Δ is of black enamel. In jeweled badges, the Δ is set with stones and may also carry a stone in the center. The pledge insignia is formed in the shape of a Δ in colors of red, white, and black with a gold X in the lower background, completing the Greek symbol of the fraternity.

Formed as a law fraternity, the Delta Chi ritual is based on concepts of justice and contains no religious inferences.

Headquarters 314 Church Street. P.O. Box 110, Iowa City, Iowa 52244. Phone: (319) 337-4811.

Membership Graduate/Alumni chapters 14. Total living membership 42,336. Total undergraduate membership 3,496. Houses owned 48. Active chapters 97. Inactive chapters 44. Colonies 24. Total number of initiates 61,013. Chapter roll:

1890	Cornell, Cornell
1891	*New York Univ., N.Y.U.* (1943)
1892	*Albany, Albany Law* (1894)
1892	DePauw, DePauw (1894-1928)
1892	Michigan, Michigan
1892	Minnesota, Minnesota (1943-1945)
1893	*Dickinson, Dickinson* (1933)
1893	*Northwestern, Northwestern* (1909)
1896	*Chicago-Kent Law, Chicago-Kent Law* (1934)
1897	Buffalo, SUNY, Buffalo (1935-1979)
1897	*Osgoode Hall, Toronto* (1975)
1899	*Syracuse, Syracuse* (1917-1967) (1970)
1901	Union, Union (NY)
1902	*New York, New York Law* (1907)
1902	Ohio State, Ohio State (1983-1989)
1902	*West Virginia, West Virginia* (1909)
1903	*Chicago, Chicago* (1929)
1903	*Georgetown, Georgetown U* (1943)
1904	*Penn, Penn* (1917-1929) (1949)
1905	*Stanford, Stanford* (1970)
1905	*Virginia, Virginia* (1936)
1906	*Washington Univ., Washington (MO)* (1909)
1907	Texas, Texas (1970-1989)
1908	Washington (WA), Washington (WA)
1909	*Nebraska, Nebraska* (1953)
1910	Abracadabra, Cal, Berkeley (1969-1978)
1910	Southern Calif., USC
1912	Iowa, Iowa
1913	*Kentucky, Kentucky* (1954-1975) (1981)
1923	*Columbia, Columbia (NY)* (1943)
1923	Illinois, Illinois
1923	Iowa State, Iowa State
1923	Kansas, Kansas
1924	Idaho, Idaho
1925	Arizona, Arizona
1925	Indiana, Indiana
1926	Florida, Florida
1927	Alabama, Alabama
1927	Oklahoma, Oklahoma (1961-1985)
1927	Purdue, Purdue
1927	*S.M.U., Southern Methodist* (1985)
1929	Penn State, Penn State

1931   Oregon State, Oregon State
1932   Miami, Miami (OH)
1934   *U.C.L.A., U.C.L.A.* (1958)
1935   Michigan State, Michigan State
1941   L.S.U., L.S.U. (1953-1965) (1966-1984)
1941   *Rollins, Rollins* (1970)
1943   Washington State, Washington State
       (1972-1988)
1948   Hobart, Hobart
1948   Oklahoma State, Oklahoma State
1949   Arizona State, Arizona State (1971-1988)
1950   *Lake Forest, Lake Forest* (1966)
1950   *Miami Univ., Miami (FL)* (1951)
1951   Auburn, Auburn (1986-1990)
1951   Missouri, Missouri (1966-1978) (1985-1988)
1952   Lehigh, Lehigh
1955   Connecticut, Connecticut
1955   Southern Illinois, Southern Illinois
       (1972-1976)
1955   Western Michigan, Western Michigan
       (1971-1984)
1956   Kansas Medical Center, Missouri, Kansas
       City
1956   *Wayne State, Wayne State (MI)* (1974)
1958   Ball State, Ball State
1959   Northern Ariz., Northern Arizona
       (1976-1986)
1961   Florida State, Florida State (1972-1982)
1961   *Texas Western, Texas, El Paso* (1966)
1963   *Oregon, Oregon* (1971)
1964   *Kansas State, Kansas State* (1981)
1964   Mississippi State, Mississippi State
       (1983-1985)
1965   *Georgia, Georgia* (1983)
1965   *Parsons, Parsons* (1972)
1966   Troy, Troy
1967   Eastern Illinois, Eastern Illinois
1967   Fullerton, Cal State, Fullerton
1967   Livingston, Livingston
1968   Jacksonville State, Jacksonville (AL)
1968   Long Beach, Cal State, Long Beach
1968   Valdosta, Valdosta
1969   Denison, Denison
1969   Gorham State, Southern Maine
1969   Massachusetts, Massachusetts
1969   Oshkosh, Wisconsin, Oshkosh (1981-1986)
1969   San Diego, San Diego U
1969   Tri-State, Tri-State
1970   Cal Poly, Pomona, Cal Poly, San Luis
       Obispo (1973-1989)
1970   Creighton, Creighton (1981-1987)
1970   *Idaho State, Idaho State* (1981)
1970   *Milwaukee, Wisconsin, Milwaukee* (1973)
1970   Northern Iowa, Northern Iowa
1970   Whitewater, Wisconsin, Whitewater
       (1982-1987)
1970   *Youngstown State, Youngstown State* (1976)

1971   Central Missouri State, Central Missouri
       State
1971   Gannon, Gannon
1971   *Northeastern, Northeastern* (1983)
1971   Northwest Missouri, Northwest Missouri
1971   Sacramento, Cal State, Sacramento
       (1973-1983)
1971   Windsor, Windsor
1972   Embry Riddle, Embry Riddle (FL)
1972   Johnstown, Pitt, Johnstown
1972   Montevallo, Montevallo
1972   West Liberty, West Liberty
1973   *East Texas, East Texas* (1981)
1973   Illinois State, Illinois State (1986-1990)
1974   California Of PA, California (PA)
1974   *Edwardsville, Southern Illinois,
       Edwardsville* (1979)
1976   *Missouri Western, Missouri Western* (1979)
1977   Huntsville, Alabama, Huntsville
1977   Marquette, Marquette
1977   Southeast Missouri, Southeast Missouri
1978   Northeast Missouri, Northeast Missouri
1979   *Jacksonville, Jacksonville* (1986)
1980   *Columbus, Columbus* (1986)
1981   New Haven, New Haven
1982   Louisville, Louisville
1983   Augusta, Augusta
1983   Colorado, Colorado
1983   Texas Tech, Texas Tech.
1983   West Virginia Tech, West Virginia Tech
1984   Eastern Washington, Eastern Washington
1984   Northern Colorado, Northern Colorado
1986   Appalachian St., Appalachian
1986   Clarion, Clarion
1986   New Hampshire, New Hampshire
1986   Southwest Missouri, Southwest Missouri
1987   Chico, Cal State, Chico
1987   Louisiana Tech., Louisiana Tech
1988   Central Michigan, Central Michigan
1988   Tarleton, Tarleton
1988   Texas A & M, Texas A & M
1989   Northern Illinois, Northern Illinois
1990   Behrend, Behrend
1990   Cal State, Hayward, Cal State, Hayward
1990   Clemson, Clemson
1990   Kent, Kent
1990   North Carolina State, North Carolina State

Colonies: Wisconsin, Madison, Houston, Georgia
Southern, Maryland, SUNY Col., Fredonia,
Maryland, North Dakota, Northern Michigan,
Albany State, Bryant, Cal, Davis, Elmhurst,
Florida International, Frostburg, Montclair,
Nevada, Western Illinois, Western Ontario,
Delaware, Edinboro, Georgia Tech, Mankato,
Southwestern (TX), Virginia Commonwealth

Delta Kappa Epsilon

ACTIVE PIN

PLEDGE PIN

DELTA KAPPA EPSILON was founded at Yale on June 22, 1844, by 15 members of the class of 1846 in protest against what they perceived to be the injustices and limitations of the society system then prevailing at the university. Opposed to the societies' constrained membership criteria, the founders of DKE emphasized a more fraternal community of tastes and interests: in the words of one of them, Edward Bartlett, who wrote at length on the beginnings of DKE, "the candidate most favored was he who combined in the most equal proportions the gentleman, the scholar, and the jolly good fellow"—criteria which have remained unchanged throughout the years.

The spirit of brotherhood which established DKE and guided its selection of members soon found expression in the objectives of the fraternity, which are "the cultivation of general literature and social culture, the advancement and encouragement of intellectual excellence, the promotion of honorable friendship and useful citizenship, the development of a spirit of tolerance and respect for the rights and views of others, the maintenance of gentlemanly dignity, self-respect, and morality in all circumstances, and the union of stout hearts and kindred interests to secure to merit its due reward."

Growth At the very first meeting, the Deke badge, grip, secret motto, and open Greek motto— "From the heart, friends forever" in translation— were established, but the fraternity was founded as a purely local group and it was not expected that it would take root anywhere else. It happened, however, that one founder, Elisha Shapleigh, had a friend at Bowdoin College, John S. H. Fogg, and, following a summer correspondence between the two men, an autumn contingent of Yale Dekes arrived at Bowdoin to install a branch of the fraternity. On November 6, 1884, five months after its founding, DKE had begun to expand. Its next effort, at Princeton in 1845, subsequently succumbed to the university's anti-fraternity laws, but in the years before the Civil War 27 charters were granted, and the fraternity's constitution was altered to make the new organizations independent chapters, instead of merely branches of the original group at Yale. (Princeton returned in 1987.)

Delta Kappa Epsilon is the first international secret college fraternity of New England origin, and it was the first fraternity to colonize heavily in the South, due in part to the large percentage of southern men then attending Yale. (In fact, in its early days, DKE was known in New England as "the Southern Fraternity.")

Nowhere is this geographical diversity more clearly shown than by the DKE experience in the Civil War. Out of a total membership of some 2500, 725 Dekes fought for the South, and 817 for the North; the first Union officer killed (and, so far as records show, the first soldier to give his life on either side) was a Deke from Yale, Theodore Winthrop, and a Princeton Deke, Philip Spence, was the last Confederate commander to surrender, six weeks after Appomattox. (A Rutgers Deke, John Gibbs, was the first U.S. officer killed in the Spanish-American War, and the first American to lose his life at the front when the U.S. entered World War I was Paul Osborn, a Dartmouth Deke.)

The end of the Civil War brought an end to several southern chapters and, indeed, to the colleges themselves, but DKE continued to grow. In 1852 the fraternity had begun to move "West" with the establishment of chapters at Miami University in Oxford, and Kenyon College in Gambier, Ohio. In 1854 the Kenyon chapter built the first fraternity lodge in America, a log structure forty by twenty and ten feet high, in a woods about a mile from the campus. (In 1861 the Yale chapter constructed the first college fraternity "tomb", which remained in use for over half a century.)

In 1876 the first West Coast chapter, at the University of California at Berkeley, was chartered, and, in 1898, DKE became international with the establishment of its first Canadian chapter at the University of Toronto. Though some chapters fell by the wayside (notably Harvard, despite such alumni as J. P. Morgan, William Randolph Hearst, and Theodore Roosevelt) DKE had 40 active chapters at the turn of the century. (Harvard returned in 1991.)

Growth since that time has been slower, as the fraternity has traditionally preferred judicious development to aggressive expansion. In recent years, however, as the result of a number of chapters lost during the campus unrest of the 1960s, DKE has embarked upon a vigorous program to establish new chapters and revive its inactive ones.

Government During the early days of DKE, its administration was largely vested in the mother chapter at Yale, which granted or refused charters, corresponded with the chapters, ran conventions, and generally managed the fraternity's affairs. The first DKE convention was held in 1846 at New Haven, but it was not until 1855 that the status and authority of the convention was formalized as the instrument for determining fraternity policy.

For many years thereafter, the business of DKE was transacted at the annual convention (now held every other year). The convention, in the absence of a central authority, embodied both legislative and executive responsibilities, but, gradually, a need began to be felt for a stronger, centralized executive body to govern the fraternity and, in 1881, the Council of Delta Kappa Epsilon was established.

Originally consisting of five alumni members and a secretary, the Council's function was, at the start, largely clerical and advisory; it supervised publications, received charter applications and reported on them to the convention, encouraged the formation of local alumni organizations, and attended to other administrative matters. The Council was incorporated by a special legislative act in 1884, and its membership (later increased to ten) rotated among the chapters, Yale alone having a permanent representative. In time, the Council assumed more responsibilities, and its close organization and consistent, continuing policies, gave DKE greater cohesion and increased effectiveness.

In 1910 the Council was enlarged to allow permanent alumni representation from every chapter, its powers and jurisdiction were increased, and a system of field and alumni secretaries was perfected. The president of the Council was renamed the president of DKE, and in 1921 the office of honorary president, to be elected at each convention in tribute to long-standing service to DKE, was established. Today, the title of president has been phased out (although that of honorary president still continues). The fraternity's top volunteer officer is now the chairman of the board, and the top DKE professional is the executive director.

The DKE Council maintained its legislative function until 1973, at which time the DKE constitution was amended to provide for a more streamlined 12-man board of directors. At the 1984 convention a new organization was created: the fraternity was divided into seven regions, each region to be represented by a director, who becomes a member of the International Board, in addition to seven directors-at-large, each having some functional, rather than geographical, responsibility. One of the directors-at-large is a Deke undergraduate, elected by the convention to serve until the next convention. This 15-man board elects the officers of the fraternity, and employs DKE's professional staff.

Traditions and Awards Closely aligned with the fraternity is the Delta Kappa Epsilon Club, a private club for Deke alumni founded in 1885 "to promote social intercourse among the members and to provide a pleasant place of convenient resort for their entertainment and improvement." The club progressed through a number of improving clubhouses until, in 1932, it joined forces with the somewhat younger Yale Club of New York; since that time, the club has operated on the Yale Club premises at 50 Vanderbilt Avenue, New York City, where its members have full use of all Yale Club facilities. In addition to the DKE Club, the fraternity has a number of regional alumni associations and Deke luncheon groups.

Each year the fraternity presents a special award, the Lion Trophy, to that chapter adjudged by the board to be the most outstanding in DKE. In addition, awards are given to chapters which have excelled in the specific areas of scholarship, alumni relations, community service, and chapter improvement. The Deke Leadership Award is presented annually to the undergraduate judged the best all-around Deke in that academic year on the basis of his contribution to his chapter and college.

DKE presents to outstanding alumni its Presidents Award, named for DKE's four U. S. Presidents (Hayes, T. Roosevelt, Ford, Bush); and the William M. Henderson Award, named for DKE's honorary president and long-time executive director and *Deke Quarterly* editor, is given each year to an alumnus for distinguished service to a chapter of DKE (not necessarily his own).

Insignia The badge is gold, of diamond shape, displaying a star in each corner on a ground of black enamel and a scroll in white bearing the letters ΔKE. The recognition pin is a gold rampant lion, and the alumni charm is a small replica of the badge. The DKE colors are crimson, blue, and gold; the flag is composed of vertical stripes of blue, gold, and crimson, with the center, gold, stripe bearing a rampant lion in black. The pledge pin is a small triangle bearing the DKE colors. The fraternity has an extensive system of armorial bearings, with each chapter having its own crest, relating in design to that of the arms of DKE.

Publications The first catalogues of DKE were issued in 1851 and 1855—both small pamphlets with the names and addresses of members. Others followed in 1858, 1863, 1867, and 1871. In 1874 a more complete version containing biographical data appeared, and in 1890 a massive, comprehensive edition was published. A directory of more modest proportions appeared in 1926, and in 1985 a modern directory containing updated information on all living Dekes was published. For many years, DKE membership records have been computerized, and continually updated listings of alumni by chapter, year of graduation, or other categories, are provided at short notice to chapters and alumni groups.

From the first, DKE has been a singing fraternity, and numerous editions of its song books have been published, the earliest dating from 1857. (A number of chapters have published their own song books as well). A recent innovation has been the production of a recorded cassette, "The Songs of DKE" containing a number of old favorites professionally rendered.

The fraternity magazine, *The Deke Quarterly* has been published since January, 1883. DKE publishes a number of leadership guides and manuals concerning chapter and alumni activities, a detailed *Deke Education Manual*, primarily for pledges, and a comprehensive looseleaf manual on chapter operations, as well as specific brochures in such areas as rushing, and alcohol awareness.

Funds and Philanthropies DKE's public charity is the Rampant Lion Foundation. It supersedes the Deke Foundation, a private charity founded in 1951, with which it merged in 1988. Having as its mission the promotion of intellectual excellence and civic and social responsibility, the Rampant Lion

Foundation serves DKE in several ways. Each year it awards a number of scholarships to deserving undergraduate Dekes on the basis of financial need, academic merit, and contribution to university and chapter activities; scholarship winners are required to use these funds for academic purposes, and must present documentation that this has been done.

In addition, the Foundation helps to fund the educational activities of the Fraternity through charitable grants to those DKE programs qualifying as educational; and it invests capital resources in an endowment fund secured by mortgages on DKE chapter real estate to provide the income to fund the Fraternity grants. Through various tax-deductible giving methods, the Rampant Lion Foundation builds endowment income from individual donors, groups of donors, trusts, and private foundations. The Foundation is administered by a board of trustees which meets at regular intervals.

The Rampant Lion Foundation is the owner of the Shant, an historic 1879 neo-Gothic meeting hall designed by William Jenny, known as "the father of the skyscraper" for his early use of steel construction. Restored and refurbished, the Shant now houses the DKE Archives, and is used by the Foundation for educational and cultural activities, among them DKE Leadership Conferences, held in off-Convention years under the aegis of the Foundation.

Headquarters 35 McKinley Place, Grosse Pointe Farms, MI 48236. Phone: (313) 886-2400.

Membership Total living membership 40,000. Total undergraduate membership 2,500. Active chapters 54. Inactive chapters 27. Colonies 2. Houses owned 40. Total number of initiates 75,000. Chapter roll:

1844 Phi, Yale
1844 Theta, Bowdoin
1845 Zeta, Princeton (1857-1987)
1846 Sigma, Amherst (1980-1986)
1846 *Xi, Colby* (1984)
1847 Gamma, Vanderbilt
1847 Psi, Alabama (1859-1885)
1850 *Chi, Mississippi* (1911-1929) (1985)
1850 *Upsilon, Brown* (1963)
1851 *Alpha, Harvard* (1856-1863) (1891)
1851 Beta, North Carolina (1861-1887)
1852 *Delta, South Carolina* (1861)
1852 Eta, Virginia
1852 Kappa, Miami (OH) (1873-1889) (1980-1988)
1852 Lambda, Kenyon
1852 *Omega, Oakland (MS)* (1861)
1853 *Pi, Dartmouth* (1970)
1854 Alpha Alpha, Middlebury (1969-1985)
1854 Iota, Centre College
1855 *Epsilon, Williams* (1961)
1855 Omicron, Michigan
1855 Rho, Lafayette

1856 Beta Phi, Rochester
1856 Mu, Colgate
1856 *Nu, CCNY* (1973)
1856 Tau, Hamilton
1856 *Theta Chi, Union (NY)* (1869)
1857 *Kappa Psi, Cumberland (TN)* (1874)
1858 *Alpha Delta, Jefferson Col.* (1862)
1858 Zeta Zeta, L.S.U.
1861 *Kappa Phi, Troy (NY)* (1865)
1861 *Phi Chi, Rutgers* (1985)
1861 *Tau Delta, Union (TN)* (1862)
1866 Psi Phi, DePauw
1867 *Eta Alpha, Washington and Lee* (1871)
1867 Gamma Phi, Wesleyan (CT)
1867 *Psi Omega, R.P.I.* (1965)
1868 Beta Chi, Case Western Reserve (1970-1989)
1870 Delta Chi, Cornell
1871 Phi Gamma, Syracuse
1874 *Gamma Beta, Columbia (NY)* (1935)
1876 Theta Zeta, Cal, Berkeley
1879 *Alpha Chi, Trinity (CT)* (1990)
1879 Delta Delta, Chicago (1947-1989)
1889 Phi Epsilon, Minnesota
1890 Sigma Tau, M.I.T.
1898 Alpha Phi, Toronto
1898 Tau Lambda, Tulane
1899 Delta Kappa, Penn
1900 *Tau Alpha, McGill* (1989)
1901 Sigma Rho, Stanford
1904 *Delta Pi, Illinois* (1964-1969) (1986)
1906 *Rho Delta, Wisconsin, Madison* (1954)
1910 *Kappa Epsilon, Washington (WA)* (1965)
1912 Omega Chi, Texas
1925 Alpha Tau, Manitoba
1932 Delta Phi, Alberta
1932 *Theta Rho, UCLA* (1952)
1948 *Delta Epsilon, Northwestern* (1959)
1948 *Lambda Delta, Southern Methodist* (1961)
1949 Phi Alpha, British Columbia
1952 *Kappa Delta, Maryland* (1960)
1953 Rho Lambda, Oklahoma (1971-1990)
1969 Tau Delta, Sewanee
1970 Psi Delta, Wake Forest
1971 Sigma Alpha, V.P.I.
1972 Phi Delta, Western Ontario (1977-1988)
1973 Sigma Phi, Villanova
1976 *Pi Beta, Troy* (1986)
1982 Alpha Mu, Glassboro
1983 Epsilon Rho, Duke
1983 Nu Zeta, Pace
1984 Alpha Omega, Louisiana Tech
1985 Theta Upsilon, Arizona State
1990 Alpha Rho, Temple
1990 Iota Mu, Fordham
1991 Chi Rho, Bloomsburg
1991 Phi Rho, Penn State
1991 Phi Sigma, Bryant
1991 Zeta Chi, Bentley
1991 Zeta Upsilon, Cal, Davis

COAT OF ARMS

Delta Phi†

ACTIVE PIN

PLEDGE PIN

DELTA PHI, third in order of establishment of American college fraternities, was founded November 17, 1827, at Union College, Schenectady, New York, by Benjamin Burroughs of Savannah, Georgia, clergyman in the Presbyterian Church; William H. Fondey of Albany, New York, who later practiced law in Albany; Samuel L. Lamberson, of Jamaica, New York, who became a clergyman of the Presbyterian Church; David H. Little, LL.D., of Rochester, New York, who was later a justice of the New York Supreme Court; Samuel C. Lawrison, M.D., of Pensacola, Florida, who was later a surgeon in the United States Navy; Thomas C. McLaury, D.D., of Lisbon, New York, a clergyman; John Mason, of Baltimore, Maryland, a clergyman; Joseph G. Masten, of Buffalo, New York, who was the mayor of that city from 1843 to 1846, and William Wilson, D.D., LL.D., president of the College of Cincinnati and bishop in the Protestant Episcopal Church.

These nine founders were all members of the class of 1828; five of them were members of Phi Beta Kappa. The objects and purposes of the founders were "to consolidate their interest and at the same time mutually benefit each other, to maintain high standing as students and gentlemen, and to foster cordial and fraternal interest."

Delta Phi, with Kappa Alpha and Sigma Phi, which were established in the fall of 1825 and the spring of 1827, respectively, have been known as the Union Triad. The new societies after a few years met with opposition from the college faculty. The defense of fraternities was taken up by Delta Phi, and John Jay Hyde of the class of 1834 as spokesman presented the case before the faculty and trustees, stating the aims and objects of the fraternities so well that their hearers were convinced that the continuance of fraternities such as Delta Phi would be beneficial to the college.

Growth The Harvard chapter became inactive in 1848, was revived in 1885, but its charter was withdrawn in 1901. The Princeton charter was withdrawn on account of the anti-fraternity regulations of the faculty. The Michigan chapter was withdrawn in 1874, re-established in 1923, and be-

† This chapter narrative is repeated from the 19th edition; no current information was provided.

came inactive again in 1936. The North Carolina charter became inactive in 1861, all but one of its members serving in the Confederate Army.

In 1917 a charter was granted to the oldest local society in existence, located at Trinity, which was established as the Corax Club shortly after the foundation of Trinity, then called Washington College. In 1829 this was developed into the I. K. A. Society.

Government Executive power is vested in the Board of Governors, one-third of whom are elected at each annual convention.

Traditions and Insignia Delta Phi has closely adhered to its aim and purpose and has kept true to its traditions. It has been conservative in its establishment of chapters up to 1967. The 139th convention issued a mandate to expand as opportunities and finances permit. No limitation as to geographical location of new chapters restricts this expansion policy. The westernmost chapter now is at Illinois.

The badge is a maltese cross of gold, in the center of which is an elliptical disc, displaying the letters ΔΦ; the arms of the cross display a scroll and quill, an antique lamp, clasped hands, and a constellation of stars. This badge was adopted in 1832. The colors are blue and white.

Publications Catalogues were published in 1845, 1851, 1868, 1875, 1883, 1887, 1893, 1897, 1907, 1927, 1949, and 1965. All of the early editions were compiled in the former manner of college triennials, with Latin headings and sub-titles. In the edition of 1847 the names of the members of the Harvard chapter, which was then sub rosa, were printed in Hebrew. In the edition of 1851 each page had a border of characteristic emblems, the Harvard chapter being surrounded with designs of Bunker Hill monument, the Pennsylvania chapter with the name of William Penn, etc. Pocket directories were published in 1913, 1915, 1920, 1926, 1935, and 1939.

A quarterly magazine, the *Delta Phi Record*, is published as the official organ. It began February 14, 1903, and varied in size until in 1960 a standard size of 8 inches by 11 was adopted.

Headquarters 317 W. State Street, Ithaca, NY 14850. Phone: (607) 277-3888.

Membership City/Area alumni associations 4. Total living membership 7,828. Total undergraduate membership 817. Houses owned 7. Active chapters 16. Inactive chapters 8. Total number of initiates 12,250. Chapter roll:

1827   Alpha, Union (NY)
1838   Beta, Brown (1962-1983)
1841   Gamma, N.Y.U.
1842   Delta, Columbia (NY)
1845   Epsilon, Rutgers
1845   *Zeta, Harvard* (1848-1885) (1901)
1849   Eta, Penn
1854   *Theta, Princeton* (1877)
1855   *Iota, Michigan* (1874-1923) (1936)

1855	*Kappa, North Carolina* (1861)
1864	Lambda, R.P.I.
1874	*Mu, Colgate* (1876)
1884	Nu, Lehigh
1885	Xi, Johns Hopkins
1889	*Omicron, Sheffield Scientific* (1925)
1891	Pi, Cornell
1908	Rho, Virginia
1917	Sigma, Trinity (CT) (1965-1982)
1920	Tau, Illinois
1926	*Upsilon, Williams* (1962)
1940	Phi, Kenyon
1950	Chi, Hamilton
1960	Psi, Penn State (1974-1986)
1968	Omega, Pitt
1987	Omega Alpha, William and Mary

Delta Psi

ACTIVE PIN

DELTA PSI was founded at Columbia College, January 17, 1847, by Edward Forbes Travis and Charles Arms Budd. The chapter was called Alpha. The fraternity was founded on a basis of good fellowship, and a good social position has usually been demanded as a qualification for membership.

The southern chapters became extinct in the Civil War, and only those at the University of Mississippi and the University of Virginia were revived at its close. The Mississippi chapter became inactive in 1912 as a result of anti-fraternity legislation, but was revived in 1926. The North Carolina chapter, extinct during the Civil War, was revived in 1926. The chapter at New York University was absorbed in 1853 by the Columbia chapter. The Burlington chapter was transferred to the University of Pennsylvania in 1854.

Each chapter owns its St. Anthony Hall, all but one including dormitory accommodations. In New York City, Philadelphia, and Boston the alumni have formed St. Anthony Clubs which are separate from the undergraduate chapters in those cities. There are also more than 25 graduate associations.

The latest catalogue of members was issued in 1957.

Government The chapters of Delta Psi are largely self-governing. The traditional character of the fraternity has changed in recent years in that women have been accepted into membership in half the chapters.

Headquarters P.O. Box 876, Ithaca, NY 14851. Phone: (607) 272-3344.

Membership Active chapters 10: Inactive chapters 9. Total number of initiates 4,600. Chapter roll:

1847	Alpha, Columbia (NY)
1847	*Beta, N.Y.U.* (1853) (Transferred to Alpha)
1848	*Gamma, Rutgers* (1850)
1849	Delta, Burlington (Charter transferred to Pennsylvania, 1854)
1850	Epsilon, Trinity (CT)
1850	*Eta, South Carolina* (1861)
1851	*Iota, Rochester* (1895)
1851	Theta, Princeton (1852-1986)
1852	Kappa, Brown (1853-1983)
1853	*Lambda, Williams* (1970)
1853	*Sigma, Randolph, Macon* (1861)
1854	Delta, Penn
1854	Xi, North Carolina (1861-1926)
1855	Phi, Mississippi (1912-1926)
1858	*Psi, Cumberland (KY)* (1861)
1860	Upsilon, Virginia
1868	Sigma, Sheffield Scientific School, Yale
1869	*Beta, Washington and Lee* (1888)
1889	Tau, M.I.T.

COAT OF ARMS

Delta Sigma Phi

ACTIVE PIN

PLEDGE PIN

DELTA SIGMA PHI was founded at the College of the City of New York on December 10, 1899, by a group of idealistic young students inspired by the promise of the dawning twentieth century. Within a period of four years, the first chapter was joined by two more, one at Columbia University, the other at New York University, thus forming an initial triad still in the fraternity insignia.

Growth In its first 15 years, the fraternity added seventeen new chapters, many of which were located on campuses in the south, including the pioneer chapter at Southern Methodist University. In 1915 this initial expansion reached the Pacific coast with a chapter at the University of California. Growth has continued steadily over the years, except for periods during the Depression, World War II, the Korean Conflict and the Vietnam Conflict, leading to the establishment of chapters in 38 of the 50 states.

Prior to 1906, the chapters were given names derived from their individual locale, i.e., "Insula" at the College of the City of New york, "Keystone" at Pennsylvania State College, and so on. Since that time, an alphabetical Greek-letter nomenclature has been used.

Most of the groups chartered from 1906 to World War II were local fraternities; some had been in existence for many years before affiliation. Two, for example, were older than the national fraternity: the University of Michigan chapter from the Knickerbocker Club, founded 1888; and the Stetson University chapter from Phi Kappa Delta, founded 1898. Since World War II a number of new chapters have come from colonies developed and nurtured to maturity by the national fraternity.

Government Government of the fraternity is vested in a board of directors known as the Grand Council. Members of the Council are elected by the national convention, which with the exception of the World War II years has met biennially since 1919 (previously it met annually). An endowment committee of three administrates a substantial endowment fund, which is invested largely in chapter properties. Routine business of the fraternity is conducted by an executive director from the national office.

For administrative purposes, the fraternity is divided into some twenty districts supported by a district governor and one or two deputy governors. These officers visit the chapters under their jurisdiction as often as circumstances may require. Also, each chapter receives at least one visit per year from a chapter leadership consultant of the professional staff. Each chapter has the guidance, on the local level, of a chapter supervisor appointed by the executive director. An alumni control board elected from and by the alumni of the chapter works with the supervisor. This board is incorporated under the laws of the state in which the chapter is located and usually holds title to the real property of the chapter.

Traditions and Insignia An unusual feature of Delta Sigma Phi is Engineered Leadership, a dynamic program of personal growth for chapter members.

Certificates of appreciation are awarded to members who perform special services for the fraternity. The Harvey Hebert Award is the distinguished service medal of Delta Sigma Phi. The "Mr. Delta Sig" award is the highest award granted for service to the fraternity while the Career Achievement Award recognizes distinguished and significant accomplishments in a professional career.

The outstanding social functions of the chapters are the "Sailors' Ball," a costume party, and the "Carnation Ball," a formal event.

The badge is a diamond displaying in gold Greek letters ΔΣΦ along its short diagonal, on a background of black enamel. At the upper apex is a circle of white containing a pyramid of green. At the lower apex is a sphinx in gold. Jeweled pins are worn only by alumni, mothers, wives, or sweethearts. The pledge pin is a green pyramid in a white circle.

The fraternity colors are nile green and white. The flower is the white carnation. The official flag is made of nile green bunting with the pledge symbol in green and white resting in the upper left corner, while the Greek letters ΔΣΦ run diagonally across the right half from top to bottom. The official pennant is of wool, with the coat of arms of the fraternity in hand-tooled leather in official colors.

The coat of arms is a shield with chevron and three symbols, a lyre, a knot, and a lamp, below which is a pyramid. An open book on the chevron contains the date 1899. Above the shield are scaraeaeus wings and a sphinx head.

Publications The exoteric publication, the *Carnation*, is published quarterly. It has appeared regularly since 1907. Beginning in 1951, a system of universal life membership has furnished the *Carnation* to each initiate as a life subscription. An esoteric publication, the *Sphinx*, first appeared in 1923 and has been issued subsequently as needed. In 1925 the fraternity first issued its Pledge Manual. Now called *The Gordian Knot*, the most recent edition is that of 1979. The *Fraternity Manual*, a guide to operation on chapter, alumni and national levels, was first published in 1928, with several subsequent editions, the most recent in 1978. *The Ritual*, first issued in 1914, remained substantially unchanged, with the exception of minor revisions in 1923 until a major revision in 1981. *The Songbook*, first published in 1932, was reissued in 1954. Other manuals prepared by the national fraternity include those dealing with rushing, pledge education, Engineered Leadership and alumni corporations.

Foundation The Delta Sigma Phi Foundation was established in 1951 and granted status as a nonprofit educational foundation in 1958. It provides scholarships to students with high academic achievement, and supports other educational programs of the fraternity.

Headquarters 1331 North Delaware Street, Indianapolis, IN 46202. Phone (317) 634-1899. The present headquarters is a National Historic property, the former home of Indianapolis mayor and U.S. senator Thomas Taggart. Delta Sigma Phi moved to Indianapolis in 1981 from Denver, Colorado, the headquarters location for 30 years.

Membership Graduate/alumni chapters 42. City/area alumni associations 5. Total living membership 51,549. Total undergraduate membership 5,400. Houses owned 83. Active chapters 124. Inactive chapters 57. Colonies 8. Total number of initiates 81,064. Chapter roll:

1899	*Alpha, CUNY, Brooklyn*	(1914)
1901	*Beta, Columbia (NY)*	(1913)
1902	*Gamma, N.Y.U.*	(1934)
1904	*Delta, M.I.T.*	(1908)
1905	Epsilon, Penn State	
1906	*Zeta, Washington and Lee*	(1914)
1907	Eta, Texas	
1907	*Theta, Cornell*	(1943)
1908	*Iota, Penn*	(1942)
1908	Kappa, Auburn	
1909	*Lambda, Trinity (TX)*	(1909-1915) (1983)
1910	*Mu, Chicago*	(1932)
1910	Nu, Waynesburg	

Year	Chapter
1912	*Omicron, Cumberland (TN)* (1918-1931) (1960)
1915	Hilgard, Cal, Berkeley
1915	*Pi, Furman* (1953)
1915	Rho, North Carolina State
1915	Sigma, Thiel
1915	Tau, Hillsdale
1915	Upsilon, Franklin and Marshall
1916	*Chi, Tulane* (1963)
1916	Omega, Pitt
1916	Phi, St. Louis (1970-1984)
1916	*Psi, Wofford* (1981)
1917	Alpha Tau, Albion
1919	Alpha Alpha, Illinois
1920	*Alpha Beta, Boston U.* (1941)
1920	Alpha Delta, North Carolina (1933-1986)
1920	Alpha Epsilon, Duke
1920	Alpha Eta, Ohio Northern
1920	Alpha Gamma, Georgia Tech
1920	Alpha Iota, Ohio State (1971-1988)
1920	*Alpha Kappa, Wisconsin, Madison* (1932-1948) (1952)
1920	Alpha Theta, Michigan (1974-1986)
1920	Alpha Zeta, Alfred
1921	Alpha Mu, Virginia (1933-1963)
1922	Alpha Nu, Oglethorpe (1942-1985)
1922	*Alpha Omicron, McGill* (1972)
1924	Alpha Pi, Michigan State
1924	Alpha Rho, Colorado (1964-1988)
1924	Alpha Sigma, Maryland
1925	Alpha Chi, Stetson
1925	Alpha Phi, USC
1925	*Alpha Psi, Nebraska* (1984)
1925	Alpha Upsilon, Kansas State
1926	*Alpha Omega, Washington (WA)* (1959)
1927	Beta Alpha, Iowa State
1927	Beta Beta, Missouri
1927	Beta Gamma, U.C.L.A.
1928	*Beta Delta, Birmingham-Southern* (1961)
1928	*Beta Epsilon, Oregon State* (1985)
1930	Beta Zeta, Florida
1931	Beta Theta, Lehigh (1985-1990)
1932	Beta Iota, Wittenberg
1932	Beta Kappa, Alabama (1958-1984)
1938	Beta Lambda, Wake Forest
1941	Beta Mu, Transylvania
1947	Beta Tau, Western Michigan (1973-1986)
1948	*Beta Chi, Samford* (1966)
1948	*Beta Omega, Arizona* (1963)
1948	Beta Omicron, Central Michigan (1970-1986)
1948	Beta Phi, St. Francis (PA)
1948	Beta Pi, Michigan Tech
1948	Beta Psi, Arizona State
1948	*Beta Rho, Hartwick* (1990)
1948	*Beta Sigma, Louisiana Tech* (1954)
1948	*Beta Upsilon, Southwestern Louisiana* (1974)
1948	*Beta Xi, Cal, Santa Barbara* (1963)
1948	Gamma Alpha, San Diego State
1948	*Gamma Beta, Arkansas* (1954)
1949	Gamma Delta, Washington State
1949	Gamma Epsilon, San Jose (1973-1984)
1949	*Gamma Gamma, Miami (FL)* (1958)
1949	Gammma Zeta, Rutgers
1950	*Gamma Eta, Washington (MO)* (1961)
1950	Gamma Iota, Idaho
1950	Gamma Kappa, Western Illinois
1950	*Gamma Lambda, Nevada* (1951)
1950	Gamma Theta, Detroit
1951	*Gamma Mu, Toronto* (1963)
1952	*Gamma Nu, Northern Arizona* (1984)
1952	Gamma Tau, Eastern Michigan
1952	Gamma Xi, North Texas
1953	Gamma Omicron, Fort Hays
1953	Gamma Pi, Indiana (PA)
1954	*Gamma Phi, Alma* (1973)
1954	Gamma Rho, Gannon
1954	Gamma Sigma, Cal, Davis
1954	Gamma Upsilon, South Dakota Mines
1956	Delta Delta, Purdue
1956	Delta Epsilon, Missouri, Rolla
1956	Delta Eta, Montana State
1956	*Delta Gamma, Kansas* (1969)
1956	*Delta Theta, Montana* (1973)
1956	Delta Zeta, High Point
1956	Gamma Chi, Drexel
1956	Gamma Psi, Morningside
1958	Delta Iota, Atlantic Christian
1958	Delta Kappa, Humboldt (1971-1989)
1959	*Delta Lambda, Utah State* (1970)
1959	Delta Nu, Edinboro
1959	Delta Omicron, Western Carolina
1959	*Delta Xi, East Texas* (1965)
1960	Delta Pi, Stephen F. Austin
1962	*Delta Chi, Lambuth* (1974)
1962	Delta Phi, California (PA)
1962	Delta Psi, Eastern Illinois
1962	Delta Rho, St. Mary's, San Antonio
1962	*Delta Sigma, Youngstown State* (1973)
1962	Delta Tau, Ferris
1962	Delta Upsilon, Northern Michigan (1976-1987)
1963	Delta Omega, Cleveland
1965	*Epsilon Alpha, Alberta* (1971)
1965	Epsilon Beta, Wisconsin, Oshkosh (1978-1984)
1966	Epsilon Delta, Wisconsin, Platteville
1966	Epsilon Gamma, Parsons (1973-1984) (Transferred to Peru)
1967	*Epsilon Epsilon, Old Dominion* (1982)
1967	*Epsilon Eta, Wisconsin, Whitewater* (1973)
1967	Epsilon Iota, Wisconsin, La Crosse
1967	*Epsilon Theta, St. John's (NY)* (1977-1979) (1985)
1967	Epsilon Zeta, Clarkson
1968	Epsilon Kappa, Loyola, Chicago
1968	Epsilon Lambda, Northwest Missouri
1968	*Epsilon Mu, Wyoming* (1972)
1968	*Epsilon Nu, Monmouth (NJ)* (1989)
1968	*Epsilon Omicron, Wisconsin, Stevens Point* (1974)
1968	*Epsilon Xi, Seton Hall* (1970)
1969	Epsilon Rho, Cal Poly, San Luis Obispo

1969 Epsilon Sigma, Nevada, Las Vegas
      (1977-1987)
1970 *Epsilon Psi, Bryant* (1974)
1970 Epsilon Tau, Grand Valley (1973-1990)
1971 *Epsilon Chi, Valdosta* (1974)
1971 Epsilon Omega, Illinois State
1971 Epsilon Phi, East Carolina
1971 Epsilon Upsilon, Nicholls
1972 Zeta Alpha, New York Tech
1973 Zeta Beta, Murray State
1973 Zeta Gamma, Valparaiso
1976 Zeta Delta, L.S.U., Shreveport
1976 Zeta Epsilon, Cal State, Fullerton
1977 Zeta Eta, Sam Houston
1977 Zeta Zeta, Texas Tech.
1979 *Zeta Theta, Southern Colorado* (1985)
1981 Zeta Iota, Rochester
1981 Zeta Kappa, Northern Colorado
1982 Zeta Lambda, Rose-Hulman
1982 *Zeta Mu, Longwood* (1989)
1982 *Zeta Nu, Southwest Missouri* (1990)
1983 Zeta Xi, St. Cloud
1984 Zeta Omicron, Cal State, Hayward
1984 Zeta Pi, Northeast Louisiana
1984 *Zeta Rho, Auraria* (1987)
1984 Zeta Sigma, Cal, San Diego
1984 Zeta Tau, Lake Superior
1985 Zeta Upsilon, Eureka
1986 Zeta Chi, Alabama, Birmingham
1986 Zeta Omega, North Carolina, Wilmington
1986 Zeta Phi, Slippery Rock
1986 Zeta Psi, SUNY Col., Brockport
1987 Eta Alpha, Milwaukee Engineering
1987 Eta Beta, Cal State, San Bernadino
1987 Eta Delta, Florida Institute
1987 Eta Epsilon, Northern Illinois
1987 Eta Eta, Rochester Tech
1987 Eta Gamma, East Stroudsburg
1987 Eta Iota, Cal State, Sacramento
1987 Eta Kappa, Michigan, Dearborn
1987 Eta Theta, Aurora
1987 Eta Zeta, LaVerne
1989 Eta Lambda, Chapman
1989 Eta Mu, New York Tech
1989 Eta Nu, Sonoma State
1989 Eta Omicron, Wisconsin, Eau Claire
1989 Eta Xi, Towson
1990 Eta Pi, Dayton
1990 Eta Rho, North Carolina, Charlotte
1990 Eta Sigma, Cal Poly, Pomona

Colonies: Millikin, New Mexico, Cal State, Fresno, Cal State, Chico, Oklahoma, Houston, Loyola Marymount, Los Angeles, Woodbury

COAT OF ARMS

Delta Tau Delta

ACTIVE PIN

PLEDGE PIN

DELTA TAU DELTA was founded at Bethany College in the spring of 1858. Bethany was then located in Virginia, but with the creation of the State of West Virginia, it now lies in the northern panhandle of that State. The Founders of Delta Tau Delta were Richard H. Alfred, Eugene Tarr, John C. Johnson, Alexander C. Earle, William R. Cunningham, John L. N. Hunt, Jacob S. Lowe and Henry K. Bell. All were members of Bethany's Neotropian Literary Society seeking to correct the abuses of another fraternity in the Society's election. From this literary base the fraternity has grown to serve as a constructive adjunct to higher education by contributing to the moral, spiritual, and social development of its members.

Growth The new organization became strongly established at Bethany and new chapters were founded at nearby West Liberty College and Monongalia Academy, which later became West Virginia University. The outlook of the nascent organization was decidedly southern and the gathering storm of the Civil War cast a shadow on further expansion.

During the 1860-61 school year, the ranks of the three chapters started to thin as military units formed calling young men to the ranks. Delta Tau Delta was in danger of extinction. Before this could happen, two students from Jefferson College, Rhodes S. Sutton and Samuel S. Brown, rode 27 miles from Canonsburg, Pennsylvania, to Bethany on horseback to be initiated into Delta Tau Delta. They had met earlier with John Thorton of the West Liberty Chapter. The fourth chapter was thus established at Jefferson, the only chapter to survive the wartime years. The Jefferson Chapter showed remarkable vitality by placing chapters at other Pennsylvania colleges, as well as in Ohio, Michigan, and other parts of the country.

Growth after the Civil War was managed by the governing Alpha Chapters. In the next 15 years, 29 chapters were added as the fraternity grew in size and sophistication. Traditionally divided into four geographic divisions, Delta Tau Delta held the first regional training meetings in the fraternity world during the spring of 1881. These division conferences continue to this day and each elects a division president who serves on the Arch Chapter.

Lengthy negotiations with the Rainbow, or W.W.W. Fraternity, culminated in a merger in 1886 which brought chapters at Mississippi and Vanderbilt into Delta Tau Delta. The Rainbow traced its founding to 1848 at Mississippi and was the first distinctly Southern fraternity. This accelerated expansion in the South. Meanwhile, Delta Tau Delta pioneered the Greek system on many campuses by being the first fraternity at Illinois, Iowa State, Penn State, Michigan State, Colorado, and other schools.

The fraternity has since grown to international proportions with chapters in 40 of the United States and one Canadian province. Expansion continues at a conservative pace with emphasis on reopening inactive chapters and expanding to high quality academic institutions.

Government For the first 25 years of its existence, Delta Tau Delta was governed by a principal chapter designated as Alpha. Bethany first served in this role until the onset of the Civil War when Jefferson assumed this role. The Alpha power was transferred to Ohio Wesleyan at the time of the merger of Washington and Jefferson College. From Ohio Wesleyan, the Alpha designation was shifted to Allegheny College, where it remained after an elected alumni Executive Committee assumed power in 1884 after the adoption of a new *Constitution*. In 1888 the Executive Committee evolved into the nine-man, all-alumni governing board renamed the Arch Chapter. Five members are elected at the biennial convention, called the Karnea, and four positions are filled by the division presidents, elected by their respective division conferences. In 1924, Delta Tau Delta added a tenth member to the Arch Chapter, the director of academic affairs, becoming the first fraternity to have a governing board member whose sole responsibility is the promotion of academic achievement. Delta Tau Delta was also one of the first fraternities to outlaw hazing, with a constitutional amendment in 1928. Recently, Delta Tau Delta has pioneered the placement of small computers in chapter houses and has been in the forefront of the crusade against alcohol abuse.

Delegates of undergraduate and alumni chapters meet biennially at the Karnea. By custom, the location of the Karnea is rotated between the four geographic divisions of the Fraternity. These divisions hold biennial conferences in the spring after the Karnea and regional conferences on a smaller scale are held in the spring immediately preceding a Karnea. Each division elects its officers, gives awards, writes its own bylaws and sets its dues so as to be financially independent of the international fraternity.

The Arch Chapter is the governing body of the fraternity between sessions of the Karnea. It oversees the day-to-day administration of the fraternity which is carried out by the staff of the Central Office. Delta Tau Delta's Central Office was first established in 1913 and now has evolved into an 18-person professional operation. The staff includes the executive vice president, the director of chapter service, the director of program development, the editor, chapter consultants, and administrative assistants.

Each undergraduate chapter has a chapter adviser, house corporation, and division vice president who assists the chapter with their programs and operations. The house corporation generally confines its activities to housing and maintaining a scholastic atmosphere. Many chapters also have graduate students who serve as resident advisers who focus their attention on academics for members and pledges.

Traditions and Insignia Delta Tau Delta has traditionally emphasized scholarship through an elaborate array of individual and chapter merit awards administered by the Scholarship Advisory Committee. This has led to a focus on graduate resident advisers, chapter libraries, and computer and terminals within chapter Shelters for the use of members. "Delta Shelter" is the best known of the fraternity's songs. It was written by Stuart MacLean, Sewanee '94, who also authored the Delta Creed, the first pledge manual, entitled *The Good Delt*, and many other pieces of the *Ritual* and literature of Delta Tau Delta.

The badge of the fraternity is a square shield with concave sides. On the black enameled shield are emblazoned the gold letters ΔTΔ with gold stars in each corner with an eye above and a crescent below the Greek letters. The pledge badge is similarly shaped with a white field and four gold stars with a square in the center. The fraternity flower is the purple iris, which contains the fraternity colors of purple, white and gold. The coat of arms is restricted to use by initiated members only. The flag carries white Greek letters ΔTΔ on a gold field bordered in purple. A special flag is awarded each year to those chapters judged as winners of the Hugh Shields Award for Chapter Excellence, named in honor of the fraternity's executive officer who served from 1926-65.

Publications The fraternity's journal, THE RAINBOW, was first published in September, 1877, and is the third oldest fraternity magazine. Originally named THE CRESCENT, the name was changed in 1886 to honor the union with the Rainbow Fraternity.

The fraternity publishes and constantly updates a broad array of operational manuals, bulletins and other publications for undergraduate and alumni chapters. Prominent among these is the 1985 edition of *The Good Delt*, the fraternity's pledge manual, *The Delt Development Program*, and the *Chapter Management Guide*. The latest membership directory was published in 1985, continuing a series of ten catalogs dating back to 1886.

Funds and Philanthropies The funds of the fraternity are administered by the Board of Directors, a five-man sub-group of the Arch Chapter. Included is a general operating fund and the Loyalty and Centennial Development Funds which endow the operations of the fraternity. The Delta Tau Delta Educational Foundation was created in 1981 as a public foundation to support educational and leadership activities, including scholarships and undergraduate loans.

Headquarters 8250 Haverstick Road #150, Indianapolis, IN 46240. Phone: (317) 259-1187.

Membership Active chapters 123. Inactive chapters 35. Colonies 4. Total number of initiates 121,545. Chapter roll:

1859	*Gamma Prime, West Liberty* (1862)
1859	Theta, Bethany (WV) (1895-1966)
1860	Gamma Delta, West Virginia
1861	Gamma, Washington and Jefferson
1862	Beta, Ohio
1864	Alpha, Allegheny
1864	Gamma Sigma, Pitt
1865	*Mu Prime, Waynesburg* (1866)
1865	*Zeta Prime, Monmouth (IL)* (1871)
1866	Mu, Ohio Wesleyan
1867	Kappa, Hillsdale
1868	*Lambda Prime, Lombard* (1885)
1870	Beta Alpha, Indiana
1871	Beta Beta, DePauw
1871	*Chi Prime, Franklin* (1877)
1872	Beta Psi, Wabash
1872	Beta Upsilon, Illinois
1872	Delta, Michigan
1872	Iota, Michigan State (1897-1947)
1872	*Phi Prime, Hanover* (1895)
1872	Tau, Penn State (1965-1977)
1873	Eta, Akron (1895-1972)
1873	*Xi, Simpson* (1894)
1874	*Nu, Lafayette* (1988)
1874	Rho, Stevens Tech
1874	*Tau Prime, Franklin and Marshall* (1895)
1875	*Beta Alpha Prime, Abingdon* (1876)
1875	Beta Zeta, Butler
1875	*Chi Second, Iowa Wesleyan* (1880)
1875	Gamma Pi, Iowa State
1875	*Sigma Prime, Mount Union* (1886)
1876	Epsilon, Albion
1877	*Beta Epsilon Prime, Illinois Wesleyan* (1880)
1878	*Beta Iota Prime, Adrian* (1884)
1879	Upsilon, R.P.I.
1880	Omicron, Iowa
1880	*Psi, Wooster* (1914)
1881	Chi, Kenyon
1882	Beta Delta, Georgia
1882	Beta Epsilon, Emory (1984-1989)
1882	*Gamma Epsilon, Columbia (NY)* (1928)
1882	Zeta, Western Reserve
1883	Beta Eta, Minnesota
1883	*Beta Kappa, Colorado* (1989)
1883	Beta Theta, U of the South
1886	*Lambda, Vanderbilt* (1930)
1886	*Pi, Mississippi* (1942)
1888	Beta Gamma, Wisconsin, Madison (1970-1979)
1889	Beta Iota, Virginia (1946-1971)

1889	Beta Mu, Tufts
1889	Beta Nu, M.I.T.
1889	Beta Sigma, Boston U. (1893-1990)
1889	*Beta Xi, Tulane* (1990)
1890	Beta Omicron, Cornell
1891	*Sigma, Williams* (1896)
1893	Beta Pi, Northwestern (1981-1984)
1893	Beta Rho, Stanford
1893	Beta Tau, Nebraska
1894	Beta Phi, Ohio State
1896	Beta Chi, Brown (1969-1983)
1896	Phi, Washington and Lee
1897	*Omega, Penn* (1971)
1898	Beta Omega, Cal, Berkeley (1972-1981)
1898	*Gamma Alpha, Chicago* (1935)
1901	Gamma Beta, Illinois Tech
1901	*Gamma Gamma, Dartmouth* (1960)
1902	*Gamma Zeta, Wesleyan (CT)* (1971-1979) (1989)
1903	Gamma Eta, George Washington
1903	Gamma Theta, Baker
1904	Gamma Iota, Texas
1905	Gamma Kappa, Missouri
1907	Gamma Lambda, Purdue
1908	Gamma Mu, Washington (WA)
1908	Gamma Nu, Maine
1909	Gamma Xi, Cincinnati
1910	Gamma Omicron, Syracuse (1935-1948)
1913	Gamma Rho, Oregon
1914	Gamma Tau, Kansas
1916	Gamma Upsilon, Miami (OH)
1918	*Gamma Phi, Amherst* (1946)
1919	Gamma Chi, Kansas State
1921	Gamma Omega, North Carolina (1935-1972)
1921	Gamma Psi, Georgia Tech
1922	Delta Alpha, Oklahoma
1923	Delta Beta, Carnegie-Mellon
1924	Delta Delta, Tennessee
1924	Delta Epsilon, Kentucky
1924	Delta Gamma, South Dakota
1925	Delta Eta, Alabama
1925	Delta Zeta, Florida
1926	Delta Iota, UCLA (1973-1976)
1926	Delta Theta, Toronto
1928	Delta Kappa, Duke
1930	Delta Lambda, Oregon State
1931	Delta Mu, Idaho
1935	Delta Nu, Lawrence
1935	Delta Xi, North Dakota
1939	Delta Omicron, Westminster (MO)
1941	Delta Pi, USC (1981-1984)
1948	Delta Rho, Whitman
1948	Delta Sigma, Maryland
1948	Delta Tau, Bowling Green
1948	Delta Upsilon, Delaware
1949	Delta Chi, Oklahoma State
1949	Delta Phi, Florida State (1970-1979)
1949	*Delta Psi, Cal, Santa Barbara* (1966-1982) (1988)
1950	Delta Omega, Kent
1952	Epsilon Alpha, Auburn
1955	Epsilon Beta, Texas Christian

1956 Epsilon Gamma, Washington State
1957 Epsilon Delta, Texas Tech.
1959 Epsilon Epsilon, Arizona
1960 Epsilon Zeta, Sam Houston
1961 Epsilon Eta, East Texas
1963 Epsilon Iota, GMI
1963 Epsilon Theta, Willamette
1966 Epsilon Kappa, L.S.U.
1966 Epsilon Lambda, Texas A & I
1966 Epsilon Mu, Ball State
1966 Epsilon Nu, Missouri, Rolla
1967 Epsilon Omicron, Colorado State
 (1972-1990)
1967 Epsilon Xi, Western Kentucky
1968 Epsilon Pi, South Florida
1968 Epsilon Rho, Texas, Arlington
1968 *Epsilon Sigma, Athens* (1979)
1968 *Epsilon Tau, Wisconsin, Milwaukee* (1982)
1968 Epsilon Upsilon, Marietta
1969 *Epsilon Chi, Northern Michigan* (1972)
1969 Epsilon Omega, Georgia Southern
1969 Epsilon Phi, Southeastern Louisiana
1969 Epsilon Psi, Southwestern Louisiana
1970 *Zeta Alpha, Marquette* (1979)
1970 Zeta Beta, LaGrange
1970 Zeta Delta, Southwest Texas
1970 *Zeta Epsilon, Tennessee Tech.* (1976)
1970 Zeta Gamma, Lamar
1970 Zeta Zeta, Morehead
1971 Zeta Eta, Mankato (1976-1990)
1971 Zeta Theta, Villanova
1972 Zeta Iota, West Florida
1972 Zeta Kappa, Middle Tennessee
1972 Zeta Lambda, Western Illinois
1973 Zeta Mu, Robert Morris
1973 *Zeta Nu, Jacksonville (AL)* (1980)
1974 *Zeta Xi, West Georgia* (1980)
1975 Zeta Omicron, Central Florida
1976 Zeta Pi, Indiana (PA)
1981 Zeta Rho, Eastern Illinois
1982 *Zeta Sigma, Texas A & M* (1985)
1984 Zeta Phi, Temple
1984 Zeta Tau, North Carolina, Wilmington
1984 Zeta Upsilon, Wyoming
1987 Theta Alpha, Western Ontario
1988 Theta Beta, Cal, San Diego
1988 Theta Gamma, Arizona State
1988 Zeta Chi, Southern Mississippi
1988 Zeta Omega, Bradley
1988 Zeta Psi, Stephen F. Austin

Colonies: Lehigh, American, San Diego U, South Carolina

COAT OF ARMS

Delta Upsilon

ACTIVE PIN

PLEDGE PIN

DELTA UPSILON, the first non-secret fraternity, established in 1834, was formed in part as an organized student protest movement against the domination in college affairs of the small groups forming early secret societies. In time the character of these secret, sub-rosa groups altered, their purposes and membership became known, and Delta Upsilon evolved to its present non-secret position of today.

Influences that affected the formation of Delta Upsilon at Williams College, Williamstown, Massachusetts, in November of 1834, in addition to opposition to secrecy, included the nineteenth century renaissance in thought and letters, the growth of literary societies, and the appearance of fraternal organizations on college campuses.

Founders of Delta Upsilon believed that, under the veil of secrecy and mystery and with the vantage ground of compact union, students entered the college secret societies and quickly assumed unfair control of both the organizations and the destinies of the college. They charged that these students gained influence and election to class offices and prominence at commencement for reasons other than merit.

In the first Constitution, framed in 1836, the founders stated:

"We the members of Williams College, feeling a deep interest in the peace and prosperity of the College to which we belong, and believing that all combinations and societies not founded upon liberal principles are calculated to destroy the harmony of the College, do hereby form ourselves into a society for the purpose of counteracting the evil tendency of association of which we disapprove and for the purpose of literary, mutual and social improvement."

The concept of the merit of the individual as the single criterion for selection to membership, and the emphasis on the worth of the individual that remains paramount in Delta Upsilon is noted in the 1838 statement of purpose:

"We would invest no class of our fellow students with advantage, but would place all upon an equal footing in running the race of honorable distinction. The only superiority which we acknowledge is the superiority of merit.

"We agree to form ourselves into a Society for maintaining and diffusing liberal principles, and for promoting the great objects of social and literary improvement."

At the time of the founding of the fraternity, sharp protests were being registered on the campus against previously accepted standards and ideals. There were many students not a part of the sub-rosa secret societies from which the founders could draw for members. These students were often influenced by the general movement in society for change and reform a part of that era.

There was also popular opposition at the time to secrecy, manifesting itself in the public hostility to the Freemasons for alleged violence against members who betrayed the secrets of the lodge. While it is reasonable to assume that this position and sentiment was known to students at the time of the founding, there is no record in the annals of early Delta Upsilon to indicate that anti-Masonry was a motivation for the formation of the new fraternity.

The opposition to secret societies began to spread from one campus to another, and the chapters were first linked together in an organization known as the Anti-Secret Confederation. It was that group that began the evolution from anti-secret to the present non-secret position of Delta Upsilon.

Justice was and is the guiding principle of Delta Upsilon from the earliest days. One of the first symbols of the Anti-Secret Confederation was the A.S.C. key that carried the balance scales of justice as a principle charge. The motto, Διχαια Υποθηχη, which means "Justice Our Foundation," and the name Delta Upsilon were in use before the formal adoption and even before the later adoption of the monogram badge of the Delta superimposed over the Upsilon.

The name Anti-Secret Confederation remained in use until 1846, when the convention voted to adopt the name Delta Upsilon on a formal basis. Before 1846, the chapters used such names as Equitable Union or Equitable Fraternity.

First rituals of initiation conducted as part of the meetings, enunciated the purposes of the fraternity. They are: the advancement of justice, promotion of friendship, diffusion of liberal culture, and the development of character. Chapter meetings were open to invited students, and discussed the literary and social issues of the day.

Growth The first Delta Upsilon chapter was formed at Williams College when thirty men from the freshmen, sophomore and junior classes met in the Freshman Recitation Room in West College Hall. The building remains in use to this day. Declaring themselves to be opposed to distinctions not founded upon merit, the records of the founders gives evidence of their determination for excellence and high personal achievement.

Seventeen of the founders became clergymen, two were educators, three lawyers, and two journalists.

Stephen J. Field was the first fraternity man to be named to the U.S. Supreme Court, and served one of the longest tenures there, while William Bross was editor of *The Chicago Tribune* and lieutenant governor of the State of Illinois. Both men were elected presidents of the fraternity. Eleven became valedictorians during the chapter's first twenty-seven years.

The second chapter at Union College had sought affiliation with Williams as early as 1840. Thereafter granting of new charters was subject to ballot among the few members of the young fraternity. There was no special power appertaining to the parent chapter, and the first convention was held at Schenectady, New York on July 10, 1847, with three chapters represented. In November of the same year, when the fraternity met at Troy, New York, there were four chapters in attendance.

In terms of continuous existence, the Hamilton Chapter has the longest unbroken record in the fraternity. It was Hamilton that gave life to many early Delta Upsilon chapters and pushed for continuing fraternity growth.

Establishment of the Wisconsin Chapter in 1885 marked the start of the westward movement for the fraternity. Extension into Canada followed in 1898. Most of the chapters established in the early days of the fraternity were organized as local groups first. Today, most Delta Upsilon new chapters begin as Alpha Delta Upsilon colonies with the "Alpha" dropped when the group qualifies for installation.

Delta Upsilon's contemporary growth program aims to add outstanding college and university sites to the fraternity's chapter rolls. The board of directors is authorized to approve chapters.

Primary features of the non-secret aspect of Delta Upsilon are that the fraternity's motto is public and can be explained, as well as the insignia of the fraternity and its symbolism. Each pledge is given this information at the time of pledging, and there is no secret grip or sign of recognition.

For many years, the fraternity has admitted its new members through a non-secret initiation ritual. While it is non-secret, the ceremonies are generally considered a private event. Some Delta Upsilon chapters, by local tradition and choice, invite parents of initiates, friends and honored members of the college faculty and administrative staff to attend the ceremonies. In similar fashion, chapter meetings are open, by invitation, but they are considered private events as well, although guests invited and included when appropriate.

The 1834 Alpha Delta Upsilon colony program includes special field staff service, an extended seminar for colonies before the start of each academic year, and monthly progress reports. The plan aims to develop a fully competitive chapter, with programs and activities, involving alumni and undergraduates in the plan. Alpha Delta Upsilon groups have their own ritual, patterned after the fraternity ritual, and their own insignia and flag for use during the colony period.

Government Delta Upsilon was incorporated in the State of New York in 1909, under a law signed into being by Governor Charles Evans Hughes, a member of the fraternity, who also served as one of the incorporators and later president of Delta Upsilon.

A unique bicameral legislative structure, the only one in the fraternity world, was formed. Legislation is initiated in the undergraduate convention where each undergraduate chapter is entitled to representation and must be approved by the fraternity's graduate legislative body, the Assembly of Trustees, that meets following the convention.

The fraternity has a president who is the chief ritual spokesman and is responsible for the appointment of alumni deputies for each chapter as well as province governors. The president also serves as the presiding officer of the Assembly. A chairman of the board of directors is the chief volunteer executive officer of Delta Upsilon. He presides at the meetings of the directors, and conducts the oversight of the operations of the fraternity, while being responsible for the convention.

Membership in Delta Upsilon may be terminated by resignation which must have both the chapter and the board of directors approval, or by expulsion. Members of the fraternity are barred from membership in all other social societies represented in more than one institution of learning; professional, honor and recognition societies being the exception. They are also barred from membership in any college societies whose principles are inconsistent with those of the fraternity. Chapters are entitled to initiate male members of the faculty and administrative staff of the college by special approval of their alumni and the board of directors.

Since 1882 the fraternity has published the *Delta Upsilon Quarterly*, the fraternity journal, on a continuous basis, and various membership plans have provided for subscriptions. Members receive an engraved membership certificate suitable for framing, membership card and manual as part of their fees.

In between the meetings of the convention and Assembly, policy is made by a board of nine directors and general officers. There are six standing committees, each chaired by a member of the board. Two are of special interest.

The Graduate Activities Committee is responsible for all phases of alumni programs in the fraternity, from the advisement and counseling teams for each chapter to chartered alumni clubs that meet regularly all over the world. The Graduate Activities Committee encourages the celebration of Founders' Day, and conducts orientation and educational programs for deputies, alumni advisors, corporation officers and directors, and province governors.

Chartered Delta Upsilon Alumni Clubs are entitled to send a delegate to the convention who may vote on all matters except the admission of new chapters, withdrawal of charters and amendments to the laws of the fraternity.

Undergraduate affairs and chapter status and condition are the province of the Undergraduate Activities committee. The committee includes undergraduate members, and meets twice a year to review progress and programs.

The Presidents Forum Seminar, annual leadership conference, and seven regional leadership seminars held in the provinces are all under the purview of the Undergraduate Activities Committee.

Funds and Philanthropies The fraternity's endorsed philanthropic project is The Villages, Inc., a group home network for abused and abandoned children founded by Dr. Karl Menninger.

The Delta Upsilon Educational Foundation, established in 1949, has as its purpose aiding, encouraging, promoting and contributing to the education of persons enrolled as students in any college or university in Canada or the United States.

A board of trustees manages the affairs of the tax-exempt corporation. It solicits gifts and bequests to further educational purposes and activities.

Traditions and Insignia The official badge of the fraternity is a monogram of the letters, the Delta superimposed over the Upsilon. This design was adopted in 1858. In 1912, the standard size and gold badge was adopted.

Colors of the fraternity are old gold and sapphire blue. There is no official flower, but flowers with gold and blue hues are considered appropriate. The pledge pin or button is a triangle forming a Delta with stylized Upsilon within. The letters are formed being of gold on blue enameled background. The sister pin is a miniature badge mounted on a gold bar background. It is worn exclusively by wives, mothers, sisters or fiancees, who may also wear the badge. By tradition, only officers or upperclass members wear jeweled badges.

November fourth is celebrated annually as Founders' Day, commemorating the establishment of the first chapter in 1834.

The flag consists of three vertical stripes, the two outer ones of blue, the middle one of yellow, upon which is surcharged the fraternity monogram in blue.

Alpha Delta Upsilon colony insignia includes the colony member's badge which is triangular in shape with three stars, one on each side of the triangle, a gold border and blue center with the numerals 1834 imposed in gold in the blue triangle. Colony pledge insignia is similar in design, except it does not have the three stars of the member badge. The colony flag is blue and gold in three parts with the numerals 1834 superimposed on the face of the flag.

Publications The fraternity headquarters publishes numerous guides and operating publications for chapters, graduate groups and others who may be concerned with the operation of the fraternity.

Fifteen editions of the *Delta Upsilon Songbook* have been published, first in 1866 and the most recent in 1967. The *Delta Upsilon Annual Report* is a report of the proceedings of the convention and Assembly and is published by the fraternity for members.

The first known, semi-annual fraternity publication called *Our Record*, was published from 1867 to 1870. There are copies extant in the fraternity archives. In 1934, at the time of the fraternity's centennial, the fraternity published an historical record of the genesis and growth of the society under the title *Delta Upsilon, One Hundred Years*. That custom was repeated at the time of the 150th anniversary when Delta Upsilon published a history of the society titled *Challenge, Conflict and Change*.

Complete membership directories were published by the fraternity for many years, and the first fraternity central office was established to assist in this work. This activity of directory publishing has been supplanted by more frequent chapter alumni listings.

The Delta Upsilon Manual, now titled *Our Record*, from the earlier fraternity publication of that name, is the basic information handbook about the fraternity for pledges and members. The twenty-second edition was published in 1985, the first being published in 1886 as "Our Record" an annual publication for the college year 1885-'86, of statistics and information concerning the fraternity.

December of 1882 marked the publication of the *Delta Upsilon Quarterly*, a small quarto of 16 pages. In 1884 it was adopted by the fraternity and changed to the usual magazine format. The magazine has been continuously published since 1882.

Operating standards for chapters are found as part of the copyrighted Delta Upsilon Superior Chapter Program that includes the *Minimum Chapter Standards*, superior chapter program checklist, progress and achievement reports, and program development guides. When leadership consultants visit the chapters for diagnostic consulting, their reporting follows the five basic areas of chapter operations identified in the Delta Upsilon Superior Chapter Program.

The Delta Upsilon Pledge-Member Development Program pioneered several new concepts of fraternity education and total membership development. Tenets of the program are an entirely positive approach to developing a member from a pledge; use of the pre-initiation conference as an integral part of the program; and involvement of outside resource personnel to make presentations as a part of the program.

Nine separate monthly operating bulletins are published for constituencies ranging from chapter presidents, corporation officers, and chapter house managers. Alumni supporting members of the fraternity receive the regular publication *The Graduate Report* quarterly, in addition to special bulletins on various giving societies.

Educational Programs The Delta Upsilon Educational Foundation, the not-for-profit educational foundation, established in 1949, has sponsored annual career and life planning programs for chapters and leaders; funded annual scholarships for the Indiana University Interfraternity Institute; developed reading and study skills materials; as well as membership development manuals. The foundation has placed unabridged dictionaries in chapter libraries, and has sponsored graduate research into student groups.

Headquarters 8705 Founders Road, P.O. Box 68942, Indianapolis, IN 46268. Phone: (317) 875-8900. The fraternity built the first fraternity headquarters building designed for that purpose in Indianapolis on Founders Road in an area zoned exclusively for the headquarters of collegiate organizations. Since that time two men's and five women's fraternity headquarters have located their headquarters buildings or purchased lots there. The Delta Upsilon international headquarters is a contemporary building with exterior of rubble-cut native Indiana limestone, and houses archives, museum collections, conference facilities and the executive offices of the fraternity.

Membership Total living membership 66,000. Undergraduate membership 4,500. Active chapters 91. Inactive chapters 41. Colonies 12. Houses owned 61. Graduate/Alumni chapters 75. City/Area alumni associations 23. Total number of initiates 96,570. Chapter roll:

1834 *Williams, Williams* (1964)
1838 Union, Union (NY) (1844-1845) (1864-1870)
1847 *Amherst, Amherst* (1862-1870) (1971)
1847 Hamilton, Hamilton
1850 *Vermont, Vermont* (1854)
1850 *Wesleyan, Wesleyan (CT)* (1852-1919) (1953)
1851 Western Reserve, Case Western Reserve (1853-1866)
1852 *Colby, Colby* (1865-1878) (1984)
1856 Middlebury, Middlebury
1857 *Bowdoin, Bowdoin* (1861-1892) (1952)
1858 Rutgers, Rutgers
1860 *Washington and Jefferson, Washington And Jefferson* (1871)
1865 Colgate, Colgate
1865 *New York, N.Y.U.* (1945)
1868 Brown, Brown (1966-1986)
1868 Miami, Miami (OH) (1873-1908)
1869 Cornell, Cornell
1870 Marietta, Marietta
1870 *Princeton, Princeton* (1871)
1870 *Trinity, Trinity (CT)* (1876)
1873 Syracuse, Syracuse (1971-1976)
1874 *Manhattan, CUNY, Brooklyn* (1878)
1876 Michigan, Michigan
1880 Northwestern, Northwestern
1881 *Harvard, Harvard* (1942)
1885 *Columbia, Columbia (NY)* (1964)
1885 *Lafayette, Lafayette* (1988)
1885 Lehigh, Lehigh
1885 Wisconsin, Madison, Wisconsin, Madison
1886 Tufts, Tufts
1887 DePauw, DePauw

1888 Penn, Penn (1972-1980) (1986-1990)
1891 Technology, M.I.T.
1894 Swarthmore, Swarthmore
1896 California, Cal, Berkeley
1896 *Stanford, Stanford* (1987)
1898 McGill, McGill (1971-1984)
1898 Nebraska, Nebraska
1899 Toronto, Toronto
1901 Chicago, Chicago
1904 Ohio State, Ohio State
1905 Illinois, Illinois
1910 Washington (WA), Washington (WA)
1911 Penn State, Penn State
1913 Iowa State, Iowa State
1914 Purdue, Purdue
1915 Indiana, Indiana
1917 Carnegie-Mellon, Carnegie-Mellon
1920 Kansas, Kansas
1922 Oregon State, Oregon State
1922 Virginia, Virginia (1943-1949)
1924 Missouri, Missouri
1925 Iowa, Iowa
1926 *Dartmouth, Dartmouth* (1966)
1927 Oklahoma, Oklahoma
1928 Johns Hopkins, Johns Hopkins
1929 *California-Los Angeles, UCLA* (1952)
1929 Manitoba, Manitoba
1930 *Washington And Lee, Washington And Lee* (1971)
1931 Western Ontario, Western Ontario
1933 Washington State, Washington State
1934 Oregon, Oregon (1969-1988)
1935 Alberta, Alberta
1935 *British Columbia, British Columbia* (1972)
1948 Kent, Kent (1971-1990)
1948 San Jose, San Jose (1969-1984)
1949 Bowling Green, Bowling Green
1949 *Denison, Denison* (1984)
1949 Louisville, Louisville
1949 Michigan State, Michigan State (1972-1979)
1949 Texas, Texas
1950 Bucknell Demosthenean, Bucknell
1951 Bradley, Bradley
1953 Colorado, Colorado
1953 North Carolina, North Carolina
1955 Ohio, Ohio
1956 Kansas State, Kansas State
1957 Florida, Florida
1957 Georgia Tech, Georgia Tech
1959 *Arizona, Arizona* (1970)
1959 *Pacific, Pacific (CA)* (1973)
1959 *Ripon, Ripon* (1984)
1959 Wichita, Wichita
1960 Oklahoma State, Oklahoma State
1961 *Auburn, Auburn* (1970)
1961 Clarkson, Clarkson
1961 North Dakota, North Dakota
1964 *San Fernando, Cal State, Northridge* (1971)
1964 *Simpson, Simpson* (1976)
1966 *Davis, Cal, Davis* (1971)
1966 Northern Illinois, Northern Illinois
1968 Fresno, Cal State, Fresno

1968 Northern Iowa, Northern Iowa
1968 San Diego, San Diego State
1969 Arlington, Texas, Arlington
1969 Creighton, Creighton
1969 *Platteville, Wisconsin, Platteville* (1975)
1969 Tennessee, Tennessee
1970 *Central Missouri State, Central Missouri State* (1989)
1970 *Delaware, Delaware* (1983)
1970 *Eastern Kentucky, Eastern Kentucky* (1983)
1970 Maine, Maine
1970 *Marquette, Marquette* (1975)
1970 North Dakota State, North Dakota State
1970 *Oshkosh, Wisconsin, Oshkosh* (1977)
1971 *Colorado State, Colorado State* (1974-1981) (1987)
1971 *Dayton, Dayton* (1982)
1971 South Dakota, South Dakota
1971 *Southern Illinois, Southern Illinois* (1980)
1971 *Tyler Junior, Tyler Junior* (1989)
1972 Maryland, Maryland
1972 *Southwest Texas, Southwest Texas* (1977)
1973 Houston, Houston
1974 Western Illinois, Western Illinois
1974 *Wilmington, North Carolina, Wilmington* (1977)
1975 Arkansas, Arkansas
1977 North Carolnia State, North Carolina State
1978 Baylor, Baylor
1979 *L.S.U., L.S.U.* (1983)
1980 Massachusetts, Massachusetts
1981 Southwest Missouri, Southwest Missouri
1983 South Carolina, South Carolina
1983 VPI, V.P.I.
1985 *Texas Tech, Texas Tech.* (1986)
1986 Michigan Tech, Michigan Tech
1987 Bakersfield, Cal State, Bakersfield
1987 Long Beach, Cal State, Long Beach
1988 Culver-Stockton, Culver-Stockton
1988 Santa Barbara, Cal, Santa Barbara
1989 Guelph, Guelph
1989 Northern Colorado, Northern Colorado
1990 Calgary, Calgary

Colonies: Iona, Texas A & M, Rochester, Minnesota, Western Michigan, Cal Poly, San Luis Obispo, Arizona State, Florida State, McMaster, Temple, Tri-State, Western Maryland

FarmHouse

ACTIVE PIN

PLEDGE PIN

FARMHOUSE Fraternity was founded at the University of Missouri on April 15, 1905, by D. Howard Doane, Robert F. Howard, Claude B. Hutchison, Henry H. Krusekopf, Earl W. Rusk, Henry P. Rusk, and Melvin E. Sherwin. The idea was conceived by D. Howard Doane, who, in making the president's address to the 1931 conclave, said, "Twenty-six years ago FarmHouse started unconsciously the job of man building. The apparent objective was the closer association of a group of men who through that association might be of mutual help. Through successive years the goal of FarmHouse has been and is now, the best in American manhood."

Membership eligibility is open to students whose subjects can be applied toward a degree in agriculture or related sciences or who come from a rural background and whose grades are equal to or above the averages of their respective classes. Many chapters of the fraternity practice programs of deferred membership selection, giving the student an opportunity to adjust to the new environment in which he finds himself before involving him in the programs of the organization.

The objective of the fraternity is the building of the whole man which includes the encouragement of high academic achievement, maintenance of the dignity of the individual, an abiding concern for the welfare of others, participation in extracurricular activities, an awareness of the moral standards of our culture and a strong desire to seek for the best in every phase of university and personal life.

Government   Government is vested in the biennial conclave in which each chapter and each association has a vote. In the interim between conclaves, administration is vested in the International Executive Board, consisting of eight alumni members. The election of four at each conclave provides continuity. In addition, one director comes from the undergraduate chapters for a one-year term on a rotating basis by charter dates. Elected board members choose from their members a president and a vice president. One man, not an elected board member, is named by the board to serve as executive director and as editor of the international magazine. He serves ex officio on the executive board and on all committees.

Traditions and Insignia   The official jewelry consists of the membership badge, recognition button, pledge button, coat of arms, and sister pin. The membership badge consists of a gold shield bordered with pearls and rubies and displays the raised letters F and H, a white star and a black crescent.

Publications   The official publication is *Pearls and Rubies.*

Headquarters   510 Francis St., Suite #314, St. Joseph, Missouri 64501. Phone: (816) 232-1864.

Membership   Total living membership 13,939. Total undergraduate membership 899. Active chapters 33. Inactive chapters 3. Colonies 2. Houses owned 23. Graduate/Alumni chapters 29. Total number of initiates 17,638. Chapter roll:

1905	Missouri, Missouri
1911	Nebraska, Nebraska
1914	Illinois, Illinois
1921	Kansas State, Kansas State
1921	*Wisconsin, Madison, Wisconsin, Madison* (1927)
1927	Iowa State, Iowa State
1928	Oklahoma State, Oklahoma State
1931	Minnesota, Minnesota
1936	Michigan State, Michigan State
1949	Colorado State, Colorado State
1950	Wyoming, Wyoming
1951	Kentucky, Kentucky
1952	Purdue, Purdue
1954	Arkansas, Arkansas
1954	North Carolina State, North Carolina State
1955	North Dakota State, North Dakota State
1955	Washington State, Washington State
1957	Idaho, Idaho
1959	Tennessee, Tennessee
1964	Mississippi State, Mississippi State
1964	Oregon State, Oregon State
1965	*Georgia, Georgia* (1974)
1966	South Dakota State, South Dakota State
1971	Auburn, Auburn
1974	Alberta, Alberta
1978	Texas Tech, Texas Tech.
1979	Montana State, Montana State
1981	*West Virginia, West Virginia* (1987)
1982	Cal Poly-Pomona, Cal Poly, Pomona
1983	Illinois State, Illinois State
1983	Tennessee Tech, Tennessee Tech.
1985	Nebraska-Curtis, Nebraska, Curtis
1987	Cal Davis, Cal, Davis
1987	New Mexico State, New Mexico State
1988	Morehead State, Morehead
1989	Wisconsin, Platteville, Wisconsin, Platteville

Colonies: Lincoln (MO), Texas A & M

Iota Phi Theta

IOTA PHI THETA Fraternity, Inc. was founded at Morgan State College, Baltimore, Maryland in 1963. It's twelve founders were young men, diversified individuals who bound together to achieve common goals and a unique blend of brotherhood not found by them in other organizations on campus.

Our fraternity is the fifth largest Black fraternity with 51 undergraduate and 18 graduate chapters located in 14 states and Washington, D.C. Our current membershis is over 5,000.

Our achievements are steadily growing. Among them are Associate Membership with the Southern Christian Leadership Conference (SCLC) and Life Membership with the National Association for the Advancement of Colored People (NAACP). On the local level, many of our chapters are involved within their communities working with such organizations as senoir citizen groups and Big Brother associations. Iota is considered a national fraternity; this is acknowledged by our membership in the National Interfraternity Conference (NIC).

Iota Phi Theta Fraternity, Inc. is looking for inspired young men to join our efforts. We are looking to achieve our primary goal of assisting in and making a contribution to the betterment of mankind by standing up to our motto "Buildiung a tradition, not resting on one."

Headquarters P.O. Box 1459, Laurel, MD 20707. Phone (301) 792-2192.

Membership Active chapters 83. Colonies 9. Graduate/Alumni chapters 23. Total number of initiates 10,000. Chapter roll:

Alpha, Morgan State
Beta, Hampton Inst
Gamma, Delaware State
Delta, Norfolk State
Epsilon, Jersey City State
Zeta, North Carolina A & T
Eta, Virginia State
Theta, District of Columbia
Iota, Elizabeth City State
Kappa, Winston-Salem State
Lambda, Prairie-View A & M
Mu, Bowie State
Nu, Maryland, College Park
Xi, Fayetteville State
Omicron, Northwestern
Pi, Boston
Rho, Towson State
Sigma, Boston College
Tau, American International
Upsilon, Southern Illinois
Phi, Glassboro State
Chi, Boston State
Psi, Coppin State
Omega, Western New England
Alpha Alpha, Stockton State
Alpha Beta, Southern Illinois, Edwardsville
Alpha Gamma, Morris Brown
Alpha Delta, Rutgers
Alpha Epsilon, North Carolina Central
Alpha Zeta, C W Post
Alpha Eta, Southern
Alpha Theta, Salem State
Alpha Iota, Wilberforce
Alpha Kappa, Dillard
Alpha Lambda, Illinois
Alpha Mu, Central State
Alpha Nu, Bridgewater State
Alpha Xi, Westfield State
Alpha Omicron, Kentucky State
Alpha Pi, Morehouse
Alpha Rho, Illinois State
Alpha Tau, Howard
Alpha Upsilon, Northeastern Illinois
Alpha Phi, New York Metro
Alpha Chi, San Francisco State

Alpha Psi, Rutgers, New Brunswick
Beta Alpha, William Patterson
Beta Beta, Massachusetts
Beta Gamma, Eastern Illinois
Beta Delta, Wilmington
Beta Epsilon, Cincinnati
Beta Zeta, Hartford
Beta Eta, Wyoming
Beta Theta, J C Smith
Beta Iota, Urbana
Beta Kappa, Kutztown
Beta Lambda, Delaware

Graduate Chapters:
Alpha Omega, Baltimore, MD
Beta Omega, Washington, DC
Gamma Omega, Hampton, VA
Delta Omega, Boston, MA
Epsilon Omega, Atlanta, GA
Zeta Omega, Atlantic City, NJ
Eta Omega, Chicago, IL
Theta Omega, Norfolk, VA
Iota Omega, Charlotte, NC
Kappa Omega, Urbana, IL
Lambda Omega, Carbondale, IL
Mu Omega, East St. Louis, IL
Nu Omega, Greensboro, NC
Xi Omega, San Francisco, CA
Omicron Omega, Richmond, VA
Pi Omega, New York, NY
Pho Omega, Springfield, MA
Sigma Omega, New Orleans, LA
Tau Omega, Hartford, CT
Upsilon Omega, Los Angeles, CA
Phi Omega, North Jersey, NJ
Chi Omega, Philadelphia, PA
Psi Omega, Columbia, MD

Colonies: Akron, Bloomfield College, DePaul, Kegne College, North Carolina, Charlotte, North Carolina State, Northern Illinois, Ohio State, Westchester State

Kappa Alpha Order†

ACTIVE PIN

KAPPA ALPHA ORDER is the outgrowth of a fraternity organized as Phi Kappa Chi at Washington College, now Washington and Lee University, Lexington, Virginia, in December. 1865. This fraternity was conceived by James Ward Wood of Lost River, West Virginia, and was founded with William Nelson Scott and Stanhope McClelland Scott, both of Lexington, and William Archibald Walsh of Rich-

† This chapter narrative is repeated from the 19th edition; no current information was provided.

mond, Virginia. Phi Kappa Chi, the name given to the new society, symbolized in those Greek letters the sentiments of personal loyalty and kindliness which were conceived to be the basis of lasting friendship. However, the name chosen, because of its similarity to Phi Kappa Psi already on the campus, gave way to Kappa Alpha. The new letters were chosen "as they summed up vastly better the great moral truths for which the fraternity contended," as is stated in the 1891 *History and Catalogue*. Wood designed the first badge and compiled the first ritual.

Growth The parent chapter was inactive from June, 1870, to March, 1875, and again in 1878. It was revived in October, 1885. The Virginia Military Institute chapter was suppressed by anti-fraternity laws in 1888, but existed sub rosa for many years. Its charter was withdrawn in 1913, but it continues as the Beta Commission and each year initiates many outstanding VMI graduates. The first Theta at Oglethorpe University died with the institution in December, 1873; but after the re-establishment of the university in Atlanta, the chapter was revived as Beta Nu in 1918 and existed until 1938, the designation Theta, meanwhile, having been given a chapter established at the University of Kentucky. The second Theta at South Carolina Military Academy was sub rosa and was suppressed in 1883, then revived in 1887; it finally succumbed to anti-fraternity legislation in 1890. The chapter at Furman University was inactive from the fall of 1875 to May, 1879, and was barred by anti-fraternity laws from 1898 to 1927, when it was revived. The chapter at Stanford University was dormant from 1899 to 1903. The University of Mississippi chapter was inactive from 1912 to 1926, due to anti-fraternity legislation; the Wofford College chapter, for the same reasons from 1909 to 1915.

The first Mu Chapter died with the return of Newberry College from Walhalla to Newberry, South Carolina. The second Mu, at Erskine College, existed sub rosa until faculty opposition ceased in 1885. In the fall of 1893, anti-fraternity laws brought about the extinction of the second Mu Chapter. The third Mu at Emory and Henry College also succumbed to anti-fraternity laws in 1893. The first Nu Chapter at the Pennsylvania College of Dental Surgery, Philadelphia (now a part of the University of Pennsylvania), was established by a graduate of the Virginia Military Institute Chapter, and died when the last of its three initiates graduated in 1879.

The first Xi Chapter at Virginia Polytechnic Institute immediately met with anti-fraternity laws, and conducted no initiations. Xi Chapter at Southwestern University of Texas was established sub rosa, but was recognized by the faculty in September, 1887. The first Omicron Chapter at Bethel Academy was almost immediately withdrawn, because of anti-fraternity laws and the decision of the order not to retain chapters in colleges that gave no de-

grees. The second Omicron, at the University of Texas, was suspended from 1887 to 1891.

The first Pi Chapter at the Gordon Institute was ordered to surrender its charter because the institution awarded no degrees. The second Pi, at the University of Tennessee, was inactive from 1887 to 1893. Rho at the University of South Carolina was inactive from 1892 to 1895, and was suppressed by state legislation from 1897 to 1927, when it revived; while being suppressed by state legislation, however, the chapter operated for a portion of the time, sub rosa. Tau, at Wake Forest College, established sub rosa, was suppressed in 1884; it was revived in 1889, suppressed in 1891, and finally revived in 1922, on the repeal of the anti-fraternity regulations. The chapter at the University of North Carolina was inactive from 1888 to 1891. Under the impression that Southern University was to close, Phi Chapter disbanded in 1882, but was reorganized in 1883 and withdrawn in 1914, due to lack of material. Phi was revived in 1922 at Birmingham-Southern College, successor to Southern University. Psi Chapter, at the University of Louisiana, died in 1883 on account of anti-fraternity laws and other opposition.

In February, 1886, Psi was re-established at Tulane University, which is a continuation of the older institution. The Johns Hopkins chapter, Alpha. Lambda, was inactive from 1910 to 1915. Alpha Xi Chapter at the University of California was inactive from 1896 to 1897. The first Alpha Psi Chapter was merged with Beta Zeta when Florida State College was consolidated with the University of Florida, and the designation Alpha Psi was later given to the chapter at Rollins College, in Winter Park, Florida. Alpha Iota Chapter at Centenary College was withdrawn in 1903, when the college was moved to Shreveport, Louisiana; it was revived in 1909, withdrawn in 1913, and finally revived in 1922. The charter of Omega Chapter at Centre College was withdrawn in 1933 for lack of material as was that of Beta Mu Chapter at St. John's College in Maryland, during the second World War.

Alpha Nu Chapter at George Washington University was inactive from 1953 to 1954; it was revived in 1954 and its charter was recalled in 1959, due to lack of material. Alpha Omicron Chapter at the University of Arkansas was inactive from 1902 to 1904 and again during the second World War; it was revived after the war until 1960, when its charter was suspended. The decline in the 1960s and resurgence in the 1970s are reflected in the Order's chapter roll.

More than fifty alumni chapters had been chartered prior to 1934, and today alumni chapters are spread throughout the United States. Times for the meetings are set by the local groups and all of them hold an annual meeting on or around January 19.

Government The executive authority of Kappa Alpha Order is vested in the Knight Commander and six Councilors, known as the Executive Council. The administrative work of the order is conducted by its national administrative office under the direction of the executive director and members of his staff.

Territorial supervision of Kappa Alpha's active chapters is exercised by Province Commanders, and the order presently consists of fifteen provinces. Province commanders are elected by the active chapters in the respective provinces and they, in turn, appoint other province officers qualified to assist them in the execution of their duties. The province commanders and the general officers compose the advisory council of the order.

The province commanders are aided in the territorial supervision of the active chapters by traveling officers, appointed by the executive council and known as traveling chapter advisors. They regularly visit all active chapters during the school year to advise the chapters' officers in their duties and functions; during the summer months the traveling advisors aid the national administrative office in its service to and collaboration with the alumni chapters.

The national scholarship officer is appointed by the knight commander to promote higher scholastic standing throughout the order. He gathers information regarding the scholastic standings of the active chapters directly from the officials of the various colleges and universities where the chapters are located. It is the purpose of the National Scholarship Officer to keep each chapter aware of its scholastic standing and to encourage it to achieve significant improvement in scholarship through the attainment of higher individual scholarship.

Traditions and Insignia Samuel Zenas Ammen of Fincastle, Virginia, who was initiated with six other new men in October, 1866, is credited with conceiving a ritualistic foundation and pattern of tradition for the development of Kappa Alpha Order. He sought in rewriting the ritual to stimulate in the hearts and minds of those who experienced its ceremonies, high regard for personal honor, sincere appreciation for the value of learning, and Christian respect for womankind. Because Robert E. Lee, the president of Washington College under whose influence the founders lived and learned, nobly exemplified those qualities, they took him as the exemplar for students brought into the order. Thus, General Lee was accepted as the spiritual founder of the order and the basic tenets he himself held dear have remained the foundation of membership. With Ammen's complete revision of the ritual Kappa Alpha Order was given an identity which set it apart from any other collegiate organization at that time and which still sets it apart.

Kappa Alpha's roll includes men from every part of the nation, and alumni chapters are organized throughout the continental United States. The territorial expansion of active chapters, however, has been limited by policy, though there is nothing of a sectional nature in either the ritual or Constitution which would prohibit further expansion into any section of the country.

The original badge consisted of a single gold shield, unjeweled, in the center of which was a circle of black enamel enclosing a Latin cross in gold, and above which was a plain arched band of gold, enclosing the letters KA in black enamel. The present badge consists of one gold shield superimposed upon another; it has a Greek cross of gold within the circle and above are the letters KA in gold, on a black field. All members are supplied with an official badge at the time of their initiation. The colors are crimson and old gold; the flowers, the magnolia blossom and the red rose. The flag consists of three bars, crimson, white and old gold, of equal width, placed parallel with the staff, the crimson bar next to the staff, the gold at the flowing end. In the center of the white bar is the crimson cross in Greek form. The pledge button is silver and of the same general design as the official badge. A quartered circle, the parts of which are alternately crimson and gold, replaces the gold cross and black circle described as a device upon the official badge. The letters KA remain on a black field.

Publications Nine catalogues have been issued by the order; the present records show a total membership of 76,276 members, The first two catalogues were published at Macon, Georgia, by J. L. Hardeman in 1873 and 1875, the former showing a membership of 270 and the latter of 370. The *Kappa Alpha History and Catalogue* was published in the fall of 1891, at Nashville, Tennessee, by J. S. Chick. It contained 375 pages, showed a membership of 2,282 inclusive of 1890, and gave a history of the Order and of the several chapters. The seventh catalogue, in 1922, was a volume of 1,335 pages and it showed a membership of over 13,000 as of December 1, 1921. In 1950, the administrative office, then in Louisville, Kentucky, issued a geographical listing of all living members to date as a special issue of the official magazine. The ninth *Directory* was published in 1966, contained 612 pages, and showed a membership of 58,994.

The constitution was revised by the convention of 1911, and an entirely new one was adopted in 1936. New editions were printed in 1921, 1926, 1936, 1947, 1956, 1963, and 1974. Songbooks were published in 1907, 1914, 1953, and 1968. Nine editions of the ritual have been issued.

The first official publication was the *Kappa Alpha Journal*, a quarterly published from Richmond, Virginia; it was published in February, August, and December of 1879, the latter date at which publication was suspended. 'The first volume of the *Journal* included general literature as well as fraternity matters. In November, 1883, the *Kappa Alpha Magazine*, also a quarterly, appeared. In October, I 885, the magazine was succeeded by the *Kappa Alpha Journal*, Volume III, and it since has appeared regularly under that name. For a while it was a monthly, then a bimonthly, then the Convention of 1911 made it a quarterly. The *Journal* is edited by the publications editor of the order. The order issues a confidential publication known as *Special Messenger*, for members only.

The Varlet, a pledge education manual, is issued and a copy presented to each pledge at the beginning of his preparation for initiation. Each college chapter is provided with an officers' handbook and each alumni chapter with an operation manual.

Funds and Philanthropies Kappa Alpha Scholarship Fund, Inc., was established and chartered as an independent corporation in 1948. It provides incentives for scholarship improvements and makes educational loans and grants to needy and deserving students. The Fund annually awards a trophy to the undergraduate chapter which maintains the highest competitive scholastic standing among all the order's undergraduate chapters for the previous year. The Freshman Scholarship Citation also is presented annually by the Fund to the freshman in each chapter who attains the highest scholastic average among its first-year members.

Fraternity Housing Corporation, Inc., was established in 1948 to assist the order's undergraduate chapters in procuring and maintaining adequate housing. This is done by purchasing and owning houses for individual chapters and by making adequately secured loans to alumni house corporations for that purpose. While the order owns all the stock of the Fraternity Housing Corporation, its operations are conducted by a group of alumni, who function as an independent board of directors.

A War Memorial to all KAs who served their country during World War I, World War II, and the Korean War has been established in the George C. Marshall Research Library in Lexington, Virginia. The memorial was dedicated during the Centennial Convention on August 27, 1965.

Headquarters P.O. Box 1865, Lexington, VA 24450. Phone: (703) 463-1865.

Membership Active chapters 117. Total number of initiates 107,441. Chapter roll:††

1865 Alpha, Washington and Lee (1870-1875) (1878-1885)
1868 *Beta, V.M.I.* (1913)
1868 Gamma, Georgia
1869 Delta, Wofford (1909-1915)
1869 Epsilon, Emory
1870 Eta, Richmond
1871 *Theta-Prime, Oglethorpe* (1873) (see Beta Nu)
1872 *Iota, Furman* (1875-1879) (1898-1927) (1963)
1873 Kappa, Mercer
1873 Lambda, Virginia
1873 *Mu-Prime, Newberry* (1874)
1877 *Nu-Prime, Pennsylvania Dental* (1879)
1877 *Xi-Prime, V.P.I.* (1877)
1878 *Omicron-Prime, Bethel Academy (VA)* (1879)

†† This chapter roll is repeated from the 19th edition; no current information was provided.

1879 *Pi-Prime, Gordon Institute (GA)* (1883)
1880 Rho, South Carolina (1892-1895) (1897-1927)
1880 Sigma, Davidson
1881 Tau, Wake Forest (1884-1889) (1891-1922)
1881 Upsilon, North Carolina (1888-1891)
1882 *Phi, Birmingham-Southern* (1882) (1883-1922) (1974)
1882 Psi, Tulane (1883-1886)
1882 *Theta-Second, South Carolina Military Academy* (1890)
1883 Alpha Alpha, U of the South
1883 Chi, Vanderbilt
1883 *Mu-Second, Erskine* (1885-1893) (1893)
1883 Nu, Auburn
1883 *Omega, Centre College* (1933)
1883 Omicron, Texas (1887-1891)
1883 Pi, Tennessee (1887-1893)
1883 Xi, Southwestern (TX)
1885 Alpha Beta, Alabama
1885 Alpha Gamma, L.S.U.
1887 Alpha Delta, William Jewell
1887 Alpha Epsilon, Southwestern, Memphis
1890 Alpha Eta, Westminster (MO)
1890 Alpha Zeta, William and Mary
1891 Alpha Iota, Centenary (1903-1909) (1913-1922)
1891 Alpha Kappa, Missouri
1891 *Alpha Lambda, Johns Hopkins* (1910-1915) (1975)
1891 Alpha Theta, Transylvania
1893 Alpha Mu, Millsaps
1893 *Mu-Third, Emory and Henry* (1895)
1893 Theta, Kentucky
1894 *Alpha Nu, George Washington* (1953-1954) (1954-1959)
1895 *Alpha Omicron, Arkansas* (1902-1904) (1960)
1895 Alpha Pi, Stanford (1899-1903)
1895 *Alpha Xi, California* (1896-1897) (1970)
1897 Alpha Rho, West Virginia
1899 Alpha Sigma, Georgia Tech
1899 Alpha Tau, Hampden-Sydney
1900 Alpha Upsilon, Mississippi (1912-1926)
1901 *Alpha Phi, Duke* (1970)
1902 *Alpha Chi, Kentucky Wesleyan* (1907)
1903 Alpha Omega, North Carolina State
1903 *Alpha Psi-Prime, Florida State* (1905)
1903 Beta Alpha, Missouri, Rolla
1903 Beta Beta, Bethany
1904 Beta Delta, Georgetown Col.
1904 Beta Epsilon, Delaware
1904 *Beta Gamma, Charleston (SC)* (1939)
1904 Beta Zeta, Florida
1905 Beta Eta, Oklahoma
1905 *Beta Theta, Washington (MO)* (1965)
1906 Beta Iota, Drury
1914 Beta Kappa, Maryland
1915 Beta Lambda, Southern Methodist
1916 *Beta Mu, St. John's (MD)* (1942)
1918 *Beta Nu, Oglethorpe* (1938)
1920 *Beta Xi, Oklahoma State* (1972)

1921 *Beta Omicron, Louisville* (1960)
1924 Beta Pi, Presbyterian
1924 Beta Rho, Roanoke
1926 Beta Sigma, USC
1927 Alpha Psi, Rollins
1927 Beta Tau, Mississippi State
1927 Beta Upsilon, Marshall
1929 Beta Phi, New Mexico
1930 Beta Chi, West Virginia Wesleyan
1931 *Beta Psi, UCLA* (1953-1956) (1960)
1936 Beta Omega, Washington (MD)
1937 Mu, Tulsa
1947 Gamma Alpha, Louisiana Tech
1947 Gamma Beta, Southwest Missouri
1948 *Gamma Delta, San Jose* (1959)
1948 Gamma Gamma, Memphis State
1949 *Gamma Epsilon, Arizona* (1961)
1949 Gamma Eta, Florida State
1949 Gamma Zeta, Southern Mississippi
1950 *Gamma Iota, San Diego State* (1961)
1950 *Gamma Theta, Miami (FL)* (1963)
1952 Gamma Kappa, Oklahoma City
1953 Gamma Lambda, North Texas
1956 *Gamma Mu, Houston* (1960)
1957 Gamma Nu, Northeast Louisiana
1957 Gamma Omicron, Lambuth
1957 *Gamma Xi, Lamar* (1970)
1958 Gamma Pi, Florida Southern
1958 Gamma Rho, East Carolina
1959 Gamma Sigma, West Texas
1960 Gamma Phi, Southwestern Louisiana
1960 Gamma Tau, Sam Houston
1960 Gamma Upsilon, East Texas
1961 Gamma Chi, Texas Tech.
1963 Gamma Psi, Northwestern Louisiana
1964 Delta Alpha, Western Carolina
1964 Gamma Omega, Midwestern
1965 Delta Beta, Delta State
1965 Delta Gamma, Old Dominion
1966 Delta Delta, East Tennessee
1966 Delta Epsilon, Newberry
1967 Delta Eta, Arkansas State
1967 *Delta Zeta, Spring Hill* (1970)
1968 Delta Iota, Texas, Arlington
1968 Delta Kappa, Stephen F. Austin
1968 Delta Theta, Georgia Southern
1969 Delta Lambda, Middle Tennessee
1969 Delta Mu, Eastern Kentucky
1969 Delta Nu, Murray State
1969 Delta Xi, McNeese
1969 Zeta, Randolph, Macon
1970 Delta Omicron, Clemson
1971 Delta Pi, Missouri Southern
1972 Delta Rho, Valdosta
1972 Delta Sigma, Houston Baptist
1974 Delta Tau, Francis Marion
1975 Delta Upsilon, Tennessee, Martin
1976 Delta Chi, L.S.U., Shreveport
1976 Delta Omega, Baylor
1976 Delta Phi, Jacksonville (AL)
1976 Delta Psi, Appalachian
1977 Epsilon Alpha, South Alabama

1977 Epsilon Beta, Nicholls

Colonies: Cal, Davis, Cal, Riverside, Henderson, Texas A & M, V.P.I.

Kappa Alpha Psi

ACTIVE PIN

KAPPA ALPHA PSI FRATERNITY was founded at Indiana University on January 5, 1911, by Elder W. Diggs, Byron K. Armstrong, John M. Lee, Henry T. Asher, Marcus P. Blakemore, Guy L. Grant, Paul Caine, George W. Edmunds, Ezra D. Alexander, and Edward G. Irvin. Its purposes are to encourage honorable achievement in every field of human endeavor, to unite in a fraternal bond college men of culture, patriotism, and high sense of honor, and to promote the social, intellectual, and moral welfare of its members.

The early years of the fraternity's existence were difficult, and expansion was slow. In recent years growth has been more rapid and certain.

Chapters are grouped geographically to constitute twelve provinces, each headed by a Province Polemarch. Membership is conferred by initiation only. To be eligible for initiation, one must have completed at least one-fourth of the requirements for graduation from his institution.

Government Legislative power is vested in the Grand Chapter which meets biannually and executive power in the Grand Board of Directors and staff. A full-time national executive secretary and staff administer the day-to-day affairs of the fraternity from the National Executive Office.

Traditions and Insignia The principal service project of the fraternity is the Guide Right Program, initiated in 1922, which is a national movement conducted on a year-round basis in order to provide for youth the greatest opportunity for discovering and developing their potentialities. This program is largely aimed at nonfraternity youth, while another program, the National Leadership Conference, is held annually for indoctrination of undergraduate chapter officers. Advisers for this are selected graduate specialists, but the undergirding of the conference is by undergraduate leaders.

To stimulate and reward outstanding achievement among members the fraternity set up a system of honors, the highest of which is the Laurel Wreath for extra-meritorious achievement on a national basis. In the fifty years of its existence this award has been bestowed upon only sixteen members.

At the Fiftieth Anniversary celebration in August, 1961, a $300,000 Elder W. Diggs Memorial shrine was dedicated on the campus of Indiana University. It houses a memorial library and shrine dedicated to the ten founders. Also it contains 30 double study rooms, sleeping accommodations for 80 men, music room, lounge and reception rooms, and a refectory. It was erected through contributions from members and chapters throughout the country, is owned by the national body, and managed by a national Memorial Housing Management Committee, Alpha Chapter at Indiana University, and the national staff.

An Achievement Commission promotes competition between undergraduate and graduate chapters and awards suitable trophies for scholarship rating, chapter finances, outstanding achievement, etc. It also administers the Elder W. Diggs Award FOR EXTRA MERITORIOUS contributions to the fraternity or to society on less than a national basis, being superseded only by the Laurel Wreath. The Guy Levis Grant Award, adopted in 1974, is named for a revered founder. It is the fraternity's paramount honor reserved exclusively for undergraduate members. The Humanitarian Award was created by the Grand Board of Directors in 1976 to honor individuals, without regard to membership, who have extended America's bounteous life to its disadvantaged citizens.

The official badge is diamond-shaped displaying the initial letters of the fraternity's name on a raised black scroll in the middle of the pin. Official colors are crimson and cream.

Publications The official publicity organ of the fraternity is the *Kappa Alpha Psi Journal*, published quarterly. It is supplemented by an esoteric organ, the *Kappa Alpha Psi Bulletin* issued quarterly to members only.

Funds A housing fund assists local chapters in the acquisition of homes. Funds for making student scholarship loans, scholarship awards, and student aid loans have been established.

Kappa Alpha Psi also has established the Elder W. Diggs Memorial Foundation for the purpose of research and study in the educational, scientific, and literary field and with a view toward the building of a better understanding and relationship between different social groups throughout the world.

Headquarters c/o PBTC, #1304-06, 5070 Parkside Avenue, Philadelphia, PA 19131. Phone: (215) 228-7184.

The National Headquarters is a three-story acquired building which houses the administrative offices on the second floor and the clerical offices and reception and work areas on the first floor and basement. The third floor is reserved for records and a library.

Membership Active chapters 326. Inactive chapters 7. Total number of initiates 80,000. Chapter roll:

	Iota Chi, Miami (FL)
	Iota Psi, Salisbury
1911	Alpha, Indiana
1913	Beta, Illinois
1914	Gamma, Iowa
1915	Delta, Wilberforce
1915	Epsilon, Lincoln (Pa.)
1915	Zeta, Ohio State
1916	Eta, Nebraska
1917	Theta, Northwestern
1918	Iota, Chicago
1919	Kappa, Meharry Medical
1920	*Lambda, Temple* (1960)
1920	Mu, Kansas
1920	Nu, Purdue
1920	Xi, Howard Payne
1921	Omicron, Columbia (NY)
1921	Pi, Morehouse
1921	Rho, Washburn
1922	Sigma, Michigan
1923	Tau, West Virginia State
1923	Upsilon, UCLA
1924	*Chi, Boston U.* (1951)
1924	*Phi, SUNY, Buffalo* (1925)
1924	Psi, Minnesota
1925	Omega, Drake
1927	Alpha Beta, Wayne State (MI)
1927	Alpha Delta, Fisk
1927	Alpha Epsilon, Johnson C. Smith
1927	Alpha Gamma, Virginia Union
1928	*Alpha Zeta, Indiana State* (1938)
1929	Alpha Eta, Creighton and Omaha
1931	Alpha Iota, Morgan State
1931	Alpha Kappa, North Carolina Central
1931	Alpha Lambda, South Carolina State
1931	Alpha Theta, Tennessee Agricultural
1931	Beta Theta, Colorado
1932	Alpha Mu, Lincoln (MO)
1933	Alpha Nu, North Carolina A & T
1933	Alpha Omicron, Louisville
1933	Alpha Pi, Langston
1933	Alpha Xi, Florida A & M
1934	Alpha Rho, Lewis
1935	Alpha Chi, Wiley
1935	Alpha Phi, Virginia State, Norfolk
1935	Alpha Sigma, Southern
1935	Alpha Tau, Bluefield
1935	Alpha Upsilon, Kentucky State
1936	Alpha Omega, Western Reserve
1936	Alpha Psi, Pittsburg State, Kansas
1937	Beta Beta, Texas Col
1937	Beta Delta, Morris Brown (1951-1955)
1937	Beta Epsilon, Pitt
1937	Beta Gamma, Dillard
1938	Beta Zeta, Alabama State
1939	Beta Eta, Cincinnati
1939	*Beta Iota, Xavier (OH)* (1953)
1940	Beta Kappa, D. C. Teachers
1940	Beta Lambda, Lane
1940	Beta Mu, LeMoyne-Owen
1942	Beta Nu, Harris-Stowe
1942	Beta Xi, Toledo
1946	*Beta Omicron, Wisconsin, Madison* (1952)
1946	Beta Pi, Youngstown State
1947	Beta Chi, Hampton Inst.

1947	Beta Omega, USC		1965	Epsilon Iota, Evansville
1947	Beta Phi, Knoxville		1965	Epsilon Kappa, Long Beach State
1947	Beta Psi, Kansas State		1966	Epsilon Lambda, Ohio
1947	Beta Rho, Allen		1966	Epsilon Mu, Florida Memorial
1947	Beta Sigma, Delaware State		1968	Epsilon Nu, Southern
1947	Beta Tau, Philander Smith		1968	Epsilon Omicron, Northern Illinois
1947	Beta Upsilon, Texas Southern		1968	Epsilon Pi, West Texas
1947	Gamma Alpha, Cal, Oakland		1968	Epsilon Xi, Northern Michigan
1948	Gamma Beta, Western Michigan		1969	Epsilon Rho, Western Kentucky
1948	*Gamma Delta, Livingstone* (1953)		1969	Epsilon Sigma, Bowie
1948	Gamma Epsilon, Tuskegee		1969	Epsilon Tau, Ferris
1948	Gamma Eta, Washington (WA)		1969	Epsilon Upsilon, Northern Arizona
1948	Gamma Gamma, Talladega		1970	Epsilon Chi, West Virginia
1948	Gamma Iota, Arizona State		1970	Epsilon Omega, Voorhees
1948	Gamma Kappa, Clark Col., Atlanta (1952-1956)		1970	Epsilon Phi, McNeese
1948	Gamma Theta, Bethune-Cookman		1970	Epsilon Psi, Paine
1948	Gamma Zeta, Fort Valley		1970	Gamma Chi, Savannah
1949	Gamma Lambda, Huston-Tillotson		1970	Gamma Psi, Grambling
1949	Gamma Mu, Benedict		1970	Zeta Alpha, Indiana
1949	Gamma Nu, Claflin		1970	Zeta Beta, Prairie View
1949	Gamma Omicron, St. Augustine's		1970	Zeta Delta, North Carolina, Charlotte
1949	Gamma Pi, Alcorn		1970	Zeta Epsilon, South Carolina
1949	Gamma Rho, Tougaloo		1970	Zeta Gamma, Coppin
1949	Gamma Sigma, Arkansas		1970	Zeta Zeta, Mississippi Valley
1949	Gamma Tau, Kent		1971	Zeta Eta, California (PA)
1949	Gamma Xi, Maryland, Eastern Shore		1971	Zeta Iota, Georgia
1950	Delta Alpha, Oregon		1971	Zeta Kappa, Tennessee, Martin
1950	Gamma Omega, Cheyney State		1971	Zeta Lambda, Morehead
1950	Gamma Phi, Alabama A & M		1971	Zeta Mu, Western Illinois
1950	Gamma Upsilon, Southern Illinois		1971	Zeta Nu, Bowling Green
1951	Delta Beta, Syracuse		1971	Zeta Theta, Oklahoma State
1951	Delta Delta, Jackson (MS)		1971	Zeta Xi, Jarvis Christian
1951	Delta Epsilon, San Diego State		1972	Zeta Omicron, Rust
1951	Delta Gamma, Shaw		1972	Zeta Phi, Florida
1952	Delta Eta, Penn		1972	Zeta Pi, Southern Illinois
1952	Delta Theta, Penn State		1972	Zeta Rho, Northeastern (OK)
1952	Delta Zeta, Central State (OH)		1972	Zeta Sigma, Barber-Scotia
1953	Delta Iota, Ball State		1972	Zeta Tau, Central Missouri State
1954	Delta Kappa, Marquette		1972	Zeta Upsilon, North Texas
1954	Delta Lambda, St. Paul's		1973	Eta Alpha, Eastern Kentucky
1955	Delta Mu, Long Island		1973	Eta Beta, Murray State
1955	Delta Nu, Eastern Michigan		1973	Eta Gamma, Middle Tennessee
1956	Delta Omicron, Arizona		1973	Zeta Chi, South Florida
1956	Delta Pi, Michigan State		1973	Zeta Omega, Oklahoma
1956	Delta Rho, San Jose		1973	Zeta Psi, Lamar
1956	Delta Sigma, Bishop		1974	Eta Delta, Trenton
1956	Delta Xi, Albany State		1974	Eta Epsilon, Rutgers
1957	Delta Tau, Miles		1974	Eta Eta, GMI
1958	Delta Phi, Indiana Tech.		1974	Eta Iota, Charleston (SC)
1958	Delta Upsilon, Wichita		1974	Eta Kappa, Culver-Stockton
1960	Delta Chi, Winston-Salem		1974	Eta Lambda, Houston
1960	Delta Psi, Edward Waters		1974	Eta Mu, Jacksonville (AL)
1961	Delta Omega, Missouri		1974	Eta Nu, South Alabama
1961	Epsilon Alpha, Elizabeth City		1974	Eta Omicron, Cameron
1962	Epsilon Beta, Fayetteville		1974	Eta Pi, Northeast Louisiana
1962	Epsilon Delta, Marshall		1974	Eta Rho, Central Michigan
1963	Epsilon Epsilon, Stillman		1974	Eta Sigma, Virginia
1963	Epsilon Eta, Northeast Missouri		1974	Eta Tau, Texas A & I
1963	Epsilon Gamma, Central State (OK)		1974	Eta Theta, Columbus
1963	Epsilon Zeta, Norfolk		1974	Eta Xi, Virginia Commonwealth
1964	Epsilon Theta, Idaho State		1974	Eta Zeta, Cal, Riverside
			1975	Eta Chi, Alabama

1975 Eta Omega, Old Dominion	1980 Kappa Pi, Washington State
1975 Eta Phi, East Texas	1980 Kappa Theta, Georgia State
1975 Eta Psi, East Carolina	1980 Kappa Xi, North Carolina State
1975 Eta Upsilon, Mississippi State	1980 Kappa Zeta (Graduate), Atlanta
1975 Theta Alpha, Henderson	1981 Kappa Chi, American
1975 Theta Beta, Austin Peay	1981 Kappa Omega, Shippensburg
1975 Theta Delta, Auburn	1981 Kappa Phi, Illinois, Chicago
1975 Theta Eata, Florida State	1981 Kappa Psi, Cal State, Chico
1975 Theta Epsilon, Arkansas, Little Rock	1981 Kappa Rho, SUNY, Albany
1975 Theta Gamma, Eastern Illinois	1981 Kappa Sigma, Western Carolina
1975 Theta Iota, M.I.T.	1981 Kappa Tau, Kentucky
1975 Theta Kappa, West Georgia	1981 Kappa Upsilon, Oakland
1975 Theta Lambda, Northwestern Louisiana	1981 Lambda Alpha, Bloomsburg
1975 Theta Mu, Arkansas State	1982 Lambda Beta, Cal, Irvine
1975 Theta Nu, Southwestern Louisiana	1982 Lambda Delta, Georgia Tech
1975 Theta Theta, Maryland	1982 Lambda Epsilon, Morris
1975 Theta Zeta, Chicago State	1982 Lambda Eta, IUPUI
1976 Theta Chi, Maryland, Baltimore County	1982 Lambda Gamma, Winthrop
1976 Theta Omicron, North Carolina	1982 Lambda Iota, Tennessee, Chattanooga
1976 Theta Phi, Troy	1982 Lambda Kappa, Southern Arkansas
1976 Theta Pi, Mercer	1982 Lambda Lambda, Paul Quinn
1976 Theta Rho, Louisiana Tech	1982 Lambda Theta, Southwest Texas
1976 Theta Sigma, Nevada, Las Vegas	1982 Lamda Zeta, Towson
1976 Theta Tau, Howard	1983 Lambda Mu, Frostburg
1976 Theta Upsilon, North Alabama	1983 Lambda Nu, Stanford
1976 Theta Xi, Texas, El Paso	1983 Lambda Omicron, New Orleans
1977 Iota Alpha, Texas, Arlington	1983 Lambda Phi, Valdosta
1977 Iota Beta, Cal State, Sacramento	1983 Lambda Pi, Mississippi
1977 Iota Delta, Texas	1983 Lambda Rho, Occidental
1977 Iota Gamma, Central Arkansas	1983 Lambda Sigma Society, Nicholls
1977 Theta Omega, New Mexico State	1983 Lambda Tau, Millersville
1977 Theta Psi, V.P.I.	1983 Lambda Upsilon, Indiana (PA)
1978 Iota Epsilon, Montclair	1983 Lambda Xi, Brown
1978 Iota Eta, West Virginia Tech	1984 Lambda Chi, Florida Institute
1978 Iota Iota, Oregon State	1984 Lambda Omega, Central Florida
1978 Iota Kappa, Bradley	1984 Lambda Psi, Georgia Southwestern
1978 Iota Lambda, Lewis	1984 Mu Alha, Emporia
1978 Iota Mu, Dayton	1984 Mu Beta, East Stroudsburg
1978 Iota Theta, Livingston	1984 Mu Delta, SUNY Col., Brockport
1978 Iota Zeta, East Tennessee	1984 Mu Gamma, DeVry Tech
1979 Iota Nu, Baldwin-Wallace	1985 Mu Epsilon, Southwest Missouri
1979 Iota Omicron, Hofstra	1985 Mu Eta, Northwest Missouri
1979 Iota Phi, Cornell	1985 Mu Iota, North Carolina, Greensboro
1979 Iota Pi, Georgia Southern	1985 Mu Kappa, SUNY, Binghamton
1979 Iota Rho, Fordham	1985 Mu Lambda, Weber
1979 Iota Sigma, Cal, Davis	1985 Mu Mu, George Mason
1979 Iota Tau, Arkansas	1985 Mu Nu, North Carolina, Wilmington
1979 Iota Upsilon, Texas Tech	1985 Mu Theta, Francis Marion
1979 Iota Xi, Duke	1985 Mu Zeta, Southeast Missouri
1980 Iota Omega, Missouri, Rolla	1986 Mu Omicron, SUNY Col., Old Westbury
1980 Kappa Alpha, Illinois State	1986 Mu Phi, Clarion
1980 Kappa Beta, Memphis State	1986 Mu Pi, St John's (NY)
1980 Kappa Delta, Miami (OH)	1986 Mu Rho, Tennessee
1980 Kappa Epsilon, Texas Christian	1986 Mu Sigma, Stephen F. Austin
1980 Kappa Eta, Arkansas, Monticello	1986 Mu Tau, Mars Hill
1980 Kappa Gamma, West Chester	1986 Mu Upsilon, Appalachian
1980 Kappa Iota, Southern Mississippi	1986 Mu Xi, Wittenberg
1980 Kappa Kappa, Alabama, Birmingham	1987 Mu Chi, Dartmouth
1980 Kappa Lambda, Clemson	1987 Mu Omega, Sonoma State
1980 Kappa Mu, SUNY Col., New Paltz	1987 Mu Psi, Georgia Col
1980 Kappa Nu, Sam Houston	1987 Nu Alpha, Texas A & M
1980 Kappa Omicron, Cal Poly, Diamond Bar	1987 Nu Beta, Southern Methodist

1987	Nu Delta, Emory
1987	Nu Epsilon, Missouri, Kansas City
1987	Nu Gamma, Yale
1987	Nu Zeta, Edinboro
1988	Nu Eta, Delta State
1988	Nu Iota, L.S.U.
1988	Nu Kappa, Northern Iowa
1988	Nu Lambda, Madison Col
1988	Nu Mu, Alabama, Huntsville
1988	Nu Nu, South Carolina, Aiken
1988	Nu Theta, Elon
1989	Nu Omicron, Pembroke
1989	Nu Phi, Lock Haven
1989	Nu Pi, R.P.I.
1989	Nu Rho, Vanderbilt
1989	Nu Sigma, Cal State, Hayward
1989	Nu Tau, Massachusetts
1989	Nu Upsilon, Michigan, Dearborn
1989	Nu Xi, Delaware
1990	Nu Chi, Wofford
1990	Nu Psi, Connecticut

Kappa Alpha Society†

ACTIVE PIN

KAPPA ALPHA SOCIETY is the oldest secret brotherhood of a social and literary character which has had a continuous existence in American colleges, and is the forerunner of the present vast system of American college fraternities.

For some years previous to 1825 there had existed at Union College an organized company of students for purposes of outdoor exercise and military drill. In the fall of that year, however, the interest in this organization died out, and the time was ripe for a new departure. An inspiration came from John Hart Hunter, Thomas Hun, and Isaac W. Jackson, of the class of 1826. They conceived the idea of a new secret society of a literary and social order, and gained the interest of four other seniors, John McGeoch, Orlando Meads, James Proud-fit, and Joseph A. Constant, and two juniors, Arthur Burtis, Jr., and Joseph Law. These nine founders held their first formal meeting on November 26, 1825, at which the organization was perfected, the name of the novel society decided upon, and a constitution adopted. On December 3, 1825, they held the first initiation, when Charles Clark Young, Andrew E. B. Knox, and Solon Grout, all seniors, were formally admitted to membership, the secret proceedings being followed by an "adjournment to the well-known dining-room at Knight's boarding house—down

† This chapter narrative is repeated from the 19th edition; no current information was provided.

town—where a supper was made enjoyable without extra stimulants of any kind, name, or nature."

On December 10 Levi Hubbell, of 1827, was initiated in similar fashion. In 1826 nine additional upperclassmen were initiated, and thirteen in 1827. Thus was started a movement destined to be the most powerful and universal factor of a social nature in American college life.

This first group of Kappa Alpha men at Union stamped a character and conservatism upon the society which it has retained. The founders possessed both zeal and an aptitude for their work, and but slight additions have been made to the ceremonial features of the society; not a few among their associates were men whose names became noted.

The new society encountered natural opposition, largely on account of its secrecy. Individuals, and even the college authorities, took up the cause; nevertheless, Kappa Alpha flourished from the beginning. Other societies of like character soon made their appearance, and within a few years the era of college fraternities was fully inaugurated at Union.

Growth In 1833 a petition for a charter from Kappa Alpha was presented by a number of students at Williams College led by Azariah S. Clark of the class of 1834. This being granted, the Williams chapter was established in that year, the first on the ground, Sigma Phi following in 1834. Here even sharper opposition was encountered than at Union, the "Social Fraternity" or "Equitable Fraternity" being founded in 1834, with the view of overthrowing the secret society system. The hostilities finally ended in 1839, when the withdrawal of several of the extremely influential members of the anti-secret organization to join Kappa Alpha led to an assault upon the meetings place of the fraternity, which was, however, successfully repelled. After this, with the founding and growth of other fraternity chapters at the college, the power of the "Social Fraternity" as an anti-secret force steadily declined until it disappeared, the body becoming the parent chapter of Delta Upsilon.

In 1844 a chapter was founded at Geneva (now Hobart) College, which was withdrawn in 1854, owing to a decline in the affairs of the college, but was re-established in 1879. The Princeton chapter, founded in 1852, had a brief, but brilliant career, brought to a close by the persistent attitude of hostility assumed toward secret societies by the college authorities. As an honorable continuance of the chapter was soon rendered impossible under the restrictions imposed, its members decided to surrender their charter, and withdrew from the college with the graduation of the class of 1856. The chapter at the University of Virginia, founded in 1857, grew out of the suppression of fraternities at Princeton, its founder being Joseph Hodgson of the Princeton chapter. This chapter also was destined for a short life. Upon the breaking out of the Civil War, many of its members left the university to join the army of the Confederacy, meetings became gradually less frequent. and in 1861 the chapter was suspended. After the close of the war no attempt was made to revive the fraternity there.

The Cornell chapter was founded in November, 1868, following the opening of the university the previous month. The Lehigh chapter was founded in 1893, and the Pennsylvania chapter in 1913. Kappa Alpha established a chapter at Toronto in Canada in 1892, at McGill in 1899, at Western Ontario in 1948, and at Wesleyan University in 1967.

Kappa Alpha was the first of the college fraternities either to occupy or own a chapter house in the modern sense of the expression. At Williams College its chapter purchased a lot and dwelling house in 1864, and completed in 1876 a handsome chapter house which the fraternity occupied until 1907.

Government Government of the fraternity is invested in the Executive Council, composed of four officers and two alumni members from each chapter.

Traditions and Insignia During the first thirty or forty years of its existence the chapter at Union occasionally held public exercises. The chapter celebrated the 25th, the 50th, the 75th, 100th, 125th, and 150th anniversaries of the founding of the fraternity with appropriate well-attended ceremonies in 1850, 1875, 1900, 1925, 1950, and 1975. Also in 1833 the semicentennial of the Williams chapter was held at Williamstown, at which Governor Henry M. Hoyt, of Pennsylvania, delivered the address. The inaugurations of the Toronto chapter, held at Ithaca, and of the Lehigh chapter at New York, of the McGill chapter at Williamstown, and of the Pennsylvania chapter at Ithaca and Williamstown were the occasions of large and enthusiastic gatherings of the members of Kappa Alpha.

The centennial anniversary of the founding of Kappa Alpha Society was celebrated with elaborate ceremonies at Schenectady, New York, on November 6–8, 1925, and was attended by about one-quarter of the living members. One of the interesting features of the celebration was the laying of the cornerstone of a handsome stone and iron gateway erected to commemorate the first centennial of an American college fraternity. This gateway is at the entrance to "Captain Jack's Garden," given to Union College by Isaac W. Jackson, a Kappa Alpha founder.

The sesquicentennial celebration was held at Union College in September. 1975. The event was attended by over 300 members. A plaque commemorating the 150th anniversary of the founding of the Society and the American College Fraternity System was dedicated in the same garden where, fifty years earlier, Kaps had dedicated the entrance gateway during the centennial ceremony.

The emblem of the fraternity is a golden key, on one side of which are the signs of the zodiac encircling the letters KA; on the other side are a rising sun and other symbols. It was adopted on July 9, 1827, and was the first emblem to be used by any of the now existing social fraternities. The fraternity possesses eight of these original emblems. It was in the form of a square medal with a ring attached to its upper corner and was worn as a watch charm. In 1833 members of the Williams chapter added a hollow barrel with square steel insert to its lower corner and used it to wind their old-fashioned watches; thus the emblem was converted into a key. Kappa Alpha is the only men's social fraternity whose emblem is in the form of a key; all others use a pin badge. The society color is scarlet.

Publications Catalogues of Kappa Alpha have been published in 1830, 1832, 1835, 1838, 1842, 1845, 1850, 1852, 1859, 1874, 1892, 1902, 1913, 1926, 1929, 1937, 1941, 1955, 1960, and 1977. The 1830 edition was the first issued by any Greek-letter fraternity. One copy survives which is in the archives of the Union chapter. It supplies the names of members, certain mystic symbols, dates of initiation, places of domicile, and class numerals. In the earlier editions of these catalogues much of the information was printed in Latin and in cipher. The *Kappa Alpha Record* of 1892, 1902, and 1913 contains full biographical accounts of the members of the fraternity, with illustrations and valuable historical matter. The centennial edition of the *Record*, published in 1926, is a quarto volume of 800 pages containing comprehensive biographical sketches of members, nearly 200 illustrations, valuable historical articles relative to the early days of the fraternity, histories of the individual chapters, and a geographical index. The latest edition of the *Record* was published in February, 1977.

Other publications of the fraternity include songbooks, a biographical record of the Williams chapter, published in 1881, with supplements in 1882 and 1890, and periodic news-bulletins, *Kappa Alpha Newsletter,* which go to every member.

Funds and Philanthropies The fraternity possesses a substantial endowment fund proposed and inaugurated during the celebration of centennial at Union in 1925. Its purpose is to render financial assistance in the building, purchase, or improvement of chapter houses, to provide scholarship aid for members, and to meet other general requirements.

Headquarters 317 West State Street, Ithaca, NY 14850. Phone: (607) 277-3888.

Membership Living membership 5,114. Active chapters 10. Inactive chapters 4. Houses owned 3. City/Area alumni associations 4, Total number of initiates 8,900. Chapter roll:

1825	C.C., Union (NY)	
1833	C.G., Williams	
1844	C.H., Hobart (1854-1879)	
1852	*C.N.C., Princeton* (1856-1984) (1984)	
1857	*V.V., Virginia* (1861)	
1868	V.C., Cornell	
1892	V.T., Toronto	
1894	V.L., Lehigh	
1899	V.M., McGill (1971-1987)	
1913	V.P., Penn	
1948	V.O.O., Western Ontario	

1967 *V.W., Wesleyan (CT)* (1980)
1989 V.A., Alberta

COAT OF ARMS

Kappa Delta Phi

ACTIVE PIN

PLEDGE PIN

KAPPA DELTA PHI was founded at the Bridgewater Normal School (which is now Bridgewater State College). Bridgewater, Massachusetts, on April 14, 1900. It was incorporated under the laws of Massachusetts on May 29, 1929.

It is a fraternity open to those who manifest a keen interest in higher education and philanthropy.

In its educational aspect, it is the purpose of this fraternity to foster the highest educational ideals and to labor for new truths and insights.

In its second aspect, the fraternity aims to strengthen and preserve the bonds of fellowship through united philanthropic services.

The fraternity actively supports the fight against discrimination on the basis of race, color or creed.

Patterned upon democratic ideals with provision for elected representative government of the national body, the government of the national body serves as a model for local chapter government.

Government The national officers, chairman of the board, vice-chairman, treasurer, and secretary are elected from the seven-member Board of Directors which governs the fraternity. Two board members are undergraduates elected by the active chapters for a one-year term.

Traditions and Insignia The official badge of Kappa Delta Phi has a gold diamond-shaped base, and mounted upon it is a smaller black diamond-shaped panel with the three Greek letters ΚΔΦ. Jeweled pins are also provided in the same design with twenty jewels mounted upon the diamond-shaped base. The official pledge pin is diamond-shaped in the vertical position and is divided across the short midpoints, the upper panel being gold and the lower panel black, the colors of the fraternity.

Publications In 1950 a yearbook was published entitled *"The Golden Year of Kappa Delta Phi."* In 1962, "Kappa Delta Phi Anniversary Book" was published. *"The Crow"* is an alumni publication issued semiannually. *"Kappa Talk"* an inter-chapter quarterly newsletter, has been published since 1968.

Headquarters 186 Finch Avenue, North Providence, RI 02904. Phone: (401) 724-3634.

Membership Total living membership 1,200. Total undergraduate membership 318. Active chapters 14. Inactive chapters 11. Graduate/Alumni chapters 3. Total number of initiates 1,220. Chapter roll is not available.

COAT OF ARMS

Kappa Delta Rho

ACTIVE PIN

PLEDGE PIN

The National Fraternity of KAPPA DELTA RHO, Inc. was founded on May 17, 1905 on the campus of Middlebury College in Middlebury, Vermont. It was incorporated under the New York Membership Corporation Law on February 10, 1954. The official colors are Middlebury Blue and Princeton Orange and the fraternity flower is the red rose.

History Kappa Delta Rho was started at the turn of the century on the campus of Middlebury College in Middlebury, Vt. The school had experienced rising enrollment during the post Civil War years but there had been no new fraternities permanently organized during this period of growth. The result of this lack of fraternal expansion was the development of a large diverse group called the Commons Club. George E. Kimball, president of the Commons Club found that the club was too casual and informal to develop the congenial friendships and bonds of brotherhood that he and a few of his peers were seeking. George E. Kimball, along with fellow club members Irving T. Coates and John Beecher met in Room 14 of Old Painter Hall on May 17, 1905 and outlined the foundations for creating a new fraternity. With the addition of Chester M. Walch, Gino A. Ratti, Thomas H. Bartley, Benjamin E. Farr, Pierce W. Darrow, Roy D. Wood, and Gideon R. Norton, officers were elected and the ritual and constitution were ratified, and Alpha Chapter of Kappa Delta Rho was born.

Most other fraternities had named their officers using names from the City-States of ancient Greece. The founders of Kappa Delta Rho decided instead to emulate the stern virtues of the ancient Roman Republic and the chapter officers are titled with their Roman equivalents. The open Latin motto, "Honor Super Omnia," which translates into "Honor Before All Things" was selected by the founders as a guide for the future.

With the foundation set, the Ten Founders channeled their energies into molding a brotherhood whose aims would be achieving the highest standards of respect, manhood and brotherly love. These concerns would take precedent above all other character attributes including social distinction, athletic prowess, and even high scholarship.

The motto, "Honor Super Omnia," ("Honor Before All Things") reflects the noble standards that the founders set for themselves and for others to follow and has guided each member of Kappa Delta Rho throughout his life. these strict ideals are also reflected in Kappa Delta Rho's National Policy Against Hazing, one of the first documents of its kind in the fraternity system.

Growth Because of strict attention to the founder's standards, Kappa Delta Rho was very conservative and sluggish in expansion during its early years. In 1913, Harold A. Severy, an alumnus of Alpha Chapter, attended Cornell to complete his graduate studies. While he was there he sparked the interest of a local group of undergraduates, and Beta Chapter was soon established. Gamma Chapter, established at New York State Teachers College at Albany, followed in 1915 and Delta Chapter was formed at Colgate in 1917. Delta Chapter had the fortune to fall under the leadership of Dr. Frank Carman Ewart. It was Dr. Ewart's vision and philosophies that helped mold Kappa Delta Rho from a small confederation of chapters into a fraternity national in scope. Through the efforts of Dr. Ewart and Alpha alumnus Arthur Ottman, both serving as National Presidents, KΔP expanded from five to twenty chapters, making 1919-1928 one of the most prosperous periods in Kappa Delta Rho's early history.

The Depression and WWII took its toll on the Greek System and KΔP was no exception. After WWII, the fraternity reorganized and reactivated many of its dormant chapters. With the post war prosperity of the 50's and early 60's, KΔP enjoyed another period of steady growth. But during the late 60's another blow fell on the Greek System and Kappa Delta Rho watched itself shrink to under twenty chapters. This period of stagnation and decline for the Greek System affected all Greek organizations and would last until the early 70's.

The 80's brought forth a more conservative campus attitude and Greek systems began to flourish again. Since 1980, Kappa Delta Rho has undergone restructuring and has experienced phenomenal growth. Several dormant chapters were reactivated and reorganized with many new ones springing up. This positive growth is credited to a Penn State KΔP alumnus, Donald L. Stohl, who has been the Executive Director of the fraternity since 1980. His leadership and implementation of a new expansion policy has seen Kappa Delta Rho grow from fifteen chapters to nearly sixty, recording KΔP as the fastest growing fraternity of the 80's.

Government In 1905, the Ten Founders drafted and ratified a constitution for the new fraternity. The document saw minor changes until 1932 when it was redrafted to conform to the newly revised Membership Corporation Law of New York. The Na-

tional Convention felt that it would be wise to overhaul the constitution and by-laws to allow for eventual incorporation under the new law. On February 10, 1954 the fraternity was incorporated as the "National Fraternity of Kappa Delta Rho, Inc."

The legislative body of Kappa Delta Rho is the National Convention. National Convention meetings are held annually and representatives from all chapters and alumni corporations are required to attend. There is also a fifteen member Board of Directors, elected on even year conventions. Ten of the members of the Board of Directors are elected to four year terms, while the remaining five board members are elected to term positions of two years. Of these two year terms, no less than three and no more than four are undergraduates. From the Board of Directors the National Officers are elected. They are the President, the Executive Vice-President, the Vice-President for Development, the Vice-President for Finance, the Secretary and the Treasurer.

The voting strength of the National Convention is as follows:

Chapters . . . . Five Votes
Alumni Corporations . . . . Three Votes
Directors . . . . One Vote
Alumni Clubs . . . . One Vote

Publications *The Quill and Scroll,* a quarterly alumni magazine

The Sentry, a monthly newsletter issued to chapters

The Pathfinder, the pledge information manual

The Kappa Delta Rho Gentleman, a guide to common courtesies

Position Statements of the National Fraternity of Kappa Delta Rho, Inc.

The Alumni Newsletter, a quarterly alumni newsletter

The Alumni Corporation Update, a quarterly publication issued to alumni corporations

The Song Book of Kappa Delta Rho

Insignia The badge is a raised monogram formed by the gold letters Kappa and Rho joined side by side. A pearl set Delta of the same letter size is imposed over the Kappa and Rho with the Delta's base slightly lower than the other letters.

The Coat of Arms consists of a shield supported by crossed Roman swords with the points downward. The helmet atop the crest has the visor closed, indicating the secret nature of the order. The field is orange and is charged with a scale and dagger, an open book and a lamp, all in gold. The ordinary is a blue bend with the letters Kappa, Delta, and Rho emblazoned on it in gold. The motto scroll contains the Latin phrase "Honor Super Omnia," which translated means "Honor Before All Things."

The pledge pin is a miniature shield with a blue field and an orange bend. The only devices present are the letters Kappa, Delta, and Rho emblazoned in gold on the bend.

Traditions Each chapter holds a formal dance each year called the Rose Formal. At this function all of the chapter's pinmates are serenaded as a group and the Chapter Sweetheart is named. Other traditions are Founder's Day, celebrated each May 17, and Charter Day, celebrated by each chapter on the date it received its charter.

Headquarters The National Fraternity of Kappa Delta Rho, Inc., 331 South Main Street, Greensburg, PA 15601. Phone: (412) 838-7100, FAX: (412) 838-7101.

Membership Total living membership 13,425. Undergraduate membership 1,419. Active chapters 43. Inactive chapters 11. Colonies 10. Houses owned 15. City/Area alumni associations 3. Total number of initiates 18,201. Chapter roll:

Chi Colony, Florida (1952)
1905	Alpha, Middlebury
1913	Beta, Cornell
1917	Delta, Colgate (1972-1985)
1919	Epsilon, Franklin
1920	Zeta, Penn State
1921	Eta, Illinois
1921	Iota, Bucknell
1921	Theta, Purdue
1922	*Kappa, Ohio State* (1976)
1924	Lambda, Cal, Berkeley
1925	*Mu, Michigan* (1940)
1926	Nu, Indiana
1926	*Xi, Colby* (1983)
1928	*Omicron, Butler* (1937)
1928	Rho, Lafayette
1928	Sigma, Oregon State
1930	Tau, Carnegie-Mellon (1939-1987)
1939	*Upsilon, Cal State, Fresno* (1956)
1950	*Phi, Oklahoma* (1954)
1953	Psi, Lycoming
1955	Omega, Indiana (PA)
1958	Alpha Alpha, Lock Haven (1985-1988)
1960	*Beta Alpha, C. W. Post* (1975-1981) (1988)
1967	*Gamma Alpha, Bradley* (1980)
1969	*Delta Alpha, Rhode Island* (1973)
1971	*Epsilon Alpha, Lewis* (1979)
1971	*Zeta Alpha, Dayton* (1973)
1981	Eta Alpha, Robert Morris
1981	Theta Alpha, Slippery Rock
1982	Iota Alpha, Pitt, Johnstown
1982	Kappa Alpha, Illinois State
1982	Lambda Alpha, Gannon
1982	Nu Alpha, Columbia (NY)
1984	Omicron Alpha, Rutgers
1984	Pi Alpha, Toledo
1985	Rho Alpha, Bryant
1985	Sigma Alpha, Hofstra
1985	Tau Alpha, Radford
1985	Upsilon Alpha, Parks (IL)
1985	Xi Alpha, Temple
1986	Alpha Beta, Delaware
1986	Psi Alpha, Behrend
1987	Chi Alpha, Pitt, Greensburg
1987	Omega Alpha, Virginia Commonwealth
1987	Phi Alpha, Clarion
1989	Beta Beta, Ball State

1989	Delta Beta, West Liberty
1989	Epsilon Beta, Old Dominion
1989	Gamma Beta, V.P.I.
1989	Zeta Beta, Tarleton
1990	Eta Beta, West Chester
1990	Iota Beta, Rochester Tech
1990	Theta Beta, New York Tech

Colonies: Edinboro, Fordham, Frostburg, Madison Col, Pitt, Syracuse, William Paterson, SUNY, Albany, Gettysburg, West Virginia

COAT OF ARMS

Kappa Sigma

ACTIVE PIN

PLEDGE PIN

KAPPA SIGMA as an American college fraternity was established at the University of Virginia on December 10, 1869, by friends imbued with a tradition of Jeffersonian democracy.

In this atmosphere every student tended to be a freeman in spirit and a man in mental development. Kappa Sigma thus began its existence at this institution as a fraternity for good fellows, good company, good manners, good morals, bright minds, and the wit, spirit, and leadership of gentlemen. The founders were William Grigsby McCormick, George Miles Arnold, Edmund Law Rogers, Jr., Frank Courtney Nicodemus, and John Covert Boyd.

Kappa Sigma in America was established in a sense as an extension of, and was named for, a secret university organization at the University of Bologna in Italy. Three of the founding group at Virginia had studied at Bologna and had been associated with this society, which maintained a number of chapters on the continent of Europe and traced its beginnings to Bologna. There in the year 1400 under the leadership of a Greek scholar, a society of students is said to have organized for protection against the wicked governor of the city. It soon spread to other universities in Europe, and at length in America its example was combined with the idealism of Thomas Jefferson to inspire the establishment of Kappa Sigma.

Growth By 1874, Kappa Sigma had installed chapters at eight universities. Kappa Sigma was the first Southern fraternity to expand into the North. At the end of the first 25 years, the chapter roll had grown to 39, with a membership of 2,320. On the fraternity's 75th birthday in 1944, 110 chapters and 50,666 initiates were on the rolls. By the centennial in 1969, the fraternity had 158 chapters and 93,390 living initiates.

Government Kappa Sigma is governed in accordance with its constitution, by-laws, and rules. These basic rules have been formulated by—and can be modified only by—the voting at the Grand Conclaves held every two years. Top administration is in the hands of a supreme executive committee of five members elected every two years at the grand conclaves. These five are worthy grand master, worthy grand procurator, worthy grand master of ceremonies, worthy grand scribe, and worthy grand treasurer.

Each of the fraternity's undergraduate chapters selects its own members, elects its own officers, and formulates its own by-laws and regulations, subject to the requirements of its university and of Kappa Sigma. An alumnus adviser, usually a former chapter officer, is available for advice and counsel. The alumnus advisers, in turn, are appointed by and report to their district grand masters. The district grand masters, one for each of the fraternity's 40 districts in the United States and Canada, are appointed by and report to the supreme executive committee, which also appoints the following commissioners: editor, comptroller, ritualists, historian, legal commissioners, and commissioners in charge of alumni, house prizes, conclave, endowment fund, housing, leadership award, pledge training, public relations, rushing, scholarship, songbook, and special projects.

Insignia The badge is a crescent surmounted by a 5-point star, within which are the letters KΣ, the general surface being convex in form. On the crescent, a skull and bones are above the star, crossed swords are on one side, and crossed keys are on the other side. The pledge button is a triangle bearing the caduceus surmounted by a circle with the letters KΣ enclosed.

The colors are scarlet, white, and green. The flower is the lily-of-the-valley. The flag consists of three equal-width vertical bars of scarlet, white, and green in the order named, with the coat of arms on the middle bar. The coat of arms includes a shield with a 5-starred bend sinister and a crescent moon, a circle-surmounted caduceus over the shield, and the letters AEKΔB on a ribbon under the shield.

Publications The fraternity magazine is the *Caduceus*, and the esoteric magazine is the *Star and Crescent*, both quarterly. Other publications include directories, histories, manuals, and songbooks.

Funds and Philanthropies The fraternity has basically three funds. The *Caduceus* Funds provide capital from which the magazine is issued on a lifetime basis. The Endowment Fund provides scholarship-leadership awards, graduate counselor stipends and chapter house loans. The Memorial Foundation provides leadership training to undergraduates and alumni members and sponsors international philanthropic programs. The funds,

starting with $10,000 in 1921, totaled more than $3,500,000 in 1977.

Since the funds were established, almost 200 chapter-house loans totaling almost two and a half million dollars have been made. About $70,000 is available annually to members as awards for scholarship.

Headquarters The administrative office of Kappa Sigma is housed on the second floor of its International Memorial building which is located on Highway 250 west two miles from the University of Virginia. The address is Box 5066, Charlottesville, Virginia 22905. The three-story white colonial mansion was built in 1922 and stands on a hill surrounded by seventeen acres of rolling countryside.

Membership Total living membership 140,000. Total deceased membership 30,000. Active chapters 207. Inactive chapters 51. Colonies 7. Most chapters own their own homes. A few others are at colleges where college rules forbid chapter houses. Still others rent satisfactory homes. Total number of initiates 176,291. Chapter roll:

1869 Zeta, Virginia
1873 Eta Prime, Duke (1873-1879)
1873 Mu, Washington and Lee (1970-1980)
1874 *Alpha-Alpha, Maryland, Baltimore County (1918)*
1874 Alpha-Alpha, Maryland (1988-1990)
1874 Alpha-Beta, Mercer
1874 Nu Prime, V.P.I. (1889-1971)
1874 *Omicron, Emory and Henry (1895)*
1874 *Xi, V.M.I. (1884)*
1877 Kappa, Vanderbilt
1880 *Alpha-Chi, Lake Forest (1967)*
1880 *Gamma, Cumberland (TN) (1884)*
1880 Lambda, Tennessee
1880 *Psi, Bethel (1882)*
1880 *Sigma, Episcopal High School (1881)*
1882 *Alpha-Iota, U.S. Grant (1898)*
1882 *Omega, U of the South (1970)*
1882 Phi, Rhodes (1981-1983)
1883 Gamma-Phi, West Virginia
1883 Upsilon, Hampden-Sydney
1884 Tau, Texas
1885 Chi, Purdue
1885 *Delta, Maryland Mil & Naval (1887)*
1885 Epsilon, Centenary (1904-1939)
1885 *Rho, North Georgia (1891)*
1886 Iota, Southwestern (TX)
1886 Psi, Maine (1979-1981)
1886 *Sigma, Ohio Northern (1888)*
1887 *Alpha-Delta-Theta, Emory (1891-1925) (1935)*
1887 Beta-Theta, Indiana
1887 Gamma, L.S.U.
1887 *Theta, Cumberland (TN) (1917)*
1888 *Beta, Thatcher Inst (1891)*
1888 Eta, Randolph, Macon (1987-1988)
1888 *Pi, Swarthmore (1962)*
1889 Sigma, Tulane
1890 Chi-Omega, South Carolina

1890	Delta, Davidson (1971-1988)
1890	Nu, William and Mary
1890	Xi, Arkansas
1891	Alpha-Gamma, Illinois
1891	*Beta, Butler* (1892-1949) (1980)
1892	Alpha-Delta, Penn State
1892	Alpha-Epsilon, Penn (1981-1987)
1892	Alpha-Eta, George Washington
1892	Alpha-Kappa, Cornell
1892	*Alpha-Theta, Union (TN)* (1908)
1892	Alpha-Zeta, Michigan
1893	Alpha-Lambda, Vermont
1893	Alpha-Mu, North Carolina
1894	Alpha-Nu, Wofford
1894	*Alpha-Omicron, Transylvania* (1901)
1894	*Alpha-Xi, Maine* (1902)
1895	Alpha-Pi, Wabash
1895	*Alpha-Rho, Bowdoin* (1965)
1895	Alpha-Sigma, Ohio State
1895	Alpha-Tau, Georgia Tech
1895	Alpha-Upsilon, Millsaps
1896	Alpha-Phi, Bucknell
1897	*Alpha-Omega, William Jewell* (1936)
1897	Alpha-Psi, Nebraska
1898	Beta-Alpha, Brown (1968-1983)
1898	Beta-Beta, Richmond
1898	Beta-Delta, Washington and Jefferson
1898	Beta-Epsilon, Wisconsin, Madison
1898	Beta-Gamma, Missouri (1986-1988)
1899	Beta, Alabama
1899	Beta-Zeta, Stanford (1981-1983)
1900	Beta-Eta, Auburn
1900	Beta-Iota, Lehigh
1901	Beta-Kappa, New Hampshire
1901	Beta-Lambda, Georgia
1901	Beta-Mu, Minnesota
1901	Beta-Nu, Kentucky
1901	Beta-Xi, Cal, Berkeley
1902	Beta-Omicron, Denver
1902	Beta-Pi, Dickinson
1902	Beta-Rho, Iowa (1936-1969)
1902	Beta-Sigma, Washington (MO) (1934-1948)
1903	Beta-Chi, Missouri, Rolla
1903	*Beta-Phi, Case Tech* (1934)
1903	Beta-Psi, Washington (WA)
1903	Beta-Tau, Baker
1903	Beta-Upsilon, North Carolina State
1904	Beta-Omega, Colorado Col
1904	Gamma-Alpha, Oregon
1904	*Gamma-Beta, Chicago* (1947)
1904	*Gamma-Delta, Massachusetts* (1984)
1904	Gamma-Gamma, Colorado Mines
1905	*Gamma-Epsilon, Dartmouth* (1980)
1905	*Gamma-Eta, Harvard* (1933)
1905	Gamma-Theta, Idaho
1906	Gamma-Iota, Syracuse (1978-1987) (-1989)
1906	Gamma-Kappa, Oklahoma
1909	Gamma-Lambda, Iowa State
1909	Gamma-Mu, Washington State
1909	Gamma-Nu, Washburn
1911	Gamma-Xi, Denison
1912	Gamma-Omicron, Kansas

1914	Gamma-Pi, M.I.T.
1915	Gamma-Rho, Arizona (1973-1980)
1915	Gamma-Sigma, Oregon State
1916	Gamma-Tau, Colorado
1918	Gamma-Upsilon, Rutgers
1919	Gamma-Chi, Kansas State
1920	Alpha-Alpha, Johns Hopkins (1941-1988)
1920	Gamma-Omega, Pitt (1941-1967)
1920	Gamma-Psi, Oklahoma State
1921	Delta-Alpha, Carnegie-Mellon
1921	*Delta-Beta, Lafayette* (1986)
1921	Delta-Gamma, Wyoming
1922	Delta-Delta, Florida (1970-1973)
1924	*Delta-Epsilon, Toronto* (1987)
1925	Delta-Eta, USC
1925	*Delta-Theta, Emory* (1935)
1925	Delta-Zeta, New Mexico (1972-1981)
1926	*Delta-Iota, South Dakota* (1941)
1926	*Delta-Kappa, Ohio Wesleyan* (1982)
1926	Delta-Lambda, Montana State
1926	Delta-Mu, North Dakota
1926	Delta-Nu, UCLA (1964-1976)
1926	Delta-Xi, Mississippi
1927	*Delta-Omicron, Montana* (1937)
1927	Delta-Pi, Southern Methodist
1928	Delta-Rho, Franklin and Marshall
1928	Delta-Sigma, Utah
1929	Delta-Tau, Union (NY) (1964-1979)
1933	Delta-Upsilon, Occidental (1963-1986)
1935	Delta-Phi, Hobart
1936	Delta-Chi, Mississippi State
1937	Delta-Omega, Wake Forest
1937	Delta-Psi, Michigan State (1981-1982)
1939	Epsilon-Alpha, Alberta
1939	Epsilon-Beta, Miami (FL) (1973-1986)
1941	Epsilon-Delta, Northwestern
1941	Epsilon-Epsilon, British Columbia
1942	Epsilon-Zeta, Connecticut (1951-1982)
1943	Epsilon-Gamma, Louisiana Tech
1947	Epsilon-Eta, Bowling Green
1947	Epsilon-Iota, San Diego U
1947	*Epsilon-Kappa, Utah State* (1964)
1947	*Epsilon-Theta, Cal, Santa Barbara* (1970)
1948	Epsilon-Lambda, Puget Sound
1948	Epsilon-Mu, Tulsa
1948	Epsilon-Nu, Southern Mississippi
1949	Alpha-Iota, Tennessee, Chattanooga
1949	*Epsilon-Omicron, Butler* (1980)
1949	Epsilon-Xi, Texas, El Paso
1950	Epsilon-Pi, Memphis State
1950	*Epsilon-Rho, Kent* (1983)
1951	Alpha, Cal State, Fresno (1970-1981)
1951	Beta-Phi, Cal, Davis (1976-1980)
1951	Epsilon-Sigma, Florida State
1952	Epsilon-Upsilon, North Texas
1953	Epsilon-Phi, Texas Tech.
1955	Theta, Texas Christian
1956	Epsilon-Chi, Southwestern Louisiana
1958	Epsilon-Omega, Georgia State
1958	Epsilon-Psi, Lambuth
1959	*Theta-Alpha, Florida Southern* (1969)
1959	Theta-Beta, Cal State, Long Beach

1959	Theta-Gamma, Midwestern
1961	Theta-Delta, Willamette
1961	Theta-Epsilon, Portland State
1962	Theta-Zeta, Eastern New Mexico
1963	Rho, Arizona State
1963	Theta-Eta, Arkansas, Little Rock
1965	Theta-Iota, San Jose
1965	Theta-Kappa, Texas A & I
1965	Theta-Theta, Western Kentucky
1966	Gamma-Beta Prime, Millikin
1966	Theta-Lambda, Southwest Texas (1987-1990)
1966	Theta-Mu, Northwestern Louisiana
1966	Theta-Nu, Ashland
1966	Theta-Omicron, Muskingum
1966	Theta-Pi, East Carolina
1966	Theta-Rho, McNeese
1966	*Theta-Tau, Cal State, Los Angeles* (1969)
1966	Theta-Xi, Tri-State
1967	Kappa-Alpha, Nevada, Las Vegas
1967	Theta-Chi, Northeast Louisiana
1967	Theta-Omega, Texas, Arlington
1967	Theta-Phi, Wichita
1967	Theta-Psi, Oklahoma City
1967	*Theta-Sigma, Spring Hill* (1969)
1967	Theta-Upsilon, Miami (OH)
1968	*Kappa-Beta, Indiana State* (1984)
1968	Kappa-Delta, South Florida
1968	*Kappa-Epsilon, Pan American* (1988)
1968	Kappa-Eta, Widener
1968	Kappa-Gamma, Northern Arizona
1968	Kappa-Theta, Indiana (PA)
1968	Kappa-Zeta, Georgia Southern
1969	Kappa-Iota, Middle Tennessee
1969	Kappa-Kappa, Georgia Southwestern
1969	Kappa-Lambda, Shippensburg
1969	Kappa-Mu, Tennessee Tech.
1969	Kappa-Nu, South Alabama
1969	Kappa-Omicron, LaGrange
1969	Kappa-Pi, Central State (OK)
1969	Kappa-Rho, Boise
1969	*Kappa-Xi, Lowell* (1978)
1970	Kappa-Chi, Charleston (SC)
1970	Kappa-Omega, North Carolina, Charlotte
1970	Kappa-Phi, George Mason
1970	*Kappa-Psi, Villanova* (1974)
1970	*Kappa-Tau, Youngstown State* (1978)
1970	Kappa-Upsilon, Clemson
1970	*Lambda-Alpha, Northern Michigan* (1976)
1971	*Lambda-Beta, East Tennessee* (1984)
1971	Lambda-Delta, West Georgia
1971	Lambda-Epsilon, Central Florida
1971	Lambda-Gamma, Jacksonville (AL)
1971	Lambda-Zeta, Virginia Commonwealth
1972	Lambda-Eta, Lamar
1972	*Lambda-Theta, Dallas Baptist* (1980)
1973	Lambda-Iota, Arkansas Col
1973	Lambda-Kappa, Eastern Montana
1973	Lambda-Lambda, Elon
1973	Lambda-Mu, New Hampshire Col
1974	Lambda-Nu, Appalachian
1974	Lambda-Xi, Georgia Col

1975	Lambda-Omicron, North Alabama
1975	Lambda-Pi, Delta State
1975	*Lambda-Rho, Nathaniel Hawthorne* (1982)
1976	Lambda-Sigma, Madison Col
1976	Lambda-Tau, Baylor
1977	Lambda-Upsilon, Emporia
1978	Lambda-Phi, Sam Houston
1979	Lambda-Chi, College of Idaho
1980	Lambda-Omega, Lander
1980	Lambda-Psi, St. Mary's, San Antonio
1981	Mu-Alpha, Southern Colorado
1982	Mu-Beta, Huntingdon
1982	Mu-Delta, Cal, Irvine
1982	Mu-Gamma, Texas A & M
1983	Mu-Epsilon, Linfield
1983	Mu-Eta, Louisville
1983	Mu-Iota, Gallaudet
1983	*Mu-Theta, Davis and Elkins* (1990)
1983	Mu-Zeta, North Carolina, Wilmington
1984	Mu-Kappa, SUNY, Buffalo
1984	Mu-Lambda, Calgary
1984	Mu-Omicron, L.S.U., Shreveport
1984	Mu-Rho, Southwest Missouri
1984	Mu-Xi, Cal State, Fullerton
1985	*Mu-Phi, Yale* (1987)
1985	Mu-Sigma, Towson
1985	Mu-Tau, Austin Peay
1985	Mu-Upsilon, Northern Iowa
1987	Mu Psi, Boston U.
1989	Mu-Omega, Southeastern Louisiana
1989	Nu-Alpha, Cal Poly, San Luis Obispo
1989	Nu-Beta, Northern Illinois
1990	Nu-Delta, Alabama, Birmingham
1990	Nu-Epsilon, New Mexico State
1990	Nu-Gamma, Pratt

Colonies: N.Y.U., Fort Hays, Hofstra, Morehead, Central Arkansas, N.Y.U., Wisconsin, Oshkosh

COAT OF ARMS

Lambda Chi Alpha

ACTIVE PIN

PLEDGE PIN

LAMBDA CHI ALPHA was founded at Boston University November 2, 1909, by Warren Albert Cole. The account of the first three years of the fraternity is the story of Cole's singular persistence. While the earliest organizers envisioned a society of national scope, no chapters were added until 1912. The first to receive a charter from the parent chapter was a group at the University of Massachusetts. Members from this chapter and the third, granted at the University of Pennsylvania, brought new elements into the personnel of the rapidly developing society that were to give it the spiritual appeal for its members that has become the foundation stone of Lambda Chi Alpha's progress. From the beginning the fraternity has been based on democratic and progressive principles.

Chief among the early workers who contributed to the idealism and organization of the fraternity was John E. Mason, an English scholar and philologist, who was the principal author of the ritual and designer of the coat of arms, flag, and other emblems. Samuel Dyer of Maine, Louis F. Robbins of Brown, and Albert Cross of Pennsylvania are also honored as important early workers.

Growth The period of the first World War and directly afterward marked a period of tremendous growth, although 90 per cent of the fraternity's 2,500 members at the time were in military service. Gains made by the fraternity resulted in a series of significant developments, including: establishing a central office directed by a full-time secretary in 1920; chartering of first alumni association in Indianapolis in 1921; employing full-time traveling secretaries in 1924 with a two-visit a year policy for the chapters; installing a chapter at the University of Toronto in 1927; purchasing a modern headquarters building; creating in 1947 an alumni office with a full-time secretary in charge and completely mechanizing the central office; incorporating in 1950 a charitable and educational foundation; in 1972 adopting the concept of associate membership to replace pledgeship, and in 1970 the creation of a 12-member student advisory committee whose chairman serves on the Grand High Zeta.

Lambda Chi Alpha's size and strength were greatly increased by a merger in 1939 with the national fraternity Theta Kappa Nu which had 37 chapters. Memberships were respectively 21,000 and 7,000. The new fraternity possessed 106 undergraduate chapters, where it had only 78 before. Chapters of either fraternity existed on nine campuses.

Government The convention, or general assembly, is the chief legislative authority of the fraternity. Between biennial sessions of this body, a board of ten officers, the Grand High Zeta, administers the affairs of the fraternity. Alumni are represented at convention through what is known as the alumni conference, which is permitted to elect a number of members as delegates to the assembly up to a maximum of 18 votes. Votes in the assembly are given to one delegate from each chapter and colony, delegates from the alumni conference, current members of the Grand High Zeta, past members of the Grand High Zeta, and members of the Order of Merit.

The Grand High Zeta is made up of the following officers: grand high alpha, president; grand high beta, vice-president; grand high pi, chancellor; grand high gamma, secretary; grand high tau, treasurer; and five directors: grand high delta, grand high epsilon, grand high kappa, grand high phi, and grand high sigma.

The board of councilors is made up of past members of the Grand High Zeta and former national officers of Theta Kappa Nu. Its function is advisory and its members enjoy franchise at the general assembly.

In nonconvention years the fraternity holds leadership seminars for undergraduates, consisting of a five-day course in training for chapter leadership.

The executive director is in charge of the office of administration. The administrative staff consists of 15 administrative officers and nine clerical workers, and is directed by the Grand High Zeta. The senior staff includes directors of business affairs, chapter services, and development and communication, and the visitation staff which includes eight educational leadership consultants.

Traditions and Insignia Founders' Day is celebrated on March 22 in recognition of John E. Mason, who developed the new ritual and emblems, and his co-workers, whose efforts led to the adoption of the ritual and insignia on this day in 1913. The fraternity maintains at international headquarters the John E. Mason Library of Fraternity Literature, in which may also be found rare 17th century volumes on heraldry and knighthood.

High scholarship is traditionally fostered by Lambda Chi Alpha. Scholarship is promoted through a national scholarship committee which guides local committees in each chapter. Graduate scholarships are awarded annually to qualifying members, the present program providing several awards of $1,000 or more. Scholarship and activity keys are awarded annually to outstanding undergraduates. Awards are made annually for scholastic excellence and improvement, publications, and public affairs.

Other awards include the Grand High Alpha Award for chapter excellence, the Phoenix Award for chapter improvement, and the Cyril F. "Duke" Flad outstanding undergraduate award. In 1983 the Standards for Chapter Excellence Program was developed to better focus the energy of chapters upon the implementation of substantial, long-lasting ideals. Chapters making exemplary use of the program receive the Bruce Hunter McIntosh Award.

The badge of the fraternity is a pearl-set crescent with horns turned toward the left, and enclosing a monogram of the Greek letters, ΛΧΑ. The center of the crescent bears the Greek letters ΔΡ in gold on black enamel. The associate member button is gold and black. The button consists of a gothic arch superimposed upon the silhouette of the Theta Kappa Nu official badge of four triangles. The flag consists of a purple ground displaying between three five-pointed stars in chevron, a cross, behind the right and bottom arms of which is a rising crescent, and upon the intersection is a shield bearing the Greek letters ΛΧΑ. The shield is in green, and the cross, crescent, stars, and letters are in gold. The chapter letter is frequently placed in the inner chief. The colors are purple, green, and gold. The flower is the white rose.

The coat of arms described in the terminology of heraldry consists of the following elements: escutcheon: quarterly 1, vert, a lighted Greek lamp, or; 2, or, an open book proper, bearing on its face the letters Chi, Omicron, Alpha, Zeta; 3, sable, a balance or; 4, vert, a pair of clasped hands argent, between three mullets in chevron or; over all an inescutcheon argent, a lion rampant holding a white rose slipped proper. Behind the escutcheon a pair of swords in saltire, points downward, argent, pommels, and hilts or. Mantling vert, lined, or. Encircling the escutcheon a riband purpure, edged argent, bearing the Greek motto Chalepa Ta Kala surrounded by an olive wreath which bears pendant the badge of the brotherhood. Below the escutcheon a scroll with the Latin motto *Vir Quisque Vir*. Crest: issuant from a crown celestial or, ensigning a gentleman's helmet proper, a crucicrescent rayonne or, Latin motto *Per Crucem Crescens*, on scroll.

Publications   An open magazine, *The Cross and Crescent*, has been published since 1914; it was originally called the *Purple, Green, and Gold*. Theta Kappa Nu's *Theta News*, established in 1924, was discontinued with the union. A private periodical, *Inescutcheon*, had appeared more or less regularly since 1914, but was discontinued in 1942. It was originally called *The Cross and Crescent*, later *Delta Pi*, and finally *Inescutcheon*, to continue the name of the Theta Kappa Nu secret bulletin. Directories were published in 1913, 1914, 1917, 1919, 1923, and 1930. A chapter officers' manual called *The Expositor* made its appearance in 1922.

Manuals are published for chapter officers. New editions of the laws are published every two years, or following each biennial convention. Five editions of a songbook have appeared. *A Membership Manual*, titled *Paedagogus*, is revised biennially. Still other publications include regular bulletins to chapters, called *Em'phasis*, and bulletins for chapter advisers and house corporations.

Funds and Philanthropies   In 1950 the John E. Mason Memorial Foundation was incorporated under the laws of the State of New York for the purpose of aiding in educational, literary, scientific, and charitable pursuits. In 1968, the foundation was renamed the Lambda Chi Alpha Educational Foundation, Inc.

The foundation continues the tradition begun in 1926 by Theta Kappa Nu of awarding scholarships for graduate study. To date more than $250,000 has been awarded to 261 men from 122 chapters. The foundation also funds educational workshops to develop leadership potential and foster personal development of undergraduates. The alcohol education of the fraternity begun in 1976 and the drug education program begun in 1980 have been funded by the foundation. More recently, university research of interfraternal value has been supported.

Headquarters   8741 Founders Road, Indianapolis, Indiana 46268. Phone: (317) 872-8000. Constructed in 1974, the headquarters building houses the executive offices.

Membership   Total living membership 125,000. Total undergraduate membership 15,000. Active chapters 224. Inactive chapters 61. Colonies 2. Houses owned 181. Graduate/Alumni chapters 214. Total number of initiates 195,583. Chapter roll:

1909	Alpha, Boston U. (1970-1983)	
1912	*Epsilon, Penn* (1956)	
1912	Gamma, Massachusetts (1976-1980)	
1912	*Iota, Brown* (1968)	
1912	Lambda, M.I.T.	
1912	Zeta, Penn State	
1913	Delta, Bucknell (1983-1985)	
1913	Mu, Cal, Berkeley	
1913	Omicron, Cornell	
1913	*Phi, Rutgers* (1988)	
1913	*Pi, Worcester Tech* (1988)	
1913	Sigma, Michigan	
1914	Eta, Rhode Island	
1914	Tau, Washington State	
1914	*Theta, Dartmouth* (1931)	
1914	Upsilon, L.S.U.	
1915	Alpha-Alpha, Butler	
1915	Chi, Illinois	
1915	*Kappa, Knox* (1934)	
1915	Nu, Georgia (1987-1990)	
1915	Omega, Auburn	
1915	Psi, Purdue	
1915	*Rho, Union (NY)* (1940)	
1915	Xi, DePauw	
1916	*Alpha-Epsilon, Harvard* (1932)	
1916	Alpha-Gamma, South Dakota	
1916	*Alpha-Zeta, Colgate* (1968)	
1917	*Alpha-Beta, Wisconsin, Madison* (1941-1946) (1968)	
1917	Alpha-Delta, Missouri, Rolla	
1917	Alpha-Eta, Oklahoma State	
1917	Alpha-Iota, Northwestern	
1917	Alpha-Lambda, Oregon State	
1917	Alpha-Mu, Texas (1930-1932) (1936-1940)	
1917	Alpha-Omicron, Indiana	
1917	Alpha-Phi, Alabama	
1917	Alpha-Pi, Denver	
1917	*Alpha-Sigma, Cumberland (TN)* (1948)	
1917	Alpha-Tau, Iowa State (1934-1948)	
1917	*Alpha-Theta, Franklin and Marshall* (1980)	
1918	Alpha-Chi, Richmond	
1918	Alpha-Kappa, Wabash	
1918	*Alpha-Nu, Case Western Reserve* (1963)	
1918	Alpha-Omega, Ohio (1937-1950) (1968-1975)	
1918	Alpha-Psi, Washington (WA)	
1918	*Alpha-Rho, Colby* (1984)	
1918	Alpha-Upsilon, Syracuse	
1918	Alpha-Xi, New Hampshire	
1919	Gamma-Alpha, Akron	
1919	Gamma-Epsilon, Pitt (1964-1981)	
1919	Gamma-Gamma, Cincinnati (1985-1988)	

1919	Gamma-Iota, Denison
1919	Gamma-Zeta, Washington and Jefferson
1920	*Gamma-Lambda, Chicago* (1937)
1921	Gamma-Beta, Nebraska (1939-1974)
1921	Gamma-Sigma, Southern Methodist
1922	*Gamma-Delta, Vanderbilt* (1938)
1922	Gamma-Omicron, Michigan State
1922	Gamma-Phi, Washington and Lee
1922	Gamma-Pi, Colorado State
1923	Gamma-Mu, Colorado (1937-1947) (1971-1985)
1923	Gamma-Tau, Ohio State (1982-1985)
1924	*Gamma-Eta, Hamilton* (1958)
1924	*Gamma-Theta, Duke* (1969)
1924	Gamma-Upsilon, North Carolina State
1924	Gamma-Xi, Kansas State (1937-1948)
1924	Theta-Alpha, Samford
1924	*Theta-Beta, Baker* (1934)
1924	Theta-Delta, Oklahoma City (1937-1946)
1924	Theta-Eta, Millsaps
1924	*Theta-Gamma, Rollins* (1970)
1924	*Theta-Iota, Iowa Wesleyan* (1974)
1924	Theta-Lambda, Simpson
1924	*Theta-Mu, Birmingham-Southern* (1984)
1924	*Theta-Omicron, Westminster (MO)* (1933)
1924	Theta-Pi, Gettysburg
1924	Theta-Sigma, Drury
1924	*Theta-Tau, Wake Forest* (1984)
1924	Theta-Zeta, Hanover (1983-1986)
1925	Gamma-Chi, Arkansas
1925	*Gamma-Omega, Minnesota* (1938-1947) (1959)
1925	Kappa-Alpha, Marietta
1925	*Kappa-Beta, Oglethorpe* (1934)
1925	Kappa-Gamma, Franklin (1932-1942)
1925	Kappa-Sigma, Alfred
1925	Theta-Chi, Eureka
1925	Theta-Kappa, Rose-Hulman
1925	Theta-Psi, Louisiana Tech
1925	*Theta-Rho, Centenary* (1958)
1925	*Theta-Theta, Clark* (1970)
1925	Theta-Upsilon, New York Tech
1925	Theta-Xi, Thiel
1926	Gamma-Kappa, Missouri
1926	Gamma-Nu, North Carolina (1985-1986)
1926	Gamma-Psi, Lehigh
1926	Gamma-Rho, Oklahoma (1937-1946)
1926	Kappa-Eta, Hampden-Sydney
1926	Kappa-Mu, Culver-Stockton
1926	*Kappa-Omicron, Wofford* (1950)
1926	Kappa-Phi, Baldwin-Wallace (1976-1979)
1926	Kappa-Tau, Randolph, Macon
1927	Epsilon-Alpha, William and Mary
1927	Epsilon-Epsilon, Toronto
1927	Epsilon-Gamma, Idaho (1946-1958) (1985-1990)
1927	*Kappa-Upsilon, Bradley* (1989)
1928	Epsilon-Zeta, North Dakota
1928	Kappa-Omega, Georgetown Col
1929	*Epsilon-Beta, Emory* (1937)
1929	Epsilon-Iota, Nevada
1929	*Epsilon-Lambda, Carnegie-Mellon* (1935)
1930	Epsilon-Phi, Kentucky
1930	Epsilon-Sigma, UCLA
1930	*Kappa-Psi, College Of Idaho* (1935)
1931	Epsilon-Delta, Montana State
1931	*Nu-Epsilon, Muhlenberg* (1937-1940) (1978)
1932	Epsilon-Omicron, Tennessee
1932	*Epsilon-Pi, Maryland* (1974)
1932	Nu-Zeta, Wittenberg
1933	Epsilon-Mu, Florida
1934	*Epsilon-Tau, Colorado Col* (1942)
1937	Epsilon-Eta, R.P.I. (1971-1975)
1937	*Epsilon-Theta, Washington (MD)* (1973)
1937	Epsilon-Upsilon, Tulsa
1938	Epsilon-Xi, Florida Southern (1962-1979)
1939	Epsilon-Chi, Mississippi State
1940	Epsilon-Omega, Miami (FL)
1941	Epsilon-Kappa, Drexel
1942	Beta-Kappa, Georgia Tech
1942	Epsilon-Nu, William Jewell
1945	Epsilon-Psi, South Carolina
1945	Epsilon-Rho, Alberta
1946	Zeta-Alpha, Coe
1946	Zeta-Epsilon, Texas, El Paso (1980-1986)
1946	Zeta-Gamma, New Mexico State (1971-1978)
1946	Zeta-Zeta, Marshall
1947	Zeta-Beta, Arizona (1971-1981)
1947	Zeta-Iota, Kansas
1947	Zeta-Lambda, Connecticut (1950-1955) (1970-1988)
1948	Zeta-Delta, USC (1979-1981)
1948	Zeta-Omicron, Oregon (1965-1985)
1948	Zeta-Phi, Tennessee, Chattanooga
1948	Zeta-Pi, San Diego U (1988-1989)
1948	Zeta-Sigma, Louisville
1949	Zeta-Eta, Cal, Santa Barbara
1949	Zeta-Mu, New Mexico (1965-1969)
1949	Zeta-Tau, Stetson
1949	Zeta-Theta, Memphis State (1982-1984)
1950	*Zeta-Chi, Norwich* (1960)
1950	*Zeta-Kappa, Utah* (1962-1982) (1989)
1950	*Zeta-Nu, San Jose* (1970)
1950	Zeta-Omega, Mercer
1950	Zeta-Rho, Florida State
1950	Zeta-Upsilon, Miami (OH)
1950	*Zeta-Xi, British Columbia* (1962)
1951	Iota-Alpha, Ball State
1951	Zeta-Psi, Arizona State
1952	Iota-Epsilon, Indiana State
1952	Iota-Gamma, Cal State, Fresno
1952	Iota-Zeta, North Texas
1953	Iota-Beta, Lycoming
1953	Iota-Iota, McGill
1953	*Iota-Lambda, West Virginia* (1976)
1954	Iota-Delta, Nebraska, Omaha
1954	Iota-Phi, High Point
1954	Iota-Sigma, Valparaiso
1956	Iota-Mu, Evansville
1956	Iota-Omicron, East Tennessee (1984-1987)
1956	Iota-Pi, Texas Christian
1957	Iota-Eta, Susquehanna
1957	*Iota-Tau, Houston* (1959-1975) (1986)
1959	Iota-Theta, Arkansas State

1959 Iota-Upsilon, East Carolina
1960 Iota-Xi, West Texas
1962 Iota-Chi, Iowa
1962 Iota-Kappa, East Texas
1962 Iota-Omega, Southwestern Louisiana
1963 Iota-Nu, U of the South
1963 Iota-Psi, Ferris
1963 *Iota-Rho, Parsons* (1973)
1964 Lambda-Alpha, New Orleans
1964 Lambda-Epsilon, GMI
1964 Lambda-Gamma, Lock Haven
1964 Lambda-Zeta, Union (TN)
1965 Lambda-Beta, Delaware
1965 Lambda-Iota, Wisconsin, Whitewater
1965 Lambda-Lambda, Western Kentucky
1966 Lambda-Phi, Southwest Texas
1966 *Lambda-Sigma, Steubenville* (1973)
1967 Lambda-Pi, Central Missouri State
1968 Lambda-Eta, Murray State
1968 Lambda-Mu, South Florida
1968 *Lambda-Omicron, Eastern Washington* (1976)
1968 Lambda-Tau, Western Michigan
1968 Lambda-Theta, South Dakota State
1968 Lambda-Upsilon, Northern Michigan
1968 Lambda-Xi, Slippery Rock
1969 Lambda-Chi, Pittsburg State, Kansas
1970 Beta-Alpha, Angelo
1970 Beta-Epsilon, Texas A & I
1970 Beta-Gamma, Indiana (PA)
1970 Beta-Zeta, Western Carolina
1970 *Lambda-Kappa, West Chester* (1980)
1970 *Lambda-Nu, Windsor* (1970)
1970 Lambda-Omega, Central Michigan
1970 *Lambda-Psi, West Liberty* (1985)
1970 *Lambda-Rho, Cal State, Los Angeles* (1985)
1971 Beta-Beta, Glenville
1971 Beta-Delta, Edinboro
1971 Beta-Eta, Central Florida
1971 Beta-Iota, Villanova
1971 Beta-Lambda, Morehead
1971 Beta-Mu, Tennessee Tech.
1971 Beta-Omicron, Illinois State
1971 *Beta-Phi, Florida Atlantic* (1976)
1971 *Beta-Pi, Point Park* (1972)
1971 *Beta-Sigma, Lamar* (1977)
1971 Beta-Tau, Western Illinois
1972 Beta-Chi, Widener
1972 Beta-Nu, Florida Institute
1972 Beta-Omega, Mansfield
1972 Beta-Psi, Southwest Missouri
1972 Beta-Rho, Cal State, Northridge
1972 *Beta-Theta, Missouri Western* (1985)
1972 Beta-Upsilon, North Carolina, Charlotte
1972 Beta-Xi, Bloomsburg
1972 Sigma-Alpha, Vincennes
1972 Sigma-Epsilon, Montevallo
1972 Sigma-Gamma, Kutztown (1976-1979)
1973 Sigma-Beta, St. Mary's, San Antonio
1973 Sigma-Iota, Old Dominion
1973 Sigma-Lambda, V.P.I.
1973 Sigma-Zeta, Texas Wesleyan

1974 *Sigma-Delta, North Alabama* (1981)
1974 Sigma-Omicron, Stephen F. Austin
1974 Sigma-Phi, Embry Riddle (FL)
1974 *Sigma-Pi, Dallas Baptist* (1980)
1974 *Sigma-Sigma, Georgia Southwestern* (1990)
1975 Sigma-Chi, Alabama, Birmingham
1975 Sigma-Eta, Dayton
1975 *Sigma-Mu, Sam Houston* (1985)
1975 Sigma-Tau, Troy
1975 Sigma-Theta, Methodist
1975 Sigma-Upsilon, Appalachian
1975 Sigma-Xi, Southern Tech
1976 Sigma-Kappa, Eastern Michigan
1976 Sigma-Nu, Texas Tech.
1976 *Sigma-Omega, Northern Colorado* (1988)
1976 Sigma-Psi, Baylor
1976 Sigma-Rho, Missouri, Kansas City
1977 Phi-Alpha, Eastern Illinois
1977 Phi-Epsilon, Cal State, Fullerton
1977 *Phi-Gamma, South Alabama* (1982)
1977 Phi-Iota, Shepherd
1977 Phi-Zeta, Arkansas Tech
1978 Phi-Beta, Eastern Kentucky
1978 Phi-Lambda, St. Joseph's (PA)
1979 Phi-Sigma, Cal Poly, San Luis Obispo
1980 Phi-Delta, Maryland, Baltimore County
1980 Phi-Phi, Michigan Tech
1980 Phi-Pi, Cal State, Sacramento
1981 Phi-Omicron, Northern Illinois
1982 Phi-Eta, Madison Col
1982 Phi-Mu, Bowling Green
1982 Phi-Tau, Shippensburg
1983 Phi-Theta, North Carolina, Greensboro
1983 Phi-Upsilon, Texas, San Antonio
1984 Phi-Chi, Cal State, Chico
1984 Phi-Kappa, Auburn, Montgomery
1984 Phi-Omega, Towson
1984 Phi-Xi, Southern Indiana
1985 *Phi-Nu, Adams* (1988)
1986 Phi-Psi, Northeast Missouri
1986 Phi-Rho, Tarleton
1987 Delta-Alpha, North Florida
1987 Delta-Epsilon, Georgia State
1987 Delta-Gamma, Cal, Davis
1988 Delta-Iota, South Carolina, Spartanburg
1988 Delta-Zeta, Calgary

Colonies: Clemson, Elon, Maine, Mankato, Nevada, Las Vegas, North Carolina, Wilmington, Northeastern (OK), Southeast Missouri, Spring Hill, Texas A & M

Lambda Phi Epsilon

On February 25, 1981 LAMBDA PHI EPSILON was founded at the University of California at Los Angeles (U.C.L.A.). Its founder, Craig Ishigo, felt that the existing Asian American fraternity was too large and impersonal. His reasoning was that a fraternity should be of moderate size so members would have close personal ties, creating true brotherhood.

Five years later, two Asian American groups, one from U.C. Davis, and the other from U.C. Santa Barbara were seeking to form Asian American fraternities. They began to search for an existing fraternity, which to model themselves. They chose Lambda Phi Epsilon, citing that the ideology of the fraternity had greater merits than those of others.

At this time, the existing chapters did not feel the need to recruit. Due to its ideology, Lambda Phi Epsilon required dedicated members. It was their logic, therefore, that groups seeking new charters should be equally dedicated. It so happens that there were three new groups who were.

Within a period of eighteen months, three new chapters were started. Groups from Cal., U.C. Irvine, and Texas went to Los Angeles, driving as much as sixty hours, to get a charter. Founding father Craig Ishigo was much impressed with their determination and granted them charters.

Until recently, the chapters of Lambda Phi Epsilon were separate and autonomous entities. Robert Mimaki, presently Executive President, felt that greater unity was needed and that a new, National constitution should be drafted and adopted. On February 16, 1990 the chapters of Lambda Phi Epsilon met to set an agenda for a convention later in the year. The chapters discussed goals for the fraternity and how best to achieve them. Among these topics were adopting a new constitution, and membership in the National Interfraternity Conference. The discussion ended by having each delegate go back to their chapters to discuss the topics at hand.

The convention was held on Memorial Day Weekend, 1990. The issues were debated and voted upon. At the end of the convention, the delegates had agreed upon a National Constitution for the Lambda Phi Epsilon Fraternity. The convention formally ended with the announcement of the host of the second annual convention. It was announced it will be hosted by the Alpha Chapter as it celebrates its 10th year anniversary.

Headquarters P.O. Box 73602, Davis, CA 95617. Phone: (916) 756-5438.

Membership Membership information is not available.

COAT OF ARMS

Phi Delta Theta

ACTIVE PIN

PLEDGE PIN

PHI DELTA THETA was founded at Miami University, Oxford, Ohio, December 26, 1848, by Robert Morrison, 1849; John McMillan Wilson, 1849; Robert Thompson Drake, 1850; John Wolfe Lindley, 1850; Ardivan Walker Rodgers, 1851; and Andrew Watts Rogers, 1851. Morrison first proposed the organization to Wilson, and they were joint authors of "The Bond of the Phi Delta Theta," a statement of the principles of the fraternity which has never been changed. Together they chose the name of the fraternity, and Morrison selected and arranged the secret motto.

The first meeting of the founders of Phi Delta Theta was in Wilson's room in the north dormitory, which still stands. At the semicentennial celebration of the fraternity, in 1898, this room was marked with a granite tablet. Though the new fraternity had the support of members of the Miami faculty, the early members thought they could best accomplish their objects by remaining sub rosa. Meetings were usually held in the rooms of members, but when the active members numbered 11, all could not assemble in any available room without attracting attention. Some of them, therefore, petitioned for a charter to establish a second chapter at Miami, and the petition was granted in April, 1852. At the following commencement the members decided to make the fraternity's existence publicly known, and began wearing badges openly.

Growth The founders of Phi Delta Theta intended that it should be extended to other institutions. Before the first anniversary a chapter had been established at Indiana University, and in the second year a chapter was installed at Centre College in Kentucky. Kentucky Alpha, established at Centre College in 1850, followed the example of the Miami chapter, and divided when its membership reached 19. The charter of the second chapter at Centre was granted in 1855, and was surrendered in the same year. The members of the second chapters at Miami and Centre affiliated again with their original chapters.

Other chapters were soon established and the fraternity had laid the foundation for substantial growth when the War Between the States checked further development and caused the suspension of the chapters at Wisconsin, Lawrence, Northwestern, Ohio Wesleyan, and Franklin. Although a charter was granted for a chapter at Hanover in 1861 it was not then organized.

At the close of the war the only functioning chapters were those at Indiana, Centre, Wabash, Butler, and Michigan. The last named, chartered in 1864, and the Chicago chapter, chartered in 1865, were the only chapters established from 1860 to 1868. In its third decade, 1869-79, the fraternity entered many southern institutions, and in its fourth decade, 1879-89, it established chapters in eastern institutions, making itself national in extent. The Lombard chapter was formed in 1878 from the parent and the only surviving chapter of Phi Sigma. It passed out of existence as a separate chapter when Lombard College in 1930 was absorbed by Knox College and the Lombard chapter was combined with the Knox chapter under the title of Illinois Delta-Zeta.

All the attendant members of the Centre chapter were graduated in 1879, but the chapter was continued by the absorption, in the fall, of the Centre chapter of one of the last remaining chapters of Delta Kappa. In 1885 the active members of the W.W.W., or Rainbow chapters, at the University of Texas, were initiated into the chapter of Phi Delta Theta there. Phi Delta Theta was established at Southwestern University by initiating the members of the Southwestern chapter of W.W.W. These two chapters had disagreed with the others in regard to the policy of uniting with Delta Tau Delta.

Kentucky Delta was established at Central University in 1885. In 1901 Centre College and Central University were consolidated under the former name, and the chapters at the two institutions were combined under the name of Kentucky Alpha-Delta. In 1887 Kappa Sigma Kappa, a fraternity having chapters in Virginia, disintegrated. Its chapters at Washington and Lee, Virginia Military Institute, Randolph-Macon, and Richmond united with Phi Delta Theta.

In 1865 an Indiana state convention was held at Indianapolis. It was the first state convention with chapter representation held by any fraternity. It addition, multi-province meetings are held annually in most areas.

In 1876 the first alumni club was organized at Franklin, Indiana. Charters have since been granted to alumni in Canada, Mexico, China, the Phillipine Islands, and 49 states.

The chapter at the University of the South in 1884, the next year after its establishment, built the first house owned by Phi Delta Theta.

Soon after the turn of the century Phi Delta Theta extended its already broad domain into Canada by establishing chapters at McGill University in 1902 and at the University of Toronto in 1906. Canadian representation was extended from coast to coast when the fraternity entered the universities of Alberta, British Columbia, Dalhousie, and Manitoba in 1930.

Government The original plan of government provided that the parent chapter at Miami should be the presiding chapter, should have the right to charter other chapters in Ohio and to charter the first chapter in each other state. The first chapter in each state was granted the right to charter other chapters in the same state.

The presiding chapter was called the Grand Chapter until 1868 when an executive committee was established. It had a president, a secretary, and a varying number of members. In 1872 its powers were enlarged, and a grand banker was added. From 1876 to 1880 it was composed of a president, a secretary, a grand banker, and one member chosen by the national Grand Chapter. Until 1878 the first chapter in each state was the presiding chapter in that area and was called the state grand chapter. In 1880 the executive committee was changed to the General Council, composed of a president, a secretary, a treasurer, and a historian, and the fraternity was divided into provinces. Full executive powers were then conferred on the General Council. In 1896 an officer known as a reporter was added to the General Council. The five councilors constitute the board of trustees, which acts as a court of appeals to decide questions of legal concern. In 1922 the offices of secretary and historian were abolished and these two officers became members-at-large of the General Council. In 1881 the fraternity was incorporated under the laws of Ohio.

On December 1, 1947, the fraternity completed, and took occupancy of its impressive Memorial Library and General Headquarters Building in Oxford, Ohio. This memorial shrine, done in the tradition of Williamsburg and the Tidewater country of Virginia, provides working quarters for an executive vice president and his staff; a spacious assembly room for conferences; an expansive library of more than 3,500 books and periodicals by and about famous Phis; a room dedicated to the founders, where treasured items of memorabilia are displayed; and guest rooms to accommodate the officers and other members of the fraternity from time to time. The memorial building was formally dedicated on September 5, 1948, at the celebration of Phi Delta Theta's Centennial.

Traditions and Insignia In 1880 Alumni Day was designated as a day for universal observance throughout the fraternity, and in 1910 Founders' Day also was designated to be celebrated annually. In 1891 Alumni Day was discontinued but Founders' Day is still celebrated on March 15, the birthday of Robert Morrison, one of the founders. On this day every year it is the traditional custom for each alumni club to have a social and business meeting, a dinner, and a discussion of fraternity topics. The members of college chapters wear the colors and celebrate the occasion with ritualistic exercises to which all resident alumni are invited.

The badge, consisting of a shield with a scroll bearing the letters ΦΔΘ in the lower part of the field and an eye in the upper part, was adopted in

1849. In 1866 an addition to it was made of a sword attached to the shield by a chain. Argent and azure were selected as fraternity colors in 1871. A coat of arms was adopted in 1866, and the design was changed in 1898. A fraternity flag, adopted in 1889, was redesigned in 1891 and 1896. The latest (1906) design consists of three vertical bars of equal width with the outer bars blue and the middle bar white; each of the outer bars charged with three white five-pointed stars; the middle bar charged with ΦΔΘ letters in blue, reading downward; the width of the whole being two thirds of the length. In 1891 the white carnation was adopted as the fraternity flower. A fraternity cheer was adopted in 1891 and a fraternity whistle in 1894.

Publications Eleven editions of the fraternity catalogues have been issued, beginning in 1860 with 292 names. The 1973 edition, printed in commemoration of the fraternity's 125th year, listed the names of over 130,000 initiates. The most recent edition, published in 1985, lists the names of living members, with a total in excess of 125,000.

Also, directories of the members residing in New York, Philadelphia, Washington, Indianapolis, Chicago, Denver, Portland, Kansas City, and other cities have been published by the alumni clubs of those areas. A yearbook containing a report and a list of the alumni and active members of each chapter was issued annually from 1905 to 1912.

A detailed and complete history of the fraternity from 1848 to 1906, compiled by Walter B. Palmer, was published in the latter year. It is an octavo volume of 966 pages, with 387 illustrations. In 1975, *From Six at First*, a history of Phi Delta Theta, 1848-1973, written by Walter E. Havighurst, was published to commemorate the 125th anniversary.

Two editions of *A Manual of Phi Delta Theta*, containing an historical sketch of the fraternity, college statistics, and other matter, were issued in 1886 and 1897. A third edition, a book of over 300 pages, *Olympian*, was printed in 1912. The fourth edition, published in 1929, is called *The Phikeia— His Book*. A fifth edition was published in 1932. A revised edition, *The Manual of Phi Delta Theta*, was published in 1938. There followed subsequent editions of *Phikeia—The Manual of Phi Delta Theta* in 1940 through 1984, making a total of 27 editions.

A preliminary edition of the fraternity songbook was issued in 1874. Ten editions of the songbook have since been published, the most recent in 1958. A supplement of quartet arrangements was issued in 1938. Several pieces of sheet music inscribed to the fraternity have been published. Over the years, numerous phonograph records and tape recordings, containing fraternity songs, have been produced.

The fraternity journal, called *The Scroll of Phi Delta Theta*, was first issued in January, 1875. In 1875 and 1876 it was a quarterly magazine published at Indianapolis, Indiana. During 1876-78 it was suspended. In 1878 it was revived as a monthly paper. In 1880 it was changed to magazine form again. In 1889 it became a bimonthly. Until 1884 *The Scroll* was a sub rosa periodical. From 1889 to 1917 it was published five times a year, from 1923 to 1933 eight times a year, and from 1933 to 1970 five times a year. Since 1970 it has been published quarterly. *The Palladium*, a quarterly bulletin devoted to the private affairs of the fraternity, was printed from 1884 to 1974. Journals are published by a number of chapters.

Funds and Philanthropies In 1910, the Frank J. R. Mitchell Fund was established to provide for a life subscription to *The Scroll* and *Palladium*. In 1922 the Walter B. Palmer Fund was established to assist chapters and chapter house corporations in purchasing, constructing, and refurnishing houses. In 1946 there was organized the Arthur R. Priest Fund, in memory of the first executive secretary. Part of the principal was used for student loans and the income was used for scholarships. The Phi Delta Theta Educational Foundation, legislated by the 1958 Convention, was incorporated in 1960. The purpose of the foundation is to provide for the advancement of learning, particularly in colleges and universities where chapters of the fraternity are located. This is accomplished through the granting of scholarships or other aid to deserving students in such colleges and universities and through the extension of financial or other aid in the furtherance of educational activities conducted at such colleges or universities. The Priest Fund was merged with the foundation in 1970.

The David D. Banta Memorial Library is located in the General Headquarters Building in Oxford, Ohio. It contains large collections of the works of Phi authors, many of them rare, and items of fraternity memorabilia. There are files of all publications of Phi Delta Theta and many of other fraternities. Included also is a large collection of reference books on higher education and descriptive material about North American colleges and universities. There is a considerable collection of texts referring to the Greek-letter fraternity system. An endowment fund, designed to support the library, was established in 1955. It was merged with the Phi Delta Theta Foundation in 1984.

Headquarters Phi Delta Theta General Headquarters, 2 South Campus Avenue, Oxford, OH 45056. Phone: (513) 523-6345.

Membership Total living membership 127,389. Total undergraduate membership 9,479. Active chapters 180. Inactive chapters 36. Colonies 11. Houses owned 125. City/Area alumni associations 85. Total number of initiates 174,930. Chapter roll:

1848 Ohio Alpha, Miami (OH) (1857-1865) (1873-1885)
1849 Indiana Alpha, Indiana
1850 Indiana Beta, Wabash
1850 *Kentucky Alpha, Centre College* (1901) (Merged with Kentucky Delta, 1901)
1852 *Ohio Gamma Prime, Wittenberg* (1854)
1853 *Texas Alpha Prime, Austin* (1854)

1854	*Kentucky Beta, Kentucky Military* (1856)
1857	*Kentucky Gamma, Georgetown Col.* (1876)
1857	Wisconsin Alpha, Wisconsin, Madison (1861-1880) (1970-1977)
1859	Illinois Alpha, Northwestern (1861-1886)
1859	Indiana Gamma, Butler
1859	Wisconsin Beta, Lawrence (1859-1934)
1860	Indiana Delta, Franklin
1860	Ohio Beta, Ohio Wesleyan (1861-1871) (1877-1879)
1861	Indiana Epsilon, Hanover
1864	Michigan Alpha, Michigan
1865	Illinois Beta, Chicago (1871-1897)
1868	Indiana Zeta, DePauw
1868	Ohio Gamma, Ohio (1976-1980)
1869	Indiana Eta, Indiana State (1870-1969)
1869	*Virginia Alpha, Roanoke* (1896)
1870	Missouri Alpha, Missouri
1871	Georgia Alpha, Georgia
1871	*Georgia Alpha Prime, Oglethorpe* (1872)
1871	Georgia Beta, Emory
1871	*Illinois Delta, Knox* (1930) (Merged with Illinois Zeta, 1930)
1871	*Illinois Gamma, Monmouth (IL)* (1884)
1871	Iowa Alpha, Iowa Wesleyan
1872	Georgia Gamma, Mercer
1872	New York Alpha, Cornell (1876-1886)
1872	*Ohio Delta, Wooster* (1897)
1873	California Alpha, Cal, Berkeley
1873	Michigan Beta, Michigan State (1898-1931)
1873	Pennsylvania Alpha, Lafayette
1873	Virginia Beta, Virginia
1874	Virginia Gamma, Randolph, Macon
1875	Nebraska Alpha, Nebraska
1875	Ohio Epsilon, Akron (1869-1924)
1875	Pennsylvania Beta, Gettysburg
1875	Pennsylvania Gamma, Washington and Jefferson
1875	Virginia Delta, Richmond (1895-1939)
1876	*Missouri Beta Prime, Central* (1878)
1876	Pennsylvania Eta, Lehigh (1877-1887)
1876	Tennessee Alpha, Vanderbilt
1877	Alabama Alpha, Alabama
1877	Mississippi Alpha, Mississippi (1912-1926)
1878	*Illinois Epsilon, Illinois Wesleyan* (1897)
1878	*Illinois Zeta, Lombard* (1930) (Merged with Illinois Delta, 1930)
1878	North Carolina Alpha, Duke (1879-1926)
1878	*Texas Alpha, Trinity (TX)* (1883)
1878	*Virginia Epsilon, V.M.I.* (1889)
1879	Alabama Beta, Auburn
1879	Pennsylvania Delta, Allegheny
1879	*South Carolina Alpha, Wofford* (1885)
1879	Vermont Alpha, Vermont
1880	Missouri Beta, Westminster (MO)
1880	Pennsylvania Epsilon, Dickinson
1881	Minnesota Alpha, Minnesota
1882	Iowa Beta, Iowa
1882	Kansas Alpha, Kansas
1882	*Michigan Gamma, Hillsdale* (1898)
1882	South Carolina Beta, South Carolina (1893-1964)
1883	New York Beta, Union (NY)
1883	Ohio Zeta, Ohio State
1883	Pennsylvania Zeta, Penn
1883	Tennessee Beta, Sewanee
1883	Texas Beta, Texas
1884	*Maine Alpha, Colby* (1986)
1884	*New Hampshire Alpha, Dartmouth* (1960)
1884	*New York Delta, Columbia (NY)* (1935)
1884	*New York Gamma, CUNY, Brooklyn* (1891)
1885	*Kentucky Delta, Central* (1901) (Merged with Kentucky Alpha, 1901)
1885	North Carolina Beta, North Carolina
1886	*Massachusetts Alpha, Williams* (1966)
1886	Texas Gamma, Southwestern (TX)
1887	*Alabama Gamma, Southern* (1896)
1887	New York Epsilon, Syracuse
1887	Virginia Zeta, Washington and Lee
1888	*Massachusetts Beta, Amherst* (1956)
1889	*Louisiana Alpha, Tulane* (1970)
1889	*Rhode Island Alpha, Brown* (1968)
1891	California Beta, Stanford
1891	Missouri Gamma, Washington (MO)
1893	Illinois Eta, Illinois
1893	Indiana Theta, Purdue
1896	Ohio Eta, Case Tech
1898	Ohio Theta, Cincinnati
1900	Washington Alpha, Washington (WA)
1901	Kentucky Alpha Delta, Centre College (Merger of Centre College and Central University)
1901	Kentucky Epsilon, Kentucky
1902	Colorado Alpha, Colorado
1902	Georgia Delta, Georgia Tech
1902	Quebec Alpha, McGill (1974-1978)
1904	Pennsylvania Theta, Penn State
1906	Ontario Alpha, Toronto
1906	South Dakota Alpha, South Dakota
1908	Idaho Alpha, Idaho
1910	Kansas Beta, Washburn
1912	Oregon Alpha, Oregon
1913	Colorado Beta, Colorado Col
1913	Iowa Gamma, Iowa State
1913	North Dakota Alpha, North Dakota
1914	Ohio Iota, Denison
1914	Utah Alpha, Utah
1914	Washington Beta, Whitman
1918	New York Zeta, Colgate
1918	Oklahoma Alpha, Oklahoma
1918	Oregon Beta, Oregon State
1918	Pennsylvania Iota, Pitt (1964-1971)
1918	*Pennsylvania Kappa, Swarthmore* (1958)
1918	Washington Gamma, Washington State
1920	Colorado Gamma, Colorado State (1938-1952) (1976-1988)
1920	Kansas Gamma, Kansas State
1920	Montana Alpha, Montana
1922	Arizona Alpha, Arizona
1922	Texas Delta, Southern Methodist
1924	California Gamma, UCLA
1924	Florida Alpha, Florida
1926	West Virginia Alpha, West Virginia
1928	North Carolina Gamma, Davidson

1930	Alberta Alpha, Alberta
1930	British Columbia Alpha, British Columbia
1930	Illinois Delta Zeta, Knox (Merger of Lombard and Knox)
1930	Manitoba Alpha, Manitoba
1930	Maryland Alpha, Maryland
1930	Nova Scotia Alpha, Dalhousie
1932	Massachusetts Gamma, M.I.T.
1934	Florida Beta, Rollins (1943-1968)
1934	Wyoming Alpha, Wyoming
1938	Louisiana Beta, L.S.U.
1946	*New Mexico Alpha, New Mexico* (1982)
1946	Oklahoma Beta, Oklahoma State
1946	Oregon Gamma, Willamette
1948	Arkansas Alpha, Arkansas
1948	California Delta, USC
1950	Florida Gamma, Florida State
1950	*Illinois Theta, Lake Forest* (1961)
1950	Ohio Kappa, Bowling Green
1952	Washington Delta, Puget Sound
1953	Texas Epsilon, Texas Tech.
1954	California Epsilon, Cal, Davis
1954	*Florida Delta, Miami (FL)* (1982)
1954	Indiana Iota, Valparaiso
1954	Ohio Lambda, Kent (1972-1988)
1955	Texas Zeta, Texas Christian
1958	Arizona Beta, Arizona State
1959	Kansas Delta, Wichita
1960	Wisconsin Gamma, Ripon
1961	Iowa Delta, Drake
1962	Ontario Beta, Western Ontario (1976-1984)
1962	Texas Eta, Stephen F. Austin
1963	Tennessee Gamma, Tennessee
1964	*Kentucky Zeta, Kentucky Wesleyan* (1974)
1964	Michigan Delta, GMI
1964	Minnesota Beta, Mankato
1964	Texas Theta, West Texas
1965	Texas Iota, Lamar
1966	California Zeta, Cal State, Northridge
1966	Kentucky Eta, Western Kentucky
1966	Nebraska Beta, Kearney
1966	Ohio Mu, Ashland
1967	California Eta, Cal, Santa Barbara
1967	Florida Epsilon, South Florida
1968	Florida Zeta, Jacksonville
1968	Kansas Epsilon, Emporia
1968	Louisiana Gamma, Southwestern Louisiana (1982-1985)
1968	*Montana Beta, Montana State* (1976)
1968	Texas Kappa, Texas, Arlington
1969	Indiana Kappa, Ball State
1969	Kentucky Theta, Eastern Kentucky
1969	Tennessee Delta, Tennessee Tech.
1970	*Alberta Beta, Calgary* (1976)
1970	South Carolina Gamma, Clemson
1971	Georgia Epsilon, Georgia Southern
1971	Maryland Beta, Western Maryland
1971	Oklahoma Gamma, Southwestern State (OK)
1972	Nevada Alpha, Nevada
1972	Virginia Eta, V.P.I.
1973	*Florida Eta, West Florida* (1974)
1973	*Ohio Nu, Youngstown State* (1978)

1975	California Theta, Cal, Irvine
1975	Georgia Zeta, Georgia Col
1977	Texas Lambda, Baylor
1978	California Iota, San Jose
1979	Florida Theta, Tampa
1979	Louisiana Delta, L.S.U., Shreveport
1980	Texas Mu, Southwest Texas
1981	Florida Iota, Central Florida
1982	California Kappa, Cal, San Diego
1982	Oregon Delta, Oregon Tech
1983	Michigan Epsilon, Northwood (MI)
1983	Missouri Delta, St. Louis
1983	New Hampshire Beta, New Hampshire
1984	Pennsylvania Lambda, Indiana (PA)
1985	Missouri Epsilon, Southwest Missouri
1985	Pennsylvania Mu, Widener
1985	Texas Nu, Texas A & M
1986	California Lambda, Pacific (CA)
1986	Indiana Lambda, Southern Indiana
1986	New York Eta, Rochester Tech
1987	California Mu, Cal, Riverside
1987	California Nu, Cal Poly, Pomona
1987	West Virginia Beta, Marshall
1988	British Columbia Beta, Victoria (BC)
1988	California Omicron, Cal State, Sacramento
1988	California Xi, Cal State, Chico
1988	Florida Kappa, Florida International
1988	New Jersey Alpha, Rutgers
1988	North Carolina Delta, North Carolina State
1988	Pennsylvania Nu, West Chester
1988	Wisconsin Delta, Marquette
1989	California Pi, San Diego U
1989	New Mexico Alpha, New Mexico
1990	Massachusetts Delta, Bentley
1990	Ontario Gamma, McMaster
1990	Texas Xi, Texas, San Antonio

Colonies: North Carolina, Marquette, Nevada, Las Vegas, SUNY Col., Oneonta, Washington (MD), Mississippi State, SUNY Col., Buffalo, Cameron, York (PA), Sam Houston, Eastern Washington

Phi Gamma Delta

ACTIVE PIN

PHI GAMMA DELTA was founded in the room of John Templeton McCarty in "Fort" Armstrong, a dormitory of Jefferson College, Canonsburg, Pennsylvania, on the night of April 22, 1848. A constitution was adopted on May 1, 1848, which is recognized as Founders' Day. The founders were: John Templeton McCarty, 1848; James Elliot, Jr., 1848; Daniel Webster Crofts, 1848; Samuel Beatty Wilson, 1848; Ellis Bailey Gregg, 1848, and Naaman Fletcher, 1849. McCarty was a student at Miami University in 1845 and 1846. He enrolled at Jefferson in 1847. Fletcher had been admitted to the bar before entering Jefferson. The first meeting of the organization provided for the establishment of "foreign chapters." The patronage of Jefferson College being largely from southern states, it was natural that expansion should be in the South; of the first 16 chapters organized prior to the Civil War, 11 were in southern states.

The McMillan Log Cabin, the first Jefferson College building at Canonsburg, is in the perpetual care of the fraternity and bears a bronze tablet in memory of the founders. In 1952, the centennial year of Phi Kappa Psi, that other member of the "Jefferson Duo" accepted the invitation to share in the custody of the cabin. In 1909 the graves of all the founders of the fraternity were marked by suitable memorials.

Growth The Washington chapter, Beta, established the same year as Alpha, became consolidated with that chapter when the two colleges were united as Washington and Jefferson College. Gamma, situated at the University of Nashville, lived but a year. Delta at Union (Tennessee), Epsilon at North Carolina, Theta at Alabama, Kappa at Baylor, Mu at Howard (Alabama), and Rho at Transylvania were killed by the Civil War. Xi at Gettysburg and Pi at Allegheny had almost their entire membership enrolled in the army on the Union or the Confederate side.

Anti-fraternity laws killed the chapters at Monmouth, Georgia, and Wooster. The charters of the Hampden-Sydney, Roanoke, College of the City of New York, Bethel, and Trinity chapters were surrendered because of the decline in the number of eligible candidates for membership. Currently the fraternity is renewing its ties with these institutions and, in 1966, had established colonies at Georgia and Hampden-Sydney (now chapters). The second Chi chapter at Racine College, died with that institution closed its doors.

Government The Ekklesia, or convention, which meets every two years, is the fraternity's supreme governing body. A leadership training school for chapter officers, known as the Fiji Academy, is convened in years between Ekklesiai. Section conventions are held annually by the section chief in each of the fraternity's 35 sections.

Until 1868 when the faculty abolished secret fraternities, Alpha at Jefferson College was the grand chapter and thus was the center of the fraternity's government during the recess of conventions. Later the grand chapter was transferred to New York. In 1898 the system of government was entirely changed so that the Ekklesia, meeting biennially and consisting of elected delegates from the undergraduate and graduate chapters, supplanted the old grand chapter form of government.

Between Ekklesiai, certain administrative matters of the fraternity are handled by seven general officers, elected by and answerable to the Ekklesiai, and known as the Archonate. The seven Archons include a president, vice-president, secretary, treasurer, and three councilors. The executive director, editor of *The Phi Gamma Delta*, director of chapter services, director of programs, and five field secretaries are employed in full-time service as the staff of the fraternity's general headquarters office.

Traditions and Insignia The fraternity was the first to advance the chapter tutor plan; it also pioneered the vocational placement plan through the Fiji Vocational Bureau.

Distinguished Fiji Awards are presented annually to six outstanding members of the fraternity. Yearly the most outstanding senior undergraduate member is chosen to receive to receive the Cecil J. Wilkinson (Ohio Wesleyan '17) Award. The Francis M. Durrance (Washington & Lee '07) Award is given each year to the outstanding Purple Legionnaire, or chapter adviser. Other awards include the Archon's Trophy, the Baker Social Service Cup, the Cheney Efficiency Cup, the Condon Cup, the Coulter Cup, the Brightman Trophy and Brightman Awards, the Jordan Bowl, the Coon Plaque, the Owen Scholarship Cup, and the McCarty Awards.

The badge, known as the founders' badge, is lozenge shaped, having a black background and displaying the letters ΦΓΔ, above which is a single star in white enamel, and below, the letters αωμη. The color is royal purple, and the flower is the purple clematis. The flag is rectangular in shape and bears the Greek letters, ΦΓΔ across the face upon a royal purple background. In the upper right-hand corner is a white star. The pledge pin or button is a five-pointed star in white enamel. The recognition pin is the same shape as the badge, with a length of five-sixteenths of an inch. Its exposed face is of enamel, showing a white star in the center of a black background. Beginning in 1884, individual coats of arms for each chapter were used secretly, until the publication of the catalogue of 1895.

Publications Catalogues of membership were published in 1856, 1862, 1870, 1878, 1895, 1898, 1907, 1913, 1925, 1930, and 1940, the fraternity having pioneered the idea of publishing membership rolls as an issue of its magazine. Departing from this custom, the 1962 directory of membership was a separate volume of more than 200,000 listings and was the first published in 22 years. It was followed by a similar directory in 1979.

The journal, a quarto in form, was first issued as a monthly in 1879, under the auspices of the Ohio Wesleyan chapter, and was called *Phi Gamma Delta*. In 1884 it was reduced in size to octavo. After two years the name was changed to the *Phi Gamma Delta Quarterly*. In 1889 its name became *The Phi Gamma Delta*. In 1961 the size was changed to 8½ x 11. Every living member receives the magazine for life.

The first songbook was issued in 1886. Subsequent editions were published in 1898, 1908, 1922, 1932, 1959, and 1967. In 1960 the fraternity issued a record album, *The Songs of Phi Gamma Delta*, which is now available as a tape.

A comprehensive history in two volumes of 350 octavo pages each is the work of William F. Chamberlin (Denison '93). Tomos Alpha and Tomos Beta, as they are called, have been published. A thesaurus is updated annually, and numerous guidebooks on fraternity affairs have been published.

Funds and Philanthropies Although an entity separate from the international fraternity, the Phi Gamma Delta Educational Foundation was chartered as an educational nonprofit corporation by the regents of the University of the State of New York 1n 1945, and it maintains its principal office in Washington, D.C. The foundation annually provides from six to eight fellowship grants for graduate study as well as undergraduate achievement awards and promotes the educational and cultural objectives of Phi Gamma Delta.

Separate from the Educational Foundation, a substantial endowment of the fraternity is administered by a board of trustees, who are the fraternity's fiscal and legal agents. The board consists of six graduate brothers.

A Chapter Loan Fund is administered by the Archons for loans to chapter house corporations seeking second mortgage funds for construction and/or renovation of chapter house.

Headquarters P.O. Box 4599, Lexington, KY 40544. Phone: (606) 255-1848. The handsome international headquarters building is custom-designed and has been occupied by the fraternity since April, 1985.

Membership Total living membership 83,500. Total undergraduate membership 6,500. Active chapters 126. Inactive chapters 38. Colonies 2. Houses owned 84. Graduate/Alumni chapters 77. Total number of initiates 131,134. Chapter roll:

1848 Alpha, Washington and Jefferson
1850 *Gamma, Nashville State* (1850)
1851 *Delta, Union (TN)* (1873)
1851 Epsilon, North Carolina
1852 *Zeta, Washington (TN)* (1852)
1855 *Eta, Marietta* (1897)
1855 Theta, Alabama
1856 *Iota, Centre College* (1856)
1856 Kappa, Baylor (1886-1978)
1856 Lambda, DePauw
1856 *Mu, Howard (AL)* (1861)
1856 *Nu, Bethel* (1912)
1858 Xi, Gettysburg
1859 Omicron, Virginia
1860 Pi, Allegheny
1860 *Rho, Transylvania* (1862)
1864 Tau, Hanover
1865 Phi, Baker (1868-1931)
1865 *Upsilon, CUNY, Brooklyn* (1906)
1866 Alpha Deuteron, Illinois Wesleyan
1866 *Beta Deuteron, Roanoke* (1905)
1866 *Chi, Waco* (1868)
1866 Omega, Columbia (NY)
1866 Psi, Wabash
1867 Delta Deuteron, Northwestern (1869-1931)

1867 *Epsilon Deuteron, Muhlenberg* (1894)
1867 Gamma Deuteron, Knox
1868 *Eta Deuteron, Mississippi* (1879)
1868 Zeta Deuteron, Washington and Lee
1869 *Chi, Monmouth (IL)* (1871)
1869 *Iota Deuteron, Cumberland (TN)* (1878)
1869 Theta Deuteron, Ohio Wesleyan
1870 Delta Deuteron, Hampden-Sydney (1904-1967)
1871 Kappa Deuteron, Georgia (1891-1968)
1871 Zeta, Indiana
1872 *Lambda Deuteron, Thiel* (1873)
1873 Mu Deuteron, Iowa
1875 *Nu Deuteron, Yale* (1965)
1876 Xi Deuteron, Case Western Reserve
1878 Omicron Deuteron, Ohio State
1878 Phi Deuteron, Maryland (1883-1979)
1880 *Chi, Racine* (1887)
1880 *Iota, Williams* (1913-1913) (1965)
1881 Beta, Penn
1881 Delta Xi, Cal, Berkeley (1884-1886)
1881 Pi Deuteron, Kansas
1882 Delta, Bucknell
1882 *Rho Deuteron, Wooster* (1913)
1883 Sigma Deuteron, Lafayette
1883 Tau Deuteron, Texas
1884 Sigma, Wittenberg
1885 Alpha Phi, Michigan
1885 Lambda Deuteron, Denison
1886 Zeta Phi, William Jewell
1887 Beta Chi, Lehigh
1887 *Theta Psi, Colgate* (1969-1976) (1988)
1888 Gamma Phi, Penn State
1888 Kappa Nu, Cornell (1987-1991)
1889 Iota Mu, M.I.T.
1890 Kappa Tau, Tennessee
1890 Mu Sigma, Minnesota
1890 Rho Chi, Richmond
1891 Beta Mu, Johns Hopkins
1891 *Lambda Sigma Society, Stanford* (1971)
1891 Pi Iota, Worcester Tech
1892 Nu Epsilon, N.Y.U.
1893 *Alpha Chi, Amherst* (1962)
1893 Chi, Union (NY)
1893 Mu, Wisconsin, Madison
1893 *Tau Alpha, Trinity (CT)* (1922)
1897 Chi Iota, Illinois
1898 Lambda Nu, Nebraska
1899 Chi Mu, Missouri
1899 Omega Mu, Maine
1900 Sigma Tau, Washington (WA)
1901 *Delta Nu, Dartmouth* (1965)
1901 Sigma Nu, Syracuse
1902 Chi Upsilon, Chicago
1902 Lambda Iota, Purdue
1902 *Pi Rho, Brown* (1968)
1907 Alpha Iota, Iowa State
1908 Chi Sigma, Colorado Col
1911 Epsilon Omicron, Oregon (1969-1977)
1912 Beta Kappa, Colorado (1969-1976)
1916 Nu Omega, Oklahoma
1916 Pi Sigma, Pitt

1917 Nu Beta, Rutgers
1919 Gamma Sigma, Sewanee
1920 Mu Iota, Idaho
1921 Kappa Omicron, Oregon State
1923 Delta Kappa, Davidson
1923 Tau Kappa, Toronto
1926 Gamma Tau, Georgia Tech
1926 *Omega Kappa, Occidental* (1969)
1929 Pi Gamma, British Columbia
1931 Lambda Alpha, UCLA (1971-1979)
1931 Upsilon Alpha, Arizona
1940 Upsilon Phi, Florida
1948 Beta Rho, L.S.U.
1948 Delta Tau, Southern Methodist
1948 *Mu Kappa, McGill* (1968)
1948 *Phi Mu, Westminster (MO)* (1988)
1948 Sigma Chi, USC
1950 Kappa Rho, Rhode Island
1950 Pi Mu, Washington State
1954 Lambda Tau, Texas Tech.
1957 Mu Upsilon, Miami (OH)
1958 *Lambda Kappa, Lawrence* (1988)
1958 *Upsilon Kappa, Kentucky* (1983)
1959 Epsilon Lambda, Michigan State
1960 *Kappa Upsilon, Kent* (1980)
1962 Alpha Upsilon, Auburn
1962 Sigma Omicron, Oklahoma State
1964 Alpha Gamma, G.M.I.
1965 Alpha Sigma, Arizona State
1965 Delta Gamma, Emory
1966 Alpha Nu, New Mexico
1966 Alpha Omega, Ohio
1966 *Tau Omicron, Puget Sound* (1971)
1967 *Lambda Upsilon, Wyoming* (1975)
1967 Phi Sigma, Florida State
1968 Chi Deuteron, Kansas State
1968 Lambda Omega, Western Ontario
1968 Phi Kappa, Colorado State
1968 Phi Tau, Texas, Arlington
1968 Upsilon Sigma, Utah State
1969 Beta Upsilon, Vermont
1969 Phi Alpha, Arkansas
1969 Rho Phi, Rose-Hulman
1970 Epsilon Alpha, Alberta
1970 Sigma Mu, Mississippi State
1971 Chi Omicron, Cincinnati
1971 Iota Sigma, Indiana State
1971 *Kappa Phi, South Florida* (1981)
1972 Kappa Mu, Western Michigan
1972 Mu Tau, Memphis State
1972 Rho Alpha, V.P.I.
1974 *Chi Alpha, Clemson* (1988)
1974 Mu Alpha, West Virginia
1974 Phi Upsilon, North Alabama
1975 Epsilon Chi, Wisconsin, Eau Claire
1975 *Phi Iota, Idaho State* (1983)
1977 Rho Upsilon, Cal, Riverside
1978 Omega Deuteron, Old Dominion
1979 Alpha Mu, Texas A & M
1980 Tau Chi, Texas Christian
1981 *Delta Upsilon, Denver* (1990)
1981 Theta Tau, Tennessee Tech.

1982 Beta Pi, Bradley
1982 Iota Chi, Cal, Irvine
1982 Tau Upsilon, Tulane
1983 Delta Phi, Jacksonville
1984 Beta Gamma, Bowling Green
1984 Tau Nu, R.P.I.
1984 Upsilon Chi, Calgary
1985 Gamma Kappa, Colorado Mines
1985 Upsilon Lambda, LaSalle
1986 Alpha Omicron, Akron
1986 Sigma Delta, San Diego U
1987 Phi Chi, Cal State, Fresno
1987 Upsilon Mu, Montana
1988 Sigma Lambda, Utah
1989 San Jose
1990 Villanova

Colonies: Cal State, Long Beach, Southwest Texas

COAT OF ARMS

Phi Kappa Psi†

ACTIVE PIN

PLEDGE PIN

PHI KAPPA PSI was founded at Jefferson College in Canonsburg, Pennsylvania, on February 19, 1852. That winter there had been an outbreak of typhoid fever that struck the town and the college. William Henry Letterman of Canonsburg and Charles Page Thomas Moore of Mason County, Virginia, tended the stricken and through long days and nights of selfless labor came to understand "the great joy of serving others." Already friends, they were inspired to give lasting form to their experience through the creation of a new fraternity, whose principles, ideals, and purposes would express the highest standard of brotherhood. Thus, when they met at the Letterman home on February 19, their intention from the beginning was to found an order that would grow to include men of honor and good will at colleges throughout America.

Moore entered the law school at the University of Virginia and established the fraternity's second chapter there in 1853. Letterman enrolled at the Jefferson Medical College in Philadelphia in 1854 and entrusted the stewardship of Phi Kappa Psi to his brothers, foremost of whom was Thomas Cochran Campbell, who had grown up in India. It was Campbell who created the essential ritual of the fraternity, conducted much of its business, wrote its documents, and vitally influenced its early de-

† This chapter narrative is repeated from the 19th edition; no current information was provided.

velopment. At the start of the Civil War, the fraternity numbered eight northern chapters and nine southern ones; the conflict closed the southern chapters, although five were eventually revived. However, it was nearly a century before the fraternity reestablished itself in the southeastern states on a broad scale.

During the mid-1860s, the fraternity expanded vigorously into the middle west, then advanced to the northeast, the plains states, the upper middle west in the 1870s and '80s, and reached the far west as well as New England in the 1890s.

Its policy was not to form chapters at every institution or in every state, but at respected colleges and universities, private and public alike, and to do so gradually and deliberately. Hence the careful, steady pace of the fraternity's extension is often characterized as conservative. From the Depression until the end of World War II, only two chapters were formed, but in recent years the rate of growth has markedly increased. The fraternity's practice has been to establish only those chapters it could responsibly support; it has also worked to reestablish lapsed chapters. The fraternity restricts its chapters to North America, although admission to membership is open to foreign nationals. For that matter, it has from its origin been free of exclusionary conditions, requiring only that prospective members be "educated men of talent and virtue."

Government Since 1853, the fraternity has vested its supreme authority in the Grand Arch Council, which is composed of three delegates from each chapter, one of whom is an alumnus. The alumni associations are also entitled to voting representatives, but the balance between undergraduates and alumni is usually more than seven to one. Until 1886, the interim governing body between the biennial GACs was the Grand Chapter, which was one of the regular collegiate chapters selected by the GAC to conduct the general fraternity's affairs. The inefficiency of this arrangement led to the adoption in 1886 of a new constitution, which provided for the election of the Executive Council, composed of both alumni and undergraduate officers. Today the Executive Council consists of four alumni members who serve as general officers elected to two-year terms by the G.A.C., and six undergraduate officers, titled Archons, each of whom is elected to a two-year term at one of the fraternity's six District Councils. Thus, Phi Kappa Psi is distinctive in its undergraduate authority and, in theory, control because in the Grand Arch Council, the District Councils, and the Executive Council undergraduate members form the majority over the alumni.

The author of the fraternity's constitution and system of government was William Clayton Wilson, whose work remains substantially unchanged to the present. The Executive Council also includes a number of appointive officers who discharge prescribed duties but serve without vote: attorney general, mystagogue, scholarship director, director of fraternity education, director of alumni relations, director of chapter finance, and others as necessary. All officers, elective and appointive, undergraduate and alumni, serve the fraternity as volunteers.

Traditions Since its early years, Phi Psi alumni have returned to their chapters to meet undergraduates and to celebrate reunion. This custom, still widely carried on, is called "symposium." The fraternity's Founders Day is celebrated each year on or about February 19 at alumni associations and chapters throughout America. The fraternity sponsors the Woodrow Wilson Leadership Schools in connection with the six District Councils, which are conducted on campuses every two years. The Schools are for the benefit of undergraduates, chapter and faculty advisers, and alumni.

Within the fraternity there is a secret society, "The Order of S.C.," which has no counterpart among other fraternities. Founded in 1920, it comprises loyal Phi Psis who regularly attend the GACs.

The fraternity colors are cardinal red and hunter's green, and the flower the Jacqueminot rose. The official anthems are "Amici usque ad aras" and "Noble Fraternity."

Phi Kappa Psi is a private, voluntary society of educated men. In keeping with its character, it encourages discretion and restraint in the use of its badge, letters, coat of arms, colors, songs, and flag. It disapproves of public display, commercial exploitation, or any unsuitable use of its name and insignia. By mandate of the Grand Arch Council, it does not allow its chapters to form auxiliary organizations for young women. Since the end of the Civil War, Phi Kappa Psi has consistently opposed the practice of hazing, regularly issuing instructions to that effect. The fraternity was also a pioneer in the movement toward interfraternity cooperation as one of the founders of the National Interfraternity Conference.

Foundations The Endowment Fund of Phi Kappa Psi was established in 1914 to provide loans to worthy brothers in need of assistance to complete their studies. Since that time the Endowment Fund has broadened its purposes to encourage achievement in scholarship, leadership, and service through a variety of programs, grants, and awards. These include the Founders Fellowships, the Solon E. Summerfield Scholarships, the Tutors-in-Residence grants, and the Mary Pickford Rogers Scholarship, among a number.

The Endowment Fund is led by three alumni trustees elected by the GAC and administered by its staff. It is a public, tax-exempt foundation maintained by voluntary contributions. It also sustains the headquarters building and related properties.

The Permanent Fund, established in 1930 and also led by three alumni trustees, sustains many of the fraternity's programs. The General Fund derives its income from initiation and pledge fees, disbursements from the Endowment and Permanent

Funds, and from the sale of merchandise approved by the Executive Council. It supports the operations and services of the fraternity headquarters, the Executive Council, and the fraternity at large.

Publications *The Shield of Phi Kappa Psi* was established in 1879 by Edgar Fahs Smith. First published in Philadelphia, the magazine has been issued as a monthly, ten-times per year, and now as a quarterly periodical. It is sent to all members under a lifetime subscription included in the initiation fee. An educational journal, *The Shield* regularly carries articles about current developments in higher education and the fraternity movement, reviews of books by Phi Psi authors, news about noteworthy Phi Psis and the activities of the general fraternity, newsletters from the chapters and alumni associations, obituaries, historical articles, and essays. It maintains one of the largest circulations among fraternity journals.

Published in 1902, *The History of the Phi Kappa Psi Fraternity 1852–1902* by Charles Liggett Van Cleve was the first official record. It was succeeded in 1952 by *The Centennial History of The Phi Kappa Psi Fraternity 1852–1952* by J. Duncan Campbell and Harry S. Gorgas, published in two volumes. *The Manual of Phi Kappa Psi Fraternity* was edited by Henry S. Griffing and first published in 1931; several editors have brought out later revisions, and *The Manual* is now in its 15th edition. It is presented to each pledge at the time of his formal induction into a chapter's pledge class.

"The Mystic Friend," an esoteric letter established by Thomas Cochran Campbell, is issued irregularly to initiates. *The Lamplighter*, a newsletter written by the fraternity's executive director, appears frequently and is circulated to members involved in the leadership of the fraternity. Phi Kappa Psi occasionally prints new editions of *The Ritual and Ceremonies* and *The Constitution and By-Laws*, which are private documents for the exclusive use of its initiates.

From time to time, the fraternity publishes special booklets on chapter management and finance, rushing, scholarship, etiquette, and subjects related to higher education and fraternity life. The fraternity's annual report is made available in *The Shield*. *The Grand Catalogue of Phi Kappa Psi*, which includes names of all initiates, current addresses, a geographical directory, and chapter rosters, was first issued in 1860. Later editions include chronological lists of officers; the thirteenth was published in 1991.

Fraternity Headquarters The first professional executive officer of Phi Kappa Psi was C. F. (Dab) Williams, who served as secretary from 1930 to 1956. His successor was Ralph D. (Dud) Daniel, who was secretary, executive secretary, and executive director from 1956 to 1979. The current executive director is Terrence G. Harper, who took office in 1990.

The original offices were established in 1929 in Cleveland, Ohio, and were moved in 1978 to a restored nineteenth century townhouse on Lockerbie Street in downtown Indianapolis, Indiana. The headquarters building contains, in addition to administrative officers, the Woodrow Wilson Library, the Thomas Cochran Campbell Sanctum, museum displays, and archives. The fraternity also owns a nearby residence for the use of its Educational Leadership Consultants, a staff of recent graduates who provide skilled guidance to chapters throughout the country during the academic year.

The headquarters building is the site of the Executive Council's winter meeting and is frequently used by chapters, alumni associations, other men's fraternities, and women's fraternities. Visitors are welcome, and guided tours are available to larger groups with advance arrangements.

The address is 510 Lockerbie Street (corner of East and Lockerbie streets), Indianapolis, IN 46202. Phone: (317) 632-1852.

Membership Living membership 47,442. Active chapters 94. Inactive chapters 32. Colonies 8. Houses owned 50. City/Area Alumni associations 76. Chapter roll:

1852	PA Alpha, Washington and Jefferson (1868-1873) (united with Washington, 1864)
1853	VA Alpha, Virginia (1861-1865)
1855	PA Beta, Allegheny
1855	*PA Delta, Washington College* (1864) (united with Jefferson College)
1855	PA Epsilon, Gettysburg
1855	PA Gamma, Bucknell (1988-1991)
1855	VA Beta, Washington and Lee (1861-1865)
1855	*VA Gamma, Hampden-Sydney* (1861-1865) (1900)
1857	MS Alpha, Mississippi (1861-1881) (1912-1930)
1857	SC Alpha, South Carolina (1872-1884) (1892-1972)
1859	PA Zeta, Dickinson
1859	*TN Alpha, LaGrange* (1860)
1859	*VA Delta, Bethany (WV)* (1882)
1860	*MS Beta, Mississippi Col.* (1861)
1860	PA Eta, Franklin and Marshall
1860	*TN Beta, Cumberland (TN)* (1861-1867) (1879)
1861	OH Alpha, Ohio Wesleyan
1864	IL Alpha, Northwestern (1870-1878)
1865	IL Beta, Chicago (1869-1880) (1886-1894) (1970-1985)
1865	IN Alpha, DePauw
1865	*KY Alpha, Transylvania* (1866)
1866	OH Beta, Wittenberg
1867	IA Alpha, Iowa (1876-1885)
1868	*IA Gamma, Cornell Col. (IA)* (1871)
1869	IN Beta, Indiana
1869	MO Alpha, Missouri (1876-1908)
1869	NY Alpha, Cornell (1877-1886)
1869	PA Theta, Lafayette
1870	IN Gamma, Wabash (1901-1948)
1870	*TN Gamma, Nashville State* (1875)

1871 *IL Gamma, Monmouth (IL)* (1884)
1871 OH Gamma, Wooster (1892)
1871 *VA Epsilon, Randolph, Macon* (1879)
1872 NY Gamma, Columbia (NY) (1876-1892)
1875 *WI Alpha, Wisconsin, Madison* (1894-1897)
         (1939)
1876 KS Alpha, Kansas
1876 MI Alpha, Michigan (1972-1983)
1876 *WI Beta, Racine* (1877)
1877 PA Iota, Penn (1973-1978)
1879 MD Alpha, Johns Hopkins (1969-1975)
1880 OH Delta, Ohio State
1881 *CA Alpha, Pacific (CA)* (1892)
1881 *NY Delta, Hobart* (1892)
1881 WI Gamma, Beloit (1970-1978)
1882 *IA Delta, Simpson* (1889)
1883 *MN Alpha, Carleton* (1888)
1884 NY Beta, Syracuse
1887 *NY Epsilon, Colgate* (1982)
1888 MN Beta, Minnesota
1889 *PA Kappa, Swarthmore* (1963)
1890 WV Alpha, West Virginia
1891 CA Beta, Stanford
1891 *NY Zeta, Brooklyn Tech* (1912)
1895 *MA Alpha, Amherst* (1948)
1895 NE Alpha, Nebraska
1896 *NH Alpha, Dartmouth* (1967)
1899 CA Gamma, Cal, Berkeley (1978-1984)
1901 IN Delta, Purdue
1901 TN Delta, Vanderbilt
1902 RI Alpha, Brown (1978-1984)
1904 IL Delta, Illinois
1904 TX Alpha, Texas
1906 OH Epsilon, Case Western Reserve
1912 PA Lambda, Penn State
1913 IA Beta, Iowa State
1914 CO Alpha, Colorado
1914 WA Alpha, Washington (WA)
1920 OK Alpha, Oklahoma
1923 OR Alpha, Oregon
1927 CA Delta, USC
1927 *PA Mu, Carnegie-Mellon* (1934)
1931 CA Epsilon, UCLA
1934 NC Alpha, Duke
1947 AZ Alpha, Arizona (1962-1977)
1948 OR Beta, Oregon State
1950 NY Eta, SUNY, Buffalo (1970-1984)
1950 OH Eta, Toledo
1950 OH Zeta, Bowling Green
1953 IN Epsilon, Valparaiso
1953 TX Beta, Texas Tech.
1954 MI Beta, Michigan State
1956 *CT Alpha, Trinity (CT)* (1970)
1960 *MO Beta, Westminster (MO)* (1976)
1962 AZ Beta, Arizona State
1962 FL Alpha, Florida State (1969-1987)
1964 AL Alpha, Alabama
1964 CA Zeta, Cal, Santa Barbara (1972-1982)
1965 NE Beta, Creighton
1965 NJ Alpha, Rider
1966 CA Eta, Cal Poly, San Luis Obispo
1966 LA Alpha, L.S.U.

1966 OH Theta, Ashland
1966 RI Beta, Rhode Island (1988-1990)
1967 CA Theta, Cal State, Northridge
1967 FL Beta, Florida (1971-1977)
1967 NJ Beta, Monmouth (NJ)
1967 *OK Beta, Oklahoma State* (1991)
1967 TN Epsilon, Tennessee
1969 *LA Beta, Southwestern Louisiana* (1991)
1969 MN Gamma, Mankato
1969 NM Alpha, Eastern New Mexico
1969 TX Gamma, Southwest Texas
1970 OH Iota, Akron
1970 PA Nu, Indiana (PA)
1970 *TN Zeta, Memphis State* (1985)
1971 IN Zeta, Butler
1971 *OH Kappa, Kent* (1978)
1972 OH Lambda, Miami (OH)
1974 *AL Beta, Auburn* (1988)
1975 *MT Alpha, Montana* (1983)
1976 GA Alpha, Georgia
1976 VA Zeta, V.P.I.
1979 *AR Alpha, Arkansas* (1991)
1979 CA Iota, Cal, Davis
1984 PA Xi, Edinboro
1985 DE Alpha, Delaware
1985 IL Epsilon, Illinois State
1985 PA Omicron, Lehigh
1987 IN Eta, Indiana State
1987 NJ Gamma, Rutgers
1987 PA Pi, Temple
1988 KY Beta, Kentucky
1988 MD Beta, Maryland, Baltimore County
1988 TX Delta, Southern Methodist
1990 NJ Delta, Trenton
1991 MA Beta, Brandeis

Colonies: George Washington, East Carolina, Loyola, New Orleans, Rochester Tech, Cal, Irvine, CUNY, York, Wisconsin, Madison

Phi Kappa Sigma

ACTIVE PIN

PLEDGE PIN

PHI KAPPA SIGMA was founded at Philadelphia August 16, 1850, by Samuel Brown Wylie Mitchell, who developed the principles to be incorporated in its ritual and constitution, selected its name, and designed its badge and other insignia. Associated with Mitchell in the enterprise were six other youthful students of the University of Pennsylvania: Alfred Victor du Pont, Charles Hare Hutchinson, a member of Phi Beta Kappa, James Bayard Hodge, Andrew Adams Ripka, John Thorn Stone, and Duane Williams. These seven organized Alpha Chapter and so announced to their faculty and fellow students on October 19, 1850.

Growth From the beginning the founders envisioned a national intercollegiate society. However, in the autumn of 1852 the University of Pennsylvania faculty banned all secret societies from its campus, and this prohibition continued until Henry Vethake was advanced to the office of provost in 1855. At this time, however, the members of Phi Kappa Sigma were permitted to continue sub rosa, using the rooms of Dr. Mitchell as their headquarters. These were located in the Philadelphia Hospital, where he was serving as assistant physician and later as resident physician. In these sub rosa years Mitchell and his colleagues succeeded in establishing chapters at six institutions: at Princeton and Lafayette in 1853 and at Virginia, Jefferson (now Washington and Jefferson), Dickinson, and Franklin and Marshall in 1854. After the removal of faculty restraints. Alpha chapter resumed its operations at Pennsylvania and thereafter enjoyed an unbroken existence.

Most of Phi Kappa Sigma's expansion after 1854 and until the outbreak of the War Between the States took place in the South. This was a natural consequence of the fact that many students from that area, while studying at Pennsylvania institutions, became members. After graduating, they returned to their home communities with enthusiasm for developing new chapters. In these southern chapters the custom developed of wearing badges with skulls made of silver, leading to the designation of Phi Kaps as the "Silver Skulls." The zeal of one of these brothers, James W. Barrow, resulted in the only instance of a college being named in honor of a Greek-letter fraternity: The Phi Kappa Sigma Male College at Monticello, Arkansas. This was chartered by the legislature, February 21, 1859, as the first institution of that state to offer collegiate instructions. It continued in operation, graduating two classes, until the buildings were taken over by the Confederate Government as storehouses for war supplies, and were subsequently destroyed by a raid of Union forces through the area in 1864.

The war also meant the destruction of a majority of the chapters, of which 15 were flourishing when the conflict began. Five of the eight located in the area of the Confederacy never reopened, but in due course those at the University of Virginia, the University of North Carolina, and Tulane University were reestablished effectively. For a period the fraternity limited its extension almost exclusively to the Atlantic seaboard, but in 1872 a charter was granted at Northwestern University, providing a base for further expansion in the Middle West. In 1895 the fraternity became international with the establishment of a Canadian chapter at the University of Toronto, and in 1903 the first Pacific Coast petition was approved for the University of California. In the 20th century the carefully planned growth of the fraternity has continued at a conservative pace and in accordance with policies formulated by the Grand Chapter.

Government The term Grand Chapter describes a convention of the fraternity, in which are vested all general legislative and executive powers of government. While all members are welcome to attend grand chapter sessions, voting is limited to accredited delegates from each undergraduate chapter, delegates of each alumni chapter, chapter advisers and the grand officers. On certain matters, such as amending the constitution, only representatives of student chapters may vote, except in case of tie. The grand chapter, providing for a democratic system of government based on chapter representation, was created in 1869. It superseded the Supreme Consistory and High Arch Tribunal, established in 1858, to provide for the executive, legislative, and judicial functions originally exercised by Alpha Chapter. According to the first constitution, the mother chapter was authorized to issue charters to new chapters, and its officers served, in effect, as officers for the fraternity as a whole.

Provision in 1869 was also made for the Executive Board, organized to carry into effect policies adopted by the grand chapter and to conduct the general business of the fraternity between conventions. As constituted, the Executive Board includes 10 grand officers, elected at sessions of the Grand Chapter, plus living past grand alphas. It is presided over by a grand alpha, who is the chief administrative officer of the fraternity. The other officers, designated with Greek-letter titles, as are those of student chapters, serve as supervisors of fraternity affairs in defined geographical jurisdictions and also have specialized assignments with respect to finance, extension, records, publications, and the like.

To represent the Executive Board locally at each campus where a chapter is chartered, a chapter visitor system was inaugurated by the grand chapter in 1903. Chapter visitors are appointed by the Executive Board and serve, as do the grand officers themselves, without compensation. In recent years this plan for supervision and counseling has been strengthened by the appointment of one or more assistant advisers or faculty advisers, who may give special assistance in chapter programs for improved scholarship, finance, or pledge education. At campuses where independent housing for chapters is permitted and deemed desirable, homeowning corporations have been formed. Alumni, serving on their boards of trustees, provide for continuity and maturity in the financing and building of chapter homes and for the prudent handling of their insurance and taxes. All plans for financing and major construction are submitted to the Executive Board for review and approval.

The Executive Board conducts a comprehensive program of personal visits to the chapters by grand officers and by their appointed representatives. The Leadership Conference provides opportunity each year for representatives of all chapters to gather and to discuss problems and programs of mutual interest.

Traditions and Insignia The tradition has developed for all chapters to celebrate October 19, 1850—the day when establishment of the fraternity was announced—as Founders' Day. However, the actual day of founding, August 16, has added significance. In 1828 it marked the birth and in 1879 the death of Dr. Mitchell, whose career set an inspiring example of continuing service to the fraternity and of devotion to scholarly, patriotic, and fraternal ideals. He was regarded as a brilliant student, earning the A.B. degree in 1852, the M.D. in 1854, and the M.A. in 1855, and then distinguishing himself in the practice of his profession. When the call to arms sounded in 1861, he threw himself wholeheartedly into the defense of the Republic, earning the rank of lieutenant colonel and a citation for his "gallant and meritorious service." To perpetuate the loyalties and comradeships of the war years, he became a founder and an officer of the Military Order of the Loyal Legion of the United States, designing its seal and badge. His talent for organizational matters found further expression in Masonic and other fraternal societies, in a variety of civic and professional associations, and as the presiding officer of his district board of school directors and of his unit of the Grand Army of the Republic.

Dr. Mitchell remained active in the affairs of his own chapter throughout life and helped many other chapters to become established and chartered. As an alumnus he held several important offices, and he was serving as a member of the fraternity's Executive Board at the time of his death.

The achievements and example of Dr. Mitchell as a continuing force in the progress of the fraternity and as a tradition were recognized at the Centennial Convention at Philadelphia August 31 and September 1 and 2, 1950. At St. Stephens Church, where the remains of Dr. Mitchell lie buried, delegates assembled to pay respectful tribute to the memory of their founder, who "dreamed and builded better than he knew." Another feature of the centennial celebration was the dedication of a General Headquarters Building, provided for by the gifts of hundreds of loyal members.

Alumni activity and concern for undergraduate welfare are a long tradition. Several unofficial alumni groups were established by Phi Kaps prior to and during the War Between the States, including the Vagabond Club at Baton Rouge, Louisiana; the Orphan Club at Baltimore, Maryland; and the Sub-Epsilon Chapter at Cumberland, Maryland. The last-named was organized to provide an opportunity for brothers wearing the blue or the gray to mingle socially within the bonds of the fraternity. Its records show how Confederate members were cleared through the Union lines in order that they might dine and dance with their northern "enemy" brothers at the St. Nicholas Hotel in Cumberland. The first regularly constituted alumni chapter was organized in 1869 at New York.

Phi Kappa Sigma's badge is a gold cross patteé with black enameled border, displaying a skull and crossed bones in the center. In the upper arm of the cross is a six-pointed star and in the other arms are the Greek letters, ΦΚΣ. The pledge pin also displays these letters on a square black background with gold border. The coat of arms is a shield displaying the symbols of the fraternity on the four quarters; a badge is centered on the shield, and the crest is formed by the skull and bones; at its base is the motto, *Stellis Aequus Durando*. The fraternity colors are old gold and black. The official flag has a black background; on it, in old gold, are displayed the skull and crossed bones at the upper left-hand corner and the Greek letters of the fraternity at center.

Publications *The Phi Kappa Sigma Magazine* was published by Alpha chapter in 1857, 1858, and 1859, first as a monthly and then as a quarterly, and presented reports from all of the chapters as well as news of fraternity-wide interest. In 1891 the Executive Board began publication of *The Phi Kappa Sigma Quarterly* on a subscription basis. This was succeeded in 1901 by *The Phi Kappa Sigma News Letter*, which has been distributed quarterly since that time to all members.

Printed catalogs of members were issued by the individual chapters in 1859 and 1860, inspiring the publication of the first *General Register* in 1872. This contained biographical data about all members. Supplements were published in 1873 and 1876, followed by a series of completely revised editions, the most recent containing 1,023 pages. The Executive Board has also published a number of *Membership Directories*, containing convenient lists of all members by their chapter and by place of residence. Other serial publications include the *Minutes* of each session of the grand chapter, the latest being the 82nd. Official publications have also included several editions of manuals for the guidance of chapter officers, including a comprehensive guide for chapter programming and management.

Funds and Philanthropies The Samuel Brown Wylie Mitchell Scholarship in English Literature was established by members of the fraternity in 1888. This award was probably the first scholastic award offered by a fraternity in any American college or university, and its acceptance by the University of Pennsylvania Board of Trustees represented the first official recognition of fraternities at that institution.

A program of voluntary annual giving, through the Alumni Fund, was begun in 1923. The response has been such that the fraternity requires no compulsory dues aside from the initiation fee.

As a memorial to Benjamin Lee, II, a permanent trust fund was established in 1920, and through its emergency loans and scholarships awards, scores of worthy young men have been assisted toward the completion of their educational plans. Today, the Phi Kappa Sigma Educational Fund, incorporated in the state of Delaware, provides for a program of scholarships and grants to encourage students of demonstrated academic and leadership potential.

Through the years a majority of chapter housing ventures have received some financial aid in the form of loans from either the Phi Kappa Sigma Foundation or the Endowment Fund.

Headquarters Two Office Colony, Suite 2-301, P.O. Box 947, Valley Forge, PA 19481. Phone: (215) 783-7222.

Membership Total living membership 29,000. Undergraduate membership 2,309. Active chapters 68. Inactive chapters 31. Colonies 2. Houses owned 33. Graduate/Alumni chapters 10. City/Area alumni associations 5. Total number of initiates 46,000. Chapter roll:

1850	Alpha, Penn
1853	*Beta, Princeton (1881)*
1853	*Gamma, Lafayette (1885)*
1854	Delta, Washington and Jefferson
1854	Epsilon, Dickinson (1984-1989)
1854	Eta, Virginia
1854	Zeta, Franklin and Marshall
1855	*Iota, Columbia (NY) (1934)*
1855	*Theta, Centenary (1861)*
1856	*Kappa, Emory and Henry (1861)*
1856	Lambda, North Carolina
1858	Mu, Tulane
1859	*Nu, Cumberland (KY) (1861)*
1859	*Xi, Mississippi (1861)*
1860	*Omicron, Centre College (1862)*
1865	*Pi, Harvard (1867)*
1865	*Rho, Austin (1865)*
1870	*Sigma, Lehigh (1889)*
1872	Tau, Randolph, Macon
1872	Upsilon, Northwestern
1873	*Chi, Racine (1875)*
1873	Phi, Richmond
1876	*Psi, Long Island (1880)*
1884	*Omega, Haverford (1890)*
1890	Psi, Penn State
1892	Rho, Illinois
1893	*Kappa, Lake Forest (1895)*
1895	Alpha Alpha, Washington and Lee
1895	Alpha Beta, Toronto
1896	Alpha Gamma, West Virginia
1898	Alpha Delta, Maine
1898	Alpha Epsilon, Illinois Tech
1899	Alpha Zeta, Maryland
1901	*Alpha Eta, Charleston (SC) (1905)*
1901	Alpha Theta, Wisconsin, Madison (1959-1988)
1902	Alpha Iota, Vanderbilt
1903	Alpha Kappa, Alabama
1903	Alpha Lambda, Cal, Berkeley
1903	Alpha Mu, M.I.T.
1904	Alpha Nu, Georgia Tech
1905	*Alpha Omicron, Michigan (1963)*
1905	Alpha Xi, Purdue

1906	*Alpha Pi, Chicago (1943)*
1911	Alpha Rho, Cornell
1915	*Alpha Sigma, Minnesota (1943)*
1915	*Alpha Tau, Stanford (1972)*
1919	Alpha Upsilon, Washington (WA)
1920	*Alpha Phi, Iowa (1990)*
1925	Alpha Chi, Ohio State (1983-1990)
1926	Alpha Psi, UCLA
1929	*Alpha Eta, South Carolina (1989)*
1929	*Kappa, Dartmouth (1938)*
1929	Omicron, Oklahoma
1936	Alpha Omega, British Columbia
1936	Nu, Duke
1937	Theta, Kenyon
1940	Sigma, Texas
1948	*Beta Alpha, Oregon (1964)*
1949	*Beta Beta, Kansas (1984)*
1949	*Beta Delta, Michigan State (1971)*
1949	*Beta Epsilon, Oregon State (1975)*
1949	Beta Gamma, Denver
1953	*Beta Zeta, Ohio (1973)*
1955	Beta Eta, North Texas
1955	Beta Theta, Texas Christian
1959	Beta Iota, St. Lawrence
1964	*Beta Kappa, Drury (1983)*
1968	Beta Lambda, Northern Illinois
1968	Beta Mu, South Alabama
1969	Beta Nu, Adrian
1971	Beta Xi, New Orleans
1973	Beta Omicron, V.P.I.
1975	*Beta Pi, Louisiana Tech (1990)*
1978	Beta Rho, Cal, Riverside
1978	*Beta Sigma, Salisbury (1980)*
1979	Beta Tau, Towson
1979	Beta Upsilon, SUNY Col., Potsdam
1981	Beta Chi, Clarkson
1981	Beta Phi, SUNY Col., Geneseo
1982	Beta Omega, Radford
1982	Beta Psi, Washington State
1983	Gamma Alpha, SUNY Col., Buffalo
1983	Gamma Beta, Drexel
1984	Gamma Delta, Texas A & M
1984	Gamma Gamma, Carthage
1986	Gamma Epsilon, Seton Hall
1986	Gamma Theta, West Chester
1987	Gamma Eta, SUNY Col., Fredonia
1987	Gamma Kappa, SUNY Col., Oneonta
1987	Gamma Lambda, North Carolina, Charlotte
1987	Gamma Zeta, California (PA)
1988	Gamma Iota, Millersville
1988	Gamma Mu, Southwest Texas
1989	Gamma Nu, SUNY, Albany
1989	Gamma Xi, George Mason
1990	Gamma Omicron, Rutgers, Camden
1990	Gamma Pi, Wesley
1990	Gamma Rho, Bryant
1990	Gamma Sigma, Rutgers

Colonies: New Hampshire, St. Leo's

COAT OF ARMS

Phi Kappa Tau

ACTIVE PIN

PLEDGE PIN

PHI KAPPA TAU was founded at Miami University, Oxford, Ohio, on March 17, 1906. Conceived by a group of four men, William H. Shideler, Clinton D. Boyd, Taylor A. Borradaile, and Dwight I. Douglass, Phi Kappa Tau traces its earliest beginnings to the spring of 1904 when the first meetings of the founders were held to form a campus society to combat undemocratic practices and ideas of false aristocracy.

The generic origins of Phi Kappa Tau lie deep in the evolution of the ideals of American Democracy. Shortly after organization, the Miami men aligned themselves with two other fraternities and independent men to reform campus elections. After completing the task of educating the student body to the value of electing logical men to office, the group realized that in its efforts it had developed all the elements of fundamental brotherhood on the highest plane and the continuance of these associations was the evolution of Phi Kappa Tau.

Historians of the fraternity have stressed three fundamental characteristics which guided the founders in establishing Phi Kappa Tau: emphasis upon innate worth as a qualification for membership, the democratic nature of the fraternity, and its Christian ideals.

At the meeting held on March 17, 1906, the founders of the fraternity, along with 17 other members, known as foundation members, approved the first constitution and provided for the continuation of the organization.

Growth At the time the reform at Miami University was taking place, similar movements were in process in neighboring colleges and universities. As a result there was an affiliation of groups of similar purposes and ideals in Ohio University, Ohio State University, Centre College, Mount Union College, and the University of Illinois. The earliest chapters bore no Greek-letter names and the organization was known as the National Phrenocon Association, a national college fraternity. A decision of the Miami chapter to adopt a Greek-letter name was readily approved by all other chapters.

In 1917, the fraternity named its first full-time secretary and the foundation was laid for what was to develop into an outstanding system of Central

Office administration and assistance to chapters. Located first in Alliance, Ohio, the office was later in Indianapolis, Indiana.

In 1931, the Memorial Headquarters Building, known as the Phi Kappa Tau National Headquarters, was completed in Oxford, Ohio, and Phi Kappa Tau became the second national fraternity to occupy a structure specifically designed for use as a fraternity headquarters.

At the Fraternity's 46th National Convention in 1983, the building was renamed the Ewing T. Boles National Headquarters Building in honor of Honorary Founding Father Ewing T. Boles who has been a leader in the fraternity since his initiation in 1914.

Government The supreme law of the fraternity is the national constitution. The supreme legislative body is the biennial national convention which consists of an undergraduate and a graduate delegate from each chapter. Elected by the conventions are the national president, vice president, and nine councilors, three of whom are undergraduates. These eleven persons plus the immediate past national president and the president of Phi Kappa Tau Foundation (the latter ex-officio, non-voting) form the national council which is the board of directors of the organization. This body has the responsibility and authority to fulfill the wishes of the convention.

The administration of the fraternity is under direction of the executive director, whose staff includes an administrative assistant, business manager, director of field operations and alumni development, director of publications, and chapter leadership consultants. As chief executive officer, he is responsible to the national council and the national conventions for the sound operation of the chapters and the administration of the national fraternity.

In addition to the executive office staff members, national officers include an educational director, housing and financial adviser, a national chaplain, and 25 regional officers known as domain directors with responsibilities for geographical regions.

In 1982, the fraternity established a not-for-profit national housing corporation known as Phi Kappa Tau Properties Incorporated. It is incorporated in the State of Ohio and functions to provide housing management assistance and resources for the procurement of chapter housing facilities.

The executive director of the fraternity serves as the executive vice president and secretary of the corporation. Other officers include a president, vice president, treasurer and an at-large-member of the executive committee. Officers are selected by the board of directors at the annual meeting.

Each of the chapters is divided into two councils. The members in college constitute the resident council; graduates and members who have left school constitute the graduate council. Although the two councils operate separately, close supervision of resident groups is maintained through the board of governors, a committee composed of officers of both councils. This practice has been in effect since 1920.

Traditions and Insignia The oldest and most widely observed tradition of the fraternity is the Annual Founder's Day Banquet, held each year on or near March 17. The first such banquet was held in 1907, at which time Dean E. E. Brandon, then faculty adviser for the organization and later to become national president of Phi Kappa Tau, emphasized the educational partnership that existed between Phi Kappa Tau and Miami University in remarks to Miami's president.

The badge of the fraternity is an irregular elongated octagon. The center is a black enameled oval bearing a white star and the gold letters ΦΚΤ. A border of 16 pearls with a diamond set in the star is the only combination of jewels permitted. The associate member badge is a shield with a white border surrounding a gold field with a raised star in the center.

The coat of arms, or arms of alliance, consists of a crest: a laurel wreath encircling a mullet on a blank field; a bow: to the force of six turns; an escutcheon: a shield thrice quartered with a chevron bearing three mullets; and the Greek motto: some words of which are omitted for secrecy.

Publications A quarterly magazine, *The Laurel of Phi Kappa Tau*, published continuously since 1919, and published from 1906 to 1919 as *Sidelights*, is provided to all members. *The Golden Jubilee History of Phi Kappa Tau*, a 409-page volume, was published in 1957. The sixth and current issue of the *Songbook* was published in 1964. A third reprint of the Ritual of the fraternity was issued in 1971. A membership manual is revised and published periodically. The President's Weekly Planning Kit is produced each year to provide chapter presidents and treasurers an all encompassing chapter planning and administration guide and workbook. In addition, there are numerous manuals for undergraduate and graduate officers and members.

Funds The Phi Kappa Tau Foundation is an educational foundation. Gifts to the fund may be considered as deductions for the purpose of federal income tax. Earnings of the foundation are used for scholarship grants and loans to individuals and institutions.

The assets of the Foundation have been greatly increased by the addition of funds acquired through the $3.2 million capital campaign called "The Decision for Phi Kappa Tau" which was completed in 1985. This campaign is believed to have been the most successful capital campaign ever launched by a fraternity or fraternity foundation.

Headquarters 15 North Campus Avenue, P.O. Box 30, Oxford, OH 45056. Phone: (513) 523-4193.

Membership Total living membership 52,351. Total undergraduate membership 3,809. Active chapters 86. Inactive chapters 38. Colonies 6. Houses owned 48. Graduate/Alumni chapters 118.

City/Area alumni associations 7. Total number of initiates 60,968. Chapter roll:

1906	Alpha, Miami (OH)	
1911	Beta, Ohio	
1912	Gamma, Ohio State	
1914	Delta, Centre College	
1915	Epsilon, Mount Union	
1916	Eta, Muhlenberg	
1916	Zeta, Illinois	
1919	Theta, Transylvania	
1920	Iota, Coe	
1920	Kappa, Kentucky	
1920	Lambda, Purdue	
1920	Mu, Lawrence	
1921	Nu, Cal, Berkeley	
1921	Xi, Franklin and Marshall	
1922	Omicron, Penn State	
1922	*Pi, USC* (1988)	
1922	Rho, R.P.I.	
1922	*Sigma, Syracuse* (1957)	
1923	Chi, North Carolina State	
1923	Phi, Bethany (WV)	
1923	Tau, Michigan (1971-1984)	
1923	Upsilon, Nebraska Wesleyan	
1924	Alpha Alpha, Michigan State (1973-1986)	
1924	*Alpha Beta, N.Y.U.* (1943)	
1924	Alpha Gamma, Delaware	
1924	Omega, Wisconsin, Madison (1940-1986)	
1924	Psi, Colorado	
1925	Alpha Delta, Case Western Reserve	
1925	Alpha Epsilon, Kansas State	
1925	*Alpha Zeta, Oregon State* (1982-1985) (1987)	
1926	Alpha Eta, Florida	
1926	*Alpha Iota, Penn* (1942)	
1927	Alpha Kappa, Washington State	
1927	Alpha Lambda, Auburn	
1928	*Alpha Mu, Ohio Wesleyan* (1958)	
1928	Alpha Nu, Iowa State	
1928	*Alpha Omicron, Lafayette* (1975)	
1928	*Alpha Xi, West Virginia* (1943)	
1929	Alpha Pi, Washington (WA)	
1929	Alpha Rho, Georgia Tech	
1929	Alpha Sigma, Colorado State	
1930	Alpha Tau, Cornell	
1937	*Alpha Upsilon, Colgate* (1971)	
1938	Alpha Chi, Mississippi State	
1938	Alpha Phi, Akron	
1941	Alpha Psi, Texas, El Paso	
1942	Alpha Omega, Baldwin-Wallace	
1943	*Beta Alpha, Texas* (1971-1985) (1988)	
1947	Beta Beta, Louisville	
1947	Beta Gamma, Idaho	
1948	*Beta Delta, Miami (FL)* (1963)	
1948	Beta Epsilon, Southern Mississippi	
1948	*Beta Eta, New Mexico* (1954)	
1948	Beta Zeta, New Mexico State	
1949	Beta Iota, Florida State	
1949	Beta Kappa, Oklahoma State	
1949	Beta Lambda, Indiana	
1950	*Beta Nu, San Diego U* (1953)	

1950 Beta Omicron, Maryland (1986-1988)
1950 *Beta Pi, Middlebury* (1972)
1950 *Beta Rho, UCLA* (1959-1984) (1987)
1950 *Beta Sigma, Idaho State* (1961)
1950 Beta Tau, Bowling Green
1950 Beta Xi, Georgia
1952 Beta Phi, Westminster (PA)
1952 *Beta Upsilon, Hobart* (1985)
1953 *Beta Chi, Southern Illinois* (1979)
1956 Beta Psi, Cal State, Long Beach
1958 Beta Omega, Cal State, Chico
1959 Gamma Alpha, Michigan Tech
1960 Gamma Gamma, St. John's (NY)
        (1976-1987)
1961 Gamma Delta, Northern Michigan
1961 *Gamma Epsilon, Pacific (CA)* (1978)
1961 *Gamma Zeta, Connecticut* (1971)
1962 Gamma Eta, East Carolina
1962 *Gamma Theta, Western Michigan* (1974)
1963 *Gamma Iota, Cal State, Sacramento* (1987)
1964 *Gamma Kappa, C. W. Post* (1974)
1965 *Gamma Lambda, Central Michigan* (1989)
1965 Gamma Mu, Bradley
1966 Gamma Nu, Rochester Tech
1966 Gamma Omicron, Cal State, Fullerton
1966 Gamma Xi, East Central State
1967 Gamma Pi, Youngstown State
1967 Gamma Rho, Kearney
1967 *Gamma Sigma, Cal, Davis* (1971)
1967 *Gamma Tau, Old Dominion* (1973)
1967 Gamma Upsilon, Spring Hill
1968 *Delta Alpha, Iowa Wesleyan* (1984)
1968 Delta Beta, Evansville
1968 Gamma Chi, Delta State (1978-1990)
1968 *Gamma Omega, LaSalle* (1971)
1968 Gamma Phi, Northeastern (1976-1988)
1968 *Gamma Psi, Southwest Texas* (1988)
1969 Delta Delta, Bryant (1971-1990)
1969 *Delta Epsilon, St. Cloud* (1979)
1969 Delta Gamma, Mississippi
1970 *Delta Eta, Marshall* (1971)
1970 *Delta Iota, New Mexico Highlands* (1975)
1970 Delta Theta, Georgetown Col
1970 *Delta Zeta, Emporia* (1977)
1971 Delta Kappa, Tennessee
1971 Delta Lambda, Muskingum
1972 *Delta Mu, Santa Fe* (1983)
1975 Delta Nu, Wright State
1975 *Delta Omicron, Pan American* (1986)
1975 *Delta Xi, Cleveland* (1990)
1982 *Delta Pi, Murray State* (1987)
1982 Delta Rho, Eastern Kentucky
1982 Delta Sigma, Webber
1984 Delta Tau, Cal Poly, Pomona
1984 *Delta Upsilon, Tennessee, Martin* (1989)
1985 Delta Chi, Rochester
1985 Delta Phi, Arkansas
1986 Delta Psi, Rider
1987 Delta Omega, Northeast Missouri
1987 Epsilon Alpha, Texas A & M
1987 Epsilon Beta, West Virginia Tech
1988 Epsilon Delta, Virginia Wesleyan

1988 Epsilon Gamma, Trenton
1989 Epsilon Epsilon, William Paterson
1989 Epsilon Eta, SUNY Col., Oswego
1989 Epsilon Zeta, SUNY Col., Buffalo
1990 Epsilon Theta, San Francisco State

Colonies: William and Mary, Kansas, Kent, Cincinnati, North Carolina, New Mexico State

Phi Kappa Theta

ACTIVE PIN

PLEDGE PIN

PHI KAPPA THETA was founded in 1889. It officially lists its place of founding as both Brown and Lehigh Universities, since it is the consolidation on an equal basis of two predecessor national fraternities—Phi Kappa and Theta Kappa Phi—founded at those institutions. The union, which had developed separately over the years, was voted by concurrent conventions held on September 8, 1958, at the Student Union Building at Ohio State University in Columbus and became operative on April 29, 1959, at simultaneous "Charter Day celebrations" at each active chapter where the combined initiation ceremonial was demonstrated and a new charter document was presented by a national legate. However, the members of the two uniting fraternities were not reinitiated at these ceremonies: all automatically became members of the consolidated fraternity, and the "charter" documents did not replace the original charters but merely amended them by substituting the name of the new fraternity.

Phi Kappa was founded at Brown University on October 1, 1889, by 13 students, using the name Phi Kappa Sigma. Upon learning of the existence of a national fraternity of that name, they adopted the name Phi Kappa in 1900 and on April 29, 1902, obtained a corporate charter from the state of Rhode Island.

Theta Kappa Phi was formed on October 22, 1919, at Lehigh as the outgrowth of a club called the "X Club" formed in the fall of 1914 by a group of Newman Club members who sought a more intimate association.

In its membership, the homogeneous nature of the original bands at Lehigh and Brown has been maintained, since the national fraternity rests on a singleness of faith and purpose, a belief in the unique destiny of man and his consequent human dignity and worth, holding fast to the same basic spiritual concepts upon which the founding fathers built this nation under God. The organization is founded upon spiritual, educational, social, and fraternal ideals. It aims to promote scholarship-achievement, character formation, loyalty to God, country, campus and fraternity.

The fraternity was one of the earliest to adopt a specific colonization procedure. A local is formed under a standard name and ritual. Thus the group is already unified in the standards of the national fraternity by the time the charter is granted and installation takes place. Members of local groups awaiting chartered chapter status may achieve full initiation into the national fraternity at the completion of a probation and training period as individuals and need not wait until the event of installation to become Phi Kappa Thetas.

Government The biennial national convention is the supreme authority with one vote for each undergraduate chapter, alumni chapter, and board of trustee member. A 10 member board of trustees administers the fraternity: two are undergraduate members and are elected at convention, while eight alumni members have overlapping four-year terms.

Besides the usual regional and chapter adult supervisors, each chapter, as well as the national board, has a chaplain to promote spiritual and moral values.

Traditions and Insignia The solemn ceremonial of Phi Kappa Theta is based mainly on a ceremony written by an initiate of Sigma Alpha Epsilon, Bard College chapter, for the infant Lehigh group—Monsignor Michael Andrew Chapman, a Catholic priest who had been a minister of the Episcopal Church.

The fraternity traditionally initiates certain members of the faculty and clergy connected with each institution. In areas of lower alumni concentration, college trained nonfraternity men may be initiated who are interested in the fraternity's ideals and willing to serve on its chapters' alumni supervisory bodies.

The badge, pledge pin, and coat of arms were completely redesigned for the 1959 consolidation. The badge used the inner black enamel shield of Theta Kappa Phi superimposed on the characteristic quatrefoil outer shape of Brown-founded group. The standard badge has four rubies in the corners of the quatrefoil. An optional model with 16 pearls added is also approved. Use of a miniature badge (sweetheart pin) is an accepted national custom. The pledge pin uses the shield outline of the Brown group with the "sun" symbol of the Lehigh group. The coat of arms is quartered, using two of the four quadrants to contain important symbols of each of the original national fraternities. The fraternity flower is the red tea rose.

Publications The magazine, a quarterly called *The Temple*, sent for life to all members, grew out of a publication founded in 1914. The esoteric newsletter is called *The Sun* and it is issued but once or twice each year. *The Sun* had been the name of the magazine of the Lehigh-founded group before merger. *The Temple* was the name of the Phi Kappa quarterly. Instructional manuals on various topics and a regular series of administrative bulletins are sent to the chapters and their supervisory alumni. A pledge manual entitled *The Journey* instructs neophyte members in history and lore.

Funds and Philanthropies The National Fraternity of Phi Kappa Theta is incorporated in Ohio and there are two separate associated corporations also incorporated there.

One of these, named PKT National Properties, Inc., operates as a real estate holding corporation.

The second, Phi Kappa Theta National Foundation, Inc., is organized to receive tax-deductible donations for scholarships, libraries, and other religious or educational activities.

The fraternity has pioneered in international student and cultural exchange programs. In 1937 a delegate attended the international student congress in Paris, and a year later at the world conclave in Liubiana, Slovenia, a member of the fraternity was elected international president of IMCS, the first American so honored. In 1938 at the interfederal assembly held in the Palace of Franz Josef, the reigning sovereign of Liechtenstein, Phi Kappa Theta was affiliated to the international secretariat (Fribourg, Switzerland) of the international movement of university students and graduates.

Headquarters The Executive Offices are located at 3901 W. 86th Street, Suite #290, Indianapolis, IN 46268. Phone: (317) 872-9934. Prior to moving the offices to Indianapolis in April of 1985, they were located in Worcester, Massachusetts.

Membership Active chapters 78. Inactive chapters 17. Colonies 1. Total number of initiates 45,000. Chapter roll:††

1889	*RI Alpha, Brown*	(1930)
1912	IL Beta Delta, Illinois	
1913	PA Beta Gamma, Penn State	
1914	*IA Delta, Iowa*	(1932-1947) (1963)
1915	KS Epsilon, Kansas	
1918	IN Zeta, Purdue	
1918	MA Eta, M.I.T.	
1919	PA Alpha, Lehigh	
1920	OH Gamma Theta, Ohio State	
1921	KS Iota, Kansas State	
1923	MO Kappa Upsilon, Missouri	(1935-1947)
1923	PA Mu, Pitt	
1923	WI Lambda, Wisconsin, Madison	
1924	IA Xi, Iowa State	
1924	*MI Nu, Michigan*	(1935)
1924	NH Epsilon, New Hampshire	
1925	*NE Pi, Nebraska*	(1934)
1925	NY Eta, CCNY	
1925	NY Sigma, R.P.I.	
1925	*NY Tau, Syracuse*	(1935)
1925	OH Omicron, Cincinnati	
1925	OH Zeta, Ohio Northern	
1926	*ME Upsilon, Maine*	(1935)
1926	PA Rho, Carnegie Tech	
1927	*CO Phi, Denver*	(1933-1949) (1957)
1927	*NY Theta, Cornell*	(1931)
1928	OH Psi, Ohio	
1928	*PA Chi, Bucknell*	(1933)

†† This chapter roll is repeated from the 19th edition; no current information was provided.

1930 DC Omega, Catholic
1932 PA Iota, Temple
1934 OK Kappa, Oklahoma
1935 MA Lambda, Worcester Tech
1936 MO Mu, Missouri Mines
1937 OK Nu, Oklahoma State
1938 LA Xi, L.S.U.
1939 IN Alpha Alpha, Indiana
1941 LA Omicron, Southwestern Louisiana
1941 OH Alpha Beta, Case Tech
1946 WA Alpha Delta, Washington State
1947 *MN Alpha Epsilon, Minnesota* (1961)
1948 MO Pi, St. Louis
1948 *MS Rho, Mississippi State* (1960)
1949 *MA Sigma, Boston* (1953)
1949 OH Phi, Kent
1949 PA Tau, St. Francis
1950 NY Alpha Eta, Manhattan
1950 *WY Alpha Zeta, Wyoming* (1963)
1951 AZ Alpha Iota, Arizona
1951 MS Chi, Mississippi
1951 OR Alpha Theta, Oregon State
1953 *IN Alpha Kappa, Butler* (1976)
1954 IL Psi, Northern Illinois
1955 AL Alpha Lambda, Spring Hill
1956 CA Alpha Nu, Loyola Marymount, Los Angeles
1956 TX Alpha Mu, Houston
1957 MI Omega, Detroit
1957 PA Alpha Xi, Duquesne
1958 *AZ Alpha Omicron, Northern Arizona* (1975)
1959 NC Alpha Rho, Belmont Abbey
1959 TX Alpha Pi, Texas
1962 LA Alpha Phi, L.S.U., New Orleans
1962 MA Omega, Merrimack
1962 NJ Phi Beta, Seton Hall
1963 CA Phi Delta, San Diego State
1963 IN Chi Rho, Indiana Tech.
1965 IL Sigma Alpha, Loyola, Chicago
1965 NY Omega, St. John's (NY)
1966 LA Nu Omega, Nicholls
1967 CT Epsilon Kappa, Fairfield
1967 GA Delta Rho, Georgia
1967 IL Kappa Phi, Lewis
1967 IN Alpha Gamma, Tri-State
1967 TX Kappa Theta, North Texas
1968 *Canada Alpha, Loyola, Montreal* (1976)
1968 IL Theta Delta, DePaul
1968 MI Alpha Alpha, Ferris
1968 MI Chi Rho, Michigan Tech
1968 MO Mu Sigma, Northeast Missouri
1968 PA Kappa Epsilon, LaSalle
1968 TX Alpha Omega, Lamar
1969 GA Gamma Tau, Georgia Tech
1969 IN Gamma Omega, Purdue, Calumet
1969 LA Alpha Sigma, Loyola, New Orleans
1969 *LA Delta Tau, Southeastern Louisiana*
1969 NS Sigma Mu, St. Mary's (NS)
1969 TN Chi Nu, Memphis State
1969 WI Mu, Marquette
1970 TX Epsilon Tau, East Texas

1970 TX Tau Mu, Pan American
1972 GA Alpha Chi, Armstrong State
1972 LA Lambda Tau, McNeese
1973 FL Omega Alpha, Florida
1973 NM Phi Alpha, Santa Fe
1973 TX Kappa Tau, Texas A & I
1974 PA Kappa Theta, Indiana (PA)

Colonies: Cal State

Phi Lambda Chi†

ACTIVE PIN

PLEDGE PIN

PHI LAMBDA CHI was founded at Arkansas State Teachers College, Conway, on March 15, 1925, as a fraternity of local character known as the Aztecs. The founders were Robert L. Taylor, Robert Clark, Wendell Collums, Grant Collar, William Huddleston, Howard Perrin, Louis Moles, Marvin Crittenden, Jeff Shemwell, Doyle Patton, Lester Adair, and Evan Douglas.

In 1928 the college decided to allow fraternities to assume Greek-letter names and in 1930 the name Aztec was dropped in favor of Phi Lambda Chi. In 1934 national affiliation was permitted. Five years later, on January 19, 1939, a provisional national council was set up to grant charters to new chapters and to form a constitution. A purpose was expressed to develop the fraternity as a national organization along lines that would qualify it for admission into the Association of Teachers College Fraternities. The first national conclave was held in March, 1940, at Conway.

Government The Grand Council is the supreme power in the fraternity. It is comprised of the national officers and chapter delegates. The national conclave is held each fall at the residence of one of the college chapters. Government during the interim is by the board of governors. The national office is the scene of the general administrative work, which is directed by the executive officer. The chapter officers school is held in connection with each convention. A chapter rushing school is held in September of each year on a regional basis.

Traditions and Insignia The fraternity has always encouraged scholarship, and the National Scholastic Cup is presented to the chapter attaining the highest scholastic rank. The James Lester Award is given to an outstanding alumnus of the fraternity. The emblem of the fraternity is a shield with the Greek letters ΦΛΧ inscribed on a diagonal bar which separates the eye in the upper right corner from the crossed sabers in the lower left corner.

The coat of arms is an armorial bearing de-

† This chapter narrative is repeated from the 19th edition; no current information was provided.

scribed: two vicious lions poised on either side against a shield, which has at its upper extremity a Grecian helmet and at its lower extremity a scroll bearing the Greek name of the fraternity. Diagonally across the shield is a solid bar separating the eye in the upper right corner from the crossed sabers in the lower left corner. The pledge badge is a disc of gold centered with blue. The colors are blue and gold. The flower is the white carnation.

Funds and Philanthropies The fraternity maintains a fund for loans to the undergraduate chapters and a memorial fund for educational and benevolent purposes.

Publications The national journal, *The Aztec*, is published during each school year and distributed to all interested members. Each chapter and national officer is furnished a *Fraternity Manual, the Pledgemaster's Manual, Rushing Brochure, Leadership Manual,* and *Pledge Manual.* A *Directory* is published at intervals.

Headquarters P.O. Box 4843, Little Rock, AR 72214. Phone: (618) 675-3699.

Membership Active chapters 5. Inactive chapters 6. Colonies 1. Total number of initiates 2,992. Chapter roll:††

1925   Alpha, Arkansas State, Conway
1939   Beta, Northeastern (OK)
1940   Gamma, Arkansas, Monticello
1941   *Delta, Southeastern Louisiana* (1948)
1946   Epsilon, Henderson
1950   *Zeta, Kansas State, Pittsburg* (1960)
1954   *Eta, Central State (OK)* (1959)
1958   *Theta, Little Rock* (1961)
1959   *Iota, Northwest Missouri* (1965)
1960   Kappa, Northwestern Oklahoma
       (1961-1964)
1977   Lambda, Arkansas Tech

Colonies: Southern Arkansas

Phi Mu Delta

ACTIVE PIN

PLEDGE PIN

PHI MU DELTA was founded March 1, 1918, at a conclave of the National Federation of Commons Clubs which met at Massachusetts Agricultural College at Amherst. Clarence Dexter Pierce conceived and promoted the concept of Phi Mu Delta and the 1918 conclave convened to create the new fraternity.

The vote of the conclave was in favor of all Commons Clubs becoming member chapters of Phi Mu

†† This chapter roll is repeated from the 19th edition; no current information was provided.

Delta and four clubs immediately did so: University of Connecticut, University of New Hampshire, University of Vermont and Union College. The alumni of the Union Commons Club refused to allow the undergraduates to join Phi Mu Delta and the three others persisted alone as the founding chapters.

The new fraternity was founded on the ideal justice embodied in the characteristics of brotherhood, service and democracy. The Founders' Creed of Phi Mu Delta calls for service to the college and community; recognition of the intrinsic worth of every man; and recognizes no creed, race or position in the application of the democracy of the order.

Government Phi Mu Delta is governed in accordance with its constitution, by-laws, trust and foundation rules as published in *The Governing Rules.* Chapters, alumni associations and chartered alumni clubs send delegates to national conclaves which meet biennially. The conclaves chart the course of the order for the following two-year period, elect the eight-man national council, approve actions of the executive committee, and devise such statutes and rule amendments as may be necessary. After election by the conclave, the national council organizes itself. There are eight positions on the national council.

Between conclaves the national council, national executive committee and the appointed executive secretary are vested with the governing powers of the order. The council appoints the trustees of the Triangle Trust Fund and the Phi Mu Delta Foundation as well as the executive secretary, editor and President's Cabinet.

Each of Phi Mu Delta's undergraduate chapters selects its own members, makes its own rules and formulates by-laws, subject to the national constitution and regulations of the host institution, and is afforded wide latitude in the conduct of its own affairs. Each chapter has an active alumni association with an elected governing board which advises and assists the undergraduates. All chapters are legally incorporated in their individual states of operation; Phi Mu Delta is nationally incorporated under Pennsylvania statutes.

Traditions Phi Mu Delta has had a conservative growth partly due to its recent founding, but also due to the desire of its members. Great stress is placed on service from national officers, staff and facilities to the respective chapters and associations. Thus the fraternity limits the number of new groups admitted according to the policy set by each conclave.

March 1 is celebrated each year as Founders' Day. At this time, chapters, alumni associations and alumni clubs conduct programs and social gatherings nationwide.

Between conclave years, the fraternity conducts leadership training conferences to educate and to inform officers and members who exhibit leadership potential.

Each year several awards are granted to acknowledge accomplishments of the chapters. Of particular interest are the Perce R. Appleyard Award for public service and relations, top scholarship awards, and the Walter Hahn Award for most improved chapter scholarship.

Two honorary chapters, The Distinguished Alumni Chapter and The Distinguished Service Chapter, were created in 1964 at the 31st conclave to honor the great men of Phi Mu Delta.

Insignia The badge of the fraternity is a black triangular field, bordered with pearls, and containing the letters of the fraternity name in gold about a sapphire center. The coat of arms is a lion bearing a shield, under which runs a ribbon bearing the Greek letters ΦΜΔ. The pledge pin is a triangular shield with three fields, each bearing one of the colors of the fraternity and each enclosing the scales of justice. The colors are Princeton orange, black and white. The flower is the jonquil.

Publications *The Triangle*, published once a year, and the *Lion Line*, which is published two times a year, are the official publications. Officers' manuals, manual for pledgeship, periodic directories, chapter guides, conclave minutes and rushing material are also published.

Funds and Philanthropies The Triangle Trust Fund was established in 1924 to provide continuing income for the publication of *The Triangle* and since 1965 has also been used as a housing trust.

The Phi Mu Delta Foundation was devised at the 27th conclave in 1956; federal tax exemption was received in 1964. The foundation is permitted to engage in educational, literary, scientific and charitable pursuits. It grants scholarships, makes educational grants, and supports leadership and vocational guidance programs from privately contributed funds.

Headquarters P.O. Box 296, State College, PA 16804. Phone: (814) 234-0626.

Membership Active chapters 11. Inactive chapters 19. Seven chapters own their houses, all others lease. Total number of initiates 9,000+. Chapter roll:

1918 *Nu Alpha, Connecticut* (1947)
1918 *Nu Beta, New Hampshire* (1981)
1918 Nu Gamma, Vermont (1936-1957)
1921 *Gamma Alpha, Northwestern* (1948)
1922 *Gamma Beta, Michigan* (1933)
1922 *Nu Delta, M.I.T.* (1977)
1923 *Gamma Gamma, Illinois* (1939)
1923 *Nu Epsilon, Maine* (1974)
1924 Mu Alpha, Susquehanna
1925 *Pi Alpha, Cal, Oakland* (1934)
1926 Mu Beta, Ohio Northern
1926 *Mu Gamma, Ohio State* (1960)
1927 *Nu Zeta, Boston U.* (1929)
1929 *Nu Eta, Rhode Island* (1977)
1929 Nu Theta, R.P.I.
1930 *Mu Delta, Wittenberg* (1977)
1930 Mu Epsilon, Penn State (1940-1954)
1931 *Pi Beta, Oregon State* (1935)
1934 *Nu Iota, Tufts* (1941)

1935 *Nu Kappa, N.Y.U.* (1937)
1953 Nu Zeta, Massachusetts
1964 *Gamma Epsilon, Minnesota, Morris* (1988)
1966 Nu Lambda, Trinity (CT)
1969 Mu Zeta, Lock Haven
1970 Nu Omicron, Keene
1972 *Mu Kappa, Slippery Rock* (1980)
1974 *Mu Omega, Toledo* (1977)
1975 *Gamma Psi, Tarkio* (1976)
1975 Nu Xi, Southern Maine
1985 Mu Pi, California (PA)

COAT OF ARMS

Phi Sigma Kappa

ACTIVE PIN

PLEDGE PIN

PHI SIGMA KAPPA was founded on the evening of March 15, 1873, after considerable preliminary planning by six sophomores at the Massachusetts Agricultural College, now the University of Massachusetts. The idea of the fraternity was conceived in the chemical laboratory, and its first quarters were located in Old North Hall, where a memorial tablet, The Shrine, was placed on the occasion of the fiftieth anniversary of the founding. When Old North Hall was demolished in the early fifties and replaced by Machmer Hall at the university, the shrine was embedded in the wall at the entrance of the latter. In 1973, on the occasion of the 100th anniversary of the founding, a plaque commemorating the centennial was placed next to the original tablet.

The founders, Joseph F. Barrett, William P. Brooks, Frederick G. Campbell, Xenos Y. Clark, Jabez W. Clay and Henry Hague, were leaders in college activities and in scholarship. They recognized the need on the Massachusetts campus for closer companionship among students of promise. Founded upon the teachings of the Golden Rule, the fraternity has as its objectives: the promotion of Brotherhood, the Stimulation of Scholarship and the Development of Character—qualities known to its members as Cardinal Principles.

Growth In 1888 the first move was made toward a national organization when Beta Chapter was established at Union College. In the earlier years the majority of the chapters were established through new groups of students at privately endowed colleges. In later years a larger number of new chapters has resulted from absorbing previously organized local fraternities at land grant colleges. The original conservative expansion policy, under the guidance of effective administration, maintained the society in good condition until the early twenties when conservatism gave way to relatively rapid expansion, especially during the years 1920 to 1930, when twenty-one new chapters were installed; again from 1940 to 1950, when twenty-one petitions were accepted and chapters installed; and again from 1960 to 1970, during which period thirty-three chapters were added to the roster.

Phi Sigma Kappa's size and strength were greatly increased by a merger in 1985 with the national fraternity Phi Sigma Epsilon which had thirty-six active chapters at the time of the merger. The current size is membership of over 110,000. The new Fraternity now possesses 114 active undergraduate chapters and colonies. Cornell University was the only campus with an active chapter of both fraternities. The Phi Sigma Epsilon chapter was released and later affiliated with another national fraternity. An account of Phi Sigma Epsilon appears in the Fraternities That Are No More section.

Government Phi Sigma Kappa was originally incorporated under the laws of the State of New York and then in 1959 reincorporated under the laws of the State of Delaware. The legislative power is vested in the general convention which meets biennially. Voting strength at the convention for active active chapters and alumni clubs is based upon membership, with each national officer having a single vote. The executive function of the Fraternity is vested in the Council, or board of directors. This body consists of the Grand President and six Directors. The Grand President is elected for a two-year term and the Directors to staggered four-year terms. The country is divided into provinces, each headed by a province president who is appointed by the Grand Council. An undergraduate province vice-president is elected at each biennial province conclave to assist the province president. The Court of Honor is composed of all living past grand presidents and is utilized in an advisory capacity. The Court at the time of the general convention elects a chancellor, who is the presiding officer of the Court, and a recorder. The chancellor also appoints and chairs the nominating committee for the election of Grand President and Grand Council. Other officers of the Fraternity include the executive director and editor of *The Signet*, a chaplain and a historian appointed by the Council. Other appointive officers are the director of member services, foundation executive director, director of expansion, director of business affairs, leadership consultants, director of alumni and a chapter advisor for each chapter. In the larger provinces a district governor may be appointed to supervise two or more chapters. The appointments are made by the Grand President. In the case of the district governors and chapter advisors, recommendations are made to the Grand President by the province president.

The convention is held in odd-numbered years. A leadership school for undergraduates and national officers is held in conjunction with each general convention. Biennially, in non-convention years, a conclave is held in each of the provinces.

The alumni are organized in the principal cities of the United States and function as chartered clubs. These clubs hold weekly or monthly luncheons, rushing dinners, annual Founders' Day banquets, and other meetings designed to maintain the interest of the membership.

Traditions and Insignia The official pin consists of the three Greek letters (ΦΣK). The letter Φ may be plain gold or crown set with fifteen whole pearls and is superimposed upon a rose engraved and rose finished chased gold Σ to the left and K to the right. As a mark of distinction, Council members may wear a ruby instead of a pearl as the center jewel and national presidents are presented with a badge set with diamonds instead of pearls, with a ruby as the center jewel. Appointive officers may wear an emerald instead of a pearl as their center jewel. (The red button is a round red field surrounded by a silver band in which the original Three T characters of the society are inset in silver. The circle and triple t's characters are then circumscribed in a triangle of silver.) The colors are silver and red. The official flowers are the red carnation and the white tea rose. The flag consists of three horizontal bars, red top and bottom, with a silver bar in the middle upon which is woven in the center ΦΣK in red, with the Three T characters and triangle displayed in silver in the upper left corner of the top bar. The popular name is Phi Sig.

Publications *The Signet*, published since 1879, is the official magazine of the Fraternity, issued four times a year during the collegiate year, and has its editorial offices at the international headquarters. Under the present laws of the Fraternity, each initiate automatically becomes a life subscriber to *The Signet* with the payment of his initiation fee. The Fraternity also issues a handbook for associates and members known as *Hills and A Star*, handbooks for each chapter officer, a chapter adviser's handbook, *Grand Chapter Policy Manual*, *Membership Education Manual*, and the *Constitution and Bylaws of the Grand Chapter*. In addition, rushing folders and posters are available. Much material on all phases of operation is available to the chapters, alumni clubs and officers through the library of the international headquarters.

Funds and Philanthropies The Phi Sigma Kappa Foundation, Inc., incorporated under the laws of the State of Delaware, was established in 1947. Its funds are utilized to advance the Fraternity's second cardinal principle—the Stimulation of Scholarship . . . providing fellowships and scholastic awards directed toward the maintenance of high scholastic achievement among the chapters and their members. The foundation also provides funding for the educational programs of the fraternity.

Headquarters 8777 Purdue Road, Suite 201, Indianapolis, Indiana 46268. Phone: (317) 875-5575. From 1938 to 1956 the national headquarters was maintained in offices in Chicago, Illinois. In 1956 the offices were moved to Drexel Hill, Pennsylvania. In 1976 the Executive Offices were moved to Indianapolis, Indiana, and is now called the International Headquarters. The more centralized location allows for increased chapter services, more rapid expansion and unlimited interaction with many other national headquarters located in Indianapolis, including the National Interfraternity Conference. The efficient professional staff consists of the executive vice president and editor of *The Signet*, a director of member services, foundation executive director, director of business affairs, director of expansion, director of publications, 2 leadership consultants, 2 administrative assistants, a membership records coordinator, a member services assistant, a bookkeeper and a special projects assistant.

Membership Total living membership 80,000. Total deceased membership 4,000. Active chapters 135. Inactive chapters 71. Colonies 7. Total number of initiates 105,000. Chapter roll:

Dubuque (1990)
1873 Alpha, Massachusetts
1888 Beta, Union (NY)
1889 Gamma, Cornell
1891 Delta, West Virginia
1893 *Epsilon, Yale* (1929)
1896 *Zeta, CUNY, Brooklyn* (1973)
1897 Eta, Maryland
1897 *Theta, Columbia (NY)* (1933)
1899 Iota, Stevens Tech
1899 Kappa, Penn State
1899 Lambda, George Washington
1900 Mu, Penn
1901 Nu, Lehigh
1902 Omicron, M.I.T.
1902 Xi, St. Lawrence
1903 Pi, Franklin and Marshall
1903 *Rho, Queens (ONT)* (1914)
1903 *Sigma, St. John's (MD)* (1940)
1905 *Tau, Dartmouth* (1955)
1906 *Chi, Williams* (1966)
1906 Phi, Swarthmore
1906 *Upsilon, Brown* (1939)
1907 Psi, Virginia
1909 Omega, Cal, Berkeley
1910 Alpha Deuteron, Illinois
1910 *Alpha Epsilon, Emporia* (1989)
1910 Beta Deuteron, Minnesota
1911 *Gamma Deuteron, Iowa State* (1939)
1915 Delta Deuteron, Michigan
1915 Epsilon Deuteron, Worcester Tech
1917 Eta Deuteron, Nevada
1917 *Zeta Deuteron, Wisconsin, Madison* (1935-1954) (1973)
1921 Theta Deuteron, Oregon State (1973-1989)
1923 *Iota Deuteron, Kansas State* (1941)
1923 Kappa Deuteron, Georgia Tech
1923 Lambda Deuteron, Washington (WA)
1923 *Mu Deuteron, Montana* (1972)

1923 *Nu Deuteron, Stanford* (1973)
1925 Omicron Deuteron, Alabama
1925 Pi Deuteron, Ohio State (1935-1946)
1925 Rho Deuteron, Gettysburg (1985-1989)
1925 *Sigma Deuteron, Nebraska* (1940)
1925 Xi Deuteron, Tennessee
1926 Chi Deuteron, Washington State
1926 Phi Deuteron, Kentucky
1926 *Psi Deuteron, Oregon* (1966)
1926 *Tau Deuteron, Carnegie-Mellon* (1940)
1926 *Upsilon Deuteron, North Carolina* (1935)
1927 Beta Epsilon, Pittsburg State, Kansas
1928 *Alpha Triton, Wesleyan (CT)* (1952)
1928 *Beta Triton, Knox* (1953)
1928 Gamma Epsilon, Northeast Missouri
1928 Omega Deuteron, USC
1929 *Gamma Triton, South Carolina* (1962)
1930 Delta Triton, Purdue
1930 Epsilon Delta, Eastern Illinois
1930 Epsilon Epsilon, Northeastern (OK)
1930 Epsilon Zeta, Fort Hays
1931 *Epsilon Eta, Southeastern Oklahoma* (1985)
1931 Epsilon Iota, Central Missouri State
1931 Epsilon Kappa, Wisconsin, Stevens Point
1934 Epsilon Lambda, Eastern Michigan
1935 Epsilon Mu, Central Arkansas
1936 Epsilon Triton, American
1938 Epsilon Nu, Northwest Missouri
1938 Epsilon Theta, Northern Iowa
1939 Zeta Triton, Montana State
1941 Epsilon Xi, Central Michigan
1942 Eta Triton, Akron
1943 Epsilon Pi, Western Illinois
1946 Epsilon Rho, Henderson
1947 Epsilon Sigma, Northern Illinois
1947 *Iota Triton, Connecticut* (1972)
1947 *Kappa Triton, Cal State, Fresno* (1959)
1947 *Theta Triton, Texas* (1976)
1948 Epsilon Tau, Ball State
1948 Lambda Triton, Rhode Island
1948 *Mu Triton, Boston U.* (1953)
1948 *Nu Triton, Hartwick* (1955)
1948 *Omicron Triton, Cal, Davis* (1973)
1948 *Pi Triton, Eastern Washington* (1953)
1948 *Xi Triton, San Jose* (1966)
1949 Chi Triton, Arizona State
1949 *Epsilon Phi, Wisconsin, Milwaukee* (1970)
1949 Phi Triton, Idaho State
1949 *Rho Triton, San Diego U* (1959)
1949 *Sigma Triton, Indiana* (1972)
1949 *Tau Triton, Baldwin-Wallace* (1954)
1949 *Upsilon Triton, Muhlenberg* (1955)
1950 *Alpha Tetarton, Linfield* (1954)
1950 Beta Tetarton, Kent
1950 Epsilon Chi, SUNY Col., Oswego (1954-1977)
1950 Epsilon Upsilon, Wisconsin, Whitewater
1950 Gamma Tetarton, R.P.I.
1950 Omega Triton, Florida Southern
1950 Psi Triton, Hobart
1951 *Delta Tetarton, Florida* (1959)
1952 *Epsilon Omega, Wisconsin, Stout* (1985)

1952	*Epsilon Psi, SUNY Col., Geneseo* (1954)
1952	Phi Beta, Wisconsin, Eau Claire
1954	Zeta Tetarton, East Tennessee
1955	Phi Delta, Black Hills (1961-1970)
1956	Eta Tetarton, Houston
1956	Phi Epsilon, Rider
1956	Phi Gamma, Western Michigan
1956	*Phi Lambda, Parsons* (1972)
1957	*Iota Tetarton, Tufts* (1976)
1957	Kappa Tetarton, Southern Illinois
1957	*Theta Tetarton, Detroit* (1973)
1958	*Lambda Tetarton, Wagner* (1982)
1958	*Mu Tetarton, Youngstown State* (1984)
1958	Phi Zeta, Illinois
1959	Nu Tetarton, Rutgers
1959	*Omicron Tetarton, Tennessee Wesleyan* (1979)
1959	Phi Eta, Clarion
1959	Phi Iota, Northland
1959	*Phi Kappa, West Virginia Wesleyan* (1985)
1959	Phi Theta, Shippensburg
1959	*Rho Tetarton, Loyola Marymount, Los Angeles* (1989)
1959	*Xi Tetarton, Michigan State* (1973)
1960	Phi Mu, Concord
1960	*Phi Pi, Wisconsin, Superior* (1976)
1960	*Phi Tetarton, Pacific (CA)* (1966)
1960	*Pi Tetarton, C. W. Post* (1971)
1960	*Sigma Alpha, Wisconsin, La Crosse* (1989)
1960	Sigma Chi, Shepherd
1960	Sigma Tetarton, Midwestern
1960	Tau Tetarton, Tennessee, Martin
1960	Upsilon Tetarton, Rochester Tech
1961	Chi Tetarton, Western Michigan
1961	Phi Omicron, St. Cloud
1962	Omega Tetarton, Cal State, Los Angeles
1962	Phi Nu, Mansfield
1962	Phi Xi, Winona
1963	*Alpha Pentaton, New Mexico* (1977)
1963	Beta Pentaton, East Stroudsburg
1963	Delta Pentaton, Northeastern (-1989)
1963	Gamma Pentaton, Utah
1963	Phi Rho, Chadron
1963	*Phi Tau, Cornell* (1985)
1964	*Epsilon Pentaton, American International* (1969)
1964	Phi Upsilon, Valparaiso
1964	Zeta Pentaton, Pan American
1965	Eta Pentaton, Drexel
1965	*Phi Phi, Wisconsin, Oshkosh* (1976)
1965	*Phi Sigma, Hillsdale* (1989)
1965	Theta Pentaton, Indiana (PA)
1966	Iota Pentaton, Cal State, Fullerton
1966	Kappa Pentaton, Cal, Santa Barbara
1966	*Lambda Pentaton, Ferris* (1978)
1966	*Mu Pentaton, Wisconsin, Milwaukee* (1971)
1967	Nu Pentaton, Clarion
1967	Omicron Pentaton, Edinboro

1967	Pi Pentaton, Northern Illinois
1967	*Rho Pentaton, Northwestern* (1976)
1967	Sigma Beta, Southwest Missouri
1967	*Xi Pentaton, Cal State, Northridge* (1970)
1968	*Chi Pentaton, Eastern Michigan* (1977)
1968	Phi Pentaton, Arizona
1968	Sigma Delta, St. Norbert
1968	Sigma Epsilon, Ferris
1968	*Sigma Pentaton, Quinnipiac* (1976)
1968	Sigma Zeta, Wisconsin, River Falls
1968	*Tau Pentaton, Mansfield* (1985)
1968	*Upsilon Pentaton, Hartford* (1972)
1969	Psi Pentaton, Memphis State
1969	Sigma Eta, Southeast Missouri
1969	Sigma Gamma, Wayne State (NE)
1969	Sigma Iota, Wisconsin, Platteville
1969	Sigma Kappa, LaSalle
1969	Sigma Lambda, Minnesota, Morris
1969	Sigma Mu, Manhattan
1969	Sigma Theta, Hofstra
1970	*Omega Pentaton, Bethel* (1973)
1970	*Phi Chi, Bemidji* (1976)
1970	Phi Omega, Moorhead
1970	Phi Psi, St. Thomas
1970	Sigma Nu, Slippery Rock
1970	Sigma Xi, Bloomsburg
1971	*Alpha Hexaton, Salem (WV)* (1974)
1971	Beta Hexaton, Purdue, Calumet
1971	Delta Hexaton, Susquehanna
1971	Gamma Hexaton, Robert Morris (1977-1986)
1971	Sigma Tau, Missouri Western
1972	Epsilon Hexaton, V.P.I.
1972	Eta Hexaton, Dayton
1972	*Zeta Hexaton, LaSalle* (1978)
1973	Iota Hexaton, Fairleigh Dickinson, Teaneck
1973	Theta Hexaton, Nicholls
1974	Kappa Hexaton, Stetson
1976	Lambda Hexaton, St. Joseph's (PA)
1976	Mu Hexaton, Radford
1976	*Nu Hexaton, West Liberty* (1977)
1976	Xi Hexaton, Clinch Valley
1977	*Omicron Hexaton, Oregon Tech* (1981)
1979	Pi Hexaton, Occidental
1981	Rho Hexaton, Northern Arizona
1982	Sigma Hexaton, Illinois State
1983	Tau Hexaton, Monmouth (NJ)
1984	Upsilon Hexaton, Fairleigh Dickinson, Madison
1985	Phi Hexaton, Towson
1988	Chi Hexaton, Virginia Commonwealth
1990	Alpha Septaton, Pitt
1990	Beta Septaton, Florida State
1990	Gamma Septaton, Bowling Green

Colonies: Cal Poly, San Luis Obispo, Frostburg, Wisconsin, Green Bay, Washington (MD), Waynesburg, McGill, Bowling Green

COAT OF ARMS

Pi Kappa Alpha

ACTIVE PIN

PLEDGE PIN

PI KAPPA ALPHA was founded at the University of Virginia, March 1, 1868, by Frederick Southgate Taylor, Julian Edward Wood, Littleton Waller Tazewell, Robertson Howard, James Benjamin Sclater, and William Alexander. Three of the founders had attended Virginia Military Institute during the War Between the States. Finding themselves together at the University of Virginia after the war, they decided to perpetuate their friendship with the addition of three others who had family or friendship ties. The founders included the three former cadets, a former Union hospital officer, a Confederate veteran, and a repatriate. In short, they were from a variety of backgrounds. The first pledge was Augustus Washington Knox, who was initiated on May 1, 1868.

Growth Although the chaotic conditions in the colleges of the South following the War made the early life of Pi Kappa Alpha difficult, plans were soon under way for establishing chapters in other institutions. Exactly one year after the founding, the mother chapter placed Beta Chapter at Davidson, and two years later, on February 27, 1871, Gamma Chapter was installed at William and Mary. Seven chapters were founded in the first ten years, six of which are active at the present time, although all except Theta had periods of inactivity in their early days.

During the period from 1868 and 1889, the Alpha Chapter was the governing body, granting charters, installing chapters, and determining policies, though for a time Theta exercised certain governing prerogatives.

In 1889 only four chapters were actively functioning: Alpha at Virginia, Theta at Rhodes, Iota at Hampden-Sydney, and Lambda at The Citadel. A call for a convention was sent out, and delegates from three of the four chapters met on December 20-23, 1889, at Hampden-Sydney. This convention is generally known as the "junior founding" and marked the beginning of the era of prosperity and substantial growth of Pi Kappa Alpha. The convention, led by Howard Bell Arbuckle, Iota, and Theron H. Rice, Theta, revised the constitution, providing government by conventions and a council form of government between conventions. This, with some

modifications, remains in effect today. Within a few years the fraternity began a solid growth.

The fraternity was not, as is sometimes stated, founded as a sectional organization. The convention of 1889, however, limited expansion to the southern states. The convention of 1904 authorized the granting of charters in the southwestern states, and the New Orleans convention in 1909 lifted the remaining ban and permitted charters to be granted anywhere in the United States. In 1933 the constitution was amended to permit chapters in Canada.

Room 47, West Range, University of Virginia, where the fraternity was founded, is now suitably furnished as a memorial and kept open to visitors daily. It is marked with a bronze plaque. Founders' Memorial Hall, erected largely by general fraternity funds, houses the mother chapter. At the Centennial Convention, the fraternity furnished the Interfraternity Council room at Virginia. The Beta Delta Chapter hall, owned by the New Mexico chapter, is a replica of the Pueblo Indian council chamber or estufa. It is situated on the campus of the University of New Mexico, and only initiates are permitted to enter.

The 1946 convention at Mackinac Island, Michigan, endorsed plans for the erection of a war memorial shrine at Memphis, Tennessee, to house trophies and books associated with Pi Kappa Alpha, and the national offices of the fraternity. This memorial building was completed in 1954 at a cost of about $300,000 and was dedicated September 5, 1954.

The record of Pi Kappa Alpha in all the wars of the country has been imposing. That was true particularly in the two World Wars. In World War I, one out of every six members of the fraternity was in the armed forces and over half a hundred of them made the supreme sacrifice. In World War II about 15,000 of the 33,000 active members were in the armed forces, including General Courtney H. Hodges, commander of the First Army. More than 400 Pi Kappa Alphas lost their lives in World War II.

In both of the World Wars, the fraternity remained active. In World War II, the fraternity had one of its greatest periods of prosperity, financially and otherwise.

Government The fraternity is governed between conventions by the Supreme Council, consisting of the national president, four national vice-presidents, two undergraduate vice-presidents, and a non-voting legal counsel. The national chaplain, the national historian, and the national editor and other national officers are appointed by the Supreme Council. National conventions are held biennially.

The executive vice-president, who is business manager of the fraternity, presides over the national office.

For administrative purposes, the country is divided into regions, each presided over by a regional president and appointed by the Supreme Council. Regional conferences are held annually.

The convention of 1924 in St. Louis established the one-term initiation rule making it compulsory for a pledge satisfactorily to complete one scholastic term before initiation. The same convention forbade organized horseplay or mock initiations of any description at all times, and the convention of 1928 reaffirmed this action. Mock initiations within the 24-hour period before initiation had been forbidden as early as 1911.

Traditions and Insignia Scholarship has always been encouraged. The convention of 1915 in San francisco established the Pi Kappa Alpha Scholarship Cup to be awarded the chapter with the highest average each year. The fraternity also awards plaques to chapters leading in scholarship on their respective campuses. Several regions have traveling scholarship cups and a number of chapters have cups or plaques for individual scholarship achievements.

The ritual was rearranged and amplified somewhat at the 1894 convention in Nashville, and rewritten in 1936 and 1952. The charge, of such antiquity that its authorship is unknown, is still retained. A uniform pledge ceremony is used by the chapters. The badge, designed by Founder William Alexander in 1868, is, with slight changes to permit copyrighting, in use today. The original coat of arms was revised in 1906, and slightly changed later for copyright.

The design of the badge is a shield of white surmounted by a diamond in black. Upon the diamond are the three capitals ΠΚΑ in gold. In the four corners of the shield are the small Greek letters φφχα. The colors of the fraternity are garnet and old gold, and the flower is the lily of the valley. The pledge button is a garnet shield with a gold Π in the center. The flag is garnet with the coat of arms and the letters ΠΚΑ in gold in the center and the letter of φφχα in gold, one in each corner.

Publications The magazine of Pi Kappa Alpha is the *Shield and Diamond*, founded in 1891 and continuously published since that time. The convention of 1926 established the Shield and Diamond Endowment Fund, providing for a life subscription to the magazine, payable at the time of initiation. The income is today used for the fraternity's leadership development program. The fund is administered by a board of three trustees.

In 1886 Daniel J. Brimm prepared *The Index*, which because of lack of money was not printed, but it served as the forerunner of the *Journal*. In 1889 Joseph Thompson McAllister, an initiate of Iota, but then a member of Alpha, published one issue of the *Bulletin*. In 1891 Robert Adger Smythe undertook on his own responsibility the publication of a bimonthly known as the *Pi Kappa Alpha Journal*, which appeared throughout one year. In 1892 the Grand Council started the *Shield and Diamond*, which has been regularly published as a quarterly or five times a year ever since. In 1898 the publica-

tion of a secret journal called the *Dagger and Key*, containing the minutes of the convention, was begun and has been maintained without interruption. In 1891 Robert Adger Smythe compiled a catalogue of the fraternity. In 1908 Lloyd Randolph Byrne published on his own responsibility the *Manual of Pi Kappa Alpha*, which is an historical treatise. In 1916 John Graham Sale published the *Pi Kappa Alpha Fraternity Register*, a book of 900 pages containing complete and exhaustive lists of members, together with a short history of each chapter and of the fraternity. Freeman H. Hart wrote the 450-page *History of Pi Kappa Alpha*, published in 1934. Jerome V. Reel, Jr. wrote *The Oak: A History of Pi Kappa Alpha*, which was published in 1980. In 1934 J. Harold Johnston published the *Pledge Manual*, later revised. Directories arranged alphabetically, geographically, and by chapters have been issued periodically since 1923. The Pi Kappa Alpha songbook has been issued regularly since 1921. "The Dream Girl of ΠΚΑ," by B. E. Shields, is one of the most popular among fraternity songs.

Forum, a biweekly newsletter to officers, chapters, and alumni associations, was launched in 1975 following six years of the *Weekend* and *Monthly Reports* and seven years of *Pi-Ties*. Officers' manuals serve areas of housing and pledge orientations while a series of modular information white papers entitled *ModuLogue* covers such subjects as alumni relations, kitchen management, management and leadership techniques for officers, and suggestions for community service and social programming. The *Garnet & Gold Membership Manual* (revised edition) and *Fraternity Bicentennial History: 200 Years of Freedom and Fraternity* were published in 1976.

Funds and Philanthropies At a national convention of Pi Kappa Alpha in 1907, a national chapter house loan fund was established. It now contains approximately $3,600,000 and has assisted more than 80 per cent of the undergraduate chapters of the fraternity in building or purchasing residence halls and lodges.

The Memorial Foundation of the fraternity administers extensive scholarship loan funds and scholarship grants. The 1966 convention established "Project Centennial," a fund-raising campaign with a $250,000 over-all objective. The foundation has assets of over $1,000,000.

In 1976 Pi Kappa Alpha adopted Big Brothers of America as its national focus in community service and developed the National Collegiate Superstar Championships to raise about $1,000,000 per year for BBA.

Headquarters 8347 West Range Cove, Memphis, TN 38138. Phone: (901) 748-1868.

Membership Living membership 116,271. Active chapters 180. Inactive chapters 49. Colonies 5. Houses owned 117. Graduate/Alumni chapters 35. City/Area alumni associations 40. Total number of initiates 163,765. Chapter roll:

1868	Alpha, Virginia
1869	Beta, Davidson
1871	*Delta, Birmingham-Southern* (1969)
1871	Gamma, William and Mary
1873	Epsilon, V.P.I.
1873	Zeta, Tennessee
1878	Eta, Tulane
1878	Theta, Rhodes
1885	Iota, Hampden-Sydney
1888	Kappa, Transylvania
1889	*Lambda, Citadel* (1890)
1890	Mu, Presbyterian
1891	Nu, Wofford
1891	Omicron, Richmond
1891	Xi, South Carolina
1892	Pi, Washington and Lee
1892	*Rho, Cumberland (KY)* (1908)
1893	Sigma, Vanderbilt
1895	Tau, North Carolina
1895	Upsilon, Auburn
1896	*Phi, Roanoke* (1909)
1898	*Chi, U of the South* (1910)
1900	*Psi, North Georgia* (1933)
1901	Alpha Alpha, Duke
1901	Omega, Kentucky
1902	*Alpha Beta, Centenary* (1951)
1902	Alpha Gamma, L.S.U.
1904	Alpha Delta, Georgia Tech
1904	Alpha Epsilon, North Carolina State
1904	Alpha Eta, Florida
1904	Alpha Theta, West Virginia
1904	Alpha Zeta, Arkansas
1905	Alpha Iota, Millsaps
1905	Alpha Kappa, Missouri, Rolla
1906	Alpha Lambda, Georgetown Col
1908	Alpha Mu, Georgia
1909	Alpha Nu, Missouri
1910	Alpha Omicron, Southwestern (TX)
1910	Alpha Xi, Cincinnati
1911	Alpha Pi, Samford
1912	Alpha Rho, Ohio State
1912	Alpha Sigma, Cal, Berkeley
1912	Alpha Tau, Utah
1912	*Alpha Upsilon, N.Y.U.* (1932)
1913	Alpha Chi, Syracuse
1913	Alpha Omega, Kansas State
1913	Alpha Phi, Iowa State
1913	*Alpha Psi, Rutgers* (1959)
1913	Beta Alpha, Penn State
1914	Beta Beta, Washington (WA)
1914	Beta Gamma, Kansas
1915	Beta Delta, New Mexico
1915	*Beta Epsilon, Western Reserve* (1959)
1916	Beta Zeta, Southern Methodist
1917	Beta Eta, Illinois
1917	*Beta Iota, Beloit* (1964)
1917	Beta Theta, Cornell
1919	Beta Kappa, Emory
1920	*Beta Lambda, Washington (MO)* (1961)
1920	Beta Mu, Texas
1920	Beta Nu, Oregon State
1920	Beta Omicron, Oklahoma
1920	Beta Pi, Penn
1920	Beta Xi, Wisconsin, Madison
1921	*Beta Rho, Colorado Col* (1933)
1921	Beta Sigma, Carnegie-Mellon
1922	Beta Chi, Minnesota (1936-1986)
1922	Beta Phi, Purdue
1922	*Beta Tau, Michigan* (1974)
1922	*Beta Upsilon, Colorado* (1969)
1923	*Beta Psi, Mercer* (1941)
1924	*Beta Omega, Lombard* (1930)
1924	Gamma Alpha, Alabama
1924	*Gamma Beta, Nebraska* (1977)
1925	Gamma Delta, Arizona
1925	Gamma Epsilon, Utah State
1925	*Gamma Gamma, Denver* (1972)
1926	*Gamma Eta, USC* (1972)
1926	*Gamma Zeta, Wittenberg* (1983)
1927	Gamma Iota, Mississippi
1927	Gamma Theta, Mississippi State
1928	Gamma Kappa, Montana State
1929	Gamma Lambda, Lehigh
1929	Gamma Mu, New Hampshire
1929	Gamma Nu, Iowa
1929	Gamma Xi, Washington State
1930	Gamma Omicron, Ohio (1974-1987)
1931	Gamma Pi, Oregon (1984-1990)
1932	Gamma Rho, Northwestern
1934	Gamma Sigma, Pitt
1935	Gamma Tau, R.P.I.
1936	Gamma Upsilon, Tulsa
1939	Gamma Chi, Oklahoma State
1939	Gamma Phi, Wake Forest
1940	Gamma Omega, Miami (FL)
1940	Gamma Psi, Louisiana Tech
1942	Delta Beta, Bowling Green
1947	Delta Delta, Florida Southern (1984-1989)
1947	*Delta Epsilon, Tennessee, Chattanooga* (1990)
1947	Delta Gamma, Miami (OH)
1947	Delta Zeta, Memphis State
1948	Delta Eta, Delaware
1948	Delta Iota, Marshall
1948	*Delta Kappa, San Diego U* (1987)
1948	Delta Theta, Arkansas State
1949	*Delta Lambda, Florida State* (1988)
1949	Delta Mu, Southern Mississippi
1950	Delta Nu, Wayne State (MI)
1950	Delta Omicron, Drake
1950	Delta Pi, San Jose
1950	Delta Rho, Linfield
1950	Delta Sigma, Bradley
1950	Delta Xi, Indiana
1951	*Delta Phi, Colorado Mines* (1963)
1951	Delta Tau, Arizona State
1951	*Delta Upsilon, Stetson* (1989)
1952	Delta Chi, Nebraska, Omaha
1952	Delta Psi, Maryland
1953	Delta Omega, High Point
1953	Epsilon Alpha, Trinity (CT)
1953	Epsilon Beta, Valparaiso
1953	Epsilon Gamma, Texas Tech.
1955	Epsilon Delta, North Texas

1955   Epsilon Epsilon, Toledo
1955   Epsilon Zeta, East Tennessee
1956   Epsilon Eta, Houston
1956   Epsilon Theta, Colorado State
1958   Epsilon Iota, Southeast Missouri
1958   Epsilon Kappa, Lamar
1958   Epsilon Lambda, Murray State
1958   *Epsilon Mu, East Carolina* (1973) (1986)
1960   Epsilon Nu, Georgia State
1960   Epsilon Omicron, Stephen F. Austin
1960   Epsilon Xi, Case Western Reserve
1961   Epsilon Pi, Sam Houston
1961   *Epsilon Rho, Idaho State* (1970)
1961   Epsilon Sigma, Tennessee, Martin
1962   *Epsilon Tau, Eastern New Mexico* (1990)
1962   Epsilon Upsilon, Gannon
1963   Epsilon Chi, Pittsburg State, Kansas
1963   Epsilon Omega, East Central State
1963   Epsilon Phi, Central Arkansas
1963   Epsilon Psi, Western Michigan
1963   Zeta Alpha, GMI
1963   Zeta Beta, Delta State
1964   *Zeta Delta, Parsons* (1973)
1964   Zeta Gamma, Eastern Illinois
1965   Zeta Epsilon, Western Kentucky
1965   Zeta Eta, Arkansas, Little Rock
1965   Zeta Theta, Southwest Texas
1965   *Zeta Zeta, Southwestern State (OK)* (1990)
1966   *Zeta Iota, Old Dominion* (1985)
1966   Zeta Kappa, Ferris
1966   *Zeta Lambda, Adrian* (1977)
1966   Zeta Mu, Idaho
1966   *Zeta Nu, Eastern Washington* (1978)
1967   Zeta Omicron, Cal State, Northridge
1967   Zeta Xi, Western Carolina
1968   Zeta Pi, South Florida
1968   Zeta Rho, North Dakota
1968   Zeta Sigma, Florida Tech
1969   Zeta Chi, Southwest Missouri
1969   *Zeta Omega, Southwestern Louisiana* (1990)
1969   Zeta Phi, Missouri, St. Louis
1969   *Zeta Psi, Nicholls* (1987)
1969   Zeta Tau, Eastern Kentucky
1969   *Zeta Upsilon, Concord College* (1986)
1970   Eta Alpha, Clemson
1970   Eta Beta, Seton Hall
1970   *Eta Delta, M.I.T.* (1982)
1970   *Eta Gamma, Windsor* (1972)
1971   Eta Epsilon, Angelo
1971   *Eta Eta, Morehead* (1984)
1971   *Eta Iota, Woodbury* (1975)
1971   Eta Kappa, South Alabama
1971   *Eta Lambda, Robert Morris* (1973)
1971   *Eta Mu, Armstrong State* (1980)

1971   Eta Nu, Northern Illinois
1971   Eta Theta, Weber
1971   Eta Zeta, Middle Tennessee
1972   Eta Omicron, Northeast Louisiana
1972   *Eta Pi, West Florida* (1982)
1972   Eta Rho, Northern Kentucky
1972   Eta Sigma, West Georgia
1972   Eta Tau, Austin Peay
1972   *Eta Xi, Alabama, Birmingham* (1984)
1973   *Eta Chi, Valencia* (1977)
1973   Eta Phi, Central Florida
1973   *Eta Psi, Texas Wesleyan* (1982)
1973   Eta Upsilon, Texas, Arlington
1974   *Eta Omega, Pembroke* (1986)
1974   Theta Alpha, North Alabama
1974   Theta Beta, Montevallo
1974   Theta Delta, Francis Marion
1974   Theta Gamma, Georgia Col
1975   Theta Epsilon, Northeastern (OK)
1975   Theta Zeta, Northern Iowa
1976   Theta Eta, Loyola Marymount, Los Angeles
1976   *Theta Iota, Tyler Junior* (1986)
1976   Theta Theta, Texas A & M
1977   Theta Kappa, Indiana Southeast
1977   Theta Lambda, Creighton
1977   Theta Mu, Massachusetts
1977   Theta Nu, Baylor
1978   Theta Xi, East Texas
1979   Theta Omicron, Indiana State
1979   Theta Pi, Alabama, Huntsville
1980   Theta Rho, Northern Arizona
1980   Theta Sigma, Winthrop
1981   Theta Tau, Cal State, Sacramento
1981   Theta Upsilon, Tennessee Tech.
1982   Theta Phi, Wichita
1984   Theta Chi, Villanova
1985   Theta Omega, Cal, Davis
1985   Theta Psi, Chapman
1986   Iota Alpha, Wyoming
1986   Iota Beta, Cal State, Fresno
1987   Iota Gamma, Kearney
1988   Iota Delta, Rose-Hulman
1988   Iota Epsilon, Cal State, Long Beach
1988   Iota Eta, Nevada
1988   Iota Zeta, Randolph, Macon
1989   Iota Iota, Michigan State
1989   Iota Kappa, Cal, Santa Barbara
1989   Iota Theta, Cal Poly, San Luis Obispo
1990   Iota Lambda, Columbia (NY)
1990   Iota Mu, Southern Illinois
1990   Iota Nu, St. Louis
1990   Iota Xi, Chicago

Colonies: Montana, Santa Clara, St. Joseph's (PA), UCLA, George Washington

Pi Kappa Phi

ACTIVE PIN

PLEDGE PIN

PI KAPPA PHI was founded at the College of Charleston, Charleston, South Carolina, December 10, 1904, by Andrew Alexander Kroeg, Jr., Simon Fogarty, Jr., and Lawrence Harry Mixson. The three had enjoyed friendship since their early school days in one of the South's most historic and significant cities. In 1907, the year of the fraternity's incorporation as a national organization, Beta Chapter was established at the Presbyterian College in Clinton, South Carolina. The following year, Gamma Chapter was established at the University of California, in Berkeley, California, making the fraternity truly national.

The goals of the fraternity, as stated in its mission statement entitled "Strong Enough to Care," include "the expression of shared values and ideals; the pursuit of brotherhood through scholarship, leadership, service and social experiences; the achievement of personal excellence in each member and collective excellence; and a lifelong brotherhood of its members." Membership may be conferred only by collegiate or alumni initiation through secret ritual. There are no honorary members. Members are commonly designated as "Pi Kapps."

Growth Pi Kappa Phi is the only national fraternity founded in the Carolinas, and with the exception of the California chapter, grew largely in the Southeast in its first two decades. Northern and Midwestern expansion became priorities in the 1920's as chapters were added at large public institutions in those states. Great strides were made in West Coast and Northeastern expansion in the 1970's and 1980's. By 1991, the fraternity had chapters and associate chapters in 33 states. Pi Kappa Phi remains as one of the few national fraternities to maintain its Alpha (first) chapter in continuous existence since the fraternity's founding.

Government Government is vested in a Supreme Chapter (convention) which meets biennially. Every 25 years, this meeting returns to Charleston to commemorate the founding. The Supreme Chapter is composed of duly elected representatives of the undergraduate and alumni chapters and the present and past national and undergraduate chapter officers. The overwhelming majority of votes at' the Supreme Chapter rest with the undergraduate delegates. To the National Council, elected at the Supreme Chapter meetings, and consisting of seven national officers—president, vice president, treasurer, secretary, chaplain, chancellor and past president—is delegated the responsibilities and duties of interpretation and administration of Supreme Law between Supreme Chapter meetings. The Council employs and supervises the work of an executive director who directs the administrative office staff. There is an assistant executive director; directors of communications, educational programming, expansion and business affairs; an office manager; leadership consultants; secretaries and clerical assistants.

For administrative purposes, the country is divided into 10 areas, each with an area governor reporting to the National Council. A leadership "conclave" meeting is held in each area annually each spring. Each chapter is required to have an alumnus who serves as chapter advisor, encouraging adherence to national policy, promoting scholarship of collegiate members and offering advice and counsel to individuals as needed.

Awards are given annually to those chapters in each area demonstrating the greatest scholastic achievement and academic improvement. The fraternity also honors a "Student of the Year." The fraternity operates on a master chapter rating system, ranking chapters semi-annually according to their achievement of the fraternity's "Six Objectives for Chapter Excellence."

Traditions and Insignia Pi Kappa Phi was among the first fraternities to have a national scholarship program and committee. It was one of the first fraternities to implement a leadership consultant program and to conduct a nationwide leadership school, Pi Kapp College, for emerging collegiate fraternity leaders. In addition, the fraternity annually sponsors two Mid-Year Leadership Conferences—one in Charlotte, the other in St. Louis—for collegiate officer training. Members seeking initiation are called "associate members," not "pledges."

The badge is a diamond-shaped emblem bearing a scroll, with the Greek capitals ΠΚΦ across the shorter diagonal and with a five-pointed gold star upon a black field above the scroll and a student's lamp on the black field below. The associate member pin is a white enamel diamond with gold edges and a gold scroll across the shorter diagonal. The fraternity's colors are gold, white and blue. The flower is the red rose. Each chapter owns a large brass bell, the public symbol of the fraternity, which rings in the start of each official chapter function. Typically, a chapter celebraties "Founders Day" each December and sponsors an annual spring formal called "Rose Ball."

All of the fraternity's symbols can be traced to the history of Charleston, South Carolina. The fraternity's motto is "Nothing Shall Ever Tear Us Asunder."

Publications *The Star and Lamp* is the fraternity's quarterly magazine, issued under a life subscription plan two or four times a year to all living initiates (frequency depending on annual giving). *The Pi Kappa Phi Journal* is a monthly publication highlighting chapter achievements from around the country. *The White Diamond* is the fraternity's associate member education manual.

Philanthropies In 1977, the national fraternity created its own unique national service project, PUSH, People Understanding the Severely Handicapped. The non-profit organization seeks to provide adaptive play environments for those with disabilities while promoting collegiate volunteerism and disability awareness programs. Through its support of PUSH, Pi Kappa Phi became the first collegiate fraternity to raise more than $1 million for a single charitable organization in 1989. The service corporation is completely funded by local undergraduate fund-raising initiatives.

PUSH frequently sponsors hands-on service weekends where undergraduates travel to designated locations to construct play facilities for disabled children. One such "Give-a-PUSH Weekend" built the first fully-accessible park in the state of Indiana in 1990. In addition, PUSH sponsors teams of traveling interns who perform "The Kids on the Block," an innovative puppet show which promotes disability awareness to elementary-aged children. Fraternity members reached more than 20,000 children between 1989–1991.

PUSH America is a coast-to-coast bicycle trek undertaken annually by as many as 50 Pi Kapp collegiates in an effort to raise money and awareness for Americans with disabilities. Since 1988, hundreds of collegiates have given their summers to cycle across the U.S., and the PUSH America project has raised more than a half-million dollars for awareness programs for the disabled. The PUSH America project, more than any other, has earned the fraternity tremendous media exposure and national acclaim.

Headquarters P.O. Box 240526, Charlotte, NC 28224. Phone: (704) 523-6000. On a large wooded lot, a "low country" style building of unfinished cypress is placed in a natural setting in the city limits of the largest city in the Carolinas. The building also houses the following subsidiaries: The Pi Kappa Phi Foundation; Pi Kapp Properties (the national housing corporation); Continuing Alumni Relations, Inc.; PUSH, Inc.; and the Pi Kappa Phi Insurance Escrow.

The Pi Kappa Phi Foundation is active in promoting numerous collegiate educational projects in areas such as alcohol awareness, sexual abuse prevention and appreciation of diversity. The fraternity received national recognition for its sexual abuse prevention programming when it received the Golden Gazelle Award from the National Organization of Women (N.O.W.) and subsequent coverage in *Time Magazine*.

The fraternity's executive director, Durward Owen, was the driving force behind the creation of the Fraternity Insurance Purchasing Group (F.I.P.G.), the most comprehensive risk management initiative in the history of the American Greek movement, serving as its first president from 1987–1991.

Membership Total living membership 44,131. Undergraduate membership 6,100. Active chapters 127. Inactive chapters 41. Colonies 14. Houses owned 78. Graduate/Alumni chapters 22. Total number of initiates 61,500. Chapter roll:

1904	Alpha, Charleston (SC)
1907	Beta, Presbyterian
1909	Delta, Furman (1963-1984)
1909	Gamma, Cal, Berkeley
1910	Sigma, South Carolina
1911	Zeta, Wofford
1912	*Epsilon, Davidson* (1970)
1912	*Eta, Emory* (1957)
1913	Iota, Georgia Tech
1913	*Theta, Cincinnati* (1913)
1914	Kappa, North Carolina
1915	Lambda, Georgia
1915	Mu, Duke (1970-1991)
1915	Nu, Nebraska (1972-1985)
1916	Xi, Roanoke
1917	Omicron, Alabama
1917	*Pi, Oglethorpe* (1943)
1920	Rho, Washington and Lee
1920	Tau, North Carolina State
1921	Chi, Stetson
1921	*Phi, Tulsa* (1926)
1921	Psi, Cornell (1986-1990)
1921	Upsilon, Illinois
1922	Omega, Purdue
1923	Alpha Alpha, Mercer
1923	*Alpha Beta, Tulane* (1935)
1923	Alpha Gamma, Oklahoma (1984-1988)
1924	Alpha Delta, Washington (WA) (1975-1990)
1924	Alpha Epsilon, Florida
1924	Alpha Zeta, Oregon State
1925	Alpha Eta, Samford
1925	Alpha Theta, Michigan State
1926	Alpha Iota, Auburn
1927	Alpha Kappa, Michigan (1934-1987)
1927	*Alpha Lambda, Mississippi* (1949)
1927	Alpha Mu, Penn State
1927	*Alpha Nu, Ohio State* (1936)
1928	Alpha Xi, New York Poly
1929	Alpha Omicron, Iowa State
1929	*Alpha Pi, U of the South* (1935)
1930	Alpha Rho, West Virginia (1938-1978)
1931	Alpha Sigma, Tennessee
1931	Alpha Tau, R.P.I.
1933	Alpha Upsilon, Drexel
1935	Alpha Phi, Illinois Tech
1947	*Alpha Chi, Miami (FL)* (1969)
1947	*Alpha Omega, Oregon* (1972)
1947	Alpha Psi, Indiana
1948	Beta Alpha, New Jersey Tech
1948	Beta Beta, Florida Southern
1949	Beta Delta, Drake
1949	Beta Epsilon, Missouri, Columbia
1949	Beta Gamma, Louisville (1966-1984)
1950	Beta Eta, Florida State

1950 *Beta Zeta, Simpson* (1952)
1951 Beta Iota, Toledo
1951 *Beta Theta, Arizona* (1963)
1954 Beta Kappa, Georgia State (1986)
1955 Beta Lambda, Tampa
1955 Beta Mu, McNeese
1956 *Beta Nu, Houston* (1959)
1956 *Beta Omicron, Northwestern* (1981)
1956 *Beta Xi, Central Michigan* (1975)
1957 *Beta Pi, Eastern Michigan* (1962)
1957 *Beta Rho, Clarkson* (1963)
1958 *Beta Sigma, Northern Illinois* (1960)
1959 Beta Tau, Valdosta
1961 Beta Upsilon, Virginia
1963 Beta Chi, East Texas
1963 Beta Phi, East Carolina
1964 *Beta Omega, East Tennessee* (1987)
1964 *Beta Psi, Tennessee Wesleyan* (1982)
1964 Gamma Alpha, Livingston
1964 Gamma Beta, Old Dominion
1966 Gamma Delta, Memphis State
1966 Gamma Epsilon, Western Carolina
1966 Gamma Gamma, Troy
1967 *Gamma Eta, Athens* (1967)
1967 Gamma Zeta, West Virginia Tech
1968 *Gamma Iota, L.S.U.* (1972)
1968 Gamma Kappa, Georgia Southern
1968 Gamma Lambda, Missouri, Rolla
1968 Gamma Theta, North Carolina, Wilmington
1969 Gamma Mu, Belmont Abbey
1969 Gamma Nu, LaGrange
1969 *Gamma Omicron, Bethel (TN)* (1977)
1969 Gamma Xi, Georgia Southwestern
1970 *Gamma Pi, Northwestern State* (1974)
1970 Gamma Rho, Lander
1970 *Gamma Sigma, Armstrong* (1984)
1970 *Gamma Tau, North Texas* (1975)
1970 Gamma Upsilon, Oklahoma State
1971 Delta Alpha, V.P.I.
1971 Delta Beta, North Georgia
1971 Gamma Chi, Jacksonville (AL) (1980-1989)
1971 Gamma Omega, Montevallo
1971 Gamma Phi, South Alabama
1971 Gamma Psi, Augusta
1972 Delta Delta, Northeast Missouri
1972 Delta Epsilon, Jacksonville (AL)
1972 *Delta Gamma, Nebraska, Omaha* (1990)
1973 Delta Eta, Morehead
1973 *Delta Iota, Middle Tennessee* (1980)
1973 *Delta Kappa, Pembroke* (1981-1984) (1991)
1973 Delta Lambda, North Carolina, Charlotte
1973 *Delta Theta, Mars Hill* (1979)
1973 Delta Zeta, Appalachian
1974 *Delta Mu, Methodist* (1981)
1974 *Delta Nu, Western Kentucky* (1984)
1974 *Delta Xi, North Alabama* (1984)
1975 *Delta Omicron, Nicholls* (1983)
1976 *Delta Pi, Wright State* (1983)
1976 *Delta Rho, USC* (1983)
1976 Delta Sigma, Bowling Green
1977 Delta Tau, James Madison

1978 Delta Chi, Kansas State
1978 Delta Phi, Radford
1978 Delta Psi, Texas, Arlington (1985-1989)
1978 Delta Upsilon, Pitt
1979 Delta Omega, Texas A & M
1979 *Epsilon Alpha, Elon* (1989)
1979 Epsilon Beta, Grand Valley
1979 Epsilon Gamma, Longwood
1980 Epsilon Delta, Auburn, Montgomery
1980 Epsilon Epsilon, Clinch Valley
1980 Epsilon Eta, Winthrop
1980 Epsilon Theta, Seton Hall
1980 *Epsilon Zeta, Central Arkansas* (1990)
1981 Epsilon Iota, North Carolina, Greensboro
1981 Epsilon Kappa, Southern Tech
1981 *Epsilon Lambda, South Carolina, Spartanburg* (1988)
1982 Epsilon Mu, Bradley
1982 Epsilon Nu, Cal State, Sacramento
1982 Epsilon Omicron, Villanova
1982 Epsilon Xi, LaSalle
1983 Epsilon Pi, Virginia Commonwealth
1983 Epsilon Rho, Lenoir-Rhyne
1983 Epsilon Sigma, Christian Brothers
1983 Epsilon Tau, St. Joseph's
1984 Epsilon Upsilon, Georgia Col.
1985 *Epsilon Chi, Denver* **(1987)**
1985 **Epsilon Phi, Alabama**, Birmingham
1985 Epsilon Psi, Slippery Rock
1986 Epsilon Omega, Texas Tech.
1986 Zeta Beta, Cal, San Diego
1986 Zeta Delta, Shippensburg
1986 Zeta Epsilon, George Mason
1986 Zeta Gamma, North Dakota
1987 Zeta Zeta, North Florida
1988 Zeta Alpha, Clemson
1988 Zeta Eta, South Florida
1988 Zeta Iota, Indiana (PA)
1988 Zeta Kappa, Stockton
1988 Zeta Lambda, Cal. State, Chico
1988 Zeta Theta, Texas
1989 Zeta Mu, Cal. State, Northridge
1989 Zeta Nu, West Chester University
1989 Zeta Omicron, SUNY, Cortland
1989 Zeta Pi, Marshall University
1989 Zeta Xi, Averett College
1990 Zeta Phi, Colorado State
1990 Zeta Chi, Albright College
1990 Zeta Rho, Cal. State, Fullerton
1990 Zeta Sigma, Cal. State, Davis
1990 Zeta Tau, Barton College
1990 Zeta Upsilon, Bloomsburg
1991 Zeta Omega, Towson State University
1991 Zeta Psi, IUPUI

Colonies: Bryant, Cal, Irvine, Colorado, Concord, Elon, Francis Marion, Indiana State, Kennesaw, Maryland, North Carolina Wesleyan, Queens (NC), San Francisco, South Carolina, Spartanburg, Wright State

COAT OF ARMS

Pi Lambda Phi

ACTIVE PIN

PLEDGE PIN

PI LAMBDA PHI was founded at Yale University, March 21, 1895, by Henry Mark Fisher, Louis Samter Levy, and Frederick Manfred Werner. As undergraduates of different faiths, conscious of the greed, aggressions, and bad feeling rampant in the world and sensing the need for greater understanding among men, these men "met to consider a college fraternity on lines broader and more liberal than those employed" at that time. It was their purpose to establish "not a narrow esoteric fraternity, but a fraternity in which all men were brothers, no matter what their religion, a fraternity in which ability, open-mindedness, far-sightedness, and a progressive, forward-looking attitude" would be "recognized as the basic attributes."

As a consequence Pi Lambda Phi was established in part as a protest against the formation of college groups which excluded Jewish men, and in part as a protest against the further establishment of exclusively Jewish groups. Thus the founders sought to exemplify a philosophy of fraternity which would not be contrary to the ideals of fraternity, nor to the formal principles of democracy. These men stated their purpose in the preamble of the constitution of the new society in these words: "We, students pursuing courses at American colleges, appreciating the need of a fraternity which shall eliminate all prejudice and sectarianism and desirous of affiliating ourselves in spirit, in feeling, and in action, do hereby associate ourselves in this Pi Lambda Phi Fraternity."

Growth   In the following year, 1896, other chapters were established. The initial growth of the fraternity was rapid, as groups of men in nine different colleges welcomed the idea of a nonsectarian fraternity. A conservative policy of development was instituted. New chapters were admitted only as they could be absorbed and upon the fulfillment of specific entrance requirements which included faculty endorsement.

A large step was taken on February 1, 1941, when a merger was effected with Phi Beta Delta, a national fraternity founded at Columbia University in 1912. The united fraternity possessed 33 undergraduate chapters, deducting the duplicates. The ideologies and purposes of Pi Lambda Phi and Phi Beta Delta were similar. The Greek-letter designation of undergraduate chapters were altered by prefixing the names of the states in which the chapters were located. The method of designation of the inactive chapters was not changed. Inactive chapters at Fordham, Brooklyn Polytechnic Institute, Worcester Polytechnic Institute, Tufts, Iowa, Drake, Minnesota and Alabama were not regarded as chapters of Pi Lambda Phi; nevertheless, the alumni of these chapters became members under the merger terms. Delta Nu Chapter (1897-1900) has been superseded by the Massachusetts Theta Chapter.

Another historic step in Pi Lambda Phi's expansion took place on November 1, 1960, when the National Councils of Pi Lambda Phi and Beta Sigma Tau, a nonsectarian national fraternity, founded at Chicago in 1948, entered an agreement to merge.

On December 12, 1972, Beta Sigma Rho merged with Pi Lambda Phi, whose ideals were quite similar, in that the former was in fact and the latter is a nonsectarian organization.

Government   The national convention is the supreme governing body. In the interim between conventions, the National Council, elected by the national convention, governs the fraternity. Officers are elected annually by members of the Council. Each chapter has an alumnus, appointed by National Council, acting as chapter supervisor.

The fraternity provides complete financial supervision and control of chapters. Title to real estate is not vested in the active chapters. In the case of a new chapter, provision is automatically made for a building fund, administered by the trustees of the permanent Endowment Fund, so that each new chapter established is sure of having a home reasonably soon.

Two types of alumni chapters are provided for: the chapter alumni association and the geographical alumni association. Either type of group can be chartered when recognized by the National Council, and both types when thus chartered are entitled to vote at conventions.

The National Executive Office is directed by the national executive secretary who with an assistant and a clerical force of four devote their time to visiting chapters, issuing publications, and conducting the other business of the fraternity.

Traditions and Insignia   Pi Lambda Phi was one of the first fraternities in the country to include complete supervision of scholarship as one of the major activities of the National Executive Office. As a result, the fraternity has always finished high in the annual scholastic records of the National Interfraternity Conference. A close check is kept by the National Executive office by means of detailed scholastic records for every undergraduate member.

Encouragement of scholarship is given by awards to chapters and individual members of undergraduate classes. Many awards are made each year for achievements in various phases of activity, both scholastic and extracurricular. National Council awards are made annually to chapters that have made the best all-around record accomplishment in scholarship, extracurricular activity, sound finances, and national fraternity cooperation.

The New Horizons program was established to make the fraternity a vital force in the growth of the members by providing opportunities for planned study groups, discussions, forums, panels on subjects of vital interest, which effect a closer tie between the college and the fraternity in carrying out cultural and fraternal projects.

The open motto is *Nostros Amemus.* Colors are purple and gold. The flower is the woodbine. The popular name is Pilam.

The present badge, redesigned in 1973, replaces the one is use since 1941. It is a pentagon-shaped pin with gold border, bright gold finish, royal blue enameled panel, Greek letters ΠΛΦ in black appearing on band of gold, bright finish, running diagonally from upper left to lower right corner of panel, lamp in upper field, a mullet in lower field, profile of a rampant lion's head turned left, superimposed on center of border, with shepherd's staff and a sword crossing diagonally, corner to corner, behind a shield. The previous badge of 1928, which resembled the shield of the fraternity, and the original diamond-shaped badge of 1895 were discarded. The official badge of initiation is the plain badge; the wearing of pearl-bordered badges is optional. The pledge button is pentagon-shaped, with a pearly circle surrounded by a small golden circle set in the center, and a vertical golden bar in the center. The recognition button is a miniature gold replica of the official crest, or the Greek letters ΠΛΦ.

Publications The official publications are: "Notes from National," quarterly exoteric magazine; the official directory of members; *National Pledge Manual; National Rush Booklet; National Rushing Manual; Guide for a Successful Scholarship Committee; Chapter Manual; Guide to Successful Pledge Training; Alumni Organization Manual; Code of Pi Lambda Phi; Manual for Chapter Supervisors;* and *National Song Book.* Most of the undergraduate chapters publish newsletters and directories for distribution to their alumni.

Funds and Philanthropies The permanent Endowment Fund is a separate corporation, membership in which was formerly obligatory upon all members; it is administered by a board of five trustees. The principal of the fund is invested, and the interest is used for lending money on mortgages to chapters, subsidizing official publications, and for any other specific purpose deemed worthy by the trustees.

The Foundation is a separate corporation established to grant scholarships and fellowships for the study of social conditions, and group relations at colleges, universities, and other educational institutions; to develop and supervise chapter educational programs; to endow chairs of professorships, and to foster the ideals of humanitarianism and good citizenship.

In 1960, Pi Lambda Phi sponsored a National Merit Scholarship through the Scholarship Program of the National Merit Scholarship Corporation, under the auspices of the Pi Lambda Phi Foundation. It is anticipated that each year Pi Lambda Phi will sponsor a college scholarship for a son of a member of the fraternity.

The National Council makes the following awards: National Council Key (CK), the highest award to an alumnus for meritorious service to the fraternity; Certificate of Merit to an alumnus for outstanding service to the fraternity; Certificate of Recognition to undergraduates for outstanding service; Bit Pi to alumni by virtue of civic, academic, or personal achievement; a jewel to a holder of the National Council Key for continuous services to the fraternity; Rafer Johnson-Upsilon Achievement Award—annually to an undergraduate brother who most exemplifies the outstanding qualities of Rafer Johnson; Alumni Achievement Award—annually to the alumnus who has done the most for Pi Lambda Phi in the preceding year; and Humanitarian Award, a gold medal presented to that individual who has gained world-wide recognition as an exponent of true humanitarianism and brotherhood.

Headquarters 1 Center Avenue, Norwalk, Connecticut 06851. Phone: (203) 847-5294.

Membership Living membership 20,000. Active chapters 51. Inactive chapters 60. Colonies 9. Houses owned 20. Graduate/Alumni chapters 30 Total number of initiates 33,614. Chapter roll:

	CA Tau Alpha, San Francisco State (1990)
1895	*Iota, Yale (1932)*
1896	*Alpha, Columbia (NY) (1964)*
1896	*NY Beta, CCNY (1935-1959) (1971)*
1896	*NY Delta, Cornell (1976)*
1896	*NY Gamma, N.Y.U. (1973)*
1896	*Nu, Harvard (1900)*
1896	PA Epsilon Zeta, Penn
1897	MA Theta, M.I.T.
1897	*Xi, Union (NY) (1900)*
1913	*PA Beta Sigma Beta, Penn State (1984)*
1914	PA Gamma Sigma, Pitt
1915	PA Lambda, Lehigh
1916	NJ Theta, Stevens Tech
1918	*Beta, Fordham (1934)*
1919	*IL Omicron, Chicago (1949)*
1919	*NY Delta Delta, CUNY, Brooklyn (1934)*
1920	*CA Kappa, USC (1952)*
1921	Canada Eta, McGill (1942-1988)
1921	*MO Pi, Washington (MO) (1967)*
1922	CA Tau, Cal., Berkeley
1922	*CA Upsilon, UCLA (1969)*
1922	*Canada Kappa, Toronto (1966-1980) (1989)*
1922	*MA Rho, Worcester Tech (1932)*
1922	*OK Iota, Oklahoma (1963)*
1922	PA Beta Zeta, Carnegie-Mellon
1922	*WV Mu, West Virginia (1959)*
1924	*MA Xi, Tufts (1931)*
1924	*NH Pi, Dartmouth (1971)*
1925	FL Delta, Florida

1925	*IA Psi, Drake* (1930)
1925	MD Rho, Johns Hopkins (1943-1980)
1926	*CO Alpha Beta, Denver* (1967)
1926	WI Omega, Wisconsin, Madison (1968-1983)
1927	*AL Alpha Eta, Alabama* (1940)
1927	*IA Phi, Iowa* (1937)
1927	*OH Alpha Epsilon, Ohio State* (1977)
1927	PA Alpha Delta, Temple
1927	*Upsilon, Amherst* (1931)
1928	*IN Alpha Theta, Indiana* (1959)
1928	*NE Chi, Creighton* (1952)
1928	*SC Alpha Zeta, South Carolina* (1950)
1929	*CO Alpha Iota, Colorado* (1963)
1929	*RI Phi, Brown* (1963)
1929	VA Psi, William and Mary
1932	*VA Omega Alpha, Virginia* (1945-1966)
1934	IL Tau Delta, Illinois
1935	*NJ Beta Theta, Rutgers, Newark* (1983)
1939	*NC Omega Beta, North Carolina* (1984)
1940	*PA Sigma, Lafayette* (1983)
1942	PA Omega Gamma, Penn State
1943	NY Omega Epsilon, SUNY, Buffalo (1968-1988)
1945	Canada Kappa Iota, Western Ontario (1968-1983)
1946	*FL Omega Eta, Miami (FL)* (1963)
1947	PA Tau Omega, Franklin and Marshall
1948	*OH Beta Sigma, Ohio Wesleyan* (1968)
1948	OH Beta Tau, Baldwin-Wallace
1948	*PA Omega Kappa, Washington and Jefferson* (1981)
1949	*Beta Sigma Kappa, Kentucky* (1953)
1949	*MA Alpha Epsilon, Lowell* (1986)
1949	NY Beta Lambda, Syracuse
1951	*NY Omega Mu, N.Y.U.* (1966)
1954	NY Kappa Tau, R.P.I.
1958	IN Alpha Delta, Indiana State
1958	*NY Sigma Tau, CUNY, Brooklyn* (1973)
1959	*ME Beta Chi, Colby* (1984)
1959	VA Lambda Kappa, Roanoke
1961	*NY Alpha Lambda, Rutgers* (1969)
1963	NY Phi Lambda, Adelphi
1965	PA Delta Iota, Drexel
1966	*CT Alpha Chi, Hartford* (1969)
1967	*MA Kappa Nu, Massachusetts* (1981)
1967	*NY Alpha Mu, Hunter* (1970)
1967	*NY Delta Epsilon, Long Island* (1970)
1967	*NY Lambda Delta, Queens (NY)* (1971)
1968	*CT Delta Kappa, Bridgeport* (1971)
1968	*CT Tau Kappa, Quinnipiac* (1975)
1968	*NM Sigma Chi, New Mexico Highlands* (1972)
1968	NY Beta Omicron, St. John's (NY)
1968	*NY Eta Chi, Hobart* (1975)
1968	*PA Gamma Chi, West Chester* (1977)
1968	*PA Phi Delta, Alliance* (1988)
1968	*TX Alpha Sigma, Texas* (1973)
1969	PA Phi Sigma, Philadelphia Pharmacy
1970	*ME Kappa Beta, Ricker* (1976)
1970	*RI Sigma Upsilon, Rhode Island* (1974)
1971	FL Delta Tau, Jacksonville
1971	*NC Delta Zeta, East Carolina* (1978)
1971	PA Omega Delta, Penn State, Altoona
1972	*TX Alpha Omega, Texas Tech.* (1978)
1978	NC Omega Zeta, Western Carolina
1982	PA Beta Upsilon, East Stroudsburg
1983	NC Zeta Alpha, North Carolina, Asheville
1984	MI Mu Delta, Michigan State
1984	*PA Alpha Xi, King's* (1988)
1984	PA Sigma Upsilon, Shippensburg
1984	VA Omega Rho, Virginia Commonwealth
1984	VA Omicron Zeta, V.P.I.
1985	MD Pi Phi, Towson
1985	NY Kappa Alpha, SUNY, Albany
1986	MA Kappa Theta, Boston U.
1986	MD Kappa Delta, Salisbury
1986	MI Alpha Omega, Siena Heights
1986	NY Kappa Gamma, SUNY Col., Cortland
1987	Canada Kappa Kappa, Windsor
1987	DL Kappa Eta, Widener
1987	FL Kappa Epsilon, Florida Atlantic
1988	PA Kappa Omega, Albright
1989	MI Delta Beta, Ferris
1989	PA Delta Phi, Edinboro
1990	NY Omicron Rho, SUNY, Binghamton

Colonies: Auburn, Delaware, Florida Institute, Winona, Appalachian, Fairleigh Dickinson, Rutherford, Hofstra, Michigan, Cincinnati

COAT OF ARMS

Psi Upsilon

ACTIVE PIN

PLEDGE PIN

PSI UPSILON was founded at Union College in November, 1833, an outgrowth of an association of young men who had banded together for moral, intellectual, and social growth. The founders were Samuel Goodale, 1836; Sterling G. Hadley, 1836; Edward Martindale, 1836; George W. Tuttle, 1836; Robert Barnard, 1837; Charles Harvey, 1837; and Merwin N. Stewart, 1837. Two were from Massachusetts, the others from New York. Three of the seven received Phi Beta Kappa keys, six their A. B. in course, and the seventh afterwards attained scholastic honors.

The Honorable William Taylor, Theta 1838, in *The History of the Psi Upsilon Fraternity*, writes:

"Several students of Union College, members of the Sophomore class of 1833 and belonging to the Delphian Institute . . . being desirous of a more close and friendly union than afforded by that association, determined to unite themselves into a club or secret society. The first record of their meeting is in the following words:

> We, the undersigned, having determined to form a secret society, and having some conversation upon the subject, do now and hereby pledge our sacred honors that we will keep all that has been said and done a most profound secret and that, if we please, at or before the beginning of the next term, we will meet and form a society. Signed: M. H. Stewart, R. Barnard, Sterling G. Hadley, Geo. W. Tuttle, Edw. Martindale, C. W. Harvey, Sam'l Goodale.

And so, on the evening of November 24th, 1833, in a quaint Dutch settlement on the banks of the Mohawk River, Psi Upsilon came into being."

Growth The early days of Psi Upsilon were by no means smooth. The formation of the Fraternity was, at first, kept secret in an effort to forestall opposition until such time as the organization was strong enough to resist. Not until June, 1834, was the badge worn publicly. The members hand-picked new associates in an effort to ensure the stability of the organization.

Rival organizations did what they could to hinder Psi Upsilon's growth and progress. They made agreements among themselves to exclude all of Psi Upsilon's members from Phi Beta Kappa, but this step seemed, to college president Dr. Eliphalet Nott, very unjust, so he informed the members of Phi Beta Kappa to dissolve the agreement. If the agreement was not dissolved, he declared the faculty would nominate the members of Psi Upsilon to Phi Beta Kappa. This threat was actually carried out, and Psi U secured fair representation in Phi Beta Kappa.

The chapter name Theta was not given until 1838, at which time Psi Upsilon embarked upon its policy of conservative expansion. Maunsell Van Rennselaer, who later became President of Hobart College, suggested the special title Theta for the mother chapter. The Union chapter was the first fraternity at that school to have representation from the four undergraduate classes. The Delta Chapter had already been established at the University of the City of New York (later changed to New York University) in 1837. The third chapter, Beta, was instituted at Yale in 1839 by the brilliant and versatile William B. Robinson, who aided in establishing the Sigma at Brown in 1840, and the Gamma at Amherst in 1841. Two more chapters, the Zeta at Dartmouth and the Lambda at Columbia, were formed in 1842. In the year following, Psi Upsilon grew by ten, with the admission of the Kappa, the Psi, and the Xi, at Bowdoin, Hamilton, and Wesleyan, respectively. Within a decade of its inception and well before many of the Greek letter organizations of today were in existence, Psi Upsilon had become a widely spread intercollegiate fraternity, for those days.

From 1843 to the Semi-Centennial in 1883 Psi Upsilon enjoyed a period of virtually uninterrupted success. It was a period of a slowly growing chapter roll. Only eight chapters were added in the entire forty years—the Alpha (Harvard), the Upsilon (Rochester), the Iota (Kenyon), the Phi (Michigan), the Omega (Chicago), the Pi (Syracuse), the Chi (Cornell), and the Beta Beta (Trinity).

From 1883 to 1949, the Fraternity witnessed remarkable growth not only within the United States, but into Canada as well. The Eta (Lehigh), the Tau (Pennsylvania), the Mu (Minnesota), the Rho (Wisconsin), the Epsilon (California at Berkeley), the Omicron (Illinois), the Delta Delta (Williams), the Theta Theta (Washington), the Nu (Toronto), the Epsilon Phi (McGill), the Zeta Zeta (British Columbia), the Epsilon Nu (Michigan State), and the Epsilon Omega (Northwestern) were all successfully established as chapters during that period.

Psi U growth during the latter years, though, has mainly been the result of the expansion efforts of the Executive Council and the international office. The last forty years have brought the Theta Epsilon (Southern California), the Nu Alpha (Washington and Lee), the Gamma Tau (Georgia Tech), the Chi Delta (Duke), the Zeta Tau (Tufts), the Epsilon Iota (Rensselaer), the Phi Beta (William and Mary), and the Kappa Phi (Pennsylvania State) into the chain of Psi Upsilon chapters.

A consequence of the extension of the chapter roll is the growth of alumni organizations. Active alumni associations have been formed in a number of large cities including New York, Washington, D.C., Chicago, and Philadelphia. Founders Day, initiations, homecomings, and commencements find the alumni of each chapter assembled in reunion in growing numbers to carry on the traditions, sing the songs, and keep alive the friendships which abound so joyously in our brotherhood.

The minute book of the Theta reveals that the first Constitution of the Fraternity was adopted on January 10, 1834. This important document was signed by the seven original founders and thirteen other members of the Fraternity and is now in the Fraternity archives. The undated manuscript was missing for a number of years before being discovered in a shop dealing in rare documents in 1936.

Psi Upsilon has had a distinguished history over its 158 years. In many areas it set the pace for the fraternity movement, being the first to hold a fraternity Convention (1840), print a membership catalogue (1843), publish a fraternity history (1843), print a fraternity songbook (1849), and issue a fraternity magazine (1850).

All of the founders, with the exception of Stewart, lived to see the maturation of Psi Upsilon. Bernard lived until 1855, when there were eleven chapters and 1,660 members. Harvey, who died in 1886, saw growth to nineteen chapters and 6,600 members. The last surviving founder, Martindale, lived to 1904 when there were twenty-three chapters and more than 11,000 members. Their dream today has grown to an International Fraternity of over thirty active chapters and 20,000 members.

Psi Upsilon is affiliated with the NIC, FEA, CFEA, and is a member of the Fraternity Insurance Purchasing Group.

Government In 1869 the Executive Council of five members, subsequently increased to twenty-five, became the administrative head of the Fraternity. While generously endowed by the Conventions with substantial power, the Executive Council guides the Fraternity through tradition and precedence, relying on the chapters and their alumni to maintain and deserve the high privilege of membership in Psi Upsilon.

The Executive Council is comprised of nine to eleven alumni term members who are elected by the Convention. In addition, the Chairman and Vice Chairman of the Undergraduate Advisory Board, the Chairman of the Alumni Advisory Board, and the Executive Director all serve as full voting members. Also serving the Council are life members (former Presidents of the council) and honorary life members (Executive Council members who have served for fifteen or more years). The Executive council meets four times annually.

An administrative office is maintained in Paoli, Pennsylvania (suburban Philadelphia). The professional staff includes the Executive Director, the Director of Chapter Services, two Field Directors (traveling chapter consultants) a Financial Manager, and an Administrative Assistant. The Fraternity's archives are located at the office facility.

Insignia The badge is a lozenge, displaying across its shorter diagonal the emblem of the clasped hands, with the Ψ above and the Υ below. Colors are garnet and gold, these also being used on the pledge button.

The arms of the Fraternity are described in heraldic terms as a black shield bearing hands and letters of gold as in the badge, around which emblems run what is known as a double tressure, flory counter flory, of silver. The 'double tressure' alludes to the 'tie that binds' the secrets, ideals, and aims of the Fraternity.

Publications The *History of the Psi Upsilon Fraternity* by William Taylor, Theta '38, was published in 1843 and contains a thorough history of the Fraternity until that time. Willard Fiske, Psi '51, wrote *The Story of the Psi Upsilon Fraternity* in 1875 and had his account of the fraternity's history published in 1895. The *Epitome*, published in 1884 by Albert P. Jacobs, Phi '73, contains a full and interesting account of the history, organization, government, membership, social life, and property of the fraternity down to that date. A history of the Upsilon Chapter by George A. Coe was published in 1883, and a bibliography by Professor Fiske, Psi '51, of Cornell in 1882. A history of the Xi Chapter by Karl P. Harrington, Xi '82, was published in 1935, and a history of the Tau Chapter by William

P. Harberson, Tau '06, in 1942. Histories of the chapters appear in the *Annals of Psi Upsilon,* published in 1941. A directory of addresses has been published nineteen times, with the most recent publication occurring in 1988. Favorite Psi Upsilon songs, written by members of the Fraternity, were recorded on a set of 78 rpm records around 1930. A Psi Upsilon Quartette, composed of Harold E. Winston, Xi, '14; John Barnes Wells, Pi, '01; Reinald Werrenrath, Delta, '05; and Cyrille Carreau, Delta, '04, sang the songs for the recording.

The Diamond, the journal of the fraternity, was first issued in January, 1878, in four-page newspaper style, and as a monthly, at Ithaca, New York, by private enterprise. In December of the same year it was surrendered to the Executive Council, which issued but only one in March 1880. In March 1881, *The Diamond* was revived by a member of the Union chapter, and in November 1883, a brown cover was added. In November, the publication was moved to New York City and given a more conventional magazine format. *The Diamond* then became a quarterly edited by a committee of members. After a career of nearly three years it suspended publication with the first number of Volume VI (May, 1887). In 1895 an unofficial journal, *Psi Upsilon Review*, was issued by an alumnus of the Michigan chapter. It was discontinued in June 1896, after six numbers. In November 1920 (Volume VII, No. 1), *The Diamond* was revived by the Psi Upsilon Club of Chicago as a quarterly. In 1926 it was incorporated and is now published quarterly under the auspices of the Executive Council. The Executive Council also publishes the *Psi U View* newsletter on a quarterly basis, alternating between issues of *The Diamond.*

Funds and Philanthropies The Psi Upsilon Foundation, Inc. was founded and incorporated in Rhode Island, in 1958, for educational purposes. Donations to the Foundation are tax-exempt in the United States. All funds from donations beyond minimal expenses are invested carefully. All income must be expended each year. For the past twenty years awards have been made in the form of scholarships to undergraduates. The foundation also supports the annual Psi Upsilon Leadership Institute in conjunction with the Fraternity.

The affairs of the Foundation are managed by its board of directors separately from the affairs of the Fraternity. The day-to-day operations of the administrative office (located in Paoli, Pennsylvania) are carried out by the Foundation's Executive Director and an Administrative Assistant.

Headquarters Two Station Square, Paoli, PA 19301. Phone: (215) 647-4830.

Membership Twenty-seven chapters have their own houses. Provisional Chapters 3. Active chapters 31. Colonies 1. Chapter roll:

1833　Theta, Union (NY)
1837　*Delta, N.Y.U.* (1989)
1839　*Beta, Yale* (1934)

1840 Sigma, Brown (1969-1985)
1841 Gamma, Amherst
1842 Lambda, Columbia (NY)
1842 Zeta, Dartmouth
1843 Kappa, Bowdoin
1843 Psi, Hamilton
1843 Xi, Wesleyan (CT)
1850 *Alpha, Harvard* (1873)
1858 Upsilon, Rochester
1860 Iota, Kenyon
1865 Phi, Michigan
1869 Omega, Chicago
1875 Pi, Syracuse
1876 Chi, Cornell (1982-1985)
1880 Beta Beta, Trinity (CT)
1884 Eta, Lehigh
1891 Mu, Minnesota
1891 *Tau, Penn* (1990)
1896 *Rho, Wisconsin, Madison* (1971-1978) (1987)
1902 Epsilon, Cal, Berkeley (1972-1986)
1910 Omicron, Illinois
1913 *Delta Delta, Williams* (1968)
1916 Theta Theta, Washington (WA)
1920 Nu, Toronto (1973-1980)
1928 Epsilon Phi, McGill (1971-1978)
1935 Zeta Zeta, British Columbia
1943 Epsilon Nu, Michigan State
1949 Epsilon Omega, Northwestern
1952 *Theta Epsilon, USC* (1962)
1970 Gamma Tau, Georgia Tech
1970 *Nu Alpha, Washington and Lee* (1974)
1973 Chi Delta, Duke
1981 Zeta Tau, Tufts
1982 Epsilon Iota, R.P.I.
1984 Phi Beta, William and Mary
1989 Kappa Phi, Penn State
1990 Beta Alpha, Miami (OH)
1990 Beta Kappa, Washington State
1990 Upsilon Tau, Texas

Colonies: Bucknell

COAT OF ARMS

Sigma Alpha Epsilon

ACTIVE PIN

PLEDGE PIN

SIGMA ALPHA EPSILON was founded March 9, 1856, at the University of Alabama at Tuscaloosa. Its eight founders included five seniors, Noble Leslie DeVotie, John Barratt Rudulph, Nathan Elams Cockrell, John Webb Kerr and Wade Foster, and three juniors, Samuel Marion Dennis, Abner Edwin Patton and Thomas Chappell Cook. Their leader was DeVotie who had written the ritual, devised the grip and chosen the name. The badge was designed by Rudulph. Of all existing general fraternities today, Sigma Alpha Epsilon is the only one founded in the ante-bellum South.

Founded in a time of growing and intense sectional feeling, Sigma Alpha Epsilon, although it determined at the outset to extend to other colleges, confined its growth to the southern states. Extension was vigorous, however, and by the end of 1857 the fraternity counted seven chapters. Its first national convention met in the summer of 1858 at Murfreesboro, Tennessee, with four of its eight chapters in attendance. By the time of the outbreak of the Civil War in 1861, fifteen chapters had been established.

The fraternity had fewer than four hundred members when the Civil War began. Of those, 369 went to war for the Confederacy and seven fought with the Union forces. Every member of the chapters at Hampden-Sydney, Georgia Military Institute, Kentucky Military Institute and Oglethorpe University fought for the gray. Members from Columbian College, William and Mary and Bethel (Ky.) were in both armies. Seventy members of the fraternity lost their lives in the War, including Noble Leslie DeVotie, who is officially recorded in the annals of the War as the first man on either side to give his life.

The miracle in the history of Sigma Alpha Epsilon is that it survived that great sectional conflict. When the smoke of battle had cleared, only one chapter, at tiny Columbian College in Washington, D.C., survived, and it died soon thereafter.

When a few of the young veterans returned to the Georgia Military Institute and found their little college burned to the ground, they decided to go to Athens, Georgia, to enter the state university there. It was the founding of the University of Georgia chapter at the end of 1865 that led to the fraternity's revival. Soon other chapters came back to life, and in 1867 the first post-war convention was held at Nashville, Tennessee, where a half dozen revived chapters planned the fraternity's future growth.

The Reconstruction years were cruel to the South, and southern colleges and their fraternities shared in the general malaise of the region. In the 1870s and early 1880s more than a score of new chapters were founded, some of them in exceedingly frail institutions. Older chapters died as fast as new ones were established. By 1886 the fraternity had chartered 49 chapters, but scarcely a dozen could be called active. Two of the 49 were in the North. After much discussion and not a little dissent, the first northern chapter had been established at Pennsylvania College, now Gettysburg College, in 1883, and a second was placed at Mt. Union College in Ohio two years later.

It was in 1886 that things took a turn for the better. That autumn a 16-year-old youngster by the name of Harry Bunting entered Southwestern Presbyterian University in Clarksville, Tennessee, and was initiated by the young Tennessee Zeta chapter there that had previously initiated two of his brothers. When Sigma Alpha Epsilon took in Harry Bunting, it caught a comet by the tail.

In just eight years, under the enthusiastic guidance of Harry Bunting and his younger brother, George, Sigma Alpha Epsilon experienced a renaissance. Together they prodded ΣAE chapters to enlarge their membership; they wrote encouraging articles in the fraternity's quarterly journal, *The Record*, promoting better chapter standards; and above all they undertook an almost incredible program of expansion of the fraternity, resurrecting old chapters in the South (including the mother chapter at Alabama) and founding new ones in the North and West. In an explosion of growth, the Buntings singlehandedly were responsible for nearly fifty chapters of ΣAE.

When Harry Bunting founded the Northwestern University chapter in 1894, he initiated as a charter member William Collin Levere, a remarkable young man whose enthusiasm for the fraternity matched Bunting's. To Levere Bunting passed the torch of leadership, and for the next three decades it was the spirit of "Billy" Levere that dominated ΣAE and brought the fraternity to maturity.

"Billy" did everything. He was twice elected national president, served as the fraternity's first full-time executive secretary and chapter visitation officer (1912–27), edited its quarterly magazine and several editions of the catalog and directory of membership and published a monumental three-volume history of the fraternity in 1911. It is small wonder than when Levere died February 22, 1927, the fraternity's supreme council decided to name their new national headquarters building the Levere Memorial Temple. Construction of the Temple, an immense Gothic structure located a stone's throw from Lake Michigan and across from the Northwestern University campus, was started in 1929, and the building was dedicated at Christmastime, 1930.

When the supreme council met regularly in the early 1930s at the Temple, educator John O. Moseley, the fraternity's national president, lamented that "we have in the Temple a magnificent schoolhouse. Why can we not have a school?" Accordingly, the economic depression notwithstanding, in the summer of 1935 the fraternity's first leadership school was held under the direction of Dr. Moseley. The first such workshop in the fraternity world, it was immensely successful, and today nearly every fraternity holds such a school. The leadership is unquestionably the best service ΣAE provides to its undergraduates who come to Evanston in regimental numbers each year.

It was probably John Moseley more than any other whose leadership carried Sigma Alpha Epsilon forward during the next twenty years until his untimely death in 1955. The last years of his life he served the fraternity as its executive secretary, capping a distinguished academic career that had included two college presidencies.

Since the Second World War the fraternity has grown much larger, and it has changed in a number of ways, some quite obvious and others quite subtle. Its growth in chapters and membership has been quite spectacular, and its total number of initiates continues to be the higher in the fraternity world. More than a hundred chapter charters have been granted in 45 years. A few chapters have died or have been suspended, but a number of older ones have been revived, including two pre-Civil War chapters (Baylor and Oglethorpe). The number of undergraduate members in each chapter has remained remarkably steady, averaging approximately seventy men each.

Qualitative changes in recent decades have been profound. Alongside their colleges chapters have democratized. Membership today is far more heterogeneous than it was a generation ago as chapters have welcomed increasing numbers of men from religious, ethnic and racial minorities, enriching chapters with an unprecedented cultural diversity. One has but to peruse the roster of the 600 or so delegates at the annual Leadership School to confirm the dimensions of change.

The fraternity enjoyed the "happy days" of the 1950s, endured to survive the campus revolt of the 1960s and early 1970s, and it tried to steer an even course in the turbulence that marked the late 1970s and the 1980s. Together with its fellow collegiate Greek-letter societies it wrestles today with problems attendant upon risk management, the war against hazing, alcohol abuse and sexual misconduct rife on our campuses. Never before have the challenges been so great or the opportunities so rich. Accordingly, the fraternity has undertaken a thorough program of reform and rejuvenation, seeking to assist its undergraduate members to make a reaffirmation of faith in their best, most wholesome traditions while seeking to adapt creatively to a new and invigorating college climate. Sigma Alpha Epsilon looks to a future full of promise.

Government In its early days the government of the fraternity was vested in one chapter, designated the Grand Chapter, which was responsible only to the general convention. In 1885 this plan was replaced by government by a Supreme Council of six members, later reduced to five, and the creation of regional units called provinces, each presided over by an Archon. After 1920 a Board of Trustees was created to manage the fraternity's endowment funds. For many years national conventions were held annually, but since 1894 they have met biennially. In alternate years province conventions meet, and at the present time there are twenty-eight provinces in the United States and Canada. Employment of a full-time executive secretary was authorized by the Nashville national convention in 1912.

Housing Sigma Alpha Epsilon's chapters are on the whole well housed. One hundred sixteen of the undergraduate chapters own their own homes, and a number of others are housed in college-owned buildings.

The first chapter of the fraternity to have a house of its own was at the University of the South, Sewanee, Tennessee. In order to get the funds to start this project the members contracted to carry the university mail all through one winter. The money earned helped build their house.

In 1904 the fraternity erected a building at Tuscaloosa, Alabama, as a memorial to Noble Leslie DeVotie and the other seven founders. Latr a chapter house was attached to it, and the entire structure served for many years as a home for the original chapter. This was replaced in 1953 by a larger structure on a new site and was dedicated at the fraternity's centennial celebration on March 9, 1956.

The fraternity's national headquarters is maintained at the Levere Memorial Temple in Evanston, Illinois. Honoring all the members of the fraternity who have served their countries on land or sea or in the air since 1856, it was dedicated on December 28, 1930. The temple also contains what is considered the most complete library pertaining to Greek-letter fraternities and sororities. The museum on the second floor is devoted to a collection of interesting historical photographs, pictures and collections from private sources. The walls of the building are hung with oil portraits of distinguished members. The basement contains the Panhellenic Room, in the ceiling of which are the coats-of-arms of forty college fraternities and seventeen sororities, while the niches on the north side contain large murals showing the founding of Phi Beta Kappa in 1776 and that of Sigma Alpha Epsilon in 1856, together with other murals depicting episodes in the history of the fraternity. The most outstanding mural in the Panhellenic Room is the reproduction of Raphael's "School of Athens," painted by Johannes Waller in the 1930s.

The building continues to be used for ceremonies and receptions by the various fraternities and sororities and honor societies at Northwestern University. National fraternities frequently meet there in convention or conclave. The impressive chapel of the temple, with its soaring vaulted ceiling and stained glass windows by Tiffany, is used regularly for religious services and is the scene of many weddings of Evanstonians and members of Sigma Alpha Epsilon. In fact, the entire building is open to the public for patriotic, religious and educational purposes, while the library is also free to scholars seeking material pertaining to the history of any or all college fraternities and college organizations.

Insignia The badge of the fraternity is diamond-shaped, a little less than an inch long and bears on a background of nazarene blue enamel the device of Minerva, with a lion crouching at her feet, above which are the letters ΣAE in gold. Below are the letters ΦA on a white ground in a wreath. The colors are royal purple and old gold. The flower is the violet. The colors of the pledge pin are nazarene blue, white and gold with ΦA in letters surrounded by a wreath.

The flag is royal purple with a corner of old gold, the size and shape of the corner being the same as the blue field in the flag of the United States. Upon the gold field appear the letters ΦA in royal purple. In the center of the purple field which constitutes the rest of the flag are the letters ΣAE in gold. Immediately beneath the gold corner are the eight golden stars in a circle, one for each founder.

Publications The catalogue of the fraternity has been published twelve times: in 1859, compiled by the North Carolina chapter and printed in Washington; in 1870, 1872, 1877, with a supplement in 1880, 1886, 1893, 1904, 1918, 1929, 1981, 1986 and 1991. In 1906 was begun the publication annually of letters from the chapters accompanied by chapter lists forming a catalogue. A manual of the fraternity, edited by Dr. George H. Kress, was published at Los Angeles in 1904. A songbook, originally published in 1891, has passed through nine editions, the latest issued in 1991. In 1911 a detailed history of the fraternity was published in three large octavo volumes with many illustrations. The work of William C. Levere, it sold out in less than a month. Research for a centennial history of the fraternity, carrying Levere's history forward from 1910 to 1956, was undertaken in 1956 by archivist Lauren Foreman. In 1972 the fraternity's historian, Joseph W. Walt, completed and saw to the publication of *The Era of Levere*, a history of ΣAE from 1910 to 1930, covering the two decades when fraternities were at their zenith. A second volume by Walt is in preparation, covering the years from 1930 to 1956.

In 1912 William C. Levere brought out *Who's Who in Sigma Alpha Epsilon*, a series of biographical sketches of living men prominent in the fraternity. Among other books are *A Paragraph History of Sigma Alpha Epsilon*, which passed through eleven editions between 1912 and 1946, *The Original Minutes of Alabama Mu*, *The Memory Book of Sigma Alpha Epsilon*, William C. Levere's lenghty account of the First World War, *Sigma Alpha Epsilon in the World War*, *The Sigma Alpha Epsilon Pledge Manual*, edited by O. K. Quivey, and *The Phoenix*, the fraternity's present pledge manual, the most recent edition of which was published in 1988, edited by Joseph W. Walt.

The fraternity's magazine, *The Record*, was founded in 1880 by Major Robert H. Wildberger of Kentucky Military Institute chapter. It is published quarterly, and at least one issue per year is sent to all living initiates of the fraternity. Its circulation of more than 140,000 is thought to be the largest among fraternity publications.

In 1891 Harry and George Bunting started a publication they called *The Hustler,* a secret, or at least private, magazine. In 1894 its name was changed to *Phi Alpha,* and it is a regularly issued secondary magazine of the fraternity. Today *The Hustler* is a publication of the annual Leadership School. Every chapter in the fraternity publishes a regular newspaper for its alumni and friends.

Headquarters   1856 Sheridan Road, P.O. Box 1856, Evanston, Illinois 60204-1856. Phone: (708) 475-1856.

Membership   Reported deceased membership 38,536. Active chapters 206. Inactive chapters 44. Colonies 4. Active alumni associations 130. Total number of initiates 219,190. Chapter roll:

1856   Alabama Mu, Alabama
1857   *Georgia Pi, Georgia Military Col.* (1865)
1857   *North Carolina Xi, North Carolina* (1990)
1857   Tennesee Nu, Vanderbilt
1857   Tennessee Eta, Union (TN)
1857   Virginia Kappa, William and Mary
1857   Virginia Omicron, Virginia
1858   *Kentucky Iota, Bethel* (1920)
1858   Texas Theta, Baylor
1858   Washington City Rho, George Washington
1859   Georgia Eta, Oglethorpe
1860   *Kentucky Chi, Kentucky Military* (1887)
1860   *Louisiana Tau, Centenary* (1861)
1860   *Tennessee Lambda, Cumberland (KY)* (1949)
1860   Virginia Upsilon, Hampden-Sydney
1865   Georgia Beta, Georgia
1866   Mississippi Gamma, Mississippi
1867   Louisiana Epsilon, L.S.U.
1867   Virginia Sigma, Washington and Lee
1868   South Carolina Phi, Furman
1869   *Mississippi Zeta, Mississippi Col.* (1872)
1870   *Alabama Beta-Beta, Howard College* (1876)
1870   *Georgia Psi, Mercer* (1989)
1874   *Virginia Theta, V.M.I.* (1911)
1876   *North Carolina Rho-Rho, Carolina Military* (1877)
1877   *Kentucky Alpha, Forest Academy* (1878)
1878   Alabama Alpha-Mu, Auburn
1878   Alabama Iota, Birmingham-Southern
1879   *Georgia Delta, North Georgia* (1888)
1879   Tennessee Kappa, Tennessee
1881   Georgia Epsilon, Emory
1881   South Carolina Upsilon, Charleston (SC)
1881   Tennessee Omega, U of the South
1882   Kentucky Kappa, Centre College
1882   South Carolina Delta, South Carolina
1882   Tennessee Zeta, Rhodes
1882   Texas Rho, Texas
1883   North Carolina Theta, Davidson
1883   Pennsylvania Delta, Gettysburg
1883   *South Carolina Lambda, South Carolina Military* (1895)
1884   Florida Upsilon, Florida
1884   Missouri Alpha, Missouri
1884   *South Carolina Mu, Erskine* (1894)
1884   *Virginia Pi, Emory And Henry* (1896)

1884   Virginia Tau, Richmond
1885   *Kentucky Alpha-Epsilon, South Kentucky* (1887)
1885   Ohio Sigma, Mount Union
1885   South Carolina Gamma, Wofford
1886   *Louisiana Zeta, Thatcher Inst* (1888)
1887   Michigan Alpha, Adrian
1887   Mississippi Theta, Mississippi State
1887   *Pennsylvania Omega, Allegheny* (1990)
1887   *Texas Psi, Southwestern (TX)* (1888)
1887   *Texas Theta (II), Buffalo Gap* (1888)
1888   Ohio Delta, Ohio Wesleyan
1889   Iowa Sigma, Simpson
1889   Michigan Iota-Beta, Michigan
1889   Ohio Epsilon, Cincinnati
1890   Georgia Phi, Georgia Tech
1890   Pennsylvania Sigma-Phi, Dickinson
1891   Colorado Chi, Colorado
1891   Colorado Zeta, Denver
1891   New York Alpha, Cornell
1892   California Alpha, Stanford
1892   *Connecticut Alpha, Trinity (CT)* (1899)
1892   Indiana Alpha, Franklin
1892   Massachusetts Beta-Upsilon, Boston Col
1892   Massachusetts Iota-Tau, M.I.T.
1892   Missouri Beta, Washington (WA)
1892   Ohio Theta, Ohio State
1892   Pennsylvania Alpha-Zeta, Penn State
1893   Indiana Beta, Purdue
1893   *Massachusetts Gamma, Harvard* (1979)
1893   Nebraska Lambda-Pi, Nebraska
1893   Pennsylvania Zeta, Bucknell
1894   Arkansas Alpha-Upsilon, Arkansas
1894   California Beta, Cal, Berkeley
1894   Illinois Psi-Omega, Northwestern
1894   Massachusetts Delta, Worcester Tech
1895   *New York Mu, Columbia (NY)* (1960)
1895   *New York Sigma-Phi, Bard* (1942)
1897   Louisiana Tau-Upsilon, Tulane
1899   Illinois Beta, Illinois
1900   Kentucky Epsilon, Kentucky
1901   Maine Alpha, Maine
1901   Pennsylvania Theta, Penn
1902   Minnesota Alpha, Minnesota
1903   Colorado Lambda, Colorado Mines
1903   *Illinois Theta, Chicago* (1941)
1903   Kansas Alpha, Kansas
1903   Wisconsin Alpha, Wisconsin, Madison
1905   Iowa Beta, Iowa
1905   Iowa Gamma, Iowa State
1905   Ohio Rho, Case Western Reserve
1906   Washington Alpha, Washington (WA)
1907   Indiana Gamma, Indiana
1907   New York Delta, Syracuse
1908   New Hampshire Alpha, Dartmouth
1909   *Oklahoma Kappa, Oklahoma* (1989)
1911   Illinois Delta, Millikin
1911   South Dakota Sigma, South Dakota
1913   Kansas Beta, Kansas State
1913   Pennsylvania Chi-Omicron, Pitt
1915   Oregon Alpha, Oregon State
1915   Washington Beta, Washington State

Year	Chapter	Year	Chapter
1915	Wisconsin Phi, Beloit	1958	*Wisconsin Beta, Ripon* (1980)
1917	Arizona Alpha, Arizona	1959	Ohio Alpha, Youngstown State
1917	Colorado Delta, Colorado State	1961	Arizona Beta, Arizona State
1917	Nevada Alpha, Nevada	1961	Michigan Delta, Western Michigan
1917	New Hampshire Beta, New Hampshire	1963	*Illinois Alpha, Monmouth (IL)* (1981)
1917	Wyoming Alpha, Wyoming	1963	New Mexico Alpha, Eastern New Mexico
1919	Idaho Alpha, Idaho	1963	*Tennessee Alpha, East Tennessee* (1983)
1919	Montana Alpha, Montana State	1965	*Arkansas Beta, Arkansas, Little Rock* (1980)
1919	New York Rho, St. Lawrence	1965	California Mu, Cal State, Los Angeles
1919	Ohio Mu, Denison	1965	Iowa Chi, Northern Iowa
1919	Ohio Tau, Miami (OH)	1965	Kentucky Beta, Western Kentucky
1919	Oregon Beta, Oregon	1965	Michigan Epsilon, GMI
1919	Pennsylvania Gamma, Lafayette	1965	Mississippi Sigma, Southern Mississippi
1919	Pennsylvania Phi, Carnegie-Mellon	1965	Oregon Delta, Lewis and Clark
1921	California Gamma, USC	1966	*Illinois Gamma, Northern Illinois* (1988)
1921	Iowa Delta, Drake	1967	California Nu, Cal State, Northridge
1923	North Dakota Alpha, North Dakota	1967	California Xi, Cal State, Sacramento
1923	Texas Delta, Southern Methodist	1967	Illinois Epsilon, Bradley
1927	Michigan Gamma, Michigan State	1967	Indiana Zeta, Ball State
1927	Montana Beta, Montana	1967	Kansas Gamma, Wichita
1927	*Vermont Alpha-Sigma-Pi, Norwich* (1960)	1967	*Minnesota Beta, Mankato* (1975)
1929	California Delta, UCLA	1967	Virginia Alpha, Randolph, Macon
1929	Rhode Island Alpha, Rhode Island	1968	Florida Delta, South Florida
1929	Vermont Beta, Vermont	1968	Louisiana Alpha, Southwestern Louisiana
1931	California Epsilon, Occidental	1968	Nebraska Iota, Creighton
1931	North Carolina Nu, Duke	1969	California Pi, Cal State, Fullerton
1931	Oklahoma Mu, Oklahoma State	1969	California Sigma, San Francisco
1935	*Maryland Rho-Delta, St. John's (NY)* (1943)	1969	*Connecticut Lambda, Hartford* (1974)
1935	North Dakota Beta, North Dakota State	1969	Indiana Sigma, Indiana State
1937	*Massachusetts Kappa, Massachusetts* (1982)	1969	*New York Beta, C. W. Post* (1977)
1939	*Utah Upsilon, Utah State* (1989)	1969	*New York Sigma, Adelphi* (1974)
1941	New Mexico Phi, New Mexico State	1969	Tennessee Beta, Middle Tennessee
1943	Connecticut Beta, Connecticut	1969	Tennessee Delta, Tennessee Tech.
1943	Maryland Beta, Maryland	1969	*West Virginia Beta, Bethany (WV)* (1983)
1945	Ohio Kappa, Bowling Green	1970	California Rho, Pacific (CA)
1946	Florida Alpha, Miami (OH)	1970	Colorado Alpha, Northern Colorado
1946	New Mexico Tau, New Mexico	1970	South Carolina Nu, Clemson
1947	California Zeta, San Jose	1971	Alabama Chi, South Alabama
1947	North Carolina Alpha, North Carolina State	1971	Kentucky Gamma, Morehead
1947	Texas Gamma, Texas, El Paso	1971	*New Mexico Sigma, New Mexico Highlands* (1975)
1949	California Eta, Cal, Santa Barbara	1971	Pennsylvania Epsilon, Drexel
1949	California Iota, Cal State, Fresno	1971	South Dakota Theta, South Dakota State
1949	California Theta, San Diego State	1972	Missouri Delta, Rockhurst
1949	Florida Beta, Florida State	1972	Tennessee Tau, Tennessee, Martin
1949	Florida Gamma, Florida Southern	1972	Utah Sigma, Weber
1949	Illinois Delta, DePauw	1973	Florida Epsilon, Central Florida
1949	Missouri Gamma, Westminster (MO)	1973	Florida Sigma, West Florida
1949	Oregon Gamma, Willamette	1973	Georgia Sigma, Valdosta
1949	Utah Phi, Utah	1973	Kentucky Delta, Eastern Kentucky
1951	New York Epsilon, R.P.I.	1973	Michigan Zeta, Ferris
1951	Washington Gamma, Puget Sound	1975	Arizona Gamma, Northern Arizona
1952	*California Kappa, Cal, Davis* (1989)	1975	*Oklahoma Tau, Oklahoma City* (1986)
1953	Ohio Gamma, Ohio	1975	Virginia Zeta, V.P.I.
1953	Ohio Lambda, Kent	1977	Maryland Sigma, Salisbury
1953	Ohio Nu, Toledo	1980	Alabama Epsilon, Troy
1953	Tennessee Sigma, Memphis State	1981	Maryland Alpha, Towson
1953	Texas Alpha, Texas Tech.	1981	North Carolina Delta, North Carolina, Wilmington
1953	*West Virginia Alpha, Marshall* (1982)	1981	Texas Tau, Texas A & M
1955	California Lambda, Cal State, Long Beach	1982	Florida Chi, Tampa
1955	Texas Beta, Texas Christian		
1956	Texas Epsilon, Houston		
1957	Indiana Epsilon, Evansville		

1982   *Indiana Theta, Indiana, Evansville* (1984)
1983   Illinois Alpha-Omega, Loyola, Chicago
1983   Louisiana Rho, Louisiana Tech
1983   New Jersey Alpha, Princeton
1984   California Tau, Cal Poly, San Luis Obispo
1984   Michigan Delta-Tau, Alma
1985   California Upsilon, LaVerne
1985   Nevada Beta, Nevada, Las Vegas
1986   California Phi, Santa Clara
1986   New York Omega, SUNY, Binghamton
1987   California Chi, Cal, San Diego
1987   California Psi, Cal, Irvine
1987   Maryland Omicron-Pi, Maryland, Baltimore County
1987   South Carolina Sigma, Winthrop
1988   Connecticut Omega, Yale
1988   Texas Kappa, North Texas
1989   Alabama Nu, North Alabama
1989   California Omega, Cal, Santa Cruz
1989   Tennessee Rho, Christian Brothers College
1990   California Alpha-Alpha, Sonoma State
1990   California Omicron, Cal, Riverside
1990   Illinois Tau-Alpha, Illinois State
1990   Mississippi Delta, Millsaps
1990   New York Pi, SUNY, Albany

Colonies: Frostburg, Georgia Southern, St. Leo, Western Ontario

COAT OF ARMS

Sigma Alpha Mu

ACTIVE PIN

PLEDGE PIN

SIGMA ALPHA MU was founded on November 26, 1909, by eight students of the College of the City of New York. Their purpose as stated in the preamble to the fraternity's constitution, was "to foster and maintain among its sons a spirit of fraternity, a spirit of mutual moral aid and support; to instill and maintain in the hearts of its sons love for and loyalty to *alma mater* and its ideals as will result in actions worthy of the highest precepts of true manhood, democracy, and humanity."

The eight founders of Sigma Alpha Mu were all of the Jewish faith and it naturally followed that they attracted to the brotherhood men of like faith. The fraternity has always acknowledged with deep appreciation the ethical values of Judaism which have enriched its life. With the advent of the mid-twentieth century, expressions of liberalism suggested that constitutional limitations of membership to any particular religious group was not in keeping with the ideal of democracy expressed in the fraternity's creed. Responsive to this thinking, Sigma Alpha Mu at its 1953 convention amended its constitution and revised its rituals to make eligible for membership any male student of good moral character.

Government The supreme legislative body is the annual convention which consists of delegates from each chapter and each chartered alumni club, representatives of each chapter alumni body, and the national and regional officers. The convention elects eight directors, seven from the alumni to two-year terms, one undergraduate to a one-year term. This board, the Octagon, chooses from its number the Supreme council of four alumni. The recognized head of the fraternity is the supreme prior.

Chapters are grouped geographically to constitute provinces, each headed by a governor appointed by the board of directors. Regional conclaves, held annually in the spring of the year, stress leadership training and efficient chapter operation. Each chapter is under the direct supervision of an alumni advisory board, the chairman of which is designated as the chapter adviser.

Much of the administrative work is delegated to the executive director and his staff. Under his direction chapters are visited by one or more field secretaries, their trips being supplemented by those regional and national officers.

Insignia The badge of the fraternity is octagonal in shape, containing a center octagon of black enamel with the letters ΣAM inlaid in gold, and bordered with 16 pearls. The standard pin is similar except the pearls are replaced by eight oblong trapezoids of purple enamel. The candidate button is octagon in shape, with a silver Σ in a field of blue enamel. The colors of the fraternity are purple and white. The flower is the purple aster.

Publications *The Octagonian*, published quarterly since 1912, serves as a mirror of activities of chapters, alumni clubs and individual alumni. It is essentially an organ of brotherhood, the backbone of the fraternity's archives A candidate handbook and chapter operation manual are among the other national publications.

Funds and Philanthropies An endowment fund, established in 1928, renders effective assistance to chapters seeking to acquire or improve chapter homes. This fund has been accumulated through life membership collections. The alumni dues are voluntary. The seven trustees of the endowment fund serve also on the board of trustees of the Sigma Alpha Mu Foundation. Chartered in 1945, the foundation has been built up through contributions and bequests so that its primary objective, namely to extend financial assistance to any deserving undergraduate member in order that he may complete his college education, has already been achieved. This is accomplished through educational loans bearing no interest, and annual scholarships.

Scholarship is encouraged through a program directed by the national scholarship chairman. Cash prizes are presented to undergraduates outstanding in academic work, and scholarship is given greatest weight in the annual competition for the Founders Cup, the highest chapter award. Serious effort is made to promote a chapter environment conducive to study.

The Sigma Alpha Mu Achievement Medal is presented annually to a member of the fraternity who has distinguished himself in his special field of endeavor. It is popularly called the "Man of the Year Award" and has been presented to eminent jurists, clergymen, authors, scientists, industrialists, and educators.

To point up its interest in community endeavors and with a view to encouraging future community leaders, the fraternity honors those alumni whose services to their community exemplify the ideals of the fraternity. They receive the "Certificate of Merit."

Honorary membership is not permitted in Sigma Alpha Mu.

Headquarters 651 N. Range Line Road, Carmel, IN 46032. Phone: (317) 846-0600. On November 26, 1969, the 60th anniversary of the fraternity, the executive offices were moved from New York to Indianapolis. In 1982, the present headquarters building was purchased.

Membership Living membership 37,801. Deceased membership 3,136. Active chapters 68. Inactive chapters 46. Colonies 3. Total number of initiates 43,367. Chapter roll:

1909 *Alpha, CCNY (1983)*
1911 Beta, Cornell (-1982)
1911 *Delta, Long Island (1934)*
1911 Gamma, Columbia (NY)
1912 *Epsilon, Columbia Medical (1922)*
1912 *Zeta, Cornell (1915)*
1913 Eta, Syracuse
1914 Theta, Penn
1915 *Iota, Kentucky (1924)*
1915 Kappa, Minnesota
1916 Lambda, Harvard (1936-1989)
1916 Nu, SUNY, Buffalo
1917 Omicron, Cincinnati
1917 *Pi, Yale (1934)*
1917 *Xi, M.I.T. (1973)*
1918 Rho, Illinois
1919 *Chi, McGill (1986)*
1919 Phi, Washington (MO)
1919 Psi, Pitt
1919 *Sigma, Dickinson (1920)*
1919 *Tau, Alabama (1961)*
1919 *Upsilon, Utah (1951)*
1920 *Omega, Toronto (1972)*
1920 *Sigma Alpha, Oklahoma (1982)*
1920 Sigma Beta, Ohio State
1920 Sigma Gamma, Tulane (1971-1976) (1980-1987)
1921 Sigma Delta, Rutgers
1922 *Sigma Epsilon, Illinois Tech (1952)*
1922 *Sigma Eta, Purdue (1989)*

1922 Sigma Theta, Texas
1922 Sigma Zeta, Indiana
1923 Sigma Iota, Michigan
1923 Sigma Kappa, Lehigh
1923 *Sigma Lambda, Kansas (1936)*
1926 Sigma Nu, Washington (WA) (1983-1988)
1926 Sigma Omicron, Nebraska
1926 Sigma Pi, UCLA
1926 Sigma Xi, Manitoba
1928 Sigma Rho, Missouri
1929 Sigma Sigma, Cal, Berkeley
1930 *Sigma Tau, Oregon (1962)*
1930 *Sigma Upsilon, Dartmouth (1935)*
1932 Sigma Phi, Bucknell
1933 Sigma Chi, Maryland
1937 *Sigma Psi, Mississippi State (1950)*
1938 Sigma Omega, North Carolina State
1939 *Mu Alpha, Southern Methodist (1976)*
1941 *Mu Beta, Alberta (1972)*
1945 Mu Gamma, Case Western Reserve
1946 Mu Epsilon, Miami (FL) (1970-1987)
1947 Mu Eta, Drexel
1947 *Mu Zeta, Washington State (1950)*
1948 *Mu Iota, Butler (1957)*
1948 *Mu Kappa, Wayne State (MI) (1971)*
1948 Mu Theta, USC
1949 Mu Lambda, Penn State (1970-1983)
1949 Mu Omicron, N.Y.U. (1966-1989)
1949 *Mu Xi, British Columbia (1959)*
1953 *Mu Pi, Colorado (1960)*
1955 *Mu Sigma, Queens (NY) (1973)*
1957 Mu Rho, Rochester
1957 Mu Upsilon, CUNY, Brooklyn (1971-1988)
1958 *Mu Phi, Long Island (1987)*
1959 Mu Chi, Michigan State (1983-1986)
1959 Mu Psi, Miami (OH)
1961 Mu Omega, Toledo
1962 *Beta Alpha, Texas, El Paso (1972)*
1962 *Beta Beta, Ferris (1979)*
1962 Beta Gamma, Arizona (1964-1988)
1963 Beta Delta, San Jose
1965 *Beta Zeta, St. Mary's, San Antonio (1967)*
1966 Beta Eta, Cal State, Northridge (1971-1984)
1966 Beta Iota, Wisconsin, Madison (1972-1983)
1966 *Beta Kappa, Hunter (1971)*
1966 *Beta Lambda, CUNY, Lehman (1970)*
1966 *Beta Theta, New Orleans (1972)*
1967 *Beta Nu, Portland State (1971)*
1967 Beta Omicron, George Washington (1971-1987)
1967 *Beta Pi, Northwestern (1973-1989) (1990)*
1967 Beta Rho, Houston (1972-1989)
1967 *Beta Sigma, North Texas (1987)*
1968 *Beta Chi, Eastern Michigan (1971)*
1968 *Beta Phi, Youngstown State (1975)*
1968 Beta Psi, Virginia
1968 Beta Tau, Northeastern (1978-1988)
1968 Beta Upsilon, Boston U. (1971-1986)
1969 Beta Omega, Kentucky Wesleyan
1969 *Gamma Alpha, Oglethorpe (1974)*
1969 *Gamma Beta, Monmouth (NJ) (1977)*
1969 *Gamma Delta, Northern Michigan (1975)*

1969 *Gamma Gamma, Southampton* (1976)
1970 Gamma Epsilon, Illinois, Chicago
1970 *Gamma Zeta, Ohio* (1972)
1971 *Gamma Eta, Southern Illinois* (1973)
1979 Gamma Theta, Cal, Davis
1980 Gamma Iota, Towson
1982 Gamma Kappa, Texas A & M
1982 Gamma Lambda, Northern Illinois
1983 Gamma Nu, San Diego U (1984-1989)
1984 *Gamma Xi, Cal State, Fullerton* (1990)
1985 Gamma Omicron, Iowa
1986 Gamma Pi, SUNY, Albany
1986 Gamma Rho, Cal, San Diego
1986 Gamma Sigma, SUNY, Binghamton
1986 Gamma Tau, Florida
1986 Gamma Upsilon, Stanford
1987 Gamma Chi, Brandeis
1987 Gamma Phi, Arizona State
1987 Gamma Psi, Temple
1988 Delta Alpha, Hofstra
1988 Gamma Omega, South Florida
1989 Delta Beta, American
1989 Delta Delta, Alfred
1989 Delta Gamma, SUNY Col., Oneonta

Colonies: Louisville, Massachusetts, Hartford

COAT OF ARMS

Sigma Chi

ACTIVE PIN

PLEDGE PIN

SIGMA CHI is the third of the Miami Triad, as three fraternities originating at Miami University, Ohio, are called, the first being Beta Theta Pi and the second Phi Delta Theta. It was established June 28, 1855, by Thomas Cowan Bell, James Parks Caldwell, Daniel William Coopr, Benjamin Piatt Runkle, Franklin Howard Scobey, Isaac M. Jordan, and William Lewis Lockwood, who, with the exception of the last named, had been members of the Kappa Chapter of Delta Kappa Epsilon.

A disagreement arose in that chapter over the election of one of its members to the office of poet in Erodelphian Literary Society. The Dekes named refused to cast their votes for their brother, alleging as their reason the superior abilities of another student for the position. The chapter stood divided on the subject, thus punishment could not be meted out to the recalcitrants, and the trouble ended by the final withdrawal of the six persons named.

They immediately organized another society under the name of Sigma Phi. The founders apparently were unacquainted with the eastern fraternity of the same name. The standard with which the fraternity began its career was declared by Isaac M. Jordan to be that "of admitting no man to membership in Sigma Chi who is not believed to be a man of good character, a student of fair ability, of ambitious purposes, and congenial disposition, possessed of good morals, having a high sense of honor and deep sense of personal responsibility." The statement came to be known as "The Jordan Standard."

The badges were worn for the first time publicly on June 28, 1855, and that date was taken as marking the origin of the fraternity. In 1856 a new constitution and ritual were prepared, and the name of Sigma Chi adopted. Previous to this time a charter had been granted to petitioners from Ohio Wesleyan University, and on Christmas Eve, 1855, the new chapter was instituted under the name Gamma.

Growth All of the Southern chapters were killed by the Civil War.[1] Those at the Universities of Virginia and Misissippi were revived; the latter became inactive from anti-fraternity legislation. The Erskine chapter was sub rosa during its brief existence. The Nu chapter, at Washington College, lost most of its membes by their enlistment in the army, and it was not revived after its extinction in 1863, in view of the approaching union of the college with Jefferson College. The chapters at Princeton, the University of Georgia, Howard College, Mississippi College, Monmouth College, the University of Alabama, V.M.I., Wooster, and the University of Illinois were killed by anti-fraternity laws, the last chapter being revived in 1891 and the Alabama chapter in 1914 (by absorption of a local society called Phi Epsilon). The Princeton chapter was first established in 1869. About a year thereafter it was disbanded owing to a belief on the part of its members that its charter had been withdrawn. It was reorganized in 1875, and became inactive, owing to the prevalent hostility to the fraternities.

The chapter at the Polytechnic College of Pennsylvania was permitted by its charter to initiate

[1]A circumstance in the history of Sigma Chi without parallel was the existence during the Civil War of a chapter in the Confederate Army, composed of members serving under General Joseph E. Johnston in the Army of Tennessee. It was called the Constantine Chapter, and was organized by Harry St. John Dixon, Virginia 1861, and several Sigma Chi comrades for the purpose of perpetuating the fraternity in the South, whatever might be the outcome of the war. On the occasion of the Constantine Chapter's 75th anniversary in 1939, the fraternity dedicated a huge marble memorial on the site of its founding near Jonesboro, Georgia. Several chapter houses proudly display a reproduction of an oil painting of the historic Constantine Chapter by Milton Caniff, Ohio State 1930, the noted artist and cartoonist.

Again during World War II, one of the most unusual groups to function in the war was the Santo Thomas Concentration Camp Chapter, which was organized by the late Royal Arch Gunnison, Washington '31, author and war correspondent, and other prisoners of the Japanese. Sigma Chi made a notable contribution toward the winning of this war. Of the nearly 10,000 Sigs in uniform, 738 made the supreme sacrifice. Capt. Maurice L. Britt, Arkansas '41, was acclaimed as the second most decorated officer of the war, and forty-three generals were Sigma Chis. A large number of Sigma Chis also served valiantly in the Korean War, with forty-three losing their lives.

students from the University of Pennsylvania. In 1875 these petitioned to be made a distinct chapter, and their withdrawal weakened the parent chapter to such an extent that it quite soon became inactive. The University of Pennsylvania died also a few years later, but was revived in 1896. The Denison chapter was sub rosa for many years, owing to faculty opposition. The chapters at George Washington University, Hampden-Sydney College, Cumberland University and Richmond College became inactive from what the members of the chapter deemed lack of suitable material to carry them on. The first two have been revived. The Hampden-Sydney chapter was revived in 1890, died in 1902, and was later revived. The North Carolina chapter became inactive in 1900 and was revived in 1914 by the absorption of a local Sigma Kappa Delta. The Tulane chapter is a continuation of the University of Louisiana chapter.

The Theta chapter in 1874 absorbed a chapter of Upsilon Beta, located at the Pennsylvania College, and indirectly caused the disruption of that entire fraternity. The Kappa chapter was formed from a local socity called the Iota, the Wabash chapter from a similar organization called the "Athenaeum," and the Beloit chapter from a local called Omega Sigma Theta. The Omega chapter was formerly a chapter of Kappa Phi Lambda, the Sigma Chi petitioners having first obtained a charter from that fraternity in order to maintain their organization. The Washington University, Albion, and Chicago chapters were formed from local organizations not bearing Greek names.

The Purdue chapter was the means of bringing the question of faculty opposition to the fraternities to a judicial determination, and its long struggle with the college authorities and its final triumph form a most interesting chapter in the history of fraternities.

The chapter at the Southern University became inactive by reason of the failure of any of its members to return to college after the close of vacation, and the same reason may be assigned for the death of the chapters at Roanoke, Randolph-Macon, and North Carolina. The charter at Hillsdale was withdrawn.

Government Until 1882, executive government of the fraternity was vested in the parent chapter subordinate to the decrees of the general convention and to the votes of a majority of the chapters during the recess of the assembly. Since 1882, the system of government has been through a biennial convention called the Grand Chapter, with ad interim government by the Grand Council, made up of general officers, an Executive Committee, and an undergraduate member from each region. The officials are named by designations peculiar to Sigma Chi. The fraternity was incorporated in 1898 under the laws of Illinois as "The Grand Council of the Sigma Chi Fraternity."

Until 1913 fraternity business was handled exclusively by volunteers; then the fraternity engaged an Executive Secretary, and the next year saw the establishment of a headquarters office in Chicago devoted exclusively to fraternity business.

The Fraternity's governing law prohibiting and defining hazing and improper activities during the preparation for membership period was adopted and issued in 1977, and is one of the most comprehensive and definitive statements on the subject.

Sigma Chi's Leadership Training Workshop was originiated in 1947. An annual training session for chapter officers, its major divisions are for chapter presidents, vice presidents, treasurers, pledge trainers, rush chairmen and chapter advisors. By 1990, the Workshop had grown to attract an attendance of nearly 1,400 members and had achieved participation by 100 percent of its active chapters four times during the 1985–1990 period.

In 1988, the Fraternity established a separately-constituted Risk Management Foundation, for the purpose of providing educational programs on risk management and liability loss prevention to chapters and members and making liability insurance coverage available at reasonable rates. In 1990, a for-profit corporation known as Constantine Capital, Inc., was formed to provide financing and assistance for campus chapter house building and improvements.

Traditions and Insignia The tradition of Sigma Chi's founding is perpetuated in the Founder's Memorial Chapter House at Miami University. A movement to place monuments on the graves of the seven founders was begun in 1921 and concluded in 1933. Oil paintings of the founders are hung in the headquarters.

An unparalleled tradition asset of the fraternity is "The Sweetheart of Sigma Chi" song composed by F. Dudleigh Vernor and Byron K. Stokes in 1911, their sophomore year at Albion College.

Both alumni support and loyalty and wife-and-sweetheart support and loyalty are cherished tradition. Although Sigma Chi is not the largest fraternity in terms of either number of chapters or membership, it has long been the largest in terms of active alumni groups. There are more than 150 active, organized alumni chapters located in cities in America, Canada, and England.

The badge of the fraternity is a cross of gold and white enamel. In the center is an elliptical plate of black enamel displaying the letters ΣX in gold. On the upper arm of the cross are two crossed keys; on the left arm, a scroll, and on the right, an eagle's head. On the lower arm is a pair of clasped hands above seven stars. Two small chains connect the upper arm of the cross with the horizontal arms.

The fraternity colors are blue and old gold. The flower is the white rose. The flag consists of two bars, blue and gold, displaying the Sigma Chi white cross. The colors of the pledge button are blue and white.

In 1983, the fraternity created a new tradition, an annual, fraternity-wide celebration of "Brother's Day." All chapters are urged to stage fraternal and social events during the same weekend each February, with emphasis on holding events with brothers of different ages and chapters.

Publications A preliminary catalogue was published in 1872, followed by the first regular edition in 1876. It contained a list of 1,750 names. The next edition, issued in 1890, contained a history of the fraternity and rather complete data concerning each members. A residence directory, published in 1902, contained chapter rolls, geographical and alphabetical indexes, and the history brought up to date. A combined manual and directory was published in Chicago in 1908. Similar volumes were issued at the same place in 1910, 1912, 1916, 1922, and 1933. In 1950 the directory was published in an elaborate volume of 832 pages. Another directory, a three-volume, loose leaf perpetual formal issue, made its appearance early in 1962, with chapter, alphabetical, and geographical sections. Later directories were published in 1978 and 1987, the latter a volume of nearly 1,200 pages. A handbook, a manual of information for members only, appeared in 1905. A pledge manual called *The Norman Shield* made its appearance in 1929, and enlarged new editions have been published biennially.

A songbook was published in 1872 under the auspices of the Lafayette chapter. Later editions were issued by the general fraternity n 1884, 1894, 1898, 1909, and 1923. *Sigma Chi Sings* made its appearance in 1952, and *Five Score and Five*, the current edition, in the 1960s.

The first volume of *The History of Sigma Chi* appeared in June, 1925. Written by Joseph Cookman Nate, D.D., for nearly a half-century a worker in Sigma Chi and interfraternity circles, it set a high standard in this type of fraternity literature. The second volume was published in May, 1928, the third and fourth in 1931. Dr. Nate died in 1933. At Bloomington, Illinois, an impressive memorial symbolizes the fraternity's deep affection for him. *The Centennial History of Sigma Chi*, the work of Grand Historian Robert M. Collett, Denison '15, was issued in book form at the Centennial Grand Chapter in June, 1955, at Cincinnati. In 1990, the Fraternity published *The History of the Sigma Chi Fraternity 1955 to 1980* by Grand Historian Douglas R. Carlson, Minnesota '73.

A journal, *The Sigma Chi*, was issued under the editorship of Theta Chapter in 1881 as a bimonthly. In 1887 the name was changed to *The Sigma Chi Quarterly*. In 1926 it was again changed to *The Magazine of Sigma Chi* to permit a greater frequency of issue. A publication endowment fund was established at the same time, and the sales of life subscriptions commenced.

In 1887 a secret monthly journal called *The Sigma Chi Bulletin*, printed on thin paper, was sent to members in sealed envelopes. It is believed to be the first, and now oldest, esoteric publication produced by a general fraternity. This contained matters deemed too private for insertion in the magazine. *The Bulletin* is still devoted to internal business, and is usually published as a section of the magazine.

A three-reel motion picture with sound was made of the highlights of the fraternity's Diamond Jubilee in 1930. "Significant Sigs," a three-reel sound picture of celebrities, was produced in 1934 largely for rushing purposes. Another historical picture was made in 1939. Still another one was produced a a record of the Centennial Grand Chapter. In 1967 a sound film strip, "This is Sigma Chi," was produced. In 1980, a special film was produced in celebration of the Fraternity's 125th anniversary.

Funds and Philanthropies The Sigma Chi Foundation, a nonprofit educational and charitable corporation, was organized and incorporated in 1939 and in 1990 had assets in excess of $7,000,000. It has as its purposes: aid to the American system of collegiate education, assistance to worthy Sigma Chis enabling them to complete their college education, scholarships and fellowships for members of the fraternity and other qualified students, and vocational and professional placement service for Sigma Chis.

Since 1929 the fraternity has had a plan of international and province awards, emblematic of the highest undergraduate honors attainable on the four-way basis of personality, scholarship, fraternity service and campus activities. They bear the name of their donor, L.G. Balfour, Indiana '07, 1939–41 chairman of the National Interfraternity Conference and past president of Sigma Chi. In 1952 the Charles G. Ross Chapter Publication Award was announced for competition among the undergraduate chapters to replace a similar award which had existed since 1931. The James E. Montgomery Award similarly was created for the best alumni publication.

Significant Sig Medals were created in 1935 by the Grand Chapter for alumni whose achievements have brought honor and prestige to the fraternity. The Daniel William Cooper Scholarship Trophy, named for a founder, replaced in 1940 numerous awards for chapter scholastic achievement. Annually an award is given to the best alumni chapter officer. Another award, the Order of Constantine Medal, was created in 1948 to honor members who had rendered long and exceptional service to the fraternity.

Other major Sigma Chi awards are the J. Dwight Peterson Significant Chapter Award, given annually to those chapters which meet comprehensive but attainable standards; Jay E. Minton Best Alumni Chapter Officer Award; Sigma Chi Alumni Community Service Award; Edna Boss Housemother Award; William T. Bringham House Corporation Officer Award; Dr. Erwin E. LeClerg Chapter Advisor Award; Sigma Chi Sportsman of the Year Award; and Sigma Chi Foundation Graduation Persistence Award, given to schools to present to that fraternity on its campus which has graduated the highest percentage of its pledge class.

Sigma Chi was one of the first of the men's general fraternities to embark upon a fraternity-wide service project, and the first to sustain such a project over the years. From the project's origin in 1967 to 1990, Sig chapters had raised nearly one million dollars for the Wallace Village for Children, a school for children with minimal brain dysfunction located in Colorado. These funds supported building of the "Sigma Chi Gym" dedicated there in August, 1976, and have been utilized for educational programs and scholarships since then. In 1986, the fraternity expanded the scope of its recommended projects to include the National Center for Missing and Exploited Children.

Headquarters 1714 Hinman Avenue, P.O. Box 469, Evanston, IL 60204. Phone: (708) 869-3655. In June, 1966, Sigma Chi moved into a new headquarters building at that address, especially designed for the purpose. Located on the edge of downtown Evanston, two blocks south of the Northwestern campus, the structure houses the offices of the fraternity and the Sigma Chi Foundation and a number of imposing public rooms such as a main lounge, the Fred Millis Memorial Library, and a museum.

A long and significant fraternal career concluded on December 31, 1989, with the retirement of long-time Executive Secretary and Executive Vice President William T. Bringham Sr. He was the Fraternity's longest serving employee and Executive Secretary, having held the position for nearly 36 years. Upon retirement, he remained active in interfraternity affairs.

Membership Living initiates 170,000. Active chapters 217. Active alumni associations and chapters 140. Total number of initiates 208,499. Chapter roll:

Year	Chapter
1855	Alpha, Miami (OH)
1855	Gamma, Ohio Wesleyan
1856	*Epsilon, Western Military Institute* (1857) (Original)
1857	Eta, Mississippi
1858	*Iota, Jefferson Col.* (1869)
1858	Lambda, Indiana
1859	*Nu, Washington (PA)* (1863) (Original)
1859	Omicron, Dickinson
1859	Xi, DePauw
1860	*Pi, Erskine* (1861) (Original)
1860	Psi, Virginia
1860	*Sigma, LaGrange Synodical (TN)* (1861) (Original)
1863	Theta, Gettysburg
1864	Epsilon, George Washington
1864	Kappa, Bucknell
1865	Rho, Butler
1865	*Upsilon, Poly Tech Of PA* (1876)
1866	Zeta, Washington and Lee
1867	Phi, Lafayette
1868	Mu, Denison
1869	Omega, Northwestern
1869	*Sigma, Princeton* (1882)
1871	Chi, Hanover
1872	Delta, Georgia
1872	*Nu, Cumberland (TN)* (1880)
1872	Pi, Samford
1872	Sigma Sigma, Hampden-Sydney
1872	Tau, Roanoke
1873	*Beta, Wooster* (1913)
1873	*Beta Beta, Mississippi Col.* (1874)
1874	*Epsilon Epsilon, Monmouth (IL)* (1878)
1874	*Gamma Gamma, Randolph, Macon* (1901)
1874	*Psi Psi, Michigan* (1875) (Original)
1875	Delta Delta, Purdue
1875	Phi Phi, Penn
1876	Iota Iota, Alabama
1876	Zeta Zeta, Centre College
1877	Theta Theta, Michigan
1879	*Chi Chi, South Alabama* (1882)
1880	*Alpha Beta, Richmond* (1882) (Original)
1880	Delta Chi, Wabash
1881	Kappa Kappa, Illinois
1882	Alpha Eta, Iowa
1882	Alpha Gamma, Ohio State
1882	Alpha Theta, M.I.T.
1882	Alpha Zeta, Beloit
1882	*Chi Psi, Louisiana* (1883)
1882	Zeta Psi, Cincinnati
1883	*Alpha Delta, Stevens Tech* (1891)
1883	Alpha Epsilon, Nebraska
1883	Alpha Iota, Illinois Wesleyan
1883	Alpha Kappa, Hillsdale
1884	Alpha Lambda, Wisconsin, Madison
1884	*Alpha Mu, V.M.I.* (1885)
1884	Alpha Nu, Texas
1884	Alpha Xi, Kansas
1886	Alpha Beta, Cal, Berkeley
1886	Alpha Omicron, Tulane
1886	Alpha Pi, Albion
1887	Alpha Rho, Lehigh
1888	Alpha Sigma, Minnesota
1889	Alpha Tau, North Carolina
1889	Alpha Upsilon, USC
1890	Alpha Phi, Cornell
1891	Alpha Chi, Penn State
1891	Alpha Omega, Stanford
1891	Alpha Psi, Vanderbilt
1892	Alpha Alpha, Hobart
1893	*Eta Eta, Dartmouth* (1960)
1893	Lambda Lambda, Kentucky
1894	Nu Nu, Columbia (NY)
1895	Mu Mu, West Virginia
1896	Xi Xi, Missouri
1897	*Omicron Omicron, Chicago* (1952)
1902	Rho Rho, Maine
1903	Tau Tau, Washington (MO)
1903	Upsilon Upsilon, Washington (WA)
1904	Psi Psi, Syracuse
1905	Beta Gamma, Colorado Col
1905	Omega Omega, Arkansas
1906	Beta Delta, Montana
1908	Beta Epsilon, Utah
1909	Beta Eta, Case Western Reserve
1909	Beta Theta, Pitt
1909	Beta Zeta, North Dakota

1910	Beta Iota, Oregon
1912	Beta Kappa, Oklahoma
1912	Beta Lambda, Duke
1914	Beta Mu, Colorado
1914	Beta Nu, Brown
1916	Beta Omicron, Iowa State
1916	Beta Pi, Oregon State
1916	Beta Xi, New Mexico
1917	Beta Rho, Montana State
1917	Beta Sigma, Tennessee
1919	Beta Tau, Colorado State
1919	Beta Upsilon, Washington State
1921	Beta Chi, Emory
1921	Beta Phi, Arizona
1922	Beta Omega, Toronto-Ryerson Tech
1922	Beta Psi, Georgia Tech
1922	Gamma Delta, Oklahoma State
1923	Gamma Epsilon, Whitman
1923	Gamma Zeta, Union (NY)
1924	Gamma Eta, Idaho
1924	Gamma Theta, Florida
1925	Gamma Iota, L.S.U.
1926	Gamma Kappa, Utah State
1927	Gamma Lambda, McGill
1928	*Gamma Mu, Wesleyan (CT)* (1959)
1929	Gamma Nu, South Carolina
1930	Gamma Omicron, Colgate
1930	Gamma Xi, Wyoming
1932	Gamma Pi, Rochester
1933	Gamma Rho, Dalhousie, St. Mary's (NS)
1934	Gamma Sigma, Auburn
1934	Gamma Tau, North Dakota State, Tri-College
1938	Gamma Upsilon, Mississippi State
1942	Gamma Chi, Maryland
1942	Gamma Phi, Miami (FL)
1942	Gamma Psi, Michigan State
1943	Delta Epsilon, North Carolina State
1943	Gamma Omega, Connecticut
1947	Delta Eta, UCLA
1947	Delta Iota, Denver
1947	Delta Kappa, Bowling Green
1947	Delta Theta, Tennessee, Chattanooga
1947	Delta Zeta, Willamette
1948	*Delta Lambda, Davidson* (1969)
1948	Delta Mu, Southern Methodist
1948	Delta Nu, Wake Forest
1949	Delta Omicron, British Columbia, Simon Fraser
1949	Delta Pi, Ohio
1949	Delta Rho, Bradley
1949	Delta Sigma, Rhode Island
1949	Delta Tau, Westminster
1949	Delta Upsilon, Kansas State
1949	Delta Xi, San Diego State
1950	Delta Phi, Puget Sound
1950	Delta Psi, R.P.I.
1951	Delta Omega, Tulsa
1951	*Epsilon Zeta, Florida State* (1988)
1952	Epsilon Eta, Cal State, Fresno
1952	Epsilon Theta, San Jose
1953	Epsilon Iota, St. Lawrence
1954	Epsilon Kappa, Memphis State
1955	Epsilon Lambda, Ripon
1955	Epsilon Mu, Texas Christian
1955	Epsilon Nu, Texas Tech.
1956	Epsilon Xi, Houston
1957	Epsilon Omicron, Western Ontario
1958	Epsilon Pi, Northern Colorado
1958	Epsilon Rho, Richmond
1959	Epsilon Sigma, Florida Southern
1959	Epsilon Tau, Murray State
1960	Epsilon Phi, Southeast Missouri
1960	Epsilon Upsilon, Arizona State
1961	*Epsilon Chi, Lamar* (1983)
1961	Epsilon Psi, Sam Houston
1962	Epsilon Omega, Ball State
1963	*Beta Alpha, Western Reserve* (1970)
1963	Zeta Eta, East Texas
1963	Zeta Theta, GMI
1964	Zeta Iota, Kansas State, Pittsburg
1965	Zeta Kappa, Cal, Santa Barbara
1965	Zeta Lambda, Kent
1965	Zeta Mu, Western Kentucky
1966	Zeta Nu, Western Michigan
1966	Zeta Xi, Cal State, Northridge
1967	Zeta Omicron, Northern Arizona
1967	Zeta Pi, Texas A & I
1967	Zeta Rho, Central Michigan
1967	Zeta Sigma, Eastern New Mexico
1967	Zeta Tau, Fort Hays
1968	*Zeta Phi, New Mexico State* (1985)
1968	Zeta Upsilon, William and Mary
1969	Zeta Chi, Nevada, Las Vegas
1969	Zeta Omega, East Tennessee
1970	Eta Alpha, Eastern Kentucky
1970	Eta Beta, Cal State, Long Beach
1970	Eta Delta, Tennessee Tech.
1970	Eta Epsilon, South Alabama
1970	Eta Gamma, Middle Tennessee
1970	Eta Theta, Georgia Southwestern
1970	Eta Zeta, Georgia Southern
1971	Eta Iota, Embry Riddle (FL)
1971	Eta Kappa, Southwest Missouri
1971	Eta Lambda, V.P.I.
1971	Eta Mu, Eastern Illinois
1972	Eta Nu, Northern Illinois
1973	Eta Omicron, Indiana (PA)
1973	Eta Xi, Austin Peay
1974	Eta Pi, Central Florida
1974	Eta Rho, North Alabama
1975	Eta Sigma, Cal, Irvine
1975	Eta Tau, Stephen F. Austin
1976	Eta Upsilon, Texas A & M
1977	Eta Chi, Youngstown State
1977	Eta Phi, Troy
1977	Eta Psi, Clemson
1978	Eta Omega, Baylor
1978	Theta Alpha, Clarion
1979	Theta Beta, South Florida
1980	Theta Gamma, Drake
1981	Theta Delta, Southern Mississippi
1982	Theta Epsilon, North Georgia
1983	Theta Eta, Missouri, Rolla

1983	Theta Zeta, Bridgewater
1984	Theta Iota, St. Louis
1984	Theta Kappa, Texas, Arlington
1984	Theta Lambda, San Diego State
1984	Theta Mu, Spring Hill
1984	Theta Nu, Alma
1985	Theta Omicron, Cal, Davis
1985	Theta Pi, Indiana State
1985	Theta Rho, Illinois State
1985	Theta Sigma, Cal Poly, Pomona
1985	Theta Xi, Cal State, Sacramento
1986	Theta Phi, Cal Poly, San Luis Obispo
1986	Theta Tau, Southwest Texas
1986	Theta Upsilon, Yale
1987	Iota Alpha, Cal State, San Bernadino
1987	Iota Beta, James Madison
1987	Theta Chi, Arkansas State
1987	Theta Omega, Elon
1987	Theta Psi, Waterloo
1988	Iota Delta, SUNY, Albany
1988	Iota Epsilon, Charleston (SC)
1988	Iota Eta, Western Connecticut
1988	Iota Gamma, Jacksonville
1988	Iota Kappa, Fairleigh Dickinson, Madison
1988	Iota Theta, Dayton
1988	Iota Zeta, Clarkson
1989	Iota Lambda, Louisville
1989	Iota Mu, Wilfrid Laurier
1989	Iota Nu, Furman
1989	Iota Omicron, Western Illinois
1989	Iota Pi, Marquette
1989	Iota Xi, George Mason
1990	Iota Phi, North Texas
1990	Iota Rho, Bishop's (QB)
1990	Iota Sigma, Valparaiso
1990	Iota Tau, St. Thomas
1990	Iota Upsilon, Boston U.
1991	Iota Chi, Cal, San Diego
1991	Iota Omega, Loyola Marymount, Los Angeles
1991	Iota Psi, Rutgers

Sigma Nu

ACTIVE PIN

PLEDGE PIN

SIGMA NU was founded on January 1, 1869, at the Virginia Military Institute, Lexington, Virginia, by three cadets, James Frank Hopkins, Greenfield Quarles, and James McIlvaine Riley. Organization proceeded from the membership of V. M. I.'s Legion of Honor, a secret society of students drawn together around Hopkins and dedicated to the eradication of hazing and other immature practices. The greek letter accouter-ments were adopted January 1, 1869, which is regarded as the founding date.

The three founders were from what was then the nation's western frontier, being attracted to V. M. I. because of its high reputation and the cultural advantages of Lexington. Founder Hopkins was a native of Arkansas and a veteran of the Civil War. Greenfield Quarles, who served under his uncle, General William A. Quarles, during the Civil War and had been captured and imprisoned, came to V. M. I. from his home in Arkansas. James McIlvaine Riley came from Missouri.

Growth At the conclusion of its first year, Sigma Nu's membership embraced residents of twelve states, the widespread representation giving impetus to extension activities, beginning with the granting of a charter at the University of Virginia in 1870. At the end of the first decade the roll numbered nine chapters, but most of these had been nominal foundings resulting from authority given members upon leaving the parent society, and had become defunct, forced by hostile faculties into inactivity or sub rosa existence.

The permanent growth of the fraternity began early in its second decade with the establishment of chapters at North Georgia College, then located in a prosperous gold field and a leading college of its day, and at Washington and Lee University. With the three chapters cooperating, *The Delta*, the fraternity's magazine, was established in 1883, the name recognizing the triangular relationship of the three chapters. Through other revivals and foundings, principally resulting from activities of the North Georgia and Washington and Lee chapters, the roll of living chapters numbered eight at the time of the first national convention in 1884 at Nashville, Tennessee.

In 1884 Sigma Nu grew out of the South, moving westward to the University of Kansas. In 1885 the East was opened with the establishment of a chapter at Lehigh University. In 1886 the Kansas chapter became the administrative head of the fraternity and for eight years dominated its extension policy. The chapter at Stanford University was installed at the time the institution itself was opened, and Sigma Nu was the first to enter the state universities of Washington, Oregon, Montana, and Nevada. The chapter at the University of Missouri, where Sigma Nu was an early contender, took an important part in establishing the fraternity in the West.

Supported by its strength in western territory and in the South, Sigma Nu spread throughout the central states with great rapidity and with marked success. The fraternity's development closely followed a policy determined by early leaders; namely that Sigma Nu should establish itself in the West before attempting eastern growth, enabling the fraternity in due time to enter the East with confidence and security. In

1949 Sigma Nu installed a chapter at the University of Toronto, its first in Canada.

Government The Grand Chapter, the national convention, is the legislative branch and supreme authority of the fraternity. Until 1884 government was through the Grand Lodge, whose executive officers, called regent and vice-regent, were elected every five years by state presidents chosen by the chapters. In 1884 the High Council was substituted and remains as the policy-making agency of the fraternity between Grand Chapters. The High Council, elected by the Grand Chapter, consists of six alumni officers: regent, vice-regent, grand treasurer, and three councilmen. The regent and vice-regent are elected for two years each; the grand treasurer for six years; the three grand councilmen for two years each.

Grand Chapters are held every two years in the even-numbered years, with control placed in the hands of the collegiate chapters, each of which may send two Voting delegates. Alumni chapters are authorized for each collegiate chapter and, if organized and represented, each may have one vote. The division commanders, subordinate administrative officers having jurisdiction over the fraternity's fifty-six divisions, and members of the High Council have one vote each. The three members of the Board of Trustees and each former regent in attendance has a vote; no proxies are permitted.

The Law, Fundamental Principles and *Ancient Customs* serve as the constitution and can be amended only by action of the Grand Chapter.

In 1915 the system was amended by placing administration in the hands of an executive secretary, appointed by the High Council. His title was changed to Executive Director in 1976.

The chapter officers (who bear military titles adopted by the founders at V. M. I.) are elected by the collegiate membership and perform such duties as the chapter prescribes.

A leadership conference is held in odd-numbered years when the Grand Chapter does not meet.

Traditions and Insignia Sigma Nu's founders adopted Honor as the cardinal principle and from the beginning a code of honor, jealously guarded, has grown and been nourished by generations of Sigma Nus. The honor system operates in every chapter, a code of behavior which is looked upon as an all-pervading belief in personal integrity and as the fundamental attribute to character. The honor code requires each member to conform strictly to the duty imposed by conscience; it directs a course of life responding to a sense of what is right, just, and true. The code is taught by the personal example of the student and thus becomes a tradition handed down.

The founders struck the badge in a shape resembling the French medal, the *legion d'honour.* Sigma Nu's five-armed cross with its serpent, crossed swords, and gold letters, is the outward manifestation of a code which has governed the fraternity since its inception.

The remaining two cardinal principles are Truth and Love.

The Sigma Nu Creed, composed by Walter James Sears, was adopted in 1907. The coat-of-arms was designed by Ellwood N. McClelland and adopted in 1915. Sigma Nu's colors are black, white, and gold; the pledge button is a coiled serpent on a circular shield. The white rose is the flower and the official song is "The White Star of Sigma Nu." The official flag consists of three horizontal bars of equal width, black at the top, white in the center and gold at the bottom, with a coiled golden serpent in the center. The fraternity has elected forty-two members into the Sigma Nu Hall of Honor, the highest single tribute it can bestow.

In the early years, chapters were designated by Roman numerals in order of their establishment but in 1886 the chapter designation was changed to assign each chapter a Greek-letter name.

Early meetings of the parent chapter at V. M. I. were held at a limestone outcropping on the military school's campus, the name of the spot being known thereafter as The Rock of Sigma Nu. When campus expansion necessitated the destruction of the meeting place, fragments of the rock were buried for safekeeping and in 1959 a segment of the original rock was enshrined within an enclosure on the grounds of the headquarters in Lexington, Virginia. A cutting from the original rosebush that produced the first Sigma Nu White Rose has also been planted on the headquarters grounds and the two symbols—the Rock and the Rose—attract numerous chapters and alumni pilgrimages each year.

Publications Sigma Nu's magazine, *The Delta,* was first published in April, 1883, by John Alexander Howard, at Dahlonega, Georgia, as a monthly publication, but soon became a quarterly journal. The magazine has been published continually since. In 1958 a new payment plan was adopted which guaranteed a lifetime subscription for all new members.

A history, *The Story of Sigma Nu,* by John C. Scott, was published in 1927 and reprinted in 1936. For his authorship the fraternity named Scott to membership in the Hall of Honor.

Catalogues are published periodically. The first songbook was published in 1910 by Dr. Isadore Dyer, and in 1932 the first series of songbooks published by the general offices appeared.

A new pledge manual, *The Way of Honor,* written by Dick Vaughan, was published in 1961, and a companion workbook, *Steps Along the Way,* was issued in 1962. These two books were replaced by a new *Sigma Nu: A Pledge Education* in 1972.

The Sigma Nu Educational Foundation has underwritten research and publication in the field of group dynamics and organizational management and, by the end of 1976, had five monographs available: *Honor, An Ideal in Practice* (1970) and *Grouping for Solutions* (1971) by Amiott; *An Experiential Self-Development Program* (1973) by Hawkins; *Brotherhood: Myth or Mystique* (1975) by Amiott and Cottingham; and *Leadership and Communication* (1976) by Capps. The foundation also makes some $20,000 of scholarship grants annually. It cooperates with the fraternity in sponsoring and conducting an annual leadership institute and internship.

A set of accounting books and monthly statements is provided for the chapters; also periodic printings of The Law, the constitution and by-laws adopted by the membership at Grand Chapter; as well as several manuals covering phases of chapter management.

Funds In December, 1920, the Permanent Endowment Fund was formed to meet the need for chapter house financing and to provide an endowment for the magazine. Valued at more than $2,000,000, the fund is administered by five trustees, composed of the regent and grand treasurer, as well as three alumni appointed by the High Council for terms of six years, staggered, one every two years.

In 1946 the Sigma Nu Educational Foundation was incorporated to qualify for a bequest of more than a quarter million dollars from the estate of former Regent William P. Yates. Subsequent gifts and bequests have been received and the foundation annually provides scholarships to members. A self-perpetuating board of directors is headed by alumni members who are nationally prominent educators.

Headquarters In 1915 the fraternity established general offices in Indianapolis, Indiana, where it remained until 1957. In 1954 a headquarters committee was appointed and the site of a new general headquarters in Lexington, Virginia, near the scene of the founding, was ratified. In 1957 Sigma Nu purchased a large home situated upon a seven-acre tract of land. The building was restored and remodeled and occupied in February, 1958, and dedicated on June 9, 1960. As a result of contributions from collegiate chapters, the fraternity constructed a museum wing and a matching library-archives wing. The three units were dedicated in 1969, the centennial year. Headquarters address: Box 1869, Lexington, Virginia 24450. Phone: (703) 463-1869.

Membership Active chapters 212. Total number of initiates 167,169. Chapter roll:††

1869 *Alpha, V.M.I.* (1911)
1870 Beta, Virginia (1891-1900)
1871 *Gamma, Bailey Law* (1871), 1931, Duke
1873 Mu, Georgia
1874 Theta, Alabama
1879 Iota, Howard

†† This chapter roll is repeated from the 19th edition; no current information was provided.

1881 Kappa, North Georgia (1933-1972)
1882 Lambda, Washington and Lee
1883 Epsilon, Bethany (1885-1899)
1883 *Zeta, Central* (1901)
1884 Eta, Mercer (1932-1948)
1884 Nu, Kansas
1884 *Omicron, Bethel* (1904)
1884 Xi, Emory
1885 Pi, Lehigh
1886 Delta, South Carolina (1897-1928)
1886 Rho, Missouri
1886 Sigma, Vanderbilt
1886 *Tau, South Carolina Military Academy* (1891)
1886 Upsilon, Texas
1887 Phi, L.S.U.
1888 Beta Phi, Tulane (1935-1962)
1888 *Chi, Cornell Col. (IA)* (1913)
1888 Psi, North Carolina
1889 *Beta Alpha, Yale* (1892)
1889 Beta Omicron, Sewanee (1893-1921)
1890 Beta Beta, DePauw
1890 Beta Theta, Auburn
1891 *Beta Chi, Stanford* (1963)
1891 *Beta Delta, Drake* (1895)
1891 Beta Epsilon, Upper Iowa (1894-1954), Coe
1891 Beta Gamma, Missouri Valley (1896-1931)
1891 Beta Nu, Ohio State
1891 Beta Zeta, Purdue
1891 *Delta Theta, Lombard* (1930), 1930, Knox
1892 Beta Eta, Indiana
1892 Beta Iota, Mount Union
1892 *Beta Kappa, Southwestern (KS)* (1897), 1913, Kansas State
1892 *Beta Lambda, Central (MO)* (1902)
1892 Beta Psi, California
1893 Beta Mu, Iowa
1894 Beta Rho, Penn (1895-1897) (1898-1904)
1894 Beta Xi, William Jewell
1895 *Beta Pi, Chicago* (1898) (see Gamma Rho)
1895 Beta Tau, North Carolina State
1895 Beta Upsilon, Rose Tech
1895 Gamma Gamma, Albion
1896 Gamma Alpha, Georgia Tech
1896 Gamma Chi, Washington (WA)
1898 Beta Sigma, Vermont
1898 Gamma Beta, Northwestern
1900 Gamma Delta, Stevens
1900 Gamma Epsilon, Lafayette
1900 Gamma Zeta, Oregon
1901 Gamma Eta, Colorado Mines
1901 Gamma Theta, Cornell
1902 Gamma Iota, Kentucky
1902 Gamma Kappa, Colorado
1902 *Gamma Lambda, Wisconsin, Madison* (1962)
1902 Gamma Mu, Illinois
1902 Gamma Nu, Michigan
1903 Gamma Omicron, Washington (MO)
1903 Gamma Xi, Missouri Mines
1904 Gamma Pi, West Virginia
1904 *Gamma Rho, Chicago* (see Beta Pi, 1934)

1904	Gamma Sigma, Iowa State
1904	Gamma Tau, Minnesota
1904	Gamma Upsilon, Arkansas
1905	Gamma Phi, Montana
1906	*Gamma Psi, Syracuse* (1970)
1907	Delta Alpha, Case Tech
1907	*Delta Beta, Dartmouth* (1961)
1908	Delta Gamma, Columbia
1909	Delta Delta, Penn State
1909	Delta Epsilon, Oklahoma
1909	Delta Eta, Nebraska
1909	*Delta Zeta, Western Reserve* (1953)
1910	Delta Iota, Washington State
1910	Delta Kappa, Delaware
1912	*Delta Lambda, Brown* (1964)
1913	Delta Mu, Stetson
1913	Delta Nu, Maine
1914	Delta Xi, Nevada
1915	Delta Omicron, Idaho
1915	Delta Pi, George Washington
1915	Delta Rho, Colorado State
1916	Delta Sigma, Carnegie Tech (1938-1940)
1917	Delta Phi, Maryland
1917	Delta Tau, Oregon State
1917	*Delta Upsilon, Colgate* (1968)
1918	*Delta Chi, Trinity* (1972)
1918	*Delta Psi, Bowdoin* (1970)
1918	Epsilon Alpha, Arizona
1919	Epsilon Beta, Drury
1920	Epsilon Delta, Wyoming
1920	Epsilon Epsilon, Oklahoma State
1920	*Epsilon Gamma, Wesleyan* (1961)
1920	Epsilon Zeta, Florida
1921	Epsilon Eta, Tennessee
1922	Epsilon Iota, William and Mary (1936-1952)
1922	*Epsilon Theta, M.I.T.* (1974)
1923	Epsilon Kappa, North Dakota
1924	Epsilon Lambda, Utah
1926	Epsilon Mu, Butler
1927	Epsilon Nu, Miami (OH)
1927	Epsilon Xi, Mississippi
1930	Epsilon Omicron, USC
1930	Epsilon Pi, UCLA
1934	Epsilon Rho, Michigan State
1934	Epsilon Sigma, Southwestern, Memphis
1937	*Epsilon Tau, Rollins* (1972)
1938	Epsilon Upsilon, Utah State
1943	*Epsilon Phi, Connecticut* (1951)
1946	Epsilon Chi, Bowling Green
1947	Epsilon Psi, Westminster (PA)
1948	Zeta Alpha, Puget Sound
1948	*Zeta Beta, Miami (FL)* (1967)
1949	Zeta Delta, Toronto
1949	*Zeta Epsilon, Norwich* (1960)
1949	*Zeta Gamma, Kent* (1970)
1950	Zeta Eta, Tufts
1950	Zeta Zeta, Florida State
1951	Zeta Iota, San Jose
1951	Zeta Kappa, Cal State, Fresno
1951	Zeta Lambda, Tulsa
1951	Zeta Mu, Ohio
1951	Zeta Theta, Presbyterian

1952	Zeta Nu, Montana State
1952	Zeta Xi, Cal, Davis
1953	Zeta Omicron, North Texas
1953	Zeta Pi, Texas Tech.
1954	Zeta Rho, Rhode Island
1954	Zeta Sigma, Gettysburg
1954	*Zeta Tau, Ripon* (1976)
1955	Zeta Phi, Bradley
1955	Zeta Upsilon, Arizona State
1956	Zeta Chi, Houston
1957	Zeta Psi, Lamar
1958	*Eta Alpha, Davidson* (1971)
1959	Eta Beta, East Carolina
1959	Eta Delta, West Texas
1959	Eta Gamma, Georgia State
1960	Eta Epsilon, Kentucky Wesleyan
1961	Eta Eta, Idaho State
1961	Eta Zeta, Louisiana Tech
1962	Eta Iota, Northern Arizona
1962	Eta Theta, North Dakota State
1963	Eta Kappa, San Diego State
1963	*Eta Lambda, Cincinnati* (1973)
1963	Eta Mu, G.M.I.
1963	Eta Nu, Southwestern Louisiana
1963	Eta Xi, Little Rock
1964	Eta Omicron, Wofford
1965	Eta Pi, Hampden-Sydney
1965	Eta Rho, Western Kentucky
1966	Eta Phi, Cal State, Los Angeles
1966	Eta Sigma, Eastern New Mexico
1966	Eta Tau, Southwest Texas
1966	Eta Upsilon, Midwestern
1967	Eta Chi, Old Dominion
1967	Eta Psi, Ashland
1967	Theta Alpha, South Florida
1968	Theta Beta, South Dakota
1968	Theta Gamma, Southern Mississippi
1969	Theta Delta, Murray State
1969	Theta Epsilon, Johns Hopkins
1970	Theta Eta, Northern Illinois
1970	Theta Iota, Middle Tennessee
1970	Theta Kappa, Georgia Southern
1970	*Theta Lambda, Eastern Washington* (1973)
1970	Theta Mu, South Alabama
1970	Theta Theta, Eastern Kentucky
1970	Theta Zeta, Clemson
1971	Theta Nu, Ball State
1971	Theta Xi, V.P.I.
1972	Theta Omicron, Weber
1972	Theta Pi, West Georgia
1972	Theta Rho, Illinois State
1972	Theta Sigma, Southwest Missouri
1973	Theta Chi, East Tennessee
1973	Theta Phi, Lander
1973	Theta Psi, Armstrong
1973	Theta Tau, Morehead
1973	Theta Upsilon, New Mexico State
1974	Iota Alpha, Indiana (PA)
1974	Iota Beta, Virginia Wesleyan
1974	Iota Delta, Madison Col
1974	Iota Epsilon, Missouri Southern
1974	Iota Eta, Nebraska, Omaha

1974 Iota Gamma, Mississippi State
1974 Iota Iota, Valley City
1974 Iota Theta, Southern Methodist
1974 Iota Zeta, Vincennes
1975 Iota Kappa, Cal State, Chico
1975 Iota Lambda, Jacksonville (AL)
1975 Iota Mu, Nevada, Las Vegas
1975 Iota Nu, Maine, Portland-Gorham
1976 Iota Omicron, Texas, Arlington
1976 Iota Pi, Southern Tech
1976 Iota Rho, Charleston
1976 Iota Xi, Salisbury

COAT OF ARMS

Sigma Phi Epsilon

ACTIVE PIN

PLEDGE PIN

SIGMA PHI EPSILON was founded at Richmond College, now the University of Richmond, Virginia, on November 1, 1901. Carter Ashton Jenkens, an initiate of Chi Phi at Rutgers College where his father was pastor of the Baptist Church, enrolled at Richmond College in September, 1900, and he quickly found himself as the leader of a group of compatible young men, most of them ministerial candidates, who sought brotherhood. Kappa Alpha Order, Phi Kappa Sigma, Phi Gamma Delta, Pi Kappa Alpha, and Kappa Sigma were there but they did not often accept ministerial students. Jenkens addressed a petition for a chapter to Chi Phi and when the request was denied he and his group persuaded a committee of the faculty to allow them to attempt to establish a fraternity to be called Sigma Phi Epsilon. Jenkens chose the name *Sigma Phi* at first, to which he added *Epsilon* when faculty reference to BAIRD'S MANUAL revealed that a Sigma Phi already existed. Jenkens sought a principle from the New Testament which would serve as the foundation of the new fraternity and chose Matthew 22: 37–40; namely: *Thou shalt love the Lord thy God with all thy heart, and with all thy soul, and with all thy mind. This is the first and great commandment. And the second is like unto it, Thou shalt love thy neighbor as thyself.*" Jenkens said, "I read Matthew 22: 37–40, where the truth of eternity is summed up in the finest philosophy the world has ever known, the profoundest truth it has ever had . . . and I said to these boys who were planning with me, 'There is the rock, there is the rock.' " The five students who with Jenkens planned the fraternity were Benjamin Donald Gaw, '04; William Hugh Carter, '02; William Andrew Wallace, '03; Thomas

Temple Wright, '04; and William Lazell Phillips, '03. These men invited six others into their group who are also recognized as founders—Lucian Baum Cox, '02; Richard Spurgeon Owens, '04; Edgar Lee Allen, '02; Robert Alfred McFarland, '02; Franklin Webb Kerfoot, '02; and Thomas Vaden McCaul, '02. Jenkens devised the symbolism and conceived the badge as heart-shaped, consistent with the theme of *agape*—Christian love. Previously these students had called themselves "The Saturday Night Club," but now they were dubbed "The Sacred Hearts."

The decision to convert the local fraternity thus established into a national fraternity was made in October, 1902, by the small band of eight members who returned for that session—Gaw and Wright of the founders and six others, including Charles W. Dickinson, Jr., secretary of the group, who prepared the application for the charter. During that session charters were granted at the Medical College of Virginia, Washington and Jefferson College, Roanoke College, Bethany College, and the University of West Virginia.

Growth Several of the early chapters were formed for the purpose of becoming chapters of Sigma Phi Epsilon, but later many local clubs or fraternities became chapters. Virginia Beta was a local called Phi Iota Sigma. Pennsylvania Delta was organized to form a chapter of Sigma Phi Epsilon, but when the chapter of Omega Pi Alpha resigned from that fraternity, twelve of its fifteen members were initiated into Sigma Phi Epsilon. The Pennsylvania Gamma chapter became a chapter of the medical fraternity Alpha Kappa Kappa. The Syracuse chapter was the local Adelphian society and Randolph-Macon the Night Marauders. The Georgia Tech chapter was a local social club and the Delaware chapter a local called Delta Chi. The Arkansas chapter, as a local, was for a number of years called Alpha Zeta Phi and then Alpha Delta. The Lehigh chapter was formed by the resigning members of Omega Pi Alpha. The Cornell chapter existed for five years as a chapter of Theta Lambda Phi. By mutual agreement the law students withdrew and the remaining members became the New York Beta chapter. The Ohio Northern chapter, had been a Theta Nu Epsilon chapter.

In 1938 Sigma Phi Epsilon merged with Theta Upsilon Omega national fraternity, founded at Lewisburg, Pennsylvania, in February, 1924. By this merger chapters were added at Worcester Tech, Muhlenberg, Rensselaer, Bucknell, Westminster (PA), Temple, and Stevens, while the Theta Upsilon Omega chapters at Illinois, George Washington, California, and Auburn merged with existing Sigma Phi Epsilon chapters. Dormant at the time were the Monmouth and Miami chapters, both subsequently re-established as chapters of Sigma Phi Epsilon in 1948. The Westminster chapter was originally the mother chapter of the national fraternity Pi Rho Phi, founded in 1854, which joined Theta Upsilon Omega in 1924 at the dissolution of the former.

Government Government of the fraternity was vested in the mother chapter until December, 1903, when the first convention assembled. This convention vested government in the grand chapter, composed of delegates from undergraduate and alumni chapters, grand officers, and district governors as the legislative body. This group meets biennially in a conclave in major U.S. cities. In the interim between conclaves, the fraternity was until 1961 governed by an executive committee elected at each conclave. At the 1961 conclave in Chicago, a recodification of the constitution and by-laws was accepted which re-constituted the executive committee in a new way and designated it as the national board of directors. Officers of the grand chapter are now ten national directors—the grand president, the grand treasurer, and eight directors without other title; two of these are elected as student members. The grand president, grand treasurer, and two student members are elected to the board to serve two-year terms, while the term of office of the others is six years, the terms being staggered, so that the terms of two of them expire every two years, coincident with the biennial conclave. The president is eligible for election to three two-year terms, while the treasurer may be re-elected to two-year terms without limit. The directors elect a "secretary of the corporation" from among their number.

The administrative office of secretary was first established in April, 1908, the title changed to grand secretary, and later to executive director. A traveling secretary was employed in 1922. In 1916 the Purdue chapter surrendered all its property to the alumni who devised a plan of operation, known as the Purdue Plan, which placed the financial affairs of the chapters entirely in the hands of the alumni.

The district governor system was authorized by the grand chapter in 1932; the fraternity is divided into 28 districts, each with a governor. Regional leadership schools, supported by the Sigma Phi Epsilon Educational Foundation, are customarily held in the spring. A brother, who may or may not be a faculty member but who must be an alumnus of a chapter, serves as the chapter counselor. Administration is also greatly assisted through the work of such committees as the housing committee and by such individuals as the director of scholarship.

A national leadership school, called the Academy, was launched in 1964 on a trial basis. It was continued until 1972 when it became a regional program, with regional academies being held in February of each year.

Traditions and Insignia The heart is in the background of every phase of the program of the fraternity and the basis of all its traditions. Chief traditional events are the annual Founders' Day banquets held throughout the nation on November 1. Another tradition is the red chapter-house door. The popular name is Sig Ep or SPE.

The badge is heart-shaped, displaying the skull and crossbones and the letters ΣΦΕ in gold or silver on a background of black enamel. Only pearls and diamonds are permitted in the mounted badges. Colors are purple and red, and the two flowers are the violet and the dark red rose. The pledge badge is red and gold. The recognition button is a small gold crown. In 1933 the coat of arms which was adopted in 1908 was revised so as to make it heraldicly correct. The fraternity flag has a background of purple with a red bar extending diagonally from the upper left-hand corner to the lower right-hand corner. A five-pointed gold star is mounted on the red bar at the middle of the flag. The letters ΣΦΕ are placed in the upper right-hand corner and the Greek letter of the chapter in the lower left. In 1972 the red heart, displaying the Greek letters ΣΦΕ, was adopted as a fraternity symbol.

Publications The *Sigma Phi Epsilon Journal* has been published at least quarterly since March, 1904. *Educating for Brotherhood*, a book for pledge education accenting spiritual values and human understanding, first introduced in 1965, was succeeded in 1974 by *Guide to Brotherhood Development*. Among other publications are *Journal* supplements, manuals in various areas of operation, a *Songbook*, and a *Directory*, the most recent edition of which appeared in 1977.

Funds and Philanthropies Sigma Phi Epsilon's life membership plan, effective since August 1, 1924, entitles every member in good standing to a subscription to the *Journal* and all rights and benefits of the fraternity. An endowment fund was established in 1923. This fund was conceived as a guarantee and safeguard of the perpetuity of Sigma Phi Epsilon.

The Student Loan and Fellowship Fund was established in 1930 for the purpose of aiding worthy members to complete their college education. At the conclave in 1947, the name of this fund was changed to the Charles L. Yancey Student Loan Fund. A Chapter Investment Fund was authorized at the 1959 conclave. High scholastic attainment is encouraged and recognized by the awarding of the Grand Chapter Scholarship Cup to those chapters that rank in first place scholastically among the fraternities on their respective campuses, by awarding the Clifford B. Scott Memorial Key to the highest ranking man scholastically in each chapter each year, and by awarding the Ulysses Grant Dubach Scroll to the member of each chapter each year who shows the greatest improvement in scholarship.

The Benjamin Hobson Frayser Memorial Plaque is awarded each year to the undergraduate chapter which issues the most meritorious chapter publication for that year. The Carter Ashton Jenkens Award is made each year to the outstanding undergraduate *Journal* contributor.

The Order of the Golden Heart is the highest honor which can be bestowed upon an alumnus. This medallion is given to distinguished alumni who have performed outstanding service to the fraternity which has required conspicuously dedicated effort. The Sigma Phi Epsilon Citation is given to alumni who have risen to a lofty place in chosen professions. Brothers who have served on a local level for a minimum of five years may be recognized.

The Sigma Phi Epsilon Educational Foundation, Inc., was established in 1943 to provide scholarships for worthy students in chapters of Sigma Phi Epsilon who need and deserve supplementary financial help in obtaining an education, and to encourage such students "to develop physically, morally, intellectually, and socially." It was originally named the William L. Phillips Foundation in memory of the founder who served as grand secretary for 34 years and who personally planned the installation of most of its chapters prior to World War II and saw to their development.

The fraternity's camp program for underprivileged boys was begun in 1950 with contributions turned over to the University Camp for Boys at Green Lane, Pennsylvania. In 1952 the program was broadened to include additional camps. The Heart Fund was adopted as an official philanthropy at the 1959 Conclave.

Headquarters P.O. Box 1901, Richmond, VA 23215. Phone: (804) 353-1901. A two-story structure of traditional design was erected on a large attractive plot at Richmond in 1967. Faced with red brick and adorned with a portico supported by six white columns, the building stands on a high bluff overlooking the intersection of Highways 1, 301, and Interstate 95 the main routes into Richmond from Washington, D.C.

Membership Total living members 120,106. Undergraduate members 15,600. Active chapters 254. Inactive chapters 64. Chapter houses owned 206. Total number of initiates 178,908. Chapter roll:

1901 Virginia Alpha, Richmond
1902 *Pennsylvania Alpha, Washington and Jefferson* (1906)
1902 Virginia Beta, Virginia Commonwealth (1905-1971)
1903 Illinois Alpha, Illinois (1913-1917)
1903 *Pennsylvania Beta, Jefferson Medical* (1912)
1903 *Pennsylvania Gamma, Pitt* (1912-1949) (1963)
1903 *Virginia Gamma, Roanoke* (1905)
1903 *West Virginia Alpha, Bethany (WV)* (1905)
1903 West Virginia Beta, West Virginia
1904 Colorado Alpha, Colorado
1904 Pennsylvania Delta, Penn
1904 South Carolina Alpha, South Carolina (1906-1929) (1938-1951)
1904 Virginia Delta, William and Mary (1938-1961)
1905 Indiana Alpha, Purdue
1905 New York Alpha, Syracuse
1905 North Carolina Beta, North Carolina State
1905 Ohio Alpha, Ohio Northern

1905 *Ohio Beta, Wittenberg* (1906)
1906 Virginia Epsilon, Washington and Lee (1940-1960)
1906 Virginia Zeta, Randolph, Macon
1907 Arkansas Alpha, Arkansas (1938-1948)
1907 Delaware Alpha, Delaware (1981-1985)
1907 Georgia Alpha, Georgia Tech
1907 Pennsylvania Epsilon, Lehigh
1907 Virginia Eta, Virginia
1908 Alabama Alpha, Auburn
1908 Ohio Gamma, Ohio State
1908 *Pennsylvania Zeta, Allegheny* (1909)
1908 *Vermont Alpha, Norwich* (1960)
1908 *Virginia Theta, V.M.I.* (1912)
1909 D.C. Alpha, George Washington
1909 New Hampshire Alpha, Dartmouth (1970-1981)
1909 North Carolina Gamma, Duke (1960-1968)
1910 California Alpha, Cal, Berkeley (1972-1984)
1910 Kansas Alpha, Baker
1911 Nebraska Alpha, Nebraska
1912 Massachusetts Alpha, Massachusetts
1912 Michigan Alpha, Michigan
1912 New York Beta, Cornell
1912 *Ohio Delta, Wooster* (1914)
1912 *Rhode Island Alpha, Brown* (1919)
1912 Washington Alpha, Washington State
1913 Colorado Beta, Denver (1973-1990)
1913 *Iowa Alpha, Iowa Wesleyan* (1976)
1913 Tennessee Alpha, Tennessee
1914 Missouri Alpha, Missouri
1915 Colorado Gamma, Colorado State
1915 Ohio Epsilon, Ohio Wesleyan
1915 Pennsylvania Eta, Penn State
1915 Wisconsin Alpha, Lawrence (1976-1980)
1916 Iowa Beta, Iowa State
1916 Minnesota Alpha, Minnesota (1941-1949) (1958-1978)
1917 Iowa Gamma, Iowa
1918 Kansas Beta, Kansas State
1918 Montana Alpha, Montana
1918 Oregon Alpha, Oregon State
1920 Oklahoma Alpha, Oklahoma State
1920 Wisconsin Beta, Wisconsin, Madison
1921 North Carolina Delta, North Carolina (1939-1947)
1922 Washington Beta, Washington (WA)
1923 Colorado Delta, Colorado Mines
1923 Kansas Gamma, Kansas
1925 Florida Alpha, Florida
1925 *Pennsylvania Theta, Carnegie-Mellon* (1937)
1925 *Vermont Beta, Middlebury* (1941-1949) (1971-1983) (1990)
1926 Oregon Beta, Oregon
1927 Alabama Beta, Alabama
1928 California Beta, USC
1928 Mississippi Alpha, Mississippi (1976-1988)
1929 Louisiana Alpha, Tulane (1941-1990)
1929 Maryland Alpha, Johns Hopkins
1929 Missouri Beta, Washington (MO) (1941-1949)

1929	New Mexico Alpha, New Mexico	1952	*Wisconsin Delta, Wisconsin, Stevens Point* (1983)
1930	*Alabama Gamma, Samford* (1935)	1953	Florida Zeta, Tampa (1976-1985)
1930	New York Gamma, N.Y.U. (1970-1980)	1953	Indiana Gamma, Ball State
1930	North Carolina Epsilon, Davidson	1953	Mississippi Gamma, Southern Mississippi
1930	Texas Alpha, Texas	1953	*Missouri Zeta, Southeast Missouri* (1989)
1931	Indiana Beta, Indiana (1938-1947)	1953	*North Carolina Eta, High Point* (1965)
1933	Kentucky Alpha, Kentucky	1953	*North Carolina Theta, Lenoir-Rhyne* (1984)
1936	Utah Alpha, Utah State	1953	*Ohio Lambda, Kent* (1983)
1938	Massachusetts Beta, Worcester Tech	1954	Arizona Beta, Arizona
1938	Mississippi Beta, Mississippi State	1954	Arkansas Beta, Henderson
1938	New Jersey Alpha, Stevens Tech	1954	Indiana Delta, Indiana State
1938	New York Delta, R.P.I.	1954	*Iowa Epsilon, Morningside* (1985)
1938	Pennsylvania Iota, Muhlenberg	1954	*New York Epsilon, SUNY, Buffalo* (1971-1979) (1989)
1938	Pennsylvania Kappa, Bucknell	1954	Ohio Mu, Youngstown State
1938	Pennsylvania Lambda, Westminster (PA)	1954	Tennessee Gamma, East Tennessee
1938	*Pennsylvania Mu, Temple* (1972)	1955	Arkansas Gamma, Arkansas State
1940	North Carolina Zeta, Wake Forest	1955	Georgia Beta, Georgia State
1940	*Wisconsin Gamma, Carroll* (1983)	1955	Indiana Epsilon, Evansville
1943	*Wyoming Alpha, Wyoming* (1963)	1955	Michigan Beta, Western Michigan
1944	New Jersey Beta, Rutgers	1955	*Texas Gamma, Texas Christian* (1976)
1946	Oklahoma Beta, Oklahoma	1956	Connecticut Alpha, Connecticut (1973-1980)
1946	*Oklahoma Gamma, Tulsa* (1959)	1956	Indiana Zeta, Valparaiso
1947	California Delta, Cal, San Diego	1956	*Iowa Zeta, Parsons* (1973)
1947	California Gamma, Cal, Santa Barbara (1972-1978)	1956	Michigan Delta, Detroit
1947	Kentucky Beta, Louisville (1958-1978)	1956	Michigan Gamma, Central Michigan
1947	Missouri Gamma, Missouri, Rolla	1956	Texas Delta, Houston (1971-1984)
1947	West Virginia Gamma, Marshall	1957	Missouri Eta, Southwest Missouri
1948	Illinois Beta, Illinois Tech	1957	Oregon Gamma, Lewis and Clark
1948	Illinois Gamma, Monmouth (IL)	1957	Texas Epsilon, Lamar
1948	Iowa Delta, Drake	1958	*California Epsilon, San Jose* (1973)
1948	Maine Alpha, Maine	1958	*Idaho Alpha, Idaho State* (1972)
1948	Ohio Eta, Miami (OH)	1958	Kansas Zeta, Fort Hays
1948	Ohio Zeta, Baldwin-Wallace	1958	North Carolina Iota, Atlantic Christian
1948	Pennsylvania Nu, Thiel	1959	Kansas Eta, Wichita
1949	Florida Beta, Stetson	1959	Kentucky Gamma, Kentucky Wesleyan
1949	*Florida Delta, Florida Southern* (1990)	1960	*Georgia Gamma, Valdosta* (1974)
1949	Florida Gamma, Miami (FL) (1976-1983)	1960	Michigan Epsilon, Michigan State (1974-1980)
1949	Illinois Delta, Bradley	1960	*Tennessee Delta, Tennessee Wesleyan* (1982)
1949	Maryland Beta, Maryland (1974-1985)	1960	West Virginia Epsilon, West Virginia Tech
1949	*Missouri Delta, Drury* (1988)	1961	*Louisiana Beta, L.S.U.* (1979)
1949	Ohio Theta, Cincinnati	1961	*Montana Beta, Montana State* (1987)
1949	Tennessee Beta, Memphis State	1961	North Carolina Kappa, East Carolina
1949	West Virginia Delta, Davis and Elkins	1961	*Texas Zeta, East Texas* (1988)
1950	Florida Epsilon, Florida State	1962	Michigan Zeta, Ferris
1950	*Massachusetts Gamma, Boston U.* (1970)	1962	*Nevada Alpha, Nevada* (1963)
1950	Ohio Iota, Toledo	1962	Texas Eta, Sam Houston
1950	Ohio Kappa, Bowling Green	1963	California Eta, Cal, Davis
1950	Utah Beta, Utah	1963	California Sigma, Cal State, Northridge (-1989)
1950	Vermont Gamma, Vermont	1963	California Theta, Cal State, Sacramento
1951	Kansas Delta, Washburn	1963	*California Zeta, Cal State, Long Beach* (1973)
1951	Kansas Epsilon, Emporia	1963	Georgia Delta, Georgia
1951	Nebraska Beta, Nebraska, Omaha	1963	Indiana Eta, Indiana Tech
1952	Arizona Alpha, Arizona State	1964	*Ohio Nu, Cleveland* (1990)
1952	*Colorado Epsilon, Northern Colorado* (1980)	1964	Pennsylvania Omicron, Philadelphia Textiles
1952	Massachusetts Delta, M.I.T.	1965	Michigan Eta, Michigan Tech
1952	Missouri Epsilon, Culver-Stockton (1986-1988)		
1952	*Oklahoma Delta, Oklahoma City* (1961)		
1952	*Pennsylvania Xi, Indiana (PA)* (1974)		
1952	Texas Beta, North Texas		

1965	Nebraska Gamma, Kearney
1965	North Carolina Lambda, Belmont Abbey
1965	Rhode Island Beta, Rhode Island
1967	Florida Eta, Rollins
1967	Kentucky Delta, Western Kentucky
1967	Ohio Xi, Ohio (1980-1988)
1967	*Wisconsin Epsilon, Wisconsin, Oshkosh (1976)*
1968	*California Iota, Cal State, Chico (1987)*
1968	Florida Iota, South Florida
1968	Florida Theta, Jacksonville
1968	Indiana Theta, Tri-State
1968	Missouri Theta, Central Missouri State
1969	*Georgia Epsilon, Georgia Southern (1989)*
1969	Kentucky Epsilon, Murray State
1969	*Tennessee Epsilon, Tennessee Tech. (1988)*
1970	Kentucky Zeta, Morehead
1970	New Jersey Gamma, Seton Hall (1985-1990)
1970	Ohio Omicron, Defiance
1970	South Carolina Beta, Clemson
1970	Texas Iota, Texas Tech.
1970	Texas Theta, St. Mary's, San Antonio
1970	Virginia Iota, Madison Col
1970	Virginia Kappa, V.P.I.
1970	*West Virginia Zeta, Charleston (WV) (1987)*
1970	*Wisconsin Zeta, Marquette (1985)*
1971	Illinois Epsilon, Northern Illinois
1971	Illinois Zeta, Illinois State
1971	Michigan Theta, Lawrence Tech
1971	Tennessee Zeta, Lambuth
1971	*Wisconsin Eta, Wisconsin, Stout (1979)*
1972	*California Kappa, Northrop (1976)*
1972	Florida Kappa, Miami-Dade
1972	Georgia Zeta, North Georgia
1972	Indiana Iota, Vincennes
1972	*Pennsylvania Pi, Duquesne (1976)*
1972	Texas Kappa, Texas, Arlington
1972	*Texas Lambda, Tyler Junior (1988)*
1973	Illinois Eta, Southern Illinois, Edwardsville
1973	Kansas Theta, Pittsburg State, Kansas
1973	*Missouri Iota, Missouri Western (1982)*
1973	North Carolina Mu, Elon
1973	North Carolina Nu, North Carolina, Charlotte
1973	*Tennessee Eta, Austin Peay (1976)*
1973	Texas Mu, Texas A & M
1973	Texas Nu, Texas Wesleyan
1973	*Texas Xi, West Texas (1984)*
1974	Arizona Gamma, Northern Arizona
1974	Arkansas Delta, Arkansas, Little Rock
1974	Iowa Eta, Loras
1974	*New Jersey Delta, Fairleigh Dickinson, Madison (1976)*
1974	Ohio Pi, Wright State
1974	Texas Omicron, Angelo
1975	*Alabama Delta, Alabama, Birmingham (1989)*
1975	California Lambda, Santa Clara
1975	North Carolina Xi, Appalachian
1976	*Illinois Iota, Lewis (1984)*
1976	Illinois Theta, Western Illinois
1976	Texas Pi, Stephen F. Austin (1983-1989)
1976	Texas Rho, Baylor
1977	Alabama Epsilon, Auburn, Montgomery
1977	Arkansas Epsilon, Arkansas Tech
1977	Indiana Kappa, IUPU, Fort Wayne
1977	Missouri Kappa, Missouri, Kansas City
1977	Pennsylvania Rho, Villanova
1977	Tennessee Theta, Middle Tennessee
1978	Alabama Zeta, Huntingdon
1978	*Idaho Beta, Boise (1990)*
1978	Massachusetts Epsilon, Bentley
1978	Michigan Iota, Northwood (MI)
1978	Virginia Lambda, Longwood
1979	Illinois Kappa, Southern Illinois
1979	*Maryland Gamma, Towson (1985)*
1979	New York Eta, Buffalo State College
1979	New York Zeta, Marist
1979	Pennsylvania Sigma, York (PA)
1979	Pennsylvania Tau, West Chester
1979	South Carolina Delta, Winthrop
1979	South Carolina Epsilon, Coastal Carolina
1979	South Carolina Gamma, Francis Marion
1979	Texas Sigma, Texas, San Antonio
1980	California Mu, Cal Poly, Pomona
1980	Missouri Lambda, Northwest Missouri
1980	New Jersey Epsilon, Glassboro
1980	New York Iota, SUNY Col., Fredonia
1980	New York Theta, SUNY Col., Geneseo
1980	*Tennessee Iota, Lincoln Memorial (TN) (1984)*
1980	Virginia Mu, George Mason
1981	California Nu, Chapman
1981	California Xi, San Francisco State
1981	Florida Lambda, St. Leo's
1981	Georgia Eta, Southern Tech
1981	Missouri Mu, Northeast Missouri
1981	New York Kappa, Daemen
1981	Texas Tau, Southwest Texas
1981	Virginia Nu, Radford
1982	Kentucky Eta, Northern Kentucky
1982	New York Lambda, Canisius
1982	*New York Mu, SUNY Col., Cortland (1990)*
1982	North Carolina Omicron, North Carolina, Greensboro
1982	Pennsylvania Upsilon, Clarion
1983	Louisiana Gamma, Loyola, New Orleans
1983	Maryland Delta, Western Maryland
1983	Michigan Kappa, Grand Valley
1983	New Hampshire Beta, New England
1983	North Carolina Pi, Western Carolina
1984	California Omicron, UCLA
1984	New Hampshire Gamma, New Hampshire
1984	Pennsylvania Phi, Susquehanna
1985	California Pi, Stanford
1985	Florida Mu, Central Florida
1985	Massachusetts Zeta, Tufts
1985	Texas Upsilon, Southern Methodist
1985	Virginia Xi, Old Dominion
1986	Nebraska Delta, Creighton
1986	New York Nu, SUNY, Binghamton
1986	New York Xi, Rochester
1987	Alabama Eta, South Alabama
1987	Florida Nu, Florida International

1987   Nevada Beta, Nevada, Las Vegas
1987   New York Omicron, SUNY, Albany
1987   Pennsylvania Chi, Albright
1988   Arkansas Zeta, Central Arkansas
1988   California Rho, Cal, San Diego
1988   New York Pi, SUNY Col., Oswego
1988   Pennsylvania Psi, St. Joseph's (PA)
1989   Alabama Theta, Jacksonville
1989   Connecticut Beta, Hartford
1989   Illinois Lambda, Northwestern
1989   Michigan Lambda, Eastern Michigan
1989   Rhode Island Gamma, Bryant
1990   California Tau, Cal Poly, San Luis Obispo
1990   New York Rho, St. John's (NY)

COAT OF ARMS

Sigma Phi Society

ACTIVE PIN

PLEDGE PIN

SIGMA PHI SOCIETY was founded at Union College in Schenectady, New York, on March 4, 1827. Its founding members were Thomas F. Bowie, 1827, John T. Bowie, 1829, Thomas S. Witherspoon, 1828, and Charles T. Cromwell, 1827. It is the second oldest of the Greek-letter fraternities, but the oldest in continuous national existence. Sigma Phi was the first fraternity to establish a branch chapter on another college campus. Each chapter is incorporated under the laws of its own state. The fraternity itself has been incorporated under the laws of the State of New York since 1885.

Three chapters have failed in the society's 160-year history. The Gamma of New York (New York University, 1835–1848) surrendered its charter in the belief that a successful chapter could not be maintained at a city college where the students met only at recitation. Along with the entire Greek community, the Alpha of New Jersey (Princeton, 1853–1858) was the victim of systematic anti-fraternity regulation by the university. The Alpha of Massachusetts (1834–1968) was closed when the fraternity system was outlawed on the Williams College campus.

Several Sig chapters had their roots in local eating or social groups on campus. The Williams chapter was formed from a local society called Phi Alpha, the Lehigh chapter from a similar organization called Beta Beta, the California chapter from the local La Junta Club, and the Virginia chapter from a campus organization known as the Serpentine Club.

Growth   The fraternity has grown very slowly.

In the matter of expansion, Sigma Phi has exhibited an intense conservatism. Its expansion criteria continued to require 1) interest demonstrated by an existing local group, 2) support of and participation by a substantial alumni group, 3) the presence of a friendly host university or college, and 4) proximity to an existing chapter.

Government   The government of the fraternity is vested jointly in both the local alumni corporations and a standing national organization. The continuity and physical operation of each chapter are the responsibilities of its local alumni group. The society's national organization is responsible for establishing the philosophical tone for the society, as well as developing and administering functional guidelines.

In the fall of each year, a national convention is held. Such conventions are hosted by the ten chapters on a rotating basis in founding order. In the interim, affairs of national significance are conducted by the Standing and Advisory Committee. That committee is composed of a Chairman (term of office: three years), an Executive Committee, and delegates appointed by each chapter. This committee maintains a central office and a general secretary. Prior to 1887, annual conventions were invariably held in Schenectady on or around March 4.

Traditions and Insignia   Founders Day (March Fourth) Banquets are frequently held in Berkeley, Buffalo, Burlington, Chicago, Clinton (N.Y.), Detroit, Pittsburgh, and Washington, D.C. Alumni reunions are held in each of the cities where the society has a chapter, as well as on the campus of Williams College.

The badge is a monogram of the letters made by placing a Σ over the Φ. The former is usually set with pearls, occasionally with precious stones. The society's colors are sky blue and white, as are the colors shown on the pledge button.

Publications   The *Catalogue* of the society was issued for the first time in 1834, and fifteen times thereafter in the nineteenth century. More recently, it was published in 1915, 1927, 1949, and again in 1977. It continues to be *the* reference manual for the history and the membership of the fraternity. Sigma Phi was the first fraternity to print a geographical distribution of its membership in its catalogue.

Collections of songs are published periodically; the last such songbook *(The Signet)* was printed in 1963. Beginning in 1887, Sigma Phi published an annual report. This gave way in 1920 to an annual magazine called the *Sigma Phi Flame*. The *Flame* is supplemented twice yearly by a smaller publication called the *Bulletin*.

Funds and Philanthropies   The society's national organization administers the Francis S. Viele Scholarship Program each year. Named for a member of the Hobart chapter initiated in 1885, the Viele Trust distributes about $50,000 per year to qualifying graduate and undergraduate Sig students.

Headquarters P.O. Box 99416, Troy, MI 48099. Phone: (313) 362-3266.

Membership Active chapters 10. Inactive chapters 3. Houses owned 10. Alumni Chapters 11. City Alumni Associations 5. Total number of initiates 9,825. Chapter roll:

1827 Alpha of NY, Union (NY)
1831 Beta of NY, Hamilton
1834 *Alpha of MA, Williams* (1968)
1835 *Gamma of NY, N.Y.U.* (1848)
1840 Delta of NY, Hobart
1845 Alpha of VT, Vermont
1853 *Alpha of NJ, Princeton* (1858)
1858 Alpha of MI, Michigan
1887 Alpha of PA, Lehigh
1890 Epsilon of NY, Cornell
1909 Alpha of WI, Wisconsin, Madison
1912 Alpha of CA, Cal, Berkeley
1953 Alpha of VA, Virginia

Sigma Pi

ACTIVE PIN

PLEDGE PIN

SIGMA PI was founded as the Tau Phi Delta Society at Vincennes (Indiana) University on February 26, 1897. The university, the oldest institution of learning west of the Alleghenies and north of the Ohio, was established by General Henry Harrison in 1801, endowed by the Federal Government with 23,000 acres of public land in 1804, and chartered in 1806 by the first general assembly of the Indiana Territory. In 1822 the State of Indiana wrongfully seized and sold the university's land and diverted the proceeds to another institution. This led to a long course of litigation in which the university was represented by the distinguished jurist Chancellor Kent. Although the U.S. Supreme Court acted in the university's favor in 1852, it was 100 years later, however, before the state began to make redress. As a consequence, the university was reduced to the status of a junior college, which it has since remained.

The founders of Sigma Pi were Rolin Rosco James, William Raper Kennedy, James Thompson Kingsbury, and George Martin Patterson. The year 1905 found seven alumni members of Tau Phi Delta at Indiana University and two at the University of Illinois. The group at Indiana attempted to organize a Beta Chapter of Tau Phi Delta, but they were not encouraged by the Vincennes local. A short time later, the two alumni at Illinois organized the Sphinx Club for the purpose of affiliating with the Vincennes local.

On February 11, 1907, Tau Phi Delta at Vincennes University changed its name to "Alpha Chapter of the Sigma Pi Fraternity of the United States" and declared its intent to become a national fraternity. This was accomplished the following year by the chartering of chapters at Illinois and Ohio State. In 1911, Sigma Pi, with six chapters, was admitted into full membership by the National Interfraternity Conference. It was in that same year, however, that Sigma Pi's Alpha Chapter became inactive when the student enrollment fell below 100.

Despite the dormancy of Alpha Chapter in 1961, Vincennes University made the national fraternity an outright gift of one of the finest country estates in southern Indiana in appreciation for the contributions and dedication of its members during the 14 years of its early existence. This property, known as "Shadowwood," is now the International headquarters of Sigma Pi. In 1965 the university and the Grand Chapter of the fraternity also joined in a petition to the National Interfraternity Conference for a special dispensation to permit the revival of the mother chapter. Such permission was granted and on February 26, 1965—the 68th anniversary of the founding of the fraternity—Alpha Chapter was reactivated. It then had the distinction of being the only chapter of a nationally recognized college fraternity on a junior college campus.

Several of the local organizations chartered by Sigma Pi antedated the founding of the parent chapter at Vincennes. The group at California which became Iota Chapter was established in 1894; the organization at Cornell which became Mu Chapter traced back to 1895; the local at Franklin and Marshall which became Nu Chapter had its origin in 1897; and the group at Purdue which became Eta Chapter came into being the following year. Sigma Pi was the pioneer at Vincennes and Temple.

Sigma Pi and its members were called to play important roles in the Spanish-American War and the two World Wars. The outbreak of war with Spain in 1898 almost caused the untimely death of the fraternity within a year after its establishment. The attendance at Vincennes University was nearly depleted when most of the male students enlisted as a unit for service in the Spanish-American War. Founder James, however, was able to surround himself with a group of new members, who were accorded sympathetic support by the faculty, and they succeeded in preserving and perpetuating the fraternity.

In June of 1964, Sigma Pi demonstrated its commitment to expansion when it gained four chapters and one colony through a merger with the small national fraternity, Delta Kappa.

Sigma Pi again made strides in expansion when it chartered its Zeta-Iota Chapter at Western Ontario in Canada on March 2, 1985. As a result, The Sigma Pi Fraternity of the U.S. became The Sigma Pi Fraternity, International, Inc.

Government Conventions, called convocations, are held biennially. The Grand Chapter, in convention assembled, is the supreme governing body of the fraternity and consists of elected delegates from active chapters and chartered alumni groups together with the grand officers. Between convocations, the government is vested in the Executive Council, consisting of the seven grand officers. The various chapters are divided geographically into provinces, with each province operating under the supervision of an archon. Provinces are divided into regions and hold biennial conventions during the years between the international convocations.

The college chapters operate on what is known as the uniform system of chapter finances which provides for a finance board to administer and supervise chapter finances. Noteworthy features of the finance system include uniform continuous records, a chapter budget based on actual operating expenses, equal distribution of the cost of operation among actives and pledges, supervision by alumni, and audit, as well as preparation of monthly and annual reports.

The fraternity is incorporated under the laws of Indiana and maintains a central administrative office called the Executive Office, with a full-time executive director, an assistant executive secretary, a director of chapter services, *The Emerald* editor, and a group of chapter consultants.

Traditions and Insignia An educational committee, in addition to supervising scholarship, which has always been encouraged, promotes and provides ways and means whereby the fraternity and its chapters may contribute to the well-rounded development of the individual members. A scholarship trophy is awarded annually to the chapter maintaining the highest competitive scholastic standing throughout the year, and a key is awarded each year to the pledge in each province who attains the highest scholastic grade.

The badge is a Greek cross of gold, bearing a raised oval of blue enamel with a crown set emerald at its center between the letters Σ and Π. The arms of the cross display, respectively, a scroll, a balance, a wreath, and ten stars arranged as a perfect triangle. The pledge button is purple and white in color and shaped like the shield of the coat of arms with the bar reversed. The flag has a lavender field, with the letters Σ and Π and the coat of arms emblazoned thereon in white. The colors are lavender and white, with gold as an auxiliary. The flower is the lavender orchid, with the lilac and white rose together as alternates.

Publications *The Emerald of Sigma Pi*, a quarterly magazine, has been published continuously since July, 1911, as the esoteric journal of the fraternity. *Keryx*, an esoteric publication, first appeared in July of 1931; it is published by the Grand Council as occasion demands. Each chapter endeavors to publish a periodical for circulation among its alumni, and a number of alumni clubs do likewise. Editions of the constitution have been printed as and when needed. Six catalogues of all members have been published, the last one, the 85th anniversary edition, in 1982. In addition, each chapter periodically publishes its own roster of members, and chapters within a given province or area often publish a joint directory. Two separate editions of a songbook have been published. *The Sigma Pi Manual* (1983) relates the history of Sigma Pi as a story. It is currently being updated for release in 1986. Illustrations within the book serve to emphasize the ideals upon which the fraternity was founded. The *Officer's Handbook* is made available to chapter and alumni officers.

Funds and Philanthropies A scholarship fund was started in late 1947 by Byron R. Lewis, an alumnus. It has been perpetuated through the generosity of alumni like Dr. Lothar I. Iversen, whose 1984 contribution was the second largest single gift left to any college fraternal educational fund. Known as The Sigma Pi Educational Fund, incorporated under the laws of the State of Indiana, it is used exclusively for charitable and educational purposes, both income and principal being available to help deserving students and to advance education in general. The Educational Fund is exempt from income tax and contributions are deductible by donors for income tax purposes.

An endowment fund, called The Sigma Pi Foundation, to which every new member subscribes, was established and incorporated under the laws of Indiana in 1923. It is administered by a board of directors, consisting of eight directors nominated by the Grand Chapter. Over 80 percent of the members are subscribers to the endowment fund. Paid-up life members number 2,004. The income from the endowment fund is used to defray operating expenses of the Grand Chapter and the cost of an *Emerald* subscription for every foundation subscriber. This income amounts to approximately one-tenth of the annual budget requirements of the Grand Chapter and helps to reduce the cost of membership to undergraduates. The principal of the fund is held intact and loaned to chapters for the purpose of building, repairing, or refinancing chapter houses as the need arises.

At the 1982 Biennial Convocation, Sigma Pi adopted Multiple Sclerosis as its national philanthropy. Each chapter is encouraged to perform one philanthropic project each year to benefit MS, a disease which primarily strikes young adults between the ages of 18 and 34.

Headquarters P.O. Box 1897, Vincennes, IN 47591. Phone: (812) 882-1897. On August 30, 1962, in conjunction with the national convocation, the Grand Chapter dedicated "Shadowwood" as a memorial to the four founders. It was officially opened as the Executive Office on July 1, 1963. The building and property were given to the fraternity by Vincennes University.

Membership Total living membership 45,249. Total undergraduate membership 5,247. Active chapters 131. Inactive chapters 44. Colonies 8.

Houses owned 82. Graduate/Alumni chapters 32. Total number of initiates 59,083. Chapter roll:

1897	Alpha, Vincennes (1910-1965)
1908	Gamma, Ohio State
1908	Phi, Illinois
1909	*Delta, Penn* (1913-1914) (1938)
1909	Kappa, Temple (1918-1931)
1910	*Epsilon, Ohio* (1943-1970) (1982)
1912	Eta, Purdue
1912	Theta, Penn State
1912	Zeta, Ohio Northern
1913	Iota, Cal, Berkeley (1967-1975)
1916	*Lambda, Kenyon* (1970)
1917	Mu, Cornell
1918	Nu, Franklin and Marshall
1918	Xi, Iowa (1938-1961)
1920	*Omicron, Tulane* (1952-1964) (1973)
1920	*Pi, Utah* (1976)
1921	Rho, North Carolina State
1922	Sigma, Iowa State (1943-1955) (1974-1990)
1922	*Tau, Wisconsin, Madison* (1932-1984) (1988)
1923	*Chi, Pitt* (1960)
1923	Upsilon, UCLA
1924	Beta, Indiana
1924	*Omega, Oregon State* (1942-1948) (1985)
1924	Psi, Emory
1925	*Alpha-Beta, Michigan* (1952-1966) (1970)
1926	Alpha-Delta, Auburn
1926	Alpha-Gamma, Washington (WA) (1958-1982)
1927	Alpha-Epsilon, Mercer (1940-1985)
1930	Alpha-Zeta, St. Lawrence
1931	Alpha-Eta, William and Mary
1931	Alpha-Theta, Beloit
1933	Alpha-Iota, Missouri, Rolla
1936	Alpha-Kappa, L.S.U. (1952-1957) (1977-1986)
1937	Alpha-Lambda, Mississippi State
1938	Alpha-Mu, New Jersey Tech
1940	Alpha-Nu, Wake Forest
1948	*Alpha-Omicron, Cal, Santa Barbara* (1972-1973) (1976)
1948	*Alpha-Phi, Georgia* (1988)
1948	Alpha-Pi, Arkansas State
1948	Alpha-Rho, Southwest Missouri
1948	*Alpha-Sigma, Arkansas* (1977)
1948	Alpha-Tau, Southwestern Louisiana (1956-1989)
1948	Alpha-Upsilon, Rhode Island (1968-1982)
1948	*Alpha-Xi, Cal State, Fresno* (1959)
1949	Alpha-Chi, Maryland
1949	Alpha-Omega, San Diego U (1961-1963) (1974-1976)
1949	*Alpha-Psi, Utah State* (1962)
1949	Beta-Gamma, Eastern Illinois
1950	*Beta-Delta, Kansas* (1961)
1950	*Beta-Epsilon, Syracuse* (1953)
1950	Beta-Eta, San Jose (1977-1990)
1950	Beta-Theta, Drexel
1950	*Beta-Zeta, Miami (FL)* (1964)
1951	Beta-Iota, Northern Arizona
1951	Beta-Kappa, Arizona State (1965-1984)
1953	Beta-Lambda, Lycoming
1953	Beta-Mu, Mississippi (1971-1974)
1955	Beta-Nu, Southern Illinois (1977-1980)
1955	Beta-Omicron, Cal State, Long Beach
1955	*Beta-Xi, New Mexico State* (1966-1967) (1971-1980) (1986)
1959	Beta-Pi, Virginia
1959	*Beta-Rho, Atlantic Christian* (1982)
1959	Beta-Sigma, Northern Illinois
1960	Beta-Chi, Loyola, Chicago
1960	Beta-Phi, Rochester Tech
1960	Beta-Tau, Valparaiso
1960	Beta-Upsilon, Shippensburg
1961	*Beta-Omega, Lock Haven* (1988)
1961	Beta-Psi, East Stroudsburg
1962	Gamma-Alpha, Detroit
1962	*Gamma-Beta, Eastern Michigan* (1972)
1962	Gamma-Delta, Slippery Rock
1962	Gamma-Gamma, Central Missouri State
1963	Gamma-Epsilon, Fairmont
1964	*Delta-Omicron, Wisconsin, Milwaukee* (1972)
1964	*Delta-Sigma, Wisconsin, Stout* (1972)
1964	Gamma-Eta, Rutgers
1964	*Gamma-Zeta, Parsons* (1973)
1965	*Delta-Chi, Western State (CO)* (1972)
1965	Gamma-Iota, Worcester Tech
1965	*Gamma-Theta, Texas* (1972)
1966	Gamma-Kappa, Indiana Tech
1966	*Gamma-Lambda, Wisconsin, Stevens Point* (1976)
1966	Gamma-Mu, Wisconsin, Oshkosh (1976-1984)
1966	Gamma-Nu, Akron
1967	Gamma-Omicron, Findlay
1967	Gamma-Pi, Indiana State
1967	Gamma-Rho, Western Michigan
1967	*Gamma-Sigma, Missouri* (1990)
1967	Gamma-Xi, West Virginia Tech
1968	*Delta-Gamma, Milton* (1977)
1968	*Gamma-Chi, Quinnipiac* (1972)
1968	*Gamma-Phi, Wisconsin, Whitewater* (1977)
1968	*Gamma-Tau, Georgia Southern* (1989)
1968	Gamma-Upsilon, Murray State
1969	Delta-Alpha, Central Michigan
1969	Delta-Beta, Monmouth (NJ) (1975-1989)
1969	Delta-Epsilon, Seton Hall
1969	*Delta-Eta, Youngstown State* (1975)
1969	Delta-Zeta, Missouri, St. Louis
1969	Gamma-Omega, Wayne State (MI)
1969	*Gamma-Psi, St. Louis* (1973-1974) (1982)
1970	Delta-Iota, Wisconsin, Platteville
1970	Delta-Lambda, Louisiana Tech
1970	Delta-Mu, Salem (WV)
1970	Delta-Nu, Ball State (1977-1983)
1970	*Delta-Pi, Bloomsburg* (1973)
1970	*Delta-Theta, Corpus Christi* (1973)
1970	*Delta-Xi, Southern Utah* (1973)
1971	*Delta-Phi, Wisconsin, La Crosse* (1986)
1971	Delta-Psi, Troy

1971 Delta-Rho, Morehead
1971 *Delta-Tau, Indiana, South Bend* (1988)
1971 Delta-Upsilon, V.P.I. (1977-1990)
1972 Delta-Omega, Southern Illinois, Edwardsville
1972 Epsilon-Alpha, Southern Tech
1973 Epsilon-Beta, Kentucky
1975 *Epsilon-Delta, Columbus* (1986)
1975 Epsilon-Gamma, Illinois Wesleyan
1976 Epsilon-Epsilon, Emporia
1976 Epsilon-Zeta, Western Illinois
1977 Epsilon-Eta, Illinois State
1977 Epsilon-Iota, Cal State, Northridge
1977 Epsilon-Kappa, Southern Arkansas
1977 Epsilon-Theta, Elon
1978 Epsilon-Lambda, Eastern Kentucky
1978 Epsilon-Mu, Madison Col
1978 Epsilon-Nu, Cal State, Fullerton
1979 Epsilon-Omicron, SUNY, Buffalo
1979 Epsilon-Xi, Fairleigh Dickinson, Rutherford
1981 Epsilon-Pi, Christopher Newport
1982 Epsilon-Phi, Embry Riddle (AZ)
1982 Epsilon-Rho, Drury
1982 Epsilon-Sigma, Loyola Marymount, Los Angeles
1982 Epsilon-Tau, Tennessee, Martin
1982 Epsilon-Upsilon, Cal, Davis (1986-1989)
1983 Epsilon-Chi, San Diego U
1983 Epsilon-Omega, SUNY Col., Potsdam
1983 Epsilon-Psi, Widener
1984 Zeta-Alpha, West Chester
1984 Zeta-Beta, Embry Riddle (FL)
1984 Zeta-Delta, Colorado
1984 Zeta-Epsilon, Michigan Tech
1984 Zeta-Gamma, Millersville
1984 Zeta-Zeta, Florida
1985 Zeta Iota, Western Ontario
1985 Zeta Kappa, Cal State, Bakersfield
1985 Zeta Lambda, USC
1985 Zeta Nu, Villanova
1985 *Zeta Xi, Southeastern Oklahoma* (1988)
1985 Zeta-Eta, Santa Clara
1985 Zeta-Theta, SUNY Col., Plattsburgh
1986 Zeta Omicron, Lawrence Tech
1986 Zeta Pi, Oakland
1986 Zeta Rho, Edinboro
1986 Zeta Sigma, North Carolina Wesleyan
1987 Zeta Phi, Southwestern Louisiana
1987 Zeta Tau, Northern Colorado
1987 Zeta Upsilon, Cal, San Diego
1988 Eta Alpha, Cal State, Sacramento
1988 Eta Beta, Southern Connecticut
1988 Eta Delta, Cal Poly, San Luis Obispo
1988 Eta Epsilon, Florida State
1988 Eta Gamma, Hofstra
1988 Zeta Chi, Glassboro
1988 Zeta Omega, Nevada
1988 Zeta Psi, West Virginia
1989 Eta Eta, Bridgewater
1989 Eta Zeta, Western Connecticut
1990 Eta Kappa, East Carolina
1990 Eta Lambda, SUNY, Albany

1990 Eta Mu, Missouri Southern

Colonies: Averett, Bridgeport, Cal State, Dominguez Hills, Clark, North Carolina, Asheville, St. Leo's, Texas A & M, Toronto, Towson, Wesley, York (PA)

Sigma Tau Gamma

ACTIVE PIN

PLEDGE PIN

SIGMA TAU GAMMA was born "during the month of roses" at Central Missouri State University in 1920 out of the desire of seventeen men to perpetuate their friendships and to found a fraternity "dedicated to the highest ideals of manhood, brotherhood and citizenship." June 28 is commemorated as the date of establishment.

Four of the founders; Emmett Ellis, Leland Thornton Hoback, Edward George Grannert, and William Glenn Parsons, had enlisted and served their country together during the First World War in France. Parsons commented that in founding the fraternity they wanted to sustain a "sense of service, responsibility and affection for their companions." These four, together with Allen Ross Nieman, Edward Henry McCune, Carl Nelson Chapman, Buell Wright McDaniel, George Eugene Hartrick, A. Barney Cott, Chiles Edward Hoffman, Rodney Edward Herndon, William Edward Billings, Clarence Willard Salter, Alpheus Oliphant Fisher, and Daniel Frank Fisher, founded the fraternity.

Growth The founders envisioned a national college fraternity serving what were then known as teachers colleges and extension was originally confined constitutionally to approved degree granting teachers colleges, but this restriction was later removed. During the formative period, the fraternity grew rapidly in fulfilling the demand for national fraternity membership in such colleges. Sigma Tau Gamma has pioneered fifty-two campuses. All of the early chapters were once local fraternities. Not until 1956 was the first colonization undertaken.

Several of the early chapters had their origins of earlier date than the fraternity. The second chapter, chartered in 1921, was the former Kappa Tau Epsilon, founded February 12, 1894, at Northeast Missouri State University. The third chapter chartered was Beta Alpha Tau, which had been organized in 1916 at Emporia State University.

The founders had provided that when five chapters had been established a meeting would be held to perfect a national organization, rewrite the constitution and ritual, and elect a set of officers to replace the provisional ones, all Alpha Chapter alumni. On May 3 and 10, 1924, the fourth and fifth chapters were installed. Accordingly, the first conclave was called for May 30, 1925, in Warrensburg, Missouri, home of Alpha Chapter. On November 28–29, 1924, a planning meeting was held in Emporia, Kansas, which enabled the delegates to the first conclave to expedite their work and to lay a solid foundation for extension, which resulted in eleven additional chapters in the second five years. At the third conclave, held at Emporia in 1927, a central office was authorized and the *SAGA of Sigma Tau Gamma* was adopted as the official name of the fraternity's magazine.

Growth was slowed during the Depression with just two chapters installed between 1930 and 1938. Rho Chapter at Buffalo State College was installed in 1933 and was to serve as a foundation for further growth in New York. All five New York chapters were closed in 1954 as a result of an adverse ruling by the State University of New York Board of Trustees regarding national fraternity affiliation. Rho chapter was later reorganized in 1977. Kappa Phi Sigma Fraternity, originally formed as the Owls Fraternity in 1915, was installed in 1934 as the Sigma Chapter at the University of Central Arkansas.

Chapter extension resumed at a sustained pace with the installation of two chapters in 1938. In the same year the central office was moved from Kirksville, Missouri, where it had been under the part time stewardship of Thomas Hutsell, to Buffalo, New York, where D. Kenneth Winebrenner began serving as executive secretary, also on a part-time basis but with full-time clerical assistance. Continued growth required the employment of a full-time field staff in 1949. In 1953 the central office was moved to Webster Groves, Missouri, where E. Kennedy Whitesitt became the first full-time chief executive.

In 1970 the central office was moved to Warrensburg, Missouri, in anticipation of constructing a permanent headquarters on the founding site of the fraternity. In 1977, the 5600 square foot Marvin Millsap Headquarters Building was built, which houses the fraternity and foundation offices, Founders Library and historical archives.

Government The Grand Chapter, supreme legislative authority, meets biennially. Representatives of the college chapters, alumni chapters, alumni associations, members of the Board of Directors, and past presidents of the fraternity are entitled to attend and vote at the Grand Chapter. The Board of Directors is the governing body, elected by the Grand Chapter, and is made up of the president, president-elect, four directors, and the two immediate past presidents. The secretary and treasurer are elected by and from among the directors. The executive director is appointed by the Board of Directors and is the chief administrative officer.

Territorial supervision of the college chapters is exercised by regional directors, volunteer alumni officers appointed by the Board of Directors. Regional directors are assisted by; district governors, who directly supervise one or two chapters, regional leadership consultants, who conduct regional educational workshops, regional expansion directors, who coordinate chapter extension, and regional alumni directors, who supervise alumni chapters. Regional directors appoint the assisting volunteer alumni officers with the advice and consent of the Board of Directors. College chapters are served by a four-member advisory board of which the chairman is appointed by the district governor.

The Sigma Tau Gamma Foundation was organized by Grand Chapter legislation in 1966. It is governed by a board of eighteen trustees elected by the Board of Directors and is administered by the executive director. The foundation conducts the annual Brotherhood College, a values clarification and investigation educational program for undergraduates and alumni. The foundation also sponsors chapter and individual scholarship programs, chapter library grants, leadership education publications and workshops, chapter advisors seminars, and maintains historical archives and the Founders Library.

Traditions and Insignia Founders Day is celebrated on June 28 or as near that date as possible. Since most schools are closed for summer break by that date, Founders Day has become primarily an alumni chapter and alumni association event. Fellowship Day is celebrated on February 26, the anniversary of the birth of Dr. Wilson C. Morris who was the sponsor and advisor to the founders and who is regarded as the "spiritual founder" of the fraternity. The Society of the Seventeen is the fraternity's highest honor for life long leadership and service on a national level. Membership in the society is limited to seventeen living persons, commemorating the number of founders. The Winebrenner Medal and Millsap Medal recognize distinguished service to the fraternity and foundation respectively. The Wilson C. Morris Fellowship recognizes significant foundation donors. The Ellsworth C. Dent "Man of the Year" and Edward H. McCune Distinguished Chapter awards go to the top undergraduate leader and top college chapter, respectively. Other awards include: Emmett Ellis Chapter Scholarship, Ronald Roskens Individual Scholarship, Stan Musial Sportsmanship, Al Hurt Performing Arts, E. Kennedy Whitesitt Newsletter, Thomas M. Hutsell Chapter Efficiency, W. T. Hembree Foundation Projects, and Robert Nagel Jones Charitable Projects awards. Most chapters choose a White Rose Sweetheart on the occasion of the annual White Rose prom or ball.

The badge is a four-pointed shield with a sword thrust diagonally through it from upper left to lower right, with a gold chain connecting the hilt of the sword with the point. The face of the badge is of blue enamel with a chevron of black, faced with gold and displaying the letters ΣΤΓ. Below the chevron is a Grecian lamp of gold. The pledge button is a four-pointed shield of silver divided into two equal vertical parts, the left of which is blue and the right silver. The flag is a rectangle divided diagonally, from lower left to upper right, into a field of blue at the right and a field of white at the left. The blue field contains an oval eighteen link chain in white. The white field contains the letters ΣΤΓ in blue. The colors are azure (blue) and white. The flower is the white rose.

Publications The *SAGA of Sigma Tau Gamma* is the quarterly esoteric magazine. There is an esoteric publication, also the *A Chain of Honor* membership manual, membership directory, and guides and handbooks for chapter operations. The foundation has published *Teacher, Immortal, the Enduring Influence of Wilson C. Morris*, a biography.

Headquarters Administrative office are located in the Marvin Millsap Headquarters Building, a brick colonial building constructed in 1977 on the fraternity's founding site at 101 Ming, P.O. Box 54, Warrensburg, Missouri 64093-0054. Phone: (816) 747-2222.

Membership Living membership 42,604. Active chapters 72. Inactive chapters 44. Colonies 8. Graduate chapters 56. City Alumni Associations 25. Houses owned 35. Total number of initiates 49,677. Chapter roll:

1920	Alpha, Central Missouri State
1921	Beta, Northeast Missouri
1922	Delta, Emporia
1924	Epsilon, Pittsburg State, Kansas
1924	*Zeta, Northeastern (OK)* (1990)
1926	*Eta, Fort Hays* (1983)
1927	*Gamma, Northwestern Oklahoma* (1962)
1927	*Iota, Kent* (1947-1971) (1987)
1927	Theta, Northwest Missouri
1928	*Kappa, Wisconsin, Whitewater* (1970)
1928	Lambda, Black Hills
1929	Mu, Southeastern Oklahoma
1929	Nu, Northwestern Louisiana
1929	*Xi, Fairmont* (1980)
1930	Omicron, Ball State
1930	*Pi, Indiana (PA)* (1986)
1933	Rho, SUNY Col., Buffalo (1954-1979)
1934	Sigma, Central Arkansas
1938	Tau, East Central State
1938	Upsilon, Arkansas, Monticello
1939	Phi, Southeastern Louisiana
1940	*Chi, Western Michigan* (1970)
1941	Alpha Alpha, Eastern Illinois
1941	*Omega, Southwest Missouri* (1987)
1941	Psi, Central Michigan (1974-1990)
1942	*Alpha Beta, Harris-Stowe* (1975)
1943	*Alpha Delta, Western Illinois* (1967)
1943	*Alpha Gamma, Cal, Santa Barbara* (1956)
1946	Alpha Epsilon, Henderson
1946	Alpha Zeta, Clarion (1972-1990)
1947	*Alpha Eta, Northern Iowa* (1978)
1948	*Alpha Iota, Keene* (1954)

1948	Alpha Kappa, Wisconsin, Stout
1948	*Alpha Theta, Eastern Michigan* (1975)
1949	Alpha Lambda, Concord
1950	*Alpha Mu, Chadron* (1982)
1950	*Alpha Nu, SUNY Col., Oneonta* (1954-1989)
1950	*Alpha Xi, Glenville* (1956)
1951	*Alpha Omicron, SUNY Col., Oswego* (1954)
1951	*Alpha Pi, Wayne State (MI)* (1955)
1951	*Alpha Rho, SUNY Col., New Paltz* (1954)
1951	Alpha Sigma, Southern Illinois (1962-1970)
1952	Alpha Phi, Southeast Missouri
1952	*Alpha Tau, SUNY Col., Cortland* (1954)
1952	*Alpha Upsilon, Marietta* (1956)
1953	Alpha Chi, Illinois
1956	Alpha Omega, Missouri, Rolla
1956	Alpha Psi, Penn State
1958	Beta Alpha, Missouri (1962-1981) (1988-1990)
1959	*Beta Beta, Alliance* (1987)
1959	*Beta Delta, Wisconsin, Eau Claire* (1977)
1959	Beta Epsilon, Shippensburg
1959	*Beta Eta, Alma* (1966)
1959	*Beta Gamma, Youngstown State* (1976)
1959	Beta Iota, California (PA)
1959	Beta Theta, Purdue (1965-1986)
1959	Beta Zeta, Central State (OK)
1960	*Beta Kappa, Wisconsin, La Crosse* (1986)
1960	Beta Lambda, Valparaiso (1968-1970)
1960	*Beta Mu, Wisconsin, Oshkosh* (1980)
1960	*Beta Nu, Northeast Louisiana* (1983)
1960	*Beta Omicron, Northland* (1983)
1960	Beta Pi, Frostburg (1971-1986)
1960	*Beta Rho, Moorhead* (1987)
1960	*Beta Sigma, St. Cloud* (1974)
1960	*Beta Xi, Winona* (1987)
1961	*Beta Tau, Slippery Rock* (1971)
1961	Beta Upsilon, Cleveland
1962	Beta Chi, Kearney
1962	Beta Phi, Southwestern State (OK)
1964	Beta Omega, Edinboro
1964	*Beta Psi, Wisconsin, Superior* (1986)
1965	Gamma Alpha, Mansfield
1965	Gamma Beta, Wisconsin, Stevens Point
1966	*Gamma Delta, Minot* (1988)
1966	Gamma Gamma, St. Norbert (1970-1986)
1968	*Gamma Epsilon, West Chester* (1976)
1968	Gamma Eta, Seton Hall
1968	Gamma Theta, Missouri, St. Louis
1968	*Gamma Zeta, Northern Arizona* (1979)
1969	*Gamma Iota, Windsor* (1970)
1969	*Gamma Kappa, Nicholls* (1971)
1969	Gamma Lambda, Wayne State (NE) (1978-1988)
1969	Gamma Mu, Missouri, Kansas City
1969	*Gamma Nu, Wisconsin, River Falls* (1978)
1969	Gamma Xi, Wisconsin, Platteville
1970	Gamma Omicron, Salem (WV)
1970	Gamma Pi, Stephen F. Austin
1972	*Gamma Rho, Cameron* (1978)
1972	*Gamma Sigma, Nebraska, Omaha* (1987)
1972	Gamma Tau, Millersville
1973	Gamma Phi, Southern Indiana

1973 Gamma Upsilon, Point Park
1974 Gamma Chi, Michigan Tech
1975 Gamma Psi, Illinois State
1977 Gamma Omega, Baylor
1978 Delta Alpha, East Carolina
1978 Delta Beta, Duquesne
1978 Delta Gamma, Texas
1979 *Delta Delta, North Carolina, Greensboro*
     (1987)
1983 Delta Epsilon, Southwest Texas
1984 Delta Eta, Arkansas
1984 Delta Zeta, Virginia Commonwealth
1985 Delta Iota, Southern Arkansas
1985 Delta Kappa, Missouri Western
1985 Delta Lambda, Iowa
1985 Delta Mu, Akron
1985 Delta Nu, Sam Houston
1985 Delta Theta, North Texas
1987 Delta Omicron, Christopher Newport
1987 Delta Xi, Carnegie-Mellon
1988 Delta Pi, Pitt, Johnstown
1990 Delta Tau, Indiana State
1990 Delta Upsilon, Penn State, Behrend

Colonies: Bridgewater, Fitchburg, Georgia, Miami (OH), Murray State, Robert Morris, South Florida, Temple, Texas Tech., Texas, San Antonio

Tau Delta Phi

ACTIVE PIN

PLEDGE PIN

TAU DELTA PHI is a college fraternity founded on June 22, 1910 and incorporated in the State of New York in 1916. The founders, close friends from the Community Center of Greenwich Village, New York City, founded chapters at the College of the City of New York, the New York College of Dentistry, and New York University.

The College of the City of New York Chapter was founded by Maximilian A. Coyne, Milton J. Goodfriend, and Alexander B. Siegel. The New York College of Dentistry Chapter was founded by Leo Epstein and Gustave Scheib. The New York University Chapter was founded by Maxwell S. Goldman, Max Klaye, Samuel Klaye, and Benjamin Gray. The Fraternity was local in character from 1910 through 1916. The Fraternity became a national organization in 1917 when college men outside New York became interested in the organization. Stone by stone the Pyramid grew to 19 chapters in 1933. In 1934, Omicron Alpha Tau National Fraternity, having similar ideals, merged with Tau Delta Phi retaining the rituals and name of Tau Delta Phi.

Government Tau Delta Phi is governed by the Grand Chapter. The Grand Chapter is composed of all the members of the Fraternity. Those with vot-

ing rights are the Executive Council Officers, delegates from each undergraduate chapter, and delegates from each chartered alumni association. The Grand Chapter meets at least every two years at a National Convention. In the interim, the administration of the fraternity is entrusted to the Executive Council, the board of directors of the fraternity.

For administrative purposes, the Fraternity is divided into regions. Each region is supervised by a Regional Vice Consul (RVC). The RVC is responsible for chapters in his region, oversees his District Chiefs, and reports directly to the Executive Council. A region is subdivided into Districts. Each district is directed by a District Chief who meets with the chapters on an ongoing basis and reports directly to the RVC.

Traditions and Insignia The fraternity's popular name is Tau Delt. Founder's Day is celebrated on July 16.

The seal is of circular form, bearing two flaming torches interlocked in a square. Within the square is a pyramid and a star. On the outside perimeter of the seal is the circular inscription "TAU DELTA PHI FRATERNITY—GRAND CHAPTER."

The coat of arms is a shield of blue and white divided into four corner sections and one diamond shaped center section. The center section depicts a pyramid and a mullet in the left northern area of the section. The upper left-hand corner section contains the fraternity's pledge pin. The upper right-hand corner section bears the symbol of a ship. The lower left-hand corner section has two mullets. The lower right-hand corner section has a rampant lion. The portion of the coat of arms above the shield is composed of an owl's head protruding from the rook. Below the crest is a legend spelling out "TAU DELTA PHI" in full Greek.

The pledge pin is a square diamond. A vertical line divides the pledge pin into two colors the left is white and the right is navy blue.

The traditional fraternity colors are blue and white.

Awards At each convention the Executive Council awards a General Achievement Cup to the chapter that has attained the highest standard in the proceeding year. The Scholarship Cup is awarded to the chapter that has distinguished itself by maintaining the highest scholarship standing for the year among all chapters. The Scholarship Improvement Trophy is awarded to the chapter that has made the greatest measure of improvement in scholarship since the last convention. The Executive Council awards, each year, the Past Grand Council Trophies for chapter and personal achievement, these being contributed by past presidents of the fraternity. These trophies are awarded for national relations, national expansion, outstanding chapter publication, extracurricular activities, and for outstanding chapter officer. Distinguished service certificates for exceptional service to the fraternity, certificates of award, and scholarship certificates are also awarded by the Executive Council.

The highest award in the fraternity, the Convention Key, is granted by unanimous vote of the Executive Council and a 2/3 vote of the Grand Chapter to the member who in the judgement of the Council, has attained eminence in the fraternity because of unusual achievement and effort for Tau Delta Phi nationally as well as locally.

Publications   The Fraternity's official magazine is *The Pyramid*. It was first published in December, 1920 and is published annually. It contains a thorough report of the year's activities. The first issue of the professional listings directory was published in 1920, listing the membership geographically, alphabetically, and professionally. In 1930, a Pledge Manual was published as a handbook of fraternity information for new members, a second edition being printed in 1934, a third edition in 1947, a fourth edition in 1953, and a fifth edition in 1953. A song book of 108 pages containing 30 fraternity songs and the more popular college songs was issued in 1929. In 1933, *The Administrative Guide* was printed. This book, consisting of four books in a single volume, is intended as an aid to those in charge of the administrative and executive operations of the fraternity, both local and national. Every phase of fraternity management is covered in the guide. The guide has undergone a series of revisions and a revised one will be published in 1991.

Funds and Philanthropies   The Tau Delta Phi Foundation, incorporated in 1945 with funds from its members, was originally established to provide scholarships for those veterans returning from the War. It has developed into an organization that is involved with student loans, libraries, and scholarships for its members. Alumni Associations also have scholarship programs for their undergraduate chapters. Participation by each chapter and its members in charitable and community volunteer programs is highly encouraged by the Executive Council.

Headquarters   Send correspondence to Tau Delta Phi Fraternity, P.O. Box 4169, Great Neck, NY 11027-4169. Phone: (718) 366-0512.

Membership   Active chapters 56. Colonies 1. Total number of initiates 15,000. Chapter roll:

1914	Alpha, CUNY, Brooklyn
1914	Beta, New York Medical
1914	Gamma, N.Y.U.
1916	Delta, Columbia (NY)
1917	Epsilon, Boston U.
1918	Zeta, Harvard
1919	Eta, M.I.T.
1920	Iota, Penn
1920	Kappa, Cincinnati
1920	Theta, Armour Inst
1921	Lambda, Chicago
1921	Mu, Vanderbilt
1922	Nu, Michigan, Flint
1923	Xi, Northwestern

1924	Omicron, Ohio State
1924	Pi, Illinois
1926	Rho, Texas
1927	Sigma, USC
1927	Tau, Lehigh
1928	Chi, UCLA
1928	Phi, Minnesota
1929	Psi, Carnegie-Mellon
1929	Upsilon, North Dakota
1932	Omega, Manitoba
1933	Tau Alpha, Colby
1934	Tau Beta, Cornell
1934	Tau Gamma, Rutgers
1935	Alpha Delta, Baruch
1943	Gamma Upsilon, N.Y.U.
1947	Tau Delta, Arizona
1947	Tau Epsilon, New Jersey Tech
1949	Tau Zeta, Syracuse
1950	Tau Eta, Loyola, Chicago
1950	Tau Theta, Norwich
1951	Tau Iota, Rutgers
1952	Tau Kappa, Queens College
1952	Tau Lambda, Alfred
1952	Tau Mu, Miami (FL)
1952	Tau Nu, Hunter
1956	Tau Omicron, Temple
1956	Tau Xi, Long Island
1957	Tau Pi, Roosevelt
1959	Tau Rho, CUNY, Brooklyn
1962	Tau Sigma, Pratt
1965	Tau Tau, Penn State
1966	Tau Upsilon, Michigan State
1967	Tau Phi, Seton Hall
1968	Tau Chi, Illinois, Chicago
1968	Tau Omega, Corpus Christi
1968	Tau Psi, C. W. Post
1969	Delta Beta, Maryland, College Park, Pharmacy
1969	Delta Delta, New York Poly
1969	Delta Epsilon, Paterson State
1969	Delta Gamma, Widener
1975	Delta Eta, Cooper Union
1976	Delta Zeta, SUNY Col. Tech, Farmingdale

Colonies: SUNY, Stony Brook

Tau Epsilon Phi

ACTIVE PIN

PLEDGE PIN

TAU EPSILON PHI was founded at Columbia University on October 19, 1910, by ten young men in the School of Pharmacy, Robert L. Blume, Julius M. Breitenbach, Charles M. Driesen, Ephraim Freedman, Leo H. Fried, Harold Goldsmith, Samuel Greenbaum, Julius Klauber, Israel Schwartz, and Julius Slofkin, who had become imbued with the idea that friendships acquired during collegiate days should be bound together through some means for the remainder of one's life and who found admission to the existing two fraternities barred because of their adherence to the Hebrew faith. They therefore decided, then and there, in light of the latter fact, that their fraternity must never bar anyone by reason of race, color, or creed.

Growth The fraternity started as a professional group, but the addition of a chapter at New York University in 1912 changed this, and the fraternity developed as a collegiate social organization. For the first seven years expansion was the result of members transfering to other colleges in the New York area, but after the first grand chapter meeting held in 1917 set up a national organization, the fraternity extended its expansion policy and was welcomed by groups of students throughout the country who desired fraternity affiliation. The fraternity is nonsectarian.

Alumni clubs are maintained in large cities. Alumni may contribute voluntarily to what is known as the National Chapter, or become life members of that organization.

Government Legislation is invested in the biennial convention, known as the grand chapter meeting. The grand chapter is composed of one delegate from each undergraduate chapter and each organized alumni club. In the interim, judicial and executive control is placed in the hands of a twenty-five-man Grand Council chosen by the grand chapter. The chapters and alumni clubs are divided geographically into fourteen regions. The administrative head of each is a regional consul, chosen by the Grand Council upon the recommendation of the delegates from his region, but responsible to the Grand Council. Regional conferences are held annually.

In 1932 the grand chapter created the position of executive secretary, and since that time the fraternity has had a full-time official and field staff. The executive secretary administers the chapters and the central office, edits the fraternity publications, and visits each chapter and alumni club annually.

Traditions and Insignia The popular name is Tau Ep or TEP.

The badge is a vertically long rectangle on raised black enamel, bearing the gold letters TEΦ vertically, and surrounded by eighteen pearls with four emeralds, one in each corner. Undergraduates may wear an alternate badge, bearing a gold bevel in place of the jewels. The pledge button is a dark lavender enamel piece shaped in the outline of a shield, bearing a white helmet upon its center. The sister pin is a replica of the jeweled pin, arranged horizontally without enamel. The colors are lavender and white.

Publications The first official directory, or *Geographic*, appeared in 1917. Since that time there have been new editions every six years; the fifth edition in 1939 listed all members alphabetically, by chapters, and geographically, together

with their profession or business. In 1917 the first edition of the *Bulletin* was published. This appeared five times yearly until December, 1923, when it took magazine form and became *The Plume of Tau Epsilon Phi*, which is issued quarterly as the official exoteric publication; the esoteric publication of the fraternity is the *Bulletin*, published monthly and sent to all members of the National Chapter. There are an official songbook, a fraternity history, and a series of manuals concerned with the administration of chapters and alumni clubs. In 1937 the first pledge manual of the fraternity, *The Portals of Tau Epsilon Phi*, appeared. It is issued to each pledge.

Funds and Philanthropies An endowment fund was established in 1922. This is enlarged by a portion of each initiation fee and furnishes a source or working capital for the erection, furnishing, and remodeling of chapter houses.

The Grand Council awards trophies to outstanding chapters for chapter efficiency, improvement, scholarship, chapter publications, and general attainment, and keys to the four outstanding campus leaders and also to the two members attaining the highest scholastic records in the undergraduate fraternity. Keys are also awarded to chapter officers for outstanding chapter service.

The Tau Epsilon Phi Scholarship and Student Aid Fund, Inc., a tax-exempt, tax-deductible scholarship foundation is designed to provide student aid in the form of scholarships and loans for anyone, regardless of membership in the fraternity.

Headquarters 3088 Mercer University Drive, #200, Atlanta, GA. Phone: (404) 454-8377.

Membership Active chapters 48. Colonies 5. Total number of initiates 37,600. Chapter roll:

1913	Delta, Cornell	
1919	Mu, Emory (-1991)	
1919	Nu, Georgia	
1919	Xi, M.I.T.	
1921	Rho, Penn (-1981)	
1922	Sigma, Syracuse	
1924	Omega, North Carolina	
1924	Psi, Illinois	
1925	Tau Alpha, Florida	
1925	Tau Beta, Maryland	
1926	Tau Gamma, USC (-1990)	
1927	Tau Delta, Ohio State (-1989)	
1929	Tau Zeta, Maine	
1932	Tau Mu, Connecticut (-1988)	
1932	Tau Theta, George Washington (-1986)	
1936	Tau Nu, Virginia (-1988)	
1947	Rho Delta Rho, Illinois Tech	
1947	Tau Epsilon, UCLA (-1989)	
1947	Tau Psi, New Jersey Tech.	
1955	Epsilon Eta, Drexel	
1956	Epsilon Theta, Queens (NY) (-1988)	
1957	Epsilon Iota, R.P.I. (-1989)	
1958	Epsilon Lambda, CUNY, Brooklyn	
1959	Epsilon Kappa, Tulane	
1959	Epsilon Nu, Rochester Tech	

1959   Phi Eta, Johns Hopkins
1960   Alpha Beta, American (-1990)
1960   Epsilon Pi, Marietta
1961   Epsilon Xi, Clark (-1989)
1961   Kappa Zeta Phi, Northeastern (-1988)
1962   Epsilon Tau, Bradley
1963   Alpha Kappa, Adelphi (-1989)
1963   Epsilon Phi, Penn State
1965   Alpha Phi, Rutgers (-1987)
1966   Sigma Epsilon, Rutgers, Camden
1967   Phi Beta, South Florida
1967   Phi Mu, Hartford (-1989)
1967   Sigma Lambda, Bryant
1967   Tau Alpha Kappa, Lehigh
1968   Lambda Phi Epsilon, Clarkson
1969   Phi Omicron, Western New England
1969   Sigma Alpha Sigma, Hofstra (-1981)
1969   Tau Omega, Rhode Island
1970   Rhi Pi, SUNY, Binghamton (-1988)
1970   Tau Eta Epsilon, SUNY Col., New Paltz
         (-1987)
1976   Omega Upsilon Chi, Husson
1986   Alpha Sigma, SUNY, Albany
1987   Beta Delta, Florida International

Colonies: Marist, Roger Williams, William
Paterson, Maryland, Baltimore County, SUNY Col.,
Oneonta

COAT OF ARMS

Tau Kappa Epsilon

ACTIVE PIN   PLEDGE PIN

TAU KAPPA EPSILON was founded as the Knights
of Classic Lore on January 10, 1899, at Illinois Wesleyan University, the outgrowth of an idea first expressed by ministerial student Joseph L. Settles for
an organization which should aid development of
character and ability of its members. The first
meeting included four others—James C. McNutt,
Owen I. Truitt, Clarence A. Mayer, and C. Roy Atkinson—in an upper room of a private residence at
504 E. Locust Street, Bloomington, Illinois. A constitution was adopted and a custom established setting aside a portion of each meeting for discussion
of the classics.

The present name was adopted in September,
1902, with acquisition of the first fraternity house
on campus. Nationalization was proclaimed in a
new constitution February 15, 1909, and two
months later a local was chartered at Millikin. National organizers were Lester H. Martin, W. G. Mc-
Cauley, L. W. Tuesburg, and William Wilson.
Illinois, added in 1912, gave the fraternity three
chapters geographically situated to form an equilateral triangle, which had been chosen earlier as its
chief symbol.

Growth   A fourth chapter was added in late
1912, also in Illinois at Knox. With Iowa State in
1915 began a steady, conservative growth lasting
through ecnomic depression years which made the
fraternity medium-sized among nationals. Several
chapters of Sigma Mu Sigma were absorbed in 1934
and, after World War II, entry into the South was
aided by additions from Alpha Lambda Tau. Accelerated growth in the postwar period included pioneering in the newer state universities and rising
small colleges. Many long established locals, some
of them older than the fraternity, became chapters.
These included groups with histories tracing back
to 1868 at Culver-Stockton, 1877 at Boston U., 1893
at Eastern Michigan and 1898 at Louisiana Polytechnic. In 1958 Tau Kappa Epsilon established in
Canada, and in 1959 it became the largest international fraternity.

Tau Kappa Epsilon granted its 200th charter during 1962, becoming the first NIC fraternity to do
this. Chapters are located in 45 states and the District of Columbia and one province of Canada.

Committed to continued growth, the fraternity
nevertheless maintains high standards of membership, leadership, scholarship, and finances as prerequisites to the granting of a charter.

Government   Supreme authority of the fraternity is exercised in biennial conclaves of the grand
chapter, composed of past and grand presidents,
eight international officers, and delegates from
each undergraduate and alumni association. Interim policy is vested in the Grand Council of eight
elected officers and interim administration in the
executive vice-president, who appoints both regional officers and chapter advisers from qualified
alumni and employs a professional staff of approximately 25 people to assist him. Leadership conferences are held annually in each area and each
conclave is preceded by an international leadership
session.

Tau Kappa Epsilon is incorporated under the laws
of Illinois but maintains international headquarters
in Indianapolis, Indiana. The fraternity operates on
an unit responsibility basis with promotion to
higher office strictly dependent on accomplishment
in previously held lower positions. A vigorous
chapter visitation and inspection program is utilized to assist in the maintenance of adequate manpower, sound finances, good scholarship, and
competitive housing. The chapters are encouraged
to leadership and excellence by an awards program.
Scholarship and loyalty to alma mater are especially stressed. All chapters participate in campus
projects and community service.

Traditions and Insignia   Members are known as
Tekes. Founders' Day celebrations are observed
each year as near as possible to January 10.

The badge adopted in 1900 has been retained without change. It is a skull and bones on an equilateral triangle above a scroll with letters TKE. The flag is cherry with a gray diagonal stripe bearing five triangles. Official flower is the red carnation, jewel the white pearl, colors cherry and gray.

Coat of arms: gules on a bend argent, five equilateral triangles, bendwise of the first voided; crest, above a peer's helmet, a death's head, three-quarters profile, proper; mantling, gules, double argent; motto, ΠΑΩΕΑ.

Publications *The Teke*, official exoteric magazine, was launched January, 1908. It is published quarterly. In 1949 the fraternity commemorated its 50th anniversary with publication of a history volume, *The Golden Book of Tau Kappa Epsilon*.

The *Teke Guide*, pledge manual, and the rush booklet were revised in 1984, together with chapter officer manuals and the *Black Book* which contains the fraternity's constitution and laws. Most of the undergraduate chapters publish newsletters and directories for distribution to their alumni.

Funds The general fraternity maintains an investment reserve fund in addition to a house fund established in 1949 for loans to chapters. All chapters are required to have their own building funds for house improvements as well. A Founders' Fund for individual student loans has provided such loans since 1924. A separate educational foundation operates to assist the fraternity in educational activities.

Headquarters 8645 Founders Road, Indianapolis, IN 46268. Phone: (317) 872-6533. A white stucco building, constructed in 1971, located in the College Park area, houses the headquarters. Facilities include a conference room, general offices, mail room, print shop, and computer department.

Membership Active chapters 322. Inactive chapters 124. Colonies 12. Total number of initiates 182,142. Chapter roll:

Belmont Abbey (-1988)
Brandeis (-1987)
Cal State, Dominguez Hills (-1989)
Cal State, Long Beach (-1989)
California (PA) (-1988)
Colorado (-1987)
Concord (-1987)
Culver-Stockton (-1990)
Fairleigh Dickinson, Madison (-1988)
Kentucky (-1987)
Marist (-1988)
Nebraska, Omaha (-1987)
Northern Arizona (-1989)
Rollins (-1989)
Salisbury (-1987)
Tarleton (-1988)
Oregon
Wagner (-1989)
Wake Forest (-1989)
Windsor (-1990)
Wisconsin, River Falls (-1987)

	Alpha Upsilon, Fort Hays (-1987)
	Lambda, Wisconsin, Madison (-1990)
	Theta Iota, Northern Michigan (-1987)
1899	Alpha, Illinois Wesleyan
1909	Beta, Millikin
1912	Delta, Knox
1912	Gamma, Illinois
1915	Epsilon, Iowa State
1916	Zeta, Coe
1917	*Eta, Chicago* (1935)
1917	Iota, Eureka
1917	Kappa, Beloit
1917	*Theta, Minnesota* (1987)
1919	Mu, Carroll
1919	Nu, Cal, Berkeley
1920	Xi, Washington (MO)
1921	Omicron, Ohio State
1922	Pi, Penn State
1923	Rho, West Virginia
1923	Scorpion, Cornell
1924	Tau, Oregon State
1925	Phi, Nebraska
1925	Upsilon, Michigan
1926	Chi, Washington (WA)
1926	Omega, Albion
1926	Psi, Gettysburg
1927	Alpha Alpha, Wabash
1927	*Alpha Beta, Ohio* (1977)
1927	Alpha Delta, Idaho
1927	Alpha Gamma, Washington State
1928	Alpha Epsilon, Monmouth (IL)
1928	Alpha Zeta, Purdue
1930	Alpha Eta, Rutgers
1930	*Alpha Iota, Hamilton* (1971)
1930	*Alpha Kappa, Penn* (1943)
1930	Alpha Theta, Whitman
1931	Alpha Lambda, Kansas State
1931	Alpha Mu, Ohio Wesleyan
1932	*Alpha Nu, New Hampshire* (1989)
1932	Alpha Xi, Drake
1934	Alpha Omicron, New Mexico State
1935	Alpha Pi, George Washington
1937	Alpha Rho, Rhode Island
1938	Alpha Sigma, North Dakota
1939	Alpha Tau, Drexel
1942	Alpha Chi, Louisville
1942	Alpha Phi, Kansas
1942	Alpha Upsilon, Fort Hays (-1987)
1946	Alpha Psi, Davis And Elkins
1946	Beta Alpha, Bradley
1947	Alpha Omega, UCLA
1947	Beta Beta, North Carolina State
1947	Beta Delta, Maryland
1947	Beta Epsilon, Tri-State
1947	Beta Eta, Missouri, Rolla
1947	*Beta Gamma, Oklahoma State* (1971)
1947	*Beta Iota, Iowa Wesleyan* (1954)
1947	Beta Kappa, Oregon (-1987)
1947	Beta Lambda, Auburn
1947	Beta Mu, Bucknell
1947	Beta Nu, Marshall
1947	Beta Theta, Missouri

1947	Beta Zeta, Louisiana Tech	1956	*Epsilon Delta, Massachusetts* (1972)
1948	*Beta Omicron, Wayne State (MI)* (1979)	1956	Epsilon Epsilon, Nebraska, Omaha (-1987)
1948	Beta Pi, Georgia Tech	1956	Epsilon Eta, Southwestern State (OK)
1948	Beta Rho, Akron	1956	*Epsilon Gamma, Moravian* (1965)
1948	Beta Sigma, USC	1956	Epsilon Iota, Youngstown State
1948	*Beta Tau, Florida Southern* (1985)	1956	Epsilon Kappa, Loyola, Chicago
1948	Beta Upsilon, Maine	1956	*Epsilon Lambda, Missouri, Kansas City* (1980)
1948	Beta Xi, Arizona State		
1949	Beta Chi, Southern Illinois	1956	*Epsilon Mu, Northeast Louisiana* (1988)
1949	Beta Omega, Southwest Missouri	1956	Epsilon Nu, Wisconsin, Stevens Point
1949	Beta Phi, L.S.U.	1956	*Epsilon Pi, Colgate* (1972)
1949	Beta Psi, Arkansas State	1956	Epsilon Rho, Northern Arizona (-1989)
1949	*Gamma Alpha, Wyoming* (1977)	1956	Epsilon Theta, Southeastern Oklahoma
1949	*Gamma Beta, Colorado State* (1975)	1956	Epsilon Xi, Shepherd
1949	Gamma Delta, Miami (FL)	1956	*Epsilon Zeta, Rider* (1987)
1949	Gamma Epsilon, R.P.I.	1956	Epsion Omicron, Houston
1949	*Gamma Eta, Idaho State* (1987)	1957	Epsilon Chi, SUNY Col., Buffalo
1949	Gamma Gamma, Texas, El Paso	1957	*Epsilon Omega, Minot* (1983)
1949	*Gamma Zeta, Hartwick* (1982)	1957	*Epsilon Phi, Detroit* (1975)
1950	Gamma Iota, Colorado (-1987)	1957	*Epsilon Psi, McNeese* (1977)
1950	Gamma Kappa, Indiana	1957	Epsilon Sigma, Central State (OK)
1950	Gamma Lambda, San Diego State	1957	Epsilon Tau, Rochester
1950	Gamma Mu, Furman	1957	Epsilon Upsilon, Northwestern Louisiana
1950	Gamma Nu, Toledo	1957	Zeta Alpha, Wagner (-1989)
1950	Gamma Omicron, Virginia	1957	Zeta Beta, Evansville
1950	Gamma Theta, Florida	1957	Zeta Delta, Alma
1950	*Gamma Xi, New Mexico* (1964)	1957	Zeta Gamma, Nebraska Wesleyan
1951	*Gamma Chi, Valparaiso* (1988)	1958	Zeta Epsilon, Waynesburg
1951	Gamma Phi, Emporia	1958	Zeta Eta, Muhlenberg
1951	*Gamma Pi, Parsons* (1973)	1958	*Zeta Iota, Manitoba* (1981)
1951	Gamma Psi, Butler	1958	Zeta Kappa, Portland State
1951	Gamma Rho, Indiana State	1958	*Zeta Lambda, Bowling Green* (1985)
1951	Gamma Sigma, Kentucky (-1987)	1958	Zeta Theta, Western Illinois
1951	*Gamma Tau, Denver* (1978)	1958	Zeta Zeta, Wisconsin, Milwaukee
1951	Gamma Upsilon, Texas	1959	Zeta Chi, Murray State
1952	Delta Alpha, Western Michigan	1959	Zeta Mu, Worcester Tech
1952	*Delta Beta, Lake Forest* (1972)	1959	Zeta Nu, Valdosta
1952	Delta Gamma, Connecticut (-1990)	1959	*Zeta Omega, California (PA)* (1982)
1952	Gamma Omega, Eastern Illinois	1959	Zeta Omicron, Western Carolina
1953	Delta Delta, Northern Colorado	1959	Zeta Phi, Rollins (-1989)
1953	Delta Epsilon, Cleveland	1959	Zeta Pi, Culver-Stockton (-1990)
1953	*Delta Eta, Northern Illinois* (1982)	1959	*Zeta Psi, Hamline* (1982)
1953	*Delta Zeta, Southeast Missouri* (1990)	1959	*Zeta Rho, American International* (1984)
1954	Delta Iota, Lenoir-Rhyne	1959	Zeta Sigma, Marietta
1954	*Delta Kappa, High Point* (1966)	1959	Zeta Tau, Shippensburg
1954	Delta Lambda, Central Missouri State	1959	*Zeta Upsilon, Alliance* (1987)
1954	*Delta Mu, Pittsburg State, Kansas* (1988)	1959	Zeta Xi, Boston U.
1954	Delta Nu, Northwest Missouri	1960	*Theta Alpha, Loyola Marymount, Los Angeles* (1967)
1954	Delta Omicron, Central Michigan		
1954	Delta Theta, Cal State, Long Beach (-1989)	1960	*Theta Beta, Belmont Abbey* (1988)
1954	Delta Xi, Miami (OH)	1960	Theta Delta, Fairmont
1955	Delta Chi, Gannon	1960	*Theta Epsilon, Humboldt* (1977)
1955	*Delta Omega, Western State (CO)* (1989)	1960	Theta Eta, South Dakota
1955	Delta Phi, St. Francis (PA)	1960	Theta Gamma, Lock Haven
1955	Delta Pi, Eastern Michigan	1960	*Theta Theta, Cal State, Los Angeles* (1977)
1955	Delta Psi, North Dakota State	1960	Theta Zeta, Rutgers, Newark
1955	Delta Rho, Indiana (PA)	1961	Theta Kappa, C. W. Post
1955	*Delta Sigma, Morningside* (1987)	1961	*Theta Lambda, Widener* (1987)
1955	Delta Tau, Northern Iowa	1961	Theta Mu, New Orleans
1955	Delta Upsilon, Missouri Valley	1961	Theta Nu, Southeastern Louisiana
1955	Epsilon Alpha, St. Louis	1961	Theta Omicron, Adrian
1955	*Epsilon Beta, Tampa* (1979)	1961	Theta Pi, Cal State, Chico

1961 Theta Rho, St. Cloud
1961 Theta Sigma, St. John's (NY)
1961 *Theta Tau, Mankato* (1980)
1961 Theta Upsilon, Cal State, Sacramento
1961 Theta Xi, Arkansas
1962 *Iota Alpha, Wisconsin, Superior* (1982)
1962 *Iota Beta, Susquehanna* (1982)
1962 *Iota Delta, Southern Oregon* (1976)
1962 Ioto Gamma, Northeast Missouri
1962 *Theta Chi, Frostburg* (1988)
1962 Theta Omega, Charleston (SC)
1962 *Theta Phi, Wisconsin, La Crosse* (1983)
1962 *Theta Psi, Ferris* (1987)
1963 *Iota Epsilon, Moorhead* (1988)
1963 *Iota Eta, Slippery Rock* (1987)
1963 Iota Iota, LaSalle
1963 Iota Kappa, Clarkson
1963 *Iota Lambda, Indiana Tech* (1982)
1963 Iota Mu, Findlay
1963 Iota Nu, Hillsdale
1963 Iota Omicron, Wisconsin, Whitewater
1963 Iota Pi, Kent
1963 Iota Rho, Seton Hall
1963 Iota Sigma, Wisconsin, Eau Claire
1963 Iota Theta, Centenary
1963 *Iota Xi, Concord* (1987)
1963 Iota Zeta, Syracuse
1964 *Iota Chi, New Mexico Highlands* (1975)
1964 Iota Omega, Glenville
1964 Iota Phi, Defiance
1964 *Iota Psi, Dickinson State* (1988)
1964 Iota Tau, East Stroudsburg
1964 Iota Upsilon, Livingston
1964 *Kappa Alpha, Franciscan* (1989)
1964 *Kappa Beta, Pan American* (1983)
1965 Kappa Delta, Old Dominion
1965 *Kappa Epsilon, Northland* (1983)
1965 Kappa Eta, New Jersey Tech
1965 *Kappa Gamma, Catholic* (1977)
1965 *Kappa Theta, Adelphi* (1990)
1965 *Kappa Zeta, Hobart* (1979)
1966 Kappa Iota, Hartford
1966 Kappa Kappa, Monmouth (NJ)
1966 *Kappa Lambda, Minnesota, Morris* (1987)
1966 Kappa Mu, Edinboro
1966 Kappa Nu, Rockhurst
1966 *Kappa Omicron, Philadelphia Textiles* (1977)
1966 *Kappa Pi, San Diego U* (1980)
1966 *Kappa Sigma, CUNY, Brooklyn* (1974)
1966 *Kappa Xi, Black Hills* (1974)
1967 Kappa Chi, Concordia U. (QB)
1967 *Kappa Omega, Washburn* (1979)
1967 *Kappa Phi, Wisconsin, Oshkosh* (1978)
1967 Kappa Psi, Quinnipiac
1967 *Kappa Tau, Arizona* (1986)
1967 *Kappa Upsilon, Villanova* (1980)
1967 *Lambda Alpha, South Florida* (1984)
1967 *Lambda Beta, Lewis* (1983)
1967 Lambda Delta, Southern Maine
1967 Lambda Epsilon, Clarion
1967 Lambda Gamma, Cincinnati

1967 Lambda Zeta, Troy
1968 Lambda Chi, Wayne State (NE)
1968 Lambda Eta, Iowa
1968 Lambda Iota, Florida State
1968 *Lambda Kappa, DePaul* (1979)
1968 Lambda Lambda, Utica
1968 *Lambda Mu, Elon* (1989)
1968 *Lambda Nu, Wisconsin, Stout* (1978)
1968 Lambda Omega, Georgia State
1968 *Lambda Omicron, North Texas* (1983)
1968 Lambda Phi, Bryant
1968 Lambda Pi, Northeastern Illinois
1968 Lambda Psi, East Carolina
1968 *Lambda Rho, Plymouth* (1978)
1968 Lambda Sigma Society, Keene
1968 Lambda Tau, Northrop
1968 *Lambda Theta, Santa Fe* (1977)
1968 Lambda Upsilon, Georgia Southern
1968 *Lambda Xi, Sul Ross* (1983)
1969 *Mu Alpha, West Chester* (1990)
1969 Mu Beta, Eastern Kentucky
1969 Mu Delta, Athens
1969 Mu Epsilon, Lowell
1969 Mu Eta, Northeastern
1969 Mu Gamma, Midwestern
1969 *Mu Iota, Western New England* (1983)
1969 *Mu Kappa, New Haven* (1983)
1969 Mu Lambda, Michigan Tech
1969 Mu Mu, Hofstra
1969 Mu Nu, Wisconsin, Platteville
1969 Mu Omicron, Tennessee Tech.
1969 *Mu Phi, Corpus Christi* (1974)
1969 *Mu Pi, Southampton* (1972)
1969 *Mu Rho, Bethel* (1978)
1969 Mu Sigma, Morehead
1969 Mu Tau, Madison Col
1969 Mu Theta, Lycoming
1969 Mu Upsilon, Illinois State
1969 *Mu Xi, Cal State, Fullerton* (1989)
1969 Mu Zeta, Nicholls
1970 *Mu Chi, North Carolina, Wilmington* (1985)
1970 Mu Omega, George Mason
1970 Mu Psi, Southeastern Massachusetts
1970 *Nu Alpha, Niagara* (1977)
1970 Nu Beta, Albright
1970 *Nu Delta, Southern Colorado* (1979)
1970 Nu Epsilon, Suffolk
1970 *Nu Eta, Boise* (1990)
1970 *Nu Gamma, St. Thomas* (1984)
1970 *Nu Iota, Illinois, Chicago* (1987)
1970 Nu Kappa, Winona (-1989)
1970 Nu Lambda, Southern Indiana
1970 Nu Mu, South Alabama
1970 *Nu Theta, Utah* (1978)
1970 Nu Zeta, Elmhurst
1971 Nu Chi, Bentley
1971 Nu Nu, Windsor (-1990)
1971 Nu Omega, William Paterson
1971 Nu Omicron, Bridgeport
1971 *Nu Phi, Duquesne* (1982)
1971 Nu Pi, Delaware
1971 *Nu Psi, West Liberty* (1977)

1971 *Nu Rho, Salem (WV)* (1983)
1971 *Nu Sigma, Upper Iowa* (1985)
1971 Nu Tau, Mansfield
1971 *Nu Upsilon, Texas A & I* (1982)
1971 *Nu Xi, Stephen F. Austin* (1988)
1971 *Xi Alpha, North Adams* (1975)
1971 Xi Beta, Southern Illinois
1971 Xi Delta, Fairleigh Dickinson, Rutherford
1971 *Xi Epsilon, Huron* (1975)
1971 *Xi Eta, Missouri Western* (1983)
1971 Xi Gamma, New York Tech
1971 Xi Iota, Central Florida
1971 Xi Theta, West Georgia
1971 *Xi Zeta, Bluefield* (1977)
1972 *Xi Kappa, Baker* (1976)
1972 Xi Lambda, Georgia
1972 Xi Mu, Dayton
1972 Xi Nu, Miami-Dade
1972 Xi Omicron, William Penn
1972 *Xi Pi, Valley City* (1987)
1972 *Xi Rho, Lander* (1978)
1972 Xi Xi, Southwest Texas
1973 Omicron Alpha, Appalachian
1973 *Omicron Beta, St. Mary's (MN)* (1980)
1973 Omicron Delta, Pembroke
1973 Omicron Epsilon, Bemidji
1973 *Omicron Gamma, Central Connecticut* (1982)
1973 Omicron Zeta, Weber
1973 Xi Chi, Southern Tech
1973 Xi Omega, V.P.I.
1973 *Xi Phi, Kutztown* (1977)
1973 *Xi Psi, South Dakota State* (1990)
1973 *Xi Sigma, Milton* (1977)
1973 Xi Tau, Arkansas
1973 Xi Upsilon, Rochester Tech
1974 *Omicron Eta, West Virginia Tech* (1978)
1974 Omicron Iota, Glassboro
1974 *Omicron Kappa, Southwestern Louisiana* (1988)
1974 *Omicron Lambda, Broward Comm. Col.* (1988)
1974 Omicron Theta, Newberry
1975 Omicron Mu, Husson
1975 Omicron Nu, Florida Institute
1975 Omicron Xi, Alabama
1976 Omicron Omicron, Missouri, St. Louis
1976 Omicron Pi, Baylor
1976 Omicron Rho, Texas Tech.
1976 Omicron Sigma, Indiana Southeast
1977 Omicron Chi, Robert Morris
1977 Omicron Omega, Radford
1977 *Omicron Phi, Oklahoma* (1987)
1977 *Omicron Psi, Lakeland* (1988)
1977 Omicron Tau, Columbus
1977 Omicron Upsilon, York (PA)
1978 Pi Alpha, Ashland
1978 Pi Beta, Bloomsburg
1979 Pi Delta, Alabama, Birmingham
1979 Pi Gamma, East Tennessee
1981 Pi Epsilon, Christian Brothers
1981 Pi Eta, Texas A & M

1981 Pi Theta, Texas, San Antonio
1981 *Pi Zeta, Auburn* (1988)
1982 Pi Iota, Nevada
1982 *Pi Kappa, Mesa* (1983)
1982 Pi Lambda, Nevada, Las Vegas
1982 Pi Mu, SUNY Col., Buffalo
1983 Pi Nu, Fairleigh Dickinson, Rutherford
1983 Pi Omicron, Northern Kentucky
1983 Pi Xi, San Diego State
1984 *Pi Pi, Cameron* (1988)
1984 Pi Rho, Babson
1984 Pi Sigma, Stockton
1985 Pi Chi, Rutgers, Camden
1985 Pi Phi, Maine
1985 Pi Tau, Iona
1985 *Pi Upsilon, Towson* (1989)
1986 Pi Omega, SUNY, Albany
1986 Pi Psi, Southern Mississippi
1986 Rho Alpha, Winthrop
1986 Rho Beta, Michigan State
1986 Rho Delta, Cal Poly, Cucamonga
1986 Rho Epsilon, Northwood (MI)
1986 Rho Gamma, North Carolina, Greensboro
1986 Rho Zeta, Montclair
1987 Rho Eta, SUNY, Stony Brook
1987 Rho Iota, Tarkio
1987 Rho Kappa, Longwood
1987 Rho Lambda, SUNY Col., Oswego
1987 Rho Mu, SUNY, Binghamton
1987 Rho Nu, San Francisco State
1987 Rho Omicron, Cal Poly, San Luis Obispo
1987 Rho Pi, Rio Grande
1987 Rho Rho, Sam Houston
1987 Rho Sigma, Grand Valley
1987 Rho Theta, Lake Superior
1987 Rho Xi, San Jose
1988 Rho Chi, Lebanon Valley
1988 Rho Omega, South Carolina, Columbia
1988 Rho Phi, SUNY Col., Cortland
1988 Rho Psi, Millersville
1988 Rho Tau, Michigan, Dearborn
1988 Rho Upsilon, Franklin
1988 Sigma Alpha, Florida International
1989 Sigma Beta, SUNY Col., Brockport
1989 Sigma Delta, Penn State
1989 Sigma Epsilon, SUNY Col., Oneonta
1989 Sigma Eta, Cal State, San Bernadino
1989 Sigma Gamma, SUNY Col., Plattsburgh
1989 Sigma Theta, St. Leo
1989 Sigma Zeta, South Carolina, Aiken
1990 Connecticut
1990 Sigma Iota, Pace
1990 Sigma Kappa, Merrimack
1990 Sigma Lambda, Northeastern (OK)
1990 Sigma Mu, Marquette
1990 Sigma Nu, SUNY Col., New Paltz
1990 Sigma Omicron, Middle Tennessee
1990 Sigma Xi, St. Norbert

Colonies: Cal, Davis, Florida Atlantic, N.Y.U., Spring Garden, Winona, Hunter, Jersey City, Johnson & Wales, Michigan, Flint, Muskingum, North Carolina, Charlotte, Sonoma State

Theta Chi

COAT OF ARMS

ACTIVE PIN

PLEDGE PIN

THETA CHI was founded at Norwich University, then situated at Norwich but now at Northfield, Vermont, on April 10, 1856, by Frederick Norton Freeman and Arthur Chase. Although its constitution provided for more than one chapter, it remained a local society for 46 years. It was incorporated in 1888. Its Beta chapter was established in 1902. The oath and ritual written by the founders, whose forebears were Episcopalian pioneers, reflect the influence of that faith.

The early years of the group were tenuous largely because the existence of the University itself was indeterminate. In 1866 a fire destroyed Old South Barracks, causing the removal of the institution to Northfield. The acting president of the University, Charles Dole, a Theta Chi, kept up operations by meeting deficits out of his own funds. However, enrollment in the fall of 1881 had sunk to 15. This number included only one Theta Chi, a junior named James Michael Holland; seven members of Theta Chi's rival society, Alpha Sigma Pi; one independent, and six entering freshmen. Among those six were Phil Sheridan Randall and Henry Blanchard Hersey, who, learning of the history of Theta Chi and its possible extinction, decided to ignore the bid offered by Alpha Sigma Pi and became Theta Chis.

Growth The example of Randall and Hersey in saving the group from extinction inspired another initiate of Alpha, a 17-year-old freshman, to make the fraternity a national organization as the founders had planned. Park Valentine Perkins left Norwich University at the end of his first year to transfer to Massachusetts Institute of Technology, and here he organized a local to petition for a charter. Through the years Alpha Chapter had grown strong along with Norwich University and it had refused all offers to become part of some established fraternity or grant charters to petitioning groups. Young Perkins persisted and the aid he secured from influential Boston alumni made possible the installation of Beta Chapter in 1902.

There were 56 chapters when in 1942 Beta Kappa Fraternity, founded at Hamline University in 1901, merged with Theta Chi. Seventeen of its once 47 chapters immediately became units of Theta Chi, and three more were added later, as well as many alumni from those chapters and others which had become inactive in the depression and war periods. Over 6,000 Beta Kappa undergraduate and alumni members became Theta Chis at the time of the union.

Government Legislation for the fraternity is determined by conventions. These were held annually until 1932, thereafter, biennially. The first convention was held at Norwich, Vermont, August 12, 1857. Conventions were held in connection with the annual commencements at Norwich University for 45 years, after which they were held in various sections of the country.

Alpha Chapter granted the first charters and served as the executive branch of the fraternity until February 22, 1908, when the Grand Chapter was organized and national officers were elected. The Grand Chapter, composed of eight graduate members, possesses administrative, executive, and judicial authority, legislative power still being vested in the fraternity convention.

Financial management of undergraduate chapters is governed by the Theta Chi finance plan. Alumni financial supervisors appoint and supervise the undergraduate treasurers. Each chapter has an alumnus advisor. Individual chapters have alumni corporations, which hold and administer the chapter real estate. A number of chapters have established endowments for student loans.

In 1934 the administration of the fraternity was organized on a regional basis, the country being divided into 10 regions, each in charge of a regional counselor assisted by one or more deputy counselors. There are now 16 regions. Regional conferences are held each year and include training sessions for chapter officers and forums for the discussion of chapter, regional, and national fraternity problems.

The executive office was established in New York in 1923, and a traveling secretary was appointed to make three-day visits with each chapter. On the creating of the position of executive secretary in 1928, the office was removed to Huntington, West Virginia. An auditor was added to the staff in 1931. Since 1932 the office has been in Trenton, New Jersey. In addition to the executive director, the assistant executive director, and five field representatives, the fraternity employs a secretarial and clerical staff of seven.

The school of fraternity practices is held in conjunction with each national convention. This is an intensive course in leadership training conducted by experienced leaders. A Chapter Leadership Conference is sponsored in non-convention year summers.

Traditions and Insignia Although Theta Chi was established at a semimilitary institution, its founders and those who built up its traditions in succeeding years introduced nothing into its ritual, its constitution, its nomenclature, its customs, its character, or its symbolism that suggests the military in any way. And yet because of the semimilitary character of Norwich University, it was not surprising that practically all Theta Chis, alumni and undergraduates, participated in the War Between the States, either for the North or the South. Many members saw service in the Spanish-American War. Sixty-three percent of the fraternity's membership served under American or Allied Colors between 1917 and 1919.

In World War II practically all the physically qualified undergraduate members over 18 years of age were in the service and a high percentage of alumni also were in uniform. More than 400 Theta Chis gave their lives in World War II. Many also served in Korea and 40 Theta Chis died in Vietnam.

Founders' Day, April 10, is celebrated annually throughout the country by undergraduates and alumni. As early as 1941 a Theta Chi chapter observed Mother's Day as a fraternity event; the day is now generally observed throughout the fraternity. From this observance has developed a large number of mothers' and parents' clubs.

Those who have proved their loyalty to their fraternity in their membership of more than 50 years are made a part of the Golden Guard. Similar recognition in the Silver Legion is provided for those who have shown an interest throughout a quarter of a century.

The badge displays a gold rattlesnake, with a ruby-set eye. The rattlesnake is fashioned to form a Θ, with swords crossed diagonally over the Θ to form a X. The pledge button is a red oval surrounded by and crossed diagonally with narrow white stripes presenting a close resemblance to the fraternity badge. The coat of arms is described as follows: or, on a bend gules, a nowed serpent between two swords, points downward, palewise, all of the first; on an esquire's helmet the crest, an eagle is displayed or. The flower is the red carnation. The flag is a rectangular field of white charged in the center with the Greek letters ΘX. A coiled serpent and the year 1856 are displayed in the lower right and upper lefthand corners respectively. The fraternity anthem is entitled *It Is to Thee, Dear Old Theta Chi*. The fraternity colors are military red and white.

Publications *The Rattle of Theta Chi* first appeared in 1912 as the private venture of Ralph C. Heath and Percy C. Seamon. It was taken over by the fraternity at the end of its first year and was published as a quarterly until 1928, when it changed to eight issues, appearing monthly through the college year until 1933. There are now four issues a year.

The first *Roster of Members* was published in 1894, and another in 1906, on the occasion of the fraternity's fiftieth anniversary. The 125th Anniversary Director of Members was published in 1981.

A History of Theta Chi, a volume of 322 pages edited by Robert H. Hoge, was published by the fraternity in 1927. Theta Chi songs were printed in pamphlet form in 1918, but the first songbook was published in 1926. It was superseded later by a songbook which contained songs of the various institutions at which the fraternity is represented as well as the fraternity songs. *Songs of Theta Chi* appeared in 1932; it contains both fraternity and college songs. A revised edition appeared in 1958. *The*

Theta Chi Confidential News is circulated only among members of the fraternity. *The Objectives of Theta Chi Fraternity*, written and published in 1935, definitely presents to members and the public the specific aims, program, and policies of the fraternity. It contains statements explaining the relationship of the fraternity with educational institutions of which Theta Chi is a part, and the relationship with members, pledges, alumni, other chapters, other fraternities, and parents. In 1939 the fraternity first published *The Handbook of Theta Chi Fraternity*. This included revised and enlarged manuals previously published and much new material on fraternity administration and fraternity practices. *The Manual of Theta Chi Fraternity* was first published in 1947. This 214-page illustrated book which includes both general and specific information about the fraternity is a guidebook for pledges, undergraduate members, and alumni members. The most recent edition was completed in 1984.

Funds and Philanthropies Convention legislation in 1928 established the National Endowment Fund to be made up of national initiation fees, *Rattle* life subscriptions, gifts, and bequests. Loans from this fund may be made to undergraduate chapter building corporations for the purchase, refinancing, or erection of chapter houses. Ten per cent of the fund is used for loans to assist in temporarily financing the education of worthy seniors, juniors, and sophomores. The income from the fund is used for the publication of the fraternity magazine and other fraternity purposes. The fund is administered by the National Board of Trustees, appointed by the Grand Chapter and approved by the convention. All members initiated since 1928 have become automatically life subscribers to the fraternity magazine.

The War Emergency Fund was established in anticipation of the financial problems of World War II. As a benefit of it, 44 chapters affected were reactivated by 1950. The fund a few years later was named the Frederick Whiting Ladue Memorial Fund and increased to more than $350,000; it continues to serve the chapters in emergencies.

The Foundation Chapter of Theta Chi, Inc. was established in 1953 to promote an educational program by scholarships and research grants.

Other encouragement for scholarship is given annually by awards to the four chapters that lead their respective campuses, which are divided into four categories on the basis of size; recognition of individuals and chapters within the various regions; and the publication of *The Theta Chi Scholar*, designed to help members and chapters improve scholastic standards. The publication is edited by the scholarship director.

The Distinguished Service Award was established by the Grand Chapter in 1938. It is presented to an alumnus of the fraternity who by reason of outstanding national service, personal effort, and unselfish interest has made distinguished contributions to the lasting good and general welfare of Theta Chi. Very occasionally someone other than a Theta Chi is similarly honored. The Theta Chi for Life Award is now the fraternity's second highest and is presented to members with a lifetime of dedicated service. The Alumni Award is presented for meritorious contributions to the local, regional, or national general welfare of the fraternity. The Active Chapter Service Award is presented annually to the man who has contributed most to the welfare of the chapter. The Appreciation Award is presented only to women who have rendered outstanding service to the fraternity or to the general fraternity cause. The Citation of Honor is presented to those in and out of the fraternity for outstanding service to the fraternity or the fraternity movement.

Headquarters 8275 Allison Pointe Trail #300, Indianapolis, IN 46250. Phone: (317) 579-5080.

Membership Total living membership 96,787. Total undergraduate membership 7,100. Active chapters 160. Inactive chapters 35. Colonies 8. Houses owned 101. Graduate/Alumni chapters 51. Total number of initiates 122,236. Chapter roll:

1856	*Alpha, Norwich* (1960)
1902	Beta, M.I.T.
1907	Gamma, Maine
1908	Delta, R.P.I.
1909	Epsilon, Worcester Tech
1910	Zeta, New Hampshire (1974-1984)
1911	Eta, Rhode Island (1988-1990)
1911	*Theta, Massachusetts* (1983) (1988)
1912	Iota, Colgate
1912	*Kappa, Penn* (1960)
1912	Lambda, Cornell (1983-1985)
1913	Mu, Cal, Berkeley
1914	Nu, Hampden-Sydney
1914	Xi, Virginia
1915	Omicron, Richmond
1916	Pi, Dickinson
1916	Rho, Illinois (1973-1989)
1916	Sigma, Oregon State
1916	Tau, Florida
1917	Phi, North Dakota State
1917	Upsilon, N.Y.U. (1968-1988)
1918	Chi, Auburn
1918	Psi, Wisconsin, Madison
1919	Alpha Beta, Pitt
1919	Alpha Gamma, Michigan
1919	Omega, Penn State
1920	Alpha Delta, Purdue
1920	*Alpha Epsilon, Stanford* (1988)
1920	Alpha Eta, North Carolina (1938-1949) (1963-1985)
1920	Alpha Zeta, Rochester
1921	Alpha Iota, Indiana
1921	Alpha Kappa, West Virginia (1936-1940)
1921	Alpha Lambda, Ohio State
1921	*Alpha Theta, Dartmouth* (1952)
1922	Alpha Mu, Iowa State
1923	Alpha Nu, Georgia Tech

1923	*Alpha Xi, Delaware* (1989)
1924	Alpha Omicron, Washington State
1924	Alpha Pi, Minnesota
1925	Alpha Rho, Washington (WA)
1925	Alpha Sigma, Oregon
1925	Alpha Tau, Ohio
1925	Alpha Upsilon, Nebraska (1939-1949)
1926	Alpha Phi, Alabama
1928	Alpha Chi, Syracuse
1929	Alpha Psi, Maryland
1930	Alpha Omega, Lafayette
1931	Beta Alpha, UCLA
1932	Beta Delta, Rutgers
1932	*Beta Gamma, North Dakota* (1989)
1937	Beta Epsilon, Montana
1939	Beta Zeta, Michigan State
1940	Beta Eta, Washington (MD)
1940	Beta Theta, Drexel (1963-1969)
1941	*Beta Iota, Arizona* (1972)
1942	Beta Chi, Allegheny
1942	Beta Kappa, Hamline
1942	Beta Lambda, Akron
1942	*Beta Mu, Middlebury* (1970)
1942	Beta Nu, Case Western Reserve
1942	Beta Omega, Susquehanna
1942	Beta Omicron, Cincinnati
1942	*Beta Phi, Nevada* (1971)
1942	Beta Pi, Monmouth (IL)
1942	Beta Psi, Presbyterian
1942	Beta Rho, Illinois Wesleyan
1942	Beta Sigma, Lehigh
1942	Beta Tau, USC
1942	Beta Upsilon, Cal State, Fresno
1942	Beta Xi, Birmingham-Southern
1942	*Gamma Alpha, Tennessee* (1960)
1942	*Gamma Beta, Furman* (1964)
1946	Gamma Delta, Florida Southern
1946	Gamma Epsilon, Western State (CO)
1947	Gamma Eta, Bucknell (1983-1986)
1947	Gamma Theta, San Diego U
1947	*Gamma Zeta, Oklahoma State* (1968)
1948	*Gamma Iota, Connecticut* (1966)
1948	Gamma Kappa, Miami (OH)
1948	*Gamma Lambda, Denver* (1980)
1948	Gamma Mu, Bowling Green
1948	Gamma Nu, New Mexico State
1948	Gamma Omicron, Wake Forest
1948	Gamma Xi, San Jose
1949	Delta Alpha, Linfield
1949	Delta Beta, Georgia
1949	Gamma Chi, Randolph, Macon
1949	*Gamma Omega, Vanderbilt* (1960)
1949	Gamma Phi, Nebraska Wesleyan
1949	Gamma Pi, SUNY, Buffalo (1972-1989)
1949	*Gamma Psi, Puget Sound* (1980)
1949	Gamma Rho, Florida State
1949	Gamma Sigma, Duke
1949	Gamma Tau, Drake
1949	Gamma Upsilon, Bradley
1950	*Delta Epsilon, Miami (FL)* (1963)
1950	*Delta Eta, Colorado State* (1972)
1950	Delta Gamma, West Virginia Wesleyan

1950	Delta Iota, Northwestern
1950	Delta Theta, Toledo (1979-1987)
1950	Delta Zeta, Nebraska, Omaha
1951	Delta Kappa, Ball State
1951	*Delta Lambda, Colorado Mines* (1961)
1951	Delta Mu, Texas (1964-1989)
1951	*Delta Nu, Vermont* (1985)
1952	Delta Omicron, Gettysburg
1952	Delta Pi, Indiana State
1952	Delta Rho, North Carolina State
1952	Delta Sigma, Clarkson
1952	Delta Xi, Valparaiso
1953	Delta Tau, Kent (1971-1987)
1953	Delta Upsilon, Arizona State
1954	Delta Chi, Lenoir-Rhyne
1954	Delta Omega, Ripon
1954	Delta Phi, North Texas
1954	Delta Psi, Kansas (1972-1982)
1954	Epsilon Alpha, High Point
1955	Epsilon Beta, Lycoming
1956	Epsilon Delta, Youngstown State
1956	Epsilon Gamma, Widener
1957	Epsilon Eta, Indiana (PA)
1957	Epsilon Theta, Tufts
1957	Epsilon Zeta, Tampa
1958	Epsilon Iota, East Carolina (1971-1988)
1959	Epsilon Kappa, Idaho
1959	*Epsilon Lambda, Lewis and Clark* (1971)
1960	Epsilon Mu, Eastern Michigan
1960	*Epsilon Nu, Cal State, Los Angeles* (1975)
1960	Epsilon Omicron, Waynesburg
1960	Epsilon Xi, Clarion
1961	Epsilon Pi, Northern Illinois
1961	Epsilon Rho, Rider
1961	Epsilon Sigma, Wagner
1961	Epsilon Tau, Stephen F. Austin
1962	Epsilon Phi, Central Missouri State
1962	Epsilon Upsilon, Central Michigan
1963	*Epsilon Chi, Missouri, Rolla* (1974)
1963	Epsilon Psi, New Jersey Tech
1964	Epsilon Omega, Cal State, Sacramento (1975-1990)
1964	*Zeta Alpha, Slippery Rock* (1988)
1964	Zeta Beta, Adrian
1965	Zeta Delta, St. Cloud
1965	Zeta Epsilon, Cal State, Long Beach
1965	*Zeta Eta, Northern Michigan* (1986)
1965	Zeta Gamma, Alberta
1966	*Zeta Iota, Dickinson State* (1982)
1966	Zeta Kappa, Ohio Northern
1966	Zeta Lambda, Westminster (PA)
1966	*Zeta Mu, American International* (1972)
1966	*Zeta Theta, Troy* (1985)
1967	*Zeta Nu, Parsons* (1973)
1967	Zeta Xi, Cal, Davis
1968	*Zeta Omicron, Shippensburg* (1988)
1968	Zeta Pi, Old Dominion
1968	Zeta Rho, Kentucky
1968	Zeta Sigma, Wisconsin, River Falls
1969	Zeta Phi, Cal Poly, San Luis Obispo
1969	Zeta Tau, Michigan, Flint (1974-1990)
1969	Zeta Upsilon, Hartford (1972-1986)

1970	Eta Alpha, Clemson
1970	*Zeta Chi, Bryant* (1972)
1970	Zeta Omega, West Chester
1970	Zeta Psi, Western Illinois
1971	Eta Beta, Eastern Kentucky
1971	Eta Delta, Babson
1971	*Eta Epsilon, Marquette* (1973)
1971	Eta Gamma, Morehead
1971	Eta Zeta, Edinboro
1972	Eta Iota, Newberry
1972	*Eta Kappa, Madison Col* (1989)
1972	Eta Lambda, V.P.I.
1972	Eta Mu, Findlay
1972	*Eta Theta, Chadron* (1985)
1973	Eta Nu, Alma
1973	Eta Omicron, Northwestern Louisiana
1973	Eta Xi, Tarkio
1974	Eta Pi, East Stroudsburg
1977	Eta Rho, Centenary
1977	Eta Sigma, Arkansas Tech
1979	Eta Tau, Cal State, Stanislaus
1980	Eta Upsilon, Texas A & M
1981	Eta Phi, Oakland
1982	Eta Chi, George Mason
1982	Eta Omega, Cal State, Chico
1982	Eta Psi, Alabama, Birmingham
1984	Theta Alpha, Cal State, Northridge
1986	Theta Beta, Trenton
1987	Theta Delta, Santa Clara
1987	Theta Epsilon, Kennesaw
1988	Theta Gamma, Northwood (MI)
1988	Theta Zeta, North Carolina, Asheville
1989	Theta Eta, Sam Houston
1989	Theta Iota, Cal, Santa Cruz
1990	Theta Kappa, Bloomsburg
1990	Theta Lambda, Texas Tech.

Colonies: Adelphi, Bridgewater, Cal State, Hayward, SUNY, Albany, Southwest Texas, Glassboro, Mars Hill, Virginia Commonwealth

Theta Delta Chi

ACTIVE PIN

PLEDGE PIN

THETA DELTA CHI was founded at Union College, October 31, 1847, by Abel Beach, Andrew H. Green, Theodore B. Brown, William G. Akin, William Hyslop, and Samuel F. Wile, all of the class of 1849, of whom four were members of Phi Beta Kappa. It was the sixth Greek-letter fraternity founded at Union and the eleventh "secret" fraternity to be organized, although it ties for ninth place with Zeta Psi and Delta Psi, as those two with Theta Delta Chi were all established in 1847. While the founders discussed their ideals for the organization of a new fraternity practically all through the year of 1847,

October 31 is officially recognized as the foundation date, since it was not until that month that deliberations were completed and the fraternity had duly announced its birth. Union College was at its zenith of prosperity in 1848, and the class of 1849 was the largest the college had known. Andrew H. Green was the chief compiler of the constitution and ritual, the latter having been retained unchanged.

Growth The charter of the Union charge was surrendered in 1867, owing to lack of suitable material. The charter of Beta Proteron, at the Ballston Law School, was withdrawn in 1849, and the members affiliated to Alpha. Delta, at Rensselaer Polytechnic Institute, ceased to exist in 1870. It was revived November 2, 1883, and again surrendered its charter in 1896. Gamma, at Vermont, died in 1857 from lack of interest and isolation. Epsilon, at William and Mary, was killed by the Civil War. It was revived about 1870, but lived only a short time. It was again revived in 1904 by the active members of a chapter of the fraternity of Mu Pi Lambda, which disbanded. Zeta, at Brown, was inactive between 1878 and 1887. It was originally formed by ex-members of Delta Psi, who had resigned because of a misunderstanding with their fraternity. The Rochester charge was inactive for a number of years. Eta, at Bowdoin, died in 1866, but was reestablished in 1872. Iota retired with other Harvard societies in 1862. It was revived in 1880 and died in 1889, but was reestablished June 8, 1892, and died in 1916. Mu, at North Carolina, and Nu, at Virginia, were killed by the war, the latter being revived in 1910.

Sigma, at Dickinson, became inactive in 1876, was reestablished in 1881, and surrendered its charter in 1896. Tau, at Princeton, and Upsilon, at Bucknell (then called Lewisburg University), were withdrawn on account of anti-fraternity laws. The Cornell charge was at first called Alpha Delta, but received its present name in 1871. The Pi Deuteron, at the College of the City of New York, was composed largely of ex-members of the extinct fraternity Delta Beta Phi; the Upsilon Deuteron, at Wabash College, of ex-members of Delta Tau Delta. There were no initiates made by this charge there being fewer students at Wabash in 1879–80 than at any time in its history.

The Kappa Charge at Tufts and Xi Charge at Hobart are the oldest two charges in continuous existence, the former since 1856 and the latter since 1857. Nineteen of the remaining thirty charges have enjoyed continuous existence for more than fifty years.

Government Government was in the hands of Alpha Charge until the convention of 1867. The Grand Lodge was then created, composed of one graduate and two undergraduate members, the graduate member being president. In 1909 a graduate secretary and graduate treasurer were added. The members are elected by the annual convention of delegates, two undergraduates and one graduate

from each charge. Theta Delta Chi appears to have been the first fraternity to form an executive governing body. Since the administration of 1882 the official annual visitation of charges and graduate associations by the president, in later years by his assistant, and, since 1957, by the executive secretary, has become an upbuilding force of the fraternity.

The employment of a full-time executive secretary to operate the central fraternity office, supervise the annual visitations to all the charges and to graduate associations, and to coordinate all administrative phases of the fraternity government was first undertaken directly after World War II and discontinued in 1950. The post was revived in 1957, and the executive secretary is business manager of the quarterly magazine, *The Shield* and directs the annual alumni giving program, called Voluntary Graduate Dues, which was begun in 1929 and has brought almost $750,000 to the fraternity.

In 1959 regional operation was introduced, with volunteer governors handling some visitations and Organizing annual spring conferences in their respective regions, under the guidance of the executive secretary. The 34 active charges are currently broken down into five regions, and alumni within their boundaries are invited to the regional conferences along with two delegates per charge.

There is an educational adviser appointed by the Grand Lodge; and on their visits the regional governors and the executive secretary also emphasize the necessity of maintaining scholarship and stress the vital importance of utilizing fraternity association to develop character and personality; all charges receive graded ratings on a record of official visitation of the entire condition of the charge.

This record of visitation, or "R.O.V.," is used as the annual check-up and report.

Traditions and Insignia The annual birthday of the fraternity, October 31, is celebrated throughout the world on the eve of the official date, as the 31st is Halloween. All of the charges and graduate associations hold banquets or luncheons on this day. The key dinner is held in New York City, to which all groups celebrating send cables and telegrams of greeting. Theta Delta Chi was one of the first to inaugurate the universal observance of its birthday.

There are graduate associations located in different parts of the United States and Canada. Many of these hold monthly luncheons and observe the annual Founders' Day.

The centennial of the fraternity was observed on June 27–30, 1947, at the Sagamore Hotel, Lake George, New York, when more than 500 members and their families gathered. On Sunday afternoon, June 29, a pilgrimage was made to the birthplace where a commemoration service was held in the memorial chapel of Union College, followed by the entire assemblage crossing the campus to Old North College. There a bronze tablet was placed on the wall of this historic building and dedicated by the president of the fraternity, who made the presentation, and was received by Dr. Carter Davidson, president of Union, for the college. The tablet was unveiled by Miss Gertrude Brown, niece of one of the founders, Theodore B. Brown.

The charge that scores the highest percentage on "R.O.V." is awarded the Victory Cup at the annual convention. The Guy C. Pierce Improvement Cup is awarded to the charge that improves most in its percentage.

The badge is a shield of gold with a face of black enamel displaying the letters ΘΔΧ surmounted by two five-pointed gold stars with diamond centers; below are two arrows crossed. The border of the shield is studded with pearls. There is also an official plain badge. The pledge button is a triangle with the colors, which are black, white, and blue. The ruby is the official jewel, and the red carnation is the flower of the fraternity.

Publications   The fraternity magazine is *The Shield*. The convention of 1868 directed the publication of a periodical by that name, and one number was issued under date of June, 1869. Failing to receive adequate support, it was discontinued. In January, 1884, a periodical under the same name was started in Boston and was published there for two years. It was then moved to New York, where it was published until 1889, when the sole editorial and business control was given over by the convention to Clay W. Holmes of Elmira, New York, who continued to edit and publish it until 1898. The volume for 1899 was published by Prof. E. W. Huffcut of Cornell. It has been successively edited in various places, and the business management is now in the Theta Delta Chi Press, incorporated in 1907 as a New York business corporation. Theta Delta Chi was the first secret fraternity to publish a magazine. In 1924 *Shield* life subscriptions were made mandatory for all active members at the time of their initiation. The resulting fund is invested by the Theta Delta Chi Founders' Corporation, and its income is paid to the Theta Delta Chi Press.

A manuscript catalogue was prepared by John W. Little of New York in 1859. The first of thirteen printed catalogues was published in 1867 by Col. William L. Stone of New York. The second in 1875 was illustrated with a series of unique charge cuts, each representing the Greek letter by which the charge is known. A more elaborate catalogue, compiled and published in 1891, embodied in addition to the regular charge lists an alphabetical list and also a geographical index. Since that time ten successively improved editions have been issued, the latest in 1959.

The first songbook was published in 1869 by the Xi Charge under the management of Robert C. Scott. Several editions have followed; many of the songs now in use were written for and dedicated to Theta Delta Chi. The fraternity's most noted song is "Stars Ablaze," composed by Richmond K. Fletcher, Harvard, '08, who also wrote "Convention Days"

and "The Fraternal Hymn," as well as the "Centennial Song."

In 1898 Clay W. Holmes edited and published the *Memorial History* at Elmira, New York, commemorating the golden jubilee of the fraternity and containing a complete history of the first half-century. In 1900 the Cornell charge published a history and biographical catalogue and also an album containing portraits of all but six of its members. Other publications include the *Historical Quiz Book* in 1921, a *Pledge Manual* in 1934, and a rushing pamphlet in 1939. These publications are revised as needed.

Come My Boys, the memoirs of Norman H. Hackett, Michigan, '98, a leader of the fraternity for many years, was published in 1960, not long after Hackett's death.

Funds and Philanthropies   The Association of Theta Delta Chi was incorporated in 1909 under the laws of the State of New York to advance the interests of the fraternity, chiefly by the accumulation of money through gifts and bequests. It is believed that this was one of the first, if not the first, fraternity endowment corporation established. In 1912 this corporation was merged with the Theta Delta Chi Founders' Corporation, also incorporated in New York. It holds in trust all fraternity funds, bequests, and donations, and is managed by a board of directors composed of the three graduate members of the Grand Lodge and twelve other graduate members of the fraternity. Its assets have a market value of approximately $1,000,000.

The Educational Foundation of Theta Delta Chi was established in 1944 for the purpose of making yearly awards for academic achievement "to further sound learning, contribute to the attainment of higher educational standards among undergraduates and the development of high standards of honor, integrity, character, and leadership, and to establish the ideals of the fraternity as a moving force in higher education." The foundation has already raised approximately $250,000 for this objective. Grants for charge house libraries were begun in 1966. The first scholarship award for graduate study of $1,000 was made at the centennial banquet in 1947, and since that time two, three, or four annual awards have been made at each successive convention. Undergraduate awards were begun in 1961.

Three scholarship prizes are awarded at the annual convention from income from a fund for that purpose given to the fraternity in 1913 by Frank E. Compton, former president. One prize goes to the charge which stands highest above the all-men's average in scholarship; a second to the charge that stands first among the fraternities on its campus in scholarship; and a third to the charge that shows the most improvement in scholarship. One mileage cup is awarded to the charge whose undergraduates at convention, exclusive of the two delegates, have traveled the most mileage to convention. Another goes to the charge with the most alumni present. The Charles P. Schmid graduate loyalty trophy is presented to the charge whose graduates had the highest dollar average in responding to voluntary graduate dues. In 1955 a new award was presented, the Norman Hackett Charge Service Trophy, whose purpose is to encourage charges to consider and perform more services for the collegiate institution and the community in which they are located in any form that reflects credit to the fraternity system as a whole and to Theta Delta Chi in particular. Also in 1955 a Fraternity Achievement Award and Theta Delt of the Year Award were introduced. They are presented at the closing Convention banquet.

Headquarters 135 Bay State Road, Boston, Massachusetts 02215. Phone: (617) 262-2815. A five-story brownstone in Boston's Back Bay purchased in 1971 provides a permanent administrative office, archives, club facility, and meeting headquarters. It also provides apartments and rooms for graduate students, visiting alumni, and undergraduates on a nightly, weekly, or yearly basis.

Membership Total living membership 21,231. Total undergraduate membership 1,372. Active chapters 33. Inactive chapters 27. Colonies 1. Houses owned 23. Graduate/Alumni chapters 31. City/Area alumni associations 12. Total number of initiates 35,095. Chapter roll:

1847 Alpha, Union (NY) (1867-1923)
1849 *Beta Proteron, Ballston Law* (1851)
1853 *Delta, R.P.I.* (1871-1883) (1896)
1853 Epsilon, William and Mary (1861-1871) (1872-1904)
1853 Zeta, Brown (1877-1887) (1971-1975)
1854 Eta, Bowdoin (1863-1872)
1854 *Theta, Kenyon* (1861-1870) (1898)
1856 *Iota, Harvard* (1857-1885) (1916)
1856 Kappa, Tufts
1856 *Lambda Grad., CCNY* (1857)
1856 *Mu, North Carolina* (1860)
1857 Nu, Virginia (1859-1873) (1881-1910)
1857 *Omicron, Wesleyan (CT)* (1863)
1857 Xi, Hobart
1858 *Pi, Washington and Jefferson* (1865)
1859 *Rho Proteron, South Carolina* (1859)
1861 *Sigma, Dickinson* (1873-1881) (1895)
1863 Tau, Princeton (1867-1984)
1865 *Upsilon, Bucknell* (1871-1968) (1977)
1867 Chi, Rochester (1880-1892)
1867 Phi, Lafayette (1886-1889)
1868 Psi, Hamilton
1869 Omicron Deuteron, Dartmouth
1869 *Rho, Washington and Lee* (1872)
1870 Beta, Cornell
1877 *Lambda, Boston U.* (1912)
1879 *Upsilon Deuteron, Wabash* (1882)
1881 *Pi Deuteron, CUNY, Brooklyn* (1931)
1883 *Rho Deuteron, Columbia (NY)* (1929)
1884 Nu Deuteron, Lehigh
1885 Mu Deuteron, Amherst (1969-1986)
1887 *Epsilon Deuteron, Yale* (1900)

1889 Gamma Deuteron, Michigan
1890 Theta Deuteron, M.I.T. (1892-1906)
1891 *Iota Deuteron, Williams* (1985-1988) (1990)
1892 *Tau Deuteron, Minnesota* (1984)
1895 Sigma Deuteron, Wisconsin, Madison
1896 Chi Deuteron, George Washington (1956-1987)
1900 Delta Deuteron, Cal, Berkeley
1901 *Zeta Deuteron, McGill* (1972)
1903 Eta Deuteron, Stanford
1908 Kappa Deuteron, Illinois (1970-1982)
1912 Lambda Deuteron, Toronto
1913 Xi Deuteron, Washington (WA)
1915 *Phi Deuteron, Penn* (1934)
1919 Beta Deuteron, Iowa State
1929 Psi Deuteron, UCLA
1951 *Kappa Triton, Northwestern* (1989)
1954 Sigma Triton, Penn State
1961 Epsilon Triton, Arizona State
1963 Omicron Triton, Rhode Island
1964 Gamma Triton, Michigan State
1968 *Psi Triton, Cal, Santa Barbara* (1980)
1968 *Zeta Triton, Calgary* (1970)
1970 Nu Triton, V.P.I.
1970 Rho Triton, Virginia Commonwealth
1972 *Phi Proteron, Florida Institute* (1972)
1972 *Pi Triton, California (PA)* (1979)
1978 *Beta Triton, Lake Forest* (1981)
1990 Delta Triton, Northeastern

Colonies: Vermont

COAT OF ARMS

Theta Xi

ACTIVE PIN

PLEDGE PIN

THETA XI was founded on April 29, 1864, at Rensselaer Polytechnic Institute, Troy, New York, by Peter Henry Fox, Ralph Gooding Packard, Christopher Champlin Waite, George Bradford Brainerd, Samuel Buel, Jr., Henry Harrison Farnum, Thomas Cole Raymond, and Nathaniel Henry Starbuck. It was the only college fraternity to be founded during the period of the Civil War. All the founders had been members of Sigma Delta, a local fraternity established in 1859 to rival Theta Delta Chi, the only secret society then at Rensselaer. Dissension had crept into the ranks of Sigma Delta's 13 members. The eight members who were to become the founders of Theta Xi considered such a condition incompatible with their ideas of unity and fellowship and determined to build anew for their future unity and fellowship and to form a fraternity which would be national in scope. Accordingly, at meetings held April 1 and April 6, 1864, all preliminary preparations were made, and the monogram Theta Xi was chosen over Theta Psi because of the reported existence at Yale of a local society called Theta Psi. On the night of April 29, the eight former members of Sigma Delta met for the purpose of founding Theta Xi. The constitution, by-laws and rules of order which had been drawn up previously were read and adopted without a dissenting vote. The oath of initiation was then taken by the founders in a body, following which they signed the constitution alphabetically by classes. On that same night, Edward H. Morrison was unanimously selected as the first pledge.

Growth The founders decided that their chapter would be called the Alpha Chapter, and that each succeeding chapter would be designated by the following letter of the Greek alphabet. Within a matter of a few months, the members of Alpha Chapter began negotiations with a group at the Sheffield Scientific School at Yale. These negotiations culminated in the installation of Beta Chapter at Yale in April, 1865. Because of the close friendship which existed between them, these two chapters formed the nucleus from which the activities of the fraternity were directed for many years.

The six chapters established by Theta Xi during the first 40 years of its existence (Yale University, Stevens Institute of Technology, Massachusetts Institute of Technology, Columbia University, Cornell University, and Lehigh University) were all located within approximately 200 miles of Rensselaer, and it was not until 1905 that it began its westward expansion with the chartering of Theta Chapter at Purdue University in February of that year, and Iota Chapter at Washington University in St. Louis a month later. The fraternity established its first west coast chapter in 1910 on the Berkeley campus of the University of California, moved into the southwest three years later with the location of a chapter at the University of Texas, and entered the Pacific northwest in 1915 with the establishment of a chapter at the University of Washington.

During the fraternity's early days, the constitution had been interpreted as having placed limitations on the qualifications for membership. As a consequence, throughout the first 62 years of its history, Theta Xi functioned as a social-engineering fraternity whose membership was generally confined to students enrolled in courses leading to a degree in engineering. On April 9, 1926, the members of the fraternity indicated by a majority of five to one their desire that Theta Xi become a general fraternity and select future members from the undergraduate student body at large.

The fraternity's chapter roll was increased substantially in 1962 when 21 chapters of the Kappa Sigma Kappa national fraternity merged with Theta Xi. Since several of its chapters were located at unaccredited institutions, Kappa Sigma Kappa could not qualify for membership in the NIC. Its officers were seeking ways and means of qualifying for such membership, and it was concluded during an informal meeting of representatives of Theta Xi and Kappa Sigma Kappa in March of that year that a merger would prove beneficial to both organizations. Special committees were appointed by each fraternity to study and discuss the possibility of such a merger. Following a series of meetings, the terms of the proposed merger were agreed upon on June 30, and were subsequently ratified by the governing bodies of the two fraternities. The merger agreement was approved unanimously by Kappa Sigma Kappa at its 1962 convention, and the 21 chapters of Kappa Sigma Kappa which were located at accredited institutions were formally merged with Theta Xi on August 20, 1962. These chapters, none of which was located on a campus having a previously established Theta Xi chapter, had a total membership of 4,079.

Alumni clubs, which have been established in many principal cities, are each entitled to be represented at the national convention by a delegate who is empowered to vote on all matters brought before the convention. These alumni clubs have proved to be successful in promoting fraternity unity and interest throughout the country.

Government The government of the fraternity is vested in the national convention. Held annually from 1864 until 1933, conventions were then held on a biennial basis from 1934 until 1972. The decision was made to hold annual conventions once again from 1974 until 1980. At that time the convention schedule was again revised and biennial conventions have been held since 1982. In its early years, the convention met with each chapter in turn serving as host; then, for a period of 20 years, it was held in New York City. In more recent years, conventions have been held throughout the country at locations selected by the Grand Lodge.

In the interim between conventions, the fraternity is governed by the Grand Lodge, composed of the president, vice president, treasurer, and five directors elected by the convention. At the time of his election, one of the five directors must be an undergraduate chapter member. The Grand Lodge serves as the fraternity's board of directors. The Grand Lodge employs a full-time executive director who is responsible for overseeing the operations of the national headquarters and its staff. The fraternity was incorporated under the General Not For Profit Corporation Act of Missouri on April 29, 1960.

Undergraduate chapters are grouped into six geographical regions. Educational conferences of representatives from the various chapters in each region are held annually. Between conferences, the activities of chapters within each region are monitored by an alumnus who is appointed as regional director.

An alumni advisor is appointed for each chapter. In the early days of the fraternity, the advisor was charged with seeing that the ritual, which was not then reduced to writing, was properly carried out. Today, as his title implies, the advisor consults with and advises the chapter officers and members on various matters.

Traditions and Insignia The name Theta Xi is popularly shortened to the English version, "TX." Alumni members of the fraternity and the undergraduate chapters pay tribute to the founders of Theta Xi with appropriate celebrations on each anniversary of its founding date. Since the merger with Kappa Sigma Kappa in 1962, September 28 has been observed as Emblem Day to commemorate the founding of Kappa Sigma Kappa on that date in 1867.

The Memorial Trophy is awarded annually to the outstanding chapter, and the General Improvement Trophy to the chapter making the greatest over-all improvement during the same period in the outstanding chapter competition.

As a means of honoring members for prolonged and meritorious service, the fraternity established the Order of the Unicorn at its Diamond Jubilee Convention in September, 1939. This award constitutes the highest honor that can be conferred upon a Theta Xi, and only 37 of its members have been so honored to date. The fraternity's Distinguished Service Award was authorized in 1941 for presentation to members in recognition and appreciation of outstanding services rendered to the fraternity. Upon the attainment of their 50th anniversary as a member of Theta Xi, members are elevated to the Order of the Golden Star.

The badge of the fraternity is a monogram made by inclining the Θ upon the Ξ. The rim of the Θ is set with 20 graduated pearls and its bars with a single stone, either a ruby or diamond. The associate member pin is a small shield taken from the coat of arms, with a field of blue diagonally crossed by a band of white.

The flag is composed of three bars of equal width, parallel with the staff. The outer bars are blue and the center bar is white. The white letter Θ is on the upper half of the bar next to the staff, the white Ξ letter is on the lower half of the outer bar, and a unicorn's head in bay color is in the middle of the center bar.

The colors of the fraternity are azure blue and silver, and the official flower is the blue iris.

Publications The first membership directory was published in 1892 and the 12th edition was published in 1984.

The official magazine, *The Unicorn of Theta Xi*, is published under direction of the Grand Lodge. It was first issued as *The Theta Xi quarterly* by Charles W. Hoyt in 1892 and has been published continuously since. The name was changed to *The Unicorn of Theta Xi* in 1928.

The first edition of the *Pledge Manual of Theta Xi* was published in November, 1930. In 1962, following the merger of Theta Xi with Kappa Sigma Kappa, the title of the manual was changed to *The Quest for Theta Xi Fraternity*.

Various songs have been printed at different times in the magazine and in sheet music form. Songbooks were issued at various times, with the most recent edition issued in 1955.

Funds and Philanthropies In 1915, a life membership plan, which eliminated the payment of annual national dues and provided a lifetime subscription to the fraternity's magazine, was adopted. All money received from the payment of life memberships is placed in the Life Membership Fund, a permanent endowment fund.

The Unicorn Housing Loan Fund, a permanent revolving loan fund, was established in 1929 by setting aside a portion of each national initiation fee received. It is available in the form of loans to alumni associations to assist them in providing and improving chapter housing.

The Theta Xi Foundation was created in January, 1947, for the purpose of providing scholarships, fellowships, grants, and loans to deserving undergraduates, graduate students, and faculty members requiring such assistance. The foundation was established as a private foundation and converted to public charity status in 1982. Today, in addition to meeting the purposes listed above, the foundation also provides funding to assist the fraternity and its members in providing leadership opportunities and educational programs.

The National Multiple Sclerosis Society was adopted as the fraternity's national service project in 1974.

Headquarters Currently located at 9974 Old Olive Street Road, St. Louis, MO 63141, Phone: (314) 993-6294. Theta Xi has maintained its national headquarters in St. Louis, Missouri, since 1924 when the headquarters was transferred from New York City and the first Grand Lodge office devoted exclusively to the business of the fraternity was established. In 1960, the purchase of a site for the location of a permanent national headquarters building was authorized. Ground for the new building, which was financed entirely by contributions from members, was broken on July 8, 1983, and it was formally dedicated on April 29, 1964, the 100th anniversary of the founding of the fraternity.

Membership Total living membership 39,474. Total undergraduate membership 2,587. Active chapters 54. Inactive chapters 44. Colonies 18. Houses owned 36. Graduate/Alumni chapters 37. City/Area alumni associations 25. Total number of initiates 53,136. Chapter roll:

1864 Alpha, R.P.I.
1865 *Beta, Yale* (1936)
1874 Gamma, Stevens Tech
1885 Delta, M.I.T.
1899 *Epsilon, Columbia (NY)* (1933)
1903 *Zeta, Cornell* (1970)
1904 Eta, Lehigh
1905 Iota, Washington (MO)
1905 Theta, Purdue
1907 Kappa, Rose-Hulman

1907 Lambda, Penn State (1974-1985)
1909 Mu, Iowa State
1910 Nu, Cal, Berkeley (1965-1977)
1912 Omicron, Penn
1912 Pi, Carnegie-Mellon
1912 *Xi, Iowa (1960-1986)*
1914 *Sigma, Michigan (1986)*
1914 Tau, Stanford
1915 *Upsilon, Washington (WA) (1990)*
1917 *Phi, Wisconsin, Madison (1941)*
1920 *Chi, Ohio State (1957)*
1920 *Psi, Minnesota (1966)*
1921 Alpha Alpha, L.S.U.
1921 *Omega, Washington State (1989)*
1922 Alpha Beta, Illinois
1922 Alpha Gamma, Illinois Tech
1927 *Alpha Delta, Oregon State (1972)*
1927 Alpha Epsilon, Nebraska
1928 Alpha Zeta, UCLA
1929 Alpha Eta, Colorado (1941-1946) (1961-1987)
1931 Alpha Iota, Kansas State (1965-1972)
1931 *Alpha Theta, Lafayette (1972)*
1932 *Alpha Kappa, Northwestern (1988)*
1932 *Alpha Lambda, Alabama (1982)*
1932 *Alpha Mu, Amherst (1957)*
1939 *Kappa Alpha, Youngstown State (1974)*
1940 Alpha Nu, USC
1940 *Alpha Xi, Mississippi State (1960)*
1942 *Kappa Beta, Arkansas, Monticello (1988)*
1943 *Alpha Pi, Connecticut (1972)*
1945 Kappa Gamma, Fairmont
1946 Alpha Omicron, Southwestern Louisiana
1946 *Kappa Delta, Indiana Tech (1975)*
1946 *Kappa Epsilon, Concord (1978)*
1947 *Kappa Eta, Glenville (1986)*
1947 Kappa Kappa, Ball State
1947 Kappa Theta, Western Illinois
1947 *Kappa Zeta, Morris Harvey (1977)*
1948 Alpha Sigma, Bradley
1949 *Alpha Chi, Trinity (CT) (1970)*
1949 *Alpha Phi, South Dakota (1962)*
1949 Alpha Psi, Missouri, Rolla
1949 *Alpha Rho, Oklahoma (1960)*
1949 *Alpha Tau, Indiana (1979)*
1949 *Alpha Upsilon, Louisiana Tech (1984)*
1949 *Kappa Lambda, Old Dominion (1972)*
1949 Kappa Mu, Rochester Tech
1949 Kappa Nu, Defiance
1949 *Kappa Xi, Detroit (1976)*
1950 *Alpha Omega, Michigan State (1959)*
1950 Kappa Omicron, Lenoir-Rhyne
1951 Beta Alpha, Georgia Tech
1951 *Beta Beta, San Jose (1970)*
1951 Beta Delta, Southern Illinois (1974-1986)
1951 *Beta Gamma, Bowling Green (1953)*
1951 *Kappa Pi, Wayne State (MI) (1972)*
1951 *Kappa Rho, Ferris (1977)*
1952 Beta Epsilon, Cal, Davis
1954 Beta Zeta, Auburn
1954 Kappa Sigma, GMI
1955 Kappa Tau, West Virginia Wesleyan

1956 *Kappa Upsilon, Utica (1978)*
1957 *Beta Iota, Missouri (1964)*
1957 *Beta Theta, Western Michigan (1974)*
1958 *Beta Kappa, Clarkson (1988)*
1958 Kappa Phi, Western Carolina
1961 Beta Lambda, Indiana (PA)
1962 *Beta Mu, Central Arkansas (1982)*
1962 Beta Nu, Kearney
1963 Beta Pi, Southeastern Louisiana
1963 *Beta Rho, Emporia (1970)*
1963 Beta Xi, New Orleans
1965 Beta Sigma, California (PA)
1965 Beta Tau, Southwest Texas
1966 Beta Phi, West Liberty
1966 Beta Upsilon, Slippery Rock (1978-1987)
1968 *Beta Chi, Lawrence Tech (1977)*
1968 *Kappa Chi, Lawrence Tech (1977)*
1969 *Beta Psi, Merrimack (1972)*
1972 Beta Omega, V.P.I.
1972 Gamma Alpha, Shepherd
1973 Gamma Beta, Florida Institute
1974 *Gamma Gamma, South Alabama (1984)*
1976 Gamma Delta, Loyola, Chicago
1984 Gamma Epsilon, Southeast Missouri
1987 Gamma Zeta, Valdosta
1988 Gamma Theta, Lake Superior
1989 Gamma Eta, Nicholls

Colonies: Cal Poly, San Luis Obispo, Edinboro, Embry Riddle (AZ), Florida State, Illinois, Chicago, Indiana Southeast, Montclair, SUNY Col., Oneonta, Northern Colorado, Henderson, Central Michigan, Texas, Henderson, Northern Colorado
1963 Beta Omicron, Clarion

Triangle

COAT OF ARMS

ACTIVE PIN

PLEDGE PIN

TRIANGLE, the fraternity of engineers, architects, and scientists, was founded at the University of Illinois by 16 civil engineering students who planned to live together during their senior year. Recognizing the advantages of a continuing organization, they incorporated April 15, 1907. The date, designated Founders' Day, is appropriately celebrated by chapters and alumni groups each year.

Similar groups at Purdue and Ohio State were installed as Triangle chapters in 1909 and 1911, making the fraternity a national organization. Triangle expanded slowly until the establishment of a full-time office in 1962 and the development of an aggressive extension program.

Until the end of 1920, membership was drawn entirely from civil engineering students. A national referendum resulted in admission of students enrolled in architecture and in all types of engineering. In 1961, science students in mathematics, physics, and chemistry became eligible. As technical courses of study incorporating several areas began to proliferate, local chapters sought to include them. An approved courses committee recommends to the National Council those courses having sufficient technical content to be on a level with engineering. Each chapter has its own list of approved courses. In 1981 computer science was added to the group of approved sciences.

Government The eight members of National Council, elected by the fraternity membership acting on the recommendation of a nominating committee, form the executive and judicial body of Triangle. National convention is the legislative body.

National Council appoints the executive director, a full-time employee who manages the national office and also serves as national secretary/treasurer and member of Council. Council appoints the trustees of several funds, the directors of the Triangle Fraternity Educational Foundation, National Council Representatives (to particular chapters), National Service Volunteers and the chairmen and members of national committees. The editor and business manager of *Triangle Review* are appointed by National Council.

Conventions were held annually except for a four-year period during World War II when none were held. Conventions were held on odd numbered years from 1957-63. Beginning with 1975, the fraternity has held a basic national meeting each year consisting of Leadership School, an Awards Luncheon, a Foundation Seminar and a National Banquet. These two-day meetings are supplemented on odd numbered years by factoring in an additional day of meetings devoted to legislative matters so as to create a biennial national convention.

Traditions and Insignia The goal of Triangle is to give its members the best of the social fraternity, as well as to function as a service fraternity for the educational institutions at which it is located. Scholarship, a chief traditional objective, is under the supervision of the national director of scholarship, the chapter advisors, and the undergraduate scholarship officers. The scholarship cup is awarded annually to the chapter with the highest scholastic standing and the scholarship plaque is awarded to the chapter showing the greatest improvement over the previous year's cumulative average.

The official badge is a gold equilateral triangle, upon which a transit is superimposed, with a T in the middle of the triangle. Official colors of the fraternity are old rose and gray; official flower is the white chrysanthemum.

Publications *Triangle review* is the quarterly publication. Manuals in various areas of chapter management for undergraduates, for alumni officers and for advisors also are issued.

Funds and Philanthropies A student loan fund was established as a memorial to Triangles who lost their lives in World War II. It is now incorporated into the Triangle Fraternity Education Foundation where students who have completed two years of college may obtain interest free loans to help them complete their education. The foundation underwrites the Leadership School and the regional workshops, presents a foundation seminar featuring outstanding speakers at each annual meeting and supports educational activities of the fraternity.

The Permanent Fund manages the investments of the fraternity and channels its income into approved purposes of education and housing. The Building Loan Fund assists chapters in financing new houses, in remodeling existing structures and in coping with emergency repairs.

The Service Key is awarded to members who have performed pre-eminent work in developing the national organization.

Other awards are the Triangle Citation, presented occasionally to a member whose career has reflected significantly on Triangle, and the Outstanding Alumnus Award to alumni nominated by their chapters. The Certificate of Service is awarded for above-average national or regional service. Prominent members are designated as Top Triangles and are entitled to wear a distinctive red and gold recognition pin.

Headquarters 2909 West Central Avenue, Toledo, Ohio 43606.

Membership Living membership 15,647. Active chapters 34. Inactive chapters 7. Colonies 3. Houses owned 29. Graduate/Alumni chapters 34. City/Area alumni associations 4. Total number of initiates 19,643. Chapter roll:

1907	Illinois, Illinois
1909	Purdue, Purdue
1911	Ohio State, Ohio State
1913	Wisconsin, Madison, Wisconsin, Madison
1920	*Kentucky, Kentucky* (1983)
1921	Cincinnati, Cincinnati
1922	*Iowa, Iowa* (1948)
1922	Minnesota, Minnesota
1923	Armour, Illinois Tech
1924	*Missouri, Missouri* (1933)
1925	Michigan, Michigan
1927	Kansas, Kansas
1927	Missouri Mines, Missouri, Rolla
1928	Penn State, Penn
1930	South Dakota Mines, South Dakota Mines
1935	*Northwestern, Northwestern* (1987)
1937	Marquette, Marquette
1941	Louisville, Louisville
1942	*Cornell, Cornell* (1985)
1955	Michigan State, Michigan State
1957	*Clarkson, Clarkson* (1970)
1957	UCLA, UCLA
1963	Nebraska, Nebraska
1964	Iowa State, Iowa State
1964	Kansas State, Kansas State
1964	Oklahoma State, Oklahoma State

1965	MSOE, Milwaukee Engineering
1967	CSU, Colorado State
1967	RIT, Rochester Tech
1968	Rose, Rose-Hulman
1969	*Colorado, Colorado* (1970)
1970	Pitt, Pitt
1970	UWM, Wisconsin, Milwaukee
1971	Toledo, Toledo
1972	Mississippi State, Mississippi State
1979	Oklahoma, Oklahoma
1980	V.P.I., VPI
1982	Connecticut, Connecticut
1986	UTA, Texas, Arlington
1988	MTU, Michigan Tech
1988	TAMU, Texas A & M

Colonies: Southern Illinois, Maryland, Tri-State

COAT OF ARMS

Zeta Beta Tau

ACTIVE PIN

PLEDGE PIN

ZETA BETA TAU was founded on December 29, 1898, in New York City. Inspired by Rabbi Gustav Gottheil, who was then the spiritual head of Temple Emanu-El, and his son, Richard J. H. Gottheil, professor of languages at Columbia University, a group of young men attending several universities in New York City, gathered at the Jewish Theological Seminary and formed an organization which was originally called Z.B.T. For the first year and a half its membership roll grew. Within two years' time the older members had scattered. The organization's original Zionist objective was eliminated, and in its place a social college fraternity came into being.

Growth On October 28, 1907, it was granted a charter by the Secretary of the State of New York as a nonprofit-sharing membership organization, with the existing units receiving chapter charters. On October 21, 1906, alterations in its constitution included the change of its name to Zeta Beta Tau Fraternity. Zeta Beta Tau is the pioneer historical American and Canadian college social fraternity of Jewish men, although since 1954 the fraternity has been nonsectarian by word and deed. No unwritten rule or understanding exists to stop a chapter from initiating any man whom it desires to include in its membership.

In 1903, the first chapter was formed at C.C.N.Y., the constitution having been amended to permit the establishment of chapters in colleges and universities throughout North America. A new unit was formed later that year at Long Island Medical College. In 1904, chapters were started at N.Y.U. and Columbia, and in 1907, others were established at Pennsylvania, Cornell, and Jefferson Medical College. In 1909, a chapter was established at Tulane University and, from this beginning came many future new units in the South. In 1913, the fraternity entered Canada by establishing a chapter at McGill University.

In 1969, Zeta Beta Tau merged with Phi Sigma Delta Fraternity (which had previously merged with Phi Alpha Fraternity). In 1970 Zeta Beta Tau merged with Phi Epsilon Pi Fraternity (which had previously merged with Kappa Nu Fraternity).

In 1988, Zeta Beta Tau eliminated the institution of pledging and all secondary classes of membership in the Fraternity, becoming the first Fraternity to do so. While its constitution and policies never required pledging to be initiated. the Fraternity concluded that, in order to eliminate hazing, it had to eliminate its root cause, pledging. ZBT's Brotherhood Program was instituted in the Fall of 1989 to replace pledging with a program that stressed full and equal rights and responsibilities by all members of the Fraternity.

Alumni clubs are situated in fifty geographical locations.

Government Until 1905, the government of Zeta Beta Tau was wholly in the hands of the "home fraternity." Since that time, this responsibility and authority has been exercised by an elected Supreme Council. Elections to the Council are held in even numbered years at the annual conventions, where officers, who are included in the Council, are also elected.

Since 1924, all administrative matters have been managed by an executive director (Executive Vice President), who is also the managing editor of the Fraternity's publications. Field secretaries (chapter consultants) have been employed since 1940.

The elected officers include a national president, two national vice presidents, a treasurer and a secretary. The Supreme Council includes the five National Officers, five elected members-at-large, five appointed (by the president) members-at-large, and five appointed undergraduate members-at-large.

Annual conventions have been held since 1907. Each chapter has one full vote, and each alumni association has one third of a vote.

The Supreme Council meets three to four times each year, between the annual conventions. Leadership schools, practice clinics, and discussion groups occupy three days of each national convention. Leadership schools are also conducted as part of several Regional Conclaves held each year.

Traditions and Insignia Zeta Beta Tau, as the occasion arises, presents the Richard J. H. Gottheil Medal. This is given to a person or persons who has bettered human understanding among people. The Fraternity also presents a Man of the Year Award. Many brothers of national recognition have received this valued award. Additionally, it awards its Riegelman-Jacobs Award to those non-ZBTs in the interfraternity community who have demonstrated commitment to the common standards of all Greek letter organizations.

Zeta Beta Tau annually awards a number of trophies, awards, and prizes to chapters and individuals for accomplishments in various fields, including scholarship, campus, and chapter activities.

The badge is in the shape of a diamond, edged with whole pearls. In the center, which is slightly raised, are the Greek letters ZBT in gold on a black background, running along the short axis. Above the letters appear a skull and crossbones in white, and below is the six-pointed star of hope in light blue.

In 1911, the crest was established having been designed by Herbert Lippman and Harold Goldman of the Columbia Chapter.

The Fraternity also awards individual undergraduates for their accomplishments through the College of Honors, comprised of the Six Orders of Zeta Beta Tau. The Orders are based upon the tenets of the fraternity. Each Order is represented by a unique lapel pin; Service (gold torch on blue background); Charity (gold extended hand on green background); Truth (gold greek temple on white background); Justice (gold balanced censers on black background); Wisdom (gold lamp on red background); and Brotherhood (gold clasped hands on purple background).

Publications Directories of members were published in 1910, 1911, 1912, 1924, 1932, 1937, 1948, 1958, and 1988.

In 1913, Zeta Beta Tau began the publication of the *Zeta Beta Tau Quarterly*. In the war period its format was changed from magazine to newspaper style, and its name was changed to the *Duration News*. The magazine format was resumed in June, 1946. In 1969, the fraternity changed the name of its alumni magazine to the *Deltan*, the name of the former Phi Sigma Delta alumni publication.

In 1923, on the occasion of its silver anniversary, *The First 25 Years* was published. The *First Fifty-three Years* was printed as an issue of the magazine in December, 1951. Recent publications include *An Introduction to Membership; Chapter Operations Manual; Good & Welfare*, the chapter newsletter; and *Brotherhood Development Director's Manual* in support of the non-pledging initiative. Other publications include a variety of educational and programming materials in support of the operations and programming of the fraternity.

Funds and Philanthropies In December, 1929, at the New Orleans convention, the National Permanent Endowment Fund was established. On November 13, 1939, it was incorporated as the N.P.E.F. Corporation. The members of the Supreme Council are the membership of the N.P.E.F. Corporation, the four purposes of which are: the endowing of expenses for the operation of Zeta Beta Tau; loans to individual Zeta Beta Tau undergraduates for room, board, tuition, and books; scholarships to individual undergraduates; loans to, and loan guarantees for, chapters for the purchase or building of chapter homes.

The Zeta Beta Tau Foundation Inc., an additional corporation of the fraternity, was founded in 1950, also as a nonprofit membership organization, incorporated in New York State. It awards scholarships every year to worthy undergraduates on the basis of need, scholarship, and chapter activity.

In 1970, ZBT Enterprises, Inc., was founded to manage the Fraternity's merchandising programs. It is a for-profit stock corporation, the Supreme Council of the Fraternity holding all the stock.

Headquarters 505 Eighth Avenue, 8th Floor, New York, NY 10018. Phone: (212) 629-0888.

Membership Deceased membership 1,847. Active chapters 78. Inactive chapters 112. 51 chapters are housed and 23 own their homes. Total number of initiates 110,756. Chapter roll:

1898	*Home Fraternity* (1903)
1903	*Alpha, CCNY* (1971)
1903	*Beta, Long Island* (1914)
1904	Delta, Columbia (NY) (1972-1974)
1904	Gamma, N.Y.U., Heights (1972-1989)
1907	*Jefferson Medical* (1909)
1907	Kappa, Cornell (1982-1988)
1907	Theta, Penn
1908	*Mu, Boston U.* (1989)
1909	Eta, Union (1971-1974)
1909	Lambda, Case Western Reserve
1909	*Pi, L.S.U.* (1989)
1909	Sigma, Tulane
1910	*Iota, CUNY, Brooklyn* (1920)
1911	Alpha, Rochester (1970-1980)
1911	*Nu, Ohio State* (1989)
1911	Omicron, Syracuse (1986-1987)
1911	Xi, M.I.T.
1912	Rho, Illinois
1913	*Upsilon, McGill* (1969)
1914	Alpha, George Washington (1969-1974)
1914	*Iota, Dickinson* (1985)
1914	*Tau, Harvard* (1933)
1915	*Chi, Virginia* (1985)
1915	*Delta, Union (NY)* (1925)
1915	*Mu, Georgia* (1985)
1916	*Alpha Beta, Chicago* (1975)
1916	Eta, Michigan (1970-1977)
1916	*Gamma, Georgetown U.* (1947)
1916	Omicron, Tufts (1969-1989)
1916	*Pi, Maine* (1925)
1916	Psi, Alabama
1916	*Sigma, Brown* (1918)
1916	*Tau, Auburn* (1920)
1916	*Upsilon, Connecticut* (1970)
1916	Xi, Georgia Tech
1917	Omega, Missouri
1917	Zeta, SUNY, Buffalo (1925-1980)
1918	*Alpha Delta, USC* (1972)
1918	Alpha Gamma, Vanderbilt
1918	Kappa Nu Kappa, R.P.I. (1969-1988)
1919	Beta Alpha Theta, Colorado (1983-1987)

1919 Epsilon, Maryland
1920 *Alpha Alpha, Dartmouth* (1922)
1920 *Alpha Epsilon, Washington and Lee* (1988)
1920 *Alpha Lambda, Yale* (1933)
1920 Gamma, Northwestern (1971-1975)
1920 Iota, Denver
1920 Lambda, Texas
1920 *Omega, Cincinnati* (1935)
1921 *Alpha Beta, Iowa* (1971)
1921 Alpha Eta, Cal, Oakland (1974-1975)
1922 Alpha Kappa, Wisconsin, Madison
       (1983-1987)
1922 Alpha Mu, Washington (WA) (1973-1974)
1922 *Alpha Theta, Nebraska* (1962)
1923 Alpha Xi, Washington (MO)
1924 *Nu, Clark* (1969)
1924 *Omicron, New Hampshire* (1962)
1925 *Rho, Richmond* (1972)
1925 *Tau, Lehigh* (1933)
1926 Alpha Omicron, Arizona (1969-1983)
1927 *Alpha Pi, North Carolina* (1985)
1927 Alpha Rho, UCLA
1927 *Chi, Trinity* (1929)
1927 Phi, Duquesne
1927 *Tau, William and Mary* (1954)
1927 *Upsilon, West Virginia* (1978)
1928 *Alpha Nu, Tennessee* (1969)
1928 Alpha Theta, South Carolina
1929 Alpha Beta, Temple
1930 *Alpha Gamma, Wayne State (MI)* (1970)
1930 *Alpha Lambda, Detroit* (1942)
1931 *Alpha Tau, Franklin and Marshall* (1988)
1932 Alpha Nu, Muhlenberg
1932 *Bemta Kappa, Arkansas* (1955)
1933 Kappa Phi, Alfred
1935 *Alpha Epsilon, Duke* (1971)
1935 *Alpha Sigma, Mississippi* (1985)
1936 Alpha Phi, Miami (OH) (1974-1989)
1937 *Alpha Epsilon, St. John's (MD)* (1947)
1938 *Alpha Zeta, St. John's (NY)* (1959)
1938 *Phi, Vermont* (1969)
1941 *Alpha Theta, Washington (MD)* (1942)
1942 Alpha Chi, British Columbia (1970-1979)
1942 *Alpha Iota, Kentucky* (1973)
1943 *Alpha Rho, Ohio* (1969)
1946 Alpha Omega, Miami (FL)
1946 Alpha Psi, Penn State (1971-1988)
1947 Beta Delta, Rutgers
1947 *Beta Epsilon, Michigan State* (1971)
1947 Beta Gamma, Indiana
1947 *Delta Beta, Connecticut* (1969)
1948 *Alpha Zeta, Florida* (1987)
1948 Beta Eta, Bowling Green
1948 *Beta Theta, Manitoba* (1972)
1949 *Beta Iota, Minnesota* (1970)
1950 *Alpha Chi, Nebraska, Omaha* (1955)
1951 Beta Lambda, San Diego State (1968-1988)
1952 *Alpha Eta, Colorado State* (1975)
1955 *Alpha Kappa, Utah* (1961)
1956 *Alpha Omicron, Pratt* (1971)
1956 *Beta Alpha, Houston* (1966)
1957 Alpha Kappa, Lehman

1957 *Alpha Mu, Massachusetts* (1972)
1957 Beta Mu, Rider
1958 *Beta Nu, Johns Hopkins* (1990)
1960 *Beta Pi, Cal State, Long Beach* (1975)
1960 Beta Xi, CUNY, Brooklyn (1973-1990)
1961 *Beta Rho, N.Y.U., Square* (1972)
1961 *Beta Zeta, Philly Textiles* (1983)
1961 Rho Iota, Rhode Island
1962 Beta Phi, Pitt
1962 *Beta Upsilon, Youngstown State* (1979)
1963 *Beta Iota, Long Island* (1968)
1963 Beta Psi, American (1971-1984)
1963 Gamma Alpha, Washington and Jefferson
1964 Gamma Beta, Cal State, Northridge
1964 *Gamma Delta, C. W. Post* (1990)
1965 *Gamma Epsilon, Marshall* (1978)
1965 *Gamma Zeta, Louisville* (1972)
1966 *Alpha Phi, Parsons* (1972)
1966 *Beta Xi, Baruch* (1968)
1966 *Gamma Eta, Bradley* (1973)
1966 *Gamma Theta, Queens (NY)* (1973)
1967 *Gamma Iota, Western Michigan* (1971)
1967 *Gamma Kappa, Adelphi* (1972)
1967 Gamma Lambda, Hartford (1967-1985)
1967 *Gamma Mu, Memphis State* (1972)
1967 *Lambda, DePaul* (1927)
1968 *Beta Phi, West Chester* (1973)
1968 *Beta Tau, Widener* (1988)
1968 Gamma Nu, Cal State, Los Angeles
1968 *Gamma Omicron, Wisconsin, Milwaukee*
       (1972)
1968 Gamma Xi, Cal, Santa Barbara (1970-1985)
1968 *Zeta Tau, Seton Hall* (1989)
1969 *Beta Pi, Western New England* (1980)
1969 *Beta Psi, Drake* (1976)
1969 Gamma Beta, New Haven
1969 Gamma Chi, South Florida (1970-1986)
1969 *Gamma Omega, Northern Illinois* (1971)
1969 Gamma Phi, Hofstra
1969 *Gamma Psi, Northeastern* (1984)
1969 *Gamma Rho, Eastern New Mexico* (1972)
1969 *Gamma Sigma, Lamar* (1979)
1969 *Gamma Tau, Arizona State* (1972)
1969 *Gamma Upsilon, Northeast Louisiana*
       (1973)
1970 *Delta Alpha, Kent* (1971)
1970 *Delta Gamma, Oklahoma* (1972)
1970 *Delta Theta, Charleston (SC)* (1989)
1970 *Delta Zeta, Rutgers, Newark* (1972)
1971 *Delta Kappa, Calumet* (1986)
1971 Delta Lambda, Monmouth (IL)
1971 *Delta Mu, Wisconsin, Superior* (1973)
1971 *Delta Nu, Southampton* (1978)
1972 *Delta Iota, Wisconsin, Oshkosh* (1975)
1972 *Delta Omicron, Tampa* (1984)
1972 Delta Pi, Fairleigh Dickinson, Teaneck
1972 *Delta Xi, V.P.I.* (1983)
1973 *Delta Rho, Monmouth (NJ)* (1975)
1973 *Delta Sigma, Marquette* (1983)
1974 *Delta Tau, Carnegie-Mellon* (1985)
1974 *Delta Upsilon, Trenton* (1989)
1976 Delta Chi, Bentley

1976 Delta Omega, Babson
1976 *Delta Phi, LaSalle* (1982)
1977 Delta Psi, SUNY, Stony Brook
1978 *Epsilon Alpha, Oregon Tech* (1983)
1980 *Epsilon Zeta, Keene* (1985)
1980 Kappa Nu, San Francisco
1982 Epsilon Theta, Delaware
1983 *Epsilon Eta, Glassboro* (1989)
1983 *Epsilon Kappa, East Carolina* (1988)
1983 *Epsilon Lambda, North Carolina State* (1985)
1983 *Epsilon Omega, SUNY Col., Cortland* (1985)
1983 *Epsilon Sigma, William Paterson* (1988)
1984 Epsilon Mu, Kansas
1984 Epsilon Omicron, Fairleigh Dickinson, Rutherford
1984 Epsilon Tau, Fairleigh Dickinson, Madison
1985 Epsilon Beta, Cal, San Diego
1986 Epsilon Gamma, SUNY, Albany
1987 Epsilon Delta, SUNY, Binghamton
1987 Epsilon Iota, Hunter
1988 *Epsilon Nu, SUNY Col., Oneonta* (1989)
1988 *Epsilon Phi, Brandeis* (1989)
1989 Beta Alpha Chi, York (PA)
1989 Epsilon Chi, Cal, Davis
1989 Epsilon Psi, Montclair
1990 Zeta Alpha, Florida State
1990 Zeta Delta, Ramapo
1990 Zeta Gamma, Texas A & M

Zeta Psi

ACTIVE PIN

PLEDGE PIN

ZETA PSI, counting itself the eleventh of the national college fraternities in order of foundation, was the first to be founded at an urban university. On June 1, 1847, John B. Yates Sommers, aged 17, William Henry Dayton, 19, and John M. Skillman, 16, students at New York University, met in Sommers' home, 82 Madison Street, New York City, and established the "Alpha of New York," later called the Phi Chapter. Less than three months after the founding, Dayton, intending for health reasons to transfer to Chapel Hill, N.C., where his uncle was president of the university, died on his way there. Undaunted, Sommers and Skillman persevered and were fortunate in securing successors even more zealous than themselves in spreading the fraternity. The early propagation of the fraternity beyond New York is rich in lore. Within 10 years the chapter roll had been increased to 13 units of which all but three survive, five without interruption.

"The aim of the fraternity was and is to develop the member as a social being through intimate relations with a limited number of congenial friends who are bound together in an organization where loyalty, truth, honor, and fraternal affection are the guiding principles," runs a classical statement of the original purpose.

Growth Three periods of expansion may be distinguished. The initial burst of growth, slowed by the Civil War, culminated in two pioneering efforts, the first Greek-letter society chapters on the Pacific coast (University of California, 1870) and in Canada (University of Toronto, 1879). For the next 80 years, conservative growth characterized Zeta Psi with new charters averaging but two per decade.

In the quarter-century from 1960, 20 charters were granted, but this high rate is now expected to decline sharply as efforts are directed towards consolidation at a size conducive to internal cohesion. The chief criterion for the limited expansion of the forthcoming period will remain the stature of the college or university. Currently, the active chapter roll is balanced evenly between private and public institutions.

Extensive disruption was occasioned by the Civil War, when a number of chapters were compelled to suspend operations on account of enlistment of the members. The Brown, Union, North Carolina, and Pennsylvania (Gettysburg) chapters contributed nearly their entire personnel to the war. This stress and heroism have been the experience of wars since, but the imprint of the first, and most poignant, conflict in the fraternity history has never been effaced. The premiere Zeta Psi song recalls it.

Over a long history conditions inevitably change, from favorable to unfavorable and back again, often at the same location. The chapters at Princeton and Harvard are examples of the influence of the times. Highly prosperous in the early life of the fraternity, they finally succumbed to the anti-fraternity forces at those universities toward the end of the 19th century. Both these chapters have been revived in the favorable conditions of the 1980's. Despite its restrained expansion policy, Zeta Psi has always had a marked interest in reviving inactive chapters. This objective has been achieved in all the presently feasible ancient sites, including, in a unique accomplishment, the entire Ivy League.

The second oldest chapter, that at Williams, ceased activity in 1972 after it had operated as an "underground" chapter for a number of years following a ban on fraternities by the administration of Williams College in the mid-1960's. Of the 67 charters thought to have been given, 12 other than Williams' are inactive though only five of these 12 were active more than five years. Some of the remainder were of doubtful real existence.

In addition to its antiquity at Princeton, Harvard, Berkeley, and Toronto, Zeta Psi is the oldest fraternity at Tufts, Cornell, McGill, Case, Stanford, Manitoba, British Columbia, Alberta, and Calgary. The prominence of Canadian chapters in this list reflects the special influence of that country and its culture on the fraternity. Whether fortuitously or presciently, the official public name of the fraternity since well before the Toronto foundation has been "The Zeta Psi Fraternity of North America." This title embodies a sense of special obligation in linking the university men of Canada and the United States.

Government Each active chapter has seven traditional officers (in order of precedence: president, vice-president, secretary, corresponding secretary, treasurer, historian, and sergeant-at-arms), an executive committee ("Supreme Council"), and each has a corresponding elder chapter. Relations within these dual active/elder units are regulated by the international fraternity's bylaws, but the local organizations are expected to be self-sustaining and autonomous. They adopt their own supplementary bylaws. The International's criteria for membership have never been other than that the candidate be male and a student in good standing at the chartered institution.

The general organization of the fraternity was at first loose, without a centralized national organization. The business of the fraternity as a whole was carried on at annual conventions of the "Grand Chapter," composed of delegates from each local unit. The first of these was held at Williamstown, Massachusetts, in August, 1849. Since that year, conventions have been held annually, though sometimes abbreviated or dislocated due to wars.

Gradually, however, the loose national organization was strengthened. This movement reached a climax in 1910 when, through the immediate influence of William A. Comstock, Michigan '99, a centralized board of trustees was created with large powers. International headquarters were opened in New York City, and graduates were employed to keep in touch with the various chapters and carry on the work of the International.

The Board of Delegates of the Grand Chapter, consisting of the independent representatives of all the active and elder chapters and of the geographical elder associations, is the supreme governing authority. It elects Grand Officers who, with four other elected members, constitute an Executive Committee with substantial powers. This committee meets semi-annually. The Executive Committee's work is supplemented significantly by several other committees, made up of its members and others, appointed by the president of the Grand Chapter ("the Phi Alpha").

Traditions and Insignia The Zeta Psi badge is formed of a monogram of the two Greek letters Z and Ψ, the Z over the Ψ (1849). The Ψ is decorated with a star on the right arm and a Roman fasces on the left (1852); each of the three bars of the Z is set with seven gems, commonly pearls, but emeralds, rubies, or diamonds may be used. Above the lower bar of the Z is an A, and below the upper bar an O (1850). The color is white (1876). The flag is white with Z and Ψ in gold. The flower is the white carnation.

The pledge pin is a circular plain white button

with a narrow gold rim. An elaborate escutcheon, emblazoned in vivid colors and bearing prominently the letters ΤΚΦ, is widely used. These latter letters, employed so frequently that they seem a virtual second name of the fraternity, refer, in fact, to an esoteric motto. Chapters are named with one or two Greek letters without regard to alphabetical order.

A notable characteristic of recent years has been a revival of strong interest in and cultivation of the traditionally secret aspects of the fraternity and an assiduous performance of the demanding but beautiful ritual. Awards are made to members demonstrating by examination superior knowledge of these matters.

The nickname "Zete" goes far back into the 19th century and is the only term for members used in ordinary speech.

Publications As early as 1859, a formal catalogue of the fraternity was issued, and periodically thereafter formal rosters of membership appeared. The issue of 1899 was a compendious volume containing a brief biographical sketch of each member, even then a prodigious task. The most recent general directory was issued in 1987.

Monthly and quarterly magazines were published by private interests in the 1880's. In 1909 the fraternity itself undertook publication of a magazine, the *Circle*, which has continued without interruption.

Several songbooks have been published, the most recent in 1958. In 1927 a 700-page volume, the *Story of Zeta Psi*, appeared. It remains authoritative for the first 80 years. The pledge manual and guides for each of the chapter officers and usual committees are revised from time to time.

Funds and Philanthropies The Zeta Psi Educational Foundation was chartered by the State of New York in 1944. It is a public foundation under United States law. The parallel Zeta Psi Foundation of Canada is a charitable organization recognized by the Canadian federal government. These organizations award scholarships and bursaries to students, conduct leadership and other training seminars, and publish educational materials. While the local chapters are encouraged to sponsor and participate in charitable activities of all kinds, the international organization is confirmed in its proper and primary mission, the strengthening of the moral, spiritual, and social character of the men of the leading American and Canadian colleges and universities.

Headquarters 15 S. Henry Street, Pearl River, NY 10965. Phone: (914) 735-1847. A relocation to Westchester County, a northern suburb, followed the repeal in 1982 of a long-standing bylaw requiring the Central Office to be in the City of New York, the site of the founding.

Membership Total living membership 22,000. Total undergraduate membership 1,800. Active chapters 51. Inactive chapters 16. Houses owned 46. Graduate/Alumni chapters 53. City/Area alumni associations 7. Total number of initiates 46,100. Chapter roll:

1847 Phi, N.Y.U.
1848 Delta, Rutgers
1848 Zeta, Williams (1852-1881) (1982)
1850 *Chi, Colby* (1988)
1850 Omicron Epsilon, Princeton (1882-1983)
1850 Sigma, Penn
1852 *Alpha, Dickinson* (1871)
1852 *Epsilon, Brown* (1987)
1852 Rho Epsilon, Harvard (1892-1985)
1853 Psi Epsilon, Dartmouth (1864-1871) (1873-1920)
1855 Kappa, Tufts
1856 *Theta, Union (NY)* (1871)
1857 Tau, Lafayette
1858 *Pi, Amherst* (1859)
1858 Upsilon, North Carolina (1871-1885)
1858 Xi, Michigan
1861 *Eta, Pennsylvania College* (1872)
1861 *Gamma, Georgia Military Col.* (1865)
1864 *Omega, Chicago* (1887)
1865 Pi, R.P.I. (1893-1951)
1867 Lambda, Bowdoin
1868 Beta, Virginia (1881-1893)
1868 Psi, Cornell
1870 Iota, Cal, Berkeley
1874 *Gamma, Navy* (1874)
1875 Gamma, Syracuse (1887-1905)
1879 Alpha, Columbia (NY) (1936-1981)
1879 Theta Xi, Toronto
1883 Alpha Psi, McGill (1970-1978)
1884 Nu, Case Western Reserve
1889 Eta, Yale
1892 *Mu, Stanford* (1987)
1899 Alpha Beta, Minnesota (1982-1987)
1909 Alpha Epsilon, Illinois
1910 *Lambda Psi, Wisconsin, Madison* (1932)
1920 Phi Lambda, Washington (WA)
1921 Pi Epsilon, Manitoba
1924 Sigma Zeta, UCLA
1926 Sigma Epsilon, British Columbia (1970-1979)
1930 Mu Theta, Alberta
1938 *Alpha Mu, Dalhousie* (1971-1979) (1988)
1947 Omega, Northwestern
1947 Theta Phi, Western Ontario
1956 Rho, Middlebury
1958 Omicron, Nebraska Wesleyan
1960 Pi Sigma, Penn State
1960 Theta, Connecticut
1962 *Omicron Sigma, Oregon State* (1970)
1967 Chi Gamma, Calgary
1968 Tau Gamma, Purdue
1969 *Delta Chi, American* (1971)
1969 Pi Kappa, Bloomsburg
1970 Sigma Phi, Illinois, Chicago
1973 Tau Delta, Lehigh
1975 Alpha Pi, V.P.I.
1975 Upsilon Mu, Massachusetts
1976 Phi Epsilon, Maryland

1976 Pi Tau, Worcester Tech
1977 Beta Tau, Tulane
1979 Iota Alpha, Texas
1979 *Psi Zeta, Ohio State* (1983)
1979 Rho Alpha, M.I.T.
1981 Iota Delta, Cal, Davis
1984 Alpha Omega, Villanova
1984 Kappa Phi, Cooper Union
1990 Delta Alpha, Colorado
1991 Alpha Nu, Claremont College

NPHC Member Fraternities

Alpha Phi Alpha†

ACTIVE PIN

ALPHA PHI ALPHA, a fraternity originally established for Negro college men, was founded at Cornell University on December 4, 1906. It was the first intercollegiate Greek-letter fraternity in the United States established for Negro college men, but in recent years the designation "Negro" has been removed from its constitution and ritual. The fraternity is now interracial, with several white brothers taking active parts in the program. At the 40th general convention, held in Miami, Florida, December, 1954, a white brother delivered the undergraduate address, marking the first time a white brother had participated fully in the program of the convention.

The founders of the fraternity were: George B. Kelley, Henry A. Callis, Charles N. Chapman, Nathaniel A. Murray, Vertner W. Tandy, Robert H. Ogle, and Eugene Kinckle Jones, who were students at Cornell. The first idea was the establishment of a social study club in the school year of 1905–06.

The certificate of incorporation of the fraternity was filed and recorded in the office of the secretary of state of New York as Alpha Phi Alpha Fraternity on January 29, 1908. The fraternity was again incorporated on April 3, 1914, under the laws of the District of Columbia. The purpose and object of the fraternity was declared to be "educational and for the mutual uplift of its members."

In the constitution adopted on December 14, 1907, provision was made that, following the establishment of the fourth chapter of the fraternity, the general organization of the fraternity should be set up. This first general convention assembled on December 28, 1908, at Howard University, Washington, D.C. This convention expressed the hope that

† This chapter narrative is repeated from the 19th edition; no current information was provided.

"the influence of Alpha Phi Alpha would reach every Negro college and university in the land, to bring together under one band and with one bond of fraternal love all the worthy leading college men wherever found, to form, as it were, a link to join them together." The constitution, the ritual, and plans for expansion were drawn up. This and subsequent conventions have continuously exhorted chapters and members to remember that "manly deeds, scholarship, and love for all mankind" are the aims of the fraternity.

Growth In rapid succession chapters were established: Epsilon at the University of Michigan, Zeta at Yale University, and Eta at Columbia University in 1909. The next year the fraternity expanded with Theta at the University of Chicago, Iota at Syracuse University, and Kappa at Ohio State University.

National conventions were held first annually and then biennially, but within recent years a return has been made to annual meetings. Significant steps in the expansion and internal development were undertaken.

Traditions and Insignia The first World War made its impression upon the fraternity. Leaders in Alpha Phi Alpha began to plan for the leadership of college men in training officers for the army. Beta Chapter was the source of a movement which led to the establishment of an officers' training camp. The camp, ultimately established at Fort Des Moines, Iowa, was the result. By June 15, 1917, there were 58 brothers of the fraternity in the ranks of the officer trainees, a far larger representation than from any other fraternity or club.

In 1919, when new chapters had been established in various communities and colleges, a campaign known as "The Go-to-High-School, Go-to-College Movement" was inaugurated. This was regarded as one of the significant contributions of the fraternity in the education of Negroes in the United States.

A further campaign was inaugurated by the fraternity with the slogan, "Education and Citizenship." This campaign was conducted in order to acquaint Negroes with their rights as citizens and their responsibility to make use of these rights. This campaign was inaugurated at the 26th convention at St. Louis in 1933.

The economic condition of the Negro in the United States had been a serious consideration of the members of the fraternity for a number of years, and this resulted in the establishment in 1939 at the 27th general convention of a committee on employment opportunities for Negroes.

Alpha Phi Alpha has continued to broaden its program to keep up with the changing times. In the field of civil rights the fraternity has taken an active part starting with the Henderson case, the suit against the southern railroads to force removal of the jim crow curtain used in the dining cars to discriminate against Negroes. It has participated in many cases, fighting for first class education and

equal pay for all, as well as in the programs of the American Council on Human Rights, the NAACP, and other organizations with the same goal.

The 40th general convention, held in Miami, Florida, December, 1954, adopted the report given by Dr. Charles Wesley for the Committee on Human Relations entitled "Suggested Next Steps in School Integration." This report, published in book form and widely distributed over the country, deals with the historic decision of the U. S. Supreme Court and provides an avenue for the successful transition from a segregated to an integrated way of life.

The later years of the fraternity's history have been characterized by a growing evidence of a militant liberalism, a cooperation in anti-segregation activities, and progressive movements which have continued into the sixties. These movements were: the emphasis upon world brotherhood on the basis of the actions of leadership; Thirty-eighth General Convention and a joint convention of fraternities and sororities, Cleveland, 1952, with a united purpose toward Civil Rights goals; emphasis on human relations, racial integration, and the publication of the report on "Next Steps in School Integration"; the establishment of a National Headquarters; and the encouragement of Alpha men to become more active in public affairs in their communities. Recently Alpha Phi Alpha Fraternity, using the international theme of Brotherhood, conducted its 70th Anniversary Convention in New York City, New York (Phase I) and Monrovia, Liberia, West Africa (Phase II). This two-phase convention was a highlight in the history of Alpha.

The insignia of the fraternity are a shield and a badge. The design on the shield consists of a torch and a dove in the upper left-hand corner, fasces which run diagonally across from upper right to lower left, and a sphinx head in the lower right-hand corner. Beneath this emblem are the Greek letters AΦA. The badge is a pin with the letter Φ superimposed on the letters A and A, with seven jewels spaced in the center and along the upper lines. The colors of the fraternity are black and gold.

Publications The official organ of the fraternity is *The Sphinx*, launched in February, 1914, and published four times a year.

The history of the fraternity was published in 1929 in a bound volume of 294 pages with 59 illustrations. It was entitled *The History of Phi Alpha Alpha: A Development in Negro College Life*, by Dr. Charles H. Wesley, professor of history at Howard University, Washington, D.C. Subsequent editions followed.

Funds and Philanthropies The Alpha Phi Alpha Foundation was created in recognition of the increasing educational, economic, and social needs of the Negro people in the United States. This program was planned to make permanent the features of the older "Go-to-High-School, Go-to-College" Campaign and was to be conducted in addition to it. It was directed by a board of seven members. The budget of the foundation for the first two-year period was placed at $2,400. An annual fellowship of $900 was awarded for mature research and graduate study. Three annual scholarships were planned, to be awarded and allocated to the eastern, western, and southern jurisdictions. Thirty-seven members subscribed $100 each toward the establishment of the Alpha Phi Alpha Foundation. Its purposes are to assist in the encouragement, maintenance, and development of scholarship; to promote research; to aid in the publication of literary, scientific, and professional materials prepared by Negroes; and to foster a program of educational guidance and placement.

Headquarters 4433 Martin Luther King, Jr. Drive, Chicago, Illinois 60653.

Membership Active chapters 259. Inactive chapters 16. Graduate chapters 259. Total number of initiates 74,250. Chapter roll:††

Beta Psi, London (England) (1958)
1906	Alpha, Cornell
1907	Beta, Howard
1907	Gamma, Virginia Union
1909	Epsilon, Michigan
1909	Eta, Columbia
1909	*Zeta, Yale (1957)*
1910	Iota, Morris Brown
1910	Kappa, Ohio State
1910	Theta, Chicago
1912	Mu, Minnesota
1912	Nu, Lincoln (PA)
1912	Xi, Wilberforce
1913	Omicron, Pitt
1914	Pi, Western Reserve
1914	Rho, Temple
1915	Sigma, Boston
1917	Tau, Illinois
1917	Upsilon, Kansas
1919	Chi, Meharry Medical
1919	Phi, Ohio (1922-1950)
1920	Alpha Alpha, Cincinnati
1920	Psi, Penn
1921	Alpha Beta, Talladega
1921	Alpha Delta, U.S.C.
1921	*Alpha Gamma, Brown (1948)*
1921	Alpha Zeta, West Virginia State
1922	Alpha Epsilon, California
1922	Alpha Eta, Harris Teachers (MO)
1922	Alpha Iota, Denver
1922	*Alpha Kappa, Amherst (1949)*
1922	Alpha Mu, Northwestern
1922	*Alpha Nu, Iowa State (1949)*
1922	*Alpha Theta, Iowa (1948)*
1923	Alpha Omicron, Johnson C. Smith
1923	*Alpha Pi, Louisville (1960)*
1924	Alpha Rho, Morehouse
1925	Alpha Sigma, Wiley
1925	Alpha Tau, Akron

1926	Alpha Upsilon, Wayne State
1926	Beta Alpha, Morgan State
1926	Beta Gamma, Virginia State, Petersburg
1927	Alpha Chi, Fisk
1927	Alpha Phi, Clark Col., Atlanta
1927	*Beta Beta, Nebraska (1958)*
1929	Beta Delta, South Carolina State
1929	Beta Epsilon, North Carolina A & T
1929	Beta Zeta, North Carolina Teachers, Elizabeth City
1930	Alpha Psi, Lincoln (MO)
1932	Beta Kappa, Langston
1932	Beta Mu, Kentucky State
1932	Beta Nu, Florida A & M
1932	Beta Theta, Bluefield
1934	Beta Eta, Southern Illinois
1934	Beta Omicron, Tennessee A & I
1934	Beta Xi, LeMoyne-Owen
1935	Beta Iota, Winston-Salem Teachers
1936	Beta Pi, Lane
1936	Beta Rho, Shaw
1936	Beta Sigma, Southern
1936	*Beta Tau, Xavier (LA) (1955)*
1936	Beta Upsilon, Alabama State
1938	Beta Chi, Philander Smith
1938	Beta Phi, Dillard
1938	*Beta Psi, Oregon (1952)*
1939	*Alpha Xi, Washington (1958)*
1939	Delta, Huston-Tillotson
1941	Gamma Alpha, Texas Col
1941	Gamma Beta, North Carolina Central
1946	Gamma Delta, Arkansas A. M. & N.
1946	Gamma Epsilon, Wisconsin, Madison
1946	Gamma Gamma, Allen
1946	Gamma Zeta, Fort Valley
1947	Gamma Eta, Indiana
1947	Gamma Iota, Hampton Inst.
1947	Gamma Kappa, Miles
1947	Gamma Mu, Livingstone
1947	Gamma Nu, Penn State
1947	Gamma Omicron, Knoxville
1947	Gamma Pi, Benedict
1947	Gamma Theta, Dayton
1947	*Gamma Xi, UCLA (1959)*
1948	Delta Alpha, Claflin
1948	Delta Beta, Bethune-Cookman
1948	Delta Delta, Albany State
1948	Delta Gamma, Alabama A & M
1948	*Gamma Chi, Kansas State, Pittsburg (1953)*
1948	Gamma Phi, Tuskegee
1948	Gamma Psi, St. Augustine's
1948	Gamma Rho, Purdue
1948	Gamma Sigma, Delaware State
1948	Gamma Tau, Michigan State
1948	Gamma Upsilon, Tougaloo Southern Christian
1949	Delta Epsilon, Buffalo
1949	Delta Eta, Savannah
1949	*Delta Zeta, Syracuse (1952)*
1950	*Delta Iota, Rutgers (1960)*
1950	Delta Kappa, Alcorn
1950	*Delta Mu, Wichita (1961)*

†† This chapter roll is repeated from the 19th edition; no current information was provided.

1950	Delta Nu, Maryland, Eastern Shore
1950	Delta Theta, Texas Southern
1951	Delta Omicron, Stanford
1951	Delta Pi, Cheyney State
1951	Delta Xi, Central State (OH)
1952	Delta Rho, Rockhurst
1952	Delta Sigma, Grambling
1952	Delta Tau, St. Paul's
1953	Delta Chi, CUNY, Brooklyn
1953	Delta Phi, Jackson (MS)
1953	Delta Upsilon, Miami
1954	Delta Psi, Florida N & I
1954	Epsilon Alpha, Toledo
1957	Epsilon Beta, Cal State, Fresno
1957	Epsilon Delta, Kent
1957	Epsilon Gamma, Bishop
1958	Epsilon Epsilon, Oklahoma State
1959	Epsilon Eta, Eastern Michigan
1959	Epsilon Zeta, Fayetteville
1960	Epsilon Theta, Cleveland
1961	Epsilon Iota, Texas
1962	Epsilon Kappa, Bradley
1962	Epsilon Mu, San Jose
1962	Epsilon Nu, Stillman
1962	Epsilon Xi, Western Michigan
1963	Epsilon Omicron, Washburn
1963	Epsilon Pi, Virginia State, Norfolk
1963	Epsilon Rho, Lamar
1964	Epsilon Phi, Southern
1964	Epsilon Sigma, St. Mary's, San Antonio
1964	Epsilon Tau, Wisconsin, Milwaukee
1964	Epsilon Upsilon, Northern Illinois
1965	Epsilon Chi, Kentucky
1965	Epsilon Psi, Missouri, Rolla
1966	Zeta Alpha, Missouri
1966	Zeta Beta, Ferris
1966	Zeta Delta, Northern Michigan
1966	Zeta Gamma, Central Missouri State
1967	Zeta Epsilon, Barber-Scotia
1967	Zeta Zeta, Oklahoma
1968	Zeta Eta, Columbia
1968	Zeta Iota, Wisconsin, Whitewater
1968	Zeta Kappa, Texas, El Paso
1968	Zeta Mu, Georgia State
1968	Zeta Nu, Eastern Illinois
1968	Zeta Theta, Arizona
1968	Zeta Xi, Southwestern Louisiana
1969	Zeta Omicron, Murray State
1969	Zeta Pi, Georgia
1969	Zeta Rho, Indiana State
1970	Eta Alpha, Paine
1970	Eta Beta, Wisconsin, Platteville
1970	Eta Delta, Miami (FL)
1970	Eta Epsilon, North Texas
1970	Eta Gamma, Prairie View
1970	Zeta Chi, Texas, Arlington
1970	Zeta Phi, Mississippi Valley
1970	Zeta Psi, West Chester
1970	Zeta Sigma, Oklahoma, Edmond
1970	Zeta Tau, Texas, Commerce
1970	Zeta Upsilon, Northeastern (OK)
1971	Eta Eta, Western Illinois
1971	Eta Iota, Voorhees
1971	Eta Kappa, Louisiana Tech
1971	Eta Mu, Texas, Houston
1971	Eta Nu, East Carolina
1971	Eta Omicron, North Carolina State
1971	Eta Pi, Wisconsin, Oshkosh
1971	Eta Theta, East Central State
1971	Eta Xi, Detroit
1971	Eta Zeta, Bowie
1972	Eta Chi, Northeast Louisiana
1972	Eta Phi, Tennessee, Chattanooga
1972	Eta Psi, Texas Christian
1972	Eta Rho, Western Kentucky
1972	Eta Sigma, San Diego State
1972	Eta Tau, Illinois State
1972	Eta Upsilon, Texas Tech.
1972	Theta Alpha, Jarvis Christian
1972	Theta Beta, Columbus
1972	Theta Delta, South Alabama
1972	Theta Epsilon, Adelphi
1972	Theta Eta, Cal, Davis
1972	Theta Gamma, South Florida
1972	Theta Zeta, Dartmouth
1973	Iota Alpha, Washington and Lee
1973	Iota Beta, Virginia
1973	Iota Gamma, Rust
1973	Theta Chi, Northwestern Louisiana
1973	Theta Iota, V.P.I.
1973	Theta Kappa, Henderson
1973	Theta Mu, Sam Houston
1973	Theta Nu, South Carolina
1973	Theta Omicron, Millikin
1973	Theta Phi, L.S.U.
1973	Theta Pi, Austin Peay
1973	Theta Psi, State College of Arkansas
1973	Theta Rho, Virginia Commonwealth
1973	Theta Sigma, Florida
1973	Theta Tau, G.M.I.
1973	Theta Theta, McNeese
1973	Theta Upsilon, Arkansas State
1973	Theta Xi, Ball State
1974	Iota Chi, Redlands
1974	Iota Delta, Florida State
1974	Iota Epsilon, Grand Valley
1974	Iota Eta, Mercer
1974	Iota Iota, Trenton
1974	Iota Kappa, Paul Quinn
1974	Iota Mu, Stephen F. Austin
1974	Iota Nu, Alabama
1974	Iota Omicron, Southern Methodist
1974	Iota Phi, Mount Union
1974	Iota Pi, Southern Illinois, Edwardsville
1974	Iota Psi, Cal Poly, Pomona
1974	Iota Rho, New Jersey Tech.
1974	Iota Sigma, Millersville
1974	Iota Tau, Eastern Washington
1974	Iota Theta, St. Joseph's Calumet
1974	Iota Upsilon, Utah State
1974	Iota Xi, Northeast Missouri
1974	Iota Zeta, Maryland
1974	Kappa Alpha, Alabama
1974	Kappa Beta, Mississippi State

1975	Kappa Chi, Francis Marion
1975	Kappa Delta, Connecticut
1975	Kappa Epsilon, Cameron
1975	Kappa Eta, Memphis State
1975	Kappa Gamma, North Alabama
1975	Kappa Iota, Southern Arkansas
1975	Kappa Kappa, Arkansas
1975	Kappa Mu, Nicholls
1975	Kappa Nu, Southeastern Louisiana
1975	Kappa Omicron, Duke
1975	Kappa Phi, Liberia
1975	Kappa Pi, William and Mary
1975	Kappa Rho, C. W. Post
1975	Kappa Sigma, West Texas
1975	Kappa Tau, Kansas State
1975	Kappa Theta, Vanderbilt
1975	Kappa Upsilon, Edward Waters
1975	Kappa Xi, Middle Tennessee
1975	Kappa Zeta, Utica
1976	Kappa Psi, Arkansas, Little Rock
1976	Mu Alpha, Emory
1976	Mu Beta, Tennessee, Martin
1976	Mu Delta, Georgia Southwestern
1976	Mu Epsilon, Carthage
1976	Mu Eta, Arizona State
1976	Mu Gamma, Georgia Col
1976	Mu Iota, Tennessee
1976	Mu Kappa, Cal, Santa Barbara
1976	Mu Theta, West Florida
1976	Mu Zeta, North Carolina

Kappa Alpha Psi

See listing in the NIC Member Fraternities for history and chapter roll.

Omega Psi Phi†

ACTIVE PIN

OMEGA PSI PHI was founded at Howard University, Washington, D.C., on November 17, 1911, being the first Greek-letter organization for men on this campus. The founders—Edgar A. Love, Oscar J. Cooper, Frank Coleman, and Ernest E. Just—established the fraternity on a foundation of faith in the basic ethical standards and in the ultimate victory of right, and upon trust in the destiny of the Negro people. The bonds that existed among these founders were among the strongest bonds that bind, being based on religion, culture, and tradition. The faith of these founders has endured and has ad-

† This chapter narrative is repeated from the 19th edition; no current information was provided.

vanced a college fraternity that has benefited thousands of men who have followed the leadership during the past fifty years.

Government The government of the fraternity, between grand conclaves, is vested in the supreme council, elected by the grand conclave. The supreme council consists of the grand basileus, first vice-grand basileus, second vice-grand basileus, and the grand keeper of records and seal, the grand keeper of finance, the editor of *The Oracle*, the grand counselor, and the immediate outgoing grand basileus. The realm of the fraternity is divided into eleven districts with each district having a district representative responsible to the grand basileus.

The national meeting of the fraternity is known as the grand conclave and meets every eighteen months, December and August alternately. Meetings of the various districts are known as district conferences and are annual.

The housing authority of the fraternity has the power to purchase undergraduate housing at institutions of learning. Eight such houses are owned by the fraternity.

Development and Growth In 1949 the fraternity deleted from its constitution and ritual any reference to race, creed, or color, and it boasts of some 150 members of other than Negro descent.

Several national programs are sponsored. Achievement Week is observed by all chapters with public programs, radio and television shows dealing with the achievement of mankind. The National High School Essay Contest, open to high-school students throughout the country, is a part of Achievement Week. Cash prizes are offered for the three essays judged the best. The memorial service is designed to pay homage and respect to the departed brothers. The Social Action Program is designed to keep the chapters informed of public and local issues affecting civil rights. Under the Scholarship Program awards are made to worthy brothers for research and continued studies.

Traditions and Insignia The cardinal principles of the fraternity—Manhood, Scholarship, Perseverance, and Uplift—were adopted at the first initiation following the first meeting.

The badge of the fraternity is a small gold shield around the edge of which are pearls. On a purple enamel plate are gold letters ΩΨΦ. Above these is a star and below a Greek lamp. The fraternity colors are purple and gold.

Publications The official publication is *The Oracle*, published quarterly since its inception in 1919. Chapter letters are published monthly by the Office of the National Executive Secretary, and district news letters are published by the various districts.

Headquarters 2714 Georgia Avenue, N.W., Washington, D.C. 20001. In 1949 the fraternity established a national headquarters with fulltime executive secretary.

Membership   Active chapters 194. Graduate chapters 247. Chapter roll:††

1911	Alpha, Howard
1914	Beta, Lincoln
1916	Gamma, Boston
1919	Delta, Meharry Medical
1919	Epsilon, New York City
1919	Zeta, Virginia Union
1920	Mu, Philadelphia
1921	Gamma Psi, Talladega
1921	Nu, Penn State
1921	Rho, Johnson C. Smith
1922	Phi, Michigan
1922	Psi, Morehouse
1922	Tau, Atlanta
1922	Theta, Wiley
1922	Theta Psi, West Virginia State
1923	Beta Psi, Clark Col., Atlanta
1923	Delta Psi, Shaw
1923	Iota, Chicago
1923	Lambda, Los Angeles
1923	Pi, Morgan State
1923	Upsilon, Wilberforce
1924	Zeta Psi, CUNY, Brooklyn
1925	Epsilon Psi, San Francisco
1925	Eta Psi, Fisk
1926	Iota Psi, Ohio State
1926	Kappa Psi, Howard
1927	Lambda Psi, Livingstone
1927	Mu Psi, North Carolina A & T
1927	Nu Psi, Virginia State
1927	Xi Psi, South Carolina State
1928	Omicron Psi, Pitt
1928	Pi Psi, Illinois
1930	Rho Psi, Tennessee State
1932	Phi Psi, Langston
1932	Tau Psi, North Carolina College, Durham
1932	Upsilon Psi, Florida Normal
1933	Chi Psi, LeMoyne-Owen
1934	Psi Psi, Kentucky State
1935	Alpha Sigma, Morris Brown
1936	Beta Sigma, Southern
1936	Eta Sigma, Lincoln (MO)
1936	Gamma Sigma, Alabama A & M
1936	Theta Sigma, Dillard
1936	Zeta Sigma, Bluefield
1938	Lambda Sigma, Claflin
1938	Mu Sigma, Allen

†† This chapter roll is repeated from the 19th edition; no current information was provided.

1938	Nu Sigma, Wayne State
1940	Kappa Sigma, Lane
1942	Pi Sigma, Philander Smith
1942	Rho Sigma, Purdue
1942	Sigma Sigma, Texas Col
1942	Tau Sigma, Arkansas A. M. & N.
1946	Beta Epsilon, Knoxville
1946	Upsilon Sigma, Fort Valley
1947	Epsilon Epsilon, Benedict
1947	Eta Epsilon, Miles
1947	Gamma Epsilon, Hampton Inst.
1947	Iota Epsilon, Cincinnati
1947	Kappa Epsilon, St. Augustine's
1947	Lambda Epsilon, Tuskegee
1947	Theta Epsilon, Brown
1947	Zeta Epsilon, Indiana
1948	Mu Epsilon, Winston-Salem Teachers
1948	Nu Epsilon, Alabama A & M
1948	Omicron Epsilon, Bethune-Cookman
1948	Pi Epsilon, Maryland State
1948	Rho Epsilon, Tougaloo
1948	Tau Epsilon, Texas Southern
1949	Alpha Gamma, Savannah
1949	Chi Epsilon, Albany State
1949	Phi Epsilon, Buffalo
1949	Psi Epsilon, Delaware State
1949	Upsilon Epsilon, Jackson (MS)
1950	Alpha Psi, Huston-Tillotson
1950	Beta Gamma, Cheyney State
1950	Eta, Alcorn A & M (MS)
1951	Delta Gamma, Fayetteville
1951	Epsilon Gamma, St. Paul's
1951	Eta Gamma, Central State (OH)
1951	Gamma Gamma, Grambling
1951	Zeta Gamma, Youngstown State
1952	Iota Gamma, Cal State, Fresno
1952	Theta Gamma, Ypsilanti
1954	Kappa Gamma, Florida Normal
1954	Lambda Gamma, Elizabeth City
1955	Omicron Sigma, St. Louis
1957	Mu Gamma, Bishop
1959	Nu Gamma, Detroit Tech
1961	Chi, Edward Waters
1961	Sigma, Michigan State
1962	Omicron Gamma, D. C. Teachers
1962	Pi Gamma, Virginia State, Norfolk
1962	Xi Gamma, San Jose
1963	Rho Gamma, Stillman
1965	Sigma Gamma, New Mexico
1965	Tau Gamma, Illinois Southern

COAT OF ARMS

Phi Beta Sigma

ACTIVE PIN

PHI BETA SIGMA Fraternity, Inc. was founded at Howard University, January 9, 1914 by A. Langston Taylor, Leonard F. Morse and Charles I. Brown.

These African American males, felt the need of embracing the principles of brotherhood, scholarship and service which are crystallized and expressed in the Fraternity's Motto "Culture for Service and Service for Humanity."

Three illustrious members of the Phi Beta Sigma Fraternity, Inc. are among African Americans the U.S. Postal Services has honored with commemorative stamps, A. Phillip Randolph, Founder of the Brotherhood of sleeping car porters, a member of the Executive Board of AFL-CIO.

James Weldon Johnson, first African American admitted to the state bar in Florida after the Civil War and the collaborated with his Brother in writing "Life Every Voice and Sing," which has become widely known as the Black National Anthem.

Dr. Alain Leroy Locke, a philosopher, author, professor, and social critic became the first black Rhodes Scholar in 1907.

Dr. George Washington Carver, perhaps the greatest American Botanist invented over 100 products from the peanut and sweet potato. Born into slavery as a child, he single-handedly rejuvenated the agricultural systems of the South.

Growth The Fraternity has a honorary chapter, the Distinguished Service Chapter, to which members are elected on the basis of their achievements either scholastically or through community and national service and distinction.

Government Government is by the biennial conclave. During the interim between conclave, the authority is vested in the General Board, and the business of the organization is carried on through the National Headquarters Office of the National Executive Director.

Traditions and Insignia The fraternity sponsors three major programs: Bigger and Better Business, inaugurated in 1925 for the purpose of encouraging the idea of thrift among minority groups and of stimulating the establishment and expansion of small business enterprises; Social Action, organized in 1945 for the purpose of securing and protecting the civil liberties and human rights

of minority groups; Education, a program instituted with the founding of the fraternity, designed to encourage scholarship among all students. The official badge of the fraternity is a monogram made of three Greek letters ΦΒΣ with twelve pearls set in the Φ. The colors are blue and white. The flower is the white carnation.

Since our founding in January 9, 1914, we have expanded through the establishment of a National Educational Foundation, Inc., National Housing Foundation, Inc., National Outreach Foundation, Inc., and Federally-Chartered Credit Union.

Publications *The Crescent,* the official Publication—Quarterly; Biennial—Newsletter—*The Crescent Extra.*

Headquarters 145 Kennedy Street, N.W., Washington, D.C. 20011, FAX (202) 882-1681, Telephone (202) 726-5424. National Executive Director, Dr. Lawrence Miller. National President, Carter D. Womack.

Membership Active chapters 371. Graduate Chapters 258. Total number of initiates 90,000. Chapter roll:

Alpha, Howard
Alpha Alpha, Wilberforce
Alpha Alpha Alpha, Virginia State, Norfolk
Alpha Alpha Beta, Chicago State
Alpha Alpha Gamma, Lock Haven
Alpha Alpha Xi, SUNY, Binghamton
Alpha Beta, Jackson (MS)
Alpha Delta, CUNY, Brooklyn
Alpha Epsilon, Johnson C. Smith
Alpha Eta, Florida A & M
Alpha Gamma, Fisk
Alpha Iota, Bluefield
Alpha Kappa, Tillotson
Alpha Lambda, Xavier (OH)
Alpha Mu, Maryland, Eastern Shore
Alpha Omicron, Allen
Alpha Pi, Fort Valley
Alpha Rho, Austin Peay
Alpha Theta, West Virginia State
Alpha Upsilon, Inglewood, CA
Alpha Zeta, Alcorn
Beta, Wiley
Beta Alpha, Boston Citywide
Beta Chi, Lincoln (MO)
Beta Delta, Texas Southern
Beta Epsilon, Langston
Beta Eta, Knoxville
Beta Gamma, Hampton Inst.
Beta Iota, University of Buffalo
Beta Kappa, Tuskegee
Beta Lambda, CUNY, Brooklyn
Beta Mu, Benedict
Beta Nu, Cleveland
Beta Omicron, Seattle
Beta Phi, Texas
Beta Pi, Florida Institute
Beta Psi, Albany State
Beta Rho, Tougaloo

Beta Tau, Oakland
Beta Theta, Arkansas, Pine Bluff
Beta Upsilon, Bethune-Cookman
Beta Xi, St. Augustine's
Beta Zeta, LeMoyne-Owen
Chi, Morehouse
Delta, Kansas State
Delta Alpha, Winston-Salem
Delta Beta, Cal State, Hayward
Delta Chi, Eastern Illinois
Delta Delta, Coppin
Delta Epsilon, Lane
Delta Eta, Southern
Delta Gamma, UCLA
Delta Iota, Virginia College, Lynchburg
Delta Kappa, Michigan State
Delta Lambda, Redlands
Delta Mu, Bowie
Delta Nu, Memphis State
Delta Omicron, Ohio State
Delta Phi, Mississippi Valley
Delta Pi, Selma
Delta Psi, Baltimore Citywide
Delta Rho, Michigan
Delta Tau, Southern Illinois
Delta Theta, Prairie View
Delta Upsilon, Richmond
Delta Xi, York (PA)
Delta Zeta, Norfolk
Epsilon, Temple
Epsilon Alpha, Dillard
Epsilon Beta, Paine
Epsilon Chi, Illinois State
Epsilon Delta, Miami (FL)
Epsilon Epsilon, Kent
Epsilon Eta, Southern
Epsilon Gamma, Northern Illinois
Epsilon Iota, Indiana
Epsilon Kappa, Pitt
Epsilon Lambda, Central Missouri State
Epsilon Mu, Michigan, Flint
Epsilon Nu, Lamar
Epsilon Omicron, Ohio
Epsilon Phi, Bowling Green
Epsilon Pi, Southern Illinois, Edwardsville
Epsilon Psi, Maryland
Epsilon Rho, McIntoch, Alabama
Epsilon Tau, Talladega
Epsilon Theta, Western Kentucky
Epsilon Upsilon, Stephen F. Austin
Epsilon Xi, Illinois
Epsilon Zeta, Jarvis Christian
Eta, North Carolina A & T
Eta Alpha, South Carolina State
Eta Beta, Mississippi
Eta Delta, Furman
Eta Epsilon, Alabama
Eta Gamma, Missouri
Eta Zeta, East Texas
Gamma, Morgan State
Gamma Beta, Alabama State
Gamma Chi, Stillman

Gamma Delta, Denver
Gamma Epsilon, Alabama A & M
Gamma Eta, Harris-Stowe
Gamma Gamma, North Carolina Central
Gamma Iota, Wayne State (MI)
Gamma Kappa, Paul Quinn
Gamma Lambda, District of Columbia
Gamma Mu, Bishop
Gamma Nu, Wichita
Gamma Omicron, Cheyney State
Gamma Pi, Edward Waters
Gamma Psi, Rust
Gamma Rho, Elizabeth City
Gamma Tau, St. Petersburg
Gamma Theta, Atlanta
Gamma Upsilon, Delaware State
Gamma Xi, Cal State, Fresno
Gamma Zeta, Savannah
Iota, Shaw
Iota Alpha, Chicago Metropolitan
Iota Beta, Akron
Iota Chi, Western Illinois
Iota Delta, Eastern Kentucky
Iota Epsilon, Saginaw Valley
Iota Eta, Lewis
Iota Gamma, Bucknell
Iota Iota, Southern Louisiana
Iota Kappa, Washington (MO)
Iota Lambda, New Orleans
Iota Mu, Middle Tennessee
Iota Nu, Northwestern
Iota Omicron, Johns Hopkins
Iota Phi, Rochester Tech
Iota Pi, Central Arkansas
Iota Psi, Northern Colorado
Iota Rho, Central Florida
Iota Tau, L.S.U.
Iota Theta, Dayton
Iota Upsilon, Brown
Iota Xi, SUNY Col., Geneseo
Iota Zeta, Morris
Kappa, Meharry Medical
Kappa Alpha, Cal State, Northridge
Kappa Beta, Frostburg
Kappa Chi, Tennessee
Kappa Delta, Valdosta
Kappa Epsilon, Montclair
Kappa Eta, Delaware
Kappa Gamma, Simpson
Kappa Iota, South Carolina
Kappa Kappa, Northeast Louisiana
Kappa Lambda, Washington (WA)
Kappa Mu, Mansfield
Kappa Nu, Catonsville Comm. Col.
Kappa Omicron, Tennessee, Martin
Kappa Phi, Coker
Kappa Pi, Evansville
Kappa Psi, Iowa
Kappa Rho, Wisconsin, Madison
Kappa Tau, Southern Methodist
Kappa Theta, Northwood (MI)
Kappa Upsilon, Arkansas

Kappa Xi, Cornell
Kappa Zeta, Auburn
Lambda, Virginia Union
Lambda Alpha, Kansas City Osteopathic
Lambda Beta, Ball State
Lambda Chi, Upsala
Lambda Delta, Wisconsin, La Crosse
Lambda Epsilon, Toledo
Lambda Eta, State (AR)
Lambda Gamma, Central Michigan
Lambda Iota, San Diego U.
Lambda Kappa, Cal, Davis
Lambda Lambda, Penn State
Lambda Mu, Indiana (PA)
Lambda Nu, Massachusetts
Lambda Omicron, Illinois Wesleyan
Lambda Phi, SUNY Col., Old Westbury
Lambda Pi, Central State (OK)
Lambda Psi, Charleston (SC)
Lambda Rho, St. John's (NY)
Lambda Tau, Florida International
Lambda Theta, Cincinnati
Lambda Upsilon, West Chester
Lambda Xi, Arizona State
Lambda Zeta, Arkansas, Monticello
Mu, Lincoln (PA)
Mu Alpha, Fitchburg
Mu Beta, Central Connecticut
Mu Chi, Winthrop
Mu Delta, SUNY, Stony Brook
Mu Epsilon, Florida State
Mu Eta, Sangamon
Mu Gamma, Nashville State
Mu Iota, SUNY, Albany
Mu Kappa, Livingston
Mu Lambda, San Jose
Mu Mu, Colorado
Mu Nu, V.P.I.
Mu Omicron, Richmond
Mu Phi, Mobile
Mu Pi, Kean (NJ)
Mu Psi, Rutgers
Mu Rho, Texas
Mu Tau, Northeast Missouri
Mu Theta, Kentucky
Mu Upsilon, LaSalle
Mu Xi, Cal State, San Bernadino
Mu Zeta, Rutgers
Nu, Central State (OH)
Nu Alpha, Nicholls
Nu Beta, Georgia Tech
Nu Chi, Winthrop
Nu Delta, UCLA
Nu Epsilon, Capital
Nu Eta, William Paterson
Nu Gamma, Grand Valley
Nu Iota, Pembroke
Nu Kappa, C. W. Post
Nu Lambda, Adelphi
Nu Mu, Allegheny
Nu Nu, Lawrence Tech
Nu Omicron, Kingsville, TX

Nu Phi, West Georgia
Nu Pi, Amarillo
Nu Psi, Wagner
Nu Rho, SUNY Col., Purchase
Nu Theta, Presbyterian
Nu Upsilon, UCLA
Nu Xi, Colorado State
Nu Zeta, Baylor
Omicron, Clafin
Omicron Alpha, Utica
Omicron Chi, Tulane
Omicron Delta, SUNY Col., Brockport
Omicron Epsilon, SUNY Col., New Paltz
Omicron Eta, Cal State, Sacramento
Omicron Gamma, Iona
Omicron Iota, Old Dominion
Omicron Kappa, South Carolina, Sumter
Omicron Lambda, Clemson
Omicron Nu, Ponchatoula, Louisiana
Omicron Omicron, Oakland
Omicron Phi, Loyola, Chicago
Omicron Pi, Cal Poly, San Luis Obispo
Omicron Psi, Cal, Berkeley
Omicron Rho, Longwood
Omicron Tau, Texas, El Paso
Omicron Theta, Southern Connecticut
Omicron Upsilon, Vincennes
Omicron Xi, Murray State
Omicron Zeta, San Francisco State
Phi, Philander Smith
Pi, Fayetteville
Pi Alpha, Georgia State
Pi Beta, East Stroudsburg
Pi Chi, Francis Marion
Pi Delta, Cal State, Chico
Pi Epsilon, Southwest Georgia
Pi Eta, Minnesota
Pi Gamma, California (PA)
Pi Iota, Baptist, Charleston
Pi Kappa, Jacksonville (AL)
Pi Lambda, Georgia Col
Pi Mu, Western Carolina
Pi Nu, Madison Col
Pi Omicron, Aurora
Pi Phi, Culver-Stockton
Pi Pi, Clarion
Pi Rho, Georgia Southern
Pi Tau, NY Tech-Central Iolip NY
Pi Theta, Queens (NY)
Pi Upsilon, Wisconsin, Madison
Pi Xi, Southwest Texas
Pi Zeta, Nevada, Las Vegas
Psi, Clark Col., Atlanta
Rho, Southern
Rho Alpha, DeVry Tech
Rho Beta, North Carolina, Greensboro
Rho Chi, Southwest Missouri
Rho Delta, Missouri Valley
Rho Epsilon, North Carolina, Wilmington
Rho Eta, Oregon
Rho Gamma, North Carolina, Charlotte
Rho Iota, Wichita

Rho Kappa, Loras
Rho Lambda, Georgia Col
Rho Mu, Citywide Miami, FL
Rho Nu, Indiana Tech
Rho Omicron, Indiana Tech
Rho Phi, Arkansas Baptist
Rho Pi, West Liberty
Rho Rho, Charleston (SC)
Rho Tau, George Mason
Rho Theta, West Virginia
Rho Upsilon, Marshall
Rho Xi, SUNY Col., Oswego
Rho Zeta, Radford
Sigma, Miles
Tau, Louisville
Theta, Tillotson
Theta Alpha, Henderson
Theta Beta, Wisconsin, Whitewater
Theta Chi, Texas, Arlington
Theta Delta, Alabama
Theta Epsilon, Monmouth (IL)
Theta Eta, Southern Mississippi
Theta Gamma, CCNY
Theta Iota, Mississippi State
Theta Kappa, Salisbury
Theta Lambda, Pace
Theta Mu, Milwaukee Engineering
Theta Nu, Southern Arkansas
Theta Omicron, Towson
Theta Phi, Niagara
Theta Pi, Louisiana Tech
Theta Psi, Glassboro
Theta Rho, Sam Houston
Theta Tau, Montgomery
Theta Theta, Mississippi Industrial
Theta Upsilon, Cal State, Fullerton
Theta Xi, Syracuse
Theta Zeta, Columbus
Upsilon, Livingstone
Xi, Grambling
Xi Alpha, Baruch
Xi Beta, Delta State
Xi Chi, Millersville
Xi Delta, Oklahoma
Xi Epsilon, Long Island
Xi Eta, McNeese
Xi Gamma, North Carolina
Xi Iota, Southeast Missouri
Xi Kappa, Houston
Xi Lambda, Kentucky State
Xi Mu, Stillwater, OK
Xi Nu, East Carolina
Xi Omicron, Fairleigh Dickinson, Rutherford
Xi Phi, Southeastern Louisiana
Xi Pi, Trenton
Xi Psi, SUNY Col. Tech, Farmingdale
Xi Rho, St. Paul's
Xi Tau, Jersey City
Xi Theta, New Jersey Tech.
Xi Upsilon, Tennessee, Chattanooga
Xi Xi, Barber-Scotia
Xi Zeta, North Carolina State

Zeta, Morris Brown
Zeta Alpha, Tennessee State
Zeta Beta, North Texas
Zeta Chi, Boston U.
Zeta Delta, Western Michigan
Zeta Epsilon, Eastern Michigan
Zeta Eta, Virginia
Zeta Gamma, Voorhees
Zeta Iota, Northwestern Louisiana
Zeta Kappa, Florida
Zeta Lambda, Connecticut
Zeta Mu, Bradley
Zeta Nu, Georgia
Zeta Omicron, Kansas
Zeta Phi, Purdue
Zeta Pi, Loyola Marymount, Los Angeles
Zeta Psi, Indiana State
Zeta Rho, Mainland
Zeta Tau, Cal State, Long Beach
Zeta Theta, Ferris
Zeta Upsilon, Maryland, Baltimore County
Zeta Xi, South Florida
Zeta Zeta, Houston

Other Men's National Fraternities

Delta Phi Kappa[†]

DELTA PHI KAPPA first made its appearance in 1869 as a debating society on the campus of the University of Deseret (now University of Utah). It was known as Delta Phi and its chief sponsor was John R. Park, the president of the University. Activity ceased about the time the University of Utah moved to its present site in 1900.

During the autumn of 1920, two or three returned missionaries attending the University saw the need of holding the missionaries together in their religious ideals. Calling upon John A. Widtsoe, president of the University, they were given hearty approval to organize a club which at first they termed the Friars. The founding date is November 24, 1920.

On April 29, 1927, chapters of the society were established at Weber College in Ogden and the Utah State Agricultural College in Logan. A group at Brigham Young University was installed in January, 1929. By then the Friars Club was the largest collegiate organization in the state.

The linking step between the original Delta Phi and the Friars Club was taken in April, 1931, when the two organizations amalgamated. The name Delta Phi was selected because Greek letters form the nomenclature of practically all national fraternities, and because much of the richness in tradition and ideals associated with the old Delta Phi

† This chapter narrative is repeated from the 19th edition; no current information was provided.

could be utilized. The original Delta Phi was the oldest of western college fraternities. The name was changed to Delta Phi Kappa in January, 1962, so that the society would not be confused with the Delta Phi established as the third member of the Union triad in 1827.

Government The authority of the fraternity is invested in the National Council, composed of national president, executive vice-president, first national vice-president, national tribune, executive secretary, historian, editor, and the elected delegates from each active and alumni chapter. Two regular National Council meetings are scheduled each year.

Traditions and Insignia Members are charged to keep ever paramount in their lives "the high and worthy ideals of manhood which become a servant of the Master." They are to encourage scholarship and a search for truth. While a member does not have to belong to the Latter Day Saints Church, he must have done six months service as a missionary, exclusive of other activities, for a Christian denomination, or be a student of divinity at a recognized school of divinity, and have done religious service which is the equivalent of six months exclusive missionary work. It is the worthy goal of members to support the LDS Institute program and to provide for church service opportunities.

The official pin consists of a fourteen-carat yellow gold French shield, the face of which is enameled black, except for the border and the Greek letters ΔΦΚ, which are placed on the shield immediately below the center. A four-cornered star of eighteen-carat white gold, set with a white sapphire, is superimposed upon the face of the shield directly above the center. A partially concealed Latin cross of the same gold as the shield protrudes above the shield in the upper right corner and below the shield to the left of the lower point. The center of the crosspiece of the cross is set with a reconstructed ruby. A chain hangs from the top of the cross to the bottom of the shield.

The coat of arms consists of a large shield mounted with jeweled four-cornered star. The shield is divided into portions by a wide band with a French shield in the center. Behind the French shield is a partially concealed Latin cross from upper right to lower left, and superimposed on it is a lighted urn. The upper portion of the large shield is crossed by horizontal parallel bars upon which is placed a fasces. The large shield rests upon a scroll upon which, to the left of the point, is placed the Greek Δ and to the right of the point the Greek Φ.

The colors are white (as significant of purity) and green (as significant of growth). Two songs are "Delta Phi Song" and "Dream Girl of Delta Phi."

Publications The *Clarion* is published three times a year as the official journal and is distributed without charge to all undergraduate and alumni members. It is the duty of the national historian to prepare and keep current a book of history

of the fraternity and a scrapbook of items of Delta Phi Kappa interest.

Funds and Philanthropies The John A. Widtsoe Scholarship Foundation was established in 1953 following the death of the founder. As originally instituted, a scholarship of $200 each year is to be given to a student who has completed his freshman year; another $200 scholarship is given to a student who has completed the lower division courses; and a third scholarship of $500 is given to a graduate returned missionary to assist him to carry forward his graduate studies.

In April, 1949, the fraternity established the Delta Phi Holding Corporation for the purpose of collecting and legally controlling money and property which the fraternity has accumulated.

Membership Active chapters 3. Inactive chapters 5. Chapter roll:††

1920 *Utah* (1975)
1927 Utah State
1927 *Weber* (1965)
1929 *Brigham Young* (1976)
1949 Ricks
1951 *Arizona State* (1955)
1965 Southern Utah
1966 *Idaho State*

Sigma Beta Kappa†

SIGMA BETA KAPPA was founded in 1943 at St. Bernard's College, St. Bernard's, Alabama, for the purpose of instilling a strong sense of Christian morality and to create a solid basis of true friendship among a group of students there. The founder is Father Louis Funk, Benedictine priest who for many years served on the faculty. St. Bernard's, the birthplace of the fraternity, has since become inactive.

Traditions and Insignia Sigma Beta Kappa is a Catholic social fraternity, but has extended the hand of brotherhood to men of every race and creed. According to the national constitution one-half of the charter members of any chapter must profess the Roman Catholic faith. However, there can be no applicant refused admission solely because of color or religious belief. Also by constitutional edict, each chapter must adopt a secondary purpose; namely, some form of Catholic action. As a result, most chapters have volunteered their services to a neighboring orphanage, or needy organization. No active participation in any religious functions are required of any non-Catholic brother, but the fraternity strongly urges interest in his particular church activities.

†† This chapter roll is repeated from the 19th edition; no current information was provided.
† This chapter narrative is repeated from the 19th edition; no current information was provided.

Motto, *Esse Quam Videri (To be rather than seem to be)*.

Membership　Active chapters 3. Inactive chapters 5. Total number of initiates 15,800. Chapter roll:††

1943　*St. Bernard's (AL)*
1945　*Catholic* (1964)
1947　LaSalle
1948　*Manhattan*
1948　*St. Francis (PA)* (1957)
1953　Merrimack
1958　St. Michael's (NM)
1960　*St. Norbert* (1976)

Sigma Gamma Chi

SIGMA GAMMA CHI was founded November 4, 1967, in Salt Lake City. It is sponsored by the Church of Jesus Christ of Latter-day Saints, to serve young men on campuses in the western part of the United States. The first officers were E. La-Mar Buckner, president; A. Carlisle Hunsaker, vice-president; and William Rolfe Kerr, executive secretary.

Sigma Gamma Chi is a social and service fraternity dedicated to promoting *brotherhood, service, spirituality, leadership, scholarship,* and *patriotism* in its members. Membership is open to all college men, regardless of race, creed, or color, who are willing to live the ideals and standards set forth in the constitution and by-laws.

Traditions and Insignia　The pin or "crimson shield" is a representation of the "Whole armor of God" spoken of by Paul the apostle. It consists of the shield of faith (an oval shield of crimson and gold), having on it the helmet of salvation (a warrior's helmet in gold), the sword of the Spirit (a silver sword), and the breastplate of righteousness (a white breast-plate with the Greek letters ΣΓΧ in gold). The colors are blue, gold, and crimson. The motto is, service to God and Country.

Publications　*The Sword and Shield*, reference manual; *The Bulletin*, quarterly publication: and *Songs of Sigma Gamma Chi*.

Headquarters　50 East North Temple, 8th floor, Salt Lake City, Utah 84150.

Membership　Active chapters 20. Total number of initiates 5,000. Chapter roll:††

Arizona State
Dixie (UT)
Eastern Utah
El Camino Junior
Idaho State
L.D.S. Business (UT)
Mesa Community (AZ)
Northern Arizona
Riverside (CA)
San Bernardino Valley
Southern Utah
Utah State
Utah Tech, Provo
Utah Tech, Salt Lake City
Utah
Weber
Wyoming

†† This chapter roll is repeated from the 19th edition; no current information was provided.

Part IV

The Womens Fraternities

NPC Member Fraternities (Sororities)

COAT OF ARMS

Alpha Chi Omega

ACTIVE PIN

PLEDGE PIN

ALPHA CHI OMEGA was founded at DePauw University, October 15, 1885, by seven undergraduate founders, all music students, assisted by Professor James Hamilton Howe, dean of the School of Music, and Dr. James G. Campbell, a member of Beta Theta Pi. The charter members were: Anna Allen (Smith); Olive Burnett (Clark), Bertha Deniston (Cunningham), Amy DuBois (Reith), Nellie Gamble (Childe), Bessie Grooms (Keenan), and Estelle Leonard.

Since its beginning Alpha Chi Omega has maintained an unusual interest in the fine arts. Although Alpha Chi Omega has always been a social and never a professional fraternity, music was regarded as the particular muse of members throughout the early years. Until 1915 *The Constitution* required that a certain percentage of the members be studying music in some form. To date Alpha Chi Omega has enjoyed 100 years of sisterhood; her members continue to support the allied arts while pursuing their own individual interests.

Growth Growth through extension has always been a top priority for Alpha Chi Omega. Within six years of the founding of its Alpha chapter, three more chapters had been established at Albion College in Michigan, Northwestern University in Illinois, and Allegheny College in Pennsylvania. In 1895 the major step of establishing a chapter on the west coast was taken. The Epsilon chapter at the University of Southern California made Alpha Chi Omega a truly national fraternity. The first 24 chapters were named in the order of the Greek alphabet and are referred to as the "single letter chapters." Of these, only one is inactive—Zeta, at the New England Conservatory of Music. It was closed to comply with the NPC ruling that chapters of a member group could only be present at four-year institutions of higher learning.

Government Since 1887 when the second chapter was established, supreme power has been vested in the national convention. Alpha chapter at DePauw University acted as the governing body between national assemblies until 1896. At that time the constitutional form was adopted whereby the convention became the governing body. It is composed of one delegate from each collegiate chapter, one from each alumnae chapter, the Province Collegiate Chairmen, the Province Alumnae Chairmen, Past National Presidents and current members of the National Council. Since Alpha Chi Omega is a collegiate-based organization, votes at the national convention are weighted so that those representing the collegiate field will always be in the majority. The national convention meet biennially.

In the interim between national conventions, the administration of the fraternity is vested in the National Council, which is composed of six members, elected by the national convention delegates. They are the national president, national vice president alumnae, national vice president collegians, national vice president finance, national vice president membership and national vice president secretary. The National Panhellenic conference delegate and the executive director attend National

Council meetings with voice but no vote. National Council meetings are held triannually.

A governmental system of dividing the country into geographical areas called provinces was adopted in 1912 to relieve the National Council of some of its growing duties. Each area elects a province alumnae chairman and a province collegiate chairman. The province collegiate chairmen visit and counsel the collegiate chapters in their area. They serve under the direction of the three directors of collegians. The province alumnae chairmen visit alumnae chapters and clubs within the province promoting alumnae support for the collegiate chapters and for the fraternity at large. They serve under the direction of the three directors of alumnae. Other directors include: directors of alumnae, and collegiate, and financial programming; director of colonizations; director of extension; directors of finance; director of housing; and director of rush.

Traditions and Insignia Among special Alpha Chi days are Founders' Day, October 15, celebrated by all collegiate and alumnae groups; Hera Day (named for the Greek goddess, Hera), observed on March 1 as a day to be set aside by every member "for personal service to the needy and lonely."

Alpha Chi Omega was the first collegiate fraternity to require the attainment of a scholastic average for initiation; it was also the first to appoint alumnae advisors to collegiate chapters. Both of these innovations have now long been required by all the members of the National Panhellenic Conference.

The badge is a Grecian lyre, jeweled in pearls or diamonds, displaying the letters AXΩ on a scroll placed diagonally across the strings. The colors are scarlet and olive green. The flower is the scarlet carnation with smilax. The pledge pin is diamond-shaped, half red and half olive green enamel, with a gold outline of the lyre superimposed.

In 1910 the honor pin (Hera head) was adopted as a token of appreciation by the fraternity to National Council members who had served one full term. A similar honor was accorded province collegiate and province alumnae chairmen in 1945 when a special service pin was adopted for them. The recognition pin is a tiny gold lyrebird or the three Greek letters in gold.

The coat of arms, adopted in 1908, utilizes the symbols of the fraternity. It is crested by the lyrebird, and the scroll underneath the shield bears the fraternity's open motto in Greek—"Together let us seek the heights".

The Award of Achievement, to honor members who have distinguished themselves in their chosen fields or professions, is presented at national conventions as is the Alumnae Appreciation Award, presented in recognition of outstanding service to the fraternity on the local level.

Publications *The Lyre*, a quarterly magazine, was authorized by the national convention of 1894, and the first issue appeared that June. It has been published continuously since 1896. Membership in the fraternity includes a life subscription. *The Tri-Star Tribune* debuted in fall 1984, and is mailed to the membership in the fall and spring of each school year.

The Heraeum, a publication for members only, has been published since 1911. *The Constitution, Membership Manual, Policies and Procedures Manual,* and officer guides for collegiate and alumnae chapter officers are among other publications. A new edition of *The History of Alpha Chi Omega* was introduced at the 1985 Centennial Convention.

Funds and Philanthropies The Alpha Chi Omega Foundation, established in its present form in 1978, is the number one altruism of the fraternity. It is the fund raising arm of Alpha Chi Omega. Through contributions to the foundation by individual members, collegiate chapters, alumnae chapters and clubs, and other individuals and groups, a wide variety of altruisms are supported. Prominent among these is the first national philanthropy of Alpha Chi Omega, the MacDowell Colony at Peterborough, New Hampshire. This altruism in the field of creative arts was adopted in 1909. The MacDowell Colony was established in 1907 by Marian Nevins MacDowell in honor of her husband, Edward MacDowell, famous musician and composer. In 1911 Alpha Chi Omega built, and later endowed, a studio at this colony retreat for artists in all fields. In addition, an annual fellowship has also been given since 1935 to make it possible for some young person of proven ability to work in his or her art at any one of the colony's studios. The Fay Barnaby Kent Fellowship Fund, established in 1961, makes several additional awards available annually.

The Alpha Chi Omega Foundation also supports aid to handicapped children through contributions to the National Easter Seal Society for Crippled Children and Adults and to the Cystic Fibrosis Foundation.

One of the main activities of the Foundation is the funding and awarding of a large variety of fellowships and scholarships. These include the Hannah Keenan Undergraduate Scholarships, named for Alpha Chi Omega's past Executive Secretary of 30 years, the daughter of Founder Bessie Grooms Keenan. Numerous other undergraduate scholarships have been endowed by individual alumnae and by alumnae groups. Fellowships are available for graduate study in the fields of fine arts, law, social service and for the pursuit of a Masters or Doctors degree. A Revolving Student Loan Fund is available at a low rate of interest to graduate and undergraduate members of Alpha Chi Omega; the Estelle McFarlane Dunkle Loan Fund lends money without interest to juniors and seniors in need of financial assistance. The Continuing Education for Women Grants are intended to help women over 30 years of age who wish to continue or update their education because of the changing demands on their lives. Alpha Chi Omega believes that by thus providing the finances for the educational needs of outstanding women we contribute to the creation of a better world. The foundation also provides financial assistance to members of the fraternity in their later years if they are in need. This is done through gifts from the Olive Burnett Clark Alumnae Fund available to members over 60 years of age.

Quite apart from the Foundation, the Fraternity itself maintains the Alta Allen Loud Clearinghouse Fund from which collegiate chapters may borrow to build or remodel chapter houses.

Headquarters Alpha Chi Omega National Headquarters is located at 8335 Allison Pointe Trail, #200, Indianapolis, IN 46250-1686. Phone: (317) 579-5050. The building serves as the business office for both the fraternity and the foundation, as well as the meeting facility for committees of both entities. Professional personnel for the fraternity includes the executive director, administrative services director, collegiate services director, financial services director, public relations director and thirteen other staff members. The foundation maintains a staff consisting of a development director and three other staff members. The fraternity field staff includes collegiate field consultants and area collegiate consultants and the National Headquarters serves as their home base.

The headquarters building also houses living quarters for visiting officers, kitchen facilities and a conference room. Although a headquarters building was not purchased until 1960, Alpha Chi Omega has maintained a central business office since 1919; it has been located in Indianapolis since 1929.

Membership Total living membership 102,300. Total undergraduate membership 8,679. Active chapters 134. Inactive chapters 30. Colonies 2. Houses owned 88. Graduate/Alumni chapters 94. City/Area alumni associations 131, Total number of initiates 133,786. Chapter roll:

1885	Alpha, DePauw
1887	Beta, Albion
1890	Gamma, Northwestern
1891	Delta, Allegheny
1895	Epsilon, USC
1895	*Zeta, New England Conservatory* (1950)
1898	Eta, Bucknell
1898	Theta, Michigan
1899	Iota, Illinois
1903	Kappa, Wisconsin, Madison
1906	Lambda, Syracuse
1907	Mu, Simpson
1907	Nu, Colorado (1973-1979)
1907	Omicron, Baker
1907	Xi, Nebraska
1909	Pi, Cal, Berkeley (1972-1977)
1910	Rho, Washington (WA)
1911	Sigma, Iowa
1911	Tau, Brenau
1913	Upsilon, Millikin
1914	Phi, Kansas
1915	Chi, Oregon State
1916	Omega, Washington State

1916	Psi, Oklahoma
1918	Alpha Beta, Purdue
1918	Alpha Gamma, New Mexico
1919	Alpha Delta, Cincinnati
1919	Alpha Epsilon, Penn (1969-1989)
1920	Alpha Eta, Mount Union
1920	Alpha Zeta, Washington (MO) (1975-1985)
1921	Alpha Iota, Vermont
1921	Alpha Kappa, Oregon
1921	Alpha Lambda, Minnesota
1921	*Alpha Theta, Drake* (1933)
1922	Alpha Mu, Indiana
1922	Alpha Nu, Missouri
1923	Alpha Omicron, Ohio State
1923	Alpha Pi, North Dakota (1938-1968)
1923	*Alpha Xi, Montana* (1952)
1924	Alpha Phi, Texas
1924	*Alpha Rho, Idaho* (1988)
1924	*Alpha Sigma, Ohio Wesleyan* (1977)
1924	Alpha Tau, New Hampshire
1924	Alpha Upsilon, Alabama
1925	Alpha Chi, Butler
1926	Alpha Omega, Birmingham-Southern
1926	Alpha Psi, UCLA
1926	*Beta Gamma, L.S.U.* (1970)
1927	Beta Delta, William and Mary
1928	Beta Epsilon, Michigan State
1928	*Beta Zeta, Whitman* (1983)
1929	Beta Eta, Florida State
1930	*Beta Iota, Toronto* (1953)
1930	*Beta Kappa, Wyoming* (1979)
1930	Beta Lambda, Arizona (1969-1981)
1930	*Beta Theta, Lawrence* (1980)
1932	Beta Mu, Penn State
1934	Beta Nu, Utah
1934	Beta Xi, Utah State
1936	Beta Omicron, Florida Southern
1937	Beta Pi, Washington (MD)
1937	Beta Rho, American
1938	Beta Sigma, Georgia
1941	Beta Tau, Miami (OH)
1942	*Beta Upsilon, Duke* (1976)
1944	Beta Chi, Willamette
1944	Beta Phi, Bowling Green
1944	Beta Psi, Louisiana Tech
1945	Beta Omega, Toledo
1946	*Gamma Delta, Denver* (1987)
1947	Gamma Epsilon, Oklahoma State
1947	Gamma Zeta, Kansas State
1948	*Gamma Eta, San Jose* (1974)
1948	Gamma Theta, Maryland
1949	Gamma Iota, Florida
1950	*Gamma Kappa, Idaho State* (1984)
1950	*Gamma Lambda, Kent* (1973)
1950	Gamma Mu, Ball State
1950	Gamma Nu, San Diego State
1951	Gamma Xi, Western Michigan
1952	Gamma Omicron, Marshall
1954	Gamma Pi, Tampa (1977-1982)
1954	Gamma Rho, Texas Tech.
1955	Gamma Sigma, Rhode Island
1955	Gamma Tau, Oklahoma City (1979-1988)

1956	Gamma Phi, Lamar	
1956	Gamma Upsilon, Houston	
1957	Gamma Chi, Stetson	
1958	Delta Epsilon, Southeast Missouri	
1958	Delta Zeta, Central Michigan	
1958	*Gamma Omega, Miami (FL)* (1970)	
1958	*Gamma Psi, Wichita* (1984)	
1959	*Delta Eta, Queens (NC)* (1965)	
1959	*Delta Iota, Emory* (1988)	
1959	Delta Kappa, Sam Houston	
1959	Delta Lambda, Ripon	
1959	*Delta Theta, Maine* (1988)	
1961	Delta Mu, Massachusetts	
1961	Delta Nu, Iowa State	
1961	Delta Omicron, Portland	
1961	Delta Pi, Tennessee	
1961	*Delta Rho, Arkansas* (1977)	
1961	Delta Xi, Denison (1969-1986)	
1962	Delta Sigma, Pacific (CA)	
1965	Delta Chi, William Woods	
1965	*Delta Phi, Texas A & I* (1978)	
1965	Delta Psi, Cal, Santa Barbara	
1965	Delta Tau, Mankato	
1965	Delta Upsilon, Colorado State	
1966	*Delta Omega, Kentucky* (1976)	
1967	Epsilon Eta, Stephen F. Austin	
1967	Epsilon Theta, Cal State, Sacramento	
1967	Epsilon Zeta, Auburn	
1968	*Epsilon Iota, Northern Iowa* (1987)	
1968	Epsilon Kappa, Cal State, Fullerton	
1969	Epsilon Lambda, Texas, Arlington	
1970	*Epsilon Mu, Northern Illinois* (1974)	
1970	Epsilon Nu, Boise	
1971	Epsilon Omicron, Indiana State	
1971	Epsilon Xi, Nevada	
1972	*Epsilon Pi, Georgia Southwestern* (1987)	
1972	Epsilon Rho, Delaware	
1973	*Epsilon Sigma, Central Florida* (1984)	
1973	*Epsilon Tau, V.P.I.* (1974)	
1974	*Epsilon Upsilon, Mississippi State* (1984)	
1975	Epsilon Phi, Georgia Tech	
1977	Epsilon Chi, North Carolina	
1977	Epsilon Psi, Cal, Irvine	
1978	Epsilon Omega, Cal Poly, San Luis Obispo	
1978	Zeta Eta, Bradley	
1979	*Zeta Iota, Stanford* (1982)	
1979	Zeta Kappa, New Mexico State	
1979	Zeta Theta, Brown	
1980	Zeta Lambda, Virginia	
1980	Zeta Mu, Dartmouth	
1981	Zeta Nu, Texas A & M	
1982	Zeta Omicron, Vanderbilt	
1982	Zeta Pi, Arizona State	
1982	Zeta Xi, North Carolina, Greensboro	
1983	Zeta Rho, Northwood (MI)	
1983	Zeta Sigma, Southwest Missouri	
1983	Zeta Tau, Villanova	
1983	Zeta Upsilon, Case Western Reserve	
1984	Zeta Chi, Muhlenberg	
1984	Zeta Phi, Cornell	
1984	Zeta Psi, Loyola, New Orleans	
1985	Theta Iota, Baylor	

1985	Theta Kappa, Memphis State
1985	Theta Lambda, Clemson
1985	Theta Mu, Eastern Montana
1985	Zeta Omega, Western Carolina
1986	Theta Nu, Santa Clara
1986	Theta Omicron, M.I.T.
1986	Theta Pi, Cal, Davis
1986	Theta Xi, Cal State, Northridge
1987	Theta Rho, Madison Col
1987	Theta Sigma, North Florida
1988	Theta Phi, Colgate
1988	Theta Tau, Rutgers
1988	Theta Upsilon, South Carolina
1989	Theta Chi, Lehigh
1989	Theta Omega, Marquette
1989	Theta Psi, Columbia (NY)
1990	Iota Kappa, Eastern Kentucky

Colonies: Texas Christian, Cal, San Diego

Alpha Delta Pi

COAT OF ARMS

ACTIVE PIN

PLEDGE PIN

ALPHA DELTA PI, as the first secret sisterhood for college women, had its birthplace at Wesleyan Female College, Macon, Georgia, oldest women's college in the world and the first of such institutions to grant academic degrees to women.

On May 15, 1851, 19 young women as charter members organized this secret group under the name Adelphean Society, and the organization has continued to function without interruption down through the years to the present time. From its inception it possessed all of the attributes of such secret orders including ritual, badge, motto, grip, and password, and its membership was highly selective. From the day of its founding, the fraternity has been bound by the covenant that only girls could be taken into the membership who "may commend themselves for their intellectual and moral worth, dignity of character, and propriety of deportment." There was also a scholastic requirement.

The founders' group, organized by Eugenia Tucker (Fitzgerald), included 19 young women. The other members were: Octavia Andrew (Rush), two of whose great granddaughters are now members of Alpha Delta Pi, Ann Burkhalter (Colquitt), Octavia Douglass (Fell), Maria J. Easterling, Mary Evans (Glass), Mary Everett (Fenn), Mary Finn (Hawkins), Josephine Freeman, Oceana Goodall (Pollard), Mary Harris (Jarrell), Anna L. Jeffers, Julia Jones (Ross), Ella Pierce (Turner), whose great granddaughter also is a member, Sara Simms (Comer), Mary J. Snow, Mary M. Tucker, Elizabeth Williams (Mitchell), and Sophronia Woodruff (Dews). Eugenia Tucker Fitzgerald was elected president and outlived all of the founders, her death occurring in January, 1929. These Adelphean founders chose as open motto for the society, "we live for each other," and their avowed purpose was that of bettering themselves "morally, mentally, and socially." Their first badge was a white satin riband, consisting of a bar with streamers. On one end was the name Adelphean, on the other end the design of clasped hands, and in the center the motto, "We live for each other." Within the first year this was replaced by a silver badge and then a gold one, diamond-shaped, which bore the name Adelphean Society, the motto, the clasped hands, and two stars. Except for slight modifications and change in size, this badge has come down unchanged to the present membership.

A replica of the original room at Wesleyan was maintained in the Old Conservatory building until the fall of 1962 when Wesleyan College, now moved to a new location outside the city of Macon, sold its old properties to the government for a post office site. The room has been reassembled and is now on display in the Sidney Lanier chapter house, United Daughters of the Confederacy, in Macon, as a tribute to the founding of Alpha Delta Pi and the beginning of the sorority system. Beautiful antique furnishings, many of them from the original meeting room, have been used in this Adelphean Room where handsome portraits of the various founders also are displayed, as well as original badges.

Growth It was not until August, 1904, that a policy of expansion was adopted, and the original unit of the society therefore became Alpha Chapter. Accordingly, the organization was incorporated under the laws of Georgia as the Adelphean Society, and in July, 1905, it amended its charter "by inserting after its name wherever it occurs in said charter, as a symbol for said name, the following Greek letters, ΑΔΦ." In 1913 the name was changed to Alpha Delta Pi.

Anti-fraternity rulings by the faculties at Wesleyan, Winston-Salem, and Mary Baldwin resulted in the inactive status of these first three chapters. Chapters have been formed in two ways, from strong pre-existing locals or through careful colonization.

Government The supreme power is vested in its biennial convention where collegiate chapters have the balance of power. The Grand Council is the governing board between conventions. Members of this council, elected at convention, include the grand president, an executive officer; three grand vice presidents of collegiate chapters; the grand vice president of alumnae; the grand secretary; and the grand treasurer. These elected officers appoint the National Panhellenic Conference delegate who is the eighth member of Grand Council.

Geographically there are 34 province presidents each of whom directs the affairs within her province, generally consisting of three to five collegiate chapters. Regional alumnae supervisors direct the work of 300 alumnae associations under the guidance of the grand vice president of alumnae. Further, each state and each Canadian province has a membership chairman who works in both collegiate and alumnae fields.

A number of standing committee chairmen further carry out the work of the sorority.

Wherever property is held by a chapter, a Corporation is formed under the laws of that state.

Traditions and Insignia Alpha Delta Pi's World War II program is a source of traditional pride. While hundreds of members donned the uniforms of the various armed services, the fraternity's home-front effort was equally determined. When the Thumbs Up campaign for British War Relief was inaugurated long before Pearl Harbor, Alpha Delta Pi's war service program marched step by step with the changing needs of the conflict. From the maintenance of an ambulance to assist blitz victims in Great Britain, the national effort turned to the making and filling of thousands of Red Cross kit bags as the United States entered the fight and American service men embarked for foreign shores. With the return of early wounded, gift boxes for convalescent veterans were filled and distributed in military hospitals all over the country. When the advance of American armies brought certainty of eventual victory, thought turned to rehabilitation of returning servicemen. Both undergraduate chapters and alumnae groups concentrated their efforts upon aid for hospitalized and handicapped veterans, with special emphasis upon individual community needs rather than a centralized program.

Many of the traditions and much of the ritual of Alpha Delta Pi are the same today as in 1851. The pledge itself has come down through the years almost unchanged.

The badge is a diamond of black enamel displaying, along the longest diagonal, clasped hands on each side of which is a star, and beneath are the letters ΑΔΠ. The pledge pin is a bar of gold bearing the Greek letters ΒΥΑ, surmounted by the lion head.

The fraternity has two official recognition pins, one a miniature replica of the crest in gold, the other the interlocking Greek letters ΑΔΠ in gold. The colors are azure blue and white, and the flower is the single purple violet.

Publications Publications of the fraternity include *The Adelphean*, a quarterly magazine, established in 1907. A secret journal, known as the *Adelphean Chronicle*, was first published in 1851 in the handwriting of the various members. After a number of years, it was discontinued and was not revived until 1915, when it was issued by the national secretary. In the years from 1921 to 1923, it was issued from the office of the national president. Since the establishment of the Executive Office, it has been issued from that office regularly as a private bulletin to collegiate chapters and alumnae associations.

Alpha Delta Pi has various manuals which are of informational and instructional value. The *Golden*

Lion Pledge Book offers a modular type of study to the provisional members; and various other notebooks detail the operational procedures recommended for collegiate chapters and alumnae associations.

Three editions of sorority history have been published to date. Jessica North McDonald of Chicago compiled and wrote two historical surveys which were published in 1929 and revised in 1931. A third edition of history was compiled by Virginia Lee Nelson, former editor *The Adelphean*, and was published in two hard-bound volumes in 1965. A third hard-bound volume covering the years between 1965 and 1985 is being written by Maxine Blake, Grand President Emeritus.

Funds and Philanthropies The fraternity has three national funds of prominence. The 125th Anniversary Fund makes scholarships available for graduate as well as collegiate work for members who are willing to serve an Alpha Delta Pi chapter as a resident counselor. The Abigail Davis Student Loan Fund is available to aid members in completing their undergraduate education. The Abigail Davis Student Loan Fund was named for a former national officer who had been instrumental in the growth of the fraternity; at the 1917 convention, the fund was established in her memory. On February 11, Miss Davis's birthday, collegiate chapters and alumnae groups throughout the fraternity each year give parties or other benefit affairs to swell this fund. The Building and Loan Fund is an available source of funds for chapters to build, renovate or redecorate their chapter houses, lodges or chapter rooms.

The Alpha Delta Pi Foundation, Inc., a Georgia non-profit corporation, was established in 1982. Five trustees manage the foundation. The purposes of the foundation include providing scholarships, loans and grants in aid to qualified and deserving Alpha Delta Pi collegians and alumnae as they complete or further their education; supporting charitable interests of Alpha Delta Pi such as Ronald McDonald Houses; and providing counseling to Alpha Delta Pi collegians and advisors in the areas of scholarship, leadership and citizen training, career development, and alcohol and drug abuse prevention. The Foundation grants a $1,000 undergraduate scholarship, a $2,000 graduate scholarship and a $1,000 continuing education scholarship each year, as well as administering a number of restricted funds from which scholarships are awarded to members of various chapters.

In 1979 Alpha Delta Pi officially adopted Ronald McDonald Houses as its service project. Ronald McDonald Houses provide a unique opportunity for collegians and alumnae to help children throughout the United States and Canada. There are over 70 Ronald McDonald Houses which provide temporary lodging for families of critically-ill, hospitalized children in a home-like atmosphere. Since Alpha Delta Pi's support began, sorority members have contributed more than $100,000 a year to these fa-

cilities. In addition to contributing dollars for building and maintaining the houses, Alpha Delta Pi members give time. They staff the houses as volunteers: answering the telephone, admitting families, cleaning, repairing, babysitting, and helping out as they can. With a wealth of love and assistance from Alpha Delta Pi, in addition to civic clubs, businesses and other concerned volunteers, Ronald McDonald Houses continue to open throughout North America and the world as secure havens for special children and their loved ones.

Leadership conferences are held for collegiate delegates in the years between conventions.

Headquarters Alpha Delta Pi Memorial Headquarters Building, 1386 Ponce De Leon Avenue North East, Atlanta, Georgia 30306. This beautiful structure, which houses the Executive Office and sorority historical materials, was formally dedicated in the spring of 1955. Beautifully furnished in the Georgian era, it provides social space for local events as well as meeting rooms for official conferences and Grand Council meetings. Of special interest is the Archives Room with its display of memorabilia of interest to the entire fraternity world.

The Executive Office when first established in 1925 was directed by an executive secretary, whose duties were those of secretary-treasurer, registrar, and business manager of *The Adelphean*. It was first located in Ames, Iowa, where it remained until 1934, when it was moved to Berkeley, California. From 1948 to June, 1954, the office was in Kansas City, Missouri.

Membership Total living membership 109,695. Total undergraduate membership approximately 12,00. Active chapters 134. Inactive chapters 51. Houses owned 55. Graduate/Alumni chapters 257. Total number of initiates 133,998. Chapter roll:

1851 *Alpha, Wesleyan (GA)* (1916)
1905 *Beta, Salem (NC)* (1909)
1906 Delta, Texas
1906 *Epsilon, Tulane* (1977)
1906 *Gamma, Mary Baldwin* (1910)
1907 Eta, Alabama (1910-1931)
1907 Zeta, Southwestern (TX)
1908 *Theta, Lawrence* (1969)
1909 Iota, Florida State
1910 Kappa, Samford
1910 Lambda, Brenau
1910 *Mu, Women's College (AL)* (1913)
1910 *Nu, Randolph, Macon* (1960)
1911 Omicron, Duke
1911 Pi, Iowa State
1911 Rho, Boston U. (1965-1987)
1912 Sigma, Illinois
1912 Tau, Kansas
1912 Upsilon, Washington State
1913 Chi, Wittenberg
1913 Phi, Hanover
1913 Psi, Cal, Berkeley
1914 *Alpha Alpha, Colorado* (1972-1981) (1985)

1914	*Omega, L.S.U.* (1985)
1914	Xi, Ohio
1915	Alpha Beta, Iowa
1915	*Alpha Delta, Colby* (1974)
1915	Alpha Epsilon, Nebraska (1934-1963)
1915	Alpha Eta, Kansas State
1915	Alpha Gamma, Missouri
1915	Alpha Zeta, Southern Methodist
1917	Alpha Theta, Washington (WA)
1920	Alpha Iota, Pitt (1943-1946)
1920	Alpha Kappa, Tennessee
1920	*Alpha Lambda, Oregon* (1986)
1920	*Alpha Mu, Wisconsin, Madison* (1934)
1920	*Alpha Nu, New Mexico* (1982)
1921	Alpha Omicron, Oklahoma State (1936-1939)
1921	Alpha Xi, Ohio State
1922	*Alpha Pi, George Washington* (1968)
1923	*Alpha Rho, Minnesota* (1987)
1923	*Alpha Sigma, Ohio Wesleyan* (1937-1949) (1967)
1924	*Alpha Tau, Syracuse* (1935-1946) (1971)
1924	*Alpha Upsilon, West Virginia* (1987)
1925	Alpha Chi, UCLA
1925	*Alpha Phi, Butler* (1933)
1925	Alpha Psi, USC
1926	Alpha Omega, Oregon State
1926	Beta Alpha, Indiana (1952-1984)
1926	Beta Beta, Tennessee, Chattanooga
1927	*Beta Delta, Hunter* (1964)
1927	*Beta Gamma, Utah* (1974)
1928	Beta Epsilon, South Carolina
1929	Beta Eta, Michigan
1929	*Beta Zeta, Toronto* (1943)
1930	Beta Theta, Manitoba
1931	Beta Iota, Queens (NC)
1931	Beta Kappa, British Columbia
1931	*Beta Lambda, CUNY, Brooklyn* (1972)
1932	*Beta Mu, Montana State* (1935)
1933	Beta Nu, Georgia
1933	*Beta Xi, Montana* (1943)
1935	*Beta Omicron, St. Lawrence* (1983)
1935	Beta Pi, Cincinnati
1936	*Beta Rho, Lake Forest* (1961)
1937	Beta Sigma, Mercer
1938	Beta Tau, Akron
1939	Beta Upsilon, North Carolina
1940	*Beta Chi, Queens (NY)* (1971)
1940	Beta Phi, Maryland
1941	Beta Psi, Kentucky
1942	Beta Omega, Auburn
1943	*Gamma Alpha, Connecticut* (1970)
1945	*Gamma Beta, Northwestern* (1971)
1946	Gamma Gamma, Florida Southern
1947	*Gamma Delta, Miami (FL)* (1976)
1947	Gamma Epsilon, Purdue
1947	Gamma Eta, Memphis State
1947	Gamma Theta, Mount Union
1947	*Gamma Zeta, Oklahoma* (1970)
1948	Gamma Iota, Florida
1948	Gamma Kappa, West Virginia Wesleyan
1948	Gamma Lambda, Rhode Island
1949	Gamma Mu, Southwest Missouri
1949	Gamma Nu, William Jewell
1950	Gamma Omicron, Susquehanna
1950	Gamma Pi, Wagner
1950	Gamma Rho, Arizona State
1950	Gamma Xi, Cal, Santa Barbara
1951	*Gamma Sigma, Bowling Green* (1990)
1951	Gamma Tau, Vermont
1953	Gamma Upsilon, North Texas
1954	Gamma Phi, East Tennessee
1955	Gamma Chi, Texas Christian
1956	Delta Beta, Lamar
1956	*Gamma Omega, Michigan State* (1978)
1956	*Gamma Psi, Houston* (1960)
1957	Delta Delta, Arkansas
1957	Delta Epsilon, Morningside
1957	Delta Gamma, Arizona
1958	Delta Eta, McNeese
1958	Delta Iota, Waynesburg
1958	*Delta Kappa, Penn State* (1975)
1958	*Delta Lambda, West Texas* (1984)
1958	Delta Theta, Valdosta
1958	*Delta Zeta, Wayne State (MI)* (1972)
1959	Delta Alpha, Emory
1959	Delta Mu, Sam Houston
1959	Delta Nu, Southeast Missouri
1959	*Delta Xi, Pittsburg State, Kansas* (1973)
1960	Delta Omicron, East Carolina
1960	Delta Pi, Ripon
1961	Delta Rho, Gettysburg
1961	Delta Sigma, Mississippi
1961	*Delta Tau, East Texas* (1982)
1961	Delta Upsilon, Tennessee, Martin
1962	Delta Chi, Northern Colorado
1962	Delta Phi, Missouri, Kansas City
1964	Delta Omega, Northern Illinois
1964	*Delta Psi, Eastern New Mexico* (1987)
1964	*Epsilon Alpha, Moorhead* (1984)
1965	*Epsilon Beta, Texas A & I* (1986)
1965	Epsilon Delta, Western Kentucky
1965	*Epsilon Gamma, Marquette* (1984)
1966	Epsilon Epsilon, Texas Tech.
1966	*Epsilon Eta, Mississippi State* (1983-1985) (1988)
1966	*Epsilon Iota, Indiana (PA)* (1975-1977) (1978)
1966	*Epsilon Theta, West Liberty* (1983)
1966	Epsilon Zeta, Southwest Texas
1967	Epsilon Kappa, Troy
1967	Epsilon Lambda, South Florida
1967	Epsilon Mu, Northern Iowa
1967	Epsilon Nu, Ashland
1968	Epsilon Omicron, Murray State
1968	Epsilon Pi, Georgia Southern
1968	Epsilon Rho, Nevada, Las Vegas
1968	*Epsilon Sigma, Maine* (1984)
1968	Epsilon Xi, Northern Arizona
1969	Epsilon Chi, Longwood
1969	Epsilon Omega, Jacksonville
1969	Epsilon Phi, Eastern Kentucky
1969	Epsilon Psi, Tennessee Tech.
1969	Epsilon Tau, Middle Tennessee

1969 *Epsilon Upsilon, Winona* (1984)
1970 Zeta Alpha, Cal State, Fullerton
1971 Zeta Beta, North Carolina State
1971 Zeta Delta, Montevallo
1971 Zeta Gamma, North Carolina, Charlotte
1972 Zeta Epsilon, West Florida
1972 *Zeta Zeta, Augusta* (1983)
1973 Zeta Eta, North Alabama
1973 Zeta Theta, Illinois State
1974 Zeta Iota, Georgia Col
1974 *Zeta Kappa, Radford* (1977)
1975 Zeta Lambda, Texas A & M
1975 Zeta Mu, Appalachian
1976 Zeta Nu, Clemson
1977 Zeta Omicron, Georgia Tech
1977 Zeta Pi, San Diego U
1977 Zeta Xi, Virginia
1978 Zeta Rho, Vanderbilt
1979 Zeta Sigma, Charleston (SC)
1979 Zeta Tau, Winthrop
1980 Zeta Chi, Baylor
1980 Zeta Phi, Francis Marion
1980 Zeta Upsilon, Oakland
1981 Zeta Psi, North Carolina, Greensboro
1982 Zeta Omega, Central Florida
1983 Eta Alpha, North Carolina, Wilmington
1983 Eta Beta, Allegheny
1983 Eta Delta, Southern Tech
1983 Eta Gamma, Austin Peay
1984 Eta Epsilon, Miami (OH)
1985 Eta Zeta, Southern Mississippi
1986 Eta Eta, South Dakota Mines
1987 Eta Lambda, Albright
1987 Eta Theta, North Carolina, Asheville
1988 Eta Iota, LaVerne
1988 Eta Kappa, Cal State, San Bernadino
1988 Eta Mu, Cal State, Sacramento
1988 Eta Nu, St. Louis
1990 Eta Omicron, Western Connecticut
1990 Eta Pi, V.P.I.
1990 Eta Rho, Cal State, Chico
1990 Eta Xi, Presbyterian

Alpha Epsilon Phi

ACTIVE PIN

PLEDGE PIN

ALPHA EPSILON PHI was founded at Barnard College on October 24, 1909, by Ida Beck, Lee Ries, Helen Phillips, Rose Salmowitz, Stella Straus, Rose Gerstein, and Augustina Hess. These young women decided to form their own social group to meet and discuss issues of common interest. With dedication to fellowship and intellectual growth, the seeds of Alpha Epsilon Phi were planted.

Growth Within a very short time, young women at other universities in the same geographical area approached this original group with the idea of forming similar chapters and maintaining a close relationship with this founding group of women at Barnard. New chapters sprung up across the country. By 1921, only 12 years later, Alpha Epsilon Phi had truly become a national organization as it had established chapters on the campuses of outstanding universities from coast to coast.

The ritual of Alpha Epsilon Phi has its foundations in the Old Testament. The Jewish founders of Alpha Epsilon Phi created an organization where members could be selected on the basis of fellowship, character, intelligence, personality, leadership ability, and other special talents.

Government National Conventions are held biennially, and province conclaves are scheduled in alternate years. The governing body is a National Council of nine members, elected for two-year terms. These sorors are elected by the convention body; no officer except the NPC representative may serve more than three consecutive terms in any one office on the council, nor can she serve more than 12 consecutive years on the council. However, the national president may serve more than 12 years to fulfill a six-year term. The convention body—composed of delegates from each collegiate and alumnae chapter, chapter advisors, province directors, national chairmen, and the National Council—may decide on such items of national business as have been brought before it according to the constitution and bylaws and the rules of the convention. The council makes policy and governs the sorority between conventions.

The chapters are divided geographically into provinces, each headed by a province director, who is responsible for annual chapter visitation and evaluation. Chapters have local alumnae advisory boards to guide them on a daily basis. The alumnae chapters may be formed by members of each chapter, and alumnae associations are established in cities where there are a number of alumnae from various chapters. A national alumnae association, Phi Ever Alums has been established for sorors who may not have access to an alumnae chapter or association. The Phi Connection is an alumnae network to assist alumnae as they establish themselves in new cities. The Talent Bank provides career assistance and resource information to sorors. All alumnae programming is under the supervision of the vice-president of alumnae, a National Council position. National chairmen, appointed by National Council, provide a resource to chapter officers in each area of chapter programming such as philanthropy, academic excellence, pledge education, rush, activities, ritual, house corporations, and heritage.

Traditions and Insignia The badge of Alpha Epsilon Phi displays the letters ΑΕΦ jeweled in pearls, arranged in even horizontal order on a narrow gold bar. The pledge pin is a facade of a Greek temple in gold. The recognition pin is the three letters slanted on a gold bar. The colony pin is a green and white diamond. The alumnae award for national service, a lily-of-the-valley engraved on a leaf-shaped gold disc, is given at each convention. The National Council pin is a brown enamel circle, bordered in pearls with the letters ΑΕΦ inscribed horizontally. Only initiated members may wear the Greek letters ΑΕΦ on jewelry and clothing. The colors are green and white, the flower is the lily-of-the-valley, and the jewel is the pearl.

Founders' Day is celebrated by each collegiate and alumnae chapter on October 24. In addition, each chapter commemorates its own birthday with a special event for its collegiate and alumnae members. Chapter and Alumnae awards are presented at each convention for excellence in academic performance, total programming, parents clubs, philanthropy, Panhellenic participation, and activities. In addition, the Blanche Z. Greenberger Award recognizes the outstanding collegiate member and the Dorothy Gribetz Shapiro Award recognizes an outstanding alumna member. Alpha Epsilon Phi gives special recognition to alumnae who have distinguished themselves in outstanding community service. In addition, the Susan Rudd Cohen Award recognizes a collegiate and an alumna for outstanding service in the Jewish community.

Publications The *Columns* has been published since 1917. It received a National Interfraternity Foundation award for excellence most recently in 1983. Other publications cover every facet of chapter operations and include a songbook, ready reference, pledge manual, "For Officers Only," chapter guide, rushing manual, house director's manual, national officer manual(s), "Let's Talk AEPhi," and regular office bulletins.

Funds and Philanthropies Each chapter is encouraged to raise funds and donate service to local community service projects of their choice. In addition, Chaim Sheba Medical Center in Israel was adopted as a national philan thropy in 1975. In the past 10 years, Alpha Epsilon Phi collegiates and alumnae have donated funds to fully equip three rehabilitation rooms at this outstanding non-denominational research and healing center.

The Alpha Epsilon Phi Foundation was incorporated in June, 1959, to channel gift-giving through this tax-free corporation. Scholarships are granted each year to collegiate and alumnae members of Alpha Epsilon Phi, as well as mature women students who return to the university campus to further their education and/or desire to change careers. The Phi-Delity Fund provides capital for educational development and programming within Alpha Epsilon Phi.

Headquarters 6100 Channingway Blvd., #302, Columbus, OH 43232.

Membership Total living membership 36,721. Total undergraduate membership 2,472. Active chapters 47. Inactive chapters 48. Colonies 1. Graduate/Alumni chapters 110. Total number of initiates 50,000. Chapter roll:

1909	*Alpha, Barnard* (1914)
1909	*Beta, Hunter* (1970)
1915	*Gamma, Columbia (NY)* (1917)
1916	Delta, Adelphi
1916	Epsilon, Tulane
1917	Eta, SUNY, Albany (1955-1985)
1917	*Theta, Penn* (1931-1959) (1970)
1917	Zeta, N.Y.U. (1970-1986)
1919	Iota, Syracuse
1920	Kappa, Cornell
1920	*Lambda, Denver* (1924)
1920	Mu, Illinois
1920	Nu, Pitt
1921	*Omicron, Northwestern* (1988)
1921	Pi, Michigan
1921	Rho, Ohio State
1921	Sigma, Wisconsin, Madison (1972-1983)
1921	Xi, USC (1985-1990)
1923	Tau, Cal, Berkeley
1924	Phi, UCLA
1924	*Upsilon, Akron* (1931)
1925	*Chi, Vanderbilt* (1965)
1925	Omega, Texas
1925	Psi, Washington (MO) (1934-1960)
1927	*Alpha Alpha, Toronto* (1955)
1929	Alpha Beta, Missouri
1930	Alpha Gamma, George Washington (1937-1959) (1970-1985)
1932	*Alpha Delta, Washington (WA)* (1987)
1934	Alpha Epsilon, Duke (1965-1975)
1937	*Alpha Zeta, Penn State* (1978)
1938	Alpha Eta, Miami (FL)
1938	*Alpha Iota, Minnesota* (1978)
1938	*Alpha Theta, L.S.U.* (1984)
1940	Alpha Kappa, Miami (OH) (1980-1986)
1940	Alpha Lambda, Arizona
1943	Alpha Mu, Maryland
1944	*Alpha Nu, Carnegie-Mellon* (1971)
1944	*Alpha Xi, Connecticut* (1970)
1945	*Alpha Omicron, Vermont* (1970)
1945	*Alpha Pi, South Carolina* (1949-1967) (1978)
1945	*Alpha Rho, Alabama* (1967)
1948	*Alpha Sigma, Tennessee* (1977)
1948	Alpha Tau, Florida
1948	*Alpha Upsilon, Purdue* (1951-1968) (1976)
1951	Alpha Chi, Boston U. (1974-1985)
1951	*Alpha Phi, Ohio* (1971-1981) (1984)
1952	*Alpha Omega, Drake* (1973)
1952	Alpha Psi, Colorado (1971-1990)
1952	*Epsilon Alpha, Michigan State* (1973)
1954	*Epsilon Beta, CUNY, Brooklyn* (1976)
1956	*Epsilon Delta, Queens (NY)* (1971)
1956	*Epsilon Gamma, Oklahoma* (1979)
1958	Epsilon Epsilon, Indiana
1958	*Epsilon Zeta, Arizona State* (1972)
1959	Epsilon Eta, Emory
1959	Epsilon Theta, American (1970-1987)
1962	*Epsilon Iota, N.Y.U.* (1965)
1962	*Epsilon Kappa, Rhode Island* (1965-1980) (1986)
1962	*Epsilon Lambda, Texas, El Paso* (1969)

1962   *Epsilon Mu, C. W. Post* (1972)
1964   *Epsilon Nu, San Diego U* (1971)
1965   *Epsilon Xi, Kent* (1970-1980) (1984)
1966   *Epsilon Omicron, CUNY, Brooklyn* (1971)
1966   *Epsilon Pi, Cal State, Long Beach* (1971)
1966   *Epsilon Rho, San Jose* (1968)
1968   *Epsilon Chi, Bradley* (1983)
1968   *Epsilon Phi, Iowa* (1974)
1968   *Epsilon Sigma, Cal State, Northridge* (1971)
1968   *Epsilon Tau, Cal, Santa Barbara* (1971)
1969   *Epsilon Omega, Southern Methodist* (1971)
1969   *Epsilon Psi, South Florida* (1979)
1969   *Phi Alpha, Eastern Michigan* (1972)
1969   *Phi Beta, Old Dominion* (1977)
1970   *Phi Gamma, Kansas* (1971)
1976   *Phi Delta, Florida State* (1979)
1980   Phi Epsilon, Cal, Davis
1982   Phi Eta, Jacksonville
1982   *Phi Zeta, Southern Illinois* (1989)
1984   Phi Iota, Hartford
1984   Phi Theta, Temple
1985   Phi Kappa, Glassboro
1985   Phi Lambda, SUNY, Buffalo
1985   Phi Mu, SUNY, Binghamton
1985   Phi Nu, SUNY Col., Oswego
1987   *Phi Omicron, York (ON)* (1990)
1987   Phi Pi, SUNY Col., Oneonta
1988   Phi Rho, Cleveland
1988   Phi Sigma, Wayne State (MI)
1988   Phi Tau, SUNY Col., Plattsburgh
1988   Phi Xi, Fairleigh Dickinson, Rutherford
1989   Phi Chi, Delaware
1989   Phi Phi, SUNY Col., New Paltz
1989   Phi Psi, Bridgeport
1989   Phi Upsilon, Hofstra
1990   Phi Omega, Northeastern

Colonies: Emerson

COAT OF ARMS

Alpha Gamma Delta

ACTIVE PIN

PLEDGE PIN

ALPHA GAMMA DELTA was founded on May 30, 1904, at Syracuse University by Jennie C. Titus, Marguerite Shepard, Estelle Shepard, Ethel Brown, Flora Knight, Georgia Otis, Emily H. Butterfield, Georgia Dickover, Mary Louise Snider, Edith MacConnell, and Grace Mosher, with the encouragement and guidance of Wellesley P. Coddington, professor of philosophy and a Greek scholar.

The Certificate of Incorporation was recorded in New York State on June 3, 1905. As stated at that time, the object of the corporation was "to perpetuate among a group of college women a spirit of mutual assistance and understanding; to maintain high standards of scholarship, to develop womanhood and to strive for the attainment of high ideals in college, community and personal life and to train for leadership and a sense of responsibility for the welfare of others."

Growth Having been founded as a national fraternity, Alpha Gamma Delta proceeded to span the continent within five years, with chapters chartered in Connecticut, Minnesota, Kentucky, Ohio, Indiana, Maryland, and Washington. Alpha Gamma Delta became international in 1919 with the establishment of a chapter at the University of Toronto, the first of an eventual seven Canadian chapters.

During the next 50 years, Alpha Gamma Delta expanded steadily in number of chapters with an accompanying growth in alumnae organizations. In 1959, Theta Sigma Upsilon Sorority merged with Alpha Gamma Delta, adding 13 chapters to the existing 70. From 1959 to the present, the addition of chapters to the roll has been dramatically accelerated to the present 142 installed chapters and over 250 alumnae organizations.

Government Government is by biennial convention and the Grand Council of seven officers. For administrative efficiency, undergraduate chapters and alumnae organizations are grouped into 20 geographical provinces.

The grand vice president-undergraduates directs the activities of the undergraduate chapters, aided by province directors-undergraduates and three area supervisors. Undergraduate services are provided by officers or committees to supervise scholarship, pledge education, membership building and selection, finance, chapter bylaws and chapter house administration. A special committee gives support and supervision to colonies and new chapters.

Area conferences are held biennially to promote undergraduate officer and adviser training and leadership skills. Chapters receive at least one visit per year by international, province or other officers.

Alumnae organizations are directed by the grand vice president-alumnae, with the assistance of province directors-alumnae and three area supervisors. Alumnae services provided are bylaw assistance, meeting programming, career networking and special newsletters to those isolated by distance from other fraternity members.

International committees direct fraternity programs of extension, philanthropy, chapter housing and ritual.

Traditions and Insignia A traditional objective of Alpha Gamma Delta is to maintain high standards of personal and chapter achievement. Measurement of undergraduate chapter achievement is accomplished through the Merit Program, which is the basis for the majority of awards given at conventions. Two of the most coveted are the Annulet Award, given for all-around chapter excellence, and the silver Rose Bowls for scholastic achievement. In addition, special awards are given for unusual and creative programming, gracious living, and philanthropic support. The alumnae Achievement Program is the basis for major alumnae awards. Others are given for newsletter quality, philanthropic endeavors and support to undergraduate chapters. Adviser support to chapters is also recognized through special awards.

Distinguished Citizen Awards are granted to alumnae members who have made outstanding contributions to their professions, to civic or public affairs and the arts.

The value of volunteer support to the fraternity was first recognized in 1919 when the Honors of Epsilon Pi were established to be conferred upon members who had rendered faithful, continued and outstanding service to the fraternity. The honors, three arcs, two crescents and the circle, are jeweled with pearls or diamonds, and are worn as badge guards.

International Reunion Day is an annual gathering celebrated traditionally on the third Saturday in April.

The Alpha Gamma Delta name, badge and coat of arms were first trademarked in 1928.

The badge design was officially approved in 1904. It is a monogram design with the Delta plain, the Gamma chased and the Alpha superimposed upon the two and set with pearls or left unjeweled. Diamonds may also be used as badge jewels, except that the all diamond badge is reserved as a lifetime gift to grand presidents at the time of their installations.

The pledge pin is a shield, the field divided per pale and per fess executed in red, buff, and green enamel.

Other official jewelry includes: the recognition pin, the three Greek letters in drop formation; the mother's pin, a gold rose flanked by three leaves, each set with a pearl; the rose bracelet and rose drop, the design of which embodies elements of the armorial bearings; the 50 year pin or charm, a design of two roses within a circle.

Fraternity colors are red, buff, and green, and the flowers are red and buff roses, with green fern.

The armorial bearings were designed and executed by Emily Butterfield, one of the fraternity's founders and a recognized authority on fraternity heraldry. In heraldic terms the description of the Alpha Gamma Delta coat of arms is: gules, on a bend, or, between two billets, or, three annulets, vert; crest, on a royal helmet a buff and crimson rose between epsilon pi, proper.

Publications The *Alpha Gamma Delta Quarterly*, the fraternity magazine, has been published continuously since November, 1909. Manuals of fraternity education have been in use since 1919. The manuals and the Constitution and Standing Rules,

along with officer handbooks, brochures, and other materials are updated and published regularly. Newsletters for undergraduates, advisers, alumnae and fraternity officers and committees are provided. The most recent addition to the publication is "It's Okay to care!"—information and programming on alcohol use, drugs, eating disorders, and other health and social issues.

Funds and Philanthropies An international altruistic project was started in 1920 with the establishment of a summer camp for underprivileged children at Jackson, Michigan. During the 27 years of conducting this camp and a later camp at Welland, Ontario, a total of $90,000 was expended, with volunteer staffs of Alpha Gamma Deltas bringing happiness to about 8,500 children.

A project of benefiting the cerebral palsied and physically handicapped was adopted in 1947. Contributions were made through the National Society for Crippled Children and Adults and provided fellowships for trainees in a counselor training program which was the only one of its kind at the time.

In 1964, the Alpha Gamma Delta Founders Memorial Foundation received federal approval. The objects and purposes for which the trust is formed are to promote and support religious, charitable, scientific, literary, and educational organizations and activities. The foundation is administered by six trustees, aided by a scholarship committee. The first charitable contributions were in the area of minimal brain dysfunction, along with the continuation of an annual grant given to Syracuse University to finance symposiums on cleft palate habilitation.

In 1979, the Juvenile Diabetes Foundation was selected the fraternity's international philanthropy. At the local level, fraternity members raise around $100,000 annually which is channeled by the Founders Memorial and Juvenile Diabetes Foundations toward research for a cure for diabetes.

The Founders Memorial Foundation also grants undergraduate and graduate scholarships, provides scholarship incentives to chapters, assists in the funding of leadership training conferences and workshops, provides educational facilities in chapter houses, and aids members in emergency financial need.

Headquarters Alpha Gamma Delta was one of the women's fraternities to establish a central office in the 1920's with a full-time executive secretary. The leased office space was in New York City from 1927 to 1954 when it was moved to Chatham, New Jersey. The 1964 convention authorized the purchase of a headquarters building in Indianapolis. The renovated Georgian colonial home provided ample space for the office, as well as meeting rooms for international officers and committees. In 1979, a permanent new headquarters building was completed at 8701 Founders Road, Indianapolis, Indiana 46268. The new headquarters provided more efficient office space with room for growth, as well as meeting facilities. In the intervening years the number of professional staff has increased to care for the editing of the *Quarterly* and other printed materials, audio visual development, undergraduate chapter programming, extension assistance, and financial services.

Membership   Total living membership 70,822. Graduate/Alumni chapters 5,795. Active chapters 116. Inactive chapters 42. Colonies 3. Houses owned 43. Graduate/Alumni chapters 128. City/Area alumni associations 120. Total number of initiates 99,332. Chapter roll:

1904 Alpha, Syracuse
1905 *Beta, Wisconsin, Madison* (1987)
1906 *Gamma, Wesleyan (CT)* (1912)
1908 Delta, Minnesota
1908 Epsilon, Kentucky
1908 Eta, DePauw
1908 *Theta, Goucher* (1950)
1908 Zeta, Ohio
1909 Iota, Washington (WA)
1912 Kappa, Allegheny
1913 Lambda, Northwestern
1913 Mu, Brenau
1913 *Nu, Boston U* (1961)
1914 Xi, Illinois Wesleyan
1915 Omicron, Cal, Berkeley
1917 *Pi, Coe* (1964)
1917 Rho, Iowa State
1918 Sigma, Illinois
1919 Tau, Toronto
1919 Upsilon, Oklahoma
1921 Chi, Michigan State
1921 Phi, Oregon State
1921 Psi, Alabama
1922 *Alpha Alpha, SUNY, Buffalo* (1972)
1922 Alpha Beta, Michigan
1922 Epsilon Alpha, Missouri (1975-1981)
1922 Epsilon Beta, Kansas
1922 Omega, Akron
1923 *Alpha Gamma, Cincinnati* (1971)
1923 *Delta Alpha, USC* (1986)
1923 Delta Beta, Washington State
1923 Gamma Alpha, Georgia
1924 *Alpha Delta, Ohio Wesleyan* (1984)
1924 *Delta Delta, Oregon* (1969)
1924 Delta Gamma, Montana State
1925 Alpha Epsilon, Westminster (PA)
1925 *Delta Epsilon, UCLA* (1982)
1925 Gamma Beta, Florida State
1927 Beta Alpha, Nebraska Wesleyan
1928 Epsilon Gamma, Denver
1930 *Alpha Zeta, McGill* (1985)
1930 Beta Beta, North Dakota State
1930 Beta Gamma, Manitoba
1930 Delta Zeta, British Columbia
1930 *Gamma Gamma, Queens (NC)* (1977)
1932 Alpha Eta, Dalhousie
1937 *Alpha Theta, Hunter* (1963)
1939 Gamma Delta, Auburn
1940 Alpha Iota, Baldwin-Wallace
1940 Epsilon Delta, Texas (1972-1985)

1945 Alpha Kappa, Bowling Green
1945 *Gamma Epsilon, North Carolina* (1965)
1946 Alpha Lambda, Ohio State (1971-1979)
1946 Epsilon Epsilon, William Jewell
1947 Alpha Mu, Penn State
1947 *Alpha Nu, Kent* (1978)
1947 Alpha Xi, Maryland (1989-1990)
1947 Beta Delta, Indiana
1947 Gamma Zeta, Memphis State
1948 Alpha Omicron, West Virginia Wesleyan
1948 Epsilon Zeta, Arkansas State
1949 Delta Eta, San Diego U.
1952 Beta Epsilon, Carroll
1955 *Epsilon Eta, Texas Christian* (1977)
1955 Gamma Eta, High Point
1957 Beta Eta, Southern Illinois
1957 *Beta Zeta, Parsons* (1973)
1958 Delta Theta, Idaho
1958 *Epsilon Theta, Colorado* (1972-1984) (1988)
1958 *Gamma Theta, Florida Southern* (1976)
1959 Alpha Pi, Wayne State (MI)
1959 *Alpha Rho, Temple* (1979)
1959 Alpha Sigma, Indiana (PA)
1959 Alpha Tau, Edinboro
1959 Alpha Upsilon, Central Michigan
1959 *Beta Theta, Wisconsin, Whitewater* (1980)
1959 Delta Iota, Cal State, Chico
1959 *Epsilon Iota, Northern Colorado* (1980)
1959 Epsilon Kappa, Pittsburg State, Kansas
1959 Epsilon Lambda, Central Missouri State
1959 Epsilon Mu, Fort Hays
1959 *Gamma Kappa, Northwestern Louisiana* (1963)
1959 Gamma Lambda, Longwood
1959 Gamma Mu, Madison Col
1960 Gamma Iota, Mercer
1961 Alpha Chi, Thiel
1961 *Alpha Phi, Marietta* (1975)
1961 Beta Iota, Eastern Illinois
1961 Epsilon Nu, Central State (OK)
1961 Gamma Nu, Tennessee
1963 *Alpha Psi, Ferris* (1979)
1964 Beta Kappa, Iowa (1977-1985)
1964 *Delta Kappa, Alberta* (1979)
1966 *Beta Lambda, South Dakota* (1970)
1966 Gamma Xi, Murray State
1967 *Beta Mu, Mankato* (1973)
1968 *Beta Nu, Northern Iowa* (1979)
1968 Beta Xi, Purdue
1968 Epsilon Xi, East Central State
1968 Gamma Omicron, Eastern Kentucky
1969 *Gamma Pi, Middle Tennessee* (1985)
1970 Gamma Rho, Armstrong
1971 Alpha Omega, Duquesne
1971 Gamma Sigma, Troy
1971 Gamma Tau, West Georgia
1972 Gamma Phi, Georgia Tech
1972 Gamma Upsilon, Montevallo
1973 Beta Omicron, Illinois State
1974 *Epsilon Omicron, Southwestern State (OK)* (1990)
1974 *Gamma Chi, Nicholls* (1983)

1974   Zeta Alpha, Eastern Michigan
1975   Epsilon Rho, Texas A & M
1976   Zeta Beta, Lehigh
1976   Zeta Gamma, Gannon
1977   *Delta Lambda, Eastern Montana* (1979)
1977   *Epsilon Sigma, Cameron* (1987)
1977   *Epsilon Tau, Colorado Mines* (1982)
1977   Gamma Psi, North Alabama
1978   Gamma Omega, Alabama, Birmingham
1979   *Beta Pi, St. Thomas* (1985)
1979   *Theta Alpha, L.S.U.* (1985)
1979   Theta Beta, Auburn, Montgomery
1979   Zeta Delta, Towson (1985-1988)
1979   Zeta Epsilon, Michigan Tech
1980   *Theta Gamma, Georgia Southern* (1984)
1980   Zeta Eta, R.P.I.
1980   Zeta Zeta, Worcester Tech
1981   *Delta Mu, Cal, Santa Barbara* (1984)
1981   Zeta Theta, Lafayette
1982   Zeta Iota, Miami (OH)
1982   Zeta Kappa, Pitt, Johnstown
1983   Delta Nu, Calgary
1983   Theta Delta, North Georgia
1983   *Zeta Lambda, Findlay* (1985)
1984   Theta Epsilon, South Alabama
1985   Beta Rho, Southern Indiana
1985   *Epsilon Chi, Kansas State* (1989)
1985   Epsilon Phi, Texas Woman's
1985   Epsilon Upsilon, Tarleton
1985   Zeta Mu, Stockton
1985   Zeta Nu, Alma
1985   Zeta Xi, Cornell
1986   Beta Sigma, Creighton
1986   Zeta Omicron, GMI
1987   Delta Xi, Arizona State
1987   Theta Zeta, Randolph, Macon
1987   Zeta Pi, St. Joseph's (PA)
1988   Beta Tau, Ball State
1988   Zeta Rho, Quinnipiac
1988   Zeta Sigma, Northwood (MI)
1989   Delta Omicron, Nevada, Las Vegas
1989   Theta Eta, Tennessee, Martin
1989   Theta Theta, Mississippi State
1989   Zeta Tau, Seton Hall
1989   Zeta Upsilon, Northern Michigan
1990   Theta Iota, Western Kentucky
1990   Theta Kappa, Virginia
1990   Theta Lambda, West Florida

Colonies: McMaster, North Carolina, Wilmington, San Francisco State

Alpha Omicron Pi

ACTIVE PIN

PLEDGE PIN

ALPHA OMICRON PI was founded at Barnard College of Columbia University on January 2, 1897, by four members of "the great and glorious Class of '98." The founders were Jessie Wallace Hughan, Helen St. Clair (Mrs. George V. Mullan), Stella George Stern (Mrs. George H. Perry), and Elizabeth Heywood Wyman. Each of these dynamic women would later distinguish herself in her respective field. Jessie, listed in *Who's Who in America*, became a writer and educator. Helen, a Phi Beta Kappa, graduated from New York University Law School as the top member of her class and was later one of the most prominent lawyers in America. Stella, writer and poet and also listed in *Who's Who in America*, was the author of more than 20 books. Elizabeth (Bess), educator and writer, served on a New Jersey Board of Education, one of the first two women so honored. Founders' Day is celebrated December 8, Stella's birthday, to commemorate the founders' determination to create a democratic, unostentatious, simple society.

Growth   The second chapter of Alpha Omicron Pi was founded at Newcomb College in New Orleans, home of one of the founders. AOΠ expanded rapidly to the west coast with the founding of Sigma chapter at the University of California at Berkeley in 1907. The University of Tennessee-Knoxville chapter has had the longest continuous existence. In 1930, the international movement began at the University of British Columbia.

AOΠ was a pioneer in the area of chapter services and was one of the first to implement the services provided by traveling secretaries.

AOΠ was one of the first sororities to establish an international philanthropic program. AOΠ has been a recognized leader in sorority programming.

Government   The government is vested in the Council, which is made up of the international officers, past presidents, chairmen of standing committees and directors of projects; regional directors; presidents of collegiate and alumnae chapters, alumnae advisers of collegiate chapters, and regional extension officers. Between sessions, affairs are administered by the Executive Board, composed of international president, vice president/operations, vice president/development, vice president/finance, and four directors.

Conventions are held biennially with the governing body selecting the meeting place. Leadership conferences are in alternate years of convention. Collegiate chapters are organized into eight regions and the alumnae chapters are similarly allocated.

Traditions and Insignia   The badge is a monogram of the Greek letters AOΠ, with a ruby in the apex of the A. The badge may be plain or jeweled. The color is cardinal, the flower is the Jacqueminot rose and the jewel is the ruby. The pledge pin is a golden sheaf of wheat bearing the letters of the name, and the recognition pin is a gold rose bearing the letters of the name. The founders chose simplicity as a guide for the organization of Alpha Omicron Pi.

Four awards in tribute to the founders are given biennially. A loving cup, known as the J.W.H. Cup, is awarded to the collegiate chapter which has been of the greatest service to its college and community during the preceding two years. The Elizabeth Heywood Wyman silver platter is awarded to an alumna who has distinguished herself in her profession, the arts, or to service to humanity. The Perry Award is given to the most outstanding chapter president. For distinguished service within the fraternity, the Helen St. Clair Mullan award is given.

An additional award is the McCausland Cup which is earned by the chapter with the highest scholastic average for the proceding two years.

Publications   *To Dragma*, The official magazine, has been published quarterly since 1905. *The Piper* is published monthly. Numerous chapters also have periodicals of local interest.

Funds and Philanthropies   Arthritis research is the international philanthropy and was adopted at the 1967 convention. Research grants are awarded annually; more than $250,000 has been awarded through 1985. The Frontier Nursing Service had been the philanthropy since 1931, but the funding of this organization had grown and its needs provided.

The Ruby Fund is used to assist members who may need financial assistance and was established at the 1946 convention. A nonprofit foundation for the purpose of granting scholarships and engaging in other charitable works was established at the 1959 Convention. It is the Diamond Jubliee Foundation, with specific goals for the 1972 diamond anniversary of the fraternity.

Headquarters   9025 Overlook Blvd., Brentwood, TN 37027. Phone: (615) 370-0920.

Membership   Total living membership 72,920. Total undergraduate membership 6,348. Active chapters 112. Inactive chapters 50. Colonies 2. Houses owned 53. City/Area alumni associations 213. Total number of initiates 98,849. Chapter roll:

1897	*Alpha, Barnard* (1915)
1898	Pi, Tulane (1976-1985)
1900	*Nu, N.Y.U.* (1961)
1902	Omicron, Tennessee
1903	*Kappa, Randolph, Macon* (1960)
1903	Zeta, Nebraska
1907	Sigma, Cal, Berkeley
1907	Theta, DePauw (1979-1983)

1908	Beta, Brown
1908	Delta, Tufts (1969-1987)
1908	Epsilon, Cornell (1962-1989)
1908	Gamma, Maine
1909	*Rho, Northwestern* (1973)
1910	*Lambda, Stanford* (1944)
1911	Iota, Illinois
1912	Tau, Minnesota
1914	Chi, Syracuse (1958-1985)
1915	*Nu Kappa, Southern Methodist* (1942)
1915	Upsilon, Washington (WA)
1916	Beta Phi, Indiana
1917	Alpha Phi, Montana State
1917	*Eta, Wisconsin, Madison* (1942)
1917	Nu Omicron, Vanderbilt
1918	Phi, Kansas (1969-1980)
1918	*Psi, Penn* (1958)
1919	Omega, Miami (OH)
1921	Omicron Pi, Michigan (1973-1978)
1923	*Alpha Sigma, Oregon* (1989)
1924	Pi Delta, Maryland
1924	*Xi, Oklahoma* (1933)
1925	Kappa Omicron, Rhodes
1925	*Kappa Theta, UCLA* (1973)
1925	Tau Delta, Birmingham-Southern
1926	Alpha Rho, Oregon State
1927	*Beta Theta, Butler* (1940)
1927	Chi Delta, Colorado
1928	*Alpha Pi, Florida State* (1980)
1929	Epsilon Alpha, Penn State (1973-1982)
1929	*Theta Eta, Cincinnati* (1958)
1930	*Alpha Tau, Denison* (1970)
1930	Beta Tau, Toronto
1932	Alpha Gamma, Washington State (1936-1961)
1932	*Beta Kappa, British Columbia* (1984)
1933	*Delta Phi, South Carolina* (1937-1978) (1982)
1934	Beta Gamma, Michigan State (1969-1989)
1935	Lambda Sigma Society, Georgia
1938	*Alpha Omicron, L.S.U.* (1980)
1938	Sigma Tau, Washington (MD)
1939	Kappa Phi, McGill (1973-1989)
1941	*Pi Kappa, Texas* (1973)
1944	Theta Psi, Toledo
1945	*Nu Lambda, USC* (1962-1976) (1990)
1946	Delta Delta, Auburn
1946	Kappa Gamma, Florida Southern
1947	*Chi Sigma, Centenary* (1951)
1948	Delta Sigma, San Jose (1970-1988)
1948	Gamma Omicron, Florida
1949	Sigma Omicron, Arkansas State
1950	*Iota Alpha, Idaho State* (1981)
1950	*Phi Omicron, Hanover* (1985)
1951	Chi Lambda, Evansville
1951	Kappa Rho, Western Michigan (1970-1985)
1951	Theta Pi, Wagner
1952	Kappa Kappa, Ball State
1952	Sigma Chi, Hartwick
1953	Kappa Alpha, Indiana State
1955	*Phi Alpha, East Tennessee* (1978)
1956	Beta Lambda, Illinois Wesleyan

1956	Gamma Sigma, Georgia State	
1957	Omega Omicron, Lambuth	
1957	*Phi Lambda, Youngstown State* (1982)	
1958	Lambda Tau, Northwestern Louisiana	
1958	Nu Beta, Mississippi	
1958	Phi Delta, Wisconsin, Milwaukee	
1959	*Beta Chi, Kentucky Wesleyan* (1981)	
1959	Upsilon Alpha, Arizona (1982-1989)	
1960	*Chi Omicron, Central State (OK)* (1966)	
1960	*Gamma Tau, Utah State* (1970)	
1960	Zeta Psi, East Carolina	
1961	Delta Omega, Murray State	
1961	*Phi Kappa, Morris Harvey* (1978)	
1961	*Rho Sigma, Portland State* (1972)	
1961	*Sigma Lambda, Wisconsin, La Crosse* (1981)	
1962	*Beta Pi, Eastern Michigan* (1979)	
1962	Delta Pi, Central Missouri State	
1963	Kappa Tau, Southeastern Louisiana	
1963	Phi Upsilon, Purdue	
1963	Theta Omega, Northern Arizona	
1964	*Nu Sigma, Parsons* (1966)	
1965	Alpha Chi, Western Kentucky	
1965	*Beta Rho, Montana* (1987)	
1965	Lambda Beta, Cal State, Long Beach	
1966	Gamma Beta, Indiana (PA)	
1966	*Iota Tau, Wisconsin, Stout* (1984)	
1966	Kappa Pi, Ohio Northern	
1966	*Rho Alpha, Pan American* (1971)	
1966	Sigma Rho, Slippery Rock	
1966	*Sigma Sigma, St. Norbert* (1968)	
1966	Tau Omicron, Tennessee, Martin	
1966	Theta Chi, Morningside	
1967	Alpha Delta, Alabama	
1967	*Lambda Phi, Wisconsin, Whitewater* (1973)	
1967	Sigma Phi, Cal State, Northridge	
1968	Iota Sigma, Iowa State	
1969	*Alpha Beta, Florida Atlantic* (1971)	
1969	Alpha Theta, Coe	
1969	*Beta Sigma, Boise* (1987)	
1969	*Chi Pi, Northeastern* (1973)	
1969	Gamma Delta, South Alabama	
1969	*Nu Zeta, Chadron* (1977)	
1969	Phi Beta, East Stroudsburg	
1969	Phi Sigma, Kearney	
1970	*Gamma Iota, Southern Illinois* (1973)	
1970	*Omega Xi, Morehead* (1984)	
1970	Sigma Iota, Western Illinois	
1970	*Theta Kappa, West Chester* (1974)	
1971	*Beta Epsilon, Bemidji* (1984)	
1971	Lambda Chi, LaGrange	
1971	*Lambda Omega, Northwest Missouri* (1982)	
1972	Delta Chi, Delaware	
1972	*Epsilon Iota, Eastern Illinois* (1974)	
1973	*Alpha Kappa, North Alabama* (1983)	
1975	Chi Alpha, Cal, Davis	
1976	Sigma Delta, Huntingdon	
1977	Lambda Iota, Cal, San Diego	
1978	Gamma Alpha, George Mason	
1978	Upsilon Lambda, Texas, San Antonio	
1979	Delta Upsilon, Duke	
1981	*Kappa Delta, Wright State* (1985)	

1982	Chi Beta, Virginia	
1982	Kappa Omega, Kentucky	
1983	Pi Alpha, Louisville	
1984	Delta Theta, Texas Woman's	
1984	Lambda Upsilon, Lehigh	
1984	Tau Lambda, Shippensburg	
1985	Beta Delta, Villanova	
1985	Gamma Theta, South Florida	
1985	Kappa Lambda, Calgary	
1985	Phi Chi, Chicago	
1985	Rho Omicron, Middle Tennessee	
1986	Alpha Beta Tau, Thomas More	
1986	Chi Psi, Cal Poly, San Luis Obispo	
1986	Delta Alpha, Missouri	
1986	Gamma Upsilon, St. Leo	
1986	Iota Chi, Western Ontario	
1986	Pi Omicron, Austin Peay	
1986	Rho Beta, Virginia Commonwealth	
1986	Sigma Alpha, West Virginia	
1986	Theta Beta, Towson	
1987	Epsilon Chi, Elon	
1987	Epsilon Omega, Eastern Kentucky	
1987	Nu Delta, Canisius	
1987	Tau Omega, Transylvania	
1987	Zeta Pi, Alabama, Birmingham	
1988	Alpha Lambda, Georgia Southern	
1988	Omega Upsilon, Ohio	
1988	Upsilon Epsilon, Parks (IL)	
1989	Alpha Psi, Bowling Green	
1989	Delta Psi, SUNY, Albany	
1989	Lambda Eta, Grand Valley	
1989	Tau Gamma, Eastern Washington	
1990	Delta Epsilon, Jacksonville	

Colonies: Northern Illinois, Southwestern Louisiana

COAT OF ARMS

Alpha Phi

ACTIVE PIN

PLEDGE PIN

ALPHA PHI was founded at Syracuse University in 1872 by Rena Michaels Atchison, Clara Bradley Burdette, Martha Foote Crow, Kate Hogoboom Gilbert, Louise Shepard Hancock, Jane Sara Higham, Ida Gilbert Houghton, Florence Chidester Lukens, Elizabeth Grace Hubbell Shults, and Clara Sittser Williams. Several of them had distinguished careers and three were listed in *Who's Who in America*. Colleges were gradually and grudgingly opening their doors to women, and these girls felt the need of a close, congenial group on the campus. Asking "Why can't we have a society like the men?", three of the leaders invited all the women at the university, about 20, to meet and discuss the possibilities. Shortly after this, the original Ten met again and bound themselves together in a fraternity which they intended from the first to be national or international. October 10 is celebrated with appropriate ceremonies by collegiate and alumnae members throughout the fraternity as Founder's Day.

Growth Alpha Phi has been a pioneer among women's fraternities in many ways. It was the first to build a chapter house; the first to adopt a plan for supervision of its chapters by visiting officers; the first to have an endowment fund of $50,000; the first to publish a history of its first 50 years. Alpha Phi called an intersorority conference in 1902, and the organization formed at this meeting is now the National Panhellenic Conference.

The first alumnae chapters were organized in 1889 in Boston and in Chicago. Many of the early alumnae chapters were state-wide organizations. Today approximately 235 alumnae chapters are established in most of the principal cities, as well as in smaller communities of the United States and Canada.

Government Government is vested in the biennial convention composed of one delegate from each collegiate and alumnae chapter and ex-officio delegates consisting of the members of the Executive Board, the district governors, district alumnae chairmen, administrative officers, and the Board of Trustees.

The Executive Board of six members, elected at each convention, administers the affairs of the fraternity between conventions. Executive Board members are the president, vice-president collegiate operations, vice-president program development, vice-president alumnae, vice-president finance, and vice-president extension. Financial affairs are administered by the Board of Trustees of three members elected by convention.

The fraternity is divided geographically into 13 districts, with supervision by district governors of collegiate chapters and district alumnae chairmen for alumnae groups. Leadership seminars are usually planned in the alternate years between general conventions. Field representatives work with chapters and aid with organization.

Traditions and Insignia The official badge is a Greek letter Φ with the Greek letter A superimposed upon it, the Φ bearing the small Greek letters αοσ in black. Pins may be either plain or jeweled in white stones. The recognition pin is a duplicate of the official badge in miniature size. The pledge pin is any ivy leaf of silver or gold with the letters ΑΦ upon it.

The crest or coat of arms incorporates the various fraternity symbols: Ursa Major or the Big Dipper, the Roman lamp, the ivy, and the public motto, the translation of which is "Union hand in hand."

The colors are bordeaux and silver gray. The flowers are the forget-me-not and the lily of the valley.

Publications The *Alpha Phi Quarterly*, official magazine, was first published in 1888 and has not missed a single issue since. The *Song Book*, first published in 1892, and the *History*, in 1922, have been amplified with the growth of the fraternity. The fraternity also publishes manuals and handbooks for the use of collegiate and alumnae members.

Funds and Philanthropies Through a general endowment fund, Alpha Phi provides low-interest loans to chapters for housing or furnishings, and educational grants to members who need financial assistance.

Several thousand dollars in scholarships are also awarded annually to members through the Alpha Phi Foundation, created in 1957 to give financial aid to deserving students and to charitable causes.

Since 1946, when heart projects were adopted as its philanthropy, the fraternity has raised and donated over $4 million, and two million hours of volunteer time have been given by members of Alpha Phi. The fraternity has twice been honored by the American Heart Association, receiving the highest tribute, the Heart and Torch Award.

Headquarters Alpha Phi Executive House, 1930 Sherman Drive, Evanston, Illinois 60201. The fraternity owns its own building, designed and built by Alpha Phi in 1975. It contains conference rooms, a memorabilia room, and an archives room in addition to modern, efficient office space.

Membership Total living membership 83,307. Total undergraduate membership 6,672. Active chapters 130. Inactive chapters 48. Houses owned 75. Graduate/Alumni chapters 227. Total number of initiates 89,016. Chapter roll:

	Beta Gamma deuteron, Colorado (-1990)
	Beta Rho deuteron, Washington State (-1990)
1872	Alpha, Syracuse
1881	Beta, Northwestern
1883	*Eta, Boston U* (1970)
1887	Gamma, DePauw
1889	Delta, Cornell
1890	Epsilon, Minnesota
1891	*Zeta, Goucher* (1950)
1892	Theta, Michigan
1896	Iota, Wisconsin, Madison
1899	*Kappa, Stanford* (1944)
1901	Lambda, Cal, Berkeley
1903	*Mu, Barnard* (1916)
1906	Nu, Nebraska
1906	Xi, Toronto
1910	Omicron, Missouri
1911	Pi, North Dakota
1912	Rho, Ohio State
1914	Sigma, Washington (WA)
1915	Tau, Oregon
1916	Upsilon, Washburn
1917	Phi, Oklahoma

1918	Chi, Montana
1920	Omega, Texas
1920	Psi, South Dakota
1922	Beta Alpha, Illinois
1922	Beta Beta, Michigan State
1924	Beta Delta, UCLA
1924	*Beta Gamma, Colorado* (1982)
1926	Beta Epsilon, Arizona
1928	Beta Eta, Manitoba
1928	Beta Zeta, Idaho
1929	Beta Theta, British Columbia
1930	Beta Iota, West Virginia
1930	*Beta Kappa, Denison* (1979)
1931	*Beta Lambda, Rollins* (1988)
1932	*Beta Mu, Alabama* (1963)
1935	*Beta Nu, Duke* (1970)
1937	*Beta Xi, American* (1944)
1943	Beta Omicron, Bowling Green
1945	Beta Pi, USC
1945	*Beta Rho, Washington State* (1985)
1946	*Beta Sigma, Utah* (1965)
1947	Beta Tau, Indiana
1947	Beta Upsilon, Oregon State
1948	*Beta Chi, Bucknell* (1978)
1948	Beta Omega, Kent
1948	*Beta Phi, Whitman* (1979)
1948	Beta Psi, Cal State, San Jose
1949	Gamma Alpha, Cal, San Diego
1950	Gamma Beta, Cal, Santa Barbara
1950	*Gamma Delta, Kansas* (1989)
1950	*Gamma Gamma, Drury* (1983)
1952	*Gamma Epsilon, Lake Forest* (1961)
1953	Gamma Zeta, Puget Sound
1954	Gamma Eta, North Texas
1954	*Gamma Theta, Colorado Col* (1961)
1955	Gamma Iota, Texas Tech
1956	Gamma Kappa, Cal State, Long Beach
1956	*Gamma Lambda, Houston* (1960)
1956	*Gamma Mu, Georgia State* (1978)
1957	Gamma Nu, Miami (OH)
1958	Gamma Omicron, Drake
1958	Gamma Pi, Arizona State
1958	Gamma Rho, Penn State
1958	Gamma Sigma, Wisconsin, Stout
1958	*Gamma Tau, Willamette* (1978)
1958	*Gamma Upsilon, Wisconsin, Milwaukee* (1972)
1958	Gamma Xi, Wichita
1959	*Gamma Chi, Portland State* (1973)
1959	Gamma Omega, Midwestern
1959	*Gamma Phi, Florida State* (1972)
1959	*Gamma Psi, Ripon* (1970)
1960	Delta Alpha, East Carolina
1960	Delta Beta, East Texas
1960	Delta Gamma, Northern Colorado
1961	Delta Delta, Oklahoma City
1961	Delta Epsilon, Iowa
1961	Delta Eta, Adrian
1961	Delta Zeta, Maryland
1962	*Delta Iota, Roanoke* (1978)
1962	Delta Theta, Western Michigan
1963	Delta Kappa, Wisconsin, La Crosse

1963	*Delta Lambda, Memphis State* (1976)
1963	Delta Mu, Purdue
1963	Delta Nu, Maine
1963	Delta Xi, Kearney
1964	*Delta Omicron, St. Cloud* (1978)
1964	Delta Pi, Indiana State
1964	Delta Rho, Ball State
1964	*Delta Sigma, Wisconsin, Stevens Point* (1983)
1964	Delta Upsilon, Baldwin-Wallace
1965	Delta Chi, William Woods
1965	*Delta Phi, Indiana (PA)* (1983)
1965	*Delta Tau, L.S.U.* (1980)
1966	*Delta Omega, Moorhead* (1988)
1966	*Delta Psi, Wisconsin, Oshkosh* (1979)
1967	Epsilon Alpha, Ashland
1967	Epsilon Beta, Butler
1968	Epsilon Gamma, Cal State, Sacramento
1969	Epsilon Delta, Northern Illinois
1969	*Epsilon Epsilon, Longwood* (1978)
1969	*Epsilon Zeta, Central Michigan* (1970)
1970	Epsilon Eta, Old Dominion
1970	Epsilon Iota, Duquesne
1970	Epsilon Theta, Northern Iowa
1971	Epsilon Kappa, West Chester
1971	*Epsilon Lambda, Texas, Arlington* (1983)
1972	Epsilon Mu, Lander
1972	Epsilon Nu, Delaware
1973	*Epsilon Omicron, Austin Peay* (1983)
1974	*Epsilon Pi, Evansville* (1983)
1974	Epsilon Rho, Cal, Davis
1974	*Epsilon Sigma, Dallas Baptist* (1978)
1974	*Epsilon Tau, L.S.U., Shreveport* (1981)
1974	Epsilon Upsilon, Cal State, Northridge
1974	Epsilon Xi, Southern Illinois, Edwardsville
1975	Epsilon Chi, Cal Poly, San Luis Obispo
1975	*Epsilon Omega, Texas A & M* (1987)
1975	*Epsilon Phi, North Carolina State* (1982)
1975	Epsilon Psi, Lehigh
1976	Zeta Alpha, Eastern Illinois
1976	Zeta Beta, Loyola Marymount, Los Angeles
1976	Zeta Gamma, Santa Clara
1977	Zeta Delta, Iowa State
1978	Kappa deuteron, Stanford
1978	Zeta Epsilon, Indiana Southeast
1978	*Zeta Eta, Newberry* (1981)
1978	Zeta Iota, Virginia
1978	Zeta Theta, Tufts
1978	*Zeta Zeta, Murray State* (1990)
1979	*Zeta Kappa, Southwest Texas* (1989)
1979	*Zeta Lambda, New Hampshire Col* (1986)
1979	Zeta Mu, Colorado State
1979	*Zeta Nu, Texas Christian* (1989)
1980	Zeta Xi, Elmhurst College
1981	Zeta Omicron, Johns Hopkins
1982	Zeta Pi, Case Western Reserve
1982	Zeta Rho, Bentley
1982	Zeta Sigma, Franklin and Marshall
1983	Zeta Tau, Illinois State
1983	Zeta Upsilon, Washington (MO)
1984	Eta deuteron, Boston U
1984	Zeta Chi, Columbia (NY)

1984 Zeta Phi, M.I.T.
1985 *Zeta Omega, Northwood (MI)* (1987)
1985 Zeta Psi, Dayton
1986 Eta Alpha, New Hampshire
1986 Eta Beta, Cal State, San Bernadino
1986 Eta Gamma, Akron
1987 Eta Delta, Cal State, Hayward
1987 Eta Epsilon, Villanova
1987 Eta Zeta, SUNY, Binghamton
1988 Epsilon Omega deuteron, Texas A & M
1988 Eta Eta, Seton Hall
1988 Eta Iota, Penn
1988 Eta Kappa, Cal, Irvine
1988 Eta Lambda, George Mason
1988 Eta Theta, San Francisco State
1989 Eta Chi, Bishop
1989 Eta Mu, Marquette
1989 Eta Nu, SUNY, Albany
1989 Eta Omicron, V.P.I.
1989 Eta Phi, SUNY, Stony Brook
1989 Eta Pi, Richmond
1989 Eta Rho, San Diego U
1989 Eta Sigma, Lafayette
1989 Eta Tau, SUNY Col., Cortland
1989 Eta Upsilon, Chapman
1989 Eta Xi, North Carolina, Wilmington
1990 Eta Omega, Towson
1990 Eta Psi, Eastern Washington
1990 Theta Alpha, Linfield
1990 Theta Beta, Bryant
1990 Theta Delta, Creighton
1990 Theta Epsilon, SUNY Col., Buffalo
1990 Theta Gamma, Northeast Missouri

COAT OF ARMS

Alpha Sigma Alpha

ACTIVE PIN

PLEDGE PIN

ALPHA SIGMA ALPHA was founded November 15, 1901, at State Normal School, Farmville, Virginia, now Longwood College, by Virginia Lee Boyd, Juliette Jefferson Hundley, Mary Williamson Hundley, Louise Burks Cox, and Calva Hamlet Watson. The sorority was chartered on February 13, 1903, in the Circuit Court of Prince Edward County, Virginia. The founders conceived Alpha Sigma Alpha as a national organization. The philosophy of the sorority was expressed explicitly by Louise Cox (Carper) in her statement: "The fundamental object of a sorority is to cultivate those qualities which will help its members to meet more successfully the events of life. A sorority is the training ground for the culti-

vation of the art of living in harmony with other people. Cooperation cannot be had where affection and trust are not. The first duty of the sorority is, then, the nurture of the atmosphere of mutual love and fellowship in a common venture. Alpha Sigma Alpha has a definite work to perform throughout the lives of its members and through them a beneficient influence upon society at large."

Growth   Beta Chapter was established at Lewisburg Female Institute, Lewisburg, West Virginia, in 1903. By 1905 there were six Alpha Sigma Alpha chapters. The first convention was called Thanksgiving weekend, 1905. By 1913, the mother chapter, Alpha, prospering in the first teacher training institution in the commonwealth of Virginia, became a dominant factor in the fraternity's decision to alter its general program to serve young women who were primarily preparing to enter the teaching profession. Accordingly, in convention, 1914, the chapter roll was restricted to teachers' colleges, departments, and colleges of education in universities. In July, 1915, Alpha Sigma Alpha established its identification with its chosen field by organizing with Sigma Sigma Sigma the Association of Education Sororities.

A ruling to limit chapter grants to four-year colleges and universities antedates a similar ruling made by A.E.S. in 1921. Expansion in some departments and colleges of education in universities, such as Drake, and particularly those in the State of Ohio, fulfilled a need for many years, but finally resulted in withdrawal of charters because of circumstances involved with changes and developments in the educational world. These changes and developments gradually led to the merging of the fields in which National Panhellenic Conference and the Association of Education Sororities functioned separately. Admitted to associate membership in 1947, Alpha Sigma Alpha became a full NPC member in 1951.

Government   The National Convention is the highest governing body of the sorority. Official alumnae and collegiate chapter delegates, national councilors, national officers, and collegiate chapter advisors comprise the voting delegation. Any member in good standing of Alpha Sigma Alpha may attend these meetings, which are held biennially. The National Council is the governing body of the sorority during the interim between conventions. Composed of seven voting members and an advisory president emerita, the Council directs the growth, coordinates the activities, and supervises the finances of the sorority. The members include the president, vice president of program, vice president of development, vice president of collegians, vice president of alumnae, vice president of finance, and secretary.

Special officers appointed by the Council are the National Panhellenic Conference delegate and alternate delegate, the national editor, and headquarters executive officer. National chairmen, appointed by the president, and approved by the Council, supervise specific areas of sorority programming. Chairmen are appointed for: alumnae development, advisors, colonies, constitution, housing, philanthropy, ritual, rush, scholarship, and standards. Chapter consultants, who are recent college graduates, are selected to travel extensively visiting collegiate chapters, to assist with program development, officer training, chapter management, and membership recruitment and education. Collegiate and alumnae chapters are divided into geographic areas for administrative purposes. Appointed province directors supervise and coordinate activities within a given province. The directors work together in planning area meetings between collegiate and alumnae chapters. These province/state days provide opportunities for leadership development and fellowship.

Traditions and Insignia The pledge pin, a tiny silver shield with four concave sides, displays the sorority letters raised against a conventional design of the rising sun. The membership badge is a black enameled shield with four concave sides superimposed upon a similarly-shaped shield of gold, displaying the sorority letters, a star, and a crown. The badge may be set with 16 pearls, or 12 pearls, with rubies set in the four corners. There are two badges which may be worn by non-members. The Crown Degree is an honor accorded to a mother, advisor, or sponsor, who has devoted time and support to the sorority. The badge is a gold crown-shaped pin set with four pearls. The Phoenix recognition pin, a gold badge, in the image of a phoenix rising from flames, is given in any situation when a recipient is to be honored.

The jewels are the pearl and the ruby. The colors are crimson red and pearl white, supplemented by palm green and gold. The fall flower is the aster, and the spring flower is the narcissus. The coat of arms of Alpha Sigma Alpha is a shield, quartered in crimson red and white, bearing a phoenix rising from lambent flames and surmounted by a gold crown. The riband below the shield carries an open motto, "Aspire, Seek, Attain", in Greek. The aim is the four-fold development of its members, spiritually, intellectually, socially, and physically.

Four significant days are celebrated by Alpha Sigma Alphas: Founders' Day is celebrated on November 15, with a program centered around the beginning of the sorority, and the phases of its growth. The national president issues an annual proclamation which is used by all chapters on this special occasion. The Christmas celebration is observed as near Christmas as possible and centers around Christ as an exemplar. St. Valentine's Day is celebrated on February 14 with appropriate traditional activities. Hermes' Day, May 25, marks the beginning and end of the Alpha Sigma Alpha year.

Publications *The Phoenix*, issued weekly, in mimeographed form, from November, 1914, to October, 1918, is the official journal of the sorority. It is now published quarterly. Every life member of the sorority is entitled to receive it. Other official publications include: *The Ritual of Alpha Sigma Alpha; The Constitution; The Years Behind Us*, a history of ASA; *The Years Behind Us, 1951- 1976*, a history supplement; *The Encounter, Membership Manual; Alumnae in Action*, handbook for alumnae chapters; *Alumnae Ritual for Alpha Sigma Alpha; Stars in My Crown*, handbook for collegiate chapter advisors; *Alpha Sigma Alpha Songbook*; and *The Symbolism of Alpha Sigma Alpha*.

Funds and Philanthropy The financial structure of Alpha Sigma Alpha consists of six principal funds, of which three provide for the general operating expenses of the sorority. They are: General Expense Fund, the *Phoenix* Fund, and the Convention Fund. The Endowment Fund, established in 1916 in a bequest from Eva Doyle Reed, Alpha Beta Chapter, former national secretary, is increased by the receipt of all money which is not designated for, or allocated to, any specific fund, according to the constitution. The fund may be invested in collegiate chapter loans, and other sound investments unanimously approved by the National Council. The Philanthropic Fund, established in 1926, provides the basis for the program as it has evolved; it is maintained by individual contributions from collegiate and alumnae chapters. In 1967, the loan program in effect since the 1940s was discontinued, and the scholarship program was revised and enlarged.

Alpha Sigma Alpha has chosen as its national philanthropy aid to the mentally retarded. More specifically, the sorority is committed to supporting the Special Olympics program as volunteers. On the local level, alumnae and collegiate chapters work with the mentally retarded in school or institutional settings and during Special Olympics events. In addition to their work with the mentally retarded, many ASA chapters extend their philanthropic endeavors to charitable organizations in their communities, as well as to state and federal programs in need of volunteers.

Nationally, the philanthropic program provides financial assistance through a scholarship program for qualified collegiate and alumnae members and non-members. Scholarships which are given annually are: Amy M. Swisher Scholarship for graduate and undergraduate study. Established in 1952 by Miss Swisher, professor of art education, Miami University, Ohio, and for many years the advisor of Alpha Alpha Chapter; Mary Turner Gallagher Scholarship for undergraduate work, established in 1967, by Mrs. Gallagher, first initiate, and advisor of Chi Chi Chapter; Wilma Wilson Sharp Scholarship, established in 1970 in honor of Mrs. Sharp, president emerita; Martha Dimond Scholarship, for graduate study in any field, to be awarded to an alumnae of ASA, established in 1977, by Mrs. Dimond; National Philanthropic Scholarship for graduate or undergraduate study in any field was established in honor of the national organization. Special Education Scholarships are available to members or non-members pursuing graduate or undergraduate work in the field of special education.

The National Council annually recognizes outstanding members through the presentation of collegiate and alumnae awards for sorority and community service: The Elizabeth Bird Small Award is given in memory of Mrs. Small, a former advisor of Pi Pi Chapter, and a former national councilor. It is the highest honor the sorority bestows upon an undergraduate member and recognizes outstanding leadership within the chapter and on the campus, high scholarship, and personality. The Frost Fidelity Award is based on intangible fraternity values, including exceptional loyalty and unusual service to Alpha Sigma Alpha. This undergraduate award was established through the generosity of Mr. and Mrs. (Emma Coleman) Donald Donald Frost III. The Ideal Pledge Award recipient has demonstrated certain qualities of spirit and enthusiasm during her pledge period, including a willingness to accept responsibility, awareness of her sorority obligations and traditions, and potential leadership. The Wilma Wilson Sharp Award is presented in convention years in the name of Mrs. Sharp. This award recognizes an alumna member who has distinguished herself through service to her community and to her profession, and has shown outstanding qualities of leadership, and has evidenced her loyalty to Alpha Sigma Alpha. The Recognition of Imminence Award, while similar to the Sharp Award, is designed to honor those alumnae whose professional or community achievements have attracted recognition far beyond the circle of Alpha Sigma Alpha. Created in celebration of the fiftieth anniversary of the sorority, it is awarded at the discretion of the National Council. The Evelyn G. Bell Award, instituted at the 1980 Buffalo Convention, is given annually to a member who has shown outstanding leadership and loyalty as a collegian, alumna, and national officer. The Helen F. Corey Convention Award is presented at each National Convention in honor of Miss Corey who served as Alpha Sigma Alpha convention chairman for 30 years. It recognizes outstanding contributions for convention planning and preparation, and for long-time devotion in making conventions successful. Other awards include 50- year Membership Awards, *Phoenix* Awards, Philanthropic Service Awards, Panhellenic Cooperation Awards, Membership Examination Award, Scholastic Achievement and Improvement Awards, and National Council Award for Collegiate Officer Efficiency.

Headquarters The national headquarters is located at 1201 East Walnut Street, Springfield, Missouri 65802. A three-storied brick residence was purchased in 1966 and was extensively remodeled. It was officially dedicated in 1967. The building houses the general offices of the sorority, and Alpha Sigma Alpha Memorial Room, Archives, and quarters for the chapter consultants, who reside there for specific periods of their employment. Here, the operation of sorority is centralized to provide services to members. Its operation and staff are supervised by the headquarters executive officer.

Membership   Chapter roll:

Year	Chapter
1901	Alpha, Longwood
1903	*Beta, Lewisburg (WV) (1904)*
1904	*Gamma, Columbia (SC) (1909)*
1905	*Delta, Mary Baldwin (1907)*
1905	*Epsilon, Fauquier Institute (1907)*
1905	*Eta, Ward Seminary (1909)*
1905	*Zeta, Fairmont Seminary (1906)*
1908	*Iota, Randolph, Macon (1913)*
1909	*Gamma Beta Sigma, St. Mary's (NC) (1910)*
1909	*Kappa Phi, Mount Union (1914)*
1909	*Sigma Phi Epsilon, Brenau (1914)*
1910	*Nu, Shorter (1912)*
1911	*Chi Iota, Hamilton (DC) (1912)*
1914	*Alpha Alpha, Miami (OH) (1936-1950)*
1914	Alpha Beta, Northeast Missouri
1914	*Alpha Gamma, Indiana (PA) (1919-1928)*
1916	Beta Beta, Colorado State, Greeley
1916	*Gamma Gamma, Northwestern Oklahoma (1952)*
1917	*Delta Delta, Ohio (1932)*
1918	Epsilon Epsilon, Emporia
1919	Zeta Zeta, Central Missouri State
1920	Eta Eta, Kansas State, Pittsburg
1921	Theta Theta, Boston
1922	*Iota Iota, Drake (1936)*
1922	Kappa Kappa, Temple
1922	*Lambda Lambda, Ohio State (1934)*
1924	*Mu Mu, Michigan, Ypsilanti (1943)*
1925	Nu Nu, Drexel
1926	*Omicron Omicron, Kent (1939)*
1926	*Pi Pi, SUNY, Buffalo (1954)*
1926	*Xi Xi, UCLA (1951)*
1927	Rho Rho, Marshall
1927	*Sigma Sigma, Western State (CO) (1971)*
1928	Chi Chi, Butler (1933), in 1936 Ball State
1928	Phi Phi, Northwest Missouri
1928	*Tau Tau, Fort Hays (1961)*
1928	*Upsilon Upsilon, Denison (1930)*
1930	*Psi Psi, Northwestern Louisiana (1971)*
1932	*Omega Omega, San Diego State (1939)*
1937	Beta Gamma, Northeastern (OK)
1938	Beta Delta, Southern Mississippi
1939	Beta Epsilon, Madison Col
1940	Beta Zeta, Southwestern Louisiana
1941	Beta Eta, North Dakota State, Dickinson
1941	Beta Theta, Central
1942	Beta Iota, Radford
1943	Beta Kappa, Western Illinois
1944	Beta Lambda, Arkansas State, Conway
1946	Beta Mu, Henderson
1946	Beta Nu, Murray State
1946	*Beta Xi, SUNY Col., Oneonta (1954)*
1946	*Gamma Clio, SUNY Col., Cortland (1953)*
1947	Beta Pi, Concord
1947	Beta Sigma, Southwest Missouri
1947	*Rho Chi, Wayne State (1959)*
1948	Beta Rho, Northern Illinois
1951	*Beta Tau, SUNY Col., Oswego (1954)*

1951 Beta Upsilon, Indiana State
1952 *Beta Chi, Arizona State* (1964)
1952 Beta Phi, Wisconsin, Stout
1953 *Beta Omega, Bucknell* (1964)
1953 *Beta Psi, Western Michigan* (1976)
1955 *Gamma Alpha, Creighton* (1971)
1956 Gamma Beta, Wisconsin, Stevens Point
1957 *Gamma Delta, Queens (NY)* (1971)
1958 *Gamma Epsilon, Wisconsin, Milwaukee* (1973)
1961 Gamma Zeta, Arkansas A & M
1962 Gamma Eta, Penn State
1964 Gamma Iota, Rochester Tech
1964 *Gamma Kappa, Glenville* (1975)
1964 Gamma Lambda, Loyola, Chicago
1964 *Gamma Theta, Syracuse* (1970)
1965 Gamma Mu, Adrian
1966 Gamma Xi, Slippery Rock
1967 Gamma Omicron, Clarion
1967 Gamma Pi, Missouri Valley
1968 Gamma Rho, East Stroudsburg
1968 *Gamma Sigma, Nicholls* (1974)
1968 *Gamma Tau, C. W. Post* (1974)
1968 *Gamma Upsilon, New Mexico Highlands* (1974)
1969 *Delta Alpha, Tampa* (1971)
1969 *Delta Beta, Tennessee Tech.* (1971)
1969 *Delta Gamma, West Chester* (1973)
1969 Gamma Omega, Eastern Illinois
1969 *Gamma Phi, St. John's (NY)* (1972)
1969 Gamma Psi, Edinboro
1970 Delta Epsilon, Mansfield
1971 Delta Eta, DePaul
1971 *Delta Zeta, Wisconsin, Whitewater* (1976)
1972 Delta Iota, Delaware
1972 Delta Kappa, Indiana, Evansville
1972 Delta Theta, Southern Illinois
1974 Delta Lambda, V.P.I.
1975 Delta Nu, G.M.I.
1975 Delta Xi, Dallas Baptist
1976 Delta Omicron, York
1977 Delta Pi, West Virginia State
1977 Delta Rho, Elon

Alpha Sigma Tau

COAT OF ARMS

ACTIVE PIN

ALPHA SIGMA TAU was founded at the Michigan State Normal College, Ypsilanti, Michigan, on November 4, 1899, initially as one of the oldest educational sororities by a group of eight college women: Helene Rice, May Gephart, Mayene Tracy, Mable Chase, Harriet Marx, Eva O'Keefe, Adriance Rice, and Ruth Dutcher. Mrs. Effie E. Lyman was the first patroness. In the next few growing years, Miss

Ada A. Norton and Miss Abigail Pearce joined Mrs. Lyman in advising the sorority.

Through the many years of its existence, Alpha Sigma Tau has bestowed its purpose to promote the ethical, cultural, and social development of its members, specifically: "to develop the character of each member through a study of ethics so that she will show in all her relationships sincerity, honesty, love and understanding; to help each member enjoy the cultural advantages in life so that she will know how to select those things which are most worthwhile, and to develop in each member the social graces to the extent that she will be able to take her place in life with true dignity and poise."

Growth Because the advisers believed that they should proceed cautiously in their choice of new chapters and because two of the early chapters were disbanded by college authorities, nationalization did not take place until October 8, 1925. Having fulfilled the necessary requirements, Alpha Sigma Tau was made a member of the Association of Education Sororities in April, 1926. In December, 1951, Alpha Sigma Tau, along with the other AES sororities, became a member of the National Panhellenic Conference.

Government The constitution and bylaws may be revised or amended only at a national convention. Between conventions business is conducted by the National Council composed of the national president, secretary, treasurer, NPC delegate, and the directors of collegiate chapters, alumnae, expansion, fraternity programs, and publications.

The chapters are grouped into geographic districts. Each district is supervised by a district president who annually visits the chapters within her district. Each collegiate chapter is also served by its own chapter advisers, consultant, and advisory board. Collegiate chapter officers and staff have a national counterpart. These national committee chairmen formulate chapter programs and review chapter reports on the programming. They are available for consultation to the collegiate chapters. In addition to the above alumnae volunteers, Alpha Sigma Tau may employ traveling/resident counselors to provide on-site assistance to colonies and chapters.

Traditions and Insignia The badge of Alpha Sigma Tau is a six-pointed shield of black enamel and gold, bordered with pearls and displaying the sorority letters in the center. The coat of arms is a shield divided into four parts with the following symbols: in the upper left, a crown; in the upper right, a book; in the lower right, an anchor; and in the lower left, six stars. Above is a candle with its spreading rays, and below appears on a band the Greek inscription, Alpha Sigma Tau. The pledge pin is a monogram of gold; the flower, the yellow rose; the jewel, the pearl; the colors, emerald and gold; the open motto, "Active, Self-Reliant, Trustworthy."

Publications The official magazine of Alpha Sigma Tau is *The Anchor*, and the alumnae newsletter is *The Crest*, both of which are published two times a year. Other publications are the sorority songbook, a pledge manual, constitution, national handbook, a housing manual, and a treasurer's guide.

Funds and Philanthropies The Effie E. Lyman Student Loan Fund provides money for loans to members of collegiate chapters for college expenses. The Endowment Fund is available to collegiate chapters wishing to borrow money for housing.

Alpha Sigma Tau members, nationally, by chapter, by pledge classes, and individually, have always been concerned about their fellow man. Throughout the years of existence, many philanthropies have been promoted and accomplished by contributions. A variety of altruisms have been undertaken by the national organization, such as assistance to Pine Mountain Settlement School in Bledsoe, Kentucky; Penland School of Handicrafts, Penland, North Carolina; contributions to our nation's war efforts; supporting Michigan Association for Emotionally Disturbed children with a major scholarship program, and assistance to the education of an American Indian through the Mary Alice Peterson Grant, in addition to other donations.

Pine Mountain School has challenged and continued to interest Alpha Sigma Tau members through a variety of programs it has offered to children and adults in the area of Appalachia. We have made contributions to Pine Mountain since 1945. The school's programs have adapted to the changing needs of the mountain people. It has evolved from a boarding school, to pre-school programs that went to foster the national Head Start program, to its environmental education program that exists today.

There are two scholarships available to sorority women of ΑΣΤ. J. O. Pollack Social Service Scholarship is given to women who contribute greatly to social service endeavors that involve her chapter, campus, community of sisters, national social service project, and her home town. The other scholarship, Lenore S. King Scholarship, named after one of the national presidents, is given to college women of the sorority, basically according to financial need and academic achievement.

Headquarters P.O. Box 59252, Birmingham, AL 35216.

Membership Membership information is not available.

COAT OF ARMS

Alpha Xi Delta

ACTIVE PIN

PLEDGE PIN

ALPHA XI DELTA was formally established at Lombard College on April 17, 1893, by ten young women to provide a source of continuing friendships and pleasant associations among women students.

The ten were: Alice Bartlett Bruner, Bertha Cook Evans, Julia Maude Foster, Harriet L. McCollum, Lewie Strong Taylor, Cora Bollinger Block, Almira Lowry Cheney, Frances Elizabeth Cheney, Eliza Curtis Everton, and Lucy W. Gilmer.

For nine years Alpha Xi Delta was an integral part of the Lombard campus, strengthened each year by new members who as alumnae continued their close relationship with the group. During the year 1901-02, with the interested cooperation of Sigma Nu, chapter members developed a constitution which declared the nationalization of Alpha Xi Delta, and this document, formally adopted in 1902, still serves.

When Lombard merged with Knox College in 1930, Alpha Chapter oriented itself to its new setting and continued its life.

Alpha Xi Delta has a Beta Chapter which originated as a society earlier than the Alpha Chapter. When in 1902 the P.E.O. Sisterhood decided to limit its expansion to the adult field, its Chapter S (founded 1869, Iowa wesleyan College, Mount Pleasant, Iowa) became Beta Chapter of Alpha Xi Delta. The two organizations have been closely allied with many overlapping memberships ever since. Gamma Chapter was installed two months later, and the three chapters met for the first national convention in 1903.

In 1907 the fraternity was incorporated under the laws of the State of Ohio.

Government Jurisdiction over all chapters and members is vested in the National chapter which meets biennially. Between conventions, the National Council governs; it is composed of seven officers, each with specific areas of responsibility.

To facilitate more direct support for college and alumnae chapters, a regional system has been developed. There are five regions, and 24 provinces are grouped geographically into these regions. Each region is designated by a Roman numeral I—V. Each region has a collegiate director and an alumnae director who are appointed by National Council. These officers do not have a vote in National Chapter.

A regional collegiate director is responsible for the development and implementation of the collegiate program in her region. She directs resource coordinators who are appointed by National Council. Resource coordinators work within a region with a specified group of collegiate chapters, primarily through training and development of chapter advisory boards.

A regional alumnae director is responsible for the development and implementation of the alumnae program in her region. She directs the province presidents who are elected in the year following national convention. Province president's work with the alumnae groups in the province and plan and coordinate province convention which is held for the election of province officers and review of goals and objectives.

Alpha Xi Delta has maintained a business office since 1918, being one of the first women's fraternities to realize the need to centralize the administration of fraternity business. The executive director and staff provide college and alumnae chapter services, and coordinate national convention and leadership training schools.

Traditions and Insignia Founders' Day is observed on April 17 of each year. It has become traditional on that day, in consideration of the needs of others, to contribute to the national philanthropic program. In November, similar gifts are made as a thank-offering for the many benefits and rewards of membership.

The badge of the fraternity is the quill; it may be obtained either jeweled or plain; set with pearls and diamonds, alone or in combination. The fraternity colors chosen by the founders were light and dark blue, but when nationalization was achieved, gold was added as a third color. The pink rose is the flower, having been chosen in complement to the white rose of Sigma Nu.

Publications *The Quill of Alpha Xi Delta*, official publication, has been published continuously since 1904. There are currently four issues each year. *Quill Points*, issued at the discretion of National Council to members only, is designed to keep Alpha Xi Delta members abreast of current fraternity trends.

Other publications include convention minutes, *Chaplain's Manual, Constitution and Bylaws, Foundation Notebook, Manual for Chapter Officers, Membership Manual, Pledge Educator's Manual, Policy and Procedure Manual, Quest Manual, Scholarship Chairman's Manual, Colony Development Manual, Blueprint for Alumnae Chapter Officers*, and *Province President's Manual*.

Funds and Philanthropies Established in 1956, the Alpha Xi Delta Foundation exists for educational, literary, and charitable purposes. All affairs of the foundation are administered by a board of trustees consisting of eight elected trustees, the na-

tional president of Alpha Xi Delta Fraternity, the fraternity executive director, and national philanthropy chairman.

The fraternity is the parent organization to the foundation, and, as such, is itself the primary beneficiary. The foundation supports specific educational programs of the fraternity, as well as offering the members scholarships, grants, and awards. Another important segment of support goes to the national philanthropy.

Through the years, time and monetary support have gone to: the Carcassone School in the Kentucky mountains in the 1930s; Red Cross for equipment during World War II; Noordwyck-by-the-Sea, a Dutch village adopted by Alpha Xi Delta from 1947-1952; disadvantaged children through Howell House in Chicago, and Pittman Hall, Albany, NY, from 1949-1978. Since 1978, the Alpha Xi Delta Foundation has expanded its involvement and commitment to the field of respiratory health. The program includes special projects with the American Lung Association such as the Aspiration of Foreign Bodies project and the Superstuff Program, a self-help program for asthmatic children.

Headquarters 8702 Founders Road, Indianapolis, IN 46268.

Membership Total living membership 74,476. Total undergraduate membership 5,549. Active chapters 97. Inactive chapters 75. Houses owned 44. Graduate/Alumni chapters 194. Total number of initiates 95,439. Chapter roll:

1893 *Alpha, Knox (1973)*
1902 Beta, Iowa Wesleyan
1903 Delta, Bethany (WV)
1903 Epsilon, South Dakota
1903 Gamma, Mount Union
1904 Eta, Syracuse
1904 Zeta, Wittenberg
1905 Iota, West Virginia
1905 Kappa, Illinois
1905 Theta, Wisconsin, Madison (1972-1980)
1907 *Lambda, Jackson (MS) (1957)*
1907 *Mu, Minnesota (1960-1983) (1987)*
1907 Nu, Washington (WA) (1974-1979)
1908 Xi, Kentucky
1909 *Omicron, Cal, Berkeley (1969)*
1911 Pi, Ohio
1912 Rho, Nebraska
1912 Sigma, Iowa
1914 Tau, New Hampshire
1915 Phi, Albion
1915 *Upsilon, Vermont (1947)*
1916 Chi, Kansas (1935-1991)
1916 Psi, Ohio State
1917 Omega, Stetson
1918 *Alpha Alpha, Pitt (1935)*
1918 *Alpha Beta, Cornell (1964)*
1918 *Alpha Gamma, Coe (1974)*
1919 Alpha Delta, Oregon State (1964-1979)
1920 Alpha Epsilon, Michigan
1921 Alpha Eta, Purdue

1921 *Alpha Iota, Drake* (1976)	1960 Gamma Phi, East Carolina
1921 *Alpha Theta, Northwestern* (1972)	1960 *Gamma Upsilon, Georgia* (1974)
1921 *Alpha Zeta, Oklahoma* (1952-1984) (1985)	1961 Delta Alpha, Wisconsin, La Crosse
1922 Alpha Kappa, Kansas State	1961 *Gamma Chi, Tennessee Wesleyan* (1979)
1922 *Alpha Lambda, Oregon* (1968)	1961 Gamma Omega, Henderson
1924 *Alpha Mu, Ohio Wesleyan* (1979)	1961 Gamma Psi, Frostburg
1924 *Alpha Nu, Montana* (1938)	1962 *Delta Beta, Southwestern State (OK)* (1970)
1924 *Alpha Xi, UCLA* (1980)	1962 Delta Delta, Northern Michigan
1925 *Alpha Omicron, Hunter* (1971)	1962 Delta Epsilon, New Orleans
1925 *Alpha Pi, Middlebury* (1965)	1962 *Delta Gamma, Kearney* (1969)
1926 *Alpha Rho, Allegheny* (1970)	1962 *Delta Zeta, C. W. Post* (1977)
1926 Alpha Sigma, Washington State (1943) (1968-1973)	1963 *Delta Eta, California (PA)* (1981)
1927 *Alpha Phi, Penn* (1966)	1963 *Delta Iota, Chadron* (1980)
1927 *Alpha Tau, Alabama* (1972-1981) (1988)	1963 Delta Kappa, Slippery Rock (1981-1987)
1927 *Alpha Upsilon, Brenau* (1941)	1963 Delta Lambda, Rochester Tech
1928 *Alpha Chi, Randolph, Macon* (1946)	1963 Delta Nu, Indiana (PA)
1929 *Alpha Omega, Florida State* (1980)	1963 *Delta Omicron, Fairmont* (1982)
1929 *Alpha Psi, Denver* (1952)	1963 *Delta Theta, St. Cloud* (1977)
1929 Beta Alpha, Texas (1943-1963)	1963 Delta Xi, Georgia State
1929 *Beta Beta, Washington (MO)* (1963)	1964 Delta Mu, Old Dominion
1931 *Beta Delta, Denison* (1949)	1964 Delta Pi, Defiance
1931 *Beta Gamma, Centenary* (1977)	1964 Delta Rho, Cal State, Northridge
1932 *Beta Epsilon, Monmouth (IL)* (1980)	1964 Delta Sigma, Ferris
1932 *Beta Zeta, Lake Forest* (1961)	1965 Delta Chi, Northern Iowa
1934 Beta Eta, Maryland	1965 *Delta Omega, Winona* (1984)
1934 Beta Theta, Michigan State	1965 *Delta Phi, Morris Harvey* (1983)
1938 *Beta Iota, L.S.U.* (1988)	1965 Delta Psi, Southwest Texas
1941 Beta Kappa, Baldwin-Wallace	1965 Delta Tau, Wisconsin, Oshkosh (1972-1986)
1942 Beta Lambda, Penn State	1965 *Delta Upsilon, Wisconsin, Superior* (1981)
1943 Beta Mu, Bowling Green	1965 Epsilon Alpha, Wisconsin, Eau Claire
1943 Beta Nu, Culver-Stockton	1965 *Epsilon Beta, Findlay* (1977)
1945 Beta Omicron, Missouri Valley	1965 *Epsilon Epsilon, Cal State, Sacramento* (1970)
1945 Beta Xi, Marietta	1966 *Epsilon Delta, Indiana State* (1985)
1946 Beta Pi, Indiana (1970-1987)	1966 Epsilon Gamma, Western Carolina
1947 *Beta Rho, Utah* (1953-1969) (1977)	1966 Epsilon Theta, West Liberty
1947 Beta Sigma, West Virginia Wesleyan	1966 *Epsilon Zeta, Eastern Washington* (1971)
1947 Beta Tau, Kent	1967 Epsilon Iota, Newberry
1948 *Beta Phi, Connecticut* (1951)	1967 Epsilon Kappa, Western Kentucky
1948 Beta Psi, Carroll	1967 Epsilon Lambda, Rider
1948 Beta Upsilon, Rhode Island	1967 Epsilon Mu, Northern Colorado
1949 Beta Chi, Gettysburg	1968 Epsilon Eta, South Dakota State
1949 *Beta Omega, Memphis State* (1977)	1968 Epsilon Nu, Hartford (1972-1985)
1949 Gamma Alpha, San Diego State	1968 *Epsilon Omicron, Oklahoma State* (1981)
1950 Gamma Beta, Marshall	1968 Epsilon Pi, Jacksonville (AL)
1950 Gamma Delta, Nebraska, Omaha	1968 Epsilon Rho, Maine, Portland-Gorham
1951 *Gamma Gamma, Arizona* (1961)	1968 *Epsilon Sigma, Georgia Southern* (1979)
1952 Gamma Epsilon, Cal State, Fresno	1968 Epsilon Xi, Missouri, St. Louis
1954 Gamma Eta, Georgia Tech	1969 *Epsilon Chi, Villanova* (1977)
1954 Gamma Zeta, Eastern Michigan	1969 *Epsilon Omega, North Texas* (1989)
1956 *Gamma Theta, East Tennessee* (1978)	1969 Epsilon Phi, Iowa State
1957 *Gamma Iota, Lambuth* (1984)	1969 *Epsilon Psi, Boise* (1973)
1957 *Gamma Kappa, Susquehanna* (1983)	1969 *Epsilon Tau, Central Missouri State* (1990)
1958 Gamma Lambda, Tennessee	1969 *Epsilon Upsilon, Woodbury* (1975)
1958 *Gamma Mu, Ripon* (1971-1977) (1987)	1970 *Zeta Alpha, Jacksonville* (1977)
1958 Gamma Nu, Southeast Missouri	1970 *Zeta Beta, Clarion* (1985)
1958 *Gamma Xi, Valdosta* (1982)	1970 *Zeta Delta, Indiana, South Bend* (1977)
1959 *Gamma Omicron, Central Michigan* (1976)	1970 *Zeta Epsilon, Edinboro* (1982)
1959 *Gamma Pi, Northern Illinois* (1985)	1970 *Zeta Zeta, Northern State* (1978)
1959 *Gamma Rho, Parsons* (1972)	1971 Zeta Eta, West Chester
1959 Gamma Sigma, Thiel	1971 *Zeta Gamma, Mississippi* (1976)
1959 Gamma Tau, Ohio Northern	1972 Zeta Theta, Wright State

1973 Zeta Iota, Arkansas
1973 *Zeta Kappa, Pitt, Johnstown* (1979)
1974 *Zeta Mu, Methodist* (1987)
1975 Zeta Lambda, Texas Wesleyan
1980 Zeta Nu, Miami (OH)
1980 Zeta Xi, Auburn
1981 Zeta Omicron, Florida
1983 *Zeta Pi, Lincoln Memorial (TN)* (1985)
1983 *Zeta Rho, North Carolina State* (1990)
1983 Zeta Sigma, Hillsdale
1983 Zeta Tau, North Carolina, Asheville
1986 Zeta Upsilon, Alma
1987 Zeta Chi, North Carolina, Wilmington
1987 Zeta Phi, SUNY, Binghamton
1987 Zeta Psi, Virginia
1989 Theta Beta, Sonoma State
1989 Zeta Omega, West Georgia
1990 Theta Alpha, Millersville
1990 Theta Delta, Towson
1990 Theta Gamma, Delaware

Chi Omega

ACTIVE PIN

PLEDGE PIN

CHI OMEGA was organized as a fraternal order at the University of Arkansas on April 5, 1895, by Ina Mae Boles, Jobelle Holcomb, Alice Simonds, Jean Vincen heller. They were assisted by Dr. Charles Richardson, an alumnus of Kappa Sigma, a regent of the university, and who, in consideration of this service, was made the sole honorary member of the fraternity.

The value of Chi Omega lies in its consistent challenge to women to grow, to develop, and to strive for excellence in all aspects of their lives. The inspiration of the fraternity is total belief in each individual member, and its success rests in each member's belief in the high ideals of Chi Omega. Personal growth is an essential element of the fraternity—from pledgeship through alumnae involvement.

Growth   At the time Chi Omega was founded no Greek-letter organizations for women had been developed in the colleges and universities of the South. This fact not only gave Chi Omega the advantage of pioneering in this section of the nation, but was also responsible in part for the distinctive leitmotif in the fraternity's program to be national in the best sense of the word. In addition to this national outlook, Chi Omega had the advantage of beginning its career after there had been a great advance in the educational standards for women. Chi Omega has been a contributing member of the National Panhellenic Conference since 1903.

Chi Omega's growth has been consistent since its founding in 1895. By 1920, 46 collegiate chapters were listed on the national roll; by 1950, the number had swelled to 109. The membership has continued to increase and in 1985 there were 168 collegiate chapters, more than 400 alumnae chapters and clubs, and over 170,000 in total membership.

Government   Government of Chi Omega is vested in the biennial convention; during the intervals between conventions, this power is delegated to the Governing Council, which is composed of five members. The executive office, originally established in 1915 in Lexington, Kentucky, moved to Cincinnati in 1924 where it has remained to the present. All administrative duties of the fraternity are managed in this office.

Traditions and Insignia   The open declaration of Chi Omega is "Hellenic Culture and Christian Ideals." The fraternity's colors are cardinal and straw. The official flower is the white carnation. There is an official flag, a banner, and a seal of Chi Omega.

The badge of the fraternity is a monogram of the Greek letters—the letter Chi is superimposed over the letter Omega in raised gold. The badge carries 14 stones, always pearls or diamonds, six on one bar of the X and eight on the other. The Greek letters PBYHΣ are written across the top of the Ω, with a skull and crossbones on the right side and an owl on the left. No one but an initiated member may wear the Chi Omega badge.

The pledge pin of Chi Omega is a black enamel oval edged in gold, with the gold letters X and Ω in the center.

Publications   *The Eleusis of Chi Omega* was established in 1899 by Ida Pace Purdue. Published quarterly, the magazine includes newsworthy items as well as thought-provoking articles pertinent to the interests and concerns of Chi Omegas across the nation. *The Eleusis* serves as a record of the growth and successes of the fraternity.

During World War I, Chi Omega began building a Service Fund, the income of which was directed toward financing the Service Fund Publications which began in the 1920's. Nationally and locally, Chi Omega has always encouraged the development of the educational aspect of fraternity life. Hence, Chi Omega has consistently devoted its resources to the issuing of publications of an educational or research nature with the hope that they will contribute to the understanding of those issues of special interest to women. Through the years, there have been nine Service Fund Publications.

In 1928, the first volume of the *History of Chi Omega* was published. In 1929, the second volume which catalogued the members to date was printed; the third in 1957; and the fourth in 1976.

In 1984-85, the fraternity introduced the *Chi Omega Cares Series*. The purpose of the series is to provide thorough research, information for discussions, and viable solutions to some of concerns of contemporary Chi Omegas. The five initial volumes ar the *Eating Disorders Handbook*, the *Personal Growth Plan*, the *Substance Awareness Handbook*, *Lasting Impressions: The Matter of Manners*, and the *Financial Management Handbook*. *Cross-Roads—Career Planning* is scheduled for release in 1986.

Funds and Philanthropies The Chi Omega Foundation is a non-profit, tax-exempt corporation whose purpose is to promote and support education, educational pursuits, and educational institutions. The foundation fosters intellectual excellence through scholarships, leadership training lectures and programs, publications, and other programs. Such funds as the **Mary** Love Collins memorial Scholarship, the Elizabeth Carmichael Orman Scholarship, and the Christelle Ferguson Leadership Fund are administered by the foundation.

The Mary Love Collins Memorial Scholarships are awarded each year to Chi Omegas who are pursuing graduate studies. The Elizabeth Carmichael Orman Scholarships are given to active members of Chi Omega to help defray the costs of their senior years in college. The Christelle Ferguson Leadership Fund finances leadership training programs for active chapter officers, advisors, and alumnae chapters.

The Chi Omega Greek Theater on the University of Arkansas campus was constructed as "an expression of appreciation of its founding and as a symbol of its devotion to the human struggle for enlightenment."

The first gift by a fraternity to the institution of its founding, the Greek Theater is the only structure of its kind in the United States. It is almost an exact replica of one built by Dionysus at the foot of the Acropolis 2,400 years ago. The original cost of this gift was borne by the national fraternity with no assessments of individual members. Preservation of this theater is made possible through contributions to the **Chi Omega Greek Theater Preservation Fund**.

In 1930, Chi Omega established the National Achievement Award, a gold medallion presented periodically to American women of notable accomplishments. The award has been given for service in the areas of public affairs, art, law, business and finance, education, and literature.

Chi Omega members possess the desire to serve the community and recognize the needs of those less fortunate. Therefore, active and alumnae Chi Omegas undertake numerous and varied philanthropic projects which serve the immediate needs of the local communities and allow members to choose worthwhile activities according to their particular interests.

Headquarters Chi Omega Fraternity Executive Office, 3111 Carew Tower, Cincinnati, OH 45202.

Membership Total living membership 158,481. Total undergraduate membership 14,682. Active chapters 176. Inactive chapters 32. Houses owned 84. City/Area alumni associations 402. Total number of initiates 196,799. Chapter roll:

1895	Psi, Arkansas
1898	*Chi (Old), Jessamine Female Institute* (1901)
1899	Chi, Transylvania
1899	*Phi (Old), Hellmuth Woman's College* (1900)
1899	Rho, Tulane
1899	*Sigma, Randolph, Macon Woman's* (1960)
1899	Tau, Mississippi (1911-1926)
1899	*Upsilon (Old), Ward-Belmont* (1900)
1900	Omicron, Illinois
1900	Pi, Tennessee
1901	Xi, Northwestern
1902	Lambda, Kansas
1902	Mu, Cal, Berkeley
1902	Nu, Wisconsin, Madison
1903	Kappa, Nebraska
1903	*Phi Alpha, George Washington* (1968)
1904	Iota, Texas
1905	Eta, Michigan
1905	Theta, West Virginia
1906	*Beta, Colby* (1984)
1906	Zeta, Colorado
1907	*Delta, Dickinson* (1971)
1907	*Epsilon (Old), Barnard* (1913)
1908	Gamma, Florida State
1909	Alpha, Washington (WA)
1909	Psi Alpha, Oregon
1910	Chi Alpha, Tufts (1971-1977)
1911	Upsilon Alpha, Syracuse
1913	Pi Alpha, Cincinnati
1913	Rho Alpha, Missouri
1913	Sigma Alpha, Miami (OH)
1913	Tau Alpha, Ohio
1914	Lambda Alpha, Kentucky
1914	Omicron Alpha, Coe
1914	Xi Alpha, Utah
1915	Kappa Alpha, Kansas State
1915	Mu Alpha, New Hampshire
1915	*Nu Alpha, Stanford* (1944)
1916	Iota Alpha, Southern Methodist
1917	Eta Alpha, Oregon State
1917	Theta Alpha, Cornell (1963-1987)
1919	Beta Alpha, Penn
1919	Chi Beta, Purdue
1919	Delta Alpha, Tennessee, Chattanooga
1919	Epsilon Alpha, Oklahoma
1919	*Gamma Alpha, Swarthmore* (1932)
1919	Phi Beta, Pitt
1919	Psi Beta, Iowa
1919	*Upsilon Beta (Old), Hollins* (1929)
1919	Zeta Alpha, Ohio State
1920	Sigma Beta, Montana State
1920	Tau Beta, Oklahoma State
1921	Omicron Beta, William and Mary
1921	*Pi Beta, Minnesota* (1989)
1921	Rho Beta, Drake
1921	Xi Beta, Maine
1922	Eta Beta, Iowa State
1922	*Iota Beta (Old), Hunter* (1940)
1922	Kappa Beta, Rhodes
1922	Lambda Beta, Rhode Island

1922 Mu Beta, Georgia	1950 Gamma Delta, San Diego U.
1922 Nu Beta, Alabama	1951 Chi Epsilon, Evansville
1922 Theta Beta, Indiana	1951 Psi Epsilon, Arizona State
1922 Zeta Beta, Arizona	1952 Phi Epsilon, Ball State
1923 Alpha Beta, Auburn	1953 Alpha Alpha, North Texas
1923 Beta Beta, Washington State	1953 *Tau Epsilon, Puget Sound* (1982)
1923 Chi Gamma, Marietta	1954 Sigma Epsilon, Vanderbilt
1923 *Delta Beta, Maryland* (1923)	1955 Pi Epsilon, Roanoke
1923 Epsilon Beta, North Carolina	1955 Rho Epsilon, Texas Christian
1923 Gamma Beta, UCLA	1956 Psi Zeta, Houston
1923 *Psi Gamma (Old), North Dakota, Sioux Falls* (1941)	1957 Chi Zeta, Colorado State
1924 Phi Gamma, L.S.U.	1958 Phi Zeta, McNeese
1924 Rho Gamma, Hillsdale	1958 Upsilon Zeta, West Texas
1924 *Sigma Gamma (Old), Oglethorpe* (1945) (Reactivated as Delta Theta in 1969)	1959 Sigma Zeta, East Texas
1924 Tau Gamma, Wittenberg	1959 Tau Zeta, Emory
1924 Upsilon, Union (TN)	1960 Pi Zeta, Western Michigan
1924 Upsilon Gamma, South Dakota	1960 Rho Zeta, East Carolina
1925 *Kappa Gamma, Ohio Wesleyan* (1975)	1961 Lambda Zeta, Missouri, Kansas City
1925 *Omicron Gamma, Westminster (PA)* (1987)	1961 Mu Zeta, Adrian
1925 Pi Gamma, New Mexico	1961 Nu Zeta, Emporia
1926 Nu Gamma, Penn State	1961 Omicron Zeta, Arkansas State
1926 Xi Gamma, Michigan State	1961 Xi Zeta, Tennessee, Martin
1927 Lambda Gamma, Virginia (1965-1977)	1962 Eta Zeta, Brenau
1927 Mu Gamma, Culver-Stockton	1962 Iota Zeta, Kearney
1928 *Delta Gamma, Denison* (1969)	1962 Kappa Zeta, Texas Tech
1928 Eta Gamma, South Carolina	1962 Theta Zeta, Eastern New Mexico
1928 Iota Gamma, Centenary	1963 Epsilon Zeta, Stephen F. Austin
1928 Theta Gamma, Queens (NC)	1963 Zeta Zeta, Samford
1928 Zeta Gamma, Charleston (SC)	1964 Alpha Zeta, Southwest Texas
1929 Beta Gamma, Louisville	1964 *Beta Zeta, Chadron* (1981)
1929 Epsilon Gamma, Tulsa	1964 Gamma Zeta, Arkansas, Little Rock
1930 Alpha Gamma, Utah State	1964 Phi Theta, East Central State
1931 Upsilon Beta, Rollins	1964 Psi Theta, Old Dominion
1933 Psi Delta, Wyoming	1964 *Upsilon Theta, Texas A & I* (1985)
1934 Chi Delta, Millsaps	1965 Chi Theta, Western Kentucky
1936 Phi Delta, Mississippi State	1965 Sigma Theta, Sam Houston
1936 *Upsilon Delta, Miami (FL)* (1984)	1965 Tau Theta, William Woods
1937 Tau Delta, Gettysburg	1966 Nu Theta, West Liberty
1938 *Sigma Delta, Lake Forest* (1961)	1966 Omicron Theta, Midwestern
1939 Pi Delta, New Mexico State	1966 *Pi Theta, Eastern Washington* (1977)
1939 Rho Delta, Texas, El Paso	1966 *Rho Theta, Wisconsin, Oshkosh* (1979)
1940 Epsilon, SUNY, Buffalo	1967 *Kappa Theta, Northern Illinois* (1985)
1940 Phi, USC	1967 Lambda Theta, Akron
1941 Iota Beta, Massachusetts	1967 Mu Theta, Southwestern Louisiana
1943 Psi Gamma, Mercer	1967 Xi Theta, South Dakota State
1944 Omicron Delta, Carnegie-Mellon	1968 *Iota Theta, Northern Michigan* (1982)
1944 Xi Delta, Toledo	1968 Theta Theta, South Florida
1945 *Nu Delta, Willamette* (1972)	1969 *Alpha Theta, Wayne State (NE)* (1983)
1947 Kappa Delta, Bowling Green	1969 Beta Theta, South Alabama
1947 Lambda Delta, Kent	1969 Delta Theta, Oglethorpe
1947 Mu Delta, Bradley	1969 Epsilon Theta, Morehead
1948 Eta Delta, Florida	1969 Gamma Theta, Eastern Kentucky
1948 Iota Delta, San Jose	1969 Zeta Theta, Middle Tennessee
1948 *Sigma Gamma, Davis and Elkins* (1984)	1970 Chi Kappa, George Mason
1948 Theta Delta, Carroll	1970 Psi Kappa, Clemson
1949 Alpha Delta, Indiana State	1971 Phi Kappa, West Georgia
1949 Epsilon Delta, Southern Mississippi	1971 Tau Kappa, Montevallo
1949 Zeta Delta, Nebraska, Omaha	1972 Sigma Kappa, Austin Peay
1950 Beta Delta, Thiel	1974 Pi Kappa, Appalachian
1950 Delta Delta, Cal, Santa Barbara	1974 Rho Kappa, Illinois State
	1975 Omicron Kappa, Cal, Davis
	1975 Xi Kappa, Texas A & M

1976	Lambda Kappa, Huntingdon
1976	Mu Kappa, Duke
1976	Nu Kappa, Georgia Southern
1977	Iota Kappa, Troy
1977	Kappa Kappa, Alabama, Huntsville
1977	Theta Kappa, Baylor
1979	Eta Kappa, Missouri, Rolla
1981	Epsilon Kappa, St. Lawrence
1981	Zeta Kappa, North Carolina, Greensboro
1982	Delta Kappa, North Carolina, Charlotte
1983	Beta Kappa, Cal Poly, Pomona
1983	Gamma Kappa, Western Illinois
1984	Alpha Kappa, North Carolina State
1984	Psi Lambda, Valdosta
1985	Chi Lambda, Winthrop
1987	Phi Lambda, Franklin and Marshall
1987	Sigma Lambda, V.P.I.
1987	*Tau Lambda, Richmond* (1988)
1987	Upsilon Lambda, Hanover
1988	Pi Lambda, Centre College
1988	Rho Lambda, Delaware
1989	Birmingham-Southern
1989	Omicron Lambda, Birmingham-Southern
1989	Xi Lambda, Washington and Lee
1990	Mu Lambda, Dayton
1990	Nu Lambda, North Carolina, Wilmington

COAT OF ARMS

Delta Delta Delta

ACTIVE PIN

PLEDGE PIN

DELTA DELTA DELTA was founded at Boston University on Thanksgiving Eve, 1888. Two friends and seniors, Sarah Ida Shaw and Eleanor Dorcas Pond, conceived the establishment of Delta Delta Delta, composing the ritual, defining the structure, and planning for national and international expansion. They invited two other members of the class of 1889, Florence Isabelle Stewart and Isabelle Morgan Breed, to join with them. These four, honored as the founders, and 14 initiated upperclassmen, formed the Alpha Chapter charter group. These early members gave the new society its ideals and character.

Growth Before the first decade had ended, 17 chapters had been established in 13 states from New England to the Midwest and South. Consistent expansion policy has resulted in a wide distribution of chapters throughout the United States and Canada.

From the first, provision was made for the formation of alumnae chapters. An alumnae degree of ini-

tiation is included in the ritual and administered to qualified members.

Tri Delta has been identified with the Panhellenic movement since its beginning in 1891 in Boston.

Government The supreme governing body of the fraternity is the biennial general convention (triennial from 1912 to 1936). Only elected delegates from collegiate and alumnae chapters and designated national officers may vote at a convention, but any member has the privilege of the floor and may speak at any meeting.

During the interim between conventions, the Executive Board, consisting of five elected officers, is the governing body of the fraternity. The officers who comprise the Executive Board are the president, collegiate vice-president, alumnae vice-president, membership director, and finance director. They are assisted by six elected associate directors who are assigned to specific areas of responsibility by each Executive Board. Three special officers, standing committees, appointed chairmen and district officers also assist the Board in carrying out its responsibilities. The legal and business affairs of the fraternity are managed by Delta Delta Delta, a not-for-profit corporation, chartered by the State of Illinois January 7, 1916. The Executive Board is the board of directors of the corporation.

Collegiate chapters are grouped into districts and are under the supervision of the collegiate vice-president and district presidents, while alumnae chapters are supervised by the alumnae vice-president and district chairmen. Area financial assistants supervise chapter finances under the direction of the finance director. Advisory committees of local alumnae support the collegiate chapters.

The executive offices are under the supervision of the executive director. Centralization of reports, publications, and supplies dates back to the establishment of Trident offices at Galva, Illinois, in 1905. The first executive offices were established in Chicago in 1912. Since 1972, they have been located in Arlington, Texas, and now occupy the fraternity's own building.

Traditions and Insignia In 1955 Tri Delta held its initial leadership school for collegiate officers and advisers, the first of its kind to be held on a national scale by a women's group. Since then, similar schools have been planned for years alternating with conventions. State or district meetings are also held every two years.

The official badge is three stars set with pearls within a 300° crescent of gold bearing three Δ's. The pledge pin is an inverted delta surrounded by three Δ's all in green enamel.

The colors are silver, gold and blue (cerulean); the flower is the pansy; the tree is the pine; the jewel is the pearl. Other emblems include the trident and the dolphin. The coat of arms, adopted in 1906, is a quartered shield with a pansy crest.

Publications Plans for a magazine were made early in the history of Delta Delta Delta with the result that the first number of the first volume of

The Trident was issued on Thanksgiving Eve, 1891, the third anniversary of the founding. Only one number, 3 of Volume II, was ever omitted. Directories were published from 1894 to 1925.

The first history was published in 1907, a cloth-bound volume of 268 pages, entitled *A Detailed Record of Delta Delta Delta, 1888-1907*. In 1932 a second edition similarly bound, of 690 pages, bringing the history up to 1931, was issued. A third edition will be issued in 1988.

Manual covering the various phases of the fraternity program have been in use since 1927. These include the *Bylaws of Delta Delta Delta Fraternity* and manuals for collegiate chapters, advisory committees, alumnae chapters, house corporations, district officers, and house directors. The *Pledge Manual* is published for pledge-members, and a pamphlet for parents, *Your Daughter and Delta Delta Delta*, is sent to the parents of each pledge-member.

The songs of Delta Delta Delta had as their nucleus a collection made by Alpha Chapter in the first year of its history. The third volume of published songs is now in its 13th edition with a 14th edition scheduled for publication in 1988.

Funds and Philanthropies In addition to the general operating expense fund each year, the fraternity maintains certain special funds: the National Endowment Fund, Collegiate Chapter Reserve Fund, the Three Star Fund, the Fiftieth Anniversary Fund, the Service Projects Fund, the Crescent Fund, Collegiate Chapter and Alumnae Chapter Convention Reserve Funds, The Delta Century Fund, and the Loyalty Fund.

The Fiftieth Anniversary Fund was established through individual contributions in celebration of the Fiftieth Anniversary of the founding. The annual income provides graduate fellowships for members.

Tri Delta's principal philanthropy provides scholarships to worthy women students on campuses where the fraternity has chapters. The project was established in 1942, and by 1985, approximately $1,289,000 had been awarded to more than 5,800 women. Awards are made annually, usually in the spring, with the cooperation of student personnel deans, and are based on merit and need, regardless of race, color, creed, or fraternity affiliation or nonaffiliation.

The Crescent Fund, derived from contributions made to it by members, chapters and others, provides confidential aid to loyal alumnae.

The Delta Century Fund was established in 1964 to accumulate funds for a special project to celebrate Tri Delta's 100th anniversary in 1988. The 1982 convention selected the National Humanities Center, located in Research Triangle Park, North Carolina, to be the recipient. Beginning in 1988, two Delta Delta Delta fellows will be named "in perpetuity" with special consideration being given to candidates from institutions where the fraternity has chapters. As a tangible reminder of the monetary gift, a wildflower garden has been presented to the Center. The garden was dedicated in April 1985.

During both World War I and World War II, Delta Delta Delta made its contribution to foreign relief. In the first war, the fraternity assumed support of the YWCA Foyer at Tours and maintained it for many months after the armistice until the women of France were able to take it over. A reconstruction school at Guny was then materially aided for a number of months; and in 1928 the unexpended balance in the war service chest was voted to endow a student room in the American dormitory of the Cite' Universitaire in Paris. In World War II, more than $12,000 was contributed to United China Relief, with a portion of the funds designated for scholarships for women in Chinese universities. This project gave impetus to the scholarship program adopted as the national philanthropy in 1942. In addition to national projects, collegiate and alumnae chapters support a wide variety of local philanthropies.

Tri Delta's second national philanthropy was adopted by the 1974 convention. The first Tuesday in December is Tri Delta's annual "Sleighbell Day," designated for contributions to support research and treatment of cancer in children, oncology and hematology. More than $1,800,000 has been contributed to Sleighbell projects over a ten-year period from 1974 to 1984.

Headquarters 2313 Brookhollow Plaza Drive, P.O. Box 5987, Arlington, Texas 76006.

Membership Total living membership 128,527. Total undergraduate membership 11,288. Active chapters 132. Inactive chapters 27. Houses owned 81. Graduate/Alumni chapters 334. Total number of initiates 162,128. Chapter roll:

1888	Alpha, Boston U (1970-1984)	
1889	Delta, Simpson	
1889	Epsilon, Knox	
1890	*Gamma, Adrian* (1946)	
1890	Omega Delta, Iowa State (1892-1912)	
1891	Beta, St. Lawrence	
1892	Zeta, Cincinnati	
1893	Eta, Vermont	
1894	Iota, Michigan	
1894	Kappa, Nebraska	
1894	Theta, Minnesota	
1895	Lambda, Baker	
1895	*Sigma, Connecticut Wesleyan* (1913)	
1895	Upsilon, Northwestern	
1896	Nu, Ohio State	
1896	Omicron, Syracuse	
1898	Mu, Wisconsin, Madison	
1898	*Xi, Goucher* (1941)	
1900	Pi, Cal, Berkeley	
1903	*Rho, Barnard* (1913)	
1904	Chi, Mississippi (1910-1926)	
1904	Phi, Iowa	
1904	Psi, Penn (1970-1986)	
1904	Tau, Bucknell	
1905	*Alpha Xi, Randolph, Macon* (1960)	

1908	*Alpha Upsilon, Colby* (1964)
1908	Beta Zeta, Transylvania
1908	Delta Alpha, DePauw
1908	Omega, Stanford (1944-1985)
1909	Theta Alpha, Washington (WA)
1910	Theta Beta, Colorado
1910	Theta Delta, Oregon
1910	Theta Gamma, Oklahoma
1911	Alpha Alpha, Adelphi
1911	Delta Beta, Miami (OH)
1911	Delta Gamma, Vanderbilt
1911	Theta Epsilon, Southwestern (TX)
1912	*Delta Delta, Wooster* (1913)
1912	Delta Epsilon, Millikin
1912	Delta Eta, Coe
1912	Delta Zeta, Franklin
1912	Theta Zeta, Texas
1913	Alpha Beta, Cornell
1913	Alpha Delta, Stetson
1913	*Alpha Gamma, Georgia Wesleyan* (1914)
1913	Delta Iota, Arkansas
1913	Delta Kappa, Drury
1913	*Delta Theta, Judson* (1919)
1913	Theta Eta, Wyoming
1913	Theta Theta, Nevada
1914	Alpha Epsilon, Brenau
1914	*Alpha Zeta, Hollins* (1929)
1914	Delta Lambda, Butler
1914	Delta Mu, Alabama
1914	Delta Nu, Mount Union
1915	Delta Xi, Missouri
1915	Theta Iota, Kansas State
1916	Alpha Eta, Florida State
1916	Alpha Theta, Pitt
1916	Theta Kappa, Southern Methodist
1917	*Alpha Iota, Middlebury* (1969)
1917	Alpha Kappa, Maine
1917	Delta Omicron, Indiana
1917	Theta Lambda, Colorado State
1918	Theta Mu, Oregon State
1918	Theta Nu, Washington State
1920	Delta Pi, Illinois
1921	Theta Xi, USC
1923	Delta Rho, Kentucky
1923	Delta Sigma, Tennessee
1923	Theta Omicron, Whitman
1925	*Delta Tau, Beloit* (1963)
1925	Delta Upsilon, Ohio Wesleyan
1925	Theta Pi, UCLA
1926	*Delta Phi, Washington (MO)* (1954)
1926	*Theta Rho, Montana* (1971)
1928	Alpha Lambda, South Carolina
1928	Alpha Mu, William and Mary
1929	Delta Chi, Denison
1929	Theta Sigma, North Dakota
1929	Theta Tau, Idaho
1930	Canada Alpha, Toronto
1931	Alpha Nu, Charleston (SC)
1931	Alpha Omicron, Duke
1931	*Canada Beta, Manitoba* (1952)
1931	Delta Psi, Rhodes
1931	Theta Upsilon, Tulsa
1932	*Canada Gamma, Alberta* (1959)
1932	Theta Phi, Utah
1933	*Theta Chi, South Dakota* (1938)
1934	Alpha Pi, Maryland
1934	Alpha Rho, Georgia
1934	Delta Omega, L.S.U.
1938	*Theta Psi, Texas, El Paso* (1977)
1943	Alpha Sigma, North Carolina
1944	Alpha Tau, Carnegie-Mellon
1944	Phi Alpha, Toledo
1946	*Phi Beta, Arizona* (1984)
1946	Theta Omega, Kansas
1947	Alpha Phi, Penn State
1948	*Alpha Chi, Miami (FL)* (1980)
1948	Alpha Psi, Florida
1948	Phi Gamma, Michigan State
1949	Phi Delta, New Mexico
1951	Phi Epsilon, Southern Mississippi
1952	Phi Zeta, Puget Sound
1953	Phi Eta, Texas Tech
1954	Phi Theta, Auburn
1955	Phi Iota, West Virginia
1955	Phi Kappa, Cal State, Long Beach
1955	Phi Lambda, Texas Christian
1957	Phi Mu, Southeast Missouri
1957	Phi Nu, Southwestern Louisiana
1958	Phi Omicron, Northern Arizona
1958	Phi Xi, Wichita
1959	Alpha Omega, Emory
1959	*Phi Pi, Utah State* (1974)
1959	Phi Rho, Pacific (CA)
1961	*Phi Sigma, Portland State* (1964)
1961	*Phi Tau, Rhode Island* (1982)
1962	Phi Phi, Delta State
1962	Phi Upsilon, Oklahoma State
1963	Phi Chi, Arkansas, Little Rock
1965	Phi Omega, Arizona State
1965	*Phi Psi, Mankato* (1975)
1966	Beta Alpha, South Florida
1967	Beta Beta, Cal State, Northridge
1968	*Beta Delta, Indiana State* (1985)
1968	Beta Gamma, Jacksonville
1969	Beta Epsilon, Texas, Arlington
1969	*Beta Eta, Boise* (1984)
1970	Beta Iota, West Georgia
1970	Beta Theta, Clemson
1972	*Beta Kappa, North Carolina, Charlotte* (1977)
1972	Beta Lambda, Central Florida
1972	Beta Mu, Mississippi State
1972	Beta Xi, Stephen F. Austin
1973	Beta Nu, V.P.I.
1974	Beta Omicron, Illinois State
1974	Beta Pi, Cal, Davis
1975	Beta Rho, L.S.U., Shreveport
1975	Beta Sigma, Virginia
1977	Beta Tau, Baylor
1979	Beta Upsilon, Cal, Irvine
1980	Beta Chi, Ball State
1980	Beta Phi, Centre College
1981	Beta Omega, Trinity
1981	Beta Psi, Union (NY)

1981   Gamma Alpha, Texas A & M
1982   Gamma Beta, Villanova
1984   Gamma Gamma, Dartmouth
1985   Gamma Delta, Spring Hill
1986   Gamma Epsilon, Dickinson
1986   Gamma Zeta, Millsaps
1987   Gamma Eta, Richmond
1987   Gamma Theta, Cal, Santa Barbara
1988   Gamma Iota, Purdue
1989   Gamma Kappa, Wake Forest
1989   Gamma Lambda, Cal, San Diego

Delta Gamma

COAT OF ARMS   ACTIVE PIN   PLEDGE PIN

DELTA GAMMA was founded in December, 1873, at the Lewis School for girls located at Oxford, Mississippi. The founders were Anna Boyd, Eva Webb, and Mary Comfort, three students who were weatherbound at the school during the Christmas holidays. Without consulting anyone, they chose their name and badge and wrote their constitution and ritual. As soon as school resumed in January, 1874, they admitted four more members to what they called the Delta Gamma Club. All three founders graduated at the end of the school year, leaving their club in the hands of others, but it continued to grow and become quite prominent in Oxford. When the first chapter charter was granted at Water Valley Seminary, the Mother chapter took the name Psi.

Growth   During the first few years, chapters were added from time to time in other female seminaries in the South. These were short-lived, with none surviving more than three years due to faculty opposition and the decline of women's colleges. A chance meeting between a Mississippi Phi Delta Theta and a fraternity brother from the North, George Banta, brought about the important move by Delta Gamma onto campuses in the Midwest. Mr. Banta was initiated by Delta Gamma's Psi chapter in 1878 and deputized to install a chapter at Franklin College, Franklin, Indiana. His fiancée, Lillie Vawter, was a charter member of this group. The couple provided contacts and encouragement for a number of other early chapters in the region.

Although originally strongest in the Midwest, Delta Gamma had chapters in both New York and California by 1887. It became international in 1913 when it installed its first Canadian chapter at the University of Toronto. Its national outlook was demonstrated when it became a charter member of the Intersorority Conference in 1902, now the National Panhellenic Conference. Despite its far-flung chapters, however, the fraternity was noted for its extremely conservative expansion policies until the Second World War. At that time the expansion rate accelerated dramatically. New chapters were installed at the average rate of three a year through the 1950s, although 1946 alone saw the advent of six new chapters. This rate of growth was equalled in the 1980s.

The first alumnae chapter was organized at Cleveland, Ohio, in 1888 when all the women at Adelbert College were expelled by an act of the administration. Today, alumnae groups are found in every state and in several foreign countries as well. Alumnae are organized into chapters, which meet certain requirements for numbers of members and frequency of meetings, and which have a vote at convention, and associations, which are smaller and are not represented at convention. Informal Hope Groups are frequently found in more isolated areas where there are not enough alumnae to maintain an association.

Government   Delta Gamma was governed by the Mother chapter until 1881. The first convention, held that year, transferred this authority to the convention body, with business between conventions to be conducted by a Grand and a Deputy chapter chosen by convention. Fraternity officers were elected from the designated chapters.

A period of transition from 1888 to 1895 replaced the Grand and Deputy chapters with a Council of alumnae members elected by the convention. Council currently consists of seven members: president, four vice-presidents, secretary-treasurer, and NPC delegate. The fraternity was incorporated in 1951 under the laws of Ohio as "Delta Gamma Fraternity."

As the supreme governing body, convention is composed of one delegate from each collegiate chapter and each alumnae chapter, the members of Council, the executive secretary, the province officers, the foundation director, and such chairman and directors as may be designated by Council.

For purposes of administration, alumnae and collegiate chapters are grouped geographically into provinces. Each area is served by a province collegiate chairman who supervises the activities of the collegiate chapters and a province alumnae chairman who directs alumnae activities in the same area.

General fraternity affairs are handled by chairman with regard to the changing needs of the fraternity. These areas include awards, constitutions, rituals, scholarship, convention, fraternity and pledge education, and public relations. This list varies from time to time and often includes committees with special assignments.

In the years between conventions, Delta Gamma offers unparalleled leadership training to its alumnae, collegiate, and national officers through Province Leadership Schools, held in the spring, and the Officers' Training School, held in the summer. These are supplemented by yearly seminars for collegiate chapter advisers. Often, collegiate officers and alumnae officers are included as seminar participants. Similar training is part of the program of each convention.

Traditions and Insignia Founders' Day is observed March 15 every year with collegiate and alumnae gatherings and candlelighting ceremonies. The date honors the founding of the oldest existing chapter, Eta, at the University of Akron. Among its achievements, Eta spearheaded the first convention in 1881, and originated the quarterly journal, *The Anchora*.

It is customary for national alumnae awards to be made at Founders' Day. All 50-year members receive special certificates. The Cable Award goes to members who have demonstrated outstanding loyalty and service to the fraternity. The Anchor Award honors those whose fraternity service has made a unique and lasting impact on the national level. The Oxford Award recognizes alumnae for sustained commitment and service to the community, thereby exemplifying the Delta Gamma philosophy of service. The Shield Award is presented to members who have achieved distinction in their community or state through noteworthy accomplishments in their chosen field. The Rose Award is reserved for members who have made distinguished contributions to the nation and the world in their chosen fields, and whose achievements have been given national recognition.

National awards for outstanding collegiate and alumnae chapters are presented at each convention. Similar awards on the province level are also presented at convention, as well as at the Province Leadership Schools.

The first Delta Gamma badge was a gold letter H with ΔΓ in enamel on the crossbar. By 1877, the anchor, in a larger, flatter form than we know it today, became the official badge. It was often embellished with colored stones and accompanied by a stickpin bearing the chapter letter.

Today the official badge of the fraternity is a plain gold anchor, the crossbar of which displays the letters TΔH in gold on white enamel. Above the flukes is a white enamel shield bearing the gold letters ΔΓ. Decorative stones are restricted to pearls and diamonds. The Council badge adds a scroll set with emeralds below the flukes of the anchor.

The pledge pin is a white enamel shield with the letters ΠΑ on it in gold. Recognition pins are small anchors, or the letters ΔΓ. A special rose pin may be worn only by 50-year members.

The fraternity colors are bronze, pink, and blue. The crest may be used by initiated members only. The flower is the cream colored rose. A rose fitting this description was developed by a Texas rose-grower and named "Delta Gamma" in 1977.

Publications The Anchora, second oldest sorority publication, originated in1 1884. The quarterly journal is received through life subscription by all initiated members and by others who subscribe annually. It celebrated its centennial in 1984 with a special history issue. Delta Gamma has a policy of regularly updating the fraternity history. Previous histories have appeared as special issues of *The Anchora* in 1915, 1934, 1945, 1955, 1966, and 1973. A catalog of the membership first appeared in 1881, followed by a second one in 1888. A membership directory was published in 1901, 1904, 1914, and 1922. Membership records are now kept by computer at Executive Offices.

Delta Gamma is known for the quality and range of the handbooks it produces. The cornerstones of its publication program are the *Collegiate Chapter Officers Manual* and the *Alumnae Officers Manual*, which detail relevant fraternity policies. Pledges have received pledge manuals since the 1930s. In 1968 this publication became known as *The Shield of Delta Gamma*. Like all the handbooks, it is updated regularly.

Other handbooks include those for Activities Chairman/Historian, Advisory Board, Anchor Splash, Foundation, Fraternity Education for collegians and alumnae, House Corporation, House Directors, Officer Slating, Election and Transition, Pledge Education, Public Relations, Rituals, Rush, Scholarship, Social, Sponsorship, and Treasurer. Other notable publications include the notebook and poster kit for *Options*, the alcohol awareness program, the inspirational *Think Anchor Deep*, and the instructional *DG Project Eye Alert*. Two poster kits dealing with the foundation and with famous Delta Gammas are also available. Except for *The Anchora*, nearly all Delta Gamma publications are printed in-house at Executive Offices.

Executive Offices also maintains a library of slide programs which are available for rental. One ties in with the *Options* program. Others deal with the history and programs of the fraternity, foundation, and Executive Offices. Two others survey the activities of collegiate chapters and show collegians involved with their most successful philanthropic fund raiser, the Anchor Splash.

Funds and Philanthropies The original motto of three founders was to "Do Good," giving Delta Gamma a philanthropic orientation from its earliest days. Greater efficiency in conducting international projects was achieved when Delta Gamma became the first sorority to establish an independent philanthropic foundation. "The Delta Gamma Foundation" was incorporated in Ohio in 1951. Its business is conducted by an appointed director and three chairmen. A Board of Trustees composed of the Council of Delta Gamma Fraternity guides their work. The foundation has three major programs: grants and loans, sight conservation, and aid to the blind.

The grants and loans program began in 1909, although a national loan fund had been proposed as early as 1881. The first loan was made in 1910. The ensuing years have seen thousands of people, both members and nonmembers, given financial assistance with their college and graduate school expenses. In a recent year, a total of $71,190.00 in grants and loans was distributed by the foundation.

Educational loans are available to upperclass and graduate members. A minimum of four graduate study fellowships are awarded each year, although there may be many more depending upon the availability of patron-sponsored fellowships. Senior Scholarships aid outstanding college seniors to finish their last year of school. The number awarded each year varies as well, with more than 65 recently granted in a single year. Dawson loans are available for siblings and children of Delta Gammas for any level of schooling. The Ruth Billow Fund provides aid for blind Delta Gammas, as well as for members who are pursuing professional training in working with the blind. In the past, fellowships were also available to members and nonmembers for graduate study in social work and orthoptics.

Since 1924 when $57,000 was raised for the Golden Jubilee Convention to endow this fund, nearly $1-million has been awarded in scholarships, fellowships, and educational loans.

Like most other groups, Delta Gamma dropped its usual projects during the two World Wars in order to provide more support to the war efforts. During World War I, all conventions and conferences were suspended to make these funds available for war work. A seaside home for ailing and destitute children who had been victims of the war was financed in Holland, and a Delta Gamma Orphanage was established in Marchiennes, Belgium. For this project, the Belgian government decorated the chairman of the fund raising campaign. After the war, Delta Gamma turned the operation and ownership of the orphanage over to the town of Marchiennes. During World War II, however, the fraternity resumed its support, once again earning a decoration from the Belgian government.

The International Education program was a logical outgrowth of the desire for peace following World War II, when a great demand for exchange education on the college level developed. At this time Delta Gamma, working with the Institute of International Education, made available free room and board in chapter houses for women studying in this country. As universities tightened their budgets for scholarships for foreign students, the demand for the program lessened. The International Education program was terminated in 1973.

The success of the World War I projects and the fundraising efforts of 1924 gave Delta Gammas a desire for another international project, something into which collegians and alumnae could channel their energies in a united effort. In 1936, the theme, "Aiding the Blind" was chosen. The title was revised to "Sight Conversation and Aid to the Blind" in 1942. As each area grew in complexity, it became advisable to divide them in 1973 to facilitate administration.

From the beginning of "Aiding the Blind," collegiate and alumnae groups have chosen projects that benefit their own communities. These range from the Blind Children's Center in Los Angeles, founded in 1938 and owned and supported by Southern California alumnae, to a mobile vision screening clinic in Dallas, to the popular DG Project Eye Alert, in which members teach children to teach younger children about eye care and safety. Alumnae in many cities are noted for their work of vision screening preschool children. Glaucoma screening is also a growing project. Many Delta Gammas on campus provide personal services for the blind such as reading, recording, and shopping. In addition, may state affiliates of the National Society to Prevent Blindness have been started and supported by Delta Gammas.

As part of Delta Gamma's centennial celebration in 1972, a $50,000 grant to establish a program in pediatric ophthalmology went to Children's Mercy Hospital in Kansas City. Another $50,000 was given to the National Society for Prevention of Blindness to provide initial financing for a Home Vision Testing Kit. Since then, the foundation has made many major grants to organizations such as the NSPB, the United States Association of Blind Athletes, the National Accreditation Council, the National Children's Eye Care Foundation, and the Association of Radio Reading Services.

Delta Gamma is proud of its record of philanthropy. Yearly fund raising in the name of the foundation passed the $1-million mark in the 1981-82 fiscal year. Today, Delta Gammas give 750 hours of service to their communities every day of every year.

Headquarters Executive Offices, 3250 Riverside Drive, Columbus, OH 43221.

An executive secretary appointed by Council manages the Delta Gamma Executive Offices and supervises the work of more than twenty full- and part-time employees. The offices include fraternity, foundation, and collegiate chapter accounting, collegiate administration, membership records, expansion, *Anchora*, and publications, orders and supplies, graphic design and printing, merchandising, convention and meeting coordination, and the fraternity archives. Field consultants, who are recent graduates, also work out of the office under the supervision of Council. Traveling from coast to coast, they ensure that each collegiate chapter is visited once a year.

The Central Office itself was established in rented office space in 1942 in response to war-time needs. Delta Gamma became the first women's group to build its own headquarters when it completed the current Executive Offices building in 1961. The Georgian-style building employs historical items throughout its decor, and features a museum room displaying documents, photographs, and memorabilia of the fraternity. Located next door is the guest house, used to accommodate visiting officers and others.

Membership Total living membership 106,229. Total undergraduate membership 8,968. Active chapters 129. Inactive chapters 31. Houses owned 62. City/Area alumni associations 237. Total number of initiates 125,840. Chapter roll:

1873	*Psi I, Lewis* (1889)
1877	*Theta I, Fairmont* (1880)
1878	*Phi I, Franklin* (1885)
1878	*Upsilon I, Southwest Baptist* (1881)
1879	Eta, Akron
1880	*Delta, Trinity (TX)* (1881)
1881	*Delta II, Hanover* (1887)
1881	Omega, Wisconsin, Madison
1882	*Alpha, Mount Union* (1908)
1882	Lambda, Minnesota
1882	*Pi I, Fulton Synodical* (1885)
1882	Sigma, Northwestern
1883	*Theta II, Adelbert* (1888)
1883	*Zeta, Albion* (1987)
1884	*Upsilon II, St. Lawrence* (1887)
1885	Chi, Cornell
1885	Xi, Michigan
1886	Phi, Colorado
1886	Tau, Iowa
1886	Upsilon, Stanford
1887	*Delta III, USC* (1897)
1888	Kappa, Nebraska
1891	*Psi II, Goucher* (1950)
1898	Theta, Indiana
1901	Rho, Syracuse
1903	Beta, Washington (WA)
1906	Iota, Illinois
1907	Gamma, Cal, Berkeley
1908	Omicron, Adelphi
1909	Mu, Missouri
1911	Epsilon, Ohio State
1911	Nu, Idaho
1911	Pi, Montana
1912	*Alpha Beta, Swarthmore* (1934)
1913	Alpha Delta, Oregon
1913	*Alpha Gamma, Toronto* (1976)
1914	Alpha Epsilon, Washington (MO) (1973-1990)
1915	Alpha Zeta, Lawrence
1916	Alpha Eta, Whitman
1916	Alpha Theta, North Dakota
1918	Alpha Iota, Oklahoma
1920	Alpha Kappa, Washburn
1921	Alpha Lambda, Drake
1922	*Alpha Mu, Beloit* (1963)
1922	Alpha Nu, USC
1922	Alpha Xi, West Virginia
1923	Alpha Omicron, Miami (OH)
1923	Alpha Pi, Arizona
1924	Alpha Rho, Ohio Wesleyan
1925	Alpha Sigma, UCLA
1925	Alpha Tau, Butler
1926	Alpha Upsilon, Southern Methodist
1927	Alpha Psi, Mississippi
1928	Alpha Phi, British Columbia
1930	Alpha Chi, Penn State
1930	Alpha Omega, Arkansas
1931	*Beta Alpha, McGill* (1973)
1931	Beta Beta, Alberta
1932	Beta Delta, Colorado Col
1932	Beta Gamma, Utah
1936	Beta Epsilon, American
1938	Beta Zeta, Denison
1939	Beta Eta, Texas
1939	Beta Lambda, Gettysburg
1939	Beta Theta, Duke (1974-1986)
1940	Beta Iota, Purdue
1941	Beta Kappa, Kansas
1943	Beta Mu, Bowling Green
1944	Beta Nu, Carnegie-Mellon
1945	Beta Pi, Willamette
1945	Beta Rho, George Washington (1982-1990)
1945	Beta Sigma, Maryland
1946	Beta Chi, Denver
1946	Beta Omega, Washington State
1946	*Beta Phi, Penn* (1958)
1946	Beta Tau, Miami (FL)
1946	Beta Upsilon, Oregon State
1946	Beta Xi, Michigan State
1947	*Beta Psi, Alabama* (1978)
1947	Gamma Alpha, Tennessee
1947	Gamma Beta, Tulsa
1947	Gamma Epsilon, Kent
1948	Gamma Delta, Montana State
1948	Gamma Eta, San Jose
1948	*Gamma Gamma, Texas Western* (1959)
1948	Gamma Zeta, L.S.U.
1949	Gamma Iota, DePauw
1949	Gamma Theta, Florida
1950	Gamma Kappa, Cal, Santa Barbara
1951	Gamma Lambda, Cal State, Fresno
1951	Gamma Mu, Florida State
1953	*Gamma Nu, North Texas* (1976)
1954	Gamma Omicron, Indiana State
1954	Gamma Xi, Texas Tech
1955	Gamma Pi, Roanoke
1956	Gamma Rho, Wittenberg
1956	Gamma Sigma, Houston
1956	Gamma Tau, Texas Christian
1958	Gamma Phi, Arizona State
1958	Gamma Upsilon, Wichita
1959	Delta Epsilon, Pacific (CA)
1959	Gamma Chi, Cal State, Long Beach
1959	Gamma Psi, Emory (1968-1989)
1960	*Gamma Omega, St. Lawrence* (1970)
1961	*Delta Alpha, New Mexico* (1973)
1962	Delta Beta, Kentucky
1965	Delta Zeta, Memphis State
1966	Delta Eta, Cal State, Sacramento
1967	Delta Iota, Georgia
1967	*Delta Theta, Georgia State* (1987)
1968	Delta Kappa, South Florida
1969	Delta Lambda, Mississippi State
1969	*Delta Mu, Florida Atlantic* (1976)
1969	Delta Nu, Northern Illinois
1970	Delta Omicron, Morehead
1970	*Delta Xi, Ball State* (1985)
1971	Delta Pi, Southern Mississippi
1971	Delta Rho, V.P.I.
1972	*Delta Sigma, Auburn* (1988)
1972	*Delta Tau, Missouri Southern* (1984)
1973	Delta Upsilon, IUPU, Fort Wayne
1974	Delta Phi, Cal, Irvine
1975	Delta Chi, Cal, Davis

1977 Delta Omega, William Woods
1977 *Delta Psi, Baylor* (1986)
1978 Epsilon Alpha, Union (NY)
1978 Epsilon Beta, Bucknell
1978 Epsilon Gamma, Virginia
1979 Epsilon Delta, Washington and Jefferson
1980 Epsilon Epsilon, Tennessee Tech
1981 Epsilon Eta, Indiana (PA)
1981 Epsilon Iota, Cal, San Diego
1981 Epsilon Kappa, Clemson
1981 Epsilon Theta, Tampa
1981 Epsilon Zeta, Loyola Marymount, Los Angeles
1982 Epsilon Lambda, Lehigh
1982 Epsilon Mu, William and Mary
1982 Epsilon Nu, Madison Col
1982 Epsilon Xi, Lafayette
1983 *Epsilon Omicron, Wyoming* (1985)
1983 Epsilon Pi, Connecticut
1984 Epsilon Phi, Loyola, New Orleans
1984 Epsilon Rho, Western Michigan
1985 Epsilon Chi, South Carolina
1985 Epsilon Psi, Rutgers
1985 Epsilon Sigma, San Diego U.
1985 Epsilon Tau, Central Florida
1985 *Epsilon Upsilon, Bradley* (1987)
1986 Epsilon Omega, Louisiana Tech
1986 Zeta Alpha, Villanova
1987 Zeta Beta, Dartmouth
1987 Zeta Delta, Rochester
1987 Zeta Epsilon, Santa Clara
1987 Zeta Gamma, Richmond
1988 Zeta Eta, Southwest Texas
1988 Zeta Theta, Columbia (NY)
1988 Zeta Zeta, Boston U
1989 Zeta Iota, Chapman
1990 Zeta Kappa, Johns Hopkins
1990 Zeta Lambda, Cal, Riverside

Delta Phi Epsilon

ACTIVE PIN

PLEDGE PIN

DELTA PHI EPSILON was founded at New York University Law School on March 17, 1917, by Minna Goldsmith Mahler, Ida Bienstock Landau, Sylvia Stierman Cohen, Eva Effron Robin, and Dorothy Cohen Schwartzman.

Government Government is vested in the Executive Council, which is composed of members elected at each biennial convention. The fraternity is divided geographically into several areas, each having a province director. Chairmen for special activities and interests are appointed. the convention is held biennially for the election of officers, consideration of policy, and all matters of national im-

portance. The Central Office is supervised by the executive director, with her staff and several field consultants.

Traditions and Insignia Each year, on March 17, undergraduates and alumnae celebrate Founders' Day, and on this day each chapter must undertake some special charitable activity.

The Delta Phi Epsilon Cup is awarded biennially to the undergraduate chapter attaining the highest ranking based on scholarship and achievement, both in collegiate and community activities, and cooperation with the Executive Council. The Triangle Plaque is awarded to the chapter with the second best rating. The Scrapbook Gavel is a permanent award presented to the chapter having the finest scrapbook of chapter activities. The Progress Plaque is awarded to the chapter having made the greatest progress in the two years prior to the biennial convention. The Ethel B. Gerson Community Service Cup is presented to the chapter outstanding in community and campus activities. Community Service and Scholarship Certificates are given to the most deserving chapters. The areas of rush, pledge education, house management, alumnae service, and inter-sorority cooperation are also recognized.

The badge is an equilateral gold triangle bordered with 21 pearls, supporting a raised triangle of black enamel, on which the Greek letters ΔΦE are embossed in gold, with a gold ribbon inscribed with the motto beneath the base. The pledge pin is a plain equilateral triangle of purple enamel, bearing the Greek letters ΔΦE in gold. The recognition pin is small and dull in color with the Greek letters ΔΦE arranged vertically. The flower is the iris; the jewel is the pearl; and the colors are royal purple and pure gold.

Publications The *Delta Phi Epsilon Triad*, the official magazine, is published twice a year. Membership in the fraternity includes a life subscription. Other publications are the *Manual*, which includes the history, traditions, and procedures; the *Song Book; Rush Guide; Pledge Guide;* and Alumnae Newsletter.

Funds and Philanthropies The Edith Barash Stern Fund, established in 1944 for the support of a war orphan, has, from 1959 to 1984, raised funds for the Foundation for Mental Health and the Juvenile Diabetes Foundation. A new recipient will be chosen at the 1985 convention. Since 1955 the official Delta Phi Epsilon Philanthropic Project has been the support of the Cystic Fibrosis Research Foundation. In 1985, the fraternity added Anorexia Nervosa and Related Disorders Foundation as a philanthropy.

The Delta Phi Epsilon Scholarship Foundation, created in recognition of the Fraternity's 50th anniversary, provides grants and loans to members and their families.

Headquarters 832 Bedford Street, Stamford, CT 06901.

Membership Total living membership 24,455.

Total undergraduate membership 1,310. Active chapters 71. Inactive chapters 43. Houses owned 11. Graduate/Alumni chapters 21. City/Area alumni associations 41. Total number of initiates 25,421. Chapter roll:

Alpha Beta, Cooper Union (1990)
Alpha Theta, Stockton (1990)
1917   Alpha, N.Y.U. (1966-1983)
1920   *Beta, Barnard* (1922)
1921   Gamma, Syracuse (1923-1949)
1922   *Delta, Hunter* (1969-1971) (1983)
1922   Epsilon, McGill
1924   *Zeta, Toronto* (1958)
1925   Eta, Pitt (1944-1966)
1925   *Iota, Florida State* (1950-1968) (1971)
1926   *Kappa, Winnipeg* (1954)
1926   *Lambda, Adelphi* (1937-1958) (1971)
1926   *Mu, Cincinnati* (1951)
1926   *Nu, Penn* (1970)
1926   *Theta, Denver* (1957)
1926   *Xi, Brenau* (1930)
1927   *Omicron, Louisville* (1951)
1927   *Pi, Alabama* (1932-1953) (1973)
1927   Rho, Illinois (1933-1945)
1928   Sigma, Ohio State (-1948) (1987-1990)
1929   *Tau, Minnesota* (1932)
1930   *Upsilon, Long Island* (1934-1962) (1970)
1931   *Phi, CUNY, Brooklyn* (1970-1972) (1984)
1934   *Chi, Texas* (1990)
1935   Psi, Georgia
1939   *Delta Alpha, Vermont* (1954)
1939   Omega, Miami (FL) (1980-1987)
1940   *Delta Beta, Colorado* (1966)
1946   *Delta Delta, Indiana* (1952)
1946   Delta Gamma, British Columbia (1972-1981)
1947   *Delta Epsilon, Drexel* (1951)
1948   *Delta Zeta, Cal, Berkeley* (1968)
1954   Delta Eta, Michigan (1971-1985)
1955   Delta Iota, Queens (NY) (1980-1990)
1955   Delta Kappa, Florida
1955   *Delta Theta, Wayne State (MI)* (1971)
1956   *Delta Lambda, UCLA* (1971)
1958   *Delta Mu, Georgia State* (1960)
1959   Delta Nu, Temple
1960   *Delta Omicron, NYU-Heights* (1968)
1960   *Delta Pi, Penn State* (1966)
1960   *Delta Rho, Cornell* (1988)
1960   Delta Xi, Maryland
1962   Delta Sigma, Rider
1963   *Delta Tau, Washington (MO)* (1971)
1965   *Delta Upsilon, Tampa* (1976)
1966   Delta Chi, George Washington (1971-1987)
1966   *Delta Phi, Oklahoma* (1969)
1967   Delta Omega, Monmouth (NJ)
1967   *Phi Alpha, CCNY* (1972)
1967   *Phi Beta, Baruch* (1970)
1968   *Delta Psi, Hartford* (1977)
1968   *Phi Delta, Eastern Michigan* (1970)
1968   *Phi Epsilon, Lehman* (1972)
1968   Phi Eta, Northeastern

1968   Phi Gamma, Indiana (PA) (1974-1989)
1968   *Phi Theta, Oglethorpe* (1973)
1969   *Phi Zeta, North Texas* (1973)
1971   *Phi Iota, Edinboro* (1982)
1974   Phi Kappa, North Carolina
1977   Phi Lambda, Emory
1977   *Phi Mu, Newcomb* (1980-1982) (1986)
1977   Phi Pi, Widener
1978   *Phi Nu, Missouri* (1984)
1978   Phi Xi, Illinois Tech
1979   Phi Omicron, Worcester Tech
1980   *Phi Rho, Bucknell* (1982)
1981   Phi Sigma, Northern Illinois
1981   Phi Tau, Rutgers, Camden
1982   Phi Phi, Towson
1982   Phi Upsilon, Robert Morris
1983   Phi Chi, Maryland, Baltimore County
1983   *Phi Omega, Lowell* (1987)
1983   Phi Psi, Keene
1984   *Epsilon Alpha, Dartmouth* (1990)
1984   Epsilon Beta, East Stroudsburg
1985   Epsilon Delta, SUNY, Binghamton
1985   Epsilon Gamma, Stevens Tech
1985   Epsilon Zeta, LaSalle
1986   Epsilon Epsilon, SUNY, Albany
1986   Epsilon Eta, SUNY Col., Fredonia
1986   Epsilon Iota, SUNY Col., Geneseo
1986   Epsilon Theta, Fairleigh Dickinson, Rutherford
1987   Epsilon Kappa, SUNY Col., Cortland
1987   Epsilon Lambda, Michigan Tech
1987   Epsilon Mu, SUNY Col., Brockport
1987   Epsilon Nu, SUNY Col., Oneonta
1987   Epsilon Omicron, Clarion
1987   Epsilon Xi, SUNY Col., Oswego
1988   Epsilon Pi, SUNY Col., Plattsburgh
1988   Epsilon Rho, Hofstra
1988   Epsilon Sigma, Gallaudet
1988   Epsilon Tau, Bentley
1988   Epsilon Upsilon, Humboldt
1989   Alpha Alpha, West Chester
1989   Alpha Delta, Seton Hall
1989   Alpha Epsilon, Kennesaw
1989   Alpha Eta, Montclair
1989   Alpha Gamma, Florida International
1989   Alpha Iota, San Francisco
1989   Alpha Lambda, York (PA)
1989   Alpha Nu, SUNY Col., New Paltz
1989   Alpha Xi, St. Thomas
1989   Alpha Zeta, Lake Superior
1989   Epsilon Chi, William Paterson
1989   Epsilon Omega, Barry (FL)
1989   Epsilon Phi, Philadelphia Textiles
1989   Epsilon Psi, Millersville
1990   Alpha Kappa, Fairleigh Dickinson, Madison
1990   Alpha Mu, Michigan, Dearborn
1990   Alpha Omicron, Fairleigh Dickinson, Teaneck
1990   Alpha Pi, Southern Connecticut
1990   Alpha Rho, Pace
1990   Alpha Sigma, St. Francis (NY)

COAT OF ARMS

Delta Zeta

ACTIVE PIN

PLEDGE PIN

DELTA ZETA was founded at Miami University, Oxford, Ohio, in 1902. Its founders, who were among the first women admitted to full collegiate status under a new administration, were: Alfa Lloyd (Mrs. Orison Hayes), Anne Simmons (Mrs. Justus F. Friedline), Anna Keen (Mrs. George H. Davis), Mabelle Minton (Mrs. Henry Hagemann), Julia Bishop (Mrs. John M. Coleman), and Mary Collins (Mrs. George Galbraith). They had the active assistance of Dr. Guy Potter Benton, president of the university and a former national president of Phi Delta Theta. Because of his continued interest, Dr. Benton was made grand patron.

Government The national convention, which meets biennially, is the highest governing body. In the interim, administration is by the National Council elected at the national convention. The Council is composed of an Executive Board of six members. The remaining members are national directors with designated responsibilities. A past national president and a national Panhellenic delegate are appointed to Council, and additional members can be appointed. There are a National Headquarters staff assigned to specific tasks and national field representatives. All collegiate and alumnae chapters are grouped into provinces supervised by appointed directors. The editor of *The Lamp* and other national committees chairmen are appointed by National Council.

Traditions and Insignia October 24, the date of the official charter granted by the State of Ohio, is designated as Founders' Day and is observed with appropriate ceremonies by college and alumnae groups annually.

Traditionally, Delta Zeta seeks to promote within its chapters a program of fine cultural training, which since 1936 has been supervised by a national committee. A national committee on scholarship has been in operation since 1914. Committees to develop campus participation and civic responsibilities also work with all chapters.

Appropriate awards are given at each national convention for outstanding achievement: Founders' Award (1936), based on general chapter excellence; Council Award (1936), based on responsibility and service; Gertrude Houk Fariss Award (1954), honoring the former national president, to recognize outstanding alumnae-collegiate chapter programming and activity; Alice Huenefeld Award, to an outstanding college chapter director; and Betty Heusch Agler Award, honoring a former national president, to an outstanding collegiate chapter.

Through the union with Delta Sigma Epsilon sorority in 1956, two of its traditional awards were incorporated in the Delta Zeta program: See Loving Cup for outstanding chapter improvement, and the Genevieve Schmitt Memorial Plaque for highest chapter scholarship.

Annual individual achievement awards include: Florence Hood Miner Award (1946), named for a former national vice president, to an outstanding junior collegian; and the Grace Mason Lundy Award (1946), honoring a former national president, to an outstanding senior collegian in recognition of exceptional leadership and service.

The colors of Delta Zeta are old rose and green; the flower is the pink rose. The badge is a Roman lamp, resting upon an Ionic column and having upon each side three wings of Mercury. The official jeweling is a diamond in the flame, and four pearls at the base of the lamp. The lamp bears the Greek letters ΔZ in black enamel. The diamond-shaped pledge pin of black enamel bears the Roman lamp in gold. The daughter-grand-daughter pendant was adopted at the 1962 convention. There are two recognition pins: one, a monogram of the two Greek letters, ΔZ; the other, a miniature version of the Roman lamp. There are special insignia for chapter advisers and others. The Order of the Golden Rose, established at the time of the 50th golden anniversary (1952), honors members on their 50th anniversary. The Order of the Laurel (1966) was established to honor those members for sorority service of exceptional merit covering a period of many years.

Publications *The Lamp*, a quarterly magazine, has been published since 1910. Other publications include several editions of the songbook entitled *Delta Zeta Sings*, and manuals for alumnae and collegiate programs.

The Delta Zeta Pledge Book first appeared in 1919 and is revised periodically.

There have been five editions of history: a small volume in 1923, an enlarged and complete one in 1934, a two-volume edition in 1952, a summary history released in 1967, and the 1902-82 issue.

Funds and Philanthropies In 1917, a student loan fund was established to assist undergraduates in completing college course. The Elizabeth Coulter Stephenson Fund, honoring a former national president, has offered working funds since 1940 to outstanding undergraduates for special studies or training. A fund for qualified graduate students was created through the merger of Delta Zeta and Beta Phi Alpha Sorority in 1941.

There have been continuous social service projects since 1922. These "Adventures in Friendship" include the support of a school in the mountain regions of Kentucky; "Foreign Friendships," a national project during World War II in which college and alumnae chapters and mothers' clubs united to provide gifts of food, clothing, money, and other necessities to a children's hospital in Holland, and to Norway's children through the personal interest of the late Crown Princess Martha, a member of Delta Zeta.

In 1943, one of the local projects moved into national acceptance, the Hearing Helps Program. At the 1954 convention, Gallaudet College in Washington, D.C., exclusively for the hearing impaired, was added to the program. A gift of $10,000 was given by chapters to furnish the new library. The Delta Zeta-Gallaudet Endowment Scholarship Fund was established at Gallaudet in 1975 to provide financial support to Gallaudet students. Additionally, Delta Zeta contributes to the Gallaudet Dance Program. A program for patients at the United States Public Health Service Hospital, Carville, Louisiana, is also a part of Delta Zeta's social service program.

In 1959, $5,000, a gift of chimes, was given for the Sesquicentennial Chapel at Miami University (Ohio) honoring the founders of Delta Zeta and Delta Sigma Epsilon. With the merger of Theta Upsilon, assistance to the Navajo Indianas was added to the "Adventures in Friendship" program.

On March 17, 1961, the Delta Zeta Foundation was established to promote educational and charitable purposes of the sorority. In 1976, in honor of Delta Zeta's six founders, a Founders Memorial Fund was established for undergraduates. The first six scholarships from this fund were awarded at the 1977 Diamond Jubilee National Convention.

In 1979, the Delta Zeta Foundation and Founders Memorial Fund were merged to form the Delta Zeta Founders Memorial Foundation, a public non-profit corporation. Recognizing that hearing loss and the related difficulties receive less attention than other major health problems, the Founders Memorial Foundation supports a variety of national organizations and local projects concerned with speech and hearing. These include the National Association of the Deaf, the Better Hearing Institute, and Council for Better Hearing and Speech Month. The foundation also makes annual grants to Delta Zeta alumnae chapters to assist with local service projects in hearing centers, schools, and clinics. The Founders Memorial Foundation provides a wide variety of scholarships for both members and nonmembers helping to meet the growing need for financial assistance and encouragement.

The Norma Minch Andrisek Leadership Conferences for Continuing Education in leadership for an individual or group training was established in 1983 to honor this former national president.

National Headquarters Through the years the national headquarters had been in various locations near the national president's residence. The 1981 convention voted to move national headquarters "back home to Oxford." Following purchase and renovation of an historical Victorian home, the National Historical Museum and National Headquarters at 202 East Church Street at Campus Avenue, Oxford, Ohio 45056, was dedicated over the 1983 Founders' Day Weekend.

Membership Total living membership 121,518. Total undergraduate membership 8,158. Active chapters 165. Inactive chapters 106. Colonies 3. Houses owned 58. City/Area alumni associations 237. Total number of initiates 137,813. Chapter roll:

1902 Alpha, Miami (OH)
1908 *Beta, Cornell* (1932)
1909 Delta, DePauw (1985-1988)
1909 Epsilon, Indiana
1910 *Eta, Baker* (1934)
1910 *Zeta, Nebraska* (1937-1966) (1971)
1911 Theta, Ohio State
1913 Iota, Iowa (1984-1984)
1914 Kappa, Washington (WA) (1976-1983)
1915 *Lambda, Kansas* (1935-1963) (1976)
1915 *Mu, Cal, Berkeley* (1969)
1915 *Nu, Knox* (1964)
1916 *Delta Omicron, Northwestern Oklahoma* (1988)
1916 Delta Xi, Northern Colorado
1916 Omicron, Pitt
1916 *Xi, Cincinnati* (1977)
1917 *Delta Pi, Emporia* (1982)
1917 Rho, Denver (1951-1982)
1917 Sigma, L.S.U.
1918 *Tau, Wisconsin, Madison* (1971)
1919 *Chi, Oregon State* (1977)
1919 *Delta Rho, New Mexico Highlands* (1978)
1919 *Phi, Washington State* (1958)
1919 *Upsilon, North Dakota* (1983)
1920 Alpha Alpha, Northwestern
1920 Omega, Oregon (1969-1986)
1920 *Psi, Franklin* (1990)
1921 Alpha Beta, Illinois (1988-1988)
1921 Delta Sigma, Northeast Missouri
1921 Delta Tau, Temple (1968-1987)
1922 *Alpha Delta, George Washington* (1930)
1922 Alpha Epsilon, Oklahoma State (-1941) (1988-1988)
1922 Alpha Gamma, Alabama
1922 *Alpha Zeta, Adelphi* (1978)
1922 Delta Upsilon, Marshall
1923 Alpha Eta, Michigan (1953-1990)
1923 *Alpha Iota, USC* (1953)
1923 Alpha Theta, Kentucky
1923 Delta Phi, Northeastern (OK)
1923 *Gamma, Minnesota* (1965)
1924 *Alpha Kappa, Syracuse* (1957)
1924 *Alpha Lambda, Colorado* (1934)
1924 *Alpha Mu, St. Lawrence* (1930)
1924 *Alpha Nu, Butler* (1935)
1924 *Alpha Omicron, Brenau* (1978)
1924 Alpha Pi, Samford (1983-1983)
1924 Alpha Sigma, Florida State
1924 *Alpha Tau, Texas* (1977)

1924   Alpha Upsilon, Maine (1936-1947)
       (1984-1985)
1924   *Alpha Xi, Randolph, Macon (1938)*
1924   Delta Chi, Cal State, Chico
1925   Alpha Chi, UCLA (1979-1984)
1925   Delta Omega, Fort Hays
1925   *Delta Psi, Cal, Santa Barbara (1967)*
1925   *Epsilon Alpha, Western State (CO) (1970)*
1926   *Alpha Omega, Millsaps (1936)*
1926   *Alpha Phi, Kansas (1936)*
1926   *Alpha Psi, Southern Methodist (1970)*
1927   *Epsilon Beta, Northwestern Louisiana*
       (1985)
1927   Epsilon Gamma, Central Missouri State
1928   Beta Alpha, Rhode Island
1928   *Beta Beta, Mississippi (1953)*
1928   Beta Delta, South Carolina
1928   *Beta Epsilon, Penn (1934)*
1928   Beta Gamma, Louisville
1928   *Beta Upsilon, Tulane (1961)*
1928   *Beta Zeta, Utah (1940)*
1928   Epsilon Delta, Concord
1928   Epsilon Epsilon, Cal State, Fresno
       (1975-1981)
1928   *Epsilon Eta, Harris-Stowe (1975)*
1928   Epsilon Zeta, Drexel
1930   *Beta Eta, Swarthmore (1934)*
1930   *Beta Iota, Arizona (1935-1966) (1978)*
1930   *Beta Phi, Oglethorpe (1949-1980) (1986)*
1930   *Beta Theta, Bucknell (1978)*
1931   Beta Chi, Wittenberg
1931   Beta Kappa, Iowa State
1932   Epsilon Theta, Clarion
1933   Beta Lambda, Tennessee (1982-1985)
1934   *Beta Psi, Charleston (SC) (1953)*
1934   Epsilon Iota, Fairmont
1935   *Beta Omega, N.Y.U. (1969)*
1936   Epsilon Kappa, Wisconsin, Whitewater
1937   *Beta Mu, Florida Southern (1979)*
1939   *Beta Nu, Miami (FL) (1978)*
1939   *Epsilon Lambda, Southwestern State (OK)*
       (1968)
1940   *Beta Pi, Albion (1970)*
1940   Beta Xi, Auburn
1940   Epsilon Mu, Southern Mississippi
       (1984-1984)
1941   *Beta Rho, Michigan State (1979)*
1941   Epsilon Nu, Southwest Missouri
       (1968-1990)
1941   Gamma Alpha, Baldwin-Wallace
1942   Beta Tau, Nebraska Wesleyan
1943   Gamma Beta, Connecticut (1972-1980)
1944   Epsilon Xi, Central Arkansas
1945   *Beta Sigma, Colorado State (1978)*
1945   *Gamma Gamma, Missouri Valley (1980)*
1946   Epsilon Omicron, Western Illinois
1946   Epsilon Pi, Henderson
1946   Gamma Delta, Penn State (1977-1988)
1946   *Gamma Epsilon, Drake (1979)*
1946   *Gamma Eta, Hunter (1971)*
1946   Gamma Zeta, Southwestern (TX)
1947   Epsilon Rho, Northwest Missouri

1947   Epsilon Sigma, Wayne State (MI)
1947   Gamma Theta, Carroll
1948   Gamma Iota, Memphis State
1948   Gamma Kappa, Kent
1948   Gamma Lambda, San Jose (1971-1979)
1948   *Gamma Mu, Illinois Tech (1969)*
1949   Epsilon Tau, Longwood
1949   Gamma Nu, Eastern Illinois
1949   Gamma Xi, New Mexico State
1950   Epsilon Upsilon, Central State (OK)
1950   Gamma Omicron, San Diego U. (1973-1989)
1950   Gamma Pi, Western Michigan
1950   Gamma Rho, Northern Illinois
1950   Gamma Tau, Bowling Green
1951   *Gamma Upsilon, Oklahoma City (1987)*
1952   *Epsilon Phi, Detroit (1973)*
1952   Gamma Phi, Indiana (PA)
1953   Gamma Chi, Ball State (1984-1985)
1953   Gamma Omega, Southern Illinois
1953   Gamma Psi, Central Michigan
1954   Delta Alpha, Cal State, Long Beach
1954   Delta Beta, Tampa (1964-1981)
1954   *Delta Gamma, Transylvania (1954)*
1955   Delta Delta, Georgia State
1955   *Delta Epsilon, Queens (NY) (1980)*
1955   Gamma Sigma, Eastern Michigan
       (1974-1989)
1956   *Delta Eta, East Tennessee (1986-1989)*
       (1989)
1956   *Delta Iota, Tufts (1970)*
1956   *Delta Kappa, Southwestern Louisiana*
       (1977)
1956   Delta Theta, Houston
1956   Epsilon Omega, Wisconsin, Eau Claire
1956   *Epsilon Psi, St. Louis (1971)*
1957   *Delta Lambda, Lamar (1985)*
1957   *Delta Mu, Morningside (1979)*
1957   *Delta Nu, Parsons (1971)*
1957   *Zeta Alpha, Bradley (1983-1983) (1987)*
1957   Zeta Beta, Wisconsin, Stout
1958   *Epsilon Chi, Wisconsin, Milwaukee (1978)*
1958   *Zeta Delta, Wagner (1967)*
1958   Zeta Epsilon, California (PA)
1958   *Zeta Eta, Southeastern Oklahoma (1974)*
1958   *Zeta Gamma, McNeese (1965)*
1958   Zeta Zeta, West Texas
1959   *Zeta Iota, Humboldt (1971)*
1959   Zeta Kappa, Ohio Northern
1959   *Zeta Theta, Sam Houston (1989)*
1960   Zeta Lambda, East Carolina
1961   *Zeta Mu, Portland State (1965)*
1961   Zeta Nu, Ferris
1961   *Zeta Omicron, Wisconsin, La Crosse (1986)*
1961   Zeta Pi, Georgia (1971-1987)
1961   Zeta Rho, William Jewell
1961   Zeta Xi, Lenoir-Rhyne
1962   *Theta Alpha, Simpson (1977)*
1962   *Theta Beta, Birmingham-Southern (1974)*
1962   *Theta Delta, Westminster (PA) (1980)*
1962   Theta Epsilon, Louisiana Tech (1974-1979)
       (1983-1984)
1962   Theta Eta, Creighton

1962	Theta Gamma, New Hampshire		1971	Kappa Theta, V.P.I.
1962	Theta Iota, Western Carolina		1972	Kappa Beta, Northern Kentucky
1962	Theta Theta, DePaul		1972	Kappa Epsilon, Plymouth
1962	*Theta Zeta, Akron* (1980)		1972	Kappa Iota, Wright State
1962	*Zeta Tau, Charleston (WV)* (1985)		1972	*Kappa Omega, Limestone* (1980)
1962	*Zeta Upsilon, Winona* (1983)		1972	*Kappa Omicron, Elon* (1973)
1963	*Theta Chi, Lock Haven* (1977)		1972	*Kappa Pi, Keene* (1974)
1963	Theta Kappa, New Orleans		1972	Kappa Psi, Shippensburg
1963	*Theta Lambda, St. Norbert* (1970)		1972	Kappa Rho, Kutztown
1963	Theta Nu, Moorhead		1972	*Kappa Upsilon, Quinnipiac* (1979)
1963	Theta Xi, Glenville		1972	Lambda Epsilon, Pitt, Johnstown
1963	*Zeta Chi, Wisconsin, Stevens Point* (1983)		1972	*Lambda Zeta, Southern Maine* (1985)
1963	*Zeta Omega, Northern Michigan* (1982)		1973	Kappa Mu, Shepherd
1963	Zeta Phi, Slippery Rock		1973	*Lambda Omega, William Paterson* (1980)
1963	Zeta Psi, Stephen F. Austin		1973	Lambda Phi, Appalachian
1963	*Zeta Sigma, Kearney* (1967)		1973	Lambda Rho, Illinois State
1964	Iota Alpha, Southwest Texas		1974	Lambda Pi, Georgia College
1965	Iota Delta, Edinboro		1975	Lambda Omicron, Angelo
1965	Theta Omega, Atlantic Christian		1975	*Lambda Psi, Columbus* (1985)
1965	Theta Psi, Ashland		1975	Lambda Theta, Michigan Tech
1965	*Theta Sigma, Steubenville* (1983)		1975	Lambda Xi, Texas A & M
1965	Theta Tau, Findlay		1976	Lambda Beta, Southern Indiana
1966	*Iota Beta, Dickinson State* (1981)		1977	Lambda Alpha, Arkansas Tech
1966	*Iota Epsilon, Wisconsin, Oshkosh* (1972)		1977	Lambda Delta, Virginia
1966	*Iota Gamma, Alliance* (1979)		1977	Lambda Gamma, Jacksonville (AL)
1966	Iota Tau, West Liberty		1977	Lambda Iota, Rochester
1966	Iota Theta, Mansfield		1977	Lambda Kappa, Alabama, Huntsville
1966	*Iota Zeta, St. John's (NY)* (1978)		1977	Lambda Lambda, Trenton
1966	Theta Mu, St. Cloud		1977	Lambda Nu, Auburn, Montgomery
1966	Theta Omicron, Pan American		1977	Lambda Sigma Society, Winthrop
1966	Theta Phi, Old Dominion		1978	Xi Kappa, Glassboro
1966	Theta Rho, Cal State, Los Angeles		1979	Xi Theta, North Carolina, Wilmington
1967	Iota Iota, Middle Tennessee		1981	Xi Alpha, Massachusetts
1967	*Iota Kappa, Rider* (1988)		1981	Xi Chi, Robert Morris
1967	*Iota Lambda, South Florida* (1978)		1982	Xi Beta, Eastern Kentucky
1967	*Iota Mu, Monmouth (NJ)* (1971)		1983	Xi Delta, Radford
1967	Iota Pi, West Virginia Tech (1976-1982)		1983	Xi Lambda, San Francisco
1967	Iota Psi, Texas, Arlington		1984	Xi Eta, Northwood (MI)
1967	*Iota Sigma, Philadelphia Textiles* (1971)		1984	Xi Iota, Muhlenberg
1967	*Theta Pi, Minot* (1985)		1985	Xi Nu, Tarleton
1968	*Iota Chi, Northland College* (1969)		1986	Xi Omicron, Loyola Marymount, Los Angeles
1968	Iota Nu, Georgia Southern (1987-1990)			
1968	*Iota Omega, Jacksonville* (1986)		1986	Xi Rho, Clarkson
1968	Iota Phi, Nevada, Las Vegas		1987	Xi Phi, Missouri, Kansas City
1968	Iota Upsilon, Cal State, Fullerton		1987	Xi Psi, Grand Valley
1968	Iota Xi, Missouri, St. Louis		1988	Xi Omega, Purdue
1968	Kappa Alpha, Nicholls		1988	Xi Sigma, North Carolina
1968	Kappa Zeta, North Texas		1988	Xi Tau, Millersville
1969	*Iota Omicron, Niagara* (1970)		1989	Omicron Alpha, St. Mary's (NS)
1969	Iota Rho, West Chester		1989	Xi Pi, Lehigh
1969	Kappa Xi, Duquesne (1978-1988)		1989	Xi Upsilon, Northeastern
1970	Kappa Chi, Youngstown State		1989	Xi Xi, North Georgia
1970	Kappa Tau, Morehead		1990	Omicron Beta, Stockton
1971	*Kappa Lambda, Livingston* (1983)		1990	Omicron Gamma, Ohio
1971	*Kappa Nu, Missouri Western* (1980)			
1971	Kappa Phi, North Carolina, Charlotte			

Colonies: Eureka, Ohio Wesleyan, Bryant

COAT OF ARMS

Gamma Phi Beta

ACTIVE PIN

PLEDGE PIN

GAMMA PHI BETA was founded November 11, 1874, at Syracuse University by Helen M. Dodge, Frances E. Haven, E. Adeline Curtis, and Mary A. Bingham. The sorority was founded by these four women who realized Gamma Phi Beta's objective "to develop the highest type of womanhood through education, social life, and service to country and humanity."

Growth Gamma Phi Beta expanded cautiously, in the beginning believing that only through cautious and gradual growth could strength be achieved. In 1882, a second chapter was placed at the University of Michigan, followed in 1885 by another in Wisconsin. The next ten years saw chapters in other eastern and midwestern colleges. In 1894, Gamma Phi Beta expanded to the West Coast, to the University of California and then into Washington, Oregon, and Idaho. Establishment of a chapter at the University of Toronto, in Canada in 1919 made the sorority international.

Government Government of the sorority is vested in the Grand Council of six members: grand president, alumnae vice president, collegiate vice president, director of finance, National Panhellenic Conference delegate and the executive secretary-treasurer. All are elected by the convention except the executive secretary-treasurer who is appointed by the elective officers and who is the supervisor of the Central Office. In addition, there are numerous international committee chairmen and other international officers, as well as traveling collegiate consultants, director of extension, director of services, and the editor of *The Crescent*.

The area financial advisors are appointed to assist the director of finance in supervising the financial operation and administration of the chapters and house corporation boards. The first convention was held in Syracuse in 1883, and there were annual sessions thereafter until 1907, when they became biennial. Conventions are held in various locations throughout the continent, alumnae and collegiate chapters near the convention site serving on the committees. An international convention coordinator is appointed each biennium by the Grand council. During the summer of off-convention years, a Leadership Training School is held.

The collegiate chapters, alumnae chapters and crescent circles are grouped geographically in 16 provinces, with each province having an alumnae director and a collegiate director.

Traditions and Insignia Self-discipline and individual responsibility in the achievement of high scholarship and of social and cultural maturity are traditional. There is a scholarship requirement for initiation, and awards are given locally to recognize scholarship achievement. The Chancellor E. O. Haven Awards are presented at convention to chapters attaining high scholarship. Other awards are the Efficiency Awards, the McCormick Medallion Award for a high degree of cooperative participation in campus activities, Panhellenic Award to Greek-letter chapters for outstanding Panhellenic service, the Golden Crescent Award to members initiated 50 years. Alumnae members who have given long and devoted service are recognized by membership on the sorority's Service Roll, for international service and the Merit Roll, for local service, and those members who have created and developed a service to the sorority that has contributed notably over the years to the fulfillment of the aims of the organization are honored with a permanent place on the sorority's Honor Roll. The Carnation Award recognizes women whose accomplishments have brought honor and distinction to themselves and the sorority; it was established in 1974.

The official badge consists of a black enamel crescent enclosing a monogram of the three Greek letters. Gamma Phi Beta was the first women's Greek-letter organization to use the term "sorority." In 1882 this word was coined for the Syracuse chapter by one of the Latin professors on that faculty. Prior to that time, Gamma Phi Beta was known as a society; it has never been known as a fraternity. The symbol is the crescent moon; the flower is the pink carnation; the colors are light and dark brown; the open motto is "Founded on a rock."

In 1974 the TranSISter Service was created and its name and logo patented for Gamma Phi Beta use only. This unique service provides assistance to members moving into new communities and bed and breakfast to traveling members. Over 400 TranSISters are listed each spring in THE CRESCENT.

Gamma Phi Beta's career network, SisterLink, was established in 1984 to assist members in career planning and to provide job contacts within the membership.

Publications *The Crescent*, official magazine, published quarterly, first appeared in June, 1900, and has been published regularly since that time. Other publications include *The History of Gamma Phi Beta* (first in 1921 and rewritten for the 1962, 1965, 1975 and 1985 editions); *Songs of Gamma Phi Beta* (first edition 1887, last revision 1964); *Guide for Pledges; President's Book; Bylaws, and Rules and Procedures; Alumnae Advisory Committee Manual; Alumnae Recommendations Committee Manual; House Corporation Board Manual; House-*

mother's Manual; Membership Chairman's Manual; Province Directors' Manuals; Scholarship Manual; and *Crescent Communique.*

Funds and Philanthropies All philanthropic funds are channeled through the Gamma Phi Beta Foundation established in 1959 and directed by seven trustees. Under its supervision, the sorority maintains a camp in British Columbia for underprivileged girls where the counselors are Gamma Phi Betas who volunteer their services. Through the foundation's "Adopt a Camp, Adopt a Camper, Adopt a Counselor" program, local chapters provide support for camping for special girls.

Through the foundation's financial aid program, assistance is available to members through scholarships, fellowships and grants-in-aid.

An Endowment Fund, established in 1915, and the Loan Fund are maintained for the development and security of the sorority. These two funds are held in a trust and administered by a board of seven members. Substantial loans are made to house corporations from this trust fund for building, major repairs and furnishings. Various educational programs of the sorority are also funded through this trust.

The Opportunity Fund, comprised of member donations, helps to fund sorority individual development programs such as Personal and Chapter Enrichment (PACE).

Service to country and humanity is stressed in the sorority's Articles of Incorporation, and to this end members contributed to the war efforts of the United States and Canada during both World Wars I and II. Gamma Phi Beta containers, placed in strategic public locations around the country, were the means of collecting funds for the U.S. Government's "Committee for Belgium Relief." At the close of the war these funds were directed to the support of French War orphans. In 1929 the sorority adopted its local camping programs as its national philanthropy, concentrating its major efforts in the field of child welfare. During World War II funds were raised for a Mobile Canteen for Great Britain and contributions were made to American Red Cross, Queen's Fund of Canada, and the Army and Navy Relief Societies. The sorority sponsored the "Bonds Buy Mercy" campaign which resulted in four drives netting $14-million and two U.S. Treasury citations for distinguished service rendered in behalf of the War Finance Program.

Headquarters Central Office, 7395 East Orchard Road, Suite 200, Englewood, CO 80111.

Membership Total living membership 62,078. Total undergraduate membership 6,156. Active chapters 107. Inactive chapters 29. Colonies 1. Houses owned 50. Graduate/Alumni chapters 174. City/Area alumni associations 41. Total number of initiates 103,688. Chapter roll:

Year	Chapter
1874	Alpha, Syracuse
1882	Beta, Michigan
1885	Gamma, Wisconsin, Madison
1887	Delta, Boston U (1970-1985)
1888	Epsilon, Northwestern
1893	*Zeta, Goucher* (1950)
1894	Eta, Cal, Berkeley
1897	Theta, Denver
1901	*Iota, Barnard* (1915)
1902	Kappa, Minnesota
1903	Lambda, Washington (WA)
1908	Nu, Oregon
1910	Xi, Idaho
1913	Omicron, Illinois
1914	Pi, Nebraska
1915	Rho, Iowa
1915	Sigma, Kansas
1915	Tau, Colorado State
1916	*Upsilon, Hollins* (1929)
1917	Phi, Washington (MO)
1918	Chi, Oregon State
1918	Omega, Iowa State
1918	Psi, Oklahoma
1919	Alpha Alpha, Toronto
1920	Alpha Beta, North Dakota
1921	Alpha Delta, Missouri
1921	Alpha Gamma, Nevada
1922	Alpha Epsilon, Arizona
1922	*Alpha Zeta, Texas* (1988)
1923	*Alpha Eta, Ohio Wesleyan* (1984)
1924	Alpha Iota, UCLA
1924	Alpha Theta, Vanderbilt
1925	*Alpha Kappa, Manitoba* (1975)
1928	Alpha Lambda, British Columbia
1928	*Alpha Mu, Rollins* (1971)
1929	Alpha Nu, Wittenberg
1929	Alpha Xi, Southern Methodist
1930	Alpha Omicron, North Dakota State
1930	*Alpha Pi, West Virginia* (1938-1959) (1984)
1930	*Alpha Rho, Birmingham-Southern* (1957)
1930	*Alpha Sigma, Randolph, Macon Woman's* (1951)
1931	Alpha Tau, McGill
1932	Alpha Phi, Colorado Col
1932	Alpha Upsilon, Penn State
1933	Alpha Chi, William and Mary
1934	*Alpha Psi, Lake Forest* (1961)
1936	Alpha Omega, Western Ontario
1938	Beta Alpha, USC
1940	Beta Beta, Maryland
1943	Beta Gamma, Bowling Green
1944	Beta Delta, Michigan State
1947	Beta Epsilon, Miami (OH)
1947	*Beta Zeta, Kent* (1972)
1948	Beta Eta, Bradley
1948	*Beta Theta, San Jose* (1984)
1949	*Beta Iota, Idaho State* (1985)
1949	Beta Kappa, Arizona State (1988-1990)
1949	Beta Lambda, San Diego State
1950	Beta Mu, Florida State
1950	*Beta Nu, Vermont* (1974)
1951	Beta Omicron, Oklahoma City
1951	*Beta Xi, Ohio State* (1967)
1952	Beta Pi, Indiana State
1954	Beta Rho, Colorado

1955	Beta Sigma, Washington State
1956	Beta Tau, Texas Tech
1957	Beta Phi, Indiana
1957	Beta Upsilon, Kansas State
1958	Beta Chi, Wichita
1958	Beta Omega, Northern Arizona
1958	Beta Psi, Oklahoma State
1958	*Gamma Alpha, Memphis State* (1984)
1959	Gamma Beta, Gettysburg
1960	Gamma Gamma, Wisconsin, Milwaukee
1961	*Gamma Delta, Wyoming* (1973)
1961	Gamma Epsilon, Puget Sound
1962	Gamma Eta, Cal State, Long Beach
1962	Gamma Zeta, East Texas
1963	Gamma Iota, Midwestern
1963	Gamma Kappa, Kearney
1963	*Gamma Theta, Pacific (CA)* (1972)
1964	*Gamma Lambda, L.S.U.* (1977)
1964	Gamma Mu, Moorhead
1965	Gamma Nu, Lamar
1965	*Gamma Xi, Tennessee* (1977)
1966	*Gamma Omicron, Kentucky* (1982)
1966	Gamma Pi, Mankato
1966	Gamma Rho, Wisconsin, Oshkosh (1976-1985)
1967	Gamma Tau, St. Louis
1968	Gamma Chi, Southwest Texas
1968	*Gamma Phi, Auburn* (1983)
1968	Gamma Psi, Northern Iowa
1968	*Gamma Sigma, Western Michigan* (1975)
1968	*Gamma Upsilon, Drake* (1983)
1969	*Delta Alpha, Wisconsin, River Falls* (1984)
1969	Gamma Omega, Wisconsin, Platteville
1970	Delta Beta, Boise
1970	*Delta Gamma, Nebraska, Omaha* (1976)
1971	Delta Delta, Cal State, Fullerton
1973	Delta Epsilon, Texas Wesleyan
1973	*Delta Zeta, Southwestern State (OK)* (1989)
1974	Delta Eta, Cal, Irvine
1975	Delta Iota, Purdue
1975	Delta Theta, Cal Poly, San Luis Obispo
1976	Delta Kappa, Lehigh
1976	Delta Lambda, Cal, Riverside
1977	Delta Mu, Rutgers
1977	Delta Nu, Southwest Missouri
1978	Delta Xi, Bucknell
1980	Delta Omicron, Southern Tech
1980	Delta Pi, Illinois State
1980	*Delta Rho, Dickinson* (1987)
1981	Delta Sigma, Florida Institute
1981	Delta Tau, Colgate
1983	Delta Chi, Cal State, Sacramento
1983	Delta Phi, Cal State, Bakersfield
1983	Delta Psi, Cal, Santa Barbara
1983	Delta Upsilon, Georgia
1983	Epsilon Alpha, LaSalle
1984	Delta Omega, Oakland
1984	Epsilon Beta, Alma
1984	Epsilon Gamma, San Diego U
1986	Epsilon Delta, Creighton
1986	Epsilon Epsilon, Union (NY)
1987	Epsilon Eta, Bridgewater

1987	Epsilon Zeta, Jacksonville (AL)
1988	Epsilon Iota, Christopher Newport
1988	Epsilon Kappa, Cal State, Chico
1988	Epsilon Theta, Clemson
1989	Epsilon Lambda, Alabama
1989	Epsilon Mu, Loyola, New Orleans
1989	Epsilon Nu, Chapman
1989	Epsilon Xi, Rhodes
1990	Epsilon Omicron, Cal, Santa Cruz
1990	Epsilon Pi, George Mason
1990	Epsilon Rho, Stephen F. Austin

Colonies: Stanford

COAT OF ARMS

Kappa Alpha Theta

ACTIVE PIN

PLEDGE PIN

KAPPA ALPHA THETA was organized at Indiana Asbury University (now DePauw University) in Greencastle, Indiana, on January 27, 1870. The founding and early progress of the fraternity were the inspiration of Betty Locke, the daughter of a professor at Asbury who was the first woman admitted to the university in 1867. Associated with her in this pioneering venture were Alice Allen, Bettie Tipton and Hanna Fitch. Kappa Alpha Theta was the first Greek-letter society of women organized with principles and methods like those of men's fraternities.

The strong doubts which then prevailed as to the advisability of higher education for women, the small number of colleges which were then admitting women to equal educational facilities with men, and the difficulties faced by those women who chose to avail themselves of this new privilege made the establishment of such a society something of an experiment. Kappa Alpha Theta was founded in a coeducational institution, where the same needs which led to the establishment of Greek-letter fraternities among men were felt by women students.

Growth The chapters were named on a state system until 1881, when the present system was adopted. In the spring of 1870, a number of students from Indiana University established the second chapter. The first Gamma Chapter, established at Moore's Hill College, succumbed to anti-fraternity laws in 1871. Delta, at Illinois Wesleyan, was the first chapter established outside Indiana. After 20 years, it was transferred to the University of Illinois. Gamma, at Ohio Wesleyan University, which was disbanded in 1881, was re-established in 1924 as Gamma Deuteron. The Wooster, Brown, Barnard, Swarthmore and Stanford chapters were killed by anti-fraternity laws. The Stanford and Brown chapters were re-established in 1979 and 1984, respectively. The chapters at Goucher and Randolph Macon College were disbanded when sororities were banned by the administrations.

Kappa Alpha Theta has continued to grow, with a wide geographical distribution and a mix of private and public institutions.

Government   Until 1883, the government of the fraternity was in the hands of Alpha Chapter. It was then vested in the Grand Chapter, composed of one member from each college chapter. Alpha remained the permanent head of the fraternity, and the secretaryship was held by the other chapters in rotation. In 1891 all legislative and judicial powers were vested in the biennial Grand Convention. This continues today. A Grand Council of seven members, elected at each convention, is the policy-making and executive board of the fraternity. Special officers are appointed to supervise specific areas of operation. For purposes of administration, there are 18 districts. Each district is supervised by one or more college district presidents and one or more alumnae district presidents. There are state and province chairmen, who assist the grand vice president alumnae in her work with alumnae organizations. There are 91 alumnae chapters and 203 alumnae clubs.

As the fraternity grew, programming was developed to meet the needs of members. Officers were elected or appointed to plan and develop supportive activities and programs. A national Leadership Conference was instituted in the early 1960s to be held in the non-convention years so that all chapter presidents would have an opportunity for participation in the national programming of the fraternity. As the need became apparent, a program in alcohol education became a part of chapter and individual support programming. "The Theta Connection," a networking program which links undergraduate members and alumnae in an interactive process of benefit to both, is a part of both collegiate chapter and alumnae group programming. Alumnae volunteers serve as advisory board personnel for college chapters and as officers of chapter house corporation boards. The alumnae program provides continuing fraternity associations and an opportunity for worthwhile community service.

Traditions and Insignia   The badge is kite-shaped, having four sides. It is of black enamel, inlaid with a white chevron on which are displayed the letters KAΘ. Above this are two diamond stars, and below are the letters XΩO. The colors are black and gold and the flower is the black and gold pansy. The colors of the pledge pin are black and gold, divided diagonally in a small square.

Publications   Catalogues were published in 1888, 1890, 1895, 1902, 1904, 1908, 1916, and 1924. The magazine is the *Kappa Alpha Theta*, a quarterly. Its publication began in 1885 under the direction of Kappa Chapter at the University of Kansas.

Other publications include a songbook, first published in 1888, with the latest edition published in 1978, the constitution and bylaws, a variety of manuals and handbooks for college and alumnae chapter officers and advisors, and three histories: *Sixty Years in Kappa Alpha Theta*, by Estelle Riddle Dodge, and *We Who Wear Kites*, Volumes I and II, by Carol Green Wilson.

Funds and Philanthropies   The Kappa Alpha Theta Foundation, an Indiana not-for-profit corporation, was established May 26, 1961. There are 14 voting members of the foundation and the management and administration are vested in a board of trustees. Currently, over $65,000 is awarded each year to graduate and undergraduate students in scholarships, including Educational Trust Fund Scholarships administered by the Foundation. Biennially, a fellowship is awarded to a Theta or non-Theta pursuing a Ph.D.

The fraternity's major philanthropy, supported by contributions to the foundation by members, is the Institute of Logopedics, Wichita, Kansas, which serves children and adults with communication handicaps. Contributions provide for the maintenance of the Theta Court, a unit of living quarters within the Institute, the Institute Scholarship Fund and the research program.

Biennially, grants are made to qualifying philanthropies recommended by Thetas who are active in support of them locally, and to two universities in recognition of the excellence of Theta chapters on those campuses.

The foundation supports several educational programs of the fraternity such as the chapter consultant program, leadership development and fraternity archival development and preservation.

Headquarters   Central Office is located in the Headquarters, 8740 Founders Road, Indianapolis, IN 46268.

Membership   Total living membership 105,660. Active chapters 118. Inactive chapters 26. Colonies 1. Houses owned 68. Graduate/Alumni chapters 92. City/Area alumni associations 205. Total number of initiates 123,860. Chapter roll:

1870	Alpha, DePauw
1870	Beta, Indiana
1870	*Cincinnati Wesleyan, Cincinnati Wesleyan (1871)*
1871	*Indiana Gamma, Moore's Hill (1874)*
1871	*Millersburg, Millersburg (KY) (1872)*
1874	Gamma, Butler (1886-1906)
1875	*Delta I, Illinois Wesleyan (1895)*
1875	*Epsilon, Wooster (1913)*
1876	*Zeta, Ohio (1886)*
1879	*Eta, Michigan (1886-1993)*
1880	*Theta, Simpson (1991)*
1881	Gamma deuteron, Ohio Wesleyan (1882-1924)

1881 Iota, Cornell (1965-1980)	1931 Beta Phi, Penn State
1881 Kappa, Kansas	1932 Beta Omega, Colorado Col
1881 Lambda, Vermont	1932 Beta Psi, McGill
1881 Mu, Allegheny	1933 Gamma Gamma, Rollins
1882 Nu, Hanover (1899-1959)	1937 Gamma Delta, Georgia
1883 Xi, Connecticut (1887-1989)	1937 Gamma Epsilon, Western Ontario
1887 Omicron, USC (1895-1917)	1942 Gamma Zeta, Connecticut (1971-1979)
1887 Pi, Albion (1908-1955)	1943 *Gamma Eta, Massachusetts* (1979)
1887 Rho, Nebraska (1891-1896)	1944 Gamma Theta, Carnegie-Mellon
1887 *Sigma, Toronto* (1889-1905) (1941)	1945 Gamma Iota, Kentucky
1887 Tau, Northwestern	1946 *Gamma Kappa, George Washington* (1975)
1889 Chi, Syracuse	1947 *Gamma Lambda, Beloit* (1970)
1889 Phi, Pacific (CA) (1892-1959)	1947 Gamma Mu, Maryland
1889 Upsilon, Minnesota (1891-1892)	1947 Gamma Nu, North Dakota State
1890 Omega, Cal, Berkeley	1948 *Gamma Omicron, New Mexico* (1978)
1890 Psi, Wisconsin, Madison	1948 Gamma Pi, Iowa State
1891 *Alpha Beta, Swarthmore* (1934)	1948 *Gamma Xi, San Jose* (1975)
1892 Alpha Gamma, Ohio State	1950 Gamma Rho, Cal, Santa Barbara
1892 Phi deuteron, Stanford (1944-1978)	1951 Gamma Sigma, San Diego U.
1895 Delta, Illinois	1951 Gamma Tau, Tulsa
1896 *Alpha Delta, Goucher* (1950)	1951 Gamma Upsilon, Miami (OH)
1897 Alpha Epsilon, Brown (1912-1984)	1953 Gamma Chi, Cal State, Fresno
1898 *Alpha Zeta, Barnard* (1915)	1953 Gamma Phi, Texas Tech
1904 Alpha Eta, Vanderbilt	1955 Gamma Psi, Texas Christian
1904 Alpha Theta, Texas	1957 Delta Delta, Whitman
1906 *Alpha Iota, Washington (MO)* (1973)	1957 Gamma Omega, Auburn
1907 *Alpha Kappa, Adelphi* (1951)	1959 Delta Epsilon, Arizona State
1908 Alpha Lambda, Washington (WA)	1959 Delta Zeta, Emory
1909 Alpha Mu, Missouri	1961 Delta Eta, Kansas State
1909 Alpha Nu, Montana	1962 Delta Theta, Florida
1909 Alpha Omicron, Oklahoma	1963 Delta Iota, Puget Sound
1909 Alpha Xi, Oregon	1963 Delta Kappa, L.S.U.
1911 Alpha Pi, North Dakota	1965 *Delta Lambda, Utah* (1988)
1912 Alpha Rho, South Dakota	1965 *Delta Mu, Rhode Island* (1973)
1913 Alpha Sigma, Washington State	1966 *Delta Nu, Arkansas* (1989)
1913 Alpha Tau, Cincinnati	1966 Delta Xi, North Carolina
1914 Alpha Phi, Tulane	1967 Delta Omicron, Alabama
1914 Alpha Upsilon, Washburn	1969 *Delta Pi, Tennessee* (1985)
1915 Alpha Chi, Purdue	1969 *Delta Rho, South Florida* (1980)
1915 Alpha Omega, Pitt	1970 Delta Sigma, Ball State
1915 Alpha Psi, Lawrence	1971 *Delta Tau, Montana State* (1983)
1916 *Beta Beta, Randolph, Macon Woman's* (1960)	1972 Delta Phi, Clemson
1917 Beta Delta, Arizona	1972 Delta Upsilon, Eastern Kentucky
1917 Beta Epsilon, Oregon State	1976 Delta Chi, Virginia
1917 Beta Gamma, Colorado State	1976 Delta Omega, Texas A & M
1919 Beta Eta, Penn (1970-1988)	1976 Delta Psi, Cal, Riverside
1919 Beta Zeta, Oklahoma State	1976 Epsilon Epsilon, Baylor
1920 Beta Theta, Idaho	1979 Epsilon Zeta, Mississippi
1921 Beta Iota, Colorado	1980 Epsilon Eta, Centre College
1921 Beta Kappa, Drake	1981 Epsilon Theta, Stetson
1922 Beta Lambda, William and Mary	1982 Epsilon Iota, Westminster (MO)
1922 Beta Mu, Nevada	1982 Epsilon Kappa, Dartmouth
1924 Beta Nu, Florida State	1982 Epsilon Lambda, Dickinson
1925 Beta Xi, UCLA	1983 Epsilon Mu, Princeton
1926 Beta Omicron, Iowa	1983 Epsilon Nu, V.P.I.
1926 Beta Pi, Michigan State	1983 Epsilon Xi, Villanova
1928 Beta Rho, Duke	1984 Epsilon Omicron, Randolph, Macon
1929 Beta Sigma, Southern Methodist	1984 Epsilon Pi, Bucknell
1929 Beta Tau, Denison	1984 Epsilon Rho, Lehigh
1930 *Beta Upsilon, British Columbia* (1980)	1985 Epsilon Sigma, Cal, Irvine
1931 Beta Chi, Alberta	1986 Epsilon Phi, Chicago
	1986 Epsilon Upsilon, Columbia (NY)

1987 Epsilon Chi, Guelph
1987 Epsilon Psi, Richmond
1988 Epsilon Omega, Washington and Jefferson
1988 Zeta Zeta, Colgate
1989 Zeta Eta, Wofford
1989 Zeta Iota, Washington and Lee
1989 Zeta Theta, Cal Poly, San Luis Obispo
1990 Zeta Kappa, South Carolina
1990 Zeta Lambda, Charleston (SC)

Colonies: Yale

COAT OF ARMS

Kappa Delta

ACTIVE PIN

PLEDGE PIN

KAPPA DELTA was founded October 23, 1897, at Longwood College, Farmville, Virginia, then the Virginia State Normal School, by Mary S. Sparks, Julia G. Tyler, Lenora D. Ashmore, and Sara Turner. It was incorporated under the laws of the Commonwealth of Virginia in 1902. The objective of the sorority is the formation and perpetuation of good fellowship, friendship, and sisterly love among its members; the encouragement of literature and education; the promotion of social interest; and the furtherance of charitable and benevolent purposes.

Growth   In 1912 the sorority became a member of the National Panhellenic Conference by surrendering those of its chapters which existed in subcollegiate institutions. These chapters were situated at Longwood College, Fairmount Seminary, and Gunston Institute. Those at the Chatham Episcopal, St. Mary's School, Presbyterian College, Caldwell, Women's College of Alabama, Judson's College, Hollins, Oglethorpe, and Randolph-Macon Woman's College became inactive when these institutions abolished sororities.

The chartered alumnae associations enjoy all the privileges of the college chapters except that of initiating new members.

Government   Government is by a convention and a council. The supreme governing body is the national convention, which meets biennially. In the interim between conventions the sorority is governed by the National Council, consisting of six members usually elected for four-year terms. This council also meets annually to transact the sorority business and attend to administrative matters. Annual conventions were held from 1904 to 1913. Since that time they have been held biennially.

In 1972, Kappa Delta's membership records were converted to computer processing and the chapter accounting records transferred in 1976. The sorority purchased and installed its own computer in 1984. A national insurance program was instituted in 1975 and all chapters participate in the general liability coverage.

The chapters are grouped into provinces according to geographical location. A province president, under the direct supervision of the national collegiate vice president and regional chapter director, is in charge of each province.

In 1908, chapters were inspected for the first time. Now, each chapter is visited annually by a member of the National Council, by the province president, or by another national officer. The national alumnae vice president supervises the province alumnae officers and work of the alumnae associations.

In 1925, a central office was established to act as a general clearing house for all routine business of the sorority.

Traditions and Insignia   Scholarship, cultural, and educational projects are promoted each year for the development of college chapter and alumnae association members.

Collegiate awards presented at convention are: Council; Merit; Achievement: Progress, Mileage; Magazine; *Angelos;* Pledge Education; Chapter Education; Gracious Living; Membership; White Rose; Diamond; Philanthropy; Scholarship; NPC. Alumnae awards include Outstanding Alumnae Association, Alumnae Advisory Board, Special Recognition, Programming, Press/PR, Chapter Assistance, Philanthropy, and Membership.

October 23 is Founders' Day, and is celebrated by the alumnae associations and the college chapters with a special ritualistic service.

The present form of the badge, the second-degree pledge pin, and the coat of arms were perfected in 1898. The diamond badge displays a dagger, the sorority's Greek letters, and the letters AOT in gold on a background of black enamel. The first-degree pledge pin is a small Norman shield of green and white enamel bearing three gold stars. The second-degree pledge pin is an open equilateral triangle of gold superimposed upon a dagger with straight lines connecting the center of the base with the center of each side. The recognition pin is a small gold dagger. The flag is a thrice barred and dentate pennant, olive and white, displaying a white rose, a dagger, and three gold stars. The sorority colors are olive green and pearl white. The flower is the white rose. The open motto is *Ta Kala Diokomen*, meaning, "Let us strive for that which is honorable, beautiful, and highest."

Publications   Since 1904 the sorority has published a quarterly magazine, *The Angelos*. A secret publication, *Ta Takta*, is issued at the discretion of the National Council, generally following each convention, when it contains the proceedings of the convention and the reports. *The Katydid* is the convention newsletter. *The Kappa Delta Songbook* was first published in 1914; since then there have been many revised editions, as there have been of the *Directory*, first published in 1912.

Other sorority publications include *Vice President's Guide for Pledge Education, House Director's Manual, The Norman Shield* (pledge manual), *National Officers' Handbook, Alumnae Advisory Board Manual, Chapter Treasurer's Guide, Rushing Manual, Alumnae Association Guide, Chapter Housing and House Corporation Manual, Province Presidents' Guide, Province Alumnae Officers' Guide, Anniversary Planning Guide, Media Relations Handbook, Miss Gracious Living*. All of these manuals have been revised from time to time.

The first *History of Kappa Delta*, in two volumes, was issued at the 1937 convention in Richmond, Virginia. A history of the years 1937-47 appeared as a special number of *The Angelos*, in 1953. *A History of Kappa Delta Sorority, 1897-1972* by Genevieve Forbes Morse was published in two volumes in 1973. *This is Kappa Delta* has been published and revised several times. A 20-minute full-color sound movie *This is Kappa Delta* was produced in 1976.

Foundations and Philanthropies The Kappa Delta Foundation, Inc., was created in 1981 and received its IRS determination as a non-profit educational and charitable foundation in 1982. It has a seven-member Board of Directors.

The sorority had a war service project in 1942 for the purpose of supplying recreational equipment for the men and women in service. A repatriation fund was also established to assist members who were confined to enemy camps.

In 1917, the Kappa Delta Student Loan Fund was established as a source of loans for worthy Kappa Deltas who would thus be able to complete their college courses.

In 1973, Founder's Scholarships were awarded for the first time. Fifteen cash awards are given to outstanding and deserving members and are presented annually.

Two graduate fellowships have been awarded annually since 1979 and the Alumna Grant for Continuing Education was created in 1982. The Kappa Delta Foundation currently underwrites the sorority's scholarship program.

The Chapter House Fund was established at the 1919 convention. Chapters may borrow from the fund, and they also have the privilege of investing their savings with the house fund, receiving interest on their deposits. This fund is administered by a committee which also supervises the operation of chapter houses.

Many chapters own their own homes while others own lodges. Several lease property or maintain rooms or apartments.

The national magazine project was inaugurated at the 1939 convention, the proceeds from which are known as the Nancy B. Hall Magazine Fund. This fund is to be invested in the chapter House Fund and used for building chapter houses.

Kappa Delta's legacy to the world is her philanthropic work with children. Initially starting with Crippled Children's Hospital in Richmond, Va., the work has now spread to include not only the hospital but also the National Committee for Prevention of Child Abuse.

A national philanthropy was considered as early as 1916, but it wasn't until Kappa Delta's 25th anniversary that the National Council, with the guidance and inspiration of National President Elizabeth Corbett Gilbert, determined a permanent philanthropy. The selection of the hospital honors the founders and the state of founding.

The hospital changed its named in 1982, dropping the word "crippled" because it now treats children with a variety of medical needs. It also selected a new symbol to denote health, activity, vitality, and growth. Children's Hospital dedicated its new addition in June, 1984, to which the sorority contributed $100,000 for a new surgical suite.

In 1981, Kappa Delta became the first fraternal organization to support the National Committee for Prevention of Child Abuse (NCPCA) on a national level. The pamphlet, "The Disabled Child and Child Abuse" was underwritten by the sorority.

Kappa Delta's attention was first drawn to NCPCA by the late Donna Stone Pesch, a sorority sister who founded the organization. Donna presented the needs of this organization to the sorority, and from the small beginning collegiate chapters and alumnae associations have recognized the necessity for financial and volunteer assistance for child abuse prevention programs and are providing support to local community agencies.

The sorority has undertaken an annual March fund raiser for the benefit of child abuse programs. Members collect monies in the respective communities and 80 per cent of the funds remain in the local area while 20 per cent are forwarded to the National Committee for Prevention of Child Abuse.

Kappa Delta's work with Children's Hospital began in 1921 when $1,200 was pledged to support two beds. The sorority continues to provide support, both monetarily and with special gifts from collegians and alumnae. On Founders' Day, the sorority presents its annual check to the hospital. These monies have purchased dental x-ray equipment;, air conditioners, closed circuit TV sets, auditorium sound systems and draperies, mobile x-ray machines, recreational therapy supplies, auditory trainers, playground equipment and video equipment.

The sorority has only one annual appeal to its members to support its philanthropies. Each fall a sheet of Christmas seals, designed by a Kappa Delta, is sent to all alumnae, informing them of the projects and suggesting a tax-exempt contribution for the seals. Receipts from the Christmas seal mailing are used to fund hospital and NCPCA projects.

These funds also provide the orthopaedic research grants given each year by Kappa Delta through her affiliation with the American Academy of Orthopaedic Surgeons. Since the first presentation in 1951, more than $100,000 has been given for research. The sorority also provides a monetary grant for orthopaedic work at Children's Hospital, Denver, Colo., site of the national headquarters.

A permanent Endowment Fund, added to annually, which represents the accumulated savings of the sorority, was established in 1923. Its purpose is to ensure the financial stability of the sorority; to assist in financing the chapter houses; and to ensure for the life membership initiates the permanent publication of the magazine, *The Angelos.*

In 1952, the Diamond Anniversary Fund was established to honor the 75th anniversary of Kappa Delta's founding. The 1973 convention voted to use the monies to purchase a national headquarters building. The sorority also has created an alumnae Crisis Fund, Headquarters Fund, Archives Fund and Century Fund, the latter to honor Kappa Delta's centennial.

Headquarters 2211 S. Josephine Street, Denver, CO 80210. In March, 1976, Central Office was moved to Denver, and occupies a former Kappa Delta chapter house near the University of Denver campus. This building of prestressed concrete vaults affords an efficient business office, a repository for memorabilia and records in the archives section, National Council meeting room, editorial offices for *The Angelos,* and living accommodations for visiting national officers.

Membership Active chapters 124. Inactive chapters 57. Houses owned 62. City/Area alumni associations 440. Total number of initiates 108,379. Chapter roll:

1897	Alpha, Longwood (1912-1949)
1902	*Beta, Chatham (1904)*
1902	*Gamma, Hollins (1912)*
1902	*Old Epsilon, Elizabeth City (1904)*
1902	*Sigma, Gunston Hall (1912)*
1903	*Phi Psi, Fairmont (1912)*
1903	*Theta, Randolph, Macon Woman's (1960)*
1904	Kappa Alpha, Florida State
1904	*Phi Delta, St. Mary's School (1910)*
1904	*Rho Omega Phi, Judson (1919)*
1904	Zeta, Alabama
1905	*Delta, Presbyterian (1910)*
1907	*Iota, Caldwell (1908)*
1907	Lambda, Northwestern
1908	Omicron, Illinois Wesleyan
1908	Sigma Sigma, Iowa State
1909	Epsilon, L.S.U.
1909	Epsilon Omega, Kentucky
1911	*Alpha Gamma, Coe (1966)*
1912	Sigma Delta, Duke (1967-1976)
1913	*Eta, Hunter (1964)*
1913	*Kappa, Women's College (AL) (1913)*
1913	Omega Xi, Cincinnati
1914	*Chi, Denver (1974)*
1914	Mu, Millsaps
1914	Rho, Wyoming
1915	*Phi Tau, Bucknell (1970)*

1916	Phi Epsilon, Colorado State
1916	*Sigma Alpha, Southern Methodist (1937-1964) (1975)*
1917	Omega Chi, Cornell (1969-1975)
1917	*Phi, Cal, Berkeley (1969)*
1917	*Theta Sigma, USC (1964)*
1918	*Psi, Lawrence (1968)*
1918	*Sigma Beta, Minnesota (1972)*
1919	Nu, Oklahoma State
1920	Pi, Nebraska (1943-1947)
1920	Sigma Gamma, Kansas State
1920	*Tau, Wisconsin, Madison (1973)*
1920	*Upsilon, Beloit (1970)*
1920	Xi, Pitt (1933-1979)
1921	Sigma Epsilon, Texas (1934-1981)
1921	*Sigma Eta, St. Lawrence (1969)*
1921	Sigma Theta, Penn
1921	*Sigma Zeta, Michigan (1969)*
1922	Sigma Iota, Washington (WA)
1922	Sigma Kappa, Ohio State
1922	Sigma Lambda, Auburn
1922	*Sigma Mu, George Washington (1968)*
1923	*Sigma Nu, Syracuse (1971)*
1923	Sigma Omicron, Illinois
1923	Sigma Pi, Albion
1923	*Sigma Rho, Iowa (1933)*
1923	Sigma Tau, Washington State
1923	Sigma Upsilon, Indiana (1941-1955)
1923	Sigma Xi, Bethany (WV)
1924	Alpha Alpha, Michigan State
1924	*Alpha Beta, Mount Union (1943)*
1924	*Sigma Chi, Montana (1942)*
1924	Sigma Omega, Montana State
1924	Sigma Phi, Georgia
1924	Sigma Psi, North Dakota State
1925	Alpha Delta, Rhodes
1925	Alpha Epsilon, Tennessee
1925	*Alpha Zeta, Ohio Wesleyan (1944)*
1926	*Alpha Eta, DePauw (1933)*
1926	Alpha Iota, UCLA
1926	Alpha Kappa, Oregon State
1926	*Alpha Lambda, Oregon (1933)*
1926	*Alpha Theta, Vermont (1937)*
1927	Alpha Mu, Mississippi
1927	Alpha Nu, Wittenberg
1928	Alpha Omicron, Queens (NC)
1928	Alpha Pi, William and Mary
1928	Alpha Xi, Louisville
1929	Alpha Rho, Maryland
1929	*Alpha Sigma, New Hampshire (1962)*
1930	*Alpha Tau, Oglethorpe (1943-1969) (1974)*
1930	Alpha Upsilon, Birmingham-Southern
1931	Alpha Chi, Louisiana Tech
1931	*Alpha Omega, Butler (1935)*
1931	Alpha Phi, Westminster (PA)
1931	Alpha Psi, Drury
1932	Beta Alpha, Virginia (1966-1978)
1933	*Beta Beta, CUNY, Brooklyn (1969)*
1936	Beta Gamma, Monmouth (IL)
1937	Beta Delta, Utah State
1937	Beta Epsilon, Tulsa
1940	*Beta Eta, Middlebury (1956)*

1940 Beta Zeta, South Carolina
1941 Beta Theta, Penn State
1943 *Beta Iota, American* (1974)
1945 *Beta Kappa, Tennessee, Chattanooga* (1963)
1946 Beta Lambda, Georgetown Col
1946 Beta Mu, Bowling Green
1946 Beta Nu, Toledo (1977-1983)
1947 Beta Xi, Colorado (1962-1984)
1948 Beta Pi, Florida
1949 Beta Rho, San Diego U.
1949 Beta Sigma, Southern Mississippi
1949 Beta Tau, Vanderbilt
1950 Beta Upsilon, Susquehanna
1951 Beta Chi, North Carolina
1951 Beta Phi, West Virginia
1952 Beta Psi, Arizona State
1952 Gamma Alpha, Northern Illinois
1954 *Gamma Beta, North Texas* (1975)
1954 Gamma Delta, East Tennessee
1955 Gamma Epsilon, Florida Southern
1955 *Gamma Eta, Ohio* (1975)
1955 Gamma Gamma, High Point
1955 Gamma Theta, Oklahoma
1955 Gamma Zeta, Texas Christian
1956 Gamma Iota, San Jose (1966-1978)
1956 Gamma Kappa, Southwestern Louisiana
1956 *Gamma Lambda, Lamar* (1983)
1958 Gamma Mu, Valdosta
1958 Gamma Nu, Miami (OH)
1958 Gamma Omicron, Wayne State (MI)
1958 Gamma Xi, Kentucky Wesleyan
1959 *Gamma Pi, Emory* (1985)
1959 Gamma Rho, Sam Houston
1960 *Gamma Sigma, East Carolina* (1984)
1960 *Gamma Tau, Ripon* (1967)
1960 Gamma Upsilon, East Texas
1961 *Gamma Phi, Tennessee Wesleyan* (1978)
1962 Gamma Chi, Lenoir-Rhyne
1962 Gamma Psi, Delta State
1963 Gamma Omega, Slippery Rock
1964 *Delta Alpha, Texas, El Paso* (1976)
1964 *Delta Beta, Eastern Illinois* (1984)
1965 Delta Gamma, Western Kentucky
1966 Delta Delta, Troy
1966 Delta Epsilon, Pan American
1967 Delta Eta, South Florida
1967 *Delta Iota, Murray State* (1984)
1967 Delta Zeta, Northeast Louisiana
1968 Delta Kappa, Arkansas State
1968 Delta Lambda, Georgia Southern
1968 Delta Mu, Newberry
1968 Delta Nu, Indiana (PA)
1968 Delta Omicron, Eastern Kentucky
1968 *Delta Theta, Samford* (1985)
1968 *Delta Xi, Eastern New Mexico* (1974)
1969 Delta Phi, Georgia Southwestern
1969 Delta Pi, Middle Tennessee
1969 *Delta Rho, Madison Col* (1981)
1969 Delta Sigma, South Alabama
1969 Delta Tau, Morehead
1969 Delta Upsilon, Tennessee Tech
1971 Delta Chi, LaGrange

1971 Delta Omega, Mississippi State
1971 Delta Psi, West Georgia
1972 Epsilon Alpha, Missouri, Rolla
1973 *Epsilon Beta, West Texas* (1980)
1973 Epsilon Delta, Austin Peay
1973 Epsilon Epsilon, Appalachian
1973 Epsilon Eta, Illinois State
1973 Epsilon Gamma, North Georgia
1973 Epsilon Zeta, Pembroke
1975 *Epsilon Theta, South Dakota State* (1978)
1976 Epsilon Iota, Missouri
1976 Epsilon Kappa, Cal Poly, San Luis Obispo
1977 Epsilon Lambda, Alabama, Huntsville
1977 *Epsilon Mu, Methodist* (1982)
1977 *Epsilon Nu, Idaho State* (1985)
1977 Epsilon Xi, Houston Baptist
1978 Epsilon Omicron, Central Florida
1979 Epsilon Pi, V.P.I.
1979 Epsilon Rho, Rochester
1979 Epsilon Sigma, Wofford
1980 Epsilon Tau, Clemson
1981 Epsilon Upsilon, Cal Poly, Pomona
1982 Epsilon Phi, Cal, Santa Barbara
1983 Epsilon Chi, Baylor
1985 Epsilon Psi, Francis Marion
1987 Zeta Alpha, Texas Tech.
1989 Zeta Gamma, Arkansas
1990 Zeta Beta, Union (TN)
1990 Zeta Delta, Connecticut
1990 Zeta Epsilon, Kansas
1990 Zeta Zeta, Cal State, San Bernadino

COAT OF ARMS

Kappa Kappa Gamma

ACTIVE PIN

PLEDGE PIN

KAPPA KAPPA GAMMA was organized at Monmouth College, Monmouth, Illinois, in March, 1870, by Mary Louise Bennett, Hannah Jeanette Boyd, Mary Moore Stewart, and Anna Elizabeth Willits. They aspired to a Greek-letter fraternity and believed they had established the first one for women. October 13, the date of their first group appearance wearing their little golden keys in the college chapel, is observed as Founders' Day. The 1930 convention added to the list of founders the names of Mary Louisa Stevenson and Susan Burley Walker who became members prior to October 13, 1870.

Government   From 1870 to 1881, government was by grand chapter. With the election of the Grand Council at the 1881 convention, Kappa Kappa Gamma became the first woman's fraternity to adopt this form of government. The biennial convention has supreme legislative and judicial power.

Fraternity officers consist of president, vice-president, treasurer, and directors of alumnae, chapters, field representatives, membership, personnel, and philanthropies. Appointed officers are the National Panhellenic Conference delegate and traveling consultants. The executive secretary is selected by and is responsible to the Council of which she is a member ex officio, without vote. The fraternity is grouped geographically into 17 provinces, with supervision by elected province directors of chapters for undergraduate chapters and province directors of alumnae for alumnae groups. The province officers constitute the Associate Council which confers with the Council regarding the business of the fraternity and effective operation of the provinces. They assist the Council in the interpretation of conditions and trends within the provinces and make recommendations for the better functioning of the chapter and alumnae groups. Province meetings are held in the alternate years between general conventions. The fraternity is further supported by 12 standing committees and such others as deemed necessary by the Council.

The alumnae began to organize in 1887 and the first delegate was seated at the 1892 convention. Thus was born the second phase of membership within the fraternity. Under the fraternity director of alumnae and province directors of alumnae, they actively support local and international projects including Kappa's rehabilitation services, general fraternity projects, and the entire scholarship aid and educational programs. The alumnae groups give assistance to the undergraduate chapters and serve as advisers and members of the house corporations. There are organizations in over 430 principal cities of the United States and Canada, as well as London, England.

Fraternity business is centralized in a headquarters supervised by the executive secretary. The present building is a mid-Victorian residence in Columbus, Ohio, and listed on the national Register of Historic Places. It serves as an office building, as living quarters for officers during committee meetings, conferences, and as the fraternity museum. A central office has been maintained since 1922.

Traditions and Insignia   Awards named for distinguished members are given at biennial conventions to undergraduate chapters showing outstanding achievement in standards, efficiency, scholarship, gracious living, culture, pledge training, advisory board relations, fraternity appreciation, Panhellenic leadership, finance, publications, house board relations, and scholarship improvement. Similar awards for exceptional accomplishment are presented to alumnae associations and clubs. Achievement awards are given at each biennial convention to alumnae who have excelled in their chosen profession or career. A Loyalty award, considered to be the highest honor which the fraternity can bestow upon a member, is presented bi-

ennially to an alumna whose work and devotion have enriched the fraternity and inspired its members.

The fraternity badge is a golden key one inch in length, plain or jeweled, with KKΓ on the stem and ΑΩΟ on the ward. A small golden key, approximately half the size of the badge, is used as a recognition pin. Colors are light and dark blue; the flower is the fleur-de-lis; the jewel is the sapphire. The pledge pin is a Greek Δ in dark blue, enclosing a Σ in light blue. Minerva, with her bird, the owl, is the patron goddess. The coat of arms incorporates the various fraternity symbols.

Publications   The convention of 1881 authorized the first women's fraternity publication, *The Golden Key*. Now known as *The Key*, it is the official magazine, a quarterly. Other publications include *The History of Kappa Kappa Gamma Fraternity 1870-1930; History,* published 1975; *History 1975-1985; Kappa Notebook; Constitution, Bylaws and Standing Rules; Song Book; Finance Manual for Chapters; Public Relations Manual; Keys To Membership Selection; Keys to Housing; Province Officers Manual; Guide Post for Alumnae Officers; Nominations and Elections; Advisers Book of Knowledge; Adventures in Leadership; Proceedings; Style Guide; Social Survival; A Guide to Scholarship; Choices* (career information); *Professional Directory* (career networking) and *Graphics Manual.*

Funds and Philanthropies   Fraternity funds include the Loyalty Fund which is an annual giving program to the operation and management of the fraternity. The Museum Loyalty Fund maintains the historical headquarters facility, preserves the priceless archives and fraternity memorabilia, and creates educational programs and displays. The Rose McGill Fund provides confidential aid for members in need; the Educational Endowment Fund is used exclusively for the advancement of education, especially scholarships in the field of rehabilitation and special research grants. The Student Aid Fund provides scholarships for chapter consultants, foreign language study, undergraduate scholarships, graduate fellowships, and emergency scholarships. The graduate fellowships and rehabilitation scholarships are also open to nonmembers provided they are students or alumnae of colleges where there are Kappa chapters. Circle Key Grants are awarded to alumnae desiring to return to school to pursue careers or advanced education.

The 1952 convention officially launched the Kappa Rehabilitation Services as the fraternity philanthropy. This area was chosen because of the possibilities of adjusting such a program to the capabilities of small alumnae clubs as well as the larger associations. Its flexibility also made it possible to serve the needs of any community. Alumnae and actives would be enabled to work in a broad, yet flexible, service in cooperation with highly diversified local organizations dedicated to the rehabilitation of the handicapped. Assistance could be offered in the form of money, gifts, scholarship funds and volunteer service. In 1971 the fraternity was awarded the Organizational Award by the National Rehabilitation Association in recognition of outstanding contributions made in this field.

The Centennial Committee recommended in 1966 that a special scholarship recipient, to be known as a Centennial Scholar, be selected on each Kappa campus. A surplus remained in the Centennial Fund which enabled the fraternity to provide an additional $107,000 for specific projects in rehabilitation. As Kappa chapters reach the century mark, the fraternity donates a scholarship to the university in honor of 100 years of cooperation with the institution. Nineteen chapters have been so honored.

In the 1982-1984 biennium, the fraternity awarded over $400,000 in scholarship aid to Kappas and non-members. This does not include the hundreds of thousands of hours in volunteer service and donations made on the local level.

Headquarters 530 East Town Street, P.O. Box 2079, Columbus, OH 43216.

Membership Active chapters 120. Inactive chapters 19. Total number of initiates 150,000. Chapter roll:

1870	Alpha, Monmouth (IL) (1884-1934)
1871	*Beta, St. Mary's (IL)* (1874)
1872	Delta, Indiana
1872	*Gamma, Smithson* (1875)
1873	Epsilon, Illinois Wesleyan
1874	*Zeta, Rockford Seminary* (1876)
1875	Eta, Wisconsin, Madison
1875	Iota, DePauw
1875	Theta, Missouri
1876	*Beta Gamma, Wooster* (1914)
1877	Lambda, Akron
1878	Mu, Butler
1879	*Nu, Franklin* (1884)
1880	Chi, Minnesota
1880	Omicron, Simpson (1890-1990)
1880	Pi, Cal, Berkeley (1885-1897)
1880	Rho, Ohio Wesleyan (1884-1925)
1881	Beta Beta, St. Lawrence (1903-1915)
1881	Kappa, Hillsdale
1881	*Tau, LaSalle* (1882)
1882	Beta Zeta, Iowa
1882	*Phi, Boston U.* (1971)
1882	Upsilon, Northwestern
1882	*Xi, Adrian* (1944)
1883	Beta Tau, Syracuse
1883	Omega, Kansas
1883	Psi, Cornell (1969-1977)
1884	Sigma, Nebraska
1885	Beta Rho, Cincinnati (1885-1914)
1888	Beta Nu, Ohio State
1888	Gamma Rho, Allegheny
1890	*Beta Alpha, Penn* (1977)
1890	Beta Delta, Michigan
1891	*Beta Epsilon, Barnard* (1917)

1892	Beta Eta, Stanford (1944-1978)
1893	*Beta Iota, Swarthmore* (1934)
1899	Beta Lambda, Illinois
1901	Beta Mu, Colorado
1902	Beta Xi, Texas
1904	Beta Omicron, Tulane
1905	Beta Pi, Washington (WA)
1905	*Beta Sigma, Adelphi* (1954)
1906	Beta Upsilon, West Virginia
1909	Beta Phi, Montana
1910	Beta Chi, Kentucky
1911	Beta Psi, Toronto
1913	Beta Omega, Oregon
1914	Beta Theta, Oklahoma
1916	Beta Kappa, Idaho
1916	Gamma Alpha, Kansas State
1918	Gamma Beta, New Mexico
1918	Gamma Gamma, Whitman
1919	Gamma Delta, Purdue
1919	Gamma Epsilon, Pitt
1920	Gamma Eta, Washington State
1920	Gamma Zeta, Arizona
1921	Gamma Iota, Washington (MO)
1921	Gamma Theta, Drake
1923	Gamma Kappa, William And Mary
1923	*Gamma Lambda, Middlebury* (1969)
1924	Gamma Mu, Oregon State
1925	Gamma Nu, Arkansas
1925	Gamma Xi, UCLA
1927	Gamma Omicron, Wyoming
1927	Gamma Pi, Alabama
1928	*Gamma Sigma, Manitoba* (1976)
1929	Gamma Chi, George Washington
1929	Gamma Omega, Denison
1929	Gamma Phi, Southern Methodist
1929	Gamma Psi, Maryland
1929	*Gamma Tau, North Dakota State* (1985)
1929	Gamma Upsilon, British Columbia
1930	Delta Alpha, Penn State
1930	Delta Beta, Duke
1930	Delta Delta, McGill
1930	Delta Gamma, Michigan State
1932	Delta Epsilon, Rollins
1932	Delta Eta, Utah
1932	Delta Zeta, Colorado Col
1933	*Delta Theta, Goucher* (1942)
1935	Delta Iota, L.S.U.
1938	Delta Kappa, Miami (FL)
1940	Delta Lambda, Miami (OH)
1942	Delta Mu, Connecticut
1942	Delta Nu, Massachusetts
1944	Delta Xi, Carnegie-Mellon
1946	Delta Omicron, Iowa State
1946	Delta Pi, Tulsa
1947	Delta Rho, Mississippi
1947	Delta Sigma, Oklahoma State
1947	Delta Tau, USC
1948	*Delta Chi, San Jose* (1972)
1948	Delta Phi, Bucknell
1948	Delta Upsilon, Georgia
1953	Delta Psi, Texas Tech
1954	Delta Omega, Cal State, Fresno

1955	Epsilon Alpha, Texas Christian	
1956	Epsilon Beta, Colorado State	
1958	Epsilon Gamma, North Carolina	
1959	Epsilon Delta, Arizona State	
1959	Epsilon Epsilon, Emory	
1961	Epsilon Zeta, Florida State	
1963	Epsilon Eta, Auburn	
1963	*Epsilon Theta, Arkansas, Little Rock* (1981)	
1966	Epsilon Iota, Puget Sound	
1967	Epsilon Kappa, South Carolina	
1967	Epsilon Lambda, Tennessee	
1970	Epsilon Mu, Clemson	
1973	Epsilon Nu, Vanderbilt	
1974	Epsilon Xi, Cal State, Northridge	
1975	Epsilon Omicron, Cal, Davis	
1976	Epsilon Pi, Cal, Riverside	
1976	Epsilon Rho, Texas A & M	
1976	Epsilon Sigma, Virginia	
1977	*Epsilon Tau, Mississippi State* (1984)	
1977	Epsilon Upsilon, Baylor	
1978	Epsilon Chi, Dartmouth	
1978	Epsilon Phi, Florida	
1978	Epsilon Psi, Cal, Santa Barbara	
1979	Epsilon Omega, Dickinson	
1980	Zeta Alpha, Babson	
1980	Zeta Beta, Lafayette	
1980	Zeta Delta, Vermont	
1980	Zeta Gamma, Centre College	
1981	Zeta Epsilon, Lawrence	
1982	Zeta Eta, Cal, Irvine	
1982	Zeta Iota, Villanova	
1982	Zeta Theta, Trinity (CT)	
1982	Zeta Zeta, Westminster (MO)	
1983	Zeta Kappa, Bowling Green	
1984	Zeta Lambda, Washington and Jefferson	
1985	Zeta Mu, V.P.I.	
1985	Zeta Nu, San Diego U.	
1987	Zeta Omicron, Richmond	
1987	Zeta Pi, Idaho	
1987	Zeta Xi, Yale	
1988	Zeta Rho, Colgate	
1989	Zeta Sigma, North Texas	
1990	Zeta Upsilon, Georgia Southern	

Phi Mu

ACTIVE PIN

PLEDGE PIN

PHI MU was founded as the Philomathean Society at Wesleyan Female College, Macon, Georgia, on January 4, 1852, by Mary DuPont Lines, Mary Myrick Daniel, and Martha Hardaway Redding. Phi Mu

and its sister sorority, Alpha Delta Pi, which was founded at Wesleyan as the Adelphean Society, have the longest continuous existence of any college organizations for women.

For several years around the turn of the century, there was repeated discussion among the Philomatheans about becoming a national organization and expanding the society's scope to other college campuses. In 1900 they adopted the Greek name, Phi Mu, which symbolized the Philomathean Society secret motto. In the 1903-04 school year, the 55 college members of the Philomathean Society, which had flourished for 52 years at Wesleyan, petitioned for a national charter. It was granted on August 1, 1904, by the State of Georgia, and the original membership became Alpha Chapter of Phi Mu Fraternity.

Growth Immediately Beta chapter was established at Hollins College, Hollins, Virginia, launching a period of expansion that resulted in eight chapters by the first national convention in June, 1907. Essential to future growth, however, was entrance into National Panhellenic Conference. This was sought and attained in December 1911, after the unselfish sacrifice of four early chapters whose campuses did not meet NPC standards.

The pattern of Phi Mu's development was far-flung. Chapters established within 10 years after the first national convention were not only in neighboring southern states but also in eastern states of Maine and New York, and the district of Columbia; mid-northern states of Ohio, Illinois, Indiana, Missouri, Iowa, and Wisconsin; southwestern states of New mexico and Texas, and western states of Washington and California.

Although Depression years of the 1930s had a slowing effect, Phi Mu had installed 73 chapters by 1939, the year it merged with Alpha Delta Theta, an NPC group founded in 1919. The most rapid period of expansion occurred in the 1960s, when 39 chapters were installed, despite campus disruptions and demonstrations by militant students.

Government Government of Phi Mu is by the biennial national conventions, voting membership of which consists of delegates (one each) from the collegiate chapters and alumnae chapters, the National Council, directors and other officers, chairmen of standing committees, past national presidents, and president of Phi Mu Foundation. During the period between conventions, governing responsibility is vested in the National Council: president, collegiate and alumnae vice-presidents, finance director, extension director, and two members-at-large, voted to Council membership by the national convention; and the NPC delegate and public relations director appointed by the elected members of the National Council. Administration is facilitated through division into geographical areas which are supervised by area coordinators who direct activities of area alumnae directors, collegiate directors, and finance directors.

Area Leadership Conferences also are on a biennial schedule, alternating with National Conventions. In addition, where local members wish, state meetings ("State Days") are held annually to promote social fellowship and to keep members abreast of fraternity trends. A "Magic Carpet District" embraces all members beyond the continental limits of the United states.

An executive office, among the first such offices in the fraternity world, was established in 1919 and has been maintained continuously since—first in New Orleans, then in Chicago and Evanston, Illinois, until 1954 when the headquarters was moved to Memphis. It has been located in Phi Mu's founding state since 1977 when a move was made to Atlanta.

An executive director supervises a staff of approximately 10 in carrying out all routine business of the fraternity, handling membership records, publications, supplies, historical records, secretarial and financial services, and auditing chapter accounts. Chapter consultants (field representatives) receive training from the executive office staff and National Council, and their schedules are supervised by area coordinators.

Traditions and Insignia Form of initiation, secret password, sign, grip and motto adopted by the founders are the same today as in 1852. The membership badge carries the same symbolism and has changed essentially, only in size. The first Philomathean badges were large shields of gold, sometimes elaborately engraved but not jeweled. The smaller size of today and the option of adding jewels were changes that came with nationalization in 1904, to be in keeping with current fraternity badges. The badge is a quatrefoil shape of black enamel displaying a hand holding a heart. Above is a band of gold bearing the letters ΦM, and below is a band bearing three stars. The provisional member (pledge) pin, a black and gold shield with the Greek letter Φ, is of the same shape as the badge but smaller. The coat of arms features a red shield bearing a badge and three stars, surmounted by two gold lions, a lamp of knowledge atop the shield, and a banner below bearing the open motto, "Les Soeurs Fideles." The colors are rose and white, and the flower is the rose carnation.

Wesleyan College, the birthplace of Phi Mu, has been the recipient of three commemorative gifts—a memorial gateway on the occasion of the college's 100th anniversary; three chandeliers for the college dining hall as memorials to Phi Mu's founders, given on the fraternity's 100th anniversary, and a scholarship awarded annually to a deserving undergraduate student at Weseleyan. The early Philomathean Hall at Wesleyan was restored and refurnished as a Philomathean Memorial Room in 1941. When Wesleyan completed its move to a new location in Macon, the Old Wesleyan buildings were sold and razed, and the Philomathean Room was moved to the Cannon Ball House, an historic home in the heart of Macon restored as a museum. The house is open to public tours.

The traditional observance most widely cherished by all Phi Mus is Founders' Day, celebrated each year on March 4, the anniversary of the announcement to the public of the Philomathean Society's founding. All collegiate and alumnae members contribute Founders' Day Pennies—one for each year of Phi Mu's life—as a gift to the Alpha Memorial Fund (for student loans and scholarships).

Recognition awards are made at national conventions to the chapters and to individual Phi Mus. Collegiate chapters are honored for scholarship, campus leadership, social service, and progress in various other fraternity activities, while alumnae chapters are honored for social service, membership, and other noteworthy activities. Outstanding alumnae are nominated each biennium for contributions to fraternity, to community and to profession or career, and one in each field receives an achievement award. Fifty-year pins are presented to all Phi Mus when they reach the golden anniversary of their membership in the fraternity. The gavel to convene each national convention once belonged to Alpha chapter at Wesleyan and was passed to Delta chapter at Sophie Newcomb College, New Orleans, when Alpha ceased operation in 1914 because of trustee action banning all Greek organizations from the campus. The fraternity has marked the graves of the three founders with large monuments in the shape of the Phi Mu badge.

Publications Phi Mu's principal publication is *The Aglaia*, a quarterly magazine. It is the outgrowth of *The Philomathean Gazette*, which was published continuously from 1857 to 1890. Phi Mu's first comprehensive history was published in 1927 and focused on Alpha chapter and its members. A 300-page hard-bound history published in 1982 recounts events of the first 130 years of Phi Mu, from 1852 to 1982.

The Song Book of Phi Mu has been reissued several times in updated editions since the first one was published in 1907-08. Other publications include *The Philomathean*, containing convention minutes and reports; the *Ritual of Phi Mu, Constitution and Bylaws, Standing Rules and Procedures*, and numerous manuals for collegiate chapter officers, alumnae chapter officers, alumnae advisory councils, house corporations, house directors, and national officers. An inter-officer bi-monthly publication, *Inside Info*, communicates to all national and area officers, and an alumnae advisory council newsletter keeps advisers informed.

In 1981 the *Phi Mu Professional Directory* was published, listing members by careers and professions. A directory of the complete membership was published in 1985. "Carnation Ball," a color and sound movie about Phi Mu, was produced in 1967 and received wide distribution not only among Phi Mu chapters but for Panhellenic events and in extension work.

Funds and Philanthropies The financial structure of Phi Mu consists of several funds which support the general operation of the fraternity and national conventions. Philanthropic and educational support is provided through two fraternity funds—the Social Service Endowment Fund and Alpha Memorial Fund—and through funds of the Phi Mu Foundation. The foundation was incorporated in 1957 as a separate entity from the fraternity. Its purpose is the furtherance of charitable and educational objectives. More than 50 scholarships and educational grants are awarded annually, in amounts from $300 to $1500, from undesignated funds and approximately 30 named funds. Scholarship charms are awarded by the foundation to every Phi Mu making straight A grades. The foundation publishes *The Cornerstone* quarterly for members, collegiate and alumnae chapters. The Philomathean Memorial Room in Macon is under management of the Phi Mu Foundation. Phi Mu chapter contributions to Project HOPE are administered by the foundation.

In the Civil War, the Philomatheans made bandages, helped in hospitals and promoted benefits for the troops. During World War I and again during World War II, members repeated these efforts, engaging in more extensive war service activities. A member who was a trained social worker was sponsored by Phi Mu as the fraternity's contribution to YWCA war-time activities in France in the first World War.

The 1921 National Convention adopted the Phi Mu Healthmobile as a national philanthropy, and the clinic on wheels was built and equipped in less than a year to travel the entire state of Georgia bringing medical care and nutrition and health education to the state's remote areas. It served thousands of children and adults annually until 1944. In 1946 Phi Mu's philanthropy became Toy Carts, placed in local hospital pediatric wards. Since 1963 Phi Mu has given its support to Project HOPE, which takes medical treatment, supplies and teaching to isolated and neglected areas overseas and in the United states. As important as treatment is the up-to-date training of local medical and paramedical personnel to meet the health needs of the country being visited by the HOPE staff. Local alumnae and collegiate chapters support numerous other philanthropic endeavors in their communities, most of them centered around children and health care.

Assisting members and non-members through scholarships dates from 1909. Phi Mu sponsored A.A.U.W. International Fellowships beginning in 1923, "Reconstruction" scholarships in nursing, nutrition and medicine in support of World War II, and International Study Grants from 1946 to 1964. Since the establishment of the Phi Mu Foundation in 1956 scholarships have grown enormously in both number and amount.

Headquarters   3558 Habersham at Northlake, Tucker, GA 30084.

Membership   Total living membership 102,398. Total undergraduate membership 7,358. Active chapters 130. Inactive chapters 74. Colonies 1. Houses owned 55. Graduate/Alumni chapters 146.

City/Area alumni associations 140. Total number of initiates 107,801. Chapter roll:

1852	*Alpha, Wesleyan College* (1914)	
1904	*Beta, Hollins* (1929)	
1906	Delta, Tulane	
1906	*Gamma, Winston-Salem* (1909)	
1906	*Upsilon Delta, St. Mary's (NC)* (1910)	
1907	*Eta, Hardin-Simmons* (1911)	
1907	*Theta, Belmont* (1911)	
1907	*Zeta, Chevy Chase* (1910)	
1908	Kappa, Tennessee	
1908	*Xi Kappa, Southwestern (TX)* (1982)	
1910	*Lambda, Randolph, Macon* (1960)	
1910	Mu, Brenau	
1911	*Nu, Shorter* (1912)	
1911	*Xi, New Mexico* (1978)	
1912	*Omicron, Akron* (1978)	
1912	Pi, Maine	
1912	*Sigma, Knox* (1989)	
1913	*Chi, Missouri* (1944)	
1913	*Phi, Texas* (1965)	
1913	*Psi, Adelphi* (1973)	
1913	Rho, Hanover	
1913	*Tau, Whitman* (1955)	
1913	Upsilon, Ohio State	
1914	Epsilon, Millsaps	
1914	*Iota, Lawrence* (1935)	
1914	*Omega, Iowa Wesleyan* (1943)	
1915	*Beta Alpha, George Washington* (1950)	
1915	Epsilon Alpha, Southern Methodist	
1915	*Iota Sigma, USC* (1950)	
1916	Eta Alpha, Cal, Berkeley (1971-1980)	
1916	Zeta Alpha, Baker	
1917	Eta Beta, Washington (WA)	
1918	*Beta Beta, Colby* (1944)	
1919	*Beta Delta, Dickinson* (1967)	
1919	*Beta Epsilon, Swarthmore* (1934)	
1919	Beta Gamma, New Hampshire	
1919	*Zeta Beta, Wisconsin, Madison* (1941)	
1920	*Beta Theta, Pitt* (1961)	
1920	*Beta Zeta, Syracuse* (1969)	
1920	Delta Alpha, Indiana	
1921	Alpha Alpha, Georgia	
1921	Delta Beta, Illinois	
1921	Zeta Gamma, Nebraska	
1922	Beta Kappa, Bucknell (1986-1987)	
1922	*Zeta Delta, Drake* (1952)	
1923	Alpha Beta, Arkansas (1933-1978)	
1923	*Epsilon Beta, Oklahoma* (1943-1955) (1965)	
1923	*Zeta Epsilon, Washington (MO)* (1966)	
1924	Alpha Gamma, Samford	
1924	*Delta Gamma, Ohio Wesleyan* (1937)	
1925	*Beta Lambda, Middlebury* (1952)	
1925	*Zeta Eta, Minnesota* (1935-1946) (1970)	
1925	*Zeta Theta, Iowa* (1941)	
1926	Alpha Delta, Mississippi	
1926	Gamma Alpha, William and Mary	
1927	Delta Delta, Ohio	
1927	*Eta Delta, UCLA* (1972-1981) (1987)	
1927	*Eta Gamma, Oregon* (1937)	
1927	*Gamma Beta, West Virginia* (1942)	

1929 Alpha Epsilon, Florida State	1964 *Delta Sigma, Marquette* (1973)
1929 Alpha Omega, Rollins	1964 Gamma Lambda, North Carolina
1929 Beta Mu, Penn State	1965 Delta Tau, Western Kentucky
1929 Delta Epsilon, Purdue	1965 *Delta Upsilon, Loyola, Chicago* (1971)
1929 Gamma Gamma, Queens (NC)	1965 Kappa Beta, Valdosta
1930 *Eta Epsilon, Utah* (1987)	1966 Beta Chi, Fairmont
1931 Alpha Zeta, Alabama	1966 Beta Phi, Marshall
1931 *Delta Zeta, Cincinnati* (1951)	1966 Kappa Delta, Athens
1932 Zeta Iota, North Dakota State	1966 Kappa Epsilon, Delta State
1933 Gamma Delta, American	1966 Kappa Gamma, Troy
1934 Alpha Eta, L.S.U.	1967 Epsilon Zeta, Texas, Arlington
1934 *Gamma Epsilon, Duke* (1987)	1967 *Eta Kappa, Humboldt* (1976)
1937 *Alpha Theta, Tennessee, Chattanooga* (1970)	1967 *Eta Lambda, Nevada, Las Vegas* (1973)
1938 Alpha Iota, Mercer	1967 Kappa Eta, Nicholls
1939 Alpha Kappa, Charleston (SC)	1967 Kappa Zeta, Atlantic Christian
1939 Beta Nu, Bethany (WV)	1968 Delta Phi, Ashland
1939 Delta Theta, Transylvania	1968 *Gamma Kappa, North Carolina, Wilmington* (1974)
1939 *Epsilon Gamma, Tulsa* (1989)	1968 Gamma Mu, Western Carolina
1939 *Zeta Kappa, Nebraska Wesleyan* (1977-1980) (1984)	1968 Kappa Iota, Northwestern Louisiana
1942 Delta Iota, Baldwin-Wallace	1968 Kappa Mu, Georgia Southern
1943 Alpha Lambda, Louisiana Tech	1968 *Kappa Theta, Tennessee Wesleyan* (1978)
1943 *Beta Xi, Connecticut* (1963)	1968 *Zeta Nu, Wisconsin, Oshkosh* (1978)
1945 *Beta Pi, Gettysburg* (1970)	1969 Delta Eta, Georgetown Col
1946 Alpha Mu, Auburn	1969 *Epsilon Eta, Sul Ross* (1976)
1946 Delta Kappa, Bowling Green	1969 Kappa Nu, Lambuth
1947 Kappa Lambda, Memphis State	1969 Kappa Omega, South Alabama
1949 *Alpha Nu, Florida* (1987)	1969 Kappa Omicron, Armstrong
1949 Alpha Xi, Stetson	1969 Kappa Pi, Tennessee Tech
1949 Beta Rho, Davis and Elkins	1969 Kappa Xi, Livingston
1950 Alpha Omicron, Southern Mississippi	1969 *Zeta Mu, Wayne State (NE)* (1983)
1950 Beta Sigma, Indiana (PA)	1970 *Kappa Rho, Florida Atlantic* (1975)
1951 Epsilon Delta, Arkansas State	1970 Kappa Sigma, Jacksonville (AL)
1951 Eta Zeta, Cal State, Fresno	1970 *Zeta Pi, Missouri Western* (1987)
1952 Delta Lambda, Evansville	1971 Gamma Nu, Elon
1952 Delta Mu, Youngstown State	1971 Gamma Rho, West Georgia
1953 Gamma Zeta, High Point	1971 Kappa Phi, LaGrange
1954 Alpha Tau, Florida Southern	1971 Kappa Tau, Lander
1954 Beta Tau, Drexel	1971 *Zeta Omicron, Southwest Missouri* (1974)
1955 Delta Nu, Michigan State	1972 *Beta Omega, Robert Morris* (1974)
1955 Gamma Eta, Roanoke	1972 Beta Psi, Southern Maine
1955 Kappa Kappa, East Tennessee	1972 Epsilon Theta, Texas Wesleyan
1956 Alpha Pi, Houston	1972 Gamma Omicron, George Mason
1956 Alpha Rho, Northeast Louisiana	1972 *Gamma Xi, Old Dominion* (1985)
1956 Alpha Sigma, Southwestern Louisiana	1972 Kappa Chi, Montevallo
1956 *Eta Theta, San Jose* (1966)	1973 Delta Chi, Eastern Kentucky
1957 *Delta Xi, Michigan* (1964)	1973 Delta Psi, Wright State
1958 Alpha Upsilon, McNeese	1973 Gamma Pi, V.P.I.
1958 *Delta Omicron, Wisconsin, Milwaukee* (1973)	1973 Gamma Sigma, Georgia Col
1959 *Alpha Chi, Texas Tech* (1981)	1973 *Kappa Psi, West Florida* (1987)
1959 *Alpha Phi, Emory* (1973)	1973 Kappa Upsilon, North Georgia
1960 *Gamma Theta, Madison Col* (1987)	1973 Theta Alpha, North Alabama
1961 Beta Upsilon, Westminster (PA) (1972-1990)	1974 Eta Mu, Cal, Davis
1961 *Gamma Iota, Longwood* (1983)	1974 *Gamma Upsilon, Francis Marion* (1982)
1961 Zeta Lambda, Northwest Missouri	1975 *Epsilon Kappa, Texas A & M* (1981)
1962 Alpha Psi, Southeastern Louisiana	1975 *Zeta Rho, Wisconsin, La Crosse* (1990)
1962 Delta Pi, Western Michigan	1976 Beta Eta, Miami (OH)
1962 *Eta Iota, Arizona* (1977)	1977 Epsilon Lambda, Arkansas Tech
1962 Kappa Alpha, Mississippi State	1978 Epsilon Mu, Houston Baptist
1964 *Delta Rho, Steubenville* (1970)	1979 Epsilon Nu, Oklahoma State
	1981 Gamma Chi, North Carolina, Greensboro
	1981 Gamma Omega, Virginia

1982 Gamma Tau, Johns Hopkins
1982 Lambda Alpha, Randolph, Macon
1983 Lambda Beta, Appalachian
1984 Beta Iota, Clarkson
1984 *Beta Omicron, Massachusetts* (1990)
1984 Epsilon Xi, L.S.U., Shreveport
1985 Delta Omega, Case Western Reserve
1985 Rho Delta, Central Michigan
1986 Phi Beta, Albright
1987 Theta Beta, Georgia State
1987 Theta Delta, Spring Hill
1988 Theta Gamma, Florida International
1989 Lambda Gamma, Virginia Commonwealth
1989 Phi Alpha, Western Maryland
1989 Phi Delta, Salisbury
1989 Phi Epsilon, Widener
1989 Phi Gamma, Maryland, Baltimore County
1989 Rho Alpha, IUPUI
1989 Rho Beta, Michigan, Dearborn
1989 Theta Epsilon, Kennesaw
1989 Theta Zeta, Georgia Tech
1989 Zeta Sigma, Wisconsin, River Falls
1990 Lambda Delta, South Carolina, Aiken
1990 Rho Epsilon, Albion
1990 Rho Gamma, Ball State

Colonies: Fairleigh Dickinson, Teaneck

Phi Sigma Sigma

ACTIVE PIN   PLEDGE PIN

PHI SIGMA SIGMA was founded on November 26, 1913, by a group of 10 Hunter College women who realized the only way they could belong to the same sorority was to found one of their own. They established a group whose ritual was nonsectarian. The founders were motivated by a desire to promote scholarship among women pursuing a higher education, by a desire to advance womanhood through a close union of congenial friends of high character and intelligence, and by a desire to engage in philanthropic service. These three goals continue to inspire members of Phi Sigma Sigma to this day.

Government Phi Sigma Sigma held its first convention in New York City in 1918, at which time the fraternity elected its first Supreme Council. The Council, which serves as the fraternity's executive body, is composed of the Grand Archon, Grand Vice-Archon, Director of Alumnae, Director of Extension, Director of Finance, Director of Housing, Director of Programming, Director of Undergraduates, Foundation President and National Panhellenic Conference Delegate.

In addition to the Supreme Council, the fraternal governing body includes Grand Council and other national personnel. Chaired by the Grand Vice-Archon, the Grand Council includes all personnel serving the areas of alumnae, programming, and undergraduates. Grand Council meets once each year at the fraternity's summer conclave; Supreme Council meets then and three times during the academic year.

Phi Sigma Sigma brought the Division Councils into being during the mid 1920's. The fraternity was divided into geographic regions to facilitate discussion and solution of problems unique to each division. Each division has its own undergraduate and alumnae presidents to serve the needs of the collegiate and alumnae chapters. Today the number of Divisions has grown to 12, indicative of the fact that the fraternity has grown in size and geographic distribution. Each division holds an annual division conference, which enables many more sisters to attend workshops and experience the bonds of national sisterhood.

The fraternity was admitted to the National Panhellenic Conference in 1951, and since that time it has been committed to serving the Greek community. Clarisse Markowitz, Past Grand Archon, was Phi Sigma Sigma's first NPC Delegate. She continued to serve in that office for well over 30 years. Phi Sigma Sigma began a 6–year term of service on the Conference's Executive Committee, culminating in the 1989–1991 biennium, when the fraternity's NPC Delegate, Louise E. Kier, assumed the office of NPC Chairman.

In recent years, new programs that the fraternity established include *Opportunity*, a career advisory and networking program, and a comprehensive health and wellness curriculum developed through the auspices of the Phi Sigma Sigma Foundation. In a cooperative effort between the Phi Sigma Sigma Foundation and the Association of Fraternity Advisors (AFA), a nationwide peer education program for Greek letter organizations, ANGLE (Advocates for National Greek Leadership and Education), was launched with a two-year commitment from the U.S. Department of Education—Fund for the Improvement of Post-Secondary Education.

Traditions and Ideals Phi Sigma Sigma celebrates its founding each year on November 26. This occasion causes the fraternity to rededicate itself to its sisterhood and ideals. At the Silver Jubilee, held in 1938, the founders and Alpha Chapter sisters were honored with an award established in their name: a cash prize given each year to a Hunter College student selected by the college administration.

The original fraternity badge was a Sphinxhead with sapphire eyes on a gold base, bearing the Greek letters ΦΣΣ in blue enamel. Later the fraternity developed a jeweled badge, a gold pyramid which bears three sapphires in each corner and on which the original Sphinxhead is imposed. The pledge pin is a blue pyramid with a border of gold, on which is written Phi Sigma Sigma's open motto, *Diokete Hupsala*, which translates as "Aim High." The colors of the fraternity are king blue and gold, and the flower is the American Beauty Rose. The coat of arms is a Sphinxhead surmounting a ribbon bearing the Greek letters ΦΣΣ, set on a shield of seven bendlets of blue and white, the whole being superimposed on a pyramid with a rose at its apex and twin scrolls bearing the legend *Diokete Hupsala* and the year 1913 en plaque at the base below.

Publications *The Sphinx* of Phi Sigma Sigma was first published in 1922. In addition to *The Sphinx*, the fraternity publishes numerous other education pamphlets and manuals for its own use, including *The Rose*, a biannual alumnae newsletter.

Funds and Philanthropies The Phi Sigma Sigma Foundation has supported many philanthropic activities, including the establishment of the Phi Sigma Sigma cardiology laboratory at the Albert Einstein School of Medicine in New York; support for the medical centers at UCLA and Johns Hopkins; and educational grants for sisters pursuing their graduate and undergraduate educations.

The Foundation has adopted the National Kidney Foundation (NKF) as its national philanthropy project. In conjunction with NKF, Foundation has supported the publication and distribution of an NKF pamphlet on high blood pressure, the leading cause of kidney disease. It has underwritten the production of "From Treatment to Cure," an audiovisual presentation being shown across the country describing the activities of NKF.

In commemoration of the 75th anniversary of Phi Sigma Sigma, Foundation awarded a Phi Sigma Sigma/NKF Fellowship that provides support for pediatric nephrology research at Washington University Medical Center in St. Louis. An additional anniversary gift has underwritten the cost of an education pamphlet for family members of patients with kidney disease. Several of our undergraduate chapters actively support the NKF organ donor program.

Foundation's 1990 gift to NKF made it possible for six children with kidney disease to attend summer camps in Texas, Arkansas, Pennsylvania, Colorado, Virginia, and Maine. These children undergo dialysis on a regular basis, so leaving home for a week at camp is usually not possible. Kidney Kamps are specially equipped and staffed so that summer camping activities are available to children who would otherwise be homebound. In 1991, the foundation is supporting a unique camping program—a family camp in Michigan. This weekend experience provides an opportunity for kidney patients of all ages and their families to share the fun and adventure of a family camping vacation.

In 1988, the Phi Sigma Sigma "Rock-a-thon" was adopted by undergraduate chapters as a coordinated national philanthropy effort to raise funds for the Foundation. This 24–hour rocking chair marathon collects money based on pledges from friends and relatives as well as donations from campus passersby. This annual fundraiser is not only fun for the participants, but it is also financially successful and spotlights the philanthropic efforts of Phi Sigma Sigma. Rock-a-thons have become me-

dia events for chapters across the country, with feature stories in the press and coverage by local TV and radio stations

Headquarters 23123 State Road #7, Suite 250, Boca Raton, FL 33428

Membership Active chapters 80. Inactive chapters 45. Colonies 13. Graduate/Alumni chapters 26. Total number of initiates 33,357. Chapter roll:

1913 *Alpha, Hunter (1976)*
1918 *Gamma, N.Y.U. (1963)*
1920 Delta, SUNY, Buffalo (-1984)
1920 *Epsilon, Adelphi*
1921 *Zeta, UCLA*
1922 *Eta, Michigan*
1923 Theta, Illinois
1924 *Iota, Pitt*
1924 Kappa, George Washington (1971-1986)
1926 *Lambda, Cincinnati (1971)*
1926 *Mu, Cal, Berkeley (1966)*
1926 Nu, Penn
1926 Xi, Temple
1927 *Omicron, L.S.U. (1933)*
1927 Pi, Syracuse
1928 *Rho, Ohio State (1958)*
1929 *Sigma, Long Island*
1929 *Tau, Texas (1933)*
1930 *Phi, Wisconsin, Madison (1969)*
1930 *Upsilon, Manitoba (1955)*
1932 *Chi, Utah (1943)*
1934 *Psi, Tulane (1946)*
1935 *Omega, Missouri (1955)*
1936 Beta Alpha, Maryland
1940 *Beta Beta, Washington (WA)*
1941 Beta Delta, Ohio (1951-1991)
1941 *Beta Gamma, Boston U (1966)*
1943 *Beta Epsilon, Connecticut*
1945 *Beta Zeta, USC (1953)*
1946 *Beta Eta, Penn State (1970)*
1947 *Beta Iota, Southern Methodist (1953)*
1947 *Beta Kappa, Florida Southern (1953)*
1947 *Beta Theta, Miami (FL) (-1985)*
1950 *Beta Lambda, Wayne State (MI) (1970)*
1952 *Beta Mu, Kentucky (1957)*
1954 *Beta Nu, CUNY, Brooklyn (1969)*
1954 *Beta Xi, Cornell (1969)*
1956 *Beta Pi, Queens (NY) (1967)*
1961 Beta Rho, Drexel
1962 Beta Upsilon, American (-1983)
1965 *Beta Phi, Georgia State*
1965 *Beta Tau, Cal State, Northridge*
1966 *Beta Chi, Wisconsin, Milwaukee*
1967 Beta Psi, Florida
1968 *Alpha Alpha, Lehman*
1969 Beta Omega, Portland State
1970 Gamma Beta, Suffolk
1971 Gamma Delta, Rutgers, Camden
1971 Gamma Gamma, Clarion
1972 *Gamma Epsilon, Waynesburg*
1973 *Gamma Zeta, Rhode Island*
1976 *Gamma Eta, Tennessee, Chattanooga*

1976 Gamma Theta, R.P.I.
1977 Gamma Iota, Worcester Tech
1977 Gamma Kappa, Towson
1977 *Gamma Lambda, Wisconsin, Superior*
1977 Gamma Mu, Clarkson (-1983)
1978 Gamma Nu, Rutgers
1978 Gamma Xi, Widener
1979 *Gamma Omicron, Fort Hays* (1983)
1979 Gamma Pi, Maryland, Baltimore County
1979 *Gamma Rho, Rochester Tech*
1979 Gamma Sigma, Virginia Commonwealth
1979 Gamma Tau, Northern Kentucky
1979 *Gamma Upsilon, New England* (1983)
1980 Gamma Phi, Fairleigh Dickinson,
      Rutherford
1981 *Delta Alpha, Eastern Michigan* (1983)
1981 Delta Beta, Rochester
1981 Delta Delta, Linfield
1981 Delta Epsilon, Windsor
1981 Delta Gamma, San Francisco State
1981 Gamma Omega, East Stroudsburg
1981 Gamma Psi, Western Maryland
1982 Delta Eta, Delaware
1982 Delta Zeta, Stevens Tech
1983 Delta Theta, Oakland
1984 Delta Iota, Central Michigan
1984 Delta Kappa, Florida International
1984 Delta Lambda, Muhlenberg
1985 Delta Mu, William Paterson
1985 Delta Nu, Iona
1985 Delta Omicron, Eastern Illinois
1985 Delta Xi, SUNY, Binghamton
1986 *Delta Pi, Dayton*
1986 *Delta Rho, Rio Grande*
1987 Delta Chi, Shippensburg
1987 Delta Omega, Pace
1987 Delta Phi, Monmouth (NJ)
1987 Delta Psi, West Florida
1987 Delta Sigma, SUNY Col., Brockport
1987 Delta Tau, SUNY, Albany
1987 Delta Upsilon, Siena Heights
1988 Epsilon Alpha, Illinois State
1988 Epsilon Beta, Ferris
1988 Epsilon Delta, Chapman
1988 Epsilon Epsilon, Bakersfield
1988 Epsilon Eta, SUNY, Stony Brook
1988 Epsilon Gamma, Millersville
1988 Epsilon Theta, Montclair
1988 Epsilon Zeta, Bloomsburg
1989 Epsilon Iota, Bridgewater
1989 Epsilon Kappa, Hofstra
1989 Epsilon Lambda, Frostburg
1989 Epsilon Mu, Hamilton
1989 Epsilon Nu, SUNY Col., Oswego
1989 Epsilon Pi, Southern Connecticut
1989 Epsilon Rho, York (PA)
1989 Epsilon Xi, SUNY Col., Oneonta
1990 Epsilon Chi, Indiana Southeast
1990 Epsilon Omega, Utica
1990 Epsilon Omicron, St. John's (NY)
1990 Epsilon Phi, Radford
1990 Epsilon Psi, Western Illinois

1990 Epsilon Sigma, Virginia Wesleyan
1990 Epsilon Tau, California (PA)
1990 Epsilon Upsilon, SUNY Col., Buffalo
1990 Zeta Alpha, Woodbury

Colonies: Averett, Canisius, Fitchburg State
College, Florida Atlantic, Johnson & Wales,
Indiana (PA), Univ. of Pittsburgh at Johnstown,
Rutgers, Newark, St. Leo College, Slipper Rock of
Pennsylvania, Trenton, Tufts, Western Connecticut

Pi Beta Phi

ACTIVE PIN

PLEDGE PIN

PI BETA PHI, the first national college fraternity for women, was founded at Monmouth College on April 28, 1867, as the I.C. Sorosis. It was conceived by 12 young women who wished to establish an organization for college women modeled after a man's Greek-letter fraternity, with the aim of providing strength and inspiration in closer bonds of friendship, assistance to colleges where its chapters might exist, and development of philanthropic service. The Greek letters ΠΒΦ were used as a secret motto from the beginning; however the Greek name was not adopted officially until 1888. The founders were Libbie Brook, Clara Brownlee, Emma Brownlee, Ada Bruen, Nancy Black, Jennie Horne, Inez Smith, Margaret Campbell, Fannie Whitenack, Rosa Moore, Jennie Nicol, and Fannie Thompson.

Growth   In 1868, one year after the founding a second chapter was established at Iowa Wesleyan College. By 1889 when Pi Beta Phi was incorporated under the laws of Illinois, 27 chapters had been established. Nineteen years later, Pi Beta Phi became international with the admission of Ontario Alpha. The first alumnae group was formed in Des Moines, Iowa, in 1882 and a national alumnae department was organized in 1892. As the oldest of the charter members of National Panhellenic Conference in 1902, Pi Beta Phi was placed first in the order of rotation to the chairmanship.

Government   Since 1884, authority in legislative matters has been vested in the convention which is biennial. National officers are elected at convention and in the interim a seven-member Grand Council administers affairs. Nine national directors serve as programming and operational specialists.

Pi Beta Phi is divided geographically into 20 collegiate and 26 alumnae provinces with province officers elected to direct and supervise activities and programs. Traveling and resident graduate consultants are chosen by the Grand Council to serve the fraternity for one year following graduation. Standing committees are appointed by the grand president.

Traditions and Insignia April 28 is designated as Founders' Day and is appropriately celebrated by all chapters and alumnae clubs. January 9, the birthday of Carrie Chapman Catt, is Chapter Loyalty Day in special recognition of the example set by Mrs. Catt in her unusual loyalty to her chapter, Iowa Gamma.

In 1939, the fraternity purchased Holt House, the house in Monmouth in which the founding took place. It has been completely restored as an early Victorian home, and is maintained with a resident hostess, as a memorial to the founders. It is used for community activities by Monmouth, Illinois, residents, and for fraternity functions by neighboring chapters and alumnae clubs.

The Balfour Cup, the Stoolman Vase, the Philadelphia Bowl, and the Directors' Award are given annually in recognition of excellence to the collegiate chapters which best meet their responsibilities to their colleges, their national organization, and themselves. Chapter achievements in scholarship, pledge education, community service, Panhellenic participation, standards, and efficiency are recognized annually, as are outstanding alumnae club achievements.

Amy Burnham Onken awards are given annually to the senior in each province who stands highest in scholarship, personality, fraternity service and character; with the national awards being given to the woman who ranks highest among province winners. A similar pattern is followed for a chapter service award and an alumnae club service award.

The badge of the fraternity is a golden arrow bearing the letters ΠΒΦ transversely on the feather, with a loop chain pendant from the shaft. The pledge pin is an arrow head of burnished gold with the Greek letter B in polished gold. The colors are wine and silver blue, the flower is the wine carnation.

Publications The fraternity's national magazine, *The Arrow*, published quarterly, originated as a publication in May, 1885, in Lawrence, Kansas, under the editorship of Kansas Alpha. Since 1908, the grand president has appointed an alumnae member of the fraternity as editor.

The first membership directory was published in 1887, the most recent in 1984. Complete histories in volume form were reprinted in 1915 and 1936. The Centennial History was released in 1967, with a supplement in 1977. A national pledge manual is printed for each pledge. Other publications include the *Idea Bank* for chapters and *The Chain* for alumnae clubs as well as manuals for chapters, chapter officers, chapter advisors, alumnae clubs and officers, standing committees, national officers, and other specific areas. An alcohol awareness pro-

gram, Friend To Friend, was published in 1984, and will be updated regularly for collegiate and alumnae use.

Funds and Philanthropies The fraternity has several endowment funds which support scholarship and loan programs for both graduate and undergraduate members. The Emma Harper Turner Fund provides loans from its principal for chapter housing and confidential assistance to needy Pi Phis from its interest. Endowment funds are maintained for the magazine, chapter house loans, and the Settlement School. Endowment funds are controlled by the Board of Trustee Funds. Donations are given to the Canadian Northern Libraries Project in the Yukon and Northwest Territories.

Pi Beta Phi's major philanthropy, established in 1912 in Gatlinburg, Tennessee, is owned and operated by the fraternity. In the early years the Settlement School provided education and health services for this remote Appalachian community. When the involvement with basic education was phased out, the fraternity built the Arrowmont School of Arts and Crafts to commemorate the centennial of Pi Beta Phi's founding. Through an agreement with the University of Tennessee, courses are offered for graduate or undergraduate credit, as well as for personal enrichment. Dormitory space and meal plans are offered to students. Scholarships for study at Arrowmont are made available through the fraternity to members and non-members.

A second phase of Pi Beta Phi's endeavor with the people of Gatlinburg has been to provide an outlet for the work of native craftsmen and weavers of the Smoky Mountains through local sales in the Arrowcraft Shop in Gatlinburg and nationwide sales by alumnae clubs and collegiate chapters. The preservation of traditional crafts and the development of contemporary work are attributable to marketing and educational programs carried out by the Arrowcraft Shop and the Arrowmont School. Any profits from sales are used to help support the school.

Headquarters 7730 Carondelet #333, St. Louis, MO 63105

Membership Active chapters 128. Inactive chapters 36. Chapter roll:

1867 Illinois Alpha, Monmouth (IL) (1884-1927)
1868 Iowa Alpha, Iowa Wesleyan
1870 *Indiana Alpha, DePauw (1879)*
1870 *Zeta, Baptist Young Ladies Seminary (1871)*
1872 *Illinois Beta, Lombard (1872) (See Illinois Delta)*
1873 Kansas Alpha, Kansas
1874 Iowa Beta, Simpson
1877 Iowa Gamma, Iowa State (1891-1906)
1881 *Dearborn Seminary (1883)*
1881 *Iowa Epsilon, South Iowa Normal (1887)*
1881 *Phi, Jacksonville Female Academy (1884)*
1881 *Xi, Iowa East Normal (1892)*
1882 *Illinois Gamma, Carthage (1888)*

1882   Iowa Zeta, Iowa
1884   Colorado Alpha, Colorado
1884   Illinois Delta, Knox
1884   *Nebraska Alpha, York (PA) (1888)*
1885   *Wesleyan (CT) (1886)*
1885   *Colorado Beta, Denver (1980)*
1886   *Iowa Lambda, Callanan (1889)*
1887   Michigan Alpha, Hillsdale
1887   *Nebraska Beta, Hastings (1887)*
1888   Indiana Alpha, Franklin
1888   Michigan Beta, Michigan
1889   *D.C. Alpha, George Washington (1968)*
1889   Ohio Alpha, Ohio
1890   Minnesota Alpha, Minnesota (1897-1905)
1891   Louisiana Alpha, Tulane
1892   *Pennsylvania Alpha, Swarthmore (1934)*
1893   California Alpha, Stanford (1897-1905)
       (1944-1978)
1893   Indiana Beta, Indiana
1893   *Vermont Alpha, Middlebury (1969)*
1894   Illinois Epsilon, Northwestern
1894   Ohio Beta, Ohio State
1894   Wisconsin Alpha, Wisconsin, Madison
       (1970-1986)
1895   Illinois Zeta, Illinois
1895   Nebraska Beta, Nebraska
1895   Pennsylvania Beta, Bucknell
1896   *Massachusetts Alpha, Boston U (1985)*
1896   New York Alpha, Syracuse (1984-1988)
1897   Indiana Gamma, Butler
1897   *Maryland Alpha, Goucher (1950)*
1898   Vermont Beta, Vermont
1899   Missouri Alpha, Missouri
1900   California Beta, Cal, Berkeley
1902   Texas Alpha, Texas
1903   Pennsylvania Gamma, Dickinson
1904   *New York Beta, Barnard (1915)*
1907   Missouri Beta, Washington (MO)
1907   Washington Alpha, Washington (WA)
1908   Ontario Alpha, Toronto
1909   Arkansas Alpha, Arkansas
1910   *Ohio Gamma, Wooster (1913)*
1910   Oklahoma Alpha, Oklahoma
1910   Wyoming Alpha, Wyoming
1912   Illinois Eta, Millikin
1912   Washington Beta, Washington State
1913   Florida Alpha, Stetson
1913   *Virginia Alpha, Randolph, Macon Woman's*
       (1960)
1914   Missouri Gamma, Drury
1914   New York Gamma, St. Lawrence
1915   Kansas Beta, Kansas State
1915   Nevada Alpha, Nevada
1915   Oregon Alpha, Oregon
1916   Texas Beta, Southern Methodist
1917   Arizona Alpha, Arizona
1917   California Gamma, USC
1917   Oregon Beta, Oregon State
1917   *Virginia Beta, Hollins (1930)*
1918   *Pennsylvania Delta, Pitt (1931)*
1918   West Virginia Alpha, West Virginia
1919   New York Delta, Cornell

1919   Oklahoma Beta, Oklahoma State
1919   *Wisconsin Beta, Beloit (1971)*
1920   Maine Alpha, Maine
1921   Florida Beta, Florida State
1921   Indiana Delta, Purdue
1921   Montana Alpha, Montana State
1921   North Dakota Alpha, North Dakota
1923   Idaho Alpha, Idaho
1923   North Carolina Alpha, North Carolina
1923   *Tennessee Alpha, Tennessee, Chattanooga*
       (1989)
1925   Kentucky Alpha, Louisville
1925   Ohio Delta, Ohio Wesleyan
1925   Virginia Gamma, William and Mary
1927   *Alabama Alpha, Birmingham-Southern*
       (1989)
1927   California Delta, UCLA
1927   South Dakota Alpha, South Dakota
1929   *Florida Gamma, Rollins (1970)*
1929   *Manitoba Alpha, Manitoba (1976)*
1929   Utah Alpha, Utah
1930   Illinois Beta-Delta, Knox
1931   Alberta Alpha, Alberta
1931   *South Carolina Alpha, South Carolina*
       (1985)
1933   North Carolina Beta, Duke
1934   *Nova Scotia Alpha, Dalhousie (1976)*
1934   Ontario Beta, Western Ontario
1936   Louisiana Beta, L.S.U.
1939   Georgia Alpha, Georgia
1940   Tennessee Beta, Vanderbilt
1940   *Wisconsin Gamma, Lawrence (1983)*
1942   Indiana Epsilon, DePauw
1943   Connecticut Alpha, Connecticut
1944   Maryland Beta, Maryland
1944   *Massachusetts Beta, Massachusetts (1973)*
1944   Oregon Gamma, Willamette
1945   Michigan Gamma, Michigan State
1945   Ohio Epsilon, Toledo
1945   Ohio Zeta, Miami (OH)
1946   New Mexico Alpha, New Mexico
1947   Illinois Theta, Bradley
1948   Tennessee Gamma, Tennessee
1948   Washington Gamma, Puget Sound
1949   Alabama Beta, Alabama
1949   California Epsilon, San Diego U.
1950   California Zeta, Cal, Santa Barbara
1950   *West Virginia Beta, Davis and Elkins*
       (1955)
1952   Indiana Zeta, Ball State
1953   Pennsylvania Epsilon, Penn State
1953   Texas Gamma, Texas Tech
1954   Colorado Gamma, Colorado State
1954   Ohio Eta, Denison
1956   Texas Delta, Texas Christian
1957   Alabama Gamma, Auburn
1959   *Michigan Delta, Albion (1985)*
1960   *Oregon Delta, Portland State (1980)*
1961   Mississippi Alpha, Southern Mississippi
1962   Kentucky Beta, Kentucky
1962   Mississippi Beta, Mississippi
1962   Tennessee Delta, Memphis State

1963   Arkansas Beta, Arkansas, Little Rock
1965   Arizona Beta, Arizona State
1965   Virginia Delta, Old Dominion
1968   *West Virginia Gamma, Bethany (WV)*
        (1981)
1969   Florida Delta, Florida (1977-1985)
1972   New Mexico Beta, New Mexico State
1974   California Eta, Cal, Irvine
1974   Illinois Iota, Illinois State
1974   Indiana Eta, IUPU, Fort Wayne
1975   Virginia Epsilon, Virginia
1976   Kentucky Gamma, Eastern Kentucky
1976   South Carolina Beta, Clemson
1976   Texas Epsilon, North Texas
1977   Texas Zeta, Baylor
1979   Pennsylvania Zeta, Washington and
        Jefferson
1980   California Theta, Davis and Elkins
1980   Pennsylvania Eta, Lafayette
1981   Florida Epsilon, Central Florida
1981   Virginia Zeta, V.P.I.
1983   Iowa Eta, Drake
1984   New York Epsilon, R.P.I.
1985   Texas Eta, Texas A & M
1986   California Iota, Cal State, Chico
1986   Colorado Delta, Colorado Mines
1986   New York Zeta, Colgate
1986   Ohio Theta, Bowling Green
1987   California Kappa, Cal, San Diego
1987   Virginia Eta, Richmond
1988   California Lambda, Cal, Riverside
1989   Connecticut Beta, Yale
1989   Ohio Iota, Dayton
1990   Arizona Gamma, Northern Arizona
1990   New Jersey Alpha, Princeton
1990   Pennsylvania Theta, Villanova

COAT OF ARMS

Sigma Delta Tau

ACTIVE PIN

PLEDGE PIN

SIGMA DELTA TAU was founded at Cornell University, March 25, 1917, by Inez Dane Ross, Amy Apfel Tishman, Regene Freund Cohane, Marian Gerber Greenberg, Dora Bloom Turteltaub, Lenore Blanche Rubinow, and Grace Srenco Grossman. In organizing the sorority and in formulating its ideals and ambitions, the founders were aided by Nathan Caleb House, ritualist.

Government of the fraternity is by biennial convention with each collegiate chapter sending two delegates, each having one vote, and each alumnae league sending one delegate who has one vote. In the interim, government is vested in the National Council which is composed of the national officers, the national advisers, and committee chairmen.

Each undergraduate chapter has an alumnae board, and an alumna adviser responsible to the national president.

The first convention was held in New York in 1920 and has been held biennially since.

Traditions and Insignia *Multae Patriae Spes Una* is the motto, and it is symbolized by the spade, the sword, and the Star of David. The motto is not secret, nor are the Bylaws. The initiation ritual, however, is considered a private affair.

The pledge pin is a gold torch on a round enamel pin of old blue and gold. The official badge is a jeweled torch. Five pearls adorn the cross bar of the torch and one the handle. Above the five pearls are the Greek letters ΣΔΤ. A diamond brightens the flame of the torch. The sorority flower is the tea rose; the jewel, the lapis lazuli; and the colors, cafe au lait and old blue.

Publications The magazine is *The Torch*, which is semiannual.

Funds and Philanthropies The national philanthropy is the prevention of child abuse. Alumnae interests and projects are directed by a national chairman, who is assisted by a chairman in those cities where alumnae leagues (chapters) exist. National philanthropic work is directed by a national chairman. Annual donations are made to the Sigma Delta Tau Foundation. The foundation is a source of scholarship grants and of contributions to Brandeis University for the Leah Affron Kartman Scholarship Fund in the field of Human Relations. There is a scholarship loan committee which makes loans to students who are in need. There is a scholarship requirement for initiation and there is an award for outstanding scholarship among the chapters.

Headquarters 401 Pennsylvania Parkway, Suite 110, Indianapolis, IN 46280. Phone: (317) 846-7747.

Membership Active chapters 48. Inactive chapters 32. Colonies 2. Chapter roll:

1917   Alpha, Cornell
1920   Beta, Penn
1921   Delta, SUNY, Buffalo (1976-1983)
1921   Gamma, Ohio State
1923   Epsilon, Cincinnati
1924   Eta, Georgia
1924   *Zeta, L.S.U. (1969)*
1925   *Theta, Nebraska (1970)*
1926   *Iota, McGill (1971)*
1926   Kappa, Illinois
1927   *Lambda, UCLA (1987)*
1927   *Mu, USC (1935)*
1929   Nu, Minnesota
1929   *Xi, Oklahoma (1975)*
1933   *Pi, Iowa (1971-1982) (1988)*
1934   *Omicron, West Virginia (1969)*

1935 Rho, Alabama
1938 *Sigma, Northwestern* (1983)
1939 Tau, Texas
1940 Upsilon, Indiana
1943 Phi, Penn State (1971-1978)
1944 Chi, Michigan
1945 Psi, Massachusetts
1946 Alpha Beta, Rhode Island
1946 Omega, Syracuse (1977-1984)
1947 *Alpha Delta, Colorado* (1971)
1948 *Alpha Epsilon, Purdue* (1953)
1950 Alpha Zeta, Pitt
1951 *Alpha Eta, Washington (MO)* (1973)
1952 Alpha Theta, Maryland
1955 Alpha Iota, Newcomb
1957 *Alpha Kappa, South Carolina* (1962)
1957 *Alpha Lambda, Missouri* (1968)
1957 Alpha Mu, Miami (FL)
1958 Alpha Nu, Wisconsin, Madison (1971-1982)
1959 Alpha Omicron, CUNY, Brooklyn
1959 Alpha Pi, Arizona (1974-1988)
1959 Alpha Xi, Boston U. (1962-1986)
1960 *Alpha Rho, N.Y.U.* (1970)
1960 *Alpha Sigma, Hunter* (1973)
1961 Alpha Tau, George Washington (1971-1985)
1962 *Alpha Phi, Memphis State* (1976)
1962 Alpha Upsilon, Bradley
1963 *Alpha Chi, Miami (OH)* (1987)
1963 *Alpha Psi, Akron* (1970)
1964 *Alpha Omega, Toledo* (1976)
1964 Beta Beta, Michigan State (1972-1984)
1965 *Beta Alpha, Denver* (1984)
1965 *Beta Gamma, Houston* (1971)
1966 *Beta Epsilon, Colorado State* (1968)
1967 *Beta Delta, Parsons* (1969)
1967 *Beta Eta, Northern Illinois* (1975)
1967 *Beta Iota, Missouri, Kansas City* (1971)
1967 *Beta Theta, C. W. Post* (1972)
1967 Beta Zeta, Queens (NY) (1971-1986)
1968 *Beta Sigma, Lehman* (1973)
1969 *Beta Kappa, Wayne State (MI)* (1971)
1969 *Beta Lambda, West Chester* (1970)
1975 *Beta Nu, Florida* (1983)
1977 Beta Xi, Union (NY)
1978 Beta Pi, Rochester
1981 *Beta Rho, Virginia* (1988)
1981 Beta Tau, Rutgers
1983 Beta Upsilon, Stanford
1984 Beta Phi, SUNY, Stony Brook
1985 Beta Chi, Kansas
1985 Gamma Alpha, SUNY, Binghamton
1985 Gamma Beta, SUNY, Albany
1986 Gamma Gamma, Hofstra
1987 Gamma Delta, American
1988 Gamma Epsilon, SUNY Col., Oneonta
1988 Gamma Eta, South Florida
1988 Gamma Theta, SUNY Col., Cortland
1988 Gamma Zeta, SUNY Col., Buffalo
1989 Gamma Iota, Hartford
1989 Gamma Kappa, SUNY Col., Oswego
1989 Gamma Lambda, Florida State
1989 Gamma Nu, SUNY Col., New Paltz

1990 Gamma Mu, Northeastern
1990 Gamma Xi, Montclair

Colonies: York (PA), Tampa

COAT OF ARMS

Sigma Kappa

ACTIVE PIN

PLEDGE PIN

SIGMA KAPPA was founded at Colby College, Waterville, Maine, November 9, 1874. The founders were Mary Low Carver, who enrolled in 1871 and was the only woman student until 1874, and Louise Helen Coburn, Elizabeth Gorham Hoag, Ida Mabel Fuller, and Frances Elliott Mann, who in that year were the next four women students to enroll. The purposes of the organization are to promote service, cultural development, spiritual standards, scholarship, and intellectual life among its members. Sigma Kappa was the first New England sorority.

Growth Until the fall of 1890, the number of girls in college was small, never more than 20 at one time, so that the plan of admitting all to Sigma Kappa presented no difficulties. In 1894, however, 15 women entered and all could not be admitted to Alpha chapter because of the membership limit of 25 set in 1879. It was decided to establish another chapter of the sorority on the campus, and the following year the girls were divided between Alpha and Beta, meetings always being held jointly. In 1892, a third chapter, Gamma, also on the Colby campus, was instituted to meet the needs of the class of 1896. A decision was reached to initiate no more girls into Beta and Gamma and to look beyond Colby for additional members. In 1904, a chapter was established at Boston, and, in 1905, another at Syracuse. Thus the sorority grew steadily and soundly.

Sigma Kappa and Pi Kappa Sigma, an NPC group founded in 1894 at Michigan State Normal College as a pioneer in the pedagogical field as a social educational sorority, merged in 1959.

Government The governing power of the sorority is vested in the Grand chapter and the National Council, a body of seven—six of whom are elected at national convention and one, the National Panhellenic Conference delegate, appointed. This council has the responsibility of managing the organization's business between conventions and of carrying out convention action. The council consists of the national president, the national vice-president for alumnae, the national vice-president for collegiate chapters, the national vice-president for expansion, national secretary, national treasurer, and the National Panhellenic Conference delegate. Other national officers include district directors, NPC alternate delegates, traveling consultants, graduate consultants, editor of the *Triangle*, province officers, director of chapter programs and resources, national historian, director of chapter corporation and finance, and permanent convention chairman. Standing committees include past national presidents, endowment, college loan fund, archives, awards, housing, loyalty fund, philanthropy, public relations, state/regional conferences, parents' club, magazine agency, and bylaws chairmen.

National conventions are held biennially. In the alternating years, a college chapter officers' training school, called COTS, is held. These began in 1957. In 1924, the convention authorized a central office, which is supervised by the executive director.

Traditions and Insignia Awards at convention and college chapters' training school include the recognition of high scholarship, the Budd Award for college chapter excellence in its gerontology program, the most cooperative chapter award for general excellence in all areas, the teamwork trophy for outstanding college-alumnae relations, the Triangle award for the best college chapter reporting to the *Triangle*, the Edna B. Dreyfus award for contributions to philanthropies, the National Council trophies for most improved chapters, the Panhellenic awards for college and alumnae chapters, and the national sisterhood awards for chapters who helped another chapter. Other awards include those for outstanding leadership, membership selection, pledge programs and initiation of all pledges.

A National Council member, at the close of her first year's service, is given an alternate diamond and pearl badge in recognition of her position and her service to Sigma Kappa.

The colors of the sorority are maroon and lavender, its flower is the violet. The Sigma Kappa jewel is the pearl. The open motto is *One Heart, One Way*. The Sigma Kappa badge is an equilateral gold triangle supporting a raised triangle of maroon enamel bearing the Greek letters ΣK in gold. The pledge pin is gold, the letter K with a serpent entwined through it in the form of an S.

Publications The *Sigma Kappa Triangle*, a quarterly magazine, has been published continuously since 1907. An annual bulletin reports official business for chapters and members. Since 1918 manuals have been issued for the guidance of chapters and officers. *The History* was first published in 1924, and at the 100th anniversary convention a *Centennial History* was published. *An Anthology of Verse* by Sigma Kappas was published in 1936, commemorating the 60th anniversary. Other publications include an *Advisory Board Handbook*, *Constitution and Bylaws*, *National Policies*, *Songs of Sigma Kappa*, *The Brave Maroon II*, *Pledge Manual*, and *Speaking of Sigma Kappa*.

Funds and Philanthropies The Sigma Kappa College Loan Fund was established in 1922 to aid members in completing their college work; it is supported by voluntary contributions. In 1924, the General Endowment Fund was set up to provide housing funds. In 1962, a foundation was set up to raise funds from which to grant annual scholarships to qualified applicants studying in some phase of the gerontology or geriatrics field.

The sorority's oldest philanthropy is the Maine Sea Coast Missionary Society, adopted in 1918 to commemorate the founding at Colby College in Waterville, Maine. Alumnae and college chapters, as well as individual members, have provided many thousands of dollars for the use of the mission, in addition to hundreds of Christmas gifts annually, and special gifts such as wheel chairs, vitamin pills, and volunteer summer workers. The society serves the residents of the 2,500 islands scattered along the coast of Maine, bringing educational opportunities, religious services, and medical and dental care to Island folk who otherwise would not have them.

The 1946 convention established an overseas philanthropy, connected with education, known as the American Farm School, Thessaloniki, Greece, which is an educational program for girls from Greek rural communities. Several scholarships have been awarded annually to assist Greek girls in acquiring basic skills and badly needed educational advantages.

In 1954, the sorority took on the philanthropy of gerontology and geriatrics. This highly important field, gaining recognition each year, is one in which Sigma Kappa has pioneered. Recognition of the sorority's work has included representation at the White House Conference on Aging. Each college and alumnae chapter has a local gerontology or geriatrics project of their choice and many outstanding ones have received local and regional recognition. At Sigma Kappa's 1984 convention, Alzheimer's Disease and Related Disorders was adopted as part of their Gerontology philanthropy.

Headquarters 8733 Founders Road, Indianapolis, IN 46268. Phone: (317) 872-3275.

Membership Total living membership 74,873. Total undergraduate membership 6,182. Active chapters 115. Inactive chapters 62. Colonies 7. Houses owned 37. Graduate/Alumni chapters 174. City/Area alumni associations 61. Total number of initiates 92,661. Chapter roll:

1874 *Alpha, Colby* (1984)
1905 Epsilon, Syracuse (1973-1990)
1906 Eta, Illinois Wesleyan
1906 Theta, Illinois (1941-1946) (1968-1975)
1906 Zeta, George Washington (1967-1988)
1908 Iota, Denver (1967-1989)
1908 *Kappa, Brown* (1911)
1910 Lambda, Cal, Berkeley
1910 Mu, Washington (WA)

1911	*Nu, Middlebury* (1969)
1913	*Omicron, Tufts* (1956-1977) (1980)
1913	Xi, Kansas
1915	*Pi, Stanford* (1931)
1917	*Rho, Randolph, Macon Woman's* (1941)
1917	*Sigma, Southern Methodist* (1963)
1918	Tau, Indiana
1918	Upsilon, Oregon State
1919	*Chi, Ohio State* (1940)
1919	Phi, Rhode Island
1919	*Psi, Wisconsin, Madison* (1959)
1920	*Alpha Beta, SUNY, Buffalo* (1964)
1920	Omega, Florida State
1921	Alpha Delta, Tennessee
1921	Alpha Epsilon, Iowa State
1921	*Alpha Eta, Minnesota* (1961)
1921	Alpha Gamma, Washington State
1921	*Alpha Zeta, Cornell* (1956)
1922	Alpha Iota, Miami (OH)
1922	Alpha Theta, Louisville
1923	*Alpha Kappa, Nebraska* (1973)
1923	*Alpha Lambda, Adelphi* (1977)
1924	Alpha Mu, Michigan (1934-1955) (1971-1984)
1924	*Alpha Nu, Montana* (1982)
1924	Alpha Xi, Iowa (1934-1981)
1925	Alpha Omicron, UCLA (1971-1975)
1925	*Alpha Pi, Ohio Wesleyan* (1941)
1926	*Alpha Rho, Vanderbilt* (1941)
1926	Alpha Sigma, Westminster (PA)
1927	Alpha Tau, Michigan State
1928	*Alpha Upsilon, North Dakota* (1937)
1929	Alpha Chi, Georgetown Col
1931	*Alpha Psi, Duke* (1967)
1932	Alpha Omega, Alabama (1943-1989)
1932	*Beta Beta, South Carolina* (1943)
1933	*Beta Gamma, Manitoba* (1956)
1939	*Beta Delta, Miami (FL)* (1969)
1940	Beta Epsilon, Louisiana Tech
1940	Beta Zeta, Maryland
1944	Beta Eta, Massachusetts
1944	Beta Theta, Marietta
1945	*Beta Iota, Carnegie-Mellon* (1968)
1947	Beta Kappa, Colorado State (1973-1990)
1947	*Beta Lambda, Utah State* (1971)
1947	Beta Mu, Culver-Stockton
1947	Beta Nu, Bradley
1947	*Beta Pi, Illinois Tech* (1960)
1947	Beta Xi, Memphis State
1948	*Beta Rho, San Jose* (1971)
1948	Beta Sigma, Purdue
1949	Beta Tau, Florida
1949	Beta Upsilon, Ohio
1950	Beta Chi, Cal, Santa Barbara (1971-1990)
1950	Beta Omega, Nebraska, Omaha
1950	*Beta Phi, Idaho State* (1965)
1950	Beta Psi, San Diego U. (1979-1981)
1950	Gamma Alpha, Northern Colorado
1950	Gamma Beta, Western Michigan (1974-1988)
1951	Gamma Gamma, Indiana State
1952	Gamma Delta, Thiel
1952	Gamma Epsilon, Indiana (PA)
1954	Gamma Eta, Ball State
1954	Gamma Theta, Cal State, Long Beach (1972-1985)
1954	Gamma Zeta, Northern Illinois
1955	*Gamma Iota, Texas Tech* (1985)
1955	Gamma Kappa, Southern Illinois
1956	Gamma Lambda, East Tennessee
1956	Gamma Mu, Eastern Illinois
1956	Gamma Nu, Gettysburg
1957	Gamma Xi, Lambuth
1958	Gamma Pi, Kentucky Wesleyan
1958	Gamma Rho, Western Carolina
1959	Delta Alpha, Eastern Michigan
1959	*Delta Beta, Marshall* (1983)
1959	Delta Chi, Central State (OK)
1959	Delta Delta, Central Michigan
1959	*Delta Epsilon, Emporia* (1974)
1959	Delta Eta, Central Missouri State
1959	*Delta Gamma, Northwestern Oklahoma* (1975)
1959	Delta Iota, Cal State, Chico
1959	*Delta Kappa, Black Hills* (1969)
1959	*Delta Lambda, Wayne State (MI)* (1974)
1959	Delta Mu, Northwestern Louisiana
1959	Delta Nu, Longwood
1959	Delta Omega, Waynesburg
1959	*Delta Omicron, Fort Hays* (1976)
1959	*Delta Phi, Fairmont* (1974)
1959	Delta Pi, Lock Haven
1959	Delta Psi, Radford (1979-1989)
1959	Delta Rho, Madison Col
1959	Delta Sigma, Western Illinois
1959	Delta Tau, Central Arkansas
1959	Delta Theta, Northeast Missouri
1959	Delta Upsilon, Southwest Missouri
1959	*Delta Xi, Western State (CO)* (1970)
1959	*Delta Zeta, Southeastern Oklahoma* (1987)
1959	*Gamma Sigma, Carroll* (1968)
1959	Gamma Tau, Midwestern
1959	Gamma Upsilon, California (PA)
1960	*Gamma Chi, Stephen F. Austin* (1989)
1960	Gamma Phi, North Carolina State
1961	Gamma Psi, Tennessee Wesleyan
1962	Epsilon Alpha, Lenoir-Rhyne (1984-1990)
1962	Epsilon Beta, New Orleans
1962	*Epsilon Gamma, Southwestern State (OK)* (1990)
1962	Gamma Omega, Wittenberg
1964	Epsilon Delta, Susquehanna
1964	Epsilon Epsilon, Georgia
1965	Epsilon Eta, Findlay
1965	Epsilon Zeta, Western Kentucky
1966	*Epsilon Iota, Athens* (1972)
1966	*Epsilon Kappa, Transylvania* (1985)
1966	*Epsilon Theta, Southwestern Louisiana* (1972
1967	*Epsilon Lambda, Cal State, Sacramento* (1975)
1968	Epsilon Mu, Missouri (1973-1990)
1968	*Epsilon Nu, Maine* (1985)
1969	*Epsilon Omicron, Southwest Texas* (1984)

1969 *Epsilon Pi, Northern Michigan* (1973)
1969 *Epsilon Xi, Adrian* (1984)
1970 *Epsilon Rho, Eastern Washington* (1977)
1970 *Epsilon Sigma, Armstrong State* (1985)
1971 *Epsilon Phi, Southern Indiana* (1983)
1971 Epsilon Tau, Cal State, Fullerton
1972 *Epsilon Chi, V.P.I.* (1988)
1972 *Epsilon Psi, Purdue, Calumet* (1982)
1973 Epsilon Omega, Cal Poly, San Luis Obispo
1973 Zeta Alpha, Indiana Southeast
1974 *Zeta Beta, Arkansas, Monticello* (1979)
1974 *Zeta Delta, Tennessee, Martin* (1988)
1976 Epsilon Upsilon, Missouri Western
1976 Zeta Epsilon, Cal State, Northridge
1976 Zeta Zeta, Babson
1977 *Zeta Eta, Cal State, Stanislaus* (1981)
1977 Zeta Iota, Elmhurst
1977 Zeta Kappa, Angelo
1977 *Zeta Lambda, Dartmouth* (1988)
1977 *Zeta Theta, Tri-State* (1983)
1978 Zeta Mu, Cal, San Diego
1978 Zeta Nu, Texas, San Antonio
1978 Zeta Omicron, Arizona
1978 *Zeta Xi, C. W. Post* (1984)
1980 Zeta Pi, Colorado Mines
1980 *Zeta Rho, Lafayette* (1990)
1980 *Zeta Sigma, Alabama, Birmingham* (1985)
1980 *Zeta Tau, Southern Colorado* (1984)
1981 Zeta Upsilon, Cal Poly, Pomona
1982 Zeta Chi, Florida Institute
1982 Zeta Phi, Rutgers
1983 Zeta Psi, Cleveland
1984 Zeta Omega, L.S.U.
1985 Theta Alpha, Appalachian
1986 Theta Beta, LaVerne
1986 Theta Delta, Delaware
1986 Theta Epsilon, Cal, Riverside
1986 Theta Gamma, Northeast Louisiana
1987 Theta Eta, Nevada, Las Vegas
1987 Theta Iota, SUNY Col., Fredonia
1987 Theta Theta, Albright
1987 Theta Zeta, Virginia
1989 Theta Kappa, USC
1989 Theta Lambda, M.I.T.
1989 Theta Mu, North Carolina, Charlotte
1989 Theta Nu, Baylor
1989 Theta Omicron, Arizona State
1989 Theta Pi, SUNY Col., Geneseo
1989 Theta Xi, Auburn
1990 Theta Rho, Kentucky
1990 Theta Sigma, Hartford

Colonies: Auburn, Baylor, M.I.T., North Carolina, Charlotte, USC, Boston U, Oregon

COAT OF ARMS

Sigma Sigma Sigma

ACTIVE PIN

PLEDGE PIN

SIGMA SIGMA SIGMA was the second of four national women's fraternities founded at Farmville, Virginia. The "Mother of Sororities," now known as Longwood College, is one of the oldest teacher training institutions in the country. Dedicated primarily to perpetuating lasting bonds of friendship while emphasizing the educated "new woman" among college students, Sigma Sigma Sigma operated as a general social sorority. From 1915 to 1947, however, its field of operation was limited to teacher colleges of first rank.

Products of post-Civil War hardships, the founders braved social stigma as they reached out to become contributors of the rebuilding of the nation. Opting for the relatively uncharted academic world, newly available to females, the founders—Margaret Batten, Louise Davis, Martha Featherston, Isabella Merrick, Sallie Michie, Lelia Scott, Elizabeth Watkins, and Lucy Wright—formed the S. S. S. Club in 1897. Kindred spirits dedicated to high standards of behavior, all were excellent students in search of intellectual and social advancement.

Growth   An innovation which separated the liberal arts sorority from the professional (education) sorority led Sigma Sigma Sigma to be a co-founder of the Association of Education Sororities in 1915. A merger of the two fields occurred in 1947 when the broadening curricula of the teachers college made logical one association for all national Greek-letter organizations for women. Thus it was that Tri Sigma became a part of the National Panhellenic Conference. For more than 87 years the sorority has contributed to women's needs in the changing academic world. Continuing to serve campus needs, Sigma Sigma Sigma offers a worthwhile heritage in keeping with the ideals of its founders. Since affiliating with NPC, Tri Sigma continues to charter chapters in accredited institutions contributing to the enrichment of the student body through lifelong national sorority affiliation.

Government   Convention is the supreme governing body. Between conventions, the Executive Council administers the business of the sorority. The council is assisted by chairmen of various standing committees appointed for the triennium.

All interim business is voted upon at the next convention.

Since 1933, Tri Sigma has operated on a triennial plan of national contact: convention, regional meetings, and national visitors. Conventions have been held since 1903 except for the war years (1939-1947). The first central office was established in Woodstock, Virginia, prior to 1925.

National standards are outlined through a long established officers' notebook system. Sorority programs emphasize scholarship as well as leadership and community service.

A Collegiate Advisory Board meets annually at national headquarters. Made up of Tri Sigma presidents of award-winning chapters and the most outstanding Tri Sigma collegian that year, the board advises the national president of the collegians' point of view and discusses matters of collegiate concern.

Alumnae serve college chapters as members of advisory boards or as chapter advisors. They give counsel and practical help where needed, even as they furnish the college itself with responsible alumnae whose sorority affiliation results in closer alma mater relationships.

Traditions and Insignia Leadership and character development are encouraged by the entire national program. Members are given practical experiences through democratic, normal chapter life. Programs about fraternity ideals and development, scholarship, social and cultural topics, and professional career networking are provided periodically for chapters.

Sigma Send-On is a spring social event hosted by the alumnae to welcome collegians to alumnae life. Outstanding chapter members are honored and alumnae relationships are emphasized.

Leadership schools for new national and chapter officers are held regularly to insure representative and trained sorority leaders locally and nationally.

Regional Alumnae/Collegiate Conferences are fall weekend meetings which offer alumnae and collegians the opportunity to participate in a series of workshops and seminars.

The official badge is an indented equilateral triangle upon the raised inner black enamel portion of which appear a skull and crossed bones in the center and a Sigma in each angle; the pledge pin is a silver triangle with a Sigma in each angle superimposed upon three arcs. The official flag has a purple ground crossed from upper left to lower right by a white band upon which appear three Sigmas with a white circle in the upper-half and in the lower a white indented triangle. The flower is the purple violet. The jewel is the pearl. Official colors are royal purple and white. Tri Sigma's open motto is "Faithful unto Death."

Publications The official magazine of the sorority is *The Triangle of Sigma Sigma Sigma*, which celebrated its 80th anniversary of continuous publication in 1985. Formerly a quarterly publication sent to every member of the sorority, it is now pub-

lished three times a year. Other publications include *The Rituals of Sigma Sigma Sigma; Constitution and Bylaws; Songs Sigmas Sing; To Be A Sigma* (pledgebook); *The Angle* (convention daily); *Chapter Officer Notebook; Handbook for National Officers; Welcome to Walton House; This is Sigma Sigma Sigma; Alumnae Chapter Notebook; Sigma Sigma Sigma Rush Manual; Something to Smile About* (social service); rush and alumnae publications; extension brochures and colony notebooks.

The Directory, first published in 1907, was discontinued in 1937 when the "living directory file" was established at Executive Office. *The Years Remembered*, the history of the sorority, was published in 1956, 1963, and 1971. A subsequent volume, *The Path from Farmville*, was published in 1981.

Foundations and Philanthropies The Sigma Sigma Sigma Educational Foundation has scholarships available to the membership for further academic advancement. The Mable Kane Stryker Memorial Scholarship Fund offers loans for graduate study and the Mabel Lee Walton Memorial Scholarship Fund offers scholarship grants to qualified Tri Sigmas who have shown leadership potential, have given service to the sorority and are above average in scholarship.

The Endowment Fund is available for collegiate chapter scholarships and financial assistance and loans for housing.

The social service department of the sorority has been called the Robbie Page Memorial Foundation since 1954. Robbie, the son of a past national president, died of polio in 1951. A fund for polio research was established as Tri Sigma's social service program.

After the Salk vaccine success in eliminating polio, the sorority began a program to support sick and crippled children projects. The "Sigma Serves Children" theme describes this social service work. In 1956 Tri Sigma began to direct its philanthropic efforts toward the field of Play Therapy for hospitalized children. Tri Sigma funds have been used to support projects in the Pediatrics Departments of the North Carolina Memorial Hospital in Chapel Hill and Children's Medical Center in Dallas. Sigma giving has made possible playrooms for hospitalized children, an isolation unit, a hospital school room and teachers, a staff conference room, intensive care unit for infants and children, and special facilities for teenagers' recreation.

In addition, Tri Sigma is providing graduate assistantships in recreation therapy to train play therapists for work with hospitalized children.

Headquarters At 225 North Muhlenberg, Drawer 466, Woodstock, Virginia 22664, stands the Mabel Lee Walton House, named for Tri Sigma's former national president and president emerita. Purchased as the national headquarters in 1963, it is a gracious home which provides facilities for conferences and sorority house-party gatherings. Some remodeling provided suitable space for Executive Office, which is maintained and supervised by the executive secretary.

Membership   Total living membership 50,101. Total undergraduate membership 2,040. Active chapters 70. Inactive chapters 58. Graduate/ Alumni chapters 121. Total number of initiates 62,543. Chapter roll:

1898   Alpha, Longwood
1903   *Beta, Lewisburg Female (1908)*
1904   *Delta, George Peabody (1911)*
1904   *Gamma, Randolph, Macon Woman's (1911)*
1905   *Alpha Delta (Texas), Southwestern (TX) (1911)*
1905   *Epsilon, Hollins (1914)*
1905   *Eta, Searcy Female (1907)*
1906   *Theta, Hood (1907)*
1909   *Sigma Phi, Union (TN) (1924)*
1911   Kappa, Miami (OH) (1935-1950)
1911   *Zeta, SUNY Col, Buffalo (1953)*
1912   *Phi, Ohio (1931)*
1915   *Iota, Northern Colorado (1940-1947) (1984)*
1915   Lambda, Indiana (PA) (1919-1928)
1915   Mu, Northeast Missouri
1915   Nu, Central Missouri State
1915   *Xi, Northwestern Oklahoma (1963)*
1917   Omicron, Eastern Michigan
1917   Pi, Emporia
1920   *Rho, Florida State (1935-1960) (1990)*
1921   *Tau, New Mexico Highlands (1964)*
1922   Chi, Pittsburg State, Kansas (1954-1956)
1922   Psi, Marshall
1922   *Upsilon, East Central State (1956)*
1925   Alpha Alpha, Concord
1925   *Alpha Beta, Kent (1947-1975) (1981)*
1925   Alpha Gamma, Fort Hays
1925   *Sigma, Western State (CO) (1982)*
1926   *Alpha Delta, Drexel (1974)*
1927   Alpha Epsilon, Northwest Missouri
1928   *Alpha Eta, Butler (1933)*
1928   Alpha Zeta, Northwestern Louisiana
1929   Alpha Iota, Northeastern (OK)
1929   Alpha Theta, Radford
1930   Alpha Kappa, Fairmont (1937-1947)
1930   *Alpha Lambda, Harris-Stowe (1975)*
1931   Alpha Mu, Southwestern Louisiana
1931   Alpha Nu, Southern Illinois (1977-1986)
1932   Alpha Xi, Wisconsin, Whitewater
1935   Alpha Omicron, Central Arkansas
1935   Alpha Pi, Clarion
1935   Alpha Rho, Lock Haven
1937   *Alpha Sigma, Southern Mississippi (1985)*
1938   *Alpha Tau, District of Columbia (1954)*
1939   Alpha Upsilon, Madison Col
1942   Alpha Chi, Murray State
1942   Alpha Phi, Central Michigan
1942   Alpha Psi, Eastern Illinois
1944   Beta Alpha, Northern Illinois
1945   Beta Beta, Southwest Missouri
1945   Beta Delta, Shepherd (1948-1960) (1985-1988)

1945   Beta Gamma, Ball State
1946   Beta Epsilon, Western Illinois
1946   *Beta Eta, Henderson (1974)*
1946   *Beta Zeta, SUNY Col., Cortland (1953-1980) (1982)*
1947   *Beta Iota, Minot (1988)*
1949   *Beta Theta, Pitt (1964-1977)*
1950   Beta Kappa, Arizona State
1950   *Beta Lambda, Wisconsin, Milwaukee (1987)*
1950   *Beta Mu, Central State (OK) (1979)*
1951   *Beta Nu, Cal State, Fresno (1956)*
1951   Beta Xi, Southeast Missouri
1952   Beta Pi, Wisconsin, Stout
1952   Beta Rho, Western Michigan
1953   *Beta Omicron, Wayne State (MI) (1959)*
1953   *Beta Sigma, Tampa (1963)*
1953   Beta Tau, Detroit
1954   Beta Upsilon, Penn State (1969-1989)
1955   *Beta Phi, Florida Southern (1975)*
1957   *Beta Chi, Queens (NY) (1971)*
1957   *Beta Psi, Youngstown State (1981)*
1957   *Gamma Alpha, Illinois (1965-1979) (1987)*
1960   Gamma Beta, East Carolina
1960   Gamma Gamma, California (PA)
1961   *Gamma Delta, Adrian (1989)*
1961   *Gamma Epsilon, Creighton (1972-1978) (1984)*
1961   Gamma Zeta, Slippery Rock
1962   *Gamma Eta, Loyola, New Orleans (1981)*
1962   *Gamma Theta, Bradley (1966)*
1963   Gamma Iota, Massachusetts
1963   Gamma Kappa, Marietta
1963   Gamma Lambda, Wisconsin, Eau Claire
1964   Gamma Mu, Southeastern Louisiana (1982-1987)
1965   *Gamma Nu, St. Cloud (1982)*
1965   Gamma Xi, Atlantic Christian
1966   *Gamma Omicron, Northern Iowa (1972)*
1967   Gamma Pi, Nicholls
1967   *Gamma Rho, Edinboro (1976)*
1968   *Gamma Sigma, Wisconsin, Superior (1974)*
1968   *Gamma Tau, West Virginia Tech (1989)*
1969   *Gamma Chi, Tennessee Tech (1977)*
1969   Gamma Phi, Wisconsin, River Falls
1969   Gamma Psi, Morehead
1969   *Gamma Upsilon, Marquette (1985)*
1970   Delta Alpha, Glenville
1970   Delta Beta, Elon
1970   *Delta Delta, North Carolina (1989)*
1970   *Delta Epsilon, Northern Michigan (1979)*
1970   *Delta Gamma, Minnesota, Morris (1980)*
1971   Delta Zeta, Bloomsburg
1972   *Delta Eta, Southern Indiana (1986)*
1974   Delta Theta, Pembroke
1975   *Delta Iota, Valley City (1984)*
1977   *Delta Kappa, South Carolina (1983)*
1978   *Delta Lambda, Mesa (1983)*
1978   *Delta Mu, Rutgers (1983)*
1978   Delta Nu, Franklin and Marshall
1978   *Delta Xi, Loyola Marymount, Los Angeles (1984)*
1979   *Delta Omicron, Gettysburg (1990)*

1979   Delta Pi, Winthrop
1979   *Delta Rho, Averett* (1981)
1980   *Delta Sigma, Oklahoma* (1982)
1981   *Delta Tau, Lincoln Memorial (TN)* (1987)
1982   Delta Chi, Virginia
1982   Delta Phi, Kansas State
1982   Delta Upsilon, Widener
1983   Delta Psi, St. Joseph's (PA)
1984   Epsilon Alpha, Cal State, Hayward
1984   Epsilon Beta, Arkansas, Monticello
1984   Epsilon Gamma, Grand Valley
1985   Epsilon Delta, Gannon
1985   Epsilon Epsilon, Stockton
1986   Epsilon Eta, East Stroudsburg
1986   Epsilon Zeta, Southern Arkansas
1987   Epsilon Iota, St. Mary's
1987   Epsilon Kappa, Wisconsin, Oshkosh
1987   Epsilon Lambda, Hofstra
1987   Epsilon Theta, Oglethorpe
1988   Epsilon Mu, Glassboro
1989   Epsilon Nu, North Carolina
1989   Epsilon Omicron, Illinois State
1989   Epsilon Xi, Indiana
1990   Epsilon Pi, Presbyterian
1990   Epsilon Rho, Mankato

Theta Phi Alpha

ACTIVE PIN

PLEDGE PIN

THETA PHI ALPHA was founded at the University of Michigan on August 30, 1912, as a sorority for Catholic women. Under the guidance of the Right Reverend Edward D. Kelley, then Auxiliary Bishop of Detroit, Amelia McSweeney, Mildred M. Connely, May C. Ryan, Selma Gilday, Camilla Ryan Sutherland, Helen Ryan Quinlan, Katrina Caughey Ward, Dorothy Caughey Phalan, Otilia Leuchtweis O'Hara, and Eva Stroh Bauer founded a sorority which would provide an environment for college girls which resembled the Catholic homes from which they came. Today, the sorority opens its membership to girls of all races, creeds, and nationalities, but chooses its members from women students of good moral conduct and scholastic potential, who understand and accept its ideals and traditions. The sorority stresses the educational and spiritual development of its members, and provides for them a group social life built on close comradeship. It strives to develop the leadership potential of each member, so she can fulfill her role as an educated woman, with a strong religious heritage, in today's world.

Growth   Theta Phi Alpha functioned as a local organization until early in 1918, by which time inquiries had been received from women's groups on other campuses. Inspectors were sent to these groups and plans for nationalization begun. In 1919, Theta Phi Alpha became a national fraternity with the addition of chapters at the University of Illinois, Ohio State, Ohio University, and the University of Cincinnati; and the first national convention was held that year. Thereafter, national conventions were held annually until 1926, since when, with rare exceptions, they have been biennial.

In 1941, Theta Phi Alpha began establishing chapters at Catholic universities, because the number of women students at these schools had greatly increased, and many were seeking national affiliations. Chapters at Marquette University, Milwaukee; Loyola of Chicago; the University of Detroit; Creighton University, Omaha; Quincy College, Quincy, Illinois; St. Louis University; The Catholic University of America, Washington, D.C.; Loyola of the South, New Orleans; St. John's University, Hillcrest, N.Y.; and the College of Steubenville, Steubenville, Ohio, followed.

Another milestone in fraternity growth was the merger, ratified by both organizations in 1952, with Pi Lambda Sigma, a sorority for Catholic women, established in 1921, at Boston University.

Government   The supreme governing body is the national convention, to which each active chapter and each chartered alumnae association is entitled to send one voting delegate; it is open to all members. In the interim, authority is vested in the Grand Council, elected at each biennial convention. The council consists of the national president, first and second vice-presidents (responsible, respectively, for active and alumnae groups), the executive secretary, and the treasurer. The council is assisted by the five-member board of trustees, also elected at convention, which advises the council on matters of national policy and is directly responsible for all national awards to chapters and to individuals. Other officers are the directors of extension and of probationary chapters, and the national editor. National chairmen supervise specific areas of fraternal activity, such as scholarship, rushing, housing, convention, music, constitution, ritual, and membership.

Chapters are grouped into provinces, each administered by a province governor and a secretary-treasurer.

Locally, each active chapter is governed by its board of directors, made up of an equal number of alumnae and active members, plus a chairman, who is an alumna.

Alumnae are organized into geographic units, associations being chartered when a sufficient number are present within an area to carry out a meaningful program.

Traditions and Insignia   Theta Phi Alpha's traditional national awards include the Guard of Honor (a guard pin in the shape of a Tudor rose, gold with sapphire center) which is the highest recognition given by the fraternity. It is presented to alumnae for distinguished service to the national organization over a long period of time. Compass Club membership is limited to those alumnae who have attended at least five national conventions of the fraternity.

National awards are traditionally presented at the Fraternity Night Banquet, during the national convention. At this festive affair, open only to initiated members, are given such undergraduate awards as the scholarship cup, the President's cup (to the outstanding chapter), the cooperation tray, the publicity cup, rushing award and trophies for special service projects to the fraternity, to the university and to the community. Alumnae groups also receive trophies for service projects.

Outstanding senior students who have demonstrated leadership, excellence of character, and scholarship, are honored each spring when the sorority observes its Founders' Day. Each collegiate chapter, through its board of directors, may nominate its most deserving senior for the Senior Service Award.

At the Silver Jubilee Convention in Ann Arbor in 1937, Theta Phi Alpha established its most cherished award, the Siena Medal, which is presented to an outstanding Catholic woman in public life, not a member. The medal is named for the Patron Saint of Theta Phi Alpha, St. Catherine of Siena, whose motto, *"Nothing great is ever achieved without much enduring,"* has been adopted by Theta Phi Alpha. Founders' Day is the feast day of St. Catherine—April 30.

The fraternity flower is the white rose; the jewel is the sapphire; and the colors are silver, gold, and blue.

The badge is a solid gold letter Theta, set with pearls, superimposed upon plain gold letters Phi and Alpha in that order.

The coat of arms is described as follows: Azure, a bend, between a double cross crosslet fitchy degreed, and a Tudor rose or, latter seeded sable. Mantling, azure doubled or. Over an esquire's helmet, the crest, an open book argent, edged or, charged with two fleurs-de-lis azure. Motto, Theta Phi Alpha in Greek.

The pledge pin is a square badge in black enamel with a gold border and a gold compass in the center.

Publications The quarterly magazine is the *Compass*, sent to all initiated members for life. Informational guides are issued regularly.

Funds and Philanthropies The Founders' Foundation was established in 1958 to honor the founders of Theta Phi Alpha and those of Pi Lambda Sigma; it administers all the monetary activities in the areas of philanthropy and aid. Its functions are to present scholarships to outstanding members; to make, as needed, housing loans to active chapters and loans to undergraduate members; and to assist financially the fraternity's national philanthropy, the Glenmary Missioners, of Glendale, Ohio, adopted in 1950. These orders of priests, brothers, and women religious are dedicated to teaching and social service work in backward areas of the United States, where they aid the needy without regard for race, color, or creed.

Headquarters 9101 Lancer, St. John, IN 46373.

Membership Active chapters 30. Inactive chapters 27. Colonies 2. Total number of initiates 14,794. Chapter roll:

1912	*Alpha, Michigan*	(1944)
1919	*Beta, Illinois*	(1953)
1919	*Delta, Ohio*	(1933-1957) (1971)
1919	Epsilon, Cincinnati	
1919	*Gamma, Ohio State*	(1944)
1920	*Zeta, Indiana*	(1959)
1921	*Eta, Boston U.*	(1970)
1921	*Iota, Kansas*	(1955)
1921	*Theta, Missouri*	(1927)
1922	Kappa, Pitt	
1923	*Lambda, Syracuse*	(1968)
1924	*Mu, Nebraska*	(1937)
1926	*Nu, Wisconsin, Madison*	(1955)
1926	*Omicron, Denver*	(1951)
1926	*Pi, UCLA*	(1954)
1926	*Xi, Iowa*	(1934)
1929	*Rho, Penn State*	(1969)
1931	*Sigma, Akron*	(1987)
1941	*Tau, Marquette*	(1969)
1943	*Upsilon, Loyola, Chicago*	(1990)
1951	*Phi, Detroit*	(1972)
1952	Chi, Creighton	
1954	*Psi, Quincy*	(1960)
1955	*Omega, St. Louis*	(1973)
1956	*Alpha Alpha, Catholic*	(1970)
1959	Alpha Beta, Loyola, New Orleans	
1960	*Alpha Delta, St. Norbert*	(1971)
1960	Alpha Epsilon, St. John's (NY)	
1960	Alpha Gamma, DePaul	
1963	Alpha Zeta, Steubenville	
1968	*Alpha Eta, Thomas More*	(1974)
1968	*Alpha Theta, Wisconsin, Stevens Point* (1972)	
1970	Alpha Iota, Purdue, Calumet	
1970	*Alpha Kappa, St. Peter's*	(1971)
1970	*Alpha Lambda, Gannon*	(1972)
1974	Alpha Mu, Northern Kentucky	
1974	Alpha Nu, GMI	
1979	Alpha Xi, Cleveland	
1983	Alpha Omicron, Xavier (OH)	
1985	Alpha Pi, Wayne State (NE)	
1985	Alpha Rho, Robert Morris	
1985	Alpha Sigma, California (PA)	
1986	Alpha Chi, Monmouth (NJ)	
1986	Alpha Phi, St. Mary's (MN)	
1986	Alpha Tau, Embry Riddle (FL)	
1986	Alpha Upsilon, Indiana (PA)	
1987	Alpha Omega, Wisconsin, Platteville	
1987	Alpha Psi, Dayton	
1987	Beta Alpha, SUNY, Stony Brook	
1988	Beta Beta, Trenton	
1988	Beta Delta, Muskingum	
1988	Beta Gamma, Fairleigh Dickinson, Madison	
1990	Beta Epsilon, Southeastern Louisiana	

1990 Beta Eta, Bryant
1990 Beta Iota, Fairleigh Dickinson, Teaneck
1990 Beta Theta, St. Francis (PA)
1990 Beta Zeta, New York Tech

Colonies: Clarion, Michigan, Flint

COAT OF ARMS

Zeta Tau Alpha

ACTIVE PIN

PLEDGE PIN

ZETA TAU ALPHA was founded on October 15, 1898, at Longwood College, Farmville, Virginia (then the State Female Normal School), by Maud Jones (Horner), Alice Bland Coleman, Ethel Coleman (Van Name), Ruby Leigh (Orgain), Frances Yancey Smith, Della Lewis (Hundley), Helen Crafford, Alice Welsh, and Mary Jones (Batte). However, informal meetings looking toward organization were held in 1897. These nine young women desired to perpetuate beyond college days the very close friendships they had formed in the warm, congenial atmosphere at Farmville, and they hoped to extend these benefits to girls in other colleges.

The founding is linked with the early organizational development of the South. A study of the southern field at the end of the 19th century revealed it as practically untouched, for, while northern nationals had passed the experimental and trial stages, they had left the southern field to its own resources. Thus, in helping meet the organization needs in that part of the country, this Virginia-born fraternity came into existence, and for many years confined its expansion to campuses in the South.

For several months after the date of founding, while the founders were carefully selecting a Greek name, the group was known as the ? ? ?—the Three Question Marks. They were aided in organization by two brilliant students from William and Mary College—brothers of Maud Jones and Frances Y. Smith. The Greek name was adopted before April, 1889, and the fraternity was chartered as a legal corporation by the Virginia legislature on March 15, 1902, at which time Zeta Tau Alpha became the first woman's fraternity to be chartered by the state of Virginia, and the first ever to be chartered by a special act of the legislature.

Growth The first selected locations were women's colleges and seminaries, then the favored types of educational institutions for women in a state in which coeducation was still far off. Three

new chapters, two in Virginia and one in Maryland, were added in 1902, soon after the state charter grant. The first chapter placed in a coeducational institution was in 1903 at the University of Arkansas, followed the next year by an installation at the University of Tennessee. Twelve charters had been granted by the end of the first decade. In 1909, Zeta Tau Alpha became the 13th organization to join the National Panhellenic Conference (then the Intersorority Conference). Movement toward the North came that same year when a chapter was placed at Drury College, Springfield, Missouri, with Rho chapter, installed at Boston University, in 1912, being heralded as Zeta's "first full-fledged northern chapter." Zeta Tau Alpha became international in 1929 when a chapter was established at the University of Manitoba.

Government From 1898 to 1902, the date on which the first Arch Chapter met, government was vested in Alpha Chapter. From 1902, until the time of the first national convention, in 1903, government was vested in the Arch Chapter, which hereafter became known as Grand Chapter, the executive branch of the fraternity. The national convention, which meets biennially (triennial for a time, until 1926) is the legislative branch, the supreme governing body of the fraternity. In 1941, to meet the increasing demands for more personnel to handle the affairs of the expanding fraternity, Grand Chapter was supplanted by an enlarged National Council, which, in 1978 consisted of a national president, vice president collegiate I, vice president collegiate II, vice president collegiate III, vice president alumnae I, vice president alumnae II, secretary-treasurer, NPC delegate and extension director. Administration is in the hands of this body between conventions.

The fraternity is divided into 35 provinces in which the collegiate chapters are located, and 26 districts which comprise the alumnae world, thus facilitating direction and administration. Each province and each district has its own president. Collegiate chapters are visited annually; alumnae groups biennially. Each college chapter has an alumnae advisory board. Alumnae-sponsored Zeta Days are annual events in many states, while the national organization holds workshops for national officers, college chapter officers and their advisers in the years between national conventions.

The national office, set up in 1920, serves as a general clearing house for fraternity business such as the auditing of chapter and house corporation accounts and as a repository for records.

Traditions and Insignia A bronze plaque in the rotunda of Longwood College, dedicated on October 15, 1948, the golden anniversary year, in ceremonies attended by five founders, national officers and friends, commemorates the fraternity's founding and honors the founders. To celebrate the Diamond Anniversary, a ceremonial mace was given to the College.

The Alumnae Certificate of Merit is awarded on

Zeta Days to alumnae who do not qualify for the Honor Ring, but whose service to the organization has been sustained and significant. The 50-year membership citation is the Order of the Shield, the recipient of which is entitled to wear the miniature white violet pin, which belongs exclusively to 50-year members.

Among the traditional awards presented at convention are the Helen Margaret Harrison Award (a silver tray) for superior chapter attainment; the Achievement Award (a silver bowl) presented to the chapter showing the greatest progress in the combined phases of chapter life, a Golden Anniversary Scholarship Cup, a Merit Award, a Standards Award, the Martha Edens Helms Award, the Vallera Clough Ross Award, an Activities Award, special National Council recognition awards, membership selection awards, and the Louise Kettler Helper Memorial Award. Major alumnae awards include: membership, public relations programming, Panhellenic service and the Betty McGehee Schuessler Award. In 1983, the Crown Chapter Award was introduced to recognize on an annual basis those collegiate chapters maintaining a high standard of excellence in the areas of membership, finances, activities, programming, and fraternity operations. This award was introduced for alumnae chapters in 1984 and is given at convention.

The badge is a shield with a smaller black shield raised upon it. In the center is the symbolic five-pointed crown, flanked by the initials ZTA. Below, in Greek, is the word Θέμισ. A chapter guard, the use of which is optional, consists of the Greek letter or letters of the wearer's chapter. The torch guard is worn by National Council officers. The pledge pin is a carpenter's square in silver and turquoise blue, with silver markings. The recognition pin is a diminutive gold crown of five points. A gold monogram pin is an alternate choice. The miniature white violet pin worn by 50-year members bears the significant "50." The Mother's Pin is a small turquoise and silver crown with a white violet on it. The Honor Ring, awarded to alumnae of distinguished service, is an oblong-octagonal ring in either silver or white gold. Upon the turquoise mounting rests the coat of arms, while on one side is an open book and on the other a five-pointed crown, both in relief. The colors are turquoise blue and steel gray. The flower is the white violet.

The technical description of the coat of arms is: quarterly argent and azure; in two and three a cinquefoil of the first; nine billets in sable bend. Crest: above a crown (radiate) or, a chain of five links fess-wise argent. Motto: "Zeta Tau Alpha" in Greek upper and lower case. The official banner is a rectangle field bordered on all sides with turquoise blue. The inner rectangle holds three divisions; the upper left section is a triangle of steel gray, containing a large A of turquoise blue, the central division is a rhombus of blue across which are the letters Θέμισ in steel gray; the lower righthand corner completes the rectangle with another triangle of steel gray on which is pictured a burning torch. On the official flag the coat of arms is placed on a steel gray field bordered by a band of turquoise blue. The Greek letters of the chapter flying it appear in the left-hand corner. The fraternity has a secret motto as well as an open one, the latter being *Seek the Noblest.*

Publications The quarterly publication, *Themis,* was first published in 1903. *The Link* first appeared in 1911 as a mimeographed esoteric publication of the national office when it was known as *The Secret Letter.*

The two-volume *History of Zeta Tau Alpha,* by Shirley Kreasan Strout, editor-historian, appeared in the 30th anniversary year (Vol. I, May 1, 1928; Vol II, July, 1929). The fourth printing was made in 1940. The 913-page *History of Zeta Tau Alpha* (1898-1948 and Supplement), covering the full 50 years of the fraternity's existence, was distributed at the 1956 convention. Printed first in the Summer, 1960, issue of *Themis, The Sixth Decade* of *Zeta Tau Alpha* (1948-1958), brought the total number of Zeta histories, by the same author, to four. The Seventh Decade (1958-68), written by Betty McGehee Schuessler, and the Eighth Decade (1968-78), written by LaVerne Porterfield Skipper, complete the coverage of Zeta's first 80 years.

Other publications have included: Constitution and Bylaws; songbooks; and a series of manuals—general and pledge; Guide to Collegiate Chapters, House Corporations, Associations, and House Director; in addition to numerous manuals and publications for the guidance of national, province, district, and chapter officers, and advisors.

Funds and Philanthropies In 1958, the convention authorized the consolidation of funds, the major one being the General Fund, used to operate the fraternity. The Themis Endowment Fund, created in 1923 to offset the expenses of the publication, remained part of the General Fund from 1958 to 1980. The interest from other from other funds in the name of chapters and individuals are used for scholarships and housing.

The Zeta Tau Alpha Fraternity Housing Corporation, chartered as a separate, non-profit corporation by the State of Indiana, was established in 1977 to provide guidance and assistance to local alumnae in securing and maintaining competitive housing for collegiate chapters. This assistance may include approval of bylaws; approval of construction plans, loans to local corporations, advice on decorating or insurance, and even total property management.

In 1983, the Zeta Tau Alpha Foundation, a corporation chartered by the State of Illinois in 1954, merged with the Crown Development Trust Fund, Inc., a corporation chartered by the State of Indiana in 1980. The merger provided the fraternity with a broader base for tax deductible contributions. Income is derived from gifts, bequests, grants and contributions, and earnings from the investment and reinvestment of funds. Funds from the

Crown Development Trust Fund, Inc. are used exclusively for charitable, educational and literary purposes. Scholarships are given annually to undergraduate and graduate students. Educational programs are also sponsored. The service fund is operated by the corporation and it supports the national service project.

The fraternity conducted a mountain health center near Marion, Virginia, from 1928-1946. In 1947, however, a new philanthropic project was adopted: that of assistance to and work with the National Society for Crippled Children and Adults, Inc. This continued until 1970, when the convention delegates voted to support educational projects of the Association for Retarded Citizens. Every college and alumnae chapter has additional local service projects.

Headquarters 3330 Founders Road, Indianapolis, IN 46268.

Membership Total living membership 97,952. Total undergraduate membership 9,149. Active chapters 150. Inactive chapters 55. Houses owned 46. City/Area alumni associations 239. Total number of initiates 102,407. Chapter roll:

1898 Alpha, Longwood (1906-1949)
1902 *Delta, Randolph, Macon Woman's* (1960)
1902 *Gamma, Hanna Moore Academy* (1904)
1902 *Original Beta, Richmond Women's College* (1903)
1903 Epsilon, Arkansas (1942-1946)
1904 *Eta, Mary Baldwin* (1906)
1904 Gamma, N.Y.U., Heights (1972-1989)
1904 Zeta, Tennessee
1905 *Beta (new), Judson* (1919)
1905 *Iota, Richmond College* (1908)
1905 Theta, Bethany (WV)
1906 Kappa, Texas
1906 Lambda, Southwestern (TX)
1907 Theta, Penn
1909 Mu, Drury
1910 Nu, Alabama
1910 *Xi, USC* (1961)
1911 *Nu, Ohio State* (1989)
1911 *Pi, Wesleyan (GA)* (1914)
1912 *Rho, Boston U* (1934-1959) (1968)
1912 Sigma, Baker
1912 Tau, Millikin
1915 *Chi, Pitt* (1965)
1915 Phi, Duke
1915 *Upsilon, Cal, Berkeley* (1969)
1916 Omega, Southern Methodist
1917 Psi, Washington (WA) (1974-1978)
1918 *Alpha Alpha, Iowa Wesleyan* (1943-1946) (1987)
1918 *Alpha Beta, Penn* (1954)
1920 *Alpha Delta, Butler* (1956)
1920 Alpha Gamma, Michigan (1951-1956)
1920 Gamma, Northwestern (1971-1975)
1921 *Alpha Epsilon, Denver* (1934)
1921 Alpha Eta, Cincinnati
1921 *Alpha Iota, Lawrence* (1939)

1921 Alpha Kappa, Illinois
1921 *Alpha Lambda, Hollins* (1929)
1921 Alpha Theta, Purdue (1934-1947)
1921 Alpha Zeta, Ohio State
1922 Alpha Mu, Washburn
1922 Alpha Nu, Birmingham-Southern
1922 Alpha Omicron, Iowa
1922 *Alpha Pi, Ohio* (1985)
1922 *Alpha Theta, Nebraska* (1962)
1922 Alpha Xi, Indiana
1923 *Alpha Phi, Northwestern* (1969)
1923 *Alpha Rho, Syracuse* (1976)
1923 *Alpha Sigma, Oregon State* (1933-1960) (1970)
1923 *Alpha Tau, Minnesota* (1959)
1923 Alpha Upsilon, Oklahoma State
1924 Alpha Chi, Kentucky
1924 *Alpha Omega, Ohio Wesleyan* (1934-1949) (1968)
1924 Alpha Psi, Missouri (1934-1945)
1924 *Beta Alpha, George Washington* (1969)
1924 *Beta Beta, Dickinson* (1967)
1924 Beta Gamma, Florida State
1924 *Omicron, New Hampshire* (1962)
1926 Beta Delta, Miami (OH)
1926 *Beta Epsilon, UCLA* (1966-1977) (1986)
1926 Beta Zeta, Iowa State (1939-1974)
1927 *Alpha Pi, North Carolina* (1985)
1927 *Beta Eta, Nebraska* (1937-1956) (1980)
1927 Beta Iota, Centenary
1927 *Beta Kappa, Tulane* (1952)
1927 *Beta Lambda, Louisville* (1943-1945) (1977)
1927 Beta Theta, Franklin
1928 *Beta Mu, Washington State* (1939)
1928 Beta Nu, New Mexico State
1929 Beta Omicron, South Carolina
1929 *Beta Pi, Oregon* (1943-1945) (1971)
1929 Beta Rho, Manitoba
1929 *Beta Sigma, Rhodes* (1977)
1929 *Beta Tau, Albion* (1968)
1929 *Beta Xi, Akron* (1972)
1931 *Beta Chi, Washington (MO)* (1957)
1931 Beta Phi, Michigan State
1931 *Beta Upsilon, Kansas State* (1940)
1932 Alpha Nu, Muhlenberg
1934 Beta Psi, Stetson
1935 Beta Omega, Union (TX)
1938 *Gamma Alpha, Miami (FL)* (1969)
1938 Gamma Beta, Washington (MD)
1938 Gamma Gamma, Texas, El Paso
1939 *Gamma Delta, Mississippi* (1986)
1939 Gamma Epsilon, Penn State
1940 Gamma Zeta, Mississippi State
1943 *Alpha Rho, Ohio* (1969)
1946 *Gamma Eta, Toledo* (1981)
1947 *Gamma Theta, Colorado* (1972)
1949 Gamma Iota, Florida
1949 Gamma Kappa, Madison Col
1949 *Gamma Lambda, Hartwick* (1963)
1949 Gamma Pi, Georgia
1950 *Alpha Chi, Nebraska, Omaha* (1955)

1950	Gamma Mu, Nebraska, Omaha
1951	Gamma Omicron, Central Michigan
1951	Gamma Rho, Auburn (1970-1976)
1951	Gamma Xi, Indiana (PA)
1952	Gamma Nu, Virginia
1952	*Gamma Sigma, Tampa* (1977)
1953	Gamma Chi, Indiana State
1953	Gamma Phi, North Texas
1953	Gamma Tau, Texas Tech
1953	Gamma Upsilon, Oklahoma (1965-1982)
1955	Gamma Psi, Texas Christian
1956	*Delta Alpha, Cal State, Long Beach* (1974)
1956	Gamma Omega, Houston
1957	Delta Beta, Florida Southern
1957	Delta Delta, Baldwin-Wallace
1957	Delta Gamma, High Point
1958	*Delta Epsilon, Wagner* (1970-1973) (1985)
1958	Delta Eta, West Texas
1959	Delta Kappa, L.S.U.
1959	Delta Theta, Ohio Northern
1959	Delta Zeta, Sam Houston
1960	Delta Iota, Clarion
1961	*Beta Rho, N.Y.U.* (1972)
1961	Delta Lambda, Georgia State
1961	Delta Mu, Tennessee, Martin
1961	Delta Nu, L.S.U., Shreveport
1961	*Delta Xi, California (PA)* (1978)
1962	Delta Omicron, Lenoir-Rhyne
1962	Delta Pi, Eastern New Mexico
1963	*Delta Rho, Eastern Michigan* (1976)
1963	Delta Sigma, Lamar
1963	Delta Tau, Davis and Elkins
1963	Delta Upsilon, West Virginia Wesleyan
1964	Delta Chi, William Jewell
1964	Delta Omega, Westminster (PA)
1964	*Delta Phi, Millsaps* (1974)
1964	Delta Psi, Samford
1964	Zeta Alpha, Evansville
1964	Zeta Beta, Thiel
1964	Zeta Gamma, Youngstown State
1965	*Zeta Delta, Northeast Louisiana* (1986)
1965	*Zeta Epsilon, Texas A & I* (1988)
1966	*Alpha Phi, Parsons* (1972)
1966	*Zeta Eta, Slippery Rock* (1982)
1966	Zeta Iota, Western Carolina
1966	Zeta Theta, East Central State
1966	*Zeta Zeta, Athens* (1982)
1967	*Zeta Kappa, Louisiana Tech* (1981)
1967	Zeta Lambda, Rider
1968	Zeta Mu, Jacksonville
1968	Zeta Nu, Lock Haven
1968	Zeta Omicron, Arkansas State
1968	*Zeta Pi, Woodbury* (1977)
1968	Zeta Xi, Georgia Southern
1969	Gamma Beta, New Haven
1969	*Gamma Omega, Northern Illinois* (1971)
1969	*Gamma Psi, Northeastern* (1984)
1969	*Gamma Upsilon, Northeast Louisiana* (1973)
1969	Zeta Chi, Tennessee Tech
1969	Zeta Phi, South Alabama
1969	Zeta Psi, Jacksonville (AL)

1969	Zeta Sigma, Texas, Arlington
1969	*Zeta Tau, North Carolina, Wilmington* (1975)
1970	*Delta Gamma, Oklahoma* (1972)
1970	Eta Alpha, Georgia Southwestern
1970	Eta Beta, Duquesne
1970	Eta Gamma, West Chester
1970	Zeta Omega, Ferris
1970	*Zeta Rho, Morehead* (1982)
1970	Zeta Upsilon, Edinboro
1971	Delta Lambda, Monmouth (NJ)
1971	*Eta Delta, Livingston* (1978)
1971	Eta Epsilon, Mansfield
1971	*Eta Eta, McNeese* (1982)
1971	Eta Iota, Valdosta
1971	Eta Kappa, Central Florida
1971	Eta Zeta, Elon
1972	Eta Lamda, Charleston (SC)
1972	Eta Mu, Augusta
1972	Eta Nu, Radford
1972	Eta Xi, V.P.I.
1973	*Delta Rho, Monmouth (NJ)* (1975)
1973	*Eta Omicron, Western Illinois* (1979)
1973	Eta Pi, Wright State
1973	Eta Rho, North Alabama
1973	Eta Sigma, Pembroke
1973	Eta Theta, Missouri, Rolla
1974	Eta Chi, Francis Marion
1974	Eta Phi, Illinois State
1974	Eta Tau, North Carolina, Charlotte
1974	Eta Upsilon, Missouri Southern
1975	Eta Omega, L.S.U., Shreveport
1975	Eta Psi, Cal Poly, San Luis Obispo
1975	Theta Alpha, Cal State, Chico
1975	Theta Delta, Salisbury
1975	Theta Gamma, Texas A & M
1976	*Theta Beta, Eastern Washington* (1978)
1977	Theta Eta, Stephen F. Austin
1977	Theta Iota, North Florida
1977	Theta Kappa, Missouri, St. Louis
1977	Theta Omicron, Baylor
1977	Theta Theta, Arkansas Tech
1978	*Epsilon Alpha, Oregon Tech* (1983)
1978	*Theta Lambda, Belmont Abbey* (1980)
1978	*Theta Mu, Bowling Green* (1980)
1978	Theta Nu, Auburn, Montgomery
1978	Theta Pi, Cal State, Northridge
1978	Theta Sigma, Winthrop
1978	Theta Xi, Rutgers
1978	Theta Zeta, Wofford
1979	Theta Epsilon, San Diego U
1979	Theta Phi, Cal State, Fullerton
1979	Theta Tau, North Carolina
1979	*Theta Upsilon, Santa Clara* (1983)
1980	Iota Alpha, Robert Morris
1980	Theta Chi, George Mason
1980	Theta Omega, Cal Poly, Pomona
1980	Theta Psi, Southwest Texas
1981	Iota Delta, Towson
1981	Iota Gamma, Trenton
1983	*Epsilon Lambda, North Carolina State* (1985)

1983	Iota Zeta, New Mexico
1984	Iota Epsilon, Hartford
1984	Iota Eta, Nevada, Las Vegas
1984	Iota Iota, Fairleigh Dickinson, Madison
1984	Iota Theta, Georgia Tech
1985	Iota Kappa, Delta State
1985	Iota Lambda, Southeast Missouri
1985	Iota Mu, Central Missouri State
1987	Iota Pi, Dayton
1987	Iota Rho, East Carolina
1987	Iota Sigma, Old Dominion
1988	*Epsilon Nu, SUNY Col., Oneonta* (1989)
1988	Iota Upsilon, Portland
1989	Epsilon Psi, Montclair

Colonies: Susquehanna, Lander, Christian Brothers

NPHC Member Sororities

COAT OF ARMS

Alpha Kappa Alpha

ACTIVE PIN

ALPHA KAPPA ALPHA, the first Greek letter sorority among Negro college women, was founded at Howard University, Washington, DC, on January 16, 1908. Ethel Hedgeman (Lyle), who originated the idea and whose efforts were greatly assisted by Miss Ethel Robinson, a member of the faculty, was joined in the enterprise by Lillian Burke, Beulah Burke, Margaret Flagg (Holmes), Marie Woolfolk (Taylor), Lavinia Taylor, Anna Brown, Lucy Stowe, and Margery Hill. Their avowed purpose for organizing was "to cultivate and encourage high scholastic and ethical standards, improve the social status of the race, promote unity and friendship among college women, and keep alive within the alumnae an interest in college life and progressive movements emanating therefrom." In 1930 the organization was incorporated under the laws of the District of Columbia, at which time the original unit became Alpha Chapter and a policy of expansion began.

In 1946 the Boule approved a policy which provides that race, color, or creed shall not be included in the qualifications of membership. A phase of the organization's activities is its study, purchase, and maintenance of houses for undergraduates on campuses where the need is found.

Government   Government is vested in the convention which is held biennially and is known as the boule; during the intervals between conventions the Directorate (Board of Directors), composed of seventeen national officers, administers the affairs of the sorority. Chapters are grouped geographically into ten regions, including an international region, with a director in charge of each.

Traditions and Insignia   The badge is shaped like an ivy leaf with a green enamel center bordered with pearls and the letters AKA in gold, one letter at each point of the leaf. In the center of the pin are the letters Ω and Υ. The pledge pin is a small ivy leaf of green enamel. A special pin of three small ivy leaves enclosed in a circle of pearls with a letter on each leaf is worn by the honorary members. The colors are salmon pink and apple green, and the flower is the tea rose.

Publications   The official publication is a quarterly magazine, *The Ivy Leaf.* A *Manual of Procedures* is also published. Newsletters from the Supreme Basileus (International President) and the Undergraduate Activities Committee are mailed periodically to all members.

Funds and Philanthropies   In keeping with its declared purpose Alpha Kappa Alpha has engaged in a varied program of civic, social, and educational service. Among these undertakings are the large number of scholarships, varying in amounts from $25 to $1,000 and more, awarded annually by chapters to high school girls to make it possible for them to continue their education. The National Body awards $2,000 annually for undergraduate member scholarships or for graduate member foreign fellowships. A health program, sponsored by the National Body, is promoted through each of its local chapters to educate for and to encourage better standards of living, to increase service and health facilities for all groups, and to cooperate with established health agencies to bring the benefits of their services more fully to every segment of the population. This program is the outgrowth of the volunteer Mississippi Health Project, which has carried out by means of a mobile clinic in Holmes County, Mississippi from 1935 to 1940. Another activity is the American Council on Human Rights, which is sponsored cooperatively with five other Greek-letter organizations. As a result of global sensitization, chapters across the country have adopted African villages where they have supported the construction of wells, health clinics, schools and other projects.

Headquarters   5656 South Stony Island Avenue, Chicago, Illinois 60637

Membership   Chapters in 46 states, West Africa, the Bahamas, the Virgin Islands, Germany, South Korea and Bermuda. Active chapters 330. Inactive chapters 36. Total number of initiates 113,000. Chapter roll:

Delta Nu, St. Thomas
Omicron Chi, Rhodes
Omicron Phi, North Carolina, Wilmington

Omicron Rho, East Tennessee
Omicron Sigma, Lynchburg
Omicron Tau, Texas, San Antonio
Omicron Upsilon, SUNY, Stony Brook
Zeta Chi, Jarvis Christian (1971)

1908	Alpha, Howard
1914	Gamma, Illinois
1916	Delta, Kansas
1916	Epsilon, Tufts
1916	Zeta, Wilberforce
1918	Iota, Pitt
1920	Kappa, IUPUI
1921	Omicron, Cincinnati
1921	*Pi, Meharry Medical* (1927)
1921	Theta, Ohio State
1922	*Eta, St. Paul, Minnesota* (1964)
1922	*Mu, Temple* (1945)
1922	Nu, West Virginia
1922	Rho, Cal, Berkeley
1922	Tau, Indiana
1923	*Upsilon, Washburn* (1978)
1923	*Xi, Detroit* (1947)
1924	Chi, Talladega
1924	Phi, Wiley
1925	*Alpha Beta, Fort Valley* (1933)
1925	Alpha Delta, Morgan State
1925	Alpha Gamma, UCLA
1925	Omega, Cleveland
1925	*Psi, Penn* (1947)
1926	Alpha Epsilon, Virginia State, Norfolk
1926	*Alpha Zeta, Rhode Island, Brown* (1939)
1927	Alpha Eta, Virginia Union
1927	*Alpha Theta, Nebraska* (1951)
1927	Pi, Fisk
1928	Alpha Iota, Lincoln (MO)
1928	Alpha Lambda, Toledo
1930	*Alpha Mu, Sam Houston* (1955)
1930	*Alpha Nu, Michigan State* (1959)
1930	Alpha Pi, Clark
1930	*Alpha Rho, Wichita* (1951)
1930	Alpha Xi, Livingstone
1931	Alpha Chi, North Carolina
1931	*Alpha Omicron, San Francisco State* (1951)
1931	Alpha Phi, North Carolina A & T
1931	Alpha Psi, Tennessee State
1931	*Alpha Tau, Dayton* (1939)
1931	*Alpha Upsilon, Pitt* (1952)
1932	Beta Alpha, Florida A & M
1932	*Beta Beta, Akron* (1962)
1932	Beta Epsilon, Louisville
1932	Beta Eta, Michigan
1932	*Beta Gamma, Des Moines, Iowa* (1974)
1932	Beta Zeta, Kentucky State
1934	*Alpha Beta, Kansas State* (1941)
1934	*Beta Iota, Portsmouth, Ohio* (1951)
1935	*Beta Kappa, San Diego U* (1953)
1936	Beta Lambda, D. C. Teachers
1936	Beta Mu, Wayne State (MI)
1937	*Beta Nu, Kansas State* (1986)
1937	*Beta Xi, Cornell* (1952)
1938	Beta Omicron, Bluefield
1938	*Beta Phi, Xavier (OH)* (1968)
1938	Beta Pi, Alabama State
1938	Beta Rho, Shaw
1938	Beta Sigma, South Carolina State
1938	Beta Tau, LeMoyne-Owen
1938	Beta Upsilon, Dillard
1939	Alpha Tau, Tyler Junior
1939	Alpha Zeta, Langston
1939	Beta Chi, Lane
1940	Beta Psi, Southern
1940	Gamma Alpha, Philander Smith
1941	Alpha Beta, Fort Valley
1942	Gamma Gamma, Morris Brown
1944	Gamma Delta, Johnson C. Smith
1946	Gamma Eta, Knoxville
1947	Gamma Theta, Hampton Inst.
1947	Mu, Allen
1947	Psi, Benedict
1947	Xi, Eastern Michigan
1948	Gamma Kappa, Tuskegee
1948	Gamma Zeta, Seton Hall
1949	Gamma Lambda, Winston-Salem
1949	Gamma Mu, Alabama A & M
1949	Gamma Nu, Claflin
1949	Gamma Omicron, Tougaloo
1949	*Gamma Pi, Iowa State* (1970)
1949	Gamma Rho, Jackson (MS)
1949	Gamma Sigma, Albany State
1949	Gamma Tau, Bethune-Cookman
1949	Gamma Upsilon, Savannah
1949	Gamma Xi, St. Augustine's
1950	*Gamma Chi, Dayton* (1968)
1950	Gamma Phi, Alcorn
1950	Gamma Psi, Texas Southern
1951	Alpha Omicron, Maryland, Eastern Shore
1951	Alpha Rho, Arkansas
1951	Alpha Theta, Grambling
1951	*Beta Iota, Evansville* (1969)
1952	Alpha Upsilon, St. Paul's
1952	Beta Xi, Central State (OH)
1952	Delta Alpha, Fayetteville
1952	Delta Beta, Southern Illinois
1953	Beta Kappa, Huston-Tillotson
1953	Beta Kappa, Huston-Tillotson
1953	Delta Delta, Youngstown State
1953	*Delta Epsilon, Detroit* (1962)
1953	Delta Gamma, Penn State
1954	*Delta Eta, Florida Institute* (1954)
1954	Delta Eta, Florida Memorial
1954	Delta Iota, Cheyney State
1954	Delta Theta, North Carolina Teachers
1954	Delta Zeta, Michigan State
1955	Delta Kappa, Bishop
1955	Delta Lambda, Delaware State
1955	Delta Mu, Temple
1959	Alpha Nu, Cal State, Fresno
1959	Delta Xi, Texas
1960	Delta Omicron, Northern Illinois
1961	Delta Pi, Akron
1962	Beta Beta, Oklahoma
1962	Delta Epsilon, Norfolk
1963	Delta Sigma, Stillman
1964	Delta Phi, Ohio

1964	Delta Tau, Missouri		1972	Eta Zeta, Marshall
1965	Delta Chi, Western Michigan		1972	Zeta Psi, San Jose
1966	Delta Psi, Barber-Scotia		1973	Eta Chi, Northwestern Louisiana
1967	Epsilon Alpha, Wichita		1973	Eta Nu, Voorhees
1967	Epsilon Beta, Southwestern Louisiana		1973	Eta Omicron, West Virginia
1968	Beta Phi, Ball State		1973	Eta Phi, Texas A & I
1968	Epsilon Delta, Wisconsin, Madison		1973	*Eta Pi, East Central State* (1984)
1968	Epsilon Epsilon, Memphis State		1973	Eta Psi, Middle Tennessee
1968	Epsilon Eta, Bradley		1973	Eta Rho, Morehead
1968	Epsilon Gamma, Kent		1973	Eta Tau, Drake
1968	Epsilon Zeta, Western Kentucky		1973	Eta Upsilon, Arkansas
1968	Gamma Chi, Northwestern		1973	Eta Xi, Georgia
1969	*Beta Iota, Northern Michigan* (1982)		1973	Theta Alpha, East Carolina
1969	Epsilon Iota, Southern Illinois		1973	Theta Beta, Oklahoma
1969	Epsilon Kappa, Coppin		1973	Theta Delta, Southwest Texas
1969	Epsilon Lambda, Houston		1973	Theta Epsilon, Sam Houston
1969	Epsilon Mu, North Texas		1973	Theta Eta, Henderson
1969	Epsilon Nu, Lincoln (PA)		1973	Theta Gamma, South Carolina
1969	*Epsilon Omicron, Stetson* (1982)		1973	Theta Iota, West Chester
1969	Epsilon Pi, Mississippi Valley		1973	Theta Kappa, Virginia
1969	Epsilon Rho, Purdue		1973	Theta Lambda, Louisiana Tech
1969	Epsilon Theta, Iowa Wesleyan		1973	Theta Theta, Paul Quinn
1969	Epsilon Xi, Indiana State		1973	Theta Zeta, Northeast Louisiana
1969	Eta, Bowie		1974	Beta Gamma, West Florida
1970	Epsilon Phi, Arkansas		1974	Iota Alpha, Brown
1970	Epsilon Psi, Edinboro		1974	Iota Beta, USC
1970	Epsilon Sigma, East Texas		1974	Iota Delta, Wisconsin, Milwaukee
1970	Epsilon Tau, Xavier (OH)		1974	*Iota Epsilon, National Col. Of Ed.* (1982)
1970	Epsilon Upsilon, South Alabama		1974	Iota Eta, Mercer
1970	Gamma Pi, Miles		1974	Iota Gamma, Northeastern
1970	Zeta Alpha, Arizona State		1974	*Iota Theta, GMI* (1984)
1970	Zeta Beta, Lamar		1974	Iota Zeta, Southern Arkansas
1970	Zeta Delta, Tennessee		1974	Theta Chi, Radford
1970	Zeta Gamma, Prairie View		1974	Theta Mu, Arkansas
1971	Zeta Epsilon, Ferris		1974	Theta Nu, Maryland
1971	Zeta Eta, Paine		1974	Theta Omicron, Eureka
1971	Zeta Iota, Western Illinois		1974	Theta Phi, V.P.I.
1971	Zeta Kappa, Tennessee, Chattanooga		1974	Theta Pi, North Carolina
1971	Zeta Lambda, Tennessee, Martin		1974	Theta Psi, Mississippi
1971	Zeta Mu, Texas, Arlington		1974	Theta Rho, Virginia Commonwealth
1971	Zeta Nu, Eastern Kentucky		1974	Theta Sigma, Alabama
1971	Zeta Omicron, Florida State		1974	Theta Tau, Detroit
1971	Zeta Phi, Indiana		1974	Theta Upsilon, Rust
1971	Zeta Pi, McNeese		1974	*Theta Xi, Tulsa* (1986)
1971	Zeta Rho, Central Michigan		1975	*Iota Chi, Millersville* (1984)
1971	Zeta Sigma, Trenton		1975	Iota Iota, Bowling Green
1971	Zeta Tau, Texas Tech		1975	Iota Kappa, Southern Mississippi
1971	Zeta Theta, Southern		1975	Iota Lambda, Florida
1971	Zeta Upsilon, South Florida		1975	Iota Mu, Duke
1971	Zeta Xi, Bennett		1975	Iota Nu, Miami (FL)
1971	Zeta Zeta, Murray State		1975	Iota Omicron, Charleston (SC)
1972	Eta Alpha, Illinois State		1975	Iota Phi, Alabama, Birmingham
1972	Eta Beta, Vanderbilt		1975	*Iota Pi, Baptist, Charleston* (1986)
1972	Eta Delta, Texas, El Paso		1975	Iota Psi, Rutgers
1972	Eta Epsilon, Stephen F. Austin		1975	Iota Rho, Utica
1972	Eta Eta, L.S.U.		1975	Iota Sigma, Kentucky
1972	Eta Gamma, Eastern Illinois		1975	Iota Tau, Arizona
1972	Eta Iota, Columbus		1975	Iota Upsilon, Syracuse
1972	Eta Kappa, L.S.U.		1975	Iota Xi, Francis Marion
1972	Eta Lambda, Cal State, Sacramento		1975	Kappa Alpha, Western Carolina
1972	Eta Mu, Georgia		1975	Kappa Beta, California (PA)
1972	Eta Theta, Loyola, New Orleans		1975	Kappa Delta, C. W. Post

1975	Kappa Epsilon, Adelphi		1979	Mu Chi, Salisbury
1975	Kappa Gamma, Old Dominion		1979	Mu Psi, Texas Wesleyan
1976	Kappa Chi, Auburn		1979	Mu Sigma, Emporia
1976	Kappa Eta, Georgia		1979	Mu Tau, Northeast Missouri
1976	Kappa Iota, Arkansas		1979	Mu Upsilon, Cornell
1976	Kappa Kappa, North Carolina, Charlotte		1979	Nu Alpha, Emory
1976	Kappa Lambda, Texas Christian		1979	Nu Beta, Georgia Tech
1976	Kappa Mu, Southern Methodist		1979	Nu Delta, Birmingham-Southern
1976	Kappa Nu, Texas Woman's		1979	Nu Gamma, Morris
1976	Kappa Omicron, North Carolina		1980	Nu Epsilon, Christopher Newport
1976	Kappa Phi, Hofstra		1980	Nu Eta, Rider
1976	Kappa Pi, Kansas		1980	Nu Iota, Edward Waters
1976	Kappa Psi, Oklahoma		1980	Nu Kappa, Fairleigh Dickinson, Teaneck
1976	Kappa Rho, Austin Peay		1980	Nu Omicron, North Alabama
1976	Kappa Sigma, Washington (WA)		1980	Nu Pi, West Virginia Tech
1976	Kappa Tau, West Georgia		1980	Nu Rho, North Carolina
1976	Kappa Theta, Cal, Riverside		1980	Nu Theta, Grand Valley
1976	Kappa Upsilon, Valdosta		1980	Nu Xi, Auburn
1976	Kappa Xi, Nevada, Las Vegas		1980	Nu Zeta, Georgia Southwestern
1976	Kappa Zeta, Clarion		1981	Nu Chi, William and Mary
1976	Lambda Alpha, Cal State, Long Beach		1981	Nu Phi, Oakland
1977	Lambda Beta, Towson		1981	Nu Psi, SUNY, Albany
1977	Lambda Delta, Longwood		1981	Nu Sigma, Southeast Missouri
1977	Lambda Epsilon, Frostburg		1981	Nu Upsilon, Capital
1977	Lambda Eta, Mississippi		1981	Xi Alpha, Tennessee Tech
1977	Lambda Gamma, Delaware		1981	Xi Beta, Stanford
1977	Lambda Iota, Millsaps		1981	Xi Delta, Missouri
1977	Lambda Kappa, Georgia Southern		1981	Xi Epsilon, Kendall
1977	Lambda Lambda, Lander		1981	Xi Gamma, Atlantic Christian
1977	Lambda Mu, Miami (OH)		1982	Xi Eta, Colorado
1977	Lambda Nu, Cal Poly, San Luis Obispo		1982	Xi Iota, Cameron
1977	Lambda Omicron, Southeastern Louisiana		1982	Xi Kappa, Chicago
1977	Lambda Phi, Maryland, Baltimore County		1982	Xi Theta, SUNY Col., Brockport
1977	Lambda Pi, Jacksonville		1982	Xi Zeta, Illinois Wesleyan
1977	Lambda Rho, Glassboro		1983	Xi Lambda, Dartmouth
1977	Lambda Sigma Society, Cal, Irvine		1983	Xi Mu, SUNY Col., New Paltz
1977	Lambda Tau, Connecticut		1983	Xi Xi, Lehman
1977	Lambda Theta, Clemson		1984	Xi Omicron, Greater New Haven
1977	Lambda Upsilon, M.I.T.		1984	Xi Phi, Michigan
1977	Lambda Xi, Wisconsin, Madison		1984	Xi Pi, Cal, Oakland
1977	Lambda Zeta, American		1984	Xi Rho, SUNY, Binghamton
1978	Lambda Chi, Madison Col		1984	Xi Sigma, SUNY Col., Buffalo
1978	Lambda Psi, Lewis		1984	Xi Tau, Johns Hopkins
1978	Mu Alpha, Troy		1984	Xi Upsilon, Cal, Torrance
1978	Mu Beta, Marquette		1985	Omicron Alpha, Aurora
1978	Mu Delta, George Washington		1985	Xi Psi, Texas A & M
1978	Mu Epsilon, Christian Brothers		1986	Omicron Gamma, Houston
1978	Mu Eta, Livingston		1987	Omicron Delta, Jacksonville
1978	Mu Gamma, Delta State		1987	Omicron Epsilon, Elon
1978	Mu Kappa, Cal, Davis		1987	Omicron Iota, George Mason
1978	Mu Lambda, South Carolina, Aiken		1987	Omicron Kappa, Appalachian
1978	Mu Mu, Montevallo		1987	Omicron Theta, Marymount Manhattan
1978	Mu Nu, Pacific (CA)		1987	Omicron Zeta, Alabama, Huntsville
1978	Mu Omicron, Slippery Rock		1988	Omicron Lambda, Pembroke
1978	Mu Pi, Spelman		1988	Omicron Mu, Samford
1978	Mu Theta, North Florida		1988	Omicron Nu, Princeton
1978	Mu Xi, Winthrop		1988	Omicron Omicron, Lambuth
1978	Mu Zeta, Augusta			

Delta Sigma Theta†

ACTIVE PIN

DELTA SIGMA THETA was founded at Howard University in 1913 and incorporated under the laws of the District of Columbia on February 18 of that year.

The sorority is a member of the National Council of Negro Women.

Government Authority is vested in the biennial convention. In the interim the powers are vested in the Executive Board. Work of the organization is implemented by the Executive Director, the Executive Committee, and the National Committees under the President.

Traditions and Insignia Founders' Day is celebrated by the chapters in January.

The basic and continuing thread of the organization's public service program is its five-point Project, through which each undergraduate and alumnae chapter in 562 communities develops action programs in response to local needs. These five are educational development, economic development, community and international development, housing and urban development, and mental health.

Historically Delta has sought to widen the educational horizons of children and adults through the improvement of library services. In 1965, the organization presented a $5,000 collection of books by and about Negroes to the Omaha, Nebraska, Public Library.

With a strong base of the membership in the teaching profession, Delta has long recognized the need for Negro youth to be better prepared for the world of work. Conferences for Counselors of Minority Youth have been sponsored in conjunction with major universities.

For the eighth year, Delta has been funded by the Department of Health, Education, and Welfare, Office of Education, to conduct a Talent Search Program. Its purpose is to identify and motivate low-income high school students into appropriate post-secondary programs. The sorority was funded for three years by the National Coalition and Health Careers Information Project in thirty urban communities. Many community programs and public workshops are sponsored with the assistance of the Delta Research and Educational Foundation, established in 1970.

Delta women are active volunteers with the YWCA, NAACP, Urban League, Girl Scouts, Red Cross, and the United Community Funds. Through participation in the Women in Community Service,

Inc. program, members recruit and screen girls for Job Corps Centers.

Projects have included scholarships to women in Uganda and India, financial aid to hurricane-devastated Haiti, and construction of the Delta Maternity Wing at a hospital in Thika, Kenya.

The social action program provides legislative and other related information to the membership for the projection and implementation of projects concerning civic and human relations issues. In addition to conducting voter registration and voter education campaigns, the sorority sponsors Social Action Seminars. One of the new program thrusts of Delta is in the area of Arts and Letters.

The badge is made up of the three Greek letters ΔΣΘ in sequence, the Σ bearing nine jewels.

Publications The sorority publication is called *The Delta* which is published seven times a year.

Headquarters 1707 New Hampshire Avenue, N.W., Washington, D.C. 20009.

Membership Chapters situated in 45 states, the District of Columbia, the Virgin Islands, and Republics of Haiti and Liberia. Active chapters 292. Graduate/Alumni chapters 264. Total number of initiates 85,000. Chapter roll:††

1913	Alpha,	Howard
1914	Beta,	Wilberforce
1918	Gamma,	Penn
1919	Delta,	Iowa
1919	Epsilon,	Ohio State
1920	Zeta,	Cincinnati
1921	Kappa,	California
1921	Mu,	Pitt
1921	Nu,	Michigan
1922	Iota,	Boston
1922	Omicron,	Nebraska
1922	Xi,	Louisville
1924	Pi,	USC
1924	Rho,	CCNY
1924	Sigma,	Clark
1924	Tau,	Wayne State
1924	Upsilon,	USC
1925	Alpha Alpha,	Kansas City (KS)
1925	Alpha Beta,	Fisk
1925	Alpha Gamma,	Morgan State
1925	Chi,	Indianapolis
1925	Omega,	Cleveland
1925	Phi,	Drake
1925	Phi,	Kansas
1927	Alpha Epsilon,	Pitt
1927	Alpha Zeta,	Talladega
1929	Alpha Eta,	Virginia State
1929	Alpha Theta,	Lincoln
1930	Alpha Iota,	Wiley
1930	Alpha Kappa,	Huston-Tillotson
1932	Alpha Delta,	West Virginia State
1932	Alpha Mu,	North Carolina A & T
1932	Alpha Nu,	Illinois

† This chapter narrative is repeated from the 19th edition; no current information was provided.

†† This chapter roll is repeated from the 19th edition; no current information was provided.

1932 Alpha Omicron, Seattle	1950 Delta Iota, Grambling
1934 Alpha Chi, Tennessee A & I	1950 Delta Theta, Cal State, Sacramento
1934 Alpha Phi, Wichita	1951 Delta Kappa, Central State
1934 Alpha Pi, Kentucky State	1951 Delta Lambda, Youngstown
1934 Alpha Rho, Shaw	1952 Delta Mu, Maryland State
1934 Alpha Tau, Southern	1952 Delta Nu, Savannah
1934 Alpha Upsilon, LeMoyne-Owen	1952 Delta Omicron, St. Paul's
1934 Alpha Xi, South Carolina State	1952 Delta Pi, Jackson (MS)
1935 Alpha Omega, Harris Teachers	1952 Delta Rho, Albany State
1935 Beta Delta, Dallas	1952 Delta Xi, Fayetteville
1936 Beta Zeta, Kansas State Teachers	1953 Delta Chi, Elizabeth City
1937 Beta Alpha, Florida A & M	1953 Delta Phi, Ball State
1937 Beta Epsilon, Virginia Union	1953 Delta Tau, Cheyney State
1937 Beta Eta, Alabama State	1953 Delta Upsilon, Western Michigan
1937 Beta Gamma, Dillard	1954 Delta Psi, Detroit
1937 Beta Iota, D. C. Teachers	1955 Delta Omega, Bishop
1937 Beta Theta, Phoenix	1958 Epsilon Alpha, Delaware State
1938 Beta Lambda, Toledo	1960 Epsilon Beta, Texas
1938 Beta Mu, San Diego State	1960 Epsilon Delta, Temple
1938 Beta Nu, Gary	1960 Epsilon Epsilon, Michigan State
1938 Beta Omicron, Corpus Christi	1960 Epsilon Gamma, Penn State
1938 Beta Pi, Bluefield	1962 Epsilon Eta, Stillman
1938 Beta Rho, Fort Worth	1962 Epsilon Theta, Virginia State
1938 Beta Tau, Milwaukee	1962 Epsilon Zeta, Los Angeles State College
1939 Beta Chi, Lane	1963 Epsilon Iota, Ohio
1939 Beta Phi, Denver	1963 Epsilon Kappa, Memphis State
1939 Beta Upsilon, Langston	1964 Epsilon Mu, Kent
1940 Beta Psi, Portland	1965 Epsilon Omicron, Bowling Green
1941 Alpha Lambda, North Carolina, Durham	1966 Epsilon Chi, Southern, New Orleans
1941 Gamma Delta, Galveston	1966 Epsilon Omega, Barber-Scotia
1941 Gamma Gamma, Philander Smith	1966 Epsilon Psi, Missouri
1942 Gamma Beta, Washburn	1968 Zeta Delta, Bowie
1942 Gamma Epsilon, Texas Col	1968 Zeta Epsilon, Coppin
1942 Gamma Eta, East St. Louis (IL)	1968 Zeta Eta, North Texas
1942 Gamma Zeta, Morris Brown	1968 Zeta Gamma, Youngstown State
1943 Gamma Kappa, Buffalo	1968 Zeta Iota, Northern Illinois
1943 Gamma Lambda, Johnson C. Smith	1968 Zeta Theta, Purdue
1944 Eta, Fort Valley	1968 Zeta Zeta, Northeast Missouri
1946 Gamma Theta, Dayton	1969 Eta Alpha, Mississippi Valley
1946 Theta, Duquesne	1969 Eta Beta, Prairie View
1947 Beta Kappa, Livingstone	1969 Eta Gamma, Kansas State
1947 Gamma Iota, Hampton Inst.	1969 Zeta Chi, Southern Illinois
1947 Gamma Mu, Knoxville	1969 Zeta Kappa, Northern Michigan
1947 Gamma Nu, Indiana	1969 Zeta Lambda, Central Missouri State
1947 Gamma Xi, Omaha	1969 Zeta Mu, Miami (OH)
1947 Lambda, Chicago	1969 Zeta Nu, Indiana State
1948 Gamma Chi, Claflin	1969 Zeta Omega, Lincoln (PA)
1948 Gamma Omicron, Evanston	1969 Zeta Omicron, Greensboro
1948 Gamma Phi, Winston-Salem Teachers	1969 Zeta Phi, Georgia State
1948 Gamma Pi, Allen	1969 Zeta Pi, Denver
1948 Gamma Rho, St. Augustine's	1969 Zeta Psi, Georgia
1948 Gamma Tau, Tuskegee	1969 Zeta Rho, Ferris
1948 Gamma Upsilon, Benedict	1969 Zeta Sigma, Houston
1949 Delta Alpha, Bethune-Cookman	1969 Zeta Tau, Florida Memorial
1949 Delta Beta, Michigan State Normal	1969 Zeta Upsilon, San Antonio
1949 Delta Delta, Alabama A & M	1969 Zeta Xi, Wisconsin
1949 Delta Epsilon, Alcorn A & M	1970 Eta Chi, Nevada
1949 Delta Gamma, Texas Southern	1970 Eta Delta, Fort Worth
1949 Delta Zeta, Newark	1970 Eta Epsilon, West Texas
1949 Gamma Omega, Meharry Medical	1970 Eta Eta, Western Illinois
1949 Gamma Psi, Tougaloo Southern Christian	1970 Eta Iota, New Mexico
1950 Delta Eta, Arkansas A. & M. and N.	1970 Eta Kappa, Atlanta

1970	Eta Lambda, Texas Tech.	
1970	Eta Nu, Miles	
1970	Eta Omega, San Jose College	
1970	Eta Omicron, Morehead	
1970	Eta Phi, Voorhees	
1970	Eta Pi, Missouri, St. Louis	
1970	Eta Psi, Lamar	
1970	Eta Rho, Eastern Kentucky	
1970	Eta Sigma, Tulsa	
1970	Eta Tau, Virginia Commonwealth	
1970	Eta Theta, Paine	
1970	Eta Upsilon, Murray State	
1970	Eta Xi, Tennessee, Martin	
1970	Eta Zeta, Western Kentucky	
1970	Gamma Alpha, Xavier	
1971	Iota Alpha, Madison Col	
1971	Theta Alpha, Northwestern	
1971	Theta Beta, Pitt	
1971	Theta Chi, Camden	
1971	Theta Delta, Illinois State	
1971	Theta Epsilon, Bradley	
1971	Theta Eta, Cleveland State	
1971	Theta Gamma, Stephen F. Austin	
1971	Theta Iota, North Carolina	
1971	Theta Kappa, Jarvis Christian	
1971	Theta Lambda, Kansas State, Emporia	
1971	Theta Mu, Oklahoma State	
1971	Theta Nu, East Texas	
1971	Theta Omega, Marshall	
1971	Theta Omicron, Culver-Stockton	
1971	Theta Phi, Columbus	
1971	Theta Pi, Rust	
1971	Theta Psi, Los Angeles	
1971	Theta Rho, Tennessee	
1971	Theta Tau, Valdosta	
1971	Theta Theta, Central Michigan	
1971	Theta Upsilon, William Paterson	
1971	Theta Xi, Southwestern Louisiana	
1971	Theta Zeta, Eastern Illinois	
1971	Theta sigma, Georgia Southwestern	
1972	Iota Beta, Trenton	
1972	Iota Delta, Henderson	
1972	Iota Epsilon, Eureka	
1972	Iota Eta, Texas Christian	
1972	Iota Gamma, Texas	
1972	Iota Iota, Catholic	
1972	Iota Kappa, Arizona State	
1972	Iota Lambda, Alabama	
1972	Iota Mu, Northwestern Louisiana	
1972	Iota Nu, Mobile	
1972	Iota Omicron, Central State (OK)	
1972	Iota Pi, Miami (FL)	
1972	Iota Rho, North Carolina, Charlotte	
1972	Iota Theta, L.S.U.	
1972	Iota Xi, California State (PA)	
1972	Iota Zeta, Illinois Wesleyan	
1973	Iota Chi, South Carolina	
1973	Iota Omega, Southwest Texas	
1973	Iota Phi, Oak Park	
1973	Iota Psi, Southeastern Oklahoma	
1973	Iota Sigma, Mercer	
1973	Iota Tau, Middle Tennessee	

1973	Iota Upsilon, Austin Peay
1973	Kappa Alpha, Oklahoma
1973	Kappa Beta, Jacksonville (AL)
1973	Kappa Delta, West Georgia
1973	Kappa Eta, Wisconsin, Milwaukee
1973	Kappa Gamma, Lander
1973	Kappa Iota, South Florida
1973	Kappa Kappa, Baldwin-Wallace
1973	Kappa Lambda, Syracuse
1973	Kappa Mu, Sam Houston
1973	Kappa Nu, Indiana State
1973	Kappa Omicron, North Carolina
1973	Kappa Pi, Delta State
1973	Kappa Rho, Virginia
1973	Kappa Sigma, East Carolina
1973	Kappa Tau, Texas A & I
1973	Kappa Theta, Wisconsin, Oshkosh
1973	Kappa Xi, Arkansas State
1973	Kappa Zeta, Millikin
1974	Delta, Iowa
1974	Kappa Chi, Louisiana Tech
1974	Kappa Omega, Cal, Santa Barbara
1974	Kappa Phi, Maryland
1974	Kappa Psi, Frostburg
1974	Kappa Upsilon, Auburn
1974	Lambda Alpha, Wisconsin, Whitewater
1974	Lambda Beta, Clarion
1974	Lambda Delta, Idaho State
1974	Lambda Epsilon, Missouri
1974	Lambda Eta, Old Dominion
1974	Lambda Gamma, Millersville
1974	Lambda Iota, Providence
1974	Lambda Kappa, Maryland, Baltimore County
1974	Lambda Lambda, Ashland
1974	Lambda Mu, Southern State
1974	Lambda Nu, Paul Quinn
1974	Lambda Omicron, Charleston (SC)
1974	Lambda Pi, Grand Valley
1974	Lambda Rho, Northeast Louisiana
1974	Lambda Tau, Pacific (CA)
1974	Lambda Theta, Arkansas
1974	Lambda Upsilon, State College of Arkansas
1974	Lambda Xi, Cal, Davis
1974	Lambda Zeta, Alabama
1975	Lambda Chi, Texas
1975	Lambda Omega, Duke
1975	Lambda Phi, Marquette
1975	Lambda Psi, Florida
1975	Mu Alpha, V.P.I.
1975	Mu Beta, George Washington
1975	Mu Delta, Findlay
1975	Mu Epsilon, Kentucky
1975	Mu Eta, Arizona
1975	Mu Gamma, Ithaca
1975	Mu Iota, Florida Tech
1975	Mu Kappa, Arkansas
1975	Mu Lambda, New Mexico State
1975	Mu Mu, Towson
1975	Mu Nu, Southern Mississippi
1975	Mu Omicron, North Carolina State
1975	Mu Pi, Delaware

1975   Mu Rho, Peabody College & Vanderbilt
1975   Mu Sigma, Cameron
1975   Mu Theta, Lewis
1975   Mu Xi, Augusta
1975   Mu Zeta, Knoxville
1976   Mu Chi, Cal, Rialto
1976   Mu Omega, Georgia Medical
1976   Mu Phi, Flint
1976   Mu Psi, Johns Hopkins
1976   Mu Tau, New Orleans
1976   Mu Upsilon, William and Mary
1976   Nu Alpha, American
1976   Nu Beta, Mississippi State
1976   Nu Delta, Southeastern Louisiana
1976   Nu Epsilon, Minneapolis
1976   Nu Eta, Indiana Northwest
1976   Nu Gamma, Northwest Missouri
1976   Nu Iota, Southern Methodist
1976   Nu Kappa, West Florida
1976   Nu Theta, Troy
1976   Nu Zeta, Southeastern Massachusetts

Sigma Gamma Rho

ACTIVE PIN

PLEDGE PIN

SIGMA GAMMA RHO was organized on November 12, 1922 in Indianapolis, Indiana by Mary Lou Allison (Mrs. Little) and six other teachers: Dorothy Hanley (Mrs. Whiteside), Vivian White (Mrs. Marbury), Nannie Mae Gahn (Mrs. Johnson), Hattie Mae Dulin (Mrs. Redford), Bessie M. Downey (Mrs. Martin), and Cubena McClure. The charter members are the founders of Sigma Gamma Rho. The group became an incorporated national collegiate sorority on December 30, 1929, when a charter was granted Alpha Chapter at Butler University.

Growth   The first three years were devoted to organizing. The first call for a national boule (convention) was held in Indianapolis, December 27-29, 1925. The second was held in Louisville, Kentucky, at which time Fannie O'Bannon became the grand basileus.

The first grand basileus, Mary Lou Little wrote the sorority pledge. The pin was designed by Cubena McClure. The slogan, Greater Service, Greater Progress, was written by Bertha Black Rhoda, a past grand basileus. Members of the Delta Chapter wrote the words of the sorority song, which has since been set to music by Zenobia Laws Bailey of Chicago. The Aurora Club ceremony was written by Ruth Cooper Armstrong, a former national organizer. Fannie O'Bannon, the second grand basileus designed the sorority coat of arms.

In keeping with the ideals of Sigma Gamma Rho, the national organization maintains membership in and/or supports the following: National Association for the Advancement of Colored People, National Council of Negro Women, National Panhellenic Council, Leadership Conference on Civil Rights, National Association for the Study of Afro-American Life and History, National Urban League, March of Dimes Birth Defects Foundation, National Mental Health Association, United Negro College Fund, Martin Luther King Center for Non-Violent Social Change, Black Women's Agenda, and American Association of University Women.

Government   For administrative purposes, the chapters are divided into five regions, according to their geographical locations. Each region elects a regional director (syntaktes), undergraduate chapter coordinator, and a youth services coordinator who is an undergraduate. The regional syntaktes who is in charge of each region, looks after much of the detail and routine work of the respective chapters. The undergraduate chapter coordinator works closely with her in planning and conducting campus chapter activities in the region. The second grand anti-basileus (a college soror) assists youth services coordinators with undergraduate activities as duties are assigned. All regional officers are under the direct supervision of the first grand anti-basileus. National and/or regional officers are available to visit chapters, upon request, when information and workshops are needed on operational procedure.

Traditions and Insignia   Activities are encouraged that will further, in every way possible, the advantages of members socially, morally, and intellectually. To this end the membership assumes the responsibility: (a) to provide an atmosphere in which friendship and social contacts may be developed, (b) to assist each member in developing social graces by emphasizing the value of poise and personal dignity, (c) to encourage and promote high scholastic attainment, (d) to develop leadership abilities and individual talents, (e) to maintain interest and attitudes in harmony with modern thought and changing educational outlook. To be eligible for membership an undergraduate student must: (a) be matriculated on a four-year accredited college campus and working toward a bachelor's degree, (b) maintain high scholastic standing, (c) give evidence of interests and abilities for growth in leadership, social, and democratic principles, (d) maintain high standards of character and reputation acceptable to the school and organization.

The alumnae chapters function as advisory and financial resources. They give guidance in organizational structure, school adjustment, and the transition from school to careers. They provide financial assistance through grants of scholarships, fellowships, and loans. They sponsor the annual financial and cultural project of Sigma Gamma Rho, "Rhomania," an activity in which all chapters are required to participate. This project creates opportunities for leadership, social development, and an atmosphere where social graces and democratic principles may be practiced. It may take any one of the following forms: extravaganza in music by graduate, undergraduate, or local talent; presentation of outstanding artists (Sigma if possible); teas, fashion shows; plays (with chapter or other talent).

Leadership training programs for teenagers and youth are sponsored at the national and local levels as means of implementing the national project of the sorority which is known as National Youth Projects. These programs are geared around youth and their development. In their various forms they include Guidance Clinics, Youth Programs, Community Activities, and any other program and or activity geared to the education and development of youth. Some activities are designed to assist in combating juvenile delinquency and preparing youth for leadership by furnishing workshops where youth of 13 to 18 may spend their leisure time studying and also enjoying such worthwhile activities as handicraft, music, dramatics, painting, drawing, and other forms of creative endeavor.

Leadership training for all chapters is conducted during area meetings and regional conferences that are held annually. These training programs are evaluated at each boule where professional consultants in leadership training help to direct the workshops which are important features of the convention.

During the month of November every chapter observes Founders Week. The program may consist of the presentation of prominent speakers, radio and TV programs, or any representative program designed to acquaint the general public with the program of Sigma Gamma Rho. Founders Day is celebrated November 12 with re-dedication services as a means of strengthening the spirit of the sorority and re-emphasizing its goals and purposes.

The flower is the tea rose; the colors are royal blue and gold. The Coat-of-Arms consists of the Lamp of Learning, a quill, a serpent, two stars, skull and crossbone, and a bundle of sticks with an ax.

The pin is an open book representing knowledge. The foundation of the whole pin is a torch which represents the existence of the organization. There are ten pearls on the edge of the book and two rubies at the base. The grand basileus' pin is a replica of the sorority's pin encircled by a laurel wreath which signifies the highest esteem of the membership; a gavel for the guard represents supreme authority. There is also a past grand basileus' pin. Honorary members are privileged to wear the sorority pin without a guard.

Awards The most coveted honor is the Blanche Edwards Award which is bestowed at each convention upon the most outstanding Sigma of the year for achievement of national scope. Other national awards include:

Annie W. Neville Talent Award—A trophy given to the winner of the undergraduate talent competition.

Evelyn Hawkins Hood Distinguished Service to Mankind Award—A plaque, given to an outstanding person in the community whom the sorority recognizes for outstanding achievement in human and community service.

Dr. Annie Lane Lawrence Mental Health Achievement Award—A trophy given to a member for outstanding service in providing Mental Health Education to the general public.

Dr. Lorraine A. Williams Award—A trophy given to the chapter and soror who contributed the greatest amount of historical materials during the past biennial.

Dr. Rejesta V. Perry Project Reassurance Award—An award given for the best documentation of a local chapter Project Reassurance Project.

Sigma Torch Award—A trophy presented at the Boule to the outstanding campus chapter for increased membership.

The Mary Lou Allison Loving Cup Award—Presented to the chapter reporting the most successful program.

Hattie Redford Awards—Two plaques—awarded to the graduate and undergraduate chapters for the best implementation of national theme exhibited by chapter report, scrapbook and exhibits.

The Gwendolyn Cherry Medallion—An award given for excellence in government service.

Publications The Aurora, the official quarterly of Sigma Gamma Rho, was begun in 1930. Its purpose is to keep chapters informed on chapter news and Sigma accomplishments. Copies are also made available in college libraries where chapters are located. The Handbook is for members and chapters to follow as a pattern of procedure.

The first edition of a Directory was published in 1948; revisions have followed keeping pace with the growth of the sorority.

Funds and Philanthropies In 1984 the Sigma Gamma Rho National Education Fund was established as a separate corporation. Its mission includes providing scholarship assistance to deserving youth (male and females of all races,) and supporting programs and research related to education and health. It is a 501 (c) 3 fund which gives thousands of dollars in scholarships annually, five of which are regional awards given to eligible undergraduate members.

Sigma Gamma Rho awards annually a fellowship to an eligible member for study towards a higher degree. In addition to this, each chapter presents annual scholarships and awards to outstanding high school and college students in its community.

Each Boule year, the sorority selects a national theme. This theme emphasizes the involvement of the membership in community service projects, human relations, and civil rights activities as well as upon the paramount objective of motivation and assistance to young people in attaining higher education.

Sigma Gamma Rho, in its quest to expand its area of service, actively participates in the sponsoring of national and international programs designed for the improved welfare of all people. These include, but are not limited to: (1) Support of Project Africa—a program in conjunction with Africare, a leading Washington agency, that provides African women with agricultural assistance. (2) Financial contribution to The Vocational Guidance and Workshop Center of New York City, which has 501 (c) 3 status and is designed to service youth 9-19 years of age, who need tutorial service, GED preparation and/or career counseling. (3) Endorsement of our nation's programs of Mental Health and Human Relations, implemented by local, state, regional, and national sorority representation and participation in these programs. (4) Annual observance of George Washington Carver Day by all chapters in order to project to the larger community the scientific and humanitarian contributions made by this renowned scientist. (5) Sponsoring jointly with the March of Dimes Birth Defects Foundation a health education program where counseling support and educational information is distributed to teenagers, their parents and grand-parents. (Project Reassurance)

Headquarters 8800 S. Stony Island Avenue, Chicago, Illinois 60617. The staff includes the Executive Secretary and other full-time administrative and clerical employees.

Membership Active chapters 172. Inactive chapters 48. Graduate/Alumni chapters 169. Inactive alumnae chapters 21. Total number of initiates 71,000. Chapter roll:

Year	Chapter
1922	Alpha, Butler
1923	Beta, Indiana State
1929	Zeta, Cleveland
1936	Alpha Theta, Lewis
1937	Alpha Delta, Harris-Stowe
1937	Alpha Mu, Lincoln (MO)
1938	Alpha Eta, Wayne State (MI)
1938	Alpha Lambda, Texas Southern
1938	Alpha Omicron, LeMoyne-Owen
1938	Alpha Phi, Howard
1938	Alpha Zeta, Virginia State, Petersburg
1938	Psi, Southern Illinois
1939	Alpha Gamma, Lane
1939	Eta, Northwestern
1940	Alpha Tau, Jackson (MS)
1940	Mu, Ball State
1940	Omicron, Dillard
1941	Delta, Xavier (OH)
1941	Iota, Langston
1942	Alpha Beta, Tennessee State
1943	Alpha Chi, Arkansas
1943	Alpha Xi, Philander Smith
1945	Alpha Omega, Huston-Tillotson
1945	Alpha Upsilon, Fisk
1946	Alpha Epsilon, Florida A & M
1946	Beta Beta, Alcorn
1946	Beta Gamma, Wiley
1947	Beta Epsilon, Benedict
1947	Lambda, Kentucky State
1948	Beta, D. C. Teachers
1949	Alpha Iota, Savannah
1950	Beta Alpha, Southern
1950	Beta Eta, Bethune-Cookman
1950	Beta Iota, Allen
1950	Beta Theta, Shaw
1950	Nu, St. Augustine's
1950	Theta, Claflin
1951	Beta Kappa, Texas Col.
1951	Gamma, North Carolina A & T
1951	Rho, Winston-Salem
1951	Tau, Virginia Union
1952	Beta Lambda, Morris Brown
1952	Beta Nu, St. Paul's
1952	Beta Omicron, North Carolina Central
1952	Beta Pi, Arizona State
1952	Phi, Clark
1954	Beta Tau, Morgan State
1955	Beta Upsilon, Johnson C. Smith
1956	Gamma Pi, L.S.U.
1957	Beta Phi, Cheyney State
1958	Beta Chi, Alabama State
1960	Beta Omega, Grambling
1960	Gamma Alpha, Monrovia
1962	Gamma Delta, Bishop
1962	Gamma Epsilon, Kent
1962	Gamma Gamma, Knoxville
1964	Gamma Iota, Paul Quinn
1964	Gamma Nu, Norfolk
1964	Gamma Xi, Florida Memorial
1966	Epsilon, Indiana Northwest
1968	Gamma Chi, Memphis State
1968	Gamma Omega, Michigan State
1968	Gamma Phi, Coppin
1968	Gamma Upsilon, Southern
1968	Nu Psi, Southern Illinois
1969	Delta Alpha, Prairie View
1969	Delta Rho, Illinois
1969	Gamma Kappa, Cal State, Long Beach
1969	Gamma Psi, Emporia
1970	Chi, Wichita (1973)
1970	Delta Epsilon, Eastern Michigan
1970	Delta Eta, Miles
1970	Delta Iota, Fayetteville
1970	Delta Kappa, Northeast Missouri
1970	Delta Nu, Minnesota
1970	Delta Omicron, Paine
1970	Delta Pi, Central Missouri State
1970	Delta Tau, Elizabeth City
1970	Delta Zeta, Ferris
1971	Beta Beta, Indiana State
1971	Delta Beta, Eastern Illinois
1971	Delta Omega, Central State (OH)
1971	Delta Phi, Ohio State
1971	Delta Upsilon, Edward Waters
1971	Delta Xi, Barber-Scotia
1971	Epsilon Chi, Indiana
1971	Kappa, Wilberforce
1972	Beta Gamma, Wiley
1972	Delta Chi, Talladega
1972	Epsilon Beta, Western Illinois
1972	Epsilon Delta, Florida State
1972	Epsilon Gamma, Purdue
1972	Epsilon Tau, Alcorn
1972	Epsilon Zeta, Virginia Commonwealth

1972	Kappa Upsilon, Jarvis Christian
1973	Alpha Rho, Missouri
1973	Delta Mu, Oregon
1973	Epsilon Eta, Spellman
1973	Epsilon Lambda, Bowie
1973	Epsilon Omicron, San Jose
1973	Epsilon Phi, Cal State, Northridge
1973	Epsilon Pi, Houston
1973	Epsilon Theta, Tuskegee
1973	Epsilon Xi, Wisconsin, Madison
1973	Gamma Epsilon, Kent
1973	Gamma Rho, Illinois State
1973	Zeta Alpha, Bowling Green
1974	Epsilon Omega, Wisconsin, Whitewater
1974	Zeta Delta, Delaware State
1974	Zeta Epsilon, Louisiana Tech
1974	Zeta Kappa, South Carolina State
1974	Zeta Mu, Lewis
1974	Zeta Theta, South Carolina
1975	Zeta Chi, Alabama
1975	Zeta Lambda, St. Thomas
1975	Zeta Nu, Northern Illinois
1975	Zeta Phi, Bradley
1975	Zeta Pi, Fort Valley
1975	Zeta Psi, Albany State
1975	Zeta Xi, Hampton Inst.
1976	Epsilon Iota, Nebraska Wesleyan
1976	Eta Alpha, North Texas
1976	Eta Beta, Maryland
1976	Eta Chi, Purdue, Calumet
1976	Eta Epsilon, Western Michigan
1976	Eta Iota, Kansas
1976	Zeta Omicron, West Virginia State
1976	Zeta Rho, Northwest Missouri
1976	Zeta Upsilon, Northern Colorado
1977	Eta Kappa, Stillman
1977	Eta Lambda, Cal State, Bakersfield
1977	Eta Mu, East Carolina
1977	Eta Omicron, Voorhees
1977	Eta Pi, Saginaw Valley
1977	Eta Xi, Towson
1978	Epsilon Rho, Akron
1978	Eta Phi, Western Kentucky
1978	Eta Tau, Southern Mississippi
1978	Eta Upsilon, Rutgers
1978	Nu Gamma, Cincinnati
1979	Eta Nu, Texas Woman's
1979	Eta Omega, Louisville
1979	Theta Alpha, Wisconsin, Oshkosh
1980	Eta Psi, Ohio
1980	Iota Psi, Michigan
1980	Theta Epsilon, USC
1980	Theta Gamma, Tougaloo
1980	Theta Kappa, Baldwin-Wallace
1980	Theta Lambda, Missouri
1980	Theta Mu, Glassboro
1980	Theta Zeta, Marquette
1981	Theta Eta, Drake
1981	Theta Omicron, Delaware
1981	Theta Pi, Central State (OH)
1981	Theta Rho, Cleveland
1981	Theta Tau, Syracuse

1981	Theta Upsilon, South Florida
1982	Iota Zeta, Missouri, Kansas City
1982	Kappa Beta, Bakers
1982	Theta Chi, Old Dominion
1982	Theta Omega, Stockton
1982	Theta Phi, Mississippi State
1982	Theta Psi, Iowa State
1983	Iota Eta, Morris
1983	Kappa Delta, Marshall
1983	Kappa Epsilon, Long Island
1983	Kappa Eta, Iowa
1983	Kappa Lambda, Indiana (PA)
1983	Kappa Zeta, Texas Tech
1983	Theta Nu, Pitt
1984	Kappa Mu, Sam Houston
1984	Kappa Nu, Northeastern
1985	Kappa Chi, Mississippi Valley
1985	Kappa Psi, V.P.I.
1986	Kappa Gamma, Tennessee, Martin
1986	Kappa Theta, Northeast Louisiana
1987	Kappa Iota, Alabama A & M
1987	Kappa Omega, North Carolina
1987	Kappa Omicron, SUNY Col., New Paltz
1987	Kappa Pi, SUNY Col., Buffalo
1987	Kappa Rho, Penn State
1987	Kappa Xi, SUNY Col., Old Westbury
1988	Lambda Alpha, Millersville
1988	Lambda Beta, Valdosta
1988	Lambda Delta, Georgia
1988	Lambda Epsilon, West Georgia
1989	Lambda Eta, Southeast Missouri
1989	Lambda Gamma, West Virginia
1989	Lambda Iota, James Madison
1989	Lambda Kappa, Winthrop
1989	Lambda Theta, Northwestern Louisiana
1989	Lambda Zeta, SUNY, Binghamton
1990	Lambda Chi, Middle Tennessee
1990	Lambda Lambda, Texas A & M
1990	Lambda Mu, Central Florida
1990	Lambda Omega, SUNY, New York
1990	Lambda Omicron, Cornell
1990	Lambda Phi, Maryland, Baltimore County
1990	Lambda Pi, Trenton
1990	Lambda Rho, Florida
1990	Lambda Tau, SUNY, Stony Brook
1990	Lambda Upsilon, Oklahoma
1991	Lambda Nu, Stephen F. Austin
1991	Lambda Psi, North Carolina
1991	Lambda Xi, Central Arkansas
1991	Mu Alpha, UCLA
1991	Mu Beta, Tennessee
1991	Mu Delta, West Chester
1991	Mu Gamma, Charleston (SC)

Metropolitan Chapters:

1938	Alpha Pi, New York, NY
1947	Beta Delta, Philadelphia, PA
1950	Alpha Nu, Los Angeles, CA
1954	Beta Rho, Chicago, IL
1957	Beta Psi, Berkeley, CA
1961	Gamma Beta, East St. Louis, IL
1962	Gamma Zeta, Indianapolis, IN

1963 Gamma Theta, Newark, NJ
1964 Gamma Mu, Baltimore, MD
1965 Gamma Eta, Oklahoma City, OK
1966 Gamma Omicron, Denver, CO
1967 Gamma Tau, Little Rock, AR
1970 Delta Gamma, San Diego, CA
1971 Delta Lambda, Shreveport, LA
1972 Delta Psi, Tallahassee, FL
1973 Epsilon Mu, Compton, CA
1975 Zeta Tau, Beaumont, TX
1976 Zeta Iota, Chattanooga, TN
1977 Eta Delta, San Diego, CA
1977 Eta Zeta, Milwaukee, WI
1978 Eta Rho, Knoxville, TN
1979 Epsilon Mu, San Antonio, TX
1980 Iota Gamma, Longview, TX
1980 Omega Tau, Houston, TX
1980 Psi Delta, Seattle, WA
1980 Theta Delta, Galveston, TX
1981 Theta Xi, Omaha, NE
1983 Kappa Tau, Tulsa, OK
1984 Kappa Phi, Stockton, CA

Colonies: Cal State, Long Beach, Bradley, Central Michigan, Kansas, Oakland, South Suburban Chicago

Zeta Phi Beta†

ZETA PHI BETA was organized at Howard University on January 16, 1920, as the result of the encouragement given the five founders by Charles Robert Samuel Taylor, a Phi Beta Sigma Fraternity leader, who felt that the campus would profit by his chapter having a sister organization. In 1915 A. Langston Taylor had recommended to Phi Beta Sigma that it should help in the establishment of a sorority, and in 1919 the general board of the fraternity passed his recommendation without a dissenting vote.

As a result, Arizona Cleaver, Viola Tyler, Myrtle Tyler, Pearl Neale, and Fannie Pettie became founders of Zeta Phi Beta, aided by Charles Taylor, and thus it with Phi Beta Sigma became the first Greek-letter sister and brother organization. Zeta Phi Beta held its first boule (convention) jointly with the Phi Beta Sigma conclave in December, 1920, in Washington, D.C. It was the idea of the founders that the sorority would reach college women in all parts of the country who were sorority-minded and desired to follow the ideal of finer womanhood that Zeta Phi Beta had set up.

The new sorority was introduced to the Howard University community by a formal reception at the Whitelaw Hotel, Washington, D.C., by Langston and Charles Taylor and by a meeting in the assembly room of Miner Hall at Howard University by Alpha Kappa Alpha and Delta Sigma Theta, other Negro sororities.

† This chapter narrative is repeated from the 19th edition; no current information was provided.

The first president of Zeta Phi Beta was Arizona Cleaver (Stemons), who in the first forty-six years of the organization has watched it spread to all sections of the United States and parts of Africa with undergraduate and graduate chapters divided into eight regions, with honorary members of renown, and with the strength and means to contribute to the encouragement of higher scholarship and to those organizations working for the betterment of communities and the world.

As a nonprofit corporation incorporated in Washington, D.C., and also in the state of Illinois, the sorority is supported only by annual dues paid by its members for operating expenses. Scholarships are donated annually from a special fund contributed by chapter members.

Government In 1922 Zeta Phi Beta found it necessary to establish the National Board to take over the responsibilities which had been carried on by Alpha Chapter, and by June, 1927, the growth of the organization made possible its first regional meeting, held at Howard University. The chapters are grouped into eight regions. Atlantic, Eastern, Southeastern, South-Central, Great Lakes, Midwestern, Pacific, and Southern, each with an appointed director.

Zeta Phi Beta was incorporated under the laws of the District of Columbia on March 30, 1923. The incorporators were Myrtle Tyler, Gladys Warrington, Joanna Houston, Josephine Johnson, and Goldie Smith.

Traditions The objectives of finer womanhood, sisterly love, and scholarship have brought together women from all parts of the country—women who have similar tastes and aspirations, similar potentialities for highest attainments, and similar desires for concerted action which will bring results in removing or blocking movements intended to retard the growth and progress of this group of women, especially in the field of academic and literary attainments.

The membership of Zeta Phi Beta includes women in the professions of medicine, law, dentistry, pharmacy, the fine arts, invention, music, painting, and all of the fields of higher learning. These women have become an integral part of the community life of the country and have interested themselves in civic and social betterment throughout the country. Wherever adverse legislation affecting minority groups has been proposed Zeta Phi Beta has been active in making its voice heard in protestation and appeal for fair play, in telegrams, letters to congressmen and senators, and public protest meetings. Zeta has been outstanding in carrying its share of community relief work, in participation in voluntary war services, in the armed forces here and abroad, in contributing to organized charity, as well as in granting scholarships to deserving women students. The sorority sponsored a national juvenile delinquency project the first forty-five years of its existence. Different aspects were highlighted through special projects such as: foster home care, youth conferences, vocational guidance clinics, tinker shops, and the development of youth groups. Other special projects are demonstrated locally: parental clinics, Finer Womanhood Week, cotillions for youth, youth camps and campership, volunteers to numerous social and health agencies, leadership conferences.

During the forty-fifth anniversary boule, the membership voted to extend, and expand the national project, Welfare, Education, and Health Services (WEHS), with emphasis on lifting the levels of the local community in the areas of leadership, as well as an individual attack upon poverty, ignorance, education and self-help.

There has been a six-point African project jointly conducted by the chapters in America and Africa. The Domestic Science Center in Monrovia, Africa, is a partnership undertaking which involves American Zetas, Liberian Zetas, CARE, and the students who will benefit.

Zeta Phi Beta sponsors a parent training program with satellite centers as a part of family life education under Operation Bootstrap in Goldsboro, North Carolina.

Publications The first official organ, the *X-Ray*, made its appearance in 1923 but in 1930 gave way to *The Archon* as the national publication which is issued twice yearly, in April and November. In 1930 and again in 1936, the *Blue Book*, a compilation of outstanding achievements of Zeta sorors, was published by the sorority. Another publication, no longer issued, was *Chapter Chatters*.

Headquarters 1734 New Hampshire Avenue, N. W., Washington, D.C. 20009. The building of red brick, decorated with gray stone, has three stories and a basement. The first floor contains approximately 5,000 square feet of usable space, including the master ballroom, two large parlors, and other facilities. The second floor consists of a conference room and five other large rooms, one of which is used for the National Office. Other rooms are shared by the grand basileus and executive secretary for living quarters. The third floor contains eight bedrooms, and attendant facilities. A complete recreation room, kitchen, a powder room, men's lounge, and several storage rooms make up the basement. Other features include a rathskeller room and patio and a four-car garage.

Membership Active and inactive undergraduate chapters 85. Total number of initiates 11,300. Chapter roll:††

Alpha, Howard
Alpha Alpha, Chicago
Alpha Beta, Dillard
Alpha Gamma, Elizabeth City
Beta, Morris Brown
Beta Alpha, Southern
Beta Beta, Arkansas, Pine Bluff

†† This chapter roll is repeated from the 19th edition; no current information was provided.

Beta Gamma, Oklahoma City
Chi, Cheyney State
Chi Alpha, Trenton
Chi Beta, Central State (OH)
Delta, San Antonio
Delta Alpha, Texas Col
Delta Beta, Fort Valley
Delta Gamma, Camden
Epsilon, New York City
Epsilon Alpha, Tennessee State
Epsilon Beta, Alabama State
Epsilon Gamma, Stillman
Eta, Philadelphia
Eta Alpha, Kentucky State
Eta Beta, Maryland, Eastern Shore
Eta Gamma, Tulsa
Gamma, Morgan State
Gamma Alpha, Florida A & M
Gamma Beta, San Francisco
Gamma Gamma, North Carolina College
Iota, Talledega
Iota Alpha, Florida Normal and Industrial
Iota Beta, West Virginia State
Iota Gamma, Rust
Kappa, Johnson C. Smith
Kappa Alpha, D. C. Teachers
Kappa Beta, Benedict
Kappa Gamma, Fisk
Lambda, Allen
Lambda Alpha, Langston
Lambda Beta, Jackson (MS)
Lambda Gamma, McNeese
Mu, Claflin
Mu Alpha, Bluefield
Mu Beta, Bethune-Cookman
Mu Gamma, Edward Waters
Nu, Union (VA)
Nu Alpha, Texas Southern
Nu Beta, Tougaloo
Nu Gamma, Baltimore
Omega, Winston-Salem
Omega Beta, Fayetteville
Omicron, Shaw
Omicron Alpha, Hollis (NY)
Omicron Beta, Brooklyn
Phi, Virginia State, Petersburg
Phi Alpha, St. Louis
Phi Beta, St. Augustine's
Pi, Knoxville
Pi Alpha, LeMoyne-Owen
Pi Beta, Albany State
Psi, Clark Col., Atlanta
Psi Alpha, South Carolina State
Psi Beta, Grambling
Rho, Bishop
Rho Alpha, Hampton Inst.
Rho Beta, Savannah
Sigma, Livingstone
Sigma Alpha, Cincinnati
Sigma Beta, Alabama A & M
Tau, Philander Smith
Tau Alpha, Omaha

Tau Beta, Paul Quinn
Theta, Wiley
Theta Alpha, Boston
Theta Beta, Tuskegee Inst.
Theta Gamma, Barber-Scotia
Upsilon, Dover
Upsilon Alpha, Huston-Tillotson
Upsilon Beta, Monrovia (Liberia)
Xi, Detroit
Xi Alpha, Los Angeles
Xi Beta, Lincoln (MO)
Zeta, Alcorn A & M
Zeta Alpha, North Carolina A & T
Zeta Beta, Southern, New Orleans
Zeta Gamma, Virginia State, Norfolk

Other Women's Sororities

Ceres

CERES International Women's Fraternity was founded on August 17, 1984, at the FarmHouse International Fraternity Conclave held in Fort Collins, Colorado. The three founding colonies—Colorado State University, University of Alberta, and California State Polytechnic University—were aware that some persons still demean the role of farmers in society. Moreover, women were not duly recognized as significant contributors to the field of Agriculture. With this in mind, the name CERES was chosen to signify the membership of the organization, and to indicate pride in, and the importance of agricultural heritage.

CERES, the Roman Goddess of Agriculture—grain, harvest, fruit, flowers and fertility of the earth—represents the historic involvement in and importance of the role of women in Agriculture. The name, CERES, is one of the few non-Greek names among women's fraternities and is proudly retained for reasons that led to its selection. Although CERES is an Agricultural women's fraternity, members study in a variety of academic fields including Agriculture, Home Economics, Education, Business, Arts, and Science. Members demonstrate qualities of character, scholarship, and professional excellence and generally come from a rural background or share an Agricultural interest.

Although most women's social groups are commonly known as sororities, they are legally incorporated as fraternities for women. CERES has chosen to retain the fraternal title to exemplify a commitment to uniqueness. As a group of women whose roots or interest in Agriculture has brought them together, the CERES commitment to Agriculture sets it apart from other women's social groups; so does the name—CERES Fraternity.

Growth CERES currently receives its staff support from the FarmHouse Fraternity staff and holds a Biennial Conclave and series of workshops in conjunction with FarmHouse gatherings. This will continue to occur until a change of relationships occur between the two organizations. Additionally, an emphasis placed on expansion finds CERES looking to continue and broaden its past growth.

Government The governing body is the Biennial Conclave to which each active chapter and association selects a voting delegate. When the Conclave is not in session, an International Executive Board of Directors is empowered to decide all questions pertaining to the welfare of the Fraternity and its membership.

Locally, each chapter receives counseling and guidance from a Chapter Advisory Committee and an Alumnae Association.

Traditions and Insignia The Conclave recognizes and awards chapters who have excelled in five different areas of Chapter Achievement as well as an award for Outstanding Chapter. Also recognized and honored at Conclave is a "Friend of Ceres" selected by the International Executive Board for their unselfish contributions to the betterment of CERES Fraternity.

The Fraternity flower is the sterling silver rose; the gemstones are amethyst and pearl; and the colors are violet and gold.

The badge is a gold pin with 3 amethysts across the top and a pearl at the bottom. The word "CERES" in gold is printed on a white enamel banner positioned diagonally from upper left to lower right. The banner separates an etched rose above and an etched scroll below.

The pledge pin is a gold pin with an etched "C" bordered by etched wheat stalks.

Publications The quarterly magazine is *The Rose and Scroll* sent to all initiated members for life.

Headquarters The Pioneer Building; 510 Francis, Suite #314; St. Joseph, MO 64501.

Membership Active chapters 6. Total number of initiates 225. Chapter roll:

1985 Colorado State
1986 Alberta
1986 Cal Poly, Pomona
1987 Cal State, Fresno
1989 Montana State
1989 Wisconsin, Platteville

Kappa Beta Gamma[†]

KAPPA BETA GAMMA was founded at Marquette University as the first sorority on that campus, on January 22. 1917, by Tess Jermain, Myra Thewalt, Jeanie Lee, Mary Weimar, and eight other young women.

Their purpose was to foster and unite in the eternal bond of sisterly confidence and affection the friendships developed among their members during their college days; to improve and aid their members socially, morally, and intellectually: to foster and perpetuate support of college, university, and alma mater, and of God and country.

Government Officers are elected to the National Executive Board at the biennial convention and serve for a two-year term. Each chapter drafts and maintains a constitution of its own consistent with the provisions of the national constitution.

Traditions and Insignia An outstanding tradition is the Star Cake Ceremony held at the last rush tea. Each point of the star signifies one of the five ideals of the sorority.

The official pin consists of a wreath of six pearls and six sapphires encircling the Greek letters KBΓ. The pledge pin resembles the center of the member pin.

The coat of arms and seal is a shield containing a torch with a heart on each side and each heart connected to the torch by a linked chain. The forget-me-not flower, which is the official flower, rests above the shield. A scroll beneath the shield bears the Greek letters KBΓ.

Membership Active chapters 4. Inactive chapters 5. Chapter roll[††]:

1917 *Beta, Marquette*
1947 *Alpha, St. Louis*
1948 Delta, Detroit
1948 *Gamma, Creighton* (1953)
1954 Epsilon, Loyola, Chicago
1961 Eta, U of Americas
1961 *Zeta, Loyola, New Orleans*
1963 *Theta, St. Norbert*
1969 Iota, St. John's

Lambda Delta Sigma

LAMBDA DELTA SIGMA was founded in Salt Lake City, Utah, in 1967. Dr. Frank Bradshaw, Alfred C. Nielsen, and Elaine A. Cannon were called to prepare materials and recommendations pertaining to the organization of this women's sorority for the Church of Jesus Christ of Latter-day Saints. After extensive research, a constitution was adopted and a slate of national officers was established at the first national convention in Salt Lake City.

Lambda Delta Sigma is a social service organization for college women based on the highest principles of Christian living. It provides an opportunity for sisterhood and personal growth. Its philosophy is based on five ideals: *spirituality, sisterhood, scholarship, the supporting role of woman,* and *service.* Membership is open to all college women, regardless of race, color, or creed, who are willing to live the ideals and standards according to the constitution and by-laws.

Traditions and Insignia The pin consists of three stacked gold Greek letters with the Sigma centered and jeweled with five blue sapphires symbolizing the five ideals. The artistically designed crest, bearing the symbols of the stone on a peaceful palm, a quill pen, a lighted lamp, and a heart, is superimposed on an oval background. These symbols are topped with a gold crown, and cupping the bottom of the crest are the Greek words Lambda Delta Sigma. The colors are azure, gold, and white. The yellow chrysanthemum is the official flower. The motto is, "Upon one strength another is built."

Publications *The Quill* is the official publication and is issued quarterly. The national office has monthly communication with chapter officers through a one-page publication, *The Hotline.* A collection of music was made into a booklet in 1974. The pledge manual was first published in 1971 and has twice been revised. Instruction manual with officers' duties, first published in 1974, is continually updated.

Headquarters 50 East North Temple, Salt Lake City, Utah 84150, 8th floor of the office building of the Church of Jesus Christ of Latter-day Saints.

Membership Chapters installed on 22 campuses between March, 1969, and January, 1977. Active chapters 47. Total number of initiates 11,000. Chapter roll:[††]

Arizona State
Arizona
Boise
Cal State, Long Beach
Cal State, Los Angeles
Cerritos Junior College (CA)
Dixie
Eastern Arizona
Eastern Utah
El Camino Junior
Fullerton Junior College (CA)
Glendale Junior College (CA)
Grossmont Junior College (CA)
Idaho State
Idaho
Latter-day Saints Business College
Los Angeles Valley Junior College
Mesa Community (AZ)
Mount San Antonio (CA)
Nevada

† This chapter narrative is repeated from the 19th edition; no current information was provided.
†† This chapter roll is repeated from the 19th edition; no current information was provided.

New Mexico State
Northern Arizona
Ohio State
Orange Coast Junior College (CA)
Pierce Junior College (CA)
Ricks
Riverside City College (CA)
San Bernadino Valley
San Fernando Valley

Santa Monica City College (CA)
Snow (UT)
Southern Utah
Texas, El Paso
Utah State
Utah Tech, Provo
Utah
Weber
Wyoming

Part V

The Professional Fraternities

Alpha Chi Sigma

(CHEMISTRY)

ACTIVE PIN

PLEDGE PIN

ALPHA CHI SIGMA was founded at the University of Wisconsin in December, 1902, by J. Howard Mathews, Joseph G. Holty, Frank J. Petura, Alfred E. Kundert, Harold E. Eggers, James C. Silverthorn, Bart Eldred McCormick, E. G. Mattke, and R. T. Conger. Its membership is drawn from students of chemistry or chemical engineering who intend to make some phase of chemistry their life work. Members of noncompetitive undergraduate fraternities are admitted, providing they fulfill the requirements for admission, but the fraternity discontinued the election of honorary members many years ago. Graduate chemists of merit may be elected to active membership through affirmative joint action of a collegiate chapter and a professional chapter.

In 1970, the fraternity law was changed to eliminate the word "male" and any related words, effective September 1, 1971. Since that date women have been admitted to membership. Thus, no restrictions for membership apply except the professional requirement of enrollment in a curriculum in chemistry or a related science or practice of chemistry or a related science.

From the date of its founding until 1922, the fraternity was made up of collegiate chapters for alumni groups, but in 1922 it was organized into two general branches, Collegiate and Professional. The Professional Branch is made up of professional chapters in various chemical industrial centers and membership is confined to collegiate chapter alumni.

The fraternity is incorporated under the laws of the State of Wisconsin as a nonprofit organization and also legalized to operate as a nonprofit organization in the State of Indiana. It is also affiliated with the National Safety Council, and is a charter member of the Professional Interfraternity Conference.

A large number of Alpha Chi Sigma's collegiate chapters recognize scholarship and chemical achievement within their departments by means of chemical handbooks, plaques, cups, medals, cash, and American Chemical Society memberships.

All collegiate chapters support a National Safety Program in the interests of laboratory safety. The program objective is to teach safe practice in chemical and chemical engineering laboratories. There is instruction and education in safe practices, reporting details of all accidents, operation of safety committees, surveys of laboratories and equipment, instruction and education in industrial hygiene, checking condition of first aid and fire-fighting equipment, and elimination of explosion hazards. The fraternity has also developed and distributed thousands of safety posters in support of this program which is guided by a national committee made up of professional members experienced in safety work.

Of national consequence to the professional (alumni) chapters of the fraternity is the financial sponsorship of the American Chemical Society Award in Pure Chemistry. This award was established by the American Chemical Society to give yearly recognition to outstanding young chemists not over 35 years of age. It is a citation certificate by the society for outstanding accomplishment and a stipend of $3,000 plus a travel allowance furnished yearly by Alpha Chi Sigma, which in 1985 was in its 26th year of such support.

In 1966 an Alpha Chi Sigma award in chemical engineering research was established. It is for recognition of outstanding accomplishments by an individual in fundamental or applied research in the field of chemical engineering. It consists of a certificate of recognition and a stipend of $2,000; a travel allowance is also provided. This award is administered by the awards committee of the American Institute of Chemical Engineers.

The two foregoing awards are financed through the Alpha Chi Sigma Educational Foundation by voluntary contributions from professional members.

In 1961, becoming operative in 1962, the fraternity established the "John R. Kuebler Award," a "man of the year" selection of a member of the fraternity who had performed distinguished services to advance the fraternity and the chemical profession. The award, with no age restrictions, consists of a suitably inscribed scroll and traveling expenses to and from the place of presentation.

Government Government is vested in a Grand Chapter consisting of a duly elected representative from each chapter (collegiate and professional), the district officers, and the national officers. This body meets in biennial conclaves, although legislation, except amendments to the Constitution and Bylaws, may be handled by this body by mail between conclaves.

Executive administration of fraternity affairs is in the hands of an Executive Committee (board of directors) of the Grand Chapter, consisting of the four elected national officers. The fraternity's national secretary-treasurer and editor of *The Hexagon* are appointed by this board, the president of which has charge of general administration and fraternity expansion. One board member directs the collegiate branch, another the professional branch, and one is national ritualist.

Immediate chapter supervision is obtained through dividing the fraternity into districts, each containing collegiate and professional chapters, and each district under the direction of a district counselor who is responsible to those members of the board of directors in charge of the collegiate and professional branches.

Biennial conventions (Grand Chapter meetings) have been held since 1904. The 50th anniversary was celebrated in 1952 at the 22nd biennial conclave held at the University of Wisconsin, the site of the fraternity's founding. In 1958, at the 24th biennial conclave at Houston, Texas, the Grand Chapter experienced its first instance of a chapter installation at a national conclave: its 63rd collegiate chapter (Beta Omicron) at the University of Houston.

Publications The fraternity publishes a journal known as *The Hexagon*, established in 1910 and printed as a quarterly until 1920. During 1920-22,

the magazine was issued monthly, then reverted to eight monthly appearances during the collegiate year. Currently it is again appearing as a quarterly. In 1927 the *History of Alpha Chi Sigma Fraternity*, by Harry A. Curtis, was published. The fraternity has published directories upon infrequent occasions. It issues also a yearly official *Proceedings of the Grand Chapter* varying from 200-400 pages; a Manual of Procedure for Collegiate Chapter Officers; a Pledge Manual; and Constitution and Bylaws edition after each biennial conclave.

Traditions and Insignia Traditions are (1) lasting friendship (2) advancement of chemistry as a science and profession and (3) to aid its members by any honorable means in the attainment of their ambitions as chemists.

The insignia are: an official badge which is a gold hexagon displaying in gold on a field of black enamel the Greek letters AXΣ, a skull and crossbones, two stars, and clasped hands; a crest composed of the gold letters, AXΣ, on a blue background, surmounted by a hexagon with blue background and a wivern on the lower section, a band of alchemical symbols slanting across the center and three stars on the top portion, and the hexagon is surmounted by an ornamental design and alchemical symbol; and a pledge button carrying one alchemical symbol. The flower is the dark red carnation. There is an official flag and in 1928, a miniature of the official badge was adopted as a sister pin. In 1934, a professional charm, an enlarged replica of the official badge suspended by a swivel ring, was adopted for wearing by the alumni.

In 1969, a replica of the official badge mounted as a tie-tac was accepted as a substitute for the official badge and, in 1971, an insignia for women was authorized consisting of a pendant bearing the insignia of the official badge, mounted on an 18-inch fine-link chain. At this same time, wearing of the professional charm on a charm bracelet was authorized.

Funds The Alpha Chi Sigma Reserve Fund is a consolidation of a former Alpha Chi Sigma Trust Fund and a Hexagon Reserve Fund. In 1962, an Alpha Chi Sigma House Fund was established. Members contributing at least $150 to either fund are exempt from further obligation for alumni dues. A Ritual Fund is maintained for the purpose of financing chapter installations and regalia and ritual replacements.

The general operating expenses of the fraternity are met by the General Fund which accrues from miscellaneous sources, but primarily from yearly dues by collegiate and professional members, pledge fees, initiation fees and contributions. All alumni are solicited annually for professional dues and additional contributions for operating expenses and about two-thirds of the income of the fraternity comes from this source. In 1975, IRS reclassified the fraternity and in 1977 issued a group exemption for the chapters as educational and charitable organizations to which all contributions were deductible to the donor.

A Counselors' Citation Fund accrued from contributions of the District Counselors pays for various recognition awards for outstanding chapter performance.

Headquarters In 1926 the fraternity consolidated its secretary-treasurer and editorial offices and assured its appointee a reasonable permanence, thereby establishing its first definite national headquarters at 5503 East Washington Street, Indianapolis, Indiana 46219, where the headquarters remained until August 1, 1977, when new offices were occupied in Indianapolis at 11 South Kitley Avenue.

In 1973, a campaign was launched to raise funds to build a new national headquarters building in Indianapolis. A lot was purchased at 2141 N. Franklin Road on the city's far northeast side. Design was approved in early 1981 and construction begun in the fall of that year. Dedication of the new building took place in the spring of 1982.

Membership Total living membership 36,148. Total undergraduate membership 1,602. Active chapters 43. Inactive chapters 38. Houses owned 14. City/Area alumni associations 12. Total number of initiates 46,965. Chapter roll:

1902	Alpha, Wisconsin, Madison
1904	Beta, Minnesota
1906	Gamma, Case Western Reserve (1971-1979)
1907	Delta, Missouri
1908	Epsilon, Indiana
1908	*Eta, Colorado* (1972)
1908	Zeta, Illinois
1909	Iota, Rose-Hulman (1938-1984)
1909	Kappa, Kansas
1909	*Theta, Nebraska* (1934)
1910	*Lambda, Ohio State* (1936)
1911	*Mu, New Hampshire* (1971)
1911	Nu, Penn State
1911	*Xi, Maine* (1941)
1912	*Omicron, Harvard* (1945)
1912	Pi, Syracuse
1912	Rho, North Carolina
1913	*Phi, Allegheny* (1934)
1913	Sigma, Cal, Berkeley
1913	Tau, Cornell
1913	*Upsilon, Northwestern* (1968)
1914	*Chi, Yale* (1968)
1914	*Psi, L.S.U.* (1986)
1915	*Omega, Pitt* (1934)
1916	*Alpha Alpha, Stanford* (1955)
1916	Alpha Beta, Michigan
1917	*Alpha Delta, Cincinnati* (1974)
1917	*Alpha Epsilon, Washington (MO)* (1972)
1917	*Alpha Gamma, Kentucky* (1970)
1919	*Alpha Eta, Oklahoma* (1969)
1919	Alpha Zeta, M.I.T. (1949-1978)
1921	*Alpha Iota, Penn* (1972)
1921	Alpha Theta, Iowa
1922	Alpha Kappa, Virginia

1923	*Alpha Lambda, Dartmouth* (1933)
1923	*Alpha Mu, Lafayette* (1935)
1924	*Alpha Nu, Colgate* (1955)
1925	*Alpha Xi, Utah* (1957)
1926	*Alpha Omicron, Montana State* (1959)
1926	*Alpha Pi, George Washington* (1973)
1927	Alpha Rho, Maryland
1928	Alpha Sigma, Arkansas
1928	*Alpha Tau, Tulane* (1971)
1928	*Alpha Upsilon, Michigan State* (1962-1978) (1985)
1929	*Alpha Chi, Iowa State* (1968)
1929	Alpha Phi, Tennessee (1985-1986)
1930	*Alpha Psi, Illinois Tech* (1985)
1932	Alpha Omega, Georgia Tech (1953-1979)
1932	*Beta Alpha, Bucknell* (1969)
1933	Beta Beta, Washington State (1974-1986)
1935	Beta Gamma, UCLA
1936	Beta Delta, Missouri, Rolla
1939	*Beta Epsilon, Clemson* (1956)
1952	Beta Eta, North Texas
1952	*Beta Theta, Texas* (1985)
1952	*Beta Zeta, Alabama* (1965)
1953	*Beta Iota, Florida* (1974)
1954	*Beta Kappa, Delaware* (1965)
1954	*Beta Lambda, Akron* (1984)
1954	Beta Mu, Occidental (1972-1982)
1955	Beta Nu, Purdue
1955	*Beta Xi, Wayne State (MI)* (1972)
1958	Beta Omicron, Houston
1960	Beta Pi, Pacific (CA)
1965	Beta Rho, Kansas State
1966	Beta Sigma, Rochester Tech
1967	Beta Tau, Arizona
1969	Beta Upsilon, American (1977-1983)
1970	Beta Phi, South Dakota Mines
1971	Beta Chi, Hampden-Sydney
1975	Beta Omega, Arizona State
1975	*Beta Psi, Southern Illinois* (1984)
1976	*Gamma Alpha, Johns Hopkins* (1981)
1978	Gamma Beta, Florida State
1980	*Gamma Gamma, Eastern Michigan* (1986)
1981	Gamma Delta, Charleston (SC)
1981	Gamma Epsilon, Vanderbilt
1982	Gamma Zeta, Cal Poly, San Luis Obispo
1985	Gamma Eta, Marshall
1985	Gamma Theta, Northeast Missouri
1987	Gamma Iota, V.P.I.

Alpha Delta Theta†

(MEDICAL TECHNOLOGY)

ALPHA DELTA THETA was established by Tau Sigma of Marquette University and Alpha Delta Tau of the University of Minnesota on February 1, 1944. As a national professional fraternity of medical technologists its purpose is to unite all women en-

† This chapter narrative is repeated from the 19th edition; no current information was provided.

tering into or engaging in the field of medical technology, to promote social and intellectual fellowship among its members, and to raise the prestige of medical technologists by inspiring the members to greater group and individual effort. Eligibility for membership is based on high scholastic rank, high moral ideals, and an active enthusiasm for medical technology. All members shall have received or be working towards a degree in medical technology through an approved curriculum of an accredited college.

Growth Alpha Delta Theta became a member of the Professional Panhellenic Association in 1952. The fraternity is steadily expanding.

Government The Executive Council is made up of ten national officers. Conventions are held annually at a city determined by the executive council. All judicial and legislative powers are vested in the national officers and delegates of the convention.

Traditions The colors of Alpha Delta Theta are green (of medicine) and gold (of science). The fraternity flower is the daffodil. The official pin is six-sided with a black background and bears the Greek letters ΑΔΘ. A pledge pin is also recognized.

Publications The *Scope* is the national publication and is published twice annually. It is supplemented by newsletters from the president and other national officers.

Headquarters P. O. Box 7241, Milwaukee, Wisconsin 53213.

Membership Active chapters 23. Inactive chapters 3. Graduate/Alumni chapters 3. Individual alumna 250. Total number of initiates 662. Chapter roll:††

1944	*Alpha, Marquette*
1944	Beta, Minnesota
1945	Delta, Michigan State
1945	Gamma, Macalester
1946	Epsilon, Wisconsin, Madison
1946	Zeta, Kansas State
1948	Eta, Indiana, Indianapolis
1948	Iota, Mount Mary
1948	*Theta, St. Scholastica*
1949	*Kappa, Wyoming*
1950	Lambda, Wayne State
1950	*Mu, Colorado*
1951	Nu, St. Louis
1952	Xi, Denver
1953	Omicron, Marycrest (IA)
1954	Pi, North Dakota
1954	Rho, St. Teresa
1956	Sigma, Augsburg
1957	Tau, West Virginia
1959	Upsilon, Ohio State
1960	Phi, Temple
1961	Chi, Wisconsin, Oshkosh
1961	Omega, Mercy (MI)
1961	Psi, Marian (WI)

†† This chapter roll is repeated from the 19th edition; no current information was provided.

1962	Alpha Alpha, Albany (NY)
1962	Alpha Beta, St. John's (NY)
1963	Alpha Delta, Loyola, New Orleans
1963	Alpha Gamma, Edgewood
1965	Alpha Epsilon, Wisconsin, Milwaukee
1965	Alpha Eta, St. Norbert
1966	Alpha Theta, Drake
1967	Alpha Iota, Philadelphia Pharmacy
1967	Alpha Kappa, Wisconsin, Superior
1968	Alpha Lambda, Massachusetts
1969	Alpha Mu, Dayton
1969	Alpha Nu, Xavier (LA)

Alpha Kappa Psi

(BUSINESS AND COMMERCE)

ACTIVE PIN

PLEDGE PIN

ALPHA KAPPA PSI, the first professional business fraternity, was founded on October 5, 1904, in the School of Commerce, Accounts, and Finance at New York University and incorporated under the laws of New York on May 20, 1905. The fraternity recognizes ten founders: George Lester Bergen, Irving Linwood Camp, Robert Stuart Douglas, Daniel Vincent Duff, Howard McNayr Jefferson, Nathan Lane, Jr., Frederic Ranney Leach, Morris Sidney Rachmil, William Owskey Tremaine, and Herbert McKeehan Wright.

The objects of the fraternity are: to further the individual welfare of its members; to foster scientific research in the fields of commerce, accounts, and finance; to educate the public to appreciate and demand higher ideals therein; and to promote and advance in institutions of collegiate rank courses leading to degrees in business administration.

Membership is restricted to regularly enrolled students working for degrees in business and to faculty members in schools and departments of business, or their equivalent, in colleges and universities of the United States and Canada which confer a degree in economics, commerce or business administration, and which promote a course of study in these subjects of not less than two years in length. To be eligible for initiation a student must possess a scholastic average not lower than the average required for graduation by the school in which the chapter is located. Another membership classification provides for honorary members who may be initiated by a chapter provided prior approval is obtained from the chapter advisor, district director, regional director, and national president in the order named.

Growth Although the fraternity was established in 1904, it was not until 1910 that Beta Chapter at the University of Denver was added, followed in 1911 by Gamma Chapter at Northwestern University and in 1912 by Delta Chapter at the University of Pittsburgh.

Government Government is by a national chapter composed of representatives from college and alumni chapters assembled in biennial conventions. It elects the national president and three national vice presidents of the fraternity, and enacts legislation. In the interim between conventions, the affairs of the fraternity are administered by a board of directors, consisting of the national president, three national vice presidents, and 13 regional directors. The board of directors in turn vests authority for supervising the business and administrative routine of the fraternity in an executive committee consisting of the national president and two other members, elected either from the board of directors or from the fraternity at large.

The chapters are divided into 13 geographical regions, each of which elects a regional director to represent it on the board of directors and to be responsible for its supervision, guidance, and visitation. The regional director may appoint district directors to assist him to supervise and perform the visitation and inspection duties of assigned districts of his region. Also each chapter has a chapter advisor, appointed by the regional director from among its alumni or faculty members.

All chapters are encouraged to conduct a program of professional activities including talks by business people and educators, industrial tours, service to the school or community, and local research projects.

In 1923 an administrative office was established at Indianapolis with a full-time executive secretary-treasurer in charge to conduct and administer the routine and business affairs of the fraternity. The office was moved to Denver, Colorado, in 1942, but was returned to Indianapolis in 1949. In 1951, the fraternity purchased its own national headquarters building at 111 East 38th Street, Indianapolis.

Forty-two national conventions have been held: 13 in New York; four in Chicago; four in Denver; three in Atlanta; three in Minneapolis; two in Detroit; two in Milwaukee; and one each in Boston, Cincinnati, Asheville, Houston, Wawasee (Indiana), Pocono (Pennsylvania), Pittsburgh, Las Vegas, Memphis, Seattle, and Orlando.

Traditions and Insignia The official badge is a monogram of the Greek letters AKΨ. In the gold official badge the letter Ψ is engraved with symbolic fraternity designs; in the jeweled badge these symbols are replaced by 13 blue sapphires. The pledge button is a gold Phoenician galley with the sail in blue enamel. The recognition button is a miniature replica of the coat of arms. Official colors are gold and navy blue. The official flower is the yellow rose.

Publications The official publication is *The Diary of Alpha Kappa Psi*, published four times each college year in the spring, summer, autumn, and winter, with a special convention-proceedings issue after each biennial national convention. The executive director is also the editor of this magazine. The publication was originally established in 1908 as *The Alpha Diary* and issued each month. In 1913, the name was changed to *The Diary of Alpha Kappa Psi Fraternity* and, in 1917, to *The Alpha Kappa Psi Diary*. In 1929, by action of the national chapter, the present name was adopted. As the magazine has been expanded in size and scope as the fraternity has developed. Published without interruption during World War II, *The Diary* was sent to all members in the armed forces without charge. Another publication, the *Alpha Kappa Psi Alumni News*, established in 1937, is issued annually and mailed to all alumni members.

In 1916, the *Handbook of Alpha Kappa Psi*, a small manual of history and fraternity information, was issued. In 1919, *Gleanings of Alpha Kappa Psi*, a pamphlet, was published. In 1923, *Alpha Kappa Psi, Its Aims and Ideals*, a booklet containing historical data on the fraternity and on business education, made its appearance. In 1934, 1937, 1948, 1956, and 1963, the essential parts of these earlier publications were included in new editions of the *Handbook of Alpha Kappa Psi*, containing comprehensive information on Alpha Kappa Psi, education for business, and the American fraternity system. Published in 1941 was a booklet titled *Alpha Kappa Psi*, containing information on the fraternity and designed both for the information of non-members and for the instruction of future members. This booklet is now replaced by three leaflets, *This is Alpha Kappa Psi*, *It's Good Business To Be an Alpha Kappa Psi*, and *Why Alpha Kappa Psi?*

In 1927, a membership directory was issued and in 1958 publication of another such directory was started by including listings of members alphabetically by states in issues of *The Diary*. In 1984, an alumni directory was published commemorating the 80th anniversary of Alpha Kappa Psi. In 1927, the first songbook was published followed by larger and more complete editions in subsequent years. In 1945, two other manuals were issued, one titled *Organization and Administration of an A. K. Psi Alumni Chapter* and, the other, *Obtaining and Operating a Chapter House*. The *Constitution and Statutory Code* of Alpha Kappa Psi is published every three years. Other publications include *The A. K. Psi Pledge Manual*, *The A. K. Psi Performance Evaluation for College Chapters*, and still others.

Funds and Philanthropies At the 1922 Cincinnati convention, a convention fund was established for the purpose of defraying the transportation expenses of college chapter delegates to national convention; a similar fund for alumni chapter delegates was established by the 1950 Minneapolis Convention. At the 1929 silver anniversary convention held in Denver, a magazine endowment fund, life memberships, alumni dues, and a fund to defray the expenses of regional officials in visiting their chapters were established. At the 1933 convention held in Chicago, a fund to defray the transportation expenses of college chapter delegates to the triennial regional conferences was established.

The 1931 Asheville Convention established the Alpha Kappa Psi Scholarship Award which is presented annually in each school of business where a chapter is located. The recipient is the student of the senior class who has the highest grade average for three full years of scholastic work in that institution, whether or not he or she is a member of Alpha Kappa Psi. The 1933 convention in Chicago established the Alpha Kappa Psi Service Award to be given to members for extraordinary services rendered the fraternity or their chapters. In 1940, the Student Loan fund was established; this is available to junior, senior, and graduate student members of the fraternity and to faculty members working for higher degrees. The life membership plan of the fraternity, established in 1929, now has 15,000 life members.

In 1926-27 a research project, directed by Dean Everett W. Lord of Boston University for the purpose of determining the relation of education and income, was conducted. The results of this study were published in 1928 in a booklet entitled *The Relation of Education and Income* and had a wide distribution. In 1930-1931, another research project to determine the books on economic subjects of greatest value to business men was sponsored. The results of this study were published in booklet form in 1932 under the title *Books for Business Men*, and it, too, enjoyed a wide and popular distribution. Other national research projects conducted by the fraternity include *A Survey of General Business Curricula in 64 Undergraduate Schools of Commerce and Business Administration (1937 and 1948), Student Persistence in American Colleges (1938), The Value of Practical Versus Theoretical College Courses in the Business Curriculum (1942), and Business Books for Serious Reading and Study* (1945, 1953, 1961). The policy of the fraternity is to conduct one major research project of national scope at regular intervals with individual chapters conducting projects of local nature annually.

In 1951 the Alpha Kappa Psi Foundation was incorporated in the State of Illinois. The purposes of the foundation, a non-profit organization, are charitable, civic, patriotic, literary, scientific, research, and professional. They include the promotion of a higher level of economic literacy so that all citizens may better understand the American system of free enterprise.

In 1952, the foundation established an award to be made annually to an individual for outstanding and meritorious work in the field of accounting. In 1956, another award was established for the best article on marketing published in *The Journal of Marketing* in the preceding year. In 1956, an award was also established to be made annually to the American business firm or organization which renders distinguished service to higher education. These awards are now made under the auspices of the Alpha Kappa Psi Foundation.

Headquarters 3706 Washington Boulevard, Indianapolis, Indiana 46205. In 1923 an administrative office was established in Indianapolis. The office was moved to Denver in 1942 but was returned to Indianapolis in 1949. In 1951, Alpha Kappa Psi was the first professional fraternity to purchase its own headquarters building.

Membership   Chapter roll:††

1904	Alpha, N.Y.U.
1910	Beta, Denver
1911	*Gamma, Northwestern* (1968)
1912	*Delta, Pitt* (1964)
1913	Epsilon, Illinois
1914	Eta, Cincinnati
1914	*Theta, Oregon State* (1933)
1914	Zeta, Nebraska
1915	Iota, Texas (1960-1962)
1915	Kappa, Oregon
1915	*Lambda, Oklahoma* (1933)
1915	Mu, Ohio State
1916	*Nu, Boston* (1964)
1916	*Xi, Harvard* (1918)
1917	Omicron, Montana
1917	Pi, Georgia State
1919	Rho, Washington
1919	*Sigma, Colorado Col* (1966)
1920	Chi, Columbia
1920	Phi, Michigan
1920	Psi, Kansas
1920	Tau, Oklahoma State
1920	Upsilon, Missouri
1921	*Alpha Beta, California* (1968)
1921	Alpha Gamma, Virginia
1921	*Omega, William and Mary* (1936)
1922	*Alpha Delta, Washington and Lee* (1929)
1922	Alpha Epsilon, Georgia
1922	Alpha Eta, Minnesota
1922	Alpha Iota, Utah
1922	Alpha Theta, Utah State
1922	Alpha Zeta, USC
1923	Alpha Kappa, Idaho (1943-1963)
1923	Alpha Lambda, Washington (MO)
1923	Alpha Mu, Wisconsin, Madison
1923	Alpha Nu, Arizona
1923	*Alpha Omicron, Syracuse* (1969)
1923	*Alpha Pi, Southern Methodist* (1962)
1923	Alpha Xi, Iowa
1924	Alpha Rho, Alabama
1924	*Alpha Sigma, Lehigh* (1971)
1925	Alpha Tau, North Carolina
1926	*Alpha Chi, Emory* (1963)

†† This chapter roll is repeated from the 19th edition; no current information was provided.

1926	Alpha Omega, Kansas State
1926	Alpha Phi, Florida
1926	*Alpha Psi, Marquette* (1972)
1926	Alpha Upsilon, UCLA
1927	Beta Gamma, Indiana
1928	*Beta Delta, Brigham Young* (1952)
1928	*Beta Epsilon, Chicago* (1934)
1928	Beta Zeta, Arkansas
1929	*Beta Eta, Duke* (1966)
1930	Beta Theta, Detroit
1931	*Beta Iota, Buffalo* (1969)
1931	*Beta Kappa, Western Ontario* (1947)
1932	Beta Lambda, Washington State
1933	Beta Mu, George Washington
1936	Beta Nu, Wyoming
1939	Beta Xi, V.P.I.
1941	Beta Omicron, Wayne State
1941	Beta Pi, Miami (FL)
1943	*Beta Rho, West Virginia* (1969)
1947	*Beta Sigma, St. John's* (1970)
1948	*Beta Tau, New Mexico* (1970)
1948	*Beta Upsilon, South Carolina* (1955)
1949	*Beta Chi, L.S.U.* (1961)
1949	Beta Omega, Samford
1949	Beta Phi, Drake
1949	Beta Psi, Florida State
1950	*Gamma Delta, Wake Forest* (1970)
1950	Gamma Epsilon, Penn State
1950	Gamma Zeta, Colorado
1951	Gamma Eta, Toledo
1951	Gamma Theta, Bradley
1952	Gamma Iota, Loyola
1952	Gamma Kappa, Portland
1952	Gamma Lambda, Cal State, Fresno
1952	Gamma Mu, Michigan State
1953	Gamma Nu, Babson Institute
1953	Gamma Omicron, Norwich
1953	*Gamma Xi, Lewis and Clark* (1972)
1954	*Gamma Phi, Tulsa* (1972)
1954	Gamma Pi, Seton Hall
1954	*Gamma Rho, Rockhurst* (1955)
1954	Gamma Sigma, Regis
1954	Gamma Tau, Western Michigan
1954	Gamma Upsilon, Wichita
1955	Delta Epsilon, Cal State, Los Angeles
1955	Delta Eta, Boston College
1955	*Delta Theta, Carroll* (1971)
1955	Delta Zeta, Richmond
1955	*Gamma Chi, Miami (OH)* (1969)
1955	Gamma Omega, Seattle
1955	Gamma Psi, Niagara
1956	Delta Iota, Waynesburg
1956	Delta Kappa, David Lipscomb
1956	Delta Lambda, Mississippi State
1956	Delta Mu, John Carroll
1956	Delta Nu, Dayton
1956	Delta Omicron, Cal State, Long Beach
1956	*Delta Xi, Hamline* (1963)
1957	Delta Phi, Wisconsin, Milwaukee
1957	*Delta Pi, Creighton* (1972)
1957	Delta Rho, St. Thomas
1957	Delta Sigma, St. Louis
1957	Delta Tau, Canisius
1957	Delta Upsilon, Idaho State
1958	*Delta Chi, Clarkson* (1973)
1958	*Delta Omega, Iowa State* (1972)
1958	Delta Psi, Illinois Wesleyan
1958	Epsilon Eta, Baylor
1958	Epsilon Zeta, Detroit (Downtown)
1959	Epsilon Iota, West Texas
1959	Epsilon Kappa, Southern Illinois
1959	Epsilon Lambda, Old Dominion
1959	Epsilon Mu, Kansas State, Pittsburg
1959	Epsilon Nu, Puget Sound
1959	*Epsilon Theta, Birmingham-Southern* (1969)
1959	Epsilon Xi, Gustavus Adolphus
1960	Epsilon Omicron, Arkansas State
1960	*Epsilon Pi, Alaska* (1972)
1961	*Epsilon Rho, Penn* (1973)
1962	Epsilon Phi, Little Rock
1962	Epsilon Sigma, Georgia Tech
1962	Epsilon Tau, Jacksonville
1962	Epsilon Upsilon, Carson-Newman
1963	Epsilon Chi, Upsala
1963	Epsilon Omega, Portland State
1963	Epsilon Psi, Fordham
1963	Zeta Eta, Pacific Lutheran
1963	Zeta Theta, St. Mary's
1964	Zeta Iota, St. Francis (NY)
1964	Zeta Kappa, Eastern Michigan
1964	Zeta Lambda, Tennessee
1964	Zeta Mu, Bloomfield
1964	Zeta Nu, St. Francis (PA)
1964	Zeta Xi, Central Michigan
1965	Zeta Chi, Tennessee, Martin
1965	*Zeta Omega, St. John's, Jamaica* (1973)
1965	Zeta Omicron, Southeast Missouri
1965	Zeta Phi, Austin Peay
1965	Zeta Pi, Ft. Hays
1965	Zeta Psi, Middle Tennessee
1965	Zeta Rho, Marshall
1965	Zeta Sigma, Millikin
1965	Zeta Tau, Western Kentucky
1965	Zeta Upsilon, Tennessee Tech.
1966	Eta Iota, Murray State
1966	Eta Kappa, Hardin-Simmons
1966	Eta Lambda, Nevada Southern
1966	Eta Mu, Stephen F. Austin
1966	Eta Nu, Michigan, Dearborn
1966	*Eta Omicron, East Carolina* (1969)
1966	Eta Pi, Adrian
1966	Eta Rho, Illinois (Chicago Circle)
1966	*Eta Sigma, Fordham (Intown)* (1969)
1966	Eta Theta, Texas Tech.
1966	Eta Xi, Youngstown State
1967	Eta Chi, Northern Michigan
1967	Eta Phi, Eastern Washington
1967	Eta Tau, Louisiana Tech
1967	Eta Upsilon, Montevallo
1968	Eta Omega, North Carolina, Charlotte
1968	*Eta Psi, Drexel* (1973)
1968	Theta Iota, Gannon
1968	Theta Kappa, Michigan Tech

1968   Theta Lambda, Western New England
1968   Theta Mu, Stetson
1969   Theta Nu, South Alabama
1969   *Theta Pi, St. Bernard* (1971)
1969   Theta Rho, Pan American
1969   Theta Xi, Tri-State
1970   Theta Chi, West Georgia
1970   Theta Omega, Pfeiffer
1970   Theta Phi, Indiana State
1970   Theta Psi, Memphis State
1970   Theta Sigma, Southwest Texas
1970   Theta Upsilon, Point Park
1971   Iota Kappa, AIC
1971   Iota Lambda, Benedictine
1971   *Iota Mu, Pacific* (1973)
1971   Iota Nu, West Liberty
1972   Iota Omicron, Cal State, San Bernadino
1972   Iota Pi, Christopher Newport
1972   Iota Rho, Montclair
1972   Iota Xi, Arizona State
1976   Iota Sigma, Sam Houston

Alpha Omega

(DENTISTRY)

ACTIVE PIN

PLEDGE PIN

ALPHA OMEGA, a professional dental fraternity, was established in 1909 by the union of the Ramach Fraternity, founded at the Pennsylvania College of Dental Surgery in 1906, and the Alpha Omega Dental Fraternity, founded at the University of Maryland in 1907. It is incorporated under the laws of Maryland.

The objectives of the fraternity are to promote the profession of dentistry; to establish, foster, and develop high standards of fellowship among all its members; to create and bind together a body of professional men, who, by scholarly attainment, faithful service, and the maintenance of ethical ideals and principles, have achieved distinction; to honor achievement in others; to strive for breadth of vision, unity in action, and accomplishment of ideals; to commend all worthy deeds, and if fraternal welfare demands to call on and counsel with its members.

Government   The fraternity is governed by the International Council, composed of the president, president-elect, secretary, treasurer, editor, immediate past president and trustees. For administrative purposes, the world is divided into 27 districts or regencies. Each regency is under the direction and supervision of a regent appointed by the International Council. He is in intimate contact with the several chapters that comprise his regency. Conventions are held annually between the period of Christmas and New Year's in alternating sections of the country.

Traditions and Insignia   The official badge of the fraternity is a jeweled pin, diamond in shape. The outer border contains ten crown pearls, blue and white sapphires in two corners; and within the border, superimposed on a black enamel background in gold are the Greek letters A and Ω. The official colors are gold and black. The official pledge pin is diamond-shaped, the upper half being black enamel and the lower half gold enamel. The official recognition pin displays the monogrammed letters AΩ in gold. The official banner of the fraternity is of black felt, in the center of which is the seal of the fraternity in gold, above it the name of the fraternity and below it the name of the chapter.

Publications   The periodicals published by the fraternity include: *The Alpha Omegan,* a quarterly magazine, which is in every dental library in the United States, Canada, and most foreign countries; the *Directory,* whose contents include an alphabetical and geographical listing of the entire membership together with a coded legend designating their fraternal and professional status; the *Constitution,* frequently revised and brought up to date; the *Undergraduate and Alumni Guide,* prepared for the instruction of subordinate chapter officers and containing information on organization, program planning, membership, protocol, etc.; the *Membership Newsletter* from the secretary's office, which is sent to all chapters, maintaining their information on fraternity matters current; the *History,* a periodically revised word and picture story of Alpha Omega, the *50th Year History;* and *The Scope,* a brochure depicting Alpha Omega's aims and accomplishments, its responsibilities, its position in the dental world.

Funds and Philanthropies   Through the years, Alpha Omega has inaugurated the awarding of a number of medals and plaques in recognition of the contribution to the arts and sciences of dentistry as a whole—and for outstanding achievement in the affairs of the fraternity. These awards include: the Alpha Omega Achievement Medal, the meritorious award given to an Alpha Omegan for his outstanding achievement for the fraternity during the year; the Alpha Omega Scholarship Award, a beautiful medal mounted on an ebony base, presented at each of the dental schools in the United States and Canada annually to its outstanding senior; the Past National President's Undergraduate Chapter Efficiency Award, presented annually at the convention to the undergraduate chapter which has displayed the highest degree of cooperation, efficiency, promptness, accomplishment, and initiative; the Undergraduate Scholarship Award Certificate given to a member in each chapter attaining the highest scholastic average for the first three years in the dental school; and certificates of award of which two may be presented annually to individuals rendering outstanding service to the fraternity. Many additional awards are made at the various dental colleges in memory of departed brothers.

Alpha Omega was a pioneer founder of a student aid fund. Tuition loans are made from its funds to needy and deserving undergraduates. These loans are non-interest bearing. Also supported is a Clinicians and Essayists Bureau which assigns outstanding practitioners to give clinics at chapters.

In 1953 Alpha Omega founded a modern dental school at the Hebrew University, Ein Karem, Jerusalem, Israel. In August, 1964, this school was formally dedicated. Alpha Omegans had contributed in excess of $1,500,000, thereby providing academic and research facilities for dental health needs of Israel.

Headquarters 267 Fifth Avenue, New York, New York 10016. The office is staffed by a fulltime executive director and assistants.

Membership Total living membership 11,000. Total undergraduate membership 1,000. Active chapters 45. Inactive chapters 7. Graduate/Alumni chapters 89. Total number of initiates 18,000. Chapter roll:

1910 Beta, Penn
1911 Gamma, Tufts
1911 Iota, N.Y.U.
1912 Delta, Harvard
1914 Eta, Columbia (NY)
1914 Theta Ramach, Temple
1916 Alpha, SUNY, Buffalo
1917 Epsilon, Georgetown U
1918 Kappa, Pacific, Surgeons, Dentistry
1920 Nu, Cal, Berkeley
1920 *Omicron, Pitt* (1988)
1921 Pi, Toronto
1922 Rho, Minnesota
1923 Zeta Mu, Maryland
1924 Tau, USC
1924 *Upsilon, Marquette* (1987)
1925 *Phi, Louisville* (1987)
1926 Chi, Michigan
1926 Psi, Ohio State
1928 Alpha Alpha, Illinois
1928 Alpha Beta, Virginia Medical
1928 *Alpha Delta, Emory* (1988)
1928 Alpha Gamma, Indiana
1931 Alpha Iota, Kansas Medical Center
1932 Alpha Kappa, Northwestern
1932 Alpha Lambda, Loyola, Chicago
1932 Alpha Theta, Loyola, New Orleans
1933 Alpha Nu, Detroit
1935 *Alpha Zeta, Tennessee* (1984)
1936 Omega, Western Reserve
1945 Alpha Chi, Baylor (-1988)
1946 Alpha Phi, Washington (MO)
1956 Alpha Pi, McGill
1958 Alpha Sigma, Hebrew
1959 Alpha Psi, New Jersey Medicine and Dentistry
1959 Alpha Rho, Manitoba

1959 National Undergraduate, Howard
1970 Alpha Tau, UCLA
1971 Beta Alpha, Meharry Medical
1974 Beta Beta, Florida
1975 *Beta Chi, Howard* (1988)
1976 Beta Delta, Western Ontario
1977 Beta Epsilon, Boston U
1979 *Beta Eta, Texas, Dentistry* (1988)
1980 Beta Gamma, Texas, San Antonio
1980 Beta Iota, Colorado
1982 Beta Kappa, Tel Aviv
1984 Beta Lambda, Connecticut
1986 Sigma Beta, SUNY, Stony Brook
1987 Delta Rho, Fairleigh Dickinson, Rutherford
1990 Beta Upsilon, Buenos Aires
1990 Sigma Alpha, Witwatersrand

Alpha Rho Chi

(ARCHITECTURE)

ACTIVE PIN

PLEDGE PIN

ALPHA RHO CHI was founded on April 11, 1914, by the union of the Arcus Society at the University of Illinois and Sigma Upsilon at the University of Michigan. It is a fraternity limiting its membership to students registered in professional courses of architecture and allied arts leading to a Bachelor's Degree or equivalent. Its objective is to organize and unite for educational and professional development purposes the students of architecture and allied arts in the universities and colleges of America to promote the artistic, scientific and practical proficiency of its membership and the profession. Membership is divided into five classes consisting of Active Members, Non-Graduate, Alumni, Faculty and Honorary. The title of Master Architect is conferred upon individuals who have gained national prominence in the field of architecture.

Government The fraternity is governed by delegates at the annual convention and at all other times by the officers of the Grand Council.

Traditions and Insignia Chapters are named for ancient Greek or Roman architects and select cadency marks to distinguish each chapter. The badge is of gold with an Egyptian triangle surmounted by a Romanesque arch of nine pearls, supporting an Ionic column and capital and displaying sundry architectural elements. The letters APAPX are placed in triangular position around a diamond-set star on a black enamel cartouche. Five pearls appear at the base of the triangle and a single pearl at the base of the badge.

The pledge pin is in the shape of an Egyptian pyramid enameled in the fraternity colors, maroon and navy blue. The fraternity flower is the white rose. The coat of arms appear on a Norman shield, quarterly sanguine and azure, in second a rose argent, a bend argent with nine mullets of eight sable, created with a gothic finial with radiate mantling dancette of eleven points all argent, and sponsored by a ribbon bearing the motto, *Fidelitas, Amor et Artes.* Gold cadency marks are placed in the shield to distinguish each chapter.

The flag is square and duplicates the arrangement of the shield in the coat of arms.

Publications The fraternity's magazine is called "The Archi" and, along with The Alpha Rho Chi Letter, is published by the Grand Council. The fraternity issues a Pledge Manual, a Handbook and a pamphlet entitled An Introduction to Alpha Rho Chi.

Funds and Philanthropies The bronze Alpha Rho Chi Medal was established in 1931 and is awarded to a graduating senior of each accredited or approved school of architecture who has shown ability for LEADERSHIP, performed willing SERVICE for the school and department and gives promise of real professional MERIT through attitude and personality. The student is nominated by the departmental faculty and, upon recommendation of the Grand Council, the medal is delivered to the university for presentation at its awards banquet or commencement ceremony.

Individual chapters and alumni associations sponsor scholarship funds at their respective universities. Alpha Rho Chi maintains a rotating National Scholastic Achievement Award plaque presented at each convention to the chapter with the best overall grade point average.

Membership Total living membership 2,960. Total undergraduate membership 210. Active chapters 12. Inactive chapters 8. Houses owned 8. Graduate/Alumni chapters 11. Total number of initiates 4,500. Chapter roll:

1914	Anthemios, Illinois	
1914	Iktinos, Michigan (1972-1985)	
1915	Demetrios, Ohio State	
1916	Mnesicles, Minnesota	
1922	Andronicus, USC	
1922	*Kallikrates, Virginia (1933-1948) (1961)*	
1923	*Paeonios, Kansas State (1935)*	
1924	*Dinocrates, Texas (1936-1964) (1971)*	
1924	*Polyklitos, Carnegie-Mellon (1936)*	
1926	Theron, Oklahoma State (1933-1990)	
1955	Vitruvius, Penn State (1972-1976)	
1962	*Satyros, Arizona State (1970)*	
1969	*Metagenes, V.P.I. (1989)*	
1970	*Xenocles, Texas, Arlington (1989)*	
1972	*Cleisthenes, Houston (1982)*	
1980	Daedalus, Cal Poly, Pomona	
1981	Daphnis, Arkansas	
1981	Heracleides, Oklahoma	
1984	Rhoecus, Kansas	
1986	Apollodorus, Florida	

Alpha Tau Delta

(NURSING)

ALPHA TAU DELTA National Fraternity for Professional Nurses was founded February 15, 1921, at the University of California, Berkeley. Its purposes are to further professional educational standards for men and women in the nursing profession; to inaugurate projects that strengthen the specific field of professional nursing; to develop character and leadership; to encourage high ethical standards of professional conduct in which members may develop sound professional philosophies; to encourage excellence of individual performance and develop the highest possible scholastic attainments; to organize the social life of its members as a contributing factor of their educational program, and maintain an interfraternity spirit of cooperation; to foster a close bond of friendship, fellowship, mutual helpfulness and understanding among those in the nursing profession.

Growth Alpha Tau Delta invites duly accredited university schools of nursing offering a baccalaureate degree or higher to petition for membership in the only professional fraternity for nurses.

To be eligible for membership, one must be a student in attendance at or a graduate of a fully accredited baccalaureate collegiate school of nursing and shall maintain a good academic standing as is required by the institution.

Government National officers include a president, vice president, secretary, and treasurer which comprise the National Council. Officers are elected by representatives from each chapter who are delegates at the biennial national convention. A national editor is appointed by the National Council. The individual chapters have their own constitutions and bylaws, which fall within the requirements of the national fraternity. ATD is a member of the professional Fraternity Association.

Traditions and Insignia The colors of the fraternity are yellow, white, gold, and blue; the flower is the yellow rose; the jewel is the pearl. The A.T.D. pin is composed of the three letters of the fraternity arranged as follows: Δ is the background and is of hammered gold; T is superimposed on Δ and is of plain gold. A is formed of plain gold or with seven small pearls on each side with one pearl forming the crossbar of the letter. The pledge pin and coat of arms are symbols which represent the purposes, services, and ideals of the fraternity. The insignia are registered in the U.S. Patent Office.

Publications The fraternity has two publications, *CAP'tions of Alpha Tau Delta*, which is published two times in the college year, and the *President's Letter*, published twice per year.

Funds and Philanthropies Annual awards, scholarships, or grant funds are available to members in need of financial assistance to complete their education. Each chapter may also provide assistance, financial and in-kind, to local charities of its choice.

Headquarters 14631 N. 2nd Drive, Phoenix, Arizona 85023.

Membership Active chapters 20. Inactive chapters 5. Chapter roll:††

1921 *Alpha, California* (1946)
1927 Beta, Minnesota
1928 *Delta, Idaho* (1936)
1928 Gamma, UCLA
1931 *Zeta, USC* (1956)
1932 Eta, Oregon, Medical, Dentistry
1936 Delta, Washington
1938 Iota, Marquette
1938 Theta, Duquesne
1939 Kappa, St. Scholastica
1940 Lambda, Montana State
1945 Mu, Pitt
1945 Nu, Seattle College
1948 *Seattle University* (1965)
1953 Epsilon, Ohio State
1957 *Omicron, Utah* (1965)
1957 Xi, Loyola, Chicago
1958 Rho, Illinois, Chicago
1959 Sigma, Wisconsin, Madison
1961 Tau, Portland
1965 Phi, Cal State, Los Angeles
1965 Upsilon, Illinois Wesleyan
1966 Chi, Evansville
1966 Omega, Cal State, Long Beach
1976 Alpha Gamma, Wisconsin, Milwaukee

Delta Omicron

(MUSIC)

ACTIVE PIN

PLEDGE PIN

DELTA OMICRON, international music fraternity, was founded September 6, 1909, at the Cincinnati Conservatory of Music by Lorena Creamer, Mabel Dunn, and Hazel Wilson. The only national music fraternity to have been established by undergraduate students, Delta Omicron was from its very beginning envisioned as a national organization and, on December 13, 1909, was incorporated under the laws of the State of Ohio.

Delta Omicron was founded to create and foster fellowship through music, to develop character and leadership, to encourage the highest possible scholastic attainment and an excellence of individual performance, to stimulate the appreciation of good

†† This chapter roll is repeated from the 19th edition; no current information was provided.

music, to give material aid to needy and worthy students, and to manifest interest in musicians entering the professional world. The fraternity has increased the breadth and scope of its purposes to include the promotion of American music and musicians, the furtherance of the work of composers, the strengthening of good international relations through greater understanding of cultures of all nations, the encouragement of high ethical standards of professional conduct, and the doing of any and all things conducive to the service, betterment, and ultimate welfare of musicians.

Collegiate membership is open to students of high scholastic average seriously pursuing the study of music in schools where chapters of the fraternity are located. Professional membership is extended to faculty members, graduates of recognized music schools, concert artists, and other professional musicians. National honorary membership may be conferred upon women musicians who have attained national or international recognition. Patrons and patronesses may be inducted on the national or local level.

Growth Delta Omicron has expanded consistently and steadily, according to its purposes. In 1958, with chartering of chapters in three universities of the Orient, it became the first music fraternity with chapters abroad. Also, in 1979, to conform to Title IX, Delta Omicron became coeducational and opened its membership to men.

Government Legislative powers are vested in the Delta Omicron triennial conference, composed of elected and appointed national and province officers and delegates from each collegiate and alumnae chapter. Thirty-two national and eight international conferences have been held. Interim business is conducted by the Delta Omicron Board of Directors, consisting of seven elected national officers and appointed executive secretary and treasurer. Geographically, the fraternity is divided into 13 provinces with each under the supervision of a province president. An executive office has been maintained since 1943.

Traditions and Insignia The badge is a lyre of gold with raised letters ΔO on a scroll across the strings. The pledge pin is silver with the Greek letters ΔO linked together. Fifty-year-members wear a gold miniature lily-of-the-valley. A senior honor pin is given to each chapter senior excelling in scholarship. The fraternity colors are old rose and gray. The flower is the lily-of-the-valley. The 1920 convention adopted a coat of arms and the open motto: Continually striving, we attain.

Delta Omicron is a charter member of the Professional Fraternity Association and is also affiliated with the National Music Council, National Association of Schools of Music, Music Teachers National Association, Music Educators National Conference, National Association for Music Therapy, American String Teachers Association, National Association for American Composers and Conductors, National

Federation of Music Clubs, and National Council of Professional Music Fraternities.

Publications Official publications are: *The WHEEL of Delta Omicron*, quarterly magazine; *The Whistle*, and alumnae newsletter; *The History; Delta Omicron Songbook; Catalogue of Delta Omicron Composers Library; Roster of National Honorary Members and National Patrons*. An instruction book and manuals for province presidents, chapter advisers, and pledges are provided.

Funds and Philanthropies The Delta Omicron Foundation, a nonprofit corporation chartered in 1958, and the Endowment Fund established in 1925, finance the philanthropic program of the fraternity, which includes loans, scholarships, grants, and awards. A Delta Omicron studio for the use of creative artists was built and endowed at the MacDowell Colony in Peterborough, New Hampshire. Seats of $1,000 each have been endowed at the Metropolitan Opera Company, Lincoln Center, New York City, and at the John F. Kennedy Center for the Performing Arts, Washington, D.C.

An International Composition Competition open to all composers and with a monetary award is sponsored triennially. A Delta Omicron Composers Library has on file the works of member composers, catalogued and available for loan.

The fraternity encourages high school music students through scholarships and awards at summer youth music camps. Gifts are made to the American Foundation for the Blind in Korea and to the rehabilitation program of Europe and the Orient. Several Korean members have been assisted for study in the United States. Rotating grants are awarded annually to ten collegiate chapters according to Greek alphabet sequence, and to four alumnae chapters. Summer scholarships are awarded to the Brevard Music Center, Interlochen Institute, as well as two open scholarships to be used at the school of the recipients choice.

Headquarters Executive Office, 1352 Redwood Court, Columbus, Ohio 43229.

Membership Active chapters 90. Inactive chapters 17. Chapter roll:††

1909 Alpha, Cincinnati Conservatory of Music
1911 Beta, Detroit Institute of Musical Art
1911 *Gamma, Southern Seminary* (1916)
1915 *Delta, Denison* (1953)
1917 *Epsilon, Morrey School of Music* (1942)
1918 *Eta, Cincinnati Conservatory of Music* (1950)
1918 Zeta, Louisville (1929-1950)
1921 Theta, Nebraska
1922 *Iota, Gulf Park* (1925)
1922 *Kappa, Des Moines* (1931)
1923 *Lambda, Northwestern* (1956)
1923 Mu, Miami (OH)
1925 *Nu, Marquette* (1931)

1925 Omicron, Western State (CO)
1925 *Pi, Bush Conservatory* (1941)
1925 *Rho, Eastman* (1956)
1925 *Xi, Michigan* (1936)
1926 Sigma, Illinois Wesleyan
1927 *Tau, Millikin* (1933)
1928 Chi, Ohio State
1928 *Phi, Lawrence* (1934)
1928 Upsilon, Colorado State
1929 *Delta Alpha, Peabody Conservatory* (1938)
1929 *Omega, Denver Conservatory* (1935)
1929 Psi, American Conservatory
1931 *Delta Beta, L.S.U.* (1962)
1932 Delta Gamma, Colorado State, Greeley
1933 Delta Delta, Georgetown
1936 Delta Epsilon, Wisconsin Music
1940 *Delta Zeta, USC* (1947)
1941 Delta Eta, Wisconsin, Milwaukee
1943 Delta Theta, Wayne State
1944 Delta Iota, Central Michigan
1945 Delta Kappa, Marshall
1947 Delta Lambda, Penn
1948 Delta Mu, South Carolina
1948 Delta Nu, Southwestern
1949 Delta Omicron, Michigan State
1950 Delta Xi, New England Conservatory
1951 Delta Pi, Hunter
1952 Delta Rho, Adelphi
1953 Delta Sigma, Indiana (PA)
1954 Delta Chi, Nebraska State, Kearney
1954 Delta Phi, Auburn
1954 Delta Tau, William and Mary
1954 Delta Upsilon, Kent
1955 Delta Omega, Jacksonville (AL)
1955 Delta Psi, Judson
1955 Omicron Alpha, Otterbein
1956 Omicron Beta, Lamar
1956 Omicron Delta, Southeastern Louisiana
1956 Omicron Epsilon, Northeast Louisiana
1956 Omicron Gamma, Samford
1957 Omicron Eta, Western Maryland
1957 Omicron Theta, Columbia (SC)
1957 Omicron Zeta, East Tennessee
1958 Kappa Alpha, Ewha (Korea)
1958 Kappa Beta, Sook Myung (Korea)
1958 Kappa Gamma, Seoul National (Korea)
1958 Omicron Iota, Mercer
1958 Omicron Kappa, Mississippi College
1959 Omicron Lambda, Queens (NC)
1959 Omicron Mu, Louisiana Col.
1960 Omicron Nu, Iowa Wesleyan
1961 Omicron Omicron, Western Kentucky
1961 Omicron Xi, Omaha
1963 Omicron Pi, Queens (NY)
1963 Omicron Rho, Philadelphia Musical
1964 Omicron Sigma, William Carey
1964 Omicron Tau, Trenton
1965 Alpha Alpha, Wisconsin, Stevens Point
1965 Omicron Chi, Wisconsin, Oshkosh
1965 Omicron Omega, Illinois State
1965 Omicron Phi, Wisconsin, Whitewater
1965 Omicron Psi, Middle Tennessee

†† This chapter roll is repeated from the 19th edition; no current information was provided.

1965 Omicron Upsilon, Glassboro
1966 Alpha Beta, Indiana
1966 Alpha Delta, Howard Payne
1966 Alpha Epsilon, Converse
1966 Alpha Gamma, Carson-Newman
1966 Alpha Zeta, Maryville
1967 Alpha Eta, Eastern Kentucky
1967 Alpha Iota, Kentucky Wesleyan
1967 Alpha Kappa, Texas A & I
1967 Alpha Lambda, Henderson
1967 Alpha Mu, Livingston State
1967 Alpha Nu, Bethel
1967 Alpha Omicron, McMurry
1967 Alpha Pi, Wyoming
1967 Alpha Rho, Southern Colorado
1967 Alpha Theta, Frostburg
1967 Alpha Xi, Richmond Professional
1968 Alpha Sigma, Findlay
1969 Kappa Delta, Yonsei (Korea)
1970 Alpha Tau, Mars Hill
1971 Alpha Upsilon, Incarnate Word
1972 Alpha Chi, Hope
1972 Alpha Phi, Florida Southern
1972 Alpha Psi, Newberry
1973 Gamma Alpha, Rosary Hill (NY)
1973 Gamma Beta, Morris Brown
1973 Gamma Gamma, Alverno
1974 Kappa Epsilon, Han Sung (Korea)
1974 Kappa Zeta, Chung Ang (Korea)
1975 Gamma Delta, Tennessee, Chattanooga
1976 Gamma Epsilon, Oakland
1976 Gamma Zeta, Alabama State

Delta Psi Kappa

(PHYSICAL EDUCATION)

ACTIVE PIN

DELTA PSI KAPPA, a professional physical education fraternity, was founded at the Normal College of the American Gymnastic Union, October 23, 1916, by Mary Browning, Eliza Bryan, Nelle Fuller, Euphemia Fosdick, Florence Johnson, Elsa Heilich, Sylvia Handler, Rose Quinn, Alice Morrow, and Ella Sattinger, and was incorporated under the laws of the State of Indiana, February 16, 1917. Its purpose is to recognize worthy members in the field of physical education, to advance the aims and ideals of physical education and to develop interest therein, and to promote greater fellowship among individuals in this field of activity. Membership is open to persons in the fields of health, physical education, recreation, and dance who have attained standards above average and have given evidence of potential leadership in the profession. Chapters may be es-

tablished only in schools with major departments in physical education, meeting the standards set forth by the American Alliance for Health, Physical Education, Recreation and Dance with which it is affiliated.

Phi Delta Pi, national professional physical education fraternity, was brought into union with Delta Psi Kappa in March, 1970.

Government Government is entrusted to the Board of Directors, composed of president, president-elect, vice president for undergraduates, vice president for alumni, executive director, province directors and the student inter-province chairman. The chapters are divided by area into provinces. Conventions are held biennially and in conjunction with the national or a district convention of the America Alliance for Health, Physical Education, Recreation and Dance.

Traditions and Insignia The flower is the yellow tea rose and the colors are turquoise and old gold. The open motto is: "A sound mind in a sound body."

Publications *The Foil*, published semi-annually, is the official publication. *The Psi Kap Shield*, a newsletter of chapters and members, is also published.

Funds and Philanthropies The first national project was completed in 1939 when equipment was presented to the Nashville (Tennessee) Home for Crippled Children. The project adopted at the 1940 convention in Indianapolis was the biennial awarding of a research fellowship to a person doing research in the field of health, physical education, recreation or dance. The recipient of the research award is chosen by a committee who are members of A.A.H.P.E.R.D. The fraternity also adopts a service project in which all collegiate and alumni chapters participate. An Educational Loan Fund has been in existence since 1924 to enable members needing financial aid to finish their education. The Delta Psi Kappa Foundation was established in 1984 for charitable and educational purposes.

Headquarters 1226 West Michigan, Indianapolis, IN 46202.

Membership Chapter roll:††

1916 Alpha, Indianapolis
1917 *Beta, Stetson*
1918 *Delta, Posse School of Gymnastics, Kendall Green*
1918 Epsilon, USC
1918 *Gamma, Oklahoma*
1919 *Eta, Battle Creek School of Physical Education*
1919 *Theta, Panzer, Newark*
1919 *Zeta, Washington (MO)*
1920 *Iota, Oregon State*
1920 *Kappa, American College of Physical Education, Chicago*

†† This chapter roll is repeated from the 19th edition; no current information was provided.

1920 *Lambda, Chicago Normal School of Physical Education*
1920 *Mu, Montana*
1920 *Nu, Pitt*
1926 *Omicron, Brenau*
1926 *Xi, Southern Methodist*
1927 *Pi, North Dakota Agricultural*
1928 Rho, North Texas
1928 *Sigma, George Peabody*
1928 Tau, Temple
1929 *Upsilon, Akron*
1930 Chi, Northern Arizona
1930 Phi, Wisconsin, La Crosse
1931 *Psi, Ithaca School of Physical Education*
1932 *Omega, Mary Hardin-Baylor*
1933 *Alpha Alpha, William and Mary*
1938 *Alpha Beta, Moorhead*
1939 Alpha Gamma, L.S.U.
1945 Alpha Delta, Butler
1946 Alpha Epsilon, Michigan State
1946 Alpha Zeta, Kansas State, Pittsburg
1947 Alpha Eta, West Virginia Wesleyan
1947 *Alpha Theta, South Carolina*
1948 *Alpha Iota, Arkansas State, Conway*
1948 Alpha Kappa, Southwest Texas
1948 Alpha Lambda, Northern Illinois
1948 Alpha Mu, Baylor
1949 Alpha Nu, North Dakota
1950 Alpha Omicron, Kent
1950 Alpha Xi, Stephen F. Austin
1952 Alpha Pi, Bowling Green
1952 *Alpha Rho, Occidental*
1953 Alpha Sigma, Southwest Missouri
1953 Alpha Tau, Central Michigan
1954 Alpha Upsilon, Texas Western
1956 Alpha Phi, Slippery Rock
1958 Alpha Chi, Lamar
1959 Alpha Psi, Arizona
1961 Alpha Omega, Kentucky
1962 Beta Alpha, Northwest Missouri
1963 Beta Beta, East Texas
1963 Beta Delta, Eastern Michigan
1963 Beta Gamma, Central Missouri State
1964 Beta Epsilon, Trenton
1964 Beta Zeta, West Texas
1965 Beta Eta, Miami (OH)
1967 Beta Iota, Texas Tech.
1967 Beta Theta, Central State (OK)
1968 Beta Kappa, Indiana State
1968 Beta Lambda, Longwood
1968 Beta Mu, Grambling
1968 Beta Nu, Southwestern Louisiana
1969 Beta Omicron, Wisconsin, River Falls
1969 Beta Pi, Southern Connecticut
1969 Beta Xi, Eastern Illinois
1970 Beta Phi, Georgetown Col
1970 Beta Rho, West Liberty
1970 Beta Tau, Miami (FL)
1970 Beta Upsilon, Florida State
1971 Beta Chi, Northwestern Louisiana
1971 Beta Sigma, Texas Christian
1972 Beta Omega, Kansas State

1972 Beta Psi, Indiana
1972 Gamma Alpha, Nicholls
1973 Gamma Beta, Georgia Southern
1973 Gamma Delta, Houston
1973 Gamma Gamma, Eastern Kentucky
1975 Gamma Epsilon, Old Dominion
1975 Gamma Zeta, V.P.I.

Delta Sigma Pi

(COMMERCE AND
BUSINESS ADMINISTRATION)

ACTIVE PIN

PLEDGE PIN

DELTA SIGMA PI is a professional fraternity in the field of commerce and business administration and was founded at New York University School of Commerce, Accounts, and Finance, on November 7, 1907, by Alexander F. Makay, H. Albert Tienken, Harold V. Jacobs, and Alfred Moysello to foster the study of business in universities; to encourage scholarship, social activity, and the association of students for their mutual advancement by research and practice; to promote closer affiliation between the commercial world and students of commerce; and to further a higher standard of commercial ethics and culture, and the civic and commercial welfare of the community.

Collegiate chapters may be established only in those leading universities and colleges having professional schools, colleges, or departments of commerce and business administration offering courses leading to a diploma or a degree in this field. To be eligible for membership in the fraternity, the student must be regularly enrolled in such professional courses.

Growth The growth of Delta Sigma Pi was relatively slow until the early '20s during which period 29 chapters were installed, a national headquarters established and such things as ritual, insignia and publications were standardized. Expansion continued at a rapid rate until the depression of the '30s. The real growth of the fraternity, however, did not take place until after World War II when over 50 per cent of the collegiate chapters were installed. Much of this was a direct result of the tremendous growth of schools of business administration throughout the country.

Government The government of the fraternity is vested in a Grand Chapter composed of the delegates of all active collegiate and alumni chapters. The national meeting of the Grand Chapter is known as the Grand Chapter Congress, which meets every odd-numbered year in August or September. The Board of Directors of 26 members is elected by the Grand Chapter Congress, and the Board of Directors administers the affairs of the fraternity between meetings of the Grand Chapter Congress.

The chapters of the fraternity are divided into 17 geographic regions within four provinces for administrative purposes. Meetings are held biennially in each region at regular intervals between meetings of the Grand Chapter Congress. The fraternity sponsors a chapter efficiency index each year.

All affairs of the fraternity are conducted from a central office, which is in the charge of the executive director, who is appointed by the board. He has a full-time staff of 12. This office serves as a depository for all fraternity records, a source of all jewelry and supplies, the administrative headquarters for all national meetings, the editorial office for all publications, and the public relations center for the fraternity.

Traditions and Insignia In 1912, the fraternity established a scholarship award, open to any student in the professional schools of commerce and business administration. It is known as the Delta Sigma Pi Scholarship Key. This key is supplied annually by the national fraternity to each university where an active chapter is maintained, and the key is awarded by the local faculty to that senior who upon graduation ranks highest in scholarship for the entire course in the professional school of commerce and business administration, regardless of fraternal affiliation. Since 1912, over 3,000 keys have been presented by the fraternity; about one-third of them have been won by its members. A number of chapters also provide local awards for scholarship, and much is done throughout the fraternity to encourage high scholarship and professional achievement. The National Endowment Fund was created in 1930; a portion of the annual revenues of the fraternity are set aside in this trust fund, the purpose of which is to endow the fraternity. These funds are invested under certain restricted conditions. A certain percentage of the fund is available for chapter loans and for loans to qualified undergraduate members to complete their college education. The income from this fund may be appropriated by the fraternity for any of the following purposes: to subsidize in whole or in part any or all of the national activities of the fraternity, including the operation of the central office and the development of the publications of the fraternity; and the encouragement of high scholarship and professional achievement. The National Endowment Fund is administered by the National Executive committee of the fraternity. Through the operation of this fund, the fraternity has assisted many collegiate members to complete their college education and has also assisted others to pursue graduate study.

The fraternity published in 1924 the *Survey of Universities Offering an Organized Curriculum in Commerce and Business Administration,* and has brought this up to date biennially. This has become the accepted authority in its field and has a large distribution. For many years, the fraternity has aided in the standardization of professional degrees in the schools of commerce and business administration. Many chapters sponsor local research projects, field trips, and comprehensive professional programs.

Feeling that one of the most important and valuable activities in the fraternity is the successful and effective operation of organized alumni activity, the fraternity directs considerable attention to its alumni program in order to foster an increased spirit of loyalty among its members for the purpose of professional and social contacts and to bring about the united support of its membership for development of a more effective fraternity. Through the central office of the fraternity, prompt attention is given to all alumni correspondence; general information is disseminated; and alumni groups are organized if a sufficient number of alumni reside in the same territory.

The official badge of Delta Sigma Pi is a skull and crossbones superimposed on a wreath of leaves, with the letters ΔΣΠ inscribed on the skull and crossbones, amethyst eyes in the skull, a crown at the top of the design, and the entire design surrounded by a crescent suitably engraved. The jeweled badge contains 19 jewels, with pearls, rubies, or diamonds, in the crescent design. Official colors of the fraternity are old gold and royal purple. The official flower of the fraternity is a red rose. The pledge pin is a true Greek-letter Δ of gold, with a field of red containing a crown of gold. The fraternity has two flags, one with a reproduction of the coat of arms in colors on a field of white, the other containing the Greek letters in purple on a field of gold, with a solid field of purple on each side. The coat of arms of Delta Sigma Pi is a shield in which is reproduced the badge of the fraternity, a cornucopia, and a ship. In the border of the shield are four stars, and at the top is a crowned helmet with an open visor.

Funds and Philanthropies In 1953, the Delta Sigma Pi Educational Foundation was established to further expand many of the services the fraternity provides in the field of business education and to develop additional projects in business research. It is incorporated as a nonprofit organization and is sustained by voluntary contributions. Specifically, the purposes of the foundation are to carry out the originally announced purposes of the fraternity and, in addition, to encourage, aid, and assist students of business, both undergraduate and graduate; to make available to students of business, financial assistance by way of scholarships, fellowships, and loans of money or other property; and to encourage and assist worthy educational and scientific projects and scientific business research.

Publications The fraternity publishes a quarterly magazine known as *The Deltasig* of Delta Sigma Pi, now in its 74th volume. National membership directories were published in 1917, 1919,

1922, 1924, 1927, 1934, and 1982; The *Manual for Pledge Education* is constantly updated as necessary. The *Manual for Chapter Operations*, first published in 1926, has been revised several times. The *Manual of Alumni Chapter Operation* and the *Anniversary Booklet* have also been published. The fraternity published, in 1924, a standard accounting system especially designed for the use of its chapters. Several fraternity songs have been published. A comprehensive system of chapter reports enables the officers of the fraternity to keep in close touch with the condition of all chapters which are inspected at regular intervals.

Headquarters   330 South Campus Avenue, Oxford, Ohio 45056. The Central Office came into existence during the fall of 1926 and was located at 222 West Adams Street, Chicago. Construction of a $95,000 building in Oxford was completed in the fall of 1956. It is of colonial brick and of modified Georgian design in keeping with the motif of Miami University structures. In 1970 two symmetrical wings were added at a cost of $100,000, doubling square footage. About an acre of ground surrounds the building.

Membership   Total living membership 100,035. Total undergraduate membership 7,352. Active chapters 170. Inactive chapters 55. Houses owned 4. City/Area alumni associations 51. Total number of initiates 146,939. Chapter roll:

1907	Alpha, N.Y.U.
1914	*Beta, Northwestern* (1977)
1916	Gamma, Boston U (1961-1965) (1969-1988)
1920	Delta, Marquette (1969-1978)
1920	Epsilon, Iowa (1935-1946)
1920	*Eta, Kentucky* (1933-1950) (1968)
1920	*Zeta, Northwestern* (1967)
1921	Iota, Kansas (1941-1947) (1978-1986)
1921	Kappa, Georgia State
1921	Lambda, Pitt (1936-1955)
1921	Mu, Georgetown U (1969-1979)
1921	Nu, Ohio State
1921	*Theta, Detroit* (1968)
1921	Xi, Michigan (1965-1982)
1922	Chi, Johns Hopkins
1922	*Omicron, Vanderbilt* (1927)
1922	Phi, USC (1941-1950) (1961-1980)
1922	Pi, Georgia (1972-1973)
1922	Rho, Cal, Berkeley (1961-1964) (1969-1984)
1922	*Sigma, Utah* (1942-1950) (1979)
1922	*Tau, McGill* (1927)
1922	Upsilon, Illinois (1930-1949)
1923	Alpha Beta, Missouri
1923	Alpha Gamma, Penn State
1923	Omega, Temple (1971-1984)
1923	Psi, Wisconsin, Madison
1924	Alpha Delta, Nebraska
1924	Alpha Epsilon, Minnesota
1924	Alpha Eta, South Dakota
1924	Alpha Iota, Drake
1924	Alpha Theta, Cincinnati (1938-1940) (1942-1949)

1924	Alpha Zeta, Tennessee (1977-1979)
1925	Alpha Kappa, SUNY, Buffalo (1936-1948)
1925	Alpha Lambda, North Carolina (1935-1937) (1970-1971)
1925	*Alpha Mu, North Dakota* (1943-1947) (1974)
1925	*Alpha Nu, Denver* (1990)
1925	Alpha Omicron, Ohio (1935-1951)
1925	Alpha Pi, Indiana
1925	*Alpha Xi, Virginia* (1935-1951) (1970)
1926	Alpha Rho, Colorado
1926	Alpha Sigma, Alabama
1927	*Alpha Chi, Washington (MO)* (1936-1948) (1953)
1927	Alpha Phi, Mississippi (1932-1937)
1927	Alpha Tau, Mercer (1933-1982)
1927	Alpha Upsilon, Miami (OH)
1928	Alpha Omega, DePaul
1928	*Alpha Psi, Chicago* (1946)
1929	*Beta Delta, North Carolina State* (1938)
1929	Beta Epsilon, Oklahoma (1932-1936)
1929	Beta Eta, Florida (1942-1948)
1929	Beta Gamma, South Carolina
1929	Beta Zeta, L.S.U.
1930	Beta Iota, Baylor (1971-1981)
1930	Beta Kappa, Texas
1930	*Beta Theta, Creighton* (1975)
1931	Beta Lambda, Auburn
1931	*Beta Mu, Dalhousie* (1937)
1932	Beta Nu, Penn (1968-1988)
1934	Beta Xi, Rider
1937	*Beta Omicron, Rutgers* (1972)
1942	Beta Pi, Kent
1942	Beta Rho, Rutgers
1946	*Beta Sigma, St. Louis* (1968)
1947	*Beta Tau, Case Western Reserve* (1970)
1947	Beta Upsilon, Texas Tech
1948	Beta Chi, Tulsa (1965-1967)
1948	Beta Omega, Miami (FL)
1948	Beta Phi, Southern Methodist
1948	Beta Psi, Louisiana Tech
1949	Gamma Delta, Mississippi State (1968-1974)
1949	Gamma Epsilon, Oklahoma State
1949	*Gamma Eta, Nebraska, Omaha* (1978)
1949	Gamma Iota, New Mexico
1949	*Gamma Kappa, Michigan State* (1974)
1949	Gamma Lambda, Florida State
1949	*Gamma Mu, Tulane* (1963)
1949	Gamma Theta, Wayne State (MI) (1974-1979)
1949	Gamma Zeta, Memphis State (1984-1985)
1950	*Gamma Nu, Wake Forest* (1972)
1950	Gamma Omicron, San Francisco (1980-1982)
1950	Gamma Pi, Loyola, Chicago
1950	*Gamma Rho, Detroit* (1985-1986) (1987)
1950	Gamma Sigma, Maryland
1950	Gamma Tau, Southern Mississippi
1950	*Gamma Xi, Santa Clara* (1971)
1951	*Gamma Chi, St. Bonaventure* (1953)
1951	Gamma Omega, Arizona State
1951	Gamma Phi, Texas, El Paso
1951	Gamma Psi, Arizona

1951	*Gamma Upsilon, Babson* (1981)	1968	Eta Kappa, Troy
1954	Delta Epsilon, North Texas	1968	*Eta Lambda, Weber* (1982)
1955	*Delta Zeta, East Carolina* (1972)	1968	Eta Mu, Northern Illinois
1956	Delta Eta, Lamar	1968	Eta Nu, Missouri, St. Louis
1956	*Delta Theta, Oklahoma City* (1971-1982) (1983)	1968	Eta Xi, Philadelphia Textiles
1957	Delta Iota, Florida Southern (1985-1987)	1969	*Eta Chi, Cal Poly, Pomona* (1989)
1957	*Delta Kappa, Boston Col* (1975)	1969	Eta Omicron, Northeast Louisiana
1957	*Delta Lambda, Ithaca* (1971)	1969	*Eta Phi, Eastern Michigan* (1982-1983) (1984)
1958	*Delta Mu, U of Americas* (1975)	1969	Eta Pi, Wayne State (NE)
1958	Delta Nu, Loyola, New Orleans	1969	Eta Psi, Houston
1958	Delta Xi, East Tennessee	1969	Eta Rho, Wisconsin, La Crosse
1959	Delta Omicron, San Francisco State	1969	*Eta Sigma, Southern Illinois* (1986)
1959	Delta Pi, Nevada (1974-1976)	1969	Eta Tau, McNeese
1959	Delta Rho, Ferris	1969	Eta Upsilon, West Florida
1959	Delta Sigma, Loyola Marymount, Los Angeles (1966-1968)	1970	Eta Omega, Virginia Commonwealth
1959	Delta Tau, Indiana State	1970	Theta Iota, Connecticut
1959	Delta Upsilon, Texas Christian	1970	Theta Kappa, Akron
1960	*Delta Chi, Washburn* (1990)	1970	Theta Lambda, Xavier (OH)
1960	Delta Omega, West Liberty	1970	*Theta Mu, Columbus* (1984)
1960	*Delta Phi, East Texas* (1987)	1970	*Theta Nu, Arkansas* (1975)
1960	*Delta Psi, Suffolk* (1988)	1970	Theta Omicron, St. Ambrose
1960	*Epsilon Eta, Eastern New Mexico* (1987)	1970	Theta Pi, Bowling Green
1960	Epsilon Iota, Mankato (1975-1981)	1970	Theta Rho, Duquesne
1960	Epsilon Theta, Cal State, Chico	1970	Theta Sigma, Central Florida
1960	*Epsilon Zeta, Midwestern* (1974)	1970	Theta Tau, St. Cloud
1961	Epsilon Kappa, Shepherd	1970	Theta Xi, Wisconsin, Whitewater
1961	*Epsilon Lambda, Rochester Tech* (1983)	1971	Theta Chi, San Jose
1962	*Epsilon Mu, Sam Houston* (1975)	1971	Theta Phi, South Florida
1962	Epsilon Nu, New Orleans	1971	Theta Psi, Indiana Northwest
1962	*Epsilon Omicron, Western Michigan* (1970)	1971	Theta Upsilon, Siena
1962	*Epsilon Pi, Monmouth (NJ)* (1971)	1972	Theta Omega, St. Edward's (1975-1981)
1962	Epsilon Xi, Ball State	1974	Iota Kappa, Madison Col
1963	Epsilon Chi, Georgia Southern	1977	Iota Lambda, IUPU, Fort Wayne
1963	Epsilon Phi, Cal State, Sacramento	1977	*Iota Mu, Georgia Col* (1988)
1963	Epsilon Rho, Tampa	1978	Iota Nu, Northeast Missouri
1963	Epsilon Sigma, LaSalle	1979	Iota Omicron, Central Missouri State
1963	Epsilon Tau, Dayton (1973-1981)	1979	Iota Pi, San Diego U.
1963	Epsilon Upsilon, New Mexico State	1979	*Iota Xi, Winston-Salem* (1987)
1964	Epsilon Omega, Eastern Illinois	1980	Iota Chi, Illinois State
1964	Epsilon Psi, Christian Brothers	1980	Iota Phi, Cal State, Fresno
1964	Zeta Eta, St. Peter's	1980	Iota Rho, Howard
1964	Zeta Iota, Mississippi Col	1980	Iota Sigma, Evansville
1964	Zeta Theta, Western Kentucky	1980	Iota Tau, Robert Morris
1965	Zeta Kappa, Western State (CO)	1980	Iota Upsilon, Cal State, Northridge
1965	*Zeta Lambda, Georgia Tech* (1973)	1981	Iota Omega, North Carolina, Greensboro
1965	Zeta Mu, Texas, Arlington	1981	Iota Psi, Corpus Christi
1965	Zeta Nu, Texas A & I	1981	Kappa Lambda, SUNY, Binghamton
1965	Zeta Omicron, C. W. Post	1981	Kappa Mu, Cal Poly, San Luis Obispo
1965	*Zeta Pi, St. Joseph's (PA)* (1983)	1981	Kappa Nu, Longwood
1965	Zeta Xi, Lewis	1981	Kappa Omicron, Southwest Missouri
1966	*Zeta Chi, Manhattan* (1971)	1981	Kappa Pi, North Florida
1966	*Zeta Phi, Florida Atlantic* (1990)	1981	Kappa Xi, Southwestern Louisiana
1966	*Zeta Rho, Menlo* (1983)	1982	Kappa Rho, Adelphi
1966	*Zeta Sigma, Southeastern Louisiana* (1984)	1982	Kappa Sigma, IUPUI
1966	*Zeta Tau, Cal State, Hayward* (1976)	1982	Kappa Tau, Clemson
1966	Zeta Upsilon, VPI	1983	Kappa Chi, Savannah
1967	Eta Iota, Nicholls	1983	Kappa Phi, Valparaiso
1967	Eta Theta, Angelo	1983	Kappa Psi, Bellarmine
1967	Zeta Omega, Northern Arizona	1983	Kappa Upsilon, Winona
1967	Zeta Psi, SUNY, Albany	1984	Kappa Omega, Purdue
		1984	Lambda Mu, Pacific (CA)

1985   Lambda Nu, Texas A & M
1986   Lambda Omicron, Western Illinois
1986   Lambda Pi, San Diego U.
1986   Lambda Rho, Livingston
1986   Lambda Sigma Society, Cal State, Fullerton
1986   Lambda Xi, Grand Valley
1987   Lambda Tau, Bentley
1988   Lambda Phi, Cal State, Long Beach
1988   Lambda Upsilon, St. Mary's
1989   Lambda Chi, Cal, Riverside
1989   Lambda Omega, Quincy
1989   Lambda Psi, Hawaii, Hilo
1989   Mu Nu, Nevada, Las Vegas
1990   Mu Omicron, Houston, Victoria
1990   Mu Xi, LaRoche

Delta Theta Phi

(LAW)

ACTIVE PIN

PLEDGE PIN

DELTA THETA PHI, a law fraternity, was formed on September 26, 1913, in Chicago, Illinois, by the amalgamation of three law fraternities: Delta Phi Delta, Alpha Kappa Phi, and Theta Lambda Phi. Delta Phi Delta was founded in 1900 (from which date Delta Theta Phi dates its founding) at the Cleveland Law School of Baldwin-Wallace College (now Cleveland State University) in Cleveland, Ohio, by Eugene Quigley, Charles E. Schmick, William F. Mackay, John Lawrence Barrett, Arthur W. Born, John H. Orgill, John H. Redhead and Fred W. Sinram. Alpha Kappa Phi was founded in 1902 at the Northwestern University School of Law, Chicago, Illinois, by Charles G. Rose, Frank B. Schaefer, Manfred S. Block, Jesse E. Eschbach, Joseph L. Shaw and Harry A. Swigert. Theta Lambda Phi was founded in 1903 at the Dickinson School of Law, in Carlisle, Pennsylvania, by Thomas S. Lanard and Walter P. Bishop.

Membership in Delta Theta Phi is open to all students enrolled in fully accredited law schools. There are no restrictions based upon race, sex, or religion.

In recognition of the growing international character of the fraternity, with active senates in Canada and Iceland, the word "International" was added to the name of the fraternity in August, 1983.

Government   The executive functions of the fraternity are exercised by the Supreme Senate (board of directors), composed of nine international officers who are elected by the International Senate (supreme legislative body) in convention assembled every two years. Seven of those nine officers are alumni members, and two are student members when elected. The chancellor (president), as the chief executive officer, and the master of rolls (secretary-treasurer), as the officer responsible for the day-to-day operations of the International Headquarters Office, are the two principal alumni officers of the Supreme Senate.

The International Senate is the supreme legislative body of the fraternity. It is a continuing body, and transacts its business by correspondence as well as during the biennial conventions. The International Senate is composed of over 220 members having one vote each: all past chancellors (presidents), all members of the Supreme Senate, each tribune (corresponding secretary) of the student senates (chapters), and each tribune (corresponding secretary) of the alumni senates (chapters).

The judicial functions of the fraternity are exercised by a Supreme Court composed of five alumni members elected by the International Senate in convention assembled.

For purposes of administration, the country is divided into regional areas and into districts. Each district is under the supervision of a district chancellor appointed by the chancellor.

Traditions and Insignia   The Delta Theta Phi Scholarship Certificate and Key are awarded to each member who, at the completion of his or her junior year, stands within the top seven and one-half percent of his or her class, or who, upon receiving his or her law degree, has attained a scholarship standing in the top fifteen percent of the graduating class. The fraternity also has a scholarship cup, for which the various student senates contest annually. Delta Theta Phi claims to be the first law fraternity to award a key on the basis of scholarship only.

An illustration of the recognition pin worn by law school members, and of the membership badge which can be purchased separately (by student and alumni members) and worn either in conjunction with, or in place of, the recognition pin, are included with this article. The alumnus badge, which may be worn by members who have graduated from law school and otherwise, is crowned with three full-set pearls. The sister/brother pin is the same as the plain badge, but is surrounded by twelve small crown-set pearls. Members who have rendered distinguished service to the fraternity or who have attained distinction in the practice or in the teaching of the law, may, by vote of the International Senate, be permitted to crown the badge with a setting of diamonds. The official pledge button is a white geometric shield with the dexter in green across the shield. The colors of the fraternity are green and white. The flower is a white carnation, with a background of green leaves.

Publications   *The Paper Book*, published quarterly, is the official magazine. Two editions of a songbook have been published, and ten editions of a directory, the latter in 1917, 1922, 1929, 1937, 1948, 1953, 1958, 1961, 1965, and—1981.

International Headquarters Office 666 High Street, Worthington, Ohio 43085-4106.

Membership Active law school senates 165. Inactive law school senates 14. Alumni senates, 102. Total membership, 90,374. Chapter roll:

1901	Ranney, Cleveland-Marshall
1902	*Wigmore, Northwestern* (1951)
1903	Cooley, Detroit Law
1903	*Finch, Cornell* (1953)
1903	Holmes, Dickinson Law (-1984)
1904	Bleckley, Georgia (-1981)
1904	*Freeman, Tennessee* (1913)
1904	Harlan-McKusick, South Dakota
1904	Warvelle, DePaul (-1985)
1905	Mitchell, Minnesota (-1981)
1906	Day, Case Western Reserve (-1979)
1907	*Kent, New York Law* (1955)
1907	*Lurton, Tennessee, Chattanooga* (1942)
1908	Douglas, Stephen, John Marshall Law, Chicago
1908	Epsilon, Arkansas (Merged with Robinson 1913)
1909	Burks-Laughlin, Washington and Lee
1909	*Lincoln, Chicago* (1934)
1909	Magruder, Chicago-Kent Law (Combined with Webster)
1910	Marshall, Ohio Northern
1910	*Parker, Union* (1915)
1910	Ramsey-Amdahl, William Mitchell Law (-1981)
1910	*Von Moschzisker, Penn* (1928)
1910	White, E.D., Georgetown U.
1911	Jefferson, Thomas, Richmond
1912	Benton, Washington (MO)
1912	Bryan, William Jennings, Creighton
1912	Christiancy, Michigan (-1980)
1912	Field, USC
1912	Fuller, Fordham
1912	Ingalls, Washburn
1913	Chase, Ohio State (-1972)
1913	Deady, Oregon
1914	*Dwight, Columbia (NY)* (1932)
1914	Wayne, Atlanta
1915	Adams, Boston U
1915	Howat, Utah
1915	*Pitney, New Jersey* (1953) (Now Rutgers)
1915	Snyder, Missouri, Kansas City
1915	Webster, Chicago-Kent Law
1916	Brewer, Kansas
1916	Gibson, John B., Pitt
1916	Hosmer, Detroit Law (-1981)
1916	Houston, Texas
1916	*Russell, N.Y.U.* (1916)
1916	Wilson, George Washington (-1974)
1919	Lee, Robert E., Virginia
1919	McKinley, John Marshall
1921	Bliss, Missouri (-1980)
1921	Cole, Drake (-1981)
1921	Dillon, Iowa
1921	Eschweiler, Marquette
1921	Jackson, Memphis State
1921	Williams, Lewis and Clark
1922	Bakewell, St. Louis
1922	Hamilton, Brooklyn Law
1922	Keeble, Vanderbilt
1922	Maxwell, Nebraska
1922	*McEnerney, Cal, Oakland* (1941)
1922	Root, Stanford
1922	Taney, Maryland
1923	*Hohfeld, Yale* (1929)
1923	Story, Washington (WA)
1923	Voorhees, IUPUI (1942-1981)
1924	Battle, North Carolina
1925	Davis, David, Illinois (-1981)
1925	McKenna, Loyola, Chicago
1926	Farrar, Loyola, New Orleans
1926	*Fleming, Colorado* (1932)
1927	Harmon, Cincinnati (-1985)
1927	Hemphill, Southern Methodist
1928	Banta, Indiana (-1981)
1928	Jay, St. John's (NY) (-1985)
1928	Lamar, Mercer
1928	Warren, Charles Beecher, Wayne State (MI) (-1979)
1928	Wolverton, Willamette (-1983)
1940	Gavin, Tulsa
1941	Davis, John W., American (-1979)
1941	Hughes, National (Merged with George Washington)
1941	Robinson, Arkansas
1941	Taft, Toledo
1947	Byrnes, Duke
1947	Edmondson, Oklahoma
1947	Hart, William McKinley
1947	Vinson, Florida
1948	Clay, Louisville
1948	Green, Samford
1948	Lohnes, Columbus (Merged with Catholic University)
1948	Warren, Fuller, Stetson (-1984)
1949	Alexander, Baylor
1949	Cardozo, Miami (FL)
1949	Evans, Wisconsin, Madison
1949	Rentner, Valparaiso
1949	Traynor, Hastings Law
1949	White, Stephen M., Loyola Marymount, Los Angeles
1950	Bickett, St. Mary's, San Antonio
1950	*Loring* (merged with Ramsey-Mitchell College of Law)
1955	Cullen, Houston
1956	Townes, South Texas Law
1964	Kerr, Oklahoma City
1965	Hughes, Catholic
1966	Barkley, Kentucky
1966	Brandeis, San Diego U
1966	Catron, Tennessee
1967	Davis, Jefferson, Mississippi
1968	Buford, Florida State
1969	Lindsey, Texas Tech
1969	Morrow, Tulane
1969	Simpson, Suffolk

1970 Hayes, Howard
1970 Kozuch, New England Law
1970 McComb, Southwestern Law
1970 Pabon, Inter-American
1970 deHostos, Catholic, Puerto Rico
1971 Kingsley, UCLA
1971 McClellan, Arkansas, Little Rock
1971 Musmanno, Duquesne
1971 Thomas, Arizona State
1972 Black, Stetson
1972 Jaeger, New Mexico
1972 Lenoir, Southern
1972 MacLean, New England Law (-1980)
1972 McKissick, North Carolina Central
1972 O'Neill, Capital
1973 Ellender, L.S.U.
1973 Johnson, Northern Kentucky
1973 Pepperdine, Pepperdine (-1979)
1973 Rankin, Emory
1973 Seiberling, Akron
1973 Snaevarr, Iceland
1973 Tucker, William and Mary (-1981)
1973 Vanderveer, Puget Sound (-1983)
1975 Patterson, Mississippi Col
1975 Power, Thomas M. Cooley
1975 Wolcott, Delaware
1976 Almond, George Mason
1976 Brown, Brigham Young
1976 Douglas, William O., Potomac
1976 Stevens, Western State, San Diego
1976 Williston, Western State, Fullerton
1977 Blackmun, Pace
1977 Coke, Northern Illinois
1977 Corman, LaVerne
1977 Ellsworth, Bridgeport
1977 Tobriner, Whittier
1978 Mathews, Alabama
1978 Shores, Miles
1979 Bryan, Robert C., Campbell
1979 Egly, LaVerne
1979 Van Sickle, North Dakota
1980 Hall, Northrop
1982 Baine, Denver
1982 Best, San Joaquin
1982 Jefferson, Bernard S., West Los Angeles
1982 Kuhio, Hawaii
1982 LeBaron, Woodrow Wilson
1982 Lee, Thomas E. Jr., Nova
1982 Lesar, Southern Illinois
1982 O'Connor, Ventura
1982 Thurmond, South Carolina
1982 Warren, Earl, Lincoln Law
1983 Alverson, Georgia State
1983 Bennett, New Brunswick, Canada
1983 Billings, Vermont
1983 Digges, Baltimore U.

1983 Ehrlich, San Francisco
1983 Fuchsberg, Touro
1983 Gibson, Phil S., Monterey
1983 Gordon, Pacific (CA)
1983 Hathaway, Wyoming
1983 Magnuson, Hamline
1983 Menard, Idaho
1983 Moorhead, Glendale
1983 Nelson-Leary, Old College
1983 Westwick, Santa Barbara
1984 Cordon, Santa Clara
1985 Blackstone, John F. Kennedy
1985 Feinstein, Humphreys
1985 Murphy, St. Thomas
1985 Williams-Berkowitz, Wake Forest

Gamma Iota Sigma

Chapter narrative is not available.
Membership Active chapters 27. Inactive chapters 3. Total number of initiates 2,500. Chapter roll:

1966 Alpha, Ohio State
1967 Beta, Bowling Green
1969 Gamma, Cincinnati
1970 *Delta, Orange Coast* (1977)
1972 Epsilon, Alabama
1973 Zeta, Georgia State
1975 Eta, Georgia
1975 Iota, Florida State
1975 *Kappa, Arizona State* (1984)
1975 *Theta, L.S.U.* (1984)
1976 Lambda, South Carolina
1976 Mu, Mississippi
1977 Nu, Central Michigan (1980-1990)
1978 Omicron, Arkansas State
1978 Pi, Mississippi State
1978 Xi, Connecticut
1979 Rho, Appalachian
1980 Sigma, Temple
1981 Tau, Howard
1981 Upsilon, Ferris
1982 Chi, Drake
1982 Phi, Ball State
1983 Psi, Eastern Kentucky
1984 Omega, Middle Tennessee
1986 Alpha Alpha, Olivet
1989 Penn State
1989 Alpha Beta, Penn State
1989 Alpha Delta, LaSalle
1989 Alpha Gamma, Penn
1990 Alpha Epsilon, Indiana State

COAT OF ARMS

Kappa Delta Epsilon

(EDUCATION)

KAPPA DELTA EPSILON was founded on March 26, 1933, in Washington, D.C., as an organization for undergraduate and graduate women students in education. It was chartered under the laws of Georgia in 1935. In 1978, the sorority became a professional education society to include men and women students at undergraduate and graduate levels. The purpose of the society is to promote the cause of education by fostering high standards of scholastic achievement, a spirit of fellowship, and professional ideals among its members.

Growth Beginning in 1933 with six founding chapters, the society has chartered a total of 70 chapters in the United States and Mexico. Kappa Delta Epsilon is a member of the Professional Fraternity Association.

Government A biennial convention is held in odd-numbered years, with regional meetings held in off convention years on the campus of one of the colleges or universities included in the organization. The convention; the National Executive Board, comprised of the duly elected officers; the National Executive Council, composed of the national officers; the chapter advisors, and representatives to the Council of Chapter Delegates; the Past Presidents' Council; and the Founders' Council are the governing bodies.

Traditions and Insignia The official colors are purple and white. The key is in the shape of a shield with the Greek word, Λουσσ, written across the top and the letters KΔE on a scroll across the key. The flower is the purple iris.

Publications A bi-monthly publication, *The Current*, carries national and chapter news of the society. The *Handbook* contains the history, insignia, duties of the officers, and responsibilities of membership, and also states the aims, purposes, and ideals of the society.

Funds and Philanthropies Four scholarships are given annually to student members of high scholastic ability needing assistance to complete their education.

Headquarters 9 Arcadia Drive, Tuscaloosa, Alabama 35404.

Membership Total undergraduate membership 27,710. Active chapters 35. Inactive chapters 41. Graduate/Alumni chapters 11. City/Area alumni associations 6. Total number of initiates 31,973. Chapter roll:

1933 *Alpha, Allegheny* (1979)
1933 Beta, Birmingham-Southern
1933 Delta (Emory Alumni)
1933 Epsilon, Illinois State
1933 *Gamma, Cornell* (1960)
1933 *Zeta, Temple* (1973)
1936 *Eta, Hamline* (1952)
1938 *Theta, Bucknell* (1960)
1939 *Iota, Gettysburg* (1960)
1940 Kappa, Mercer
1941 *Lambda, Millsaps* (1978)
1946 Mu, Mississippi for Women
1950 *Nu, Arizona State* (1954)
1950 Omicron, Birmingham-Southern
1950 Pi, South Carolina
1950 Rho, Belhaven
1950 *Xi, Emory and Henry* (1971)
1951 *Sigma, Furman* (1985)
1952 *Tau, Penn* (1969)
1952 *Upsilon, N.Y.U.* (1969)
1953 *Phi, Southern Connecticut* (1981)
1954 *Alpha Alpha, Idaho State* (1960)
1954 Chi, Jacksonville
1954 Omega, Samford
1954 Psi, Point Loma
1955 Alpha Beta, Columbia (NY)
1955 *Alpha Delta (South Carolina Alumni)* (1956)
1955 *Alpha Gamma, American* (1967)
1956 Alpha Epsilon, Georgia
1956 *Alpha Eta, Wittenberg* (1979)
1956 *Alpha Zeta, Limestone* (1988)
1957 Alpha Iota (Samford Alumni)
1957 Alpha Kappa, Duquesne
1957 *Alpha Theta, Moravian* (1974)
1958 *Alpha Lambda, Georgia Southern* (1979)
1958 Alpha Mu, Vanderbilt
1959 Alpha Nu, Eastern Montana
1959 Alpha Omicron, Wesleyan (CT)
1959 *Alpha Xi, Emory* (1974-1981) (1986)
1960 Alpha Pi (Philadelphia Alumni)
1960 *Alpha Rho, SUNY, Albany* (1966)
1961 Alpha Sigma, Alabama
1963 *Alpha Tau, Johnson State* (1976)
1965 *Alpha Phi (Macon Alumni)* (1973)
1965 *Alpha Upsilon, Louisiana Col* (1971)
1966 *Alpha Chi, Maine, Portland-Gorham* (1984)
1968 *Alpha Omega, Miami (OH)* (1978)
1968 *Alpha Psi, Boston Col.* (1970)
1968 *Beta Alpha, SUNY Col., Plattsburgh* (1971)
1968 *Beta Beta, Georgia State* (1984-1988) (1989)
1968 *Beta Gamma, Loyola, Chicago* (1975)
1969 Beta Delta, L.S.U.
1970 *Beta Epsilon, California (PA)* (1983)
1970 *Beta Zeta, Holy Cross* (1972)
1974 *Beta Eta (Gorham Alumni)* (1984)
1974 *Beta Theta (Southern Connecticut Alumni)* (1977)
1975 Beta Iota, Alabama, Birmingham
1975 *Beta Kappa, Carlow* (1981-1989)
1975 *Beta Lambda, Southern* (1982-1989)

1978 *Beta Mu, Steubenville* (1983)
1979 *Beta Nu (Greenburg Alumni)* (1984)
1980 *Beta Xi (Pittsburgh Alumni)* (1982)
1982 *Beta Omicron, Mercer* (1989)
1982 Beta Pi, Clark
1982 Beta Rho, Judson (1987-1989)
1982 *Beta Tau, Regiomontana* (1985)
1983 *Beta Phi (Washington (D.C.) Alumni)* (1984)
1983 Beta Sigma (Alabama Alumni)
1983 Beta Upsilon, Mobile
1985 Beta Chi (L.S.U. ALUMNI)
1986 Beta Omega, Alabama, Birmingham
1986 Beta Psi, Spelman
1988 Gamma Alpha, Alice Lloyd
1988 Gamma Beta, Jacksonville
1989 Gamma Delta, Nevada, Las Vegas
1989 Gamma Gamma, Caldwell

Kappa Epsilon

(PHARMACY)

ACTIVE PIN

KAPPA EPSILON was founded in Iowa City, Iowa, on May 13, 1921, by Professor Zada M. Cooper and representatives of the women's pharmacy clubs of the University of Minnesota, University of Nebraska and the University of Iowa. The clubs became Alpha, Beta and Gamma Chapters, respectively, and their members became charter members of Kappa Epsilon Fraternity. The purpose of the fraternity is to promote the cause of pharmacy by fostering a spirit of fellowship, high standards of scholastic attainment, and professional ideals among its members. The fraternity is a member of the Professional Fraternity Association.

Government The governing body is the convention which meets biennially in odd-numbered years. It is composed of elected delegates from each collegiate and alumnae chapter and the Grand Council. In the interim between conventions, the fraternity is directed by the Grand Council which is composed of the president, four vice presidents, secretary, treasurer and two past presidents.

Insignia The official badge is composed of the Greek letters, K and E. The gold E is the foundation of the badge on which is superimposed the K, usually set in pearls. The pledge pin is a black enamel diamond-shaped pin, superimposed with a gold mortar and pestle engraved with KE in the center. The official colors are red and white. The official flower is the red rose.

Publications *The BOND of Kappa Epsilon Fraternity* is the official publication. It is published twice a year and distributed to all members in good standing.

Awards Zada M. Cooper Scholarships are given an-

nually to collegiate members. The Nellie Wakeman Fellowship is given annually to a member pursuing graduate study in one of the pharmaceutical sciences. Scholastic achievement is recognized by awards presented to collegiate members with the highest scholastic average for an academic year and for her collegiate career. The Key of Excellence is a special award given to a member selected by the biennial convention for her distinguished achievement and her outstanding contribution to Kappa Epsilon Fraternity and to the profession of pharmacy.

Headquarters Executive Office, P.O. Box 11, Boonville, Missouri 65233.

Membership Active chapters 35. Inactive chapters 8. Colonies 1. Graduate/Alumni chapters 14. Total number of initiates 14,715. Chapter roll:

1921 Alpha, Minnesota
1921 Beta, Nebraska
1921 Gamma, Iowa
1922 Delta, Montana State
1926 Epsilon, Ohio State
1926 *Zeta, Wisconsin, Madison* (1985)
1928 *Eta, Western Reserve* (1949)
1930 Iota, North Dakota State
1930 *Theta, Colorado* (1937-1955) (1986)
1939 Kappa, Florida
1940 Lambda, North Carolina
1942 Mu, Kansas
1942 *Nu, Loyola, New Orleans* (1965)
1943 Xi, Texas
1945 Omicron, Philadelphia Pharmacy
1948 Pi, Purdue
1949 Rho, Cincinnati
1952 Sigma, Arizona
1953 Tau, Virginia Medical
1953 Upsilon, Houston
1956 Chi, South Dakota State
1956 Phi, Auburn
1957 Psi, Ohio Northern
1958 Omega, Missouri, Kansas City
1959 *Alpha Alpha, Utah* (1981)
1960 Alpha Beta, Southwestern State (OK)
1960 Alpha Delta, Mercer
1960 Alpha Epsilon, Northeast Louisiana
1960 Alpha Gamma, Mississippi
1961 *Alpha Zeta, George Washington* (1964)
1962 *Alpha Eta, Puerto Rico, Rio Piedras* (1968)
1964 Alpha Theta, Arkansas, Little Rock
1965 Alpha Iota, Oklahoma
1965 *Alpha Kappa, Wyoming* (1987)
1966 Alpha Lambda, South Carolina
1968 Alpha Mu, New Mexico
1970 Alpha Nu, Xavier (LA)
1971 Alpha Xi, Florida A & M
1980 Alpha Omicron, St. Louis Pharmacy
1984 Alpha Pi, Howard
1987 Alpha Rho, Campbell
1988 Alpha Sigma, Southeastern Pharm. (FL)
1988 Alpha Tau, Massachusetts Pharmacy

Colonies: Albany Pharmacy

Kappa Kappa Psi

(BAND)

ACTIVE PIN

KAPPA KAPPA PSI, a college recognition society for band members, was founded at Oklahoma Agricultural and Mechanical College, November 27, 1919, by William A. Scroggs, Raymond D. Shannon, Carl A. Stevens, Clyde Haston, Clayton Soule, William Coppedge, Asher Hendrickson, Dick Hurst, A. Frank Martin, and Hawthorne Nelson. Led by William A. Scroggs, these founders did most of the early work with the cooperation of Bohumil Makovsky, director of the Oklahoma A&M College Band. Immediately after the installation of Alpha Chapter an expansion program was started.

The society was founded for the primary purpose of encouraging good fellowship, leadership, scholarship, and musical ability among college band members.

From 1923 until 1930, the society enjoyed a healthy growth, chartering more than 35 chapters. In the period known as the Depression, a few chapters became inactive. With the reorganization of the National Council in 1937, however, new plans made it possible for these inactive chapters to be revived and an extended expansion program to be carried out. At the biennial convention in 1939 at Cincinnati, Ohio, steps were taken to make the Kappa Kappa Psi society international. Invitations were extended to colleges and universities in Canada and in South America. Since the end of World War II, the "band fraternity," as it has come to be known, has continued to enjoy a steady but significant growth.

Government   The society is governed in the interim between conventions by the National Council, which is composed of the five national officers: national president, national first vice president, national second vice president, national secretary-treasurer, and national member-at-large. The work of the society is done through a national headquarters office administered by an executive director, who is also executive director of Tau Beta Sigma. Conventions are held biennially in the odd-numbered years at the same time and place as the Tau Beta Sigma convention. Kappa Kappa Psi/Tau Beta Sigma commission a musical work to be premiered by the National Intercollegiate Band at the biennial convention of Kappa Kappa Psi/Tau Beta Sigma. The National Intercollegiate Band (NIB) originated in 1935 and is sponsored by the two societies. Membership in the NIB is open only to highly qualified band members.

Traditions and Insignia   The badge is the shape of an ancient Venetian harp, with lines and spaces running horizontally, the lines in gold and the space in black enamel. In the upper left corner, the Greek letters AEA are displayed on a background of black enamel; running obliquely from right to left and through the harp is a golden baton; perpendicularly across the lines and spaces, the Greek letters KKΨ are displayed in gold; the bar across the top of the badge contains five crown-set pearls; the lower part of semi-circle may contain either ten crown-set pearls or other jewels. The pledge pin is rectangular in shape with a bass clef showing quarter notes on spaces AEA. The spaces are blue enamel; the lines and notes of the staff are silver. The colors are blue and white; the flower is the cardinal carnation.

Publications   The official publication is *The Podium*, which is also the official publication of Tau Beta Sigma. It is edited by the executive director of both societies, the expenses being pro-rated.

Headquarters   122 Seretean Center for the Performing Arts, Oklahoma State University, Stillwater, Oklahoma 74078.

Membership   Chapter roll:††

Year	Chapter
1919	Alpha, Oklahoma State
1920	Beta, Montana State
1921	Delta, Oklahoma
1923	Eta, Ohio State
1924	Iota, Georgia Tech
1924	Lambda, Arkansas
1925	Nu, Michigan
1925	Omicron, West Virginia
1925	Xi, Colorado Mines
1927	Sigma, Ohio Northern
1928	Upsilon, Cincinnati
1929	Omega, Arizona
1929	Psi, UCLA
1931	Alpha Delta, Ohio
1931	Alpha Eta, Florida
1931	Alpha Theta, Northern Colorado
1931	Alpha Zeta, Indiana
1932	Alpha Iota, Colorado
1935	Alpha Mu, North Dakota State
1937	Alpha Omicron, Texas Tech
1938	Alpha Rho, Northeastern (OK)
1941	Alpha Sigma, Tampa
1941	Alpha Tau, Texas
1941	Alpha Upsilon, USC
1947	Alpha Chi, Texas, El Paso
1947	Alpha Psi, West Texas
1948	Alpha Omega, Pitt
1948	Beta Alpha, Baylor
1948	*Beta Beta, Mississippi*
1948	Beta Delta, Sam Houston
1948	Beta Gamma, L.S.U.
1949	Beta Kappa, Bowling Green
1949	Beta Lambda, Eastern New Mexico
1949	*Beta Mu, Emory*
1949	Beta Nu, Vandercook, Chicago

†† This chapter roll is repeated from the 19th edition; no current information was provided.

1949 Beta Omicron, Arizona State
1949 Beta Xi, Sul Ross
1950 Beta Sigma, Houston
1950 Beta Tau, Wichita
1951 Beta Psi, Kent
1951 Gamma Alpha, Midwestern
1953 Gamma Delta, Wayne (NE)
1954 Gamma Eta, New Mexico State
1954 Gamma Kappa, Northern Arizona
1954 Gamma Lambda, Doane
1954 Gamma Zeta, Lamar
1955 Gamma Nu, Florida State
1955 Gamma Xi, Maryland
1956 Gamma Pi, Purdue
1957 Delta Alpha, Langston
1957 Gamma Chi, Southern Mississippi
1957 Gamma Omega, Texas Southern
1957 Gamma Phi, Stephen F. Austin
1957 Gamma Sigma, Texas Christian
1958 Delta Delta, Arkansas Tech
1958 Delta Gamma, Missouri, Rolla
1960 Delta Iota, Florida A & M
1962 Delta Omicron, Connecticut
1962 Delta Pi, Mississippi Valley
1962 Delta Xi, Emporia
1964 Delta Rho, Arkansas State
1964 Delta Sigma, Texas, Arlington
1964 Delta Tau, Adams
1965 Delta Phi, Xavier
1965 Delta Upsilon, Eastern Michigan
1966 Delta Chi, Southern State
1966 Delta Omega, Ferris
1966 Delta Psi, Prairie View A & M
1967 Epsilon Beta, Central Arkansas
1967 Epsilon Delta, Texas A & I
1967 Epsilon Epsilon, Southwestern State (OK)
1967 Epsilon Gamma, Alabama State
1967 Epsilon Zeta, Oklahoma Baptist
1968 Epsilon Iota, Mansfield
1968 Epsilon Kappa, Angelo
1968 Epsilon Theta, Northeast Louisiana
1969 Epsilon Lambda, Western Carolina
1969 Epsilon Nu, Massachusetts
1970 Epsilon Chi, Arkansas, Pine Bluff
1970 Epsilon Phi, Clarion
1970 Epsilon Pi, Kansas State
1970 Epsilon Psi, Southwest Missouri
1970 Epsilon Rho, Grambling
1970 Epsilon Sigma, Cal State, Sacramento
1970 Epsilon Tau, Oral Roberts
1970 Epsilon Upsilon, Maine
1970 Epsilon Xi, Miami
1971 Zeta Alpha, Bloomsburg
1971 Zeta Beta, Howard Payne
1971 Zeta Delta, Southwest Baptist
1971 Zeta Epsilon, Michigan State
1971 Zeta Eta, South Carolina State
1971 Zeta Gamma, Texas Lutheran
1971 Zeta Zeta, Arkansas, Monticello
1972 Zeta Iota, Land
1972 Zeta Kappa, East Texas
1972 Zeta Lambda, Marshall

1972 Zeta Theta, West Virginia Tech
1973 Zeta Mu, Kutztown
1973 Zeta Nu, Southern
1973 Zeta Omicron, Akron
1973 Zeta Pi, Tennessee State
1973 Zeta Xi, Tyler Junior
1974 Zeta Chi, South Carolina
1974 Zeta Phi, Tuskegee
1974 Zeta Sigma, North Carolina Central
1974 Zeta Tau, Cameron
1974 Zeta Upsilon, Troy State
1975 Eta Alpha, Lock Haven
1975 Zeta Omega, Weber
1975 Zeta Psi, Virginia State
1976 Eta Beta, V.P.I.
1976 Eta Delta, Eastern Illinois
1976 Eta Gamma, Morgan State

Kappa Psi†

(PHARMACY)

ACTIVE PIN

PLEDGE PIN

KAPPA PSI Pharmaceutical Fraternity was founded by F. Harvey Smith at the Russell Military Academy in New Haven, Connecticut, on May 30, 1879. Originally an academic society, it expanded into several other institutions, chapters being installed at the Cheshire Military Academy, Cheshire, Connecticut (1879) and at Hillhouse Academy, New Haven, Connecticut (1894). In 1896, with visions of a national organization, representatives from the three chapters organized a grand chapter which they called Alpha Chapter. The first collegiate chapter, Delta, was founded at the University of Maryland in the fall of 1898 by members of the Hillhouse Chapter, who had entered the study of medicine at that institution. Other members, who had undertaken the study of pharmacy, formed Gamma Chapter at Columbia University in 1898, and still others in 1900, organized Beta Chapter at the University College of Medicine in Richmond, Virginia. By 1902 the organization included six chapters and had held tour conventions.

Growth In 1903 Kappa Psi was incorporated as a national fraternity, and for many years thereafter existed as a joint medical pharmaceutical fraternity, chartering chapters in both medical and pharmacy schools and colleges.

The fraternity in 1925 was reorganized by mutual agreement, dividing into two distinct organizations. Under provisions of the agreement the pharmacy division retained the name Kappa Psi

† This chapter narrative is repeated from the 19th edition; no current information was provided.

and later was incorporated under the title of Kappa Psi Pharmaceutical Fraternity. The medical division adopted the name Theta Kappa Psi for the new medical fraternity. At present Kappa Psi is strictly a professional fraternity, limiting its collegiate chapters to those schools and colleges of pharmacy which meet the requirements for accreditation by the American Council on Pharmaceutical Education.

The constituent divisions are: Alpha Chapter, collegiate chapters, and graduate chapters.

Government The supreme governing body, the grand council, consisting of representatives from the constituent divisions, meets in grand council (national) convention every two years. The executive committee composed of eleven members, is the chief legislative body of the fraternity between sessions of the grand council. Alpha Chapter consists of seven national officers who are elected every two years. For the purpose of mutual helpfulness the fraternity is divided geographically into ten provinces each of which is composed of all the chapters within the boundary of !he province.

Traditions and Insignia The fraternity colors are scarlet and cadet gray. The flower is the red carnation. The badge is in the shape of a rhombus, having a black enamel center of similar shape displaying a mask raised from the face of the black enamel center. The Greekletters K and Ψ appear one above and one below the mask. The eyes of the mask and the border of the badge may be jeweled.

Publications *The Mask*, the official magazine, is published quarterly.

Headquarters Suite 402, 275 Union Boulevard, St. Louis, Missouri 63108.

Membership Total deceased membership 3,750. Active chapters 52. Inactive chapters 5. Graduate/Alumni chapters 22. Inactive graduate chapters 5. Total number of initiates 22,278. Chapter roll:††

1896 Alpha, Grand Chapter
1902 Eta, Philadelphia Pharmacy
1907 Mu, Massachusetts Pharmacy
1909 *Tau, USC* (1940)
1909 Upsilon, Kentucky
1910 Beta Delta, Union (Albany Pharmacy)
1910 Beta Gamma, California
1910 Chi, Illinois
1911 Beta Epsilon, Rhode Island
1911 Beta Zeta, Oregon State
1913 Beta Kappa, Pitt
1913 Psi, Tennessee
1915 Beta Xi, North Carolina
1916 Beta Omicron, Washington
1916 Beta Pi, Washington State
1919 Beta Psi, Wisconsin, Madison
1920 Gamma Delta, Ohio Northern
1920 Gamma Epsilon, Nebraska
1920 Gamma Eta, Montana State

1921 Gamma Iota, Buffalo
1921 *Gamma Omicron, Oklahoma* (1958)
1921 Theta, Virginia Medical
1923 Beta Sigma, North Dakota State
1924 Omega, Rutgers
1925 Beta Eta, West Virginia
1925 Beta Lambda, Toledo
1925 Xi, Ohio State
1926 *Beta Nu, Creighton* (1935)
1926 Beta Rho, Mississippi
1926 Sigma, Maryland (1941-1967)
1927 Beta Phi, Cincinnati
1927 Iota, South Carolina Medical
1927 Mu Omicron Pi, Wayne State
1928 Epsilon, Minnesota
1928 Nu, Connecticut
1928 Pi, Purdue
1930 Beta Chi, Drake
1930 Beta Omega, Temple
1930 Beta Upsilon, Butler
1932 Rho, Kansas (1957-1967)
1934 Gamma Gamma, Texas
1935 Gamma Zeta, Howard
1946 Gamma Pi, St. Louis Pharmacy
1948 Gamma Rho, New Mexico
1949 Gamma Sigma, Florida
1950 *Gamma Tau, George Washington* (1963)
1950 Gamma Upsilon, Arizona
1951 Gamma Phi, Georgia
1952 Gamma Chi, Ferris
1953 Gamma Psi, Mercer
1955 Gamma Omega, Arkansas
1957 Gamma Theta, Kansas City
1958 Gamma Lambda, Northeastern
1959 Gamma Mu, Northeast Louisiana
1960 Gamma Nu, Pacific
1961 Gamma Xi, South Carolina
1963 Delta Beta, Southwestern State (OK)
1963 Delta Delta, Houston
1963 Delta Gamma, Auburn
1967 Delta Epsilon, Duquesne
1968 Gamma Kappa, South Dakota State
1989 Gamma, Columbia

Lambda Kappa Sigma

(PHARMACY)

ACTIVE PIN

LAMBDA KAPPA SIGMA was first organized as a social club for women pharmacy students at the Massachusetts College of Pharmacy in Boston on October 14, 1913. The librarian, Ethel J. Heath, along with eight women students, were the charter members. In 1918, it became a secret and closed so-

†† This chapter roll is repeated from the 19th edition; no current information was provided.

ciety and began to expand nationally by establishing chapters at other pharmacy schools across the country. The Council of Alpha Chapter conducted the national affairs of the sorority (now fraternity) until May, 1922, when the first Graduate Grand Council was organized. The first national convention was held in 1926, beginning the biennial convention schedule. Regional meetings were added in 1941 and are held within the five regions in the years without conventions. The fraternity became international with the addition of a chapter at the University of British Columbia in 1956. In 1964, the fraternity adopted Project Hope as its international philanthropy, an affiliation which continues to this day. The fraternity promotes the profession of pharmacy among women.

Growth The fraternity has greatly grown in numbers, doubling in size within the last decade, as the number of women in pharmacy schools has nearly doubled. In 1980, an international office was established and in 1984, the position of executive director was established to aid in administration and programming.

Government The authority of Lambda Kappa Sigma is vested in an international convention which meets biennially. During the interim, the government is the Grand Council, composed of nine members elected from the alumnae and associate members by the delegates in attendance at each biennial convention.

Traditions and Insignia Founders' Day is celebrated each October 14 with a special candlelight ceremony, and greetings are sent to the living founders. On March 15 of each year, Hygeia Day is observed with a special professional program to honor Hygeia, who, according to the Greek mythology, was the first woman pharmacist. This is an open meeting and non-members are welcome to attend. Each chapter may annually present an honor key to any graduating fraternity member in good standing who has attained a cumulative scholastic rank in the upper 10 per cent of all the candidates for graduation in her school or college of pharmacy. Each chapter may present a Ruth Davies Flaherty Award annually, recognizing outstanding chapter activity and fraternity loyalty. Biennially, at convention, alumnae may be recognized with the Award of Merit for outstanding professional accomplishment or the Distinguished Service Citation for outstanding fraternity loyalty and activity. Both graduate and undergraduate grants are traditionally awarded annually to members who qualify. The Cora E. Craven Undergraduate and Dr. B. Olive Cole Graduate Educational Grants are funded by the Lambda Kappa Sigma Educational Trust, founded in 1974.

Insignia Hygeia design jewelry is available to members in addition to traditional jewelry. The pledge pin is a small cutout triangle in medium blue enamel on gold with the Greek letter initials in the corners. The badge is a small double ellipse, the inner one raised and bearing the Greek initials in gold on black enamel. The outer ellipse is either plain gold, set in half pearls, or whole pearls. There is a recognition pin in the shape of a mortar and pestle with the three initials in the center of the mortar. There is a special honorary member pin in the shape of a triangle with acorns embellishing each corner and the three Greek initials in the center. The Ethel J. Heath Scholarship Key is a triangular shaped key with a Caduceus embossed upon it and the three Greek letters appearing at the sides and bottom.

Publications *The Blue and Gold Triangle*, established in 1926 and issued six times during a biennium, is the official publication. In addition, various handbooks of information and manuals of operation are issued. A bimonthly chapter newsletter *LinKS* began in 1984.

Membership Total living membership 13,000. Total deceased membership 1,450. Active chapters 39. Inactive chapters 4. Colonies 2. Graduate/Alumni chapters 25. City/Area alumni associations 1. Total number of initiates 16,479. Chapter roll:

1913 Alpha, Massachusetts Pharmacy
1918 Beta, Albany Pharmacy
1918 Delta, Pitt
1918 Gamma, Illinois (1973-1978)
1919 Epsilon, Maryland (1974-1988)
1919 Zeta, Cal Medical, San Francisco (1974-1985)
1920 Eta, Philadelphia Pharmacy
1920 Theta, Creighton (1974-1978)
1921 Lambda, USC
1922 Mu, Washington State
1925 Nu, Drake
1927 Xi, Rhode Island
1930 Omicron, Wayne State (MI)
1930 Pi, Rutgers
1930 Rho, Oregon State
1931 *Sigma, Columbia (NY)* (1969)
1932 Tau, Duquesne
1936 Upsilon, Idaho State
1938 Phi, Butler
1941 Chi, Washington (WA)
1947 *Psi, Detroit Tech* (1956)
1948 Alpha Alpha, Temple
1948 Omega, South Carolina Medical (1953-1979)
1949 Alpha Beta, Connecticut
1950 *Alpha Delta, Michigan* (1968)
1950 Alpha Gamma, Samford
1951 Alpha Epsilon, Tennessee
1951 Alpha Eta, Long Island (1969-1987)
1951 Alpha Zeta, St. Louis Pharmacy
1952 Alpha Theta, SUNY, Buffalo
1953 Alpha Iota, Ferris
1954 Alpha Kappa, Georgia
1956 Alpha Lambda, British Columbia
1956 Alpha Mu, Toledo
1958 Alpha Nu, Kentucky
1959 Alpha Xi, Pacific (CA)
1960 Alpha Omicron, West Virginia
1961 Alpha Pi, St. John's (NY)

Mu Phi Epsilon

(MUSIC)

ACTIVE PIN

PLEDGE PIN

MU PHI EPSILON was established at the Metropolitan College of Music November 13, 1903, by Winthrop S. Sterling with Elizabeth Mathias. It was incorporated under the laws of the State of Ohio on May 18, 1905, as a music sorority and became a fraternity in 1977 when membership was opened to men.

The fraternity has as its purpose the advancement of music in America and throughout the world, the promotion of musicianship and scholarship, loyalty to alma mater, and the development of a true bond of friendship.

Election to Mu Phi Epsilon is made on the basis of scholarship, musicianship, character, and personality. The grade average for election is formulated by each chapter within the national eligibility requirement, with the approval of the faculty adviser, the director of the music department, and the National Council of the fraternity; and chapters are required to adhere to this average.

Collegiate members are music majors or minors enrolled as candidates for a degree who show excellence in scholarship and musicianship. Persons in the professional field who show evidence of unusual musical talent and who meet the academic qualifications for membership in the collegiate chapter may become members by special election with approval of National Council. Music faculty members are eligible at all times if not a member of another professional music fraternity.

Mu Phi Epsilon maintains memberships in the Music Teachers National Association, the Music Educators National Conference, the National Federation of Music Clubs, the National Association for Music Therapy, the National Association of Composers and Conductors, National Music Council, National Council on the Arts and Government, and National Association of the Schools of Music.

Government Authority of Mu Phi Epsilon is vested in a triennial national convention to which each chapter sends a delegate and between conventions is directed by the National Council composed of six elected officers (the national president and five vice-presidents) and two appointed officers (the national editor and the national executive secretary-treasurer). The National Council meets annually. In the convention year the National Council meets in pre- and post-convention sessions. The fraternity maintains a national executive office under the direction of the national executive secretary-treasurer. A province governor directs general fraternity matters in each of the geographically divided 13 provinces. The chapters are further divided into 32 districts (regardless of province boundaries) for the purpose of meeting in district conferences once each triennium and are in the charge of district directors.

Traditions and Insignia The fraternity sponsors a biennial original composition contest and a biennial musicological research contest with monetary awards in several classifications. Annual awards are made to the senior member who in the opinion of National Council has best served the campus and the fraternity who has maintained high scholarship through college.

A Service Award is offered annually to the collegiate and alumni chapter most conscientious in fulfilling duties to fraternity, school, and community. In addition, chapters award scholarships either as gifts or in the form of loans to worthy students. Mu Phi Epsilon maintains a file of its artist members.

The badge is a triangle enclosing a lyre and displaying the letters ΜΦΕ, one on each side of the triangle. The pledge pin has only the triangle enclosing a lyre. Colors are royal purple and white; the flower, the violet. The open motto is *Seeketh not her own.*

Publications The quarterly magazine, *The Triangle*, is the official publication of the fraternity. Other publications are Constitution and Bylaws; manuals for collegiate chapter officers and advisers, alumni chapter officers, province governors, and district directors; *Pledge Handbook*; Ritual; a bi-annual chapter newsletter, *Metronome-Opus*; *Songs of Mu Phi Epsilon*; *Mu Phi Epsilon Composers and Authors*, a catalog of compositions and books by members of Mu Phi Epsilon; a Mu Phi Epsilon Information Bulletin; Patron Bulletin; *About Installing a Chapter of Mu Phi Epsilon*; Mu Phi Epsilon Memorial Foundation *Guide*, and Brochure.

Funds and Philanthropies In 1953, the fraternity's 50th anniversary, a Mu Phi Epsilon Scholarship Lodge was presented to National Music Camp, Interlochen, Michigan, the rental income of which provides annual scholarships to students at camp. The fraternity maintains the Mu Phi Epsilon School of Music at Gads Hill Center, Chicago, and contributes to other settlement schools: $4,000 has been granted in scholarships to schools offering courses in music therapy, and has provided for the publication of "Abstracts of Research in Music Therapy." Music for the blind has been aided by the underwriting of an issue of the *Braille Musician*. Gifts of money, instruments, music, and books go to such international destinations as Silliman University, Philippine Women's University, and University of the Philippines in the Philippines.

Mu Phi Epsilon Memorial Foundation, established in 1963, will continue and expand the philanthropic activities of the fraternity. The Mu Phi Epsilon Artist Concerts is a unique venture of the foundation whose purpose is to give aspiring young members, selected in triennial auditions judged by eminent musicians, an opportunity to gain performing experience. Chapters of Mu Phi Epsilon located throughout the country traditionally present the winners in concert.

In observance of the 75th anniversary, the Mu Phi Epsilon Chair of Composition has been endowed at Brevard Music Center in North Carolina. A recognized composer will be selected each summer session to compose, teach, and hold seminars: in addition, his/her works will be presented by various performing groups of the Center.

Headquarters   833 Laurel Ave., Highland Park, Illinois 60035.

Membership   Chapter roll:††

1903	*Alpha, Metropolitan Music, Cincinnati* (1930)
1903	Beta, New England Conservatory
1904	Gamma, Michigan
1905	*Delta, Detroit Conservatory* (1942)
1905	Epsilon, Toledo
1905	*Eta, Syracuse* (1916)
1905	Zeta, DePauw
1906	*Iota, Chicago Conservatory* (1909)
1906	Kappa, Butler
1906	*Theta, Kroeger Music, St. Louis* (1954)
1909	*Lambda, Ithaca Conservatory* (1942-1966)
1910	*Iota Alpha, Chicago Conservatory* (1954)
1911	Mu, Brenau
1911	Nu, Oregon
1911	Xi, Kansas
1912	*Omicron, Coombs Conservatory, Philadelphia* (1932)
1912	*Pi, Lawrence* (1942)
1914	*Rho, von Unschuld (DC)* (1917)
1914	*Sigma, Northwestern* (1968)
1915	*Chi, Pennsylvania Music, Meadville* (1942)
1915	Phi, Mount Union
1915	Tau, Washington
1915	*Upsilon, Cincinnati Conservatory of Music* (1955)
1916	Psi, Bucknell
1917	Mu Alpha, Simpson
1917	Omega, Drake
1918	*Rho Beta, Washington Music (DC)* (1934)
1919	Mu Beta, Washington State
1919	*Mu Delta, Kansas City Conservatory (MO)* (1959)

†† This chapter roll is repeated from the 19th edition; no current information was provided.

1919	Mu Gamma, Nebraska
1920	*Mu Epsilon, MacPhail, Minneapolis* (1967)
1920	Mu Eta, Pacific
1920	Mu Theta, Texas
1920	Mu Zeta, Whitman
1921	*Mu Iota, Columbia Music, Chicago* (1938)
1922	Mu Kappa, Oklahoma
1922	*Mu Lambda, Wisconsin, Madison* (1930)
1922	Mu Mu, Kansas State
1923	Mu Nu, USC
1923	*Mu Omicron, Cincinnati Conservatory of Music* (1955)
1923	Mu Pi, Ohio Wesleyan
1923	Mu Rho, Denver
1923	Mu Xi, American Conservatory
1924	*Mu Sigma, Louisville Conservatory* (1940)
1924	Mu Tau, South Dakota
1925	Mu Upsilon, Eastman, Rochester
1926	Mu Chi, Southern Methodist
1926	*Mu Omega, Atlanta Conservatory* (1940)
1926	Mu Phi, Baldwin-Wallace
1926	Mu Psi, Coe
1926	*Tau Alpha, New York City* (1946)
1927	*Phi Alpha, Miami (FL)* (1932)
1927	*Phi Beta, Minnesota* (1945)
1927	Phi Gamma, Peabody Conservatory
1928	*Phi Delta, Missouri* (1938)
1929	*Phi Epsilon, College of Emporia* (1974)
1929	Phi Zeta, Morningside
1931	*Phi Eta, Michigan State* (1942)
1932	Phi Theta, Lindenwood
1935	Phi Iota, Concordia (MO)
1935	Phi Kappa, Wayne State
1938	Phi Lambda, Willamette
1938	Phi Mu, San Jose
1938	Phi Nu, UCLA
1939	Phi Omicron, Cleveland Music
1939	Phi Xi, Baylor
1941	Phi Pi, Wichita
1944	*Phi Rho, Minneapolis Music* (1959)
1944	Phi Sigma, DePaul
1945	Phi Chi, Cal State, Fresno
1945	*Phi Phi, Kansas City* (1959)
1945	Phi Tau, North Texas
1945	Phi Upsilon, Boston
1946	*Epsilon Alpha, St. Catherine* (1958)
1946	*Epsilon Beta, Queens (NC)* (1952)
1946	Phi Omega, Westminster (PA)
1946	Phi Psi, Mary Washington
1947	Epsilon Delta, Lewis and Clark
1947	Epsilon Gamma, Belhaven
1948	Epsilon Epsilon, Texas Christian
1948	Epsilon Eta, George Pepperdine
1948	Epsilon Zeta, Hendrix
1949	Epsilon Iota, Eastern Washington
1949	Epsilon Theta, Linfield
1950	Epsilon Kappa, Southern Illinois
1950	Epsilon Lambda, Eastern Michigan
1950	Epsilon Mu, Utah
1950	Epsilon Nu, West Virginia
1951	Epsilon Omicron, Indiana
1951	Epsilon Xi, Illinois

1952 Epsilon Pi, Texas Tech.
1952 Epsilon Rho, Montana
1953 Epsilon Phi, Friends
1953 Epsilon Sigma, Pacific Lutheran
1953 Epsilon Tau, Washington (MO)
1953 Epsilon Upsilon, Duquesne
1955 Alpha Alpha, Cincinnati
1955 *Epsilon Chi, Brigham Young* (1960)
1955 Epsilon Omega, San Francisco State
1955 Epsilon Psi, Juilliard
1956 Alpha Beta, Hartt (CT)
1957 Alpha Gamma, Southern Mississippi
1958 Alpha Delta, Cal State, Sacramento
1959 Alpha Epsilon, Holy Names
1959 Alpha Eta, American
1959 Alpha Iota, Midwestern
1959 Alpha Kappa, Kansas City
1959 Alpha Lambda, Portland State
1959 Alpha Theta, Penn State
1959 Alpha Zeta, Radford
1960 Alpha Mu, Southwest Missouri
1960 Alpha Nu, West Texas
1960 Alpha Omicron, Roosevelt
1960 Alpha Xi, North Carolina, Greensboro
1961 Alpha Pi, Southwest Texas
1962 Alpha Rho, Phillips
1962 Alpha Sigma, Abilene Christian
1962 Alpha Tau, Philippine Women's
1963 Alpha Phi, Maryhurst
1963 Alpha Upsilon, Furman
1964 Alpha Chi, Southwestern (KS)
1965 Alpha Omega, Stephen F. Austin
1965 Alpha Psi, Whitworth
1965 Beta Alpha, Cal State, Fullerton
1965 Beta Beta, Jacksonville
1965 Beta Delta, Cal, Santa Barbara
1965 Beta Gamma, Alabama
1966 Beta Epsilon, Nazareth
1966 Beta Eta, Cal State, Hayward
1966 Beta Iota, Southern Illinois
1966 Beta Theta, Tennessee Tech.
1966 Beta Zeta, Southern
1967 Beta Kappa, Trinity
1967 Beta Lambda, Cal State, Chico
1967 Beta Mu, Dickinson State
1967 Beta Mu, East Texas
1967 Beta Xi, Philippines
1968 Beta Omicron, Western Illinois
1968 Beta Pi, Nebraska Wesleyan
1968 Beta Rho, Wartburg
1968 Beta Sigma, Oregon College of Education
1969 Beta Chi, Florida State
1969 Beta Omega, Ball State
1969 Beta Phi, Seattle Pacific
1969 Beta Psi, Indiana Central
1969 Beta Tau, Georgia State
1969 Beta Upsilon, Towson
1971 Gamma Alpha, Evangel
1972 Gamma Beta, Augustana
1972 Gamma Delta, Pan American
1972 Gamma Epsilon, Oral Roberts
1972 Gamma Eta, Central State (OH)

1972 Gamma Gamma, Southwestern State (OK)
1972 Gamma Zeta, Delta State
1973 Gamma Iota, Dallas Baptist
1973 Gamma Kappa, Boise
1973 Gamma Theta, Bridgeport
1974 Gamma Lambda, Loretto Heights (CO)
1974 Gamma Mu, Cal, Riverside
1974 Gamma Nu, Chicago State
1974 Gamma Xi, New Orleans
1975 Gamma Omicron, Olivet
1975 Gamma Pi, Shorter
1976 Gamma Rho, North Carolina A & T
1976 Gamma Sigma, Cal State, Dominguez Hills
1976 Gamma Tau, St. Thomas (TX)

Omega Tau Sigma†

(VETERINARY MEDICINE)

ACTIVE PIN

PLEDGE PIN

OMEGA TAU SIGMA was founded at the University of Pennsylvania School of Veterinary Medicine in 1906 by Frank A. Lentz, George A. Schwartz, Edward A. Parker, Jr., Howard H. Custes, William G. Haines, and Gerrett P. Judd. Membership is limited to students of Veterinary medicine. In 1914 the fraternity became international when a chapter was installed at the Ontario Veterinary College.

Government   The international governing body is the Grand Council. This group is composed of two undergraduate members from each chapter and elected graduate members. The first meeting was held on April 1, 1911, at Philadelphia. At the present time the Grand Council meets annually in the month of October. 'The Grand Council officers are president, vice-president, secretary, treasurer, and historian—elected from graduate members.

Traditions and Insignia   The purposes of the fraternity are: to encourage and foster the development of well-rounded, ethical veterinarians and through them create a better profession on the basis of friendship, cooperation, and respect for fellow men; to impart to its members a desire to serve faithfully and zealously the varied needs of the animal kingdom and to inspire these members with the fact that the knowledge of a job well done and the regard of clientele and colleague far surpasses financial gain; to give aspiring young veterinary students a chance to survey analytically the veterinary profession in order that they may be sure that their best talents will be utilized in this profession before they have invested the valuable God-given assets, youth, time, and ambition, in the

† This chapter narrative is repeated from the 19th edition; no current information was provided.

pursuance of an occupation that may leave their best talents dormant; to instill the principles of honesty, morality, resourcefulness, and brotherly love in all its members; and to give these young embryonic veterinarians a chance to learn the much valued trait of living happily with a group for the mutual benefit of all.

The official pin is a diamond-shaped yellow gold badge with a small black diamond in the center. Inside the black diamond is a small square with the Greek letters ΩΤΣ.

Membership   Active chapters 8. Total number of initiates 7,517. Chapter roll:††

1906	*Alpha, Penn*	
1911	Beta, Cornell	
1911	Gamma, Ohio State	
1914	Delta, Ontario Veterinary	
1940	Zeta, Auburn	
1948	Eta, Georgia	
1956	Theta, Illinois	
1958	Iota, Oklahoma State	
1965	Kappa, Iowa State	

Phi Alpha Delta

(LAW)

ACTIVE PIN

PLEDGE PIN

PHI ALPHA DELTA is unique in that it is the only law fraternity whose roots were nurtured in a legal controversy. It was on November 4, 1987, that the Supreme Court of Illinois adopted a rule for admission to the Illinois Bar which seriously affected many of the students then preparing for admission. To protect their rights they organized the "Law Students League." This League secured the passage of an act by the Illinois Legislature which exempted the students then studying for the Bar from certain requirements of the rule. The Illinois Supreme Court, however, refused to recognize these exemptions, whereupon a test case was taken directly to the Supreme Court of Illinois (see in re Application of Henry M. Day, et al., 181 Ill. 73). The League was partially successful in this new undertaking.

The realization that more could be accomplished by a unified group and the close association formed in this common struggle led the members of the League to seek a way in which to preserve the relationship thus formed. Accordingly, in 1898 they formed the Lambda Epsilon Fraternity, Lambda standing for "law" and Epsilon for "equity."

The founders of Lambda Epsilon undoubtedly

†† This chapter roll is repeated from the 19th edition; no current information was provided.

meant to establish a fraternity, but, unfortunately, their fears that the organization might pass into the control of those who might not have the same lofty ideals, and their ambition to be known as the fathers of what they had hoped to be a great law fraternity, led them into errors which were not possible to correct.

This finally led to a rebellion within the fraternity and, after four stormy years of existence, delegates to the convention held at the Colonial Tavern in South Haven, Michigan, on July 26, 1902, unanimously adopted a resolution dissolving Lambda Epsilon. On the next day, the "South Haven Articles" which were to be the foundation of Phi Alpha Delta were signed. A committee was appointed to suggest a method of procedure. After several months of arduous work, a meeting was held in Chicago on November 8, 1902, and the articles, constitution, ritual, and rules governing the organization of Phi Alpha Delta were proposed and formally adopted together with the name of Phi Alpha Delta.

Growth   Within a month, Blackstone, Story, Fuller, Webster and Marshall Chapters were installed. By 1910, the roster of chapters had increased to 23 in number.

Subsequently, Phi Alpha Delta, secure in its principles and purpose, has weathered war and depression and has proceeded along a steady, conservative policy of expansion. The fraternity has more law school chapters than any other law fraternity, and these chapters are restricted to law schools accredited by the American Bar Association, a high standard peculiar only to Phi Alpha Delta.

A merger with Phi Delta Delta, women's professional law fraternity, became effective August 12, 1972, during concurrent conventions for the two fraternities at San Diego, California. Phi Delta Delta by that time had initiated more than 5,000 members and 57 law school chapters. All members of Phi Delta Delta automatically became members of Phi Alpha Delta, and all chapters of Phi Delta Delta were automatically merged into chapters of Phi Alpha Delta. The governing board of latter was expended by two positions which were assigned to members of Phi Delta Delta. The Phi Alpha Delta headquarters serves as headquarters of the merged organizations.

Government   Phi Alpha Delta is governed by a nine person International Executive Board composed of an international justice, international vice justice, international second vice justice, international advocate, international secretary, international treasurer, international historian, international marshal, and an international advocate. This board is elected every two years by the delegates which the law school and alumni chapters send to the international convention.

The country is divided into 24 districts and the international justice appoints a district justice for each district whose duty it is to supervise activities of law school and alumni chapter in that district.

Within each district are located the law school and alumni chapters themselves. Each chapter is governed by a set of elected officers which includes a justice, vice justice, clerk, treasurer, and marshal. An alumni advisor selected by the chapter and its district justice aids and advises on all phases of activities.

Insignia. The badge is an oblong hexagonal shield with concave sides displaying in vertical order a balance and the letters ΦΑΔ. The alumni key is hexagon shaped with a balance above the letters ΦΑΔ. A special badge is presented to all new members which is a pin which may be worn in the lapel or on a blouse or coat. It consists of the logo of the organization with the crest in the center. There is no pledge status. Colors are old gold and purple; the flower is the red carnation.

Publications The interchange of law business is facilitated through fraternity directories published in 1901, 1906, 1910, 1913, 1917, 1923, 1927, 1932, 1935, 1950, 1955, 1960, 1965, 1970, 1975, 1979, and 1981-82. In these, each member's name is listed alphabetically and geographically. Also is shown the year the person was admitted to the bar and the nature of his or her law practice. A publication called the *Phi Alpha Delta Quarterly* was begun in 1906 and continued uninterruptedly until 1930 when the name of the magazine was changed to *The Reporter*. In 1946, the format of the publication was changed from that of a magazine to that of a tabloid and this format has been continued.

Endowment Fund Phi Alpha Delta has an Endowment Fund which is utilized primarily for the making of loans to deserving law students to assist them in the completion of their law school education.

Headquarters The International Executive Office is located at 10722 White Oak Avenue, Granada Hills, California 91344-0217, where it has been situated since 1955.

Membership Total undergraduate membership 7,800. Active chapters 243. Pre-law chapters 76. Graduate/Alumni chapters 84. Total number of initiates 120,000. Chapter roll:

1902	Blackstone, Chicago-Kent Law
1902	Fuller, Northwestern
1902	Marshall, Chicago
1902	Story, DePaul
1902	Webster, Loyola, Chicago
1904	Ryan, Wisconsin, Madison
1905	Campbell, Michigan
1906	Garland, Arkansas
1906	Hay, Case Western Reserve
1907	Benton, Missouri, Kansas City
1908	Chase, Cincinnati
1908	Hammond, Iowa
1908	Williams, Oregon
1909	Calhoun, Yale
1909	Green, Kansas
1909	Lawson, Missouri
1909	Rapallo, N.Y.U.
1909	Taft, Georgetown U.
1910	Gunter, Colorado
1910	Jefferson, Virginia
1911	Corliss, North Dakota
1911	Field, Cal, Berkeley
1911	Holmes, Stanford
1911	Ross, USC
1911	Temple, Hastings
1912	Staples, Washington and Lee
1913	Hughes, Denver
1914	Borah, Idaho
1914	Clay, Kentucky
1914	Dunbar, Washington (WA)
1915	Brewer, Stetson
1915	Reese, Nebraska
1916	Harlan, Oklahoma
1916	Livingston, Columbia (NY)
1916	McReynolds, Tennessee
1920	Jay, George Washington
1920	MacLean, New England Law
1921	Benson, Washburn
1921	Cole, Drake
1921	Lurton, Vanderbilt
1921	McKinley, Ohio State
1921	T. Ruffin, North Carolina
1922	C. Clark, Washington (MO)
1922	Mitchell, Minnesota
1922	Morgan State, Alabama
1922	Nu, Brooklyn Law
1923	Burr, Dickinson Law
1923	Knox, Arizona
1924	Fletcher, Florida
1924	Lusk, Willamette
1924	Martin, Tulane
1925	Watson, Pitt
1925	Willey, West Virginia
1925	Wilson, Cornell
1926	Begbie, British Columbia
1926	Sutherland, Utah
1927	Doyle, South Dakota
1927	Keener, Emory
1928	Fish, Mercer
1929	Lamar, Mississippi
1932	Taney, Southern Methodist
1935	Vinson, Louisville
1937	Ford, Loyola Marymount, Los Angeles
1938	M. Sullivan, San Francisco
1939	Roberts, Temple
1946	Rasco, Miami (FL)
1946	Rutledge, Duke
1947	A. H. Stephens, Georgia
1947	Halleck, Valparaiso
1947	T. C. Clark, Texas
1947	Timberlake, Wake Forest
1948	Hamill, Indiana
1948	Henry, Richmond
1949	Baylor, Baylor
1949	Hull, Samford
1949	J. Sullivan, St. Louis
1949	Pinckney, South Carolina
1950	Brantly, Montana
1950	More, Creighton

1951	McKenna, UCLA		1974	Truman, Puget Sound
1953	Lincoln, John Marshall Law, Chicago		1975	Arthur, Vermont
1953	Wythe, William and Mary		1975	Christiancy, Thomas M. Cooley
1954	Carmody, Syracuse		1975	Fleming, Nova
1954	Hardy, Tulsa		1975	Monroe, Hamline
1955	Hoffman, Northern Kentucky		1975	Read, Delaware
1955	Jackson, Rutgers, Newark		1975	Waite, Dayton
1957	deBracton, St. John's (NY)		1976	Kennedy, Hofstra
1958	Darrow, Maryland		1976	Munoz, Inter-American
1959	Cooley, Wayne State (MI)		1977	Hoynes, Notre Dame
1959	Houston, South Texas Law		1978	Dooley, Northern Illinois
1960	Brandeis, American		1978	Humphrey, Detroit
1960	Coke, Toledo		1979	A. L. Stephens, Whittier
1960	Vaught, Oklahoma		1979	Homburger, Pace
1960	Willis, Ohio Northern		1979	Iredell, Campbell
1961	McCormick, San Diego U.		1979	Rockefeller, Albany Law
1962	Beaumont, Cal Western		1979	Vallarta, Regiomontana
1962	Butler, William Mitchell Law		1980	Griffith, Mississippi
1962	Cardozo, Catholic		1980	Lowenstein, Yeshiva
1962	Grant, Akron		1980	Tureaud, Southern
1962	Meck, Cleveland		1980	Wm. Douglas, Bridgeport
1963	Egan, Duquesne		1981	G. L. Ruffin, Harvard
1963	Hickman, Houston		1981	Pre Law, Southwest Missouri
1963	White, L.S.U.		1981	Pre Law, Walsh Accountancy
1964	Paterson, Seton Hall		1982	Pre Law, Drury
1964	Wormser, Fordham		1982	Pre Law, Kent
1965	Burton, Boston U.		1982	Pre Law, Louisville
1965	Frankfurter, Suffolk		1982	Pre Law, Marshall
1965	O'Niell, Loyola, New Orleans		1982	Pre Law, Morehead
1966	Adams, Indiana		1982	Pre Law, Ohio
1966	Edmonds, Santa Clara		1982	Pre Law, San Diego U
1966	Frelinghuysen, Rutgers, Camden		1983	Pre Law, Alabama
1966	LaFollette, Marquette		1983	Pre Law, Canisius
1966	Langston, Howard		1983	Pre Law, Capital
1966	McKellar, Memphis State		1983	Pre Law, Catholic, Puerto Rico
1967	Robinson, Arkansas, Little Rock		1983	Pre Law, Northern Arizona
1968	Alden, SUNY, Buffalo		1983	Pre Law, Ohio State
1968	Connelly, Gonzaga		1983	Pre Law, Richmond
1968	Murphy, Detroit		1983	Pre Law, Southwest Baptist
1968	Terrell, Florida State		1983	Pre Law, USC
1968	Tilden, New York Law		1983	Touro, Touro
1969	Engle, Pacific (CA)		1984	Blume, Wyoming
1969	Greener, Texas Southern		1984	Pre Law, Arizona State
1969	Hayes, Capital		1984	Pre Law, Bowling Green
1969	MacDonald, Windsor		1984	Pre Law, Cal State, Dominguez Hills
1969	Rayburn, Texas Tech		1984	Pre Law, Cal State, Sacramento
1969	deDiego, Catholic, Puerto Rico		1984	Pre Law, Catholic
1970	Garner, St. Mary's (CA)		1984	Pre Law, Cincinnati
1970	Sammis, Southwestern Law		1984	Pre Law, DePaul
1971	Watkins, North Carolina Central		1984	Pre Law, Evansville
1972	Black, Arizona State		1984	Pre Law, George Washington
1972	Dirksen, Golden Gate		1984	Pre Law, Georgia
1972	Juarez, Cal, Davis		1984	Pre Law, Illinois
1972	Llewellyn, Lewis and Clark		1984	Pre Law, Indiana
1972	Shepherd, Pepperdine		1984	Pre Law, Mississippi Col
1973	LaBrum, Baltimore U.		1984	Pre Law, Missouri
1973	Starr, Connecticut		1984	Pre Law, Niagara
1974	Cowley, Brigham Young		1984	Pre Law, Northern Illinois
1974	Kenealy, Boston Law		1984	Pre Law, Oklahoma
1974	Kenison, Franklin Pierce		1984	Pre Law, Radford
1974	Middleton, Western New England		1984	Pre Law, South Alabama
1974	S. Douglas, Southern Illinois		1984	Pre Law, Tennessee

1984	Pre Law, Western Carolina	
1984	Pre Law, Wisconsin, Madison	
1984	Ramos, Puerto Rico, Rio Piedras	
1984	Russell, Georgia State	
1985	Pre Law, Akron	
1985	Pre Law, Arkansas, Monticello	
1985	Pre Law, Arkansas	
1985	Pre Law, Cal, Irvine	
1985	Pre Law, David Lipscomb	
1985	Pre Law, Dayton	
1985	Pre Law, Detroit	
1985	Pre Law, Marquette	
1985	Pre Law, Mercer	
1985	Pre Law, Nevada	
1985	Pre Law, North Carolina	
1985	Pre Law, Oklahoma City	
1985	Pre Law, Oklahoma State	
1985	Pre Law, South Dakota	
1985	Pre Law, St. Louis	
1985	Pre Law, Stetson	
1985	Pre Law, Washington (WA)	
1985	Pre Law, Weber	
1985	Pre Law, West Texas	
1986	Pre Law, Arizona	
1986	Pre Law, Central Arkansas	
1986	Pre Law, Florida	
1986	Pre Law, Golden Gate	
1986	Pre Law, Inter-American	
1986	Pre Law, Nova	
1986	Pre Law, Pepperdine	
1986	Pre Law, Seton Hall	
1986	Pre Law, South Carolina	
1986	Pre Law, V.P.I.	
1986	Pre Law, Washington (MO)	
1986	Pre Law, Willamette	
1986	Pre Law, Xavier (OH)	
1987	Pre Law, Central Michigan	
1987	Pre Law, Montclair	
1987	Pre Law, Texas	
1987	Pre Law, Tulsa	

Phi Beta

(MUSIC AND SPEECH)

ACTIVE PIN

PHI BETA, national professional fraternity for women in music and speech, was founded May 5, 1912, at Northwestern University, Evanston, Illinois, by Gladys Burnside, Elsie Schultz, and Josephine Mack.

Growth In 1914 the fraternity was chartered by the state of Illinois. At the time of its founding there was no thought of expansion but in 1917 a group at Chicago Musical College petitioned for a charter and became Beta Chapter. Subsequently Phi Beta has continued a steady and consistent growth.

Since its inception Phi Beta has followed the objectives of its founders: to promote the best in music and speech; to develop the highest type of womanhood; to advance its members intellectually and socially; to live a life of service, giving aid to members and nonmembers who need it and who are worthy; to foster college spirit and loyalty to each chosen campus. Phi Beta has always encouraged fine scholarship and performance and has continued to inspire the members to work for the highest ideals of professional achievement.

The fraternity voted in December, 1976, to open its collegiate membership to all qualified persons, regardless of sex.

Members of a collegiate chapter are elected on the basis of talent, character, and scholastic standing, and must be students of music or speech in the college, university or conservatory where a chapter is located. Before their initiation they must prove their professional and scholastic abilities. Membership may be conferred upon women of real professional ability who are actively engaged in their field of music or speech. National honorary membership may be conferred upon women artists of national reputation. Chapters may induct as patrons those men or women who are prominent and actively interested in the arts.

Phi Beta has been a member of the Professional Panhellenic Association since its founding in 1925. The fraternity is also a member of American National Theatre and Academy, Speech Communications Association, American Theatre Association through Children's Theatre Association of America, Professional Panhellenic Association, National Federation of Music Clubs, National Music Council and Interfraternity Research and Advisory Council.

Government The legislative power of Phi Beta is vested in a national convention which meets triennially and is attended by the National Council and delegates from collegiate and alumna chapters. The National Council meets annually in the interim to formulate policies of the fraternity. To correlate the Phi Beta program collegiate and alumnae counselors are appointed to supervise the respective areas of fraternity work within geographical divisions of the United States, designated as fraternity provinces.

Insignia The badge is a monogram of the two Greek letters in the name of the organization. The O and bar may be set with pearls; the bar may be set with diamonds. The pledge pin is a small gold Φ. The recognition pin is a small gold laurel wreath, through the middle of which is placed a baton in gold. The flower is the rose; the colors are violet and gold. 'The open motto is: "Είναί μάλλων η Φενέσθί," meaning *To be rather than to seem to be.*

Publications The publications of the fraternity include a quarterly magazine, *The Baton; The Prospectus; the Song Book;* Pledge Manuals and Handbooks.

Philanthropies In 1931 a stone cottage, known as the Phi Beta Studio, was built at the MacDowell Colony at Peterborough, New Hampshire, and endowed with a permanent maintenance fund. Its use for creative artists is directed by the Edward Mac-Dowell Association. In 1934 a practice studio was erected by Phi Beta at the National Music Camp, Interlochen, Michigan.

From early 1951 through 1965, Phi Beta offered voluntary assistance to the recreational program of the U.S. armed forces. During these years many chapters wrote, directed, and performed in shows and programs around the world—all arranged through the Armed Forces Professional Entertainment Branch.

Between the late '60s and mid-'70s, Phi Beta conducted two successful projects of help to individual music program activities in Mexico; these included contributions of time, financial aid, music, and instruments. An earlier project included the gift of a music library to the Philippine Islands. An annual grant is made to a foreign visitor to the Children's Theatre Conference of ATA. Study awards to members, both collegiate and alumni, are available annually. The fraternity also collaborates in a project of hand-enlarging music for the use of partially sighted persons; this is carried out in cooperation with the Library of Congress.

Headquarters 1397 Maetzel Drive, Columbus, Ohio 43227.

Membership Active chapters 21. Graduate/Alumni chapters 31. Total number of initiates 15,000+. Chapter roll:††

1912   Alpha, Northwestern
1917   *Beta, Chicago Conservatory* (1954)
1918   Delta, Cincinnati
1919   *Gamma, American Conservatory* (1963)
1920   *Zeta, Cosmopolitan School of Music* (1963)
1921   Eta, Stetson
1923   *Theta, Rollins* (1967)
1925   *Iota, Bush Conservatory*
1925   *Kappa, Kentucky* (1973)
1925   Lambda, USC
1925   *Mu, UCLA* (1969)
1926   *Nu, Knox* (1967)
1927   Xi, Wisconsin, Madison
1928   Omicron, William Woods
1929   Pi, Oregon
1929   Rho, Minnesota
1929   *Sigma, Illinois* (1952)
1931   Tau, Central Methodist
1931   *Upsilon, Butler*
1932   *Chi, Arkansas State*
1932   Phi, Capital
1932   *Psi, Carroll*
1933   *Omega, Cincinnati Conservatory of Music*
1939   *Alpha Alpha, L.S.U.*
1939   Alpha Beta, Virginia Intermont

†† This chapter roll is repeated from the 19th edition; no current information was provided.

1939   Epsilon, Loyola of the South
1947   *Alpha Gamma, Santa Barbara* (1967)
1948   *Alpha Delta, Transylvania* (1972)
1948   Alpha Epsilon, Houston
1950   *Alpha Zeta, Pepperdine* (1970)
1951   *Alpha Eta, Sacred Heart Dominican* (1960)
1953   Alpha Theta, Portland
1954   Alpha Iota, Centenary
1955   *Alpha Kappa, Cal State, Long Beach* (1970)
1955   *Alpha Lambda, San Francisco State* (1969)
1956   *Alpha Mu, Stanford* (1969)
1959   *Alpha Nu, Northeast Louisiana* (1973)
1962   Alpha Omicron, Louisiana Tech
1962   *Alpha Pi, Hofstra* (1965)
1962   *Alpha Rho, Portland State* (1970)
1962   *Alpha Xi, St. Mary's (LA)* (1973)
1963   Alpha Sigma, Whittier
1965   *Alpha Tau, Cal State, Fullerton* (1970)
1967   *Alpha Phi, Puget Sound* (1922)
1967   *Alpha Upsilon, Pacific Lutheran* (1975)
1968   Alpha Chi, Seattle
1970   Alpha Psi, Ursuline
1974   Beta Beta, George Mason
1975   Beta Gamma, Augsburg

Phi Chi

(MEDICINE)

ACTIVE PIN

PLEDGE PIN

PHI CHI Medical Fraternity is the result of the union of two local medical societies, an "eastern" and a "southern" organization, which had, for some unknown, unexplained and unrecorded reasons, essentially the same name at the time of their unification in 1905. An eastern group, named The Phi Chi Society, had been organized by Caleb Wakefield Clark at the University of Vermont Medical School, March 31, 1889; while a southern group, The Phi Chi Fraternity (Medical), was organized on October 26, 1894, by a group of medical students of which Dr. A. Harris Kelly was president and Linn L. Kennedy, secretary, at the Louisville Medical College. New chapters were developed at medical schools in the area by each organization and, when the two groups met in Baltimore, Maryland, on March 5, 1905, for amalgamation, there were five eastern and 16 southern chapters. Principal agreements and concessions of the union provided that the Vermont chapter would be designated as the "Alpha" of Phi Chi and the one at Louisville Medical School "Alpha Alpha." Provisions were made for the combining of the two constitutions, the redesigning of the badge to symbolize the two groups and their unity, as well as a revision and consolidation of the rituals.

Growth and Progress For 20 years, conventions of

representatives of each chapter of the combined order were held annually at various locations. New chapters were being organized rapidly at various medical schools and by 1916, as a result of the newly chartered groups and others resulting from medical school mergers, reorganizations and expansions, there were 34 active chapters. The medical school development of this era is well reflected in the fraternity's active/inactive chapter roster. The Louisville chapter, Alpha Alpha, is an example of the instability of medical schools of these years in that it became a composite group of five chapters from closed schools. Beta Delta, originally instituted as Beta of the northern group at the Baltimore Medical College, had three names before it became a chapter at the University of Maryland with 897 alumni, all from the former Baltimore area chapters except Kappa Delta (Johns Hopkins University). (Continued organizational changes, however, eventually led Delta to become inactive.) The chapters Beta, Gamma, Delta, and Epsilon continued the names of the original chapters with those names during the years of medical college reorganization. Sigma, Phi Rho, Upsilon Pi, Upsilon Iota, Kappa Rho, Mu, and Theta Eta are all combined chapters: Upsilon combined with Sigma, Kappa Psi with Phi Rho, Chi Theta with Upsilon Pi, Phi Beta with Upsilon Iota, Psi Rho Sigma with Kappa Rho, and Theta with Eta.

Following a period of somewhat decreased reorganizational activities, on October 14, 1922, the Pi Mu Medical Fraternity, established in 1892 at the University of Virginia, merged with Phi Chi, affording Phi Chi nine additional chapters and a transfer to the Phi Chi membership rolls of those Pi Mu alumni who so desired it.

Later, in January, 1948, the Phi Alpha Gamma Medical Fraternity (founded March 25, 1884, at the New York Homeopathic Medical College) merged with Phi Chi. Its Alpha chapter (New York) and Gamma chapter (Philadelphia) became, respectively, the Phi Alpha and Phi Alpha Gamma chapters of Phi Chi. Alumni members or groups were afforded Phi Chi alumni recognition for those who desired it.

A constructive step forward occurred in 1950 when the Phi Chi Welfare Association was established as an incorporated not-for-profit entity of the fraternity to provide assistance to student members and chapters from a fund to be developed from voluntary alumni contributions. This has enabled the fraternity to provide low interest emergency loans to junior and senior student members to enable them to graduate without layouts for financial reasons.

The last restrictive membership clause was removed in 1973, when by unanimous vote of the Grand Chapter, membership was made available to women.

Government The government of the fraternity is vested in a convention—an assembly of an elected representative of each active chapter and alumni association, designated the Grand Chapter. The constitution provides for a three- to five-day meeting every two or more years at selected and varied locations. The Grand Chapter elects national officers who, along with two additional elected members, constitute a body known as the executive trustees. The executive trustees have executive and administrative powers for all actions and activities during the interim between conventions. A national headquarters known as The Central Office of Phi Chi was established in 1917 as an organizational advancement. A few years later, in an effort to effect greater efficiency and provide improved continuity of administrative service to the chapters and the alumni, the terms of office of the grand secretary-treasurer and chairman of the executive trustees were increased from two to ten years. In 1948, in an organizational expansion, a new Bureau of Publications, Publicity and Programming, including promotion of alumni liaison and postgraduate meetings, was established.

Traditions The official gold badge of the fraternity symbolizes the union of the two original Phi Chi groups. It consists of a skull above crossed bones resting upon the Greek letters Φ and X in the form of a monogram, the Φ nuggeted and X polished gold. The eyes of the skull are rubies and the letters EΦA are engraved on the forehead of the skull. Embellished badges have jewels in the Φ and may be of varied stones, pearls usually. The badge design is patented and the coat of arms copyrighted. The official colors are white and olive green and the flower, lily-of-the valley. The pledge pin is a green medical (Greek) cross displaying a silver caduceus on the vertical between the letters Φ and X on the horizontal arms of the cross.

The fraternity has two ceremonial days, Founders' Day on February 26 when banquets are held honoring the founders, and a Memorial Day on November 15 when members wear a white carnation in respect to Phi Chi dead.

The fraternity has no honorary members but strives to maintain true fraternal friendships, enduring peer relationships and the opportunity to recognize after-graduation honors and successes by means of associated membership with nominations coming from chapter members. Student proficiency is recognized by two national awards each year—the Eben J. Carey Award for achieving the highest grades in anatomy during the freshman year and the Michael J. Carey senior award for leadership and fraternal contributions.

Headquarters Grant Secretary-Treasurer, P.O. Box 2035, Valdosta, GA 31604; Chairman, Executive Trustees, 1129 S. Second St., Springfield, IL 62704.

Membership Chapter roll:††

---

†† This chapter roll is repeated from the 19th edition; no current information was provided.

1889	*Alpha, Vermont*
1894	Alpha Alpha, Louisville
1895	*Beta Delta, Maryland* (1895)
1899	Theta Eta, Virginia Medical
1902	*Kappa, Georgetown*
1903	Chi, Jefferson
1903	Mu, Indiana
1903	Omicron, Tulane
1903	Zeta, Texas
1904	*Iota, Alabama*
1904	Phi, George Washington
1905	*Pi, Vanderbilt*
1905	Psi, Michigan
1905	*Rho, Rush* (1944)
1905	Sigma, Emory
1905	*Sigma Theta, North Carolina*
1906	*Alpha Theta, Western Reserve* (1941)
1907	*Phi Sigma, Loyola, Chicago*
1907	Xi, Southwestern (TX)
1908	*Pi Delta Phi, California*
1908	*Upsilon Pi, Penn*
1909	*Kapa Delta, Johns Hopkins*
1909	*Theta Upsilon, Temple*
1910	Phi Rho, St. Louis
1911	*Sigma Upsilon, Stanford* (1937)
1913	*Beta, Oregon* (1931)
1913	*Delta, Tufts*
1913	*Gamma, Ohio State*
1914	Alpha Beta, Tennessee
1914	*Epsilon, Wayne State* (1942)
1915	*Kappa Upsilon, Kansas*
1915	*Lambda Rho, Arkansas*
1916	Chi Upsilon, Creighton
1916	Upsilon Nu, Nebraska
1918	*Upsilon Iota, Illinois*
1918	*Upsilon Zeta, Cincinnati*
1920	*Delta Pi, Utah* (1945)
1920	Kappa Chi, Minnesota
1920	*Kappa Rho, Northwestern*
1920	*Upsilon Sigma, Columbia*
1921	*Beta Chi, Colorado* (1937)
1921	*Beta Upsilon, Boston*
1921	*Epsilon Chi, Marquette*
1921	*Eta Upsilon, Harvard* (1935)
1921	*Rho Delta, Cornell*
1921	*Sigma Delta, South Dakota* (1942)
1921	Tau Beta, Wisconsin, Madison
1922	*Beta Mu, McGill* (1944)
1922	*Epsilon Delta, Washington (MO)* (1939)
1922	*Gamma Sigma, Yale* (1943)
1922	*Omicron Kappa, Oklahoma*
1922	*Pi Mu, Virginia*
1922	*Tau Omicron, Toronto*
1923	*Mu Gamma, Iowa*
1926	Theta Pi, Mississippi
1927	Sigma Kappa, South Carolina
1928	Nu Sigma, Dalhousie
1929	*Delta Kappa Upsilon, Kansas*
1929	*Delta Phi, USC*
1929	*Theta Beta Pi, Syracuse* (1944)
1930	Alpha Phi Sigma, Georgia
1930	*Delta Upsilon, Duke*

1932	Lambda Sigma, L.S.U.
1933	*Gamma Chi, West Virginia*
1934	*Omega Upsilon Phi, Buffalo*
1935	*Tau Kappa, Wake Forest*
1938	*Alpha Mu, SUNY, Downstate Medical*
1943	Xi Chi, Baylor
1948	*Epsilon Kappa, Washington*
1948	*Phi Alpha, New York Medical*
1948	*Phi Alpha Gamma, Hahnemann Med.*
1952	*Epsilon Beta, UCLA*
1953	Beta Alpha, Miami (FL)
1955	*Mu Sigma, Missouri*
1960	Omega, Mexico
1962	*Upsilon Beta, Puerto Rico, San Juan*
1963	*Phi Sigma Gamma, California College of Medicine*
1970	*Upsilon Tau, Texas, San Antonio*

Phi Chi Theta

(BUSINESS ADMINISTRATION AND ECONOMICS)

ACTIVE PIN

PHI CHI THETA grew out of the consolidation of two national professional sororities having mutual aims and purposes, Phi Theta Kappa and Phi Kappa Epsilon. At a meeting on May 16, 1924, at Pittsburgh, Pennsylvania, representatives from the chapters completed details of the alliance; but agreed that the actual date and place of the merger was to be June 17, 1924, at Chicago, Illinois, immediately following the biennial convention of Phi Theta Kappa, previously scheduled. Six founders are recognized: Mary Stoddard Duggan and Nina Miller, New York Alpha Chapter, Columbia University; Anna E. Hall, Colorado Alpha Chapter, Denver University; Edna Blake Davis, New York Beta Chapter, New York University; Alice Wyman Schulze, Delta Chapter, Northwestern University; and Nell McKenry, Epsilon Chapter, University of Pittsburgh. On July 27, 1973, Epsilon Eta Phi was merged into Phi Chi Theta.

The purpose of Phi Chi Theta is to promote the cause of higher business education and training for all women; to foster high ideals for women in business careers; to encourage fraternity and cooperation among people preparing for such careers; to stimulate the spirit of sacrifice and unselfish devotion to the attainment of such ends. Chapters are established in universities or colleges whose schools of business are accredited by the American Association of Collegiate Schools of Business, or in universities or colleges which are accredited by the regional accrediting association and in which a course of study in business is approved by the Phi Chi Theta Committee on Admissions. Membership is extended to students fully matriculated in the school of business who have expressed the intention to complete the course and receive a degree. The fraternity was incorporated December 9, 1925, under the laws of the State of New York, was registered in 1956 under the U.S. Trademark Act, and was a charter member of the Professional Panhellenic Association, a predecessor of the Professional Fraternity Association. Each chapter is encouraged to select an honorary member each year.

Government The governing body is the national chapter, which meets biennially and is composed of the national officers and one national councillor from each collegiate and alumni chapter. The national officers constitute the Executive Council which administers affairs between the biennial meetings. The chapters are divided into ten geographical regions. A district director, who is elected for each region at the biennial meeting, is responsible for the supervision, guidance, and visitation. The district director may appoint one or more assistants to assist with these responsibilities. All chapters are encouraged to hold professional meetings and to conduct projects which will benefit the university, town, members, and other business students.

Traditions and Insignia An efficiency rating program was established in 1953. Certificates are awarded annually to the winning chapters in each district, and a plaque goes to the chapter winning the biennial National Award. Each collegiate chapter annually awards a scholarship key to a student in the chapter's college selected by a committee composed of chapter members and faculty members from the university. Various alumni chapters award scholarships annually to a collegiate chapter member.

The badge is of yellow gold forming the Greek letters ΦΧΘ with the Χ jeweled in pearls. The pledge pin, also in yellow gold, is of rectangular shape with the Greek letters raised in perpendicular line. The crest, in pin form, is presented to and worn by honorary members. The flower is the iris; the colors are lavendar and gold.

Publications The official publication is *The Iris of Phi Chi Theta*, published quarterly since 1927. Additional publications include the *Efficiency Rating Program, Pledge Manual,* and *Officer Manuals.*

Funds and Philanthropies In 1966, the Phi Chi Theta Foundation was established to carry out the original purpose of the fraternity. It is sustained by voluntary contributions.

Headquarters In 1981, a permanent national headquarters was established at 3703 Washington Blvd., Indianapolis, IN 46205.

Membership Total undergraduate membership 2,334. Active chapters 49. Inactive chapters 82. Colonies 1. Total number of initiates 36,401. Chapter roll:

1924	*Colorado Alpha, Denver* (1962)
1924	*Delta, Northwestern* (1972)
1924	Epsilon, Pitt (1987)
1924	Gamma, Oregon State
1924	*New York Alpha, Columbia (NY)* (1951)
1924	New York Beta, N.Y.U.
1924	*Oregon Beta, Oregon* (1981)
1924	*Zeta, Boston U* (1964)
1925	*Eta, Cal, Berkeley* (1984)
1925	Iota, Wisconsin, Madison
1925	*Kappa, North Dakota* (1956-1958) (1959)
1925	*Lambda, Kansas* (1980)
1925	*Mu, Utah* (1968)
1925	*Xi, USC* (1985)
1926	Omicron, Missouri
1926	*Pi, Idaho* (1957)
1927	Rho, Nebraska
1927	*Sigma, Illinois* (1958)
1928	*Tau, Ohio State* (1985)
1929	Upsilon, Georgia State (1984-1985)
1936	*Phi, Colorado* (1938)
1938	*Alpha Alpha, UCLA* (1970)
1938	*Chi, Alabama* (1983)
1938	*Psi, Brigham Young* (1965)
1939	*Alpha Beta, Marquette* (1976)
1944	*Alpha Gamma, Southern Methodist* (1986)
1947	*Alpha Delta, Washington State* (1976)
1947	Alpha Epsilon, Georgia
1947	*Alpha Zeta, Montana* (1974)
1948	*Alpha Eta, St. Louis* (1980)
1955	Alpha Iota, Penn State
1955	*Alpha Kappa, Pepperdine* (1967)
1955	*Alpha Lambda, Michigan* (1969)
1955	*Alpha Mu, Maryland* (1986)
1956	*Alpha Omicron, Florida* (1986)
1956	*Alpha Xi, Tulane* (1962-1965) (1965)
1957	Alpha Nu, North Texas
1957	*Alpha Pi, Kansas State* (1984)
1957	*Alpha Rho, Florida State* (1983)
1958	*Alpha Sigma, Birmingham-Southern* (1963)
1958	Alpha Tau, Arizona
1959	Alpha Phi, Nebraska, Omaha
1959	Alpha Upsilon, Bradley
1960	*Alpha Chi, Samford* (1987)
1960	*Alpha Omega, Rutgers* (1986)
1960	*Alpha Psi, Morningside* (1967)
1961	*Beta Alpha, Southern Mississippi* (1987)
1961	*Beta Beta, Portland* (1986)
1962	Beta Delta, St. John's (NY) (1985-1987)
1962	*Beta Epsilon, McNeese* (1987)
1962	*Beta Gamma, Loyola, New Orleans* (1975)
1963	*Beta Eta, Carson-Newman* (1988)
1963	Beta Iota, New Orleans
1963	Beta Theta, Sam Houston
1963	Beta Zeta, Texas Christian
1964	Beta Kappa, Cal State, Fresno
1964	*Beta Lambda, East Texas* (1980)
1964	*Beta Mu, Cal State, Los Angeles* (1979)
1964	Beta Nu, Midwestern
1965	Beta Omicron, Rider
1965	*Beta Xi, Puget Sound* (1984)
1966	Beta Chi, Tennessee, Martin

1966 *Beta Phi, Seattle* (1975)
1966 *Beta Pi, Mississippi State* (1984)
1966 Beta Rho, Florida Southern
1966 *Beta Sigma, Pacific Lutheran* (1979)
1966 *Beta Tau, Wisconsin, Milwaukee* (1974)
1966 *Beta Upsilon, Cal State, Northridge* (1979)
1967 *Beta Omega, Eastern Washington* (1983)
1967 *Beta Psi, Loyola, Chicago* (1973)
1967 Gamma Alpha, Tennessee
1968 *Gamma Beta, Western Kentucky* (1975)
1968 Gamma Delta, Stephen F. Austin
1968 *Gamma Gamma, Arizona State* (1979)
1969 *Gamma Epsilon, Cal State, Long Beach* (1976)
1969 Gamma Zeta, South Alabama
1970 *Gamma Eta, Idaho State* (1982)
1970 Gamma Theta, Stetson
1971 Gamma Iota, Colorado, Denver
1972 *Gamma Kappa, Alabama A & M* (1984)
1972 *Gamma Lambda, San Francisco* (1986)
1972 *Gamma Mu, South Florida* (1980)
1973 *Gamma Nu, Cal Poly, Pomona* (1986)
1973 *Gamma Omicron, Central Florida* (1981)
1973 Gamma Phi, Waynesburg
1973 *Gamma Pi, Southern Illinois, Edwardsville* (1979)
1973 *Gamma Rho, Washburn* (1978)
1973 *Gamma Sigma, St. Ambrose* (1976)
1973 Gamma Tau, Montevallo
1973 Gamma Upsilon, Duquesne
1973 Gamma Xi, Pace
1974 *Delta Alpha, Austin Peay* (1981)
1974 *Delta Beta, St. Francis (PA)* (1987)
1974 *Delta Delta, Upsala* (1986)
1974 *Delta Epsilon, Pan American* (1977)
1974 *Delta Eta, Louisiana Tech* (1985)
1974 Delta Gamma, Montclair
1974 *Delta Iota, Metropolitan State (CO)* (1987)
1974 Delta Theta, St. Cloud
1974 *Delta Zeta, Fairleigh Dickinson, Madison* (1988)
1974 *Gamma Chi, Louisville* (1980)
1974 *Gamma Omega, Auburn* (1985)
1974 *Gamma Psi, Indiana Northwest* (1978)
1975 *Delta Kappa, Suffolk* (1984)
1975 *Delta Lambda, Akron* (1981)
1975 Delta Mu, Texas
1975 *Delta Nu, Menlo* (1977)
1975 Delta Omicron, Southwest Texas (1983-1985)
1975 Delta Xi, Central Michigan
1976 Delta Chi, Cal State, Chico
1976 Delta Phi, Trenton
1976 Delta Pi, St. Elizabeth
1976 Delta Rho, San Francisco State (1980-1988)
1976 Delta Sigma, Madison Col (1985-1987)
1976 *Delta Tau, L.S.U.* (1985)
1976 *Delta Upsilon, Western State (CO)* (1984)
1977 Delta Omega, Slippery Rock
1977 *Delta Psi, Seton Hall* (1987)
1977 Epsilon Alpha, Carlow
1978 Epsilon Beta, St. Joseph's (PA)

1978 Epsilon Gamma, Western Michigan
1979 *Epsilon Delta, Connecticut* (1983)
1979 *Epsilon Epsilon, New Hampshire* (1983)
1981 Epsilon Zeta, San Jose
1982 Epsilon Iota, Cincinnati
1982 *Epsilon Kappa, Northwood (MI)* (1987)
1982 *Epsilon Theta, South Carolina State* (1986)
1983 *Epsilon Eta, Florida Atlantic* (1983)
1986 Epsilon Mu, St. John's (NY)
1987 Epsilon Lambda, Juniata
1987 Epsilon Nu, Notre Dame (OH)

Colonies: Southeastern (DC)

Phi Delta Chi

(PHARMACY)

ACTIVE PIN

PHI DELTA CHI was founded in the Department of Pharmacy at the University of Michigan, November 2, 1883, by Charles E. Bond, F. H. Frazee, Llewellyn H. Gardner, Charles P. Godfrey, Arthur G. Hoffman, A. G. Hopper, G. P. Lemon, A. S. Rogers, Azor Thurston, A. T. Waggoner, and Charles F. Hueber. At first it was called Phi Chi. It was sponsored from the beginning by Dr. A. B. Prescott, who was then the dean of the College of Pharmacy and who was the first honorary member. At the second meeting of the society, a motion was made to change the name to Phi Delta Chi. It was defeated but was reconsidered in March 1909, and the change was then made. In 1887, the society was reorganized into a Greek-letter fraternity, with symbols, signs, ritual, and regalia being adopted.

Growth   Phi Delta Chi grew slowly at first, as did pharmacy education itself. No new chapters were established until 1896; however, between then and 1928, 30 chapters were founded in schools of pharmacy from coast to coast. Following the second World War, another growth spurt saw 20 new chapters founded, bringing the total number of Phi Delta Chi chapters to 53 by 1960.

While two new chapters were founded in 1981 and 1982, recent activity has focused more on reactivation of Phi Delta Chi chapters. Recent reactivations include Alpha (1984), Mu (1980) Rho (1979), Tau (1980) and Alpha Lambda (1983). Only nine chapters remain inactive, and three of those are at universities that no longer have schools of pharmacy.

Government   Government is by a representative body called the grand council, consisting of one alumnus and one active member from each chapter, which meets, biennially. Between sessions, the Executive Council administers affairs.

Traditions and Insignia The badge is a plain gold triangle with the point at the bottom, displaying the letters ΦΔΧ. The flower is the red carnation. Colors are old gold and dregs of wine.

Publication A quarterly, *The Communicator of Phi Delta Chi,* is published.

Funds and Philanthropies Phi Delta Chi has an extensive Achievement Awards program, and part of this program involves scholarships and awards to chapters for excellence in service projects, publications, scholarship, brotherhood, and window displays. At least $700 per year is allocated to this program for monetary awards from the Albert B. Prescott Scholarship Fund. Additionally, the chapter accruing the most points in the program is given the Emory W. Thurston Grand President's Award for that year.

From 1981 until 1983, Phi Delta Chi conducted a national service project on aging. At least 10 chapters reported geriatric service projects to the national office during this period.

Headquarters Pharmacy/Association Services, Post Office Box 5770, Washington, D.C. 20814.

Membership Total living membership 20,000. Total undergraduate membership 1,623. Active chapters 51. Inactive chapters 7. Houses owned 18. Graduate/Alumni chapters 33. Total number of initiates 33,599. Chapter roll:

1883 Alpha, Michigan (1968-1984)
1896 Beta, Northwestern
1898 *Gamma, Columbia (NY)* (1940)
1900 Delta, Wisconsin, Madison (1903-1971)
1901 Epsilon, Philadelphia Pharmacy
1902 Eta, Massachusetts Pharmacy
1902 Zeta, Cal Medical, San Francisco
1904 Theta, Minnesota
1905 Iota, Maryland
1905 Kappa, Washington (WA)
1905 Lambda, Texas (1933-1956)
1907 Mu, Pitt (1974-1980)
1907 Nu, Iowa
1908 Xi, Ohio State
1909 Omicron, USC
1912 *Pi, Nebraska* (1924)
1913 Rho, Oklahoma (1972-1979)
1914 Sigma, Colorado
1916 Tau, Purdue (1926-1979)
1917 *Upsilon, Kansas* (1930)
1920 *Phi, Creighton* (1971)
1921 Chi, Auburn (1931-1953)
1921 Psi, Drake
1922 Omega, Tennessee
1923 *Alpha Alpha, Western Reserve* (1937)
1923 Alpha Beta, Kentucky
1923 Alpha Gamma, North Carolina
1925 Alpha Delta, Virginia Commonwealth
1927 Alpha Epsilon, Mississippi
1928 Alpha Eta, Wayne State (MI)
1928 Alpha Zeta, Idaho State
1931 Alpha Theta, Albany Pharmacy
1937 Alpha Iota, Georgia

1947 Alpha Kappa, South Carolina Medical
1949 Alpha Lambda, Connecticut (1965-1983)
1949 Alpha Mu, Wyoming
1950 Alpha Nu, Arizona
1951 Alpha Omicron, Temple
1951 Alpha Pi, Utah
1951 Alpha Rho, Mercer
1951 Alpha Xi, Ferris
1952 Alpha Sigma, Illinois, Chicago
1953 Alpha Tau, Houston
1955 Alpha Phi, Butler
1955 Alpha Upsilon, Ohio Northern
1956 *Alpha Chi, Samford* (1987)
1956 Alpha Omega, Southwestern State (OK)
1956 Alpha Psi, Pacific (OR)
1958 Beta Alpha, St. John's (NY)
1959 Beta Beta, Northeast Louisiana
1960 Beta Delta, St. Louis Pharmacy
1960 Beta Epsilon, Missouri, Kansas City
1960 Beta Gamma, Duquesne
1963 *Beta Zeta, Long Island* (1981)
1967 Beta Eta, Arkansas
1981 Beta Theta, South Carolina
1982 Beta Iota, Oregon State
1988 Beta Kappa, Campbell

Phi Delta Phi[†]

(LAW)

ACTIVE PIN

PHI DELTA PHI, international legal fraternity, was founded at the University of Michigan on December 13, 1869, in the old Gregory House in Ann Arbor. The first meeting had been held earlier on November 22. The founders did not realize at the time that they were organizing the first professional Greek-letter fraternity in America and sent numerous letters to eastern colleges hoping to become affiliated with an established society of similar purpose. Two of the founders, John M. Howard and Arthur M. Monteith, had been roommates at Monmouth College before coming to Michigan. Howard was a charter member of the Phi Gamma Delta chapter at Monmouth and had been commissioned to organize a chapter at Michigan, but had given up the project because of his inability to find suitable material. He, Monteith, and John B. Cleland decided to form a secret society within the Webster Debating Society to control politics and put them on a basis of merit. They approached only men of highest scholastic leadership and among them were three of the four prize-winning debaters of the year, Eugene E. Al-

† This chapter narrative is repeated from the 19th edition; no current information was provided.

len, Joseph D. Ronan, and Frederick F. Wendell. They added James E. Howell, W. S. Beebe, Alfred E. Hawes, and Robert J. Hill to their ranks. Three days after founding the first initiation was held for Charles S. Thomas, Frank Butterworth, and John L. Starkweather. The policy of Phi Delta Phi has always been to encourage members of college fraternities who are enrolled for the study of law to join its ranks, and no conflict of allegiance has been experienced.

The chapters are called inns and are of two classes: barrister inns, composed of alumni members and located in the principal cities of Canada and the United States; and student inns, located in the principal law schools of Canada and the United States.

Most of the inns maintain meeting rooms, some of them with law libraries; but, because of the maturity of the membership and dual membership in college fraternities, few of the inns lease or own their own homes.

Growth   Expansion began in 1875. Inns were established at the University of Pennsylvania in 1875, at Illinois Wesleyan in 1878, at Northwestern University in 1880, and at Columbia University also in 1880. By 1900 thirty active inns had been established. In the next ten years fourteen more inns were added. Then during and for a period following World War I fewer new inns were admitted, but activity continued in all established inns, and additional inns were admitted between World Wars I and II. During the latter, all the inns remained active on a restricted basis although law school enrollments dropped to almost nothing. Thus almost before the fighting had ceased the fraternity sprang back to full strength and entered into another period of rapid expansion.

Government   The sovereignty and legislative power of the fraternity are vested in a biennial convention composed of delegates from the inns, and administrative control rests in the five-member Council, which manages, controls, and supervises the fraternity subject to the constitution and the directions of the general convention.

Traditions and Insignia   The principal purpose of the organization is to promote a higher standard of professional ethics and culture in the schools and in the profession at large. To encompass these ends the inns conduct aggressive programs of moot court competition, appellate arguments, legal debates, legal aid projects, and addresses on practical subjects relating to law. Purely social functions are held frequently.

The official badge was adopted in 1882 and is a monogram. The colors are claret red and pearl blue. The flower is the Jacqueminot rose. The flag is a pennant with three diagonal panels, the upper and lower ones plain and claret red in color, the middle one pearl blue displaying the letters ΦΔΦ in claret red. The great seal is a circle centered with the illuminated symbols C, C, and S of ritualistic significance in a circular band bearing the inscription

"International Legal Fraternity of Phi Delta Phi, 1869."

Awards and Loans   Phi Delta Phi awards two $100 scholarships each academic year to the two members of each chapter who have best exhibited the highest degree of scholarship as well as service to their inn and law school. The Graduate of the Year Award honors the student who ranks highest in scholarship, ability, and service to Phi Delta Phi. Each student inn selects its own candidate; the winner is invited, at fraternity expense. to attend and address the biennial convention.

Publications   *The Brief* is a quarterly professional journal devoted to the advancement of law and of the legal profession and to the interests of the fraternity. The *Centennial History* was published in 1971.

Headquarters   1750 N Street, N.W., Washington. D.C. 20036. The headquarters building is a five-story townhouse. A fulltime executive director and professional staff of five are employed.

Membership   Active student inns 95. Inactive inns 9. Total number of initiates 95,000. Inn roll:

1869   Kent, Michigan
1878   *Benjamin, Illinois Wesleyan* (1928)
1880   Booth, Northwestern
1881   Story, Columbia (1913-1922)
1882   Cooley, Washington
1884   *Jay, Albany Law* (1912)
1884   Marshall, George Washington
1885   *Webster, Boston* (1956)
1886   *Gibson, Penn* (1934)
1886   Hamilton, Cincinnati (1925-1927)
1887   *Choate, Harvard* (1909)
1887   Waite, Yale
1888   Conkling, Cornell
1888   Field, New York
1890   Minor, Virginia
1890   Tiedeman, Missouri
1891   Chase, Oregon
1891   *Daniels, Buffalo* (1942)
1891   Dillon, Minnesota
1891   Harlan, Wisconsin, Madison
1893   McClain, Iowa
1893   Swan, Ohio State
1895   Lincoln, Nebraska
1896   Fuller, Chicago-Kent Law
1896   Osgoode, Osgoode Hall Law (1899-1909)
1897   Green, Kansas
1897   Miller, Stanford
1899   Comstock, Syracuse
1899   Dwight, New York Law
1900   Foster, Indiana
1901   Langdell, Illinois
1901   Ranney, Case Western Reserve
1902   Brewer, Denver
1903   Douglas, Chicago (1942-1957)
1907   Ballinger, Washington
1907   Beatty, USC
1907   Evarts, Brooklyn Law
1907   Malone, Vanderbilt

1907 Thomas, Colorado
1908 *Reed, Maine* (1919)
1908 Tucker, Washington and Lee
1909 Roberts, Texas
1909 *Shiras, Pitt* (1959)
1911 Ames, South Dakota
1911 Bruce, North Dakota
1911 Holmes, Oklahoma
1911 White, Tulane
1913 Jones, Cal, Berkeley
1919 Cockrell, Florida
1919 Roosevelt, Tennessee
1919 Vance, North Carolina
1922 Brooke, West Virginia
1922 Clayberg, Montana
1922 Wilson, Georgia
1922 deGraffenried, Alabama
1923 Lamar, Emory
1925 Breckinridge, Kentucky
1925 *Weldon, Dalhousie* (1940)
1927 Calhoun, South Carolina
1927 Martin, L.S.U.
1927 Mayes, Mississippi
1929 Pattee, Arizona
1931 Hughes, Duke
1931 Taft, St. John's (NY)
1937 Aggeler, Loyola Marymount, Los Angeles
1937 Conwell, Temple
1942 Powell, Kansas City
1947 Bryan, Miami (FL)
1947 Cardozo, Stetson
1947 Johnson, Utah
1947 McNary, Willamette
1947 Ruffin, Wake Forest
1947 Scott, Georgetown
1947 Willkie, Indiana
1949 Hemphill, Baylor
1949 Murphy, St. Louis
1949 Tarlton, St. Mary's
1950 Beasley, Rutgers
1951 Pound, UCLA
1953 Hutcheson, Houston
1957 Stone Inn, Marquette
1959 Monteith Inn, Southern Methodist
1959 Rogers Inn, Tulsa
1959 Stephens Inn, San Francisco
1961 Learned Hand Inn, Oklahoma City
1962 Madison Inn, Richmond
1962 Wigmore Inn, San Diego U.
1964 Brandeis Inn, Cal Western
1964 George Inn, Mercer
1965 Jefferson Inn, William and Mary
1965 Kennedy Inn, American
1965 Robinson Inn, Samford
1965 Stevenson Inn, Memphis State
1968 Ladd, Florida State
1969 Shields, Pacific (CA)
1970 Gibson, Cal, Davis
1971 McFarland, Arizona State
1972 Warren, Texas Tech
1973 Velasco, Escuela Libre de Derecho
1974 Landon, Washburn

1975 Salinas, Universidad de Monterrey
1976 Ford, Vermont Law
1976 Rehnquist, Suffolk
1983 Pomeroy, Hastings Law

Phi Gamma Nu

(BUSINESS AND ECONOMICS)

ACTIVE PIN

PLEDGE PIN

PHI GAMMA NU was founded at Northwestern University, School of Commerce, February 17, 1924, by Mary Chard, Elizabeth Conroy, Marge McInerney, Sylvia Pekar, Helen Vogel, and Celeste Weyl. It is incorporated under the state laws of Michigan. The objects are: to foster the study of business in colleges and universities; to uphold the interests of our alma maters through the encouragement of high scholarship, participation in school activities, and the association of students for their mutual advancement; to promote professional competency and achievement in the field of business; and to further a high standard of commercial ethics and culture in civic and professional enterprises.

Only students who have completed at least six semester hours of pre-business subjects, including economics, retailing, management, political science, data processing, food management, etc., are eligible for membership. Classifications of membership are collegiate members, honorary members, alumnae members, associate members, sustaining members, faculty members, and professional members.

Government The national chapter congress, the supreme power, is composed of one representative from each active and each alumnae chapter and the national officers. It meets triennially. The supreme executive and legislative body during the interval between the meetings of the congress is the National Council.

Traditions and Insignia The badge is a monogram of the letters, Φ, Γ, N, encircled by pearls and having one ruby in the corner of the Gamma. The pledge pin is a shield with one half of gold and the other half of cardinal red. The flower is the red rose. The colors are cardinal red and gold. The banner is a reproduction of the official coat of arms in gold on a field of cardinal red. The motto is *Esse Quam Videri*.

Publications Under the direction of the national editor, *The Magazine of Phi Gamma Nu* is published once each college year.

Funds and Philanthropies Phi Gamma Nu Educational Foundation now awards the Phi Gamma Nu Educational Grant, the Phi Gamma Nu Scholarship Key, and the Phi Gamma Nu Scholarship Cup.

Each year the Phi Gamma Nu Scholarship Key is presented by the National Council at each college or university where a chapter is located. This key is awarded to the senior woman business major to be graduated with the highest scholastic average. The Phi Gamma Nu Scholarship Cup is an annual award presented to the collegiate chapter attaining the highest cumulative scholastic average for the current school year. The Phi Gamma Nu Scholarship Certificate is annually awarded to the member of each collegiate chapter who has attained the highest scholastic average.

The Phi Gamma Nu Chapter Performance Rating Achievement Contest was inaugurated during the 1955-57 biennium. This annual competition serves to outline the major areas of local activity for which the chapter is responsible and provides a yardstick by which it may measure its activities and performance against reasonable goals set by the National Council.

The National Council of Phi Gamma Nu adopted a new national project at the 1983 Convention. Phi Gamma Nu now supports a project consisting of educating people about drug and alcohol abuse.

Headquarters　6745 Cheryl Ann Drive, Seven Hills, Ohio 44131.

Membership　Chapter roll:††

1924	Alpha, Northwestern
1927	*Beta, Boston*
1928	Delta, Iowa
1928	*Gamma, Denver*
1929	*Epsilon, Temple*
1931	*Eta, DePaul*
1931	Theta, Wyoming
1931	Zeta, Detroit
1944	*Iota, Baylor*
1946	*Kappa, Limestone*
1949	Lambda, Texas Tech.
1949	*Mu, New Mexico*
1949	Nu, Wayne State
1950	Omicron, Michigan State
1950	*Pi, Arkansas*
1950	Xi, Mississippi
1951	Rho, Kent
1951	Sigma, Memphis State
1953	Tau, West Texas
1954	Upsilon, Drake
1955	Phi, Texas Western
1961	Chi, Eastern New Mexico
1961	Psi, West Liberty
1962	Omega, Canisius
1963	Alpha Alpha, St. Mary-Of-The-Woods
1963	*Alpha Beta, Dyke*
1966	*Alpha Delta, Upsala*
1966	Alpha Epsilon, Temple Community College
1966	Alpha Gamma, Creighton
1967	*Alpha Eta, Adrian* (1973)
1967	Alpha Iota, Central State

1967	Alpha Kappa, Southeast Missouri
1967	Alpha Lambda, Rochester Tech
1967	Alpha Nu, Ferris
1967	Alpha Theta, Eastern Michigan
1967	Alpha Xi, Nevada, Las Vegas
1968	*Alpha Omicron, Southern Illinois* (1972)
1968	Alpha Pi, Florida Atlantic
1968	Alpha Rho, Tennessee Tech.
1968	*Alpha Sigma, Drexel* (1974)
1968	Alpha Tau, Roosevelt
1969	Alpha Chi, Xavier
1969	Alpha Omega, Texas A & I
1969	Alpha Phi, Dayton
1969	Alpha Psi, Ohio
1969	Alpha Upsilon, Western Illinois
1971	Beta Alpha, New Mexico State
1972	Beta Beta, Shepherd
1972	Beta Delta, Dillard
1972	Beta Gamma, Tampa
1973	Beta Epsilon, Houston
1973	Beta Eta, Michigan, Dearborn
1973	Beta Zeta, Wisconsin, La Crosse
1973	Gamma Beta, St. Mary's
1974	Beta Iota, Troy
1974	Beta Kappa, Ball State
1974	Beta Lambda, Texas, Arlington
1974	*Beta Nu, Weber* (1975)
1974	Beta Omicron, Lewis
1974	Beta Pi, Illinois
1974	Beta Theta, SUNY, Albany
1974	Beta Xi, American International
1975	Beta Chi, Illinois Wesleyan
1975	Beta Phi, Niagara
1975	Beta Rho, LaSalle
1975	*Beta Sigma, Oklahoma* (1975)
1975	Beta Tau, Delaware State
1975	*Beta Upsilon, Cal State, Sacramento*
1976	Beta Omega, Federal City
1976	Beta Psi, St. Francis
1976	Gamma Gamma, Eastern Illinois

†† This chapter roll is repeated from the 19th edition; no current information was provided.

Phi Mu Alpha— Sinfonia

(MUSIC)

ACTIVE PIN

PHI MU ALPHA, commonly called Sinfonia, was organized as the Sinfonia Club of the New England Conservatory of Music on October 6, 1898, by Ossian E. Mills and thirteen conservatory students. It was decided in 1900 to expand the club and form a national fraternity for men in music in schools and conservatories of approved excellence, and the first national convention was held April 16–20, 1901 in Boston. The Greek letters Phi Mu Alpha were adopted in 1905, and the fraternity evolved from "Sinfonia-Phi Mu Alpha" to the present-day "Phi Mu Alpha Sinfonia Fraternity of America." The purposes of Phi Mu Alpha Sinfonia are to encourage and actively promote the highest standards of creativity, performance, education and research in music in America; to develop and encourage loyalty to the Alma Mater; to foster the mutual welfare and brotherhood of students of music; to develop the truest fraternal spirit among its members; and to instill in all people an awareness of music's important role in the enrichment of the human spirit.

Growth Four chapters had been installed at the time of the fraternity's first national convention in Boston in April of 1900, although only three were represented there. By 1909 Sinfonia had more than doubled, adding six new chapters. Eight additional chapters were installed from 1910 to 1919, although during World War I Sinfonia survived largely through the efforts of a few administrators, with no charters being added between 1915 and 1919.

The first major boom in fraternity expansion occurred in the post-war decade of 1920–29, which saw the installation of 37 new chapters. Growth was steady but slight in the Depression era, with 20 charters granted between 1930 and 1939. World War II again thinned Sinfonia's ranks and threatened its survival. Only ten charters were granted between 1940 and 1942, but the post-war period resulted in 32 new chapters, making the forties the period of greatest expansion to that time. Under the leadership of Archie Jones, whose ten-year term as national president remains the longest in the history of the fraternity, 60 new chapters were added between 1950 and 1959. Sinfonia enjoyed its greatest period of growth by far in the era of 1960–69, however, chartering 131 chapters during those years. The ensuing period was difficult for all fraternities, and Phi Mu Alpha was no exception. Only 56 chapters were added from 1970–79, and fourteen have been chartered from 1980–1985.

Government Phi Mu Alpha Sinfonia is governed by a seven-member National Executive Committee which meets twice each year and at all National Assemblies. The fraternity is divided geographically into 36 provinces, each under the direction of a province governor who is appointed by the national president, and a collegiate province representative, who is elected at-large from among the collegiate membership of the province. The National Executive Committee consists of the national president, who serves as chairman, the national vice president, the elected chairmen of the Council of Province Governors and the Council of Collegiate Province Representatives, a National Collegiate Representative elected from among the collegiate delegates to the National Assembly, each serving a three-year term, and two Executive Committeemen elected at-large to six-year terms.

Sinfonia enacts legislation at its National Assembly. The National Assembly was held annually from 1900–1920, biennially from 1920–1964, and triennially from 1964 to the present. In 1964 the assembly was changed from one delegate representing each collegiate chapter to a representative format, with one collegiate delegate elected to represent each province. Delegates to the National Assembly currently include the members of the National Executive Committee, the province governors and the collegiate province representatives.

Between National Assemblies, matters pertaining to the constitution are referred to the National Council, consisting of the National Executive committee, the province governors, and the president of each active collegiate chapter. The main governing documents are the *Constitution* and the *General Regulations for Chapters*.

Traditions and Insignia Each chapter is required to give at least one program annually consisting solely of American music. Chapters are urged to undertake projects of benefit to the sheltering institution, the campus community and the community at-large of a musical, social and service nature.

The badge is a triangle with the point at the top. It displays an Old English script letter 'S' in the center, with the letters ΦΜΑ displayed at each point beginning at the top and continuing counterclockwise. The letters are gold on a black enamel background. The badge is surrounded either by a gold border with scrollwork or by eighteen stones, twelve pearls and six contrasting garnets. The pledge pin is also a triangle with the point at the top. The center of the pledge pin is a black triangle outlined in gold, which is surrounded by a red triangular border, also outlined in gold.

The colors of the fraternity are red, black, gold and white. The official flower is the chrysanthemum. Founder's Day is celebrated on October 6. Each chapter additionally celebrates Chapter Day on the anniversary of its charter.

Publications The fraternity publishes four issues of *The Sinfonian* annually. The magazine is sent to all collegiate and alumni members in good standing. The fraternity also publishes *The Red & Black*, a newsletter for collegiate members, roughly five times each year. In addition, the fraternity publishes *Sinfonian Songs*, a songbook with words and music by the members, *Themes for Brotherhood*, a fraternity education handbook for probationary members, and the constitution and *General Regulations for Chapters*. A general revision of fraternity publications was begun in 1985, including work on a manual for chapter officers, a directory, and numerous manuals on general chapter operations, which are expected to be published during 1986. The fraternity employs a full-time director of publications to edit and oversee its ongoing program of published educational and informative material.

Funds and Philanthropies The philanthropic

arm of Phi Mu Alpha Sinfonia is the Sinfonia Foundation, established in 1952. The foundation is governed by a non-salaried Board of Trustees, which consists of the National Executive Committee of the fraternity and up to four trustees elected at-large.

The Sinfonia Foundation commissions new works of music from American composers, provides annual grants for research in American music by competent scholars, matching grants to fraternity chapters for special projects beyond the scope of normal activities, and awards scholarships to schools hosting the chapters earning the Charles E. Lutton Province Merit Award each triennium.

Headquarters "Lyrecrest," 10600 Old State Road, Evansville, Indiana 47711-1399. Lyrecrest, a gracious fourteen room home on the northern outskirts of Evansville, was dedicated in 1970. The more than five acres of rolling wooded land and a small lake form a picturesque setting for the base of operations of America's largest fraternal organization in music. Headquarters operations are managed by a salaried national executive director.

Membership Eta merged with Omicron in 1955 to become Eta-Omicron. Delta Chi charter was withdrawn at the time of the merger of Minneapolis College of Music with McPhail School of Music and rechartered at McPhail as Theta Omega. In 1967 Theta Omega merged into Alpha Mu at the University of Minnesota. Epsilon Mu merged with Alpha Psi in 1959. Kappa Omega merged in 1969 with Beta Epsilon. Beta Zeta charter was withdrawn when the College of Emporia closed in 1973.

Total living membership 84,248. Total deceased membership 4,720. Active chapters 204. Inactive chapters 179. Houses owned 3. Graduate/Alumni chapters 3. Total number of initiates 104,396. Chapter roll:

1898   *Alpha, New England Conservatory* (1970)
1900   Beta, Combs (1930-1960)
1900   *Gamma, American Conservatory* (1901)
1901   Delta, Ithaca
1902   *Epsilon, Michigan* (1967)
1902   *Zeta, Chicago Conservatory* (1904)
1903   *Eta, Cincinnati Conservatory of Music* (1955)
1904   *Gamma, Detroit Conservatory* (1911)
1904   *Theta, Syracuse* (1977)
1907   Zeta, Missouri
1910   Iota, Northwestern
1911   *Kappa, Peabody Conservatory* (1915-1958) (1985)
1911   *Lambda, DePauw* (1913-1924) (1982)
1912   Mu, Oklahoma
1912   *Nu, Denison* (1949-1958) (1969)
1914   *Omicron, Cincinnati Conservatory of Music* (1955)
1914   Xi, Kansas
1915   Pi, Simpson
1920   *Rho, American Conservatory* (1983)
1921   Chi, Washington State (1984)
1921   *Phi, Wisconsin, Madison* (1975)

1921   *Psi, Oregon* (1974)
1921   *Sigma, Washington (WA)* (1974)
1921   *Tau, Kansas State* (1934-1960) (1985)
1921   Upsilon, Nebraska
1922   Alpha Beta, Drake
1922   Alpha Delta, Iowa State
1922   *Alpha Gamma, Kentucky* (1977-1979) (1989)
1922   *Omega, Ohio Wesleyan* (1982)
1923   *Alpha Epsilon, USC* (1985)
1923   *Alpha Eta, Denver College of Music* (1932)
1923   Alpha Zeta, Penn State
1924   Alpha Iota, Texas
1924   Alpha Kappa, Ohio
1924   Alpha Lambda, Illinois Wesleyan
1924   *Alpha Mu, Minnesota* (1974)
1924   Alpha Theta, Miami (OH)
1925   Alpha Nu, Eastman School
1925   Alpha Omicron, Arkansas (1933-1949)
1925   *Alpha Pi, Bucknell* (1950)
1925   Alpha Xi, Illinois
1926   Alpha Rho, North Carolina
1926   *Alpha Sigma, Butler* (1986)
1927   *Alpha Chi, Tulsa* (1974)
1927   Alpha Phi, Fort Hays
1927   *Alpha Psi, Kansas Medical Center* (1987)
1927   Alpha Tau, Wittenberg
1927   *Alpha Upsilon, Arizona* (1977-1983) (1987)
1928   Alpha Omega, Carnegie-Mellon
1928   *Beta Delta, Pittsburg State, Kansas* (1984)
1928   *Beta Epsilon, N.Y.U.* (1980)
1928   *Beta Gamma, Columbia (NY)* (1976)
1929   *Beta Eta, San Jose* (1977-1980) (1981)
1929   Beta Theta, Millikin
1929   *Beta Zeta, Emporia* (1941-1954) (1973)
1930   Beta Iota, Albion
1930   Beta Kappa, Coe
1930   *Beta Lambda, Muskingum* (1969)
1930   Beta Mu, Central Missouri State
1931   Beta Nu, Northern Iowa
1931   Beta Omicron, Mansfield
1931   Beta Pi, Pacific (CA)
1931   Beta Xi, Ohio State (1975-1986)
1934   *Beta Rho, Northern Colorado* (1984)
1936   *Beta Sigma, Idaho* (1975)
1937   *Beta Chi, Colorado* (1976-1980) (1985)
1937   *Beta Phi, Baldwin-Wallace* (1985)
1937   *Beta Psi, UCLA* (1973)
1937   Beta Tau, Miami (FL)
1937   *Beta Upsilon, Emporia* (1984)
1938   Beta Omega, L.S.U.
1938   Gamma Delta, Murray State
1938   Gamma Epsilon, Michigan State
1938   Gamma Eta, Furman (1940-1955)
1938   Gamma Zeta, Lawrence
1940   Gamma Iota, Baylor
1940   *Gamma Kappa, Davidson* (1969)
1940   *Gamma Lambda, Hendrix* (1955)
1940   Gamma Mu, Bethany (KS)
1940   *Gamma Nu, Western Reserve* (1947)
1940   Gamma Theta, North Texas

1941	Gamma Omicron, Wayne State (MI) (1978-1981)
1941	*Gamma Pi, Cal State, Fresno (1983)*
1941	Gamma Xi, Morningside
1942	Gamma Rho, Northwestern Louisiana
1947	Delta Epsilon, Southwestern Louisiana
1947	*Gamma Chi, Texas Wesleyan (1987)*
1947	Gamma Omega, Indiana State
1947	Gamma Phi, Southwest Texas (1977-1978)
1947	*Gamma Psi, George Peabody (1981)*
1947	*Gamma Sigma, Wichita (1979-1982) (1985)*
1947	Gamma Tau, Indiana (1982-1990)
1947	*Gamma Upsilon, Phillips (1983)*
1948	*Delta Eta, Youngstown State (1987)*
1948	Delta Iota, Western Michigan
1948	*Delta Kappa, South Dakota (1986)*
1948	Delta Lambda, Ball State
1948	Delta Mu, Texas Christian
1948	Delta Nu, Bradley
1948	*Delta Omicron, Boston U (1975)*
1948	*Delta Rho, Wisconsin, Milwaukee (1984)*
1948	*Delta Theta, Montana (1981)*
1948	*Delta Xi, Eastern Michigan (1988)*
1948	*Delta Zeta, Oklahoma City (1979)*
1949	*Delta Chi, Minneapolis College of Music (1959)*
1949	Delta Omega, Southeastern Louisiana
1949	*Delta Phi, Lewis and Clark (1973)*
1949	Delta Pi, Redlands
1949	Delta Psi, Auburn
1949	Delta Sigma, South Carolina
1949	Delta Tau, Oklahoma State (1981-1989)
1949	*Delta Upsilon, Southern Methodist (1979-1984) (1986)*
1949	Epsilon Eta, Puget Sound (1969-1989)
1949	Epsilon Iota, Florida State
1949	Epsilon Kappa, Southern Illinois
1949	*Epsilon Theta, Roosevelt (1973)*
1949	*Epsilon Zeta, Denver (1977-1981) (1985)*
1950	Epsilon Lambda, Georgia
1950	*Epsilon Mu, Kansas Medical Center (1959)*
1950	Epsilon Nu, Jacksonville (AL)
1950	Epsilon Omicron, San Diego U.
1950	Epsilon Pi, Hartwick (1986-1989)
1950	*Epsilon Rho, Northern Illinois (1983)*
1950	*Epsilon Sigma, West Virginia (1985)*
1950	*Epsilon Tau, Eastern Washington (1974)*
1950	*Epsilon Xi, Idaho State (1958)*
1951	*Epsilon Chi, Pepperdine (1970)*
1951	Epsilon Omega, Nebraska, Omaha
1951	Epsilon Phi, Capital
1951	*Epsilon Psi, Wyoming (1982)*
1951	Epsilon Upsilon, Evansville
1952	*Zeta Eta, Marshall (1978)*
1952	Zeta Iota, Howard (1973-1977)
1952	*Zeta Kappa, Louisville (1985)*
1952	*Zeta Theta, Wagner (1989)*
1953	*Zeta Lambda, Brigham Young (1973)*
1953	*Zeta Nu, Washington (MO) (1967)*
1953	Zeta Omicron, Georgia Southern
1953	*Zeta Pi, Loyola, New Orleans (1967)*
1953	*Zeta Rho, Fisk (1979-1984) (1987)*
1953	Zeta Sigma, Texas Tech
1953	Zeta Tau, Indiana (PA)
1953	*Zeta Xi, Lincoln (MO) (1977)*
1954	*Zeta Mu, Sam Houston (1990)*
1954	*Zeta Phi, Friends (1983)*
1954	Zeta Upsilon, Cal State, Los Angeles (1978-1988)
1955	Eta Iota, Northeast Louisiana
1955	*Eta Kappa, Occidental (1985)*
1955	Eta Omicron, Cincinnati
1955	*Eta Theta, Catholic (1982)*
1955	Zeta Chi, McNeese
1955	*Zeta Omega, Hartt School of Music (1976)*
1955	Zeta Psi, East Carolina
1956	*Eta Lambda, Moorhead (1986)*
1956	Eta Mu, Lamar
1956	Eta Nu, St. Mary's (MN)
1956	*Eta Pi, Willamette (1976)*
1956	Eta Xi, Tennessee State
1957	Eta Phi, Southern Mississippi
1957	*Eta Rho, Park (MO) (1974)*
1957	*Eta Sigma, San Francisco State (1972-1975) (1981)*
1957	*Eta Tau, Cal State, Sacramento (1974-1980) (1987)*
1957	Eta Upsilon, Centenary (1969-1980)
1958	*Eta Chi, Minnesota (1975)*
1958	Eta Omega, Florida
1958	*Eta Psi, Maryland (1976)*
1958	Theta Iota, SUNY Col., Potsdam
1959	*Theta Kappa, Mississippi Col (1985)*
1959	Theta Lambda, Hardin-Simmons
1959	*Theta Mu, Midwestern (1981)*
1959	Theta Nu, Northern State
1959	Theta Omicron, Tennessee (1976-1978) (1979-1981)
1959	Theta Pi, Morehead
1959	Theta Rho, Memphis State
1959	Theta Sigma, Florida Southern
1959	Theta Tau, Austin Peay
1959	*Theta Xi, Drury (1987)*
1960	Iota Kappa, Lebanon Valley
1960	Iota Lambda, Duquesne
1960	Iota Mu, Western Kentucky
1960	Iota Nu, Troy
1960	Iota Omicron, Bowling Green
1960	Iota Pi, West Texas
1960	Iota Rho, Southwest Missouri
1960	Iota Sigma, Union (TN)
1960	Iota Tau, Old Dominion
1960	*Iota Xi, Kearney (1986)*
1960	*Theta Chi, Dickinson (1971)*
1960	*Theta Omega, MacPhail (MN) (1967)*
1960	*Theta Phi, Eastern New Mexico (1986)*
1960	Theta Psi, Georgetown Col (1980-1984)
1960	Theta Upsilon, Delta State
1961	*Iota Chi, Evangel (1986)*
1961	*Iota Omega, Hope (1982)*
1961	*Iota Phi, New Mexico (1974)*
1961	Iota Psi, Southeast Missouri
1961	Iota Upsilon, Wayland Baptist

Year	Chapter
1961	*Kappa Lambda, Cal State, Northridge* (1976)
1961	Kappa Mu, William Jewell
1961	Kappa Nu, Arizona State (1980-1984)
1961	Kappa Omicron, Cal State, Long Beach
1961	*Kappa Pi, Manhattan* (1982)
1961	Kappa Rho, Washburn
1961	Kappa Sigma, Valparaiso
1961	*Kappa Tau, Central State (OK)* (1984)
1961	*Kappa Upsilon, Juilliard* (1971)
1961	Kappa Xi, Northern Arizona (1985-1988)
1962	Kappa Chi, Del Mar
1962	*Kappa Omega, N.Y. College of Music* (1969)
1962	*Kappa Phi, DePaul* (1983)
1962	Kappa Psi, Western Illinois
1962	Lambda Mu, Montclair
1962	*Lambda Nu, Trenton* (1980)
1962	Lambda Xi, Mississippi (1982-1985)
1963	Lambda Chi, Minot
1963	Lambda Omega, Carson-Newman
1963	*Lambda Omicron, Livingston* (1982)
1963	Lambda Phi, Mississippi State
1963	Lambda Pi, Boston Conservatory
1963	Lambda Psi, Mercer
1963	Lambda Rho, Northwest Mississippi
1963	Lambda Sigma Society, East Tennessee (1976-1979)
1963	*Lambda Tau, Mankato* (1973-1978) (1979)
1963	*Lambda Upsilon, Kentucky Wesleyan* (1973-1978) (1986)
1964	Mu Nu, Louisiana Tech
1964	Mu Omicron, Ouachita Baptist
1964	*Mu Pi, Lewis* (1984)
1964	*Mu Rho, New Mexico State* (1972)
1964	Mu Xi, Stephen F. Austin
1965	*Mu Chi, Pacific (OR)* (1982)
1965	*Mu Omega, Buena Vista* (1989)
1965	*Mu Phi, Union (KY)* (1983)
1965	Mu Psi, Southern
1965	*Mu Sigma, Southwestern (KS)* (1978)
1965	*Mu Tau, Philadelphia Musical* (1977)
1965	*Mu Upsilon, Belhaven* (1983)
1965	*Nu Chi, Mount Union* (1985)
1965	Nu Omega, Howard Payne
1965	*Nu Omicron, Illinois State* (1984)
1965	*Nu Phi, Orlando Junior* (1970)
1965	Nu Pi, Central Michigan
1965	Nu Psi, Shenandoah Conservatory
1965	*Nu Rho, Southern Colorado* (1982)
1965	Nu Sigma, William and Mary
1965	Nu Upsilon, Hillsdale (1983-1987)
1965	*Nu Xi, William Carey* (1986)
1965	Xi Omicron, Wisconsin, Stevens Point
1965	Xi Pi, Wisconsin, Whitewater
1966	*Nu Tau, Wisconsin, Oshkosh* (1984)
1966	Omicron Chi, Jacksonville
1966	Omicron Phi, Alabama
1966	Omicron Pi, Cal State, Fullerton
1966	Omicron Rho, Belmont (1984-1985)
1966	*Omicron Sigma, Portland State* (1982)
1966	Omicron Tau, Middle Tennessee
1966	Omicron Upsilon, Houston
1966	Xi Chi, Tennessee Tech
1966	Xi Omega, Frostburg
1966	*Xi Phi, Iowa Wesleyan* (1974)
1966	Xi Psi, Westminster (PA)
1966	*Xi Rho, Maryville (TN)* (1977-1980) (1985)
1966	*Xi Sigma, Bethel (TN)* (1982)
1966	Xi Tau, Southern Illinois, Edwardsville (1976-1984)
1966	Xi Upsilon, Eastern Illinois
1967	Omicron Omega, Arkansas State
1967	Omicron Psi, Eastern Kentucky
1967	*Pi Chi, Texas A & I* (1988)
1967	*Pi Omega, Gettysburg* (1989)
1967	*Pi Phi, Cal State, Hayward* (1974)
1967	Pi Psi, East Texas
1967	Pi Rho, Mars Hill
1967	Pi Sigma, Samford
1967	Pi Tau, Oklahoma Baptist
1967	Pi Upsilon, Colorado State
1967	Rho Chi, SUNY Col., Fredonia
1967	Rho Omega, Virginia Commonwealth
1967	*Rho Phi, Kent* (1982)
1967	*Rho Psi, Wake Forest* (1977)
1967	Rho Sigma, West Chester
1967	Rho Tau, Appalachian
1967	*Rho Upsilon, Temple* (1980)
1967	*Sigma Tau, Towson* (1976)
1967	*Sigma Upsilon, Adrian* (1983)
1968	Sigma Chi, Henderson
1968	Sigma Omega, Texas, Arlington (1984-1986)
1968	Sigma Phi, Brevard Comm. Col.
1968	Sigma Psi, Tennessee, Martin
1968	*Tau Chi, Arkansas, Little Rock* (1978)
1968	*Tau Omega, Northern Michigan* (1990)
1968	Tau Phi, Southwestern State (OK)
1968	*Tau Psi, St. Cloud* (1976)
1968	*Tau Upsilon, Findlay* (1979)
1968	Upsilon Chi, Northwest Missouri
1968	*Upsilon Omega, North Dakota* (1975)
1968	Upsilon Phi, Northeast Missouri
1968	Upsilon Psi, South Florida (1982-1986)
1969	Beta Alpha, Tennessee, Chattanooga
1969	*Chi Omega, Northeastern Illinois* (1984)
1969	*Chi Psi, American* (1977)
1969	*Delta Alpha, Cumberland (KY)* (1987)
1969	Delta Beta, Alabama State
1969	*Delta Gamma, Houston Baptist* (1988)
1969	Gamma Alpha, Madison Col
1969	Gamma Beta, Wisconsin, Eau Claire
1969	*Phi Chi, Georgia State* (1976)
1969	Phi Omega, Dayton
1969	*Phi Psi, Nebraska Wesleyan* (1984)
1969	*Psi Omega, Knoxville* (1983)
1970	*Epsilon Alpha, Toledo* (1973)
1970	*Epsilon Beta, Abilene Christian* (1985)
1970	*Epsilon Delta, South Alabama* (1983)
1970	Epsilon Gamma, Central Missouri State
1970	*Zeta Alpha, Glassboro* (1980)
1970	Zeta Beta, Augustana (IL)
1970	*Zeta Delta, North Central* (1983)
1970	Zeta Epsilon, Shorter
1970	Zeta Gamma, Valdosta (1976-1981)

1971	Eta Alpha, Georgia Col
1971	Eta Beta, Pembroke
1971	Eta Delta, Grambling
1971	*Eta Epsilon, Augustana (SD)* (1980)
1971	*Eta Gamma, Southern Arkansas* (1983)
1971	Eta Zeta, Newberry
1971	*Theta Alpha, Kean (NJ)* (1986)
1971	*Theta Beta, Richmond* (1976)
1971	*Theta Delta, Southern Oregon* (1984)
1971	Theta Gamma, Fort Valley
1972	Iota Alpha, Alma (1976-1986)
1972	Iota Beta, North Carolina A & T
1972	Iota Gamma, Iowa
1972	*Iowa Delta, Central Connecticut* (1984)
1972	Theta Eta, Wright State
1972	*Theta Zeta, Indianapolis* (1984)
1973	Iota Epsilon, North Carolina
1973	Iota Eta, Central State (OH)
1973	*Iota Theta, Salem (WV)* (1982)
1973	*Iota Zeta, Bridgeport* (1980)
1973	Kappa Alpha, David Lipscomb
1973	Kappa Beta, Morris Brown
1974	Kappa Delta, Texas Southern
1974	Kappa Epsilon, Olivet
1974	Kappa Gamma, Berry (GA)
1974	*Kappa Zeta, West Virginia Wesleyan* (1982)
1975	Kappa Eta, Arkansas Tech
1975	*Kappa Theta, Pan American* (1978)
1976	Kappa Iota, Central Arkansas
1976	*Lambda Alpha, Trinity (CT)* (1988)
1976	Lambda Beta, Susquehanna
1976	*Lambda Delta, Boise* (1978)
1976	*Lambda Epsilon, Dickinson State* (1987)
1976	Lambda Gamma, Edinboro
1976	*Lambda Zeta, Limestone* (1987)
1976	*Theta Epsilon, Wartburg* (1976)
1977	Lambda Eta, Western Oregon
1978	*Lambda Iota, Mount Senario* (1984)
1978	Lambda Kappa, Carthage
1978	*Lambda Theta, Xavier (LA)* (1980)
1978	*Mu Alpha, V.P.I.* (1980)
1978	Mu Gamma, Angelo
1979	*Mu Beta, Winston-Salem* (1987)
1979	Mu Delta, Longwood
1979	Mu Eta, Central Florida
1979	Mu Theta, Tarleton
1979	*Mu Zeta, Western Connecticut* (1986)
1980	*Mu Iota, Transylvania* (1983)
1980	*Mu Lambda, Atlantic Christian* (1984)
1980	*Nu Alpha, Augusta* (1983)
1980	Nu Beta, West Georgia
1981	Nu Gamma, Missouri Western
1982	*Nu Delta, Northwestern Oklahoma* (1984)
1982	*Nu Epsilon, Arkansas, Monticello* (1984)
1982	*Nu Eta, Texas, San Antonio* (1987)
1982	*Nu Zeta, Cal State, Stanislaus* (1986)
1983	*Nu Theta, Kennesaw* (1987)
1984	Nu Iota, South Carolina State
1985	Nu Kappa, Winthrop
1985	Nu Lambda, Texas, El Paso
1985	*Nu Mu, McMurry* (1988)
1986	Xi Alpha, Hastings

1987	Xi Beta, Benedict
1988	Xi Gamma, Columbus
1989	Xi Delta, Nevada

Phi Rho Sigma†

(MEDICINE)

ACTIVE PIN

PLEDGE PIN

PHI RHO SIGMA was founded at Northwestern University Medical School, then the Chicago Medical College, October 31, 1890, by Milbank Johnson, assisted by T. J. Robeson, N. H. Forline, and J. A. Poling.

Alpha Chapter granted charters to Beta and Gamma chapters and was the head of the fraternity until early in 1896 when three members from each of the then existing chapters were appointed to take charge of administrative affairs. These nine representatives were elected yearly, and the body was known as the Grand Chapter. They elected their own officers and had full power to grant charters, enact laws, and perform other duties devolving upon them. By this body charters were granted to Delta, Epsilon, and Zeta. A revised constitution was adopted March 20, 1899. In accordance with this act the first general convention was called to Chicago in 1899.

Growth On April 6, 1929, articles of amalgamation were signed at Cincinnati by the proper authorities of Chi Zeta Chi and Phi Rho Sigma. The invested funds of Chi Zeta Chi were set aside in a trust fund to be known as the Jesse Ansley Griffin Memorial Fund, thus honoring the founder of Chi Zeta Chi.

Government The constitution was replaced by the Laws of Phi Rho Sigma Fraternity in 1934. Conventions are now held biennially. In the interim between conventions the executive power of the fraternity is vested in the Executive Council. In 1921 there was established a Chapter International of which all graduates automatically become members. In the same year a central office was established. The name was changed to Phi Rho Sigma Medical Society in April, 1976.

Traditions and Insignia In 1946 the plan was inaugurated of presenting two gold medals to outstanding alumni. One of these is known as the Jesse Ansley Griffin Medal and is presented to an alumnus who has made an outstanding contribution to the fraternity. The other is the Irving S. Cutter Medal, in honor of a past national president, and is presented to an alumnus who has made an out-

---

† This chapter narrative is repeated from the 19th edition; no current information was provided.

standing contribution to medicine. 'These awards are made at every regular biennial convention. Many undergraduate chapters sponsor scholarship awards and lectureships.

In 1960 the Grand Chapter established a group of national student research awards. Each biennium, awards are given to the medical students who submit the best reports of their personal research in basic science and clinical areas. Winners of the top awards in each area are invited to present papers on their research at the biennial Grand Chapter Convention.

The official badge is a gold monogram outline of the letters ΦΡΣ, the Φ being placed on a separate plane above the other two letters and its face set with pearls. Colors are scarlet and gold. The coat of arms: per pale or and gules, a fess cotised and couped sable, between three crosses pommee counter charged. Mantling; or doubled gules. Crest: on a peer's helmet and a wreath of the colors two lozenges voided gules and or, interlaced upon a branch of laurel proper, palewise. Motto Phi Rho Sigma in upper and lower case old English letters. The pledge button is a scarlet oval with the Greek letters, Φ, Ρ, Σ, appearing separately from above down. The recognition button is a small Greek-letter Φ in gold. There is an official alumnus key designed from the original badge.

Funds and Philanthropies The fraternity sponsors the Student Loan Fund maintained by a dollar contribution from each undergraduate, made at the time of his initiation. It was established in 1924 at the suggestion of Dr. Ralph W. Elliott, national secretary and treasurer from 1921 to 1946. The fund is also supported by many alumni contributions. It is available upon recommendation of the faculty and chapter officers of the applicant's school.

Publications The Journal of Phi Rho Sigma was first published in 1901. After some irregularity in issue it became a quarterly. In 1919, after World War I, it was published twice a year until in 1923 it was changed to a monthly. The form and style of a tabloid newspaper were adopted at that time. The Journal goes regularly to every living member and now appears quarterly. In 1912 a history and directory edited by Dr. D. E. W. Wenstrand was published. In the fall of 1925 a geographical catalogue was issued. In 1928 a service leaflet was published, How to Choose an Internship, by Dr. H. A. Christian. This was followed by several other service leaflets, among them How to Choose and to Approach a Community for the Practice of Medicine, War and Nutrition, and The Health of the Medical Student, all by Dr. Jonathan Forman. In the summer of 1929 the Manual of Phi Rho Sigma was issued under the editorship of Dr. Forman. In 1937 The History and Directory, edited by Dr. Ralph W. Elliott, was published. This supplements the 1912 History, which is out of print. In the summer of 1938 Dr. Forman edited a book, The Medical Student, which was published and distributed to the undergraduates and many alumni. In 1940 a brief history

entitled Fifty Years of Phi Rho Sigma was compIled by Dr. Paul L. McLain for the fiftieth anniversary celebration. Two editions of the Phi Rho Sigma Song Book have been published, the first appearing in 1920 and the second in 1942. Fraternitas, an indoctrination manual for pledges, appeared first in 1949, was reprinted in 1954, and again in 1961; it was prepared by a committee headed by Dr. William Bromme. A rushing brochure, The Facts on Phi Rho Sigma, was written by Dr. Paul L. McLain and Dr. C. H. William Ruhe and was published in 1953. In 1966 Careers in Medicine was published under the editorship of Dr. McLain in honor of the 75th anniversary.

Headquarters The central office address is P. O. Box 10886, Pittsburgh, Pennsylvania 15236.

Membership Active chapters 13. Inactive chapters 36. Total number of initiates 29,000. Chapter roll:††

Year	Chapter
1890	Alpha, Northwestern
1894	Beta, Illinois (1969) (Beta-Gamma since 1936)
1895	Gamma, Chicago (merged with Beta 1936)
1896	Delta, USC (1969)
1897	Epsilon, Wayne State (1965)
1897	Zeta, Michigan
1900	Eta, Creighton (1973)
1900	Theta Tau, Minnesota
1901	Iota, Nebraska
1901	Kappa, Western Reserve
1901	Lambda Phi, Penn (1973)
1902	Mu, Iowa
1902	Nu, Harvard (1923)
1903	Chi Alpha, Georgia
1903	Omicron, Marquette (1921)
1903	Pi, Indiana
1903	Xi, Johns Hopkins (1904)
1904	Chi Beta, Emory (1959)
1904	Chi Gamma, Maryland (1936)
1904	Rho, Jefferson (1965)
1904	Sigma, Virginia (1929)
1906	Chi Delta, South Carolina
1906	Chi Epsilon, Tennessee
1906	Chi Eta, St. Louis
1906	Chi Zeta, Arkansas (1939)
1906	Upsilon, Virginia Medical (1943)
1907	Skull and Sceptre, Yale (1919)
1908	Chi, Pitt (1970)
1909	Psi, Colorado (1972)
1911	Alpha Omega Delta, Buffalo (1931)
1913	Alpha Beta, Columbia (1932)
1913	Alpha Gamma, McGill (1938)
1913	Omega, Ohio State (1943)
1918	Delta Omicron Alpha, Tulane (1950)
1921	Alpha Delta, Washington (1944)
1922	Alpha Epsilon, Toronto (1942)
1923	Alpha Zeta, Stanford (1959)
1924	Chi Theta, Wake Forest (1965)

†† This chapter roll is repeated from the 19th edition; no current information was provided.

1925   Alpha Eta, Dalhousie
1927   *Alpha Theta, Cincinnati* (1935)
1929   *Alpha Iota, Manitoba* (1944)
1932   *Alpha Kappa, Rochester* (1938)
1933   Alpha Lambda, Temple
1935   *Alpha Mu, L.S.U.* (1941)
1939   Alpha Nu, Texas
1939   *Alpha Omicron, Southwestern Medical*
         (1944-1956)
1948   *Alpha Pi, Utah* (1965)
1958   *Alpha Rho, Seton Hall* (1969)
1964   *Iota Gamma, California College of*
         Medicine (1974)

Pi Sigma Epsilon†

(MARKETING AND SALES MANAGEMENT)

ACTIVE PIN

PI SIGMA EPSILON was founded at the Atlanta Division of the University of Georgia, now Georgia State College, in the fall of 1951. The idea of a professional fraternity for undergraduates in the fields of marketing, sales management, and selling was proposed by Lloyd Antle, Atlanta educator and business man, and advanced by Henry G. Baker and William G. Harris of the College and by Lewis F. Gordon, a founder of the Atlanta Sales Executives Club.

After the first organizational meeting on November 1, 1951, purposes were set forth as follows: "To create a collegiate brotherhood of men who are interested in the advancement of marketing, sales management, and selling as a career and a profession; to promote the study of marketing, sales management, selling and related subjects in colleges and universities; to bring together academically qualified students who express a desire to enter these career fields; to encourage in colleges and universities the establishing of courses preparing men for such careers; to stimulate research and improved methods and techniques in these fields; to instill in its members the highest possible ethical standards of the profession." Alpha Chapter was established at the College on June 2, 1952.

Government   The governing power of the fraternity is vested in a National Council, elected biennially by the chapters at their national convention, in accordance with the constitution and bylaws adopted in April, 1952. The Council is composed of the president, educator vice-president, professional vice-president, secretary, treasurer, and past presidents. The board of directors is made up of out-standing educators and executives from various parts of the nation. Operations of the fraternity are conducted through the national office under the direction of an executive director selected by the National Council.

At the time of the founding of a chapter, any given number of men from the sponsoring club may be taken in as professional founding members. After a chapter has become operative, however, no chapter may nominate more than six men in any one year as professional members.

Traditions and Insignia   One of the most basic activities of all chapters is to engage in sales projects which are both fundraising and "laboratories" in which men engaged may obtain practical experience. Principles of marketing and selling are applied objectively to specific commodities and services.

At each national convention, a trophy and cash award of $200 are given by "The Council on Opportunities in Selling" to the chapter having conducted the "Top Sales Projects of the Year." A Top Chapter Award, trophy and $350; a "PSE Top Salesman of the Year" trophy and cash award of $250; a "Top Faculty Advisor" Award, Lamp of Knowledge electric clock and cash award of $100; are also given. There is also a "Top SME Sponsor Club" Award annually.

The official key has a gold book as a background, symbolizing *Knowledge;* on the open pages are a blue oval with the Greek letters ΠΣΕ and symbols representing the basic principles of the fraternity. The recognition button is the blue oval extracted from the key.

Funds and Philanthropies   On May 12, 1967, the Pi Sigma Epsilon National Educational Foundation was chartered under the laws of the State of Georgia. The purposes of the Foundation, a non-profit organization, are charitable, scientific, research and aid in the advancement of education and curricula in the areas of marketing, sales management and selling. Among other activities scholarships are made available to deserving members, both at the undergraduate and postgraduate level.

Publications   The official publication is *Dotted Lines,* a comprehensive magazine. The fraternity also issues a bi-monthly newsletter.

Headquarters   612 Georgia Savings Bank Building, Atlanta, Georgia 30303.

Membership   Active chapters 46. Inactive chapters 1. Total number of initiates 7,000. Chapter roll:††

1952   Alpha, Georgia State
1953   *Beta, Utah* (1955)
1954   Gamma, Georgia
1956   Delta, Southern Mississippi
1956   Epsilon, Auburn
1957   Zeta, Northeast Louisiana

---

† This chapter narrative is repeated from the 19th edition; no current information was provided.

†† This chapter roll is repeated from the 19th edition; no current information was provided.

1958	Eta, Florida
1958	Iota, Arizona State
1958	Kappa, Memphis State
1958	Lambda, Adelphi
1958	Theta, Hofstra
1959	Mu, St. John's (NY)
1960	Nu, CCNY
1960	Omicron, Buffalo
1960	Pi, Detroit
1960	Rho, Cal State, Long Beach
1960	Xi, LaSalle
1961	Chi, Pace
1961	Phi, Los Angeles State
1961	Sigma, New York, Washington Square
1961	Tau, Puerto Rico
1961	Upsilon, Hawaii
1962	Alpha Alpha, Detroit Tech
1962	Alpha Beta, Southern Illinois
1962	Alpha Delta, Arlington (TX)
1962	Alpha Epsilon, Marquette
1962	Alpha Gamma, Georgia Tech
1962	Omega, American
1962	Psi, Minnesota
1963	Alpha Iota, Evansville
1963	Alpha Lambda, Arizona State
1963	Alpha Theta, Mississippi
1963	Alpha Zeta, Mississippi State
1963	Alpha Zeta, Villanova
1964	Alpha Kappa, Richmond Professional
1964	Alpha Nu, CCNY
1965	Alpha Mu, Cal State, Fresno
1965	Alpha Omicron, Western Kentucky
1965	Alpha Pi, Middle Tennessee
1965	Alpha Xi, Wisconsin, Milwaukee
1966	Alpha Rho, South Carolina
1966	Alpha Sigma, Boston Col
1966	Alpha Tau, Seton Hall
1967	Alpha Chi, Xavier (OH)
1967	Alpha Phi, Little Rock
1967	Alpha Psi, Nicholls
1967	Alpha Upsilon, Gannon

Psi Omega

(DENTISTRY)

ACTIVE PIN   PLEDGE PIN

PSI OMEGA was organized at the Baltimore College of Dental Surgery in 1892. The fraternity aims to maintain the standards of the profession, to encourage scientific investigation and literary culture. Psi Omega is dentistry's largest professional fraternity.

Growth Psi Chapter was formerly at the Ohio-Starling Medical College, which institution was taken over by the Ohio State University. Delta Tau Chapter was merged into Psi when the institutions were consolidated. In the same manner Gamma Xi merged with Gamma Omicron; Gamma with Zeta; Sigma with Eta; Pi with Phi. Phi was then combined with Alpha and became known as Phi-Alpha, and at a later date Phi-Alpha became known as Alpha Chapter. Tau merged with Gamma Iota and later became known as Gamma Tau Chapter. Delta Phi merged with Delta Rho in 1920 and later became Phi Rho Chapter when the two colleges combined under the name of The Kansas City-Western Dental College, now a part of the University of Kansas City. Gamma Nu Chapter was dissolved when the Vanderbilt University School of Dentistry was discontinued in 1926. Mu Chapter became inactive when the Denver School of Dentistry was closed in 1932. Psi Alpha was dissolved in 1935. Lambda Chapter became Zeta Kappa Chapter; Rho Chapter was discontinued when the Ohio College of Dental Surgery was closed in 1926; Beta Gamma was combined with Beta Theta; Theta was dissolved in 1912 and Beta Eta in 1909. Beta Epsilon was combined with Delta Omega, and the Gamma Pi was merged with Beta Zeta in 1912.

Government Government is through a triennial convention called the grand chapter with a recess administration by a board of officers as the National Council.

Traditions and Insignia The badge is an heraldic shield of gold with a slightly curved field of black enamel on which are displayed a caduceus, the letter ΨΩ, and three ivy-leaves. Colors are blue and white.

Publications The quarterly journal, *The Frater of Psi Omega*, was first published in 1900.

Headquarters 1030 Lincoln Avenue, Prospect Park, Pennsylvania 19076.

Membership Chapter roll:††

1892	Alpha, Baltimore Dental Surgery
1893	Beta, New York Dentistry
1894	*Gamma, Pennsylvania Dental* (1910)
1895	*Delta, Tufts* (1938-1941) (1965)
1896	Epsilon, Western Reserve
1896	Eta, Temple
1896	Iota, Northwestern
1896	Kappa, Loyola Dental
1896	*Lambda, Minnesota* (1903)
1896	Zeta, Penn
1897	*Mu, Denver* (1932)
1897	*Mu Delta, Harvard* (1965)
1897	Nu, Pitt
1897	Omicron, Louisville Dental
1897	Xi, Marquette
1898	Beta Sigma, San Francisco P & S
1898	*Pi, Baltimore Medical* (1913)
1899	*Rho, Ohio Dental* (1926)
1899	*Sigma, Medico-Chirurgical* (1917)
1900	Chi, Oregon

†† This chapter roll is repeated from the 19th edition; no current information was provided.

1900   *Phi, Maryland* (1924)
1900   *Tau, Atlanta Dental* (1918)
1900   Upsilon, USC
1901   Psi, Ohio State
1901   *Theta, Buffalo* (1912)
1903   Beta Alpha, Chicago
1903   Beta Delta, California
1903   *Beta Epsilon, New Orleans Dentistry* (1926)
1903   *Beta Gamma, George Washington* (1919)
1903   Beta Zeta, St. Louis Dental
1903   Omega, Indiana Dental
1904   *Beta Eta, Keokuk Dental* (1909)
1904   Beta Theta, Georgetown
1904   *Gamma Iota, Southern Dental, Atlanta* (1918)
1905   *Gamma Kappa, Michigan* (1936-1958)
1906   Gamma Lambda, Dental and Oral Surgery, New York
1906   Gamma Mu, Iowa
1906   *Gamma Nu, Vanderbilt* (1926)
1907   *Gamma Xi, Virginia Medical* (1913)
1908   Gamma Omicron, Virginia Medical
1909   *Gamma Pi, Washington (MO)* (1912)
1910   *Delta Rho, Kansas City Dental* (1920)
1912   *Delta Tau, Wisconsin P & S* (1912)
1913   Delta Upsilon, Texas, Dentistry
1914   *Delta Phi, Western Dental, Kansas City* (1920)
1918   Gamma Tau, Emory
1918   Zeta Kappa, Minnesota
1919   Delta Chi, Royal College of Dental Surgeons
1920   Delta Psi, Baylor
1920   Phi Rho, Kansas (formerly Kansas City-Western)
1921   Delta Omega, Loyola, New Orleans
1921   *Psi Alpha, Creighton* (1935)
1921   *Psi Beta, McGill* (1930)
1924   *Phi Alpha, Maryland* (1939)
1926   Psi Gamma, Tennessee
1929   *Psi Delta, Dalhousie* (1932)
1939   Delta Mu, Detroit
1947   Theta Xi, Washington
1951   Chi Tau, Alabama
1951   Chi Upsilon, North Carolina
1958   Sigma Eta, New Jersey Medicine And Dentistry
1962   Sigma, West Virginia
1973   Sigma Chi, Charleston (SC)
1974   Sigma Alpha, San Antonio, TX
1975   Gamma Gamma, Gainesville, FL

Rho Pi Phi

(PHARMACY)

ACTIVE PIN

PLEDGE PIN

RHO PI PHI, a nonsectarian fraternity, was founded in 1919 at the Massachusetts College of Pharmacy, Boston. The charter members were Joseph Dunn, Robert Goodless, Samuel Greenberg, Samuel Nannis, Ralph Polian, Eli Rodman, Joseph Rosenberg, Max Stoller, Israel Stone, Louis Tankel, Isaac Weiser, Hyman Wolf, and I. Zolotoy.

The preamble of the constitution reads:

"Whereas it has become imperative that a fraternity, composed of students in pharmacy and pharmaceutical chemistry, and based on the principles and precepts of ethical practice, should be organized to maintain the ethical standards and dignity of, and pride in this most ancient and honorable profession;

"And whereas a pharmaceutical fraternity can do much to contribute toward the welfare of all students in pharmacy, morally, socially, and intellectually, therefore the Rho Pi Phi Fraternity has been formed to accomplish the above purposes."

In 1921, chapters were organized in other colleges of pharmacy. In 1926, the opening of Nu Chapter at the Ontario College of Pharmacy made the fraternity international.

Government   The Supreme Council, elected at the annual convention, is the governing body. Delegates from each active chapter and each graduate chapter have the deciding votes, although any member present may speak on a proposed subject. Supreme Council meetings are held every two months. The chapters are divided into geographical sections and are responsible to regional directors appointed by the Supreme Council. The regional directors attend the Supreme Council meetings.

Traditions and Insignia   The badge is diamond-shaped, gold, and inlaid with black enamel. The Greek letters are inscribed in gold. It has 13 pearls, 12 around outline and one protruding from black background. Official colors are blue and white.

Publications   *Rope Newsletter* is published quarterly and sent to all members. A convention journal is also sent annually.

Foundations and Philanthropies   The Rho Pi Phi Foundation was established in 1953 under the laws of New York State. The Supreme Council awards scholarships to each chapter annually. Many of the chapters have also established scholarships at their colleges which are given annually. Some chapters do charity work on a local basis.

Headquarters 9280 Hamlin, Des Plaines, Illinois 60016.

Membership Active chapters 26. Houses owned 3. Graduate/Alumni chapters 12. Total number of initiates 10,000. Chapter roll:

1919	Alpha, Massachusetts Pharmacy	
1921	Beta, Albany Pharmacy	
1921	Gamma, Columbia (NY)	
1922	Delta, Rhode Island	
1922	Epsilon, SUNY, Buffalo	
1923	Eta, Ohio Northern	
1923	Kappa, USC	
1923	Zeta, Ohio State	
1924	Iota, St. John's (NY)	
1925	Eta, Rutgers	
1925	Theta, Long Island	
1926	Mu, Connecticut	
1926	Nu, Toronto	
1928	Xi, Wayne State (MI)	
1932	Pi, St. Louis Pharmacy	
1940	Rho, Fordham	
1952	Beta Galen, Philadelphia Pharmacy	
1952	Gamma Galen, Temple	
1956	Sigma, Florida	
1957	Tau, Northeastern	
1959	Delta Kappa Sigma, Illinois	
1962	Phi Alpha, Maryland	
1978	Nu Beta Kappa, Montreal	
1978	Phi, Michigan	
1984	Upsilon Tau, Toledo	
1988	Sigma Epsilon, Southeastern Pharmacy-Miami	

Sigma Alpha

(WOMEN'S AGRICULTURAL FRATERNITY)

SIGMA ALPHA is a professional sorority for women in agriculture. The name "Sigma Alpha" represents "Sisters in Agriculture". It is the purpose of Sigma Alpha to promote women in all facets of agriculture and to strengthen the bonds of friendship among them. It is the object of its members to strive for achievement in scholarship, leadership and service.

The first Sigma Alpha chapter was established at The Ohio State University on January 26, 1978. Five undergraduate women in the OSU College of Agriculture were looking for an alternative to the programs offered by the agricultural fraternities and the traditional sororities.

The founders of the sorority were: Ann Huling Mathews, Marilyn Burns, Jennifer McMillan, Cindie Davis and Amy Mathews. The idea of Sigma Alpha was conceived on February 26, 1977. It took the founders nearly a full year to be recognized as an official student organization to become the Alpha Chapter of Sigma Alpha Sorority.

The National Board began very informally in 1980 by the five founders of the sorority. Early goals of the National Board were to provide guidance and continuity for the Alpha Chapter and to develop new chapters at other universities.

Changing needs of the Alpha Chapter as well as varying requirements for student organization constitutions at other universities dictated the first revision of the constitution.

The first annual Sigma Alpha National Convention was held in 1985 in Columbus, Ohio. During the 1987 National Convention it was voted upon to hold the National Convention in November. Thereafter the convention date was established as the first weekend in November.

The Articles of Incorporation were filed and recorded in the office of the Secretary of the State of Ohio in February 1991. The certificate of incorporation of Sigma Alpha Sorority was approved April 8, 1991. The three incorporators were: Holly Downing Stacy, Jodi Plummer Black and Holly Stickel.

Growth After six years of building a foundation the Beta Chapter was Chartered at Purdue University on April 14, 1984. This began a rapid successions of chapter establishments. The Gamma, Delta, Epsilon, Zeta, Eta, Theta, Iota, Kappa, Lambda, Mu and Nu Chapters were all chartered between 1985 and May 1991.

Traditions and Insignia The insignia of the sorority are a crest and a badge. The crest is diamond shaped with the top half being geometrically larger than the bottom half. The greek letters of Sigma and Alpha appear in the middle of the diamond with an etching of a chrysanthemum to the right of the letters and a yoke to the left. Above the letters appears two rows of greek letters. The top ones are Eta, Beta, Mu, Delta, Mu. The second ones are Omicron, Sigma, Upsilon. Below the larger Sigma and Alpha in the middle is a etching symbolizing a sunrise and shafts of wheat. Immediately below this are the greek letters Rho and Beta. The badge is a pin identical to the crest, with an emerald in each of the four points of the diamond shape and pearls positioned between them to edge the crest. The colors of the sorority are Emerald and Maize. The jewel is the emerald and the flower is the yellow chrysanthemum. The mascot is the baby bull.

Publications The national organization began printing a newsletter, "Sigma Alpha News", to be sent to alumni and active chapters as their first form of a publication. This newsletter has continued over the years. In 1991 the "Emerald & Maize" was developed and printed. This one page brief style format newsletter was established to be an administrative update from the National Board to all active and alumni chapters on an every other month bases. The "Sigma Alpha News" continues to deliver news about the national board and also from the chapters. It is sent to all paid alumni members.

Headquarters At this point a Post Office Box serves as a central mailing address. Each volunteer National Board member works out of her home. The board president's address is 8550 North County Road 51, Green Springs, Ohio 44836.

Membership The National Board consist of 7 volunteer alumni members who are elected into their positions during the National Convention. Active and alumni membership is currently 750. Chapter roll:

1978	Alpha, The Ohio State University
1984	Beta, Purdue University
1985	Gamma, Michigan State University –reactivated in 1990
1986	Delta, Iowa State University
1989	Epsilon, Penn State University
1989	Zeta, Louisiana State University
1990	Eta, University of Connecticut
1990	Theta, University of Tennessee
1990	Iota, University of Arkansas
1990	Kappa, California Polytechnic State University
1990	Lambda, University of California, Davis
1991	Mu, University of Vermont
1991	Nu, Colorado State University

Sigma Alpha Iota

(MUSIC)

ACTIVE PIN

SIGMA ALPHA IOTA was established at The University of Michigan School of Music, Ann Arbor, June 12, 1903, by Elizabeth Campbell, Frances Caspari, Minnie Davis, Leila Farlin, Georgina Potts, and Mary Storrs. It was incorporated as an "honorary sorority," the Articles of Association being signed December 1, 1904.

In 1928, the corporate name was changed to Sigma Alpha Iota, International Music Fraternity. In changing the corporate name, no change was made in objectives or in standards for membership. In 1981, the Office for Civil Rights declared Sigma Alpha Iota exempt from the provisions of Title IX. Therefore, college chapter membership is open only to women.

Sigma Alpha Iota is an organization which promotes interaction between those who share a commitment to music. The objectives are: to raise the standard of productive music work at music schools across the United States; to uphold the highest ideals of a musical education; to further the develop-

ment of music in America; to promote stronger bonds of musical interest and understanding between foreign countries and the United States; to give inspiration and material aid to its members; to cooperate with the ideals and aims of the alma mater and to adhere to the highest standards of American citizenship and democracy.

College members are students enrolled as music majors or minors on campuses with Sigma Alpha Iota chapters. They must be recommended by the faculty and show excellence in scholarship and musicianship. They may be professional musicians approved by the director of the school. Specific scholastic requirements for membership are set by each college chapter with the approval of the director of the school.

Patroness members are women interested and active in the musical life of the community and are affiliated with college chapters.

There are three categories of honorary membership: Honorary Members are outstanding women performing artists or composers who are nationally or internationally known; National Arts Associates are men and women who are nationally or internationally recognized for distinguished contributions to the arts; Friends of the Arts are men and women who are interested, supporting or actively participating in the arts at the local or regional level.

Sigma Alpha Iota is a member of the National Music Council, the National Federation of Music Clubs, the National Association of Schools of Music, and the Professional Fraternity Association. Sigma Alpha Iota is a founding member of the National Council of Professional Music Fraternities and cooperates actively with the Music Educators National Conference and the Music Teachers National Association.

Government Authority is vested in the national triennial convention to which each chapter sends one voting delegate. The National Executive Board is composed of five elected and three appointed officers who meet in the convention interim to direct the regular business of the fraternity and to recommend fraternity policies. The National Council has jurisdiction over matters of general fraternity interest and is composed of the National Executive Board and the officers of the geographically determined provinces. The National Officers' Conference includes all national and province officers as well as the project directors. A National Executive Office is maintained. The office and staff are directed by the national executive secretary who is appointed by the five elected members of the National Executive Board.

Traditions and Insignia Sigma Alpha Iota is deeply committed to the promotion of music by American composers. The Inter-American Music Awards offer prizes to composers of the Americas for important new works. Since 1978, the competitions have been open only to women composers. The judges of the competition are American composers who are commissioned to write works for the fraternity. The winning works and the compositions by the IAMA Composer-Judges are subsequently published in the prestigious Inter-American Music Awards Series through the C. F. Peters Corporation. Sigma Alpha Iota also sponsors the Modern Music Series published by Carl Fischer, Inc.

In 1918, a colonial two-story residence, "The Sigma Alpha Iota Cottage" (formerly known as "Pan's Cottage") was built by Sigma Alpha Iota at the MacDowell Colony for Creative Artists at Peterboro, New Hampshire. The cottage is equipped for summer and winter use. Yearly maintenance expense of the cottage has been paid by Sigma Alpha Iota since its construction.

The Sigma Alpha Iota member badge is seven Roman gold pan pipes encircled by a jewelled ellipse bearing the letters ΣAI in gold on black enamel. The pledge pin is the pan pipes alone. The colors are crimson and white; the flower, the red rose; and the jewel, the pearl. The open motto is *"Vita brevis, ars longa."*

Publications The Sigma Alpha Iota Quarterly is *Pan Pipes.* The winter issue of this journal includes yearly updates on American composers' new works, performances and publications. The fraternity also publishes a *Manual for Members,* College and Alumnae Chapter Manuals, the *Sigma Alpha Iota Songbook,* and Songbook Supplements(s). Slide-tape programs are available on the SAI Cottage and on Women in Music History.

Funds and Philanthropies Sigma Alpha Iota Philanthropies, Inc., was established in 1974, combining the programs of the fraternity's International Music Fund and the Sigma Alpha Iota Foundation. SAI Philanthropies, Inc., sponsors many significant projects, including the Inter-American Music Awards and the Sigma Alpha Iota Cottage at the MacDowell Colony. The People-to-People Music Committee is funded by SAI Philanthropies, Inc., and assists musicians, schools and music organizations in developing countries with instruments, books, scores and teaching materials. Gifts of American music are made to performers in other countries, and a variety of services are provided to musicians in many parts of the world. Other SAI Philanthropies-sponsored projects include: national scholarships for undergraduate and graduate study in diverse fields of music; scholarships for summer music study; low interest student loans for members, and chapter Seed Money Grants for special projects. In 1985, the establishment of a $5,000 SAI Impact Grant was announced, available as a matching-fund grant to college or university music departments in cooperation with Sigma Alpha Iota chapters. The grant is awarded for major projects in music, the results to benefit those beyond the campus and chapter membership.

Through a broad program of outreach, music needs are served through projects such as Bold Note Music for the partially sighted, Braille Services of Sigma Alpha Iota, Community Action Music,

Music for the Hearing Impaired, Music Therapy and SAI Strings. Numerous gifts have been made to organizations of national importance and special grants have been made to college music departments. All gifts and bequests to Sigma Alpha Iota Philanthropies, Inc., are fully tax deductible.

Headquarters Sigma Alpha Iota National Executive Office, 4119 Rollins Avenue, Des Moines, Iowa 50312.

Membership   Chapter roll:††

1903	Alpha, Michigan
1904	Beta, Northwestern
1906	Gamma, American Conservatory
1907	*Delta, Detroit Conservatory* (1967)
1909	Epsilon, Ithaca
1911	Zeta, Butler
1914	*Eta, Cincinnati Conservatory of Music* (1955)
1914	Theta, Washburn
1915	*Iota, Cincinnati Conservatory of Music* (1955)
1915	Kappa, Nebraska
1915	Lambda, New England Conservatory
1916	Mu, North Dakota
1917	Nu, Millikin
1917	Xi, Lawrence
1920	Omicron, North Dakota State
1920	Pi, Drake
1921	Rho, Wisconsin, Madison
1921	*Sigma, Detroit Institute of Musical Art* (1946), *Wayne State in* 1953 (1973)
1922	*Tau, Kansas City Conservatory (MO)* (1959)
1923	*Chi, Macalester* (1941)
1923	*Phi, MacPhail, Minneapolis* (1953)
1923	Psi, Knox
1923	*Upsilon, Nebraska Wesleyan* (1933)
1924	Omega, Chicago Conservatory
1924	Sigma Alpha, Illinois Wesleyan
1924	Sigma Beta, Ohio
1924	Sigma Delta, Illinois
1924	*Sigma Epsilon, Wisconsin Conservatory* (1913)
1924	Sigma Eta, Redlands (1935-1949)
1924	Sigma Gamma, Tulsa
1924	Sigma Zeta, Idaho
1925	Sigma Iota, Syracuse
1925	*Sigma Kappa, Wyoming* (1942)
1925	Sigma Lambda, Iowa State
1925	Sigma Mu, Hillsdale
1925	*Sigma Nu, Louisville* (1961)
1925	Sigma Omicron, Arkansas
1925	Sigma Theta, Eastman, Rochester
1925	Sigma Xi, UCLA
1926	Sigma Chi, Miami (FL)
1926	Sigma Phi, L.S.U.
1926	*Sigma Pi, MacMurray* (1935)
1926	*Sigma Rho, Montana* (1933)
1926	Sigma Sigma, Minnesota

†† This chapter roll is repeated from the 19th edition; no current information was provided.

1926	Sigma Tau, USC	1951	Beta Lambda, Valparaiso
1926	*Sigma Upsilon, Denver* (1953)	1951	Beta Mu, Northern Illinois
1927	Alpha Alpha, Bethany (KS)	1951	*Beta Nu, Immaculate Heart* (1969)
1927	Alpha Beta, Arizona	1951	Beta Xi, Texas
1927	Sigma Omega, Susquehanna	1952	Beta Omicron, Hartwick
1927	*Sigma Psi, Beloit* (1935)	1953	Beta Pi, Houston
1928	Alpha Delta, Wittenberg	1953	Beta Rho, Georgia Col
1928	*Alpha Epsilon, Columbia, Chicago* (1937) (merged with Omega)	1953	Beta Sigma, Tampa
1928	Alpha Eta, Oklahoma Baptist	1954	Beta Phi, Catholic
1928	*Alpha Gamma, Muskingum* (1961)	1954	Beta Tau, N.Y.U.
1928	Alpha Zeta, Oklahoma City	1954	Beta Upsilon, Cal State, Los Angeles
1929	Alpha Iota, Oklahoma	1955	Beta Chi, McNeese
1929	Alpha Theta, Columbia (1943-1965)	1955	*Beta Omega, Mount Mary's (CA)* (1968)
1930	Alpha Kappa, Kansas State, Pittsburg	1955	Beta Psi, East Carolina
1930	Alpha Lambda, Michigan State (1942-1965)	1955	Eta-Iota, Cincinnati Conservatory of Music
1930	Alpha Mu, Carnegie Tech	1955	Gamma Alpha, Boston
1930	Alpha Nu, Youngstown State (1942-1945)	1955	Gamma Beta, Stanford
1930	*Alpha Xi, Chicago Conservatory* (1953)	1957	Gamma Delta, Crane Conservatory (NY)
1931	Alpha Omicron, Occidental	1957	Gamma Epsilon, Maryland
1931	Alpha Pi, Fort Hays	1957	Gamma Gamma, Shenandoah Conservatory
1934	Alpha Rho, Our Lady Of The Lake	1957	Gamma Zeta, Old Dominion
1935	Alpha Sigma, New Mexico	1958	*Gamma Eta, Agnes Scott* (1968)
1935	Alpha Tau, Carthage	1958	Gamma Iota, Madison Col
1936	Alpha Chi, U.S.A.O., Chickasha	1958	Gamma Theta, Georgia Southern
1936	Alpha Phi, Colorado	1959	Gamma Kappa, Longwood
1936	*Alpha Psi, Texas Fine Arts, Austin* (1941)	1959	Gamma Lambda, Wesleyan (GA)
1936	Alpha Upsilon, Iowa State, Cedar Falls	1959	Gamma Mu, Arizona State
1937	Alpha Omega, Mississippi	1959	Gamma Nu, Eastern New Mexico
1938	Iota Alpha, Oklahoma State	1959	Gamma Omicron, Bowling Green
1939	Iota Beta, Murray State	1959	Gamma Pi, Cal State, Long Beach
1939	Iota Delta, San Diego State	1959	Gamma Xi, Moorhead
1939	Iota Epsilon, Indiana	1959	Tau-Sigma, Kansas City Conservatory (MO)
1939	Iota Gamma, Emporia	1960	Gamma Rho, Tennessee
1940	Iota Zeta, Georgia	1960	Gamma Sigma, Union (TN)
1941	Iota Kappa, Mississippi For Women	1960	Gamma Tau, Northern State
1941	Iota Lambda, Missouri	1960	Gamma Upsilon, Morehead
1941	Iota Theta, North Texas	1961	Delta Alpha, Lebanon Valley
1942	Iota Mu, Drury	1961	Gamma Chi, San Fernando Valley
1942	*Iota Nu, Seton Hill* (1975)	1961	*Gamma Omega, Webster* (1970)
1942	*Iota Xi, Central YMCA, Chicago* (1948)	1961	Gamma Phi, Hardin-Simmons
1943	Iota Eta, Indiana State	1961	Gamma Psi, William Jewell
1943	Iota Omicron, Southwestern Louisiana	1962	Delta Beta, Memphis State
1943	Iota Pi, Albion	1962	Delta Gamma, Florida
1945	Iota Rho, Mary Hardin-Baylor	1963	Delta Delta, Montclair
1946	Iota Chi, Ball State	1963	Delta Epsilon, Southeast Missouri
1946	Iota Phi, George Peabody	1963	Delta Eta, Northern Arizona
1946	*Iota Sigma, Kansas City* (1959)	1963	Delta Zeta, Troy
1946	*Iota Tau, North Carolina* (1955)	1964	Delta Kappa, Minot
1946	Iota Upsilon, Benedictine	1964	Delta Lambda, SUNY Col., Fredonia
1947	Beta Alpha, Florida State	1964	Delta Mu, Temple
1947	Iota Omega, Texas Woman's	1964	*Delta Theta, Mankato* (1972)
1947	Iota Psi, Minnesota, Duluth	1965	Delta Nu, Howard
1948	Beta Beta, Kansas	1965	Delta Pi, Austin Peay
1948	Beta Delta, Puget Sound	1965	Delta Rho, North Central
1948	Beta Epsilon, Evansville	1965	Delta Sigma, Dayton
1948	Beta Gamma, Bradley	1965	Delta Tau, Augustana (IL)
1949	Beta Eta, Western Michigan	1965	*Delta Xi, Pacific (OR)* (1970)
1949	Beta Zeta, Meredith	1966	Delta Chi, South Florida
1950	Beta Iota, Northwestern Louisiana	1966	*Delta Psi, Lincoln (MO)* (1974)
1950	Beta Kappa, Texas Wesleyan	1966	*Delta Upsilon, Union (KY)* (1971)
1950	Beta Theta, Sam Houston	1967	Delta Omega, Kentucky
		1967	Delta Phi, Mansfield

1967   Epsilon Alpha, Texas, El Paso
1967   Epsilon Beta, Gettysburg
1967   Epsilon Delta, Ouachita Baptist
1967   Epsilon Gamma, Arkansas State
1968   Epsilon Epsilon, West Chester
1968   Epsilon Eta, Eastern Illinois
1968   Epsilon Theta, Appalachian
1968   Epsilon Zeta, Boston Conservatory
1969   Epsilon Iota, Tennessee, Martin
1969   Epsilon Kappa, Louisiana Tech
1969   Epsilon Lambda, Belmont
1969   Epsilon Mu, Northern Michigan
1969   Epsilon Nu, Hawaii
1969   Epsilon Omicron, Wisconsin, Eau Claire
1969   Epsilon Pi, Northeast Missouri
1969   Epsilon Xi, St. Cloud
1970   Epsilon Rho, Northeastern Illinois
1970   Epsilon Sigma, Colorado College for Women
1971   Epsilon Chi, Mississippi State
1971   Epsilon Omega, Central Missouri State
1971   Epsilon Phi, Northwest Missouri
1971   Epsilon Psi, Fairmont
1971   Epsilon Tau, Arkansas, Little Rock
1971   Epsilon Upsilon, Adrian
1971   Zeta Alpha, Wichita
1972   Zeta Delta, Houston Baptist
1972   Zeta Epsilon, Iowa
1972   Zeta Eta, West Virginia Wesleyan
1972   Zeta Gamma, South Alabama
1972   Zeta Theta, Valdosta
1972   Zeta Zeta, Kean (NJ)
1973   Zeta Beta, Wayland Baptist
1973   Zeta Iota, Wright State
1973   Zeta Kappa, Southern Oregon
1973   Zeta Lambda, Southern State
1973   Zeta Mu, Western Connecticut
1974   Zeta Nu, Texas, Arlington
1974   Zeta Omicron, David Lipscomb
1974   Zeta Xi, Berry (GA)
1975   Zeta Pi, Central Connecticut
1975   Zeta Rho, Arkansas Tech
1975   Zeta Sigma, Angelo
1976   Zeta Tau, Florida Tech
1976   Zeta Upsilon, Edinboro
1977   Zeta Phi, St. Rose (NY)

Sigma Phi Delta[†]

(ENGINEERING)

ACTIVE PIN

SIGMA PHI DELTA Fraternity was founded April 11, 1924, at the University of Southern California

† This chapter narrative is repeated from the 19th edition; no current information was provided.

to promote the advancement of the engineering profession; to foster the advancement of engineering education; to instill a greater spirit of cooperation among engineering students and organizations; to inculcate in its members the highest ideals of Christian manhood, good citizenship, obedience to law, and brotherhood, and to encourage excellence in scholarship. It was the outgrowth of a third attempt at the university to launch a professional engineering fraternity. At least two previous attempts had been made, but both groups thus formed had become social fraternities.

Growth In 1922 a group of engineers at the University of South Dakota organized Delta Pi Sigma. On April 11, 1926, Delta Pi Sigma accepted a tentative plan of joining Sigma Phi Delta. With the installation of Delta Pi Sigma on May 23, 1926, the idea that Sigma Phi Delta should found a new national engineering fraternity seemed to be realized. The name Sigma Phi Delta was retained; the group at Southern California became Alpha Chapter, the one at the University of South Dakota, Beta Chapter. The constitution provided for five members on the Supreme Council, and Alpha Chapter was to elect the grand president, the grand secretary-treasurer, and one council member-at-large. Beta Chapter was to elect the grand vice-president and the remaining council member-at-large.

Delta Pi at North Dakota Agricultural College was founded in 1913 as an honor engineering fraternity. This status was maintained until World War I when every member entered the service. Delta Pi was reorganized in 1919, and the group became a professional fraternity rather than an honor society, although scholastic standing still remains one of the principal requisites for membership. It was installed as Epsilon Chapter on May 21, 1928.

The second general convention was held at the University of Texas in 1929, when it was felt desirable to make constitutional changes and amendments. By the fall of 1930 satisfactory changes had been made. When Theta Chapter was installed at the University of British Columbia, Vancouver, on April 24, 1932, the fraternity became international.

Government The government of the fraternity is vested in the Supreme Council, an executive secretary, and representatives from active and alumni chapters. The executive functions are vested in a grand president, assisted by the Supreme Council and executive secretary, who is appointed by the grand president and who maintains the national office. The chief legislative body consists of a general convention, which meets biennially and which, through correspondence, is maintained in session at all times. The general convention is made up of the Supreme Council, executive secretary, and one representative from each active and alumni chapter. Subordinate legislation is enacted by the Supreme Council, which consists of the grand president, grand vice-president, editor of the Castle, and the province councillors, there being three provinces, eastern, central, and western. The judicial functions are vested in the general convention.

Responsibility for the fraternity's expansion program is in the hands of the grand vice-president, assisted by the province councillors. Appointed chapter councillors handle the routine administrative functions for chapters under the guidance of the province councillors.

Traditions and Insignia   The fraternity has constantly recognized the need for a professional engineering fraternity which favors in its expansion both the large university and the small college. It has a well-defined professional program and a controlled program of social activities. Dual membership was permitted at first and prevailed for a few years, but this was eliminated at the general convention held in 1929. The fraternity does not tolerate proselyting and early took steps for the abolition of Hell Week. The fraternity believes in cooperating to the fullest extent with school authorities. Believing that membership in the organization should be available to engineers without regard to race, creed, or color, the fraternity has eliminated all such barriers and numbers among its membership representatives from many of the nations of the earth.

A key is awarded annually by each chapter to the individual who, scholastically and through service, has contributed most to the fraternity.

An efficiency contest has been in effect since 1933. Major revisions in the rules of the contest were made in 1953. A plaque is awarded annually to the chapter which scores the highest in the contest.

The standard badge consists of a triangle having concave corners on which are superimposed three smaller triangles having concave sides and having their vertices at the center of the badge in which is placed a ruby. The smaller triangles, which contain the letters ΣΦΔ are black, the background between them being white. The gold border is engraved. Jeweled badges, with rubies and pearls in the borders, are also available. The crest contains the symbolic castle, retorts, bolt of lightning, and other symbols which play an important part in the ritual. The pledge button displays a red triangular background on which is a black castle, the whole bordered in gold. The recognition button is a gold castle. The fraternity colors are red and black; the flower is the American beauty rose. The motto of the fraternity is "Pro Bono Professionis."

Publications   The Castle is published twice each year. A directory was published last in 1975. The Castle is an exoteric publication. The Star, an esoteric publication of current information for members, is edited by the grand president not fewer than three times each year. Manual of Procedure, first distributed in 1927, has been revised as needed, as has the Pledge Manual, first issued in 1953.

Funds   The endowment funds are administered by the Board of Trustees, consisting of the grand

president and two members elected for four-year terms. With the exception of the trustees, all officers are elected for two-year terms.

Headquarters   438 Smithfield Street, East Liverpool, Ohio 43920.

Membership   Active chapters 11. Inactive chapters 8. Graduate/Alumni chapters 12. Total number of initiates 6,000. Chapter roll:††

1924   Alpha, USC
1926   *Beta, South Dakota*
1927   *Gamma, Texas*
1928   Delta, Illinois
1928   Epsilon, North Dakota State
1929   *Zeta, Tulane*
1931   Eta, Marquette
1932   Theta, British Columbia
1935   *Iota, Chicago Tech* (1976)
1947   Kappa, Tri-State
1951   Lambda, Indiana Tech.
1951   *Mu, UCLA* (1965)
1952   *Nu, California* (1969)
1953   Xi, Manitoba
1958   *Omicron, Michigan State* (1969)
1960   Pi, Embry Riddle (FL)
1965   Rho, Bradley
1969   *Sigma, Cal State, Long Beach* (1974)
1970   Tau, Loyola Marymount, Los Angeles

Tau Beta Sigma

(BAND)

ACTIVE PIN

TAU BETA SIGMA, recognition society for persons in college and university bands, was established at Texas Technological College in the fall of 1939. The founders were a group of band women who felt that a society along the lines of Kappa Kappa Psi, the recognition society for band men, would serve a useful purpose. It became a national organization under a charter at Oklahoma Agricultural and Mechanical College, March 26, 1946, with its national executive director and headquarters the same as Kappa Kappa Psi, by which it was adopted as a sister organization.

Its purposes are to promote high standards of band work on the part of college students, to encourage musical ability and cooperation in musical organizations, and to help new members of the band to adjust to new environments when entering college. The organization is formed on a parallel line with Kappa Kappa Psi. Together with this soci-

†† This chapter roll is repeated from the 19th edition; no current information was provided.

ety, it sponsors both a commissioned work and the National Intercollegiate Band, activities internationally recognized in musical circles.

Government The society is governed in the interim between conventions by the National Council, which is composed of five national officers: national president, national first vice president, national second vice president, national treasurer, and national secretary. The work of the society is done through a national headquarters office administered by an executive director, who is also by law the executive director of Kappa Kappa Psi. Conventions are held biennially in the odd-numbered years at the same time and place as the national convention of Kappa Kappa Psi.

Traditions and Insignia The badge is briolette in shape, with the center panel of the badge in black enamel, upon the panel space is shown the lyre; at the base of the panel is a five-pointed star; in the center of the panel are the three Greek letter symbols, TBΣ. The badge may be circled with crown-set pearls or other jewels. The pledge pin is rectangular in shape with a white background and the treble clef and two notes in gold. The colors and blue and white; the flower is the red rose.

Publication The official publication is *The Podium*, which is also the official publication of Kappa Kappa Psi. It is edited by the executive director of both societies, the expenses being prorated.

Headquarters 122 Seretean Center for the Performing Arts, Oklahoma State University, Stillwater, Oklahoma 74078.

Membership Chapter roll:††

1946   Alpha, Oklahoma State
1946   Beta, Texas Tech
1946   Delta, Oklahoma
1946   Gamma, Colorado
1947   Theta, Cincinnati
1948   Iota, Baylor
1948   Kappa, Texas, El Paso
1948   Lambda, Michigan
1949   Rho, Indiana
1949   Sigma, Arizona State
1949   Xi, West Texas
1950   Alpha Alpha, Northern Colorado
1950   Chi, Ohio State
1950   Omega, Arizona
1950   Psi, Arkansas
1950   Tau, Houston
1950   Upsilon, Eastern New Mexico
1951   Alpha Delta, Ohio
1951   Alpha Epsilon, Midwestern
1951   Alpha Gamma, Kent
1951   Alpha Theta, North Dakota State
1952   Alpha Lambda, L.S.U.
1952   Alpha Mu, Wichita
1952   Alpha Omicron, Sam Houston

†† This chapter roll is repeated from the 19th edition; no current information was provided.

1952   Alpha Xi, Bowling Green
1953   Alpha Pi, Wayne State
1954   Alpha Chi, Northern Arizona
1954   Alpha Psi, Doane
1954   Alpha Upsilon, Lamar
1955   Alpha Omega, Florida State
1956   Beta Beta, New Mexico State
1956   Beta Alpha, Sul Ross
1957   Beta Delta, Texas Christian
1957   Beta Eta, Maryland
1957   Beta Gamma, Texas
1957   Beta Kappa, Southern Mississippi
1957   Beta Zeta, Stephen F. Austin
1958   Beta Nu, Arkansas Tech
1958   Beta Omicron, Texas Southern
1958   Beta Xi, Florida
1959   Beta Sigma, Purdue
1959   Beta Tau, Mississippi
1960   Beta Phi, Florida A & M
1960   Beta Upsilon, Montana State
1962   Gamma Eta, Mississippi Valley
1962   Gamma Zeta, Emporia
1964   Gamma Kappa, Connecticut
1964   Gamma Lambda, Adams
1964   Gamma Mu, Ohio Northern
1965   Gamma Nu, Texas, Arlington
1965   Gamma Xi, Arkansas State
1966   Gamma Omicron, Southern State
1966   Gamma Pi, Ferris
1967   Gamma Rho, Eastern Michigan
1967   Gamma Tau, Central Arkansas
1968   Gamma Chi, Mansfield State
1968   Gamma Phi, Southwestern State (OK)
1969   Delta Alpha, Langston
1969   Delta Beta, West Virginia
1969   Delta Delta, Massachusetts
1969   Delta Epsilon, Miami (OH)
1969   Gamma Omega, Pitt
1969   Gamma Psi, Northeastern (OK)
1970   Delta Kappa, Kansas State
1970   Delta Lambda, Cal State, Sacramento
1970   Delta Mu, Oral Roberts
1970   Delta Nu, Maine
1970   Delta Omicron, Clarion State
1970   Delta Pi, Arkansas, Pine Bluff
1970   Delta Rho, Southwest Missouri
1970   Delta Sigma, Northeast Louisiana
1970   Delta Theta, Alabama State
1970   Delta Xi, Missouri, Rolla
1970   Delta Zeta, Texas A & I
1971   Delta Chi, Tampa
1971   Delta Omega, Bloomsburg
1971   Delta Phi, Texas Lutheran
1971   Delta Psi, Southwest Baptist
1971   Delta Tau, Angelo
1971   Epsilon Alpha, South Carolina
1972   Epsilon Beta, East Texas
1972   Epsilon Delta, Marshall
1972   Epsilon Gamma, Lane
1973   Epsilon Epsilon, Kutztown
1973   Epsilon Eta, Tyler Junior
1973   Epsilon Iota, Akron

1973   Epsilon Kappa, UCLA
1973   Epsilon Theta, Georgia Tech
1973   Epsilon Zeta, Oklahoma Baptist
1974   Epsilon Lambda, North Carolina Central
1974   Epsilon Mu, Arkansas, Monticello
1974   Epsilon Nu, VanderCook College of Music
1974   Epsilon Omicron, USC
1974   Epsilon Pi, Cameron
1974   Epsilon Xi, Troy
1975   Epsilon Chi, South Carolina State
1975   Epsilon Phi, Western Carolina
1975   Epsilon Rho, Virginia State
1975   Epsilon Sigma, Norfolk
1975   Epsilon Tau, Weber
1975   Epsilon Upsilon, Lock Haven
1976   Epsilon Omega, Morgan State
1976   Epsilon Psi, Prairie View A & M
1976   Zeta Alpha, Illinois State
1976   Zeta Beta, Tuskegee

Theta Tau

(ENGINEERING)

ACTIVE PIN

PLEDGE PIN

THETA TAU was founded as the Society of Hammer and Tongs at the University of Minnesota on October 15, 1904, by Erich J. Schrader, Elwin L. Vinal, William M. Lewis and Isaac B. Hanks. Mr. Schrader devoted his life to the fraternity, serving on the Executive Council until his death in 1962. The other founders also continued to follow the progress of the fraternity closely throughout their lives. Although all four founders were students in mining engineering, the policy from the beginning was to have membership include those in all branches of engineering and geology. Since 1964, only those in engineering have been eligible for initiation. The object was to form a fraternity for engineers like professional fraternities existing then only within other fields. The purpose of Theta Tau is to develop and maintain a high standard of professional interest among its members and to unite them in a strong bond of fraternal fellowship. In 1911, the Greek letters which had always appeared on its badge were adopted as the Fraternity's official name.

Growth   The Rhombohedron Club, established in 1903 at Michigan College of Mining and Technology, became the fraternity's Beta Chapter in 1906. As a student at Colorado School of Mines, Founder Lewis established Gamma Chapter in 1907. Seven additional chapters, ranging from coast to coast, were established during the next ten years. A total of 21 chapters had been installed by the fraternity's Silver Anniversary in 1929. A period of very conservative extension began during the Depression years and continued until 1959 with charters generally being granted only to petitioning locals which had been long established. An active program of extension was inaugurated in 1959, but a conservative policy remains in that only carefully selected engineering schools with accredited degree-granting programs are considered. In 1964, a colony program was established providing an optional intermediate step toward becoming a chapter.

The formation of alumni clubs is encouraged. These have developed into alumni associations chartered by the Executive Council in major centers of engineering activity.

It is a fraternity policy for each chapter to maintain a permanent headquarters in the form of a chapter house or a chapter room where meetings and other activities may be held. About three-fourths of the chapters maintain houses.

Government   Sovereignty rests with the convention, held biennially beginning in 1911. After the convention in 1941, the series was interrupted by World War II, and resumed in 1946. Beginning in 1980, the national fraternity has met annually. The mid-biennium meeting is called a national conference, and has replaced the regional conferences previously held at that time. Chapters and alumni associations are represented at conventions and conferences. The convention elects seven alumni and one student member to two-year terms on the Executive Council which directs the fraternity during the interim between national meetings. The immediate past grand regent (national president) also serves on the Executive Council ex-officio as delegate-at-large.

Traditions and Insignia   The badge is a gold gear wheel jeweled with pearls on the rim and a dark red garnet at the hub. The lower part of the wheel is crossed by a hammer and a pair of tongs. The letters Θ and T are displayed on the upper part of the wheel. This badge was adopted in 1911 replacing the former gold skull bearing the letters on its forehead, and displaying the hammer and tongs below its jaw. Only members may wear the badge. Other items of official jewelry include a sister pin which resembles the badge but is smaller and without the hammer and tongs; a pledge insigne which features a dark red gear wheel on a triangular gold shield; and a recognition button which is of the same design as the pledge insigne, but reduced in size. The coat of arms includes as a crest a hand grasping a hammer and tongs; a shield displaying three gear wheels on the chief, a bridge with three arches below; and the Greek-letter name on a ribbon below the shield. The flag is divided into four quadrants, the upper right and lower left being fields of gold, and the others dark red with the coat of arms in full color on the upper left and the Greek letters in gold on the lower right quadrant. The colors are dark red and gold. The flower is the Jacqueminot or dark red rose.

To maintain close fraternal ties among the members, the fraternity limits to a maximum of fifty the number of student members in a chapter at any one time. Only a very limited number of honorary members may be elected to membership in accord with a prescribed procedure involving alumni approval. Other national engineering fraternities are considered competitive, but members are free to affiliate with general fraternities.

In 1928, Theta Tau was a founding member of the Professional Interfraternity Conference which merged in 1977 to form the Professional Fraternity Association.

The student chapter delegates to a convention or conference select one of their number of receive the designation "Outstanding Delegate," the fraternity's highest student honor. The Erich J. Schrader Award (named for the fraternity's principal founder) is presented biennially to the outstanding chapter. The Founders' Award, also presented biennially, goes to the chapter making the greatest improvement. Annual national awards go to chapters for best newsletter, best photograph, best presentation, best display, and greatest member miles in attending the national meeting. Regional awards are presented to the best delegations.

Plans are being developed for a national professional paper competition with a scholarship award and for an Alumni Hall of Fame.

Publications *The Gear of Theta Tau*, the official magazine, was launched in 1907. Publication was begun by Beta Chapter, but a few years later became a function of the national fraternity. Each initiate is provided, free of additional charge, a lifetime subscription. On the occasion of the fraternity's 75th Anniversary, a history was published, and publication of a national directory was resumed at five-year intervals. The *Executive Council Bulletin* has been issued a few times each year since 1971 for chapter officers and advisers, alumni organization officers, national officers and alumni field secretaries. The Pledge and Membership Manual and the Chapter Officers Manual are revised and distributed as required.

Headquarters A Central Office was established in 1963. Since 1983, it has been located at 9974 Old Olive Street Road, St. Louis, MO 63141-5984.

Membership Total living membership 19,182. Total undergraduate membership 489. Active chapters 25. Inactive chapters 16. Colonies 5. Houses owned 13. City/Area alumni associations 15. Total number of initiates 25,030. Chapter roll:

1904 Alpha, Minnesota
1906 Beta, Michigan Tech
1907 *Gamma, Colorado Mines* (1985)
1911 *Delta, Case Western Reserve* (1990)
1911 *Epsilon, Cal, Berkeley* (1975)
1912 *Eta, M.I.T.* (1930)
1912 Zeta, Kansas
1914 *Theta, Columbia (NY)* (1957-1963) (1970)
1916 *Iota, Missouri, Rolla* (1975)
1916 *Kappa, Illinois* (1939)

1920 *Lambda, Utah* (1974)
1922 Mu, Alabama
1922 *Nu, Carnegie-Mellon* (1948)
1923 Omicron, Iowa (1945-1947)
1923 Pi, Virginia (1976-1988)
1923 Xi, Wisconsin, Madison (1929-1947)
1924 Rho, North Carolina State
1924 Sigma, Ohio State
1925 *Tau, Syracuse* (1989)
1928 Phi, Purdue
1928 Upsilon, Arkansas
1930 Chi, Arizona
1932 Omega, South Dakota Mines
1932 *Psi, Montana Mines* (1988)
1935 Gamma Beta, George Washington (1979-1989)
1939 *Delta Beta, Louisville* (1978)
1947 Xi Beta, Lawrence Tech
1951 Epsilon Beta, Wayne State (MI)
1960 *Zeta Beta, Utah State* (1966)
1961 *Eta Beta, Houston* (1988)
1963 *Theta Beta, Washington (WA)* (1971)
1964 Iota Beta, Detroit
1964 Kappa Beta, Mississippi State
1968 Lambda Beta, Tennessee Tech
1969 *Mu Beta, GMI* (1983)
1975 Nu Beta, Wisconsin, Platteville
1988 Omicron Beta, Michigan, Dearborn
1989 Rho Beta, Ohio
1989 Sigma Beta, Wisconsin, Milwaukee
1990 Tau Beta, Southern Methodist
1990 Upsilon Beta, Old Dominion

Colonies: Houston, Oakland, Texas, Toledo, Windsor

Xi Psi Phi

(DENTISTRY)

ACTIVE PIN   PLEDGE PIN

XI PSI PHI was organized February 8, 1889, at the University of Michigan by Arthur A. Deyoe, Lewis C. Thayer, William F. Gary, Walter H. Booth, Gordon C. McCoy, and Eldon Waterloo. Fifteen others are counted as associate founders. On February 6, 1906, the Supreme Chapter was incorporated under the laws of Illinois.

Traditions and Insignia The official insignia is a four-leaf gold pin; in each leaf are set three pearls. The center of the pin is surmounted by a diamond-shaped black-enamel piece bearing the three Greek letters ΞΨΦ. The official crest consists of two rampant lions holding between them the official insignia of the fraternity, surmounted by the helmet of the supreme chapter. Below is a ribbon bearing the motto of the fraternity, "Hospitality is the life of friendship" (in Greek letters). Above the crest is a spray of red roses, the official flower of the fraternity. The official colors of the fraternity are lavender and cream.

Publications   Catalogues were issued in 1901, 1903, and 1906. The journal, *Xi Psi Phi Quarterly*, first issued in 1901, is published at Fulton, Missouri.

Headquarters   Xi Psi Phi Fraternity, 1005 East Main Street, Suite 7, Medford, Oregon 97501.

Membership   Chapter roll:††

1889   *Alpha, Michigan* (1950)
1893   *Beta, N.Y.U.* (1972)
1893   *Delta, Baltimore Dental Surgery* (merged with Maryland, June, 1923, and with Eta)
1893   *Epsilon, Iowa* (1951)
1893   Eta, Maryland
1893   Gamma, Temple
1893   Theta, Indiana
1893   *Zeta, Pennsylvania Dental* (merged with Pennsylvania, 1909, and with Pi)
1894   Iota, California
1896   Kappa, Ohio State
1896   Lambda, Loyola Dental
1896   *Mu, Buffalo* (1966)
1899   *Nu, Harvard*
1899   Omicron, Royal College, Toronto
1899   *Pi, Penn* (1959)
1900   Rho, Northwestern
1901   Tau, Washington
1902   *Sigma, Illinois* (1955)
1904   *Xi, Virginia Medical* (1962)
1905   Chi, Kansas City
1905   *Omega, Vanderbilt* (college discontinued June, 1926)
1905   Phi, Minnesota (reorganized 1942)
1905   *Phi, Nebraska* (1971)
1905   *Upsilon, Ohio Dental* (college discontinued July, 1926)
1906   *Alpha Alpha, Detroit Medical* (college discontinued June, 1909)
1906   *Alpha Beta, Baltimore Medical* (merged with Maryland 1912, and with Eta)
1908   *Alpha Delta, New Orleans Dentistry* (1926) (reorganized as Alpha Nu)
1908   Alpha Epsilon, Oregon
1912   Alpha Eta, Emory (formerly Atlanta-Southern)
1912   *Alpha Zeta, Southern Dental* (merged with Atlanta-Southern 1917, and Alpha Eta)
1913   *Alpha Theta, USC* (1967)
1914   *Alpha Iota, Louisville* (1959)
1915   Alpha Kappa, Creighton
1917   *Alpha Lambda, Jersey City* (college discontinued, 1920)
1917   *Alpha Mu, George Washington* (college discontinued, 1920)

1918   *Alpha Nu, Tulane* (college discontinued, 1926)
1919   *Alpha Xi, Georgetown* (1969)
1921   Alpha Omicron, Tennessee (-1947)
1921   Alpha Pi, Baylor
1922   *Alpha Rho, Colorado Dental* (college discontinued, 1931)
1922   *Alpha Sigma, Western Reserve*
1924   *Alpha Tau, Columbia*
1924   *Alpha Upsilon, Pitt*
1926   *Alpha Phi, College of Physicians and Surgeons, School of Dentistry* (1973)
1930   Alpha Chi, Loyola
1930   Alpha Psi, Texas
1943   *Alpha Omega, St. Louis* (1974)
1947   *Beta Alpha, Washington* (1973)
1952   Beta Beta, North Carolina
1953   *Beta Gamma, Alabama* (1961)
1954   *Beta Delta, Tufts* (1952)
1957   *Beta Epsilon, Detroit* (1967)
1959   *Beta Zeta, Seton Hall* (1973)
1962   *Beta Eta, Puerto Rico* (1972)
1962   Beta Theta, West Virginia
1963   Beta Iota, Winnipeg, Manitoba
1972   Beta Kappa, South Carolina
1973   Beta Lambda, Texas

Zeta Phi Eta†

(COMMUNICATIONS ARTS AND SCIENCES)

ACTIVE PIN

ZETA PHI ETA, the first national professional fraternity in the speech arts field, was founded on October 10, 1893, at Northwestern University.

The idea of a friendly society of service which might eventually become a national and vital force in the speech arts was the germ of its founding. The five founders were Edith DeVore Tiffany, Maud Newell Wilson, Mollie Connor Hackney, Leila Little Heckler, and Laurine Wright Bartlett. The fraternity was incorporated under the laws of the state of Illinois, June 25, 1902.

In 1908 Zeta Phi Eta affiliated with Phi Eta Sigma, a local organization founded in 1901 at Emerson College, Boston. In the affiliation the chapter at Boston became Alpha, and the one at Evanston, Beta. In 1952 Omega Upsilon disbanded, and its members affiliated with Zeta Phi Eta.

Since the 1950s the field of speech arts has broadened to include communication arts and sciences. However, Zeta Phi Eta still has as its purpose, as stated in its constitution: to band together

†† This chapter roll is repeated from the 19th edition; no current information was provided.

† This chapter narrative is repeated from the 19th edition; no current information was provided.

groups of selected college students interested in maintaining high standards of speech and drama; to promote and maintain a better understanding among colleges and universities teaching the speech arts; to build a professional philosophy for members engaged in the profession; to stimulate and encourage all worthy enterprises in the speech fields; and to make the fraternity a professional aid and stimulus after graduation.

Zeta Phi Eta is affiliated with the American Theatre Association, the Professional Panhellenic Association, the Speech Communication Association, and the Children's Theatre Association.

Government Conventions are held triennially. At the Boston convention in 1908 government was entrusted to the National Council composed of five members. This has since been enlarged to a membership of eight.

Traditions and Insignia Each active chapter fosters one worth-while activity or more in the professional field. The project must be of service to the speech or drama department of the institution in which the chapter is located or to the community and must offer the members professional experience and training. Included among the projects are children's theatres, speech clinics, little theatres, puppet shows, programs, shows for the crippled children, the aged, and taping for the blind.

The badge is a rose-colored cameo carved with the Greek letters ΣΦΗ in white, surrounded by twenty-three pearls. The pledge pin is a small gold shield etched with the initials ΣΦΗ. Colors are rose and white. The flower is the LaFrance rose.

Publications The quarterly magazine is the *Cameo*. It contains articles of professional interest, reports of prominent members who are active in the various fields of speech arts. and chapter and alumnae news. In addition the fraternity publishes the *Prospectus, Pledge Manual,* and other manuals.

Funds and Philanthropies Institution of the Zeta Phi Eta Foundation was authorized at the 1955 convention.

Four awards are presented at each national convention. The Pearl Bennett Broxam award, given in memory of a former national president, is granted to that active chapter showing the most outstanding professional achievement.

The Omega Upsilon Recognition Award is presented to the chapter which has made outstanding progress during the interim between national conventions. The National Council Award is presented to the chapter which distinguishes itself by planning and executing programs of value to individual members, the chapter, the department, and the community. The Lorraine Jackson Memorial Award, named for a former national president, is given to a deserving chapter to present to one of the departments in the university in which the chapter is located. The Chapter Achievement Award is given to that chapter that has shown superiority in scholarship, activities, financial status, and chapter projects. The award is in the form of a plaque.

From the Foundation, the annual Winifred Ward Prize is given through the Children's Theatre Association to a new community theatre which has done outstanding work and shows promise for the future. Other grants include those to: Gallaudet College; Hadley School for the Blind; John F. Kennedy Center for the Performing Arts, and the McCord Theatre Museum at Southern Methodist University. In 1960, Zeta Phi Eta was approved by the Library of Congress as the first national organization to provide volunteer readers for the Library's taping program. Alumnae members read selected books onto tape. The books become part of the permanent collection loaned to blind people throughout the country by the Library of Congress.

Headquarters Box 1201, Evanston, Illinois 60201.

Membership Active chapters 20. Inactive chapters 26. Total number of initiates 15,000. Chapter roll:††

1893	Beta, Northwestern
1908	Alpha, Emerson
1914	Delta, Syracuse
1917	Epsilon, Brenau
1919	Zeta, Southern Methodist
1921	Eta, USC
1921	Gamma, Drake
1924	*Theta, Coe (1937)*
1926	*Iota, North Dakota (1942)*
1928	*Kappa, Washington (MO) (1936)*
1930	*Lambda, Michigan (1968)*
1930	*Mu, Washington (1974)*
1930	*Nu, UCLA*
1931	*Xi, Alabama (1951)*
1932	*Omicron, Wisconsin, Madison*
1934	*Pi, Minnesota (1969)*
1934	*Rho, Alabama State (1972)*
1936	*Sigma, Iowa*
1937	Tau, Illinois
1937	*Upsilon, Florida State*
1939	*Phi, Arizona*
1941	*Chi, Ohio State*
1943	Psi, Georgia
1945	*Alpha Alpha, Science and Arts (OK) (1974)*
1945	*Alpha Beta, Denver*
1945	*Alpha Gamma, Utah*
1945	Omega, Texas Woman's
1947	Alpha Delta, South Dakota
1947	*Alpha Epsilon, Occidental*
1950	Alpha Zeta, Wichita
1951	*Alpha Eta, Mary Washington*
1952	Alpha Theta, Marquette
1956	*Alpha Iota, Southern Illinois*
1958	*Alpha Kappa, Miami (FL)*
1958	*Alpha Lambda, Florida*
1959	*Alpha Mu, American*
1959	*Alpha Nu, Oklahoma*
1962	*Alpha Xi, Portland*

†† This chapter roll is repeated from the 19th edition; no current information was provided.

1966 *Alpha Omicron, Southern Illinois, Edwardsville* (1975)
1967 Alpha Pi, Oregon State
1968 Alpha Rho, West Virginia
1969 Alpha Sigma, Western Kentucky
1970 Alpha Tau, Baylor
1972 *Alpha Upsilon, Missouri, Kansas City* (1974)
1974 Alpha Phi, Wisconsin, Whitewater
1975 Alpha Chi, Texas, Arlington
1976 Alpha Psi, Texas Southern

Osteopathic Organizations

Atlas Club†

ACTIVE PIN

THE ATLAS CLUB is the oldest Osteopathic Organization. It was founded December 10, 1898, by Henry S. Bunting, Homer Wollery, K. K. Smith, Norman Mattison, T. E. Reagan, Forrest Webber, H. B. McIntyre, William Laughlin, and C. E. Still. The organization is controlled by the Grand Council, which meets at the annual convention of the American Osteopathic Association. The official publication is the *Atlas Bulletin*, and since 1922, when it suspended publication as a semi-professional monthly, it has been issued annually in the form of reports and directory. The name and form of the pin are taken from the first vertebra of the spinal column. The colors are red and white.

Membership Active chapters 6. Chapter roll††:

1898 Axis, Kirksville Osteopathic
1914 Hyoid, Chicago Osteopathy
1918 Cricoid, Los Angeles Osteopathic
1918 Xyphoid, Osteopathic Medicine, Des Moines
1923 Mastoid, Kansas City Osteopathic
1924 Styloid, Philadelphia Osteopathic

† This chapter narrative is repeated from the 19th edition; no current information was provided.
†† This chapter roll is repeated from the 19th edition; no current information was provided.

Delta Omega†

ACTIVE PIN

DELTA OMEGA was organized at the American School of Osteopathy, Kirksville, Missouri, October 15, 1904. It is a national professional organization, whose local chapters are organized in colleges recognized by the American Osteopathic Association.

Specifically the purposes are: "The closer study of all osteopathic work, the promotion of the cause of pure osteopathy and the maintenance of its principles. the maintenance of friendship and a high standard of ethics among all osteopaths, the elevation of all moral, intellectual, and social conditions of our fellow men, and the promotion of love, loyalty, and charity among our members."

The members of Delta Omega consist of five classes: active, pledge, active field, associate, and honorary. Active members are women of high character in attendance at an accredited osteopathic college who have been initiated according to the ritual of Delta Omega. Pledged members include those who have taken the pledge oath, but have not been initiated. Active field members are those members who have been graduated and are engaged in the active practice of osteopathy. Associate members include all those in good standing who have for some good reason discontinued the study or practice of osteopathy. Honorary members included women who are unanimously elected by the active members of the chapter, according to the ritual.

The Grand Chapter of the fraternity holds an annual meeting in conjunction with the national convention of the American Osteopathic Association. Its chief projects are: financial contributions to osteopathic research funds, publication of the fraternity magazine, *The Alpha*, and presentation of awards to members of local chapters who achieve high scholastic standing. The local chapters are required each year to complete some major project that will benefit either the community or the profession.

Traditions and Insignia The fraternity emblem is a kite-shaped shield displaying a skull and crossbones on a green field and the fraternity letters on a white chevron. The colors are green and gold. The flower is the chrysanthemum, and the jewel is the diamond.

Membership Active chapters 5. Inactive chapters 1. Total number of initiates 55. Chapter roll††:

1904 Alpha, Kirksville Osteopathic
1912 Beta, Osteopathic Medicine, Des Moines
1914 *Gamma, Los Angeles Osteopathic* (1925)

1921   Delta, Chicago Osteopathy
1953   Zeta, Kansas City Osteopathic
1966   Iota, Philadelphia Osteopathic

Iota Tau Sigma[†]

ACTIVE PIN

IOTA TAU SIGMA was founded in Kirksville, Missouri, December 2, 1902, by L. K. Tuttle, W. C. Hall, O. S. Miller, F. R. Graham, R. L. Starkweather, H. M. Gifford, L. A Myers, R H. Switzer, and A. F. McWilliams. It was the first osteopathic organization to call itself a fraternity. It is controlled by the Supreme Council which meets annually at the convention of the American Osteopathic Association.

Publication and Insignia   The official publication is the *Gozzle Nipper Magazine* and is issued semiannually. The official emblem is illustrated. Colors are green and white, and the flower is the white carnation.

Membership   Total living membership 2,200. Total deceased membership 735. Active chapters 4. Inactive chapters 2. Total number of initiates 2,935. Chapter roll[††]:

1902   Alpha, Kirksville Osteopathic
1903   *Beta, Osteopathic Medicine, Des Moines*
1908   *Gamma, Los Angeles Osteopathic* (1964)
1909   Delta, Philadelphia Osteopathic
1911   Zeta, Chicago Osteopathy
1916   Eta, Kansas City Osteopathic

Lambda Omicron Gamma[†]

LAMBDA OMICRON GAMMA was organized in 1924 at Philadelphia, Pennsylvania, by David Bachrach, Herman Kohn, Sydney M. Kanev, Samuel Getlen, Edward M. Grossman, and Alexander Levitt. The fraternity is controlled by the National Chapter which meets several times during the year at a place designated by the executive officers. There is a convention which is held annually.

The official publications are the *L.O.G. Book*, issued two times a year, and the *Directory*, published annually. Each of these is sent to each member of the fraternity.

Membership   Active chapters 3. Inactive chap-

[†] This chapter narrative is repeated from the 19th edition; no current information was provided.
[††] This chapter roll is repeated from the 19th edition; no current information was provided.

---

ters 2. Graduate/Alumni chapters 5. Total number of initiates 850. Chapter roll[††]:

1929   *Astra Chapter, Los Angeles Osteopathic* (1964)
1929   Caduceus Chapter, Philadelphia Osteopathic
1938   *Calvaria Chapter, Osteopathic Medicine, Des Moines*
1939   Claviculae Chapter, Chicago Osteopathy
1964   Cardia Chapter, Kansas City Osteopathic

Phi Sigma Gamma[†]

ACTIVE PIN

PHI SIGMA GAMMA was organized April 28, 1915, through the union of the Phi Sigma Beta and the Phi Omicron Gamma fraternities, which already had chapters in osteopathic colleges. The union of the two added strength to the organization which began with five chapters; a sixth was added within two years. The fraternity is controlled by the Grand Council, which meets annually at the time of the convention of the American Osteopathic Association. The official publication is the *Speculum*, issued annually. The official emblem is illustrated. Colors are navy blue and white, and the flower is the white carnation.

Membership   Active chapters 4. Inactive chapters 3. Total number of initiates 2,375. Chapter roll[††]:

1915   *Alpha, Kirksville Osteopathic*
1915   Beta, Los Angeles Osteopathic
1915   Delta, Osteopathic Medicine, Des Moines
1915   Epsilon, Kansas City Osteopathic
1915   *Gamma, Chicago Osteopathy*
1917   Zeta, Philadelphia Osteopathic
1918   *Eta, Massachusetts Osteopathy*

Psi Sigma Alpha[†]

ACTIVE PIN

PSI SIGMA ALPHA, national osteopathic scholastic honor society, was founded in 1924 at the Kirksville College of Osteopathy and surgery at Kirksville, Missouri, by Drs. A. C. Hardy, F. J. Cohen, E. C. Petermyer. T. A. Martwell, H. R. Holloway, H. V. Tollerton, T. D. Gregory, and O. C. Hudson. The founders of Psi Sigma Alpha, recognizing the need for a true honor society within the osteopathic colleges, agreed that the purpose of Psi Sigma Alpha would be to recognize and encourage scholarship, friendship, cultural interest and osteopathic progress. It was their decision that membership should not be based on scholarship alone, but that other attributes should be considered for membership.

After the establishment of the chapter at the Kirksville College of Osteopathy and Surgery, chapters were formed in two of the other osteopathic colleges.

Government The government of Psi Sigma Alpha is vested in the Grand Council which meets each year at the time of the annual convention of the American Osteopathic Association. Its central headquarters is at the office of Dr. John W. Hayes, 203 West Fifth Street, East Liverpool, Ohio 43920.

Publication The official publication of Psi Sigma Alpha is *The Skull*, issued bi-annually.

Membership Active chapters 2. Inactive chapters 2. Total number of initiates 843. Chapter roll††:

1924 Alpha, Kirksville Osteopathic
1930 Beta, Kansas City Osteopathic
1932 *Gamma, Osteopathic Medicine, Des Moines*
1943 *Delta, Los Angeles Osteopathic*

Sigma Sigma Phi†

ACTIVE PIN

SIGMA SIGMA PHI SOCIETY, honor organization in osteopathy, was organized in 1921 at Kirksville, Missouri, by A. W. King, P. L. Etter, R. M. Embry, J. J. Grace, R. J. Tell, N. J. McDonald, F. M. Stoffer, J. A. Atkinson, and Herbert Weber. The society is governed by the Grand Chapter which meets annually at the time of the convention of the American Osteopathic Association. The official publication is the *Year Book of Sigma Sigma Phi*. The emblem is copied from the anatomical sword, the sternum, as illustrated. Colors are red and blue, and the flower is the red carnation.

Membership Active chapters 5. Total number of initiates 953. Chapter roll††:

† This chapter narrative is repeated from the 19th edition; no current information was provided.

†† This chapter roll is repeated from the 19th edition; no current information was provided.

1921 Alpha, Kirksville Osteopathic
1925 Beta, Osteopathic Medicine, Des Moines
1930 Gamma, Los Angeles Osteopathic
1932 Delta, Kansas City Osteopathic
1939 Epsilon, Chicago Osteopathy

Theta Psi†

ACTIVE PIN

THETA PSI was founded May 21, 1903, at Kirksville, Missouri, by W. W. Johonnett, H. W. Conklin, C. S. Green, G. P. Long, R. H. Long, E. T. Hall, Kendall Achorn, Ray Hamilton, Fred Hamilton, W. H. Richardson, and C. F. Cook. The fraternity is controlled by the Theta Psi Alumni Association, which meets annually at the time of the convention of the American Osteopathic Association. The official publication is the *Signet*, issued annually. The official emblem is as illustrated.

Membership Active chapters 1. Inactive chapters 3. Total number of initiates 720. Chapter roll††:

1903 Alpha, Kirksville Osteopathic
1919 *Beta, Chicago Osteopathy (1943)*
1922 *Gamma, Philadelphia Osteopathic (1943)*
1939 *Epsilon, Los Angeles Osteopathic*

Other Professional Fraternities

Alpha Alpha Gamma†

(ARCHITECTURE)

ALPHA ALPHA GAMMA was founded as a national fraternity of women in architecture and related arts, at Washington University, St. Louis, Missouri, on January 28, 1922. It was an outgrowth of the local organization "Confrerie Alongiv." The charter members were: Edith Balson (Mrs. Wilfred Verity), Ann Coffman (Mrs. C. F. Kistenmacher), Bernice Goedde, Mildred L. Graf (Mrs. E. R. Ravenscroft), Elsa M. Greiser (Mrs. M. J. Bussard), Elizabeth Harter (Mrs. D. C, Walmsley), Helen Milius (Mrs. I. A. Baum, deceased), Jane Pelton, May Steinmesch, and Evelyn Webb. The fraternity was founded with the object of promoting the exchange of ideas, mutual encouragement, and friendship among women with common problems, interests, and ideals.

Members in an undergraduate chapter are students registered in these schools of higher learning offering comprehensive programs, or granting degrees in architecture, architectural engineering, interior design, industrial design, landscape design, textile design, ceramic design, sculpture, mural painting, and such arts as the association as a whole shall deem allied to architecture. To be eligible for membership the student must have completed one year of work toward her degree or certificate. As the chief object of the organization is professional, prospective members are considered for their scholastic and professional qualifications rather than social or personal eligibility.

Association of Women in Architecture   Around 1927 there began to be so many ΑΑΓ alumnae who wished to continue the ties and friendship of the organization that several alumnae chapters were formed. These became the strength of the organization and increased their professional status by opening their membership to other women active in the fields of architecture and the allied arts. As a result of this continuous growth and expansion, the alumnae groups were reclassified at the 1948 convention in San Francisco as professional chapters of the Association of Women in Architecture, the undergraduates retaining the title of Alpha Alpha Gamma. As membership increased, co-ordination of architecture with its allied arts became more necessary. It is for this purpose that members are striving today, and each year brings satisfaction in gradually approaching this end.

Members in professional chapters may be former members of undergraduate chapters, or women actively or formerly engaged in architecture or architectural engineering, interior design, industrial design, landscape design, textile design, ceramics, sculpture, mural painting, and such other arts as the chapter shall deem allied to architecture.

Government   Government is by the Arch Chapter consisting of national officers and committee chairmen. National conventions have been held biennially since the organization was founded. They are held in even-numbered years the first week in July at the location of a professional or undergraduate chapter. National officers are elected from the professional membership at the convention and serve for a two-year term, except for the historian, who was elected to permanent office in 1952.

Traditions and Insignia   Membership offers participation in the activities of the largest and oldest architectural organization for women. It offers an avenue of contact between women of similar backgrounds with common problems, ideals, and interests. In addition, the organization provides instructive programs, stimulating ideas, an incentive for self-improvement, and a broadened outlook through the understanding of those in allied fields.

The purchase and wearing of pins for either undergraduate or professional members is optional. The colors are blue and gold.

Publications   The official journal is *The Keystone;* frequency of issue is left to the discretion of the editor.

Funds and Philanthropies   In 1948 the student Loan Fund was established and is available to women students in accredited schools of architecture and the related arts, as determined and approved by Arch Chapter. In 1956 the restrictions for use of this fund were lessened to allow it to be lent for chapter and national projects to benefit the organization and its objectives. Since 1950 a book prize has been awarded annually by the St. Louis Professional Chapter to the outstanding woman student in the School of Architecture at Washington University, selected by the faculty.

Membership   Active chapters 7. Active professional chapters 9. Total number of initiates 1,145. Chapter roll:††

1922   Alpha, Washington (MO)
1922   Beta, Minnesota
1922   *Delta, California*
1922   Gamma, Texas
1925   *Epsilon, Illinois*
1928   *Zeta, Michigan*
1935   Eta, Cornell
1950   Theta, Kansas State
1956   *Iota, Auburn*
1957   Kappa, UCLA
1966   Lambda, Kansas

Alpha Beta Alpha†

(LIBRARY SCIENCE)

ACTIVE PIN

ALPHA BETA ALPHA was founded at Northwestern State College of Louisiana on May 3, 1950. It is the first co-educational undergraduate library science fraternity to be established.

The idea of such an organization was first discussed at a banquet on the campus in 1945 at which were present some forty library science students and librarians and several dignitaries, including Nora Beust, of the U.S. Office of Education, Sue Hefley, Louisiana State Supervisor of School Libraries, and Mary W. Harris, Assistant State Librarian.

The purposes of the fraternity to be exemplified by its members are: To maintain an abiding interest in librarianship, and to acquire a true professional spirit and a deep sense of responsibility to the profession; to seek a sincere, sympathetic, and full understanding of the work and problems of human beings.

†† This chapter roll is repeated from the 19th edition; no current information was provided.
† This chapter narrative is repeated from the 19th edition; no current information was provided.

The first biennial convention was held in Natchitoches, Louisiana, March 15–16, 1952.

Government The fraternity is governed by the Executive Council, comprised of the president, vice-president, treasurer, executive secretary, and a councilman from each of the five regional districts. All officers are elected for one-year terms.

Insignia The badge is in the shape of a closed book, behind which a quill pen is placed vertically; diagonally across the book are the letters ABA. The pledge button is in the shape of a shield and is crossed by a diagonal line.

The blazon of the official coat of arms is as follows: arms—purpure, on a bend argent, three Greek letters ABA, of the first, between; in chief, a white rose-leaved vert; and, in base, the reproduction of the ABA key. Crest—on a wreath of the colors, a candle holder argent holding a candle purpure, flamed and resplendent or. The motto is *Books, People, Service, Life.*

The fraternity colors are purple and white; and the official flower is a white rose. The official seal is round in shape with a reproduction of the badge in the center and with the name of the fraternity and the date encircling the badge.

Publications *The Alphabet* is the official magazine of the fraternity.

Headquarters Milner Library. Illinois State University, Normal, Illinois 61761.

Membership Active chapters 37. Inactive chapters 11. Total number of initiates 1,600. Chapter roll:††

1950 Alpha, Northwestern Louisiana
1950 Beta, Mississippi for Women
1952 Gamma, Indiana State
1953 Delta, Alabama
1953 Epsilon, Murray State
1953 Eta, Texas Woman's
1953 *Iota, San Jose* (1968)
1953 *Theta, Arizona State* (1970)
1953 Zeta, Concord
1954 *Kappa, Millersville* (1972)
1954 Lambda, L.S.U.
1956 Mu, Illinois State
1956 *Nu, Marshall* (1975)
1956 *Xi, Northern Iowa* (1971)
1957 Omicron, Florida A & M
1957 *Pi, Our Lady Of The Lake* (1967)
1957 Rho, Kutztown
1958 *Sigma, Western Michigan* (1971)
1958 *Tau, Northern Illinois* (1964)
1958 Upsilon, Shepherd
1960 *Chi, North Texas* (1973)
1960 *Omega, Tennessee* (1968)
1960 *Phi, Central Michigan* (1970)
1960 Psi, Southeast Missouri
1961 Alpha Alpha, Madison Col
1961 Alpha Beta, Nicholls

1962 Alpha Gamma, Morehead
1963 Alpha Delta, Oklahoma State
1963 Alpha Epsilon, Florence State (AL)
1965 Alpha Zeta, Shippensburg
1966 Alpha Theta, Louisiana Tech
1967 Alpha Eta, East Carolina
1968 Alpha Iota, Glassboro
1968 Alpha Kappa, Central State (OK)
1969 Alpha Lambda, Edinboro
1969 Alpha Mu, Northwest Missouri
1969 Alpha Nu, Radford
1969 Alpha Omicron, West Virginia Wesleyan
1969 Alpha Xi, Eastern Illinois
1970 Alpha Pi, Mansfield
1970 Alpha Rho, Austin Peay
1970 Alpha Sigma, Sam Houston
1970 Alpha Tau, Slippery Rock
1970 Alpha Upsilon, State College of Arkansas
1971 Alpha Phi, Jackson (MS)
1972 Alpha Chi, Wisconsin, Whitewater
1972 Alpha Psi, Western Illinois
1973 Alpha Omega, South Carolina State

Alpha Epsilon Rho†

(THE NATIONAL HONORARY BROADCASTING SOCIETY)

ALPHA EPSILON RHO was founded on December 1, 1941, as Beta Epsilon Phi, but on April 30, 1943, the name was changed to Alpha Epsilon Rho.

The organization took place at the Institute for Education by Radio, Columbus, Ohio. Although originally annual meetings were held with the Institute, since 1962 they have been held in various metropolitan areas throughout the country. The founders were student groups from Stephens College, Columbia, Missouri, Syracuse University, and the University of Minnesota.

In 1975 the organization became "The National Honorary Broadcasting Society—Alpha Epsilon Rho" and changed from a recognition to a professional society. Greek-letter names for chapters were dropped.

Alpha Epsilon Rho encourages interest in and high standards of broadcasting. To be eligible for membership students must have B grades or better in radio and television courses and at least C grades in other college courses. Within these limits members are selected on the basis of quantity and quality of service to the school broadcasting. Both men and women are eligible.

Government The national officers, constituting the executive committee, are national president, vice president for regional development, vice president for professional/alumni relations, vice president for public information, and the national executive secretary. All legislation is in the hands

†† This chapter roll is repeated from the 19th edition; no current information was provided.

† This chapter narrative is repeated from the 19th edition; no current information was provided.

of the National Council, consisting of the Executive Council and a representative of each chapter.

Traditions and Insignia The emblem is a stylized frame of single-sprocket film with one-half a polydirectional microphone combined with one-half of the front turret of a three-lens camera combined as a symbol imposed on the stylized motion picture-film frame. Society colors are red and green, with red symbolizing the energy and courage which a student in broadcasting employs in setting his standards and goals, and green symbolizing faithfulness and integrity.

Headquarters College of Journalism, University of South Carolina, Columbia, South Carolina 29208.

Membership Active chapters 56. Total number of initiates 11,600. Chapter roll:††

1941	Stephens College
1943	Syracuse
1945	Alabama
1946	Nebraska
1946	Utah
1950	Miami (FL)
1952	Kansas State
1954	USC
1956	Kentucky
1958	San Diego State
1958	Washington
1959	Kansas
1959	Tulsa
1960	Ithaca
1960	Murray State
1965	Detroit
1967	Cal State, Long Beach
1968	Southern Illinois
1969	Central Missouri State
1969	Memphis State
1970	San Bernadino Valley
1970	South Carolina
1970	Texas Tech
1970	Wisconsin, Oshkosh
1971	Arizona State
1971	CUNY, Brooklyn
1971	South Carolina Professional Chapter
1972	Central Michigan
1972	SUNY Col., Oswego
1973	Cal State, Northridge
1973	Indiana
1973	Oklahoma State
1974	Delta State
1974	Northeast Louisiana
1975	Morehead
1975	N.Y.U.
1975	Northern Illinois
1976	Arkansas State
1976	Auburn
1976	Glassboro
1976	James Madison
1976	Norfolk
1976	SUNY Col., Buffalo
1976	Shaw
1976	Southwest Texas
1976	V.P.I.
1976	Winthrop
1976	St. Clair County Community
1977	Appalachian
1977	Arkansas, Little Rock
1977	Black Hawk College
1977	Boston Col
1977	Cincinnati
1977	Gannon
1977	Towson
1977	Youngstown State

Alpha Eta Rho[†]

(AVIATION)

ACTIVE PIN

ALPHA ETA RHO was established in 1929 at the University of Southern California by Prof. Earl W. Hill, who was teaching aviation, with the purpose in mind of a closer band of knowledge and understanding among those students of aviation, regardless of color, race, or creed.

Government Government is by the Board of Directors composed of the national president, national vice-president, and national secretary-treasurer. Regional management is coordinated through the western regional governor, midwestern regional governor, and the eastern regional governor.

Traditions and Insignia The fraternity emblem is patterned after the historically famous five-cylinder radial engine. A scholarship key is awarded annually to the outstanding member of each collegiate chapter.

Publication *The Beam* is issued periodically.

Headquarters Parks College, St. Louis University, Parks Airport, East St. Louis, Illinois 62201.

Membership Associate membership is offered those industry leaders who have participated in undergraduate chapter activities. Active chapters 16. Inactive chapters 12. Total number of initiates 3,800. Chapter roll:††

† This chapter narrative is repeated from the 19th edition; no current information was provided.

†† This chapter roll is repeated from the 19th edition; no current information was provided.

1929 Alpha, USC
1936 *Beta, UCLA*
1936 *Gamma, Northwestern (1942)*
1939 *Delta, San Diego State (1942)*
1939 *Epsilon, Duke (1942)*
1940 Eta, San Jose
1940 *Zeta, Pasadena City College (1942)*
1946 Iota, USC, Santa Maria
1949 *Kappa, Denver (1965)*
1950 Lambda, Northrop Aeronautical
1950 *Mu, Riverside (1952)*
1950 Nu, Mt. San Antonio College
1950 Pi, Parks (IL)
1950 *Rho, Tennessee*
1951 *Sigma, Los Angeles City Col.*
1954 Chi, Illinois
1954 *Omicron, American*
1956 Tau, College of San Mateo
1956 Xi, San Bernardino Valley
1957 *Alpha Rho, Norwich (1965)*
1957 Phi, SUNY Col. Tech, Farmingdale
1957 *Psi, Stephens (MO) (1965)*
1959 Omega, National (Korea)
1961 Epsilon Rho, Embry Riddle (FL)
1962 Beta, Purdue
1963 Sigma, Southern Illinois
1966 Delta, North Dakota
1966 Gamma, Auburn

Alpha Kappa Kappa†

(MEDICINE)

ACTIVE PIN

PLEDGE PIN

ALPHA KAPPA KAPPA was founded September 29, 1888, at Dartmouth by a group of seventeen medical students led by the enthusiasm of Dixi Crosby, 1891, who was the son and grandson of professors of the Dartmouth Medical School. In 1889 the fraternity was incorporated by sPecial act of the New Hampshire legislature, and soon thereafter assumed national status. It became international in 1904 when a chapter was installed at McGill University.

Dr. George Cook of Concord, New Hampshire, became interested in the aims and ideals of the fraternity and was elected grand president in 1898. Under his leadership chapters were installed at the leading medical schools.

Government The Council, composed of eight alumni members and elected at the biennial convention, is the governing body of the fraternity. Supervision of the various chapters is maintained by annual visitations by council members in cooperation with the chapter district deputy and the alumni advisory committee.

Traditions and Insignia The badge is a gold crescent between the horns of which is held a book bearing the chapter letters. On the crescent are the letters AKK and around it are coiled two serpents facing each other. The crescent and book are set with emeralds and pearls exemplifying the colors, Dartmouth green and white. The pledge button consists of a crescent, half green and half white. The coat of arms and letters AKK are used as recognition insignia.

Publications *The Centaur*, the official publication, is published quarterly.

Headquarters Prather Road, Box 153, Ellettsville, Indiana 47429.

Membership Active chapters 10. Inactive chapters 56. Total number of initiates 35,612. Chapter roll:††

1888 *Alpha, Dartmouth Medical (1962)*
1893 *Gamma, Tufts Medical (1931)*
1894 *Delta, Vermont (1932)*
1896 *Zeta, Long Island Medical (1952)*
1897 *Theta, Maine Medical (school discontinued 1920)*
1898 Psi, Minnesota
1899 *Beta, P & S, San Francisco (school discontinued 1918)*
1899 *Eta, Illinois (1969)*
1899 *Iota, Syracuse (1965)*
1899 *Sigma, California (1963)*
1900 Epsilon, Jefferson Medical
1900 *Kappa, Marquette (1968)*
1901 *Lambda, Cornell (1941)*
1901 *Mu, Penn (1956)*
1901 *Nu, Rush (1964)*
1901 *Omicron, Cincinnati (1969)*
1901 *Xi, Northwestern (1968)*
1902 *Pi, Ohio State (1972)*
1903 *Alpha Beta, Tulane (1972)*
1903 *Chi, Vanderbilt (1954)*
1903 Omega, Tennessee
1903 *Phi, Nashville (school discontinued 1910)*
1903 *Rho, Colorado (1912)*
1903 *Tau, Sewanee (school discontinued 1909)*
1903 *Upsilon, Oregon (1964)*
1904 *Alpha Delta, McGill (1965)*
1904 Alpha Gamma, Georgia
1905 *Alpha Epsilon, Toronto (1961)*
1905 *Alpha Zeta, George Washington (1941)*
1906 Alpha Eta, Yale (1938-1943)
1906 *Alpha Iota, Michigan (1961)*
1906 Alpha Kappa, Virginia Medical
1906 Alpha Theta, Texas
1908 *Alpha Lambda, South Carolina Medical (1969)*
1909 *Alpha Mu, St. Louis (1969)*

† This chapter narrative is repeated from the 19th edition; no current information was provided.

†† This chapter roll is repeated from the 19th edition; no current information was provided.

1909 *Alpha Nu, Louisville* (1976)
1909 *Alpha Xi, Case Western Reserve* (1957)
1911 *Alpha Omicron, Kansas City Medical*
      (school discontinued 1912)
1911 *Alpha Pi, Pitt* (1912)
1912 *Alpha Rho, Harvard Medical* (1951)
1913 *Alpha Sigma, USC* (1955)
1914 *Alpha Tau, Emory* (1963)
1917 *Alpha Phi, Missouri* (1935)
1917 *Alpha Upsilon, Johns Hopkins* (1948)
1920 *Alpha Chi, Oklahoma* (1942)
1921 Alpha Psi, Iowa
1921 *Beta Gamma, Nebraska* (1955)
1922 *Beta Delta, Virginia* (1939)
1922 *Beta Epsilon, Boston* (1966)
1922 *Beta Zeta, Wisconsin, Madison* (1933)
1923 *Beta Eta, Maryland* (1928)
1923 *Beta Iota, North Carolina* (1964)
1923 *Beta Theta, Washington (MO)* (1935)
1924 *Beta Kappa, Western Ontario* (1974)
1925 *Beta Lambda, Columbia* (1948)
1928 *Beta Mu, Georgetown* (1932)
1931 *Beta Nu, Duke* (1955)
1932 Beta Omicron, Temple
1932 *Beta Xi, Stanford* (1962)
1934 *Beta Pi, L.S.U.* (1954)
1937 *Beta Rho, New York Medical* (1969)
1947 Beta Sigma, Mississippi
1947 *Beta Tau, Washington* (1963)
1948 *Beta Phi, Hahnemann Medical* (1964)
1948 *Beta Upsilon, Baylor* (1970)
1953 Beta Chi, Miami (FL)

Alpha Psi†

(VETERINARY MEDICINE)

ACTIVE PIN

ALPHA PSI was founded at the College of Veterinary Medicine, Ohio State University, January 18, 1907, by twenty-two students of that college. The purpose of the organization is "to promote a stronger bond between the veterinary colleges of the United States and Canada, to create a better feeling among the students of all veterinary colleges, and to infuse a deeper interest in the study of veterinary science."

The Delta and Gamma chapters became inactive when the institutions supporting them were closed.

Government Government during the interim of annual conventions is by the National Council.

Traditions and Insignia The badge is diamond-shaped, with the letters AΨ arranged along the

shorter diagonal. Below is a horseshoe and above is a star. Colors are dark blue and bright gold. The flower is the red carnation.

Publications Publication of the *Alpha Psi Quarterly* was begun in 1915. The *Directory* was first issued in 1912, again in 1942, after which revisions were prepared which included a pledge manual.

Headquarters Michigan State University, East Lansing, Michigan 48823.

Membership Active chapters 8. Inactive chapters 5. Total number of initiates 7,231. Chapter roll:††

1907 Alpha, Ohio State
1907 Beta, Cornell
1907 *Gamma, Chicago Veterinary* (1920)
1908 *Delta, Kansas City Veterinary* (1918)
1908 Epsilon, Penn
1910 *Zeta, Colorado State*
1912 *Eta, Kansas State*
1912 Theta, Auburn
1915 *Iota, Michigan State*
1915 Kappa, Washington State
1949 Lambda, Georgia
1954 Mu, Oklahoma State
1956 Nu, Minnesota

Alpha Tau Alpha†

(AGRICULTURAL EDUCATION)

ALPHA TAU ALPHA was founded at the University of Illinois in 1921 by Aretas W. Nolan and a group of his students in agricultural education. The fraternity aims "to develop a true professional spirit in the teaching of agriculture. to help prepare teachers of agriculture who shall be rural leaders in their communities, and to foster a fraternal spirit among prospective teachers of vocational agriculture."

Government The conclave is held each year to transact the business of the fraternity and is customarily held in Kansas City, Missouri, immediately preceding the national convention of Future Farmers of America. One delegate from each chapter makes up the official conclave body. A written constitution serves as the guide to all chapters. Officers are elected from advisers who are members of the teacher training staffs at the colleges or universities in which local chapters are active.

Traditions and Insignia The emblem is in the shape of an equilateral triangle, each side representing the physical, the intellectual, the spiritual. The three sides are tied together by the ATA bond of friendship. The lamp of knowledge, open book, and two sheaves of wheat complete the emblem.

Headquarters Agricultural Education, 435

---

† This chapter narrative is repeated from the 19th edition; no current information was provided.

†† This chapter roll is repeated from the 19th edition; no current information was provided.

GCB. University of Missouri, Columbia, Missouri 65201.

Membership   Active chapters 32.   Inactive chapters 9.   Total number of initiates 13,767. Chapter roll:††

1921   Alpha, Illinois
1925   Beta, Nebraska (1930-1956)
1925   Gamma, California (1926-1951)
1928   *Delta, George Peabody* (1937)
1929   *Epsilon, Florida* (1963)
1930   *Lambda, Arkansas State Teachers* (1940)
1930   Zeta, Colorado State
1931   Eta, Penn State
1931   Theta, Wyoming (1933-1949)
1932   Iota, L.S.U.
1932   Kappa, Clemson Agricultural
1934   Mu, Texas A & I
1934   Nu, Missouri
1935   Xi, Illinois State
1938   *Omicron, Mississippi State* (1956)
1940   *Pi, New Mexico A & M* (1972)
1940   *Rho, College of A & M Mayaguez, Puerto Rico* (1941-1950) (1954)
1949   Sigma, Utah State
1950   *Delta, Tennessee Tech* (1957)
1950   Tau, West Virginia
1951   Phi, Arizona
1951   Upsilon, Washington State
1954   Chi, Arkansas
1955   Psi, Southern
1957   *Eta-A, Philippines* (1966)
1962   Omega, Purdue
1963   Alpha Alpha, Minnesota
1963   Alpha Beta, Oklahoma
1964   Alpha Gamma, Arkansas State
1965   Alpha Delta, Kansas
1966   Alpha Epsilon, Arkansas, Pine Bluff
1968   Alpha Zeta, Rutgers
1969   Alpha Eta, Prairie View
1969   Alpha Theta, Florida A & M
1971   Alpha Iota, Maryland, Eastern Shore
1971   Alpha Kappa, Cal State, Fresno
1972   Alpha Lambda, V.P.I.
1973   Alpha Mu, Wisconsin, River Falls
1973   Alpha Nu, Alcorn A & M
1973   Alpha Xi, North Carolina
1975   Alpha Omicron, South Dakota State

†† This chapter roll is repeated from the 19th edition; no current information was provided.

Alpha Zeta

(AGRICULTURE)

ACTIVE PIN

ALPHA ZETA was established November 4, 1897, at the College of Agriculture of The Ohio State University by Charles W. Burkett and John F. Cunningham. It grew from the realization of a need for fellowship among students dedicated to the cause of agriculture.

Today, it is a fraternity of men and women whose educational objectives and/or careers fall within a broadly defined agriculture. Its purpose is to foster high standards of scholarship, leadership, character, and fellowship. It also strives to promote the profession and serve the students and agricultural divisions on its university campuses.

The fraternity's active chapters are encouraged to develop a character that will, within those broad objectives, best serve their individual campuses. As a result, there is substantial diversity within the fraternity. Three chapters own and operate chapter houses. That diversity has bred vitality and responsiveness to change, on its campuses and within the profession.

Students selected for membership must be enrolled in agriculture or one of its related fields of study, have completed at least one year of classes, rank in the upper two-fifths of their class, and evidence good character and qualities of leadership.

Since 1946, the fraternity and many of its chapter have given scholarships to superior agricultural students. Nationally that program is now sponsored by the Alpha Zeta Foundation, Inc., a not-for-profit charitable organization. Chapters nominate candidates for scholarships annually. Alpha Zeta alumni provide a majority of the foundation's resources.

Government   Student members represent their chapters in biennial conclaves which establish general policies, elect the High Council, and transact other fraternity business. The seven-member High Council is the executive body of the fraternity and includes one student representative. It employs a staff responsible for day-to-day operation of the national office, liaison with student and alumni chapters, and publication of the *AZ News*.

Insignia   The badge is a monogram of the A over the Z. The key is gold and black, shaped as two overlapping circles. Superimposed on the black interior is the A over Z monogram. Colors are mode (old gold) and sky blue.

Publications   The *AZ News* is the fraternity's principal publication. This quarterly newsletter is mailed to all members, student, and alumni, for whom addresses are known.

Headquarters P.O. Box 595, Lafayette, Indiana 47902.

Membership   Chapter roll:††

1897	Townshend, Ohio State
1898	Morrill, Penn State
1900	Morrow, Illinois
1901	Cornell, Cornell
1902	Kedzie, Michigan State
1903	Granite, New Hampshire
1904	Nebraska, Nebraska
1904	North Carolina, North Carolina State
1905	Green Mountain, Vermont
1905	*La Grange, Minnesota* (1973)
1905	Wilson, Iowa State
1906	Babcock, Wisconsin, Madison
1906	Centennial, Colorado State
1906	Maine, Maine
1907	Elliott, Washington State
1907	Missouri, Missouri
1908	*California Alpha, California* (1957)
1908	Purdue, Purdue
1909	Dacotah, North Dakota State
1909	Kansas, Kansas State
1912	Morgan, Tennessee
1912	Scovell, Kentucky
1914	Georgia, Georgia
1916	Louisiana, L.S.U.
1916	Oklahoma, Oklahoma State
1917	Arkansas, Arkansas
1918	Oregon, Oregon State
1920	Idaho, Idaho
1920	Maryland, Maryland
1922	Cook, Rutgers
1922	Florida, Florida
1922	Montana, Montana State
1922	West Virginia, West Virginia
1924	South Dakota, South Dakota State
1927	Arizona, Arizona
1927	New Mexico, New Mexico State
1928	Mississippi, Mississippi State
1930	South Carolina, Clemson
1930	Utah, Utah State
1932	Virginia, V.P.I.
1933	Wyoming, Wyoming
1936	Rhode Island, Rhode Island
1937	*California Beta, UCLA* (1961)
1940	California Gamma, Cal, Davis
1941	Alabama, Auburn
1949	Delaware, Delaware
1951	Texas Alpha, Texas A & M
1951	Texas Beta, Texas Tech
1952	Connecticut, Connecticut
1956	Massachusetts, Massachusetts
1959	California Delta, Cal Poly
1959	Puerto Rico, Puerto Rico, Mayaguez

1960	Illinois Beta, Southern Illinois
1962	California Epsilon, Cal State, Fresno
1963	Nevada, Nevada
1964	Arizona Beta, Arizona State
1964	Louisiana Beta, Southwestern Louisiana
1966	California Zeta, Cal Poly
1966	Illinois Gamma, Western Illinois
1970	Utah Beta, Brigham Young
1971	Wisconsin Beta, Wisconsin, Platteville
1972	Texas Gamma, Tarleton
1972	Wis. Gamma, Wisconsin, River Falls
1974	Illinois Delta, Illinois State
1974	Louisiana Gamma, Louisiana Tech
1976	Tennessee Beta, Tennessee, Martin
1977	Texas Delta, West Texas

Alpha Zeta Omega†

(PHARMACY)

ALPHA ZETA OMEGA, a pharmaceutical fraternity, was founded at the Philadelphia College of Pharmacy in December, 1919. The fraternity was founded upon the principles of intimate association with one another and the practice of the virtues of mutual trust, sympathy, faithfulness, and unselfishness. It was first known as the "Dead Men's Club."

Government   The Supreme National Officers are elected by the fraternity at large each summer at the annual convention. The Supreme Chapter consists of the directorum, the subdirectorum, the signare, the excheque, the bellarum, the *Azoan* editor, supreme historian, supreme deputy, supreme chaplain, supreme board of directors, supreme insurance signare, and supreme justices.

Two regional meetings are also held annually. The fraternity is divided into six districts.

Publications   The official organ, *The Azoan*, formerly called the *Hazy-O*, is published three times a year. One issue is devoted to items of professional interest and is rather scientific in nature.

Funds and Philanthropies   The Supreme Cultural Foundation was established in July, 1939. The year 1958 saw completion of the fraternity's drive to raise $100,000 for an AZΩ library at the Hebrew University College of Pharmacy in Israel. THe Alpha Zeta Omega Achievement Medal is presented annually "for meritorious contribution to pharmacy and its allied sciences."

Headquarters   80 Nottingham Court, Montvale, NJ 07645.

Membership   Active chapters 43. Total number of initiates 8,250. Chapter roll:

---

†† This chapter roll is repeated from the 19th edition; no current information was provided.

† This chapter narrative is repeated from the 19th edition; no current information was provided.

1921   Beta, Philadelphia Pharmacy
1922   Gamma, Temple
1923   Delta, McGill
1923   Epsilon, Rutgers
1923   Kappa, Maryland
1923   Lambda, Kentucky
1923   Zeta, Columbia (NY)
1924   Eta, Cincinnati
1926   Philadelphia Alumni
1926   Theta, Western Reserve
1928   Iota, Arnold & Marie Schwartz College
1928   Mu, Pitt
1929   Nu, Connecticut
1929   Xi, Fordham
1930   Omicron, Detroit Tech
1930   Pi, George Washington
1931   Pittsburgh Alumni
1942   Rho, St. Louis Pharmacy
1949   Omega Chi, Virginia Medical
1950   Connecticut Alumni
1950   Sigma, Toledo
1950   Tau, Hampton Inst.
1951   New York City Alumni
1951   Phi, Wayne State (MI)
1951   Upsilon, Northeastern
1951   Virginia Alumni
1952   Theta Alpha, Ohio Northern
1953   Miami (FL) Alumni
1955   Detroit Alumni
1957   Boston Alumni
1957   Louisville Alumni
1957   Maryland Alumni
1958   California Alumni
1960   Omega, Hebrew Pharmacy
1960   Western MA Alumni
1961   St. Louis Alumni
1963   Milwaukee Alumni
1963   Phoenix Alumni
1963   Southern CN Alumni
1965   Chicago Alumni
1966   Long Island Alumni
1968   Kansas City Alumni
1969   Epsilon Chi, Missouri
1971   Zeta Phi, Iowa
1974   Omicron Alpha, Ferris
1975   Eta Upsilon, St. John's (NY)
1975   West Florida Alumni
1979   Toledo Alumni
1985   Theta Beta, Ohio State

Beta Alpha Psi†

(ACCOUNTING)

ACTIVE PIN

BETA ALPHA PSI, a professional accounting fraternity, was organized February 12, 1919, at the University of Illinois. Its purpose, as expressed in its constitution, is "to instill in its members desire for self-improvement; to foster high moral and ethical standards in its members; to encourage and give recognition to scholastic and professional excellence; to cultivate a sense of responsibility and service in its members; to promote the collegiate study of accountancy; and to provide opportunities for association among its members and practicing accountants."

Government   The governing body is the National Council, consisting of the national president, two most recent past national presidents, national secretary-treasurer, and three councilors, all of whom are ranking faculty members at schools where chapters are located.

Membership   Active chapters 107. Inactive chapters 4. Total number of initiates 70,000. Chapter roll:††

1919   Alpha, Illinois
1921   Beta, Oregon
1921   Delta, Washington
1921   Gamma, Northwestern
1923   Epsilon, Oregon State
1923   *Eta, Boston U.* (1927)
1923   Zeta, North Dakota
1924   Theta, Texas
1925   Iota, USC
1925   Lambda, California
1926   Mu, N.Y.U.
1927   *Kappa, William and Mary* (1939)
1927   Nu, Colorado
1929   Omicron, Ohio State
1929   Xi, Syracuse
1930   Pi, Case Western Reserve
1931   Rho, Minnesota
1932   Sigma, Wisconsin, Madison
1936   Tau, Maryland
1938   Upsilon, Florida
1939   Chi, Oklahoma State
1939   Phi, L.S.U.
1942   Omega, Miami (OH)
1942   Psi, Marquette

† This chapter narrative is repeated from the 19th edition; no current information was provided.
†† This chapter roll is repeated from the 19th edition; no current information was provided.

1948 Alpha Beta, Alabama
1949 Alpha Delta, Penn
1949 Alpha Gamma, CCNY
1950 Alpha Epsilon, Southern Methodist
1950 Alpha Zeta, Denver
1951 Alpha Eta, Michigan
1951 Alpha Iota, Arkansas
1951 Alpha Lambda, Tennessee
1951 Alpha Theta, Mississippi
1952 Alpha Kappa, Ohio
1952 Alpha Mu, Kentucky
1953 Alpha Nu, Creighton
1954 Alpha Omicron, Michigan State
1954 Alpha Pi, Iowa
1954 Alpha Xi, Detroit
1955 Alpha Rho, Baylor
1955 Alpha Sigma, Cincinnati
1955 *Alpha Tau, Pitt* (1967)
1955 Alpha Upsilon, Bowling Green
1956 Alpha Chi, Louisiana Tech
1956 Alpha Phi, Temple
1957 Alpha Omega, Fordham
1957 Alpha Psi, West Virginia
1957 Beta Alpha, Indiana
1958 Beta Gamma, DePaul
1959 Beta Delta, Texas Tech
1959 Beta Epsilon, Lehigh
1959 Beta Zeta, Loyola
1960 Beta Eta, San Diego State
1960 Beta Iota, Loyola
1960 Beta Kappa, Mississippi State
1960 Beta Theta, Penn State
1961 Beta Lambda, Cal State, Los Angeles
1961 Beta Mu, Georgia State
1961 Beta Nu, Tulane
1961 Beta Xi, Miami (FL)
1962 Beta Omicron, Arizona
1962 Beta Pi, North Texas
1962 Beta Rho, Florida State
1962 Beta Sigma, Notre Dame
1963 Beta Tau, Arizona State
1963 Beta Upsilon, Georgia
1964 Beta Chi, San Francisco State
1964 Beta Phi, Cal State, Sacramento
1964 Beta Psi, Kent
1965 Beta Omega, Texas Christian
1965 Gamma Alpha, Brigham Young
1965 Gamma Beta, South Carolina
1966 Gamma Delta, Houston
1966 Gamma Epsilon, Toledo
1966 Gamma Zeta, Southern Illinois
1967 Drake University
1967 Gamma Eta, Akron
1967 *Gamma Iota, UCLA* (1971)
1967 Gamma Kappa, Omaha
1967 Gamma Lambda, V.P.I.
1967 Gamma Theta, Missouri
1968 Northeastern
1969 Cal State, Fresno
1969 San Jose
1971 Colorado State
1971 Memphis State

1971 New Orleans
1971 Northern Illinois
1971 Rhode Island
1971 Texas, Arlington
1971 Western Michigan
1972 Cal State, Fullerton
1972 Cal State, Long Beach
1972 Missouri, St. Louis
1972 South Florida
1972 Wyoming
1973 Cal State, Chico
1973 Seattle
1973 Washington State
1974 Hawaii
1974 Montana
1974 New Mexico State
1974 Texas A & M
1975 Massachusetts
1975 Texas Southern
1975 Virginia
1976 Drexel
1976 Eastern Washington
1976 Hofstra
1976 Nebraska
1976 Pacific Lutheran

Delta Kappa Phi†

(TEXTILES)

ACTIVE PIN

DELTA KAPPA PHI was founded at the Philadelphia Textile Institute, Philadelphia, Pennsylvania, October, 1899, by a group of eight students. Membership is confined to students in textile schools or to colleges with textile departments. The founders were John Paul Jones, Charles E. Washburn, Harris A. Soloman, Leon H. Buck, Raymond J. Doyle, Yasujiro Yamaji, William J. Montgomery, and George A. Kerr. The plan at first was to join a national fraternity, but since their interests were especially in textiles, they decided to form their own fraternIty. This was the first textile fraternity in America and became a national in 1902 when the second chapter, Beta, was formed at Lowell Textile Institute, Massachusetts. The fraternity was incorporated at Philadelphia in 1905.

Government Government is vested in the Supreme Council, which consists of the supreme consul, supreme pro-consul, supreme annotator, and supreme custodian. A convention is held annually in a city where a chapter is located.

Traditions and Insignia The purpose of the fra-

† This chapter narrative is repeated from the 19th edition; no current information was provided.

ternity varies somewhat in the different localities. All have an interest in textiles. The three chapters in the North are social in nature. The chapter at Raleigh is professional, and the chapter at Atlanta requires very high scholarship as an entrance requirement.

The pin is diamond in shape. The center is of black enamel, bearing in gold the letters ΔKΦ perpendicularly on its longer axis. In the left portion of the shorter axis is a shield. Said personifications are surrounded by a plain gold binding or border of precious stones. The colors of the fraternity are royal purple and white.

Publications A bulletin is issued to the membership with items of interest in regards to pledging and social activities of the various chapters and with reports from the Supreme Council. A report on the annual convention is also issued to all members.

Headquarters Philadelphia College of Textiles and Sciences, Philadelphia, Pennsylvania 19144.

Membership Active chapters 5. Inactive chapters 1. Graduate/Alumni chapters 4. Total number of initiates 3,086. Chapter roll:††

1899 Alpha, Philadelphia Textiles
1902 Beta, Lowell Tech
1917 Delta, New Bedford Institute of Textiles and Technology
1917 *Gamma, Rhode Island Design*
1948 Kappa, North Carolina State
1949 Theta, Georgia Tech

Delta Pi Epsilon[†]

(BUSINESS EDUCATION)

ACTIVE PIN

DELTA PI EPSILON, graduate fraternity in business education, was founded at New York University in 1936 under the sponsorship of Paul S. Lomax, chairman of the Department of Business Education. It was incorporated under the laws of the State of New York on December 3, 1937.

The purposes of the fraternity are: to encourage research in the field of business education; to acquaint the profession with research achievement; to develop leadership in business education; to render service to members and the profession; to further the welfare of those in business education; to further the professional influence of Delta Pi Epsilon.

Candidates for membership must be graduates of an accredited college or university and have com-

pleted at least eight points of semester hours of graduate work with an average of at least B in the institution where the chapter has been formed. Each candidate must have declared his major interest to be in business education.

The classes of membership are: active, honorary, and life.

A chapter may be organized at any institution of higher learning which meets the standards set by various scholastic boards that are acceptable to the national council and which offers graduate work in the field of business education. The institution must offer a year-round program in business education on the graduate level and have at least two full-time instructors in business education.

Government The legislative body of Delta Pi Epsilon is the national council, which is composed of the national officers and a delegate from each chapter. A regular biennial meeting of the council is held.

The national officers elected by the national council form the National Executive Board. This board functions continually during the two-year interval between council meetings. The national officers are: president, vice-president, secretary, treasurer, historian, and past president. An executive secretary is appointed by the board.

Traditions Each chapter of the fraternity conducts a program of professional activity designed to develop among its members and to contribute to the improvement of business education. Some chapters conduct research projects; some sponsor conferences, clinics, and seminars; and some engage in other actIvIties that are designed to contribute to the professional growth and development of members and of business educators in general.

Publications Continuing publications include: *Business Education Index*, published yearly since 1940; *Delta Pi Epsilon Journal*, a quarterly devoted to research results; and a *Newsletter*. Special items published include: *Research in Business Education, Implications of Research for Teaching Typewriting,* and *Index to Doctoral Dissertations in Business Education 1900–1975*. The publications are made available at cost to libraries and persons interested in business education.

Headquarters Delta Pi Epsilon National Office, Gustavus Adolphus College, St. Peter, Minnesota 56082.

Membership Active chapters 75. Total number of initiates 19,009. Chapter roll:††

1936 Alpha, N.Y.U.
1938 Beta, Oklahoma State
1940 Gamma, Pitt
1942 Delta, Cincinnati
1942 Epsilon, Boston U.
1942 Eta, Denver
1942 Zeta, North Carolina, Greensboro

---

† This chapter narrative is repeated from the 19th edition; no current information was provided.

†† This chapter roll is repeated from the 19th edition; no current information was provided.

1945   Iota, Syracuse
1945   Theta, Indiana
1946   Kappa, Michigan
1946   Lambda, Northwestern
1946   Mu, Tennessee
1947   Omicron, Iowa
1947   Xi, Florida
1948   Pi, Ball State
1948   Rho, Ohio State
1949   Sigma, Oklahoma
1950   Tau, Columbia
1951   Chi, Penn State
1951   Phi, Minnesota
1951   Upsilon, Mississippi
1953   Omega, George Peabody
1953   Psi, USC
1954   Alpha Alpha, Northern Colorado
1955   Alpha Beta, Illinois
1956   Alpha Gamma, Houston
1957   Alpha Delta, Emporia
1957   Alpha Epsilon, North Texas
1958   Alpha Eta, Wisconsin
1958   Alpha Zeta, Temple
1959   Alpha Iota, Colorado
1959   Alpha Theta, Texas
1960   Alpha Kappa, San Francisco State
1961   Alpha Lambda, Michigan State
1963   Alpha Mu, SUNY, Albany
1963   Alpha Nu, North Dakota
1964   Alpha Omicron, UCLA
1964   Alpha Xi, Hunter
1965   Alpha Pi, Wayne State
1966   Alpha Rho, Cal State, Fresno
1966   Alpha Sigma, Arizona State
1966   Alpha Tau, Northern Iowa
1966   Alpha Upsilon, Nebraska
1967   Alpha Phi, Northern Illinois
1968   Alpha Chi, Rider
1969   Alpha Omega, Brigham Young
1969   Alpha Psi, Mankato
1969   Beta Alpha, Indiana (PA)
1969   Beta Beta, Southern Illinois
1969   Beta Delta, Georgia
1969   Beta Epsilon, San Jose
1969   Beta Gamma, V.P.I.
1971   Beta Eta, Bowling Green
1971   Beta Iota, Illinois State
1971   Beta Kappa, Portland State
1971   Beta Theta, Wisconsin, Madison
1971   Beta Zeta, Indiana State
1972   Beta Lambda, Shippensburg
1972   Beta Mu, Central Connecticut
1972   Beta Nu, Utah State
1972   Beta Omicron, Southern Illinois
1972   Beta Pi, Cal State
1972   Beta Xi, Memphis State
1973   Beta Rho, Western Michigan
1973   Beta Sigma, Wisconsin, Eau Claire
1973   Beta Tau, Georgia State
1974   Beta Chi, Western Illinois
1974   Beta Phi, Montclair
1974   Beta Upsilon, Kansas State, Pittsburg

1975   Beta Omega, Louisiana Tech
1975   Beta Psi, Eastern Illinois
1975   Gamma Alpha, Eastern Michigan
1976   Gamma Beta, Trenton
1976   Gamma Gamma, Virginia Commonwealth

Delta Sigma Delta[†]

(DENTISTRY)

ACTIVE PIN

PLEDGE PIN

DELTA SIGMA DELTA, the first fraternity to limit its membership to dental students and practitioners, was founded at the University of Michigan on November 15, 1882. Its charter members were Louis M. James, Charles W. Howard, Louis J. Mitchell, Clarence J. Hand, Ezra L. Kern, L. L. Davis, Frank Cassidy, D. D. McGill, William Cleland, and C. P. Weinrich.

The objective is to keep high the standards of dentistry by inculcating in the minds of dental students and practitioners a spirit of fraternal cooperation toward scientific, ethical, and professional progress.

Government   The supreme chapter, composed of graduate members, meets annually and is the governing body. The supreme council of nine graduate members acts as an ad interim committee between annual meetings.

There are 44 graduate chapters that hold regular meetings in the principal cities in America. There are four chapters in Europe, four in Australia, and one in New Zealand. Graduate chapters operate both as local clubs and as state organizations. They have jurisdictional authority over graduate members in their respective districts and may initiate dental practitioners. Undergraduate chapters are divided into seven conclave districts, each district holding one meeting each year.

Publication   The fraternity has published *Desmos*, a quarterly magazine, without interruption since October, 1894.

Funds   Delta Sigma Delta operates an educational foundation for the purpose of granting loans for dental research and student aid.

Tradition and Insignia   The badge is a monogram, the Σ being superimposed over the two crossed Δ's. A crown set with 1/8 carat diamond is added for graduate members. The colors are turquoise blue and garnet.

Headquarters   2317 Westwood Avenue, P.O. Box 6272, Richmond, Virginia 23230.

Membership   Total deceased membership 8,521.

† This chapter narrative is repeated from the 19th edition; no current information was provided.

Active chapters 38. Supreme chapter initiates
1,557. Houses owned 13. Graduate/Alumni chapters 51. Total number of initiates 42,510. Chapter roll:

1882 Alpha, Michigan
1885 Beta, Loyola, Chicago
1891 Epsilon, Penn
1891 *Gamma, Harvard* (1944)
1891 Zeta, California
1892 Eta, Northwestern
1894 Theta, Minnesota
1895 *Iota, Detroit Medical* (1908)
1896 *Kappa, Vanderbilt* (1926)
1897 Lambda, Western Reserve
1897 *Mu, Tufts*
1898 Nu, Kansas City
1900 Xi, Indiana
1901 *Omicron, St. Louis*
1901 *Pi, Buffalo*
1901 Rho, Illinois
1903 Sigma, Pitt
1904 *Tau, Ohio Dental* (1932)
1904 Upsilon, Washington (MO)
1906 Chi, USC
1906 *Phi, Colorado Dental* (1932)
1907 Psi, Oregon
1910 Omega, Creighton
1912 Alpha Alpha, Georgetown
1913 *Beta Beta, Nebraska*
1914 Epsilon Epsilon, Louisville
1914 Gamma Gamma, Iowa
1917 Zeta Zeta, Loyola, New Orleans
1918 Eta Eta, Marquette
1921 Kappa Kappa, Tennessee
1921 Theta Theta, Emory
1922 Lambda Lambda, Baylor
1926 Mu Mu, Ohio State
1926 Nu Nu, San Francisco P & S
1931 Omicron Omicron, Virginia Medical
1931 *Xi Xi, Maryland* (1938)
1939 Pi Pi, Detroit
1945 Rho Rho, Temple
1947 Sigma Sigma, Washington
1947 Tau Tau, Texas
1951 Upsilon Upsilon, North Carolina
1952 Phi Phi, Alabama
1961 Chi Chi, West Virginia
1963 *Psi Psi, Puerto Rico*
1969 Omega Omega, UCLA
1972 Alpha Alpha, South Carolina
1973 Alpha Chi, Texas
1975 Alpha Gamma, Florida
1976 Alpha Delta, Colorado

Graduate Chapters:
 Arizona
 Arkansas
 Badger
 Boston
 Buffalo
 Chicago

Cincinnati-Dayton
Cleveland
Columbus
Connecticut
Denver
Des Moines
Detroit
European Continental
Florida
Georgia
Greater Washington
Hawaii
Holland
Houston
Indiana
Kansas City
London
Los Angeles
Nebraska
New Orleans
New South Wales, Australia
New York
New Zealand
North Carolina
Oregon
Paris
Philadelphia
Pittsburgh
Rochester
Salt Lake City
San Francisco
Scandinavian
Seattle
South Australian
Southern Colorado
Spokane
St. Louis
The Queensland (Australia)
Twin City
Victorian (Australia)
Virginia
West Virginia
Worcester

Delta Sigma Theta†

(PHARMACY)

DELTA SIGMA THETA is the outgrowth of the Mortar and Pestle Club, established at the Brooklyn College of Pharmacy in the fall of 1914 by a group of six men of whom A. Bertram Lemon was the leader. It began its organization on December 11, 1915, and one year later was incorporated in the state of New York as Alpha Chapter of Delta Sigma Theta.

It is an international fraternity of the healing arts which embraces pharmacy, medicine, and den-

† This chapter narrative is repeated from the 19th edition; no current information was provided.

tistry. It espouses such fundamental ideals as the furthering of the brotherhood and equality of man, religious liberty and tolerance, and the elevation of the pharmaceutical and allied professions.

Government   The organization is directed by the Supreme Royal Council.

Headquarters   39 Broadway, New York, New York.

Membership   Active chapters 14. Inactive chapters 3. Chapter roll:††

1917	Alpha, Brooklyn College of Pharmacy
1917	Beta, Columbia Dental
1917	Gamma, New York Dentistry
1923	Delta, Columbia Pharmacy
1924	Epsilon, Rutgers Pharmacy
1924	Eta, New York Flower Hospital Medical
1924	*Iota, Temple Dentistry*
1924	Kappa, Long Island Medical
1924	*Lambda, Massachusetts College of Pharmacy*
1924	Theta, Tufts Medical
1924	Zeta, Pennsylvania Dentistry
1927	Mu, St. John's Pharmacy
1927	Rho, Rome Medical
1927	Sigma, American, Beirut
1927	Tau, Edinburgh
1952	Chi, St. Louis
1953	Omega, New England Pharmacy (now Northeastern U.)
1958	Phi, Hampden College (MA)

Gamma Eta Gamma†

(LAW)

ACTIVE PIN   PLEDGE PIN

GAMMA ETA GAMMA was founded at the law school of the University of Maine on February 25, 1901, by Charles Vey Holman, Charles Hickson Reid, Jr., and Harold Dudley Greeley. These men wrote in their own handwriting into the preamble of our Constitution: "We the undersigned, students of the Law School of the University of Maine, with a view of establishing in this and other schools of law, as well as in the general practice of the profession, an elevated standard of personal deportment, a high code of professional ethics and a broad and catholic development of mental culture and moral character, do associate ourselves in the lasting

†† This chapter roll is repeated from the 19th edition; no current information was provided.

† This chapter narrative is repeated from the 19th edition; no current information was provided.

bonds of a fraternal union under the name of Gamma Eta Gamma."

Undergraduate chapters are limited to law schools on the approved list of the American Bar Association.

Government   The convention, called the "Witan," was held annually for sixteen years, the first having assembled on May 29, 1901, but it is now held biennially. During the interim between sessions of the Witan the fraternity is governed by a council of twelve members called the "Curia," composed of the four elective executive officers and the eight province presidents appointed by them. Eight of the twelve members of the Curia must be alumni. Province conferences are held in off-Witan years to discuss chapter problems. They have no legislative powers.

Traditions and Insignia   Founders' Day is generally celebrated on February 25 by the chapters, although some observe the original tradition by holding the Prandium Cancellari on June 7, the date on which the fraternity's first banquet was tendered in 1901 to the sixteen members of the organization by Holman.

At the Founders' Day dinner of 1962, in Baltimore, Harold Dudley Greeley, the sole surviving founder, addressed the attending members from Washington and Baltimore metropolitan areas, as well as the members of the active chapters from Catholic University, Georgetown, and George Washington Universities in Washington. and from the host chapter, University of Maryland Law School at Baltimore, and visiting brothers from New Orleans, New York, and Detroit.

The badge is a shield displaying a lamp, a star, and a fasces above the motto and a triangle encloses the letter "Π." On two sides of the triangle are the letters "Γ" "Γ." Beneath the triangle is a balance. The official badge contains twenty pearls surrounding the shield. The high chancellor's badge, presented to each national president upon his retirement from office, has a diamond border. The pledge button is circular, the letters "Γ" "Η" "Γ" appearing in a circle on a red field, imposed on a triangle, with the rest of the button black. The fasces key. for alumni graduated with a degree in law. is a gold fasces with the letters "Γ" "Η" "Γ" embedded on the face of the key. The fraternity colors are red and black.

Publications   The quarterly magazine is called *The Rescript:* it was started as an annual in 1912 and in 1920 was put on a quarterly basis. Separate editions of the directory. used by many alumni for the reference of legal business, were published in 1922, 1924, 1926, 1928, and 1933. Songbooks were published in 1909, 1915, and 1924. *The Pledge Institutes*, a pledge manual of fifty-six pages containing brief histories of Gamma Eta Gamma and the fraternity movement, a chapter on how to study law effectively, a chapter on etiquette, and general fraternity information, was published in 1932.

Headquarters 12500 Swirl Lane, Bowie, Maryland 20715.

Membership Active chapters 24. Inactive chapters 9. Total number of initiates 7,364. Chapter roll:††

1901	*Alpha, Maine*
1902	Beta, Boston
1904	Gamma, Albany Law
1908	*Delta, Syracuse* (1932)
1909	*Epsilon, Cornell* (1918)
1911	Eta, Indiana
1911	*Zeta, Michigan* (1929)
1912	Theta, Creighton
1914	Iota, Georgetown
1915	*Kappa, Oregon* (1917)
1919	Lambda, Northwestern
1919	Mu, Detroit
1920	Nu, Chicago
1920	Omicron, Maryland
1920	Xi, Fordham
1921	*Pi, Illinois* (1931)
1922	Rho, Ohio State
1922	Sigma, USC
1922	*Tau, Vanderbilt* (1928)
1923	Phi, Iowa
1923	Upsilon, Wisconsin, Madison
1924	Chi, Minnesota
1924	Psi, California
1925	*Omega, Washington (MO)* (1929)
1927	Beta Gamma, Wake Forest
1929	Beta Delta, Duke
1930	Beta Epsilon, L.S.U.
1930	*Beta Zeta, Western Reserve* (1932)
1931	Beta Eta, George Washington
1931	Beta Kappa, Catholic
1931	Beta Theta, Santa Clara
1934	Beta Mu, DePaul
1950	Beta Nu, Virginia

Kappa Alpha Mu†

(PHOTOJOURNALISM)

ACTIVE PIN

KAPPA ALPHA MU was founded on the University of Missouri campus by Cliff Edom, director of photojournalism in the School of Journalism, in 1944 for the purpose of raising standards in photojournalism. To be eligible for membership a student must have higher than average grades in that subject and at least average grades in all other subjects. The professional fraternity became na-

tional with the installation of Beta Chapter at the University of Oklahoma a year later, and since then has placed chapters in various institutions which offer a curriculum in photojournalism. Its chapters often are responsible for photography shows of both professional and amateur work.

The fraternity, in conjunction with the National Press Photographers Association, and with the assistance of the National Geographic Society and the School of Journalism, University of Missouri, each year sponsors the National College Photo Competition, which selects the College Photographers of the Year.

Membership Active chapters 9. Inactive chapters 16. Chapter roll:††

1944	Alpha, Missouri
1945	*Beta, Oklahoma* (1957)
1946	*Gamma, Syracuse* (1947)
1947	*Alpha Alpha, New Mexico* (1955)
1947	*Chi, Kent* (1954)
1947	*Delta, Everett Junior College (WA)* (1948)
1947	*Epsilon, Stephens College* (1955)
1947	*Eta, Texas Tech*
1947	*Nu, Michigan State* (1961)
1947	*Phi, Bowling Green* (1955)
1947	Pi, Miami (FL) (1948-1955)
1947	*Rho, Nebraska* (1960)
1947	Tau, Houston
1947	Upsilon, Ohio
1947	Zeta, Texas Woman's
1954	*Alpha Delta, Bradley*
1954	Alpha Epsilon, Kansas
1954	*Alpha Eta, Boston U.* (1955)
1954	*Alpha Gamma, Southern Illinois*
1954	*Alpha Zeta, Indiana* (1957)
1956	*Alpha Theta, Florida State* (1958)
1957	Alpha Iota, San Jose
1957	Alpha Kappa, Minnesota
1959	*Alpha Mu, Maryland*
1960	Alpha Nu, Kansas State

Kappa Beta Pi

(LAW)

ACTIVE PIN

PLEDGE PIN

KAPPA BETA PI was founded at Chicago-Kent College of Law, Chicago, Illinois, in the autumn of 1908 by Mrs. Alice Craig Edgerton, Mary A. Sellers, Claire L. Gleason, Phyllis M. Kelley, Nettie Rothblum, Charlotte Doolittle, Mrs. Alice A. Prince, Anna Knabjohann, Sue M. Brown, and Mrs. Kather-

---

† This chapter narrative is repeated from the 19th edition; no current information was provided.

†† This chapter roll is repeated from the 19th edition; no current information was provided.

ine S. Clark. The sorority was incorporated under the laws of Illinois, December 15, 1908. This date is celebrated annually by all chapters as Founders' Day. At the 1973 convention, the name of the organization was changed to Kappa Beta Pi Legal Association International. At a special convention in Columbus, Ohio, in May, 1976, all references were eliminated which might indicate a restriction of membership to women.

The purposes of the organization are to encourage scholarship, to promote a higher professional standard among law students and lawyers, and to strengthen by educational and social enjoyments the ties of friendship between law students and lawyers.

The association maintains a high scholastic requirement for members. Since 1925, admission of new chapters has been rigidly limited to American schools meeting the requirements for membership in the Association of American Law Schools or to schools on the approved list of the American Bar Association and to foreign law schools meeting equivalent requirements. The association is a member of the Professional Fraternity Association.

Government The order transacts most of its business at biennial conventions of chapter delegates. In the intermediate years, province conventions are held, the continent of North America being divided for this purpose into six provinces. The government and management are vested in the Board of Directors with the international president as the chief executive officer.

Traditions and Insignia The badge is a monogram with the K jeweled and superimposed over the letters B and Π, which are embellished with scroll work. The pledge pin is an irregularly shaped shield enameled in turquoise and old gold. On the coat of arms the turquoise blue appears in the upper left-hand field, while the lower right-hand field is white. The open book and scales are gold. The helmet shown "proper," i.e., in the natural color, is a knight's, shown full face with the visor open and is of steel with silver ornaments. The helmet symbolizes the protection of the law, as the helmet protected the head of the warrior, and also inspires the membership to knightly conduct. The flower is the yellow tea rose. The colors are turquoise blue and old gold. The official song, "To Kappa Beta Pi," was written in 1941 by Alice Craig Edgerton.

Publications Publications include, *The Kappa Beta Pi Quarterly*, published four times in the scholastic year. This magazine is listed in the Index of Legal Periodicals of the American Association of Law Libraries. *The Secret Bulletin*, an esoteric issue of the *Quarterly*, is published after each biennial convention. A directory is printed periodically. A comprehensive handbook was published in 1972 and includes the sorority constitution and by-laws, model chapter by-laws, official song rituals, historical sketch, chapter roll, names of founders and of grand deans, and statements concerning the professional Panhellenic Association and Inter-American

Bar Association. A copy of this handbook is presented to each new member at the time of her initiation. *The History of Kappa Beta Pi*, Volume I, written by Mrs. Alice Craig Edgerton, one of the founders and the first dean, was published in 1937, and Volume II by Mrs. Edgerton was published in 1941. Volume III by Miss Elizabeth F. Reed was published in December, 1948. In 1958, as a part of the observance of the fiftieth anniversary of the founding of the order, *The Golden Anniversary History of Kappa Beta Pi 1908-1958, December 15, 1958* was published. It was prepared by Ora Marshino, Nu, Agnes McWhinnie, Epsilon, and Elizabeth F. Reed, Epsilon, grand historian.

Funds and Philanthropies The association maintains a fund for scholarships and loans and also awards honor pins to those members in the upper 10 per cent of each year's graduating classes. Each of the chapters encourages high scholarship in some concrete way. Several of the larger chapters also maintain annual scholarships. Chapters hold monthly meetings in the school year at which time subjects of interest to the legal profession are discussed. Prominent members of the bench and bar are frequently guest speakers on these occasions.

Headquarters 10435 Edgewood Ave., Silver Spring, MD 20901.

Membership Chapter roll:

Year	Chapter
1908	Alpha, Chicago-Kent Law
1915	*Beta, Northwestern*
1916	*Delta, Chicago*
1916	Epsilon, American
1916	*Eta, Texas*
1916	Gamma, DePaul
1916	Zeta, John Marshall Law, Chicago
1917	Iota, California (1945-1946)
1917	Theta, Kansas City
1920	*Kappa, Yale* (1929)
1920	Lambda, Detroit
1920	Mu, Detroit Law (1939-1959)
1920	Nu, George Washington
1921	*Chi, Oregon*
1921	*Omicron, National Law* (school merged with George Washington)
1921	*Phi, Illinois*
1921	*Pi, Washington (MO)*
1921	*Psi, Wisconsin, Madison*
1921	*Rho, Iowa*
1921	*Sigma, Cornell* (1939)
1921	*Tau, Boston*
1921	*Upsilon, Syracuse*
1921	Xi, Michigan
1923	Alpha Alpha, John Marshall Law, Cleveland
1923	*Alpha Beta, Minnesota*
1923	*Omega, USC* (1949)
1924	Alpha Delta, Buffalo
1924	*Alpha Epsilon, Chicago-Kent Law* (school closed 1935)
1924	*Alpha Eta, Hastings Law* (1957)
1924	*Alpha Gamma, Southwestern, Los Angeles*

1924 Alpha Theta, Loyola, Chicago
1924 *Alpha Zeta, Marquette*
1925 *Alpha Iota, St. Louis*
1925 *Alpha Kappa, Creighton*
1925 Alpha Mu, Osgoode Hall Law
1926 Alpha Nu, Ohio State
1926 Alpha Xi, Oklahoma
1927 Alpha Omicron, Paris (France)
1930 *Alpha Pi, Tulane*
1931 *Alpha Rho, Alabama*
1931 Alpha Sigma, Denver
1931 *Alpha Tau, North Dakota*
1932 Alpha Phi, Arizona
1932 *Alpha Upsilon, West Virginia*
1934 Alpha Chi, Columbia (1938-1957)
1940 Alpha Omega, Drake
1940 Alpha Psi, Southern Methodist
1940 Beta Alpha, London (England)
1945 Alpha Lambda, Nebraska (1942-1951)
1946 Beta Beta, Missouri (1950-1951)
1946 *Beta Delta, San Francisco*
1946 Beta Gamma, Columbus Law (DC)
1947 *Beta Zeta, Shanghai (China)*
1948 Beta Eta, South Dakota
1949 Beta Iota, Emory (1952-1953)
1949 Beta Theta, Miami (FL)
1950 *Beta Kappa, Virginia*
1952 Beta Lambda, St. Mary's, San Antonio
1953 Beta Mu, Georgetown
1954 Beta Nu, West Germany
1955 Beta Xi, Houston
1956 Beta Omicron, Toledo
1958 *Beta Pi, Boston Law*
1960 *Beta Rho, Kentucky*
1962 Beta Sigma, Seton Hall
1962 *Beta Tau, Rutgers (1970)*
1963 *Beta Chi, Kentucky (1971)*
1963 *Beta Phi, Fordham (1970)*
1963 *Beta Upsilon, Howard (1974)*
1964 *Beta Psi, Puerto Rico (1973)*
1966 Beta Omega, Ohio Northern
1966 *Gamma Alpha, Colorado (1972)*
1967 *Gamma Beta, Franklin (OH) (1973)*
1967 Gamma Delta, Arkansas, Little Rock
1967 Gamma Gamma, Arkansas
1968 *Gamma Epsilon, New Brunswick (1973)*
1970 Gamma Zeta, Mississippi
1971 Gamma Eta, Texas Tech.
1972 *Gamma Iota, Duquesne (1973)*
1972 *Gamma Theta, Pitt (1973)*
1973 Gamma Kappa, Windsor
1974 Gamma Lambda, Ottawa

Kappa Delta Phi

NATIONAL AFFILIATED SORORITY, INC.
(EDUCATION AND PHILANTHROPY)

COAT OF ARMS   ACTIVE PIN   PLEDGE PIN

KAPPA DELTA PHI National Affiliated Sorority was founded at Husson College, Bangor, Maine, on December 6, 1971. The National Constitution was ratified at Castleton State College, Castleton, Vermont on May 7, 1977. It was incorporated under the laws of New Hampshire on July 17, 1979. It is an educational and philanthropic sorority. It is educational in the sense that the sorority fosters the maximization of educational potential through a variety of individual and chapter scholarships and awards. The sorority is philanthropic in that it sponsors national and local fundraisers for organized charities and provides labor for college and community philanthropic activities.

Patterned upon democratic ideals with provision for elected representative government of the national body, the government of the national body serves as a model for local chapter government. The sorority opposes discrimination and promotes a bond of sisterhood through a cooperate effort aimed at the fulfillment of the sorority's ideals.

Government The national officers, chairperson of the board, vice chairperson, treasurer and secretary, are elected from the five-member Board of Directors which governs the sorority. The Board members are alumnae elected by the undergraduates for two-year terms.

Traditions and Insignia The official badge is oval in shape and consists of an oval shaped panel of black enamel on which appears the Greek letter "K" in gold. The official pledge pin is also oval in shape. The pin is divided equally from one tip to the other by a gold strand. One half of the pin is black, the other gold. A jeweled badge is available to alumnae. It has the design of the official badge but is bordered in pearls. The colors of the sorority are black and gold. The national mascot is a crow. The national flower is a yellow rose.

Publications *The Kappa Rose* is the inter-chapter and alumnae newsletter. *Alumnae Gold* is an annual newsletter for alumnae.

Headquarters 186 Finch Avenue, North Providence, RI 02904

Membership Total living membership 1,200. Total undergraduate membership 318. Active chapters 14. Inactive chapters 1. Graduate/Alumni chapters 3. Total number of initiates 1,220. Chapter roll:

1900 *Alpha, Bridgewater* (1976)
1914 *Beta, Salem State (MA)* (1980)
1921 Gamma, Keene
1927 *Delta, Boston U.* (1960)
1928 Epsilon, Rhode Island Col.
1931 Eta, Maine, Machias
1931 *Zeta, Maine, Farmington* (1971)
1938 Iota, Southern Maine (1968-1976)
1938 *Theta, Edinboro* (1960)
1950 *Kappa, Southern Connecticut* (1967)
1952 Lambda, Husson
1952 Mu, Maine, Presque Isle
1960 Nu, Thomas
1960 Xi, Lyndon
1961 Omicron, North Adams
1966 *Pi, Hyannis* (1973)
1966 Rho, Maine, Fort Kent (1979-1982)
1966 Sigma, Plymouth
1968 Chi, New Hampshire Col
1968 Phi, Maine, Augusta (1978-1989)
1968 Tau, Castleton
1968 *Upsilon, Lowell* (1979-1981) (1983)
1969 *Psi, Framingham* (1976-1980) (1982)
1971 *Omega, Unity* (1975)
1972 *Alpha Alpha, Maine* (1974)

Kappa Phi Kappa[†]

(EDUCATION)

ACTIVE PIN

KAPPA PHI KAPPA was incorporated April 25, 1922, under the laws of New Hampshire, by Riverda H. Jordan, Arthur D. Wright, Adam C. Gilliland, James G. Stevens, Wesley R. Jones, and Thomas J. Bryne. The incorporation of the national body preceded the organization of local chapters, a situation unique among fraternities. February 27, 1922, is celebrated as Founders' Day, as it was on that day that the first meeting was held to work out detailed plans for organization. It is a professional education fraternity, confining its activity to institutions with well developed departments of education. It admits to membership persons belonging to the undergraduate Greek-letter fraternities and does not bar its members from belonging to honor or graduate organizations. Membership is limited to those students who are taking, or have taken, courses in the department of education, and includes graduate students and faculty members. Provision is made for alumni and honorary memberships.

The Ohio State chapter was formed from a chapter of Sigma Delta Sigma, a fraternity of similar aims with two chapters.

In lieu of honorary membership the fraternity has provided the Omega Chapter-at-large for those persons who become members, but are not affiliated with any individual collegiate chapter. The membership in this Omega Chapter is confined to a few outstanding leaders in the field of education.

Government The government of the fraternity is through a biennial general assembly of delegates from all of the chapters. In the interim between meetings of the general assembly the business of the fraternity is handled by the National Council, made up of the five national officers and six other members.

Traditions and Insignia The badge is a charm in the form of a key displaying an open book, in dull gold, with the letters KΦKdone in black enamel in relief across the pages of the book. The colors of the fraternity are green and white, and the flower is the white carnation.

Publications For general distribution the fraternity publishes a magazine known as *The Open Book Magazine of Kappa Phi Kappa* quarterly. The "house organ" is known as the *Closed Book* and is circulated only among undergraduate members.

Headquarters Dr. Frank A. Peake, 1920 Southwood Road, Birmingham, Alabama 35216.

Membership Active chapters 40. Inactive chapters 30. Graduate/Alumni chapters 4. Chapter roll:[††]

1922 Alpha, Dartmouth (1937-1950)
1922 Beta, Lafayette
1923 *Delta, Colby* (1937)
1923 Epsilon, Gettysburg
1923 Eta, Wittenberg
1923 Gamma, Maine (1936-1948)
1923 Zeta, Allegheny (1937-1950)
1924 Iota, Emory and Henry (1950-1951)
1924 Kappa, Birmingham-Southern
1924 Lambda, Penn
1924 *Theta, Millikin* (1936)
1925 *Mu, Middlebury* (1939)
1925 Nu, Syracuse
1925 *Omicron, Washington and Lee* (1936)
1925 *Pi, William and Mary* (1936)
1925 *Rho, Drake* (1936)
1925 Xi, Miami (OH)
1926 *Phi, Hamline* (1954)
1926 *Sigma, Wake Forest* (1936)
1926 Tau, Pitt
1926 *Upsilon, Rochester* (1936)
1927 Alpha Alpha, Temple
1927 Alpha Beta, Penn State (1950-1951)
1927 *Alpha Delta, Centre College* (1929)
1927 *Alpha Epsilon, Emory* (1954)
1927 Alpha Gamma, Vermont
1927 Chi, New York Teachers

† This chapter narrative is repeated from the 19th edition; no current information was provided.

†† This chapter roll is repeated from the 19th edition; no current information was provided.

1927   *Psi, Muhlenberg* (1953)
1928   Alpha Eta, Ohio State
1928   *Alpha Theta, Colgate* (1946)
1928   *Alpha Zeta, Boston* (1937)
1929   Alpha Iota, Howard
1929   *Alpha Kappa, Maryland* (1936)
1929   *Alpha Lambda, Florida* (1935)
1929   Alpha Mu, Mercer
1929   *Alpha Nu, Illinois* (1935)
1930   Alpha Omicron, N.Y.U.
1930   *Alpha Pi, South Carolina* (1947)
1930   *Alpha Rho, Wooster* (1932-1935) (1939)
1930   Alpha Xi, Bucknell
1931   Alpha Sigma, North Carolina State
        (1935-1939)
1931   *Alpha Tau, Illinois Normal* (1939)
1932   Alpha Upsilon, Southern Illinois State
        (1952)
1934   *Alpha Chi, Rutgers* (1946-1948) (1955)
1934   *Alpha Phi, Cornell* (1956)
1934   Alpha Psi, L.S.U.
1937   *Beta Alpha, Coe* (1939)
1937   Beta Beta, Moravian
1940   Beta Epsilon, Peabody Conservatory
1948   Beta Eta, Jacksonville (AL)
1948   Beta Zeta, Pasadena
1949   *Beta Iota, Southern Methodist* (1952)
1949   *Beta Theta, New York Teachers, Oswego*
        (1953)
1950   *Beta Kappa, Arizona State*
1950   *Beta Lambda, Villanova*
1951   Beta Mu, Furman
1951   Beta Nu, Clemson
1952   *Beta Xi, Texas Tech* (1954)
1953   *Beta Omicron, Virginia State* (1953)
1954   Beta Pi, Duquesne
1954   Beta Rho, American
1954   Beta Sigma, Idaho State
1955   Beta Tau, St. Louis
1956   Beta Phi, Southern
1956   Beta Upsilon, Georgia
1957   Beta Chi, Georgia Southern
1958   Beta Psi, Eastern Montana
1960   Gamma Alpha, St. Michael's
1962   Gamma Beta, Johnson State
1965   Gamma Gamma, Louisiana Col.
1967   Gamma Delta, Boston Col.
1969   Gamma Zeta, California State (PA)

Kappa Pi Sigma†

(COMMERCE AND BUSINESS ADMINISTRATION)

ACTIVE PIN

KAPPA PI SIGMA, a professional fraternity with honor requirements in business administration or commerce, was established at Our Lady of the Lake College, San Antonio, Texas, February 12, 1945. The founders were Wanda Jean Butcher Tassos, Lorraine Cody Hatch, Sylvia Cohen Slapper, Rose Marie Helton, Joan McClung, Sarah Forbes Shipper, and Dolores Tough Schafer.

Government   The aims and purposes of Kappa Pi Sigma are: to promote standards of high scholarship in the field of commerce; to bind the members into closer friendship and loyalty to one another; to dignify the profession of commerce; to extend the feeling of tolerance and understanding; to encourage participation in school activities; and to uphold the interests of the alma mater.

Membership is open to students specializing in business administration or commerce in standard four-year accredited institutions offering a major in business administration or commerce leading to a recognized degree. Such students must be of at least junior standing, must have completed a minimum of twelve semester hours in business administration or commerce courses, with a rating not lower than B, or its equivalent, and must have a satisfactory average in all other courses.

The Grand Council, consisting of a president, vice-president, executive secretary, recording secretary, and treasurer, is the governing body during the interim between national conventions, held biennially; the Grand Council with two delegates from each active and alumni chapter make up the supreme governing body while the convention is in session.

Traditions and Insignia   The fraternity coat of arms is a shield surmounted by two intersecting laurel branches. The shield is divided horizontally by the cross bar of the letter Π; the lower portion of the shield is divided vertically by the lines which form the base of the Greek character. In the left-hand section of the upper part of the shield is the letter K; in the right, the letter Σ. In the center is a carnation, below which are three links joined to form a chain. A burning torch is displayed in the center between the parallel lines of the letter Π. The lower left-hand portion is a ground of diagonal lines upon which is superimposed a white triangu-

† This chapter narrative is repeated from the 19th edition; no current information was provided.

lar field, indicating the blue and silver of the fraternity. In the right-hand section is a ship. the symbol of commerce. Beneath the shield is a scroll, bearing the closed motto.

The official key of the fraternity is a modified shield, displaying the gold letters ΚΠΣ upon a black-enamel field. A band of gold borders each side. Two laurel branches, supporting a pearl at their intersection, are found below the Greek characters. Placed diagonally behind the key so that only the ends are visible is a gold quill.

The official pin of the fraternity is a modified shield, displaying the gold letters ΚΠΣ upon a black-enamel field. A band of gold, jeweled with six pearls, borders each side. Two laurel branches, supporting another pearl at their intersection, are found below the Greek characters. Placed diagonally behind the badge so that only the ends are visible is a gold quill.

The official pledge pin is an open sterling silver chain link, displaying the Greek-letters ΚΠΣ vertically along the closed side of the link.

The open motto of Kappa Pi Sigma is *Knowledge and Personality for Success.* The closed motto is *Ever Onward! Ever Upward!* The official flower is the white carnation. The official colors are blue and silver.

Publications   *The Kappa Pi Sigman* is the official publication and is issued and distributed to members through their respective chapters. It carries a résumé of activities and news.

Headquarters   Our Lady of the Lake College, San Antonio, Texas 78207.

Membership   Active chapters 7. Inactive chapters 1. Total number of initiates 950. Chapter roll:††

1945   Alpha, Our Lady of the Lake
1945   Beta, St. Mary's, San Antonio
1945   *Gamma, Trinity (TX)* (1957)
1948   Delta, Georgian Court (NJ)
1949   Epsilon, St. Scholastica
1954   Zeta, Incarnate Word
1955   Eta, Mount St. Vincent (NS)
1959   Theta, Sacred Dominican (TX)

†† This chapter roll is repeated from the 19th edition; no current information was provided.

Keramos†

(CERAMIC ENGINEERING)

ACTIVE PIN

KERAMOS was founded at the Ohio State University in the fall of 1902 under the name of Beta Pi Kappa. The founders were A. F. Greaves-Walker, C. H. Griffin, Roy H. Minton, and W. B. Harris, students in the department of ceramic engineering. In 1915 a ceramic professional fraternity having exactly the same objectives was organized at the University of Illinois under the name of Keramos. In February, 1932, Beta Pi Kappa and Keramos were consolidated under the name of Keramos and incorporated under the laws of Illinois.

Ceramic engineering in 1902 was an entirely new and practically unknown branch of engineering, and the primary object of the organization was to promote the professional interests of the students and graduates. It was, therefore, as far as is known, the first professional ceramic engineering fraternity organized in the United States.

Membership is limited to undergraduate and graduate students who have conferred honor on their *alma mater* by distinguished scholarship and exemplary character. The purpose is given in the by-laws as follows: "To provide a professional fraternity open to students in the schools, departments. and divisions of Ceramic Engineering, Technology, and Science in universities and colleges of the United States and Canada. To promote and emphasize scholarship and character in the thoughts of Ceramic students, to stimulate mental development. and to promote interest in the professional aspects of ceramic engineering, technology and science. To bind alumni more closely to their Alma Mater and to the alumni of other universities and colleges having schools, departments, or divisions of Ceramic Engineering. Technology, and Science and to furnish an additional tie of college friendship."

Government   The fraternity is governed between its biennial convocations by the Executive Council, consisting of the national president, national vice-president, national recording secretary, national treasurer, national herald, general secretary, and the immediate past national president.

Sub-chapters are provided for in those departments of ceramic engineering not considered large enough or strong enough to Support an active chapter. These sub-chapters are governed by the Executive Council and cannot initiate members. They have a similar status as colonies in a social fraternity.

Traditions and Insignia   The badge has four concave sides composed of one fourth of the circumference

† This chapter narrative is repeated from the 19th edition; no current information was provided.

of four tangent circles of two different diameters surrounding a new moon and five stars and the Greek word, Keramos. The center of the badge is black enamel surrounded by a narrow frame of gold. The key is of the same design, but does not have the black background. The colors are cobalt blue and gold.

Publications The publication is the *Keragram*, issued several times a year.

Headquarters NYS College of Ceramics, Alfred University. Alfred, New York 14802.

Membership Active chapters 13. Total number of initiates 3,542. Chapter roll:††

1902	Ohio, Ohio State
1915	Illinois, Illinois
1924	North Carolina, North Carolina State
1926	New York, Alfred
1941	Iowa, Iowa State
1941	Virginia, V.P.I.
1947	Missouri, Rolla
1947	New Jersey, Rutgers
1948	Pennsylvania, Penn State
1950	Georgia, Georgia Tech
1952	Washington, Washington
1958	South Carolina, Clemson
1976	Florida, Florida

Nu Beta Epsilon

(LAW)

NU BETA EPSILON is a national legal fraternity made up of men, but more recently including some women, who entered a law school with the express purpose of following a legal career. The emphasis has ever been on this idea, and the very name of the fraternity itself carries this out. The fraternity motto is *Nomus Barcilia Esta* (Law is king).

The fraternity is an organization resulting from a merger of two substantially identical groups. one called Nu Beta Epsilon organized in 1919 at Northwestern University, Chicago, Illinois, by Barnet Hodes with the encouragement of the late Dean Wigmore and Supreme Court Justice Brandeis, and the other known as Alpha Kappa Sigma, founded in 1918 at the University of Maryland, Baltimore, by H. Edwin Siff. Representatives from the midwest and eastern groups met at Columbus, Ohio, in 1939, and the merger was effected in 1940, the merged organization adopting the name, motto, and seal of the old Nu Beta Epsilon group.

Nu Beta Epsilon is nonsectarian, and bars none because of race, providing all other standards are met. Emphasis at the undergraduate level is placed upon scholarship. Leadership in activities related to the law such as debating, writing for the law reviews, and moot court. On the alumnus level emphasis is placed upon assistance and guidance for undergraduates and newly licensed lawyers, workshops in law and office problems, symposia, and encouragement of high ideals in the legal profession.

Government The governing body of the fraternity is the national convention which convenes yearly at various cities throughout the United States and has all of the governmental powers. It acts through its national officers. known as the Grand Council, which, besides the national grand chancellor, vice-chancellors, etc., includes six regional vice-grand chancellors, responsible for fraternity business in the various parts of the United States. The fraternity is composed of undergraduate chapters and active alumni clubs, the chancellors or presidents of which have representative capacity in the national convention, over all policy and jurisdiction rest in the national convention based upon a written constitution and a set of by-laws, but the individual chapters and alumni clubs are autonomous in their form of government, dues, and requirements for admission to and maintenance of membership. Until quite recently no one could join except as an undergraduate, but now practicing lawyers can become members through special provisions of the constitution.

Traditions and Insignia There are three awards made annually, the Barnet Hodes Award, a key given to the alumnus performing the most outstanding service for the fraternity on a national level; the National Pledge Essay Award, a set of law books and a cup awarded for the best legal essay written by a pledge; and the Ben Rubin Endowment, a cash award given to an undergraduate within the most progressive undergraduate chapter for scholarship and the like, the chapter receiving a trophy.

The fraternity crest or seal includes various symbols all associated with the legal profession and the bonds existing between members of the fraternity.

Publications The fraternity publishes a directory intermittently; the official newspaper. issued four times a year, is *The Nu Bate*.

Membership Active chapters 10. Inactive chapters 5. Graduate/Alumni chapters 7. Total number of initiates 1,750. Chapter roll:††

1918	Alpha, Maryland
1919	*Brandeis, Northwestern*
1919	*Delta, Temple*
1919	*Epsilon, Newark*
1923	Cardozo, DePaul
1924	Benjamin, Chicago-Kent Law
1928	Marshall, Washington (MO)
1929	*Chicago, Chicago*
1929	Horner, Illinois
1931	Beta Gamma, George Washington and Georgetown
1932	Loyola, Loyola, Chicago
1933	Zeta, Atlanta Law Emory University, John Marshall Law School, Atlanta
1941	Coleman, USC
1946	Theta, Miami (FL)
1950	Currie, UCLA

†† This chapter roll is repeated from the 19th edition; no current information was provided.

Omega Epsilon Phi†

(OPTOMETRY)

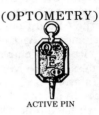

ACTIVE PIN

OMEGA EPSILON PHI was formed in answer to a need for a nonsectarian fraternity at the School of Optometry at Columbia University on October 12, 1919, by Drs. Alexander J. Broder, Abraham L. Graubart, and Daniel D. Weiss. The aim of the fraternity is to promote the cause of optometry by striving for higher ethical and educational standards within the profession. The establishment of chapters is limited to those schools which have obtained an "A" rating. Membership in the chapters is open to optometric students of sound moral character, high scholastic standing and promise of ability. Candidates for membership may be members of collegiate social fraternities. but not of any other active optometric fraternity. Honorary membership may be extended to those who have attained distinction in the field of optometry and its associated subjects.

Traditions and Insignia   Each local chapter has its individual award which is presented to that student who in the opinion of the faculty deserves such a prize. The national body presents yearly the Omega Epsilon Phi Award to that individual who has done most in the field of optometry the previous year. The award may be presented to nonmembers as well as to members.

The badge is a key displaying the raised letters ΩΕΦ diagonally across the key with a raised eye in the upper right corner. Colors are blue and white.

Headquarters   1022 Hamilton Street, Allentown, Pennsylvania 18101.

Membership   roll:
Active chapters 7. Inactive chapters 7. Total number of initiates 3,827. Chapter roll:††

1919   Alpha, Columbia
1925   Beta, Rochester
1927   *Gamma, Northern Illinois*
1939   Delta, Southern College
1940   *Epsilon, Los Angeles Optometry*
1941   *Eta, Ohio State*
1941   *Zeta, Massachusetts Optometry*
1948   Iota, Chicago College of Optometry
1948   *Theta, Pacific University*
1949   Kappa, California
1950   *Lambda, Penn State*

† This chapter narrative is repeated from the 19th edition; no current information was provided.
†† This chapter roll is repeated from the 19th edition; no current information was provided.

1954   *Gamma Iota, Illinois College of Optometry*
1954   Mu, Centro Escolar (Philippines)
1955   *Nu, Indiana*

Phi Alpha Tau†

(FORENSIC ARTS)

ACTIVE PIN

PHI ALPHA TAU Fraternity was founded in 1902 at the Emerson College of Oratory by Walter Bradley Tripp. The fraternity became national in 1904 with the acquisition of a Beta chapter at the University of Wisconsin. First arid foremost in the mind of the founder was debate, but as the organization grew, it eventually included chapters which specialized in additional areas of forensic art. When the national organization was dissolved in 1937, the chapter at Emerson College remained as the only active chapter.

As the years passed the fraternity came to emphasize social as well as honor aspects. Interests expanded beyond forensics to include music, painting, and journalism. In this way Phi Alpha Tau evolved into a broad communicative arts fraternity.

The fraternity is secret in character, and prefers the pin symbol over the key. Fraternity members are selected from those young men who show a strong inclination toward the communicative arts.

Government   In 1967 the fraternity became national, for a second time, with the acquisition of a newly acquired Beta chapter at Suffolk University in Boston. The national council of the fraternity has supreme authority, the seat of which is in Boston.

The national council is required to hold monthly business meetings and a national convention once a year. Eight elected officers include: national rayis, national naib rais, national katib, national hazing, national pledgemaster, national corresponding secretary, national historian, and national dabit.

Traditions   The fraternity maintains an official seal for charters and other documents. A major traditional change took place in 1957 when an official blazer was adopted bearing a newly adopted symbol of a torch and a book. This is the public symbol of the fraternity as opposed to the secret one. The torch is used to represent endurance while the book stands for knowledge. The major objectives of the fraternity are: (1) To promote the communicative arts; (2) To help the school of the local chapter; (3) To foster brotherhood.

Publications   Alpha chapter's *The Torch*, is pub-

† This chapter narrative is repeated from the 19th edition; no current information was provided.

lished quarterly. The national council plans a publication that will be sent out to all alumni.

Awards The Joseph E. Connor Memorial Award, formerly an Alpha chapter function, was made a national tradition in 1968.

The award is given each year to an individual of national or international recognition, whom, in the opinion of the fraternity, best represents the drive and determination in communications of Joseph E. Connor, an outstanding brother. Recipients of the award have included: Edward R. Murrow, William Cunningham, Joseph Welch, Elliot Norton, Carlos P. Romulo, Elia Kazan, Robert Frost, Arthur Fiedler, Red Skelton, Robert W. Sarnoff, Edward W. Brooke, Walter Cronkite, and Erwin D. Canham.

Headquarters 130 Beacon Street, Boston, Massachusetts 02116.

Membership Active chapters 2. Inactive chapters 17. Total number of initiates 550. Chapter roll[1]††:

1902 Alpha, Emerson Oratory
1904 *Beta, Wisconsin, Madison*
1907 *Epsilon, Stanford*
1907 *Gamma, Nebraska*
1915 *Kappa, Syracuse*
1916 *Iota, Kansas*
1916 *Omicron, Kansas State*
1916 *Xi, Michigan*
1922 *Pi, Arkansas*
1967 Beta, Suffolk

Phi Beta Gamma†

(LAW)

ACTIVE PIN

PHI BETA GAMMA, legal fraternity. was organized at Georgetown University School of Law in April, 1922, and is incorporated under the laws of the District of Columbia. Membership is extended only to law students at such institutions where a chapter may exist. In addition to secret ritualistic degrees, the fraternity has formulated and adopted a set of

[1]Name and year of establishment of a number of chapters were lost when the fraternity's official records were lost. Chapters were known to exist, however, at John Carroll, Northwestern College (now called North Central), University of the Pacific, Oklahoma, Minnesota, Puget Sound, and Dartmouth.

"Canons of Ethics and Rules of Conduct," which are public. Under these canons:

Each chapter is required to establish and maintain a high standard of scholarly attainment as an essential requirement for admission and controlling rule of conduct for members.

It is the paramount duty of the national and chapter officers to establish contacts between student members and eminent and exemplary members of the legal profession; encourage the active participation of members in institutional affairs, both political and social; foster close cooperation with the faculty for the improvement of educational facilities and the standing of the institution; and take such other steps as shall be helpful and necessary to strengthen the character and fire the ambition of each member.

Graduate members are required to observe and obey the canons and ethics of their profession and to so shape their conduct that they may be qualified in all respects. both moral and professional, to minister in the forum of justice.

Government Government is vested in the national conventions which convene biennially, ad interim authority being vested in the Supreme Executive Council.

Traditions and Insignia Members are privileged to wear the badge pin or the official watch key. This key is plain gold. in form an inverted triangle, bearing the Greek letters ΦΒΓ. The scholarship key may be worn only by the student member of each chapter who graduated with the highest average during the entire course of study. This key takes the form of an open book upon which is raised the coat of arms of the order. The fraternity also has a chapter scholarship award, made annually by the national administration to the chapter whose members maintain the highest standing in their classes.

Publications The quarterly publication is *The Advocate*.

Headquarters The Law Building, 425 St. Paul Place, Baltimore, Maryland 21202.

Membership Active chapters 7. Inactive chapters 4. Graduate/Alumni chapters 7. Total number of initiates 2,500. Chapter roll:††

1922 Alpha, Georgetown
1924 *Beta, National (DC)*
1925 Delta, St. Paul
1925 *Epsilon, George Washington*
1925 Gamma, Minnesota
1926 *Zeta, Loyola, New Orleans*
1927 *Eta, Cumberland*
1929 Theta, Jefferson (KY)
1932 Iota, Baltimore U.
1932 Kappa, Miami (FL)
1939 Lambda, Tulsa

†† This chapter roll is repeated from the 19th edition; no current information was provided.
† This chapter narrative is repeated from the 19th edition; no current information was provided.

Phi Beta Pi
and
Theta Kappa Psi†

(MEDICINE)

ACTIVE PIN   ACTIVE PIN

PHI BETA PI Fraternity, founded on March 10, 1891, and Theta Kappa Psi, founded on November 30, 1879. were officially merged on February 8, 1961, retaining the names of the two fraternities.

Phi Beta Pi was founded at Western Pennsylvania Medical College, now the Medical School of the University of Pittsburgh; but its history as a national fraternity really began April 1, 1898, when Beta Chapter was installed at the University of Michigan, and the first general assembly was held at Ann Arbor, Michigan, January 6 to 8, 1900. The fraternity has consistently made an effort to advance sound medicine in its widest social and professional implications. Phi Beta Pi has constantly endeavored to provide opportunity for practitioners, teachers of medicine, and medical students to consider together the problems of medicine and their relationship to the general welfare.

Theta Kappa Psi was founded at New Haven, Connecticut, as the "Society of Kappa Psi." The fraternity was reorganized at the University of Maryland, School of Medicine, Baltimore, on November 18, 1898, by William C. Bennett, Perry L. Boyer, William F. Clark, James E. Cathill, Edwin J. Frosher, Thompson D. Gilbert, J. Dawson Reeder, Press W. Eldridge, and F. Harvey Smith. On January 15, 1925, the fraternity was reorganized and the name changed to Theta Kappa Psi. It is composed of medical graduates, members of medical school faculties, and students of medicine. There are two classes of chapters: collegiate, limited to recognized medical colleges, and graduate, composed of medical graduates and practitioners. Both classes of chapters have the same and equal rights and privileges in all matters.

Growth   Theta Kappa Psi on November 17, 1917, absorbed Delta Omicron Alpha medical fraternity founded in the college of medicine at Tulane University in 1904. Again, on January 26, 1918, the fraternity absorbed Phi Delta medical fraternity founded at the Long Island Hospital Medical College in 1901.

Phi Beta Pi amalgamated in 1934 with Omega Upsilon Phi medical fraternity.[2]

Consolidation and discontinuance of medical schools was responsible for the death of a considerable number of chapters. In 1906 there were 162 medical schools in the United States and Canada; in 1954 there were 79.

Government   A Joint Constitutional Committee was named following the merger, and this six-man body has guided the formation of a gradually integrated administration. Phi Beta Pi has governed through the general assembly held biennially and in the interim by the Supreme Council of officers. In Theta Kappa Psi the governing body, called the Grand Chapter, occupied the first place on the chapter roll as Alpha. This body met in annual conventions from 1898 to 1908, and after that triennially. Administration was in the hands of the executive council and the grand officers.

The Joint Constitutional Committee of the two merged fraternities is made up of three officers from each. The Supreme Officers include the archon, moderator, first vice-archon, second vice-archon, secretary-treasurer, editor, and co-editor. Other bodies include a nine-man council, which includes most of the above officers and two councilors elected at large; a board of trustees; an editorial board; and an alumni advisory council.

Traditions and Insignia   The ideals as well as the policies of the two fraternities are the same. Phi Beta Pi lectureships have been established on many campuses by the local chapters. Phi Beta Pi bookshelves are prominent in many medical school libraries, and some chapters have music libraries.

The Phi Beta Pi badge is a diamond of gold with emerald corners and pearl sides; the center is black enamel displaying in gold the skull and pelvis and the letters ΦΒΠ. The colors are green and white: the flower is the white chrysanthemum.

The Theta Kappa Psi badge is a shield displaying a gold caduceus raised from the face of, the black enamel center, the Greek letters ΘΚΨ appearing above the caduceus; the corners of the enamel center contain three emeralds, and the border of the badge may be jeweled. The colors are gold and green. The flower is the red rose.

Publications   The two fraternities issue *The Asklepion of Phi Beta Pi-Theta Kappa Psi Medical Fraternity.* Phi Beta Pi had formerly issued a magazine called *The Quarterly of Phi Beta Pi Medical Fraternity.* Directories were published in 1909, 1920, 1927, 1938, and 1951. Supplements to the directory were published yearly in the May issue of the *Quarterly.*

Theta Kappa Psi formerly published *The Messenger* as a quarterly. From 1903 until 1907 the journal was issued each month of the college year. A directory known as *The Register* was published annually from 1903 until 1910, and after that less frequently.

---

† This chapter narrative is repeated from the 19th edition; no current information was provided.

[2]Omega Upsilon Phi is described in Fraternities That Are No More.

Headquarters Suite 110, 24655 Southfield Road, Southfield, Michigan 48075.

Membership Active collegiate chapters of Phi Beta Pi and Theta Kappa Psi 8; inactive 51; alumni chapters 4; total membership 27,000. The chapter roll of Phi Beta Pi is:††

1891	Alpha, Pitt
1898	*Beta, Michigan (1945)*
1900	*Gamma, Starling (1905)*
1901	*Delta, Chicago (formerly Rush Medical College)*
1901	*Epsilon, McGill (1908)*
1901	*Zeta, Maryland*
1902	*Eta, Jefferson*
1902	Iota, Illinois
1902	*Theta, Northwestern*
1903	Kappa, Wayne State
1903	Lambda, St. Louis
1903	Mu, Washington (MO)
1904	*Nu, Kansas (1913)*
1904	*Xi, Minnesota*
1905	*Omicron (Omicron Alpha Zeta), Indiana*
1905	Pi, Iowa State
1906	*Chi, Georgetown (1934)*
1906	*Omega, Cooper Medical (1912)*
1906	*Phi (Phi Psi), Virginia*
1906	*Psi (Phi Psi), Virginia Medical*
1906	*Rho, Vanderbilt (1944)*
1906	*Sigma, Alabama*
1906	*Tau, Missouri*
1906	*Upsilon, Western Reserve (1911)*
1907	*Alpha Alpha, Creighton*
1907	*Alpha Beta, Tulane (1929)*
1907	*Alpha Delta (Alpha Sigma), Medico-Chirurgical*
1907	*Alpha Epsilon, Marquette (1942)*
1907	*Alpha Gamma, Syracuse (1918)*
1908	*Alpha Zeta (Omicron Alpha Zeta), Indiana*
1909	*Alpha Eta, Virginia*
1909	*Alpha Theta, Penn (1913)*
1910	*Alpha Iota, Kansas* (Combined with Alpha Upsilon as Alpha Iota Upsilon, 1962)
1910	Alpha Kappa, Texas
1912	*Alpha Lambda, Oklahoma*
1913	*Alpha Mu, Louisville*
1913	*Alpha Nu, Utah*
1913	*Alpha Omicron, Johns Hopkins*
1913	*Alpha Xi, Harvard*
1915	*Alpha Pi, Wisconsin, Madison (1953-1960) (1962)*
1915	*Alpha Rho, Oakland (1918)*
1919	*Alpha Sigma, Penn*
1919	*Alpha Tau, California (1936)*
1920	*Alpha Chi, Colorado*
1920	*Alpha Iota Upsilon, Kansas*
1920	*Alpha Phi Alpha, Baylor*
1920	Alpha Phi Beta, Southwestern Medical
1920	*Alpha Psi, Nebraska (1939)*
1921	*Alpha Omega, Loyola, Chicago*
1922	*Beta Alpha, West Virginia*
1923	*Beta Beta, Emory (1934)*
1928	*Beta Gamma, Tennessee*
1930	*Beta Delta, USC (1938)*
1931	*Beta Epsilon, Duke (1938)*
1933	*Beta Zeta, L.S.U.*
1934	*Beta Eta, Temple*
1938	*Beta Theta, Arkansas*
1947	*Beta Iota, Washington (1953)*
1947	*Beta Kappa, Hahnemann Med.*
1948	*Beta Lambda, North Dakota*
1950	*Beta Mu, Chicago Medical (1954)*
1955	*Beta Nu, Oregon*
1955	*Beta Xi, Miami (FL)*

Of the 59 chapters installed by Theta Kappa Psi, only one remains active—Gamma Kappa (Georgia). Chapter roll of Theta Kappa Psi:††

1879	*Alpha, Grand Chapter*
1888	*Mu Sigma Alpha, Michigan (1940)*
1898	*Delta, Maryland (1931)*
1900	*Beta, Virginia Medical*
1901	*Chi, Illinois (1916)*
1901	*Epsilon, Maryland Medical College (school discontinued 1914)*
1901	*Phi Delta, Long Island (1950)*
1902	*Zeta, Georgetown (1942)*
1903	Beta Epsilon, Ohio State (1943-1960)
1905	*Beta Pi, Sioux City Medical (school discontinued 1909)*
1905	*Beta Xi, University Medical (1910)*
1905	*Beta Zeta, Washington (MO) (1912)*
1905	*Gamma, Albany*
1905	*Gamma Eta, Michigan M & S (school discontinued 1907)*
1905	*Iota, Alabama*
1906	*Kappa, Birmingham Medical (school discontinued 1913)*
1907	*Lambda, Vanderbilt (1919)*
1907	*Nu, South Carolina Medical*
1908	*Kappa Phi, Minnesota*
1908	*Omicron, Nashville (school discontinued 1911)*
1908	*Pi, Tulane*
1908	*Xi, West Virginia*
1909	*Rho, Emory (1953)*
1909	*Sigma, Baltimore P & S (merged with University of Maryland 1915)*
1909	*Tau, USC (1942)*
1910	*Omega, Southern Methodist (school discontinued in 1915)*
1910	*Psi, Southwestern Medical*
1912	*Beta Eta, Jefferson*
1913	*Beta Lambda, George Washington*
1913	*Beta Mu, Louisville*
1913	*Beta Theta, Tennessee (1943)*
1915	*Upsilon, North Carolina (1939)*
1917	*Beta Rho, Loyola, Chicago*
1917	*Beta Sigma, Ft. Worth (school discontinued 1918)*

†† This chapter roll is repeated from the 19th edition; no current information was provided.

1917 *Beta Tau, Marquette* (1924)
1918 *Beta Phi, Texas*
1919 *Beta Chi, Cincinnati* (1928)
1919 *Gamma Delta, Wisconsin, Madison* (1924)
1920 *Beta Omega, Johns Hopkins* (1926)
1920 *Gamma Gamma, Columbia*
1920 Gamma Kappa, Georgia
1920 *Gamma Theta, Tufts* (1928)
1920 *Gamma Zeta, Toronto* (1940)
1921 *Gamma Lambda, Penn* (1929)
1921 *Gamma Mu, Oregon* (1949)
1921 *Gamma Nu, Harvard*
1922 *Gamma Xi, St. Louis* (1929)
1923 *Gamma Pi, Wake Forest*
1923 *Gamma Rho, Arkansas* (1949)
1923 *Gamma Sigma, N.Y.U. and Bellevue Hospital Medical College*
1923 *Gamma Tau, Manitoba*
1924 *Gamma Upsilon, Indiana* (1944)
1926 *Beta Gamma, Mississippi*
1928 *Eta, Rush* (1930)
1929 *Beta Nu, McGill* (1944)
1930 *Beta Kappa, Duke*
1931 *Beta Iota, L.S.U.* (1943)
1931 *Phi, Northwestern*
1942 *Gamma Phi, Baylor* (1950)

Phi Delta Epsilon†

(MEDICINE)

ACTIVE PIN

PLEDGE PIN

PHI DELTA EPSILON was founded October 13, 1904, at the Cornell University Medical College, by Michael H. Barsky, Henry Aronson, Aaron Brown, Abraham L. Garbat, Phillip Frank, Bernard H. Eliasberg, Irving H. Engel, and William I. Wallach. Of this number the late Aaron Brown was designated as the founder.

Government Government is vested in the senate and the Board of Trustees. The senate is composed of one representative from each chapter and club and meetings are held annually. The Board of Trustees consists of past grand officers.

Traditions and Insignia The fraternity celebrated its Golden Jubilee Anniversary at the fiftieth annual convention in New York City, December, 1954.

The fraternity sponsors lectureships and awards scholarship prizes at the various medical schools. It maintains a student loan fund for needy undergraduates and a higher education loan program to assist men just going into practice.

The Aaron Brown Educational Foundation, Inc., was established in 1945 to perpetuate the memory of the founder of the fraternity and supports the annual lectureships. There is also a placement committee for the exchange of information on positions wanted or available.

The official gold badge is a triangular arrangement of the three Greek letters ΦΔE; the Δ at the apex is jeweled with pearls and amethysts. The gold torch connecting the three letters has a ruby at its base. An elaborate system of jewels for the center of the Δ is used to designate the various grand offices. The pledge button is a triangle divided perpendicularly and in two colors, purple and white. A special key. displaying the official coat of arms, is worn by members who have been active 25 years or more.

Publications The fraternity has published several directories, yearbooks, songbooks, and histories of its members. It publishes a quarterly magazine called *The Phi Delta Epsilon News* and the *Bulletin*. Colors are royal purple and white. The coat of arms is copyrighted.

Headquarters 145 East 52nd Street, New York, New York 10022.

Membership Active chapters 39. Inactive chapters 25. Graduate/Alumni chapters 42. Total number of initiates 20,000. Chapter roll:††

1904 *Alpha, Cornell* (1955)
1905 *Gamma, Columbia* (1959)
1906 *Zeta, Long Island College Hospital* (1958)
1907 Kappa Pi, Penn
1907 *Theta, Fordham* (1921)
1909 *Lambda, Johns Hopkins* (1933)
1911 Nu, Pitt
1912 Delta Epsilon, Maryland
1913 Omicron, New York Medical
1913 *Xi, Loyola* (1918)
1916 Mu, Jefferson
1916 *Rho, Harvard* (1933)
1916 Sigma, Temple
1918 Alpha Alpha, Illinois
1918 Alpha Beta, Northwestern
1918 Alpha Delta, Wayne State
1918 Alpha Eta, USC
1918 *Alpha Gamma, Chicago* (1949) (formerly Rush Medical)
1918 Alpha Iota, Tulane
1918 Alpha Theta, Tufts
1919 *Tau, Syracuse* (1942-1943) (1958)
1919 Upsilon, Case Western Reserve
1920 Psi, George Washington
1921 Chi, Ohio State
1921 Omega, Michigan
1921 Phi, Louisville
1922 *Alpha Kappa, Washington (MO)* (1959)
1922 Alpha Lambda, Marquette
1923 Alpha Mu, Virginia Medical

† This chapter narrative is repeated from the 19th edition; no current information was provided.

†† This chapter roll is repeated from the 19th edition; no current information was provided.

1923   Alpha Nu, Texas
1923   Alpha Omicron, Boston
1923   Alpha Xi, Minnesota
1924   Alpha Pi, St. Louis
1924   *Alpha Rho, Yale* (1960)
1924   Alpha Sigma, Toronto
1924   *Alpha Tau, Indiana* (1956)
1924   *Alpha Upsilon, Virginia* (1946)
1925   *Alpha Chi, Creighton* (1936-1945) (1959)
1925   Alpha Phi, California
1926   *Alpha Omega, Oregon* (1936)
1926   Alpha Psi, Wisconsin, Madison
1926   Beta Beta, Colorado
1926   *Beta Delta, McGill* (1933)
1926   *Beta Gamma, Kansas* (1932)
1928   Beta Epsilon, Cincinnati
1929   *Beta Eta, Tennessee* (1956)
1929   Beta Iota, Georgia
1929   *Beta Kappa, Iowa* (1942)
1929   Beta Theta, Baylor
1929   Beta Zeta, Hahnemann Med.
1930   *Beta Lambda, Vermont* (1939-1943) (1961)
1930   *Beta Mu, Dalhousie* (1947)
1930   Beta Nu, Emory
1935   Beta Xi, Georgetown
1938   Beta Omicron, L.S.U.
1943   Beta Pi, Southwestern (TX)
1944   *Beta Rho, Nebraska* (1954)
1949   *Beta Sigma, South Carolina* (1959)
1949   Beta Tau, Chicago
1951   *Beta Upsilon, Buffalo* (1953)
1953   Beta Chi, Miami (FL)
1953   Beta Phi, UCLA
1955   *Beta, N.Y.U.* (1965)
1962   Kappa Rho, California College of Medicine (L.A.)

Phi Epsilon Kappa†

(PHYSICAL EDUCATION)

PLEDGE PIN

PHI EPSILON KAPPA is a national professional fraternity for men who are engaged in or preparing themselves to engage in teaching supervision, and administration in the related fields of health, physical education, and recreation. The fraternity, incorporated under the laws of Indiana, was founded at the Normal College of the American Gymnastic Union, April 12, 1913.

The stated purposes of the fraternity are: to inculcate the principles of peace, friendship, and brotherly love; to promote and enhance the happiness of its members; to elevate the standards, ideals, and ethics for those engaged in teaching health, physical education, and recreation; to support the undergraduate chapters; to perpetuate itself as a fraternal organization; and to provide for its government.

Government The fraternity is governed by three independent co-ordinated departments comprised of the legislative. the executive, and the judicial. Judicial power is vested in the national and subordinate tribunals; executive power is vested in the elected national officers and the district counselors appointed by the president; legislative power is vested in the National Council, composed of the national officers and the district counselors.

There are but two classes of membership: honorary, which may be conferred only by a three-fourths vote of the national chapter, and active membership, which may be conferred on the collegiate level, alumni level, or on an unaffiliated basis.

Traditions Upon recommendation of a chapter, a scholarship key is awarded to members of collegiate or alumni chapters who have satisfactorily met the requirements prescribed by the education committee and are approved by the national chapter. An honor award may also be granted by the national chapter to any member whose accomplishments in the profession have[een such as to have brought honor to himself, to the profession, and to the fraternity.

Publications Principal publication is *The Physical Educator*, a professional journal issued quarterly. At least three issues are circulated annually of *Black and Gold*, esoteric journal. The fraternity also publishes its constitution and by-laws, its rituals, its pledge manual, and *Index and Abstracts of Foreign Physical Education Literature*.

Headquarters 4000 Meadows Drive, Suite L-24, Indianapolis, Indiana 46205.

Membership The Alpha Chapter emerged as Alpha Chapter of Indiana University with the assimilation of the Normal College by Indiana University. The Beta Chapter was transferred to De Paul University, Chicago, when that institution assimilated American College. Zeta Chapter, originally established at the Savage School for Physical Education, was transferred to Teachers College, Columbia University, in 1946.

Total undergraduate membership 1,300. Active chapters 43. Inactive chapters 7. Total number of initiates 10,000. Chapter roll:††

1913   Alpha, Normal College of the American Gymnastic Union, Indianapolis
1920   Beta, American College of Physical Education, Chicago
1921   Gamma, Temple
1923   *Delta, Panzer (NJ)* (1943)
1924   *Epsilon, Akron* (1937)

---

† This chapter narrative is repeated from the 19th edition; no current information was provided.

†† This chapter roll is repeated from the 19th edition; no current information was provided.

1924   Eta, Trenton
1924   *Zeta, Columbia*
1925   Iota, Iowa
1925   Kappa, Michigan
1925   Theta, Wisconsin, Madison
1926   Lambda, UCLA
1926   Mu, Ithaca
1926   Nu, Wisconsin, La Crosse
1927   *Xi, Wyoming*
1928   Omicron, Oregon
1928   Pi, Montana
1929   Rho, Illinois
1930   Phi, Kansas State
1930   Sigma, Minnesota
1930   Tau, Nebraska
1930   Upsilon, Cincinnati
1931   Chi, Occidental
1931   *Psi, Ohio Wesleyan*
1932   *Omega, Ohio State* (1936)
1934   Alpha Alpha, Indiana
1934   Alpha Beta, Penn State
1934   Alpha Delta, Kent
1934   Alpha Gamma, Washington State
1935   *Sigma Alpha, USC* (1952)
1939   Alpha Epsilon, San Jose
1941   *Alpha Zeta, Boston* (1956)
1943   Alpha Eta, Manhattan
1948   *Alpha Theta, Utah State* (1953)
1949   Alpha Iota, Miami (OH)
1949   Alpha Kappa, North Dakota
1949   Alpha Lambda, Wake Forest
1950   Alpha Mu, Michigan State
1950   Alpha Nu, Buffalo
1950   Alpha Omicron, Syracuse
1950   Alpha Xi, Brooklyn
1951   Alpha Pi, Northeast Louisiana
1951   Alpha Rho, Cal State, Los Angeles
1953   Alpha Sigma, Pacific (CA)
1953   Alpha Tau, Bowling Green
1956   Alpha Chi, Southeastern Louisiana
1956   Alpha Phi, Arizona State
1956   Alpha Upsilon, Washington
1957   Alpha Omega, Idaho
1957   Alpha Psi, Kansas
1957   Beta Alpha, Cal State, Long Beach
1958   Beta Beta, Florida State
1960   Beta Gamma, Texas Tech
1961   Beta Delta, Central Michigan

Phi Lambda Kappa[†]

(MEDICINE)

ACTIVE PIN

PLEDGE PIN

PHI LAMBDA KAPPA, a medical fraternity, was founded at the University of Pennsylvania in 1907. The organization stems from an eastern branch, the Aleph Yod He Fraternity, organized in 1907, and the western branch of Chicago whose name Phi Lambda Kappa was acquired during the amalgamation in Pittsburgh in 1922. In 1924 policy was altered to permit graduate members to hold national offices. This led to the National Directorate as the governing board, which still functions. It meets four times a year to establish ruling policies.

The membership consists of honorary, graduate, and undergraduate members.

Government   Administrative affairs are mapped in convention by graduate and undergraduate members. At the 1952 convention the constitution was modified to put membership on a nonsectarian basis. A convention meets yearly.

Traditions and Insignia   Lectureships in the medical colleges are sponsored yearly.

The badge is diamond-shaped with a blue field. On the upper corner of this field is a skull and crossbones. The name is in the middle and situated below this is a six-pointed star. The corners of the badge are set with rubies and four pearls intervene between each two rubies. Colors are blue and white.

Publications   The *Quarterly* is the official magazine.

Funds and Philanthropies   A student loan fund to extend loans to needy undergraduate members is a conspicuous part of the program. The following awards are given annually: the Bronx Alumni Club Award for the best article by an undergraduate on Jewish cultural or historic medicine; the Quarterly Award for the best non-scientific article; and the Undergraduate Essay Award to the undergraduate who submits the best thesis on a scientific subject.

The Grand Scientific Award is offered annually at each convention to that physician who has contributed most to the advancement of medical sciences. The award which extends beyond the limits of membership in the fraternity has been granted 44 times.

Other awards include the Max Thorek Award for the best surgical research essay by a Phi Lambda Kappa student, intern, resident, or recent graduate; the Alvin Behrens Award for best paper on ophthalmology by a student; best chapter award; best

† This chapter narrative is repeated from the 19th edition; no current information was provided.

scribe award; Maury D. Sanger award to ladies' auxiliary; and Louis Edeiken address at convention.

Headquarters Room 1401, 1015 Chestnut, Philadelphia, Pennsylvania 19107.

Membership Total living membership 4,800. Active chapters 17. Inactive chapters 24. Chapter roll:††

1907	Alpha, Penn
1908	Alpha Alpha, Illinois
1909	Beta, Jefferson
1912	*Delta, Rush Medical*
1912	Gamma, Loyola
1914	*Epsilon, Northwestern*
1919	Eta, N.Y.U., Bellevue
1919	Theta, Long Island
1919	*Zeta, Columbia P & S*
1920	Iota, Tufts
1920	Kappa, Buffalo
1922	*Mu, Pitt*
1922	Nu, Boston
1922	Omicron, Wayne State
1922	*Pi, Michigan*
1922	*Xi, Maryland*
1923	*Rho, George Washington*
1923	*Sigma, Virginia Medical*
1924	*Chi, Albany Medical*
1924	*Phi, Georgetown*
1924	Psi, Tulane
1924	*Tau, St. Louis*
1924	Upsilon, Virginia
1925	*Lambda, Yale*
1925	*Omega, Tennessee*
1926	Alpha Gamma, Case Western Reserve
1927	*Alpha Delta, Harvard*
1927	*Alpha Epsilon, Kansas*
1927	*Alpha Eta, Washington (MO)*
1927	*Alpha Zeta, South Carolina Medical*
1928	*Alpha Iota, Temple*
1928	*Alpha Kappa, Cornell*
1928	*Alpha Theta, Ohio State*
1929	Alpha Mu, New York Medical
1930	*Alpha Nu, Louisville*
1933	*Alpha Lambda, California*
1933	*Alpha Xi, Baylor*
1936	*Alpha Omicron, L.S.U.*
1939	Alpha Rho, Chicago Medical
1949	Hebrew, Hadassah (Israel)

†† This chapter roll is repeated from the 19th edition; no current information was provided.

Phi Psi†

(TEXTILE ARTS)

ACTIVE PIN

PHI PSI was founded March 18, 1903, at the Philadelphia Textile School, now the Philadelphia College of Textiles and Science, by Harold H. Hart, Charles A. Kalenbach, Henry W. Eddy. Robert M. Baeny, and Paul Benninghoffen. It was incorporated under the laws of the Commonwealth of Pennsylvania on April 14, 1905. The aims and goals expressed by the founders are regarded as the foundation of the organization. These are: (1) to promote fellowship among men of textile colleges and universities with textile departments; (2) to encourage high standards in textile work; and (3) to assist, by every honorable means, the advancement of its members.

Government Each chapter is governed by its elected officers. Nationally, the government is vested in the Grand Council, composed of five elected officers chosen from the various active alumni members. To its annual meetings are brought all matters concerning the welfare of the fraternity. The national convention is held in a different section of the country each year, when an opportunity is afforded for undergraduate and alumni members to gather and exchange ideas of both fraternal and general textile interest.

Traditions and Insignia The standard pin of the fraternity is a diamond-shaped emblem with a gold border and four perpendicular gold bars on a black face, which contains the Greek letters ΦΨ in gold. The coat of arms is the eighteenth century shield, quartered. surmounted with a crown of Denmark on a roll of the colors of the fraternity, black and gold. The motto is *Semper ad perfectum.* The yellow tea rose is the official flower.

Publications The official organ is the *Phi Psi Quarterly,* which carries reports from each of the undergraduate and alumni chapters and from the Grand Council and also contains articles of an informative nature which are of value to all those, whether associated with this fraternity or not, who are interested in the textile industry.

Headquarters Philadelphia College of Textiles and Science, Schoolhouse Lane and Henry Avenue, Philadelphia, Pennsylvania 19144.

Membership Since 1914, when the first alumni chapter was formed at Boston, twelve alumni chapters have been organized in the important textile centers of the country, with the purpose of

† This chapter narrative is repeated from the 19th edition; no current information was provided.

strengthening the bonds of business associations in later years.

The newest chapter, Mu, formed on May 5. 1961, is situated at a graduate school, the Institute of Textile Technology. Many of these Phi Psi brothers are alumni of undergraduate chapters; the remainder are graduates of various engineering schools who have chosen to do their graduate work in textiles.

Phi Psi confines its membership to men and women undergraduate and graduate students in a textile curriculum. It is the largest professional textile fraternity in the world. Active chapters 10. Graduate/Alumni chapters 12. Total number of initiates 6,000. Chapter roll:††

1903   Alpha, Philadelphia Textiles
1904   Beta, Southeastern Massachusetts
1904   Gamma, Lowell Tech
1909   Delta, Bradford Durfee
1924   Eta, North Carolina State
1925   Theta, Georgia Tech
1927   Iota, Clemson
1931   Kappa, Texas Tech
1936   Lambda, Auburn
1961   Mu, ITT (VA)

Phi Sigma Pi†

(EDUCATION)

ACTIVE PIN

PHI SIGMA PI is an undergraduate professional honor fraternity for men in institutions of college rank who are preparing for professional careers. It was founded at the Central Missouri State Teachers College, Warrensburg, Missouri, February 14, 1916. The charter roll included names of three faculty members, President E. L. Hendricks, Dean C. A. Phillips, Professor C. H. McClure; and of ten students, Alfred V. Thayer, J. A. Leach, Roland W. Grinstead, Ray F. Perkins, W. C. Fowler, R. G. Bigelow, Arthur Kresge, John Doak, Harold Patterson, and Harry Hill.

The founders, some of whom were members of Phi Delta Kappa, were interested in establishing an organization in undergraduate teachers colleges which would challenge men to attain the same high scholastic standing and professional leadership that Phi Delta Kappa was encouraging in the universities and graduate schools. In 1921 the national organization was completed when provision was made for installing Beta and Gamma chapters.

The fraternity was chartered as a nonprofit organization in Illinois in 1949. It was chartered as a nonprofit national honor fraternity in Pennsylvania in 1966.

Phi Sigma Pi is distinctly professional in nature, being founded upon the basis of high scholarship and with the avowed purpose of advancing educational ideals through the promotion of scholarship, professional leadership, and fellowship.

Government The Grand Chapter holds regular meetings every year. It consists of the National Council, the regional directors, and the authorized representatives of the local chapters. The National Council, consisting of six national officers who are charged with the executive and administrative work of the fraternity, is authorized to meet at least once a year. These officers are president, vice-president, secretary, treasurer, counselor, historian, and student representative.

Traditions and Insignia The fraternity is social only inasmuch as it exists to meet the needs of close fellowship and social intercourse among men of like interests in four-year colleges. The professional programs consist of a variety of activities—some of which are: (1) Group and individual study of educational problems; (2) Meeting prominent men and discussing problems with these men as leaders; (3) Directing a wider interest in literature concerning college education; (4) Contacting alumni, and using their experience in the educational growth of the college student.

The badge is a monogram of the letters ΦΣΠ linked diagonally. Chapter presidents and secretaries who perform their duties faithfully and efficiently are awarded distinguished service keys, bearing the coat of arms, by the National Council. Other members who render particularly meritorious service to the fraternity may be awarded service keys by the grand chapter. The colors are purple and gold.

Publications A newsletter, *Purple and Gold*, published several times a school year, is edited by the national secretary.

Headquarters State College, Millersville, Pennsylvania 17551.

Membership Active chapters 13. Inactive chapters 8. Total number of initiates 5,266. Chapter roll:††

1916   Alpha, Central Missouri State
1921   Beta, Northeast Missouri
1921   Gamma, Bradley
1925   Delta, Kansas State
1926   Epsilon, George Peabody
1927   Zeta, General Beadle State (SD)
1929   Eta, Indiana (PA)
1930   Iota, Bloomsburg
1930   Kappa, California (PA)
1930   Lambda, Clarion

† This chapter narrative is repeated from the 19th edition; no current information was provided.

†† This chapter roll is repeated from the 19th edition; no current information was provided.

1930 Mu, Slippery Rock
1930 Theta, Mansfield
1931 Nu, New Mexico Western
1931 Omicron, Shippensburg
1931 Xi, Northwestern Oklahoma
1932 Pi, Dickinson State
1934 Rho, D. C. Teachers
1934 Sigma, Millersville
1936 Tau, East Carolina
1938 Upsilon, Edinboro
1961 Beta Gamma, Farmington State (ME)

Pi Lambda Theta†

(EDUCATION)

ACTIVE PIN

PI LAMBDA THETA, a national honor and professional association for persons in education, was founded in July, 1917, at Columbia, Mo. Its purposes are to: recognize persons of superior scholastic achievement and high potential for professional leadership; foster creativity and academic excellence at all educational levels; support, extend, and interpret the function of education in a democracy; demonstrate the power of competence in the body of knowledge unique to the profession; stimulate, conduct, and utilize research; accept responsibility for evaluation and improvement of the profession of teaching; contribute to the solution of educational, social, and cultural problems of national and international concern; promote professional fellowship and cooperation as a means to positive action; foster leadership among women; and endeavor to improve the status of women in education.

College or university chapters elect to membership promising students and teachers in the field of education; field chapters are composed of former members of college or university chapters. Over a period of years, the membership has come to include not only teachers but persons in all areas of education. These persons of diversified backgrounds and experiences in education are united through the purpose of Pi Lambda Theta.

Prior to 1975 membership was restricted to women only; however, since that time membership has been open to men as well as women.

About the year 1900, deans of departments of education in universities and colleges realized the need for organizations that would recognize academic achievement and give students a sense of preparing for a distinct profession.

Although the earliest of these organizations were

for men, the development of women's groups followed quickly. Between 1910 and 1916, such associations for women were founded at Missouri, Syracuse, Kansas, Pittsburgh, Minnesota, Washington, and Pennsylvania.

Even in their beginnings. the local groups seemed to realize that their common goals and interests would lead them to form a national organization. Through correspondence and some exchange of representatives, the seven organizations achieved mutual respect and a realization of their unity of purpose. At the meeting of the Department of Superintendence in February, 1917, the deans of schools of education proposed a meeting of all groups interested in founding a national association for women in education. The University of Missouri group invited the others to a conference at Columbia, Missouri, on July 2, 1917. The delegates to that meeting became the founders of Pi Lambda Theta. They were: Louise Nardin, University of Missouri (Alpha Chapter); Ruth Austin, Syracuse University (Beta Chapter); Helen Rhoda Hoopes and Iva Testerman Spangler, University of Kansas (Gamma Chapter); Mary Jane Chambers Dury and Katharine Foulke, University of Pittsburgh (Delta Chapter); Helen Larsen Stevens, University of Minnesota (Epsilon Chapter); Virginia Athen Noland, University of Washington (Zeta Chapter); and Ruth Immel, University of Pennsylvania (Eta Chapter).

The problems of organization were completed; a constitution was written, submitted to the chapters, and approved by the last of the seven chapters on March 3, 1918.

Growth It is the policy of Pi Lambda Theta to grant charters to groups in (1) universities with a strong department, school, or college of education and with a full research program; (2) teachers colleges which meet the necessary criteria; and (3) liberal arts colleges having a strong department of education and offering at least a master's degree.

Any group of twenty or more members of Pi Lambda Theta may petition the Board of Directors to grant a charter for a field chapter.

Government Pi Lambda Theta is a nonprofit corporation, chartered under the laws of the State of Indiana. The Board of Directors consists of the national officers. The officers are a president, a first vice-president, six vice-presidents (two of whom are student vice-presidents), a treasurer and a secretary. All officers, except the secretary, are elected by the chapters from a slate prepared by the nominating committee. Officers, except the secretary, are elected for a two-year term, except for one student vice-president who is selected by the delegates to the National Council. The executive director serves as secretary.

The National Council, made up of the Board of Directors and one delegate from each chapter, meets biennially. The Council receives reports and acts upon recommendations made by the Board of Directors, adopts a budget for the biennium, re-

---

† This chapter narrative is repeated from the 19th edition; no current information was provided.

views and evaluates the association's program, and makes plans for the future.

The national staff, under the direction of the executive director, is responsible for the execution of the policies established by the National Council and the national board.

Each chapter, college (or university) or field, adopts by-laws for its own government which are in harmony with the national constitution and by-laws of Pi Lambda Theta. A chapter, through its duly elected officers, may present to the national board any matter of policy or business for its consideration and action. Each chapter in good Standing is entitled to send one voting delegate or her alternate to the National Council.

Chapter meetings are held at regular intervals, thus providing for continuity and growth. College or university chapters meet five times during the academic year, and field chapters meet at least four times a year. In addition to business and professional matters, programs include opportunity for fellowship.

Publications *Educational Horizons*, the official publication of Pi Lambda Theta, is published quarterly. The *Newsletter*, containing organizational material, is also a quarterly.

Awards The Ella Victoria Dobbs Award, which originated with a founder and early president, recognizes unique or outstanding research by a member. The Distinguished Research Award is given annually to a woman who has completed a superior doctoral research study in education. The Anna Tracey Memorial Award is given to help finance a communications medium that will develop a positive attitude toward older citizens.

Educational Conferences Pi Lambda Theta is represented at major educational conferences and also co-sponsors professional meetings. It has co-sponsored comparative education seminars to the Soviet Union, India, Hungary, and Japan.

Headquarters 4101 East Third Street, P.O. Box A-850, Bloomington, Indiana 47401.

Membership Active chapters 67. Field chapters 37. Total number of initiates 101,727. Chapter roll:††

1918	Alpha, Missouri
1918	Beta, Syracuse
1918	Delta, Pitt
1918	Epsilon, Minnesota
1918	Eta, Penn
1918	Gamma, Kansas
1918	Zeta, Washington
1920	Iota, Indiana
1920	Theta, Iowa
1921	Kappa, Oregon
1921	Lambda, Chicago

†† This chapter roll is repeated from the 19th edition; no current information was provided.

1922	Nu, Ohio State
1922	Xi, Michigan
1923	Omicron, Nebraska
1923	Pi, Washington State
1924	Rho, N.Y.U.
1925	Tau, North Dakota
1926	Chi, Johns Hopkins
1927	Omega, California
1927	Psi, Texas
1928	Alpha Alpha, Arizona
1930	Alpha Beta, Wisconsin, Madison
1930	Alpha Gamma, Boston
1931	Alpha Delta, UCLA
1932	Alpha Epsilon, Columbia
1933	Alpha Eta, Harvard
1933	Alpha Zeta, Northwestern
1935	Alpha Iota, Claremont
1935	Alpha Theta, George Washington
1936	Alpha Kappa, Penn State
1939	Alpha Mu, New Mexico
1939	*Alpha Nu, SUNY Col., Buffalo* (1971)
1940	Alpha Xi, Tennessee
1941	Alpha Omicron, North Colorado
1945	Alpha Pi, Wayne State
1950	Alpha Sigma, Texas Woman's
1954	Alpha Tau, Ball State
1955	Alpha Phi, Florida
1955	Alpha Upsilon, Southern Illinois
1956	Alpha Chi, Cal State, Long Beach
1957	Alpha Psi, Cal State, Los Angeles
1958	Alpha Omega, Bradley
1961	Beta Alpha, San Jose
1962	Beta Beta, San Diego State
1962	Beta Gamma, San Francisco State
1963	Beta Delta, Northern Illinois
1963	Beta Epsilon, Wisconsin, Milwaukee
1964	Beta Zeta, Hawaii
1965	Beta Eta, Toledo
1966	Beta Theta, Kansas State Teachers
1967	Beta Kappa, Arizona State
1968	Beta Lambda, Akron
1969	Beta Mu, Whitworth
1969	Beta Nu, Redlands
1970	Beta Omicron, Millersville
1970	Beta Xi, St. Louis
1971	Beta Pi, Indiana State
1972	Beta Rho, Portland State
1972	Beta Sigma, Connecticut
1973	Beta Chi, William Paterson
1973	Beta Phi, Marquette
1973	Beta Tau, Evansville
1973	Beta Upsilon, Missouri, Kansas City
1974	Beta Omega, Western Connecticut
1974	Beta Psi, Tennessee Tech
1974	Gamma Alpha, Mississippi State
1975	Gamma Beta, Hayward State
1976	Gamma Delta, Indiana Southeast
1976	Gamma Gamma, Indiana, Kokomo

Scarab[†]

(ARCHITECTURE)

ACTIVE PIN

SCARAB was founded in 1909 at the University of Illinois by a small group of architectural students who felt the need of closer communication than that provided in the classrooms and drafting rooms. The first meetings were entirely casual and perhaps more social In aspect than professional. However, since architects the world over cannot refrain from talking shop and discussing or criticizing current buildings, the professional trend became predominant. The fraternity was entirely local for five years, but selected members only from students enrolled in the course of architecture. In later years membership was extended to Include architectural engineers and landscape architects. Upon the addition of other chapters, the rather loose organization became more defined. A ritual was developed, a constitution and by-laws were adopted, and a membership certificate and official badge designed.

Government The government is through an annual general convention and the Supreme Council. Chapter delegates, one from each chapter, and members of the Supreme Council have one vote each. The Supreme Council has power and responsibility of making all decisions between conventions and is charged with carrying out and administering the actions of the general convention.

Traditions and Insignia In the earlier years after additional chapters were taken in, a traveling exhibit of the architectural design work of the schools where Scarab was established was sponsored and administered. Later this was supplanted by a traveling sketch exhibit, consisting of sketches submitted by any architectural students enrolled in schools where Scarab maintained chapters. Prizes were given for the best entries. The sketch exhibit was subsequently discontinued on account of the apparent lack of interest in sketching among architectural students.

A Gold Medal Recognition Award is made by the convention to persons who have made substantial contributions to the architectural profession or outstanding service to the fraternity.

The ritual is based upon Egyptian background and terminology. The badge or key (either form optional) is rectangular in shape with a raised gold scarab (Egyptian beetle) on a black background. Chapters are referred to as temples and are named after Egyptian temples.

† This chapter narrative is repeated from the 19th edition; no current information was provided.

Publications The publication is *The Hieratic*, published twice during the academic year by the national historian. In 1935 Scarab published Louis Sullivan's *Kindergarten Chats* in a limited edition of one thousand copies.

Headquarters Headquarters are at the address of the current national secretary-treasurer, 306 Marvin Hall, Lawrence, Kansas 66044.

Membership Active chapters 7. Inactive chapters 6. Chapters are not allowed to live in houses as a social group. Total number of initiates 5,238. Chapter roll:††

1909	Illinois
1914	*Washington (MO)*
1915	*Illinois Tech*
1916	Penn State
1920	*Carnegie Tech*
1921	Kansas
1921	*M.I.T.*
1926	*George Washington*
1926	*Minnesota*
1927	*USC*
1928	*Virginia*
1929	Cincinnati
1932	Auburn
1932	Washington State
1954	Cal Poly
1955	*R.P.I.*

The Society of Professional Journalists

Sigma Delta Chi[†]

(JOURNALISM)

ACTIVE PIN

THE SOCIETY OF PROFESSIONAL JOURNALISTS, SIGMA DELTA CHI, is the largest, oldest, and most representative organization serving the field of journalism. It is a not-for-profit, voluntary association with a world-wide membership of men and women engaged in every field of journalism. It began at DePauw University on April 17, 1909. The founders were: Leroy H. Millikan, Gilbert B. Clippinger, Charles A. Fisher, William M. Glenn, Marion H. Hedges, L. Aldis Hutchens, Edward H. Lockwood, Eugene C. Pulliam, Paul M. Riddick, and Laurence H. Sloan.

Although founded as a fraternity, Sigma Delta

†† This chapter roll is repeated from the 19th edition; no current information was provided.

Chi changed its designation in 1960 to that of a professional society of journalists. It adopted its present name in 1973.

Sigma Delta Chi is dedicated to the highest ideals of journalism and is comparable to those professional organizations serving the fields of medicine and the law.

SPJ, SDX is the only professional organization that embraces all kinds of journalism as well as all ranks of journalists. It is also the only organization that conducts an extensive program of professional enrichment among journalism students—juniors, seniors, and graduates—at colleges and universities throughout the United States.

In this role, the Society consistently endeavors to raise the standards of competence of its members, to recognize outstanding achievement by journalists, to recruit and hold able young talent for journalism, to advance the cause of freedom of information, and to elevate the prestige of journalism in every respect.

Professional membership is by invitation, following nomination by a chapter and election by the National Board of Directors. Undergraduate membership is by invitation, following election by a student chapter.

There are three classes of membership: undergraduate—the student member elected as a sophomore, junior, or senior major in journalism, with definite intent upon entering journalism as a career, of good character, and having exhibited journalistic proficiency; and professional persons elected from the professional field by undergraduate or professional chapters; and those members initiated as undergraduate who have qualified by having engaged in journalism (as defined by the society) at least one year following graduation, and are so engaged at any given time; fellows—those on whom the society wishes to confer high honor in recognition of their achievements in the profession of journalism. Election is by the national convention. Fellows may be elected from within or without the membership. The maximum number of fellows who may be elected each year shall be three.

Government Government is through an annual convention of delegates and national officers with recess governmental authority in the Board of Directors consisting of five national officers, twelve regional directors, and the past president *(ad hoc)*. Administration is supervised by a fulltime officer.

Traditions and Insignia The emblem is a key bearing a scroll centered over a perpendicular quill, displaying a lamp of learning on the left and a five-pointed Star on the right.

Publication *The Quill.* a professional magazine for journalists of all media, is published twelve months of the year under the direction of a fulltime editor.

Headquarters 35 East Wacker Drive, Chicago, Illinois 60601.

Membership Active chapters 155. Inactive

chapters 15. Total number of initiates 75,000. Chapter roll:††

1909	DePauw
1910	*Denver* (1924)
1910	Kansas
1910	Michigan
1910	*Virginia* (1922)
1911	Ohio State
1911	Oklahoma
1911	Purdue
1911	Washington
1911	Wisconsin, Madison
1912	Illinois
1912	Iowa
1912	*Penn* (1929)
1913	Missouri
1913	Oregon
1913	Texas
1913	*Toronto* (1929)
1914	Indiana
1914	Iowa State
1914	Nebraska
1915	*Beloit* (1926)
1915	*Chicago* (1917)
1915	Kansas State
1915	L.S.U.
1915	*Maine* (1924)
1915	Montana
1915	*Stanford* (1962)
1916	*Miami (OH)* (1924)
1916	Minnesota
1917	*Case Western Reserve* (1933)
1917	*Knox* (1927)
1919	Colorado
1919	*Columbia* (1925)
1919	Grinnell
1919	*Pitt* (1935)
1920	*Cornell* (1959)
1920	Marquette
1920	*North Carolina* (1922)
1920	Oregon State
1922	North Dakota
1922	Northwestern
1924	Drake
1924	Washington State
1925	California (1933-1943)
1926	Butler
1926	*South Dakota* (1932)
1926	Syracuse
1927	*Kentucky* (1936)
1928	Georgia
1928	*South Carolina* (1935)
1929	Baylor (1931-1946)
1929	Florida
1929	Washington and Lee
1930	Temple
1931	Southern Methodist
1932	Ohio

†† This chapter roll is repeated from the 19th edition; no current information was provided.

1932	Penn State		1968	George Washington
1934	USC		1968	Northern Arizona
1937	South Dakota State		1969	Georgia State
1940	Michigan State		1969	New Mexico State
1941	*Emory* (1953)		1969	San Francisco State
1946	Oklahoma State		1970	Cal State, Long Beach
1947	Boston U.		1970	Colorado State
1947	Miami (FL)		1970	Fordham
1947	Nevada		1970	Hawaii
1948	Alabama		1970	Toledo
1948	Idaho		1970	Wichita
1949	Houston		1971	Arkansas State
1949	New Mexico		1971	Cal Poly, Pomona
1952	American		1971	Central Michigan
1952	Kent		1971	College of White Plains
1952	Wayne State		1971	Northeastern
1954	North Texas		1971	Southern Colorado
1954	San Jose		1972	Bridgeport
1954	Texas A & M		1972	Central State University
1954	UCLA		1972	East Tennessee
1954	Utah		1972	Florida Tech
1956	Kentucky		1972	Lincoln (PA)
1956	Maryland		1972	Loyola
1956	Southern Illinois		1972	Marshall
1956	Tennessee		1972	*Pepperdine*
1957	San Diego State		1972	Texas Southern
1958	Bradley		1972	Virginia Commonwealth
1958	Duquesne		1972	Wisconsin, Oshkosh
1958	North Carolina		1972	Wisconsin, Whitewater
1958	Sam Houston		1973	Murray State
1958	Texas Tech		1973	Nebraska, Omaha
1959	Brigham Young		1973	Pepperdine
1959	West Virginia		1973	Point Park
1960	Arizona State		1973	South Florida
1960	South Carolina		1973	Southern Illinois, Edwardsville
1960	Texas Christian		1973	Texas, Arlington
1960	Tulsa		1974	Alaska, Anchorage
1961	East Texas		1974	Central Missouri State
1961	Wyoming		1974	Middle Tennessee
1962	Long Island		1974	Western Kentucky
1963	Arizona		1974	Wisconsin, Eau Claire
1963	Detroit		1975	Arkansas
1963	Cal State, Fresno		1975	Arkansas, Little Rock
1963	Mississippi		1975	Southern Mississippi
1963	San Fernando Valley		1975	Texas, El Paso
1963	Trinity		1975	Utah State
1965	Bowling Green		1975	Wisconsin, River Falls
1965	Cal Poly		1976	Cal State, Hayward
1965	Indiana State		1976	Humboldt
1965	Wisconsin, Milwaukee		1976	Northern Colorado
1966	Ball State		1976	St. Cloud
1966	Cal State, Los Angeles		1976	Stephen F. Austin
1966	Memphis State		1976	Suffolk
1966	St. Bonaventure		1976	Troy
1966	St. Thomas		1977	Florida Southern
1967	Northern Illinois		1977	Rider
1967	Cal State, Sacramento		1977	Wisconsin, La Crosse
1968	Cal State, Fullerton			

Sigma Delta Kappa[†]

(LAW)

ACTIVE PIN

PLEDGE PIN

SIGMA DELTA KAPPA, intercollegiate law fraternity, was founded on August 14, 1914, at the University of Michigan, Ann Arbor.

The objectives of this fraternity are to bring together congenial members of the legal profession and those fitting themselves to become such for mutual association in a business and professional way; to enable students of recognized law schools to meet and associate with other students of character and ability from their own schools and other institutions teaching law; to perpetuate the friendships formed in college; and to aid and assist each other throughout life in every possible way, both socially and professionally.

Government   Each active chapter is represented in the grand chapter by two delegates and each alumni chapter by the delegates. A distinctive feature is the Supreme Council, consisting of a chief justice and eight associate justices, one from each district. Their function is to decide all questions pertaining to the constitution and by-laws of the fraternity and to advise the Executive Committee. Each district is in charge of a grand vice-president reporting to the Executive Committee. During recess of the grand chapter, government is by the Executive Committee, consisting of the grand president, the grand secretary, and three grand trustees, who have authority to grant and withdraw charters and to transact all business for the fraternity not prohibited by the constitution.

Traditions and Insignia   The fraternity's fundamental requirements are scholarship and high character. To encourage scholarship, a scholarship key is awarded to each chapter for the member with the best scholastic record for the year. Numerous awards are made by the active chapters. Each year the Executive Committee awards to a member of Sigma Delta Kappa for some outstanding services rendered to the fraternity a meritorious service award key which is specially designed.

Alumni chapters have been established in fourteen cities. These chapters give invaluable assistance to the college chapters by serving them in an advisory capacity. Another principal function of the alumni chapters is to place graduate members of the fraternity in law offices wherever possible, and otherwise to help them get established in the practice.

† This chapter narrative is repeated from the 19th edition; no current information was provided.

The badge is a coffin-shaped shield, displaying the letters ΣΔK in gold on a black background. The coat of arms is a checkered shield, diagonally across which are six consecutive stars, and over which rests an owl supporting in his beak a pair of balance scales, and surrounding the above is a folded wreath. The flower is a red rose; the colors are red and black.

Publications   The fraternity publishes an official magazine, *Si-De-Ka.*

Headquarters   Suite 414, Arlington Executive Building, 2009 North 14th Street, Arlington, Virginia 22201.

Membership   Active chapters 18. Inactive chapters 31. Graduate/Alumni chapters 13. Total number of initiates 18,350. Chapter roll:

1914	*Alpha, Michigan*
1914	*Beta, Chicago-Kent Law* (school discontinued)
1915	*Delta, Hamilton Law, Chicago*
1915	*Epsilon, Benton Law, St. Louis*
1915	Gamma, Indiana, Indianapolis
1916	Zeta, Valparaiso
1917	Eta, Indiana, Indianapolis
1917	Theta, Chattanooga
1920	*Iota, Washington and Lee*
1921	Kappa, Atlanta Law
1921	Lambda, Detroit
1921	*Mu, National (DC)*
1921	*Nu, Northwestern*
1922	Omicron, Ohio Northern
1922	*Pi, Cumberland* (moved to Birmingham, AL, 1962)
1922	*Xi, Georgia*
1925	Rho, San Francisco
1925	*Sigma, USC*
1926	*Chi, Alabama*
1926	*Phi, Hastings Law*
1926	*Tau, DePaul*
1926	*Upsilon, Minnesota Law, Minneapolis*
1927	*Alpha Alpha, Illinois*
1927	*Alpha Beta, Westminster Law (CO)*
1927	*Alpha Gamma, Mississippi*
1927	*Omega, Chicago-Kent Law* (school discontinued)
1927	*Psi, St. Joseph Law (MO)*
1928	*Alpha Delta, St. John's, Law*
1928	*Alpha Epsilon, Louisville*
1928	*Alpha Eta, Knoxville Law*
1928	*Alpha Theta, Tennessee*
1928	*Alpha Zeta, John R. Neal Law, Knoxville* (school discontinued)
1929	Alpha Iota, Baltimore U.
1929	*Alpha Kappa, Lake Erie Law* (school discontinued)
1929	*Alpha Lambda, Wake Forest*
1929	*Alpha Mu, Columbus (DC)*
1929	*Alpha Nu, Des Moines*
1930	*Alpha Xi, Los Angeles Law*
1931	*Alpha Omicron, Jefferson Law, Dallas*
1932	Alpha Pi, Indiana

1933 Alpha Rho, Washington Law (DC)
1933 Alpha Sigma, Jones Law (AL)
1933 Alpha Tau, Woodrow Wilson (GA)
1936 Alpha Phi, Birmingham Law
1937 *Alpha Psi, Philadelphia*
1938 Alpha Chi, John Marshall Law, Atlanta
1951 *Alpha Omega, Jackson Law (MS)*
1953 Beta Alpha, Augusta Law
1960 Beta Beta, Baltimore Law
1963 Pi, Samford
1966 Massey Law (GA)
1966 Beta Chi, Memphis State

Sigma Nu Phi

(LAW)

SIGMA NU PHI Fraternity (Legal) was founded in 1902 at National University Law School in Washington, D.C. The founding members aspired to create a national organization of strength, with integrity, zeal and efficacy in promoting the study of law and of upholding the ethics of the legal profession. The foundation of those principles was grounded in the ancient English Order of the Coif. The principles being uppermost, include wisdom, justice, truth, friendship, tolerance and reverence, which are the principles ingrained in the fabric of American life.

Government Authority is vested in the Executive Council which is composed of the lord high chancellor, two lord vice chancellors and six other executive officers. The High Court of Chancery is held biennially in Washington, D.C. Each active chapter is represented at the High Court of Chancery by two delegates who have one vote for their chapter. The Executive Council does not vote at the High Court of Chancery, the voting being limited to the active chapters and all past chapter chancellors, who retain a lifetime voting privilege.

Traditions Founders' Day is Lincoln's Birthday, February 12. The badge is a shield within a circle of pearls. A crossed axe and key and three white carnations are shown in the background, with an owl, lamp, law book and Greek letters in the foreground.

Publications The official published magazine is the *Owl*.

The Adelphia Law Journal is a law journal published by the fraternity chapters on a rotating basis. The first issue was published by the Syracuse University of Law. The second issue was published by Detroit College of Law. The third issue was published by Cumberland School of Law. The fourth issue is being published by the chapter at Hamline School of Law. The publishing of these law journals has provided the fraternity with a great deal of favorable publicity. Each issue has been a professional report concerning recent cases.

Headquarters The National Office is located at

Suite 1500, 625 Fourth Avenue South, Minneapolis, Minnesota 55415.

Membership Total living membership 400. Total undergraduate membership 80. Active chapters 10. Inactive chapters 13. Graduate/Alumni chapters 2. City/Area alumni associations 2. Total number of initiates 2,000. Chapter roll:

1902 *Joseph H. Choate Alpha, Nat'l. U. School of Law, Washington D.C. (1943)*
1903 *Chas. E. Hughes Beta, Georgetown U. (1944)*
1904 *Oliver Wendell Holmes Theta, American (1944)*
1916 *Nathan Green Delta, Cumberland (TN) (1940)*
1916 Wm. H. Taft Gamma, Detroit Law
1917 *Gavin Craig Epsilon, USC (1941)*
1921 *Jefferson Davis Zeta, Richmond (1940)*
1921 John Marshall Eta, Stetson
1922 *Champ Clark Iota, St. Louis (1943)*
1922 *James J. Jenkins Kappa, Marquette (1946)*
1923 *Richard Pearson Lambda, Duke (1935)*
1923 *William Mitchell Nu, William Mitchell Law (1940)*
1925 *Edward Douglas Omicron, Loyola, New Orleans (1940)*
1925 *Steven A. Douglas Xi, Loyola, Chicago (1943)*
1975 H. A. Blackmun Alpha Beta, Hamline
1980 Howard J. Munson Alpha Eta, Syracuse
1980 Orville Richardson Alpha Epsilon, St. Louis
1980 Roscoe Pound Alpha Zeta, Nebraska
1981 Marion Griffith Alpha Theta, Vanderbilt
1982 Allen D. Vestal, Iowa
1982 Louis D. Brandeis, Cal Western
1982 Nathan Green Delta, Samford, Law

Tau Epsilon Rho†

(LAW)

ACTIVE PIN

TAU EPSILON RHO was established in 1921 by the amalgamation of Lambda Eta Chi, founded at Western Reserve University Law School in 1919, and Phi Epsilon Rho, founded at Ohio State University Law School in 1920. The fraternity places undergraduate chapters only in day schools having the entrance and curricular requirements of the Association of American Law Schools.

Graduate chapters have been established in various cities, these being composed of men who during

† This chapter narrative is repeated from the 19th edition; no current information was provided.

their residence at law school were members of an undergraduate chapter.

All chapters may admit honorary members. Graduate chapters may include as associate members lawyers who were never members of the fraternity, provided they are of good character and high standards. Honorary members consist of lawyers who are judges, law professors, or notables.

Government The national officers now consist of the following: honorary supreme chancellor, supreme chancellor, supreme vice-chancellors (3), supreme master of the rolls, supreme bursar, supreme graduate bursar, supreme pledgor. supreme scholar, supreme historian, supreme recorder, and supreme editor.

The Supreme Council now consists of the above officers and all past supreme chancellors; one supreme councillor, elected by each graduate chapter; and three undergraduate supreme councillors, elected to represent all of the undergraduate chapters.

Publications The fraternity publishes a quarterly newspaper, the *Summons*. The first *Directory* appeared in 1948 and new editions have been brought out at regular intervals.

Funds The fraternity now has a scholarship foundation made up of a general fund and four memorial funds. The purpose of the foundation is to make loans to undergraduates at a low rate of interest, payable a stated number of years after graduation.

Headquarters Washington Lane and Rugby Street, Philadelphia, Pennsylvania 19138.

Membership Active chapters 12. Inactive chapters 6. Graduate chapters are maintained at Chicago, Cleveland, Columbus, Detroit, Miami, Milwaukee, Philadelphia, and Pittsburgh. Total number of initiates 6,000. Chapter roll:††

1919	Alpha, Case Western Reserve
1920	*Beta, Ohio State*
1924	*Delta, Dickinson Law* (1935)
1924	*Gamma, Columbia* (1936)
1926	Epsilon, Michigan
1926	Eta, Pitt
1926	*Zeta, Denver* (1937)
1927	*Theta, Penn* (1943)
1929	*Iota, Boston*
1929	*Kappa, Albany Law* (1938)
1930	*Lambda, Toronto* (1940)
1931	Mu, Wisconsin, Madison
1934	Nu, Temple
1936	*Delta Rho, Northwestern*
1936	*Xi, Marquette*
1937	*Omicron, Wayne State*
1947	Sigma, Detroit Law
1951	Phi, Miami (FL)

†† This chapter roll is repeated from the 19th edition; no current information was provided.

Women in Communications†

WOMEN IN COMMUNICATIONS is a professional organization of women and men in all fields of communications, founded at the University of Washington, April 8, 1909, as Theta Sigma Phi. (Theta Sigma Phi was founded as an honor society for women in journalism.) Its objectives are: to work for a free and responsible press; to unite women engaged in all fields of communications; to recognize distinguished achievement of woman journalists; to maintain high professional standards; to encourage members to greater individual effort.

There are approximately 75 professional chapters and 75 student chapters across the United States. Chapters go through a petitioning period of approximately two years before receiving their charters. Members of the petitioning chapters can become full-fledged members of the national WICI organization, however, before the petitioning period is completed. Male members have been accepted since 1972.

Government Women in Communications, Inc., is incorporated as a nonprofit organization under the laws of the state of Texas. It is governed by the annual meeting and by the Board of Directors composed of the elected officers of the corporation: the president; the president-elect, who coordinates work of eight regional vice-presidents: the first vice-president, who plans national professional programs and the annual national meeting; the second vice-president, who is concerned with long-term development; the third vice-president. who promotes expansion; the fourth vice-president, who works with student chapters; treasurer; and eight regional vice-presidents.

Traditions and Insignia Most WICI chapters sponsor special events in the spring to honor members and community leaders who have distinguished themselves in communications or who have made contributions in advancing the purposes of Women in Communications.

One national research grant of $1,000 is presented each year to a member or group of members for independent research for the benefit of WICI or the communications industry. In addition, many local chapters give scholarships and awards. The National Headliner Awards, given each year at the national meeting, recognize outstanding professional achievements of members. WICI also sponsors the annual Clarion Awards competition for excellence in communications. Clarion plaques and certificates are awarded at the national meeting.

The badge is a replica in gold or silver of the organization's logo, a "W" encircled by a "C."

Publications A quarterly magazine, *Matrix*, is

† This chapter narrative is repeated from the 19th edition; no current information was provided.

published in January, April, August, and November. A national Newsletter is published eight times annually. WICI also publishes a career booklet for students and a 22-chapter short course for public school journalism teachers.

Headquarters 8305A Shoal Creek Boulevard, Austin, Texas 78758.

Membership The Greek name, Theta Sigma Phi, and the Greek chapter name were laid aside in 1972. Installed as WICI chapters (inactive chapters excluded): Arizona State, Ball State, Boston University, Bowling Green State, California State-Fullerton, California State-Long Beach, California State-Northridge, Central Michigan, Detroit, Duquesne. Fordham, Georgia State, Hampton Institute, Long Island University, Miami (Ohio), Mississippi University for Women, Northern Illinois, Pepperdine University, Southwest Texas State, Suffolk University, Trinity University, Tulsa, Utah, Washington State, Wichita State, Xavier University. Active chapters 72. Chapter roll:††

1909	Alpha, Washington
1910	Beta, Wisconsin, Madison
1911	Gamma, Missouri
1913	Delta, Indiana
1913	Epsilon, Kansas
1913	Eta, Ohio State
1915	Theta, Oregon
1915	Zeta, Oklahoma
1916	Kappa, Montana
1916	Lambda, Nebraska
1916	Mu, Kansas State
1917	Omicron, Iowa State

†† This chapter roll is repeated from the 19th edition; no current information was provided.

1918	Pi, Illinois
1918	Rho, Iowa
1919	Sigma, DePauw
1919	Xi, Texas
1920	Chi, Kentucky
1923	Alpha Beta, Northwestern
1923	Alpha Gamma, Marquette
1925	Alpha Eta, Oregon State
1925	Alpha Zeta, Washington State
1926	Alpha Theta, Michigan
1927	Alpha Iota, Butler
1927	Alpha Kappa, L.S.U.
1927	Alpha Lambda, Colorado
1930	Alpha Mu, Southern Methodist
1930	Alpha Omicron, USC
1930	Alpha Xi, Georgia
1932	Alpha Pi, Texas Woman's
1932	Alpha Rho, Drake
1933	Alpha Sigma, Temple
1934	Alpha Tau, Penn State
1941	Alpha Phi, Ohio
1941	Alpha Upsilon, Texas Tech
1942	Alpha Chi, Oklahoma State
1944	Alpha Psi, Michigan State
1946	Alpha Omega, Franklin
1949	Beta Delta, South Dakota State
1950	Beta Epsilon, Houston
1951	Beta Zeta, Kent
1952	Beta Eta, Mississippi
1953	Beta Kappa, North Texas
1954	Beta Lambda, Purdue
1955	Beta Nu, Idaho
1957	Beta Omicron, American
1962	Beta Phi, Duquesne
1967	Beta Omega, Texas Christian

Part VI

ACHS Member Societies

Alpha Chi

(SCHOLARSHIP)

ACTIVE PIN

ALPHA CHI had its origin as a local scholarship society on the campus of Southwestern University, Georgetown, Texas. The effects there were so noteworthy that other colleges and universities became interested. As a result, there was a movement led by the late Dr. Harry Yandell Benedict, then dean of the College of Arts and Sciences of the University of Texas and later president of the university, which led to the establishment, on February 22, 1922, of a statewide organization bearing the name "Scholarship Societies of Texas."

In time, colleges in Louisiana and Arkansas were admitted to membership, and at a meeting of the society Council on February 26, 1927, the name was changed to "Scholarship Societies of the South." In order to provide an organization better suited to wider opportunities, a new constitution was adopted at a meeting of the Council on February 22, 1934. At this meeting the name was changed to Alpha Chi, the initial letters of the Greek words meaning truth and character. In February, 1955, Alpha Chi became a member of the ACHS.

Purpose   To encourage sound scholarship and devotion to truth, not only among its members but among all the students on campuses on which there are chapters. It is opposed to bigotry, narrowness, and discrimination on any basis other than that of genuine worth.

Major Activities   An outstanding feature of Alpha Chi chapters is their activity and close affiliation with the faculty. The Constitution calls for regular chapter meetings at which there will be activities promoting and recognizing scholarly achievement. Visiting speakers are presented; student papers are read; faculty-led discussions are held. Free tutoring is done by some chapters; some recognize achievement by granting scholarships. At regional and national meetings, student members take part in presenting papers, musical and entertainment features, panel discussions, and in voting on policies and actions.

Government   There are at present seven regions of Alpha Chi, each governed by a regional council composed of a faculty and a student representative from each chapter. Alpha Chi really heads up in the National Council which is composed of not fewer than twelve faculty members, eight of whom are elected by the National Convention, and six student members elected by the regional conventions. Election to National Council membership is for a term of four years. Officers of the National Council are a president, a vice-president, and a secretary-treasurer who is also the executive officer of Alpha Chi. Chapters which are not located in a region are under the direct supervision of the National Council.

A college or university, to be eligible for a chapter, must offer a full four-year liberal arts academic curriculum and be a member of its regional accrediting association. The granting of a new chapter is done by a vote of the National Council.

Classes of membership are active and honorary. High scholarship is the prime requisite but it must be accompanied by good character and reputation. Election to active and alumnus membership is decided by the faculty sponsors; honorary membership is awarded by vote of the National Council.

Eligibility Active membership is restricted to not more than the top-ranking ten percent of members of the junior and senior classes with the provision that a student may qualify for membership at the time of graduation with the baccalaureate degree. The faculty of a given institution may set higher standards. A candidate for membership must have been a regular student in the electing institution for not less than one academic year prior to election and must have completed not less than one half of the hours required for graduation. High scholarship is the primary requisite for membership, but good character and reputation are considerations.

Traditions and Insignia The badge or key is a shield bearing on its front an academic lamp and raised initial letters of the society. On the back in small block letters are the name of the person entitled to wear the key and the name or official initials of the college or university which he was attending when elected to membership. At the bottom in raised letters appears the date of the founding of the Society, Feb. 22, 1922. The presidents and the secretary-treasurers of the National Council and the regional councils are entitled to wear the key which, for them, is set with a chip diamond. The colors of the society are emerald green, signifying victory, and sapphire blue, signifying truth.

Publication The *Alpha Chi Recorder* is published annually.

Headquarters Harding College, Searcy, Arkansas 72143.

Membership Active chapters 273. Graduate/Alumni chapters 2. Total number of initiates 172,000. Chapter roll:††

1922	Texas Alpha, Southwestern (TX)
1922	Texas Beta, Mary Hardin-Baylor
1922	*Texas Delta, Texas Presbyterian*
1922	Texas Epsilon, Trinity (TX)
1922	Texas Eta, North Texas
1922	Texas Gamma, Baylor
1922	Texas Iota, Southwest Texas
1922	Texas Kappa, Austin
1922	Texas Lambda, East Texas
1922	Texas Mu, Texas Wesleyan
1922	Texas Nu, Our Lady of the Lake
1922	Texas Theta, Texas Woman's
1922	Texas Zeta, West Texas
1923	Texas Omicron, Sam Houston
1923	*Texas Xi, Texas Christian*
1925	Texas Pi, Howard Payne
1925	Texas Rho, Hardin-Simmons
1926	Arkansas Alpha, Hendrix
1926	Louisiana Alpha, Centenary
1926	Texas Chi, Sul Ross
1926	Texas Phi, Incarnate Word
1926	Texas Sigma, Stephen F. Austin
1926	Texas Tau, St. Edward's

†† This chapter roll is repeated from the 19th edition; no current information was provided.

1926	Texas Upsilon, McMurry
1927	Texas Omega, Texas A & I
1927	Texas Psi, Abilene Christian
1928	Arkansas Beta, Ouachita
1928	*Texas Alpha Alpha, Texas Tech.*
1929	Louisiana Beta, Louisiana Col.
1932	Arkansas Delta, Ozarks
1932	Arkansas Gamma, Central Arkansas
1937	Oklahoma Alpha, Northeastern (OK)
1937	Texas Alpha Beta, Texas Western
1947	Massachusetts Alpha, American International
1947	Nebraska Alpha, Hastings
1950	Oklahoma Beta, Central State (OK)
1951	Texas Alpha Gamma, Midwestern
1953	Arkansas Epsilon, Henderson
1956	Arkansas Zeta, Arkansas A & M
1956	Texas Alpha Delta, Texas Lutheran
1957	Arkansas Eta, Harding
1957	South Carolina Alpha, Lander
1957	Utah Alpha, Westminster
1958	Arkansas Theta, Southern Arkansas
1958	Georgia Alpha, Valdosta
1958	Texas Alpha Epsilon, Pan American
1958	Texas Alpha Eta, Wayland Baptist
1958	Texas Alpha Zeta, East Texas Baptist
1959	Indiana Alpha, Anderson
1959	Mississippi Alpha, Mississippi Col.
1960	Arkansas Iota, Arkansas Col.
1960	Iowa Alpha, Wartburg
1960	Nebraska Beta, Dana
1960	Tennessee Alpha, Tusculum
1962	North Carolina Alpha, Appalachian
1962	Tennessee Beta, Union (TN)
1963	Maine Alpha, Nasson
1963	Oklahoma Gamma, East Central State
1964	Michigan Alpha, Adrian
1964	Ohio Alpha, Steubenville
1965	Iowa Beta, William Penn
1965	Kansas Alpha, Sterling
1965	Kentucky Alpha, Murray State
1966	Indiana Beta, Huntington
1966	Iowa Gamma, Westmar
1966	Oklahoma Delta, Langston
1966	Oklahoma Epsilon, Oklahoma Christian
1966	South Dakota Alpha, Sioux Falls
1967	Colorado Alpha, Southern Colorado
1967	Kentucky Beta, Nazareth (KY)
1967	Missouri Alpha, William Woods
1967	North Carolina Beta, East Carolina
1968	Alabama Alpha, Talladega
1968	California Alpha, Pepperdine
1968	Florida Alpha, Tampa
1968	Kansas Beta, St. Mary of the Plains
1968	Kentucky Gamma, Kentucky Wesleyan
1968	Maine Beta, Maine, Farmington
1968	Maine Gamma, Ricker
1968	Michigan Beta, Olivet
1968	North Carolina Delta, Elon
1968	North Carolina Gamma, Atlantic Christian
1968	Tennessee Delta, Carson-Newman
1968	Tennessee Epsilon, Lincoln Memorial (TN)

1968	Tennessee Gamma, Tennessee Wesleyan
1968	Texas Alpha Iota, Angelo
1968	Texas Alpha Theta, Texas, Arlington
1968	West Virginia Alpha, Davis and Elkins
1969	Arkansas Kappa, Arkansas Tech
1969	California Beta, Cal Baptist
1969	California Gamma, Azusa, Pacific (CA)
1969	Connecticut Alpha, New Haven
1969	Georgia Beta, Berry (GA)
1969	Illinois Alpha, Eureka
1969	Iowa Delta, St. Ambrose
1969	Minnesota Alpha, St. Scholastica
1969	Pennsylvania Alpha, Widener
1969	Texas Alpha Kappa, Tarleton
1969	Washington Alpha, Fort Wright
1969	West Virginia Beta, Concord
1970	Hawaii Alpha, Brigham Young, Hawaii
1970	Iowa Epsilon, Buena Vista
1970	Louisiana Gamma, Dillard
1970	Massachusetts Beta, North Adams
1970	South Carolina Beta, Voorhees
1971	Arizona Alpha, Grand Canyon
1971	Georgia Gamma, Oglethorpe
1971	Illinois Beta, Blackburn
1971	Illinois Gamma, Parks (IL)
1971	Mexico Alpha, U of Americas
1971	Mississippi Beta, William Carey
1971	New Jersey Alpha, Caldwell
1971	New York Alpha, Ladycliff
1971	North Carolina Epsilon, Mars Hill
1971	North Carolina Zeta, Gardner-Webb
1971	Ohio Beta, Defiance
1971	Oregon Alpha, Warner Pacific
1971	Pennsylvania Beta, Lincoln (PA)
1971	Tennessee Eta, Belmont
1971	Tennessee Zeta, Lee
1971	Texas Alpha Lambda, Houston Baptist
1971	Virginia Alpha, George Mason
1971	West Virginia Delta, Bluefield
1971	West Virginia Gamma, West Virginia Tech
1972	Michigan Gamma, Lake Superior State
1972	Missouri Beta, Culver-Stockton
1972	Missouri Gamma, Southwest Baptist
1972	New York Beta, St. Thomas Aquinas
1972	North Carolina Eta, Shaw
1972	North Carolina Theta, North Carolina A & T
1972	Oklahoma Zeta, Panhandle State
1972	Texas Alpha Mu, Lubbock Christian
1972	Texas Alpha Nu, Dallas Baptist
1972	Virginia Beta, Averett
1972	Virginia Gamma, Bridgewater
1974	Connecticut Beta, Hartford
1974	Kansas Gamma, Marymont
1974	Kentucky Delta, Brescia
1974	Virginia Delta, Roanoke
1974	Virginia Epsilon, Old Dominion
1975	Alabama Beta, South Alabama

1975	Arkansas Lambda, John Brown
1975	California Delta, Menlo
1975	Georgia Delta, Tift
1975	Georgia Epsilon, Piedmont
1975	Louisiana Delta, Our Lady of Holy Cross
1975	Louisiana Epsilon, Southern
1975	Maryland Alpha, Bowie
1975	Mississippi Gamma, Jackson (MS)
1975	Missouri Delta, Westminster
1975	New York Delta, White Plains
1975	New York Epsilon, Mercy
1975	New York Gamma, Medaille
1975	North Carolina Iota, Elizabeth City
1975	North Carolina Kappa, Pembroke
1975	North Dakota Alpha, Jamestown
1975	Ohio Gamma, Mount St. Joseph
1975	Tennessee Theta, Christian Brothers
1976	Maine Delta, Thomas
1976	Missouri Epsilon, Columbia (MO)
1976	North Carolina Lambda, Johnson C. Smith
1976	North Carolina Mu, Methodist
1976	North Carolina Nu, High Point
1976	Pennsylvania Delta, York (PA)
1976	Pennsylvania Gamma, Spring Garden
1976	Tennessee Iota, Freed-Hardeman
1976	Texas Alpha Xi, Texas Eastern
1976	Virginia Zeta, Christopher Newport

Alpha Delta Mu

(SOCIAL WORK)

ALPHA DELTA MU was founded in 1976 at Morgan State University. The Society was admitted to ACHS as an associate in 1983 and reached full membership in 1986.

Purpose To advance excellence in social work practice and to encourage, stimulate, and maintain scholarship of the individual members in all fields, particularly in social work.

Eligibility A student must be a Social Work or Social Welfare major or majoring in a program that is accredited by the Council on Social Work Education. For a junior or senior undergraduate, a grade point average of 3.0 or above is required. A graduate student must have achieved a grade point average of 3.5 or above. Both graduate and undergraduate must have earned a minimum of six semester hours or equivalent in social work.

Major Activities Publications, national conventions, local chapter activities, and Alpha Delta Mu Annual Scholarships.

Publication The *Alpha Delta Mu Journal*.

Membership Active chapters 88. Total number of initiates 8,350. Chapter roll is not available.

Alpha Epsilon

(AGRICULTURAL ENGINEERING)

ACTIVE PIN

ALPHA EPSILON, honor society of agricultural engineering, was founded at the University of Missouri in the spring of 1959. Its purpose is to promote the high ideals of the engineering profession, to give recognition to those agricultural engineers who manifest worthy qualities of character, scholarship, and professional attainment, and to encourage and support such improvements in the agricultural engineering profession to make it an instrument of greater service to mankind.

Eligibility　Membership shall be based on scholarship, leadership, and character. Active members shall be undergraduate and graduate students enrolled in agricultural engineering. A senior must be in the upper third of the college class in which enrolled. A junior must be in the upper quarter of the college class in which enrolled. Graduate students must have completed seven semester hours of graduate course work with a minimum grade average of 3.25 on a 4.0 point scale, or have been eligible as an undergraduate.

Growth　Alpha Epsilon has had a steady growth since its formation in 1959. A national organization of Alpha Epsilon was established by the adoption of a national constitution and bylaws on December 11, 1963, by delegates from Missouri Alpha, Minnesota Gamma, Illinois Delta, Arkansas Epsilon, Indiana Zeta, and Virginia Eta chapters.

An annual meeting is held in conjunction with the American Society of Agricultural Engineers winter meeting. This meeting is purely for convenience as there is no connection between Alpha Epsilon and the American Society of Agricultural Engineers.

Government　The national officers are president, vice-president, and secretary/treasurer. National officers are elected at the annual convention, each officer holding office for one year.

The National Council is made up of the national officers and selected chapter delegates. Each chapter has full autonomy in its direction of program and growth at the chapter level. Each chapter is responsible to the national organization to stay within the limits of the constitution and bylaws and Executive Committee policy.

Traditions and Insignia　There are no prevalent traditions that exist throughout all chapters. Each chapter sets its own policies regarding certain special traditions. The accepted insignia consists of a key and a crest.

Chapters often develop traditional activities concerning the development of high academic standards. These are often done by offering special tutoring service to other students and promoting high-level scholastic services to others in the profession.

The official badge of the society is a watch key. The initials of the owners, the name of the chapter, and the year of the member's initiation are engraved on the reverse side of the key. The official colors of the society are black and gold. The jewelry consists of gold plated keys, tie tacs, key pin, and lapel pin. The Alpha Epsilon crest consists of a shield with a banner showing the words "Alpha Epsilon." In the shield are three symbols representing the "horn of plenty," a "plow," and a "T-square and compass." These symbols represent the place of agricultural engineering in the production of food and fiber. At the top of the shield is the center portion of the key with the letters "AE."

The seal consists of two concentric circles, bearing at the top of the region between the two circles, the words "Alpha Epsilon Founded 1959 University of Missouri."

Publication　Alpha Epsilon has no official or formal publication.

Headquarters　Headquarters location is determined by the residency of the secretary/treasurer. The headquarters will unofficially reside at the Department of Agricultural Engineering, University of Florida, Gainesville, FL 32611.

Membership　Active chapters 27. Total number of initiates 4,291. Chapter roll:††

1959	Alpha, Missouri
1960	Delta, Illinois
1960	Gamma, Minnesota
1961	Epsilon, Arkansas
1962	Zeta, Indiana
1963	Eta, Virginia
1964	Theta, North Dakota
1965	Iota, Ohio
1966	Kappa, South Dakota
1966	Lambda, Nebraska
1966	Mu, North Carolina
1969	Nu, Colorado
1969	Xi, Texas
1970	Omicron, Penn
1971	Pi, Iowa
1971	Rho, West Virginia
1973	Sigma, Michigan
1974	Tau, Wisconsin, Madison
1976	Chi, California
1976	Phi, Texas
1976	Upsilon, Oregon
1977	Omega, Kentucky
1977	Psi, Maryland

†† This chapter roll is repeated from the 19th edition; no current information was provided.

Alpha Epsilon Delta

(PREMEDICAL)

ACTIVE PIN

ALPHA EPSILON DELTA, the national premedical honor society, was founded at the University of Alabama, University, Alabama, April 28, 1926, by W. S. Britt, James Cameron, Joseph G. Cocke, C. S. Cotlin, J. W. Cummins, William Deramus, James Dean, H. G. Franklin, R. L. Garrard, Eugene Johnson, Thomas Lavender, Champ Lyons, S. A. Mitchell, C. P. Powell, W. C. Simpson and Jack P. Montgomery.

Dr. Montgomery acted as adviser in organizing the society and aided in the formulation of the constitution and ritual. The purpose of the society is to encourage and recognize excellence in premedical scholarship; to stimulate an appreciation of the importance of premedical education in the study of medicine; to promote cooperation and contacts between medical and premedical students and educators in developing an adequate program of premedical education; to bind together similarly interested students; and to use its knowledge for the benefit of health organizations, charities, and the community.

In addition to an extensive program of chapter activities, the society is actively engaged in a number of projects in further service to its members and other premedical students. Symposia on premedical education were held at the meetings of the American Association for the Advancement of Science annually from 1946 to 1972. A National Conference on Pre-Medical Education was held on October 21-22, 1950, in cooperation with the Association of American Medical Colleges. Beginning at the University of Louisville in 1947, the society has held numerous regional conferences pertaining to preprofessional education; papers from these meetings have been published in *The Scalpel*. The 1954 convention authorized the sponsorship of four regional conferences to consider the report, "Preparation for Medical Education in the Liberal Arts College." These were held in Berkeley, California; New York City; Chicago, and Birmingham, Alabama, during the academic year 1954-55.

In 1954, the society made the first presentation of the Alpha Epsilon Delta Distinguished Service Award to Dean Aura E. Severinghaus, Columbia University, for his outstanding contributions to premedical education. Dr. Emmett B. Carmichael, Medical College of Alabama, a former AED president, was the recipient in 1966. This award was presented in 1968 to Dr. Jack Caughey, Case Western Reserve School of Medicine, and in 1970 to Dr. Ward Darley, University of Colorado, and formerly executive director of the Association of America Medical Colleges.

Since 1964 the society has presented annually a number of Alumni Scholarships, and since 1981 five Moore Scholarships per year.

The society is a member of the Association of College Honor Societies and an affiliated member of the American Association for the Advancement of Science.

Government The government of the society is by a convention held biennially. In the biennium, administration is controlled by the national officers: national president, vice-president, secretary, treasurer and councilor.

A chapter may be established at any accredited four-year university or college. The membership of the chapters is composed of undergraduate, active alumni and honorary members. Undergraduate members are chosen from the student body of the institution where a chapter is located; active alumni members are individuals chosen from the scientific or medical profession who may become affiliated with the chapter; honorary members are elected by approval of the national officers as outstanding members of the scientific or medical professions.

Membership is open to men and women, the requirements for eligibility being: (1) the student shall be engaged in courses leading to the study of medicine; (2) the student shall have completed at least three semesters or five quarters of premedical work with a general scholastic average of at least 3.0 on a 4.0 scale for "A," and also with an average of 3.0 in the sciences and rank in the upper 35 per cent of the class in general scholarship; (3) character, general ability and personality are considered carefully in selection of every member.

Traditions and Insignia The badge consists of a hexagonal key or pin on the face of which is inscribed AEΔ in longitudinal column. The key is reminiscent of the benzene ring, while the border is emblematic of the continuity of premedical science. Colors are ultraviolet and infrared.

Publications The official magazine, *The Scalpel*, is published at least two times, the *AED Newsletter* at least four times during the college year as well as *Notes to Alumni*.

Headquarters The central office of the society is managed by the national secretary and is located in Garrett Hall, University of Virginia, Charlottesville, Virginia 22903.

Membership Active chapters 140. Total number of initiates 92,000. Chapter roll:††

†† This chapter roll is repeated from the 19th edition; no current information was provided.

1926	Alabama Alpha
1928	Alabama Beta, Samford
1928	South Carolina Alpha, South Carolina
1929	Texas Alpha, Texas
1929	Texas Beta, Baylor
1930	Florida Alpha, Florida
1931	West Virginia Alpha, West Virginia
1932	Alabama Gamma, Auburn
1932	Georgia Alpha, Georgia
1934	Colorado Alpha, Colorado
1934	Missouri Alpha, Central Methodist
1935	Mississippi Alpha, Millsaps
1935	*Pennsylvania Alpha, Lehigh* (1970)
1936	North Carolina Alpha, Davidson
1936	North Carolina Beta, North Carolina
1936	Oklahoma Alpha, Oklahoma
1936	*Virginia Alpha, Emory and Henry* (1969)
1937	*Illinois Alpha, Illinois Wesleyan* (1960)
1938	Arkansas Alpha, Arkansas
1938	Mississippi Beta, Mississippi
1938	Mississippi Gamma, Mississippi State
1938	Nevada Alpha, Nevada
1938	Pennsylvania Beta, Penn State
1938	South Carolina Beta, Furman
1938	Texas Gamma, Texas Tech.
1939	California Alpha, USC
1939	*California Beta, Redlands* (1975)
1939	*Idaho Alpha, Idaho* (1962)
1939	Utah Alpha, Utah State
1939	Wyoming Alpha, Wyoming
1940	Ohio Alpha, Ohio
1941	Michigan Alpha, Detroit
1941	Washington Alpha, Seattle
1945	Kentucky Alpha, Louisville
1946	*Florida Beta, Florida State* (1969)
1946	*New York Alpha, Cornell* (1972)
1946	*Tennessee Alpha, Tusculum* (1969)
1947	New York Beta, Syracuse
1947	Ohio Beta, Toledo
1948	Florida Gamma, Miami (FL)
1948	*Illinois Beta, Carthage* (1964)
1948	North Carolina Gamma, Wake Forest
1948	Ohio Gamma, Otterbein
1948	Pennsylvania Gamma, Pitt
1948	Tennessee Beta, Tennessee
1948	Virginia Beta, Washington and Lee
1948	Washington Beta, Washington (WA)
1949	Indiana Alpha, Indiana
1949	Mississippi Delta, Southern Mississippi
1949	New Hampshire Alpha, New Hampshire
1949	Ohio Delta, Bowling Green
1950	Indiana Beta, Purdue
1950	Louisiana Alpha, Louisiana
1950	Ohio Epsilon, Denison
1950	Pennsylvania Delta, LaSalle
1950	*Tennessee Gamma, Chattanooga* (1960)
1950	Utah Beta, Utah
1950	West Virginia Beta, Marshall
1951	Mississippi Epsilon, Mississippi for Women
1951	*Ohio Zeta, Muskingum* (1968)
1951	Pennsylvania Epsilon, Penn

1952	New York Gamma, Adelphi
1954	Louisiana Beta, L.S.U.
1954	Rhode Island Alpha, Providence
1955	Louisiana Gamma, Centenary
1956	Maryland Alpha, Johns Hopkins
1956	Texas Delta, Houston
1957	Arkansas Beta, Hendrix
1957	New York Delta, Long Island
1958	Louisiana Delta, Tulane
1958	*Quebec Alpha, McGill* (1972)
1959	Kentucky Beta, Kentucky
1959	New York Epsilon, Hofstra
1960	Arizona Alpha, Arizona State
1960	*California Gamma, Pacific (CA)* (1974)
1960	Michigan Beta, Hope
1960	*Vermont Alpha, St. Michael's* (1971)
1962	Connecticut Alpha, Fairfield
1962	*Georgia Beta, Emory* (1969)
1962	Ohio Eta, Dayton
1963	Indiana Gamma, Notre Dame
1963	Ohio Theta, John Carroll
1964	New Jersey Alpha, Seton Hall
1964	Virginia Gamma, Virginia
1965	*Massachusetts Alpha, Holy Corss* (1972)
1965	Mississippi Zeta, Mississippi Col.
1965	New York Zeta, Yeshiva
1966	Colorado Beta, Denver
1966	*New York Eta, Fordham* (1974)
1966	Oklahoma Beta, Oklahoma State
1967	Arizona Beta, Arizona
1968	Illinois Gamma, Millikin
1968	Kentucky Gamma, Western Kentucky
1968	Pennsylvania Eta, St. Joseph's (PA)
1968	Pennsylvania Zeta, Villanova
1968	Wisconsin Alpha, Marquette
1969	Illinois Delta, Illinois
1969	Utah Gamma, Brigham Young
1970	Utah Delta, Weber
1971	South Carolina Gamma, Clemson
1972	District of Columbia Alpha, George Washington
1973	Pennsylvania Theta, Duquesne
1974	District of Columbia Beta, American
1974	Indiana Delta, Valparaiso
1974	Louisiana Epsilon, Northeast Louisiana
1974	Louisiana Zeta, Louisiana Tech
1975	California Delta, San Diego
1975	Florida Delta, South Florida
1975	*Illinois Epsilon, Northwestern* (1976)
1975	North Carolian Delta, North Carolina State
1976	Illinois Zeta, Elmhurst
1976	Kansas Alpha, Kansas State
1976	Louisiana Eta, Xavier (LA)
1976	Nevada Beta, Nevada, Las Vegas
1976	New York Theta, R.P.I.
1976	North Carolina Epsilon, East Carolina
1976	Pennsylvania Iota, Scranton
1976	Texas Epsilon, Houston Baptist
1977	Illinois Eta, Loyola, Chicago
1977	Massachusetts Beta, Boston Col
1977	Virginia Delta, V.P.I.

Alpha Kappa Delta

(SOCIOLOGY)

ACTIVE PIN

ALPHA KAPPA DELTA, a national sociology honor society, was established at the University of Southern California in the fall of 1920 under the leadership of Prof. Emory S. Bogardus. The purpose of the society is the promotion of the study of sociology, the advancement of sound research, and general service to mankind. Administration is by eight officers and ten regional representatives, which operate for the united chapters. The business affairs are conducted annually at the time of the annual meeting of the American Sociological Society.

Charters are granted to colleges and universities in which at least three professors devote full-time to teaching sociology. The school must also offer graduate work leading to at least the master's degree in sociology, and have an active sociology club. In addition, the institution must offer at least ten semester courses in sociology, or 30 semester hours, with at least one course required in methods and theory.

Eligibility For students classified as undergraduate: Must be an officially declared sociology major or demonstrate a serious interest in sociology within an official program of the host institution. Must be at least a junior (third year) by standards of the host institution. Must have accumulated the equivalent of an overall grade point average of 3.0 on a four point scale where A=4. Must have maintained the equivalent of a 3.0 grade point average in sociology courses taken at the host institution prior to initiation. Must have completed at least four regular courses in sociology prior to initiation (exclusive of extension or courses graded pass/fail).

Barring unusual circumstances, graduate students are eligible for membership in Alpha Kappa Delta. Election to Alpha Kappa Delta shall be without regard to race, creed, or national origin.

Insignia The official insignia is the Alpha Kappa Delta key or key pin.

Publication *Sociological Inquiry* and *AKD Newsletter* are published four times a year.

Headquarters Department of Sociology, P.O. Box 10026, Lamar University, Beaumont, TX 77710.

Membership Active chapters 351. Total number of initiates 47,000. Chapter roll:††

†† This chapter roll is repeated from the 19th edition; no current information was provided.

1920	Alpha of California, USC
1922	Alpha of Wisconsin, Wisconsin, Madison
1923	Alpha of Illinois, Northwestern
1923	Alpha of Washington, Washington (WA)
1925	Alpha of Minnesota, Hamline
1925	Alpha of New York, Cornell
1925	Alpha of Ohio, Miami (OH)
1926	Alpha of Iowa, Morningside
1926	Alpha of Nebraska, Omaha
1926	Alpha of Oregon, Oregon
1926	Beta of Ohio, Ohio
1927	Alpha of Michigan, Michigan
1927	Alpha of Missouri, Missouri
1928	Alpha of Texas, Baylor
1928	Beta of Illinois, Loyola, Chicago
1928	Beta of New York, Syracuse
1928	Gamma of Illinois, Illinois
1929	Gamma of Ohio, Ohio State
1930	Gamma of California, Pomona
1931	Alpha of North Carolina, North Carolina
1932	Beta of Texas, Southern Methodist
1932	Delta of Ohio, Ohio Wesleyan
1932	Gamma of New York, N.Y.U.
1933	Beta of Missouri, Washington
1934	Epsilon of Ohio, Cincinnati
1934	Gamma of Texas, Texas
1936	Alpha of Indiana, Indiana
1936	Alpha of Pennsylvania, Pitt
1936	Beta of Nebraska, Nebraska
1936	Delta of Texas, Texas Woman's
1938	Alpha of Alabama, Alabama
1939	Alpha of New Hampshire, New Hampshire
1939	Beta of Michigan, Wayne State (MI)
1939	Beta of Washington, Washington State
1939	Beta of Wisconsin, Marquette
1940	Alpha of New Mexico, New Mexico
1943	Delta of New York, Brooklyn
1945	Alpha of Tennessee, Fisk
1946	Alpha of Georgia, Atlanta
1946	Alpha of Maryland, Maryland
1946	Alpha of South Carolina, Winthrop
1946	Beta of Pennsylvania, Bucknell
1947	Alpha of Colorado, Denver
1947	Delta of Illinois, Southern Illinois
1947	Epsilon of New York, St. Lawrence
1948	Beta of Indiana, DePauw
1949	Alpha of Florida, Florida State
1949	Alpha of Oklahoma, Tulsa
1949	Gamma of Pennsylvania, Penn State
1950	Alpha of Arkansas, Arkansas
1950	Alpha of West Virginia, Marshall
1950	Beta of Florida, Florida
1950	Beta of Iowa, Drake
1950	Beta of North Carolina, North Carolina State
1950	Delta of Iowa, Iowa
1950	Gamma of Florida, Miami (FL)
1950	Gamma of Iowa, Iowa State
1952	Alpha of District of Columbia, George Washington
1952	Alpha of Kansas, Wichita (1956-1959)
1952	Alpha of Massachusetts, Tufts

1952	Beta of District of Columbia, Howard
1952	Beta of Louisiana, L.S.U.
1952	Gamma of North Carolina, North Carolina
1952	Zeta of New York, Buffalo
1953	Alpha of Arizona, Arizona
1953	Alpha of Louisiana, Tulane
1953	Delta of California, San Diego State
1953	Eta of Ohio, Bowling Green
1953	Gamma of Michigan, Michigan State
1954	Alpha of Delaware, Delaware
1954	Alpha of Mississippi, Mississippi State
1954	Gamma of Indiana, Purdue
1954	Theta of Ohio, Kent
1955	Epsilon of California, Occidental
1956	Beta of Georgia, Emory
1956	Beta of Minnesota, Minnesota
1956	Epsilon of Texas, Houston
1957	Eta of California, Whittier
1958	Alpha of Montana, Montana
1958	Beta of Oklahoma, Oklahoma
1958	Delta of Pennsylvania, Duquesne
1958	Eta of Texas, Sam Houston
1959	Alpha of Kentucky, Kentucky
1959	Alpha of Rhode Island, Rhode Island
1959	Theta of Texas, North Texas
1960	Epsilon of Illinois, Northern Illinois
1960	Iota of California, Los Angeles State
1960	Theta of California, San Jose
1961	Beta of Arizona, Arizona State
1961	Beta of Colorado, Colorado
1961	Beta of Kansas, Kansas
1961	Iota of Texas, Texas A & M
1962	Alpha of Utah, Brigham Young
1962	Alpha of Virginia, Virginia State
1962	Epsilon of Iowa, Grinnell
1962	Epsilon of Pennsylania, Penn
1962	Eta of New York, Adelphi
1963	Delta of Indiana, Indiana State
1963	Gamma of Wisconsin, Wisconsin, Oshkosh
1963	Iota of Ohio, Western Reserve
1963	Kappa of California, San Fernando Valley
1963	Kappa of Texas, East Texas
1963	Lambda of California, Cal Western
1963	Zeta of Pennsylvania, Temple
1964	Alpha of New Jersey, Rutgers
1964	Alpha of North Dakota, North Dakota
1964	Beta of Massachusetts, Northeastern
1964	Delta of Wisconsin, Carroll
1964	Gamma of Colorado, Colorado State
1964	Gamma of Louisiana, Southern
1964	Gamma of Missouri, Southwest Missouri
1964	Kappa of Ohio, Denison
1964	Lambda of Ohio, Toledo
1964	Mu of California, San Francisco State
1964	Theta of New York, St. John's (NY)
1965	Delta of Michigan, Detroit
1965	Epsilon of Michigan, Western Michigan
1965	Epsilon of Wisconsin, Mount Mary
1965	Gamma of Georgia, Georgia
1965	Gamma of Minnesota, Macalester
1965	Gamma of Washington, Eastern Washington
1965	Iota of New York, Fordham

1965	Lambda of Texas, Texas Christian
1966	Beta of Tennessee, Tennessee
1966	Delta of Georgia, Georgia State
1966	Delta of North Carolina, East Carolina
1966	Zeta of Illinois, Illinois Wesleyan
1967	Kappa of New York, SUNY, Albany

Alpha Kappa Mu

(SCHOLARSHIP)

ACTIVE PIN

ALPHA KAPPA MU Honor Society began with the meeting of representatives of five local honor societies in Negro colleges at Tennessee Agricultural and Industrial State University, Nashville, November 26–27, 1937. The idea was first conceived by Dr. George W. Gore, Jr., then dean of that school and sponsor of Phi Beta Tau, the host honor society, now president emeritus of Florida A & M University.

The following institutions were represented: Alpha Delta Sigma of West Virginia State College; Gamma Tau of the Agricultural and Technical College of North Carolina; Alpha Epsilon of Bennett College; Beta Tau Upsilon of Tuskegee Institute; and Phi Beta Tau.

The name of the organization as adopted at the 1937 convention was "Federation of Honorary Scholastic Societies." The name was changed to Alpha Kappa Mu Honor Society at the 1939 session at Arkansas State College in Pine Bluff, at which time Dean I. A. Derbigny of Tuskegee Institute became the first president of the society.

Purpose To promote high scholarship, to encourage sincere and zealous endeavor in all fields of knowledge and service, to cultivate a high order of personal living; and to develop an appreciation for scholarship and scholarly endeavor in others.

Election to membership in a chapter of Alpha Kappa Mu is a recognition of intellectual capacities well employed in acquiring an education in liberal arts and sciences or in applied sciences. Since its organization members of Alpha Kappa Mu have been leaders in undergraduate life and winners of advanced degrees.

Eligibility Election to membership in a chapter of Alpha Kappa Mu is limited to students of junior or senior classification, who have earned a minimum of thirty hours at the institution a year prior to induction, with a cumulative grade point ratio of 3.3 or better (A=4), fifty percent or more of the hours needed for graduation must have been completed. In addition to academic requirements, good character and one's reputation are considered for membership. First-year graduate students are eligible if they meet the requirements for undergraduates. A continuing graduate student must have been admitted as a matriculated student and must have earned fifteen hours with a GPA of 3.7 or better.

Most chapters of the society hold monthly meetings at which time a literary or cultural program is presented. At least once a year chapters hold an honors day convocation on their campus at which time an address is delivered on some phase of scholarship, and students who have distinguished themselves in scholarship are presented. Each chapter endeavors to make itself felt on its campus. In some instances, the chapter makes available tutoring services for deficient students.

Traditions and Insignia The official emblem of the society is a gold key engraved with the letters AKM, the torch symbolic of the light that knowledge brings, the open book of knowledge, and the chapter identity. Keys are issued in two sizes, a large size and a small size and they may be gold-filled or 10–carat gold, or pin-on type.

Publications The official publications of the society include the *Proceedings of Annual Conventions*, *News Letters*, the *Official Handbook*, and *A K M Journal*.

Headquarters South Carolina State College, Orangeburg, South Carolina 29117.

Membership Active chapters 77. Graduate/Alumni chapters 6. Total number of initiates 21,600. Chapter roll:††

1937	Alpha Delta Sigma, West Virginia State
1937	*Alpha Epsilon, Bennett* (1973)
1937	Beta Tau Upsilon, Tuskegee
1937	Gamma Tau, North Carolina A & T
1937	Phi Beta Tau, Tennessee State
1938	Alpha Beta Tau, Arkansas, Pine Bluff
1938	Eta Sigma Tau, Knoxville
1939	Alpha Kappa Sigma, Johnson C. Smith
1940	Alpha Omicron, Shaw
1940	Alpha Pi Mu, Prairie View
1940	Kappa Delta, Hampton Inst.
1940	Kappa Gamma, North Carolina Central
1940	Pi Lambda Psi, Morgan State
1940	Pi Sigma Kappa, Philander Smith
1940	Rho Beta Chi, Fayetteville
1940	Zeta Phi Rho, Xavier
1940	*Zeta Rho Chi, Bluefield* (1966)
1941	Kappa Alpha, Southern
1941	Kappa Eta, Virginia Union
1942	Alpha Kappa, Elizabeth City
1942	Delta Eta Sigma, Dillard
1944	Kappa Beta, LeMoyne-Owen
1944	Kappa Iota, Florida A & M

†† This chapter roll is repeated from the 19th edition; no current information was provided.

1944	Kappa Theta, Clark College
1945	Kappa Kappa, Morris Brown
1945	Kappa Lambda, Wilberforce
1945	Kappa Mu, Wiley
1945	Kappa Nu, Kentucky State
1945	*Kappa Xi, Houston-Tillotson* (1952)
1947	Kappa Omicron, Alabama State
1947	Kappa Pi, Benedict
1947	Kappa Rho, Paine
1948	Kappa Sigma, Alabama A & M
1948	Kappa Tau, Central State (OH)
1949	*Kappa Chi, Allen* (1974)
1949	Kappa Phi, Jackson (MS)
1949	Kappa Upsilon, Alcorn
1950	Alpha Alpha, St. Augustine's
1950	Alpha Beta, Texas Southern
1950	Alpha Gamma, Lincoln
1950	Kappa Epsilon, Winston-Salem
1950	Kappa Iota, Bethune-Cookman
1950	Kappa Zeta, Grambling
1951	Alpha Delta, Texas Col
1951	Alpha Eta, Virginia State
1951	Alpha Theta, Claflin
1951	Alpha Zeta, Bishop
1951	Kappa Psi, South Carolina State
1952	Alpha Iota, Albany State
1952	Alpha Mu, Fort Valley
1952	Alpha Nu, Savannah
1953	Alpha Xi, Jarvis Christian
1954	Alpha Phi, Florida Memorial
1954	Alpha Pi, St. Paul's
1954	Alpha Rho, Tougaloo
1954	Alpha Tau, Barber-Scotia
1955	Alpha Lambda, Maryland, Eastern Shore
1956	Alpha Sigma, Miles
1956	Alpha Upsilon, Stillman
1957	Alpha Chi, Langston
1962	Alpha Omega, Lane
1962	Alpha Psi, Livingstone
1963	Alpha Alpha Mu, Houston, TX, Alumni
1963	Mu Alpha, Delaware State
1963	Mu Beta, Coppin
1965	Mu Gamma, Bowie
1966	Beta Alpha Mu, Nashville, TN, Alumni
1966	Gamma Alpha Mu, Little Rock, AR, Alumni
1967	Delta Alpha Mu, East Texas Alumni (Tyler)
1967	Epsilon Alpha Mu, Montgomery, AL, Alumni
1967	Eta Alpha Mu, Savannah, GA, Alumni
1967	Zeta Alpha Mu, Birmingham, AL, Alumni
1969	Mu Delta, Mississippi Valley
1969	Mu Epsilon, Voorbees
1970	Mu Zeta, Norfolk
1973	Mu Eta, Cheyney State
1975	Mu Iota, Paul Quinn
1975	Mu Theta, Rust
1976	Mu Kappa, Mississippi, Hattiesburg

Alpha Lambda Delta

(FRESHMAN SCHOLARSHIP)

ACTIVE PIN

ALPHA LAMBDA DELTA was established at the University of Illinois, May 31, 1924, by Dean Maria Leonard and Miss Gladys Pennington (Mrs. Arthur M. Houser, Jr.) assistant dean of women, to interest freshman women in the pursuit of learning and in high scholastic achievement. Two years later Alpha Lambda Delta became a national organization and was chartered in other educational institutions which were members of the Association of American Universities.

The purpose of the society as stated in the constitution is: to encourage superior scholastic achievement among students in their first year in institutions of higher education, to promote intelligent living, and a continued high standard of learning, and to assist women and men in recognizing and developing meaningful goals for their roles in society.

Membership is based upon superior scholastic accomplishment. The student must be registered for a course of study leading to a bachelor's degree for an amount of work equal to an average full load (usually 15 hours). The scholastic average required for membership is a grade exactly halfway between the two highest grades given by the institution. Scholastic eligibility may be obtained on the grades of one full curricular period, i.e., semester, trimester, quarter, or term or two of these or the cumulative average of the total hours earned within the first year in college.

The chapters initiate their own particular activity programs. The National Council favors the groups' sponsoring only such activities as foster a wholesome respect for and achievement of scholarship. The purpose of membership is to recognize in freshman students potentiality for scholarly development and to encourage them in the pursuit of learning.

Government The National Council is composed of 14 members, the officers (president, vice-president, national secretary), nine district advisers, and *The Flame* Editor. The executive director meets with the Council.

National Awards Senior Certificates are given to all Alpha Lambda Delta seniors who, at graduation, have the cumulative gradepoint average required for membership. A Book Award is presented to the graduating senior in each chapter with the highest cumulative gradepoint average. The national Council annually awards 15 $3,000 graduate fellowships. Any member graduating with a cumulative average of Alpha Lambda Delta initiation standard is eligible. Graduating seniors may apply if they have achieved this average at the end of the first semester (or first quarter) of the senior year.

Publication Alpha Lambda Delta publishes *The Flame*.

Headquarters P.O. Box 88, Muncie, IN 47305.

Membership Active chapters 208. Inactive chapters 30. Total number of initiates 390,352. Chapter roll:

1924	Illinois
1926	Purdue
1927	DePauw
1928	*Michigan* (1974)
1929	Oklahoma
1930	Alabama
1930	*George Washington* (1976)
1930	Mississippi
1930	Penn State
1930	South Dakota
1931	Cincinnati
1931	Doane
1931	Indiana
1931	Montana State
1931	Nebraska
1931	Southern Methodist
1931	*Washington (MO)* (1982)
1932	Maryland
1932	Tennessee (1982-1984)
1933	Idaho
1933	L.S.U.
1933	Northwestern
1933	Oregon State
1933	Texas Woman's
1933	*Utah* (1982)
1934	Birmingham-Southern
1934	Georgia
1934	*Lake Forest* (1962)
1935	Denver
1935	Texas
1936	Montana
1936	Seton Hill
1937	Incarnate Word
1937	Wittenberg
1938	Bucknell
1938	Coe
1938	Drake
1939	Montevallo
1939	USC
1940	Albion
1940	Kentucky
1940	UCLA
1941	Akron
1941	*Florida State* (1986)
1941	Ohio
1942	*Arkansas* (1982)
1942	Kalamazoo
1945	*Iowa* (1977)
1945	Ohio State
1947	Mount Union

1947	Tennessee, Chattanooga		1961	William and Mary
1948	Nebraska		1962	*Evansville* (1987)
1948	Willamette		1962	Howard Payne
1949	Butler		1962	South Carolina
1949	Drury		1962	Texas Christian
1949	Illinois Wesleyan		1962	Western Michigan
1949	Lindenwood		1963	San Jose
1949	Texas Tech		1963	*Washington (WA)* (1974)
1950	*Brigham Young* (1977)		1964	*Colorado* (1974)
1950	Florida		1964	Connecticut
1950	Miami (FL)		1964	North Dakota State
1950	North Dakota		1965	Arkansas State
1950	Oklahoma Science and Arts		1965	DePaul
1951	*Beloit* (1969)		1965	East Tennessee
1951	Bradley		1965	Houston
1951	*Vermont* (1978)		1965	Illinois, Chicago
1952	Auburn		1965	Mississippi State
1952	North Texas		1965	Northeast Louisiana
1953	Hanover		1965	Northwestern Louisiana
1953	*Marshall* (1976)		1965	Southern Nazarene
1953	Oregon		1965	Southwestern Louisiana
1953	Utah State		1966	Bowling Green
1954	Alfred		1966	Cal State, Long Beach
1955	Georgia State		1966	Charleston (WV)
1955	Trinity (TX)		1966	Hawaii
1955	Valparaiso		1966	Illinois State
1956	Colorado State		1966	Longwood
1956	East Texas		1966	Moorhead
1956	MacMurray		1966	Ohio Northern
1956	Monmouth (IL)		1966	South Dakota State
1956	*San Diego U.* (1977)		1966	Winthrop
1956	Southern Illinois		1966	Wisconsin, Oshkosh
1957	Colorado Col		1967	Cal, Santa Barbara
1957	Iowa State		1967	Eastern New Mexico
1957	*Lake Erie* (1988)		1967	Indiana State
1957	*Michigan State* (1980)		1967	Lamar
1957	Southern Mississippi		1967	Murray State
1957	William Jewell		1967	Oklahoma State
1958	Arizona State		1967	Wayne State (NE)
1958	*Arizona* (1981)		1968	Carson-Newman
1958	Baylor		1968	Carthage
1958	Central Methodist		1968	Georgetown Col
1958	Kansas State		1968	Nicholls
1958	Memphis State		1968	*Washington State* (1985)
1958	Regis (MA)		1969	Texas A & I
1958	*SUNY, Buffalo* (1985)		1969	*Tift* (1987)
1958	Samford		1969	Vanderbilt
1959	Fort Hays		1969	West Georgia
1959	Marygrove		1970	Anderson
1959	Morningside		1970	Maine
1960	Kent		1970	North Carolina State
1960	Massachusetts		1970	Sam Houston
1960	Miami (OH)		1970	*Syracuse* (1978)
1960	Mississippi Col		1970	*V.P.I.* (1978)
1960	Otterbein		1970	Wisconsin, Platteville
1960	Pacific (CA)		1971	Alabama, Birmingham
1960	Temple		1971	Angelo
1960	Texas, El Paso		1971	Clemson
1961	*Central Michigan* (1987)		1971	Elizabethtown
1961	*Central Missouri State* (1978)		1971	*New Orleans* (1985)
1961	*Cornell* (1986)		1971	South Alabama
1961	Oklahoma Baptist		1971	Stephens

1971　Wisconsin, Eau Claire
1972　Midland Lutheran
1972　SUNY Col., Fredonia
1972　Tulane
1972　*West Chester* (1988)
1972　Western Carolina
1973　Central State (OK)
1973　Oral Roberts
1973　Radford
1973　Tennessee Tech
1973　Valdosta
1973　*Western Illinois* (1982)
1974　Alabama, Huntsville
1974　Midwestern
1974　North Alabama
1974　Southwest Texas
1974　Texas Lutheran
1974　Troy
1974　West Virginia Wesleyan
1974　Wichita
1975　Tennessee State
1975　Texas A & M
1975　Toledo
1976　Georgia Southwestern
1976　Maryville (TN)
1976　Rider
1976　Roanoke
1977　Jackson (MS)
1977　Susquehanna
1978　Ball State
1978　North Carolina A & T
1979　Salem (WV)
1980　Austin Peay
1980　Brenau
1980　Millikin
1980　Penn State, Altoona
1980　Texas Wesleyan
1981　American
1981　Texas, San Antonio
1982　Converse
1982　Morgan State
1982　Tougaloo
1983　Simpson
1984　Hiram
1984　New Haven
1984　Southern Oregon
1985　Columbia (NY)
1985　IUPUI
1985　McNeese
1985　Rio Grande
1985　St. Joseph's (PA)
1985　Wisconsin, Green Bay
1986　Heidelberg
1986　Liberty
1986　Northern Arizona
1986　Salem State (MA)
1986　Spelman
1987　Wesleyan (GA)
1987　Wright State
1988　Cumberland (KY)
1988　North Carolina, Greensboro
1988　Pitt, Bradford

1988　Rose-Hulman
1988　Southern Colorado

Alpha Phi Sigma

(CRIMINAL JUSTICE)

ALPHA PHI SIGMA was founded in 1942 at Washington State University and admitted to ACHS in 1981.

Purpose　The purpose of Alpha Sigma Phi is to recognize and promote high scholarship among students actively engaged in collegiate preparation for professional services; to keep abreast of the advances in scientific research; to elevate the ethical standards of the Criminal Justice professions; and to establish in the public mind the benefit and necessity of education.

Eligibility　All students must have completed one-third of the credit hours required for graduation by a college or university accredited by the appropriate regional accrediting organization. They also must be recommended by a local chapter advisor or faculty member. Undergraduates must maintain a 3.0 cumulative GPA and a 3.2 GPA in the Criminal Justice field while graduate students are required to have a 3.4 GPA in all graduate courses. Students must rank in the top thirty-five percent of their class.

Major Activities　Alpha Phi Sigma holds a National Convention.

Publication　The Society publishes the *National Newsletter*.

Membership　Active chapters 129. Total number of initiates 17,500. Chapter roll is not available.

Alpha Pi Mu

(INDUSTRIAL ENGINEERING)

ACTIVE PIN

ALPHA PI MU was founded at the Georgia Institute of Technology, Atlanta, on January 25, 1949, by nine students of industrial engineering under the leadership of James T. French. The founders were: Alphonse Boissy, Jr., Ernest T. Sturgis, Charles O. Fiveash, Jr., George M. Lane, James L. Elrod, William R. P. Wilson, William A. Granberry, Alan E. Thomas, and James T. French. It was chartered in the State of Georgia on March 17, 1949, and the founders set out immediately to make it a national organization. The second chapter was installed on May 7 at Ohio State University.

Purpose (1) Confer recognition upon students of Industrial Engineering who have shown exceptional academic interest and abilities in their field; (2) Encourage the advancement and quality of Industrial Engineering education; (3) Unify the student body of the Industrial Engineering department in presenting its needs and ideals to the faculty.

Eligibility Students of Industrial Engineering who rank scholastically in the upper one-third of the senior Industrial Engineering class and the upper one-fifth of the junior Industrial Engineering class are considered for membership on the basis of leadership, ethics, sociability, character, and breadth of interest. Graduate students and alumni may be elected to membership if they meet the requirements. Faculty members and professional industrial engineers may be elected to faculty and honorary membership respectively have proven themselves outstanding professionals in the field.

At the chapter level the many projects conducted are classified in three basic categories: for the betterment of the field; for the betterment of the school; and for the betterment of the chapter. Examples of these projects are engineering educational programs in high schools, preparation of directories of industrial engineering terms, curriculum rating, free tutoring service, participation in honor councils and student councils, preparation of exhibits for Engineers' Week and special meetings, presentation of awards to outstanding students, publishing of special publications, and the sponsoring of student-faculty meetings, special speakers' meetings, and conferences for all students.

At the national level in addition to coordinating and planning chapter and alumni activities, several specific projects are undertaken. Some of these are: a chapter awards program, the promotion of the field of industrial engineering and the publication of related explanatory literature, standardization of industrial engineering terms and curricula, and a program for interesting industrial engineers in registration.

Government The Executive Council consists of a president, vice-president, executive secretary, editor, associate editor, seven regional directors, and a three-member advisory board. The ultimate authority rests in the national convention, which meets biennially. The national officers are elected at each convention. The advisory board consists of the three past national presidents.

Publication The national publication is *The Cogwheel*.

Headquarters P.O. Box 934, Blacksburg, VA 24063-0934.

Membership Active chapters 69. Total number of initiates 30,000. Chapter roll:††

†† This chapter roll is repeated from the 19th edition; no current information was provided.

1949	Alabama, Alabama
1949	Georgia Tech, Georgia Tech
1949	*N.Y.U., N.Y.U.* (1971)
1949	Ohio State, Ohio State
1949	Virginia Tech, Virginia Tech
1950	*Washington (MO)* (1965)
1950	Penn State, Penn State
1951	Columbia, Columbia
1951	Oklahoma State, Oklahoma State
1951	Phi Alpha Mu, Syracuse
1952	Lehigh University, Lehigh
1953	Texas Tech, Texas Tech.
1954	Tennessee, Tennessee
1955	North Carolina State, North Carolina State
1955	West Virginia, West Virginia
1956	Arkansas, Arkansas
1957	California, California
1957	Columbia, Columbia
1957	Michigan, Michigan
1958	*Northwestern U., Northwestern* (1974)
1958	Pittsburgh, Pitt
1958	Southern California, USC
1958	Texas A & M, Texas A & M
1959	Lamar Tech, Lamar
1959	Purdue, Purdue
1960	Houston, Houston
1960	Northeastern University, Northeastern
1962	Arizona State, Arizona State
1963	Missouri, Missouri
1964	Bradley, Bradley
1964	N.C.E., Newark Engineering
1965	I.I.T., Illinois Tech.
1965	Rutgers, Rutgers
1966	Massachusetts, Massachusetts
1967	Florida, Florida
1968	Auburn, Auburn
1968	*Cornell, Cornell* (1972)
1968	Oklahoma, Oklahoma
1969	Kansas State, Kansas State
1969	Oregon State, Oregon State
1970	Texas, Texas, Arlington
1971	Mississippi State, Mississippi State
1971	Toledo, Toledo
1972	New Mexico State, New Mexico State
1972	Puerto Rico, Puerto Rico
1973	Cal Poly, Cal Poly
1973	Florida Tech, Florida Tech
1973	Louisiana Tech, Louisiana Tech
1973	Montana State, Montana State
1974	Nebraska, Nebraska
1976	Gamma Epsilon Sigma, Iowa State
1976	Illinois, Illinois

Alpha Sigma Mu

(METALLURGICAL AND MATERIALS ENGINEERING)

ACTIVE PIN

ALPHA SIGMA MU was established in 1932 by the faculty of Metallurgical Engineering at the Michigan College of Mining and Technology (now Michigan Technological University), at Houghton, Michigan. Early operation was effective on the three campuses where chapters were established, but it appeared that the society needed assistance to accomplish truly widespread growth. In 1956, the national officers approached the American Society for Metals as to that society's willingness to assume the business management of the fraternity. A careful study was made as to Alpha Sigma Mu's potential and the professional needs for such an Organization. 'The American Society for Metals agreed that both the potentials and the possible influence on education were sufficiently important to justify interest in, and support of, the society's efforts to expand its activities. From 1957 to 1963 the American Society for Metals' national officers served also as the governing board of Alpha Sigma Mu, and used the full influence of that society to further the interests of the honor society. By 1963 enough growth and strengthening had occurred that Alpha Sigma Mu developed a new constitution and undertook its own management. Provision is made for election of members-at-large from schools that do not have chapters. Honorary members may be elected from the outstanding members of the profession.

Purpose To honor those students of metallurgy, metallurgical engineering and materials engineering who attain high rank in scholarship and who possess to a high degree the qualities of exemplary integrity, leadership and initiative.

Eligibility There are three classes of membership: *Distinguished Life Members, Regular,* and *Honorary. Distinguished Life Members* shall have achieved and maintained, throughout a long career, a distinguished international standing in metallurgy, metallurgical engineering, materials science, or materials engineering professions, either through academic, research, or industrial activity. Election to Distinguished Life Membership shall be made by unanimous action of the Board of Trustees. An *Honorary Member* shall have achieved exceptionally high standing in the metallurgy, metallurgical engineering, materials science, or materials engineering professions either through academic, research, or industrial activity. A *Regular Member*

shall be either an outstanding undergraduate or graduate student possessing the qualities of integrity, leadership, and initiative, at a recognized college or university in a pertinent curriculum, or a practicing scientist or engineer who has attained high stature in the field of metallurgical or materials engineering, either through outstanding scholarly activity, research, or service to the profession.

An undergraduate student shall be of junior or senior status, shall have completed at least nine semester credit hours, or the equivalent in his major area, and shall have attended the approved college or university for at least two full quarters or one semester. He shall be in the cumulative upper one-third scholastically of all students working toward a degree in the pertinent curriculum. A graduate student shall have completed at least nine semester hours or the equivalent at the graduate level and must meet the above qualities. A practicing scientist or engineer shall be well-known and respected nationally or regionally for his contributions to science or engineering in fields related to metallurgy and/or materials.

Government It is governed by a national board of trustees of nine members operating under and being elected by an annual meeting of the membership. Most correspondence is carried out through the office of the national secretary.

Major Activities Alpha Sigma Mu Lecture given at the Annual Meeting of the Society.

Traditions and Insignia The original emblem of the fraternity consisted of a gold nugget on a key with the letters Alpha Sigma Mu encrusted on the nugget. Upon reorganization in 1957, the Trustees authorized a key emblem showing a steel time-temperature-transformation diagram, intended to represent the transition of the metallurgical field from an art to a science.

Publications The Alpha Sigma Mu *Newsletter* is published annually and a descriptive brochure is produced at three-year intervals.

Headquarters The International Headquarters is maintained in the office of the national secretary; currently at the University of Missouri at Rolla, Rolla, Missouri 65401.

Membership Active chapters 24. Inactive chapters none. Total number of initiates 6,850. Chapter roll:††

1932	Alpha, Michigan Tech
1940	Beta, Illinois
1941	Gamma, V.P.I.
1958	Missouri Alpha, Missouri, Rolla
1960	Maryland Alpha, Maryland
1960	Michigan Beta, Wayne State (MI)
1960	New York Alpha, N.Y.U.
1960	New York Beta, Brooklyn Polytech
1961	Alabama Alpha, Alabama
1961	New York Gamma, R.P.I.

†† This chapter roll is repeated from the 19th edition; no current information was provided.

1961 Ohio Alpha, Case Tech
1962 Indiana Alpha, Notre Dame
1962 North Carolina Alpha, North Carolina State
1962 Ohio Beta, Ohio State
1962 Pennsylvania Alpha, Drexel Institute
1962 Quebec Alpha, Ecole Polytechnique
1963 Indiana Beta, Purdue
1965 Colorado Alpha, Colorado Mines
1965 Texas Alpha, Texas, El Paso
1966 Florida Alpha, Florida
1968 Colorado Beta, Denver
1969 Kentucky Alpha, Kentucky
1969 Ohio Gamma, Cincinnati
1969 Wisconsin Alpha, Wisconsin, Madison
1971 Michigan Gamma, Michigan
1973 New York Alpha, New York
1974 Illinois Gamma, Northwestern
1974 New Mexico Alpha, New Mexico
1974 Pennsylvania Beta, Penn State
1976 Ohio Delta, Youngstown
1976 Tennessee Alpha, Vanderbilt

Alpha Sigma Nu

(GENERAL SCHOLARSHIP—JESUIT)

ACTIVE PIN

ALPHA SIGMA NU, national honor society of the Jesuit colleges and universities, was established at Marquette University in 1915 by the Rev. John A. Danihy, S.J. The society (originally Alpha Sigma Tau) continued as a local organization until 1921 when a chapter was installed at Creighton University. Subsequently, invitations were extended to St. Louis University and the University of Detroit where chapters were installed in 1923 and 1924.

The first national convention was held in Milwaukee, Wisconsin, on February 13-17, 1925; William Hebard was elected the first national president. In 1973 the society merged with Gamma Pi Epsilon, a Jesuit honor society for women, with chapters on 15 campuses, to form the present Alpha Sigma Nu society.

Candidates are selected by the chapter's active members from lists of junior and senior students from all the departments or colleges; those nominated must have demonstrated superior scholarship, loyalty and service to the college or university. The final elections are made with the approval of the deans and the president of the college or university. No more than four per cent of the population may be elected and they must rank in the top 15 per cent of their class and have not less than a "B" average. In addition, the president of each college or university is accorded, each year,

the privilege of nominating from the eligibility list not more than three students whom he deems qualified for membership.

Purpose To honor students of Jesuit colleges and universities who distinguish themselves in scholarship, loyalty, and service; to band together and encourage those so honored both as students and as alumni to understand, to appreciate, and to promote the ideals of Jesuit education.

Government A triennial convention elects a national board of directors which in turn elects its own officers. An executive committee administers the affairs of the society between board meetings through an executive director.

Traditions and Insignia The society is dedicated to the recognition of outstanding students and to the promotion of the ideals of Jesuit education. Membership is open to members of other honor societies and fraternities, to both men and women, and to qualified persons of any race, color, or creed.

The chapters are autonomous in adapting their programs to their own campuses; some schedule lecture series or sponsor outstanding lectures; others participate in honor convocations and still other prepare special reports for the college or university president.

The society's emblem is a shield with the Greek letters over the eye of wisdom. It is available as a key or pin.

Publications The *ASN Newsletter* is published semi-annually and distributed to all members. In addition, a monthly bulletin is circulated to all faculty advisers and chapters, *Faculty Advisers Bulletin.*

Major Activities The national organization funds Gesu Awards through the Jesuit Institute for the Arts, three Annual Book Awards for the best books written by faculty or administrators in Jesuit colleges or universities, and annual undergraduate scholarships. Each chapter is to a large degree autonomous and may undertake such activities as may promote the intellectual and cultural interests of its membership and the college or university and such activities as are appropriate to the aims and purpose of the Society. Some schedule special lecture series or sponsor outstanding lecturers; others participate in a special way in honors convocations; and still others prepare special reports for the college or university president and sponsor tutorial programs.

Headquarters 1324 W. Wisconsin Avenue, Milwaukee, Wisconsin 53233.

Membership Active chapters 29. Graduate/Alumni chapters 3. Total number of initiates 27,000. Chapter roll:††

1915 Marquette
1921 Creighton

†† This chapter roll is repeated from the 19th edition; no current information was provided.

1923	St. Louis
1924	Detroit
1936	Loyola, New Orlens
1937	Spring Hill
1938	Loyola, Chicago
1939	Boston Col
1939	Gonzaga
1939	John Carroll
1939	Loyola Marymount, Los Angeles
1939	St. Joseph's (PA)
1939	Xavier (OH)
1940	Holy Cross
1941	San Francisco
1942	Loyola (MD)
1942	Santa Clara
1943	Scranton
1950	Georgetown
1951	LeMoyne-Owen
1953	Rockhurst
1955	Canisius
1959	Wheeling (WV)
1961	Fairfield
1966	Regis (CO)
1967	St. Peter's
1975	Sogang (Korea)

Beta Gamma Sigma

(BUSINESS AND MANAGEMENT)

ACTIVE PIN

BETA GAMMA SIGMA is a national scholastic honor society for men and women in schools and colleges of commerce and business administration. Its purpose is to encourage and reward scholarship and accomplishment among student's of business administration, to promote the advancement of education in the art and science of business, and to foster integrity in the conduct of business operations.

It was founded February 26, 1913, by the union of three local societies for men in commerce and economics: Beta Gamma Sigma at the University of Wisconsin, the Economics Club at the University of California, and Delta Kappa Chi at the University of Illinois.

In 1919 it was designated by the American Association of Collegiate Schools of Business as "the scholarship society" for students in commerce and business administration. Chapters are eligible only in those schools of business accredited by AACSB.

Growth In 1933 it effected a merger with Gamma Epsilon Pi, which was founded in 1918 as an honor organization for women, corresponding to

Beta Gamma Sigma for men. Beta Gamma Sigma now admits men and women on equal terms.

Eligibility Limited to those majoring in business and management. The upper 10 percent of undergraduate students, the upper 20 percent of master's students, and doctoral students who have completed all requirements for that degree may be inducted. Undergraduates may be inducted as early as their junior year.

Government Government is by convention held biennially and an intermediate administration by the Board of Governors, consisting of the five national officers, the immediate past national president, the chief executive officer of the Directors' Table, and twelve additional members (six being elected by each biennial convention for four-year terms).

Major Activities Beta Gamma Sigma provides $2,500 scholarships for undergraduate and master's students and contributes $20,000 to the National Doctoral Fellowship Program, which provides fellowship support for a doctoral student as well as support for the institution.

Insignia The emblem is a gold key displaying a rectangular shield with the society's name on a diagonal band.

Headquarters 750 Office Parkway, Suite 50, St. Louis, Missouri 63141.

Membership Active chapters 253. Inactive chapters 3. Graduate/Alumni chapters 1. Total number of initiates 275,000. Chapter roll:††

1913	Alpha of California, California
1913	*Alpha of Illinois, Illinois*
1913	Alpha of Wisconsin, Wisconsin, Madison
1916	Alpha of Pennsylvania, Penn
1917	Alpha of New York, Columbia (NY)
1918	Alpha of Georgia, Georgia
1918	Alpha of Washington, Washington (WA)
1920	Alpha of Iowa, Iowa
1920	Beta of Illinois, Northwestern
1920	Beta of Pennsylvania, Pitt
1921	Alpha of Minnesota, Minnesota
1921	Alpha of Missouri, Washington (MO)
1921	Alpha of Oregon, Oregon
1922	Alpha of Ohio, Cincinnati
1922	Alpha of Texas, Texas
1922	Beta of New York, Syracuse
1922	Beta of Ohio, Ohio State
1923	Alpha of Indiana, Indiana
1923	Beta of California, USC
1924	Alpha of Nebraska, Nebraska
1925	Alpha of Massachusetts, Boston
1926	Alpha of Colorado, Denver
1926	Alpha of Kansas, Kansas
1926	Alpha of Louisiana, Tulane
1926	*Alpha of North Dakota, North Dakota*
1927	*Beta of Georgia, Georgia Tech* (1933)
1928	Alpha of Kentucky, Kentucky

†† This chapter roll is repeated from the 19th edition; no current information was provided.

1929	Alpha of Virginia, Virginia	1962	Zeta of Pennsylvania, Duquesne
1929	Beta of Wisconsin, Marquette	1963	Alpha of South Carolina, South Carolina
1930	Alpha of Florida, Florida	1963	Beta of Arizona, Arizona State
1930	Alpha of Michigan, Michigan	1963	Beta of Indiana, Notre Dame
1931	Alpha of Alabama, Alabama	1963	Beta of Nebraska, Creighton
1931	Beta of Missouri, Missouri	1963	Delta of Louisiana, Louisiana Tech
1932	Alpha of Arkansas, Arkansas	1963	Delta of Massachusetts, Northeastern
1932	Gamma of New York, Buffalo	1963	Gamma of Florida, Florida State
1933	Alpha of North Carolina, North Carolina	1963	Gamma of Missouri, St. Louis
1933	Alpha of Oklahoma, Oklahoma	1963	Theta of California, San Francisco
1933	Beta of Louisiana, L.S.U.	1963	Zeta of Illinois, Southern Illinois
1933	Beta of Texas, Southern Methodist	1964	Beta of Utah, Brigham Young
1933	Beta of Virginia, Washington and Lee	1964	Eta of Illinois, Roosevelt
1933	Delta of New York, N.Y.U.	1964	Eta of New York, Rochester
1935	Epsilon of New York, CCNY	1964	Eta of Texas, Houston
1935	Gamma of Pennsylvania, Temple	1964	Gamma of Oklahoma, Tulsa
1939	Beta of Colorado, Colorado	1964	Iota of California, Cal State, Sacramento
1939	Zeta of New York, Fordham	1964	Iota of Ohio, Kent
1940	Alpha of Maryland, Maryland	1964	Zeta of Texas, Texas Christian
1940	Gamma of California, UCLA	1965	Gamma of Nebraska, Omaha
1940	Gamma of Illinois, Chicago	1965	Gamma of Virginia, Richmond
1942	Alpha of New Jersey, Rutgers, Newark	1965	Kappa of California, Cal State, Fullerton
1944	Alpha of Mississippi, Mississippi	1966	Gamma of Washington, Seattle
1946	Alpha of Utah, Utah	1967	Alpha of Delaware, Delaware
1947	Alpha of Tennessee, Tennessee	1967	Delta of Virginia, V.P.I.
1947	Gamma of Ohio, Miami (OH)	1967	Kappa of Ohio, Akron
1948	Alpha of Arizona, Arizona	1968	Drexel
1950	Delta of Pennsylvania, Lehigh	1968	East Carolina
1950	Gamma of Georgia, Emory	1968	Hawaii
1951	Alpha of South Dakota, South Dakota	1968	San Jose
1951	Beta of Washington, Washington State	1968	Texas Southern
1951	Beta of Oregon, Oregon State	1969	Hofstra
1951	Delta of Ohio, Ohio	1969	Missouri, Kansas City
1952	Alpha of Montana, Montana	1969	New Orleans
1952	Beta of Michigan, Detroit	1969	Northern Arizona
1953	Beta of Iowa, Drake	1969	Rhode Island
1954	Gamma of Michigan, Michigan State	1969	San Francisco State
1955	Alpha of West Virginia, West Virginia	1969	St. John's
1955	Delta of California, Santa Clara	1969	Texas, Arlington
1955	Epsilon of Ohio, Bowling Green	1969	Wichita
1955	Zeta of Ohio, Toledo	1970	Bridgeport
1957	Alpha of Wyoming, Wyoming	1970	Colorado State
1957	Beta of Massachusetts, Boston Col	1970	Memphis State
1957	Epsilon of Pennsylvania, Penn State	1970	Northern Illinois
1958	Beta of Florida, Miami (FL)	1970	Purdue
1958	Delta of Illinois, DePaul	1970	South Florida
1958	Eta of Ohio, Western Reserve	1970	Wisconsin, Milwaukee
1958	Gamma of Louisiana, Loyola, New Orleans	1970	Wisconsin, Oshkosh
1959	Alpha of Connecticut, Connecticut	1971	Missouri, St. Louis
1959	Beta of Oklahoma, Oklahoma State	1971	N.Y.U.
1959	Gamma of Massachusetts, Massachusetts	1971	Pacific Lutheran
1959	Gamma of Texas, Texas	1971	Western Michigan
1960	Delta of Georgia, Georgia State	1972	Cal State, Long Beach
1960	Delta of Texas, Baylor	1972	Illinois, Chicago
1960	Epsilon of California, Cal State, Fresno	1972	John Carroll
1960	Zeta of California, San Diego State	1973	Alabama, Birmingham
1961	Beta of Mississippi, Mississippi State	1973	Cal State, Chico
1961	*Beta of North Carolina, Wake Forest*	1973	Kansas State
1961	Eta of California, Cal State, Los Angeles	1973	New Mexico State
1962	Alpha of Nevada, Nevada	1973	Northeast Louisiana
1962	Epsilon of Illinois, Loyola, Chicago	1973	William and Mary
1962	Epsilon of Texas, North Texas	1974	Cleveland State

1974   Maine
1974   Utah State
1975   Atlanta
1975   Eastern Michigan
1975   Fort Lewis
1975   Old Dominion
1975   Wisconsin, Whitewater
1976   Cal State, Bakersfield
1976   East Texas
1976   Eastern Washington
1976   Idaho State
1976   Southern Illinois, Edwardsville
1976   Stephen F. Austin
1976   Villanova
1976   Wright State
1977   Arkansas, Little Rock
1977   Auburn
1977   Howard
1977   Murray State
1977   North Florida
1977   South Alabama
1977   Southern Mississippi
1977   St. Cloud
1977   Wayne State

Beta Kappa Chi

(NATURAL SCIENCES AND MATHEMATICS)

ACTIVE PIN

BETA KAPPA CHI was founded at Lincoln University (Pennsylvania) in 1923 by a group of undergraduate science students who were strongly supported and encouraged by the Science Faculty. The original organization was more or less a scientific club at Lincoln. Officers of this club undertook to write other colleges regarding the increased interest in science on their respective campuses and the harnessing of this potential in a common cause. It existed as a local organization until 1926, at which time a chapter was established at West Virginia State College. Three years later, in 1929, a third chapter was founded at Howard University. In May, 1929, the society was incorporated in the State of Pennsylvania through the efforts of the chapter at Lincoln University. Since then expansion has been steady.

The purpose of Beta Kappa Chi is to stimulate undergraduate and graduate education in the natural sciences and mathematics; to inspire the continued pursuit of knowledge and achievement, and the capture of scientific truths during the entire career of each member.

There are two classes of elective membership: undergraduate and graduate student members and professional graduate members. High scholarship is the prime requisite. Undergraduate and graduate student members are chosen from the student body of the institution where a chapter is located. Professional graduate members are elected by approval of the national officers from among men and women who have made outstanding contributions to the scientific and mathematical professions.

Eligibility   Undergraduate students are eligible for membership if they rank in the upper fifth of their class and have completed at least sixty-four semesters hours of college work, seventeen semester hours of which shall be in one of the sciences recognized by Beta Kappa Chi with a grade average of at least B in the science area and a general college average of at least B; graduate students are eligible if they have completed at least fifteen semester hours in one of the sciences recognized by the Society with a grade average of A in at least one-third of the hours and at least B in the remaining two-thirds semester hours.

Government   The government of the society is by a convention held annually. During the interim, the administration is controlled by the Executive Council: national president, the vice-presidents of each of the five regions, executive secretary, treasurer, editor-in-chief, and assistant editor of the official magazine.

Traditions and Insignia   The badge consists of a key in the form of a benzene ring with the letters BKX across the middle; above the B is a clover leaf, the symbol of botany; above the K is a skull and crossed bones, the symbol of anatomy; and above the X is a circle, the symbol of astronomy. Below the B is a retort, the symbol of chemistry; below the K is a balance, the symbol of physics; and below the X is a scroll with stencils extending from each end, the symbol of mathematics.

Major Activities   Publishes the *Beta Kappa Chi Bulletin*, two issues a year, and a Booklet of Information; sponsors, stimulates, and encourages a variety of program activities through local chapters; conducts an annual national convention to transact Society business and for the presentation of reports on research conducted by undergraduate and graduate members.

Publication   The official magazine, the *Beta Kappa Chi Bulletin*, is published two times in the college year.

Headquarters   Hampton University, Hampton, Virginia 23668.

Membership   Active chapters 57. Total number of initiates 9,600. Chapter roll:††

1923   Lincoln (PA)
1926   West Virginia State
1929   Howard
1931   Johnson C. Smith
1932   Lincoln (MO)

†† This chapter roll is repeated from the 19th edition; no current information was provided.

1933 Virginia Union
1934 Morgan State
1935 Virginia State
1943 Hampton Inst.
1943 *Lane* (1960)
1943 *Wilberforce* (1955)
1944 North Carolina College
1944 Philander Smith
1944 Southern
1944 Tennessee A & I
1944 Tuskegee
1945 D.C. Teachers
1945 Fisk
1945 Kentucky State
1945 LeMoyne-Owen
1945 *Livingstone* (1960)
1945 Wiley
1946 North Carolina A & T
1947 *Alabama State* (1960)
1947 Bluefield
1947 Prairie View
1948 *Benedict* (1960)
1948 Bennett
1948 Central State (OH)
1948 South Carolina State
1951 Bethune-Cookman
1951 Fort Valley
1952 Arkansas A & M
1952 Atlanta University Center
1952 *Bishop* (1960)
1952 *Shaw* (1960)
1952 *St. Augustine's* (1960)
1952 Texas Southern
1953 Florida A & M
1953 *Savannah State* (1960)
1953 *Texas Col.* (1960)
1956 Grambling
1956 Talladega
1957 Dillard
1958 Knoxville
1958 Tougaloo Southern Christian

Beta Phi Mu

(LIBRARY SCIENCE)

BETA PHI MU was founded in August, 1948, at the University of Illinois. The society was proposed by a group of leading librarians and library educators who felt such an organization might offer much in the service of librarianship and library education. The first initiation was held in the spring of 1949. The society was admitted to ACHS in 1969.

Purpose Recognition of superior academic achievement in library and information science; sponsorship of professional and scholarly projects.

Government The society is governed by a national Executive Council composed of the president and president-elect who hold two-year terms, a treasurer, six directors-at-large elected for three-

year terms. It also includes the appointed offices of executive secretary and administrative secretary. The council meets twice a year.

Membership is granted to graduates of library school programs accredited by the American Library Association who fulfill the following requirements: (1) Complete the course requirements leading to a fifth-year or other advanced degree in librarianship with a scholastic average of A-minus. This provision also applies to planned programs beyond the fifth year that do not culminate in a degree but which require full-time study for one or more academic years. (2) Receive a letter of recommendation from their respective library schools attesting to their demonstrated fitness of successful professional careers.

Major Activities The society has developed a scholarship program for beginning library school students and for Beta Phi Mu members who wish to engage in continuing education or foreign study. The *Monograph* publications program is a major activity of the society. The national organization sponsors an annual initiation during the summer American Library Association Convention.

Award An annual award, conferred through the American Library Association, is made to a person in or out of the professional who has made an outstanding contribution to education for librarianship through tools, methods, or classroom techniques. The award consists of a citation and a cash sum.

Insignia The insignia is the dolphin and the anchor, mark of the Venetian printer Aldus Manutius, who not only created beautiful editions of the classics but who also dedicated his life to making his works accessible to many. Gold and black keys and pins bearing the insignia are available to members. The motto is *Aliis Inserviendo Consumor* ("We are consumed in the service to all.")

Publications A newsletter is circulated semi-annually. The society also sponsors a series of chapbooks designed to create a beautiful combination of text and format in the interest of the graphic arts.

Headquarters University of Pittsburgh, School of Library and Information Science, Pittsburgh, Pennsylvania 15260.

Membership Active chapters 49. Inactive chapters 5. Total number of initiates 24,700. Chapter roll:

1949 Alpha, Illinois
1956 Beta, USC
1957 Epsilon, North Carolina
1957 Gamma, Florida State
1959 Pi Lambda Sigma Society, Syracuse
1960 Zeta, Atlanta
1962 Theta, Pratt
1964 Iota, Catholic
1964 Iota, Maryland
1966 *Kappa, Western Michigan* (1983)
1967 Lambda, Oklahoma
1967 Mu, Michigan

1967	Nu, Columbia (NY)
1967	Pi, Pitt
1968	Rho, Kent
1968	Xi, Hawaii
1969	Sigma, Drexel
1969	*Tau, SUNY Col., Geneseo* (1983)
1970	Chi, Indiana
1970	Omicron, Rutgers
1970	*Phi, Denver* (1985)
1970	Upsilon, Kentucky
1971	Beta Alpha, Queens (NY)
1971	Psi, Missouri
1972	Omega, San Jose
1973	Beta Beta, Simmons
1973	Beta Delta, SUNY, Buffalo
1973	Beta Epsilon, Emporia
1973	Beta Gamma, Oregon
1974	Beta Eta, Texas
1974	Beta Zeta, L.S.U.
1975	Beta Kappa, Alabama
1975	Beta Theta, Brigham Young
1976	Beta Iota, Rhode Island
1976	Beta Lambda, North Texas
1976	Beta Lambda, Texas Woman's
1976	Beta Mu, Long Island
1976	Beta Xi, North Carolina Central
1977	Beta Nu, St. John's (NY)
1977	Beta Omicron, Tennessee
1977	Beta Pi, Arizona
1978	Beta Rho, Wisconsin, Milwaukee
1979	*Beta Tau, Wayne State (MI)* (1985)
1980	Beta Phi, South Florida
1980	Beta Sigma, Clarion
1980	*Beta Upsilon, Alabama A & M* (1981)
1981	Beta Psi, Southern Mississippi
1982	Beta Omega, South Carolina
1983	Beta Beta Delta, Cologne—West Germany
1983	Beta Beta Gamma, Rosary (IL)
1984	Beta Beta Epsilon, Wisconsin, Madison
1984	Beta Beta Zeta, North Carolina, Greensboro
1985	Beta Beta Alpha, UCLA
1988	Beta Beta Theta, Iowa

Chi Epsilon

(CIVIL ENGINEERING)

ACTIVE PIN

IN 1922 two groups of civil engineering students at the University of Illinois simultaneously began the work of organizing a departmental honor fraternity. Finding the existence of one another, they pooled their efforts and on May 20, 1922, Chi Epsilon Fraternity was formed. On February 13, 1923, the fraternity was incorporated in the State of Illinois. Shortly thereafter, on March 29, 1923, the second chapter of Chi Epsilon was formed at the Armour Institute of Technology, now Illinois Institute of Technology, and the fraternity was on its way to becoming a national organization. Basic steps to create a firm foundation for future growth were taken at the first conclave, held at Armour Institute in 1924 and furthered by the second conclave in 1926 at the University of Illinois.

The purpose of Chi Epsilon is to place a mark of distinction upon the student of civil engineering who exemplifies the four traits of the successful engineer, the cornerstones upon which Chi Epsilon is founded: scholarship, character, practicality, and sociability. Only those students are eligible for active membership who have maintained an average grade in scholarship in the highest one-third of the class of those who are eligible to Chi Epsilon honors, namely those students duly registered in the civil engineering course, or directly associated courses whose curricula have been approved, and who have completed at least one-half of the required work for their bachelor's degree.

Government The society is governed by national conclaves held biennially, and by the Supreme Council which acts between conclaves. The Supreme Council consists of 12 members, ten of whom represent geographical sections of the United States, a secretary-treasurer, and the editor of *The Transit.*

Traditions and Insignia Activities of the society at the chapter level include such projects as establishing reading rooms for all civil engineering students; awarding a prize to the outstanding freshman civil engineering student; setting up exhibits of civil engineering working models for Engineer Day shows, etc.; surveys of curricula and teaching methods in civil engineering; talks to high school students, telling them about civil engineering; surveys of physical plant, such as lighting of class and drafting rooms and fire protection; and study-help programs for underclassmen.

Chapter activities are undertaken with the thought of assisting the department in its work and in promoting faculty-student relations. Each chapter occasionally selects an outstanding civil engineer to be an honor member of that chapter. At each biennial national conclave, one such chapter honor member may be elevated to national honor member by petition of the nominating chapter and election of the Supreme Council. This is the highest honor which Chi Epsilon can confer.

National projects include the preparation and distribution of a scholarship survey, including scholarships, fellowships, and assistantships available to civil engineering students. Distribution is made to all interested organizations and all engineering schools without regard to membership in the society.

Colors are purple and white. The badge for all except national honor members is a yellow gold key made to resemble a full front view of an engineer's transit with the superimposed letters XE between the standards of the transit. In the space representing the objective of the transit is set a red jewel. The badge of national honor members is a white gold key, in all other respects the same as described above.

Publication   The society magazine, *The Transit*, is published semiannually.

Headquarters   College of Engineering, Tennessee Tech University, Cookeville, Tennessee 38505.

Membership   Total living membership 55,000. Total undergraduate membership 2,000. Active chapters 109. Inactive chapters 2. Graduate/ Alumni chapters 1. Total number of initiates 62,581. Chapter roll:

1922	Illinois
1923	Illinois Tech
1923	Minnesota
1924	USC
1925	Cal, Berkeley
1925	Cornell
1925	Wisconsin, Madison
1927	Penn State
1928	M.I.T.
1929	Colorado
1929	Purdue
1934	Missouri
1934	Texas
1937	Mississippi
1938	Auburn
1940	Iowa
1940	R.P.I.
1941	Georgia Tech
1941	Oklahoma State
1941	V.P.I.
1948	Alabama
1948	Michigan Tech
1948	Michigan
1948	North Carolina State
1948	Utah
1949	CUNY, Brooklyn
1949	Connecticut
1949	Cooper Union
1949	Manhattan
1949	New York Poly
1949	Ohio State
1949	Tennessee
1949	West Virginia
1950	Cincinnati
1950	Colorado State
1950	Detroit
1950	Marquette
1950	Missouri, Rolla
1951	Clarkson
1951	Michigan State
1951	New Mexico
1951	Norwich
1952	Lehigh
1953	Drexel
1954	*N.Y.U.* (1973)
1955	Southern Methodist
1956	Wayne State (MI)
1956	*Yale* (1964)
1957	Hawaii
1958	New Jersey Tech
1960	Kansas State
1961	Maryland
1961	Nebraska
1961	South Dakota State
1961	Worcester Tech
1962	Arkansas
1962	Kentucky
1962	Texas A & M
1964	Duke
1965	Iowa State
1965	Northeastern
1966	Notre Dame
1967	Kansas
1967	San Diego U.
1967	Vanderbilt
1968	L.S.U.
1968	Lamar
1968	New Mexico State
1969	Bradley
1969	SUNY, Buffalo
1969	Texas, Arlington
1970	Cal State, Los Angeles
1970	Pitt
1970	Rutgers
1970	Vermont
1971	Mississippi State
1971	Montana State
1971	San Jose
1971	Wisconsin, Platteville
1972	Houston
1973	Cal State, Long Beach
1973	Tri-State
1974	Clemson
1975	Tennessee Tech
1975	Texas Tech
1976	Louisiana Tech
1976	Texas, El Paso
1977	Virginia
1978	Louisville
1978	Syracuse
1979	Old Dominion
1980	Maine
1980	South Carolina
1982	Cal Poly, Pomona
1982	Carnegie-Mellon
1982	Colorado, Denver
1982	Columbia (NY)
1982	Villanova
1983	Lowell
1983	Oklahoma
1983	Washington (WA)
1984	Miami (OH)
1984	South Florida
1985	Arizona State
1985	Delaware
1985	Southwestern Louisiana
1986	Cal Poly, San Luis Obispo
1988	Cal, Irvine
1988	Massachusetts
1988	Nebraska, Omaha
1988	Rhode Island

Delta Epsilon Sigma

(SCHOLARSHIP)

ACTIVE PIN

DELTA EPSILON SIGMA is a national scholastic honor society for students, faculty, and alumni of colleges and universities with a Catholic tradition. It was begun at the suggestion of Rev. E. A. Fitzgerald, dean of studies at Loras College, Dubuque, Iowa, who in October, 1938, surveyed Catholic colleges and universities concerning their interest in initiating such a society.

In 1939 a committee of founders under the chairmanship of Father Fitzgerald was appointed to draw up a general plan of organization. Subcommittees on constitution, on name and motto, and on insignia were all appointed. A constitutional convention was held at Hotel President, Kansas City, Missouri, in March, 1940; a provisional constitution was adopted.

National meetings between 1941 and 1945 were infrequent because of the war situation, but the society was kept alive through the efforts of Father Fitzgerald, the national secretary-treasurer. In 1947 the society initiated its official publication, the *Delta Epsilon Sigma Bulletin*.

The first major revision of the constitution and bylaws was adopted in April, 1959. On May 28, 1976, in the bicentennial year of the United States of America, a new constitution, by-laws, and induction ritual were approved by a national conclave held at Rosemont College, Philadelphia.

Purpose The purposes of this Society shall be to recognize academic accomplishments, to foster scholarly activities, and to encourage a sense of intellectual community among its members.

Eligibility To be eligible for membership in the Society, candidates must be persons who have a record of outstanding academic accomplishment, who have shown dedication to intellectual activity, and who have accepted their responsibility of service to others. Undergraduate students shall have completed at least fifty percent of the credit requirements for their baccalaureate degrees with a distinction of performance which, if continued, would make them eligible for graduation *cum laude*. Graduate students shall have completed at least one-half of the credit requirements for their degrees, with an average performance which, if continued would make them eligible for their degrees. Faculty members are eligible for election to membership. Alumni of an institution are eligible for election to membership if they have graduated *cum laude* or have received a graduate degree or have fulfilled the general requirements of membership in some other manner.

Government An Executive Committee of six members is elected by the annual convention.

Insignia The official key bears the inscription ΔΕΣ in the upper right-hand corner, and the lamp of the catacombs in the lower left.

Publication The official organ of the society is the *Delta Epsilon Sigma Bulletin*, published four times a year. In addition, the society publishes a handbook for members and some publicity material.

Headquarters Loras College, Dubuque, Iowa 52001.

Membership Active chapters 99. Total number of initiates 42,000. Chapter roll:††

1940	Alpha, Loras
1940	Alpha Alpha, Loyola, Chicago
1940	Alpha Beta, Siena Heights
1940	Alpha Delta, Notre Dame (MD)
1940	Alpha Epsilon, Immaculata
1940	Alpha Eta, St. Mary's, San Antonio
1940	Alpha Gamma, St. Norbert
1940	Alpha Zeta, Niagara
1940	Beta, St. Mary's (MN)
1940	Chi, St. Francis (PA)
1940	Delta, Fontbonne
1940	Epsilon, St. Joseph's (NY)
1940	Eta, St. Francis (IL)
1940	Gamma, Carroll (MT)
1940	Iota, Regis (MA)
1940	Kappa, Emmanuel
1940	Lambda, Dayton
1940	Mu, St. John's (MN)
1940	Nu, Immaculate Heart
1940	Omega, St. Benedict (MN)
1940	Omicron, Portland
1940	Phi, St. Vincent
1940	Pi, Loyola (LA)
1940	Psi, Maryland (MO)
1940	Rho, Clarke
1940	Sigma, St. Mary-of-the-Woods
1940	Tau, St. Anselm's
1940	Theta, Providence
1940	Upsilon, St. Scholastica
1940	Xi, St. Ambrose
1940	Zeta, Mount St. Mary's (MD)
1941	Alpha Iota, Holy Cross
1941	Alpha Theta, DePaul
1942	Alpha Chi, St. Rose (NY)
1942	Alpha Kappa, Our Lady of the Elms
1942	Alpha Lambda, St. Mary (KS)
1942	Alpha Mu, Seton Hall
1942	Alpha Nu, St. Michael's
1942	Alpha Omega, St. Francis (IN)
1942	Alpha Omicron, Rosemount (PA)
1942	Alpha Phi, Good Counsel (NY)
1942	Alpha Pi, Rockhurst
1942	Alpha Psi, Mount Mercy (PA)

†† This chapter roll is repeated from the 19th edition; no current information was provided.

1942	Alpha Rho, Mount Mary
1942	Alpha Sigma, St. Thomas
1942	Alpha Tau, Mount St. Vincent (NY)
1942	Alpha Upsilon, Chestnut Hill
1942	Alpha Xi, Marcyhurst
1942	Beta Beta, College Misericordia (PA)
1943	Beta Gamma, Barat (IL)
1944	Beta Delta, Caldwell
1944	Beta Epsilon, Marywood
1945	Beta Eta, Marian (IN)
1945	Beta Zeta, Barry (FL)
1946	Beta Iota, Saint Mary's (LA)
1946	Beta Theta, St. Theresa (MO)
1948	Beta Lambda, Rivier
1948	Beta Mu, Sacred Heart (LA)
1948	Beta Nu, Cardinal Stritch
1948	Beta Omicron, Our Lady of Mercy (ME)
1948	Beta Xi, Mount St. Mary's (CA)
1949	Beta Pi, Alverno
1949	Beta Sigma, Marycrest (IA)
1949	Beta Tau, Annhurst
1950	Beta Upsilon, Aquinas
1951	Beta Phi, Mercy (MI)
1953	Beta Chi, Villanova
1954	Beta Psi, Siena
1955	Beta Omega, St. Thomas (TX)
1955	Gamma Alpha, Catholic
1956	Gamma Beta, Assumption
1956	Gamma Delta, St. Joseph's (IN)
1956	Gamma Epsilon, Rosary Hill (NY)
1956	Gamma Eta, Quincy
1956	Gamma Gamma, Anna Maria
1956	Gamma Theta, National Chapter-at-Large
1956	Gamma Zeta, Duchesne (NE)
1959	Gamma Iota, Belmont Abbey
1959	Gamma Kappa, St. Bonaventure
1959	Gamma Lambda, St. Bernard (AL)
1959	Gamma Mu, Bellarmine
1959	Gamma Nu, Marymount (NY)
1960	Gamma Omicron, Stonehill
1960	Gamma Xi, Marillac (MO)
1961	Gamma Pi, Edgewood
1962	Gamma Rho, Albuquerque
1963	Gamma Sigma, King's
1965	Gamma Chi, Lewis
1965	Gamma Phi, St. Mary (OH)
1965	Gamma Tau, St. John Fisher
1965	Gamma Upsilon, Great Falls
1968	Delta Alpha, Salve Regina
1968	Delta Beta, San Diego College
1968	Gamma Omega, Molloy
1968	Gamma Psi, Catholic, Puerto Rico
1970	Delta Gamma, Sacred Heart (CT)
1971	Delta Delta, Allentown
1971	Delta Epsilon, Iona
1971	Delta Zeta, Notre Dame (CA)
1972	Delta Eta, St. Francis (ME)
1976	Delta Theta, Biscayne (FL)

Delta Mu Delta

(BUSINESS ADMINISTRATION)

ACTIVE PIN

DELTA MU DELTA was established at New York University on November 13, 1913, as the result of action taken by five professors on the faculty of the School of Commerce, Accounts and Finance: Dean Joseph French Johnson, Prof. George Burton Hotchkiss, Prof. Charles W. Gerstenberg, Prof. Edward J. Kilduff, and Prof. John R. Weldmon. These men strongly believed that recognition should be given to outstanding students of business subjects. This recognition should be similar to that given by honor societies in the various fields of scholastic endeavor. At that time, there were no honor societies for business students.

In 1951, a national charter was applied for and a National Council established under bylaws and standing rules. This was done for the purpose of binding the individual chapters into a cohesive unit to carry forward the aims of the society. In 1963, the society became a member of The Association of College Honor Societies.

Purpose To promote higher scholarship in training for business and to recognize and reward scholastic attainment in business subjects.

Government The national officers and the faculty advisor from each chapter are members of the National Council. Each council member has one vote. National Council meetings are held triennially. The Executive Council meets at least once in each 18-month period. The officers consist of president, vice-president, executive secretary, and treasurer whose terms of office are three years. The chairman for the committee on expansion and development and four members-at-large are elected national officers.

Under the national bylaws, each chapter can admit into membership in Delta Mu Delta those scholastically qualified students of good character. Undergraduate members are restricted to those students registered in the programs of business administration who are candidates for the baccalaureate degree and who have completed at least half of the work required for this degree and who have achieved an cumulative average qualified grade record of .2 above a B or better and are in the top 20 percent of their class. The local chapters must model their bylaws after the national bylaws and may raise their standards but may not lower them.

Candidates who are graduate students studying for the master's degree, and who have attained a scholastic average not less than .25 above a B are eligible for membership provided they have one-half of the work completed and are in the top 20 percent of their class in cumulative grades.

The society grants annual scholarships to students in the business program at schools where there is a chapter of Delta Mu Delta.

Insignia The emblem is a gold key in the form of a Greek letter Δ, on one side of which appears a full-rigged ship with sails set and colors flying, symbolizing the activity of business. Below the ship are the letters ΔMΔ. The key and the engraved certificate are presented upon induction. The motto is *Through Knowledge Power.*

Publication A newsletter from the National Council is circulated annually.

Headquarters 800 Oakton, Apt. 3, Evanston, Illinois 60202.

Membership Active chapters 122. Inactive chapters 12. Total number of initiates 57,252. Chapter roll:

1921	*Alpha, Pitt* (1960)
1922	*Beta, Northwestern* (1970)
1925	Gamma, Cincinnati
1932	*Delta, St. John's (NY)* (1968)
1932	Epsilon, Bucknell
1948	Zeta, Baldwin-Wallace
1954	Eta, DePaul
1959	*Theta, Georgia State* (1960)
1960	Sigma, Quinnipiac
1961	*Iota, Memphis State* (1970)
1963	Kappa, Lincoln (MO)
1963	Lambda, Elmhurst
1964	*Mu, Texas Southern* (1982)
1964	Nu, C. W. Post
1964	*Xi, Atlanta* (1973)
1966	*Omicron, Kansas State* (1974)
1966	*Pi, Iona* (1988)
1966	Rho, Ithaca
1967	*Phi, Middle Tennessee* (1984)
1967	Tau, Eastern Illinois
1967	Upsilon, Roanoke
1968	Alpha Alpha, West Liberty
1968	Chi, Pittsburg State, Kansas
1968	Omega, Scranton
1968	Psi, Chaminade
1970	Alpha Beta, Wagner
1970	*Alpha Delta, Kansas Wesleyan* (1982)
1970	Alpha Epsilon, South Carolina State
1970	Alpha Eta, Bryant
1970	Alpha Gamma, Andrews
1970	Alpha Iota, Athens (1982-1983)
1970	Alpha Kappa, Manhattan
1970	Alpha Lambda, William Jewell
1970	Alpha Mu, High Point
1970	Alpha Theta, West Virginia Wesleyan
1970	Alpha Zeta, Western New England
1971	*Alpha Chi, Cal State, Hayward* (1984)
1971	Alpha Nu, North Park
1971	Alpha Omicron, Jackson (MS)
1971	Alpha Phi, Northern Michigan
1971	Alpha Pi, Nicholls
1971	Alpha Rho, Delaware State
1971	Alpha Sigma, Alabama A & M
1971	Alpha Tau, Moorhead
1971	Alpha Upsilon, Harding
1971	Alpha Xi, New York Tech
1972	Alpha Omega, St. Augustine's
1972	Alpha Psi, Slippery Rock
1972	Beta Alpha, Tuskegee
1973	Beta Beta, Grove City
1973	Beta Delta, Western Connecticut
1973	Beta Epsilon, Alfred
1973	Beta Eta, Bloomsburg
1973	Beta Gamma, Benedict
1973	Beta Iota, Ohio Northern
1973	Beta Kappa, St. Edward's
1973	Beta Theta, Daemen
1973	Beta Zeta, Prairie View (1982-1988)
1974	Beta Lambda, Lewis and Clark
1974	Beta Mu, Grand Valley
1974	Beta Nu, Nicholls
1974	Beta Xi, Adelphi
1975	Beta Omicron, Franklin
1975	Beta Pi, Mount Mary's (CA)
1975	Beta Rho, Delta State
1975	Beta Sigma, Salem State (MA)
1975	Beta Tau, Wartburg
1975	Beta Upsilon, Mercy (NY)
1976	Beta Chi, Radford
1976	Beta Omega, Pace
1976	Beta Phi, Tennessee State
1976	Beta Psi, Central Methodist
1976	Gamma Beta, Fayetteville
1977	Gamma Delta, Mount Vernon Nazarene
1977	Gamma Epsilon, Alabama State
1977	Gamma Eta, Walsh Accountancy
1977	Gamma Gamma, Stonehill
1977	Gamma Iota, Trenton
1977	Gamma Kappa, Bowie
1977	Gamma Theta, Tri-State
1977	Gamma Zeta, Anderson
1978	Gamma Alpha, Suffolk
1978	Gamma Lambda, Fairleigh Dickinson, Rutherford
1978	Gamma Mu, Morgan State
1978	Gamma Nu, New Hampshire Col
1978	Gamma Omicron, Baltimore U.
1979	Gamma Pi, Eastern
1979	Gamma Sigma, Bethany Nazarene
1979	Gamma Tau, SUNY Col., Oswego
1979	Gamma Xi, Dakota State
1980	Gamma Phi, Southampton
1980	Gamma Rho, Meredith
1980	Gamma Upsilon, Susquehanna
1981	Gamma Chi, Illinois Col
1981	Gamma Omega, Eastern New Mexico
1981	Gamma Psi, Cal Poly, Pomona
1982	Delta Alpha, Salisbury
1982	Delta Beta, Texas A & M
1982	Delta Gamma, Monmouth (IL)
1983	Delta Epsilon, LeMoyne-Owen
1983	Delta Eta, Central Connecticut
1983	Delta Iota, Hawaii Pacific

1983   Delta Theta, SUNY Col., Geneseo
1983   Delta Zeta, St. Mary's, San Antonio
1984   Delta Kappa, St. Francis (PA)
1984   Delta Lambda, Our Lady of the Lake
1984   Delta Pi, Dowling
1984   Delta Sigma, Taylor
1984   Delta Xi, Northwood (MI)
1985   Delta Mu, St. Bonaventure
1985   Delta Omega, Eastern Connecticut
1985   Delta Omicron, Marcyhurst
1985   Delta Phi, SUNY Col., Fredonia
1985   Delta Psi, Indianapolis
1985   Delta Rho, Freed-Hardeman
1985   Delta Tau, St. Catherine
1985   Delta Upsilon, Philadelphia Textiles
1986   Delta Chi, York (PA)
1986   Delta Nu, Ramapo
1986   Epsilon Alpha, St. Thomas Aquinas
1986   Epsilon Beta, Ashland
1986   Epsilon Gamma, Madonna
1987   Epsilon Delta, Sacred Heart
1987   Epsilon Eta, Florida Institute
1987   Epsilon Zeta, Georgian Court
1988   Epsilon Lambda, Fontbonne
1988   Epsilon Theta, Mid-America Nazarene
1989   Epsilon Kappa, Augsburg
1989   Epsilon Mu, Cal State, Dominguez Hills
1989   Epsilon Nu, Southeastern Massachusetts
1989   Epsilon Xi, Roosevelt
1990   Epsilon Iota, Mount Mary's (MD)
1990   Epsilon Omicron, King's
1990   Epsilon Pi, Fisk

Delta Sigma Rho-Tau Kappa Alpha

(FORENSICS)

ACTIVE PIN

DELTA SIGMA RHO-TAU KAPPA ALPHA was founded at Denver, Colorado, on August 18, 1963, through merger of societies established at Chicago, Illinois, on April 13, 1906, and Indianapolis, Indiana, May 13, 1908, respectively.

Delta Sigma Rho was conceived by Prof. E. E. McDermott of the University of Minnesota. He discussed the desirability of a forensic honor society with his friends in the public speaking departments of neighboring universities for several years. The final steps leading to its organization were suggested simultaneously by him and Prof. Henry E. Gordon of Iowa.

Tau Kappa Alpha originated in the state house of Indiana in the chamber of the lieutenant-governor,

Hugh T. Miller. Oswald Ryan, a young debater of Butler University, was the father, founder, and first secretary of the society.

The purposes of Delta Sigma Rho-Tau Kappa Alpha are "to promote interest in, and to award suitable recognition for, excellence in forensics and original speaking; and to foster respect for, and an appreciation of, freedom of speech as a vital element of democracy."

To become a member a student must have participated at a high level of excellence in at least two years of intercollegiate (or equivalent) forensics or original speaking activity, supervised by the faculty sponsor of a campus chapter or by qualified members of the forensic staff. However, when the forensic or original speaking activity was commenced in the senior year as an undergraduate, one year of such participation shall be acceptable. In any case, the student shall have completed at least three semesters of five quarters of college prior to initiation, and shall rank in the upper 35 per cent of his college class.

Traditions   The society sponsors annual national and regional conferences at which students discuss and debate current vital national issues. A National Student Council involves undergraduate members in the operation of the society.

Annual awards are made to the "Speaker of the Year," who exemplifies the characteristics of "effective, intelligent, and responsible communication in a democracy," to Distinguished Alumni, and to the winners in the National Forensic League nationwide high school tournament.

Insignia   The emblem is the gold key bearing the initials of the society and a five-point star.

Publication   The society publishes a journal, *The Speaker and the Gavel*, and has published a textbook, *Argumentation and Debate*.

Headquarters   University of Georgia, Athens, Georgia 30602.

Membership   Active chapters 192. Total number of initiates 58,000. Chapter roll:††

1906   Chicago
1906   Illinois
1906   Michigan
1906   Minnesota
1906   Nebraska
1906   Northwestern
1906   Wisconsin, Madison
1907   Ohio Wesleyan
1908   Butler
1908   Cincinnati
1908   George Washington
1908   Indiana
1908   Miami (OH)
1908   Missouri
1908   Notre Dame
1908   Virginia

†† This chapter roll is repeated from the 19th edition; no current information was provided.

1909	Beloit	1917	Washington and Jefferson
1909	Brown	1917	Wyoming
1909	Denver	1919	Rhode Island
1909	Harvard	1920	Middlebury
1909	Iowa State	1920	Pitt
1909	North Carolina	1921	Bucknell
1909	Penn	1921	Utah State
1909	Texas	1921	William and Mary
1909	Vanderbilt	1921	Wittenburg
1909	Yale	1922	Brigham Young
1910	Colgate	1922	Emory
1910	Colorado	1922	Hamilton
1910	Dartmouth	1922	Oregon State
1910	Kansas	1922	Roanoke
1910	Montana State	1922	Washington (MO)
1910	N.Y.U. (U. Heights)	1922	Wooster
1910	Ohio State	1923	Hampden-Sydney
1910	Syracuse	1924	Berea
1910	Utah	1924	Denison
1910	Wesleyan	1924	West Virginia
1910	Williams	1925	Bridgewater
1911	Albion	1925	Ursinus
1911	Carleton	1926	Florida
1911	Cornell	1926	New Hampshire
1911	North Dakota	1926	Willamette
1911	Stanford	1927	Birmingham-Southern
1911	Western Reserve	1928	Evansville
1912	L.S.U.	1928	Pomona
1912	Muskingum	1928	Waynesburg
1912	New York, Washington Square	1928	Western Michigan
1912	Richmond	1929	Capital
1912	Vermont	1929	Earlham
1913	Allegheny	1929	Rutgers
1913	Amherst	1930	Marquette
1913	Iowa State, Cedar Falls	1931	Elmira
1913	Kentucky	1932	American
1913	Oklahoma	1933	Rockford
1913	Randolph, Macon	1934	Creighton
1913	Wabash	1935	Auburn
1913	Washington and Lee	1935	Boston
1914	Arkansas	1936	Hanover
1914	DePauw	1936	Lincoln Memorial (TN)
1914	Duke	1936	Manchester
1914	Oregon	1936	Oberlin
1914	USC	1937	Pacific
1915	Alabama	1937	Wayne State
1915	Bates	1938	New Mexico
1915	Dickinson	1940	Brooklyn
1916	Clark	1940	Mercer
1916	Colorado Col	1941	Alma
1916	Ohio	1941	Cal, Santa Barbara
1916	Purdue	1941	Indiana State
1916	South Dakota	1941	Murray State
1916	St. Lawrence	1941	Wichita State
1916	Tennessee	1942	Case Tech
1916	Westminster	1947	Hawaii
1917	Emory and Henry	1948	Loyola (MD)
1917	Mississippi	1948	Nevada
1917	Occidental	1949	Mundelein
1917	Penn State	1950	Ball State
1917	Southern Methodist	1950	Temple
1917	Washington State	1950	V.P.I.

1951 Florida State
1951 Grinnell
1951 Kansas State
1951 SUNY, Albany
1952 Connecticut
1953 Cal State, Long Beach
1953 Davidson
1953 Texas Tech.
1954 Mount Mercy
1955 Mankato
1955 Morgan State
1955 Tufts
1956 M.I.T.
1956 South Carolina
1956 Xavier
1958 Bellarmine
1958 Howard
1958 John Carroll
1958 Maryland
1958 Miami (FL)
1958 Michigan State
1959 Morehouse
1959 Rochester Tech
1960 Lehigh
1960 Loyola, Chicago
1960 New Mexico Highlands
1960 SUNY Col., Fredonia
1960 St. Anselm's
1960 Tulane
1960 Western Kentucky State
1961 Kings
1961 San Francisco State
1961 Southwest Missouri
1961 Yeshiva
1962 Hiram
1962 Wisconsin, Milwaukee
1963 Wake Forest
1964 C. W. Post
1964 Eastern Kentucky State
1964 Georgia
1964 Massachusetts
1964 Queens (NY)
1964 St. May's (TX)
1965 Clemson
1965 Weber
1965 Whittier
1966 Hampton Inst.
1966 Harpur (NY)
1966 Hartford
1966 Samford
1966 Spring Hill
1967 Emerson

Eta Kappa Nu

(ELECTRICAL ENGINEERING)

ACTIVE PIN

PLEDGE PIN

ETA KAPPA NU, an honor society among students of electrical engineering and others practicing that profession, was organized at the University of Illinois October 28, 1904, by ten men under the leadership of M. L. Carr. Its purpose is to confer honor and bring into closer union, whereby mutual benefits may be derived, those men in the profession of electrical engineering who by their attainments in college or in practice have manifested a deep interest and marked ability in their chosen life work. Election to the society is based upon scholarship and the personal qualities that indicate probability of success in the profession. Although until 1940 there were four classes of membership, undergraduate, graduate, associate, and honorary, and those to whom certificates in the last three mentioned classes were issued continue to hold these certificates, since 1940 members are undergraduate students, graduate students, faculty, men in industry and the profession, and eminent members. This last-named category includes individuals who by their technical attainments and contributions to society have shown themselves to be outstanding leaders in the field of electrical engineering and great benefactors of their fellow men. To be elected an eminent member a person must receive the unanimous approval of the members of the National Executive Council, the approval of the majority of the members of the national advisory board, and the approval of at least three-fourths of the college chapters. Eminent members and members-at-installation of a new chapter are inducted by the national president; all other members by the college chapters.

For an undergraduate student to be eligible for election to membership, he must be in the upper fourth of his junior electrical engineering class or upper third of his senior electrical engineering class.

Purpose "That those in the profession of electrical engineering, who by their attainment in college or practice, have manifested a deep interest and marked ability in their chosen life work, may be brought into closer union so as to foster a spirit of liberal culture in the engineering colleges and to mark in an outstanding manner those who, as students in electrical engineering, have conferred honor on their alma mater by distinguished scholarship, activities, leadership, and exemplary character and to help these students progress by association with alumni who have attained prominence."

Eligibility For a junior to be eligible for election he must be in the top quarter of his EE class; for a senior, in the top third. All must have acceptable character and show marked ability and personality. There is no discrimination as to sex, race or creed and/or membership in or affiliation with other recognized societies. Men and women in industry and the profession may become members on national approval. Engineers of exceedingly high attainment are made "Eminent Members."

Government Government of the society is generally by an annual convention by mail proxy-ballot, although provision is made for holding an assembled convention if one is deemed necessary. In the annual mail convention the executive secretary, in the fall of each year, calls for nominations for offices that will become vacant the following July 1 and writes college and alumni chapters to submit proposals of new legislation. These are compiled and mailed to the chapters, and a prepared proxy-ballot must be filled out by the chapter officers after consideration by the chapter. In the meantime, any member or chapter is free to write the chapters to influence their voting. This has been the practice since 1931. It has been very successful and has saved each student an assessment of at least $7.50 a year, which was the average assessment as his share of the cost of financing the assembled conventions. However, in 1954 Eta Kappa Nu celebrated its 50th anniversary by an assembled convention in Urbana, Illinois. In the 1956 mail convention an amendment to the constitution was ratified to provide for an assembled convention each five years beginning with 1959.

Eta Kappa Nu was incorporated in 1951 under the laws of Delaware, and the proxy-ballots now are counted and the election declared at its corporate annual meeting. The three officers of the National Executive Council, board of directors of the corporation, are voted powers of proxy, but the meeting is open to any member.

Interim government is by the National Executive Council composed of three members: the national president, who succeeds from national vice-president; the national vice-president, elected at each convention; and an executive secretary, elected for a three-year term. The office of the executive secretary is the national headquarters of the society, and the position is a full-time one. The national advisory board, composed of six members elected three a year for a two-year term and the most recent living past president, has the dual responsibility of being adviser to the National Executive Council and of serving in the capacity of "supreme court" to decide constitutionality.

Major Activities In furthering the purpose, the members of the college chapter try to help themselves and their fellow students by departmental and campus activities. Among many others, these sometimes include: Collaborate with IEEE student branches to develop interesting and instructive meetings. Sponsor annual survey of student opinion of individuals of EE faculty—this to be a guide to the individual teacher and not to the department head. Encourage underclass scholarship by making an appropriate award to the outstanding EE sophomore. Sponsor noon luncheons or evening meetings at which cultural and civic subjects are discussed with people from other departments and from industry. Sponsor social events with other honor societies, such as spring picnics, fall banquets, and dances. However, there is no regimentation; the chapters are informed of possible activities through regular meetings and *The Bridge*, and then make a choice. Nationally, the Association periodically undertakes a salary survey of its members. Each year it recognizes the Most Outstanding EE Teacher, the Most Outstanding Young Electrical Engineer, and also the Most Outstanding Jr. and Sr. EE Student.

Traditions and Insignia In furthering the purpose of the society, the members of the college chapters try to help themselves and their fellow students by departmental and campus activities. The alumni chapters undertake activities that help student chapters and members, such as employment assistance in the 1930s and employment counseling at present. The seven college chapters in the vicinity of New York City and the alumni chapter there have formed a metropolitan council to exchange ideas and to perform activities of mutual advantage.

In addition to the chartered chapters, in 1953 the faculty of electrical engineering departments who were members of Eta Kappa Nu were authorized to organize a branch of Eta Chapter on their campuses. Eta Chapter does not have a student list of officers, but the officers of the National Executive Council are the officers thereof. The members of Eta Kappa Nu on the faculty at a branch of Eta Chapter each year nominate senior electrical engineering students in the upper third of their class. These nominations, with data on the men, are sent to the National Executive Council which, if it approves unanimously, notifies the chairman of the faculty group to arrange with the nearest chartered college chapter to give these men the ritual for the school's branch of Eta Chapter. At present these are authorized branches for Eta Chapter as shown at the bottom of the chapter list.

The purpose of these branches of Eta is to give worthy men in smaller schools the opportunity of becoming members, the same as the worthy men in the larger schools.

The Eta Kappa Nu Recognition of Outstanding Young Electrical Engineers was established in 1936 to select and honor young electrical engineers for exceptional achievement in their chosen work, coupled with meritorious contributions to civic, social, cultural, and professional activities. Any man who has been graduated not more than ten years from the regular (baccalaureate) electrical engineering course of a recognized American college or university and is not more than 35 years of age is eligible for this annual recognition. The winner's name is engraved on a bronze bowl on permanent display in the Engineering Societies Building, New York City. A smaller replica bowl is presented to each winner, also a certificate of citation. Certificates of citation for honorable mention are also presented to three or four others each year. The citations are presented at an annual dinner held the first Monday evening of the mid-winter conference of the American Institute of Electrical Engineers.

As a 50th anniversary project, the society co-sponsored with the moving-picture unit of the University of Illinois a movie, "Engineering—A Career for Tomorrow," which has been shown by the chapters, industrial companies, and others to high-school students to acquaint them with the opportunities in engineering.

The badge is a Wheatstone bridge bearing in the center an oval representation of a galvanometer displaying the letters H, K, and N in the early Greek form. The colors are navy blue and scarlet.

Publication A quarterly publication, *The Bridge,* was first published as a yearbook in May, 1909, was changed to a quarterly in October, 1919, to a bi-monthly in November, 1929, and again to a quarterly in 1951.

Headquarters Department of Electrical Engineering, University of Illinois, Urbana, Illinois.

Membership Active chapters 180. Graduate/Alumni chapters 5. Total number of initiates 150,000. Chapter roll:

1904 Alpha, Illinois
1906 Beta, Purdue
1907 Gamma, Ohio State
1909 Delta, Illinois Tech
1909 Epsilon, Penn State
1910 Theta, Wisconsin, Madison
1910 Zeta, Case Western Reserve
1911 Iota, Missouri
1912 Kappa, Cornell
1913 Lambda, Penn
1915 Mu, Cal, Berkeley
1916 Nu, Iowa State
1920 Omicron, Minnesota
1920 Xi, Auburn
1921 Pi, Oregon State
1922 Rho, Colorado
1923 Sigma, Carnegie-Mellon
1923 Tau, Cincinnati
1925 Upsilon, USC
1926 Chi, Lehigh
1926 Phi, Union (KY)
1928 Psi, Texas
1930 Omega, Oklahoma State
1935 Beta Alpha, Drexel
1936 Beta Beta, CUNY, Brooklyn (Merged to become Zeta Sigma in 1974)
1936 Beta Gamma, Michigan Tech
1937 Beta Delta, Pitt
1937 Beta Epsilon, Michigan

1938 Beta Eta, North Carolina State
1938 Beta Zeta, N.Y.U. (Merged to become Zeta Sigma in 1974)
1939 Beta Iota, Iowa
1939 Beta Kappa, Kansas State
1939 Beta Theta, M.I.T.
1940 Beta Lambda, V.P.I.
1941 Beta Mu, Georgia Tech
1942 Beta Nu, R.P.I.
1942 Beta Xi, Oklahoma
1945 Beta Omicron, Marquette
1946 Beta Pi, CUNY, Brooklyn
1947 Beta Rho, West Virginia
1947 Beta Sigma, Detroit
1948 Beta Phi, Tennessee
1948 Beta Tau, Northwestern
1948 Beta Upsilon, Kentucky
1949 Beta Chi, South Dakota Mines
1949 Beta Omega, Connecticut
1949 Beta Psi, Nebraska
1950 Gamma Alpha, Manhattan
1950 Gamma Beta, Northeastern
1950 Gamma Delta, Worcester Tech
1950 Gamma Epsilon, Rutgers
1950 Gamma Gamma, Clarkson
1951 Gamma Eta, Syracuse
1951 Gamma Zeta, Michigan State
1952 Gamma Iota, Kansas
1952 Gamma Theta, Missouri, Rolla
1953 Gamma Kappa, New Jersey Tech
1954 Gamma Lambda, Columbia (NY)
1955 Gamma Mu, Texas A & M
1956 Gamma Nu, Texas Tech
1957 Gamma Omicron, Southern Methodist
1957 Gamma Pi, Virginia
1957 Gamma Rho, South Dakota State
1957 Gamma Xi, Maryland
1958 Gamma Sigma, Utah
1958 Gamma Tau, North Dakota State
1958 Gamma Upsilon, Johns Hopkins
1959 Gamma Chi, New Mexico State
1959 Gamma Omega, Mississippi State
1959 Gamma Phi, Arkansas
1959 Gamma Psi, Lafayette
1960 Delta Alpha, Wayne State (MI)
1960 Delta Beta, Lamar
1960 *Delta Delta, Denver* (1975)
1960 Delta Epsilon, Ohio
1960 Delta Eta, Massachusetts
1960 Delta Gamma, Louisiana Tech
1960 Delta Zeta, Washington (MO)
1961 Delta Iota, L.S.U.
1961 Delta Kappa, Maine
1961 Delta Lambda, Duke
1961 Delta Mu, Villanova
1961 Delta Theta, Pratt
1962 Delta Chi, Cooper Union
1962 Delta Nu, Alabama
1962 Delta Omicron, New Mexico
1962 Delta Phi, South Carolina
1962 Delta Pi, Colorado State
1962 Delta Rho, North Dakota

1962	Delta Sigma, Notre Dame
1962	Delta Tau, Southwestern Louisiana
1962	Delta Upsilon, Bradley
1962	Delta Xi, Air Force Inst
1963	Delta Omega, Hawaii
1963	*Delta Psi, St. Louis* (1974)
1963	Epsilon Alpha, Cleveland
1963	Epsilon Beta, Arizona State
1963	Epsilon Gamma, Toledo
1964	Epsilon Delta, Tufts
1964	Epsilon Epsilon, Houston
1964	Epsilon Zeta, Lowell
1965	Epsilon Eta, Rose-Hulman
1965	Epsilon Iota, San Jose
1965	Epsilon Kappa, Miami (FL)
1965	Epsilon Theta, Cal State, Long Beach
1966	Epsilon Lambda, Vanderbilt
1966	Epsilon Mu, Texas, Arlington
1966	Epsilon Nu, Cal State, Los Angeles
1966	Epsilon Omicron, Delaware
1966	Epsilon Xi, Wichita
1967	*Epsilon Pi, Princeton* (1978)
1967	Epsilon Rho, Tennessee Tech
1967	Epsilon Sigma, Florida
1969	Epsilon Tau, Cal, Santa Barbara
1969	Epsilon Upsilon, Tuskegee
1971	Epsilon Chi, Louisville
1971	Epsilon Omega, Mississippi
1971	Epsilon Phi, Cal Poly, Pomona
1971	Epsilon Psi, Santa Clara
1971	Zeta Alpha, Monmouth (IL)
1971	Zeta Beta, Texas A & I
1971	Zeta Delta, Texas, El Paso
1971	Zeta Epsilon, Florida Institute
1971	Zeta Eta, Brigham Young
1971	Zeta Gamma, Rhode Island
1971	Zeta Zeta, Akron
1972	Zeta Iota, Clemson
1972	Zeta Theta, Cal Poly, Pomona
1973	Zeta Kappa, Tennessee State
1973	Zeta Lambda, Prairie View
1973	Zeta Mu, Northrop
1973	Zeta Nu, Tulsa
1974	Zeta Omicron, West Virginia Tech
1974	Zeta Pi, SUNY, Buffalo
1974	Zeta Rho, New Haven
1974	Zeta Sigma, New York Poly
1974	Zeta Tau, San Diego U.
1974	Zeta Xi, Southeastern Massachusetts
1975	Zeta Chi, Central Florida
1975	Zeta Phi, Tri-State
1975	Zeta Upsilon, Old Dominion
1976	Theta Alpha, Tulane
1976	Zeta Omega, Cal, Irvine
1976	Zeta Psi, Southern
1977	Theta Beta, Portland
1977	Theta Delta, Naval Postgraduate
1977	Theta Gamma, Fairleigh Dickinson, Rutherford
1978	Theta Epsilon, GMI
1978	Theta Eta, Alabama, Huntsville
1978	Theta Zeta, Colorado, Denver

1979	Theta Iota, George Washington
1979	Theta Kappa, Cal State, Fresno
1979	Theta Lambda, South Alabama
1979	Theta Mu, SUNY, Stony Brook
1979	Theta Theta, SUNY Col. Tech, Farmingdale
1980	Theta Nu, North Carolina A & T
1980	Theta Omicron, Southern Illinois, Edwardsville
1980	Theta Pi, Missouri, Kansas City
1980	Theta Xi, Norwich
1981	Theta Rho, Rice
1981	Theta Sigma, Bridgeport
1981	Theta Tau, Michigan, Dearborn
1982	Theta Chi, Colorado, Colorado Springs
1982	Theta Omega, Pacific (CA)
1982	Theta Phi, V.M.I.
1982	Theta Psi, Nevada
1982	Theta Upsilon, Lawrence Tech
1983	Iota Alpha, Alabama, Birmingham
1983	Iota Beta, Milwaukee Engineering
1983	Iota Delta, Stevens Tech
1984	Iota Epsilon, Hartford
1984	Iota Gamma, UCLA
1985	Iota Zeta, Cal State, Chico

Gamma Theta Upsilon

(GEOGRAPHY)

ACTIVE PIN

GAMMA THETA UPSILON, a geographical honor society, was founded at the Illinois State Normal University, Normal, in 1928, under the sponsorship of Dr. Robert G. Buzzard, then head of the Department of Geography.

The purposes of the fraternity are to further professional interest in geography by providing a common organization for persons interested in this field; to strengthen professional training through experiences other than those of the classroom and laboratory; to advance the status of geography as a cultural and practical discipline for study and investigation; to encourage student research of high quality and to promote an outlet for publication; and to create and administer a scholarship and loan fund for furthering graduate study and research in geography.

Membership may be extended to any student regularly enrolled in the institution in which a chapter is located and who has completed at least six semester hours or the equivalent in geography, provided that the average grade of all geography courses shall be higher than the median grade of the college and that the student signifies his intention of completing at least twelve semester hours in the subject. Associate and honorary membership is also provided for persons who can qualify academically or who have contributed materially to the field of geography. All alumni may join the international Alumni Chapter (Omega Omega).

Government The fraternity is governed by the Executive Committee, elected by chapter delegates at the annual convention, consisting of president, first vice-president, second vice-president, secretary, treasurer, treasurer of the Loan Fund, historian, and two student representatives. Loans are made to members for graduate study or for research in geography. Allotment of loans is controlled by the Loan Fund Committee, appointed by the president. The society publishes an annual Newsletter and a biennial journal, the *Geographical Bulletin*.

Awards An undergraduate and a graduate scholarship are awarded each year. Individuals must be members and nominated by their geography departments.

Traditions and Insignia Each chapter of the fraternity conducts a program of professional activity in geography, designed to develop leadership among its members and to create interest in and desire for graduate study. The insignia of the fraternity is a gold key, designed as a seven-sided shield, on the beveled edge of which are the initials of the seven great land masses of the earth, with the central area of the key showing five wavy blue lines significant of the five great bodies of water, over which is a white star, signifying Polaris, and above this three Greek letters, Γ, Θ, and Υ. The colors of the fraternity are brown for the earth, blue for the oceans, and gold for the sunlight.

Headquarters Geography Department, University of Arkansas, Fayetteville, Arkansas 72701.

Membership Active chapters 216. Graduate/Alumni chapters 1. Total number of initiates 37,000. Chapter roll:

1928	Alpha, Illinois State
1928	Beta, Northern Iowa
1930	Gamma, Sam Houston
1931	Delta, Bloomsburg
1931	Epsilon, Southwest Missouri
1932	Theta, Arizona State
1932	Zeta, Slippery Rock
1933	Eta, Moorhead
1933	Iota, Montclair
1934	Kappa, Valley City
1936	Lambda, Southern Illinois
1936	Mu, Minnesota, Duluth
1937	Nu, Emory and Henry
1937	Omicron, Shippensburg
1937	Xi, Concord
1940	Pi, Wilson
1940	Rho, Eastern Illinois
1948	Chi, Oklahoma State
1948	Omega, East Stroudsburg
1948	Phi, Stanford
1948	Psi, North Dakota
1948	Sigma, Kentucky
1948	Tau, Indiana
1948	Upsilon, Bowling Green
1949	Alpha Alpha, North Texas
1949	Alpha Beta, Tennessee
1949	Alpha Delta, Miami (FL)
1949	Alpha Epsilon, Utah
1949	Alpha Eta, Chadron
1949	Alpha Gamma, Western Michigan
1949	Alpha Theta, Washington State
1949	Alpha Zeta, Columbia (NY)
1950	Alpha Iota, Oklahoma
1950	Alpha Kappa, Virginia
1950	Alpha Lambda, East Tennessee
1950	Alpha Mu, Wisconsin, Milwaukee
1950	Alpha Nu, Kent
1950	Alpha Omicron, Northwestern
1950	Alpha Pi, East Central State
1950	Alpha Xi, Valparaiso
1951	Alpha Rho, St. Louis
1951	Alpha Sigma, Clark
1951	Alpha Tau, Penn State
1951	Alpha Upsilon, Cal State, Long Beach
1952	Alpha Chi, Mexico City
1952	Alpha Phi, Nebraska
1953	Alpha Omega, West Texas
1953	Alpha Psi, Colorado
1953	Beta Alpha, SUNY, Buffalo
1953	Beta Beta, Washington (WA)
1953	Beta Gamma, Western Illinois
1954	Beta Delta, Towson
1954	Beta Epsilon, Southern
1954	Beta Zeta, Ohio State
1955	Beta Eta, Eastern New Mexico
1955	Beta Iota, East Carolina
1955	Beta Kappa, Morgan State
1955	Beta Lambda, Southern Oregon
1955	Beta Mu, Iowa
1955	Beta Nu, Marshall
1955	Beta Omicron, Mansfield
1955	Beta Theta, Miner Teachers
1955	Beta Xi, Missouri
1956	Beta Pi, Carroll
1956	Beta Rho, Stetson
1956	Beta Sigma, Florida State
1956	Beta Tau, District of Columbia
1957	Beta Chi, Michigan State
1957	Beta Phi, Maryland
1957	Beta Upsilon, Oregon State
1959	Beta Omega, Cal State, Chico
1959	Beta Psi, Kansas State
1959	Gamma Beta, Edinboro
1960	Gamma Alpha, Austin Peay
1961	Gamma Delta, California (PA)
1961	Gamma Epsilon, Morehead
1961	Gamma Gamma, San Jose
1962	Gamma Zeta, Eastern Michigan
1963	Gamma Eta, West Chester
1963	Gamma Kappa, Arkansas
1963	Gamma Lambda, Southern Illinois, Edwardsville
1963	Gamma Mu, San Diego U.
1963	Gamma Omicron, Texas

1964	Gamma Chi, Nebraska, Omaha
1964	Gamma Omega, Indiana (PA)
1964	Gamma Phi, Frostburg
1964	Gamma Rho, Western Washington
1964	Gamma Xi, Elmhurst
1965	Gamma Pi, North Carolina Central
1965	Gamma Psi, Kutztown
1965	Gamma Sigma, Grambling
1965	Gamma Tau, Central Washington
1965	Gamma Upsilon, Wisconsin, Whitewater
1965	Iota Alpha, Southern Mississippi
1965	Iota Beta, Cincinnati
1965	Iota Chi, Harris-Stowe
1965	Iota Eta, Denver
1965	Iota Gamma, Northern Illinois
1965	Iota Iota, Jackson (MS)
1966	Gamma Nu, Georgia
1966	Iota Epsilon, Prairie View
1966	Iota Kappa, Miami (OH)
1966	Iota Lambda, Central Missouri State
1966	Iota Mu, Michigan
1966	Iota Nu, Central Michigan
1966	Iota Omicron, San Francisco State
1966	Iota Phi, Florida
1966	Iota Psi, Murray State
1966	Iota Rho, Boston State
1966	Iota Sigma, Maine, Farmington
1966	Iota Theta, Tennessee
1967	Iota Pi, Northeastern Illinois
1967	Iota Tau, Akron
1967	Iota Upsilon, Kansas
1967	Iota Xi, Central Arkansas
1967	Iota Zeta, Briar Cliff
1967	Kappa Alpha, Brigham Young
1967	Kappa Beta, Waterloo Lutheran
1967	Kappa Chi, Texas Tech
1968	Iota Omega, Ball State
1968	Kappa Delta, Central Connecticut
1968	Kappa Epsilon, Texas Christian
1968	Kappa Eta, Jacksonville
1968	Kappa Gamma, Stephen F. Austin
1968	Kappa Iota, Alabama
1968	Kappa Kappa, South Florida
1968	Kappa Lambda, St. Cloud
1968	Kappa Mu, Western Kentucky
1968	Kappa Omicron, Radford
1968	Kappa Theta, Cal State, Fresno
1968	Kappa Xi, New Mexico State
1968	Kappa Zeta, Northern Colorado
1969	Delta Alpha, Northern Arizona
1969	Delta Delta, Peru
1969	Delta Gamma, New Mexico
1969	Kappa Nu, Indiana State
1969	Kappa Omega, Nevada, Las Vegas
1969	Kappa Phi, North Carolina, Greensboro
1969	Kappa Pi, Wisconsin, Stevens Point
1969	Kappa Psi, South Carolina
1969	Kappa Sigma, Clarion
1969	Kappa Tau, SUNY, Albany
1969	Kappa Upsilon, Southwest Texas
1970	Delta Beta, Boston U
1970	Delta Epsilon, Wittenberg

1970	Delta Eta, Western Oregon
1970	Delta Iota, Illinois, Chicago
1970	Delta Theta, Chicago State
1970	Delta Zeta, South Dakota State
1970	Kappa Rho, Wisconsin, Superior
1971	Delta Mu, Mary Washington
1971	Delta Nu, Lock Haven
1971	Delta Omicron, Charleston (WV)
1971	Delta Rho, Pitt
1971	Delta Tau, Wisconsin, Eau Claire
1972	Delta Phi, Weber
1972	Delta Pi, Aquinas
1973	Delta Lambda, South Alabama
1973	Epsilon Alpha, Nevada
1973	Epsilon Beta, West Georgia
1974	Epsilon Delta, West Liberty
1974	Epsilon Epsilon, Illinois
1974	Epsilon Eta, Wisconsin, La Crosse
1974	Epsilon Gamma, Memphis State
1974	Epsilon Theta, Houston
1974	Epsilon Zeta, Appalachian
1975	Epsilon Iota, Idaho
1975	Epsilon Kappa, Macalester
1975	Epsilon Lambda, Southern Connecticut
1975	Epsilon Mu, William Paterson
1975	Epsilon Nu, Eastern Kentucky
1975	Epsilon Xi, Northeast Louisiana
1976	Epsilon Omicron, Wisconsin, Platteville
1976	Epsilon Pi, St. Anselm's
1976	Epsilon Rho, Framingham
1976	Epsilon Sigma, Hawaii, Hilo
1976	Epsilon Upsilon, Missouri, Kansas City
1977	Epsilon Chi, Trenton
1977	Epsilon Omega, SUNY Col., Plattsburgh
1977	Epsilon Phi, Cal State, Northridge
1977	Epsilon Psi, Colgate
1977	Epsilon Tau, Carthage
1978	Zeta Alpha, North Adams
1978	Zeta Delta, Lethbridge
1978	Zeta Epsilon, Bradley
1978	Zeta Gamma, Jacksonville (AL)
1979	Zeta Zeta, Texas A & M
1980	Zeta Eta, Salisbury
1980	Zeta Iota, Rutgers
1980	Zeta Kappa, Connecticut
1980	Zeta Lambda, New Orleans
1980	Zeta Mu, Cheyney State
1980	Zeta Nu, North Alabama
1980	Zeta Theta, Northwest Missouri
1981	Zeta Xi, Toledo
1982	Zeta Omicron, Worcester Tech
1982	Zeta Pi, Utah State
1982	Zeta Rho, SUNY, Binghamton
1982	Zeta Sigma, Kearney
1983	Zeta Tau, North Carolina
1983	Zeta Upsilon, Arizona
1984	Zeta Omega, North Carolina, Charlotte
1984	Zeta Phi, Mankato
1985	Eta Alpha, Vermont
1985	Eta Beta, Texas, San Antonio
1985	Zeta Chi, Old Dominion
1985	Zeta Psi, Bemidji

1986 Eta Gamma, SUNY Col., Geneseo
1987 Eta Delta, Maryland
1987 Eta Epsilon, Indiana Southeast
1987 Eta Eta, Wyoming
1987 Eta Iota, Alaska, Fairbanks
1987 Eta Theta, Auburn
1987 Eta Zeta, V.P.I.
1988 Eta Kappa, Salem State (MA)
1988 Eta Lambda, Villanova
1988 Eta Mu, Texas Southern
1988 Eta Nu, Bridgewater
1989 Eta Omicron, George Mason
1989 Eta Pi, Wisconsin, River Falls
1989 Eta Xi, Wisconsin, Green Bay

Kappa Delta Pi

(EDUCATION)

ACTIVE PIN

KAPPA DELTA PI grew out of a local society, the Illinois Education Club, founded at the University of Illinois in 1909, March 8, 1911; it was incorporated under the laws of Illinois as the educational fraternity, Kappa Delta Pi. On October 4, 1932, this title was changed to Kappa Delta Pi, an honor society in education, and was so registered in the office of the secretary of state at Springfield, Illinois. Membership consists of juniors, seniors, and graduate students, both men and women, whose general scholarship is above the upper quintile point of the institution. Work in courses in education must have been completed to the extent of six semester hours for juniors and twelve semester hours for seniors and graduate students. A limited number of faculty members and honorary members may be elected.

As stated in the by-laws of the society: "The purpose of Kappa Delta Pi shall be to encourage high professional, intellectual, and personal standards and to recognize outstanding contributions to education. To this end it shall invite to membership such persons as exhibit commendable personal qualities, worthy educational ideals, and sound scholarship. It shall endeavor to maintain a high degree of professional fellowship among its members and to quicken professional growth by honoring achievement in educational work."

The roll includes chapters at state colleges and universities, municipal universities, state teachers colleges, privately endowed universities, and liberal arts colleges. It is an honor society which has the unique distinction of maintaining the Laureate Chapter, composed of outstanding educators, the intention being to make this in essence an academy of educators similar to the Academy of Science or the Academy of Fine Letters. This chapter may have no more than sixty members at any one time.

Eligibility Undergraduate students with at least full junior collegiate standing and/or graduate students, all preparing to be certified to teach, with grade point indices in the upper fifth of the institution.

Government A biennial convocation is held, and in the year between convocations there are regional conferences.

Insignia The key is a scroll and stylus upon which are the three Greek letters of the society's name, the letter Δ being placed upon a beehive.

Publications The society publishes *The Educational Forum* and the *Kappa Delta Pi Record*, each four times for the school year. It also publishes a biennial volume in the Kappa Delta Pi Lecture Series, written by Prominent educators.

Headquarters P.O. Box A, West Lafayette, Indiana 47906.

Membership Active chapters 417. Inactive chapters 22. Graduate/Alumni chapters 35. Total number of initiates 50,800. Chapter roll:††

1911 Alpha, Illinois
1912 Beta, Colorado
1915 Gamma, Oklahoma
1916 Delta, Texas (1932-1963)
1917 Epsilon, Drake
1917 Zeta, Cincinnati
1919 Eta, Purdue
1920 Iota, Emporia
1920 Kappa, Columbia
1920 Theta, Colorado State, Greeley
1921 Lambda, Oklahoma State
1922 Mu, Illinois State (Normal)
1922 Nu, Miami (OH)
1922 Omicron, Northern State
1922 Pi, Eastern Michigan
1922 Rho, Central Missouri State
1922 Xi, Alabama
1923 Alpha Alpha, Ohio Wesleyan
1923 Chi, Western State (CO)
1923 Omega, Ohio
1923 Phi, Marshall
1923 Psi, Iowa State, Cedar Falls
1923 *Sigma, Penn State* (1936)
1923 Tau, Northeast Missouri
1923 Upsilon, Florida
1924 Alpha Beta, Arkansas
1924 Alpha Gamma, Kentucky
1925 Alpha Delta, Florida State
1925 Alpha Epsilon, Western Illinois
1925 Alpha Eta, Southeast Missouri
1925 Alpha Theta, Akron
1925 Alpha Zeta, Kansas State, Pittsburg
1926 Alpha Iota, North Texas
1926 Alpha Kappa, Indiana State
1926 Alpha Lambda, Denver

†† This chapter roll is repeated from the 19th edition; no current information was provided.

1926   Alpha Mu, Wyoming
1926   Alpha Nu, Cal State, Chico
1927   *Alpha Omicron, Franklin* (1940)
1927   Alpha Pi, George Peabody
1927   Alpha Rho, Cal, Santa Barbara
1927   Alpha Sigma, San Diego State
1927   Alpha Tau, Duke
1927   Alpha Upsilon, West Virginia
1927   Alpha Xi, William and Mary
1928   Alpha Chi, Madison Col
1928   Alpha Omega, Oregon State
1928   Alpha Phi, Auburn
1928   Alpha Psi, Heidelberg
1928   Beta Alpha, San Jose
1928   *Beta Beta, New Hampshire* (1965)
1928   Beta Delta, Southeastern Oklahoma
1928   Beta Epsilon, Longwood
1928   Beta Eta, Oklahoma Baptist
1928   Beta Gamma, Indiana (PA)
1928   Beta Zeta, Idaho
1929   Beta Iota, Western Michigan
1929   Beta Kappa, Georgia
1929   Beta Lambda, Alabama College, Montevallo
1929   Beta Mu, Peru
1929   Beta Nu, Black Hills
1929   Beta Theta, Wisconsin, Oshkosh
1929   Beta Xi, Baylor
1930   Beta Chi, Northern Arizona
1930   Beta Omicron, Wisconsin, Milwaukee
1930   Beta Phi, Arizona State
1930   Beta Pi, N.Y.U.
1930   Beta Rho, Mansfield
1930   *Beta Sigma, Georgia State Teachers* (1932)
1930   Beta Tau, Wisconsin, La Crosse
1930   Beta Upsilon, Washington (MO)
1931   Beta Omega, Fairmont
1931   Beta Psi, Eastern Illinois
1931   Gamma Alpha, Radford
1931   Gamma Beta, Bloomsburg
1931   Gamma Delta, North Dakota State
1931   Gamma Epsilon, Montclair
1931   Gamma Eta, New Mexico Western
1931   Gamma Gamma, Moorhead
1931   Gamma Iota, C.C.N.Y.
1931   Gamma Kappa, Tulsa
1931   Gamma Lambda, Harris Teachers (MO)
1931   Gamma Mu, SUNY, Buffalo
1931   Gamma Nu, Butler
1931   Gamma Theta, Ball State
1931   Gamma Xi, East Stroudsburg
1931   Gamma Zeta, Trenton
1932   Gamma Omicron, Maine
1932   Gamma Pi, St. Cloud
1932   Gamma Rho, Wichita
1934   Gamma Phi, Northwestern (LA)
1934   *Gamma Sigma, San Francisco State* (1965)
1934   Gamma Tau, Winona
1934   Gamma Upsilon, L.S.U.
1935   Delta Alpha, Eastern Kentucky State
1935   Delta Beta, Kent
1935   Delta Delta, Winthrop
1935   Delta Epsilon, Northern Illinois

1935   Delta Gamma, Concord
1935   Delta Zeta, Northern Michigan
1935   Gamma Chi, Massachusetts State, Worcester
1935   Gamma Omega, Central State (OK)
1935   Gamma Psi, Cal State, Fresno
1936   Delta Eta, Northwestern Oklahoma
1936   Delta Iota, Southwestern Louisiana
1936   Delta Kapps, Eastern Washington
1936   Delta Lambda, D. C. Teachers
1936   Delta Theta, Sam Houston
1937   Delta Mu, Westminister (PA)
1938   Delta Nu, Wisconsin, Whitewater
1938   Delta Omicron, Central Washington
1938   Delta Pi, Henderson
1938   Delta Rho, Rutgers, Newark
1938   Delta Sigma, Lock Haven
1938   Delta Tau, Slippery Rock
1938   Delta Upsilon, Jersey City
1938   Delta Xi, Rutgers
1939   Delta Chi, Southern Illinois
1939   Delta Omega, Murray State
1939   Delta Phi, Bowling Green
1939   Delta Psi, Shepherd
1940   Epsilon Alpha, Maryland State, Towson
1940   Epsilon Beta, Tulane
1940   Epsilon Gamma, Florida Southern
1941   Epsilon Delta, California (PA)
1941   Epsilon Epsilon, Shippensburg
1941   Epsilon Eta, Central Michigan
1941   Epsilon Zeta, Kutztown
1942   Epsilon Iota, Massachusetts State,
         Bridgewater
1942   Epsilon Kappa, Michigan State
1942   Epsilon Lambda, Texas Western
1942   Epsilon Theta, Moorehead
1943   Epsilon Mu, Central Connecticut
1943   Epsilon Nu, Willimantic State (CT)
1943   Epsilon Omicron, Wisconsin, Eau Claire
1943   Epsilon Pi, Keene
1943   Epsilon Xi, Danbury State (CT)
1944   Epsilon Phi, Alpha State, Jacksonville
1944   Epsilon Rho, Rhode Island College of
         Education
1944   Epsilon Sigma, SUNY Col., Oneonta
1944   Epsilon Tau, SUNY Col., Geneseo
1944   Epsilon Upsilon, SUNY Col., Potsdam
1945   Epsilon Chi, SUNY Col., Cortland
1945   Epsilon Omega, SUNY Col., Oswego
1945   Epsilon Psi, Alabama State, Florence
1945   Zeta Alpha, Paterson State (NJ)
1946   Zeta Beta, Minnesota, Duluth
1946   Zeta Delta, Sul Ross
1946   Zeta Epsilon, Toledo
1946   Zeta Gamma, Alabama State, Troy
1946   Zeta Zeta, SUNY Col., New Paltz
1947   Zeta Eta, Mississippi
1947   Zeta Iota, East Tennessee
1947   *Zeta Theta, Samford* (1966)
1948   Zeta Kappa, Southeastern Louisiana
1948   Zeta Lambda, Northwest Missouri
1948   Zeta Mu, East Texas
1948   Zeta Nu, Beaver

1948	Zeta Xi, North Dakota State, Minot		1959	Iota Epsilon, Virginia State
1949	Zeta Omicron, Delaware		1959	Iota Eta, Louisiana Col.
1949	Zeta Pi, SUNY Col., Brockport		1959	Iota Gamma, Stephen F. Austin
1949	Zeta Rho, Loyola, New Orleans		1959	Iota Zeta, Carroll
1950	Zeta Chi, Tennessee A & I		1960	Iota Iota, Massachusetts State, Westfield
1950	Zeta Phi, Miami		1960	Iota Kappa, Ohio Northern
1950	Zeta Sigma, North Dakota State, Valley City		1960	Iota Lambda, Augustana
1950	Zeta Tau, Stetson		1960	Iota Mu, Hampton
1950	Zeta Upsilon, SUNY Col., Fredonia		1960	Iota Theta, West Texas
1951	Eta Alpha, Seattle		1961	Iota Nu, Bucknell
1951	Eta Beta, Western Washington		1961	Iota Omicron, Southern Oregon
1951	Eta Delta, Arkansas State		1961	Iota Xi, Kansas State
1951	Eta Epsilon, McMurry		1962	Iota Chi, Dubuque
1951	Eta Eta, Macalester		1962	Iota Phi, Cal State, Los Angeles
1951	Eta Gamma, Georgia State, Statesboro		1962	Iota Pi, Berea
1951	Eta Iota, Edinboro		1962	Iota Psi, DePaul
1951	Eta Kappa, Virginia		1962	Iota Rho, Wisconsin, Platteville
1951	Eta Theta, Brooklyn		1962	Iota Sigma, Rhode Island
1951	Eta Zeta, Southwest Texas		1962	Iota Tau, Grambling
1951	Zeta Omega, Houston		1962	Iota Upsilon, Maryland
1952	The Laureate Chapter		1963	Iota Omega, St. Ambrose
1952	Eta Lambda, Wisconsin, River Falls		1963	Kappa Alpha, Hiram
1952	Eta Mu, Southern A & M (LA)		1963	Kappa Beta, Wayne State (NE)
1952	Eta Nu, Tennessee Tech.		1963	Kappa Gamma, Queens (NY)
1952	Eta Xi, Youngstown		1964	Kappa Delta, Elizabeth City
1953	Eta Chi, East Carolina		1964	Kappa Epsilon, Morris Harvey
1953	Eta Omicron, Louisville		1964	Kappa Eta, St. John's (NY)
1953	Eta Phi, Nebraska State, Kearney		1964	Kappa Zeta, Northeastern
1953	Eta Pi, Denison		1965	Kappa Iota, Wartburg
1953	Eta Psi, Glassboro		1965	Kappa Kappa, Mercy (MI)
1953	Eta Rho, Austin Peay		1965	Kappa Lambda, Massachusetts
1953	Eta Sigma, Langston		1965	Kappa Mu, High Point
1953	Eta Tau, Lynchburg		1965	Kappa Theta, Illinois Wesleyan
1953	Eta Upsilon, Vermont		1966	Kappa Chi, Framingham
1954	Eta Omega, Omaha		1966	Kappa Nu, Ashland
1954	Theta Alpha, Howard		1966	Kappa Omega, Baldwin-Wallace
1954	Theta Beta, Hofstra		1966	Kappa Omicron, Glenville
1954	Theta Delta, Delta State		1966	Kappa Phi, West Chester
1954	Theta Epsilon, Abilene Christian		1966	Kappa Pi, Arizona
1954	Theta Gamma, Southern Mississippi		1966	Kappa Psi, Texas Southern
1954	Theta Zeta, Phillips		1966	Kappa Rho, Northeastern (OK)
1955	Theta Eta, National Col. of Ed.		1966	Kappa Sigma, Gonzaga
1955	Theta Iota, Florida A & M		1966	Kappa Tau, Tampa
1955	Theta Kappa, SUNY Col., Plattsburgh		1966	Kappa Upsilon, Texas Christian
1955	Theta Lambda, Willamette		1966	Kappa Xi, L.S.U., New Orleans
1955	Theta Mu, South Dakota State		1966	Lambda Alpha, Plymouth
1955	Theta Theta, Richmond		1966	Lambda Beta, Southwest Missouri
1956	Theta Nu, Nebraska Wesleyan		1967	Lambda Delta, Tuskegee
1956	Theta Omicron, Middle Tennessee		1967	Lambda Epsilon, Bridgeport
1956	Theta Pi, Cal State, Sacramento		1967	Lambda Eta, Clarion
1956	Theta Rho, Illinois Teachers, Chicago		1967	Lambda Gamma, Memphis State
1956	Theta Sigma, D. C. Teachers		1967	Lambda Iota, Appalachian
1956	Theta Xi, Morgan State		1967	Lambda Kappa, Rollins
1957	Theta Tau, North Carolina A & T		1967	Lambda Theta, Southern Illinois
1958	Iota Alpha, Hunter		1967	Lambda Zeta, West Virginia State
1958	Theta Chi, Mississippi State		1968	Lambda Lambda, Mankato
1958	Theta Omega, Ouachita Baptist		1968	Lambda Mu, Pepperdine
1958	Theta Phi, Catawba		1968	Lambda Nu, Daeman
1958	Theta Psi, St. Mary's (LA)		1968	Lambda Omicron, Maine, Farmington
1958	Theta Upsilon, Howard Payne		1968	Lambda Pi, Arkansas Tech
1959	Iota Beta, Mississippi Col.		1968	Lambda Rho, Carson-Newman
1959	Iota Delta, Connecticut		1968	Lambda Sigma, Valparaiso

1968	Lambda Tau, South Florida
1968	Lambda Xi, Fordham
1969	Lambda Chi, Cal State, Long Beach
1969	Lambda Omega, Trinity (TX)
1969	Lambda Phi, Wright State
1969	Lambda Psi, Pan American
1969	Lambda Upsilon, Adrian
1969	Mu Alpha, Tennessee, Chattanooga
1969	Mu Beta, Midwestern
1969	Mu Gamma, Angelo
1970	Mu Delta, Missouri
1970	Mu Epsilon, Prairie View A & M
1970	Mu Eta, Western Carolina State
1970	Mu Iota, Missouri, St. Louis
1970	Mu Kappa, Southwestern State (OK)
1970	Mu Theta, Savannah State
1970	Mu Zeta, West Virginia Wesleyan
1971	Mu Lambda, Virginia Commonwealth
1971	Mu Mu, Alabama, Birmingham
1971	Mu Nu, Nevada, Las Vegas
1971	Mu Omicron, Nicholls
1971	Mu Pi, Iowa State
1971	Mu Rho, Douglass (NJ)
1971	Mu Sigma, Manhattan
1971	Mu Tau, Anderson
1971	Mu Xi, Lehman
1972	Mu Chi, Texas A & M
1972	Mu Omega, Alabama A & M
1972	Mu Phi, Western Montana
1972	Mu Psi, Indiana Southeast
1972	Mu Upsilon, Clemson
1972	Nu Alpha, George Mason
1973	Nu Beta, Olivet Nazarene
1973	Nu Delta, Tennessee
1973	Nu Epsilon, Alabama State
1973	Nu Gamma, Boston State Col
1974	Nu Eta, Old Dominion
1974	Nu Zeta, Armstrong State
1975	Nu Iota, Southern Methodist
1975	Nu Kappa, Dallas
1975	Nu Lambda, Harding
1975	Nu Mu, Drury
1975	Nu Nu, Adelphi
1975	Nu Omicron, Albany State
1975	Nu Pi, Texas A & I
1975	Nu Theta, Cheyney
1975	Nu Xi, Mary Washington
1976	Nu Chi, Arkansas, Little Rock
1976	Nu Phi, Belmont
1976	Nu Psi, Barry (FL)
1976	Nu Rho, William Woods
1976	Nu Sigma, Texas Tech.
1976	Nu Tau, Monmouth (NJ)
1976	Nu Upsilon, Rutgers, Camden
1977	Nu Omega, West Virginia College of Graduate Studies
1977	Xi Alpha, Texas, Arlington
1977	Xi Beta, Bowie
1977	Xi Delta, West Liberty State
1977	Xi Epsilon, Furman
1977	Xi Gamma, Seton Hall
1977	Xi Zeta, V.P.I.

Kappa Mu Epsilon

(MATHEMATICS)

ACTIVE PIN

KAPPA MU EPSILON was founded at Northeastern State College, Tahlequah, Oklahoma, April 18, 1931, under the direction of Kathryn Wyant and Prof. L. P. Woods. Members of this first group were: Dee Casey, Theodore Casey, Mary Lou Chilcoat, Ano Davis, Lorene Davis, Beth DeLay, Clara Green, Harold J. Hudson, Marguerite Jones, Ethel Ruth DeLay, Earl O. Layton, Paul Lewis, Iva King, Velma McCormick, Charles Nussbaum, Cherry Saunders, Helen Scott, Margaret Smith, Beulah Turner, Howell Wiggins, Nell Woodard, Prof. L. P. Woods, and Kathryn Wyant.

Purpose To further the interests of mathematics in those schools which place their primary emphasis on the undergraduate program; to recognize and honor outstanding scholastic achievement of undergraduate students in mathematics.

Eligibility Active members must be or have been a faculty member or a regularly enrolled student at an institution which has a Kappa Mu Epsilon Chapter; must have completed at least three semesters (or five quarters) of the college course and rank in the upper thirty-five percent of his class; must have completed at least three college courses in mathematics including at least one semester (or two quarters) of calculus and attained an average of B or better in all mathematics courses.

Government The national officers of Kappa Mu Epsilon are: president, vice-president, treasurer, secretary, historian, and past president. These officers are elected at the national convention which is held every two years. The officers constitute the National Council, which serves as a general executive committee in the interim between conventions. Each chapter is governed by chapter by-laws which may not be at variance with the national constitution.

Major Activities The local chapters plan their programs for the regular meetings which provide opportunities for members to present papers and hear visiting lecturers. Local chapters often award scholarships and other awards. Student papers selected from those submitted by the chapters are presented at the national biennial convention and at regional meetings.

Traditions and Insignia The badge of the society is a pentagon with the sides slightly concave, on the upper half the five-leaf rose, and on the lower half the letters KME. 'The colors of the society are rose-pink and silver; the flower is the wild rose.

Publication   The official publication is *The Pentagon*, published semiannually.

Headquarters   Central Michigan University, Mt. Pleasant, Michigan 48859.

Membership   Active chapters 107. Inactive chapters 29. Total number of initiates 53,903. Chapter roll:

1931   Iowa Alpha, Northern Iowa
1931   Oklahoma Alpha, Northeastern (OK)
1932   Kansas Alpha, Pittsburg State, Kansas
1932   Mississippi Alpha, Mississippi for Women
1932   Mississippi Beta, Mississippi State
1932   Missouri Alpha', Southwest Missouri
1933   *Illinois Alpha, Illinois State* (1981)
1933   Nebraska Alpha, Wayne State (NE)
1934   Kansas Beta, Emporia
1935   *Alabama Alpha, Athens* (1953)
1935   Alabama Beta, North Alabama
1935   Illinois Beta, Eastern Illinois
1935   New Mexico Alpha, New Mexico
1936   *Louisiana Alpha, L.S.U.* (1947)
1937   Alabama Gamma, Montevallo
1937   Michigan Alpha, Albion (1975-1977)
1937   Ohio Alpha, Bowling Green
1938   Missouri Beta, Central Missouri State
1940   Iowa Beta, Drake
1940   Kansas Gamma, Benedictine
1940   *New Jersey Alpha, Upsala* (1969)
1940   *South Carolina Alpha, Coker* (1962)
1940   Texas Alpha, Texas Tech
1940   Texas Beta, Southern Methodist
1941   *Ohio Beta, Wooster* (1954)
1941   Tennessee Alpha, Tennessee Tech
1942   *Illinois Gamma, Chicago State* (1975)
1942   Michigan Beta, Central Michigan
1942   New York Alpha, Hofstra
1944   New Jersey Beta, Montclair
1945   Illinois Delta, St. Francis (IL) (1979-1981)
1946   *Michigan Gamma, Wayne State (MI)* (1958)
1947   Kansas Delta, Washburn
1947   Missouri Gamma, William Jewell
1947   Ohio Gamma, Baldwin-Wallace
1947   *Texas Delta, Texas Christian* (1959)
1947   Texas Gamma, Texas Woman's
1947   Wisconsin Alpha, Mount Mary
1948   *California Alpha, Pomona* (1963)
1948   Colorado Alpha, Colorado State
1948   *Missouri Delta, Kansas Medical Center* (1952)
1949   Mississippi Gamma, Southern Mississippi
1949   Missouri Epsilon, Central Methodist
1950   Indiana Alpha, Manchester
1950   Pennsylvania Alpha, Westminster (PA)
1951   *Louisiana Beta, Southwestern Louisiana* (1968)
1951   *North Carolina Alpha, Wake Forest* (1982)
1951   *Texas Epsilon, North Texas* (1982)
1952   Indiana Beta, Butler
1952   Kansas Epsilon, Fort Hays

1953   Pennsylvania Beta, LaSalle
1954   *California Beta, Occidental* (1969)
1955   Virginia Alpha, Virginia State, Norfolk
1957   Indiana Gamma, Anderson
1957   *New York Beta, SUNY, Albany* (1969)
1958   California Gamma, Cal Poly, San Luis Obispo
1959   Nebraska Beta, Kearney
1959   *New York Gamma, SUNY Col., Oswego* (1979)
1959   Pennsylvania Gamma, Waynesburg
1959   Tennessee Beta, East Tennessee
1959   Virginia Beta, Radford
1960   *Florida Alpha, Stetson* (1974)
1960   Indiana Delta, Evansville
1960   *Ohio Delta, Wittenberg* (1963)
1960   Ohio Epsilon, Marietta
1961   *Alabama Delta, Howard* (1969)
1961   Missouri Zeta, Missouri, Rolla
1961   *New York Delta, Utica* (1979)
1962   Nebraska Gamma, Chadron
1962   *New York Epsilon, Ladycliff* (1981)
1963   Illinois Epsilon, North Park
1963   Maryland Alpha, Notre Dame (MD)
1964   California Delta, Cal Poly, Pomona
1964   Oklahoma Beta, Tulsa
1964   Pennsylvania Delta, Marywood
1965   Alabama Epsilon, Huntingdon (1975-1979)
1965   Arkansas Alpha, Arkansas State
1965   Iowa Gamma, Morningside
1965   Maryland Beta, Western Maryland
1965   Pennsylvania Epsilon, Kutztown
1965   Pennsylvania Zeta, Indiana (PA)
1965   Tennessee Gamma, Union (TN)
1965   Wisconsin Beta, Wisconsin, River Falls
1966   *New York Zeta, Colgate* (1975)
1967   *Connecticut Alpha, Southern Connecticut* (1986)
1967   Illinois Zeta, Rosary (IL)
1967   Pennsylvania Eta, Grove City
1967   South Carolina Beta, South Carolina State
1967   *Texas Zeta, Tarleton* (1979)
1968   Massachusetts Alpha, Assumption
1968   Missouri Eta, Northeast Missouri
1968   New York Eta, Niagara
1969   Illinois Eta, Western Illinois
1969   *New York Theta, St. Francis (NY)* (1987)
1969   Ohio Zeta, Muskingum
1969   Pennsylvania Iota, Shippensburg
1969   Pennsylvania Theta, Susquehanna
1970   *Maryland Gamma, St. Joseph's (PA)* (1973)
1970   Mississippi Delta, William Carey
1971   Colorado Beta, Colorado Mines
1971   Kentucky Alpha, Eastern Kentucky
1971   Missouri Theta, Evangel
1971   New York Iota, Wagner
1971   Pennsylvania Kappa, Holy Family
1971   Tennessee Delta, Carson-Newman
1972   South Carolina Gamma, Winthrop
1973   Iowa Delta, Wartburg
1973   Oklahoma Gamma, Southeastern Oklahoma
1973   Pennsylvania Lambda, Bloomsburg

1974   New York Kappa, Pace
1975   Georgia Alpha, West Georgia
1975   Missouri Iota, Missouri Southern
1975   *North Carolina Beta, Western Carolina*
       (1982)
1975   Texas Eta, Hardin-Simmons
1975   West Virginia Alpha, Bethany (WV)
1976   Florida Beta, Florida Southern
1978   Maryland Delta, Frostburg
1978   Wisconsin Gamma, Wisconsin, Eau Claire
1979   Illinois Theta, Illinois Benedictine
1979   Pennsylvania Mu, St. Francis (PA)
1980   *Texas Theta, Southwest Texas* (1986)
1981   Alabama Zeta, Birmingham-Southern
1981   Connecticut Beta, Eastern Connecticut
1983   New York Lambda, C. W. Post
1984   Missouri Kappa, Drury
1985   Colorado Gamma, Fort Lewis
1986   Nebraska Delta, Nebraska Wesleyan
1987   New York Mu, St. Thomas Aquinas
1987   Ohio Eta, Ohio Northern
1987   Pennsylvania Nu, Ursinus
1987   Texas Iota, MacMurray
1987   Virginia Gamma, Liberty
1990   Colorado Delta, Mesa
1990   North Carolina Gamma, Elon
1990   Oklahoma Delta, Oral Roberts
1990   Pennsylvania Xi, Cedar Crest

Kappa Tau Alpha

(JOURNALISM AND MASS
COMMUNICATIONS)

ACTIVE PIN

KAPPA TAU ALPHA completed seventy-five years of service dedicated to the promotion of the highest ideals of scholarship in the field of journalism and mass communications in 1985. The society was founded at the University of Missouri, where its first constitution, bearing the 1910 date, was adopted. Begun at the suggestion of Walter Williams, dean and founder of the first journalism school, Kappa Tau Alpha from the first had as its major purpose the recognition of high achievement in scholarship. The second official chapter was chartered in 1925 at the University of Illinois. In 1930 three new chapters were admitted. Although there are no chapters in foreign countries, nationals of other countries have been admitted to membership.

Purpose   The recognition and encouragement of high scholarship and professional standards among students of journalism in the better schools and departments of journalism and communication in American colleges and universities.

Eligibility   Limited to the upper ten percent of the junior-senior group and exceptional graduate students.

Government   The society is governed by the National Council, composed of the chapter advisers of each chapter. The executive committee is made up of the president, vice-president, secretary and treasurer, who are elected biennially. The annual meeting of the National Council is held in connection with that of the Association for Education in Journalism and Mass Communication (AEJMC).

Traditions and Insignia   Kappa Tau Alpha fulfills its function of rewarding and recognizing scholarship by electing to membership undergraduate and graduate students, faculty members, and distinguished scholars in the field; by rewarding outstanding research; by sponsoring a distinguished annual lecture; and by publication. The annual Frank Luther Mott Research Award has been presented each year since 1944 to the author of an outstanding piece of scholarly research in the field. The Kappa Tau Alpha Lecture, inaugurated in 1950, has become a regular part of the annual convention program of the AEJMC. The *Year Book of Kappa Tau Alpha* appeared from 1946 to 1984 and served as an archive of the society's activities. The *Newsletter* was started in 1983.

The letters KTA stand for γρχτυ ξι το χλτφεσ— *The truth will prevail.* The Greek letters also suggest three English words: *knowledge, truth, accuracy.* The emblem is the gold key bearing a quill and the initials of the society in black. The colors are blue and gold.

Publication   Kappa Tau Alpha publishes *KTA Newsletter.*

Headquarters   c/o Executive Director Dr. William H. Taft, 107 Sondra Ave., Columbia, Missouri 65202.

Membership   Active chapters 85. Total number of initiates 32,000. Chapter roll:

1910   Missouri
1925   Illinois
1930   Georgia
1930   Marquette
1930   Ohio
1930   West Virginia
1931   Kentucky
1931   Michigan
1931   Southern Methodist
1934   Colorado
1936   Arkansas
1936   Iowa
1936   Nevada
1936   Ohio State
1945   Washington (WA)
1946   N.Y.U.
1947   Nebraska
1948   Minnesota
1949   Northwestern

1951	Florida
1951	Oklahoma
1951	Utah
1952	Brigham Young
1952	Tennessee
1953	Montana
1954	Oklahoma State
1955	North Carolina
1955	Penn State
1955	San Jose
1956	Michigan State
1958	Miami (FL)
1958	Southern Illinois
1960	Oregon
1961	Texas
1962	Duquesne
1962	Maryland
1962	South Dakota State
1964	Bradley
1966	American
1967	Kansas
1967	Long Island
1967	Texas Tech
1968	Ball State
1968	South Carolina
1970	Arizona
1970	Cal State, Northridge
1971	Bowling Green
1971	Drake
1971	Northern Illinois
1972	North Texas
1972	San Diego U.
1973	Memphis State
1974	Alabama
1974	St. Bonaventure
1974	Temple
1975	Cal State, Long Beach
1976	Oregon State
1977	Arkansas, Little Rock
1977	South Florida
1977	Syracuse
1978	Hawaii, Manoa
1978	L.S.U.
1978	Mississippi
1978	Virginia Commonwealth
1979	Texas Christian
1979	Wisconsin, Eau Claire
1979	Wisconsin, Oshkosh
1981	Arkansas State
1981	Central State (OK)
1981	Hampton Inst.
1981	Southwest Texas
1981	Western Kentucky
1983	Eastern Illinois
1983	Eastern Kentucky
1983	Northern Arizona
1983	Texas A & M
1984	Texas, Arlington
1985	Cal State, Fullerton
1985	Madison Col
1986	Abilene Christian
1986	Humboldt

1986	Iowa State
1986	North Dakota
1986	Northeastern
1986	V.P.I.
1987	Cal State, Fresno
1987	New Mexico
1988	Northeast Louisiana
1988	Southeast Missouri
1990	Central Missouri State
1990	Kent
1990	Loyola, New Orleans
1990	Massachusetts
1990	Southern Mississippi
1990	Winthrop

Lambda Iota Tau

(LITERATURE)

ACTIVE PIN

LAMBDA IOTA TAU was founded in December, 1953, by Prof. Warren L. Fleischauer at Michigan State College. Friends at other institutions recognized the value of an honor society in literature, and within a few months there were chapters at a number of other colleges in Michigan and throughout the northern Midwest. On Saturday, March 6, 1954, representatives from these six early chapters met at East Lansing to celebrate the incorporation of the society. At this meeting the address was given by Prof. Louis I. Bredvold of the University of Michigan.

Professor Fleischauer served as the first executive secretary. The society became international with the founding of the first chapter outside the United States in 1960. In 1965 Lambda Iota Tau was admitted into membership in the Association of College Honor Societies.

Purpose To recognize and promote excellence in the study of literature.

Chapters are encouraged to hold regular meetings and to sponsor events and activities which will bring the study of literature to the attention of the campus at large. The society holds regional conferences as well.

Eligibility Members are majors or minors in literature, no matter in what language that literature may be written, who (1) are in the upper thirty-five percent of their class in cumulative grade average, (2) have attained at least a full B average in at least twelve semester credit hours or eighteen term hours of literature and all prerequisites thereto; (3) are enrolled in at least their fifth college semester or seventh college term, and (4) have presented an initiation paper on a literary topic or of a creative nature.

Government There are three geographical regions of Lambda Iota Tau—the East, the Midwest, and the West and South. Chapters outside the United States are assigned to these regions depending on their location and direction. Chapters in each region elect one member to the International Board of Moderators, which is the legislative body of the society. The executive officers of the society are the international executive secretary, the assistant international executive secretary, and such associate international executive secretaries as the executive secretary may appoint.

Chapters may be founded only at four-year degree-granting institutions which are fully accredited by the appropriate regional accrediting agency. Petitions from new chapters must be approved by the International Board of Moderators. There are three classes of membership—active, alumni, and honorary. Alumni members are those who were active members during their undergraduate or graduate academic careers; they may form alumni chapters. Honorary membership is awarded by the International Board of Moderators on nomination by the local chapters.

The society bestows an honorary presidency upon some figure in the world of literature who has distinguished himself both as a creator and as a critic. Past honorary presidents of the society include such authors as Archibald MacLeish, W. H. Auden, Robert Penn Warren, Saul Bellow, Joyce Carol Oates, and others.

Traditions and Insignia The insignia of the society is a lozenge-shaped badge which comes in two forms: A pin with a wide gold border around the badge and a lapel button with a narrower border. Both badges are black and bear the Greek initials of the society. The colors of the society are purple, standing for the magnificence of literature, and gold. which stands for the "realms of gold" into which the poet Keats has said literature takes us. The flower of the society is the pansy, which, according to Shakespeare's Ophelia, is for thought.

Publications *LIT*, a journal containing essays, stories, poems, and plays by members, as well as a bibliography of master's theses in literature, is published annually. The *Lambdan*, a newsletter for alumni members, also appears annually and contains information about college teaching opportunities and about scholarly and critical journals to which members may subscribe at reduced prices. The Lambda Iota Tau *Newsletter* appears twice a year and is sent to all active and alumni members

Headquarters Aquinas College, Grand Rapids, Michigan 49506.

Membership Active chapters 102. Inactive chapters 1. Colonies 3. Graduate/Alumni chapters 1. Total number of initiates 30,000. Chapter roll:

	Alpha Chi (Alumni)
1954	Alpha Iota, West Virginia State
1954	Beta, Aquinas
1954	Gamma, Sioux Falls
1954	Gamma Lambda, Purdue
1954	Lambda, Siena Heights
1954	Mu, Alma
1954	Nu, Nazareth
1954	Omega, Baldwin-Wallace
1955	Alpha Xi, Lambuth
1955	Chi, St. Scholastica
1955	Omicron, Augsburg
1955	Pi, Wheaton
1955	Tau, Anna Maria
1955	Upsilon, Mount Mary's (CA)
1956	Alpha Alpha, Adrian
1956	Alpha Delta, Southern Mississippi
1956	Alpha Mu, Mount Mary
1956	Alpha Pi, John Carroll
1956	Alpha Theta, Morgan State
1956	Alpha Zeta, Fort Hays
1956	*Beta Mu, Colorado State* (1960)
1957	Alpha Rho, Mount Mary's (MD)
1957	Alpha Sigma, Gordon
1957	Alpha Tau, Immaculata
1957	Alpha Upsilon, Marian (IN)
1958	Beta Delta, Florida A & M
1958	Beta Epsilon, Misericordia
1958	Beta Zeta, LaSalle
1959	Alpha Epsilon, Holy Family
1960	Xi, Madonna
1961	Alpha Omicron, Southern Illinois
1961	Beta Eta, Ladycliff
1964	Alpha Omega, Florida Memorial
1964	Alpha Phi, Kansas Wesleyan
1964	Alpha Psi, Geneva
1964	Beta Kappa, Shinshu
1964	Beta Lambda, Marywood
1964	Delta, Weber
1964	Epsilon, South Dakota
1964	Rho, Tokyo Kyoiku
1965	Alpha Gamma, Rosary Hill (NY)
1965	Beta Iota, Grove City
1965	Beta Tau, Aichi
1965	Iota, Morehead
1965	Psi, Barry (FL)
1966	Alpha Lambda, Arkansas State
1966	Beta Alpha, St. Teresa
1966	Beta Chi, Illinois
1966	Beta Phi, Racine (Dominican)
1966	Beta Psi, Utah State
1966	Beta Sigma, Cabrini
1966	Eta Theta, Longwood
1966	Gamma Alpha, Grambling
1966	Gamma Beta, Knoxville
1966	Gamma Epsilon, North Adams
1967	Alpha Beta, Hillsdale
1967	Beta Beta, Tuskegee
1967	Gamma Gamma, William Carey
1967	Gamma Iota, Moravian
1968	Beta Rho, Rosary Hill (NY)
1968	Eta, Mary Washington

1968	Sigma, Chicago State
1968	Theta, Annhurst
1968	Zeta, Kentucky Wesleyan
1969	Alpha Eta, Lewis-St. Francis
1969	Alpha Kappa, Carroll
1969	Alpha Nu, Centenary
1969	Beta Gamma, Carlow
1969	Beta Theta, Seattle Pacific
1970	Beta Nu, Bethany (KS)
1970	Beta Omicron, Wisconsin State
1970	Beta Pi, Columbus
1970	Gamma Delta, Loras
1970	Gamma Theta, Georgia State
1971	Gamma Eta, Westfield
1971	Gamma Kappa, Tsuda
1971	Gamma Mu, Florida
1971	Gamma Nu, Evansville
1971	Gamma Xi, Hope
1971	Gamma Zeta, Dickinson State
1972	Gamma Phi, Alabama
1972	Gamma Pi, Malloy
1972	Gamma Rho, Ball State
1972	Gamma Sigma, Marion
1972	Gamma Tau, Florida State
1972	Gamma Upsilon, Bethany (WV)
1973	Delta Alpha, Texas Southern
1973	Delta Beta, Towson
1973	Delta Gamma, Western Carolina
1973	Gamma Chi, Fisk
1973	Gamma Omega, Maryville (TN)
1973	Gamma Psi, Tennessee
1974	Delta Delta, Dillard
1974	Delta Epsilon, Alverno
1974	Delta Eta, Shepherd
1974	Delta Iota, Delta State
1974	Delta Theta, Worcester Tech
1974	Delta Zeta, St. Cloud
1975	Delta Kappa, North Central
1975	Delta Lambda, Utah
1975	Delta Mu, Montana State
1977	Phi, Pikeville

Colonies: Mount Saint Vincent, St. Mary's College, Westminster College

Lambda Sigma Society

(SOPHOMORE LEADERSHIP)

LAMBDA SIGMA SOCIETY, a sophomore society for women and men, was founded at the University of Pittsburgh in 1922. Its purpose is "to pursue leadership, scholarship, fellowship, and the spirit of serving among members of the sophomore class, to promote leadership among freshmen and to serve and promote the interests of the college or university in every way possible. Lambda Sigma is the former Cwens, the leadership and service honor society for sophomore women founded in 1922. When Cwens disbanded as a single-sex society in the summer of 1976, Lambda Sigma (L for leadership and S

for service) accepted its structure (and history) and the added purpose of functioning as a sophomore society for men as well as women.

Not more than 50 students or 10 per cent of the freshmen class may be chosen. Selection is made on the basis of scholarship, promise of leadership, a marked interest in student activities and a spirit of service to the school. Members serve as guides and assistants for freshmen during the orientation week, proctor freshman tests, help at registration, hold get-acquainted dances for the freshmen, conduct campus tours for visitors and tutor interested freshmen.

Government Lambda Sigma is proud of its tradition of student representation on its National Executive Board. The board consists of four elected officers, an appointed executive secretary and a treasurer, three representatives who are chapter advisors and two students. The national convention is held every two years and regional meetings are held annually.

Publications The *Diamond* is the annual publication which is sent to all members. The *Carbon Copy* is a newsletter published twice a year to supplement the *Diamond* and report chapter news.

Funds and Philanthropies Lambda Sigma chapters support the national fund for a scholarship given annually to a current or former Lambda Sigma member who has shown outstanding contributions in keeping with the ideals of the society.

Headquarters 126 Seventeenth Street, Atlanta, Georgia 30309.

Membership Total undergraduate membership 1,018. Active chapters 33. Inactive chapters 10. Total number of initiates 31,964. Chapter roll:

1922	Alpha, Pitt
1925	Beta, Miami (OH)
1925	*Gamma, Missouri* (1936)
1927	*Delta, Penn State* (1977)
1927	Epsilon, Allegheny
1928	Zeta, Muskingum
1929	Eta, Carnegie-Mellon
1931	Theta, Kentucky
1941	Iota, Mississippi
1945	*Kappa, Seton Hill* (1956)
1945	Lambda, Westminster (PA)
1948	Mu, Eastern Kentucky
1952	*Nu, Louisville* (1984)
1953	*Xi, Grove City* (1978)
1954	Omicron, Northern Illinois
1957	Pi, Auburn
1959	Rho, Thiel
1959	*Sigma, Alfred* (1977)
1961	*Phi, Union (KY)* (1980)
1961	Tau, Kansas
1961	*Upsilon, Morehead* (1985)
1964	Chi, Louisiana Tech
1965	Omega, Pittsburg State, Kansas
1965	Psi, Central Missouri State
1966	Alpha Alpha, Mount Union
1969	Alpha Beta, Oklahoma

1969 Alpha Gamma, Duquesne
1970 Alpha Delta, Southern Mississippi
1970 Alpha Eta, Penn State, Behrend
1972 Alpha Zeta, Texas A & M
1974 Alpha Epsilon, Mansfield
1974 Alpha Theta, Slippery Rock
1978 Alpha Iota, Mississippi State
1978 Alpha Kappa, Georgia Tech
1981 Alpha Lambda, D'Youville
1981 Alpha Mu, Berry (GA)
1982 Alpha Nu, Butler
1983 Alpha Omicron, Penn State, Beaver
1984 Alpha Pi, Lawrence
1984 Alpha Xi, Texas Tech
1987 Alpha Rho, Robert Morris
1987 Alpha Sigma, Gannon
1988 Alpha Tau, Alabama

Mortar Board

(NATIONAL SENIOR HONOR SOCIETY
SERVICE, SCHOLARSHIP, LEADERSHIP)

ACTIVE PIN

MORTAR BOARD, the first and only national organization of senior women, began its career as an outstanding factor in American collegiate life in February, 1918, at Syracuse, New York, through the pioneering efforts of four local senior women's honor societies at Cornell University, the University of Michigan, the Ohio State University and Swarthmore College. The choice of the name Mortar Board, which had been that of two of the local groups represented, the selection of the pin and drafts of the ritual, the constitution and the expansion policy were accomplishments of the first convention.

Growth By the 1920's Mortar Board had expanded to the west coast and to the south. Expansion was continual with considerable numbers of chapters added in the '60s and '70s. In October, 1975, a special conference was convened in Kansas City, Missouri. At that conference the delegates voted to select male members as well as females. Today there are over 190 chapters throughout the continental United States and Hawaii. In addition approximately 50 alumni clubs have been formed in cities throughout the United States.

Government The National Conference is the governing body of Mortar Board. At each conference members of the National Council are elected by the active chapter delegates to conduct the business of the society in the time between conferences. At the 1985 National Conference the delegates voted to change from triennial conferences to biennial conferences and to add a student representative to the eight alumni officers composing the Council. For ease of administration the chapters are grouped geographically into 22 sections, each supervised by a section coordinator.

Purpose and Traditions The purpose of the society is to facilitate cooperation among senior honor societies, to contribute to the self-awareness of its members, to promote equal opportunities among all peoples, to emphasize the advancement of the status of women, to support the ideals of the university, to advance a spirit of scholarship, to recognize and encourage leadership, to provide service, and to establish the opportunity for a meaningful exchange of ideas as individuals and as a group.

The qualifications for membership are service, scholarship and leadership. The acceptance of membership commits every wearer of the Mortar Board pin to continue serving the ideals of discriminating service, responsible leadership, and the application of scholarly principles to personal and general problems, not only through the senior year but after graduation from college.

New members are elected to Mortar Board in the spring from among students who are at least in their junior year or have attained equivalent status. Each candidate for active membership shall meet the scholarship standard of the upper 35 percent of the junior class, but no lower than a B average. It is suggested chapters have no more than 35 nor fewer than five members.

Honorary membership, being the highest honor given by the Mortar Board chapter, may be conferred only upon a person who has made a distinguished contribution toward the advancement of the goals and purpose of Mortar Board, Inc., within the college or university and community or region.

Each chapter performs services of value for its campus. National Mortar Board requires no definite activities in which the chapters must participate since campuses differ and have their own peculiar needs, but a National Project (Organ Donor Awareness) was established at the 26th National Conference. Each chapter shall recognize its responsibility as part of the national organization of Mortar Board, Inc., by implementing in its own way those resolutions passed during and since the most recent National Conference.

The badge is a small black enameled mortarboard with gold edgings and tassel, bearing the Greek letters ΠΣΑ. Mortar Board colors are gold and silver.

Publication The national publication is the *Mortar Board FORUM*. It is published at least three times a year.

Funds By action of the 1941 convention a national fellowship was established and named the Katherine Wills Coleman Fellowship as a tribute to a past national president. It carries one or more awards of one thousand dollars ($1,000) each and is given to members who can qualify as candidates for advanced studies. As many as fourteen fellowships have been awarded in one year.

At the convention in 1949, the gift membership, which may be awarded annually in each chapter to a candidate for membership who otherwise would be financially unable to accept membership in the Mortar Board, was named the Coral Vanstrum Stevens Membership in honor of the retiring national president.

The Mortar Board Foundation Fund was established by action of the 1955 convention in response to inquiries from members, alumni and friends of Mortar Board as a means by which they might contribute funds and/or other property, either by outright gift, bequests or devises for the general purpose of the organization. The primary purpose of foundation monies is the awarding of grants to members to assist in their graduate study.

Awards Individual chapters may confer a Chapter Citation upon a person in recognition of an important contribution to an individual Mortar Board chapter or the community in which it is located. A National Citation may be given to a person in recognition of distinguished contribution to the nation within the ideals of service, scholarship and leadership.

Headquarters 1250 Chambers Road, #170, Columbus, Ohio 43212.

Membership Total undergraduate membership 5,000. Active chapters 198. City/Area alumni associations 48. Disaffiliated chapters 4. Total number of initiates 142,000. Chapter roll:

1918	Der Hexenkreis, Cornell
1918	Friars, Missouri
1918	Mortar Board, Ohio State
1918	Mortarboard, Michigan
1918	Phi Delta Psi, Illinois
1918	*Pi Sigma Chi, Swarthmore* (1965)
1919	DePauw
1919	Sigma Tau, Minnesota
1920	Knox
1920	Wisconsin, Madison
1920	Staff & Crown, Kentucky
1921	Indiana
1921	Penn
1921	Black Masque, Nebraska
1922	Northwestern
1922	Washington (MO)
1922	Iota, Lawrence
1922	Pleiade, Miami (OH)
1923	Idaho
1923	Alpha Lambda Nu, Pitt
1923	Eta, Carnegie-Mellon
1923	Gamma Tau, Washington State
1923	Scroll & Script, Oregon
1923	Visor, Texas
1924	Colorado
1924	Akraia, Vermont
1924	Laurel, West Virginia
1924	Torch, Kansas
1925	Owl & Triangle, Oklahoma
1925	Theta Gamma, Cal, Berkeley
1925	Tolo, Washington (WA)

1925	Torch, Iowa State
1926	Purdue
1926	Whitman
1926	Pi Sigma Alpha, Arizona
1926	Staff & Circle, Iowa
1927	Penetralia, Montana
1927	Pi Sigma Alpha, Montana State
1928	*Banshee, Middlebury* (1985)
1928	Keystone, South Dakota
1928	Virginia Gamma, William and Mary
1928	XIX, Kansas State
1929	Hypatia, Alabama
1929	Torch & Tassel, USC
1929	Women's Boosters, Ohio Wesleyan
1930	Pomona
1930	Pi Alpha, Westhampton
1931	Hoasc, Agnes Scott
1931	Torchbearer, Florida State
1932	Decima, Southern Methodist
1932	Mystic Thirteen, Cincinnati
1932	Quo Vadis, North Dakota
1933	Cap & Gown, Oregon State
1933	Cap & Gown, Wyoming
1933	Order of the Acorn, Utah
1934	Adele H. Stamp, Maryland
1934	Blazer, L.S.U.
1934	Sphinx, Michigan State
1935	Archousai, Penn State
1935	Scroll, Birmingham-Southern
1936	Cap & Gown, Denison
1936	Maia, New Mexico
1937	Cap & Gown, Tennessee
1937	Cap and Gown, Grinnell
1937	Kedros, Denver
1938	Cap and Gown, New Hampshire
1938	Cresset, Ohio
1938	*Hour Glass, George Washington* (1979)
1939	Agathai, UCLA
1939	Parthenian, Georgia
1940	Achofoa, Oklahoma State
1940	Bachelor Maids, Vanderbilt
1940	Octagon, Arkansas
1941	Bucknell
1941	Chevron, Albion
1942	Star & Sceptor, Mississippi for Women
1942	Tassels, Mississippi
1943	Torch, Cornell Col. (IA)
1947	Dranzen, Occidental
1948	Keystone, Hood
1949	Laurels, Connecticut
1949	Pallas, Louisville
1950	Senior Staff, Tulsa
1951	Carleton
1951	Senior Bench, Beloit
1952	Gold Key, Wayne State (MI)
1952	LUX, Case Western Reserve
1953	Quadrangle, Tennessee, Chattanooga
1954	Wichita
1954	Margaret Fuller/Sieve & Shears, Drake
1955	Isogon, Massachusetts
1955	*Kalon, St. Lawrence* (1976)
1955	Sphinx, Auburn

1955	Target, Westminster (PA)
1955	W.E.B.S., Redlands
1956	Scarlet Quill, Butler
1957	Forum, Texas Tech
1957	Hood & Tassel, Chatham
1958	Alpha Sigma Sigma, Tulane
1958	Cap & Gown, Willamette
1958	The Honor, Stetson
1959	Cap & Gown, Mary Washington
1959	Otlah, Puget Sound
1960	Tassell, Delaware
1960	Trianon, Florida
1961	Alcor, Hope
1961	Tau Iota Omega, Colorado State
1963	Arista, Western Michigan
1963	Pleiades, Arizona State
1964	Pierian, Akron
1964	Senior Staff, North Dakota State
1964	Torch, Rhodes
1965	Aglaia, Augustana (IL)
1965	Cap & Gown, San Diego U.
1965	Crown & Scepter, Cal, Santa Barbara
1965	Hui Po'Okela, Hawaii, Manoa
1965	Nu Kappa Tau, Miami (FL)
1966	Skiff, Drury
1967	Alpha Order, South Carolina
1967	Arrow & Mask, Wittenberg
1967	Gavel, Converse
1967	Knolens, Pacific (CA)
1967	Laurels, Rhode Island
1967	Mu Beta, New Mexico State
1967	Wakapa, Bradley
1968	Cap & Gown, American
1968	Cap and Gown, MacMurray
1968	Meritum, North Texas
1968	Zeta Chi, Oklahoma Baptist
1969	Cap & Gown, Bowling Green
1969	Gown & Gavel, Valparaiso
1969	Tassels, Wake Forest
1969	Women's Honor Organization, Emory
1970	Ampersand, Texas Christian
1970	Cap & Gown, Houston
1970	Sigma Phi Eta, Utah State
1971	Clavia, Ball State
1971	Laurel, Baylor
1971	Pleiades, Northern Illinois
1971	Senior Women's Honor Board, Northern Arizona
1971	Women's Leadership Organization, Fort Hays
1972	Adahi, Eastern Michigan
1972	Alpha Theta Mu, Grove City
1972	Athenaeum, South Florida
1972	Cap & Gown, Cal State, Long Beach
1972	Chenrizig, Texas, El Paso
1972	Crimson Key, Georgia State
1972	Crown & Sceptre, Wesleyan (GA)
1972	Delphi, Texas Woman's
1972	Gold Key, Northern Colorado
1972	Laurels, Kent
1972	Sigma Lambda Sigma Society, South Dakota State
1972	Silver Tassel, Idaho State
1972	Tau Pi, Monmouth (IL)
1973	Alpha Sigma Chi, Berea
1973	Delta Alpha, Missouri
1973	Scho-Lea, Trinity (TX)
1973	Senior Women's Honor Board, Central Michigan
1973	Tassel, Memphis State
1974	Alpha Tau Delta, Louisiana Tech
1974	Cap and Crown, Boston U
1974	Panathenees, Carson-Newman
1975	Aurora, Ohio Northern
1975	Cap and Gown, Evansville
1975	Gold Circle, Tennessee Tech
1975	Gold Key Honor Society, Fisk
1975	Honoratae, Wisconsin, Milwaukee
1975	Laurel Society, Lake Erie
1976	Arista, Western Illinois
1976	Gold Caps, Wisconsin, Eau Claire
1976	Haught Honor Society, West Virginia Wesleyan
1976	Red Tassel, Illinois State
1976	Sigma Lambda Delta, Duquesne
1976	Tassels, Hanover
1977	Order of Athena, Clemson
1977	Percy Warren Senior Honor Society, James Madison
1977	Senior Board, Northeast Louisiana
1977	Sigma Lambda Sigma Society, V.P.I.
1978	Bronze Key, Central State (OK)
1978	Cap and Gown, Mississippi Col
1978	Panaegis, William Jewell
1979	Cap and Gown, Texas A & M
1979	Gold Key, South Alabama
1979	Spires Honor Society, Troy
1979	Telion, Northern Michigan
1980	Chi Sigma, Bethany Nazarene
1981	Cap and Gown, Midwestern
1982	Pamarista, Indiana State
1983	Cap and Gown, Western Carolina
1983	Collegiate Pentacle, Eastern Kentucky
1983	Peppers Honor Society, Toledo
1984	Arete, Salem (NC)
1984	Tassels, Central Missouri State
1985	Crescent Honor Society, Coe
1985	Scribes Honor Society, West Texas

Omega Chi Epsilon

(CHEMICAL ENGINEERING)

ACTIVE PIN

OMEGA CHI EPSILON, national chemical engineering honor society, was founded in 1931 at the University of Illinois by a group of chemical engineering students to recognize those juniors and seniors who displayed academic excellence and leadership in their profession. With the counsel of Professors D. B. Keyes and Norman Krase, they designed a key, petitioned for and received recognition from the university administration and became the Alpha Chapter of Omega Chi Epsilon.

Omega Chi Epsilon promotes high scholarship, encourages original investigation in chemical engineering, and recognizes the valuable traits of character, leadership and integrity. It fosters meaningful dialog within the chemical engineering department.

Growth The society grew slowly at first. By 1957, there were only six chapters, three of them inactive. Interest was revived in the 1960s and reached a sustained high level in the 1970s. Twenty-three of the present 47 chapters received their charters since 1975. Membership in the spring of 1985 reached 10,400 members.

A constitutional amendment in 1966 permitted women to become members. The Society joined the Association of College Honor Societies in 1967.

Eligibility Active membership is limited to chemical engineering juniors, seniors, and graduate students. Juniors must have completed three hours of chemical engineering course work and be in the upper one-fourth of their class. Seniors must be in the upper one-third of their class. Graduate students must have completed nine hours of chemical engineering courses. All those elected must have traits and characteristics of leadership that make them likely to succeed as professional engineers. Associate membership consists of professors or other members of the staff of the institution who have shown noteworthy achievement in chemical engineering.

Government The annual meeting is held at the same time and place as the annual meeting of the American Institute of Chemical Engineers. The national officers are the president, vice president, executive secretary and treasurer. With the past president, these officers constitute the Executive Committee and have general oversight of the society. The executive secretary is appointed to a two-year term at the annual meeting in even-numbered years. The other national officers are elected to two-year terms in the spring of even-numbered years and are eligible for re-election.

Each chapter formulates its own program and activities. It operates under bylaws established at the time its charter is granted.

Traditions and Insignia Traditions prevail at the chapter level rather than at the national level. Generally these are built around service to the chemical engineering department.

The badge consists of a black maltese cross background upon which is superimposed a circular crest. The crest bears the letters $\Omega X E$ on a white band across a horizontal diameter. Above the white band are two crossed retorts in gold on a maroon background. Below the white band, also on a maroon background, are a gold integral sign and a bolt of lightning. These symbols represent the roles of chemistry, mathematics and physics in chemical engineering.

The seal consists of two concentric circles, bearing at the top of the region between the two circles the words "Omega Chi Epsilon" and the words "Founded, 1931" at the bottom. The letters of the society appear in the center of the seal. The colors of the society are black, white and maroon.

Headquarters Executive Secretary, Dr. Edwin O. Eisen, Department of Chemical Engineering, McNeese State University, Lake Charles, Louisiana 70609.

Membership Active chapters 47. Inactive chapters 2. Total number of initiates 12,860. Chapter roll:

1931	*Alpha, Illinois* (1936)
1932	Beta, Iowa State (1938-1956)
1934	*Gamma, Minnesota* (1938)
1941	Delta, Clarkson
1941	Epsilon, Texas
1943	Zeta, Purdue
1957	Eta, New Jersey Tech
1958	Theta, West Virginia
1959	Iota, Pitt
1960	Kappa, New York Tech
1964	Lambda, CUNY, Brooklyn
1964	Mu, Oklahoma State
1965	Nu, Detroit
1965	Xi, Northeastern
1967	Omicron, Lamar
1969	Pi, Rose-Hulman
1970	Rho, Texas A & M
1970	Sigma, Arkansas
1971	Phi, Louisiana Tech
1971	Tau, Alabama
1971	Upsilon, Kentucky
1973	Chi, Maryland
1974	Omega, Missouri, Rolla
1974	Psi, USC
1975	Alpha Alpha, Auburn
1975	Alpha Beta, Northwestern
1975	Alpha Delta, Houston
1975	Alpha Gamma, Lowell
1976	Alpha Epsilon, Kansas State

1977 Alpha Zeta, Michigan State
1978 Alpha Eta, Mississippi State
1978 Alpha Iota, Tulane
1978 Alpha Theta, Youngstown State
1979 Alpha Kappa, South Carolina
1979 Alpha Lambda, Southwestern Louisiana
1979 Alpha Mu, New Mexico State
1980 Alpha Nu, Tri-State
1980 Alpha Xi, Colorado
1981 Alpha Omicron, Texas Tech
1982 Alpha Pi, Howard
1983 Alpha Rho, Georgia Tech
1983 Alpha Sigma, Connecticut
1984 Alpha Chi, V.P.I.
1984 Alpha Phi, Iowa
1984 Alpha Tau, Colorado State
1984 Alpha Upsilon, Cal Poly, Pomona
1985 Alpha Psi, Manhattan
1988 Alpha Omega, L.S.U.
1988 Beta Alpha, Penn State

Omega Rho

(OPERATIONS RESEARCH AND MANAGEMENT SCIENCE)

OMEGA RHO was founded at the TIMS/ORSA Meeting in Philadelphia, PA in April, 1976. The society was admitted to the Association of College Honor Societies as an associate in 1983 and received full membership in 1986.

Purpose To encourage the study of operations research and management science related disciplines, to recognize and honor excellence in such studies, and to further professional interests.

Eligibility Undergraduates must rank in the top twenty-five percent of the class and have completed at least five semesters or seven quarters of the curricular requirements. Graduate students must have at least a 3.5 average on a 4.0 scale in all graduate courses; shall have no failures; and shall have completed at least one-third of the residency requirements for the master's degree. Men and women in industry, academia, and the profession may be made Honorary Members upon approval of the Executive Committee of the Society. Faculty teaching in the field may be elected faculty members.

Major Activities Each chapter plans its own activities. The Society sponsors the annual Omega Rho Distinguished Lecture as a plenary session at the fall Joint ORSA/TIMS Meeting, and the annual Omega Rho Student Paper Competition at the spring Joint TIMS/ORSA Meeting.

Membership Chapter roll is not available.

Omicron Delta Epsilon

(ECONOMICS)

ACTIVE PIN

OMICRON DELTA EPSILON, national Greek-letter recognition society in economics, is the outgrowth of a union of Omicron Chi Epsilon and The Order of Artus, which became effective on January 1, 1963.

The Order of Artus (Omicron Delta Gamma) was the older of these societies, having been established on May 7, 1915, when a merger was formed of the Economics Society of the University of Wisconsin and the Undergraduate Society of Economics of Harvard University. Prof. T. K. Urdahl had sponsored the Wisconsin Society and Prof. Frank W. Taussig the Harvard Society.

The younger partner in the union, Omicron Chi Epsilon, was founded in 1956 by a group of students at the City College of New York who felt the need for such a society among students in American colleges and universities in order to both stimulate interest in economics and to provide a means of conferring suitable honors on the more promising students working in this field. Its principal founder was Alan A. Brown. The society aimed to provide a forum for academic intercourse between graduate and undergraduate students of economics across the country, and thus facilitate cross-fertilization of ideas among budding members of the profession.

Purpose The objectives of Omicron Delta Epsilon are recognition of scholastic attainment and the honoring of outstanding achievements in economics; the establishment of closer ties between students and faculty in economics within colleges and universities and among colleges and universities; the publication of the official journal, *The American Economist;* the sponsoring of panels at professional meetings and the Irving Fisher and Frank W. Taussig competitions.

Eligibility Undergraduates must have an overall scholastic average of at least a "B" or better. They do not necessarily have to be economics majors, but they must have an average of better than "B" and are eligible after completing one semester of full-time work. There are no admission requirements for faculty members.

Awards The Irving Fisher Graduate Monograph Award pays $1,000 and provides for publication of the award-winning manuscript by Cambridge University Press and/or the publication of an article in the *American Economic Review.* This competition is open to Omicron Delta Epsilon graduate students in economics or those members who have received their Ph.D. not more than two years prior to entering the competition.

The Frank W. Taussig Undergraduate Article Award, awarded annually, pays $250 to the winner, $100 to his/her chapter and provides for publication in *The American Economist.*

Publication An official journal, *The American Economist,* is published semiannually by the society. Its purpose is two-fold: (1) to provide an outlet for meritorious essays and papers written by graduate and undergraduate students, of a nature not normally catered for by existing professional journals, but of sufficient interest and merit to warrant publication, and (2) to provide a means of acquainting would-be economists, particularly undergraduates contemplating a career in economics, with some idea of modern developments in pure and applied economics.

Headquarters P.O. Drawer AS, University, AL 35456.

Membership Total undergraduate membership is estimated to be three-fourths of total membership. Active chapters 501. Inactive chapters 112. Total number of initiates 100,000+. Chapter roll:

AK Alpha, Alaska, Fairbanks
AK Beta, Alaska, Anchorage
AL Alpha, Auburn
AL Beta, Alabama
AL Delta, Alabama, Huntsville
AL Epsilon, North Alabama
AL Eta, Alabama A & M
AL Gamma, Alabama, Birmingham
AL Iota, Troy
AL Theta, Spring Hill
AL Zeta, Auburn, Montgomery
AR Alpha, Arkansas State
AR Beta, Arkansas
AZ Alpha, Arizona State
AZ Beta, Arizona
AZ Gamma, Northern Arizona
Australia Alpha, Western Australia
Australia Beta, Macquarie
Australia Gamma, New South Wales Tech
BC Alpha, Simon Fraser
CA Alpha, USC
CA Alpha-Beta, Cal Poly, Pomona
CA Alpha-Delta, Cal State, San Bernadino
CA Alpha-Epsilon, St. Mary's (CA)
CA Alpha-Eta, Whittier
CA Alpha-Gamma, Pepperdine
CA Alpha-Iota, Cal Poly, San Luis Obispo
CA Alpha-Kappa, Loyola Marymount, Los Angeles
CA Alpha-Theta, Cal State, Bakersfield
CA Alpha-Zeta, Mills
CA Beta, Cal State, Fresno
CA Chi, Cal Tech
CA Delta, Cal, Berkeley
CA Epsilon, Occidental
CA Eta, Cal State, Los Angeles
CA Gamma, San Diego U.

CA Iota, Cal State, Sacramento
CA Kappa, Cal State, Fullerton
CA Lambda, Cal, Riverside
CA Mu, Claremont
CA Nu, Cal State, Hayward
CA Omega, San Diego U
CA Omicron, Cal, Davis
CA Phi, Pacific (CA)
CA Pi, Cal, Santa Barbara
CA Psi, Stanford
CA Rho, Cal State, Chico
CA Sigma, Cal State, Northridge
CA Tau, Cal State, Long Beach
CA Theta, UCLA
CA Upsilon, Redlands
CA Xi, Claremont
CA Zeta, Cal State, San Jose
CO Alpha, Air Force Inst
CO Beta, Colorado
CO Delta, Colorado State
CO Epsilon, Metropolitan State (CO)
CO Eta, Denver
CO Gamma, Southern Colorado
CO Theta, Colorado, Denver
CO Zeta, Northern Colorado
CT Alpha, Connecticut
CT Beta, Yale
CT Delta, Fairfield
CT Epsilon, Central Connecticut
CT Eta, Southern Connecticut
CT Gamma, Hartford
CT Theta, Western Connecticut
CT Zeta, Eastern Connecticut
DC Alpha, George Washington
DC Beta, Howard
DC Delta, Georgetown U
DC Gamma, American
DE Alpha, Delaware
Egypt Alpha, American, Cairo (1986)
FL Alpha, Miami (FL)
FL Beta, Tampa
FL Delta, Florida
FL Epsilon, Florida Atlantic
FL Eta, Florida Southern
FL Gamma, Florida State
FL Iota, Central Florida
FL Kappa, Rollins
FL Lambda, Eckerd
FL Mu, South Florida
FL Nu, Florida International
FL Theta, North Florida
FL Zeta, Rollins
France Alpha, Paris
GA Alpha, Georgia
GA Beta, Georgia State
GA Delta, West Georgia
GA Epsilon, Spelman
GA Eta, Berry (GA)
GA Gamma, Georgia Southern
GA Iota, Morehouse
GA Kappa, Georgia Tech
GA Theta, LaGrange

GA Zeta, Emory
HI Alpha, Hawaii
IA Alpha, Iowa
IA Beta, Luther
IA Delta, Drake
IA Epsilon, Coe
IA Eta, Loras
IA Gamma, Iowa State
IA Zeta, Northern Iowa
ID Alpha, Idaho State
ID Beta, Boise
IL Alpha, Illinois
IL Beta, Southern Illinois
IL Delta, Northern Illinois
IL Epsilon, Western Illinois
IL Eta, Chicago
IL Gamma, Bradley
IL Kappa, Eastern Illinois
IL Lambda, Loyola, Chicago
IL Mu, Purdue
IL Mu, Wheaton
IL Nu, Rockford
IL Omicron, MacMurray
IL Phi, Illinois Wesleyan
IL Pi, DePaul
IL Rho, Lake Forest
IL Sigma, Northeastern Illinois
IL Tau, Illinois Col
IL Theta, Illinois State
IL Upsilon, Sangamon
IL Xi, Northwestern
IL Zeta, Illinois, Chicago
IN Alpha, DePauw
IN Beta, Notre Dame
IN Delta, Valparaiso
IN Epsilon, Butler
IN Eta, Indiana State
IN Gamma, Indiana
IN Iota, Indiana Northwest
IN Kappa, Wabash
IN Lambda, Southern Indiana
IN Mu, Purdue
IN Theta, Indiana, South Bend
IN Zeta, Ball State
KS Alpha, Wichita
KS Beta, Kansas State
KS Delta, Pittsburg State, Kansas
KS Epsilon, Washburn
KS Gamma, Benedictine
KS Zeta, Fort Hays
KY Alpha, Kentucky
KY Beta, Berea
KY Delta, Transylvania
KY Epsilon, Western Kentucky
KY Eta, Bellarmine
KY Gamma, Centre College
KY Zeta, Eastern Kentucky
LA Alpha, Tulane
LA Beta, Southwestern Louisiana
LA Delta, Louisiana Tech
LA Epsilon, New Orleans
LA Eta, Southeastern Louisiana

LA Gamma, L.S.U.
LA Theta, Xavier (LA)
LA Zeta, Northeast Louisiana
MA Alpha, Harvard
MA Alpha-Alpha, Massachusetts
MA Beta, Tufts
MA Chi, Suffolk
MA Delta, Brandeis
MA Epsilon, Boston U
MA Eta, Clark
MA Gamma, Boston Col
MA Iota, Northeastern
MA Kappa, Nicholls
MA Lambda, Regis (MA)
MA Mu, Worcester Tech
MA Omega, Merrimack
MA Omicron, Wheaton
MA Phi, Stonehill
MA Pi, Bentley
MA Psi, Fitchburg (1986)
MA Rho, Mount Holyoke
MA Sigma, Massachusetts
MA Tau, Babson
MA Theta, American International
MA Upsilon, Gordon
MA Xi, Framingham
MA Zeta, Holy Cross
MD Alpha, Maryland
MD Beta, Western Maryland
MD Delta, Navy
MD Epsilon, Maryland, Baltimore County
MD Eta, Hood
MD Gamma, Loyola (MD)
MD Theta, Frostburg (1980)
MD Zeta, Johns Hopkins
ME Alpha, Maine
MI Alpha, Northern Michigan
MI Beta, Albion
MI Delta, Wayne State (MI)
MI Epsilon, Central Michigan
MI Eta, Eastern Michigan
MI Gamma, Michigan State
MI Iota, Oakland
MI Kappa, Michigan, Dearborn
MI Lambda, Andrews
MI Mu, Michigan
MI Nu, Michigan, Flint
MI Theta, Hope
MI Xi, Aquinas
MI Zeta, Alma
MN Alpha, Macalester
MN Beta, St. Olaf
MN Delta, Minnesota, Duluth
MN Epsilon, Minnesota
MN Eta, Gustavus Adolphus
MN Gamma, St. Thomas
MN Iota, St. Cloud
MN Kappa, Mankato
MN Theta, St. John's (MN)
MN Zeta, St. Catherine
MO Alpha, Washington (MO)
MO Beta, Missouri

MO Delta, Missouri, St. Louis
MO Epsilon, Southwest Missouri
MO Eta, Park (MO)
MO Gamma, Central Missouri State
MO Iota, Missouri, Rolla
MO Kappa, Lincoln (MO)
MO Lambda, Northwest Missouri
MO Mu, St. Louis
MO Nu, Southeast Missouri
MO Theta, Missouri Southern
MO Zeta, Missouri, Kansas City
MS Alpha, Southern Mississippi
MS Beta, Mississippi State
MS Delta, Millsaps
MS Gamma, Mississippi
MT Alpha, Montana
Mexico Alpha, U of Americas
NC Alpha, North Carolina A & T
NC Beta, Davidson
NC Delta, North Carolina
NC Epsilon, North Carolina, Asheville
NC Eta, Wake Forest
NC Gamma, North Carolina State
NC Iota, North Carolina, Greensboro
NC Kappa, Appalachian
NC Lambda, Western Carolina
NC Mu, St. Andrews Presbyterian
NC Nu, Fayetteville
NC Omicron, Lenoir-Rhyne
NC Theta, North Carolina, Charlotte
NC Xi, Duke
NC Zeta, East Carolina
ND Alpha, North Dakota
NE Alpha, Creighton
NE Beta, Nebraska, Omaha
NE Delta, Nebraska Wesleyan
NE Epsilon, Kearney
NE Gamma, Nebraska
NH Alpha, Dartmouth
NH Beta, New Hampshire
NH Gamma, St. Anselm's
NJ Alpha, Princeton
NJ Beta, St. Peter's
NJ Delta, Fairleigh Dickinson, Rutherford
NJ Epsilon, Seton Hall
NJ Eta, Rider
NJ Gamma, Fairleigh Dickinson, Madison
NJ Iota, Fairleigh Dickinson, Teaneck
NJ Kappa, Jersey City
NJ Lambda, Rutgers, Camden
NJ Mu, Kean (NJ)
NJ Nu, Drew
NJ Omicron, Trenton
NJ Pi, William Paterson
NJ Rho, Stockton
NJ Sigma, Ramapo
NJ Theta, Rutgers
NJ Xi, Montclair
NJ Zeta, Rutgers, Newark
NM Alpha, New Mexico
NM Beta, New Mexico State
NV Alpha, Nevada

NV Beta, Nevada, Las Vegas
NY Alpha, CUNY, Brooklyn
NY Alpha-Beta, Union (NY)
NY Alpha-Chi, Adelphi
NY Alpha-Delta, Russell Sage
NY Alpha-Epsilon, SUNY, Albany
NY Alpha-Eta, Vassar
NY Alpha-Gamma, SUNY, Buffalo
NY Alpha-Iota, Hunter
NY Alpha-Kappa, SUNY, Binghamton
NY Alpha-Lambda, SUNY Col., Oneonta
NY Alpha-Mu, Hartwick
NY Alpha-Nu, SUNY Col., Cortland
NY Alpha-Omega, LeMoyne-Owen
NY Alpha-Omicron, St. John Fisher
NY Alpha-Phi, Yeshiva
NY Alpha-Pi, Mt. St. Vincent
NY Alpha-Psi, Touro
NY Alpha-Rho, Pace
NY Alpha-Sigma, SUNY Col., Plattsburgh
NY Alpha-Tau, Rochester Tech
NY Alpha-Theta, SUNY Col., Buffalo
NY Alpha-Upsilon, Ithaca
NY Alpha-Xi, Hobart
NY Alpha-Zeta, Skidmore
NY Beta, Manhattan
NY Beta-Alpha, St. Bonaventure
NY Beta-Beta, Utica
NY Beta-Delta, New York Tech
NY Beta-Epsilon, Niagara
NY Beta-Eta, SUNY Col., Brockport
NY Beta-Gamma, Long Island
NY Beta-Theta, Hamilton
NY Beta-Zeta, Baruch
NY Chi, St. Lawrence
NY Delta, Queens (NY)
NY Epsilon, Hofstra
NY Eta, St. Francis (NY)
NY Gamma, Fordham
NY Iota, N.Y.U.
NY Kappa, Cornell
NY Lambda, Syracuse
NY Mu, Colgate
NY Nu, Iona
NY Omega, Rochester
NY Omicron, Dowling
NY Phi, SUNY Col., Oswego
NY Pi, Lehman
NY Psi, SUNY Col., Potsdam
NY Rho, SUNY Col., Geneseo
NY Sigma, Long Island
NY Tau, SUNY Col., Fredonia
NY Theta, St. John's (NY)
NY Upsilon, R.P.I.
NY Xi, SUNY, Stony Brook
NY Zeta, Columbia (NY)
OH Alpha, Muskingum
OH Alpha-Beta, Baldwin-Wallace
OH Alpha-Delta, Wright State
OH Alpha-Epsilon, Wittenberg
OH Alpha-Gamma, Wooster
OH Beta, Miami (OH)

OH Chi, Cleveland
OH Delta, Ohio State
OH Epsilon, John Carroll
OH Eta, Cincinnati
OH Gamma, Kent
OH Iota, Akron
OH Kappa, Denison
OH Lambda, Bowling Green
OH Mu, Ohio Wesleyan
OH Nu, Kenyon
OH Omega, Hiram
OH Omicron, Xavier (OH)
OH Phi, Ashland
OH Pi, Otterbein
OH Psi, Mount Union
OH Rho, Marietta
OH Sigma, Ohio
OH Tau, Dayton
OH Theta, Youngstown State
OH Upsilon, Ohio Northern
OH Xi, Toledo
OH Zeta, Case Western Reserve
OK Alpha, Oklahoma
OK Beta, Oklahoma State
OK Gamma, Central State (OK)
ON Alpha, Waterloo
ON Beta, Windsor
OR Alpha, Southern Oregon
OR Beta, Linfield
OR Gamma, Oregon State
PA Alpha, Pitt
PA Alpha-Beta, Wilkes
PA Alpha-Delta, Lafayette
PA Alpha-Epsilon, West Chester
PA Alpha-Eta, Muhlenberg
PA Alpha-Gamma, Indiana (PA)
PA Alpha-Iota, Chatham
PA Alpha-Kappa, Shippensburg
PA Alpha-Lambda, Gettysburg
PA Alpha-Theta, St. Joseph's (PA)
PA Alpha-Zeta, Dickinson
PA Beta, Penn State
PA Chi, California (PA)
PA Delta, Lehigh
PA Epsilon, Duquesne
PA Eta, Widener
PA Gamma, Penn
PA Iota, Bucknell
PA Kappa, Franklin and Marshall
PA Lambda, Villanova
PA Mu, Lycoming
PA Nu, Westminster (PA)
PA Omega, Clarion
PA Omicron, Carnegie-Mellon
PA Phi, LaSalle
PA Pi, Gannon
PA Psi, Waynesburg
PA Rho, Ursinus
PA Sigma, Albright
PA Tau, Bloomsburg
PA Theta, Temple
PA Upsilon, Lincoln (PA)

PA Xi, Scranton
PA Zeta, Washington and Jefferson
PR Alpha, Puerto Rico, San Juan
QB Gamma, McGill
RI Alpha, Rhode Island
RI Beta, Brown
RI Delta, Providence
RI Gamma, Bryant
SC Alpha, South Carolina
SC Beta, Clemson
SC Delta, Charleston (SC)
SC Epsilon, Francis Marion
SC Zeta, Winthrop
SD Alpha, Minuteman Graduate
SD Beta, South Dakota
SD Delta, Northern State
SD Gamma, South Dakota State
Scotland Alpha, Strathclyde
South Africa Alpha, Cape Town
South Africa Beta, Natal
South Africa Gamma, Rhodes
TN Alpha, Fisk
TN Beta, Tennessee
TN Delta, Memphis State
TN Epsilon, Vanderbilt
TN Eta, Tennessee Tech
TN Gamma, U of the South
TN Iota, Austin Peay
TN Kappa, Middle Tennessee
TN Theta, Rhodes
TN Zeta, Tennessee, Chattanooga
TX Alpha, Baylor
TX Beta, Texas
TX Chi, Texas, El Paso
TX Delta, Southern Methodist
TX Epsilon, St. Mary's, San Antonio
TX Eta, Texas Christian
TX Gamma, Houston
TX Iota, Sam Houston
TX Kappa, Texas A & M
TX Lambda, St. Thomas (TX)
TX Mu, Texas, Arlington
TX Nu, West Texas
TX Omicron, North Texas
TX Omicron, Texas Woman's
TX Phi, Trinity (TX)
TX Pi, Prairie View
TX Rho, Dallas
TX Sigma, Texas, San Antonio
TX Tau, Lamar
TX Theta, Stephen F. Austin
TX Upsilon, Rice
TX Xi, East Texas
TX Zeta, Texas Tech
UT Alpha, Brigham Young
UT Beta, Weber
UT Delta, Utah State
UT Gamma, Utah
VA Alpha, Virginia
VA Beta, Mary Washington
VA Delta, Roanoke
VA Epsilon, V.P.I.

VA Eta, Old Dominion
VA Gamma, Washington and Lee
VA Iota, Hampden-Sydney
VA Kappa, Virginia Commonwealth
VA Lambda, Richmond
VA Mu, Mary Baldwin
VA Nu, Virginia State, Norfolk
VA Omicron, Madison Col
VA Pi, Hollins
VA Rho, Norfolk
VA Sigma, Christopher Newport
VA Tau, Emory and Henry
VA Theta, George Mason
VA Upsilon, Radford
VA Xi, William and Mary
VA Zeta, V.M.I.
VT Alpha, Middlebury
VT Beta, Norwich
VT Delta, St. Michael's
VT Gamma, Vermont
WA Alpha, Washington (WA)
WA Beta, Washington State
WA Delta, Seattle
WA Epsilon, Gonzaga
WA Eta, Pacific Lutheran
WA Gamma, St. Martin's
WA Theta, Puget Sound
WA Zeta, Western Washington
WI Alpha, Wisconsin, Madison
WI Beta, Wisconsin, River Falls
WI Delta, Wisconsin, Milwaukee
WI Epsilon, Lawrence
WI Eta, St. Norbert
WI Gamma, Wisconsin, Platteville
WI Iota, Wisconsin, Whitewater
WI Kappa, Ripon
WI Lambda, Marquette
WI Theta, Wisconsin, Eau Claire
WI Zeta, Wisconsin, Oshkosh
WV Alpha, Bethany (WV)
WV Beta, West Virginia
WV Delta, Marshall
WV Epsilon, West Virginia Wesleyan
WV Gamma, West Liberty
WV Zeta, West Virginia State
WY Alpha, Wyoming

Omicron Nu

(HOME ECONOMICS)

ACTIVE PIN

OMICRON NU was established at the Michigan Agricultural College, now Michigan State University, East Lansing, on April 23, 1912, by Maude Gilchrist, at that time dean of home economics.

Purpose Omicron Nu recognizes superior graduate achievement in addition to undergraduate scholastic excellence. The program of each chapter, while flexible, emphasizes the purposes of Omicron Nu—the promotion of graduate study and research and the stimulation of scholarship and leadership toward the well-being of individuals and families throughout the world.

Eligibility Fifteen percent of those with junior ranking who have at least a B average; twenty percent of those with senior ranking (including those already elected as juniors) with at least a B average; graduate students who have completed at least half of their work and have a grade point average halfway between the maximum and minimum grade point average acceptable for the degree.

Government The government of the organization is vested in the grand council and the Executive Committee. The grand council consists of the five national officers and three conclave delegate representatives who comprise the Executive Committee, and a representative from each of the active chapters. The Executive Committee meets in the alternate year and conducts all matters of business between sessions of the grand council.

Major Activities Omicron Nu provides four $2,250 Research Fellowships per biennium for doctoral study and two $2,000 Eileen C. Maddex master's Fellowships. A biennial Conclave provides student members with an opportunity for leadership training and involvement in national decision making. Omicron Nu is a member of the American Home Economics Association's Coordinating Council of Home Economics Honor Societies.

Traditions and Insignia The emblem is a gold key displaying the plain Greek letter O superimposed on an embellished N. There is no pledge emblem.

Publication *The Omicron Nu* is published four times a year, also the *Home Economics FORUM*.

Headquarters Human Ecology Building, Michigan State University, East Lansing, Michigan 48824.

Membership Active chapters 138. Inactive chapters 34. Total number of initiates 25,716. Chapter roll:

1651 *Kappa Alpha Kappa, Southern Illinois*
      (1985)
1912 Omicron Alpha, Michigan State
1913 Omicron Beta, N.Y. State Teachers
1913 Omicron Delta, Purdue
1913 Omicron Gamma, Iowa State
1914 Omicron Epsilon, Illinois
1914 Omicron Zeta, Nebraska
1915 Omicron Eta, Wisconsin, Madison
1915 Omicron Iota, Kansas
1915 Omicron Theta, Kansas State
1919 Omicron Kappa, Washington State
1919 Omicron Lambda, Oregon State
1919 Omicron Mu, Cornell
1920 Omicron Nu, Colorado State
1921 Omicron Xi, Oklahoma State
1922 Kappa Alpha, Northwest Missouri
1922 Omicron Omicron, Washington (WA)
1922 Omicron Pi, Florida State
1923 Kappa Beta, Central Missouri State
1923 Omicron Rho, Minnesota
1923 Omicron Sigma, Indiana
1924 Kappa Gamma, Fort Hays (1933-1951)
1924 Omicron Tau, Penn State
1924 Omicron Upsilon, Texas
1925 Kappa Delta, Southeast Missouri
1925 Omicron Chi, UCLA
1925 Omicron Phi, Vermont
1926 Kappa Epsilon, Marshall
1926 Omicron Psi, Oklahoma
1927 *Kappa Eta, Arizona (1942)*
1927 Kappa Iota, Texas A & I
1927 *Kappa Zeta, West Texas (1961)*
1928 *Kappa Kappa, Emporia (1967)*
1928 *Kappa Lambda, Oklahoma for Women*
      (1938)
1928 *Kappa Theta, Cal, Santa Barbara (1961)*
1928 Omicron Omega, Ohio State
1929 *Kappa Mu, Southwestern (KS) (1977)*
1930 *Kappa Nu, Peru (1945)*
1930 *Kappa Xi, Ohio Wesleyan (1931)*
1930 Omicron Alpha Alpha, Iowa
1931 Omicron Alpha Beta, Maine
1931 Omicron Alpha Gamma, Montevallo
1933 Omicron Alpha Delta, Utah
1934 *Kappa Omicron, William and Mary (1946)*
1935 Omicron Alpha Epsilon, Tennessee
1936 Kappa Pi, New Mexico
1937 Omicron Alpha Zea, Maryland
1938 *Kappa Rho, Florida Southern (1949)*
1938 Omicron Alpha Eta, Drexel
1939 *Kappa Sigma, Louisiana Col (1952)*
1939 Omicron Alpha Theta, Cincinnati
1940 Kappa Tau, Indiana (PA)
1941 Omicron Alpha Iota, Syracuse
1942 *Kappa Upsilon, Concord (1979)*
1942 Omicron Alpha Kappa, North Carolina,
      Greensboro
1943 *Kappa Phi, Our Lady of the Lake (1976)*
1944 Kappa Chi, Immaculata
1944 Omicron Alpha Lambda, Cal, Davis
1945 Kappa Psi, Southwest Missouri

1947 Kappa Alpha Alpha, Marywood
      (1947-1975)
1948 Kappa Alpha Beta, Mansfield
1948 Kappa Alpha Gamma, Seton Hill
1949 *Kappa Alpha Delta, Carthage (1962)*
1949 *Kappa Alpha Epsilon, Mount Mary (1965)*
1949 *Kappa Alpha Eta, Marcyhurst (1958)*
1949 *Kappa Alpha Zeta, St. Mary-of-the-Woods*
      (1976)
1950 Kappa Alpha Theta, Eastern Illinois
1951 *Kappa Alpha Iota, Regis (MA) (1956)*
1951 Kappa Alpha Lambda, Southern Mississippi
1951 Kappa Alpha Mu, Illinois State
1951 Omicron Alpha Mu, Rhode Island
1951 Omicron Alpha Nu, Auburn
1952 Omicron Alpha Omicron, West Virginia
1952 Omicron Alpha Pi, Massachusetts
1952 Omicron Alpha Xi, Carnegie-Mellon
1955 Kappa Alpha Nu, Kent
1955 Kappa Alpha Omicron, Kearney
1955 *Kappa Alpha Xi, Pepperdine (1981)*
1956 Kappa Alpha Pi, Middle Tennessee
1959 Omicron Alpha Rho, Chapter At Large
1961 *Kappa Alpha Rho, Lindenwood (1964)*
1961 Kappa Alpha Sigma, Murray State
1961 Kappa Alpha Tau, Bradley
1961 Omicron Alpha Sigma, Arizona
1961 Omicron Alpha Tau, Brigham Young
1962 *Kappa Alpha Chi, Mary Washington (1968)*
1962 Kappa Alpha Phi, Sam Houston
1962 Kappa Alpha Psi, Montana
1962 *Kappa Alpha Upsilon, Longwood (1988)*
1962 Kappa Beta Alpha, Samford
1963 Kappa Beta Beta, North Alabama
1963 Kappa Beta Delta, Shepherd
1963 Kappa Beta Epsilon, Prairie View
1963 *Kappa Beta Gamma, Puget Sound (1963)*
1963 Omicron Alpha Phi, Howard
1963 Omicron Alpha Upsilon, Delaware
1964 Kappa Beta Eta, Virginia State, Petersburg
1964 *Kappa Beta Zeta, Mercy (MI) (1986)*
1965 *Kappa Beta Iota, St. Joseph's (MD) (1972)*
1965 Kappa Beta Kappa, Western Illinois
1965 Kappa Beta Theta, Lamar
1967 Kappa Beta Lambda, Grambling
1968 Kappa Beta Mu, Tennessee Tech
1968 Kappa Beta Nu, Northeast Missouri
1968 Kappa Beta Omicron, Morehead
1968 Kappa Beta Xi, Carson-Newman
1969 *Kappa Beta Pi, Austin Peay (1972)*
1969 Kappa Beta Rho, East Tennessee
1969 Omicron Alpha Chi, Radford
1969 Omicron Alpha Psi, Cal State, Long Beach
1970 Kappa Beta Sigma, Tennessee State
1971 Kappa Beta Tau, West Virginia Wesleyan
1971 *Kappa Beta Upsilon, Georgetown Col*
      (1986)
1972 Kappa Beta Chi, McNeese
1972 Kappa Beta Phi, Mississippi State
1972 *Kappa Beta Psi, Lincoln (MO) (1984)*
1972 Kappa Gamma Alpha, Alcorn
1972 *Kappa Gamma Beta, Barry (FL) (1977)*

1972 Omicron Alpha Omega, Missouri
1973 Kappa Gamma Delta, Delta State
1973 Kappa Gamma Epsilon, North Carolina Central
1973 Kappa Gamma Eta, Mississippi
1973 *Kappa Gamma Gamma, Whittier* (1987)
1973 Kappa Gamma Iota, Albright
1973 Kappa Gamma Theta, Baylor
1973 Kappa Gamma Zeta, Central Michigan
1973 Omicron Beta Alpha, Rutgers
1974 Kappa Gamma Kappa, Memphis State
1974 Kappa Gamma Lambda, Adrian
1974 *Kappa Gamma Mu, CUNY, Brooklyn* (1983)
1974 Kappa Gamma Nu, Northeast Louisiana
1974 Kappa Gamma Xi, Dayton
1975 *Kappa Gamma Omicron, Northern Michigan* (1980)
1975 Kappa Gamma Pi, Southwestern Louisiana
1975 Kappa Gamma Rho, Alabama A & M
1975 Kappa Gamma Sigma, South Carolina State
1976 Kappa Delta Alpha, Minnesota, Duluth
1976 Kappa Delta Beta, Hood
1976 Kappa Gamma Chi, Bethel, McPherson, Sterling
1976 Kappa Gamma Phi, Northwestern Louisiana
1976 Kappa Gamma Psi, Tennessee, Chattanooga
1976 Kappa Gamma Tau, Valparaiso
1976 Kappa Gamma Upsilon, Appalachian
1976 Omicron Beta Beta, Louisiana Tech
1976 Omicron Beta Gamma, Northern Illinois
1977 Kappa Delta Delta, Butler
1977 Kappa Delta Epsilon, Tuskegee
1977 Kappa Delta Gamma, Akron
1977 Omicron Beta Delta, L.S.U.
1978 Kappa Delta Eta, Rosary (IL)
1978 Kappa Delta Iota, Emporia
1978 Kappa Delta Kappa, Glassboro
1978 Kappa Delta Mu, North Carolina A & T
1978 *Kappa Delta Theta, St. Mary's (LA)* (1984)
1978 Kappa Delta Zeta, St. Catherine
1979 Kappa Delta Lambda, Cheyney State
1979 Omicron Beta Epsilon, Cal State, Northridge
1980 Kappa Delta Nu, Hampton Inst.
1980 Kappa Delta Xi, Morgan State
1981 Kappa Delta Omicron, Meredith
1982 Kappa Delta Pi, Nicholls
1982 Kappa Delta Rho, Olivet Nazarene
1984 Kappa Delta Sigma, Ashland
1985 Kappa Delta Tau, Christian Heritage
1985 Kappa Delta Upsilon, Maryland, Eastern Shore
1985 Omicron Beta Zeta, V.P.I.
1987 Kappa Delta Phi, Nevada
1987 Omicron Beta Eta, Puerto Rico, San Juan
1989 Omicron Beta Theta, Montclair
1990 Kappa Delta Chi, Andrews
1990 Kappa Delta Psi, Arkansas, Pine Bluff
1990 Kappa Epsilon Alpha, Abilene Christian

Phi Alpha Theta

(HISTORY)

ACTIVE PIN

PHI ALPHA THETA, international honor society in history, was founded at the University of Arkansas, March 14, 1921; the Beta Chapter was established exactly one year later at the University of Pittsburgh. N. Andrew Cleven, David Y. Thomas and Frederick H. Alder were responsible for the founding of the society. Incorporated under the laws of Pennsylvania on October 13, 1925, the society registered its name and emblems in the United States Patent Office in 1933.

Primarily organized for the purpose of recognizing excellence in the study of history, its requirements for eligibility to membership are exacting and definite. An undergraduate to be eligible must have completed at least twelve semester hours in history with an average grade in all history courses of between the highest and the second highest grade in the working scale, a grade of at least the second highest grade in the working scale in two-thirds of the remainder of the work, and must rank in the upper 35 per cent of the class. A graduate student must have completed 30 per cent of the residence requirements for the master's degree with more than half of the grades of the highest grade in the working scale.

Government Government is by national convention, meeting biennially, which elects the National Council of eleven members, one of whom, the national secretary-treasurer, is the executive secretary of the society.

Traditions and Insignia A placement bureau is part of the work of the society, and scholarship and research funds are available for further study. Additional grants for outstanding papers by both undergraduate student members and graduate student members are made each year. Two annual Book Awards are made, each of $500—one for the best book published by a member as their first book published in the field of history, the other award for the best book published by a member as a subsequent book in the field of history.

An award given, usually annually, is the Manuscript Award, covering the publication costs of a manuscript selected because it makes a significant contribution to historical knowledge either by offering a challenging new interpretation, or by presenting important new material on subjects already researched, and by the proper evaluation and interpretation of primary sources which are being used for the first time, or by breaking ground in heretofore neglected areas of history.

The biennial convention of December 27–30, 1981, established a new category of awards known as the Donald B. Hoffman Scholarship Awards. These awards are funded by voluntary contributions of individuals and chapters with a total funding of $25,000.

First category of awards is a $1,000 grant to a faculty advisor who has served in that position for a total of five or more years and is awarded for any special activity such as research and writing assistance and travel for the advancement of their career or for other programs involving further participation by the faculty member. The second grant is for an advanced graduate student to assist in the completion of requirements for the Ph.D. Degree.

Every grant is awarded yearly and in the amount of $1,000.

The emblem is a six-pointed star, laid on a circular base of gold. This emblem is also mounted on a key. Colors are madonna red and blue. The flower is the red rose.

Publications The journal of the society, *The Historian*, was launched in 1938; formerly issued semiannually it was changed in 1956 to quarterly with issues in November, February, May, and August. A newsletter is issued three times yearly.

Headquarters 2333 Liberty Street, Allentown, Pennsylvania 18104.

Membership Total undergraduate membership varies yearly between 6,000 and 7,500. Active chapters 698. Inactive chapters 10. Total number of initiates 159,201. Chapter roll:

1921	Alpha, Arkansas
1922	Beta, Pitt
1923	Gamma, Penn
1926	Delta, Florida State
1927	Epsilon, Illinois
1927	Eta, Southern Methodist
1927	Zeta, Ohio State
1928	Theta, Denison
1929	Iota, Northern Colorado
1929	Kappa, Muhlenberg
1930	Lambda, Pittsburg State, Kansas
1932	Mu, Central Arkansas
1932	Nu, Oklahoma State
1932	Xi, USC
1934	Omicron, Nebraska, Omaha
1934	Pi, Northwestern Louisiana
1934	Rho, Southwestern State (OK)
1936	Sigma, New Mexico
1937	Phi, Minnesota
1937	Tau, Kentucky
1937	Upsilon, Waynesburg
1938	Chi, Cal, Berkeley
1938	Psi, Kent
1939	Omega, Gettysburg
1940	Alpha Alpha, Lehigh
1941	Alpha Beta, Wooster

1941	Alpha Delta, Marquette
1941	Alpha Gamma, Bucknell
1942	Alpha Epsilon, Southeast Missouri
1942	Alpha Zeta, Stetson
1943	Alpha Eta, Upsala
1944	Alpha Theta, Hofstra
1945	Alpha Iota, Nevada
1945	Alpha Kappa, Toledo
1945	Alpha Lambda, North Texas
1946	Alpha Mu, CUNY, Brooklyn
1946	Alpha Nu, Henderson
1946	Alpha Omicron, Kansas
1946	Alpha Pi, Augustana (IL)
1946	Alpha Rho, Utah
1946	Alpha Xi, Westminster (PA)
1947	Alpha Chi, Cedar Crest
1947	Alpha Omega, Rhode Island
1947	Alpha Phi, Michigan State
1947	Alpha Psi, Muskingum
1947	Alpha Sigma, Washington and Jefferson
1947	Alpha Tau, Winthrop
1947	Alpha Upsilon, Temple
1947	Alpha-Omega, Rhode Island
1947	Beta Alpha, Texas
1947	Beta Beta, Stanford
1947	Beta Gamma, William Jewell
1948	Beta Chi, Drury
1948	Beta Delta, Puerto Rico, Rio Piedras
1948	Beta Epsilon, Colorado
1948	Beta Eta, Columbia (SC)
1948	Beta Iota, Brigham Young
1948	Beta Kappa, San Diego U.
1948	Beta Lambda, San Jose
1948	Beta Mu, Richmond
1948	Beta Nu, Davis and Elkins
1948	Beta Omega, Maryland
1948	Beta Omicron, Alabama
1948	Beta Phi, Monmouth (IL)
1948	Beta Pi, Georgetown U
1948	Beta Psi, Montana
1948	Beta Rho, Carroll
1948	Beta Sigma, Franklin
1948	Beta Tau, Queens (NY)
1948	Beta Theta, Franklin and Marshall
1948	Beta Upsilon, North Dakota
1948	Beta Xi, Lafayette
1948	Beta Zeta, Otterbein
1948	Gamma Alpha, Rutgers
1949	Gamma Beta, Bradley
1949	Gamma Delta, North Carolina, Greensboro
1949	Gamma Epsilon, Texas, El Paso
1949	Gamma Eta, Florida
1949	Gamma Gamma, Mississippi for Women
1949	Gamma Iota, Cal, Santa Barbara
1949	Gamma Kappa, Tulane
1949	Gamma Theta, Minnesota, Duluth
1949	Gamma Zeta, Wittenberg
1950	Gamma Chi, Marshall
1950	Gamma Lambda, St. Thomas (MN)
1950	Gamma Mu, Marietta
1950	Gamma Nu, Mississippi State
1950	Gamma Omega, Texas A & I

1950	Gamma Omicron, Hope	1956	Zeta Gamma, Howard
1950	Gamma Phi, Inter-American	1956	Zeta Zeta, Lycoming
1950	Gamma Pi, Cincinnati	1957	Zeta Iota, Texas Tech
1950	Gamma Psi, Washington State	1957	Zeta Kappa, Houston
1950	Gamma Rho, Wichita	1957	Zeta Lambda, Loras
1950	Gamma Sigma, Georgetown Col	1957	Zeta Mu, South Dakota
1950	Gamma Tau, Westminster (MO)	1957	Zeta Nu, Nebraska
1950	Gamma Upsilon, Bowling Green	1957	Zeta Theta, Oklahoma
1950	Gamma Xi, Utica	1958	Zeta Chi, Augustana (SD)
1951	Delta Alpha, Miami (FL)	1958	Zeta Omega, Arizona
1951	Delta Beta, Occidental	1958	Zeta Omicron, Park (MO)
1951	Delta Delta, Doane	1958	Zeta Phi, North Georgia
1951	Delta Epsilon, Indiana	1958	Zeta Pi, Eastern New Mexico
1951	Delta Eta, Dayton	1958	Zeta Psi, Wayland Baptist
1951	Delta Gamma, Heidelberg	1958	Zeta Rho, Philippines, Quezon City
1951	Delta Iota, Washington (WA)	1958	Zeta Sigma, Detroit
1951	Delta Theta, Manhattan	1958	Zeta Tau, Northeastern
1951	Delta Zeta, Ozarks	1958	Zeta Upsilon, West Texas
1952	Delta Kappa, Tulsa	1958	Zeta Xi, Albion
1952	Delta Lambda, Salem (NC)	1959	Eta Alpha, John Carroll
1952	Delta Mu, Boston U	1959	Eta Beta, East Texas
1952	Delta Nu, West Virginia	1959	Eta Delta, Peru
1952	Delta Omicron, Connecticut	1959	Eta Epsilon, Greenville
1952	Delta Pi, North Carolina	1959	Eta Eta, Northern Illinois
1952	Delta Xi, Utah State	1959	Eta Gamma, West Virginia State
1953	Delta Chi, Akron	1959	Eta Iota, Salisbury
1953	Delta Omega, Mount Mary	1959	Eta Kappa, Texas Christian
1953	Delta Phi, Wisconsin, Milwaukee	1959	Eta Lambda, Western Reserve
1953	Delta Psi, Union (TN)	1959	Eta Theta, Emmanuel
1953	Delta Rho, Iowa	1959	*Eta Zeta, Pepperdine* (1983)
1953	Delta Sigma, Kansas State	1960	Eta Chi, Arkansas State
1953	Delta Tau, Dubuque	1960	Eta Mu, Texas Lutheran
1953	Delta Upsilon, Baldwin-Wallace	1960	Eta Nu, Texas Woman's
1953	Epsilon Alpha, North Carolina	1960	Eta Omega, Morgan State
1954	Epsilon Beta, Ohio	1960	Eta Omicron, Mary Hardin-Baylor
1954	Epsilon Delta, Judson	1960	Eta Phi, Harding
1954	Epsilon Epsilon, Central State (OH)	1960	Eta Pi, Western Kentucky
1954	Epsilon Eta, McPherson	1960	Eta Psi, Fort Hays
1954	Epsilon Gamma, Wilmington	1960	Eta Rho, Lewis and Clark
1954	Epsilon Iota, Wagner	1960	Eta Sigma, Stephen F. Austin
1954	Epsilon Kappa, Oregon State	1960	Eta Tau, East Stroudsburg
1954	Epsilon Theta, Hunter	1960	Eta Upsilon, Denver
1954	Epsilon Zeta, Ohio Wesleyan	1960	Eta Xi, Cal State, Los Angeles
1955	Epsilon Lambda, Citadel	1960	Theta Alpha, Boston Col
1955	Epsilon Mu, Eastern Illinois	1961	Theta Beta, Towson
1955	Epsilon Nu, Memphis State	1961	Theta Delta, Austin Peay
1955	Epsilon Omicron, Catholic, Puerto Rico	1961	Theta Epsilon, Carson-Newman
1955	Epsilon Xi, Southwestern Louisiana	1961	Theta Eta, Creighton
1956	Epsilon Chi, David Lipscomb	1961	Theta Gamma, Tampa
1956	Epsilon Omega, Long Island	1961	Theta Iota, Montevallo
1956	Epsilon Phi, Duquesne	1961	Theta Theta, William and Mary
1956	Epsilon Pi, Georgia	1961	Theta Zeta, Mississippi Col
1956	Epsilon Psi, American	1962	Theta Chi, Colorado State
1956	Epsilon Rho, Samford	1962	Theta Kappa, Southern Mississippi
1956	Epsilon Sigma, Wake Forest	1962	Theta Lambda, Suffolk
1956	Epsilon Tau, Northeast Louisiana	1962	Theta Mu, Southwest Missouri
1956	Epsilon Upsilon, Penn State	1962	Theta Nu, St. Francis (NY)
1956	*Zeta Alpha, Immaculate Heart* (1981)	1962	Theta Omicron, Catholic
1956	Zeta Beta, Abilene Christian	1962	*Theta Phi, Newton of the Sacred Heart* (1981)
1956	Zeta Delta, Adelphi		
1956	Zeta Epsilon, Thiel	1962	Theta Pi, Cal State, Fullerton
1956	Zeta Eta, L.S.U.	1962	Theta Rho, Aquinas

1962   Theta Sigma, Southern Arkansas
1962   Theta Tau, Cal State, Northridge
1962   Theta Upsilon, UCLA
1962   Theta Xi, Old Dominion
1963   Iota Alpha, Miami (OH)
1963   Iota Beta, Guilford
1963   Iota Delta, Wisconsin, Stevens Point
1963   Iota Epsilon, Rider
1963   Iota Gamma, Arizona State
1963   Iota Zeta, Arkansas, Little Rock
1963   Theta Omega, Moravian
1963   Theta Psi, Mount Mary's (MD)
1964   Iota Eta, West Virginia Tech
1964   Iota Iota, Frostburg
1964   Iota Kappa, Rutgers, Newark
1964   Iota Lambda, Canisius
1964   Iota Mu, Troy
1964   Iota Nu, Western State (CO)
1964   Iota Omicron, Monmouth (NJ)
1964   Iota Pi, Fort Lewis
1964   Iota Rho, Mount Mary's (CA)
1964   Iota Theta, Beaver
1964   Iota Xi, Belhaven
1965   Iota Chi, Ripon
1965   Iota Omega, Centre College
1965   Iota Phi, Pikeville
1965   Iota Psi, Bloomfield
1965   Iota Sigma, Marywood
1965   Iota Tau, Rosary (IL)
1965   Iota Upsilon, Colgate
1965   Kappa Alpha, Mississippi
1965   Kappa Beta, Albright
1965   Kappa Delta, Bridgeport
1965   Kappa Epsilon, Columbia Union
1965   Kappa Eta, Wisconsin, Oshkosh
1965   Kappa Gamma, Whittier
1965   Kappa Iota, Iowa State
1965   Kappa Kappa, Texas Southern
1965   Kappa Lambda, Central Missouri State
1965   Kappa Mu, American International
1965   Kappa Nu, Xavier (OH)
1965   Kappa Omicron, Westfield
1965   Kappa Phi, San Francisco State
1965   Kappa Pi, Auburn
1965   Kappa Rho, Dallas
1965   *Kappa Sigma, St. Joseph's (MD)* (1973)
1965   Kappa Tau, Tennessee Tech
1965   Kappa Theta, Northern Arizona
1965   Kappa Upsilon, Roosevelt
1965   Kappa Xi, Mary Baldwin
1965   Kappa Zeta, St. Mary's, San Antonio
1966   Kappa Chi, Buena Vista
1966   Kappa Omega, Holy Cross
1966   Kappa Psi, Rhode Island
1966   Lambda Alpha, Alberta
1966   Lambda Beta, Mankato
1966   Lambda Chi, Spring Hill
1966   Lambda Delta, Tarkio
1966   Lambda Epsilon, Seton Hall
1966   Lambda Eta, East Carolina
1966   Lambda Gamma, Syracuse
1966   Lambda Iota, Macalester

1966   Lambda Kappa, Susquehanna
1966   Lambda Lambda, St. Mary's (MN)
1966   *Lambda Mu, Fort Wright* (1982)
1966   Lambda Nu, Wisconsin, River Falls
1966   Lambda Omega, Luther
1966   Lambda Omicron, Wisconsin, Eau Claire
1966   Lambda Phi, Chaminade
1966   Lambda Pi, Tennessee, Chattanooga
1966   Lambda Psi, Alma
1966   Lambda Rho, Louisiana Tech
1966   Lambda Sigma Society, Thomas More
1966   Lambda Tau, Eastern
1966   Lambda Theta, Sul Ross
1966   Lambda Upsilon, Santa Clara
1966   Lambda Xi, Wisconsin, Madison
1966   Lambda Zeta, Merrimack
1966   Mu Alpha, St. Louis
1967   Mu Beta, Ball State
1967   Mu Chi, Lamar
1967   Mu Delta, King's
1967   Mu Epsilon, Bethany (WV)
1967   Mu Eta, Lewis
1967   Mu Gamma, Graceland
1967   *Mu Iota, Massachusetts Pharmacy* (1983)
1967   Mu Kappa, Dana
1967   Mu Lambda, Northwestern Oklahoma
1967   Mu Mu, Olivet
1967   Mu Nu, Lincoln Memorial (TN)
1967   Mu Omega, St. Joseph's (PA)
1967   Mu Omicron, Ottawa
1967   Mu Phi, Western Washington
1967   Mu Pi, SUNY, Stony Brook
1967   Mu Psi, Bloomsburg
1967   Mu Rho, Scranton
1967   Mu Sigma, Norwich
1967   Mu Tau, Georgia State
1967   Mu Theta, Jacksonville
1967   Mu Upsilon, Illinois State
1967   Mu Xi, Kutztown
1967   Mu Zeta, Marist
1967   Nu Alpha, Wyoming
1967   Nu Beta, Wisconsin, Whitewater
1967   Nu Delta, Transylvania
1967   Nu Epsilon, Mount St. Vincent
1967   Nu Gamma, Illinois Wesleyan
1967   Nu Zeta, Olivet Nazarene
1968   Nu Chi, Northeast Missouri
1968   Nu Eta, Pace
1968   Nu Iota, St. Mary-of-the-Woods
1968   Nu Kappa, Ohio Northern
1968   Nu Lambda, N.Y.U.
1968   Nu Mu, Kentucky Wesleyan
1968   Nu Nu, Bridgewater
1968   Nu Omega, Purdue
1968   Nu Omicron, SUNY Col., Cortland
1968   Nu Phi, Washington (MD)
1968   Nu Pi, Notre Dame (MD)
1968   Nu Psi, LaSalle
1968   Nu Rho, Stonehill
1968   Nu Sigma, West Chester
1968   Nu Tau, Charleston (WV)
1968   Nu Theta, Hartwick

1968	Nu Upsilon, St. Elizabeth
1968	Nu Xi, Louisville
1968	Xi Alpha, Belmont
1968	Xi Beta, Indiana (PA)
1968	Xi Delta, Brigham Young, Hawaii
1968	Xi Epsilon, Lander
1968	Xi Eta, St. Mary's (NE)
1968	Xi Gamma, Gonzaga
1968	Xi Iota, Carthage
1968	Xi Kappa, Barry (FL)
1968	Xi Lambda, Murray State
1968	Xi Mu, Quincy
1968	Xi Nu, St. Vincent
1968	Xi Omicron, Southwestern State (OK)
1968	Xi Pi, Upper Iowa
1968	Xi Theta, Eastern Kentucky
1968	Xi Xi, Concordia (IL)
1968	Xi Zeta, Angelo
1969	*Omicron Alpha, Alaska Methodist* (1981)
1969	Omicron Beta, Indiana, South Bend
1969	Omicron Chi, Nicholls
1969	Omicron Delta, Fairleigh Dickinson, Rutherford
1969	Omicron Epsilon, Berry (GA)
1969	Omicron Eta, Clarkson
1969	Omicron Gamma, Chadron
1969	Omicron Iota, Notre Dame (OH)
1969	Omicron Kappa, Texas, Arlington
1969	Omicron Lambda, Andrews
1969	Omicron Mu, Northern Michigan
1969	Omicron Nu, St. Francis (IL)
1969	Omicron Omega, Central Michigan
1969	Omicron Omicron, Western Illinois
1969	Omicron Phi, Appalachian
1969	Omicron Pi, Elizabethtown
1969	Omicron Psi, Cal State, Long Beach
1969	Omicron Rho, SUNY Col., Geneseo
1969	Omicron Sigma, Winona
1969	Omicron Tau, Adrian
1969	Omicron Theta, Albany State
1969	Omicron Upsilon, Chicago State
1969	Omicron Xi, Siena
1969	Omicron Zeta, Ashland
1969	Pi Alpha, Georgia Southern
1969	Pi Beta, Loyola Marymount, Los Angeles
1969	Xi Chi, Ithaca
1969	Xi Omega, Florida Atlantic
1969	Xi Phi, South Carolina
1969	Xi Psi, Millsaps
1969	Xi Rho, West Georgia
1969	Xi Sigma, Findlay
1969	Xi Tau, SUNY Col., Fredonia
1969	Xi Upsilon, Fitchburg
1970	Pi Chi, Loyola Marymount, Los Angeles
1970	Pi Delta, Eastern Montana
1970	Pi Epsilon, Shepherd
1970	Pi Eta, St. Lawrence
1970	Pi Gamma, Northeastern Illinois
1970	Pi Iota, Defiance
1970	Pi Kappa, California (PA)
1970	Pi Lambda, Northern Iowa
1970	Pi Mu, East Texas Baptist
1970	Pi Nu, Kearney
1970	Pi Omega, San Diego U
1970	Pi Omicron, Salem (WV)
1970	Pi Phi, Missouri, Kansas City
1970	Pi Pi, St. Peter's
1970	Pi Psi, Western Carolina
1970	Pi Rho, Russell Sage
1970	Pi Sigma, Middle Tennessee
1970	Pi Tau, Butler
1970	Pi Theta, Idaho
1970	Pi Upsilon, CUNY, Lehman
1970	Pi Xi, V.P.I.
1970	Pi Zeta, Sonoma State
1970	Rho Alpha, William Paterson
1970	Rho Beta, North Alabama
1970	Rho Delta, Lambuth
1970	Rho Epsilon, Morehouse
1970	Rho Eta, Morehead
1970	Rho Gamma, Northeastern (OK)
1970	Rho Iota, Slippery Rock
1970	Rho Kappa, Tennessee State
1970	Rho Theta, South Alabama
1970	Rho Zeta, New Mexico State
1971	Rho Chi, Winston-Salem
1971	Rho Lambda, Central State (OK)
1971	Rho Mu, West Virginia Wesleyan
1971	Rho Nu, South Florida
1971	*Rho Omega, St. Bernard* (1979)
1971	Rho Omicron, William Penn
1971	Rho Phi, Southeastern Louisiana
1971	Rho Pi, Portland
1971	Rho Psi, Notre Dame
1971	Rho Rho, Jersey City
1971	Rho Sigma, Wright State
1971	Rho Tau, William Woods
1971	Rho Upsilon, Southern
1971	Rho Xi, Cal State, Sacramento
1971	Sigma Alpha, Southern, Seventh-Day Adventists
1971	Sigma Beta, McMurry
1971	Sigma Delta, St. Teresa
1971	Sigma Epsilon, Our Lady of the Elms
1971	Sigma Eta, Western Connecticut
1971	Sigma Gamma, St. Bonaventure
1971	Sigma Iota, West Florida
1971	Sigma Kappa, Southern Illinois
1971	Sigma Lambda, Bowie
1971	Sigma Mu, Mundelein
1971	Sigma Nu, Indiana Southeast
1971	Sigma Omicron, Oklahoma City
1971	Sigma Pi, Millikin
1971	Sigma Rho, Texas A & M
1971	Sigma Sigma, Oglethorpe
1971	Sigma Tau, Delaware State
1971	Sigma Theta, Armstrong
1971	Sigma Xi, St. John Fisher
1971	Sigma Zeta, Southwest Texas
1972	Sigma Chi, Mount St. Joseph
1972	Sigma Omega, St. Anselm's
1972	Sigma Phi, Sam Houston
1972	Sigma Psi, West Liberty
1972	Sigma Upsilon, San Francisco

1972	Tau Alpha, Cleveland		1975	Phi Omicron, Meredith
1972	Tau Beta, Baylor		1975	Phi Phi, Lincoln (PA)
1972	Tau Delta, Delta State		1975	Phi Pi, McNeese
1972	Tau Epsilon, Cal State, Dominguez Hills		1975	Phi Psi, Metropolitan State (CO)
1972	Tau Eta, Brenau		1975	Phi Rho, Pfeiffer
1972	Tau Gamma, Midwestern		1975	Phi Sigma, Asbury
1972	Tau Iota, Central Washington		1975	Phi Tau, Emory
1972	Tau Kappa, Radford		1975	Phi Upsilon, Columbus
1972	Tau Lambda, CUNY, York		1975	Phi Xi, New Haven
1972	Tau Mu, Baltimore U.		1976	Chi Alpha, SUNY, Buffalo
1972	Tau Nu, Edinboro		1976	Chi Beta, North Carolina, Charlotte
1972	Tau Omicron, Gwynedd-Mercy		1976	Chi Delta, SUNY, Albany
1972	Tau Pi, Madison Col		1976	Chi Epsilon, Oral Roberts
1972	Tau Rho, Pan American		1976	Chi Eta, Franklin Pierce
1972	Tau Sigma, Oklahoma Christian		1976	Chi Gamma, Clarion
1972	Tau Theta, Jacksonville (AL)		1976	Chi Iota, Central Connecticut
1972	Tau Xi, Nebraska Wesleyan		1976	Chi Kappa, Shippensburg
1972	Tau Zeta, Lakeland		1976	Chi Lambda, Georgia
1973	Tau Chi, Colorado, Colorado Springs		1976	Chi Mu, Loyola, Chicago
1973	Tau Omega, Alabama, Huntsville		1976	Chi Nu, Newberry
1973	Tau Phi, Villanova		1976	Chi Omicron, Alabama, Birmingham
1973	Tau Psi, Trenton		1976	Chi Pi, Rutgers
1973	Tau Tau, New Mexico Highlands		1976	Chi Rho, Idaho State
1973	Tau Upsilon, Westmar		1976	Chi Sigma, St. Olaf
1973	Upsilon Alpha, Framingham		1976	Chi Tau, Mars Hill
1973	Upsilon Beta, Loyola (MD)		1976	Chi Theta, Ouachita Baptist
1973	Upsilon Delta, Mary Washington		1976	Chi Upsilon, Hillsdale
1973	Upsilon Epsilon, Arkansas, Pine Bluff		1976	Chi Xi, Birmingham-Southern
1973	Upsilon Eta, Bethany (KS)		1976	Chi Zeta, Valparaiso
1973	Upsilon Gamma, St. Thomas		1976	*Phi Omega, St. Mary's (LA)* (1985)
1973	Upsilon Iota, Indiana State		1977	Chi Chi, St. John's (NY)
1973	Upsilon Kappa, Carnegie-Mellon		1977	Chi Omega, Michigan, Flint
1973	Upsilon Lambda, Cal Poly, Pomona		1977	Chi Phi, Fordham
1973	Upsilon Mu, Virginia		1977	Chi Psi, Auburn, Montgomery
1973	Upsilon Nu, Ozarks		1977	Psi Alpha, Texas Col
1973	Upsilon Omicron, St. Mary of the Plains		1977	Psi Beta, Valley City
1973	Upsilon Pi, Montana State		1977	Psi Delta, Maryland, Baltimore County
1973	Upsilon Rho, Worcester Tech		1977	Psi Epsilon, Fairleigh Dickinson, Rutherford
1973	Upsilon Sigma, Montclair		1977	Psi Eta, North Florida
1973	Upsilon Tau, Dillard		1977	Psi Gamma, St. Augustine's
1973	Upsilon Theta, Salem State (MA)		1977	Psi Iota, Glassboro
1973	Upsilon Xi, Rust		1977	Psi Kappa, Hollins
1973	Upsilon Zeta, North Carolina A & T		1977	Psi Theta, Fairfield
1974	Phi Alpha, Illinois		1977	Psi Zeta, Cal State, Bakersfield
1974	Phi Beta, Portland State		1978	Psi Chi, Redlands
1974	Phi Delta, DePaul		1978	Psi Lambda, St. Mary's (NE)
1974	Phi Epsilon, Prairie View		1978	Psi Mu, Coastal Carolina
1974	Phi Eta, Westminster (UT)		1978	Psi Nu, Elon
1974	Phi Gamma, Maine		1978	Psi Omega, C. W. Post
1974	Phi Iota, Sacred Heart		1978	Psi Omicron, Fairmont
1974	Phi Kappa, Texas, Permian Basin		1978	Psi Phi, Valdosta
1974	Phi Theta, North Carolina, Asheville		1978	Psi Pi, New Hampshire
1974	Phi Zeta, Mercy (NY)		1978	Psi Psi, Missouri, Saint Louis
1974	Upsilon Chi, Lincoln (MO)		1978	Psi Rho, Hampden-Sydney
1974	Upsilon Omega, Roanoke		1978	Psi Sigma, Nevada, Las Vegas
1974	Upsilon Phi, Hampton Inst.		1978	Psi Tau, Elmira
1974	Upsilon Psi, Cabrini		1978	Psi Upsilon, Point Loma
1974	Upsilon Upsilon, Cumberland (KY)		1978	Psi Xi, Erskine
1975	Phi Chi, George Washington		1979	Omega Alpha, Kean (NJ)
1975	Phi Lambda, Pepperdine		1979	Omega Beta, Jackson (MS)
1975	Phi Mu, St. Joseph's (NY)		1979	Omega Delta, Houghton
1975	Phi Nu, Fort Valley		1979	Omega Epsilon, Delaware

1979	Omega Eta, Carroll	1985	Alpha Beta Pi, Florida International
1979	Omega Gamma, SUNY Col., Oswego	1985	Alpha Beta Psi, Simpson
1979	Omega Theta, Grand Valley	1985	Alpha Beta Rho, Oklahoma Panhandle
1979	Omega Zeta, Texas Wesleyan	1985	Alpha Beta Sigma, Clemson
1980	Omega Iota, Wilkes	1985	Alpha Beta Tau, Keene
1980	Omega Kappa, Navy	1985	Alpha Beta Upsilon, Lynchburg
1980	Omega Lambda, Wayne State (MI)	1985	Alpha Gamma Alpha, SUNY Col., Plattsburgh
1980	Omega Mu, Wisconsin, Parkside		
1980	*Omega Nu, Yankton* (1985)	1985	Alpha Gamma Beta, Youngstown State
1980	Omega Omicron, Boise	1985	Alpha Gamma Delta, Berea
1980	Omega Pi, Virginia Wesleyan	1985	Alpha Gamma Epsilon, Mesa
1980	Omega Rho, Drexel	1985	Alpha Gamma Eta, Briar Cliff
1980	Omega Xi, North Central	1985	Alpha Gamma Gamma, Colorado, Denver
1981	Alpha Alpha Alpha, Biola	1985	Alpha Gamma Iota, LeMoyne-Owen
1981	Alpha Alpha Beta, St. Francis (PA)	1985	Alpha Gamma Kappa, Queens (NC)
1981	Alpha Alpha Gamma, Northwest Missouri	1985	Alpha Gamma Theta, Presbyterian
1981	Omega Chi, Seattle Pacific	1985	Alpha Gamma Zeta, Emporia
1981	Omega Omega, Cal, Davis	1986	Alpha Gamma Lambda, SUNY Col., Brockport
1981	Omega Phi, Charleston (SC)		
1981	Omega Psi, Eastern Washington	1986	Alpha Gamma Mu, V.M.I.
1981	Omega Sigma, Talladega	1986	Alpha Gamma Nu, Cal, Irvine
1981	Omega Tau, Trinity	1986	Alpha Gamma Omicron, Weber
1981	Omega Upsilon, Western Maryland	1986	Alpha Gamma Pi, Southern Maine
1982	Alpha Alpha Delta, Rio Grande	1986	Alpha Gamma Rho, Mount Mary
1982	Alpha Alpha Epsilon, Kennesaw	1986	Alpha Gamma Xi, Eastern Oregon
1982	Alpha Alpha Eta, Virginia State, Norfolk	1987	Alpha Delta Alpha, Rockford
1982	Alpha Alpha Iota, Liberty	1987	Alpha Delta Beta, St. Joseph's (PA)
1982	Alpha Alpha Kappa, Cameron	1987	Alpha Delta Delta, Tennessee, Martin
1982	Alpha Alpha Lambda, Grove City	1987	Alpha Delta Gamma, U of the South
1982	Alpha Alpha Mu, Pan American	1987	Alpha Gamma Omega, Wisconsin, Green Bay
1982	Alpha Alpha Nu, Coppin		
1982	Alpha Alpha Theta, South Dakota State	1987	Alpha Gamma Phi, Ursinus
1982	Alpha Alpha Xi, Mobile	1987	Alpha Gamma Psi, Hardin-Simmons
1982	Alpha Alpha Zeta, Michigan	1987	Alpha Gamma Sigma, Hastings
1983	Alpha Alpha Chi, Rockhurst	1987	Alpha Gamma Tau, L.S.U.
1983	Alpha Alpha Omega, Centenary	1987	Alpha Gamma Upsilon, George Mason
1983	Alpha Alpha Omicron, Drew	1988	Alpha Delta Epsilon, Whitman
1983	Alpha Alpha Phi, North Carolina State	1988	Alpha Delta Eta, Evansville
1983	Alpha Alpha Pi, Iona	1988	Alpha Delta Iota, Niagara
1983	Alpha Alpha Psi, Vermont	1988	Alpha Delta Kappa, Southern Indiana
1983	Alpha Alpha Rho, Immaculata	1988	Alpha Delta Lambda, Oregon
1983	Alpha Alpha Sigma, Molloy	1988	Alpha Delta Mu, LaGrange
1983	Alpha Alpha Tau, Whitworth	1988	Alpha Delta Nu, Cal State, San Bernadino
1983	Alpha Alpha Upsilon, Indianapolis	1988	Alpha Delta Omicron, Cal State, Chico
1983	Alpha Beta Alpha, Randolph, Macon	1988	Alpha Delta Pi, Ramapo
1983	Alpha Beta Beta, Washburn	1988	Alpha Delta Theta, SUNY, Buffalo
1983	Alpha Beta Gamma, Alaska, Anchorage	1988	Alpha Delta Xi, Pembroke
1984	Alpha Beta Delta, Western Michigan	1988	Alpha Delta Zeta, Georgian Court
1984	Alpha Beta Epsilon, Hawaii, Manoa	1989	Alpha Delta Chi, Linfield
1984	Alpha Beta Eta, Massachusetts	1989	Alpha Delta Omega, Michigan, Dearborn
1984	Alpha Beta Iota, Vanderbilt	1989	Alpha Delta Phi, Christian Brothers
1984	Alpha Beta Kappa, Washington (MO)	1989	Alpha Delta Psi, McKendree
1984	Alpha Beta Lambda, Athens	1989	Alpha Delta Rho, Houston, Clear Lake
1984	Alpha Beta Mu, Eastern Michigan	1989	Alpha Delta Sigma, Caldwell
1984	Alpha Beta Nu, Missouri	1989	Alpha Delta Tau, Skidmore
1984	Alpha Beta Theta, SUNY Col., Potsdam	1989	Alpha Delta Upsilon, East Texas
1984	Alpha Beta Xi, Goshen	1990	Alpha Epsilon Alpha, Missouri Southern
1984	Alpha Beta Zeta, Dickinson	1990	Alpha Epsilon Beta, CUNY, Brooklyn
1985	Alpha Beta Chi, Tarleton	1990	Alpha Epsilon Delta, Rhodes
1985	Alpha Beta Omega, North Adams	1990	Alpha Epsilon Epsilon, East Tennessee
1985	Alpha Beta Omicron, Hawaii, Hilo	1990	Alpha Epsilon Eta, Furman
1985	Alpha Beta Phi, Northern Kentucky	1990	Alpha Epsilon Gamma, Yale

1990   Alpha Epsilon Iota, Mount Holyoke
1990   Alpha Epsilon Kappa, Wheaton
1990   Alpha Epsilon Lambda, Cal State,
       Stanislaus
1990   Alpha Epsilon Mu, Army
1990   Alpha Epsilon Theta, Purdue, Calumet
1990   Alpha Epsilon Zeta, Atlantic Union

Phi Eta Sigma

(FRESHMAN SCHOLARSHIP)

ACTIVE PIN

PHI ETA SIGMA was founded at the University of Illinois on March 22, 1923, to encourage and reward high scholastic attainment among the male members of the freshman class. Founders were Dean of Men Thomas Arkle Clark, Dean K. C. Babcock of the College of Liberal Arts and Sciences, and Dean C. M. Thompson of the College of Commerce and Business Administration. In 1974 the constitution was amended to admit women. Admitted to the Association of College Honor Societies in 1937.

The purpose of the society is to stimulate interest in scholarship in first-year students and to provide activities and projects that will promote academic excellence on the local campus.

All freshman men and women who have a cumulative scholarship average equivalent to or better than 3.5 (on a 4.0 scale) at the conclusion of any term of their freshman year are eligible for membership. Chapters are placed in accredited four-year degree-granting colleges or universities upon petition of not fewer than ten undergraduate students from a single class other than the senior class who meet requirements for initiation. The petition must be approved by the president of the institution. It is then transmitted to the Grand Secretary-Treasurer with proper information on the institution; the petition is then sent to members of the Executive Committee for approval.

Government   The control of the society is exercised by a biennial convention composed of student delegates from each chapter and members of the Executive Committee. Conduct of the local chapter is guided by a faculty adviser and elected local officers. The one-time national membership fee of $8 provides each member with a key, a membership certificate, and a copy of the magazine; it also supports the national convention and the operation of the national office and provides for unlimited copies of a study pamphlet for distribution on chapter campuses and a 50-cents-per-member contribution to the scholarship fund. Local chapters assess additional dues to cover local expenses.

Grand Chapter Activities   National finances a national convention every two years, paying the expenses of chapter delegates; this convention is the governing body of the society. Three students elected at the convention serve on the National Executive Committee.

Chapter Activities   Chapters engage in numerous activities of their own choosing designed to promote and recognize high scholarship. These include funding local scholarships, offering tutoring services, sponsoring faculty lectures, offering book and other awards, publishing scholarship information, inviting advanced placement high school students to campus, promoting academic honesty campaigns, and nominating chapter members for national scholarships.

Traditions and Insignia   The emblem of the society is an oblong key in the form of a golden scroll bearing the three Greek letters ΦΗΣ in black enamel.

Publications   The FORUM OF PHI ETA SIGMA, established in 1930, contains articles of interest for members, carries the annual audit of the national society and the directory of chapters, honors scholarship winners, documents the installation of new chapters, reports convention proceedings, and carries profiles of faculty advisers. The eight-page pamphlet *Hints on How to Study* is furnished free to each chapter for distribution to all new students at its institution. Phi Eta Sigma also provides a brochure, *Questions and Answers*, for chapters to send to students who are eligible for induction.

Scholarship Funds   The Founders Scholarship Fund, created in 1937 in honor of the founders and distinguished members of the Society, currently provides income each year for nine or more $1000 scholarships and 30 or more $500 scholarships to selected senior members for the first year of graduate or professional work.

Headquarters   Dean James E. Foy, 228 Foy Union Building, Auburn University, Alabama 36849.

Membership   Active chapters 252. Inactive chapters 41. Total number of initiates 438,432. Chapter roll:

1923   Illinois
1926   *Lake Forest* (1968)
1926   *Michigan* (1978)
1926   Missouri
1927   Oklahoma
1927   Wisconsin, Madison
1928   Miami (OH)
1928   Ohio State
1929   Catholic
1929   DePauw
1929   George Washington
1929   Penn State
1930   Alabama
1930   Florida
1930   Georgia Tech
1930   Indiana

1930	Lehigh
1930	Mississippi
1930	*Montana State* (1981)
1930	North Carolina State
1930	North Dakota
1930	South Dakota
1930	Tennessee
1931	Arkansas
1931	Butler
1931	Oklahoma State
1931	*Southern Methodist* (1990)
1931	Texas
1931	*Washington (MO)* (1974)
1932	Duke
1932	L.S.U.
1932	Mercer
1932	Northwestern
1933	*Cincinnati* (1976)
1934	Idaho
1935	Mississippi State
1936	Ohio
1936	UCLA
1936	*USC* (1976)
1936	Utah
1937	Pitt
1937	Washington and Lee
1938	Georgia
1938	Wittenberg
1939	Bucknell
1940	Akron
1940	Clemson
1940	Maryland
1945	Iowa
1946	Kentucky
1946	Texas Tech
1947	Brigham Young
1947	*Cal, Berkeley* (1962)
1947	Iowa State
1947	North Carolina
1947	Tennessee, Chattanooga
1947	Willamette
1948	*Beloit* (1970)
1948	Illinois Tech
1948	Marshall (1985-1990)
1948	Nebraska, Omaha
1948	Purdue
1948	*San Jose* (1974)
1948	Tulsa
1948	Virginia (1976-1990)
1948	*Washington State* (1985)
1949	*Albion* (1988)
1949	Doane
1949	Oregon State
1949	Oregon
1949	Texas A & M
1950	Auburn
1950	Miami (FL)
1950	Northern Arizona
1950	Southern Mississippi
1950	Vanderbilt
1951	Bradley
1951	Drury

1952	*Arizona State* (1980)
1952	New Jersey Tech
1953	North Texas
1954	Bowling Green
1954	*Michigan State* (1976)
1954	Michigan Tech
1954	Southern Illinois
1954	Tulane
1955	Florida State
1955	*Massachusetts* (1981)
1955	San Diego U.
1956	Birmingham-Southern
1956	Georgia State
1957	Drake
1957	Hanover
1957	Kansas State
1957	*Kent* (1974)
1958	Fort Hays
1958	Oklahoma Baptist
1959	Arizona
1959	Louisville
1959	SUNY, Buffalo
1959	*Washington (WA)* (1980)
1960	Arkansas State
1960	East Texas
1960	Nebraska
1960	*St. Joseph's (IN)* (1961)
1960	Wisconsin, Platteville
1961	*Cornell* (1973)
1961	Southwestern Louisiana
1961	*St. Michael's* (1970)
1961	Toledo
1961	*Utah State* (1976)
1962	*Baylor* (1984)
1962	*Davidson* (1986)
1962	*DePaul* (1986)
1962	*Temple* (1974)
1962	*Texas Christian* (1976)
1962	Western Michigan
1963	Missouri, Rolla
1963	Northwestern Louisiana
1963	*Pacific (CA)* (1974)
1963	Wisconsin, Milwaukee
1964	*Detroit* (1980)
1964	*Ferris* (1985)
1964	Hawaii
1964	Montana
1964	North Dakota State
1964	*San Francisco State* (1967)
1965	Colorado State
1965	Houston
1965	Illinois State
1965	*Kalamazoo* (1978)
1965	New Mexico Highlands
1965	Otterbein
1965	Spring Hill
1965	William and Mary
1966	Anderson
1966	Cal State, Long Beach
1966	*Cal State, Northridge* (1974)
1966	Central Michigan
1966	*Northern Illinois* (1977)

1966	Ohio Northern
1966	South Carolina
1966	V.P.I.
1966	Wisconsin, Eau Claire
1966	*Wisconsin, Oshkosh* (1974)
1967	Cal State, Chico
1967	*Georgetown U.* (1973)
1967	Illinois Wesleyan
1967	Illinois, Chicago
1967	*Moorhead* (1976)
1967	Morningside
1967	New Orleans
1967	St. Ambrose
1967	Syracuse (1974-1987)
1968	*Angelo* (1976)
1968	Lamar
1969	*Carroll* (1986)
1969	Drexel
1969	*Redlands* (1976)
1969	South Alabama
1969	Wichita
1970	Western Kentucky
1971	Carson-Newman
1971	Nicholls
1972	Central Missouri State
1972	Northeast Louisiana
1972	Samford
1973	*Eastern New Mexico* (1990)
1973	New Mexico
1973	North Alabama
1973	Southwest Texas
1973	West Georgia
1973	West Texas
1973	Western Illinois
1974	Campbell
1974	Central State (OK)
1974	Memphis State
1974	SUNY Col., Fredonia
1974	Tennessee, Martin
1974	Troy
1975	East Carolina
1975	Midwestern
1975	Richmond
1975	Tampa
1975	Widener
1976	Evansville
1977	Delta State
1977	Indiana Southeast
1977	Texas, Arlington
1978	Armstrong State
1978	Pace, Pleasantville
1978	SUNY Col., Cortland
1978	Stetson
1978	Wisconsin, Whitewater
1979	Baker
1979	GMI
1979	North Carolina, Wilmington
1979	Prairie View
1979	Rhode Island
1980	Edinboro
1980	Jacksonville (AL)
1980	Lynchburg
1980	Pitt, Johnstown
1980	Stephen F. Austin
1981	Auburn, Montgomery
1981	Eastern Washington
1981	Frostburg
1981	Indiana, South Bend
1981	Millsaps
1981	Oklahoma City
1981	Tarleton
1981	Wisconsin, Stevens Point
1982	Coe
1982	Colgate
1982	Florida International
1982	Furman
1982	Maine, Presque Isle
1982	Morgan State
1982	Northern Iowa
1982	Northwest Missouri
1982	Pepperdine
1982	Slippery Rock
1982	Southern Illinois, Edwardsville
1982	Southwest Missouri
1982	Western New Mexico
1983	Castleton
1983	Clarion
1983	Duquesne
1983	Grand View
1983	Morris Brown
1983	North Carolina, Charlotte
1983	Pikeville
1983	SUNY Col., Oswego
1983	SUNY Col., Plattsburgh
1983	Salisbury
1983	Tri-State
1983	Vermont
1983	Virginia Commonwealth
1983	Virginia Wesleyan
1983	West Chester
1983	Westminster (UT)
1984	C. W. Post
1984	College of Idaho
1984	Culver-Stockton
1984	Florida Southern
1984	Indiana Northwest
1984	Kearney
1984	Kennesaw
1984	*South Florida* (1988)
1984	Southeast Missouri
1984	Wingate
1985	Cameron
1985	Columbia Union
1985	IUPUI
1985	Livingston
1985	North Carolina Wesleyan
1985	Ohio Wesleyan
1985	Pace
1985	West Florida
1986	Abilene Christian
1986	Appalachian
1986	Huntingdon
1986	Marcyhurst
1986	Methodist

1986   Rutgers
1986   Wayne State (MI)
1986   West Virginia State
1987   Alabama State
1987   Averett
1987   Florida A & M
1987   Gannon
1987   Monmouth (NJ)
1987   Rollins
1988   Adrian
1988   Carnegie-Mellon
1988   Missouri Southern
1988   North Carolina, Asheville
1988   Oglethorpe
1988   St. Louis
1989   Arkansas Tech
1989   Central Florida
1989   Columbus
1989   North Georgia
1989   SUNY Col., Potsdam
1989   Southeastern Louisiana
1989   Youngstown State
1990   Bluefield
1990   Centenary
1990   Coastal Carolina
1990   Elmira
1990   Loyola, New Orleans
1990   Northeast Missouri
1990   Northern State

Phi Kappa Phi

(SCHOLARSHIP)

ACTIVE PIN

PHI KAPPA PHI is an honor society recognizing and encouraging superior scholarship in colleges and universities, without restriction as to area of study. It elects from letters, arts, science, humanities, and the various applied professional fields of study. No more than ten percent of any class may be elected, and in most chapters the actual quota is less. Membership is also open to superior graduate students and to faculty members who merit distinction. An occasional honorary or distinguished member may be elected by a chapter, with approval of the Board of Directors.

In 1897 a group of ten students at the University of Maine at Orono, who perceived a need for an honor society on broader lines than any then in existence, was assisted by interested professors to organize the Lambda Sigma Eta Society. A year or so later the name was changed to the Morrill Society, in honor of the sponsor of the Congressional Act which provided for land-grant colleges. In 1900 it

was transformed into a national society by action of a committee composed of the presidents of the University of Maine at Orono, the University of Tennessee and Pennsylvania State College (now Pennsylvania State University). The chapters in these institutions are the founding chapters. The society was renamed Phi Kappa Phi, from the initial letters of the Greek words forming its adopted motto: Philosophía Krateîtō Phōtôn, "Let the love of learning rule mankind." Phi Kappa Phi currently has chapters in institutions from Maine to the Philippines and from Alaska to Puerto Rico.

Government   The society is governed ultimately by the Triennial Convention, supplemented by any interim—though rare—special conventions deemed necessary. Each chapter may send one official delegate to a convention. Between conventions, the business of the society is conducted by the Board of Directors, composed of twelve directors, of whom eight are elective (president, president-elect, a national vice president, four regional vice-presidents and the immediate past president) and four are appointive (executive director of the Society, regent, editor of *National Forum*, and director of fellowships). The executive director is in charge of the society's national office.

Traditions and Insignia   The primary objective of the national Honor Society of Phi Kappa Phi is the recognition and encouragement of superior scholarship in all academic disciplines. The society is convinced that in recognizing and honoring those persons of good character who have excelled in scholarship, in whatever field, it will stimulate others to strive for excellence. Moreover, the society serves the interests of the student capable of excellence by insisting that in order to acquire a chapter of Phi Kappa Phi, an institution provide the means and atmosphere conducive to academic excellence.

Every chapter must hold at least two meetings a year and is encouraged to be active in various ways. Many chapters cite students for excellence as early as the freshman year. Some sponsor an annual Honors Day. Many of them grant awards or give scholarships to students and researchers doing work of scholarly quality. Some also extend recognition to superior teachers. The aim, however, is not to give the recipient something which may encourage complacency, but to challenge the member to continued excellence.

The Phi Kappa Phi Foundation was incorporated in 1969 to promote academic excellence and achievement by means of scholarships and fellowships. To support first-year graduate work, the society offers annually through the Foundation 50 Fellowships and 30 Honorable Mention Awards, on a competitive basis, to graduating students who have been initiated into the society and who have also been nominated by their chapters for the competition. Many chapters also have their own local scholarship program.

The badge of this society, which appears on the key, is a globe against the background of the sun, whose rays form an expansive corona and radiate in a number of symmetrical concentrations from behind the globe. These signify equivalence among the various branches of learning and represent the dissemination of truth as light. Encircling the globe is a band containing the Greek letters ΦΚΦ and symbolizing a fraternal bond which girds the earth and binds the lovers of wisdom in a common purpose.

Publications The society publishes a quarterly journal for distribution to its active membership. Each issue of *National Forum: The Phi Kappa Phi Journal* is devoted to a significant theme and addresses prominent issues of the day from an interdisciplinary perspective. The journal features articles by scholars inside and outside the academic community. In addition to timely articles, each issue of *National Forum* contains selected poetry and reviews of current books and periodical literature. Active members of the society also receive bimonthly issues of the *Phi Kappa Phi Newsletter*. The *Newsletter* features new items of interest to members on both national and local levels. A year's subscription to these publications, a membership certificate and a society emblem (key) are included in the initiation fee.

Headquarters Post Office Box 16000, Louisiana State University, Baton Rouge, Louisiana 70893.

Membership Active chapters 253. Inactive chapters 4. Colonies 1. Graduate/Alumni chapters 1. Total number of initiates 500,000+. Chapter roll:

	Kennesaw
1897	Maine
1899	Tennessee
1900	Penn State
1904	Massachusetts
1905	Delaware
1911	Iowa State
1912	Florida
1912	Nevada
1913	Nebraska Wesleyan
1913	North Dakota State
1913	Rhode Island
1914	Auburn
1914	Georgia Tech
1915	Kansas State
1916	Arizona
1916	New Mexico
1916	Syracuse (1978-1988)
1919	Washington State
1920	Cornell (1979-1983)
1920	Maryland
1920	Missouri, Rolla
1920	Oklahoma State
1920	Utah State
1920	Wisconsin, Madison
1921	V.P.I.
1922	Butler
1922	Illinois Wesleyan
1922	Montana State
1922	New Hampshire
1922	Utah
1922	Wyoming
1923	Georgia
1923	North Carolina State
1924	Dakota Wesleyan
1924	Oregon State
1924	USC
1925	Coe
1925	Florida State
1926	*Michigan* (1970-1979) (1980)
1927	Colorado State
1927	Michigan State
1928	*Parsons* (1976)
1930	Hawaii
1930	L.S.U.
1933	*Carnegie-Mellon* (1984)
1933	Illinois
1933	Philippines, Quezon City
1936	Drexel
1938	Clemson
1942	Louisville
1947	Indianapolis Alumni
1949	Houston
1949	Millikin
1949	South Dakota State
1949	Texas A & M
1951	Brigham Young
1951	Connecticut
1951	Louisiana Tech
1951	Mississippi State
1951	Pacific (CA)
1951	Southwestern Louisiana
1952	Toledo
1953	Berea
1953	Cal State, Fresno
1953	Northwestern Louisiana
1954	Arizona State
1954	Cal, Davis
1954	Fort Hays
1954	Miami (FL)
1954	*Montana* (1984)
1954	San Jose
1955	Michigan Tech
1956	Ohio
1956	Southeastern Louisiana
1956	Southern Illinois
1956	Texas Tech
1957	Mississippi for Women
1959	Mississippi
1959	Northern Arizona
1960	Idaho
1960	Wisconsin, Milwaukee
1962	Cal State, Chico
1962	New Mexico State
1962	Texas
1963	Bradley
1963	Cal State, Long Beach
1963	Cal State, Sacramento
1963	Evansville
1963	Northeastern
1964	American

1964	Bowling Green
1964	Central Michigan
1964	Winthrop
1964	Southern California Alumni
1965	Cal Poly, San Luis Obispo
1965	Cal State, Los Angeles
1965	Lamar
1965	San Diego U.
1966	Nebraska, Omaha
1967	Nevada, Las Vegas
1967	Ohio Northern
1967	Southern Mississippi
1968	Cal State, Fullerton
1969	Missouri, Kansas City
1969	New Mexico Highlands
1969	Puerto Rico, San Juan
1969	Radford
1969	Wesleyan (GA)
1969	Wisconsin, Eau Claire
1969	Wisconsin, Whitewater
1970	Alfred
1970	Drake (1974-1984)
1970	East Carolina
1970	East Tennessee
1970	Idaho State
1970	New Orleans
1970	Northeast Louisiana
1970	Rochester Tech
1970	Tennessee Tech
1970	Wichita
1971	Eastern Kentucky
1971	Eastern New Mexico
1971	Florida Atlantic
1971	Georgia Southern
1971	Georgia State
1971	McNeese
1971	Memphis State
1971	North Alabama
1971	Purdue
1971	South Florida
1971	Tennessee, Martin
1971	Troy
1971	Washburn
1971	Weber
1972	Arkansas State
1972	Arkansas, Little Rock
1972	Central Missouri State
1972	Clarkson
1972	Delta State
1972	Longwood
1972	Miami (OH)
1972	Missouri
1972	Northern Michigan
1972	Samford
1972	Western Carolina
1972	Western Illinois
1972	Youngstown State
1973	Alabama, Huntsville
1973	Cal Poly, Pomona
1973	Eastern Michigan
1973	Georgia Col.
1973	Illinois, Chicago
1973	Morehead
1973	Ohio State
1973	West Florida
1973	West Georgia
1973	Wisconsin, Platteville
1974	Appalachian
1974	Augusta
1974	Boise
1974	Cal State, Northridge
1974	Madison Col
1974	Mankato
1974	Minnesota
1974	Nicholls
1974	Northern Illinois
1974	Salisbury
1974	Southwest Missouri
1974	St. Cloud
1974	Texas, El Paso
1974	Valdosta
1974	Villanova
1975	Alabama, Birmingham
1975	Cameron
1975	Campbell
1975	Hood
1975	Jacksonville
1975	Kansas
1975	Lock Haven
1975	North Georgia
1975	Puget Sound
1975	Russell Sage
1975	Southern Maine
1975	West Virginia
1976	Alaska, Fairbanks
1976	Austin Peay
1976	Central Washington
1976	Charleston (SC)
1976	Columbus
1976	Duquesne
1976	Jackson (MS)
1976	Montclair
1976	Salem State (MA)
1976	Virginia Commonwealth
1976	Westmont
1977	Bloomsburg
1977	Elmhurst
1977	Ithaca
1977	Kean (NJ)
1977	Lewis and Clark
1977	Navy
1977	Old Dominion
1977	South Alabama
1977	West Virginia Wesleyan
1978	Army
1978	Florida International
1978	Francis Marion
1978	Montevallo
1978	Southern Illinois, Edwardsville
1978	Trenton
1978	V.M.I.
1979	Bridgeport
1979	Cal State, San Bernadino
1979	Citadel

1979 Lycoming
1979 Millersville
1979 Pittsburg State, Kansas
1979 Widener
1980 Emporia
1980 Grand Valley
1980 Houston, Clear Lake
1980 Indiana State
1980 Missouri, St. Louis
1980 North Carolina, Charlotte
1980 North Carolina, Wilmington
1980 North Florida
1980 Plymouth
1980 Portland State
1980 Southern Oregon
1980 Western Oregon
1981 Texas Woman's
1982 Arkansas
1982 Central Florida
1982 Eastern Washington
1982 Houston, Victoria
1982 Mercer
1982 Moorhead
1982 North Texas
1983 Fordham
1983 Pan American
1983 SUNY Col., Cortland
1983 Western Kentucky
1984 Cal State, Dominguez Hills
1985 L.S.U., Shreveport
1987 Humboldt
1987 Middle Tennessee
1987 Wisconsin, Stevens Point
1988 Wisconsin, River Falls
1989 Andrews
1989 Western Michigan
1989 Western Washington
1990 Alaska
1990 Auburn, Montgomery
1990 Oklahoma
1990 Tulsa
1990 Wright State

Colonies: Alabama

Phi Sigma

(BIOLOGICAL SCIENCES)

ACTIVE PIN

PHI SIGMA was founded at Ohio State University on March 17, 1915, and was designed from the outset to be national in scope. It had been designated as an honor biological research society from the date of its founding up until the 1928 convention at New York. At this convention the constitution was so altered that the society should now be considered as a working guild of biologists, interested in research: in effect, election to Phi Sigma should be an opportunity for better work, rather than merely election to an honor society. Any student of good moral character enrolled in a college or university, so equipped with facilities for research in biological sciences that at least one degree beyond the bachelor's degree may be earned for biological research, shall be eligible to active membership if he has shown research interest ad has received an equivalent of at least two years of college credit, of which at least one fourth is in biological science. In accordance with ACHS requirements the student must be in the upper 35 per cent of his class in general scholarship; this minimum requirement is modified by most chapters to a minimum B average. In addition, any competent biologist who is engaged in biological activity near an institution having a chapter is eligible for membership. Faculty and honorary memberships are also granted.

Purpose Devoted to the promotion of research and academic excellence in the biological sciences.

Government Since 1924, when the first national convention was held, and until 1954, national meetings were held biennially In connection with the meetings of the American Association for the Advancement of Science, which granted the society official recognition as an affiliated organization. Prior to 1924, government was vested in a council composed of the president, past president, vice-president, and executive secretary-treasurer. Since 1954 meetings have been held with the American Institute of Biological Sciences, in which the society holds full membership and has representation on the Governing Board.

In 1950 the society became a member of the ACHS.

Major Activities Each chapter plans its own programs with a wide variety of activities, ranging from the presentation of papers by the members and lectures by outside speakers to field trips, laboratory demonstrations, and projects. Biennial meetings are held at which delegates from each active chapter meet with the Council for the purpose of formulating policies and transacting all important business of the Society. The national organization annually cooperates with each school that maintains an active chapter in presenting award certificates to one outstanding undergraduate and one outstanding graduate student in any of the biological sciences, pure or applied. A number of chapters supplement these certificates with monetary awards.

Traditions and Insignia Since the spring of 1938 scholarship medals or certificates for excellence in biology have been awarded each college year in cooperation with each institution where there is an active chapter. The recipients are selected by a faculty committee appointed by the president of each institution. The students selected need not be members. Several chapters award scholarships each year, most of them for students attending biological stations.

The emblem is a key displaying the Greek letter Φ superimposed on the letter Σ.

Publication The society publishes quarterly *The Biologist*, in which are presented official communications, editorials, special articles, special papers, and items of general biological interest.

Headquarters Virginia Polytechnic Institute, 1305 Hillcrest Drive, Blacksburg, Virginia 24060.

Membership Active chapters 32. Inactive chapters 16. Total number of initiates 67,500. Chapter roll:††

1915 *Alpha, Ohio State* (1924)
1916 Beta, Michigan
1917 *Delta, Maine* (1935)
1917 Epsilon, Denver
1917 *Zeta, Wisconsin, Madison* (1962)
1921 Eta, Akron
1921 *Iota, Washington* (1939)
1921 Kappa, Kansas
1921 Lambda, Montana
1921 *Theta, Michigan State* (1937)
1922 *Mu, California* (1944)
1922 Nu, Washington and Jefferson
1924 *Omicron, North Dakota* (1929)
1924 *Xi, Neraska* (1935)
1925 Pi, Emory
1925 Rho, Illinois
1925 Sigma, Florida
1926 Phi, New Hampshire
1926 *Tau, Duke* (1942)
1926 Upsilon, Miami (OH)
1927 *Chi, Montana* (1967)
1927 Psi, Washington
1928 Alpha Alpha, USC
1928 Alpha Beta, Mount Union
1928 Alpha Gamma, South Dakota (1933-1970)
1928 Omega, Oklahoma
1929 Alpha Delta, Lawrence
1929 *Alpha Epsilon, Pitt* (1966)
1930 Alpha Eta, Oklahoma State
1930 *Alpha Theta, Washington State* (1943)
1930 Alpha Zeta, William and Mary
1931 Alpha Iota, Bucknell
1931 Alpha Kappa, Hunter
1932 Alpha Lambda, Utah
1933 Alpha Mu, Oregon State
1935 Alpha Nu, New Mexico
1935 Alpha Xi, Rhode Island
1938 Alpha Omicron, Marquette
1941 Alpha Pi, Colorado
1945 *Alpha Rho, Arkansas* (1960)
1946 *Alpha Sigma, Texas*
1947 *Alpha Tau, National, Mexico*
1947 *Alpha Upsilon, UCLA* (1954)
1948 Alpha Phi, Puget Sound
1949 Alpha Chi, Philippines

1949 Alpha Psi, V.P.I.
1951 Alpha Omega, Georgia
1955 Beta Alpha, Penn State
1956 Beta Beta, Florida State
1957 Beta Gamma, Long Island
1958 Bea Delta, Virginia
1960 Beta Epsilon, Northern Illinois
1961 Beta Zeta, Maryland
1962 Beta Eta, Idaho
1963 Beta Theta, North Carolina State
1964 Beta Iota, Duquesne
1965 Beta Kappa, Texas Christian
1966 Beta Lambda, Illinois State
1967 Beta Mu, Southwestern Louisiana
1968 Beta Nu, Northeastern
1969 Beta Omicron, Colorado, Denver
1969 Beta Xi, Tennessee
1970 Beta Pi, Eastern Illinois
1970 Beta Rho, Texas A & M
1971 Beta Sigma, Central Washington
1973 Beta Tau, South Florida
1974 Beta Upsilon, Texas, San Antonio
1975 Beta Chi, Michigan Tech
1975 Beta Phi, Texas, Arlington
1976 Beta Omega, Wayne State
1976 Beta Psi, Eastern Kentucky
1976 Gamma Alpha, Southern

Phi Sigma Iota

(FOREIGN LANGUAGES)

ACTIVE PIN

PHI SIGMA IOTA was founded in October, 1922, by members of the Department of Romance Languages at Allegheny College under the leadership of Prof. Henry Ward Church. It existed as a local organization until 1925, at which time the Beta Chapter was established at Pennsylvania State University.

Chapters are established only in high-grade colleges and universities in which there are strong departments of Romance languages.

Purpose The recognition of outstanding ability and attainments in the field of foreign languages, literatures, and cultures, including classics, linguistics, philology, and comparative literature; the stimulation of advanced work and individual research in any of these languages and literatures; and the promotion of a sentiment of international amity.

Eligibility Membership is based on scholastic attainment. At the time of election to membership, undergraduates must have at least a B average in all of their language courses and be enrolled in a third- or fourth-year language course. They must

†† This chapter roll is repeated from the 19th edition; no current information was provided.

have a cumulative average of B for all of their college work and must rank in the upper thirty-five percent of their class in general scholarship at that date. As a rule, undergraduates are not elected to membership prior to their junior year, but sophomores of exceptional ability who have met the stated minimum requirements and completed at least three semesters or five quarters of their college course may also be elected. Graduate students of one or more languages may also be elected to membership after one quarter or semester of graduate residence, provided they have attained at least a B-plus average in their graduate studies. Individual chapters are at liberty to increase the requirements for membership if they so desire.

Growth In November, 1935, Phi Sigma Iota, having then twenty chapters, merged with Alpha Zeta Pi, a society founded at the University of Denver in 1917 by Dr. Etienne Renaud and with aims and ideals similar to those of Phi Sigma Iota. The nine active chapters of Alpha Zeta Pi have since the merger been indicated by double Greek letters, and new chapters are named Phi Alpha, Phi Beta, and so on.

Traditions and Insignia The Phi Sigma Iota Scholarships, in honor of Henry Ward Church and Anthony S. Corbiere, are awarded yearly for the encouragement of continuing study in languages and literatures, to active student members whose essays, submitted to the National Scholarship Committee, are judged by its members. Awards of up to $500 per student are made.

The badge is a gold key, containing the letters ΦΣΙ and superimposed on a five-pointed star. The star is surrounded by an ivy wreath.

Publication The official journal, the *Phi Sigma Iota Newsletter*, in 1975 became the Phi Sigma Iota *Forum*.

Headquarters Department of Modern Foreign Languages, Boston University, 718 Commonwealth Avenue, Boston, Massachusetts 02215.

Membership Active chapters 180. Inactive chapters 15. Total number of initiates 30,000. Chapter roll:

	Beta Delta, Santa Clara
	Beta Delta, Santa Clara
1917	Alpha Alpha, Denver
1922	Alpha, Allegheny
1922	Beta Beta, Missouri
1923	Zeta Zeta, Northern Colorado
1925	Beta, Penn State
1926	Delta, Iowa
1926	Epsilon, Drake
1926	Eta, Illinois Wesleyan
1926	Gamma, Wooster
1926	Kappa, Bates
1926	Theta, Beloit
1926	Zeta, Coe
1927	Delta Delta, Texas Christian
1927	Iota, Lawrence
1928	Lambda, Muhlenberg
1928	Theta Theta, Wyoming

1929	Mu, Lake Forest
1929	Nu, Morningside
1929	Omicron-1, Colby
1929	Xi, South Dakota
1930	Pi, DePauw
1930	Sigma, Emory
1931	Tau, Gettysburg
1931	Upsilon, Birmingham-Southern
1933	Lambda Lambda, New Mexico Highlands
1933	Phi, Otterbein
1936	Phi Alpha, L.S.U.
1936	Phi Beta, Wittenberg
1936	Phi Epsilon, Northwestern
1938	Phi Delta, Nebraska
1938	Phi Gamma, Vanderbilt
1939	Phi Zeta, Washington (WA)
1940	Phi Eta, Hobart
1945	Phi Theta, William Jewell
1946	Phi Iota, Syracuse
1947	Phi Kappa, Tulane
1948	Phi Mu, New Mexico
1948	Phi Nu, Muskingum
1950	Phi Lambda, Kentucky
1950	Phi Omicron, Mary Washington
1950	Phi Pi, Centenary
1950	Phi Xi, St. Louis
1952	Phi Rho, Indiana
1954	Phi Sigma, Hiram
1955	Phi Chi, North Central
1955	Phi Phi, Texas Woman's
1955	Phi Tau, Indiana State
1955	Phi Upsilon, Willamette
1956	Phi Omega, Boston U
1956	Phi Psi, Case Western Reserve
1957	Sigma Alpha, Ripon
1958	Sigma Delta, Wake Forest
1958	Sigma Gamma, Furman
1961	Sigma Epsilon, Rollins
1963	Sigma Zeta, Iowa State
1964	Sigma Eta, Madison Col
1964	Sigma Iota, Michigan
1964	Sigma Kappa, Michigan State
1965	Sigma Lambda, Heidelberg
1965	Sigma Theta, Colorado State
1966	Sigma Omicron, Wesleyan (CT)
1966	Sigma Xi, Ohio
1967	Mu, SUNY, Stony Brook
1967	Rho, Rochester
1967	Sigma Pi, Colorado Col
1967	Sigma Rho, Utah
1967	Sigma Tau, SUNY, Stony Brook
1969	Sigma Pi, Hartford
1969	Sigma Sigma, Rutgers
1969	Sigma Tau, Alfred
1969	Sigma Upsilon, East Carolina
1970	Sigma Chi, Pace
1971	Sigma Omega, Duquesne
1971	Sigma Psi, Holy Cross
1972	Iota Alpha, V.P.I.
1974	Iota Beta, Mercy (NY)
1974	Iota Gamma, South Carolina
1975	Iota Delta, Maine

1975	Iota Epsilon, Richmond		1982	Alpha Omega, West Georgia
1976	Iota Eta, Centre College		1982	Beta Epsilon, SUNY Col., Oneonta
1976	Iota Theta, Bloomsburg		1982	Beta Gamma, Rhode Island Col.
1976	Iota Zeta, Northeastern		1983	Delta Alpha, Ursinus
1977	Iota Iota, St. Francis (PA)		1983	Delta Beta, Providence
1977	Iota Mu, Texas, Arlington		1983	Delta Gamma, Alaska
1977	Iota Nu, Hamilton		1983	Delta Iota, Holy Family
1978	Chi, Fort Lewis		1983	Delta Kappa, Sacred Heart
1978	Delta, Northern Illinois		1983	Delta Lambda, Moravian
1978	Eta, Southwest Texas		1983	Delta Sigma, Southern Oregon
1978	Iota, Wabash		1984	Delta Epsilon, Pace, Pleasantville
1978	Iota Omicron, Adams		1984	Delta Phi, Lehigh
1978	Iota Pi, Eastern		1984	Delta Pi, L.S.U., Shreveport
1978	Iota Xi, Ohio Wesleyan		1984	Delta Zeta, High Point
1978	Nu, Lincoln (PA)		1984	Eta Alpha, San Francisco State
1978	Omicron, Union (NY)		1984	Eta Gamma, Cal State, Fresno
1978	Pi, Southern		1985	Eta Delta, Western Oregon
1978	Zeta, Gordon		1985	Eta Epsilon, Texas Southern
1979	Alpha Gamma, Central State (OK)		1985	Kappa Alpha, Agnes Scott
1979	Chi Chi, Rhode Island		1985	Kappa Beta, Allentown
1979	Eta Eta, Mercer		1985	Kappa Gamma, Methodist
1979	Gamma Gamma, Alabama		1985	Sigma Beta, Immaculate Heart
1979	Kappa Kappa, Hampden-Sydney		1986	Kappa Delta, Jacksonville
1979	Mu Mu, Northern Michigan		1986	Kappa Epsilon, Weber
1979	Nu Nu, Portland State		1986	Kappa Eta, SUNY Col., Oswego
1979	Omega, Nevada		1986	Kappa Iota, LaSalle
1979	Omicron Alpha, Skidmore		1986	Kappa Lambda, Butler
1979	Pi Pi, Albertus Magnus		1986	Kappa Mu, San Jose
1979	Psi, St. Norbert		1986	Kappa Zeta, Middle Tennessee
1979	Psi Psi, North Texas		1987	Delta Theta, North Alabama
1979	Rho Rho, Michigan, Flint		1987	Kappa Chi, Caldwell
1979	Tau Tau, Cal, Berkeley		1987	Kappa Nu, Southern Maine
1979	Upsilon Upsilon, Austin		1987	Kappa Omega, SUNY Col., New Paltz
1979	Xi Xi, Pitt		1987	Kappa Omicron, Susquehanna
1980	Alpha Beta, Millikin		1987	Kappa Phi, Bradley
1980	Alpha Delta, Radford		1987	Kappa Pi, Northern Arizona
1980	Alpha Epsilon, Bridgeport		1987	Kappa Psi, Washburn
1980	Alpha Eta, Gallaudet		1987	Kappa Rho, St. Joseph's (PA)
1980	Alpha Iota, SUNY Col., Buffalo		1987	Kappa Sigma, Paris
1980	Alpha Kappa, Illinois Col		1987	Kappa Tau, Lynchburg
1980	Alpha Lambda, North Carolina State		1987	Kappa Theta, St. Mary's, San Antonio
1980	Alpha Nu, Morris Brown		1987	Kappa Upsilon, Kutztown
1980	Alpha Theta, Lebanon Valley		1987	Kappa Xi, Rosemont
1980	Alpha Xi, Maryland		1988	Delta Eta, Navy
1980	Alpha Zeta, Virginia		1988	Delta Mu, St. Thomas Aquinas
1980	Omega Omega, New Rochelle		1988	Delta Nu, Fort Hays
1981	Alpha Chi, West Texas		1988	Delta Omicron, Gannon
1981	Alpha Mu, New Hampshire		1988	Delta Rho, Cameron
1981	Alpha Omicron, Central Arkansas		1988	Delta Tau, Virgin Islands
1981	Alpha Phi, SUNY Col., Geneseo		1988	Delta Xi, Emory and Henry
1981	Alpha Pi, Plymouth		1989	Delta Chi, Lycoming
1981	Alpha Psi, Millersville		1989	Delta Omega, Illinois Benedictine
1981	Alpha Rho, Converse		1989	Delta Psi, Salem (WV)
1981	Alpha Sigma, Kentucky Christian		1989	Delta Upsilon, Hastings
1981	Alpha Tau, Regiomontana		1989	Iota Kappa, Metropolitan State (CO)
1981	Alpha Upsilon, Niagara			

Phi Sigma Tau

(PHILOSOPHY)

ACTIVE PIN

PHI SIGMA TAU was founded at Muhlenberg College in 1930 as Alpha Kappa Alpha, with chapters at colleges in Pennsylvania and Maryland. It remained in this regional status until October 21, 1955, when it was incorporated as Phi Sigma Tau, a national honor society in philosophy. Its essential purpose was and is to promote ties between philosophy departments in accredited institutions and students in philosophy nationally. The organization is intended to be instrumental in developing and honoring academic excellence and philosophical interest on the local and national level.

Phi Sigma Tau's stated purpose is to serve as a means of awarding distinction to students having high scholarship and personal interest in philosophy; to promote student interest in research and advanced study in this field; to provide opportunities for the publication of student research papers of merit; to encourage a professional spirit and friendship among those who have displayed marked ability in this field; to popularize an interest in philosophy among the general collegiate public.

Growth   The parent chapter is Baldwin-Wallace College, Berea, Ohio. In 1955, Phi Sigma Tau included the chapters drawn from Ohio, Pennsylvania, Tennessee, Maryland, Washington, the District of Columbia, New Mexico, California, Oregon and Louisiana. By 1958 ten more chapters had been added, including those which had formerly constituted Alpha Kappa Alpha and the date of the later's organization was taken as Phi Sigma Tau's founding date.

Phi Sigma Tau was admitted to ACHS in 1958.

Eligibility   Undergraduate students are eligible for active membership if they have completed three semesters or five quarters of the college course, rank in the upper thirty-five percent of their class, and have completed at least two semester courses or three quarter courses in philosophy with an average grade of over the second highest grade of the working scale. Graduate students are eligible if they meet the requirements established for undergraduates; or have completed at least one-third of the residence requirements of the master's degree with a grade average of at least half on the highest grade of the working scale and half in the second highest grade.

Government   The first national convention was held at Gettysburg College in 1960 and thereafter as called.

The national officers of the society consist of a president, vice-president and secretary-treasurer, elected from graduate members of the society. The general supervision of chapter and society affairs is the responsibility of the secretary-treasurer The Executive Council consists of three national officers, plus four other members who are called councillors. The councillors serve for periods of three years, one term of office expiring each year at the spring meeting of the Council.

A large amount of autonomy remains with individual chapters, both for direction of programs and growth of the organization. The secretary-treasurer serves as liaison officer, supervising publications, finances, convention arrangements and such matters.

Traditions and Insignia   Local chapters serve the schools in which they are functioning by promoting the highest ideals in philosophical education. Meetings involve student presentation of papers, outside speakers, debates and symposia on philosophical issues.

The emblem of the society is a pentagon with the letters ΦΣΤ placed in the center. Each of the five angles contains a symbol representing each of the five streams of world thought: Chinese, Indian, Islamic, Hebrew and Greek. Its key displays the emblem of the society and is worn only by duly initiated members of the organization. The seal of the society is the reverse side of the Athenian silver tetradrachma, 480–400 B.C., bearing the owl, olive spray and small crescent. The margin of the seal carries the following legend, "Phi Sigma Tau, 1930."

The colors of the society are white and purple, the latter identified as 84-24-7 in terms of International Printing Institute Code.

Publications   Beginning in 1930, annual meetings were held at which student papers were read, discussed, then published in an annual volume, *Philosoph*. Since 1956 the society has published semiannually an official journal, *Dialogue*, which includes articles in the entire field of philosophy, whether or not the authors are members of Phi Sigma Tau or come from institutions having chapters of the society. Articles are accepted from undergraduate students, but not from those whose academic work is completed and who are now teaching. The organization also publishes a quarterly *Newsletter* which goes to all active members nationally.

Headquarters   Philosophy Department, Marquette University, Milwaukee, Wisconsin 53232.

Membership   Active chapters 74. Inactive chapters 39. Graduate/Alumni chapters 1. National Alumni chapters 218. Total number of initiates 17,621. Chapter roll:

1941   Washington and Jefferson
1955   Baylor

1955	Bucknell
1955	Mississippi
1955	Morgan State
1955	New Mexico
1955	Pacific (CA)
1955	St. Lawrence
1955	Wichita
1956	Loyola, Chicago
1960	Detroit
1961	Marquette
1962	Akron
1962	Nebraska
1962	San Jose
1962	Wheaton
1963	Bowling Green
1963	Cal State, Chico
1963	Clark
1963	Florida State
1963	Providence
1963	Texas Christian
1964	Bellarmine
1964	Cal State, Long Beach
1964	USC
1965	East Carolina
1965	Suffolk
1966	Muskingum
1967	Centre College
1967	Lindenwood
1967	North Park
1967	Whittier
1968	Carson-Newman
1968	Dayton
1968	Florida Atlantic
1968	Lewis
1968	Milligan
1968	Rockhurst
1969	Loras
1969	Westminster (PA)
1971	Creighton
1971	Wittenberg
1972	IUPUI
1972	Winthrop
1973	Fairfield
1973	Georgia
1973	Northern Illinois
1973	Olivet
1973	San Diego U
1973	Tulane
1973	Villanova
1973	Wisconsin, Whitewater
1974	Long Island
1974	Westmont
1974	William Jewell
1975	St. Michael's
1976	Christopher Newport
1976	Monmouth (NJ)
1976	SUNY Col. Tech, Farmingdale
1976	Spring Hill
1976	St. Joseph's (PA)
1976	Wisconsin, Parkside
1977	Wilkes
1978	Central State (OH)

1978	LaSalle
1978	Sacred Heart
1979	Agnes Scott
1979	Albion
1979	Belmont Abbey
1979	Coastal Carolina
1979	Emory
1979	Holy Cross (MA)
1979	King's
1979	Molloy
1979	Rider
1979	SUNY, Stony Brook
1979	Siena Heights
1979	St. Mary-of-the-Woods
1979	V.P.I.
1979	Washington (MD)
1979	West Chester
1979	Wisconsin, La Crosse
1980	Baker
1980	Illinois
1980	Lycoming
1980	Mercy (MI)
1980	St. Peter's
1980	Westminster (MO)
1981	Lake Forest
1981	Madison Col
1981	Mercer
1981	Mount Mary's (MD)
1982	Boston U
1982	Iona
1982	LeMoyne-Owen
1982	Mundelein
1982	Richmond
1982	Scranton
1982	Southwest Texas
1983	Asbury
1983	George Mason
1983	Salisbury
1983	Wooster
1984	C. W. Post
1984	Slippery Rock
1985	Catholic

Phi Upsilon Omicron

(HOME ECONOMICS)

ACTIVE PIN

PHI UPSILON OMICRON was founded at the University of Minnesota in February, 1909. The society was admitted to the Association of College Honor Societies in 1979.

Purpose To recognize and encourage academic excellence, professional service and leadership, and good character, as well as a commitment to advance the profession of home economics and to further the professional development of Phi Upsilon Omicron members.

Eligibility Membership in Phi Upsilon Omicron is open to men and women who, as undergraduate students, have completed 40 semester hours, 60 quarter hours, or the equivalent, with a major in home economics or one of its specialized areas. Students must rank well in general ability and have a minimum grade point average of 3.0 on a 4.0 scale. In addition to scholarship, membership eligibility shall be based on: potential professional and community leadership, and good character as exemplified by personal integrity and professional attitude. A graduate student in home economics is eligible when the student has completed twelve semester hours, or its equivalent, in home economics courses with a grade point average of 3.2 on a 4.0 scale.

Major Activities The Society awards twelve undergraduate scholarships, one Leadership Award, and the Orinne Johnson Writing Award annually. Six fellowships are granted annually to graduate students in home economics. Additionally, the National Council recognizes outstanding chapter professional projects. A Biennial Conclave and District Workshops provide an opportunity for members to participate with the National Council in leadership development and policy formation. Two Awards recognize outstanding alumni who have provided distinguished service and leadership to home economics. The Phi Upsilon Omicron Educational Foundation is supported by the collegiate and alumni members of the honor society.

Publication Phi Upsilon Omicron publishes *The Candle* semiannually and an *Alumni Newsletter*.

Membership Active chapters 67. Graduate/ Alumni chapters 45. Total number of initiates 62,600. Chapter roll:††

1909   Alpha, Minnesota
1914   Beta, North Dakota State
1915   Delta, Wyoming
1915   Gamma, Ohio State
1917   Epsilon, Montana State
1918   Zeta, Idaho
1920   Eta, Kansas State, Pittsburg
1921   Theta, Ohio
1922   Iota, Kentucky
1923   Kappa, Utah State
1923   Lambda, West Virginia
1923   Mu, SUNY Col., Buffalo
1925   Nu, Wisconsin, Madison
1925   Xi, Nebraska
1926   Omicron, Iowa State
1926   Pi, Illinois
1929   Rho, Missouri
1931   Sigma, L.S.U.
1933   Tau, Wisconsin, Stout
1934   Phi, South Dakota State

†† This chapter roll is repeated from the 19th edition; no current information was provided.

1934   Upsilon, Winthrop
1936   Chi, Georgia
1936   Psi, Alabama
1937   Omega, Texas Tech
1938   Alpha Alpha, Texas Woman's
1940   Alpha Beta, Mississippi for Women
1941   Alpha Gamma, Wayne State
1943   Alpha Delta, Arkansas
1944   Alpha Epsilon, North Dakota
1945   Alpha Zeta, New Hampshire
1946   Alpha Eta, Georgia Col.
1946   *Alpha Theta, Case Western Reserve* (1966)
1947   Alpha Iota, North Texas
1948   Alpha Kappa, Penn State
1948   Alpha Lambda, Connecticut
1949   *Alpha Mu, Ohio Wesleyan* (1971)
1950   Alpha Nu, Oklahoma State
1952   *Alpha Omicron, Regis (MA)* (1968)
1952   *Alpha Pi, Hunter* (1965)
1952   Alpha Xi, Bowling Green
1955   Alpha Rho, San Jose
1956   Alpha Sigma, Ball State
1960   Alpha Chi, Kansas State
1960   Alpha Phi, Indiana State
1960   Alpha Tau, Houston
1960   Alpha Upsilon, Arizona State
1962   Alpha Psi, Iowa
1963   Alpha Omega, Miami (OH)
1964   Beta Alpha, Hawaii
1965   Beta Beta, Cal Poly
1965   Beta Gamma, Mankato
1966   Beta Delta, Western Kentucky
1967   Beta Epsilon, SUNY Col., Plattsburgh
1968   Beta Eta, East Carolina
1968   Beta Theta, Cal State, Los Angeles
1968   Beta Zeta, Texas Christian
1969   Beta Iota, Southern
1969   Beta Kappa, Northern
1969   Beta Lambda, V.P.I.
1969   Beta Mu, Georgia Southern
1970   Beta Nu, Northern Iowa
1970   Beta Xi, Southwest Texas
1971   Beta Omicron, SUNY Col., Oneonta
1971   Beta Pi, Framingham
1972   Beta Rho, Idaho State
1972   Beta Sigma, Tennessee, Martin
1973   Beta Phi, San Diego State
1973   Beta Tau, Eastern Kentucky
1973   Beta Upsilon, Stephen F. Austin
1975   Beta Chi, Cal State, Fresno

Pi Alpha Alpha

(PUBLIC AFFAIRS AND ADMINISTRATION)

PI ALPHA ALPHA is the national honor society for public affairs and administration. Those universities and colleges which are members of the National Association of Schools of Public Affairs and Administration (NASPAA) are eligible to establish a PAA Chapter.

Established in 1974, PAA membership is open to undergraduate and graduate students in schools of public affairs and administration, faculty members, alumni, scholars and public officials who have made significant contributions to the field.

Purpose The purpose of this Society shall be to encourage and recognize outstanding scholarship and accomplishment in public affairs and administration, to promote the advancement of education and practice in the art and science of public affairs and administration, and to foster integrity, professionalism and creative performance in the conduct of governmental and related public service activities.

Eligibility Membership is limited to persons who demonstrate academic achievement in public affairs and administration programs in NASPAA member schools and/or outstanding public service, and who fall within the following classes: student, alumni, faculty, and honorary. All membership is national membership with local chapter affiliation.

Government The government of the society is vested in the National Council and a four member Executive Committee. The National Council consists of ten national officers and a president, vice president and two former presidents. Five Council members are elected every four years and the president serves a two year term.

Local Chapter and National Activities
Activities vary from chapter to chapter. Chapters may choose to sponsor orientation activities for incoming public administration students, provide tutoring services, schedule seminars, leadership conferences or lecture series. At the National level, PAA sponsors an annual "Best Student Manuscript Award in Public Administration" competition. PAA is a member of the Association of College Honor Societies, a national organization dedicated to encouraging general and specialized honor societies in establishing and maintaining high standards, scholarship and achievement of their members.

Biennial meetings are held in conjunction with the National Association of Schools of Public Affairs and Administration. During this meeting, a distinguished person of national stature, who has made outstanding contributions to the profession, is nominated by the National Council for honorary membership in the Society. The national office maintains communication with chapters, prepares certificates, publishes a chapter roster and annual report.

Headquarters NASPAA, 1120 G. Street, NW, Suite 520, Washington, DC 20005, (202) 628-8965, National Director, Alfred M. Zuck.

Membership Active chapters 78. Total number of initiates 7,800. Chapter roll:

American
Arizona State
Arizona
Baltimore U.
C. W. Post
CUNY, Baruch
CUNY, John Jay

Cal State, Bakersfield
Cal State, Dominguez Hills
Cal State, Long Beach
Carnegie-Mellon
Central Florida
Colorado, Colorado Springs
Colorado
Connecticut
Cookingham Inst
Dayton
Drake
Fairleigh Dickinson, Rutherford
Florida Atlantic
Florida International
Florida State
George Washington
Georgia Southern
Georgia State
Georgia
Houston, Clear Lake
Howard
Indiana
Kansas
Kean (NJ)
Kent
Kentucky
Madison Col
Maine
Marywood
Michigan State
Mississippi State
Mississippi
Missouri
New Mexico
New School/Social Research
North Carolina State
North Carolina, Charlotte
North Texas
Northern Illinois
Ohio State
Oklahoma
Old Dominion
Oregon
Pace
Pacific (CA)
Penn State, Capitol
Russell Sage
Rutgers, Newark
SUNY, Albany
SUNY, Binghamton
San Diego U.
South Florida
Southwest Texas
Suffolk
Tennessee State
Texas A & M
Texas Tech
Troy, European Region
USC
Utah
Wayne State (MI)
West Florida
West Virginia

Pi Delta Phi

(FRENCH)

ACTIVE PIN

PI DELTA PHI, college recognition society in French for men and women, was founded at the University of California in 1906 and remained a local organization for nineteen years before it installed a second chapter. Admitted to ACHS in 1967.

Purpose To recognize outstanding scholarship in the French language and literature; to increase knowledge of the contribution of France to world culture; to stimulate and encourage such cultural activities that will lead to a deeper appreciation of France and its people.

Eligibility There are three classes of membership. *Regular* members include those college and university students who are nominated in recognition of their academic achievement in French. They must rank in the upper thirty-five percent of their class in general studies as well as have a B average in French. Graduate students who are candidates for an advanced degree in French are also eligible for Regular membership. *Honorary* members include the French faculty of the sponsoring institution, members of the faculty-at-large, and community leaders who have manifested interest in French culture. *Associate* members include those students who actively support French culture in the community or are known for their interest in things French, but do not qualify as yet for Regular Membership.

Government Government is vested in an executive committee composed of national president, five vice-presidents, and executive secretary. The first triennial convention of the society was held in 1934 at Berkeley.

Major Activities On a national level, the Society awards scholarships. On the local level, each chapter is free to develop and sponsor any activity which will promote interest in French culture, either in the academic milieu or in the community.

Traditions and Insignia The badge is an oblong key displaying the society's name on a vertical band. The flower is the fleur-de-lis.

Publication *News-Letter.*

Headquarters 6923 North Kilpatrick, Lincolnwood, Illinois 60646.

Membership Active chapters 248. Total number of initiates 55,000. Chapter roll:††

1906　Alpha, California

†† This chapter roll is repeated from the 19th edition; no current information was provided.

1925　Beta, USC
1926　Gamma, UCLA
1927　Delta, Mississippi for Women
1927　Epsilon, Illinois
1928　Zeta, Oregon
1930　Eta, Kansas
1930　Theta, Rice
1934　Iota, Stanford
1936　Kappa, Cornell
1936　Lambda, Alabama College
1936　Mu, Dominican
1938　Nu, San Francisco Women's
1938　Omicron, Florida State
1938　Xi, Penn
1941　Pi, Arizona
1944　Rho, Texas
1946　Sigma, Hunter
1948　Chi, Kent
1948　Phi, Notre Dame (MD)
1948　Psi, Southwestern Louisiana Institute
1948　Tau, Southern Methodist
1948　Upsilon, N.Y.U. (Heights)
1949　Alpha Alpha, Barat (IL)
1949　Alpha Beta, Denison
1949　Alpha Delta, St. Catherine
1949　Alpha Epsilon, Mount Mary's (CA)
1949　Alpha Eta, Miami (OH)
1949　Alpha Gamma, Tennessee
1949　Alpha Theta, Brooklyn
1949　Alpha Zeta, Lincoln Memorial (TN)
1949　Omega, St. Joseph's (MD)
1950　Alpha Iota, North Texas
1950　Alpha Kappa, Southern Mississippi
1950　Alpha Lambda, Iowa
1950　Alpha Mu, Winthrop
1950　Alpha Nu, Adrian
1950　Alpha Omicron, West Virginia
1950　Alpha Xi, Minnesota
1951　Alpha Chi, St. Teresa
1951　Alpha Phi, Texas Western
1951　Alpha Pi, Marquette
1951　Alpha Psi, La Salle
1951　Alpha Rho, Bucknell
1951　Alpha Sigma, Maryhurst (OR)
1951　Alpha Tau, Rosary (IL)
1951　Alpha Upsilon, Marshall
1952　Alpha Omega, Yeshiva
1952　Beta Alpha, North Carolina
1952　Beta Beta, Houston
1952　Beta Delta, C.C.N.Y.
1952　Beta Epsilon, William and Mary
1952　Beta Gamma, Miami
1952　Beta Zeta, Howard
1953　Beta Eta, Detroit
1953　Beta Theta, Southern Arkansas
1954　Beta Iota, Temple
1954　Beta Kappa, Webster
1955　Beta Lambda, North Carolina A & T
1955　Beta Mu, Carson-Newman
1955　Beta Nu, Wisconsin, Eau Claire
1956　Beta Omicron, Tennessee A & I
1956　Beta Pi, West Virginia State

1956	Beta Rho, Judson	1967	Epsilon Eta, Utah
1956	Beta Sigma, Georgetown Col.	1967	Epsilon Iota, Lamar
1956	Beta Tau, Toledo	1967	Epsilon Kappa, Mansfield
1956	Beta Upsilon, Morehouse	1967	Epsilon Lambda, Frostburg
1956	Beta Xi, Texas Tech.	1967	Epsilon Mu, Wisconsin, Whitewater
1957	Beta Chi, St. Teresa (MO)	1967	Epsilon Nu, Cal State, Los Angeles
1957	Beta Pi, Millsaps	1967	Epsilon Theta, San Diego College for Women
1958	Beta Omega, Cincinnati	1967	Epsilon Xi, Chattanooga
1958	Beta Psi, DePaul	1967	Epsilon Zeta, San Diego State
1958	Gamma Alpha, Beaver	1968	Epsilon Omicron, Fontbonne
1959	Gamma Beta, Holy Names	1968	Epsilon Pi, Southern Colorado
1959	Gamma Gamma, Adelphi	1968	Epsilon Rho, SUNY Col., Fredonia
1960	Gamma Delta, Woman's College (NC)	1968	Epsilon Sigma, Wichita
1960	Gamma Epsilon, Texas Southern	1968	Epsilon Tau, Southwest Texas
1960	Gamma Zeta, Mundelein	1968	Epsilon Upsilon, Indiana (PA)
1962	Gamma Eta, St. Thomas (TX)	1969	Epsilon Chi, Ohio Northern
1962	Gamma Iota, Bowling Green	1969	Epsilon Omega, Marymount College
1962	Gamma Kappa, Montclair	1969	Epsilon Phi, Little Rock
1962	Gamma Lambda, Holy Names (WA)	1969	Epsilon Psi, Maryville (MO)
1962	Gamma Mu, Hope	1969	Zeta Alpha, Susquehanna
1962	Gamma Mu, Oregon State	1969	Zeta Beta, Cal State, Sacramento
1962	Gamma Omicron, Dickinson	1969	Zeta Delta, Southern Illinois, Edwardsville
1962	Gamma Theta, North Carolina College	1969	Zeta Epsilon, Fairfield
1962	Gamma Xi, Trinity (DC)	1969	Zeta Eta, Akron
1963	Gamma Chi, Regis (CO)	1969	Zeta Gamma, SUNY, Albany
1963	Gamma Omega, Loyola, Chicago	1969	Zeta Iota, Portland
1963	Gamma Phi, Appalachian	1969	Zeta Theta, Cal State, Long Beach
1963	Gamma Pi, Emporia	1969	Zeta Zeta, Georgia
1963	Gamma Psi, Brigham Young	1970	Zeta Kappa, Nevada
1963	Gamma Rho, Hofstra	1970	Zeta Lambda, Buena Vista
1963	Gamma Sigma, Slippery Rock	1970	Zeta Mu, Morris Harvey
1963	Gamma Tau, Purdue	1970	Zeta Nu, Southwestern (TX)
1963	Gamma Upsilon, Marcyhurst	1970	Zeta Omicron, Murray State
1964	Delta Alpha, Kearney State	1970	Zeta Pi, Lindenwood
1964	Delta Beta, Georgian Court	1970	Zeta Rho, Georgia Southern
1964	Delta Delta, Notre Dame (OH)	1970	Zeta Sigma, Lehman
1964	Delta Epsilon, Western Kentucky	1970	Zeta Tau, Whittier
1964	Delta Eta, Oklahoma Women	1970	Zeta Upsilon, Randolph, Macon
1964	Delta Gamma, Maryville (TN)	1970	Zeta Xi, Cal State, San Bernardino
1964	Delta Zeta, Marygrove	1971	Eta Alpha, Dominican (TX)
1965	Delta Iota, Nazareth	1971	Eta Beta, West Texas
1965	Delta Kappa, Trinity (TX)	1971	Eta Delta, St. Lawrence
1965	Delta Lambda, Memphis State	1971	Eta Epsilon, Georgia Southwestern
1965	Delta Mu, Mississippi State	1971	Eta Gamma, Edinboro
1965	Delta Nu, Baylor	1971	Eta Zeta, Armstrong
1965	Delta Omicron, Glassboro	1971	Zeta Chi, California Lutheran
1965	Delta Pi, St. John's (NY)	1971	Zeta Omega, Central Michigan
1965	Delta Rho, Westminster (PA)	1971	Zeta Phi, Rhode Island
1965	Delta Sigma, Connecticut	1971	Zeta Psi, East Texas
1965	Delta Tau, Auburn	1972	Eta Eta, Thiel
1965	Delta Theta, Drury	1972	Eta Iota, Sam Houston
1965	Delta Upsilon, Kentucky	1972	Eta Kappa, Pace
1965	Delta Xi, Hawaii	1972	Eta Lambda, Roanoke
1966	Delta Chi, Marillac (MO)	1972	Eta Mu, George Washington
1966	Delta Omega, Mississippi	1972	Eta Theta, St. Bonaventure
1966	Delta Phi, Radford	1973	Eta Nu, St. John Fisher
1966	Delta Psi, Illinois State Normal	1973	Eta Omicron, Delaware
1966	Epsilon Alpha, Austin	1973	Eta Phi, Pepperdine
1966	Epsilon Beta, Montana	1973	Eta Pi, Bethany (KS)
1966	Epsilon Gamma, Rider	1973	Eta Rho, Southwest Missouri
1967	Epsilon Delta, St. Louis	1973	Eta Sigma, Alabama
1967	Epsilon Epsilon, Queens (NY)	1973	Eta Xi, St. Augustine's

1974   Eta Chi, Cal State, Dominguez Hills
1974   Eta Psi, North Carolina, Asheville
1974   Eta Tau, Hobart-William Smith
1974   Eta Upsilon, Cal, Davis
1975   Eta Omega, Arkansas
1975   Theta Alpha, Clemson
1975   Theta Beta, South Carolina
1975   Theta Delta, SUNY Col., Oswego
1975   Theta Epsilon, Wright State
1975   Theta Eta, Salve Regina
1975   Theta Gamma, Columbia (SC)
1975   Theta Zeta, Louisville
1976   Theta Iota, Texas A & M
1976   Theta Kappa, Hood
1976   Theta Lambda, Santa Barbara
1976   Theta Mu, Eastern Illinois
1976   Theta Nu, Valdosta
1976   Theta Theta, East Tennessee

Pi Gamma Mu

(SOCIAL SCIENCE)

ACTIVE PIN

PI GAMMA MU, the national social science honor society, was founded by Dean Leroy Allen, Southwestern College, Winfield, Kansas, and Dean William A. Hamilton, College of William and Mary, Williamsburg, Virginia, on December 1, 1924. Seventeen charter chapters were organized simultaneously. The purpose of the society is to encourage young men and women in the scientific study of all social problems and to promote cooperation among the several branches of social science. It is an interdepartmental honor society, initiating members from the five core fields of history, political science, sociology/anthropology, economics, international relations and other social science disciplines. In 1980 the name of the organization was officially changed to Pi Gamma Mu, International Honor Society in Social Science. It is incorporated under the laws of Colorado as a non-profit-seeking society.

In 1940 the society became associated with and in 1947 affiliated with the American Association for the Advancement of Science. Pi Gamma Mu was admitted to the Association of College Honor Societies in 1953.

Eligibility   Any person of good moral character may be invited or may petition to join an active chapter of Pi Gamma Mu when he/she is a junior, senior, or graduate student; is in the upper 35 percent of the class; has at least 20 semester hours of social science; and has a grade average of "B" or better. Faculty and administrators may also accept the privileges and responsibilities of membership in a collegiate chapter.

Government   It is governed by international officers operating under a board of trustees. There is a governor who presides over the activities of the society in each state, and several states are grouped into regions with a chancellor in charge of each. The collegiate chapters are semi-autonomous; activities vary from campus to campus. Each is expected to initiate members annually following at least the minimal standards set for membership.

Insignia   The running figure on the emblem is reminiscent of the ancient Greek torch race. A key, as well as a year's subscription to the publications, is included in the initiation fee. The motto is *Ye shall know the truth, and the truth shall make you free*. The colors are blue and white. The flower is the cineraria.

Publications   The society publishes a quarterly journal, *International Social Science Review*, and the *Pi Gamma Mu Newsletter*, six times a year.

Lectureships and Scholarships   Guest lectureships are available to chapters upon application. These grants are to bring persons with special qualifications to advance the social sciences on the various campuses.

The Pi Gamma Mu scholarship program was initiated in 1951 to aid members in first year graduate work in the five core social sciences. To date, 130 Pi Gamma Mu scholars have been awarded grants totaling over $115,000.

Headquarters   1717 Ames, Winfield, Kansas 67156.

Membership   Active chapters 189. Inactive chapters 173. Total number of initiates 148,571. Chapter roll:

1924   *AL Alpha, Birmingham-Southern* (1940)
1924   *CA Alpha, Pacific (CA)* (1958)
1924   *IA Alpha, Iowa State* (1939)
1924   *IL Alpha, North Central* (1969)
1924   KS Alpha, Southwestern (KS)
1924   *KS Beta, Washburn* (1958)
1924   KY Alpha, Berea
1924   MN Alpha, Hamline
1924   *MT Alpha, Montana* (1939-1952) (1954)
1924   *OH Alpha, Akron* (1939)
1924   OH Beta, Toledo
1924   *OR Alpha, Willamette* (1978)
1924   *TX Alpha, Southwestern (TX)* (1978)
1924   *TX Beta, Baylor* (1969)
1924   *VA Alpha, William and Mary* (1938)
1924   *WI Alpha, Lawrence* (1937)
1924   *WY Alpha, Wyoming* (1939)
1925   *MO Alpha, Drury* (1964)
1925   *SD Alpha, Dakota Wesleyan* (1937)
1926   *ME Alpha, Colby* (1954)
1926   *MS Alpha, Mississippi State* (1942)
1926   NE Alpha, Nebraska Wesleyan
1926   *NY Alpha, Union (NY)* (1937)
1926   PA Alpha, Grove City
1926   *PA Beta, Gettysburg* (1939)

1926 SC Alpha, Furman (1941-1973)
1926 *SD Beta, South Dakota (1931)*
1926 *TX Gamma, Texas Christian (1939)*
1926 *VA Beta, Randolph, Macon Woman's (1940)*
1926 *WV Alpha, Marshall (1937)*
1927 *CO Alpha, Denver (1983)*
1927 *IL Beta, Knox (1937)*
1927 *IL Delta, Illinois Col (1938)*
1927 IL Gamma, Bradley
1927 *KS Delta, Emporia (1946)*
1927 *KS Gamma, Pittsburg State, Kansas (1937)*
1927 *KY Beta, Louisville (1938)*
1927 *MO Beta, Northwest Missouri (1942-1968)
       (1972-1980) (1987)*
1927 *ND Alpha, North Dakota State (1942)*
1927 *NY Beta, Elmira (1943)*
1927 *NY Delta, SUNY, Albany (1971)*
1927 NY Gamma, Alfred
1927 PA Delta, Penn
1927 PA Gamma, Susquehanna
1927 *TX Delta, Texas Tech (1937)*
1927 *TX Epsilon, North Texas (1937)*
1927 VA Gamma, Longwood
1928 *AL Beta, Alabama (1939)*
1928 AL Gamma, Samford
1928 *CO Beta, Western State (CO) (1937)*
1928 FL Alpha, Florida Southern
1928 *GA Alpha, Brenau (1937)*
1928 *IA Beta, Simpson (1953)*
1928 *IA Gamma, Northern Iowa (1984)*
1928 *KS Epsilon, Kansas Wesleyan (1946)*
1928 *LA Alpha, Louisiana Tech (1939)*
1928 LA Beta, Centenary (1940-1990)
1928 LA Gamma, Southwestern Louisiana
1928 *MS Beta, Mississippi for Women (1982)*
1928 *NE Beta, Hastings (1946)*
1928 *NM Alpha, New Mexico (1940)*
1928 *OH Delta, Wilmington (1937)*
1928 *OH Gamma, Muskingum (1950)*
1928 *OK Alpha, Oklahoma City (1950-1964)
       (1965)*
1928 *OK Beta, Southwestern State (OK) (1941)*
1928 *PA Epsilon, Penn State (1971)*
1928 *PA Zeta, Albright (1959)*
1928 *TN Alpha, Tennessee, Chattanooga (1981)*
1928 TX Eta, Southwest Texas
1928 TX Zeta, Mary Hardin-Baylor (1953-1978)
1928 VA Delta, Emory and Henry (1957-1989)
1928 VA Epsilon, Radford
1928 *WA Alpha, Puget Sound (1968)*
1928 *WA Beta, Washington State (1938)*
1928 WV Beta, Fairmont
1929 CA Beta, Cal State, Fresno
1929 DC Alpha, Catholic
1929 *FL Beta, Florida (1939)*
1929 *FL Gamma, Stetson (1942)*
1929 *GA Beta, Georgia Col (1971)*
1929 *HI Alpha, Hawaii (1960)*
1929 *IA Delta, Morningside (1960)*
1929 *IL Epsilon, DePaul (1986)*
1929 *IL Zeta, Loyola, Chicago (1966)*
1929 *IN Alpha, Evansville (1973)*

1929 *MN Beta, Gustavus Adolphus (1946)*
1929 *MO Delta, Lindenwood (1949)*
1929 *MO Gamma, Southwest Missouri (1954)*
1929 NC Alpha, Elon
1929 *NE Gamma, Peru (1941)*
1929 *NY Epsilon, Adelphi (1958)*
1929 *NY Zeta, Syracuse (1955)*
1929 *OH Epsilon, Baldwin-Wallace (1938)*
1929 OK Delta, Tulsa (1964-1975)
1929 *OK Epsilon, Oklahoma Baptist (1937)*
1929 *OK Gamma, Oklahoma State (1958)*
1929 OR Beta, Linfield
1929 *PA Eta, Temple (1954)*
1929 *PA Theta, Slippery Rock (1971)*
1929 SD Gamma, South Dakota State
1929 TX Theta, Hardin-Simmons (1937-1950)
1929 *WI Beta, Carroll (1942)*
1930 *AR Alpha, Ouachita Baptist (1937)*
1930 *DC Beta, George Washington (1959)*
1930 IL Eta, Wheaton (1980-1990)
1930 IL Theta, Illinois State (1968-1989)
1930 IN Beta, Hanover (1937-1951) (1963)
1930 *KS Eta, Bethany (KS) (1942)*
1930 *KS Zeta, Ottawa (1943)*
1930 MO Epsilon, William Jewell
1930 *PA Iota, Clarion (1971)*
1930 *SD Delta, Yankton (1938)*
1930 *TN Beta, U of the South (1962)*
1930 *TX Iota, Trinity (TX) (1938)*
1931 *DC Gamma, American (1978)*
1931 *IL Iota, Illinois Wesleyan (1952)*
1931 IN Gamma, Ball State
1931 *KS Theta, Fort Hays (1954)*
1931 *MO Zeta, Missouri Valley (1979)*
1931 *NY Eta, N.Y.U. (1937)*
1931 PA Kappa, Mansfield (1940-1969)
1931 TX Kappa, Sam Houston
1932 CA Delta, UCLA
1932 *CA Gamma, San Diego U. (1939)*
1932 *CO Delta, Colorado (1957)*
1932 *CO Gamma, Colorado State (1965)*
1932 *DC Delta, Georgetown U. (1951)*
1932 *FL Delta, Rollins (1973)*
1932 *IN Delta, Indiana State (1971)*
1932 *IN Epsilon, Valparaiso (1958)*
1932 *MA Alpha, Boston U. (1955)*
1932 *MI Alpha, Eastern Michigan (1962)*
1932 NY Theta, Keuka
1932 *ONT Alpha, Toronto (1941)*
1932 PHIL Alpha, Philippines, Quezon City
1932 SD Epsilon, Huron
1932 *TN Gamma, Peabody (1970)*
1932 *VT Alpha, Vermont (1942)*
1932 *WV Gamma, Concord (1957)*
1933 *AZ Alpha, Northern Arizona (1940)*
1933 *NC Beta, Duke (1943)*
1933 NE Delta, Wayne State (NE)
1933 PA Lambda, California (PA) (1951-1971)
1934 AR Beta, Arkansas State
1934 *AR Gamma, Henderson (1939)*
1934 *IA Epsilon, Iowa (1941)*
1934 OH Zeta, Mount Union

1934	*TN Delta, YMCA Graduate* (1941)
1934	*UT Alpha, Utah State* (1952)
1935	*LA Delta, L.S.U.* (1958)
1935	*MO Eta, Westminster (MO)* (1942)
1935	MO Kappa, Central Methodist
1935	*SC Beta, South Carolina* (1949)
1936	CT Alpha, Trinity (CT)
1936	*MA Beta, Springfield* (1946)
1937	PA Mu, Franklin and Marshall
1937	*TX Lambda, Our Lady of the Lake* (1983)
1938	*IA Zeta, Coe* (1958)
1938	*MI Beta, Western Michigan* (1967)
1938	*NC Gamma, Davidson* (1943)
1938	PA Nu, Lebanon Valley
1938	*SC Gamma, Winthrop* (1952)
1938	*WV Eta, Bethany (WV)* (1946-1985)
1939	*AZ Beta, Arizona State* (1946)
1939	OH Eta, Kent (1971-1987)
1939	SC Delta, Wofford
1940	*NJ Alpha, Drew* (1960)
1941	MN Gamma, St. Catherine (1966-1978) (1982-1989)
1941	NH Alpha, New Hampshire
1941	OK Epsilon, Oklahoma Science and Arts
1946	KS Iota, Kansas State
1946	*MN Delta, Macalester* (1965)
1947	*MI Delta, Michigan State* (1973)
1947	*MO Lambda, St. Louis* (1949)
1947	PA Xi, Seton Hill
1948	*PA Omicron, Lehigh* (1960)
1948	VA Zeta, Mary Washington
1949	*MN Epsilon, St. Olaf* (1965)
1949	NY Pi, Hofstra (1969-1989)
1949	*VA Eta, Randolph, Macon* (1971-1983) (1984)
1950	ID Alpha, Idaho
1950	MN Zeta, St. Thomas (1957-1985)
1950	*PA Rho, Allegheny* (1984)
1950	PA Sigma, Ursinus
1951	*DC Epsilon, Dunbarton Holy Cross* (1973)
1951	*DC Zeta, Trinity (DC)* (1968)
1951	NE Epsilon, Nebraska (1958-1979)
1951	*NM Alpha, New Mexico Highlands* (1983)
1951	*OK Zeta, Oklahoma* (1958)
1952	MA Beta, Regis (MA)
1953	IL Kappa, Rosary (IL)
1953	*MN Eta, St. Teresa* (1989)
1953	*PA Tau, Duquesne* (1959)
1953	*TX Mu, Midwestern* (1967)
1954	CA Epsilon, Holy Names
1954	*CT Beta, Bridgeport* (1968)
1954	*NY Rho, Hobart* (1979)
1954	NY Sigma, LeMoyne-Owen
1955	*CA Zeta, Pepperdine* (1966)
1955	*IL Lambda, Western Illinois* (1969)
1955	*KY Beta, Union (KY)* (1966)
1955	*MS Gamma, Southern Mississippi* (1982)
1955	NC Delta, North Carolina Central
1955	PR Alpha, Catholic
1956	CO Epsilon, Colorado Col
1956	MD Alpha, Morgan State (1960-1984)
1956	MN Theta, Minnesota, Duluth
1956	*NE Zeta, Kearney* (1972)
1956	OH Theta, Ohio
1957	*CA Eta, Cal State, Long Beach* (1963)
1957	LA Epsilon, Southern
1957	MN Iota, Concordia Col. (MN)
1957	NC Epsilon, Appalachian
1957	*NM Beta, New Mexico State* (1972)
1957	*TN Epsilon, Maryville (TN)* (1985)
1958	CA Theta, Redlands
1958	MS Delta, Delta State
1958	MS Epsilon, Mississippi Col
1958	NY Omicron, Long Island
1958	TN Zeta, Middle Tennessee
1958	*TX Nu, St. Mary's, San Antonio* (1981)
1959	*AL Epsilon, Jacksonville (AL)* (1975)
1959	GA Delta, LaGrange
1959	GA Gamma, Wesleyan (GA)
1959	*IL Mu, Monmouth (IL)* (1981)
1959	*IL Nu, MacMurray* (1961)
1959	MN Kappa, Augsburg
1959	MO Mu, Park (MO)
1959	*NJ Beta, Glassboro* (1973)
1959	NY Phi, Nazareth
1959	NY Upsilon, St. John Fisher
1959	*OH Iota, Marietta* (1965)
1959	*PA Upsilon, Dickinson* (1971-1985) (1988)
1959	WI Alpha, Marquette
1960	MD Beta, Western Maryland
1961	KS Zeta, Sterling
1961	*MN Lambda, St. Scholastica* (1976)
1961	NY Chi, Daemen
1961	TN Eta, East Tennessee
1961	*WA Beta, Pacific Lutheran* (1970)
1962	*FL Epsilon, Florida A & M* (1985)
1962	IL Xi, Elmhurst
1962	*MO Nu, Fontbonne* (1974)
1962	NH Beta, St. Anselm's
1962	NM Gamma, Western New Mexico
1962	PA Pi, Indiana (PA)
1962	*TN Iota, Tusculum* (1971)
1962	*TN Theta, Tennessee Wesleyan* (1970)
1963	CA Iota, Loyola Marymount, Los Angeles
1963	*CO Zeta, Northern Colorado* (1964)
1963	GA Epsilon, Shorter (1971-1985)
1963	*MN Mu, Bethel (MN)* (1981)
1963	NC Eta, Bennett
1963	*NY Psi, Yeshiva* (1976)
1963	OH Iota, Hiram
1963	WV Delta, Charleston (WV)
1965	*IN Epsilon, Anderson* (1977)
1965	*NC Theta, Greensboro* (1967)
1965	NJ Gamma, Montclair
1965	*NY Omega, SUNY Col., Oswego* (1970)
1965	OK Zeta, Northeastern (OK)
1965	*WA Delta, Eastern Washington* (1972)
1966	CA Kappa, Cal Poly, Pomona
1966	KS Eta, Baker
1966	NJ Delta, Rider
1967	*CA Lambda, Cal State, Hayward* (1969)
1967	LA Zeta, Southeastern Louisiana
1967	PA Omega, West Chester
1967	SD Zeta, Dakota Wesleyan

1967 TX Xi, Austin
1968 *CA Mu, California Lutheran* (1981)
1968 CA Nu, Cal Poly, San Luis Obispo
1968 NC Theta, Atlantic Christian
1968 *NY Alpha Beta, SUNY Col., Oneonta* (1979)
1968 NY Tau, Pace (1970-1984)
1969 CA Xi, LaVerne
1969 GA Zeta, West Georgia
1969 MS Zeta, William Carey
1969 *NM Delta, Santa Fe* (1975)
1969 *PA Alpha Gamma, Alliance* (1979)
1969 VA Theta, James Madison
1970 *IA Delta, Upper Iowa* (1982)
1970 MA Gamma, Suffolk
1970 MN Xi, St. Mary's (MN)
1970 SC Epsilon, Converse
1971 KY Gamma, Morehead
1971 LA Eta, Grambling
1971 *PA Alpha Delta, Gannon* (1990)
1971 PA Alpha Epsilon, Scranton
1972 *CA Omicron, Mount Mary's (CA)* (1980)
1972 MO Omicron, Evangel
1972 NC Rho, Belmont Abbey
1972 PA Alpha Eta, Marywood
1972 PA Alpha Zeta, Widener
1972 SC Zeta, Baptist, Charleston
1972 TX Omicron, West Texas
1972 WV Epsilon, West Virginia Wesleyan
1973 *NC Sigma, Warren Wilson* (1981)
1973 NC Tau, Winston-Salem
1974 GA Eta, Savannah
1974 KS Theta, Kansas Newman
1974 *NC Upsilon, Fayetteville* (1985)
1974 SC Iota, Claflin
1975 AL Zeta, Alabama State
1975 NY Alpha Gamma, Siena
1975 PA Alpha Theta, Waynesburg
1975 SC Kappa, South Carolina State
1975 TX Pi, St. Thomas (TX)
1976 CA Pi, Pepperdine
1976 CA Rho, Cal State, Northridge
1976 FL Zeta, Florida State
1976 IN Zeta, Indiana Wesleyan
1976 NC Phi, Methodist
1976 NY Iota, Mercy (NY)
1976 PA Alpha Iota, Eastern
1976 TN Kappa, Union (TN)
1976 TX Rho, Howard Payne
1977 MO Pi, Missouri Southern
1977 *NC Zeta, Guilford* (1979)
1977 SC Lambda, Francis Marion
1978 CT Gamma, Western Connecticut
1978 OK Eta, East Central State
1978 PA Phi, Lycoming
1979 FL Eta, South Florida
1979 WV Zeta, Glenville
1980 GA Theta, Valdosta
1980 IL Omicron, Illinois Benedictine
1980 NC Iota, Johnson C. Smith
1980 NC Kappa, Salem (NC)
1980 SD Eta, Northern State
1981 CA Sigma, Humboldt

1981 NH Gamma, Plymouth
1981 UT Beta, Weber
1981 VA Iota, Roanoke
1981 VT Beta, Norwich
1982 GA Iota, Clark Col., Atlanta
1982 MO Theta, Maryville (MO)
1982 MS Mu, Jackson (MS)
1982 PA Chi, Millersville
1982 TX Sigma, Angelo
1982 VA Kappa, Sweet Briar
1983 MD Gamma, Salisbury
1983 NC Lambda, Western Carolina
1983 NC Mu, Campbell
1983 NY Kappa, St. Bonaventure
1983 OR Gamma, Oregon
1983 SC Lambda, Western Carolina
1983 SC Mu, Campbell
1984 MD Delta, Baltimore U.
1984 MN Nu, Southwest State (MN)
1984 NC Nu, St. Andrews Presbyterian
1985 SC Eta, Presbyterian
1987 IA Eta, Wartburg
1987 MD Epsilon, Coppin
1987 NY Lambda, St. Thomas Aquinas
1989 MA Delta, Wheelock
1989 NY Mu, Dominican
1989 TX Tau, Texas Wesleyan
1990 CO Eta, Metropolitan State (CO)
1990 FL Theta, Barry (FL)
1990 PHIL Beta, LaSalle
1990 TX Upsilon, Houston

Pi Kappa Lambda

(MUSIC)

ACTIVE PIN

PI KAPPA LAMBDA was organized in April, 1918 at Northwestern University by Carl M. Beecher, Louis Norton Dodge and Walter Allen Stults. The society is dedicated to the furtherance of music in education and education in music in colleges, universities, and other institutions of higher learning which offer programs in musical instruction in one or more fields.

Eligibility Membership in the Society is open to juniors, seniors, graduate students, and faculty in accordance with established restrictions. A graduating senior must be considered by the faculty committee of the chapter to be outstanding in scholarly achievement and musicianship, must have been in residence the equivalent of at least four semesters prior to graduation, and must rank not lower than the highest twenty percent of the graduating class (including students elected in the junior year) as determined by GPA or by class rank when no grades are assigned. A junior must rank not lower than the highest ten percent of the junior class. A graduate student must have no less than two thirds of his graduate credit hours as "A" or the equivalent when letter grades are nonexistent.

Government The government is vested in the Board of Regents, which consists of the national past presidents and general officers of the national organization. Conventions are held biennially. The chapters, subject to the approval of the Board of Regents, may elect honorary members.

Traditions and Insignia The badge is a gold key in the form of the Grecian lyre at the base of which are the letters ΠΚΛ on a black enamel background. The symbols of music and drama, Pan's pipes and mask and foils, are on each side of the three strings of the lyre. The badge is worn as a pin or pendant. The colors of each chapter correspond to the colors of the institution.

Publications Pi Kappa Lambda publishes a series of studies in American Music. A newsletter is published twice a year.

Headquarters School of Music, Northwestern University, Evanston, Illinois 60201.

Membership Active chapters 170. Inactive chapters 4. Chapter roll:

1918	Alpha, Northwestern
1920	Beta, Nebraska
1921	Delta, Pacific (CA)
1921	Gamma, Knox
1923	Epsilon, Ohio Wesleyan
1923	Eta, USC
1923	Zeta, Illinois
1926	Theta, Oberlin
1927	Iota, New England Conservatory
1927	Kappa, Kansas
1927	*Lambda, Louisville* (1933)
1928	Mu, Drake
1929	*Nu, Grinnell* (1970)
1935	Xi, Rollins
1936	Omicron, DePauw
1936	Pi, Cincinnati
1938	Rho, Converse
1938	Sigma, Redlands
1940	Tau, North Carolina
1941	Upsilon, Wooster
1943	Phi, Florida State
1945	Chi, Michigan
1948	Alpha Alpha, North Texas
1948	Alpha Beta, Indiana
1948	Alpha Delta, Howard
1948	Alpha Gamma, Cornell Col. (IA)
1948	Omega, Texas
1948	Psi, Montevallo
1949	Alpha Epsilon, Rhodes
1949	Alpha Zeta, Southern Mississippi
1950	Alpha Eta, Southern Methodist
1951	Alpha Theta, Lawrence
1955	Alpha Iota, Ball State
1955	Alpha Kappa, Boston U

1955	Alpha Lambda, Oklahoma
1956	Alpha Mu, Central Missouri State
1956	Alpha Nu, Ithaca
1957	Alpha Omicron, Millikin
1957	Alpha Pi, Alabama
1957	Alpha Rho, Ohio State
1957	Alpha Xi, Willamette
1958	Alpha Sigma, Minnesota
1958	Alpha Tau, Colorado
1960	Alpha Phi, Iowa
1960	Alpha Upsilon, Oklahoma City
1961	*Alpha Chi, New Mexico* (1973)
1962	Alpha Psi, Missouri, Kansas City
1963	Alpha Omega, Montana
1963	Beta Alpha, Michigan State
1963	Beta Beta, Miami (FL)
1963	Beta Gamma, Stetson
1964	Beta Delta, St. Olaf
1964	Beta Epsilon, Idaho
1964	*Beta Eta, Cal, Santa Barbara* (1986)
1964	Beta Iota, Syracuse
1964	Beta Theta, Oregon
1964	Beta Zeta, East Carolina
1965	Beta Kappa, Walla Walla
1965	Beta Lambda, L.S.U.
1965	Beta Mu, Southern Illinois
1965	Beta Nu, Tulsa
1965	Beta Xi, Cleveland Music
1966	Beta Omicron, Wyoming
1966	Beta Pi, Eastman School
1968	Beta Rho, Catholic
1968	Beta Sigma, Western Michigan
1968	Beta Tau, Georgia
1968	Beta Upsilon, Sam Houston
1969	Beta Chi, Brigham Young
1969	Beta Omega, Cal State, Fullerton
1969	Beta Phi, Ohio
1969	Beta Psi, Tennessee
1970	Gamma Alpha, Carson-Newman
1970	Gamma Beta, Furman
1970	Gamma Delta, Kentucky
1970	Gamma Epsilon, Texas Christian
1970	Gamma Gamma, Missouri
1970	Gamma Gamma, Missouri
1970	Gamma Zeta, Florida
1971	Gama Theta, South Carolina
1971	Gamma Eta, Appalachian
1971	Gamma Iota, Memphis State
1971	Gamma Kappa, Cal State, Northridge
1971	Gamma Theta, South Carolina
1972	Gamma Lambda, Northern State
1973	Gamma Mu, Meredith
1973	Gamma Nu, Iowa State
1973	Gamma Xi, Northern Colorado
1974	Gamma Chi, Hofstra
1974	Gamma Omicron, Samford
1974	Gamma Phi, Wisconsin, Stevens Point
1974	Gamma Pi, Spelman
1974	Gamma Rho, Miami (OH)
1974	Gamma Sigma, Northern Iowa
1974	Gamma Tau, Baylor
1974	Gamma Upsilon, Illinois Wesleyan

1975	Delta Alpha, Queens (NY)
1975	Gamma Omega, Anderson
1975	Gamma Psi, Boston Conservatory
1976	Delta Beta, Southern Illinois, Edwardsville
1976	Delta Delta, Southwestern Louisiana
1976	Delta Epsilon, Virginia Commonwealth
1976	Delta Gamma, Morehead
1976	Delta Zeta, Butler
1977	Delta Eta, Westminster Choir
1977	Delta Iota, Stephen F. Austin
1977	Delta Kappa, Midwestern
1977	Delta Lambda, Kansas State
1977	Delta Mu, Indiana State
1977	Delta Nu, Eastern New Mexico
1977	Delta Omicron, Bowling Green
1977	Delta Theta, Wisconsin, Eau Claire
1977	Delta Xi, Cal State, Sacramento
1978	Delta Pi, Maryland
1978	Delta Rho, Glassboro
1978	Delta Sigma, West Chester
1978	Delta Tau, Cleveland
1979	Delta Phi, Washington State
1979	Delta Upsilon, Evansville
1980	Delta Chi, Kent
1980	Delta Omega, SUNY Col., Fredonia
1980	Delta Psi, Immaculata
1981	Epsilon Alpha, Birmingham-Southern
1981	Epsilon Beta, Shorter
1981	Epsilon Delta, Ouachita Baptist
1981	Epsilon Epsilon, Augustana
1981	Epsilon Gamma, Hartford
1982	Epsilon Eta, Belmont
1982	Epsilon Iota, Moorhead
1982	Epsilon Kappa, Andrews
1982	Epsilon Theta, West Virginia
1982	Epsilon Zeta, Alabama State
1983	Epsilon Lambda, Wayne State (MI)
1983	Epsilon Mu, Albion
1983	Epsilon Nu, Wisconsin, Madison
1983	Epsilon Omicron, Peabody Conservatory
1983	Epsilon Xi, Cal State, Long Beach
1984	Epsilon Phi, N.Y.U.
1984	Epsilon Pi, Hardin-Simmons
1984	Epsilon Rho, Jacksonville
1984	Epsilon Sigma, Arkansas
1984	Epsilon Tau, Southwest Texas
1984	Epsilon Upsilon, Hawaii
1985	Epsilon Chi, Illinois State
1985	Epsilon Omega, Luther
1985	Epsilon Psi, Evangel
1986	Zeta Alpha, Texas, El Paso
1986	Zeta Beta, Southwest Missouri
1986	Zeta Gamma, Northern Illinois
1987	Zeta Delta, Hope
1987	Zeta Epsilon, Marywood
1987	Zeta Eta, DePaul
1987	Zeta Zeta, Southwest Baptist
1988	Zeta Iota, Penn State
1988	Zeta Kappa, Arkansas State
1988	Zeta Lambda, Capital
1988	Zeta Mu, SUNY Col., Potsdam
1988	Zeta Nu, Colorado State

1988	Zeta Omicron, Houghton
1988	Zeta Theta, Duquesne
1988	Zeta Xi, Tennessee Tech
1989	Zeta Chi, Gustavus Adolphus
1989	Zeta Phi, Connecticut
1989	Zeta Pi, Oklahoma Baptist
1989	Zeta Psi, SUNY Col., Buffalo
1989	Zeta Rho, Delta State
1989	Zeta Sigma, Maine
1989	Zeta Tau, Houston
1989	Zeta Upsilon, Rhode Island
1990	Eta Alpha, West Texas
1990	Eta Beta, Rutgers
1990	Eta Delta, Valparaiso
1990	Eta Gamma, Auburn
1990	Zeta Omega, Arizona State

Pi Omega Pi

(BUSINESS EDUCATION)

ACTIVE PIN

PI OMEGA PI, national business teacher education society for men and women, was founded at the Northeast Missouri State Teachers College, Kirksville, June 13, 1923, by Dr. P. O. Selby, head of the department of business education. Edwin Myers, a charter member, designed the badge.

The original constitution provided that Alpha Chapter should rule the organization until five chapters had been established. The additional four came at the rate of about one a year. In December, 1927, Alpha Chapter called a meeting of the others in Kansas City to form a national organization. At this convention a constitution was adopted, officers were elected, and biennial student delegate meetings were provided for. The policy of meeting the same week and in the same city as the National Business Teachers Association convention was adopted.

Purpose To create and encourage interest and promote scholarship in business education. To foster high ethical standards in business and professional life among teachers. To encourage civic responsibility. To create a fellowship among teachers of business subjects. To teach the ideal of service as the basis of worthy enterprise.

Eligibility Each candidate must be enrolled in a business teacher education curriculum and must have expressed an intention of becoming a teacher of business subjects. Each candidate must possess the following qualifications: (a) Completion of at least three semesters or five quarters of college courses including at least fifteen semester hours or twenty-two quarter hours in business and/or education subjects; (b) Attainment of general scholarship sufficient to place him within the upper thirty-five percent of his college class (sophomore, junior, senior, graduate) and the achievement of an average grade of B or higher, or its equivalent in other grading systems, in all courses in business and/or education.

Major Activities   Each year the National Council selects ten chapters for special recognition; the first place chapter is presented a plaque and has its name inscribed on a traveling trophy; the remaining nine chapters receive certificates signed by the National Council. A national convention is held biennially to conduct Society business. Fifty-year chapters receive Golden Awards and sponsors in service five or more years receive Distinguished Service Awards.

Traditions and Insignia   The emblem is a gold key bearing the Greek letters ΠΩΠ horizontally arranged, surmounted by the lamp of learning. The colors are blue and silver.

Publications   The Society publishes a newsletter, *Here and There*, dealing with activities in various chapters four times a year. An information booklet, *This Is Your Society*, is published biennially.

Headquarters   Department of Business Education, Murray State University, Murray, Kentucky 42071.

Membership   Active chapters 101. Inactive chapters 50. Total number of initiates 50,009. Chapter roll:

1923	Alpha, Northeast Missouri
1924	Beta, Northwest Missouri
1925	Gamma, Northern Iowa
1927	Delta, Peru
1927	*Epsilon, Iowa (1980)*
1928	Eta, North Texas
1928	Theta, Illinois State
1928	Zeta, Northern Colorado
1929	*Iota, Northern State (1968)*
1929	Kappa, Indiana (PA)
1929	Lambda, Fort Hays
1929	Mu, Emporia
1929	*Nu, Kearney (1979)*
1929	Xi, Ball State
1930	*Omicron, Pittsburg State, Kansas (1978)*
1930	Pi, Valley City
1930	*Rho, Northeastern (OK) (1967)*
1931	Sigma, Southeastern Oklahoma
1931	*Tau, Northern Arizona (1977)*
1934	*Alpha Alpha, San Jose (1978)*
1934	Chi, Indiana State
1934	Omega, Western Illinois
1934	Phi, Sam Houston
1934	Psi, Wisconsin, Whitewater
1934	Upsilon, Trenton
1935	Alpha Beta, Eastern Kentucky
1935	Alpha Delta, Bloomsburg
1935	Alpha Gamma, Mississippi for Women
1936	Alpha Epsilon, Mary Washington
1937	Alpha Zeta, Southwest Missouri
1938	*Alpha Eta, Oklahoma State (1970)*
1938	Alpha Iota, Arizona State
1938	Alpha Theta, Chadron
1939	Alpha Kappa, Arkansas State

1939	*Alpha Lambda, Oklahoma (1972)*
1939	Alpha Mu, Central State (OK)
1939	Alpha Nu, Northwestern Louisiana
1939	Alpha Omicron, St. Cloud
1939	Alpha Pi, Mississippi State
1939	*Alpha Xi, Ohio State (1963)*
1940	Alpha Chi, Eastern Illinois
1940	Alpha Phi, Duquesne
1940	Alpha Rho, Wayne State (NE)
1940	Alpha Sigma, Southern Mississippi
1940	*Alpha Tau, USC (1961)*
1940	*Alpha Upsilon, Miami (OH) (1972)*
1941	*Alpha Omega, Drexel (1970)*
1941	Alpha Psi, Bowling Green
1941	*Beta Delta, N.Y.U. (1964)*
1941	*Beta Gamma, Tennessee (1963)*
1941	Beta Zeta, Southern Illinois
1942	Beta Alpha, George Peabody
1942	*Beta Beta, Akron (1968)*
1942	Beta Epsilon, Montana State
1942	Beta Eta, SUNY, Albany
1942	*Beta Iota, Wayne State (MI) (1963)*
1942	*Beta Theta, New Mexico Highlands (1978)*
1944	Beta Kappa, East Carolina
1944	Beta Lambda, Shippensburg
1945	*Beta Mu, Tennessee Tech (1981)*
1945	Beta Nu, Madison Col
1946	*Beta Xi, Boston U (1968)*
1947	Beta Omicron, Arizona
1948	*Beta Pi, Concord (1960)*
1948	Beta Rho, Central Missouri State
1948	Beta Sigma, Montclair
1949	*Beta Chi, San Diego U. (1971)*
1949	Beta Phi, Eastern Michigan
1949	Beta Tau, East Texas
1949	*Beta Upsilon, Central Methodist (1977)*
1950	*Beta Omega, New Jersey State Teachers (1956)*
1950	Beta Psi, Tennessee State
1950	Gamma Alpha, Western Michigan
1950	Gamma Beta, West Liberty
1950	*Gamma Delta, Cal State, Chico (1978)*
1950	*Gamma Gamma, Florida State (1976)*
1951	Gamma Epsilon, North Dakota
1951	Gamma Eta, Bluefield
1951	*Gamma Iota, South Dakota (1982)*
1951	Gamma Kappa, Southwest Texas
1951	*Gamma Lambda, V.P.I. (1964)*
1951	Gamma Theta, Lincoln Memorial (TN)
1951	*Gamma Zeta, Penn State (1962)*
1952	Gamma Mu, Marshall
1952	Gamma Nu, Georgia
1952	Gamma Omicron, Central Arkansas
1952	Gamma Xi, Texas Tech
1953	*Gamma Pi, Kent (1980)*
1953	*Gamma Rho, Bethune-Cookman (1976)*
1953	*Gamma Sigma, Cal State, Fresno (1971)*
1953	*Gamma Tau, UCLA (1961)*
1953	Gamma Upsilon, Murray State
1954	*Gamma Chi, Middle Tennessee (1980)*
1954	Gamma Phi, North Carolina A & T
1955	Gamma Omega, Texas

1955	*Gamma Psi, Appalachian* (1973)
1956	*Delta Alpha, Salem (WV)* (1981)
1956	*Delta Beta, Miami (FL)* (1971)
1956	*Delta Gamma, Cal State, Long Beach* (1970)
1957	*Delta Delta, Michigan State* (1974)
1957	Delta Epsilon, Northern Illinois
1957	*Delta Eta, Detroit* (1970)
1957	Delta Zeta, Southeast Missouri
1958	*Delta Iota, Georgia Southern* (1981)
1958	*Delta Theta, Hawaii* (1960)
1959	Delta Kappa, West Texas
1959	Delta Lambda, Southern
1960	Delta Mu, Delta State
1960	Delta Nu, Virginia State, Petersburg
1960	Delta Omicron, Cal State, Sacramento
1960	*Delta Xi, Kansas* (1966)
1961	Delta Pi, Ferris
1961	Delta Rho, Longwood
1961	*Delta Sigma, Baylor* (1967)
1961	*Delta Tau, Colorado State* (1972)
1962	Delta Phi, Houston
1962	*Delta Upsilon, Mississippi* (1976)
1963	Delta Chi, Temple
1964	Delta Omega, Minot
1964	*Delta Psi, Mary Hardin-Baylor* (1966)
1964	*Epsilon Alpha, Edgewood* (1976)
1966	Epsilon Beta, Southern Illinois, Edwardsville
1966	Epsilon Gamma, Norfolk
1967	Epsilon Delta, Northern Michigan
1968	Epsilon Epsilon, Rider
1968	Epsilon Zeta, Radford
1970	Epsilon Eta, Mankato
1970	Epsilon Theta, Western Kentucky
1971	Epsilon Iota, Texas Southern
1972	Epsilon Kappa, Moorhead
1973	Epsilon Lambda, Fayetteville
1973	Epsilon Mu, Wichita
1973	Epsilon Nu, Bishop
1973	Epsilon Omicron, Prairie View
1973	Epsilon Xi, Jackson (MS)
1974	Epsilon Pi, Jarvis Christian
1974	Epsilon Rho, Grambling
1974	Epsilon Sigma, Wisconsin, Eau Claire
1974	Epsilon Tau, New Hampshire
1975	Epsilon Phi, Pan American
1975	*Epsilon Upsilon, Mississippi Valley* (1976)
1976	Epsilon Chi, Northeast Louisiana
1976	Epsilon Psi, Missouri Southern
1977	Epsilon Omega, Wiley
1977	Zeta Alpha, Florida A & M
1978	*Zeta Beta, Mississippi* (1979)
1978	Zeta Delta, Alabama State
1978	Zeta Gamma, South Alabama
1979	Zeta Epsilon, Central Michigan
1981	Zeta Zeta, Alabama
1983	Zeta Eta, Kansas State

Pi Sigma Alpha

(POLITICAL SCIENCE)

ACTIVE PIN

PI SIGMA ALPHA was founded at the University of Texas in 1920 as a national honor society in political science. Prof. C. Perry Patterson, of the Department of Government, University of Texas, was chiefly responsible for the organization of the society. Admitted to ACHS in 1949.

Purpose To stimulate productive scholarship and intelligent interest in the subject of government among men and women students at institutions of higher learning in which chapters are maintained.

Eligibility Juniors, seniors, and graduate students are eligible for membership if they possess the following qualifications: Completion of fifteen quarter hours or ten semester hours of work in government, political science, international relations, or public administration, including at least one course not open to students in the first two years of collegiate work; Maintenance of an average of B or higher in all courses in government, political science, international relations, and public administration, and the maintenance of general scholarship sufficient to place them within the upper third of their college class; and Fulfillment of such additional academic requirements as may have been prescribed by the local chapters. Any member of the faculty of the department of political science or government at any institution at which a local chapter is located may be elected as a member by any local chapter or by the national convention. Membership in the Society may be secured also through election as an honorary member. Only distinguished persons who have made valuable contributions to political science or government are eligible for election into honorary membership. Each chapter may elect not more than two persons in a year for this class of membership.

Government Conventions are held biennially in the even-numbered years at the time and place of the meeting of the American Political Science Association. Between conventions the national officers constitute a council with full authority to conduct the business of the society.

Major Activities Biennial national convention to transact Society business and consider any matters within the field of the Society's activities. Intellectual activity through sponsorship of speakers, forums, conferences, and chapter awards and grants for best activity program and best student.

Publication Interchange of ideas and information regarding political science and chapter activities through circulation of a quarterly *Newsletter*. Publication of a series of books, monographs, and symposiums by leading political scientists.

Headquarters Bureau of Governmental Research, University of Maryland, College Park, Maryland 20740.

Membership Active chapters 380. Inactive chapters 1. Total number of initiates 105,000. Chapter roll:

1920	Alpha, Texas
1922	Beta, Oklahoma
1922	Gamma, Kansas
1923	Delta, Kentucky
1923	Epsilon, UCLA
1926	Eta, Stanford
1926	Iota, Cal, Berkeley
1926	Kappa, Washington (MO)
1926	Theta, L.S.U.
1926	Zeta, Southern Methodist
1927	Lambda, USC
1928	Nu, Washington (WA)
1928	Xi, Pitt
1929	Chi, New Mexico
1929	Mu, Columbia (NY)
1929	Omicron, Ohio State
1929	Pi, Wisconsin, Madison
1930	Rho, Bucknell
1931	Sigma, Wayne State (MI)
1931	Tau, Nebraska
1932	Alpha Alpha, Akron
1932	Phi, DePauw
1932	Upsilon, Ohio Wesleyan
1935	Omega, San Francisco
1935	Psi, Washington and Jefferson
1937	Alpha Beta, Indiana
1937	Alpha Gamma, Marshall
1938	Alpha Delta, Wichita
1938	Alpha Epsilon, Emory
1938	Alpha Zeta, Maryland
1939	Alpha Eta, Texas Tech
1939	Alpha Theta, Washington State
1946	Alpha Iota, Utah State
1946	Alpha Kappa, Utah
1947	Alpha Lambda, Wooster
1947	Alpha Mu, Bowling Green
1947	Alpha Nu, Denison
1947	Alpha Xi, Wittenberg
1948	Alpha Omicron, Michigan State
1948	Alpha Pi, Georgia
1948	Alpha Rho, Mississippi
1949	Alpha Chi, North Carolina
1949	Alpha Phi, Idaho State
1949	Alpha Psi, St. Lawrence
1949	Alpha Sigma, Tulane
1949	Alpha Tau, Bradley
1949	Alpha Upsilon, Michigan
1950	Alpha Omega, Kent
1950	Beta Alpha, Vanderbilt
1950	Beta Beta, Case Western Reserve
1950	Beta Delta, Cal, Santa Barbara
1950	Beta Epsilon, Syracuse
1950	Beta Eta, N.Y.U.
1950	Beta Gamma, Florida
1950	Beta Kappa, Queens (NY)
1950	Beta Zeta, Tennessee
1951	Beta Iota, Citadel
1951	Beta Theta, Oregon
1952	Beta Lambda, Texas Christian
1952	Beta Mu, Brigham Young
1953	Beta Nu, Valparaiso
1953	Beta Omicron, Rutgers
1953	Beta Pi, Penn State
1953	Beta Rho, Yale
1953	Beta Sigma, Knox
1953	Beta Tau, Penn
1953	Beta Xi, Richmond
1954	Beta Chi, Iowa
1954	Beta Omega, Washington and Lee
1954	Beta Phi, New Hampshire
1954	Beta Psi, American
1954	Beta Upsilon, North Texas
1954	Gamma Alpha, Florida State
1955	Gamma Beta, Colgate
1955	Gamma Delta, Notre Dame
1955	Gamma Epsilon, Rhode Island
1955	Gamma Eta, Baylor
1955	Gamma Gamma, Connecticut
1955	Gamma Iota, Southern Illinois
1955	Gamma Theta, Duke
1955	Gamma Zeta, Missouri
1956	Gamma Chi, South Dakota
1956	Gamma Kappa, Howard
1956	Gamma Lambda, Atlanta
1956	Gamma Mu, Illinois
1956	Gamma Nu, South Dakota
1956	Gamma Omicron, Alabama
1956	Gamma Xi, Boston U
1957	Gamma Pi, West Virginia
1957	Gamma Rho, Johns Hopkins
1958	Gamma Sigma, U of the South
1959	Gamma Phi, Colorado
1959	Gamma Tau, Whittier
1959	Gamma Upsilon, San Diego U.
1960	Delta Alpha, Hunter
1960	Delta Beta, Louisville
1960	Delta Delta, San Francisco State
1960	Delta Gamma, Northeastern
1960	Gamma Omega, Cal State, Los Angeles
1961	Delta Epsilon, Claremont
1961	Delta Eta, Georgetown U
1961	Delta Theta, Arizona State
1961	Delta Zeta, Fordham
1962	Delta Iota, Arizona
1963	Delta Kappa, Oklahoma State
1963	Delta Lambda, Massachusetts
1964	Delta Mu, Miami (OH)
1964	Delta Nu, Lehigh
1964	Delta Xi, Nevada
1965	Delta Omicron, Cal State, Long Beach
1965	Delta Pi, Miami (FL)
1965	Delta Rho, Temple
1965	Delta Sigma, Cal State, Northridge
1966	Delta Chi, Macalester

1966	Delta Phi, Colorado State	1975	Eta Zeta, Missouri
1966	Delta Psi, Eastern Illinois	1976	Eta Chi, Southwest Missouri
1966	Delta Tau, Western Washington	1976	Eta Lambda, Clemson
1966	Delta Upsilon, Cal, Davis	1976	Eta Mu, East Tennessee
1967	Delta Omega, Purdue	1976	Eta Nu, St. Joseph's (PA)
1967	Epsilon Alpha, CUNY, Brooklyn	1976	Eta Omega, Sam Houston
1967	Epsilon Beta, Wyoming	1976	Eta Omicron, Westminster (PA)
1967	Epsilon Delta, Maine	1976	Eta Phi, Augustana (SD)
1967	Epsilon Epsilon, Texas, El Paso	1976	Eta Pi, Hofstra
1967	Epsilon Gamma, SUNY, Albany	1976	Eta Psi, Roanoke
1968	Epsilon Eta, Cal State, Fullerton	1976	Eta Rho, William and Mary
1968	Epsilon Iota, San Jose	1976	Eta Sigma, Kean (NJ)
1968	Epsilon Theta, Arkansas	1976	Eta Tau, Appalachian
1968	Epsilon Zeta, Northern Illinois	1976	Eta Upsilon, Muhlenberg
1969	Epsilon Kappa, St. Louis	1976	Eta Xi, Wisconsin, River Falls
1969	Epsilon Lambda, East Carolina	1977	Theta Alpha, Creighton
1969	Epsilon Mu, Montana	1977	Theta Beta, Mississippi State
1970	Epsilon Nu, Auburn	1977	Theta Delta, Missouri, St. Louis
1970	Epsilon Omicron, Marquette	1977	Theta Epsilon, North Carolina, Charlotte
1970	Epsilon Pi, Iowa State	1977	Theta Eta, Detroit
1970	Epsilon Xi, Wisconsin, Milwaukee	1977	Theta Gamma, Shippensburg
1971	Epsilon Rho, New Orleans	1977	Theta Iota, Cal State, San Bernadino
1971	Epsilon Sigma, Lake Forest	1977	Theta Kappa, Indiana, South Bend
1971	Epsilon Tau, CUNY, Lehman	1977	Theta Lambda, Northeastern Illinois
1971	Epsilon Upsilon, V.P.I.	1977	Theta Mu, San Diego U
1972	Epsilon Chi, Providence	1977	Theta Nu, Alma
1972	Epsilon Omega, Villanova	1977	Theta Theta, Midwestern
1972	Epsilon Phi, Western Illinois	1977	Theta Xi, Susquehanna
1972	Epsilon Psi, Cal State, Sacramento	1977	Theta Zeta, Wright State
1972	Zeta Alpha, Carroll	1978	Iota Alpha, Canisius
1972	Zeta Beta, Western Kentucky	1978	Iota Beta, Wisconsin, La Crosse
1972	Zeta Delta, SUNY Col., Cortland	1978	Iota Delta, Seton Hall
1972	Zeta Epsilon, North Carolina State	1978	Iota Epsilon, Stephen F. Austin
1972	Zeta Eta, Memphis State	1978	Iota Eta, Arkansas State
1972	Zeta Gamma, East Texas	1978	Iota Gamma, Montana State
1972	Zeta Iota, Ball State	1978	Iota Theta, Pittsburg State, Kansas
1972	Zeta Kappa, Colby	1978	Iota Zeta, Ohio
1972	Zeta Theta, SUNY, Binghamton	1978	Theta Chi, St. Peter's
1972	Zeta Zeta, Dayton	1978	Theta Omega, Eastern Kentucky
1973	Zeta Lambda, Lamar	1978	Theta Omicron, Hampden-Sydney
1973	Zeta Mu, Loyola, Chicago	1978	Theta Phi, Nevada, Las Vegas
1973	Zeta Nu, Middle Tennessee	1978	Theta Pi, Northern Arizona
1973	Zeta Omicron, Central Missouri State	1978	Theta Psi, Texas A & M
1973	Zeta Pi, South Florida	1978	Theta Rho, Pembroke
1973	Zeta Xi, Delaware	1978	Theta Sigma, Elizabethtown
1974	Eta Alpha, Jersey City	1978	Theta Tau, Northeast Missouri
1974	Eta Beta, George Washington	1978	Theta Upsilon, Northeastern (OK)
1974	Zeta Chi, Montclair	1979	Iota Chi, East Stroudsburg
1974	Zeta Omega, Old Dominion	1979	Iota Iota, Hawaii
1974	Zeta Phi, Murray State	1979	Iota Kappa, William Paterson
1974	Zeta Psi, Morgan State	1979	Iota Lambda, Monmouth (IL)
1974	Zeta Rho, Drew	1979	Iota Mu, Arkansas, Little Rock
1974	Zeta Sigma, Tulsa	1979	Iota Nu, Lycoming
1974	Zeta Tau, Eastern Michigan	1979	Iota Omega, Frostburg
1974	Zeta Upsilon, Union (NY)	1979	Iota Omicron, Evansville
1975	Eta Delta, Florida Atlantic	1979	Iota Phi, Cal Poly, Pomona
1975	Eta Epsilon, Loyola, New Orleans	1979	Iota Pi, Auburn, Montgomery
1975	Eta Eta, New Mexico	1979	Iota Psi, Spring Hill
1975	Eta Gamma, Holy Cross	1979	Iota Rho, Southeast Missouri
1975	Eta Iota, Boston State	1979	Iota Sigma, Charleston (SC)
1975	Eta Kappa, Hope	1979	Iota Tau, SUNY Col., New Paltz
1975	Eta Theta, SUNY, Stony Brook	1979	Iota Upsilon, Thiel

1979   Iota Xi, Kansas State
1979   Kappa Alpha, Rider
1979   Kappa Beta, Pitt, Johnstown
1980   Kappa Delta, North Carolina, Wilmington
1980   Kappa Epsilon, Navy
1980   Kappa Eta, Austin Peay
1980   Kappa Gamma, Oregon State
1980   Kappa Iota, Scranton
1980   Kappa Kappa, Indiana State
1980   Kappa Mu, South Alabama
1980   Kappa Nu, SUNY Col., Potsdam
1980   Kappa Omicron, Fairleigh Dickinson,
         Rutherford
1980   Kappa Phi, Grand Valley
1980   Kappa Pi, Texas, Arlington
1980   Kappa Rho, Sonoma State
1980   Kappa Sigma, Illinois State
1980   Kappa Tau, Drake
1980   Kappa Theta, Grambling
1980   Kappa Upsilon, Mary Washington
1980   Kappa Xi, Madison Col
1980   Kappa Zeta, IUPUI
1981   Kappa Chi, Fairfield
1981   Kappa Omega, Lenoir-Rhyne
1981   Kappa Psi, Virginia State, Norfolk
1981   Mu Alpha, Illinois, Chicago
1981   Mu Beta, Radford
1981   Mu Delta, Hartwick
1981   Mu Epsilon, Mars Hill
1981   Mu Eta, Rutgers, Camden
1981   Mu Gamma, Baltimore U.
1981   Mu Iota, Mount Mary's (CA)
1981   Mu Kappa, Southeastern Massachusetts
1981   Mu Lambda, Central Washington
1981   Mu Mu, Weber
1981   Mu Nu, Westfield
1981   Mu Omicron, C. W. Post
1981   Mu Phi, Duquesne
1981   Mu Pi, Winthrop
1981   Mu Rho, Hanover
1981   Mu Sigma, Central Florida
1981   Mu Tau, Tennessee, Martin
1981   Mu Theta, Catholic
1981   Mu Upsilon, John Carroll
1981   Mu Xi, Tri-State
1981   Mu Zeta, Baldwin-Wallace
1982   Mu Chi, Albion
1982   Mu Omega, Texas Woman's
1982   Mu Psi, St. Mary's (NS)
1982   Nu Alpha, Long Island
1982   Nu Beta, SUNY Col., Oswego
1982   Nu Delta, Alabama
1982   Nu Epsilon, West Georgia
1982   Nu Eta, Harding
1982   Nu Gamma, Eastern Washington
1982   Nu Iota, Trenton
1982   Nu Kappa, South Carolina, Spartanburg

1982   Nu Lambda, Toledo
1982   Nu Mu, Northwestern
1982   Nu Nu, St. Mary's
1982   Nu Omicron, Central Connecticut
1982   Nu Pi, Portland State
1982   Nu Rho, SUNY Col., Brockport
1982   Nu Sigma, Jackson (MS)
1982   Nu Tau, Kennesaw
1982   Nu Theta, Adelphi
1982   Nu Xi, North Dakota
1982   Nu Zeta, Wake Forest
1983   Nu Chi, L.S.U., Shreveport
1983   Nu Omega, Oakland
1983   Nu Phi, Georgia State
1983   Nu Psi, Gettysburg
1983   Nu Upsilon, Tampa
1983   Xi Alpha, Dickinson
1983   Xi Beta, Fairleigh Dickinson, Madison
1983   Xi Delta, Virginia
1983   Xi Epsilon, Ramapo
1983   Xi Eta, Chaminade
1983   Xi Gamma, West Chester
1983   Xi Iota, DePaul
1983   Xi Kappa, North Georgia
1983   Xi Lambda, George Mason
1983   Xi Mu, Southern
1983   Xi Nu, Georgia Southwestern
1983   Xi Theta, SUNY Col., Buffalo
1983   Xi Zeta, Centre College
1984   Omicron Alpha, St. Olaf
1984   Omicron Beta, Connecticut Col
1984   Omicron Delta, Lafayette
1984   Omicron Epsilon, Manhattan
1984   Omicron Eta, Maryland, Baltimore County
1984   Omicron Gamma, Birmingham-Southern
1984   Omicron Iota, Northwest Missouri
1984   Omicron Theta, Cal Poly, Pomona
1984   Omicron Zeta, Washburn
1984   Xi Chi, Boise
1984   Xi Omega, Northern Kentucky
1984   Xi Omicron, Trinity (TX)
1984   Xi Pi, Virginia Commonwealth
1984   Xi Psi, King's
1984   Xi Xi, SUNY Col., Geneseo
1985   Omicron Kappa, West Virginia State
1985   Omicron Lambda, Illinois Wesleyan
1985   Omicron Mu, Loyola (MD)
1985   Omicron Nu, Western Maryland
1985   Omicron Omicron, Puget Sound
1985   Omicron Pi, West Liberty
1985   Omicron Rho, Marist
1985   Omicron Sigma, Colorado, Denver
1986   Omicron Phi, Sul Ross
1986   Omicron Tau, Tennessee, Chattanooga
1986   Omicron Upsilon, Wisconsin, Eau Claire
1986   Omicron Xi, Lynchburg

Pi Tau Sigma

(MECHANICAL ENGINEERING)

ACTIVE PIN

PI TAU SIGMA is a mechanical engineering society whose purpose is to establish a closer bond of fellowship which will result in mutual benefit to those men in the study and in the profession of mechanical engineering who by their academic or practical achievements manifest a real and marked ability in their chosen work.

Active members are chosen on the basis of high scholastic achievement, engineering ability, and personality. Students are not eligible until their junior year in a college whose mechanical engineering curriculum has been accredited by the Engineers' Council for Professional Development. Not more than 25 per cent of the members who complete their junior year are eligible, and not more than 35 per cent of the seniors are eligible. Membership is also available to graduate students who have fulfilled the requirements for membership in their undergraduate days. Honorary membership is based upon successful achievements by practicing engineers and professors of mechanical engineering.

With the Twentieth Century came the realization that honor societies made a definite contribution to the department and that membership required active participation. Pi Tau Sigma came into being on March 16, 1915, at the University of Illinois. A similar organization embarked November 15, 1915, at Wisconsin. The formal merger of the two groups into a national organization with the name Pi Tau Sigma took place in Chicago on March 12, 1916, with Oliver C. K. Hutchinson and John B. Wilkinson as co-chairmen.

Growth   In ten years Pi Tau Sigma grew to six chapters in the middle west (Illinois Alpha, Wisconsin Alpha, Purdue Beta, Minnesota Gamma, Illinois Delta, and Missouri Epsilon). In 1925 the expansion continued to the east with the Penn State Zeta Chapter being installed. Six years later the Texas Kappa Chapter and the following year the Colorado Mu Chapter established chapters in the south and west. Also in 1932 the expansion continued southeast to include Georgia Tech Nu Chapter. It was not until nine years later that the first chapter was installed on the Pacific coast (Oregon State Omega). In twenty-six years Pi Tau Sigma became a truly national honorary mechanical engineering fraternity with a total of twenty-five chapters. During the succeeding four years nine additional chapters were installed.

From 1947 to 1958 forty new chapters were installed.

Government   Government is by annual convention in which one undergraduate delegate from each chapter and the members of the National Council constitute the voting members. The National Council is composed of national officers consisting of a president, three vice-presidents, and a secretary-treasurer, who are elected by the national convention for terms to insure continuity of organization. The council acts as a recess government by carrying out the policies of the society.

Traditions and Insignia   Each chapter presents an award annually to the sophomore mechanical engineer with the highest scholastic average at that institution. The national organization annually makes two awards at the American Society of Mechanical Engineers' national convention. The Pi Tau Sigma Gold Medal Award is given to a young mechanical engineer for outstanding achievement in his profession within ten years after graduation from a mechanical engineering curriculum of an American college or university accredited by the Engineers' Council for Professional Development. The Charles Russ Richards Memorial Award is given to a mechanical engineer who has demonstrated outstanding achievement within a period of not less than 20 years or more than 25 years following graduation from a mechanical engineering curriculum of an American college or university accredited by the Engineers' Council for Professional Development. This award is named after Charles Russ Richards, the founder of Pi Tau Sigma.

The insignia is a key or pin with the Carnot cycle predominate. The colors are murrey and azure; the flower is the white rose.

Publications   An annual publication, *The Condenser*, is sent to each new member. The magazine contains messages from the national officers, proceedings of the national annual convention, reports on activities of the various chapters, and biographies of new honorary members. Periodically a booklet is published, *The Story of Pi Tau Sigma*, so that each member receives an up-to-date history of all chapters and the constitution.

Headquarters   Box S 161, Tennessee Technological University, Cookeville, Tennessee 38501.

Membership   Active chapters 142. Total number of initiates 86,000. Chapter roll:††

1916	Illinois Alpha, Illinois
1916	Wisconsin Alpha, Wisconsin
1922	Minnesota Gamma, Minnesota
1922	Purdue Beta, Purdue
1924	Illinois Delta, Illinois Tech
1925	Missouri Epsilon, Missouri
1925	Penn State Zeta, Penn State
1926	Cincinnati Eta, Cincinnati
1927	Lehigh Theta, Lehigh

†† This chapter roll is repeated from the 19th edition; no current information was provided.

1930 Carnegie Iota, Caregie Tech
1931 Oklahoma Lambda, Oklahoma State
1931 Texas Kappa, Texas
1932 Colorado Mu, Colorado
1932 Georgia Tech Nu, Georgia Tech
1933 Drexel Xi, Drexel Tech
1935 Iowa Omicron, Iowa
1938 Nebraska Pi, Nebraska
1939 Kansas State Rho, Kansas State
1940 Auburn Chi, Auburn
1940 Oklahoma Sigma, Oklahoma
1940 Pittsburgh Tau, Pitt
1940 Rensselaer Phi, R.P.I.
1940 Virginia Tech Upsilon, V.P.I.
1941 Kansas Psi, Kansas
1941 Oregon State Omega, Oregon State
1942 CCNY Pi Beta, C.C.N.Y.
1942 Iowa State Pi Epsilon, Iowa State
1942 Marquete Pi Delta, Marquette
1942 North Carolina Pi Alpha, North Carolina
1942 West Virginia Pi Gamma, West Virginia
1943 Detroit Pi Eta, Detroit
1943 NYU Pi Zeta, N.Y.U.
1943 Northwestern Pi Theta, Northwestern Tech
1944 Duke Pi Iota, Duke
1947 Kentucky Pi Lambda, Kentucky
1947 M.I.T. Pi Kappa, M.I.T.
1948 Alabama Pi Omicron, Alabama
1948 Brooklyn Poly Pi Pi, Brooklyn Tech
1948 Connecticut Pi Psi, Connecticut
1948 Cornell Pi Tau, Cornell
1948 Michigan Pi Rho, Michigan
1948 N.D.S.U. Pi Upsilon, North Dakota
      Agricultural
1948 New Mexico Pi Sigma, New Mexico
1948 Ohio State Pi Mu, Ohio State
1948 Syracuse Pi Nu, Syracuse
1948 Utah Pi Xi, Utah
1949 California Pi Omega, California
1949 Cooper Union Pi Phi, Cooper Union
1949 John Hopkins Tau Alpha, Johns Hopkins
1949 Southern California Tau Beta, USC
1949 Washington Pi Chi, Washington (MO)
1950 Clarkson Tau Gamma, Clarkson
1950 M.S.U. Tau Epsilon, Michigan State
1950 New Mexico Tau Delta, New Mexico A & M
1950 Tennessee Tau Eta, Tennessee
1951 L.S.U. Tau Zeta, L.S.U.
1951 Newark Tau Theta, Newark Engineering
1952 Northeastern Tau Kappa, Northeastern
1952 Rutgers Tau Iota, Rutgers
1955 Missouri Tau Lambda, Missouri Mines
1956 Maryland Tau Mu, Maryland
1957 Louisiana Tech Tau Xi, Louisiana Tech
1957 Mississippi State Tau Nu, Mississippi State
1958 Montana State Tau Rho, Montana State
1958 Pratt Tau Omicron, Pratt
1958 S.M.U. Tau Sigma, Southern Methodist
1958 Villanova Tau Pi, Villanova
1959 Arkansas Tau Upsilon, Arkansas
1959 W.P.I. Tau Tau, Worcester Tech
1960 Wayne State Tau Phi, Wayne State

1961 Bradley Tau Omega, Bradley
1961 Colorado State Tau Psi, Colorado State
1961 South Dakota Tau Chi, South Dakota
1961 U.S.L. Sigma Alpha, Southwestern
      Louisiana
1962 Notre Dame Sigma Beta, Notre Dame
1964 Arizona State Sigma Gamma, Arizona State
1964 Texas A & M Sigma Delta, Texas A & M
1966 California Sigma Eta, Cal, Long Beach
1966 Houston Sigma Zeta, Houston
1967 Michigan Tech Sigma Iota, Michigan Tech
1967 San Diego State Sigma Theta, San Diego
      State
1968 Sigma Kappa, UCLA
1968 Sigma Lambda, Rose-Hulman
1968 Sigma Mu, Penn
1968 Sigma Nu, Tennessee
1968 Sigma Omicron, Florida
1968 Sigma Xi, Lamar
1969 Sigma Pi, Hawaii
1969 Sigma Rho, Texas
1969 Sigma Sigma, Washington State
1969 Sigma Tau, Manhattan
1970 Sigma Chi, Tulane
1970 Sigma Phi, Rhode Island
1970 Sigma Psi, Tuskegee
1970 Sigma Upsilon, Miami (FL)
1971 Delta Alpha, Vanderbilt
1971 Delta Beta, Cal Poly, Pomona
1971 Delta Gamma, Texas
1971 Sigma Omega, Lafayette
1972 Delta Delta, Tri-State
1972 Delta Epsilon, North Carolina
1973 Delta Eta, Hartford
1973 Delta Theta, West Virginia
1973 Delta Zeta, New Haven
1974 Delta Iota, Toledo
1975 Delta Kappa, Northrop
1975 Delta Lambda, N.Y.U.
1975 Delta Mu, Southern

Psi Chi

(PSYCHOLOGY)

ACTIVE PIN

PSI CHI, the national honor society in psychology, was founded on September 4, 1929, at Yale University during the Ninth International Congress of Psychology. The purpose of the society is to encourage, stimulate, and maintain excellence in scholarship of the individual members in all fields, particularly in psychology; and to advance the science of psychology.

Each chapter is known by the college or university in which it is located. Chapters elect members from among men and women who qualify according to the Psi Chi laws. Distinguished membership is bestowed on persons who have national or international reputations because of the contributions they have made to psychology and Psi Chi. The chapters or a member of the National Council nominate persons for distinguished membership and the National Council elects them.

The Council of the Association of College Honor Societies (ACHS) voted to classify Psi Chi as an honor society at its meeting at Madison, Wisconsin, February 1963, with certain changes to be made in the Psi Chi laws. The changes were made in 1964, and Psi Chi became a member of ACHS in 1965 at the annual ACHS meeting in Chicago.

Eligibility For active student membership, the student must be enrolled in an accredited college or university and must have completed twelve quarter (eight semester) hours of psychology, or nine quarter (six semester) hours and registered for at least three quarter (two semester) hours of psychology in addition, or equivalent credits in psychology. He or she must be registered for major or minor standing in psychology or for a program psychological in nature which is equivalent to such standing. Undergraduate students must rank not lower than the highest thirty-five percent of their class in general scholarship; graduate students must have an average grade of B in all graduate courses. All must have high standards of personal behavior and the vote of two-thirds of those present at a regular meeting of the chapter.

Government A National Council is elected by the chapters and guides the affairs of the society. Psi Chi holds a national convention annually in conjunction with the convention of the American Psychological Association (APA). In addition, Psi Chi holds annual conventions in each of its six regions. Graduate and undergraduate research competitions are held annually.

Traditions and Insignia The badge is a key or pin formed by superimposing the letter Ψ on the letter X.

Publications The *Psi Chi Newsletter* is published quarterly and the *Psi Chi Handbook* biannually. The history is published annually and compiled by decades.

Headquarters 1400 North Uhle Street, Arlington, VA 22201, in the APA Virginia building.

Membership Active chapters 684. Inactive chapters 21. Total number of initiates 195,000. Chapter roll:

1929 Alabama
1929 *Arkansas* (1977)
1929 *Chicago* (1948)
1929 Denver
1929 Drake
1929 Iowa State
1929 Kansas
1929 Nebraska

1929 Ohio
1929 Rutgers
1929 UCLA
1929 USC (1981-1987)
1929 Washington State
1929 Wittenberg
1930 Georgia
1930 Montana
1930 Nebraska Wesleyan
1930 Penn State
1930 Penn
1930 Southern Methodist
1930 Washington (WA)
1930 *Washington and Lee* (1976)
1930 Wyoming
1932 Syracuse
1933 N.Y.U.
1934 Missouri
1934 Tulane
1936 Minnesota
1936 Oklahoma
1939 Beaver
1939 Illinois
1939 Morningside
1939 Utah
1940 Miami (OH)
1941 Cal, Berkeley
1941 Kent
1941 Pittsburg State, Kansas
1942 Baylor
1942 Wisconsin, Madison
1945 L.S.U.
1946 Denison
1946 Tulsa
1947 Bowling Green
1947 CUNY, Baruch
1947 Howard
1947 Occidental
1947 Roosevelt (1959-1988)
1948 Cornell
1948 Indiana
1948 Louisville
1948 Marshall
1948 New Mexico Highlands
1948 North Texas
1948 Oklahoma State (1982-1986)
1948 San Jose
1948 Temple
1948 Utah State
1948 West Virginia
1948 Western Michigan (1982-1986)
1948 Wichita
1949 Case Western Reserve
1949 Colorado
1949 George Washington
1949 Gettysburg
1949 Louisiana Col
1949 New Hampshire
1949 Pitt
1950 Adelphi
1950 Akron
1950 Bucknell

1950	Colgate		1959	Duke
1950	Delaware		1959	Florida State
1950	Duquesne		1959	Hawaii
1950	Hofstra		1959	Hollins
1950	Hunter		1959	Muhlenberg
1950	Miami (FL)		1959	Redlands
1950	*Michigan State* (1980)		1959	Southwestern Louisiana
1950	Nevada		1959	Trinity (CT)
1950	Richmond		1960	Alma
1950	San Diego U.		1960	Clark
1950	Texas		1960	Georgia State
1950	Tufts		1960	Lafayette
1951	Arizona State		1960	Lake Forest
1951	CUNY, Brooklyn		1960	MacMurray
1951	Cal State, Fresno		1960	Marquette
1951	Hartwick		1960	Texas Tech
1951	Ohio State		1961	Auburn
1951	Ohio Wesleyan		1961	CUNY, Brooklyn
1951	Queens (NY)		1961	Concordia Col. (MN)
1951	Wayne State (MI)		1961	Florida
1952	Loyola, Chicago		1961	Kentucky
1952	North Carolina		1961	Long Island
1952	Pepperdine		1961	North Carolina Central
1952	Rhodes (1976-1987)		1961	North Dakota
1952	South Carolina		1961	Southern
1952	Upsala		1961	Virginia Commonwealth
1952	Willamette		1961	William and Mary
1953	Boston U		1962	Central Washington
1953	*Oregon* (1971)		1962	Eastern Washington
1954	Brigham Young		1962	Florida Southern
1954	Cal State, Long Beach		1962	Hampden-Sydney
1954	*DePauw* (1982)		1962	*New Mexico State* (1977)
1954	Mary Washington		1962	New Orleans
1954	*Memphis State* (1978)		1962	West Virginia Wesleyan
1954	Yeshiva		1962	Westminster (PA)
1955	Detroit		1962	*Whitworth* (1966)
1955	*Illinois Tech* (1968)		1962	Xavier (OH)
1955	Lehigh		1963	Bridgeport
1955	Maryland		1963	Columbia (NY)
1955	Missouri, Kansas City		1963	Fairleigh Dickinson, Rutherford
1955	St. Lawrence		1963	Northern Illinois
1955	St. Louis		1963	Southern Mississippi
1955	*Stanford* (1957)		1963	Winthrop
1956	Baldwin-Wallace		1963	Wisconsin, Oshkosh
1956	Cal State, Los Angeles		1964	Albion
1956	Texas Christian		1964	Alfred
1957	Arizona		1964	Benedictine College
1957	Berea		1964	Cal State, Chico
1957	*Johns Hopkins* (1980)		1964	Colorado State
1957	Stetson		1964	Emporia
1957	Texas, El Paso		1964	Evansville
1958	American (1976-1988)		1964	LaSalle
1958	Cal State, Sacramento		1964	Lebanon Valley
1958	Catholic		1964	Monmouth (NJ)
1958	Houston		1964	Purdue
1958	Minnesota, Duluth		1964	San Francisco State
1958	Morgan State		1964	St. John's (NY)
1958	North Carolina, Greensboro		1964	Tampa
1958	Wisconsin, Milwaukee		1964	Wisconsin, Eau Claire
1959	C. W. Post		1965	Carson-Newman
1959	Cincinnati		1965	Elmhurst
1959	Dayton		1965	*Emmanuel* (1979)

1965	Holy Cross	1968	Wheeling
1965	Hope	1969	Augustana (IL)
1965	Huntingdon	1969	CUNY, Lehman
1965	Jacksonville	1969	Davis and Elkins
1965	John Carroll	1969	Eastern Illinois
1965	Michigan State	1969	Florida A & M
1965	Montana State	1969	Hartford
1965	Murray State	1969	Northeast Louisiana
1965	Nebraska	1969	Northwestern Louisiana
1965	Rider	1969	Pace
1965	Springfield	1969	Rutgers, Newark
1965	Stephen F. Austin	1969	Scranton
1965	Virginia State, Norfolk	1969	Seton Hall
1966	DePaul	1969	Skidmore
1966	East Carolina	1969	St. Cloud
1966	Marywood	1969	St. Mary's (MN)
1966	SUNY, Albany	1969	Western Illinois
1966	Toledo	1970	Bloomsburg
1966	Towson	1970	Central Arkansas
1966	Trinity (TX)	1970	Central Michigan
1966	Wagner	1970	East Texas
1966	Westmar	1970	Fort Hays
1967	American International	1970	Indiana (PA)
1967	Cal State, Fullerton	1970	*Jamestown* (1982)
1967	Cal State, Northridge	1970	Kansas State
1967	Central Missouri State	1970	Marymount (NY)
1967	Eastern New Mexico	1970	Nevada, Las Vegas
1967	Fairleigh Dickinson, Teaneck	1970	Ripon
1967	Lake Erie	1970	SUNY Col., Geneseo
1967	Loyola, New Orleans	1970	Slippery Rock
1967	Massachusetts Pharmacy	1970	Southwest Missouri
1967	Missouri, St. Louis	1970	Texas A & M
1967	Oklahoma City	1970	Texas Woman's
1967	*Parsons* (1972)	1970	Trenton
1967	SUNY Col., Cortland	1970	West Florida
1967	South Dakota	1970	Western Carolina
1967	South Florida	1971	David Lipscomb
1967	St. Bonaventure	1971	Edinboro
1967	Ursinus	1971	Elmira
1967	Wabash	1971	Furman
1968	Bellarmine	1971	Madison Col
1968	*Bradley* (1970)	1971	Montclair
1968	Central Connecticut	1971	Regis (MA)
1968	Eastern Kentucky	1971	*Tarkio* (1978)
1968	Fairleigh Dickinson, Madison	1971	Utica
1968	Hamline	1971	West Texas
1968	Holy Family	1971	Western Connecticut
1968	Iona	1972	Cal State, Dominguez Hills
1968	Muskingum	1972	Carthage
1968	*Nasson* (1983)	1972	Eastern Montana
1968	North Carolina State	1972	Kutztown
1968	Northeastern Illinois	1972	Middle Tennessee
1968	Notre Dame (1971-1987)	1972	Monmouth (IL)
1968	Oklahoma Baptist	1972	Old Dominion
1968	Rutgers, Camden	1972	Pitt, Johnstown
1968	SUNY Col., Oswego	1972	Presbyterian
1968	SUNY Col., Plattsburgh	1972	Russell Sage
1968	Southern Colorado	1972	South Alabama
1968	Southern Illinois, Edwardsville	1972	South Florida
1968	Susquehanna	1972	Southern Connecticut
1968	Washburn	1972	St. Mary's, San Antonio
1968	West Chester	1972	St. Olaf

1972 Stevens Tech	1975 New Rochelle
1973 Adrian	1975 Norfolk
1973 Alverno	1975 *SUNY Col., Brockport* (1978)
1973 Columbus	1975 San Diego U
1973 Dillard	1975 Smith
1973 Drexel	1975 Southwestern (TX)
1973 Georgetown U	1975 Texas Lutheran
1973 Kearney	1976 Austin
1973 King's	1976 Cal State, San Bernadino
1973 Loyola (MD) (1974-1986)	1976 Central State (OK)
1973 Mansfield	1976 Emory
1973 Maryland, Baltimore County	1976 Frostburg
1973 Molloy	1976 Harding
1973 North Carolina, Asheville	1976 Louisiana Tech
1973 Sam Houston	1976 Lycoming
1973 San Francisco	1976 Moravian
1973 Southeastern Louisiana	1976 Mount Mary's (MD)
1973 *St. John's (MN)* (1976)	1976 New Haven
1973 Tennessee State	1976 Northeast Missouri
1973 Thiel	1976 Northern Arizona
1973 Western Kentucky	1976 Shippensburg
1974 Barry (FL) (1979-1987)	1976 St. Francis (PA)
1974 Birmingham-Southern	1976 Tennessee, Chattanooga
1974 Bowie	1976 Troy
1974 CUNY, John Jay	1976 Waynesburg
1974 Canisius	1976 Whittier (1983-1987)
1974 Catawba	1976 William Paterson
1974 George Mason	1977 Alabama, Huntsville
1974 Hood	1977 Ball State
1974 Kean (NJ)	1977 *Capital* (1982)
1974 Metropolitan State (CO)	1977 Cheyney State
1974 Midwestern	1977 Clark
1974 Mundelein	1977 Dowling
1974 New York Tech	1977 East Tennessee
1974 North Central	1977 Elizabethtown
1974 North Dakota State	1977 Fairfield
1974 Notre Dame (MD)	1977 Franklin and Marshall
1974 SUNY Col., Fredonia	1977 Hamilton
1974 Salisbury	1977 Hanover
1974 Spelman	1977 Hillsdale
1974 St. Joseph's (PA)	1977 Immaculata
1974 Tennessee, Martin	1977 Pepperdine
1974 Weber	1977 St. Mary-of-the-Woods (1979-1986)
1974 Western Maryland	1977 St. Thomas (TX)
1974 Western New England	1977 V.P.I.
1975 Avila (1978-1988)	1977 Westfield
1975 Baltimore U.	1977 Wisconsin, Stevens Point
1975 CUNY, York	1978 American International
1975 Carnegie-Mellon	1978 Andrews
1975 Clarion	1978 CUNY, Staten Island
1975 Clemson	1978 Drury
1975 Colorado, Colorado Springs	1978 East Central State
1975 Dickinson	1978 Eastern Michigan
1975 Florida International	1978 Francis Marion
1975 Hampton Inst.	1978 Georgian Court
1975 Houston Baptist	1978 Idaho
1975 Illinois Wesleyan	1978 Indiana Northwest
1975 Indiana, South Bend	1978 Mercy (NY)
1975 Manhattan	1978 Pembroke
1975 Mary Baldwin	1978 Roger Williams
1975 Meredith	1978 Southeast Missouri
1975 Michigan, Flint	1978 Spring Arbor

1978	Suffolk	1981	Aquinas
1978	Tennessee	1981	Bethune-Cookman
1978	Texas, Permian Basin	1981	Biola
1978	Villanova	1981	Central Florida
1979	Alaska, Fairbanks	1981	Chestnut Hill
1979	Arkansas State	1981	Colby
1979	Cal, Santa Barbara	1981	Delaware State
1979	Cardinal Stritch	1981	Fisk
1979	Charleston (SC)	1981	Florida Institute
1979	Claremont	1981	Georgia Southern
1979	Creighton	1981	IUPUI
1979	Illinois Benedictine	1981	Lewis
1979	Jersey City	1981	Marietta
1979	Loyola Marymount, Los Angeles	1981	Marymount (NY)
1979	Manhattanville	1981	Mercy (MI)
1979	Marist	1981	Montevallo
1979	Marymount Manhattan	1981	New Mexico
1979	Massachusetts	1981	North Carolina, Wilmington
1979	Missouri, Rolla	1981	Northern Kentucky
1979	Morehead (1981-1987)	1981	Pacific Union
1979	Nazareth	1981	Texas, Arlington
1979	Nicholls	1981	Vanderbilt
1979	North Carolina A & T	1981	Washington and Jefferson
1979	Ohio Dominican	1981	Westminster (MO)
1979	Olivet	1981	Wilkes
1979	Radford	1981	Worcester Tech
1979	SUNY Col., Buffalo	1982	Appalachian
1979	SUNY Col., Oneonta	1982	Beloit
1979	Siena	1982	Cal Poly, Pomona
1979	South Carolina State	1982	Cal, Davis
1979	South Dakota State	1982	Central State (OH)
1979	St. Catherine	1982	Eastern Connecticut
1979	St. Joseph's (IN)	1982	Eastern Oregon
1979	Stockton	1982	Gannon
1979	Tennessee Tech	1982	Hastings
1979	Texas Wesleyan	1982	Kennesaw
1979	Transylvania	1982	Lincoln (PA)
1979	Trinity (IL)	1982	Michigan
1979	Union College	1982	Mount St. Vincent
1979	Virginia Wesleyan	1982	North Georgia
1979	Virginia	1982	Northeastern (OK)
1980	Alaska, Anchorage	1982	Northern Colorado
1980	Bethany (WV)	1982	Northwest Missouri
1980	Carroll	1982	Pfeiffer
1980	Dominican	1982	SUNY, Binghamton
1980	Drew	1982	Southern Maine
1980	East Stroudsburg	1982	Southern Oregon
1980	Fordham	1982	Southwest Texas
1980	Indiana State	1982	Stephens
1980	Jackson (MS)	1982	Washington (MD)
1980	Michigan, Dearborn	1983	Augusta
1980	Missouri Southern	1983	Biscayne
1980	Mount Holyoke	1983	Cabrini
1980	Roanoke	1983	Connecticut
1980	Rosary (IL)	1983	East Texas
1980	Salem State (MA)	1983	Fitchburg
1980	St. Ambrose	1983	Fordham
1980	St. Norbert	1983	Linfield
1980	Wesleyan (GA)	1983	Lock Haven
1980	Western Oregon	1983	Marian (IN)
1980	Wisconsin, Whitewater	1983	Methodist
1980	Youngstown State	1983	Mobile

1983	Niagara		1987	Briar Cliff
1983	North Carolina Wesleyan		1987	Cal, Riverside
1983	Northern Iowa		1987	Christian Brothers
1983	Pan American		1987	Doane
1983	SUNY, Buffalo		1987	Gardner-Webb
1983	Seton Hill		1987	Johnson C. Smith
1983	Stonehill		1987	Pacific Lutheran
1983	Western Washington		1987	Sacred Heart
1984	Bloomfield		1987	Southwest State (MN)
1984	Cal State, Stanislaus		1987	St. Mary's (MD)
1984	Cleveland		1987	Wake Forest
1984	Colorado, Denver		1987	Wheaton
1984	Eastern		1987	Williams
1984	Heidelberg		1987	Wisconsin, Platteville
1984	Humboldt		1987	Wisconsin, River Falls
1984	Illinois State		1988	Cal, Irvine
1984	Maine, Farmington		1988	Chapman
1984	Minnesota, Morris		1988	Charleston (WV)
1984	Mississippi		1988	Conception
1984	Moorhead		1988	Connecticut Col
1984	Morehouse		1988	Covenant
1984	Mount Mary's (CA)		1988	Gustavus Adolphus
1984	New York Tech		1988	High Point
1984	Oakland		1988	Liberty
1984	Plymouth		1988	Long Island
1984	Rhode Island		1988	Longwood
1984	Saginaw Valley		1988	Mesa
1984	Southern Indiana		1988	Neumann
1984	Spalding		1988	North Alabama
1984	Washington (MO)		1988	Pomona
1984	West Virginia State		1988	SUNY, Stony Brook
1984	Wisconsin, La Crosse		1988	Sonoma
1985	Athens		1988	Texas Col
1985	Forest		1988	Thomas More
1985	Houston, Clear Lake		1989	Cal, Santa Cruz
1985	Iowa		1989	California (PA)
1985	Merrimack		1989	Carroll
1985	Miami Psych		1989	Christopher Newport
1985	North Florida		1989	Columbia Union
1985	North Park		1989	Corpus Christi
1985	Oglethorpe		1989	Eastern Nazarene
1985	Puget Sound		1989	Franciscan
1985	Seattle		1989	Georgetown Col
1985	St. Peter's		1989	Georgia Southwestern
1985	St. Xavier		1989	Holy Names
1985	Texas Southwestern, Medical		1989	Houston, Victoria
1985	Texas, San Antonio		1989	Idaho State
1985	Webster		1989	Indiana Southeast
1985	Wheaton		1989	Keene
1985	Xavier (LA)		1989	Lynchburg
1986	Auburn, Montgomery		1989	Millersville
1986	Berry (GA)		1989	Missouri Western
1986	Bridgewater		1989	Northern State
1986	Illinois, Chicago		1989	Regis (CO)
1986	Lamar		1989	William Jewell
1986	Lander		1990	Agnes Scott
1986	Lewis and Clark		1990	Albright
1986	Maine		1990	Allegheny
1986	Mid-America		1990	Austin Peay
1986	Quinnipiac		1990	Brandeis
1986	Wisconsin, Parkside		1990	Cedar Crest
1987	Allentown		1990	Coastal Carolina

1990 Grand Valley
1990 LaVerne
1990 Lowell
1990 Luther
1990 Mississippi Col.
1990 North Carolina, Charlotte
1990 Pitzer
1990 Point Park
1990 Randolph, Macon
1990 Rice
1990 Sangamon
1990 Southern Utah
1990 Spring Hill
1990 St. Anselm's
1990 Trinity, Vermont

Rho Chi

(PHARMACY)

ACTIVE PIN

RHO CHI was founded at the University of Michigan in May, 1922, to encourage high scholastic attainment and fellowship among students in pharmacy and to promote the pharmaceutical sciences. The organization evolved from the Aristolochite Society which had been established there in 1908. Institutional membership is limited to colleges of pharmacy that are members in good standing of the American Association of Colleges of Pharmacy, or meet the minimum standards of the Association of Faculties of Pharmacy of Canada. Alumni chapters may be established in any locality where there is no active chapter. Those eligible to election as active members in a chapter are: undergraduate students who have completed a minimum of 75 hours of scholastic work, are in the highest 20 percent of their class, and have attained a scholastic average equivalent to the second highest letter grade, and who have shown a capacity for achievement in the science and art of pharmacy as evidenced by character, personality and leadership; graduate students majoring in one or more of the areas of pharmaceutical study who have completed one full academic year of courses carrying approved graduate credit; faculty who hold regular, research or administrative appointments and are permitted to vote in faculty matters in a school or college of pharmacy.

On March 1, 1947, Rho Chi Society was admitted to membership in the Association of College Honor Societies.

Government Government is by convention held at the same time each year as the meeting of the American Association of Colleges of Pharmacy. In the interim of conventions government is vested in the Executive Council, consisting of four national officers and eight elected members. A revised constitution was published in 1984. Progress is reported to the chapters by means of an annual publication, *Report of Rho Chi.*

Traditions and Insignia Local chapters of the society have established a number of scholarship prizes. The national society awards two graduate scholarships annually for $1,000 each and sponsors two awards to the two chapters which successfully compete for the best overall program of activities and the best new program ($600 and $400 respectively).

The badge is in the form of an old-fashioned key embodying the Greek letters PX in a definite configuration, raised on an oblong eight-sided base. The colors are purple and white.

Headquarters Mercer University School of Pharmacy, 345 Boulevard, N.D., Atlanta, Georgia 30312.

Membership Active chapters 72. Inactive chapters 7. Total number of initiates 46,500. Chapter roll:

1922 Alpha, Michigan (Alpha or Aristolochite Society, 1908 to 1922)
1922 Beta, Oregon State (Beta of Aristolochite 1919 to 1922)
1922 Gamma, Oklahoma
1923 Delta, Iowa
1925 Epsilon, Washington State
1925 Eta, Wisconsin, Madison
1925 Theta, USC
1925 Zeta, Auburn
1928 Iota, Florida
1928 Kappa, North Dakota State
1929 Lambda, Virginia Commonwealth
1929 Xi, North Carolina
1930 Mu, Minnesota
1930 Nu, Texas
1930 Omicron, Maryland
1931 *Pi, North Pacific* (1941)
1931 Rho, Washington (WA)
1931 *Sigma, Case Western Reserve* (1950)
1931 Tau, South Dakota State
1934 Phi, Illinois, Chicago
1934 Upsilon, Ohio State
1937 Chi, Mississippi
1939 Psi, Massachusetts Pharmacy
1940 Omega, SUNY Col., Buffalo
1941 Alpha Alpha, Creighton
1941 Alpha Beta, Duquesne
1942 *Alpha Delta, Loyola*
1942 Alpha Gamma, Connecticut
1943 Alpha Epsilon, Nebraska
1945 Alpha Zeta, Purdue
1947 Alpha Eta, Rutgers
1947 Alpha Iota, South Carolina Medical
1947 Alpha Theta, Colorado
1948 Alpha Nu, Tennessee
1949 Alpha Kappa, Georgia

1949 Alpha Lambda, Cal, San Francisco
1949 Alpha Mu, West Virginia
1949 Alpha Xi, Kentucky
1950 Alpha Omicron, Pitt
1951 *Alpha Pi, Arizona* (1958) (alumni)
1951 Alpha Rho, Kansas
1951 Alpha Sigma, Drake
1951 Alpha Tau, Philadelphia Pharmacy
1951 Alpha Upsilon, Idaho State
1953 Alpha Chi, Wayne State
1953 Alpha Phi, Butler
1954 Alpha Omega, Missouri, Kansas City
1954 Alpha Psi, Arizona
1954 Beta Alpha, South Carolina
1954 Beta Beta, Samford
1954 Beta Delta, St. John's
1954 *Beta Gamma, Columbia (NY)* (1976)
1955 Beta Epsilon, Utah
1955 Beta Eta, Toledo
1955 Beta Iota, Arkansas
1955 Beta Kappa, St. Louis Pharmacy
1955 Beta Lambda, Temple
1955 Beta Mu, Ferris
1955 Beta Theta, Long Island
1955 *Beta Zeta, George Washington* (1964)
1956 Beta Nu, Cincinnati
1956 *Beta Xi, Fordham*
1958 Beta Omicron, Houston
1959 Beta Pi, Rhode Island
1960 Beta Rho, Montana
1960 Beta Sigma, Howard
1961 Beta Chi, Northeast Louisiana
1961 Beta Phi, Wyoming
1961 Beta Tau, Northeastern
1961 Beta Upsilon, Southwestern State (OK)
1962 Beta Psi, Ohio Northern
1964 Beta Omega, Pacific (CA)
1967 Gamma Alpha, Mercer
1968 Gamma Beta, New Mexico
1976 Gamma Gamma, Albany Pharmacy
1977 Gamma Delta, Texas Southern
1977 Gamma Epsilon, Xavier
1980 Gamma Zeta, Florida

Sigma Delta Pi

(SPANISH)

ACTIVE PIN

SIGMA DELTA PI, the only national honor society exclusively for students of Spanish, men and women, in four-year colleges and universities, originated in the mind of Ruth Barnes, a student at the University of California at Berkeley; and in her home the evening of November 14, 1919, she and six other students of the university (Miriam Burt, Ferdinand V. Custer, Anna Krause, Margaret Priddle, Ruth Rhodes and Vera Stump) by unanimous vote founded the society. Although most honor societies were formed by university professors or administrators, it should be noted that Sigma Delta Pi was conceived, planned and founded entirely by students; and for the first ten years of its existence they directed its activities and made it a national society with sixteen chapters in highly respected universities throughout the land. Its growth has been steady: in 1945, 50 chapters; in 1955, 100; in 1967, 150; in 1969, 200; in 1973, 250; in 1977, 300; and in 1985, 391.

Its purposes are: To honor those who seek and attain excellence in the study of Spanish language and in the study of the literature and the culture of the Spanish-speaking people; to honor those who strive to make the Hispanic contributions to modern culture better known to the English-speaking peoples; to encourage college and university students to acquire a greater interest in, and a deeper understanding of Hispanic culture; and to foster friendly relations and mutual respect between the nations of Hispanic speech and those of English speech.

Government The officers are a national president; five regional vice presidents for the Northeast, the Southeast, the Midwest, the Southwest, and the West; and an executive secretary, all of whom are elected at a triennial convention. They and the immediate past president constitute the Executive Council, which conducts the affairs of the society between conventions, including the admission of new chapters. The editor and the national artist are appointed by the national president. Upon the recommendation of the vice presidents, the president of the society appoints a director for each state. The individual chapters are semiautonomous: each prepares its own constitution, but this must incorporate at least the minimal standards and the regulations governing memberships and awards, as set forth in the national constitution.

Traditions and Insignia The insigne is the coat of arms of Castile at the time of Ferdinand and Isabel bearing two castles and two lions rampant, one in each quadrant. In the center oval are the Greek letters ΣΔΠ arranged vertically and representing the name of the society. The shield is surmounted by a crown and is set up in the traditional form of a key.

In addition to the ordinary membership categories (active, associate, and alumus), Honorary Membership is granted by the chapters; Distinguished Membership, granted only by the national office, and memberships in the Optimates Chapter, granted only by the national office. Also, there are two honorary orders, that of Don Quijote and that of Los Descubridores, each symbolized by a gold key bearing the image of the corresponding notable. Membership in the former is the society's highest award. Outstanding students of Spanish may be recommended by their chapter for the coveted Gabriela Mistral Prize.

Activities A rich and varied series of activities pertaining to Hispanic culture is carried out by chapters, including, among other things, the offering of local awards and scholarships, the giving of lecture series, movies and other characteristic entertainments, such as programs celebrating important moments in Hispanic life, including *El Diá de la Raza* or Columbus Day (October 12), *El Diá del Idioma* or Cervantes Day (April 23), and Pan American Day (April 14). Many other imaginative and informative projects are carried out by local chapters in an effort to bring information concerning Hispanic civilization to the entire campus community.

Sigma Delta Pi sponsors annually a national scholarship contest. Any active member who is a Spanish major and a full-time student may enter. In the year 1984–85, with the help of grants from the Southland Corporation and the Instituto de Cooperación Iberoamericana, and with the society's own funds, a total of $10,700 was awarded in scholarships. Four were for a summer school in Spain, one for a summer school in Mexico, and three were to be used according to the wishes of the winner in furthering his education and/or research.

Publications The society publishes a newsletter called *Entre Nosotros*. From two to four issues are printed each academic year depending upon the judgement of the editor. A copy is furnished for each active member of the society. The newsletter is one of the chief means used by Sigma Delta Pi to convey important news and information to all its members. The society has also published a Handbook for Chapter Advisers, a set of Instructions for Initiation Ceremonies and Chapter Installations, a formal Ritual followed in initiation and installation ceremonies, and several minor publications intended to assist chapters in their activities.

Headquarters P.O. Box 55125, Riverside, CA 92517

Membership Active chapters 397. Total number of initiates 85,000. Chapter roll:††

1919	Alpha, California
1921	Beta, Missouri
1922	Delta, Maryland (1931-1958)
1922	*Gamma, Oregon* (1966)
1924	Epsilon, Wooster
1925	Eta, USC
1925	*Theta, Idaho* (1940)
1925	Zeta, Texas
1926	Iota, UCLA
1926	*Kappa, Stanford* (1963)
1926	Lambda, Illinois
1927	*Mu, Middlebury* (1945)
1928	Nu, Baylor
1928	Xi, Hunter

†† This chapter roll is repeated from the 19th edition; no current information was provided.

1929	Omicron, C.C.N.Y.
1930	Pi, Arizona
1931	Chi, South Carolina (1936-1967)
1931	Omega, Davidson
1931	Phi, Denison
1931	Psi, Wisconsin, Madison
1931	Rho, Chattanooga
1931	Sigma, Mary Hardin-Baylor
1931	Tau, Adelphi
1931	*Upsilon, Dominican* (1969)
1932	Alpha Alpha, Miami (OH)
1934	Alpha Beta, Rutgers
1935	Alpha Delta, Florida State
1935	Alpha Epsilon, San Jose State
1935	Alpha Gamma, Cal State, Fresno
1935	Alpha Zeta, Western State (CO)
1936	Alpha Eta, Southern Methodist
1936	Alpha Theta, Duke
1937	Alpha Iota, Texas Western
1937	*Alpha Kappa, Stetson* (1970)
1937	Alpha Lambda, L.S.U.
1937	*Alpha Mu, San Francisco Women's* (1969)
1937	Alpha Nu, Baldwin-Wallace
1938	*Alpha Omicron, Louisiana Col.* (1945)
1938	Alpha Pi, Texas
1938	Alpha Xi, Vanderbilt
1940	Alpha Rho, Southwestern Louisiana
1941	Alpha Sigma, Hofstra
1941	Alpha Tau, North Carolina Woman's
1943	Alpha Upsilon, Bucknell
1944	Alpha Chi, Miami (FL)
1944	*Alpha Omega, Louisiana Tech* (1970)
1944	Alpha Phi, Texas Tech.
1944	Alpha Psi, Tennessee
1945	Beta Alpha, Alabama
1945	Beta Beta, Michigan State
1945	Beta Gamma, Brooklyn
1946	Beta Delta, Judson
1946	Beta Epsilon, Toledo
1947	Beta Eta, New Mexico State
1947	Beta Theta, N.Y.U. (Heights)
1947	*Beta Zeta, Willamette* (1970)
1948	*Beta Iota, British Columbia* (1953)
1948	*Beta Kappa, Marshall* (1970)
1948	Beta Lambda, Kent
1948	Beta Mu, Bowling Green
1948	*Beta Nu, Buffalo* (1970)
1948	*Beta Omicron, Michigan* (1970)
1948	Beta Xi, Rosary (IL)
1949	Beta Chi, West Virginia State
1949	Beta Phi, Southern Mississippi (1950-1967)
1949	Beta Pi, Kansas
1949	*Beta Rho, Florida* (1950)
1949	Beta Sigma, Hardin-Simmons
1949	Beta Tau, Barat (IL) (1950-1967)
1949	Beta Upsilon, Northern Illinois
1950	*Beta Omega, Washington (MO)* (1969)
1950	*Beta Psi, Lincoln Memorial (TN)* (1970)
1950	*Gamma Alpha, Iowa* (1951)
1950	Gamma Beta, St. Teresa
1950	Gamma Delta, Memphis State
1950	Gamma Epsilon, Arkansas

1950 Gamma Gamma, Marquette	1965 Epsilon Psi, Stphen F. Austin
1950 Gamma Zeta, Columbia	1965 Epsilon Rho, College of the Holy Name (CA)
1951 Gamma Eta, Tennessee A & I	1965 Epsilon Sigma, Salve Regina
1951 Gamma Iota, Drury	1965 Epsilon Tau, Westminster (PA)
1951 *Gamma Theta, Oklahoma* (1970)	1965 Epsilon Upsilon, Kentucky
1952 Gamma Kappa, West Texas	1966 Epsilon Omega, Trinity (TX)
1952 Gamma Lambda, Texas A & I	1966 Zeta Alpha, Arlington State
1952 Gamma Mu, Washington and Jefferson	1966 *Zeta Beta, dropped* (1966)
1952 Gamma Nu, Wichita	1966 Zeta Delta, University of the Pacific
1952 *Gamma Omicron, Penn* (1970)	1966 Zeta Gamma, Utah
1952 Gamma Pi, William and Mary	1967 Zeta Epsilon, Centre College
1952 Gamma Rho, Houston	1967 Zeta Eta, Eastern Illinois
1952 Gamma Xi, Wofford	1967 *Zeta Iota, Maryville (TN)* (1967)
1953 Gamma Phi, Marietta	1967 Zeta Kappa, Maine
1953 Gamma Sigma, Georgetown Col	1967 Zeta Lambda, Wisconsin, Whitewater
1953 Gamma Tau, Cincinnati	1967 Zeta Mu, Florida Presbyterian
1953 *Gamma Upsilon, Rice* (1969)	1967 Zeta Nu, Rider
1954 Delta Alpha, Queens (NY)	1967 Zeta Omicron, Nevada
1954 *Delta Beta, Midwestern* (1955)	1967 Zeta Pi, Cal State, San Bernardino
1954 Gamma Chi, Carson-Newman	1967 Zeta Theta, St. Francis (NY)
1954 Gamma Omega, Connecticut	1967 Zeta Xi, Montana
1954 Gamma Psi, Cal State, Los Angeles	1967 Zeta Zeta, Virginia
1955 Delta Delta, New Mexico State	1968 Eta Alpha, SUNY Col, Fredonia
1955 Delta Gamma, Georgia	1968 Eta Beta, Cal State, San Diego
1956 *Delta Epsilon, DePaul* (1969)	1968 *Eta Delta, Texas Wesleyan* (1970)
1956 Delta Eta, George Washington	1968 Eta Epsilon, Transylvania
1956 Delta Theta, Emporia	1968 Eta Eta, Ohio Northern
1956 Delta Zeta, Monmouth	1968 Eta Gamma, Towson
1957 Delta Iota, Mississippi	1968 Eta Iota, Lamar
1958 Delta Kappa, Temple	1968 Eta Kappa, Akron
1959 Delta Lambda, Oregon State	1968 Eta Lambda, Southwest Missouri State
1959 Delta Mu, Portland	1968 Eta Theta, Mansfield State
1959 Delta Nu, Howard	1968 Eta Zeta, San Diego State
1959 Delta Omicron, Mount Mary's (CA)	1968 *Zeta Chi, Fontbonne* (1970)
1959 Delta Pi, Brigham Young	1968 Zeta Omega, Cal, Riverside
1959 Delta Xi, Mississippi for Women	1968 Zeta Phi, Georgia Southern
1960 *Delta Rho, D'Youville (NY)* (1969)	1968 Zeta Psi, North Carolina
1960 Delta Sigma, Purdue	1968 Zeta Rho, Millsaps
1960 Delta Tau, West Virginia	1968 Zeta Sigma, Little Rock
1960 Delta Upsilon, Butler	1968 Zeta Tau, Fairfield
1961 Delta Chi, Montclair	1968 Zeta Upsilon, Murray State
1961 Delta Omega, Austin	1969 Eta Chi, College of the Ozarks
1961 Delta Phi, Marygrove	1969 Eta Mu, Eastern Kentucky
1961 Delta Psi, Wisconsin, Eau Claire	1969 Eta Nu, Angelo
1962 Epsilon Alpha, Thiel	1969 Eta Omega, Georgia State
1962 Epsilon Beta, Southwest Texas	1969 Eta Omicron, Gordon College
1962 Epsilon Delta, Dickinson	1969 Eta Phi, C. W. Post
1962 Epsilon Epsilon, Winthrop	1969 Eta Pi, Monmouth
1962 *Epsilon Gamma, Mississippi State* (1967)	1969 Eta Psi, SUNY, Albany
1962 Epsilon Zeta, Pomona	1969 Eta Rho, Central State
1963 Epsilon Eta, Alabama State	1969 *Eta Sigma, Wisconsin, Madison* (1969)
1963 Epsilon Iota, Wisconsin, Milwaukee	1969 Eta Tau, Dayton
1963 Epsilon Kappa, St. John's (NY)	1969 Eta Upsilon, Illinois State
1963 Epsilon Theta, Wisconsin, La Crosse	1969 Eta Xi, South Jersey
1964 Epsilon Lambda, Georgian Court	1969 Theta Alpha, Lehman
1964 Epsilon Mu, Western Kentucky	1969 Theta Beta, Rhode Island
1964 Epsilon Nu, Slippery Rock	1969 Theta Delta, Auburn
1964 Epsilon Omicron, Appalachian	1969 Theta Epsilon, Arizona State
1964 Epsilon Xi, Kansas State	1969 Theta Eta, Northern Iowa
1965 Epsilon Chi, Augustana (IL)	1969 Theta Gamma, New Hampshire
1965 Epsilon Phi, Texas Southern	1969 Theta Zeta, East Texas
1965 Epsilon Pi, Hope	1970 *Theta Iota, Prairie View* (1970)

1970	Theta Kappa, Concordia Col. (MN)
1970	Theta Lambda, College of St. Catherine (MN)
1970	Theta Mu, St. Lawrence
1970	Theta Nu, Colorado
1970	Theta Omicron, Edinboro
1970	Theta Pi, East Tennessee
1970	Theta Rho, Seton Hall
1970	Theta Sigma, Mars Hill (NC)
1970	Theta Theta, Central Michigan
1970	Theta Xi, Howard
1971	Iota Alpha, Iona
1971	Iota Beta, Davis and Elkins
1971	Iota Delta, Southwestern (TX)
1971	Iota Epsilon, Pembroke
1971	Iota Eta, Colby
1971	Iota Gamma, Park (MO)
1971	Iota Iota, CUNY, York
1971	Iota Kappa, Cal State, Sacramento
1971	Iota Lambda, College of New Rochelle
1971	Iota Theta, Chapman
1971	Iota Zeta, SUNY, New York
1971	Theta Chi, Fort Wayne
1971	Theta Omega, St. Thomas (TX)
1971	Theta Phi, Southern State (AR)
1971	Theta Psi, Oakland
1971	Theta Tau, Hawaii
1971	Theta Upsilon, Newberry (SC)
1972	Iota Chi, SUNY, Plattsburgh
1972	Iota Mu, Indiana (PA)
1972	Iota Nu, Indiana State
1972	Iota Omega, Wright State
1972	Iota Omicron, Cleveland
1972	Iota Phi, Clemson
1972	Iota Pi, Ithaca
1972	Iota Psi, Frostburg
1972	Iota Rho, Marymount (CA)
1972	Iota Sigma, Loyola, Chicago
1972	Iota Tau, Glassboro
1972	Iota Upsilon, Northern Arizona
1972	Iota Xi, Lindenwood
1973	Kappa Alpha, Stetson
1973	Kappa Beta, Spring Hill
1973	Kappa Delta, Wagner
1973	Kappa Epsilon, Dominican (TX)
1973	Kappa Eta, Roanoke
1973	Kappa Gamma, Georgia Southwestern
1973	Kappa Iota, Florida Southern
1973	Kappa Kappa, Worcester Tech
1973	Kappa Lambda, East Texas Baptist
1973	Kappa Mu, Bates
1973	Kappa Nu, Dillard
1973	Kappa Omicron, Lowell
1973	Kappa Theta, Morris Harvey
1973	Kappa Xi, Bethany (WV)
1973	Kappa Zeta, Sam Houston
1974	Kappa Chi, Baruch
1974	Kappa Omega, St. Louis
1974	Kappa Phi, Friends
1974	Kappa Pi, Notre Dame (MD)
1974	Kappa Psi, Georgia Col
1974	Kappa Rho, Oral Roberts

1974	Kappa Sigma, Albertus Magnus
1974	Kappa Tau, Fort Lewis
1974	Kappa Upsilon, Delaware
1974	Lambda Beta, Georgetown
1975	Lambda Delta, Hood
1975	Lambda Epsilon, McMurry
1975	Lambda Eta, Knox
1975	Lambda Gamma, North Carolina
1975	Lambda Iota, Wittenberg
1975	Lambda Theta, Cornell
1975	Lambda Zeta, Valparaiso
1976	Lambda Chi, Old Dominion
1976	Lambda Kappa, Northwestern Louisiana
1976	Lambda Lambda, Wheaton
1976	Lambda Mu, Columbia (SC)
1976	Lambda Nu, Spelman
1976	Lambda Omicron, Hamline
1976	Lambda Phi, Montana State
1976	Lambda Pi, South Alabama
1976	Lambda Psi, V.P.I.
1976	Lambda Rho, Stonehill
1976	Lambda Sigma, Northeast Louisiana
1976	Lambda Tau, Texas A & M
1976	Lambda Upsilon, Bethany Nazarene (OK)
1976	Lambda Xi, Colgate

Sigma Gamma Tau

(AEROSPACE ENGINEERING)

ACTIVE PIN

SIGMA GAMMA TAU, national college honor society in aerospace engineering for men, and women, was founded in 1953 through the merger of two aeronautical engineering societies, Gamma Alpha Rho and Tau Omega. Tau Omega was founded in 1927 at the University of Oklahoma and Gamma Alpha Rho was founded in 1947 at Rensselaer Polytechnic Institute. The society is incorporated in the state of Oklahoma.

Purpose To recognize and honor those individuals in the field of aeronautics and astronautics who have through scholarship, integrity, and outstanding achievement been a credit to their profession. The Society seeks to foster a high standard of ethics and professional practices and to create a spirit of loyalty and fellowship, particularly among students of aeronautical engineering.

Eligibility *Student members* must have completed at least five quarters or three semesters of their undergraduate college work for the bachelor's degree, be enrolled in an accredited department of aerospace engineering, be in the upper one-third of their senior or upper one-quarter of their junior class or upper one-fifth of their sophomore class, and must meet residence requirements. They must also have shown aualities of high moral character and have an active interest in aeronautics and/or astronautics. Graduate students must be in good standing and have met similar requirements.

Special members must be in the aerospace engineering profession. They may be elected if they have made worthy contributions toward the advancement of the aerospace profession, if they are teachers of aerospace engineering or related subjects, or if they have made a significant contribution to science that may be deemed worthy of membership in the Society.

Government   Authority for the society is vested in the national convention, the accredited delegates at which conduct such business as is placed on the agenda, and an executive council composed of a national president and a national vice-president. The president and the vice-president are elected by chapter ballot, and in turn they elect an executive secretary-treasurer who maintains the national headquarters in his office.

The first convention was held in 1953 at Purdue. National conventions are held at least biennially or on the approved call of a chapter or the executive council. Between conventions, business matters are submitted directly to chapters.

The collegiate chapters hold an annual election of officers and these officers have the responsibility of administrating the affairs of their respective chapters consistent with the purposes of the national society.

Activities   Promote better understanding between students and staff, act as a means of organizing aeronautical and astronautical activities both scientific and social in nature, and in general to promote ethical and professional betterment of the field as stated in the purpose of the society. Annually award eight honor awards consisting of a monetary award and plaque, one to the outstanding member in each of the seven regions and one to the outstanding member in the country. The purpose of these awards is to recognize "excellence."

Publications   A publication, which has been issued with such titles as *Contact* and *Mach*, is published occasionally on a volunteer basis. Other publications are *History-Constitution* and *Newsletter*.

Insignia   The emblem of the society is a key of conventional type which displays the Greek letters ΣΓΤ as part of a symbolic arrangement which is appropriate to the nature of the society.

Headquarters   Office of the National Secretary-Treasurer, Department of Mechanical and Aerospace Engineering, North Carolina State University, Raleigh, North Carolina 27607.

Membership   Active chapters 43. Inactive chapters 3. Total number of initiates 12,000. Chapter roll:††

†† This chapter roll is repeated from the 19th edition; no current information was provided.

1953	*Alabama*
1953	*Carnegie Tech* (1966)
1953	Georgia Tech
1953	Illinois
1953	Iowa State
1953	Kansas
1953	Minnesota
1953	Ohio State
1953	Oklahoma
1953	Purdue
1953	Rensselaer
1953	V.P.I.
1953	Wichita State
1954	West Virginia
1955	New York Poly
1957	*N.Y.U. (Heights)*
1957	Penn State
1957	Texas A & M
1957	Texas
1965	Auburn
1966	Maryland
1968	Cincinnati
1970	North Carolina State
1970	Texas, Arlington
1971	Mississippi State
1974	Colorado
1974	Missouri-Rolla
1974	Northrop

Sigma Lambda Alpha

(LANDSCAPE ARCHITECTURE)

SIGMA LAMBDA ALPHA was founded in 1977 at the University of Minnesota. The Society was admitted to the Association of College Honor Societies as Associate in 1983 and Full Membership in 1986.

Purpose   To encourage, recognize, and reward academic excellence in preparation for the profession of landscape architecture. The society elects, in addition, those who have achieved professionally. Honorary and Distinguished Memberships; students, faculty/staff, and professionals are recognized. Leadership and sound character are emphasized. Preserving the valuable traditions and customs consonant with the wise husbandry of the land are sought, and a spirit of amiability is fostered among those of marked ability in this discipline.

Eligibility   Undergraduates, preferably juniors, and seniors of sound character, with a 3.2 GPA on a four-point scale are eligible. Graduate students who have completed at least one-third of the degree credit requirements with a 3.5 GPA on the same point-scale are eligible, both MLA and doctoral candidates.

Major Activities   ΣΛΑ and its members are obligated to nourish, recognize, and reward scholarship in all ways possible. Collegiate chapter activities that serve that end are stressed. Service to the school, the program, and all students in it, is encouraged. Promoting the high ideals in professional education and assisting the worthy endeavors of landscape architecture are required; social functions are incidental. The chapters sponsor lectureships, tutorials, seminars, design competitions, and exhibits of student projects. A national scholarship of one thousand dollars is given annually to a graduate and an undergraduate member; the first was given in 1985.

Membership Active chapters 36. Total number of initiates 2,700. Chapter roll:††

1977	Alpha Founders', Chapter At Large Chapter comprised of 37 original signatories and 30 members who have been designated SLA Distinguished Members.
1978	Beta, Idaho
1978	Epsilon, L.S.U.
1978	Gamma, Michigan State
1979	Delta, Texas A & M
1979	Eta, Minnesota
1979	Iota, Arizona
1979	Kappa, Texas Tech
1979	Lambda, Penn State
1979	Mu, Cal Poly, Pomona
1979	Nu, SUNY Col., Forestry, Syracuse
1979	Omicron, Florida
1979	Theta, Cal Poly, San Luis Obispo
1979	Xi, Purdue
1979	Zeta, Utah State
1980	Pi, Washington State
1980	Rho, Ohio State
1980	Sigma, Georgia
1981	Phi, Kansas State
1981	Tau, Ball State
1981	Upsilon, Rutgers
1982	Chi, Cal, Davis
1982	Omega, V.P.I.
1982	Psi, Illinois
1983	Alpha Alpha, Morgan State
1984	Alpha Beta, West Virginia
1985	Alpha Delta, Oklahoma State
1985	Alpha Epsilon, Auburn
1985	Alpha Gamma, Wisconsin, Madison
1987	Alpha Zeta, Arizona
1988	Alpha Eta, Texas, Arlington
1988	Alpha Iota, Arkansas
1988	Alpha Lambda, Mississippi State
1988	Alpha Theta, Colorado, Denver
1989	Alpha Mu, Kentucky
1989	Alpha Nu, Colorado State
1990	Alpha Kappa, Washington (WA)
1990	Alpha Omicron, Massachusetts
1990	Alpha Xi, Michigan

†† This chapter roll is repeated from the 19th edition; no current information was provided.

Sigma Lambda Chi

(CONSTRUCTION MANAGEMENT)

SIGMA LAMBDA CHI was admitted to the Association of College Honor Societies in 1991.

Purpose The fundamental purpose of Sigma Lambda Chi shall be the recognition of outstanding students in construction.

Eligibility Limited to those majoring in construction management. The upper 20 percent of undergraduates and the upper 30 percent of graduate students who have completed other requirements for membership may be inducted.

Membership Active chapters 33. Total number of initiates 7,000. Chapter roll is not available.

Sigma Pi Sigma

(PHYSICS)

ACTIVE PIN

SIGMA PI SIGMA had its origin in a group of five undergraduate students and four faculty members at Davidson College. These physics majors and their teachers in the departments of mathematics and physics felt a need for an organization designed specifically for students in the field of physics. The group began its formal activities on December 11, 1921, and this date is recognized as the founding date. The late J. M. Douglas, head of the physics department at Davidson, was one of the chief guiding faculty members.

Sigma Pi Sigma is the only national honor society in physics. It is also the only specialized honor society to function as a component of the student organization of the professional society in its field. Sigma Pi Sigma chapters are restricted to colleges and universities of recognized standing which offer a strong physics major. The objectives of the society are: to recognize high scholarship and potential achievement in physics among outstanding students; to encourage and assist students interested in physics to develop the knowledge, competence, enthusiasm and social responsibility that are essential to the advancement of physics; to stimulate interest in advanced study and research in physics; to develop friendship among physics students and faculty members; and to promote public interest in physics.

The chapters of the society receive into membership undergraduate and graduate physics students, faculty members and a few others in closely related fields, irrespective of their membership in other organizations. Students elected to membership must attain high standards of general scholarship, outstanding achievement in physics and promise of professional merit. Membership is conferred upon no basis of selection other than scholastic or professional record. Both men and women students are eligible for membership.

Growth In 1925, the movement to nationalize the society started when the Davidson Chapter, under the leadership of undergraduates M. W. Trawick, Davidson '25, and R. W. Graves, Davidson, '26, began contacting other nearby physics departments.

At its first national convention in April, 1928, at Davidson, the first real consciousness of a national unity was induced. A group of aggressive national officers quickly developed a strong expansion and internal development policy. A headquarters organization was established that was placed under the direction of an executive secretary, Marsh W. White, at the second national convention held at the University of Kentucky in November, 1931. At the third national convention, at Purdue University in October, 1934, all elements of secrecy were removed from the procedure for the reception of new members and the original designation "fraternity" changed to "society."

At its eighth national convention at Purdue University in December 1967, approval was given for the formation of a new organization, the Society of Physics Students, through the union of Sigma Pi Sigma and the Student Sections of the American Institute of Physics. The Articles of Agreement were signed on April 22, 1968. Sigma Pi Sigma continues to operate as an honor society within the framework of the Society of Physics Students, a general membership organization open to all those interested in physics.

The number of chapters increased dramatically following the union. In the first two years, the number of chapters increased by 50 percent to over 200. Steady growth has continued in the past fifteen years to bring the number of chapters to 358 in 1985.

Government The annual meeting of the Society of Physics Students Council is designated as a convention for Sigma Pi Sigma. The council consists of twelve councillors (faculty members), twelve associate councillors (students), and the Executive Committee members. The councillors, who serve three-year terms, and the associate councillors, who serve one-year terms, are elected by chapters. The six-member Executive Committee has responsibility for operations between Council meetings. The general administrative officer of Sigma Pi Sigma is now the executive director of the Society of Physics Students.

Traditions and Insignia Although a major purpose of the society is the recognition of high scholarship in physics, a strong emphasis is placed upon the objective of maintaining the chapters as work-

ing organizations throughout the academic year. Each chapter is expected to function as an integral part of the physics department in the promotion of a number of worthwhile extracurricular activities. Yet Sigma Pi Sigma was founded by students and continues to exist as a student's physics society.

Members of Sigma Pi Sigma, particularly those newly received, are encouraged and financially assisted in joining one or more of the professional physics organizations. One of the important objectives of the society is a systematic program for the installation of a more professional spirit among the members. To this end the society offers financial and other assistance in obtaining memberships in most of the member societies of the American Institute of Physics.

The symbolism of the insignia may be explained to anyone that is interested.

Sigma Pi Sigma became a member of the ACHS in 1945, and is an affiliated society of Sections B (physics), A (mathematics), L (history and philosophy of science) and Q (education) of the American Association for the Advancement of Science. In 1951 it was designated as an affiliated society of the American Institute of Physics. It is now part of the Education Division of the American Institute of Physics.

Publications The exoteric magazine is *The Radiations of Sigma Pi Sigma*, edited by the executive secretary. A handbook for chapter officers has been prepared. An information leaflet is available for new members and others interested in the history and the activities of the society. Information concerning the organization of petitioning groups and the installation of chapters is available. Other publications of the Society are *Physics Today, Journal of Undergraduate Research in Physics* and *SPS Newsletter*.

Headquarters Society of Physics Students-Sigma Pi Sigma, American Institute of Physics, 335 East 45th Street, New York, New York 10017.

Membership Active chapters 350. Inactive chapters 53. Colonies 30. Total number of initiates 61,941. Chapter roll:

	Keene
1921	Davidson
1925	Duke
1926	Penn State (1976-1977)
1927	*Centenary* (1935-1961) (1977)
1927	Furman (1932-1985)
1927	William and Mary
1929	Ohio Wesleyan (1943-1949) (1952-1982)
1929	*St. Lawrence* (1973)
1929	Tennessee, Chattanooga
1929	West Virginia
1930	Colorado
1930	Kentucky (1951-1982)
1930	Lake Forest (1953-1974)
1930	Morningside
1930	Oklahoma
1930	*Park (MO)* (1937-1970) (1979)

1930	*Washington (WA)* (1934)
1930	William Jewell
1930	*Wooster* (1943)
1931	Wheaton
1932	*Chicago* (1934)
1932	Miami (OH)
1932	*Philippines, Quezon City* (1962)
1932	Purdue
1932	Richmond
1933	*Syracuse* (1960)
1934	Denver
1934	Oregon State (1969-1977)
1935	Michigan State (1964-1984)
1936	Brigham Young
1936	*George Washington* (1974)
1936	Ohio State
1937	Berea
1937	N.Y.U.
1937	Stetson (1947-1965)
1938	Franklin and Marshall
1938	Pitt (1957-1979)
1939	Fort Hays
1939	*Wayne State (MI)* (1955)
1940	*Muskingum* (1982)
1940	San Diego U.
1941	Citadel (1960-1979)
1941	*Georgia* (1963-1968) (1974)
1944	Western Kentucky
1946	Texas
1947	Marquette (1967-1978)
1947	Nebraska Wesleyan
1947	*Redlands* (1951)
1947	South Dakota State (1961-1979)
1947	*South Dakota* (1959)
1947	*Tufts* (1957)
1948	Arkansas
1948	*Bucknell* (1974)
1948	Colby
1948	Emory
1948	Manchester
1948	Maryland
1948	Occidental
1948	Oklahoma State
1948	*Oregon* (1952)
1948	Utah (1965-1969)
1949	Alabama
1949	Clemson
1949	Delaware
1949	Evansville
1949	Georgia Tech
1949	*Gettysburg* (1961)
1949	Howard
1949	*Illinois Tech* (1966)
1949	Maine
1949	Southern Illinois
1949	*Trinity (CT)* (1977)
1949	V.P.I.
1949	*Wyoming* (1974)
1950	Arizona
1950	Auburn
1950	Connecticut
1950	Kansas
1950	L.S.U.
1950	Missouri, Rolla
1950	*New Hampshire* (1957)
1950	St. Olaf
1950	Tulane
1951	Hofstra
1951	Manhattan
1951	South Dakota Mines
1951	St. Joseph's (PA)
1951	Virginia State, Petersburg
1952	Louisville
1953	Boston Col
1953	North Carolina State
1953	UCLA
1954	Florida State
1954	*Hawaii* (1963)
1954	Loyola, New Orleans
1954	Temple
1954	Tennessee
1954	Texas Tech
1954	*Upsala* (1977)
1955	*Wabash* (1964)
1956	Houston
1956	South Carolina (1962-1985)
1957	Florida
1958	Nevada
1958	Ohio
1958	U of the South
1958	*Utica* (1965)
1958	Wichita
1959	Baylor
1959	Linfield
1959	New York Poly
1959	Texas A & M
1959	Utah State
1959	Western Illinois
1959	Westminster (PA)
1960	Idaho
1960	*N.Y.U.* (1973)
1960	New Mexico State
1960	SUNY, Albany
1960	Southwestern Louisiana
1960	St. Bonaventure
1960	Washburn
1962	Adelphi
1962	Clark
1962	Colorado State
1962	Indiana
1962	McMurry
1962	*Providence* (1986)
1962	Texas, Abilene
1963	*Cal State, Los Angeles* (1974)
1963	Detroit
1963	Illinois Benedictine
1963	Murray State
1963	Oklahoma City
1963	R.P.I.
1963	Rhodes
1963	Texas Christian
1963	Tulsa
1963	Xavier (OH)
1964	*Albion* (1974)

1964	*Nebraska* (1965)	1969	Morgan State
1964	*Rutgers, Newark* (1965)	1969	New Orleans
1964	St. Mary's	1969	North Carolina, Wilmington
1965	Drexel	1969	Pittsburg State, Kansas
1965	*Duquesne* (1973)	1969	Rhode Island
1965	Lamar	1969	Ripon
1965	North Texas	1969	Rochester Tech (1974-1981)
1965	Sam Houston	1969	Rutgers, Camden
1966	Cal State, Northridge	1969	SUNY, Stony Brook
1966	*Cal, Santa Barbara* (1976)	1969	Santa Clara
1966	DePauw	1969	Scranton
1966	Emporia	1969	Seton Hall
1966	Navy	1969	Southeast Missouri
1966	Roanoke	1969	Southwestern State (OK)
1966	Rose-Hulman	1969	St. Peter's
1966	South Florida	1969	Toledo
1966	Stephen F. Austin	1969	Wisconsin, Oshkosh
1966	Texas, Arlington	1969	Wisconsin, Platteville
1966	*Trinity (DC)* (1977)	1969	Wisconsin, Whitewater
1966	Trinity (TX)	1969	Wright State
1966	V.M.I.	1969	Yeshiva
1966	Virginia	1970	Bloomsburg
1967	*Loma Linda* (1974)	1970	*Boston State* (1983)
1967	Louisiana Tech	1970	Cal State, Sacramento
1967	Memphis State	1970	Cal, Irvine
1967	Monmouth (NJ)	1970	Central Missouri State
1967	*Morehead* (1977)	1970	Central State (OK)
1967	*Pan American* (1986)	1970	East Stroudsburg
1968	Ball State	1970	Eastern Illinois
1968	Carson-Newman	1970	Elizabethtown
1968	*Cooper Union* (1986)	1970	Fordham
1968	Dayton	1970	George Mason
1968	Denison	1970	Grove City
1968	Dickinson	1970	Holy Cross
1968	Johns Hopkins	1970	Hunter
1968	Lowell	1970	Indiana State
1968	Moravian	1970	Iona
1968	Northeast Louisiana	1970	Jacksonville
1968	Northern Arizona	1970	Mississippi Col
1968	*Pacific Union* (1986)	1970	Mississippi State
1968	*Salem (WV)* (1972)	1970	Northwestern
1968	Widener	1970	*Pratt* (1972)
1968	Wisconsin, Superior	1970	Rice
1969	Akron	1970	SUNY Col., Fredonia
1969	Alabama, Huntsville	1970	Tennessee Space Inst
1969	Appalachian	1970	Thomas More
1969	Augustana	1970	Worcester Tech
1969	Austin Peay	1971	American
1969	*Birmingham-Southern* (1977)	1971	Arkansas State
1969	Bowling Green	1971	Bemidji
1969	Cal Poly, Pomona	1971	Benedictine
1969	Cal Poly, San Luis Obispo	1971	Bradley
1969	Cal State, Long Beach	1971	Bridgeport
1969	Cincinnati	1971	Eastern New Mexico
1969	Clarkson	1971	Edinboro
1969	*Cleveland* (1986)	1971	Grambling
1969	Florida Southern (1975-1984)	1971	*Jamestown* (1979)
1969	Florida Tech	1971	Loyola (MD)
1969	Georgia State	1971	Missouri, Kansas City
1969	Hanover	1971	New York Tech
1969	Idaho State	1971	Northwestern Louisiana
1969	Miami (FL)	1971	Old Dominion

1971	Ottawa (1988)
1971	SUNY, Buffalo
1971	Seattle
1971	Southern Mississippi
1971	Thiel
1971	Wake Forest
1971	West Virginia Tech
1972	Austin
1972	DePaul
1972	Dordt
1972	East Carolina
1972	East Texas
1972	Gannon
1972	Indiana (PA)
1972	Kansas Wesleyan (1986)
1972	Kent
1972	Lawrence Tech
1972	Lynchburg
1972	Muhlenberg (1977)
1972	Nebraska, Omaha (1977)
1972	Puget Sound
1972	SUNY Col., Geneseo
1972	Southern Arkansas
1972	Southern
1972	Southwest Missouri
1972	USC
1972	Youngstown State
1973	Abilene Christian
1973	Concordia Col. (MN) (See North Dakota State)
1973	Frostburg
1973	Henderson
1973	Lycoming
1973	Moorhead (1986) (See North Dakota State)
1973	North Dakota State
1973	Northern Illinois
1973	SUNY Col., Oswego
1973	Saginaw Valley
1973	Shippensburg
1973	St. John's (NY)
1973	Texas A & I
1973	Wagner (1977)
1973	West Florida
1974	Andrews
1974	Cameron
1974	Montana State
1974	New Mexico Highlands
1974	North Carolina, Charlotte
1974	Prairie View
1974	SUNY, Binghamton
1974	Siena
1974	Southern Colorado
1974	Trenton
1975	Heidelberg
1975	John Carroll
1975	Juniata
1975	Kearney
1975	Lewis
1975	Midwestern
1975	Rollins
1975	SUNY Col., Oneonta
1975	Slippery Rock
1975	Towson
1975	Union
1975	Wisconsin, River Falls
1976	Augsburg
1976	Central Michigan
1976	Eastern Oregon
1976	Florida International
1976	Iowa State
1976	Kansas State
1976	Massachusetts Pharmacy
1976	Michigan Tech
1976	Morehouse
1976	North Alabama
1976	North Georgia
1976	Southwest Texas
1976	Tennessee Tech
1976	Western Washington
1977	Angelo
1977	Guilford
1977	North Carolina, Greensboro
1977	Valparaiso
1977	Villanova
1978	Cal State, Hayward
1978	Colorado Mines
1978	Jackson (MS)
1978	Northeastern (OK)
1978	SUNY Col., Cortland
1978	Southern Methodist
1978	Valdosta
1978	Virginia Commonwealth
1979	Elmhurst
1979	Loyola Marymount, Los Angeles
1979	Minnesota
1979	Mississippi
1979	South Alabama
1979	Wilkes
1979	Wisconsin, Eau Claire
1980	Loyola, Chicago
1980	Maryland, Baltimore County
1980	Olivet Nazarene
1980	SUNY Col., Plattsburgh
1980	SUNY Col., Potsdam
1980	Vanderbilt
1981	Alma
1981	Arkansas, Little Rock
1981	Boston U
1981	Cal, Davis
1981	Cal, Santa Cruz (1986)
1981	Georgia Southern
1981	Millersville
1981	San Francisco
1981	Southern Oregon
1981	Ursinus
1982	Cal State, Fresno
1982	Creighton
1982	Hope
1982	M.I.T.
1982	Presbyterian
1982	Stockton
1983	Arizona State
1983	Benedict
1983	Cal State, Chico

1983 Central Arkansas
1983 Columbia (NY)
1983 Iowa
1983 Madison Col
1983 North Carolina
1983 Northern Iowa
1983 Southeastern Massachusetts
1984 Cal, Berkeley
1984 Dallas
1984 Eastern Kentucky
1984 Luther
1984 Principia
1984 Texas Southern
1985 Randolph, Macon
1985 West Georgia

Colonies: Penn State, Behrend, Eastern Michigan, Hampton Inst., North Carolina, Asheville, Army, Colorado, Colorado Springs, Francis Marion, Lewis and Clark, Mary Washington, Michigan, Mount Union, Northeastern, West Chester, Central Washington, Charleston (SC), Lincoln (PA), Middle Tennessee, Northeast Missouri, San Jose, Carroll, Drew, Gonzaga, Millsaps, Rutgers, Susquehanna, Wellesley, Keene, Mesa, Transylvania, Wyoming

Sigma Tau Delta

(ENGLISH)

ACTIVE PIN

SIGMA TAU DELTA, national English honor society, was founded December 12, 1922, as the English Club of the Dakota Wesleyan University, Mitchell, South Dakota. It seeks to promote the mastery of written expression, encourage worthwhile reading, and foster a spirit of fellowship among men and women professionally engaged in the study or teaching of the English language and literature. It endeavors to stimulate among its members a desire to express life in terms of truth and beauty and to make first-hand contacts with literary masterpieces. Active membership is limited to upperclassmen, graduate students, and faculty elected on the basis of high scholarship.

Under the leadership of Prof. Judson Quincy Owen, Dakota Wesleyan University, who founded the first chapter and wrote the national constitution, Prof. Frederic Fadner, Lombard College, who prepared the ritual, and Prof. P. C. Somerville, Kansas Wesleyan University, the fraternity became a national organization in May, 1924. It held its first national convention April 3 and 4, 1925. At this meeting it formally chartered its first twelve chapters, adopted its insignia, and provided for the regular publication of *The Rectangle,* a literary magazine published twice a year, and *The Newsletter,* also published twice a year.

In 1972 Sigma Tau Delta became a member of the Association of College Honor Societies.

National conventions have been held in 1970 at Northern Illinois University, in 1972 at Kearney State College, in 1974 at Baylor University, and in 1976 at the University of Mississippi.

Purpose To confer distinction for high achievement in undergraduate, graduate, and professional studies in English language and literature; to provide cultural stimulation on college campuses through its local chapters; to furnish community interest within English departments through its local chapters; and to encourage creative and critical writing.

Eligibility Undergraduate students must have either a major or minor in English, must have taken at least two literature courses beyond the freshman requirements, must have a B average in English, must rank in the highest thirty-five percent of the class in general scholarship (cumulative scholastic record), and must have completed three semesters or five quarters of the college course. Graduate students must have graduated with scholastic rating within the upper twenty percent of the class.

Government A Board of Directors from five area regions, an executive committee of president, vice-president, executive secretary, treasurer, and historian, and a student advisory council from the five area regions govern the national organization. The Board plus the executive committee and the student advisory council meets in the spring and fall to transact most of the business of the society. Other business is handled at national and regional conventions.

Major Activities Sigma Tau Delta activities include awarding of the annual Judson Q. Owen Graduate Fellowship of $1,000 in creative writing, the Eleanor B. North Undergraduate Award of $200 in poetry, the Frederic Fadner First National President Award of $200 in critical writing, and the Herbert L. Hughes Award of $200 in short story; conducting of the biennial international convention and regional conventions; awarding of annual scholarships of $1,000 each; and awarding of several "Outstanding Chapter" awards of $100 each.

Traditions and Insignia The emblem is a gold badge or a key design jeweled to indicate the wearer's degree of professional attainment.

Publications Publication of *The Rectangle,* a literary magazine, biannually; publication of *The Newsletter,* biannually; publication of the *Scholars' Essay Series.*

Headquarters Department of English, Northern Illinois University, DeKalb, Illinois 60115.

Membership Active chapters 392. Inactive chapters 79. Total number of initiates 68,500. Chapter roll:††

†† This chapter roll is repeated from the 19th edition; no current information was provided.

Ashland (1969)
Marymount (1969)
New Orleans (1969)
Pasadena College (1969)
Southeastern Louisiana (1969)
Eta, Alliance
Iota, Howard Payne
Phi Delta, Western Illinois
Phi Kappa, West Virginia Wesleyan
Rho Iota, Clarion
Upsilon Kappa, Campbellsville College
Xi Kappa, Mississippi State
Xi Theta, Findlay
1922 Alpha, Dakota Wesleyan (1930-1961)
1924 *Beta Alpha, Grand Island* (1929)
1924 Delta Alpha, Westmar (formerly Western Union College)
1924 *Gamma Alpha, Lombard* (1929)
1925 *Epsilon Alpha, Parsons* (1930)
1925 Eta Alpha, Georgetown Col (1932-1938) (1942-1946) (1950-1969)
1925 *Iota Alpha, Jamestown* (1936)
1925 Kappa Alpha, Simpson
1925 Lambda Alpha, Baylor
1925 Mu Alpha The Grand Chapter
1925 *Nu Alpha, Drake* (1946)
1925 Omicron Alpha, Iowa Wesleyan (1931-1950)
1925 *Pi Alpha, Drury* (1934)
1925 *Theta Alpha, College of Idaho* (1940)
1925 *Xi Alpha, Chattanooga* (1929)
1925 *Zeta Alpha, Kansas Wesleyan* (1931)
1926 Chi Alpha, Texas Christian (1956-1976)
1926 Omega Alpha, Muskingum
1926 Phi Alpha, Nebraska, Peru
1926 *Psi Alpha, Washington* (1927)
1926 *Rho Alpha, Monmouth* (1969)
1926 Sigma Alpha, Kansas State, Pittsburg
1926 Tau Alpha, Upper Iowa
1926 *Upsilon Alpha, Redlands* (1969)
1927 *Alpha Beta, Southwestern (TX)* (1940)
1927 *Beta Beta, Western Reserve* (1969)
1927 Delta Beta, Mary Hardin-Baylor
1927 *Epsilon Beta, Bucknell* (1969)
1927 Eta Beta, St. Mary-of-the-Woods
1927 Gamma Beta, Morningside
1927 *Zeta Beta, Hillsdale* (1938)
1928 Iota Beta, Columbia (SC) (1956-1977)
1928 *Kappa Beta, Lindenwood* (1944)
1928 *Lambda Beta, Iowa State Teachers* (1944-1951) (1969)
1928 *Mu Beta, William Jewell* (1930-1951) (1960)
1928 *Nu Beta, Lynchburg* (1946)
1928 *Omicron Beta, Duke* (1930)
1928 Theta Beta, Hunter
1928 Xi Beta, Nebraska, Kearney
1929 Phi Beta, Harris Teachers
1929 Pi Beta, Nebraska, Wayne
1929 *Rho Beta, Albright* (1959)
1929 *Sigma Beta, Nebraska, Chadron* (1945-1961) (1963)
1929 Tau Beta, Durant State (OK)

1929 Upsilon Beta, East Texas
1930 *Alpha Gamma, General Beadle State (SD)* (1932)
1930 *Chi Beta, Shurtleff*
1930 *Delta Gamma, Fresno State* (1945)
1930 Epsilon Gamma, Northwest Missouri (1950-1977)
1930 *Eta Gamma, Lake Forest* (1940)
1930 Iota Gamma, Doane (1932-1976)
1930 Omega Beta, Ouachita Baptist (1931-1954)
1930 *Psi Beta, Wisconsin, Stevens Point* (1969)
1930 *Theta Gamma, New Mexico Normal* (1936)
1930 *Zeta Gamma, New Mexico Western* (1959)
1931 Kappa Gamma, Omaha (1950-1964)
1931 *Lambda Gamma, Carroll* (1950)
1931 *Mu Gamma, Moorhead* (1941)
1931 *Nu Gamma, Wisconsin, Whitewater* (1944)
1931 *Omicron Gamma, North Dakota* (1933)
1931 *Pi Gamma, Coker* (1970)
1931 Rho Gamma, Louisiana Tech
1931 Xi Gamma, Northern State (SD) (1934-1974)
1932 *Sigma Gamma, North Central (IL)* (1956)
1932 Tau Gamma, Arizona State (1940-1953)
1932 Upsilon Gamma, Eastern Illinois
1933 *Chi Gamma, Central State (OK)* (1940-1953) (1969)
1933 *Psi Gamma, Youngstown* (1950)
1934 Alpha Delta, Southeast Missouri
1934 *Beta Delta, Marquette* (1969)
1935 Delta Delta, Sam Houston (1942-1971)
1935 *Epsilon Delta, D. C. Teachers* (1947)
1935 Eta Delta, Slippery Rock
1935 Gamma Delta, Trinity (TX) (1937-1956)
1935 Zeta Delta, Butler
1936 *Iota Delta, McKendree (IL)* (1969)
1936 Kappa Delta, Bowling Green
1936 Lambda Delta, Illinois State
1936 Theta Delta, Alabama State, Florence
1937 *Mu Delta, Our Lady of the Lake* (1969)
1937 Nu Delta, Buena Vista
1938 *Omicron Delta, Ball State* (1969)
1938 Xi Delta, Northern Illinois
1939 *Pi Delta, Dusquesne* (1969)
1939 *Rho Delta, Southern Illinois* (1942)
1940 *Sigma Delta, Central Michigan* (1969)
1940 Tau Delta, North Texas
1941 Chi Delta, Oklahoma Baptist
1941 Upsilon Delta, Waynesburg
1943 Psi Delta, Texas Tech
1944 *Omega Delta, Marywood* (1969)
1945 *Alpha Epsilon, Mary Washington* (1969)
1945 Beta Epsilon, Texas Woman's
1946 Gamma Epsilon, Oklahoma State
1947 *Delta Epsilon, Central* (1969)
1947 *Eta Epsilon, Dickinson State* (1952)
1947 Iota Epsilon, Anderson
1947 *Kappa Epsilon, Centenary* (1969)
1947 Lambda Epsilon, Davis and Elkins
1947 *Zeta Epsilon, Briar Cliff* (1969)
1948 *Mu Epsilon, Florida* (1952)
1948 Nu Epsilon, Missouri Valley

1949	Omicron Epsilon, Mississippi for Women

1949 Omicron Epsilon, Mississippi for Women
1949 Pi Epsilon, Alabama State, Jacksonville
1949 Xi Epsilon, Hardin-Simmons
1950 *Rho Epsilon, Florida State* (1969)
1950 Sigma Epsilon, Eastern Kentucky (1953-1971)
1950 Tau Epsilon, Abilene Christian
1950 *Upsilon Epsilon, Seattle Pacific* (1959)
1951 Chi Epsilon, Mount Mary
1951 Phi Epsilon, McMurry
1951 *Psi Epsilon, Florida Southern* (1969)
1952 Omega Epsilon, Southwest Texas
1954 Alpha Zeta, Sul Ross
1955 Beta Zeta, Northeast Louisiana
1955 Delta Zeta, East Stroudsburg
1955 Gamma Zeta, Stetson
1956 Epsilon Zeta, Carthage
1956 Kappa Zeta, Athens
1956 Lambda Zeta, Southwestern Louisiana
1956 Mu Zeta, David Lipscomb
1956 Nu Zeta, Texas Wesleyan
1956 Omicron Zeta, Long Island
1956 Pi Zeta, McNeese
1956 Rho Zeta, Tampa
1956 Theta Zeta, Wisconsin, Eau Claire
1956 *Xi Zeta, Penn State* (1972)
1957 *Alpha Theta, Nicholls* (1969)
1957 Beta Theta, C. W. Post
1957 Chi Zeta, Caldwell
1957 *Omega Zeta, L.S.U.* (1969)
1957 *Phi Zeta, Catholic, Puerto Rico* (1969)
1957 Psi Zeta, Mississippi Col.
1957 Tau Zeta, Tennessee Tech
1957 *Upsilon Zeta, Greenville* (1969)
1958 Delta Theta, California (PA)
1958 Gamma Theta, Central Missouri State
1959 Epsilon Theta, Southern Arkansas
1959 Eta Theta, Wayland Baptist
1959 Zeta Theta, Samford
1960 *Iota Theta, Bethany* (1969)
1960 Kappa Theta, Auburn
1960 Lambda Theta, Wisconsin, Milwaukee
1960 Mu Theta, Arlington State (TX)
1961 *Nu Theta, Kansas City* (1969)
1961 Omicron Theta, East Carolina
1961 *Pi Theta, Colorado State* (1969)
1961 *Rho Theta, Southern Methodist* (1969)
1961 Sigma Beta, Sterling
1962 Chi Theta, West Texas
1962 Omega Theta, Tennessee, Martin
1962 Phi Theta, Texas Lutheran
1962 Tau Theta, Olivet Nazarene
1962 Upsilon Theta, St. Mary's (NB)
1963 *Texas A & M* (1969)
1963 Beta Iota, Marshall
1963 Delta Iota, Ohio Northern
1963 Epsilon Iota, Culver-Stockton
1963 Gamma Iota, Muhlenberg
1963 Pi Iota, Western Kentucky
1963 Theta Iota, Keuka
1964 Northwestern Louisiana
1964 Oglethorpe

1964 Beta Omega, Fairmont
1964 Chi Iota, Mankato
1964 Delta Kappa, Indiana State
1964 Mu Iota, Northeastern (OK)
1964 Omega Iota, Georgia State
1964 *Omicron Iota, Steubenville* (1969)
1964 *Phi, Minot* (1969)
1964 Psi Iota, Yeshiva
1964 Xi Iota, Carson-Newman
1965 Alpha Zeta, Stephen F. Austin
1965 Epsilon Kappa, Berry (GA)
1965 Iota Kappa, Morris Harvey
1966 *Our Lady of the Elms* (1969)
1966 Eta Kappa, Radford
1966 *Kappa Kappa, Westhampton* (1969)
1966 Kappa Tau, Marian (WI)
1966 *Lambda Kappa, West Virginia Tech* (1969)
1966 Theta Kappa, Bloomsburg
1966 Xi Kappa, Cedar Crest
1967 *Mt. Angel College* (1970)
1967 *South Carolina* (1969)
1967 *St. Martin's* (1969)
1967 Lambda Kappa, Montevallo
1967 *Rho Gamma, College of Artesia* (1971)
1970 Alpha Kappa, Cardinal Stritch
1970 Alpha Lambda, Northeast Missouri
1970 Beta Lambda, Bradley
1971 Delta Lambda, Houston Baptist
1971 Epsilon Lambda, Frostburg
1971 Eta Lambda, Arkansas Col.
1971 Gamma Lambda, Gardner-Webb
1971 Iota Lambda, SUNY Col., Geneseo
1971 Kappa Lambda, Savannah
1971 Lambda Lambda, St. Augustine's
1971 Mu Lambda, Central Methodist
1971 Theta Lambda, Eureka
1971 Zeta Lambda, IUPUI
1972 Alpha Mu, Heidelberg
1972 Beta Mu, East Texas Baptist
1972 Chi Lambda, Elmhurst
1972 Delta Mu, Wagner
1972 Epsilon Mu, Tarkio
1972 Eta Mu, William Woods
1972 Gamma Mu, Southampton
1972 Nu Lambda, Navy
1972 Omega Lambda, Clinch Valley
1972 Omicron Lambda, Fayetteville
1972 Phi Lambda, Coppin
1972 Pi Lambda, Troy
1972 Psi Lambda, Evangel
1972 Rho Lambda, Lewis
1972 Sigma Lambda, Lane
1972 Tau Lambda, Mississippi Valley
1972 Upsilon Lambda, Prairie View
1972 Xi Lambda, Johnson C. Smith
1972 Zeta Mu, Kentucky State
1973 Iota Mu, Winthrop
1973 Kappa Mu, Union
1973 Lambda Mu, Wisconsin, Oshkosh
1973 Mu Mu, Alverno
1973 Nu Mu, Ozarks
1973 Theta Mu, Winston-Salem

1973   Xi Mu, Kent
1974   Alpha Nu, Glenville
1974   Beta Nu, Alabama A & M
1974   Chi Mu, Salem College
1974   Delta Nu, Southwest Missouri
1974   Gamma Nu, Lamar
1974   Omega Mu, South Florida
1974   Omicron Mu, Henderson
1974   Phi Mu, Miami (FL)
1974   Pi Mu, Harding
1974   Psi Mu, Maryland, Eastern Shore
1974   Rho Mu, Oklahoma Christian
1974   Sigma Mu, Georgian Court
1974   Tau Mu, Missouri Western
1974   Upsilon Mu, Alabama, Huntsville
1975   Epsilon Nu, Middle Tennessee
1975   Eta Nu, Mississippi
1975   Iota Nu, Elizabeth City
1975   Kappa Nu, Puget Sound
1975   Lambda Nu, Kutztown
1975   Theta Nu, Georgia Southwestern
1975   Zeta Nu, Arkansas, Pine Bluff
1976   Chi Nu, Miami (OH)
1976   Mu Nu, Midland Lutheran
1976   Nu Nu, Bowie
1976   Omicron Nu, West Liberty
1976   Phi Nu, Lehigh
1976   Pi Nu, Angelo
1976   Rho Nu, Virginia Union
1976   Sigma Nu, Benedict
1976   Tau Mu, Wofford
1976   Upsilon Nu, Morehouse
1976   Xi Nu, Norfolk

Sigma Theta Tau

(NURSING)

ACTIVE PIN

SIGMA THETA TAU, the only national honor society of nursing, was founded at Indiana University Training School for Nurses in 1922. The founders were six students in the School who chose the name Sigma Theta Tau to represent the initials of the Greek words Storga, Tharos, Tima, meaning Love, Courage, Honor. October 5 is officially recognized as the anniversary date.

Purpose   The purpose of Sigma Theta Tau is (1) To recognize superior achievement. (2) To recognize the development of leadership qualities. (3) To foster high professional standards. (4) To encourage creative work. (5) To strengthen commitment on the part of individuals to the ideals and purposes of the profession.

Eligibility   Candidates for membership shall have demonstrated superior scholastic achievement and evidence of professional leadership potential. Undergraduate members are selected from junior and senior students in basic professional programs in nursing. Nurses matriculated for graduate study and full-time faculty members of the educational unit may also be selected. In addition, nurses who have received a baccalaureate or higher degree and have shown marked achievement in the field of nursing are eligible for election. Student membership is restricted to the upper one-third of a class.

Government   The national society is composed of its constituent local chapters and of honorary members who are chosen nationally. Local chapters consist of members initiated by the chapter and accepted by transfer from other chapters. The House of Delegates, composed of the national officers and two delegates from each local chapter, constitutes the voting body of the society. Regular meetings of the House of Delegates are held biennially in the odd years, with local chapters serving as hosts.

Traditions and Insignia   The insignia is a key described as follows: the cup denotes the satisfaction of professional life. The circle of gold with its six stars represents the six founders. The Greek letters in black—Sigma, Theta, Tau—represent the charge: *Storga, Tharos, Tima* (Love, Courage, Honor). The lamp is the lamp of learning. The key may be jeweled with amethyst stars and a circle of pearls. The colors of the society are orchid and fuschia. The flower is the orchid.

Major Activities   The society awards research grants to nurses engaged in nursing research; holds biennial conventions; conducts national and international research conferences; conducts Regional Assemblies and programs, and is currently engaged in developing a Center for Nursing Scholarship. Local chapters fund local grants, research and scholarships; initiate projects that contribute to their school and community; sponsor programs of significance to the profession; act as hosts to national programs; and participate in honor convocations and other campus activities.

Funds   The purpose of the Research Committee is to encourage qualified nurses to contribute to the advancement of nursing through research, and to administer the Research Fund. Applicants for awards must have received formal preparation for research at the graduate level, and have a well-defined research project pertinent to nursing. Allocation of funds is based on the quality of the proposed research, the past performance, and future promise of the applicant, and the research budget.

The amount of a grant is determined by the amount of funds requested, the number of requests, and the amount of funds available during the grant period. The maximum limit is $3,000. The allocation of funds is determined by the Research Committee and the national treasurer. Applications are due March 1.

Publications   Sigma Theta Tau publishes the journal *Image: Journal of Nursing Scholarship* four times a year and the newsletter *Reflections* four times a year, and monographs of scholarly papers.

Headquarters School of Nursing Building, Indiana University, Indianapolis, Indiana 46202.

Membership Active chapters 263 (3 outside U.S.). Inactive chapters 2. Total number of initiates 130,000. Chapter roll:††

1922   Alpha, Indiana
1927   *Beta, Washington*
1929   Gamma, Iowa
1931   Delta, Kansas (1957-1965)
1932   Epsilon, Ohio State
1934   Zeta, Minnesota
1946   Eta, Pitt
1953   Iota, Vanderbilt
1953   Kappa, Catholic
1953   Lambda, Wayne
1953   Theta, Boston
1955   Mu, Connecticut
1958   Nu, Alabama
1958   Xi, Penn
1959   Omicron, Syracuse
1959   Pi, Maryland
1959   Rho, Michigan
1960   Sigma, St. Joseph
1960   Tau, Georgetown
1961   Phi, South Dakota State
1961   Upsilon, New York
1962   Alpha Alpha, North Carolina
1962   Chi, St. Catherine's
1962   Omega, DePauw
1962   Psi, Washington
1963   Alpha Beta, Loyola, Chicago
1963   Alpha Delta, Texas Medical
1963   Alpha Gamma, San Jose
1964   Alpha Epsilon, Emory
1964   Alpha Eta, Cal, San Francisco
1964   Alpha Iota, Missouri
1964   Alpha Theta, Florida
1964   Alpha Zeta, Columbia
1966   Alpha Kappa, Colorado, Denver
1966   Alpha Lambda, Illinois, Chicago
1966   Alpha Nu, Villanova
1966   Alpha Omicron, St. Xavier, Chicago
1966   Alpha Pi, Wyoming
1966   Alpha Rho, West Virginia
1966   Alpha Sigma, Seattle
1966   Alpha Xi, South Carolina
1966   Mu, Western Reserve
1968   Alpha Tau, Rutgers
1968   Alpha Upsilon, Cornell
1970   Alpha Chi, Boston
1970   Alpha Omega, Adelphi
1970   Alpha Phi, Hunter
1970   Alpha Psi, Michigan
1970   Beta Alpha, Texas Christian
1970   Beta Alpha, Texas Woman's
1970   Beta Delta, Oklahoma

†† This chapter roll is repeated from the 19th edition; no current information was provided.

1970   Beta Gamma, San Francisco
1972   Beta Epsilon, Duke
1972   Beta Eta, Wisconsin
1972   Beta Iota, Cincinnati
1972   Beta Kappa, Virginia
1972   Beta Theta, Tennessee
1972   Beta Zeta, Massachusetts
1974   Beta Lambda, Avila
1974   Beta Mu, Arizona
1974   Beta Nu, East Carolina
1974   Beta Omicron, Georgia Medical
1974   Beta Pi, Florida State
1974   Beta Rho, Ball State
1974   Beta Sigma, Penn
1974   Beta Tau, Miami
1974   Beta Xi, Delaware
1976   Beta Chi, Northwestern
1976   Beta Omega, Northern Illinois
1976   Beta Phi, Alabama, Huntsville
1976   Beta Psi, Oregon
1976   Beta Upsilon, Arizona State
1976   Gamma Alpha, Loma Linda
1976   Gamma Beta, Howard
1976   Gamma Delta, Pittsburgh State
1976   Gamma Epsilon, Northeastern
1976   Gamma Gamma, San Diego State
1976   Gamma Zeta, North Carolina, Greensboro

Tau Beta Pi

(ENGINEERING)

ACTIVE PIN

TAU BETA PI was founded at Lehigh University on June 15, 1885, by Prof. Edward Higginson Williams, Jr. Its purpose, as stated in the preamble of its constitution, is: "To mark in a fitting manner those who have conferred honor upon their *alma mater* by distinguished scholarship and exemplary character as undergraduates in engineering, or by their attainments as alumni in the field of engineering, and to foster a spirit of liberal culture in engineering colleges." When a chapter becomes established it may confer its key upon its alumni and students of earlier years. Membership may be offered to graduates of engineering colleges where there is no chapter, provided the recipient fulfilled the regular eligibility requirements as a student. Membership may also be offered to other outstanding engineers. Undergraduates with scholastic averages placing them in the top eighth of the junior class or the top fifth of the senior class are further considered on the basis of character, leadership and campus service.

The society was incorporated under the laws of

Tennessee in 1947, and the Executive Council was enlarged from three to five members to conform with law.

Government Conventions are held each year. Between conventions the Executive Council of five alumni administers the affairs of the society. These persons are elected from the same locality and hold frequent meetings.

Until 1947 a secretary-treasurer was appointed by the Executive Council to conduct the routine business of the society. The 1946 convention approved the employment of a full-time, permanent secretary-treasurer and editor, and the post was filled in 1947. Twenty years later, the post of assistant secretary-treasurer was added.

Traditions and Insignia The badge is a watch key in the form of the bent of a trestle. It displays certain secret characters and the name and chapter of the owner. The colors are seal brown and white.

Publications The society publishes a quarterly magazine called *The Bent*, which was first issued in 1906. In 1985, circulation exceeded 93,000 subscribers. Another publication, *The Bulletin*, was launched in 1924 and is distributed to undergraduate members. A catalogue was published by the Executive Council in 1898, and a new edition in 1911 in looseleaf form, followed by a similar edition in 1916. Others were published in 1927, 1932 and 1939.

Funds and Fellowships A fellowship program was instituted in 1929 to give outstanding members a year of graduate work in the field and at the institution of their choice. To date 558 fellowships have been awarded with grants totaling over $1,200,000.

In 1953 a cooperative industry-Tau Beta Pi fellowship program was inaugurated under which Tau Beta Pi awards fellowship stipends that are paid by industrial firms. Through its regular fellowship procedures Tau Beta Pi selects these winners and administers this full program, leaving only the donation of the annual stipend currently $5,000 for each winner, for the cooperating company.

A student loan program was inaugurated in 1932, and thus far 1,350 undergraduate and graduate student members have borrowed a total of $425,000 from the society.

Programs A district program was established in 1978. Sixteen volunteer national officers (a program director and fifteen district directors) attend chapter functions and train student officers in chapter management.

Major awards are given each year to the outstanding chapter and the most improved chapter in the nation through the chapter awards program. A laureate program was established in 1984 to recognize annually up to five students who outstandingly exemplify a spirit of liberal culture in engineering colleges.

Through a greater interest in government program, cash grants up to $750 each are awarded annually to chapters for unique projects performed in the public interest.

Merger with Sigma Tau Sigma Tau Fraternity was founded in 1904 at the University of Nebraska and grew to include 34 collegiate chapters and 45,000 initiated members. In the belief that a single, strong honor society would serve the engineering profession better than two competing societies, the governing boards of Sigma Tau and Tau Beta Pi recommended merger of the two organizations. The collegiate chapters of both approved, and the merger became effective January 1, 1974. All Sigma Tau chapters were converted to or merged into Tau Beta Pi chapters early in 1974; the Sigma Tau headquarters was then closed and its records transferred to Tau Beta Pi's central office. Tau Beta Pi continues to provide customary membership services to Sigma Tau alumni, all of whom may become members of Tau Beta Pi if they choose. The merger is commemorated in the annual award of a Tau Beta Pi-Sigma Tau graduate fellowship.

Headquarters University of Tennessee, Knoxville, Tennessee, 37916. The headquarters office suite, built for the society by the university in 1963 and occupied on a rental basis by Tau Beta Pi's salaried staff of eleven persons, is named for R. C. Matthews, who served as secretary-treasurer from 1905 to 1947.

Membership Active chapters 201. Inactive chapters 5. Graduate/Alumni chapters 57. Total number of initiates 349,248. Chapter roll:

1885	PA Alpha,	Lehigh
1892	MI Alpha,	Michigan State
1893	IN Alpha,	Purdue
1896	NJ Alpha,	Stevens Tech
1897	IL Alpha,	Illinois
1899	WI Alpha,	Wisconsin, Madison
1900	OH Alpha,	Case Western Reserve
1902	KY Alpha,	Kentucky
1902	MO Alpha,	Missouri
1902	NY Alpha,	Columbia (NY)
1904	MI Beta,	Michigan Tech
1905	CO Alpha,	Colorado Mines
1905	CO Beta,	Colorado
1906	IL Beta,	Illinois Tech
1906	MI Gamma,	Michigan
1906	MO Beta,	Missouri, Rolla
1906	NY Beta,	Syracuse
1907	CA Alpha,	Cal, Berkeley
1907	IA Alpha,	Iowa State
1908	NY Gamma,	R.P.I. (1916-1936)
1909	IA Beta,	Iowa
1909	MN Alpha,	Minnesota
1910	MA Alpha,	Worcester Tech
1910	NY Delta,	Cornell
1911	ME Alpha,	Maine
1912	PA Beta,	Penn State
1912	WA Alpha,	Washington (WA)
1914	AR Alpha,	Arkansas
1914	KS Alpha,	Kansas
1915	OH Beta,	Cincinnati
1916	PA Gamma,	Carnegie-Mellon
1916	TX Alpha,	Texas

1921	AL Alpha, Auburn	
1921	CA Beta, Cal Tech	
1921	MD Alpha, Johns Hopkins	
1921	OH Gamma, Ohio State	
1921	PA Delta, Penn	
1921	PA Epsilon, Lafayette	
1921	VA Alpha, Virginia	
1922	MA Beta, M.I.T.	
1922	MO Gamma, Washington (MO)	
1922	WV Alpha, West Virginia	
1923	CT Alpha, Yale	
1923	*MA Gamma, Harvard* (1936)	
1923	WA Beta, Washington State	
1924	OR Alpha, Oregon State	
1925	GA Alpha, Georgia Tech	
1925	NC Alpha, North Carolina State	
1926	AL Beta, Alabama	
1926	AZ Alpha, Arizona	
1926	MT Alpha, Montana State	
1926	OK Alpha, Oklahoma	
1927	MA Delta, Tufts	
1928	IN Beta, Rose-Hulman	
1928	MS Alpha, Mississippi State	
1928	*NC Beta, North Carolina* (1938)	
1928	SC Alpha, Clemson	
1929	MD Beta, Maryland	
1929	TN Alpha, Tennessee	
1930	PA Zeta, Drexel	
1931	*NY Epsilon, N.Y.U.* (1974)	
1931	*NY Zeta, New York Poly* (1974)	
1932	WI Beta, Marquette	
1933	DE Alpha, Delaware	
1933	UT Alpha, Utah	
1933	VA Beta, V.P.I.	
1934	NJ Beta, Rutgers	
1935	CA Gamma, Stanford	
1936	LA Alpha, L.S.U.	
1936	LA Beta, Tulane	
1937	TX Beta, Texas Tech	
1940	NY Eta, CUNY, Brooklyn	
1940	TX Gamma, Rice	
1941	IL Gamma, Northwestern	
1941	MA Epsilon, Northeastern	
1941	MI Delta, Detroit	
1941	NJ Gamma, New Jersey Tech	
1941	NY Theta, Clarkson	
1946	TN Beta, Vanderbilt	
1947	CA Delta, USC	
1947	NY Iota, Cooper Union	
1947	NY Kappa, Rochester	
1947	PA Eta, Bucknell	
1948	NC Gamma, Duke	
1948	TX Delta, Texas A & M	
1949	CT Beta, Connecticut	
1950	ND Alpha, North Dakota State	
1950	NH Alpha, New Hampshire	
1951	LA Gamma, Louisiana Tech	
1951	MI Epsilon, Wayne State (MI)	
1952	CA Epsilon, UCLA	
1952	NY Lambda, Pratt	
1953	OH Delta, Ohio	
1953	OH Epsilon, Cleveland	

1954	*CO Gamma, Denver* (1975)	
1954	OH Zeta, Toledo	
1954	RI Alpha, Brown	
1954	RI Beta, Rhode Island	
1956	CA Zeta, Santa Clara	
1956	DC Alpha, Howard	
1956	MA Zeta, Massachusetts	
1958	SC Beta, South Carolina	
1958	VT Alpha, Vermont	
1959	OH Eta, Air Force Inst	
1960	IN Gamma, Notre Dame	
1960	LA Delta, Southwestern Louisiana	
1961	FL Alpha, Florida	
1961	OH Theta, Dayton	
1961	PA Theta, Villanova	
1962	DC Beta, Catholic	
1962	TX Epsilon, Houston	
1963	AZ Beta, Arizona State	
1963	DC Gamma, George Washington	
1963	IN Delta, Valparaiso	
1964	CA Eta, San Jose	
1964	FL Beta, Miami (FL)	
1964	IL Delta, Bradley	
1964	NY Mu, Union (NY)	
1964	UT Beta, Brigham Young	
1965	CA Theta, Cal State, Long Beach	
1965	KS Beta, Wichita	
1965	VT Beta, Norwich	
1966	WA Gamma, Seattle	
1967	CA Iota, Cal State, Los Angeles	
1967	NY Nu, SUNY, Buffalo	
1967	NY Xi, Manhattan	
1968	CA Kappa, Cal State, Northridge	
1968	PA Iota, Widener	
1968	TN Gamma, Tennessee Tech	
1968	TX Zeta, Lamar	
1969	CA Lambda, Cal, Davis	
1969	MS Beta, Mississippi	
1969	PR Alpha, Puerto Rico, San Juan	
1969	TX Eta, Texas, Arlington	
1969	TX Theta, Texas, El Paso	
1970	NY Omicron, SUNY, Stony Brook	
1971	MI Zeta, G.M.I.	
1971	NY Pi, Rochester Tech	
1971	OK Beta, Tulsa	
1972	CA Mu, Cal Poly, San Luis Obispo	
1972	CA Nu, Cal Poly, Pomona	
1972	NJ Delta, Princeton	
1972	WV Beta, West Virginia Tech	
1973	CA Xi, San Diego U.	
1973	OH Iota, Ohio Northern	
1973	WI Gamma, Wisconsin, Milwaukee	
1974	CA Omicron, Loyola Marymount, Los Angeles	
1974	CA Pi, Northrop	
1974	CA Rho, Cal State, Fresno	
1974	CO Delta, Colorado State	
1974	FL Gamma, South Florida	
1974	ID Alpha, Idaho	
1974	KS Gamma, Kansas State	
1974	KY Beta, Louisville	
1974	ND Beta, North Dakota	

1974	NE Alpha, Nebraska
1974	NM Alpha, New Mexico State
1974	NM Beta, New Mexico
1974	NV Alpha, Nevada
1974	NY Rho, New York Poly
1974	OH Kappa, Akron
1974	OH Lambda, Youngstown State
1974	OK Gamma, Oklahoma State
1974	PA Kappa, Swarthmore
1974	PA Lambda, Pitt
1974	SD Alpha, South Dakota Mines
1974	SD Beta, South Dakota State
1974	TN Delta, Christian Brothers
1974	TX Iota, Southern Methodist
1974	TX Kappa, Prairie View
1974	TX Lambda, Texas A & I
1974	UT Gamma, Utah State
1974	WY Alpha, Wyoming
1975	AK Alpha, Alaska
1975	IN Epsilon, Tri-State
1975	MA Eta, Boston U
1976	IL Epsilon, Southern Illinois
1977	AL Gamma, Alabama, Birmingham
1977	FL Delta, Central Florida
1977	TN Epsilon, Memphis State
1978	MI Eta, Lawrence Tech
1979	MI Theta, Oakland
1979	NC Delta, North Carolina, Charlotte
1979	VA Gamma, Old Dominion
1980	AL Delta, Alabama, Huntsville
1981	AZ Gamma, Northern Arizona
1981	CA Sigma, Cal, Santa Barbara
1981	SC Gamma, Citadel
1982	CA Tau, Cal, Irvine
1982	MI Iota, Michigan, Dearborn
1984	CA Upsilon, Cal State, Sacramento
1984	IL Zeta, Illinois, Chicago
1984	MD Gamma, Navy
1984	MT Beta, Montana Mines
1985	CO Epsilon, Colorado, Denver
1985	FL Epsilon, Florida Atlantic
1985	MA Theta, Lowell
1985	NM Gamma, New Mexico Tech
1986	FL Zeta, Florida Institute
1986	NC Epsilon, North Carolina A & T
1988	CA Phi, Pacific (CA)
1989	MI Kappa, Western Michigan
1990	AL Epsilon, South Alabama
1990	OH Mu, Wright State
1990	TN Zeta, Tennessee, Chattanooga
1990	WI Delta, Milwaukee Engineering

Tau Sigma Delta

(ARCHITECTURE AND ALLIED ARTS)

ACTIVE PIN

TAU SIGMA DELTA, a national honor society in architecture and allied arts, was organized in May, 1913, at the proposal and under the direction of the faculty members of the Departments of Architecture and Landscape Design at the University of Michigan. The organization was first known as the Honor Society in Architecture and Landscape Design. However, as the architectural departments at many of the universities have been set up as separate colleges of architecture with expanded curricula it became advisable for Tau Sigma Delta to make its elections include also students in these colleges majoring in courses directly allied with architecture. This led to the designation given above.

All the chapters of Tau Sigma Delta are established in five-year, degree-granting colleges and universities where the colleges or departments of architecture are accredited by the National Architectural Accrediting Board.

The society has been incorporated under the laws of Michigan as the Tau Sigma Delta Association. To quote from the constitution, its purpose is "to recognize and encourage high scholastic attainment among students of architecture, landscape architecture, and the allied arts of design, rewarding talent and marked ability through election to membership."

Purpose To stimulate mental achievement, effort, and initiative; to emphasize leadership and character; and to reward students who attain high scholastic standing in architecture, landscape architecture, and the allied arts of design with the reward of membership.

Eligibility To be eligible for undergraduate membership, a candidate must be a bona fide student enrolled in a course of study leading to the initial degree in Architecture, Landscape Architecture, or the Allied Arts of Design. The candidate must have completed a minimum of two and one-half academic years (five semesters or eight quarters) of the initial degree program and shall have completed the major prerequisites of the degree program established by the Faculty of the college, school, or department in which the chapter is domiciled. Any eligible transfer student shall have been enrolled in residence a minimum of the academic year in the institution where his selection for membership is considered. The candidate must have maintained a high academic standard as determined by the faculty of the college, school, or department in which the chapter is maintained. Specific requirements for scholarship shall be set up as a guide by the Grand Chapter in the Manual of Instructions.

Government Three elected officers govern the society in the interim between meetings of the Advisory Council. The council is made up of faculty members, normally deans or heads of the departments of member schools. Meetings are held annually in conjunction with the national convention of the Association of Collegiate Schools of Architecture. Officers are elected for four-year terms and are voting members of the council.

Major Activities To be of service to the school in which the chapter is functioning; to promote high ideals in architectural education; and to provide a collegiate organization which might assist in worthy endeavors for the benefit of the profession in architecture and the allied arts. The social functions of the chapters are incidental, and may be held in connection with initiations, dinners, meetings, lectures, exhibitions of work, awarding of prizes to undergraduates, etc. Institutional chapters are chartered only at such four-year or more degree granting American colleges and universities whose department, school, or college of architecture is on the accredited list of the National Architectural Accrediting Board which is jointly organized by the American Institute of Architects, the Association of Collegiate Schools of Architecture, and the National Council of Architectural Registration Boards.

Publication *Newsletter.*

Headquarters College of Architecture, Clemson University, Clemson, South Carolina 29631.

Membership Active chapters 34. Inactive chapters 11. Total number of initiates 13,000. Chapter roll:††

1913 *Alpha, Michigan*
1917 Beta, Minnesota (1934-1967)
1917 *Chi, Illinois* (1918)
1918 *Delta, Syracuse*
1918 *Epsilon, Penn*
1918 *Gamma, Carnegie Tech*
1920 *Eta, California* (1937)
1920 *Zeta, Liverpool, England* (1924)
1922 *Theta, Ohio State* (1935)
1924 Iota, Washington
1930 Kappa, Iowa State
1931 *Lambda, USC*
1931 *Mu, Texas*
1947 Nu, V.P.I.
1949 Eta Alpha (Xi), Tulane
1950 Omicron, Kansas State
1950 Pi, Kansas
1956 Rho, Georgia Tech
1961 Sigma, Notre Dame
1961 Tau, William Marsh Rice

†† This chapter roll is repeated from the 19th edition; no current information was provided.

1962 Upsilon, Texas Tech
1963 Phi, Clemson
1965 Psi, Nebraska
1966 Omega, Florida
1968 Xi, Oklahoma
1970 Alpha Alpha, Texas A & M
1971 Alpha Beta, Howard
1971 Alpha Gamma, Oklahoma State
1974 Alpha Delta, North Dakota
1974 Alpha Epsilon, Kent State
1975 Alpha Chi, Kentucky
1977 Alpha Eta, Arkansas
1977 Alpha Zeta, Louisiana

Theta Alpha Kappa

(RELIGIOUS STUDIES—THEOLOGY)

THETA ALPHA KAPPA was established at Manhattan College in Riverdale, New York City, during the fall semester of 1976 by the members of the Religious Studies faculty. The department chairman at that time was Albert Clark, F.S.C. It is an honor society whose purpose is to bring students, teachers and authors of Religious Studies and Theology together both intellectually and socially; to encourage excellence in research, learning, teaching and publication and to foster the exchange of thought among scholars. Membership in Theta Alpha Kappa is based upon excellence in academic pursuits with the completion of at least three semesters or five quarters at the institution where the inducting chapter is located; the completion of a minimum of twelve credits in Religious Studies/Theology with a grade index of 3.5 [B+]; a cumulative index of 3.0 [B]and a standing among the upper 35 percent of the candidate's class.

Government The government of the society is vested in the National Board of Directors. This is composed of the president, secretary, treasurer, editor of the *Journal of Theta Alpha Kappa* and three national delegates who represent the various chapters in accord with their undergraduate enrollment: [less than 1700; 1700–4000; over 4000]. The Board of Directors meets twice each year and conducts all matters of business between the annual general meetings.

Local chapters sponsor such activities as forums, debates, and seminars, along with other gatherings to promote informal and social communication among members.

Insignia The emblem is a gold key upon which is displayed the three Greek-letters of the society: Theta Alpha Kappa. The intertwine of these letters is the official insignia for all certificates of membership, stationery and public documents.

Publications National activities include the mailing of newsletters and the publication of *The Journal of Theta Alpha Kappa.* This is published twice during each academic year. Journal acticles are authored by professors and students. Past issues have featured works on the nature of religion, biblical and moral questions, the role of women in the Church, as well as poetry and book reviews.

Headquarters Department of Religious Studies, Manhattan College, Riverdale, New York 10471.

Membership Total undergraduate membership 1,600. Active chapters 63. Inactive chapters 5. Total number of initiates 2,392. Chapter roll:

1977	Alpha, Manhattan
1977	Beta, King's
1977	Delta, St. Elizabeth
1977	Epsilon, Iona
1977	Eta, Mount St. Vincent
1977	Gamma, Caldwell
1977	Iota, Portland
1977	Kappa, Barry (FL)
1977	Lambda, Dayton
1977	Mu, James Madison
1977	Nu, San Francisco
1977	*Omicron, Kenrick* (1978)
1977	Pi, St. Edward's
1977	Rho, DePaul (1978-1990)
1977	Sigma, Georgian Court
1977	Tau, St. Francis (NY)
1977	Theta, Marquette
1977	Upsilon, Loyola, Chicago
1977	*Xi, LaSalle* (1985)
1977	Zeta, Fairfield
1978	*Chi, St. Teresa* (1989)
1978	Omega, Villanova
1978	Phi, New Rochelle
1978	*Psi, Shenandoah Conservatory* (1986)
1979	Alpha Alpha, St. John's (NY)
1979	*Alpha Beta, Allentown* (1979)
1979	Alpha Delta, St. Catherine
1979	Alpha Epsilon, Evangel
1979	Alpha Eta, John Carroll
1979	Alpha Gamma, St. Francis (PA)
1979	Alpha Iota, St. Peter's
1979	Alpha Kappa, Carroll
1979	Alpha Lambda, Atlantic Christian
1979	Alpha Mu, Molloy
1979	Alpha Theta, North Carolina Wesleyan
1979	Alpha Zeta, St. Louis
1980	Alpha Nu, Scranton
1980	Alpha Omicron, Seton Hall
1980	Alpha Pi, Cabrini
1980	Alpha Xi, St. Joseph's (PA)
1981	Alpha Rho, Seton Hill
1981	Alpha Sigma, Loyola Marymount, Los Angeles
1981	Alpha Tau, Elon
1981	Alpha Upsilon, Niagara
1982	Alpha Alpha Alpha, Lewis
1982	Alpha Alpha Beta, Canisius
1982	Alpha Alpha Gamma, Mount Mary's (MD)
1982	Alpha Chi, San Diego U
1982	Alpha Omega, Loyola (MD)
1982	Alpha Phi, Santa Clara
1982	Alpha Psi, Marywood
1983	Alpha Alpha Delta, Duquesne
1983	Alpha Alpha Epsilon, Salve Regina
1983	Alpha Alpha Eta, Gonzaga
1983	Alpha Alpha Theta, Lourdes
1983	Alpha Alpha Zeta, Rosary (IL)
1984	Alpha Alpha Iota, Notre Dame
1985	Alpha Alpha Kappa, Loyola, New Orleans
1985	Alpha Alpha Lambda, Richmond
1986	Alpha Alpha Mu, Baylor
1986	Alpha Alpha Nu, Western Evangelical
1987	Alpha Alpha Omicron, Emory
1987	Alpha Alpha Pi, Houston Baptist
1987	Alpha Alpha Rho, Andrews
1987	Alpha Alpha Xi, St. Thomas
1989	Alpha Alpha Sigma, Mobile
1989	Alpha Alpha Tau, Mount Mary
1990	Alpha Alpha Ypsilon, Allentown

Xi Sigma Pi

(FORESTRY)

ACTIVE PIN

XI SIGMA PI, forestry honor society, was founded at the University of Washington on November 24, 1908. It existed as a local honor society until 1915, when a constitution which opened a wider field was adopted. The society today has chapters stretching across the nation.

The objects of Xi Sigma Pi are "to secure and maintain a high standard of scholarship in forestry education, to work for the improvement of the forestry profession and to promote a fraternal spirit among those engaged in activities related to the forest."

Eligibility Juniors, seniors, and transfer students regularly registered in forest resource management curriculum or similarly named instructional entities are eligible for membership under the following conditions: completion of seventy-four semesters hours or one hundred ten quarter hours of credit; rank scholastically in the upper twenty-five percent of his or her class or have a B average (chapters may impose higher requirements at their discretion); and transfer students must have been regularly registered for at least one semester or one and one-half quarters.

Graduate students must have completed ten or more semester hours or fifteen or more quarter hours of credit in forest resource management credits and have an outstanding academic record at the graduate level.

Government The governing body of the society consists of the Executive Council, composed of a forester, an associate forester, and a secretary-fiscal agent, who are elected for a term of two years by the delegates at the biennial conventions, and a member elected from each chapter.

The society holds biennial conventions in conjunction with the annual meetings of the Society of American Foresters. Each of the individual chapters schedules various activities including speakers, civic programs, and professional service. A Scholarship Fund allows for the awarding of a $350 scholarship to each of ten regional winners every year. Criteria for selection include activities in the Society, leadership in community or campus organization, professional activities, academic achievement, and financial need. Each region consists of seven or more chapters.

Insignia The badge of the society is a key or pin, identical except as to mounting.

Headquarters Department of Forestry and Range Management, Washington State University, Pullman, Washington 99164.

National Headquarters is rotated biennially among the chapters with faculty members of those chapters serving as national officers.

Membership Total undergraduate membership 1,855. Active chapters 42. Inactive chapters 1. Total number of initiates 24,000. Chapter roll:

1908	Alpha, Washington (WA)
1916	Beta, Michigan State
1917	Gamma, Maine
1920	Delta, Minnesota
1920	Epsilon, Idaho
1921	Zeta, Oregon State
1924	Eta, Penn State
1924	Theta, Cal, Berkeley
1927	*Iota, Penn State* (1929)
1934	Kappa, Purdue
1939	Lambda, Utah State
1940	Mu, North Carolina State
1940	Nu, L.S.U.
1941	Xi, Georgia
1943	Omicron, Colorado State
1948	Pi, Florida
1952	Rho, West Virginia
1952	Sigma, Auburn
1952	Tau, Missouri
1958	Upsilon, Michigan
1960	Phi, Montana State
1962	Chi, V.P.I.
1962	Psi, Massachusetts
1964	Omega, Southern Illinois
1965	Alpha Alpha, Illinois
1965	Alpha Beta, Clemson
1965	Alpha Gamma, Iowa State
1966	Alpha Delta, Washington State
1966	Alpha Epsilon, New Hampshire
1968	Alpha Zeta, Stephen F. Austin
1971	Alpha Eta, Michigan Tech
1971	Alpha Theta, Mississippi State
1972	Alpha Kappa, Tennessee
1973	Alpha Lambda, Humboldt
1973	Alpha Mu, Oklahoma State

1974	Alpha Nu, Wisconsin, Madison
1975	Alpha Omicron, Vermont
1975	Alpha Pi, Northern Arizona
1975	Alpha Xi, Wisconsin, Stevens Point
1976	Alpha Rho, Kentucky
1978	Alpha Sigma, Texas A & M
1980	Alpha Tau, Alberta
1980	Alpha Upsilon, Cal Poly, Pomona

Other Honor Societies

Alpha Omega Alpha[†]

(MEDICINE)

ACTIVE PIN

ALPHA OMEGA ALPHA, a nonsecret, college medical honor society, was founded by a third-year medical student, William W. Root. The society was organized at the College of Medicine of the University of Illinois, August 25, 1902, and is the only order of its kind in medical schools on this continent. Race, color, creed, sex or social standing are of no consideration in the selection of members.

Undergraduate membership is based entirely on scholarship, personal honesty, and potential leadership; the total number of student members elected from any class may not exceed one-sixth of the total number expected to graduate in that class.

Alumnus membership is granted for distinctive achievement in the art and practice of scientific medicine, honorary membership to eminent leaders in medicine and the allied sciences. A chapter may, with advice of its counselor, elect each year to membership one member from the faculty of medicine with which the chapter is affiliated and three alumnus members.

The society is closely allied with the Council on Medical Education and Hospitals of the American Medical Association and the Association of American Medical Colleges. Only medical schools of the highest rank may be granted charters of Alpha Omega Alpha. The motto of the society is "Αξιος 'ωφελεῖν τοὺς ἀλγοῦντας (*To Be Worthy to Serve the Suffering*)."

Chapter meetings are often devoted to the presentation of clinical cases and scientific papers, with discussion. Public addresses, by distinguished physicians, are given each year under chapter auspices.

Government Administration is vested in a Governing Council, made up of the chapter counselor of

† This chapter narrative is repeated from the 19th edition; no current information was provided.

each constituent chapter, the board of directors elected by the Governing Council, and the general officers elected by the board of directors.

Each chapter elects its own officers; the secretary and the counselor must be members of the faculty and of the society. At least two meetings shall be held each school year. All members of the chapter, whether students or graduates, may vote at chapter meetings. Chapters are urged to engage in activities in which undergraduates may take part since the society in its inception was an undergraduate organization.

Traditions and Insignia The society's badge is a golden key, fashioned after the Manubrium Sterni. The letters AΩA and the date 1902 are on one side, with the reverse bearing name of the college, the member and his year of election. Each member receives also a certificate of membership, signed by the national president and secretary of the society.

Publications General directories were published in 1922, 1936, and 1956, containing the history, constitution, and biographical data. The society's official publication, *The Pharos*, was first printed in 1938.

Headquarters 2 Palo Alto Square, Palo Alto, California 94304.

Membership Active chapters 105. Total number of initiates 56,469. Chapter roll:††

SUNY, Medical
1902 Alpha of Illinois, Illinois
1902 Beta of Illinois, Chicago
1903 Alpha of Ohio, Western Reserve
1903 Alpha of Pennsylvania, Jefferson Medical
1903 Beta of Pennsylvania, Penn
1903 Gamma of Illinois, Northwestern
1905 Alpha of Missouri, Washington (MO)
1906 Alpha of California, California
1906 Alpha of Maryland, Johns Hopkins
1906 Alpha of Massachusetts, Harvard
1906 Alpha of Ontario, Toronto
1907 Alpha of Michigan, Michigan
1907 Alpha of New York, Columbia (NY)
1908 Alpha of Minnesota, Minnesota
1910 Beta of New York, Cornell
1911 Alpha of Quebec, McGill
1911 Gamma of New York, SUNY, Upstate Medical
1914 Alpha of Louisiana, Tulane
1914 Alpha of Nebraska, Nebraska
1916 Alpha of Indiana, Indiana
1916 Beta of Ohio, Cincinnati
1916 Gamma of Pennsylvania, Pitt
1919 Alpha of Virginia, Virginia
1920 Alpha of Connecticut, Yale
1920 Alpha of Iowa, Iowa
1920 Alpha of Texas, Texas
1923 Alpha of Oregon, Oregon
1923 Alpha of Tennessee, Vanderbilt

1923 Delta of New York, N.Y.U.
1924 Beta of Missouri, St. Louis
1924 Epsilon of New York, Buffalo
1926 Alpha of Colorado, Colorado
1926 Alpha of Georgia, Georgia
1926 Alpha of Kentucky, Louisville
1926 Alpha of Wisconsin, Wisconsin, Madison
1929 Beta of California, Stanford
1929 Zeta of New York, Rochester
1930 Alpha of Kansas, Kansas
1931 Alpha of North Carolina, Duke
1933 Gamma of Ohio, Ohio State
1934 Delta of Pennsylvania, Woman's Medical (PA)
1939 Beta of Georgia, Emory
1940 Beta of Massachusetts, Tufts
1940 Beta of Virginia, Virginia Medical
1941 Beta of Tennessee, Tennessee
1942 Beta of Michigan, Wayne State (MI)
1942 Beta of Ontario, Western Ontario
1948 Eta of New York
1948 Gamma of Massachusetts, Boston
1949 Alpha of Utah, Utah
1949 Beta of Louisiana, L.S.U.
1949 Beta of Maryland, Maryland
1949 Beta of North Carolina, Bowman Gray
1949 Beta of Texas, Baylor
1949 Beta of Wisconsin, Marquette
1949 Gamma of California, USC
1949 Theta of New York, Albany Medical
1950 Alpha of Alabama, Alabama Medical
1950 Alpha of Washington, Washington (WA)
1950 Epsilon of Pennsylvania, Temple
1950 Gamma of Texas, Southwestern Medical (TX)
1952 Alpha of Vermont, Vermont
1952 Zeta of Pennsylvania, Hahnemann Med.
1953 Alpha of Oklahoma, Oklahoma
1953 Alpha of South Carolina, South Carolina Medical
1954 Alpha of British Columbia, British Columbia
1954 Alpha of District of Columbia, George Washington
1954 Beta of District of Columbia, Georgetown U.
1954 Gamma of North Carolina, North Carolina
1955 Alpha of Arkansas, Arkansas
1955 Gamma of District of Columbia, Howard
1956 Alpha of Puerto Rico, Puerto Rico
1956 Delta of California, UCLA
1957 Alpha of Mississippi, Mississippi
1957 Beta of Nebraska, Creighton
1957 Epsilon of California, Loma Linda
1957 Gamma of Missouri, Missouri
1957 Gamma of Tennessee, Meharry Medical
1957 Iota of New York, New York Medical
1958 Alpha of Alberta, Alberta
1958 Alpha of Lebanon, American, Beirut
1958 Alpha of Nova Scotia, Dalhousie
1959 Alpha of Florida, Miami (FL)
1959 Kappa of New York, Albert Einstein Medicine

†† This chapter roll is repeated from the 19th edition; no current information was provided.

1960   Beta of Florida, Florida
1962   Alpha of West Virginia, West Virginia
1964   Beta of Kentucky, Kentucky
1965   Delta of Illinois, Chicago Medical
1968   Alpha of New Mexico, New Mexico
1970   Lambda of New York, Mount Sinai Medicine
1971   Alpha of Arizona, Arizona
1971   Gamma of Ontario, Ottawa
1971   Zeta of California, Cal, Irvine
1972   Eta of California, Cal, Davis
1973   Alpha of New Hampshire, Dartmouth Medical
1973   Gamma of Louisiana, L.S.U., Shreveport
1973   Zeta of Illinois, Rush Medical
1974   Delta of Ohio, Ohio Medical
1975   Alpha of New Jersey, Rutgers Medical
1975   Delta of Texas, Texas, Houston
1975   Epsilon of Texas, Texas, San Antonio
1976   Gamma of Florida, South Florida
1977   Beta of Alabama, South Alabama
1977   Beta of New Jersey, New Jersey Medicine and Dentistry

Delta Phi Delta[†]

(ART)

ACTIVE PIN

DELTA PHI DELTA is the outgrowth of an art club known as the "Palette Club," founded at the University of Kansas January 10, 1909. On May 28, 1912, plans to form a national organization were completed and the group adopted the name, Delta Phi Delta. Since that time the official name has become Delta Phi Delta National Honor Art Fraternity, Inc. The purposes are to promote art in the United States, to encourage high scholarship, and to recognize superior accomplishment in the fine arts and related arts. Chapters are located in schools of higher education that grant four-year degrees in the various phases of art.

Traditions and Insignia   The key is in the form of a palette and the badge is of similar design. Laureate members receive an especially designed key.

Delta Phi Delta has honored the following well known artists with Laureate memberships: Foster Gribble, the founder, Ruth Raymond, Birger Sandzen, Edwin O. Christensen, Frances D. Whittemore, William Griffith, Lorado Taft, Levon West, Oscar B. Jacobson, Jon Jonson, Grant Wood, Board-man Robinson, Raymond Johnson, Wayman Adams, Dwight Kirsch, John Rood, Abraham Rattner, Bruce Haswell, Muriel Sibell Wolle, Eugene Francis Savage, Buckminster Fuller, and Bruce Goff.

Publications   The fraternity publishes the *Palette*, annual magazine; *News Letter*, semiannual, and the *Manual*.

     Headquarters   1106 Cody, Hays, Kansas 67601.

     Membership   Active chapters 38. Total number of initiates 13,450. Chapter roll:[††]

1909   Alpha, Kansas
1918   *Beta, Montana*
1919   Gamma, Minnesota
1920   Delta, Bethany (KS)
1920   Epsilon, Washburn
1921   *Eta, Wisconsin, Madison*
1921   Zeta, Chicago Art Institute
1922   Iota, Ohio
1922   Kappa, North Dakota
1922   Lambda, Drake
1922   Theta, Ohio Wesleyan
1924   Mu, Missouri
1926   *Nu, James Millikin*
1928   Omicron, Iowa State
1929   *Phi, California*
1930   Rho, Colorado
1930   Sigma, Washington State
1930   Tau, Miami (OH)
1931   *Upsilon, USC*
1932   Chi, Edinboro
1932   Phi, Montana State
1936   *Alpha Alpha, New Mexico*
1936   Omega, Oklahoma
1936   Psi, Nebraska
1938   Alpha Beta, California Arts and Crafts
1938   Alpha Gamma, Colorado State, Greeley
1939   Alpha Delta, Ohio State
1940   Alpha Epsilon, Texas Woman's
1941   Alpha Zeta, Cincinnati
1944   Alpha Eta, Ball State
1945   Alpha Theta, Southwest Missouri
1946   Alpha Kappa, San Jose
1946   Alpha Lambda, Indiana (PA)
1948   Alpha Mu, Michigan State
1948   Alpha Nu, Illinois Wesleyan
1948   Alpha Xi, Bowling Green
1949   Alpha Omicron, Puget Sound
1951   Alpha Pi, Bradley
1952   Alpha Rho, Kansas State
1956   Alpha Sigma, Mount Mary
1959   Alpha Tau, St. Mary's (NE)
1960   Alpha Phi, East Carolina
1960   Alpha Upsilon, Purdue
1964   Alpha Chi, St. Catherine
1964   Alpha Psi, Northern State

[†] This chapter narrative is repeated from the 19th edition; no current information was provided.

[††] This chapter roll is repeated from the 19th edition; no current information was provided.

Gamma Sigma Delta†

(AGRICULTURE)

ACTIVE PIN

GAMMA SIGMA DELTA, an honor society in agriculture, resulted from a series of movements. In 1905 the professional fraternity, Delta Theta Sigma, was organized at Ohio State University. Chapters of this fraternity were subsequently established at Iowa State, Pennsylvania State, Oregon State, and Utah State colleges and at the University of Missouri. Ohio State withdrew in 1913, and the remaining chapters adopted the name, Gamma Sigma Delta. Chapters were established at Kansas State College in 1914 and at Alabama Polytechnic Institute in 1916 under the new name.

In 1917 Gamma Sigma Delta amalgamated with The Honor Society of Agriculture, which had been organized in 1915 at the University of Minnesota. The new constitution made the fraternity strictly an honor society and established the broad principles of faculty control and eligibility of membership to graduating seniors, graduate students, alumni, and faculty.

The objectives of Gamma Sigma Delta, are to advance agriculture in all its phases, to maintain and improve relations of agriculture to other industries, and to recognize the responsibility of its members to their fellow men. It seeks to encourage high standards of scholarship, worthy attainment, and high degree of excellence in the practice of agricultural pursuits.

Each year a national Gamma Sigma Delta Distinguished Service Award is given to a member making the greatest contribution in the field of agricultural science. National certificates of merit are issued each year to outstanding senior and sophomore students at each of the chapters.

Government The government of the society is vested in a biennial legislative council. Between meetings of the council, the officers constitute an executive committee in charge of administration of the organization. A new constitution and bylaws were adopted in 1960.

Traditions and Insignia The emblem of the Society is a key bearing the words "The Honor Society of Agriculture" in small Roman letters and the Greek letters, ΓΣΔ, as its insigne. These are the initial letters for the Greek words, Gaea (Ge-'a), Syndesmos (Syn-des'mos), and Demeter (De-Me-'ter) which have been chosen as symbolic of the organization.

The Greek meaning is "*The binding together of earth, the mother of all, and the practice of agriculture, and the arts relating thereto for the welfare of mankind.*"

Publications Publications include the *News Letter,* which is issued once a year, and a brochure prepared by the international officers to provide information on the history, objectives, and activities of Gamma Sigma Delta.

Headquarters Director's Office, 104 Patterson Hall, North Carolina State University, Raleigh, North Carolina 27607.

Membership Active chapters 36. Inactive chapters 2. Total number of initiates 41,000. Chapter roll:††

1905	Ohio State
1907	Iowa State
1908	Penn State
1909	Missouri
1909	*Oregon State* (1943)
1909	*Utah State* (1922)
1914	Kansas State
1916	Auburn
1917	Minnesota
1918	Nebraska
1923	Illinois
1938	Puerto Rico
1954	Arkansas
1954	Connecticut
1955	Florida
1955	Kentucky
1955	North Carolina State
1957	Philippines
1957	South Carolina
1957	South Dakota
1958	Arizona
1959	West Virginia
1961	Georgia
1961	L.S.U.
1961	Wyoming
1963	Colorado
1964	Mississippi
1964	Tennessee
1965	Texas A & M
1966	Nevada
1967	California (Kellogg-Voorhis)
1967	Wisconsin, Madison
1968	Hawaii
1970	Virginia
1972	Purdue
1972	Texas Tech.
1974	North Carolina A & T

---

† This chapter narrative is repeated from the 19th edition; no current information was provided.

†† This chapter roll is repeated from the 19th edition; no current information was provided.

Iota Sigma Pi†

(CHEMISTRY—WOMEN)

ACTIVE PIN

IOTA SIGMA PI was founded in 1900 and as now constituted is the outgrowth of a merger of three organizations: Alchemi, founded at the University of California in 1900 and extended later to the University of Southern California and to Stanford University; a national honor chemical society for women established at the University of Washington in 1911; and Iota Sigma Pi, established at the University of Nebraska in 1912. The later two groups were merged in 1913 and were joined in 1916 by Alchemi under the name of Iota Sigma Pi.

Government Government is vested in general conventions and the National Council of six members: president, vice-president, secretary, treasurer, editor, and coordinator of regional directors.

Publication The *Iotan* has been published annually since 1941.

Traditions and Insignia A Research Award to an outstanding woman in chemistry or allied fields was initiated at the 1951 triennial convention and the award has been granted once each three years. The emblem is a hexagonal gold key displaying a crescent, circle, and letters IΣΠ. The colors are white, gold, and cedar green. The flower is the white narcissus.

Headquarters Nutrition Research Institute, Oregon State University, Corvallis, Oregon 97331.

Membership Active chapters 25. Inactive chapters 6. Total number of initiates 7,468. Chapter roll:††

1900	Hydrogen, California
1911	Oxygen, Washington
1912	*Nitrogen, Nebraska*
1913	Carbon, Stanford
1914	Sulfur, USC
1917	*Phosphorus, Michigan*
1918	Iodine, Illinois
1918	Tungsten, Colorado
1920	Aurum, Iowa State
1920	*Ytterbium, Yale*
1921	Helium, Oklahoma
1923	Mercury, Minnesota
1923	Radium, Cincinnati
1924	*Kalium, Kansas*
1924	Platinum, Denver

† This chapter narrative is repeated from the 19th edition; no current information was provided.
†† This chapter roll is repeated from the 19th edition; no current information was provided.

1925	Fluorine, Western Reserve
1926	Iridium, Iowa
1930	*Indium, Indiana*
1930	Palladium, Penn
1930	Tellurium, Texas
1937	Polonium, George Washington
1939	Aurum Iodide, Chicago (alumnae)
1947	Columbium, Columbia
1947	Uranium, Texas State
1949	Chlorine, L.S.U.
1951	Manganese, Hunter
1960	Niobium, Oregon State
1963	Osmium, Ohio State
1963	Plutonium, Purdue
1965	Vanadium, Fordham
1966	Neptunium, Houston

Kappa Gamma Pi†

(LEADERSHIP)

KAPPA GAMMA PI is a national scholastic and leadership honor society for women graduates of Catholic colleges. Its purpose is to strive for a high standard of personal Christian excellence and scholarship among members; to encourage participation in local and national Church and community affairs; and to awaken a spirit of Catholic leadership among undergraduates of Kappa-affiliated colleges.

It was founded in June, 1926, at the Conference of Deans of the National Catholic Educational Association, meeting in St. Louis. Membership requirements stress undergraduate lay leadership and include a scholastic requirement of graduation with honors. Not more than 10 per cent of a graduating class may be nominated. In order to nominate new members, the 124 affiliated colleges must hold full constituent membership in the National Catholic Educational Association.

Government The Executive Board consists of 8 national officers, an executive secretary, 4 regents and 1 standing chairman. National conventions are biennial and national executive board meetings are scheduled in the intervening years.

Insignia The official key has Greek letters standing for "Catholic Women Leaders" on a diagonal panel, separating a cross (faith) in the lower left corner from a wheel (service) in the upper right corner.

Publication The official publication is the *Kappa Gamma Pi News*, issued five times a year.

Headquarters 2415 Hillcrest Drive, Stow, Ohio 44224.

Membership 21 chapters are located in metropolitan areas. Total number of initiates 18,000. Chapter roll:††

Akron, OH (1967)
Albany
Baltimore, MD (1968)
Boston, MA (1972)
Buffalo, NY
Scranton
Chicago, IL
Cincinnati, OH
Cleveland, OH
Columbus, OH
Dallas, TX (1969)
Davenport, IA
Dayton, OH (1973)
Denver, CO
Detroit, MI
Erie, PA
Grand Rapids, MI
Kansas City, MO (1969)
Long Beach, CA (1972)
Los Angeles, CA
Louisville, KY
Milwaukee, WI (1969)
Minneapolis, MN
Newark, NJ (1968)
Oakland, CA (1972)
Omaha, NE (1977)
Philadelphia, PA (1971)
Pittsburgh, PA (1973)
Portland, OR
San Diego, CA
San Francisco, CA (1972)
San Jose, CA (1972)
San Mateo, CA (1972)
Seattle, WA
Spokane, WA
St. Louis, MO (1976)
Toledo, OH
Trenton, NJ (1969)
Washington, DC (1971)
Wilkes-Barre, PA

†† This chapter roll is repeated from the 19th edition; no current information was provided.

National Collegiate Players†

(DRAMATICS)

ACTIVE PIN

NATIONAL COLLEGIATE PLAYERS, an honor society in dramatics for men and women, was founded in June, 1922, through the coalition of Pi Epsilon Delta and Associated University Players. The purposes of this society are: to affiliate closely the college groups which are working for the betterment of drama in their own institutions and thus in America; to stand as a national college unit on all nationwide dramatic movements; to raise dramatic standards and achievements through encouraging the best individual and group efforts in playwriting, acting, directing, stage designing, and research in dramatic technique and literature.

The first chapter of Pi Epsilon Delta was established on June 8, 1919, at the University of Wisconsin, fostered by a group of seniors interested in dramatics. Its purpose was to recognize and encourage all phases of dramatic endeavor. It wished to organize the dramatic forces already at work, to support every movement for the advancement of dramatics in whatever institution it entered. Besides the encouragement of participation in dramatic performances, the writing of plays, and the study of dramatic problems in regularly organized courses, particular emphasis was placed upon research in theatre problems and the application of the drama to the situations peculiar to the school and the community. Pi Epsilon Delta aimed to encourage leadership in these fields. Meanwhile Associated University Players, another national organization, was founded in 1913 at the University of Illinois. This group had similar ideals and purposes, and in June, 1922, the two groups became one and adopted the name, National Collegiate Players. Several other changes were necessary, but the ideals and scope of the society were in no way changed from those set down by Pi Epsilon Delta, The key and the motto of Pi Epsilon Delta were retained as was the substance of the ceremonies of this group. Members are admitted through a point system based upon distinctive work done in writing, acting, directing, stage designing, and completion of accredited courses in dramatic art and literature. Only upperclass men and women are eligible.

The society sponsors a junior organization in ju-

† This chapter narrative is repeated from the 19th edition; no current information was provided.

nior colleges, Junior Collegiate Players, which has the same aims and purposes as the senior organization. It was founded in 1949 at Stephens College.

National Collegiate Players became an honor society in February, 1963, when it was accepted into membership by the Association of College Honor Societies at Madison, Wisconsin, during the annual meeting of its Council.

The membership emblem is a key bearing two masques and the letters ΠΕΔ. The motto is *Palamay en Drama (Art in Drama).*

Publication *Players Magazine*, established in 1924, is edited and published eight times a year at Northern Illinois University, DeKalb. It strives to be an educationally significant journal in the field of drama in university, college, high school, and community theatre. Circulation is international.

Headquarters Department of Speech and Theatre Arts, University of Akron, Akron, Ohio 44325.

Membership Active chapters 44. Inactive chapters 44. Total number of initiates 15,000. Chapter roll:††

1922	Illinois
1922	Minnesota
1922	*Northwestern* (1932)
1922	Ohio (1930-1941)
1922	*Oregon* (1960)
1922	*Washington (MO)* (1958)
1922	Wisconsin
1923	DePauw
1923	*Iowa State* (1934)
1923	Oregon State
1923	Washington State
1924	Nebraska
1926	Arizona
1926	*Butler* (1935)
1926	*Denver* (1950)
1926	North Dakota
1926	USC
1926	*Adelbert, Western Reserve* (1945)
1927	Kansas
1927	Lawrence
1927	Muskingum
1927	Southwest Texas
1927	*Flora Mather, Western Reserve* (1945)
1928	Grinnell (1943-1950)
1929	Earlham
1929	Monmouth
1930	*Cornell Col. (IA)* (1941)
1932	*Iowa* (1950)
1935	Wichita
1936	Alabama, Montevallo
1936	*Texas Woman's* (1950)
1937	*Alabama* (1951)
1938	Hamline

1938	*Wayne State* (1950)
1941	St. Olaf
1941	Tulane
1942	St. Catherine
1943	MacMurray
1945	George Washington (1947-1958)
1945	Kansas State
1945	Louisiana Tech
1946	Drury
1947	Arkansas
1947	Beloit
1947	*George Pepperdine* (1957)
1947	Maryland
1947	Wisconsin, Eau Claire
1948	Florida
1948	South Dakota
1948	Southeast Missouri
1948	Southern Illinois
1948	Wooster
1949	*Florida Southern* (1953)
1949	Gustavus Adolphus
1949	*Northern Idaho* (1952)
1950	Mankato
1951	Capital
1951	Emporia
1951	Hope
1951	Macalester
1951	Toledo
1951	Vermont
1952	Montana
1952	Ohio State
1954	Wisconsin, Milwaukee
1956	Elmira
1957	Southeastern Louisiana
1958	Augsburg
1958	Milikin
1959	Southern Connecticut
1959	St. Cloud
1960	Cornell
1961	Arkansas Tech
1961	Ouachita Baptist
1961	Queens (NY)
1961	Wisconsin, Oshkosh
1962	Akron
1962	Winona
1963	Arizona State
1963	Cal State, Long Beach
1963	Missouri, Kansas City
1963	Wake Forest
1964	Western Illinois
1965	Stephens College
1965	Stephens
1966	Cal State, Fresno
1966	East Carolina
1966	West Virginia
1967	Cal State, Sacramento
1969	Northern Illinois
1974	Wartburg

†† This chapter roll is repeated from the 19th edition; no current information was provided.

The National Order of Omega

History The Order of Omega was founded at the University of Miami in the fall of 1959 by a group of outstanding fraternity men, who felt that individuals in the Greek community should be recognized for their service to the fraternity system and the university.

The Chapter at Miami had long desired for their organization to expand to other colleges and universities. The Chapter gave its sanction to Dean Patrick W. Halloran to make initial inquiries and to further grant charters to universities that were accredited and interested in the purpose of The Order of Omega. On February 9, 1967, a Chapter was chartered at the University of Southern Mississippi. There are now over two hundred seventy chapters in the United States and Canada.

The idea of an honorary for fraternity men at the University of Miami is attributed to Parker F. Enwright, the advisor to fraternities at the time. Enwright was later to accept a position at the University of Pittsburgh. He was also responsible for the founding of the Omega Chapter at the University of Pittsburgh in the spring of 1964.

The original constitution was approved by the Organizations Committee at the University of Miami on April 14, 1959, the recognized founding date.

Since then a National Constitution has been constructed to guide the Order's affairs. Chapter charters and membership certificates have been designed. The ritual and regalia, since revised, serve as a foundation upon which this honorary is being built. The Order of Omega voted to become a co-ed organization in the spring of 1977.

Many institutions have inquired concerning membership in the Order. Colonization procedures have been implemented to further the growth of this honorary.

Considering the age of the American college fraternity, the "active honorary" concept is long overdue. There must continue to be a common means by which the most outstanding fraternity men and women can stand united to further the philosophy of the college fraternity.

Purpose To recognize those fraternity men and women who have attained a high standard of leadership in interfraternity activities, to encourage them to continue along this line, and to inspire others to strive for similar conspicuous attainment;

To bring together outstanding fraternity men and women to create an organization which will help to mold the sentiment of the institution on questions of local and intercollegiate fraternity affairs;

To bring together members of the faculty, alumni, and student members of the institution's fraternities and sororities on a basis of mutual interest, understanding and helpfulness;

To help create an atmosphere where ideas and issues can be discussed openly across Greek lines and to help work out solutions.

Government The governing body for The National Order of Omega is made up of the members of the Executive Committee and Board of Directors. The members of the Executive Committee constitute the Executive Director, President, Vice President, Secretary/Treasurer, and Editor. The Board of Directors is made up of nine members connected with higher education, one of which is a student member of The Order of Omega. These members, with the exception of the student, serve three-year rotating terms. The student member serves a one-year term. The Executives and Board of Directors meet at least one time per year as provided in the National Constitution and Bylaws.

Publication The official newsletter for the National Order of Omega is the *Omega Trends*. This publication is sent quarterly to all of the chapters in the Order.

Awards The National Order of Omega wishes to recognize some of our outstanding members by conferring a number of scholarships to help these students continue in either graduate or professional work upon graduation. In addition to student scholarships there are two advisor fellowships—one for a Greek advisor working on a master's degree and one for a Greek advisor working on a doctoral degree. The candidates are selected by a scholarship committee chaired by the Vice President of the Order.

Headquarters The National Office of The Order of Omega is located at 1408 W. Abram, Suite 205, Arlington, Texas, 76013-1789.

Membership Chapter roll:
- Adrian College
- Akron
- Alabama
- Alabama in Birmingham
- Alabama in Huntsville
- Alberta (Canada)
- Albion College
- Allegheny College
- American University
- Appalachian State
- Arizona
- Arizona State
- Arkansas
- Arkansas at Little Rock
- Arkansas Technological
- Ashland College
- Auburn
- Austin Peay State
- Baldwin-Wallace College

Ball State
Baylor
Bentley College
Birmingham-Southern College
Boston
Bowling Green State
Bradley
Bucknell
California, Berkeley
California, Irvine
California, Los Angeles
California, Riverside
California, San Diego
California, Santa Barbara
California Polytechnic State, San Luis
  Obispo
California State Polytechnic, Pomona
California State, Chico
California State, Fresno
California State, Fullerton
California State, Northridge
California State, Sacramento
California State, San Bernardino
Carnegie Mellon
Case Western Reserve
Central Arkansas
Central Florida
Central Michigan
Central Missouri State
Centre College
Christopher Newport College
Cincinnati
Clarkson
Clemson
Colorado
Colorado State
Connecticut
Cornell
Culver-Stockton College
Dartmouth College
Dayton
Delaware
Delta State
Denver
DePauw
Drake
Drexel
Duke
East Carolina
East Tennessee State
East Texas State
Eastern Illinois
Eastern Kentucky
Eastern Michigan
Eastern New Mexico
Elmhurst College
Emory
Evansville
Ferris State College
Florida
Florida Institute of Technology
Florida International

Florida Southern College
Florida State
Fort Hays State
Frostburg State
George Washington University
Georgia
Georgia Institute of Technology
Georgia Southern
Georgia State
Gettysburg College
GMI Engineering & Management Institute
Hartford
Hartwick College
Heidelberg College
Henderson State
Hofstra
Houston
Idaho
Illinois
Illinois at Chicago
Illinois State
Indiana State
Indiana
Indiana University of Pennsylvania
Iowa
Iowa State
Jacksonville State
Jacksonville
James Madison
Johns Hopkins
Kansas
Kansas State
Kent State
Kentucky
Lamar University—Beaumont
Lehigh
Lock Haven
Longwood College
Louisiana State
Louisville
Loyola Marymount
Loyola University in New Orleans
Maine at Orono
Mankato State
Marshall
Maryland at College Park
Massachusetts Amherst
McNeese State College
Memphis State
Mercer
Miami
Miami of Ohio
Michigan
Michigan State
Midwestern State
Millikin
Millsaps College
Minnesota
Mississippi
Mississippi State
Missouri-Columbia
Monmouth College

Montana State
Morehead State
Muhlenberg College
Murray State
Nebraska at Kearney
Nebraska Wesleyan
Nevada at Las Vegas
New Hampshire
New Mexico
New Mexico State
New Orleans
New York at Fredonia
New York at Plattsburgh
Nicholls State
North Alabama
North Carolina at Charlotte
North Carolina at Wilmington
North Carolina State
North Dakota
North Dakota State
North Texas
Northeast Missouri State
Northeastern
Northern Arizona
Northern Colorado
Northern Illinois
Northern Iowa
Northern Kentucky
Northwest Missouri State
Northwestern
Ohio Northern
Ohio State
Ohio
Ohio Wesleyan
Oklahoma
Oklahoma State
Old Dominion
Oregon
Oregon State
Otterbein College
Pacific
Pennsylvania
Pennsylvania State
Pittsburg State
Pittsburgh
Puget Sound
Purdue
Queens College (North Carolina)
Radford
Rensselaer Polytechnic Institute
Rhode Island
Rhodes College
Richmond
Rider College
Robert Morris College
Rochester
Rochester Institute of Technology
Rutgers (New Brunswick)
Saint Louis
Sam Houston State
San Diego
San Diego State

San Jose State
Santa Clara
Shippensburg
Slippery Rock, Pennsylvania
South Alabama
South Carolina
South Dakota
South Dakota State
South Florida
Southeast Missouri State
Southeastern Louisiana
Southeastern Oklahoma State
Southern California
Southern Illinois at Carbondale
Southern Indiana
Southern Methodist
Southern Mississippi
Southwest Missouri State
Southwest Texas State
Southwestern Louisiana
Stanford
Stephen F. Austin State
Stetson
Susquehanna
Syracuse
Tampa
Tarleton State
Temple
Tennessee at Knoxville
Tennessee at Martin
Tennessee Technological
Texas A & M
Texas at Arlington
Texas at Austin
Texas at El Paso
Texas Christian
Texas Tech
Texas Wesleyan
Toledo
Transylvania
Tufts
Tulane
Tulsa
Union College
Utah
Utah State
Valdosta State College
Valparaiso
Vermont
Villanova
Virginia
Virginia Commonwealth
Virginia Polytechnic Institute
Washington
Washington State
Washington
West Chester
West Georgia College
West Texas State
West Virginia
Western Carolina
Western Illinois

Western Kentucky
Western Michigan
Wichita State
Widener
Willamette
William Jewell College
William Woods College
Wisconsin-LaCrosse
Wisconsin-Madison
Wisconsin-River Falls
Wisconsin-Whitewater
Wittenberg
Worcester Polytechnic Institute
Wyoming

Omicron Kappa Upsilon†

(DENTISTRY)

ACTIVE PIN

OMICRON KAPPA UPSILON was organized May 21, 1914, by the faculty of Northwestern University Dental School to encourage and develop a spirit of emulation among students in dentistry and to recognize in an appropriate manner students who distinguish themselves by a high grade of scholarship. The founders were Dr. Charles R. E. Koch, Dr. G. V. Black, Dr. Thomas L. Gilmer, Dr. Edmund Noyes, Dr. James H. Prothero, Dr. I. B. Sellery, Dr. E. S. Willard, Dr. Harry I. Van Tuyl, Dr. George C. Poundstone, Dr. Fred W. Gethro, Dr. Herbert A. Potts, and Dr. Arthur D. Black. The name and key of the society are built upon three words which represent the dental ideal—conservation of teeth and health: soteria for conservation, odous for teeth, and hygeia for health.

The faculty members of each component chapter may elect from each graduating class a number of students not exceeding 12 per cent of the entire class, provided that if 12 per cent be less than three, three members may be chosen, in the following manner: At a time subsequent to the final examinations, the secretary of each component chapter shall obtain from the dean of the school a list containing the names of at least the upper 20 per cent of the senior class who rank highest in scholarship for the entire period they have been in attendance at the school. From any on this list, a number constituting not more than 12 per cent of the senior class who in addition to scholarship have demonstrated exemplary traits of character and potential qualities of future professional growth and attainments may be elected to alumni membership by the faculty members of the component chapter. Graduates of any school where there is a component chapter who would have been eligible in their respective classes under the provisions prescribed are eligible for membership. Dental members of the faculty of a school holding a charter may become eligible for membership after three years of fulltime or five years of part-time teaching. Members of the dental profession and others not members of the profession who have made similar contributions to the advancement of dentistry may be elected to honorary membership, provided that no component chapter shall elect more than one such honorary member during any one year and the supreme chapter may also elect to honorary membership members of the dental profession who have attained distinction, provided that only one such honorary member shall be elected at any annual meeting.

Government Government is by the supreme chapter, consisting of one faculty member delegate, or an alternate, from each component chapter. The officers of the supreme chapter include president, president-elect, vice-president and secretary treasurer, who constitute the Executive Committee and are chosen at the annual convention holding office until their successors are duly elected and qualified. The annual meeting is held the week of the meeting of the American Association of Dental Schools in the same city.

Insignia The insignia is a key upon which a monogram of the letters of the name of the society is superimposed on a large Σ standing for conservation.

Headquarters P.O. Box 64, Esparto, California 95627.

Membership Active chapters 50. Inactive chapters 1. Total number of initiates 14,500. Chapter roll:††

1914	Alpha, Northwestern
1916	Beta, Pitt
1916	Delta, Oregon, Portland
1916	Epsilon, Creighton
1916	Eta, Penn
1916	Gamma, Washington (MO)
1916	*Iota, Vanderbilt* (1965)
1916	Theta, Ohio State (1936-1965)
1916	Zeta, USC
1921	Lambda, Emory
1923	Mu, Iowa
1924	Kappa, Virginia Medical
1924	Nu, Louisville
1924	Xi, Marquette
1925	Omicron, Baylor
1925	Pi, Loyola, Chicago
1928	Sigma, Illinois
1929	Rho, Western Dental, Kansas City

† This chapter narrative is repeated from the 19th edition; no current information was provided.

†† This chapter roll is repeated from the 19th edition; no current information was provided.

1929   Tau, Loyola, New Orleans
1929   Upsilon, Western Reserve
1930   Alpha Alpha, Nebraska
1930   Beta Beta, Minnesota
1930   Chi, Michigan
1930   Gamma Gamma, Harvard
1930   Omega, NYU
1930   Phi, Maryland, Baltimore, Dentistry
1930   Psi, Tennessee
1933   Delta Delta, Pacific, Surgeons, Dentistry
1934   Epsilon Epsilon, Columbia
1934   Eta Eta, St. Louis
1934   Theta Theta, Indiana
1934   Zeta Zeta, Georgetown
1937   Kappa Kappa, Temple
1937   Lambda Lambda, Buffalo
1940   Mu Mu, Texas
1941   Nu Nu, Detroit
1944   Xi Xi, Tufts
1945   Omicron Omicron, Meharry Medical
1948   Pi Pi, Howard
1948   Rho Rho, California
1950   Sigma Sigma, Washington
1950   Tau Tau, Toronto
1953   Upsilon Upsilon, North Carolina
1954   Phi Phi, Alabama
1956   Chi Chi, Medical Evangelists (CA)
1957   Omega Omega, Seton Hall
1957   Psi Psi, Fairleigh Dickinson
1961   Alpha Beta, West Virginia
1961   Beta Gamma, Puerto Rico
1961   Gamma Delta, Manitoba
1966   Delta Epsilon, Kentucky

Order of the Coif†

(LAW)

ORDER OF THE COIF, an honor society for law students, was formed from an order originally called Theta Kappa Nu, founded at the University of Illinois in 1902. Its initiates are taken from the upper 10 per cent of the graduating class and there is special provision for the election of faculty members and honorary members.

The preamble of the constitution of the order provides that its purpose is "to foster a spirit of careful study and to mark in a fitting manner those who have attained a high grade of scholarship." Government is by convention and the Executive Committee.

Awards   Coif confers each three years an award or awards upon the author or authors of outstanding legal publications evidencing creative talent of the highest level. The National Executive Committee is by the Coif constitution also authorized to make other awards designed to recognize outstand-

ing merit in legal writing or in service to the legal profession.

Insignia   The badge is a key bearing on one side the words, *Order of the Coif,* and in relief a representation of the bust of a sergeant-at-law wearing a wig and coif, and, on the opposite side, the owner's name, chapter, and year of his admission to membership.

Membership   Active chapters 56. Total number of initiates 25,000.   Chapter roll:††

1902   Illinois
1904   Nebraska
1905   Missouri
1906   Virginia
1907   Northwestern
1907   Wisconsin, Madison
1908   Iowa
1911   Chicago
1911   Stanford
1913   Western Reserve
1914   Cornell
1914   Ohio State
1914   Penn
1915   Minnesota
1915   Yale
1924   Kansas
1924   Washington
1925   Indiana
1925   Michigan
1925   North Dakota
1925   Oklahoma
1925   West Virginia
1926   George Washington
1927   California
1927   Pitt
1927   Texas
1928   Cincinnati
1928   North Carolina
1929   USC
1931   Kentucky
1931   Tulane
1933   Duke
1934   Oregon
1937   Washington (MO)
1938   Maryland
1942   Colorado
1942   L.S.U.
1948   Vanderbilt
1950   Washington and Lee
1952   Drake
1952   Syracuse
1952   Tennessee
1953   Utah
1954   Hastings Law
1954   UCLA
1956   Florida
1958   N.Y.U.
1961   Villanova

† This chapter narrative is repeated from the 19th edition; no current information was provided.

†† This chapter roll is repeated from the 19th edition; no current information was provided.

1963   Boston Col
1967   Southern Methodist
1970   Alabama
1970   Arizona
1971   Emory
1971   New Mexico
1972   Cal, Davis
1974   Texas Tech.

Phi Beta Kappa[†]

(SCHOLARSHIP)

ACTIVE PIN

PHI BETA KAPPA was founded on December 5, 1776, at the College of William and Mary, in Williamsburg, Virginia. It was the first society to have a Greek-letter name, and in its initial period at William and Mary it introduced the essential characteristics of such societies: an oath of secrecy, a badge, mottoes in Latin and Greek, a code of laws, an elaborate form of initiation, a seal, and a special handclasp or grip. Regular meetings were held at which chief attention was given to literary exercises, especially to composition and debating. According to the original records, preserved at the College of William and Mary and printed at Williamsburg in 1896, the first members debated such subjects as "The cause and origin of Society," "Whether a wise state hath any interest nearer at Heart than the Education of the Youth," "Whether anything is more dangerous to Civil Liberty in a Free State than a standing army in time of Peace," and "Whether Theatrical Exhibitions are advantageous to States or ye Contrary." Fraternal sentiments were fostered, occasional meetings were held for social purposes, and anniversaries were celebrated, as they again are since the restoration of Colonial Williamsburg, in the Apollo Room of the Raleigh Tavern.

The emblem adopted at the first meeting was a square silver medal, engraved on one side with the letters ΣP, the initials of the Latin words *Societas Philosophiae*, and on the other with ΦBK, the initials of the Greek motto Φίλοσοφία Βίου Κυβερνήτης, "Love of wisdom the guide of life."[1] The pointing finger and the three stars symbolized the ambition of the young scholars and the three distinguishing principles of their society: friendship, morality, literature (learning). Later a stem was attached to the medal, converting it into a watchkey. On the gold key of today the letters ΣP and the

original symbols, the finger and the stars, are kept virtually unchanged.

Growth   The original society at William and Mary had an active life of only four years, ending when the approach of Cornwallis' army forced the college to close its doors.[2] During this brief Period, however, 67 meetings were held, 50 men were admitted to membership, and charters were granted for new branches or alphas, as the chapters were at first called.

A charter was granted to Harvard by vote on December 4, 1779, and another to Yale five days later. They were entrusted to Elisha Parmele, a graduate of Harvard, who upon his return to New England in the following year delivered them to groups at New Haven and Cambridge; thus were established the Alpha of Connecticut at Yale on November 13, 1780, and the Alpha of Massachusetts at Harvard on September 5, 1781. Both documents are preserved—the Harvard charter with its original ribbons described in the minutes of 1782 as "pink and sky blue," colors still used by a few chapters. The Alpha at Harvard has had an uninterrupted existence of 196 years, and the Alpha at Yale was inactive only from 1871 to 1884. These two alphas largely determined the permanent character of Phi Beta Kappa and shaped its policy in the establishment of new alphas.

The two New England branches preserved the essential qualities of the Virginia brotherhood with some changes in procedure to suit local conditions. Shortly before the close of the college year the members selected from the junior class a small group of leading students who in the following year constituted the "immediate society." At Harvard in 1782 faculty and students were invited to the celebration of the first anniversary, which was fittingly observed in the college chapel. The custom thus inaugurated has led to many significant contributions to American prose and poetry. In these first years, also, a few men from earlier classes were elected to alumni membership, and, beginning at Yale in 1790 and at Harvard in 1813, still others to honorary membership. Thus very soon the members who were no longer in college came to outnumber the undergraduate or immediate members and by their continued interest assured the permanence and added to the prestige of the society.

Fifty years after the society's entry into New England only four additional chapters had been founded, in each case by concurrent action of those already chartered: Alpha of New Hampshire at Dartmouth, 1787; Alpha of New York at Union, 1817; Alpha of Maine at Bowdoin, 1825; and Alpha of Rhode Island at Brown, 1830. The term "chapter" came into use shortly after the organization in 1845 of Beta and Gamma of Connecticut at Trinity

---

[†] This chapter narrative is repeated from the 19th edition; no current information was provided.

[1] The motto of the key has been supplemented by another, which appears on the seal of the United Chapters, *Per aspera ad astra*.

[2] The Alpha at William and Mary was revived in 1851, but became again inactive early in the Civil War; it was reorganized in 1893.

and Wesleyan. There were fifteen additional chapters established in the succeeding thirty years.[3]

Three important changes marked the first century of Phi Beta Kappa's history. The anti-Masonic agitation of the 1820s led at Dartmouth, Harvard, and Yale, to much discussion of the Phi Beta Kappa oath. In 1831 the alpha at Harvard, under the leadership of Edward Everett, Joseph Story, and John Quincy Adams, removed the requirement of secrecy. Although most of the other branches retained the formal obligation for many years, the Harvard action probably saved the society from further open criticism, as well as from rivalry with the fraternities which made their appearance about that time; and with the organization of the United Chapters in 1883 the last vestiges of secrecy disappeared. A second change was more fundamental. Originally Phi Beta Kappa had been a society of congenial spirits, similar in its basis of membership to the present day fraternity, and in the character of its meetings to a debating or literary club. As time passed, it tended more and more to become an "honor" society. Although undergraduate activity continues in some chapters, most chapters now meet only two or three times a year for election and initiation of members and for a dinner, followed often by public exercises with a scholarly address and occasionally a poem.

Another innovation was the admission of women. The Alpha at the University of Vermont, finding in 1875 that two women had met the scholastic requirements, admitted them. The following year, four women were elected by Gamma of Connecticut at Wesleyan. Although this step, taken when Phi Beta Kappa was just attaining its centenary, was regarded in some quarters as revolutionary, it aroused no formal protest; and a few years later, when a general constitution and bylaws were adopted, the right of women to membership was accepted without question.

In 1877 members of Phi Beta Kappa living in New York City formed an association, which ever since has met three or four times annually for lectures, discussion, friendly intercourse. Later, similar groups were formed in other cities, until in 1947 there were 112. To many graduates such organizations have been a means of their finding new friends and keeping still active their concern with things of the mind. Moreover, these associations often have opportunities of influencing public opinion in support of liberal education. Some have undertaken especially to foster scholarship in secondary schools. In 1977 there were more than fifty active associations.

In the 107 years from the founding of the society in 1776 to the organization of the United Chapters in 1883, 25 chapters had been chartered and approximately 14,000 persons had been elected to membership. At the centennial celebration of Alpha

of Massachusetts, on June 30, 1881, to which the other chapters had been invited to send representatives, a proposal was made by the delegate from Hobart, a member at Harvard, to effect a closer union. After full discussion then and in later meetings, a constitution was prepared, adopted, and duly ratified, and on September 5, 1883, the first National Council of the United Chapters of Phi Beta Kappa began its sessions. A revision of the constitution in 1937 strengthened this union of the chapters, at the same time safeguarding the rights and liberties of the individual chapters.

Government and Administration The legislative body of the society is the council, comprised of delegates elected for a term of three years. Each chapter may elect three delegates. Each accredited association of 25 or more members may elect one delegate; each of 200 or more, two. The association delegates may vote on all matters except the granting of charters and other questions requiring a vote by chapters.

The council has sole power to charter new chapters and to legislate for the society as a whole.

The Senate, or permanent executive body, consists of 24 members elected by the council, 12 at each triennial session for terms of six years. The Senate meets annually in December and, if necessary, at other times in special session.

The Senate elects a standing committee on qualifications composed of six members, which both supervises the standards of existing chapters and, after thorough examination of non-member institutions, invites those considered qualified for charters to submit applications. The committee reports its recommendations to the chapters, the district conferences, and the Senate. The Senate refers these recommendations as approved to the council, which invites the institution to accept a charter, much as a chapter invites an individual to accept membership. The committee on qualifications has exerted upon hundreds of American colleges and universities a very direct and substantial influence in raising their standards of scholarship and in encouraging support of the liberal arts and sciences. Known to be stricter than any accrediting agency, it has been widely commended for placing its emphasis not upon quantitative measurements, but rather upon the spirit of a college, the quality of its work, the achievements of its graduates.

Services and Publications The national offices of the United Chapters assist the chapters, the graduate associations, and the more than 325,000 members of the society. The executive secretary and his staff carry out the directives of the various council and senate committees. They also publish the membership quarterly, *The Key Reporter*, as well as numerous booklets and pamphlets required by chapters and associations.

The editorial offices of *The American Scholar*, published for general circulation by Phi Beta Kappa, are in the national offices of the United Chapters. Founded in 1931, this periodical has

---

[3]Alpha of Alabama, organized in 1851, was disbanded at the outbreak of the Civil War and was not reorganized until 1912.

made rapid strides editorially and financially in recent years. Guided by a "working" editorial board of fifteen members, elected by the Phi Beta Kappa Senate, this "quarterly for the independent thinker" has won the high regard of an ever-widening and influential circle of readers.

In 1924 the Phi Beta Kappa Foundation was chartered by the University of the State of New York as a corporation empowered to hold and administer trust funds, accruing through gifts and bequests for the general purpose of encouraging scholarship. The foundation expended $100,000 for the erection of the Phi Beta Kappa Hall at the College of William and Mary in honor of the founders of Phi Beta Kappa and in commemoration of the 150th anniversary of the society. The sesquicentennial celebration led to the restoration of Colonial Williamsburg. That extraordinary imaginative feat of historical reconstruction was first conceived by a member of Phi Beta Kappa, the late Dr. W. A. R. Goodwin, rector of Bruton Parish Church, Williamsburg, and was made a reality through the munificence of another member and former Phi Beta Kappa senator, John D. Rockefeller, Jr.

The foundation has already received more than two million dollars toward an endowment, the income from which is used to maintain general headquarters and to make the society more useful to its members and more influential.

The Phi Beta Kappa Associates were organized in 1940 by an unofficial group of members living in New York City. The purpose of the organization is "to foster and advance the welfare of the Phi Beta Kappa Society and the ideals for which it stands." The active membership is limited to 200, without geographical restrictions. These men and women, by annual contributions of $100 to be paid over a period of ten years, constitute a "living endowment" for Phi Beta Kappa. Upon the completion of all contributions an associate enters life membership, leaving his place in the active group to be taken by another.

In 1942 when the founding membership of 200 was completed, the Associates opened a Phi Beta Kappa National Lectureship which, functioning through the United Chapters, aims to secure for each chapter and association annually one or more distinguished speakers. Endowed from Associates funds to supplement small local treasuries, the lectureship places its emphasis on "the urgent problems of discovering, educating, and training the young men and women needed for positions of responsibility in the post-war world."

For over a century and a half, election to Phi Beta Kappa has been a recognition of intellectual capacities well employed, especially in the acquiring of an education in the liberal arts and sciences. And because of the remarkably high proportion of famous names on the roll of Phi Beta Kappa, admission to its ranks may reasonably be held to indicate also potentialities of future distinction. No society has a monopoly of merit or talent. Still, when all allowances are made, it remains true that election to Phi Beta Kappa is a fair augury of intellectual achievement in the service of the American commonwealth.

Headquarters   1811 Q Street, N.W., Washington, D.C. 20009.

Membership   Active chapters 225. Total number of initiates 325,000. Chapter roll:††

1776	Alpha of Virginia, William and Mary (1780-1851) (1860-1893)
1780	Alpha of Connecticut, Yale (1871-1884)
1781	Alpha of Massachusetts, Harvard
1787	Alpha of New Hampshire, Dartmouth
1817	Alpha of New York, Union (NY)
1825	Alpha of Maine, Bowdoin
1830	Alpha of Rhode Island, Brown
1845	Beta of Connecticut, Trinity (CT)
1845	Gamma of Connecticut, Wesleyan (CT)
1847	Alpha of Ohio, Western Reserve, Adelbert, Flora Stone Mather
1848	Alpha of Vermont, Vermont
1851	Alpha of Alabama, Alabama
1853	Beta of Massachusetts, Amherst
1858	Beta of New York, N.Y.U. (Heights and Square)
1858	Beta of Ohio, Kenyon
1860	Gamma of Ohio, Marietta
1864	Gamma of Massachusetts, Williams
1867	Gamma of New York, CCNY
1868	Beta of Vermont, Middlebury
1869	Alpha of New Jersey, Rutgers
1869	Delta of New York, Columbia (NY), Barnard
1870	Epsilon of New York, Hamilton
1871	Zeta of New York, Hobart
1878	Eta of New York, Colgate
1882	Theta of New York, Cornell
1887	Alpha of Pennsylvania, Dickinson
1887	Beta of Pennsylvania, Lehigh
1887	Iota of New York, Rochester
1889	Alpha of Indiana, DePauw
1890	Alpha of Illinois, Northwestern
1890	Alpha of Kansas, Kansas
1890	Gamma of Pennsylvania, Lafayette
1892	Alpha of Minnesota, Minnesota
1892	Delta of Massachusetts, Tufts
1892	Delta of Pennsylvania, Penn
1895	Alpha of Iowa, Iowa
1895	Alpha of Maryland, Johns Hopkins
1895	Alpha of Nebraska, Nebraska
1896	Beta of Maine, Colby
1896	Epsilon of Pennsylvania, Swarthmore
1896	Kappa of New York, Syracuse
1898	Alpha of California, California
1898	Beta of Indiana, Wabash
1899	Alpha of Wisconsin, Wisconsin, Madison
1899	Beta of Illinois, Chicago
1899	Beta of New Jersey, Princeton
1899	Delta of Ohio, Cincinnati

†† This chapter roll is repeated from the 19th edition; no current information was provided.

1899 Epsilon of Massachusetts, Boston
1899 Lambda of New York, St. Lawrence
1899 Mu of New York, Vassar
1899 Zeta of Pennsylvania, Haverford
1901 Alpha of Missouri, Missouri
1901 Alpha of Tennessee, Vanderbilt
1902 Eta of Pennsylvania, Allegheny
1904 Alpha of Colorado, Colorado
1904 Alpha of North Carolina, North Carolina
1904 Beta of California, Stanford
1904 Beta of Colorado, Colorado Col
1904 Epsilon of Ohio, Ohio State
1904 Eta of Massachusetts, Wellesley
1904 Zeta of Massachusetts, Smith
1905 Alpha of Texas, Texas
1905 Beta of Maryland, Goucher
1905 Theta of Massachusetts, Mount Holyoke
1907 Alpha of Michigan, Michigan
1907 Eta of Ohio, Ohio Wesleyan
1907 Gamma of Illinois, Illinois
1907 Zeta of Ohio, Oberlin
1908 Beta of Iowa, Grinnell
1908 Beta of Virginia, Virginia
1908 Theta of Pennsylvania, Franklin and Marshall
1909 Alpha of Louisiana, Tulane
1910 Alpha of West Virginia, West Virginia
1911 Beta of Wisconsin, Beloit
1911 Gamma of Indiana, Indiana
1911 Gamma of Virginia, Washington and Lee
1911 Iota of Ohio, Miami (OH)
1911 Theta of Ohio, Denison
1914 Alpha of Georgia, Georgia
1914 Alpha of North Dakota, North Dakota
1914 Alpha of Washington, Washington (WA)
1914 Beta of Minnesota, Carleton
1914 Beta of Missouri, Washington (MO)
1914 Gamma of California, Pomona
1914 *Gamma of Wisconsin, Lawrence* [4]
1914 Iota of Massachusetts, Radcliffe
1917 Delta of Illinois, Knox
1917 Delta of Virginia, Randolph, Macon Woman's
1917 Gamma of Maine, Bates
1920 Alpha of Oklahoma, Oklahoma
1920 Beta of North Carolina, Duke
1920 Beta of Washington, Whitman
1920 Nu of New York, Hunter
1923 Alpha of Oregon, Oregon
1923 Delta of Iowa, Cornell
1923 Delta of Maine, Maine
1923 Gamma of Iowa, Drake
1923 Gamma of North Carolina, Davidson
1923 Iota of Pennsylvania, Gettysburg
1923 Zeta of Virginia, Randolph, Macon
1926 Alpha of Idaho, Idaho
1926 Alpha of Kentucky, Kentucky
1926 Alpha of South Carolina, South Carolina
1926 Alpha of South Dakota, South Dakota

1926 Beta of Georgia, Agnes Scott
1926 Beta of Tennessee, Sewanee
1926 Delta of California, Occidental
1926 Kappa of Ohio, Wooster
1929 Beta of Texas, Rice
1929 Epsilon of California, USC
1929 Epsilon of Virginia, Richmond
1929 Gamma of Georgia, Emory
1929 Gamma of Washington, Washington State
1929 Lambda of Ohio, Ohio
1929 Zeta of California, Mills
1932 Alpha of Arizona, Arizona
1932 Alpha of Arkansas, Arkansas
1932 Epsilon of Illinois, Illinois Col
1932 Kappa of Massachusetts, Wheaton
1932 Xi of New York, Wells
1935 Alpha of Florida, Florida State
1935 Alpha of Utah, Utah
1935 Delta of Connecticut, Connecticut Col.
1937 Beta of Alabama, Birmingham-Southern
1937 Kappa of Pennsylvania, Washington and Jefferson
1937 Lambda of Pennsylvania, Penn State
1938 Alpha of the D. of C., George Washington
1938 Beta of Florida, Florida
1938 Beta of Oregon, Reed
1938 Eta of California, UCLA
1938 Gamma of Minnesota, St. Catherine
1938 Omicron of New York, Buffalo
1940 Alpha of Wyoming, Wyoming
1940 Beta of Michigan, Albion
1940 Gamma of Colorado, Denver
1940 Mu of Pennsylvania, Bucknell
1940 Pi of New York, Elmira
1941 Beta of South Carolina, Wofford
1941 Delta of North Carolina, Wake Forest
1941 *Delta of Wisconsin, Milwaukee-Downer* [5]
1942 Beta of District of Columbia, Catholic
1949 Delta of Minnesota, St. Olaf
1949 Epsilon of Iowa, Coe
1949 Eta of Virginia, Hampden-Sydney
1949 Gamma of Tennessee, Southwestern, Memphis
1949 Gamma of Texas, Southern Methodist
1950 Nu of Pennsylvania, Wilson
1950 Rho of New York, Brooklyn
1950 Sigma of New York, Queens (NY)
1950 Theta of Virginia, Sweet Briar
1950 Zeta of Illinois, Augustana (IL)
1952 Alpha of Hawaii, Hawaii
1952 Beta of New Hampshire, New Hampshire
1952 Epsilon of Wisconsin, Ripon
1953 Delta of Tennessee, Fisk
1953 Eta of Illinois, Rockford
1953 Gamma of District of Columbia, Howard
1953 Gamma of Michigan, Wayne State (MI)
1953 Lambda of Massachusetts, Clark
1953 Xi of Pennsylvania, Pitt
1956 Alpha of Delaware, Delaware

[4]In 1954, Lawrence College and Milwaukee-Downer merged as Lawrence University. The Gamma Chapter at Lawrence and the Delta Chapter at Downer combines as Gamma-Deta of Wisconsin.

[5]In 1954, Lawrence College and Milwaukee-Downer merged as Lawrence University. The Gamma Chapter at Lawrence and the Delta Chapter at Downer combines as Gamma-Deta of Wisconsin.

1956	Epsilon of Connecticut, Connecticut
1956	Epsilon of North Carolina, North Carolina, Greensboro [6]
1958	Delta of Michigan, Kalamazoo
1962	Iota of Virginia, Hollins
1962	Mu of Massachusetts, Brandeis
1962	Omicron of Pennsylvania, Chatham
1962	Tau of New York, Fordham
1962	Theta of California, Scripps
1962	Theta of Illinois, Lake Forest
1964	Gamma of Maryland, Maryland
1964	Gamma-Delta of Wisconsin, Lawrence
1965	Alpha of New Mexico, New Mexico
1965	Delta of D.C., Georgetown U.
1965	Delta of Indiana, Earlham
1965	Epsilon of Tennessee, Tennessee
1965	Iota of California, Cal, Riverside
1965	Nu of Massachusetts, Massachusetts
1968	Delta of Georgia, Morehouse
1968	Epsilon of Indiana, Notre Dame
1968	Epsilon of Michigan, Michigan State
1968	Epsilon of Minnesota, Macalester
1968	Gamma of Missouri, St. Louis
1968	Kappa of California, Cal, Davis
1968	Pi of Pennsylvania, Muhlenberg
1971	Beta of Kentucky, Centre College
1971	Chi of New York, Lehman
1971	Delta of Texas, Texas Christian
1971	Epsilon of D.C., Trinity (DC)
1971	Kappa of Virginia, Mary Washington
1971	Lambda of Virginia, Mary Baldwin
1971	Mu of Ohio, Hiram
1971	Omicron of Massachusetts, Boston Col
1971	Phi of New York, Skidmore
1971	Psi of New York, SUNY, Binghamton
1971	Upsilon of New York, Manhattan
1971	Xi of Massachusetts, M.I.T.
1971	Zeta of Indiana, Purdue
1971	Zeta of Michigan, Hope
1971	Zeta of Wisconsin, Marquette
1973	Beta of Arizona, Arizona State
1973	Delta of Colorado, Colorado State
1973	Gamma of South Carolina, Furman
1973	Omega of New York, Hofstra
1973	Zeta of Iowa, Iowa State
1974	Alpha Alpha of N.Y., SUNY, Albany
1974	Alpha Beta of N.Y., SUNY, Stony Brook
1974	Beta of Kansas, Kansas State
1974	Epsilon of Texas, Trinity (TX)
1974	Eta of Wis., Wisconsin, Milwaukee
1974	Mu of California, Cal, Irvine
1974	Nu of California, San Diego State
1974	Pi of Massachusetts, Holy Cross
1974	Rho of Pennsylvania, Temple
1974	Zeta of Minnesota, Hamline
1977	Cal State, Long Beach [7]
1977	Cal, San Diego[3]
1977	Redlands[3]
1977	Santa Clara[3]

1977	Beta of Louisiana, L.S.U.
1977	Beta of Rhode Island, Rhode Island
1977	Iota of Illinois, Chicago Circle
1977	Mu of Virginia, V.P.I. and State Univ.
1977	Nu of Ohio, Kent
1977	Zeta of Texas, Baylor
1977	San Francisco State[3]

Pi Mu Epsilon[†]

(MATHEMATICS)

ACTIVE PIN

PI MU EPSILON was incorporated May 25, 1914, under the laws of New York by E. D. Roe, Jr., F. F. Decker, Helen L. Applebee, P. J. Bentley, Olive E. Jones, Florence A. Lane, Helen M. Barnard, E. J. Cottrell, and A. Sussman. The society developed out of the Mathematics Club of Syracuse University, E. D. Roe, Jr., taking the initiative. Syracuse remained the sole chapter until 1919 when Ohio State University became a member. From that time on chapters have applied for membership regularly. Pi Mu Epsilon is an honor society, confining its activity to institutions with well-developed departments of mathematics which offer graduate as well as undergraduate work.

The requirements for individual membership in local chapters are somewhat elastic. Those persons are eligible for membership who stand scholastically in the upper fourth of the student body taking mathematics and the upper third of the student body as a whole. They must also have completed at least two years of college mathematics, and they must possess the academic ranking of a junior.

Government The government of the organization rests in the hands of the national officers, all of whom are elected by the vote of each member chapter for a three-year period. The convention is usually held in conjunction with the Mathematical Association of America.

Traditions and Insignia Each chapter carries on its own program, independent in detail from the program of other member chapters, the only society stipulation being that it must be of a scholarly, creative nature. Many chapters carry on research projects; others establish loan and scholarship funds for needy students; still others use the program as a means of supplementing classroom activity with mathematical lectures and contests. The emblem is a gold key bearing a vertical panel which displays the Greek letters ΠΜΕ superimposed on an equilateral triangle.

[6]Chartered as a section of the Alpha of North Carolina on December 12, 1934; elevated to chapter status in 1956.
[7]Greek name not yet assigned.

† This chapter narrative is repeated from the 19th edition; no current information was provided.

Publication *The Pi Mu Epsilon Journal* is devoted to mathematical articles and news of interest to members.

Headquarters Department of Mathematics, University of Maryland, College Park, Maryland 20742.

Membership Active chapters 185. Inactive chapters 14. Total number of initiates 55,000. Chapter roll:††

1914	New York Alpha, Syracuse
1919	Ohio Alpha, Ohio State
1921	Pennsylvania Alpha, Penn
1922	Alabama Alpha, Alabama
1922	Missouri Alpha, Missouri
1923	Iowa Alpha, Iowa State
1924	Illinois Alpha, Illinois
1925	California Alpha, UCLA
1925	Missouri Beta, Washington (MO)
1925	Montana Alpha, Montana
1925	New York Beta, Hunter
1925	Pennsylvania Beta, Bucknell
1927	Kentucky Alpha, Kentucky
1927	Ohio Beta, Ohio Wesleyan
1928	Kansas Alpha, Kansas
1928	Nebraska Alpha, Nebraska
1929	Oklahoma Alpha, Oklahoma
1929	Pennsylvania Gamma, Lehigh
1930	*California Beta, California*
1930	Pennsylvania Delta, Penn State
1931	Arkansas Alpha, Arkansas
1931	Oregon Alpha, Oregon
1931	Washington Alpha, Washington State
1932	North Carolina Alpha, Duke
1932	Washington Beta, Washington (WA)
1933	New York Delta, Courant Institute, N.Y.U.
1933	New York Gamma, Brooklyn
1933	Wisconsin Alpha, Marquette
1934	Georgia Alpha, Georgia
1935	Kansas Beta, Kansas State
1935	New York Epsilon, St. Lawrence
1936	*Colorado Alpha, Colorado*
1936	Ohio Gamma, Toledo
1937	*New York Zeta, Columbia (NY)*
1938	Oklahoma Beta, Oklahoma State
1938	Oregon Beta, Oregon State
1939	Louisiana Alpha, L.S.U.
1939	Wisconsin Beta, Wisconsin, Madison
1940	Michigan Alpha, Michigan State
1941	Arizona Alpha, Arizona
1941	Delaware Alpha, Delaware
1944	Illinois Beta, Northwestern
1945	Missouri Gamma, St. Louis
1947	Pennsylvania Epsilon, Carnegie-Mellon
1948	New Hampshire Alpha, New Hampshire
1948	North Carolina Beta, North Carolina
1948	Virginia Alpha, Richmond
1949	Ohio Delta, Miami (OH)
1950	Colorado Beta, Denver

†† This chapter roll is repeated from the 19th edition; no current information was provided.

1950	Kansas Gamma, Wichita
1951	D. of C. Alpha, Howard
1951	Florida Alpha, Miami (FL)
1951	New York Eta, SUNY, Buffalo
1953	Alabama Beta, Auburn
1953	New York Theta, Cornell
1954	New Jersey Alpha, Rutgers
1955	Nevada Alpha, Nevada
1956	Florida Beta, Florida State
1956	Illinois Gamma, DePaul
1956	Indiana Alpha, Purdue
1956	Alpha, Maryland
1956	Ohio Epsilon, Kent
1957	California Gamma, Sacramento State Col
1957	Illinois Delta, Southern Illinois
1959	Georgia Beta, Georgia Tech
1959	Montana Beta, Montana State
1959	South Carolina Alpha, South Carolina
1959	Texas Alpha, Texas Christian
1960	Louisiana Beta, Southern
1960	North Carolina Gamma, North Carolina State
1960	New Mexico Alpha, New Mexico State
1960	New York Iota, Brooklyn Tech
1960	New York Kappa, R.P.I.
1960	Ohio Zeta, Dayton
1960	Pennsylvania Zeta, Temple
1960	South Dakota Alpha, South Dakota
1960	Utah Alpha, Utah
1960	Washington Gamma, Seattle
1961	Louisiana Gamma, Tulane
1961	Minnesota Alpha, Carleton
1961	New York Lambda, Manhattan
1961	New York Mu, Yeshiva
1961	Ohio Eta, Cleveland State
1961	Virginia Beta, V.P.I.
1962	Ohio Theta, Xavier (OH)
1962	Rhode Island Alpha, Rhode Island
1962	Utah Beta, Utah State
1963	California Delta, Cal, Santa Barbara
1963	California Epsilon, Harvey Mudd, Claremont
1963	Connecticut Alpha, Connecticut
1963	Ohio Iota, Denison
1963	Oregon Gamma, Portland State
1963	Pennsylvania Eta, Franklin and Marshall
1963	Washington Delta, Western Washington
1964	D.C. Beta, Georgetown U.
1964	Indiana Beta, Indiana
1964	Louisiana Delta, Southeastern Louisiana
1964	Louisiana Epsilon, McNeese
1964	Minnesota Beta, St. Catherine
1964	New York Nu, N.Y.U.
1964	New York Xi, Adelphi
1965	California Zeta, Cal, Riverside
1965	Florida Delta, Florida
1965	Florida Gamma, Eckerd
1965	Maine Alpha, Maine
1965	Michigan Beta, Detroit
1965	New York Omicron, Clarkson
1965	New York Pi, SUNY Col., Fredonia
1965	New York Rho, St. John's (NY)

1965	Ohio Lambda, John Carroll
1965	Texas Beta, Lamar
1966	*Colorado Gamma, U.S. Air Force Academy*
1966	D.C. Gamma, George Washington
1966	Florida Epsilon, South Florida
1966	Indiana Delta, Indiana State
1966	Indiana Gamma, Rose-Hulman
1966	Louisiana Zeta, Southwestern Louisiana
1966	Massachusetts Alpha, Worcester Tech
1966	Pennsylvania Theta, Drexel
1967	Alabama Gamma, Samford
1967	California Eta, Santa Clara
1967	Massachusetts Beta, Holy Cross
1967	New Jersey Gamma, Rutgers, Camden
1967	New Mexico Beta, New Mexico Tech, Socorro
1967	New York Sigma, Pratt
1967	North Dakota Alpha, North Dakota State
1967	Pennsylvania Iota, Villanova
1967	Rhode Island Beta, Rhode Island Col.
1967	Tennessee Alpha, Memphis State
1967	West Virginia Alpha, West Virginia
1968	Arizona Beta, Arizona State
1968	Louisiana Eta, Nicholls
1968	Minnesota Gamma, Macalester
1968	Mississippi Alpha, Mississippi
1968	New Jersey Delta, Seton Hall
1968	New Jersey Epsilon, St. Peter's
1968	New York Tau, Lehman
1968	North Carolina Delta, East Carolina
1968	Utah Gamma, Brigham Young
1968	Washington Epsilon, Gonzaga
1969	California Theta, Occidental
1969	North Carolina Epsilon, North Carolina, Greensboro
1969	N.Y. Phi, SUNY Col., Potsdam
1969	New Jersey Zeta, Fairleigh Dickinson
1969	New York Chi, SUNY, Albany
1969	New York Upsilon, Ithaca
1969	Ohio Mu, Ohio
1969	Ohio Nu, Akron
1969	Texas Gamma, Prairie View
1970	Louisiana Iota, Grambling
1970	Louisiana Theta, Loyola, New Orleans
1970	Maryland Beta, Morgan State
1970	Michigan Gamma, Andrews
1970	Pa. Kappa, West Chester
1970	S.D. Beta, South Dakota Mines
1970	Texas Delta, Stephen F. Austin
1970	Texas Epsilon, Sam Houston
1970	West Virginia Beta, Marshall
1971	Colorado Delta, Northern Colorado
1971	New York Psi, Iona
1971	Pennsylvania Lambda, Clarion
1971	Tenn. Beta, Tennessee, Chattanooga
1971	Tenn. Gamma, Middle Tennessee
1971	Texas Zeta, Angelo
1971	Virginia Gamma, Madison Col
1972	Alabama Delta, South Alabama
1972	Alabama Epsilon, Tuskegee
1972	California Iota, USC
1972	Florida Zeta, Florida Atlantic

1972	Illinois Epsilon, Northern Illinois
1972	Kentucky Beta, Western Kentucky
1972	Massachusetts Gamma, Bridgewater
1972	Michigan Delta, Hope
1972	Texas Eta, Texas A & M
1972	Virginia Delta, Roanoke
1973	Ill. Zeta, Southern Illinois, Edwardsville
1973	Louisiana Kappa, Louisiana Tech
1973	Nebraska Beta, Creighton
1973	Pennsylvania Mu, Scranton
1973	South Carolina Beta, Clemson
1974	Florida Eta, North Florida
1974	Georgia Gamma, Armstrong
1974	Mississippi Beta, Mississippi Col.
1974	North Carolina Zeta, North Carolina, Wilmington
1974	Pennsylvania Nu, Edinboro
1974	Rhode Island Gamma, Providence
1974	Texas Theta, Houston
1975	California Kappa, Loyola Marymount, Los Angeles
1975	Kentucky Gamma, Murray State
1975	Missouri Delta, Westminster (MO)
1975	Pennsylvania Xi, St. Joseph's (PA)
1975	Texas Iota, Texas, Arlington
1975	Texas Kappa, West Texas
1975	Texas Lambda, Texas
1976	Alabama Zeta, Alabama State
1976	Arkansas Beta, Hendrix
1976	North Carolina Eta, Appalachian
1976	Virginia Epsilon, Longwood
1958	New Jersey Beta, Douglass (NJ)

Sigma Epsilon Sigma[†]

(SCHOLARSHIP—FRESHMAN WOMEN)

ACTIVE PIN

SIGMA EPSILON SIGMA was established in the fall of 1927 at the University of Wisconsin by a group of women students who felt the need of a society that would recognize and encourage high scholarship in freshman women. Organizational meetings were held, the name Sigma Epsilon Sigma chosen, the constitution and ritual drawn up, and a pin selected. The first initiation was held on December 8 that year.

To be eligible for membership, a woman must be of good character and have maintained a 3.5 out of a possible 4.0 grade-point average in her freshman year.

Headquarters Adviser to Sigma Epsilon Sigma, University of Wisconsin, Madison, Wisconsin

† This chapter narrative is repeated from the 19th edition; no current information was provided.

Traditions and Insignia   The name comes from the motto which signifies Wisdom, Independence, and Self-control.

The pin is a symbol of scholarship; its gold represents man's best desires; its shape, brotherhood; and its lamp, the light of learning.

Membership   Active chapters 4. Inactive chapters 5. Total number of initiates 1,000. Chapter roll:††

1927   Alpha, Wisconsin, Madison
1928   Beta, Missouri
1929   *Gamma, Colorado*
1930   Delta, North Dakota
1930   Epsilon, Minnesota
1933   Eta, Washington
1941   *Wisconsin, Milwaukee*
1941   Theta, Carroll
1950   *Iota, Arizona State*

Sigma Gamma Epsilon†

(EARTH SCIENCES)

ACTIVE PIN

SIGMA GAMMA EPSILON was founded at the University of Kansas in 1915, its object being "the scholastic, and scientific, advancement of its members; the extension of the relations of friendship and assistance between the university and scientific schools of the United States and Canada; and the advancement of the earth sciences." High scholarship and active interest in the pursuit of work in the earth sciences are fundamental requirements for membership.

Government   A general convention, held biennially, is the governing body; authority rests with the Grand Council of seven members in the interim.

Traditions and Insignia   The badge is diamond-shaped, bearing hammer, shovel, and compass. The colors are blue, gold, and silver.

Publication   *The Compass* is published quarterly.

Headquarters   830 Van Vleet Oval, Room 163, University of Oklahoma, Norman, Oklahoma 73019.

Membership   Active chapters 60. Inactive chapters 26. Total number of initiates 2,400. Chapter roll:††

1915   Alpha, Kansas
1915   *Beta, Pitt*

†† This chapter roll is repeated from the 19th edition; no current information was provided.
† This chapter narrative is repeated from the 19th edition; no current information was provided.

1916   Gamma, Oklahoma
1917   *Delta, Nebraska*
1919   *Epsilon, Missouri* (1939)
1920   Zeta, Texas
1921   Eta, Missouri Mines (1926-1951)
1921   *Iota, Michigan*
1921   Theta, Cornell
1922   *Kappa, Penn State*
1922   Lambda, Colorado Mines
1922   *Mu, Utah*
1922   *Nu, Minnesota*
1924   *Omicron, California* (1940)
1924   *Pi, Nevada* (1936)
1924   *Xi, Washington State*
1926   Rho, Indiana
1926   *Sigma, Ohio State*
1927   *Tau, George Washington* (1947)
1927   Upsilon, West Virginia
1928   Chi, Kentucky
1928   *Phi, Colgate* (1940)
1929   *Psi, Idaho*
1932   *Alpha Alpha, North Carolina*
1932   Alpha Beta, Texas Tech
1932   *Alpha Delta, Cincinnati*
1932   *Alpha Gamma, U.C.L.A.* (1947)
1932   Omega, USC
1934   *Alpha Eta, Colorado*
1934   Alpha Theta, Miami (OH)
1934   *Alpha Zeta, Oregon State* (1953)
1938   Alpha Iota, Augustana (IL)
1939   *Alpha Kappa, Johns Hopkins* (1947)
1940   Alpha Lambda, Texas Western
1942   *Alpha Mu, V.P.I.*
1947   Alpha Nu, Kansas State
1947   *Alpha Rho, Michigan State*
1947   *Alpha Xi, Chicago* (1948)
1948   Alpha Sigma, Brigham Young
1948   *Alpha Tau, Emory*
1948   Alpha Upsilon, Mississippi State
1949   Alpha Chi, Alabama
1949   Alpha Omega, Oklahoma State
1949   Alpha Phi, Purdue
1949   Alpha Psi, Arkansas
1950   *Beta Alpha, Washington* (1955)
1950   *Beta Beta, Upsala*
1950   *Beta Delta, Montana*
1950   Beta Epsilon, Centenary
1950   Beta Eta, Tulane
1950   Beta Gamma, Utah State
1950   Beta Zeta, North Dakota
1951   Beta Iota, Houston
1951   *Beta Theta, Massachusetts*
1952   *Beta Kappa, Virginia*
1953   *Beta Lambda, Tulsa*
1953   Beta Mu, New Mexico
1954   Beta Nu, Southwestern Louisiana
1955   Beta Omicron, Redlands
1955   *Beta Xi, Louisiana Tech*
1957   *Beta Pi, Cornell Col. (IA)*
1957   *Beta Rho, Michigan Tech*
1958   Beta Sigma, Rice
1959   Beta Tau, Arizona

1959   Beta Upsilon, Bowling Green
1960   Beta Chi, Arizona State
1960   *Beta Phi, Southern State*
1962   Beta Psi, Florida
1965   Beta Omega, Arlington State (TX)
1966   Gamma Alpha, Wisconsin, Superior
1966   Gamma Beta, Wichita
1967   Gamma Gamma, Tennessee
1968   Gamma Delta, Northern Arizona
1968   *Gamma Epsilon, East Texas*
1968   Gamma Zeta, Kent
1969   Gamma Theta, Iowa
1970   Gamma Iota, Northeast Louisiana
1971   Gamma Kappa, Albion College
1972   Gamma Lambda, Indiana State
1972   Gamma Mu, Mississippi
1972   Gamma Nu, Nevada, Las Vegas
1972   Gamma Omicron, New Orleans
1973   Gamma Pi, Chadron
1973   *Gamma Xi, Texas A & M*
1974   Gamma Chi, Eastern Illinois
1974   Gamma Phi, Stephen F. Austin
1974   Gamma Rho, Boise
1974   Gamma Sigma, Northern Iowa
1974   *Gamma Tau, New Mexico Highlands*
1974   Gamma Upsilon, West Texas
1975   Delta Alpha, William and Mary
1975   Delta Beta, Auburn
1975   Delta Gamma, Washington (MO)
1975   Gamma Omega, New Mexico State
1975   Gamma Psi, Western Carolina
1976   Delta Delta, Nicholls
1976   Delta Epsilon, Wright State
1976   Delta Zeta, Indiana (PA)
1977   Delta Eta, South Alabama

Sigma Xi†

(SCIENTIFIC RESEARCH)

ACTIVE PIN

THE SOCIETY OF THE SIGMA XI was founded at Cornell University in November, 1886, by Henry S. Williams, William A. Day, William H. Riley, Frank Van Vleck, Henry E. Smith, William A. Mosscrop, Charles B. Wing, John Knickerbacker, John J. Berger, and Edwin N. Sanderson, with the intention of establishing in scientific and technical institutions a society, the badge of which would have the same significance of scholarly merit in science as that of Phi Beta Kappa among classical students. It is not a secret society. The object is to encourage original investigation in science, pure and applied, by the holding of meetings for the discussion of scientific subjects; the establishment of fraternal relations among investigators at the scientific centers; the granting of membership to investigating students who have, in their college course, given special promises of future achievement; the publication of such scientific matter as may be deemed desirable in the society's quarterly, *American Scientist;* the support of grants-in-aid for research; the presentation of national lectureships.

The society adopted the name, Sigma Xi, The Scientific Research Society of North America, in January, 1973. At that time a merger with the Scientific Research Society of America (RESA) was effected. Sigma Xi accepted into membership fifty former RESA Branches which had been established between 1949 and 1967 situated at important scientific research centers throughout the nation.

The membership of institutional chapters is composed of members and associate members who are actively connected with the staff or student body of the institution and of affiliated members and associate members who, on presenting satisfactory credentials, become affiliated with the chapter.

Those eligible to election as members in a chapter are: any professor, instructor, or other member of the staff of the institution who has shown noteworthy achievement as an original investigator in some branch of pure or applied science; any student in the institution who, as judged by his actual work of investigation, has exhibited an aptitude for scientific research.

Those eligible to election as associate members are: any graduate student who has shown marked excellence in one or more departments of pure or applied science; any undergraduate student who has completed two and one-half years of undergraduate work and who has shown marked excellence in two or more departments of pure or applied science.

A chapter may be established at any educational institution in which scientific research is cultivated and promoted, or at any research institution which allows the same unrestricted rights of publication as educational institutions, provided that no institution shall be considered unless its permanency is shown to be reasonably assured by private endowment or state support. A club may be established at any place where the object of the society would be furthered. Clubs have all the rights and privileges of institutional chapters, except that they do not elect to membership.

Government   The control of the society is by an annual convention. Between its sessions administration is by the officers with cooperation and approval of the Executive Committee of ten.

Traditions and Insignia   The insigne for a member is a watch chain pendent key-pin, or ring, formed of the letters Σ and Ξ. Associate members display Σ only. Colors are electric-blue and white.

Publications   The constitution was published in 1887, 1893, 1904, 1907, 1911, 1912, 1915, 1922,

† This chapter narrative is repeated from the 19th edition; no current information was provided.

and 1942. A general catalogue was published in 1888, a *Quarter Century and History* in 1912, *Half Century* in 1936. A number of adresses and other pamphlets have also been published. An important quarterly, the *American Scientist*, is published by the society and also a biennial publication, *Science in Progress* (Yale University Press), containing material presented in the Sigma Xi National Lectureships by eminent research scientists.

Funds In 1921 the society founded a research fund from which grants-in-aid are awarded annually to research workers in any field of science. The award is made by a committee on award.

Headquarters 155 Whitney Avenue, Yale University, New Haven, Connecticut 06510.

Membership Active chapters 201. Total number of initiates 200,000. Chapter roll:††

1886	Cornell
1887	R.P.I.
1887	Union
1890	Kansas
1895	Yale
1896	Minnesota
1897	Nebraska
1898	Ohio State
1899	Penn
1900	Brown
1900	Iowa
1901	Stanford
1902	California
1902	Columbia
1903	Chicago
1903	Michigan
1904	Case Tech
1904	Indiana
1905	Colorado
1905	Missouri
1906	Northwestern
1906	Syracuse
1907	Washington
1907	Wisconsin, Madison
1908	Worcester Tech
1909	Purdue
1910	Washington (MO)
1915	District of Columbia
1915	Texas
1920	Mayo Foundation
1920	North Carolina
1920	North Dakota
1921	Iowa State
1922	Idaho
1922	Kentucky
1922	McGill
1922	Rutgers
1923	Oregon
1923	Swarthmore
1924	Cal Tech
1924	Johns Hopkins

†† This chapter roll is repeated from the 19th edition; no current information was provided.

1924	Virginia
1926	Cincinnati
1926	N.Y.U.
1927	Michigan State
1928	Arizona
1928	Illinois, Chicago Medicine
1928	Kansas State
1928	Lehigh
1928	Maryland
1930	Oklahoma
1930	Penn State
1930	Rochester
1930	Washington State
1930	Wyoming
1931	Harvard
1931	Pitt
1932	Princeton
1932	Western Reserve
1933	Duke
1933	U.C.L.A.
1934	M.I.T.
1934	Tulane
1935	Smith
1935	Wesleyan
1936	Buffalo
1936	Carleton
1937	Carnegie Tech
1937	George Washington
1937	Oregon State
1937	Utah
1938	Florida
1938	Massachusetts
1938	Rice
1938	Wellesley
1939	Alabama
1939	West Virginia
1940	USC
1940	V.P.I.
1941	Bryn Mawr
1941	Oberlin
1942	Illinois Tech
1942	L.S.U.
1942	Utah State
1943	Brooklyn Tech
1943	Radcliffe
1943	Tufts
1944	Emory
1944	North Carolina State
1944	St. Louis
1944	Vanderbilt
1944	Wayne State
1945	Catholic
1945	Connecticut
1946	Georgia
1946	Vermont
1947	Cal, Davis
1947	Hawaii
1948	Maine
1949	Oklahoma State
1949	Temple
1950	Amherst
1950	Auburn

1950	Brigham Young	1966	Houston
1950	Denver	1966	Idaho State
1950	Montana State	1966	Mississippi State
1950	Tennessee	1966	Southern Illinois
1951	Texas A & M	1967	Georgetown
1952	Boston	1967	Jefferson Medical
1952	Notre Dame	1967	Kent
1952	Oregon Medical & Dental	1967	Mississippi Medical
1953	Arkansas	1967	Mount Holyoke
1953	Colorado State	1967	Texas Christian
1953	Georgia Tech	1968	Baylor
1953	Rhode Island	1968	Dartmouth
1954	Brooklyn	1968	Manhattan College
1954	Missouri Mines	1968	Queens College
1954	New Hampshire	1968	Manitoba
1954	New Mexico	1969	Hunter
1954	Stevens Tech	1969	Indiana, Indianapolis Medical
1954	Texas, Medical	1969	Miami (FL)
1955	Florida State	1969	Northern Illinois
1955	Louisville	1969	SUNY, Downstate Medical
1955	Loyola, Chicago	1969	Akron
1956	Tennessee Medical	1969	Nevada
1957	Alabama Medical	1970	Cal, Santa Barbara
1957	Howard	1970	SUNY, Albany
1957	New Mexico State	1971	City of the CUNY
1957	South Dakota State	1971	Clarkson College of Tech.
1958	Fordham	1971	Michigan Tech.
1958	Rockefeller Institute	1972	Drexel
1958	South Carolina	1972	Miami (OH)
1958	U.S. Navy Postgraduate School	1972	Texas, Arlington
1959	Delaware	1972	Mississippi
1960	Marquette	1973	Cal, Northridge
1960	Texas Tech	1974	East Carolina
1961	Ohio	1974	Portland State
1961	South Dakota State	1974	Tuskegee Institute
1962	Chicago Medical	1975	Bowling Green
1963	Arkansas, Little Rock	1975	Georgia Medical
1963	Cal, Riverside	1975	Herbet H. Lehman
1963	Virginia Medical	1975	Oakland
1963	North Dakota State	1975	Texas, El Paso
1964	Montana	1975	Dayton
1965	Arizona State	1976	Loma Linda
1965	Colorado Mines	1976	New Jersey Tech.
1965	Hamilton	1976	Oklahoma Health Science Center
1965	Northeastern	1976	Southern Methodist
1965	South Dakota Mines	1976	Toledo
1965	Wake Forest	1977	Abbott Laboratories
1966	Boston College	1977	Guelph
1966	Clemson		

Part VII

The Recognition Societies

Service Fraternities and Societies

Alpha Phi Omega†

ACTIVE PIN

ALPHA PHI OMEGA, a National Service Fraternity, was founded at Lafayette College, December 16, 1925 by Frank Reed Horton and 13 other undergraduates. The purpose of the Fraternity is to assemble college and university students in the fellowship and principles of Leadership, Friendship, and Service. Chapter activities can include many service projects, especially in the four fields of service to chapter, school, community, and nation.

Over 300 types of service activities are conducted each year by the chapters. Typical sponsorships include blood mobiles, Special Olympics, major disease telethons, freshman orientations, escort services for co-eds, used book exchanges, monitor campus elections, working with youth and elderly, Boy Scout and Girl Scout activities.

There are three basic requirements for active membership. The student must want to exhibit the principles of Leadership, Friendship and Service, as exemplified in the Boy Scout Oath and Law. Second, exhibit a real desire to give service within the Fraternity. Third, the student should have a satisfactory scholastic standing. Advisory and honorary membership may be conferred upon educators, scouters, and other members of the community.

† This chapter narrative is repeated from the 19th edition; no current information was provided.

Membership in no way affects a membership in any other organization, either social, professional, or honorary. The members of Alpha Phi Omega are comprised of young men and women in colleges and universities within the United States in over 300 chapters.

Government The collegiate chapters constitute the supreme authority of the organization. Chapters register their views by vote of their official delegates at national conventions and by referendum vote between conventions. The governing body between conventions is the National Executive Board, composed of eight national officers selected at each national convention to serve two-year terms, all past national presidents, life members of the Board, as well as ten Regional Directors elected to serve two-year terms. National conventions are held biennially in even-numbered years. Sectional Conferences are held annually in most of the 50 sections of the fraternity.

Traditions and Insignia National Founders' Day is observed on December 16 each year.

The motto is *Be a leader, be a friend, be of service.*

The badge is formed by three equilateral triangles of blue superimposed on a shield of gold bearing a sun, surrounded by a circle of pearls. The Greek letters AΦΩ in gold are placed one on each triangle. Either the pin or key, plain or jeweled, may be worn by members. The recognition pin is of trefoil design, bearing the three Greek letters and a letter S in the center, standing for service. The pledge pin is similar with a letter P in the center.

The colors are blue and gold; the flower is the forget-me-not; the tree is the sturdy oak; the jewel is the diamond; and the bird is the Golden Eagle.

Publications The magazine is *The Torch and Trefoil*, published four times in each college year. Other publications include *Questions and Answers*, an information pamphlet; *The Pledge Manual*, and

Leadership Series for officers and advisors; and a monthly national newsletter.

Headquarters 14901 East 42nd Street, Independence, Missouri 64055.

Membership Active chapters 657. Total number of initiates 225,000. Chapter roll:

1902	Minnesota Alpha, Minnesota
1925	Alpha, Lafayette
1927	Beta, Pitt
1927	Delta, Auburn
1927	Epsilon, Northeast Missouri
1927	Gamma, Cornell
1928	Eta, Northern Illinois
1928	Zeta, Stanford
1929	Iota, Park College
1929	Kappa, Carnegie-Mellon
1929	Lambda, Kansas
1929	Mu, Indiana
1929	Nu, Upsala
1929	Theta, Virginia
1930	Omicron, Iowa
1930	Pi, Kansas State
1930	Rho, North Carolina
1930	Xi, Iowa State
1931	Chi, UCLA
1931	Omega, Drake
1931	Phi, Syracuse
1931	Psi, Cal, Santa Barbara
1931	Sigma, Northwestern
1931	Tau, Florida
1931	Upsilon, Wisconsin, Milwaukee
1932	Alpha Alpha, Illinois, Chicago, Medical
1932	Alpha Beta, Penn State
1932	Alpha Delta, San Diego State
1932	Alpha Epsion, L.S.U.
1932	Alpha Gamma, Purdue
1933	Alpha Zeta, Kentucky
1934	Alpha Eta, Missouri, Kansas City
1934	Alpha Iota, Ohio State
1934	Alpha Kappa, USC
1934	Alpha Lambda, North Dakota State
1934	Alpha Mu, William Jewell
1934	Alpha Theta, Nebraska, Omaha
1935	Alpha Nu, St. Norbert
1935	Alpha Omicron, Southern Methodist
1935	Alpha Pi, Miami (OH)
1935	Alpha Rho, Texas
1935	Alpha Sigma, Nebraska
1935	Alpha Xi, Washington State
1936	Alpha Chi, M.I.T.
1936	Alpha Omega, Kirksville Osteopathic
1936	Alpha Phi, Washington (WA)
1936	Alpha Psi, Lehigh
1936	Alpha Tau, Butler
1936	Alpha Upsilon, DePauw
1937	Beta Alpha, Wichita
1937	Beta Beta, Michigan State
1937	Beta Delta, East Texas
1937	Beta Gamma, Central YMCA
1938	Beta Epsilon, Northern Iowa
1938	Beta Eta, Missouri

1938	Beta Iota, N.Y.U.
1938	Beta Kappa, Central Missouri State
1938	Beta Lambda, Indiana State
1938	Beta Mu, Southwest Missouri
1938	Beta Nu, Northeastern (OK)
1938	Beta Theta, Wisconsin, Madison
1938	Beta Xi, Westminster (MO)
1938	Beta Zeta, Georgia
1939	Beta Chi, Oklahoma City
1939	Beta Omega, Oklahoma Baptist
1939	Beta Omicron, Missouri, Rolla
1939	Beta Phi, Southwestern Louisiana
1939	Beta Pi, Tulsa
1939	Beta Psi, Southeast Missouri
1939	Beta Rho, Arkansas
1939	Beta Sigma, Texas Tech
1939	Beta Upsilon, Northwest Missouri
1939	Gamma Alpha, Washington (WA)
1939	Gamma Beta, San Jose
1939	Gamma Delta, Baruch
1939	Gamma Epsilon, CUNY, Brooklyn
1939	Gamma Gamma, Cal, Berkeley
1939	Gamma Zeta, Georgia Tech
1940	Beta Tau, Washburn
1940	Gamma Eta, Springfield Tech
1940	Gamma Iota, CUNY, Brooklyn
1940	Gamma Lambda, Clemson
1940	Gamma Mu, Evansville
1940	Gamma Omicron, Queens (NY)
1940	Gamma Pi, Michigan
1940	Gamma Sigma Pet Grp, Chicago
1940	Gamma Xi, Rockhurst
1941	Gamma Chi, Samford
1941	Gamma Nu, Idaho
1941	Gamma Phi, Western Michigan
1941	Gamma Tau, Louisiana Tech
1941	Gamma Theta, Colorado
1941	Gamma Upsilon, Tulane
1942	Delta Alpha, Cincinnati
1942	Delta Beta, Oklahoma
1942	Delta Gamma, Ohio
1942	Gamma Omega, N.Y.U., University Heights
1942	Gamma Psi, Minnesota
1942	Gamma Rho, North Texas
1944	Delta Delta, St. Louis
1945	Delta Epsilon, Illinois Tech
1945	Delta Zeta, Penn
1946	Delta Eta, Oregon State
1946	Delta Iota, Mercer
1946	Delta Kappa, Emory
1946	Delta Lambda, Coe
1946	Delta Mu, Pittsburg State, Kansas
1946	Delta Nu, Yale
1946	Delta Theta, Louisville
1947	Delta Chi, Texas A & I
1947	Delta Omega, Houston
1947	Delta Omicron, Wabash
1947	Delta Phi, Johnson C. Smith
1947	Delta Pi, Trinity (TX)
1947	Delta Psi, Eastern Illinois
1947	Delta Rho, Rutgers
1947	Delta Sigma, Connecticut

1947	Delta Tau, New Mexico		1949	Eta Nu, St. John's (NY)
1947	Delta Upsilon, East Stroudsburg		1949	Eta Omega, Montana
1947	Delta Xi, Ball State		1949	Eta Omicron, Brigham Young
1947	Epsilon Alpha, Emporia		1949	Eta Phi, American
1947	Epsilon Beta, Central Michigan		1949	Eta Pi, Detroit
1947	Epsilon Delta, Central Connecticut		1949	Eta Psi, Cal State, Chico
1947	Epsilon Epsilon, Missouri Valley		1949	Eta Rho, Marquette
1947	Epsilon Eta, West Georgia		1949	Eta Sigma, Illinois Col
1947	Epsilon Gamma, Alfred		1949	Eta Tau, West Texas
1947	Epsilon Iota, Mississippi State		1949	Eta Theta, Idaho State
1947	Epsilon Kappa, Willamette		1949	Eta Upsilon, Marshall
1947	Epsilon Lambda, Michigan Tech		1949	Eta Xi, Central Washington
1947	Epsilon Mu, Maryland		1949	Eta Zeta, Montana State
1947	Epsilon Nu, SUNY Col., Oswego		1949	Theta Alpha, Stevens Tech
1947	Epsilon Theta, North Dakota		1949	Theta Beta, Cleveland
1947	Epsilon Xi, Colorado State		1949	Theta Delta, Waynesburg
1947	Epsilon Zeta, R.P.I.		1949	Theta Epsilon, Illinois State
1948	Epsilon Chi, Los Angeles City		1949	Theta Eta, Health Sciences
1948	Epsilon Omega, Mississippi		1949	Theta Gamma, Hendrix
1948	Epsilon Omicron, Long Island		1949	Theta Iota, Arizona
1948	Epsilon Phi, Youngstown State		1949	Theta Kappa, SUNY, Binghamton
1948	Epsilon Pi, Southern Illinois, Edwardsville		1949	Theta Lambda, Rice
1948	Epsilon Psi, Kent		1949	Theta Theta, Centre College
1948	Epsilon Rho, Eastern Washington		1949	Theta Zeta, New Hampshire
1948	Epsilon Sigma, SUNY, Buffalo		1950	Gamma Kappa, Texas Christian
1948	Epsilon Tau, Alabama		1950	Iota Alpha, Tennessee
1948	Epsilon Upsilon, Wisconsin, Oshkosh		1950	Iota Beta, Pacific Lutheran
1948	Eta Alpha, Santa Clara		1950	Iota Delta, Hiram
1948	Eta Beta, Simpson		1950	Iota Epsilon, Central State (OH)
1948	Eta Delta, Keene		1950	Iota Eta, American International
1948	Eta Gamma, Union College		1950	Iota Gamma, Towson
1948	Zeta Alpha, Bradley		1950	Iota Iota, Portland State
1948	Zeta Beta, V.P.I.		1950	Iota Kappa, Bucknell
1948	Zeta Chi, Centenary		1950	Iota Lambda, North Carolina State
1948	Zeta Delta, Miami (OH)		1950	Iota Theta, Rutgers, Newark
1948	Zeta Epsilon, Gustavus Adolphus		1950	Iota Zeta, LeMoyne-Owen
1948	Zeta Eta, Tennessee		1950	Theta Chi, George Washington
1948	Zeta Gamma, Valparaiso		1950	Theta Mu, Vanderbilt
1948	Zeta Iota, Temple		1950	Theta Nu, Hamline
1948	Zeta Kappa, Bowling Green		1950	Theta Omega, Randolph, Macon
1948	Zeta Lambda, Toledo		1950	Theta Omicron, Georgia Southwestern
1948	Zeta Mu, Catholic		1950	Theta Phi, Millsaps
1948	Zeta Nu, Southern Illinois		1950	Theta Pi, Indianapolis
1948	Zeta Omega, Baylor		1950	Theta Psi, Bridgeport
1948	Zeta Omicron, Cal Poly, Pomona		1950	Theta Rho, Sam Houston
1948	Zeta Phi, Howard		1950	Theta Sigma, Oklahoma State
1948	Zeta Pi, Wayne State (MI)		1950	Theta Tau, Texas, Arlington
1948	Zeta Psi, Oregon		1950	Theta Upsilon, Case Western Reserve
1948	Zeta Rho, Wittenberg		1950	Theta Xi, Parks (IL)
1948	Zeta Sigma, Delaware		1951	Iota Chi, Northern Michigan
1948	Zeta Tau, Central Methodist		1951	Iota Mu, South Carolina
1948	Zeta Theta, Drexel		1951	Iota Nu, Wisconsin, Milwaukee
1948	Zeta Upsilon, Boston U		1951	Iota Omega, SUNY Col., Brockport
1948	Zeta Xi, Southern Oregon		1951	Iota Omicron, Gettysburg
1948	Zeta Zeta, Graceland		1951	Iota Phi, Cal, Davis
1949	Eta Chi, Hardin-Simmons		1951	Iota Pi, City College of San Francisco
1949	Eta Epsilon, Millikin		1951	Iota Psi, Utah
1949	Eta Eta, Arizona State		1951	Iota Rho, Florida State
1949	Eta Iota, Millersville		1951	Iota Sigma, Midwestern
1949	Eta Kappa, Wisconsin, Stout		1951	Iota Tau, St. Olaf
1949	Eta Lambda, Wisconsin, Eau Claire		1951	Iota Upsilon, Slippery Rock
1949	Eta Mu, Utica		1951	Iota Xi, Edinboro

1951 Kappa Alpha, Lamar	1958 Mu Omicron, Clarkson
1951 Kappa Beta, Polytech	1958 Mu Pi, Colorado School of Mines
1952 Kappa Delta, Florida A & M	1958 Mu Xi, High Point
1952 Kappa Epsilon, Wagner	1959 Mu Chi, Indiana (PA)
1952 Kappa Eta, Southern Mississippi	1959 Mu Phi, Fort Hays
1952 Kappa Gamma, Wisconsin, La Crosse	1959 Mu Rho, Upper Iowa
1952 Kappa Iota, Hanover	1959 Mu Sigma, South Dakota State
1952 Kappa Kappa, Western New Mexico	1959 Mu Tau, West Virginia Tech
1952 Kappa Lambda, Southern	1959 Mu Upsilon, Washington and Jefferson
1952 Kappa Mu, Johns Hopkins	1960 Mu Omega, Tampa
1952 Kappa Nu, Grinnell	1960 Mu Psi, Niagara
1952 Kappa Omicron, Massachusetts	1960 Nu Alpha, Quinnipiac
1952 Kappa Pi, Wiley	1960 Nu Beta, Hope
1952 Kappa Rho, Seattle	1960 Nu Delta, Lebanon Valley
1952 Kappa Sigma, Cal State, Sacramento	1960 Nu Epsion, Georgia Southern
1952 Kappa Theta, Wake Forest	1960 Nu Gamma, Southwest Texas
1952 Kappa Xi, Xavier (LA)	1960 Nu Zeta, Abilene Christian
1952 Kappa Zeta, Southeastern Oklahoma	1961 Nu Eta, Cal Medicine, Irvine
1953 Kappa Chi, Creighton	1961 Nu Iota, Bethune-Cookman
1953 Kappa Omega, Cooper Union	1961 Nu Kappa, Campbell
1953 Kappa Phi, St. Lawrence	1961 Nu Lambda, Moravian
1953 Kappa Psi, North Carolina A & T	1961 Nu Mu, Minnesota, Duluth
1953 Kappa Tau, Citadel	1961 Nu Nu, Eastern New Mexico
1953 Kappa Upsilon, East Carolina	1961 Nu Omicron, Troy
1953 Lambda Alpha, East Tennessee	1961 Nu Pi, Mankato
1953 Lambda Beta, Houghton	1961 Nu Rho, William and Mary
1953 Lambda Delta, New Jersey Tech	1961 Nu Sigma, Stephen F. Austin
1953 Lambda Epsion, St. Cloud	1961 Nu Theta, Glassboro
1953 Lambda Gamma, Manhattan	1961 Nu Xi, Birmingham-Southern
1954 Lambda Eta, Lehman	1962 Nu Chi, Davidson
1954 Lambda Iota, New Mexico State	1962 Nu Omega, Alaska
1954 Lambda Kappa, Loras	1962 Nu Phi, Chadron
1954 Lambda Lambda, Shippensburg	1962 Nu Psi, Montclair
1954 Lambda Mu, Cal State, Los Angeles	1962 Nu Tau, Cal State, Northridge
1954 Lambda Theta, Columbia (NY)	1962 Nu Upsilon, Princeton
1954 Lambda Zeta, Ripon	1962 Xi Alpha, Muhlenberg
1955 Lambda Nu, Duke	1962 Xi Beta, Kearney
1955 Lambda Omicron, West Virginia	1962 Xi Delta, Texas A & M
1955 Lambda Pi, LaSalle	1962 Xi Epsilon, Wyoming
1955 Lambda Rho, Augustana (IL)	1962 Xi Gamma, Adams
1955 Lambda Xi, Pan American	1963 Xi Eta, Brown
1956 Lambda Chi, Memphis State	1963 Xi Iota, Susquehanna
1956 Lambda Omega, California (PA)	1963 Xi Kappa, Fairleigh Dickinson, Madison
1956 Lambda Phi, Eastern Michigan	1963 Xi Lambda, Bloomsburg
1956 Lambda Psi, Northern Colorado	1963 Xi Mu, Lock Haven
1956 Lambda Sigma Society, Wisconsin, Stevens Point	1963 Xi Nu, Texas Wesleyan
	1963 Xi Omicron, Tarleton
1956 Lambda Tau, Salem-Teikyo	1963 Xi Pi, Lycoming
1956 Lambda Upsilon, Ursinus	1963 Xi Rho, SUNY Col., Oneonta
1956 Mu Alpha, Georgetown U.	1963 Xi Sigma, Carson-Newman
1956 Mu Beta, Colgate	1963 Xi Theta, Ferris
1956 Mu Delta, Great Falls	1963 Xi Xi, Fordham
1956 Mu Gamma, Morgan State	1963 Xi Zeta, Rochester Tech
1956 Mu Zeta, San Francisco State	1964 Omicron Alpha, Kutztown
1957 Mu Epsilon, Hawaii	1964 Omicron Beta, Marietta
1957 Mu Eta, Albright	1964 Omicron Delta, MacMurray
1957 Mu Iota, Lynchburg	1964 Omicron Epsilon, Union (NY)
1957 Mu Kappa, Pratt	1964 Omicron Eta, Suffolk
1957 Mu Theta, Luther College	1964 Omicron Gamma, West Virginia State
1958 Mu Lambda, Rochester	1964 Omicron Iota, Worcester Tech
1958 Mu Mu, Oglethorpe	1964 Omicron Theta, Monmouth (NJ)
1958 Mu Nu, Western Illinois	1964 Omicron Zeta, Cal State, Hayward

1964 Xi Chi, Greensboro	1967 Rho Pi, Cal, San Diego
1964 Xi Omega, Murray State	1967 Rho Psi, Chabot
1964 Xi Phi, New Haven	1967 Rho Rho, Cal, Irvine
1964 Xi Psi, Western Kentucky	1967 Rho Sigma, Point Park
1964 Xi Tau, Tidewater	1967 Rho Tau, Imperial Valley
1964 Xi Upsilon, Mount Union	1967 Rho Upsilon, Cumberland (KY)
1965 Omicro Upsilon, West Chester	1967 Rho Xi, Penn Valley
1965 Omicron Chi, Walker	1967 Sigma Alpha, Missouri, St. Louis
1965 Omicron Kappa, Los Angeles Harbor	1967 Sigma Beta, Redlands
1965 Omicron Lambda, Calumet	1967 Sigma Chi, Miami-Dade Community College
1965 Omicron Mu, Carthage	1967 Sigma Delta, Oakland
1965 Omicron Nu, Puerto Rico, San Juan	1967 Sigma Epsilon, El Centro
1965 Omicron Omega, East Texas Baptist	1967 Sigma Eta, Villanova
1965 Omicron Omicron, Pfeiffer	1967 Sigma Gamma, San Antonio
1965 Omicron Phi, Richmond	1967 Sigma Iota, Valdosta
1965 Omicron Pi, Fairleigh Dickinson, Teaneck	1967 Sigma Kappa, Eastern
1965 Omicron Psi, Fitchburg	1967 Sigma Lambda, Marritt
1965 Omicron Rho, North Carolina Wesleyan	1967 Sigma Mu, Virginia Union
1965 Omicron Sigma, St. Peter's	1967 Sigma Nu, Delaware Valley
1965 Omicron Tau, Alma	1967 Sigma Omega, Lincoln (PA)
1965 Omicron Xi, Denison	1967 Sigma Omicron, Howard Payne
1965 Pi Alpha, Philander Smith	1967 Sigma Phi, Notre Dame
1965 Pi Beta, Dubuque	1967 Sigma Pi, Prairie View
1965 Pi Delta, Western Carolina	1967 Sigma Psi, Tusculum
1965 Pi Epsilon, Alabama A & M	1967 Sigma Rho, Elon
1965 Pi Gamma, Baldwin-Wallace	1967 Sigma Sigma, Illinois, Chicago
1965 Pi Zeta, Tuskegee	1967 Sigma Tau, Chapman
1966 Pi Chi, Duquesne	1967 Sigma Theta, St. Mary's (MN)
1966 Pi Eta, Loyola, Chicago	1967 Sigma Upsilon, North Carolina, Charlotte
1966 Pi Iota, Wofford	1967 Sigma Xi, Maine
1966 Pi Kappa, Pace	1967 Sigma Zeta, Mars Hill
1966 Pi Lambda, Wisconsin, Green Bay	1967 Tau Alpha, Davis and Elkins
1966 Pi Mu, Mobile	1967 Tau Beta, Appalachian
1966 Pi Nu, Guilford	1967 Tau Delta, North Carolina Central
1966 Pi Omega, Kentucky State	1967 Tau Epsilon, Tennessee Tech
1966 Pi Omicron, Emory and Henry	1967 Tau Gamma, Southern
1966 Pi Phi, Union	1968 Tau Eta, SUNY Col. Ag & Tech, Cobleskill
1966 Pi Pi, College of the Ozarks	1968 Tau Iota, Louisiana Col.
1966 Pi Psi, Winona	1968 Tau Kappa, Lansing Community College
1966 Pi Rho, Rider	1968 Tau Lambda, Rose-Hulman
1966 Pi Sigma, San Mateo	1968 Tau Mu, South Florida
1966 Pi Tau, St. Peter's (eves)	1968 Tau Nu, Humboldt
1966 Pi Theta, Otero Junior	1968 Tau Omega, Ocean County
1966 Pi Upsilon, Drew	1968 Tau Omicron, IUPUI
1966 Pi Xi, Lincoln Memorial (TN)	1968 Tau Pi, Delaware State College
1966 Rho Alpha, Paul Smiths	1968 Tau Psi, Middlesex
1966 Rho Beta, Armstrong	1968 Tau Rho, Del Mar
1966 Rho Delta, Rhode Island	1968 Tau Sigma, Brandywine
1966 Rho Epsion, Savannah	1968 Tau Tau, Wilmington
1966 Rho Eta, Grayson County Junior College	1968 Tau Theta, Wayland Baptist
1966 Rho Gamma, Cal State, Long Beach	1968 Tau Upsilon, Wisconsin, Platteville
1966 Rho Iota, Augusta	1968 Tau Xi, Westminster (PA)
1966 Rho Kappa, Milligan	1968 Tau Zeta, Texas Southern
1966 Rho Lambda, St. Edward's	1968 Upsilon Alpha, Austin Peay
1966 Rho Theta, Capital	1969 Phi Alpha, Morton
1966 Rho Zeta, Hiwassee	1969 Phi Beta, Spartanburg Methodist
1967 Rho Chi, Gannon	1969 Phi Delta, Cal Poly, Pomona
1967 Rho Mu, Belmont Abbey	1969 Phi Epsion, Maine Maritime Academy
1967 Rho Nu, Sierra	1969 Phi Eta, Ohio State, Newark
1967 Rho Omega, San Bernardino Valley Col.	1969 Phi Gamma, Texas Lutheran
1967 Rho Omicron, Maryland, Eastern Shore	1969 Phi Iota, Dallas Baptist
1967 Rho Phi, Dominican	1969 Phi Kappa, North Carolina, Greensboro

1969	Phi Lambda, North Virginia Comm. Coll.	1971	Chi Upsilon, Dillard
1969	Phi Theta, Arkansas Tech	1971	Chi Xi, Central Texas
1969	Phi Zeta, Fort Valley	1972	Chi Omega, McKendree
1969	Tau Chi, Winston-Salem	1972	Psi Alpha, Berry (GA)
1969	Tau Phi, Wingate	1972	Psi Beta, Illinois Central
1969	Upsilon Beta, St. Francis (PA)	1972	Psi Delta, Maine, Machias
1969	Upsilon Chi, Clark Col., Atlanta	1972	Psi Epsilon, Delgado (LA)
1969	Upsilon Delta, Kean (NJ)	1972	Psi Eta, Inter-American
1969	Upsilon Epsilon, Central Oregon Comm. Col.	1972	Psi Gamma, Wentworth Military
1969	Upsilon Eta, Texas, El Paso	1972	Psi Iota, Blinn
1969	Upsilon Gamma, Lake Michigan	1972	Psi Theta, Moorhead
1969	Upsilon Iota, DePaul	1972	Psi Zeta, Bishop
1969	Upsilon Kappa, St. Augustine's	1973	Psi Kappa, Chattanooga State Tech
1969	Upsilon Lambda, Sterling	1973	Psi Lambda, Rust
1969	Upsilon Mu, Puerto Rico, Mayaguez	1973	Psi Mu, Mary Hardin-Baylor
1969	Upsilon Nu, North Carolina, Wilmington	1973	Psi Nu, Benedict
1969	Upsilon Omega, Tarrant County Junoir Col	1973	Psi Xi, Alabama State
1969	Upsilon Omicron, Alabama, Birmingham	1974	Omega Rho, Inter-American
1969	Upsilon Phi, IUPU, Fort Wayne	1974	Psi Omicron, Morehouse
1969	Upsilon Pi, Cameron	1974	Psi Pi, Penn State, Hazleton
1969	Upsilon Psi, Nevada	1974	Psi Rho, North Florida
1969	Upsilon Rho, Baptist, Charleston	1974	Psi Sigma, Albany State
1969	Upsilon Sigma, Western State (CO)	1974	Psi Tau, Virginia State, Norfolk
1969	Upsilon Tau, Shenandoah Conservatory	1974	Psi Upsilon, Southwestern State (OK)
1969	Upsilon Theta, Cal State, Sono	1975	Omega Alpha, Tarkio
1969	Upsilon Xi, Arapahoe Comm. Coll.	1975	Psi Chi, South Alabama
1969	Upsilon Zeta, Boston Col	1975	Psi Omega, Central Florida
1969	Upsion Upsilon, St. Thomas	1975	Psi Phi, Tennessee State
1970	Chi Alpha, Mohawk Valley Comm. Coll.	1975	Psi Psi, Arkansas, Pine Bluff
1970	Chi Beta, Gloucester County Coll.	1976	Omega Beta, Augsburg
1970	Chi Delta, Pepperdine	1976	Omega Delta, Fairfield
1970	Chi Epsilon, Richard Bland	1976	Omega Epsion, Illinois Wesleyan
1970	Chi Gamma, James Madison	1976	Omega Eta, Loyola, Chicago
1970	Chi Zeta, Tennessee, Martin	1976	Omega Gamma, Angelo
1970	Phi Chi, Missouri Western	1976	Omega Theta, Lon Morris
1970	Phi Mu, Norfolk	1976	Omega Zeta, Durham
1970	Phi Nu, Midland Lutheran	1977	Omega Iota, Marion
1970	Phi Omega, Herkimer County Comm. Coll.	1977	Omega Kappa, Coastal Carolina
1970	Phi Omicron, Ferrum	1977	Omega Lambda, Fisk
1970	Phi Phi, Florida Memorial	1977	Omega Mu, Clarion
1970	Phi Pi, Langston	1977	Omega Nu, New Hampshire Col
1970	Phi Psi, Lehigh County Comm. Coll.	1977	Omega Omicron, Concordia
1970	Phi Rho, Westminster Choir	1977	Omega Xi, Cornell Col. (IA)
1970	Phi Sigma, Catholic, Puerto Rico	1978	Omega Phi, Tougaloo
1970	Phi Tau, Fayetteville	1978	Omega Pi, Arkansas State
1970	Phi Upsilon, Amarillo	1978	Omega Sigma, California State (PA)
1970	Phi Xi, Austin	1978	Omega Tau, Beloit
1971	Chi Chi, Central Arkansas	1978	Omega Upsilon, Florida International
1971	Chi Eta, Tarrant County Junior Coll.	1979	Alpha Alpha Alpha, Maryville (TN)
1971	Chi Iota, Bemidji	1979	Alpha Alpha Beta, Long Island
1971	Chi Kappa, North Carolina, Asheville	1979	Omega Chi, Jacksonville (AL)
1971	Chi Lambda, Elizabeth City	1979	Omega Omega, Gallaudet
1971	Chi Mu, Henry Ford Comm. Coll.	1979	Omega Psi, Jackson (MS)
1971	Chi Nu, Grambling	1980	Alpha Alpha Delta, Salisbury
1971	Chi Omicron, Connors State	1980	Alpha Alpha Epsilon, Charleston (SC)
1971	Chi Phi, Oakland	1980	Alpha Alpha Eta, MacMurray
1971	Chi Pi, SUNY Col., Fredonia	1980	Alpha Alpha Gamma, Weber
1971	Chi Psi, Kean (NJ)	1980	Alpha Alpha Iota, Barber-Scotia
1971	Chi Rho, Kemper Military	1980	Alpha Alpha Kappa, Snow College
1971	Chi Sigma, Allegheny	1980	Alpha Alpha Lambda, Alcorn
1971	Chi Tau, Lee	1980	Alpha Alpha Rho, Incarnate Word
1971	Chi Theta, Columbus	1980	Alpha Alpha Theta, St. Ambrose

1980	Alpha Alpha Zeta, St. Mary's (NE)
1981	Alpha Alpha Mu, Scranton
1981	Alpha Alpha Nu, Palm Beach Junior College
1981	Alpha Alpha Omicron, Longwood
1981	Alpha Alpha Pi, Westminster (PA)
1981	Alpha Alpha Sigma, Northeast Louisiana
1981	Alpha Alpha Tau, Tallahassee Comm. Coll.
1981	Alpha Alpha Upsilon, Mount Mary's (CA)
1981	Alpha Alpha Xi, Pacific (CA)
1982	Alpha Alpha Chi, Fairmont
1982	Alpha Alpha Phi, Columbia (NY)
1982	Alpha Alpha Psi, Eastfield
1983	Alpha Alpha Omega, Middle Tennessee
1983	Alpha Beta Alpha, Indiana Southeast
1983	Alpha Beta Beta, St. Bonaventure
1984	Alpha Beta Delta, Widener
1984	Alpha Beta Epsilon, Arkansas, Monticello
1984	Alpha Beta Eta, College of the Southwest
1984	Alpha Beta Gamma, Knox
1984	Alpha Beta Zeta, Radford
1985	Alpha Beta Iota, St. Joseph's (IN)
1985	Alpha Beta Lambda, Wright State
1985	Alpha Beta Theta, Morris
1986	Alpha Beta Kappa, New Orleans
1986	Alpha Beta Mu, Grove City
1986	Alpha Beta Nu, Penn State, Behrend
1986	Alpha Beta Omicron, Elmhurst
1986	Alpha Beta Xi, SUNY Col., Geneseo
1987	Alpha Beta Chi, SUNY Col., Plattsburgh
1987	Alpha Beta Phi, Concordia Lutheran
1987	Alpha Beta Pi, Lenoir-Rhyne
1987	Alpha Beta Rho, Pitt, Bradford
1987	Alpha Beta Sigma, Robert Morris
1987	Alpha Beta Tau, Washington and Lee
1987	Alpha Beta Upsion, Broward Comm. Col.
1988	Alpha Beta Omega, Old Dominion
1988	Alpha Beta Psi, Roanoke
1989	Alpha Gamma Alpha, Dickinson
1989	Alpha Gamma Beta, Clark
1989	Alpha Gamma Gamma, Hunter
1990	Alpha Gamma Delta, SUNY Col., New Paltz
1990	Alpha Gamma Epsilon, DeVry Tech
1990	Alpha Gamma Eta, Vermont
1990	Alpha Gamma Theta, Columbus State Comm. Col.
1990	Alpha Gamma Zeta, Houston Baptist

Gamma Sigma Sigma†

GAMMA SIGMA SIGMA was founded in 1953 following a meeting during the preceding fall at the Beekman Towers in New York of a group of young women from Drexel Institute of Technology, Boston University, Brooklyn College, Los Angeles City College, New York University, Queens College, University of Houston, and Miami University. The name Gamma Sigma Sigma was chosen because of the common usage of GSS standing for girls' service so-

rority. Although each organIzatIon represented at the meeting varied in its history, organization, and activities, all were based and operated on the same principle—service.

The purpose of the sorority is to assemble college and university women in the spirit of service to humanity. The sorority serves to develop friendship among women of all races and creeds, through working side by side by side through the fulfillment of these goals common to all. It is the policy of the sorority to include both social sorority members and nonmembers.

Government The supreme authority of Gamma Sigma Sigma is vested in the national convention which meets in June of odd-numbered years. The governing body between conventions is the National Executive Board. This consists of the seven national officers elected at convention, plus the parliamentarian who is appointed.

Traditions and Insignia The traditional goal of the sorority is expressed by the motto, *Unity in Service*. Members of chapters aid at registration of new students, conduct student elections, usher at assemblies and special functions, work on campus chest drives, and participate in every type of useful campus project. The badge is the chevron superimposed on a triangle. In one corner of the triangle is engraved the Greek letter O, symbolizing equality, another the rose of friendship, and in the third the staff of service. The pledge pin is a maroon and white triangle.

Publications The *Gamma Gossip* is published and distributed to each member three times during the academic year. A *Pledge Handbook* is kept up to date while a *Questions and Answers* booklet is designed for prospective chapters.

Headquarters 403 Sheffield Road, Apt. 212, Waukesha. Wisconsin 53186.

Membership Active chapters 128. Inactive chapters 5. Total number of initiates 12,500. Chapter roll:††

1953	Alpha, Houston (1958-1966)
1953	Beta, Brooklyn
1953	Delta, N.Y.U.
1953	Epsilon, Boston U.
1953	*Gamma, Los Angeles City College*
1953	*Iota, Detroit*
1953	Theta, Queens (NY)
1953	Zeta, Drexel
1955	*Kappa, California*
1955	Lambda, Hunter (Bronx)
1956	Mu, Upsala
1956	Nu, Connecticut
1957	Omicron, Minnesota
1957	Pi, CCNY
1957	Rho, Hunter (Manhattan)
1957	*Sigma, Valparaiso*
1957	Tau, Penn State

† This chapter narrative is repeated from the 19th edition; no current information was provided.

†† This chapter roll is repeated from the 19th edition; no current information was provided.

1957	Xi, Maryland
1958	Chi, Georgia
1958	*Phi, City College of San Francisco*
1958	Upsilon, Miami (FL)
1959	Omega, Wisconsin, Eau Claire
1959	Psi, Great Falls
1960	Alpha Alpha, Wisconsin, Oshkosh
1961	Alpha Beta, St. Cloud
1961	Alpha Gamma, Northwest Missouri
1963	Alpha Delta, Southern
1963	Alpha Epsilon, Southern Illinois
1963	Alpha Eta, Howard
1963	Alpha Iota, Minnesota
1963	Alpha Kappa, Florida State
1963	Alpha Lambda, Mankato
1963	Alpha Theta, Massachusetts
1963	Alpha Zeta, Youngstown State
1964	Alpha Mu, Northern Michigan
1964	Alpha Nu, Central Connecticut
1964	Alpha Xi, Morgan State
1965	Alpha Omicron, Carthage
1965	Alpha Pi, Wisconsin, Stout
1965	Alpha Rho, American
1965	Alpha Sigma, Northeastern (OK)
1965	Alpha Tau, Xavier (LA)
1966	Alpha Chi, Wisconsin, Madison
1966	Alpha Omega, Cal Poly
1966	Alpha Phi, Westfield
1966	Alpha Psi, Southeast Missouri
1966	Alpha Upsilon, Marietta
1967	Beta Alpha, Campbell
1967	Beta Beta, Albright
1967	Beta Delta, Wisconsin, La Crosse
1967	Beta Epsilon, Edinboro
1967	Beta Eta, Suffolk
1967	Beta Gamma, Delaware
1967	Beta Iota, Tarleton
1967	Beta Theta, Texas Wesleyan
1967	Beta Zeta, Tuskegee
1968	Beta Kappa, Wisconsin, Green Bay
1968	Beta Lambda, North Carolina A & T
1968	Beta Mu, Bucks County Community
1968	Beta Nu, Oklahoma
1968	Beta Omicron, Missouri Valley
1968	Beta Pi, Rider
1968	Beta Rho, Lincoln Memorial (TN)
1968	Beta Sigma, Western Kentucky
1968	Beta Xi, SUNY Col., Oneonta
1969	Beta Chi, Lebanon Valley
1969	Beta Phi, Lynchburg
1969	Beta Psi, Indiana (PA)
1969	Beta Tau, St. Peter's
1969	Beta Upsilon, New Mexico
1969	Gamma Alpha, Florida A & M
1969	Gamma Beta, Wisconsin, Milwaukee
1969	Gamma Delta, Duquesne
1969	Gamma Eta, Utica
1969	Gamma Gamma, Wiley
1970	Gamma Iota, Savannah
1970	Gamma Kappa, Tennessee
1970	Gamma Lambda, Puerto Rico, Rio Piedras
1970	Gamma Mu, Maryland State
1970	Gamma Nu, Alabama A & M
1970	Gamma Omicron, Ball State
1970	Gamma Pi, Carson-Newman
1970	Gamma Rho, Pitt
1970	Gamma Theta, Stephen F. Austin
1970	Gamma Xi, Alabama, Huntsville
1971	Delta Alpha, Appalachian
1971	Delta Beta, West Texas
1971	Gamma Chi, Southwest Texas
1971	Gamma Omega, Cameron
1971	Gamma Phi, St. Francis
1971	Gamma Psi, Cal State, Chico
1971	Gamma Sigma, Alma
1971	Gamma Tau, Winston-Salem
1971	Gamma Upsilon, North Carolina Central
1972	Delta Delta, SUNY Col., Brockport
1972	Delta Epsilon, East Texas
1972	Delta Eta, Texas, El Paso
1972	Delta Gamma, Arkansas
1972	Delta Iota, North Virginia Community
1972	Delta Kappa, North Carolina
1972	Delta Lambda, Ocean County (NJ)
1972	Delta Mu, Central Michigan
1972	Delta Nu, Maine
1972	Delta Theta, Fort Valley
1972	Delta Xi, Southwest Missouri
1972	Delta Zeta, Auburn
1973	Delta Omicron, Louisville
1973	Delta Pi, Monmouth (NJ)
1973	Delta Rho, Fayetteville
1973	Delta Sigma, Samford
1973	Delta Tau, East Tennessee
1973	Delta Upsilon, SUNY Col., Potsdam
1974	Delta Chi, East Carolina
1974	Delta Omega, LaSalle
1974	Delta Phi, Dillard
1974	Delta Psi, Texas, Arlington
1974	Epsilon Alpha, St. Augustine's
1974	Epsilon Beta, Clemson
1974	Epsilon Gamma, McKendree (IL)
1975	Epsilon Delta, Delgado (LA)
1975	Epsilon Epsilon, Tennessee, Martin
1975	Epsilon Eta, Florida Memorial
1975	Epsilon Iota, Bishop
1975	Epsilon Kappa, Kentucky State
1975	Epsilon Lambda, Alabama State
1975	Epsilon Mu, Chattanooga State Tech
1975	Epsilon Theta, Durham
1975	Epsilon Zeta, North Carolina, Greensboro
1976	Epsilon Nu, Bethune-Cookman
1976	Epsilon Omicron, ASC (GA)
1976	Epsilon Xi, Moravian
1977	Epsilon Pi, Central Missouri State
1977	Epsilon Rho, Dubuque

COAT OF ARMS

Intercollegiate Knights†

IN 1919, a group of University of Washington students organized a society dedicated to the highest ideals of manhood and collegiate loyalty. The name of the society, Knights of the Hook, alluded to the ideals of service, sacrifice, and loyalty, as exemplified in the legends of King Arthur and his knights.

On March 13, 1922, the university administration granted the Knights permission to form a national organization which would include all the universities and colleges of the northwest and Pacific Coast. After two years extension would continue to eastern schools.

Growth On April 12, 1922, the Intercollegiate Knights was incorporated under the laws of the state of Washington. Lester Foran, first Royal King of the Order, chartered chapters at the University of Idaho, Washington State College (later W.S.U.), the University of Oregon, Montana State College, and Montana State University. The first convention was held in April, 1924, on the campus of Washington State. Thirteen delegates were present from the charter chapters and Oregon State Agricultural College. The constitution and ritual were adopted and plans formulated for administration and expansion.

Government The government of the fraternity is that of a corporation with all members of the fraternity having the right to vote every year through their local chapter for a chapter delegate, who is a member of the General Assembly of the fraternity. The General Assembly is the supreme authority of the fraternity and has all legislative power. The assembly elects an Executive Council composed of five student officers, and two faculty members and four regional directors. This body is the executive and judicial branch of the corporation. One of the faculty members is the national advisor and the other is the national executive secretary, who supervises the activities and administers policy. The student officers supervise such areas as publications, finances, ritual, etc. The royal king, national president, is the executive head of the fraternity.

Traditions and Insignia Founder's Day is observed on April 12. The motto is: "Service, Sacrifice, and Loyalty." The Intercollegiate Knights have a tradition of service to alma mater. This objective is stressed through the rendition of outstanding student leadership in scholarship and collegiate extracurricular activities.

The badge of the fraternity is a shield with two charges separated by a band crossing from upper right to left, with the letters I and K in the charges and a mounted knight ready to do battle in the center of the Shield. A golden cup encircled by a halo on the top of the Shield, a horse under the cup and at the bottom of the shield a banner with the motto. In the background of the shield a battle ax and a broad-sword. The colors are red, blue, white, black, and gold.

The national colors are red and blue. The national flag has a blue color background with coat of arms in center and the year of foundation at the bottom.

The pledge pin is a plain divided shield enameled red and blue, with gold letters I and K.

Publications The Magazine is *The Shield,* published four times in each college year. Other publications include *Guide Book for Chapter Officers, Page Manual,* and *I. K. Newsletter.*

Headquarters P.O. Box 11045, Salt Lake City, Utah 84147.

Membership Active chapters 37. Total number of initiates 35,000. Chapter roll:††

1922	Idaho
1922	Washington State
1924	Utah State
1932	Idaho State
1932	Lewis-Clark (ID)
1935	Central Washington
1935	College of Idaho
1937	Eastern Washington
1937	Utah
1939	Linfield
1940	Boise
1940	Seattle
1941	Brigham Young
1946	Puget Sound
1947	Pacific
1949	Humboldt
1949	Southern Utah
1951	Denver
1951	Eastern Oregon
1951	Westminster
1953	Colorado State
1953	Olympic
1959	Eastern Montana
1959	Eastern Utah
1959	Pan American
1959	Snow
1960	Nevada Southern
1960	Oregon College
1960	Portland State
1961	Oklahoma State
1961	Ventura
1962	Church (HI)
1964	Missouri, Rolla
1964	Pacific Lutheran
1964	Yakima
1975	Texas

---

† This chapter narrative is repeated from the 19th edition; no current information was provided.

†† This chapter roll is repeated from the 19th edition; no current information was provided.

The National Spurs†

ACTIVE PIN

THE NATIONAL SPURS, sophomore women's service recognition society, was founded on the campus of Montana State College in 1922. Sponsored by the local Mortar Board chapter, the group was established to meet the need for student service to the college.

Spurs strive toward their goal to serve wherever needed. Their purpose is to promote school spirit, to support all activities in which the student body participates, to foster among the women of the college or university a spirit of loyalty and helpfulness, and to uphold the traditions of the college.

Members are selected on the basis of interest and participation in college activities, dependability, sense of honor, sense of democracy, unselfishness, and scholarship rating equal to at least accumulative C plus average.

Government The officers are college students, with the exception of the executive secretary-treasurer, who is a Spur alumna member. In addition to her duties as secretary-treasurer she acts as an adviser to the group.

Spurs officers are chosen every two years at the national convention by the outgoing executive council and a special committee of convention delegates. They serve as national officers during their junior and senior college years. The executive council consists of the national president, two national vice-presidents, national editor, eleven regional directors, and the executive secretary-treasurer.

Traditions and Insignia The motto is *At Your Service.* Members traditionally help with freshman orientation. Service projects on the campus and in the community include ushering at plays, concerts, and ball games, helping at election booths, participating in the conduct of Homecoming, tutoring, and providing entertainment for old and young in nursing homes and institutions for handicapped.

Founders' Day is observed February 14. The emblem is a small gold spur to which a chain is attached.

Publication *The Spur,* a newsletter, is published quarterly. The National Spurs Kit is the official workbook and guide for all chapters.

Headquarters 921 East Maple, Post Falls, Idaho 83854.

Membership About 1,300 new members are tapped each year. About 1,300 new members are tapped each year. Active chapters 40. Chapter roll:††

Adams
Arizona
Brigham Young
Butler
Cal State, Chico
California Lutheran
Carroll
Colorado State
Colorado Women's College
Denver
Eastern New Mexico
Fort Hays
Idaho State
Idaho
Jamestown
Emporia
Kansas State
Kearney
Linfield (ID)
Montana Mines
Montana State
Montana, Eastern
Montana
Moorhead
Nevada
New Mexico Highlands
New Mexico State
New Mexico
Northern Arizona
Northern Colorado
Northern Montana
Pacific Lutheran
Puget Sound
Redlands
Texas Western
Texas, El Paso
Utah State
Washington State
Western Montana
Whitman
Wichita
Wyoming

† This chapter narrative is repeated from the 19th edition; no current information was provided.

†† This chapter roll is repeated from the 19th edition; no current information was provided.

Recognition Societies

Alpha Phi Sigma[†]

(SCHOLARSHIP)

ALPHA PHI SIGMA was founded on the campus of the Northeast Missouri State University in February, 1930, primarily through the efforts of the late Byron D. Cosby. It is a national scholastic honor society conferring membership on outstanding students in all fields. Any fully accredited four year institution is eligible for the installation of a chapter.

Government Governing power is vested in national conventions which meet every two years. A president, vice president, and historian are elected at each convention. A National Advisory Council composed of elected officers and past national presidents can be called into session by the president.

Publication *The Key* is published as occasion requires.

Traditions and Insignia The motto is Joy, Vision, and Service. The purpose of the society is to recognize scholarship and to encourage a further love of learning. 'The official key bears the lamp of learning and three emeralds on a gold background. The colors of the society are green and gold. The official flower is the yellow rose.

Headquarters Department of Social Science, Mayville State College, Mayville, North Dakota 58257.

Membership Active chapters 8. Total number of initiates 15,000. Chapter roll:††

1930	Alpha, Northeast Missouri	
1930	Gamma, Mary Washington	
1930	Zeta, Western Carolina	
1934	Iota, Southwestern State (OK)	
1939	Nautilus, Bemidji	
1956	Omicron, Mayville State (ND)	
1956	Xi, Cheyney State	
1957	Tau, Chadron	

† This chapter narrative is repeated from the 19th edition; no current information was provided.

†† This chapter roll is repeated from the 19th edition; no current information was provided.

Alpha Psi Omega[†]

(DRAMA)

ACTIVE PIN

ALPHA PSI OMEGA, men's and women's national recognition society in dramatics, was organized August 12, 1925, at Fairmont State College by Dr. Paul F. Opp for the purpose of providing a reward for students distinguishing themselves in college dramatic productions. Students qualify for membership by faithful work in playing a certain number of major and minor roles in the plays of the regular dramatic club of the college. Provision is also made for crediting other kinds of dramatic work on the technical and business side of play production as equivalent to major and minor roles. Membership has always been open to men and women on an equal basis. Nationally the society provides a wide fellowship for college directors of dramatics and students interested in promoting dramatic activities. The national magazine provides information upon the problems of selecting and staging plays suitable for schools and colleges. Each chapter is called a cast, as the society is distinctly dramatic in its organization and ritual.

A number of chapters provide tuition scholarships for students who are majoring in speech and drama.

Government Between conventions government is vested in an executive council of three national officers called the Grand Cast.

Publications The society publishes a national constitution, a national directory, a book of ceremonies, and songs, as well as the official magazine, *The Playbill*.

Traditions and Insignia The official badge is a monogram of the Greek-letter symbols of the society. The coat of arms is a crest or design representing the stage of a Greek theater. The colors are amber and moonlight blue, two colors much used in theatrical lighting effects. These colors are worn in lieu of a pledge button. The flower is the violet.

Membership Active chapters 395. Inactive chapters 2. Total number of initiates 50,175. Chapter roll:††

1925	Alpha, Fairmont	
1925	Beta, Marshall	
1925	Delta, Acadia (Canada)	
1925	Gamma, Washington and Lee	
1926	Chi, Buena Vista	
1926	Epsilon, Lynchburg	
1926	Iota, Johns Hopkins	
1926	Kappa, Ottawa	

1926 Lambda, Washington and Jefferson
1926 *Mu, Texas* (1939)
1926 Nu, Houston
1926 Omicron, Wilmington
1926 Phi, Colorado State, Greeley
1926 Pi, West Virginia
1926 Rho, Lincoln Memorial (TN)
1926 Sigma, Linfield
1926 Tau, Texas Tech
1926 Theta, Baker
1926 Upsilon, Kansas Wesleyan
1926 Xi, Cal State, Chico
1926 Zeta, Western State (CO)
1927 Alpha Alpha, Mississippi
1927 Alpha Beta, Coker
1927 Alpha Delta, Tarkio
1927 Alpha Epsilon, Westminster (MO)
1927 Alpha Eta, Moorhead
1927 Alpha Gamma, Morningside
1927 Alpha Iota, Berea
1927 Alpha Kappa, Tampa
1927 Alpha Lambda, Wisconsin, Superior
1927 Alpha Mu, Emory and Henry
1927 Alpha Nu, Colgate
1927 Alpha Omicron, Bloomsburg
1927 Alpha Theta, McKendree (IL)
1927 Alpha Xi, Arkansas College
1927 Alpha Zeta, Central
1927 Omega, Iowa Wesleyan
1927 Psi, Lindenwood
1928 Alpha Omega, Augustana
1928 Alpha Phi, Wisconsin, La Crosse
1928 Alpha Pi, Millsaps
1928 Alpha Rho, West Virginia Wesleyan
1928 Alpha Sigma, Louisiana Col.
1928 Alpha Tau, Mount Union
1928 Alpha Upsilon, Clarion
1928 Beta Alpha, Humboldt
1928 Beta Beta, Lafayette
1928 Beta Delta, New York, Washington Square
1928 Beta Epsilon, Rutgers
1928 Beta Eta, Huntington
1928 Beta Gamma, Bethany (WV)
1928 Beta Iota, Valparaiso
1928 Beta Kappa, Upper Iowa
1928 Beta Lambda, Delaware
1928 Beta Mu, Union (TN)
1928 *Beta Theta, Georgia*
1928 Beta Zeta, East Central State
1929 Beta Chi, Defiance
1929 Beta Nu, Arizona State, Flagstaff
1929 Beta Omicron, California State (PA)
1929 Beta Phi, Stephen F. Austin
1929 Beta Pi, William Jewell
1929 Beta Psi, Kent
1929 Beta Rho, Nebraska State, Wayne
1929 Beta Tau, Newberry
1929 Beta Upsilon, Western New Mexico
1929 Beta Xi, Concord
1930 Beta Omega, Keuka
1930 Gamma Alpha, Southeastern Oklahoma
1930 Gamma Beta, Trinity (TX)

1930 Gamma Delta, New Mexico Highlands
1930 Gamma Epsilon, Murray State
1930 Gamma Eta, Lenoir-Rhyne
1930 Gamma Gamma, Alabama
1930 Gamma Iota, Sul Ross
1930 Gamma Kappa, Edinboro
1930 Gamma Lambda, Baylor
1930 Gamma Mu, Muhlenberg
1930 Gamma Theta, Indiana Central
1930 Gamma Zeta, Colorado State
1931 Delta Alpha, New Brunswick
1931 Gamma Chi, Southwestern State (OK)
1931 Gamma Nu, Georgia State
1931 Gamma Omega, Montana State
1931 Gamma Omicron, Alton Center (IL)
1931 Gamma Phi, Rocky Mountain
1931 Gamma Pi, Bessie Tift
1931 Gamma Psi, Roanoke
1931 Gamma Rho, Northwestern Oklahoma
1931 Gamma Sigma, Cascade (OR)
1931 Gamma Tau, South Carolina
1931 Gamma Upsilon, Northern Illinois
1932 Delta Beta, Alma
1932 Delta Delta, Hampden-Sydney
1932 Delta Epsilon, North Central
1932 Delta Eta, Northwestern Louisiana
1932 Delta Gamma, Alderson-Broaddus
1932 Delta Zeta, Dubuque
1933 Delta Iota, Centenary
1933 Delta Kappa, Mary Hardin-Baylor
1933 Delta Lambda, Northwestern (IA)
1933 Delta Mu, Winthrop
1933 Delta Nu, Florida Southern
1933 Delta Theta, North Dakota State, Minot
1933 Delta Xi, R.P.I.
1934 Delta Chi, Panhandle A & M
1934 Delta Omega, Judson
1934 Delta Omicron, Doane
1934 Delta Phi, Slippery Rock
1934 Delta Pi, Cal Tech
1934 Delta Psi, Mississippi State
1934 Delta Rho, Russell Sage
1934 Delta Sigma, Bethel (KS)
1934 Delta Tau, Ursinus
1934 Delta Upsilon, Texas Christian
1935 Zeta Alpha, Abilene Christian
1935 Zeta Beta, Wisconsin, Stout
1935 Zeta Delta, Arkansas State
1935 Zeta Epsilon, Delta State
1935 Zeta Eta, Norwich
1935 Zeta Gamma, Simpson
1935 Zeta Iota, Drexel Tech
1935 Zeta Kappa, Ozarks
1935 Zeta Lambda, Central Missouri State
1935 Zeta Theta, Hardin-Simmons
1935 Zeta Zeta, Bethany (KS)
1936 Zeta Chi, Union (KY)
1936 Zeta Mu, Ashland
1936 Zeta Nu, SUNY Col., Geneseo
1936 Zeta Omicron, Hendrix
1936 Zeta Phi, Eastern Kentucky
1936 Zeta Pi, Mercer

1936	Zeta Rho, Alabama State, Florence
1936	Zeta Sigma, Stonehill
1936	Zeta Tau, Texas Western, El Paso
1936	Zeta Upsilon, Heidelberg
1936	Zeta Xi, LaVerne
1937	Eta Alpha, Marietta
1937	Eta Beta, Carson-Newman
1937	Eta Delta, Wisconsin, Stevens Point
1937	Eta Epsilon, Spring Hill
1937	Eta Eta, Mary Washington
1937	Eta Gamma, V.P.I.
1937	Eta Zeta, Upsala
1937	Zeta Omega, West Virginia State
1937	Zeta Psi, Ball State
1938	Eta Iota, West Texas
1938	Eta Kappa, Northern Montana
1938	Eta Lambda, Eastern Montana
1938	Eta Mu, Little Rock
1938	Eta Nu, Meredith
1938	Eta Omicron, Carthage
1938	Eta Theta, Washburn
1938	Eta Xi, Thiel
1939	Eta Chi, Furman
1939	Eta Phi, Youngstown State
1939	Eta Pi, Mississippi State
1939	Eta Rho, West Liberty
1939	Eta Sigma, Alabama State
1939	Eta Tau, Carroll
1939	Eta Upsilon, Bridgewater
1940	Eta Omega, Harding
1940	Eta Psi, Pacific
1940	Theta Alpha, Glenville
1940	Theta Beta, Georgia State
1940	Theta Delta, Tennessee
1940	Theta Epsilon, McPherson
1940	Theta Eta, Hood
1940	Theta Gamma, LaGrange
1940	Theta Theta, Waynesburg
1940	Theta Zeta, Lock Haven
1941	Theta Iota, Western Carolina
1941	Theta Kappa, San Francisco State
1941	Theta Lambda, Georgia Southern
1941	Theta Mu, Minnesota, Duluth
1941	Theta Nu, Oakland City
1941	Theta Omicron, Texas Wesleyan
1941	Theta Xi, George Peabody
1942	Theta Chi, Eastern Oregon
1942	Theta Phi, Susquehanna
1942	Theta Pi, Pacific Lutheran
1942	Theta Psi, Hastings
1942	Theta Rho, Whitworth
1942	Theta Sigma, Missouri Valley
1942	Theta Tau, Southwestern Louisiana
1942	Theta Upsilon, Radford State
1943	Iota Alpha, Pembroke
1943	Iota Beta, Wisconsin, River Falls
1943	Iota Delta, McMurry
1943	Iota Gamma, Cedar Crest
1943	Theta Omega, SUNY Col., Fredonia
1944	Iota Epsilon, Southwest Texas
1944	Iota Eta, C. W. Post
1944	Iota Iota, Sam Houston
1944	Iota Kappa, Davidson
1944	Iota Lambda, Westmar
1944	Iota Mu, Arkansas A. M. & N.
1944	Iota Nu, Immaculata
1944	Iota Theta, Moravian
1944	Iota Xi, Incarnate Word
1944	Iota Zeta, Marcyhurst
1945	Iota Chi, Columbia (SC)
1945	Iota Omega, Davis and Elkins
1945	Iota Omicron, East Stroudsburg
1945	Iota Phi, American
1945	Iota Pi, Our Lady of the Lake
1945	Iota Psi, Manchester
1945	Iota Rho, Coe
1945	Iota Sigma, Maryland State, Towson
1945	Iota Tau, Longwood
1945	Iota Upsilon, Belhaven
1946	Kappa Alpha, Berry (GA)
1946	Kappa Beta, Gannon
1946	Kappa Delta, Bethel (TN)
1946	Kappa Epsilon, Briar Cliff
1946	Kappa Eta, Ferris
1946	Kappa Gamma, Southwest Missouri
1946	Kappa Iota, Southwestern, Memphis
1946	Kappa Theta, Central Michigan
1946	Kappa Zeta, Fenn (OH)
1947	Kappa Chi, Lewis and Clark
1947	Kappa Kappa, Portland
1947	Kappa Lambda, St. Andrews Presbyterian (NC)
1947	Kappa Mu, Oregon College of Education
1947	Kappa Nu, West Virginia Tech
1947	Kappa Omicron, Belmont
1947	Kappa Pi, Greensboro
1947	Kappa Psi, Clemson
1947	Kappa Psi, Texas A & I
1947	Kappa Rho, Georgetown Col.
1947	Kappa Sigma, Northwest Missouri
1947	Kappa Tau, Idaho State
1947	Kappa Upsilon, Eastern New Mexico
1947	Kappa Xi, Maryland State, Frostburg
1948	Kappa Omega, Wayland Baptist
1948	Lambda Alpha, Blue Mountain (MS)
1948	Lambda Beta, Keene
1948	Lambda Delta, Morris Harvey
1948	Lambda Epsilon, East Tennessee
1948	Lambda Eta, Drew
1948	Lambda Gamma, Middle Tennessee
1948	Lambda Iota, Midland (NE)
1948	Lambda Kappa, Wagner
1948	Lambda Lambda, Arkansas State
1948	Lambda Mu, Wartburg
1948	Lambda Nu, Southern Mississippi
1948	Lambda Theta, Anderson
1948	Lambda Zeta, Appalachian
1949	Lambda Chi, Omaha
1949	Lambda Omega, SUNY Col., Oneonta
1949	Lambda Omicron, Elon
1949	Lambda Phi, Dickinson
1949	Lambda Pi, Villanova
1949	Lambda Psi, Tusculum
1949	Lambda Rho, Central State (OK)

1949	Lambda Sigma, South Dakota State		1955	Tenn. Eta, Milligan
1949	Lambda Tau, Emmanuel		1956	Pi Nu, Marygrove
1949	Lambda Upsilon, Mansfield		1956	Pi Omicron, Lamar
1949	Lambda Xi, Fort Hays		1956	Pi Xi, Nebraska State, Chadron
1949	Mu Alpha, Hillsdale		1957	Pi Chi, Mississippi Col.
1949	Mu Beta, Emory		1957	Pi Omega, Sterling
1949	Mu Gamma, Northeastern (OK)		1957	Pi Phi, Springfield
1950	Mu Delta, New Mexico A & M		1957	Pi Pi, Converse
1950	Mu Epsilon, Adams		1957	Pi Psi, Westfield
1950	Mu Eta, East Texas		1957	Pi Rho, Friends
1950	Mu Iota, SUNY Col., Oswego		1957	Pi Sigma, Mercy (MI)
1950	Mu Kappa, Cal State, Sacramento		1957	Pi Tau, Shippensburg
1950	Mu Lambda, Western Kentucky		1957	Pi Upsilon, Tennessee Tech.
1950	Mu Mu, Beaver		1957	Vermont Eta, Norwich
1950	Mu Nu, Nicholls		1958	Rho Alpha, Pfeiffer
1950	Mu Omicron, Memphis State		1958	Rho Beta, Boston State
1950	Mu Theta, John Carroll		1958	Rho Delta, Black Hills
1950	Mu Xi, Boston		1958	Rho Epsilon, Valdosta
1950	Mu Zeta, American, Cairo		1958	Rho Gamma, Tennessee, Martin
1951	Mu Chi, Adelphi		1958	Rho Zeta, South Dakota Northern, Aberdeen
1951	Mu Epsilon, Lycoming		1959	Okla. Gamma, Oklahoma City
1951	Mu Omega, Duquesne		1960	Okla. Gamma, Oklahoma City
1951	Mu Phi, Southern Arkansas		1960	Rho Eta, Lebanon Valley
1951	Mu Pi, Creighton		1960	Rho Theta, Paterson State (NJ)
1951	Mu Psi, Hofstra		1960	Tenn. Zeta, Tennessee Wesleyan
1951	Mu Rho, Rhode Island Education		1961	Rho Iota, Eastern Washington
1951	Mu Sigma, Albright		1961	Rho Lambda, Framingham
1951	Mu Tau, Central Washington		1961	Rho Mu, West Chester
1951	Nu Alpha, Alabama State, Livingston		1962	Rho Kappa, Worcester Tech
1951	Nu Beta, Parsons		1962	Rho Nu, Glassboro
1952	Nu Delta, St. Mary's (MN)		1962	Rho Omicron, Sioux Falls
1952	Nu Epsilon, Evansville		1962	Rho Pi, Notre Dame (NY)
1952	Nu Eta, Niagara		1962	Rho Rho, Monmouth (NJ)
1952	Nu Gamma, Westminster (PA)		1962	Rho Sigma, Millersville
1952	Nu Iota, Hartwick		1962	Rho Tau, Luther
1952	Nu Kappa, Austin		1962	Rho Xi, Loyola, Chicago
1952	Nu Lambda, Notre Dame (MO)		1963	Rho Chi, St. Joseph's (PA)
1952	Nu Theta, Hamilton		1963	Rho Omega, Notre Dame (OH)
1952	Nu Zeta, Trinity (DC)		1963	Rho Phi, Grand Canyon
1953	Nu Mu, Marylhurst (OR)		1963	Rho Psi, Erskine
1953	Nu Nu, Findlay		1963	Rho Upsilon, Kutztown
1953	Nu Omicron, Indiana (PA)		1964	Sigma Alpha, Oklahoma Christian
1953	Nu Xi, St. Mary's (LA)		1964	Sigma Beta, Principia (IL)
1954	Nu Chi, Northeastern		1964	Sigma Delta, Viterbo (WI)
1954	Nu Epsilon, Nebraska State, Kearney		1964	Sigma Epsilon, East Carolina
1954	Nu Omega, St. Teresa		1964	Sigma Eta, Merrimack
1954	Nu Phi, Morgan State		1964	Sigma Gamma, North Texas
1954	Nu Pi, North Georgia		1964	Sigma Zeta, Randolph, Macon
1954	Nu Psi, Rutgers, Newark		1965	Sigma Iota, Dana
1954	Nu Rho, Emporia		1965	Sigma Kappa, Cal. Western
1954	Nu Sigma, Lake Forest		1965	Sigma Theta, Xavier
1954	Nu Tau, Wisconsin, Platteville		1966	Sigma Lambda, L.S.U., Medical
1954	Pi Alpha, Eastern Michigan		1966	Sigma Mu, Pan American
1954	Scarlet Masque, Wabash		1966	Sigma Nu, Steubenville
1955	Kentucky Lambda, Kentucky Wesleyan		1966	Sigma Omicron, Emerson
1955	Pi Beta, Mount Mary		1966	Sigma Xi, Oklahoma College, Chickasha
1955	Pi Delta, Midwestern		1967	Sigma Chi, William Carey
1955	Pi Epsilon, Gettysburg		1967	Sigma Phi, Elizabethtown
1955	Pi Eta, Southern Oregon		1967	Sigma Pi, Caltech (Kellogg-Voorhis)
1955	Pi Gamma, McNeese		1967	Sigma Psi, Miami (Wright State campus)
1955	Pi Theta, Newark Engineering		1967	Sigma Rho, California Lutheran
1955	Pi Zeta, Washington (MO)			

1967 Sigma Sigma, San Francisco College for
      Women
1967 Sigma Tau, Cumberland (KY)
1967 Sigma Upsilon, Guam

Angel Flight†

(AIR FORCE)

ACTIVE PIN

THE ANGEL FLIGHT is an organization of college women who have the interests of the United States Air Force, the Air Force Reserve Officers Training Corps program, and the Arnold Air Society at heart. Angel Flight exists for the same purpose that the Arnold Air Society exists; that is, to further the cause of the United States Air Force by promoting the interest of the college man in the AFROTC program. Angel Flights, through their many activities, aid the progress of the Arnold Air Society and serve as a symbol of appreciation for the importance and the dignity of Air Force life.

The first Angel Flight was founded at the University of Omaha in February, 1952, and was called "The Sponsor Corps." Until 1957 the Angel Flight was a national idea with many names, uniforms, and activities. On April 18, 19, and 20 of that year various associate member groups of the Arnold Air Society sent delegates to New York to the eighth annual conclave of the Arnold Air Society to join their purposes under a National Co-ordinating Headquarters. Sibyl Klak from the University of Maryland was hostess Angel and Patricia Choonmaker from Pennsylvania State was chairman of the meeting. The fifteen schools represented were: Auburn, Ball State, Indiana, Pennsylvania State, Maryland, North Carolina, Colorado A. and M., Allegheny, Detroit, Southern Illinois, Minnesota, Louisville, George Washington, San Diego State, and Brooklyn.

The representatives reported on their respective organizations so they could compare the differences. At that time the flights ranged from memberships of thirteen to ninety. No flight wore the same uniform nor was there any uniformity in means of selection and in the activities of individual flights. The national name, Angel Flight, was chosen at this time. Pennsylvania State was selected as the first national headquarters.

Government The Angel Flights are sponsored by the Arnold Air Society. The provision. as stated in the Arnold Air Society Manual, is: "Provisions are hereby made for sponsorship of an Angel Flight to the Arnold Air Society, the members of which shall be known as Associate Members of the Arnold Air Society. Organization, chartering, management, and activities of these Associate Member groups shall be as prescribed in individual squadron bylaws."

The National Commander is elected by the general assembly of the Angel Flight at the annual conclave which convenes in conjunction with that of the Arnold Air Society. Other officers who may be appointed by the National Commander at her discretion are the national executive officer, national administrative services officer, national comptroller, national informations officer, and national operations officer. The national publications officer is not appointed by the Commander. She is always from the Angel Flight at Texas Technological College and is selected by that flight. Texas Tech is designated as the National Publications Headquarters for both the Arnold Air Society and Angel Flight.

For both the Arnold Air Society and the Angel Flight, the country is divided into seventeen geographical areas, each of which is commanded by an Arnold air area staff and an Angel Flight staff. The purpose of these areas and their staffs is to act as a liaison between the national headquarters and the local units, and also to carry on the majority of the administrative work that would otherwise have to be done by the national officers.

Traditions and Insignia Several years ago, a national Angel Flight uniform was designed and adopted. However, due to problems with many of the flights, it was decided that it was not a compulsory matter. No flights are obligated to adopt this as their uniform. No flights wear the same uniform, although many are similar. It is standardized as far as it is required that all uniforms be blue and white.

The badge is a horizontal double wing with a star in the center. The pin is silver. The crest displays double wings pointing upwards with a shield of the United States and a torch superimposed on the shield. A band under the wings bears the name ANGEL FLIGHT. The flag in a blue field with white fringe surrounding the edge with the official crest in gold in the center. The flower is the white rose. The colors are blue and white. A gold or silver key may be awarded to a member at the discretion of the individual flight in recognition of a service or honor.

Headquarters The National Headquarters for Angel Flight is elected biannually. The address of the permanent headquarters is 1750 Pennsylvania Avenue NW, Washington. D.C. 20006. Its official title is Angel Flight—Arnold Air Society National Administrative Headquarters.

Membership Active flights 135. Flight list:††

Akron
Allegheny

---

† This chapter narrative is repeated from the 19th edition; no current information was provided.

†† This chapter roll is repeated from the 19th edition; no current information was provided.

Arizona State
Arizona
Arkansas
Auburn
Ball State
Baylor
Boston
Bowling Green
Bradley
Brigham Young
Buffalo
Butler
California
Capital
Case Tech
Catholic
Central Washington
Cincinnati
Clemson
Colorado
Colorado State
Colorado State, Greeley
Connecticut
Detroit
Douglass
Drake
Duquesne
East Carolina
East Texas
Evansville
Florida State
Florida
Fordham
Cal State, Fresno
George Washington
Georgia
Georgetown
Grove City
Hawaii
Howard
Idaho
Illinois
Indiana
Iowa State
Iowa
Kansas State
Kansas
Kent
Kentucky
L.S.U.
Louisiana Tech
Louisville
Lowell Tech
M.I.T.
Maryland State
Maryland
Massachusetts
Memphis State
Miami (FL)
Miami (OH)
Michigan State
Michigan Tech

Minnesota, Duluth
Minnesota
Mississippi State
Mississippi
Missouri
Montana
N.Y.U.
Nebraska
New Hampshire
New Mexico State
New Mexico
North Carolina A & T
North Carolina State
North Carolina
North Dakota State
North Texas
Occidental
Ohio State
Ohio Wesleyan
Ohio
Oklahoma State
Oklahoma
Omaha
Oregon State
Oregon
Otterbein
Pembroke (Brown)
Penn State
Pitt
Portland
Puget Sound
Purdue
SUNY
San Diego State
San Francisco State
San Jose
South Carolina
South Dakota State
Southern Illinois
Southern Methodist
Southwest Texas
Southwestern Louisiana
St. Louis
St. Olaf
St. Thomas
Stanford
Syracuse
Tennessee A & I
Tennessee
Texas Christian
Texas Tech.
Texas
Tulane
Tulsa
Tuskegee
UCLA
Utah State
Utah
Washburn
Washington (MO)
Washington (WA)
Washington State

West Virginia
Wichita
Willamette
Wisconsin State
Wisconsin, Madison
Wyoming

Arnold Air Society†

(AIR FORCE)

ACTIVE PIN

PLEDGE PIN

THE ARNOLD AIR SOCIETY for college men was conceived in the spring and summer of 1947. The first efforts for the organization were made by Lt. Col. James F. Pierce, Maj. Victor J. Sampson, and Capt. James L. Nollkamper, all assistant professors of military science and tactics at the University of Cincinnati.

At a general meeting in October, 1947, a committee of cadets was formed to consider a constitution and to take such actions as the University of Cincinnati would require for campus recognition. Additional consideration was given to the many phases any organization must undergo in the embryonic stage: by-laws, rituals, activities, and a suitable name to replace that of Arnold Airmen; that chosen was the Arnold Society of Air Cadets, unanimously decided upon to honor General H. H. Arnold.

Cadets associated with the society at this time constantly sought the recognition of the U.S. Air Force. They corresponded with the Air Material Command at Wright Field in Dayton, Ohio, and made this, their nearest Air Force contact, aware of their activities and interest. April 6, 1948, General C. B. Stone III formally notified the Arnold Society of Air Cadets of its official recognition by the U.S. Air Force.

Shortly thereafter the society became a project of the Air Defense Command, whose duty it was to see that the local group became nationalized. In September, 1948, the Air Defense Command sent copies of the society's constitution to all universities and colleges throughout the nation, that maintained an AFROTC unit.

The first national officers, as well as their successors, were chosen from the University of Cincinnati until 1954. Cincinnati remained national headquarters during the early years of expansion. Paul T. Johns, who later lost his life in a tragic summer camp accident, became the first national commander. Since his death, a Paul T. Johns Award has been awarded each year by the national adviser to

† This chapter narrative is repeated from the 19th edition; no current information was provided.

the outstanding cadet of the Hap Arnold national headquarters squadron. With the death of General Arnold, a vacancy was brought about among the national officers; General James Doolittle was chosen by unanimous consent to serve as honorary national commander.

The Sabre Flight, a drill organization for basic cadets sponsored by the Omaha A.A.S. squadron, merged with the Arnold Air Society in April, 1954.

Angel Flight, a co-ed auxiliary, was given national status at the Los Angeles Conclave in November, 1952.

Government The annual national conclave is the supreme power, authority being delegated to these national officers: national commander, national executive officer, national adjutant recorder, national comptroller, national public information officer, national publications officer, national operations officer, and national adviser.

Publication *The Arnold Air Letter,* launched in 1949, is the official monthly publication, with headquarters at Texas Technological College, Lubbock, Tex. In 1954 an executive board was formed, composed of all area commanders and the national commander.

The country was originally divided into six permanent areas numbered clockwise corresponding to the United States Air Force Areas, for purposes of administration. However, at the Los Angeles conclave in 1952, the number was increased to eleven, lettered from A to K, with each maintaining a headquarters at a chosen college. In 1954, a plan was begun to rotate the national headquarters each year to the university which was host to the last conclave.

The office of executive secretary, authorized in 1954, was created in 1955. Affiliation with the Air Force Association was voted in 1956.

Traditions and Insignia The Arnold Air Society has grown into the largest organization open to ROTC cadets, embracing squadrons on campuses in the United States, including Hawaii, and Puerto Rico.

The Arnold Memorial Scholarship, a cash award of $300, is given annually in rotation among the areas to the outstanding first-year member of the various squadrons eligible.

The badge is an Air Force star of white with a cardinal ball resting on opposed wings of the Air Force in gold, under which are two gold bars with the inscription, Arnold Air Society superimposed thereon. The insignia worn by an active member on his uniform is a blue and gold fourragère of the society. The ribbon is regulation size utilizing four colors. In the center are alternating stripes of red and blue: two active blue, one red bounded by white, with yellow-orange border stripes.

Administrative Headquarters 1750 Pennsylvania Avenue, Washington, D.C. 20006.

Membership Active Squadrons 168. Squadron

list (top squadron in each area is area headquarters):††

AREA A-1

Boston
Brown
Colby
Connecticut
Lowell
M.I.T.
Massachusetts
New Hampshire
St. Michael's
Trinity
Tufts

AREA A-2

Fordham
Manhattan
N.Y.U. (Heights)
N.Y.U., Washington Square
Rensselaer
Union

AREA B-1

Catholic
Georgetown
Gettysburg
Howard
Lehigh
Maryland, Eastern Shore
Maryland
Newark Engineering
Rutgers
St. Joseph's (PA)
Stevens Tech
Virginia

AREA B-2

Duke
East Carolina
North Carolina A & T
North Carolina State
North Carolina
V.P.I.

AREA C-1

Citadel
Clemson
Emory
Florida Staate
Georgia Tech
Georgia
Miami (FL)
Puerto Rico
Sewanee

South Carolina
Tuskegee

AREA C-2

Alabama
Auburn
L.S.U.
Memphis State
Mississippi State
Mississippi
Southwestern Louisiana
Tulane

AREA D-1

Capital
Cincinnati
Denison
Kenyon
Miami (OH)
Ohio State
Ohio Wesleyan
Ohio
Otterbein

AREA D-2

Ball State
Bradley
Butler
DePauw
Evansville
Illinois Tech
Illinois
Indiana
Kentucky
Louisville
Purdue
Tennessee A & I
Tennessee

AREA E-1

Allegheny
Buffalo
Colgate
Cornell
Duquesne
Grove City
Hobart
Penn State
Pitt
Rochester
Syracuse
West Virginia

AREA E-2

Akron
Bowling Green
Case Tech
Detroit
Kent

†† This chapter roll is repeated from the 19th edition; no current information was provided.

Michigan State
Michigan
Notre Dame

AREA F-1

Michigan Tech
Minnesota, Duluth
Minnesota
North Dakota State
South Dakota State
St. Olaf
St. Thomas
Wisconsin, Superior

AREA F-2

Drake
Illinois Tech
Iowa State
Iowa
Lawrence
Nebraska
Omaha
Wisconsin

AREA G-1

Arkansas
Baylor
East Texas
Louisiana Tech
Missouri
North Texas
Oklahoma State
Oklahoma
Southern Methodist
Southwest Texas
Texas Christian
Texas Tech.
Texas
Tulsa

AREA G-2

Kansas State
Kansas
Parks (IL)
Southern Illinois
Washburn
Washington (MO)
Wichita

AREA H-1

Brigham Young
Colorado State, Greeley
Colorado State
Colorado
Utah State
Utah
Wyoming

AREA H-2

Central Washington
Montana State
Montana
Oregon State
Oregon
Portland
Puget Sound
Washington State
Washington
Willamette

AREA I

Arizona State
Arizona
Cal State, Fresno
California
Hawaii
Loyola Marymount, Los Angeles
New Mexico State
New Mexico
Occidental
San Diego State
San Francisco State
San Jose
Stanford
UCLA
USC

Beta Beta Beta†

(BIOLOGY)

ACTIVE PIN

BETA BETA BETA Biological Society was organized at Oklahoma City University in 1922 by Prof. Frank G. Brooks for the purpose of supplying for the biological sciences an undergraduate recognition society that would promote interest in and further the objectives of the science. It attempts to do this by reserving its membership for college men and women who meet certain scholastic standards and who have completed a required amount of work in biology. It has as additional objectives the spread of biological information and the advancement of science by new discoveries. It emphasizes, therefore, a three-fold program, namely: sound scholarship, dissemination of scientific truth, and research.

The constitution provides for four types of membership. National honorary members are elected by the biennial convention of the society and this membership is reserved for persons of outstanding

† This chapter narrative is repeated from the 19th edition; no current information was provided.

accomplishment and stature in one or more of the biological sciences or persons rendering outstanding service to Beta Beta Beta. Chapter honorary members are elected by a chapter in recognition of accomplishment as biologists or outstanding service to an individual chapter. Active members are undergraduate majors in biology who have completed a minimum of three courses in biology with an average grade of **B** or its equivalent and are in good academic standing. Associate members are those with a significant interest in the life sciences but who are not or not yet eligible for active status.

Beta Beta Beta is an affiliated society of the American Association for the Advancement of Science and of the AIBS.

Growth   New chapters are installed only after application by the school desiring the chapter, an inspection by national officers, consideration and approval by the national executive committee, and a vote of approval by the majority of the chapters of the district where the school is located. Beta Beta Beta does not solicit for new chapters but will consider applications from any accredited four-year college.

Government   Government is by a biennial convention which is arranged for by the national officers at a time and place which will allow as many student delegates to attend as possible and will also provide for the student delegates significant biological experiences such as field trips, major scientific meetings (AAAS, AIBS, WSN, etc.) or contacts with research workers at an important research center.

Traditions and Insignia   Regional and district conferences are held each year with programs featuring distinguished biologists, research papers by members, and field trips. The Frank G. Brooks District Award Plaque is given in each district to the student giving the best research presentation. A further award is the McClung Award given annually for the best research report by an undergraduate member published in *Bios*. The Bertholf Award Plaque for chapter efficiency is presented annually.

The key has a coiled snake and the initials of the society on a gold shield. The crest contains a shield of the same shape, several symbolic figures, and the motto, *Blepein Basin Biou*. The colors are green and red. 'The flower is the red American beauty rose.

Publications   The quarterly journal, *Bios*, contains articles of general interest to undergraduate biologists and serves as a medium for the publication of papers and research reports by active members.

Headquarters   Drew University, Madison, New Jersey 07940.

Membership   Active chapters 256. Inactive chapters 30. Total number of initiates 71,500. Chapter roll:††

†† This chapter roll is repeated from the 19th edition; no current information was provided.

1922	Alpha, Oklahoma City
1925	Beta, Simpson
1925	Delta, Southwestern (KS) (1939-1950)
1925	Gamma, Western State (CO)
1926	Eta, Iowa Wesleyan
1926	Iota, Marietta
1927	Kappa, Thiel
1927	Lambda, William Jewell (1939-1950)
1927	Mu, Carroll
1928	*Nu, Birmingham-Southern* (1939)
1928	Pi, Nebraska State, Peru
1928	Rho, Gettysburg
1928	Sigma, Chattanooga
1928	*Tau, Morningside*
1928	Upsilon, Mississippi for Women
1928	Xi, Wittenberg
1929	Chi, Drury
1929	*Omega, Knox* (1942)
1929	Psi, Winthrop
1930	Epsilon, Carthage
1931	Beta Tau, Baylor
1931	Omicron, Pacific (CA)
1931	*Phi, Brigham Young* (1974)
1931	Theta, Colorado State
1932	Alpha Mu, Western Maryland
1932	*Alpha Upsilon, American* (1976)
1932	Sigma Tau, Southern Methodist (1938-1965)
1933	*Beta Gamma, Brenau* (1941)
1934	Delta Iota, Northern Iowa
1935	*Gamma Kappa, Nebraska State, Kearney*
1935	Lambda Phi, Lake Forest
1936	*Mu Sigma, Mississippi State*
1937	*Beta Alpha, Spring Hill* (1972)
1937	Epsilon Iota, Cornell Col. (IA)
1937	Gamma Nu, North Central
1937	Gamma Xi, Missouri Valley
1937	Upsilon Delta, Drew
1939	Beta Theta, Richmond
1939	Gamma Omicron, Hamline
1940	Beta Iota, Alabama College
1941	Alpha Theta, Canisius
1941	Beta Kappa, Mississippi (1958-1972)
1941	*Epsilon Gamma, Santa Barbara*
1942	Alpha Iota, St. Lawrence
1942	Beta Lambda, Tulane
1942	*Epsilon Delta, San Jose* (1974)
1943	Alpha Lambda, Hofstra
1943	*Epsilon Zeta, Portland* (1972)
1944	Kearney
1944	Beta Mu, West Virginia Wesleyan
1945	Alpha Nu, Randolph, Macon
1945	Gamma Pi, Monmouth
1945	Zeta Alpha, Puerto Rico A & M
1945	Zeta Beta, Inter-American
1946	Beta Nu, Huntingdon
1946	Delta Epsilon, Texas Woman's
1947	Alpha Omicron, Hood
1947	Alpha Xi, Notre Dame (MD)
1947	Beta Omicron, Miami (FL)
1947	Beta Pi, Murray State
1947	Beta Xi, Stetson
1947	Delta Eta, Arkansas State

1947 Delta Zeta, North Texas	1957 Eta Zeta, Grove City
1947 Gamma Rho, Drake	1957 Gamma Beta, Alma
1948 Alpha Pi, Mary Baldwin	1957 Gamma Gamma, Greenville
1948 Alpha Sigma, Westminster (PA)	1958 Eta Iota, Emory and Henry
1948 Beta Rho, Wake Forest	1958 Eta Kappa, Western Michigan
1948 Gamma Sigma, Augustana (IL)	1958 Eta Mu, Southern
1949 Alpha Phi, Bethany	1958 Eta Nu, Samford
1949 *Alpha Rho, Toledo* (1973)	1958 Eta Xi, Louisiana Tech
1949 *Alpha Tau, DePauw* (1973)	1959 Epsilon Tau, Northern Arizona
1949 Delta Theta, Northeast Louisiana	1959 Eta Omicron, Nazareth
1949 Epsilon Kappa, Whitworth	1959 Eta Pi, Austin Peay
1949 *Epsilon Theta, Nevada* (1958)	1959 Eta Rho, Emmanuel
1950 Alpha Alpha, Albion	1959 Gamma Epsilon, St. Mary's (MN)
1950 Alpha Chi, Edinboro	1959 Gamma Zeta, Augustana (SD)
1950 Alpha Eta, Hope	1960 *Epsilon Mu, Redlands*
1950 Alpha Omega, Hartwick	1960 Eta Sigma, Elmira
1950 Beta Chi, Southern Mississippi	1960 Eta Tau, Carson-Newman
1950 Beta Delta, Delta State	1960 Gamma Mu, Wisconsin, Whitewater
1950 *Beta Sigma, Peabody Teachers* (1974)	1960 Gamma Psi, Kansas State, Pittsburg
1950 Beta Upsilon, Georgetown Col.	1960 Zeta Delta, Catholic, Puerto Rico
1950 Delta Kappa, Emporia	1961 Delta Gamma, East Texas
1950 Gamma Eta, Harris Teachers (MO)	1961 Delta Lambda, Stephen F. Austin
1951 Beta Gamma, North Carolina Women's	1961 Eta Upsilon, Wagner
1951 Epsilon Lambda, Cal State, Fresno	1961 *Gamma Omega, Wisconsin, River Falls* (1975)
1951 Gamma Chi, Nebraska State, Chadron	
1951 Gamma Delta, Northwestern	1961 Gamma Theta, Eastern Illinois
1951 Gamma Lambda, Wartburg	1961 Theta Alpha, Mount Mary
1951 *Gamma Tau, DePaul* (1958)	1961 Theta Beta, Wisconsin, Platteville
1952 Alpha Beta, Bowling Green	1962 *Parsons* (1973)
1952 *Alpha Delta, Rutgers*	1962 Delta Nu, Ouachita Baptist
1952 Alpha Gamma, Pitt	1962 *Eta Omega, Tennessee Wesleyan* (1973)
1952 Alpha Kappa, Hiram	1962 *Theta Delta, D'Youville*
1952 *Beta Phi, Vanderbilt*	1962 Theta Epsilon, New Rochelle
1952 Delta Sigma, Southwestern State (OK)	1962 *Theta Eta, Fort Hays* (1972)
1952 Epsilon Pi, Cal Tech	1962 Theta Gamma, Albany State
1952 Zeta Gamma, Puerto Rico, Rio Piedras	1962 Theta Kappa, Dayton
1953 Alpha Zeta, Lebanon Valley	1962 *Theta Lambda, Luther*
1953 Beta Zeta, Alabama State, Florence	1962 Theta Zeta, Central Michigan
1954 Alpha Epsilon, St. Elizabeth (NJ)	1963 Delta Delta, Langston
1954 Beta Epsilon, Berea	1963 Delta Omicron, Lamar
1954 Beta Omega, Mercer	1963 *Delta Pi, Panhandle A & M* (1973)
1954 Beta Psi, Appalachian	1963 Delta Xi, West Texas
1954 Delta Beta, Oklahoma Baptist	1963 Epsilon Pi, Cal Poly, Pomona
1954 Delta Mu, Midwestern	1963 Eta Chi, Elizabeth City
1954 Epsilon Tau, Arizona State	1963 Eta Phi, Maryville
1955 Alpha Psi, Delaware	1963 Theta Mu, North Park
1955 Beta Eta, Florida Southern	1963 Theta Nu, Upsala
1955 *Eta Alpha, Western Reserve*	1963 Theta Omicron, Mundelein
1955 Eta Beta, Heidelberg	1963 *Theta Pi, Dunbarton* (1973)
1955 *Eta Gamma, Virginia*	1963 Theta Theta, St. Ambrose
1955 Gamma Iota, Western Illinois	1963 Theta Xi, Iona
1955 Zeta, Michigan State	1964 Delta Rho, Austin
1956 Epsilon Beta, Arizona	1964 *Eta Psi, Georgia State*
1956 Eta Lambda, Loyola, New Orleans	1964 *Theta Phi, St. Joseph* (1973)
1956 Gamma Alpha, St. Catherine (MN)	1964 Theta Rho, Illinois Wesleyan
1956 Gamma Phi, Central Missouri State	1964 Theta Sigma, Manchester
1956 Gamma Upsilon, Central Methodist	1964 Theta Tau, Nebraska Wesleyan
1957 Delta Alpha, New Mexico State	1964 Theta Upsilon, Rosary Hill (NY)
1957 *Eta Delta, Utica* (1972)	1965 Delta Tau, Sam Houston
1957 Eta Epsilon, Adelphi	1965 Delta Upsilon, Texas Southern
1957 Eta Eta, Roanoke	1965 Iota Alpha, Elmhurst
1957 Eta Theta, Fairmont	1965 Kappa Alpha, Shorter

1965	Theta Chi, Loyola (MD)
1965	Theta Psi, Cedar Crest
1966	*Delta Chi, Texas Tech.* (1976)
1966	Delta Phi, Texas, El Paso
1966	Iota Beta, Northwest Missouri
1966	Kappa Beta, Alabama
1966	Kappa Gamma, Georgia
1966	Lambda Alpha, Aquinas
1966	Lambda Beta, Rider
1966	Lambda Delta, Rutgers, Newark
1966	Lambda Eta, Kent
1966	Lambda Gamma, Ohio Northern
1966	Lambda Zeta, Keene
1966	Theta Omega, Gannon
1967	Delta Omega, Houston
1967	Delta Psi, Hardin-Simmons
1967	Iota Delta, Ripon
1967	Kappa Delta, Middle Tennessee
1967	Kappa Zeta, Southwest Texas
1967	Lambda Mu, Fairleigh Dickinson, Madison
1967	Lambda Nu, Frostburg
1967	Lambda Pi, Adrian
1967	Lambda Xi, SUNY Col., Potsdam
1968	Sigma Alpha, Jacksonville
1968	Sigma Beta, Georgia Tech
1968	Sigma Chi, Prairie View A & M
1968	Sigma Delta, Tarleton
1968	Sigma Epsilon, Jackson (MS)
1968	Upsilon Chi, SUNY Col., Fredonia
1968	Upsilon Eta, Towson
1968	Upsilon Gamma, Mount Marty (SD)
1968	Upsilon Iota, Pace
1968	Upsilon Kappa, Maine, Farmington
1969	Iota Chi, St. Louis
1969	Kappa Chi, New Orleans
1969	Kappa Epsilon, Old Dominion
1969	Kappa Eta, Mars Hill
1969	Omicron Alpha, San Francisco
1969	Sigma Eta, Barry (FL)
1969	Sigma Gamma, Erskine
1969	Upsilon Lambda, Fairleigh Dickinson, Teaneck
1969	Upsilon Mu, Mount Mary's (CA)
1969	Upsilon Nu, Muskingum
1969	Upsilon Omega, Regis
1970	Epsilon Chi, New Mexico Institute of M & T
1970	Iota Eta, Kansas Wesleyan
1970	Iota Kappa, Westminster (MO)
1970	Lambda Chi, Holy Family
1970	Lambda Epsilon, Juniata
1970	Lambda Iota, Central State
1970	Lambda Kappa, Alliance
1970	Lambda Lambda, Slippery Rock
1970	Lambda Omega, Loyola, Chicago
1970	Mu Alpha, Memphis State
1970	Mu Chi, South Alabama
1970	*Mu Delta, Clinch Valley* (1974)
1970	Mu Eta, Virginia State
1971	Mu Beta, Mississippi Col.
1971	Upsilon Phi, Colgate
1971	Upsilon Pi, Marcyhurst
1971	Upsilon Rho, Villa Maria
1972	Epsilon Omega, Sul Ross
1972	Epsilon Xi, Eastern New Mexico
1972	Iota Lambda, William Woods
1972	Iota Mu, Doane
1972	Lambda Psi, Salisbury
1972	Mu Gamma, Western Kentucky
1972	Upsilon Sigma, Manhattanville
1972	Upsilon Tau, Vassar
1973	*Dominican* (1974)
1973	Epsilon Phi, Texas A & I, Corpus Christi
1973	Epsilon Psi, Texas Lutheran
1973	Iota Nu, Missouri Southern
1973	Kappa Iota, Dillard
1973	Kappa Kappa, Augusta
1973	Lambda Omicron, Wisconsin, Stevens Point
1973	Sigma Iota, Florida Institute
1974	Iota Omega, Nebraska, Omaha
1974	Iota Omicron, Marycrest
1974	Kappa Lambda, Longwood
1974	Kappa Mu, West Virginia
1974	Lambda Rho, Cabrini
1974	Mu Epsilon, Troy
1974	Mu Iota, Grambling
1974	Upsilon Psi, C. W. Post
1974	Zeta Epsilon, Puerto Rico, Cayey
1975	Beta Kappa, Millsaps
1975	Chi Alpha, Russell Sage
1975	Chi Beta, CUNY, York
1975	Chi Delta, New Haven
1975	Chi Epsilon, Manhattan
1975	Iota Phi, Wisconsin, Oshkosh
1975	Iota Pi, Illinois Benedictine
1975	Kappa Omega, Alcorn
1975	Kappa Phi, Southern Missionary
1975	Kappa Psi, Birmingham-Southern
1975	Lambda Sigma, Susquehanna
1975	Lambda Tau, Geneva
1975	Lambda Theta, Mount Mary's
1975	Omicron Beta, Occidental
1976	Chi Eta, Monmouth (NJ)
1976	Iota Psi, Hillsdale
1976	Kappa Omicron, Southern, New Orleans
1976	Kappa Rho, Henderson
1976	Kappa Sigma, Judson
1976	Kappa Tau, Tennessee Tech.
1976	Kappa Theta, Averett
1976	Mu Kappa, Oral Roberts
1976	Omicron Chi, Whittier

Blue Key†

(STUDENT ACTIVITIES)

ACTIVE PIN

BLUE KEY, recognition society for upperclass males of outstanding character and ability who have won campus distinction for scholarship and non-political attainments in service and leadership, was founded at the University of Florida, October, 1924, by Dean B. C. Riley—who passed away in 1962.

The society was established in order that through organized effort among student leaders in American colleges and universities: (1) The belief in God will be perpetuated and intensified, the government of the United States will be supported and defended, and the established institutions of society and the principles of good citizenship will be preserved; (2) An ambition for intellectual attainment and a desire to serve college and fellows will be fostered among students in institutions of higher learning; (3) Student problems may be studied, student life may be enriched, and the progress and best interests of the institutions in which the organization is found may be stimulated and promoted; (4) Students may become adults who will encourage and promote the welfare of the community in which they reside and live so as to reflect credit upon their college.

Honorary membership is extended to a limited number of distinguished faculty and alumni.

Government The legislative powers of the society are vested in the membership of a national chapter, composed of the national officers and one member elected by each chapter. Conventions are held biennially. The national administrative council is made up of five members.

Traditions and Insignia The badge is an oblong key of gold on the surface of which appears a gold oval with a raised border. Within the oval in gold relief appears a cross; on the surface of the cross appears a spread eagle; at the feet, on the lower point of the cross is a star. Outside of the oval in which these symbols appear, the corners of the key are brilliant azure blue.

Headquarters P.O. Box 8487, Metairie, Louisiana 70011.

Membership Active chapters 141. Total number of initiates 80,000. Chapter roll:††

1925 Emory and Henry
1925 Wabash

† This chapter narrative is repeated from the 19th edition; no current information was provided.
†† This chapter roll is repeated from the 19th edition; no current information was provided.

1926 Butler
1926 Chattanooga
1926 Colorado Mines
1926 Georgia
1926 Idaho
1926 Loyola, Chicago
1926 Nevada
1926 North Dakota
1926 Northeast Missouri
1926 Oglethorpe
1926 Pacific (OR)
1926 Trinity (TX)
1927 DePaul
1927 Drexel Tech
1927 Franklin
1927 Iowa Wesleyan
1927 Michigan State
1927 Midland (NE)
1927 Nebraska Wesleyan
1927 North Dakota State
1927 Ohio
1927 Sewanee
1927 South Carolina
1928 Arkansas
1928 Mercer
1928 Mississippi State
1928 North Carolina State
1928 South Dakota State
1928 Wittenberg
1928 Wofford
1929 Indiana
1930 Roanoke
1930 UCLA
1930 USC
1931 Loyola, New Orleans
1932 Ball State
1932 Brigham Young
1932 Case Tech
1932 Catholic
1932 Clemson
1932 Concord
1932 Hope
1932 Kent
1932 Michigan Tech
1932 Nebraska State, Chadron
1932 New Mexico State
1932 Oklahoma State
1932 Presbyterian
1932 Rose-Hulman
1932 San Diego State
1932 Southeastern Oklahoma
1932 Southern Methodist
1932 Southwestern Louisiana
1932 St. Olaf
1932 Utah State
1933 Arizona
1933 Missouri, Rolla
1933 Northern Colorado
1933 Oklahoma City
1934 Kansas State
1934 Oregon State
1936 Alfred

1936	Cal State, Chico
1936	Cal State, Fresno
1939	Indiana State
1940	Santa Barbara
1941	Arizona State
1941	Hendrix
1942	Detroit
1943	Illinois Wesleyan
1948	Augustana (SD)
1948	Furman
1948	San Jose
1948	Southwestern Louisiana
1949	Lewis and Clark
1949	Northern Arizona
1950	Cal State, Los Angeles
1950	North Texas
1950	Pacific (CA)
1951	Babson
1951	Cal, Davis
1951	Georgia State
1951	Newberry
1951	Pacific Lutheran
1951	Portland
1952	Cal Tech
1952	Toledo
1954	Arkansas Tech
1954	Colorado Col
1956	Cal State, Sacramento
1956	Carson-Newman
1956	McNeese
1956	Monmouth
1956	New Mexico State
1957	New Mexico
1958	Abilene Christian
1958	Cal State, Northridge
1958	Gannon
1959	Idaho State
1959	Northwestern Louisiana
1960	Adams
1960	Cal State, Long Beach
1960	Lynchburg
1960	Mount Union
1960	Northern State
1960	Northwest Missouri
1961	Colorado
1961	Emporia
1961	Lamar
1961	Northern Michigan
1961	Ouachita Baptist
1962	Morningside
1962	N.Y.U.
1963	Cal Western
1963	Howard Payne
1964	Eastern Oregon
1964	Evansville
1964	Weber
1964	Western Illinois
1965	Belmont
1965	CCNY
1965	Northwestern Oklahoma
1966	Florida Tech
1966	Morehead
1966	Oregon College of Education
1966	Wayne State
1967	Cal State, Fullerton
1967	Livingston
1967	Wisconsin, La Crosse
1968	Cal Poly
1968	Carthage
1969	Cleveland
1969	Eastern New Mexico
1970	Florida Atlantic
1970	Georgia Southwestern
1970	Illinois Benedictine
1971	Illinois Wesleyan
1971	Lander
1972	Our Lady of Holy Cross
1973	Philadelphia Textiles
1974	St. Joseph's
1975	Southwestern (TX)
1976	Southwestern Louisiana
1976	Trenton
1976	West Georgia

Cardinal Key†

(ACTIVITIES)

ACTIVE PIN

CARDINAL KEY was organized by B. C. Riley, dean of the general extension division of the University of Florida, in the spring of 1932. The useful purpose of Blue Key, an activities organization for men which Dean Riley had founded at the University in 1924, suggested to campus leaders in many places that a similar society be instituted for women.

Government Control of the society, as specified in the Constitution and Bylaws adopted in 1939, is by a National Board of Governors and National Director. In 1946 the constitution was changed permitting the individual chapters to establish membership qualifications with respect to race.

Traditions and Insignia The word *Cardinal* is suggested by the four cardinal points of the compass as well as the four principal virtues as set forth by Socrates and Plato: Prudence, Fortitude, Temperance, and Justice. Young women taking upon themselves the obligations of membership pledge service of the highest type to college, family, community, and government through faith in God and Christianity. The first phrase of the Pledge reads: "I, believing in God . . . "

The emblem is an oblong key-charm on whose surface appears an oval with raised border; within the oval is a cross; on the top of the cross appears a

† This chapter narrative is repeated from the 19th edition; no current information was provided.

spread eagle; in the mouth of the eagle is a wreath of laurel; at the feet of the eagle on the lower point of the cross is a star. The numerous rays of gold which run from the outer edge of the circle to the cross symbolize the chapters. The red enamel is symbolic of the ideals in their entirety.

Headquarters Northern Arizona University, Flagstaff, Arizona 86001.

Membership Active chapters 24. Inactive chapters 4. Total number of initiates 6,233. Chapter roll:††

1932	*Auburn*
1932	Midland (NE)
1933	Kent
1933	New Mexico Western
1934	*Idaho*
1934	Mercer
1934	Northeast Missouri
1934	Oklahoma City
1935	Doane
1937	Cal State, Chico
1937	Southeastern Oklahoma
1938	Concord
1938	Nebraska State, Chadron
1941	*Cumberland (TN)*
1942	Emory and Henry
1943	Phillips
1948	Nebraska Wesleyan
1948	Southwestern (TX)
1949	Arizona State, Flagstaff
1949	Hendrix
1949	Roanoke
1953	*Loyola, New Orleans*
1954	Mississippi State
1954	St. Mary's (LA)
1958	Arkansas Tech
1959	Adams
1960	Cal Poly, San Luis Obispo
1961	Lynchburg

Chi Beta Phi†

(SCIENCE)

ACTIVE PIN

CHI BETA PHI, scientific society for college men and women, was founded at Randolph-Macon College in April, 1916. The purpose of the organization is to promote interest in science through reviews of current investigations, lectures by prominent scien-

†† This chapter roll is repeated from the 19th edition; no current information was provided.
† This chapter narrative is repeated from the 19th edition; no current information was provided.

tists, papers prepared by regular members, and general discussions. To become eligible for membership a student shall have a scholastic average of 80 per cent or above in all college work; he shall have completed, with at least an 80 per cent average, twenty semester hours in the natural sciences and mathematics and shall be taking one or more additional courses in them; he shall have shown a marked interest in science.

Government Government is by national conventions, which meet biennially, and by the seven grand officers who constitute the Board of Directors. The society is chartered as a corporation in the state of West Virginia.

Traditions and Insignia In order to promote its objectives Chi Beta Phi awards a key annually to a member of each chapter who has an outstanding scholastic record, and it gives cash awards for the best papers which the *Record* publishes, presented each year by members to their chapters.

Colors are colonial blue and crimson; the flower is the cape jasmine; the motto is *Scientia Omnia Vincit.*

Publications There are two publications: *The Chi Beta Phi Record,* an annual containing about fifty pages each issue with scientific articles and book reviews in addition to editorials and chapter news; *The Chi Beta Phi NewsLetter,* also an annual, distributed to the active membership through the chapters and providing a medium for the exchange of notes on chapter programs and activities.

Membership Active chapters 24. Inactive chapters 9. Total number of initiates 4,750. Chapter roll:††

1916	Alpha, Randolph, Macon
1921	*Beta, William and Mary* (1939)
1921	*Delta, Emory* (1925)
1921	Gamma, Hampden-Sydney
1923	Epsilon, Morris Harvey
1925	*Eta, Presbyterian* (1940)
1925	*Iota, Alabama* (1940)
1925	Kappa, Marshall
1925	*Lambda, West Virginia Tech* (1931)
1925	*Theta, Wofford* (1939)
1925	Zeta, Davis and Elkins
1926	Mu, Wilmington
1928	Nu, Furman
1929	Xi, Buffalo (1933-1945)
1930	*Omicron, Centre* (1937)
1930	Pi, Concord
1933	Alpha Sigma, Agnes Scott
1935	Rho, West Liberty (1936-1939)
1935	*Sigma, Austin* (1936)
1935	Tau, Southwestern, Memphis
1940	*Upsilon, North Carolina* (1942)
1941	Iota Sigma, Radford
1941	Theta Sigma, Limestone
1945	Kappa Sigma, Mary Washington
1947	Phi, Memphis State
1948	Omega, Lynchburg
1951	*Alpha Alpha, Parsons* (1972)

1952 Alpha Beta, Lenoir-Rhyne
1953 Alpha Delta, Franklin
1953 Alpha Gamma, East Carolina
1954 Alpha Epsilon, Keuka

Chi Delta Phi†

(LITERATURE)

ACTIVE PIN

CHI DELTA PHI was founded at the University of Tennessee by Charles R. Morse on October 31, 1919, at which time its first national constitution was adopted and its first officers were elected. The sorority corresponded to a similar fraternity among men called Sigma Upsilon. The purpose of the sorority was to form groups of representative women who would by their influence and their literary interest uphold the highest ideals of a liberal education. The sorority's object is to provide a means whereby congenial groups of women of a literary inclination may meet for the purposes of informal study and entertainment; to raise the standards of productive literary work among the women students in the colleges and universities; to furnish the highest reward for conscientious efforts in furthering the best interests of literature, in the broadest sense of the term. Eligibility to membership shall be based primarily on literary interest and achievements, with due regard to the quality of congeniality. Admission to membership in any chapter shall be only by the unanimous vote of all active members of said chapter.

Government The supreme governing body of Chi Delta Phi is the national convention composed of the national officers and delegates from college and alumnae associations. The national officers are: national president, first vice-president, second vice-president, secretary, treasurer, chapterian, editor. These officers compose the National Council, elected by the national convention. The Permanent Endowment Fund Committee is composed of three members; the chairman is elected for life.

Traditions and Insignia The national emblems are the circle, star, lamp, quills, and mask. The colors are blue and gold, and the national flower is the pansy. The official pin has the symbolic lamp of learning and the Greek letters ΧΔΦ imposed in gold on a blue star mounted over the crossed quills, the whole arranged on a circular plane.

Publication The magazine is *The Litterateur*, published semiannually.

Headquarters Darby Crest, Galloway, Ohio.

Membership Active chapters 10. Inactive chapters 2. Total number of initiates 2,200. Chapter roll:††

1921 Delta, Alabama
1922 Theta, William and Mary
1925 Xi, Kentucky
1926 Alpha Epsilon, Ohio State
1930 Alpha Pi, Huntingdon
1931 *Alpha Tau, Nevada* (1955)
1932 Alpha Upsilon, Limestone
1936 *Alpha Psi, Bethel* (1956)
1938 Alpha Chi, Oklahoma for Women
1943 Beta Alpha, SUNY, Buffalo
1952 Beta Beta, Oregon
1956 Beta Gamma, Marietta

Delta Phi Alpha†

(GERMAN)

ACTIVE PIN

DELTA PHI ALPHA was founded at Wofford College, May 27, 1929, by James A. Chiles, head of the Modern Language Department. and John Olin Eidson, graduate of the class of 1929. The society aims to promote the study of the German language, literature, and civilization, to further an interest in and a better understanding of the German-speaking people, and to foster a sympathetic appreciation of German culture.

Membership is open to undergraduate and graduate students, both men and women, who have completed at least two years of college German, and whose general average is approximately 80 and average in German courses at least 85, those showing outstanding ability in the study and indicating continued interest in the German language and literature. By honoring excellence in German, the society seeks to give students an incentive for higher scholarship. Membership also includes members of the German faculty in colleges and universities having chapters and anyone showing a marked literary or scholastic achievement and interest in things German, who may be recommended by a chapter.

Government The original constitution governing the society was adopted by a vote of chapters on March 1, 1932. A new one was adopted, October, 1951, and revised October, 1965. Government is vested in the National Council of five members.

Traditions and Insignia The colors are black, red, and gold. The emblem is a shield bearing the

†† This chapter roll is repeated from the 19th edition; no current information was provided.

† This chapter narrative is repeated from the 19th edition; no current information was provided.

coat of arms in the three colors. An eagle in gold is raised on a black background. The three Greek letters, ΔΦΑ, are engraved on a small red shield in the center of the eagle's breast.

Publication The society has no official publication. A *Delta Phi Alpha Bulletin* containing the roll of members and chapter officers and news of chapter activities is issued annually, as well as a newsletter in May of each year.

Headquarters Muhlenberg College, Allentown, Pennsylvania 18104.

Membership Active chapters 108. Inactive chapters 21. Total number of initiates 23,539. Chapter roll:††

1929 Alpha, Wofford
1929 *Beta, Central Missouri State*
1929 *Gamma, Bates*
1930 Delta, Vanderbilt
1930 Epsilon, Davidson
1930 Eta, Rochester
1930 Iota, Washington
1930 Theta, Birmingham-Southern
1930 Zeta, Berea
1931 Kappa, Rutgers
1931 *Lambda, West Virginia*
1931 *Mu, Alabama, Montevallo*
1931 Nu, Wittenberg
1931 Omicron, Duke
1931 Pi, Illinois
1931 Rho, Penn
1931 Xi, Cincinnati
1932 Chi, UCLA
1932 Phi, Bucknell
1932 Psi, Washington (MO)
1932 *Sigma, South Carolina* (1938)
1932 Tau, N.Y.U., Washington Square
1932 Upsilon, Adelbert, Western Reserve
1933 Beta Alpha, Indiana
1933 *Beta Beta, Cornell*
1933 *Beta Gamma, Clark*
1934 Beta Delta, Colorado
1934 *Beta Epsilon, Buffalo*
1934 *Beta Eta, USC*
1934 *Beta Theta, Union* (1939)
1934 *Beta Zeta, Southern Methodist*
1935 Beta Iota, Colgate
1935 Beta Kappa, Miami (OH)
1936 *Beta Lambda, Oregon*
1936 *Beta Mu, Tennessee*
1936 Beta Nu, Iowa
1936 Sigma Epsilon Phi, Hunter
1937 Beta Omicron, Capital
1937 Beta Pi, Baldwin-Wallace
1937 Beta Xi, Drake
1938 Beta Rho, North Carolina
1938 *Beta Sigma, Emory*
1939 Beta Tau, Wooster
1939 Beta Upsilon, Louisville

†† This chapter roll is repeated from the 19th edition; no current information was provided.

1940 Beta Phi, Hobart and William Smith
1941 Beta Chi, Upsala
1942 Beta Psi, Albright
1942 Zeta Alpha, Gettysburg
1947 Gamma Alpha, Wabash
1948 Gamma Beta, Dickinson
1948 Gamma Epsilon, Boston
1948 *Gamma Eta, Northwestern*
1948 *Gamma Gamma, Ohio State*
1948 Gamma Theta, Oklahoma
1948 Gamma Zeta, L.S.U.
1948 Phi Gamma Phi, Syracuse
1949 Gamma Iota, Marquette
1949 Gamma Kappa, Colby
1949 Gamma Lambda, American
1949 Gamma Mu, Miami (FL)
1949 *Gamma Nu, Florida*
1949 Gamma Omicron, Temple
1949 Gamma Pi, Kansas
1949 Gamma Rho, Howard
1949 *Gamma Sigma, Georgetown*
1949 Gamma Xi, Rice
1950 Gamma Phi, Georgia
1950 Gamma Tau, Westminster (PA)
1950 Gamma Upsilon, Kent
1951 Gamma Chi, Hope
1951 Gamma Psi, Alabama
1952 Delta Alpha, Denison
1952 *Delta Beta, West Virginia State*
1952 Delta Gamma, Adelphi
1953 *Delta Delta, Emmanuel*
1954 Delta Epsilon, Johns Hopkins
1954 Delta Zeta, Columbia
1955 Delta Eta, Wagner
1955 Delta Iota, Manhattan
1955 Delta Kappa, Texas
1955 *Delta Theta, Virginia*
1956 Delta Lambda, Washington and Jefferson
1956 Delta Mu, Michigan State
1956 Delta Nu, Penn State
1956 Delta Omicron, Queens (NY)
1956 Delta Xi, Wayne State
1957 Delta Pi, Nebraska
1957 Delta Rho, Michigan
1957 Delta Sigma, Pomona
1957 Delta Tau, Ohio
1958 Delta Chi, Wake Forest
1958 Delta Phi, N.Y.U., Heights
1958 Delta Upsilon, Trinity (CT)
1959 Delta Psi, Concordia (IN)
1959 Epsilon Alpha, Thiel
1959 Epsilon Beta, Columbia
1960 Epsilon Gamma, Kentucky
1961 Epsilon Delta, Houston
1961 Epsilon Epsilon, Arizona
1961 Epsilon Eta, Muhlenberg
1961 Epsilon Zeta, Tulane
1962 Epsilon Iota, Brigham Young
1962 Epsilon Kappa, Delaware
1962 Epsilon Lambda, Southwest Texas
1962 Epsilon Mu, Hawaii
1962 Epsilon Nu, Georgetown Col.

1962　Epsilon Omicron, Mansfield
1962　Epsilon Theta, Brandeis
1962　Epsilon Xi, Texas Tech.
1962　Epsion Pi, Pitt
1963　Epsilon Rho, Western Washington
1963　Epsilon Sigma, Bowling Green
1963　Epsilon Tau, Memphis State
1964　Epsilon Upsilon, Western Kentucky
1964　Zeta Epsilon, California
1965　Epsilon Chi, Cal, Riverside
1965　Epsilon Phi, Emporia
1965　Epsilon Psi, Heidelberg
1965　Zeta Beta, Florida Presbyterian
1965　Zeta Delta, Ripon
1965　Zeta Gamma, Wyoming
1966　Zeta Eta, New Hampshire
1966　Zeta Iota, Bemidji
1966　Zeta Kappa, Lehigh
1966　Zeta Lambda, Illinois State Normal
1966　Zeta Mu, Duquesne
1966　Zeta Theta, San Diego State
1966　Zeta Zeta, Mississippi State

Delta Tau Kappa†

(SOCIAL SCIENCE)

DELTA TAU KAPPA, International Social Science Society, was formally established on April 19, 1961. The founders of the organization, eighteen in number, were either social science majors at the University of Bridgeport, or faculty members of the University. Under the supervision of Joseph S. Roucek, then chairman of the Sociology and Political Science Departments at the University, the organization laid down its general framework and pointed towards future objectives.

The membership is composed of those students who meet with the qualifications stipulated by the society. These qualifications include at least 3.20 QPR in the major field of study, as well as a minimum of twenty hours of credits in the field of social sciences. Nominations for membership are obtained through recommendation by the department chairman of each of the fields or areas which fall under the realm of the social sciences. Applications will then be subject to the approval of the executive committee; in some cases, the qualifications may be waived if the committee finds the individual deserving of this honor in all other aspects. The executive committee also approves nomination of election of outstanding scholars of other countries. Further, the executive committee has reserved the right to suspend any member of the organization who does not fulfill his obligation to the society.

The primary aim of the society is to promote the highest level of scholastic achievement and to further promote the aims of the Social Sciences. Parallel to this, is the hope that the society may assist in the fostering of interfaith, interracial, international and intercultural good will, not only on the university campus but on the community level and global level.

An annual meeting is held in the spring for the purpose of electing officers.

Membership　The chapters abroad, in Europe, Asia, and Japan, do not operate along the American formula. Each is represented by a social science scholar in England, Madrid, Barcelona, Padova, Singapore, Geneva, Berlin, Ghent, Syria, Tokyo, and Israel.

Active chapters 10. American chapter roll:††

1961　Alpha, Bridgeport
1962　Gamma, Inter-American
1964　Pearl Chidenbaram (India)
1964　Beta, Florida State
1964　Delta, Central State (OH)
1964　Mt. Sentinel, Montana
1965　Milwaukee Delta, Wisconsin, Milwaukee
1965　Tau, Wisconsin, Oshkosh
1966　Areta, Salem State (MA)
1967　Gamma Kappa, Georgian Court

Eta Mu Pi†

(RETAILING)

ETA MU PI, a recognition society for college men and women, was established at New York University School of Retailing in May, 1922. The society was founded by Robert Barnett, Herbert O. Bergdahl, Robert Jenista, and John W. Wingate; several others assisted. The purposes of the society are the promotion of ethics and science in retailing. Membership is based on high scholarship and on noteworthy performance in executive-training programs offered by stores in which students have obtained practical experience as an integral part of their college curriculum in preparation for a career in retailing. Only students in the upper 20 per cent of the class (10 per cent in some chapters) qualify for membership. Graduate students exclusively are eligible for the Alpha Chapter. Undergraduate students may become members of all other chapters.

Government　Authority of the organization is vested in an Executive Committee composed of the three national officers.

Insignia　The Greek letters comprising the name stand for Greek words meaning ETHICS, SCIENCE, and TRADE, respectively.

Headquarters　New York University School of Retailing, 24 Waverly Place, New York 3, New York.

Membership　Active chapters 12. Inactive chapters 2. Total number of initiates 2,050. Chapter roll:††

†† This chapter roll is repeated from the 19th edition; no current information was provided.
† This chapter narrative is repeated from the 19th edition; no current information was provided.

1922 Alpha, N.Y.U.
1939 Beta, N.Y.U.
1940 *Gamma, Florida* (1943)
1941 *Delta, San Jose* (1955)
1943 Epsilon, Long Island
1944 Zeta, Drexel Tech
1946 Eta, Washington (MO)
1947 Iota, CCNY
1947 Theta, Pitt
1948 Kappa, Buffalo
1949 Lambda, Marshall
1949 Mu, Oregon
1951 Nu, South Carolina
1960 Omicron, Rochester Tech

Eta Sigma Phi[†]

(CLASSICS)

ACTIVE PIN

ETA SIGMA PHI grew out of the local society Phi Sigma which was founded at the University of Chicago in 1914, became nationalized in 1924, and was incorporated in 1927 as the departmental classical society, Eta Sigma Phi. The purpose of the society is to further the spirit of cooperation and good will among members of classical departments, to stimulate interest in the study of the classics, and to increase knowledge of the art and literature of ancient Greece and Rome. Both men and women are eligible.

Government The government of the society is vested in the Executive Council, consisting of the national officers and the board of trustees (faculty members) in accordance with the constitution and the policies adopted at the annual conventions.

Traditions and Insignia The badge is an oval-shaped key of gold on which against a black background are superimposed a gold owl with ruby eyes, designed from the owl of an ancient Athenian coin, the letters ΗΣΦ, and the motto of the fraternity. The colors are gold and royal purple.

The fraternity conducts national contests annually among college students of Greek and Latin, makes available to high school teachers of Latin medals to award outstanding students in second- and fourth-year Latin and to alumni who are teaching or intend to teach Latin and/or Greek each summer, it grants two scholarships for study at the American School of Classical Studies at Athens, Greece, and the American Academy in Rome, Italy.

Publication The official journal, *Nuntius*, is published on November 15, January 15, March 15, and May 15.

Headquarters Birmingham-Southern College, Birmingham, Alabama 35204.

Membership Active chapters 72. Inactive chapters 35. Chapter roll:[††]

1924 *Alpha, Chicago*
1924 *Beta, Northwestern*
1925 *Delta, Franklin*
1925 Epsilon, Iowa
1925 Gamma, Ohio
1926 Eta, Florida State
1926 *Iota, Vermont*
1926 *Kappa, Colorado Col.*
1926 Lambda, Mississippi
1926 *Mu, Cincinnati*
1926 *Nu, Morningside*
1926 Theta, Indiana
1926 *Xi, Kansas*
1926 Zeta, Denison
1927 *Alpha Alpha, Winthrop*
1927 *Alpha Beta, Denver*
1927 *Alpha Gamma, Southern Methodist*
1927 *Chi, Coe*
1927 Omega, William and Mary
1927 *Omicron, Penn*
1927 *Phi, West Virginia*
1927 Pi, Birmingham-Southern
1927 *Rho, Drake*
1927 *Sigma, Miami (OH)*
1927 Tau, Kentucky
1927 Upsilon, Mississippi For Women
1928 Alpha Delta, Agnes Scott
1928 Alpha Epsilon, Lehigh
1928 *Alpha Eta, Michigan*
1928 *Alpha Iota, South Carolina*
1928 *Alpha Kappa, Illinois*
1928 *Alpha Lambda, Oklahoma*
1928 Alpha Mu, Missouri
1928 *Alpha Theta, Hunter*
1928 *Alpha Zeta, N.Y.U., Washington Square*
1928 Psi, Vanderbilt
1929 *Alpha Nu, Davidson*
1929 Alpha Omicron, Lawrence
1929 *Alpha Xi, Washington (MO)*
1931 Alpha Pi, Gettysburg
1932 Alpha Rho, Muhlenberg
1933 Alpha Sigma, Emory
1934 Alpha Tau, Ohio State
1934 Alpha Upsilon, Wooster
1935 Alpha Phi, Millsaps
1936 Alpha Chi, Tulane
1936 *Alpha Omega, L.S.U.*
1936 Alpha Psi, Washington and Jefferson
1938 Beta Alpha, South Dakota
1939 Beta Beta, Furman
1940 *Beta Delta, Tennessee*
1940 *Beta Epsilon, Brooklyn*

[†] This chapter narrative is repeated from the 19th edition; no current information was provided.

[††] This chapter roll is repeated from the 19th edition; no current information was provided.

1940 Beta Gamma, Richmond
1941 Beta Zeta, St. Louis
1942 *Beta Eta, Westminster (MO)*
1942 Beta Iota, Wake Forest
1942 Beta Theta, Hampden-Sydney
1949 Beta Kappa, Notre Dame (MD)
1949 Beta Lambda, Marymount
1950 Beta Mu, Butler
1950 Beta Nu, Mary Washington
1950 Beta Omicron, Mount Mary
1950 *Beta Pi, Arkansas*
1950 Beta Rho, Duke
1950 Beta Sigma, Marquette
1950 Beta Tau, Georgetown
1950 Beta Xi, Rosary
1951 Beta Chi, Loyola (MD)
1951 *Beta Phi, Adelphi*
1951 Beta Upsilon, Marshall
1952 *Beta Omega, Ball State*
1952 Beta Psi, Southwest, Memphis
1952 Gamma Alpha, Indiana State
1952 Gamma Beta, Bowling Green
1952 Gamma Delta, Yeshiva
1952 Gamma Epsilon, Wisconsin, Madison
1952 Gamma Gamma, Wisconsin, Milwaukee
1952 *Gamma Zeta, Albion*
1953 Gamma Eta, Louisiana Col.
1953 Gamma Theta, Georgetown Col.
1954 Gamma Iota, Wabash
1954 Gamma Kappa, Heidelberg
1954 Gamma Lambda, St. Mary's (MN)
1954 Gamma Mu, Westminster (PA)
1955 *Gamma Nu, Montclair*
1956 Gamma Omicron, Monmouth
1956 Gamma Xi, Howard
1957 *Gamma Pi, St. Peter's*
1958 Gamma Rho, Hope
1958 Gamma Sigma, Texas
1958 Gamma Tau, Mississippi Col.
1960 Gamma Chi, Lindenwood
1960 *Gamma Omega, Baylor*
1960 Gamma Phi, LeMoyne-Owen
1960 *Gamma Psi, Ursuline (KY)*
1960 Gamma Upsilon, Austin
1961 Delta Alpha, Randolph, Macon Woman's
1961 Delta Beta, Canisius
1962 Delta Gamma, Marywood
1963 Dellta Zeta, Colgate
1963 Delta Delta, Alberta
1963 Delta Epsilon, Belhaven
1964 Delta Eta, Seton Hill
1964 Delta Iota, St. Teresa
1964 Delta Kappa, Carroll
1964 Delta Lambda, Holy Cross
1964 Delta Theta, Dickinson
1965 Delta Mu, Illinois State Normal

Gamma Alpha[†]

(GRADUATE SCIENCE)

ACTIVE PIN

GAMMA ALPHA Graduate Scientific Fraternity for men is the outgrowth of two societies. In March, 1899, six students in the scientific departments of Cornell University organized the Society of Gamma Alpha with the object of bringing together men who were engaged in scientific work. In the fall of 1905 ten students at Johns Hopkins University organized a similar society named Alpha Delta Epsilon. In 1909 the two merged as the Gamma Alpha Graduate Scientific Fraternity. It is a nonsecret, nonprofit organization intended to unite and to promote good fellowship among men engaged in scientific work. The membership is open to men and to women as associate members specializing in the study of science and holding baccalaureate degrees from collegiate institutions of recognized standing. The fraternity is an affiliate of the American Association for the Advancement of Science.

Publication   *Gamma Alpha Record*, a quarterly journal, was established in 1908.

Headquarters   c/o Cornell Chapter, 116 Oak Avenue, Ithaca, New York 14850.

Membership   Active chapters 3. Inactive chapters 11. Total number of initiates 10,000. Chapter roll:[††]

1899 Cornell
1905 *Johns Hopkins*
1906 *Dartmouth* (1937)
1908 Chicago
1908 Illinois
1910 *Wisconsin, Madison*
1914 Michigan
1914 *Missouri*
1915 *Yale*
1916 *Minnesota*
1920 *Iowa*
1922 Ohio State
1923 *California*
1923 *Harvard*
1939 *Stanford* (1954)
1955 Cal, Davis

† This chapter narrative is repeated from the 19th edition; no current information was provided.
†† This chapter roll is repeated from the 19th edition; no current information was provided.

Gamma Sigma Epsilon

(CHEMISTRY)

GAMMA SIGMA EPSILON a recognition society in chemistry for men and women, was founded at Davidson College on December 19, 1919, by three students of chemistry: L. P. Good, Manley A. Siske, and M. R. Doubles. H. B. Arbuckle and O. J. Thies, Jr., of the chemistry department aided in the development of the constitution and ritual. It is designed to stimulate and encourage the study of chemistry among undergraduate students in colleges of recognized standing.

Government Government is by the National Council, composed of the national officers, executive president, executive recorder, executive treasurer, executive director of the archives, and executive president-elect. It administers affairs between biennial conventions.

Insignia The badge is a ten-sided shield near the top of which is an "x" ray radiating light; near the bottom is a chemical balance and across the center the Greek letters ΓΣΕ.

Headquarters Stetson University, Deland, Florida 32720.

Membership Active chapters 16. Inactive chapters 16. Total number of initiates 10,000. Chapter roll:

1919 *Alpha Alpha, Davidson* (1972)
1921 *Alpha Beta, North Carolina State* (1951)
1921 *Beta Alpha, Florida* (1965)
1923 *Delta Alpha, Auburn* (1933)
1923 *Gamma Alpha, Johns Hopkins* (1924)
1924 Delta Beta, Alabama
1926 *Alpha Gamma, Wake Forest* (1971)
1927 *Epsilon Alpha, Washington and Lee* (1931)
1929 *Zeta Alpha, Georgetown Col* (1968)
1930 *Eta Alpha, Battle Creek* (1968)
1932 Beta Beta, Stetson
1932 Iota Alpha, Tennessee, Chattanooga
1932 *Theta Alpha, Wyoming* (1965)
1933 *Kappa Alpha, St. Lawrence* (1965)
1935 Lambda Alpha, Mississippi for Women
1937 *Lambda Beta, Mississippi* (1957)
1938 *Mu Alpha, Brenau* (1960)
1939 *Beta Gamma, Florida State* (1952)
1940 Mu Beta, Georgia
1942 Mu Gamma, Mercer
1948 Epsilon Beta, Richmond
1953 *Kappa Beta, Adelphi* (1960)
1957 Nu Alpha, Ouachita Baptist
1961 *Xi Alpha, Sul Ross* (1961)
1965 Kappa Gamma, Clarkson
1965 Xi Beta, McMurry
1970 Xi Gamma, Angelo
1972 Xi Delta, Midwestern
1979 Kappa Delta, SUNY Col., Potsdam
1981 Epsilon Gamma, William and Mary
1981 Xi Epsilon, Stephen F. Austin
1983 Omicron Alpha, Eastern Illinois

Iota Lambda Sigma†

(INDUSTRIAL EDUCATION)

ACTIVE PIN

IOTA LAMBDA SIGMA was founded at the Pennsylvania State University, July 21, 1925, by a group of students preparing for positions in industrial education. The fraternity was primarily designed to bring such men closer together. An organization was effected, a constitution adopted, and a ritual developed, all of which were intended to advance the professional ideals of the group. After two years of successful operation the society was incorporated in Pennsylvania, September 2, 1927, as the Iota Lambda Sigma Fraternity, Alpha Chapter and Grand Chapter. In the meantime negotiations had been carried on with similar organizations in other institutions maintaining departments of industrial education. The fraternity became national in scope by chartering the Beta Chapter at University of Tennessee in 1929, and the first grand chapter meeting, or national convention, was held in 1930. The late F. Theodore Struck of Pennsylvania State was the first national president, followed by Professor Clyde H. Wilson of the University of Tennessee in 1931. Four additional chapters were chartered in 1930–31. Since then the organization has expanded until at the present time it numbers twenty-seven chapters in leading institutions offering specialized training in industrial education. Field chapters were authorized in 1945, and one of these has been established at Hampton, Virginia. The 1947 grand chapter passed a constitutional amendment permitting chapters 10 be chartered in any qualified institution in the Western Hemisphere. Although a field chapter was authorized in Brazil, making the fraternity international, it is no longer active. Constitutional revision has been broadened to include distributive, business, and technical education.

Traditions and Insignia The badge is a key, the shape of a keystone, bearing the letters ΙΛΣ and the symbols, a hammer, a rule, and a torch.

Headquarters Trade and Industrial Education Services Department, University of Cincinnati, Cincinnati, Ohio 45221.

Membership Active chapters 26. Inactive chapters 3. Chapter roll:††

† This chapter narrative is repeated from the 19th edition; no current information was provided.
†† This chapter roll is repeated from the 19th edition; no current infor-

1925 Alpha, Penn State
1929 Beta, Tennessee
1930 Delta, Kent
1930 Epsilon, Alabama
1930 Gamma, Clemson
1930 Zeta, Oklahoma State
1931 Eta, Colorado State
1934 Theta, Pitt
1935 *Iota, Millersville*
1939 Kappa, Florida State
1939 Lambda, Mississippi State
1940 Mu, Purdue
1940 Nu, Maryland
1941 Xi, Michigan
1946 Alpha Field, Hampton Inst.
1947 *Beta Field, Brazil*
1947 Omicron, Cincinnati
1949 Pi, Northwestern State College
1950 Rho, Illinois State Normal
1950 Sigma, Texas
1951 Tau, Georgia
1954 Upsilon, New Mexico Western
1955 Chi, Texas A & M
1955 Phi, Taiwan Teachers, Taipei, Taiwan, Formosa
1956 Psi, Southern Illinois
1958 *Omega, Southern Mississippi*
1962 Alpha Alpha, East Texas
1965 Alpha Beta, Southeast Missouri
1967 Alpha Gamma, Ohio State

Iota Tau Tau†

(LAW)

IOTA TAU TAU, international nonsectarian legal sorority, was founded November 11, 1925, at Southwestern University, Los Angeles, California. Its purpose is to create fellowship, encourage scholastic standing, and develop character. The membership is composed of students and graduates of law schools who are selected on a basis of good moral character and attainment of an average grade of B or above. The open motto is: *For the Advancement of Women in the Legal Profession.*

Government The biennial convention enacts rules for the government of the sorority in accordance with the constitution. An executive committee, composed of five members of the Supreme Council, executes all rules and manages the affairs of the sorority between conventions. Regional meetings are held annually under the supervision of the regional chancellor.

Traditions The official badge is diamond

shaped, with raised gold letters TT superimposed over the I. Colors are purple and gold. Official flowers are the yellow rose and purple violet.

Publications The official publication, *The Double Tau*, is issued every other year and is supplemented by bulletins from the supreme dean.

Funds and Philanthropies The sorority maintains the Westover Scholarship Foundation, which was established by Judge and Mrs. Myron Westover of Los Angeles, California. Loans are made to members of the sorority from the foundation funds to aid them to continue in law school during periods of financial stress. Four annual scholarship awards in the form of sorority keys are given to the members graduating from law school with the highest scholastic achievement determined by a scholarship committee. Each chapter usually rewards its honor students with a prize upon graduation.

Headquarters Office of International Supreme Dean, 1401 Benfield Road, Severna Park, Maryland 21146.

Membership Active chapters 30. Inactive chapters 4. Graduate/Alumni chapters 8. Total number of initiates 1,545. Chapter roll:††

Beta, Honorary—founders, past supreme deans
1925 Alpha, Southwestern, Los Angeles
1928 Delta, Chapter of Memory for deceased
1928 *Epsilon, Associate San Francisco Law (1940)*
1928 Gamma, San Francisco Law
1929 Eta, Indiana, Indianapolis
1929 Zeta, Cumberland-Howard (AL)
1930 Iota, St. John's (NY)
1930 *Theta, Chattanooga*
1931 Kappa, Los Angeles Law
1932 Lambda, Baltimore Law
1932 Mu, Atlanta Law (1942-1961)
1934 Nu, Pacific Coast, Los Angeles
1935 *Xi, National D.C.* (1954)
1936 Lambda Alpha Upsilon, Portia Law, Boston
1936 *Omicron, Omaha Law* (1942)
1943 Pi, Oklahoma City
1947 Rho, Philippines
1947 Sigma, Rome (Italy)
1952 Upsilon, USC
1956 Alpha Alpha, Mount Vernon (MD)
1956 Chi, John Marshall Law, Atlanta
1956 Omega, N.Y.U.
1956 Phi, Woodrow Wilson Law (GA)
1958 Alpha Gamma, UCLA
1961 Alpha Epsilon, McGeorge, Sacramento
1966 Alpha Eta, Beverly Law, Los Angeles
1966 Alpha Zeta, South Texas Law
1967 Alpha Theta, Orange Law

mation was provided.
† This chapter narrative is repeated from the 19th edition; no current information was provided.

†† This chapter roll is repeated from the 19th edition; no current information was provided.

Kappa Eta Kappa†

(ELECTRICAL ENGINEERING)

ACTIVE PIN

KAPPA ETA KAPPA, professional electrical engineering fraternity, was founded at the State University of Iowa, February 10, 1923, by C. J. Lapp, G. C. K. Johnson, Theodore Pals, H. K. Shore, and C. H. Smoke.

Government The national council includes national president, vice-president, and national secretary-treasurer.

Growth Chapters were initiated at other schools and just before World War II, the fraternity had chapters at: State University of Iowa, University of Minnesota, Kansas University, University of Wisconsin, Massachusetts Institute of Technology, Georgia Institute of Technology, and Kansas State College.

Only the chapters at the University of Minnesota, Kansas University, and the University of Wisconsin became active again after the war. One chapter has been initiated since that time, and it is at the Milwaukee School of Engineering.

Traditions and Insignia The badge is a jeweled rhomboid with a circle in the center containing the Greek letter H, one K of the name being placed above it and the other below.

Publications *The Electron* is published semiannually.

Membership Active chapters 4. Inactive chapters 4. Chapter roll:††

1923 *Alpha, Iowa*
1923 Beta, Minnesota
1923 Gamma, Kansas
1924 Delta, Wisconsin, Madison
1924 *Epsilon, M.I.T.*
1928 *Zeta, Georgia Tech*
1935 *Eta, Kansas State*
1957 Theta, M.S.O.E.

ACTIVE PIN

Kappa Pi†

(ART)

KAPPA PI was founded at the University of Kentucky in 1911 Membership is open to men and women alike and is based upon scholarship and demonstrated ability in the field of art. Either the completion of two years of courses in the art department with an average of 85 or higher, or the position of art editor on a college publication, earned by at least three years' work for the publication, may qualify for election to membership. Noted artists over the world are elected to honorary membership.

The purposes of the fraternity are to promote art interest among college students; to bring art departments of various colleges closer together through its activities; to stimulate higher scholarship; and to recognize potential and professional ability.

Traditions and Insignia The badge is palette-shaped, bordered in pearls and displaying the Greek letters ΚΠ. There is also a badge keypin. The recognition pin displays the coal of arms. The colors are purple and gold; the flower is the purple iris.

An annual traveling art exhibition and several contests are conducted for the chapters. A special service award is given to members who perform outstanding meritorious work for the fraternity or in various fields of artistic achievement. A $500 scholarship is given for high achievement.

Publication *The Sketch Book of Kappa Pi* is published annually in the spring and offers members the chance to see their art work and their written features in print.

Headquarters P.O. Box 7843, Midfield, Birmingham, Alabama 35228.

Membership Active chapters 160. Total number of initiates 50,000. Chapter roll:††

1926 Theta, Birmingham-Southern
1928 Iota, Iowa Wesleyan
1928 Kappa, Lindenwood
1928 Lambda, Oklahoma City
1932 Mu, New Mexico Western
1937 Nu, Fort Hays
1937 Omicron, Western Montana
1937 Pi, Georgia
1937 Xi, Alabama College

† This chapter narrative is repeated from the 19th edition; no current information was provided.
†† This chapter roll is repeated from the 19th edition; no current information was provided.

1938 Rho, Mississippi for Women
1938 Tau, Emporia
1938 Upsilon, Douglas, Rutgers
1939 Chi, Eastern Illinois
1939 Phi, Central State (OK)
1940 Alpha Alpha, Samford
1940 Omega, Indiana State
1940 Psi, Southern Illinois Normal
1941 Alpha Beta, Central Washington
1941 Alpha Delta, Arkansas
1941 Alpha Gamma, Northern Illinois
1942 Alpha Epsilon, Mary Hardin-Baylor
1942 Alpha Zeta, Joselyn Memorial Museum of
        Art
1944 Alpha Eta, Florida Southern
1944 Alpha Iota, DePauw
1944 Alpha Theta, Winthrop
1945 Alpha Kappa, Baylor
1945 Alpha Lambda, Sam Houston
1945 Alpha Mu, Minnesota, Duluth
1945 Alpha Nu, Albion
1946 Alpha Chi, Black Hills State
1946 Alpha Omicron, Georgetown Col.
1946 Alpha Phi, Fashion Academy (NY)
1946 Alpha Pi, Southwest Texas
1946 Alpha Rho, Brenau
1946 Alpha Sigma, Our Lady of the Lake
1946 Alpha Tau, Stetson
1946 Alpha Upsilon, Minnesota, Winona
1946 Alpha Xi, Kansas Wesleyan
1947 Alpha Alpha Alpha, Oregon College of
        Education
1947 Alpha Alpha Beta, Oklahoma Baptist
1947 Alpha Alpha Gamma, Akron Art Institute
1947 Alpha Omega, Wichita
1947 Alpha Psi, South Carolina
1948 Alpha Alpha Delta, Western State (CO)
1948 Alpha Alpha Epsilon, Southwestern (KS)
1948 Alpha Alpha Eta, USC
1948 Alpha Alpha Iota, Miami (FL)
1948 Alpha Alpha Kappa, Arkansas State
1948 Alpha Alpha Lambda, Southwestern State
        (OK)
1948 Alpha Alpha Theta, Tampa
1948 Alpha Alpha Zeta, Carthage
1949 Alpha Alpha Mu, Eastern Washington
1949 Alpha Alpha Nu, Texas Western
1949 Alpha Alpha Omicron, Eastern New Mexico
1949 Alpha Alpha Pi, Oregon State
1949 Alpha Alpha Rho, Southern Mississippi
1949 Alpha Alpha Xi, Phillips
1950 Alpha Alpha Chi, Murray State
1950 Alpha Alpha Phi, North Carolina
1950 Alpha Alpha Psi, Eastern Kentucky
1950 Alpha Alpha Sigma, New Mexico Highlands
1950 Alpha Alpha Tau, West Liberty
1950 Alpha Alpha Upsilon, Minnesota State, St.
        Cloud
1950 Beta Alpha, Baker
1951 Beta Beta, Nebraska State, Kearney
1951 Beta Delta, Alabama
1951 Beta Epsilon, North Texas

1951 Beta Eta, Marshall
1951 Beta Gamma, Southeast Missouri
1951 Beta Zeta, Heidelberg
1952 Beta Iota, Stephen F. Austin
1952 Beta Kappa, Queens (NY)
1952 Beta Theta, Nebraska State, Wayne
1954 Bea Lambda, Hofstra
1954 Beta Chi, Hardin-Simmons
1954 Beta Mu, Maryland State, Frostburg
1954 Beta Nu, Hunter
1954 Beta Omega, Seattle Pacific
1954 Beta Omicron, Lewis and Clark
1954 Beta Phi, Texas Wesleyan
1954 Beta Pi, West Texas
1954 Beta Psi, Concord
1954 Beta Rho, Northern Iowa
1954 Beta Sigma, Drew
1954 Beta Tau, Lamar
1954 Beta Upsilon, Harris-Stowe
1954 Beta Xi, Evansville
1954 Gamma Alpha, Northwest Missouri
1955 Gamma Epsilon, Houston
1958 Gamma Eta, Nebraska
1958 Gamma Iota, Eastern Oregon
1958 Gamma Theta, Montclair
1959 Gamma Beta, Fairmont
1959 Gamma Delta, Wisconsin, Eau Claire
1959 Gamma Kappa, Madison Col.
1959 Gamma Lambda, Abilene Christian
1959 Gamma Mu, Northwestern Louisiana
1959 Gamma Nu, Southwestern Louisiana
1959 Gamma Xi, Louisiana Col.
1959 Gamma Zeta, Hastings
1960 Gamma Gamma, Union (KY)
1960 Gamma Omicron, Centenary
1960 Gamma Pi, Western Kentucky
1960 Gamma Rho, Northwestern Oklahoma
1960 Gamma Sigma, Adelphi
1960 Gamma Tau, Los Angeles City Col.
1961 Delta Alpha, Northeast Louisiana
1961 Gamma Chi, Alaska Methodist, Anchorage
1961 Gamma Omega, West Virginia Wesleyan
1961 Gamma Phi, National Photographic
        Chapter, Mt. Pleasant, Iowa
1961 Gamma Psi, San Diego State
1961 Gamma Upsilon, Alaska
1962 Delta Beta, Mississippi Col
1962 Delta Delta, Western Illinois
1962 Delta Epsilon, Bridgeport
1962 Delta Gamma, Mankato
1962 Delta Zeta, SUNY Col., New Paltz
1963 Delta Eta, Northern Montana, Havre
1964 Delta Iota, Moorhead
1964 Delta Kappa, Philippines
1964 Delta Lambda, Delta State
1964 Delta Theta, Agricultural and Teachers,
        Greensboro
1965 Delta Mu, Florence State (AL)
1965 Delta Nu, Belhaven
1966 Delta Omicron, C. W. Post
1966 Delta Pi, Asheville Biltmore (NC)
1966 Delta Rho, Ottawa

1966   Delta Xi, Arkansas Tech
1967   Delta Chi, Cal State, Fullerton
1967   Delta Omega, Louisiana Tech
1967   Delta Phi, Mount St. Vincent (NY)
1967   Delta Psi, Waynesburg
1967   Delta Sigma, Keuka
1967   Delta Upsilon, Troy
1967   Epsilon Alpha, Baldwin-Wallace
1967   Epsilon Delta, Minot
1967   Epsilon Gamma, Middle Tennessee
1968   Epsilon Eta, Central Arkansas
1968   Epsilon Iota, Harding
1968   Epsilon Kappa, Montreat-Anderson (NC)
1968   Epsilon Lambda, Wyoming
1968   Epsilon Mu, Boise
1968   Epsilon Theta, McMurry
1968   Epsilon Xi, John F. Kennedy
1968   Epsilon Zeta, Dickinson State
1969   Epsilon Omicron, Lehman
1969   Epsilon Pi, Carson-Newman
1970   Epsilon Rho, Friends
1970   Epsilon Sigma, Ohio Northern
1972   Epsilon Tau, Alabama, Huntsville
1972   Epsilon Upsilon, St. Mary's (MD)
1974   Epsilon Chi, Bethany (WV)
1974   Epsilon Omega, Instituto Allende, San
        Miguel de Allende (Mexico)
1975   Epsilon Phi, Mississippi State
1976   Epsilon Psi, Mississippi
1976   Zeta Alpha, Austin
1976   Zeta Beta, Annhurst
1976   Zeta Gamma, Union (TN)

Lambda Delta Lambda[†]

(PHYSICAL SCIENCE)

ACTIVE PIN

LAMBDA DELTA LAMBDA, physical science fraternity for men and women, was organized at Fairmont State College, West Virginia, June 5. 1925, by H. F. Rogers, George L. Craig, Kenneth H. Whoolery, Kenneth Abbott, Herman Martin, Clarence Y. Ross, Robert Sloan, John F. Snodgrass, Clarence A. Brock, Dale Snodgrass, and Ross W. Meadows. Primarily it

is an honor organization, membership being conferred only after a student has completed a certain number of hours of chemistry or physics with honor grades. Charters are limited to colleges that are members of a recognized college association such as the American Association of Teachers Colleges or the North Central Association of Colleges and Secondary Schools.

Government   Government is by the Grand Council, composed of the national officers, president, vice-president, secretary-treasurer, and three directors. A national convention is held every year. Initiation and charter fees are collected by the national organization, but no annual dues are assessed.

Traditions and Insignia   The badge and key are in the shape of the benzene ring. Inside the ring is a washbottle. To the left of the bottle is the letter Λ above is the letter Δ; and on the right another letter Λ. Below is the date of founding, 1925. The colors are red, green, and blue-violet, the primary colors of the spectrum. The coat of arms is a shield at the top of which is the rising sun. Across the shield is a chevron bearing the letters $\Lambda\Delta\Lambda$. Above the chevron is a pair of balances; to the left of the balances is a graduated cylinder; and to the right of the balances, a Liebig condenser. Beneath the chevron is a washbottle. Beneath the shield is a scroll bearing the inscription Σοφία, Ἱστορία, Ἀλήθεια.

Publication   The magazine is *The Filter*.

Headquarters   Wayne State College, Wayne, Nebraska 68787.

Membership   Active chapters 13. Inactive chapters 3. Total number of initiates 5,506. Chapter roll:[††]

1925   Alpha, Fairmont
1930   Beta, Nebraska, Wayne
1931   *Delta Kappa, San Diego State* (1950)
1931   Epsilon, Nebraska, Kearney (1934-1941)
1931   Eta, Northwestern Louisiana
1931   Gamma, Western State (CO)
1931   Theta, Iowa State
1931   *Zeta, Arkansas State* (1937)
1932   Iota, Arizona State
1933   Kappa, Nebraska
1935   *Lambda, North Dakota State* (1940)
1936   Mu, Nebraska
1937   Nu, Kansas State
1940   Xi, North Dakota
1950   Omicron, Oklahoma State
1969   Rho, Mount Marty (SD)

[†] This chapter narrative is repeated from the 19th edition; no current information was provided.

[††] This chapter roll is repeated from the 19th edition; no current information was provided.

Lambda Tau†

(MEDICAL TECHNOLOGY)

ACTIVE PIN

LAMBDA TAU was established by a premedical technology group at the University of Oklahoma in 1942. A similar organization was established at the University of Tulsa in 1944. Each of these functioned alone until 1949; at that time, these two groups joined forces to form the nucleus of a national honor society for pre-medical technology students. The same year, Lambda Tau was incorporated in the state of Oklahoma. In 1953, the society was recognized by the American Society of Medical Technologists in convention as the authorized honor society in undergraduate schools.

The objectives of Lambda Tau are: (a) To develop a spirit of cooperation and unity among students entering any of the fields of medical laboratory technology, medical bacteriology, histology, parasitology and radiology; (b) To stimulate a higher type of ideal for scholastic effort, to encourage research, and to help develop the professional character of the work itself; (c) To interest other students in these fields; (d) To determine and make known the requirements of hospitals and other institutions offering training approved by the American Society of Clinical Pathologists.

Chapters may be established at any four year institution of higher learning which requires a curriculum approved by the American Society of Clinical Pathologists.

Membership consists of active, provisional, faculty, and honorary members. Active membership can be attained after one full year of prescribed course work (plus the required quality quotient). Provisional status is given after one full semester and a fulfillment of the above requirements. Faculty memberships and a limited number of honorary memberships are awarded.

Traditions and Insignia In 1967, the first annual Lambda Tau Awards were given to three members of the junior class of their respective institutions on the basis of outstanding achievements and service to the profession of medical technology. The official badge consists of a shield of gold overlaid with a black shield bearing a microscope and a balance and a gold diagonal bar bearing the Greek letters ΛT in black. The coat-of-arms consists of the same shield and a scroll beneath it bearing the motto of the society, the Greek words for Knowledge, Service, and Accuracy.

Publication The *Lambda Tau Newsletter* is published semiannually.

Headquarters Department of Biological Sciences, Southwestern Oklahoma State University, Weatherford, Oklahoma 73096.

Membership Active chapters 23. Inactive chapters 2. Total number of initiates 4,868. Chapter roll:††

1942	Alpha, Oklahoma
1944	Beta, Tulsa
1956	Gamma, Spring Hill
1961	Delta, Troy
1961	Epsilon, L.S.U.
1962	Eta, Auburn
1962	Iota, Lander
1962	Theta, Florida
1962	Zeta, Nebraska
1963	Kappa, Rhode Island
1963	Lambda, St. Mary's (NE)
1964	Mu, Quinnipiac
1965	Nu, Youngstown State
1966	Omicron, Huntingdon
1966	Xi, Rosary Hill (NY)
1967	Pi, Middle Tennessee
1967	Rho, St. Francis (IN)
1967	Sigma, Judson
1969	Tau, Southeastern Louisiana
1970	*Pi, East Carolina* (1974)
1970	Upsilon, South Dakota
1971	Chi, Mississippi for Women
1972	Psi, Kearney
1973	Omega, West Carolina
1974	Beta Alpha, Southwestern State (OK)
1975	Beta Gamma, Northeastern (OK)

Mu Beta Psi†

(MUSIC)

ACTIVE PIN

MU BETA PSI was founded at North Carolina State College, now North Carolina State University at Raleigh, on November 5, 1925, by a group of eleven college musicians who met with their director to discuss the formation of a music club. The director, P. W. Price, later decided that the club was sufficiently different from other existing groups to warrant forming a larger organization and the fraternity became national in 1929.

Although honorary by name, Mu Beta Psi is flexible in that it allows its chapters to tailor their governments and projects to fit the needs on the

† This chapter narrative is repeated from the 19th edition; no current information was provided.

†† This chapter roll is repeated from the 19th edition; no current information was provided.

various campuses. With this in mind, Mu Beta Psi has often been called "the service fraternity of music." Not only does the fraternity strive to fulfill its constitutional purposes of promoting music to its proper place as an educational subject and creating fellowship among musicians, but it also stimulates interest in music campus-wide by sponsoring open musical events at the member colleges.

Persons are eligible if they have served two years in a recognized collegiate musical organization, whether it be band, orchestra, glee club, or other. Pledges are usually admitted during the final weeks of their second year. In 1961 the membership was opened to women.

Government The fraternity is governed in the interim of conventions by the National Executive Committee, which is composed of the national officers and one member-at-large from each chapter. The national officers are elected at the conventions with the exception of the executive secretary, who serves indefinitely at the discretion of the fraternity.

Insignia The fraternity coat-of-arms consists of a badge surrounding a red field which is split into quadrants, each containing a musical instrument. This is surmounted by the traditional symbols of education: books of knowledge and the lamp of learning. A complete explanation of the coat-of-arms and its symbolism is given to all initiates. All members receive a golden key charm of the coat-of-arms. The jeweled pin is composed of a red enamel field in the shape of a rounded triangle with the letters MBΨ in the corners. This is surrounded by pearls and the chapter letter is attached with a chain. The pledge pin is the same as the field of the jeweled pin with no letters. The fraternity colors are red and white and the flower is the American Beauty Rose.

Publication *The Clef* is published semiannually for distribution to all members and to interested nonmembers. Minutes of the conventions, as well as other matters of interest, are included in the publication.

Headquarters 3401 Hickory Crest Drive, Marietta, Georgia 30064.

Membership Active chapters 5. Inactive chapters 2. Total number of initiates 1,752. Chapter roll:††

1925 Alpha, North Carolina State
1929 *Beta, Davidson* (1931)
1937 Delta, Clemson
1965 Epsilon, Washington and Lee
1967 Zeta, Michigan Tech
1970 *Eta, V.M.I.* (1971)
1973 Theta, St. Augustine's

National Block and Bridle†

(ANIMAL HUSBANDRY)

ACTIVE PIN

THE NATIONAL BLOCK AND BRIDLE CLUB, a professional fraternity in animal husbandry, was founded December 2, 1919, by student representatives of four animal husbandry clubs from the universities of Iowa, Kansas, Nebraska, and Missouri. The objectives of the fraternity are "to promote a higher scholastic standard among students of animal husbandry; to promote animal husbandry, especially all phases of student animal husbandry work in colleges and universities; and to bring about a closer relationship between students, faculty, and others engaged in animal husbandry."

Government Government is vested in the Executive Committee, consisting of the national president, the vice-president, secretary-treasurer and editor, elected by the annual convention.

Traditions and Insignia The badge consists of a large "B," with a meat block and cleaver in the upper half, and a bridle in the lower half. The colors are royal purple and navy blue. The flower is the lilac.

Publications The annual report published the first of each year contains reports of the national officers, of the annual convention, and of the college chapters.

Headquarters Animal Science Department, South Dakota State University, Brookings, South Dakota 57606.

Membership Active chapters 42. Inactive chapters 6. Total number of initiates 6,650. Chapter roll:††

1919 Iowa
1919 Kansas State
1919 Missouri
1919 Nebraska
1920 Oklahoma State
1920 West Virginia
1923 Kentucky
1924 Penn State
1928 *Washington State* (1956)
1930 Michigan State
1931 L.S.U.
1933 Texas Tech.

† This chapter narrative is repeated from the 19th edition; no current information was provided.
†† This chapter roll is repeated from the 19th edition; no current information was provided.

1935	V.P.I.
1937	Clemson
1937	Cornell
1937	Florida
1938	Connecticut
1938	Maryland
1938	Mississippi State
1938	New Mexico A & M
1946	South Dakota State
1946	Tennessee
1948	Rutgers
1949	Auburn
1950	*Cal Poly* (1955)
1950	*Utah State* (1953)
1951	Texas A & M
1954	Tennessee Tech.
1955	Illinois
1955	Louisiana Tech
1956	McNeese
1956	North Carolina State
1956	Purdue
1957	Cal State, Fresno
1957	Idaho
1959	Arkansas State
1959	Middle Tennessee
1959	Panhandle A & M
1959	Southern Illinois
1960	Georgia
1962	Oregon State
1964	Southern Illinois
1964	West Texas
1965	Delaware Valley
1965	Ohio State
1965	Western Illinois
1966	Abilene Christian
1967	Wisconsin, Madison

Phi Delta Gamma†

(GRADUATE)

ACTIVE PIN

PHI DELTA GAMMA, national fraternity for graduate women, was founded at the University of Maryland in January, 1923. It is the only Greek-letter fraternity whose membership is open to women of all professional interests who are pursuing graduate courses in the various fields of learning in colleges and universities.

The idea of organizing a fraternity for graduate women originated with Helen Gould Brooks, Catharine M. Koch, Elizabeth Miller, and Arbutus Stange, in the School of Commerce of the University of Maryland. Drawn together by mutual interests and ambitions growing out of their association in the School of Commerce, they organized a club known as the Women's Commerce Club in 1922. It soon became apparent that their ideals and aspirations were beyond the scope of their immediate circle, and the need of a more permanent and definite organization was keenly felt. They formed a new national organization. the chief aims of which, as expressed in the preamble of their constitution, were to "encourage a high standard of education for business women and to afford an opportunity for mutual helpfulness." In consequence, in January, 1923, the Women's Commerce Club became Alpha Chapter of Phi Delta Gamma.

Through the assistance of Dr. Frederick Juchhoff, a professor at both the University of Maryland and American University, contact was made with a number of graduate women at American University, Washington, D.C., with the result that Beta Chapter was installed by the officers of Alpha Chapter on June 24, 1923. The certificate of incorporation was filed in the office of the recorder of deeds in the District of Columbia on June 25, 1923, which day marks the beginning of the duly incorporated national organization.

The next step in the development of Phi Delta Gamma took place in August, 1924, when the constitution was amended to include professional women in other fields besides commerce. This was brought about because most of the graduate students of American University represented other professions and activities.

Because of a change in the status of the College of Commerce at the University of Maryland, Alpha Chapter could not find students eligible for membership. After consideration, the members decided to invite Beta to consolidate with them and to assume the name as well as the records of their chapter. Beta Chapter accepted, and on December 14, 1925, Alpha and Beta consolidated and became known as Alpha Chapter of American University. Phi Delta Gamma has since this time commemorated December 14 as Founders' Day of the Fraternity.

The purpose of Phi Delta Gamma is twofold: to promote the highest professional ideals among women of the graduate schools and to advance the social welfare and activities of women of the graduate schools. Chapters may be established only in colleges and universities of good standing where women are graduate students.

There are six classes of membership in the fraternity: active, life, associate, alumnae, inactive, and honorary.

Government The government of Phi Delta Gamma is vested in the National Council, the national executive committee, the national convention, and the national advisory committee, and such additional agencies as may be created by the national convention or the National Council. The National Council is composed of one representative

† This chapter narrative is repeated from the 19th edition; no current information was provided.

from each active chapter, the immediate past national president, the editor-in-chief of the *Phi Delta Gamma Journal*, and the national executive secretary. The last three named are non-voting members. The national executive committee is composed of the national president, the national vice-president, the national Secretary, and the national treasurer. The three non-voting members of National Council also sit with the national executive committee as non-voting members. The national advisory committee is composed of all past national presidents; its sole function is to advise the National Council.

Traditions and Insignia The badge is a monogram with the letter Φ jeweled or plain superimposed over the letters Δ and Γ. The letters Δ and Γ may be chased or in black enamel.

The colors of Phi Delta Gamma are gold, white, and black. The flower of the fraternity is the yellow rose.

Publications The official organ of the fraternity is the *Phi Delta Gamma Journal*, which is entirely professional in nature, carrying articles by members engaged in the various professions and fields of learning. *The Journal* is published annually. The *National Newsletter* is also published annually. Chapter newsletters are issued periodically by the individual chapters. The *National Directory* is published.

Funds and Philanthropies An Education and Service Fund and an Endowment Fund are maintained. From the former, a $500 study grant is made each biennium to a member who is participating in a planned program beyond the master's level. The Endowment Fund, from which only interest can be used for operating expenses in an emergency, is financed by allotment of a designated amount from each life membership fee and by endowments from members. At the National convention, which is held biennially a nonmonetary National Achievement Award is made to an out standing member selected from chapter nominations. This award is in recognition of professional excellence. A symbolic plaque is presented at a banquet honoring the award winner.

Headquarters 2752 North Lefeber Avenue, Wauwatosa, Wisconsin 53210.

Membership Active chapters 18. Inactive chapters 5. Graduate/Alumni chapters 3. Total number of initiates 5,100. Chapter roll:††

1923 Alpha, American
1927 Beta, George Washington
1928 Gamma, Johns Hopkins
1930 Delta, Ohio State
1931 *Epsilon, North Carolina* (1933)
1932 Eta, Wisconsin, Madison
1932 Theta, Western Reserve
1932 *Zeta, Columbia* (1954)
1933 Iota, Temple
1936 Kappa, Pitt

1940 *Lambda, Cornell* (1953)
1945 *Mu, Chicago* (1948)
1945 Nu, Omaha
1948 Xi, Marquette (1964)
1950 Omicron, USC
1951 Pi, Creighton
1953 Rho, Kansas State
1956 Sigma, Maryland
1960 Tau, Nebraska
1960 Upsilon, Maryland, Baltimore County
1961 Phi, Cal State, Long Beach
1967 Chi, Florida State
1967 Psi, Western Maryland

Phi Lambda Upsilon†

(CHEMISTRY)

ACTIVE PIN

PHI LAMBDA UPSILON, national college recognition society in chemistry for men, was founded as an honor society in March, 1899, at the University of Illinois. The founders—Horace C. Porter, Paul F. A. Rudnick, and Fred C. Koch, at that time seniors majoring in chemistry—were assisted by Profs. A. W. Palmer, H. S. Grindley, and S. W. Parr, who continued for many years to lend their support.

The aims and purposes are "the promotion of high scholarship and original investigation in all branches of pure and applied chemistry."

Growth The first seven years represent the founding, growth, and entrenchment of the Alpha Chapter at Illinois. The second period began in 1906, when Beta Chapter was established at the University of Wisconsin. Following Beta Chapter, five other chapters were chartered prior to June 29, 1911, the date of the Convention at Indianapolis, when the national society was organized. The third period, from 1911 on, has witnessed a continuous growth in the numbers of chapters, a steady increase in the number of members, and a gradual rise in the standards for membership.

The active membership is elected from among men graduate students, seniors, and juniors who are majoring in any branch of chemistry or chemical engineering. Honorary members are elected annually from among men of national or international reputation in pure or applied chemistry.

Government Government is by means of the Administrative Council, consisting of one councilor from each chapter, the six incumbent national officers (president, vice-president, secretary, treasurer, editor, and historian), and the two most

---

†† This chapter roll is repeated from the 19th edition; no current information was provided.

† This chapter narrative is repeated from the 19th edition; no current information was provided.

recent past national presidents. This body transacts all official business in the interim between national conventions. The convention is held triennially, with representation from each of the chapters, and functions as the deliberative and legislative body to determine policies of the society.

Traditions and Insignia The badge worn as a key is a hexagon, at the top of which are crossed retorts and a Liebig bulb. Across the center is a white band displaying the letters ΦΛΥ. Below this the letters στ appear as an abbreviation of the motto, *A Mark of Honor*. The letters on the outer band of the emblem compose the formula of an organic chemical compound. The colors are the red and blue shades of litmus.

Publication The biannual publication is called *The Register*.

Awards The society annually presents the Fresenius Award in Pure and Applied Chemistry to an outstanding chemist who has not yet reached his or her thirty-fifth birthday. Honorary membership, the highest honor the society can bestow, is awarded to persons of proven ability internationally recognized. The individual chapters offer various awards to undergraduate and graduate chemistry students who have made outstanding records in scholarship, in research, or in competitive chemistry examinations. Such awards include loving cups, medals, names engraved on plaques, chemistry reference books, and membership in the American Chemical Society. Further professional activity of the chapters includes the sponsorship of public lectures or lectures by visiting chemists of renown.

Headquarters 321 Saunders Laboratory, Department of Chemistry, Auburn University, Auburn, Alabama 36830.

Membership Active chapters 57. Total number of initiates 41,000. Chapter roll:††

1899	Alpha, Illinois
1906	Beta, Wisconsin, Madison
1909	Delta, Michigan
1909	Gamma, Columbia
1910	Epsilon, Washington
1910	Zeta, Minnesota
1911	Eta, Ohio State
1912	*Kappa, Denver*
1912	Theta, Iowa State
1913	Iota, Stanford
1914	Mu, Penn State
1917	Nu, Purdue
1920	Omicron, Illinois Tech
1920	Pi, Texas
1922	Rho, Nebraska
1922	Sigma, Rutgers
1924	Tau, West Virginia
1925	Upsilon, Iowa State
1926	Alpha Alpha, Rice

1926	Chi, Washington State
1926	Omega, Indiana
1926	Phi, Arizona
1926	Psi, USC
1927	Alpha Beta, Oregon State
1927	Alpha Gamma, Northwestern
1929	Alpha Delta, Oklahoma State
1931	Alpha Epsilon, Kansas State
1932	Alpha Eta, Johns Hopkins
1932	Alpha Zeta, Brooklyn Tech
1933	Alpha Iota, Auburn
1933	Alpha Theta, V.P.I.
1935	Alpha Kappa, UCLA
1935	Alpha Lambda, N.Y.U.
1937	Alpha Mu, L.S.U.
1938	Alpha Nu, R.P.I.
1939	Alpha Xi, Cincinnati
1942	Alpha Omicron, Michigan Tech
1944	Alpha Pi, Duke
1948	Alpha Rho, Kansas
1950	Alpha Sigma, Colorado
1951	*Alpha Chi, Georgia Tech* (1960)
1951	Alpha Phi, Connecticut
1951	Alpha Tau, Syracuse
1951	Alpha Upsilon, Penn
1952	Alpha Omega, Oklahoma
1952	Alpha Psi, Wayne State
1956	Beta Alpha, M.I.T.
1957	Beta Beta, Texas A & M
1959	Beta Gamma, Fordham
1962	Beta Delta, Louisville
1966	Beta Epsilon, Drexel Institute
1969	Beta Zeta, Worcester Tech
1970	Beta Eta, South Dakota State
1971	Beta Theta, Arizona State
1972	Beta Iota, Missouri
1975	Beta Kappa, Scranton
1976	Beta Lambda, North Carolina State
1917	Xi, Pitt

Phi Zeta†

(VETERINARY MEDICINE)

PHI ZETA was originated by a group of seniors of the class of 1925 in the New York State Veterinary College at Cornell University. The society was formally organized with the aid of a group of faculty members. Chief among the organizers was the dean of the college, Dr. Veranus A. Moore. Dean Moore was the first chapter president and when a national society was organized in 1929, he became the first national president. The first organizational meeting was held in Detroit, Mich., in 1929. Dr. V. A. Moore was elected president, Dr. L. A. Klein, vice-president, and Dr. W. A. Hagan, secretary-treasurer.

In 1929, a petition was granted to the School of Veterinary Medicine of the University of Pennsyl-

---

†† This chapter roll is repeated from the 19th edition; no current information was provided.

† This chapter narrative is repeated from the 19th edition; no current information was provided.

vania and the chapter was installed by President Moore as the Beta Chapter. In 1931, the national executive committee approved the petition of a group from Iowa State College and the Gamma Chapter was installed. Since 1931, eleven new chapters have been installed constituting fourteen chapters in all.

From its beginning, it has been the aim of Phi Zeta to stand for the constant advancement of the veterinary profession, for higher educational requirements, and for high scholarship. As stated in the national constitution, the object of the society shall be to recognize and promote scholarship and research in matters pertaining to the welfare and diseases of animals.

Membership consists of two classes, active and honorary. Those eligible as active members are: (a) Any graduate veterinarian who has been in the possession of his degree for at least two years and who is a member of the faculty or scientific staff of the institution where a chapter is located. (b) Any graduate veterinarian who is enrolled as a graduate student in an institution where a chapter is located and who has displayed ability of a high order in dealing with one or more phases of the science of Veterinary Medicine. (c) Any undergraduate student in a veterinary college where a chapter exists, who has completed two years and one term of his course of instruction and who possesses high ideals respecting professional service and conduct. If elected is junior year, he must rank in the upper 10 per cent of his class in scholarship. If elected in his senior year, he must rank in the upper 25 per cent of those in his class who are not already members of the society.

Those eligible to election an honorary members are: (a) Alumni of the institution where a chapter is located, who have been in the possession of the Veterinary degree for at least five years and who have rendered notable service to the profession. (b) Veterinarians or others not in possession of the veterinary degree, who have rendered distinguished service in the advancement of the science relating to animal industry and particularly of animal diseases.

Government The national officers call and preside at the annual meeting and issue certificates and insignia. In addition, they coordinate activities of the various chapters and are responsible for the establishment of new chapters in colleges of veterinary medicine. Meetings are held annually during the time and at the same place as the national convention of the American Veterinary Medical Association. All members of the society are urged to attend these meetings.

Traditions and Insignia The chapters recognize and encourage high scholarship and ethical standards in veterinary medicine. They recognize and honor men who have made outstanding contributions in the fields of welfare and diseases of animals. They sponsor scientific programs on local campuses for faculty, students, alumni, and the public.

The organizers of this society, when seeking a suitable name, sought the help of a learned Greek scholar, Professor George P. Bristol of Cornell University. Professor Bristol suggested a Greek word, which in the Latin form is spelled PHILOZOI which means "love for animals." The abbreviation Phi Zeta was adopted as the name.

The emblem consists of a pendant made up of the letter Φ superimposed upon the letter Z. The design was the work of Professor Louis Agassiz Feurtes, the great naturalist and artist.

Headquarters Comparative Toxicology Laboratory, Veterinary Medical Science Building, Kansas State University, Manhattan, Kansas 66506.

Membership Active chapters 19. Total number of initiates 9,300. Chapter roll:††

1925	Alpha, Cornell
1929	Beta, Penn
1931	Gamma, Iowa State
1934	Delta, Ohio State
1948	Epsilon, Auburn
1950	Eta, Texas A & M
1950	Theta, Colorado State
1950	Zeta, Michigan State
1952	Iota, Washington State
1952	Kappa, Minnesota
1953	Lambda, California
1953	Mu, Illinois
1958	Nu, Oklahoma State
1959	Xi, Georgia
1962	Omicron, Purdue
1965	Pi, Missouri
1967	Rho, Tuskegee Institute
1969	Sigma, Kansas State
1977	Tau, L.S.U.

Pi Alpha Xi†

(FLORICULTURE)

ACTIVE PIN

PI ALPHA XI, a society in the field of floriculture and ornamental horticulture for men and women, was founded at Cornell University in June, 1923. The object of the society is to promote high scholarship, to foster good fellowship among its members, to increase the efficiency of the profession, and to

†† This chapter roll is repeated from the 19th edition; no current information was provided.
† This chapter narrative is repeated from the 19th edition; no current information was provided.

establish corgial relations among its students, educators, and professional representatives.

The membership is composed of active, associate, alumni, and honorary members. Active members are undergraduate or graduate students and faculty specializing in floriculture and ornamental horticulture at an institution where there is a chapter. Associate members include those faculty members of departments other than floriculture and ornamental horticulture at an institution where there is a chapter, who are contributing to the advancement of floriculture and ornamental horticulture. Undergraduate members in good standing, upon withdrawal or graduation, automatically become alumni members. Alumni membership is also open to those who have been ineligible to active membership through causes other than scholarship, but who, after termination of their college work, display marked ability in achievement in the field. Honorary membership is confined to those persons who have rendered marked service in the advancement of the field of floriculture and ornamental horticulture, or who are engaged in teaching or research of benefit to floriculture and ornamental horticulture.

Regularly enrolled students of both sexes are eligible to membership if they are majoring or specializing in floriculture and ornamental horticulture, have an average grade of B or better for all credit hours taken in floriculture and ornamental horticulture, and have a minimum average not lower than the midpoint between B and C in courses other than those in floriculture and ornamental horticulture.

Government   The society holds a biennial national convention. National officers consist of president, vice-president, and a secretary-treasurer.

Traditions and Insignia   The badge of the society is a pin or key on which is inscribed the letters ΠΑΞ and contains a representation of an ancient stylus, an Egyptian hoe, Nymphaea caerulea or the Egyptian lotus, and an ancient vase. The official colors are lotus blue and nile green.

Publication   The official journal, *The Lotus Leaf*, is issued after every convention.

Headquarters   Cornell University.

Membership   Active chapters 8.   Total number of initiates 1,500.   Chapter roll:††

1923	Alpha, Cornell
1924	Beta, Illinois
1926	Gamma, Penn State
1929	Delta, Michigan State
1929	Epsilon, Ohio State
1933	Zeta, Rutgers
1949	Eta, Washington State
1949	Theta, Maryland
1967	Iota, V.P.I.

†† This chapter roll is repeated from the 19th edition; no current information was provided.

Pi Kappa Delta†

(FORENSICS)

ACTIVE PIN

PI KAPPA DELTA, national college recognition society for men and women in forensics, was developed from the plans of Prof. E. R. Nichols of Ripon College in cooperation with the following from the colleges named: E. A. Vaughan, Kansas State College; John A. Shields, Ottawa University; J. H. Krenmyre, Iowa Wesleyan College; C. J. Boddy, Kansas Wesleyan University; P. C. Sommerville, Illinois Wesleyan University; Arthur L. Crookham, Southwestern (Kansas) College; M. M. Maynard, Monmouth College; H. O. Pritchard, Cotner College; Dan C. Lockwood, College of Emporia; and Frank P. Johnson, Morningside College.

The purpose of the organization is to stimulate progress in and to further the interests of intercollegiate speech activities and communication in an effort to provide functional leadership training for life and at the same time encourage a spirit of fellowship, brotherly cooperation, and incentive for achievement.

Pi Kappa Delta recognizes as its special field those standard, regularly accredited colleges and universities in which forensic work of a high order is maintained. It has grown rapidly until it is now the largest of the forensic societies. Exceedingly cordial relations have been established with Delta Sigma Rho-Tau Kappa Alpha honor society. Under certain conditions members of any of these organizations are allowed to take out membership in one of the others.

Government   The society is governed by a national constitution adopted and amended by the national conventions. It provides for the National Council, which has general charge of affairs of the society. Conventions are held biennially in the odd-numbered years. In the even-numbered years a provincial convention is held in each of its ten provinces.

Traditions and Insignia   National and provincial tournaments in oratory, debating, extempore speaking, discussion, and other forms of public speaking are conducted at each of these conventions, those at its national conventions being the largest forensic tournaments held anywhere in the country. Seven volumes containing the winning debates, speeches, and orations for these tournaments have been published. They contain the winning

† This chapter narrative is repeated from the 19th edition; no current information was provided.

speeches for the national conventions held in the years 1926–38.

The badge is a pear-shaped key, displaying a trifoliate scroll, an eye, a circle, and the letters ΠΚΔ. The key is jeweled in such a way as to show the degree and the order which each member has earned.

Headquarters   Pacific Lutheran University, Tacoma, Washington 98447.

Membership   Active chapters 242. Total number of initiates 50,000. Chapter roll:††

1913	Kansas Alpha, Ottawa
1913	Kansas Beta, Washburn
1913	Nebraska Alpha, Nebraska Wesleyan
1913	Wisconsin Alpha, Ripon
1914	California Alpha, Redlands
1914	Illinois Alpha, Illinois Wesleyan
1914	Iowa Beta, Central College
1915	Colorado Alpha, Colorado State
1915	Illinois Beta, Eureka
1915	Kansas Delta, Southwestern (KS)
1915	South Dakota Alpha, South Dakota Wesleyan
1916	Oklahoma Alpha, Oklahoma State
1917	Kansas Zeta, Emporia
1918	Colorado Beta, Colorado State, Greeley
1918	Iowa Epsilon, Simpson
1918	Michigan Alpha, Kalamazoo
1918	South Dakota Beta, Huron
1919	Missouri Alpha, Westminster
1920	Illinois Gamma, Carthage
1920	Nebraska Delta, Hastings
1920	Nebraska Gamma, Doane
1920	South Dakota Delta, South Dakota State
1920	South Dakota Epsilon, Sioux Falls
1921	Illinois Delta, Bradley
1921	Indiana Alpha, Franklin
1921	Kansas Theta, Kansas State, Pittsburg
1921	Kentucky Alpha, Georgetown Col
1921	Minnesota Alpha, Macalester
1921	Missouri Gamma, Central
1921	Montana Beta, Montana State
1921	Ohio Alpha, Baldwin-Wallace
1921	Ohio Beta, Heidelberg
1921	South Dakota Zeta, Northern State
1922	California Delta, Pacific (CA)
1922	Illinois Zeta, Monmouth (IL)
1922	Iowa Eta, Upper Iowa
1922	Minnesota Beta, St. Olaf
1922	Missouri Delta, William Jewell
1922	Missouri Zeta, Culver-Stockton
1922	Ohio Delta, Akron
1922	Oklahoma Gamma, Oklahoma Baptist
1922	Tennessee Alpha, Maryville (TN)
1922	Washington Alpha, Puget Sound
1923	Arkansas Alpha, Henderson (1952-1962)
1923	California Epsilon, UCLA
1923	Illinois Eta, Illinois State Normal

1923	Iowa Theta, Coe
1923	Kansas Lambda, Sterling
1923	Minnesota Delta, Hamline
1923	Minnesota Gamma, Gustavus Adolphus
1923	Nebraska Zeta, Nebraska State, Kearney
1923	Ohio Epsilon, Otterbein
1924	Arkansas Beta, Ouachita Baptist
1924	Illinois Iota, North Central
1924	Iowa Iota, Westmar
1924	Iowa Kappa, Buena Vista (1934-1954)
1924	Kansas Nu, Fort Hays
1924	Missouri Eta, Central Missouri State
1924	Oregon Alpha, Linfield
1924	South Dakota Eta, Augustana (SD)
1924	Texas Delta, Howard Payne
1924	Texas Gamma, East Texas (1964-1966)
1924	Wisconsin Beta, Carroll
1925	Colorado Gamma, Western State (CO)
1925	Louisiana Alpha, Louisiana Col.
1925	Texas Epsilon, Mary Hardin-Baylor
1926	Iowa Mu, Drake
1926	Louisiana Beta, Centenary
1926	North Carolina Beta, Wake Forest
1926	Ohio Zeta, Marietta
1926	Texas Zeta, Texas Christian
1927	Idaho Alpha, College of Idaho
1927	Texas Eta, North Texas
1928	Texas Theta, Hardin-Simmons
1928	Wisconsin Gamma, Wisconsin, Oshkosh (1952-1957)
1930	Illinois Mu, Wheaton
1930	Louisiana Gamma, Southwestern Louisiana
1930	Missouri Theta, Northeast Missouri
1930	Ohio Eta, Bowling Green
1930	Oklahoma Eta, East Central State
1932	Illinois Nu, Western Illinois
1932	Missouri Iota, Southeast Missouri
1932	Missouri Kappa, Northwest Missouri (1958-1966)
1932	Oklahoma Theta, Southeastern Oklahoma
1932	Tennessee Gamma, East Tennessee
1934	Alabama Beta, Alabama College
1934	Arizona Alpha, Arizona State, Flagstaff (1962-1966)
1934	Illinois Pi, Northern Illinois
1934	Minnesota Eta, Concordia Col. (MN)
1934	Mississippi Beta, Mississippi State
1934	Oklahoma Iota, Central State (OK)
1934	Texas Lambda, Southwest Texas
1934	Texas Mu, Stephen F. Austin
1936	Arizona Beta, Arizona State
1936	Wisconsin Delta, Wisconsin, River Falls
1938	Florida Beta, Stetson
1938	Kansas Xi, Bethel (KS)
1938	Nebraska Eta, Nebraska State, Chadron
1940	Michigan Theta, Central Michigan
1940	Nebraska Theta, Omaha
1940	Tennessee Delta, Tennessee Tech.
1940	Tennessee Epsilon, Carson-Newman
1940	Washington Beta, Seattle Pacific
1942	Illinois Upsilon, Southern Illinois
1942	Kansas Omicron, McPherson

†† This chapter roll is repeated from the 19th edition; no current information was provided.

1942	Nebraska Iota, Nebraska State, Wayne
1943	Wisconsin Epsilon, Wisconsin, Whitewater
1944	Louisiana Delta, Louisiana Tech
1945	Missouri Nu, Drury
1947	Texas Nu, Texas A & I
1948	Illinois Phi, Illinois Col
1948	Mississippi Gamma, Mississippi For Women
1948	Missouri Xi, Rockhurst
1948	Nebraska Kappa, Midland (NE)
1948	Oregon Beta, Lewis and Clark
1949	California Eta, San Diego State
1949	Idaho Gamma, Idaho State
1949	Maine Beta, Maine
1949	Mississippi Delta, Southern Mississippi
1949	Oklahoma Kappa, Phillips
1949	Washington Epsilon, Pacific Lutheran
1950	North Carolina Epsilon, Appalachian
1950	Oklahoma Mu, Southwestern State (OK)
1950	West Virginia Beta, Marshall
1950	Wisconsin Zeta, Wisconsin, Madison
1951	Illinois Chi, Greenville
1951	Louisiana Epsilon, Northwestern Louisiana
1951	Washington Zeta, Western Washington
1952	Tennessee Zeta, Middle Tennessee
1952	Washington Eta, St. Martin's
1955	Louisiana Zeta, Southeastern Louisiana
1955	South Dakota Iota, South Dakota State
1955	Washington Theta, Whitman
1956	California Mu, Humboldt
1956	California Nu, Cal State, Fresno
1956	South Dakota Kappa, Southern State (SD)
1956	Tennessee Theta, David Lipscomb
1956	West Virginia Gamma, Morris Harvey
1957	Arkansas Zeta, Harding
1957	Montana Gamma, Eastern Montana
1958	Florida Beta, Stetson
1958	Idaho Delta, Northwest Nazarene
1958	Louisiana Eta, McNeese
1958	Mississippi Epsilon, Mississippi Col
1958	Missouri Kappa, Northwest Missouri
1959	Oklahoma Nu, Panhandle A & M
1960	Michigan Iota, Ferris
1960	Missouri Pi, Kansas City
1960	Montana Delta, Carroll
1960	Ohio Lambda, Dayton
1961	Arizona Gamma, Arizona
1961	Mississippi Zeta, Delta State
1961	Texas Chi, Midwestern
1961	Texas Psi, Texas Western
1962	Connecticut Beta, South Connecticut State, New Haven
1962	Illinois Omega, Olivet Nazarene
1962	Michigan Kappa, Northern Michigan
1962	Pennsylvania Delta, Bloomsburg
1962	Texas Omega, West Texas
1962	Virginia Beta, Old Dominion
1963	Colorado Epsilon, South Colorado State
1963	Illinois Alpha Alpha, Elmhurst
1963	Ohio Mu, Mount Union
1963	Wisconsin Eta, Wisconsin, Platteville
1964	California Rho, Cal Poly, Pomona
1964	New Mexico Alpha, New Mexico State
1964	Ohio Nu, Youngstown State
1964	Pennsylvania Eta, Clarion
1964	Pennsylvania Zeta, California (PA)
1964	Tennessee Iota, Tennessee Wesleyan
1964	Vermont Alpha, Norwich
1965	Arkansas Eta, Arkansas State, Conway
1965	Minnesota Kappa, Moorhead
1965	New York Alpha, Ithaca
1965	Texas Alpha Alpha, Texas A & M
1965	Wisconsin Iota, Wisconsin, Superior
1965	Wisconsin Kappa, Wisconsin, Stout
1966	California Tau, Cal State, Hayward
1966	California Upsilon, California
1966	Maryland Alpha, Towson
1966	Missouri Rho, Evangel
1966	New Mexico Beta, Eastern New Mexico
1966	New York Beta, SUNY Col., Geneseo
1966	Texas Alpha Beta, Texas Lutheran
1966	Texas Alpha Gamma, McMurry
1967	Illinois Alpha Gamma, Southern Illinois, Edwardsville
1967	North Dakota Delta, North Dakota State
1967	Ohio Xi, Ohio Northern
1967	Pennsylvania Theta, East Stroudsburg
1969	California Chi, Cal State, Stanislaus
1969	Iowa Pi, Northwestern (IA)
1969	Minnesota Mu, Southwest State (MN)
1969	Missouri Sigma, Southwest Baptist
1969	Montana Epsilon, Great Falls
1969	New York Delta, SUNY Col., Brockport
1969	North Dakota Epsilon, Mayville State
1969	Pennsylvania Iota, West Chester
1969	Pennsylvania Kappa, Lock Haven
1969	Texas Alpha Delta, Houston Baptist
1969	Washington Kappa, Eastern Washington
1969	Wisconsin Lambda, Wisconsin, La Crosse
1969	Wisconsin Mu, Wisconsin, Stevens Point
1971	Connecticut Gamma, Central Connecticut
1971	Georgia Delta, Georgia Southern
1971	Idaho Epsilon, Boise
1971	Louisiana Theta, Northeast Louisiana
1971	Maryland Beta, Frostburg
1971	Massachusetts Beta, Bridgewater State
1971	Michigan Mu, Adrian
1971	Minnesota Nu, Bethel (MN)
1971	Minnesota Xi, Winona
1971	New Jersey Alpha, Monmouth (NJ)
1971	New Jersey Beta, New Jersey Tech.
1971	Pennsylvania Lambda, Mansfield
1971	Tennessee Kappa, Tennessee State
1971	Texas Alpha Epsilon, Angelo
1973	Arkansas Theta, Arkansas
1973	Mississippi Eta, William Carey
1973	Montana Eta, Montana Mines
1973	Montana Zeta, Montana
1973	New York Epsilon, Plattsburgh State
1973	Ohio Rho, Rio Grande
1973	Ohio Sigma, Wright State
1973	Tennessee Lambda, Austin Peay
1973	West Virginia Delta, Shepherd
1974	New York Zeta, Hunter
1974	Tennessee Mu, Trevecca Nazarene

1975 New Jersey Gamma, Trenton
1975 Oklahoma Omicron, Cameron
1975 Pennsylvania Nu, Edinboro
1975 Pennsylvania Xi, Shippensburg
1975 Tennessee Nu, Fisk
1976 Alabama Delta, Troy
1976 Arkansas Iota, Arkansas
1976 Connecticut Delta, Coast Guard Academy
1976 Kansas Eta, St. Mary of the Plains
1976 Louisiana Iota, L.S.U.
1976 New York Pi, St. Francis (NY)
1976 New York Theta, St. Rose (NY)
1976 Pennsylvania Omicron, Wilkes College
1977 Missouri Tau, Missouri Western
1977 Pennsylvania Pi, York (PA)

Rho Epsilon[†]

(REAL ESTATE)

ACTIVE PIN

RHO EPSILON, national real estate recognition society, was founded on October 9, 1947, at the University of Southern California. The founders desired to promote the attainment of three major objectives: the advancement of the real estate calling to full professional status; the dissemination of real estate knowledge to the young men and women interested in real estate as a career, and the development of a scholarship fund for the training of instructors and professors of real estate.

The founders were a group of real estate majors who felt the need of a society which would give them as well as men of similar interests the opportunity of discussing problems and activities related to real estate with the help of practicing realtors who would lend experience, knowledge and dignity, and be the contact between the student and the business world. From an informal basis, the group took steps to organize and to adopt a Greek-letter name in 1951.

Government Government is by the Supreme Executive Board which consists of the supreme president, executive vice-president, supreme vice-president, supreme secretary, supreme treasurer, assistant treasurer, supreme editor, supreme historian, and immediate past supreme president. These officers are elected at the biennial national convention which is held on even years at the same time and place as the annual convention of the National Association of Real Estate Boards. The United States has been divided into thirteen districts. General supervision of active and alumni chapters within each district is exercised by its district director.

Traditions and Insignia The pin is a small shield with a rather wide gold border surrounding a green field. On this field are the English letters R E and crossed house keys in gold. On the pin the Greek letter P has been anglicized. The fraternity colors are green and gold.

Publication The official publication is *The Binder* which is published in October, February, and May.

Headquarters 822–15 Peachtree Street, Atlanta, Georgia 30303.

Membership Active chapters 9. Inactive chapters 4. Total number of initiates 1,260. Chapter roll:††

1947 USC
1953 Omaha
1953 *UCLA* (1957)
1959 *CCNY* (1960)
1959 *Florida* (1959)
1959 N.Y.U.
1960 American
1961 Georgia
1961 *Penn State*
1962 Southern Mississippi
1963 Tennessee
1964 San Jose
1965 Cal State, Los Angeles
1967 Colorado

Scabbard and Blade[†]

(MILITARY)

ACTIVE PIN

SCABBARD AND BLADE, a national military society for men, was founded at the University of Wisconsin in the fall of 1904 by Charles A. Taylor, Leo M. Cook, Victor R. Griggs, Harold K. Weld, and Albert W. Foster, senior officers in the cadet corps.

The organization is modeled upon that of the United States Army, the various chapters being designated "companies," organized into regiments in the order of their establishment. The national society is designated a division, composed of regiments, each containing twelve companies, except for the most recently created regiment which is not yet filled.

With a few exceptions, the life of the chapters has been continuous since the date of founding. During the period of the two World Wars, however,

†† This chapter roll is repeated from the 19th edition; no current information was provided.
† This chapter narrative is repeated from the 19th edition; no current information was provided.

the local chapters did not function, as practically the whole membership was in the military services.

The purpose of Scabbard and Blade is to raise the standard of military training in American colleges and universities, to unite in closer relationship their military departments, to encourage and foster the development of the essential qualities of good and efficient officers, and to promote intimacy and good fellowship among the cadet officers. In addition, the society attempts to hold before the college man his responsibility as the natural leader in times of national crisis and to promote preparedness for proper defense of the United States by disseminating accurate information among its members and others concerning the military needs of the nation.

The qualifications for membership are not based on scholarship alone, but also on those qualities of leadership, initiative, and character which cannot be expressed by a decimal point. With these basic requirements selection of members rests with the local company under such regulations and restrictions as it may adopt.

Members are classed as active, alumni, associate, and honorary. Active members are chosen from the cadet officers and other members of the advanced course in Army, Navy, and Air Force training. Associate members are chosen from active and retired commissioned officers of the United States Armed Forces, Reserve Components, and National Guard in Army, Navy, and Air Force. Certain authorities of the institution where a local unit is stationed are also eligible. Honorary members are chosen from those who have shown especial interest in the furthering of military science and national defense.

Government The government rests in a regular or special convention, held annually up to and including the convention of 1916, when it was made biennial. Companies are entitled to equal representation, and the national officers are delegates *ex officio*. In the interim between conventions the governing power is vested in the national officers.

Traditions and Insignia The badge is a representation, in gold of the American eagle bearing a shield, over whose breast are crossed two sheathed sabers. Upon one of the scabbards are placed five small jewels representing the five-pointed stars that appear in a similar position upon the coat of arms. The colors are red, white, and blue.

Scabbard and Blade traditionally honors its first honorary member, Col. Charles A. Curtis, U. S. Army, who was commandant of cadets at the University of Wisconsin at the time of the founding of the society, and to whose suggestions, wisdom, counsel, and support in its early days Scabbard and Blade owes a large measure of the success and growth which have marked its progress.

Publications *The Scabbard and Blade Journal,* the society's official publication, was first issued in October, 1913. It is issued quarterly during the school year.

Six general directories have been issued, one in December, 1913, the second in March, 1915, with a supplement thereto in May, 1916. The third was issued in October, 1921, and showed a total membership in all classes of 2,558. The fourth directory was published in January, 1927, and showed a total membership of 8,150. The fifth directory was published in February, 1932, showing a total membership of 16,834. The sixth directory, published in May, 1940, showed a total membership of 31,980 as of February 1, 1940. This directory was dedicated to the five founders and to Harris C. Mahin, who at the time of his death had served as a national officer continuously for twenty-three years.

Headquarters 308 First National Bank Building, Stillwater, Oklahoma 74074.

Membership Active companies 158. Inactive companies 29. Total number of initiates 108,796. List of companies (company letter follows year of establishment):††

FIRST REGIMENT:

1904 A, Wisconsin, Madison
1905 B, Minnesota
1906 C, Cornell
1906 *D, Iowa*
1908 E, Purdue
1909 F, Illinois
1911 G, Missouri
1912 H, Penn State
1914 I, Washington
1914 K, Michigan State
1914 L, Kansas State
1915 M, Ohio State

SECOND REGIMENT:

1915 A, Iowa State
1916 B, Arkansas
1916 C, West Virginia
1916 *D, Maine*
1916 E, Washington State
1920 F, Indiana
1920 G, Oregon State
1920 H, Florida
1920 I, Johns Hopkins
1920 K, Oklahoma State
1920 L, Georgia
1921 M, Georgia Tech

THIRD REGIMENT:

1921 *A, Coe*
1921 *B, North Dakota*
1921 *C, Nebraska*
1921 D, Oklahoma
1922 *E, Gettysburg*
1922 *F, Vermont*
1922 G, North Carolina State
1922 H, Lehigh
1922 *I, Maryland*

†† This chapter roll is repeated from the 19th edition; no current information was provided.

1922   K, *Northwestern*
1922   L, Penn
1922   M, North Dakota State

FOURTH REGIMENT:

1922   *A, Utah State*
1922   B, Syracuse
1922   *E, Montana*
1923   C, Cincinnati
1923   D, Kentucky
1923   F, Michigan
1923   G, Kansas
1923   H, Colorado State
1923   I, Tennessee
1923   K, Arizona
1923   *L, Emory*
1923   *M, California*

FIFTH REGIMENT:

1923   *A, DePauw*
1923   B, Davidson
1923   C, Rutgers
1923   D, Knox
1923   E, L.S.U.
1923   *F, Stanford*
1924   G, M.I.T.
1924   H, Washington
1924   I, South Dakota
1924   K, Alabama
1924   L, Auburn
1957   *M, Utah*

SIXTH REGIMENT:

1925   A, UCLA
1925   *B, Idaho*
1925   C, Akron
1925   *D, Montana State*
1926   E, N.Y.U.
1926   *F, New Hampshire*
1926   *G, Carnegie Tech*
1927   H, Rhode Island State
1927   I, South Dakota State
1928   K, Boston U
1928   L, Oregon
1928   M, Wofford

SEVENTH REGIMENT:

1928   A, Drexel Tech
1928   B, Mississippi State
1929   *C, Nevada*
1929   D, Pitt
1929   E, Wyoming
1930   F, Wichita
1932   G, Colorado Mines
1932   H, Lafayette
1932   I, Delaware
1933   K, Clemson

1938   L, V.P.I.
1938   M, Arkansas State

EIGHTH REGIMENT:

1939   A, Ohio
1940   B, Mississippi
1941   C, Duquesne
1941   D, San Francisco
1942   E, Tulane
1949   *F, Denver*
1949   G, Texas
1949   H, West Virginia State
1949   I, Hampton
1949   K, William and Mary
1949   L, North Carolina
1949   M, Kent

NINTH REGIMENT:

1949   A, Dayton
1950   B, Jacksonville State
1950   *C, Southern Methodist*
1950   D, Howard
1950   E, Toledo
1950   F, Virginia State
1950   G, Temple
1951   H, Mercer
1951   I, Georgetown
1951   L, Cal, Davis
1951   M, Cal, Santa Barbara

TENTH REGIMENT:

1951   A, Tulsa
1951   B, North Carolina A & T
1952   D, Stetson
1952   E, Connecticut
1952   F, Florida A & M
1952   G, Miami (FL)
1953   H, John Carroll
1953   I, CCNY
1953   K, Presbyterian
1953   L, Washington and Lee
1953   M, Vanderbilt
1955   *C, Wayne State*

ELEVENTH REGIMENT:

1953   A, Richmond
1953   B, St. Lawrence
1954   C, Western Kentucky
1954   D, Texas Tech
1954   E, Furman
1954   F, Georgia State
1954   G, Hofstra
1954   H, Northeastern
1954   I, Loyola
1954   K, Niagara
1954   L, Wake Forest
1955   M, East Tennessee State

TWELFTH REGIMENT:

1955   A, Santa Clara
1955   B, Kansas State, Pittsburg
1955   C, South Carolina State
1955   D, St. Peters
1955   E, Florida State
1955   F, South Dakota Mines
1956   G, Marquette
1956   H, Prairie View A & M
1956   I, North Georgia
1956   I, Pratt
1956   K, Marshall
1956   M, Texas, El Paso

THIRTEENTH REGIMENT:

1956   A, Murray State
1956   B, Northeast Louisiana
1956   C, Seattle
1956   *D, DePaul*
1956   E, Westminster
1956   F, Sam Houston
1956   *G, San Jose*
1956   H, Cal Poly
1956   I, Houston
1956   K, Brooklyn Tech
1957   L, Idaho State
1957   M, Central State

FOURTEENTH REGIMENT:

1957   A, Spring Hill
1958   B, Wisconsin, Milwaukee
1958   C, Colorado
1958   D, Gannon
1958   E, Ouachita Baptist
1959   F, Southern University A & M
1959   G, Lincoln
1959   H, Clarkson Tech
1959   I, McNeese
1959   K, Southern Mississippi
1960   L, Loyola
1960   M, Puerto Rico

FIFTEENTH REGIMENT:

1961   A, Midwestern
1961   B, Youngstown
1961   C, Tennessee Tech
1962   D, West Texas
1962   E, Arkansas Tech
1963   F, Panhandle A & M
1963   G, Henderson
1964   H, Tuskegee Institute
1964   I, Chattanooga
1964   K, Eastern Kentucky State
1964   L, Massachusetts
1964   M, N.Y.U., Washington Square

SIXTEENTH REGIMENT:

1965   A, Western Michigan
1965   B, Missouri, Rolla

1965   C, Eastern Michigan
1966   D, Worcester Tech
1966   E, Loyola, Chicago
1966   F, Ripon
1967   G, Seton Hall
1967   H, Tennessee, Martin

Sigma Delta Epsilon[†]

(GRADUATE SCIENCE)

ACTIVE PIN

SIGMA DELTA EPSILON was established at Cornell University on May 24, 1921, by a group of graduate women in science. At the Toronto meetings of the American Association for the Advancement of Science in December, 1921, representatives of Sigma Delta Epsilon met with members of a similarly formed group of women from the University of Wisconsin. It was agreed that these two clubs should unite, and thus was founded the national organization of Sigma Delta Epsilon, with Alpha Chapter at Cornell University and Beta Chapter at the University of Wisconsin. In April, 1922, this fraternity was incorporated under the statutes of New York. In 1975 the organization became Sigma Delta Epsilon, Graduate Women in Science, Inc., under the statutes of New York State.

The object of Sigma Delta Epsilon is to further interest in science, to provide an organization for the recognition of women in science. To be eligible for membership a woman must hold a degree from a recognized institution of learning and must be or have been engaged in scientific research. An elected membership-at-large was established in 1935 to make possible the inclusion of women who qualify in every way, but who have never been in attendance at an institution where membership in one of the local chapters was possible. The national honorary membership was established to show recognition of outstanding achievement in scientific research. Such a person is considered a member of the national organization and not of any particular chapter. She does not pay dues.

Sigma Delta Epsilon became an associate of the American Association for the Advancement of Science in 1936 and an affiliate in 1939. It became affiliated with the Federation of Organizations for Professional Women in 1972.

Government   The National Organization meets twice a year. One meeting is held with the American Association for the Advancement of Science; the other, the Grand Chater Meeting, is held with a

† This chapter narrative is repeated from the 19th edition; no current information was provided.

chapter. Chapters usually meet once a month from September through June. The Grand Chapter has jurisdiction over the affairs of the organization. The general executive government is vested in the National Council, which consists of the president, a vice-president, secretary, treasurer, past president, past treasurer, and such other officers as may be necessary from time to time.

Traditions and Insignia The badge is the Nile key bearing upon its crossbar the letters ΣΔΕ in black enamel. Superimposed upon the key is a benzene ring, a thunderbolt, and the nabla. The colors are those of the spectrum.

Publications The *SDE-GWIS Bulletin* and *Newsletter* are sent to all active members twice a year. A roster of members is prepared annually.

Funds and Philanthropies In 1926 Sigma Delta Epsilon established a trust fund to make possible the financing of a national research fellowship for graduate women in science. At the close of 1940 this fund had attained sufficient proportions so that the fellowship board was authorized to proceed with the awarding of the first fellowship for the spring of 1941, the year in which Sigma Delta Epsilon celebrated its twentieth anniversary.

Currently the national organization gives Sigma Delta Epsilon grants-in-aid and Eloise Gerry Fellowships to women in science who have demonstrated outstanding ability and promise in the mathematical, physical, or biological sciences.

Headquarters A national headquarters office was established in 1976 at 1346 Connecticut Avenue N.W., Washington, D.C. 20036.

Membership Active chapters 17. Inactive chapters 7. Total number of initiates 1,200. Chapter roll:††

1921 Alpha, Cornell
1922 Beta, Wisconsin, Madison
1924 *Delta, Missouri*
1924 Gamma, Illinois
1925 *Epsilon, Iowa State*
1925 *Eta, Chicago*
1927 Iota, Nebraska
1927 Theta, Ohio State
1928 Kappa, SUNY, New York
1929 *Lambda, Northwestern*
1933 *Mu, Syracuse*
1936 Nu, Penn State
1945 Xi, Minnesota
1948 Omicron, Washington, D.C.
1949 Pi, Purdue
1951 Rho, Philadelphia
1954 *Sigma, Michigan State*
1959 Tau, USC and Western Arizona
1959 Upsilon, Indiana
1968 Omega, At Large
1968 Phi, Kansas
1969 Chi, Chicago
1970 Lambda, California, Southwest U.S.
1976 Psi, Rochester

Sigma Delta Psi†

(ATHLETICS)

ACTIVE PIN

SIGMA DELTA PSI, national college recognition society in athletics for men, was organized in 1912 at Indiana University. In an address before the University Press Club, George Fitch, journalist and author, spoke of a national system of physical education he had seen in Sweden and expressed the hope that something similar might be developed in America. William Lowe Bryan, then president of the University, secured complete information from the Swedish government and asked Dr. Charles P. Hutchins, who was then director of physical education at the University, to use the Swedish rules as a basis for rules suitable to American universities. Dr. Hutchins consulted with Dr. L. J. Cooke at the University of Minnesota and Dr. W. G. Anderson of Yale University and they organized the society.

The purpose of the organization is the promotion of the total fitness of college students with emphasis on physical fitness. Students must obtain proficiency in fifteen tests to be admitted for active membership.

Insignia The emblem is a key displaying the letters ΣΔΨ.

Publication The official magazine is a newsletter issued three times each year.

Headquarters Department of University Recreation and Intramural Sports, Ohio State University, Columbus, Ohio 43210.

Membership Active chapters 169. Total number of initiates 4,522. Chapter roll:††

1912 Indiana
1912 Minnesota
1913 Springfield
1914 Yale
1916 Northwestern
1916 USC
1917 Ohio State
1918 Eastern Michigan
1918 Wisconsin, Madison
1920 Illinois
1921 Oberlin
1923 Vanderbilt
1925 Colgate
1925 Millikin
1925 Nebraska

† This chapter narrative is repeated from the 19th edition; no current information was provided.

†† This chapter roll is repeated from the 19th edition; no current information was provided.

1925	Oregon
1925	Western Reserve
1926	Occidental
1926	SUNY
1927	Arkansas
1927	William and Mary
1928	Colorado
1928	Indiana Central
1928	Juniata
1928	Knox
1928	Michigan
1928	Oklahoma
1928	Oregon State
1928	St. Olaf
1928	Tennessee
1928	Vermont
1928	Wabash
1928	Wayne State
1929	Purdue
1929	South Dakota State
1929	South Dakota
1930	Carleton
1930	Cincinnati
1930	Montana State
1931	Maryville
1931	Texas Christian
1932	Furman
1933	Allegheny
1933	Tulane
1933	West Texas
1934	Bowling Green
1934	Davidson
1934	Idaho
1934	L.S.U.
1935	Colorado Col
1935	Colorado Mines
1935	Colorado State, Greeley
1935	Hiram
1935	V.P.I.
1935	Virginia
1936	Alabama
1936	Arizona
1936	California
1936	Dubuque
1936	Florida
1936	Ithaca
1936	Michigan State
1936	New Mexico State
1936	Utah State
1936	Washington State
1937	Pacific (CA)
1938	Arizona State
1938	Hawaii
1938	Macalester
1941	Concordia
1946	Arkansas State
1946	Bradley
1946	Mississippi
1947	Branch Agricultural College
1947	Georgia Tech
1947	Mount Union
1947	Texas

1948	Alabama State
1948	Ball State
1948	Idaho State
1948	Muskingum
1948	Nevada
1949	Alaska
1949	Albion
1949	Miami (OH)
1949	St. Louis
1949	Wisconsin, La Crosse
1950	Cal State, Fresno
1950	Florida State
1950	Iowa
1950	Pitt
1950	San Diego State
1950	Washington and Lee
1950	Wofford
1951	Emory
1951	Wheaton
1953	Drake
1954	DePaul
1955	Massachusetts
1956	Baldwin-Wallace
1956	Louisville
1956	Wisconsin, Eau Claire
1957	Harding
1957	Los Angeles State
1957	Presbyterian
1957	Wake Forest
1958	Cal State, Chico
1958	Eastern New Mexico
1958	Morehouse
1958	North Carolina College
1959	Florida A & M
1959	George Peabody
1959	Lincoln University
1959	North Dakota
1959	Ohio Northern
1959	Pomona
1959	Tuskegee
1959	Virginia State
1959	West Virginia
1960	Citadel
1960	Grambling
1960	Morningside
1960	New Mexico Western
1960	Southern Mississippi
1961	Bethel
1961	Central Michigan
1961	Findlay
1961	Mankato
1961	New Mexico Mining
1963	Knoxville
1963	Southern Illinois
1964	North Arizona
1964	Phoenix Junior College
1964	Stanford
1965	East Carolina
1966	Cal State College
1966	Eastern Illinois
1966	M.I.T.
1966	San Joaquin Delta

1967 Ferris
1967 Florida Atlantic
1967 Long Beach City College
1967 Middle Tennessee
1967 Milligan
1967 Montana
1967 San Francisco State
1967 Southwest Missouri
1968 Brigham Young
1968 Duke
1968 Northern Illinois
1968 Southern Connecticut
1968 Texas A & M
1969 Miami (FL)
1969 Tennessee Tech.
1969 Washington and Jefferson
1970 East Texas
1970 Portland State
1970 South Dakota State
1970 Wisconsin, Parkside
1971 Gainesville Junior College
1971 Georgia Southern
1972 Manhattan
1972 Northern Michigan
1972 Purdue, Calumet
1973 Ricks
1973 U.S. Military Academy
1976 North Carolina
1976 Richmond

Sigma Iota Epsilon†

(MANAGEMENT)

ACTIVE PIN

SIGMA IOTA EPSILON, national college recognition society for management students of both sexes, was founded in January, 1927, at the University of Illinois. It was established through the merger of three local industrial management and management fraternities sponsored respectively by Prof. A. G. Anderson at Illinois, Prof. Maurice C. Cross at Syracuse University and Prof. Chester F. Lay at the University of Texas. Membership is conferred only after a student, graduate or undergraduate, man or woman, has completed a certain number of hours and courses in management with honor grades. Charters are limited to accredited institutions that maintain an organized management program and with an enrollment adequate to support a local chapter.

Government Government is by a national office, composed of the national officers, president and secretary, and an executive board of three past national presidents. Initiation and charter fees are collected by the international organization, but no annual dues are assessed.

Traditions and Insignia The badge is a gold key of conventional design, uncut and rectangular in shape. The letters, Σ, I, and E are arranged diagonally from upper left to lower right. In the upper right is a replica of the old Slater Textile Mill, the first factory built in the United States at Pawtucket, R.I., and symbolic of factory production where science was first applied to the work of management. In the lower left is a representation of the functional organization developed by Frederick W. Taylor, and symbolic of managerial techniques.

Publication The magazine is *The Manager's Key*, which is published semiannually in rotation by the individual chapters.

Headquarters College of Business, Florida State University, Tallahassee, Florida 32306.

Membership Active chapters 33. Inactive chapters 7. Total number of initiates 7,500. Chapter roll:††

1927 Alpha, Illinois
1927 *Beta, Syracuse*
1927 Gamma, Texas
1929 *Delta, Northwestern* (1960)
1946 *Epsilon, Illinois Tech*
1949 *Zeta, Louisiana Tech* (1960)
1951 Eta, Texas Tech
1951 Theta, Southern Methodist
1952 Iota, Tennessee Tech
1955 Kappa, Indiana
1957 Lambda, Houston
1958 Mu, Colorado
1959 Nu, Wayne State
1961 *Xi, Cincinnati*
1962 Omicron, Tulsa
1963 Pi, Arizona State
1963 Rho, Northern Illinois
1966 *Sigma, Iowa*
1966 Tau, San Diego State
1967 Upsilon, Denver
1968 *Chi, Georgia State*
1968 Phi, North Texas
1968 Psi, Trinity (TX)
1968 Sigma Alpha, Florida State
1969 Omega, Western Michigan
1969 Sigma Beta, Air Force Inst.
1970 Sigma Delta, Arkansas
1970 Sigma Gamma, Michigan State
1971 Sigma Epsilon, Central Michigan
1971 Sigma Eta, Texas A & M
1971 Sigma Iota, Western Illinois
1971 Sigma Zeta, Dallas
1972 Sigma Kappa, Baylor
1973 Sigma Lambda, U.S. Naval Academy
1973 Sigma Theta, Georgia

† This chapter narrative is repeated from the 19th edition; no current information was provided.

†† This chapter roll is repeated from the 19th edition; no current information was provided.

1975 Sigma Mu, Georgia Tech
1975 Sigma Nu, Rider College
1976 Sigma Omicron, Cal State, Fresno
1976 Sigma Rho, Florida Tech
1976 Sigma Xi, Wisconsin, Whitewater

Sigma Mu Sigma[†]

(GENERAL)

SIGMA MU SIGMA, general recognition fraternity
for men, is the outgrowth of a social fraternity of
that name which was established at Tri-State College, Angola, Indiana, on Good Friday, 1921, by
three Knights Templar and nine Master Masons.
Square and Compass, originated as a club of Master
Masons at Washington and Lee University in 1897.
These two organizations merged on August 3, 1952,
after separate careers of some distinction.

Within five years of its establishment, Sigma Mu
Sigma had established nine chapters, initiated
nearly 1,000 members, and was admitted to junior
membership in the National Interfraternity Conference. When eight of these chapters were absorbed
by Tau Kappa Epsilon in 1934, Alpha at Tri-State
returned to local status. Square and Compass, incorporated in the state of Virginia on May 12, 1917,
established 57 chapters in 11 years and initiated
5,000 men. In December, 1950, a convention held in
Richmond adopted the name Square and Compass-
Sigma Alpha Chi.

Although both fraternities originally limited
membership to Master Masons, Sigma Mu Sigma
since the merger has enrolled men of good moral
character, including those belonging to other fraternities. The purpose of the fraternity is to foster the
indoctrination of the college men of America with
the traditions of their American heritage.

Headquarters   2724 Greenhill Lane, Lynchburg,
Virginia 24503.

Membership   Active chapters 3. Inactive chapters 13. Total number of initiates 6,700. Chapter
roll:[††]

1921 *Alpha, Tri-State* (1966)
1924 *Beta, Oklahoma* (1934)
1925 *Delta, Milwaukee Engineering*
1925 *Epsilon, George Washington* (1934)
1925 *Eta, Illinois* (1934)
1925 *Gamma* (charter withdrawn)
1925 *Zeta, Purdue* (1934)
1926 *Theta, Oklahoma State* (1934)
1929 *Iota, Michigan State* (1934)
1950 *Lambada, Elon* (1969)
1951 *Mu, Virginia Medical*

† This chapter narrative is repeated from the 19th edition; no current
information was provided.
†† This chapter roll is repeated from the 19th edition; no current information was provided.

1952 *Nu, Chase Law*
1953 *Omicron, Louisville*
1953 *Xi, Joliet Junior College*
1955 *Pi, N.Y.U.*
1955 Rho, V.P.I.
1962 Sigma, Lynchburg
1967 Tau, Brandywine (DE)

Sigma Phi Alpha[†]

(DENTAL HYGIENE)

ACTIVE PIN

SIGMA PHI ALPHA, national recognition society
for women in dental hygiene, was founded in 1958
at Northwestern University. Plans for the society
were first formulated on March 25 of that year at
the business meeting of the Dental Hygiene Education section of the American Association of Dental
Schools in Detroit. All chapters are in schools of
dental hygiene. The purpose of the Society is to
promote, recognize, and honor scholarship, service,
and character among students and graduates of
oral/dental hygiene.

Classes of members include charter, faculty,
alumnae, and transfer; there is also an honorary
class. Charter members are the faculty members
who founded the chapter. Faculty members are the
instructors in a school which has a program for the
education of dental/oral hygienists who are elected
to membership after three years of fulltime or five
years of part-time teaching. Alumnae members are
the senior dental/oral hygiene students who are
elected to membership who rank highest in scholarship and character and who exhibit potential
qualities for future growth and attainment as recommended by faculty members. The membership is
limited to 10 per cent of the graduated class and
selected from a list composed of the upper 20 per
cent of the class.

Government   The business affairs of the Supreme Chapter are conducted annually by the executive council and delegates and alternates of each
chapter at the time of the annual meeting of the
American Association of Dental Schools. The officers who constitute the council are president,
president-elect, vice-president, and secretary-treasurer.

Insignia   The emblem of the society is a keypin
of simple rectangular design displaying the Greek
letters ΣΦΑ in diagonal arrangement from upper
left to lower right.

Headquarters   250 Lake Boulevard, Buffalo
Grove, Illinois 60000.

Membership   Active chapters 67. Total number of initiates 3,452. Chapter roll:††

1958	Alpha, Northwestern
1958	Beta, Baylor
1958	Delta, West Liberty
1958	Epsilon, Iowa
1958	Eta, Minnesota
1958	Gamma, Bridgeport
1958	Kappa, Temple
1958	Sigma, Washington
1958	Theta, Indiana
1958	Zeta, Ohio State
1959	Iota, Penn
1959	Lambda, Columbia
1959	Mu, Howard
1959	Nu, Michigan
1959	Xi, North Carolina
1960	Omicron, Meharry Medical
1960	Pi, Forsyth School for Dental Hygienists
1960	Rho, College of Dentistry, Memphis
1960	Tau, Marquette
1960	*Upsilon, Broome Technical*
1961	Chi, Loyola, New Orleans
1961	Phi, Vermont
1962	Alpha Alpha, Loma Linda
1962	Omega, Detroit
1962	Psi, Fairleigh Dickinson
1963	Alpha Beta, Westbrook Junior College
1963	Alpha Delta, New York City Community College
1963	Alpha Gamma, Kansas City
1964	Alpha Epsilon, Texas
1965	Alpha Eta, Pensacola Junior College
1965	*Alpha Theta, Louisville*
1965	Alpha Zeta, Rangely
1966	Alpha Iota, IUPU, Fort Wayne
1967	Alpha Kappa, Hawaii
1967	Alpha Lambda, Nebraska
1967	*Alpha Mu, State University A & T*
1967	Alpha Nu, Ferris
1967	Alpha Xi, West Virginia
1968	*Alpha Omicron, Diablo Valley*
1968	Alpha Pi, Palm Beach Junior
1968	Alpha Rho, Midlands Technical
1969	Alpha Phi, Old Dominion
1969	Alpha Sigma, Southern Illinois
1969	*Alpha Tau, Kentucky*
1969	Alpha Upsilon, St. Petersburg Junior
1970	Alpha Chi, South Dakota
1971	Alpha Alpha Alpha, Greenville Tech
1971	*Alpha Alpha Beta, Los Angeles City Col.*
1971	Alpha Alpha Gamma, Virginia Commonwealth
1971	Alpha Omega, William Rainey Harper
1971	Alpha Psi, Arkansas
1972	*Alpha Alpha Delta, Forest Park Community*
1972	Alpha Alpha Epsilon, Loyola, Maywood
1973	Alpha Alpha Eta, Maryland

1973	Alpha Alpha Theta, Wichita
1973	Alpha Alpha Zeta, Cincinnati
1974	Alpha Alpha Iota, Lakeland
1974	Alpha Alpha Kappa, Del Mar College
1974	Alpha Alpha Lambda, Baltimore Community
1974	Alpha Alpha Mu, Eastern Washington State
1974	Alpha Alpha Nu, Foothill Community
1975	Alpha Alpha Chi, L.S.U.
1975	Alpha Alpha Omicron, Indiana, South Bend
1975	Alpha Alpha Phi, Onondaga Community
1975	Alpha Alpha Pi, Normandale Community
1975	Alpha Alpha Psi, Northampton County Community
1975	Alpha Alpha Rho, Texas Woman's
1975	Alpha Alpha Sigma, New Hampshire Tech
1975	Alpha Alpha Tau, Albany Junior
1975	Alpha Alpha Upsilon, Minnesota, Duluth
1975	Alpha Alpha Xi, Clayton Junior
1976	Alpha Alpha Alpha Alpha, Tyler Junior
1976	Alpha Alpha Alpha Beta, Bristol Community
1976	Alpha Alpha Alpha Gamma, Parkland
1976	Alpha Alpha Omega, Prairie State

Sigma Zeta†

(SCIENCE AND MATHEMATICS)

ACTIVE PIN

SIGMA ZETA, men's and women's recognition society in science and mathematics, was founded at Shurtleff College, Alton, Illinois, in 1925. Profs. Elmer E. List of the biology department, J. Ellis Powell of the mathematics department, and Ralph K. Carleton of the chemistry department met with a group of ten undergraduate students who were majoring in mathematics or one of the sciences. On October 1, 1925, the name Sigma Zeta was selected, a preliminary draft of a constitution prepared, and an initiation ceremony outlined. In the spring of the following year Beta Chapter at McKendree College was formed and that June the first conclave of Sigma Zeta was held.

The society exists for the two-fold purpose of giving recognition of high scholarship to worthy undergraduate students of the sciences and mathematics, and the fostering of the continuation of knowledge of and interest in these several areas. Steady growth in the number of chapters has been experienced, with considerable autonomy of program given to the various chapters.

Two classes of membership exist. Active member-

†† This chapter roll is repeated from the 19th edition; no current information was provided.

† This chapter narrative is repeated from the 19th edition; no current information was provided.

ship is granted to those students of junior and senior rank who meet the scholastic and other qualifications of the society. Faculty members may also be elected to this class of membership. Persons of distinction in the sciences or mathematics may be elected to honorary membership.

Government Government is vested in the National Chapter, consisting of the national officers and the accredited delegates to the annual convention. In the interim between conventions the National Council, consisting of the elected national officers, conducts affairs. A convention has been held annually since the founding except during the war years.

Traditions and Insignia The badge is a gold key in the form of an opened book, with the letters Σ and Z in relief above other symbols of scientific significance.

The three founders of Sigma Zeta presented to the society in 1947 the Founders Cup. This cup is awarded at the annual convention to that chapter which has best represented the society through student papers presented to the convention and achievements on the home campus. The cup is held by the winning chapter for one year.

An Honor Award is granted by the National Council each year to not more than one person from each chapter who meets certain qualifications of scientific aptitude and achievement.

Publication *The Sigma Zetan* is published annually for distribution to all members. It includes minutes of the annual convention and of meetings of the National Council, summaries of student papers presented at the convention, and other matters of interest to members.

Funds and Philanthropies The Sigma Zeta Development Fund was established in 1954 to foster and promote the growth and development of the Society. This fund has grown from contributions in the form of gifts from interested members, and other sources.

Headquarters Anderson College, Anderson, Indiana 46011.

Membership Active chapters 43. Inactive chapters 6. Total number of initiates 13,169. Chapter roll:††

1925 *Alpha, Shurtleff* (1958)
1926 Beta, McKendree
1927 Delta, Northeast Missouri
1927 Gamma, Virginia Medical
1929 Epsilon, Otterbein
1929 Zeta, Wisconsin, Stevens Point
1932 *Eta, Southeast Missouri* (1939)
1932 *Theta, Elizabethtown* (1942)
1935 Kappa, Western Illinois
1936 Lambda, Mansfield
1937 Mu, Mankato
1937 *Mu, Northern Illinois* (1972)

1938 Xi, Ball State
1939 *Omicron, Wilson Teachers* (1942)
1943 Pi, Millikin
1943 Rho, Indiana Central
1943 Sigma, Our Lady of the Lake
1947 Tau, East Stroudsburg
1948 Phi, Eureka
1948 Upsilon, Anderson
1951 Chi, Missouri Valley (1952-1967)
1956 Psi, Central Missouri State
1961 *Alpha Alpha, SUNY Col., Oswego* (1965)
1961 Omega, Maryland, Frostburg
1963 Alpha Beta, Campbellsville (KY)
1969 Alpha Delta, Kansas Newman (KS)
1969 Alpha Epsilon, Marian (IN)
1969 Alpha Gamma, Malone College (OH)
1969 Alpha Zeta, Indiana State
1969 Alpha Zeta, Olivet
1970 Alpha Iota, Wisconsin, La Crosse
1970 Alpha Kappa, Indiana, Evansville
1970 Alpha Lambda, Suffolk
1970 Alpha Theta, Asbury
1970 Anne Arundel Associate Chapter, Anne Arundel Community (MD)
1970 Illinois Central Associate Chapter, Illinois Central
1971 Alha Nu, Oglethorpe
1971 Alpha Mu, Immaculate
1971 Alpha Omicron, Baptist, Charleston
1971 Alpha Xi, Clinch Valley
1972 Alpha Pi, Trevecca Nazarene (TN)
1972 Alpha Rho, Stonehill
1972 Alpha Sigma, Dakota Wesleyan
1973 Alpha Tau, Annhurst
1975 Alpha Phi, Marist (TN)
1975 Alpha Upsilon, Union
1976 Alpha Omega, St. Mary-of-the-Woods
1976 Alpha Chi, Eastern
1976 Alpha Psi, Hillsdale

Society for Collegiate Journalists

Pi Delta Epsilon-Alpha Phi Gamma†

(JOURNALISM)

SOCIETY FOR COLLEGIATE JOURNALISTS, national college recognition society in journalism for men and women, was created in September, 1975, upon the merger of Pi Delta Epsilon and Alpha Phi Gamma, two similar organizations. The history of these two groups is the history of the Society.

†† This chapter roll is repeated from the 19th edition; no current information was provided.

† This chapter narrative is repeated from the 19th edition; no current information was provided.

PI DELTA EPSILON, national college recognition society in journalism for men and women, was organized at Syracuse University, December 6, 1909. The founders were Sydney H. Coleman, Neil Dow Cranmer, Paul L. Benjamin, J. H. Lloyd Baxter, C. Earl Bradbury, William G. Kennedy, Willard R. Jillson, Philip S. Perkins, Wallace M. Williams, and Donald J. Wormer. These ten undergraduate men were associated on *The Syracuse Daily Orange*, and they conceived the idea of a closer bond and mutual interest in collegiate journalism which finally culminated in the founding of the organization.

The 1937 grand convention authorized revision of the constitution so as to admit women to membership. July 1, 1944, Alpha Chi Alpha, women's journalism society, petitioned and was merged with Pi Delta Epsilon; chapters of Alpha Chi Alpha were given active status.

ALPHA PHI GAMMA is a recognition fraternity for men and women in student publications. It was founded December 11, 1919, at Ohio Northern University, Ada, Ohio, by B. H. Focht, Lloyd W. Reese, R. S. Lyman, Tom B. Haber, and Fred C. Slager.

The original name of the group was Phi Alpha Gamma. It remained a campus group until 1923 when delegates from six other Ohio colleges attended a meeting, called the first national convention, in Ada, and were granted charters in the organization. Also at that meeting the first woman was initiated, making it a coeducational fraternity, and the name Alpha Phi Gamma was adopted because another fraternity was named Phi Alpha Gamma.

The fraternity was greatly strengthened in 1929 when Omega Xi Alpha, a California fraternity, merged with Alpha Phi Gamma as its western section. Activity came almost to a standstill during World War II, and the efforts of Gil A. Cowan of the *Los Angeles Examiner* were largely responsible for continued activity and post-war growth. In 1949 Cowan was named President Emeritus, the only member ever so honored.

In 1957 Alpha Delta, a journalism fraternity similar to Alpha Phi Gamma, disbanded and most of its 12 active chapters were granted charters.[1]

The Society's principal purposes are to honor and recognize individual achievement in journalism, as shown through a student's participation on a campus publication, radio station, or news bureau, and to help maintain and improve the quality of student publications.

[1] In January, 1977, seventeen inactive chapters were in process of reactivating. These were Augustana, Bucknell, California State (Chico), Carleton, Carnegie-Mellon, Fairleigh Dickinson (Teaneck), Gustavus Adolphus, Indiana (Pa.), Lehigh, Mississippi State (Columbus), Monmouth, Moravian, Northeast Missouri State, Northern Iowa, Pacific, Wisconsin (Oshkosh), and Wittenberg.

Chapters were being established on twelve campuses: Alliance (Pa.), Armstrong (Calif.), Ashland (Ohio), Buffalo State (N.Y.), Florida International, Jackson State (Miss.), Jacksonville State (Alabama), Lakeland (Wis.), Lyndon State (Vt.), Northern Kentucky, Rose-Hulman Tech (Ind.), and Spelman (Ga.).

General purposes of the fraternity are to recognize and honor individual ability and achievement in collegiate student publications; to serve, promote, and help to improve collegiate journalism; to establish cordial relationships between students and members of the profession; and to fraternally unite congenial students interested in journalism.

Membership To be eligible for active (student) membership, a student must be registered at a college or university with a Society chapter, must be in good academic standing, and must have served for at least one academic year (two semesters or three quarters) on a campus publication or other medium in the editorial or business department. Honorary memberships may be conferred by chapters on faculty members or professional journalists. Individual initiation fees are $12. There are no individual or chapter annual dues.

Charters for Society chapters are granted to petitioning groups from campuses upon approval of the national convention or by the national council.

Government Government of the Society is through a national convention held biennially. In the biennium the national council constitutes the governing body. The nine council seats are held by the president, past president, first and second vice-presidents, executive secretary-treasurer, and four chapter memberships. Officers are elected at each convention, except for the executive secretary treasurer, who is elected for four years.

Traditions and Insignia The Society sponsors an annual student publications contest for newspapers, yearbooks, and magazines in which cash awards and certificates arc presented to winning members. The Society also annually recognizes one chapter for its contributions to the Society and to journalism.

The Society's seal and pin are a circular design bearing the Society's name and founding date around the outer edge and crossed quills and an inkpot in the center. The Society's flower is a white carnation. Its colors are from its predecessor organizations, olive green and gray (Pi Delta Epsilon) and black and white (Alpha Phi Gamma).

Publications The *Collegiate Journalist*, which was the name of the Alpha Phi Gamma magazine, is the Society's quarterly magazine of general interest to student journalists. It also is a descendant of *The College Publisher*, which was the quarterly publication of Pi Beta Epsilon. In addition, the Society publishes a monthly newsletter for member chapters. It is the successor to *Epsilog* of Pi Delta Epsilon and *Black and White* of Alpha Phi Gamma.

Headquarters John David Reed. c/o Student Publications, Eastern Illinois University, Charleston, Illinois 61920.

Member Chapters Active chapters 109. Inactive chapters 186. Total number of initiates 60,000. Chapter roll:††

†† This chapter roll is repeated from the 19th edition; no current information was provided.

ORIGINAL ALPHA PHI GAMMA CHAPTERS:

1919   Alpha, Ohio Northern
1923   Beta, Akron
1923   Eta, Toledo
1923   Gamma, Wilmington
1927   Iota, Toledo
1928   Lambda, Redlands
1928   Rho, Hanover
1928   Tau, Albion
1931   Alpha Delta, Pacific (CA)
1931   Omega, Ball State
1938   Alpha Kappa, Indiana State
1948   Alpha Omega, Northern Iowa
1948   Beta Alpha, Oakland City (IN)
1949   Beta Delta, Wartburg
1957   Beta Tau, Franklin
1958   Beta Psi, Furman
1961   Gamma Zeta, Bethel (TN)
1963   Gamma Iota, Anderson
1963   Gamma Lambda, Cal Tech
1964   Gamma Mu, Morningside
1965   Gamma Omega, Eastern Michigan
1965   Gamma Phi, Tri-State
1965   Gamma Psi, Savannah
1965   Gamma Upsilon, G.M.I.
1966   Delta Beta, High Point
1967   Delta Delta, Bloomsburg
1967   Delta Epsilon, Juniata
1967   Delta Eta, Harding
1968   Eastern Kentucky
1968   Middle Tennessee
1969   East Carolina
1970   Elizabeth City
1970   South Carolina State
1970   West Virginia Wesleyan
1974   William Paterson
1975   Tennessee Tech

ORIGINAL PI DELTA EPSILON CHAPTERS:

1922   Stevens
1923   Wabash
1924   Washington and Jefferson
1926   Richmond
1930   Maryland
1930   V.P.I.
1934   Westminster (PA)
1935   William and Mary (1938-1959)
1939   Gettysburg
1939   Hampden-Sydney
1939   Southern Illinois
1940   Midland Lutheran (NE)
1944   Montevallo
1944   South Dakota
1944   Wayne State

1947   Bethany
1947   Mississippi State
1948   Dickinson
1948   John Carroll
1948   Worcester Tech
1948   Wyoming
1949   Clarkson Tech
1949   Eastern Illinois
1949   Marietta
1950   Keuka
1950   Longwood
1950   Utica, Syracuse
1951   SUNY Col., Potsdam
1951   Newark Engineering
1951   Upsala
1952   Memphis State
1953   Florida Southern
1953   Hofstra
1953   Muhlenberg
1953   Thiel
1954   Missouri Valley
1955   Bridgewater
1956   St. Francis (PA)
1957   Our Lady of Cincinnati
1960   Glassboro
1960   Kansas State, Pittsburg
1961   Linfield
1961   Valparaiso
1962   King's
1962   Nebraska State, Kearney
1962   Rider
1964   Bimidji State (MN)
1964   David Lipscomb
1964   Radford
1965   Edinboro
1965   Hartwick
1965   Millerville State (PA)
1965   Northeastern (OK)
1965   Rutgers, Newark
1965   Shippensburg
1965   Southeast Missouri
1965   St. John's (NY)
1966   Aurora
1966   California (PA)
1966   St. John's, Staten Island
1967   Evangel
1967   Mount St. Mary's (MD)
1967   Slippery Rock
1967   St. Bonaventure
1968   Northwest Missouri
1969   Texas Wesleyan
1970   Fort Hays
1971   East Stroudsburg
1972   Winthrop
1974   York (PA)

Theta Alpha Phi†

(DRAMATICS)

ACTIVE PIN

THETA ALPHA PHI, college recognition society for men and women in dramatics, was established in December, 1919, during a meeting of the National Association of the Teachers of Speech held at Chicago. Its purpose as expressed in the constitution is: "to increase interest, stimulate creativeness, and foster artistic achievement in all of the allied arts and crafts of the theatre." Students become eligible after having successfully met a prescribed minimum of experience in directing, writing, acting in, or managing plays.

Government Government is through a convention with an interim administration of the Executive Council of five national officers.

Insignia The badge is a comico-tragic mask of gold crowned with four rubies bearing the black enameled letters ΘΑΦ on the left eye, nose, and right eye, respectively.

Publication *The Cue* is a quarterly magazine established in 1922.

Membership Active chapters 54. Inactive chapters 32. Total number of initiates 22,800. Chapter roll:††

1919	Bucknell
1919	Louisiana
1919	Ohio Wesleyan
1919	*Oklahoma State* (1934)
1919	*Ripon* (1947)
1919	Stetson
1920	*Arizona* (1934)
1920	Baldwin-Wallace
1920	*Colorado Col* (1934)
1920	*Connecticut State* (1942)
1920	Dakota Wesleyan
1920	*Huron* (1937)
1920	*Missouri* (1934)
1920	*Occidental* (1930)
1920	Redlands
1920	*Tennessee* (1934)
1920	Tulsa
1920	*Utah* (1954)
1920	Willamette
1920	*Parsons* (1954)
1921	*Adrian* (1934)
1921	*Auburn* (1934)
1921	*Hawaii* (1935)

† This chapter narrative is repeated from the 19th edition; no current information was provided.
†† This chapter roll is repeated from the 19th edition; no current information was provided.

1921	*Pitt* (1934)
1921	*South Dakota* (1934)
1921	Wyoming
1922	College of the Pacific
1922	*Heidelberg* (1934)
1922	*Hillsdale* (1934)
1922	Indiana
1922	*Knox* (1934)
1922	Oklahoma Baptist
1922	*Puget Sound* (1935)
1922	Wittenberg
1923	*Carroll* (1954)
1923	*Culber-Stockton* (1940)
1923	Franklin
1923	Illinois Wesleyan
1923	Iowa State, Cedar Falls
1923	*Jamestown* (1934)
1923	*Kansas State, Pittsburg* (1934)
1923	*Montana State* (1934)
1923	Nebraska Wesleyan
1923	Park (MO)
1923	Penn State
1923	*South Dakota State, Aberdeen* (1939)
1923	*Yankton* (1934)
1924	Bradley
1924	Brigham Young
1924	Michigan State
1924	Ohio Northern
1924	*Southern Presbyterian* (1934)
1925	*Central Missouri State* (1934)
1925	*Duke* (1954)
1925	*Tulane* (1933)
1925	William and Mary
1926	Central Missouri
1926	Illinois State Normal
1926	Emporia
1927	Maryville
1927	Otterbein
1927	Utah State
1928	*College of Emporia* (1934)
1928	*New Mexico* (1945)
1929	Albion
1929	Drake
1929	Purdue
1930	Hiram
1931	Grove City (PA)
1933	*Alfred* (1954)
1933	Temple
1934	Ithaca
1936	Indiana State
1936	*Miami (FL)* (1954)
1938	Eastern Illinois State
1938	Rollins
1940	Santa Barbara
1941	Cincinnati
1945	Bowling Green
1950	Hanover
1950	Tennessee A & I
1952	Henderson
1953	Chicago City Junior College, Wilson
1953	Wisconsin State
1954	Howard (AL)
1960	Howard Payne (TX)
1960	Stevens

Part VIII

Fraternities That Are No More

Men's Fraternities

Alpha Gamma

ALPHA GAMMA was founded at Cumberland University, Lebanon, Tennessee, in 1867. It established some twenty-one chapters, the most prominent of which were at Washington and Jefferson College, Trinity University, Mercersburg College, Southwestern Presbyterian University, Cumberland University, and West Virginia University. The chapters at Trinity and West Virginia were killed by anti-fraternity laws; those at Washington and Jefferson and Southwestern Presbyterian accepted charters from Alpha Tau Omega; the remainder disbanded. The badge of the fraternity was a shield of gold displaying a globe encircled by a pennant bearing the letters AΓ and surmounted by six stars.

Alpha Gamma Upsilon

ACTIVE PIN

ALPHA GAMMA UPSILON, founded in Fort Wayne, Indiana, at Anthony Wayne Institute in 1922, was absorbed in part by Alpha Sigma Phi in May, 1965. The founders were Herbert R. Carter of Indiana, Homer H. Iden of New Mexico, Alfred C. Koeneke of North Dakota, and Dale R. Odneal of Missouri.

The aims and purpose of Alpha Gamma Upsilon were "to promote friendship, comradeship, and mutual understanding among its members; to encourage excellence in scholarship; to develop good character; to uphold the ideals of the colleges where its chapters are located; and to foster the highest ideals of Christian conduct and good citizenship."

The badge of the Alpha Gamma Upsilon Fraternity was a diamond-shaped shield of black across the center of which were superimposed in gold the Greek letters AΓΥ. In the area above the letters appear two joined links, and below is a miniature dagger. The fraternity flower was the pink rose, and the fraternity colors were black and gold. The fraternity's motto was ΑΔΕΛΦΟΣ ΑΝΔΡΙ ΠΑΡΕΙΗ.

The fraternity's publications included *Links*, first published in 1924, a review of the fraternity's activities.

Altogether, Alpha Gamma Upsilon installed fourteen chapters, as follows: Alpha, Anthony Wayne, 1922; Beta, Universal, 1927; Gamma, Detroit Tech, 1930: Delta, General Motors Institute, 1932; Beta, Indiana Tech, 1932; Epsilon, Lawrence Tech, 1933; Zeta, Detroit, 1934; Eta, Wayne State, 1947; Theta, Toledo, 1948; Iota, Eastern Michigan, 1948; Kappa, Defiance, 1949; Lambda, Tri-State, 1949; Mu, Rider, 1951; and Nu, Lycoming, 1951.

The Lycoming chapter was installed as Gamma Rho chapter of Alpha Sigma Phi on May 22, 1965. At the same time colony status was assigned the chapters at Detroit Tech, Indiana Tech, and Eastern State (Mich.). The G.M.I. chapter became inactive in 1964 and subsequently joined Phi Gamma Delta. The chapter at Lawrence Tech, an unaccredited institution, was not a participant in the merger. The chapter at Tri-State joined Sigma Phi Epsilon in 1968.

Alpha Kappa Phi

ALPHA KAPPA PHI was founded as Archania at the University of the Pacific, then situated at Santa Clara, California, in 1854 by T. H. Blaine. It was the first literary society on the Pacific Coast, its name meaning "first" and "oldest." It had a meeting hall, but not a house. In the *Narajado*, the university's yearbook, of 1889 Archania was listed as a distinctly working fraternity.

During the Civil War Archania tended to favor the South, while Rhizomia, its rival, tended to favor the North. Many stormy battles, both vocal and physical, were fought out on the campus.

In 1918 nineteen stars were added to its service flag. When the college was moved to Stockton, Archania acquired a house of its own. The house was given a formal Opening and house warming on May 1, 1926. The fraternity, then called Alpha Kappa Phi, was inactive from 1943–46. It ended its existence as a local in 1961 when granted a charter of Phi Kappa Tau.

Alpha Kappa Phi

ALPHA KAPPA PHI was founded at Centre College, Kentucky, about 1858 and established chapters at La Grange College, Cumberland University, Bethel College, Oakland College, and perhaps other places, the dates of their establishment being unknown, as the records were lost during the Civil War. After the war a few of the chapters were revived, but all soon again became dormant, except Psi chapter at the University of Mississippi, which had been re-established in 1867. After existing for some time as a local fraternity it became the Beta Beta of Beta Theta Pi in 1879. The badge of the fraternity was a shield with concave-curved sides, displaying at the top a pair of clasped hands, in the center the letters ΑΚΦ.

Alpha Kappa Pi

ACTIVE PIN

ALPHA KAPPA PI was consolidated with Alpha Sigma Phi in 1946, during the latter's centennial convention. It was organized at the Newark College of Engineering, Newark, New Jersey, January 1, 1921, and remained a local society until March 23, 1926, when the Beta chapter was placed at Wagner College, Staten Island. Prior to this date, a committee, composed of Wilson Hull, James A. Gibbons, Ralph A. Brader, and Harry W. Dierman from Newark College, Harry T. McKnight, John W. Kern and Paul Clemen from Wagner College, directed by Albert H. Wilson, New York, had worked out a complete plan for nationalization and on the date mentioned all former actions were ratified and a formal announcement of future policy was made.

The first convention was held in New York, May 22, 1926, with Wilson Hull, first grand president, in charge. *The Alpha* was the magazine.

The official badge was an unjeweled seven-pointed star bearing in its center crossed swords and the Greek letters ΑΚΠ. Only diamonds and pearls were permitted in adorning other badges. The pledge button showed the colors—white and Dartmouth green. The flower was the yellow tea rose.

At time of this union, Alpha Kappa Pi had thirty-six chapters, of which only one, Theta, as Columbia University, was inactive at an institution where Alpha Sigma Phi was represented. The alumni of Theta were added to Alpha Sigma Phi's Lambda. Only two of the remaining thirty-five were at institutions where Alpha Sigma Phi was represented: Omicron at Penn State and Sigma at the University of Illinois. These were combined with Alpha Sigma Phi's Upsilon and Eta, respectively. The remaining thirty-three chapters were added to the Alpha Sigma Phi roll as of the date of founding of the Alpha Kappa Pi chapters. Of these ten were inactive. They are shown as inactive chapters of Alpha Sigma Phi, existing as of the dates of Alpha Kappa Pi activity. The thirty-three chapters of Alpha Kappa Pi forming new chapters of Alpha Sigma Phi may be identified on the latter's chapter roll as all chapters from Alpha Rho to Alpha Psi, from Beta Alpha to Beta Psi, Gamma Alpha to Gamma Gamma. The letter Omega was not used as a chapter designation by either fraternity.

Alpha Lambda Tau

ALPHA LAMBDA TAU, the first fraternity organization at Oglethorpe University after its reorganization in 1916, disbanded with the advent of World War II. Several of its chapters were absorbed by Tau Kappa Epsilon which thus aided that fraternity's growth in the South.

It was organized as the Alpha Lambda Club, but T. V. Morrison, C. C. Mason, Marion Gaertner (the first freshmen to enter the University), O. M. Cobb, William Nunn, H. F. Whitehead, and Carl Stokes decided to build a national order. Consequently the fraternity was incorporated under the laws of the State of Georgia; the name was registered as Alpha Lambda Tau. Expansion took place mostly in the Southeast, at the average of approximately one new chapter a year. There was an idea that gained widespread publicity throughout the organization that the fraternity would never go north of the Mason-Dixon line but this was disproved in 1927 when it was brought to the floor of the convention and the move led to the chartering of Lambda chapter at the University of Illinois. In 1930 the first chapter was lost when the charter granted a little more than a year before was withdrawn from Arkansas College, where Alpha Lambda Tau had pioneered as the first national on the campus.

A central office was opened at Atlanta, Georgia, in 1927, with a secretary in charge. In 1933, *Summer News*, a regular weekly fraternity publication, was launched. Directories were published in 1926 and 1933. The official songs were "The Sweetheart of AΛT," by Tom Ellis of Eta Chapter, and "The Dreamgirl of AΛT," by Paul Crumbaugh of Omicron Chapter.

The badge was of gold having four arms on which were mounted the letters AΛOT, while the center was round, upon which was a black enamel shield containing the following figures in gold: a serpent and cross in the middle with two torches on the side, above which were three stars while a fourth star was at the bottom.

The pledge button was the same shape as the shield on the badge, being of gold and having a black enamel panel down each side and a cross and serpent in the middle. The colors were old gold and black. The flower was the American Beauty rose.

The chapter roll was:

1920	Alpha,	Oglethorpe
1922	Beta,	Auburn
1923	Gamma,	Mercer
1924	Delta,	Louisiana Tech
1925	Epsilon,	North Carolina
1925	Zeta,	North Carolina State
1926	Eta,	Howard College
1927	Iota,	Presbyterian (S.C.)
1928	Kappa,	Wofford
1928	Lambda,	Illinois
1928	Mu,	Arkansas
1929	Theta,	Georgia
1929	Nu,	Arkansas (1930)
1929	Xi,	Chattanooga
1929	Omicron,	Transylvania
1931	Pi,	Alabama
1931	Rho,	Culver-Stockton
1932	Sigma,	Kentucky
1934	Tau,	Maryland
1935	Upsilon,	Michigan State
1935	Phi,	Missouri Mines

Alpha Mu Sigma

ACTIVE PIN

ALPHA MU SIGMA during its years as a men's national fraternity installed a total of twenty-two chapters. However, progress was reversed by the economic depression and the war which followed. All chapters except Alpha at Cooper Union became inactive and the fraternity reverted to local status.

The Pratt Institute chapter withdrew to become affiliated with Tau Epsilon Phi in 1962. The end came when the C.C.N.Y. chapter was dissolved in the spring of 1963. Alpha itself gradually expired after the new decade began, with decline of the system at Cooper Union.

Alpha Mu Sigma was founded at the Cooper Union Institute of Technology on March 21, 1914, by Irwin S. Chanin, Henry Charles Dinney, Irving H. Fisher, Edward D. Fox, Henry I. Gilbert, Theodore F. Haynes, Julius Liebing, Benjamin Rothstein, Saul Shaw, Samuel H. Solodar, Jonas I. Speciner, and Joseph Spies. Its constitution and founders originally permitted induction of only male members of the Jewish faith. The chief reason for its founding was to form a common bond among young Jewish engineers setting out to gain a foothold in their profession.

In the beginning no plan for a national fraternity was envisaged. However, with the prosperity of the 1920s, the fraternity, which had established chapters at C.C.N.Y., Brooklyn Polytechnic Institute, and M.I.T., grew rapidly and with its growth dropped the religious affiliation requirement.

The emblem, used as a badge, was a shield; upon this is fixed a raised black concentric shield, in which the Greek letters A, M and Σ in gold are arranged vertically. The outer border is studded with sixteen pearls and three sapphires, so that two sapphires occupy the two upper corners of the shield and the third occupies the extreme lowest point, the pearls filling in the remainder. The pledge pin was a shield, the front covered with black enamel with a jagged white streak running through it.

Chapter roll was:

1914	Alpha,	Cooper Union (1971)
1917	Beta,	C.C.N.Y. (1963)
1919	Gamma,	Brooklyn Polytechnic (1919)
1920	Delta,	M.I.T. (1920)
1920	Epsilon,	Columbia (1920)
1921	Zeta,	N.Y.U.
1921	Eta,	Harvard (1921)
1922	Theta,	Bellevue Hospital Medical College (1922)
1922	Iota,	Yale (1922)
1929	Kappa,	Boston (1929)
1923	Lambda,	Pennsylvania (1923)
1925	Mu,	Maryland (1925)
1925	Nu,	Virginia
1927	Xi,	Union (1927)
1926	Omicron,	Southern California (1926)
1928	Pi,	Long Island University (1928)
1927	Rho,	Alabama (1927)
1930	Sigma,	Lewis Institute (1930)
1937	Tau,	George Washington (1937)
1937	Upsilon,	Brooklyn (1960)
1939	Phi (1),	St. Johns (Brooklyn) (1963)
1958	Phi (2),	Pratt (1962)

Alpha Sigma Chi

ACTIVE PIN

ALPHA SIGMA CHI FRATERNITY was organized simultaneously at Rutgers College and Cornell University in 1871 by Elbridge Van Syckel and Ellis D. Thompson. The chapter roll was: Rutgers College, Cornell University, Stevens Institute of Technology, Princeton University, St. Lawrence University, Columbia University, and the University of Maine. The St. Lawrence and Maine chapters were formed from local societies. The Columbia chapter did not agree with the remainder of the fraternity and was expelled in 1878. In 1879 after negotiations extending over some months, the active chapters of the fraternity united with Beta Theta Pi, it being part of the plan that the Princeton chapter should be allowed to die under the operation of the anti-fraternity laws. The badge was a monogram of the letters A Σ X.

American Association of Commons Clubs

ACTIVE PIN

THE AMERICAN ASSOCIATION OF COMMONS CLUBS, popularly shortened to "American Commons Club," was founded in 1921 at a convention held April 22 and 23 at Denison University. The official delegates who gathered for this purpose were T. V. Caulkins, Jr., and D. S. Cowles of the Denison Commons Club; Dennis West and W. V. Wilkerson of the Ohio University Commons Club; and Clinton Douglas and L. L. Latham of the Hillsdale Commons Club. Dr. Forbes B. Wiley, faculty adviser of the Denison Commons Club, participated in almost all of the sessions and remained a steadfast friend and wise counselor to the Commons Club until his death in 1956.

The organization's national existence ended in June, 1964, when the clubs at Cincinnati and Adrian voted to withdraw, the former becoming a colony of Tau Kappa Epsilon; and five years later the mother chapter affiliated with Delta Chi.

Founded originally as a "nonfraternity" (but never anti-fraternity) organization, the Commons Club sought to make available to all unaffiliated male students the advantages of fraternity life—

which tended to be restricted to an exclusive segment of the campus.

The mother chapter, at Denison, was founded in 1917, taking the basic name and some of its ideas from the older National Federation of Commons Clubs which was then breaking up in the east—but with which there was never any formal relationship. The Wesleyan Commons Club, in Connecticut, founded in 1903, had been the mother chapter of the Federation and based its organization on the ideas of a "House of Commons" organized on the Wesleyan campus several years previously by Woodrow Wilson. The idea of a college social organization open to all men ("Commons" vs. "nobility") thus goes back considerably farther than the American Association.

The official badge of the Association included three pearls and a central ruby, with the letters A C C in the apices. It may be bordered with pearls. The pledge pin was of the same shape (triangular, with slightly concave sides) as the official badge, and is divided equally into the two colors of the Association: cardinal red and gray. The official publication was *The American Commoner*.

The chapter roll was as follows:

1921	Denison (1969)
1921	Ohio (1921)
1921	Hillsdale (1924)
1922	Simpson (1935)
1923	Akron (1932)
1923	Rochester (1926)
1924	DePauw (1937)
1925	Wabash (1931)
1926	Cincinnati (1964)
1927	Iowa State (1936)
1928	Knox (1933)
1929	Colorado State (1956)
1931	Wittenberg (1934)
1931	Penn State (1938)
1932	Colorado Teachers (1948)
1933	Purdue (1937)
1936	Adrian (1964)
1949	Kent State (1961)

Beta Kappa

ACTIVE PIN

BETA KAPPA was founded at Hamline University, St. Paul, Minnesota, October 15, 1901, by the Rev. Daniel Paul Rader, a Sigma Nu who became a world famous religious leader. Associated with him were Edward T. Marlatte, Albert T. Spencer, and Charles H. Wallace. Beta Kappa existed as a local fraternity for twenty-one years. In 1922 Beta chapter was installed, and the fraternity expanded to include over forty chapters with a total membership of more than five thousand. It was a member of the NIC. A quarterly publication, *Beta Kappa Journal*, was issued. The badge was diamond in shape of black enamel surrounded by twenty-four pearls, a white circular disc in the center bearing a coiled serpent, above a lamp, below crossed swords and on either side the Greek letters B and K. The colors were purple and gold; the flower was the red Templar rose. Beta Kappa merged with Theta Chi in 1942. The mother chapter at Hamline became Beta Kappa chapter of Theta Chi. The Georgia Tech chapter became Beta Kappa Zeta of Lambda Chi Alpha in 1942.

Beta Phi

ACTIVE PIN

BETA PHI FRATERNITY was organized in 1911 at Chicago. It was successful for a time. In 1920 it had eight chapters: University of Chicago, Northwestern University, Armour Institute, University of Illinois, Iowa State College, University of Michigan, DePauw University, and Rose Polytechnic Institute; with a membership of 750.

Beta Sigma Rho

ACTIVE PIN

BETA SIGMA RHO was founded at Cornell University in 1910 primarily as a local organization under the name of Beta Samach, the Greek Beta and the Hebrew Samach suggesting the application of the Greek society idea to the social and cultural life of the Jewish undergraduate. The founders were M. H. Milman, M. M. Milman, Nathaniel E. Koenig, and Lester D. Krohn. Almost immediately the following men joined their group: Saul Blickman, A. B. Pollack, A. M. Fox, M. M. Wyckoff, and then others, including I. J. Elkind, Fred Kleinman, H. Z. Harris, and Jay Cohen.

Simplicity was the keynote of the founders and exhibited itself in the absence of initiation fees, dues, constitution, even formalized ideals. Time, experience, and the new ideas of a later generation, however, brought fees, a constitution, a ritual, and the other surface attributes of fraternity. Though

Beta chapter was added at Penn State University in 1913, national expansion was still far from the minds of the members.

Gamma chapter was formed at Columbia University and the name of the fraternity was changed to the all-Greek Beta Sigma Rho; then the trustees responded to a growing demand from the membership for a national attitude and a program of slow and careful expansion.

Over the years, whatever religious requirements were expressed or implied in the original thinking of the founders gradually disappeared.

On December 12, 1972, Beta Sigma Rho merged with Pi Lambda Phi.

The badge was a shepherd's staff and a sword crossed behind a shield which was surrounded by thirteen pearls and surmounted by a plumed helmet. The three Greek letters, B ΣP, appear on the shield, gold with black background. Colors were blue and gold.

The estimated total membership at the time of merger was 5,380. The chapter roll:

1910	Alpha,	Cornell
1913	Beta,	Penn State
1919	Gamma,	Columbia
1920	Delta,	Buffalo
1922	Epsilon,	Pennsylvania
1922	Zeta,	Carnegie University
1930	Eta,	Toronto
1935	Theta,	Newark (Rutgers)
1945	Iota,	Western Ontario
1949	Kappa,	Kentucky (1952)
1950	Lambda,	Syracuse
1958	Mu,	Miami (Fla.)
1962	Nu,	N.Y.U. (1965)
1964	Xi,	C.C.N.Y.
1969	Omicron,	St. John's (N.Y.)

Beta Sigma Tau

BETA SIGMA TAU was founded in May, 1948, at the National Conference of Intercultural Fraternities held in Chicago, Illinois. It was the first national interracial and interreligious college social fraternity in the United States to be organized following World War II. As mentioned in its Constitutional Preamble, Beta Sigma Tau was founded "to level, not raise barriers among people" and to have a foundation based "upon a brotherhood and democracy which transcends racial, national, and religious differences."

The existence of Beta Sigma Tau ended when it was absorbed by merger with Pi Lambda Phi in 1960. The chapter roll in 1956 was:

1948	Baldwin-Wallace
1948	Buffalo
1948	Ohio State

1948　Ohio Wesleyan
1948　Roosevelt University, Chicago
1948　Santa Barbara
1948　California
1949　Lincoln (Pa.)
1949　New Mexico Highlands (Nev.)
1949　Morgan State (Md.)
1949　Hobart
1949　Colorado
1949　Southern California
1950　Columbia
1950　Tri-State
1951　Johns Hopkins
1952　U.C.L.A.

Chi Tau

ACTIVE PIN

CHI TAU was founded at Trinity College (now Duke), North Carolina, October 3, 1920, by Henry Belk, Merrimon Teague Hipps, Samuel L. Holton, Jr., and Numa Francis Wilkerson. It existed as a local organization until May 2, 1923, when a joint meeting was held at Durham of Chi Tau and Lambda Sigma Delta, a local society at North Carolina State College. This resulted in the formal establishment of Chi Tau, which then became incorporated under the laws of North Carolina. It had chapters at Duke University, North Carolina State College, University of North Carolina, Wake Forest College, Presbyterian College of South Carolina, University of California, Columbia University, Wofford College, University of Illinois, and perhaps others. It published a quarterly magazine for some years. The motto of the fraternity was *Esse Quam Videri*, the motto of North Carolina. The badge was hexagon-shaped with the following symbols on the crest: one torch, one triangle, three stars, and the Greek letters X T. The colors were white, crimson, and gold. The flowers were white, red, and yellow rose buds. Internal dissension developing, the fraternity disintegrated in 1929.

Delta Alpha Pi

ACTIVE PIN

DELTA ALPHA PI was founded at Ohio Wesleyan University, November 22, 1919, by John H. Al-

spach, Howard C. Cameron, Carl L. Clugston, Charles Melvin Coulter, Barton R. Deming, E. Frank Francis, Douglas M. Gaither, Robert B. Hartley, Charles M. Hempstead, Frank B. Jemison, John A. King, Stanley Mullen, Donald H. Price, Allen E. Rupp, Vernie Seibert, and Donald Wogaman. The purpose of the founders was to inaugurate a type of fraternity for the development of Christian character.

In the early years of the depression, the chapters at Ohio Wesleyan, Illinois, and Butler became inactive. In 1935 arrangements were effected to merge with Phi Mu Delta, but before their completion the Purdue chapter withdrew and eventually its members joined the local chapter of Alpha Chi Rho. The remaining chapters and all the alumni joined Phi Mu Delta in October, 1935.

The magazine was the *Cross and Shield*, published semi-annually. The badge was a shield mounted upon a cross of which only the ends were visible. Upon the black background of the shield were two crossed swords, above which were the Greek letters Δ Α Π.

The chapter roll was:

1919　Alpha, Ohio Wesleyan
1921　Beta, Ohio State
1924　Gamma, Purdue
1925　Delta, N.Y.U.
1927　Epsilon, Butler
1927　Zeta, Illinois

Delta Epsilon

DELTA EPSILON was established at Roanoke College, Virginia, in 1862. The intention was to confine it entirely to Virginia colleges. After establishing three chapters, it became defunct. The last chapter joined Beta Theta Pi at Hampden-Sydney in 1868.

Delta Kappa

ACTIVE PIN

DELTA KAPPA was merged with Sigma Pi by approval of the conventions of the fraternities, in June and September, 1964, respectively.

Delta Kappa was originally founded under the name of Kappa Kappa Kappa at the State Teachers College, Buffalo, New York, in 1920. The purpose of the fraternity was to foster the development of fellowship, scholarship, and leadership through the socializing influence of fraternal life. In 1930 the one inactive and four active chapters located in the normal schools and colleges of New York state were nationalized under the corporate law of the State of New York and became recognized as a national fraternity for the teaching profession. Because of the possible mistaken identification with the Ku Klux Klan, the national convention of 1936 voted to change the name of the fraternity. The incorporation was completed in 1937, and the organization became known as Delta Kappa, the original tri-kappa symbolism being maintained by the employment of the Greek letter, Delta, signifying three. Beside changing the name of the organization, the convention of 1936 changed the scope of the organization from a professional to a social fraternity by writing into the constitution the fact that any institution of higher learning offering a bachelor's degree could become the home of a chapter of the organization.

The State University of New York, made up of twenty-one educational institutions of varied character, in 1953 forbade any of its units to permit any social fraternity or sorority chapter to be affiliated with a national organization. This forced the inactivation of twelve veteran chapters of Delta Kappa. The remaining chapters met in the fall of 1954 and decided to reincorporate in the state of Wisconsin, because the majority of them were located in the middle-west section of the country. This third incorporation included seven active undergraduate chapters.

The official badge was in the form of a triangle with a black center on which Δ and K are inscribed in gold. The official colors were maroon and white, and the official flower was the red rose. The motto was: "True leadership is possible only through honorable and upright living."

The official publication, *The Kappan*, was published annually. Consequent to the merger, the chapter at Milton, an unaccredited school, was given the status of a colony. The chapter at Wisconsin State-Oshkosh preferred not to participate in the merger but became a chapter of Delta Sigma Phi. The chapter roll:

1920	Alpha, Buffalo Teachers (N.Y.) (1953)
1925	Beta, Cortland Teachers (N.Y.) (1953)
1926	Gamma, Oswego Teachers (N.Y.) (1953)
1927	Delta, Plattsburg Teachers (N.Y.) (1953)
1931	Epsilon, Ithaca (1964)
1935	Zeta, New Paltz Teachers (N.Y.) (1953)
1946	Theta, Potsdam Teachers (N.Y.) (1953)
1948	Iota, Genesco Teachers (N.Y.) (1953)
1949	Delta Chi, Southeast Missouri State (1953)
1951	Delta Rho, Madison (Va.) (1953)
1951	Phi, Clarion State (Pa.)
1951	Sigma Phi, Frostburg Teachers (Md.)
1951	Kappa, Indiana State (Terre Haute) (1954)

1951	Sigma, Stout State (Wis.) (1964)
1952	Chi Delta, Wisconsin State (Whitewater)
1952	Eta Phi, Wisconsin State (Eau Claire) (1953)
1953	Omicron, Wisconsin-Milwaukee (1964)
1953	Chi Gamma, Milton (Wis.) (1964)
1960	Iota Alpha Sigma, Wisconsin State (Oshkosh) (1964)

Delta Kappa

ACTIVE PIN

DELTA KAPPA, founded in 1845, was the second freshman society at Yale College. It established other chapters as follows: 1848, Beta, Amherst College (1870); 1850, Gamma, University of North Carolina (1861); 1851, Delta, University of Virginia (1861); 1853, Epsilon, University of Mississippi (1862); 1860, Zeta, Dartmouth College; 1867, Eta, Centre College (1879). The southern chapters were killed by the Civil War. Eta at Centre became a chapter of Phi Delta Theta in 1879. The badge was a crescent about three-quarters of an inch in diameter bearing a star in each horn, with a white shield in its broadest part, this shield carrying a crossed key and dagger device, the letters Δ and K being on either side of the shield.

Delta Psi Theta

DELTA PSI THETA was the first local fraternity to be established at Indiana University and was probably formed by 1866. John Herschel Lemon, a member of the class of 1863, living in New Albany, Indiana, in 1933, wrote that the Deltas—as they were called—were organized at that period and that there were chapters at Indiana Asbury (DePauw) and at the Waveland Collegiate Institute on the banks of the Little Raccoon Creek, near Crawfordsville. In 1941 with the publication of Edward H. Ziegner's *Phi Gamma Delta at Wabash*, it became known that the Deltas also had a group at Crawfordsville in 1865. Deciding to petition a national fraternity, a delegate from Bloomington, Indiana, was sent to Greencastle, and he selected Phi Kappa Psi. The Wabash group entered Phi Gamma Delta. The Waveland chapter, in what is called today a secondary school, did not survive.

Delta Sigma Lambda

ACTIVE PIN

DELTA SIGMA LAMBDA, the first college fraternity composed entirely of members of the Order of DeMolay, traces its origin to the spontaneous rise throughout the country during the years 1921–24 of numerous local organizations based on the principles of the Order of DeMolay. On December 23, 1924, six of these fraternities met at Lawrence, Kansas, to consider the formation of a national DeMolay college fraternity. Those represented were Delta Sigma Lambda with chapters at the University of California and the University of Nevada; Star and Crescent at Purdue University; Scimitar Fraternity at the University of Kansas; Delta Kappa Fraternity and the Illini DeMolay Club, both at the University of Illinois; and Delta Lambda, at the University of Nebraska. Several other fraternities were invited to attend, but were unable to do so at that time. By Christmas Day the consolidation had been completed.

The name of Delta Sigma Lambda was adopted for the new organization, it being that of the oldest participating group, and the date and place of its founding were, for the same reason, defined as September 9, 1921, in San Francisco. The ritual of the California fraternity was accepted without change; but the adoption of a new badge and pledge pin was deemed desirable by the delegates.

For several years the fraternity gained in strength and chapters. In September, 1933, a merger was affected with Theta Alpha, which had been founded in 1909 and had chapters at Syracuse and Cornell. Later in the same year an agreement was concluded with the Grand Council of the Order of DeMolay , which recognized Delta Sigma Lambda as the national college fraternity for DeMolays, but that may easily have proved a handicap. Difficulties developed in the next few years. The chapters at California, Nevada, Kansas, and Carnegie Tech became inactive; The Cornell chapter, acquired through Theta Alpha, died; the Nebraska chapter withdrew to join Phi Gamma Delta; in 1937 an agreement was made by which Theta Chi absorbed the chapters at Purdue and Montana, and also the alumni of those chapters; the Arizona chapter was too weak to merge and continued as a local by the same name; the Syracuse chapter had withdrawn previously and resumed its local status as Theta Alpha. The Nebraska chapter was absorbed by Phi Gamma Delta in 1936, and the R.P.I. chapter was absorbed by Lambda Chi Alpha the same year.

The badge was a jeweled shield containing the three Greek letters Δ Σ Λ at the top, with a star and crescent in the center, and below this the Greek letters Θ A. This shield was superimposed upon a white-gold maltese cross.

The chapter roll in 1935 was:

1921	Alpha, California (1932)
1922	Beta, Arizona (1923)
1922	Gamma, Nevada
1924	Beta, Kansas
1924	Epsilon, Nebraska
1924	Zeta, Purdue
1925	Eta, Illinois
1927	Theta, Montana
1930	Delta, Arizona
1931	Iota, Carnegie Tech
1931	Kappa, Rensselaer
1933	Alpha, Syracuse
1933	Lambda, Cornell

Epsilon Alpha

EPSILON ALPHA was founded at the University of Virginia about 1855, and had chapters also at Washington College (Virginia), University of North Carolina, University of Mississippi, William and Mary, Emory and Henry, and elsewhere. All of its chapters were probably killed by the Civil War except the one at Washington College which died in 1868. Its badge was a large three-sided shield entirely covered with black enamel except for emblems in other colors, as follows: a gold star in each upper corner; a colored rainbow encircling the top of the badge, under which was a crescent in white enamel; a large bundle of arrows, with points upwards, occupied the center of the badge, on each side of which were the letters of the fraternity; at the extreme lower part of the badge in a semicircle were the words "Univ. of Va." The badge, as printed on its membership certificate, makes no reference to the University of Virginia and substitutes an upper arm and forearm, bent to fit the lower point of the badge, with the forearm, with clenched fist, extending up towards the letter A.

Gamma Tau

GAMMA TAU was founded at Howard University on March 16, 1934; several chapters were established before the fraternity became inactive. The badge was a gold triangle with garnets or rubies at the points and four pearls along each side; a triangular black and gold center had the word Excalibur flanked by the Greek letters Γ and T inlaid in gold. The colors were garnet and gold; the flower was the white carnation.

Kappa Alpha

ACTIVE PIN

KAPPA ALPHA—the first Kappa Alpha—was founded in 1812 at the University of North Carolina by four members of Phi Beta Kappa whose identity has been lost. Its constitution, ritual, and secrets were so similar to those of the original Phi Beta Kappa as to indicate strongly that it was a descendent of one of the community branches chartered by Phi Beta Kappa before its dissolution at William and Mary in 1781. Kappa Alpha's chapters, called "circles," were, so far as known, as follows: 1812, Alpha, University of North Carolina (1866); Delta, Furman University (1861); Epsilon, University of South Carolina (1861); Wofford College (1861); 1842, LaGrange College, Alabama (1855); 1848, University of Alabama (1855); Howard College, Alabama (1861); Centenary Institute, Summerfield, Alabama (1861); 1855, Florence Wesleyan University, Alabama (1861); 1855, Lambda, Centenary College, Louisiana (1858); Omicron, Louisiana College (1861); 1855, University of Mississippi (1858); Union University, Tennessee (1861); Phi, Emory and Henry College, Virginia (1861). It is thought that there were also circles at the University of Georgia, Emory College, Centre College, Western Military Institute of Tennessee, William and Mary College and Washington and Lee University. The correct order of the establishment of the circles is unknown. If they were named in alphabetical order, the Emory and Henry chapter was the twenty-first established, making a large chapter roll for those times. Circles were organized in county-seat towns, as well as in colleges. These community circles were composed of the professional and gentry classes, united for social and literary purposes.

Internal dissensions in the circle at the University of Alabama resulted in the spring of 1855 from members of the minority faction disclosing the secrets and the consequent dissolution of that and other circles. The majority faction accepted a charter from Phi Gamma Delta. The circle at Centenary accepted a charter from Delta Kappa Epsilon in January, 1858; the circle at Mississippi, a charter from the Chi Psi in the fall of 1858. The circle at South Carolina, followed by the one at Emory and Henry and others, reorganized under the name of Phi Mu Omicron in 1858. The mother circle at North Carolina also was dissolved by the exposure in 1855, and most of its members joined Chi Psi, establishing that fraternity there in that year. It was revived at North Carolina as Kappa Alpha in 1859 and was the only circle that did not suspend at the beginning of the Civil War. It died, in 1866, as a result of a second exposure of the secrets.

The badge of old Kappa Alpha, also called "Kuklos Adelphon" or the "Alpha Society," was of diamond shape, enclosing a circular band and the letter A, with openings between the inside of the diamond, the circular band, and the letter A. On the band or circle was Kuklos Adelphon in Greek; on the right leg of the letter A were the letters N E C S J A, initials of the secret Latin motto; on the crossbar of the letter A were clasped hands. The seal was an equilateral triangle containing an open eye and the letters of the fraternity. Kappa Alpha had many prominent members, among them, James K. Polk, president of the United States.

See also Phi Mu Omicron.

Kappa Nu

ACTIVE PIN

KAPPA NU was established at the University of Rochester on November 12, 1911; its life as a national fraternity by that name ended when it merged with Phi Epsilon Pi, also an NIC member, October 14, 1961.

Kappa Nu's six founders were residents of Rochester, New York. The local organization began to admit new men, the founders and older men graduating and in many instances entering graduate schools elsewhere. Several of the men had gone to New York City for professional studies where they came into contact with other Rochester men who had not belonged to Kappa Nu. These men formed new groups at New York University, Columbia University, Albany Law School, Union College, Boston University, University of Buffalo, and Harvard University.

By 1917 there were six groups. In that year a convention of delegates from these groups was held in Rochester, and Kappa Nu was established as a national college fraternity, with six chapters.

By 1952, the roster had grown to twenty-six chapters installed, but of these nine were casualties of World War I and the economic depression.

Kappa Nu as a national fraternity encouraged a great deal of freedom and flexibility in the individual chapters. The aim of the fraternity was to develop fine, upright, loyal citizens, men of scholarship and men who would be active in the community and willing to give of their time and effort to help others.

The governing body was made up of the national president, national vice-president, secretary, national treasurer, and two representatives from each chapter.

Kappa Nu's official colors were purple and white. *The Reporter,* a magazine, was published three times each year. The badge consisted of two pieces, diamond-shaped, and a base jeweled with pearls and with corners of amethysts, crown set. The center piece or panel was enameled and contained Hebrew letters above and a star below with Greek letters of Kappa Nu showing through the background in gold. The chapter roll in 1956 was:

1911	Alpha, Rochester	
1915	Beta, N.Y.U. (Heights)	
1915	Gamma, Columbia (1926)	
1915	Delta, Union University, Albany, New York (1925)	
1916	Theta, New York State, Albany (1919)	
1917	Epsilon, Boston (1934)	
1917	Zeta, Buffalo	
1917	Iota, Union	
1918	Eta, Harvard (1934)	
1918	Kappa, Rensselaer	
1919	Lambda, Western Reserve (1932)	
1919	Mu, Michigan (1953)	
1919	Nu, Pennsylvania	
1921	Xi, Pittsburgh	
1921	Omicron, Chicago (1934)	
1921	Pi, Alabama	
1921	Rho, Cincinnati (1923)	
1922	Sigma, Tulane	
1922	Tau, California	
1932	Upsilon, Arkansas (1941)	
1933	Phi, Alfred	
1939	Chi, Louisiana State (1942)	
1951	Omega, N.Y.U. (Square)	
1951	Alpha Beta, Cornell	
1952	Alpha Omega, Wayne State	
1952	Alpha Delta, U.C.L.A.	

Kappa Phi Lambda

KAPPA PHI LAMBDA FRATERNITY was founded at Jefferson College, August 3, 1862, by J. J. Belville. Chapters are known to have existed at Mount Union, Michigan, Monmouth, Northwestern, Moores Hill, Ohio Wesleyan, Virginia, Denison, and the Western University of Pennsylvania. The fraternity became extinct in 1874. The Michigan chapter joined Psi Upsilon, the Mount Union chapter Delta Tau Delta, the Northwestern chapter Sigma Chi, and the Denison chapter Beta Theta Pi. The badge was a shield displaying at the top a balance, immediately below a sunburst and mountain, and beneath a pennant bearing the letters of the fraternity. The Westminster College (Pennsylvania) chapter maintained a continuous existence, sometimes sub rosa, until it affiliated with Sigma Nu.

Kappa Sigma Kappa

ACTIVE PIN

KAPPA SIGMA KAPPA Fraternity was founded at Virginia Military Institute on September 28, 1867, by four cadets: John M. Tutwiler, James Gunnell Hurst, David Gamble Murrell, and Kenneth McDonald. The group was formed by the upperclassmen partially to assist the administration in subduing pranksters from two rival groups on campus.

The fraternity originally took the name C. E. C. Fraternity but soon changed it to Kappa Sigma Kappa, the name Tutwiler suggested. Tutwiler also designed the badge in the form of a Jerusalem cross and devised the ritual. By 1885 there were ten chapters of Kappa Sigma Kappa. The mother chapter chose Gamma as its designation and the other chapters were permitted to choose their designations.

Small college enrollments and faculty opposition to fraternities in the 1880s seriously curtailed fraternity activity. Chapters became inactive, and a long period of dormancy began for the old Kappa Sigma Kappa when the last three chapters affiliated with another fraternity by the end of 1886.

In 1935 a group of students at the University of Virginia who desired to form a fraternity reactivated the old Delta (Virginia) chapter. Led by Frederick St. Paul Henstridge, the men reconstructed the chapter roll from the university's historical files. They learned that three members of the chapter were living and that founder Kenneth McDonald and Zeta chapter members Robert J. Noell and W. L. Pierce also were living. These men formed an alumni council which gave the group permission to reactivate and to use the name, rituals, and insignia. Founder McDonald, who was eighty-five years old and living in San Francisco, helped in this work.

In 1948 brothers from three provinces meeting at Arkansas A. and M. at Monticello for the first convention divided the United States into five provinces, wrote a constitution, planned a national convention for St. Louis the following year, and elected a president.

In 1962, twenty-one of Kappa Sigma Kappa's chapters merged with Theta Xi. The delegates approved a merger agreement at the fourteenth annual convention in Detroit on August 19–22. Eight chapters at unaccredited institutions remained in the fraternity.

The badge was a Jerusalem cross of white with seven gold dots on each arm and with the fraternity's Greek letters in gold on a black disc in the center. The original name, C. E. C., which also stood for the secret motto, was engraved on the back of the badge.

The coat of arms was blazoned as follows: Purpure, on a fess azure, the Greek letters Kappa Sigma Kappa, on dexter and sinister chief, two crescents, or, in the middle base a crescent, of the same. Crest: above an esquire's helmet, a plume, or. Mantling: or. Motto: *Numine et Virtute.*

The colors of the fraternity were purple and gold and the flower was the purple iris.

Total membership at time of merger with Theta Xi 14,437. Chapter roll in 1962:

1947	Michigan Alpha, Detroit
1947	Maryland Alpha, University of Baltimore
1948	Michigan Beta, Lawrence Institute of Technology
1949	Illinois Epsilon, Chicago Technical College
1950	New York Gamma, New York Institute of Applied Sciences, Buffalo
1950	Indiana Gamma, Tri-State College
1958	New York Eta, Westchester Community College
1958	New York Theta, Hudson Valley Community College

INACTIVE IN 1962:

1867	V.M.I. (1886)
1871	Washington and Lee (1886)
1874	Virginia A & M (1886)
1875	Virginia (1886) (1935–1939)
1881	Emory and Henry (1886)
1881	Randolph-Macon (1886)
1882	Richmond (1886)
1883	Bethel Military Academy (1886)
1885	North Carolina (1886)
1885	Louisiana State (1887)
1935	Lebanon Valley (1942)
1937	Western Reserve (1942)
1937	Texas Mines (1942)
1941	Waynesburg (1959)
1946	New Mexico Highlands (1958)
1946	Fort Hays Kansas State (1962)[1]
1946	Eastern Illinois (1958)
1946	Arizona State College (1958)
1947	Northern Polytechnic Institute, England (1951)
1947	Canterbury University, New Zealand (1951)
1947	University of Hobart, Tasmania (1951)
1947	Sacramento State (1952)
1947	Central Missouri State (1962)[1]
1948	University of Manitoba (1960)
1948	Cedarville (1955)
1948	Armstrong College (Calif.)[1]
1948	Buffalo (1959)
1949	Pennsylvania Military College (1961)
1951	Hillsdale[1]

1952	Russell Sage College (1956)
1953	Agricultural and Technical Institute at Alfred, N.Y. (1955)
1953	Russell Sage College (1956)
1954	Rhode Island (1960)
1956	Northern Illinois (1961)

MERGED WITH THETA XI:

1940	Youngstown
1942	Arkansas A & M
1945	Fairmont State
1946	Indiana Tech
1946	Concord
1947	Morris Harvey
1947	Glenville State
1947	Western Illinois
1947	Henderson State
1947	Ball State
1949	Old Dominion
1949	Rochester Institute
1949	Defiance
1949	Detroit
1950	Lenoir Rhyne
1951	Wayne State
1951	Ferris
1954	General Motors Institute
1955	West Virginia Wesleyan
1956	Utica College of Syracuse U.
1958	Western Carolina

Mu Pi Lambda

MU PI LAMBDA was founded at Washington and Lee University in 1895, by M. G. Perrow, R. S. Martins, and H. H. Larimore. The following chapters were established: 1895, Washington and Lee; 1897, Virginia; 1898, Harvard; 1898, West Virginia; 1899, William and Mary. Government was an arch chapter of not more than eleven members. The badge was a five-sided shield displaying the letters M Π Λ beneath an eye and above the skull and bones. The Harvard chapter and the West Virginia chapter lived but a few months. In 1903 the University of Virginia chapter disbanded, part of its members joining Kappa Sigma and part Phi Delta Theta. In 1904 the fraternity disbanded. The Washington and Lee chapter joined Kappa Sigma, and the William and Mary chapter Theta Delta Chi.

[1]The Central Missouri State Chapter was absorbed by Theta Chi, the Fort Hays chapter by Alpha Kappa Lambda. In accordance with a special provision inserted in the constitution of Kappa Sigma Kappa at the constitutional convention held in 1961, final and permanent releases were granted by the grand council of Kappa Sigma Kappa at a meeting held on April 21, 1962; hence these two chapters did not merge with Theta Xi. Prior to the 1962 convention, Kappa Sigma Kappa had revoked the charter of California Gamma at Armstrong College. Michigan Zeta at Hillsdale did not participate in the merger but reverted to local status.

Mystic Seven

ACTIVE PIN

MYSTIC SEVEN was organized as a society in 1837 at Wesleyan University by Hamilton Brewer. In 1838 Henry Robert Branham entered Emory College as a freshman. After one year he went north to Wesleyan and in Middletown became a member of the Mystic Seven. The next year he returned to Georgia and established the Temple of the Sword of the Mystic Seven.

The Skull and Bones was established at Athens, Georgia, by a transfer student from Emory. The Temple of the Wreath was organized at Centenary College, then at Jackson, Louisiana, in 1849 by Daniel Martindale, a member of the Mystic Seven at Wesleyan, then teaching at Jackson. The Temple of the Scroll and Pen was authorized by the parent Mystic Seven Temple at Genesee College, Lima, New York [Syracuse], in 1853. The Temple of the Star was organized at the University of Mississippi about 1859. The Hands and Torch at the University of Virginia was chartered by the Genesee Temple in 1868. Cumberland University was the home of the Temple of the Serpent, probably organized by transfer students from Virginia and Mississippi in the early 1870's.

Following the Civil War, the Temple of the Wand at Wesleyan was disbanded as a four-year college society, and some of its members petitioned and won a charter of Delta Kappa Epsilon as did other members at Genesee. The Temple of the Hands and Torch at the University of Virginia then centralized control of the Mystic Seven, revised the constitution, and later adopted an alternate name, Phi Theta Alpha. The Virginia group also chartered the Sword and Shield at Davidson College in 1884 and the Temple of the Star of the South at the University of North Carolina in the same year. The three southern temples established a publication, *The Mystic Messenger*. This group also revived the Wesleyan Temple in 1889, and the next year, the living temples (Virginia, Davidson, North Carolina, and Wesleyan) formed a union with Beta Theta Pi and alumni of the Mystic Seven, and the Mystics were received into that fraternity. The Wesleyan senior society had taken the name Owl and Wand, but in 1882 became known as the Mystic Seven Society. This group published a centennial history in 1937, written by Carl F. Price of Wesleyan. In 1940 upon the celebration of the fiftieth anniversary of the Temple of the Sword and Shield and the Pi Alpha of Beta Theta Pi, Beta Theta Pi Fraternity published *The Mystics and Beta Theta Pi*. The Mystic societies were Hebrew in nomenclature instead of Greek; much was made of the number seven, and their rituals were based on Shakespeare. The badge was a seven-pointed golden star, one inch high, bearing seven Hebrew characters, a serpent, the Pleiades, a moon in the first quarter, and a comet. Below was a boiling cauldron with a ladle bearing the founding date, 1837.

Omega Pi Alpha

OMEGA PI ALPHA was organized as a men's fraternity at the College of the City of New York on January 1, 1901. It quickly established chapters at Columbia University, University of Pennsylvania, Lehigh University, Rutgers College, and Cornell University. All of these chapters except the parent one became inactive in 1907. The Cornell chapter became a local and assumed the name of Nayati which existed for some time thereafter.

Omicron Alpha Tau

ACTIVE PIN

OMICRON ALPHA TAU was founded at Cornell University in the spring of 1912 by Joseph Seidlin, James Castelle, Jack Grossman, Benjamin Brinkman, Nat Shiren, Jules Jokel, and Abraham Haibloom. They had no thought of organizing a Greek-letter fraternity which would develop into a national, but the influence of the group began to spread among the friends and brothers of those who originally joined the fraternity at Cornell and soon was extended to other institutions. The chapter roll included: 1912, Alpha, Cornell University; 1915, Beta, College of Dental and Oral Surgery (combined with Gamma); 1916, Gamma, Columbia University; 1919 Epsilon, New York University; 1919, Zeta, Syracuse University; 1928, Eta, Rutgers University; 1922, Lambda, University of Pennsylvania; 1924, Nu, Valparaiso University; 1925, Xi. University of Buffalo; 1927, Omicron, University of Alabama; 1927, Pi, University of Illinois; 1927, Rho, McGill University; 1927, Sigma, University of Chicago; 1928, Tau, George Washington University; 1928, Upsilon, Marquette University. There were alumni clubs in North New Jersey, Buffalo, Chicago, and New York. The Cornell and Syracuse chapters owned houses. *The Oath* was a publication issued three times a year. The fraternity disintegrated in 1934.

Phi Alpha

ACTIVE PIN

PHI ALPHA was founded on October 14, 1914, at George Washington University, Washington, D.C., by David Davis, Maurice H. Herzmark, Edward Lewis, Reuben Schmidt, and Hyman Shapiro. Its existence as Phi Alpha ended when a merger was consummated with Phi Sigma Delta, continuing the name of the latter, on April 6, 1959.

Government was by a national convention which met annually in the latter part of December. The fraternity began the publication of a quarterly exoteric magazine in 1917, known as the *Phi Alpha Quarterly.* An esoteric publication known as the *Phi Alpha Bulletin* was published monthly. Directories was published from time to time.

The badge was a gold plaque with the raised letters ΦA and surrounded with a row of pearls. Colors were maroon and blue. The flower was the rose. The pledge button was circular containing a blue circle within a red circle.

The chapter roll was:

1914	Alpha, George Washington	
1915	Beta, Maryland	
1916	Gamma, Georgetown	
1919	Delta, Northwestern (1924)	
1919	Epsilon, Maryland	
1920	Zeta, Yale (1925)	
1920	Eta, Johns Hopkins (1938)	
1920	Theta, N.Y.U.	
1920	Iota, Columbia (1923)	
1921	Kappa, Pennsylvania (1939–1952)	
1921	Lambda, De Paul (1927)	
1922	Mu, Virginia	
1924	Nu, Clark	
1924	Omicron, New Hampshire	
1924	Pi, Boston	
1925	Rho, Richmond	
1925	Sigma, Brooklyn Polytechnic	
1927	Tau, William and Mary	
1927	Upsilon, Chicago	
1927	Phi, Duquesne	
1927	Chi, Trinity (1929)	
1928	Psi, Tennessee (1930)	
1928	Omega, North Carolina	
1928	Alpha Alpha, West Virginia (1935)	
1929	Alpha Beta, Temple	
1930	Alpha Gamma, Wayne State	
1930	Alpha Delta, Detroit	
1937	Alpha Epsilon, St. John's College	
1938	Alpha Zeta, St. John's University	
1940	Alpha Eta, C.C.N.Y.	
1941	Alpha Theta, Washington (1942)	
1953	Alpha Iota, Cornell	

Phi Alpha Chi

PHI ALPHA CHI existed as a fraternity at a number of Virginia colleges between 1883 and 1895. Chapters were reported at Randolph-Macon, University of Virginia, and Richmond College.

Phi Beta Delta

ACTIVE PIN

PHI BETA DELTA was founded at Columbia University on April 4, 1912. A journal, *Phi Beta Delta News Letter,* and a magazine, *The Tripod of Phi Beta Delta,* were published. The badge, diamond-shaped and edged with pearls, had the Greek letters Φ B Δ in gold on a blue background; above the letters was a five-pointed star, and below were two crossed keys. The colors were blue and gold; the flower was the hyacinth. On October 1, 1940, when the fraternity had sixteen active chapters, eighteen inactive chapters and a total enrollment of over 3,000, an agreement was signed with Pi Lambda Phi to merge under the name of Pi Lambda Phi.

Phi Delta Kappa

PHI DELTA KAPPA was founded at Washington and Jefferson College in 1874, the founders being members of a chapter of Iota Alpha Kappa, which had been placed at Washington, Pennsylvania, the previous year. When Iota Alpha Kappa disbanded, this chapter resolved to continue its organization and did so. The chapters established were: Alpha, Washington and Jefferson College, 1874; Beta, Western University of Pennsylvania, 1876; Gamma, Thiel College, 1876; Delta, Lafayette College, 1876; and Epsilon, University of Louisiana, 1878. All the chapters, with the exception of Alpha, had become defunct from various causes by the year 1880. In 1881 Alpha entered Phi Gamma Delta, thus reviving the then inactive Alpha Chapter of that fraternity.

Phi Epsilon Pi

ACTIVE PIN

PHI EPSILON PI was founded at the College of the City New York on November 23, 1904, by Max Shlivek, Alvin P. Bloch, Arthur Hamburger, Siegfried F. Hartman, Arthur Hirschberg, William A. Hannig, and Abraham E. Horn. The preamble of the fraternity states that the members have undertaken to promote a love for higher learning and close friendship, to cultivate a spirit of unselfish fellowship, one unto another, and to exert throughout life an influence tending to more manly character, higher idealism, and tolerance of mind and spirit, all inspired of universal brotherhood. The fraternity was founded as a nonsectarian organization and continued to be nonsectarian in constitution and ritual. The membership, however, had always been predominantly Jewish. The fraternity was incorporated in 1914 in the State of New York.

Most of the chapters were formed from local fraternities, in many cases older than the national body itself. The chapter at the University of Georgia, for instance, was formed from the E.D.S. Society, founded in 1895, the oldest Jewish local fraternity in continuous existence. The chapters at Ohio State, Muhlenberg, and Boston University were originally chapters of the Sigma Lambda Pi Fraternity, which became extinct with the absorption of these three chapters by Phi Epsilon Pi in 1932.

Phi Epsilon Pi became an international fraternity in April, 1951, when its first chapter in Canada was established at McGill University.

In 1961 Kappa Nu and Phi Epsilon Pi entered into an agreement to merge their two fraternities under the name "Phi Epsilon Pi." Kappa Nu was founded at the University of Rochester on November 12, 1911. Phi Epsilon Pi went into the merger with thirty-eight active chapters; Kappa Nu with seventeen. Both were active at Columbia University, Pennsylvania, University of Pittsburgh, U.C.L.A., Cornell University, Brooklyn College, and C.C.N.Y.

The fraternity expired when it merged with Zeta Beta Tau in March, 1970.

The badge of the fraternity was a concave rectangular center with couped ends, domed, and with the three Greek letters emerging bendwise in gold through a black enameled background. The base was jeweled with sixteen pearls, four on each side, following the perimenter of the center piece. The pledge pin was an elongated concave rectangular shape with corners couped with a gold beveled border and the center of purple enamel through which shows a ducal coronet, a scimitar piercing it in a bendwise direction curved toward an open eye in the base. The colors were purple and gold.

The coat of arms was blazoned as follows: Arms: Argent, on a fess purpure a rising sun replendent or. In middle chief, a Phoenician galley under sail and power on a conventionalized ocean all proper, guided by a mullet on the second in dexter, and in base a scimitar piercing the field palewise emerging in the center of a single loop of rope knotted with ends couped at top, all proper. Crest: a sword fesswise surmounted by a ducal coronet all proper under three mullets or. Motto: a Greek phrase.

The fraternity was the first men's Greekletter organization to appropriate funds for activities outside of its own organization. In 1925 the fraternity endowed a $10,000 scholarship at the National Agricultural College in Doylestown, Pennsylvania. The interest on this scholarship provided for the annual expenses of a young man interested in agriculture. The fraternity also gave its International Service Award annually to the person making the most significant contribution to the essentials of brotherhood. This award was started in 1935.

The Phi Epsilon Pi Foundation was created in 1945 to implement the basic aims of the fraternity which, essentially, were to encourage the most complete personal development of its members, intellectual, physical, and social. It continues to function separately.

Total estimated membership May 31, 1967, was 26,811. The chapter roll included fifty-four active and twenty-one inactive chapters.

1904	Alpha, C.C.N.Y.
1905	Beta, Columbia (1928–1958)
1911	Kappa Alpha, Rochester
1911	Epsilon, Cornell
1913	Zeta, Pittsburgh
1914	Eta, Pennsylvania
1914	Theta, Pennsylvania State
1914	Iota, Dickinson
1914	Kappa, N.Y.U. (Square) (1922–1949)
1915	Kappa Beta, N.Y.U. (Heights)
1915	Lambda, Rutgers
1915	Mu, Georgia
1915	Nu, Virginia
1915	Kappa Delta, Union U. (1925)
1916	Xi, Georgia Tech
1916	Omicron, Tufts
1916	Pi, Maine (1925)
1916	Rho, Rhode Island State (1922)
1916	Kappa Iota, New York State (1917)
1916	Sigma, Brown University (1918)
1916	Tau, Auburn (1920)
1916	Upsilon, Connecticut (1964)
1916	Phi, Carnegie Tech (1922)
1917	Kappa Zeta, Buffalo
1917	Kappa Iota, Union
1917	Chi, Syracuse
1920	Gamma, Northwestern
1920	Delta, Washington and Lee

1920   Psi, Illinois
1920   Omega, Cincinnati (1935)
1920   Alpha Alpha, Dartmouth (1922)
1920   Alpha Beta, Iowa
1920   Alpha Epsilon, Johns Hopkins
1921   Alpha Gamma, Michigan (1942–1957)
1921   Kappa Omicron, Chicago (1934)
1921   Kappa Pi, Alabama
1921   Kappa Nu, California
1922   Kappa Sigma, Tulane (1956)
1923   Alpha Delta, Minnesota
1925   Alpha Eta, Wisconsin (1937–1966)
1926   Alpha Zeta, Harvard (1935)
1928   Alpha Theta, South Carolina
1929   Alpha Iota, Miami (Fla.)
1930   Alpha Mu, George Washington (1952)
1932   Kappa Upsilon, Arkansas (1941)
1932   Alpha Nu, Muhlenberg
1932   Alpha Omicron, Ohio State (1964)
1932   Alpha Xi, Boston
1933   Alpha Kappa, Western Reserve
          (1955–1966)
1933   Kappa Phi, Alfred
1933   Alpha Pi, Louisiana State (1958)
1933   Alpha Rho, Ohio
1935   Alpha Sigma, Mississippi
1948   Alpha Tau, Queens (L.I.)
1949   Alpha Upsilon, Memphis State (1959)
1949   Alpha Phi, North Carolina State (1962)
1950   Alpha Chi, Omaha (1955)
1951   Alpha Psi, McGill
1952   Kappa Alpha Delta, U.C.L.A.
1952   Kappa Alpha Gamma, Wayne State (1963)
1956   Beta Alpha, Houston
1957   Beta Beta, American
1958   Beta Gamma, Brooklyn
1959   Beta Delta, Rensselaer
1960   Beta Epsilon, Florida
1961   Beta Zeta, Philadelphia Textiles
1961   Beta Eta, Indiana
1962   Beta Theta, Maryland
1963   Beta Iota, Long Island U.
1965   Beta Lambda, Northern Illinois
1966   Beta Mu, C. W. Post
1966   Beta Xi, C.C.N.Y. (Baruch)
1967   Beta Omicron, DePaul
1967   Beta Sigma, Southampton

Phi Eta

PHI ETA, a fraternity founded in 1904 at the University of Pennsylvania, had as its object "the recognition of sound learning, true culture, and high attainment by the establishment of fraternal relations among male graduate students in the various universities, and by granting the privilege of membership to students who during their graduate course have shown ability in their special fields, and who, in addition, have those personal qualities which make for true culture." Five chapters were established as follows: 1904, Alpha, University of Pennsylvania; 1909, Beta, University o Wisconsin; 1914, Gamma, University of Illinois; 1915, Delta, University of Chicago; 1917, Epsilon, Columbia University. Weakened by the demands of World War I, all the chapters disbanded in the spring of 1918, and none was revived.

Phi Kappa

ACTIVE PIN

PHI KAPPA was founded on October 1, 1889, at Brown University, as a fraternity of Catholic men, and after a distinguished history was joined in a bond with Theta Kappa Phi, a fraternity of Catholic men having similar ideals and principles, on April 29, 1959. The two fraternities were unified on equal terms, choosing the name of Phi Kappa Theta.

The founders of Phi Kappa were Dennis J. Holland, Joseph Mary Killelea, Edward S. Kiley, James M. Gillrain, Edward DeV. O'Connor, James E. Smith, Arthur F. McGinn, James E. Brennan, Edward F. Cunningham, John J. Fitzgerald, Thomas P. Corcoran, Joseph Kirwen, and William H. Magill. They did not contemplate the establishment of a full-fledged Greekletter fraternity, but had in mind only the formation of a club or society. The name Phi Kappa Sigma, meaning fraternity of Catholic students, was assumed by the society. The name was changed to Phi Kappa in 1900, because there had long been the Phi Kappa Sigma Fraternity. On April 29, 1902, which date was celebrated as Founders' Day, the fraternity was incorporated under the laws of the State of Rhode Island and Providence Plantations. The charter set forth the purposes of incorporation as: "Promoting social and intellectual intercourse among its members, identifying students and alumni more closely with their college, and cultivating a spirit of loyalty to *alma mater*."

The fraternity magazine, *The Temple*, was published quarterly. Other publications included a membership directory, a songbook, *Manual for chapter Fellows* for the guidance of graduate chapter advisers residing in the chapter houses, and also the complete *Pledge Manual*.

The badge was a quatrefoil of yellow gold, the border jeweled with twelve crown-set whole pearls and four amethysts, the latter placed one on each corner. Super imposed on the center along the vertical axis were a skeleton cipher monogram of Φ K, the Φ being Roman finish and the letter K chased.

The coat of arms: Φ K, or, two bars purpure, on a chief embattled of the second. A cross-quarterly pierced between two quartrefoils argent, within a border sable. Behind the shield, two swords saltire-wise point downward, proper, pommeled or. On an esquire's helmet and a wreath of colors, or, pur-pure, the crest a façade of a Grecian temple with six Doric columns purpure. Mantling, leaves of oak, conventionalized, purpure and agent. Motto: a Greek phrase.

The pledge pin: argent, two bars purpure, a chief embattled of the second, all within a bordure or. The flag had three vertical stripes of purple, white, and gold. Upon the purple stripe the letter Φ and on the gold letter K. Upon the middle stripe (of white) a shield with two purple bars, on a chief embattled of the second, all within a gold border. This was a replica of the pledge pin.

The motto of the fraternity was *Loyalty to God and College*. Colors were purple, white, and gold. The flower was the ophelia rose.

The chapter roll was:

1889 Alpha, Brown (1930)
1912 Beta, Illinois
1913 Gamma, Pennsylvania State
1914 Delta, Iowa (1932–1947)
1915 Epsilon, Kansas
1918 Zeta, Purdue
1918 Eta, M.I.T.
1920 Theta, Ohio State
1921 Iota, Kansas State
1923 Kappa, Missouri (1935–1948)
1923 Lambda, Wisconsin
1923 Mu, Pittsburgh
1924 Nu, Michigan (1935)
1924 Xi, Iowa State
1925 Pi, Nebraska (1934)
1925 Rho, Carnegie Tech
1925 Sigma, Rennselaer
1925 Tau, Syracuse (1935)
1926 Upsilon, Maine (1935)
1927 Phi, Denver (1933–1949)
1929 Chi, Bucknell (1933)
1929 Psi, Ohio
1930 Omega, Catholic University
1939 Alpha Alpha, Indiana
1941 Alpha Beta, Case Institute
1943 Alpha Gamma (colony), Tri-State
1947 Alpha Epsilon, Minnesota
1949 Alpha Delta, Washington State
1950 Alpha Zeta, Wyoming
1950 Alpha Eta, Manhattan
1951 Alpha Theta, Oregon State
1951 Alpha Iota, Arizona
1953 Alpha Kappa, Butler
1955 Alpha Lambda, Spring Hill
1956 Alpha Mu, Houston
1956 Alpha Nu, Loyola of Los Angeles

Phi Kappa Alpha

PHI KAPPA ALPHA was the outgrowth of a society called Wayland Literary Society, founded at Brown University in 1870. In 1873 a union was effected with the Literary Union of Rochester University. The name of the society was changed to Sigma Phi. The Brown chapter was called Alpha, and the one at Rochester Beta. In 1874 the name was changed to Phi Kappa Alpha. Beta became extinct in 1879, and in 1880 Alpha entered Beta Theta Pi, reviving Kappa Chapter of that fraternity. The badge was a three-sided shield displaying the letters Φ K A above an open book. The shield was bounded by circular arcs, the upper one bearing the name of the college.

Phi Kappa Phi

PHI KAPPA PHI owed its origin to the Philozetian Literary Society, established at Baldwin Institute in 1849. In 1857 the Phreno-Cosmian Society was founded as a rival, and the two existed in healthy competition until they joined forces in 1915, two years after the present Baldwin-Wallace College had been formed by the union of Baldwin College and German Wallace College. The new fraternity was named Phi Kappa Phi. On April 18, 1941 Phi Kappa Phi became Epsilon Theta Chapter of Alpha Tau Omega.

Phi Kappa Pi

PHI KAPPA PI was founded at Monmouth College on September 21, 1885. The fraternity was known as Theta Sigma Phi until 1902 when the name Phi Kappa Pi was chosen. The badge was made up of the Greek letters Φ KΠ set with pearls and with the fraternity crest attached as a guard. The colors were red and blue. On May 3, 1947, Phi Kappa Pi became Epsilon Nu Chapter of Alpha Tau Omega.

Phi Mu Omicron

ACTIVE PIN

PHI MU OMICRON was the outgrowth of the dis-banding of several of the chapters or circles of the old southern order of Kappa Alpha. This occurred following exposure of the secrets of the order in 1855. To perpetuate the order, it was reorganized at the University of South Carolina in 1858 under the name of Phi Mu Omicron. The reorganized circle there being named Alpha, other circles were soon established, among them the following: Beta, Charleston College; Zeta, Wofford College; Kappa, Emory College; Omicron, Emory and Henry College; Sigma, Newberry College. The circles at South Carolina and Emory and Henry had been circles of Kappa Alpha, and other Phi Mu Omicron circles doubtless grew out of disbanded Kappa Alpha circles. None of them survived the Civil War. An attempt to revive the circle at Emory and Henry in 1879 resulted in several of the Kappa Alpha and Phi Mu Omicron alumni joining Kappa Sigma, which was then revived there. The badge of Phi Mu Omicron was a Maltese cross, with black enamel arms on each of which were three gold stars; and with a circular field of gold in the center on which were an open eye, clasped hands, and a dagger, the central field surrounded by a wreath. On the reverse at the top were "A.D. 1812," the year that Kappa Alpha had been founded, the owner's name across the center, and the letters Φ M O at the bottom. This is the only known instance of the name of a fraternity appearing on the reverse instead of the obverse of its badge.

Phi Phi Phi

PHI PHI PHI (TRI-PHI) was a fraternity organized at Austin College, Sherman, Texas, November 22, 1894. It was started with the idea of establishing chapters in the West and South and more especially in small colleges affording men for one good chapter. The chapter roll was as follows: 1894, Austin College; 1894. Southwestern University; 1896, Presbyterian College of South Carolina; 1896, Centenary College; 1897, University of Texas. The chapter at the University of Texas joined Phi Kappa Psi in 1904. The remaining chapters one by one became inactive. The badge was an open book of white enamel bearing a hand and an anchor of gold and resting upon two crossed lances between the heads of which extended a scroll bearing the letters Φ Φ Φ.

Phi Pi Phi

PHI PI PHI was founded on November 15, 1915, as a graduate fraternity and so remained until its Alpha chapter was established at Northwestern in 1923. It was admitted to membership in the NIC in 1924, and ended its existence as a national in 1939 when Alpha Sigma Phi absorbed its five then existing chapters at Illinois Tech, Case Institute, Baldwin-Wallace, Westminster (Pa.), and Purdue. The founders were Victor B. Scott, Fred M. Clarke, Arnold C. Van Zandt, and William B. Kinney.

The official organ, *The Quarterly of Phi Pi Phi*, was established in 1924. A songbook was published in 1927. In 1926 an endowment fund for the support of the magazine was begun. The badge was a monogram of Greek letters, the letter "Π" superimposed upon intertwined "Φ Φ." The colors were turquoise blue and black; the colors of the pledge button black and gold. The flower was the bluebell.

The chapter roll was as follows:

1923	Alpha, Northwestern
1923	Beta, Chicago
1923	Gamma, Armour Institute
1923	Delta, Illinois
1924	Epsilon, Washburn
1924	Zeta, Wisconsin
1924	Eta, Utah
1924	Theta, California
1925	Iota, Washington and Jefferson
1925	Kappa, Pennsylvania
1926	Lambda, Case Shool
1926	Mu, Baldwin-Wallace
1927	Nu, Westminster (Pa.)
1927	Xi, North Carolina State
1927	Omicron, Mississippi
1928	Pi, South Carolina
1928	Rho, St. Lawrence
1929	Sigma, Pennsylvania State
1929	Tau, Tennessee
1929	Upsilon, Oregon State

Phi Sigma

ACTIVE PIN

PHI SIGMA LEAGUE was founded at Lombard University, Galesburg, Illinois, by several students of the class of 1857. It established chapters at Knox College, Monmouth College, Northwestern University, Hedding College, Abingdon College, Eureka College, and Jefferson College, Wisconsin, but none was prosperous, and they soon died. The parent chapter joined Phi Delta Theta in 1879. There were three degrees. The two lower ones, the "Anchor" and "Harp," were for undergraduates; these emblems were worn as badges.

Phi Sigma Delta

ACTIVE PIN

PHI SIGMA DELTA was founded at Columbia University, November 10, 1909, by William L. Berk, Herbert L. Eisenberg, Maxwell Hyman, Alfred Iason, Joseph Levy, Herbert K. Minsky, Joseph Shalleck, and Robert Shapiro. These men seemed unable to find the proper opportunity for the campus fellowship they were seeking and thus determined to form their own fraternity and thereby perpetuate and nurture their comradeship. The initial meetings and gatherings were held weekly at the homes of the various founders, during which time the constitution, ritual, and design of the badge were completed. The first initiate was inducted early in 1911, and the young fraters, cognizant of prospective expansion, established a chapter home in two rooms of Hartley Hall dormitory in September of that year. The chapter, gathering strength, had twelve members when it was incorporated in the State of New York on June 1, 1912.

A merger between Phi Sigma Delta and Phi Alpha Fraternity, consummated on April 6, 1959, produced considerable impetus. At the time of the merger, Phi Alpha had sixteen active chapters, mostly located in the east. Both fraternities had chapters at three campuses; two of these conflicts were readily resolved, while the third, by mutual agreement, saw one of the groups given its release to affiliate with another national fraternity.

Phi Sigma Delta's existence as a national fraternity ended in 1969 when agreement was reached to merge with Zeta Beta Tau.

The badge of the fraternity consisted of monogram or the letters Φ Σ Δ, obliquely joined, the base being of gold with twenty-four crown pearls inset on the three Greek letters. The pledge pin was round, depicting a white palm and pyramid within a purple background. The Phi Sigma Delta Hymn, generally known as "We Sing To Thee, Phi Sigma Delta," was officially adopted in 1930.

Total membership May 31, 1967, was 19,500. The chapter roll at that time included forty-nine active and twenty-two inactive chapters.

1909	Alpha, Columbia (1933–1955)
1912	Beta, Cornell
1913	Gamma, R.P.I.
1913	Delta, N.Y.U. (Heights)
1914	Epsilon, Union
1914	Phi Alpha, George Washington
1915	Phi Beta, Maryland (Baltimore)
1916	Zeta, Pennsylvania
1916	Eta, Michigan
1916	Phi Gamma, Georgetown (1947)
1919	Phi Delta, Northwestern (1924)
1919	Phi Epsilon, Maryland (College Park)
1919	Theta, Colorado
1920	Phi Zeta, Yale (1925)
1920	Iota, Denver
1920	Kappa, Western Reserve
1920	Lambda, Texas
1921	Phi Lambda, De Paul (1927)
1921	Mu, Chicago
1921	Nu, M.I.T. (1927)
1921	Omicron, Ohio State
1922	Pi, Wisconsin
1922	Phi Mu, Virginia (1942)
1923	Rho, Johns Hopkins
1924	Phi Nu, Clark
1924	Phi Omicron, New Hampshire (1962)
1924	Phi Pi, Boston
1925	Tau, Lehigh (1933)
1925	Phi Rho, Richmond
1925	Phi Sigma, Brooklyn Polytechnic
1927	Sigma, Penn State
1927	Upsilon, West Virginia
1927	Phi Tau, William and Mary (1954)
1927	Phi Phi, Duquesne
1927	Phi Chi, Trinity (1929)
1928	Phi, Vermont
1928	Phi Psi, Tennessee (1930)
1928	Phi OMega, North Carolina (1943)
1929	Chi, Duke (1936)
1929	Psi, Alabama (1939)
1929	Phi Alpha Beta, Temple
1930	Phi Alpha Gamma, Wayne State (1942–1961)
1931	Omega, Missouri (1964)
1937	Phi Alpha Epsilon, St. John's College (1947)
1938	Phi Alpha Zeta, St. John's University (1941)
1941	Phi Alpha Eta, C.C.N.Y.
1941	Phi Alpha Theta, Washington College (1942)
1943	Alpha Alpha, Connecticut
1947	Alpha Beta, U.C.L.A.
1947	Alpha Gamma, Illinois
1948	Alpha Delta, Ohio
1949	Alpha Epsilon, Syracuse
1952	Alpha Zeta, Miami (Fla.) (1966)
1952	Alpha Eta, Colorado State
1952	Alpha Theta, Rutgers
1952	Alpha Iota, N.Y.U. (Square) (1966)
1955	Alpha Kappa, Utah (1961)
1957	Phi Alpha Kappa, Hunter
1957	Alpha Lambda, Detroit
1957	Alpha Mu, Massachusetts
1957	Alpha Nu, Wisconsin-Milwaukee
1958	Alpha Xi, C.W. Post
1959	Alpha Omicron, Pratt
1959	Phi Alpha Mu, C.C.N.Y.
1961	Kappa Nu, Brooklyn
1963	Alpha Pi, Rhode Island
1963	Alpha Rho, Washington (Mo.)
1963	Alpha Sigma, Michigan State
1964	Alpha Tau, L.I.U.
1965	Alpha Upsilon, Adelphi
1965	Alpha Phi, Parsons

Phi Sigma Epsilon

ACTIVE PIN

PLEDGE PIN

PHI SIGMA EPSILON was founded on February 20, 1910, at Kansas State Teachers College, Emporia, in answer to the dream of Fred M. Thompson and Orin M. Rhine to have a Greek letter organization on the campus. Initial membership consisted of thirteen men. Because the college administration refused to recognize the newly formed organization, it existed for some time as an outlaw organization. However, it continued to win friends by strict adherence to its principles and positive contributions to the institution and finally, in 1913, the group was officially recognized by the college. The repercussions that followed were in the nature of an obstacle which too, was overcome.

In 1927-28, the Emporia Phi Sigma Epsilon formed a union with Pi Sigma Epsilon of Kansas State Teachers College of Pittsburg, and Sigma Delta Tau of Kirksville State Teachers College, Missouri, and became the National Fraternity of Phi Sigma Epsilon. The purpose of the fraternity was "to promote bonds of fellowship among men of like mind, and to further promote the ideals of intellectual, moral, social and physical development." A further objective was "to encourage culture, to foster college spirit, to perpetuate friendship and intimate social ties within its membership, and to provide college homes for its active members."

Phi Sigma Epsilon became one of the new twentieth century college fraternities and expanded accordingly. During the 1930s the fraternity added seven chapters throughout the Midwest, admitting only well-established local fraternities at accredited teachers colleges. Growth was slow and continued during the '40s prior to World War II, when privations rendered the brotherhood all but inactive. However, when the war was over, each of the fifteen chapters was revived and several new ones added between 1946 and 1948. As the 1950s approached, Phi Sigma Epsilon leaders became aware of the need for branching out from teachers colleges into liberal arts schools. In 1952, the first colony was established. The fraternity doubled in size between 1950 and 1960. Phi Sigma Epsilon became a junior member of the NIC in 1953 and a senior member in 1965.

At the time of the merger with Phi Sigma Kappa, the Fraternity had 35 chapters, one colony and 40,000 initiates.

1910 Alpha, Kansas State, Emporia (1974)
1928 Beta, Kansas State, Pittsburg
1928 Gamma, Northeast Missouri
1929 Delta, Eastern Illinois
1929 Epsilon, Northeastern (OK)
1929 Zeta, Fort Hays
1929 Eta, Southeastern (OK) (1960-1967)
1931 Theta, Northern Iowa
1931 Iota, Central Missouri State
1932 Kappa, Wisconsin, Stevens Point
1935 Lambda, Eastern Michigan
1935 Mu, Arkansas State
1939 Nu, Northwest Missouri
1940 Xi, Central Michigan
1941 Omicron, Wayne (1950)
1941 Pi, Western Illinois
1945 Rho, Henderson
1947 Sigma, Northern Illinois (1976)
1948 Tau, Ball State
1949 Phi, Wisconsin, Milwaukee (1970)
1950 Upsilon, Wisconsin, Whitewater
1950 Chi, SUNY Col., Oswego (1954-1977)
1952 Psi, SUNY Col., Geneseo (1954)
1952 Omega, Wisconsin, Stout
1952 Phi Beta, Wisconsin, Eau Claire
1955 Phi Delta, Black Hills (1961-1970)
1956 Phi Gamma, Western Michigan
1956 Phi Epsilon, Rider
1956 Phi Lambda, Parsons (IA) (1972)
1958 Phi Zeta, Illinois (1972)
1959 Phi Eta, Clarion (1972)
1959 Phi Theta, Shippensburg
1959 Phi Iota, Northland
1959 Phi Kappa, West Virginia Wesleyan
1960 Phi Mu, Concord
1960 Sigma Chi, Shepherd
1960 Sigma Alpha, Wisconsin, LaCrosse
1961 Phi Omicron, St. Cloud
1961 Phi Pi, Wisconsin, Superior (1976)
1962 Phi Nu, Mansfield
1962 Phi Xi, Winona
1963 Phi Rho, Chadron
1963 Phi Tau, Cornell
1964 Phi Upsilon, Valparaiso
1965 Phi Sigma, Hillsdale
1965 Phi Phi, Wisconsin, Oshkosh (1976)
1967 Sigma Beta, Southwest Missouri
1969 Sigma Gamma, Wayne State (NE)
1968 Sigma Delta, St. Norbert
1968 Sigma Epsilon, Ferris
1968 Sigma Zeta, Wisconsin, River Falls
1969 Sigma Eta, Southeast Missouri
1969 Sigma Theta, Hofstra
1969 Sigma Iota, Wisconsin, Platteville
1969 Sigma Kappa, LaSalle
1970 Sigma Nu, Slippery Rock
1970 Phi Omega, Moorhead
1970 Phi Psi, St. Thomas
1970 Sigma Xi, Bloomsburg
1971 Phi Chi, Bemidji (1976)
1971 Sigma Tau, Missouri Western (1976)

Pi Epsilon Phi

ACTIVE PIN

PI EPSILON PHI Fraternity was the oldest organization on the Evansville College campus, actually older than the college itself, until on December 14, 1957, it became Indiana Epsilon of Sigma Alpha Epsilon. The society was formed in 1854 in the town of Moores Hill, Indiana, in anticipation of the funding of Moores Hill College (now Evansville College), nine months later. Prior to the founding of Moores Hill college it was known as the Philomathean Literary Society. Isaac Ward was permanent chairman of the group.

With the move to make the fraternity a part of Moores Hill College, the name was changed to the Philoneikean Library Society. It retained that name until 1929 when it became the Pi Epsilon Phi Fraternity.

In the Civil War period, with the beginning of hostilities, the fraternity, to a man, offered service to the country. One-third of these men made the supreme sacrifice. "Excelsior" was the motto of the fraternity. The colors were black and gold, the flower the yellow rose.

Pi Rho Phi

PI RHO PHI was a fraternity founded at Westminister College, Pennsylvania, in 1854. The organization was originally known as Cross of Hearts Fraternity, with Pi Rho Phi as its motto, but it gradually assumed the Greek letters of the motto as the name of the fraternity. Chapters were established at Hiram, Monmouth, Thiel, Muskingum, and Allegheny Theological Seminary, the latter being a graduate chapter. In 1868 the mother chapter at Westminster was admitted to Delta Tau Delta as Chi Chapter, but was forced to relinquish its charter in 1872 when the entire chapter was ousted from college. A year or so later Pi Rho Phi was revived and flourished as a sub rosa fraternity until 1920 when it was recognized by the college. In 1924 the Westminster chapter joined with nine other fraternities in organizing Theta Upsilon Omega, which in 1938 was absorbed by Sigma Phi Epsilon. With the exception of the Monmouth chapter, the other chapters of Pi Rho Phi disbanded. The Monmouth chapter was organized in 1907 as Tau Lambda Phi, the Pi Rho Phi installation taking place in 1910. The Pi Rho Phi tradition at Westminster is continued in a local sorority, which adopted the badge, name, and ritual.

Psi Alpha Kappa

PSI ALPHA KAPPA was a fraternity having chapters at Lehigh, Lafayette, and the Massachusetts Institute of Technology. The parent chapter joined Alpha Tau Omega and the Lafayette chapter Alpha Chi Rho.

Psi Theta Psi

PSI THETA PSI FRATERNITY was founded about the year 1885 at Washington and Lee University. It had chapters at Roanoke, Randolph-Macon, University of Virginia, Hampden-Sydney, and perhaps one or two other colleges. It disbanded in 1895. The Washington and Lee chapter entered Delta Tau Delta.

Q.T.V.

Q.T.V., was founded at Massachusetts Agricultural College in 1869, two years after the college opened. One of the first Latin letter fraternities in the country, Q.T.V. was committed to "strong academic, social and athletic leadership on campus." Its founding brothers were: Lemuel LeB. Holmes, Fred M. Somers, George Mackie, W.R. Peabody, R.W. Livermore and Edward R. Fisk.

In 1874, Q.T.V. expanded to include the Orono, Maine, chapter, followed by the Granite, New Hampshire, chapter in 1881 and the Boston alumni chapter in 1889. To keep members up to date on events, the other chapters and alumni, Q.T.V. distributed first a quarterly, then an annual publication.

Q.T.V. was originally located in South College, as were the other fraternities at M.A.C. The brothers of Q.T.V. later bought land on Lincoln Avenue on which to build a fraternity house. The college, however, wanted the land for its own use, so in 1917, Q.T.V. purchased the Henry Dana Fearing mansion for their new home. The mansion was torn down in the 1960s because it was believed to be a fire hazard. A new brick building was constructed in its place to house the 48 brothers.

Q.T.V. left campus in 1970, then returned four years later to open a new membership, mostly comprised of the local Phi Sigma chapter. Shortly thereafter, Q.T.V. closed its doors because it could not maintain the mortgage payments on the fraternity house. At that time it was the only Latin letter fraternity left in the country and one of the oldest in the nation.

Rho Lambda Phi

RHO LAMBDA PHI FRATERNITY, originally called Rhizomian Literary Fraternity, was founded on November 26, 1858, by ten students at the University of the Pacific. The purpose of the founders was to form an association for mutual improvement in elocution, composition, and debate.

For fifty years the traditions and activities of Rhizomia centered around the room in West Hall where the founders met. When West Hall burned, other quarters on the campus had to be found. In the fall of 1925, a year after the College of the Pacific moved to Stockton, the members of Rhizomia acquired their own spacious house.

The local ended its existence on December 3, 1960, when it received a charter as the Phi Tetarton chapter of Phi Sigma Kappa.

Sigma Alpha

SIGMA ALPHA (BLACK BADGE) SOCIETY was organized at Roanoke College, Salem, Virginia, in 1859. Soon after its foundation the Civil War put an end to college studies, and the society was not reorganized until 1868. Chapters were established as follows: 1859, Alpha Roanoke College (1879); 1869, Beta, Hampden-Sydney College (1873); 1871, Gamma University of Virginia (1877); 1873, Epsilon, Virginia State College (1880); 1873, Zeta, Salado College (1882); 1873, Eta, University of Maryland (1882); 1873, Theta, Washington and Lee University (1882); 1873, Iota, Kings College (1882); 1875, Xi, Somerville Institute, Miss. (1882). The initiation into the society was elaborate and consisted of several degrees. The organization was completely in the hands of the alumni and was controlled mainly by the chapter at Lynchburg. The badge was of black enamel and displayed the letter Σ, skull and bones, and crossed swords. The fraternity disbanded in 1882.

Sigma Alpha Theta

SIGMA ALPHA THETA during the Civil War and for a time thereafter maintained chapters at Indiana Asbury (DePauw), Merom Christian College, and Hanover College. The chapter at Hanover entered Delta Tau Delta in 1872 and disbanded in 1895.

Sigma Delta Pi

SIGMA DELTA PI, known also as the Vitruvian, was founded at Dartmouth College in 1858 by Benjamin A. Kimball, Augustus Livingstone, William H. Fessenden, Henry L. Bartholomew, W. U. Potter, John A. Staples, and Charles W. Thompson. The parent chapter was called Alpha. In 1871 Beta Chapter, which died in 1874, was established at Cornell University, and in 1874 Gamma Chapter, which died in 1877, was placed at the College of Wooster. The parent chapter continued in good condition until 1889 when it became a chapter of Beta Theta Pi, carrying with it its alumni.

Sigma Delta Rho

ACTIVE PIN

SIGMA DELTA RHO was founded at Miami University, January 8, 1921, by Gilbert L. Stout, Albert O. Grooms, Arthur Baker, Herbert Ansteatt, and Roe Bush. It existed for several months under the name of Delta Sigma Rho and had received recognition from the university as a local fraternity, but when plans were made for expansion into a national organization the name was changed to avoid confusion with the recognition society of that same name. Sigma Delta Rho was incorporated under the laws of Ohio and was the fifth social fraternity to be organized at Miami.

In the latter years of its existence disagreement developed among its chapters as to the policies of the fraternity. This, accentuated by financial problems brought on by the depression and by the absence of strong leadership, led to disintegration in the spring of 1935. The chapters at Franklin and Marshall, Toledo, and Cincinnati joined Alpha Kappa Pi; the Illinois chapter joined the remnants of a chapter of Beta Psi to form a revived chapter of Pi Kappa Phi. The others already threatened with dissolution, gradually disappeared.

The official badge was a cross paté formé purpure with edges or, connected by four chains of five links each; superimposed, a mascle or, inclosing the letters Σ ΔΡ on a field argent.

The chapter roll is 1935 was:

1921	Alpha, Miami (Ohio)
1922	Beta, Ohio State
1924	Gamma, Toledo
1926	Delta, Illinois
1926	Epsilon, Cincinnati
1928	Zeta, Ohio
1929	Eta, Franklin and Marshall
1934	Theta, Hillsdale
1934	Iota, Tri-State

Sigma Iota

SIGMA IOTA was established in 1904 at Louisiana State University as a secret society for Spanish-American students, under the name of Sociedad Hispano-Americana. In 1911 it was changed to a Greek-letter fraternity. Its membership was composed of Spanish-American youths studying in all the universities of America and Europe. It was organized to promote friendship and give help to the Spanish-American students attending foreign universities. The chapter roll was: Alpha Alpha, Louisiana State University; Nu Epsilon, Tulane University; Upsilon Lambda, Loyola University, New Orleans; Alpha Omega, University of Florida. Chapters were later located as follows: Nu Alpha, Alabama Polytechnic Institute; Nu Beta, Syracuse University; Nu Gamma, Rensselaer Polytechnic Institute; Nu Delta, Atlanta Medical School; Nu Zeta, University of Pennsylvania. There were also chapters in Belgium, Switzerland, and Guatemala City. Conventions were held in Baton Rouge 1928 and in New Orleans 1929.

In 1932 Sigma Iota joined Phi Lambda Alpha Fraternity, which later changed its name to Phi Iota Alpha.

Sigma Lambda Pi

SIGMA LAMBDA PI was founded at New York University in April, 1915, by Herbert J. Roeder, Mathew W. Sherman, Abraham Weinberg, and Milton R. Wein berger. It was chartered under the laws of New York as nonsectarian. It established about a dozen chapters, including those at Fordham, Columbia, West Virginia, Pennsylvania, Western Reserve, Michigan, Boston, Muhlenberg, Ohio State, and Rider College. Several of these were shortlived. In 1932 the fraternity disintegrated, its chapters at Boston, Muhlenberg, and Ohio State joining Phi Epsilon Pi; its Columbia chapter dissolving and the branch at Rider College becoming a local, being allowed to retain the name Sigma Lambda Pi. Subsequently the Rider chapter granted a charter to the Bryant and Stratton Commercial College in Providence, Rhode Island. The badge of Sigma Lambda Pi was in the shape of an arch surmounted by a crown. There were seven pearls in the arch and ten in the crown surmounted by one sapphire. The exposed gold was nugget finished, the background of the letters was sapphire blue, the letters in gold. Colors were sapphire blue and gold. The open motto was *Dum Vivimus Fratres Vivamus*, "While we live, let us live as brothers."

Sigma Mu Sigma

SIGMA MU SIGMA, founded at Tri-State College, in 1921, ceased to exist as a national in 1934 when Tau Kappa Epsilon absorbed a number of its chapters. Founded by three Master Masons on Good Friday, it was designed as a Masonic local. In 1924 it was decided to expand into a national fraternity with all the advantages of a social fraternity which would at the same time maintain the scholarship standards of Phi Beta Kappa and restrict its members to Master Masons. This was soon found to be impracticable. The PHi Beta Kappa standard was hard to maintain and was soon dropped, but the fraternity did require a high scholarship record of its pledges. In 1929, the membership requirements were changed to allow the pledging and initiation of sons and brothers of Masons. The fraternity became a junior member of NIC in 1928.

The motto was "Sincerity, Morality and Scholarship." The colors were azure and gold. The flower was the Egyptian lotus.

Chapter roll:

1921	Alpha, Tri-State	
1924	Beta, Oklahoma	
1925	Epsilon, Georgia Washington	
1925	Zeta, Purdue	
1925	Eta, Illinois	
1926	Theta, Oklahoma State College	
1929	Iota, Michigan State Teachers College	

Sigma Nu Sigma was in part revived when remnants of the former fraternity merged with Square and Compass recognition society in 1952.

Sigma Omega Psi

SIGMA OMEGA PSI was founded in 1914 at the College of the City of New York. For a time its progress was rapid and it established chapters at C.C.N.Y., New York University, Columbia, Lowell, Boston, Worcester Tech, Temple, Tufts, Syracuse, M.I.T., Harvard, Northeastern, Alabama, St. John's (Brooklyn), and Cornell. Its existence as Sigma Omega Psi ended in 1940 when a merger was effected with Alpha Epsilon Pi. At the time of the union only the chapters at Tufts, Boston, Worcester Tech, Lowell, and New York University were active. This first three became chapters of Alpha Epsilon Pi and the last was merged with Alpha Chapter. Lowell could not be installed because of an NIC ruling. Subsequently, the chapters at Syracuse, M.I.T., and C.C.N.Y. were re-activated by Alpha Epsilon Pi, and are considered to be revivals of those chapters of Sigma Omega Psi.

Sigma Phi Sigma

ACTIVE PIN

SIGMA PHI SIGMA was founded at the University of Pennsylvania in 1908 as a fraternity. The founder and first high officer was Brice Hayden Long, who enlisted the aid of two other students, Percy Hollinshed Wood and Guy Park Needham. The fraternity was national in scope; eighteen chapters were established with a total membership of approximately 4,500. The official magazine was the *Sigma Phi Sigma Monad*. The badge was a monogram of the Greek letters Σ Φ Σ, the Φ pearl- or diamond-set on two gold Σ's. The fraternity was officially dissolved by its grand assembly held at Berkeley, California, in January, 1947.

The fraternity was committed to an expansion policy of concentrating its chapters in the larger institutions, mostly state universities or large private institutions. By the onset of the depression of the 1930s, it had attained a chapter roll of only eighteen units, which was insufficient to support a strong national organization in the face of the depression years and the World War II years that followed. Only four active chapters re-opened after World War II, and the impotence of the fraternity as a national organization plus the strong desires of the remaining chapters to re-affiliate with stronger fraternity systems led to its formal dissolution by vote of its 21st grand assembly in January, 1947.

The disintegration was triggered as early as 1941 when the University of Maryland chapter withdrew and became a chapter of Sigma Chi. The Cornell chapter became defunct that same year, most of those members joined Tau Kappa Epsilon. Following the dissolution in 1947, the Oregon State chapter became Phi Kappa Psi, and the Illinois chapter merged with Tau Kappa Epsilon. At the same time, the California chapter became Phi Sigma Kappa with the provision that any other member of Sigma Phi Sigma from other chapters might likewise join the former. As a consequence most of the ex-Nevada and Wisconsin chapter members also joined Phi Sigma Kappa; moreover, at the latter institution, the alumni of both the defunct Phi Sigma Kappa and Sigma Phi Sigma chapters joined efforts in re-establishing a Phi Sigma Kappa chapter on the Wisconsin campus, which had been defunct since 1931.

At the time of dissolution vote, however, the Pennsylvania State University chapter announced it would carry on as a local fraternity and retain the name and identity as Sigma Phi Sigma. However, it maintained its existence for only a short time.

Sigma Tau Phi

SIGMA TAU PHI became a part of Alpha Epsilon Pi in March, 1947. Founded in 1918 at the University of Pennsylvania, the fraternity originally admitted only students of engineering and architecture. It established a Beta Chapter at Cincinnati in 1920, and a Gamma Chapter at Pennsylvania State in 1921, Delta at Delaware in 1925, Epsilon at Dickinson in 1926, Zeta at Temple in 1927, and Eta at New York University in 1929. At the time of the union with Alpha Epsilon Pi there were functioning: Alpha at Pennsylvania, which was combined with Gamma of Alpha Epsilon Pi; Delta, renamed Rho Deuteron; and Beta, renamed Omicron Deuteron. The Penn State Chapter was revived and named Pi Deuteron, while the Alpha Pi Chapter, established in 1956, is considered to be a reactivation of the Zeta Chapter of Sigma Tau Phi.

The Record, the official periodical, was published annually. The badge of black enamel had the Greek letters Σ T Φ in pearls. The colors were blue and gold.

Sigma Zeta

SIGMA ZETA with chapters at the University of Pennsylvania and the University of Michigan was formed by the union of Chi Delta Alpha, local at the former institution, and Delta Tau Upsilon, local at the latter. The magazine was *The Torch.* It may have established a few other chapters before it disbanded in February, 1933, other fraternities absorbing its chapters.

Square and Compass

ACTIVE PIN

SQUARE AND COMPASS (Freemasons) Fraternity was established at Washington and Lee University in 1917. Membership was limited to those who were Master Masons or the sons or other close relatives of Master Masons. The founders were Edgar F. Grossman, Thomas J. Farrar, Carl A. Foss, Lacy L. Shirey, George T. Holbrook, Fred M. Davis, Willis McD. Bristow, Malcolm L McCrae, and W. Bucy Trigg. All were students except Thomas J. Farrar, who was a member of the faculty.

The Masonic Club, of which Square and Compass is the successor, existed at least as far back as 1897. In the fall of 1916 the members of the club believed that affiliation with an intercollegiate organization would strengthen the club and secure the interest of the Masonic students of the university. As all of the members of the club were also members of Greek-letter fraternities, they found themselves unable to affiliate with Acacia, the only existing Masonic intercollegiate organization. Accordingly, they planned a new organization which would accept members of Greek-letter fraternities and would also use the Masonic method of applying for membership rather than the Greek-letter system of "bidding." It was intended from the first that the new organization should be extended to other institutions. Faculty members were placed on the same basis with student members, and a distinguishing characteristic of the fraternity was that qualified applicants must be accepted on their own application unless excellent reasons, which were satisfactory to the local group, could be given for their rejection.

The name of Square and Compass was adopted for the organization which was incorporated under the laws of Virginia on May 12, 1917. Two days later two of the officers left to enter the first ROTC, and before the end of the college year, all of the founders were in either the Army or the Navy. The necessarily postponed for the time being any extension of the fraternity. In the fall of 1919 Carl A. Foss, the secretary of the fraternity, returned to Washington and Lee to complete his education. With the help of Thomas J. Farrar and others he reorganized the fraternity. By the beginning of World War II it had nearly 4,500 members in its 57 "squares," as the groups were called. It closed "for the duration," but started up again at the close of the war, opening its membership to sons and close relatives of Masons.

Square and Compass merged with Sigma Mu Sigma, a recognition society—but originally a men's fraternity and a junior member of the NIC—on August 3, 1952.

Tau Delta Phi

ACTIVE PIN

PLEDGE PIN

TAU DELTA PHI was founded on June 22, 1910, at the College of the City of New York as a local fraternity. The group comprising the organization maintained itself as a single unit until 1912, when a division into two chapters became necessary. The local character was continued until 1917 by confining the chapters to the city of New York with the thought that only in localization could the spirit of the organization be maintained. This idea had to be changed when college men outside of New York became interested in the organization. It was from

this beginning that Tau Delta Phi grew into a national fraternity.

Tau Delta Phi was governed by the Grand Chapter composed of a national executive council and delegates from each undergraduate chapter. The executive council met every two months and the entire Grand Chapter met twice a year. For administrative purposes the fraternity was divided into regions with regional heads who sit on the national executive council.

The fraternity's popular name was Taudelt. The seal was of circular form, bearing two flaming torches interlocked in a square within the square, a pyramid, star, and the circular inscription "Tau Delta Phi Fraternity—Grand Chapter."

The coat of arms was a shield of blue and white divided into four corner and one center sections. The center section consisted of a pyramid and a mullet in the right northern area of the section. The upper lefthand corner bore the symbol of a ship. A rampant lion was in the left bottom section. The upper righthand conner contained the fraternity pledge pin. The lower right had two mullets. The crest above the shield was composed of an owl protruding from a rook. The pledge pin was a square diamond. A vertical line divided the pin into two colors; the left side, white, and the right, navy blue. Fraternity colors were navy blue and white.

The Pyramid, the official magazine, was published annually.

For a number of years, the fraternity maintained a headquarters at 269 High Street, Newark, New Jersey 07102.

Tau Delta Phi installed about fifty-five chapters during its life and, in 1977, reported fourteen active and forty-one inactive with a total membership estimated at 13,000. The fraternity continued a slow but steady decline until about 1973 when no active chapters were known to exist. The chapter roll:

1914	Alpha, C.C.N.Y.	
1914	Gamma, N.Y.U. (Square)	
1916	Delta, Columbia (1949)	
1917	Epsilon, Boston (1951)	
1918	Zeta, Harvard (1929)	
1919	Eta, M.I.T. (1929)	
1920	Theta, Armour Institute (1923)	
1920	Iota, Pennsylvania (1970)	
1920	Kappa, Cincinnati (1928)	
1921	Lambda, Chicago (1935)	
1921	Mu, Vanderbilt (1923)	
1922	Nu, Michigan (1968)	
1923	Xi, Northwestern (1968)	
1924	Omicron, Ohio State (1931)	
1924	Pi, Illinois (1975)	
1926	Rho, Texas (1975)	
1927	Sigma, Southern California (1968)	
1927	Tau, Lehigh (1973)	
1928	Chi, U.C.L.A. (1969)	
1928	Phi, Minnesota (1952)	
1929	Upsilon, North Dakota (1941)	
1929	Psi, Carnegie Tech (1973)	

1932 Omega, Manitoba (1957)
1933 Tau Alpha, Colby (1972)
1934 Tau Beta, Cornell (1971)
1934 Tau Gamma, Rutgers (1976)
1943 Gamma Upsilon, N.Y.U. (Heights) (1969)
1947 Tau Delta, Arizona (1968)
1947 Tau Epsilon, Newark Engineering
1949 Tau Zeta, Syracuse
1950 Tau Eta, Loyola (Chicago) (1968)
1950 Tau Theta, Norwich (1960)
1951 Tau Iota, Rutgers (Newark)
1952 Tau Kappa, Queens (L.I.)
1952 Tau Lambda, Alfred (1970)
1952 Tau Mu, Miami (Fla.) (1971)
1952 Tau Nu, Hunter (1968)
1956 Tau Omicron, Temple (1971)
1956 Tau Xi, Long Island (1971)
1957 Tau Pi, Roosevelt (1968)
1959 Tau Rho, Brooklyn
1962 Tau Sigma, Pratt
1965 Tau Tau, Pennsylvania State (1973)
1966 Tau Upsilon, Michigan State (1968)
1967 Tau Phi, Seton Hall
1968 Tau Chi, Chicago (1970)
1968 Tau Psi, C. W. Post (1971)
1968 Tau Omega, Corpus Christi (1972)
1969 Delta Beta, Maryland (1973)
1969 Delta Gamma, Widener (Pa.)
1969 Delta Delta, P.I.N.Y. (Brooklyn)
1969 Delta Epsilon, Paterson State
1975 Delta Eta, Cooper Union
1975 Delta Zeta, P.I.N.Y. (Farmingdale)

Theta Alpha

THETA ALPHA was organized at Syracuse University on February 22, 1909. At the time the fraternity merged with Delta Sigma Lambda in 1933 it had initiated 585 members through these four active chapters: 1909, Alpha, Syracuse University; 1914, Beta, Cornell University; 1922, Gamma, University of Illinois; 1925, Delta, University of Southern California. A periodical, *Theta Alpha*, was published by the Grand Chapter.

The Syracuse chapter was not a part of the merger and resumed its old name as a local; meanwhile by 1937 Delta Sigma Lambda, too, had disintegrated.

See also Delta Sigma Lambda.

Theta Kappa Nu

THETA KAPPA NU was founded by the union of eleven well established local fraternities at a meeting held in Springfield, Missouri, June 9, 1924. The chapters which united at this time were Phi Kappa Nu, Howard College (Birmingham); Tau Lambda Delta at Rollins College, University of Florida, and

North Carolina State College; Tri Kappa, Hanover College; Kappa Delta Psi, Iowa Wesleyan College; Sigma Delta Chi, Simpson College; Phi Beta Omega, Baker University; Phi Alpha Sigma, Drury College; Kappa Phi, Oklahoma City University; and Phi Sigma, Gettysburg College.

The leaders of the union meeting at Springfield were Professor Winslow S. Anderson, then a member of the faculty of North Carolina State College; Otho R. McAtee of Springfield, Missouri; the Reverend Jerry H. Krenmyre, a Methodist minister of Agency, Iowa; and Donald F. Lybarger an attorney of Cleveland, Ohio. More than fifty chapters were established with a total membership of almost six thousand. The magazine *Theta News*, was published quarterly. The badge, enameled in black, was formed by three equilateral triangles with vertices meeting at a center upon which was superimposed a fourth equilateral triangle with the base uppermost. The outer triangles with the base uppermost. The outer triangles displayed the Greek letters T K N in gold, the center triangle bore a Tudor rose and a mystic symbol. The colors were argent, sable, and crimson; the flower was the white rose.

Theta Kappa Nu affiliated with Lambda Chi Alpha on October 11, 1939.

Theta Kappa Phi

ACTIVE PIN

THETA KAPPA PHI was the outgrowth of the X Club at Lehigh University, organized by several men of the Newman Club in 1914, all of whose members enlisted in World War I. Three of the original group returned to Lehigh and on October 22, 1919, completed the reorganization of the X Club along fraternal lines, choosing the name and motto of Theta Kappa Phi. A few months later the Lehigh chapter amalgamated with Kappa Theta of Pennsylvania State College to form the national fraternity of Theta Kappa Phi, which possessed twenty chapters when the fraternity was consolidated with Phi Kappa on an equal basis on April 29, 1959, the resultant brotherhood being known as Phi Kappa Theta. The fraternity was based on a singleness of faith and purpose, a belief in the unique destiny of man and his consequent human dignity and worth, holding fast to the same basic spiritual concepts upon which the founding fathers built this nation under God.

The fraternity pioneered in international student and cultural exchange programs. In 1937 a delegate of Theta Kappa Phi attended the international student congress in Paris, and a year later at the world conclave in Liubiana a member of the fraternity was elected international president, the first American so honored.

In early September, 1939, Theta Kappa Phi served as federation host to an international university conference in Washington and New York. Over a thousand delegates from fifty-three countries attended. While the conference was in session hostilities broke out in Europe, and many of the delegates, principally from Eastern Europe, were prevented from returning to their native lands. The fraternity, together with other agencies, found scholarship opportunities for this first group of displaced students, thus inaugurating its relief program on behalf of student victims of the war.

Theta Kappa Phi alumni, stationed in Europe with the U.S. Armed Forces, military government, the foreign service, and United Nations agencies, formed, in 1946 the European Alumni Chapter of Theta Kappa Phi with "headquarters" in the thousand-year-old Bavarian castle of Hohenashaw, where various chapter functions and activities were held. This alumni chapter sponsored social activities for American students attending the University of Maryland (in Europe).

The official publication was *The Sun of Theta Kappa Phi*, issued quarterly. The badge was a shield displaying upon a black enamel face the letters Θ K Φ in gold over a golden heart. All this was mounted on a gold shield bordered with crown-set pearls, and four rubies in the form of a cross. The pledge button was a shield of white, bordered with a gold chain enclosing a golden sun. The colors were red, silver, and gold. The flower was the columbine.

The chapter roll was:

1919	Alpha, Lehigh	
1922	Beta, Pennsylvania State	
1922	Gamma, Ohio State	
1923	Delta, Illinois	
1924	Epsilon, New Hampshire	
1925	Zeta, Ohio Northern	
1925	Eta, C.C.N.Y.	
1927	Theta, Cornell (1931)	
1932	Iota, Temple	
1934	Kappa, Oklahoma	
1935	Lambda, Worcester Tech	
1936	Mu, Missouri Mines	
1937	Nu, Oklahoma State	
1938	Xi, Louisiana State	
1941	Omicron, Southwestern Louisiana	
1948	Pi, St. Louis	
1948	Rho, Mississippi State	
1949	Sigma, Boston	
1949	Tau, St. Francis	
1949	Upsilon, Missouri	
1949	Phi, Kent State	
1951	Chi, Mississippi	
1954	Psi, Northern Illinois State	
1953	Colony, San Jose State (1954)	
1954	Colony, Wisconsin	

Theta Nu Epsilon

THETA NU EPSILON was founded at Wesleyan University in 1870, primarily as a social fraternity for sophomores, accepting into membership members of other fraternities. In this it was similar to other fraternities of its day that started as class societies. This society was so loosely governed nationally, however, and the behavior of its membership in many institutions so unrestrained the fraternity fell into disrepute, and most fraternities prohibited their members from joining it. Some of its early chapters were formed as general social fraternities, but on discovering the poor reputation of the organization nationally, left it to become chapters of other nationals. Such a case was the Omicron Omicron Chapter at Ohio Northern University, founded 1903, which joined Sigma Phi Epsilon in 1905 as that fraternity's Ohio Alpha Chapter. In 1909 an effort was made to reorganize the fraternity along national lines that would make it more acceptable. Its new administration started publishing a journal, but by 1915 this had been discontinued. Unauthorized chapters continued to appear on many campuses (as many as eighty-three unauthorized chapters have been identified). Because of its lack of effective administration, by 1920 such discredit was being cast upon the fraternity system by the misbehavior of some of these units the National Interfraternity Council appointed a committee to look into the matter and find some solution. A convention of the fraternity was held in Philadelphia in 1923 and adopted a resolution on policy for reorganization. This took place at the beginning of the college year 1925–26, following the fifteenth convention in Louisville, December, 1925, with the recognition of an active roll of fourteen chapters and an enrollment membership of 9,200.

Government of the fraternity to 1907 had been by the Alpha Chapter. In that year of reorganization the fraternity was incorporated under the laws of New York by representatives of all chapters. The government was then changed to operate through the Grand Council of five members, who were to be elected at the biennial conventions. In 1919 a business administration was established under an executive secretary, and in 1925 it ceased clandestine activity and became an open general fraternity, forbidding the initiation of members of other fraternities. In 1920 it started publication of a magazine, *The Keys*. The fraternity, however, like many others which were founded or reorganized in the late '20s, received its death blow from the financial depression, starting to decline in 1930. In 1942 its last known chapter, the revived Omicron Omicron at Ohio Northern, joined Alpha Kappa Pi, that fraternity announcing that this was last legitimate chapter of Theta Nu Epsilon. Thus two chapters of national fraternities on that campus owe their being to Theta Nu Epsilon.

Underground chapters existed in the 1950s although there was apparently no national organization or coordination. (Recent communication with an alumnus indicates there is currently an effort being made to reorganize the organization under more legitimate principles— Editor.)

No known chapters were begun after 1929. By the time World War II started the fraternity was reduced to five chapters: Union, Rensselaer, Ohio Northern, New York University (Square), and Pennsylvania State. Of these three apparently became casualties, and the remaining two joined Alpha Kappa Pi, and with the union of that fraternity with Alpha Sigma Phi, became chapters of the latter.

The chapter roll, including the fate of each chapter, follows:

1874   Gamma, Union, inactive 1940.

1882   Lambda, Rensselaer, in 1940 became Alpha Kappa of Alpha Kappa Pi, then in 1946 became Beta Psi of Alpha Sigma Phi.

1883   Mu, Stevens Institute, became inactive 1934.

1903   Omicron Omicron, Ohio Northern, in 1905 became Ohio Alpha of Sigma Phi Epsilon (oldest on Ohio Northern campus), but Omicron Omicron was reestablished about 1923, and it in 1942 became Alpha Lambda of Alpha Kappa Pi, changed its name in 1946 to Gamma Alpha when Alpha Sigma Phi absorbed Alpha Kappa Pi.

1909   Officially, the parent chapter at Wesleyan was abolished in 1909; actually, it continued to exist sub rosa and was later brought back into the open. It serves as Wesleyan's sophomore honor society in sports.

1911   Nu Nu, Marquette, became inactive 1930 when most of its members were graduated.

1912   Upsilon Upsilon, N.Y.U., became inactive 1940–41 when most of the membership enlisted or were drafted.

1914   Alpha Beta, Buffalo, inactive 1918–26, became inactive again within a year of its re-establishment.

1922   Delta Lambda, Kansas City Western Dental, never recognized by the college, became inactive after 1928.

1924   Delta Pi, California, became inactive 1933–34.

1927   Delta Phi, Lombard, became inactive 1930 when the college died.

1927   Pi, Pennsylvania State, a re-establishment, as Pi was active there in 1888–1903; it disbanded after 1940.

1928   Mu Mu, Coe, formed May, 1928, from a local called Sigma Phi Delta, left Theta Nu Epsilon in 1933 and resumed status as the local Sigma Phi Delta, but after 1934 dissolved, its membership joining other fraternities.

1928   Xi Xi, Louisville, became inactive after 1933.

1928   Pi Pi, Illinois, became inactive after 1934.

1928   Alpha Eta, Ohio State, inactive after 1931.

1928   Alpha Mu, Southwestern University (Memphis) inactive after 1936.

Theta Upsilon Omega

THETA UPSILON OMEGA was founded December 1, 1923, at the National Interfraternity Conference, New York. On December 1–2, 1923, contemporary with the annual meeting of the Conference, there was a conference of local fraternities sponsored by the expansion committee of the Conference. Seventy-eight local fraternities were represented. It was found that the representatives of the following had a common desire for the formation of a new national organization: Delta Tau (1906) of Worcester Polytechnic Institute, Phi Kappa Pi (1906) of Stevens Institute of Technology, Zeus Fraternity (1920) of University of Illinois, Kappa Sigma Phi (1920) of Temple University, Beta Kappa Psi (1920) of Bucknell University, Kappa Tau Omega (1921) of George Washington University, Sigma Beta (1921) of University of New Hampshire, Delta Kappa Nu (1921) of Pennsylvania State College, Phi Alpha Pi (1922) of Davidson College, Phi Delta Sigma (1914) of University of Chattanooga, Everett Fraternity (1889) of Nebraska Wesleyan University, and Sigma Sigma of Iowa State College. Articles of agreement, subject to ratification by the respective local fraternities, were drawn up and signed, and the tentative organization of Phi Kappa Pi was launched. The articles of agreement, when presented to the Conference, were promptly endorsed, and were returned to Phi Kappa Pi with a pledge of support and cooperation by the Conference. Charles R. Drenk of Zeus Fraternity was elected president and Merle C. Cowden, Delta Tau, secretary-treasurer of this tentative organization.

The first nine of the above-mentioned fraternities ratified the action of their representatives to the conference of local fraternities, and on February 21–23, 1924, the delegates of these nine met at the Beta Kappa Psi house at Bucknell University, Lewisburg, Pennsylvania, and completed arrangements for the permanent organization under the name of Theta Upsilon Omega. At this constitutional convocation, Pi Rho Phi (1854) of Westminster College was admitted to the group, thus making a charter list of ten chapters with a total initial membership of 544. On May 2, 1924, at midnight the ten chapters received their charters, and their members were inducted into Theta Upsilon Omega.

In the middle 1930s there was much discussion about expansion. After considering offers from several interested groups, the fourteenth arch convocation voted to enter into a merger with Sigma Phi Epsilon. In the spring of 1938, Beta Alpha Chapter became Massachusetts Beta of Sigma Phi Epsilon; Gamma Alpha, New Jersey Alpha; Epsilon Alpha, Pennsylvania Mu; Zeta Alpha, Pennsylvania Kappa; Lambda Alpha, Pennsylvania Lambda; Delta Beta, Pennsylvania Iota; Theta Beta, New York Delta. Delta Alpha at University of Illinois, Eta Alpha at George Washington University, Gamma Beta at University of California, and Eta Beta at Alabama Polytechnic Institute merged with the existing Sigma Phi Epsilon chapters on those campuses. Iota Alpha Chapter at Pennsylvania State College merged with the local Theta Chi chapter. Theta Alpha at the University of New Hampshire reverted to local status in 1936, and resuming its old name, Sigma Beta.

The Westminster chapter (originally Pi Rho Phi) became Pennsylvania Lambda of Sigma Phi Epsilon in 1938 with the completion of the merger agreement between Sigma Phi Epsilon and Theta Upsilon Omega. At the seventy-fifth anniversary celebration of the Westminster group in 1929 a colored stained-glass memorial window was placed in the Old Main Memorial Chapel of the college to the memory of Pi Rho Phi.

The fraternity publication was *The Omegan*, issued four times in each academic year. The badge consisted of three forked triangles, bearing the letters Θ Υ Ω in gold on black with gold edge, meeting under a circular center of black containing a jewel centered nine-pointed star. Symmetrically spaced with the triangles about the center were three pairs of jewels. The pledge button was a cross fitchy of midnight blue edged with gold and the recognition pin was a dragon issuing from a mural crown done in old gold. The fraternity colors were midnight blue and gold; the floral emblem the dark red rose. The flag was of three equal vertical bands of blue, gold, and blue with a blue cross fitchy on the center gold band.

W. W. W. (or Rainbow)

ACTIVE PIN

W.W.W., or RAINBOW, was organized in 1849, at the University of Mississippi, by John B. Earle, John B. Herring, James H. Mason, Robert Buldow, Joshua L. Halbert, Marlborough Pegues, and Drew W. Bynum. These young men had been students at La Grange College, Tennessee, and had removed to the University of Mississippi. The name of the society to the members was Mystic Sons of Iris. It later became known as the Rainbow, or W.W.W. Society. Its ritual and many of its practices were based upon the number seven. The chapter roll was as follows: 1848, University of Mississippi; 1858, La Grange College (1861); 1871, Furman University (1874); 1872, Erskine College (1884); 1872, Southern Presbyterian University (1873); 1873, Wofford College (1875); 1874, Neophogen College (1874); 1880, Chamberlain-Hunt Academy (1886); 1881, Vanderbilt University; 1882, Southwestern University (1886); 1883, University of Texas (1886); 1884, Emory and Henry College (1886); 1884, University of Tennessee (1886). After a checkered career, negotiations were entered into between this fraternity and Delta Tau Delta with a view to consolidating the two fraternities; the union was effected in 1886. The journal of Delta Tau Delta, therefore called *The Crescent*, was rechristened *The Rainbow* out of compliment to the other order. At the time of the union only two Rainbow chapters, those at the University of Mississippi and Vanderbilt, were alive. The chapters at Southwestern and the University of Texas went into Phi Delta Theta. The chapter at Emory and Henry disbanded, most of its members joining Sigma Alpha Epsilon.

Webster Society

WEBSTER SOCIETY was an organization of the literary society type, established at Kansas State College before the Civil War. It had some secret features and placed chapters in a number of institutions. In 1930 Gamma Chapter of the Webster Literary Society was in existence at Purdue University, and the Men of Webster was flourishing at the University of Wichita. In 1924 this group was approached by the national president of Webster, at which time four chapters were reported, one at Park College, Parkville, Illinois, in addition to the ones already named. The founding organization still exists at Kansas State College among the literary societies. The founding organization still exists at Kansas State College among the literary societies. The Purdue chapter reported a jeweled badge and a key as insignia. The badge, roughly rectangular in shape, bore a flaming torch at the top, a scroll in the center, and a W at the bottom. The key, a green shield, with mantle about it, bore a helmet with visor closed, a lion rampant centered within four fleur-de-lis and standing upon a W.

Zeta Phi

ZETA PHI SOCIETY was founded at the University of Missouri, November 7, 1870, by Oren Root, a Sigma Phi, then a professor at the university, who modeled it after the older organization. Calling itself Alpha, it established in 1871 Sigma at William Jewel College and in 1872 Delta at Washington University. Delta Chapter disbanded voluntarily in 1874; Sigma surrendered its charter in 1886 and subsequently accepted a charter from Phi Gamma Delta. Alpha, after a prosperous career of twenty years, in 1890 became the Zeta Phi chapter of Beta Theta Pi, carrying with it into that fraternity all of its alumni. The badge was a monogram of the letters of the society name, and much resembled that of Sigma Phi. The color of the fraternity was white.

Zeta Sigma

ZETA SIGMA was founded as a national social fraternity for men May 10, 1935, at Fairmont State College, Fairmont, West Virginia. It installed a total of fourteen chapters before the national organization was disbanded following World War II and the individual chapters restored to operation as locals. The Shepherd chapter in 1956 and the mother chapter in 1960 received charters from Tau Kappa Epsilon. The Davis and Elkins group became a chapter of Sigma Phi Epsilon in 1949.

The founders of record are Rex Bradley, Park Kennis, Samuel Harris, Forrest Justis, and Harold Hohman. The object of founding was to provide for the social and fraternal needs of a large group of men not reached by the limited number of fraternity chapters then on the campus.

The fraternity published a national magazine, *The Zeta Sigma Chronicle.* The pledge pin was a plain gold star. The badge was a five-pointed star, displaying in gold letters Z Σ, surmounted by a skull and bones. The flower was the pink rose, and the fraternity colors azure, silver, and gold.

The chapter roll was:

1935	West Virginia Alpha, Fairmont (1960)	
1935	Indiana Alpha, Canterbury (1945)	
1935	Oklahoma Alpha, Oklahoma City (1948)	
1936	New Mexico Alpha, New Mexico Western, Silver City (1941)	
1937	New Mexico Beta, New Mexico Highlands (1947)	
1938	West Virginia Beta, Concord (1939)	
1939	West Virginia Gamma, Shepherd (1956)	
1940	West Virginia Delta, Davis and Elkins (1949)	
1940	West Virginia Epsilon, West Virginia (1941)	
1941	Mississippi Alpha, Southern Mississippi (1946)	
1941	Connecticut Alpha, New Haven State (1942)	
1941	New York Alpha, New York State (Plattsburg)	
1941	California Alpha, Los Angeles University	
1942	Maine Alpha, Washington State Teachers (Maine) (1960)	

Women's Fraternities

Alpha Delta Theta

ALPHA DELTA THETA was founded as a local group called Alpha Theta in the early fall of 1919 at Transylvania College, Lexington, Kentucky. The founding members were Juanita Minish, Violet Young, Martha Hall, Zenaide Harrod, Valleria Grannis, Irene Duncan, Ruth Dutt, Hazel Grow, Williebel Chilton, and Mary Owsley, with Isabel Wolf Hemenway as faculty member and Mrs. W. C. Bower as patroness. At the time Alpha Theta was organized there were only two other sororities on the campus of Transylvania, the oldest college west of the Allegheny Mountains. The new group was organized as a result of the rapid increase in women's enrollment at Transylvania and the lack of national groups to supply the needs.

The Alpha Theta members prepared their group for affiliation with a national organization but soon determined to establish an independent national of their own with its own ideals and principles. The name Alpha Delta Theta was adopted, and the new national organization was announced in the *Crimson Rambler,* a Transylvania publication, in November, 1921. The first initiation held under the name of Alpha Delta Theta took place in February, 1922. In June, 1922, Beta Chapter was installed at the University of Kentucky. The first national conventions were held in Lexington, home of both Alpha and Beta chapters. Alpha Delta Theta was admitted to the National Panhellenic Congress in January, 1926. It was the first national to be recorded as an "associate member of National Panhellenic Congress," this membership having been granted in 1923. The fraternity was incorporated under the laws of the Commonwealth of Kentucky during the winter of 1927–28.

Government was by a grand council and a convention which met first annually, then in alternate years. Under the direction of Isabel Hamenway and Violet Young, the first publication appeared in May, 1924. It was called *The Silhouette* and was issued annually for three years, then semi-annually for two years. In 1928 the name was changed to *The Portals* and it became a quarterly publication. An *Alumnae Directory and News Bulletin* was published in 1926 and 1927, then became part of *The Portals* annually through 1932. In 1926 the first pledge handbook was published. The first formal ritual book was published in May, 1929. The *Latch Key* was a convention publication in 1928 and 1930. Other publications included an officers' handbook, constitution and bylaws and song books.

The badge was a yellow-gold pin, delta in shape, bordered with fifteen pearls and with an emerald at each corner, the delta superimposed upon a gold key placed horizontally. The center of the delta was of black enamel, bearing the emblems in gold, the A in the lower left corner, the Δ in the apex, the Θ in the lower right corner, a lighted candle in the candlestick between the A and Θ with crossed palm branches above. The recognition pin was formed for small gold palm branches with an emerald in the center. The pledge pin was a vertical bar of silver bearing the raised letters A Θ one above the other. The mothers' pin was a chased gold triangle holding within its open center a candlestick with a single pearl for the flame. The coat of arms was as follows, Arms: Argent, a chief, gules, charged with three keys of the first, in the base two crossed palm branches, vert: Crest: Above a marquis helmet, a candlestick, argent, charged with a lighted candle; Mantling: Gules, doubled, argent; Supporters: Two unicorns, rampant, proper; Motto: OYK EΣTIN APXHXΩ PIΣAITIAΣ. Colors were turquoise blue, scarlet, and silver. The flower was the French sweet pea.

A merger with Phi Mu was effected in August, 1939, and the fraternity was absorbed by that organization. The merger was announced at the close of the National Panhellenic Congress meeting in November, 1939, at which Alpha Delta Theta was the hostess fraternity. National officers of both Phi Mu and Alpha Delta Theta traveled from the meeting first to Alpha Delta Theta's Alpha chapter, then to remaining chapters to install chapters and to initiate collegiate and alumnae members into Phi Mu.

Hazel Falconer Benninghoven, Alpha Delta Theta national president at the time of the merger, later served Phi Mu as national president, perhaps the only person to serve as president of two NPC groups. Alpha Delta Theta maintained a central office in Hamilton, Ohio. The chapter roll was:

1918	Alpha, Transylvania
1922	Beta, Kentucky
1923	Gamma, Cincinnati
1923	Delta, Illinois (1934)
1923	Epsilon, Butler (1933)
1923	Zeta, Nebraska
1924	Eta, Ohio State
1924	Theta, Washington
1924	Iota, California (1934)
1925	Kappa, Ohio Wesleyan (1934)
1926	Lambda, George Washington
1926	Mu, U.C.L.A.
1927	Nu, Nebraska Wesleyan
1927	Xi, Adelphi
1928	Omicron, Brenau
1929	Pi, Howard
1929	Rho, Ohio
1930	Sigma, Tulsa
1931	Tau, Minnesota
1931	Upsilon, Missouri (1933)
1931	Phi, Southern California
1932	Chi, Nevada
1932	Psi, Queens-Chicora
1932	Omega, Bethany
1934	Alpha Alpha, Charleston

Alpha Kappa Psi

ALPHA KAPPA PSI SORORITY was founded in 1904 at St. Mary's School, Raleigh, North Carolina. It had other chapters at Carnegie Institute of Technology; Fairmont Seminary, Montegle, Tennessee; Florida State College for Women' Gunston Hall, Washington, D.C.; Shorter College; Stetson University; Stuart Hall; Synodical College, Fulton, Missouri, and Wesleyan Female College. Total membership was about six hundred.

Alpha Sigma Delta

ALPHA SIGMA DELTA was founded as the Iaqua Club in 1919 at the University of California. In April, 1932, Alpha Sigma Delta merged with Lambda Omega and ceased to exist as a separate fraternity.

See also Lambda Omega.

Beta Phi Alpha

ACTIVE PIN

BETA PHI ALPHA was organized on May 8, 1909, at the University of California at Berkeley under the name of Bide-a-wee, changed after a few months to Aldebaran. In 1919 the name was changed to Kappa Phi Alpha, but when a movement toward expansion gained strength it became Beta Phi Alpha. More than thirty chapters were established with a total membership exceeding three thousand. It was a member of NPC. *Aldebaran* was the official publication. The badge was a Greek Φ outlined in pearls with B and A embossed on the black enamel at either side of the stem of the Φ. The colors were green and gold; the flower was the yellow tea rose.

On June 22, 1941, Beta Phi Alpha united with Delta Zeta and ceased to exist as a separate fraternity.

Beta Sigma Omicron

ACTIVE PIN

BETA SIGMA OMICRON was merged with Zeta Tau Alpha in August, 1964.

The sorority was founded in Columbia, Missouri, on December 12, 1888 by Eulalia Hockaday, Maud Haines, and Katherine Turner. After three years as a local fraternity, Beta Sigma Omicron installed a second chapter, Beta, at Synodical College, Fulton, Missouri, on October 9, 1891.

The first expansion of the fraternity was confined entirely to southern colleges for women. A unanimous vote at the convention of 1925, however, agreed to limit future extension to Class A colleges and universities throughout the United States.

The colors were ruby and pink; the flowers, Richmond and Killarney roses. The badge was a monogram of the Greek letters B Σ O, the Σ being superimposed. The pledge pin was triangular with a gold star in each corner and a Grecian lamp in the center.

The quarterly magazine was *The Urn*. The support of the Pine Mountain Settlement School in Harlan County, Kentucky, was adopted as a national philanthropy in 1913. In 1959, the National Kidney Disease Foundation, founded by a member of the sorority, was adopted as a second philanthropy.

During its lifetime the sorority installed sixty-one chapters and initiated nearly 15,000 members. Fifteen chapters were active at the time of the merger. Of these, the chapter at Fenn reverted to local status; the chapter at Queens elected not to affiliate with a national group and reverted to local status under the name Beta Sigma Delta; at Hunter, Beta Sigma Omicron continued to function under that name but as a local sorority. The chapter roll:

1888   Alpha, Missouri (1892)
1891   Beta, Synodical College (1928)
1892   Gamma I, Missouri Valley (1895)
1898   Delta, Sedalia High School (Mo.) (1907)
1902   Epsilon, Hardin (Mo.) (1925)
1902   Zeta, Potter (Ky.) (1909)
1903   Eta, Stephens (1925)
1903   Theta, Ward-Belmont (1914)
1903   Iota, Mary Baldwin (1907)
1904   Kappa, Fairment (D.C.) (1913)
1906   Lambda Hamilton (Kentucky) (1926)
1906   Mu, Crescent (Arkansas) (1912)
1906   Nu, Brenau (1913)
1906   Xi, Central College (Missouri) (1925)
1908   Omicron, Liberty (Missouri) (1913)
1909   Zeta II, Centenary College (1921)
1910   Gamma II, Christian (Missouri) (1915)
1911   Delta II, Woman's College (Alabama) (1913)
1913   Pi, Hollins (Virginia) (1917)
1914   Rho, Colorado Woman's College (1920)
1916   Sigma, Greenville Woman's College (South Carolina) (1930)
1916   Tau, Lindenwood (Missouri) (1920)
1916   Upsilon, Belhaven (Mississippi) (1920)
1918   Phi, Grenada (Mississippi) (1920)
1926   Alpha Alpha, Wisconsin (1933)
1926   Alpha Beta, Indiana (1937)
1926   Alpha Gamma, Kentucky (1932)
1926   Alpha Delta, Illinois Wesleyan (1936)
1926   Alpha Epsilon, U.C.L.A. (1933)
1926   Alpha Zeta, Millsaps (1964)
1926   Alpha Eta, New Mexico (1933)
1927   Alpha Theta, Southern California (1946)
1927   Alpha Iota, California (1942)
1927   Alpha Kappa, Mississippi (1932)
1927   Alpha Lambda, Northwestern (1939)
1927   Alpha Mu, Illinois (1941)
1928   Alpha Nu, Arkansas College (1936)
1929   Alpha Xi, Miami (Ohio) (1939)
1929   Alpha Omicron, Simpson (1941)
1929   Alpha Pi, Baldwin-Wallace (1964)
1929   Alpha Rho, Louisiana State (1964)
1929   Alpha Sigma, Newcomb (La.) (1959)
1930   Alpha Tau, Pittsburgh (1964)
1931   Alpha Upsilon, Nevada (1941)
1931   Alpha Phi, Washburn (1936)
1931   Alpha Chi, Oklahoma (1935)
1931   Alpha Psi, William Jewell (1964)
1932   Alpha Omega, Washington (1936)
1933   Beta Alpha, Hunter (1964)
1933   Beta Beta, Howard College (1964)
1937   Beta Gamma, Westminster (Pa.) (1964)
1941   Beta Delta, Queens (L.I.) (1964)
1946   Beta Epsilon, Pennsylvania State (1962)
1947   Beta Zeta, Florida Southern (1959)
1947   Beta Eta, Louisiana Tech (1959)
1949   Beta Theta, Evansville (1964)
1950   Beta Iota, Thiel (1964)
1951   Beta Kappa Indiana State (Pa.) (1964)
1952   Beta Lambda, Youngstown (1964)
1954   Beta Mu, Fenn (1964)
1961   Beta Nu, Waynesburg (1963)

Delta Sigma

DELTA SIGMA was the outcome of the union of Alpha Delta Sigma, a local society originating at Tufts College, and Delta Sigma, a similar local at Brown University. Its chapters and membership were as follows: 1895, Alpha, Tufts College, 77; 1896, Beta, Brown University, 68; 1902, Gamma, University of Maine, 19. The badge was a square of black enamel, with concave sides outlined in gold and displaying the letters Δ Σ in gold. This square was encircled by a jeweled golden circle. The colors were pale green and white. The Maine and Tufts chapters entered Alpha Omicron Pi, and the Brown chapter became inactive when sororities were abolished at Brown in 1911.

Delta Sigma Epsilon

DELTA SIGMA EPSILON was founded at Miami University, Oxford, Ohio, September 23, 1914, by Marie Cropper, Ruth Gabler, Josephine McIntire, Virginia Stark, Charlotte Stark, Opal Warning, and Louise

Wolf. At the time it merged with Delta Zeta in 1956, it had forty-four active chapters, eight inactive ones, and sixty-eight alumnae chapters with a total membership of 13,001. In the fall of 1940 Pi Delta Theta petitioned Delta Sigma Epsilon for membership. The merger of Pi Delta Theta with Delta Sigma Epsilon was the first and only such merger in the history of the Association of Education Sororities. It had been an NPC member.

Delta Sigma Epsilon's magazine, *The Shield*, first published in 1917, was issued quarterly. Other publications were the *Omega Phi* (for members only), a songbook, a directory, manuals, and handbooks. The badge was shield-shaped, having seven points, the background of enamel, bordered with pearls, and displaying the fraternity letters, a circle, and a cornucopia. There was a plain badge in black and gold. The pledge pin was a silver cornucopia. Colors were olive green and cream; the flower the cream tea rose; motto: *Nihil sine labore.*

1922	Delta, N.Y.U. (Square)
1922	Epsilon, New Jersey Law (1942)
1926	Zeta, Adelphi
1927	Eta, Denver (1942)
1929	Kappa, Toronto (1956)
1930	Iota, Long Island
1931	Lambda, Brooklyn
1932	Mu, Manitoba (1965)
1935	Nu, Wayne State
1938	Omicron, Queens
1942	Pi, Syracuse
1946	Rho, Miami (1956)
1946	Sigma, Temple
1947	Upsilon, Rider (1955)
1954	Phi, Illinois
1960	Psi, N.Y.U. (Heights) (1965)
1962	Beta Alpha, Penn State
1965	Beta Beta, C.C.N.Y.
1966	Beta Delta, Cornell
1966	Beta Epsilon, C.W. Post

Iota Alpha Pi

ACTIVE PIN

IOTA ALPHA PI, the oldest national sorority founded by Jewish women, began at Hunter College, then known as Normal College, in March, 1903. The founders were Hannah Finkelstein Swick, Olga Edelstein Ecker, Sadie April Glotzer, Rose Posner Bernstein, Rose Delson Hirschman, May Finkelstein Spiegel, and Frances Zellermayer Delson. These young women were motivated by a spirit of friendship and a desire to aid humanity generally. They held meetings in members' homes and engaged in settlement work in the lower East Side of New York. One of their cultural tasks was a study of women in the Bible. The sorority expanded first to chapters in the surrounding area and then to the West and to Canada.

The national organization disbanded in 1971.

The colors were red and black. The flower was the red rose. The pledge pin was diamond-shaped, having a gold shaft on a scarlet field. The recognition pin was I A Π in gold. The badge was a diamond-shaped pin, with two full-blown gold roses on each of the horizontal points, consisting of a scarlet field surrounded by a border of twenty pearls.

Total estimated membership May 31, 1967, was 6,300. There were thirteen active and ten inactive chapters.

1903	Alpha, Normal (now Hunter College) (1913)
1913	Beta, Hunter (1965)
1913	Gamma, Brooklyn Law (1941)

Lambda Omega

LAMBDA OMEGA was founded May 5, 1923, at the University of California. Its origin goes back to the Norroena Club, founded in November, 1915, at Berkeley, California, by Stella Chappell, Flossie Banks, Marcella Brinkmeyer, Frances Anne Stranahan, Sarah Fairchild, Annette Girard, Florence Koehler, Anne Wallingford, Fin Hahn, Barbara Mensing, Helen Coursen, Maude Miller, Louise Koehler, Estha Rodkey, Grace Palmer, Ethel Flood, Fannie Granger, and Maude Hudson. Norroena existed as a local house club for seven and a half years. The group lived at 1736 Oxford Street from January, 1916, to June, 1918, and at 2520 Virginia Street until the house burned on September 16, 1923. Norroena, meaning "breath of the North," developed its ritual around an Indian legend and had a Norse motif emphasizing the hardihood of the Norse people, their hospitality, economy, and friendship.

Soon after Norroena became Lambda Omega in 1923 other chapters were started.

Alpha Sigma Delta, founded also at the University of California at Berkeley as the Iaqua Club in 1919, merged with Lambda Omega in April, 1932. This union brought Lambda Omega strength for the Berkeley and Los Angeles chapters and added two new chapters: Colby College and the University of Utah.

Lambda Omega's magazine was *The Pharetra*, while Alpha Sigma Delta published an annual magazine, *The Crown*.

Lambda Omega merged with Theta Upsilon in September, 1933. It had been an associate member of NPC. Theta Upsilon, in turn, was accepted into membership by Delta Zeta, another NPC group, on May 6, 1962.

The chapter roll was:

1923	Alpha, California
1923	Beta, Illinois
1924	Gamma, Ohio State
1925	Delta, Ohio
1927	Epsilon, Northwestern
1928	Zeta, U.C.L.A.
1929	Eta, Washington
1930	Theta, Denver

Phi Omega Pi

ACTIVE PIN

PHI OMEGA PI, founded at the University of Nebraska, March 5, 1910, was originally limited to members of the Eastern Star, but in 1931 all restrictions were eliminated. In 1933 Sigma Phi Beta was amalgamated with Phi Omega Pi which became a member of NPC in October, 1933. The official publication, *The Pentagon of Phi Omega Pi*, was a quarterly magazine. The badge, an irregular pentagon of black enamel surrounded by a gold band, had a five-pointed star set with a sapphire above the Greek letters Φ Ω Π engraved in gold. The colors were sapphire blue and white; the official flower was the lily-of-the-valley.

The chapters at Iowa State Teachers College, Newark State Normal, and Montclair Teachers College were placed on the inactive list by order of the Panhellenic Congress when Phi Omega Pi joined it. In the period following, chapters were taken over by Alpha Omicron Pi, Alpha Gamma Delta, Sigma Kappa, and Kappa Alpha Theta. The group disbanded in 1946. Through an NPC committee, Delta Zeta was asked to consider the alumnae and a few chapters which remained. The society was officially absorbed by Delta Zeta on August 10, 1946.

Pi Delta Theta

PI DELTA THETA SORORITY was organized in 1925. With requests for another such sorority coming from several local groups, Mrs. Ida Shaw Martin, head of the Sorority Service Bureau, asked that three of the local organizations send their faculty advisers to meet with her in Boston, Massachusetts. In the summer of 1925 Mrs. Robert E. Brown, representing Kappa Theta Alpha of Miami University, and Miss Beulah Houlton, representing Zeta Sigma Alpha of Kansas State Teachers College, Emporia, met with Mrs. Martin in Boston. The new sorority was organized, and Mrs. Brown was made its first

president. Alpha Chapter was installed at Miami University by her on February 14, 1926. The total membership was about 1,000 in 1940, when there were four active, five inactive, and twenty alumnae chapters.

The government was vested in three bodies, the national convention, the National Council, and the Board of Advisers. The national publication was the *Thalia*, published twice a year. The badge consisted of the Greek letters Π and Θ in gold with a superimposed Δ set with pearls. Colors were white, gold with myrtle green. Flower was the marguerite.

In September, 1941, Pi Delta Theta was merged with Delta Sigma Epsilon, which in 1956 merged with Delta Zeta.

Pi Kappa Sigma

PI KAPPA SIGMA was founded November 17, 1894, at Michigan State Normal College, Ypsilanti, by Georgia Fox, a student. Thirteen other students with her comprised the first organization. It was known as J.P.N. The purpose was mainly social training. In 1897 J.P.N. was reorganized and the purpose broadened. The name was changed to Pi Kappa Sigma. In 1915 the widening opportunity for women in teaching as leaders and policy makers led to the broadening of the scope of work to be accomplished by the chapters. Objectives were to prepare members to fill these places and to give a better service in their work, to keep pace with the broadening democratic ideals, and to give opportunity for training in initiative and cooperation to more girls.

The Laurel was first issued in 1918. Up to 1927 two numbers a year were published. The convention that year increased the annual issues to three, and in 1931, to four. Life subscription was provided for in 1927, and the convention of 1931 made life subscription compulsory for each initiate. A songbook with words was published in 1945 with a revision in 1953. A pledge book and a handbook were published in 1940.

The badge was a modified triangular shield of black enamel displaying the sorority letters and a lamp and carrying a diamond surrounded by thirteen gold rays. The pledge pin was a modified triangle enameled in turquoise and carrying the sorority letters. The official insignia of office was a gold disk with thirteen gold rays. Colors were turquoise blue and gold. Flowers were forget-me-nots and jonquils.

Pi Kappa Sigma ended its existence on May 15, 1959, when absorbed by Sigma Kappa by merger.

The chapter roll in 1957 was:

1894	Alpha, Michigan State Normal
1900	Beta, Northwestern State (Okla.)
1902	Gamma, Central Michigan College
1905	Delta, Eastern Washington College (1918)

1907   Epsilon, Wisconsin State College
          (Milwaukee) (1911)
1909   Zeta, Indiana State (Pa.) (1918–1930)
1915   Eta, Miami University (1938)
1917   Theta, Cincinnati (1919)
1918   Iota, Kansas State (Emporia)
1919   Kappa, Southeastern State College (Okla.)
1920   Lambda, Central Missouri State
1920   Mu, Colorado State College of Education
1922   Nu, East Central State College (Okla.)
1923   Xi, Ohio (1933)
1923   Omicron, Marshall
1924   Pi, Northeast Missouri State
1925   Rho, New York Teachers at Buffalo (1954)
1925   Sigma, Drake (1932)
1925   Tau, Chico State (Calif.)
1925   Upsilon, Florida State (1929)
1926   Phi, U.C.L.A. (1939)
1926   Chi, Black Hills Teachers (S.D.)
1926   Psi, Kent State (1947)
1927   Omega, Southern California (1940)
1927   Alpha Alpha, Auburn (1937)
1928   Alpha Beta, Kansas State (Pittsburg)
          (1941)
1928   Alpha Gamma, Wayne State
1928   Alpha Delta, Northwestern State (La.)
1928   Alpha Epsilon, Longwood
1929   Alpha Zeta, Western State (Colo.)
1929   Alpha Eta, Millikin (1937)
1929   Alpha Theta, Stetson (1940)
1929   Alpha Iota, Butler (1937)
1930   Alpha Kappa, Harris Teachers
1930   Alpha Lambda, Wittenberg (1936)
1930   Alpha Mu, Kansas State (Fort Hays) (1940)
1935   Alpha Nu, Lock Haven State (Pa.)
1939   Alpha Xi, Southern Illinois
1939   Alpha Omicron, Madison (Va.)
1943   Alpha Pi, Western Illinois State
1944   Alpha Phi, Arkansas State Teachers
1945   Alpha Chi, Ball State
1945   Alpha Rho, Northern Illinois State
1946   Alpha Sigma, Henderson (1952)
1946   Alpha Tau, District of Columbia Teachers
1947   Theta Nu, Southwest Missouri State
1948   Alpha Omega, Fairmont (W.Va.)
1950   Alpha Upsilon, Central State (Okla.)
1951   Gamma Theta, Radford
1954   Alpha Psi, Illinois

Pi Lambda Sigma

PI LAMBDA SIGMA was founded at Boston University in June, 1921, as a national Catholic sorority, with the aid of Ida Shaw Martin, Delta Delta Delta, the Chancellery Office at Boston, and the approval of His Eminence William Cardinal O'Connell, Pi Lambda Sigma. The founders were: Theresa Talamini, Mary O'Shaughnessy Brennan, Constance Bartholomew, Mary Lyons Laffoley, Lauretta Nally Cushing, and Helen Wilson.

Chapters were maintained at Boston University, University of Cincinnati, Creighton University, and Quincy College. The members of Pi Lambda Sigma at the universities of Cincinnati and Boston become respectively members of Epsilon and Eta chapters of Theta Phi Alpha. Chi Chapter at Creighton University was initiated in the fall of 1952, and Psi at Quincy College in 1954.

Its stated purpose was "to stimulate the social, intellectual, ethical, and spiritual life of its members; and to count as a world force through services rendered to others." *The Torch,* a quarterly, was the official publication. The badge was a black enamel shield surrounded by pearls and the letters ΠΛ Σ inscribed in gold; the pledge pin, a gold Greek cross and circle; the colors, white and gold.

Pi Lambda Sigma merged with Theta Phi Alpha, also a fraternity for Catholic women, on June 28, 1952.

Sigma Phi Beta

SIGMA PHI BETA was founded at New York University November 1, 1920, by Vera Bartone Goeller and students of the junior, sophomore, and freshman classes. Until July 28, 1927, it was conducted under the name of Sigma Sigma Omicron. On January 7, 1928, Sigma Phi Beta and Phi Alpha Chi, having found their interests and purposes similar, amalgamated. The former consisted of five chapters and the latter three. Under the terms of the amalgamation the combined organizations were to be known as Sigma Phi Beta.

On October 1, 1933, this sorority was absorbed by Phi Omega Pi, which in turn was absorbed by Delta Zeta on August 10, 1946.

Sigma Sigma Omicron

SIGMA SIGMA OMICRON was founded at New York University, November 1, 1920. It had organized several chapters mainly in teachers colleges, when in 1927 it changed its name to Sigma Phi Beta, and, a year later, in combination with Phi Alpha Chi, formed the Sigma Phi Beta Sorority.

Sigma Phi Beta was absorbed by Phi Omega Pi in 1933, which was to become a part of Delta Zeta through merger in 1946.

Theta Sigma Upsilon

THETA SIGMA UPSILON was founded March 25, 1921, at Kansas State Teachers College, Emporia. Of the many earnest women whose concerted efforts made the national organization possible, special honor is given to Miss Frances Hashbarger as the founder of Theta Sigma Upsilon. It had existed from 1909 as the Sigma Society, but changed its name to Theta Sigma Upsilon when it entered the national field.

The fraternity was united with Alpha Gamma Delta June 29, 1959, under the name of the latter.

During its existence Theta Sigma Upsilon sought to establish among its members a sisterhood that had for its five-fold objective the social, intellectual, physical, ethical, and spiritual development of its members. Members were encouraged to develop a trade of ideal American womanhood: sturdy physique, alert mind, understanding spirit.

Official publications included: the *Pledge Manual; Constitution Manual; The Torch,* a bi-annual magazine circulated to the entire membership; *The Shield,* secret yearly magazine; *The Flame,* a semi-annual bulletin published by each alumnae chapter; the *Songbook; Brochure; Social Service Pamphlets; Sorority Directory;* and *History of the Sorority.*

The five badges were the pledge pin, a silver torch; the plain badge, a five-pointed shield of black enamel, displaying a torch and the Greek letters and mounted upon a beveled shield of gold similarly shaped; the jeweled badge, a shield similar to the plain badge, but jeweled with pearls and turquoises; the recognition pin, a facsimile of the coat of arms in silver or gold; the mother-patroness auxiliary badge, the flame of a torch. The flag was a rectangle of rose displaying the sorority letters in silver. The coat of arms was a shield similar to that used as the official badge and displaying as its device a torch. The crest was the helmet of Minerva with the visor closed and a riband below the shield carrying the sorority letters. The official colors were rose and silver. The flower was the rose. The jewels were pearls and turquoises. The insignia were the helmet, the shield, the spear, and the torch. The open motto was "The Higher Good." The patron was Minerva.

The chapter roll was:

1921	Alpha, Kansas State (Emporia) (1943–1947) (1947)
1923	Beta, Michigan State Normal (1942)
1924	Gamma, Temple
1924	Delta, Miami (1933)
1924	Epsilon, Kansas State (Pittsburg)
1926	Zeta, Marshall (1931)
1926	Eta, Kent State (1947)
1927	Theta, New York Teachers at Buffalo (1954)
1928	Iota, Colorado State College
1928	Kappa, Northwestern State (Louisiana)
1928	Lambda, Ohio (1931)
1928	Mu, Fort Hays State
1929	Nu, Central State (Missouri)
1929	Xi, Western State (Colorado) (1933)
1931	Omicron, Chico State (California)
1935	Pi, Indiana State (Pa.)
1936	Rho, Wisconsin State (Whitewater)
1937	Sigma, Harris Teachers (1954)
1939	Tau, Longwood
1941	Upsilon, Central Michigan
1942	Phi, Madison (Virginia)
1944	Chi, Drexel Institute
1952	Psi, Edinboro State (Pa.)

Theta Upsilon

ACTIVE PIN

THETA UPSILON was founded at the University of California in 1914, by Mildred Rau, Lillian Rhein, Ella Rau, Margua Gilbert, Celine Goethals, Marie Goethals, Grace Terry, Arline Cavins, and Olive Stevenson. The fraternity traces its beginnings back to 1909 when a group of girls rented a house on Walnut Street and named it the Walnut Shell. Later they organized formally as the Mekatina Club. Theta Upsilon was admitted to associate membership in National Panhellenic Conference in 1923 and to full membership in 1928. In September, 1933, Lambda Omega, as associate member of National Panhellenic Conference, was received into Theta Upsilon membership, adding four chapters and one thousand members to the roster.

Theta Upsilon's national aims were threefold: to foster close friendship between members; to stimulate the intellectual, social, and spiritual life of members; and to count as a world force through service to others.

Theta Upsilon's first published magazine appeared in 1924. Since that time the fraternity magazine, *The Dial,* was published quarterly. *Laurel Leaves,* an esoteric issue, was published annually. Eight membership directories were printed. The first *Theta Upsilon Song Book* was published in 1928, and a revised edition reprinted in 1951. *The Theta Upsilon Cook Book,* containing favorite recipes of members, was published in 1951.

The badge was a jeweled Θ superimposed upon a hand-chase Υ. The colors were the rainbow tints, with yellow and white for public display. The flower was the iris. The pledge pin was a conventionalized iris of sterling silver. The flag was a rectangle of white with lion rampant and border of yellow.

Theta Upsilon was taken into membership by Delta Zeta on May 6, 1962. Chapter roll:

1914	Alpha, California (1961)
1921	Beta, Brenau (1938)
1923	Gamma, Illinois (1940–1946)
1923	Delta, Ohio State (1940–1946) (1952)
1923	Epsilon, Washington State (1933)
1923	Zeta, Ohio Wesleyan (1936)

1924   Eta, Allegheny (1955)
1924   Theta, Boston (1936)
1924   Iota, Simpson
1925   Kappa, Ohio (1939)
1925   Lambda, Florida State (1939)
1925   Mu, Miami (Ohio)
1925   Nu, Ripon (1927)
1926   Xi, Birmingham-Southern
1927   Omicron, U.C.L.A. (1930)
1928   Pi, Lombard (1930)
1929   Rho, Washington (1940–1946) (1952)
1930   Sigma, Utah State (1957)
1930   Tau, New Hampshire
1931   Upsilon, Westminster
1931   Phi, Nebraska Wesleyan (1941)
1931   Chi, West Virginia (1936)
1932   Psi, Louisiana Tech
1932   Alpha Alpha, Alabama (1952)
1932   Beta Alpha, N.Y.U.
1933   Gamma Alpha, Millikin (1946)
1933   Delta Alpha, Temple
1933   Epsilon Alpha, Northwestern (1940)
1933   Zeta Alpha, Denver (1941)
1933   Theta Alpha, Colby (1935)
1935   Iota Alpha, Auburn (1956)
1939   Kappa Alpha, Akron
1947   Lambda Alpha, Colorado (1960)
1954   Mu Alpha, Creighton
1955   Nu Alpha, Western Michigan (1961)
1958   Xi Alpha, De Paul, Chicago
1960   Omicron Alpha, Western Carolina

Trianon

TRIANON was founded as a sorority at Cincinnati on December 28, 1929, at a meeting held by groups from the University of Cincinnati, Butler University, and Miami University. In 1931 a charter was granted to a chapter at Ohio State University. Membership was open upon application by the candidate. The badge was a yellow-gold chevron-like base supporting a cluster of peaks upon which the letter T in white gold was superimposed. The colors were royal blue and gold.

Other Departed Societies

Aleph Yodh He

ALEPH YODH HE (STUDENTS OF MEDICINE) was founded in 1908 at the Chicago College of Medicine and Surgery. It established eight other chapters: 1910, College of Physicians and Surgeons of Chicago; 1912, Jenner Medical College; 1913, Loyola University (Bennett Medical College); 1913, University of Pennsylvania; 1914, Jefferson Medical College; 1914, Medico-Chirurgical College,

Philadelphia; 1914, University of Maryland; 1914, Temple University. Its membership was 350. It became part of the Phi Lambda Kappa medical fraternity in 1921.

Alpha Chi Alpha

ACTIVE PIN

ALPHA CHI ALPHA, recognition society, was founded at the University of Tennessee on December 17, 1919. In 1940 it had nine active and five inactive chapters. The official organ was *Al-Cri*, published three times during each college year.

The badge was shield-shaped, bearing on a background of black enamel the Greek letters of the name, above a crossed sword and quill, which were superimposed upon a scroll, upon the upper part of which was a star. Colors were gold and white. The flower was the yellow rose.

On July 1, 1944, Alpha Chi Alpha was merged with Pi Delta Epsilon.

Alpha Delta

ALPHA DELTA was founded as a journalistic recognition society for men and women on December 28, 1929, at Rock Island, Illinois, by the editors-in-chief and business managers of three weekly newspapers which had been acknowledged leaders in the Illinois College Press Association. The founders were Newell H. Dailey and Floyd T. Johnston of the *Augustana Observer*, J. Howard Dunker and Orville W. Connett of *The Bradley Tech*, and Edward V. Hahn and Robert Aykens of the *Illinois Wesleyan Argus*. Chapters were installed immediately at the three institutions thus represented. On February 7, 1930, the National Council of the society was chartered by Illinois as "a corporation not for pecuniary profit."

Eligibility to active membership was based upon proficiency in college journalism demonstrated by actual service to a student publication. Government was vested in a national convention of delegates from the several chapters which elected the National Council.

The badge was a key, oblong with concave corners, displaying a quill, a scroll, and an hourglass grouped above the letters A Δ. The colors featured in the coat of arms were blue and silver.

Alpha Delta was absorbed by Alpha Phi Gamma, a journalistic recognition society for men and women, in the spring of 1957.

The chapter roll was:

1930 Illinois Alpha, Augustana
1930 Illinois Beta, Bradley
1930 Illinois Gamma, Illinois Wesleyan (1932)
1930 Iowa Alpha, Parsons (1931)
1930 Georgia Alpha, Brenau
1933 Illinois Delta, Wheaton (1950)
1937 Georgia Beta, Georgia State Woman's (1941)
1939 Colorado Alpha, Colorado State College
1941 Wisconsin Alpha, St. Norbert
1941 Illinois Epsilon, Western Illinois
1942 Illinois Zeta, Northern Illinois State
1947 Michigan Alpha, Central Michigan
1949 Illinois Eta, Knox
1950 Oklahoma Alpha, East Central State (Okla.)
1950 South Dakota Alpha, School of Mines and Technology, Rapid City
1951 Michigan Beta, Ferris Institute
1951 Oklahoma Beta, Phillips (Okla.)
1951 Wisconsin Beta, Wisconsin-Milwaukee
1951 Illinois Theta, Illinois State Normal

Alpha Delta Alpha

ALPHA DELTA ALPHA was founded at Coe College in 1920 as a local scientific society and became national by merging with a similar society at Iowa. In 1923 it became a general social fraternity, and in the next few years established chapters at Iowa State Teachers College (1923), Buena Vista College (1926), Simpson College (1927), Hanover College (1928), Tri-State College (1930), and Upper Iowa University (1932). The badge was an equilateral triangle with a border of twenty-one pearls. The inner triangle was of black enamel with a single pearl, a radio antenna, and the letters A Δ A. In December, 1934, at a national meeting held in Cedar Falls, Iowa, the fraternity was dissolved.

Alpha Epsilon Iota

ACTIVE PIN

ALPHA EPSILON IOTA, medical fraternity for women, was founded at the University of Michigan, February 26, 1890, by Lotta Ruth Arwine-Suverkrup, May Belle Stuckey Reynolds, Ada Fenimore Bock, Anna Ward Croacher, and Lily Mac Gowan-Fellows.

It was dissolved as a national organization in March, 1963.

The badge was a black enameled faceted pentagon, having a gold star at the apex with an emerald inset. The three upper facets contained the Greek letters A E I in gold, the two lower facets, a gold serpent. The flower was the white carnation. Colors were black, white, and green. The *Directory-Journal* was issued biennially.

Total membership was about 4,000. Chapter roll:

1890 Alpha, Michigan
1890 Beta, Chicago (1940)
1899 Gamma, Cincinnati (1933)
1899 Delta, Illinois (Chicago)
1901 Epsilon, Minnesota
1902 Zeta, Stanford
1902 Eta, Cornell (1913)
1902 Theta, Woman's Medical College of Pennsylvania
1905 Iota, California (San Francisco)
1906 Kappa, U.C.L.A.
1909 Lambda, Syracuse
1919 Mu, Tulane
1921 Nu, Oklahoma
1922 Xi, Oregon (Portland)
1922 Omicron, Kansas (1948)
1923 Pi, Medical College of Virginia
1923 Rho, Texas
1923 Sigma, Ohio State
1927 Tau, Wisconsin
1927 Upsilon, Southwestern Medical (Dallas)
1927 Phi, George Washington
1927 Chi, Washington University (Mo.)
1938 Psi, Louisiana State (New Orleans)
1940 Omega, Tennessee
1941 Alpha-Alpha, Marquette
1944 Alpha-Beta, Hahnemann
1948 Alpha Gamma, Baylor (Houston)
1948 Alpha Delta, New York Medical
1948 Alpha Epsilon, Temple
1949 Alpha Zeta, Creighton
1949 Alpha Eta, Georgia (Augusta)

Alpha Gamma Chi

ALPHA GAMMA CHI, a musical sorority established at Ottawa, Ohio, in 1898, had chapters at the New England Conservatory of Music, the Cincinnati Conservatory of Music, and possibly at Richmond, Virginia.

Alpha Omega Delta

ALPHA OMEGA DELTA was a medical fraternity founded in September, 1879, at the University of Buffalo. Other chapters were established as follows: Baltimore Medical College, Syracuse University, Detroit College of Medicine, University of Maryland, Georgetown University, and George Washington University. The society existed until 1910 when dissensions arose among the chapters, and they became inactive one by one except the parent chapter which continued to flourish and became again a local organization. In 1911 it became a chapter of Phi Rho Sigma, retaining its old name as a chapter designation. The badge was a monogram surmounting a skull and bones. The membership was about 1,500.

Alpha Phi Epsilon

ACTIVE PIN

ALPHA PHI EPSILON, forensic honor fraternity, was founded at Atlanta, Georgia, April 29, 1918, by representatives from nine southern colleges. The call for the meeting was sent out by Roy B. Smart of Alabama, who was elected first president. Originally the membership was drawn from one literary or debating society in each institution having a chapter, and all members of that society were members of the intercollegiate society. The year following the first World War was marked by the decision that such a literary society could not flourish, and in 1920 a convention, held at the University of Tennessee, changed the nature of the society in several respects. Women were admitted, and men from every recognized literary society in its component colleges became eligible to membership. The standards were set to require one and one-half collegiate years' membership in and attendance upon the meetings of a literary society, participation in at least five debates in the society, presentation of at least two original orations, and a written parliamentary law examination to be passed with a grade of at least eighty-five percent. Individual chapters were allowed to add other requirements. The adoption of these changes made the fraternity a recognized force in forensics in the South and led to expansion into other parts of the country, about thirty chapters being established. Government was vested in the Executive Council which had absolute authority between biennial conventions. There were three classes of membership: active, alumni, and honorary. A special service award, the emblem of the fraternity mounted upon a rayed background, was presented for outstanding meritorious service for the fraternity. A paper, *The Garnet and Green*, was published quarterly. The badge was of gold displaying fraternity symbols. Colors were garnet and green. The flower was a red rose. In 1935 the chapters were absorbed by Tau Kappa Alpha.

Alpha Tau Sigma

ALPHA TAU SIGMA Fraternity was founded in 1912 at the American School of Osteopathy, Kirksville, Missouri, by Charles W. Barnes, W. S. Giddings, E. E. Loose, E. E. Ruby, and W. C. Warner, The fraternity was incorporated in 1915 and, although having the power to grant additional chapters, never expanded into the other recognized colleges of osteopathy. It ceased operation in 1964.

Axis Club

AXIS CLUB was founded in 1899 at the Kirksville College of Osteopathy and Surgery. At one time it had five chapters, but with the wider business and professional opportunities for women their attendance at the osteopathic colleges decreased, and the club discontinued operations.

Chi Sigma Delta

CHI SIGMA DELTA was founded as a secret honor fraternity at Stevens Institute of Technology about 1925. It was composed of outstanding men on the campus, fraternity men being included as well as nonfraternity men. This organization, however, was excluded from the local interfraternity council. It petitioned Theta Nu Epsilon later and was incorporated in that fraternity.

Chi Zeta Chi

ACTIVE PIN

CHI ZETA CHI was founded in the Medical Department of the University of Georgia, October, 1903, by J. Ansley Griffin. Chapters originally were named after distinguished physicians who were associated with the institution at which the chapter was located, but in 1907 the alphabetical system was adopted. Membership was limited to bona fide matriculated male first-year medical students of the Caucasian race. The chapter roll was: Alpha, University of Georgia; Delta, University of Maryland, Baltimore; Lambda, University of Tennessee; Mu, Tulane University; Nu, University of Arkansas, Little Rock; Omicron, Washington University; Psi, Medical College of Virginia, Richmond; Tau, Jefferson Medical College, Philadelphia; Xi, St. Louis University; Alpha Alpha, Emory University, Atlanta; Beta Beta, University of Oklahoma; Upsilon, Baylor University, Dallas.

On April 6, 1929, the fraternity was amalgamated with Phi Rho Sigma.

Chimes

ACTIVE PIN

CHIMES was founded as a student leadership society for women in December, 1947, at Pennsylvania State University when representatives from that campus, Ohio State, Temple University, and West Virginia University met to organize a national junior society to meet a common need recognized by the four schools. When Chimes held its second national convention in September, 1950, Key and Scroll, a West Coast Society of three chapters, merged with the group.

In 1959 Chimes was dissolved. Each of its chapters reverted to the status of a local junior women's honor society for its individual school.

The purpose of Chimes was: "to honor those junior women who have shown and who will continue to show their loyalty as an individual and as a group to their college or university by giving their service and leadership to the advancement of its interests, welfare, and unity, and of stimulating scholarship and participation in extra-curricular activities."

The national publication was *Keynotes*.

The symbol was a golden bell with a cluster of three pearls forming the clapper; the name of the society was written across the base. The colors were gold, white, and dark brown. The flower was the yellow rose. The chapter roll:

1947	Pennsylvania State
1947	Ohio State
1947	Temple
1947	West Virginia
1948	Bradley
1950	Butler
1950	Southern California (Key and Scroll, 1946)
1950	Santa Barbara (Key and Scroll, 1946)
1950	U.C.L.A. (Key and Scroll, 1946)
1950	Minnesota
1950	Iowa State
1950	Washington (Mo.)
1950	Ohio
1952	Kansas
1954	Idaho State
1956	Arizona

Delta Omicron Alpha

DELTA OMICRON ALPHA was founded as a medical fraternity at Tulane University of Louisiana in 1907. It had the following chapter roll: 1907 Tulane University; 1908, Columbia University; 1910, University of Tennessee; 1910, Southwestern University; 1911, University of Alabama; 1912, Birmingham Medical College; 1912, Fort Worth School of Medicine; 1914, Chicago School of Medicine and Surgery. The chapters at Southwestern University and Birmingham Medical College ceased to exist in 1915. This fraternity merged with Theta Kappa Psi Fraternity, November 17, 1917.

Delta Phi Delta

DELTA PHI DELTA was organized as a law fraternity at the Cleveland Law School in 1900. In 1914 it united with Alpha Kappa Phi and Theta Lambda Phi to form Delta Theta Phi.

Delta Phi Upsilon

ACTIVE PIN

DELTA PHI UPSILON, the first national recognition society of early childhood education, was founded at Broadoaks, Pasadena, California, a graduate school in early childhood education, on January 8, 1923, by the following seven women who had entered the field of kindergarten-primary training and who felt the need of such an organization: Adamae Brooks, Cloyde Duval Dalzell, Helen Knudson Hose, Lulu Pickett, Marjorie Test-Loomis, Phoebe Ann Mathewson, and Winona Bassett Stevens. The society aims were "to promote professional attainments and to set a high goal of achievement before the undergraduate students." Membership was based primarily upon scholarship and such qualities as leadership, campus activities, cooperation, and professional attitude.

The society published a *Bulletin* containing news and information for the members, an alumnae directory, and a songbook.

The badge was a monogram pin, the letter Φ enclosing the monogram Δ Υ, the Υ resting upon the Δ which is of black enamel. There was an emerald at each end of the Φ. The coat of arms is: On a bend dexter three Greek letters Δ Φ Υ, over a rose slipped from dexter base to sinister chief. Colors were blue and green. The flower was the rose.

The chapter roll in 1940 was:

1923	Grand Alpha, Broadoaks Training School, Pasadena
1924	Beta, U.C.L.A.
1924	Gamma, Pestalozzi-Froedel Training School, Chicago
1925	Delta, Chico State (Calif.)

1928   Epsilon, San Francisco State (Calif.)
1928   Zeta, San Jose State
1933   Eta, Santa Barbara
1933   Theta, Temple

Epsilon Eta Phi

ACTIVE PIN

EPSILON ETA PHI was founded on May 3, 1927, at Northwestern University, Chicago, Illinois, and incorporated October 14, 1930, in the State of Illinois. The fraternity was organized to foster the study of business administration and commerce in universities; foster loyalty to alma mater; encourage scholarship; uphold high moral, social and intellectual standards; promote closer affiliation between the commercial world and women students of commerce and business administration; and further a higher standard of commercial ethics and culture and the civic and commercial welfare of the community.

Epsilon Eta Phi was merged with Phi Chi Theta, business administration and economics fraternity, member of Professional Panhellenic Association, in July, 1973.

The official flower was the rose-colored sweet pea; colors, steel gray and old rose; motto, *To be rather than to seem.* The official publication, the *Epsilon Eta Phi Magazine,* was issued annually on Founders' Day.

Total estimated membership May 31, 1967, was 900. There were five active and two inactive chapters. The chapter roll was:

1927   Alpha, Northwestern
1931   Beta, DePaul
1931   Gamma, Boston (1961)
1935   Delta, Duquesne (day)
1947   Epsilon, Duquesne (evening)
1954   Zeta, Beaver (Pa.) (1965)
1964   Eta, Hardin-Simmons

Gamma Alpha Chi

ACTIVE PIN

GAMMA ALPHA CHI, national professional advertising fraternity for women, was founded in 1920 at the University of Missouri by a group headed by Ruth Prather Midyette and under the guidance of Walter Williams, first dean of the university's journalism school.

Its purpose was three-fold: to furnish to its collegiate members opportunities for extracurricular education and activities in the field of advertising; to give honor and recognition for outstanding work done in professional advertising and to help in every way possible to raise the standards of advertising; to provide its graduates and alumnae contact with the advertising field through its thousands of members and affiliations with the Advertising Federation of America and Advertising Association of the West.

Gamma Alpha Chi merged with Alpha Delta Sigma, national advertising recognition society for men, on November 2, 1971, to form ADS. In 1973 ADS chapters were absorbed by the American Advertising Federation, thus ending the function of the society, technically, as a fraternal organization.

Gamma Alpha Chi's slogan was "Truth and Service." Its octagonal badge, pierced by a golden pen, contained the Greek letters of the fraternity's name, a globe-encircled relief map of the western hemisphere, and a star engraved in gold on a black field. The colors were gold and brown; the flower, the yellow rose.

Total estimated membership May 31, 1967, was 8,500. There were thirty-nine active and thirteen inactive chapters. The chapter roll was:

1920   Alpha, Missouri
1923   Gamma, Washington (1947–1955)
1924   Delta, Illinois (1940–1945)
1926   Epsilon, Nebraska (1941–1949)
1927   Zeta, Oregon
1928   Eta, Southern California
1929   Theta, Washington State (1945)
1929   Iota, California (1931)
1946   Lambda, Iowa
1947   Mu, Oklahoma
1947   Nu, Kansas
1948   Xi, Syracuse (1955)
1948   Omicron, Roosevelt College (1950)
1948   Pi, Indiana
1948   Rho, Butler (1954)
1948   Sigma, C.C.N.Y.
1948   Tau, U.C.L.A. (1950)
1949   Upsilon, San Jose State
1949   Phi, Colorado
1949   Chi, Ohio State
1950   Psi, Miami (Fla.)
1950   Omega, Southern Methodist
1950   Alpha Alpha, Wisconsin
1950   Alpha Beta, Houston (1954–1961)
1951   Alpha Gamma, Florida
1951   Alpha Delta, Florida State
1953   Alpha Epsilon, Fordham
1956   Alpha Zeta, Georgia
1956   Alpha Eta, Temple
1957   Alpha Theta, Marquette

1958   Alpha Iota, Arizona State (Tempe)
1958   Alpha Kappa, Michigan State
1959   Alpha Lambda, Texas Tech
1960   Alpha Mu, Arizona
1960   Alpha Nu, Texas
1961   Alpha Xi, Maryland
1962   Alpha Omicron, Long Beach State
1964   Alpha Pi, N.Y.U.
1966   Alpha Rho, Chico State

Gamma Epsilon Pi

GAMMA EPSILON PI was founded at the University of Illinois on March 26, 1918, by five junior women of the college of commerce who felt the need of an honor organization for women corresponding with Beta Gamma Sigma for men. Its chapter roll was: 1918, Alpha, University of Illinois; 1919, Beta, Northwestern University; 1920, Gamma, University of California; 1920, Delta, University of Pittsburgh; 1920, Epsilon, State University of Iowa; 1920, Zeta, University of Kansas; 1921, Eta, University of Minnesota; 1922, Theta, University of Oklahoma; 1922, Iota, Washington University; 1922, Kappa, University of Southern California; 1922, Lambda, Montana State University; 1922, Alpha Beta, University of Washington; 1922, Alpha Gamma, University of Wisconsin; 1922, Alpha Delta, University of Texas; 1922, Alpha Epsilon, Syracuse University; 1922, Alpha Zeta, New York University; 1924, Mu, University of Nebraska; 1926, Nu, Ohio State University. The badge was a key bearing the Greek letters of the name. In 1933 the sorority was merged with Beta Gamma Sigma honor society.

Gamma Pi Epsilon

ACTIVE PIN

GAMMA PI EPSILON was the national Jesuit honor society for women and was established in fourteen of the Jesuit universities of the United States.

Candidates were elected by the members from lists of junior and senior women from all colleges and departments who had demonstrated superior scholarship, loyalty, and service to the university and who had been approved by their deans. No more than five per cent of the coed population could be elected.

The society was founded at Marquette University in 1925 to honor women students who had excelled in these areas of scholarship, loyalty, and service, and also to promote all of the various activities of the school in which the society was established, especially those concerned with the welfare of women students and those concerned with the scholarship spectrum of college life.

Gamma Pi Epsilon was formally merged with Alpha Sigma Nu, the national Jesuit honor society for men, on March 30, 1973, to form the new Alpha Sigma Nu national Jesuit honor society for men and women.

The society's emblem was a gold key inscribed with the Greek letters, Γ Π Ε, and the traditional lamp of learning.

Total estimated membership March 30, 1973, was 450. There were fourteen college chapters. The chapter roll was:

1925   Marquette
1947   St. Louis
1950   Gonzaga
1951   LeMoyne
1952   Creighton
1953   Detroit
1958   San Francisco
1959   Wheeling
1962   Seattle
1963   Georgetown
1964   John Carroll
1966   Santa Clara
1971   Regis College
1971   Xavier University

Kappa Phi

KAPPA PHI was organized as a medical-pharmaceutical fraternity at the University of the South in 1909. It had the following chapters: University of the South, Lincoln Memorial University, University College of Medicine, and University of Alabama.

Omega Upsilon Phi

ACTIVE PIN

OMEGA UPSILON PHI was founded as a medical fraternity at the University of Buffalo, November 15, 1894, by Amos T. Baker, John W. Garratt, Frank O. Garrison, Lawrence Hendee, Elbert W. LeWall, George H. Minard, George S. Staniland, Edward A. Southall, Townsend Walker, Henry Joslyn, and Ross G. Loop. Chapters were established at University of Buffalo, Niagara University, Union University (Albany), University of Colorado (Denver), University and Bellevue Hospital Medical College, University of Toronto, University of Colorado, University of

Cincinnati, Cornell University, Stanford University, Columbia University, Miami Medical College, Northwestern University, Medical College of Virginia, University College of Medicine, University of North Carolina, University of Pennsylvania, Jefferson Medical College, University of Minnesota, North Carolina Medical College, Medico-Chirurgical College, Vanderbilt University, Fordham University, University of Maryland, University of California, Temple University, Georgetown University, St. Louis University, and Ohio State University. There were four degrees in the ritualistic work. Directories were published in 1901, 1912, and 1915. There was a quarterly magazine and an annual publication. The badge was a shield displaying a monogram of the letters Ω Υ Φ below an eye. Colors were crimson and gold; the flower was the red carnation.

In 1934 the fraternity was merged with Phi Beta Pi.

Phi Alpha Gamma

PHI ALPHA GAMMA was founded at the New York Homeopathic Medical College, March 25, 1894, by Thomas D. Buchanan, Thomas F. Davies, Edmund M. De Vol, Robert M. Jones, Brooks DeF. Norwood, Arthur B. Smith, and Harry S. Willard. The Minnesota and Iowa chapters were formed from the two chapters of a fraternity called Phi Kappa Tau, and the Hahnemann Medical College of Philadelphia chapter from a local fraternity named Delta Kappa Upsilon.

A number of the undergraduate chapters were combined because of the union of institutions.

A catalogue was published under authority of the grand chapter in 1899, and directories in 1905, 1920 and 1925. A history appeared in 1912. The *Quarterly* of Phi Alpha Gamma was published continuously since 1902.

The undergraduate badge was the facsimile-in-ivory of the middle phalanx of the little finger of the human hand, with the letters Φ A Γ in gold upon a field of black enamel upon the mounting of gold. The graduate key or badge consisted of a miniature of the coat of arms of the fraternity. The pledge pin was of violet enamel surrounded by a narrow band of gold. The color was violet. The flower was the violet.

The chapter roll was:

1894   Alpha, New York Homeopathic
1896   Beta, Boston (1917)
1897   Gamma, Hahnemann
1897   Delta, Minnesota (1909)
1897   Epsilon, Iowa (1920)
1897   Zeta Theta, Ohio State (1924)

1897   Eta, Chicago Homeopathic (united with Lambda)
1899   Theta, Pulte Medical (1901) (united with Zeta)
1899   Iota, Homeopathic of Missouri (1909)
1900   Kappa, Michigan (1923)
1900   Eta Lambda, Hahnemann (Chicago) (1909)
1906   Mu, Hahnemann (Pacific) (1909)
1906   Iota Nu, Hahnemann (Kansas City) (1917)

Phi Chi Delta

PHI CHI DELTA was founded in February, 1913, at Louisiana State University. The fraternity was composed largely of medical students from Latin countries. The chapter roll was: 1912, Louisiana State University (1916); 1912, Baltimore College of Physicians and Surgeons; 1912, Tulane University; 1912, Pennsylvania State College; 1913, University of Maryland; 1913, University of Michigan; 1913, Loyola University; 1913, Syracuse University; 1913, George Washington University; 1913, Medical College of Virginia; 1913, Purdue University; 1914, University of Pennsylvania; 1914, Jefferson Medical College; 1914, Medico-Chirurgical College of Philadelphia. Membership was 226. In 1914 the fraternity commenced the publication of a monthly journal in Spanish called *Mundo Latino*. It was published at San Juan, Puerto Rico. The fraternity ceased to exist in 1918.

Phi Delta

PHI DELTA was organized as a medical fraternity at the Long Island College of Medicine in 1901. The chapters were all termed "alphas." The chapter roll was: 1901, Long Island College of Medicine; 1902, Starling Medical College; 1902, Union University, Albany; 1903, Wisconsin College of Physicians and Surgeons; 1903, University Medical College, Kansas City (1910); 1903, Washington University; 1903, Michigan College of Medicine and Surgery; 1904, Sioux City Medical College (1910); 1904, Toronto Medical College (1910); 1904, Columbia University (1911); 1904, Dearborn Medical College (1908); 1904, University of Minnesota; 1905, Chicago College of Physicians and Surgeons; 1905, St. Louis Medical College; 1906, University of Illinois, Chicago; 1912, Loyola University. Of the sixteen mentioned chapters five had ceased to exist when the fraternity was merged with the Theta Kappa Psi Fraternity on January 26, 1918.

Phi Delta Delta

ACTIVE PIN

PHI DELTA DELTA, an international women's legal fraternity, was founded at the University of Southern California, College of Law, on November 11, 1911 by Georgia P. Bullock, Annett F. Hunley, Gladys Moore Brown, Sarah Patten Doherty, and Vere Radir-Norton. It was organized to promote a high standard of scholarship, professional ethics, and culture among women in law schools and in the legal profession. It was incorporated under the laws of the State of California, October 25, 1912.

The fraternity maintained a high scholastic standard as the requirement for invitation to membership. Every student initiated, either undergraduate or postgraduate, prior to invitation to membership, must have attained a grade of at least fifteen per cent higher than the passing grade of the law school in which the particular chapter was installed.

New chapters could be established only in schools or colleges of law which were members of the American Law School Association, or which appeared on the list of schools approved by the American Bar Association.

Phi Delta Delta merged with Phi Alpha Delta law fraternity, member of the Professional Interfraternity Conference, August 12, 1972. Two members of Phi Delta Delta became members of the governing board of Phi Alpha Delta.

Traditions and Insignia: The official badge and the pledge pin comprised the official jewelry. The colors were old rose and violet, and the flowers were roses and violets.

Total estimated membership, August 12, 1972, was 5,000 members at fifty-seven law school chapters. The chapter roll was:

1911	Alpha, Southern California
1913	Beta, American, Washington, D.C.
1913	Gamma, Chicago-Kent (1917)
1913	Delta, Oregon
1917	Epsilon, Washington
1918	Zeta, George Washington
1920	Eta, Portia (Boston)
1920	Theta, Kansas
1921	Kappa, Washburn
1921	Lambda, Pittsburgh
1921	Iota, Vanderbilt
1922	Mu, Missouri
1922	Nu, Brooklyn Law
1922	Xi, Northwestern (Portland, Ore.)
1923	Omicron, Dickinson
1923	Pi, Western Reserve

1923	Rho, Stetson (St. Petersburg, Fla.)
1923	Sigma, Buffalo
1924	Phi, Colorado
1924	Chi, Duquesne (1937)
1924	Tau, Temple University
1924	Upsilon, Willamette
1925	Psi, Kansas City
1926	Omega, British Columbia
1926	Alpha Alpha, Fordham
1927	Alpha Beta, Cincinnati
1927	Alpha Gamma, N.Y.U.
1927	Alpha Delta, Maryland (Baltimore)
1927	Alpha Epsilon, Minneapolis—Minnesota College of Law (1959)
1927	Alpha Zeta, Loyola, New Orleans
1927	Alpha Eta, South Dakota (1937)
1928	Alpha Theta, Loyola, Los Angeles
1928	Alpha Iota, Louisville
1928	Alpha Kappa, Wayne State
1928	Alpha Lambda, National (Washington, D.C.) (1955)
1929	Alpha Mu, Columbia (1937)
1929	Alpha Nu, Cleveland— Marshall
1929	Alpha Xi, Indiana (Indianapolis)
1929	Alpha Omicron, Tulsa
1929	Alpha Pi, Utah
1929	Alpha Rho, St. John's (N.Y.)
1930	Alpha Tau, Yale (1937)
1930	Alpha Sigma, Michigan
1930	Alpha Upsilon, St. Louis
1931	Alpha Phi, Miami (Fla.)
1931	Alpha Chi, Memphis
1931	Alpha Psi, St. Paul College of Law (1959)
1931	Alpha Omega, Louisiana State
1932	Beta Alpha, Southwestern (Los Angeles)
1933	Beta Beta, California
1936	Beta Gamma, Mississippi
1937	Beta Delta, Stanford
1947	Beta Zeta, Florida
1948	Beta Epsilon, Catholic (Washington, D.C.)
1949	Beta Eta, Georgia
1950	Beta Theta, California
1954	Beta Iota, Richmond
1954	Beta Kappa, Salmon P. Chase
1955	Beta Lambda, Georgetown
1959	Beta Mu, Alabama
1959	Alpha Epsilon Psi, William Mitchell

Phi Delta Gamma

ACTIVE PIN

PHI DELTA GAMMA was established as a forensic society in 1924 by William O. Moore and George O. Hurley, State University of Iowa; Kenneth E.

Oberholtzer, University of Illinois; Dean William A. Hamilton, College of William and Mary; Russell D. Tubaugh, Ohio University; Paul A. Lomax, University of Southern California; William Waldo Girdner, George Washington University; and Carl E. Anderson, University of Minnesota. They were members of an official committee organized through correspondence as a result of a meeting held at Urbana, Illinois, in 1922, following a movement which was started in some of the colleges and universities in the Middle West for the nationalization of literary societies. The fraternity aimed to maintain and stimulate a greater interest in the work of literary societies, debate clubs, and dramatic organizations in colleges and universities and to foster the upbuilding of literary societies. It sought to establish on a firm basis intersociety debates and forensic contests, and emphasized intersociety rather than intercollegiate forensics. The chapter roll included: 1924, State University of Iowa; 1924, University of Illinois; 1924, College of William and Mary; 1924, Ohio University; 1924, University of Southern California; 1924, George Washington University; 1924, University of Minnesota; 1925, Alabama Polytechnic Institute; 1925, University of Texas; 1927, Northwestern University; 1927, Ohio State University; 1928, Indiana University. *The Literary Scroll* was an occasional publication. In 1935 the fraternity was absorbed by Tau Kappa Alpha.

Phi Delta Pi

PHI DELTA PI, national professional physical education fraternity for women, was founded at the Normal College of the American Gymnastic Union at Indianapolis in October, 1916, and was incorporated under the laws of Indiana February 2, 1917. Charters were granted only in colleges and universities having a firmly established and approved major course in physical education.

Phi Delta Pi was a member of the American Association for Health, Physical Education, and Recreation.

Phi Delta Pi was merged with Delta Psi Kappa, women's professional physical education fraternity, Professional Panhellenic Association member, in March, 1970.

Colors were purple and gold; emblems were the purple violet, the amethyst, and the oak leaf.

Total estimated membership May 31, 1967, was 5,000. There were fourteen active and sixteen inactive chapters. The chapter roll was:

1916 Alpha, Normal College of the American Gymnastic Union, Indianapolis, Ind. (1942)
1918 Beta, Temple
1918 Gamma, Northwestern (1919)

1919 Delta, American College of Physical Education, now De Paul University, (1965)
1919 Epsilon, Kellogg School of Physical Education (Mich.)
1919 Zeta, Chicago Normal School of Physical Education (1921)
1920 Eta, Utah
1922 Theta, Ithaca School of Physical Education, New York
1924 Iota, Savage School of Physical Education, New York City (1944)
1927 Kappa, Panzer College of Physical Education, East Orange, New Jersey (1944)
1928 Lambda, Ohio (1936)
1929 Mu, Utah State
1930 Nu, Southeastern Teachers (Okla.) (1942)
1931 Xi, Brigham Young University
1933 Omicron, Santa Barbara (1943)
1935 Pi, Slippery Rock (Penn.) (1954)
1949 Rho, Wittenberg (1965)
1951 Sigma, Minnesota, (Duluth)
1952 Tau, Miami (Fla.)
1959 Upsilon, Florida State

Phi Mu Gamma

PHI MU GAMMA was organized at Hollins College, Virginia, on October 17, 1898, by Maude Johnson, Elizabeth Cooley, Pearl S. Penn, Mona House, Daisy Bell Cooley, Lois Sykes, Daisy Estes, and Elizabeth Leigh Wood. The aim was to"instill loyalty among the members and to work for mental and artistic development."

In 1900 it was decided to develop a national organization, and a policy of expansion was adopted. On March 22, 1902, Phi Mu Gamma was incorporated under the laws of Virginia under articles introduced by: "The object of said association shall be the formation and perpetuation of good fellowship among its members and the encouragement of literature."

In 1930 Phi Mu Gamma formed a merger with Lambda Phi Delta, a professional fine arts fraternity, founded at Northwestern University in 1916–1917 by Grace Brown, Fern Calvert, Rachael Parmenter, Blanche Evans, and Hazel Ingersoll. Lambda Phi Delta invited into membership women students who had shown outstanding ability in speech arts, music arts, or the dance.

The name of Phi Mu Gamma was adopted for the new merged group. The rituals and constitutions of the two organizations were revised and combined. Chapters established in schools not offering majors of degrees in the fine arts were dropped, and a relettering was made. The scope of the fraternity came thus to include the following arts: drama, music, art, creative writing, and the dance.

The badge was a black-enameled shield superimposed on a gold triangle. A small gold shield upon which were inscribed the Greek letters ΦΜΓ rested upon the black shield. The outer shield was the triangle and plain shield. The colors were gold, black, and blue; the flowers, sweetheart roses and forget-me-nots.

Phi Mu Gamma initiated an estimated 10,550 members into seventeen camps chapters. The chapter roll was:

1908	Alpha, Emerson College of Oratory, Boston
1913	Xi, Chicago Musical College
1913	Omicron, Kansas City (Kansas) Conservatory (1948)
1914	Psi, Wisconsin Conservatory of Music (1938)
1916	Beta, Northwestern (1940)
1917	Delta, Kansas State (Pittsburg) (1943)
1920	Theta, Lombard (1936)
1920	Mu, Kansas State (Emporia) 1939
1921	Gamma, Drake
1921	Zeta, Horner Institute of Fine Arts (1939)
1921	Iota, Oklahoma (1938)
1922	Nu, Millikin (1938)
1925	Epsilon, Simpson (Iowa) (1935)
1926	Eta, Washington
1928	Kappa, West Virginia (formerly New River State College)
1947	Lambda, MacPhail College of Music and Drama, Minneapolis
1956	Tau, Durham University, Durham, England

Pi Kappa Tau

PI KAPPA TAU was organized as a medical fraternity in the homeopathic department of the University of Iowa by R. E. Peck and I. B. Hoskins in October, 1905. A second chapter was established at the University of Minnesota in 1896, In 1897 the two chapters became chapters of Phi Alpha Gamma, Medical-homeopathic fraternity.

Pi Mu

ACTIVE PIN

PI MU was founded as a medical fraternity December 13, 1892, at the University of Virginia by Dr. John W. Mallet and ten associates. The chapter roll was as follows: 1892, University of Virginia; 1896, Medical College of Virginia; 1908, University of Louisville; 1908, Jefferson Medical College (1915); 1908, Medical College of South Carolina (1914);

1908, University of Nashville; 1910, Vanderbilt University; 1910, Johns Hopkins University; 1913, Columbia University. The membership was 1,500. The journal was called the *Cerebrum*. The badge was a Greek cross with skull and bones at the center and the letters Π and M. In 1920 the fraternity became part of Phi Chi.

Sigma Kappa Alpha

SIGMA KAPPA ALPHA was founded at the University of Minnesota in 1908 as a local professional fraternity restricting membership to students of mining and metallurgical engineering. In January, 1910, this local, together with Sigma Rho (1892) at the Michigan College of Mines, Mu Sigma (1909) at the Case Institute of Technology, and a new local at the South Dakota School of Mines held a meeting in Minneapolis, Minnesota, for the purpose of founding a national professional mining and metallurgical engineering fraternity, the reason of which was stated to be: "to bring more closely together the students in mining and metallurgy, to foster a spirit of honesty, to create a high standard of scholarship, and to promote a feeling of good fellowship and a lasting bond of unity among its members." Each of the mining locals was represented by two delegates, but at the last moment the delegates from Sigma Rho withdrew as their organization refused to join the new national. This withdrawal of the oldest local in the group seems to have disorganized the young fraternity from the start, and in 1910 Alpha Chapter of Sigma Kappa Alpha at Minnesota accepted a charter from Sigma Rho, thus becoming the Beta Chapter of that fraternity. The chapter at the South Dakota School of Mines never had a good start and finally died. In May, 1911, the remaining chapter of Sigma Kappa Alpha at Case Institute of Technology was chartered as Delta Chapter of Theta Tau.

Sigma Tau

ACTIVE PIN

SIGMA TAU was an honor society founded at the University of Nebraska, February 24, 1904, by fourteen faculty members and students of the College of Engineering. The motive that guided the founders was a desire to be of service to engineering education. The ideals of the society were, as far as the founders were able to determine, the ideals of engineering education.

In fixing the basis of eligibility to membership in the society, those qualities which best give promise of a successful career were selected. The members of the various chapters were chosen from those men and women who ranked in scholarship among the upper third of the juniors and seniors of a recognized engineering school. Selection of members from these men and women who qualified scholastically was on the further basis of practicality and sociability.

Each chapter recognized scholarship among freshman engineering students by presenting the Sigma Tau Medal each year to the freshman ranking highest in scholarship. One or more graduate fellowships were offered each year by the Sigma Tau Foundation to some deserving member of the organization who desired to pursue graduate study. The Sigma Tau Merit Awards were presented to members and non-members for service to engineering education.

Sigma Tau was merged with Tau Beta Pi engineering honor society January 1, 1974. The merger is commemorated in the annual award of a Tau Beta Pi-Sigma Tau graduate fellowship.

The colors of Sigma Tau Society were navy blue and white. The symbols were the pyramid and rail section.

Total estimated membership January 1, 1974, was 45,000. There were thirty-four collegiate chapters. The chapter roll was:

1904   Alpha, Nebraska
1907   Beta, Iowa (1912)
1911   Gamma, Pennsylvania
1912   Delta, South Dakota (1916)
1912   Epsilon, Kansas State
1913   Zeta, Oregon State
1913   Eta, Washington State
1914   Theta, Illinois
1914   Iota, Colorado
1915   Kappa, Pennsylvania State
1915   Lambda, Kansas
1916   Mu, Oklahoma
1916   Nu, Swarthmore
1921   Xi, George Washington
1922   Pi, North Dakota
1922   Rho, Idaho
1923   Sigma, Oklahoma State
1923   Tau, South Dakota Mines and Tech
1923   Upsilon, Florida
1924   Phi, Akron
1928   Chi, New Mexico
1930   Psi, Pittsburgh
1932   Omega, Wyoming
1935   Omicron, Louisville
1936   Alpha Alpha, Colorado State
1941   Delta, South Dakota State
1942   Alpha Beta, Southern Methodist
1949   Alpha Gamma, New Mexico A & M
1951   Alpha Delta, Utah State
1952   Alpha Epsilon, Nevada
1953   Alpha Zeta, Rice
1956   Alpha Eta, Texas A & I
1956   Alpha Theta, Youngstown

1958   Alpha Iota, Bradley
1966   Alpha Kappa, Fresno State
1954   Omega Alpha, General Chapter

Sigma Upsilon

SIGMA UPSILON was established as a literary honor society for men in 1901 through the efforts of Paul Jones of the Sopherim Club of the University of the South and Neil Cullom of the Calumet Club of Vanderbilt University. It was a federation of local honorary literary groups in Southern colleges, each chapter choosing its own name. Membership was based primarily upon literary ability and elections were usually made once a year from members of the sophomore, junior, and senior classes.

Publications included a biennial *Journal of Sigma Upsilon*, a quarterly, *The Scarab*, and an annual directory of members. The badge was a triangular shield surmounted by a dark green scarab displaying the letters E Υ. Colors were green and old gold. The flower was the jonquil.

Chapters were established in rapid succession until 1928, the last being Harveyans at Morris Harvey College in that year. After that, a decline of interest began which resulted in the gradual death of the society.

Theta Chi Delta

THETA CHI DELTA was founded as a chemical recognition society on February 2, 1921, by three professors and twelve students at Lombard College under the leadership of Prof. H. A. Geauque, head of the department of chemistry. It offered membership as a reward for high scholarship in chemistry.

The society became national in scope April 3, 1925, when representatives of five colleges met in St. Louis. Charter groups and their representatives at the meeting were: Prof. H. A. Geauque, Prof. Castle W. Foard, Hilmer C. Nelson, William Watson, Henry Miles, Lombard College; L. Burdette Wylie, William B. Duke, College of Wooster; Millard A. Wagoner, University of Louisville; Ernest Larson, Bethany College; Prof. H. A. Wycoff and Walter Swift, Missouri Wesleyan College.

Chapter membership was limited to students who had completed three semester courses in chemistry with superior scholarship, to graduates actively engaged in chemical work, and to those who had achieved distinction in the field of chemistry.

The society publication was *The Crucible*. The badge was a gold and black French enamel key, hexagon-shaped, the area inside the gold border of the key was black enamel with the letters, Θ X Δ over crossed retorts in gold. On the reverse side was a raised and modeled balance with member's name and chapter. The colors were gold, purple, and black.

The chapter roll in 1940 before the demise of the society was:

1925	Alpha Beta, Wooster
1925	Alpha Gamma, Louisville
1925	Alpha Delta, Bethany
1925	Alpha Epsilon, Birmingham-Southern
1926	Alpha Eta, Carthage
1926	Alpha Theta, William and Mary
1927	Alpha Iota, Wittenberg
1932	Alpha Nu, William Jewell

Colleges and Universities Where Fraternities Were Founded

University of Alabama

MEN'S SOCIAL
Sigma Alpha Epsilon   1856

HONOR
Alpha Epsilon Delta   1932

Allegheny College

PROFESSIONAL
Kappa Delta Epsilon   1933

HONOR
Phi Sigma Iota   1922

American Gymnastic Union Normal College

PROFESSIONAL
Delta Psi Kappa   1916
Phi Delta Pi   1916
Phi Epsilon Kappa   1913

America School of Osteopathy

PROFESSIONAL
Alpha Tau Sigma   1912
Delta Omega   1904

Anthony Wayne Institute

MEN'S SOCIAL
Alpha Gamma Upsilon   1922

University of Arkansas

WOMEN'S SOCIAL
Chi Omega   1895

HONOR
Phi Alpha Theta   1921

Arkansas State College (Conway)

MEN'S SOCIAL
Phi Lambda Chi   1925

Baltimore College of Dental Surgery

PROFESSIONAL
Psi Omega   1892

Barnard College

WOMEN'S SOCIAL
Alpha Epsilon Phi   1909
Alpha Omicron Pi   1897

Bethany College

MEN'S SOCIAL
Delta Tau Delta   1858

Boston University

MEN'S SOCIAL
Lambda Chi Alpha   1909

WOMEN'S SOCIAL
Delta Delta Delta   1888
Pi Lambda Sigma*   1921

Bridgewater State Teachers College

PROFESSIONAL
Kappa Delta Phi   1900

Brooklyn College of Pharmacy

PROFESSIONAL
Delta Sigma Theta

Brown University

MEN'S SOCIAL
Phi Kappa*   1889

Bucknell University

MEN'S SOCIAL
Theta Upsilon Omega*   1924

University of Buffalo

PROFESSIONAL
Omega Upsilon Phi*

University of California

MEN'S SOCIAL
Alpha Kappa Lambda   1914

WOMEN'S SOCIAL
Beta Phi Alpha*   1909
Lambda Omega*   1923
Theta Upsilon*   1914

PROFESSIONAL
Alpha Tau Delta   1921
Upsilon Alpha   1918

HONOR
Iota Sigma Pi   1900

RECOGNITION
Pi Delta Phi   1906
Sigma Delta Pi   1919

University of California at Los Angeles

MEN'S SOCIAL
Lambda Phi Epsilon   1981

Central Missouri State College

MEN'S SOCIAL
Sigma Tau Gamma   1920

PROFESSIONAL
Phi Sigma Pi   1916

College of Charleston

MEN'S SOCIAL
Pi Kappa Phi   1904

Chicago-Kent College of Law

PROFESSIONAL
Kappa Beta Pi   1908
Phi Alpha Delta   1897

University of Chicago

HONOR
Delta SIgma Rho   1906

*An asterisk denotes inactive school or society.

RECOGNITION
Eta Sigma Phi   1924

Cincinnati Conservatory of Music

PROFESSIONAL
Delta Omicron   1909

University of Cincinnati

RECOGNITION
Arnold Air Society   1947

Cleveland Law School

PROFESSIONAL
Delta Theta Phi   1900

Colby College

WOMEN'S SOCIAL
Sigma Kappa   1874

University of Colorado

RECOGNITION
Phi Epsilon Phi   1927

Columbia University

MEN'S SOCIAL
Delta Psi   1847
Phi Sigma Delta   1909
Phi Beta Delta*   1912
Tau Epsilon Phi   1910

PROFESSIONAL
Omega Epsilon Phi   1919
Phi Chi Theta   1924

Cooper Union

MEN'S SOCIAL
Alpha Mu Sigma   1914

Cornell University

MEN'S SOCIAL
Alpha Phi Alpha   1906
Alpha Sigma Chi*   1871
Beta Sigma Rho   1910
Delta Chi   1890
Rho Psi   1916

WOMEN'S SOCIAL
Sigma Delta Tau   1917

PROFESSIONAL
Lambda Phi Mu*   1920
Phi Delta Epsilon   1904
Sigma Delta Epsilon   1921

HONOR
Sigma Xi   1886

RECOGNITION
Gamma Alpha   1899
Pi Alpha Xi   1923

Dakota Wesleyan University

PROFESSIONAL
Sigma Tau Delta   1922

Dartmouth College

PROFESSIONAL
Alpha Kappa Kappa   1888
Kappa Phi Kappa   1922

Davidson College

HONOR
Sigma Pi Sigma   1921

RECOGNITION
Gamma Sigma Epsilon   1920

Denison University

MEN'S SOCIAL
American Association of Commons Clubs   1921

DePauw University

WOMEN'S SOCIAL
Alpha Chi Omega   1885
Kappa Alpha Theta   1870

PROFESSIONAL
Sigma Delta Chi   1909

Drake University

RECOGNITION
Psi Chi   1929

Fairmont State College

RECOGNITION
Alpha Psi Omega   1925
Lambda Delta Lambda   1925
Zeta Sigma*   1935

University of Florida

RECOGNITION
Blue Key   1924
Cardinal Key   1932

Georgetown University

PROFESSIONAL
Delta Phi Epsilon   1920
Phi Beta Gamma   1922

George Washington University

MEN'S SOCIAL
Phi Alpha*   1914

PROFESSIONAL
Sigma Nu Phi   1902

Georgia Institute of Technology

HONOR
Alpha Pi Mu   1949

Georgia State College

RECOGNITION
Pi Sigma Epsilon   1952

Hamilton College

MEN'S SOCIAL
Alpha Delta Phi   1832

Hamline University

MEN'S SOCIAL
Beta Kappa*   1901

Hollins College

PROFESSIONAL
Phi Mu Gamma   1898

Howard University

MEN'S SOCIAL
Phi Beta Sigma   1914
Omega Psi Phi   1911

WOMEN'S SOCIAL
Alpha Kappa Alpha   1908
Delta Sigma Theta   1913
Zeta Phi Beta   1920

Hunter College

WOMEN'S SOCIAL
Iota Alpha Pi   1903

Phi Sigma Sigma   1913

Illinois State Normal University

PROFESSIONAL
Gamma Theta Upsilon   1928

University of Illinois

MEN'S SOCIAL
Beta Sigma Psi   1920
Delta Rho Sigma*   1906
Triangle   1907

PROFESSIONAL
Alpha Tau Alpha   1923
Beta Alpha Psi   1919
Sigma Iota Epsilon   1926
Scarab   1909

HONOR
Alpha Lambda Delta   1924
Alpha Omega Alpha   1902
Chi Epsilon   1922
Eta Kappa Nu   1904
Kappa Delta Pi   1911
Order of the Coif   1902
Phi Eta Sigma   1923
Pi Tau Sigma   1916

RECOGNITION
Phi Lambda Upsilon   1899

Illinois Wesleyan University

MEN'S SOCIAL
Tau Kappa Epsilon   1899

Indiana University

MEN'S SOCIAL
Kappa Alpha Psi   1911

PROFESSIONAL
Phi Delta Kappa   1906

HONOR
Sigma Theta Tau   1922

RECOGNITION
Sigma Delta Psi   1912

State University of Iowa

PROFESSIONAL
Kappa Epsilon   1921
Kappa Eta Kappa   1923
National Block and Bridle   1919

Jefferson (Washington and Jefferson) College

MEN'S SOCIAL
Kappa Phi Lambda*   1862
Phi Gamma Delta   1848
Phi Kappa Psi   1852

Emporia State Teachers College

MEN'S SOCIAL
Phi Sigma Epsilon*   1910

WOMEN'S SOCIAL
Theta Sigma Epsilon*

University of Kansas

HONOR
Delta Phi Delta   1912
Sigma Gamma Epsilon   1915

University of Kentucky

RECOGNITION
Kappa Pi   1911

---

*An asterisk denotes defunct school or society.

Kirksville College of Osteopathy and Surgery

PROFESSIONAL
Axis Club*   1899
Atlas Club   1898
Iota Tau Sigma   1902
Phi Sigma Gamma   1915
Psi Sigma Alpha   1924
Sigma Sigma Phi   1921
Theta Psi   1903

Lafayette College

SERVICE
Alpha Phi Omega   1925

Lehigh University

MEN'S SOCIAL
Theta Kappa Phi*   1919

HONOR
Tau Beta Pi   1885

Lewis School, Oxford Institute (University of Mississippi)

WOMEN'S SOCIAL
Delta Gamma   1873

Lincoln University (Pa.)

HONOR
Beta Kappa Chi   1944

Lombard College (Merged with Knox College, 1930)

WOMEN'S SOCIAL
Alpha Xi Delta   1893

RECOGNITION
Theta Chi Delta*   1921

Longwood College

WOMEN'S SOCIAL
Alpha Sigma Alpha   1901
Kappa Delta   1897
Sigma Sigma Sigma   1898
Zeta Tau Alpha   1898

Loras College

HONOR
Delta Epsilon Sigma   1940

Loyola University (Chicago)

MEN'S SOCIAL
Alpha Delta Gamma   1924

University of Maine

PROFESSIONAL
Gamma Eta Gamma   1901

HONOR
Phi Kappa Phi   1900

Marquette University

PROFESSIONAL
Alpha Delta Theta   1944

University of Maryland

PROFESSIONAL
Alpha Omega   1907
Phi Delta Gamma   1923
Theta Kappa Psi   1898

Massachusetts College of Pharmacy

PROFESSIONAL
Lambda Kappa Sigma   1913

Rho Pi Phi   1919

University of Massachusetts

MEN'S SOCIAL
Phi Sigma Kappa   1873

Metropolitan College of Music

PROFESSIONAL
Mu Phi Epsilon   1903

Miami University

MEN'S SOCIAL
Beta Theta Pi   1839
Phi Delta Theta   1848
Phi Kappa Tau   1906
Sigma Chi   1855

WOMEN'S SOCIAL
Delta Sigma Epsilon*   1914
Delta Zeta   1902

Michigan State University

HONOR
Omicron Nu   1913

Michigan State Normal College (Eastern Michigan University)

WOMEN'S SOCIAL
Alpha Sigma Tau   1899
Pi Kappa Sigma*   1894

University of Michigan

MEN'S SOCIAL
Acacia   1904

WOMEN'S SOCIAL
Theta Phi Alpha   1912

PROFESSIONAL
Alpha Epsilon Iota*   1890
Delta Sigma Delta   1882
Nu Sigma Nu   1882
Phi Delta Chi   1887
Phi Delta Phi   1869
Sigma Alpha Iota   1903
Sigma Delta Kappa   1914
Xi Psi Phi   1889

HONOR
Rho Chi   1922
Tau Sigma Delta   1933

Middlebury College

MEN'S SOCIAL
Kappa Delta Rho   1905

University of Minnesota

PROFESSIONAL
Alpha Kappa Gamma   1922
Kappa Epsilon   1921
Phi Upsilon Omicron   1909
Theta Tau   1904

University of Mississippi

MEN'S SOCIAL
W.W.W. or Rainbow*   1849

University of Missouri

MEN'S SOCIAL
FarmHouse   1905

WOMEN'S SOCIAL
Beta Sigma Omicron*   1888

PROFESSIONAL
Alpha Delta Sigma   1914
Gamma Alpha Chi   1920
Kappa Alpha Mo   1947

Pi Lambda Theta   1917

HONOR
Kappa Tau Alpha

Monmouth College

WOMEN'S SOCIAL
Kappa Kappa Gamma   1870
Pi Beta Phi   1867

Montana State College

SERVICE
Spurs   1922

Muhlenberg College

HONOR
Phi Sigma Tau   1930

University of Nebraska

HONOR
Sigma Tau   1904

RECOGNITION
Pershing Rifles   1892

Newark College of Engineering

MEN'S SOCIAL
Alpha Kappa Pi*   1921

New England Conservatory of Music

PROFESSIONAL
Phi Mu Alpha-Sinfonia   1898

City College of New York

MEN'S SOCIAL
Delta Sigma Phi   1899
Phi Epsilon Pi   1904
Sigma Alpha Mu   1909
Tau Delta Phi   1910

RECOGNITION
Omicron Chi Epsilon*   1955

New York University

MEN'S SOCIAL
Alpha Epsilon Pi   1913
Zeta Psi   1847

WOMEN'S SOCIAL
Delta Phi Epsilon   1917
Sigma Phi Beta*   1920

PROFESSIONAL
Alpha Kappa Psi   1904
Delta Pi Epsilon   1936
Delta Sigma Pi   1907

HONOR
Delta Mu Delta   1913

University of North Carolina

MEN'S SOCIAL
Kappa Alpha*   1812

Northern Illinois College of Optometry

PROFESSIONAL
Omega Delta   1919

Northeast Missouri State

RECOGNITION
Pi Omega Pi   1923

Northeastern State (Okla.)

RECOGNITION
Kappa Mu Epsilon   1931

---

*An asterisk denotes defunct school or society.

Northwest Missouri State

PROFESSIONAL
Kappa Omicron Phi   1922

Northwestern State College (La.)

PROFESSIONAL
Alpha Beta Alpha   1950

Northwestern University

PROFESSIONAL
Epsilon Eta Phi   1927
Nu Beta Epsilon   1919
Omicron Kappa Upsilon   1914
Phi Beta   1912
Phi Gamma Nu   1924
Phi Rho Sigma   1890
Zeta Phi Eta   1893

HONOR
Pi Kappa Lambda   1918

RECOGNITION
Sigma Phi Alpha   1958

Norwich University

MEN'S SOCIAL
Theta Chi   1856

Ohio Northern University

RECOGNITION
Alpha Phi Gamma   1919

Ohio State University

MEN'S SOCIAL
Alpha Gamma Rho   1904

PROFESSIONAL
Alpha Psi   1907
Alpha Zeta   1897
Keramos   1902
Lambda Eta Chi*   1919

HONOR
Gamma Sigma Delta   1905
Phi Sigma   1915

Oklahoma City University

RECOGNITION
Beta Beta Beta   1922

Oklahoma State University

RECOGNITION
Kappa Kappa Psi   1919
Theta Alpha Phi   1919

Municipal University of Omaha

RECOGNITION
Angel Flight   1952

Our Lady of the Lake College

PROFESSIONAL
Kappa Pi Sigma   1945

Ottawa University

RECOGNITION
Pi Kappa Delta   1913

Pennsylvania State University

PROFESSIONAL
Iota Lambda Sigma   1925
Sigma Alpha Eta   1949

HONOR
Chimes*   1947

University of Pennsylvania

MEN'S SOCIAL
Phi Kappa Sigma   1850
Sigma Phi Sigma*   1908
Sigma Tau Phi   1918

PROFESSIONAL
Phi Lambda Kappa   1907
Omega Tau Sigma   1907

Philadelphia College of Osteopathy

PROFESSIONAL
Lambda Omicron Gamma   1929

Philadelphia College of Pharmacy

PROFESSIONAL
Alpha Zeta Omega   1919

Philadelphia Textile Institute

PROFESSIONAL
Delta Kappa Phi   1899
Phi Psi   1903

University of Pittsburgh

PROFESSIONAL
Phi Beta Pi   1891

RECOGNITION
Cwens   1922

Princeton University

MEN'S SOCIAL
Chi Phi   1824

Randolph-Macon College

RECOGNITION
Chi Beta Phi   1916

Rensselaer Polytechnic Institute

MEN'S SOCIAL
Theta Xi   1864

University of Richmond

MEN'S SOCIAL
Sigma Phi Epsilon   1901

University of Rochester

MEN'S SOCIAL
Kappa Nu*   1911

Russell Military Academy

PROFESSIONAL
Kappa Psi   1879

Rutgers University

MEN'S SOCIAL
Alpha Sigma Chi*   1871

St. Bernards College

MEN'S SOCIAL
Sigma Beta Kappa   1943

Shurtleff College

RECOGNITION
Sigma Zeta   1925

University of Southern California

PROFESSIONAL
Alpha Eta Rho   1929
Phi Delta Delta   1911
Sigma Phi Delta   1924

HONOR
Alpha Kappa Delta   1920

RECOGNITION
Rho Epsilon   1947

Southwestern College (Kan.)

HONOR
Pi Gamma Mu   1924

Southwestern University (Calif.)

PROFESSIONAL
Iota Tau Tau   1925

Southwestern University (Texas)

HONOR
Alpha Chi   1922

State University College of Education, Buffalo, N.Y.

MEN'S SOCIAL
Delta Kappa*   1920

Syracuse University

MEN'S SOCIAL
Alpha Phi Delta   1914

WOMEN'S SOCIAL
Alpha Gamma Delta   1904
Alpha Phi   1872
Gamma Phi Beta   1874

HONOR
Pi Mu Epsilon   1914

RECOGNITION
Pi Delta Epsilon   1909

Tennessee A. and I. State College

HONOR
Alpha Kappa Mu   1937

University of Tennessee

RECOGNITION
Chi Delta Phi   1919

Texas Tech University

RECOGNITION
Tau Beta Sigma   1939

University of Texas

HONOR
Pi Sigma Alpha   1920

Trinity College

MEN'S SOCIAL
Alpha Chi Rho   1895

University of Toronto

MEN'S SOCIAL
Phi Kappa Pi   1913

Tri-State College

RECOGNITION
Sigma Mu Sigma   1952

Union College

MEN'S SOCIAL
Chi Psi   1841
Delta Phi   1827
Kappa Alpha Society   1825
Psi Upsilon   1833
Sigma Phi   1827
Theta Delta Chi   1847

*An asterisk denotes defunct school or society.

University of Utah

MEN'S SOCIAL
Delta Phi Kappa   1869

University of Vermont

PROFESSIONAL
Phi Chi   1889

Vincennes University

MEN'S SOCIAL
Sigma Pi   1897

Virginia Military Institute

MEN'S SOCIAL
Alpha Tau Omega   1865
Kappa Sigma Kappa   1867
Sigma Nu   1868

University of Virginia

MEN'S SOCIAL
Kappa Sigma   1869
Pi Kappa Alpha   1868

PROFESSIONAL
Kappa Psi   1879
Pi Mu*   1892

Washington and Lee University

MEN'S SOCIAL
Kappa Alpha Order   1865
Square and Compass*   1897

HONOR
Omicron Delta Kappa   1914

Washington University

PROFESSIONAL
Alpha Alpha Gamma   1922

University of Washington

PROFESSIONAL
Theta Sigma Phi   1909

HONOR
Xi Sigma Pi   1908

SERVICE
Intercollegiate Knights   1919

Wesleyan College

WOMEN'S SOCIAL
Alpha Delta Pi   1851
Phi Mu   1852

Wesleyan University

MEN'S SOCIAL
Mystic Seven*   1837
Phi Mu Delta   1918
Theta Nu Epsilon*   1870

Westminster College (Pa.)

MEN'S SOCIAL
Pi Rho Phi*   1854

Western Reserve University

PROFESSIONAL
Tau Epsilon Rho   1921

College of William and Mary

HONOR
Phi Beta Kappa   1776

Williams College

MEN'S SOCIAL
Delta Upsilon   1834

University of Wisconsin

PROFESSIONAL
Alpha Chi Sigma   1902

HONOR
Beta Gamma Sigma   1913
Sigma Epsilon Sigma   1927

RECOGNITION
National Collegiate Players   1922
Order of Artus*   1915
Scabbard and Blade   1904

Wofford College

RECOGNITION
Delta Phi Alpha   1929

Yale University

MEN'S SOCIAL
Alpha Sigma Phi   1845
Delta Kappa Epsilon   1844
Pi Lambda Phi   1895

Campuses on Which the Fraternity System Has Died

**Abingdon College,
Abingdon, IL**

MEN'S SOCIAL
1876   Delta Tau Delta

**Austin College,
Austin, TX**

MEN'S SOCIAL
1853   Phi Delta Theta
1865   Phi Kappa Sigma
1895   Alpha Tau Omega

**Bailey Law School,
Asheville, NC***

MEN'S SOCIAL
1871   Sigma Nu

**Ballston Law School,
Ballston Spa, NY***

MEN'S SOCIAL
1849   Theta Delta Chi

**Belmont College,
Nashville, TN**

WOMEN'S SOCIAL
1903   Chi Omega
1911   Phi Mu
1914   Beta Sigma Omicron*

**Bethel Academy,
Warrenton, VA**

MEN'S SOCIAL
1875   Alpha Tau Omega

1879   Kappa Alpha Order
1882   Kappa Sigma

**Bethel College,
Hopkinsville, KY**

MEN'S SOCIAL
1872   Alpha Tau Omega
1902   Kappa Sigma
1904   Sigma Nu
1912   Phi Gamma Delta
1920   Sigma Alpha Epsilon

**Bolivar College,
Bolivar, TN**

WOMEN'S SOCIAL
1881   Delta Gamma

**Buffalo Gap College,
Buffalo, TX***

MEN'S SOCIAL
1888   Sigma Alpha Epsilon

**Burlington College,
Burlington, NJ**

MEN'S SOCIAL
1854   Delta Psi

**Caldwell College,
Danville, KY
(Now Centre College)**

WOMEN'S SOCIAL
1908   Kappa Delta

**Callanan College,
Des Moines, IA**

WOMEN'S SOCIAL
1889   Pi Beta Phi

**Carleton College
Northfield, MN**
1883   Phi Kappa Psi

**Carolina Military Institute,
Charlotte, NC***

MEN'S SOCIAL
1877   Sigma Alpha Epsilon

**Centenary College,
Cleveland, TN***

WOMEN'S SOCIAL
1921   Beta Sigma Omicron*

**Central College for Women,
Lexington, MO***

WOMEN'S SOCIAL
1925   Beta Sigma Omicron*

**Chatham Episcopal Institute,
Chatham, VA***

WOMEN'S SOCIAL
1904   Kappa Delta

**Chevy Chase College,
Chevy Chase, MD**

WOMEN'S SOCIAL
1910   Phi Mu

---

*An asterisk denotes defunct school or society.

A-6 BAIRD'S MANUAL

**Christian College,
Columbia, MO**

WOMEN'S SOCIAL
1915 Beta Sigma Omicron'

**College for Women,
Columbia, SC***

WOMEN'S SOCIAL
1910 Kappa Delta

**Colorado Woman's College,
Denver, CO**

WOMEN'S SOCIAL
1920 Beta Sigma Omicron*

**Crescent College, Eureka
Springs, AK***

WOMEN'S SOCIAL
1912 Beta Sigma Omicron*

**Cumberland College,
Virginia***

MEN'S SOCIAL
1884 Kappa Sigma

**Cumberland University,
Lebanon, TN**

MEN'S SOCIAL
1860, 1878, 1899 Beta Theta Pi
1861 Alpha Delta Phi
1861 Chi Phi
1861 Delta Psi
1861 Phi Kappa Sigma
1874 Delta Kappa Epsilon
1878 Phi Gamma Delta
1879 Phi Kappa Psi
1880 Sigma Chi
1902 Alpha Tau Omega
1908 Pi Kappa Alpha
1917 Kappa Sigma
1917 Lambda Chi Alpha
1918 Delta Sigma Phi
1947 Sigma Alpha Epsilon

**University of Edinburgh,
Scotland**

MEN'S SOCIAL
1870 Chi Phi

**Ellsworth College,
Iowa Falls, IA***

MEN'S SOCIAL
1929 Alpha Kappa Pi

**Fairmont College,
Monteagle, TN***

WOMEN'S SOCIAL
1880 Delta Gamma

**Fairmont Seminary,
Washington, DC***

WOMEN'S SOCIAL
1912 Kappa Delta
1913 Beta Sigma Omicron*

**Forest Academy,
Anchorage, KY***

MEN'S SOCIAL
1878 Sigma Alpha Epsilon

**Georgia Military Institute,
Marietta, GA**

MEN'S SOCIAL
1865 Sigma Alpha Epsilon

**Gordon Military College,
Barnesville, GA**

MEN'S SOCIAL
1883 Kappa Alpha Order

**Grenada College,
Grenada, MS***

WOMEN'S SOCIAL
1920 Beta Sigma Omicron*

**Gunston Hall,
Washington, DC**

WOMEN'S SOCIAL
1912 Kappa Delta

**Hannah Moore Academy,
Reisterstown, MD**

WOMEN'S SOCIAL
1903 Zeta Tau Alpha

**Hardin College,
Mexico, MO***

WOMEN'S SOCIAL
1925 Beta Sigma Omicron*
1911 Phi Mu

**Hellmuth Women's College,
London, ONT***

WOMEN'S SOCIAL
1900 Chi Omega

**Jamestown Collegiate Institute,
Jamestown, NY**

MEN'S SOCIAL
1871 Delta Tau Delta

**Jessamine Female Institute,
Nicholasville, KY***

WOMEN'S SOCIAL
1902 Chi Omega

**Kentucky Military Institute,
Lyndon, KY**

MEN'S SOCIAL
1856 Phi Delta Theta
1861 Delta Kappa Epsilon
1887 Sigma Alpha Epsilon
1887 Alpha Tau Omega
1883 Chi PhI

**LaGrange College,
Tennessee***

MEN'S SOCIAL
1861 Delta Tau Delta
(Rainbow)
1860 Phi Kappa Psi
1861 Sigma Chi

**Lake Shore Seminary,
North East, PA**

MEN'S SOCIAL
1875 Delta Tau Delta

**Lasell Seminary,
Auburndale, MA
(Now Lasell Junior College)**

WOMEN'S SOCIAL
1882 Kappa Kappa Gamma

**Liberty Ladies' College,
Liberty, MO***

WOMEN'S SOCIAL
1913 Beta Sigma Omicron*

**Lombard College,
Galesburg, IL**

**(Did not die but merged with
Knox)**

MEN'S SOCIAL
1885 Delta Tau Delta
1930 Phi Delta Theta
1930 Sigma Nu
1930 Pi Kappa Alpha

WOMEN'S SOCIAL
1930 Pi Beta Phi
1930 Alpha Xi Delta
1930 Delta Zeta
1930 Theta Upsilon*

**Marvin College,
Waxahachie, TX***

MEN'S SOCIAL
1884 Sigma Alpha Epsilon

**Maryland Military and Naval
Academy,
Oxford, MS***

SOCIAL
1887 Kappa Sigma

**Middle Georgia Military and
Agricultural College,
Milledgeville, GA**

MEN'S SOCIAL
1894 Alpha Tau Omega

**Nashville University,
Nashville, TN**

MEN'S SOCIAL
1861 Delta Kappa Epsilon
1850 Phi Gamma Delta
1857 Sigma Chi
1876 Sigma Alpha Epsilon
1861 Chi Phi
1875 Phi Kappa Psi
1872 Alpha Tau Omega

**New York College of Dentistry,
New York***

MEN'S SOCIAL
1927 Tau Epsilon Phi
1926 Phi Beta Delta

**Norwich University
Northfield, VT**

MEN'S SOCIAL
1856 Theta Chi
1908 Sigma Phi Epsilon
1927 Sigma Alpha Epsilon
1949 Sigma Nu
1950 Tau Delta Phi
1950 Lambda Chi Alpha

**Oxford Institute (Lewis School),
Oxford, MS**

WOMEN'S SOCIAL
1889 Delta Gamma

**Oakland College,
Mississippi**

MEN'S SOCIAL
1861 Delta Kappa Epsilon

**Parsons College,
Fairfield, IA**

MEN'S SOCIAL
1969 Phi Sigma Delta

*An asterisk denotes defunct school or society.

1972   Phi Sigma Epsilon
1972   Alpha Epsilon Pi
1972   Delta Chi
1973   Delta Sigma Phi
1973   Alpha Chi Rho
1973   Sigma Phi Epsilon
1973   Tau Kappa Epsilon
1973   Lambda Chi Alpha
1973   Pi Kappa Alpha
1973   Sigma Pi
1973   Theta Chi
1972   Zeta Beta Tau

WOMEN'S SOCIAL
1966   Alpha Omicron Pi
1969   Sigma Delta Tau
1971   Delta Zeta
1973   Alpha Gamma Delta
1972   Alpha Xi Delta

**Pennsylvania Polytechnic College,
Philadelphia, PA**

MEN'S SOCIAL
1876   Sigma Chi

**Philadelphia College of Dental
Surgery,
Philadelphia, PA**

MEN'S SOCIAL
1879   Kappa Alpha Order

**Potter College, Bowling
Green, KY***

WOMEN'S SOCIAL
1909   Beta Sigma Omicron

**Poughkeepsie Collegiate Institute,
Poughkeepsie, NY***

MEN'S SOCIAL
1867   Delta Tau Delta

**Queens University,
Kingston, ONT**

MEN'S SOCIAL
1914   Phi Sigma Kappa

**Quincy College,
Quincy, IL**

MEN'S SOCIAL
1947   Alpha Delta Gamma

WOMEN'S SOCIAL
1954   Theta Phi Alpha

**Racine College,
Racine, WI***

MEN'S SOCIAL
1875   Phi Kappa Sigma
1877   Phi Kappa Psi
1887   Phi Gamma Delta

**Randolph-Macon Woman's College,
Lynchburg, VA**

WOMEN'S SOCIAL
1900   Chi Omega
1902   Zeta Tau Alpha
1903   Alpha Omicron Pi
1903   Kappa Delta
1903   Delta Delta Delta
1910   Alpha Delia Pi
1910   Phi Mu
1910   Kappa Alpha Theta
1913   Pi Beta Phi
1917   Sigma Kappa
1923   Delta Zeta
1928   Alpha Xi Delta
1931   Beta Phi Alpha*

1930   Gamma Phi Beta

**St. John's College,
Annapolis, MD**

MEN'S SOCIAL
1874   Chi Phi
1942   Phi Sigma Kappa
1942   Kappa Alpha Order
1942   Alpha Kappa Pi

**St. Bernard College,
St. Bernard, Cullman, AL**

MEN'S SOCIAL
1954   Sigma Beta Kappa

**St. John's College,
Little Rock, AK**

MEN'S SOCIAL
1874   Chi Phi

**St. Mary's School,
Raleigh, NC**

WOMEN'S SOCIAL
1874   Kappa Kappa Gamma
1911   Kappa Delta
1910   Phi Mu

**Sedalia Seminary,
Sedalia, MO**

WOMEN'S SOCIAL
1907   Beta Sigma Omicron

**Shorter College,
Rome, GA**

WOMEN'S SOCIAL
1912   Phi Mu

**Smithson College,
Logansport, IN***

WOMEN'S SOCIAL
1875   Kappa Kappa Gamma

**South Iowa Normal School,
Bloomfield, IA**

WOMEN'S SOCIAL
1887   Pi Beta Phi

**South Kentucky College,
Hopkinsville, KY***

MEN'S SOCIAL
1887   Sigma Alpha Epsilon

**Southwest Kansas College
(Southwestern),
Winfield, KS**

MEN'S SOCIAL
1897   Sigma Nu

**Stephens College,
Columbia, MO**

WOMEN'S SOCIAL
1925   Beta Sigma Omicron

**Synodical College,
Fulton, MO***

WOMEN'S SOCIAL
1885   Delta Gamma
1928   Beta Sigma Omicron

**Thatcher Institute,
Shreveport, LA**

MEN'S SOCIAL
1888   Sigma Alpha Epsilon
1891   Kappa Sigma

**Troy University,
Troy, NY***

MEN'S SOCIAL
1862   Delta Kappa Epsilon

**United States Naval Academy,
Annapolis, MD**

MEN'S SOCIAL
1863   Beta Theta Pi
1874   Zeta Psi

**U.S. Grant University (Chattanooga
University),
Chattanooga, TN**

MEN'S SOCIAL
1898   Kappa Sigma

**Virginia Military Institute,
Lexington, VA**

MEN'S SOCIAL
1881   Alpha Tau Omega
1913   Kappa Alpha Order
1880   Beta Theta Pi
1911   Sigma Nu
1883   Kappa Sigma
1911   Sigma Alpha Epsilon
1889   Phi Delta Theta
1885   Sigma Chi
1911   Sigma Phi Epsilon

**Washington College,
Tennessee**

MEN'S SOCIAL
1852   Phi Gamma Delta

**Water Valley Seminary,
Water Valley, MS**

WOMEN'S SOCIAL
1880   Delta Gamma

**Wesleyan College
Macon, GA**

WOMEN'S SOCIAL
1851   Alpha Delta Pi
1852   Phi Mu
1854   Kappa Alpha Theta
1906   Alpha Gamma Delta
1911   Zeta Tau Alpha
1913   Delta Delta Delta

**West Liberty College,
West Virginia***

MEN'S SOCIAL
1862   Delta Tau Delta

**College of Wooster,
Wooster, OH**

MEN'S SOCIAL
1892   Phi Kappa Psi
1913   Beta Theta Pi
1897   Phi Delta Theta
1913   Sigma Chi
1913   Delta Tau Delta
1913   Phi Gamma Delta
1913   Alpha Tau Omega
1913   Sigma Phi Epsilon

WOMEN'S SOCIAL
1913   Kappa Alpha Theta
1913   Kappa Kappa Gamma
1913   Pi Beta Phi
1913   Delta Delta Delta

**York College,
York, NE**

WOMEN'S SOCIAL
1888   Pi Beta Phi

*An asterisk denotes defunct school or society.

Famous Greeks—Sports

BASEBALL HALL OF FAME

LOU BOUDREAU—*Phi Sigma Kappa*
"HAPPY" CHANDLER—*Pi Kappa Alpha*
MICKEY COCHRANE—*Lambda Chi Alpha*
EDDIE COLLINS—*Beta Theta Pi*
BILLY EVANS—*Alpha Tau Omega*
FORD FRICK—*Phi Kappa Psi*
LOU GEHRIG—*Phi Delta Theta*
WAITE HOYT—*Chi Psi*
FERGUSON JENKINS—*Lambda Chi Alpha*
HUGHIE JENNINGS—*Phi Delta Theta*
SANDY KOUFAX—*Pi Lambda Phi*

CHRISTY MATHEWSON—*Phi Gamma Delta*
LARRY McPHAIL—*Beta Theta Pi*
STAN MUSIAL—*Sigma Tau Gamma*
JIM PALMER—*Sigma Chi*
BRANCH RICKEY—*Delta Tau Delta*
EPPA RIXEY—*Delta Tau Delta*
JOE SEWELL—*Pi Kappa Phi*
GEORGE SISLER—*Delta Tau Delta*
BILL VEECK—*Beta Theta Pi*
BILLY WILLIAMS—*Lambda Chi Alpha*
TOM YAWKEY—*Phi Gamma Delta*

MAJOR LEAGUE BASEBALL PLAYERS

The following is a partial list of additional Greeks who have played major league baseball. Many later became coaches, managers and executives.

ETHAN ALLEN—*Beta Theta Pi*
BOB ASPROMONTE—*Phi Kappa Theta*
ELDON AUKER—*Phi Sigma Kappa*
EARL AVERILL, JR.—*Sigma Nu*
JEFF BALLARD—*Theta Delta Chi*
SAL BANDO—*Phi Gamma Delta*
FRANK BAUMHOLTZ—*Beta Theta Pi*
GLENN BECKERT—*Phi Kappa Psi*
JOHN BERARDINO—*Phi Kappa Tau*
CHARLIE BERRY—*Phi Delta Theta*
CURT BLEFARY—*Alpha Sigma Phi*
BOB BOONE—*Zeta Psi*
STEVE BOROS—*Phi Kappa Sigma*
JIM BOUTON—*Delta Sigma Phi*
TOMMY BRIDGES—*Sigma Alpha Epsilon*
BILL BUCKNER—*Sigma Chi*
STEVE BUECHELE—*Delta Tau Delta*
DON BUFORD—*Kappa Alpha Psi*
LEW BURDETTE—*Pi Kappa Alpha*
TOMMY BYRNE—*Pi Kappa Alpha*
KEN CAMINITI—*Sigma Alpha Epsilon*
RON CEY—*Phi Delta Theta*
DAVID CHALK—*Sigma Phi Epsilon*
CLIFF CHAMBERS—*Lambda Chi Alpha*
SPUD CHANDLER—*Alpha Gamma Rho*
SAM CHAPMAN—*Sigma Phi Epsilon*
GALEN CISCO—*Delta Upsilon*
DONN CLENDENON—*Kappa Alpha Psi*
GENE CONLEY—*Acacia*
DOUG CORBETT—*Alpha Tau Omega*
AL DARK—*Phi Delta Theta*
ART DITMAR—*Theta Chi*
CHUCK DOBSON—*Kappa Sigma*
TAYLOR DOUTHIT—*Pi Kappa Alpha*
MOE DRABOWSKY—*Alpha Chi Rho*
WALTER DROPO—*Sigma Nu*
FRANK DUFFY—*Phi Delta Theta*
DUFFY DYER—*Sigma Chi*
GEORGE EARNSHAW—*Phi Kappa Psi*
JOHN EDWARDS—*Phi Kappa Tau*

MIKE EPSTEIN—*Zeta Beta Tau*
SAMMY ESPOSITO—*Theta Chi*
CHUCK ESSEGIAN—*Delta Tau Delta*
WALTER "HOOT" EVERS—*Delta Chi*
RON FAIRLY—*Acacia*
"DOC" FARRELL—*Delta Upsilon*
DAVE "BOO" FERRISS—*Kappa Sigma*
RAY FISHER—*Chi Psi*
HORACE "HOD" FORD—*Zeta Psi*
KEN FORSCH—*Beta Theta Pi*
BILL FREEHAN—*Sigma Alpha Epsilon*
BOB FRIEND—*Sigma Chi*
JAKE GIBBS—*Pi Kappa Alpha*
JOE GIRARDI—*Alpha Tau Omega*
JOE GORDON—*Sigma Chi*
SID GORDON—*Alpha Epsilon Pi*
TOM GORMAN—*Tau Kappa Epsilon*
DALLAS GREEN—*Sigma Nu*
BOBBY GRICH—*Sigma Nu*
DICK GROAT—*Sigma Chi*
IRVING "BUMP" HADLEY—*Phi Kappa Psi*
TOM HALLER—*Theta Chi*
STEVE HAMILTON—*Sigma Alpha Epsilon*
CHUCK HARTENSTEIN—*Kappa Sigma*
GRADY HATTON—*Delta Tau Delta*
JACKIE HAYES—*Delta Tau Delta*
HARVEY "GINK" HENDRICK—*Alpha Tau Omega*
RON HERBEL—*Tau Kappa Epsilon*
TOMMY HERR—*Alpha Tau Omega*
OREL HERSHISER—*Sigma Phi Epsilon*
"PINKY" HIGGINS—*Delta Tau Delta*
ORAL HILDEBRAND—*Lambda Chi Alpha*
BILLY HITCHCOCK—*Sigma Nu*
BURT HOOTON—*Kappa Alpha Order*
DICK HOWSER—*Sigma Nu*
FRED HUTCHINSON—*Alpha Sigma Phi*
LARRY JACKSON—*Kappa Sigma*
RANDY JACKSON—*Sigma Alpha Epsilon*
JACKIE JENSEN—*Alpha Delta Phi*
TOMMY JOHN—*Alpha Tau Omega*

BOB KEEGAN—*Sigma Chi*
DON KESSINGER—*Sigma Nu*
JACK KNOTT—*Delta Sigma Phi*
HARVEY KUENN—*Delta Upsilon*
DUANE KUIPER—*Tau Kappa Epsilon*
BARRY LATMAN—*Zeta Beta Tau*
TIM LEARY—*Beta Theta Pi*
DON LEE—*Delta Chi*
CRAIG LEFFERTS—*Phi Kappa Psi*
HANK LEIBER—*Sigma Nu*
DANNY LITWILER—*Lambda Chi Alpha*
BOBBY LOCKER—*Phi Delta Theta*
JIM LONBORG—*Phi Delta Theta*
RAY MACK—*Phi Delta Theta*
TIM McCARVER—*Kappa Alpha Order*
"DOC" MEDICH—*Sigma Chi*
GENE MICHAEL—*Alpha Tau Omega*
KEITH MORELAND—*Sigma Phi Epsilon*
THURMAN MUNSON—*Delta Upsilon*
TOM MURPHY—*Beta Theta Pi*
CRAIG NETTLES—*Sigma Alpha Epsilon*
WILLARD NIXON—*Tau Kappa Epsilon*
JIM NORTHRUP—*Tau Kappa Epsilon*
ORVAL OVERALL—*Sigma Nu*
CLAUDE PASSEAU—*Kappa Sigma*
FRITZ PETERSON—*Tau Kappa Epsilon*
"BUBBA" PHILLIPS—*Kappa Alpha Order*
DEL PRATT—*Alpha Tau Omega*
HUB PRUETT—*Sigma Nu*
FRANK QUILICI—*Theta Xi*
DICK RADATZ—*Alpha Tau Omega*
BOBBY RANDALL—*Alpha Tau Omega*
STEVE RENKO—*Phi Delta Theta*
MERV RETTENMUND—*Sigma Phi Epsilon*
CARL REYNOLDS—*Phi Delta Theta*
LANCE RICHBOURG—*Alpha Tau Omega*
LEW RIGGS—*Alpha Tau Omega*
STEVE ROGERS—*Kappa Sigma*
"RED" ROLFE—*Phi Sigma Kappa*
RICH ROLLINS—*Alpha Tau Omega*
AL ROSEN—*Pi Lambda Phi*
"MUDDY" RUEHL—*Phi Delta Theta*

JOE SAMBITO—*Tau Kappa Epsilon*
RON SANTO—*Lambda Chi Alpha*
TOM SATRIANO—*Delta Chi*
RICHIE SCHEINBLUM—*Tau Kappa Epsilon*
MIKE SCHMIDT—*Beta Theta Pi*
HAL SCHUMACHER—*Alpha Tau Omega*
LUKE SEWELL—*Pi Kappa Phi*
BOB SHAW—*Alpha Tau Omega*
BILL "MOOSE" SKOWRON—*Tau Kappa Epsilon*
ROY SMALLEY, SR.—*Sigma Nu*
DON SLAUGHT—*Sigma Chi*
LARY SORENSEN—*Sigma Alpha Epsilon*
AL SPANGLER—*Kappa Sigma*
PAUL SPLITTORFF—*Delta Sigma Phi*
RIGGS STEPHENSON—*Sigma Chi*
WES STOCK—*Phi Kappa Tau*
STEVE STONE—*Alpha Epsilon Pi*
BILL STONEMAN—*Beta Theta Pi*
FRANK SULLIVAN—*Kappa Sigma*
HAYWOOD SULLIVAN—*Kappa Alpha Order*
JIM SUNDBERG—*Delta Upsilon*
EVAR SWANSON—*Sigma Nu*
GREG SWINDELL—*Sigma Nu*
ROY THOMAS—*Alpha Tau Omega*
DANNY THOMPSON—*Beta Theta Pi*
FRESCO THOMPSON—*Alpha Delta Phi*
JEFF TORBORG—*Chi Psi*
CECIL UPSHAW—*Kappa Sigma*
BOBBY VALENTINE—*Sigma Chi*
BILL VIRDON—*Kappa Alpha Order*
DICK WAKEFIELD—*Phi Gamma Delta*
GERALD "GEE" WALKER—*Sigma Chi*
CURT WALKER—*Kappa Alpha Order*
PRESTON WARD—*Tau Kappa Epsilon*
BILLY WERBER—*Sigma Chi*
SAMMY WHITE—*Sigma Alpha Epsilon*
BURGESS WHITEHEAD—*Zeta Psi*
"BUMP" WILLS—*Sigma Chi*
ROBERT "RED" WILSON—*Alpha Tau Omega*
GLENN WRIGHT—*Delta Tau Delta*
GEOFF ZAHN—*Beta Theta Pi*

PROMINENT BASEBALL EXECUTIVES

ARTHUR ALLYN—*Sigma Chi*
BILL BARTHOLOMAY—*Delta Kappa Epsilon*
"BUZZY" BAVASI—*Phi Kappa Psi*
JIMMY BRAGAN—*Kappa Alpha Order*
DR. BOBBY BROWN—*Delta Kappa Epsilon*
JOE L. BROWN—*Zeta Psi*
GEORGE W. BUSH—*Delta Kappa Epsilon*
EDDIE CHILES—*Sigma Alpha Epsilon*
BRAD CORBETT—*Alpha Sigma Phi*
POWELL CROSLEY, JR.—*Phi Delta Theta*
HARRY DALTON—*Theta Delta Chi*
ROY EISENHARDT—*Beta Theta Pi*
"CHUB" FEENEY—*Phi Kappa Psi*
DAN GALBREATH—*Psi Upsilon*
JOHN GALBREATH—*Delta Tau Delta*
BART GIAMATTI—*Delta Kappa Epsilon*
BILL GILES—*Sigma Chi*

PAT GILLICK—*Delta Chi*
GORDON GOLDSBERRY—*Zeta Psi*
DALLAS GREEN—*Sigma Nu*
CALVIN GRIFFITH—*Acacia*
FRED HANEY—*Phi Kappa Psi*
LARRY HIMES—*Delta Chi*
JEROLD HOFFBERGER—*Zeta Beta Tau*
BOB HOWSAM—*Alpha Sigma Phi*
ELI JACOBS—*Zeta Psi*
HAL KELLER—*Kappa Alpha Order*
FRED KNORR—*Alpha Tau Omega*
CONNIE MACK, JR.—*Phi Delta Theta*
LEE McPHAIL—*Delta Upsilon*
PETER O'MALLEY—*Phi Gamma Delta*
WALTER O'MALLEY—*Theta Delta Chi*
BUD SELIG—*Pi Lambda Phi*
GEORGE STEINBRENNER—*Delta Kappa Epsilon*

BILL STONEMAN—*Beta Theta Pi*
HAYWOOD SULLIVAN—*Kappa Alpha Order*
FRESCO THOMPSON—*Alpha Delta Phi*
GEORGE TRAUTMAN—*Phi Delta Theta*

PETER UEBBEROTH—*Delta Upsilon*
FAY VINCENT—*Alpha Delta Phi*
WILLIAM WRIGLEY—*Delta Kappa Epsilon*

PROMINENT COLLEGE BASEBALL COACHES

GARY ADAMS—*Phi Kappa Sigma*
"BOBO" BRAYTON—*Sigma Phi Epsilon*
LARRY COCHELL—*Sigma Chi*
FRED DECKER—*Sigma Alpha Epsilon*
ROD DEDEAUX—*Delta Chi*
LEE EILBRACHT—*Theta Xi*
"DUTCH" FEHRING—*Delta Tau Delta*
RAY FISHER—*Chi Psi*

MARK MARQUESS—*Delta Tau Delta*
GENE McARTOR—*Sigma Chi*
BOB MORGAN—*Beta Theta Pi*
DALE RAMSBURG—*Phi Sigma Kappa*
JOHN SANDERS—*Sigma Alpha Epsilon*
JOHN SKEETERS—*Delta Tau Delta*
JOHN WINKIN—*Sigma Chi*

BASKETBALL HALL OF FAME

FORREST "PHOG" ALLEN—*Phi Kappa Psi*
"RED" AUERBACH—*Tau Epsilon Phi*
JUSTIN "SAM" BARRY—*Delta Upsilon*
RICK BARRY—*Kappa Sigma*
CLAIR BEE—*Delta Sigma Phi*
DAVE BING—*Sigma Alpha Mu*
JOHN BUNN—*Beta Theta Pi*
HOWARD CANN—*Phi Gamma Delta*
H. CLIFFORD CARLSON—*Phi Gamma Delta*
WILT CHAMBERLAIN—*Kappa Alpha Psi*
EVERETT DEAN—*Alpha Tau Omega*
FORREST DeBERNARDI—*Phi Delta Theta*
ED DIDDLE—*Beta Theta Pi*
BRUCE DRAKE—*Alpha Tau Omega*
HARRY FISHER—*Theta Delta Chi*
HAROLD "BUD" FOSTER—*Kappa Sigma*
LADDIE GALE—*Phi Delta Theta*
JACK GARDNER—*Kappa Sigma*
AMORY "SLATS" GILL—*Phi Delta Theta*
CLIFF HAGAN—*Sigma Nu*
VIC HANSON—*Zeta Psi*
"TONY" HINKLE—*Alpha Tau Omega*
HOWARD HOBSON—*Phi Delta Theta*
BOB HOUBREGS—*Alpha Sigma Phi*
CHUCK HYATT—*Phi Gamma Delta*
HANK IBA—*Lambda Chi Alpha*
NED IRISH—*Delta Upsilon*
BILL JOHNSON—*Phi Delta Theta*
SAM JONES—*Kappa Alpha Psi*
ALVIN "DOGGIE" JULIAN—*Phi Kappa Psi*
BOB KURLAND—*Sigma Alpha Epsilon*
WARD "PIGGY" LAMBERT—*Delta Tau Delta*
EMIL LISTON—*Sigma Phi Epsilon*
KEN LOEFFLER—*Sigma Phi Epsilon*
ARTHUR "DUTCH" LONBORG—*Sigma Chi*

CLYDE LOVELETTE—*Sigma Chi*
JERRY LUCAS—*Beta Theta Pi*
HANK LUISETTI—*Delta Kappa Epsilon*
ED MACAULEY—*Phi Kappa Theta*
PETE MARAVICH—*Sigma Alpha Epsilon*
BRANCH McCRACKEN—*Kappa Sigma*
FRANK McGUIRE—*Phi Kappa Sigma*
WALTER MEANWELL—*Sigma Alpha Epsilon*
RAY MEYER—*Phi Kappa Theta*
RALPH MILLER—*Phi Kappa Psi*
BILL MOKRAY—*Theta Chi*
RALPH MORGAN—*Sigma Alpha Epsilon*
CHARLES "STRETCH" MURPHY—*Delta Tau Delta*
JAMES NAISMITH—*Sigma Phi Epsilon*
PETE NEWELL—*Phi Kappa Tau*
HARLAN "PAT" PAGE—*Delta Tau Delta*
BOB PETTIT—*Delta Kappa Epsilon*
ANDY PHILLIP—*Delta Tau Delta*
JIM POLLARD—*Delta Kappa Epsilon*
ERNEST QUIGLEY—*Sigma Chi*
FRANK RAMSEY—*Sigma Alpha Epsilon*
WILLIS REED—*Phi Beta Sigma*
WILLIAM REID—*Phi Gamma Delta*
OSCAR ROBERTSON—*Kappa Alpha Psi*
BILL RUSSELL—*Kappa Alpha Psi*
JOHN SCHOMMER—*Phi Kappa Sigma*
DEAN SMITH—*Phi Gamma Delta*
AMOS ALONZO STAGG—*Psi Upsilon*
LYNN ST. JOHN—*Alpha Tau Omega*
JOHN "CAT" THOMPSON—*Sigma Chi*
OSWALD TOWER—*Phi Gamma Delta*
ROBERT VAN DIVIER—*Phi Delta Theta*
JOHN WOODEN—*Beta Theta Pi*

PROMINENT PRO BASKETBALL PLAYERS, COACHES & EXECUTIVES

TOM ABERNETHY—*Sigma Nu*
BARRY ACKERLEY—*Sigma Chi*
STAN ALBECK—*Sigma Chi*
JOE AXELSON—*Phi Kappa Psi*
AL BIANCHI—*Sigma Alpha Epsilon*
ROLANDO BLACKMAN—*Kappa Alpha Psi*

BOB BOOZER—*Kappa Alpha Psi*
LARRY BROWN—*Lambda Chi Alpha*
LEN CHAPPELL—*Sigma Chi*
BARRY CLEMENS—*Phi Delta Theta*
JERRY COLANGELO—*Phi Kappa Psi*
MEL COUNTS—*Beta Theta Pi*

LOUIE DAMPIER—*Pi Kappa Alpha*
MEL DANIELS—*Omega Psi Phi*
TERRY DISCHINGER—*Sigma Alpha Epsilon*
ALEX ENGLISH—*Kappa Alpha Psi*
KEITH ERICKSON—*Beta Theta Pi*
DICK FARLEY—*Acacia*
RICHARD EVANS—*Beta Theta Pi*
DAVE GAMBEE—*Sigma Nu*
DICK GARMAKER—*Sigma Alpha Epsilon*
JOHN GIANELLI—*Sigma Alpha Epsilon*
ARTIS GILMORE—*Pi Lambda Phi*
HARRY GLICKMAN—*Sigma Alpha Mu*
MIKE GMINSKI—*Sigma Alpha Epsilon*
GAIL GOODRICH—*Beta Theta Pi*
STEVE GREEN—*Phi Gamma Delta*
KEVIN GREVEY—*Sigma Alpha Epsilon*
SCOTT HASTINGS—*Lambda Chi Alpha*
STEVE HAWES—*Psi Upsilon*
ART HEYMAN—*Zeta Beta Tau*
BOB HILL—*Sigma Chi*
DARRALL IMHOFF—*Phi Kappa Tau*
GEORGE IRVINE—*Phi Delta Theta*
DAN ISSEL—*Pi Kappa Alpha*
PHIL JACKSON—*Sigma Alpha Epsilon*
BILL KELLER—*Beta Theta Pi*
JOHNNY KERR—*Phi Kappa Psi*
HOWIE "BUTCH" KOMIVES—*Sigma Chi*
JIM KREBS—*Sigma Alpha Epsilon*
WENDELL LADNER—*Phi Kappa Tau*
RUDY LaRUSSO—*Pi Lambda Phi*
RON LEE—*Theta Chi*
BOB LEONARD—*Delta Tau Delta*
DANNY MANNING—*Kappa Alpha Psi*
JACK MARIN—*Kappa Sigma*
JACK McCLOSKEY—*Sigma Chi*
JOHN McGLOCKLIN—*Sigma Alpha Epsilon*
"BONES" McKINNEY—*Theta Chi*

DICK MOTTA—*Pi Kappa Alpha*
JEFF MULLINS—*Phi Kappa Sigma*
BILL MUSSELMAN—*Phi Gamma Delta*
WILLIE NAULLS—*Kappa Alpha Psi*
ED NEALY—*Delta Tau Delta*
BOB NETOLICKY—*Alpha Tau Omega*
JACK NICHOLS—*Sigma Nu*
TOM NISSALKE—*Lambda Chi Alpha*
DON OHL—*Beta Theta Pi*
BARRY PARKHILL—*Pi Kappa Alpha*
RAY PATTERSON—*Psi Upsilon*
ABE POLLIN—*Zeta Beta Tau*
PAT RILEY—*Sigma Nu*
RICK ROBEY—*Delta Tau Delta*
DAVE ROBISCH—*Sigma Nu*
"RED" ROCHA—*Phi Delta Theta*
JIMMY RODGERS—*Delta Upsilon*
JOHN RUDOMETKIN—*Delta Chi*
FRED SCHAUS—*Sigma Chi*
DANNY SCHAYES—*Sigma Alpha Mu*
DAVE SCHELLHASE—*Sigma Chi*
MIKE SCHULER—*Sigma Nu*
FRANK SELVY—*Sigma Alpha Epsilon*
JERRY SICHTING—*Beta Theta Pi*
JACK SIKMA—*Sigma Chi*
ADRIAN SMITH—*Lambda Chi Alpha*
DICK SNYDER—*Kappa Sigma*
BOB STEIN—*Beta Theta Pi*
MAURICE STOKES—*Tau Kappa Epsilon*
RICK SUND—*Delta Upsilon*
CHARLIE TYRA—*Phi Kappa Tau*
DARNELL VALENTINE—*Phi Beta Sigma*
DICK VAN ARSDALE—*Sigma Alpha Epsilon*
TOM VAN ARSDALE—*Sigma Alpha Epsilon*
ZOLLIE VOLCHOK—*Sigma Alpha Mu*
GEORGE YARDLEY—*Phi Kappa Psi*

PROMINENT COLLEGE BASKETBALL COACHES

DAVE BLISS—*Psi Upsilon*
JIM BOEHEIM—*Delta Upsilon*
BOB BOYD—*Phi Kappa Tau*
LARRY BROWN—*Lambda Chi Alpha*
VIC BUBAS—*Phi Kappa Psi*
LOU CARNASECCA—*Tau Kappa Epsilon*
PETE CARRIL—*Delta Tau Delta*
DENNY CRUM—*Phi Kappa Sigma*
DAVE GAVITT—*Beta Theta Pi*
RON GREENE—*Sigma Chi*
JUD HEATHCOTE—*Sigma Alpha Epsilon*
TERRY HOLLAND—*Phi Delta Theta*
GENE KEADY—*Sigma Phi Epsilon*

ROLLIE MASSIMINO—*Kappa Sigma*
RAY MEARS—*Delta Tau Delta*
ELDON MILLER—*Beta Theta Pi*
STAN MORRISON—*Phi Kappa Sigma*
GERALD MYERS—*Phi Delta Theta*
C.M. NEWTON—*Sigma Alpha Epsilon*
JOHNNY ORR—*Sigma Chi*
TOM PENDERS—*Theta Xi*
"DIGGER" PHELPS—*Tau Kappa Epsilon*
RICK PITINO—*Lambda Chi Alpha*
PAT HEAD SUMMITT—*Chi Omega*
EDDIE SUTTON—*Sigma Chi*
KAY YOW—*Delta Zeta*

NATIONAL FOOTBALL FOUNDATION
COLLEGE FOOTBALL HALL OF FAME

Over 400 fraternity members have been elected to the College Hall of Fame for their playing and coaching exploits. Due to space limitations, we have listed only those players active in college football over the past 60 years. All known Greek coaches, however, are listed.

PLAYERS

ALEX AGASE—*Tau Kappa Epsilon*
HARRY AGGANIS—*Sigma Alpha Epsilon*
FRANKIE ALBERT—*Delta Kappa Epsilon*
LANCE ALWORTH—*Pi Kappa Alpha*
WARREN AMLING—*Alpha Tau Omega*
DONNY ANDERSON—*Kappa Sigma*
DOUG ATKINS—*Sigma Phi Epsilon*
"REDS" BAGNELL—*Phi Gamma Delta*
JOHNNY BAKER—*Phi Kappa Tau*
TERRY BAKER—*Phi Delta Theta*
HUB BECHTOL—*Phi Delta Theta*
JAY BERWANGER—*Psi Upsilon*
FRED BILETNIKOFF—*Lambda Chi Alpha*
"DOC" BLANCHARD—*Sigma Nu*
ED BOCK—*Sigma Chi*
DON BOSSELER—*Sigma Chi*
VIC BOTTARI—*Kappa Sigma*
JOHN BRODIE—*Zeta Psi*
RAYMOND "TAY" BROWN—*Sigma Chi*
GEORGE CAFEGO—*Pi Kappa Alpha*
JOHN CAIN—*Phi Sigma Kappa*
HOWARD CASSADY—*Sigma Chi*
SAM CHAPMAN—*Sigma Phi Epsilon*
BOB CHAPPUIS—*Phi Delta Theta*
PAUL CHRISTMAN—*Kappa Sigma*
JACK CLOUD—*Sigma Alpha Epsilon*
DON COLEMAN—*Alpha Phi Alpha*
BILL CORBUS—*Phi Delta Theta*
FRED CRAWFORD—*Phi Delta Theta*
CARROLL DALE—*Pi Kappa Alpha*
JERRY DALRYMPLE—*Sigma Nu*
AVERELL DANIELL—*Lambda Chi Alpha*
JIM DANIELL—*Kappa Sigma*
BOBBY DAVIS—*Chi Phi*
ERNIE DAVIS—*Sigma Alpha Mu*
MIKE DITKA—*Sigma Chi*
GLENN DOBBS—*Pi Kappa Alpha*
BOBBY DODD—*Sigma Nu*
BILL DUDLEY—*Sigma Alpha Epsilon*
"TURK" EDWARDS—*Theta Chi*
"BUMP" ELLIOTT—*Sigma Chi*
RAY EVANS—*Phi Delta Theta*
TOM FEARS—*Zeta Psi*
BEATTIE FEATHERS—*Phi Gamma Delta*
BOB FENIMORE—*Sigma Nu*
JOHN FERRARO—*Kappa Alpha Order*
DAN FORTMANN—*Delta Upsilon*
SAM FRANCIS—*Sigma Alpha Epsilon*
ROD FRANZ—*Phi Delta Theta*
BOB GAIN—*Sigma Phi Epsilon*
HUGH GALLARNEAU—*Delta Upsilon*
MIKE GARRETT—*Tau Epsilon Phi*

PAUL GIEL—*Phi Kappa Theta*
FRANK GIFFORD—*Phi Sigma Kappa*
WALTER GILBERT—*Pi Kappa Alpha*
CHET GLADCHUK—*Lambda Chi Alpha*
MARSHALL GOLDBERG—*Zeta Beta Tau*
PAUL GOVERNALI—*Alpha Sigma Phi*
OTTO GRAHAM—*Alpha Delta Phi*
BOBBY GRAYSON—*Phi Delta Theta*
BOB GRIESE—*Sigma Chi*
PARKER HALL—*Kappa Sigma*
JACK HAM—*Phi Delta Theta*
BOBBY HAMILTON—*Zeta Psi*
TOM HARMON—*Phi Delta Theta*
BILL HARTMAN—*Chi Phi*
MEL HEIN—*Sigma Nu*
DON HEINRICH—*Sigma Nu*
TED HENDRICKS—*Kappa Sigma*
BOB HERWIG—*Alpha Kappa Lambda*
HERMAN HICKMAN—*Sigma Alpha Epsilon*
DAN HILL—*Sigma Chi*
CARL HINKLE—*Sigma Alpha Epsilon*
CLARKE HINKLE—*Sigma Alpha Epsilon*
JIMMY HITCHCOCK—*Sigma Nu*
E.J. HOLUB—*Phi Gamma Delta*
LES HORVATH—*Delta Tau Delta*
"DIXIE" HOWELL—*Alpha Lambda Tau*
DON HUTSON—*Sigma Chi*
CECIL ISBELL—*Phi Delta Theta*
DAROLD JENKINS—*Delta Upsilon*
JACKIE JENSEN—*Alpha Delta Phi*
CHARLEY JUSTICE—*Beta Theta Pi*
LARRY KELLEY—*Delta Kappa Epsilon*
DOUG KENNA—*Sigma Alpha Epsilon*
LEROY KEYES—*Omega Psi Phi*
"BRUISER" KINARD—*Phi Pi Phi*
NILE KINNICK—*Phi Kappa Psi*
RON KRAMER—*Sigma Chi*
MAL KUTNER—*Delta Tau Delta*
HANK LAURICELLA—*Sigma Chi*
BOB LILLY—*Sigma Phi Epsilon*
FLOYD LITTLE—*Tau Delta Phi*
RICHIE LUCAS—*Phi Delta Theta*
SID LUCKMAN—*Zeta Beta Tau*
BOB MacLEOD—*Alpha Delta Phi*
JOHNNY MAJORS—*Sigma Chi*
VAUGHN MANCHA—*Lambda Chi Alpha*
ARCHIE MANNING—*Sigma Nu*
EDGAR "EGGS" MANSKE—*Delta Tau Delta*
ED MARINARO—*Psi Upsilon*
VICTOR MARKOV—*Sigma Chi*
BILL McCOLL—*Zeta Psi*
TOMMY McDONALD—*Sigma Nu*

HUGH McELHENNY—*Chi Psi*
GENE McEVER—*Phi Gamma Delta*
BANKS McFADDEN—*Alpha Tau Omega*
MIKE McGEE—*Kappa Alpha Order*
THURMAN McGRAW—*State Sigma Nu*
MARLIN McKEEVER—*Kappa Alpha Order*
DON MEREDITH—*Phi Delta Theta*
ABE MICKAL—*Lambda Chi Alpha*
TONY MINISI—*Sigma Alpha Epsilon*
ED MOLINKSI—*Delta Sigma Phi*
CLIFF MONTGOMERY—*Delta Kappa Epsilon*
DONN MOOMAW—*Delta Sigma Phi*
GEORGE MORRIS—*Phi Delta Theta*
BILL MORTON—*Delta Kappa Epsilon*
"MONK" MOSCRIP—*Zeta Psi*
TOMMY NOBIS—*Kappa Alpha Order*
LEO NOMELLINI—*Delta Chi*
DAVEY O'BRIEN—*Sigma Phi Epsilon*
MERLIN OLSEN—*Sigma Chi*
JOHN ORSI—*Beta Theta Pi*
JIM OWENS—*Sigma Nu*
STEVE OWENS—*Kappa Sigma*
"ACE" PARKER—*Sigma Chi*
PETE PIHOS—*Beta Theta Pi*
ERNY PINCKERT—*Sigma Chi*
JOHNNY PINGEL—*Sigma Nu*
JIM PLUNKETT—*Delta Tau Delta*
MERV PREGULMAN—*Sigma Alpha Mu*
EDDIE PRICE—*Delta Sigma Phi*
BOB "HORSE" REYNOLDS—*Zeta Psi*
BOBBY REYNOLDS—*Phi Kappa Psi*
ERNEST "PUG" RENTNER—*Sigma Nu*
LES RICHTER—*Phi Gamma Delta*
JOHN RILEY—*Sigma Nu*
AARON ROSENBERG—*Zeta Beta Tau*
KYLE ROTE—*Sigma Alpha Epsilon*
GEORGE SAUER—*Delta Tau Delta*
GEORGE SAVITSKY—*Phi Sigma Kappa*
GALE SAYERS—*Kappa Alpha Psi*
JACK SCARBATH—*Sigma Alpha Epsilon*
BOB SCHLOREDT—*Alpha Delta Phi*
DAVE SCHREINER—*Phi Delta Theta*

PAUL SCHWEGLER—*Kappa Sigma*
CLYDE SCOTT—*Kappa Sigma*
TOM SCOTT—*Pi Kappa Alpha*
RON SELLERS—*Lambda Chi Alpha*
CLAUDE "MONK" SIMONS—*Phi Kappa Sigma*
FRANK SINKWICH—*Pi Kappa Alpha*
ERNIE SMITH—*Phi Sigma Kappa*
HARRY SMITH—*Kappa Sigma*
RILEY SMITH—*Phi Kappa Sigma*
VERNON "CATFISH" SMITH—*Sigma Chi*
AL SPARLIS—*Sigma Nu*
STEVE SPURRIER—*Alpha Tau Omega*
HARRISON STAFFORD—*Sigma Chi*
JOE STEFFY—*Sigma Chi*
BOB STEUBER—*Phi Delta Theta*
JOE STYDAHAR—*Kappa Sigma*
BOB SUFFRIDGE—*Pi Kappa Alpha*
STEVE SUHEY—*Sigma Pi*
JIM SWINK—*Phi Delta Theta*
GEORGE TALIAFERRO—*Kappa Alpha Psi*
FRAN TARKENTON—*Sigma Alpha Epsilon*
JOHN TAVENER—*Beta Theta Pi*
CHUCK TAYLOR—*Delta Chi*
ERIC TIPTON—*Kappa Sigma*
CHARLEY TRIPPI—*Lambda Chi Alpha*
NORM VAN BROCKLIN—*Kappa Sigma*
BILLY VESSELS—*Sigma Nu*
DOAK WALKER—*Phi Delta Theta*
COTTON WARBURTON—*Sigma Alpha Epsilon*
BOB WARD—*Phi Delta Theta*
BOB WESTFALL—*Theta Chi*
BYRON "WHIZZER" WHITE—*Phi Gamma Delta*
ED WIDSETH—*Phi Delta Theta*
DICK WILDUNG—*Phi Delta Theta*
BOBBY WILSON—*Kappa Sigma*
ALBERT WISTERT—*Phi Delta Theta*
ALVIN WISTERT—*Phi Delta Theta*
FRAN WISTERT—*Phi Delta Theta*
BOWDEN WYATT—*Sigma Chi*
RON YARY—*Phi Kappa Psi*
GUST ZARNAS—*Delta Chi*

COACHES

BILL ALEXANDER—*Kappa Sigma*
IKE ARMSTRONG—*Sigma Alpha Epsilon*
MATTY BELL—*Beta Theta Pi*
HUGH BEZDEK—*Phi Kappa Sigma*
DANA X. BIBLE—*Delta Kappa Epsilon*
BERNIE BIERMAN—*Alpha Delta Phi*
BOB BLACKMAN—*Sigma Chi*
EARL "RED" BLAIK—*Beta Theta Pi*
FRANK BROYLES—*Sigma Pi*
PAUL "BEAR" BRYANT—*Sigma Nu*
WALTER CAMP—*Delta Kappa Epsilon*
FRANK CAVANAUGH—*Alpha Delta Phi*
RICHARD COLMAN—*Phi Delta Theta*
"FRITZ" CRISLER—*Delta Sigma Phi*
DAN DEVINE—*Phi Kappa Theta*
BILL EDWARDS—*Alpha Tau Omega*
"RIP" ENGLE—*Pi Kappa Alpha*

DON FAUROT—*FarmHouse*
SID GILLMAN—*Zeta Beta Tau*
ERNIE GODFREY—*Alpha Tau Omega*
RAY GRAVES—*Sigma Nu*
ANDY GUSTAFSON—*Sigma Alpha Epsilon*
DICK HARLOW—*Phi Sigma Kappa*
HARVEY HARMAN—*Phi Gamma Delta*
JESSE HARPER—*Phi Delta Theta*
WOODY HAYES—*Sigma Chi*
BOB HIGGINS—*Beta Theta Pi*
MORLEY JENNINGS—*Sigma Chi*
THOMAS "TAD" JONES—*Delta Psi*
LLOYD JORDAN—*Sigma Alpha Epsilon*
RALPH "SHUG" JORDAN—*Theta Chi*
ANDY KERR—*Phi Kappa Sigma*
GEORGE LITTLE—*Alpha Tau Omega*
DAVE MAURER—*Beta Theta Pi*

HERB McCRACKEN—*Delta Tau Delta*
DAN McGUGIN—*Delta Upsilon*
JOHN McKAY—*Alpha Tau Omega*
ALLYN McKEEN—*Sigma Chi*
JACK MOLLENKOPF—*Sigma Alpha Epsilon*
ANDREW MOORE—*Kappa Sigma*
RAY MORRISON—*Beta Theta Pi*
GEORGE MUNGER—*Delta Psi*
CLARENCE "BIGGIE" MUNN—*Phi Kappa Sigma*
ED "HOOKS" MYLIN—*Chi Phi*
JESS NEELY—*Delta Tau Delta*
FRANK "BUCK" O'NEILL—*Delta Chi*
BENNIE OWEN—*Sigma Chi*
TOMMY PROTHRO—*Sigma Alpha Epsilon*
DICK ROMNEY—*Sigma Chi*
DARRELL ROYAL—*Delta Upsilon*

FRANCIS SCHMIDT—*Sigma Alpha Epsilon*
BEN SCHWARTZWALDER—*Kappa Alpha Order*
CLARK SHAUGHNESSY—*Sigma Chi*
ANDY SMITH—*Sigma Alpha Epsilon*
AMOS ALONZO STAGG—*Psi Upsilon*
"JOCK" SUTHERLAND—*Sigma Chi*
THAD "PIE" VANN—*Alpha Tau Omega*
WALLACE WADE—*Delta Phi*
LYNN "PAPPY" WALDORF—*Pi Kappa Alpha*
"TAD" WIEMAN—*Kappa Sigma*
JOHN WILCE—*Delta Kappa Epsilon*
HENRY WILLIAMS—*Alpha Delta Phi*
CHARLES "BUD" WILKINSON—*Psi Upsilon*
GEORGE WOODRUFF—*Psi Upsilon*
FIELDING YOST—*Sigma Chi*
BOB ZUPPKE—*Kappa Sigma*

PROMINENT COLLEGE FOOTBALL COACHES

FRED AKERS—*Sigma Chi*
DEE ANDROS—*Acacia*
CHRIS AULT—*Sigma Alpha Epsilon*
BOBBY BOWDEN—*Pi Kappa Alpha*
RICH BROOKS—*Phi Delta Theta*
MACK BROWN—*Sigma Alpha Epsilon*
EARLE BRUCE—*Chi Phi*
MILT BRUHN—*Alpha Gamma Rho*
LEE CORSO—*Alpha Tau Omega*
CARMEN COZZA—*Delta Tau Delta*
DICK CRUM—*Alpha Tau Omega*
PAUL DIETZEL—*Sigma Alpha Epsilon*
TERRY DONAHUE—*Alpha Tau Omega*
VINCE DOOLEY—*Phi Kappa Theta*
LAVELL EDWARDS—*Sigma Nu*
PETE ELLIOTT—*Sigma Chi*
JACK ELWAY—*Sigma Alpha Epsilon*
DENNIS ERICKSON—*Sigma Alpha Epsilon*
FORREST EVASHEVSKI—*Phi Gamma Delta*
KEN HATFIELD—*Sigma Chi*
LOU HOLTZ—*Delta Upsilon*
DON JAMES—*Sigma Phi Epsilon*
FRANK KUSH—*Alpha Tau Omega*

JOHN MAJORS—*Sigma Chi*
BILL MALLORY—*Phi Kappa Tau*
BILL McCARTNEY—*Pi Kappa Alpha*
DON NEHLEN—*Sigma Alpha Epsilon*
JOE PATERNO—*Delta Kappa Epsilon*
BILL PETERSON—*Delta Sigma Phi*
JOHNNY PONT—*Sigma Chi*
JOHN RALSTON—*Sigma Nu*
HAROLD "TUBBY" RAYMOND—*Phi Delta Theta*
ERK RUSSELL—*Kappa Sigma*
"BO" SCHEMBECHLER—*Sigma Alpha Epsilon*
HOWARD SCHNELLENBERGER—*Pi Kappa Alpha*
LARRY SMITH—*Phi Delta Theta*
BRUCE SNYDER—*Alpha Tau Omega*
STEVE SPURRIER—*Alpha Tau Omega*
BUDDY TEEVENS—*Beta Theta Pi*
DICK TOMEY—*Phi Kappa Psi*
JIM WACKER—*Phi Delta Theta*
JIM WALDEN—*Phi Delta Theta*
MIKE WHITE—*Delta Upsilon*
BILL YEOMAN—*Pi Kappa Alpha*
JIM YOUNG—*Sigma Chi*

PRO FOOTBALL HALL OF FAME

LANCE ALWORTH—*Pi Kappa Alpha*
DOUG ATKINS—*Sigma Phi Epsilon*
MORRIS "RED" BADGRO—*Sigma Chi*
BERT BELL—*Phi Kappa Sigma*
FRED BILETNIKOFF—*Lambda Chi Alpha*
TERRY BRADSHAW—*Tau Kappa Epsilon*
PAUL BROWN—*Delta Kappa Epsilon*
EARL "DUTCH" CLARK—*Phi Gamma Delta*
GUY CHAMBERLIN—*Beta Theta Pi*
JACK CHRISTIANSEN—*Sigma Alpha Epsilon*
JIM CONZELMAN—*Kappa Sigma*
WILLIE DAVIS—*Kappa Alpha Psi*
LEN DAWSON—*Alpha Tau Omega*
MIKE DITKA—*Sigma Chi*
JOHN "PADDY" DRISCOLL—*Sigma Alpha Epsilon*
BILL DUDLEY—*Sigma Alpha Epsilon*
GLEN "TURK" EDWARDS—*Theta Chi*

WEEB EWBANK—*Phi Delta Theta*
TOM FEARS—*Zeta Psi*
LEN FORD—*Omega Psi Phi*
DANNY FORTMANN—*Delta Upsilon*
FRANK GIFFORD—*Phi Sigma Kappa*
SID GILLMAN—*Zeta Beta Tau*
OTTO GRAHAM—*Alpha Delta Phi*
HAROLD "RED" GRANGE—*Zeta Psi*
BOB GRIESE—*Sigma Chi*
LOU GROZA—*Alpha Tau Omega*
GEORGE HALAS—*Tau Kappa Epsilon*
JACK HAM—*Phi Delta Theta*
ED HEALEY—*Sigma Chi*
MEL HEIN—*Sigma Nu*
TED HENDRICKS—*Kappa Sigma*
WILBUR "PETE" HENRY—*Alpha Tau Omega*
CLARKE HINKLE—*Sigma Alpha Epsilon*

LAMAR HUNT—*Kappa Sigma*
DON HUTSON—*Sigma Chi*
STAN JONES—*Sigma Nu*
SONNY JURGENSEN—*Kappa Alpha Order*
FRANK "BRUISER" KINARD—*Phi Pi Phi*
TOM LANDRY—*Delta Kappa Epsilon*
DANTE LAVELLI—*Delta Tau Delta*
ALPHONSE "TUFFY" LEEMANS—*Delta Tau Delta*
BOB LILLY—*Sigma Phi Epsilon*
SID LUCKMAN—*Zeta Beta Tau*
ROY "LINK" LYMAN—*Sigma Alpha Epsilon*
OLLIE MATSON—*Kappa Alpha Psi*
MIKE McCORMACK—*Sigma Nu*
HUGH McELHENNY—*Chi Psi*
MIKE MICHALSKE—*Alpha Tau Omega*
RON MIX—*Delta Chi*

BRONKO NAGURSKI—*Sigma Chi*
ERNIE NEVERS—*Kappa Alpha Order*
LEO NOMELLINI—*Delta Chi*
MERLIN OLSEN—*Sigma Chi*
JIM OTTO—*Phi Delta Theta*
CLARENCE "ACE" PARKER—*Sigma Chi*
PETE PIHOS—*Beta Theta Pi*
GALE SAYERS—*Kappa Alpha Psi*
TEX SCHRAMM—*Phi Kappa Psi*
ART SHELL—*Alpha Phi Alpha*
JOE STYDAHAR—*Kappa Sigma*
FRAN TARKENTON—*Sigma Alpha Epsilon*
CHARLEY TRIPPI—*Lambda Chi Alpha*
GENE UPSHAW—*Alpha Phi Alpha*
NORM VAN BROCKLIN—*Kappa Sigma*
ARNIE WEINMEISTER—*Alpha Tau Omega*

CANADIAN FOOTBALL HALL OF FAME

JOHN BARROW—*Sigma Phi Epsilon*
ORMAND BEACH—*Phi Gamma Delta*
TOM BROWN—*Kappa Sigma*
FRANK CLAIR—*Beta Theta Pi*
WES CUTLER—*Phi Gamma Delta*
SAM ETCHEVERRY—*Sigma Chi*
BERNIE FALONEY—*Sigma Alpha Epsilon*
JOHN FERRARO—*Pi Kappa Phi*
W. C. FOULDS—*Delta Upsilon*
TONY GABRIEL—*Phi Gamma Delta*
HARRY "BUD" GRANT—*Phi Delta Theta*
DEAN GRIFFING—*Kappa Sigma*
FRITZ HANSON—*Theta Chi*
LEW HAYMAN—*Zeta Beta Tau*
"INDIAN" JACK JACOBS—*Kappa Alpha Order*

GREG KABAT—*Lambda Chi Alpha*
JOE KAPP—*Kappa Alpha Order*
RON LANCASTER—*Phi Gamma Delta*
EARL LUNSFORD—*Sigma Nu*
FRANK McGILL—*Delta Upsilon*
PERCY MOLSON—*Zeta Psi*
ROGER NELSON—*Acacia*
"RED" O'QUINN—*Delta Sigma Phi*
KEN PLOEN—*Beta Theta Pi*
RUSS REBHOLZ—*Kappa Sigma*
PAUL ROWE—*Sigma Phi Epsilon*
JEFF RUSSELL—*Zeta Psi*
DAVE THELEN—*Beta Theta Pi*
VIRGIL WAGNER—*Delta Sigma Phi*

PRO FOOTBALL PLAYERS

DAN ABRAMOWICZ—*Tau Kappa Epsilon*
FRANKIE ALBERT—*Delta Kappa Epsilon*
DONNY ANDERSON—*Kappa Sigma*
FRED ARBANAS—*Delta Upsilon*
TRACE ARMSTRONG—*Phi Delta Theta*
JON ARNETT—*Kappa Alpha Order*
RALPH BAKER—*Sigma Pi*
SAM BAKER—*Phi Delta Theta*
JIM BAKKEN—*Sigma Chi*
BRUNO BANDUCCI—*Delta Chi*
LEM BARNEY—*Kappa Alpha Psi*
TERRY BARR—*Sigma Chi*
JIM BENTON—*Kappa Sigma*
BILL BERGEY—*Kappa Alpha Order*
FORREST BLUE—*Sigma Alpha Epsilon*
ORDELL BRAASE—*Beta Theta Pi*
BILL BRADLEY—*Lambda Chi Alpha*
GREG BREZINA—*Sigma Chi*
JOHN BRODIE—*Zeta Psi*
BILL BROWN—*Sigma Phi Epsilon*
BOBBY BRYANT—*Phi Kappa Sigma*
NORM BULAICH—*Sigma Alpha Epsilon*
CHRIS BURFORD—*Delta Tau Delta*
KEN BURROUGH—*Phi Beta Sigma*

BLAIR BUSH—*Lambda Chi Alpha*
DAVE BUTZ—*Alpha Tau Omega*
TOMMY CASANOVA—*Kappa Sigma*
HOWARD CASSADY—*Sigma Chi*
WES CHANDLER—*Alpha Phi Alpha*
PAUL CHRISTMAN—*Kappa Sigma*
CRIS COLLINSWORTH—*Alpha Tau Omega*
VINCE COSTELLO—*Sigma Nu*
FRED COX—*Lambda Chi Alpha*
LINDON CROW—*Phi Kappa Psi*
MIKE CURTIS—*Phi Delta Theta*
CARROLL DALE—*Pi Kappa Alpha*
JIM DAVID—*Sigma Chi*
JOE DEVLIN—*Sigma Alpha Epsilon*
DOUG DIEKEN—*Sigma Chi*
DAN DIERDORF—*Kappa Sigma*
GLENN DOBBS—*Pi Kappa Alpha*
DALE DODRILL—*Sigma Phi Epsilon*
BOYD DOWLER—*Delta Tau Delta*
CHUCK DRAZENOVICH—*Delta Upsilon*
RIKI ELLISON—*Phi Gamma Delta*
JOHN ELWAY—*Delta Tau Delta*
JIM EVERETT—*Sigma Chi*
KEITH FAHNHORST—*Beta Theta Pi*

BEATTIE FEATHERS—*Phi Gamma Delta*
JOE FIELDS—*Tau Kappa Epsilon*
GALEN FISS—*Sigma Chi*
PAUL FLATLEY—*Delta Upsilon*
DAVE FOLEY—*Kappa Sigma*
TIM FOLEY—*Phi Gamma Delta*
CHUCK FOREMAN—*Omega Psi Phi*
RUSS FRANCIS—*Chi Psi*
TUCKER FREDERICKSON—*Kappa Alpha Order*
BOB GAIN—*Sigma Phi Epsilon*
MIKE GARRETT—*Tau Epsilon Phi*
GARY GARRISON—*Sigma Chi*
PETE GOGOLAK—*Delta Upsilon*
MARSHALL GOLDBERG—*Phi Epsilon Pi*
JOHN GORDY—*Lambda Chi Alpha*
JEFF GOSSETT—*Sigma Pi*
JIM GRABOWSKI—*Tau Kappa Epsilon*
RANDY GRADISHAR—*Delta Upsilon*
L.C. GREENWOOD—*Phi Beta Sigma*
JACK GREGORY—*Kappa Alpha Order*
ROSEY GRIER—*Alpha Phi Alpha*
JOHN HADL—*Sigma Nu*
LEN HAUSS—*Sigma Chi*
MATT HAZELTINE—*Sigma Phi*
WALLY HILGENBERG—*Delta Upsilon*
CALVIN HILL—*Delta Kappa Epsilon*
BOB HOERNSCHEMEYER—*Theta Chi*
E.J. HOLUB—*Phi Gamma Delta*
JIM HOUSTON—*Alpha Tau Omega*
CHUCK HOWLEY—*Sigma Chi*
CLAUDE HUMPHREY—*Phi Beta Sigma*
BOBBY HUNT—*Kappa Alpha Order*
TUNCH ILKIN—*Theta Chi*
TIM IRWIN—*Sigma Chi*
CECIL ISBELL—*Phi Delta Theta*
JOHN JAMES—*Sigma Chi*
TOMMY JAMES—*Acacia*
DAVE JENNINGS—*Sigma Chi*
BILLY "WHITE SHOES" JOHNSON—
    Alpha Sigma Phi
CHARLEY JOHNSON—*Theta Chi*
NORM JOHNSON—*Sigma Nu*
JIMMY JOHNSON—*Pi Lambda Phi*
BERT JONES—*Kappa Sigma*
ED "TOO TALL" JONES—*Omega Psi Phi*
HENRY JORDAN—*Sigma Nu*
E.J. JUNIOR—*Kappa Alpha Psi*
JOE KAPP—*Kappa Alpha Order*
TOM KEATING—*Sigma Chi*
MARK KELSO—*Lambda Chi Alpha*
JACK KEMP—*Alpha Tau Omega*
BILL KOMAN—*Phi Kappa Sigma*
KEN KONZ—*Kappa Alpha Order*
JERRY KRAMER—*Sigma Nu*
RON KRAMER—*Sigma Chi*
DAVE KREIG—*Sigma Phi Epsilon*
WARREN LAHR—*Delta Kappa Epsilon*
GREG LANDRY—*Kappa Sigma*
MIKE LANSFORD—*Pi Kappa Alpha*
BILL LENKAITIS—*Phi Gamma Delta*
KEITH LINCOLN—*Phi Kappa Tau*
FLOYD LITTLE—*Tau Delta Phi*

LARRY LITTLE—*Omega Psi Phi*
JAMES LOFTIN—*Phi Delta Chi*
JERRY LOGAN—*Kappa Alpha Order*
MIKE LUCCI—*Pi Kappa Alpha*
MICK LUCKHURST—*Delta Upsilon*
TOM MACK—*Sigma Alpha Epsilon*
JOHN MACKEY—*Sigma Alpha Mu*
ARCHIE MANNING—*Sigma Nu*
RAY MANSFIELD—*Theta Chi*
CHESTER MARCOL—*Delta Sigma Phi*
ED MARINARO—*Psi Upsilon*
JIM MARSHALL—*Kappa Alpha Psi*
HARVEY MARTIN—*Kappa Alpha Psi*
TOMMY MASON—*Sigma Alpha Epsilon*
TOM MATTE—*Phi Gamma Delta*
JERRY MAYS—*Alpha Tau Omega*
TOMMY McDONALD—*Sigma Nu*
VANN McELROY—*Sigma Phi Epsilon*
THURMAN McGRAW—*Sigma Nu*
REGGIE McKENZIE—*Kappa Alpha Psi*
DON MEREDITH—*Phi Delta Theta*
WALT MICHAELS—*Delta Upsilon*
LYDELL MITCHELL—*Omega Psi Phi*
DERLAND MOORE—*Tau Kappa Epsilon*
MILT MORIN—*Kappa Sigma*
JOHNNY MORRIS—*Kappa Sigma*
LARRY MORRIS—*Kappa Alpha Order*
GUY MORRISS—*Kappa Sigma*
MARK MOSELEY—*Delta Sigma Phi*
HOWARD MUDD—*Delta Tau Delta*
CHUCK MUNCIE—*Theta Delta Chi*
JIM NANCE—*Zeta Beta Tau*
BILL NELSEN—*Phi Kappa Psi*
DARRIN NELSON—*Theta Delta Chi*
JOHN NILAND—*Phi Delta Theta*
TOMMY NOBIS—*Kappa Alpha Order*
BLAINE NYE—*Beta Theta Pi*
JOHN OFFERDAHL—*Sigma Alpha Epsilon*
JOHNNY OLSZEWSKI—*Sigma Nu*
JIMMY ORR—*Kappa Alpha Order*
DAVE OSBORNE—*Sigma Alpha Epsilon*
STEVE OWENS—*Kappa Sigma*
DAVID PARKS—*Phi Delta Theta*
BUBBA PARIS—*Phi Beta Sigma*
PRESTON PEARSON—*Kappa Alpha Psi*
BILL PELLINGTON—*Phi Gamma Delta*
GERRY PHILBIN—*Tau Kappa Epsilon*
JIM "RED" PHILLIPS—*Theta Chi*
RAY PINNEY—*Phi Delta Theta*
JIM PLUNKETT—*Delta Tau Delta*
GLENN PRESNELL—*Alpha Gamma Rho*
EDDIE PRICE—*Delta Sigma Phi*
JETHRO PUGH—*Alpha Phi Alpha*
TOM RAFFERTY—*Phi Delta Theta*
SONNY RANDLE—*Delta Kappa Epsilon*
RANDY RASMUSSEN—*Phi Delta Theta*
RICK REDMAN—*Theta Chi*
MIKE RENFRO—*Kappa Sigma*
LANCE RENTZEL—*Kappa Sigma*
JERRY RICE—*Phi Beta Sigma*
LES RICHTER—*Phi Gamma Delta*
GERALD RIGGS—*Kappa Alpha Psi*

KEN RILEY—*Alpha Phi Alpha*
JOHNNY ROBINSON—*Sigma Phi Epsilon*
JOHNNY ROLAND—*Kappa Alpha Psi*
FRAN ROGEL—*Kappa Delta Rho*
TIMM ROSENBACH—*Sigma Alpha Epsilon*
TIM ROSSOVICH—*Sigma Chi*
KYLE ROTE—*Sigma Alpha Epsilon*
JACK RUDNAY—*Sigma Chi*
ANDY RUSSELL—*Sigma Chi*
MARK RYPIEN—*Delta Tau Delta*
DICK SCHAFRATH—*Kappa Sigma*
VIC SEARS—*Phi Sigma Kappa*
RON SELLERS—*Lambda Chi Alpha*
JEFF SIEMON—*Delta Tau Delta*
PHIL SIMMS—*Tau Kappa Epsilon*
BRIAN SIPE—*Kappa Sigma*
BOB SKORONSKI—*Delta Tau Delta*
JACKIE SLATER—*Phi Beta Sigma*
NORMAN SNEAD—*Delta Sigma Phi*
GORDIE SOLTAU—*Phi Delta Theta*
LARRY STALLINGS—*Sigma Chi*
NORM STANDLEE—*Phi Delta Theta*
BILL STANFILL—*Sigma Nu*
JACK STROUD—*Sigma Chi*
SCOTT STUDWELL—*Delta Chi*
MATT SUHEY—*Phi Gamma Delta*
JERRY TAGGE—*Theta Xi*
GEORGE TALIAFERRO—*Kappa Alpha Psi*
HUGH "BONES" TAYLOR—*Sigma Pi*

R.C. THIELEMANN—*Sigma Nu*
"FUZZY" THURSTON—*Phi Delta Theta*
DAVID TREADWELL—*Sigma Alpha Epsilon*
BOB TRUMPY—*Sigma Chi*
JIM TURNER—*Sigma Chi*
HOWARD TWILLEY—*Pi Kappa Alpha*
JIM TYRER—*Alpha Tau Omega*
MARK VAN EEGHEN—*Delta Upsilon*
DANNY VILLANUEVA—*Tau Kappa Upsilon*
BOB VOGEL—*Tau Epsilon Phi*
RICK VOLK—*Beta Theta Pi*
BILLY WADE—*Beta Theta Pi*
MIKE WAGNER—*Theta Chi*
WAYNE WALKER—*Phi Delta Theta*
GENE WASHINGTON—*Delta Tau Delta*
CHARLIE WATERS—*Sigma Nu*
ROGER WEHRLI—*Phi Gamma Delta*
ED WEIR—*Acacia*
RAY WERSCHING—*Lambda Chi Alpha*
ED WHITE—*Sigma Chi*
DAVE WHITSELL—*Delta Chi*
PAUL WIGGIN—*Phi Delta Theta*
REGGIE WILLIAMS—*Alpha Phi Alpha*
AL WISTERT—*Phi Delta Theta*
DAVE WYMAN—*Delta Tau Delta*
RON YARY—*Phi Kappa Psi*
JACK YOUNGBLOOD—*Alpha Tau Omega*
ROGER ZATKOFF—*Lambda Chi Alpha*

PROMINENT PRO FOOTBALL EXECUTIVES & COACHES

ERNIE ACCORSI—*Theta Chi*
"BUD" ADAMS—*Sigma Chi*
EDWIN ANDERSON—*Sigma Chi*
NEIL ARMSTRONG—*Sigma Nu*
BILL BELICHICK—*Chi Psi*
PAT BOWLEN—*Pi Kappa Alpha*
BUD CARSON—*Phi Delta Theta*
BLANTON COLLIER—*Kappa Alpha Order*
DON CORYELL—*Beta Theta Pi*
BRUCE COSLET—*Delta Upsilon*
JIM DOOLEY—*Sigma Alpha Epsilon*
WILLIAM CLAY FORD—*Psi Upsilon*
HARRY "BUD" GRANT—*Phi Delta Theta*
JIM HANIFAN—*Psi Upsilon*
LINDY INFANTE—*Sigma Nu*
JERRY JONES—*Kappa Sigma*
MARV LEVY—*Tau Kappa Epsilon*
JOHN MECOM—*Sigma Alpha Epsilon*

"RED" MILLER—*Sigma Tau Gamma*
JIM MORA—*Alpha Tau Omega*
CLINT MURCHISON—*Sigma Alpha Epsilon*
DICK NOLAN—*Phi Delta Theta*
JACK PATERA—*Sigma Chi*
JOHN RAUCH—*Lambda Chi Alpha*
JOHN ROBINSON—*Sigma Chi*
CARROLL ROSENBLOOM—*Zeta Beta Tau*
LOU SABAN—*Sigma Chi*
HERMAN SARKOWSKY—*Zeta Beta Tau*
RANKIN SMITH, JR.—*Sigma Alpha Epsilon*
RANKIN SMITH, SR.—*Chi Phi*
HANK STRAM—*Sigma Chi*
RUSS THOMAS—*Delta Upsilon*
"SONNY" WERBLIN—*Zeta Beta Tau*
RALPH WILSON—*Phi Delta Theta*
SAM WYCHE—*Kappa Alpha Order*

PROMINENT GOLFERS

TOMMY AARON—*Kappa Alpha Order*
ANDY BEAN—*Sigma Alpha Epsilon*
JIM BENEPE—*Beta Theta Pi*
PATTY BERG—*Kappa Kappa Gamma*
SUSIE MAXWELL BERNING—*Alpha Phi*
RONNIE BLACK—*Kappa Sigma*
JANE BLALOCK—*Kappa Kappa Gamma*
MARY BUDKA—*Sigma Kappa*
SANDRA BURNS—*Kappa Kappa Gamma*

JOANNE CARNER—*Kappa Alpha Theta*
LEE ANN CASSIDY—*Kappa Alpha Theta*
BRIAN CLAAR—*Phi Delta Theta*
CHARLES COODY—*Phi Delta Theta*
ANNE CREED—*Kappa Delta*
BEN CRENSHAW—*Kappa Alpha Order*
ANNE DECKER—*Gamma Phi Beta*
DALE DOUGLAS—*Kappa Sigma*
DAVE EICHELBERGER—*Sigma Phi Epsilon*

WALTER EMERY—*Sigma Chi*
JILL ENDACOTT—*Kappa Alpha Theta*
CHICK EVANS—*Phi Delta Theta*
JIM FERREE—*Sigma Chi*
DOW FINSTERWALD—*Beta Theta Pi*
BUDDY GARDNER—*Sigma Alpha Epsilon*
AL GEIBERGER—*Kappa Alpha Order*
BOB GILDER—*Sigma Alpha Epsilon*
HUBIE GREEN—*Pi Kappa Alpha*
MARGARET GUNTHER—*Chi Omega*
FRED HAAS—*Lambda Chi Alpha*
JAY HAAS—*Kappa Sigma*
LABRON HARRIS—*Alpha Tau Omega*
JERRY HEARD—*Sigma Alpha Epsilon*
JAY HEBERT—*Kappa Sigma*
EDEAN ANDERSON IHIANFELDT—*Alpha Phi*
HALE IRWIN—*Phi Gamma Delta*
PETER JACOBSEN—*Kappa Sigma*
DON JANUARY—*Kappa Alpha Order*
BOBBY JONES—*Sigma Alpha Epsilon*
GRIER JONES—*Beta Theta Pi*
GARY KOCH—*Sigma Alpha Epsilon*
BILL KRATZERT—*Sigma Alpha Epsilon*
GIB LARSEN—*Sigma Chi*
BONNIE LAUER—*Delta Gamma*
LAWSON LITTLE—*Chi Psi*
LYNN LOTT—*Kappa Alpha Order*
MARK LYE—*Theta Chi*
DON MASSENGALE—*Sigma Alpha Epsilon*
MIKE McCULLOUGH—*Sigma Chi*
BARBARA McINTYRE—*Kappa Alpha Theta*
STEVE MELNYK—*Alpha Tau Omega*
CAREY MIDDLECOFF—*Kappa Alpha Order*
JACK MONTGOMERY—*Kappa Sigma*

GIL MORGAN—*Sigma Tau Gamma*
BOB MURPHY—*Sigma Alpha Epsilon*
JACK NICKLAUS—*Phi Gamma Delta*
KYLE O'BRIEN—*Kappa Alpha Theta*
SANDRA PALMER—*Alpha Delta Pi*
JERRY PATE—*Phi Gamma Delta*
BILLY JOE PATTON—*Kappa Alpha Order*
MIKE PECK—*Phi Delta Theta*
TOM PURTZERT—*Sigma Alpha Epsilon*
DAVE RAGAN—*Phi Delta Theta*
AMELIA RORER—*Delta Zeta*
BOB ROSBURG—*Kappa Sigma*
MASON RUDOLPH—*Kappa Sigma*
JOHN SCHROEDER—*Lambda Chi Alpha*
TOM SHAW—*Theta Chi*
DENNY SHUTT—*Phi Gamma Delta*
JAY SIGEL—*Kappa Alpha Order*
JIM SIMONS—*Kappa Alpha Order*
MARILYNN SMITH—*Kappa Alpha Theta*
J.C. SNEED—*Sigma Phi Epsilon*
HOLLIS STACY—*Kappa Kappa Gamma*
PAYNE STEWART—*Phi Gamma Delta*
DAVE STOCKTON—*Kappa Alpha Order*
BETH STONE—*Gamma Phi Beta*
CURTIS STRANGE—*Kappa Sigma*
MARLENE STEWART STREIT—
  Kappa Alpha Theta
TOMMY VALENTINE—*Sigma Alpha Epsilon*
KEN VENTURI—*Sigma Nu*
LANNY WADKINS—*Kappa Sigma*
JoANN WASHAM—*Alpha Gamnma Delta*
TOM WATSON—*Alpha Sigma Phi*
JACK WESTLUND—*Psi Upsilon*
BO WININGER—*Sigma Alpha Epsilon*

PROMINENT TENNIS PLAYERS

WILLMER ALLISON—*Delta Kappa Epsilon*
ARTHUR ASHE—*Kappa Alpha Psi*
BRUCE BARNES—*Delta Tau Delta*
TUT BARTZEN—*Kappa Sigma*
PAULINE BETZ—*Kappa Alpha Theta*
LOUISE BROUGH—*Kappa Alpha Theta*
NANCY CHAFFEE—*Kappa Kappa Gamma*
PAT DUPRE—*Zeta Psi*
HERB FLAM—*Tau Epsilon Phi*
ALTHEA GIBSON—*Alpha Kappa Alpha*
CLARK GRAEBNER—*Delta Upsilon*
"BITSY" GRANT—*Sigma Alpha Epsilon*
DORIS HART—*Kappa Kappa Gamma*
HELEN HULL JACOBS—*Kappa Alpha Theta*
GEORGE LOTT—*Psi Upsilon*
BARRY MACKAY—*Phi Gamma Delta*
TODD MARTIN—*Delta Tau Delta*
SANDY MAYER—*Zeta Psi*
FRED McNAIR—*Phi Delta Theta*
DON McNEIL—*Delta Kappa Epsilon*

MATT MITCHELL—*Zeta Psi*
HELEN WILLS MOODY—*Kappa Kappa Gamma*
GARDNER MULLOY—*Delta Chi Alpha*
WENDY OVERTON—*Kappa Kappa Gamma*
CHUCK PASARELL—*Beta Theta Pi*
DENNIS RALSTON—*Phi Sigma Kappa*
HAM RICHARDSON—*Delta Kappa Epsilon*
MARTY RIESSEN—*Sigma Alpha Epsilon*
HELEN ROARK—*Kappa Kappa Gamma*
NICK SAVIANO—*Zeta Psi*
TED SCHROEDER—*Phi Delta Theta*
VIC SEIXAS—*Chi Psi*
STAN SMITH—*Beta Theta Pi*
JANE STRATTON—*Pi Beta Phi*
CLIFF SUTTER—*Beta Theta Pi*
ROSCOE TANNER—*Zeta Psi*
BILL TILDEN—*Delta Kappa Epsilon*
TONY TRABERT—*Sigma Chi*
ELLSWORTH VINES—*Sigma Nu*

PROMINENT GREEKS IN OTHER SPORTS

MIKE ANTONOVICH—*Hockey* Beta Theta Pi
BOB BEATTIE—*Skiing* Sigma Phi Epsilon
DOUG BLUBAUGH—*Wrestling* Tau Kappa Epsilon
AVERY BRUNDAGE—*Olympics* Sigma Alpha
    Epsilon
CONRAD CALDWELL—*Wrestling* Beta Theta Pi
MARK DONAHUE—*Auto Racing* Theta Delta Chi
RENEE DUPREL—*Cycling* Sigma Kappa
NAT FLEISCHER—*Boxing* Phi Epsilon Pi
BRIAN HAYWARD—*Hockey* Delta Chi
TONY HULMAN—*Auto Racing* Alpha Tau Omega
PHIL HILL—*Auto Racing* Kappa Sigma
BERNIE JAMES—*Pro Soccer* Sigma Alpha
    Epsilon
DAVID JENKINS—*Skating* Phi Delta Theta
HAYES ALAN JENKINS—*Skating* Phi Delta Theta
KEN KRAFT—*Wrestling* Chi Psi
FRANK LEWIS—*Wrestling* Sigma Chi
JANE FAUNTZ MANSKE—*Swimming* Kappa
    Alpha Theta

TERRY McCANN—*Wrestling* Theta Xi
JOHN McCRILLIS—*Skiing* Sigma Delta Epsilon
BILL MUNCEY—*Hydroplane Racing* Lambda Chi
    Alpha
SUSAN NATTRAS—*Trap Shooting* Delta Gamma
FLOYD PATTERSON—*Boxing* Phi Kappa Theta
ROGER PENSKE—*Auto Racing* Phi Gamma Delta
BOBBY RAHAL—*Auto Racing* Phi Gamma Delta
PETER REVSON—*Auto Racing* Delta Upsilon
JACK RILEY—*Wrestling* Sigma Nu
KYLE ROTE, JR.—*Pro Soccer* Delta Tau Delta
TIM RICHMOND—*Auto Racing* Sigma Nu
MYRON RODERICK—*Wrestling* Beta Theta Pi
WILBUR SHAW—*Auto Racing* Alpha Tau Omega
DANNY SULLIVAN—*Auto Racing* Kappa Alpha
    Order
WAYNE WELLS—*Wrestling* Phi Delta Theta
JOHN ZIEGLER—*NHL Commissioner* Sigma Chi

SPORTS BROADCASTING

MIKE ADAMLE—*Phi Delta Theta*
CONNIE ALEXANDER—*Sigma Alpha Epsilon*
MEL ALLEN—*Zeta Beta Tau*
RICK BARRY—*Kappa Sigma*
BOB BEATTIE—*Sigma Phi Epsilon*
GARY BENDER—*Phi Delta Theta*
LOU BOUDREAU—*Phi Sigma Kappa*
TERRY BRADSHAW—*Tau Kappa Epsilon*
JOHN BRODIE—*Zeta Psi*
TOM BROOKSHIER—*Phi Gamma Delta*
DAVE CAMPBELL—*Sigma Alpha Epsilon*
SKIP CARAY—*Phi Gamma Delta*
JIMMY CEFALO—*Phi Gamma Delta*
BUD COLLINS—*Alpha Tau Omega*
HOWARD COSELL—*Zeta Beta Tau*
DAN DIERDORF—*Kappa Sigma*
LARRY DIERKER—*Lambda Chi Alpha*
EDDIE DOUCETTE—*Sigma Nu*
DICK ENBERG—*Phi Sigma Kappa*
BILL FLEMMING—*Delta Tau Delta*
TIM FOLEY—*Phi Gamma Delta*
FRANK GIFFORD—*Phi Sigma Kappa*
MARTY GLICKMAN—*Sigma Alpha Mu*
FRANK GLIEBER—*Theta Xi*
CURT GOWDY—*Alpha Tau Omega*
GEORGE GRANDE—*Kappa Alpha Order*
BOB GRIESE—*Sigma Chi*
TOM HARMON—*Phi Delta Theta*
ERNIE HARWELL—*Sigma Alpha Epsilon*
ALEX HAWKINS—*Pi Kappa Alpha*
FOSTER HEWITT—*Beta Theta Pi*
KEITH JACKSON—*Alpha Tau Omega*
CHARLEY JONES—*Kappa Sigma*
SONNY JURGENSEN—*Kappa Alpha Order*
HARRY KALAS—*Phi Delta Theta*

BRUCE KING—*Sigma Alpha Epsilon*
ANDREA KIRBY—*Alpha Gamma Delta*
BOB LOBEL—*Phi Gamma Delta*
BILL MACATEE—*Delta Tau Delta*
DENNY MATTHEWS—*Sigma Chi*
TIM McCARVER—*Kappa Alpha Order*
BRIAN McFARLANE—*Alpha Tau Omega*
DON MEREDITH—*Phi Delta Theta*
AL MICHAELS—*Sigma Nu*
MONTE MOORE—*Alpha Tau Omega*
PAT O'BRIEN—*Delta Tau Delta*
MERLIN OLSEN—*Sigma Chi*
FERD PACHECO—*Sigma Phi Epsilon*
JIM PALMER—*Sigma Chi*
ROSS PORTER—*Sigma Alpha Epsilon*
BOB PRINCE—*Phi Delta Theta*
MEL PROCTOR—*Kappa Sigma*
JAY RANDOLPH—*Delta Tau Delta*
BRUCE RICE—*Alpha Tau Omega*
CRAIG SAGER—*Delta Tau Delta*
DICK SCHAAP—*Zeta Beta Tau*
CHRIS SCHENKEL—*Phi Sigma Kappa*
JIM SIMPSON—*Sigma Alpha Epsilon*
BOB SNYDER—*Sigma Alpha Mu*
HANK STRAM—*Sigma Chi*
JOE TAIT—*Tau Kappa Epsilon*
FRAN TARKENTON—*Sigma Alpha Epsilon*
TONY TRABERT—*Sigma Chi*
BOB TRUMPY—*Sigma Chi*
WAYNE WALKER—*Phi Delta Theta*
GENE WASHINGTON—*Delta Tau Delta*
"BUD" WILKINSON—*Psi Upsilon*
BOB WOLF—*Sigma Nu*
BILL WORRELL—*Sigma Chi*

Famous Greeks—Science

ASTRONAUTS

JOE ALLEN—*Beta Theta Pi*
NEIL ARMSTRONG—*Phi Delta Theta*
CHARLES BASSETT—*Phi Kappa Tau*
ALAN BEAN—*Delta Kappa Epsilon*
VANCE BRAND—*Sigma Nu*
SCOTT CARPENTER—*Delta Tau Delta*
GERALD CARR—*Tau Kappa Epsilon*
EUGENE CERNAN—*Phi Gamma Delta*
LEROY CHIAO—*Phi Kappa Tau*
JAN DAVIS—*Alpha Xi Delta*
CHARLES DUKE—*Alpha Tau Omega*
RON EVANS—*Sigma Nu*
JOHN FABIAN—*Phi Sigma Kappa*
EDWARD GIBSON—*Theta Chi*
RICHARD GORDON—*Phi Sigma Kappa*
GREG HARBAUGH—*Sigma Chi*
TERRY HART—*Delta Upsilon*
HENRY HARTSFIELD—*Delta Chi*

RICK HAUCK—*Delta Upsilon*
DAVID LOW—*Phi Kappa Sigma*
KEN MATTINGLY—*Delta Tau Delta*
JON McBRIDE—*Phi Delta Theta*
RON McNAIR—*Omega Psi Phi*
STORY MUSGRAVE—*Phi Delta Theta*
STEVE NAGEL—*Alpha Delta Phi*
ELLISON ONIZUKA—*Triangle*
ROBERT OVERMYER—*Alpha Tau Omega*
DICK RICHARDS—*Lambda Chi Alpha*
WALTER SCHIRRA—*Sigma Pi*
BREWSTER SHAW—*Delta Upsilon*
DEKE SLAYTON—*Delta Kappa Epsilon*
JOHN SWIGERT—*Phi Gamma Delta*
RICHARD TRULY—*Kappa Alpha Order*
JAMES VAN HOFTEN—*Pi Kappa Alpha*
PAUL WEITZ—*Beta Theta Pi*
JOHN YOUNG—*Sigma Chi*

Famous Greeks—Arts

Thousands of fraternity men and sorority women over the years have achieved notable success in the arts. The following list is by no means complete but still gives a comprehensive picture of what Greeks have accomplished in the following areas: motion pictures, television, music, radio, the legitimate stage and writing. Included are both past and present leaders in their respective industries.

GEORGE ABBOTT—*Psi Upsilon* Playwright, producer, director, screenwriter
HARRY ACKERMAN—*Phi Delta Theta* TV producer, director
DEBORAH ADAIR—*Kappa Kappa Gamma* TV actress
CHARLES ADDAMS—*Theta Chi* Cartoonist "The Addams Family"
MARTIN AGRONSKY—*Sigma Alpha Mu* Radio and TV commentator
CLAUDE AKINS—*Lambda Chi Alpha* TV and motion picture actor
EDDIE ALBERT—*Chi Psi* TV and motion picture actor
DENISE ALEXANDER—*Pi Beta Phi* TV actress
DUANE ALLEN—*Delta Tau Delta* Vocalist with "The Oak Ridge Boys"
FRAN ALLISON—*Alpha Gamma Delta* TV actress "Kukla, Fran and Ollie"
PRESTON AMES—*Phi Gamma Delta* TV and motion picture art director
BILL ANDERSON—*Kappa Sigma* Vocalist and TV game show host
EDWARD ANDREWS—*Theta Chi* TV and motion picture actor
JOHN ANISTON—*Alpha Chi Rho* TV actor
ANN-MARGRET—*Kappa Alpha Theta* TV and motion picture actress, vocalist
DAVID ANSPAUGH—*Sigma Nu* Motion picture and TV director

JOSEPHINE ANTONIE—*Chi Omega* Opera singer
ROONE ARLEDGE—*Phi Gamma Delta* TV executive
JAMES ARNESS—*Beta Theta Pi* TV actor "Gunsmoke"
EDWARD ARNOLD—*Sigma Phi Epsilon* Motion picture actor
JOHN ASTIN—*Phi Kappa Psi* TV actor
ROBERT AURTHUR—*Sigma Nu* TV, stage and motion picture writer
DONNA AXUM—*Delta Delta Delta* TV hostess
BILL BAIRD—*Sigma Chi* TV and motion picture puppeteer
JIMMIE BAKER—*Pi Kappa Alpha* TV producer, director
JOE DON BAKER—*Sigma Phi Epsilon* Motion picture actor
LEN BAKER—*Phi Kappa Tau* Vocalist with "Sha Na Na"
BOB BALABAN—*Phi Kappa Tau* Motion picture actor, director
MARCIA BALDWIN—*Alpha Phi* Opera singer
JACK BANNON—*Sigma Alpha Epsilon* TV actor
BILL BANOWSKI—*Beta Theta Pi* Broadcasting executive
BOB BARKER—*Sigma Nu* TV game show host
JACK BARRY—*Phi Sigma Delta* TV game show host
RICHARD BARTHELMESS—*Psi Upsilon* Motion picture actor

ALAN BAXTER—*Phi Sigma Kappa* Motion picture and TV actor

JOHN BEAL—*Psi Upsilon* Motion picture actor

MORGAN BEATTY—*Kappa Alpha Order* Journalist, radio commentator

WARREN BEATTY—*Sigma Chi* Motion picture actor, director

MICHAEL BECK—*Kappa Alpha Order* Motion picture and TV actor

LEE PHILLIP BELL—*Delta Delta Delta* TV producer, writer

REBECCA BELL—*Delta Delta Delta* TV commentator

ROBERT BENCHLEY—*Delta Upsilon* Humorist, journalist, screenwriter, actor

DIRK BENEDICT—*Phi Delta Theta* TV actor "The A Team"

TEX BENEKE—*Delta Kappa Epsilon* Orchestra leader

STEPHEN VINCENT BENET—*Alpha Delta Phi* Poet

BRUCE BENNETT—*Beta Theta Pi* Motion picture actor

MEG BENNETT—*Delta Gamma* TV actress

JACK BENNY—*Zeta Beta Tau* TV and radio comedian, motion picture actor

JOHN BERADINO—*Phi Kappa Tau* TV actor "General Hospital"

CANDICE BERGEN—*Kappa Kappa Gamma* TV and motion picture actress

EDGAR BERGEN—*Delta Upsilon* Radio and TV ventriloquist, motion picture actor

DON BERNSTEIN—*Sigma Alpha Epsilon* TV executive

LEONARD BERNSTEIN—*Zeta Beta Tau* Orchestra conductor, composer

JAN BERRY—*Phi Gamma Delta* Vocalist with "Jan and Dean"

TED BESSELL—*Phi Delta Theta* TV actor, director

DAVID BIRNEY—*Sigma Nu* TV and motion picture actor

BILL BIXBY—*Phi Delta Theta* TV actor "The Incredible Hulk"

WOLF BLITZER—*Alpha Epsilon Pi* TV commentator

BILL BOGGS—*Alpha Tau Omega* TV host, producer

LOUIE BONNANO—*Tau Kappa Epsilon* Motion picture actor

PAT BOONE—*Kappa Alpha Order* Vocalist, TV host, motion picture actor

RICHARD BOONE—*Theta Xi* TV and motion picture actor

POWERS BOOTHE—*Lambda Chi Alpha* Motion picture and TV actor

MARGARET BOURKE-WHITE—*Alpha Omicron Pi* Photo Journalist

BEAU BRIDGES—*Sigma Alpha Epsilon* Motion picture actor

LLOYD BRIDGES—*Sigma Alpha Epsilon* Motion picture and TV actor

"THE BROTHERS FOUR"—*Phi Gamma Delta* Vocal group

DR. JOYCE BROTHERS—*Sigma Delta Tau* TV personality

JOE E. BROWN—*Zeta Psi* TV comedian, motion picture actor

JOHNNY MACK BROWN—*Kappa Sigma* Motion picture actor

WOODY BROWN—*Lambda Chi Alpha* Motion picture and TV actor

DAVID BRUCE—*Phi Delta Theta* Motion picture and TV actor

EDGAR BUCHANAN—*Theta Chi* Motion picture and TV actor

PEARL BUCK—*Kappa Delta* Novelist

BETTY BUCKLEY—*Zeta Tau Alpha* TV, Broadway and motion picture actress, vocalist

BOBBY BURGESS—*Sigma Pi* TV dancer, vocalist

BILL BURRUD—*Sigma Phi Epsilon* TV producer

LAUREL HURLEY BUTZ—*Sigma Kappa* Opera singer

JOANNA CAMERON—*Delta Delta Delta* Motion picture actress

JOE CAMP—*Sigma Nu* Motion picture director, producer, screenwriter

DAVID CANARY—*Sigma Chi* TV actor

STEPHEN CANNELL—*Sigma Chi* TV producer, screenwriter

MILTON CANNIFF—*Sigma Chi* Cartoonist "Steve Canyon"

MacDONALD CAREY—*Alpha Delta Phi* TV and motion picture actor

PHILIP CAREY—*Kappa Sigma* TV and motion picture actor

RICHARD CARLSON—*Phi Kappa Psi* Motion picture and TV actor

STEVE CARLSON—*Alpha Tau Omega* Motion picture actor

HOAGY CARMICHAEL—*Kappa Sigma* Songwriter, motion picture actor

LIZ CARPENTER—*Alpha Phi* Writer, columnist

JOHNNY CARSON—*Phi Gamma Delta* TV host

DIXIE CARTER—*Delta Delta Delta* TV actress "Designing Women"

ALLEN CASE—*Kappa Sigma* TV actor

BARBARA CASON—*Kappa Kappa Gamma* TV actress

TED CASSIDY—*Alpha Sigma Phi* TV and motion picture actor

HOITE CASTON—*Sigma Chi* TV producer, director

FELIX CAVALIERE—*Sigma Phi Epsilon* Vocalist "The Rascals"

FRANCES CAVANAUGH—*Delta Delta Delta* Writer

FRANK CAVETT—*Phi Delta Theta* Broadcasting executive

WILLIAM CHRISTOPHER—*Sigma Chi* TV actor "M*A*S*H*"

DICK CLARK—*Delta Kappa Epsilon* TV host, producer

FRED CLARK—*Delta Chi*   TV and motion picture actor

CHARLES COBURN—*Zeta Beta Tau*   Motion picture actor

DABNEY COLEMAN—*Phi Delta Theta*   TV and motion picture actor

NANCY COLEMAN—*Kappa Alpha Theta*   Motion picture actress

STEPHEN COLLINS—*Alpha Delta Phi*   Motion picture and TV actor

TOM COLLINS—*Sigma Chi*   Country music producer

BUD COLLYER—*Psi Upsilon*   TV game show host

MARSHALL COLT—*Sigma Chi*   Motion picture and TV actor

FORREST COMPTON—*Phi Kappa Psi*   TV and Broadway actor

MIKE CONNERS—*Phi Delta Theta*   TV and motion picture actor "Mannix"

TIM CONWAY—*Phi Delta Theta*   TV comedian, motion picture actor

FIELDER COOK—*Delta Tau Delta*   Broadway producer, director

JOAN GANZ COONEY—*Kappa Alpha Theta*   TV producer, writer

AL CORLEY—*Tau Kappa Epsilon*   TV actor "Dynasty"

ROGER CORMAN—*Sigma Alpha Epsilon*   Motion picture director, producer

ANETA CORSAUT—*Alpha Omicron Pi*   TV actress

KEVIN COSTNER—*Delta Chi*   Motion picture actor, director, producer

FRANKLIN COVER—*Kappa Sigma*   TV and motion picture actor

G. HARMON COXE—*Sigma Nu*   Novelist

"BUSTER" CRABBE—*Sigma Chi*   Motion picture and TV actor

STEPHEN CRANE—*Delta Upsilon*   Novelist

RICHARD CRENNA—*Kappa Sigma*   TV and motion picture actor

LUCILLE CRITE—*Delta Delta Delta*   Playwright

WALTER CRONKITE—*Chi Phi*   TV commentator

GARY CROSBY—*Zeta Psi*   TV and motion picture actor

KATHRYN CROSBY—*Chi Omega*   Motion picture and TV actress

MARY CROSBY—*Delta Delta Delta*   TV and motion picture actress

JOHN CULLUM—*Phi Gamma Delta*   Broadway actor

FAITH DANIELS—*Zeta Tau Alpha*   TV hostess, commentator

WILLIAM DANIELS—*Sigma Nu*   TV and motion picture actor

DON DANNEMAN—*Zeta Beta Tau*   Vocalist "The Cyrkle"

JOHN DAVIDSON—*Delta Upsilon*   TV game show host, singer, actor

JIM DAVIS—*Kappa Sigma*   Motion picture and TV actor "Dallas"

LORRAINE DAVIS—*Alpha Gamma Delta*   Magazine publishing

TOM DAWES—*Sigma Nu*   Vocalist "The Cyrkle"

DENNIS DAY—*Phi Kappa Theta*   TV actor, singer, comedian

FRED DeCORDOVA—*Phi Kappa Sigma*   TV director, producer

RICK DEES—*Pi Kappa Alpha*   TV host, singer

CARTER DeHAVEN, III—*Sigma Alpha Epsilon*   Motion picture director

ALBERT DEKKER—*Alpha Delta Phi*   Motion picture actor

BRIAN DENNEHY—*Sigma Chi*   Motion picture actor

DAVID DePATIE—*Phi Gamma Delta*   Motion picture and TV producer

JOYCE DEWITT—*Chi Omega*   TV actress "Three's Company"

JOAN DIDION—*Delta Delta Delta*   Novelist, motion picture screenwriter

LLOYD DOBYNS—*Kappa Sigma*   TV commentator

ED DODD—*Delta Tau Delta*   Cartoonist "Mark Trail"

BOB DOTSON—*Delta Tau Delta*   TV commentator

LLOYD C. DOUGLAS—*Phi Gamma Delta*   Novelist

MELVIN DOUGLAS—*Zeta Beta Tau*   Motion picture actor

PEGGY DOW—*Delta Delta Delta*   Motion picture actress

FRED DREYER—*Tau Kappa Epsilon*   TV and motion picture actor "Hunter"

ALEX DREIER—*Sigma Alpha Epsilon*   TV and radio commentator

JAMES DRURY—*Tau Kappa Epsilon*   TV actor "The Virginian"

VAL DUFOUR—*Theta Xi*   TV actor

FAYE DUNAWAY—*Pi Beta Phi*   Motion picture actress

MILDRED DUNNOCK—*Alpha Phi*   Motion picture actress

DAN DURYEA—*Tau Kappa Epsilon*   Motion picture actor

NANCY DUSSAULT—*Delta Delta Delta*   TV and Broadway actress

ROGER EBERT—*Phi Delta Theta*   Movie reviewer, TV personality

RONNIE CLAIRE EDWARDS—*Kappa Alpha Theta*   TV and motion picture actress

MICHAEL EISNER—*Delta Upsilon*   Movie and broadcasting executive

SEGER ELLIS—*Phi Delta Theta*   Vocalist and songwriter

SAM ELLIOTT—*Sigma Alpha Epsilon*   Motion picture actor

SKINNAY ENNIS—*Alpha Sigma Phi*   Orchestra leader

BERGEN EVANS—*Beta Theta Pi*   TV commentator, moderator

EVERLY BROTHERS—*Tau Kappa Epsilon*   Vocalists

TOM EWELL—*Sigma Phi Epsilon* Motion picture and TV actor
NANETTE FABRAY—*Delta Zeta* TV and motion picture actress
DONNA FARGO—*Alpha Gamma Delta* Vocalist
WILLIAM FAULKNER—*Sigma Alpha Epsilon* Novelist
WILLIAM FAWCETT—*Theta Chi* Motion picture and TV actor
BARBARA FELDON—*Kappa Kappa Gamma* TV actress "Get Smart"
CLIFF FENNEMAN—*Phi Kappa Tau* TV Producer
FERRANTE & TEICHER—*Tau Kappa Epsilon* Pianists
PAT FINLEY—*Delta Delta Delta* TV actress
MYRON FLOREN—*Tau Kappa Epsilon* Musician
HARRISON FORD—*Sigma Nu* Motion picture actor
"TENNESSEE" ERNIE FORD—*Pi Kappa Alpha* TV host, vocalist
NANCY FOREMAN—*Chi Omega* TV personality "Today Show"
FREDERIC FORREST—*Delta Tau Delta* Motion picture and TV actor
HENDERSON FORSYTHE—*Theta Xi* TV and Broadway actor
RADNEY FOSTER—*Phi Gamma Delta* Vocalist "Foster and Lloyd"
"FOUR FRESHMEN"—*Tau Kappa Epsilon* Vocalists
"FOUR LADS"—*Tau Kappa Epsilon* Vocalists
MIKE FRANKOVICH—*Zeta Psi* Motion picture producer
MARY FRANN—*Delta Gamma* TV actress "Newhart"
SQUIRE FRIDELL—*Phi Sigma Kappa* TV actor and spokesman
JANE FROMAN—*Kappa Kappa Gamma* Vocalist
ROBERT FROST—*Theta Delta Chi* Poet
GEORGE FURTH—*Phi Gamma Delta* Motion picture actor, writer
MAX GAIL—*Alpha Delta Phi* TV actor "Barney Miller"
RAY GANDOLF—*Pi Kappa Alpha* TV commentator
ROBERT GARALSKY—*Sigma Alpha Epsilon* TV commentator
JAN GARBER—*Tau Kappa Epsilon* Vocalist
ART GARFUNKEL—*Alpha Epsilon Pi* Vocalist "Simon and Garfunkel"
DAVID GATES—*Delta Tau Delta* Vocalist "Bread"
JOHN GAVIN—*Chi Psi* Motion picture actor
WILL GEER—*Lambda Chi Alpha* Motion picture and TV actor "The Waltons"
CHRISTOPHER GEORGE—*Sigma Phi Epsilon* Motion picture and TV actor
FLORENCE GEORGE—*Alpha Delta Pi* Motion picture actress
PHYLLIS GEORGE—*Zeta Tau Alpha* TV hostess, personality

LEEZA GIBBONS—*Delta Delta Delta* TV personality
SHERIDAN GIBNEY—*Delta Kappa Epsilon* Motion picture screenwriter
TERRY GILLIAM—*Sigma Alpha Epsilon* Motion picture director, producer
FRANK GILROY—*Theta Chi* TV, Broadway writer
JACK GING—*Phi Kappa Sigma* TV actor
ANN BONNER GLASSCOCK—*Delta Delta Delta* Novelist
SAMUEL GOLDWYN, JR.—*Zeta Beta Tau* Motion picture producer, director
LOUIS GOSSETT, JR.—*Alpha Phi Alpha* Motion picture and TV actor
CHESTER GOULD—*Lambda Chi Alpha* Cartoonist "Dick Tracy"
AMY GRANT—*Kappa Alpha Theta* Vocalist
PETER GRAVES—*Phi Kappa Psi* TV and motion picture actor
GLENN GRAY—*Tau Kappa Epsilon* Orchestra leader
LINDA CROCKETT GRAY—*Gamma Phi Beta* Novelist
FRANCES GREER—*Phi Mu* Opera singer
ZANE GREY—*Sigma Nu* Novelist
MERV GRIFFIN—*Tau Kappa Epsilon* TV personality, producer
CATHY GRISEDE—*Delta Delta Delta* Cartoonist
GEORGE GRIZZARD—*Kappa Alpha Order* Motion picture, Broadway, TV actor
LEWIS GRIZZARD—*Sigma Pi* Writer
DAVE GUARD—*Sigma Nu* Vocalist "The Kingston Trio"
PAULA LEE HALLER—*Gamma Phi Beta* TV producer
TOM HALLICK—*Sigma Chi* TV and motion picture actor
RICHARD HALLIDAY—*Phi Kappa Psi* TV, Broadway producer
GEORGE HAMILTON IV—*Kappa Alpha Order* Vocalist
PAMELA LONG HAMMER—*Phi Mu* TV writer
JAMES HAMPTON—*Kappa Alpha Order* TV and motion picture actor
LIONEL HAMPTON—*Alpha Phi Alpha* Orchestra leader
JOHN HARDIN—*Sigma Chi* TV executive
DEAN HARGROVE—*Phi Delta Theta* TV producer, writer
RICHARD HARKNESS—*Delta Chi* TV commentator
WOODY HARRELSON—*Sigma Chi* TV and motion picture actor "Cheers"
JENILEE HARRISON—*Alpha Chi Omega* TV actress
LORENZ HART—*Phi Sigma Delta* Composer
DAVID HARTMAN—*Sigma Chi* TV actor, host
ALEX HARVEY—*Sigma Chi* Vocalist, composer
GWEN HARVEY—*Alpha Chi Omega* TV writer, director

PAUL HARVEY—*Lambda Chi Alpha*   TV, radio commentator

BOBBY HATFIELD—*Sigma Alpha Epsilon*   Vocalist "The Righteous Brothers"

ERNEST HAYCOX—*Delta Tau Delta*   Novelist

BILL HAYES—*Lambda Chi Alpha*   TV actor "Days of Our Lives"

EDITH HEAD—*Delta Zeta*   Motion picture costume designer

EILEEN HECKART—*Pi Beta Phi*   TV and motion picture actress

VAN HEFLIN—*Phi Delta Theta*   Motion picture actor

HORACE HEIDT—*Beta Theta Pi*   Orchester leader

FLORENCE HENDERSON—*Delta Zeta*   TV and Broadway actress, vocalist

MIKE HENRY—*Kappa Sigma*   Motion picture actor

JANE HENSON—*Alpha Xi Delta*   Co-creator of "The Muppets"

WOODY HERMAN—*Sigma Phi Epsilon*   Orchestra leader

ANTHONY HERRERA—*Sigma Chi*   TV actor

EDWARD HERRMANN—*Phi Kappa Psi*   Motion picture and TV actor

JEAN HERSHOLT—*Lambda Chi Alpha*   Motion picture actor

JOEL HIGGINS—*Delta Tau Delta*   TV actor "Silver Spoons"

STEVEN HILL—*Sigma Alpha Mu*   Motion picture and TV actor

WILLIAM HINDS—*Tau Kappa Epsilon*   Cartoonist

AL HODGE—*Delta Tau Delta*   TV actor "Captain Video"

REBECCA HOLDEN—*Zeta Tau Alpha*   TV actress

JACK HOLT—*Sigma Alpha Epsilon*   Motion picture actor

BOB HOPE—*Phi Kappa Theta*   TV personality, motion picture actor

MARILYN HORNE—*Chi Omega*   Opera singer

DAVID HOROWITZ—*Alpha Epsilon Pi*   TV personality

EDWARD EVERETT HORTON—*Phi Kappa Psi*   Motion picture and TV actor

CHUCK HOWARD—*Beta Theta Pi*   TV executive

JOHN HOWARD—*Delta Kappa Epsilon*   Motion picture and TV actor

SUSAN HOWARD—*Gamma Phi Beta*   TV actress "Dallas"

ELIZABETH HUDSON—*Delta Delta Delta*   TV executive

DAGNY HULTGREEN—*Delta Gamma*   TV commentator

GAYLE HUNNICUTT—*Kappa Kappa Gamma*   TV and motion picture actress

JEFFREY HUNTER—*Phi Delta Theta*   Motion picture actor

CHET HUNTLEY—*Sigma Alpha Epsilon*   TV commentator

JIM IBBOTSON—*Sigma Alpha Epsilon*   Vocalist "Nitty Gritty Dirt Band"

WILLIAM INGE—*Sigma Nu*   Motion picture, Broadway writer

BURL IVES—*Phi Sigma Kappa*   Motion picture and TV actor, musician

KATE JACKSON—*Kappa Kappa Gamma*   TV and motion picture actress

DEAN JAGGER—*Lambda Chi Alpha*   Motion picture and TV actor

JOHN JAKES—*Sigma Alpha Epsilon*   Novelist

RENNE JARRETT—*Delta Delta Delta*   TV actress

GEORGE JENKINS—*Delta Phi*   Motion picture art director

ROY JENSON—*Delta Tau Delta*   Motion picture actor

TOM JOHNSON—*Sigma Nu*   TV executive

OLLIE JOHNSTON—*Delta Tau Delta*   Motion picture animator

ROMAIN JOHNSON—*Delta Tau Delta*   TV art director

GORDON JONES—*Theta Xi*   Motion picture actor

JEFFREY JONES—*Beta Theta Pi*   Motion picture actor

JENNIFER JONES—*Kappa Alpha Theta*   Motion picture actress

KINLEY JONES—*Sigma Alpha Epsilon*   TV commentator

MERL JONES—*Alpha Tau Omega*   TV executive

BRENDA JOYCE—*Delta Gamma*   Motion picture actress

GORDON JUMP—*Kappa Sigma*   TV actor "WKRP"

SAMMY KAYE—*Theta Chi*   Orchestra leader

STACY KEACH—*Psi Upsilon*   TV and motion picture actor

BOB KEESHAN—*Sigma Pi*   TV actor "Captain Kangaroo"

AGNES KEITH—*Alpha Gamma Delta*   Novelist

VIRGINIA KELLOGG—*Alpha Gamma Delta*   Motion picture screenwriter

GENE KELLY—*Phi Kappa Theta*   Motion picture and TV actor, dancer

ARTHUR KENNEDY—*Phi Kappa Psi*   Motion picture and Broadway actor

DOUGLAS KENNEDY—*Psi Upsilon*   Motion picture actor

STAN KENTON—*Tau Kappa Epsilon*   Orchestra leader

HANK KETCHAM—*Phi Delta Theta*   Cartoonist "Dennis The Menace"

JOYCE KILMER—*Delta Upsilon*   Poet

FLORENCE KIRK—*Chi Omega*   Opera singer

JAMES KITCHELL—*Kappa Delta Rho*   Broadcasting executive

ROBERT KLEIN—*Zeta Beta Tau*   TV comedian, motion picture actor

FLETCHER KNEBEL—*Sigma Chi*   Novelist

"FUZZY" KNIGHT—*Sigma Nu*   Motion picture actor

DON KNOTTS—*Phi Sigma Kappa*   TV actor

GAIL KOBE—*Alpha Xi Delta*   TV producer

TED KOPPEL—*Pi Kappa Alpha*   TV commentator, host

KRESKIN—*Pi Kappa Alpha* TV personality
NANCY KULP—*Pi Beta Phi* Motion picture and TV actress "The Beverly Hillbillies"
IRV KUPCINET—*Tau Delta Phi* TV host, columnist
CHARLES KURALT—*Delta Psi* TV host, commentator
KAY KYSER—*Sigma Nu* Orchestra leader
DAVID LADD—*Delta Tau Delta* Motion picture actor, executive
CHRISTINE LAHTI—*Delta Gamma* Motion picture actress
FRANKIE LAINE—*Lambda Chi Alpha* Vocalist
JIM LANGE—*Phi Gamma Delta* TV game show host
FRANK LANGELLA—*Alpha Chi Rho* Motion picture and Broadway actor
CAROL LAWRENCE—*Alpha Xi Delta* TV and Broadway actress, vocalist
CLORIS LEACHMAN—*Gamma Phi Beta* TV and motion picture actress
HARPER LEE—*Chi Omega* Novelist
RICK LENZ—*Psi Upsilon* Motion picture and TV actor
SHELDON LEONARD—*Zeta Beta Tau* TV actor, producer
DAVID LETTERMAN—*Sigma Chi* TV host
"THE LETTERMEN"—*Tau Kappa Epsilon* Vocal group
FULTON LEWIS—*Sigma Nu* Radio commentator
JERRY LEWIS—*Alpha Epsilon Pi* TV and motion picture actor, comedian
RICHARD LEWIS—*Alpha Epsilon Pi* TV actor, comedian
ROBERT Q. LEWIS—*Phi Sigma Delta* TV game show host
ART LINKLETTER—*Alpha Tau Omega* TV host, personality
JACK LINKLETTER—*Beta Theta Pi* TV personality
JOHN LITEL—*Alpha Tau Omega* Motion picture actor
GLORIA LORING—*Alpha Gamma Delta* TV actress, vocalist
GARY LOCKWOOD—*Delta Sigma Phi* Motion picture and TV actor
JOHNNY LONG—*Sigma Nu* Orchestra leader
JOSEPH LOSEY—*Delta Upsilon* Motion picture director
BOB LOSURE—*Pi Kappa Alpha* TV commentator
JAMES RUSSELL LOWELL—*Alpha Delta Phi* Poet, writer
ELMER LOWER—*Alpha Tau Omega* TV executive
JOAN LUNDEN—*Delta Gamma* TV hostess
PETER LUPUS—*Sigma Chi* TV actor "Mission Impossible"
PEG LYNCH—*Gamma Phi Beta* TV writer
PAUL LYNDE—*Phi Kappa Sigma* TV and motion picture comedian, actor
PETER MAAS—*Sigma Nu* Novelist
TED MACK—*Sigma Phi Epsilon* TV host

CATHERINE MACKIN—*Alpha Omicron Pi* TV commentator
JOHN D. MacDONALD—*Delta Tau Delta* Novelist
BARTON MacLANE—*Chi Psi* Motion picture actor
ARCHIBALD MacLEISH—*Psi Upsilon* Playwright, poet
MEREDITH MacRAE—*Delta Delta Delta* TV and motion picture actress
GEORGE MACREADY—*Delta Phi* Motion picture actor
MARJORIE MAIN—*Delta Delta Delta* Motion picture actress
JOSEPH MANKEWICZ—*Phi Sigma Delta* Motion picture producer
DELBERT MANN—*Kappa Alpha Order* Motion picture and TV director
FREDRIC MARCH—*Alpha Delta Phi* Motion picture actor
ED MARINARO—*Psi Upsilon* TV actor "Hill Street Blues"
GARRY MARSHALL—*Alpha Tau Omega* TV and motion picture producer, director, writer
FREDDY MARTIN—*Tau Kappa Epsilon* Orchestra leader
WINK MARTINDALE—*Kappa Sigma* TV game show host
JAMES MASON—*Phi Sigma Epsilon* Motion picture actor
JERRY MATHERS—*Chi Psi* TV actor "Leave it to Beaver"
LEO McCAREY—*Delta Chi* Motion picture director, producer
RUE McCLANAHAN—*Kappa Alpha Theta* TV actress "The Golden Girls"
TED McGINLEY—*Sigma Chi* Motion picture and TV actor
KERRY McCLUGGAGE—*Sigma Chi* TV executive
BOB McGRATH—*Phi Gamma Delta* TV personality "Sesame Street"
ED McMAHON—*Phi Kappa Theta* TV personality
JAMES MELTON—*Delta Tau Delta* Opera singer, TV personality
DON MEREDITH—*Phi Delta Theta* TV actor
GARY MERRILL—*Delta Kappa Epsilon* Motion picture and TV actor
DENNY MILLER—*Phi Gamma Delta* Motion picture and TV actor
GLENN MILLER—*Sigma Nu* Orchestra leader
RON MILLER—*Sigma Chi* Motion picture and TV executive
TAYLOR MILLER—*Chi Omega* TV actress "All My Children"
DONNA MILLS—*Delta Gamma* Motion picture and TV actress "Knots Landing"
MARTIN MILNER—*Phi Sigma Kappa* TV and motion picture actor
WALTER MIRISCH—*Zeta Beta Tau* Motion picture producer
PAT MITCHELL—*Phi Mu* TV personality, commentator

MARY ANN MOBLEY—*Chi Omega*   Motion picture and TV actress, hostess

VAUGHN MONROE—*Sigma Nu*   Vocalist, TV and motion picture actor

WILLIAM MONROE—*Sigma Chi*   TV moderator

EDWARD P. MORGAN—*Beta Theta Pi*   Radio commentator

RALPH MORGAN—*Phi Gamma Delta*   Motion picture actor

WILLIE MORRIS—*Delta Tau Delta*   Novelist, writer, magazine editor

BUDDY MORROW—*Tau Kappa Epsilon*   Orchestra leader

GREG MULLAVEY—*Sigma Chi*   TV and film actor

ROGER MUDD—*Delta Tau Delta*   TV commentator

EDWARD R. MURROW—*Kappa Sigma*   TV commentator

PAMELA MYERS—*Delta Delta Delta*   Broadway and TV actress

JIM NABORS—*Delta Tau Delta*   TV and movie actor, vocalist

GEORGE NADER—*Phi Gamma Delta*   Motion picture actor

CONRAD NAGEL—*Sigma Alpha Epsilon*   Motion picture actor

PATRICIA NEAL—*Pi Beta Phi*   Motion picture actress

DAVID NELSON—*Kappa Sigma*   TV actor

OZZIE NELSON—*Alpha Chi Rho*   TV actor, producer

PAUL NEWMAN—*Phi Kappa Tau*   Motion picture actor, director

JOHN NICHOLS—*Theta Delta Chi*   Novelist

LLOYD NOLAN—*Delta Kappa Epsilon*   Motion picture and TV actor

WAYNE NORTHRUP—*Sigma Chi*   TV actor

DEBORAH NORVILLE—*Delta Delta Delta*   TV hostess, commentator

ELLIOTT NUGENT—*Phi Kappa Psi*   Motion picture and Broadway actor, director

CHRIS NYBY—*Tau Kappa Epsilon*   TV director

CARROLL O'CONNOR—*Sigma Phi Epsilon*   Motion picture and TV actor "All in the Family"

OLIVER (WILLIAM SWOFFORD)—*Chi Phi*   Vocalist

DON OLIVER—*Sigma Chi*   TV commentator

CHARLES "BLACKIE" O'NEAL—*Delta Tau Delta*   TV screenwriter

ROBERT OSBORNE—*Delta Upsilon*   TV actor

RANDY OWEN—*Pi Kappa Phi*   Vocalist "Alabama"

WILLIAM PALEY—*Zeta Beta Tau*   Broadcasting executive

PETER PALMER—*Kappa Sigma*   Broadway and motion picture actor, vocalist

JOHN PALMER—*Sigma Alpha Epsilon*   TV commentator

FESS PARKER—*Pi Kappa Alpha*   Motion picture and TV actor "Davy Crockett"

JAMISON PARKER—*Tau Kappa Epsilon*   TV actor "Simon and Simon"

LARRY PARKS—*Sigma Alpha Epsilon*   Motion picture actor

GAIL PATRICK—*Delta Zeta*   TV producer and actress

LES PAUL—*Tau Kappa Epsilon*   Musician

JANE PAULEY—*Kappa Kappa Gamma*   TV hostess

E.J. PEAKER—*Delta Delta Delta*   TV actress

NORMAN VINCENT PEAL—*Phi Gamma Delta*   TV host, writer

RUTH STAFFORD PEALE—*Alpha Phi*   TV producer, writer

MARY BETH PEIL—*Gamma Phi Beta*   Broadway actress, opera singer

DREW PEARSON—*Kappa Sigma*   Radio commentator, journalist

NATE PENDLETON—*Delta Upsilon*   Motion picture actor

GEORGE PEPPARD—*Beta Theta Pi*   Motion picture and TV actor "The A Team"

WALKER PERCY—*Sigma Alpha Epsilon*   Novelist

ANTHONY PERKINS—*Kappa Alpha Order*   Motion picture actor

JO ANN PFLUG—*Kappa Kappa Gamma*   Motion picture and TV actress

JANE PICKENS—*Zeta Tau Alpha*   Motion picture actress

ROBERT PINE—*Phi Delta Theta*   TV actor

COLE PORTER—*Delta Kappa Epsilon*   Composer

TOM POSTON—*Sigma Nu*   TV actor "Newhart"

DICK POWELL—*Sigma Alpha Epsilon*   Motion picture and TV actor, producer

ELVIS PRESLEY—*Tau Kappa Epsilon*   Vocalist, motion picture actor

VINCENT PRICE—*Alpha Sigma Phi*   Motion picture and TV actor

WILLIAM PRINCE—*Alpha Delta Phi*   Motion picture and TV actor

Le ROY PRINZ—*Lambda Chi Alpha*   Motion picture producer, director

JAMES PRITCHETT—*Phi Delta Theta*   TV actor

DOROTHY PROVINE—*Alpha Gamma Delta*   TV and motion picture actress

ZEV PUTTERMAN—*Phi Kappa Tau*   TV producer

ERNIE PYLE—*Sigma Alpha Epsilon*   Journalist

WARD QUAAL—*Delta Tau Delta*   Broadcasting executive

JANE BRYANT QUINN—*Pi Beta Phi*   TV commentator, columnist

CHARLOTTE RAE—*Alpha Epsilon Phi*   TV actress "Facts of Life"

ALAN RAFKIN—*Sigma Alpha Mu*   TV director, producer

JOHN S. RAGIN—*Delta Tau Delta*   TV actor "Quincy"

MARTIN RANSOHOFF—*Phi Gamma Delta*   Motion picture executive

RONALD REAGAN—*Tau Kappa Epsilon*   Motion picture and TV actor

HARRY REASONER—*Theta Chi*   TV commentator

ROBERT REDFORD—*Kappa Sigma*   Motion picture actor, director

ROBERT REED—*Beta Theta Pi*   TV actor "The Brady Bunch"
ED REIMERS—*Alpha Sigma Phi*   TV spokesman
BURT REYNOLDS—*Phi Delta Theta*   Motion picture and TV actor
FRANK REYNOLDS—*Lambda Chi Alpha*   TV commentator
QUENTIN REYNOLDS—*Delta Tau Delta*   Journalist
VIRGINIA GARBESON RICH—*Gamma Phi Beta*   Novelist
JEFF RICHARDS—*Sigma Chi*   Motion picture and TV actor
ANN RICHARDSON—*Sigma Kappa*   TV producer
JAMES WHITCOMB RILEY—*Phi Kappa Psi*   Poet
JOHN RITTER—*Phi Gamma Delta*   TV and motion picture actor
TONY ROBERTS—*Tau Delta Phi*   Motion picture and Broadway actor
NAN ROBERTSON—*Alpha Phi*   Columnist, writer
PAT ROBERTSON—*Sigma Alpha Epsilon*   TV personality, host
ROBERT ROCKWELL—*Tau Kappa Epsilon*   TV actor
MARCIA RODD—*Kappa Kappa Gamma*   Motion picture and TV actress
RICHARD RODGERS—*Zeta Beta Tau*   Composer, Broadway producer
BUDDY ROGERS—*Phi Kappa Psi*   Motion picture actor
ANDY ROONEY—*Sigma Chi*   TV commentator
AARON ROSENBERG—*Zeta Beta Tau*   Motion picture producer
LANNY ROSS—*Zeta Psi*   Vocalist
PHILIP ROTH—*Sigma Alpha Mu*   Novelist
TIM ROSSOVICH—*Sigma Chi*   Motion picture and TV actor
GENA ROWLANDS—*Kappa Kappa Gamma*   Motion picture and TV actress
ROBERT RUARK—*Phi Kappa Sigma*   Novelist
HUGHES RUDD—*Sigma Alpha Epsilon*   TV commentator
ROBERT RYAN—*Psi Upsilon*   Motion picture actor
EVA MARIE SAINT—*Delta Gamma*   Motion picture actress
GENE SAKS—*Zeta Beta Tau*   Motion picture and Broadway director, actor
"CHIC" SALE—*Sigma Nu*   Motion picture actor
WALDO SALT—*Alpha Kappa Lambda*   Motion picture screenwriter
CHRIS SARANDON—*Phi Sigma Kappa*   Motion picture actor
BOB SARLATTE—*Delta Tau Delta*   TV comedian
DAVID SARNOFF—*Tau Delta Phi*   Broadcasting executive
GAILARD SARTAIN—*Kappa Sigma*   TV and motion picture actor
VAN GORDON SAUTER—*Phi Delta Theta*   Broadcasting executive
DORE SCHARY—*Tau Delta Phi*   Motion picture producer, director, screenwriter

ROY SCHEIDER—*Phi Kappa Psi*   Motion picture actor
BOB SCHIEFFER—*Phi Delta Theta*   TV commentator
STEPHEN SCHNETZER—*Alpha Sigma Phi*   TV actor "Another World"
RON SCHWARY—*Sigma Chi*   Motion picture producer
MARTHA SCOTT—*Delta Gamma*   Motion picture and TV actress
RANDOLPH SCOTT—*Kappa Alpha Order*   Motion picture actor
WILLARD SCOTT—*Alpha Sigma Phi*   TV personality
TOM SELLECK—*Sigma Chi*   TV and motion picture actor
DR. SEUSS (TED GEISEL)—*Sigma Phi Epsilon*   Writer, cartoonist
TED SHACKELFORD—*Phi Delta Theta*   TV actor "Knots Landing"
JOHNNY SHEFFIELD—*Delta Tau Delta*   Motion picture actor "Bomba"
GARY SHEPPARD—*Sigma Phi Epsilon*   TV Commentator
ALLAN SHERMAN—*Sigma Alpha Mu*   Vocalist
DINAH SHORE—*Alpha Epsilon Pi*   TV personality, vocalist
TOM SHIPLEY—*Alpha Sigma Phi*   Vocalist "Brewer and Shipley"
RICHARD SHOBERG—*Alpha Tau Omega*   TV actor "All My Children"
IRVING SHULMAN—*Phi Epsilon Pi*   Novelist, playwright
ANDY SIDARIS—*Sigma Alpha Epsilon*   Motion picture and TV producer, director
PAUL SIMON—*Alpha Epsilon Pi*   Vocalist "Simon and Garfunkel"
JEREMY SLATE—*Beta Theta Pi* TV   actor
JEAN SMART—*Alpha Delta Pi*   TV actress "Designing Women"
HOWARD K. SMITH—*Alpha Tau Omega*   TV commentator
KENT SMITH—*Kappa Sigma*   Motion picture and TV actor
TOM SMOTHERS—*Phi Sigma Kappa*   TV personality, vocalist "The Smothers Brothers"
STEPHEN SONDHEIM—*Beta Theta Pi*   Broadway composer, writer
STEVEN SPIELBERG—*Theta Chi*   Motion picture director, producer
LAWRENCE SPIVAK—*Sigma Alpha Mu*   TV producer
FRANK STANTON—*Phi Delta Theta*   Broadcasting executive
CHARLES STARRETT—*Psi Upsilon*   Motion picture actor "The Durango Kid"
LILIBET STERN—*Zeta Tau Alpha*   TV actress "The Young and the Restless"
GEORGE STEVENS, JR.—*Phi Gamma Delta*   Motion picture and TV producer
SHADDOE STEVENS—*Sigma Nu*   TV personality

McLEAN STEVENSON—*Phi Gamma Delta* TV actor

JAY STEWART—*Sigma Chi* TV announcer

IRVING STONE—*Phi Epsilon Pi* Novelist

MARY STUART—*Delta Delta Delta* TV actress "Search for Tomorrow"

WILLIAM STYRON—*Phi Delta Theta* Novelist

HOPE SUMMERS—*Gamma Phi Beta* TV actress "The Andy Griffith Show"

DENNIS SWANSON—*Sigma Chi* Broadcasting executive

INGA SWENSON—*Alpha Phi* TV actress "Benson"

BOOTH TARKINGTON—*Sigma Chi* Novelist, playwright

DON TAYLOR—*Sigma Nu* Motion picture actor, director

JOHN TESH—*Lambda Chi Alpha* TV personality

STEVE TESICH—*Phi Kappa Psi* Motion picture screenwriter

BRYNN THAYER—*Delta Delta Delta* TV actress

ALAN THICKE—*Delta Upsilon* TV actor "Growing Pains"

DANNY THOMAS—*Tau Kappa Epsilon* TV actor, personality

FRANK THOMAS—*Theta Delta Chi* Motion picture animator

MARLO THOMAS—*Kappa Alpha Theta* TV and motion picture actress

LOWELL THOMAS—*Kappa Sigma* Radio commentator, writer

MARSHALL THOMPSON—*Phi Gamma Delta* Motion picture and TV actor

SADA THOMPSON—*Kappa Alpha Theta* TV and Broadway actress "Family"

RICHARD THRELKELD—*Delta Upsilon* TV commentator

JAMES THURBER—*Phi Kappa Psi* Humorist, writer

KEVIN TIGHE—*Sigma Alpha Epsilon* TV actor

MARK TINKER—*Sigma Chi* TV producer

PRESTON TISCH—*Sigma Alpha Mu* Motion picture executive

"PINKY" TOMLIN—*Delta Tau Delta* Composer, motion picture actor

FRANCHOT TONE—*Alpha Delta Phi* Motion picture actor

REGIS TOOMEY—*Sigma Chi* Motion picture actor

RIP TORN—*Sigma Chi* Motion picture actor

DEAN TORRANCE—*Phi Sigma Kappa* Vocalist "Jan and Dean"

JOHN SCOTT TROTTER—*Delta Sigma Phi* Orchestra leader

LAMAR TROTTI—*Delta Tau Delta* Motion picture producer, screenwriter

BOBBY TROUP—*Sigma Alpha Epsilon* Motion picture actor, musician

DALTON TRUMBO—*Delta Tau Delta* Motion picture screenwriter, novelist

SONNY TUFTS—*Delta Kappa Epsilon* Motion picture actor

ED TURNER—*Phi Gamma Delta* Broadcasting executive

ROBERT URICH—*Lambda Chi Alpha* TV and motion picture actor

RUDY VALLEE—*Sigma Alpha Epsilon* Motion picture and TV actor, vocalist

MARILYN VanDERBER—*Pi Beta Phi* TV personality

NED VAUGHN—*Kappa Alpha Order* TV and motion picture actor

CHARLIE VENTURA—*Tau Kappa Epsilon* Orchestra leader

JESSE VINT—*Phi Gamma Delta* Motion picture actor

PHIL VOLK—*Sigma Nu* Vocalist, musician "Paul Revere and the Raiders"

HELEN WAGNER—*Kappa Kappa Gamma* TV actress "As the World Turns"

RALPH WAITE—*Lambda Chi Alpha* TV actor "The Waltons"

PHIL WALDEN—*Phi Delta Theta* Recording executive, producer

WILLIAM WALKER—*Phi Kappa Sigma* Opera singer

MARSHA WALLACE—*Delta Zeta* TV actress

MIKE WALLACE—*Zeta Beta Tau* TV commentator

WALTER WANGER—*Alpha Delta Phi* Motion picture producer

FRED WARING—*Alpha Chi Rho* Orchestra leader

JACK WARNER—*Zeta Beta Tau* Motion picture and TV producer

JOHN WAYNE—*Sigma Chi* Motion picture actor

PATRICK WAYNE—*Alpha Delta Gamma* Motion picture and TV actor

SHAWN WEATHERLY—*Delta Delta Delta* Motion picture and TV actress

MARJORIE WEAVER—*Kappa Kappa Gamma* Motion picture actress

TED WEEMS—*Delta Sigma Phi* Orchestra leader

LAWRENCE WELK—*Tau Kappa Epsilon* TV host, orchestra leader

ROB WELLER—*Beta Theta Pi* TV host

DAWN WELLS—*Alpha Chi Omega* TV actress "Gilligan's Island"

NED WERTIMER—*Phi Gamma Delta* TV and Broadway actor

ADAM WEST—*Beta Theta Pi* Motion picture and TV actor "Batman"

JAMES WESTMAN—*Delta Tau Delta* TV and motion picture director

MICHAEL WESTMORE—*Lambda Chi Alpha* Motion picture makeup artist

E.B. WHITE—*Phi Gamma Delta* Novelist

MARY WICKS—*Phi Mu* TV and motion picture actress

GENE WILDER—*Alpha Epsilon Pi* Motion picture actor

THORNTON WILDER—*Alpha Delta Phi* Novelist, playwright

TENNESSEE WILLIAMS—*Alpha Tau Omega* Playwright

DON WILSON—*Sigma Chi*   TV announcer "Jack Benny Show"
EARL WILSON—*Alpha Tau Omega*   Columnist, writer
HUGH WILSON—*Phi Delta Theta*   TV and motion picture screenwriter
WALTER WINCHELL—*Alpha Epsilon Pi*   Radio commentator, columnist
THOMAS WOLFE—*Pi Kappa Phi*   Novelist
JAMES WOODS—*Theta Delta Chi*   Motion picture actor
ROBERT WOODS—*Sigma Alpha Epsilon*   TV actor
JOANNE WOODWARD—*Chi Omega*   Motion picture and TV actress

MORGAN WOODWARD—*Pi Kappa Alpha*   Motion picture and TV actor "Dallas"
MONTE WOOLLEY—*Alpha Delta Phi*   Motion picture actor
JUDGE JOSEPH WOPNER—*Tau Epsilon Phi*   TV actor
ALEXANDRA YORK—*Phi Mu*   TV actress, personality
ROBERT YOUNG—*Sigma Alpha Epsilon*   Motion picture and TV actor "Marcus Welby"
RICHARD ZANUCK—*Phi Gamma Delta*   Motion picture producer

Famous Greeks—Olympics

Acacia	Van Bebber, Jack	USA	1932	GOLD	Wrestling
Alpha Chi Omega	Rogers, Annette	USA	1932	GOLD	Track & Field
Alpha Chi Omega	Rogers, Annette	USA	1936	GOLD	Track & Field
Alpha Delta Phi	Carpenter, Leonard	USA	1924	GOLD	Rowing
Alpha Delta Phi	Kingsbury, Howard	USA	1924	GOLD	Rowing
Alpha Delta Phi	Lindley, Alfred	USA	1924	GOLD	Rowing
Alpha Delta Phi	Wilson, Alfred	USA	1924	GOLD	Rowing
Alpha Delta Phi	Babcock, Harold	USA	1912	GOLD	Track & Field
Alpha Delta Phi	Foss, Frank	USA	1920	GOLD	Track & Field
Alpha Delta Phi	Taber, Norman	USA	1912	GOLD	Track & Field
Alpha Gamma Rho	Wigger, Lones	USA	1972	GOLD	Shooting (2)
Alpha Kappa Lambda	Richards, Bob	USA	1952	GOLD	Track & Field
Alpha Kappa Lambda	Richards, Bob	USA	1956	GOLD	Track & Field
Alpha Phi Alpha	Metcalfe, Ralph	USA	1936	GOLD	Track & Field
Alpha Phi Alpha	Owens, Jesse	USA	1936	GOLD	Track & Field (4)
Alpha Sigma Phi	Jastram, Burton	USA	1932	GOLD	Rowing
Alpha Sigma Phi	Reed, Robin	USA	1924	GOLD	Wrestling
Alpha Tau Omega	Pippin, Daniel	USA	1952	GOLD	Basketball
Alpha Tau Omega	Williams, Howard	USA	1952	GOLD	Basketball
Alpha Tau Omega	Morris, Glenn	USA	1936	GOLD	Track & Field
Alpha Tau Omega	Russell, Henry	USA	1928	GOLD	Track & Field
Alpha Tau Omega	Davies, John	AUS	1952	GOLD	Swimming
Beta Theta Pi	Counts, Mel	USA	1964	GOLD	Basketball
Beta Theta Pi	Lucas, Jerry	USA	1960	GOLD	Basketball
Beta Theta Pi	Eagan, Edward	USA	1932	GOLD	Bobsledding
Beta Theta Pi	Rimkus, Edward	USA	1948	GOLD	Bobsledding
Beta Theta Pi	Eagan, Edward	USA	1920	GOLD	Boxing
Beta Theta Pi	Clotworthy, Robert	USA	1956	GOLD	Diving
Beta Theta Pi	Miller, John	USA	1924	GOLD	Rowing
Beta Theta Pi	Thompson, William	USA	1928	GOLD	Rowing
Beta Theta Pi	Furniss, Bruce	USA	1976	GOLD	Swimming (2)
Beta Theta Pi	Harrison, George	USA	1960	GOLD	Swimming
Beta Theta Pi	Kojac, George	USA	1928	GOLD	Swimming (2)
Beta Theta Pi	Rose, Murray	AUS	1956	GOLD	Swimming (3)
Beta Theta Pi	Rose, Murray	AUS	1960	GOLD	Swimming (2)
Beta Theta Pi	Roth, Richard	USA	1964	GOLD	Swimming
Beta Theta Pi	Bragg, Don	USA	1960	GOLD	Track & Field
Beta Theta Pi	Cochran, Leroy	USA	1948	GOLD	Track & Field (2)
Beta Theta Pi	Hamm, Ed	USA	1928	GOLD	Track & Field
Beta Theta Pi	Pearce, Robert	USA	1932	GOLD	Wrestling
Beta Theta Pi	North, Lowell	USA	1968	GOLD	Yachting
Beta Theta Pi	Doe, Charles W.	USA	1920	GOLD	Rugby
Beta Theta Pi	Doe, Charles W.	USA	1924	GOLD	Rugby

Beta Theta Pi	Helffrich, Alan	USA	1924	GOLD	Track & Field
Chi Phi	Schardt, Arlie	USA	1912	GOLD	Track & Field
Chi Phi	Barton, Greg	USA	1988	GOLD	Kayaking
Chi Psi	Degener, Richard	USA	1936	GOLD	Diving
Chi Psi	Webster, Robert	USA	1960	GOLD	Diving
Chi Psi	Webster, Robert	USA	1964	GOLD	Diving
Chi Psi	Carr, Sabin	USA	1920	GOLD	Track & Field
Chi Psi	Charlton, Thomas	USA	1956	GOLD	Rowing
Chi Psi	Cooke, John P.	USA	1956	GOLD	Rowing
Chi Psi	Morey, Robert	USA	1956	GOLD	Rowing
Delta Chi	Bishop, Ralph	USA	1936	GOLD	Basketball
Delta Chi	Lubin, Frank	USA	1936	GOLD	Basketball
Delta Chi	Fuqua, Iran	USA	1932	GOLD	Track & Field
Delta Kappa Epsilon	Walsh, James	USA	1956	GOLD	Basketball
Delta Kappa Epsilon	Mason, Geoffrey	USA	1928	GOLD	Bobsledding
Delta Kappa Epsilon	Parke, Richard	USA	1928	GOLD	Bobsledding
Delta Kappa Epsilon	Rockefeller, James	USA	1924	GOLD	Rowing
Delta Kappa Epsilon	Fish, George	USA	1920	GOLD	Rugby
Delta Kappa Epsilon	Tilden, Charles	USA	1920	GOLD	Rugby
Delta Kappa Epsilon	Williams, Alan	USA	1924	GOLD	Rugby
Delta Kappa Epsilon	Schallender, Don	USA	1964	GOLD	Swimming (4)
Delta Kappa Epsilon	Schallander, Don	USA	1968	GOLD	Swimming (1)
Delta Kappa Epsilon	Baxter, Irving	USA	1900	GOLD	Track & Field (2)
Delta Kappa Epsilon	Craig, Ralph	USA	1912	GOLD	Track & Field (2)
Delta Kappa Epsilon	Dyer, Hector	USA	1932	GOLD	Track & Field
Delta Kappa Epsilon	Kiesel, Robert	USA	1932	GOLD	Track & Field
Delta Kappa Epsilon	Meredith, James	USA	1912	GOLD	Track & Field (2)
Delta Kappa Epsilon	Miller, William	USA	1932	GOLD	Track & Field
Delta Kappa Epsilon	Thompson, Earl	CAN	1920	GOLD	Track & Field
Delta Kappa Epsilon	Woodring, Allen	USA	1920	GOLD	Track & Field
Delta Kappa Epsilon	Friedrichs, George	USA	1968	GOLD	Yachting
Delta Kappa Epsilon	Jahncke, Barton	USA	1968	GOLD	Yachting
Deja Kappa Epsilon	Sheffield, Frederick	USA	1924	GOLD	Rowing
Delta Kappa Epsilon	Tucker, Nion	USA	1928	GOLD	Bobsledding
Delta Kappa Epsilon	Curtis, Thomas	USA	1896	GOLD	Track & Field
Delta Phi	Stevens, Curtis	USA	1932	GOLD	Bobsledding
Delta Psi	Carr, William	USA	1932	GOLD	Track & Field
Delta Psi	Chance, Britton	USA	1952	GOLD	Yachting
Delta Tau Delta	Jeangerard, Robert	USA	1956	GOLD	Basketball
Delta Tau Delta	Tomsic, Ron	USA	1956	GOLD	Basketball
Delta Tau Delta	Salisbury, Edwin	USA	1932	GOLD	Rowing
Delta Tau Delta	Larson, Lance	USA	1960	GOLD	Swimming
Delta Tau Delta	Saari, Roy	USA	1960	GOLD	Swimming
Delta Tau Delta	Scholes, Clark	USA	1952	GOLD	Swimming
Delta Tau Delta	Baker, Walter	USA	1956	GOLD	Track & Field
Delta Tau Delta	King, Robert	USA	1928	GOLD	Track & Field
Delta Tau Delta	Lightbody, Jim	USA	1904	GOLD	Track & Field (3)
Delta Tau Delta	Lightbody, Jim	USA	1906	GOLD	Track & Field (1)
Delta Tau Delta	Oerter, Al	USA	1956	GOLD	Track & Field
Delta Tau Delta	Oerter, Al	USA	1960	GOLD	Track & Field
Delta Tau Delta	Oerter, Al	USA	1964	GOLD	Track & Field
Delta Tau Delta	Oerter, Al	USA	1968	GOLD	Track & Field
Delta Tau Delta	Spencer, Emerson	USA	1928	GOLD	Track & Field
Delta Tau Delta	Burnand, Al	USA	1932	GOLD	Yachting
Delta Tau Delta	Cooper, William	USA	1932	GOLD	Yachting
Delta Upsilon	Anderson, John	USA	1932	GOLD	Track & Field
Delta Upsilon	Ashenfelter, Horace	USA	1952	GOLD	Track & Field
Delta Upsilon	Morrison, Allie	USA	1928	GOLD	Wrestling
Delta Upsilon	Kenney, Robert Earl	USA	1952	GOLD	Basketball
Delta Upsilon	Wolfe, Rowland	USA	1932	GOLD	Gymnastics
Gamma Phi Beta	Bauer, Sybil	USA	1924	GOLD	Swimming
Kappa Alpha	Paddock, Charles	USA	1920	GOLD	Track & Field (2)

Kappa Alpha	Scholz, Jackson	USA	1920	GOLD	Track & Field (1)
Kappa Alpha	Scholz, Jackson	USA	1924	GOLD	Track & Field (1)
Kappa Alpha	Seagren, Bob	USA	1968	GOLD	Track & Field
Kappa Alpha	Wykoff, Frank	USA	1928	GOLD	Track & Field
Kappa Alpha	Wykoff, Frank	USA	1932	GOLD	Track & Field
Kappa Alpha	Wykoff, Frank	USA	1936	GOLD	Track & Field
Kappa Alpha Psi	Russell, William	USA	1956	GOLD	Basketball
Kappa Alpha Theta	Curtis, Ann	USA	1948	GOLD	Swimming
Kappa Delta	Marshall, Ann		1976	GOLD	Swimming
Kappa Delta Rho	Osborn, Harold	USA	1924	GOLD	Track & Field (2)
Kappa Kappa Gamma	DeVarona, Donna	USA	1964	GOLD	Swimming (2)
Kappa Kappa Gamma	Wightman, Hazel	USA	1924	GOLD	Tennis (2)
Kappa Kappa Gamma	Willis, Helen	USA	1924	GOLD	Tennis (2)
Kappa Kappa Gamma	Robinson, Elizabeth	USA	1928	GOLD	Track & Field (1)
Kappa Kappa Gamma	Robinson, Elizabeth	USA	1936	GOLD	Track & Field (1)
Kappa Sigma	Gallagher, Vincent	USA	1920	GOLD	Rowing
Kappa Sigma	Farrish, Linn	USA	1924	GOLD	Rugby
Kappa Sigma	Barbuti, Ray	USA	1928	GOLD	Track & Field
Kappa Sigma	Davis, Glenn	USA	1956	GOLD	Track & Field (1)
Kappa Sigma	Davis, Glenn	USA	1960	GOLD	Track & Field (2)
Kappa Sigma	Gutterson, Al	USA	1912	GOLD	Track & Field
Kappa Sigma	Patton, Mel	USA	1948	GOLD	Track & Field (2)
Kappa Sigma	Osthoff, Oscar	USA	1904	GOLD	Weight Lifting
Kappa Sigma	Hunter, Francis	USA	1924	GOLD	Tennis
Lambda Chi Alpha	Brown, Larry	USA	1964	GOLD	Basketball
Lambda Chi Alpha	Clawson, John	USA	1968	GOLD	Basketball
Lambda Chi Alpha	Smith, Adrian	USA	1960	GOLD	Basketball
Omega Psi Phi	Ewell, Harold N.	USA	1948	GOLD	Track & Field
Phi Delta Alpha	Ashworth, Gerald	USA	1964	GOLD	Track & Field
Phi Delta Theta	Skelton, Robert	USA	1924	GOLD	Swimming
Phi Delta Theta	Toomey, William	USA	1968	GOLD	Track & Field
Phi Delta Theta	Clapp, Austin	USA	1928	GOLD	Swimming
Phi Delta Theta	Lienhard, William B.	USA	1952	GOLD	Basketball
Phi Delta Theta	Wells, Wayne	USA	1972	GOLD	Wrestling
Phi Delta Theta	Russell, Doug	USA	1968	GOLD	Swimming (2)
Phi Delta Theta	Jones, Wallace	USA	1948	GOLD	Basketball
Phi Delta Theta	Desjardins, Pete	USA	1928	GOLD	Diving (2)
Phi Delta Theta	Sitzberger, Ken	USA	1964	GOLD	Diving
Phi Delta Theta	Jenkins, David	USA	1960	GOLD	Figure Skating
Phi Delta Theta	Jenkins, Hayes	USA	1956	GOLD	Figure Skating
Phi Delta Theta	Windle, Robert	USA	1964	GOLD	Swimming
Phi Delta Theta	Wrenn, Heaton	USA	1964	GOLD	Rugby
Phi Delta Theta	Hickox, Charles	USA	1968	GOLD	Swimming (3)
Phi Delta Theta	Kiefer, Adolph	USA	1936	GOLD	Swimming
Phi Delta Theta	Medica, Jack	USA	1936	GOLD	Swimming
Phi Delta Theta	Mulliken, William	USA	1960	GOLD	Swimming
Phi Delta Theta	O'Connor, James	USA	1924	GOLD	Swimming
Phi Epsilon Pi	Clarke, Louis	USA	1924	GOLD	Track & Field
Phi Kappa Psi	Arnette, Jay	USA	1960	GOLD	Basketball
Phi Kappa Psi	Bontemps, Ronald	USA	1952	GOLD	Basketball
Phi Kappa Psi	Ford, Gilbert	USA	1956	GOLD	Basketball
Phi Kappa Psi	Pinkston, Clarence	USA	1920	GOLD	Diving
Phi Kappa Psi	Graham, Norris	USA	1932	GOLD	Rowing
Phi Kappa Psi	Valentine, Al	USA	1924	GOLD	Rugby
Phi Kappa Psi	Burton, Michael	USA	1968	GOLD	Swimming (2)
Phi Kappa Psi	Burton, Michael	USA	1972	GOLD	Swimming (1)
Phi Kappa Psi	Kinsella, John	USA	1972	GOLD	Swimming
Phi Kappa Psi	Spitz, Mark	USA	1968	GOLD	Swimming (2)
Phi Kappa Psi	Spitz, Mark	USA	1972	GOLD	Swimming (7)
Phi Kappa Psi	Schmidt, Fred	USA	1964	GOLD	Swimming
Phi Kappa Psi	Stamm, Mike	USA	1972	GOLD	Swimming
Phi Kappa Psi	Troy, Mike	USA	1960	GOLD	Swimming (2)

Phi Kappa Psi	O'Brien, Parry	USA	1952	GOLD	Track & Field (1)
Phi Kappa Psi	O'Brien, Parry	USA	1956	GOLD	Track & Field (1)
Phi Kappa Psi	Saling, George	USA	1932	GOLD	Track & Field
Phi Kappa Psi	Smith, Owen	USA	1948	GOLD	Track & Field
Phi Kappa Psi	Spellman, John	USA	1924	GOLD	Wrestling
Phi Gamma Delta	Darling, Charles	USA	1956	GOLD	Basketball
Phi Gamma Delta	Houghland, William	USA	1952	GOLD	Basketball
Phi Gamma Delta	Houghland, William	USA	1956	GOLD	Basketball
Phi Gamma Delta	Hurley, Marcus	USA	1904	GOLD	Cycling (4)
Phi Gamma Delta	Wrighson, Bernard	USA	1968	GOLD	Diving
Phi Gamma Delta	Hume, Donald	USA	1936	GOLD	Rowing
Phi Gamma Delta	Martin, Robert	USA	1948	GOLD	Rowing
Phi Gamma Delta	Moch, Robert	USA	1936	GOLD	Rowing
Phi Gamma Delta	Westlund, Warren	USA	1948	GOLD	Rowing
Phi Gamma Delta	Will, Robert	USA	1948	GOLD	Rowing
Phi Gamma Delta	Ross, Norman	USA	1920	GOLD	Swimming (3)
Phi-Gamma Delta	Mathias, Robert	USA	1948	GOLD	Track & Field
Phi Gamma Delta	Mathias, Robert	USA	1952	GOLD	Track & Field
Phi Gamma Delta	Warner, Karl	USA	1932	GOLD	Track & Field
Phi Gamma Delta	Williams, Percy	CAN	1928	GOLD	Track & Field (2)
Phi Gamma Delta	Brown, Horace	USA	1920	GOLD	Track & Field
Phi Gamma Delta	Smithson, Forrest	USA	1908	GOLD	Track & Field
Phi Gamma Delta	Breyer, Ralph	USA	1924	GOLD	Swimming
Phi Kappa Theta	Fowler, Calvin	USA	1968	GOLD	Basketball
Phi Kappa Tau	Irmhoff, Darrell	USA	1960	GOLD	Basketball
Phi Kappa Sigma	Friherger, Marcus	USA	1952	GOLD	Basketball
Phi Kappa Sigma	Mullins, Jeff	USA	1964	GOLD	Basketball
Pi Kappa Alpha	Towns, Forrest	USA	1936	GOLD	Track & Field
Pi Kappa Alpha	Dresser, Ivan	USA	1920	GOLD	Track & Field
Pi Lambda Phi	Johnson, Ralph	USA	1960	GOLD	Track & Field
Pi Upsilon	Mehringer, Pete	USA	1932	GOLD	Wrestling
Psi Upsilon	Stoddard, Laurence	USA	1924	GOLD	Rowing
Psi Upsilon	Stowe, William	USA	1964	GOLD	Rowing
Psi Upsilon	Nelson, John	USA	1968	GOLD	Swimming
Sigma Alpha Epsilon	Dischinger, Terry	USA	1960	GOLD	Basketball
Sigma Alpha Epsilon	Kurland, Robert	USA	1948	GOLD	Basketball
Sigma Alpha Epsilon	Kurland, Robert	USA	1952	GOLD	Basketball
Sigma Alpha Epsilon	Ahlgren, George	USA	1948	GOLD	Rowing
Sigma Alpha Epsilon	Goodell, Brian	USA	1976	GOLD	Swimming (2)
Sigma Alpha Epsilon	Hencken, John	USA	1972	GOLD	Swimming (1)
Sigma Alpha Epsilon	Hencken, John	USA	1976	GOLD	Swimming (2)
Sigma Alpha Epsilon	Ris, Walter	USA	1948	GOLD	Swimming
Sigma Alpha Epsilon	Ablowich, Edgar	USA	1932	GOLD	Track & Field
Sigma Alpha Epsilon	Alderman, Fred	USA	1928	GOLD	Track & Field
Sigma Alpha Epsilon	Bausch, James	USA	1932	GOLD	Track & Field
Sigma Alpha Epsilon	Cook, Edward	USA	1908	GOLD	Track & Field
Sigma Alpha Epsilon	Leconey, Jeremiah	USA	1924	GOLD	Track & Field
Sigma Chi	Anderson, Miller	USA	1948	GOLD	Diving
Sigma Chi	Anderson, Miller	USA	1952	GOLD	Diving
Sigma Chi	Browning, David	USA	1952	GOLD	Diving
Sigma Chi	Galitzen, Michael	USA	1932	GOLD	Diving
Sigma Chi	Baird, George H.	USA	1928	GOLD	Track & Field
Sigma Chi	Harlan, Bruce	USA	1948	GOLD	Diving
Sigma Chi	Kuehn, Louis	USA	1920	GOLD	Diving
Sigma Chi	Ferry, Edward	USA	1964	GOLD	Rowing
Sigma Chi	Farrell, Felix	USA	1960	GOLD	Swimming (2)
Sigma Chi	Crabb, Buster	USA	1932	GOLD	Swimming
Sigma Chi	Barnes, Lee	USA	1924	GOLD	Track & Field
Sigma Chi	Borah, Charles	USA	1928	GOLD	Track & Field
Sigma Chi	Carpenter, William	USA	1936	GOLD	Track & Field
Sigma Chi	Cleaveland, Norman	USA	1924	GOLD	Rugby
Sigma Chi	Kelly, Frederick	USA	1912	GOLD	Track & Field

Sigma Chi	Long, Maxwell	USA	1900	GOLD	Track & Field
Sigma Chi	Porter, William	USA	1948	GOLD	Track & Field
Sigma Chi	Reidpath, Charles	USA	1912	GOLD	Track & Field (2)
Sigma Chi	Lewis, Frank	USA	1936	GOLD	Wrestling
Sigma Nu	Haldorson, Burdette	USA	1956	GOLD	Basketball
Sigma Nu	Blair, James	USA	1932	GOLD	Rowing
Sigma Nu	Ewry, Ray	USA	1900	GOLD	Track & Field (4)
Sigma Nu	Ewry, Ray	USA	1904	GOLD	Track & Field (4)
Sigma Nu	Ewry, Ray	USA	1908	GOLD	Track & Field (2)
Sigma Nu	Tootell, Fred	USA	1924	GOLD	Track & Field
Sigma Nu	Young, Cyrus	USA	1952	GOLD	Track & Field
Sigma Nu	Moore, Charles	USA	1952	GOLD	Track & Field
Sigma Phi	Leavitt, Robert	USA	1906	GOLD	Track & Field
Sigma Phi Epsilon	Long, Dallas	USA	1964	GOLD	Track & Field
Sigma Phi Epsilon	Richards, Alma	USA	1912	GOLD	Track & Field
Tau Kappa Epsilon	Iness, Simeon	USA	1952	GOLD	Track & Field
Tau Kappa Epsilon	Blubaugh, Doug	USA	1960	GOLD	Wrestling
Theta Kappa Nu	Hardin, Glenn	USA	1936	GOLD	Track & Field
Theta Chi	Ayrault, Arthur	USA	1956	GOLD	Rowing
Theta Chi	Ayrault, Arthur	USA	1960	GOLD	Rowing
Theta Chi	Dally, William	USA	1928	GOLD	Rowing
Theta Chi	Mitchell, Henry	USA	1964	GOLD	Rowing
Theta Chi	Donlon, Peter	USA	1928	GOLD	Rowing
Theta Chi	Hunt, James	USA	1968	GOLD	Yachting
Theta Delta Chi	Brinck, John	USA	1928	GOLD	Rowing
Theta Delta Chi	Marsh, Edward	USA	1900	GOLD	Rowing
Theta Delta Chi	Lindberg, Edward	USA	1912	GOLD	Track & Field
Theta Nu Epsilon	Stevens, John Hubert	USA	1932	GOLD	Bobsledding
Theta Xi	McCann, Terrence	USA	1960	GOLD	Wrestling
Tiger Inn	Garrett, Robert	USA	1896	GOLD	Track & Field (2)
Zeta Psi	Fitzpatrick, James	USA	1920	GOLD	Rugby
Zeta Psi	Landon, Richmond	USA	1920	GOLD	Track & Field
Zeta Psi	Knowles, Carl	USA	1936	GOLD	Basketball
Zeta Psi	Jones, Sam S.	USA	1904	GOLD	Track & Field
Zodiac	Munson, David	USA	1904	GOLD	Track & Field

Famous Greeks—Politicians

Alpha Beta Gamma	Murray, James C.	Representative	Illinois
Acacia	Alexander, John G.	Representative	Minnesota
Acacia	Bingham, Hiram	Senator	Connecticut
Acacia	Bray, William	Representative	Indiana
Acacia	Bryan, Wm. Jennings	Representative	Nebraska
Acacia	Capper, Arthur	Senator	Kansas
Acacia	Carlson, Frank	Rep./Senator	Kansas
Acacia	Case, Francis	Rep./Senator	South Dakota
Acacia	Davis, Jacob E.	Representative	Ohio
Acacia	Fisher, Ovie	Representative	Texas
Acacia	Hutchinson, Ed	Representative	Michigan
Acacia	Kolbe, James T.	Representative	Arizona
Acacia	McKinley, Wm. Brown	Rep./Senator	Illinois
Acacia	Murray, Reid Fred	Representative	Wisconsin
Acacia	Thornberry, Wm. Homer	Representative	Texas
Acacia	Utterback	Representative	Iowa
Acacia	Wilson, George H.	Representative	Oklahoma
Acacia	Yarborough, Ralph	Senator	Texas
Alpha Chi Omega	May, Catherine	Representative	Washington
Alpha Chi Omega	Mikulski, Barbara	Representative	Maryland
AD Club	Ravenel, Arthur	Representative	
Alpha Delta Gamma	Derwinski, Ed	Representative	Illinois
Alpha Delta Phi	Aldrich, Richard	Representative	Rhode Island

Alpha Delta Phi	Allison, Wm. Boyd	Rep./Senator	Iowa
Alpha Delta Phi	Andrew, John	Representative	Massachusetts
Alpha Delta Phi	Biester, Edward G. Jr.	Representative	Pennsylvania
Alpha Delta Phi	Andrus, John	Representative	New York
Alpha Delta Phi	Bacon, Robert Low	Representative	New York
Alpha Delta Phi	Bailey, Alexander H.	Representative	New York
Alpha Delta Phi	Barbour, Lucien	Representative	Indiana
Alpha Delta Phi	Barton, Bruce	Representative	New York
Alpha Delta Phi	Bass, Perkins	Representative	New York
Alpha Delta Phi	Bassett, Edward	Representative	New York
Alpha Delta Phi	Beedy, Carroll L.	Representative	Maine
Alpha Delta Phi	Belmont, Perry	Representative	New York
Alpha Delta Phi	Bradford, Taul	Representative	Alabama
Alpha Delta Phi	Brigham, Lewis	Representative	New Jersey
Alpha Delta Phi	Brown, Lathrop	Representative	New York
Alpha Delta Phi	Chapin, Alfred	Representative	New York
Alpha Delta Phi	Chase, Ray	Representative	Minnesota
Alpha Delta Phi	Chase, Salmon	Senator	Ohio
Alpha Delta Phi	Cowles, George	Representative	New York
Alpha Delta Phi	Crapo, William	Representative	Massachusetts
Alpha Delta Phi	Crosser, Robert	Representative	Ohio
Alpha Delta Phi	Cutcheon, Byron	Representative	Michigan
Alpha Delta Phi	Davis, Lowndes	Representative	Missouri
Alpha Delta Phi	DeForest, Robert	Representative	Connecticut
Alpha Delta Phi	Delano, Charles	Representative	Massachusetts
Alpha Delta Phi	Doolittle, James	Senator	Wisconsin
Alpha Delta Phi	Douglas, Albert	Representative	Ohio
Alpha Delta Phi	Douglas, Lewis W.	Representative	Arizona
Alpha Delta Phi	Dubois, Fred	Delegate/Sen.	Idaho
Alpha Delta Phi	Ewing, Thomas	Representative	Ohio
Alpha Delta Phi	Fassett, Jacob	Representative	New York
Alpha Delta Phi	Fraselr, Don	Representative	Minnesota
Alpha Delta Phi	Frothingham, Louis	Representative	Massachusetts
Alpha Delta Phi	Gardner, Augustus	Representative	Massachusetts
Alpha Delta Phi	Gillett, Fred	Rep./Senator	Massachusetts
Alpha Delta Phi	Groesbeck, William	Representative	Ohio
Alpha Delta Phi	Guarini, Frank J.	Representative	New Jersey
Alpha Delta Phi	Hall, Osee M.	Representative	Minnesota
Alpha Delta Phi	Hancock, Clarence	Representative	New York
Alpha Delta Phi	Hill, John B.P.C.	Representative	Maryland
Alpha Delta Phi	Hitchcock, Phineas W.	Senator	
Alpha Delta Phi	Horton, Frank	Representative	Wyoming
Alpha Delta Phi	Hubbard, Richard	Representative	Connecticut
Alpha Delta Phi	Hubbell, Jay	Representative	Michigan
Alpha Delta Phi	Ingersoll, Colin M.	Representative	Connecticut
Alpha Delta Phi	Jenckes, Thomas	Representative	Rhode Island
Alpha Delta Phi	Kellogg, Stephen	Representative	Connecticut
Alpha Delta Phi	LeFevre, Jay	Representative	New York
Alpha Delta Phi	Lyman, Theodore	Representative	Massachusetts
Alpha Delta Phi	Lynde, William	Representative	Wisconsin
Alpha Delta Phi	Maynard, Horace	Representative	Tennessee
Alpha Delta Phi	Miller, Joseph	Representative	Ohio
Alpha Delta Phi	Miller, Samuel F.	Representative	New York
Alpha Delta Phi	Monagan, John S.	Representative	Connecticut
Alpha Delta Phi	Morse, Oliver	Representative	New York
Alpha Delta Phi	Morton, Thruston	Rep./Senator	Kentucky
Alpha Delta Phi	Otis, John G.	Representative	Kansas
Alpha Delta Phi	Parker, James S.	Representative	New York
Alpha Delta Phi	Parris, Stanford E.	Representative	Virginia
Alpha Delta Phi	Percy, Charles	Senator	Illinois
Alpha Debta Phi	Perkins, John Jr.	Representative	Louisiana
Alpha Delta Phi	Peters, John A.	Representative	Maine

Alpha Delta Phi	Pomeroy, Theodore	Representative	New York
Alpha Delta Phi	Pugh, George	Senator	Ohio
Alpha Delta Phi	Quarles, Joseph	Senator	Wisconsin
Alpha Delta Phi	Richardson, David P.	Representative	New York
Alpha Delta Phi	Roberts, Ellis	Representative	New York
Alpha Delta Phi	Rockwell, Francis	Representative	Massachusetts
Alpha Delta Phi	Ross, Jonathon	Senator	Vermont
Alpha Delta Phi	Sayler, Milton	Representative	Ohio
Alpha Delta Phi	Scofield, Glenni	Representative	Pennsylvania
Alpha Delta Phi	Seymour, Edward	Representative	Connecticut
Alpha Delta Phi	Sheffield, William	Representative	Rhode Island
Alpha Delta Phi	Shiel, George K.	Representative	Oregon
Alpha Delta Phi	Shiras, George	Representative	Pennsylvania
Alpha Delta Phi	Shoemaker, Lazarus	Representative	Pennsylvania
Alpha Delta Phi	Shonk, George	Representative	Pennsylvania
Alpha Delta Phi	Shorter, Eli	Representative	Alabama
Alpha Delta Phi	Simpkins, John	Representative	Massachusetts
Alpha Delta Phi	Spriggs, John T.	Representative	New York
Alpha Delta Phi	Squire, Watson	Senator	Washington
Alpha Delta Phi	Treadway, Allen	Representative	Massachusetts
Alpha Delta Phi	Welch, Adonijah	Senator	Florida
Alpha Delta Phi	White, Wallace	Rep./Senator	Maine
Alpha Delta Phi	Whitling, William	Representative	Massachusetts
Alpha Delta Phi	Willard, Charles	Representative	Vermont
Alpha Delta Phi	Williams, George	Representative	Massachusetts
Alpha Delta Phi	Willits, Edwin	Representative	Michigan
Alpha Delta Phi	Wold, John	Representative	Wyoming
Alpha Delta Phi	Zion, Roger	Representative	Indiana
Alpha Digemma	Dawes, Rufus	Representative	Ohio
Alpha Gamma Rho	Fuqua, Don	Representative	Florida
Alpha Gamma Rho	Harvey, Ralph	Representative	Indiana
Alpha Gamma Rho	Jones, Ed	Representative	Tennessee
Alpha Gamma Rho	Jones, Walter B.	Representative	North Carolina
Alpha Gamma Rho	McIntire, Clifford G.	Representative	Maine
Alpha Gamma Rho	Sikes, Robert	Representative	Florida
Alpha Gamma Rho	Smith, Charles	Representative	Florida
Alpha Kappa Alpha	Collins, Cardiss	Representative	Illinois
Alpha Omicrom Pi	Farrington, Elizabeth	Delegate	Hawaii
Alpha Phi Alpha	Brooke, Edward	Senator	Massachusetts
Alpha Phi Alpha	Dawson, William L.	Representative	Illinois
Alpha Phi Alpha	Dellums, Ronald	Representative	California
Alpha Phi Alpha	Dixon, Julian	Representative	California
Alpha Phi Alpha	Ford, Harold E.	Representative	Tennessee
Alpha Phi Alpha	Gray, William H. III	Representative	Pennsylvania
Alpha Phi Alpha	Rangel, Charles B.	Representative	New York
Alpha Phi Delta	Russo, Martin A.	Representative	Illinois
Alpha Sigma Phi	Allen, James B.	Senator	Alabama
Alpha Sigma Phi	Buffett, Howard	Representative	Nebraska
Alpha Sigma Phi	Capehart, James	Representative	West Virginia
Alpha Sigma Phi	Coffee, John	Representative	Washington
Alpha Sigma Phi	Crapo, William	Representative	Massachusetts
Alpha Sigma Phi	Fenn, Edward	Representative	Connecticut
Alpha Sigma Phi	Fowler, Charles	Representative	New Jersey
Alpha Sigma Phi	Hansen, John R.	Representative	Iowa
Alpha Sigma Phi	Hedge, Thomas	Representative	Iowa
Alpha Sigma Phi	Hubbard, Elbert	Representative	Iowa
Alpha Sigma Phi	Joy, Charles	Representative	Missouri
Alpha Sigma Phi	Kasich, John R.	Representative	Ohio
Alpha Sigma Phi	Kornegay, Horace	Representative	North Carolina
Alpha Sigma Phi	Merritt, Schuyler	Representative	Connecticut
Alpha sigma Phi	Oakman, Charles G.	Representative	Michigan
Alpha Sigma Phi	Pittenger, William	Representative	Minnesota

Alpha Sigma Phi	Platt, Thomas	Rep./Senator	New York
Alpha Sigma Phi	Porter, Peter	Representative	New York
Alpha Sigma Phi	Russell, Charles	Representative	Connecticut
Alpha Sigma Phi	Sanford, John	Representative	New York
Alpha Sigma Phi	Stewart, William	Senator	Nevada
Alpha Sigma Phi	Sweet, Edwin F.	Representative	Michigan
Alpha Sigma Phi	Taft, Charles P.	Representative	Ohio
Alpha Sigma Phi	Tollefson, Thor	Representative	Washington
Alpha Sigma Phi	West, Charles	Representative	Ohio
Alpha Sigma Phi	Wetmore, George	Senator	Rhode Island
Alpha Sigma Phi	White, Wilbur	Representative	Ohio
Alpha Sigma Phi	Wolcott, Edward	Senator	Colorado
Alpha Sigma Phi	Wolf, Frank R.	Representative	Virginia
Alpha Tau Omega	Acklen, Joseph H.	Representative	Louisiana
Alpha Tau Omega	Ainey, William	Representative	Pennsylvania
Alpha Tau Omega	Angell, Homer D.	Representative	Oregon
Alpha Tau Omega	Bayh, Birch	Senator	Indiana
Alpha Tau Omega	Benet, Christie	Senator	South Carolina
Alpha Tau Omega	Breckinridge, Clifton	Representative	Arkansas
Alpha Tau Omega	Brinson, Samuel M.	Representative	North Carolina
Alpha Tau Omega	Brown, Paul	Representative	Georgia
Alpha Tau Omega	Bryan, Nathan P.	Senator	Florida
Alpha Tau Omega	Bryan, William J.	Senator	Florida
Alpha Tau Omega	Chiles, Lawton M.	Senator	Florida
Alpha Tau Omega	Coffee, Harry	Representative	Nebraska
Alpha Tau Omega	Davis, Ewin	Representative	Tennessee
Alpha Tau Omega	DeMuth, Peter	Representative	Pennsylvania
Alpha Tau Omega	DeVries, Marion M. L.	Representative	California
Alpha Tau Omega	DuPre, Henry	Representative	Louisiana
Alpha Tau Omega	Eastland, James	Senator	Mississippi
Alpha Tau Omega	Ervin, Joseph W.	Representative	North Carolina
Alpha Tau Omega	Evans, T. Cooper	Representative	Iowa
Alpha Tau Omega	Gibbons, Sam	Representative	Florida
Alpha Tau Omega	Goodling, George A.	Representative	Pennsylvania
Alpha Tau Omega	Goodwin, Robert K.	Representative	Iowa
Alpha Tau Omega	Greever, Paul	Representative	Wyoming
Alpha Tau Omega	Gregory, William V.	Representative	Kentucky
Alpha Tau Omega	Griswold, Dwight	Senator	Nebraska
Alpha Tau Omega	Gurney, Edward	Rep./Senator	Florida
Alpha Tau Omega	Hamilton, Lee	Representative	Indiana
Alpha Tau Omega	Holland, Spessard	Senator	Florida
Alpha Tau Omega	Irby, John	Senator	South Carolina
Alpha Tau Omega	Johnson, Albert	Representative	Pennsylvania
Alpha Tau Omega	Jordan, Leonard	Senator	Idaho
Alpha Taw Omega	Kemp, Jack F.	Representative	New York
Alpha Tau Omega	Kindness, Thomas N.	Representative	Ohio
Alpha Tau Omega	Krueger, Robert C.	Representative	Texas
Alpha Tau Omega	Lafean, Daniel F.	Representative	Pennsylvania
Alpha Tau Omega	Lambertson, William P.	Representative	Kansas
Alpha Tau Omega	Larson, Oscar John	Representative	Minnesota
Alpha Tau Omega	Lea, Luke	Senator	Tennessee
Alpha Tau Omega	Loftin, Scott	Senator	Florida
Alpha Tau Omega	Logan, William T.	Representative	South Carolina
Alpha Tau Omega	Long, Clarence D. Jr.	Representative	Maryland
Alpha Tau Omega	Mansfield, Mike	Rep./Senator	Montana
Alpha Tau Omega	Marshall, James W.	Representative	Virginia
Alpha Tau Omega	Martin, Thomas	Senator	Virginia
Alpha Tau Omega	Martin, Thomas E.	Rep./Senator	Iowa
Alpha Tau Omega	Maybank, Burnet R.	Senator	South Carolina
Alpha Tau Omega	McDonald, Lawrence P.	Representative	Georgia
Alpha Tau Omega	McDuffie, John	Representative	Alabama
Alpha Tau Omega	Menges, Franklin	Representative	Pennsylvania

Alpha Tau Omega	Meyer, William H.	Representative	Vermont
Alpha Tau Omega	Milton, William H.	Senator	Florida
Alpha Tau Omega	Morris, Robert P.	Representative	Minnesota
Alpha Tau Omega	Owen, Robert	Senator	Oklahoma
Alpha Tau Omega	Paul, John	Representative	Virginia
Alpha Tau Omega	Pearson, James B.	Senator	Kansas
Alpha Tau Omega	Peterson, Hugh	Representative	Georgia
Alpha Tau Omega	Phelan, James	Representative	Tennessee
Alpha Tau Omega	Polk, Rufus	Representative	Pennsylvania
Alpha Tau Omega	Pollock, William P.	Senator	South Carolina
Alpha Tau Omega	Porter, John E.	Representative	Illinois
Alpha Tau Omega	Pou, Edward W.	Representative	North Carolina
Alpha Tau Omega	Price, Andrew B.	Representative	Louisiana
Alpha Tall Omega	Roberts, Ken	Representative	Alabama
Alpha Tau Omega	Robeson, Edward J.	Representative	Virginia
Alpha Tau Omega	Roddenbery, Seaborn	Representative	Georgia
Alpha Tau Omega	Samford, William J.	Representative	Alabama
Alpha Tau Omega	Santini, James D.	Representative	Nevada
Alpha Tau Omega	Sears, William	Representative	Nebraska
Alpha Tau Omega	Simmons, Furnifold M.	Rep./Senator	North Carolina
Alpha Tau Omega	Simpson, Alan K.	Senator	Wyoming
Alpha Tau Omega	Simpson, Milward	Senator	Wyoming
Alpha Tau Omega	Smith, H. Allen	Representative	California
Alpha Tau Omega	Stubblefield, Frank	Representative	Kentucky
Alpha Tau Omega	Taylor, Zachary	Representative	Tennessee
Alpha Tau Omega	Warren, Lindsey	Representative	North Carolina
Alpha Tau Omega	Weaver, Phillip	Representative	Nebraska
Alpha Tau Omega	West, William S.	Senator	Georgia
Alpha Tau Omega	Wilkinson, Theodore	Representative	Louisiana
Beta Alpha Sigma	Barr, Joseph	Representative	Indiana
Beta Sigma Rho	Eilbert, Joshua	Representative	Pennsylvania
Beta Sigma Rho	Joelson, Charles	Representative	New Jersey
Beta Theta Pi	Allen, John M.	Representative	Mississippi
Beta Theta Pi	Andrew, Andrew P. Jr.	Representative	Massachusetts
Beta Theta Pi	Armstrong, William	Representative	Pennsylvania
Beta Theta Pi	Aspinall, Wayne	Representative	Colorado
Beta Theta Pi	Bakewell, Charles	Representative	Connecticut
Beta Theta Pi	Barnes, George T.	Representative	Georgia
Beta Theta Pi	Baumhart, A. D.	Representative	Ohio
Beta Theta Pi	Beall, James A.	Representative	Texas
Beta Theta Pi	Beck, James B.	Rep./Senator	Kentucky
Beta Theta Pi	Begg, James T.	Representative	Ohio
Beta Theta Pi	Bennett, Thomas	Delegate	Idaho
Beta Theta Pi	Berry, Albert	Representative	Kentucky
Beta Theta Pi	Blue, Richard	Representative	Kansas
Beta Theta Pi	Boggs, Thomas H.	Representative	Louisiana
Beta Theta Pi	Booth, Newton	Senator	California
Beta Theta Pi	Borah, William E.	Senator	Idaho
Beta Theta Pi	Boutell, Henry S.	Representative	Illinois
Beta Theta Pi	Brotzman, Donald	Representative	Colorado
Beta Theta Pi	Brown, Benjamin	Senator	Missouri
Beta Theta Pi	Brown, John Y.	Representative	Kentucky
Beta Theta Pi	Brown, Norris	Senator	Nebraska
Beta Theta Pi	Brown, Webster E.	Representative	Wisconsin
Beta Theta Pi	Burton, Joseph	Senator	Kansas
Beta Theta Pi	Butler, John M.	Senator	Maryland
Beta Theta Pi	Bynum, William	Representative	Indiana
Beta Theta Pi	Byrns, Joseph	Representative	Tennessee
Beta Theta Pi	Campbell, Courtney W.	Representative	Florida
Beta Theta Pi	Campbell, James	Representative	Ohio
Beta Theta Pi	Cander, Ezekiel S.	Representative	Mississippi
Beta Theta Pi	Clarke, Frank G.	Representative	New Hampshire

Beta Theta Pi	Clark, Rush	Representative	Iowa
Beta Theta Pi	Clements, Isaac	Representative	Illinois
Beta Theta Pi	Colfax, Schuyler	Representative	Indiana
Beta Theta Pi	Comstock, Daniel W.	Representative	Indiana
Beta Theta Pi	Cooper, John S.	Senator	Kentucky
Beta Theta Pi	Cotton, Norris	Rep./Senator	New Hampshire
Beta Theta Pi	Coughlin, Clarence	Representative	Pennsylvania
Beta Theta Pi	Cowherd, William S.	Representative	Missouri
Beta Theta Pi	Cravens, William	Representative	Missouri
Beta Theta Pi	Crittenden, Thomas	Representative	Missouri
Beta Theta Pi	Cromer, George	Representative	Indiana
Beta Theta Pi	Crosby, Charles N.	Representative	Pennsylvania
Beta Theta Pi	Cumback, William	Representative	Indiana
Beta Theta Pi	Danaher, John A.	Senator	Connecticut
Beta Theta Pi	DeMotte, Mark	Representative	Indiana
Beta Theta Pi	Dodds, Ozro Jr.	Representative	Ohio
Beta Theta Pi	Edgerton, Alonzo J.	Senator	Minnesota
Beta Theta Pi	Edmunds, Paul C.	Representative	Virginia
Beta Theta Pi	Elliott, William	Representative	South Carolina
Beta Theta Pi	Ellis, Ezekiel J.	Representative	Louisiana
Beta Theta Pi	Ellsworth, Robert	Representative	Kansas
Beta Theta Pi	Field, Scott	Representative	Virginia
Beta Theta Pi	Farrington, Joseph	Delegate	Hawaii
Beta Theta Pi	Fuller, William E.	Representative	Iowa
Beta Theta Pi	Galloway, Samuel	Representative	Ohio
Beta Theta Pi	Gephardt, Richard A.	Representative	Missouri
Beta Theta Pi	Glover, John M.	Representative	Missouri
Beta Theta Pi	Goff, Abe M.	Representative	Idaho
Beta Theta Pi	Gordon, John B.	Senator	Georgia
Beta Theta Pi	Granger, Miles	Representative	Connecticut
Beta Theta Pi	Griffin, Levi	Representative	Michigan
Beta Theta Pi	Gunderson, Steven C.	Representative	Wisconsin
Beta Theta Pi	Hall, Benton J.	Representative	Iowa
Beta Theta Pi	Halleck, Charles	Representative	Indiana
Beta Theta Pi	Hanna, John	Representative	Indiana
Beta Theta Pi	Harlan, James	Senator	Iowa
Beta Theta Pi	Harris, Henry R.	Representative	Georgia
Beta Theta Pi	Hatfield, Mark	Senator	Oregon
Beta Theta Pi	Henry, Patrick	Representative	Mississippi
Beta Theta Pi	Hitt, Robert	Representative	Illinois
Beta Theta Pi	Hoffman, Henry	Representative	Maryland
Beta Theta Pi	Holland, Edward E.	Representative	Virginia
Beta Theta Pi	Howard, Jonas	Representative	Indiana
Beta Theta Pi	Ikard, Frank	Representative	Texas
Beta Theta Pi	Ireland, Clifford C.	Representative	Illinois
Beta Theta Pi	Izlar, James F.	Representative	South Carolina
Beta Theta Pi	Johnson, Martin N.	Rep./Senator	North Dakota
Beta Theta Pi	Kem, James P.	Senator	Missouri
Beta Theta Pi	Kinsey, William M.	Representative	Missouri
Beta Theta Pi	Kopp, William F.	Representative	Iowa
Beta Theta Pi	Kruse, Ed	Representative	Indiana
Beta Theta Pi	LaFollette, Robert	Senator	Wisconsin
Beta Theta Pi	Landis, Charles B.	Representative	Indiana
Beta Theta Pi	Latham, Milton S.	Rep./Senator	California
Beta Theta Pi	Lentz, John J.	Representative	Ohio
Beta Theta Pi	Letts, Fred D.	Representative	Iowa
Beta Theta Pi	Loeffler, Thomas G.	Representative	Texas
Beta Theta Pi	Lowden, Frank O.	Representative	Illinois
Beta Theta Pi	Lugar, Richard G.	Senator	Indiana
Beta Theta Pi	Marshall, Humphrey	Representative	Kentucky
Beta Theta Pi	Martin, James G.	Representative	North Carolina
Beta Theta Pi	Matson, Courtland	Representative	Indiana

Beta Theta Pi	Matthews, Stanley	Senator	Ohio
Beta Theta Pi	McCormick, John W.	Representative	Ohio
Beta Theta Pi	McDill, James	Rep./Senator	Iowa
Beta Theta Pi	McDonald, Joseph	Rep./Senator	Indiana
Beta Theta Pi	McLean, William P.	Representative	Texas
Beta Theta Pi	McMaster, William H.	Senator	South Dakota
Beta Theta Pi	Mercur, Ulysses	Representative	Pennsylvania
Beta Theta Pi	Miers, Robert	Representative	Indiana
Beta Theta Pi	Montague, Andrew	Representative	Virginia
Beta Theta Pi	Moore, Arch	Representative	West Virginia
Beta Theta Pi	Moorehead, Tom Van Horn	Representative	Ohio
Beta Theta Pi	Morrow, Dwight W.	Senator	New Jersey
Beta Theta Pi	Morton, Oliver	Senator	Indiana
Beta Theta Pi	Nelson, William	Representative	Florida
Beta Theta Pi	Newberry, John	Representative	Michigan
Beta Theta Pi	Nickles, Donald L.	Representative	Oklahoma
Beta Theta Pi	O'Connell, Jeremiah E.	Representative	Rhode Island
Beta Theta Pi	Odell, Benjamin B.	Representative	New York
Beta Theta Pi	Packwood, Robert W.	Senator	Oregon
Beta Theta Pi	Paine, Halbert E.	Representative	Wisconsin
Beta Theta Pi	Pattison, John	Representative	Ohio
Beta Theta Pi	Peirce, Robert B. F.	Representative	Indiana
Beta Theta Pi	Penrose, Boies	Senator	Pennsylvania
Beta Theta Pi	Pickett, Thomas A.	Representative	Texas
Beta Theta Pi	Pollard, Henry M.	Representative	Missouri
Beta Theta Pi	Porter, Albert G.	Representative	Indiana
Beta Theta Pi	Pritchard, George M.	Representative	North Carolina
Beta Theta Pi	Pugsley, Jacob	Representative	Ohio
Beta Theta Pi	Quay, Matthew	Senator	Pennsylvania
Beta Theta Pi	Rawlins, Joseph L.	Delegate/Sen.	Utah
Beta Theta Pi	Ray, John	Representative	New York
Beta Theta Pi	Reynolds, Robert	Senator	North Carolina
Beta Theta Pi	Reeves, Henry A.	Representative	New York
Beta Theta Pi	Rhodes, George	Representative	Pennsylvania
Beta Theta Pi	Rhodes, John	Representative	Arizona
Beta Theta Pi	Rider, Ira E.	Representative	New York
Beta Theta Pi	Rose, Charles G. III	Representative	North Carolina
Beta Theta Pi	Rouse, Arthur	Representative	Kentucky
Beta Theta Pi	Rubey, Thomas L.	Representative	Missouri
Beta Theta Pi	Schaefer, Daniel L.	Representative	Colorado
Beta Theta Pi	Scott, Charles	Representative	Kansas
Beta Theta Pi	Scott, Harvey D.	Representative	Indiana
Beta Theta Pi	Scudder, Townsend	Representative	New York
Beta Theta Pi	Seaton, Frederick A.	Senator	Nebraska
Beta Theta Pi	Sharp, Philip R.	Representative	Indiana
Beta Theta Pi	Smith, Dennis A.	Representative	Oregon
Beta Theta Pi	Smith, Frank	Representative	Mississippi
Beta Theta Pi	Smith, John M. C.	Representative	Michigan
Beta Theta Pi	Snell, Bertrand H.	Representative	New York
Beta Theta Pi	Spencer, William B.	Representative	Louisiana
Beta Theta Pi	Spratt, John M. Jr.	Representative	South Carolina
Beta Theta Pi	Springer, William	Representative	Illinois
Beta Theca Pi	Stack, Edward J.	Representative	Florida
Beta Theta Pi	Stevenson, William F.	Representative	South Carolina
Beta Theta Pi	Sutherland, Howard	Rep./Senator	West Virginia
Beta Theta Pi	Synar, Michael L.	Representative	Oklahoma
Beta Theta Pi	Teague, Charles	Representative	California
Beta Theta Pi	Townsend, Hosea	Representative	Colorado
Beta Theta Pi	Tucker, Henry St.G.	Representative	Virginia
Beta Theta Pi	Ullman, Al	Representative	Oregon
Beta Theta Pi	Upson, William H.	Representative	Ohio
Beta Theta Pi	Voorhees, Daniel	Rep./Senator	Indiana

Beta Theta Pi	Ware, John	Representative	Pennsylvania
Beta Theta Pi	Warner, John W.	Senator	Virginia
Beta Theta Pi	Watson, Walter	Representative	Virginia
Beta Theta Pi	Weaver, Claude	Representative	Oklahoma
Beta Theta Pi	Weber, Edward F.	Representative	Ohio
Beta Tneta Pi	Wherry, Ken	Senator	Nebraska
Beta Theta Pi	Whitten, Jamie	Representative	Mississippi
Beta Theta Pi	Williamson, Ben	Senator	Kentucky
Beta Theta Pi	Wilson, Joseph G.	Representative	Oregon
Beta Theta Pi	Winter, Charles E.	Representative	Wyoming
Beta Theta Pi	Wise, John S.	Representative	Virginia
Beta Theta Pi	Wyatt, Wendell	Representative	Oregon
Beta Theta Pi	Young, John S.	Representative	Louisiana
Chi Omega	Schroeder, Patricia	Representative	
Chi Omega	Smith, Virginia D.	Representative	Nebraska
Chi Phi	Appleby, Stewart	Representative	New Jersey
Chi Phi	Briggs, Clay S.	Representative	Texas
Chi Phi	Carpenter, William R.	Representative	Kansas
Chi Phi	Chase, Jackson	Representative	Nebraska
Chi Phi	Churchill, George	Representative	Massachusetts
Chi Phi	Dewalt, Arthur G.	Representative	Pennsylvania
Chi Phi	Glascock, John R.	Representative	California
Chi Phi	Hale, Fletcher	Representative	New Hampshire
Chi Phi	Hall, Edwin A. Jr.	Representative	New York
Chi Phi	Johnson, Hiram	Senator	California
Chi Phi	Jonas, Charles R.	Representative	North Carolina
Chi Phi	Kenney, Richard R.	Senator	Delaware
Chi Phi	Kinzer, John	Representative	Pennsylvania
Chi Phi	Kline, Marcus C. L.	Representative	Pennsylvania
Chi Phi	Kyros, Peter N.	Representative	Maine
Chi Phi	Moody, Malcolm A.	Representative	Oregon
Chi Phi	Moore, Robert W.	Representative	Virginia
Chi Phi	Overman, Lee S.	Senator	North Carolina
Chi Phi	Pheiffer, William T.	Representative	New York
Chi Phi	Ratchford, W. R.	Representative	Connecticut
Chi Phi	Saxbe, William B.	Senator	Ohio
Chi Phi	Saylor, John	Representative	Pennsylvania
Chi Phi	Small, John H.	Representative	North Carolina
Chi Phi	Speer, Emery	Representative	Georgia
Chi Phi	Stenger, William S.	Representative	Pennsylvania
Chi Phi	Stewart, Arthur T.	Senator	Tennessee
Chi Phi	Thomson, Vernon	Representative	Wisconsin
Chi Phi	Terry, William L.	Representative	Arkansas
Chi Psi	Allen, Charles H.	Representative	Massachusetts
Chi Psi	Burchard, Horatio C.	Representative	Illinois
Chi Psi	Cooper, James	Representative	Tennessee
Chi Psi	Croft, Theodore G.	Representative	South Carolina
Chi Psi	Davenport, Stanley W.	Representative	Pennsylvania
Chi Psi	Davis, Horace	Representative	California
Chi Psi	Earle, Joseph H.	Senator	South Carolina
Chi Psi	Fazio, Vic	Representative	California
Chi Psi	Fessenden, Thomas A.	Representative	Maine
Chi Psi	Findlay, John V. L.	Representative	Maryland
Chi Psi	Gillet, Charles	Representative	New York
Chi Psi	Hungerford, John N.	Representative	New York
Chi Psi	Lawrence, George P.	Representative	Massachusetts
Chi Psi	May, Edwin	Representative	Connecticut
Chi Psi	Minshall, William	Representative	Ohio
Chi Psi	Paige, David R.	Representative	Ohio
Chi Pst	Palmer, Thomas	Senator	Michigan
Chi Psi	Perry, William H.	Representative	South Carolina
Chi Psi	Phelps, William W.	Representative	Minnesota

Chi Psi	Proxmire, William	Senator	Wisconsin
Chi Psi	Reed, Thomas	Representative	Maine
Chi Psi	Reuss, Henry	Representative	Wisconsin
Chi Psi	Seymour, Henry	Representative	Michigan
Chi Psi	Steiger, William	Representative	Wisconsin
Chi Psi	Stewart, John W.	Rep./Senator	Vermont
Chi Psi	Stockdale, Thomas R.	Representative	Mississippi
Chi Psi	Wainwright, Stuyvesant	Representative	New York
Chi Psi	White, Harry	Representative	Pennsylvania
Cottage Club	Bond, Christopher	Senator	Missouri
Delta Chi	Bennet, William S.	Representative	New York
Delta Chi	Bradley, Frederick	Representative	Michigan
Delta Chi	Bricker, John	Senator	Ohio
Delta Chi	Church, Ralph	Representative	Illinois
Delta Chi	Craig, Larry E.	Representative	Idaho
Delta Chi	Dockweiler, John F.	Representative	California
Delta Chi	Dolliver, James I.	Representative	Iowa
Delta Chi	Duff, James H.	Senator	Pennsylvania
Delta Chi	Flannery, J. Harold	Representative	Pennsylvania
Delta Chi	Harding, John E.	Representative	Ohio
Delta Chi	Harness, Forest A.	Representative	Indiana
Delta Chi	Harter, John	Representative	New York
Delta Chi	Haskell, Reuben L.	Representative	New York
Delta Chi	Jackson, Henry M.	Rep./Senator	Washington
Delta Chi	Jefferis, Albert	Representative	Nebraska
Delta Chi	Jones, John M.	Representative	Texas
Delta Chi	Kearney, Bernard	Representative	New York
Delta Chi	Kenney, Edward A.	Representative	New Jersey
Delta Chi	Kurtz, Jacob	Representative	Pennsylvania
Delta Chi	Love, Rodney M.	Representative	Ohio
Delta Chi	Lukens, Donald	Representative	Ohio
Delta Chi	McFarlane, W. D.	Representative	Texas
Delta Chi	Murray, James E.	Senator	Montana
Delta Chi	Neely, Matthew M.	Rep./Senator	West Virginia
Delta Chi	Paddock, George A.	Representative	Illinois
Delta Chi	Pope, James P.	Senator	Idaho
Delta Chi	Reed, Daniel	Representative	New York
Delta Chi	Roush, J. Edward	Representative	Indiana
Delta Chi	Rutherford, Albert G.	Representative	Pennsylvania
Delta Chi	Sasscer, Lansdale G.	Representative	Maryland
Delta Chi	Schwellenbach, Lewis B	Senator	Washington
Delta Chi	Shelby, Richard C.	Representative	Alabama
Delta Chi	Simon, Paul	Senator	Illinois
Delta Chi	Smith, George R.	Representative	Minnesota
Delta Chi	Stratton, William	Representative	Illinois
Delta Chi	Stump, Robert	Representative	Arizona
Delta Kappa Epsilon	Aldrich, J. Frank	Representative	Illinois
Delta Kappa Epsilon	Alexander, DeAlva	Representative	New York
Delta Kappa Epsilon	Allen, Clarence	Representative	Utah
Delta Kappa Epsilon	Anderson, Chapman L.	Representative	Mississippi
Delta Kappa Epsilon	Andrew, John	Representative	Massachusetts
Delta Kappa Epsilon	Archer, Stevenson	Representative	Maryland
Delta Kappa Epsilon	Ashley, Thomas	Representative	Ohio
Delta Kappa Epsilon	Atherton, Gibson	Representative	Ohio
Delta Kappa Epsilon	Ballenger, Thomas	Representative	North Carolina
Delta Kappa Epsilon	Banks, Nathaniel	Representative	Massachusetts
Delta Kappa Epsilon	Bartlett, Franklin	Representative	New York
Delta Kappa Epsilon	Bayard, Thomas	Senator	Deleware
Delta Kappa Epsilon	Beach, Clifton B.	Representative	Ohio
Delta Kappa Epsilon	Belmont, Perry	Representative	New York
Delta Kappa Epsilon	Benson, Samuel	Representative	Maine
Delta Kappa Epsilon	Beveridge, Albert	Senator	Indiana

Delta Kappa Epsilon	Biemiller, Andrew J.	Representative	Wisconsin
Delta Kappa Epsilon	Bingham, Jonathon	Representative	New York
Delta Kappa Epsilon	Black, Frank	Representative	New York
Delta Kappa Epsilon	Blaine, James G.	Rep./Senator	Maine
Delta Kappa Epsilon	Bonynge, Robert	Representative	Colorado
Delta Kappa Epsilon	Brandegee, Augustus	Representative	Connecticut
Delta Kappa Epsilon	Brandegee, Frank	Rep./Senator	Connecticut
Delta Kappa Epsilon	Brewster, Ralph	Rep./Senator	Maine
Delta Kappa Epsilon	Brice, Calvin	Senator	Ohio
Delta Kappa Epsilon	Brigham, Elbert	Representative	Vermont
Delta Kappa Epsilon	Brown, Fred	Senator	New Hampshire
Delta Kappa Epsilon	Buck, Alfred	Representative	Alabama
Delta Kappa Epsilon	Burlingame, Anson	Representative	Massachusetts
Delta Kappa Epsilon	Burnett, Edward	Representative	Massachusetts
Delta Kappa Epsilon	Burnside, Ambrose E.	Senator	Rhode Island
Delta Kappa Epsilon	Burton, Harold	Senator	Ohio
Delta Kappa Epsilon	Bush, George	Representative	Texas
Delta Kappa Epsilon	Butler, Matthew	Senator	South Carolina
Delta Kappa Epsilon	Chafee, John	Senator	Rhode Island
Delta Kappa Epsilon	Chandler, William	Senator	New Hampshire
Delta Kappa Epsilon	Cleveland, James	Representative	New Hampshire
Delta Kappa Epsilon	Codd, George	Representative	Michigan
Delta Kappa Epsilon	Connolly, Maurice	Representative	Iowa
Delta Kappa Epsilon	Copeland, Royal	Senator	New York
Delta Kappa Epsilon	Cross, Oliver	Representative	Texas
Delta Kappa Epsilon	Davidson, Robert	Representative	Florida
Delta Kappa Epsilon	Dooley, Edwin B.	Representative	New York
Delta Kappa Epsilon	Dryden, John	Senator	New Jersey
Delta Kappa Epsilon	Dubois, Fred	Delegate/Sen.	Idaho
Delta Kappa Epsilon	Dunnell, Mark	Representative	Minnesota
Delta Kappa Epsilon	Eagleton, Thomas	Senator	Missouri
Delta Kappa Epsilon	Edwards, Don	Representative	California
Delta Kappa Epsilon	Fenn, Edward	Representative	Connecticut
Delta Kappa Epsilon	Flanagan, DeWitt C.	Representative	New Jersey
Delta Kappa Epsilon	Foote, Henry	Senator	Mississippi
Delta Kappa Epsilon	Ford, Gerald	Representative	Michigan
Delta Kappa Epsilon	Foster, David	Representative	Vermont
Delta Kappa Epsilon	Frothingham, Louis	Representative	Massachusetts
Delta Kappa Epsilon	Gardner, Augustus	Representative	Massachusetts
Delta Kappa Epsilon	Garland, Peter	Representative	Maine
Delta Kappa Epsilon	Garrison, George	Representative	Virginia
Delta Kappa Epsilon	Gibson, Paris	Senator	Montana
Delta Kappa Epsilon	Gibson, Randall	Rep./Senator	Louisiana
Delta Kappa Epsilon	Gilman, Charles	Representative	Maine
Delta Kappa Epsilon	Goodnight, Isaac	Representative	Kentucky
Delta Kappa Epsilon	Graves, Alexander	Representative	Missouri
Delta Kappa Epsilon	Grover, LaFayette	Rep./Senator	Oregon
Delta Kappa Epsilon	Haldeman, Richard	Representative	Pennsylvania
Delta Kappa Epsilon	Hale, Eugene	Rep./Senator	Maine
Delta Kappa Epsilon	Hay, James	Representative	Virginia
Delta Kappa Epsilon	Hayden, Edward	Representative	Massachusetts
Delta Kappa Epsilon	Hayes, Rutherford B.	Representative	Ohio
Delta Kappa Epsilon	Hearst, William R.	Representative	New York
Delta Kappa Epsilon	Hedge, Thomas	Representative	Iowa
Delta Kappa Epsilon	Hennings, Thomas	Rep./Senator	Missouri
Delta Kappa Epsilon	Herbert, Hilary	Representative	Alabama
Delta Kappa Epsilon	Heselton, John	Representative	Massachusetts
Delta Kappa Epsilon	Hiestand, Edgar	Representative	California
Delta Kappa Epsilon	Hill, Joseph L.	Rep./Senator	Alabama
Delta Kappa Epsilon	Hobbs, Sam	Representative	Alabama
Delta Kappa Epsilon	Hubbard, Elbert	Representative	Iowa
Delta Kappa Epsilon	Hurd, Frank	Representative	Ohio

Delta Kappa Epsilon	Husted, James	Representative	New York
Delta Kappa Epsilon	Irion, Alfred	Representative	Louisiana
Delta Kappa Epsilon	Jacobs, Ferris Jr.	Representative	New York
Delta Kappa Epsilon	Jones, William	Representative	Washington
Delta Kappa Epsilon	Jones, William A.	Representative	Virginia
Delta Kappa Epsilon	Joy, Charles	Representative	Missouri
Delta Kappa Epsilon	Kaynor, William K.	Representative	Massachusetts
Delta Kappa Epsilon	Kean, John	Rep./Senator	New Jersey
Delta Kappa Epsilon	Kent, William	Representative	California
Delta Kappa Epsilon	Keyes, Henry	Senator	New Hampshire
Delta Kappa Epsilon	Kline, Isaac C.	Representative	Pennsylvania
Delta Kappa Epsilon	Knapp, Charles	Representative	New York
Delta Kappa Epsilon	Knox, William S.	Representative	Massachusetts
Delta Kappa Epsilon	Lapham, Oscar	Representative	Rhode Island
Delta Kappa Epsilon	Latham, Louis	Representative	North Carolina
Delta Kappa Epsilon	Lee, Warren	Representative	New York
Delta Kappa Epsilon	Leonard, Fred Churchill	Representative	Pennsylvania
Delta Kappa Epsilon	Leonard, John E.	Representative	Louisiana
Delta Kappa Epsilon	Lewis, Burwell	Representative	Alabama
Delta Kappa Epsilon	Lingston, Robert L.	Representative	Louisiana
Delta Kappa Epsilon	Lodge, Henry	Rep./Senator	Massachusetts
Delta Kappa Epsilon	Long, Gillis	Representative	Louisiana
Delta Kappa Epsilon	Long, John	Representative	Massachusetts
Delta Kappa Epsilon	Long, Russell	Senator	Louisiana
Delta Kappa Epsilon	Longworth, Nicholas	Representative	Ohio
Delta Kappa Epsilon	Lowe, William	Representative	Alabama
Delta Kappa Epsilon	Martin, George	Senator	Kentucky
Delta Kappa Epsilon	Maybury, William	Representative	Michigan
Delta Kappa Epsilon	McClammy, Charles	Representative	North Carolina
Delta Kappa Epsilon	McCreary, James	Rep./Senator	Kentucky
Delta Kappa Epsilon	McKellar, Kenneth	Rep./Senator	Tennessee
Delta Kappa Epsilon	Merritt, Edwin A.	Representative	New York
Delta Kappa Epsilon	Merritt, Schuyler	Representative	Connecticut
Delta Kappa Epsilon	Metcalf, Victor	Representative	California
Delta Kappa Epsilon	Millard, Stephen	Representative	New York
Delta Kappa Epsilon	Milliken, Seth	Representative	Maine
Delta Kappa Epsilon	Moffat, Seth	Representative	Michigan
Delta Kappa Epsilon	Morey, Henry M.	Representative	Ohio
Delta Kappa Epsilon	Morton, Rogers	Representative	Maryland
Delta Kappa Epsilon	Mosier, Harold	Representative	Ohio
Delta Kappa Epsilon	O'Grady, James	Representative	New York
Delta Kappa Epsilon	O'Neal, Emmet	Representative	Kentucky
Delta Kappa Epsilon	Owens, James	Representative	Ohio
Delta Kappa Epsilon	Parsons, Herbert	Representative	New York
Delta Kappa Epsilon	Patton, John	Senator	Michigan
Delta Kappa Epsilon	Patten, Thomas G.	Representative	New York
Delta Kappa Epsilon	Peters, John	Representative	Maine
Delta Kappa Epsilon	Pettibone, Augustus	Representative	Tennessee
Delta Kappa Epsilon	Pettengill, Sam	Representative	Indiana
Delta Kappa Epsilon	Pigott, James	Representative	Connecticut
Delta Kappa Epsilon	Plaisted, Harris	Representative	Maine
Delta Kappa Epsilon	Porter, Peter	Representative	New York
Delta Kappa Epsilon	Powers, Samuel	Representative	Massachusetts
Delta Kappa Epsilon	Pray, Charles	Representative	Montana
Delta Kappa Epsilon	Quayle, Dan	Representative	Indiana
Delta Kappa Epsilon	Rathbone, Henry	Representative	Illinois
Delta Kappa Epsilon	Russell, Charles	Representative	Connecticut
Delta Kappa Epsilon	Sawyer, Lewis E.	Representative	Arkansas
Delta Kappa Epsilon	Shannon, Richard	Representative	New York
Delta Kappa Epsilon	Snow, Donald	Representative	Maine
Delta Kappa Epsilon	Spencer, Selden	Senator	Missouri
Delta Kappa Epsilon	Sprague, Charles F.	Representative	Massachusetts

Delta Kappa Epsilon	Stearns, Foster W.	Representative	New Hampshire
Delta Kappa Epsilon	Stewart, Percy H.	Representative	New York
Delta Kappa Epsilon	Storer, Bellamy	Representative	Ohio
Delta Kappa Epsilon	Strong, Theron	Representative	New York
Delta Kappa Epsilon	Sweet, Edwin F.	Representative	Michigan
Delta Kappa Epsilon	Symongton, Stuart	Senator	Missouri
Delta Kappa Epsilon	Taft, Charles P.	Representative	Ohio
Delta Kappa Epsilon	Taft, Robert	Rep./Senator	Ohio
Delta Kappa Epsilon	Taylor, Robert	Rep./Senator	Tennessee
Delta Kappa Epsilon	Tyler, Robert W.	Representative	Ohio
Delta Kappa Epsilon	Upton, Robert W.	Senator	New Hampshire
Delta Kappa Epsilon	Utter, George	Representative	Rhode Island
Delta Kappa Epsilon	Wadsworth, James	Rep./'Senator	New York
Delta Kappa Epsilon	Walker, Amasa	Representative	Massachusetts
Delta Kappa Epsilon	Wallace, William	Representative	New York
Delta Kappa Epsilon	Warner, John	Representative	New York
Delta Kappa Epsilon	Washburn, Charles	Representative	Massachusetts
Delta Kappa Epsilon	Washburn, William	Rep./Senator	Minnesota
Delta Kappa Epsilon	Webb, William R.	Senator	Tennessee
Delta Kappa Epsilon	Winslow, Sam	Representative	Massachusetts
Delta Kappa Epsilon	Woodford, Stewart	Representative	New York
Delta Kappa Epsilon	Young, Stephen	Rep./Senator	Ohio
Delta Phi	Bailey, John	Representative	New York
Delta Phi	Brewster, Daniel	Rep./Senator	Maryland
Delta Phi	Brooks, Franklin E.	Representative	Colorado
Delta Phi	Buck, Clayton D.	Senator	Delaware
Delta Phi	Chanler, John	Representative	New York
Delta Phi	Cox, Samuel	Representative	Ohio, NY
Delta Phi	Davis, Cushman	Senator	Minnesota
Delta Phi	DeWitt, David	Representative	New York
Delta Phi	Hazelton, George	Representative	Washington
Delta Phi	Miller, Thomas	Representative	Delaware
Delta Phi	Olney, Richard	Representative	Massachusetts
Delta Phi	Pell, Herbert	Representative	New York
Delta Phi	Post, Philip	Representative	Illinois
Delta Phi	Ransdell, Joseph	Rep./Senator	Louisiana
Delta Phi	Reeves, Henry	Representative	New York
Delta Phi	Ten Eyck, Peter	Representative	New York
Delta Phi	Van Auken, Daniel	Representative	Pennsylvania
Delta Phi	Voorhis, Charles	Representative	New Jersey
Delta Phi	Weideman, Carl M.	Representative	Michigan
Delta Psi	Adams, Robert Jr.	Representative	Pennsylvania
Delta Psi	Bailey, Joseph W.	Rep./Senator	Texas
Delta Psi	Bennett, Risden T.	Representative	North Carolina
Delta Psi	Catchings, Thomas C.	Representative	Mississippi
Delta Psi	Clark, Joseph	Senator	Pennsylvania
Delta Psi	Cluett, Ernest	Representative	New York
Delta Psi	Coffin, Thomas	Representative	Idaho
Delta Psi	Coughlin, Robert L. Jr	Representative	Pennsylvania
Delta Psi	Dewey, Char!es	Representative	Illinois
Delta Psi	Faulkner, Charles Jr.	Senator	West Virginia
Delta Psi	Fish, Hamilton	Representative	New York
Delta Psi	Goodwyn, Albert T.	Representative	Alabama
Delta Psi	Martin, Charles H.	Representative	North Carolina
Delta Psi	Mitchell, John M.	Representative	New York
Delta Psi	Money, Hernando DeSoto	Rep./Senator	Mississippi
Delta Psi	Morrell, Edward DeV.	Representative	Pennsylvania
Delta Psi	Newberry Truman	Senator	Michigan
Delta Psi	Perkins, James B.	Representative	New York
Delta Psi	Reyburn, William	Representative	Pennsylvania
Delta Psi	Saulsbury, Willard	Senator	Delaware
Delta Psi	Slaughter, D. French	Representative	Virginia

Delta Psi	Slayden, James L.	Representative	Texas
Delta Psi	Sullivan, William V.	Rep./Senator	Mississippi
Delta Psi	Tunney, John V.	Rep./Senator	California
Delta Psi	Wainwright, Jonathan M.	Representative	New York
Delta Psi	Wallop, Malcolm	Senator	Wyoming
Delta Psi	Whaley, Richard	Representative	South Carolina
Delta Psi	Woodford, Stewart	Representative	New York
Delta Sigma Phi	Adair, E. Ross	Representative	Indiana
Delta Sigma Phi	Brooks, Charles W.	Senator	Illinois
Delta Sigma Phi	Davis, James J.	Senator	Pennsylvania
Delta Sigma Phi	Harkin, Tom	Senator	Iowa
Delta Sigma Phi	Hebert, F. Edward	Representative	Louisiana
Delta Sigma Phi	Hughes, William J.	Representative	New Jersey
Delta Sigma Phi	Jones, Robert F.	Representative	Ohio
Delta Sigma Phi	Karst, Raymond W.	Representative	Missouri
Delta Sigma Phi	Lagomarsino, Robert J.	Representative	California
Delta Sigma Phi	Strangeland, Arlan	Representative	Montana
Delta Sigma Phi	Machen, Hervey	Representative	Maryland
Delta Sigma Phi	Miller, Louis E.	Representative	Missouri
Delta Sigma Phi	Scott, Lon A.	Representative	Tennessee
Delta Sigma Phi	Sullivan, John	Representative	Missouri
Delta Sigma Phi	Werdel, T. Harold	Representative	California
Delta Tau Delta	Allen, Henry J.	Senator	Kansas
Delta Tau Delta	Anthony, Daniel R.	Representative	Kansas
Delta Tau Delta	Atkinson, George W.	Representative	West Virginia
Delta Tau Delta	Badger, DeWitt C.	Representative	Ohio
Delta Tau Delta	Barkley, Alben W.	Rep./Senator	
Delta Tau Delta	Betts, Jackson	Representative	Ohio
Delta Tau Delta	Blanchard, James J.	Representative	Michigan
Delta Tau Delta	Borland, William P.	Representative	Missouri
Delta Tau Delta	Brown, Prentiss M.	Rep./Senator	Michigan
Delta Tau Delta	Browne, Thomas	Representative	Virginia
Delta Tau Delta	Brumm, George	Representative	Pennsylvania
Delta Tau Delta	Buck, Ellsworth	Representative	New York
Delta Tau Delta	Cable, John	Representative	Ohio
Delta Tau Delta	Carper, Thomas R.	Representative	Delaware
Delta Tau Delta	Clark, Joel	Senator	Missouri
Delta Tau Delta	Cline, Cyrus	Representative	Indiana
Delta Tau Delta	Cornwell, David	Representative	Indiana
Delta Tau Delta	Crosby, Charles N.	Representative	Pennsylvania
Delta Tau Delta	Cullop, William A.	Representative	Indiana
Delta Tau Delta	Edmiston, Andrew	Representative	West Virginia
Delta Tau Delta	Gardner, Washington	Representative	Michigan
Delta Tau Delta	Geyer, Lee E.	Representative	California
Delta Tau Delta	Hainer, Eugene J.	Representative	Nebraska
Delta Tau Delta	Hance Kent	Representative	Texas
Delta Tau Delta	Hastings, William	Representative	Oklahoma
Delta Tau Delta	Hoch, Homer	Representative	Kansas
Delta Tau Delta	Hopkins, Albert	Rep./Senator	Illinois
Delta Tau Delta	Horr, Ralph A.	Representative	Washington
Delta Tau Delta	Humphreys, Ben	Representative	Mississippi
Delta Tau Delta	Jacoway, Henderson M.	Representative	Arkansas
Delta Tau Delta	Jenner, William	Senator	Indiana
Delta Tau Delta	Johnson, Tim	Representative	South Dakota
Delta Tau Delta	Kilgore, Harley	Senator	West Virginia
Delta Tau Delta	Kimball, Henry M.	Representative	Michigan
Delta Tau Delta	MacKinnon, George E.	Representative	California
Delta Tau Delta	Main, Verner W.	Representative	Michigan
Delta Tau Delta	Mann, James	Representative	Illinois
Delta Tau Delta	McDowell, John A.	Representative	Ohio
Delta Tau Delta	McIntyre, Thomas J.	Senator	New Hampshire
Delta Tau Delta	Miller, Warren	Representative	West Virginia

Delta Tau Delta	Morrison, James	Representative	Louisiana
Delta Tau Delta	Muldrow, Henry	Representative	Mississippi
Delta Tau Delta	Norton, Miner G.	Representative	Ohio
Delta Tau Delta	Orth, Godlove	Representative	Indiana
Delta Tau Delta	Paddock, George	Representative	Illinois
Delta Tau Delta	Padgett, Lemuel	Representative	Tennessee
Delta Tau Delta	Pease, Donald J.	Representative	Ohio
Delta Tau Delta	Pepper, Irvin St. Clair	Representative	Iowa
Delta Tau Delta	Pickett, Charles	Representative	Iowa
Delta Tau Delta	Prouty, Solomon F.	Representative	Iowa
Delta Tau Delta	Purnell, Fred	Representative	Indiana
Delta Tau Delta	Richards, Charles L.	Representative	Nevada
Delta Tau Delta	Richardson, Bill	Representative	New Mexico
Delta Tau Delta	Short Dewey	Representative	Missouri
Delta Tau Delta	Simpson, Richard M.	Representative	Pennsylvania
Delta Tau Delta	Sloan, Charles H.	Representative	Nebraska
Delta Tau Delta	Steele, Leslie J.	Representative	Georgia
Delta Tau Delta	Sturgiss, George C.	Representative	West Virginia
Delta Tau Delta	Stewart, Donald W.	Senator	Alabama
Delta Tau Delta	Thomson, Charles M.	Representative	Illinois
Delta Tau Delta	Trammell Park	Senator	Florida
Delta Tau Delta	Wilson, John L.	Rep./Senator	Washington
Delta Upsilon	Aspin, Les	Representative	Wisconsin
Delta Upsilon	Avery, William H.	Representative	Kansas
Delta Upsilon	Barnes, Michael D.	Representative	Maryland
Delta Upsilon	Bassett, Edward M.	Representative	New York
Delta Upsilon	Blair, Austin	Representative	Michigan
Delta Upsilon	Case, Clifford	Rep./Senator	New Jersey
Delta Upsilon	Conlon, John B.	Representative	Arizona
Delta Upsilon	Dawes, Beman G.	Representative	Ohio
Delta Upsilon	Dennison, David	Representative	Ohio
Delta Upsilon	Dixon, Allen J.	Senator	Illinois
Delta Upsilon	Donnan, William G.	Representative	Iowa
Delta Upsilon	Douglas, Paul	Senator	Illinois
Delta Upsilon	Eliot, Thomas H.	Representative	Massachusetts
Delta Upsilon	Elston, John A.	Representative	California
Delta Upsilon	Englebright, Harry L.	Representative	California
Delta Upsilon	Farnsley, Charles R. P.	Representative	Kentucky
Delta Upsilon	Fisher, Joseph L.	Representative	Virginia
Delta Upsilon	Francis, George B.	Representative	New York
Delta Upsilon	Garfield, James	Representative	Ohio
Delta Upsilon	Griffiths, Percy W.	Representative	Ohio
Delta Upsilon	Hanrahan, Robert	Representative	Illinois
Delta Upsilon	Keating, Kenneth B.	Rep./Senator	New York
Delta Upsilon	Lafor, John	Representative	Pennsylvania
Delta Upsilon	Landis, Gerald	Representative	Indiana
Delta Upsilon	Law, Charles B.	Representative	New York
Delta Upsilon	Layton, Caleb R.	Representative	Delaware
Delta Upsilon	McCormick, Washington	Representative	Montana
Delta Upsilon	Moffett, Anthony T.	Representative	Connecticut
Delta Upsllon	Morgan, Thomas E.	Representative	Pennsylvania
Delta Upsilon	Morrill, Justin S.	Rep./Senator	Vermont
Delta Upsilon	Partridge, Frank C.	Senator	Vermont
Delta Upsilon	Payne, Sereno E.	Representative	New York
Delta Upsilon	Powers, Llewellyn	Representative	Maine
Delta Upsilon	Proctor, Redfield	Senator	Vermont
Delta Upsilon	Prouty, Winston	Rep./Senator	Vermont
Delta Upsilon	Reed, Chauncey W.	Representative	Illinois
Delta Upsilon	Rowe, Fred	Representative	New York
Delta Upsilon	Smart, James S.	Representative	New York
Delta Upsilon	Smith, Horace B.	Representative	New York
Delta Upsilon	Sperry, Lewis	Representative	Connecticut

Delta Upsilon	Stafford, Robert T.	Senator	Vermont
Delta Upsilon	Steele, Robert H.	Representative	Connecticut
Delta Upsilon	Stobbs, George Russell	Representative	Massachuetts
Delta Upsilon	Stone, Charles W.	Representative	Pennsylvania
Delta Upsilon	Vandenberg, Arthur	Senator	Michigan
Delta Upsilon	Whitehurst, George	Representative	Virginia
Delta Upsilon	Willis, Benjamin A.	Representative	New York
Delta Upsilon	Younger, Jesse	Representative	California
Delta Zeta	Neuberger, Maurine	Senator	Oregon
Delta Zeta Epsilon	Powers, David L.	Representative	New Jersey
Kappa Alpha	Abercrombie, John W.	Representative	Alabama
Kappa Alpha	Albert, Carl	Representative	Oklahoma
Kappa Alpha	Battle, Laurie	Representative	Alabama
Kappa Alpha	Bland, Schuyler	Representative	Virginia
Kappa Alpha	Boggs, J. Caleb	Rep./Senator	Delaware
Kappa Alpha Order	Borscher, Frederick	Representative	Virginia
Kappa Alpha	Bowen, David R.	Representative	Missouri
Kappa Alpha	Breckinridge, John B.	Representative	Kentucky
Kappa Alpha	Brooks, Overton	Representative	Louisiana
Kappa Alpha	Broyhill, Joel T.	Representative	Virginia
Kappa Alpha	Button, Daniel Evan	Representative	New York
Kappa Alpha	Byron, Goodloe E.	Representative	Maryland
Kappa Alpha	Candler, Milton A.	Representative	Georgia
Kappa Alpha Order	Clinger, William F. Jr.	Representative	Pennsylvania
Kappa Alpha	Coleman, Earl T.	Representative	Missouri
Kappa Alpha	Cravens, William Fadjo	Representative	Arkansas
Kappa Alpha	Davis, John William	Representative	Georgia
Kappa Alpha	Derrick, Butler C.	Representative	South Carolina
Kappa Alpha	Edwards, William J.	Representative	Alabama
Kappa Alpha	Faison, John M.	Representative	North Carolina
Kappa Alpha Order	Gordon, Barton J.	Representative	Tennessee
Kappa Alpha	Gordon, John Brown	Senator	Georgia
Kappa Alpha	Gubser, Charles	Representative	California
Kappa Alpha	Hancock, Franklin	Representative	North Carolina
Kappa Alpha	Hardy, Porter	Representative	Virginia
Kappa Alpha	Harris, William J.	Senator	Georgia
Kappa Alpha	Harrison, Burr	Representative	Virginia
Kappa Alpha	Hemphill, Robert	Representative	South Carolina
Kappa Alpha Order	Henry, Robert L.	Representative	Texas
Kappa Alpha Order	Hobson, Richmond P.	Representative	Alabama
Kappa Alpha	Hubbard, Carroll	Representative	Kentucky
Kappa Alpha	Huckaby, Thomas Jerald	Representative	Louisiana
Kappa Alpha	Jones, Robert	Representative	Alabama
Kappa Alpha	Kerr, John Hosea	Representative	North Carolina
Kappa Alpha	Ketchum, William	Representative	California
Kappa Alpha	Kitchin, Alvin	Representative	North Carolina
Kappa Alpha	Lamar, William Bailey	Representative	Florida
Kappa Alpha	Lanham, Fritz	Representative	Texas
Kappa Alpha	Lankford, Menalcus	Representative	Virginia
Kappa Alpha	Love, Francis Johnson	Representative	West Virginia
Kappa Alpha	Montgomery, Gillespie	Representative	Mississippi
Kappa Alpha	Nicholls, Samuel J.	Representative	South Carolina
Kappa Alpha	Paul, John	Representative	Virginia
Kappa Alpha	Pepper, Claude	Rep./Senator	Florida
Kappa Alpha	Radcliffe, George L.	Senator	Maryland
Kappa Alpha Order	Reid, Charles C.	Representative	Arkansas
Kappa Alpha	Sheppard, Morris	Rep./Senator	Texas
Kappa Alpha	Spence, Floyd D.	Representative	South Carolina
Kappa Alpha	Stephens, Robert Grier	Representative	Georgia
Kappa Alpha	Stoll, Philip	Representative	South Carolina
Kappa Alpha	Storke, Thomas	Senator	California
Kappa Alpha	Vinson, Carl	Representative	Georgia

Kappa Alpha	Walker, Elzar Steven	Representative	New Mexico
Kappa Alpha	Webb, Edwin Yates	Representative	North Carolina
Kappa Alpha	Wickliffe, Robert	Representative	Louisiana
Kappa Alpha	Wilson, Thomas Webber	Representative	Mississippi
Kappa Alpha Society	Allen, Thomas	Representative	Missouri
Kappa Alpha Society	Babcock, Leander	Representative	New York
Kappa Alpha Society	Beale, Charles	Representative	New York
Kappa Alpha Society	Bouck, Gabriel	Representative	Wisconsin
Kappa Alpha Society	Bragg, Edward	Representative	Wisconsin
Kappa Alpha Society	Carroll, John	Representative	New York
Kappa Alpha Society	Dixon, James	Rep./Senator	Connecticut
Kappa Alpha Society	Dunwell, Charles T.	Representative	New York
Kappa Alpha Society	Henry, Lewis	Representative	New York
Kappa Alpha Society	King, Preston	Rep./Senator	New York
Kappa Alpha Society	Mackey, Levi	Representative	Pennsylvania
Kappa Alpha Society	Norton, Jesse	Representative	Illinois
Kappa Alpha Society	Overton, Edward Jr.	Representative	Pennsylvania
Kappa Alpha Society	Steele, John	Representative	New York
Kappa Alpha Society	Wells, John	Representative	New York
Kappa Alpha Psi	Conyers, John Jr.	Representative	Michigan
Kappa Alpha Psi	Crockett, George W.	Representative	Michigan
Kappa Alpha Psi	Dymally, Mervyn	Representative	California
Kappa Alpha Psi	Stokes, Louis	Representative	Ohio
Kappa Alpha Theta	Kassebaum, Nancy	Senator	Kansas
Kappa Delta	Kelly, Edna	Representative	New York
Kappa Delta Rho	Anderson, Glenn Malcolm	Representative	California
Kappa Kappa Kappa	Baker, Henry	Representative	New Hampshire
Kappa Kappa Kappa	Burnham, Henry Eben	Senator	New Hampshire
Kappa Kappa Kappa	Burroughs, Sherman	Representative	New Hampshire
Kappa Kappa Kappa	Cass, Lewis	Senator	Michigan
Kappa Kappa Kappa	Choate, Rufus	Rep./Senator	Massachusetts
Kappa Kappa Kappa	Clark, Daniel	Senator	New Hampshire
Kappa Kappa Kappa	Drew, Irving	Senator	New Hampshire
Kappa Kappa Kappa	Flanders, Benjamin	Representative	Louisiana
Kappa Kappa Kappa	Gooch, Daniel	Representative	Massachusetts
Kappa Kappa Kappa	Hammond, Winfield S.	Representative	Minnesota
Kappa Kappa Kappa	Marsh, George Perkins	Representative	Vermont
Kappa Kappa Kappa	McCall, Samuel	Representative	Massachusetts
Kappa Kappa Kappa	Ranney, Ambrose	Representative	Massachusetts
Kappa Kappa Kappa	Webster, Daniel	Rep./Senator	Massachusetts
Kappa Kappa Kappa	Woodbury, Levi	Senator	New Hampshire
Kappa Sigma	Alexander, William V.	Representative	Arkansas
Kappa Sigma	Austin, Warren	Senator	Vermont
Kappa Sigma	Beamer, John	Representative	Indiana
Kappa Sigma	Beck, Joseph David	Representative	Wisconsin
Kappa Sigma	Bethune, Edwin R.	Representative	Arkansas
Kappa Sigma	Bosco, Douglas H.	Representative	California
Kappa Sigma	Caldwell, Millard	Representative	Florida
Kappa Sigma	Cannon, Clarence	Representative	Missouri
Kappa Sigma	Cole, Albert	Representative	Kansas
Kappa Sigma	Cooper, Jere	Representative	Tennessee
Kappa Sigma	Covington, James H.	Representative	Maryland
Kappa Sigma	Craig, William Benjamin	Representative	Alabama
Kappa Sigma	Daub, Harold J.	Representative	Nebraska
Kappa Sigma	Dole, Robert	Rep./Senator	Kansas
Kappa Sigma	Donnell, Forrest	Senator	Missouri
Kappa Sigma	Eaton, William R.	Representative	Colorado
Kappa Sigma	Ellsworth, Mathew	Representative	Oregon
Kappa Sigma	Fannin, Paul	Senator	Arizona
Kappa Sigma	Fascell, Dante	Representative	Florida
Kappa Sigma	Featherston, Winfield S	Representative	Mississippi
Kappa Sigma	Graham, William Johnson	Representative	Illinois

Kappa Sigma	Griffith, John Keller	Representative	Louisiana
Kappa Sigma	Healey, James	Representative	New York
Kappa Sigma	Hill, Samuel B.	Representative	Washington
Kappa Sigma	Horton, Frank	Representative	New York
Kappa Sigma	Hyde, DeWitt S.	Representative	Maryland
Kappa Sigma	Jenrette, John	Representative	South Carolina
Kappa Sigma	Johnson, Luther	Representative	Texas
Kappa Sigma	Kefauver, Carey Estes	Rep./Senator	Tennessee
Kappa Sigma	Lambeth, John Walter	Representative	North Carolina
Kappa Sigma	Lankford, Richard Estep	Representative	Maryland
Kappa Sigma	Lloyd, James F.	Representative	California
Kappa Sigma	Lowry, Mike	Representative	Washington
Kappa Sigma	Mayfield, Earle	Senator	Texas
Kappa Sigma	McAdoo, William Gibbs	Senator	California
Kappa Sigma	McClellan, John	Rep./Senator	Arkansas
Kappa Sigma	Moran, Edward C.	Representative	Maine
Kappa Sigma	Oliver, James	Representative	Maine
Kappa Sigma	Olpp, Archibald	Representative	New Jersey
Kappa Sigma	Pearson, Herron C.	Representative	Tennessee
Kappa Sigma	Peery, George Campbell	Representative	Virginia
Kappa Sigma	Perky, Kirtland Irving	Senator	Idaho
Kappa Sigma	Pridemore, Auburn L	Representative	Virginia
Kappa Sigma	Reeves, Albert Lee Jr.	Representative	Missouri
Kappa Sigma	Sasser, James R.	Senator	Tennessee
Kappa Sigma	Smith, Neal	Representative	Iowa
Kappa Sigma	Stockman, Lowell	Representative	Oregon
Kappa Sigma	Terry, David	Representative	Arkansas
Kappa Sigma	Thomason, Robert E.	Representative	Texas
Kappa Sigma	Treen, David C.	Representative	Louisiana
Kappa Sigma	Waggonner, Joseph	Representative	Louisiana
Kappa Sigma	Watson, Albert	Representative	South Carolina
Kappa Sigma	Wortley, George C.	Representative	New York
Lambda Chi Alpha	Abernathy, Thomas G.	Representative	Mississippi
Lambda Chi Alpha	Berry, E. Y.	Representative	South Dakota
Lambda Chi Alpha	Bible, Alan H.	Senator	Nevada
Lambda Chi Alpha	Bottum, Joseph H.	Senator	South Dakota
Lambda Chi Alpha	Breaux, John B.	Representative	Louisiana
Lambda Chi Alpha	Brown, Charles H.	Representative	Missouri
Lambda Chi Alpha	Burleson, Omar	Representative	Texas
Lambda Chi Alpha	Burnside, Maurice	Representative	West Virginia
Lambda Chi Alpha	Craley, Nathaniel N.	Representative	Pennsylvania
Lambda Chi Alpha	Danforth, John	Senator	Missouri
Lambda Chi Alpha	Coleman, Ronald	Representative	Texas
Lambda Chi Alpha	Dannemeyer, William	Representative	California
Lambda Chi Alpha	Dunn, James	Representative	Michigan
Lambda Chi Alpha	Ford, Wendell H.	Senator	Kentucky
Lambda Chi Alpha	Hall, Durwood G.	Representative	Missouri
Lambda Chi Alpha	Hanna, Richard T.	Representative	California
Lambda Chi Alpha	Hartke, Rupert Vance	Senator	Indiana
Lambda Chi Alpha	Heflin, Howell	Senator	Alabama
Lambda Chi Alpha	Johnson, Harold T.	Representative	California
Lambda Chi Alpha	Jones, James R.	Representative	Oklahoma
Lambda Chi Alpha	Kelly, Melville Clyde	Representative	Pennsylvania
Lambda Chi Alpha	Levering, Robert W.	Representative	Ohio
Lambda Chi Alpha	Lloyd, James T.	Representative	Missouri
Lambda Chi Alpha	Lovre, Harold O.	Representative	South Dakota
Lambda Chi Alpha	McGuire, John A.	Representative	Connecticut
Lambda Chi Alpha	Paul, Ron	Representative	Texas
Lambda Chi Alpha	Rich, Carl W.	Representative	Ohio
Lambda Chi Alpha	Ruffin, James E.	Representative	Missouri
Lambda Chi Alpha	Russell, Charles H.	Representative	Nevada
Lambda Chi Alpha	Taylor, Alfred A.	Representative	Tennessee

Lambda Chi Alpha	Trible, Paul S.	Rep./Senator	Virginia
Lambda Chi Alpha	Truman, Harry	Senator	Missouri
Lambda Chi Alpha	Velde, Harold H.	Representative	Illinois
Lambda Chi Alpha	Weldon, Wayne C.	Representative	Pennsylvania
Lambda Chi Alpha	Young, Clarence	Representative	Nevada
Lambda Iota	Ferriss, Orange	Representative	New York
Lambda Iota	Higby, William	Representative	California
Lambda Iota	Smith, Worthington C.	Representative	Vermont
Phi Beta Sigma	Mitchell, Arthur W.	Representative	Alabama
Phi Delta Theta	Adams, Brock	Representative	Washington
Phi Delta Theta	Allen, John B.	Delegate/Senator	Washington
Phi Delta Theta	Ammerman, Joseph S.	Representative	Pennsylvania
Phi Delta Theta	Anderson, John	Representative	Kansas
Phi Delta Theta	Austin, Albert E.	Representative	Connecticut
Phi Delta Theta	Bankhead, William	Representative	Alabama
Phi Delta Theta	Barnard, D. Douglas	Representative	Georgia
Phi Delta Theta	Bedell, Berkeley	Representative	Iowa
Phi Delta Theta	Black, James C.	Representative	Georgia
Phi Delta Theta	Black, John	Representative	Illinois
Phi Delta Theta	Blackburn, J.C.S.	Rep./Senator	Kentucky
Phi Delta Theta	Bolling, Richard	Representative	Missouri
Phi Delta Theta	Bond, Charles	Representative	New York
Phi Delta Theta	Bonin, Edward J.	Representative	Pennsylvania
Phi Delta Theta	Brantley, William	Representative	Georgia
Phi Delta Theta	Broyhill, James T.	Representative	North Carolina
Phi Delta Theta	Burtness, Olger	Representative	North Dakota
Phi Delta Theta	Cain, Harry	Senator	Washington
Phi Delta Theta	Callaway, Howard	Representative	Georgia
Phi Delta Theta	Carlyle, F. Ertel	Representative	North Carolina
Phi Delta Theta	Chelf, Frank	Representative	Kentucky
Phi Delta Theta	Chiperfield, Robert B	Representative	Illinois
Phi Delta Theta	Collins, James M.	Representative	Texas
Phi Delta Theta	Collins, Ross	Representative	Mississippi
Phi Delta Theta	Conable, Barber	Representative	New York
Phi Delta Theta	Conger, E. H.	Representative	Iowa
Phi Delta Theta	Connally, Tom	Rep./Senator	Texas
Phi Delta Theta	Cooley, Harold	Representative	North Carolina
Phi Delta Theta	Corbett, Robert	Representative	Pennsylvania
Phi Delta Theta	Courter, James A.	Representative	New Jersey
Phi Delta Theta	Darby, Harry	Senator	Kansas
Phi Delta Theta	Deal, Joseph	Representative	Virginia
Phi Delta Theta	DeConcini, Dennis W.	Senator	Arizona
Phi Delta Theta	Durno, Edwin	Representative	Oregon
Phi Delta Theta	Fenton, Lucien	Representative	Ohio
Phi Delta Theta	Fitzhenry, Louis	Representative	Illinois
Phi Delta Theta	Fletcher, Charles	Representative	California
Phi Delta Theta	Fletcher, Duncan	Senator	Florida
Phi Delta Theta	Foster, Israel M.	Representative	Ohio
Phi Delta Theta	Fowler, William W.	Representative	Georgia
Phi Delta Theta	French, Burton	Representative	Idaho
Phi Delta Theta	Fulton, James	Representative	Pennsylvania
Phi Delta Theta	Goodell, Charles	Rep./Senator	New York
Phi Delta Theta	Graff, J. V.	Representative	Illinois
Phi Delta Theta	Gray, Oscar	Representative	Alabama
Phi Delta Theta	Griffith, Francis	Representative	Indiana
Phi Delta Theta	Griggs, J. M.	Representative	Georgia
Phi Delta Theta	Grosvenor, Charles H.	Representative	Ohio
Phi Delta Theta	Hadley, Lindley H.	Representative	Washington
Phi Delta Theta	Hamilton, Andrew	Representative	Indiana
Phi Delta Theta	Hardwick, Thomas	Rep./Senator	Georgia
Phi Delta Theta	Hardy, Rufus	Representative	Texas
Phi Delta Theta	Harrison, Benjamin	Senator	Indiana

Phi Delta Theta	Hefley, Joel	Representative	Colorado
Phi Delta Theta	Hill, Wilson	Representative	Mississippi
Phi Delta Theta	Holmes, Otis H.	Representative	Washington
Phi Delta Theta	Howard, William	Representative	Georgia
Phi Delta Theta	Jarman, John	Representative	Oklahoma
Phi Delta Theta	Johnson, Roayl	Representative	South Dakota
Phi Delta Theta	Johnston, J. Bennett	Senator	Louisiana
Phi Delta Theta	Kennedy, John	Representative	Nebraska
Phi Delta Theta	Kurtz Jacob B.	Representative	Pennsylvania
Phi Delta Theta	LaFollette, Charles	Representative	Indiana
Phi Delta Theta	Lee, Gordon (J.G.)	Representative	Georgia
Phi Delta Theta	Lemke, William	Representative	North Dakota
Phi Delta Theta	Lewis, John	Representative	Kentucky
Phi Delta Theta	McCloskey, Pete	Representative	California
Phi Delta Theta	McEwen, Robert	Representative	New York
Phi Delta Theta	McLaughlin, Charles	Representative	Nebraska
Phi Delta Theta	Millikin, Eugene	Senator	Colorado
Phi Delta Theta	Minton, Sherman	Senator	Indiana
Phi Delta Theta	Mize, Chester	Representative	Kansas
Phi Delta Theta	Moore, Allen	Representative	Illinois
Phi Delta Theta	Morehead, Charles S.	Representative	Kentucky
Phi Delta Theta	Morrison, Martin	Representative	Indiana
Phi Delta Theta	Moses, Charles	Representative	Georgia
Phi Delta Theta	Muhlenberg, Fred	Representative	Pennsylvania
Phi Delta Theta	Norton, Patrick	Representative	North Dakota
Phi Delta Theta	Nunn, Sam Jr.	Senator	Georgia
Phi Delta Theta	Oliver, William B.	Representative	Alabama
Phi Delta Theta	Overstreet, James	Representative	Georgia
Phi Delta Theta	Parker, Homer	Representative	Georgia
Phi Delta Theta	Paschal, Thomas	Representative	Texas
Phi Delta Theta	Patterson, Malcolm	Representative	Tennessee
Phi Delta Theta	Philips, John	Representative	Missouri
Phi Delta Theta	Prince, George	Representative	Illinois
Phi Delta Theta	Pugh, Sam	Representative	Kentucky
Phi Delta Theta	Ramsey, Alexander	Rep./Senator	PA. & Minnesota
Phi Delta Theta	Robinson, Art	Senator	Indiana
Phi Delta Theta	Rogers, Dwight	Representative	Florida
Phi Delta Theta	Rogers, Paul G.	Representative	Florida
Phi Delta Theta	Russell, G. J.	Representative	Texas
Phi Delta Theta	Sherwin, John C.	Representative	Illinois
Phi Delta Theta	Shouse, Jouett	Representative	Kansas
Phi Delta Theta	Shriver, Garner	Representative	Kansas
Phi Delta Theta	Sittler, Edward Jr.	Representative	Pennsylvania
Phi Delta Theta	Slattery, Jim	Representative	Kansas
Phi Delta Theta	Springer, William	Representative	Illinois
Phi Delta Theta	Stevenson, Adlai	Representative	Illinois
Phi Delta Theta	Stinson, K. William	Representative	Washington
Phi Delta Theta	Sweet, Willis	Representative	Idaho
Phi Delta Theta	Swope, King	Representative	Kentucky
Phi Delta Theta	Thomas, Elbert	Senator	Utah
Phi Delta Theta	Thomas, John	Rep./Senator	Oklahoma
Phi Delta Theta	Thompson, Clark W.	Representative	Texas
Phi Delta Theta	Thomson, Edwin K.	Representative	Wyoming
Phi Delta Theta	Tompkins, Emmett	Representative	Ohio
Phi Delta Theta	Tribble Sam	Representative	Georgia
Phi Delta Theta	Underwood, Thomas	Rep./Senator	Kentucky
Phi Delta Theta	Venable, William W.	Representative	Mississippi
Phi Delta Theta	Vilas, William F.	Senator	Wisconsin
Phi Delta Theta	Vinson Fred	Representative	Kentucky
Phi Delta Theta	Walter, Francis E.	Representative	Pennsylvania
Phi Delta Theta	Ward, Thomas	Representative	Indiana
Phi Delta Theta	Widnall, William	Representative	New Jersey

Phi Delta Theta	Wilfley, X. P.	Senator	Missouri
Phi Delta Theta	Willis, Raymond	Senator	Indiana
Phi Delta Theta	Witherspoon, Samuel A.	Representative	Mississippi
Phi Delta Theta	Worley, Francis E.	Representative	Texas
Phi Kappa Psi	Acheson, Ernest F.	Representative	Pennsylvania
Phi Kappa Psi	Adams, Wilbur	Representative	Delaware
Phi Kappa Psi	Bannon, Henry	Representative	Ohio
Phi Kappa Psi	Barber, Laird	Representative	Pennsylvania
Phi Kappa Psi	Bates, Arthur	Representative	Pennsylvania
Phi Kappa Psi	Beatty, John	Representative	Ohio
Phi Kappa Psi	Belford, Joseph	Representative	New York
Phi Kappa Psi	Beltzhoover, Frank	Representative	Pennsylvania
Phi Kappa Psi	Bingham, Henry	Representative	Pennsylvania
Phi Kappa Psi	Bromwell, James	Representative	Iowa
Phi Kappa Psi	Burke, Frank W.	Representative	Kentucky
Phi Kappa Psi	Byrns, Joseph	Representative	Tennessee
Phi Kappa Psi	Calkins, William H.	Representative	Indiana
Phi Kappa Psi	Chamberlain, George	Senator	Oregon
Phi Kappa Psi	Champion, Edwin	Representative	Illinois
Phi Kappa Psi	Church, Ralph	Representative	Illinois
Phi Kappa Psi	Cooney, James	Representative	Missouri
Phi Kappa Psi	Crow, William	Representative	Pennsylvania
Phi Kappa Psi	Dale, Thomas H.	Representative	Pennsylvania
Phi Kappa Psi	Daniel, Robert W. Jr.	Representative	Virginia
Phi Kappa Psi	Davis, John W.	Representative	West Virginia
Phi Kappa Psi	Denton, Winfield	Representative	Indiana
Phi Kappa Psi	Dill, Clarence C.	Rep./Senator	Washington
Phi Kappa Psi	Dugro, Philip	Representative	New York
Phi Kappa Psi	Durborow, Allan	Representative	Illinois
Phi Kappa Psi	Ewart, Hamilton	Representative	North Carolina
Phi Kappa Psi	Faris, George W.	Representative	Indiana
Phi Kappa Psi	Finley, David	Representative	South Carolina
Phi Kappa Psi	Foraker, Joseph	Senator	Ohio
Phi Kappa Psi	Gilbert, Newton	Representative	Indiana
Phi Kappa Psi	Gwinn, Ralph	Representative	New York
Phi Kappa Psi	Hand, Thomas	Representative	New Jersey
Phi Kappa Psi	Harrison, Thomas W.	Representative	Virginia
Phi Kappa Psi	Hartman, Charles	Representative	Montana
Phi Kappa Psi	Heiner, Daniel B.	Representative	Pennsylvania
Phi Kappa Psi	Henderson, Charles B.	Senator	Nevada
Phi Kappa Psi	Henderson, Thomas J.	Representative	Illinois
Phi Kappa Psi	Henry, Charles	Representative	Indiana
Phi Kappa Psi	Hicks, Frederick C.	Representative	New York
Phi Kappa Psi	Hoblitzell, John	Senator	West Virginia
Phi Kappa Psi	Hogg, Herschel M.	Representative	Colorado
Phi Kappa Psi	Hosmer, Craig	Representative	California
Phi Kappa Psi	Hughes, Charles J.	Representative	Colorado
Phi Kappa Psi	Jenks, George A.	Representative	Pennsylvania
Phi Kappa Psi	Jones, John S.	Representative	Ohio
Phi Kappa Psi	Keifer, J. Warren	Representative	Ohio
Phi Kappa Psi	Kenyon, William S.	Senator	Iowa
Phi Kappa Psi	Kuchel, Thomas	Senator	California
Phi Kappa Psi	Legare, George S.	Representative	South Carolina
Phi Kappa Psi	Little, Edward C.	Representative	Kansas
Phi Kappa Psi	Lowndes, Lloyd	Representative	Maryland
Phi Kappa Psi	Marsh, John	Representative	Virginia
Phi Kappa Psi	Martin, Edward L.	Representative	Delaware
Phi Kappa Psi	Massingale, Samuel C.	Representative	Oklahoma
Phi Kappa Psi	McClure, Addison	Representative	Ohio
Phi Kappa Psi	McCollister, John Y.	Representative	Nebraska
Phi Kappa Psi	McCullogh, Welty	Representative	Pennsylvania
Phi Kappa Psi	McKinney, James	Representative	Illinois

Phi Kappa Psi	Miller, Clarence B.	Representative	Minnesota
Phi Kappa Psi	Mitchell, Hugh B.	Rep./Senator	Washington
Phi Kappa Psi	Mitchell, John I.	Rep./Senator	Pennsylvania
Phi Kappa Psi	Moss, Hunter	Representative	West Virginia
Phi Kappa Psi	Needham, James C.	Representative	California
Phi Kappa Psi	Noland, James	Representative	Indiana
Phi Kappa Psi	Page, Henry	Representative	Maryland
Phi Kappa Psi	Palmer, Alexander M.	Representative	Pennsylvania
Phi Kappa Psi	Perry, William H.	Representative	South Carolina
Phi Kappa Psi	Peters, Sam	Representative	Kansas
Phi Kappa Psi	Peyer, Pete	Representative	New York
Phi Kappa Psi	Pickler, John	Representative	South Dakota
Phi Kappa Psi	Price, Hugh	Representative	Wisconsin
Phi Kappa Psi	Randall, William	Representative	Missouri
Phi Kappa Psi	Rich, Robert	Representative	Pennsylvania
Phi Kappa Psi	Rogers, William	Representative	New York
Phi Kappa Psi	Seiberling, Francis	Representative	Ohio
Phi Kappa Psi	Shallenberger, William	Representative	Pennsylvania
Phi Kappa Psi	Short, Don	Representative	North Dakota
Phi Kappa Psi	Smith, Ellison	Senator	South Carolina
Phi Kappa Psi	Smyser, Martin	Representative	Ohio
Phi Kappa Psi	Stephens, Hubert D.	Rep./Senator	Mississippi
Phi Kappa Psi	Sundstrom, Frank	Representative	New York
Phi Kappa Psi	Taft, Kingsley A.	Senator	Ohio
Phi Kappa Psi	Taylor, Dean	Representative	New York
Phi Kappa Psi	Townshend, Richard W.	Representative	Illinois
Phi Kappa Psi	Tuttle, William Edgar	Representative	New York
Phi Kappa Psi	Tyler, David	Representative	Virginia
Phi Kappa Psi	Walker, James A.	Representative	Virginia
Phi Kappa Psi	Watson, James	Rep./Senator	Indiana
Phi Kappa Psi	Willey, Earle	Representative	Delaware
Phi Kappa Psi	Williams, George	Representative	Delaware
Phi Kappa Psi	Williams, James R.	Representative	Illinois
Phi Kappa Psi	Williams, Robert	Representative	Virginia
Phi Kappa Psi	Winchester, Boyd	Representative	Kentucky
Phi Kappa Psi	Winn, Edward L. Jr.	Representative	Kansas
Phi Kappa Psi	Wolverton, Simon	Representative	Pennsylvania
Phi Kappa Psi	Wooten, Dudley G.	Representative	Texas
Phi Kappa Psi	Yocum, Seth	Representative	Pennsylvania
Phi Gamma Delta	Allott, Gordon	Senator	Colorado
Phi Gamma Delta	Antony, Edwin Leroy	Representative	Texas
Phi Gamma Delta	Badham, Robert E.	Representative	California
Phi Gamma Delta	Bell , Alphonzo	Representative	California
Phi Gamma Delta	Benner, George J.	Representative	Pennsylvania
Phi Gamma Delta	Botkin, Jeremiah D.	Representative	Kansas
Phi Gamma Delta	Brand, Charles	Representative	Ohio
Phi Gamma Delta	Brown, Foster	Representative	Tennessee
Phi Gamma Delta	Buchanan, Frank	Representative	Pennsylvania
Phi Gamma Delta	Burleson, Albert S.	Representative	Texas
Phi Gamma Delta	Butler, Manley	Representative	Virginia
Phi Gamma Delta	Carr, Robert	Representative	Michigan
Phi Gamma Delta	Clarke, John Davenport	Representative	New York
Phi Gamma Delta	Darden, Colgate	Representative	Virginia
Phi Gamma Delta	Dellenback, John	Representative	Oregon
Phi Gamma Delta	Edmondson, Edmond	Representative	Oklahoma
Phi Gamma Delta	Edmondson, J. Howard	Rep./Senator	Oklahoma
Phi Gamma Delta	Ellsworth, Franklin F.	Representative	Minnesota
Phi Gamma Delta	Emerson, William	Representative	Missouri
Phi Gamma Delta	Enloe, Benjamin	Representative	Tennessee
Phi Gamma Delta	Erdman, Constantine J.	Representative	Pennsylvania
Phi Gamma Delta	Fairbanks, Charles	Senator	Indiana
Phi Gamma Delta	Fellows, Frank	Representative	Maine

Phi Gamma Delta	Ferguson, Harvey B.	Delegate/Rep.	New Mexico
Phi Gamma Delta	Ferguson, Philip	Representative	Oklahoma
Phi Gamma Delta	Follett, John F.	Representative	Ohio
Phi Gamma Delta	Frey, Louis	Representative	Florida
Phi Gamma Delta	Gould, Sam	Representative	Maine
Phi Gamma Delta	Hall, Homer W.	Representative	Illinois
Phi Gamma Delta	Henderson, John E.	Representative	Ohio
Phi Gamma Delta	Hollenbeck, Harold C.	Representative	New Jersey
Phi Gamma Delta	Hopkins, James	Representative	Pennsylvania
Phi Gamma Delta	Huffman, James W.	Senator	Ohio
Phi Gamma Delta	Hunter, Morton Craig	Representative	Indiana
Phi Gamma Delta	Jenkins, Albert	Representative	Virginia
Phi Gamma Delta	Kribbs, George	Representative	Pennsylvania
Phi Gamma Delta	Ladd, Edwin	Senator	North Dakota
Phi Gamma Delta	Lane, Henry S.	Rep./Senator	Indiana
Phi Gamma Delta	Lee, Joshua Bryan	Rep./Senator	Oklahoma
Phi Gamma Delta	Lehman, Herbert	Senator	New York
Phi Gamma Delta	Lesher, John V.	Representative	Virginia
Phi Gamma Delta	Lewis, Fred	Representative	Pennsylvania
Phi Gamma Delta	Ludlow, Louis Leon	Representative	Indiana
Phi Gamma Delta	Maffett, James	Representative	Pennsylvania
Phi Gamma Delta	Martin, John M.	Representative	Alabama
Phi Gamma Delta	Mathias, Bob	Representative	California
Phi Gamma Delta	Matyr, Gilbert DeLa	Representative	Indiana
Phi Gamma Delta	McClelland, William	Representative	Pennsylvania
Phi Gamma Delta	McSweeney, John	Representative	Ohio
Phi Gamma Delta	Miller, Ward	Representative	Ohio
Phi Gamma Delta	Monroney, Almer	Rep./Senator	Oklahoma
Phi Gamma Delta	Mouser, Grant E. Jr.	Representative	Ohio
Phi Gamma Delta	O'Hair, Frank T.	Representative	Illinois
Phi Gamma Delta	O'Hara, Barratt	Representative	Illinois
Phi Gamma Delta	Oliver, Samuel	Representative	Iowa
Phi Gamma Delta	Patterson, Thomas M.	Del./Rep./Senator	Colorado
Phi Gamma Delta	Penington, John	Representative	Delaware
Phi Gamma Delta	Pritchard, Joel M.	Representative	Washington
Phi Gamma Delta	Railsback, Thomas F.	Representative	Illinois
Phi Gamma Delta	Reams, Henry Frazier	Representative	Ohio
Phi Gamma Delta	Reid, Ogden	Representative	New York
Phi Gamma Delta	Riddle, Haywood Y.	Representative	Tennessee
Phi Gamma Delta	Robbins, Edward E.	Representative	Pennsylvania
Phi Gamma Delta	Robinson, James W.	Representative	Ohio
Phi Gamma Delta	Satterfield, Dave E.	Representative	Virginia
Phi Gamma Delta	Satterfield, David	Representative	Virginia
Phi Gamma Delta	Seerley, John Joseph	Representative	Iowa
Phi Gamma Delta	Shanks, John P. C.	Representative	Indiana
Phi Gamma Delta	Shreve, Milton	Representative	Pennsylvania
Phi Gamma Delta	Sikorsk, Gerry	Representative	Montana
Phi Gamma Delta	Sterling, John A.	Representative	Illinois
Phi Gamma Delta	Sterling, Thomas A.	Senator	South Dakota
Phi Gamma Delta	Stockdale, Thomas R.	Representative	Mississippi
Phi Gamma Delta	Tracewell, Robert	Representative	Indiana
Phi Gamma Delta	Vance, Zebulon	Rep./Senator	North Carolina
Phi Gamma Delta	Weicher, Lowell	Rep./Senator	Connecticut
Phi Gamma Delta	Welty, Benjamin F. Jr.	Representative	Ohio
Phi Gamma Delta	White, Compton	Representative	Idaho
Phi Gamma Delta	White, Stephen V. C.	Representative	New York
Phi Gamma Delta	Wilson, Eugen	Representative	Minnesota
Phi Gamma Delta	Wilson, Stanyarne	Representative	South Carolina
Phi Gamma Delta	Woods, James P.	Representative	Virginia
Phi Kappa Sigma	Brown, Clarence J.	Representative	Ohio
Phi Kappa Sigma	Busbey, Fred	Representative	Illinois
Phi Kappa Sigma	Cole, William P. Jr.	Representative	Maryland

Phi Kappa Sigma	Duncan, William A.	Representative	Pennsylvania
Phi Kappa Sigma	DuPont, Henry A.	Senator	Delaware
Phi Kappa Sigma	Ellis, Ezekiel John	Representative	Louisiana
Phi Kappa Sigma	Evins, Joseph L.	Representative	Tennessee
Phi Kappa Sigma	Fredericks, John D.	Representative	California
Phi Kappa Sigma	Haight, Charles	Representative	New Jersey
Phi Kappa Sigma	Hogg, Robert	Representative	West Virginia
Phi Kappa Sigma	Leech, James	Representative	Pennsylvania
Phi Kappa Sigma	Luhring, Oscar R.	Representative	Indiana
Phi Kappa Sigma	McComas, Louis E.	Rep./Senator	Maryland
Phi Kappa Sigma	McEnery, Samuel D.	Senator	Louisiana
Phi Kappa Sigma	Neal, John R.	Representative	Tennessee
Phi Kappa Sigma	O'Conor, Herbert R.	Senator	Maryland
Phi Kappa Sigma	O'Mahoney, Joseph	Senator	Wyoming
Phi Kappa Sigma	Revercomb, William	Senator	West Virginia
Phi Kappa Sigma	Robson, Howard	Representative	New York
Phi Kappa Sigma	Schirm, Charles R.	Representative	Maryland
Phi Kappa Sigma	Schweiker, Richard	Rep./Senator	Pennsylvania
Phi Kappa Sigma	Smathers, William H.	Senator	New Jersey
Phi Kappa Sigma	Swanson, Claude A.	Rep./Senator	Virginia
Phi Kappa Sigma	Tydings, Joseph	Senator	Maryland
Phi Kappa Sigma	Wellborn, Olin	Representative	Texas
Phi Kappa Sigma	Whitehead, Joseph	Representative	Virginia
Phi Kappa Tau	Brown, John Y. Sr.	Representative	Kentucky
Phi Kappa Tau	Lantaff, William	Representative	Florida
Phi Kappa Tau	McVey, William	Representative	Illinois
Phi Kappa Tau	McConnell, Mitchell	Senator	Kentucky
Phi Nu Theta	Jenkins, Mitchell	Represenatative	Pennsylvania
Phi Nu Theta	Hubbard, William	Represenatative	West Virginia
Phi Nu Theta	Hubbard, Chester	Represenatative	West Virginia
Phi Nu Theta	Davenport, Frederick	Represenatative	New York
Phi Nu Theta	Daddario, Emilio	Represenatative	Connecticut
Phi Sigma Epsilon	Schwengel, Fred	Represenatative	Iowa
Pi Kappa Alpha	Anderson, LeRoy	Represenatative	Montana
Pi Kappa Alpha	Andrews, Charles O.	Senator	Florida
Pi Kappa Alpha	Arends, Leslie C.	Represenatative	Illinois
Pi Kappa Alpha	Bateman, Herbert H.		Virginia
Pi Kappa Alpha	Bell, John Junior		Texas
Pi Kappa Alpha	Beville, Tom	Rep./Senator	Alabama
Pi Kappa Alpha	Blackburn, Ben	Representative	Georgia
Pi Kappa Alpha	Buchanan, John H.		Alabama
Pi Kappa Alpha	Chandler, Albert B.	Senator	Kentucky
Pi Kappa Alpha	Clark, Jerome Bayard	Representative	North Carolina
Pi Kappa Alpha	Clements, Earle C.	Rep./Senator	Kentucky
Pi Kappa Alpha	Cochran, Than	Rep./Senator	Mississippi
Pi Kappa Alpha	Colmer, William	Representative	Mississippi
Pi Kappa Alpha	Conte, Silvio		Massachusetts
Pi Kappa Alpha	Cunningham, Glenn		Nebraska
Pi Kappa Alpha	Deen, Braswell Drue		Georgia
Pi Kappa Alpha	Dirksen, Everett	Rep./Senator	Illinois
Pi Kappa Alpha	Edwards, Edwin W.	Representative	Louisiana
Pi Kappa Alpha	Ellender, Allen	Senator	Louisiana
Pi Kappa Alpha	Fishburne, John W.	Representative	Virginia
Pi Kappa Alpha	Gathings, Ezekiel		Arkansas
Pi Kappa Alpha	Hammerschmidt, John P.		Arkansas
Pi Kappa Alpha	Healy, Ned R.		California
Pi Kappa Alpha	Henderson, David		North Carolina
Pi Kappa Alpha	Hinson, Jon C.		Mississippi
Pi Kappa Alpha	Huddleston, Walter D.	Senator	Kentucky
Pi Kappa Alpha	Jones, Paul	Representative	Missouri
Pi Kappa Alpha	King, David		Utah
Pi Kappa Alpha	Kyl, Jon		Arizona

Pi Kappa Alpha	McMullen, Chester B.		Florida
Pi Kappa Alpha	Mollohan, Alan B.		West Virginia
Pi Kappa Alpha	Morse, Wayne	Senator	Oregon
Pi Kappa Alpha	Moss, Frank	Senator	Utah
Pi Kappa Alpha	O'Neal, Maston	Represenatative	Georgia
Pi Kappa Alpha	Pirnie, Alexander		New York
Pi Kappa Alpha	Pool, Joe		Texas
Pi Kappa Alpha	Rainey, Lillus Bratton		Alabama
Pi Kappa Alpha	Roberts, C. Patrick		Kansas
Pi Kappa Alpha	Robertson, A. Willis	Rep./Senator	Virginia
Pi Kappa Alpha	Rogers, Will	Representative	Oklahoma
Pi Kappa Alpha	Sparkman, John	Rep./Senator	Alabama
Pi Kappa Alpha	Spong, William	Senator	Virginia
Pi Kappa Alpha	Thurmond, James Strom	Senator	South Carolina
Pi Kappa Alpha	Tolley, Harold	Representative	New York
Pi Kappa Alpha	Underwood, Oscar W.	Rep./Senator	Alabama
Pi Kappa Alpha	Walters, Herbert	Senator	Tennessee
Pi Kappa Alpha	Williams, John Bell	Representative	Mississippi
Pi Kappa Alpha	Williams, John J.	Senator	Delaware
Phi Kappa Psi	Baker, Howard H.	Senator	Tennessee
Phi Kappa Psi	Coble, Howard	Representative	North Carolina
Phi Kappa Psi	Crane, Philip Miller		Illinois
Phi Kappa Psi	Galifianakis, Nick		North Carolina
Phi Kappa Psi	Grant, George		Alabama
Phi Kappa Psi	Hendricks, Joseph E.		Florida
Phi Kappa Psi	Herlong, Albert		Alabama
Phi Kappa Psi	Johnston, Olin	Senator	South Carolina
Phi Kappa Psi	Nelson, Gaylord	Senator	Wisconsin
Phi Kappa Psi	Poff, Richard	Representative	Virginia
Phi Kappa Psi	Preston, Prince		Georgia
Phi Kappa Psi	Starnes, Joe		Alabama
Phi Kappa Psi	Swindall, Pat		Georgia
Phi Lambda Psi	Cardin, Benjamin		Maryland
Phi Lambda Psi	Specter, Arlen	Senator	Pennsylvania
Phi Lambda Psi	Yates, Sidney R.	Representative	Illinois
Psi Upsilon	Allen, Amos Lawrence		Maine
Psi Upsilon	Arnold, Samuel Greene	Senator	Rhode Island
Psi Upsilon	Auchincloss, James C.	Representative	New Jersey
Psi Upsilon	Ayres, Stephen B.	Representative	New York
Psi Upsilon	Baldrige, Howard		Nebraska
Psi Upsilon	Barrett, William E.		Massachusetts
Psi Upsilon	Barry, William Taylor		Mississippi
Psi Upsilon	Bass, Lyman		New York
Psi Upsilon	Bean, Curtis Coe	Delegate	Arizona
Psi Upsilon	Bell, Charles Henry	Senator	New Hampshire
Psi Upsilon	Bennett, Augustus	Representative	New York
Psi Upsilon	Bingham, Hiram	Senator	Connecticut
Psi Upsilon	Buck, John Ransom	Representative	Connecticut
Psi Upsilon	Bush, Prescott	Senator	Connecticut
Psi Upsilon	Cohen, William S.	Rep./Senator	Maine
Psi Upsilon	Cole, Cornelius	Rep./Senator	California
Psi Upsilon	Colt, LeBaron Bradford	Senator	Rhode Island
Psi Upsilon	Corning, Parker	Representative	New York
Psi Upsilon	Coudert, Frederic		New York
Psi Upsilon	Dalzell, John		Pennsylvania
Psi Upsilon	Day, Stephen A.		Illinois
Psi Upsilon	Dean, Sidney		Connecticut
Psi Upsilon	Depew, Chauncey M.	Senator	New York
Psi Upsilon	Eames, Benjamin Tucker	Representative	Rhode Island
Psi Upsilon	Esty, Constantine		Massachusetts
Psi Upsilon	Ferry, O.S.	Rep./Senator	Connecticut
Psi Upsilon	Field, Walbridge Abner	Representative	Massachusetts

Psi Upsilon	Foote, Wallace Turner		New York
Psi Upsilon	Fowler, Charles		New Jersey
Psi Upsilon	Frye, William	Rep./Senator	Maine
Psi Upsilon	Goff, Guy Despard	Senator	West Virginia
Psi Upsilon	Granger, Daniel	Representative	Rhode Island
Psi Upsilon	Green, Theodore	Senator	Rhode Island
Psi Upsilon	Grow, Galusha	Representative	Pennsylvania
Psi Upsilon	Hale, Robert		Maine
Psi Upsilon	Harrison, Francis		New York
Psi Upsilon	Havens, James Smith		New York
Psi Upsilon	Hawley, Joseph Roswell	Rep./Senator	Connecticut
Psi Upsilon	Higgins, Anthony	Senator	Delaware
Psi Upsilon	Hollister, John Baker	Representative	Ohio
Psi Upsilon	Hutchins, Waldo		New York
Psi Upsilon	Johnson, Charles	Senator	Maine
Psi Upsilon	Jones, Burr W.	Representative	Wisconsin
Psi Upsilon	Kilburn, Clarence Evans		New York
Psi Upsilon	Kittredge, Alfred	Senator	South Dakota
Psi Upsilon	Leach, Robert Milton	Representative	Massachusetts
Psi Upsilon	Lee, William Henry F.		Virginia
Psi Upsilon	Lippitt, Henry F.	Senator	Rhode Island
Psi Upsilon	Loring, George Bailey	Representative	Massachusetts
Psi Upsilon	Lyman, Theodore		Massachusetts
Psi Upsilon	MacGregor, Clarence		New York
Psi Upsilon	MacCregor, Clark		Minnesota
Psi Upsilon	Mahany, Rowland B.	Representative	New York
Psi Upsilon	McClory, Robert		Illinois
Psi Upsilon	McCowan, Jonas H.		Michigan
Psi Upsilon	Millard, Charles D.		New York
Psi Upsilon	Miller, Edward Tyler		Maryland
Psi Upsilon	Moody, Arthur Blair Jr.	Senator	Michigan
Psi Upsilon	Moses, George Higgins	Senator	New Hampshire
Psi Upsilon	Newlands, Francis G.	Rep./Senator	Nevada
Psi Upsilon	Patterson, James	Rep./Senator	New Hampshire
Psi Upsilon	Pettit, John W.	Representative	Indiana
Psi Upsilon	Pike, James		New Hampshire
Psi Upsilon	Potter, Clarkson Nott		New York
Psi Upsilon	Rice, Alexander H.		Massachusetts
Psi Upsilon	Rice, William		Massachusetts
Psi Upsilon	Robinson, William E.		New York
Psi Upsilon	Sackett, Frederic M.	Senator	Kentucky
Psi Upsilon	Sanford, John	Representative	New York
Psi Upsilon	Seelye, Julius		Massachusetts
Psi Upsilon	Sibal, Abner Woodruff		Connecticut
Psi Upsilon	Spooner, John Coit	Senator	Wisconsin
Psi Upsilon	Stahlnecker, William G.	Representative	New York
Psi Upsilon	Stratton, Samuel S.		New York
Psi Upsilon	Taft, Robert Alphonso	Senator	Ohio
Psi Upsilon	Thayer, Eli	Representative	Massachusetts
Psi Upsilon	Thomas, John Parnell		New Jersey
Psi Upsilon	Tilson, John Quillin		Connecticut
Psi Upsilon	Tirrell, Charles Q.		Massachusetts
Psi Upsilon	Vilas, William F.	Senator	Wisconsin
Psi Upsilon	Vorys, John M.	Representative	Ohio
Psi Upsilon	Walcott, Frederic C.	Senator	Connecticut
Psi Upsilon	Ward, William L.	Representative	New York
Psi Upsilon	Westland, Alfred J.		Washington
Psi Upsilon	Wetmore, George P.	Senator	Rhode Island
Sigma Alpha Epsilon	Aandahl, Fred	Representative	North Dakota
Sigma Alpha Epsilon	Adams, Sherman		New Hampshire
Sigma Alpha Epsilon	Archer, William R.		Texas
Sigma Alpha Epsilon	Arnold, William W.		Illinois

Sigma Alpha Epsilon	Bankhead, John H.	Senator	Alabama
Sigma Alpha Epsilon	Bankhead, Walter W.	Representative	Alabama
Sigma Alpha Epsilon	Baucus, Max	Senator	Montana
Sigma Alpha Epsilon	Beckham, J. Crepps		Kentucky
Sigma Alpha Epsilon	Bereuter, Douglas K.		Nebraska
Sigma Alpha Epsilon	Blanchard, George	Representative	Wisconsin
Sigma Alpha Epsilon	Bonior, David E.		Michigan
Sigma Alpha Epsilon	Brand, Charles		Georgia
Sigma Alpha Epsilon	Brock, W. E.	Rep./Senator	Tennessee
Sigma Alpha Epsilon	Brown, Joseph E.	Representative	Tennessee
Sigma Alpha Epsilon	Browne, Thomas H. B.		Virginia
Sigma Alpha Epsilon	Budge, Hamer		Idaho
Sigma Alpha Epsilon	Butler, Robert		Oregon
Sigma Alpha Epsilon	Chandler, Walter		Tennessee
Sigma Alpha Epsilon	Chavez, Dennis	Rep./Senator	New Mexico
Sigma Alpha Epsilon	Clements, Newton	Representative	Alabama
Sigma Alpha Epsilon	Cobey, William W.		North Carolina
Sigma Alpha Epsilon	Combs, George H.		Missouri
Sigma Alpha Epsilon	Condon, Robert		California
Sigma Alpha Epsilon	Coon, Samuel		Oregon
Sigma Alpha Epsilon	Cox, Edward		Georgia
Sigma Alpha Epsilon	Davis, Clifford		Tennessee
Sigma Alpha Epsilon	Davis, James C.		Georgia
Sigma Alpha Epsilon	Dear, Cleveland		Louisiana
Sigma Alpha Epsilon	DeGraffenried, Edward		Alabama
Sigma Alpha Epsilon	Dent, Stanley		Alabama
Sigma Alpha Epsilon	Denton, George K.		Indiana
Sigma Alpha Epsilon	Dickinson, William L.	Alabama	
Sigma Alpha Epsilon	Domenici, Peter V.	Senator	New Mexico
Sigma Alpha Epsilon	Dorgan, Byron	Representative	North Dakota
Sigma Alpha Epsilon	Dorsey, John		Kentucky
Sigma Alpha Epsilon	Ecton, Zales	Senator	Montana
Sigma Alpha Epsilon	Elvins, Politte	Representative	Missouri
Sigma Alpha Epsilon	Fleming, William H.		Georgia
Sigma Alpha Epsilon	Flood, Daniel J.		Pennsylvania
Sigma Alpha Epsilon	Flood, Henry		Virginia
Sigma Alpha Epsilon	Flowers, Walter		Alabama
Sigma Alpha Epsilon	Flynt, John		Georgia
Sigma Alpha Epsilon	Frazier, James	Senator	Tennessee
Sigma Alpha Epsilon	Frazier, James B. Jr.	Representative	Tennessee
Sigma Alpha Epsilon	Gambrell, David H.	Senator	Georgia
Sigma Alpha Epsilon	Gekas, George W.	Representative	Pennsylvania
Sigma Alpha Epsilon	Harris, Oren		Arkansas
Sigma Alpha Epsilon	Harris, William A.	Rep./Senator	Kansas
Sigma Alpha Epsilon	Harrison, Byron Patton		Mississippi
Sigma Alpha Epsilon	Harrison, George P.	Representative	Alabama
Sigma Alpha Epsilon	Healey, Arthur D.		Massachusetts
Sigma Alpha Epsilon	Heiskell, John N.	Senator	Arkansas
Sigma Alpha Epsilon	Henry, Patrick	Representative	Mississippi
Sigma Alpha Epsilon	Hersman, Hugh S.		California
Sigma Alpha Epsilon	Hickey, John	Senator	Wyoming
Sigma Alpha Epsilon	Hunter, Richard		Nebraska
Sigma Alpha Epsilon	Hutcheson, Joseph C.	Representative	Texas
Sigma Alpha Epsilon	Jarman, Pete		Alabama
Sigma Alpha Epsilon	Johnson, James P.		Colorado
Sigma Alpha Epsilon	Johnson, Paul		Mississippi
Sigma Alpha Epsilon	Jones, Hamilton C.		North Carolina
Sigma Alpha Epsilon	Kavanaugh, William M.	Senator	Arkansas
Sigma Alpha Epsilon	Kloeb, Frank L.	Representative	Ohio
Sigma Alpha Epsilon	Knox, Philander C.	Senator	Pennsylvania
Sigma Alpha Epsilon	Lawson, John W.	Representative	Virginia
Sigma Alpha Epsilon	Lewis, Lawrence		Colorado

Sigma Alpha Epsilon	Loser, J. Carleton		Tennessee
Sigma Alpha Epsilon	Lumpkin, Alva M.	Senator	South Carolina
Sigma Alpha Epsilon	Mackie, John C.		Michigan
Sigma Alpha Epsilon	Malone, George W.	Senator	Nevada
Sigma Alpha Epsilon	McKinley, William	Rep./Senator	Illinois
Sigma Alpha Epsilon	McSween, Harold	Representative	Louisiana
Sigma Alpha Epsilon	Miller, Thomas B.		Pennsylvania
Sigma Alpha Epsilon	Mitchell, Harlan E.		Georgia
Sigma Alpha Epsilon	Mitchell, John R.		Tennessee
Sigma Alpha Epsilon	Montgomery, Samuel J.		Oklahoma
Sigma Alpha Epsilon	Morehead, John M.		North Carolina
Sigma Alpha Epsilon	Morse, Frank		Massachusetts
Sigma Alpha Epsilon	Murray, Tom		Tennessee
Sigma Alpha Epsilon	Patterson, Gilbert B.		North Carolina
Sigma Alpha Epsilon	Pittman, Key	Senator	Nevada
Sigma Alpha Epsilon	Plumley, Charles	Representative	Vermont
Sigma Alpha Epsilon	Poulson, C. Norris		California
Sigma Alpha Epsilon	Price, Robert		Texas
Sigma Alpha Epsilon	Pryor, David H.		Arkansas
Sigma Alpha Epsilon	Ragon, Hiram H.		Arkansas
Sigma Alpha Epsilon	Reames, Alfred	Senator	Oregon
Sigma Alpha Epsilon	Regula, Ralph S.	Representative	Ohio
Sigma Alpha Epsilon	Rohrbough, Edward G.	West Virginia	
Sigma Alpha Epsilon	Russell, Richard B.	Senator	Georgia
Sigma Alpha Epsilon	Sanders, Jared Y.	Representative	Louisiana
Sigma Alpha Epsilon	Scott, Byron N.		California
Sigma Alpha Epsilon	Selden, Armistead		Alabama
Sigma Alpha Epsilon	Shuford, George A.		North Carolina
Sigma Alpha Epsilon	Siler, Eugene		Kentucky
Sigma Alpha Epsilon	Simms, Albert		New Mexico
Sigma Alpha Epsilon	Sims, Hugo S. Jr.		South Carolina
Sigma Alpha Epsilon	Sisson, Thomas U.		Mississippi
Sigma Alpha Epsilon	Smathers, George	Rep./Senator	Florida
Sigma Alpha Epsilon	Stanley, Augustus O.		Kentucky
Sigma Alpha Epsilon	Stauffer, Simon W.	Representative	Pennsylvania
Sigma Alpha Epsilon	Stenholm, Charles W.		Texas
Sigma Alpha Epsilon	Stokes, James W.		South Carolina
Sigma Alpha Epsilon	Stuckey, Williamson		Georgia
Sigma Alpha Epsilon	Swift, Oscar W.		New York
Sigma Alpha Epsilon	Tucker, Jim		Arkansas
Sigma Alpha Epsilon	VanDeerlin, Lionel		California
Sigma Alpha Epsilon	Vincent, Earl W.		Iowa
Sigma Alpha Epsilon	Watson, Thomas E.	Rep./Senator	Georgia
Sigma Alpha Epsilon	Whitaker, John A.	Representative	Kentucky
Sigma Alpha Epsilon	Wilson, William L.	Representative	West Virginia
Sigma Alpha Epsilon	White, Richard		Texas
Sigma Chi	Abdnor, E. James		South Dakota
Sigma Chi	Allen, William		Ohio
Sigma Chi	Andrews, Mark		North Dakota
Sigma Chi	Anthony, Beryl F.		Arkansas
Sigma Chi	Baker, Jacob T.		New Jersey
Sigma Chi	Barden, Graham		North Carolina
Sigma Chi	Barry, Alexander	Senator	Oregon
Sigma Chi	Beall, J. Glenn	Rep./Senator	Maryland
Sigma Chi	Beard, Robin L.	Representative	Tennessee
Sigma Chi	Bilbray, James		Nevada
Sigma Chi	Burgener, Clair		California
Sigma Chi	Burke, Edward	Rep./Senator	Nebraska
Sigma Chi	Burke, James	Representative	Pennsylvania
Sigma Chi	Burlison, Bill		Missouri
Sigma Chi	Camden, Johnson	Senator	West Virginia
Sigma Chi	Cannon, Arthur P.	Representative	Florida

Sigma Chi	Cobb, Thomas R.		Indiana
Sigma Chi	Coffin, Howard		Michigan
Sigma Chi	Coombs, Frank L.		California
Sigma Chi	Cooper, George W.		Indiana
Sigma Chi	Cooper, Henry A.		Wisconsin
Sigma Chi	Courtney, William		Tennessee
Sigma Chi	Cramer, William		Florida
Sigma Chi	Curtin, Willard		Pennsylvania
Sigma Chi	Denny, Walter M.		Mississippi
Sigma Chi	Dixon, Lincoln		Indiana
Sigma Chi	Doolittle, Dudley		Kansas
Sigma Chi	Drewry, Patrick		Virginia
Sigma Chi	Duncan, Robert B.		Oregon
Sigma Chi	DuPont, Thomas	Senator	Delaware
Sigma Chi	Eckhardt, Robert	Representative	Texas
Sigma Chi	Falconer, Jacob		Washington
Sigma Chi	Faust, Charles L.		Missouri
Sigma Chi	Felch, Alpheus	Senator	Michigan
Sigma Chi	Fisher, Hubert	Representative	Tennessee
Sigma Chi	Franklin, Web		Mississippi
Sigma Chi	Fulbright, J. William	Rep./Senator	Arkansas
Sigma Chi	Garn, Jacob	Senator	Utah
Sigma Chi	Gillmore, Paul E.	Representative	Ohio
Sigma Chi	Glenn, Milton		New Jersey
Sigma Chi	Goldwater, Barry	Senator	Arizona
Sigma Chi	Hall, Tony P.	Representative	Ohio
Sigma Chi	Hansen, Orval		Idaho
Sigma Chi	Harrison, William		Wyoming
Sigma Chi	Hays, Lawrence B.		Arkansas
Sigma Chi	Himes, Joseph		Ohio
Sigma Chi	Hinshaw, Edmund		Nebraska
Sigma Chi	Hoey, Clyde	Rep./Senator	North Carolina
Sigma Chi	Hoyer, Steny H.	Representative	Maryland
Sigma Chi	Hunter, Allan		California
Sigma Chi	Hunter, Morton C.		Indiana
Sigma Chi	Hyde, Henry		Illinois
Sigma Chi	Jordan, Isaac		Ohio
Sigma Chi	Kindred, John		New York
Sigma Chi	Kleberg, Richard		Texas
Sigma Chi	Kyle, John C.		Mississippi
Sigma Chi	Langer, William	Senator	North Dakota
Sigma Chi	Lanham, Henderson	Representative	Georgia
Sigma Chi	Lassiter, Francis R.		Virginia
Sigma Chi	Lloyd, Sherman		Utah
Sigma Chi	Lucas, Wingate		Texas
Sigma Chi	Lybrand, Archibald		Ohio
Sigma Chi	Marland, Earnest W.		Oklahoma
Sigma Chi	Maverick, Fontaine M.		Texas
Sigma Chi	McCormack, Mike		Washington
Sigma Chi	McCullock, Roscoe	Rep./Senator	Ohio
Sigma Chi	McKenney, William	Representative	Virginia
Sigma Chi	McLain, Frank		Mississippi
Sigma Chi	Meiklejohn, George deRue		Nebraska
Sigma Chi	Mercer, David		Nebraska
Sigma Chi	Metcalf, Lee	Rep./Senator	Montana
Sigma Chi	Meyer, Herbert A.	Representative	Kansas
Sigma Chi	Moore, W. Henson III		Louisiana
Sigma Chi	Moores, Merrill		Indiana
Sigma Chi	Morris, Thomas		New Mexico
Sigma Chi	Mott, James W.		Oregon
Sigma Chi	Murphy, Morgan F.		Illinois
Sigma Chi	Narey, Harry		Iowa

Sigma Chi	New, Harry	Senator	Indiana
Sigma Chi	Newton, Cleveland	Representative	Missouri
Sigma Chi	O'Brien, George M.		Illinois
Sigma Chi	O'Neall, John		Indiana
Sigma Chi	Oxley, Michael G.		Ohio
Sigma Chi	Parker, Samuel W.		Indiana
Sigma Chi	Parks, Tilman		Arkansas
Sigma Chi	Patten, Harold		Arizona
Sigma Chi	Patterson, Jerry M.		California
Sigma Chi	Pence, Lafayette		Colorado
Sigma Chi	Rivers, Ralph		Alaska
Sigma Chi	Reece, B. Carroll		Tennessee
Sigma Chi	Roudebush, Richard		Indiana
Sigma Chi	Roy, William R.		Kansas
Sigma Chi	Saunders, Edward W.		Virginia
Sigma Chi	Scrugham, James G.	Rep./Senator	Nevada
Sigma Chi	Shaw, Frank T.	Representative	Maryland
Sigma Chi	Shuster, Elmer		Pennsylvania
Sigma Chi	Simonton, Charles B.		Tennessee
Sigma Chi	Skelton, Isaac N.		Missouri
Sigma Chi	Smart, James S.		New York
Sigma Chi	Smith, Robert F.		Oregon
Sigma Chi	Spight, Thomas		Mississippi
Sigma Chi	Stahlnecker, William G.		New York
Sigma Chi	Storm, John		Pennsylvania
Sigma Chi	Stout, Tom		Missouri
Sigma Chi	Swift, Alan B.		Washington
Sigma Chi	Talcott, Burt		California
Sigma Chi	Thornton, R. H. Jr.		Arkansas
Sigma Chi	Thropp, Joseph E.		Pennsylvania
Sigma Chi	Tyson, John		Alabama
Sigma Chi	Udall, Morris		Arizona
Sigma Chi	Vanderveen, Richard F.		Michigan
Sigma Chi	Venable, Edward		Virginia
Sigma Chi	Watson, David K.		Ohio
Sigma Chi	Welker, Herman	Senator	Idaho
Sigma Chi	Wilson, George A.		Iowa
Sigma Chi	Woodrum, Clifton A.	Representative	Virginia
Sigma Chi	Wydler, John W.		New York
Sigma Chi	Yaple, George		Michigan
Sigma Chi	Yound, James		Texas
Sigma Kappa	Smith, Margaret Chase	Rep./Senator	Maine
Sigma Nu	Alexander, Sydenham	Representative	North Carolina
Sigma Nu	Andrews, George W.		Alabama
Sigma Nu	Avis, Samuel		West Virginia
Sigma Nu	Ball, L. Heisler	Rep./Senator	Delaware
Sigma Nu	Barney, Samuel S.	Representative	Wisconsin
Sigma Nu	Bentsen, Lloyd M.	Rep./Senator	Texas
Sigma Nu	Bland, Oscar E.		Indiana
Sigma Nu	Boner, William H.		Tennessee
Sigma Nu	Broussard, Edwin	Senator	Louisiana
Sigma Nu	Brownson, Charles	Representative	Indiana
Sigma Nu	Burdick, Quentin	Rep./Senator	Minnesota
Sigma Nu	Carmichael, Archibald	Representative	Alabama
Sigma Nu	Clayton, Bertram		New York
Sigma Nu	Clayton, Henry		Alabama
Sigma Nu	Cole, William		New York
Sigma Nu	Cranston, Alan	Senator	California
Sigma Nu	Devine, Samuel	Representative	Ohio
Sigma Nu	Dicks, Norman		Washington
Sigma Nu	Dorsey, Frank		Pennsylvania
Sigma Nu	Edwards, Charles G.		Georgia

Sigma Nu	Ellett, Tazewell		Virginia
Sigma Nu	Evans, John M.		Montana
Sigma Nu	Favrot, George		Louisiana
Sigma Nu	Fletcher, Thomas B.		Ohio
Sigma Nu	Frear, J. Allen	Senator	Delaware
Sigma Nu	Frenzel, William B.	Representative	Minnesota
Sigma Nu	George, Walter	Senator	Georgia
Sigma Nu	Graham, Bob		Florida
Sigma Nu	Hansen, Cliff		Wyoming
Sigma Nu	Harless, Richard F.	Representative	Arizona
Sigma Nu	Heald, William H.		Delaware
Sigma Nu	Helm, Harvey		Kentucky
Sigma Nu	Hillis, Elwood H.		Indiana
Sigma Nu	Kasten, Robert	Senator	Wisconsin
Sigma Nu	Leach, James A.	Representative	Iowa
Sigma Nu	Lichtenwalner, Norton		Pennsylvania
Sigma Nu	Lott, C. Trent		Mississippi
Sigma Nu	Martin, Whitmell		Louisiana
Sigma Nu	McArthur, Clifton		Oregon
Sigma Nu	McClure, James A.		Idaho
Sigma Nu	McConnell, Samuel K.		Pennsylvania
Sigma Nu	Michel, Robert H.		Illinois
Sigma Nu	Mitchell, George J.	Senator	Maine
Sigma Nu	Moses, John		North Dakota
Sigma Nu	Norblad, Albin	Representative	Oregon
Sigma Nu	Overton, John	Rep./Senator	Louisiana
Sigma Nu	Pace, Stephen	Representative	Georgia
Sigma Nu	Patterson, Roscoe	Rep./Senator	Missouri
Sigma Nu	Robinson, Tommy	Representative	Arkansas
Sigma Nu	Robison, John	Rep./Senator	Kentucky
Sigma Nu	Schoeppel, Andrew	Senator	Kansas
Sigma Nu	Shaw, E. Clay	Representative	Florida
Sigma Nu	Stallings, Jesse		Alabama
Sigma Nu	Steagall, Henry		Alabama
Sigma Nu	Steck, Daniel	Senator	Iowa
Sigma Nu	Steiwer, Fred	Senator	Oregon
Sigma Nu	Stewart, J. George	Representative	Delaware
Sigma Nu	Sweet, Burton E.		Iowa
Sigma Nu	Symms, Steven D.		Idaho
Sigma Nu	Talmadge, Herman	Senator	Georgia
Sigma Nu	Walker, John R.	Representative	Georgia
Sigma Phi	Barbour, Henry E.		California
Sigma Phi	Bowie, Thomas F.		Maryland
Sigma Phi	Campbell, William W.		New York
Sigma Phi	Cochrane, Clarke B.		New York
Sigma Phi	Cochrane, John		New York
Sigma Phi	Cole, Orsamus		Wisconsin
Sigma Phi	Darragh, Archibald		Michigan
Sigma Phi	Davis, Thomas T.		New York
Sigma Phi	Einstein, Edwin		New York
Sigma Phi	Fleetwood, Frederick G.		Vermont
Sigma Phi	Foss, Eugene		Vermont
Sigma Phi	Gould, Norman J.		New York
Sigma Phi	Hornbeck, John W.		Pennsylvania
Sigma Phi	Ingalls, John J.	Senator	Kansas
Sigma Phi	Keith, Hastings	Representative	Massachusetts
Sigma Phi	Knox, Samuel		Missouri
Sigma Phi	Laflin, Addison		New York
Sigma Phi	Merriman, Trumann		New York
Sigma Phi	Mullin, Joseph		New York
Sigma Phi	Olin, Abraham B.		New York
Sigma Phi	Oliver, Andrew		New York

Sigma Phi	Pratt, Daniel D.	Senator	Indiana
Sigma Phi	Root, Elihu		New York
Sigma Phi	Sedgwick, Charles B.	Representative	New York
Sigma Phi	Sherman, James S.		New York
Sigma Phi	Walker, Gilbert C.		Virginia
Sigma Phi	Wemple, Edward		New York
Sigma Phi Epsilon	Bartlett, Steve		Texas
Sigma Phi Epsilon	Bkurton, Philip		California
Sigma Phi Epsilon	Byrd, Harry	Senator	Virginia
Sigma Phi Epsilon	Cochran, Thomas C.	Representative	Pennsylvania
Sigma Phi Epsilon	Cunningham, Paul		Iowa
Sigma Phi Epsilon	Flood, Joel W.		Virginia
Sigma Phi Epsilon	Frey, Oliver W.		Pennsylvania
Sigma Phi Epsilon	Gary, Julian		Virginia
Sigma Phi Epsilon	Gonzalez, Henry B.		Texas
Sigma Phi Epsilon	Hayden, Carl	Rep./Senator	Arizona
Sigma Phi Epsilon	Hickenlooper, Bourke	Senator	Iowa
Sigma Phi Epsilon	Holt, Joseph	Representative	California
Sigma Phi Epsilon	Horan, Walter		Washington
Sigma Phi Epsilon	Jennings, William		Virginia
Sigma Phi Epsilon	Matthews, Donald		Florida
Sigma Phi Epsilon	Phipps, Lawrence	Senator	Colorado
Sigma Phi Epsilon	Rogers, W. E.	Representative	Texas
Sigma Phi Epsilon	Schwert, Pius		New York
Sigma Phi Epsilon	Smith, Willis	Senator	North Carolina
Sigma Phi Epsilon	Steelman, Alan W.	Representative	Texas
Sigma Phi Epsilon	Tuck, William		Virginia
Sigma Phi Epsilon	Warburton, Herbert		Delaware
Sigma Phi Epsilon	Whitener, Basil		North Carolina
Sigma Phi Epsilon	Wiley, Alexander	Senator	Wisconsin
Sigma Pi	Bow, Frank	Representative	Ohio
Sigma Pi	Harsha, William		Ohio
Sigma Pi	Hopkins, David W.		Missouri
Sigma Pi	Mobley, William C.		Georgia
Sigma Pi	Myers, John		Indiana
Sigma Pi	Troutman, William I.		Pennsylvania
Sigma Tau Gamma	Arnold, Samuel W.		Missouri
Tau Kappa Epsilon	Byrd, Robert	Rep./Senator	West Virginia
Tau Kappa Epsilon	Hillelson, Jeffery	Representative	Missouri
Tau Kappa Epsilon	Howell, George		Illinois
Tau Kappa Epsilon	Hunt, Lester C.	Senator	Wyoming
Tau Kappa Epsilon	Jepson, Rober W.	Senator	Iowa
Tau Kappa Epsilon	Morrison, Sidney W.	Representative	Washington
Tau Kappa Epsilon	Pursell, Carl		Michigan
Tau Kappa Epsilon	Quillen, James H.		Tennessee
Tau Kappa Epsilon	Rowland, John G.		Connecticut
Tau Kappa Epsilon	Stone, Richard B.	Senator	Florida
Tau Kappa Epsilon	Tauzin, W. J.	Representative	Louisiana
Tau Kappa Epsilon	Watkins, Wes		Oklahoma
Theta Chi	Allen, John J.		California
Theta Chi	Barry, William B.		New York
Theta Chi	Christianson, Theodore		Minnesota
Theta Chi	Curtis, Carl	Rep./Senator	Nebraska
Theta Chi	Edgar, Robert W.	Representative	Pennsylvania
Theta Chi	Gibson, Ernest W.	Rep./Senator	Vermont
Theta Chi	Gibson, Ernest W.	Senator	Vermont
Theta Chi	Goodling, William F.	Representative	Pennsylvania
Theta Chi	Griffin, Robert	Rep./Senator	Michigan
Theta Chi	Hoidale, Einar	Representative	Minnesota
Theta Chi	Keough, Eugene		New York
Theta Chi	Magnuson, Warren	Rep./Senator	Washington
Theta Chi	McLoskey, Robert	Representative	Illinois

Theta Chi	Smith, Robert		New Hampshire
Theta Chi	Snyder, Melvin C.		West Virginia
Theta Chi	Spalding, Burleigh F.		North Dakota
Theta Chi	Staebler, Neil		Michigan
Theta Chi	Whittaker, Robert		Kansas
Theta Chi	Wyman, Louis C.		New Hampshire
Theta Delta Chi	Bellamy, John D.		North Carolina
Theta Delta Chi	Bentley, Alvin		Michigan
Theta Delta Chi	Buck, Frank H.		California
Theta Delta Chi	Crumpecker, Maurice E.		Oregon
Theta Delta Chi	Dixon, Nathan II	Rep./Senator	Rhode Island
Theta Delta Chi	France, Joseph I.	Senator	Maryland
Theta Delta Chi	Furlow, Allen J.		Minnesota
Theta Delta Chi	Gibson, Henry R.		Tennessee
Theta Delta Chi	Ives, Irving M.	Senator	New York
Theta Delta Chi	Kyle, Thomas B.	Representative	Ohio
Theta Delta Chi	Leggett, Robert L.		California
Theta Delta Chi	Lewis, Jerry		California
Theta Delta Chi	Lockwood, Daniel N.		New York
Theta Delta Chi	McGillicuddy, Daniel J.		Maine
Theta Delta Chi	McLachlan, James		California
Theta Delta Chi	Nicholls, John C.		Georgia
Theta Delta Chi	Sanford, Rollin		New York
Theta Delta Chi	Schneebeli, Herman T.		Pennsylvania
Theta Delta Chi	Sinnickson, Clement H.		New Jersey
Theta Delta Chi	Smith, Henry P. III		New York
Theta Delta Chi	Spooner, Henry J.		Rhode Island
Theta Delta Chi	Stevens, Frederick C.		Minnesota
Theta Delta Chi	Stiness, Walter R.		Rhode Island
Theta Xi	Adams, Alva	Senator	Colorado
Theta Xi	Aldrich, Truman	Representative	Alabama
Theta Xi	Ames, Butler		Massachusetts
Theta Xi	Church, Frank	Senator	Idaho
Theta Xi	Magnuson, Don H.	Representative	Washington
Theta Xi	McConnell, Samuel K.		Pennsylvania
Theta Xi	Thomas, W. Aubrey		Ohio
Theta Xi	Wiley, William H.		New Jersey
Zeta Beta Tau	Boschwitz, Rudolph	Senator	Minnesota
Zeta Beta Tau	Frost, J. Martin	Representative	Texas
Zeta Beta Tau	Gilman, Benjamin A.		New York
Zeta Beta Tau	Kahn, Julius		California
Zeta Beta Tau	Lehman, William		Florida
Zeta Beta Tau	Marks, Marc L.		Pennsylvania
Zeta Beta Tau	Mikva, Abner S.		Illinois
Zeta Beta Tau	Neuberger, Richard L.	Senator	Oregon
Zeta Beta Tau	Ottinger, Richard	Representative	New York
Zeta Beta Tau	Ribicoff, Abraham	Rep./Senator	Connecticut
Zeta Beta Tau	Smith, Lawrence	Representative	Florida
Sigma Alpha Mu	Downey, Thomas J.		New York
Sigma Alpha Mu	Edwards, Mickey		Oklahoma
Sigma Alpha Mu	Glickman, Daniel		Kansas
Sigma Alpha Mu	Hecht, Jacob	Senator	Nevada
Sigma Alpha Mu	Kramer, Kenneth B.	Representative	Colorado
Sigma Alpha Mu	Lantos, Thomas P.		California
Sigma Alpha Mu	Weiss, Samuel		Pennsylvania
Sigma Alpha Mu	Zorinsky, Edward	Senator	Nebraska
Alpha Epsilon Pi	Farbstein, Leonard	Representative	New York
Alpha Epsilon Pi	Isacson, Leo		New York
Alpha Epsilon Pi	Toll, Herman		Pennsylvania
Alpha Epsilon Pi	Wolff, Lester L.		New York
Alpha Chi Rho	D'Amato, Alfonse	Senator	New York
Alpha Chi Rho	Martin, David	Representative	Nebraska

Alpha Chi Rho	Scott, Hugh	Rep./Senator	Pennsylvania
Alpha Chi Rho	Stennis, John	Senator	Mississippi
Alpha Chi Rho	Weaver, James	Representative	Pennsylvania
Phi Sigma Kappa	Bachman, Carl G.		West Virginia
Phi Sigma Kappa	Bowman, Frank		West Virginia
Phi Sigma Kappa	Brown, William G. Jr.		West Virginia
Phi Sigma Kappa	Carrigg, Joseph L.		Pennsylvania
Phi Sigma Kappa	Coelho, Tony		California
Phi Sigma Kappa	Curtis, Thomas		Missouri
Phi Sigma Kappa	Denney, Robert		Nebraska
Phi Sigma Kappa	Gude, Gilbert		Maryland
Phi Sigma Kappa	Higgins, Edwin W.		Connecticut
Phi Sigma Kappa	Kee, John		West Virginia
Phi Sigma Kappa	King, Carleton		New York
Phi Sigma Kappa	Lausche, Frank	Senator	Ohio
Phi Sigma Kappa	Long, Oren		Hawaii
Phi Sigma Kappa	Martin, Thomas S.		Virginia
Phi Sigma Kappa	McLean, Donald H.		New Jersey
Phi Sigma Kappa	Michener, Earl C.	Representative	Michigan
Phi Sigma Kappa	Neely, Matthew	Rep./Senator	West Virginia
Phi Sigma Kappa	Tunney, John V.	Senator	California
Phi Sigma Kappa	Wallhauser, George M.	Representative	New Jersey
Phi Sigma Kappa	Nix, Robert		Pennsylvania
Phi Kappa Theta	Barrett, William		Massachusetts
Phi Kappa Theta	de la Garza, Kika		Texas
Phi Kappa Theta	McCarthy, Eugene	Rep./Senator	Minnesota
Zeta Psi	Allen, Henry C.	Representative	New Jersey
Zeta Psi	Benton, William B.	Senator	Connecticut
Zeta Psi	Bisbee, Horatio Jr.	Representative	Florida
Zeta Psi	Cable, Ben		Illinois
Zeta Psi	Campbell, William W.		Ohio
Zeta Psi	Coyne, James K.		Pennsylvania
Zeta Psi	Denny, Harmar		Pennsylvania
Zeta Psi	Dingley, Nelson Jr.		Maine
Zeta Psi	Edwards, Edward I.	Senator	New Jersey
Zeta Psi	Gale, Richard	Representative	Minnesota
Zeta Psi	Goodwin, Angier		Massachusetts
Zeta Psi	Goodwin, Forrest		Maine
Zeta Psi	Henderson, John S.		North Carolina
Zeta Psi	Hilborn, Samuel G.		California
Zeta Psi	Hinds, Asher C.		Maine
Zeta Psi	Hinshaw, John C. W.		California
Zeta Psi	Kirkpatrick William S.		Pennsylvania
Zeta Psi	Gearhart, Bertrand W.		California
Zeta Psi	Hitchcock, Phineas W.	Del./Senator	Nebraska
Zeta Psi	Kirkpatrick, William H.	Representative	Pennsylvania
Zeta Psi	Knowland, William	Senator	California
Zeta Psi	Longworth, Nicholas	Representative	Ohio
Zeta Psi	Nelson, Charles P.		Maine
Zeta Psi	Nelson, John E.		Maine
Zeta Psi	Pepper, George W.	Senator	Pennsylvania
Zeta Psi	Phillips, Alfred	Representative	Connecticut
Zeta Psi	Simpson, Kenneth F.		New York
Zeta Psi	Stedman, Charles M.		North Carolina
Zeta Psi	Steers, Newton		Maryland
Zeta Psi	Sumner, Charles A.		California
Zeta Psi	Swasey, John P.		Maine
Zeta Psi	Voorhis, Horace J.		California
Zeta Psi	Wilson, Pete	Senator	California

This famous greek list was compiled by Jay Langhammer, ΔΤΔ and Jon Williamson, ΛΧΑ; who have been researching greeks in the public eye for over fifteen years.

Index

Auburn University at Montgomery, II 12
Augsburg College, II 12
Augusta College, II 12
Augustana College (Rock Island, I L), II 13
Augustana College (Sioux Falls, SD), II 13
Auraria Higher Education Center, II 13
Aurora University, II 13
Austin College, II 13
Austin Peay State University, II 13
Averett College, II 13
Avila College, II 13
Axis Club *d*, VIII 38

B

Babson College of Management, II 13
Baird, William Raimond, I 7-8, I 18
Baker University, II 13-14
Bakersfield College, II 14
Baldwin-Wallace College, II 14
Ball State University, II 14
Banta, George, I 17
Banta's Greek Quarterly, I 17
Baptist College at Charleston, II 14
Barber-Scotia College, II 14-15
Bard College, II 15
Barnard College, II 15
Barry University, II 15
Baruch College, II 15
Baseball executives, A 9-10
Baseball hall of fame members, A 8
Basketball hall of fame members, A 10
Bates College, II 15
Baylor University, II 15
Beaver College, II 15
Behrend College, II 15
Belhaven College, II 16
Bellarmine College, II 16
Belmont Abbey College, II 16
Belmont College, II 16
Beloit College, II 16
Bemidji State University, II 16
Benedict College, II 16
Benedictine College, II 16
Bennett College, II 17
Bentley College, II 17
Berea College, II 17
Beta Alpha Psi (Accounting), V 73-74
Beta Beta Beta (Biology), VII 19-22
Beta Gamma Sigma (Business and Management), I 20, VI 16-18
Beta Kappa *d*, VIII 4-5
Beta Kappa Chi (Natural Sciences and Mathematics), VI 18-19
Beta Phi *d*, VIII 5
Beta Phi Alpha *d*, I 21, VIII 30
Beta Phi Mu (Library Science), VI 19-20
Beta Sigma Omicron *d*, I 21, VIII 30-31
Beta Sigma Rho *d*, I 21, VIII 5
Berry College, II 17
Beta Sigma Psi, III 25-27
Beta Sigma Tau *d*, I 21, VIII 5-6

Beta Theta Pi, I 8, I 11, I 16-18, I 21, I 26, III 27-30
Bethany College (Bethany, WV), II 17
Bethany College (Lindsborg, KS), II 17
Bethany Nazarene College, II 17
Bethel College (McKenzie, TN), II 17
Bethel College (St. Paul, MN), II 17
Bethune-Cookman College, II 17-18
Biola University, II 18
Birmingham-Southern University, II 18
Bishop College, II 18
Black Hills College, II 18
Blackburn College, II 18
Blinn College, II 18
Bloomfield College, II 18
Bloomsburg State College, II 18-19
Bluefield State College, II 19
Blue Key (Student Activities), VII 23-24
Boise State University, II 19
Boston College, II 19
Boston College of Law, II 19
Boston Conservatory of Music, II 19
Boston University, II 19
Bowdoin College, II 19
Bowie State University, II 20
Bowling Green University, II 20
Bradley University, II 20
Brandeis University, II 21
Brant, Jonathan J., I 26
Brenau College, II 21
Brescia College, II 21
Brevard Community College, II 21
Briar Cliff College, II 21
Bridgewater College, II 21
Brigham Young University, II 21-22
Brooklyn College of Pharmacy, II 98
Brooklyn College of the City University of New York, II 22
Brooklyn Law School, II 22
Broward Community College, II 22
Brown University, II 22-23
Bryant College, II 23
Bucknell University, II 23
Buena Vista College, II 23
Butler University, II 23

C

C. W. Post College of Long Island University, II 47
Cabrini College, II 24
Caldwell College for Women, II 24
California Baptist College, II 26
California College of Medicine, II 26
California Institute of Technology, II 27
California Lutheran College, II 27
California Polytechnic State University (Pamona, CA), II 27
California Polytechnic State University (San Luis Obispo, CA), II 27
California State College of Pennsylvania, II 27-28
California State College, Stanislaus, II 27
California State University, Bakersfield, II 28
California State University, Chico, II 28

M